This book may contain website addresses
to third party sites unconnected with
HarperCollins Publishers Ltd. HarperCollins
Publishers Ltd. is not responsible for, and has
no liability in relation to, the content of any
third party sites, nor does it endorse any third
party site in any way.

HarperCollins does not warrant that
www.collinsdictionary.com,
www.collinslanguage.com or any other website
mentioned in this title will be provided
uninterrupted, that any website will be error
free, that defects will be corrected, or that the
website or the server that makes it available are
free of viruses or bugs. For full terms and
conditions please refer to the site terms
provided on the website.

D0571185

GENERAL EDITOR
Gaëlle Amiot-Cadey

CONTRIBUTORS
Gabriella Bacchelli   Daphne Day

EDITORIAL COORDINATION
Susanne Reichert

SERIES EDITOR
Rob Scriven

Dictionary
hers 2007

alian Dictionary, 1982,
05, 2006, 2009

3 2

& Co. Ltd 1990
hers 1996, 1999, 2002,

trademark of
s Limited

om

his book is available

by Thomas Callan

t by
lutions, Glasgow

Spa, Lavis (Trento)

those authors and
gave permission for
e used in the Collins
so like to thank Times
viding valuable data.

Col
— POC
Ital
Dicti

HarperCollins Publish
Westerhill Road
Bishopbriggs
Glasgow
G64 2QT
Great Britain

Sixth Edition 2010

Previously published a
Collins Express Italian
© HarperCollins Publi

Based on Collins Gem
1989, 1993, 1998, 2001,

Reprint 10 9 8 7 6 5

© William Collins Sor
© HarperCollins Publi
2007, 2010

ISBN 978-0-00-732500

Collins® is a register
HarperCollins Publish

www.collinslanguage

A catalogue record fo
from the British Libr

Dictionary text types

Supplement text typ
Davidson Publishing

Printed in Italy by L

Acknowledgements
We would like to tha
publishers who kin
copyright material
Word Web. We woul
Newspapers Ltd for

William Collins' dream of knowledge for all began with the publication of his first book in 1819. A self-educated mill worker, he not only enriched millions of lives, but also founded a flourishing publishing house. Today, staying true to this spirit, Collins books are packed with inspiration, innovation, and practical expertise. They place you at the centre of a world of possibility and give you exactly what you need to explore it.

Language is the key to this exploration, and at the heart of Collins Dictionaries, is language as it is really used. New words, phrases, and meanings spring up every day, and all of them are captured and analysed by the Collins Word Web. Constantly updated, and with over 2.5 billion entries, this living language resource is unique to our dictionaries.

Words are tools for life. And a Collins Dictionary makes them work for you.

Collins. Do more.

INDICE		CONTENTS

I marchi registrati

I termini che a nostro parere costituiscono un marchio registrato sono stati designati come tali. In ogni caso, né la presenza né l'assenza di tale designazione implicano alcuna valutazione del loro reale stato giuridico.

Note on trademarks

Entered words that we have reason to believe constitute trademarks have been designated as such. However, neither the presence nor the absence of such designation should be regarded as affecting the legal status of any trademark.

INTRODUZIONE

Vi ringraziamo di aver scelto questo dizionario inglese e ci auguriamo che esso si riveli uno strumento utile e piacevole da usare nello studio, in vacanza e sul lavoro.

In questa introduzione troverete alcuni suggerimenti per aiutarvi a trarre il massimo beneficio dal vostro nuovo dizionario, ricco non solo per il suo ampio lemmario ma anche per il gran numero di informazioni contenute in ciascuna voce.

All'inizio del dizionario troverete l'elenco delle abbreviazioni usate nel testo e una guida alla pronuncia. Troverete inoltre un utile elenco delle forme dei verbi irregolari inglesi e italiani, seguito da una sezione finale con i numeri, l'ora e la data.

Come usare il dizionario

Per imparare ad usare in modo efficace il dizionario è importante comprendere la funzione delle differenziazioni tipografiche, dei simboli e delle abbreviazioni usati nel testo. Vi forniamo pertanto qui di seguito alcuni chiarimenti in merito a tali convenzioni.

I lemmi

Sono le parole in **neretto** elencate in ordine alfabetico. Il primo e l'ultimo lemma di ciascuna pagina appaiono al margine superiore.

Dove opportuno, informazioni sull'ambito d'uso o il livello di formalità di certe parole vengono fornite tra parentesi in corsivo e spesso in forma abbreviata dopo l'indicazione della categoria grammaticale (es. (*Comm*), (*inf*)).

In certi casi più parole con radice comune sono raggruppate sotto lo stesso lemma. Tali parole appaiono in neretto ma in un carattere leggermente ridotto (es. **acceptance**).

Esempi d'uso del lemma sono a loro volta in neretto ma in un carattere diverso dal lemma (es. **to be cold**).

La trascrizione fonetica

La trascrizione fonetica che illustra la corretta pronuncia del lemma è tra parentesi quadre e segue immediatamente il lemma (es. **knee** [niː]). L'elenco dei simboli fonetici è alle pagine xii-xiii.

Le traduzioni

Le traduzioni sono in carattere tondo e, quando il lemma ha più di un significato, le traduzioni sono separate da un punto e virgola. Spesso diverse traduzioni di un lemma sono introdotte da una o più parole in corsivo tra parentesi tonde: la loro funzione è di chiarire a quale significato del lemma si riferisce la traduzione. Possono essere sinonimi, indicazioni di ambito d'uso o di registro del lemma (es. **party** *(Pol)*, *(team)*, *(celebration)*; **laid back** *(inf)* ecc.).

Le 'parole chiave'

Un trattamento particolare è stato riservato a quelle parole che, per frequenza d'uso o complessità, necessitano una strutturazione più chiara ed esauriente (es. **da, di, avere** in italiano, **at, to, be, this** in inglese). Frecce e numeri vi guidano attraverso le varie distinzioni grammaticali e di significato; ulteriori informazioni sono fornite in corsivo tra parentesi.

Informazioni grammaticali

Le parti del discorso (noun, adjective ecc.) sono espresse da abbreviazioni convenzionali in corsivo (*n*, *adj* ecc.) e seguono la trascrizione fonetica del lemma.

Eventuali ulteriori informazioni grammaticali, come ad esempio le forme di un verbo irregolare o il plurale irregolare di un sostantivo, precedono tra parentesi la parte del discorso (es. **give** (*pt* **gave**, *pp* **given**) *vt*; **man** [...] (*pl* **men**) *n*).

INTRODUCTION

We are delighted that you have decided to buy this Italian Dictionary and hope you will enjoy and benefit from using it at school, at home, on holiday or at work.

This introduction gives you a few tips on how to get the most out of your dictionary – not simply from its comprehensive wordlist but also from the information provided in each entry. This will help you to read and understand modern Italian, as well as communicate and express yourself in the language.

The dictionary begins by listing the abbreviations used in the text and illustrating the sounds shown by the phonetic symbols. You will also find Italian and English verb tables, followed by a section on numbers and time expressions.

Using your dictionary

A wealth of information is presented in the dictionary, using various typefaces, sizes of type, symbols, abbreviations and brackets. The various conventions and symbols used are explained in the following sections.

Headwords

The words you look up in a dictionary – "headwords" – are listed alphabetically. They are printed in **bold type** for rapid identification. The two headwords appearing at the top of each page indicate the first and last word dealt with on the page in question.

Information about the usage or form of certain headwords is given in brackets after the part of speech. This usually appears in abbreviated form and in italics (e.g. (*fam*), (*Comm*)).

Where appropriate, words related to headwords are grouped in the same entry (e.g. **illustrare, illustrazione**) in a slightly smaller bold type than the headword.

Common expressions in which the headword appears are shown in a different bold roman type (e.g. **aver freddo**).

Phonetic spellings

Where the phonetic spelling of headwords (indicating their pronunciation) is given, it will appear in square brackets immediately after the headword (e.g. **calza** ['kaltsa]). A list of these symbols is given on pages xii-xiii.

Translations

Headword translations are given in ordinary type and, where more than one meaning or usage exists, these are separated by a semi-colon. You will often find other words in italics in brackets before the translations. These offer suggested contexts in which the headword might appear (e.g. **duro** (*pietra*) or (*lavoro*)) or provide synonyms (e.g. **duro** (*ostinato*)).

"Key" words ⭕

Special status is given to certain Italian and English words which are considered as "key" words in each language. They may, for example, occur very frequently or have several types of usage (e.g, **da, di, avere** in Italian, **at, to, be, this** in English). A combination of arrows and numbers helps you to distinguish different parts of speech and different meanings. Further helpful information is provided in brackets and italics.

Grammatical information

Parts of speech are given in abbreviated form in italics after the phonetic spellings of headwords (e.g. *vt, av, cong*).

Genders of Italian nouns are indicated as follows: *sm* for a masculine and *sf* for a feminine noun. Feminine and irregular plural forms of nouns are also shown (e.g. **uovo**, *(pl(f)* **uova**)*;* **dottore**, **essa**).

Feminine adjective endings are given, as are plural forms (e.g. **opaco, a, chi, che**).

ABBREVIAZIONI

abbreviazione	*abbr*	abbreviation
aggettivo	*adj*	adjective
amministrazione	*Admin*	administration
avverbio	*adv*	adverb
aeronautica, viaggi aerei	*Aer*	flying, air travel
aggettivo	*ag*	adjective
agricoltura	*Agr*	agriculture
amministrazione	*Amm*	administration
anatomia	*Anat*	anatomy
architettura	*Archit*	architecture
articolo determinativo	*art def*	definite article
articolo indeterminativo	*art indef*	indefinite article
attributivo	*attrib*	attributive
ausiliare	*aus, aux*	auxiliary
automobile	*Aut*	motor car and motoring
avverbio	*av*	adverb
aeronautica, viaggi aerei	*Aviat*	flying, air travel
biologia	*Biol*	biology
botanica	*Bot*	botany
inglese britannico	*BRIT*	British English
consonante	*C*	consonant
chimica	*Chim, Chem*	chemistry
commercio, finanza	*Comm*	commerce, finance
comparativo	*compar*	comparative
informatica	*Comput*	computing
congiunzione	*cong, conj*	conjunction
edilizia	*Constr*	building
sostantivo usato come aggettivo, ma mai con funzione predicativa	*cpd*	compound element: noun used as adjective and which cannot follow the noun it qualifies
cucina	*Cuc, Culin*	cookery
davanti a	*dav*	before

ABBREVIATIONS

ABBREVIAZIONI		ABBREVIATIONS
articolo determinativo	*def art*	definite article
determinativo; articolo, aggettivo dimostrativo o indefinito ecc	*det*	determiner: article, demonstrative etc
diminutivo	*dimin*	diminutive
diritto	*Dir*	law
economia	*Econ*	economics
edilizia	*Edil*	building
elettricità, elettronica	*Elettr, Elec*	electricity, electronics
esclamazione	*escl, excl*	exclamation
femminile	*f*	feminine
familiare (! da evitare)	*fam(!)*	colloquial usage (! particularly offensive)
ferrovia	*Ferr*	railways
senso figurato	*fig*	figurative use
fisiologia	*Fisiol*	physiology
fotografia	*Fot*	photography
verbo inglese la cui particella è inseparabile dal verbo	*fus*	(phrasal verb) where the particle cannot be separated from the main verb
nella maggior parte dei sensi; generalmente	*gen*	in most or all senses; generally
geografia, geologia	*Geo*	geography, geology
geometria	*Geom*	geometry
storia, storico	*Hist*	history, historical
impersonale	*impers*	impersonal
articolo indeterminativo	*indef art*	indefinite article
familiare (! da evitare)	*inf(!)*	colloquial usage (! particularly offensive)
infinito	*infin*	infinitive
informatica	*Inform*	computing

ABBREVIAZIONI		**ABBREVIATIONS**
insegnamento, sistema scolastico e universitario	*Ins*	schooling, schools and universities
invariabile	*inv*	invariable
irregolare	*irreg*	irregular
grammatica, linguistica	*Ling*	grammar, linguistics
maschile	*m*	masculine
matematica	*Mat(h)*	mathematics
termine medico, medicina	*Med*	medical term, medicine
il tempo, meteorologia	*Meteor*	the weather, meteorology
maschile o femminile	*m/f*	masculine or feminine
esercito, linguaggio militare	*Mil*	military matters
musica	*Mus*	music
sostantivo	*n*	noun
nautica	*Naut*	sailing, navigation
numerale (aggettivo, sostantivo)	*num*	numeral adjective or noun
	o.s.	oneself
peggiorativo	*peg, pej*	derogatory, pejorative
fotografia	*Phot*	photography
fisiologia	*Physiol*	physiology
plurale	*pl*	plural
politica	*Pol*	politics
participio passato	*pp*	past participle
preposizione	*prep*	preposition
pronome	*pron*	pronoun
psicologia, psichiatria	*Psic, Psych*	psychology, psychiatry
tempo passato	*pt*	past tense
qualcosa	*qc*	
qualcuno	*qn*	
religione, liturgia	*Rel*	religions, church service
sostantivo	*s*	noun
	sb	somebody

ABBREVIAZIONI		ABBREVIATIONS
insegnamento, sistema scolastico e universitario	Scol	schooling, schools and universities
singolare	sg	singular
soggetto (grammaticale)	sog	(grammatical) subject
	sth	something
congiuntivo	sub	subjunctive
soggetto (grammaticale)	subj	(grammatical) subject
superlativo	superl	superlative
termine tecnico, tecnologia	Tecn, Tech	technical term, technology
telecomunicazioni	Tel	telecommunications
tipografia	Tip	typography, printing
televisione	TV	television
tipografia	Typ	typography, printing
università	Univ	university
inglese americano	US	American English
vocale	V	vowel
verbo	vb	verb
verbo o gruppo verbale con funzione intransitiva	vi	verb or phrasal verb used intransitively
verbo pronominale o riflessivo	vpr	pronominal or reflexive verb
verbo o gruppo verbale con funzione transitiva	vt	verb or phrasal verb used transitively
zoologia	Zool	zoology
marchio registrato	®	registered trademark
introduce un'equivalenza culturale	≈	introduces a cultural equivalent

TRASCRIZIONE FONETICA

Consonanti

Consonants

NB **p, b, t, d, k, g** sono seguite da un'aspirazione in inglese.

NB **p, b, t, d, k, g** are not aspirated in Italian.

Italiano	IPA	English
padre	p	**p**uppy
bambino	b	**b**aby
tu**tt**o	t	**t**ent
da**d**o	d	**d**a**dd**y
cane **ch**e	k	**c**ork **k**iss **ch**ord
gola **gh**iro	g	**g**a**g** **gu**ess
sano	s	**s**o ri**c**e ki**ss**
svago e**s**ame	z	cou**s**in bu**zz**
scena	∫	**sh**eep **s**ugar
	ʒ	plea**s**ure bei**g**e
pe**ce** lan**ci**are	t∫	**ch**urch
giro **gi**oco	dʒ	**j**udge **g**eneral
a**f**a **f**aro	f	**f**arm ra**ff**le
vero bra**v**o	v	**v**ery re**v**
	θ	**th**in ma**th**s
	ð	**th**at o**th**er
letto a**l**a	l	**l**ittle ba**ll**
g**li**	ʎ	mi**lli**on
rete a**r**co	r	**r**at **r**a**r**e
ramo mad**r**e	m	**m**u**mm**y co**mb**
no fu**n**a**n**te	n	**n**o ra**n**
gnomo	ɲ	ca**ny**on
	ŋ	si**ng**i**ng** ba**n**k
	h	**h**at re**h**eat
bu**i**o p**i**acere	j	**y**et
uomo g**u**aio	w	**w**all be**w**ail
.	x	lo**ch**

Varie

Miscellaneous

per l'inglese: la "r" finale viene pronunciata se seguita da una vocale	ʳ	
precede la sillaba accentata	'	precedes the stressed syllable

PHONETIC TRANSCRIPTION

Vocali		**Vowels**
NB La messa in equivalenza di certi suoni indica solo una rassomiglianza approssimativa.		NB The pairing of some vowel sounds only indicates approximate equivalence.
v**i**no **i**dea	i i:	h**ee**l b**ea**d
	ɪ	h**i**t p**i**ty
st**e**lla **e**dera	e	
epoca ec**ce**tto	ɛ	s**e**t t**e**nt
m**a**mma **a**more	a æ	b**a**t **a**pple
	ɑ:	**a**fter c**a**r c**a**lm
	ã	fi**anc**é
	ʌ	f**u**n c**ou**sin
m**ü**sli	y	
	ə	**o**ver **a**bove
	ə:	**ur**n f**er**n w**or**k
r**o**sa **o**cchio	ɔ	w**a**sh p**o**t
	ɔ:	b**or**n c**or**k
p**o**nte **o**gnuno	o	
f**ö**hn	ø	
utile z**u**cca	u	f**u**ll s**oo**t
	u:	b**oo**n l**ew**d
Dittonghi		**Diphthongs**
	ɪə	b**eer** t**ier**
	ɛə	t**ear** f**air** th**ere**
	eɪ	d**a**te pl**ai**ce d**ay**
	aɪ	l**i**fe b**uy** cr**y**
	au	**ow**l f**ou**l n**ow**
	əu	l**ow** n**o**
	ɔɪ	b**oi**l b**oy** **oi**ly
	uə	p**oor** t**our**

ITALIAN PRONUNCIATION

Vowels

Where the vowel **e** or the vowel **o** appears in a stressed syllable it can be either open [ɛ], [ɔ] or closed [e], [o]. As the open or closed pronunciation of these vowels is subject to regional variation, the distinction is of little importance to the user of this dictionary. Phonetic transcription for headwords containing these vowels will therefore only appear where other pronunciation difficulties are present.

Consonants

c before "e" or "i" is pronounced like the *"tch"* in match.
ch is pronounced like the *"k"* in "kit".
g before "e" or "i" is pronounced like the *"j"* in "jet".
gh is pronounced like the *"g"* in "get".
gl before "e" or "i" is normally pronounced like the *"lli"* in "million", and in a few cases only like the *"gl"* in "glove".
gn is pronounced like the *"ny"* in "canyon"
sc before "e" or "i" is pronounced *"sh"*.
z is pronounced like the *"ts"* in "stetson", or like the *"d's"* in "bird's-eye".

Headwords containing the above consonants and consonantal groups have been given full phonetic transcription in this dictionary.

NB All double written consonants in Italian are fully sounded: e.g. the *tt* in "tutto" is pronounced as in "hat trick".

ITALIAN VERB FORMS

1 Gerundio **2** Participio passato **3** Presente **4** Imperfetto **5** Passato remoto **6** Futuro **7** Condizionale **8** Congiuntivo presente **9** Congiuntivo passato **10** Imperativo

andare 3 vado, vai, va, andiamo, andate, vanno **6** andrò *ecc.* **8** vada **10** va'!, vada!, andate!, vadano!

apparire 2 apparso **3** appaio, appari *o* apparisci, appare *o* apparisce, appaiono *o* appariscono **5** apparvi *o* apparsi, apparisti, apparve *o* apparì *o* apparse, apparvero *o* apparirono *o* apparsero **8** appaia *o* apparisca

aprire 2 aperto **3** apro **5** aprii, apristi **8** apra

AVERE 3 ho, hai, ha, abbiamo, avete, hanno **5** ebbi, avesti, ebbe, avemmo, aveste, ebbero **6** avrò *ecc.* **8** abbia *ecc.* **10** abbi!, abbia!, abbiate!, abbiano!

bere 1 bevendo **2** bevuto **3** bevo *ecc.* **4** bevevo *ecc.* **5** bevvi *o* bevetti, bevesti **6** berrò *ecc.* **8** beva *ecc.* **9** bevessi *ecc.*

cadere 5 caddi, cadesti **6** cadrò *ecc.*

cogliere 2 colto **3** colgo, colgono **5** colsi, cogliesti **8** colga

correre 2 corso **5** corsi, corresti

cuocere 2 cotto **3** cuocio, cociamo, cuociono **5** cossi, cocesti

dare 3 do, dai, dà, diamo, date, danno **5** diedi *o* detti, desti **6** darò *ecc.* **8** dia *ecc.* **9** dessi *ecc.* **10** da'!, dai!, date!, diano!

dire 1 dicendo **2** detto **3** dico, dici, dice, diciamo, dite, dicono **4** dicevo *ecc.* **5** dissi, dicesti **6** dirò *ecc.* **8** dica, diciamo, diciate, dicano **9** dicessi *ecc.* **10** di'!, dica!, dite!, dicano!

dolere 3 dolgo, duoli, duole, dolgono **5** dolsi, dolesti **6** dorrò *ecc.* **8** dolga

dovere 3 devo *o* debbo, devi, deve, dobbiamo, dovete, devono *o* debbono **6** dovrò *ecc.* **8** debba, dobbiamo, dobbiate, devano *o* debbano

ESSERE 2 stato **3** sono, sei, è, siamo, siete, sono **4** ero, eri, era, eravamo, eravate, erano **5** fui, fosti, fu, fummo, foste, furono **6** sarò *ecc.* **8** sia *ecc.* **9** fossi, fossi, fosse, fossimo, foste, fossero **10** sii!, sia!, siate!, siano!

fare 1 facendo **2** fatto **3** faccio, fai, fa, facciamo, fate, fanno **4** facevo *ecc.* **5** feci, facesti **6** farò *ecc.* **8** faccia *ecc.* **9** facessi *ecc.* **10** fa'!, faccia!, fate!, facciano!

FINIRE 1 finendo **2** finito **3** finisco, finisci, finisce, finiamo, finite, finiscono **4** finivo, finivi, finiva, finivamo, finivate, finivano **5** finii, finisti, finì, finimmo, fineste, finirono **6** finirò, finirai, finirà, finiremo, finirete, finiranno **7** finirei, finiresti, finirebbe, finiremmo, finireste, finirebbero **8** finisca, finisca, finisca, finiamo, finiate, finiscano **9** finissi, finissi, finisse, finissimo, finiste, finissero **10** finisci!, finisca!, finite!, finiscano!

giungere 2 giunto **5** giunsi, giungesti

leggere 2 letto **5** lessi, leggesti

mettere 2 messo **5** misi, mettesti

morire 2 morto **3** muoio, muori, muore, moriamo, morite, muoiono **6** morirò *o* morrò *ecc.* **8** muoia

muovere 2 mosso **5** mossi, movesti

nascere 2 nato **5** nacqui, nascesti

nuocere 2 nuociuto **3** nuoccio, nuoci, nuoce, nociamo *o* nuociamo, nuocete, nuocciono **4** nuocevo *ecc.* **5** nocqui, nuocesti **6** nuocerò *ecc.* **7** nuoccia

offrire 2 offerto **3** offro **5** offersi *o* offrii, offristi **8** offra

parere 2 parso **3** paio, paiamo, paiono **5** parvi *o* parsi, paresti **6** parrò *ecc.* **8** paia, paiamo, paiate, paiano

PARLARE 1 parlando **2** parlato **3** parlo, parli, parla, parliamo, parlate, parlano **4** parlavo, parlavi, parlava, parlavamo, parlavate, parlavano **5** parlai, parlasti, parlò, parlammo, parlaste, parlarono **6** parlerò, parlerai, parlerà, parleremo, parlerete, parleranno **7** parlerei, parleresti, parlerebbe, parleremmo, parlereste, parlerebbero **8** parli, parli, parli, parliamo, parliate, parlino **9** parlassi, parlassi, parlasse, parlassimo, parlaste, parlassero **10** parla!, parli!, parlate!, parlino!

piacere 2 piaciuto **3** piaccio, piacciamo, piacciono **5** piacqui, piacesti **8** piacci *ecc.*

porre 1 ponendo **2** posto **3** pongo, poni, pone, poniamo, ponete, pongono **4** ponevo *ecc.* **5** posi, ponesti **6** porrò *ecc.* **8** ponga, poniamo, poniate, pongano **9** ponessi *ecc.*

potere 3 posso, puoi, può, possiamo, potete, possono **6** potrò *ecc.* **8** possa, possiamo, possiate, possano

prendere 2 preso **5** presi, prendesti

ridurre 1 riducendo **2** ridotto **3** riduco *ecc.* **4** riducevo *ecc.* **5** ridussi, riducesti **6** ridurrò *ecc.* **8** riduca *ecc.* **9** riducessi *ecc.*

riempire 1 riempiendo **3** riempio, riempi, riempie, riempiono

rimanere 2 rimasto **3** rimango, rimangono **5** rimasi, rimanesti **6** rimarrò *ecc.* **8** rimanga

rispondere 2 risposto **5** risposi, rispondesti

salire 3 salgo, sali, salgono **8** salga

sapere 3 so, sai, sa, sappiamo, sapete, sanno **5** seppi, sapesti **6** saprò *ecc.* **8** sappia *ecc.* **10** sappi!, sappia!, sappiate!, sappiano!

scrivere 2 scritto **5** scrissi, scrivesti

sedere 3 siedo, siedi, siede, siedono **8** sieda

spegnere 2 spento **3** spengo, spengono **5** spensi, spegnesti **8** spenga

stare 2 stato **3** sto, stai, sta, stiamo, state, stanno **5** stetti, stesti **6** starò *ecc.* **8** stia *ecc.* **9** stessi *ecc.* **10** sta'!, stia!, state!, stiano!

tacere 2 taciuto **3** taccio, tacciono **5** tacqui, tacesti **8** taccia

tenere 3 tengo, tieni, tiene, tengono **5** tenni, tenesti **6** terrò *ecc.* **8** tenga

trarre 1 traendo **2** tratto **3** traggo, trai, trae, traiamo, traete, traggono **4** traevo *ecc.* **5** trassi, traesti **6** trarrò *ecc.* **8** tragga **9** traessi *ecc.*

udire 3 odo, odi, ode, odono **8** oda

uscire 3 esco, esci, esce, escono **8** esca

valere 2 valso **3** valgo, valgono **5** valsi, valesti **6** varrò *ecc.* **8** valga

vedere 2 visto *o* veduto **5** vidi, vedesti **6** vedrò *ecc.*

VENDERE 1 vendendo **2** venduto **3** vendo, vendi, vende, vendiamo, vendete, vendono **4** vendevo, vendevi, vendeva, vendevamo, vendevate, vendevano **5** vendei *o* vendetti, vendesti, vendé *o* vendette, vendemmo, vendeste, venderono *o* vendettero **6** venderò, venderai, venderà, venderemo, venderete, venderanno **7** venderei, venderesti, venderebbe, venderemmo, vendereste, venderebbero **8** venda, venda, venda, vendiamo, vendiate, vendano **9** vendessi, vendessi, vendesse, vendessimo, vendeste, vendessero **10** vendi!, venda!, vendete!, vendano!

venire 2 venuto **3** vengo, vieni, viene, vengono **5** venni, venisti **6** verrò *ecc.* **8** venga

vivere 2 vissuto **5** vissi, vivesti

volere 2 voglio, vuoi, vuole, vogliamo, volete, vogliono **5** volli, volesti **6** vorrò *ecc.* **8** voglia *ecc.* **10** vogli!, voglia!, vogliate!, vogliano!

ENGLISH VERB FORMS

present	pt	pp	present	pt	pp
arise	arose	arisen	feed	fed	fed
awake	awoke	awoken	feel	felt	felt
be (am, is, are; being)	was, were	been	fight	fought	fought
			find	found	found
bear	bore	born(e)	flee	fled	fled
beat	beat	beaten	fling	flung	flung
become	became	become	fly	flew	flown
begin	began	begun	forbid	forbade	forbidden
bend	bent	bent	forecast	forecast	forecast
bet	bet, betted	bet, betted	forget	forgot	forgotten
			forgive	forgave	forgiven
bid (at auction, cards)	bid	bid	forsake	forsook	forsaken
			freeze	froze	frozen
bid (say)	bade	bidden	get	got	got, (US) gotten
bind	bound	bound			
bite	bit	bitten	give	gave	given
bleed	bled	bled	go (goes)	went	gone
blow	blew	blown	grind	ground	ground
break	broke	broken	grow	grew	grown
breed	bred	bred	hang	hung	hung
bring	brought	brought	hang (execute)	hanged	hanged
build	built	built	have (has; having)	had	had
burn	burnt, burned	burnt, burned	hear	heard	heard
burst	burst	burst	hide	hid	hidden
buy	bought	bought	hit	hit	hit
can	could	(been able)	hold	held	held
cast	cast	cast	hurt	hurt	hurt
catch	caught	caught	keep	kept	kept
choose	chose	chosen	kneel	knelt, kneeled	knelt, kneeled
cling	clung	clung			
come	came	come	know	knew	known
cost	cost	cost	lay	laid	laid
cost (work out price of)	costed	costed	lead	led	led
			lean	leant, leaned	leant, leaned
creep	crept	crept			
cut	cut	cut	leap	leapt, leaped	leapt, leaped
deal	dealt	dealt	learn	learnt, learned	learnt, learned
dig	dug	dug			
do (does)	did	done	leave	left	left
draw	drew	drawn	lend	lent	lent
dream	dreamed, dreamt	dreamed, dreamt	let	let	let
			lie (lying)	lay	lain
drink	drank	drunk	light	lit, lighted	lit, lighted
drive	drove	driven			
dwell	dwelt	dwelt	lose	lost	lost
eat	ate	eaten	make	made	made
fall	fell	fallen			

present	pt	pp	present	pt	pp
may	might	—	spell	spelt, spelled	spelt, spelled
mean	meant	meant			
meet	met	met	spend	spent	spent
mistake	mistook	mistaken	spill	spilt, spilled	spilt, spilled
mow	mowed	mown, mowed			
			spin	spun	spun
must	(had to)	(had to)	spit	spat	spat
pay	paid	paid	split	split	split
put	put	put	spoil	spoiled, spoilt	spoiled, spoilt
quit	quit, quitted	quit, quitted			
			spread	spread	spread
read	read	read	spring	sprang	sprung
rid	rid	rid	stand	stood	stood
ride	rode	ridden	steal	stole	stolen
ring	rang	rung	stick	stuck	stuck
rise	rose	risen	sting	stung	stung
run	ran	run	stink	stank	stunk
saw	sawed	sawed, sawn	stride	strode	stridden
			strike	struck	struck, stricken
say	said	said			
see	saw	seen	strive	strove	striven
seek	sought	sought	swear	swore	sworn
sell	sold	sold	sweep	swept	swept
send	sent	sent	swell	swelled	swollen, swelled
set	set	set			
sew	sewed	sewn	swim	swam	swum
shake	shook	shaken	swing	swung	swung
shear	sheared	shorn, sheared	take	took	taken
			teach	taught	taught
shed	shed	shed	tear	tore	torn
shine	shone	shone	tell	told	told
shoot	shot	shot	think	thought	thought
show	showed	shown	throw	threw	thrown
shrink	shrank	shrunk	thrust	thrust	thrust
shut	shut	shut	tread	trod	trodden
sing	sang	sung	wake	woke, waked	woken, waked
sink	sank	sunk			
sit	sat	sat			
slay	slew	slain	wear	wore	worn
sleep	slept	slept	weave	wove, weaved	woven, weaved
slide	slid	slid			
sling	slung	slung			
slit	slit	slit	wed	wedded, wed	wedded, wed
smell	smelt, smelled	smelt, smelled			
			weep	wept	wept
sow	sowed	sown, sowed	win	won	won
			wind	wound	wound
speak	spoke	spoken	wring	wrung	wrung
speed	sped, speeded	sped, speeded	write	wrote	written

I NUMERI		NUMBERS
uno(a)	1	one
due	2	two
tre	3	three
quattro	4	four
cinque	5	five
sei	6	six
sette	7	seven
otto	8	eight
nove	9	nine
dieci	10	ten
undici	11	eleven
dodici	12	twelve
tredici	13	thirteen
quattordici	14	fourteen
quindici	15	fifteen
sedici	16	sixteen
diciassette	17	seventeen
diciotto	18	eighteen
diciannove	19	nineteen
venti	20	twenty
ventuno	21	twenty-one
ventidue	22	twenty-two
ventitré	23	twenty-three
ventotto	28	twenty-eight
trenta	30	thirty
quaranta	40	forty
cinquanta	50	fifty
sessanta	60	sixty
settanta	70	seventy
ottanta	80	eighty
novanta	90	ninety
cento	100	a hundred
cento uno	101	a hundred and one
duecento	200	two hundred
mille	1 000	a thousand
milleduecentodue	1 202	one thousand two hundred and two
cinquemila	5000	five thousand
un milione	1 000 000	a million

I NUMERI

NUMBERS

primo(a)	first, 1st
secondo(a)	second, 2nd
terzo(a)	third, 3rd
quarto(a)	fourth, 4th
quinto(a)	fifth, 5th
sesto(a)	sixth, 6th
settimo(a)	seventh
ottavo(a)	eighth
nono(a)	ninth
decimo(a)	tenth
undicesimo(a)	eleventh
dodicesimo(a)	twelfth
tredicesimo(a)	thirteenth
quattordicesimo(a)	fourteenth
quindicesimo(a)	fifteenth
sedicesimo(a)	sixteenth
diciassettesimo(a)	seventeenth
diciottesimo(a)	eighteenth
diciannovesimo(a)	nineteenth
ventesimo(a)	twentieth
ventunesimo(a)	twenty-first
ventiduesimo(a)	twenty-second
ventitreesimo(a)	twenty-third
ventottesimo(a)	twenty-eighth
trentesimo(a)	thirtieth
centesimo(a)	hundredth
centunesimo(a)	hundred-and-first
millesimo(a)	thousandth
milionesimo(a)	millionth

Frazioni

mezzo
terzo
due terzi
quarto
quinto
zero virgola cinque, 0,5
tre virgola quattro, 3,4
dieci per cento
cento per cento

Esempi

abita al numero dieci
si trova nel capitolo sette,
  a pagina sette
abita al terzo piano
arrivò quarto
scala uno a venticinquemila

Fractions

half
third
two thirds
quarter
fifth
(nought) point five, 0.5
three point four, 3.4
ten per cent
a hundred per cent

Examples

he lives at number 10
it's in chapter 7, on page 7

he lives on the 3rd floor
he came in 4th
scale 1:25,000

L'ORA	**THE TIME**
che ora è?, che ore sono?	*what time is it?*
è …, sono …	*it's …*
mezzanotte	midnight
l'una (di notte)	one o'clock (in the morning), one (a.m.)
le tre del mattino	three o'clock (in the morning), three (a.m.)
l'una e cinque	five past one
l'una e dieci	ten past one
l'una e un quarto, l'una e quindici	a quarter past one, one fifteen
l'una e venticinque	twenty-five past one, one twenty-five
l'una e mezzo *or* mezza, l'una e trenta	half past one, one thirty
le due meno venticinque, l'una e trentacinque	twenty-five to two, one thirty-five
le due meno venti, l'una e quaranta	twenty to two, one forty
le due meno un quarto, l'una e tre quarti	a quarter to two, one forty-five
le due meno dieci, l'una e cinquanta	ten to two, one fifty
le dodici, mezzogiorno	twelve o'clock, midday, noon
l'una, le tredici	one o'clock (in the afternoon), one (p.m.)
le sette (di sera), le diciannove	seven o'clock (in the evening), seven (p.m.)
a che ora?	*at what time?*
a mezzanotte	at midnight
all'una, alle tredici	at one o'clock
fra venti minuti	in twenty minutes
venti minuti fa	twenty minutes ago

LA DATA

DATES

oggi	today
ogni giorno, tutti i giorni	every day
ieri	yesterday
stamattina	this morning
domani notte; domani sera	tomorrow night
l'altroieri notte; l'altroieri sera	the night before last
l'altroieri	the day before yesterday
ieri notte; ieri sera	last night
due giorni/sei anni fa	two days/six years ago
domani pomeriggio	tomorrow afternoon
dopodomani	the day after tomorrow
tutti i giovedì, di *or* il giovedì	every Thursday, on Thursdays
ci va di *or* il venerdì	he goes on Fridays
"chiuso il mercoledì"	"closed on Wednesdays"
dal lunedì al venerdì	from Monday to Friday
per giovedì, entro giovedì	by Thursday
un sabato di marzo	one Saturday in March
tra una settimana	in a week's time
martedì a otto	a week next *or* on Tuesday
questa/la prossima/la scorsa settimana	this/next/last week
tra due settimane, tra quindici giorni	in two weeks *or* a fortnight
lunedì a quindici	two weeks on Monday
il primo/l'ultimo venerdì del mese	the first/last Friday of the month
il mese prossimo	next month
l'anno scorso	last year
il primo giugno	the 1st of June, June first
il due ottobre	the 2nd of October *or* October 2nd
sono nato nel 1987	I was born in 1987
il suo compleano è il 5 giugno	his birthday is on June 5th (*BRIT*) *or* 5th June (*US*)
il 18 agosto	on 18th August (*BRIT*) *or* August 18 (*US*)
nel '96	in '96
nella primavera del '94	in the Spring of '94
dal 19 al 3	from the 19th to the 3rd
quanti ne abbiamo oggi?	what's the date? *or* what date is it today?

oggi è il 15	today's date is the 15th or today is the 15th
1988 - millenovecentottantotto	1988 - nineteen eighty-eight
2005 - duemilacinque	2005 - two thousand and five
10 anni esatti	10 years to the day
alla fine del mese	at the end of the month
la settimana del 30/7	week ending 30/7
giornalmente or al giorno	daily
settimanalmente or alla settimana	weekly
mensilmente, al mese	monthly
annualmente or all'anno	annually
due volte alla settimana/al mese/ all'anno	twice a week/month/year
bimestralmente	bi-monthly
nel 4 a.C.	in 4 B.C. or B.C. 4
nel 79 d.C.	in 79 A.D or A.D. 79
nel tredicesimo secolo	in the 13th century
negli anni '80	in or during the 80s
nel 1990 e rotti	in 1990 something

La data nelle lettere
9 ottobre 2004

Headings of letters
9th October 2004 or 9 October 2004

a

A *abbr (= autostrada)* ≈ M *(motorway)*

a *(a + il = al, a + lo = allo, a + l' = all', a + la = alla, a + i = ai, a + gli = agli, a + le = alle) prep*

1 *(stato in luogo)* at; *(: in)* in; **essere alla stazione** to be at the station; **essere a casa/a scuola/a Roma** to be at home/at school/in Rome; **è a 10 km da qui** it's 10 km from here, it's 10 km away

2 *(moto a luogo)* to; **andare a casa/a scuola** to go home/to school

3 *(tempo)* at; *(epoca, stagione)* in; **alle cinque** at five (o'clock); **a mezzanotte/Natale** at midnight/Christmas; **al mattino** in the morning; **a maggio/primavera** in May/spring; **a cinquant'anni** at fifty (years of age); **a domani!** see you tomorrow!

4 *(complemento di termine)* to; **dare qc a qn** to give sth to sb

5 *(mezzo, modo)* with, by; **a piedi/cavallo** on foot/horseback; **fatto a mano** made by hand, handmade; **una barca a motore** a motorboat; **a uno a uno** one by one; **all'italiana** the Italian way, in the Italian fashion

6 *(rapporto)* a, per; *(: con prezzi)* at; **prendo 850 euro al mese** I get 850 euros *o* per month; **pagato a ore** paid by the hour; **vendere qc a 2 euro il chilo** to sell sth at 2 euros *o* per kilo

abbagli'ante [abbaʎ'ʎante] *ag* dazzling; **abbaglianti** *smpl (Aut)*:

accendere gli abbaglianti to put one's headlights on full *(BRIT) o* high *(US)* beam

abbagli'are [abbaʎ'ʎare] *vt* to dazzle; *(illudere)* to delude

abbai'are *vi* to bark

abbando'nare *vt* to leave, abandon, desert; *(trascurare)* to neglect; *(rinunciare a)* to abandon, give up; **abbandonarsi** *vpr* to let o.s. go; **abbandonarsi a** *(ricordi, vizio)* to give o.s. up to

abbas'sare *vt* to lower; *(radio)* to turn down; **abbassarsi** *vpr (chinarsi)* to stoop; *(livello, sole)* to go down; *(fig: umiliarsi)* to demean o.s.; **~ i fari** *(Aut)* to dip *o* dim *(US)* one's lights

ab'basso *escl* **~ il re!** down with the king!

abbas'tanza [abbas'tantsa] *av (a sufficienza)* enough; *(alquanto)* quite, rather, fairly; **non è ~ furbo** he's not shrewd enough; **un vino ~ dolce** quite a sweet wine; **averne ~ di qn/qc** to have had enough of sb/sth

ab'battere *vt (muro, casa)* to pull down; *(ostacolo)* to knock down; *(albero)* to fell; *(: vento)* to bring down; *(bestie da macello)* to slaughter; *(cane, cavallo)* to destroy, put down; *(selvaggina, aereo)* to shoot down; *(fig: malattia, disgrazia)* to lay low; **abbattersi** *vpr (avvilirsi)* to lose heart; **abbat'tuto, -a** *ag (fig)* depressed

abba'zia [abbat'tsia] *sf* abbey

'abbia *vb vedi* **avere**

abbi'ente *ag* well-to-do, well-off; **abbienti** *smpl* **gli abbienti** the well-to-do

abbiglia'mento [abbiʎʎa'mento] *sm* dress *no pl; (indumenti)* clothes *pl; (industria)* clothing industry

abbi'nare *vt* **~ (a)** to combine (with)

abboc'care *vi (pesce)* to bite; *(tubi)* to join; **~ (all'amo)** *(fig)* to swallow the bait

abbona'mento *sm* subscription; (*alle ferrovie ecc*) season ticket; **fare l'~** to take out a subscription (*o season ticket*)

abbo'narsi *vpr* **~ a un giornale** to take out a subscription to a newspaper; **~ al teatro/alle ferrovie** to take out a season ticket for the theatre/the train

abbon'dante *ag* abundant, plentiful; (*giacca*) roomy

abbon'danza [abbon'dantsa] *sf* abundance; plenty

abbor'dabile *ag* (*persona*) approachable; (*prezzo*) reasonable

abbotto'nare *vt* to button up, do up

abbracci'are [abbrat't∫are] *vt* to embrace; (*persona*) to hug, embrace; (*professione*) to take up; (*contenere*) to include; **abbracciarsi** *vpr* to embrace (one another); **ab'braccio** *sm* hug, embrace

abbrevi'are *vt* to shorten; (*parola*) to abbreviate

abbreviazi'one [abbrevjat'tsjone] *sf* abbreviation

abbron'zante [abbron'dzante] *ag* tanning, sun *cpd*

abbronzarsi *vpr* to tan, get a tan

abbron'zato, -a [abbron'dzato] *ag* (sun)tanned

abbrusto'lire *vt* (*pane*) to toast; (*caffè*) to roast; **abbrustolirsi** *vpr* to toast; (*fig: al sole*) to soak up the sun

abbuf'farsi *vpr* (*fam*): **~ di qc** to stuff o.s. (with sth)

abdi'care *vi* to abdicate; **~ a** to give up, renounce

a'bete *sm* fir (tree); **abete rosso** spruce

'abile *ag* (*idoneo*): **~ (a qc/a fare qc)** fit (for sth/to do sth); (*capace*) able; (*astuto*) clever; (*accorto*) skilful; **~ al servizio militare** fit for military service; **abilità** *sf inv* ability; cleverness; skill

a'bisso *sm* abyss, gulf

abi'tante *sm/f* inhabitant

abi'tare *vt* to live in, dwell in ▸ *vi* **~ in campagna/a Roma** to live in the country/in Rome; **dove abita?** where do you live?; **abitazi'one** *sf* residence; house

'abito *sm* dress *no pl*; (*da uomo*) suit; (*da donna*) dress; (*abitudine, disposizione, Rel*) habit; **abiti** *smpl* (*vestiti*) clothes; **in ~ da sera** in evening dress

abitu'ale *ag* usual, habitual; (*cliente*) regular

abitual'mente *av* usually, normally

abitu'are *vt* **~ qn a** to get sb used *o* accustomed to; **abituarsi a** to get used to, accustom o.s. to

abitudi'nario, -a *ag* of fixed habits ▸ *sm/f* regular customer

abi'tudine *sf* habit; **aver l'~ di fare qc** to be in the habit of doing sth; **d'~** usually; **per ~** from *o* out of habit

abo'lire *vt* to abolish; (*Dir*) to repeal

abor'tire *vi* (*Med*) to miscarry, have a miscarriage; (: *deliberatamente*) to have an abortion; (*fig*) to miscarry, fail; **a'borto** *sm* miscarriage; abortion

ABS [abiɛse] *sigla m* (= *Anti-Blockier System*) ABS

'abside *sf* apse

abu'sare *vi* **~ di** to abuse, misuse; (*alcool*) to take to excess; (*approfittare, violare*) to take advantage of

abu'sivo, -a *ag* unauthorized, unlawful; **(occupante) ~** (*di una casa*) squatter

▌ Attenzione! In inglese esiste la parola *abusive* che però vuol dire *ingiurioso*.

a.C. *av abbr* (= *avanti Cristo*) B.C.

a'cacia, -cie [a'kat∫a] *sf* (*Bot*) acacia

ac'cadde *vb vedi* **accadere**

acca'demia *sf* (*società*) learned society; (*scuola: d'arte, militare*) academy

acca'dere *vb impers* to happen, occur

accal'dato *ag* hot

accalo'rarsi *vpr* (*fig*) to get excited

accampa'mento *sm* camp

accamparsi *vpr* to camp

acca'nirsi *vpr* (*infierire*) to rage; (*ostinarsi*) to persist; **acca'nito, -a** *ag* (*odio, gelosia*) fierce, bitter; (*lavoratore*) assiduous, dogged; (*fumatore*) inveterate

ac'canto *av* near, nearby; **~ a** *prep* near, beside, close to

accanto'nare *vt* (*problema*) to shelve; (*somma*) to set aside

accappa'toio *sm* bathrobe

accarez'zare [akkaret'tsare] *vt* to caress, stroke, fondle; (*fig*) to toy with

acca'sarsi *vpr* to set up house; to get married

accasci'arsi [akkaʃʃarsi] *vpr* to collapse; (*fig*) to lose heart

accat'tone, -a *sm/f* beggar

accaval'lare *vt* (*gambe*) to cross

acce'care [attʃe'kare] *vt* to blind ▶ *vi* to go blind

ac'cedere [at'tʃedere] *vi* **~ a** to enter; (*richiesta*) to grant, accede to

accele'rare [attʃele'rare] *vt* to speed up ▶ *vi* (*Aut*) to accelerate; **~ il passo** to quicken one's pace; **accelera'tore** *sm* (*Aut*) accelerator

ac'cendere [at'tʃɛndere] *vt* (*fuoco, sigaretta*) to light; (*luce, televisione*) to put on, switch on, turn on; (*Aut: motore*) to switch on; (*Comm: conto*) to open; (*fig: suscitare*) to inflame, stir up; **ha da ~?** have you got a light?; **non riesco ad ~ il riscaldamento** I can't turn the heating on; **accen'dino, accendi'sigaro** *sm* (*cigarette*) lighter

accen'nare [attʃen'nare] *vt* (*Mus*) to pick out the notes of; to hum ▶ *vi* **~ a**

(*fig: alludere a*) to hint at; (*: far atto di*) to make as if; **~ un saluto** (*con la mano*) to make as if to wave; (*col capo*) to half nod; **accenna a piovere** it looks as if it's going to rain

ac'cenno [at'tʃenno] *sm* (*cenno*) sign; nod; (*allusione*) hint

accensi'one [attʃen'sjone] *sf* (*vedi verbo*) lighting; switching on; opening; (*Aut*) ignition

ac'cento [at'tʃɛnto] *sm* accent; (*Fonetica, fig*) stress; (*inflessione*) tone (of voice)

accentu'are [attʃentu'are] *vt* to stress, emphasize; **accentuarsi** *vpr* to become more noticeable

accerchi'are [attʃer'kjare] *vt* to surround, encircle

accerta'mento [attʃerta'mento] *sm* check; assessment

accer'tare [attʃer'tare] *vt* to ascertain; (*verificare*) to check; (*reddito*) to assess; **accertarsi** *vpr* **accertarsi (di)** to make sure (of)

ac'ceso, -a [at'tʃeso] *pp di* **accendere** ▶ *ag* lit; on; open; (*colore*) bright

acces'sibile [attʃes'sibile] *ag* (*luogo*) accessible; (*persona*) approachable; (*prezzo*) reasonable

ac'cesso [at'tʃɛsso] *sm* (*anche Inform*) access; (*Med*) attack, fit; (*impulso violento*) fit, outburst

accessori *smpl* accessories

ac'cetta [at'tʃetta] *sf* hatchet

accet'tabile [attʃet'tabile] *ag* acceptable

accet'tare [attʃet'tare] *vt* to accept; **accettate carte di credito?** do you accept credit cards?; **~ di fare qc** to agree to do sth; **accettazi'one** *sf* acceptance; (*locale di servizio pubblico*) reception; **accettazione bagagli** (*Aer*) check-in (desk)

acchiap'pare [akkjap'pare] *vt* to catch

acciaie'ria [attʃaje'ria] *sf* steelworks *sg*

acci'aio [at'tʃajo] *sm* steel

acciden'tato, -a [attʃiden'tato] *ag* (*terreno ecc*) uneven

accigli'ato, -a [attʃiʎ'ʎato] *ag* frowning

ac'cingersi [at'tʃindʒersi] *vpr* **~ a fare qc** to be about to do sth

acciuf'fare [attʃuf'fare] *vt* to seize, catch

acci'uga, -ghe [at'tʃuga] *sf* anchovy

ac'cludere *vt* to enclose

accocco'larsi *vpr* to crouch

accogli'ente [akkoʎ'ʎɛnte] *ag* welcoming, friendly

ac'cogliere [ak'koʎʎere] *vt* (*ricevere*) to receive; (*dare il benvenuto*) to welcome; (*approvare*) to agree to, accept; (*contenere*) to hold, accommodate

ac'colgo *ecc vb vedi* **accogliere**

ac'colsi *ecc vb vedi* **accogliere**

accoltel'lare *vt* to knife, stab

accomoda'mento *sm* agreement, settlement

accomo'dante *ag* accommodating

accomodarsi *vpr* (*sedersi*) to sit down; (*entrare*) to come in; **s'accomodi!** (*venga avanti*) come in!; (*si sieda*) take a seat!

accompagna'mento [akkompaɲɲa'mento] *sm* (*Mus*) accompaniment

accompa'gnare [akkompaɲ'ɲare] *vt* to accompany, come *o* go with; (*Mus*) to accompany; (*unire*) to couple; **~ la porta** to close the door gently

accompagna'tore, -trice *sm/f* companion; **~ turistico** courier

acconcia'tura [akkontʃa'tura] *sf* hairstyle

accondiscen'dente [akkondiʃʃen'dɛnte] *ag* affable

acconsen'tire *vi* **~ (a)** to agree *o* consent (to)

acconten'tare *vt* to satisfy; **accontentarsi** *vpr* **accontentarsi di** to be satisfied with, content o.s. with

ac'conto *sm* part payment; **pagare una somma in ~** to pay a sum of money as a deposit

acco'rato, -a *ag* heartfelt

accorci'are [akkor'tʃare] *vt* to shorten; **accorciarsi** *vpr* to become shorter

accor'dare *vt* to reconcile; (*colori*) to match; (*Mus*) to tune; (*Ling*): **~ qc con qc** to make sth agree with sth; (*Dir*) to grant; **accordarsi** *vpr* to agree, come to an agreement; (*colori*) to match

ac'cordo *sm* agreement; (*armonia*) harmony; (*Mus*) chord; **essere d'~** to agree; **andare d'~** to get on well together; **d'~!** all right!, agreed!; **accordo commerciale** trade agreement

ac'corgersi [ak'kordʒersi] *vpr* **~ di** to notice; (*fig*) to realize

ac'correre *vi* to run up

ac'corto, -a *pp di* **accorgersi** ▸ *ag* shrewd; **stare ~** to be on one's guard

accos'tare *vt* (*avvicinare*): **~ qc a** to bring sth near to, put sth near to; (*avvicinarsi a*) to approach; (*socchiudere: imposte*) to half-close; (*: porta*) to leave ajar ▸ *vi* (*Naut*) to come alongside; **accostarsi** *vpr* **accostarsi a** to draw near, approach; (*fig*) to support

accredi'tare *vt* (*notizia*) to confirm the truth of; (*Comm*) to credit; (*diplomatico*) to accredit

ac'credito *sm* (*Comm: atto*) crediting; (*: effetto*) credit

accucci'arsi [akkut'tʃarsi] *vpr* (*cane*) to lie down

accu'dire *vt* (*anche: vi* **~ a**) to attend to

accumu'lare *vt* to accumulate; **accumularsi** *vpr* to accumulate; (*Finanza*) to accrue

accu'rato, -a *ag* (*diligente*) careful; (*preciso*) accurate

ac'cusa *sf* accusation; (*Dir*) charge; **la pubblica ~** the prosecution

accu'sare *vt* **~ qn di qc** to accuse sb of sth; (*Dir*) to charge sb with sth; **~ ricevuta di** (*Comm*) to acknowledge receipt of

accusa'tore, -'trice *sm/f* accuser ▶ *sm* (*Dir*) prosecutor

a'cerbo, -a [a'tʃerbo] *ag* bitter; (*frutta*) sour, unripe; (*persona*) immature

'acero ['atʃero] *sm* maple

a'cerrimo, -a [a'tʃerrimo] *ag* very fierce

a'ceto [a'tʃeto] *sm* vinegar

ace'tone [atʃe'tone] *sm* nail varnish remover

A.C.I. ['atʃi] *sigla m* = **Automobile Club d'Italia**

'acido, -a ['atʃido] *ag* (*sapore*) acid, sour; (*Chim*) acid ▶ *sm* (*Chim*) acid

'acino ['atʃino] *sm* berry; **acino d'uva** grape

'acne *sf* acne

'acqua *sf* water; (*pioggia*) rain; **acque** *sfpl* (*di mare, fiume ecc*) waters; **fare ~** (*Naut*) to leak, take in water; **~ in bocca!** mum's the word!; **acqua corrente** running water; **acqua dolce/salata** fresh/salt water; **acqua minerale/potabile/tonica** mineral/drinking/tonic water; **acque termali** thermal waters

a'cquaio *sm* sink

acqua'ragia [akkwa'radʒa] *sf* turpentine

a'cquario *sm* aquarium; (*dello zodiaco*): **A~** Aquarius

acquascooter [akkwas'kuter] *sm inv* Jet Ski®

ac'quatico, -a, -ci, -che *ag* aquatic; (*Sport, Scienza*) water *cpd*

acqua'vite *sf* brandy

acquaz'zone [akkwat'tsone] *sm* cloudburst, heavy shower

acque'dotto *sm* aqueduct; **waterworks** *pl*, water system

acque'rello *sm* watercolour

acqui'rente *sm/f* purchaser, buyer

acquis'tare *vt* to purchase, buy; (*fig*) to gain; **a'cquisto** *sm* purchase; **fare acquisti** to go shopping

acquo'lina *sf* **far venire l'~ in bocca a qn** to make sb's mouth water

a'crobata, -i, -e *sm/f* acrobat

a'culeo *sm* (*Zool*) sting; (*Bot*) prickle

a'cume *sm* acumen, perspicacity

a'custico, -a, ci, che *ag* acoustic ▶ *sf* (*scienza*) acoustics *sg*; (*di una sala*) acoustics *pl*; **cornetto ~** ear trumpet; **apparecchio ~** hearing aid

a'cuto, -a *ag* (*appuntito*) sharp, pointed; (*suono, voce*) shrill, piercing; (*Mat, Ling, Med*) acute; (*Mus*) high-pitched; (*fig: dolore, desiderio*) intense; (: *perspicace*) acute, keen

a'dagio [a'dadʒo] *av* slowly ▶ *sm* (*Mus*) adagio; (*proverbio*) adage, saying

adatta'mento *sm* adaptation

adat'tare *vt* to adapt; (*sistemare*) to fit; **adattarsi** *vpr* **adattarsi (a)** (*ambiente, tempi*) to adapt (to); (*essere adatto*) to be suitable (for)

a'datto, -a *ag* **~ (a)** suitable (for), right (for)

addebi'tare *vt* **~ qc a qn** to debit sb with sth

ad'debito *sm* (*Comm*) debit

adden'tare *vt* to bite into

adden'trarsi *vpr* **~ in** to penetrate, go into

addestra'mento *sm* training

addes'trare *vt* to train

ad'detto, -a *ag* **~ a** (*persona*) assigned to; (*oggetto*) intended for ▶ *sm* employee; (*funzionario*) attaché; **gli addetti ai lavori** authorized personnel; (*fig*) those in the know; **addetto commerciale** commercial attaché; **addetto stampa** press attaché

ad'dio *sm, escl* goodbye, farewell

addirit'tura *av* (*veramente*) really, absolutely; (*perfino*) even; (*direttamente*) directly, right away

addi'tare *vt* to point out; (*fig*) to expose

addi'tivo *sm* additive

addizi'one *sf* addition

addob'bare *vt* to decorate; **ad'dobbo** *sm* decoration

addolo'rare *vt* to pain, grieve; **addolorarsi (per)** to be distressed (by)

addolo'rato, -a *ag* distressed, upset; **l'Addolorata** (*Rel*) Our Lady of Sorrows

ad'dome *sm* abdomen

addomesti'care *vt* to tame

addomi'nale *ag* abdominal; **(muscoli** *mpl*) **addominali** stomach muscles

addormen'tare *vt* to put to sleep; **addormentarsi** *vpr* to fall asleep

ad'dosso *av* on; **mettersi ~ il cappotto** to put one's coat on; **~ a** (*sopra*) on; (*molto vicino*) right next to; **stare ~ a qn** (*fig*) to breathe down sb's neck; **dare ~ a qn** (*fig*) to attack sb

adeguarsi *vpr* to adapt

adegu'ato, -a *ag* adequate; (*conveniente*) suitable; (*equo*) fair

a'dempiere *vt* to fulfil, carry out

ade'rente *ag* adhesive; (*vestito*) close-fitting ▶ *sm/f* follower

ade'rire *vi* (*stare attaccato*) to adhere, stick; **~ a** to adhere to, stick to; (*fig: società, partito*) to join; (*: opinione*) to support; (*richiesta*) to agree to

adesi'one *sf* adhesion; (*fig*) agreement, acceptance; **ade'sivo, -a** *ag, sm* adhesive

a'desso *av* (*ora*) now; (*or ora, poco fa*) just now; (*tra poco*) any moment now

adia'cente [adja'tʃɛnte] *ag* adjacent

adi'bire *vt* (*usare*): **~ qc a** to turn sth into

adole'scente [adoleʃ'ʃɛnte] *ag, sm/f* adolescent

adope'rare *vt* to use

ado'rare *vt* to adore; (*Rel*) to worship

adot'tare *vt* to adopt; (*decisione, provvedimenti*) to pass; **adot'tivo, -a** *ag* (*genitori*) adoptive; (*figlio, patria*) adopted; **adozi'one** *sf* adoption; **adozione a distanza** child sponsorship

adri'atico, -a, -ci, -che *ag* Adriatic ▶ *sm* **l'A~**, **il mare A~** the Adriatic, the Adriatic Sea

ADSL *sigla m* ADSL (*asymmetric digital subscriber line*)

adu'lare *vt* to adulate, flatter

a'dultero, -a *ag* adulterous ▶ *sm/f* adulterer (adulteress)

a'dulto, -a *ag* adult; (*fig*) mature ▶ *sm* adult, grown-up

a'ereo, -a *ag* air *cpd*; (*radice*) aerial ▶ *sm* aerial; (*aeroplano*) plane; **aereo da caccia** fighter (plane); **aereo di linea** airliner; **aereo a reazione** jet (plane); **ae'robica** *sf* aerobics *sg*; **aero'nautica** *sf* (*scienza*) aeronautics *sg*; **aeronautica militare** air force

aero'porto *sm* airport; **all'~ per favore** to the airport, please

aero'sol *sm inv* aerosol

'afa *sf* sultriness

af'fabile *ag* affable

affaccen'dato, -a [affattʃen'dato] *ag* (*persona*) busy

affacci'arsi [affat'tʃarsi] *vpr* **~ (a)** to appear (at)

affa'mato, -a *ag* starving; (*fig*): **~ (di)** eager (for)

affan'noso, -a *ag* (*respiro*) difficult; (*fig*) troubled, anxious

af'fare *sm* (*faccenda*) matter, affair; (*Comm*) piece of business, (business) deal; (*occasione*) bargain; (*Dir*) case;

(*fam: cosa*) thing; **affari** *smpl* (*Comm*) business *sg*; **Ministro degli Affari esteri** Foreign Secretary (*BRIT*), Secretary of State (*US*)

affasci'nante [affaʃʃi'nante] *ag* fascinating

affasci'nare [affaʃʃi'nare] *vt* to bewitch; (*fig*) to charm, fascinate

affati'care *vt* to tire; **affaticarsi** *vpr* (*durar fatica*) to tire o.s. out; **affati'cato, -a** *ag* tired

af'fatto *av* completely; **non ... ~** not ... at all; **niente ~** not at all

affer'mare *vt* (*dichiarare*) to maintain, affirm; **affermarsi** *vpr* to assert o.s., make one's name known; **affer'mato, -a** *ag* established, well-known; **affermazi'one** *sf* affirmation, assertion; (*successo*) achievement

affer'rare *vt* to seize, grasp; (*fig: idea*) to grasp; **afferrarsi** *vpr* **afferrarsi a** to cling to

affet'tare *vt* (*tagliare a fette*) to slice; (*ostentare*) to affect

affetta'trice [affetta'tritʃe] *sf* meat slicer

affet'tivo, -a *ag* emotional, affective

af'fetto *sm* affection; **affettu'oso, -a** *ag* affectionate

affezio'narsi [affettsjo'narsi] *vpr* **~ a** to grow fond of

affezio'nato, -a [affettsjo'nato] *ag* **~ a qn/qc** fond of sb/sth; (*attaccato*) attached to sb/sth

affia'tato, -a *ag* **essere molto affiatati** to get on very well

affibbi'are *vt* (*fig: dare*) to give

affi'dabile *ag* reliable

affida'mento *sm* (*Dir: di bambino*) custody; (*fiducia*): **fare ~ su qn** to rely on sb; **non dà nessun ~** he's not to be trusted

affi'dare *vt* **~ qc o qn a qn** to entrust sth *o* sb to sb; **affidarsi** *vpr* **affidarsi a** to place one's trust in

affi'lare *vt* to sharpen

affi'lato, -a *ag* (*gen*) sharp; (*volto, naso*) thin

affinché [affin'ke] *cong* in order that, so that

affit'tare *vt* (*dare in affitto*) to let, rent (out); (*prendere in affitto*) to rent; **af'fitto** *sm* rent; (*contratto*) lease

af'fliggere [af'fliddʒere] *vt* to torment; **affliggersi** *vpr* to grieve

af'flissi *ecc vb vedi* **affliggere**

afflosci'arsi [afffloʃ'ʃarsi] *vpr* to go limp

afflu'ente *sm* tributary

affo'gare *vt, vi* to drown

affol'lare *vt* to crowd; **affollarsi** *vpr* to crowd; **affol'lato, -a** *ag* crowded

affon'dare *vt* to sink

affran'care *vt* to free, liberate; (*Amm*) to redeem; (*lettera*) to stamp; (*: meccanicamente*) to frank (*BRIT*), meter (*US*)

af'fresco, -schi *sm* fresco

affrettarsi *vpr* to hurry; **~ a fare qc** to hurry *o* hasten to do sth

affret'tato, -a *ag* (*veloce: passo, ritmo*) quick, fast; (*frettoloso: decisione*) hurried, hasty; (*: lavoro*) rushed

affron'tare *vt* (*pericolo ecc*) to face; (*nemico*) to confront; **affrontarsi** *vpr* (*reciproco*) to come to blows

affumi'cato, -a *ag* (*prosciutto, aringa ecc*) smoked

affuso'lato, -a *ag* tapering

Af'ganistan *sm* **l'~** Afghanistan

a'foso, -a *ag* sultry, close

'Africa *sf* **l'~** Africa; **afri'cano, -a** *ag, sm/f* African

a'genda [a'dʒɛnda] *sf* diary

  Attenzione! In inglese esiste la parola *agenda* che però vuol dire *ordine del giorno*.

a'gente [a'dʒɛnte] *sm* agent; **agente di cambio** stockbroker; **agente**

di polizia police officer; **agente segreto** secret agent; **agen'zia** sf agency; (*succursale*) branch; **agenzia immobiliare** estate agent's (office) (*BRIT*), real estate office (*US*); **agenzia di collocamento/stampa** employment/press agency; **agenzia viaggi** travel agency

agevo'lare [adʒevo'lare] vt to facilitate, make easy

agevolazi'one [adʒevolat'tsjone] sf (*facilitazione economica*) facility; **agevolazione di pagamento** payment on easy terms; **agevolazioni creditizie** credit facilities; **agevolazioni fiscali** tax concessions

a'gevole [a'dʒevole] ag easy; (*strada*) smooth

agganci'are [aggan'tʃare] vt to hook up; (*Ferr*) to couple

ag'geggio [ad'dʒeddʒo] sm gadget, contraption

agget'tivo [addʒet'tivo] sm adjective

agghiacci'ante [aggjat'tʃante] ag chilling

aggior'nare [addʒor'nare] vt (*opera, manuale*) to bring up-to-date; (*seduta ecc*) to postpone; **aggiornarsi** vpr to bring (*o keep*) o.s. up-to-date; **aggior'nato, -a** ag up-to-date

aggi'rare [addʒi'rare] vt to go round; (*fig: ingannare*) to trick; **aggirarsi** vpr to wander about; **il prezzo s'aggira sul milione** the price is around the million mark

aggi'ungere [ad'dʒundʒere] vt to add

aggi'unsi ecc [ad'dʒunsi] vb vedi **aggiungere**

aggius'tare [addʒus'tare] vt (*accomodare*) to mend, repair; (*riassettare*) to adjust; (*fig: lite*) to settle

aggrap'parsi vpr **~ a** to cling to

aggra'vare vt (*aumentare*) to increase; (*appesantire: anche fig*) to weigh down, make heavy; (*pena*) to make worse; **aggravarsi** vpr to worsen, become worse

aggre'dire vt to attack, assault

aggressi'one sf aggression; (*atto*) attack, assault

aggres'sivo, -a ag aggressive

aggres'sore sm aggressor, attacker

aggrot'tare vt **~ le sopracciglia** to frown

aggrovigliarsi vpr (*fig*) to become complicated

aggu'ato sm trap; (*imboscata*) ambush; **tendere un ~ a qn** to set a trap for sb

agguer'rito, -a ag fierce

agi'ato, -a [a'dʒato] ag (*vita*) easy; (*persona*) well-off, well-to-do

'agile ['adʒile] ag agile, nimble

'agio ['adʒo] sm ease, comfort; **mettersi a proprio ~** to make o.s. at home o comfortable; **agi** smpl comforts; **mettersi a proprio ~** to make o.s. at home o comfortable; **dare ~ a qn di fare qc** to give sb the chance of doing sth

a'gire [a'dʒire] vi to act; (*esercitare un'azione*) to take effect; (*Tecn*) to work, function; **~ contro qn** (*Dir*) to take action against sb

agi'tare [adʒi'tare] vt (*bottiglia*) to shake; (*mano, fazzoletto*) to wave; (*fig: turbare*) to disturb; (*: incitare*) to stir (up); (*: dibattere*) to discuss; **agitarsi** vpr (*mare*) to be rough; (*malato, dormitore*) to toss and turn; (*bambino*) to fidget; (*emozionarsi*) to get upset; (*Pol*) to agitate; **agi'tato, -a** ag rough; restless; fidgety; upset, perturbed

'aglio ['aʎʎo] sm garlic

a'gnello [aɲ'ɲɛllo] sm lamb

'ago (*pl* **'aghi**) sm needle

ago'nistico, -a, -ci, -che ag athletic; (*fig*) competitive

agopun'tura sf acupuncture

a'gosto sm August

a'grario, -a ag agrarian, agricultural; (riforma) land cpd

a'gricolo, -a ag agricultural, farm cpd; **agricol'tore** sm farmer; **agricol'tura** sf agriculture, farming

agri'foglio [agri'fɔʎʎo] sm holly

agritu'rismo sm farm holidays pl

agrodolce ag bittersweet; (salsa) sweet and sour

a'grume sm (spesso al pl: pianta) citrus; (: frutto) citrus fruit

a'guzzo, -a [a'guttso] ag sharp

'ahi escl (dolore) ouch!

'Aia sf l'~ the Hague

'aids abbr m o f Aids

airbag sm inv air bag

ai'rone sm heron

aiu'ola sf flower bed

aiu'tante sm/f assistant ▶ sm (Mil) adjutant; (Naut) master-at-arms; **aiutante di campo** aide-de-camp

aiu'tare vt to help; **~ qn (a fare)** to help sb (to do); **aiutarsi** vpr to help each other; **~ qn in qc/a fare qc** to help sb with sth/to do sth; **può aiutarmi?** can you help me?

ai'uto sm help, assistance, aid; (aiutante) assistant; **venire in ~ di qn** to come to sb's aid; **aiuto chirurgo** assistant surgeon

'ala (pl 'ali) sf wing; **fare ~** to fall back, make way; **ala destra/sinistra** (Sport) right/left wing

ala'bastro sm alabaster

a'lano sm Great Dane

'alba sf dawn

alba'nese ag, sm/f, sm Albanian

Alba'nia sf l'~ Albania

albe'rato, -a ag (viale, piazza) lined with trees, tree-lined

al'bergo, -ghi sm hotel; **albergo della gioventù** youth hostel

'albero sm tree; (Naut) mast; (Tecn) shaft; **albero genealogico** family tree; **albero a gomiti** crankshaft; **albero maestro** mainmast; **albero di Natale** Christmas tree; **albero di trasmissione** transmission shaft

albi'cocca, -che sf apricot

'album sm album; **album da disegno** sketch book

al'bume sm albumen

'alce ['altʃe] sm elk

'alcol sm inv = **alcool**

al'colico, -a, -ci, -che ag alcoholic ▶ sm alcoholic drink

alcoliz'zato, -a [alkolid'dzato] sm/f alcoholic

'alcool sm inv alcohol

al'cuno, -a (det: dav sm: **alcun** + C, V, **alcuno** + s impura, gn, pn, ps, x, z; dav sf: **alcuna** + C, **alcun'** + V) det (nessuno): **non ... ~** no, not any; **alcuni, e** det pl some, a few; **non c'è alcuna fretta** there's no hurry, there isn't any hurry; **senza alcun riguardo** without any consideration ▶ pron pl **alcuni, e** some, a few

alfa'betico, -a, ci, che ag alphabetical

alfa'beto sm alphabet

'alga, -ghe sf seaweed no pl, alga

'algebra ['aldʒebra] sf algebra

Alge'ria [aldʒe'ria] sf l'~ Algeria

alge'rino, -a [aldʒe'rino] ag, sm/f Algerian

ali'ante sm (Aer) glider

'alibi sm inv alibi

a'lice [a'litʃe] sf anchovy

ali'eno, -a ag (avverso): **~ (da)** opposed (to), averse (to) ▶ sm/f alien

alimen'tare vt to feed; (Tecn) to feed; to supply; (fig) to sustain ▶ ag food cpd; **alimentari** smpl foodstuffs; (anche: **negozio di alimentari**) grocer's shop; **alimentazi'one** sf feeding; supplying; sustaining; (gli alimenti) diet

a'liquota *sf* share; (*d'imposta*) rate; **aliquota d'imposta** tax rate

alis'cafo *sm* hydrofoil

'alito *sm* breath

all. *abbr* (= *allegato*) encl.

allaccia'mento [allattʃa'mento] *sm* (*Tecn*) connection

allacci'are [allat'tʃare] *vt* (*scarpe*) to tie, lace (up); (*cintura*) to do up, fasten; (*luce, gas*) to connect; (*amicizia*) to form

allaccia'tura [allattʃa'tura] *sf* fastening

alla'gare *vt* to flood; **allagarsi** *vpr* to flood

allar'gare *vt* to widen; (*vestito*) to let out; (*aprire*) to open; (*fig: dilatare*) to extend; **allargarsi** *vpr* (*gen*) to widen; (*scarpe, pantaloni*) to stretch; (*fig: problema, fenomeno*) to spread

allar'mare *vt* to alarm

al'larme *sm* alarm; **allarme aereo** air-raid warning

allat'tare *vt* to feed

alle'anza [alle'antsa] *sf* alliance

alle'arsi *vpr* to form an alliance; **alle'ato, -a** *ag* allied ▸ *sm/f* ally

alle'gare *vt* (*accludere*) to enclose; (*Dir: citare*) to cite, adduce; (*denti*) to set on edge; **alle'gato, -a** *ag* enclosed ▸ *sm* enclosure; (*di e-mail*) attachment; **in allegato** enclosed

allegge'rire [alleddʒe'rire] *vt* to lighten, make lighter; (*fig: lavoro, tasse*) to reduce

alle'gria *sf* gaiety, cheerfulness

al'legro, -a *ag* cheerful, merry; (*un po' brillo*) merry, tipsy; (*vivace: colore*) bright ▸ *sm* (*Mus*) allegro

allena'mento *sm* training

alle'nare *vt* to train; **allenarsi** *vpr* to train; **allena'tore** *sm* (*Sport*) trainer, coach

allen'tare *vt* to slacken; (*disciplina*) to relax; **allentarsi** *vpr* to become slack; (*ingranaggio*) to work loose

aller'gia, -'gie [aller'dʒia] *sf* allergy; **al'lergico, -a, -ci, -che** *ag* allergic; **sono allergico alla penicillina** I'm allergic to penicillin

alles'tire *vt* (*cena*) to prepare; (*esercito, nave*) to equip, fit out; (*spettacolo*) to stage

allet'tante *ag* attractive, alluring

alle'vare *vt* (*animale*) to breed, rear; (*bambino*) to bring up

allevi'are *vt* to alleviate

alli'bito, -a *ag* astounded

alli'evo *sm* pupil; (*apprendista*) apprentice; (*Mil*) cadet

alliga'tore *sm* alligator

alline'are *vt* (*persone, cose*) to line up; (*Tip*) to align; (*fig: economia, salari*) to adjust, align; **allinearsi** *vpr* to line up; (*fig: a idee*): **allinearsi a** to come into line with

al'lodola *sf* (sky)lark

alloggi'are [allod'dʒare] *vt* to accommodate ▸ *vi* to live; **al'loggio** *sm* lodging, accommodation (*BRIT*), accommodations (*US*)

allonta'nare *vt* to send away, send off; (*impiegato*) to dismiss; (*pericolo*) to avert, remove; (*estraniare*) to alienate; **allontanarsi** *vpr* **allontanarsi (da)** to go away (from); (*estraniarsi*) to become estranged (from)

al'lora *av* (*in quel momento*) then ▸ *cong* (*in questo caso*) well then; (*dunque*) well then, so; **la gente d'~** people then o in those days; **da ~ in poi** from then on

al'loro *sm* laurel

'alluce ['allutʃe] *sm* big toe

alluci'nante [allutʃi'nante] *ag* awful; (*fam*) amazing

allucinazi'one [allutʃinat'tsjone] *sf* hallucination

al'ludere *vi* **~ a** to allude to, hint at

allu'minio *sm* aluminium (*BRIT*), aluminum (*US*)

allun'gare vt to lengthen; (distendere) to prolong, extend; (diluire) to water down; **allungarsi** vpr to lengthen; (ragazzo) to stretch, grow taller; (sdraiarsi) to lie down, stretch out

al'lusi ecc vb vedi **alludere**

allusi'one sf hint, allusion

alluvi'one sf flood

al'meno av at least ▶ cong (se) ~ if only; **(se) ~ piovesse!** if only it would rain!

a'logeno, -a [a'lɔdʒeno] ag **lampada alogena** halogen lamp

a'lone sm halo

'Alpi sfpl **le ~** the Alps

alpi'nismo sm mountaineering, climbing; **alpi'nista, -i, -e** sm/f mountaineer, climber

al'pino, -a ag Alpine; mountain cpd; **alpini** smpl (Mil) Italian Alpine troops

alt escl halt!, stop!

alta'lena sf (a funi) swing; (in bilico) seesaw

al'tare sm altar

alter'nare vt to alternate; **alternarsi** vpr to alternate; **alterna'tiva** sf alternative; **alterna'tivo, -a** ag alternative

al'terno, -a ag alternate; **a giorni alterni** on alternate days, every other day

al'tero, -a ag proud

al'tezza [al'tettsa] sf height; width, breadth; depth; pitch; (Geo) latitude; (titolo) highness; (fig: nobiltà) greatness; **essere all'~ di** to be on a level with; (fig) to be up to o equal to

al'ticcio, -a, -ci, -ce [al'tittʃo] ag tipsy

alti'tudine sf altitude

'alto, -a ag high; (persona) tall; (tessuto) wide, broad; (sonno, acque) deep; (suono) high(-pitched); (Geo) upper; (settentrionale) northern ▶ sm top (part) ▶ av high; (parlare) aloud,

loudly; **il palazzo è ~ 20 metri** the building is 20 metres high; **ad alta voce** aloud; **a notte alta** in the dead of night; **in ~** up, upwards; at the top; **dall'~ in o al basso** up and down; **degli alti e bassi** (fig) ups and downs; **alta fedeltà** high fidelity, hi-fi; **alta finanza/società** high finance/society; **alta moda** haute couture

altopar'lante sm loudspeaker

altopi'ano (pl **altipi'ani**) sm plateau, upland plain

altret'tanto, -a ag, pron as much; (pl) as many ▶ av equally; **tanti auguri! —grazie, ~** all the best! — thank you, the same to you

altri'menti av otherwise

⭕ **'altro, -a**
det

1 (diverso) other, different; **questa è un'altra cosa** that's another o a different thing

2 (supplementare) other; **prendi un altro cioccolatino** have another chocolate; **hai avuto altre notizie?** have you had any more o any other news?

3 (nel tempo): **l'altro giorno** the other day; **l'altr'anno** last year; **l'altro ieri** the day before yesterday; **domani l'altro** the day after tomorrow; **quest'altro mese** next month

4: **d'altra parte** on the other hand
▶ pron

1 (persona, cosa diversa o supplementare): **un altro, un'altra** another (one); **lo farà un altro** someone else will do it; **altri, e** others; **gli altri** (la gente) others, other people; **l'uno e l'altro** both (of them); **aiutarsi l'un l'altro** to help one another; **da un giorno all'altro** from day to day; (nel giro di 24 ore) from one day to the next; (da un momento all'altro) any day now

2 (sostantivato: solo maschile) something else; (: in espressioni

interrogative) anything else; **non ho
altro da dire** I have nothing else *o* I
don't have anything else to say; **più
che altro** above all; **se non altro** at
least; **tra l'altro** among other things;
ci mancherebbe altro! that's all we
need!; **non faccio altro che lavorare**
I do nothing but work; **contento?
— altro che!** are you pleased? — and
how!; *vedi* **senza**; **noialtri**; **voialtri**;
tutto

al'trove *av* elsewhere, somewhere
else

altru'ista, -i, -e *ag* altruistic

a'lunno, -a *sm/f* pupil

alve'are *sm* hive

al'zare [al'tsare] *vt* to raise, lift; (*issare*)
to hoist; (*costruire*) to build, erect;
alzarsi *vpr* to rise; (*dal letto*) to get
up; (*crescere*) to grow tall (*o* taller); **~
le spalle** to shrug one's shoulders;
alzarsi in piedi to stand up, get to
one's feet

a'maca, -che *sf* hammock

amalga'mare *vt* to amalgamate;
amalgamarsi *vpr* to amalgamate

a'mante *ag* **~ di** (*musica ecc*) fond of
▶ *sm/f* lover/mistress

a'mare *vt* to love; (*amico, musica, sport*)
to like; **amarsi** *vpr* to love each other

amareggi'ato, -a [amared'dʒato] *ag*
upset, saddened

ama'rena *sf* sour black cherry

ama'rezza [ama'rettsa] *sf* bitterness

a'maro, -a *ag* bitter ▶ *sm* bitterness;
(*liquore*) bitters *pl*

amaz'zonico, -a, ci, che
[amad'dzɔniko] *ag* Amazonian;
Amazon *cpd*

ambasci'ata [ambaʃ'ʃata] *sf*
embassy; (*messaggio*) message;
ambascia'tore, -'trice *sm/f*
ambassador/ambassadress

ambe'due *ag inv* **~ i ragazzi** both boys
▶ *pron inv* both

ambienta'lista, -i, e *ag*
environmental ▶ *sm/f*
environmentalist

ambien'tare *vt* to acclimatize;
(*romanzo, film*) to set; **ambientarsi** *vpr*
to get used to one's surroundings

ambi'ente *sm* environment; (*fig:
insieme di persone*) milieu; (*stanza*)
room

am'biguo, -a *ag* ambiguous

ambizi'one [ambit'tsjone] *sf*
ambition; **ambizi'oso, -a** *ag*
ambitious

'ambo *ag inv* both ▶ *sm* (*al gioco*)
double

'ambra *sf* amber; **ambra grigia**
ambergris

ambu'lante *ag* itinerant ▶ *sm* peddler

ambu'lanza [ambu'lantsa] *sf*
ambulance; **chiamate un ~** call an
ambulance

ambula'torio *sm* (*studio medico*)
surgery

A'merica *sf* **l'~** America; **l'~ latina**
Latin America; **ameri'cano, -a** *ag*,
sm/f American

ami'anto *sm* asbestos

ami'chevole [ami'kevole] *ag* friendly

ami'cizia [ami'tʃittsja] *sf* friendship;
amicizie *sfpl* (*amici*) friends

a'mico, -a, -ci, -che *sm/f* friend;
(*fidanzato*) boyfriend/girlfriend;
amico del cuore bosom friend

'amido *sm* starch

ammac'care *vt* (*pentola*) to dent;
(*persona*) to bruise

ammacca'tura *sf* dent; bruise

ammaes'trare *vt* (*animale*) to train

ammai'nare *vt* to lower, haul down

amma'larsi *vpr* to fall ill; **amma'lato,
-a** *ag* ill, sick ▶ *sm/f* sick person;
(*paziente*) patient

ammanet'tare *vt* to handcuff

ammas'sare *vt* (*ammucchiare*)
to amass; (*raccogliere*) to gather

together; **ammassarsi** vpr to pile up; to gather

ammat'tire vi to go mad

ammaz'zare [ammat'tsare] vt to kill; **ammazzarsi** vpr (uccidersi) to kill o.s.; (rimanere ucciso) to be killed; **ammazzarsi di lavoro** to work o.s. to death

am'mettere vt to admit; (riconoscere: fatto) to acknowledge, admit; (permettere) to allow, accept; (supporre) to suppose

amminis'trare vt to run, manage; (Rel, Dir) to administer; **amministra'tore** sm administrator; (di condominio) flats manager; **amministratore delegato** managing director; **amministrazi'one** sf management; administration

ammi'raglio [ammi'raʎʎo] sm admiral

ammi'rare vt to admire; **ammirazi'one** sf admiration

am'misi ecc vb vedi **ammettere**

ammobili'ato, -a ag furnished

am'mollo sm **lasciare in ~** to leave to soak

ammo'niaca sf ammonia

ammo'nire vt (avvertire) to warn; (rimproverare) to admonish; (Dir) to caution

ammonizi'one [ammonit'tsjone] sf (monito: anche Sport) warning; (rimprovero) reprimand; (Dir) caution

ammon'tare vi **~ a** to amount to ▶ sm (totale) amount

ammorbi'dente sm fabric conditioner

ammorbi'dire vt to soften

ammortizza'tore sm (Aut, Tecn) shock-absorber

ammucchi'are [ammuk'kjare] vt to pile up, accumulate

ammuf'fire vi to go mouldy (BRIT) o moldy (US)

ammuto'lire vi to be struck dumb

amne'sia sf amnesia

amnis'tia sf amnesty

'amo sm (Pesca) hook; (fig) bait

a'more sm love; **amori** smpl love affairs; **il tuo bambino è un ~** your baby's a darling; **fare l'~ o all'~** to make love; **per ~ o per forza** by hook or by crook; **amor proprio** self-esteem, pride

amo'roso, -a ag (affettuoso) loving, affectionate; (d'amore: sguardo) amorous; (: poesia, relazione) love cpd

'ampio, -a ag wide, broad; (spazioso) spacious; (abbondante: vestito) loose; (: gonna) full; (: spiegazione) ample, full

am'plesso sm intercourse

ampli'are vt (ingrandire) to enlarge; (allargare) to widen; **ampliarsi** vpr to grow, increase

amplifica'tore sm (Tecn, Mus) amplifier

ampu'tare vt (Med) to amputate

A.N. sigla f (= Alleanza Nazionale) Italian right-wing party

anabbagli'anti smpl dipped (BRIT) o dimmed (US) headlights

anaboliz'zante ag anabolic ▶ sm anabolic steroid

anal'colico, -a, -ci, -che ag non-alcoholic ▶ sm soft drink

analfa'beta, -i, -e ag, sm/f illiterate

anal'gesico, -a, -ci, -che [anal'dʒeziko] ag, sm analgesic

a'nalisi sf inv analysis; (Med: esame) test; **analisi del sangue** blood test sg

analiz'zare [analid'dzare] vt to analyse; (Med) to test

a'nalogo, -a, -ghi, -ghe ag analogous

'ananas sm inv pineapple

anar'chia [anar'kia] sf anarchy; **a'narchico, -a, -ci, -che** ag anarchic(al) ▶ sm/f anarchist

anarco-insurreziona'lista *ag* anarcho-revolutionary

'A.N.A.S. *sigla f* (= *Azienda Nazionale Autonoma delle Strade*) national roads department

anato'mia *sf* anatomy

'anatra *sf* duck

'anca, -che *sf* (*Anat*) hip

'anche ['anke] *cong* (*inoltre, pure*) also, too; (*perfino*) even; **vengo anch'io** I'm coming too; **~ se** even if

an'cora *av* still; (*di nuovo*) again; (*di più*) some more; (*persino*): **~ più forte** even stronger; **non ~** not yet; **~ una volta** once more, once again; **~ un po'** a little more; (*di tempo*) a little longer

an'dare *sm* **a lungo ~** in the long run ▶ *vi* to go; (*essere adatto*): **~ a** to suit; (*piacere*): **il suo comportamento non mi va** I don't like the way he behaves; **ti va di ~ al cinema?** do you feel like going to the cinema?; **andarsene** to go away; **questa camicia va lavata** this shirt needs a wash *o* should be washed; **~ a cavallo** to ride; **~ in macchina/aereo** to go by car/plane; **~ a fare qc** to go and do sth; **~ a pescare/sciare** to go fishing/skiing; **~ a male** to go bad; **come va?** (*lavoro, progetto*) how are things?; **come va? —bene, grazie!** how are you? — fine, thanks!; **va fatto entro oggi** it's got to be done today; **ne va della nostra vita** our lives are at stake; **an'data** *sf* going; (*viaggio*) outward journey; **biglietto di sola andata** single (*BRIT*) *o* one-way ticket; **biglietto di andata e ritorno** return (*BRIT*) *o* round-trip (*US*) ticket

andrò *ecc vb vedi* **andare**

a'neddoto *sm* anecdote

a'nello *sm* ring; (*di catena*) link; **anelli** *smpl* (*Ginnastica*) rings

a'nemico, -a, -ci, -che *ag* anaemic

aneste'sia *sf* anaesthesia

anfeta'mina *sf* amphetamine

'angelo ['andʒelo] *sm* angel; **angelo custode** guardian angel

anghe'ria [ange'ria] *sf* vexation

angli'cano, -a *ag* Anglican

anglo'sassone *ag* Anglo-Saxon

'angolo *sm* corner; (*Mat*) angle; **angolo cottura** (*di appartamento ecc*) cooking area

an'goscia, -sce [an'gɔʃʃa] *sf* deep anxiety, anguish *no pl*

angu'illa *sf* eel

an'guria *sf* watermelon

'anice ['anitʃe] *sm* (*Cuc*) aniseed; (*Bot*) anise

'anima *sf* soul; (*abitante*) inhabitant; **non c'era ~ viva** there wasn't a living soul; **anima gemella** soul mate

ani'male *sm, ag* animal; **animale domestico** pet

anna'cquare *vt* to water down

annaffi'are *vt* to water; **annaffia'toio** *sm* watering can

an'nata *sf* year; (*importo annuo*) annual amount; **vino d'~** vintage wine

anne'gare *vt, vi* to drown

anne'rire *vt* to blacken ▶ *vi* to become black

annien'tare *vt* to annihilate, destroy

anniver'sario *sm* anniversary; **anniversario di matrimonio** wedding anniversary

'anno *sm* year; **ha 8 anni** he's 8 (years old)

anno'dare *vt* to knot, tie; (*fig: rapporto*) to form

annoi'are *vt* to bore; **annoiarsi** *vpr* to be bored

> Attenzione! In inglese esiste il verbo *to annoy* che però vuol dire *dare fastidio a*.

anno'tare *vt* (*registrare*) to note, note down; (*commentare*) to annotate

annu'ale *ag* annual

annu'ire *vi* to nod; (*acconsentire*) to agree

annul'lare *vt* to annihilate, destroy; (*contratto, francobollo*) to cancel; (*matrimonio*) to annul; (*sentenza*) to quash; (*risultati*) to declare void

annunci'are [annun'tʃare] *vt* to announce; (*dar segni rivelatori*) to herald

an'nuncio [an'nuntʃo] *sm* announcement; (*fig*) sign; **annunci economici** classified advertisements, small ads; **annunci mortuari** (*colonna*) obituary column; **annuncio pubblicitario** advertisement

'annuo, -a *ag* annual, yearly

annu'sare *vt* to sniff, smell; **~ tabacco** to take snuff

a'nomalo, -a *ag* anomalous

a'nonimo, -a *ag* anonymous ▶ *sm* (*autore*) anonymous writer (*o painter ecc*); **società anonima** (*Comm*) joint stock company

anores'sia *sf* anorexia

ano'ressico, -a, ci, che *ag* anorexic

anor'male *ag* abnormal ▶ *sm/f* subnormal person

ANSA *sigla f* (= *Agenzia Nazionale Stampa Associata*) press agency

'ansia *sf* anxiety

ansi'mare *vi* to pant

ansi'oso, -a *ag* anxious

'anta *sf* (*di finestra*) shutter; (*di armadio*) door

An'tartide *sf* l'~ Antarctica

an'tenna *sf* (*Radio, TV*) aerial; (*Zool*) antenna, feeler; (*Naut*) yard; **antenna parabolica** satellite dish

ante'prima *sf* preview; **anteprima di stampa** (*Inform*) print preview

anteri'ore *ag* (*ruota, zampa*) front; (*fatti*) previous, preceding

antiade'rente *ag* non-stick

antibi'otico, -a, -ci, -che *ag, sm* antibiotic

anti'camera *sf* anteroom; **fare ~** to wait (for an audience)

antici'pare [antitʃi'pare] *vt* (*consegna, visita*) to bring forward, anticipate; (*somma di denaro*) to pay in advance; (*notizia*) to disclose ▶ *vi* to be ahead of time; **an'ticipo** *sm* anticipation; (*di denaro*) advance; **in anticipo** early, in advance; **occorre che prenoti in anticipo?** do I need to book in advance?

an'tico, -a, -chi, -che *ag* (*quadro, mobili*) antique; (*dell'antichità*) ancient; **all'antica** old-fashioned

anticoncezio'nale [antikontʃettsjo'nale] *sm* contraceptive

anticonfor'mista, -i, -e *ag, sm/f* nonconformist

anti'corpo *sm* antibody

antidolo'rifico, -ci *sm* painkiller

anti'doping *sm* drug testing ▶ *ag inv* **test ~** drugs (*BRIT*) *o* drug (*US*) test

an'tifona *sf* (*Mus, Rel*) antiphon; **capire l'~** (*fig*) to take the hint

anti'forfora *ag inv* anti-dandruff

anti'furto *sm* anti-theft device

anti'gelo [anti'dʒɛlo] *ag inv* **(liquido)** ~ (*per motore*) antifreeze; (*per cristalli*) de-icer

antiglobalizzazione [antiglobaliddzat'tsjone] *ag inv* **movimento ~** anti-globalization movement

An'tille *sfpl* **le ~** the West Indies

antin'cendio [antin'tʃendjo] *ag inv* fire *cpd*

anti'nebbia *sm inv* (*anche:* **faro ~**: *Aut*) fog lamp

antinfiamma'torio, -a *ag, sm* anti-inflammatory

antio'rario [antio'rarjo] *ag* **in senso ~** anticlockwise

anti'pasto *sm* hors d'œuvre

antipa'tia *sf* antipathy, dislike; **anti'patico, -a, -ci, -che** *ag* unpleasant, disagreeable

antiproi'ettile *ag inv* bulletproof
antiquari'ato *sm* antique trade; **un oggetto d'~** an antique
anti'quario *sm* antique dealer
anti'quato, -a *ag* antiquated, old-fashioned
anti'rughe *ag inv* (*crema, prodotto*) anti-wrinkle
antitraspi'rante *ag* antiperspirant
anti'vipera *ag inv* **siero ~** remedy for snake bites
antivirus [anti'virus] *sm inv* antivirus software *no pl* ▶ *ag inv* antivirus
antolo'gia, -'gie [antolo'dʒia] *sf* anthology
anu'lare *ag* ring *cpd* ▶ *sm* third finger
'anzi ['antsi] *av* (*invece*) on the contrary; (*o meglio*) or rather, or better still
anzi'ano, -a [an'tsjano] *ag* old; (*Amm*) senior ▶ *sm/f* old person; senior member
anziché [antsi'ke] *cong* rather than
a'patico, -a, -ci, -che *ag* apathetic
'ape *sf* bee
aperi'tivo *sm* apéritif
aperta'mente *av* openly
a'perto, -a *pp di* **aprire** ▶ *ag* open; **all'~** in the open (air); **è ~ al pubblico?** is it open to the public?; **quando è ~ il museo?** when is the museum open?
aper'tura *sf* opening; (*ampiezza*) width; (*Fot*) aperture; **apertura alare** wing span; **apertura mentale** open-mindedness
ap'nea *sf* **immergersi in ~** to dive without breathing apparatus
a'postrofo *sm* apostrophe
ap'paio *ecc vb vedi* **apparire**
ap'palto *sm* (*Comm*) contract; **dare/prendere in ~ un lavoro** to let out/undertake a job on contract
appannarsi *vpr* to mist over; to grow dim
apparecchi'are [apparek'kjare] *vt*

to prepare; (*tavola*) to set ▶ *vi* to set the table
appa'recchio [appa'rekkjo] *sm* piece of apparatus, device; (*aeroplano*) aircraft *inv*; **apparecchio acustico** hearing aid; **apparecchio telefonico** telephone; **apparecchio televisivo** television set
appa'rente *ag* apparent
appa'rire *vi* to appear; (*sembrare*) to seem, appear
appar'tarsi *vpr* to withdraw
apparte'nere *vi* **~ a** to belong to
ap'parvi *ecc vb vedi* **apparire**
appassio'nare *vt* to thrill; (*commuovere*) to move; **appassionarsi** *vpr* **appassionarsi a qc** to take a great interest in sth; **appassio'nato, -a** *ag* passionate; (*entusiasta*): **appassionato (di)** keen (on)
appas'sire *vi* to wither
appas'sito, -a *ag* dead
ap'pello *sm* roll-call; (*implorazione, Dir*) appeal; **fare ~ a** to appeal to
ap'pena *av* (*a stento*) hardly, scarcely; (*solamente, da poco*) just ▶ *cong* as soon as; **(non) ~ furono arrivati ...** as soon as they had arrived ...; **~ ... che** *o* **quando** no sooner ... than
ap'pendere *vt* to hang (up)
appen'dice [appen'ditʃe] *sf* appendix; **romanzo d'~** popular serial
appendi'cite [appendi'tʃite] *sf* appendicitis
Appen'nini *smpl* **gli ~** the Apennines
appesan'tire *vt* to make heavy; **appesantirsi** *vpr* to grow stout
appe'tito *sm* appetite
appic'care *vt* **~ il fuoco a** to set fire to, set on fire
appicci'care [appittʃi'kare] *vt* to stick; **appiccicarsi** *vpr* to stick; (*fig: persona*) to cling

appiso'larsi *vpr* to doze off

applau'dire *vt, vi* to applaud; **ap'plauso** *sm* applause

appli'care *vt* to apply; (*regolamento*) to enforce; **applicarsi** *vpr* to apply o.s.

appoggi'are [appod'dʒare] *vt* (*mettere contro*): **~ qc a qc** to rest sth against sth; (*fig: sostenere*) to support; **appoggiarsi** *vpr* **appoggiarsi a** to lean against; (*fig*) to rely upon; **ap'poggio** *sm* support

apposita'mente *av* specially; (*apposta*) on purpose

ap'posito, -a *ag* appropriate

ap'posta *av* on purpose, deliberately

appos'tarsi *vpr* to lie in wait

ap'prendere *vt* (*imparare*) to learn

appren'dista, -i, -e *sm/f* apprentice

apprensi'one *sf* apprehension

apprez'zare [appret'tsare] *vt* to appreciate

appro'dare *vi* (*Naut*) to land; (*fig*): **non ~ a nulla** to come to nothing

approfit'tare *vi* **~ di** to make the most of; (*peg*) to take advantage of

approfon'dire *vt* to deepen; (*fig*) to study in depth

appropri'ato, -a *ag* appropriate

approssima'tivo, -a *ag* approximate, rough; (*impreciso*) inexact, imprecise

appro'vare *vt* (*condotta, azione*) to approve of; (*candidato*) to pass; (*progetto di legge*) to approve

appunta'mento *sm* appointment; (*amoroso*) date; **darsi ~** to arrange to meet (one another); **ho un ~ con ...** I have an appointment with ...; **vorrei prendere un ~** I'd like to make an appointment

ap'punto *sm* note; (*rimprovero*) reproach ▶ *av* (*proprio*) exactly, just; **per l'~!, ~!** exactly!

apribot'tiglie [apribot'tiʎʎe] *sm inv* bottle opener

a'prile *sm* April

a'prire *vt* to open; (*via, cadavere*) to open up; (*gas, luce, acqua*) to turn on ▶ *vi* to open; **aprirsi** *vpr* to open; **aprirsi a qn** to confide in sb, open one's heart to sb; **a che ora aprite?** what time do you open?

apris'catole *sm inv* tin (*BRIT*) o can opener

APT *sigla f* (= *Azienda di Promozione Turistica*) ≈ tourist board

aquagym [akkwa'dʒim] *sf* aquaerobics

'aquila *sf* (*Zool*) eagle; (*fig*) genius

aqui'lone *sm* (*giocattolo*) kite; (*vento*) North wind

A/R *abbr* = **andata e ritorno** (*biglietto*) return ticket (*BRIT*), round-trip ticket (*US*)

A'rabia Sau'dita *sf* **l'~** Saudi Arabia

'arabo, -a *ag, sm/f* Arab ▶ *sm* (*Ling*) Arabic

a'rachide [a'rakide] *sf* peanut

ara'gosta *sf* crayfish; lobster

a'rancia, -ce [a'rantʃa] *sf* orange; **aranci'ata** *sf* orangeade; **aranci'one** *ag inv* **(color) arancione** bright orange

a'rare *vt* to plough (*BRIT*), plow (*US*)

a'ratro *sm* plough (*BRIT*), plow (*US*)

a'razzo [a'rattso] *sm* tapestry

arbi'trare *vt* (*Sport*) to referee; to umpire; (*Dir*) to arbitrate

arbi'trario, -a *ag* arbitrary

'arbitro *sm* arbiter, judge; (*Dir*) arbitrator; (*Sport*) referee; (: *Tennis, Cricket*) umpire

ar'busto *sm* shrub

archeolo'gia [arkeolo'dʒia] *sf* arch(a)eology; **arche'ologo, -a, -gi, -ghe** *sm/f* arch(a)eologist

architet'tare [arkitet'tare] *vt* (*fig: ideare*) to devise; (: *macchinare*) to plan, concoct

archi'tetto [arki'tetto] *sm* architect; **architet'tura** *sf* architecture

ar'chivio [ar'kivjo] *sm* archives *pl*;
(*Inform*) file

'arco *sm* (*arma*, *Mus*) bow; (*Archit*) arch;
(*Mat*) arc

arcoba'leno *sm* rainbow

arcu'ato, -a *ag* curved, bent

'ardere *vt, vi* to burn

ar'desia *sf* slate

'area *sf* area; (*Edil*) land, ground; **area
di rigore** (*Sport*) penalty area; **area di
servizio** (*Aut*) service area

a'rena *sf* arena; (*per corride*) bullring;
(*sabbia*) sand

are'narsi *vpr* to run aground

argente'ria [ardʒente'ria] *sf*
silverware, silver

Argen'tina [ardʒen'tina] *sf* l'~
Argentina; **argen'tino, -a** *ag, sm/f*
Argentinian

ar'gento [ar'dʒento] *sm* silver;
argento vivo quicksilver

ar'gilla [ar'dʒilla] *sf* clay

'argine ['ardʒine] *sm* embankment,
bank; (*diga*) dyke, dike

argo'mento *sm* argument; (*motivo*)
motive; (*materia*, *tema*) subject

'aria *sf* air; (*espressione*, *aspetto*) air,
look; (*Mus: melodia*) tune; (*di opera*)
aria; **mandare all'~ qc** to ruin *o* upset
sth; **all'~ aperta** in the open (air)

'arido, -a *ag* arid

arieggi'are [arjed'dʒare] *vt* (*cambiare
aria*) to air; (*imitare*) to imitate

ari'ete *sm* ram; (*Mil*) battering ram;
(*dello zodiaco*): **A~** Aries

a'ringa, -ghe *sf* herring *inv*

arit'metica *sf* arithmetic

'arma, -i *sf* weapon, arm; (*parte
dell'esercito*) arm; **chiamare alle armi**
to call up (*BRIT*), draft (*US*); **sotto le
armi** in the army (*o* forces); **alle armi!**
to arms!; **arma atomica/nucleare**
atomic/nuclear weapon; **arma da
fuoco** firearm; **armi di distruzione di
massa** weapons of mass destruction

arma'dietto *sm* (*di medicinali*)
medicine cabinet; (*in palestra ecc*)
locker; (*in cucina*) (kitchen) cupboard

ar'madio *sm* cupboard; (*per abiti*)
wardrobe; **armadio a muro** built-in
cupboard

ar'mato, -a *ag* ~ **(di)** (*anche fig*)
armed (with) ▶ *sf* (*Mil*) army; (*Naut*)
fleet; **rapina a mano armata** armed
robbery

arma'tura *sf* (*struttura di sostegno*)
framework; (*impalcatura*) scaffolding;
(*Storia*) armour *no pl*, suit of armour

armis'tizio [armis'tittsjo] *sm*
armistice

armo'nia *sf* harmony

ar'nese *sm* tool, implement; (*oggetto
indeterminato*) thing, contraption;
male in ~ (*malvestito*) badly dressed;
(*di salute malferma*) in poor health;
(*povero*) down-at-heel

'arnia *sf* hive

a'roma, -i *sm* aroma; fragrance;
aromi *smpl* (*Cuc*) herbs and spices;
aromatera'pia *sf* aromatherapy

'arpa *sf* (*Mus*) harp

arrabbi'are *vi* (*cane*) to be affected
with rabies; **arrabbiarsi** *vpr* (*essere
preso dall'ira*) to get angry, fly into a
rage; **arrabbi'ato, -a** *ag* rabid, with
rabies; furious, angry

arrampi'carsi *vpr* to climb (up)

arrangiarsi *vpr* to manage, do the
best one can

arreda'mento *sm* (*studio*) interior
design; (*mobili ecc*) furnishings *pl*

arre'dare *vt* to furnish

ar'rendersi *vpr* to surrender

arres'tare *vt* (*fermare*) to stop, halt;
(*catturare*) to arrest; **arrestarsi**
vpr (*fermarsi*) to stop; **ar'resto** *sm*
(*cessazione*) stopping; (*fermata*)
stop; (*cattura, Med*) arrest; **subire un
arresto** to come to a stop *o* standstill;
mettere agli arresti to place under

arrest; **arresti domiciliari** house arrest sg

arre'trare vt, vi to withdraw; **arre'trato, -a** ag (lavoro) behind schedule; (paese, bambino) backward; (numero di giornale) back cpd; **arretrati** smpl arrears

arric'chire [arrik'kire] vt to enrich; **arricchirsi** vpr to become rich

arri'vare vi to arrive; (accadere) to happen, occur; **~ a** (livello, grado ecc) to reach; **a che ora arriva il treno da Londra?** what time does the train from London arrive?; **non ci arrivo** I can't reach it; (fig: non capisco) I can't understand it

arrive'derci [arrive'dertʃi] escl goodbye!

arri'vista, -i, -e sm/f go-getter

ar'rivo sm arrival; (Sport) finish, finishing line

arro'gante ag arrogant

arros'sire vi (per vergogna, timidezza) to blush, flush; (per gioia, rabbia) to flush

arros'tire vt to roast; (pane) to toast; (ai ferri) to grill

ar'rosto sm, ag inv roast

arroto'lare vt to roll up

arroton'dare vt (forma, oggetto) to round; (stipendio) to add to; (somma) to round off

arrugginito, -a [arruddʒin'ito] ag rusty

'arsi vb vedi **ardere**

'arte sf art; (abilità) skill

ar'teria sf artery; **arteria stradale** main road

'artico, -a, -ci, -che ag Arctic

articolazi'one sf articulation; (Anat, Tecn) joint

ar'ticolo sm article; **articolo di fondo** (Stampa) leader, leading article

artifici'ale [artifi'tʃale] ag artificial

artigia'nato [artidʒa'nato] sm craftsmanship; craftsmen pl

artigi'ano, -a [arti'dʒano] sm/f craftsman/woman

ar'tista, -i, -e sm/f artist; **ar'tistico, -a, -ci, -che** ag artistic

ar'trite sf (Med) arthritis

a'scella [aʃʃella] sf (Anat) armpit

ascen'dente [aʃʃen'dɛnte] sm ancestor; (fig) ascendancy; (Astr) ascendant

ascen'sore [aʃʃen'sore] sm lift

a'scesso [aʃʃɛsso] sm (Med) abscess

asciugaca'pelli [aʃʃugaka'pelli] sm hair-drier

asciuga'mano [aʃʃuga'mano] sm towel

asciu'gare [aʃʃu'gare] vt to dry; **asciugarsi** vpr to dry o.s.; (diventare asciutto) to dry

asci'utto, -a [aʃʃutto] ag dry; (fig: magro) lean; (: burbero) curt; **restare a bocca asciutta** (fig) to be disappointed

ascol'tare vt to listen to

as'falto sm asphalt

'Asia sf l'~ Asia; **asi'atico, -a, -ci, -che** ag, sm/f Asiatic, Asian

a'silo sm refuge, sanctuary; **~ (d'infanzia)** nursery(-school); **asilo nido** crèche; **asilo politico** political asylum

'asino sm donkey, ass

ASL sigla f (= Azienda Sanitaria Locale) local health centre

'asma sf asthma

as'parago, -gi sm asparagus no pl

aspet'tare vt to wait for; (anche Comm) to await; (aspettarsi) to expect ▶ vi to wait; **aspettami, per favore** wait for me, please

as'petto sm (apparenza) aspect, appearance, look; (punto di vista) point of view; **di bell'~** good-looking

aspira'polvere sm inv vacuum cleaner

aspi'rare vt (respirare) to breathe in, inhale; (apparecchi) to suck (up) ▶ vi ~ **a** to aspire to

aspi'rina sf aspirin

'aspro, -a ag (sapore) sour, tart; (odore) acrid, pungent; (voce, clima, fig) harsh; (superficie) rough; (paesaggio) rugged

assaggi'are [assad'dʒare] vt to taste; **posso assaggiarlo?** can I have a taste?; **assaggino** [assad'dʒino] sm **assaggini** (Cuc) selection of first courses; **solo un assaggino** just a little

as'sai av (molto) a lot, much; (: con ag) very; (a sufficienza) enough ▶ ag inv (quantità) a lot of, much; (numero) a lot of, many; ~ **contento** very pleased

as'salgo ecc vb vedi **assalire**

assa'lire vt to attack, assail

assal'tare vt (Mil) to storm; (banca) to raid; (treno, diligenza) to hold up

as'salto sm attack, assault

assassi'nare vt to murder; to assassinate; (fig) to ruin; **assas'sino, -a** ag murderous ▶ sm/f murderer; assassin

'asse sm (Tecn) axle; (Mat) axis ▶ sf board; **asse** sf **da stiro** ironing board

assedi'are vt to besiege

asse'gnare [asseɲ'ɲare] vt to assign, allot; (premio) to award

as'segno [as'seɲɲo] sm allowance; (anche: ~ **bancario**) cheque (BRIT), check (US); **contro** ~ cash on delivery; **posso pagare con un ~?** can I pay by cheque?; **assegno circolare** bank draft; **assegni familiari** ≈ child benefit no pl; **assegno sbarrato** crossed cheque; **assegno di viaggio** traveller's cheque; **assegno a vuoto** dud cheque; **assegno di malattia/di invalidità** sick pay/disability benefit

assem'blea sf assembly

assen'tarsi vpr to go out

as'sente ag absent; (fig) faraway, vacant; **as'senza** sf absence

asse'tato, -a ag thirsty, parched

assicu'rare vt (accertare) to ensure; (infondere certezza) to assure; (fermare, legare) to make fast, secure; (fare un contratto di assicurazione) to insure; **assicurarsi** vpr (accertarsi): **assicurarsi (di)** to make sure (of); (contro il furto ecc): **assicurarsi (contro)** to insure o.s. (against); **assicurazi'one** sf assurance; insurance

assi'eme av (insieme) together; ~ **a** (together) with

assil'lare vt to pester, torment

assis'tente sm/f assistant; **assistente sociale** social worker; **assistente di volo** (Aer) steward/stewardess

assis'tenza [assis'tɛntsa] sf assistance; ~ **ospedaliera** free hospital treatment; ~ **sociale** welfare services pl; **assistenza sanitaria** health service

as'sistere vt (aiutare) to assist, help; (curare) to treat ▶ vi ~ **(a qc)** (essere presente) to be present (at sth), to attend (sth)

'asso sm ace; **piantare qn in** ~ to leave sb in the lurch

associ'are [asso'tʃare] vt to associate; **associarsi** vpr to enter into partnership; **associarsi a** to become a member of, join; (dolori, gioie) to share in; ~ **qn alle carceri** to take sb to prison

associazi'one [assotʃat'tsjone] sf association; (Comm) association, society; ~ **a delinquere** (Dir) criminal association

as'solsi ecc vb vedi **assolvere**

assoluta'mente av absolutely

asso'luto, -a ag absolute

assoluzi'one [assolut'tsjone] sf (Dir) acquittal; (Rel) absolution

as'solvere vt (Dir) to acquit; (Rel)

to absolve; (*adempiere*) to carry out, perform

assomigli'are [assomiʎ'ʎare] *vi* ~ **a** to resemble, look like; **assomigliarsi** *vpr* to look alike; (*nel carattere*) to be alike

asson'nato, -a *ag* sleepy

asso'pirsi *vpr* to doze off

assor'bente *ag* absorbent ▶ *sm*; **assorbente interno** tampon; **assorbente esterno/igienico** sanitary towel

assor'bire *vt* to absorb

assor'dare *vt* to deafen

assorti'mento *sm* assortment

assor'tito, -a *ag* assorted; matched, matching

assuefazi'one [assuefat'tsjone] *sf* (*Med*) addiction

as'sumere *vt* (*impiegato*) to take on, engage; (*responsabilità*) to assume, take upon o.s.; (*contegno, espressione*) to assume, put on; (*droga*) to consume

as'sunsi *ecc vb vedi* **assumere**

assurdità *sf inv* absurdity; **dire delle ~** to talk nonsense

as'surdo, -a *ag* absurd

'asta *sf* pole; (*vendita*) auction

as'temio, -a *ag* teetotal ▶ *sm/f* teetotaller

> Attenzione! In inglese esiste la parola *abstemious* che però vuol dire *moderato*.

aste'nersi *vpr* ~ **(da)** to abstain (from), refrain (from); (*Pol*) to abstain (from)

aste'risco, -schi *sm* asterisk

'astice ['astitʃe] *sm* lobster

astig'matico, -a, ci, che *ag* astigmatic

asti'nenza [asti'nɛntsa] *sf* abstinence; **essere in crisi di ~** to suffer from withdrawal symptoms

as'tratto, -a *ag* abstract

'astro... *prefisso*; **astrolo'gia** [astrolo'dʒia] *sf* astrology; **astro'nauta, -i, -e** *sm/f*

astronaut; **astro'nave** *sf* space ship; **astrono'mia** *sf* astronomy; **astro'nomico, -a, -ci, -che** *ag* astronomic(al)

as'tuccio [as'tuttʃo] *sm* case, box, holder

as'tuto, -a *ag* astute, cunning, shrewd

A'tene *sf* Athens

'ateo, -a *ag, sm/f* atheist

at'lante *sm* atlas

at'lantico, -a, -ci, -che *ag* Atlantic ▶ *sm* l'A~, l'Oceano A~ the Atlantic, the Atlantic Ocean

at'leta, -i, -e *sm/f* athlete; **at'letica** *sf* athletics *sg*; **atletica leggera** track and field events *pl*; **atletica pesante** weightlifting and wrestling

atmos'fera *sf* atmosphere

a'tomico, -a, -ci, -che *ag* atomic; (*nucleare*) atomic, atom *cpd*, nuclear

'atomo *sm* atom

'atrio *sm* entrance hall, lobby

a'troce [a'trotʃe] *ag* (*che provoca orrore*) dreadful; (*terribile*) atrocious

attac'cante *sm/f* (*Sport*) forward

attacca'panni *sm* hook, peg; (*mobile*) hall stand

attac'care *vt* (*unire*) to attach; (*cucendo*) to sew on; (*far aderire*) to stick (on); (*appendere*) to hang (up); (*assalire: anche fig*) to attack; (*iniziare*) to begin, start; (*fig: contagiare*) to pass on ▶ *vi* to stick, adhere; **attaccarsi** *vpr* to stick, adhere; (*trasmettersi per contagio*) to be contagious; (*afferrarsi*): **attaccarsi (a)** to cling (to); (*fig: affezionarsi*): **attaccarsi (a)** to become attached (to); **~ discorso** to start a conversation; **at'tacco, -chi** *sm* (*azione offensiva: anche fig*) attack; (*Med*) attack, fit; (*Sci*) binding; (*Elettr*) socket

atteggia'mento [atteddʒa'mento] *sm* attitude

at'tendere vt to wait for, await ▶ vi ~
a to attend to

atten'dibile ag (storia) credible;
(testimone) reliable

atten'tato sm attack; ~ **alla vita di qn**
attempt on sb's life

at'tento, -a ag attentive; (accurato)
careful, thorough; **stare ~ a qc** to pay
attention to sth; ~! be careful!

attenzi'one [atten'tsjone] sf
attention; ~! watch out!, be careful!;
attenzioni sfpl (premure) attentions;
fare ~ a to watch out for; **coprire qn di
attenzioni** to lavish attentions on sb

atter'raggio [atter'raddʒo] sm
landing

atter'rare vt to bring down ▶ vi
to land

at'tesa sf waiting; (tempo trascorso
aspettando) wait; **essere in ~ di qc** to
be waiting for sth

at'tesi ecc vb vedi **attendere**

at'teso, -a pp di **attendere**

'attico, -ci sm attic

attil'lato, -a ag (vestito) close-fitting

'attimo sm moment; **in un ~** in a
moment

atti'rare vt to attract

atti'tudine sf (disposizione) aptitude;
(atteggiamento) attitude

attività sf inv activity; (Comm)
assets pl

at'tivo, -a ag active; (Comm) profit-
making, credit cpd ▶ sm (Comm) assets
pl; **in ~** in credit

'atto sm act; (azione, gesto) action,
act, deed; (Dir: documento) deed,
document; **atti** smpl (di congressi ecc)
proceedings; **mettere in ~** to put into
action; **fare ~ di fare qc** to make as if
to do sth; **atto di morte/di nascita**
death/birth certificate

at'tore, -'trice sm/f actor/actress

at'torno av ~ **(a)** round, around, about

attrac'care vt, vi (Naut) to dock, berth

at'tracco, -chi sm (Naut) docking
no pl; berth

at'trae ecc vb vedi **attrarre**

attra'ente ag attractive

at'traggo ecc vb vedi **attrarre**

at'trarre vt to attract

at'trassi ecc vb vedi **attrarre**

attraver'sare vt to cross; (città, bosco,
fig: periodo) to go through; (fiume) to
run through

attra'verso prep through; (da una
parte all'altra) across

attrazi'one [attrat'tsjone] sf attraction

attrezza'tura sf equipment no pl

at'trezzo sm tool, instrument; (Sport)
piece of equipment

at'trice [at'tritʃe] sf vedi **attore**

attu'ale ag (presente) present; (di
attualità) topical; **attualità** sf inv
topicality; (avvenimento) current
event; **attual'mente** av at the
moment, at present

Attenzione! In inglese esiste la
parola actual che però vuol dire
effettivo.

Attenzione! In inglese esiste la
parola actually che però vuol dire
effettivamente oppure veramente.

attu'are vt to carry out

attu'tire vt to deaden, reduce

'audio sm (TV, Radio, Cine) sound

audiovi'sivo, -a ag audiovisual

audizi'one [audit'tsjone] sf hearing;
(Mus) audition

augu'rare vt to wish; **augurarsi qc** to
hope for sth

au'guri smpl best wishes; **fare gli ~
a qn** to give sb one's best wishes;
tanti ~! best wishes!; (per compleanno)
happy birthday!

'aula sf (scolastica) classroom;
(universitaria) lecture theatre; (di
edificio pubblico) hall

aumen'tare vt, vi to increase;
au'mento sm increase

au'rora sf dawn

ausili'are ag, sm, sm/f auxiliary

Aus'tralia sf l'~ Australia; **australi'ano, -a** ag, sm/f Australian

'Austria sf l'~ Austria; **aus'triaco, -a, -ci, -che** ag, sm/f Austrian

au'tentico, -a, -ci, -che ag authentic, genuine

au'tista, -i sm driver

'auto sf inv car

autoabbron'zante sm, ag self-tan

autoade'sivo, -a ag self-adhesive ▶ sm sticker

autobio'grafico, -a, ci, che ag autobiographic(al)

'autobus sm inv bus

auto'carro sm lorry (BRIT), truck

autocertificazi'one [autotʃertifikat'tsjone] sf self-declaration

autodistrut'tivo, -a ag self-destructive

auto'gol sm inv own goal

au'tografo, -a ag, sm autograph

auto'grill® sm inv motorway restaurant

auto'matico, -a, -ci, -che ag automatic ▶ sm (bottone) snap fastener; (fucile) automatic

auto'mobile sf (motor) car

automobi'lista, -i, -e sm/f motorist

autono'leggio sm car hire

autono'mia sf autonomy; (di volo) range

au'tonomo, -a ag autonomous, independent

autop'sia sf post-mortem, autopsy

auto'radio sf inv (apparecchio) car radio; (autoveicolo) radio car

au'tore, -'trice sm/f author

autoreg'gente [autored'dʒɛnte] ag **calze autoreggenti** hold ups

auto'revole ag authoritative; (persona) influential

autorici'cabile ag **scheda ~** top-up card

autori'messa sf garage

autorità sf inv authority

autoriz'zare [autorid'dzare] vt (permettere) to authorize; (giustificare) to allow, sanction

autos'contro sm dodgem car (BRIT), bumper car (US)

autoscu'ola sf driving school

autos'tima sf self-esteem

autos'top sm hitchhiking; **autostop'pista, -i, -e** sm/f hitchhiker

autos'trada sf motorway (BRIT), highway (US); **autostrada informatica** information superhighway

- **autostrade**
- You have to pay to use Italian
- motorways. They are indicated by an
- "A" followed by a number on a green
- sign. The speed limit on Italian
- motorways is 130 kph.

auto'velox® sm inv (police) speed camera

autovet'tura sf (motor) car

au'tunno sm autumn

avam'braccio [avam'brattʃo] (pl (f) **-cia**) sm forearm

avangu'ardia sf vanguard

a'vanti av (stato in luogo) in front; (moto: andare, venire) forward; (tempo: prima) before ▶ prep (luogo): **~ a** before, in front of; (tempo): **~ Cristo** before Christ ▶ escl (entrate) come (o go) in!; (Mil) forward!; (coraggio) come on! ▶ sm inv (Sport) forward; **~ e indietro** backwards and forwards; **andare ~** to go forward; (continuare) to go on; (precedere) to go (on) ahead; (orologio) to be fast; **essere ~ negli studi** to be well advanced with one's studies

avan'zare [avan'tsare] vt (spostare in avanti) to move forward; (domanda) to put forward; (promuovere) to promote; (essere creditore): **~ qc da qn** to be owed sth by sb ▶ *vi* (*andare avanti*) to move forward; (*progredire*) to make progress; (*essere d'avanzo*) to be left, remain

ava'ria *sf* (*guasto*) damage; (: *meccanico*) breakdown

a'varo, -a *ag* avaricious, miserly ▶ *sm* miser

○ **a'vere**
sm (*Comm*) credit; **gli averi** (*ricchezze*) wealth *sg*
▶ *vt*

1 (*possedere*) to have; **ha due bambini/una bella casa** she has (got) two children/a lovely house; **ha i capelli lunghi** he has (got) long hair; **non ho da mangiare** I've (got) nothing to eat, I don't have anything to eat

2 (*indossare*) to wear, have on; **aveva una maglietta rossa** he was wearing *o* he had on a red tee-shirt; **ha gli occhiali** he wears *o* has glasses

3 (*ricevere*) to get; **hai avuto l'assegno?** did you get *o* have you had the cheque?

4 (*età, dimensione*) to have; **ha 9 anni** he is 9 (years old); **la stanza ha 3 metri di lunghezza** the room is 3 metres in length; *vedi* **fame**; **paura** *ecc*

5 (*tempo*): **quanti ne abbiamo oggi?** what's the date today?; **ne hai per molto?** will you be long?

6 (*fraseologia*): **avercela con qn** to be angry with sb; **cos'hai?** what's wrong *o* what's the matter (with you)?; **non ha niente a che vedere** *o* **fare con me** it's got nothing to do with me
▶ *vb aus*

1 to have; **aver bevuto/mangiato** to have drunk/eaten

2 (+ *da* + *infinito*): **avere da fare qc** to have to do sth; **non hai che da chiederlo** you only have to ask him

aviazi'one [avjat'tsjone] *sf* aviation; (*Mil*) air force

'avido, -a *ag* eager; (*peg*) greedy

avo'cado *sm* avocado

a'vorio *sm* ivory

Avv. *abbr* = **avvocato**

avvantaggi'are [avvantad'dʒare] *vt* to favour; **avvantaggiarsi** *vpr* **avvantaggiarsi negli affari/sui concorrenti** to get ahead in business/of one's competitors

avvele'nare *vt* to poison

av'vengo *ecc vb vedi* **avvenire**

avveni'mento *sm* event

avve'nire *vi, vb impers* to happen, occur ▶ *sm* future

av'venni *ecc vb vedi* **avvenire**

avven'tato, -a *ag* rash, reckless

avven'tura *sf* adventure; (*amorosa*) affair

avventu'rarsi *vpr* to venture

avventu'roso, -a *ag* adventurous

avve'rarsi *vpr* to come true

av'verbio *sm* adverb

avverrò *ecc vb vedi* **avvenire**

avver'sario, -a *ag* opposing ▶ *sm* opponent, adversary

avver'tenza [avver'tentsa] *sf* (*ammonimento*) warning; (*cautela*) care; (*premessa*) foreword; **avvertenze** *sfpl* (*istruzioni per l'uso*) instructions

avverti'mento *sm* warning

avver'tire *vt* (*avvisare*) to warn; (*rendere consapevole*) to inform, notify; (*percepire*) to feel

avvi'are *vt* (*mettere sul cammino*) to direct; (*impresa, trattativa*) to begin, start; (*motore*) to start; **avviarsi** *vpr* to set off, set out

avvici'nare [avvitʃi'nare] *vt* to bring near; (*trattare con: persona*) to approach; **avvicinarsi** *vpr* **avvicinarsi (a qn/qc)** to approach (sb/sth), draw near (to sb/sth)

avvi'lito, -a *ag* discouraged

avvin'cente *ag* captivating

avvi'sare *vt* (*far sapere*) to inform;

b

(*mettere in guardia*) to warn;
av'viso *sm* warning; (*annuncio*)
announcement; (: *affisso*)
notice; (*inserzione pubblicitaria*)
advertisement; **a mio avviso** in
my opinion; **avviso di chiamata**
(*servizio*) call waiting; (*segnale*) call
waiting signal; **avviso di garanzia**
(*Dir*) notification (*of impending
investigation and of the right to name a
defence lawyer*)

> Attenzione! In inglese esiste la
> parola *advice* che però vuol dire
> *consiglio*.

avvis'tare *vt* to sight
avvi'tare *vt* to screw down (*o* in)
avvo'cato, -'essa *sm/f* (*Dir*) barrister
(*BRIT*), lawyer; (*fig*) defender,
advocate
av'volgere [av'voldʒere] *vt* to roll up;
(*avviluppare*) to wrap up; **avvolgersi**
vpr (*avvilupparsi*) to wrap o.s. up;
avvol'gibile *sm* roller blind (*BRIT*),
blind
av'volsi *ecc vb vedi* **avvolgere**
avvol'toio *sm* vulture
aza'lea [addza'lɛa] *sf* azalea
azi'enda [ad'dzjɛnda] *sf* business,
firm, concern; **azienda agricola** farm
azi'one [at'tsjone] *sf* action; (*Comm*)
share
a'zoto [ad'dzɔto] *sm* nitrogen
azzar'dare [addzar'dare] *vt* (*soldi,
vita*) to risk, hazard; (*domanda, ipotesi*)
to hazard, venture; **azzardarsi** *vpr*
azzardarsi a fare to dare (to) do
az'zardo [ad'dzardo] *sm* risk
azzec'care [attsek'kare] *vt* (*risposta
ecc*) to get right
azzuf'farsi [attsuf'farsi] *vpr* to come
to blows
az'zurro, -a [ad'dzurro] *ag* blue ▸ *sm*
(*colore*) blue; **gli azzurri** (*Sport*) the
Italian national team

'babbo *sm* (*fam*) dad, daddy; **Babbo
Natale** Father Christmas
baby'sitter ['beɪbɪsitəʳ] *sm/f inv*
baby-sitter
'bacca, -che *sf* berry
baccalà *sm* dried salted cod; (*fig: peg*)
dummy
bac'chetta [bak'ketta] *sf* (*verga*) stick,
rod; (*di direttore d'orchestra*) baton;
(*di tamburo*) drumstick; **~ magica**
magic wand
ba'checa, -che [ba'kɛka] *sf* (*mobile*)
showcase, display case; (*Univ, in
ufficio*) notice board (*BRIT*), bulletin
board (*US*)
baci'are [ba'tʃare] *vt* to kiss; **baciarsi**
vpr to kiss (one another)
baci'nella [batʃi'nella] *sf* basin
ba'cino [ba'tʃino] *sm* basin;
(*Mineralogia*) field, bed; (*Anat*) pelvis;
(*Naut*) dock
'bacio ['batʃo] *sm* kiss
'baco, -chi *sm* worm; **baco da seta**
silkworm
ba'dare *vi* (*fare attenzione*) to take care,
be careful; (*occuparsi di*): **~ a** to look
after, take care of; (*dar ascolto*): **~ a** to
pay attention to; **bada ai fatti tuoi!**
mind your own business!
'baffi *smpl* moustache *sg*; (*di animale*)
whiskers; **leccarsi i ~** to lick one's lips
bagagli'aio [bagaʎ'ʎajo] *sm* luggage
van (*BRIT*) *o* car (*US*); (*Aut*) boot (*BRIT*),
trunk (*US*)

ba'gaglio [ba'gaʎʎo] sm luggage no pl, baggage no pl; **fare/disfare i bagagli** to pack/unpack; **i nostri bagagli non sono arrivati** our luggage has not arrived; **può mandare qualcuno a prendere i nostri bagagli?** could you send someone to collect our luggage?; **bagaglio a mano** hand luggage

bagli'ore [baʎ'ʎore] sm flash, dazzling light; **un ~ di speranza** a ray of hope

ba'gnante [ban'nante] sm/f bather

ba'gnare [ban'nare] vt to wet; (inzuppare) to soak; (innaffiare) to water; (fiume) to flow through; (: mare) to wash, bathe; **bagnarsi** vpr to get wet; (al mare) to go swimming o bathing; (in vasca) to have a bath

ba'gnato, -a [ban'nato] ag wet

ba'gnino [ban'nino] sm lifeguard

'bagno ['banno] sm bath; (stanza) bathroom; (toilette) toilet; **bagni** smpl (stabilimento) baths; **fare il ~** to have a bath; (nel mare) to go swimming o bathing; **dov'è il ~?** where's the toilet?; **fare il ~ a qn** to give sb a bath; **mettere a ~** to soak; **~ schiuma** bubble bath

bagnoma'ria [bannoma'ria] sm **cuocere a ~** to cook in a double saucepan

bagnoschi'uma [bannoskj'uma] sm inv bubble bath

'baia sf bay

balbet'tare vi to stutter, stammer; (bimbo) to babble ▶ vt to stammer out

bal'canico, -a, ci, che ag Balkan

bal'cone sm balcony; **avete una camera con ~?** do you have a room with a balcony?

bal'doria sf **fare ~** to have a riotous time

ba'lena sf whale

ba'leno sm flash of lightning; **in un ~** in a flash

bal'lare vt, vi to dance

balle'rina sf dancer; ballet dancer; (scarpa) ballet shoe

balle'rino sm dancer; ballet dancer

bal'letto sm ballet

'ballo sm dance; (azione) dancing no pl; **essere in ~** (fig: persona) to be involved; (: cosa) to be at stake

balne'are ag seaside cpd; (stagione) bathing

'balsamo sm (aroma) balsam; (lenimento, fig) balm; (per capelli) conditioner

bal'zare [bal'tsare] vi to bounce; (lanciarsi) to jump, leap; **'balzo** sm bounce; jump, leap; (del terreno) crag

bam'bina ag, sf vedi bambino

bam'bino, -a sm/f child

'bambola sf doll

bambù sm bamboo

ba'nale ag banal, commonplace

ba'nana sf banana

'banca, -che sf bank; **banca dati** data bank

banca'rella sf stall

banca'rotta sf bankruptcy; **fare ~** to go bankrupt

ban'chetto [ban'ketto] sm banquet

banchi'ere [ban'kjɛre] sm banker

ban'china [ban'kina] sf (di porto) quay; (per pedoni, ciclisti) path; (di stazione) platform; **~ cedevole** (Aut) soft verge (BRIT) o shoulder (US)

'banco, -chi sm bench; (di negozio) counter; (di mercato) stall; (di officina) (work-)bench; (Geo, banca) bank; **banco di corallo** coral reef; **banco degli imputati** dock; **banco di prova** (fig) testing ground; **banco dei testimoni** witness box; **banco dei pegni** pawnshop; **banco di nebbia** bank of fog

'Bancomat® sm inv automated banking; (tessera) cash card

banco'nota sf banknote

'banda *sf* band; (*di stoffa*) band, stripe; (*lato, parte*) side; **banda larga** broadband

bandi'era *sf* flag, banner

ban'dito *sm* outlaw, bandit

'bando *sm* proclamation; (*esilio*) exile, banishment; **~ alle chiacchiere!** that's enough talk!; **bando di concorso** announcement of a competition

bar *sm inv* bar

'bara *sf* coffin

ba'racca, -che *sf* shed, hut; (*peg*) hovel; **mandare avanti la ~** to keep things going

ba'rare *vi* to cheat

'baratro *sm* abyss

ba'ratto *sm* barter

ba'rattolo *sm* (*di latta*) tin; (*di vetro*) jar; (*di coccio*) pot

'barba *sf* beard; **farsi la ~** to shave; **farla in ~ a qn** (*fig*) to do sth to sb's face; **che ~!** what a bore!

barbabi'etola *sf* beetroot (*BRIT*), beet (*US*); **barbabietola da zucchero** sugar beet

barbi'ere *sm* barber

bar'bone *sm* (*cane*) poodle; (*vagabondo*) tramp

'barca, -che *sf* boat; **barca a motore** motorboat; **barca a remi** rowing boat; **barca a vela** sail(ing) boat

barcol'lare *vi* to stagger

ba'rella *sf* (*lettiga*) stretcher

ba'rile *sm* barrel, cask

ba'rista, -i, -e *sm/f* barman/maid; (*proprietario*) bar owner

ba'rocco, -a, -chi, -che *ag, sm* baroque

ba'rometro *sm* barometer

ba'rone *sm* baron; **baro'nessa** *sf* baroness

'barra *sf* bar; (*Naut*) helm; (*linea grafica*) line, stroke

bar'rare *vt* to bar

barri'carsi *vpr* to barricade o.s.

barri'era *sf* barrier; (*Geo*) reef

ba'ruffa *sf* scuffle

barzel'letta [bardzel'letta] *sf* joke, funny story

ba'sare *vt* to base, found; **basarsi** *vpr* **basarsi su** (*fatti, prove*) to be based o founded on; (: *persona*) to base one's arguments on

'basco, -a, -schi, -sche *ag* Basque ▶ *sm* (*copricapo*) beret

'base *sf* base; (*fig: fondamento*) basis; (*Pol*) rank and file; **di ~** basic; **in ~ a** on the basis of, according to; **a ~ di caffè** coffee-based

'baseball ['beisbɔ:l] *sm* baseball

ba'sette *sfpl* sideburns

ba'silica, -che *sf* basilica

ba'silico *sm* basil

basket ['basket] *sm* basketball

bas'sista, -i, -e *sm/f* bass player

'basso, -a *ag* low; (*di statura*) short; (*meridionale*) southern ▶ *sm* bottom, lower part; (*Mus*) bass; **la bassa Italia** southern Italy

bassorili'evo *sm* bas-relief

bas'sotto, -a *ag* squat ▶ *sm* (*cane*) dachshund

'basta *escl* (that's) enough!, that will do!

bas'tardo, -a *ag* (*animale, pianta*) hybrid, crossbreed; (*persona*) illegitimate, bastard; (*peg*) ▶ *sm/f* illegitimate child, bastard (*peg*)

bas'tare *vi, vb impers* to be enough, be sufficient; **~ a qn** to be enough for sb; **basta chiedere** o **che chieda a un vigile** you have only to o need only ask a policeman; **basta così, grazie** that's enough, thanks

basto'nare *vt* to beat, thrash

baston'cino [baston'tʃino] *sm* (*Sci*) ski pole; **bastoncini di pesce** fish fingers

bas'tone *sm* stick; **~ da passeggio** walking stick

bat'taglia [bat'taʎʎa] *sf* battle; fight
bat'tello *sm* boat
bat'tente *sm* (*imposta: di porta*) wing, flap; (: *di finestra*) shutter; (*batacchio: di porta*) knocker; (: *di orologio*) hammer; **chiudere i battenti** (*fig*) to shut up shop
'**battere** *vt* to beat; (*grano*) to thresh; (*percorrere*) to scour ▶ *vi* (*bussare*) to knock; (*urtare*): **~ contro** to hit *o* strike against; (*pioggia, sole*) to beat down; (*cuore*) to beat; (*Tennis*) to serve; **battersi** *vpr* to fight; **~ le mani** to clap; **~ i piedi** to stamp one's feet; **~ a macchina** to type; **~ bandiera italiana** to fly the Italian flag; **~ in testa** (*Aut*) to knock; **in un batter d'occhio** in the twinkling of an eye
batte'ria *sf* battery; (*Mus*) drums *pl*
bat'terio *sm* bacterium
batte'rista, -i, -e *sm/f* drummer
bat'tesimo *sm* (*rito*) baptism; christening
battez'zare [batted'dzare] *vt* to baptize; to christen
batti'panni *sm inv* carpet-beater
battis'trada *sm inv* (*di pneumatico*) tread; (*di gara*) pacemaker
'**battito** *sm* beat, throb; **battito cardiaco** heartbeat
bat'tuta *sf* blow; (*di macchina da scrivere*) stroke; (*Mus*) bar; beat; (*Teatro*) cue; (*frase spiritosa*) witty remark; (*di caccia*) beating; (*Polizia*) combing, scouring; (*Tennis*) service
ba'tuffolo *sm* wad
ba'ule *sm* trunk; (*Aut*) boot (*BRIT*), trunk (*US*)
'**bava** *sf* (*di animale*) slaver, slobber; (*di lumaca*) slime; (*di vento*) breath
bava'glino [bavaʎ'ʎino] *sm* bib
ba'vaglio [ba'vaʎʎo] *sm* gag
'**bavero** *sm* collar
ba'zar [bad'dzar] *sm inv* bazaar
BCE *sigla f* (= *Banca centrale europea*) ECB

be'ato, -a *ag* blessed; (*fig*) happy; **~ te!** lucky you!
bec'care *vt* to peck; (*fig: raffreddore*) to catch; **beccarsi** *vpr* (*fig*) to squabble; **beccarsi qc** to catch sth
beccherò *ecc* [bekke'rɔ] *vb vedi* **beccare**
'**becco, -chi** *sm* beak, bill; (*di caffettiera ecc*) spout; lip
be'fana *sf* hag, witch; **la B~** *old woman who, according to legend, brings children their presents at the Epiphany;* (*Epifania*) Epiphany

- **Befana**
- The **Befana** is a national holiday on
- the feast of the Epiphany. It takes
- its name from **la Befana**, the old
- woman who, according to Italian
- legend comes down the chimney
- during the night leaving gifts for
- children who have been good, and
- coal for those who have not.

bef'fardo, -a *ag* scornful, mocking
'**begli** ['beʎʎi] *ag vedi* **bello**
'**bei** *ag vedi* **bello**
beige [bɛʒ] *ag inv* beige
bel *ag vedi* **bello**
be'lare *vi* to bleat
'**belga, -gi, -ghe** *ag, sm/f* Belgian
'**Belgio** ['bɛldʒo] *sm* **il ~** Belgium
'**bella** *sf* (*Sport*) decider; *vedi anche* **bello**
bel'lezza [bel'lettsa] *sf* beauty

○ '**bello, -a**
(*ag: dav sm* **bel** + *C*, **bell'** + *V*,
bello + *s impura, gn, pn, ps, x, z, pl*
bei + *C*, **begli** + *s impura ecc o V*) *ag*
◼ (*oggetto, donna, paesaggio*) beautiful, lovely; (*uomo*) handsome; (*tempo*) beautiful, fine, lovely; **le belle arti** fine arts
◼ (*quantità*): **una bella cifra** a considerable sum of money; **un bel niente** absolutely nothing
◼ (*rafforzativo*): **è una truffa bella e buona!** it's a real fraud!; **è bell'e finito** it's already finished

▶*sm*

1 (*bellezza*) beauty; (*tempo*) fine weather

2: **adesso viene il bello** now comes the best bit; **sul più bello** at the crucial point; **cosa fai di bello?** are you doing anything interesting?
▶*av* **fa bello** the weather is fine, it's fine

'**belva** *sf* wild animal

belve'dere *sm inv* panoramic viewpoint

benché [ben'ke] *cong* although

'**benda** *sf* bandage; (*per gli occhi*) blindfold; **ben'dare** *vt* to bandage; to blindfold

'**bene** *av* well; (*completamente, affatto*): **è ben difficile** it's very difficult ▶*ag inv* **gente ~** well-to-do people ▶*sm* good; **beni** *smpl* (*averi*) property *sg*, estate *sg*; **io sto ~/poco ~** I'm well/not very well; **va ~** all right; **volere un ~ dell'anima a qn** to love sb very much; **un uomo per ~** a respectable man; **fare ~** to do the right thing; **fare ~ a** (*salute*) to be good for; **fare del ~ a qn** to do sb a good turn; **beni di consumo** consumer goods

bene'detto, -a *pp di* **benedire** ▶*ag* blessed, holy

bene'dire *vt* to bless; to consecrate

benedu'cato, -a *ag* well-mannered

benefi'cenza [benefi'tʃɛntsa] *sf* charity

bene'ficio [bene'fitʃo] *sm* benefit; **con ~ d'inventario** (*fig*) with reservations

be'nessere *sm* well-being

benes'tante *ag* well-to-do

be'nigno, -a [be'niɲɲo] *ag* kind, kindly; (*critica ecc*) favourable; (*Med*) benign

benve'nuto, -a *ag, sm* welcome; **dare il ~ a qn** to welcome sb

ben'zina [ben'dzina] *sf* petrol (*BRIT*), gas (*US*); **fare ~** to get petrol (*BRIT*) o

gas (*US*); **sono rimasto senza ~** I have run out of petrol (*BRIT*) o gas (*US*); **benzina verde** unleaded (petrol); **benzi'naio** *sm* petrol (*BRIT*) o gas (*US*) pump attendant

'**bere** *vt* to drink; **darla a ~ a qn** (*fig*) to fool sb; **vuoi qualcosa da ~?** would you like a drink?

ber'lina *sf* (*Aut*) saloon (car) (*BRIT*), sedan (*US*)

Ber'lino *sf* Berlin

ber'muda *smpl* (*calzoncini*) Bermuda shorts

ber'noccolo *sm* bump; (*inclinazione*) flair

ber'retto *sm* cap

berrò *ecc vb vedi* **bere**

ber'saglio [ber'saʎʎo] *sm* target

besciamella [beʃʃa'mɛlla] *sf* béchamel sauce

bes'temmia *sf* curse; (*Rel*) blasphemy

bestemmi'are *vi* to curse, swear; to blaspheme ▶*vt* to curse, swear at; to blaspheme

'**bestia** *sf* animal; **andare in ~** (*fig*) to fly into a rage; **besti'ale** *ag* beastly; animal *cpd*; (*fam*): **fa un freddo bestiale** it's bitterly cold; **besti'ame** *sm* livestock; (*bovino*) cattle *pl*

be'tulla *sf* birch

be'vanda *sf* drink, beverage

'**bevo** *ecc vb vedi* **bere**

be'vuto, -a *pp di* **bere**

'**bevvi** *ecc vb vedi* **bere**

bianche'ria [bjanke'ria] *sf* linen; **~ da donna** ladies' underwear, lingerie; **biancheria femminile** lingerie; **biancheria intima** underwear

bi'anco, -a, -chi, -che *ag* white; (*non scritto*) blank ▶*sm* white; (*intonaco*) whitewash ▶*sm/f* white, white man/ woman; **in ~** (*foglio, assegno*) blank; (*notte*) sleepless; **in ~ e nero** (*TV, Fot*) black and white; **mangiare in ~** to follow a bland diet; **pesce in ~** boiled

fish; **andare in ~** (*non riuscire*) to fail;
bianco dell'uovo egg-white
biasi'mare *vt* to disapprove of
'**Bibbia** *sf* (*anche fig*) bible
bibe'ron *sm inv* feeding bottle
'**bibita** *sf* (soft) drink
biblio'teca, -che *sf* library; (*mobile*)
bookcase
bicarbo'nato *sm* **~ (di sodio)**
bicarbonate (of soda)
bicchi'ere [bik'kjɛre] *sm* glass
bici'cletta [bitʃi'kletta] *sf* bicycle;
andare in ~ to cycle
bidè *sm inv* bidet
bi'dello, -a *sm/f* (*Ins*) janitor
bi'done *sm* drum, can; (*anche:* **~
dell'immondizia**) (dust)bin; (*fam:
truffa*) swindle; **fare un ~ a qn** (*fam*) to
let sb down; to cheat sb
bien'nale *ag* biennial
- **Biennale di Venezia**
- The **Biennale di Venezia** is an
- international contemporary art
- festival, which takes place every
- two years at Giardini in Venice. In
- its current form, it includes exhibits
- by artists from the many countries
- taking part, a thematic exhibition
- and a section for young artists.
bifamili'are *sf* ≈ semi-detached
house
bifor'carsi *vpr* to fork
bigiotte'ria [bidʒotte'ria] *sf* costume
jewellery; (*negozio*) jeweller's (*selling
only costume jewellery*)
bigliet'taio, -a *sm/f* (*in treno*) ticket
inspector; (*in autobus*) conductor
bigliette'ria [biʎʎette'ria] *sf* (*di
stazione*) ticket office; booking office;
(*di teatro*) box office
bigli'etto [biʎ'ʎetto] *sm* (*per viaggi,
spettacoli ecc*) ticket; (*cartoncino*)
card; (*anche:* **~ di banca**) (bank)note;
biglietto d'auguri greetings card;
biglietto da visita visiting card;

biglietto d'andata e ritorno return
(ticket), round-trip ticket (*US*);
biglietto di sola andata single
(ticket); **biglietto elettronico**
e-ticket
bignè [biɲ'ɲe] *sm inv* cream puff
bigo'dino *sm* roller, curler
bi'gotto, -a *ag* over-pious
bi'kini *sm inv* bikini
bi'lancia, -ce [bi'lantʃa] *sf* (*pesa*)
scales *pl*; (: *di precisione*) balance;
(*dello zodiaco*): **B~** Libra; **bilancia
commerciale** balance of trade;
bilancia dei pagamenti balance of
payments
bi'lancio [bi'lantʃo] *sm* (*Comm*)
balance(-sheet); (*statale*) budget;
fare il ~ di (*fig*) to assess; **bilancio
consuntivo** (final) balance; **bilancio
preventivo** budget
bili'ardo *sm* billiards *sg*; billiard table
bi'lingue *ag* bilingual
bilo'cale *sm* two-room flat (*Brit*) o
apartment (*US*)
'**bimbo, -a** *sm/f* little boy (girl)
bi'nario, -a *ag* (*sistema*) binary ▶ *sm*
(*railway*) track o line; (*piattaforma*)
platform; **da che ~ parte il treno per
Londra?** which platform does the
train for London go from?; **binario
morto** dead-end track
bi'nocolo *sm* binoculars *pl*
bio... *prefisso*; **biodegra'dabile** *ag*
biodegradable; **biodi'namico, -a,
-ci, -che** *ag* biodynamic; **biogra'fia** *sf*
biography; **biolo'gia** *sf* biology
bio'logico, -a, -ci, -che *ag* (*scienze,
fenomeni ecc*}) biological; (*agricoltura,
prodotti*) organic; **guerra biologica**
biological warfare
bi'ondo, -a *ag* blond, fair
biotecnologia [bioteknolo'dʒia] *sf*
biotechnology
biri'chino, -a [biri'kino] *ag*
mischievous ▶ *sm/f* little rascal

bi'rillo *sm* skittle (*BRIT*), pin (*US*)

'biro® *sf inv* biro®

'birra *sf* beer; **a tutta ~** (*fig*) at top speed; **birra chiara/scura** ≈ lager/stout; **birre'ria** *sf* ≈ bierkeller

bis *escl, sm inv* encore

bis'betico, -a, -ci, -che *ag* ill-tempered, crabby

bisbigli'are [bisbiʎ'ʎare] *vt, vi* to whisper

'bisca, -sche *sf* gambling-house

'biscia, -sce ['biʃʃa] *sf* snake; **biscia d'acqua** grass snake

biscot'tato, -a *ag* crisp; **fette biscottate** rusks

bis'cotto *sm* biscuit

bisessu'ale *ag, sm/f* bisexual

bises'tile *ag* **anno ~** leap year

bis'nonno, -a *sm/f* great grandfather/grandmother

biso'gnare [bizoɲ'ɲare] *vb impers* **bisogna che tu parta/lo faccia** you'll have to go/do it; **bisogna parlargli** we'll (*o* I'll) have to talk to him

bi'sogno [bi'zoɲɲo] *sm* need; **ha ~ di qualcosa?** do you need anything?

bis'tecca, -che *sf* steak, beefsteak

bisticci'are [bistit'tʃare] *vi* to quarrel, bicker; **bisticciarsi** *vpr* to quarrel, bicker

'bisturi *sm* scalpel

'bivio *sm* fork; (*fig*) dilemma

biz'zarro, -a [bid'dzarro] *ag* bizarre, strange

blate'rare *vi* to chatter

blin'dato, -a *ag* armoured

bloc'care *vt* to block; (*isolare*) to isolate, cut off; (*porto*) to blockade; (*prezzi, beni*) to freeze; (*meccanismo*) to jam; **bloccarsi** *vpr* (*motore*) to stall; (*freni, porta*) to jam, stick; (*ascensore*) to stop, get stuck

blocche'rò *ecc* [blokke'rɔ] *vb vedi* **bloccare**

bloc'chetto [blok'ketto] *sm* notebook; (*di biglietti*) book

'blocco, -chi *sm* block; (*Mil*) blockade; (*dei fitti*) restriction; (*quadernetto*) pad; (*fig: unione*) coalition; (*il bloccare*) blocking; isolating, cutting-off; blockading; freezing; jamming; **in ~** (*nell'insieme*) as a whole; (*Comm*) in bulk; **blocco cardiaco** cardiac arrest; **blocco stradale** road block

blog [blog] *sm inv* blog

blu *ag inv, sm* dark blue

'blusa *sf* (*camiciotto*) smock; (*camicetta*) blouse

'boa *sm inv* (*Zool*) boa constrictor; (*sciarpa*) feather boa ▶ *sf* buoy

bo'ato *sm* rumble, roar

bob [bɔb] *sm inv* bobsleigh

'bocca, -che *sf* mouth; **in ~ al lupo!** good luck!

boc'caccia, -ce [bok'kattʃa] *sf* (*malalingua*) gossip; **fare le boccacce** to pull faces

boc'cale *sm* jug; **boccale da birra** tankard

boc'cetta [bot'tʃetta] *sf* small bottle

'boccia, -ce ['bottʃa] *sf* bottle; (*da vino*) decanter, carafe; (*palla*) bowl; **gioco delle bocce** bowls *sg*

bocci'are [bot'tʃare] *vt* (*proposta, progetto*) to reject; (*Ins*) to fail; (*Bocce*) to hit

bocci'olo [bot'tʃɔlo] *sm* bud

boc'cone *sm* mouthful, morsel

boicot'tare *vt* to boycott

'bolla *sf* bubble; (*Med*) blister; **bolla di consegna** (*Comm*) delivery note; **bolla papale** papal bull

bol'lente *ag* boiling; boiling hot

bol'letta *sf* bill; (*ricevuta*) receipt; **essere in ~** to be hard up

bollet'tino *sm* bulletin; (*Comm*) note; **bollettino meteorologico** weather report; **bollettino di spedizione** consignment note

bollicina [bolli'tʃina] *sf* bubble

bol'lire *vt, vi* to boil
bolli'tore *sm* (*Cuc*) kettle; (*per riscaldamento*) boiler
'bollo *sm* stamp; **bollo per patente** driving licence tax; **bollo postale** postmark
'bomba *sf* bomb; **bomba atomica** atom bomb; **bomba a mano** hand grenade; **bomba ad orologeria** time bomb
bombarda'mento *sm* bombardment; bombing
bombar'dare *vt* to bombard; (*da aereo*) to bomb
'bombola *sf* cylinder
bombo'letta *sf* aerosol
bomboni'era *sf* box of sweets (*as souvenir at weddings, first communions etc*)
bo'nifico, -ci *sm* (*riduzione, abbuono*) discount; (*versamento a terzi*) credit transfer
bontà *sf* goodness; (*cortesia*) kindness; **aver la ~ di fare qc** to be good o kind enough to do sth
borbot'tare *vi* to mumble
'borchia ['borkja] *sf* stud
bor'deaux [bor'do] *ag inv, sm inv* maroon
'bordo *sm* (*Naut*) ship's side; (*orlo*) edge; (*striscia di guarnizione*) border, trim; **a ~ di** (*nave, aereo*) aboard, on board; (*macchina*) in
bor'ghese [bor'geze] *ag* (*spesso peg*) middle-class; bourgeois; **abito ~** civilian dress
'borgo, -ghi *sm* (*paesino*) village; (*quartiere*) district; (*sobborgo*) suburb
boro'talco *sm* talcum powder
bor'raccia, -ce [bor'rattʃa] *sf* canteen, water-bottle
'borsa *sf* bag; (*anche: ~ da signora*) handbag; (*Econ*): **la B~ (valori)** the Stock Exchange; **borsa dell'acqua calda** hot-water bottle; **borsa nera**

black market; **borsa della spesa** shopping bag; **borsa di studio** grant; **borsel'lino** *sm* purse; **bor'setta** *sf* handbag
'bosco, -schi *sm* wood
bos'niaco, -a, ci, che *ag, sm/f* Bosnian
'Bosnia Erze'govina ['bɔsnja erdze'govina] *sf* **la ~** Bosnia Herzegovina
Bot, bot *sigla m inv* (= *buono ordinario del Tesoro*) short-term Treasury bond
bo'tanica *sf* botany
bo'tanico, -a, -ci, -che *ag* botanical ▶ *sm* botanist
'botola *sf* trap door
'botta *sf* blow; (*rumore*) bang
'botte *sf* barrel, cask
bot'tega, -ghe *sf* shop; (*officina*) workshop
bot'tiglia [bot'tiʎʎa] *sf* bottle; **bottiglie'ria** *sf* wine shop
bot'tino *sm* (*di guerra*) booty; (*di rapina, furto*) loot
'botto *sm* bang; crash; **di ~** suddenly
bot'tone *sm* button; **attaccare ~ a qn** (*fig*) to buttonhole sb
bo'vino, -a *ag* bovine; **bovini** *smpl* cattle
box [bɔks] *sm inv* (*per cavalli*) horsebox; (*per macchina*) lock-up; (*per macchina da corsa*) pit; (*per bambini*) playpen
boxe [bɔks] *sf* boxing
'boxer ['bɔkser] *sm inv* (*cane*) boxer ▶ *smpl* (*mutande*): **un paio di ~** a pair of boxer shorts
BR *sigla fpl* = **Brigate Rosse**
brac'cetto [brat'tʃetto] *sm* **a ~** arm in arm
braccia'letto *sm* bracelet, bangle
bracci'ata [brat'tʃata] *sf* (*nel nuoto*) stroke
'braccio ['brattʃo] (*pl(f)* **braccia**) *sm* (*Anat*) arm; (*pl(m)* **bracci**: *di gru, fiume*) arm; (: *di edificio*) wing; **braccio di**

mare sound; **bracci'olo** sm (appoggio) arm

'bracco, -chi sm hound

'brace ['bratʃe] sf embers pl

braci'ola [bra'tʃɔla] sf (Cuc) chop

'branca, -che sf branch

branchia ['brankja] sf (Zool) gill

'branco, -chi sm (di cani, lupi) pack; (di pecore) flock; (peg: di persone) gang, pack

bran'dina sf camp bed (BRIT), cot (US)

'brano sm piece; (di libro) passage

Bra'sile sm **il ~** Brazil; **brasili'ano, -a** ag, sm/f Brazilian

'bravo, -a ag (abile) clever, capable, skilful; (buono) good, honest; (: bambino) good; (coraggioso) brave; **~!** well done!; (a teatro) bravo!

bra'vura sf cleverness, skill

Bre'tagna [bre'taɲɲa] sf **la ~** Brittany

bre'tella sf (Aut) link; **bretelle** sfpl (di calzoni) braces

'bretone ag, sm/f Breton

'breve ag brief, short; **in ~** in short

brevet'tare vt to patent

bre'vetto sm patent; **brevetto di pilotaggio** pilot's licence (BRIT) o license (US)

'bricco, -chi sm jug; **bricco del caffè** coffeepot

'briciola ['britʃola] sf crumb

'briciolo ['britʃolo] sm (specie fig) bit

'briga, -ghe sf (fastidio) trouble, bother; **pigliarsi la ~ di fare qc** to take the trouble to do sth

bri'gata sf (Mil) brigade; (gruppo) group, party; **Brigate Rosse** (Pol) Red Brigades

'briglia ['briʎʎa] sf rein; **a ~ sciolta** at full gallop; (fig) at full speed

bril'lante ag bright; (anche fig) brilliant; (che luccica) shining ▶ sm diamond

bril'lare vi to shine; (mina) to blow up ▶ vt (mina) to set off

'brillo, -a ag merry, tipsy

'brina sf hoarfrost

brin'dare vi **~ a qn/qc** to drink to o toast sb/sth

'brindisi sm inv toast

bri'oche [bri'ɔʃ] sf inv brioche

bri'tannico, -a, -ci, -che ag British

'brivido sm shiver; (di ribrezzo) shudder; (fig) thrill

brizzo'lato, -a [brittso'lato] ag (persona) going grey; (barba, capelli) greying

'brocca, -che sf jug

'broccoli smpl broccoli sg

'brodo sm broth; (per cucinare) stock; **brodo ristretto** consommé

bron'chite [bron'kite] sf (Med) bronchitis

bronto'lare vi to grumble; (tuono, stomaco) to rumble

'bronzo ['brondzo] sm bronze

'browser ['brauzer] sm inv (Inform) browser

brucia'pelo [brutʃa'pelo]: **a ~** av point-blank

bruci'are [bru'tʃare] vt to burn; (scottare) to scald ▶ vi to burn; **bruciarsi** vpr to burn o.s.; (fallire) to ruin one's chances; **~ le tappe** (fig) to shoot ahead; **bruciarsi la carriera** to ruin one's career

'bruco, -chi sm caterpillar; grub

'brufolo sm pimple, spot

'brullo, -a ag bare, bleak

'bruno, -a ag brown, dark; (persona) dark(-haired)

'brusco, -a, -schi, -sche ag (sapore) sharp; (modi, persona) brusque, abrupt; (movimento) abrupt, sudden

bru'sio sm buzz, buzzing

bru'tale ag brutal

'brutto, -a ag ugly; (cattivo) bad; (malattia, strada, affare) nasty, bad; **~ tempo** bad weather

Bru'xelles [bry'sɛl] sf Brussels

BSE [biɛssɛ'e] *sigla f* (= *encefalopatia spongiforme bovina*) BSE

'**buca, -che** *sf* hole; (*avvallamento*) hollow; **buca delle lettere** letterbox

buca'neve *sm inv* snowdrop

bu'care *vt* (*forare*) to make a hole (*o* holes) in; (*pungere*) to pierce; (*biglietto*) to punch; **bucarsi** *vpr* (*di eroina*) to mainline; **~ una gomma** to have a puncture

bu'cato *sm* (*operazione*) washing; (*panni*) wash, washing

'**buccia, -ce** ['buttʃa] *sf* skin, peel

bucherò *ecc* [buke'rɔ] *vb vedi* **bucare**

'**buco, -chi** *sm* hole

bud'dismo *sm* Buddhism

bu'dino *sm* pudding

'**bue** *sm* ox; **carne di ~** beef

bu'fera *sf* storm

'**buffo, -a** *ag* funny; (*Teatro*) comic

bu'gia, -gie [bu'dʒia] *sf* lie; **dire una ~** to tell a lie; **bugi'ardo, -a** *ag* lying, deceitful ▶ *sm/f* liar

'**buio, -a** *ag* dark ▶ *sm* dark, darkness

'**bulbo** *sm* (*Bot*) bulb; **bulbo oculare** eyeball

Bulga'ria *sf* **la ~** Bulgaria

'**bulgaro, -a** *ag, sm/f, sm* Bulgarian

buli'mia *sf* bulimia; **bu'limico, -a, -ci, -che** *ag* bulimic

bul'lismo [bul'lizmo] *sm* bullying

bul'lone *sm* bolt

buona'notte *escl* good night! ▶ *sf* **dare la ~ a** to say good night to

buona'sera *escl* good evening!

buongi'orno [bwon'dʒorno] *escl* good morning (*o* afternoon)!

buongus'taio, -a *sm/f* gourmet

○ **bu'ono, -a**
(*ag: dav sm* **buon** + *C o* V, **buono** + *s impura, gn, pn, ps, x, z; dav sf* **buon'** + V) *ag*

1 (*gen*) good; **un buon pranzo** a good lunch; **(stai) buono!** behave!

2 (*benevolo*): **buono (con)** good (to), kind (to)

3 (*giusto, valido*) right; **al momento buono** at the right moment

4 (*adatto*): **buono a/da** fit for/to; **essere buono a nulla** to be no good *o* use at anything

5 (*auguri*): **buon anno!** happy New Year!; **buon appetito!** enjoy your meal!; **buon compleanno!** happy birthday!; **buon divertimento!** have a nice time!; **buona fortuna!** good luck!; **buon riposo!** sleep well!; **buon viaggio!** bon voyage!, have a good trip!

6: **a buon mercato** cheap; **di buon'ora** early; **buon senso** common sense; **alla buona** *ag* simple

▶ *av* in a simple way, without any fuss

▶ *sm*

1 (*bontà*) goodness, good

2 (*Comm*) voucher, coupon; **buono di cassa** cash voucher; **buono di consegna** delivery note; **buono del Tesoro** Treasury bill

buon'senso *sm* = **buon senso**

burat'tino *sm* puppet

'**burbero, -a** *ag* surly, gruff

buro'cratico, -a, ci, che *ag* bureaucratic

burocra'zia [burokrat'tsia] *sf* bureaucracy

bur'rasca, -sche *sf* storm

'**burro** *sm* butter

bur'rone *sm* ravine

bus'sare *vi* to knock

'**bussola** *sf* compass

'**busta** *sf* (*da lettera*) envelope; (*astuccio*) case; **in ~ aperta/chiusa** in an unsealed/sealed envelope; **busta paga** pay packet

busta'rella *sf* bribe, backhander

bus'tina *sf* (*piccola busta*) envelope; (*di cibi, farmaci*) sachet; (*Mil*) forage cap; **bustina di tè** tea bag

'**busto** *sm* bust; (*indumento*) corset, girdle; **a mezzo ~** (*foto*) half-length

but'tare *vt* to throw; (*anche*: **~ via**) to

throw away; **~ giù** (*scritto*) to scribble down; (*cibo*) to gulp down; (*edificio*) to pull down, demolish; (*pasta, verdura*) to put into boiling water; **buttarsi** *vpr* (*saltare*) to jump; **buttarsi dalla finestra** to jump out of the window

byte ['bait] *sm inv* byte

C

ca'bina *sf* (*di nave*) cabin; (*da spiaggia*) beach hut; (*di autocarro, treno*) cab; (*di aereo*) cockpit; (*di ascensore*) cage; **cabi'nato** *sm* cabin cruiser; **cabina di pilotaggio** cockpit; **cabina telefonica** call *o* (tele)phone box

ca'cao *sm* cocoa

'caccia ['kattʃa] *sf* hunting; (*con fucile*) shooting; (*inseguimento*) chase; (*cacciagione*) game ▶ *sm inv* (*aereo*) fighter; (*nave*) destroyer; **caccia grossa** big-game hunting; **caccia all'uomo** manhunt

cacci'are [kat'tʃare] *vt* to hunt; (*mandar via*) to chase away; (*ficcare*) to shove, stick ▶ *vi* to hunt; **cacciarsi** *vpr* **dove s'è cacciata la mia borsa?** where has my bag got to?; **cacciarsi nei guai** to get into trouble; **~ fuori qc** to whip *o* pull sth out; **~ un urlo** to let out a yell; **caccia'tore** *sm* hunter; **cacciatore di frodo** poacher

caccia'vite [kattʃa'vite] *sm inv* screwdriver

'cactus *sm inv* cactus

ca'davere *sm* (dead) body, corpse

'caddi *ecc vb vedi* **cadere**

ca'denza [ka'dɛntsa] *sf* cadence; (*ritmo*) rhythm; (*Mus*) cadenza

ca'dere *vi* to fall; (*denti, capelli*) to fall out; (*tetto*) to fall in; **questa gonna cade bene** this skirt hangs well; **lasciar ~** (*anche fig*) to drop; (*anche: ~ dal sonno*) to be falling asleep on one's feet; **~ dalle nuvole** (*fig*) to be taken aback

cadrò *ecc vb vedi* **cadere**

ca'duta *sf* fall; **la ~ dei capelli** hair loss

caffè *sm inv* coffee; (*locale*) café; **caffè corretto** espresso coffee with a shot of spirits; **caffè macchiato** coffee with a dash of milk; **caffè macinato** ground coffee

caffel'latte *sm inv* white coffee

caffetti'era *sf* coffeepot

'cagna ['kaɲɲa] *sf* (*Zool, peg*) bitch

CAI *sigla m* = **Club Alpino Italiano**

cala'brone *sm* hornet

cala'maro *sm* squid

cala'mita *sf* magnet

calamità *sf inv* calamity, disaster

ca'lare *vt* (*far discendere*) to lower; (*Maglia*) to decrease ▶ *vi* (*discendere*) to go *o* come down; (*tramontare*) to set, go down; **~ di peso** to lose weight

cal'cagno [kal'kaɲɲo] *sm* heel

cal'care *sm* (*incrostazione*) (lime)scale

'calce ['kaltʃe] *sm* **in ~** at the foot of the page ▶ *sf* lime; **calce viva** quicklime

cal'cetto [kal'tʃetto] *sm* (*calcio-balilla*) table football; (*calcio a cinque*) five-a-side (football)

calci'are [kal'tʃare] *vt, vi* to kick; **calcia'tore** *sm* footballer

'calcio ['kaltʃo] *sm* (*pedata*) kick; (*sport*) football, soccer; (*di pistola, fucile*) butt; (*Chim*) calcium; **calcio d'angolo** (*Sport*) corner (kick); **calcio**

di punizione (*Sport*) free kick; **calcio di rigore** penalty

calco'lare *vt* to calculate, work out, reckon; (*ponderare*) to weigh (up); **calcola'tore, -'trice** *ag* calculating ▶ *sm* calculator; (*fig*) calculating person; **calcolatore elettronico** computer; **calcola'trice** *sf* calculator

'**calcolo** *sm* (*anche Mat*) calculation; (*infinitesimale ecc*) calculus; (*Med*) stone; **fare i propri calcoli** (*fig*) to weigh the pros and cons

cal'daia *sf* boiler

'**caldo, -a** *ag* warm; (*molto caldo*) hot; (*fig: appassionato*) keen ▶ *sm* heat; **ho ~** I'm warm/hot; **fa ~** it's warm/hot

caleidos'copio *sm* kaleidoscope

calen'dario *sm* calendar

'**calibro** *sm* (*di arma*) calibre, bore; (*Tecn*) callipers *pl*; (*fig*) calibre; **di grosso ~** (*fig*) prominent

'**calice** ['kalitʃe] *sm* goblet; (*Rel*) chalice

Cali'fornia *sf* California

californi'ano, -a *ag* Californian

calligra'fia *sf* (*scrittura*) handwriting; (*arte*) calligraphy

'**callo** *sm* callus; (*ai piedi*) corn

'**calma** *sf* calm

cal'mante *sm* tranquillizer

cal'mare *vt* to calm; (*lenire*) to soothe; **calmarsi** *vpr* to grow calm, calm down; (*vento*) to abate; (*dolori*) to ease

'**calmo, -a** *ag* calm, quiet

'**calo** *sm* (*Comm: di prezzi*) fall; (*: di volume*) shrinkage; (*: di peso*) loss

ca'lore *sm* warmth; heat

calo'ria *sf* calorie

calo'rifero *sm* radiator

calo'roso, -a *ag* warm

calpes'tare *vt* to tread on, trample on; "**è vietato ~ l'erba**" "keep off the grass"

ca'lunnia *sf* slander; (*scritta*) libel

cal'vizie [kal'vittsje] *sf* baldness

'**calvo, -a** *ag* bald

'**calza** ['kaltsa] *sf* (*da donna*) stocking; (*da uomo*) sock; **fare la ~** to knit; **calze di nailon** nylons, (nylon) stockings

calza'maglia [kaltsa'maʎʎa] *sf* tights *pl*; (*per danza, ginnastica*) leotard

calzet'tone [kaltset'tone] *sm* heavy knee-length sock

cal'zino [kal'tsino] *sm* sock

calzo'laio [kaltso'lajo] *sm* shoemaker; (*che ripara scarpe*) cobbler

calzon'cini [kaltson'tʃini] *smpl* shorts; **calzoncini da bagno** (swimming) trunks

cal'zone [kal'tsone] *sm* trouser leg; (*Cuc*) savoury turnover made with pizza dough; **calzoni** *smpl* (*pantaloni*) trousers (*BRIT*), pants (*US*)

camale'onte *sm* chameleon

cambia'mento *sm* change

cambi'are *vt* to change; (*modificare*) to alter, change; (*barattare*): **~ (qc con qn/qc)** to exchange (sth with sb/for sth) ▶ *vi* to change, alter; **cambiarsi** *vpr* (*d'abito*) to change; **~ casa** to move (house); **~ idea** to change one's mind; **~ treno** to change trains; **dove posso ~ dei soldi?** where can I change some money?; **ha da ~?** have you got any change?; **posso cambiarlo, per favore?** could I exchange this, please?

cambiava'lute *sm inv* exchange office

'**cambio** *sm* change; (*modifica*) alteration, change; (*scambio, Comm*) exchange; (*corso dei cambi*) rate (of exchange); (*Tecn, Aut*) gears *pl*; **in ~ di** in exchange for; **dare il ~ a qn** to take over from sb

'**camera** *sf* room; (*anche: ~ da letto*) bedroom; (*Pol*) chamber, house; **camera ardente** mortuary chapel; **camera d'aria** inner tube; (*di pallone*) bladder; **camera di commercio** Chamber of Commerce; **Camera dei Deputati** Chamber of Deputies,

≈ House of Commons (BRIT), ≈ House of Representatives (US); **camera a gas** gas chamber; **camera a un letto/due letti** single/twin-bedded room; **camera matrimoniale** double room; **camera oscura** (Fot) dark room

Attenzione! In inglese esiste la parola *camera*, che però significa *macchina fotografica*.

came'rata, -i, -e sm/f companion, mate ▶ sf dormitory

cameri'era sf (domestica) maid; (che serve a tavola) waitress; (che fa le camere) chambermaid

cameri'ere sm (man)servant; (di ristorante) waiter

came'rino sm (Teatro) dressing room

'camice ['kamitʃe] sm (Rel) alb; (per medici ecc) white coat

cami'cetta [kami'tʃetta] sf blouse

ca'micia, -cie [ka'mitʃa] sf (da uomo) shirt; (da donna) blouse; **camicia di forza** straitjacket; **camicia da notte** (da donna) nightdress; (da uomo) nightshirt

cami'netto sm hearth, fireplace

ca'mino sm chimney; (focolare) fireplace, hearth

'camion sm inv lorry (BRIT), truck (US)

camio'nista, -i sm lorry driver (BRIT), truck driver (US)

cam'mello sm (Zool) camel; (tessuto) camel hair

cammi'nare vi to walk; (funzionare) to work, go

cam'mino sm walk; (sentiero) path; (itinerario, direzione, tragitto) way; **mettersi in ~** to set o start off

camo'milla sf camomile; (infuso) camomile tea

ca'moscio [ka'moʃʃo] sm chamois; **di ~** (scarpe, borsa) suede cpd

cam'pagna [kam'paɲɲa] sf country, countryside; (Pol, Comm, Mil)

campaign; **in ~** in the country; **andare in ~** to go to the country; **fare una ~** to campaign; **campagna pubblicitaria** advertising campaign

cam'pana sf bell; (anche: **~ di vetro**) bell jar; **campa'nello** sm (all'uscio, da tavola) bell

campa'nile sm bell tower, belfry

cam'peggio sm camping; (terreno) camp site; **fare (del) ~** to go camping

camper ['kamper] sm inv motor caravan (BRIT), motor home (US)

campio'nario, -a ag **fiera campionaria** trade fair ▶ sm collection of samples

campio'nato sm championship

campi'one, -'essa sm/f (Sport) champion ▶ sm (Comm) sample

'campo sm field; (Mil) field; (accampamento) camp; (spazio delimitato: sportivo ecc) ground; field; (di quadro) background; **i campi** (campagna) the countryside; **campo da aviazione** airfield; **campo di battaglia** (Mil, fig) battlefield; **campo di concentramento** concentration camp; **campo da golf** golf course; **campo profughi** refugee camp; **campo sportivo** sports ground; **campo da tennis** tennis court; **campo visivo** field of vision

'Canada sm **il ~** Canada; **cana'dese** ag, sm/f Canadian ▶ sf (anche: **tenda canadese**) ridge tent

ca'naglia [ka'naʎʎa] sf rabble, mob; (persona) scoundrel, rogue

ca'nale sm (anche fig) channel; (artificiale) canal

'canapa sf hemp; **canapa indiana** (droga) cannabis

cana'rino sm canary

cancel'lare [kantʃel'lare] vt (con la gomma) to rub out, erase; (con la penna) to strike out; (annullare) to annul, cancel; (disdire) to cancel

cancelle'ria [kantʃelle'ria] *sf* chancery; (*materiale per scrivere*) stationery

can'cello [kan'tʃɛllo] *sm* gate

'cancro *sm* (*Med*) cancer; (*dello zodiaco*): **C~** Cancer

candeg'gina [kanded'dʒina] *sf* bleach

can'dela *sf* candle; **candela (di accensione)** (*Aut*) spark(ing) plug

cande'labro *sm* candelabra

candeli'ere *sm* candlestick

candi'dare *vt* to present as candidate; **candidarsi** *vpr* to present o.s. as candidate

candi'dato, -a *sm/f* candidate; (*aspirante a una carica*) applicant

'candido, -a *ag* white as snow; (*puro*) pure; (*sincero*) sincere, candid

can'dito, -a *ag* candied

'cane *sm* dog; (*di pistola, fucile*) cock; **fa un freddo ~** it's bitterly cold; **non c'era un ~** there wasn't a soul; **cane da caccia/da guardia** hunting/guard dog; **cane lupo** Alsatian; **cane pastore** sheepdog

ca'nestro *sm* basket

can'guro *sm* kangaroo

ca'nile *sm* kennel; (*di allevamento*) kennels *pl*; **canile municipale** dog pound

'canna *sf* (*pianta*) reed; (: indica, da zucchero) cane; (*bastone*) stick, cane; (*di fucile*) barrel; (*di organo*) pipe; (*fam: droga*) joint; **canna fumaria** chimney flue; **canna da pesca** (fishing) rod; **canna da zucchero** sugar cane

cannel'loni *smpl* pasta tubes stuffed with sauce and baked

cannocchi'ale [kannok'kjale] *sm* telescope

can'none *sm* (*Mil*) gun; (*Storia*) cannon; (*tubo*) pipe, tube; (*piega*) box pleat; (*fig*) ace

can'nuccia, -ce [kan'nuttʃa] *sf* (drinking) straw

ca'noa *sf* canoe

'canone *sm* canon, criterion; (*mensile, annuo*) rent; fee

canot'taggio [kanot'taddʒo] *sm* rowing

canotti'era *sf* vest

ca'notto *sm* small boat, dinghy; canoe

can'tante *sm/f* singer

can'tare *vt, vi* to sing; **cantau'tore, -'trice** *sm/f* singer-composer

canti'ere *sm* (*Edil*) (building) site; (*cantiere navale*) shipyard

can'tina *sf* cellar; (*bottega*) wine shop; **cantina sociale** cooperative winegrowers' association

> Attenzione! In inglese esiste la parola *canteen*, che però significa *mensa*.

'canto *sm* song; (*arte*) singing; (*Rel*) chant; chanting; (*poesia*) poem, lyric; (*parte di una poesia*) canto; (*parte, lato*): **da un ~** on the one hand; **d'altro ~** on the other hand

canzo'nare [kantso'nare] *vt* to tease

can'zone [kan'tsone] *sf* song; (*Poesia*) canzone

'caos *sm inv* chaos; **ca'otico, -a, -ci, -che** *ag* chaotic

CAP *sigla m* = **codice di avviamento postale**

ca'pace [ka'patʃe] *ag* able, capable; (*ampio, vasto*) large, capacious; **sei ~ di farlo?** can you o are you able to do it?; **capacità** *sf inv* ability; (*Dir, di recipiente*) capacity

ca'panna *sf* hut

capan'none *sm* (*Agr*) barn; (*fabbricato industriale*) (factory) shed

ca'parbio, -a *ag* stubborn

ca'parra *sf* deposit, down payment

ca'pello *sm* hair; **capelli** *smpl* (*capigliatura*) hair *sg*

ca'pezzolo [ka'pettsolo] *sm* nipple

ca'pire *vt* to understand; **non capisco** I don't understand

capi'tale *ag* (*mortale*) capital; (*fondamentale*) main, chief ▶ *sf* (*città*) capital ▶ *sm* (*Econ*) capital

capi'tano *sm* captain

capi'tare *vi* (*giungere casualmente*) to happen to go, find o.s.; (*accadere*) to happen; (*presentarsi: cosa*) to turn up, present itself ▶ *vb impers* to happen; **mi è capitato un guaio** I've had a spot of trouble

capi'tello *sm* (*Archit*) capital

ca'pitolo *sm* chapter

capi'tombolo *sm* headlong fall, tumble

'capo *sm* head; (*persona*) head, leader; (: *in ufficio*) head, boss; (: *in tribù*) chief; (*di oggetti*) head; top; end; (*Geo*) cape; **andare a ~** to start a new paragraph; **da ~** over again; **capo di bestiame** head *inv* of cattle; **capo di vestiario** item of clothing; **Capo'danno** *sm* New Year; **capo'giro** *sm* dizziness *no pl*; **capola'voro, -i** *sm* masterpiece; **capo'linea** (*pl* **capi'linea**) *sm* terminus; **capostazi'one** (*pl* **capistazi'one**) *sm* station master

capo'tavola (*pl(m)* **capi'tavola**) *pl(f) inv sm/f* (*persona*) head of the table; **sedere a ~** to sit at the head of the table

capo'volgere [kapo'vɔldʒere] *vt* to overturn; (*fig*) to reverse; **capovolgersi** *vpr* to overturn; (*barca*) to capsize; (*fig*) to be reversed

'cappa *sf* (*mantello*) cape, cloak; (*del camino*) hood

cap'pella *sf* (*Rel*) chapel

cap'pello *sm* hat

'cappero *sm* caper

cap'pone *sm* capon

cap'potto *sm* (over)coat

cappuc'cino [kapput'tʃino] *sm* (*frate*) Capuchin monk; (*bevanda*) cappuccino, *frothy white coffee*

cap'puccio [kap'puttʃo] *sm* (*copricapo*) hood; (*della biro*) cap

'capra *sf* (she-)goat

ca'priccio [ka'prittʃo] *sm* caprice, whim; (*bizza*) tantrum; **fare i capricci** to be very naughty; **capricci'oso, -a** *ag* capricious, whimsical; naughty

Capri'corno *sm* Capricorn

capri'ola *sf* somersault

capri'olo *sm* roe deer

'capro *sm* ~ **espiatorio** scapegoat

ca'prone *sm* billy-goat

'capsula *sf* capsule; (*di arma, per bottiglie*) cap

cap'tare *vt* (*Radio, TV*) to pick up; (*cattivarsi*) to gain, win

carabini'ere *sm member of Italian military police force*

● **carabinieri**
● Originally part of the armed forces,
● the **carabinieri** are police who
● perform both military and civil
● duties. They include paratroopers
● and mounted divisions.

ca'raffa *sf* carafe

Ca'raibi *smpl* **il mar dei ~** the Caribbean (Sea)

cara'mella *sf* sweet

ca'rattere *sm* character; (*caratteristica*) characteristic, trait; **avere un buon ~** to be good-natured; **carattere jolly** wild card; **caratte'ristica, -che** *sf* characteristic, trait, peculiarity; **caratte'ristico, -a, -ci, -che** *ag* characteristic

car'bone *sm* coal

carbu'rante *sm* (motor) fuel

carbura'tore *sm* carburettor

carce'rato, -a [kartʃe'rato] *sm/f* prisoner

'carcere ['kartʃere] *sm* prison; (*pena*) imprisonment

carci'ofo [kar'tʃɔfo] *sm* artichoke

cardel'lino sm goldfinch

car'diaco, -a, -ci, -che ag cardiac, heart cpd

cardi'nale ag, sm cardinal

'**cardine** sm hinge

'**cardo** sm thistle

ca'rente ag ~ **di** lacking in

cares'tia sf famine; (penuria) scarcity, dearth

ca'rezza [ka'rettsa] sf caress

'**carica, -che** sf (mansione ufficiale) office, position; (Mil, Tecn, Elettr) charge; **ha una forte ~ di simpatia** he's very likeable; vedi anche **carico**

caricabatte'ria sm inv battery charger

cari'care vt (merce, Inform) to load; (orologio) to wind up; (batteria, Mil) to charge

'**carico, -a, -chi, -che** ag (che porta un peso): ~ **di** loaded o laden with; (fucile) loaded; (orologio) wound up; (batteria) charged; (colore) deep; (caffè, tè) strong ▶ sm (il caricare) loading; (ciò che si carica) load; (fig: peso) burden, weight; **persona a ~** dependent; **essere a ~ di qn** (spese ecc) to be charged to sb

'**carie** sf (dentaria) decay

ca'rino, -a ag (grazioso) lovely, pretty, nice; (riferito a uomo, anche simpatico) nice

carità sf charity; **per ~!** (escl di rifiuto) good heavens, no!

carnagi'one [karna'dʒone] sf complexion

'**carne** sf flesh; (bovina, ovina ecc) meat; **non mangio ~** I don't eat meat; **carne di maiale/manzo/pecora** pork/beef/mutton; **carne in scatola** tinned o canned meat; **carne tritata** o **macinata** mince (BRIT), hamburger meat (US), minced (BRIT) o ground (US) meat

carne'vale sm carnival

○ **carnevale**
○ **Carnevale** is the period between
○ Epiphany (Jan. 6th) and the
○ beginning of Lent. People wear
○ fancy dress, and there are parties,
○ processions of floats and bonfires. It
○ culminates immediately before Lent
○ in the festivities of **martedì grasso**
○ (Shrove Tuesday).

'**caro, -a** ag (amato) dear; (costoso) dear, expensive; **è troppo ~** it's too expensive

ca'rogna [ka'roɲɲa] sf carrion; (anche: fig: fam) swine

ca'rota sf carrot

caro'vana sf caravan

car'poni av on all fours

car'rabile ag suitable for vehicles; "**passo ~**" "keep clear"

carreggi'ata [karred'dʒata] sf carriageway (BRIT), (road)way

car'rello sm trolley; (Aer) undercarriage; (Cinema) dolly; (di macchina da scrivere) carriage

carri'era sf career; **fare ~** to get on; **a gran ~** at full speed

carri'ola sf wheelbarrow

'**carro** sm cart, wagon; **carro armato** tank; **carro attrezzi** breakdown van

car'rozza [kar'rottsa] sf carriage, coach

carrozze'ria [karrottse'ria] sf body, coachwork (BRIT); (officina) coachbuilder's workshop (BRIT), body shop

carroz'zina [karrot'tsina] sf pram (BRIT), baby carriage (US)

'**carta** sf paper; (al ristorante) menu; (Geo) map; plan; (documento) card; (costituzione) charter; **carte** sfpl (documenti) papers, documents; **alla ~** (al ristorante) à la carte; **carta assegni** bank card; **carta assorbente** blotting paper; **carta bollata** o **da bollo** official stamped caso | 41

paper; **carta (da gioco)** playing card; **carta di credito** credit card; **carta (geografica)** map; **carta d'identità** identity card; **carta igienica** toilet paper; **carta d'imbarco** (*Aer, Naut*) boarding card; **carta da lettere** writing paper; **carta da pacchi** wrapping paper; **carta da parati** wallpaper; **carta stradale** road map; **carta verde** (*Aut*) green card; **carta vetrata** sandpaper; **carta da visita** visiting card

car'taccia, -ce [kar'tattʃa] *sf* waste paper

carta'pesta *sf* papier-mâché

car'tella *sf* (*scheda*) card; (*Inform, custodia: di cartone*) folder; (: *di uomo d'affari ecc*) briefcase; (: *di scolaro*) schoolbag, satchel; **cartella clinica** (*Med*) case sheet

cartel'lino *sm* (*etichetta*) label; (*su porta*) notice; (*scheda*) card; **timbrare il ~** (*all'entrata*) to clock in; (*all'uscita*) to clock out; **cartellino di presenza** clock card, timecard

car'tello *sm* sign; (*pubblicitario*) poster; (*stradale*) sign, signpost; (*Econ*) cartel; (*in dimostrazioni*) placard; **cartello stradale** sign; **cartel'lone** *sm* (*della tombola*) scoring frame; (*Teatro*) playbill; **tenere il cartellone** (*spettacolo*) to have a long run; **cartellone pubblicitario** advertising poster

car'tina *sf* (*Aut, Geo*) map

car'toccio [kar'tɔttʃo] *sm* paper bag

cartole'ria *sf* stationer's (shop)

carto'lina *sf* postcard; **cartolina postale** ready-stamped postcard

car'tone *sm* cardboard; (*Arte*) cartoon; **cartoni animati** (*Cinema*) cartoons

car'tuccia, -ce [kar'tuttʃa] *sf* cartridge

'casa *sf* house; (*in senso astratto*) home; (*Comm*) firm, house; **essere a ~** to be at home; **vado a ~ mia/tua** I'm going home/to your house; **vino della ~** house wine; **casa di cura** nursing home; **casa editrice** publishing house; **Casa delle Libertà** *centre-right coalition*; **casa di riposo** (*old people's*) home, care home; **case popolari** ≈ council houses (*o* flats) (*BRIT*), ≈ public housing units (*US*); **casa dello studente** student hostel

ca'sacca, -che *sf* military coat; (*di fantino*) blouse

casa'linga, -ghe *sf* housewife

casa'lingo, -a, -ghi, -ghe *ag* household, domestic; (*fatto a casa*) home-made; (*semplice*) homely; (*amante della casa*) home-loving

cas'care *vi* to fall; **cas'cata** *sf* fall; (*d'acqua*) cascade, waterfall

cascherò *ecc* [kaske'rɔ] *vb vedi* cascare

'casco, -schi *sm* helmet; (*del parrucchiere*) hair-drier; (*di banane*) bunch; **casco blu** (*Mil*) blue helmet (*UN soldier*)

casei'ficio [kazei'fitʃo] *sm* creamery

ca'sella *sf* pigeon-hole; **casella e-mail** (*Comput*) mailbox; **casella postale** post office box

ca'sello *sm* (*di autostrada*) toll-house

ca'serma *sf* barracks *pl*

casset'tiera [kasset'tjɛra] *sf* chest of drawers

ca'sino (*fam*) *sm* brothel; (*confusione*) row, racket

casinò *sm inv* casino

'caso *sm* chance; (*fatto, vicenda*) event, incident; (*possibilità*) possibility; (*Med, Ling*) case; **a ~** at random; **per ~** by chance, by accident; **in ogni ~, in tutti i casi** in any case, at any rate; **al ~** should the opportunity arise; **nel ~ che** in case; **~ mai** if by chance; **caso limite** borderline case

caso'lare *sm* cottage

'**caspita** *escl* (*sorpresa*) good heavens!; (*impazienza*) for goodness' sake!

'**cassa** *sf* case, crate, box; (*bara*) coffin; (*mobile*) chest; (*involucro: di orologio ecc*) case; (*macchina*) cash register, till; (*luogo di pagamento*) checkout (counter); (*fondo*) fund; (*istituto bancario*) bank; **cassa automatica prelievi** cash dispenser; **cassa continua** night safe; **cassa mutua** o **malattia** health insurance scheme; **cassa integrazione: mettere in cassa integrazione** ≈ to lay off; **cassa di risparmio** savings bank; **cassa toracica** (*Anat*) chest

cassa'forte (*pl* **casse'forti**) *sf* safe; **lo potrebbe mettere nella ~?** could you put this in the safe, please?

cassa'panca (*pl* **cassa'panche** o **casse'panche**) *sf* settle

casseru'ola *sf* saucepan

cas'setta *sf* box; (*per registratore*) cassette; (*Cinema, Teatro*) box-office takings *pl*; **film di ~** box-office draw; **cassetta di sicurezza** strongbox; **cassetta delle lettere** letterbox

cas'setto *sm* drawer

cassi'ere, -a *sm/f* cashier; (*di banca*) teller

casso'netto *sm* wheelie-bin

cas'tagna [kas'taɲɲa] *sf* chestnut

cas'tagno [kas'taɲɲo] *sm* chestnut (tree)

cas'tano, -a *ag* chestnut (brown)

cas'tello *sm* castle; (*Tecn*) scaffolding

casti'gare *vt* to punish; **cas'tigo, -ghi** *sm* punishment; **mettere/essere in ~** to punish/be punished

cas'toro *sm* beaver

casu'ale *ag* chance *cpd*; (*Inform*) random *cpd*

catalizza'tore [kataliddza'tore] *sm* (*anche fig*) catalyst; (*Aut*) catalytic converter

ca'talogo, -ghi *sm* catalogue

catarifran'gente [katarifran'dʒɛnte] *sm* (*Aut*) reflector

ca'tarro *sm* catarrh

ca'tastrofe *sf* catastrophe, disaster

catego'ria *sf* category

ca'tena *sf* chain; **catena di montaggio** assembly line; **catene da neve** (*Aut*) snow chains; **cate'nina** *sf* (*gioiello*) (thin) chain

cate'ratta *sf* cataract; (*chiusa*) sluice-gate

ca'tino *sm* basin

ca'trame *sm* tar

'**cattedra** *sf* teacher's desk; (*di docente*) chair

catte'drale *sf* cathedral

catti'veria *sf* malice, spite; naughtiness; (*atto*) spiteful act; (*parole*) malicious o spiteful remark

cat'tivo, -a *ag* bad; (*malvagio*) bad, wicked; (*turbolento: bambino*) bad, naughty; (: *mare*) rough; (*odore, sapore*) nasty, bad

cat'tolico, -a, -ci, -che *ag, sm/f* (Roman) Catholic

cattu'rare *vt* to capture

'**causa** *sf* cause; (*Dir*) lawsuit, case, action; **a ~ di, per ~ di** because of; **fare** o **muovere ~ a qn** to take legal action against sb

cau'sare *vt* to cause

cau'tela *sf* caution, prudence

'**cauto, -a** *ag* cautious, prudent

cauzi'one [kaut'tsjone] *sf* security; (*Dir*) bail

'**cava** *sf* quarry

caval'care *vt* (*cavallo*) to ride; (*muro*) to sit astride; (*ponte*) to span; **caval'cata** *sf* ride; (*gruppo di persone*) riding party

cavalca'via *sm inv* flyover

cavalci'oni [kaval'tʃoni]: **a ~ di** *prep* astride

cavali'ere *sm* rider; (*feudale, titolo*)

knight; (*soldato*) cavalryman; (*al ballo*) partner

caval'letta *sf* grasshopper

caval'letto *sm* (*Fot*) tripod; (*da pittore*) easel

ca'vallo *sm* horse; (*Scacchi*) knight; (*Aut: anche*: ~ **vapore**) horsepower; (*dei pantaloni*) crotch; **a** ~ on horseback; **a** ~ **di** astride, straddling; **cavallo di battaglia** (*fig*) hobby-horse; **cavallo da corsa** racehorse; **cavallo a dondolo** rocking horse

ca'vare *vt* (*togliere*) to draw out, extract, take out; (: *giacca, scarpe*) to take off; (: *fame, sete, voglia*) to satisfy; **cavarsela** to manage, get on all right; (*scamparla*) to get away with it

cava'tappi *sm inv* corkscrew

ca'verna *sf* cave

'cavia *sf* guinea pig

cavi'ale *sm* caviar

ca'viglia [ka'viʎʎa] *sf* ankle

'cavo, -a *ag* hollow ▶ *sm* (*Anat*) cavity; (*corda, Elettr, Tel*) cable

cavo'letto *sm* ~ **di Bruxelles** Brussels sprout

cavolfi'ore *sm* cauliflower

'cavolo *sm* cabbage; (*fam*): **non m'importa un** ~ I don't give a damn

'cazzo ['kattso] *sm* (*fam!: pene*) prick (!); **non gliene importa un** ~ (*fig fam!*) he doesn't give a damn about it; **fatti i cazzi tuoi** (*fig fam!*) mind your own damn business

C.C.D. *sigla m* (= *Centro Cristiano Democratico*) *Italian political party of the centre*

CD *sm inv* CD; (*lettore*) CD player

CD-Rom *sigla m* [tʃidi'rɔm] *sm inv* CD-ROM

C.D.U. *sigla m* (= *Cristiano Democratici Uniti*) *Italian centre-right political party*

ce [tʃe] *pron, av vedi* **ci**

Ce'cenia [tʃe'tʃɛnja] *sf* **la** ~ Chechnya

ce'ceno, -a [tʃe'tʃɛno] *sm/f, ag* Chechen

'ceco, -a, -chi, -che ['tʃɛko] *ag, sm/f* Czech; **la Repubblica Ceca** the Czech Republic

'cedere ['tʃedere] *vt* (*concedere posto*) to give up; (*Dir*) to transfer, make over ▶ *vi* (*cadere*) to give way, subside; ~ **(a)** to surrender (to), yield (to), give in (to)

'cedola ['tʃedola] *sf* (*Comm*) coupon; voucher

'ceffo ['tʃɛffo] (*peg*) *sm* ugly mug

cef'fone [tʃef'fone] *sm* slap, smack

cele'brare [tʃele'brare] *vt* to celebrate

'celebre ['tʃɛlebre] *ag* famous, celebrated

ce'leste [tʃe'lɛste] *ag* celestial; heavenly; (*colore*) sky-blue

'celibe ['tʃɛlibe] *ag* single, unmarried

'cella ['tʃɛlla] *sf* cell; **cella frigorifera** cold store

'cellula ['tʃɛllula] *sf* (*Biol, Elettr, Pol*) cell; **cellu'lare** *sm* cellphone

cellu'lite [tʃellu'lite] *sf* cellulite

cemen'tare [tʃemen'tare] *vt* (*anche fig*) to cement

ce'mento [tʃe'mento] *sm* cement; **cemento armato** reinforced concrete

'cena ['tʃena] *sf* dinner; (*leggera*) supper

ce'nare [tʃe'nare] *vi* to dine, have dinner

'cenere ['tʃenere] *sf* ash

'cenno ['tʃenno] *sm* (*segno*) sign, signal; (*gesto*) gesture; (*col capo*) nod; (*con la mano*) wave; (*allusione*) hint, mention; **far** ~ **di sì/no** to nod (one's head)/shake one's head

censi'mento [tʃensi'mento] *sm* census

cen'sura [tʃen'sura] *sf* censorship; censor's office; (*fig*) censure

cente'nario, -a [tʃente'narjo] *ag* hundred-year-old; (*che ricorre ogni cento anni*) centennial, centenary *cpd*

▶ *sm/f* centenarian ▶ *sm* centenary

cen'tesimo, -a [tʃen'tezimo] *ag, sm* hundredth; *(di euro, dollaro)* cent

cen'tigrado, -a [tʃen'tigrado] *ag* centigrade; **20 gradi centigradi** 20 degrees centigrade

cen'timetro [tʃen'timetro] *sm* centimetre

centi'naio [tʃenti'najo] *(pl(f)* **-aia)** *sm* **un ~ (di)** a hundred; about a hundred

'cento ['tʃɛnto] *num* a hundred, one hundred

cento'mila [tʃɛnto'mila] *num* a o one hundred thousand; **te l'ho detto ~ volte** *(fig)* I've told you a thousand times

cen'trale [tʃen'trale] *ag* central ▶ *sf;* **centrale elettrica** electric power station; **centrale eolica** wind farm; **centrale telefonica** (telephone) exchange; **centrali'nista** *sm/f* operator; **centra'lino** *sm* (telephone) exchange; *(di albergo ecc)* switchboard; **centralizzato, -a** [tʃentralid'dzato] *ag* central

cen'trare [tʃen'trare] *vt* to hit the centre of; *(Tecn)* to centre

cen'trifuga [tʃen'trifuga] *sf* spin-drier

'centro ['tʃɛntro] *sm* centre; **centro civico** civic centre; **centro commerciale** shopping centre; *(città)* commercial centre

'ceppo ['tʃeppo] *sm (di albero)* stump; *(pezzo di legno)* log

'cera ['tʃera] *sf* wax; *(aspetto)* appearance

ce'ramica, -che [tʃe'ramika] *sf* ceramic; *(Arte)* ceramics *sg*

cerbi'atto [tʃer'bjatto] *sm (Zool)* fawn

cercaper'sone [tʃerkaper'sone] *sm inv* bleeper

cer'care [tʃer'kare] *vt* to look for, search for ▶ *vi* **~ di fare qc** to try to do sth; **stiamo cercando un albergo/ristorante** we're looking for

a hotel/restaurant

cercherò *ecc* [tʃerke'rɔ] *vb vedi* **cercare**

'cerchia ['tʃerkja] *sf* circle

cerchietto [tʃer'kjetto] *sm (per capelli)* hairband

'cerchio ['tʃerkjo] *sm* circle; *(giocattolo, di botte)* hoop

cereali [tʃere'ali] *smpl* cereal *sg*

ceri'monia [tʃeri'mɔnja] *sf* ceremony

ce'rino [tʃe'rino] *sm* wax match

cernia ['tʃɛrnja] *sf (Zool)* stone bass

cerni'era [tʃer'njɛra] *sf* hinge; **cerniera lampo** zip (fastener) *(BRIT)*, zipper *(US)*

'cero ['tʃero] *sm (church)* candle

ce'rotto [tʃe'rɔtto] *sm* sticking plaster

certa'mente [tʃerta'mente] *av* certainly

certifi'cato *sm* certificate; **certificato medico** medical certificate; **certificato di nascita/di morte** birth/death certificate

'certo, -a ['tʃɛrto] *ag (sicuro):* **certo (di/che)** certain o sure (of/that) ▶ *det*

1 *(tale)* certain; **un certo signor Smith** a (certain) Mr Smith

2 *(qualche: con valore intensivo)* some; **dopo un certo tempo** after some time; **un fatto di una certa importanza** a matter of some importance; **di una certa età** past one's prime

▶ *pron* **certi, e** *pl* some

▶ *av (certamente)* certainly; *(senz'altro)* of course; **di certo** certainly; **no (di) certo!, certo che no!** certainly not!; **sì certo** yes indeed, certainly

cer'vello, -i [tʃer'vɛllo] *(Anat) (pl(f)* **-a)** *sm* brain; **cervello elettronico** computer

'cervo, -a ['tʃɛrvo] *sm/f* stag/doe ▶ *sm* deer; **cervo volante** stag beetle

ces'puglio [tʃes'puʎʎo] *sm* bush

ces'sare [tʃes'sare] *vi, vt* to stop, cease;

~ di fare qc to stop doing sth
ces'tino [tʃes'tino] sm basket; (*per la carta straccia*) wastepaper basket; **cestino da viaggio** (*Ferr*) packed lunch (*o* dinner)
'cesto ['tʃesto] sm basket
'ceto ['tʃeto] sm (social) class
cetrio'lino [tʃetrio'lino] sm gherkin
cetri'olo [tʃetri'ɔlo] sm cucumber
Cfr. *abbr* (= *confronta*) cf.
CGIL *sigla f* (= *Confederazione Generale Italiana del Lavoro*) trades union organization
chat line [tʃæt'laen] sf inv chat room
chattare [tʃat'tare] vi (*Inform*) to chat online

che
[ke] pron

1 (*relativo: persona: soggetto*) who; (: *oggetto*) whom, that; (: *cosa, animale*) which, that; **il ragazzo che è venuto** the boy who came; **l'uomo che io vedo** the man (whom) I see; **il libro che è sul tavolo** the book which *o* that is on the table; **il libro che vedi** the book (which *o* that) you see; **la sera che ti ho visto** the evening I saw you
2 (*interrogativo, esclamativo*) what; **che (cosa) fai?** what are you doing?; **a che (cosa) pensi?** what are you thinking about?; **non sa che (cosa) fare** he doesn't know what to do; **ma che dici!** what are you saying!
3 (*indefinito*): **quell'uomo ha un che di losco** there's something suspicious about that man; **un certo non so che** an indefinable something
▶*det*
1 (*interrogativo: tra tanti*) what; (: *tra pochi*) which; **che tipo di film preferisci?** what sort of film do you prefer?; **che vestito ti vuoi mettere?** what (*o* which) dress do you want to put on?
2 (*esclamativo: seguito da aggettivo*)

how; (: *seguito da sostantivo*) what; **che buono!** how delicious!; **che bel vestito!** what a lovely dress!
▶*cong*
1 (*con proposizioni subordinate*) that; **credo che verrà** I think he'll come; **voglio che tu studi** I want you to study; **so che tu c'eri** I know (that) you were there; **non che, non che sia sbagliato, ma ...** not that it's wrong, but ...
2 (*finale*) so that; **vieni qua, che ti veda** come here, so (that) I can see you
3 (*temporale*): **arrivai che eri già partito** you had already left when I arrived; **sono anni che non lo vedo** I haven't seen him for years
4 (*in frasi imperative, concessive*): **che venga pure!** let him come by all means!; **che tu sia benedetto!** may God bless you!
5 (*comparativo: con più, meno*) than; *vedi anche* **più**; **meno**; **così** *ecc*
chemiotera'pia [kemjotera'pia] sf chemotherapy
chero'sene [kero'zɛne] sm kerosene

chi
[ki] pron

1 (*interrogativo: soggetto*) who; (: *oggetto*) who, whom; **chi è?** who is it?; **di chi è questo libro?** whose book is this?, whose is this book?; **con chi parli?** who are you talking to?; **a chi pensi?** who are you thinking about?; **chi di voi?** which of you?; **non so a chi rivolgermi** I don't know who to ask
2 (*relativo*) whoever, anyone who; **dillo a chi vuoi** tell whoever you like
3 (*indefinito*): **chi ... chi ...** some ... others ...; **chi dice una cosa, chi dice un'altra** some say one thing, others say another
chiacchie'rare [kjakkje'rare] vi to chat; (*discorrere futilmente*) to chatter; (*far pettegolezzi*) to gossip;

chi'acchiere *sfpl* **fare due** *o* **quattro chiacchiere** to have a chat

chia'mare [kja'mare] *vt* to call; (*rivolgersi a qn*) to call (in), send for; **chiamarsi** *vpr* (*aver nome*) to be called; **come ti chiami?** what's your name?; **mi chiamo Paolo** my name is Paolo, I'm called Paolo; **~ alle armi** to call up; **~ in giudizio** to summon; **chia'mata** *sf* (*Tel*) call; (*Mil*) call-up

chia'rezza [kja'rettsa] *sf* clearness; clarity

chia'rire [kja'rire] *vt* to make clear; (*fig: spiegare*) to clear up, explain

chi'aro, -a ['kjaro] *ag* clear; (*luminoso*) clear, bright; (*colore*) pale, light

chi'asso ['kjasso] *sm* uproar, row

chi'ave ['kjave] *sf* key ▶ *ag inv* key *cpd*; **posso avere la mia ~?** can I have my key?; **chiave d'accensione** (*Aut*) ignition key; **chiave di volta** keystone; **chiave inglese** monkey wrench

chi'azza ['kjattsa] *sf* stain; splash

'chicco, -chi ['kikko] *sm* grain; (*di caffè*) bean; **chicco d'uva** grape

chi'edere ['kjɛdere] *vt* (*per sapere*) to ask; (*per avere*) to ask for ▶ *vi* **~ di qn** to ask after sb; (*al telefono*) to ask for *o* want sb; **~ qc a qn** to ask sb sth; to ask sb for sth; **chiedersi** *vpr* **chiedersi (se)** to wonder (whether)

chi'esa ['kjɛza] *sf* church

chi'esi *ecc* ['kjɛzi] *vb vedi* **chiedere**

'chiglia ['kiʎʎa] *sf* keel

'chilo ['kilo] *sm* kilo; **chilo'grammo** *sm* kilogram(me); **chi'lometro** *sm* kilometre

'chimica ['kimika] *sf* chemistry

'chimico, -a, -ci, -che ['kimiko] *ag* chemical ▶ *sm/f* chemist

chi'nare [ki'nare] *vt* to lower, bend; **chinarsi** *vpr* to stoop, bend

chi'occiola ['kjɔttʃola] *sf* snail; (*di indirizzo e-mail*) at sign, @; **scala a ~**

spiral staircase

chi'odo ['kjɔdo] *sm* nail; (*fig*) obsession; **chiodo di garofano** (*Cuc*) clove

chi'osco, -schi ['kjɔsko] *sm* kiosk, stall

chi'ostro ['kjɔstro] *sm* cloister

chiro'mante [kiro'mante] *sm/f* palmist

chirur'gia [kirur'dʒia] *sf* surgery; **chirurgia estetica** cosmetic surgery; **chi'rurgo, -ghi** *o* **gi** *sm* surgeon

chissà [kis'sa] *av* who knows, I wonder

chi'tarra [ki'tarra] *sf* guitar

chitar'rista, -i, e [kitar'rista] *sm/f* guitarist, guitar player

chi'udere ['kjudere] *vt* to close, shut; (*luce, acqua*) to put off, turn off; (*definitivamente: fabbrica*) to close down, shut down; (*strada*) to close; (*recingere*) to enclose; (*porre termine a*) to end ▶ *vi* to close, shut; to close down, shut down; to end; **chiudersi** *vpr* to shut, close; (*ritirarsi: anche fig*) to shut o.s. away; (*ferita*) to close up; **a che ora chiudete?** what time do you close?

chi'unque [ki'unkwe] *pron* (*relativo*) whoever; (*indefinito*) anyone, anybody; **~ sia** whoever it is

'chiusi *ecc* ['kjusi] *vb vedi* **chiudere**

chi'uso, -a ['kjuso] *pp di* **chiudere** ▶ *sf* (*di corso d'acqua*) sluice, lock; (*recinto*) enclosure; (*di discorso ecc*) conclusion, ending; **chiu'sura** *sf* (*vedi* **chiudere**) closing; shutting; closing *o* shutting down; enclosing; putting *o* turning off; ending; (*dispositivo*) catch; fastener; **chiusura lampo®** zip (fastener) (*BRIT*), zipper (*US*)

C.I. *abbr* = **carta d'identità**

ci

⊘ [tʃi] (*dav lo, la, li, le, ne diventa* **ce**) *pron*

1 (*personale: complemento oggetto*) us;

(: *a noi: complemento di termine*) (to) us;
(: *riflessivo*) ourselves; (: *reciproco*) each
other, one another; (*impersonale*): **ci
si veste** we get dressed; **ci ha visti**
he's seen us; **non ci ha dato niente**
he gave us nothing; **ci vestiamo** we
get dressed; **ci amiamo** we love one
another *o* each other

2 (*dimostrativo: di ciò, su ciò, in ciò ecc*)
about (*o* on *o* of) it; **non so cosa farci**
I don't know what to do about it;
che c'entro io? what have I got to do
with it?

▶*av* (*qui*) here; (*lì*) there; (*moto attraverso
luogo*): **ci passa sopra un ponte** a
bridge passes over it; **non ci passa più
nessuno** nobody comes this way any
more; **esserci** *vedi* **essere**

cia'batta [tʃa'batta] *sf* slipper; (*pane*)
ciabatta

ciam'bella [tʃam'bɛlla] *sf* (*Cuc*) ring-
shaped cake; (*salvagente*) rubber
ring

ci'ao ['tʃao] *escl* (*all'arrivo*) hello!; (*alla
partenza*) cheerio! (BRIT), bye!

cias'cuno, -a [tʃas'kuno] (*det: dav sm:*
ciascun +*C, V*, **ciascuno** +*s impura, gn,
pn, ps, x, z; dav sf:* **ciascuna** +*C*, **ciascun'**
+*V*) *det* every, each; (*ogni*) every
▶*pron* each (one); (*tutti*) everyone,
everybody

ci'barie [tʃi'barje] *sfpl* foodstuffs

cibernauta, -i, -e [tʃiber'nauta] *sm/f*
Internet surfer

ciberspazio [tʃiber'spattsjo] *sm*
cyberspace

'cibo ['tʃibo] *sm* food

ci'cala [tʃi'kala] *sf* cicada

cica'trice [tʃika'tritʃe] *sf* scar

'cicca ['tʃikka] *sf* cigarette end

'ciccia ['tʃittʃa] (*fam*) *sf* fat

cicci'one, -a [tʃit'tʃone] *sm/f* (*fam*)
fatty

cicla'mino [tʃikla'mino] *sm* cyclamen

ci'clismo [tʃi'klizmo] *sm* cycling;

ci'clista, -i, -e *sm/f* cyclist

'ciclo ['tʃiklo] *sm* cycle; (*di malattia*)
course

ciclomo'tore [tʃiklomo'tore] *sm*
moped

ci'clone [tʃi'klone] *sm* cyclone

ci'cogna [tʃi'koɲɲa] *sf* stork

ci'eco, -a, -chi, -che ['tʃɛko] *ag* blind
▶*sm/f* blind man/woman

ci'elo ['tʃɛlo] *sm* sky; (*Rel*) heaven

'cifra ['tʃifra] *sf* (*numero*) figure;
numeral; (*somma di denaro*) sum,
figure; (*monogramma*) monogram,
initials *pl*; (*codice*) code, cipher

'ciglio, -i ['tʃiʎʎo] (*delle palpebre*) (*pl(f)*
ciglia) *sm* (*margine*) edge, verge;
(eye)lash; (eye)lid; (*sopracciglio*)
eyebrow

'cigno ['tʃiɲɲo] *sm* swan

cigo'lare [tʃigo'lare] *vi* to squeak,
creak

'Cile ['tʃile] *sm* il ~ Chile

ci'leno, -a [tʃi'leno] *ag, sm/f* Chilean

cili'egia, -gie *o* **ge** [tʃi'ljɛdʒa] *sf* cherry

cili'egina [tʃilje'dʒina] *sf* glacé cherry

cilin'drata [tʃilin'drata] *sf* (*Aut*)
(cubic) capacity; **una macchina di
grossa ~** a big-engined car

ci'lindro [tʃi'lindro] *sm* cylinder;
(*cappello*) top hat

'cima ['tʃima] *sf* (*sommità*) top; (*di
monte*) top, summit; (*estremità*) end;
in ~ a at the top of; **da ~ a fondo** from
top to bottom; (*fig*) from beginning
to end

'cimice ['tʃimitʃe] *sf* (*Zool*) bug;
(*puntina*) drawing pin (BRIT),
thumbtack (US)

cimini'era [tʃimi'njɛra] *sf* chimney;
(*di nave*) funnel

cimi'tero [tʃimi'tɛro] *sm* cemetery

'Cina ['tʃina] *sf* la ~ China

cin'cin [tʃin'tʃin] *escl* cheers!

'cinema ['tʃinema] *sm inv* cinema

ci'nese [tʃi'nese] *ag, sm/f, sm* Chinese

'cinghia ['tʃingja] sf strap; (cintura, Tecn) belt

cinghi'ale [tʃin'gjale] sm wild boar

cinguet'tare [tʃingwet'tare] vi to twitter

'cinico, -a, -ci, -che ['tʃiniko] ag cynical ▶ sm/f cynic

cin'quanta [tʃin'kwanta] num fifty; **cinquan'tesimo, -a** num fiftieth

cinquan'tina [tʃinkwan'tina] sf (serie): **una ~ (di)** about fifty; (età): **essere sulla ~** to be about fifty

'cinque ['tʃinkwe] num five; **avere ~ anni** to be five (years old); **il ~ dicembre 2008** the fifth of December 2008; **alle ~** (ora) at five (o'clock)

cinque'cento [tʃinkwe'tʃento] num five hundred ▶ sm **il C~** the sixteenth century

cin'tura [tʃin'tura] sf belt; **cintura di salvataggio** lifebelt (BRIT), life preserver (US); **cintura di sicurezza** (Aut,Aer) safety o seat belt

cintu'rino [tʃintu'rino] sm strap; **~ dell'orologio** watch strap

ciò [tʃɔ] pron this; that; **~ che** what; **~ nonostante** o **nondimeno** nevertheless, in spite of that

ci'occa, -che ['tʃɔkka] sf (di capelli) lock

ciocco'lata [tʃokko'lata] sf chocolate; (bevanda) (hot) chocolate; **cioccola'tino** sm chocolate

cioè [tʃo'ɛ] av that is (to say)

ci'otola ['tʃɔtola] sf bowl

ci'ottolo ['tʃɔttolo] sm pebble; (di strada) cobble(stone)

ci'polla [tʃi'polla] sf onion; (di tulipano ecc) bulb

cipol'lina [tʃipol'lina] sf **cipolline sottaceto** pickled onions

ci'presso [tʃi'presso] sm cypress (tree)

'cipria ['tʃiprja] sf (face) powder

'Cipro ['tʃipro] sm Cyprus

'circa ['tʃirka] av about, roughly ▶ prep about, concerning; **a mezzogiorno ~** about midday

'circo, -chi ['tʃirko] sm circus

circo'lare [tʃirko'lare] vi to circulate; (Aut) to drive (along), move (along) ▶ ag circular ▶ sf (Amm) circular; (di autobus) circle (line); **circolazi'one** sf circulation; **la ~** (Aut) (the) traffic

'circolo ['tʃirkolo] sm circle

circon'dare [tʃirkon'dare] vt to surround; **circondarsi** vpr **circondarsi di** to surround o.s. with

circonvallazi'one [tʃirkonvallat'tsjone] sf ring road (BRIT), beltway (US); (per evitare una città) by-pass

circos'petto, -a [tʃirkos'petto] ag circumspect, cautious

circos'tante [tʃirkos'tante] ag surrounding, neighbouring

circos'tanza [tʃirkos'tantsa] sf circumstance; (occasione) occasion

cir'cuito [tʃir'kuito] sm circuit

CISL sigla f (= Confederazione Italiana Sindacati Lavoratori) trades union organization

cis'terna [tʃis'tɛrna] sf tank, cistern

'cisti ['tʃisti] sf cyst

cis'tite [tʃis'tite] sf cystitis

ci'tare [tʃi'tare] vt (Dir) to summon; (autore) to quote; (a esempio) to cite

ci'tofono [tʃi'tɔfono] sm entry phone; (in uffici) intercom

città [tʃit'ta] sf inv town; (importante) city; **città universitaria** university campus

cittadi'nanza [tʃittadi'nantsa] sf citizens pl; (Dir) citizenship

citta'dino, -a [tʃitta'dino] ag town cpd; city cpd ▶ sm/f (di uno Stato) citizen; (abitante di città) townsman, city dweller

ci'uccio ['tʃuttʃo] sm (fam) comforter, dummy (BRIT), pacifier (US)

ci'uffo ['tʃuffo] sm tuft

ci'vetta [tʃi'vetta] sf (Zool) owl; (fig: donna) coquette, flirt ▶ ag inv **auto/ nave ~** decoy car/ship

'civico, -a, -ci, -che ['tʃivico] ag civic; (museo) municipal, town cpd; city cpd

ci'vile [tʃi'vile] ag civil; (non militare) civilian; (nazione) civilized ▶ sm civilian

civiltà [tʃivil'ta] sf civilization; (cortesia) civility

'clacson sm inv (Aut) horn

clandes'tino, -a ag clandestine; (Pol) underground, clandestine; (immigrato) illegal ▶ sm/f stowaway; (anche: **immigrato ~**) illegal immigrant

'classe sf class; **di ~** (fig) with class; of excellent quality; **classe operaia** working class; **classe turistica** (Aer) economy class

'classico, -a, -ci, -che ag classical; (tradizionale: moda) classic(al) ▶ sm classic; classical author

clas'sifica sf classification; (Sport) placings pl

classifi'care vt to classify; (candidato, compito) to grade; **classificarsi** vpr to be placed

'clausola sf (Dir) clause

clavi'cembalo [klavi'tʃembalo] sm harpsichord

cla'vicola sf (Anat) collar bone

clic'care vi (Inform): **~ su** to click on

cli'ente sm/f customer, client

'clima, -i sm climate; **climatizzatore** sm air conditioning system

'clinica, -che sf (scienza) clinical medicine; (casa di cura) clinic, nursing home; (settore d'ospedale) clinic

clo'nare vt to clone; **clonazione** [klona'tsjone] sf cloning

'cloro sm chlorine

club sm inv club

c.m. abbr = **corrente mese**

cm abbr (= centimetro) cm

coalizi'one [koalit'tsjone] sf coalition

'COBAS sigla mpl (= Comitati di base) independent trades unions

'coca sf (bibita) Coke®; (droga) cocaine

coca'ina sf cocaine

cocci'nella [kottʃi'nɛlla] sf ladybird (BRIT), ladybug (US)

cocci'uto, -a [kot'tʃuto] ag stubborn, pigheaded

'cocco, -chi sm (pianta) coconut palm; (frutto): **noce di ~** coconut ▶ sm/f (fam) darling

cocco'drillo sm crocodile

cocco'lare vt to cuddle, fondle

cocerò ecc [kotʃe'rɔ] vb vedi **cuocere**

co'comero sm watermelon

'coda sf tail; (fila di persone, auto) queue (BRIT), line (US); (di abiti) train; **con la ~ dell'occhio** out of the corner of one's eye; **mettersi in ~** to queue (up) (BRIT), line up (US); to join the queue (BRIT) o line (US); **coda di cavallo** (acconciatura) ponytail

co'dardo, -a ag cowardly ▶ sm/f coward

'codice ['koditʃe] sm code; **codice di avviamento postale** postcode (BRIT), zip code (US); **codice a barre** bar code; **codice civile** civil code; **codice fiscale** tax code; **codice penale** penal code; **codice segreto** (di tessera magnetica) PIN (number); **codice della strada** highway code

coe'rente ag coherent

coe'taneo, -a ag, sm/f contemporary

'cofano sm (Aut) bonnet (BRIT), hood (US); (forziere) chest

'cogliere ['kɔʎʎere] vt (fiore: frutto) to pick, gather; (sorprendere) to catch, surprise; (bersaglio) to hit; (fig: momento opportuno ecc) to grasp, seize, take; (: capire) to grasp; **~ qn in flagrante** o **in fallo** to catch sb red-handed

co'gnato, -a [koɲˈɲato] sm/f brother-/sister-in-law

co'gnome [koɲˈɲome] sm surname

coinci'denza [kointʃiˈdɛntsa] sf coincidence; (Ferr, Aer, di autobus) connection

coin'cidere [koinˈtʃidere] vi to coincide

coin'volgere [koinˈvɔldʒere] vt ~ **in** to involve in

cola'pasta sm inv colander

co'lare vt (liquido) to strain; (pasta) to drain; (oro fuso) to pour ▶ vi (sudore) to drip; (botte) to leak; (cera) to melt; ~ **a picco** vt, vi (nave) to sink

colazi'one [kolatˈtsjone] sf breakfast; **fare** ~ to have breakfast; **a che ora è servita la ~?** what time is breakfast?

co'lera sm (Med) cholera

'colgo ecc vb vedi **cogliere**

'colica sf (Med) colic

co'lino sm strainer

'colla sf glue; (di farina) paste

collabo'rare vi to collaborate; ~ **a** to collaborate on; (giornale) to contribute to; **collabora'tore, -'trice** sm/f collaborator; contributor; **collaboratore esterno** freelance; **collaboratrice familiare** home help

col'lana sf necklace; (collezione) collection, series

col'lant [kɔˈlã] sm inv tights pl

col'lare sm collar

col'lasso sm (Med) collapse

collau'dare vt to test, try out

col'lega, -ghi, -ghe sm/f colleague

collega'mento sm connection; (Mil) liaison

colle'gare vt to connect, join, link; **collegarsi** vpr (Radio, TV) to link up; **collegarsi con** (Tel) to get through to

col'legio [kolˈlɛdʒo] sm college; (convitto) boarding school; **collegio elettorale** (Pol) constituency

'collera sf anger

col'lerico, -a, -ci, -che ag quick-tempered, irascible

col'letta sf collection

col'letto sm collar

collezio'nare [kollettsjoˈnare] vt to collect

collezi'one [kolletˈtsjone] sf collection

col'lina sf hill

col'lirio sm eyewash

'collo sm neck; (di abito) neck, collar; (pacco) parcel; **collo del piede** instep

colloca'mento sm (impiego) employment; (disposizione) placing, arrangement

collo'care vt (libri, mobili) to place; (Comm: merce) to find a market for

collocazi'one [kollokatˈtsjone] sf placing; (di libro) classification

col'loquio sm conversation, talk; (ufficiale, per un lavoro) interview; (Ins) preliminary oral exam

col'mare vt ~ **di** (anche fig) to fill with; (dare in abbondanza) to load o overwhelm with

co'lombo, -a sm/f dove; pigeon

co'lonia sf colony; (per bambini) holiday camp; **(acqua di)** ~ (eau de) cologne

co'lonna sf column; **colonna sonora** (Cinema) sound track; **colonna vertebrale** spine, spinal column

colon'nello sm colonel

colo'rante sm colouring

colo'rare vt to colour; (disegno) to colour in

co'lore sm colour; **a colori** in colour, colour cpd; **farne di tutti i colori** to get up to all sorts of mischief; **vorrei un ~ diverso** I'd like a different colour

colo'rito, -a ag coloured; (viso) rosy, pink; (linguaggio) colourful ▶ sm (tinta) colour; (carnagione) complexion

'colpa sf fault; (biasimo) blame; (colpevolezza) guilt; (azione colpevole) offence; (peccato) sin; **di chi è la ~?** whose fault is it?; **è ~ sua** it's his fault; **per ~ di** through, owing to; **col'pevole** ag guilty

col'pire vt to hit, strike; (fig) to strike; **rimanere colpito da qc** to be amazed o struck by sth

'colpo sm (urto) knock; (: affettivo) blow, shock; (: aggressivo) blow; (di pistola) shot; (Med) stroke; (rapina) raid; **di ~** suddenly; **fare ~** to make a strong impression; **colpo d'aria** chill; **colpo in banca** bank job o raid; **colpo basso** (Pugilato, fig) punch below the belt; **colpo di fulmine** love at first sight; **colpo di grazia** coup de grâce; **colpo di scena** (Teatro) coup de théâtre; (fig) dramatic turn of events; **colpo di sole** sunstroke; **colpo di Stato** coup d'état; **colpo di telefono** phone call; **colpo di testa** (sudden) impulse o whim; **colpo di vento** gust (of wind); **colpi di sole** (nei capelli) highlights

'colsi ecc vb vedi **cogliere**

coltel'lata sf stab

col'tello sm knife; **coltello a serramanico** clasp knife

colti'vare vt to cultivate; (verdura) to grow, cultivate

'colto, -a pp di **cogliere** ▸ ag (istruito) cultured, educated

'coma sm inv coma

comanda'mento sm (Rel) commandment

coman'dante sm (Mil) commander, commandant; (di reggimento) commanding officer; (Naut, Aer) captain

coman'dare vi to be in command ▸ vt to command; (imporre) to order, command; **~ a qn di fare** to order sb to do

combaci'are [kombaˈtʃare] vi to meet; (fig: coincidere) to coincide

com'battere vt, vi to fight

combi'nare vt to combine; (organizzare) to arrange; (fam: fare) to make, cause; **combinazi'one** sf combination; (caso fortuito) coincidence; **per combinazione** by chance

combus'tibile ag combustible ▸ sm fuel

 'come
av

1 (alla maniera di) like; **ti comporti come lui** you behave like him o like he does; **bianco come la neve** (as) white as snow; **come se** as if, as though

2 (in qualità di) as a; **lavora come autista** he works as a driver

3 (interrogativo) how; **come ti chiami?** what's your name?; **come sta?** how are you?; **com'è il tuo amico?** what is your friend like?; **come?** (prego?) pardon?, sorry?; **come mai?** how come?; **come mai non ci hai avvertiti?** why on earth didn't you warn us?

4 (esclamativo): **come sei bravo!** how clever you are!; **come mi dispiace!** I'm terribly sorry!

▸ cong

1 (in che modo) how; **mi ha spiegato come l'ha conosciuto** he told me how he met him

2 (correlativo) as; (con comparativi di maggioranza) than; **non è bravo come pensavo** he isn't as clever as I thought; **è meglio di come pensassi** it's better than I thought

3 (appena che, quando) as soon as; **come arrivò, iniziò a lavorare** as soon as he arrived, he set to work; vedi **così**; **tanto**

'comico, -a, -ci, -che ag (Teatro) comic; (buffo) comical ▸ sm (attore) comedian, comic actor

cominci'are [komin'tʃare] vt, vi to begin, start; **~ a fare/col fare** to begin to do/by doing; **a che ora comincia il film?** when does the film start?

comi'tato sm committee

comi'tiva sf party, group

co'mizio [ko'mittsjo] sm (Pol) meeting, assembly

com'media sf comedy; (opera teatrale) play; (: che fa ridere) comedy; (fig) playacting no pl

commemo'rare vt to commemorate

commen'tare vt to comment on; (testo) to annotate; (Radio, TV) to give a commentary on

commerci'ale [kommer'tʃale] ag commercial, trading; (peg) commercial

commercia'lista, -i, e [kommertʃa'lista] sm/f (laureato) graduate in economics and commerce; (consulente) business consultant

commerci'ante [kommer'tʃante] sm/f trader, dealer; (negoziante) shopkeeper

commerci'are [kommer'tʃare] vt, vi ~ **in** to deal o trade in

com'mercio [kom'mɛrtʃo] sm trade, commerce; **essere in ~** (prodotto) to be on the market o on sale; **essere nel ~** (persona) to be in business; **commercio al dettaglio/all'ingrosso** retail/wholesale trade; **commercio elettronico** e-commerce

com'messo, -a pp di **commettere** ▶ sm/f shop assistant (BRIT), sales clerk (US) ▶ sm (impiegato) clerk; **commesso viaggiatore** commercial traveller

commes'tibile ag edible

com'mettere vt to commit

com'misi ecc vb vedi **commettere**

commissari'ato sm (Amm) commissionership; (: sede) commissioner's office; **commissariato di polizia** police station

commis'sario sm commissioner; (di pubblica sicurezza) ≈ (police) superintendent (BRIT), ≈ (police) captain (US); (Sport) steward; (membro di commissione) member of a committee o board

commissi'one sf (incarico) errand; (comitato, percentuale) commission; (Comm: ordinazione) order; **commissioni** sfpl (acquisti) shopping sg; **commissioni bancarie** bank charges; **commissione d'esame** examining board

com'mosso, -a pp di **commuovere**

commo'vente ag moving

commozi'one [kommot'tsjone] sf emotion, deep feeling; **commozione cerebrale** (Med) concussion

commu'overe vt to move, affect; **commuoversi** vpr to be moved

como'dino sm bedside table

comodità sf inv comfort; convenience

'comodo, -a ag comfortable; (facile) easy; (conveniente) convenient; (utile) useful, handy ▶ sm comfort; convenience; **con ~** at one's convenience o leisure; **fare il proprio ~** to do as one pleases; **far ~** to be useful o handy

compa'gnia [kompaɲ'ɲia] sf company; (gruppo) gathering

com'pagno, -a [kom'paɲɲo] sm/f (di classe, gioco) companion; (Pol) comrade

com'paio ecc vb vedi **comparire**

compa'rare vt to compare

compara'tivo, -a ag, sm comparative

compa'rire vi to appear

com'parvi ecc vb vedi **comparire**

compassi'one sf compassion, pity; **avere ~ di qn** to feel sorry for sb, to pity sb

com'passo sm (pair of) compasses pl; callipers pl

compa'tibile ag (scusabile) excusable; (conciliabile, Inform) compatible

compa'tire vt (aver compassione di) to sympathize with, feel sorry for; (scusare) to make allowances for

com'patto, -a ag compact; (roccia) solid; (folla) dense; (fig: gruppo, partito) united

compen'sare vt (equilibrare) to compensate for, make up for; **~ qn di** (rimunerare) to pay o remunerate sb for; (risarcire) to pay compensation to sb for; (fig: fatiche, dolori) to reward sb for; **com'penso** sm compensation payment, remuneration; reward; **in compenso** (d'altra parte) on the other hand

compe'rare vt = **comprare**

'compere sfpl **fare ~** to do the shopping

compe'tente ag competent; (mancia) apt, suitable

com'petere vi to compete, vie; (Dir: spettare): **~ a** to lie within the competence of; **competizi'one** sf competition

compi'angere [kom'pjandʒere] vt to sympathize with, feel sorry for

'compiere vt (concludere) to finish, complete; (adempiere) to carry out, fulfil; **compiersi** vpr (avverarsi) to be fulfilled, come true; **~ gli anni** to have one's birthday

compi'lare vt (modulo) to fill in; (dizionario, elenco) to compile

'compito sm (incarico) task, duty; (dovere) duty; (Ins) exercise; (: a casa) piece of homework; **fare i compiti** to do one's homework

comple'anno sm birthday

complessità sf complexity

comples'sivo, -a ag (globale) comprehensive, overall; (totale: cifra) total

com'plesso, -a ag complex ▶ sm (Psic, Edil) complex; (Mus: corale) ensemble; (: orchestrina) band; (: di musica pop) group; **in o nel ~** on the whole; **complesso alberghiero** hotel complex; **complesso edilizio** building complex; **complesso vitaminico** vitamin complex

completa'mente av completely

comple'tare vt to complete

com'pleto, -a ag complete; (teatro, autobus) full ▶ sm suit; **al ~** full; (tutti presenti) all present; **completo da sci** ski suit

compli'care vt to complicate; **complicarsi** vpr to become complicated

'complice ['kɔmplitʃe] sm/f accomplice

complicità [komplitʃi'ta] sf inv complicity; **un sorriso/uno sguardo di ~** a knowing smile/look

complimen'tarsi vpr **~ con** to congratulate

compli'mento sm compliment; **complimenti** smpl (cortesia eccessiva) ceremony sg; (ossequi) regards, compliments; **complimenti!** congratulations!; **senza complimenti!** don't stand on ceremony!; make yourself at home!; help yourself!

complot'tare vi to plot, conspire

com'plotto sm plot, conspiracy

com'pone ecc vb vedi **comporre**

compo'nente sm/f member ▶ sm component

com'pongo ecc vb vedi **comporre**

componi'mento sm (Dir) settlement; (Ins) composition; (poetico, teatrale) work

com'porre vt (musica, testo) to compose; (mettere in ordine) to arrange; (Dir: lite) to settle; (Tip) to set; (Tel) to dial; **comporsi** vpr **comporsi di** to consist of, be composed of

compor'tamento sm behaviour

compor'tare vt (implicare) to involve; **comportarsi** vpr to behave

com'posi ecc vb vedi **comporre**

composi'tore, -'trice sm/f composer; (Tip) compositor, typesetter

com'posto, -a pp di **comporre** ▶ ag (persona) composed, self-possessed; (: decoroso) dignified; (formato da più elementi) compound cpd ▶ sm compound

com'prare vt to buy; **dove posso ~ delle cartoline?** where can I buy some postcards?

com'prendere vt (contenere) to comprise, consist of; (capire) to understand

compren'sibile ag understandable

compensi'one sf understanding

compren'sivo, -a ag (prezzo): **~ di** inclusive of; (indulgente) understanding

⎸ Attenzione! In inglese esiste la parola comprehensive, che però in genere significa completo.

com'preso, -a pp di **comprendere** ▶ ag (incluso) included; **il servizio è ~?** is service included?

com'pressa sf (Med: garza) compress; (: pastiglia) tablet; vedi anche **compresso**

com'primere vt (premere) to press; (Fisica) to compress; (fig) to repress

compro'messo, -a pp di **compromettere** ▶ sm compromise

compro'mettere vt to compromise; **compromettersi** vpr to compromise o.s.

com'puter sm inv computer

comu'nale ag municipal, town cpd, ≈ borough cpd

co'mune ag common; (consueto) common, everyday; (di livello medio) average; (ordinario) ordinary ▶ sm (Amm) town council; (: sede) town hall ▶ sf (di persone) commune; **fuori del ~** out of the ordinary; **avere in ~** to have in common, share; **mettere in ~** to share

comuni'care vt (notizia) to pass on, convey; (malattia) to pass on; (ansia ecc) to communicate; (trasmettere: calore ecc) to transmit, communicate; (Rel) to administer communion to ▶ vi to communicate

comuni'cato sm communiqué; **comunicato stampa** press release

comunicazi'one [komunikat'tsjone] sf communication; (annuncio) announcement; (Tel): **dare la ~ a qn** to put sb through; **ottenere la ~** to get through; **comunicazione (telefonica)** (telephone) call

comuni'one sf communion; **comunione di beni** (Dir) joint ownership of property

comu'nismo sm communism

comunità sf inv community; **Comunità Europea** European Community

co'munque cong however, no matter how ▶ av (in ogni modo) in any case; (tuttavia) however, nevertheless

con prep with; **partire col treno** to leave by train; **~ mio grande stupore** to my great astonishment; **~ tutto ciò** for all that

con'cedere [kon'tʃɛdere] vt (accordare) to grant; (ammettere) to admit, concede; **concedersi qc** to treat o.s. to sth, to allow o.s. sth

concentrarsi vpr to concentrate

concentrazi'one sf concentration

conce'pire [kontʃe'pire] vt (bambino)

to conceive; (*progetto, idea*) to conceive (of); (*metodo, piano*) to devise

con'certo [kon'tʃɛrto] *sm* (*Mus*) concert; (: *componimento*) concerto

con'cessi *ecc* [kon'tʃɛssi] *vb vedi* **concedere**

con'cetto [kon'tʃɛtto] *sm* (*pensiero, idea*) concept; (*opinione*) opinion

concezi'one [kontʃet'tsjone] *sf* conception

con'chiglia [kon'kiʎʎa] *sf* shell

conci'are [kon'tʃare] *vt* (*pelli*) to tan; (*tabacco*) to cure; (*fig: ridurre in cattivo stato*) to beat up; **conciarsi** *vpr* (*sporcarsi*) to get in a mess; (*vestirsi male*) to dress badly

concili'are [kontʃi'ljare] *vt* to reconcile; (*contravvenzione*) to pay on the spot; (*sonno*) to be conducive to, induce; **conciliarsi qc** to gain *o* win sth (for o.s.); **conciliarsi qn** to win sb over; **conciliarsi con** to be reconciled with

con'cime [kon'tʃime] *sm* manure; (*chimico*) fertilizer

con'ciso, -a [kon'tʃizo] *ag* concise, succinct

concitta'dino, -a [kontʃitta'dino] *sm/f* fellow citizen

con'cludere *vt* to conclude; (*portare a compimento*) to conclude, finish, bring to an end; (*operare positivamente*) to achieve ▶ *vi* (*essere convincente*) to be conclusive; **concludersi** *vpr* to come to an end, close

concor'dare *vt* (*tregua, prezzo*) to agree on; (*Ling*) to make agree ▶ *vi* to agree

con'corde *ag* (*d'accordo*) in agreement; (*simultaneo*) simultaneous

concor'rente *sm/f* competitor; (*Ins*) candidate; **concor'renza** *sf* competition

concorrenzi'ale [konkorren'tsjale] *ag* competitive

con'correre *vi* ~ **(in)** (*Mat*) to converge *o* meet (in); ~ **(a)** (*competere*) to compete (for); (: *Ins: a una cattedra*) to apply (for); (*partecipare: a un'impresa*) to take part (in), contribute (to); **con'corso, -a** *pp di* **concorrere** ▶ *sm* competition; (*Ins*) competitive examination; **concorso di colpa** (*Dir*) contributory negligence

con'creto, -a *ag* concrete

con'danna *sf* sentence; conviction; condemnation

condan'nare *vt* (*Dir*) ~ **a** to sentence to; ~ **per** to convict of; (*disapprovare*) to condemn

conden'sare *vt* to condense

condi'mento *sm* seasoning; dressing

con'dire *vt* to season; (*insalata*) to dress

condi'videre *vt* to share

condizio'nale [kondittsjo'nale] *ag* conditional ▶ *sm* (*Ling*) conditional ▶ *sf* (*Dir*) suspended sentence

condizio'nare [kondittsjo'nare] *vt* to condition; **ad aria condizionata** air-conditioned; **condiziona'tore** *sm* air conditioner

condizi'one [kondit'tsjone] *sf* condition

condogli'anze [kondoʎ'ʎantse] *sfpl* condolences

condo'minio *sm* joint ownership; (*edificio*) jointly-owned building

con'dotta *sf* (*modo di comportarsi*) conduct, behaviour; (*di un affare ecc*) handling; (*di acqua*) piping; (*incarico sanitario*) country medical practice controlled by a local authority

condu'cente [kondu'tʃɛnte] *sm* driver

con'duco *ecc vb vedi* **condurre**

con'durre *vt* to conduct; (*azienda*) to manage; (*accompagnare: bambino*) to take; (*automobile*) to drive; (*trasportare: acqua, gas*) to convey, conduct; (*fig*) to lead ▶ *vi* to lead

con'dussi *ecc vb vedi* **condurre**

confe'renza [konfe'rɛntsa] *sf* (*discorso*) lecture; (*riunione*) conference; **conferenza stampa** press conference

con'ferma *sf* confirmation

confer'mare *vt* to confirm

confes'sare *vt* to confess; **confessarsi** *vpr* to confess; **andare a confessarsi** (*Rel*) to go to confession

con'fetto *sm* sugared almond; (*Med*) pill

> Attenzione! In inglese esiste la parola *confetti*, che però significa *coriandoli*.

confet'tura *sf* (*gen*) jam; (*di arance*) marmalade

confezio'nare [konfettsjo'nare] *vt* (*vestito*) to make (up); (*merci, pacchi*) to package

confezi'one [konfet'tsjone] *sf* (*di abiti: da uomo*) tailoring; (: *da donna*) dressmaking; (*imballaggio*) packaging; **confezioni per signora** ladies' wear; **confezioni da uomo** menswear; **confezione regalo** gift pack

confic'care *vt* **~ qc in** to hammer *o* drive sth into; **conficcarsi** *vpr* to stick

confi'dare *vi* **~ in** to confide in, rely on ▶ *vt* to confide; **confidarsi con qn** to confide in sb

configu'rare *vt* (*Inform*) to set

configurazi'one [konfigurat'tsjone] *sf* configuration; (*Inform*) setting

confi'nare *vi* **~ con** to border on ▶ *vt* (*Pol*) to intern; (*fig*) to confine

Confin'dustria *sigla f* (= *Confederazione Generale dell'Industria Italiana*) employers' association, ≈ CBI (*BRIT*)

con'fine *sm* boundary; (*di paese*) border, frontier

confis'care *vt* to confiscate

con'flitto *sm* conflict

conflu'enza [konflu'ɛntsa] *sf* (*di fiumi*) confluence; (*di strade*) junction

con'fondere *vt* to mix up, confuse; (*imbarazzare*) to embarrass; **confondersi** *vpr* (*mescolarsi*) to mingle; (*turbarsi*) to be confused; (*sbagliare*) to get mixed up

confor'tare *vt* to comfort, console

confron'tare *vt* to compare

con'fronto *sm* comparison; **in** *o* **a ~ di** in comparison with, compared to; **nei miei (***o* **tuoi** *ecc***) confronti** towards me (*o* you *ecc*)

con'fusi *ecc vb vedi* **confondere**

confusi'one *sf* confusion; (*chiasso*) racket, noise; (*imbarazzo*) embarrassment

con'fuso, -a *pp di* **confondere** ▶ *ag* (*vedi confondere*) confused; embarrassed

conge'dare [kondʒe'dare] *vt* to dismiss; (*Mil*) to demobilize; **congedarsi** *vpr* to take one's leave

con'gegno *sm* device, mechanism

conge'lare [kondʒe'lare] *vt* to freeze; **congelarsi** *vpr* to freeze; **congela'tore** *sm* freezer

congesti'one [kondʒes'tjone] *sf* congestion

conget'tura [kondʒet'tura] *sf* conjecture

con'giungere [kon'dʒundʒere] *vt* to join (together); **congiungersi** *vpr* to join (together)

congiunti'vite [kondʒunti'vite] *sf* conjunctivitis

congiun'tivo [kondʒun'tivo] *sm* (*Ling*) subjunctive

congi'unto, -a [kon'dʒunto] *pp di* **congiungere** ▶ *ag* (*unito*) joined ▶ *sm/f* relative

congiunzi'one [kondʒun'tsjone] *sf* (*Ling*) conjunction

congi'ura [kon'dʒura] *sf* conspiracy

congratu'larsi *vpr* **~ con qn per qc** to congratulate sb on sth

congratulazi'oni
[kongratulat'tsjoni] *sfpl*
congratulations
con'gresso *sm* congress
C.O.N.I. *sigla m* (= *Comitato Olimpico Nazionale Italiano*) Italian Olympic Games Committee
coni'are *vt* to mint, coin; (*fig*) to coin
co'niglio [ko'niʎʎo] *sm* rabbit
coniu'gare *vt* (*Ling*) to conjugate; **coniugarsi** *vpr* to get married
'coniuge ['kɔnjudʒe] *sm/f* spouse
connazio'nale [konnattsjo'nale] *sm/f* fellow-countryman/woman
connessi'one *sf* connection
con'nettere *vt* to connect, join ▶ *vi* (*fig*) to think straight
'cono *sm* cone; **cono gelato** ice-cream cone
co'nobbi *ecc vb vedi* **conoscere**
cono'scente [konoʃʃente] *sm/f* acquaintance
cono'scenza [konoʃʃentsa] *sf* (*il sapere*) knowledge *no pl*; (*persona*) acquaintance; (*facoltà sensoriale*) consciousness *no pl*; **perdere ~** to lose consciousness
co'noscere [ko'noʃʃere] *vt* to know; **ci siamo conosciuti a Firenze** we (first) met in Florence; **conoscersi** *vpr* to know o.s.; (*reciproco*) to know each other; (*incontrarsi*) to meet; **~ qn di vista** to know sb by sight; **farsi ~** (*fig*) to make a name for o.s.; **conosci'uto, -a** *pp di* **conoscere** ▶ *ag* well-known
con'quista *sf* conquest
conquis'tare *vt* to conquer; (*fig*) to gain, win
consa'pevole *ag* **~ di** aware o conscious of
'conscio, -a, -sci, -sce ['kɔnʃo] *ag* **~ di** aware o conscious of
consecu'tivo, -a *ag* consecutive; (*successivo: giorno*) following, next
con'segna [kon'seɲɲa] *sf* delivery;

(*merce consegnata*) consignment; (*custodia*) care, custody; (*Mil: ordine*) orders *pl*; (: *punizione*) confinement to barracks; **pagamento alla ~** cash on delivery; **dare qc in ~ a qn** to entrust sth to sb
conse'gnare [konseɲ'ɲare] *vt* to deliver; (*affidare*) to entrust, hand over; (*Mil*) to confine to barracks
consegu'enza [konse'gwɛntsa] *sf* consequence; **per o di ~** consequently
con'senso *sm* approval, consent; **consenso informato** informed consent
consen'tire *vi* **~ a** to consent o agree to ▶ *vt* to allow, permit
con'serva *sf* (*Cuc*) preserve; **conserva di frutta** jam; **conserva di pomodoro** tomato purée
conser'vante *sm* (*per alimenti*) preservative
conser'vare *vt* (*Cuc*) to preserve; (*custodire*) to keep; (: *dalla distruzione ecc*) to preserve, conserve
conserva'tore, -'trice *sm/f* (*Pol*) conservative
conserva'torio *sm* (*di musica*) conservatory
conservazi'one [konservat'tsjone] *sf* preservation; conservation
conside'rare *vt* to consider; (*reputare*) to consider, regard; **considerarsi** *vpr* to consider o.s.
consigli'are [konsiʎ'ʎare] *vt* (*persona*) to advise; (*metodo, azione*) to recommend, advise, suggest; **mi può ~ un buon ristorante?** can you recommend a good restaurant?; **con'siglio** *sm* (*suggerimento*) advice *no pl*, piece of advice; (*assemblea*) council; **consiglio d'amministrazione** board; **Consiglio d'Europa** Council of Europe; **Consiglio dei Ministri** (*Pol*): **il Consiglio dei Ministri** ≈ the Cabinet

consis'tente *ag* thick; solid; (*fig*) sound, valid

con'sistere *vi* ~ **in** to consist of

conso'lare *ag* consular ▶ *vt* (*confortare*) to console, comfort; (*rallegrare*) to cheer up; **consolarsi** *vpr* to be comforted; to cheer up

conso'lato *sm* consulate

consolazi'one [konsolat'tsjone] *sf* consolation, comfort

'console *sm* consul

conso'nante *sf* consonant

'consono, -a *ag* ~ **a** consistent with, consonant with

con'sorte *sm/f* consort

consta'tare *vt* to establish, verify

consu'eto, -a *ag* habitual, usual

consu'lente *sm/f* consultant

consul'tare *vt* to consult; **consultarsi** *vpr* **consultarsi con qn** to seek the advice of sb

consul'torio *sm* ~ **familiare** family planning clinic

consu'mare *vt* (*logorare: abiti, scarpe*) to wear out; (*usare*) to consume, use up; (*mangiare, bere*) to consume; (*Dir*) to consummate; **consumarsi** *vpr* to wear out; to be used up; (*anche fig*) to be consumed; (*combustibile*) to burn out

con'tabile *ag* accounts *cpd*, accounting ▶ *sm/f* accountant

contachi'lometri [kontaki'lɔmetri] *sm inv* ≈ mileometer

conta'dino, -a *sm/f* countryman/woman, farm worker; (*peg*) peasant

contagi'are [konta'dʒare] *vt* to infect

contagi'oso, -a *ag* infectious; contagious

conta'gocce [konta'gottʃe] *sm inv* (*Med*) dropper

contami'nare *vt* to contaminate

con'tante *sm* cash; **pagare in contanti** to pay cash; **non ho contanti** I haven't got any cash

con'tare *vt* to count; (*considerare*) to consider ▶ *vi* to count, be of importance; ~ **su qn** to count *o* rely on sb; ~ **di fare qc** to intend to do sth; **conta'tore** *sm* meter

contat'tare *vt* to contact

con'tatto *sm* contact

'conte *sm* count

conteggi'are [konted'dʒare] *vt* to charge, put on the bill

con'tegno [kon'teɲɲo] *sm* (*comportamento*) behaviour; (*atteggiamento*) attitude; **darsi un** ~ to act nonchalant; to pull o.s. together

contemporanea'mente *av* simultaneously; at the same time

contempo'raneo, -a *ag*, *sm/f* contemporary

conten'dente *sm/f* opponent, adversary

conte'nere *vt* to contain; **conteni'tore** *sm* container

conten'tezza [konten'tettsa] *sf* contentment

con'tento, -a *ag* pleased, glad; ~ **di** pleased with

conte'nuto *sm* contents *pl*; (*argomento*) content

con'tessa *sf* countess

contes'tare *vt* (*Dir*) to notify; (*fig*) to dispute

con'testo *sm* context

continen'tale *ag*, *sm/f* continental

conti'nente *ag* continent ▶ *sm* (*Geo*) continent; (: *terra ferma*) mainland

contin'gente [kontin'dʒente] *ag* contingent ▶ *sm* (*Comm*) quota; (*Mil*) contingent

continua'mente *av* (*senza interruzione*) continuously, nonstop; (*ripetutamente*) continually

continu'are *vt* to continue (with), go on with ▶ *vi* to continue, go on; ~ **a fare qc** to go on *o* continue doing sth

continuità *sf* continuity

con'tinuo, -a *ag* (*numerazione*) continuous; (*pioggia*) continual, constant; (*Elettr*): **corrente continua** direct current; **di ~** continually

'conto *sm* (*calcolo*) calculation; (*Comm, Econ*) account; (*di ristorante, albergo*) bill; (*fig: stima*) consideration, esteem; **il ~, per favore** can I have the bill, please?; **lo metta sul mio ~** put it on my bill; **fare i conti con qn** to settle one's account with sb; **fare ~ su qn/qc** to count o rely on sb; **rendere ~ a qn di qc** to be accountable to sb for sth; **tener ~ di qn/qc** to take sb/sth into account; **per ~ di** on behalf of; **per ~ mio** as far as I'm concerned; **a conti fatti, in fin dei conti** all things considered; **conto corrente** current account; **conto alla rovescia** countdown

con'torno *sm* (*linea*) outline, contour; (*ornamento*) border; (*Cuc*) vegetables *pl*

con'torto, -a *pp di* **contorcere**

contrabbandi'ere, -a *sm/f* smuggler

contrab'bando *sm* smuggling, contraband; **merce di ~** contraband, smuggled goods *pl*

contrab'basso *sm* (*Mus*) (double) bass

contraccambi'are *vt* (*favore ecc*) to return

contraccet'tivo, -a [kontrattʃet'tivo] *ag, sm* contraceptive

contrac'colpo *sm* rebound; (*di arma da fuoco*) recoil; (*fig*) repercussion

contrad'dire *vt* to contradict; **contraddirsi** *vpr* to contradict o.s.; (*uso reciproco: persone*) to contradict each other o one another; (: *testimonianze ecc*) to be contradictory

contraf'fare *vt* (*persona*) to mimic; (*alterare: voce*) to disguise; (*firma*) to forge, counterfeit

contraria'mente *av* **~ a** contrary to

contrari'are *vt* (*contrastare*) to thwart, oppose; (*irritare*) to annoy, bother

con'trario, -a *ag* opposite; (*sfavorevole*) unfavourable ▶ *sm* opposite; **essere ~ a qc** (*persona*) to be against sth; **in caso ~** otherwise; **avere qc in ~** to have some objection; **al ~** on the contrary

contrasse'gnare [kontrassen'nare] *vt* to mark

contras'tare *vt* (*avversare*) to oppose; (*impedire*) to bar; (*negare: diritto*) to contest, dispute ▶ *vi* **~ (con)** (*essere in disaccordo*) to contrast (with); (*lottare*) to struggle (with)

contrat'tacco *sm* counterattack

contrat'tare *vt, vi* to negotiate

contrat'tempo *sm* hitch

con'tratto, -a *pp di* **contrarre** ▶ *sm* contract

contravvenzi'one [kontravven'tsjone] *sf* contravention; (*ammenda*) fine

contrazi'one [kontrat'tsjone] *sf* contraction; (*di prezzi ecc*) reduction

contribu'ente *sm/f* taxpayer; ratepayer (*BRIT*), property tax payer (*US*)

contribu'ire *vi* to contribute

'contro *prep* against; **~ di me/lui** against me/him; **pastiglie ~ la tosse** throat lozenges; **~ pagamento** (*Comm*) on payment ▶ *prefisso*; **controfi'gura** *sf* (*Cinema*) double

control'lare *vt* (*accertare*) to check; (*sorvegliare*) to watch, control; (*tenere nel proprio potere, fig: dominare*) to control; **controllarsi** *vpr* to control o.s.; **con'trollo** *sm* check; watch; control; **controllo delle nascite** birth control; **control'lore** *sm* (*Ferr, Autobus*) (ticket) inspector

contro'luce [kontro'lutʃe] *sf inv* (*Fot*) backlit shot ▶ *av* **(in) ~** against the light; (*fotografare*) into the light

contro'mano *av* **guidare ~** to drive on the wrong side of the road; (*in un senso unico*) to drive the wrong way up a one-way street

controprodu'cente [kontroprodu'tʃɛnte] *ag* counterproductive

contro'senso *sm* (*contraddizione*) contradiction in terms; (*assurdità*) nonsense

controspio'naggio [kontrospio'naddʒo] *sm* counterespionage

contro'versia *sf* controversy; (*Dir*) dispute

contro'verso, -a *ag* controversial

contro'voglia [kontro'vɔʎʎa] *av* unwillingly

contusi'one *sf* (*Med*) bruise

convale'scente [konvaleʃʃɛnte] *ag, sm/f* convalescent

convali'dare *vt* (*Amm*) to validate; (*fig: sospetto, dubbio*) to confirm

con'vegno [kon'veɲɲo] *sm* (*incontro*) meeting; (*congresso*) convention, congress; (*luogo*) meeting place

conve'nevoli *smpl* civilities

conveni'ente *ag* suitable; (*vantaggioso*) profitable; (: *prezzo*) cheap

> Attenzione! In inglese esiste la parola *convenient*, che però significa *comodo*.

conve'nire *vi* (*riunirsi*) to gather, assemble; (*concordare*) to agree; (*tornare utile*) to be worthwhile ▶ *vb impers* **conviene fare questo** it is advisable to do this; **conviene andarsene** we should go; **ne convengo** I agree

con'vento *sm* (*di frati*) monastery; (*di suore*) convent

convenzio'nale [konventsjo'nale] *ag* conventional

convenzi'one [konven'tsjone] *sf* (*Dir*)

agreement; (*nella società*) convention

conver'sare *vi* to have a conversation, converse

conversazi'one [konversat'tsjone] *sf* conversation; **fare ~** to chat, have a chat

conversi'one *sf* conversion; **conversione ad U** (*Aut*) U-turn

conver'tire *vt* (*trasformare*) to change; (*Pol, Rel*) to convert; **convertirsi** *vpr* **convertirsi (a)** to be converted (to)

con'vesso, -a *ag* convex

convin'cente [konvin'tʃɛnte] *ag* convincing

con'vincere [kon'vintʃere] *vt* to convince; **~ qn di qc** to convince sb of sth; **~ qn a fare qc** to persuade sb to do sth; **convincersi** *vpr* **convincersi (di qc)** to convince o.s. (of sth); **~ qn di qc** to convince sb of sth; **~ qn a fare qc** to convince sb to do sth

convi'vente *sm/f* common-law husband/wife

con'vivere *vi* to live together

convo'care *vt* to call, convene; (*Dir*) to summon

convulsi'one *sf* convulsion

coope'rare *vi* **~ (a)** to cooperate (in); **coopera'tiva** *sf* cooperative

coordi'nare *vt* to coordinate

co'perchio [ko'pɛrkjo] *sm* cover; (*di pentola*) lid

co'perta *sf* cover; (*di lana*) blanket; (*da viaggio*) rug; (*Naut*) deck

coper'tina *sf* (*Stampa*) cover, jacket

co'perto, -a *pp di* **coprire** ▶ *ag* covered; (*cielo*) overcast ▶ *sm* place setting; (*posto a tavola*) place; (*al ristorante*) cover charge; **~ di** covered in o with

coper'tone *sm* (*Aut*) rubber tyre

coper'tura *sf* (*anche Econ, Mil*) cover; (*di edificio*) roofing

'copia *sf* copy; **brutta/bella ~** rough/final copy

copi'are vt to copy

copi'one sm (Cinema, Teatro) script

'coppa sf (bicchiere) goblet; (per frutta, gelato) dish; (trofeo) cup, trophy; **coppa dell'olio** oil sump (BRIT) o pan (US)

'coppia sf (di persone) couple; (di animali, Sport) pair

coprifu'oco, -chi sm curfew

copri'letto sm bedspread

copripiu'mino sm duvet cover

co'prire vt to cover; (occupare: carica, posto) to hold; **coprirsi** vpr (cielo) to cloud over; (vestirsi) to wrap up, cover up; (Econ) to cover o.s.; **coprirsi di** (macchie, muffa) to become covered in

coque [kɔk] sf **uovo alla ~** boiled egg

co'raggio [ko'raddʒo] sm courage, bravery; **~!** (forza!) come on!; (animo!) cheer up!

co'rallo sm coral

Co'rano sm (Rel) Koran

co'razza [ko'rattsa] sf armour; (di animali) carapace, shell; (Mil) armour(-plating)

'corda sf cord; (fune) rope; (spago, Mus) string; **dare ~ a qn** to let sb have his (o her) way; **tenere sulla ~ qn** to keep sb on tenterhooks; **tagliare la ~** to slip away, sneak off; **corda vocale** vocal cords

cordi'ale ag cordial, warm ▶ sm (bevanda) cordial

'cordless ['kɔːdlɪs] sm inv cordless phone

cor'done sm cord, string; (linea: di polizia) cordon; **cordone ombelicale** umbilical cord

Co'rea sf **la ~** Korea

coreogra'fia sf choreography

cori'andolo sm (Bot) coriander; **coriandoli** smpl confetti sg

cor'nacchia [kor'nakkja] sf crow

corna'musa sf bagpipes pl

cor'netta sf (Mus) cornet; (Tel) receiver

cor'netto sm (Cuc) croissant; (gelato) cone

cor'nice [kor'nitʃe] sf frame; (fig) setting, background

cornici'one [korni'tʃone] sm (di edificio) ledge; (Archit) cornice

'corno (pl(f) **-a**) sm (Zool) horn; (pl(m) **-i**: Mus) horn; **fare le corna a qn** to be unfaithful to sb

Corno'vaglia [korno'vaʎʎa] sf **la ~** Cornwall

cor'nuto, -a ag (con corna) horned; (fam!: marito) cuckolded ▶ sm (fam!) cuckold; (: insulto) bastard (!)

'coro sm chorus; (Rel) choir

co'rona sf crown; (di fiori) wreath

'corpo sm body; (militare, diplomatico) corps inv; **prendere ~** to take shape; **a ~ a ~** hand-to-hand; **corpo di ballo** corps de ballet; **corpo insegnante** teaching staff

corpora'tura sf build, physique

cor'reggere [kor'rɛddʒere] vt to correct; (compiti) to correct, mark

cor'rente ag (acqua: di fiume) flowing; (: di rubinetto) running; (moneta, prezzo) current; (comune) everyday ▶ sm **essere al ~ (di)** to be well-informed (about); **mettere al ~ (di)** to inform (of) ▶ sf (d'acqua) current, stream; (spiffero) draught; (Elettr, Meteor) current; (fig) trend, tendency; **la vostra lettera del 5 ~ mese** (Comm) your letter of the 5th of this month; **corrente alternata/ continua** alternate/direct current; **corrente'mente** av commonly; **parlare una lingua correntemente** to speak a language fluently

'correre vi to run; (precipitarsi) to rush; (partecipare a una gara) to race, run; (fig: diffondersi) to go round ▶ vt (Sport: gara) to compete in; (rischio) to run; (*pericolo*) to face; **~ dietro a qn** to run after sb; **corre voce che ...** it is rumoured that ...

cor'ressi *ecc vb vedi* **correggere**

correzi'one [korret'tsjone] *sf* correction; marking; **correzione di bozze** proofreading

corri'doio *sm* corridor; (*in aereo, al cinema*) aisle; **vorrei un posto sul ~** I'd like an aisle seat

corri'dore *sm* (*Sport*) runner; (: *su veicolo*) racer

corri'era *sf* coach (BRIT), bus

corri'ere *sm* (*diplomatico, di guerra, postale*) courier; (*Comm*) carrier

corri'mano *sm* handrail

corrispon'dente *ag* corresponding ▶ *sm/f* correspondent

corrispon'denza [korrispon'dɛntsa] *sf* correspondence

corris'pondere *vi* (*equivalere*): **~ (a)** to correspond (to) ▶ *vt* (*stipendio*) to pay; (*fig: amore*) to return

cor'rodere *vt* to corrode

cor'rompere *vt* to corrupt; (*comprare*) to bribe

cor'roso, -a *pp di* **corrodere**

cor'rotto, -a *pp di* **corrompere** ▶ *ag* corrupt

corru'gare *vt* to wrinkle; **~ la fronte** to knit one's brows

cor'ruppi *ecc vb vedi* **corrompere**

corruzi'one [korrut'tsjone] *sf* corruption; bribery

'corsa *sf* running *no pl*; (*gara*) race; (*di autobus, taxi*) journey, trip; **fare una ~** to run, dash; (*Sport*) to run a race; **corsa campestre** cross-country race

'corsi *ecc vb vedi* **correre**

cor'sia *sf* (*Aut, Sport*) lane; (*di ospedale*) ward

'Corsica *sf* **la ~** Corsica

cor'sivo *sm* cursive (writing); (*Tip*) italics *pl*

'corso, -a *pp di* **correre** ▶ *sm* course; (*strada cittadina*) main street; (*di unità monetaria*) circulation; (*di titoli, valori*) rate, price; **in ~** in progress, under way; (*annata*) current; **corso d'acqua** river, stream; (*artificiale*) waterway; **corso d'aggiornamento** refresher course; **corso serale** evening class

'corte *sf* (court)yard; (*Dir, regale*) court; **fare la ~ a qn** to court sb; **corte marziale** court-martial

cor'teccia, -ce [kor'tettʃa] *sf* bark

corteggi'are [korted'dʒare] *vt* to court

cor'teo *sm* procession

cor'tese *ag* courteous; **corte'sia** *sf* courtesy; **per cortesia ...** excuse me, please ...

cor'tile *sm* (court)yard

cor'tina *sf* curtain; (*anche fig*) screen

'corto, -a *ag* short; **essere a ~ di qc** to be short of sth; **corto circuito** short-circuit

'corvo *sm* raven

'cosa *sf* thing; (*faccenda*) affair, matter, business *no pl*; **(che) ~?** what?; **(che) cos'è?** what is it?; **a ~ pensi?** what are you thinking about?

'coscia, -sce ['kɔʃʃa] *sf* thigh; **coscia di pollo** (*Cuc*) chicken leg

cosci'ente [koʃʃɛnte] *ag* conscious; **~ di** conscious *o* aware of

⊙ **così**
   av

1 (*in questo modo*) like this, (in) this way; (*in tal modo*) so; **le cose stanno così** this is the way things stand; **non ho detto così!** I didn't say that!; **come stai? — (e) così** how are you? — so-so; **e così via** and so on; **per così dire** so to speak

2 (*tanto*) so; **così lontano** so far away; **un ragazzo così intelligente** such an intelligent boy

▶ *ag inv* (*tale*): **non ho mai visto un film**

così I've never seen such a film
▶*cong*
1 (*perciò*) so, therefore
2: **così ... come** as ... as; **non è così
bravo come te** he's not as good as you;
così ... che so ... that
cosid'detto, -a *ag* so-called
cos'metico, -a, -ci, -che *ag, sm*
cosmetic
cos'pargere [kos'pardʒere] *vt* ~ **di** to
sprinkle with
cos'picuo, -a *ag* considerable, large
cospi'rare *vi* to conspire
'cossi *ecc vb vedi* **cuocere**
'costa *sf* (*tra terra e mare*) coast(line);
(*litorale*) shore; (*Anat*) rib; **la C~
Azzurra** the French Riviera
cos'tante *ag* constant; (*persona*)
steadfast ▶ *sf* constant
cos'tare *vi, vt* to cost; **quanto costa?**
how much does it cost?; ~ **caro** to be
expensive, cost a lot
cos'tata *sf* (*Cuc*) large chop
costeggi'are [kosted'dʒare] *vt* to be
close to; to run alongside
costi'ero, -a *ag* coastal, coast *cpd*
costitu'ire *vt* (*comitato, gruppo*) to set
up, form; (*elementi, parti: comporre*) to
make up, constitute; (*rappresentare*)
to constitute; (*Dir*) to appoint;
costituirsi *vpr* **costituirsi alla polizia**
to give o.s. up to the police
costituzi'one [kostitut'tsjone] *sf*
setting up; building up; constitution
'costo *sm* cost; **a ogni** *o* **qualunque ~,
a tutti i costi** at all costs
'costola *sf* (*Anat*) rib
cos'toso, -a *ag* expensive, costly
cos'tringere [kos'trindʒere] *vt* ~ **qn a
fare qc** to force sb to do sth
costru'ire *vt* to construct, build;
costruzi'one *sf* construction,
building
cos'tume *sm* (*uso*) custom; (*foggia di
vestire, indumento*) costume; **costume**

da bagno bathing *o* swimming
costume (*BRIT*), swimsuit; (*da uomo*)
bathing *o* swimming trunks *pl*
co'tenna *sf* bacon rind
coto'letta *sf* (*di maiale, montone*) chop;
(*di vitello, agnello*) cutlet
co'tone *sm* cotton; **cotone idrofilo**
cotton wool (*BRIT*), absorbent
cotton (*US*)
'cotta *sf* (*fam: innamoramento*) crush
'cottimo *sm* **lavorare a ~** to do
piecework
'cotto, -a *pp di* **cuocere** ▶ *ag* cooked;
(*fam: innamorato*) head-over-heels in
love; **ben ~** (*carne*) well done
cot'tura *sf* cooking; (*in forno*) baking;
(*in umido*) stewing
co'vare *vt* to hatch; (*fig: malattia*) to be
sickening for; (: *odio, rancore*) to nurse
▶ *vi* (*fuoco, fig*) to smoulder
'covo *sm* den
co'vone *sm* sheaf
'cozza ['kɔttsa] *sf* mussel
coz'zare [kot'tsare] *vi* ~ **contro** to
bang into, collide with
'crampo *sm* cramp; **ho un ~ alla
gamba** I've got cramp in my leg
'cranio *sm* skull
cra'tere *sm* crater
cra'vatta *sf* tie
cre'are *vt* to create
'crebbi *ecc vb vedi* **crescere**
cre'dente *sm/f* (*Rel*) believer
cre'denza [kre'dɛntsa] *sf* belief;
(*armadio*) sideboard
'credere *vt* to believe ▶ *vi* ~ **in**, ~ **a** to
believe in; ~ **qn onesto** to believe
sb (to be) honest; ~ **che** to believe *o*
think that; **credersi furbo** to think
one is clever
'credito *sm* (*anche Comm*) credit;
(*reputazione*) esteem, repute;
comprare a ~ to buy on credit
'crema *sf* cream; (*con uova, zucchero
ecc*) custard; **crema pasticciera**

confectioner's custard; **crema solare** sun cream

cre'mare *vt* to cremate

'crepa *sf* crack

cre'paccio [kre'pattʃo] *sm* large crack, fissure; (*di ghiacciaio*) crevasse

crepacu'ore *sm* broken heart

cre'pare *vi* (*fam: morire*) to snuff it, kick the bucket; **~ dalle risa** to split one's sides laughing

crêpe [krɛp] *sf inv* pancake

cre'puscolo *sm* twilight, dusk

'crescere ['krɛʃʃere] *vi* to grow ▸ *vt* (*figli*) to raise

'cresima *sf* (*Rel*) confirmation

'crespo, -a *ag* (*capelli*) frizzy; (*tessuto*) puckered ▸ *sm* crêpe

'cresta *sf* crest; (*di polli, uccelli*) crest, comb

'creta *sf* chalk; clay

creti'nata *sf* (*fam*): **dire/fare una ~** to say/do a stupid thing

cre'tino, -a *ag* stupid ▸ *sm/f* idiot, fool

CRI *sigla f* = **Croce Rossa Italiana**

cric *sm inv* (*Tecn*) jack

cri'ceto [kri'tʃeto] *sm* hamster

crimi'nale *ag, sm/f* criminal

criminalità *sf* crime; **criminalità organizzata** organized crime

'crimine *sm* (*Dir*) crime

crip'tare *vt* (*TV: programma*) to encrypt

crisan'temo *sm* chrysanthemum

'crisi *sf inv* crisis; (*Med*) attack, fit; **crisi di nervi** attack *o* fit of nerves

cris'tallo *sm* crystal; **cristalli liquidi** liquid crystals

cristia'nesimo *sm* Christianity

cristi'ano, -a *ag, sm/f* Christian

'Cristo *sm* Christ

cri'terio *sm* criterion; (*buon senso*) (common) sense

'critica, -che *sf* criticism; **la ~** (*attività*) criticism; (*persone*) the critics *pl*; *vedi anche* **critico**

criti'care *vt* to criticize

'critico, -a, -ci, -che *ag* critical ▸ *sm* critic

cro'ato, -a *ag, sm/f* Croatian, Croat

Croa'zia [kroa'ttsja] *sf* Croatia

croc'cante *ag* crisp, crunchy

'croce ['krotʃe] *sf* cross; **in ~** (*di traverso*) crosswise; (*fig*) on tenterhooks; **Croce Rossa** Red Cross

croci'ata [kro'tʃata] *sf* crusade

croci'era [kro'tʃɛra] *sf* (*viaggio*) cruise; (*Archit*) transept

croci'fisso, -a *pp di* **crocifiggere**

crol'lare *vi* to collapse; **'crollo** *sm* collapse; (*di prezzi*) slump, sudden fall; **crollo in Borsa** *slump in prices on the Stock Exchange*

cro'mato, -a *ag* chromium-plated

'cromo *sm* chrome, chromium

'cronaca, -che *sf* (*Stampa*) news *sg*; (: *rubrica*) column; (*TV, Radio*) commentary; **fatto** *o* **episodio di ~** news item; **cronaca nera** crime news *sg*; crime column

'cronico, -a, -ci, -che *ag* chronic

cro'nista, -i *sm* (*Stampa*) reporter

cro'nometro *sm* chronometer; (*a scatto*) stopwatch

'crosta *sf* crust

cros'tacei [kros'tatʃei] *smpl* shellfish

cros'tata *sf* (*Cuc*) tart

cros'tino *sm* (*Cuc*) crouton; (: *da antipasto*) canapé

cruci'ale [kru'tʃale] *ag* crucial

cruci'verba *sm inv* crossword (puzzle)

cru'dele *ag* cruel

'crudo, -a *ag* (*non cotto*) raw; (*aspro*) harsh, severe

cru'miro (*peg*) *sm* blackleg (*BRIT*), scab

'crusca *sf* bran

crus'cotto *sm* (*Aut*) dashboard

CSI *sigla f inv* (= *Comunità Stati Indipendenti*) CIS

CSM [tʃiɛsse'emme] *sigla m* (= *consiglio superiore della magistratura*)

Magistrates' Board of Supervisors

'Cuba sf Cuba

cu'bano, -a ag, sm/f Cuban

cu'betto sm; **cubetto di ghiaccio** ice cube

'cubico, -a, -ci, -che ag cubic

cu'bista, -i, -e ag (Arte) Cubist ▶ sf (in discoteca) podium dancer

'cubo, -a ag cubic ▶ sm cube; **elevare al ~** (Mat) to cube

cuc'cagna [kuk'kaɲɲa] sf **paese della ~** land of plenty; **albero della ~** greasy pole (fig)

cuc'cetta [kut'tʃetta] sf (Ferr) couchette; (Naut) berth

cucchiai'ata [kukja'jata] sf spoonful

cucchia'ino [kukkja'ino] sm teaspoon; coffee spoon

cucchi'aio [kuk'kjajo] sm spoon

'cuccia, -ce ['kuttʃa] sf dog's bed; **a ~!** down!

'cucciolo ['kuttʃolo] sm cub; (di cane) puppy

cu'cina [ku'tʃina] sf (locale) kitchen; (arte culinaria) cooking, cookery; (le vivande) food, cooking; (apparecchio) cooker; **cucina componibile** fitted kitchen; **cuci'nare** vt to cook

cu'cire [ku'tʃire] vt to sew, stitch; **cuci'trice** sf stapler

cucù sm inv cuckoo

'cuffia sf bonnet, cap; (da infermiera) cap; (da bagno) (bathing) cap; (per ascoltare) headphones pl, headset

cu'gino, -a [ku'dʒino] sm/f cousin

'cui pron

1 (nei complementi indiretti: persona) whom; (: oggetto, animale) which; **la persona/le persone a cui accennavi** the person/people you were referring to o to whom you were referring; **i libri di cui parlavo** the books I was talking about o about which I was talking; **il quartiere in cui abito** the district

where I live; **la ragione per cui** the reason why

2 (inserito tra articolo e sostantivo) whose; **la donna i cui figli sono scomparsi** the woman whose children have disappeared; **il signore, dal cui figlio ho avuto il libro** the man from whose son I got the book

culi'naria sf cookery

'culla sf cradle

cul'lare vt to rock

'culmine sm top, summit

'culo (fam!) sm arse (BRIT!), ass (US!); (fig: fortuna): **aver ~** to have the luck of the devil

'culto sm (religione) religion; (adorazione) worship, adoration; (venerazione: anche fig) cult

cul'tura sf culture; education, learning; **cultu'rale** ag cultural

cultu'rismo sm body-building

cumula'tivo, -a ag cumulative; (prezzo) inclusive; (biglietto) group cpd

'cumulo sm (mucchio) pile, heap; (Meteor) cumulus

cu'netta sf (avvallamento) dip; (di scolo) gutter

cu'ocere ['kwɔtʃere] vt (alimenti) to cook; (mattoni ecc) to fire ▶ vi to cook; **~ al forno** (pane) to bake; (arrosto) to roast; **cu'oco, -a, -chi, -che** sm/f cook; (di ristorante) chef

cu'oio sm leather; **cuoio capelluto** scalp

cu'ore sm heart; **cuori** smpl (Carte) hearts; **avere buon ~** to be kind-hearted; **stare a ~ a qn** to be important to sb

'cupo, -a ag dark; (suono) dull; (fig) gloomy, dismal

'cupola sf dome; cupola

'cura sf care; (Med: trattamento) (course of) treatment; **aver ~ di** (occuparsi di) to look after; **a ~ di** (libro) edited by; **cura dimagrante** diet

cu'rare vt (malato, malattia) to treat;
(: guarire) to cure; (aver cura di) to take
care of; (testo) to edit; **curarsi** vpr to
take care of o.s.; (Med) to follow a
course of treatment; **curarsi di** to pay
attention to

curio'sare vi to look round, wander
round; (tra libri) to browse; ~ **nei
negozi** to look o wander round the
shops

curiosità sf inv curiosity; (cosa rara)
curio, curiosity

curi'oso, -a ag curious; **essere ~ di** to
be curious about

cur'sore sm (Inform) cursor

'curva sf curve; (stradale) bend, curve

cur'vare vt to bend ▶ vi (veicolo) to
take a bend; (strada) to bend, curve;
curvarsi vpr to bend; (legno) to warp

'curvo, -a ag curved; (piegato) bent

cusci'netto [kuʃʃi'netto] sm pad;
(Tecn) bearing ▶ ag inv **stato ~** buffer
state; **cuscinetto a sfere** ball bearing

cu'scino [kuʃʃino] sm cushion;
(guanciale) pillow

cus'tode sm/f keeper, custodian

cus'todia sf care; (Dir) custody;
(astuccio) case, holder

custo'dire vt (conservare) to keep;
(assistere) to look after, take care of;
(fare la guardia) to guard

CV abbr (= cavallo vapore) h.p.

cybercaffè [tʃiberka'fɛ] sm inv
cybercafé

cybernauta, -i, -e sm/f Internet
surfer

cyberspazio sm cyberspace

d

da
(da+il = **dal**, da+lo = **dallo**, da+l' =
dall', da+la = **dalla**, da+i = **dai**, da+gli =
dagli, da+le = **dalle**) prep

1 (agente) by; **dipinto da un grande
artista** painted by a great artist

2 (causa) with; **tremare dalla paura** to
tremble with fear

3 (stato in luogo) at; **abito da lui** I'm
living at his house o with him; **sono
dal giornalaio/da Francesco** I'm at the
newsagent's/Francesco's (house)

4 (moto a luogo) to; (moto per luogo)
through; **vado da Pietro/dal
giornalaio** I'm going to Pietro's
(house)/to the newsagent's; **sono
passati dalla finestra** they came in
through the window

5 (provenienza, allontanamento)
from; **arrivare/partire da Milano** to
arrive/depart from Milan; **scendere
dal treno/dalla macchina** to get off
the train/out of the car; **si trova a 5 km
da qui** it's 5 km from here

6 (tempo: durata) for; (: a partire da: nel
passato) since; (: nel futuro) from; **vivo
qui da un anno** I've been living here
for a year; **è dalle 3 che ti aspetto** I've
been waiting for you since 3 (o'clock);
da oggi in poi from today onwards; **da
bambino** as a child, when I (o he ecc)
was a child

7 (modo, maniera) like; **comportarsi da
uomo** to behave like a man; **l'ho fatto**

da me I did it (by) myself

8 (*descrittivo*): **una macchina da corsa** a racing car; **una ragazza dai capelli biondi** a girl with blonde hair; **un vestito da 60 euro** a 60 euro dress

dà *vb vedi* **dare**

dac'capo *av* (*di nuovo*) (once) again; (*dal principio*) all over again, from the beginning

'**dado** *sm* (*da gioco*) dice *o* die; (*Cuc*) stock (*BRIT*) *o* bouillon (*US*) cube; (*Tecn*) (screw)nut; **dadi** *smpl* (game of) dice; **giocare a dadi** to play dice

'**daino** *sm* (fallow) deer *inv*; (*pelle*) buckskin

dal'tonico, -a, -ci, -che *ag* colour-blind

'**dama** *sf* lady; (*nei balli*) partner; (*gioco*) draughts *sg* (*BRIT*), checkers *sg* (*US*)

damigi'ana [dami'dʒana] *sf* demijohn

da'nese *ag* Danish ▶ *sm/f* Dane ▶ *sm* (*Ling*) Danish

Dani'marca *sf* **la ~** Denmark

dannazi'one *sf* damnation

danneggi'are [danned'dʒare] *vt* to damage; (*rovinare*) to spoil; (*nuocere*) to harm

'**danno** *sm* damage; (*a persona*) harm, injury; **danni** *smpl* (*Dir*) damages; **dan'noso, -a** *o* **dannoso (a, per)** harmful (to), bad (for)

Da'nubio *sm* **il ~** the Danube

'**danza** ['dantsa] *sf* **la ~** dancing; **una ~** a dance

dan'zare [dan'tsare] *vt, vi* to dance

dapper'tutto *av* everywhere

dap'prima *av* at first

'**dare** *sm* (*Comm*) debit ▶ *vt* to give; (*produrre: frutti, suono*) to produce ▶ *vi* (*guardare*): **~ su** to look (out) onto; **darsi** *vpr* **darsi a** to dedicate o.s. to; **darsi al commercio** to go into business; **darsi al bere** to take to drink; **~ da mangiare a qn** to give sb

sth to eat; **~ per certo qc** to consider sth certain; **~ per morto qn** to give sb up for dead; **darsi per vinto** to give in

'**data** *sf* date; **~ limite d'utilizzo** *or* **di consumo** best-before date; **data di nascita** date of birth; **data di scadenza** expiry date

'**dato, -a** *ag* (*stabilito*) given ▶ *sm* datum; **dati** *smpl* data *pl*; **~ che** given that; **un ~ di fatto** a fact; **dati sensibili** personal information

da'tore, -'trice *sm/f*; **datore di lavoro** employer

'**dattero** *sm* date

dattilogra'fia *sf* typing

datti'lografo, -a *sm/f* typist

da'vanti *av* in front; (*dirimpetto*) opposite ▶ *ag inv* front ▶ *sm* front; **~ a** in front of; facing, opposite; (*in presenza di*) before, in front of

davan'zale [davan'tsale] *sm* windowsill

dav'vero *av* really, indeed

d.C. *adv abbr* (= *dopo Cristo*) A.D.

'**dea** *sf* goddess

'**debbo** *ecc vb vedi* **dovere**

'**debito, -a** *ag* due, proper ▶ *sm* debt; (*Comm: dare*) debit; **a tempo ~** at the right time

'**debole** *ag* weak, feeble; (*suono*) faint; (*luce*) dim ▶ *sm* weakness; **debo'lezza** *sf* weakness

debut'tare *vi* to make one's debut

deca'denza [deka'dɛntsa] *sf* decline; (*Dir*) loss, forfeiture

decaffei'nato, -a *ag* decaffeinated

decapi'tare *vt* to decapitate, behead

decappot'tabile *ag, sf* convertible

de'cennio [de'tʃɛnnjo] *sm* decade

de'cente [de'tʃɛnte] *ag* decent, respectable, proper; (*accettabile*) satisfactory, decent

de'cesso [de'tʃɛsso] *sm* death

de'cidere [de'tʃidere] *vt* **~ qc** to decide

on sth; (*questione, lite*) to settle sth; ~ **di fare/che** to decide to do/that; ~ **di qc** (*cosa*) to determine sth; **decidersi (a fare)** to decide (to do), make up one's mind (to do)

deci'frare [detʃi'frare] *vt* to decode; (*fig*) to decipher, make out

deci'male [detʃi'male] *ag* decimal

'decimo, -a ['dɛtʃimo] *num* tenth

de'cina [de'tʃina] *sf* ten; (*circa dieci*): **una ~ (di)** about ten

de'cisi *ecc* [de'tʃizi] *vb vedi* **decidere**

decisi'one [detʃi'zjone] *sf* decision; **prendere una ~** to make a decision

deci'sivo, -a [detʃi'zivo] *ag* (*gen*) decisive; (*fattore*) deciding

de'ciso, -a [de'tʃizo] *pp di* **decidere**

decli'nare *vi* (*pendio*) to slope down; (*fig: diminuire*) to decline ▶ *vt* to decline

declinazi'one *sf* (*Ling*) declension

de'clino *sm* decline

decodifica'tore *sm* (*Tel*) decoder

decol'lare *vi* (*Aer*) to take off; **de'collo** *sm* take-off

deco'rare *vt* to decorate; **decorazi'one** *sf* decoration

de'creto *sm* decree; **decreto legge** *decree with the force of law*

'dedica, -che *sf* dedication

dedi'care *vt* to dedicate; **dedicarsi** *vpr* **dedicarsi a** to devote o.s. to

dedicherò *ecc* [dedike'rɔ] *vb vedi* **dedicare**

'dedito, -a *ag* ~ **a** (*studio ecc*) dedicated *o* devoted to; (*vizio*) addicted to

de'duco *ecc vb vedi* **dedurre**

de'durre *vt* (*concludere*) to deduce; (*defalcare*) to deduct

de'dussi *ecc vb vedi* **dedurre**

defici'ente [defi'tʃɛnte] *ag* (*mancante*): ~ **di** deficient in; (*insufficiente*) insufficient ▶ *sm/f* mental defective; (*peg: cretino*) idiot

'deficit ['dɛfitʃit] *sm inv* (*Econ*) deficit

defi'nire *vt* to define; (*risolvere*) to settle; **defini'tiva** *sf* **in ~** (*dopotutto*) in the end; (*dunque*) hence; **defini'tivo, -a** *ag* definitive, final; **definizi'one** *sf* definition; settlement

defor'mare *vt* (*alterare*) to put out of shape; (*corpo*) to deform; (*pensiero, fatto*) to distort; **deformarsi** *vpr* to lose its shape

de'forme *ag* deformed; disfigured

de'funto, -a *ag* late *cpd* ▶ *sm/f* deceased

degene'rare [dedʒene'rare] *vi* to degenerate

de'gente [de'dʒɛnte] *sm/f* (*in ospedale*) in-patient

deglu'tire *vt* to swallow

de'gnare [deɲ'ɲare] *vt* ~ **qn della propria presenza** to honour sb with one's presence; **degnarsi** *vpr* **degnarsi di fare qc** to deign *o* condescend to do sth

'degno, -a *ag* dignified; ~ **di** worthy of; ~ **di lode** praiseworthy

de'grado *sm*; **degrado urbano** urban decline

'delega, -ghe *sf* (*procura*) proxy

dele'terio, -a *ag* damaging; (*per salute ecc*) harmful

del'fino *sm* (*Zool*) dolphin; (*Storia*) dauphin; (*fig*) probable successor

deli'cato, -a *ag* delicate; (*salute*) delicate, frail; (*fig: gentile*) thoughtful, considerate; (: *che dimostra tatto*) tactful

delin'quente *sm/f* criminal, delinquent; **delinquente abituale** regular offender, habitual offender; **delin'quenza** *sf* criminality, delinquency; **delinquenza minorile** juvenile delinquency

deli'rare *vi* to be delirious, rave; (*fig*) to rave

de'lirio *sm* delirium; (*ragionamento insensato*) raving; (*fig*): **andare/**

mandare in ~ to go/send into
a frenzy

de'litto sm crime

delizi'oso, -a ag delightful; (cibi)
delicious

delta'plano sm hang-glider; **volo col
~** hang-gliding

delu'dente ag disappointing

de'ludere vt to disappoint;
delusi'one sf disappointment;
de'luso, -a pp di **deludere**

'demmo vb vedi **dare**

demo'cratico, -a, -ci, -che ag
democratic

democra'zia [demokrat'tsia] sf
democracy

demo'lire vt to demolish

de'monio sm demon, devil; **il D~**
the Devil

de'naro sm money

densità sf inv density

'denso, -a ag thick, dense

den'tale ag dental

'dente sm tooth; (di forchetta) prong;
al ~ (Cuc: pasta) al dente; **denti del
giudizio** wisdom teeth; **denti da
latte** milk teeth; **denti'era** sf (set of)
false teeth pl

denti'fricio [denti'fritʃo] sm
toothpaste

den'tista, -i, -e sm/f dentist

'dentro av inside; (in casa) indoors;
(fig: nell'intimo) inwardly ▶ prep **~ (a)** in;
piegato in ~ folded over; **qui/là ~** in
here/there; **~ di sé** (pensare, brontolare)
to oneself

de'nuncia, -ce o **cie** [de'nuntʃa] sf
denunciation; declaration; **denuncia
dei redditi** (income) tax return

denunci'are [denun'tʃare] vt to
denounce; (dichiarare) to declare;
(persona, smarrimento ecc) report;
vorrei ~ un furto I'd like to report
a theft

denu'trito, -a ag undernourished

denutrizi'one [denutrit'tsjone] sf
malnutrition

deodo'rante sm deodorant

depe'rire vi to waste away

depi'larsi vpr **~ (le gambe)** (con rasoio)
to shave (one's legs); (con ceretta) to
wax (one's legs)

depila'torio, -a ag hair-removing
cpd, depilatory

dépli'ant [depli'ã] sm inv leaflet;
(opuscolo) brochure

deplo'revole ag deplorable

de'pone, de'pongo ecc vb vedi
deporre

de'porre vt (depositare) to put down;
(rimuovere: da una carica) to remove;
(: re) to depose; (Dir) to testify

depor'tare vt to deport

de'posi ecc vb vedi **deporre**

deposi'tare vt (gen, Geo, Econ) to
deposit; (lasciare) to leave; (merci) to
store; **depositarsi** vpr (sabbia, polvere)
to settle

de'posito sm deposit; (luogo)
warehouse; depot; (: Mil) depot;
deposito bagagli left-luggage office

deposizi'one [depozit'tsjone] sf
deposition; (da una carica) removal

depra'vato, -a ag depraved ▶ sm/f
degenerate

depre'dare vt to rob, plunder

depressi'one sf depression

de'presso, -a pp di **deprimere** ▶ ag
depressed

deprez'zare [depret'tsare] vt (Econ)
to depreciate

depri'mente ag depressing

de'primere vt to depress

depu'rare vt to purify

depu'tato sm (Pol) deputy, ≈ Member
of Parliament (BRIT), ≈ Member of
Congress (US)

deragli'are [deraʎ'ʎare] vi to be
derailed; **far ~** to derail

de'ridere vt to mock, deride

de'risi *ecc vb vedi* **deridere**

de'riva *sf* (*Naut, Aer*) drift; **andare alla ~** (*anche fig*) to drift

deri'vare *vi* **~ da** to derive from ▶ *vt* to derive; (*corso d'acqua*) to divert

derma'tologo, -a, -gi, -ghe *sm/f* dermatologist

deru'bare *vt* to rob

des'crivere *vt* to describe; **descrizi'one** *sf* description

de'serto, -a *ag* deserted ▶ *sm* (*Geo*) desert; **isola deserta** desert island

deside'rare *vt* to want, wish for; (*sessualmente*) to desire; **~ fare/che qn faccia** to want o wish to do/sb to do; **desidera fare una passeggiata?** would you like to go for a walk?

desi'derio *sm* wish; (*più intenso, carnale*) desire

deside'roso, -a *ag* **~ di** longing for

desi'nenza [dezi'nɛntsa] *sf* (*Ling*) ending, inflexion

de'sistere *vi* **~ da** to give up, desist from

deso'lato, -a *ag* (*paesaggio*) desolate; (*persona: spiacente*) sorry

'dessi *ecc vb vedi* **dare**

'deste *ecc vb vedi* **dare**

desti'nare *vt* to destine; (*assegnare*) to appoint, assign; (*indirizzare*) to address; **~ qc a qn** to intend sb to have sth; **destina'tario, -a** *sm/f* (*di lettera*) addressee

destinazi'one [destinat'tsjone] *sf* destination; (*uso*) purpose

des'tino *sm* destiny, fate

destitu'ire *vt* to dismiss, remove

'destra *sf* (*mano*) right hand; (*parte*) right (side); (*Pol*): **la ~** the Right; **a ~** (*essere*) on the right; (*andare*) to the right

destreggi'arsi [destred'dʒarsi] *vpr* to manoeuvre (*BRIT*), maneuver (*US*)

des'trezza [des'trettsa] *sf* skill, dexterity

'destro, -a *ag* right, right-hand

dete'nuto, -a *sm/f* prisoner

deter'gente [deter'dʒɛnte] *ag* (*crema, latte*) cleansing ▶ *sm* cleanser

Attenzione! In inglese esiste la parola *detergent* che però significa *detersivo*.

determi'nare *vt* to determine

determina'tivo, -a *ag* determining; **articolo ~** (*Ling*) definite article

determi'nato, -a *ag* (*gen*) certain; (*particolare*) specific; (*risoluto*) determined, resolute

deter'sivo *sm* detergent

detes'tare *vt* to detest, hate

de'trae, de'traggo *ecc vb vedi* **detrarre**

de'trarre *vt* **~ (da)** to deduct (from), take away (from)

de'trassi *ecc vb vedi* **detrarre**

'detta *sf* **a ~ di** according to

det'taglio [det'taʎʎo] *sm* detail; (*Comm*): **il ~** retail; **al ~** (*Comm*): retail; separately

det'tare *vt* to dictate; **~ legge** (*fig*) to lay down the law; **det'tato** *sm* dictation

'detto, -a *pp di* **dire** ▶ *ag* (*soprannominato*) called, known as; (*già nominato*) above-mentioned ▶ *sm* saying; **~ fatto** no sooner said than done

devas'tare *vt* to devastate; (*fig*) to ravage

devi'are *vi* **~ (da)** to turn off (from) ▶ *vt* to divert; **deviazi'one** *sf* (*anche Aut*) diversion

'devo *ecc vb vedi* **dovere**

de'volvere *vt* (*Dir*) to transfer, devolve

de'voto, -a *ag* (*Rel*) devout, pious; (*affezionato*) devoted

devozi'one [devot'tsjone] *sf* devoutness; (*anche Rel*) devotion

dezip'pare [dedzip'pare] *vt* (*Comput*) to unzip

di
(*di+il* = **del**, *di+lo* = **dello**, *di+l'* = **dell'**, *di+la* = **della**, *di+i* = **dei**, *di+gli* = **degli**, *di+le* = **delle**) *prep*

1 (*possesso, specificazione*) of; (*composto da, scritto da*) by; **la macchina di Paolo/ mio fratello** Paolo's/my brother's car; **un amico di mio fratello** a friend of my brother's, one of my brother's friends; **un quadro di ...** a painting by ...
2 (*caratterizzazione, misura*) of; **una casa di mattoni** a brick house, a house made of bricks; **un orologio d'oro** a gold watch; **un bimbo di 3 anni** a child of 3, a 3-year-old child
3 (*causa, mezzo, modo*) with; **tremare di paura** to tremble with fear; **morire di cancro** to die of cancer; **spalmare di burro** to spread with butter
4 (*argomento*) about, of; **discutere di sport** to talk about sport
5 (*luogo: provenienza*) from; out of; **essere di Roma** to be from Rome; **uscire di casa** to leave the house
6 (*tempo*) in; **d'estate/d'inverno** in (the) summer/winter; **di notte** by night, at night; **di mattina/sera** in the morning/evening; **di lunedì** on Mondays

▶*det* (*una certa quantità di*) some; (: *negativo*) any; (*interrogativo*) any; some; **del pane** (some) bread; **delle caramelle** (some) sweets; **degli amici miei** some friends of mine; **vuoi del vino?** do you want some o any wine?
dia'bete *sm* diabetes *sg*
dia'betico, -a, -ci, -che *ag, sm/f* diabetic
dia'framma, -i *sm* (*divisione*) screen; (*Anat, Fot, contraccettivo*) diaphragm
di'agnosi [di'aɲɲozi] *sf* diagnosis *sg*
diago'nale *ag, sf* diagonal
dia'gramma, -i *sm* diagram
dia'letto *sm* dialect
di'alisi *sf* dialysis *sg*

di'alogo, -ghi *sm* dialogue
dia'mante *sm* diamond
di'ametro *sm* diameter
diaposi'tiva *sf* transparency, slide
di'ario *sm* diary
diar'rea *sf* diarrhoea
di'avolo *sm* devil
di'battito *sm* debate, discussion
'dice ['ditʃe] *vb vedi* **dire**
di'cembre [di'tʃembre] *sm* December
dice'ria [ditʃe'ria] *sf* rumour
dichia'rare [dikja'rare] *vt* to declare; **dichiararsi** *vpr* to declare o.s.; (*innamorato*) to declare one's love; **dichiararsi vinto** to acknowledge defeat; **dichiarazi'one** *sf* declaration; **dichiarazione dei redditi** statement of income; (*modulo*) tax return
dician'nove [ditʃan'nɔve] *num* nineteen
dicias'sette [ditʃas'sɛtte] *num* seventeen
dici'otto [di'tʃɔtto] *num* eighteen
dici'tura [ditʃi'tura] *sf* words *pl*, wording
'dico *ecc vb vedi* **dire**
didasca'lia *sf* (*di illustrazione*) caption; (*Cine*) subtitle; (*Teatro*) stage directions *pl*
di'dattico, -a, -ci, -che *ag* didactic; (*metodo*) teaching; (*libro*) educational
di'eci ['djɛtʃi] *num* ten
di'edi *ecc vb vedi* **dare**
'diesel ['dizəl] *sm inv* diesel engine
dies'sino, -a *sm/f* member of the DS political party
di'eta *sf* diet; **essere a ~** to be on a diet
di'etro *av* behind; (*in fondo*) at the back ▶ *prep* behind; (*tempo: dopo*) after ▶ *sm* back, rear ▶ *ag inv* back *cpd*; **le zampe di ~** the hind legs; **~ richiesta** on demand; (*scritta*) on application
di'fendere *vt* to defend; **difendersi** *vpr* (*cavarsela*) to get by; **difendersi da/contro** to defend o.s. from/

against; **difendersi dal freddo** to protect o.s. from the cold; **difen'sore, -a** sm/f defender; **avvocato difensore** counsel for the defence; **di'fesa** sf defence

di'fesi ecc vb vedi **difendere**

di'fetto sm (mancanza): **~ di** lack of; shortage of; (di fabbricazione) fault, flaw, defect; (morale) fault, failing, defect; (fisico) defect; **far ~** to be lacking; **in ~** at fault; in the wrong; **difet'toso, -a** ag defective, faulty

diffe'rente ag different

diffe'renza [diffe'rɛntsa] sf difference; **a ~ di** unlike

diffe'rire vt to postpone, defer ▶ vi to be different

diffe'rita sf **in ~** (trasmettere) prerecorded

dif'ficile [dif'fitʃile] ag difficult; (persona) hard to please, difficult (to please); (poco probabile): **è ~ che sia libero** it is unlikely that he'll be free ▶ sm difficult part; difficulty; **difficoltà** sf inv difficulty

diffi'dente ag suspicious, distrustful

diffi'denza sf suspicion, distrust

dif'fondere vt (luce, calore) to diffuse; (notizie) to spread, circulate; **diffondersi** vpr to spread

dif'fusi ecc vb vedi **diffondere**

dif'fuso, -a pp di **diffondere** ▶ ag (malattia, fenomeno) widespread

'diga, -ghe sf dam; (portuale) breakwater

dige'rente [didʒe'rɛnte] ag (apparato) digestive

dige'rire [didʒe'rire] vt to digest; **digesti'one** sf digestion; **diges'tivo, -a** ag digestive ▶ sm (after-dinner) liqueur

digi'tale [didʒi'tale] ag digital; (delle dita) finger cpd, digital ▶ sf (Bot) foxglove

digi'tare [didʒi'tare] vt, vi (Inform) to key (in)

digiu'nare [didʒu'nare] vi to starve o.s.; (Rel) to fast; **digi'uno, -a** ag **essere digiuno** not to have eaten ▶ sm fast; **a digiuno** on an empty stomach

dignità [diɲɲi'ta] sf inv dignity

'DIGOS ['digɔs] sigla f (= Divisione Investigazioni Generali e Operazioni Speciali) police department dealing with political security

digri'gnare [digriɲ'ɲare] vt **~ i denti** to grind one's teeth

dilapi'dare vt to squander, waste

dila'tare vt to dilate; (gas) to cause to expand; (passaggio, cavità) to open (up); **dilatarsi** vpr to dilate; (Fisica) to expand

dilazio'nare [dilattsjo'nare] vt to delay, defer

di'lemma, -i sm dilemma

dilet'tante sm/f dilettante; (anche Sport) amateur

dili'gente [dili'dʒɛnte] ag (scrupoloso) diligent; (accurato) careful, accurate

dilu'ire vt to dilute

dilun'garsi vpr (fig): **~ su** to talk at length on o about

diluvi'are vb impers to pour (down)

di'luvio sm downpour; (inondazione, fig) flood

dima'grante ag slimming cpd

dima'grire vi to get thinner, lose weight

dime'nare vt to wave, shake; **dimenarsi** vpr to toss and turn; (fig) to struggle; **~ la coda** (cane) to wag its tail

dimensi'one sf dimension; (grandezza) size

dimenti'canza [dimenti'kantsa] sf forgetfulness; (errore) oversight, slip; **per ~** inadvertently

dimenti'care vt to forget; **ho dimenticato la chiave/il passaporto** I forgot the key/my passport; **dimenticarsi** vpr **dimenticarsi di qc**

to forget sth

dimesti'chezza [dimesti'kettsa] *sf* familiarity

di'mettere *vt* ~ **qn da** to dismiss sb from; *(dall'ospedale)* to discharge sb from; **dimettersi** *vpr* **dimettersi (da)** to resign (from)

dimez'zare [dimed'dzare] *vt* to halve

diminu'ire *vt* to reduce, diminish; *(prezzi)* to bring down, reduce ▶ *vi* to decrease, diminish; *(rumore)* to die down; *(prezzi)* to fall, go down

diminu'tivo, -a *ag, sm* diminutive

diminuzi'one *sf* decreasing, diminishing

di'misi *ecc vb vedi* **dimettere**

dimissi'oni *sfpl* resignation *sg*; **dare** *o* **presentare le ~** to resign, hand in one's resignation

dimos'trare *vt* to demonstrate, show; *(provare)* to prove, demonstrate; **dimostrarsi** *vpr* **dimostrarsi molto abile** to prove to be very clever; **dimostra 30 anni** he looks about 30 (years old); **dimostrazi'one** *sf* demonstration; proof

di'namica *sf* dynamics *sg*

di'namico, -a, -ci, -che *ag* dynamic

dina'mite *sf* dynamite

'dinamo *sf inv* dynamo

dino'sauro *sm* dinosaur

dintorni *smpl* outskirts; **nei ~ di** in the vicinity *o* neighbourhood of

'dio *(pl* **'dei)** *sm* god; **D~** God; **gli dei** the gods; **D~ mio!** my goodness!, my God!

diparti'mento *sm* department

dipen'dente *ag* dependent ▶ *sm/f* employee; **dipendente statale** state employee

di'pendere *vi* ~ **da** to depend on; *(finanziariamente)* to be dependent on; *(derivare)* to come from, be due to

di'pesi *ecc vb vedi* **dipendere**

di'pingere [di'pindʒere] *vt* to paint

di'pinsi *ecc vb vedi* **dipingere**

di'pinto, -a *pp di* **dipingere** ▶ *sm* painting

di'ploma, -i *sm* diploma

diplo'matico, -a, -ci, -che *ag* diplomatic ▶ *sm* diplomat

diploma'zia [diplomat'tsia] *sf* diplomacy

di'porto: imbarcazione da ~ *sf* pleasure craft

dira'dare *vt* to thin (out); *(visite)* to reduce, make less frequent; **diradarsi** *vpr* to disperse; *(nebbia)* to clear (up)

'dire *vt* to say; *(segreto, fatto)* to tell; ~ **qc a qn** to tell sb sth; ~ **a qn di fare qc** to tell sb to do sth; ~ **di sì/no** to say yes/no; **si dice che ...** they say that ...; **si ~bbe che ...** it looks (*o* sounds) as though ...; **dica, signora?** *(in un negozio)* yes, Madam, can I help you?; **come si dice in inglese...?** what's the English (word) for ...?

di'ressi *ecc vb vedi* **dirigere**

di'retta: in ~ *avv (transmettere)* live; **un incontro di calcio in ~** a live football match

di'retto, -a *pp di* **dirigere** ▶ *ag* direct ▶ *sm (Ferr)* through train

diret'tore, -'trice *sm/f (di azienda)* director: manager/ess; *(di scuola elementare)* head (teacher) *(BRIT)*, principal *(US)*; **direttore d'orchestra** conductor; **direttore vendite** sales director *o* manager

direzi'one [diret'tsjone] *sf* board of directors; management; *(senso di movimento)* direction; **in ~ di** in the direction of, towards

diri'gente [diri'dʒɛnte] *sm/f* executive; *(Pol)* leader ▶ *ag* **classe ~** ruling class

di'rigere [di'ridʒere] *vt* to direct; *(impresa)* to run, manage; *(Mus)* to conduct; **dirigersi** *vpr* **dirigersi verso** *o* **a** to make *o* head for

dirim'petto *av* opposite; **~ a** opposite, facing

di'ritto, -a *ag* straight; (*onesto*) straight, upright ▶ *av* straight, directly; **andare ~** to go straight on ▶ *sm* right side; (*Tennis*) forehand; (*Maglia*) plain stitch; (*prerogativa*) right; (*leggi, scienza*): **il ~** law; **diritti** *smpl* (*tasse*) duty *sg*; **stare ~** to stand up straight; **aver ~ a qc** to be entitled to sth; **diritti d'autore** royalties

dirotta'mento *sm*; **dirottamento (aereo)** hijack

dirot'tare *vt* (*nave, aereo*) to change the course of; (*aereo sotto minaccia*) to hijack; (*traffico*) to divert ▶ *vi* (*nave, aereo*) to change course; **dirotta'tore, -'trice** *sm/f* hijacker

di'rotto, -a *ag* (*pioggia*) torrential; (*pianto*) unrestrained; **piovere a ~** to pour; **piangere a ~** to cry one's heart out

di'rupo *sm* crag, precipice

di'sabile *sm/f* disabled person ▶ *ag* disabled; **i disabili** the disabled

disabi'tato, -a *ag* uninhabited

disabitu'arsi *vpr* **~ a** to get out of the habit of

disac'cordo *sm* disagreement

disadat'tato, -a *ag* (*Psic*) maladjusted

disa'dorno, -a *ag* plain, unadorned

disagi'ato, -a [diza'dʒato] *ag* poor, needy; (*vita*) hard

di'sagio [di'zadʒo] *sm* discomfort; (*disturbo*) inconvenience; (*fig: imbarazzo*) embarrassment; **essere a ~** to be ill at ease

disappro'vare *vt* to disapprove of; **disapprovazi'one** *sf* disapproval

disap'punto *sm* disappointment

disar'mare *vt, vi* to disarm; **di'sarmo** *sm* (*Mil*) disarmament

di'sastro *sm* disaster

disas'troso, -a *ag* disastrous

disat'tento, -a *ag* inattentive; **disattenzi'one** *sf* carelessness, lack of attention

disavven'tura *sf* misadventure, mishap

dis'capito *sm* **a ~ di** to the detriment of

dis'carica, -che *sf* (*di rifiuti*) rubbish tip *o* dump

di'scendere [diʃʃɛndere] *vt* to go (*o* come) down ▶ *vi* to go (*o* come) down; (*strada*) to go down; (*smontare*) to get off; **~ da** (*famiglia*) to be descended from; **~ dalla macchina/dal treno** to get out of the car/out of *o* off the train; **~ da cavallo** to dismount, get off one's horse

di'scesa [diʃʃesa] *sf* descent; (*pendio*) slope; **in ~** (*strada*) downhill *cpd*, sloping; **discesa libera** (*Sci*) downhill (race)

disci'plina [diʃʃi'plina] *sf* discipline

'disco, -schi *sm* disc; (*Sport*) discus; (*fonografico*) record; (*Inform*) disk; **disco orario** (*Aut*) parking disc; **disco rigido** (*Inform*) hard disk; **disco volante** flying saucer

disco'grafico, -a, ci, che *ag* record *cpd*, recording *cpd* ▶ *sm* record producer; **casa discografica** record(ing) company

dis'correre *vi* **~ (di)** to talk (about)

dis'corso, -a *pp di* **discorrere** ▶ *sm* speech; (*conversazione*) conversation, talk

disco'teca, -che *sf* (*raccolta*) record library; (*locale*) disco

discre'panza [diskre'pantsa] *sf* disagreement

dis'creto, -a *ag* discreet; (*abbastanza buono*) reasonable, fair

discriminazi'one [diskriminat'tsjone] *sf* discrimination

dis'cussi *ecc vb vedi* **discutere**

discussi'one *sf* discussion; (*litigio*) argument; **fuori ~** out of the question

dis'cutere *vt* to discuss, debate; (*contestare*) to question ▶ *vi* (*conversare*): **~ (di)** to discuss; (*litigare*) to argue

dis'detta *sf* (*di prenotazione ecc*) cancellation; (*sfortuna*) bad luck

dis'dire *vt* (*prenotazione*) to cancel; (*Dir*): **~ un contratto d'affitto** to give notice (to quit); **vorrei ~ la mia prenotazione** I want to cancel my booking

dise'gnare [disen'ɲare] *vt* to draw; (*progettare*) to design; (*fig*) to outline

disegna'tore, -'trice *sm/f* designer

di'segno [di'seɲɲo] *sm* drawing; design; outline; **disegno di legge** (*Dir*) bill

diser'bante *sm* weed-killer

diser'tare *vt, vi* to desert

dis'fare *vt* to undo; (*valigie*) to unpack; (*meccanismo*) to take to pieces; (*neve*) to melt; **disfarsi** *vpr* to come undone; (*neve*) to melt; **~ il letto** to strip the bed; **disfarsi di qn** (*liberarsi*) to get rid of sb; **dis'fatto, -a** *pp di* **disfare**

dis'gelo [diz'dʒɛlo] *sm* thaw

dis'grazia [diz'grattsja] *sf* (*sventura*) misfortune; (*incidente*) accident, mishap

disgu'ido *sm* hitch; **disguido postale** error in postal delivery

disgus'tare *vt* to disgust

dis'gusto *sm* disgust; **disgus'toso, -a** *ag* disgusting

disidra'tare *vt* to dehydrate

disimpa'rare *vt* to forget

disinfet'tante *ag, sm* disinfectant

disinfet'tare *vt* to disinfect

disini'bito, -a *ag* uninhibited

disinstal'lare *vt* (*software*) to uninstall

disinte'grare *vt, vi* to disintegrate; **disintegrarsi** *vpr* to disintegrate

disinteres'sarsi *vpr* **~ di** to take no interest in

disinte'resse *sm* indifference; (*generosità*) unselfishness

disintossi'carsi *vpr* to clear out one's system; (*alcolizzato, drogato*) to be treated for alcoholism (*o* drug addiction)

disin'volto, -a *ag* casual, free and easy

dismi'sura *sf* excess; **a ~** to excess, excessively

disoccu'pato, -a *ag* unemployed ▶ *sm/f* unemployed person; **disoccupazi'one** *sf* unemployment

diso'nesto, -a *ag* dishonest

disordi'nato, -a *ag* untidy; (*privo di misura*) irregular, wild

di'sordine *sm* (*confusione*) disorder, confusion; (*sregolatezza*) debauchery; **disordini** *smpl* (*Pol ecc*) disorder *sg*; (*tumulti*) riots

disorien'tare *vt* to disorientate

disorien'tato, -a *ag* disorientated

'dispari *ag inv* odd, uneven

dis'parte: in ~ *av* (*da lato*) aside, apart; **tenersi** *o* **starsene in ~** to keep to o.s., hold o.s. aloof

dispendi'oso, -a *ag* expensive

dis'pensa *sf* pantry, larder; (*mobile*) sideboard; (*Dir*) exemption; (*Rel*) dispensation; (*fascicolo*) number, issue

dispe'rato, -a *ag* (*persona*) in despair; (*caso, tentativo*) desperate

disperazi'one *sf* despair

dis'perdere *vt* (*disseminare*) to disperse; (*Mil*) to scatter, rout; (*fig: consumare*) to waste, squander; **disperdersi** *vpr* to disperse; to scatter; **dis'perso, -a** *pp di* **disperdere** ▶ *sm/f* missing person

dis'petto *sm* spite *no pl*, spitefulness *no pl*; **fare un ~ a qn** to play a (nasty) trick on sb; **a ~ di** in spite of;

dispet'toso, -a *ag* spiteful

dispia'cere [dispja'tʃere] *sm* (*rammarico*) regret, sorrow; (*dolore*) grief; **dispiaceri** *smpl* (*preoccupazioni*) troubles, worries *vi* ~ **a** to displease *vb impers* **mi dispiace (che)** I am sorry (that); **le dispiace se...?** do you mind if...?

dis'pone, dis'pongo *ecc vb vedi* **disporre**

dispo'nibile *ag* available

dis'porre *vt* (*sistemare*) to arrange; (*preparare*) to prepare; (*Dir*) to order; (*persuadere*): ~ **qn a** to incline *o* dispose sb towards ▶ *vi* (*decidere*) to decide; (*usufruire*): ~ **di** to use, have at one's disposal; (*essere dotato*): ~ **di** to have

dis'posi *ecc vb vedi* **disporre**

disposi'tivo *sm* (*meccanismo*) device

disposizi'one [dispozit'tsjone] *sf* arrangement, layout; (*stato d'animo*) mood; (*tendenza*) bent, inclination; (*comando*) order; (*Dir*) provision, regulation; **a ~ di qn** at sb's disposal

dis'posto, -a *pp di* **disporre**

disprez'zare [dispret'tsare] *vt* to despise

dis'prezzo [dis'prɛttso] *sm* contempt

'disputa *sf* dispute, quarrel

dispu'tare *vt* (*contendere*) to dispute, contest; (*gara*) to take part in ▶ *vi* to quarrel; ~ **di** to discuss; **disputarsi qc** to fight for sth

'disse *vb vedi* **dire**

dissente'ria *sf* dysentery

dissen'tire *vi* ~ **(da)** to disagree (with)

disse'tante *ag* refreshing

'dissi *vb vedi* **dire**

dissimu'lare *vt* (*fingere*) to dissemble; (*nascondere*) to conceal

dissi'pare *vt* to dissipate; (*scialacquare*) to squander, waste

dissu'adere *vt* ~ **qn da** to dissuade sb from

distac'care *vt* to detach, separate;

(*Sport*) to leave behind; **distaccarsi** *vpr* to be detached; (*fig*) to stand out; **distaccarsi da** (*fig: allontanarsi*) to grow away from

dis'tacco, -chi *sm* (*separazione*) separation; (*fig: indifferenza*) detachment; (*Sport*): **vincere con un ~ di ...** to win by a distance of ...

dis'tante *av* far away ▶ *ag* ~ **(da)** distant (from), far away (from)

dis'tanza [dis'tantsa] *sf* distance

distanzi'are [distan'tsjare] *vt* to space out, place at intervals; (*Sport*) to outdistance; (*fig: superare*) to outstrip, surpass

dis'tare *vi* **distiamo pochi chilometri da Roma** we are only a few kilometres (away) from Rome; **quanto dista il centro da qui?** how far is the town centre?

dis'tendere *vt* (*coperta*) to spread out; (*gambe*) to stretch (out); (*mettere a giacere*) to lay; (*rilassare: muscoli, nervi*) to relax; **distendersi** *vpr* (*rilassarsi*) to relax; (*sdraiarsi*) to lie down

dis'tesa *sf* expanse, stretch

dis'teso, -a *pp di* **distendere**

distil'lare *vt* to distil

distille'ria *sf* distillery

dis'tinguere *vt* to distinguish; **distinguersi** *vpr* (*essere riconoscibile*) to be distinguished; (*emergere*) to stand out, be conspicuous, distinguish o.s.

dis'tinta *sf* (*nota*) note; (*elenco*) list; **distinta di versamento** pay-in slip

distin'tivo, -a *ag* distinctive; distinguishing ▶ *sm* badge

dis'tinto, -a *pp di* **distinguere** ▶ *ag* (*dignitoso ed elegante*) distinguished; **"distinti saluti"** (*in lettera*) yours faithfully

distinzi'one [distin'tsjone] *sf* distinction

dis'togliere [dis'tɔʎʎere] *vt* ~ **da** to take away from; (*fig*) to dissuade from

distorsi'one *sf* (*Med*) sprain; (*Fisica, Ottica*) distortion

dis'trarre *vt* to distract; (*divertire*) to entertain, amuse; **distrarsi** *vpr* (*non fare attenzione*) to be distracted, let one's mind wander; (*svagarsi*) to amuse o enjoy o.s.; **dis'tratto, -a** *pp di* **distrarre** ▶ *ag* absent-minded; (*disattento*) inattentive; **distrazi'one** *sf* absent-mindedness; inattention; (*svago*) distraction, entertainment

dis'tretto *sm* district

distribu'ire *vt* to distribute; (*Carte*) to deal (out); (*posta*) to deliver; (*lavoro*) to allocate, assign; (*ripartire*) to share out; **distribu'tore** *sm* (*di benzina*) petrol (*BRIT*) o gas (*US*) pump; (*Aut, Elettr*) distributor; **distributore automatico** vending machine

distri'care *vt* to disentangle, unravel; **districarsi** *vpr* (*tirarsi fuori*): **districarsi da** to get out of, disentangle o.s. from

dis'truggere [dis'truddʒere] *vt* to destroy; **distruzi'one** *sf* destruction

distur'bare *vt* to disturb, trouble; (*sonno, lezioni*) to disturb, interrupt; **disturbarsi** *vpr* to put o.s. out

dis'turbo *sm* trouble, bother, inconvenience; (*indisposizione*) (slight) disorder, ailment; **scusi il ~** I'm sorry to trouble you

disubbidi'ente *ag* disobedient

disubbi'dire *vi* ~ (**a qn**) to disobey (sb)

disu'mano, -a *ag* inhuman

di'tale *sm* thimble

'dito (*pl(f)* **'dita**) *sm* finger; (*misura*) finger, finger's breadth; **dito (del piede)** toe

'ditta *sf* firm, business

ditta'tore *sm* dictator

ditta'tura *sf* dictatorship

dit'tongo, -ghi *sm* diphthong

di'urno, -a *ag* day *cpd*, daytime *cpd*

'diva *sf vedi* **divo**

di'vano *sm* sofa; divan; **divano letto** bed settee, sofa bed

divari'care *vt* to open wide

di'vario *sm* difference

dive'nire *vi* = **diventare**

diven'tare *vi* to become; ~ **famoso/ professore** to become famous/a teacher

diversifi'care *vt* to diversify, vary; to differentiate; **diversificarsi** *vpr* **diversificarsi (per)** to differ (in)

diversità *sf inv* difference, diversity; (*varietà*) variety

diver'sivo *sm* diversion, distraction

di'verso, -a *ag* (*differente*): ~ **(da)** different (from); **diversi, -e** *det pl* several, various; (*Comm*) sundry *pron pl* several (people), many (people)

diver'tente *ag* amusing

diverti'mento *sm* amusement, pleasure; (*passatempo*) pastime

diver'tire *vt* to amuse, entertain; **divertirsi** *vpr* to amuse o enjoy o.s.

di'videre *vt* (*anche Mat*) to divide; (*distribuire, ripartire*) to divide (up), split (up); **dividersi** *vpr* (*separarsi*) to separate; (*strade*) to fork

divi'eto *sm* prohibition; "~ **di sosta**" (*Aut*) "no parking"

divinco'larsi *vpr* to wriggle, writhe

di'vino, -a *ag* divine

di'visa *sf* (*Mil ecc*) uniform; (*Comm*) foreign currency

di'visi *ecc vb vedi* **dividere**

divisi'one *sf* division

'divo, -a *sm/f* star

divo'rare *vt* to devour

divorzi'are [divor'tsjare] *vi* ~ **(da qn)** to divorce (sb)

di'vorzio [di'vortsjo] *sm* divorce

divul'gare *vt* to divulge, disclose; (*rendere comprensibile*) to popularize

dizio'nario [ditsjo'narjo] *sm* dictionary

DJ [di'dʒei] *sigla m/f* (= *Disk Jockey*) DJ

do *sm* (*Mus*) C; (: *solfeggiando*) do(h)

dobbi'amo vb vedi **dovere**

D.O.C. [dɔk] abbr (= denominazione di origine controllata) label guaranteeing the quality of wine

'**doccia, -ce** ['dɔttʃa] sf (bagno) shower; **fare la ~** to have a shower

do'cente [do'tʃɛnte] ag teaching ▶ sm/f teacher; (di università) lecturer

'**docile** ['dɔtʃile] ag docile

documen'tario sm documentary

documentarsi vpr **~ (su)** to gather information o material (about)

docu'mento sm document; **documenti** smpl (d'identità ecc) papers

dodi'cesimo, -a [dodi'tʃɛzimo] num twelfth

'**dodici** ['doditʃi] num twelve

do'gana sf (ufficio) customs pl; (tassa) (customs) duty; **passare la ~** to go through customs; **dogani'ere** sm customs officer

'**doglie** ['dɔʎʎe] sfpl (Med) labour sg, labour pains

'**dolce** ['doltʃe] ag sweet; (carattere, persona) gentle, mild; (fig: mite: clima) mild; (non ripido: pendio) gentle ▶ sm (sapore dolce) sweetness, sweet taste; (Cuc: portata) sweet, dessert; (: torta) cake; **dolcifi'cante** sm sweetener

'**dollaro** sm dollar

Dolo'miti sfpl **le ~** the Dolomites

do'lore sm (fisico) pain; (morale) sorrow, grief; **dolo'roso, -a** ag painful; sorrowful, sad

do'manda sf (interrogazione) question; (richiesta) demand; (: cortese) request; (Dir: richiesta scritta) application; (Econ): **la ~** demand; **fare una ~ a qn** to ask sb a question; **fare ~ (per un lavoro)** to apply (for a job)

doman'dare vt (per avere) to ask for; (per sapere) to ask; (esigere) to demand; **domandarsi** vpr to wonder; to ask o.s.; **~ qc a qn** to ask sb for sth; to ask sb sth

do'mani av tomorrow ▶ sm **il ~** (il futuro) the future; (il giorno successivo) the next day; **~ l'altro** the day after tomorrow

do'mare vt to tame

doma'tore, -'trice sm/f (gen) tamer; **domatore di cavalli** horsebreaker; **domatore di leoni** lion tamer

domat'tina av tomorrow morning

do'menica, -che sf Sunday; **di** o **la ~** on Sundays

do'mestico, -a, -ci, -che ag domestic ▶ sm/f servant, domestic

domi'cilio [domi'tʃiljo] sm (Dir) domicile, place of residence

domi'nare vt to dominate; (fig: sentimenti) to control, master ▶ vi to be in the dominant position

do'nare vt to give, present; (per beneficenza ecc) to donate ▶ vi (fig): **~ a** to suit, become; **~ sangue** to give blood; **dona'tore, -'trice** sm/f donor; **donatore di sangue/di organi** blood/organ donor

dondo'lare vt (cullare) to rock; **dondolarsi** vpr to swing, sway; '**dondolo** sm **sedia/cavallo a dondolo** rocking chair/horse

'**donna** sf woman; **donna di casa** housewife; home-loving woman; **donna di servizio** maid

donnai'olo sm ladykiller

'**donnola** sf weasel

'**dono** sm gift

doping ['dɔpiŋ] sm doping

'**dopo** av (tempo) afterwards; (più tardi) later; (luogo) after, next ▶ prep after ▶ cong (temporale): **~ aver studiato** after having studied; **~ mangiato** va **a dormire** after having eaten o after a meal he goes for a sleep ▶ ag inv **il giorno ~** the following day; **un anno ~** a year later; **~ di me/lui** after me/him; **~, a ~!** see you later!

dopo'barba sm inv after-shave

dopodo'mani *av* the day after tomorrow

doposcì [dopoʃʃi] *sm inv* après-ski outfit

dopo'sole *sm inv* aftersun (lotion)

dopo'tutto *av* (*tutto considerato*) after all

doppi'aggio [dop'pjaddʒo] *sm* (*Cinema*) dubbing

doppi'are *vt* (*Naut*) to round; (*Sport*) to lap; (*Cinema*) to dub

'doppio, -a *ag* double; (*fig: falso*) double-dealing, deceitful ▶ *sm* (*quantità*): **il ~ (di)** twice as much (*o many*), double the amount (*o number*) of; (*Sport*) doubles *pl* ▶ *av* double

doppi'one *sm* duplicate (copy)

doppio'petto *sm* double-breasted jacket

dormicchi'are [dormik'kjare] *vi* to doze

dormigli'one, -a [dormiʎ'ʎone] *sm/f* sleepyhead

dor'mire *vt, vi* to sleep; **andare a ~** to go to bed; **dor'mita** *sf* **farsi una dormita** to have a good sleep

dormi'torio *sm* dormitory

dormi'veglia [dormi'veʎʎa] *sm* drowsiness

'dorso *sm* back; (*di montagna*) ridge, crest; (*di libro*) spine; **a ~ di cavallo** on horseback

do'sare *vt* to measure out; (*Med*) to dose

'dose *sf* quantity, amount; (*Med*) dose

do'tato, -a *ag* **~ di** (*attrezzature*) equipped with; (*bellezza, intelligenza*) endowed with; **un uomo ~** a gifted man

'dote *sf* (*di sposa*) dowry; (*assegnata a un ente*) endowment; (*fig*) gift, talent

Dott. *abbr* (= *dottore*) Dr.

dotto'rato *sm* degree; **dottorato di ricerca** doctorate, doctor's degree

dot'tore, -essa *sm/f* doctor; **chiamare un ~** call a doctor

- **dottore**
- In Italy, anyone who has a degree
- in any subject can use the title
- **dottore**. Thus a person who
- is addressed as **dottore** is not
- necessarily a doctor of medicine.

dot'trina *sf* doctrine

Dott.ssa *abbr* (= *dottoressa*) Dr.

'dove *av* (*gen*) where; (*in cui*) where, in which; (*dovunque*) wherever ▶ *cong* (*mentre, laddove*) whereas; **~ sei?/vai?** where are you?/are you going?; **dimmi dov'è** tell me where it is; **di ~ sei?** where are you from?; **per ~ si passa?** which way should we go?; **la città ~ abito** the town where *o* in which I live; **siediti ~ vuoi** sit wherever you like

do'vere *sm* (*obbligo*) duty ▶ *vt* (*essere debitore*): **~ qc (a qn)** to owe (sb) sth ▶ *vi* (*seguito dall'infinito: obbligo*) to have to; **rivolgersi a chi di ~** to apply to the appropriate authority *o* person; **lui deve farlo** he has to do it, he must do it; **quanto le devo?** how much do I owe you?; **è dovuto partire** he had to leave; **ha dovuto pagare** he had to pay; (: *intenzione*): **devo partire domani** I'm (due) to leave tomorrow; (: *probabilità*): **dev'essere tardi** it must be late; **come si deve** (*lavorare, comportarsi*) properly; **una persona come si deve** a respectable person

dove'roso, -a *ag* (right and) proper

dovrò *ecc vb vedi* **dovere**

do'vunque *av* (*in qualunque luogo*) wherever; (*dappertutto*) everywhere; **~ io vada** wherever I go

do'vuto, -a *ag* (*causato*): **~ a** due to

doz'zina [dod'dzina] *sf* dozen; **una ~ di uova** a dozen eggs

dozzi'nale [doddzi'nale] *ag* cheap, second-rate

'drago, -ghi *sm* dragon

'dramma, -i *sm* drama; **dram'matico, -a, -ci, -che** *ag* dramatic

'drastico, -a, -ci, -che *ag* drastic

'dritto, -a *ag, av* = **diritto**

'droga, -ghe *sf* (*sostanza aromatica*) spice; (*stupefacente*) drug; **droghe leggere/pesanti** soft/hard drugs

drogarsi *vpr* to take drugs

dro'gato, -a *sm/f* drug addict

droghe'ria [droge'ria] *sf* grocer's shop (*BRIT*), grocery (store) (*US*)

drome'dario *sm* dromedary

DS [di'ɛsse] *sigla mpl* (= *Democratici di Sinistra*) *Italian left-wing party*

'dubbio, -a *ag* (*incerto*) doubtful, dubious; (*ambiguo*) dubious ▶ *sm* (*incertezza*) doubt; **avere il ~ che** to be afraid that, suspect that; **mettere in ~ qc** to question sth

dubi'tare *vi* **~ di** to doubt; (*risultato*) to be doubtful of

Dub'lino *sf* Dublin

'duca, -chi *sm* duke

du'chessa [du'kessa] *sf* duchess

'due *num* two

due'cento [due'tʃento] *num* two hundred ▶ *sm* **il D~** the thirteenth century

due'pezzi [due'pɛttsi] *sm* (*costume da bagno*) two-piece swimsuit; (*abito femminile*) two-piece suit

'dunque *cong* (*perciò*) so, therefore; (*riprendendo il discorso*) well (then) ▶ *sm inv* **venire al ~** to come to the point

du'omo *sm* cathedral

■ Attenzione! In inglese esiste la parola *dome*, che però significa *cupola*.

dupli'cato *sm* duplicate

'duplice ['duplitʃe] *ag* double, twofold; **in ~ copia** in duplicate

du'rante *prep* during

du'rare *vi* to last; **~ fatica a** to have difficulty in

du'rezza [du'rettsa] *sf* hardness; stubbornness; harshness; toughness

'duro, -a *ag* (*pietra, lavoro, materasso, problema*) hard; (*persona: ostinato*) stubborn, obstinate; (*severo*) harsh, hard; (*voce*) harsh; (*carne*) tough ▶ *sm* hardness; (*difficoltà*) hard part; (*persona*) tough guy; **tener ~** to stand firm, hold out; **~ d'orecchi** hard of hearing

DVD [divu'di] *sigla m* (= *digital versatile (or) video disc*) DVD; (*lettore*) DVD player

e

e (*davV spesso* **ed**) *cong* and; **e lui?** what about him?; **e compralo!** well buy it then!

E *abbr* (= *est*) E

è *vb vedi* **essere**

eb'bene *cong* well (then)

'ebbi *ecc vb vedi* **avere**

e'braico, -a, -ci, -che *ag* Hebrew, Hebraic ▶ *sm* (*Ling*) Hebrew

e'breo, -a *ag* Jewish ▶ *sm/f* Jew/ess

EC *abbr* (= *Eurocity*) *fast train connecting Western European cities*

ecc. *av abbr* (= *eccetera*) etc

eccel'lente [ettʃel'lɛnte] *ag* excellent

ec'centrico, -a, -ci, -che [et'tʃɛntriko] *ag* eccentric

ecces'sivo, -a [ettʃes'sivo] *ag* excessive

ec'cesso [et'tʃɛsso] *sm* excess; **all'~** (*gentile, generoso*) to excess, excessively; **eccesso di velocità** (*Aut*) speeding

ec'cetera [et'tʃɛtera] *av* et cetera, and so on

ec'cetto [et'tʃɛtto] *prep* except, with the exception of; **~ che** except, other than; **~ che (non)** unless

eccezio'nale [ettʃetsjo'nale] *ag* exceptional

eccezi'one [ettʃet'tsjone] *sf* exception; (*Dir*) objection; **a ~ di** with the exception of, except for; **d'~** exceptional

ecci'tare [ettʃi'tare] *vt* (*curiosità, interesse*) to excite, arouse; (*folla*) to incite; **eccitarsi** *vpr* to get excited; (*sessualmente*) to become aroused

'ecco *av* (*per dimostrare*): **~ il treno!** here's *o* here comes the train!; (*dav pron*): **~mi!** here I am!; **~ne uno!** here's one (of them)!; (*dav pp*): **~ fatto!** there, that's it done!

ec'come *av* rather; **ti piace? — ~!** do you like it? — I'll say! *o* and how! *o* rather! (*BRIT*)

e'clisse *sf* eclipse

'eco (*pl*(*m*) **'echi**) *sm o* echo

ecogra'fia *sf* (*Med*) scan

ecolo'gia [ekolo'dʒia] *sf* ecology

eco'logico, -a, ci, che [eko'lɔdʒiko] *ag* ecological

econo'mia *sf* economy; (*scienza*) economics *sg*; (*risparmio: azione*) saving; **fare ~** to economize, make economies; **eco'nomico, -a, -ci, -che** *ag* economic; (*poco costoso*) economical

ecstasy ['ekstazi] *sf* Ecstasy

'edera *sf* ivy

e'dicola *sf* newspaper kiosk *o* stand (*US*)

edi'ficio [edi'fitʃo] *sm* building

e'dile *ag* building *cpd*

Edim'burgo *sf* Edinburgh

edi'tore, -'trice *ag* publishing *cpd* ▶ *sm/f* publisher

> Attenzione! In inglese esiste la parola *editor*, che però significa *redattore*.

edizi'one [edit'tsjone] *sf* edition; (*tiratura*) printing; **edizione straordinaria** special edition

edu'care *vt* to educate; (*gusto, mente*) to train; **~ qn a fare** to train sb to do; **edu'cato, -a** *ag* polite, well-mannered; **educazi'one** *sf* education; (*familiare*) upbringing; (*comportamento*) (good) manners *pl*; **educazione fisica** (*Ins*) physical training *o* education

> Attenzione! In inglese esiste la parola *educated*, che però significa *istruito*.

eduche'rò *ecc* [eduke'rɔ] *vb vedi* **educare**

effemi'nato, -a *ag* effeminate

efferve'scente [efferveʃʃente] *ag* effervescent

effet'tivo, -a *ag* (*reale*) real, actual; (*impiegato, professore*) permanent; (*Mil*) regular ▶ *sm* (*Mil*) strength; (*di patrimonio ecc*) sum total

ef'fetto *sm* effect; (*Comm: cambiale*) bill; (*fig: impressione*) impression; **in effetti** in fact, actually; **effetto serra** greenhouse effect; **effetti personali** personal effects, personal belongings

effi'cace [effi'katʃe] *ag* effective

effici'ente [effi'tʃente] *ag* efficient

E'geo [e'dʒɛo] *sm* **l'~, il mare ~** the Aegean (Sea)

E'gitto [e'dʒitto] *sm* **l'~** Egypt

egizi'ano, -a [edʒit'tsjano] *ag, sm/f* Egyptian

'egli ['eʎʎi] *pron* he; **~ stesso** he himself

e

ego'ismo sm selfishness, egoism;
  ego'ista, -i, -e ag selfish, egoistic
  ▶ sm/f egoist
Egr. abbr = **egregio**
e'gregio, -a, -gi, -gie [e'grɛdʒo] ag
  (nelle lettere): **E~ Signore** Dear Sir
E.I. abbr = **Esercito Italiano**
elabo'rare vt (progetto) to work out,
  elaborate; (dati) to process
elasticiz'zato, -a [elastitʃid'dzato]
  ag stretch cpd
e'lastico, -a, -ci, -che ag elastic; (fig:
  andatura) springy; (: decisione, vedute)
  flexible ▶ sm (di gomma) rubber band;
  (per il cucito) elastic no pl
ele'fante sm elephant
ele'gante ag elegant
e'leggere [e'lɛddʒere] vt to elect
elemen'tare ag elementary; **le
  (scuole) elementari** sfpl primary
  (BRIT) o grade (US) school
ele'mento sm element; (parte
  componente) element, component,
  part; **elementi** smpl (della scienza ecc)
  elements, rudiments
ele'mosina sf charity, alms pl;
  chiedere l'~ to beg
elen'care vt to list
elencherò ecc [elenke'rɔ] vb vedi
  elencare
e'lenco, -chi sm list; **elenco
  telefonico** telephone directory
e'lessi ecc vb vedi **eleggere**
eletto'rale ag electoral, election cpd
elet'tore, -'trice sm/f voter, elector
elet'trauto sm inv workshop for
  car electrical repairs; (tecnico) car
  electrician
elettri'cista, -i [elettri'tʃista] sm
  electrician
elettricità [elettritʃi'ta] sf electricity
e'lettrico, -a, -ci, -che ag electric(al)
elettriz'zante [elettrid'dzante] ag
  (fig) electrifying, thrilling
elettriz'zare [elettrid'dzare] vt to

electrify; **elettrizzarsi** vpr to become
  charged with electricity
e'lettro... prefisso;
  elettrodo'mestico, -a, -ci, -che
  ag **apparecchi elettrodomestici**
  domestic (electrical) appliances;
  elet'tronico, -a, -ci, -che ag
  electronic
elezi'one [elet'tsjone] sf election;
  elezioni sfpl (Pol) election(s)
'elica, -che sf propeller
eli'cottero sm helicopter
elimi'nare vt to eliminate
elisoc'corso sm helicopter ambulance
el'metto sm helmet
elogi'are [elo'dʒare] vt to praise
elo'quente ag eloquent
e'ludere vt to evade
e'lusi ecc vb vedi **eludere**
e-mail [i'mɛil] sf inv (messaggio,
  sistema) e-mail ▶ ag inv (indirizzo)
  e-mail
emargi'nato, -a [emardʒi'nato]
  sm/f outcast; **emarginazione**
  [emardʒinat'tsjone] sf
  marginalization
embri'one sm embryo
emenda'mento sm amendment
emer'genza [emer'dʒɛntsa] sf
  emergency; **in caso di ~** in an
  emergency
e'mergere [e'mɛrdʒere] vi to emerge;
  (sommergibile) to surface; (fig:
  distinguersi) to stand out
e'mersi ecc vb vedi **emergere**
e'mettere vt (suono, luce) to give
  out, emit; (onde radio) to send out;
  (assegno, francobollo, ordine) to issue
emi'crania sf migraine
emi'grare vi to emigrate
emis'fero sm hemisphere; **emisfero
  australe** southern hemisphere;
  emisfero boreale northern
  hemisphere
e'misi ecc vb vedi **emettere**

emit'tente *ag* (*banca*) issuing; (*Radio*) broadcasting, transmitting ▸ *sf* (*Radio*) transmitter

emorra'gia, -'gie [emorra'dʒia] *sf* haemorrhage

emor'roidi *sfpl* haemorrhoids *pl* (*BRIT*), hemorrhoids *pl* (*US*)

emo'tivo, -a *ag* emotional

emozio'nante [emottsjo'nante] *ag* exciting, thrilling

emozio'nare [emottsjo'nare] *vt* (*commuovere*) to move; (*agitare*) to make nervous; (*elettrizzare*) to excite; **emozionarsi** *vpr* to be moved; to be nervous; to be excited; **emozionato, -a** [emottsjo'nato] *ag* (*commosso*) moved; (*agitato*) nervous; (*elettrizzato*) excited

emozi'one [emot'tsjone] *sf* emotion; (*agitazione*) excitement

enciclope'dia [entʃiklope'dia] *sf* encyclopaedia

endove'noso, -a *ag* (*Med*) intravenous

'E.N.E.L. ['enel] *sigla m* (= *Ente Nazionale per l'Energia Elettrica*) *national electricity company*

ener'getico, -a, ci, che [ener'dʒetiko] *ag* (*risorse, crisi*) energy *cpd*; (*sostanza, alimento*) energy-giving

ener'gia, -'gie [ener'dʒia] *sf* (*Fisica*) energy; (*fig*) energy, strength, vigour; **energia eolica** wind power; **energia solare** solar energy, solar power; **e'nergico, -a, -ci, -che** *ag* energetic, vigorous

'enfasi *sf* emphasis; (*peg*) bombast, pomposity

en'nesimo, -a *ag* (*Mat, fig*) nth; **per l'ennesima volta** for the umpteenth time

e'norme *ag* enormous, huge

'ente *sm* (*istituzione*) body, board, corporation; (*Filosofia*) being; **enti pubblici** public bodies; **ente di ricerca** research organization

en'trambi, -e *pron pl* both (of them) ▸ *ag pl* ~ **i ragazzi** both of the boys

en'trare *vi* to go (*o* come) in; ~ **in** (*luogo*) to enter, go (*o* come) into; (*trovar posto, poter stare*) to fit into; (*essere ammesso a: club ecc*) to join, become a member of; ~ **in automobile** to get into the car; **far** ~ **qn** (*visitatore ecc*) to show sb in; **questo non c'entra** (*fig*) that's got nothing to do with it; **en'trata** *sf* entrance, entry; **dov'è l'entrata?** where's the entrance?; **entrate** *sfpl* (*Comm*) receipts, takings; (*Econ*) income *sg*

'entro *prep* (*temporale*) within

entusias'mare *vt* to excite, fill with enthusiasm; **entusiasmarsi** *vpr* **entusiasmarsi (per qc/qn)** to become enthusiastic (about sth/sb); **entusi'asmo** *sm* enthusiasm; **entusi'asta, -i, -e** *ag* enthusiastic ▸ *sm/f* enthusiast

epa'tite *sf* hepatitis

epide'mia *sf* epidemic

Epifa'nia *sf* Epiphany

epiles'sia *sf* epilepsy

epi'lettico, -a, ci, che *ag, sm/f* epileptic

epi'sodio *sm* episode

'epoca, -che *sf* (*periodo storico*) age, era; (*tempo*) time; (*Geo*) age

ep'pure *cong* and yet, nevertheless

EPT *sigla m* (= *Ente Provinciale per il Turismo*) *district tourist bureau*

equa'tore *sm* equator

equazi'one [ekwat'tsjone] *sf* (*Mat*) equation

e'questre *ag* equestrian

equi'librio *sm* balance, equilibrium; **perdere l'equilibrare** to lose one's balance

e'quino, -a *ag* horse *cpd*, equine

equipaggia'mento
[ekwipaddʒa'mento] sm (operazione:
di nave) equipping, fitting out; (: di
spedizione, esercito) equipping, kitting
out; (attrezzatura) equipment

equipaggi'are [ekwipad'dʒare] vt (di
persone) to man; (di mezzi) to equip;
equipaggiarsi vpr to equip o.s;
equi'paggio sm crew

equitazi'one [ekwitat'tsjone] sf
(horse-)riding

equiva'lente ag, sm equivalent

e'quivoco, -a, -ci, -che ag
equivocal, ambiguous; (sospetto)
dubious ▶ sm misunderstanding;
a scanso di equivoci to avoid any
misunderstanding; **giocare sull'~** to
equivocate

'equo, -a ag fair, just

'era sf era

'era ecc vb vedi **essere**

'erba sf grass; **in ~** (fig) budding; **erbe
aromatiche** herbs; **erba medica**
lucerne; **er'baccia, -ce** sf weed

erboriste'ria sf (scienza) study of
medicinal herbs; (negozio) herbalist's
(shop)

e'rede sm/f heir; **eredità** sf (Dir)
inheritance; (Biol) heredity; **lasciare
qc in eredità a qn** to leave o bequeath
sth to sb; **eredi'tare** vt to inherit;
eredi'tario, -a ag hereditary

ere'mita, -i sm hermit

er'gastolo sm (Dir: pena) life
imprisonment

'erica sf heather

er'metico, -a, -ci, -che ag hermetic

'ernia sf (Med) hernia

'ero vb vedi **essere**

e'roe sm hero

ero'gare vt (somme) to distribute; (gas,
servizi) to supply

e'roico, -a, -ci, -che ag heroic

ero'ina sf heroine; (droga) heroin

erosi'one sf erosion

e'rotico, -a, -ci, -che ag erotic

er'rato, -a ag wrong

er'rore sm error, mistake; (morale)
error; **per ~** by mistake; **ci dev'essere
un ~** there must be some mistake;
errore giudiziario miscarriage of
justice

eruzi'one [erut'tsjone] sf eruption

esacer'bare [ezatʃer'bare] vt to
exacerbate

esage'rare [ezadʒe'rare] vt to
exaggerate ▶ vi to exaggerate;
(eccedere) to go too far

esal'tare vt to exalt; (entusiasmare) to
excite, stir

e'same sm examination; (Ins) exam,
examination; **fare o dare un ~** to sit
o take an exam; **esame di guida**
driving test; **esame del sangue**
blood test

esami'nare vt to examine

esaspe'rare vt to exasperate; to
exacerbate

esatta'mente av exactly; accurately,
precisely

esat'tezza [ezat'tettsa] sf exactitude,
accuracy, precision

e'satto, -a pp di **esigere** ▶ ag (calcolo,
ora) correct, right, exact; (preciso)
accurate, precise; (puntuale)
punctual

esau'dire vt to grant, fulfil

esauri'ente ag exhaustive

esauri'mento sm exhaustion;
esaurimento nervoso nervous
breakdown

esau'rire vt (stancare) to exhaust,
wear out; (provviste, miniera) to
exhaust; **esaurirsi** vpr to exhaust
o.s., wear o.s. out; (provviste) to run
out; **esau'rito, -a** ag exhausted;
(merci) sold out; **registrare il tutto
esaurito** (Teatro) to have a full house;
e'sausto, -a ag exhausted

'esca (pl **'esche**) sf bait

'esce ['eʃʃe] *vb vedi* **uscire**

eschi'mese [eski'mese] *ag, sm/f* Eskimo

'esci ['eʃʃi] *vb vedi* **uscire**

escla'mare *vi* to exclaim, cry out

esclama'tivo, -a *ag* **punto ~** exclamation mark

esclamazi'one *sf* exclamation

es'cludere *vt* to exclude

es'clusi *ecc vb vedi* **escludere**

esclusi'one *sf* exclusion; **a ~ di, fatta ~ per** except (for), apart from; **senza ~ (alcuna)** without exception; **procedere per ~** to follow a process of elimination; **senza ~ di colpi** *(fig)* with no holds barred; **esclusione sociale** social exclusion

esclu'siva *sf (Dir, Comm)* exclusive *o* sole rights *pl*

esclusiva'mente *av* exclusively, solely

esclu'sivo, -a *ag* exclusive

es'cluso, -a *pp di* **escludere**

'esco *vb vedi* **uscire**

escogi'tare [eskodʒi'tare] *vt* to devise, think up

'escono *vb vedi* **uscire**

escursi'one *sf (gita)* excursion, trip; (: *a piedi*) hike, walk; *(Meteor)* range; **escursione termica** temperature range

esecuzi'one [ezekut'tsjone] *sf* execution, carrying out; *(Mus)* performance; **esecuzione capitale** execution

esegu'ire *vt* to carry out, execute; *(Mus)* to perform, execute

e'sempio *sm* example; **per ~** for example, for instance; **fare un ~** to give an example; **esem'plare** *ag* exemplary ▶ *sm* example; *(copia)* copy

eserci'tare [ezertʃi'tare] *vt* (*professione*) to practise (BRIT), practice (US); (*allenare: corpo, mente*) to exercise, train; (*diritto*) to exercise; (*influenza, pressione*) to exert; **esercitarsi** *vpr* to practise; **esercitarsi alla lotta** to practise fighting

e'sercito [e'zertʃito] *sm* army

eser'cizio [ezer'tʃittsjo] *sm* practice; exercising; (*fisico: di matematica*) exercise; *(Econ)* financial year; (*azienda*) business, concern; **in ~** (*medico ecc*) practising; **esercizio pubblico** *(Comm)* commercial concern

esi'bire *vt* to exhibit, display; (*documenti*) to produce, present; **esibirsi** *vpr* (*attore*) to perform; *(fig)* to show off; **esibizi'one** *sf* exhibition; (*di documento*) presentation; (*spettacolo*) show, performance

esi'gente [ezi'dʒɛnte] *ag* demanding

e'sigere [e'zidʒere] *vt* (*pretendere*) to demand; (*richiedere*) to demand, require; (*imposte*) to collect

'esile *ag* (*persona*) slender, slim; (*stelo*) thin; (*voce*) faint

esili'are *vt* to exile; **e'silio** *sm* exile

esis'tenza [ezis'tɛntsa] *sf* existence

e'sistere *vi* to exist

esi'tare *vi* to hesitate

'esito *sm* result, outcome

'esodo *sm* exodus

esone'rare *vt* to exempt

esor'tare *vt* **~ qn a fare** to urge sb to do

e'sotico, -a, -ci, -che *ag* exotic

es'pandere *vt* to expand; (*confini*) to extend; (*influenza*) to extend, spread; **espandersi** *vpr* to expand; **espansi'one** *sf* expansion; **espansione di memoria** *(Inform)* memory upgrade; **espan'sivo, -a** *ag* expansive, communicative

espatri'are *vi* to leave one's country

espedi'ente *sm* expedient

es'pellere *vt* to expel

esperi'enza [espe'rjɛntsa] *sf* experience

esperi'mento *sm* experiment

es'perto, -a *ag, sm* expert

espi'rare *vt, vi* to breathe out

es'plicito, -a [es'plitʃito] *ag* explicit

es'plodere *vi* (*anche fig*) to explode ▸*vt* to fire

esplo'rare *vt* to explore

esplosi'one *sf* explosion

es'pone *ecc vb vedi* **esporre**

es'pongo, es'poni *ecc vb vedi* **esporre**

es'porre *vt* (*merci*) to display; (*quadro*) to exhibit, show; (*fatti, idee*) to explain, set out; (*porre in pericolo, Fot*) to expose; **esporsi** *vpr* **esporsi a** (*sole, pericolo*) to expose o.s. to; (*critiche*) to lay o.s. open to

espor'tare *vt* to export

es'pose *ecc vb vedi* **esporre**

esposizi'one [espozit'tsjone] *sf* displaying; exhibiting; setting out; (*anche Fot*) exposure; (*mostra*) exhibition; (*narrazione*) explanation, exposition

es'posto, -a *pp di* **esporre** ▸ *ag* ~ **a nord** facing north ▸ *sm* (*Amm*) statement, account; (: *petizione*) petition

espressi'one *sf* expression

espres'sivo, -a *ag* expressive

es'presso, -a *pp di* **esprimere** ▸ *ag* express ▸ *sm* (*lettera*) express letter; (*anche:* **treno ~**) express train; (*anche:* **caffè ~**) espresso

es'primere *vt* to express; **esprimersi** *vpr* to express o.s.

es'pulsi *ecc vb vedi* **espellere**

espulsi'one *sf* expulsion

es'senza [es'sɛntsa] *sf* essence; **essenzi'ale** *ag* essential; **l'essenziale** the main *o* most important thing

O **'essere**
sm being; **essere umano** human being

▸*vb copulativo*

1 (*con attributo, sostantivo*) to be; **sei giovane/simpatico** you are *o* you're young/nice; **è medico** he is *o* he's a doctor

2 (+ *di: appartenere*) to be; **di chi è la penna?** whose pen is it?; **è di Carla** it is *o* it's Carla's, it belongs to Carla

3 (+ *di: provenire*) to be; **è di Venezia** he is *o* he's from Venice

4 (*data, ora*): **è il 15 agosto/lunedì** it is *o* it's the 15th of August/Monday; **che ora è?, che ore sono?** what time is it?; **è l'una** it is *o* it's one o'clock; **sono le due** it is *o* it's two o'clock

5 (*costare*): **quant'è?** how much is it?; **sono 10 euro** it's 10 euros

▸*vb aus*

1 (*attivo*): **essere arrivato/venuto** to have arrived/come; **è gia partita** she has already left

2 (*passivo*) to be; **essere fatto da** to be made by; **è stata uccisa** she has been killed

3 (*riflessivo*): **si sono lavati** they washed, they got washed

4 (+ *da* + *infinito*): **è da farsi subito** it must be *o* is to be done immediately

▸*vi*

1 (*esistere, trovarsi*) to be; **sono a casa** I'm at home; **essere in piedi/seduto** to be standing/sitting

2: **esserci: c'è** there is; **ci sono** there are; **che c'è?** what's the matter?, what is it?; **ci sono!** (*fig: ho capito*) I get it!; *vedi anche* **ci**

▸*vb impers* **è tardi/Pasqua** it's late/ Easter; **è possibile che venga** he may come; **è così** that's the way it is

'essi *pron mpl vedi* **esso**

'esso, -a *pron* it; (*riferito a persona: soggetto*) he/she; (: *complemento*) him/her

est *sm* east

es'tate *sf* summer

esteri'ore *ag* outward, external

es'terno, -a *ag* (*porta, muro*) outer, outside; (*scala*) outside; (*alunno, impressione*) external ▶ *sm* outside, exterior ▶ *sm/f* (*allievo*) day pupil; **all'~** outside; **per uso ~** for external use only; **esterni** *smpl* (*Cinema*) location shots

'estero, -a *ag* foreign ▶ *sm* **all'~** abroad

es'teso, -a *pp di* **estendere** ▶ *ag* extensive, large; **scrivere per ~** to write in full

es'tetico, -a, -ci, -che *ag* aesthetic ▶ *sf* (*disciplina*) aesthetics *sg*; (*bellezza*) attractiveness; **este'tista, -i, -e** *sm/f* beautician

es'tinguere *vt* to extinguish, put out; (*debito*) to pay off; **estinguersi** *vpr* to go out; (*specie*) to become extinct

es'tinsi *ecc vb vedi* **estinguere**

estin'tore *sm* (*fire*) extinguisher

estinzi'one *sf* putting out; (*di specie*) extinction

estir'pare *vt* (*pianta*) to uproot, pull up; (*fig: vizio*) to eradicate

es'tivo, -a *ag* summer *cpd*

es'torcere [es'tɔrtʃere] *vt* **~ qc (a qn)** to extort sth (from sb)

estradizi'one [estradit'tsjone] *sf* extradition

es'trae, es'traggo *ecc vb vedi* **estrarre**

es'traneo, -a *ag* foreign ▶ *sm/f* stranger; **rimanere ~ a qc** to take no part in sth

es'trarre *vt* to extract; (*minerali*) to mine; (*sorteggiare*) to draw

es'trassi *ecc vb vedi* **estrarre**

estrema'mente *av* extremely

estre'mista, -i, e *sm/f* extremist

estremità *sf inv* extremity, end ▶ *sfpl* (*Anat*) extremities

es'tremo, -a *ag* extreme; (*ultimo: ora, tentativo*) final, last ▶ *sm* extreme; (*di pazienza, forze*) limit, end; **estremi** *smpl* (*Amm: dati essenziali*) details, particulars; **l'~ Oriente** the Far East

estro'verso, -a *ag, sm* extrovert

età *sf inv* age; **all'~ di 8 anni** at the age of 8, at 8 years of age; **ha la mia ~** he (*o* she) is the same age as me *o* as I am; **raggiungere la maggiore ~** to come of age; **essere in ~ minore** to be under age

'etere *sm* ether

eternità *sf* eternity

e'terno, -a *ag* eternal

etero'geneo, -a [etero'dʒɛneo] *ag* heterogeneous

eterosessu'ale *ag, sm/f* heterosexual

'etica *sf* ethics *sg*; *vedi anche* **etico**

eti'chetta [eti'ketta] *sf* label; (*cerimoniale*): **l'~** etiquette

'etico, -a, -ci, -che *ag* ethical

eti'lometro *sm* Breathalyzer®

etimolo'gia, -'gie [etimolo'dʒia] *sf* etymology

Eti'opia *sf* **l'~** Ethiopia

'etnico, -a, -ci, -che *ag* ethnic

e'trusco, -a, -schi, -sche *ag, sm/f* Etruscan

'ettaro *sm* hectare (= 10,000 m²)

'etto *sm abbr* (= *ettogrammo*) 100 grams

'euro *sm inv* (*divisa*) euro

Eu'ropa *sf* **l'~** Europe

europarlamen'tare *sm/f* Member of the European Parliament, MEP

euro'peo, -a *ag, sm/f* European

eutana'sia *sf* euthanasia

evacu'are *vt* to evacuate

e'vadere *vi* (*fuggire*): **~ da** to escape from ▶ *vt* (*sbrigare*) to deal with, dispatch; (*tasse*) to evade

evapo'rare *vi* to evaporate

e'vasi *ecc vb vedi* **evadere**

evasi'one *sf* (*vedi* **evadere**) escape; dispatch; **evasione fiscale** tax evasion

eva'sivo, -a *ag* evasive

e'vaso, -a *pp di* **evadere** ▶ *sm* escapee

e'vento *sm* event

eventu'ale *ag* possible

▎ Attenzione! In inglese esiste la parola *eventual*, che però significa *finale*.

eventual'mente *av* if necessary

▎ Attenzione! In inglese esiste la parola *eventually*, che però significa *alla fine*.

evi'dente *ag* evident, obvious

evidente'mente *av* evidently; (*palesemente*) obviously, evidently

evi'tare *vt* to avoid; **~ di fare** to avoid doing; **~ qc a qn** to spare sb sth

evoluzi'one [evolut'tsjone] *sf* evolution

e'volversi *vpr* to evolve

ev'viva *escl* hurrah!; **~ il re!** long live the king!, hurrah for the king!

ex *prefisso* ex, former

'extra *ag inv* first-rate; top-quality ▸ *sm inv* extra; **extracomuni'tario, -a** *ag* from outside the EC ▸ *sm/f* non-EC citizen

extrater'restre *ag, sm/f* extraterrestrial

f

fa *vb vedi* **fare** ▸ *sm inv* (*Mus*) F; (: *solfeggiando la scala*) fa ▸ *av* **10 anni fa** 10 years ago

'fabbrica *sf* factory; **fabbri'care** *vt* to build; (*produrre*) to manufacture, make; (*fig*) to fabricate, invent

▎ Attenzione! In inglese esiste la parola *fabric*, che però significa *stoffa*.

fac'cenda [fat'tʃɛnda] *sf* matter, affair; (*cosa da fare*) task, chore

fac'chino [fak'kino] *sm* porter

'faccia, -ce ['fattʃa] *sf* face; (*di moneta*) side; **faccia a faccia** face to face

facci'ata [fat'tʃata] *sf* façade; (*di pagina*) side

fac'cina [fat'tʃina] *sf* (*Comput*) emoticon

'faccio ['fattʃo] *vb vedi* **fare**

fa'cessi *ecc* [fa'tʃessi] *vb vedi* **fare**

fa'cevo *ecc* [fa'tʃevo] *vb vedi* **fare**

'facile ['fatʃile] *ag* easy; (*disposto*): **~ a** inclined to, prone to; (*probabile*): **è ~ che piova** it's likely to rain

facoltà *sf inv* faculty; (*autorità*) power

facolta'tivo, -a *ag* optional; (*fermata d'autobus*) request *cpd*

'faggio ['faddʒo] *sm* beech

fagi'ano [fa'dʒano] *sm* pheasant

fagio'lino [fadʒo'lino] *sm* French (*BRIT*) o string bean

fagi'olo [fa'dʒɔlo] *sm* bean

'fai *vb vedi* **fare**

'fai-da-'te *sm inv* DIY, do-it-yourself

'falce ['faltʃe] *sf* scythe; **falci'are** *vt* to cut; (*fig*) to mow down

falcia'trice [faltʃa'tritʃe] *sf* (*per fieno*) reaping machine; (*per erba*) mower

'falco, -chi *sm* hawk

'falda *sf* layer, stratum; (*di cappello*) brim; (*di cappotto*) tails *pl*; (*di monte*) lower slope; (*di tetto*) pitch

fale'gname [faleɲ'ɲame] *sm* joiner

falli'mento *sm* failure; bankruptcy

fal'lire *vi* (*non riuscire*): **~ (in)** to fail (in); (*Dir*) to go bankrupt ▸ *vt* (*colpo, bersaglio*) to miss

'fallo *sm* error, mistake; (*imperfezione*) defect, flaw; (*Sport*) foul; fault; **senza ~** without fail

falò *sm inv* bonfire

falsifi'care *vt* to forge; (*monete*) to forge, counterfeit

'falso, -a *ag* false; (*errato*) wrong; (*falsificato*) forged; fake; (: *oro, gioielli*) imitation *cpd* ▶ *sm* forgery; **giurare il ~** to commit perjury

'fama *sf* fame; (*reputazione*) reputation, name

'fame *sf* hunger; **aver ~** to be hungry

fa'miglia [fa'miʎʎa] *sf* family

famili'are *ag* (*della famiglia*) family *cpd*; (*ben noto*) familiar; (*rapporti, atmosfera*) friendly; (*Ling*) informal, colloquial ▶ *sm/f* relative, relation

fa'moso, -a *ag* famous, well-known

fa'nale *sm* (*Aut*) light, lamp (*BRIT*); (*luce stradale, Naut*) light; (*di faro*) beacon

fa'natico, -a, -ci, -che *ag* fanatical; (*del teatro, calcio ecc*): **~ di** *o* **per** mad *o* crazy about ▶ *sm/f* fanatic; (*tifoso*) fan

'fango, -ghi *sm* mud

'fanno *vb vedi* **fare**

fannul'lone, -a *sm/f* idler, loafer

fantasci'enza [fantaʃʃɛntsa] *sf* science fiction

fanta'sia *sf* fantasy, imagination; (*capriccio*) whim, caprice ▶ *ag inv* **vestito ~** patterned dress

fan'tasma, -i *sm* ghost, phantom

fan'tastico, -a, -ci, -che *ag* fantastic; (*potenza, ingegno*) imaginative

fan'tino *sm* jockey

fara'butto *sm* crook

fard *sm inv* blusher

'fare
sm

1 (*modo di fare*): **con fare distratto** absent-mindedly; **ha un fare simpatico** he has a pleasant manner

2: **sul far del giorno/della notte** at daybreak/nightfall

▶ *vt*

1 (*fabbricare, creare*) to make; (: *casa*) to build; (: *assegno*) to make out; **fare un pasto/una promessa/un film** to make a meal/a promise/a film; **fare rumore** to make a noise

2 (*effettuare: lavoro, attività, studi*) to do; (: *sport*) to play; **cosa fa?** (*adesso*) what are you doing?; (*di professione*) what do you do?; **fare psicologia/italiano** (*Ins*) to do psychology/Italian; **fare un viaggio** to go on a trip *o* journey; **fare una passeggiata** to go for a walk; **fare la spesa** to do the shopping

3 (*funzione*) to be; (*Teatro*) to play, be; **fare il medico** to be a doctor; **fare il malato** (*fingere*) to act the invalid

4 (*suscitare: sentimenti*): **fare paura a qn** to frighten sb; **(non) fa niente** (*non importa*) it doesn't matter

5 (*ammontare*): **3 più 3 fa 6** 3 and 3 are *o* make 6; **fanno 3 euro** that's 3 euros; **Roma fa 2.000.000 di abitanti** Rome has 2,000,000 inhabitants; **che ora fai?** what time do you make it?

6 (+ *infinito*): **far fare qc a qn** (*obbligare*) to make sb do sth; (*permettere*) to let sb do sth; **fammi vedere** let me see; **far partire il motore** to start (up) the engine; **far riparare la macchina/costruire una casa** to get *o* have the car repaired/a house built

7: **farsi: farsi una gonna** to make o.s. a skirt; **farsi un nome** to make a name for o.s.; **farsi la permanente** to get a perm; **farsi tagliare i capelli** to get one's hair cut; **farsi operare** to have an operation

8 (*fraseologia*): **farcela** to succeed, manage; **non ce la faccio più** I can't go on; **ce la faremo** we'll make it; **me l'hanno fatta!** (*imbrogliare*) I've been done!; **lo facevo più giovane** I thought he was younger; **fare sì/no con la testa** to nod/shake one's head

▶*vi*

1 (*agire*) to act, do; **fate come volete** do as you like; **fare presto** to be quick; **fare da** to act as; **non c'è niente da fare** it's no use; **saperci fare con qn/qc** to know how to deal with sb/sth; **faccia pure!** go ahead!

2 (*dire*) to say; **"davvero?" fece** "really?" he said

3: **fare per** (*essere adatto*) to be suitable for; **fare per fare qc** to be about to do sth; **fece per andarsene** he made as if to leave

4: **farsi: si fa così** you do it like this, this is the way it's done; **non si fa così!** (*rimprovero*) that's no way to behave!; **la festa non si fa** the party is off

5: **fare a gara con qn** to compete *o* vie with sb; **fare a pugni** to come to blows; **fare in tempo a fare** to be in time to do

▶*vb impers* **fa bel tempo** the weather is fine; **fa caldo/freddo** it's hot/cold; **fa notte** it's getting dark

▶*vpr* **farsi**

1 (*diventare*) to become; **farsi prete** to become a priest; **farsi grande/vecchio** to grow tall/old

2 (*spostarsi*): **farsi avanti/indietro** to move forward/back

3 (*fam: drogarsi*) to be a junkie

far'falla *sf* butterfly

fa'rina *sf* flour

farma'cia, -'cie [farma'tʃia] *sf* pharmacy; (*negozio*) chemist's (shop) (BRIT), pharmacy; **farma'cista, -i, -e** *sm/f* chemist (BRIT), pharmacist

'farmaco, -ci *o* **chi** *sm* drug, medicine

'faro *sm* (*Naut*) lighthouse; (*Aer*) beacon; (*Aut*) headlight

'fascia, -sce ['faʃʃa] *sf* band, strip; (*Med*) bandage; (*di sindaco, ufficiale*) sash; (*parte di territorio*) strip, belt; (*di contribuenti ecc*) group, band; **essere in fasce** (*anche fig*) to be in one's infancy; **fascia oraria** time band

fasci'are [faʃʃare] *vt* to bind; (*Med*) to bandage

fa'scicolo [faʃʃikolo] *sm* (*di documenti*) file, dossier; (*di rivista*) issue, number; (*opuscolo*) booklet, pamphlet

'fascino ['faʃʃino] *sm* charm, fascination

fa'scismo [faʃʃizmo] *sm* fascism

'fase *sf* phase; (*Tecn*) stroke; **fuori ~** (*motore*) rough

fas'tidio *sm* bother, trouble; **dare ~ a qn** to bother *o* annoy sb; **sento ~ allo stomaco** my stomach's upset; **avere fastidi con la polizia** to have trouble *o* bother with the police; **fastidi'oso, -a** *ag* annoying, tiresome

> Attenzione! In inglese esiste la parola *fastidious*, che però significa *pignolo*.

'fata *sf* fairy

fa'tale *ag* fatal; (*inevitabile*) inevitable; (*fig*) irresistible

fa'tica, -che *sf* hard work, toil; (*sforzo*) effort; (*di metalli*) fatigue; **a ~** with difficulty; **fare ~ a fare qc** to have a job doing sth; **fati'coso, -a** *ag* tiring, exhausting; (*lavoro*) laborious

'fatto, -a *pp di* **fare** ▶ *ag* **un uomo ~** a grown man; **~ a mano/in casa** hand-/home-made ▶ *sm* fact; (*azione*) deed; (*avvenimento*) event, occurrence; (*di romanzo, film*) action, story; **cogliere qn sul ~** to catch sb red-handed; **il ~ sta** *o* **è che** the fact remains *o* is that; **in ~ di** as for, as far as ... is concerned

fat'tore *sm* (*Agr*) farm manager; (*Mat, elemento costitutivo*) factor; **fattore di protezione** (*di lozione solare*) factor; **vorrei una crema solare con ~ di protezione 15** I'd like a factor 15 suntan cream

fatto'ria *sf* farm; farmhouse

> Attenzione! In inglese esiste la parola *factory*, che però significa *fabbrica*.

fatto'rino *sm* errand-boy; (*di ufficio*) office-boy; (*d'albergo*) porter

fat'tura *sf* (*Comm*) invoice; (*di abito*) tailoring; (*malia*) spell

fattu'rato *sm* (*Comm*) turnover

'fauna *sf* fauna

'fava *sf* broad bean

'favola *sf* (*fiaba*) fairy tale; (*d'intento morale*) fable; (*fandonia*) yarn; **favo'loso, -a** *ag* fabulous; (*incredibile*) incredible

fa'vore *sm* favour; **per ~** please; **fare un ~ a qn** to do sb a favour

favo'rire *vt* to favour; (*il commercio, l'industria, le arti*) to promote, encourage; **vuole ~?** won't you help yourself?; **favorisca in salotto** please come into the sitting room

fax *sm inv* fax; **mandare qc via ~** to fax sth

fazzo'letto [fattso'letto] *sm* handkerchief; (*per la testa*) (head)scarf; **fazzoletto di carta** tissue

feb'braio *sm* February

'febbre *sf* fever; **aver la ~** to have a high temperature; **febbre da fieno** hay fever

'feci *ecc* ['fɛtʃi] *vb vedi* **fare**

fecondazi'one [fekondat'tsjone] *sf* fertilization; **fecondazione artificiale** artificial insemination

fe'condo, -a *ag* fertile

'fede *sf* (*credenza*) belief, faith; (*Rel*) faith; (*fiducia*) faith, trust; (*fedeltà*) loyalty; (*anello*) wedding ring; (*attestato*) certificate; **aver ~ in qn** to have faith in sb; **in buona/cattiva ~** in good/bad faith; **"in ~"** (*Dir*) "in witness whereof"; **fe'dele** *ag* **fedele (a)** faithful (to) ▸ *sm/f* follower; **i fedeli** (*Rel*) the faithful

'federa *sf* pillowslip, pillowcase

fede'rale *ag* federal

'fegato *sm* liver; (*fig*) guts *pl*, nerve

'felce ['feltʃe] *sf* fern

fe'lice [fe'litʃe] *ag* happy; (*fortunato*) lucky; **felicità** *sf* happiness

felici'tarsi [felitʃi'tarsi] *vpr* (*congratularsi*): **~ con qn per qc** to congratulate sb on sth

fe'lino, -a *ag, sm* feline

'felpa *sf* sweatshirt

'femmina *sf* (*Zool, Tecn*) female; (*figlia*) girl, daughter; (*spesso peg*) woman; **femmi'nile** *ag* feminine; (*sesso*) female; (*lavoro, giornale, moda*) woman's ▸ *sm* (*Ling*) feminine

'femore *sm* thighbone, femur

fe'nomeno *sm* phenomenon

feri'ale *ag* **giorno ~** weekday

'ferie *sfpl* holidays (*BRIT*), vacation *sg* (*US*); **andare in ~** to go on holiday *o* vacation

fe'rire *vt* to injure; (*deliberatamente: Mil ecc*) to wound; (*colpire*) to hurt; **ferirsi** *vpr* to hurt o.s., injure o.s; **fe'rita** *sf* injury, wound; **fe'rito, -a** *sm/f* wounded *o* injured man/woman

fer'maglio [fer'maʎʎo] *sm* clasp; (*per documenti*) clip

fer'mare *vt* to stop, halt; (*Polizia*) to detain, hold ▸ *vi* to stop; **fermarsi** *vpr* to stop, halt; **fermarsi a fare qc** to stop to do sth; **può fermarsi qui/all'angolo?** could you stop here/at the corner?

fer'mata *sf* stop; **fermata dell'autobus** bus stop

fer'menti *smpl* **~ lattici** probiotic bacteria

fer'mezza [fer'mettsa] *sf* (*fig*) firmness, steadfastness

'fermo, -a *ag* still, motionless; (*veicolo*) stationary; (*orologio*) not working; (*saldo: anche fig*) firm; (*voce, mano*) steady ▸ *escl* stop!; keep still! ▸ *sm* (*chiusura*) catch, lock; (*Dir*): **fermo di polizia** police detention

fe'roce [fe'rɔtʃe] *ag* (*animale*) fierce, ferocious; (*persona*) cruel, fierce;

(*fame, dolore*) raging; **le bestie feroci** wild animals

ferra'gosto *sm* (*festa*) feast of the Assumption; (*periodo*) August holidays *pl*

- **Ferragosto**
- **Ferragosto**, August 15th, is a
- national holiday. Marking the Feast
- of the Assumption, its origins are
- religious but in recent years it has
- simply become the most important
- public holiday of the summer
- season. Most people take some
- extra time off work and head out of
- town to the holiday resorts.

ferra'menta *sfpl* **negozio di ~** ironmonger's (*BRIT*), hardware shop o store (*US*)

'ferro *sm* iron; **una bistecca ai ferri** a grilled steak; **ferro battuto** wrought iron; **ferro da calza** knitting needle; **ferro di cavallo** horseshoe; **ferro da stiro** iron

ferro'via *sf* railway (*BRIT*), railroad (*US*); **ferrovi'ario, -a** *ag* railway *cpd* (*BRIT*), railroad *cpd* (*US*); **ferrovi'ere** *sm* railwayman (*BRIT*), railroad man (*US*)

'fertile *ag* fertile

'fesso, -a *pp di* **fendere** ▶ *ag* (*fam: sciocco*) crazy, cracked

fes'sura *sf* crack, split; (*per gettone, moneta*) slot

'festa *sf* (*religiosa*) feast; (*pubblica*) holiday; (*compleanno*) birthday; (*onomastico*) name day; (*ricevimento*) celebration, party; **far ~** to have a holiday; to live it up; **far ~ a qn** to give sb a warm welcome

festeggi'are [fested'dʒare] *vt* to celebrate; (*persona*) to have a celebration for

fes'tivo, -a *ag* (*atmosfera*) festive; **giorno ~** holiday

'feto *sm* breath; (*resistenza*) foetus (*BRIT*), fetus (*US*)

'fetta *sf* slice

fettuc'cine [fettut'tʃine] *sfpl* (*Cuc*) ribbon-shaped pasta

FF.SS. *abbr* = **Ferrovie dello Stato**

FI *sigla* = **Firenze** ▶ *abbr* (= *Forza Italia*) Italian centre-right political party

fi'aba *sf* fairy tale

fi'acca *sf* weariness; (*svogliatezza*) listlessness

fi'acco, -a, -chi, -che *ag* (*stanco*) tired, weary; (*svogliato*) listless; (*debole*) weak; (*mercato*) slack

fi'accola *sf* torch

fi'ala *sf* phial

fi'amma *sf* flame

fiam'mante *ag* (*colore*) flaming; **nuovo ~** brand new

fiam'mifero *sm* match

fiam'mingo, -a, -ghi, -ghe *ag* Flemish ▶ *sm/f* Fleming ▶ *sm* (*Ling*) Flemish; **i Fiamminghi** the Flemish

fi'anco, -chi *sm* side; (*Mil*) flank; **di ~** sideways, from the side; **a ~ a ~** side by side

fi'asco, -schi *sm* flask; (*fig*) fiasco; **fare ~** to fail

fia'tare *vi* (*fig: parlare*): **senza ~** without saying a word

fi'ato *sm* breath; (*resistenza*) stamina; **avere il ~ grosso** to be out of breath; **prendere ~** to catch one's breath

'fibbia *sf* buckle

'fibra *sf* fibre; (*fig*) constitution

fic'care *vt* to push, thrust, drive; **ficcarsi** *vpr* (*andare a finire*) to get to

ficcherò *ecc* [fikke'rɔ] *vb vedi* **ficcare**

'fico, -chi *sm* (*pianta*) fig tree; (*frutto*) fig; **fico d'India** prickly pear; **fico secco** dried fig

fidanza'mento [fidantsa'mento] *sm* engagement

fidan'zarsi [fidan'tsarsi] *vpr* to get engaged; **fidan'zato, -a** *sm/f* fiancé/fiancée

fi'darsi *vpr* ~ **di** to trust; **fi'dato, -a** *ag* reliable, trustworthy

fi'ducia [fi'dutʃa] *sf* confidence, trust; **incarico di** ~ position of trust, responsible position; **persona di** ~ reliable person

fie'nile *sm* barn; hayloft

fi'eno *sm* hay

fi'era *sf* fair

fi'ero, -a *ag* proud; (*audace*) bold

'fifa (*fam*) *sf* **aver** ~ to have the jitters

fig. *abbr* (= *figura*) fig.

'figlia ['fiʎʎa] *sf* daughter

figli'astro, -a [fiʎ'ʎastro] *sm/f* stepson/daughter

'figlio ['fiʎʎo] *sm* son; (*senza distinzione di sesso*) child; **figlio di papà** spoilt, wealthy young man; **figlio unico** only child

fi'gura *sf* figure; (*forma, aspetto esterno*) form, shape; (*illustrazione*) picture, illustration; **far** ~ to look smart; **fare una brutta** ~ to make a bad impression

figu'rina *sf* figurine; (*cartoncino*) picture card

'fila *sf* row, line; (*coda*) queue; (*serie*) series, string; **di** ~ in succession; **fare la** ~ to queue; **in** ~ **indiana** in single file

fi'lare *vt* to spin ▶ *vi* (*baco, ragno*) to spin; (*formaggio fuso*) to go stringy; (*discorso*) to hang together; (*fam: amoreggiare*) to go steady; (*muoversi a forte velocità*) to go at full speed; ~ **diritto** (*fig*) to toe the line; ~ **via** to dash off

filas'trocca, -che *sf* nursery rhyme

filate'lia *sf* philately, stamp collecting

fi'letto *sm* (*di vite*) thread; (*di carne*) fillet

fili'ale *ag* filial ▶ *sf* (*di impresa*) branch

film *sm inv* film

'filo *sm* (*anche fig*) thread; (*filato*) yarn; (*metallico*) wire; (*di lama, rasoio*) edge;

per ~ **e per segno** in detail; **con un** ~ **di voce** in a whisper; **filo d'erba** blade of grass; **filo interdentale** dental floss; **filo di perle** string of pearls; **filo spinato** barbed wire

fi'lone *sm* (*di minerali*) seam, vein; (*pane*) ≈ Vienna loaf; (*fig*) trend

filoso'fia *sf* philosophy; **fi'losofo, -a** *sm/f* philosopher

fil'trare *vt, vi* to filter

'filtro *sm* filter; **filtro dell'olio** (*Aut*) oil filter

fi'nale *ag* final ▶ *sm* (*di opera*) end, ending; (: *Mus*) finale ▶ *sf* (*Sport*) final; **final'mente** *av* finally, at last

fi'nanza [fi'nantsa] *sf* finance; **finanze** *sfpl* (*di individuo, Stato*) finances

finché [fin'ke] *cong* (*per tutto il tempo che*) as long as; (*fino al momento in cui*) until; **aspetta** ~ **io** (**non**) **sia ritornato** wait until I get back

'fine *ag* (*lamina, carta*) thin; (*capelli, polvere*) fine; (*vista, udito*) keen, sharp; (*persona: raffinata*) refined, distinguished; (*osservazione*) subtle ▶ *sf* end ▶ *sm* aim, purpose; (*esito*) result, outcome; **secondo** ~ ulterior motive; **in** *o* **alla** ~ in the end, finally

fi'nestra *sf* window; **fines'trino** *sm* window; **vorrei un posto vicino al finestrino** I'd like a window seat

'fingere ['findʒere] *vt* to feign; (*supporre*) to imagine, suppose; **fingersi** *vpr* **fingersi ubriaco/pazzo** to pretend to be drunk/mad; ~ **di fare** to pretend to be doing

fi'nire *vt* to finish ▶ *vi* to finish, end; **quando finisce lo spettacolo?** when does the show finish?; ~ **di fare** (*compiere*) to finish doing; (*smettere*) to stop doing; ~ **in galera** to end up *o* finish up in prison

finlan'dese *ag, sm* (*Ling*) Finnish ▶ *sm/f* Finn

Fin'landia sf la ~ Finland

'fino, -a ag (capelli, seta) fine; (oro) pure; (fig: acuto) shrewd ▶ av (spesso troncato in **fin**: pure, anche) even ▶ prep (spesso troncato in **fin**: tempo): **fin quando?** till when?; (: luogo): **fin qui** as far as here; **~ a** (tempo) until, till; (luogo) as far as, (up) to; **fin da domani** from tomorrow onwards; **fin da ieri** since yesterday; **fin dalla nascita** from o since birth

fi'nocchio [fi'nɔkkjo] sm fennel; (fam: peg: omosessuale) queer

fi'nora av up till now

'finsi ecc vb vedi **fingere**

'finta sf pretence, sham; (Sport) feint; **far ~ (di fare)** to pretend (to do)

'finto, -a pp di **fingere** ▶ ag false; artificial

finzi'one [fin'tsjone] sf pretence, sham

fi'occo, -chi sm (di nastro) bow; (di stoffa, lana) flock; (di neve) flake; (Naut) jib; **coi fiocchi** (fig) first-rate; **fiocchi di avena** oatflakes; **fiocchi di granturco** cornflakes

fi'ocina ['fjɔtʃina] sf harpoon

fi'oco, -a, -chi, -che ag faint, dim

fi'onda sf catapult

fio'raio, -a sm/f florist

fi'ore sm flower; **fiori** smpl (Carte) clubs; **a fior d'acqua** on the surface of the water; **avere i nervi a fior di pelle** to be on edge; **fior di latte** cream; **fiori di campo** wild flowers

fioren'tino, -a ag Florentine

fio'retto sm (Scherma) foil

fio'rire vi (rosa) to flower; (albero) to blossom; (fig) to flourish

Fi'renze [fi'rɛntse] sf Florence

'firma sf signature

▌ Attenzione! In inglese esiste la parola firm, che però significa ditta.

fir'mare vt to sign; **un abito firmato** a designer suit; **dove devo ~?** where do I sign?

fisar'monica, -che sf accordion

fis'cale ag fiscal, tax cpd; **medico ~** doctor employed by Social Security to verify cases of sick leave

fischi'are [fis'kjare] vi to whistle ▶ vt to whistle; (attore) to boo, hiss

fischi'etto [fis'kjetto] sm (strumento) whistle

'fischio ['fiskjo] sm whistle

'fisco sm tax authorities pl, ≈ Inland Revenue (BRIT), ≈ Internal Revenue Service (US)

'fisica sf physics sg

'fisico, -a, -ci, -che ag physical ▶ sm/f physicist ▶ sm physique

fisiotera'pia sf physiotherapy

fisiotera'pista sm/f physiotherapist

fis'sare vt to fix, fasten; (guardare intensamente) to stare at; (data, condizioni) to fix, establish, set; (prenotare) to book; **fissarsi** vpr **fissarsi su** (sguardo, attenzione) to focus on; (fig: idea) to become obsessed with

'fisso, -a ag fixed; (stipendio, impiego) regular ▶ av **guardare ~ qc/qn** to stare at sth/sb

'fitta sf sharp pain; vedi anche **fitto**

fit'tizio, -a ag fictitious, imaginary

'fitto, -a ag thick, dense; (pioggia) heavy ▶ sm depths pl, middle; (affitto, pigione) rent

fi'ume sm river

fiu'tare vt to smell, sniff; (animale) to scent; (fig: inganno) to get wind of, smell; **~ tabacco/cocaina** to take snuff/cocaine

fla'grante ag **cogliere qn in ~** to catch sb red-handed

fla'nella sf flannel

flash [flaʃ] sm inv (Fot) flash; (giornalistico) newsflash

'flauto sm flute

fles'sibile ag pliable; (fig: che si adatta) flexible

flessibili'tà sf (anche fig) flexibility

flessi'one sf (gen) bending; (Ginnastica: a terra) sit-up; (: in piedi) forward bend; (: sulle gambe) knee-bend; (diminuzione) slight drop, slight fall; (Ling) inflection; **fare una ~** to bend; **una ~ economica** a downward trend in the economy

'flettere vt to bend

'flipper sm inv pinball machine

F.lli abbr (= fratelli) Bros.

'flora sf flora

'florido, -a ag flourishing; (fig) glowing with health

'floscio, -a, -sci, -sce ['flɔʃʃo] ag (cappello) floppy, soft; (muscoli) flabby

'flotta sf fleet

'fluido, -a ag, sm fluid

flu'oro sm fluorine

'flusso sm flow; (Fisica, Med) flux; **~ e ri~** ebb and flow

fluvi'ale ag river cpd, fluvial

FMI sigla m (= Fondo Monetario Internazionale) IMF

'foca, -che sf (Zool) seal

fo'caccia, -ce [fo'kattʃa] sf kind of pizza; (dolce) bun

'foce ['fotʃe] sf (Geo) mouth

foco'laio sm (Med) centre of infection; (fig) hotbed

foco'lare sm hearth, fireside; (Tecn) furnace

'fodera sf (di vestito) lining; (di libro, poltrona) cover

'fodero sm (di spada) scabbard; (di pugnale) sheath; (di pistola) holster

'foga sf enthusiasm, ardour

'foglia ['fɔʎʎa] sf leaf; **foglia d'argento/d'oro** silver/gold leaf

'foglio ['fɔʎʎo] sm (di carta) sheet (of paper); (di metallo) sheet; **foglio di calcolo** (Inform) spreadsheet; **foglio rosa** (Aut) provisional licence; **foglio di via** (Dir) expulsion order; **foglio volante** pamphlet

'fogna ['foɲɲa] sf drain, sewer

föhn [føːn] sm inv hair dryer

'folla sf crowd, throng

'folle ag mad, insane; (Tecn) idle; **in ~** (Aut) in neutral

fol'lia sf folly, foolishness; foolish act; (pazzia) madness, lunacy

'folto, -a ag thick

fon sm inv hair dryer

fondamen'tale ag fundamental, basic

fonda'mento sm foundation; **fondamenta** sfpl (Edil) foundations

fon'dare vt to found; (fig: dar base): **~ qc su** to base sth on

fon'dente ag **cioccolato ~** plain o dark chocolate

'fondere vt (neve) to melt; (metallo) to fuse, melt; (fig: colori) to merge, blend; (: imprese, gruppi) to merge ▶ vi to melt; **fondersi** vpr to melt; (fig: partiti, correnti) to unite, merge

'fondo, -a ag deep ▶ sm (di recipiente, pozzo) bottom; (di stanza) back; (quantità di liquido che resta, deposito) dregs pl; (sfondo) background; (unità immobiliare) property, estate; (somma di denaro) fund; (Sport) long-distance race; **fondi** smpl (denaro) funds; **a notte fonda** at dead of night; **in ~ a** at the bottom of; at the back of; (strada) at the end of; **andare a ~** (nave) to sink; **conoscere a ~** to know inside out; **dar ~ a** (fig: provviste, soldi) to use up; **in ~** (fig) after all, all things considered; **andare fino in ~ a** (fig) to examine thoroughly; **a ~ perduto** (Comm) without security; **fondi di magazzino** unsold stock sg; **fondi di caffè** coffee grounds; **fondo comune di investimento** investment trust

fondo'tinta sm inv (cosmetico) foundation

fo'netica sf phonetics sg

fon'tana sf fountain

'fonte sf spring, source; (fig) source ▶ sm; **fonte battesimale** (Rel) font; **fonte energetica** source of energy

fo'raggio [fo'raddʒo] sm fodder

fo'rare vt to pierce, make a hole in; (pallone) to burst; (biglietto) to punch; **~ una gomma** to burst a tyre (BRIT) o tire (US)

'forbici ['fɔrbitʃi] sfpl scissors

'forca, -che sf (Agr) fork, pitchfork; (patibolo) gallows sg

for'chetta [for'ketta] sf fork

for'cina [for'tʃina] sf hairpin

fo'resta sf forest

foresti'ero, -a ag foreign ▶ sm/f foreigner

'forfora sf dandruff

'forma sf form; (aspetto esteriore) form, shape; (Dir: procedura) procedure; (per calzature) last; (stampo da cucina) mould; **mantenersi in ~** to keep fit

formag'gino [formad'dʒino] sm processed cheese

for'maggio [for'maddʒo] sm cheese

for'male ag formal

for'mare vt to form, shape, make; (numero di telefono) to dial; (fig: carattere) to form, mould; **formarsi** vpr to form, take shape; **for'mato** sm format, size; **formazi'one** sf formation; (fig: educazione) training; **formazione professionale** vocational training

for'mica¹, -che sf ant

formica®² ['fɔrmika] sf (materiale) Formica®

formi'dabile ag powerful, formidable; (straordinario) remarkable

'formula sf formula; **formula di cortesia** courtesy form

formu'lare vt to formulate; to express

for'naio sm baker

for'nello sm (elettrico, a gas) ring; (di pipa) bowl

for'nire vt **~ qn di qc, ~ qc a qn** to provide o supply sb with sth, supply sth to sb

'forno sm (di cucina) oven; (panetteria) bakery; (Tecn: per calce ecc) kiln; (: per metalli) furnace; **forno a microonde** microwave oven

'foro sm (buco) hole; (Storia) forum; (tribunale) (law) court

'forse av perhaps, maybe; (circa) about; **essere in ~** to be in doubt

'forte ag strong; (suono) loud; (spesa) considerable, great; (passione, dolore) great, deep ▶ av strongly; (velocemente) fast; (a voce alta) loud(ly); (violentemente) hard ▶ sm (edificio) fort; (specialità) forte, strong point; **essere ~ in qc** to be good at sth

for'tezza [for'tettsa] sf (morale) strength; (luogo fortificato) fortress

for'tuito, -a ag fortuitous, chance

for'tuna sf (destino) fortune, luck; (buona sorte) success, fortune; (eredità, averi) fortune; **per ~** luckily, fortunately; **di ~** makeshift, improvised; **atterraggio di ~** emergency landing; **fortu'nato, -a** ag lucky, fortunate; (coronato da successo) successful

'forza ['fɔrtsa] sf strength; (potere) power; (Fisica) force; **forze** sfpl (fisiche) strength sg; (Mil) forces escl come on!; **per ~** against one's will; (naturalmente) of course; **a viva ~** by force; **a ~ di** by dint of; **~ maggiore** circumstances beyond one's control; **la ~ pubblica** the police pl; **forze armate** armed forces; **forze dell'ordine** the forces of law and order; **Forza Italia** Italian centre-right political party; **forza di pace** peacekeeping force

for'zare [for'tsare] vt to force; **~ qn a fare** to force sb to do

for'zista, -i, e [for'tsista] ag of Forza

Italia ▶ *sm/f* member (*o* supporter) of Forza Italia

fos'chia [fos'kia] *sf* mist, haze

'fosco, -a, -schi, -sche *ag* dark, gloomy

'fosforo *sm* phosphorous

'fossa *sf* pit; (*di cimitero*) grave; **fossa biologica** septic tank

fos'sato *sm* ditch; (*di fortezza*) moat

fos'setta *sf* dimple

'fossi *ecc vb vedi* **essere**

'fossile *ag, sm* fossil

'fosso *sm* ditch; (*Mil*) trench

'foste *ecc vb vedi* **essere**

'foto *sf* photo; **può farci una ~, per favore?** would you take a picture of us, please? ▶ *prefisso:* **foto ricordo** souvenir photo; **foto tessera** passport(-type) photo; **foto'camera** *sf* **fotocamera digitale** digital camera; **foto'copia** *sf* photocopy; **fotocopi'are** *vt* to photocopy; **fotocopi'atrice** [fotokopja'tritʃe] *sf* photocopier; **foto'fonino** *sm* camera phone; **fotogra'fare** *vt* to photograph; **fotogra'fia** *sf* (*procedimento*) photography; (*immagine*) photograph; **fare una fotografia** to take a photograph; **una fotografia a colori/in bianco e nero** a colour/black and white photograph; **foto'grafico, -a, ci, che** *ag* photographic; **macchina fotografica** camera; **fo'tografo, -a** *sm/f* photographer; **fotoro'manzo** *sm* romantic picture story

fou'lard [fu'lar] *sm inv* scarf

fra *prep* = **tra**

'fradicio, -a, -ci, -ce ['fraditʃo] *ag* (*molto bagnato*) soaking (wet); **ubriaco ~** blind drunk

'fragile ['fradʒile] *ag* fragile; (*fig: salute*) delicate

'fragola *sf* strawberry

fra'grante *ag* fragrant

frain'tendere *vt* to misunderstand

fram'mento *sm* fragment

'frana *sf* landslide; (*fig: persona*): **essere una ~** to be useless

fran'cese [fran'tʃeze] *ag* French ▶ *sm/f* Frenchman/woman ▶ *sm* (*Ling*) French; **i Francesi** the French

'Francia ['frantʃa] *sf* **la ~** France

'franco, -a, -chi, -che *ag* (*Comm*) free; (*sincero*) frank, open, sincere ▶ *sm* (*moneta*) franc; **farla franca** (*fig*) to get off scot-free; **prezzo ~ fabbrica** ex-works price; **franco di dogana** duty-free

franco'bollo *sm* (postage) stamp

'frangia, -ge ['frandʒa] *sf* fringe

frap'pè *sm* milk shake

'frase *sf* (*Ling*) sentence; (*locuzione, Mus*) phrase; **frase fatta** set phrase

'frassino *sm* ash (tree)

frastagli'ato, -a [frastaʎ'ʎato] *ag* (*costa*) indented, jagged

frastor'nare *vt* to daze; to befuddle

frastu'ono *sm* hubbub, din

'frate *sm* friar, monk

fratel'lastro *sm* stepbrother; (*con genitore in comune*) half-brother

fra'tello *sm* brother; **fratelli** *smpl* brothers; (*nel senso di fratelli e sorelle*) brothers and sisters

fra'terno, -a *ag* fraternal, brotherly

frat'tempo *sm* **nel ~** in the meantime, meanwhile

frat'tura *sf* fracture; (*fig*) split, break

frazi'one [frat'tsjone] *sf* fraction; (*di comune*) small town

'freccia, -ce ['frettʃa] *sf* arrow; **freccia di direzione** (*Aut*) indicator

fred'dezza [fred'dettsa] *sf* coldness

'freddo, -a *ag, sm* cold; **fa ~** it's cold; **aver ~** to be cold; **a ~** (*fig*) deliberately; **freddo'loso, -a** *ag* sensitive to the cold

fre'gare *vt* to rub; (*fam: truffare*) to take in, cheat; (: *rubare*) to swipe, pinch; **fregarsene** (fam!): **chi se ne frega?** who gives a damn (about it)?

fregherò ecc [frege'rɔ] vb vedi **fregare**

fre'nare vt (veicolo) to slow down; (cavallo) to rein in; (lacrime) to restrain, hold back ▶ vi to brake; **frenarsi** vpr (fig) to restrain o.s., control o.s.

'freno sm brake; (morso) bit; **tenere a ~** to restrain; **freno a disco** disc brake; **freno a mano** handbrake

frequen'tare vt (scuola, corso) to attend; (locale, bar) to go to, frequent; (persone) to see (often)

frequen'tato, -a ag (locale) busy

fre'quente ag frequent; **di ~** frequently

fres'chezza [fres'kettsa] sf freshness

'fresco, -a, -schi, -sche ag fresh; (temperatura) cool; (notizia) recent, fresh ▶ sm **godere il ~** to enjoy the cool air; **stare ~** (fig) to be in for it; **mettere al ~** to put in a cool place

'fretta sf hurry, haste; **in ~** in a hurry; **in ~ e furia** in a mad rush; **aver ~** to be in a hurry

'friggere ['friddʒere] vt to fry ▶ vi (olio ecc) to sizzle

'frigido, -a ['fridʒido] ag (Med) frigid

'frigo sm fridge

frigo'bar sm inv minibar

frigo'rifero, -a ag refrigerating ▶ sm refrigerator

fringu'ello sm chaffinch

'frissi ecc vb vedi **friggere**

frit'tata sf omelette; **fare una ~** (fig) to make a mess of things

frit'tella sf (Cuc) fritter

'fritto, -a pp di **friggere** ▶ ag fried ▶ sm fried food; **fritto misto** mixed fry

frit'tura sf (Cuc): **frittura di pesce** mixed fried fish

'frivolo, -a ag frivolous

frizi'one [frit'tsjone] sf friction; (sulla pelle) rub, rub-down; (Aut) clutch

friz'zante [frid'dzante] ag (anche fig) sparkling

fro'dare vt to defraud, cheat

'frode sf fraud; **frode fiscale** tax evasion

'fronda sf (leafy) branch; (di partito politico) internal opposition; **fronde** sfpl (di albero) foliage sg

fron'tale ag frontal; (scontro) head-on

'fronte sf (Anat) forehead; (di edificio) front, façade ▶ sm (Mil, Pol, Meteor) front; **a ~, di ~** facing, opposite; **di ~ a** (posizione) opposite, facing, in front of; (a paragone di) compared with

fronti'era sf border, frontier

'frottola sf fib

fru'gare vi to rummage ▶ vt to search

frugherò ecc [fruge'rɔ] vb vedi **frugare**

frul'lare vt (Cuc) to whisk ▶ vi (uccelli) to flutter; **frul'lato** sm milk shake; fruit drink; **frulla'tore** sm electric mixer

fru'mento sm wheat

fru'scio [fruʃ'ʃio] sm rustle; rustling; (di acque) murmur

'frusta sf whip; (Cuc) whisk

frus'tare vt to whip

frus'trato, -a ag frustrated

'frutta sf fruit; (portata) dessert; **frutta candita** candied fruit; **frutta secca** dried fruit

frut'tare vi to bear dividends, give a return

frut'teto sm orchard

frutti'vendolo, -a sm/f greengrocer (BRIT), produce dealer (US)

'frutto sm fruit; (fig: risultato) result(s); (Econ: interesse) interest; (: reddito) income; **frutti di bosco** berries; **frutti di mare** seafood sg

FS abbr = **Ferrovie dello Stato**

fu vb vedi **essere** ▶ ag inv **il fu Paolo Bianchi** the late Paolo Bianchi

fuci'lare [futʃi'lare] vt to shoot

fu'cile [fu'tʃile] sm rifle, gun; (da caccia) shotgun, gun

'fucsia sf fuchsia

'fuga sf escape, flight; (di gas, liquidi) leak; (Mus) fugue; **fuga di cervelli** brain drain

fug'gire [fud'dʒire] vi to flee, run away; (fig: passar veloce) to fly ▶ vt to avoid

'fui vb vedi **essere**

fu'liggine [fu'liddʒine] sf soot

'fulmine sm thunderbolt; lightning no pl

fu'mare vi to smoke; (emettere vapore) to steam ▶ vt to smoke; **le dà fastidio se fumo?** do you mind if I smoke?; **fuma'tore, -'trice** sm/f smoker

fu'metto sm comic strip; **giornale** sm **a fumetti** comic

'fummo vb vedi **essere**

'fumo sm smoke; (vapore) steam; (il fumare tabacco) smoking; **fumi** smpl (industriali ecc) fumes; **i fumi dell'alcool** the after-effects of drink; **vendere ~** to deceive, cheat; **fumo passivo** passive smoking; **fu'moso, -a** ag smoky; (fig) muddled

'fune sf rope, cord; (più grossa) cable

'funebre ag (rito) funeral; (aspetto) gloomy, funereal

fune'rale sm funeral

'fungere ['fundʒere] vi ~ **da** to act as

'fungo, -ghi sm fungus; (commestibile) mushroom; **fungo velenoso** toadstool

funico'lare sf funicular railway

funi'via sf cable railway

'funsi ecc vb vedi **fungere**

funzio'nare [funtsjo'nare] vi to work, function; (fungere): ~ **da** to act as; **come funziona?** how does this work?; **la TV non funziona** the TV isn't working

funzio'nario [funtsjo'narjo] sm official; **funzionario statale** civil servant

funzi'one [fun'tsjone] sf function; (carica) post, position; (Rel) service; **in ~** (meccanismo) in operation; **in ~ di** (come) as; **fare la ~ di qn** (farne le veci) to take sb's place

fu'oco, -chi sm fire; (fornello) ring; (Fot, Fisica) focus; **dare ~ a qc** to set fire to sth; **far ~** (sparare) to fire; **al ~!** fire!; **fuoco d'artificio** firework

fuorché [fwor'ke] cong, prep except

fu'ori av outside; (all'aperto) outdoors, outside; (fuori di casa, Sport) out; (esclamativo) get out! ▶ prep ~ **(di)** out of, outside ▶ sm outside; **lasciar ~ qc/qn** to leave sth/sb out; **far ~ qn** (fam) to kill sb, do sb in; **essere ~ di sé** to be beside o.s.; ~ **luogo** (inopportuno) uncalled for; ~ **mano** remote; ~ **pericolo** out of danger; ~ **uso** old-fashioned; obsolete; **fuorigi'oco** sm offside; **fuori'strada** sm (Aut) cross-country vehicle

'furbo, -a ag clever, smart; (peg) cunning

fu'rente ag ~ **(contro)** furious (with)

fur'fante sm rascal, scoundrel

fur'gone sm van

'furia sf (ira) fury, rage; (fig: impeto) fury, violence; (fretta) rush; **a ~ di** by dint of; **andare su tutte le furie** to get into a towering rage; **furi'bondo, -a** ag furious

furi'oso, -a ag furious

'furono vb vedi **essere**

fur'tivo, -a ag furtive

'furto sm theft; **vorrei denunciare un ~** I'd like to report a theft; **furto con scasso** burglary

'fusa sfpl **fare le ~** to purr

fu'seaux smpl inv leggings

'fusi ecc vb vedi **fondere**

fu'sibile sm (Elettr) fuse

fusi'one sf (di metalli) fusion, melting; (colata) casting; (Comm) merger; (fig) merging

'fuso, -a pp di **fondere** ▶ sm (Filatura)
spindle; **fuso orario** time zone

fus'tino sm (di detersivo) tub

'fusto sm stem; (Anat, di albero) trunk;
(recipiente) drum, can

fu'turo, -a ag, sm future

g

'gabbia sf cage; (da imballaggio) crate;
gabbia dell'ascensore lift (BRIT) o
elevator (US) shaft; **gabbia toracica**
(Anat) rib cage

gabbi'ano sm (sea)gull

gabi'netto sm (Med ecc) consulting
room; (Pol) ministry; (WC) toilet,
lavatory; (Ins: di fisica ecc) laboratory

'gaffe [gaf] sf inv blunder

ga'lante ag gallant, courteous;
(avventura) amorous

ga'lassia sf galaxy

ga'lera sf (Naut) galley; (prigione)
prison

'galla sf a ~ afloat; **venire a** ~ to
surface; (fig: verità) to come out

galleggi'are [galled'dʒare] vi to float

galle'ria sf (traforo) tunnel; (Archit,
d'arte) gallery; (Teatro) circle; (strada
coperta con negozi) arcade

'Galles sm il ~ Wales; **gal'lese** ag Welsh
▶ sm/f Welshman/woman ▶ sm (Ling)
Welsh; **i Gallesi** the Welsh

gal'lina sf hen

'gallo sm cock

galop'pare vi to gallop

ga'loppo sm gallop; **al o di** ~ at a gallop

'gamba sf leg; (asta: di lettera) stem; **in**
~ (in buona salute) well; (bravo, sveglio)
bright, smart; **prendere qc sotto** ~
(fig) to treat sth too lightly

gambe'retto sm shrimp

'gambero sm (di acqua dolce) crayfish;
(di mare) prawn

'gambo sm stem; (di frutta) stalk

'gamma sf (Mus) scale; (di colori, fig)
range

'gancio ['gantʃo] sm hook

'gara sf competition; (Sport)
competition; contest; match; (: corsa)
race; **fare a** ~ to compete, vie

ga'rage [ga'raʒ] sm inv garage

garan'tire vt to guarantee; (debito)
to stand surety for; (dare per certo)
to assure

garan'zia [garan'tsia] sf guarantee;
(pegno) security

gar'bato, -a ag courteous, polite

gareggi'are [gared'dʒare] vi to
compete

garga'rismo sm gargle; **fare i**
gargarismi to gargle

ga'rofano sm carnation

'garza ['gardza] sf (per bende) gauze

gar'zone [gar'dzone] sm (di negozio)
boy

gas sm inv gas; **sento odore di** ~ I can
smell gas; **a tutto** ~ at full speed; **dare**
~ (Aut) to accelerate

ga'solio sm diesel (oil)

gas'sato, -a ag fizzy

gast'rite sf gastritis

gastrono'mia sf gastronomy

gat'tino sm kitten

'gatto, -a sm/f cat, tomcat/she-cat;
gatto delle nevi (Aut, Sci) snowcat;
gatto selvatico wildcat

'gazza ['gaddza] sf magpie

gel [dʒɛl] sm inv gel

ge'lare [dʒe'lare] *vt, vi, vb impers* to freeze

gelate'ria [dʒelate'ria] *sf* ice-cream shop

gela'tina [dʒela'tina] *sf* gelatine; **gelatina esplosiva** dynamite; **gelatina di frutta** fruit jelly

ge'lato, -a [dʒe'lato] *ag* frozen ▸ *sm* ice cream

'gelido, -a ['dʒɛlido] *ag* icy, ice-cold

'gelo ['dʒɛlo] *sm* (*temperatura*) intense cold; (*brina*) frost; (*fig*) chill

gelo'sia [dʒelo'sia] *sf* jealousy

ge'loso, -a [dʒe'loso] *ag* jealous

'gelso ['dʒɛlso] *sm* mulberry (tree)

gelso'mino [dʒelso'mino] *sm* jasmine

ge'mello, -a [dʒe'mɛllo] *ag, sm/f* twin; **gemelli** *smpl* (*di camicia*) cufflinks; (*dello zodiaco*): **Gemelli** Gemini *sg*

'gemere ['dʒɛmere] *vi* to moan, groan; (*cigolare*) to creak

'gemma ['dʒɛmma] *sf* (*Bot*) bud; (*pietra preziosa*) gem

gene'rale [dʒene'rale] *ag, sm* general; **in ~** (*per sommi capi*) in general terms; (*di solito*) usually, in general

gene'rare [dʒene'rare] *vt* (*dar vita*) to give birth to; (*produrre*) to produce; (*causare*) to arouse; (*Tecn*) to produce, generate; **generazi'one** *sf* generation

'genere ['dʒɛnere] *sm* kind, type, sort; (*Biol*) genus; (*merce*) article, product; (*Ling*) gender; (*Arte, Letteratura*) genre; **in ~** generally, as a rule; **genere umano** mankind; **generi alimentari** foodstuffs

ge'nerico, -a, -ci, -che [dʒe'nɛriko] *ag* generic; (*vago*) vague, imprecise

'genero ['dʒɛnero] *sm* son-in-law

gene'roso, -a [dʒene'roso] *ag* generous

ge'netica [dʒe'nɛtika] *sf* genetics *sg*

ge'netico, -a, -ci, -che [dʒe'nɛtiko] *ag* genetic

gen'giva [dʒen'dʒiva] *sf* (*Anat*) gum

geni'ale [dʒen'jale] *ag* (*persona*) of genius; (*idea*) ingenious, brilliant

'genio ['dʒɛnjo] *sm* genius; **andare a ~ a qn** to be to sb's liking, appeal to sb

geni'tore [dʒeni'tore] *sm* parent, father *o* mother; **i miei genitori** my parents, my father and mother

gen'naio [dʒen'najo] *sm* January

'Genova ['dʒɛnova] *sf* Genoa

'gente ['dʒɛnte] *sf* people *pl*

gen'tile [dʒen'tile] *ag* (*persona, atto*) kind; (: *garbato*) courteous, polite; (*nelle lettere*): **G~ Signore** Dear Sir; (: *sulla busta*): **G~ Signor Fernando Villa** Mr Fernando Villa

genu'ino, -a [dʒenu'ino] *ag* (*prodotto*) natural; (*persona, sentimento*) genuine, sincere

geogra'fia [dʒeogra'fia] *sf* geography

geolo'gia [dʒeolo'dʒia] *sf* geology

ge'ometra, -i, -e [dʒe'ɔmetra] *sm/f* (*professionista*) surveyor

geome'tria [dʒeome'tria] *sf* geometry

ge'ranio [dʒe'ranjo] *sm* geranium

gerar'chia [dʒerar'kia] *sf* hierarchy

'gergo, -ghi ['dʒɛrgo] *sm* jargon; slang

geria'tria [dʒerja'tria] *sf* geriatrics *sg*

Ger'mania [dʒer'manja] *sf* **la ~** Germany; **la ~ occidentale/orientale** West/East Germany

'germe ['dʒɛrme] *sm* germ; (*fig*) seed

germogli'are [dʒermoʎ'ʎare] *vi* to sprout; to germinate

gero'glifico, -ci [dʒero'glifiko] *sm* hieroglyphic

ge'rundio [dʒe'rundjo] *sm* gerund

'gesso ['dʒɛsso] *sm* chalk; (*Scultura, Med, Edil*) plaster; (*statua*) plaster figure; (*minerale*) gypsum

gesti'one [dʒes'tjone] *sf* management

ges'tire [dʒes'tire] *vt* to run, manage

'gesto ['dʒɛsto] *sm* gesture

Gesù [dʒe'zu] *sm* Jesus

gesu'ita, -i [dʒezu'ita] *sm* Jesuit
get'tare [dʒet'tare] *vt* to throw; (*anche*: **~ via**) to throw away *o* out; (*Scultura*) to cast; (*Edil*) to lay; (*acqua*) to spout; (*grido*) to utter; **gettarsi** *vpr* **gettarsi in** (*fiume*) to flow into; **~ uno sguardo su** to take a quick look at
'getto ['dʒetto] *sm* (*di gas, liquido, Aer*) jet; **a ~ continuo** uninterruptedly; **di ~** (*fig*) straight off, in one go
get'tone [dʒet'tone] *sm* token; (*per giochi*) counter; (: *roulette ecc*) chip; **gettone telefonico** telephone token
ghiacci'aio [gjat'tʃajo] *sm* glacier
ghiacci'ato, -a *ag* frozen; (*bevanda*) ice-cold
ghi'accio ['gjattʃo] *sm* ice
ghiacci'olo [gjat'tʃɔlo] *sm* icicle; (*tipo di gelato*) ice lolly (BRIT), Popsicle® (US)
ghi'aia ['gjaja] *sf* gravel
ghi'anda ['gjanda] *sf* (*Bot*) acorn
ghi'andola ['gjandola] *sf* gland
ghi'otto, -a ['gjotto] *ag* greedy; (*cibo*) delicious, appetizing
ghir'landa [gir'landa] *sf* garland, wreath
'ghiro ['giro] *sm* dormouse
'ghisa ['giza] *sf* cast iron
già [dʒa] *av* already; (*ex, in precedenza*) formerly ▸ *escl* of course!, yes indeed!
gi'acca, -che ['dʒakka] *sf* jacket; **giacca a vento** windcheater (BRIT), windbreaker (US)
giacché [dʒak'ke] *cong* since, as
giac'cone [dʒak'kone] *sm* heavy jacket
gi'ada ['dʒada] *sf* jade
giagu'aro [dʒa'gwaro] *sm* jaguar
gi'allo ['dʒallo] *ag* yellow; (*carnagione*) sallow ▸ *sm* yellow; (*anche*: **romanzo ~**) detective novel; (*anche*: **film ~**) detective film; **giallo dell'uovo** yolk
Giamaica [dʒa'maika] *sf* **la ~** Jamaica
Giap'pone [dʒap'pone] *sm* Japan; **giappo'nese** *ag, sm/f, sm* Japanese *inv*

giardi'naggio [dʒardi'naddʒo] *sm* gardening
giardini'ere, -a [dʒardi'njɛre] *sm/f* gardener
giar'dino [dʒar'dino] *sm* garden; **giardino d'infanzia** nursery school; **giardino pubblico** public gardens *pl*, (public) park; **giardino zoologico** zoo
giavel'lotto [dʒavel'lɔtto] *sm* javelin
gigabyte [dʒiga'bait] *sm inv* gigabyte
gi'gante, -'essa [dʒi'gante] *sm/f* giant ▸ *ag* giant, gigantic; (*Comm*) giant-size
'giglio ['dʒiʎʎo] *sm* lily
gilè [dʒi'lɛ] *sm inv* waistcoat
gin [dʒin] *sm inv* gin
gine'cologo, -a, -gi, -ghe [dʒine'kɔlogo] *sm/f* gynaecologist
gi'nepro [dʒi'nepro] *sm* juniper
gi'nestra [dʒi'nɛstra] *sf* (*Bot*) broom
Gi'nevra [dʒi'nevra] *sf* Geneva
gin'nastica *sf* gymnastics *sg*; (*esercizio fisico*) keep-fit exercises; (*Ins*) physical education
gi'nocchio [dʒi'nɔkkjo] (*pl(m)* **gi'nocchi**, *o pl(f)* **gi'nocchia**) *sm* knee; **stare in ~** to kneel, be on one's knees; **mettersi in ~** to kneel (down)
gio'care [dʒo'kare] *vt* to play; (*scommettere*) to stake, wager, bet; (*ingannare*) to take in ▸ *vi* to play; (*a roulette ecc*) to gamble; (*fig*) to play a part, be important; **~ a** (*gioco, sport*) to play; (*cavalli*) to bet on; **giocarsi la carriera** to put one's career at risk; **gioca'tore, -'trice** *sm/f* player; gambler
gio'cattolo [dʒo'kattolo] *sm* toy
giocherò *ecc* [dʒoke'rɔ] *vb vedi* **giocare**
gi'oco, -chi ['dʒɔko] *sm* game; (*divertimento, Tecn*) play; (*al casinò*) gambling; (*Carte*) hand; (*insieme di pezzi ecc necessari per un gioco*) set; **per ~** for fun; **fare il doppio ~ con qn** to

double-cross sb; **i Giochi Olimpici** the Olympic Games; **gioco d'azzardo** game of chance; **gioco degli scacchi** chess set

giocoli'ere [dʒokoʎ'ljɛre] *sm* juggler

gi'oia ['dʒɔja] *sf* joy, delight; (*pietra preziosa*) jewel, precious stone

gioielle'ria [dʒojelle'ria] *sf* jeweller's craft; jeweller's (shop)

gioielli'ere, -a [dʒojeʎ'ljɛre] *sm/f* jeweller

gioi'ello [dʒoˈjɛllo] *sm* jewel, piece of jewellery; **i miei gioielli** my jewels *o* jewellery; **gioielli** *smpl* (*anelli, collane ecc*) jewellery; **i gioielli della Corona** the crown jewels

Gior'dania [dʒor'danja] *sf* **la ~** Jordan

giorna'laio, -a [dʒorna'lajo] *sm/f* newsagent (BRIT), newsdealer (US)

gior'nale [dʒor'nale] *sm* (news) paper; (*diario*) journal, diary; (*Comm*) journal; **giornale di bordo** log; **giornale radio** radio news *sg*

giornali'ero, -a [dʒorna'ljɛro] *ag* daily; (*che varia: umore*) changeable ▶ *sm* day labourer

giorna'lismo [dʒorna'lizmo] *sm* journalism

giorna'lista, -i, -e [dʒorna'lista] *sm/f* journalist

gior'nata [dʒor'nata] *sf* day; **giornata lavorativa** working day

gi'orno ['dʒorno] *sm* day; (*opposto alla notte*) day, daytime; (*anche: luce del ~*) daylight; **al ~** per day; **di ~** by day; **al ~ d'oggi** nowadays

gi'ostra ['dʒɔstra] *sf* (*per bimbi*) merry-go-round; (*torneo storico*) joust

gio'vane ['dʒovane] *ag* young; (*aspetto*) youthful ▶ *sm/f* youth/girl, young man/woman; **i giovani** young people

gio'vare [dʒo'vare] *vi* **~ a** (*essere utile*) to be useful to; (*far bene*) to be good for ▶ *vb impers* (*essere bene, utile*) to be useful; **giovarsi di qc** to make use of sth

giovedì [dʒove'di] *sm inv* Thursday; **di** *o* **il ~** on Thursdays

gioventù [dʒoven'tu] *sf* (*periodo*) youth; (*i giovani*) young people *pl*, youth

G.I.P. [dʒip] *sigla m inv* (= Giudice per le Indagini Preliminari) judge for preliminary enquiries

gira'dischi [dʒira'diski] *sm inv* record player

gi'raffa [dʒi'raffa] *sf* giraffe

gi'rare [dʒi'rare] *vt* (*far ruotare*) to turn; (*percorrere, visitare*) to go round; (*Cinema*) to shoot; to make; (*Comm*) to endorse ▶ *vi* to turn; (*più veloce*) to spin; (*andare in giro*) to wander, go around; **girarsi** *vpr* to turn; **~ attorno a** to go round; to revolve round; **al prossimo incrocio giri a destra/sinistra** turn right/left at the next junction; **far ~ la testa a qn** to make sb dizzy; (*fig*) to turn sb's head

girar'rosto [dʒirar'rɔsto] *sm* (*Cuc*) spit

gira'sole [dʒira'sole] *sm* sunflower

gi'revole [dʒi'revole] *ag* revolving, turning

gi'rino [dʒi'rino] *sm* tadpole

'giro ['dʒiro] *sm* (*circuito, cerchio*) circle; (*di chiave, manovella*) turn; (*viaggio*) tour, excursion; (*passeggiata*) stroll, walk; (*in macchina*) drive; (*in bicicletta*) ride; (*Sport: della pista*) lap; (*di denaro*) circulation; (*Carte*) hand; (*Tecn*) revolution; **prendere in ~ qn** (*fig*) to pull sb's leg; **fare un ~** to go for a walk (*o* a drive *o* a ride); **andare in ~** to go about, walk around; **a stretto ~ di posta** by return of post; **nel ~ di un mese** in a month's time; **essere nel ~** (*fig*) to belong to a circle (of friends); **giro d'affari** (*Comm*) turnover; **giro di parole** circumlocution; **giro di prova** (*Aut*) test drive; **giro turistico**

sightseeing tour; **giro'collo** sm a **girocollo** crew-neck cpd

gironzo'lare [dʒirondzo'lare] vi to stroll about

'**gita** ['dʒita] sf excursion, trip; **fare una ~** to go for a trip, go on an outing

gi'tano, -a [dʒi'tano] sm/f gipsy

giù [dʒu] av down; (dabbasso) downstairs; **in ~** downwards, down; **~ di lì** (pressappoco) thereabouts; **bambini dai 6 anni in ~** children aged 6 and under; **~ per, cadere ~ per le scale** to fall down the stairs; **essere ~** (fig: di salute) to be run down; (: di spirito) to be depressed

giub'botto [dʒub'bɔtto] sm jerkin; **giubbotto antiproiettile** bulletproof vest; **giubbotto salvagente** life jacket

giudi'care [dʒudi'kare] vt to judge; (accusato) to try; (lite) to arbitrate in; **~ qn/qc bello** to consider sb/sth (to be) beautiful

gi'udice ['dʒuditʃe] sm judge; **giudice conciliatore** justice of the peace; **giudice istruttore** examining (BRIT) o committing (US) magistrate; **giudice popolare** member of a jury

giu'dizio [dʒu'dittsjo] sm judgment; (opinione) opinion; (Dir) judgment, sentence; (: processo) trial; (: verdetto) verdict; **aver ~** to be wise o prudent; **citare in ~** to summons

gi'ugno ['dʒuɲɲo] sm June

gi'ungere ['dʒundʒere] vi to arrive ▶ vt (mani ecc) to join; **~ a** to arrive at, reach

gi'ungla ['dʒungla] sf jungle

gi'unsi ecc ['dʒunsi] vb vedi **giungere**

giura'mento [dʒura'mento] sm oath; **giuramento falso** perjury

giu'rare [dʒu'rare] vt to swear ▶ vi to swear, take an oath

giu'ria [dʒu'ria] sf jury

giu'ridico, -a, -ci, -che [dʒu'ridiko] ag legal

giustifi'care [dʒustifi'kare] vt to justify; **giustificazi'one** sf justification; (Ins) (note of) excuse

gius'tizia [dʒus'tittsja] sf justice; **giustizi'are** vt to execute

gi'usto, -a ['dʒusto] ag (equo) fair, just; (vero) true, correct; (adatto) right, suitable; (preciso) exact, correct ▶ av (esattamente) exactly, precisely; (per l'appunto, appena) just; **arrivare ~** to arrive just in time; **ho ~ bisogno di te** you're just the person I need

glaci'ale [gla'tʃale] ag glacial

gli [ʎi] (davV, s impura, gn, pn, ps, x, z) det mpl the ▶ pron (a lui) to him; (a esso) to it; (in coppia con lo, la, li, le, ne: a lui, a lei, a loro ecc): **~ele do** I'm giving them to him (o her o them); vedi anche **il**

glo'bale ag overall

'**globo** sm globe

'**globulo** sm (Anat): **globulo rosso/ bianco** red/white corpuscle

'**gloria** sf glory

'**gnocchi** ['ɲɔkki] smpl (Cuc) small dumplings made of semolina pasta or potato

'**gobba** sf (Anat) hump; (protuberanza) bump

'**gobbo, -a** ag hunchbacked; (ricurvo) round-shouldered ▶ sm/f hunchback

'**goccia, -ce** ['gottʃa] sf drop; **goccio'lare** vi, vt to drip

go'dere vi (compiacersi): **~ (di)** to be delighted (at), rejoice (at); (trarre vantaggio): **~ di** to benefit from ▶ vt to enjoy; **godersi la vita** to enjoy life; **godersela** to have a good time, enjoy o.s.

godrò ecc vb vedi **godere**

'**goffo, -a** ag clumsy, awkward

gol [gɔl] sm inv (Sport) goal

'**gola** sf (Anat) throat; (golosità) gluttony, greed; (di camino) flue; (di monte) gorge; **fare ~** (anche fig) to tempt

golf sm inv (Sport) golf; (maglia) cardigan

'golfo sm gulf

go'loso, -a ag greedy

gomi'tata sf **dare una ~ a qn** to elbow sb; **farsi avanti a (forza o furia di) gomitate** to elbow one's way through; **fare a gomitate per qc** to fight to get sth

'gomito sm elbow; (di strada ecc) sharp bend

go'mitolo sm ball

'gomma sf rubber; (per cancellare) rubber, eraser; (di veicolo) tyre (BRIT), tire (US); **gomma americana o da masticare** chewing gum; **gomma a terra** flat tyre (BRIT) o tire (US); **ho una ~ a terra** I've got a flat tyre; **gom'mone** sm rubber dinghy

gonfi'are vt (pallone) to blow up, inflate; (dilatare, ingrossare) to swell; (fig: notizia) to exaggerate; **gonfiarsi** vpr to swell; (fiume) to rise; **'gonfio, -a** ag swollen; (stomaco) bloated; (vela) full; **gonfi'ore** sm swelling

'gonna sf skirt; **gonna pantalone** culottes pl

'gorgo, -ghi sm whirlpool

gorgogli'are [gorgoʎ'ʎare] vi to gurgle

go'rilla sm inv gorilla; (guardia del corpo) bodyguard

'gotico, -a, ci, che ag, sm Gothic

'gotta sf gout

gover'nare vt (stato) to govern, rule; (pilotare, guidare) to steer; (bestiame) to tend, look after

go'verno sm government

GPL sigla m (= Gas di Petrolio Liquefatto) LPG

GPS sigla m (= Global Positioning System) GPS

graci'dare [gratʃi'dare] vi to croak

'gracile ['gratʃile] ag frail, delicate

gradazi'one [gradat'tsjone] sf (sfumatura) gradation; **gradazione alcolica** alcoholic content, strength

gra'devole ag pleasant, agreeable

gradi'nata sf flight of steps; (in teatro, stadio) tiers pl

gra'dino sm step; (Alpinismo) foothold

gra'dire vt (accettare con piacere) to accept; (desiderare) to wish, like; **gradisce una tazza di tè?** would you like a cup of tea?

'grado sm (Mat, Fisica ecc) degree; (stadio) degree, level; (Mil, sociale) rank; **essere in ~ di fare** to be in a position to do

gradu'ale ag gradual

graf'fetta sf paper clip

graffi'are vt to scratch; **graffiarsi** vpr to get scratched; (con unghie) to scratch o.s.

'graffio sm scratch

gra'fia sf spelling; (scrittura) handwriting

'grafico, -a, -ci, -che ag graphic ▶ sm graph; (persona) graphic designer

gram'matica, -che sf grammar

'grammo sm gram(me)

'grana sf (granello, di minerali, corpi spezzati) grain; (fam: seccatura) trouble; (: soldi) cash ▶ sm inv Parmesan (cheese)

gra'naio sm granary, barn

gra'nata sf (proiettile) grenade

Gran Bre'tagna [-bre'taɲɲa] sf **la ~** Great Britain

'granchio ['grankjo] sm crab; (fig) blunder; **prendere un ~** (fig) to blunder

'grande (qualche volta **gran** + C, **grand'** + V) ag (grosso, largo, vasto) big, large; (alto) tall; (lungo) long; (in sensi astratti) great ▶ sm/f (persona adulta) adult, grown-up; (chi ha ingegno e potenza) great man/woman; **fare le cose in ~** to do things in style; **una gran bella donna** a very beautiful woman; **non**

è una gran cosa o **un gran che** it's nothing special; **non ne so gran che** I don't know very much about it

gran'dezza [gran'dettsa] sf (dimensione) size; magnitude; (fig) greatness; **in ~ naturale** life-size(d)

grandi'nare vb impers to hail

'grandine sf hail

gra'nello sm (di cereali, uva) seed; (di frutta) pip; (di sabbia, sale ecc) grain

gra'nito sm granite

'grano sm (in quasi tutti i sensi) grain; (frumento) wheat; (di rosario, collana) bead; **grano di pepe** peppercorn

gran'turco sm maize

'grappa sf rough, strong brandy

'grappolo sm bunch, cluster

gras'setto sm (Tip) bold (type)

'grasso, -a ag fat; (cibo) fatty; (pelle) greasy; (terreno) rich; (fig: guadagno, annata) plentiful ► sm (di persona, animale) fat; (sostanza che unge) grease

'grata sf grating

gra'ticola sf grill

'gratis av free, for nothing

grati'tudine sf gratitude

'grato, -a ag grateful; (gradito) pleasant, agreeable

gratta'capo sm worry, headache

grattaci'elo [gratta'tʃɛlo] sm skyscraper

gratta e vinci ['gratta e 'vintʃi] sm inv (biglietto) scratchcard; (lotteria) scratchcard lottery

grat'tare vt (pelle) to scratch; (raschiare) to scrape; (pane, formaggio, carote) to grate; (fam: rubare) to pinch ► vi (stridere) to grate; (Aut) to grind; **grattarsi** vpr to scratch o.s.; **grattarsi la pancia** (fig) to twiddle one's thumbs

grat'tugia, -gie [grat'tudʒa] sf grater; **grattugi'are** vt to grate; **pane grattugiato** breadcrumbs pl

gra'tuito, -a ag free; (fig) gratuitous

'grave ag (danno, pericolo, peccato ecc)

grave, serious; (responsabilità) heavy, grave; (contegno) grave, solemn; (voce, suono) deep, low-pitched; (Ling): **accento ~** grave accent; **un malato ~** a person who is seriously ill

grave'mente av (ammalato, ferito) seriously

gravi'danza [gravi'dantsa] sf pregnancy

gravità sf seriousness; (anche Fisica) gravity

gra'voso, -a ag heavy, onerous

'grazia ['grattsja] sf grace; (favore) favour; (Dir) pardon

'grazie ['grattsje] escl thank you!; **~ mille!** o **tante!** o **infinite!** thank you very much!; **~ a** thanks to

grazi'oso, -a [grat'tsjoso] ag charming, delightful; (gentile) gracious

'Grecia ['grɛtʃa] sf la ~ Greece; **'greco, -a, -ci, -che** ag, sm/f, sm Greek

'gregge ['greddʒe] (pl(f) -i) sm flock

grembi'ule sm apron; (sopravveste) overall

'grembo sm lap; (ventre della madre) womb

'grezzo, -a ['greddzo] ag raw, unrefined; (diamante) rough, uncut; (tessuto) unbleached

gri'dare vi (per chiamare) to shout, cry (out); (strillare) to scream, yell ► vt to shout (out), yell (out); **~ aiuto** to cry o shout for help

'grido (pl(m) -i, o pl(f) -a) sm shout, cry; scream, yell; (di animale) cry; **di ~** famous

'grigio, -a, -gi, -gie ['gridʒo] ag, sm grey

'griglia ['griʎʎa] sf (per arrostire) grill; (Elettr) grid; (inferriata) grating; **alla ~** (Cuc) grilled

gril'letto sm trigger

'grillo sm (Zool) cricket; (fig) whim

'grinta sf grim expression; (Sport) fighting spirit

gris'sino *sm* bread-stick
Groen'landia *sf* **la ~** Greenland
gron'daia *sf* gutter
gron'dare *vi* to pour; (*essere bagnato*):
~ di to be dripping with ▶ *vt* to drip
with
'groppa *sf* (*di animale*) back, rump;
(*fam: dell'uomo*) back, shoulders *pl*
gros'sezza [gros'settsa] *sf* size;
thickness
gros'sista, -i, -e *sm/f* (*Comm*)
wholesaler
'grosso, -a *ag* big, large; (*di spessore*)
thick; (*grossolano: anche fig*) coarse;
(*grave, insopportabile*) serious,
great; (*tempo, mare*) rough ▶ *sm* **il**
~ di the bulk of; **un pezzo ~** (*fig*) a
VIP, a bigwig; **farla grossa** to do
something very stupid; **dirle grosse**
to tell tall stories; **sbagliarsi di ~** to be
completely wrong
'grotta *sf* cave; grotto
grot'tesco, -a, -schi, -sche *ag*
grotesque
gro'viglio [gro'viʎʎo] *sm* tangle; (*fig*)
muddle
gru *sf inv* crane
'gruccia, -ce ['gruttʃa] *sf* (*per*
camminare) crutch; (*per abiti*) coat-
hanger
'grumo *sm* (*di sangue*) clot; (*di farina*
ecc) lump
'gruppo *sm* group; **gruppo**
sanguigno blood group
GSM *sigla m* (= *Global System for Mobile*
Communication) GSM
guada'gnare [gwadaɲ'ɲare] *vt*
(*ottenere*) to gain; (*soldi, stipendio*) to
earn; (*vincere*) to win; (*raggiungere*)
to reach
gua'dagno [gwa'daɲɲo] *sm* earnings
pl; (*Comm*) profit; (*vantaggio, utile*)
advantage, gain; **guadagno lordo/**
netto gross/net earnings *pl*
gu'ado *sm* ford; **passare a ~** to ford

gu'ai *escl* **~ a te** (*o* **lui** *ecc*)**!** woe betide
you (*o him ecc*)!
gu'aio *sm* trouble, mishap;
(*inconveniente*) trouble, snag
gua'ire *vi* to whine, yelp
gu'ancia, -ce ['gwantʃa] *sf* cheek
guanci'ale [gwan'tʃale] *sm* pillow
gu'anto *sm* glove
guarda'linee *sm inv* (*Sport*) linesman
guar'dare *vt* (*con lo sguardo: osservare*)
to look at; (*film, televisione*) to watch;
(*custodire*) to look after, take care
of ▶ *vi* to look; (*badare*): **~ a** to pay
attention to; (*luoghi: esser orientato*):
~ a to face; **guardarsi** *vpr* to look at
o.s.; **guardarsi da** (*astenersi*) to refrain
from; (*stare in guardia*) to beware of;
guardarsi dal fare to take care not to
do; **guarda di non sbagliare** try not to
make a mistake; **~ a vista qn** to keep a
close watch on sb
guarda'roba *sm inv* wardrobe; (*locale*)
cloakroom
gu'ardia *sf* (*individuo, corpo*) guard;
(*sorveglianza*) watch; **fare la ~ a qc/qn**
to guard sth/sb; **stare in ~** (*fig*) to be
on one's guard; **di ~** (*medico*) on call;
guardia carceraria (prison) warder;
guardia del corpo bodyguard;
Guardia di finanza (*corpo*) customs
pl; (*persona*) customs officer; **guardia**
medica emergency doctor service

● **Guardia di finanza**
● The **Guardia di Finanza** is a
● military body which deals with
● infringements of the laws governing
● income tax and monopolies. It
● reports to the Ministers of Finance,
● Justice or Agriculture, depending on
● the function it is performing.

guardi'ano, -a *sm/f* (*di carcere*)
warder; (*di villa ecc*) caretaker; (*di*
museo) custodian; (*di zoo*) keeper;
guardiano notturno night
watchman

guarigi'one [gwari'dʒone] *sf* recovery
gua'rire *vt* (*persona, malattia*) to cure;
(*ferita*) to heal ▶ *vi* to recover, be cured;
to heal (up)
guar'nire *vt* (*ornare: abiti*) to trim;
(*Cuc*) to garnish
guasta'feste *sm/f inv* spoilsport
guastarsi *vpr* (*cibo*) to go bad;
(*meccanismo*) to break down; (*tempo*)
to change for the worse
gu'asto, -a *ag* (*non funzionante*)
broken; (*: telefono ecc*) out of order;
(*andato a male*) bad, rotten; (*: dente*)
decayed, bad; (*fig: corrotto*) depraved
▶ *sm* breakdown; (*avaria*) failure;
guasto al motore engine failure
gu'erra *sf* war; (*tecnica: atomica,
chimica ecc*) warfare; **fare la ~ (a)**
to wage war (against); **guerra
mondiale** world war; **guerra
preventiva** preventive war
'gufo *sm* owl
gu'ida *sf* (*libro*) guidebook; (*persona*)
guide; (*comando, direzione*) guidance,
direction; (*Aut*) driving; (*tappeto: di
tenda, cassetto*) runner; **avete una ~
in italiano?** do you have a guidebook
in Italian?; **c'è una ~ che parla
italiano?** is there an Italian-speaking
guide?; **guida a destra/a sinistra**
(*Aut*) right-/left-hand drive; **guida
telefonica** telephone directory;
guida turistica tourist guide
gui'dare *vt* to guide; (*squadra,
rivolta*) to lead; (*auto*) to drive; (*aereo,
nave*) to pilot; **sai ~?** can you drive?;
guida'tore, -trice *sm/f* (*conducente*)
driver
guin'zaglio [gwin'tsaʎʎo] *sm* leash,
lead
'guscio ['guʃʃo] *sm* shell
gus'tare *vt* (*cibi*) to taste; (*: assaporare
con piacere*) to enjoy, savour; (*fig*) to
enjoy, appreciate ▶ *vi* ~ **a** to please;
non mi gusta affatto I don't like

it at all
'gusto *sm* taste; (*sapore*) flavour;
(*godimento*) enjoyment; **che gusti
avete?** which flavours do you
have?; **al ~ di fragola** strawberry-
flavoured; **mangiare di ~** to eat
heartily; **prenderci ~: ci ha preso ~**
he's acquired a taste for it, he's got
to like it; **gus'toso, -a** *ag* tasty; (*fig*)
agreeable

h

H, h ['akka] *sf o m inv* (*lettera*) H, h
▶ *abbr* (= *ora*) hr; (= *etto, altezza*) h; **H
come hotel** ≈ H for Harry (*BRIT*), H
for How (*US*)
ha, 'hai [a, ai] *vb vedi* **avere**
ha'cker [hæ'kəᵊ] *sm inv* hacker
hall [hɔl] *sf inv* hall, foyer
hamburger [am'burger] *sm inv* (*carne*)
hamburger; (*panino*) burger
'handicap ['handikap] *sm inv*
handicap; **handicap'pato, -a** *ag*
handicapped ▶ *sm/f* handicapped
person, disabled person
'hanno ['anno] *vb vedi* **avere**
hard discount [ardi'kaunt] *sm inv*
discount supermarket
hard disk [ar'disk] *sm inv* hard disk
hardware ['ardwer] *sm inv* hardware
hascisch [aʃʃiʃ] *sm inv* hashish
Hawaii [a'vai] *sfpl* **le ~** Hawaii *sg*

help [ɛlp] *sm inv* (*Inform*) help

'herpes ['ɛrpes] *sm* (*Med*) herpes *sg*; **herpes zoster** shingles *sg*

'hi-fi ['haifai] *sm inv, ag inv* hi-fi

ho [ɔ] *vb vedi* **avere**

'hobby ['hɔbi] *sm inv* hobby

'hockey ['hɔki] *sm* hockey; **hockey su ghiaccio** ice hockey

home page ['houm'peidʒ] *sf inv* home page

Hong Kong ['ɔkɔg] *sf* Hong Kong

'hostess ['houstis] *sf inv* air hostess (*BRIT*) *o* stewardess

hot dog ['hɔtdɔg] *sm inv* hot dog

ho'tel *sm inv* hotel

humour ['hju:mə] *sm inv* (sense of) humour

'humus *sm* humus

husky ['aski] *sm inv* (*cane*) husky *m inv*

◆

i *det mpl* the

IC *abbr* (= *Intercity*) Intercity

ICI ['itʃi] *sigla f* (= *Imposta Comunale sugli Immobili*) ≈ Council Tax

i'cona *sf* (*Rel, Inform, fig*) icon

i'dea *sf* idea; (*opinione*) opinion, view; (*ideale*) ideal; **dare l'~ di** to seem, look like; **neanche** *o* **neppure per ~!** certainly not!; **idea fissa** obsession

ide'ale *ag, sm* ideal

ide'are *vt* (*immaginare*) to think up,

conceive; (*progettare*) to plan

i'dentico, -a, -ci, -che *ag* identical

identifi'care *vt* to identify; **identificarsi** *vpr* **identificarsi (con)** to identify o.s. (with)

identità *sf inv* identity

ideolo'gia, -'gie [ideolo'dʒia] *sf* ideology

idio'matico, -a, -ci, -che *ag* idiomatic; **frase idiomatica** idiom

idi'ota, -i, -e *ag* idiotic ▸ *sm/f* idiot

'idolo *sm* idol

idoneità *sf* suitability

i'doneo, -a *ag* **~ a** suitable for, fit for; (*Mil*) fit for; (*qualificato*) qualified for

i'drante *sm* hydrant

idra'tante *ag* moisturizing ▸ *sm* moisturizer

i'draulico, -a, -ci, -che *ag* hydraulic ▸ *sm* plumber

idroe'lettrico, -a, -ci, -che *ag* hydroelectric

i'drofilo, -a *ag vedi* **cotone**

i'drogeno [i'drɔdʒeno] *sm* hydrogen

idrovo'lante *sm* seaplane

i'ena *sf* hyena

i'eri *av, sm* yesterday; **il giornale di ~** yesterday's paper; **~ l'altro** the day before yesterday; **~ sera** yesterday evening

igi'ene [i'dʒɛne] *sf* hygiene; **igiene pubblica** public health; **igi'enico, -a, -ci, -he** *ag* hygienic; (*salubre*) healthy

i'gnaro, -a [iɲ'ɲaro] *ag* **~ di** unaware of, ignorant of

i'gnobile [iɲ'ɲɔbile] *ag* despicable, vile

igno'rante [iɲɲo'rante] *ag* ignorant

igno'rare [iɲɲo'rare] *vt* (*non sapere, conoscere*) to be ignorant *o* unaware of, not to know; (*fingere di non vedere, sentire*) to ignore

i'gnoto, -a [iɲ'ɲɔto] *ag* unknown

il

(*pl(m)* **i**; diventa **lo** (*pl* **gli**) davanti a *s* impura, **gn, pn, ps, x, z**; **f la** (*pl* **le**)) *det m*

1 the; **il libro/lo studente/l'acqua** the book/the student/the water; **gli scolari** the pupils

2 (*astrazione*): **il coraggio/l'amore/la giovinezza** courage/love/youth

3 (*tempo*): **il mattino/la sera** in the morning/evening; **il venerdì** *ecc* (*abitualmente*) on Fridays *ecc*; (*quel giorno*) on (the) Friday *ecc*; **la settimana prossima** next week

4 (*distributivo*) a, an; **2 euro il chilo/paio** 2 euros a o per kilo/pair

5 (*partitivo*) some, any; **hai messo lo zucchero?** have you added sugar?; **hai comprato il latte?** did you buy (some o any) milk?

6 (*possesso*): **aprire gli occhi** to open one's eyes; **rompersi la gamba** to break one's leg; **avere i capelli neri/il naso rosso** to have dark hair/a red nose

7 (*con nomi propri*): **il Petrarca** Petrarch; **il Presidente Bush** President Bush; **dov'è la Francesca?** where's Francesca?

8 (*con nomi geografici*): **il Tevere** the Tiber; **l'Italia** Italy; **il Regno Unito** the United Kingdom; **l'Everest** Everest

ille'gale *ag* illegal

illeg'gibile [illed'dʒibile] *ag* illegible

ille'gittimo, -a [ille'dʒittimo] *ag* illegitimate

il'leso, -a *ag* unhurt, unharmed

illimi'tato, -a *ag* boundless; unlimited

ill.mo *abbr* = **illustrissimo**

il'ludere *vt* to deceive, delude; **illudersi** *vpr* to deceive o.s., delude o.s.

illumi'nare *vt* to light up, illuminate; (*fig*) to enlighten; **illuminarsi** *vpr* to light up; **~ a giorno** to floodlight; **illuminazi'one** *sf* lighting; illumination; floodlighting; (*fig*) flash of inspiration

il'lusi *ecc vb vedi* **illudere**

illusi'one *sf* illusion; **farsi delle illusioni** to delude o.s.; **illusione ottica** optical illusion

il'luso, -a *pp di* **illudere**

illus'trare *vt* to illustrate; **illustrazi'one** *sf* illustration

il'lustre *ag* eminent, renowned; **illus'trissimo, -a** *ag* (*negli indirizzi*) very reverend

imbal'laggio [imbal'laddʒo] *sm* packing *no pl*

imbal'lare *vt* to pack; (*Aut*) to race

imbalsa'mare *vt* to embalm

imbambo'lato, -a *ag* (*sguardo*) vacant, blank

imbaraz'zante [imbarat'tsante] *ag* embarrassing, awkward

imbaraz'zare [imbarat'tsare] *vt* (*mettere a disagio*) to embarrass; (*ostacolare movimenti*) to hamper

imbaraz'zato, -a [imbarat'tsato] *ag* embarrassed; **avere lo stomaco ~** to have an upset stomach

imba'razzo [imba'rattso] *sm* (*disagio*) embarrassment; (*perplessità*) puzzlement, bewilderment; **imbarazzo di stomaco** indigestion

imbar'care *vt* (*passeggeri*) to embark; (*merci*) to load; **imbarcarsi** *vpr* **imbarcarsi su** to board; **imbarcarsi per l'America** to sail for America; **imbarcarsi in** (*fig: affare ecc*) to embark on

imbarcazi'one [imbarkat'tsjone] *sf* (small) boat, (small) craft *inv*; **imbarcazione di salvataggio** lifeboat

im'barco, -chi *sm* embarkation; loading; boarding; (*banchina*) landing stage

imbas'tire *vt* (*cucire*) to tack; (*fig: abbozzare*) to sketch, outline

im'battersi *vpr* **~ in** (*incontrare*) to bump o run into

imbat'tibile *ag* unbeatable, invincible

imbavagli'are [imbavaʎ'ʎare] *vt* to gag

imbe'cille [imbe'tʃille] *ag* idiotic ▶ *sm/f* idiot; (*Med*) imbecile

imbian'care *vt* to whiten; (*muro*) to whitewash ▶ *vi* to become *o* turn white

imbian'chino [imbjan'kino] *sm* (house) painter, painter and decorator

imboc'care *vt* (*bambino*) to feed; (*entrare: strada*) to enter, turn into

imbocca'tura *sf* mouth; (*di strada, porto*) entrance; (*Mus, del morso*) mouthpiece

imbos'cata *sf* ambush

imbottigli'are [imbottiʎ'ʎare] *vt* to bottle; (*Naut*) to blockade; (*Mil*) to hem in; **imbottigliarsi** *vpr* to be stuck in a traffic jam

imbot'tire *vt* to stuff; (*giacca*) to pad; **imbottirsi** *vpr* **imbottirsi di** (*rimpinzarsi*) to stuff o.s. with; **imbot'tito, -a** *ag* stuffed; (*giacca*) padded; **panino imbottito** filled roll

imbra'nato, -a *ag* clumsy, awkward ▶ *sm/f* clumsy person

imbrogli'are [imbroʎ'ʎare] *vt* to mix up; (*fig: raggirare*) to deceive, cheat; (: *confondere*) to confuse, mix up; **imbrogli'one, -a** *sm/f* cheat, swindler

imbronci'ato, -a *ag* sulky

imbu'care *vt* to post; **dove posso ~ queste cartoline?** where can I post these cards?

imbur'rare *vt* to butter

im'buto *sm* funnel

imi'tare *vt* to imitate; (*riprodurre*) to copy; (*assomigliare*) to look like

immagazzi'nare [immagaddzi'nare] *vt* to store

immagi'nare [immadʒi'nare] *vt* to imagine; (*supporre*) to suppose; (*inventare*) to invent; **s'immagini!** don't mention it!, not at all!; **immaginazi'one** *sf* imagination; (*cosa immaginata*) fancy

im'magine [im'madʒine] *sf* image; (*rappresentazione grafica, mentale*) picture

imman'cabile *ag* certain; unfailing

im'mane *ag* (*smisurato*) enormous; (*spaventoso*) terrible

immangi'abile [imman'dʒabile] *ag* inedible

immatrico'lare *vt* to register; **immatricolarsi** *vpr* (*Ins*) to matriculate, enrol

imma'turo, -a *ag* (*frutto*) unripe; (*persona*) immature; (*prematuro*) premature

immedesi'marsi *vpr* ~ **in** to identify with

immediata'mente *av* immediately, at once

immedi'ato, -a *ag* immediate

im'menso, -a *ag* immense

im'mergere [im'mɛrdʒere] *vt* to immerse, plunge; **immergersi** *vpr* to plunge; (*sommergibile*) to dive, submerge; (*dedicarsi a*): **immergersi in** to immerse o.s. in

immeri'tato, -a *ag* undeserved

immersi'one *sf* immersion; (*di sommergibile*) submersion, dive; (*di palombaro*) dive

im'mettere *vt* ~ **(in)** to introduce (into); ~ **dati in un computer** to enter data on a computer

immi'grato, -a *sm/f* immigrant

immi'nente *ag* imminent

immischiarsi *vpr* ~ **in** to interfere *o* meddle in

im'mobile *ag* motionless, still; **immobili'are** *ag* (*Dir*) property *cpd*

immon'dizia [immon'dittsja] *sf* dirt, filth; (*spesso al pl: spazzatura, rifiuti*) rubbish *no pl*, refuse *no pl*

immo'rale *ag* immoral
immor'tale *ag* immortal
im'mune *ag* (*esente*) exempt; (*Med, Dir*) immune
immu'tabile *ag* immutable; unchanging
impacchet'tare [impakket'tare] *vt* to pack up
impacci'ato, -a *ag* awkward, clumsy; (*imbarazzato*) embarrassed
im'pacco, -chi *sm* (*Med*) compress
impadro'nirsi *vpr* ~ **di** to seize, take possession of; (*fig: apprendere a fondo*) to master
impa'gabile *ag* priceless
impa'lato, -a *ag* (*fig*) stiff as a board
impalca'tura *sf* scaffolding
impalli'dire *vi* to turn pale; (*fig*) to fade
impa'nato, -a *ag* (*Cuc*) coated in breadcrumbs
impanta'narsi *vpr* to sink (in the mud); (*fig*) to get bogged down
impappi'narsi *vpr* to stammer, falter
impa'rare *vt* to learn
impar'tire *vt* to bestow, give
imparzi'ale [impar'tsjale] *ag* impartial, unbiased
impas'sibile *ag* impassive
impas'tare *vt* (*pasta*) to knead
impastic'carsi *vpr* to pop pills
im'pasto *sm* (*l'impastare: di pane*) kneading; (*: di cemento*) mixing; (*pasta*) dough; (*anche fig*) mixture
im'patto *sm* impact
impau'rire *vt* to scare, frighten ▶ *vi* (*anche:* **impaurirsi**) to become scared *o* frightened
impazi'ente [impat'tsjɛnte] *ag* impatient
impaz'zata [impat'tsata] *sf* all'~ (*precipitosamente*) at breakneck speed
impaz'zire [impat'tsire] *vi* to go mad; ~ **per qn/qc** to be crazy about sb/sth
impec'cabile *ag* impeccable

impedi'mento *sm* obstacle, hindrance
impe'dire *vt* (*vietare*): ~ **a qn di fare** to prevent sb from doing; (*ostruire*) to obstruct; (*impacciare*) to hamper, hinder
impegnarsi *vpr* (*vincolarsi*): ~ **a fare** to undertake to do; (*mettersi risolutamente*): ~ **in qc** to devote o.s. to sth; ~ **con qn** (*accordarsi*) to come to an agreement with sb
impegna'tivo, -a *ag* binding; (*lavoro*) demanding, exacting
impe'gnato, -a *ag* (*occupato*) busy; (*fig: romanzo, autore*) committed, engagé
im'pegno [im'peɲɲo] *sm* (*obbligo*) obligation; (*promessa*) promise, pledge; (*zelo*) diligence, zeal; (*compito, d'autore*) commitment
impel'lente *ag* pressing, urgent
impen'narsi *vpr* (*cavallo*) to rear up; (*Aer*) to nose up; (*fig*) to bridle
impensie'rire *vt* to worry; **impensierirsi** *vpr* to worry
impera'tivo, -a *ag, sm* imperative
impera'tore, -'trice *sm/f* emperor/ empress
imperdo'nabile *ag* unforgivable, unpardonable
imper'fetto, -a *ag* imperfect ▶ *sm* (*Ling*) imperfect (tense)
imperi'ale *ag* imperial
imperi'oso, -a *ag* (*persona*) imperious; (*motivo, esigenza*) urgent, pressing
imperme'abile *ag* waterproof ▶ *sm* raincoat
im'pero *sm* empire; (*forza, autorità*) rule, control
imperso'nale *ag* impersonal
imperso'nare *vt* to personify; (*Teatro*) to play, act (the part of)
imperter'rito, -a *ag* fearless, undaunted; impassive
imperti'nente *ag* impertinent

'impeto sm (moto, forza) force, impetus; (assalto) onslaught; (fig: impulso) impulse; (: slancio) transport; **con ~** energetically; vehemently

impet'tito, -a ag stiff, erect

impetu'oso, -a ag (vento) strong, raging; (persona) impetuous

impi'anto sm (installazione) installation; (apparecchiature) plant; (sistema) system; **impianto elettrico** wiring; **impianto di risalita** (Sci) ski lift; **impianto di riscaldamento** heating system; **impianto sportivo** sports complex

impic'care vt to hang; **impiccarsi** vpr to hang o.s.

impicciarsi [impit'tʃarsi] vpr (immischiarsi): **~ (in)** to meddle (in); **impicciati degli affari tuoi!** mind your own business!

impicci'one, -a [impit'tʃone] sm/f busybody

impie'gare vt (usare) to use, employ; (spendere: denaro, tempo) to spend; (investire) to invest; **impie'gato, -a** sm/f employee

impi'ego, -ghi sm (uso) use; (occupazione) employment; (posto di lavoro) (regular) job, post; (Econ) investment

impieto'sire vt to move to pity; **impietosirsi** vpr to be moved to pity

impigli'arsi vpr to get caught up o entangled

impi'grirsi vpr to grow lazy

impli'care vt to imply; (coinvolgere) to involve

im'plicito, -a [im'plitʃito] ag implicit

implo'rare vt to implore; (pietà ecc) to beg for

impolve'rarsi vpr to get dusty

im'pone ecc vb vedi **imporre**

impo'nente ag imposing, impressive

im'pongo ecc vb vedi **imporre**

impo'nibile ag taxable ▶ sm taxable income

impopo'lare ag unpopular

im'porre vt to impose; (costringere) to force, make; (far valere) to impose, enforce; **imporsi** vpr (persona) to assert o.s.; (cosa: rendersi necessario) to become necessary; (aver successo: moda, attore) to become popular; **~ a qn di fare** to force sb to do, make sb do

impor'tante ag important; **impor'tanza** sf importance; **dare importanza a qc** to attach importance to sth; **darsi importanza** to give o.s. airs

impor'tare vt (introdurre dall'estero) to import ▶ vi to matter, be important ▶ vb impers (essere necessario) to be necessary; (interessare) to matter; **non importa!** it doesn't matter!; **non me ne importa!** I don't care!

im'porto sm (total) amount

importu'nare vt to bother

im'posi ecc vb vedi **imporre**

imposizi'one [impozit'tsjone] sf imposition; order, command; (onere, imposta) tax

imposses'sarsi vpr **~ di** to seize, take possession of

impos'sibile ag impossible; **fare l'~** to do one's utmost, do all one can

im'posta sf (di finestra) shutter; (tassa) tax; **imposta sul reddito** income tax; **imposta sul valore aggiunto** value added tax (BRIT), sales tax (US)

impos'tare vt (imbucare) to post; (preparare) to plan, set out; (avviare) to begin, start off; (voce) to pitch

impostazi'one [impostat'tsjone] sf (di lettera) posting (BRIT), mailing (US); (di problema, questione) formulation, statement; (di lavoro) organization, planning; (di attività) setting up; (Mus: di voce) pitch; **impostazioni** sfpl (di computer) settings

impo'tente ag weak, powerless; (anche Med) impotent

imprati'cabile ag (strada) impassable; (campo da gioco) unplayable

impre'care vi to curse, swear; ~ **contro** to hurl abuse at

imprecazi'one [imprekat'tsjone] sf abuse, curse

impre'gnare [impreɲ'ɲare] vt ~ (di) (imbevere) to soak o impregnate (with); (riempire) to fill (with)

imprendi'tore sm (industriale) entrepreneur; (appaltatore) contractor; **piccolo ~** small businessman

im'presa sf (iniziativa) enterprise; (azione) exploit; (azienda) firm

impressio'nante ag impressive; upsetting

impressio'nare vt to impress; (turbare) to upset; (Fot) to expose; **impressionarsi** vpr to be easily upset

impressi'one sf impression; (fig: sensazione) sensation, feeling; (stampa) printing; **fare ~** (colpire) to impress; (turbare) to frighten, upset; **fare buona/cattiva ~ a** to make a good/bad impression on

impreve'dibile ag unforeseeable; (persona) unpredictable

impre'visto, -a ag unexpected, unforeseen ▶ sm unforeseen event; **salvo imprevisti** unless anything unexpected happens

imprigio'nare [impridʒo'nare] vt to imprison

impro'babile ag improbable, unlikely

im'pronta sf imprint, impression, sign; (di piede, mano) print; (fig) mark, stamp; **impronta digitale** fingerprint; **impronta ecologica** carbon footprint

improvvisa'mente av suddenly; unexpectedly

improvvi'sare vt to improvise

improv'viso, -a ag (imprevisto) unexpected; (subitaneo) sudden; **all'~** unexpectedly; suddenly

impru'dente ag unwise, rash

impu'gnare [impuɲ'ɲare] vt to grasp, grip; (Dir) to contest

impul'sivo, -a ag impulsive

im'pulso sm impulse

impun'tarsi vpr to stop dead, refuse to budge; (fig) to be obstinate

impu'tato, -a sm/f (Dir) accused, defendant

in (in + il = **nel**, in + lo = **nello**, in + l' = **nell'**, in + la = **nella**, in + i = **nei**, in + gli = **negli**, in + le = **nelle**) prep

1 (stato in luogo) in; **vivere in Italia/città** to live in Italy/town; **essere in casa/ufficio** to be at home/the office; **se fossi in te** if I were you

2 (moto a luogo) to; (: dentro) into; **andare in Germania/città** to go to Germany/town; **andare in ufficio** to go to the office; **entrare in macchina/casa** to get into the car/go into the house

3 (tempo) in; **nel 1989** in 1989; **in giugno/estate** in June/summer

4 (modo, maniera) in; **in silenzio** in silence; **in abito da sera** in evening dress; **in guerra** at war; **in vacanza** on holiday; **Maria Bianchi in Rossi** Maria Rossi née Bianchi

5 (mezzo) by; **viaggiare in autobus/treno** to travel by bus/train

6 (materia) made of; **in marmo** made of marble, marble cpd; **una collana in oro** a gold necklace

7 (misura) in; **siamo in quattro** there are four of us; **in tutto** in all

8 (fine): **dare in dono** to give as a gift; **spende tutto in alcool** he spends all his money on drink; **in onore di** in honour of

inabi'tabile *ag* uninhabitable

inacces'sibile [inattʃes'sibile] *ag* (*luogo*) inaccessible; (*persona*) unapproachable

inaccet'tabile [inattʃet'tabile] *ag* unacceptable

ina'datto, -a *ag* ~ **(a)** unsuitable *o* unfit (for)

inadegu'ato, -a *ag* inadequate

inaffi'dabile *ag* unreliable

inami'dato, -a *ag* starched

inar'care *vt* (*schiena*) to arch; (*sopracciglia*) to raise

inaspet'tato, -a *ag* unexpected

inas'prire *vt* (*disciplina*) to tighten up, make harsher; (*carattere*) to embitter; **inasprirsi** *vpr* to become harsher; to become bitter; to become worse

inattac'cabile *ag* (*anche fig*) unassailable; (*alibi*) cast-iron

inatten'dibile *ag* unreliable

inat'teso, -a *ag* unexpected

inattu'abile *ag* impracticable

inau'dito, -a *ag* unheard of

inaugu'rare *vt* to inaugurate, open; (*monumento*) to unveil

inaugurazi'one [inaugurat'tsjone] *sf* inauguration; unveiling

incal'lito, -a *ag* calloused; (*fig*) hardened, inveterate; (: *insensibile*) hard

incande'scente [inkandeʃʃɛnte] *ag* incandescent, white-hot

incan'tare *vt* to enchant, bewitch; **incantarsi** *vpr* (*rimanere intontito*) to be spellbound; to be in a daze; (*meccanismo: bloccarsi*) to jam; **incan'tevole** *ag* charming, enchanting

in'canto *sm* spell, charm, enchantment; (*asta*) auction; **come per ~** as if by magic; **mettere all'~** to put up for auction

inca'pace [inka'patʃe] *ag* incapable

incarce'rare [inkartʃe'rare] *vt* to imprison

incari'care *vt* ~ **qn di fare** to give sb the responsibility of doing; **incaricarsi di** to take care *o* charge of

in'carico, -chi *sm* task, job

incarta'mento *sm* dossier, file

incar'tare *vt* to wrap (in paper)

incas'sare *vt* (*merce*) to pack (in cases); (*gemma: incastonare*) to set; (*Econ: riscuotere*) to collect; (*Pugilato: colpi*) to take, stand up to; **in'casso** *sm* cashing, encashment; (*introito*) takings *pl*

incas'trare *vt* to fit in, insert; (*fig: intrappolare*) to catch; **incastrarsi** *vpr* (*combaciare*) to fit together; (*restare bloccato*) to become stuck

incate'nare *vt* to chain up

in'cauto, -a *ag* imprudent, rash

inca'vato, -a *ag* hollow; (*occhi*) sunken

incendi'are [intʃen'djare] *vt* to set fire to; **incendiarsi** *vpr* to catch fire, burst into flames

in'cendio [in'tʃendjo] *sm* fire

inceneri'tore [intʃeneri'tore] *sm* incinerator

in'censo [in'tʃɛnso] *sm* incense

incensu'rato, -a [intʃensu'rato] *ag* (*Dir*): **essere ~** to have a clean record

incenti'vare [intʃenti'vare] *vt* (*produzione, vendite*) to boost; (*persona*) to motivate

incen'tivo [intʃen'tivo] *sm* incentive

incepparsi *vpr* to jam

incer'tezza [intʃer'tettsa] *sf* uncertainty

in'certo, -a [in'tʃɛrto] *ag* uncertain; (*irresoluto*) undecided, hesitating ▶ *sm* uncertainty

in'cetta [in'tʃetta] *sf* buying up; **fare ~ di qc** to buy up sth

inchi'esta [in'kjɛsta] *sf* investigation, inquiry

inchinarsi vpr to bend down; (per riverenza) to bow; (: donna) to curtsy

inchio'dare [inkjo'dare] vt to nail (down); **~ la macchina** (Aut) to jam on the brakes

inchi'ostro [in'kjɔstro] sm ink; **inchiostro simpatico** invisible ink

inciam'pare [intʃam'pare] vi to trip, stumble

inci'dente [intʃi'dɛnte] sm accident; **ho avuto un ~** I've had an accident; **incidente automobilistico** o **d'auto** car accident; **incidente diplomatico** diplomatic incident

in'cidere [in'tʃidere] vi **~ su** to bear upon, affect ▸ vt (tagliare incavando) to cut into; (Arte) to engrave; to etch; (canzone) to record

in'cinta [in'tʃinta] ag f pregnant

incipri'are [intʃi'prjare] vt to powder

incipriarsi vpr to powder one's face

in'circa [in'tʃirka] av **all'~** more or less, very nearly

in'cisi ecc [in'tʃizi] vb vedi **incidere**

incisi'one [intʃi'zjone] sf cut; (disegno) engraving; etching; (registrazione) recording; (Med) incision

in'ciso, -a [in'tʃizo] pp di **incidere** ▸ sm **per ~** incidentally, by the way

inci'tare [intʃi'tare] vt to incite

inci'vile [intʃi'vile] ag uncivilized; (villano) impolite

incl. abbr (= incluso) encl.

incli'nare vt to tilt; **inclinarsi** vpr (barca) to list; (aereo) to bank

in'cludere vt to include; (accludere) to enclose; **in'cluso, -a** pp di **includere** ▸ ag included; enclosed

incoe'rente ag incoherent; (contraddittorio) inconsistent

in'cognita [in'koɲɲita] sf (Mat, fig) unknown quantity

in'cognito, -a [in'koɲɲito] ag unknown ▸ sm **in ~** incognito

incol'lare vt to glue, gum; (unire con colla) to stick together

inco'lore ag colourless

incol'pare vt **~ qn di** to charge sb with

in'colto, -a ag (terreno) uncultivated; (trascurato: capelli) neglected; (persona) uneducated

in'colume ag safe and sound, unhurt

incom'benza [inkom'bɛntsa] sf duty, task

in'combere vi (sovrastare minacciando): **~ su** to threaten, hang over

incominci'are [inkomin'tʃare] vi, vt to begin, start

incompe'tente ag incompetent

incompi'uto, -a ag unfinished, incomplete

incom'pleto, -a ag incomplete

incompren'sibile ag incomprehensible

inconce'pibile [inkontʃe'pibile] ag inconceivable

inconcili'abile [inkontʃi'ljabile] ag irreconcilable

inconclu'dente ag inconclusive; (persona) ineffectual

incondizio'nato, -a [inkondittsjo'nato] ag unconditional

inconfon'dibile ag unmistakable

inconsa'pevole ag **~ di** unaware of, ignorant of

in'conscio, -a, -sci, -sce [in'kɔnʃo] ag unconscious ▸ sm (Psic): **l'~** the unconscious

inconsis'tente ag insubstantial; unfounded

inconsu'eto, -a ag unusual

incon'trare vt to meet; (difficoltà) to meet with; **incontrarsi** vpr to meet

in'contro av **~ a** (verso) towards ▸ sm meeting; (Sport) match; meeting; **incontro di calcio** football match

inconveni'ente sm drawback, snag

incoraggia'mento [inkoraddʒa'mento] sm encouragement

incoraggi'are [inkorad'dʒare] *vt* to encourage

incornici'are [inkorni'tʃare] *vt* to frame

incoro'nare *vt* to crown

in'correre *vi* ~ **in** to meet with, run into

incosci'ente [inkoʃ'ʃente] *ag* (*inconscio*) unconscious; (*irresponsabile*) reckless, thoughtless

incre'dibile *ag* incredible, unbelievable

in'credulo, -a *ag* incredulous, disbelieving

incremen'tare *vt* to increase; (*dar sviluppo a*) to promote

incre'mento *sm* (*sviluppo*) development; (*aumento numerico*) increase, growth

incresci'oso, -a [inkreʃ'ʃoso] *ag* (*incidente ecc*) regrettable

incrimi'nare *vt* (*Dir*) to charge

incri'nare *vt* to crack; (*fig: rapporti, amicizia*) to cause to deteriorate; **incrinarsi** *vpr* to crack; to deteriorate

incroci'are [inkro'tʃare] *vt* to cross; (*incontrare*) to meet ▶ *vi* (*Naut, Aer*) to cruise; **incrociarsi** *vpr* (*strade*) to cross, intersect; (*persone, veicoli*) to pass each other; ~ **le braccia/le gambe** to fold one's arms/cross one's legs

in'crocio [in'krotʃo] *sm* (*anche Ferr*) crossing; (*di strade*) crossroads

incuba'trice [inkuba'tritʃe] *sf* incubator

'incubo *sm* nightmare

incu'rabile *ag* incurable

incu'rante *ag* ~ **(di)** heedless (of), careless (of)

incurio'sire *vt* to make curious; **incuriosirsi** *vpr* to become curious

incursi'one *sf* raid

incur'vare *vt* to bend, curve; **incurvarsi** *vpr* to bend, curve

incusto'dito, -a *ag* unguarded, unattended

in'cutere *vt* ~ **timore/rispetto a qn** to strike fear into sb/command sb's respect

'indaco *sm* indigo

indaffa'rato, -a *ag* busy

inda'gare *vt* to investigate

in'dagine [in'dadʒine] *sf* investigation, inquiry; (*ricerca*) research, study; **indagine di mercato** market survey

indebi'tarsi *vpr* to run *o* get into debt

indebo'lire *vt, vi* (*anche:* **indebolirsi**) to weaken

inde'cente [inde'tʃente] *ag* indecent

inde'ciso, -a [inde'tʃizo] *ag* indecisive; (*irresoluto*) undecided

indefi'nito, -a *ag* (*anche Ling*) indefinite; (*impreciso, non determinato*) undefined

in'degno, -a [in'deɲɲo] *ag* (*atto*) shameful; (*persona*) unworthy

indemoni'ato, -a *ag* possessed (by the devil)

in'denne *ag* unhurt, uninjured

indenniz'zare [indennid'dzare] *vt* to compensate

indetermina'tivo, -a *ag* (*Ling*) indefinite

'India *sf* l'~ India; **indi'ano, -a** *ag* Indian ▶ *sm/f* (*d'India*) Indian; (*d'America*) Native American, (American) Indian

indi'care *vt* (*mostrare*) to show, indicate; (: *col dito*) to point to, point out; (*consigliare*) to suggest, recommend; **indica'tivo, -a** *ag* indicative ▶ *sm* (*Ling*) indicative (mood); **indicazi'one** *sf* indication; (*informazione*) piece of information

'indice ['inditʃe] *sm* index; (*fig*) sign; (*dito*) index finger, forefinger; **indice di gradimento** (*Radio, TV*) popularity rating

indicherò ecc [indike'rɔ] vb vedi **indicare**

indi'cibile [indi'tʃibile] ag inexpressible

indietreggi'are [indietred'dʒare] vi to draw back, retreat

indi'etro av back; (guardare) behind, back; (andare, cadere: anche: **all'~**) backwards; **rimanere ~** to be left behind; **essere ~** (col lavoro) to be behind; (orologio) to be slow; **rimandare qc ~** to send sth back

indi'feso, -a ag (città ecc) undefended; (persona) defenceless

indiffe'rente ag indifferent

in'digeno, -a [in'didʒeno] ag indigenous, native ▶ sm/f native

indigesti'one [indidʒes'tjone] sf indigestion

indi'gesto, -a [indi'dʒɛsto] ag indigestible

indi'gnare [indiɲ'ɲare] vt to fill with indignation; **indignarsi** vpr to get indignant

indimenti'cabile ag unforgettable

indipen'dente ag independent

in'dire vt (concorso) to announce; (elezioni) to call

indi'retto, -a ag indirect

indiriz'zare [indirit'tsare] vt (dirigere) to direct; (mandare) to send; (lettera) to address

indi'rizzo [indi'rittso] sm address; (direzione) direction; (avvio) trend, course; **il mio ~ è... ** my address is ...

indis'creto, -a ag indiscreet

indis'cusso, -a ag unquestioned

indispen'sabile ag indispensable, essential

indispet'tire vt to irritate, annoy ▶ vi (anche: **indispettirsi**) to get irritated o annoyed

individu'ale ag individual

individu'are vt (dar forma distinta a) to characterize; (determinare) to locate;

(riconoscere) to single out

indi'viduo sm individual

indizi'ato, -a ag suspected ▶ sm/f suspect

in'dizio [in'dittsjo] sm (segno) sign, indication; (Polizia) clue; (Dir) piece of evidence

'indole sf nature, character

indolen'zito, -a [indolen'tsito] ag stiff, aching; (intorpidito) numb

indo'lore ag painless

indo'mani sm **l'~** the next day, the following day

Indo'nesia sf **l'~** Indonesia

indos'sare vt (mettere indosso) to put on; (avere indosso) to have on; **indossa'tore, -'trice** sm/f model

indottri'nare vt to indoctrinate

indovi'nare vt (scoprire) to guess; (immaginare) to imagine, guess; (il futuro) to foretell; **indovi'nello** sm riddle

indubbia'mente av undoubtedly

in'dubbio, -a ag certain, undoubted

in'duco ecc vb vedi **indurre**

indugi'are [indu'dʒare] vi to take one's time, delay

in'dugio [in'dudʒo] sm (ritardo) delay; **senza ~** without delay

indul'gente [indul'dʒɛnte] ag indulgent; (giudice) lenient

indu'mento sm article of clothing, garment

indu'rire vt to harden ▶ vi (anche: **indurirsi**) to harden, become hard

in'durre vt **~ qn a fare qc** to induce o persuade sb to do sth; **~ qn in errore** to mislead sb

in'dussi ecc vb vedi **indurre**

in'dustria sf industry; **industri'ale** ag industrial ▶ sm industrialist

inecce'pibile [inettʃe'pibile] ag unexceptionable

i'nedito, -a ag unpublished

ine'rente ag **~ a** concerning, regarding

i'nerme *ag* unarmed; defenceless

inerpi'carsi *vpr* **~ (su)** to clamber (up)

i'nerte *ag* inert; (*inattivo*) indolent, sluggish

ine'satto, -a *ag* (*impreciso*) inexact; (*erroneo*) incorrect; (*Amm: non riscosso*) uncollected

inesis'tente *ag* non-existent

inesperi'enza [inespe'rjɛntsa] *sf* inexperience

ines'perto, -a *ag* inexperienced

inevi'tabile *ag* inevitable

i'nezia [i'nɛttsja] *sf* trifle, thing of no importance

infagot'tare *vt* to bundle up, wrap up; **infagottarsi** *vpr* to wrap up

infal'libile *ag* infallible

infa'mante *ag* defamatory

in'fame *ag* infamous; (*fig: cosa, compito*) awful, dreadful

infan'gare *vt* to cover with mud; (*fig: reputazione*) to sully; **infangarsi** *vpr* to get covered in mud; to be sullied

infan'tile *ag* child *cpd*; childlike; (*adulto, azione*) childish; **letteratura ~** children's books *pl*

in'fanzia [in'fantsja] *sf* childhood; (*bambini*) children *pl*; **prima ~** babyhood, infancy

infari'nare *vt* to cover with (*o sprinkle with o dip in*) flour; **infarina'tura** *sf* (*fig*) smattering

in'farto *sm* (*Med*) heart attack

infasti'dire *vt* to annoy, irritate; **infastidirsi** *vpr* to get annoyed *o* irritated

infati'cabile *ag* tireless, untiring

in'fatti *cong* actually, as a matter of fact

> Attenzione! In inglese esiste l'espressione *in fact* che però vuol dire *in effetti*.

infatu'arsi *vpr* **~ di** to become infatuated with, fall for

infe'dele *ag* unfaithful

infe'lice [infe'litʃe] *ag* unhappy; (*sfortunato*) unlucky, unfortunate; (*inopportuno*) inopportune, ill-timed; (*mal riuscito: lavoro*) bad, poor

inferi'ore *ag* lower; (*per intelligenza, qualità*) inferior ▶ *sm/f* inferior; **~ a** (*numero, quantità*) less *o* smaller than; (*meno buono*) inferior to; **~ alla media** below average; **inferiorità** *sf* inferiority

inferme'ria *sf* infirmary; (*di scuola, nave*) sick bay

infermi'ere, -a *sm/f* nurse

infermità *sf inv* illness; infirmity; **infermità mentale** mental illness; (*Dir*) insanity

in'fermo, -a *ag* (*ammalato*) ill; (*debole*) infirm

infer'nale *ag* infernal; (*proposito, complotto*) diabolical

in'ferno *sm* hell

inferri'ata *sf* grating

infes'tare *vt* to infest

infet'tare *vt* to infect; **infettarsi** *vpr* to become infected; **infezi'one** *sf* infection

infiam'mabile *ag* inflammable

infiam'mare *vt* to set alight; (*fig, Med*) to inflame; **infiammarsi** *vpr* to catch fire; (*Med*) to become inflamed; **infiammazi'one** *sf* (*Med*) inflammation

infie'rire *vi* **~ su** (*fisicamente*) to attack furiously; (*verbalmente*) to rage at

infi'lare *vt* (*ago*) to thread; (*mettere: chiave*) to insert; (*: anello, vestito*) to slip *o* put on; (*strada*) to turn into, take; **infilarsi** *vpr* **infilarsi in** to slip into; (*indossare*) to slip on; **~ l'uscio** to slip in; to slip out

infil'trarsi *vpr* to penetrate, seep through; (*Mil*) to infiltrate

infil'zare [infil'tsare] *vt* (*infilare*) to string together; (*trafiggere*) to pierce

'infimo, -a *ag* lowest

in'fine *av* finally; (*insomma*) in short

infinità *sf* infinity; (*in quantità*): **un'~ di** an infinite number of

infi'nito, -a *ag* infinite; (*Ling*) infinitive ▶ *sm* infinity; (*Ling*) infinitive; **all'~** (*senza fine*) endlessly

infinocchi'are [infinok'kjare] (*fam*) *vt* to hoodwink

infischi'arsi [infis'kjarsi] *vpr* **~ di** not to care about

in'fisso, -a (*pp*) *di* **infiggere** *sm* fixture; (*di porta, finestra*) frame

inflazi'one [inflat'tsjone] *sf* inflation

in'fliggere [in'fliddʒere] *vt* to inflict

in'flissi *ecc vb vedi* **infliggere**

influ'ente *ag* influential; **influ'enza** *sf* influence; (*Med*) influenza, flu; **influenza aviaria** bird flu

influen'zare [influen'tsare] *vt* to influence, have an influence on

influ'ire *vi* **~ su** to influence

in'flusso *sm* influence

infon'dato, -a *ag* unfounded, groundless

in'fondere *vt* **~ qc in qn** to instill sth in sb

infor'mare *vt* to inform, tell; **informarsi** *vpr* **informarsi (di** *o* **su)** to inquire (about)

infor'matica *sf* computer science

informa'tivo, -a *ag* informative

infor'mato, -a *ag* informed; **tenersi ~** to keep o.s. (well-)informed

informa'tore *sm* informer

informazi'one [informat'tsjone] *sf* piece of information; **prendere informazioni sul conto di qn** to get information about sb; **chiedere un'~** to ask for (some) information

in'forme *ag* shapeless

informico'larsi *vpr* to have pins and needles

infortu'nato, -a *ag* injured, hurt ▶ *sm/f* injured person

infor'tunio *sm* accident; **infortunio**

sul lavoro industrial accident, accident at work

infra'dito *sm inv* (*calzatura*) flip flop (*BRIT*), thong (*US*)

infrazi'one [infrat'tsjone] *sf* **~ a** breaking of, violation of

infredda'tura *sf* slight cold

infreddo'lito, -a *ag* cold, chilled

infu'ori *av* out; **all'~** outwards; **all'~ di** (*eccetto*) except, with the exception of

infuri'arsi *vpr* to fly into a rage

infusi'one *sf* infusion

in'fuso, -a *pp di* **infondere** ▶ *sm* infusion

Ing. *abbr* = **ingegnere**

ingaggi'are [ingad'dʒare] *vt* (*assumere con compenso*) to take on, hire; (*Sport*) to sign on; (*Mil*) to engage

ingan'nare *vt* to deceive; (*fisco*) to cheat; (*eludere*) to dodge, elude; (*fig: tempo*) to while away ▶ *vi* (*apparenza*) to be deceptive; **ingannarsi** *vpr* to be mistaken, be wrong

in'ganno *sm* deceit, deception; (*azione*) trick; (*menzogna, frode*) cheat, swindle; (*illusione*) illusion

inge'gnarsi [indʒeɲ'ɲarsi] *vpr* to do one's best, try hard

inge'gnere [indʒeɲ'ɲere] *sm* engineer; **~ civile/navale** civil/naval engineer; **ingegne'ria** *sf* engineering; **ingegnere genetica** genetic engineering

in'gegno [in'dʒeɲɲo] *sm* (*intelligenza*) intelligence, brains *pl*; (*capacità creativa*) ingenuity; (*disposizione*) talent; **inge'gnoso, -a** *ag* ingenious, clever

ingelo'sire [indʒelo'zire] *vt* to make jealous ▶ *vi* (*anche:* **ingelosirsi**) to become jealous

in'gente [in'dʒente] *ag* huge, enormous

ingenuità [indʒenui'ta] *sf* ingenuousness

in'genuo, -a [in'dʒɛnuo] *ag* naïve
Attenzione! In inglese esiste la parola *ingenious*, che però significa *ingegnoso*.

inge'rire [indʒe'rire] *vt* to ingest

inges'sare [indʒes'sare] *vt* (*Med*) to put in plaster; **ingessa'tura** *sf* plaster

Inghil'terra [ingil'tɛrra] *sf* l'~ England

inghiot'tire [ingjot'tire] *vt* to swallow

ingial'lire [indʒal'lire] *vi* to go yellow

inginocchi'arsi [indʒinok'kjarsi] *vpr* to kneel (down)

ingiù [in'dʒu] *av* down, downwards

ingi'uria [in'dʒurja] *sf* insult; (*fig: danno*) damage

ingius'tizia [indʒus'tittsja] *sf* injustice

ingi'usto, -a [in'dʒusto] *ag* unjust, unfair

in'glese *ag* English ▶ *sm/f* Englishman/woman ▶ *sm* (*Ling*) English; **gli Inglesi** the English; **andarsene** *o* **filare all'~** to take French leave

ingoi'are *vt* to gulp (down); (*fig*) to swallow (up)

ingol'farsi *vpr* to flood

ingom'brante *ag* cumbersome

ingom'brare *vt* (*strada*) to block; (*stanza*) to clutter up

in'gordo, -a *ag* ~ **di** greedy for; (*fig*) greedy *o* avid for

in'gorgo, -ghi *sm* blockage, obstruction; (*anche:* ~ **stradale**) traffic jam

ingoz'zarsi *vpr* ~ (**di**) to stuff o.s. (with)

ingra'naggio [ingra'naddʒo] *sm* (*Tecn*) gear; (*di orologio*) mechanism; **gli ingranaggi della burocrazia** the bureaucratic machinery

ingra'nare *vi* to mesh, engage ▶ *vt* to engage; ~ **la marcia** to get into gear

ingrandi'mento *sm* enlargement; extension

ingran'dire *vt* (*anche Fot*) to enlarge; (*estendere*) to extend; (*Ottica, fig*) to magnify ▶ *vi* (*anche:* **ingrandirsi**) to become larger *o* bigger; (*aumentare*) to grow, increase; (*espandersi*) to expand

ingras'sare *vt* to make fat; (*animali*) to fatten; (*lubrificare*) to oil, lubricate ▶ *vi* (*anche:* **ingrassarsi**) to get fat, put on weight

in'grato, -a *ag* ungrateful; (*lavoro*) thankless, unrewarding

ingredi'ente *sm* ingredient

in'gresso *sm* (*porta*) entrance; (*atrio*) hall; (*l'entrare*) entrance, entry; (*facoltà di entrare*) admission; **ingresso libero** admission free

ingros'sare *vt* to increase; (*folla, livello*) to swell ▶ *vi* (*anche:* **ingrossarsi**) to increase; to swell

in'grosso *av* all'~ (*Comm*) wholesale; (*all'incirca*) roughly, about

ingua'ribile *ag* incurable

'inguine *sm* (*Anat*) groin

ini'bire *vt* to forbid, prohibit; (*Psic*) to inhibit; **inibirsi** *vpr* to restrain o.s.

ini'bito, -a *ag* inhibited ▶ *sm/f* inhibited person

iniet'tare *vt* to inject; **iniezi'one** *sf* injection

ininterrotta'mente *av* non-stop, continuously

ininter'rotto, -a *ag* unbroken; uninterrupted

inizi'ale [init'tsjale] *ag, sf* initial

inizi'are [init'tsjare] *vi, vt* to begin, start; **a che ora inizia il film?** when does the film start?; ~ **qn a** to initiate sb into; (*pittura ecc*) to introduce sb to; ~ **a fare qc** to start doing sth

inizia'tiva [inittsja'tiva] *sf* initiative; **iniziativa privata** private enterprise

i'nizio [i'nittsjo] *sm* beginning; **all'~** at the beginning, at the start; **dare ~ a qc** to start sth, get sth going

innaffi'are ecc = **annaffiare** ecc

innamo'rarsi vpr ~ **(di qn)** to fall in love (with sb); **innamo'rato, -a** ag (che nutre amore): **innamorato (di)** in love (with); (appassionato): **innamorato di** very fond of ▸ sm/f lover; sweetheart

innanzi'tutto av first of all

in'nato, -a ag innate

innatu'rale ag unnatural

inne'gabile ag undeniable

innervo'sire vt ~ **qn** to get on sb's nerves; **innervosirsi** vpr to get irritated o upset

innes'care vt to prime

'inno sm hymn; **inno nazionale** national anthem

inno'cente [inno'tʃɛnte] ag innocent

in'nocuo, -a ag innocuous, harmless

innova'tivo, -a ag innovative

innume'revole ag innumerable

inol'trare vt (Amm) to pass on, forward

i'noltre av besides, moreover

inon'dare vt to flood

inoppor'tuno, -a ag untimely, ill-timed; inappropriate; (momento) inopportune

inorri'dire vt to horrify ▸ vi to be horrified

inosser'vato, -a ag (non notato) unobserved; (non rispettato) not observed, not kept

inossi'dabile ag stainless

INPS sigla m (= Istituto Nazionale Previdenza Sociale) social security service

inqua'drare vt (foto, immagine) to frame; (fig) to situate, set

inqui'eto, -a ag restless; (preoccupato) worried, anxious

inqui'lino, -a sm/f tenant

inquina'mento sm pollution

inqui'nare vt to pollute

insabbi'are vt (fig: pratica) to shelve; **insabbiarsi** vpr (arenarsi: barca) to run aground; (fig: pratica) to be shelved

insac'cati smpl (Cuc) sausages

insa'lata sf salad; **insalata mista** mixed salad; **insalata russa** (Cuc) Russian salad (comprised of cold diced cooked vegetables in mayonnaise); **insalati'era** sf salad bowl

insa'nabile ag (piaga) which cannot be healed; (situazione) irremediable; (odio) implacable

insa'puta sf all'~ **di qn** without sb knowing

inse'diarsi vpr to take up office; (popolo, colonia) to settle

in'segna [in'seɲɲa] sf sign; (emblema) sign, emblem; (bandiera) flag, banner

insegna'mento [inseɲɲa'mento] sm teaching

inse'gnante [inseɲ'ɲante] ag teaching ▸ sm/f teacher

inse'gnare [inseɲ'ɲare] vt, vi to teach; ~ **a qn qc** to teach sb sth; ~ **a qn a fare qc** to teach sb (how) to do sth

insegui'mento sm pursuit, chase

insegu'ire vt to pursue, chase

insena'tura sf inlet, creek

insen'sato, -a ag senseless, stupid

insen'sibile ag (nervo) insensible; (persona) indifferent

inse'rire vt to insert; (Elettr) to connect; (allegare) to enclose; (annuncio) to put in, place; **inserirsi** vpr (fig): **inserirsi in** to become part of

inservi'ente sm/f attendant

inserzi'one [inser'tsjone] sf insertion; (avviso) advertisement; **fare un'~ sul giornale** to put an advertisement in the paper

insetti'cida, -i [insetti'tʃida] sm insecticide

in'setto sm insect

insi'curo, -a ag insecure

insi'eme av together ▸ prep ~ **a** o **con** together with ▸ sm whole; (Mat, servizio, assortimento) set; (Moda) ensemble, outfit; **tutti ~** all together; **tutto ~** all together; (*in una volta*) at one go; **nell'~** on the whole; **d'~** (*veduta ecc*) overall

in'signe [in'siɲɲe] *ag* (*persona*) famous, distinguished; (*città, monumento*) notable

insignifi'cante [insiɲɲifi'kante] *ag* insignificant

insinu'are *vt* (*introdurre*): **~ qc in** to slip *o* slide sth into; (*fig*) to insinuate, imply; **insinuarsi** *vpr* **insinuarsi in** to seep into; (*fig*) to creep into; to worm one's way into

in'sipido, -a *ag* insipid

insis'tente *ag* insistent; persistent

in'sistere *vi* **~ su qc** to insist on sth; **~ in qc/a fare** (*perseverare*) to persist in sth/in doing

insoddis'fatto, -a *ag* dissatisfied

insoffe'rente *ag* intolerant

insolazi'one [insolat'tsjone] *sf* (*Med*) sunstroke

inso'lente *ag* insolent

in'solito, -a *ag* unusual, out of the ordinary

inso'luto, -a *ag* (*non risolto*) unsolved

in'somma *av* (*in conclusione*) in short; (*dunque*) well ▶ *escl* for heaven's sake!

in'sonne *ag* sleepless; **in'sonnia** *sf* insomnia, sleeplessness

insonno'lito, -a *ag* sleepy, drowsy

insoppor'tabile *ag* unbearable

in'sorgere [in'sordʒere] *vi* (*ribellarsi*) to rise up, rebel; (*apparire*) to come up, arise

in'sorsi *ecc vb vedi* **insorgere**

insospet'tire *vt* to make suspicious ▶ *vi* (*anche:* **insospettirsi**) to become suspicious

inspi'rare *vt* to breathe in, inhale

in'stabile *ag* (*carico, indole*) unstable; (*tempo*) unsettled; (*equilibrio*) unsteady

instal'lare *vt* to install

instan'cabile *ag* untiring, indefatigable

instau'rare *vt* to introduce, institute

insuc'cesso [insut'tʃɛsso] *sm* failure, flop

insuffici'ente [insuffi'tʃɛnte] *ag* insufficient; (*compito, allievo*) inadequate; **insuffici'enza** *sf* insufficiency; inadequacy; (*Ins*) fail; **insufficienza di prove** (*Dir*) lack of evidence; **insufficienza renale** renal insufficiency

insu'lina *sf* insulin

in'sulso, -a *ag* (*sciocco*) inane, silly; (*persona*) dull, insipid

insul'tare *vt* to insult, affront

in'sulto *sm* insult, affront

intac'care *vt* (*fare tacche*) to cut into; (*corrodere*) to corrode; (*fig: cominciare ad usare: risparmi*) to break into; (: *ledere*) to damage

intagli'are [intaʎ'ʎare] *vt* to carve

in'tanto *av* (*nel frattempo*) meanwhile, in the meantime; (*per cominciare*) just to begin with; **~ che** while

inta'sare *vt* to choke (up), block (up); (*Aut*) to obstruct, block; **intasarsi** *vpr* to become choked *o* blocked

intas'care *vt* to pocket

in'tatto, -a *ag* intact; (*puro*) unsullied

intavo'lare *vt* to start, enter into

inte'grale *ag* complete; (*pane, farina*) wholemeal (*BRIT*), whole-wheat (*US*); (*Mat*): **calcolo ~** integral calculus

inte'grante *ag* **parte ~** integral part

inte'grare *vt* to complete; (*Mat*) to integrate; **integrarsi** *vpr* (*persona*) to become integrated

integra'tore *sm* **integratori alimentari** nutritional supplements

integrità *sf* integrity

'integro, -a *ag* (*intatto, intero*) complete, whole; (*retto*) upright

intelaia'tura *sf* frame; (*fig*) structure, framework

intel'letto *sm* intellect;
intellettu'ale *ag*, *sm/f* intellectual
intelli'gente [intelli'dʒɛnte] *ag*
intelligent
intem'perie *sfpl* bad weather *sg*
in'tendere *vt* (*avere intenzione*): ~
fare qc to intend *o* mean to do sth;
(*comprendere*) to understand; (*udire*) to
hear; (*significare*) to mean; **intendersi**
vpr (*conoscere*): **intendersi di**
to know a lot about, be a connoisseur
of; (*accordarsi*) to get on (well);
intendersela con qn (*avere una
relazione amorosa*) to have an affair
with sb; **intendi'tore, -'trice** *sm/f*
connoisseur, expert
inten'sivo, -a *ag* intensive
in'tenso, -a *ag* intense
in'tento, -a *ag* (*teso, assorto*): ~ (a)
intent (on), absorbed (in) ▶ *sm* aim,
purpose
intenzio'nale [intentsjo'nale] *ag*
intentional
intenzi'one [intents'tsjone] *sf*
intention; (*Dir*) intent; **avere ~ di
fare qc** to intend to do sth, have the
intention of doing sth
interat'tivo, -a *ag* interactive
intercet'tare [intertʃet'tare] *vt* to
intercept
intercity [intəsi'ti] *sm inv* (*Ferr*)
≈ intercity (train)
inter'detto, -a *pp di* **interdire** ▶ *ag*
forbidden, prohibited; (*sconcertato*)
dumbfounded ▶ *sm* (*Rel*) interdict
interes'sante *ag* interesting;
essere in stato ~ to be expecting
(a baby)
interes'sare *vt* to interest;
(*concernere*) to concern, be of interest
to; (*far intervenire*): ~ **qn a** to draw
sb's attention to ▶ *vi* ~ **a** to interest,
matter to; **interessarsi** *vpr* (*mostrare
interesse*): **interessarsi a** to take
an interest in, be interested in;

(*occuparsi*): **interessarsi di** to take
care of
inte'resse *sm* (*anche Comm*) interest
inter'faccia, -ce [inter'fattʃa] *sf*
(*Inform*) interface
interfe'renza [interfe'rɛntsa] *sf*
interference
interfe'rire *vi* to interfere
interiezi'one [interjet'tsjone] *sf*
exclamation, interjection
interi'ora *sfpl* entrails
interi'ore *ag* interior, inner, inside,
internal; (*fig*) inner
inter'medio, -a *ag* intermediate
inter'nare *vt* (*arrestare*) to intern;
(*Med*) to commit (to a mental
institution)
inter'nauta *sm/f* Internet user
internazio'nale [internattsjo'nale]
ag international
'Internet ['internet] *sf* Internet; **in ~**
on the Internet
in'terno, -a *ag* (*di dentro*) internal,
interior, inner; (*: mare*) inland;
(*nazionale*) domestic; (*allievo*)
boarding ▶ *sm* inside, interior; (*di
paese*) interior; (*fodera*) lining; (*di
appartamento*) flat (number); (*Tel*)
extension ▶ *sm/f* (*Ins*) boarder;
interni *smpl* (*Cinema*) interior shots;
all'~ inside; **Ministero degli Interni**
Ministry of the Interior, ≈ Home
Office (*BRIT*), Department of the
Interior (*US*)
in'tero, -a *ag* (*integro, intatto*) whole,
entire; (*completo, totale*) complete;
(*numero*) whole; (*non ridotto: biglietto*)
full; (*latte*) full-cream
interpel'lare *vt* to consult
interpre'tare *vt* to interpret;
in'terprete *sm/f* interpreter;
(*Teatro*) actor/actress, performer;
(*Mus*) performer; **ci potrebbe fare
da interprete?** could you act as an
interpreter for us?

interregio'nale [interredʒo'nale] *sm* train that travels between two or more regions of Italy, stopping frequently

interro'gare *vt* to question; (*Ins*) to test; **interrogazi'one** *sf* questioning *no pl*; (*Ins*) oral test

inter'rompere *vt* to interrupt; (*studi, trattative*) to break off, interrupt; **interrompersi** *vpr* to break off, stop

interrut'tore *sm* switch

interruzi'one [interrut'tsjone] *sf* interruption; break

interur'bana *sf* trunk *o* long-distance call

inter'vallo *sm* interval; (*spazio*) space, gap

interve'nire *vi* (*partecipare*): ~ **a** to take part in; (*intromettersi: anche Pol*) to intervene; (*Med: operare*) to operate; **inter'vento** *sm* participation; (*intromissione*) intervention; (*Med*) operation; **fare un intervento nel corso di** (*dibattito, programma*) to take part in

inter'vista *sf* interview; **intervis'tare** *vt* to interview

intes'tare *vt* (*lettera*) to address; (*proprietà*): ~ **a** to register in the name of; ~ **un assegno a qn** to make out a cheque to sb

intestato, -a *ag* (*proprietà, casa, conto*) in the name of; (*assegno*) made out to; **carta intestata** headed paper

intes'tino *sm* (*Anat*) intestine

intimidazi'one [intimidat'tsjone] *sf* intimidation

intimi'dire *vt* to intimidate ▶ *vi* (*intimidirsi*) to grow shy

intimità *sf* intimacy; privacy; (*familiarità*) familiarity

'intimo, -a *ag* intimate; (*affetti, vita*) private; (*fig: profondo*) inmost ▶ *sm* (*persona*) intimate *o* close friend; (*dell'animo*) bottom, depths *pl*; **parti intime** (*Anat*) private parts

in'tingolo *sm* sauce; (*pietanza*) stew

intito'lare *vt* to give a title to; (*dedicare*) to dedicate; **intitolarsi** *vpr* (*libro, film*) to be called

intolle'rabile *ag* intolerable

intolle'rante *ag* intolerant

in'tonaco, -ci o chi *sm* plaster

into'nare *vt* (*canto*) to start to sing; (*armonizzare*) to match; **intonarsi** *vpr* (*colori*) to go together; **intonarsi a** (*carnagione*) to suit; (*abito*) to go with, match

inton'tito, -a *ag* stunned, dazed; ~ **dal sonno** stupid with sleep

in'toppo *sm* stumbling block, obstacle

in'torno *av* around; ~ **a** (*attorno a*) around; (*riguardo, circa*) about

intossi'care *vt* to poison; **intossicazi'one** *sf* poisoning

intralci'are [intral'tʃare] *vt* to hamper, hold up

intransi'tivo, -a *ag*, *sm* intransitive

intrapren'dente *ag* enterprising, go-ahead

intra'prendere *vt* to undertake

intrat'tabile *ag* intractable

intratte'nere *vt* to entertain; to engage in conversation; **intrattenersi** *vpr* to linger; **intrattenersi su qc** to dwell on sth

intrave'dere *vt* to catch a glimpse of; (*fig*) to foresee

intrecci'are [intret'tʃare] *vt* (*capelli*) to plait, braid; (*intessere: anche fig*) to weave, interweave, intertwine

intri'gante *ag* scheming ▶ *sm/f* schemer, intriguer

in'trinseco, -a, -ci, -che *ag* intrinsic

in'triso, -a *ag* ~ (**di**) soaked (in)

intro'durre *vt* to introduce; (*chiave ecc*): ~ **qc in** to insert sth into; (*persone: far entrare*) to show in; **introdursi** *vpr* (*moda, tecniche*) to be introduced; **introdursi in** (*persona: penetrare*) to enter; (*: entrare furtivamente*) to steal o slip into; **introduzi'one** sf introduction

in'troito sm income, revenue

intro'mettersi vpr to interfere, meddle; (interporsi) to intervene

in'truglio [in'truʎʎo] sm concoction

intrusi'one sf intrusion; interference

in'truso, -a sm/f intruder

intu'ire vt to perceive by intuition; (rendersi conto) to realize; **in'tuito** sm intuition; (perspicacia) perspicacity

inu'mano, -a ag inhuman

inumi'dire vt to dampen, moisten; **inumidirsi** vpr to become damp o wet

i'nutile ag useless; (superfluo) pointless, unnecessary

inutil'mente av unnecessarily; (senza risultato) in vain

inva'dente ag (fig) interfering, nosey

in'vadere vt to invade; (affollare) to swarm into, overrun; (acque) to flood

inva'ghirsi [inva'girsi] vpr ~ **di** to take a fancy to

invalidità sf infirmity; disability; (Dir) invalidity

in'valido, -a ag (infermo) infirm, invalid; (al lavoro) disabled; (Dir: nullo) invalid ▶ sm/f invalid; disabled person

in'vano av in vain

invasi'one sf invasion

inva'sore, invadi'trice [invadi'tritʃe] ag invading ▶ sm invader

invecchi'are [invek'kjare] vi (persona) to grow old; (vino, popolazione) to age; (moda) to become dated ▶ vt to age; (far apparire più vecchio) to make look older

in'vece [in'vetʃe] av instead; (al contrario) on the contrary; ~ **di** instead of

inve'ire vi ~ **contro** to rail against

inven'tare vt to invent; (pericoli, pettegolezzi) to make up, invent

inven'tario sm inventory; (Comm) stocktaking no pl

inven'tore sm inventor

invenzi'one [inven'tsjone] sf invention; (bugia) lie, story

inver'nale ag winter cpd; (simile all'inverno) wintry

in'verno sm winter

invero'simile ag unlikely

inversi'one sf inversion; reversal; **"divieto d'~"** (Aut) "no U-turns"

in'verso, -a ag opposite; (Mat) inverse ▶ sm contrary, opposite; **in senso ~** in the opposite direction; **in ordine ~** in reverse order

inver'tire vt to invert, reverse; ~ **la marcia** (Aut) to do a U-turn

investi'gare vt, vi to investigate; **investiga'tore, -'trice** sm/f investigator, detective; **investigatore privato** private investigator

investi'mento sm (Econ) investment

inves'tire vt (denaro) to invest; (veicolo: pedone) to knock down; (: altro veicolo) to crash into; (apostrofare) to assail; (incaricare) ~ **qn di** to invest sb with

invi'are vt to send; **invi'ato, -a** sm/f envoy; (Stampa) correspondent; **inviato speciale** (Pol) special envoy; (di giornale) special correspondent

in'vidia sf envy; **invidi'are** vt **invidiare qn (per qc)** to envy sb for sth; **invidiare qc a qn** to envy sb sth; **invidi'oso, -a** ag envious

in'vio, -'vii sm sending; (insieme di merci) consignment; (tasto) Return (key), Enter (key)

invipe'rito, -a ag furious

invi'sibile ag invisible

invi'tare vt to invite; ~ **qn a fare** to invite sb to do; **invi'tato, -a** sm/f guest; **in'vito** sm invitation

invo'care vt (chiedere: aiuto, pace) to cry out for; (appellarsi: la legge, Dio) to appeal to, invoke

invogli'are [invoʎ'ʎare] *vt* ~ **qn a fare** to tempt sb to do, induce sb to do

involon'tario, -a *ag* (*errore*) unintentional; (*gesto*) involuntary

in'volto *sm* (*pacco*) parcel; (*fagotto*) bundle

in'volucro *sm* cover, wrapping

inzup'pare [intsup'pare] *vt* to soak; **inzupparsi** *vpr* to get soaked

'io *pron* I ▶ *sm inv* **l'~** the ego, the self; **~ stesso(a)** I myself

i'odio *sm* iodine

l'onio *sm* **lo ~, il mar ~** the Ionian (Sea)

ipermer'cato *sm* hypermarket

ipertensi'one *sf* high blood pressure, hypertension

iper'testo *sm* hypertext; **ipertestu'ale** *ag* (*Comput*) **link ~** hyperlink

ip'nosi *sf* hypnosis; **ipnotiz'zare** *vt* to hypnotize

ipocri'sia *sf* hypocrisy

i'pocrita, -i, -e *ag* hypocritical ▶ *sm/f* hypocrite

ipo'teca, -che *sf* mortgage

i'potesi *sf inv* hypothesis

'ippica *sf* horseracing

'ippico, -a, -ci, -che *ag* horse *cpd*

ippocas'tano *sm* horse chestnut

ip'podromo *sm* racecourse

ippo'potamo *sm* hippopotamus

'ipsilon *sf o m inv* (*lettera*) Y, y; (: *dell'alfabeto greco*) epsilon

IR *abbr* (= *Interregionale*) long distance train which stops frequently

ira'cheno, -a [ira'kɛno] *ag, sm/f* Iraqi

l'ran *sm* **l'~** Iran

irani'ano, -a *ag, sm/f* Iranian

l'raq *sm* **l'~** Iraq

'iride *sf* (*arcobaleno*) rainbow; (*Anat, Bot*) iris

'iris *sm inv* iris

Ir'landa *sf* **l'~** Ireland; **l'~ del Nord** Northern Ireland, Ulster; **la Repubblica d'~** Eire, the Republic of Ireland; **irlan'dese** *ag* Irish ▶ *sm/f* Irishman/woman; **gli Irlandesi** the Irish

iro'nia *sf* irony; **i'ronico, -a, -ci, -che** *ag* ironic(al)

irragio'nevole [irradʒo'nevole] *ag* irrational; unreasonable

irrazio'nale [irrattsjo'nale] *ag* irrational

irre'ale *ag* unreal

irrego'lare *ag* irregular; (*terreno*) uneven

irremo'vibile *ag* (*fig*) unshakeable

irrequi'eto, -a *ag* restless

irresis'tibile *ag* irresistible

irrespon'sabile *ag* irresponsible

irri'gare *vt* (*annaffiare*) to irrigate; (*fiume ecc*) to flow through

irrigi'dire [irridʒi'dire] *vt* to stiffen; **irrigidirsi** *vpr* to stiffen

irri'sorio, -a *ag* derisory

irri'tare *vt* (*mettere di malumore*) to irritate, annoy; (*Med*) to irritate; **irritarsi** *vpr* to become irritated *o* annoyed; (*Med*) to become irritated

ir'rompere *vi* ~ **in** to burst into

irru'ente *ag* (*fig*) impetuous, violent

ir'ruppi *ecc vb vedi* **irrompere**

irruzi'one [irrut'tsjone] *sf* **fare ~ in** to burst into; (*polizia*) to raid

is'crissi *ecc vb vedi* **iscrivere**

is'critto, -a *pp di* **iscrivere** ▶ *sm/f* member; **per** *o* **in ~** in writing

is'crivere *vt* to register, enter; (*persona*): ~ **(a)** to register (in), enrol (in); **iscriversi** *vpr* **iscriversi (a)** (*club, partito*) to join; (*università*) to register *o* enrol (at); (*esame, concorso*) to register *o* enter (for); **iscrizi'one** *sf* (*epigrafe ecc*) inscription; (*a scuola, società*) enrolment, registration; (*registrazione*) registration

Is'lam *sm* **l'~** Islam

Is'landa *sf* **l'~** Iceland

islan'dese *ag* Icelandic ▸ *sm/f* Icelander ▸ *sm* (*Ling*) Icelandic

'isola *sf* island; **isola pedonale** (*Aut*) pedestrian precinct

isola'mento *sm* isolation; (*Tecn*) insulation

iso'lante *ag* insulating ▸ *sm* insulator

iso'lare *vt* to isolate; (*Tecn*) to insulate; (: *acusticamente*) to soundproof; **isolarsi** *vpr* to isolate o.s.; **iso'lato, -a** *ag* isolated; insulated ▸ *sm* (*gruppo di edifici*) block

ispet'tore *sm* inspector

ispezio'nare [ispettsjo'nare] *vt* to inspect

'ispido, -a *ag* bristly, shaggy

ispi'rare *vt* to inspire

Isra'ele *sm* l'~ Israel; **israeli'ano, -a** *ag*, *sm/f* Israeli

is'sare *vt* to hoist

istan'taneo, -a *ag* instantaneous ▸ *sf* (*Fot*) snapshot

is'tante *sm* instant, moment; **all'~**, **sull'~** instantly, immediately

is'terico, -a, -ci, -che *ag* hysterical

isti'gare *vt* to incite

is'tinto *sm* instinct

istitu'ire *vt* (*fondare*) to institute, found; (*porre: confronto*) to establish; (*intraprendere: inchiesta*) to set up

isti'tuto *sm* institute; (*di università*) department; (*ente, Dir*) institution; **istituto di bellezza** beauty salon; **istituto di credito** bank, banking institution; **istituto di ricerca** research institute

istituzi'one [istitut'tsjone] *sf* institution

'istmo *sm* (*Geo*) isthmus

'istrice ['istritʃe] *sm* porcupine

istru'ito, -a *ag* educated

istrut'tore, -'trice *sm/f* instructor ▸ *ag* **giudice ~** *vedi* **giudice**

istruzi'one *sf* education; training; (*direttiva*) instruction; **istruzioni** *sfpl* (*norme*) instructions; **istruzioni per l'uso** instructions for use; ~ **obbligatoria** (*Scol*) compulsory education

I'talia *sf* l'~ Italy

itali'ano, -a *ag* Italian ▸ *sm/f* Italian ▸ *sm* (*Ling*) Italian; **gli Italiani** the Italians

itine'rario *sm* itinerary

'ittico, -a, -ci, -che *ag* fish *cpd*; fishing *cpd*

Iugos'lavia = **Jugoslavia**

IVA ['iva] *sigla f* (= *imposta sul valore aggiunto*) VAT

◆

J

jazz [dʒaz] *sm* jazz

jeans [dʒinz] *smpl* jeans

jeep® [dʒip] *sm inv* jeep

'jogging ['dʒɔɡiŋ] *sm* jogging; **fare ~** to go jogging

'jolly ['dʒɔli] *sm inv* joker

joystick [dʒois'tik] *sm inv* joystick

ju'do [dʒu'dɔ] *sm* judo

Jugos'lavia [jugoz'lavja] *sf* (*Storia*): **la ~** Yugoslavia; **la ex-~** former Yugoslavia; **jugos'lavo, -a** *ag*, *sm/f* (*Storia*) Yugoslav(ian)

K l

K, k ['kappa] *sf o m inv (lettera)* K, k
▶ *abbr* (= *kilo-, chilo-*) k; *(Inform)* K;
K come Kursaal ≈ K for King
kamikaze [kami'kaddze] *sm inv*
kamikaze
karaoke [ka'raokɛ] *sm inv* karaoke
karatè *sm* karate
ka'yak [ka'jak] *sm inv* kayak
Kenia ['kenja] *sm il* ~ Kenya
kg *abbr* (= *chilogrammo*) kg
'killer *sm inv* gunman, hired gun
kitsch [kitʃ] *sm* kitsch
'kiwi ['kiwi] *sm inv* kiwi fruit
km *abbr* (= *chilometro*) km
K.O. [kappa'o] *sm inv* knockout
ko'ala [ko'ala] *sm inv* koala (bear)
koso'varo, -a [koso'varo] *ag, sm/f*
Kosovan
Ko'sovo *sm* Kosovo
'krapfen *sm inv (Cuc)* doughnut
Kuwait [ku'vait] *sm il* ~ Kuwait

l' *det vedi* **la**; **lo**; **il**
la (*dav V* **l'**) *det f* the ▶ *pron (oggetto: persona)* her; (: *cosa*) it; (: *forma di cortesia*) you; *vedi anche* **il**
là *av* there; **di là** *(da quel luogo)* from there; *(in quel luogo)* in there; *(dall'altra parte)* over there; **di là di** beyond; **per di là** that way; **più in là** further on; *(tempo)* later on; **fatti in là** move up; **là dentro/sopra/sotto** in/up (*o* on)/under there; *vedi anche* **quello**
'labbro (*pl(f)* **labbra**) *(solo nel senso Anat)* *sm* lip
labi'rinto *sm* labyrinth, maze
labora'torio *sm (di ricerca)* laboratory; *(di arti, mestieri)* workshop; **laboratorio linguistico** language laboratory
labori'oso, -a *ag (faticoso)* laborious; *(attivo)* hard-working
'lacca, -che *sf* lacquer
'laccio ['lattʃo] *sm* noose; *(legaccio, tirante)* lasso; *(di scarpa)* lace; **laccio emostatico** tourniquet
lace'rare [latʃe'rare] *vt* to tear to shreds, lacerate; **lacerarsi** *vpr* to tear
'lacrima *sf* tear; **in lacrime** in tears; **lacri'mogeno, -a** *ag* **gas lacrimogeno** tear gas
la'cuna *sf (fig)* gap
'ladro *sm* thief
laggiù [lad'dʒu] *av* down there; *(di là)* over there

la'gnarsi [laɲ'narsi] *vpr* ~ **(di)** to complain (about)

'lago, -ghi *sm* lake

la'guna *sf* lagoon

'laico, -a, -ci, -che *ag* (*apostolato*) lay; (*vita*) secular; (*scuola*) non-denominational ▶ *sm/f* layman/ woman

'lama *sm inv* (*Zool*) llama; (*Rel*) lama ▶ *sf* blade

lamentarsi *vpr* (*emettere lamenti*) to moan, groan; (*rammaricarsi*): ~ **(di)** to complain (about)

lamen'tela *sf* complaining *no pl*

la'metta *sf* razor blade

'lamina *sf* (*lastra sottile*) thin sheet (*o layer o plate*); **lamina d'oro** gold leaf; gold foil

'lampada *sf* lamp; **lampada a gas** gas lamp; **lampada da tavolo** table lamp

lampa'dario *sm* chandelier

lampa'dina *sf* light bulb; **lampadina tascabile** pocket torch (*BRIT*) *o* flashlight (*US*)

lam'pante *ag* (*fig: evidente*) crystal clear, evident

lampeggi'are [lamped'dʒare] *vi* (*luce, fari*) to flash ▶ *vb impers* **lampeggia** there's lightning; **lampeggia'tore** *sm* (*Aut*) indicator

lampi'one *sm* street light *o* lamp (*BRIT*)

'lampo *sm* (*Meteor*) flash of lightning; (*di luce: fig*) flash

lam'pone *sm* raspberry

'lana *sf* wool; **pura ~ vergine** pure new wool; **lana d'acciaio** steel wool; **lana di vetro** glass wool

lan'cetta [lan'tʃetta] *sf* (*indice*) pointer, needle; (*di orologio*) hand

'lancia ['lantʃa] *sf* (*arma*) lance; (*: picca*) spear; (*di pompa antincendio*) nozzle; (*imbarcazione*) launch; **lancia di salvataggio** lifeboat

lanciafi'amme [lantʃa'fjamme] *sm inv* flamethrower

lanci'are [lan'tʃare] *vt* to throw, hurl, fling; (*Sport*) to throw; (*far partire: automobile*) to get up to full speed; (*bombe*) to drop; (*razzo, prodotto, moda*) to launch; **lanciarsi** *vpr* **lanciarsi contro/su** to throw *o* hurl *o* fling o.s. against/on; **lanciarsi in** (*fig*) to embark on

lanci'nante [lantʃi'nante] *ag* (*dolore*) shooting, throbbing; (*grido*) piercing

'lancio ['lantʃo] *sm* throwing *no pl*; throw; dropping *no pl*; drop; launching *no pl*; launch; **lancio del disco** (*Sport*) throwing the discus; **lancio del peso** putting the shot

'languido, -a *ag* (*fiacco*) languid, weak; (*tenero, malinconico*) languishing

lan'terna *sf* lantern; (*faro*) lighthouse

'lapide *sf* (*di sepolcro*) tombstone; (*commemorativa*) plaque

'lapsus *sm inv* slip

'lardo *sm* bacon fat, lard

lar'ghezza [lar'gettsa] *sf* width; breadth; looseness; generosity; **larghezza di vedute** broad-mindedness

'largo, -a, -ghi, -ghe *ag* wide; broad; (*maniche*) wide; (*abito: troppo ampio*) loose; (*fig*) generous ▶ *sm* width; breadth; (*mare aperto*): **il ~** the open sea ▶ *sf* **stare** *o* **tenersi alla larga (da qn/qc)** to keep one's distance (from sb/sth), keep away (from sb/sth); **~ due metri** two metres wide; **~ di spalle** broad-shouldered; **di larghe vedute** broad-minded; **su larga scala** on a large scale; **di manica larga** generous, open-handed; **al ~ di Genova** off (the coast of) Genoa; **farsi ~ tra la folla** to push one's way through the crowd

'larice ['laritʃe] *sm* (*Bot*) larch

larin'gite [larin'dʒite] sf laryngitis

'larva sf larva; (fig) shadow

la'sagne [la'zaɲɲe] sfpl lasagna sg

lasci'are [laʃʃare] vt to leave; (abbandonare) to leave, abandon, give up; (cessare di tenere) to let go of ▶ vb aus ~ **fare qn** to let sb do; ~ **andare** o **correre** o **perdere** to let things go their own way; ~ **stare qc/qn** to leave sth/sb alone; **lasciarsi** vpr (persone) to part; (coppia) to split up; **lasciarsi andare** to let o.s. go

'laser ['lazer] ag, sm inv (**raggio**) ~ laser (beam)

lassa'tivo, -a ag, sm laxative

'lasso sm; **lasso di tempo** interval, lapse of time

lassù av up there

'lastra sf (di pietra) slab; (di metallo, Fot) plate; (di ghiaccio, vetro) sheet; (radiografica) X-ray (plate)

lastri'cato sm paving

late'rale ag lateral, side cpd; (uscita, ingresso ecc) side cpd ▶ sm (Calcio) half-back

la'tino, -a ag, sm Latin

lati'tante sm/f fugitive (from justice)

lati'tudine sf latitude

'lato, -a ag (fig) wide, broad ▶ sm side; (fig) aspect, point of view; **in senso ~** broadly speaking

'latta sf tin (plate); (recipiente) tin, can

lat'tante ag unweaned

'latte sm milk; **latte detergente** cleansing milk o lotion; **latte intero** full-cream milk; **latte a lunga conservazione** UHT milk, long-life milk; **latte magro** o **scremato** skimmed milk; **latte in polvere** dried o powdered milk; **latte solare** suntan lotion; **latti'cini** smpl dairy products

lat'tina sf (di birra ecc) can

lat'tuga, -ghe sf lettuce

'laurea sf degree; **laurea in ingegneria** engineering degree;

laurea in lettere ≈ arts degree

○ **laurea**
○ The **laurea** is awarded to students
○ who successfully complete their
○ degree courses. Traditionally,
○ this takes between four and six
○ years; a major element of the final
○ examinations is the presentation
○ and discussion of a dissertation.
○ A shorter, more vocational course
○ of study, taking from two to three
○ years, is also available; at the end of
○ this time students receive a diploma
○ called the **laurea breve**.

laure'arsi vpr to graduate

laure'ato, -a ag, sm/f graduate

'lauro sm laurel

'lauto, -a ag (pranzo, mancia) lavish

'lava sf lava

la'vabo sm washbasin

la'vaggio [la'vaddʒo] sm washing no pl; **lavaggio del cervello** brainwashing no pl; **lavaggio a secco** dry-cleaning

la'vagna [la'vaɲɲa] sf (Geo) slate; (di scuola) blackboard

la'vanda sf (anche Med) wash; (Bot) lavender; **lavande'ria** sf laundry; **lavanderia automatica** launderette; **lavanderia a secco** dry-cleaner's; **lavan'dino** sm sink

lavapi'atti sm/f dishwasher

la'vare vt to wash; **lavarsi** vpr to wash; ~ **a secco** to dry-clean; **lavarsi i denti** to clean one's teeth

lava'secco sm o f inv dry cleaner's

lavasto'viglie [lavasto'viʎʎe] sm o f inv (macchina) dishwasher

lava'trice [lava'tritʃe] sf washing machine

la'vello sm (kitchen) sink

lavo'rare vi to work; (fig: bar, studio ecc) to do good business ▶ vt to work; **lavorarsi qn** (persuaderlo) to work on sb; ~ **a** to work on; ~ **a maglia** to

knit; **lavora'tivo, -a** *ag* working;
lavora'tore, -'trice *sm/f* worker ▶ *ag*
working
la'voro *sm* work; (*occupazione*) job,
work *no pl*; (*opera*) piece of work,
job; (*Econ*) labour; **che ~ fa?** what do
you do?; **lavori forzati** hard labour
sg; **lavoro interinale** *o* **in affitto**
temporary work
le *det fpl* the ▶ *pron* (*oggetto*) them; (: *a
lei, a essa*) (to) her; (: *forma di cortesia*)
(to) you; *vedi anche* **il**
le'ale *ag* loyal; (*sincero*) sincere;
(*onesto*) fair
'lecca 'lecca *sm inv* lollipop
leccapi'edi (*peg*) *sm/f inv* toady,
bootlicker
lec'care *vt* to lick; (*gatto: latte ecc*) to
lick *o* lap up; (*fig*) to flatter; **leccarsi i
baffi** to lick one's lips
leccherò *ecc* [lekke'rɔ] *vb vedi* **leccare**
'leccio ['lettʃo] *sm* holm oak, ilex
leccor'nia *sf* titbit, delicacy
'lecito, -a ['lɛtʃito] *ag* permitted,
allowed
'lega, -ghe *sf* league; (*di metalli*) alloy
le'gaccio [le'gattʃo] *sm* string, lace
le'gale *ag* legal ▶ *sm* lawyer;
legaliz'zare *vt* to authenticate;
(*regolarizzare*) to legalize
le'game *sm* (*corda, fig: affettivo*) tie,
bond; (*nesso logico*) link, connection
le'gare *vt* (*prigioniero, capelli, cane*) to
tie (up); (*libro*) to bind; (*Chim*) to alloy;
(*fig: collegare*) to bind, join ▶ *vi* (*far lega*)
to unite; (*fig*) to get on well
le'genda [le'dʒɛnda] *sf* (*di carta
geografica ecc*) = **leggenda**
'legge ['leddʒe] *sf* law
leg'genda [led'dʒɛnda] *sf* (*narrazione*)
legend; (*di carta geografica ecc*) key
'leggere ['lɛddʒere] *vt, vi* to read
legge'rezza [leddʒe'rettsa] *sf*
lightness; thoughtlessness; fickleness
leg'gero, -a [led'dʒɛro] *ag* light; (*agile,

snello*) nimble, agile, light; (*tè, caffè*)
weak; (*fig: non grave, piccolo*) slight;
(: *spensierato*) thoughtless;
(: *incostante*) fickle; free and easy;
alla leggera thoughtlessly
leg'gio, -'gii [led'dʒio] *sm* lectern;
(*Mus*) music stand
legherò *ecc* [lege'rɔ] *vb vedi* **legare**
legisla'tivo, -a [ledʒizla'tivo] *ag*
legislative
legisla'tura [ledʒizla'tura] *sf*
legislature
le'gittimo, -a [le'dʒittimo] *ag*
legitimate; (*fig: giustificato, lecito*)
justified, legitimate; **legittima
difesa** (*Dir*) self-defence
'legna ['leɲɲa] *sf* firewood
'legno ['leɲɲo] *sm* wood; (*pezzo di
legno*) piece of wood; **di ~** wooden;
legno compensato plywood
le'gumi *smpl* pulses
'lei *pron* (*soggetto*) she; (*oggetto: per dare
rilievo, con preposizione*) her; (*forma di
cortesia: anche*: **L~**) you ▶ *sm* **dare del ~
a qn** to address sb as "lei"; **~ stessa** she
herself; you yourself
● **lei**
● **lei** is the third person singular
● pronoun. It is used in Italian to
● address an adult whom you do not
● know or with whom you are on
● formal terms.
lenta'mente *av* slowly
'lente *sf* (*Ottica*) lens *sg*; **lente
d'ingrandimento** magnifying glass;
lenti *sfpl* (*occhiali*) lenses; **lenti a
contatto** contact lenses; **lenti
(a contatto) morbide/rigide**
soft/hard contact lenses
len'tezza [len'tettsa] *sf* slowness
len'ticchia [len'tikkja] *sf* (*Bot*) lentil
len'tiggine [len'tiddʒine] *sf* freckle
'lento, -a *ag* slow; (*molle: fune*) slack;
(*non stretto: vite, abito*) loose ▶ *sm*
(*ballo*) slow dance

'lenza ['lɛntsa] *sf* fishing-line

lenzu'olo [len'tswɔlo] *sm* sheet

le'one *sm* lion; (*dello zodiaco*): **L~** Leo

lepo'rino, -a *ag* **labbro ~** harelip

'lepre *sf* hare

'lercio, -a, -ci, -cie ['lɛrtʃo] *ag* filthy

lesi'one *sf* (*Med*) lesion; (*Dir*) injury, damage; (*Edil*) crack

les'sare *vt* (*Cuc*) to boil

'lessi *ecc vb vedi* **leggere**

'lessico, -ci *sm* vocabulary; lexicon

'lesso, -a *ag* boiled ▶ *sm* boiled meat

le'tale *ag* lethal; fatal

leta'maio *sm* dunghill

le'tame *sm* manure, dung

le'targo, -ghi *sm* lethargy; (*Zool*) hibernation

'lettera *sf* letter; **lettere** *sfpl* (*letteratura*) literature *sg*; (*studi umanistici*) arts (subjects); **alla ~** literally; **in lettere** in words, in full

letteral'mente *av* literally

lette'rario, -a *ag* literary

lette'rato, -a *ag* well-read, scholarly

lettera'tura *sf* literature

let'tiga, -ghe *sf* (*barella*) stretcher

let'tino *sm* cot (*BRIT*), crib (*US*); **lettino solare** sunbed

'letto, -a *pp di* **leggere** ▶ *sm* bed; **andare a ~** to go to bed; **letto a castello** bunk beds *pl*; **letto a una piazza** single; **letto a due piazze** *o* **matrimoniale** double bed

let'tore, -'trice *sm/f* reader; (*Ins*) (foreign language) assistant (*BRIT*), (foreign) teaching assistant (*US*) ▶ *sm* (*Tecn*): **~ ottico** optical character reader; **lettore CD/DVD** CD/DVD player; **lettore MP3/MP4** MP3/MP4 player

let'tura *sf* reading

Attenzione! In inglese esiste la parola *lecture*, che però significa *lezione* oppure *conferenza*.

leuce'mia [leutʃe'mia] *sf* leukaemia

'leva *sf* lever; (*Mil*) conscription; **far ~ su qn** to work on sb; **leva del cambio** (*Aut*) gear lever

le'vante *sm* east; (*vento*) East wind; **il L~** the Levant

le'vare *vt* (*occhi, braccio*) to raise; (*sollevare, togliere: tassa, divieto*) to lift; (*indumenti*) to take off, remove; (*rimuovere*) to take away; (: *dal di sopra*) to take off; (: *dal di dentro*) to take out

leva'toio, -a *ag* **ponte ~** drawbridge

lezi'one [let'tsjone] *sf* lesson; (*Univ*) lecture; **fare ~** to teach; to lecture; **dare una ~ a qn** to teach sb a lesson; **lezioni private** private lessons

li *pron pl* (*oggetto*) them

lì *av* there; **di** *o* **da lì** from there; **per di lì** that way; **di lì a pochi giorni** a few days later; **lì per lì** there and then; at first; **essere lì (lì) per fare** to be on the point of doing, be about to do; **lì dentro** in there; **lì sotto** under there; **lì sopra** on there; up there; *vedi anche* **quello**

liba'nese *ag, sm/f* Lebanese *inv*

Li'bano *sm* **il ~** the Lebanon

'libbra *sf* (*peso*) pound

li'beccio [li'bettʃo] *sm* south-west wind

li'bellula *sf* dragonfly

libe'rale *ag, sm/f* liberal

liberaliz'zare [liberalid'dzare] *vt* to liberalize

libe'rare *vt* (*rendere libero: prigioniero*) to release; (: *popolo*) to free, liberate; (*sgombrare: passaggio*) to clear; (: *stanza*) to vacate; (*produrre: energia*) to release; **liberarsi** *vpr* **liberarsi di qc/qn** to get rid of sth/sb; **liberazi'one** *sf* liberation, freeing; release; rescuing

● **Liberazione**
● The **Liberazione** is a national
● holiday which falls on April 25th.
● It commemorates the liberation
● of Italy at the end of the Second
● World War.

'libero, -a *ag* free; (*strada*) clear; (*non occupato: posto ecc*) vacant; free; not taken; empty; not engaged; **~ di fare qc** free to do sth; **~ da** free from; **è ~ questo posto?** is this seat free?; **~ arbitrio** free will; **~ professionista** self-employed professional person; **~ scambio** free trade; **libertà** *sf inv* freedom; (*tempo disponibile*) free time ▶ *sfpl* (*licenza*) liberties; **in libertà provvisoria/vigilata** released without bail/on probation

'Libia *sf* **la ~** Libya; **'libico, -a, -ci, -che** *ag, sm/f* Libyan

li'bidine *sf* lust

li'braio *sm* bookseller

li'brarsi *vpr* to hover

libre'ria *sf* (*bottega*) bookshop; (*mobile*) bookcase

Attenzione! In inglese esiste la parola *library*, che però significa *biblioteca*.

li'bretto *sm* booklet; (*taccuino*) notebook; (*Mus*) libretto; **libretto degli assegni** cheque book; **libretto di circolazione** (*Aut*) logbook; **libretto di risparmio** (savings) bank-book, passbook; **libretto universitario** student's report book

'libro *sm* book; **libro di cassa** cash book; **libro mastro** ledger; **libro paga** payroll; **libro di testo** textbook

li'cenza [li'tʃɛntsa] *sf* (*permesso*) permission, leave; (*di pesca, caccia, circolazione*) permit, licence; (*Mil*) leave; (*Ins*) school leaving certificate; (*libertà*) liberty; licence; licentiousness; **andare in ~** (*Mil*) to go on leave

licenzia'mento [litʃentsja'mento] *sm* dismissal

licenzi'are [litʃen'tsjare] *vt* (*impiegato*) to dismiss; (*Comm: per eccesso di personale*) to make redundant; (*Ins*) to award a certificate to; **licenziarsi** *vpr* (*impiegato*) to resign, hand in one's notice; (*Ins*) to obtain one's school-leaving certificate

li'ceo [li'tʃɛo] *sm* (*Ins*) secondary (*BRIT*) o high (*US*) school (*for 14- to 19-year-olds*)

'lido *sm* beach, shore

Liechtenstein ['liktənstain] *sm* **il ~** Liechtenstein

li'eto, -a *ag* happy, glad; **"molto ~"** (*nelle presentazioni*) "pleased to meet you"

li'eve *ag* light; (*di poco conto*) slight; (*sommesso: voce*) faint, soft

lievi'tare *vi* (*anche fig*) to rise ▶ *vt* to leaven

li'evito *sm* yeast; **lievito di birra** brewer's yeast

'ligio, -a, -gi, -gie ['lidʒo] *ag* faithful, loyal

'lilla *sm inv* lilac

'lillà *sm inv* lilac

'lima *sf* file; **lima da unghie** nail file

limacci'oso, -a [limat'tʃoso] *ag* slimy; muddy

li'mare *vt* to file (down); (*fig*) to polish

limi'tare *vt* to limit, restrict; (*circoscrivere*) to bound, surround; **limitarsi** *vpr* **limitarsi nel mangiare** to limit one's eating; **limitarsi a qc/a fare qc** to limit o.s. to sth/to doing sth

'limite *sm* limit; (*confine*) border, boundary; **limite di velocità** speed limit

limo'nata *sf* lemonade (*BRIT*), (lemon) soda (*US*); lemon squash (*BRIT*), lemonade (*US*)

li'mone *sm* (*pianta*) lemon tree; (*frutto*) lemon

'limpido, -a *ag* clear; (*acqua*) limpid, clear

'lince ['lintʃe] *sf* lynx

linci'are *vt* to lynch

'linea *sf* line; (*di mezzi pubblici di trasporto: itinerario*) route; (*: servizio*) service; **a grandi linee** in outline; **mantenere la ~** to look after one's figure; **aereo di ~** airliner; **nave di ~** liner; **volo di ~** scheduled flight; **linea aerea** airline; **linea di partenza/ d'arrivo** (Sport) starting/finishing line; **linea di tiro** line of fire

linea'menti smpl features; (fig) outlines

line'are ag linear; (fig) coherent, logical

line'etta sf (trattino) dash; (d'unione) hyphen

lin'gotto sm ingot, bar

'lingua sf (Anat, Cuc) tongue; (idioma) language; **mostrare la ~** to stick out one's tongue; **di ~ italiana** Italian-speaking; **che lingue parla?** what languages do you speak?; **una ~ di terra** a spit of land; **lingua madre** mother tongue

lingu'aggio [lin'gwaddʒo] sm language

lingu'etta sf (di strumento) reed; (di scarpa, Tecn) tongue; (di busta) flap

'lino sm (pianta) flax; (tessuto) linen

li'noleum sm inv linoleum, lino

liposuzi'one [liposut'tsjone] sf liposuction

lique'fatto, -a pp di **liquefare**

liqui'dare vt (società, beni: persona: uccidere) to liquidate; (persona: sbarazzarsene) to get rid of; (conto, problema) to settle; (Comm: merce) to sell off, clear; **liquidazi'one** sf liquidation; settlement; clearance sale

liquidità sf liquidity

'liquido, -a ag, sm liquid; **liquido per freni** brake fluid

liqui'rizia [likwi'rittsja] sf liquorice

li'quore sm liqueur

'lira sf (Storia: unità monetaria) lira; (Mus) lyre; **lira sterlina** pound sterling

'lirico, -a, -ci, -che ag lyric(al); (Mus) lyric; **cantante/teatro ~** opera singer/house

Lis'bona sf Lisbon

'lisca, -sche sf (di pesce) fishbone

lisci'are [liʃʃare] vt to smooth; (fig) to flatter

'liscio, -a, -sci, -sce ['liʃʃo] ag smooth; (capelli) straight; (mobile) plain; (bevanda alcolica) neat; (fig) straightforward, simple ▶ av **andare ~** to go smoothly; **passarla liscia** to get away with it

'liso, -a ag worn out, threadbare

'lista sf (elenco) list; **lista elettorale** electoral roll; **lista delle spese** shopping list; **lista dei vini** wine list; **lista delle vivande** menu

lis'tino sm list; **listino dei cambi** (foreign) exchange rate; **listino dei prezzi** price list

'lite sf quarrel, argument; (Dir) lawsuit

liti'gare vi to quarrel; (Dir) to litigate

li'tigio [li'tidʒo] sm quarrel

lito'rale ag coastal, coast cpd ▶ sm coast

'litro sm litre

livel'lare vt to level, make level

li'vello sm level; (fig) level, standard; **ad alto ~** (fig) high-level; **livello del mare** sea level

'livido, -a ag livid; (per percosse) bruised, black and blue; (cielo) leaden ▶ sm bruise

Li'vorno sf Livorno, Leghorn

'lizza ['littsa] sf lists pl; **scendere in ~** to enter the lists

lo (dav s impura, gn, pn, ps, x, z; dav V **l'**) det m the ▶ pron (oggetto: persona) him; (: cosa) it; **lo sapevo** I knew it; **lo so** I know; **sii buono, anche se lui non lo è** be good, even if he isn't; vedi anche **il**

lo'cale ag local ▶ sm room; (luogo pubblico) premises pl; **locale notturno** nightclub; **località** sf inv locality

lo'canda *sf* inn
locomo'tiva *sf* locomotive
locuzi'one [lokut'tsjone] *sf* phrase, expression
lo'dare *vt* to praise
'lode *sf* praise; (*Ins*): **laurearsi con 110 e ≈** to graduate with a first-class honours degree (*BRIT*), graduate summa cum laude (*US*)
'loden *sm inv* (*stoffa*) loden; (*cappotto*) loden overcoat
lo'devole *ag* praiseworthy
loga'ritmo *sm* logarithm
'loggia, -ge ['lɔddʒa] *sf* (*Archit*) loggia; (*circolo massonico*) lodge; **loggi'one** *sm* (*di teatro*): **il loggione** the Gods *sg*
'logico, -a, -ci, -che ['lɔdʒiko] *ag* logical
logo'rare *vt* to wear out; (*sciupare*) to waste; **logorarsi** *vpr* to wear out; (*fig*) to wear o.s. out
'logoro, -a *ag* (*stoffa*) worn out, threadbare; (*persona*) worn out
Lombar'dia *sf* **la ~** Lombardy
lom'bata *sf* (*taglio di carne*) loin
lom'brico, -chi *sm* earthworm
londi'nese *ag* London *cpd* ▶ *sm/f* Londoner
'Londra *sf* London
lon'gevo, -a [lon'dʒevo] *ag* long-lived
longi'tudine [londʒi'tudine] *sf* longitude
lonta'nanza [lonta'nantsa] *sf* distance; absence
lon'tano, -a *ag* (*distante*) distant, faraway; (*assente*) absent; (*vago: sospetto*) slight, remote; (*tempo: remoto*) far-off, distant; (*parente*) distant, remote ▶ *av* far; **è lontana la casa?** is it far to the house?, is the house far from here?; **è ~ un chilometro** it's a kilometre away *o* a kilometre from here; **più ~** farther; **da** *o* **di ~** from a distance; **~ da** a long way from; **è molto ~ da qui?** is it far from here?; **alla lontana** slightly, vaguely
lo'quace [lo'kwatʃe] *ag* talkative, loquacious; (*fig: gesto ecc*) eloquent
'lordo, -a *ag* dirty, filthy; (*peso, stipendio*) gross
'loro *pron pl* (*oggetto, con preposizione*) them; (*complemento di termine*) to them; (*soggetto*) they; (*forma di cortesia: anche: L~*) you; to you; **il(la) ~, i(le) ~** *det* their; (*forma di cortesia: anche: L~*) your ▶ *pron* theirs; (*forma di cortesia: anche: L~*) yours; **~ stessi(e)** they themselves; you yourselves
'losco, -a, -schi, -sche *ag* (*fig*) shady, suspicious
'lotta *sf* struggle, fight; (*Sport*) wrestling; **lotta libera** all-in wrestling; **lot'tare** *vi* to fight, struggle; to wrestle
lotte'ria *sf* lottery; (*di gara ippica*) sweepstake
'lotto *sm* (*gioco*) (state) lottery; (*parte*) lot; (*Edil*) site

● **Lotto**
● The **Lotto** is an official lottery run
● by the Italian Finance Ministry.
● It consists of a weekly draw of
● numbers and is very popular.

lozi'one [lot'tsjone] *sf* lotion
lubrifi'cante *sm* lubricant
lubrifi'care *vt* to lubricate
luc'chetto [luk'ketto] *sm* padlock
lucci'care [luttʃi'kare] *vi* to sparkle, glitter, twinkle
'luccio ['luttʃo] *sm* (*Zool*) pike
'lucciola ['luttʃola] *sf* (*Zool*) firefly; glowworm
'luce ['lutʃe] *sf* light; (*finestra*) window; **alla ~ di** by the light of; **fare ~ su qc** (*fig*) to shed *o* throw light on sth; **~ del sole/della luna** sun/moonlight
lucer'nario [lutʃer'narjo] *sm* skylight
lu'certola [lu'tʃertola] *sf* lizard
luci'dare [lutʃi'dare] *vt* to polish

lucida'trice [lutʃidaˈtritʃe] *sf* floor polisher

'lucido, -a [ˈlutʃido] *ag* shining, bright; (*lucidato*) polished; (*fig*) lucid ▶ *sm* shine, lustre; (*disegno*) tracing; **lucido per scarpe** shoe polish

'lucro *sm* profit, gain

'luglio [ˈluʎʎo] *sm* July

'lugubre *ag* gloomy

'lui *pron* (*soggetto*) he; (*oggetto: per dare rilievo, con preposizione*) him; **~ stesso** he himself

lu'maca, -che *sf* slug; (*chiocciola*) snail

lumi'noso, -a *ag* (*che emette luce*) luminous; (*cielo, colore, stanza*) bright; (*sorgente*) of light, light *cpd*; (*fig: sorriso*) bright, radiant

'luna *sf* moon; **luna nuova/piena** new/full moon; **luna di miele** honeymoon; **siamo in ~ di miele** we're on honeymoon

'luna park *sm inv* amusement park, funfair

lu'nare *ag* lunar, moon *cpd*

lu'nario *sm* almanac; **sbarcare il ~** to make ends meet

lu'natico, -a, -ci, -che *ag* whimsical, temperamental

lunedì *sm inv* Monday; **di** *o* **il ~** on Mondays

lun'ghezza [lunˈgettsa] *sf* length; **lunghezza d'onda** (*Fisica*) wavelength

'lungo, -a, -ghi, -ghe *ag* long; (*lento: persona*) slow; (*diluito: caffè, brodo*) weak, watery, thin ▶ *sm* length ▶ *prep* along; **~ 3 metri** 3 metres long; **a ~** for a long time; **a ~ andare** in the long run; **di gran lunga** (*molto*) by far; **andare in ~** *o* **per le lunghe** to drag on; **saperla lunga** to know what's what; **in ~ e in largo** far and wide, all over; **~ il corso dei secoli** throughout the centuries

lungo'mare *sm* promenade

lu'notto *sm* (*Aut*) rear *o* back window; **lunotto termico** heated rear window

lu'ogo, -ghi *sm* place; (*posto: di incidente ecc*) scene, site; (*punto, passo di libro*) passage; **in ~ di** instead of; **in primo ~** in the first place; **aver ~** to take place; **dar ~ a** to give rise to; **luogo di nascita** birthplace; (*Amm*) place of birth; **luogo di provenienza** place of origin; **luogo comune** commonplace

'lupo, -a *sm/f* wolf

'luppolo *sm* (*Bot*) hop

'lurido, -a *ag* filthy

lusin'gare *vt* to flatter

Lussem'burgo *sm* (*stato*): **il ~** Luxembourg ▶ *sf* (*città*) Luxembourg

'lusso *sm* luxury; **di ~** luxury *cpd*; **lussu'oso, -a** *ag* luxurious

lus'suria *sf* lust

lus'trino *sm* sequin

'lutto *sm* mourning; **essere in/ portare il ~** to be in/wear mourning

m. *abbr* = **mese**; **metro**; **miglia**; **monte**

ma *cong* but; **ma insomma!** for goodness sake!; **ma no!** of course not!

'macabro, -a *ag* gruesome, macabre

macché [mak'ke] *escl* not at all!, certainly not!

macche'roni [makke'roni] *smpl* macaroni *sg*

'macchia ['makkja] *sf* stain, spot; (*chiazza di diverso colore*) spot, splash, patch; (*tipo di boscaglia*) scrub; **alla ~** (*fig*) in hiding; **macchi'are** *vt* (*sporcare*) to stain, mark; **macchiarsi** *vpr* (*persona*) to get o.s. dirty; (*stoffa*) to stain; to get stained *o* marked

macchi'ato, -a [mak'kjato] *ag* (*pelle, pelo*) spotted; **~ di** stained with; **caffè ~** coffee with a dash of milk

'macchina ['makkina] *sf* machine; (*motore, locomotiva*) engine; (*automobile*) car; (*fig: meccanismo*) machinery; **andare in ~** (*Aut*) to go by car; (*Stampa*) to go to press; **macchina da cucire** sewing machine; **macchina fotografica** camera; **macchina da presa** cine *o* movie camera; **macchina da scrivere** typewriter; **macchina a vapore** steam engine

macchi'nario [makki'narjo] *sm* machinery

macchi'nista, -i [makki'nista] *sm* (*di treno*) engine-driver; (*di nave*) engineer

Macedonia [matʃe'dɔnja] *sf* **la ~** Macedonia

mace'donia [matʃe'dɔnja] *sf* fruit salad

macel'laio [matʃel'lajo] *sm* butcher

macelle'ria *sf* butcher's (shop)

ma'cerie [ma'tʃɛrje] *sfpl* rubble *sg*, debris *sg*

ma'cigno [ma'tʃiɲɲo] *sm* (*masso*) rock, boulder

maci'nare [matʃi'nare] *vt* to grind; (*carne*) to mince (*BRIT*), grind (*US*)

macrobi'otico, -a *ag* macrobiotic ▶ *sf* macrobiotics *sg*

Ma'donna *sf* (*Rel*) Our Lady

mador'nale *ag* enormous, huge

'madre *sf* mother; (*matrice di bolletta*) counterfoil ▶ *ag inv* mother *cpd*; **ragazza ~** unmarried mother; **scena ~** (*Teatro*) principal scene; (*fig*) terrible scene

madre'lingua *sf* mother tongue, native language

madre'perla *sf* mother-of-pearl

ma'drina *sf* godmother

maestà *sf inv* majesty

ma'estra *sf vedi* **maestro**

maes'trale *sm* north-west wind, mistral

ma'estro, -a *sm/f* (*Ins: anche:* **~ di scuola o elementare**) primary (*BRIT*) *o* grade school (*US*) teacher; (*esperto*) expert ▶ *sm* (*artigiano, fig: guida*) master; (*Mus*) maestro ▶ *ag* (*principale*) main; (*di grande abilità*) masterly, skilful; **maestra d'asilo** nursery teacher; **~ di cerimonie** master of ceremonies

'mafia *sf* Mafia

'maga *sf* sorceress

ma'gari *escl* (*esprime desiderio*): **~ fosse vero!** if only it were true!; **ti piacerebbe andare in Scozia? — ~!** would you like to go to Scotland? — and how! ▶ *av* (*anche*) even; (*forse*) perhaps

magaz'zino [magad'dzino] *sm* warehouse; **grande ~** department store

Attenzione! In inglese esiste la parola *magazine* che però significa *rivista*.

'maggio ['maddʒo] *sm* May

maggio'rana [maddʒo'rana] *sf* (*Bot*) (sweet) marjoram

maggio'ranza [maddʒo'rantsa] *sf* majority

maggior'domo [maddʒor'dɔmo] *sm* butler

maggi'ore [mad'dʒore] *ag* (*comparativo: più grande*) bigger, larger; taller; greater; (: *più vecchio*: *sorella, fratello*) older, elder; (: *di grado superiore*) senior; (: *più importante*: *Mil, Mus*) major; (*superlativo*) biggest, largest; tallest; greatest; oldest, eldest ▶ *sm/f* (*di grado*) superior; (*di età*) elder; (*Mil*) major; (: *Aer*) squadron leader; **la maggior parte** the majority; **andare per la ~** (*cantante ecc*) to be very popular; **maggio'renne** *ag* of age ▶ *sm/f* person who has come of age

ma'gia [ma'dʒia] *sf* magic; **'magico, -a, -ci, -che** *ag* magic; (*fig*) fascinating, charming, magical

magis'trato [madʒis'trato] *sm* magistrate

'maglia ['maʎʎa] *sf* stitch; (*lavoro ai ferri*) knitting *no pl*; (*tessuto, Sport*) jersey; (*maglione*) jersey, sweater; (*di catena*) link; (*di rete*) mesh; **maglia diritta/rovescia** plain/purl; **magli'etta** *sf* (*canottiera*) vest; (*tipo camicia*) T-shirt

magli'one *sm* sweater, jumper

ma'gnetico, -a, -ci, -che *ag* magnetic

ma'gnifico, -a, -ci, -che [maɲ'ɲifiko] *ag* magnificent, splendid; (*ospite*) generous

ma'gnolia [maɲ'nɔlja] *sf* magnolia

'mago, -ghi *sm* (*stregone*) magician, wizard; (*illusionista*) magician

ma'grezza [ma'grettsa] *sf* thinness

'magro, -a *ag* (*very*) thin, skinny; (*carne*) lean; (*formaggio*) low-fat; (*fig*: *scarso, misero*) meagre, poor; (: *meschino*: *scusa*) poor, lame; **mangiare di ~** not to eat meat

'mai *av* (*nessuna volta*) never; (*talvolta*) ever; **non ... ~** never; **~ più** never again; **non sono ~ stato in Spagna** I've never been to Spain; **come ~?** why (*o how*) on earth?; **chi/dove/quando ~?** whoever/wherever/whenever?

mai'ale *sm* (*Zool*) pig; (*carne*) pork

'mail ['meil] *sf inv* = **e-mail**

maio'nese *sf* mayonnaise

'mais *sm inv* maize

mai'uscolo, -a *ag* (*lettera*) capital; (*fig*) enormous, huge

mala'fede *sf* bad faith

malan'dato, -a *ag* (*persona*: *di salute*) in poor health; (: *di condizioni finanziarie*) badly off; (*trascurato*) shabby

ma'lanno *sm* (*disgrazia*) misfortune; (*malattia*) ailment

mala'pena *sf* **a ~** hardly, scarcely

ma'laria *sf* (*Med*) malaria

ma'lato, -a *ag* ill, sick; (*gamba*) bad; (*pianta*) diseased ▶ *sm/f* sick person; (*in ospedale*) patient; **malat'tia** *sf* illness, disease; (*cattiva salute*) illness, sickness; (*di pianta*) disease

mala'vita *sf* underworld

mala'voglia [mala'vɔʎʎa] *sf* **di ~** unwillingly, reluctantly

Ma'laysia *sf* Malaysia

mal'concio, -a, -ci, -ce [mal'kontʃo] *ag* in a sorry state

malcon'tento *sm* discontent

malcos'tume *sm* immorality

mal'destro, -a *ag* (*inabile*) inexpert, inexperienced; (*goffo*) awkward

'male *av* badly ▶ *sm* (*ciò che è ingiusto, disonesto*) evil; (*danno, svantaggio*) harm; (*sventura*) misfortune; (*dolore fisico, morale*) pain, ache; **di ~ in peggio** from bad to worse; **sentirsi ~ to** feel ill; **far ~** (*dolere*) to hurt; **far ~ alla salute** to be bad for one's health; **far del ~ a qn** to hurt *o* harm sb; **restare** *o* **rimanere ~** to be sorry; to be disappointed; to be hurt; **andare a ~** to go bad; **come va? — non c'è ~** how are you? — not bad; **avere mal di gola/testa** to have a sore throat/a headache; **aver ~ ai piedi** to have sore feet; **mal d'auto** carsickness; **mal di**

m

cuore heart trouble; **male di dente** toothache; **mal di mare** seasickness

male'detto, -a pp di **maledire** ▸ ag cursed, damned; (fig: fam) damned, blasted

male'dire vt to curse; **maledizi'one** sf curse; **maledizione!** damn it!

maledu'cato, -a ag rude, ill-mannered

maleducazi'one [maledukat'tsjone] sf rudeness

ma'lefico, -a, -ci, -che ag (influsso, azione) evil

ma'lessere sm indisposition, slight illness; (fig) uneasiness

malfa'mato, -a ag notorious

malfat'tore, -'trice sm/f wrongdoer

mal'fermo, -a ag unsteady, shaky; (salute) poor, delicate

mal'grado prep in spite of, despite ▸ cong although; **mio** (o **tuo** ecc) ~ against my (o your ecc) will

ma'ligno, -a [ma'lippo] ag (malvagio) malicious, malignant; (Med) malignant

malinco'nia sf melancholy, gloom; **malin'conico, -a, -ci, -che** ag melancholy

malincu'ore: a ~ av reluctantly, unwillingly

malin'teso, -a ag misunderstood; (riguardo, senso del dovere) mistaken, wrong ▸ sm misunderstanding; **c'è stato un ~** there's been a misunderstanding

ma'lizia [ma'littsja] sf (malignità) malice; (furbizia) cunning; (espediente) trick; **malizi'oso, -a** ag malicious; cunning; (vivace, birichino) mischievous

malme'nare vt to beat up

ma'locchio [ma'lɔkkjo] sm evil eye

ma'lora sf **andare in ~** to go to the dogs

ma'lore sm (sudden) illness

mal'sano, -a ag unhealthy

'malta sf (Edil) mortar

mal'tempo sm bad weather

'malto sm malt

maltrat'tare vt to ill-treat

malu'more sm bad mood; (irritabilità) bad temper; (discordia) ill feeling; **di ~** in a bad mood

'malva sf (Bot) mallow ▸ ag, sm inv mauve

mal'vagio, -a, -gi, -gie [mal'vadʒo] ag wicked, evil

malvi'vente sm criminal

malvolenti'eri av unwillingly, reluctantly

'mamma sf mummy, mum; **~ mia!** my goodness!

mam'mella sf (Anat) breast; (di vacca, capra ecc) udder

mam'mifero sm mammal

ma'nata sf (colpo) slap; (quantità) handful

man'canza [man'kantsa] sf lack; (carenza) shortage, scarcity; (fallo) fault; (imperfezione) failing, shortcoming; **per ~ di tempo** through lack of time; **in ~ di meglio** for lack of anything better

man'care vi (essere insufficiente) to be lacking; (venir meno) to fail; (sbagliare) to be wrong, make a mistake; (non esserci) to be missing, not to be there; (essere lontano): **~ (da)** to be away (from) ▸ vt to miss; **~ di** to lack; **~ a** (promessa) to fail to keep; **tu mi manchi** I miss you; **mancò poco che morisse** he very nearly died; **mancano ancora 10 sterline** we're still £10 short; **manca un quarto alle 6** it's a quarter to 6

mancherò ecc [manke'rɔ] vb vedi **mancare**

'mancia, -ce ['mantʃa] sf tip; **quanto devo lasciare di ~?** how much should I tip?; **~ competente** reward

manci'ata [man'tʃata] sf handful
man'cino, -a [man'tʃino] ag (braccio) left; (persona) left-handed; (fig) underhand
manda'rancio [manda'rantʃo] sm clementine
man'dare vt to send; (far funzionare: macchina) to drive; (emettere) to send out; (: grido) to give, utter, let out; **~ a chiamare qn** to send for sb; **~ avanti** (fig: famiglia) to provide for; (: fabbrica) to run, look after; **~ giù** to send down; (anche fig) to swallow; **~ via** to send away; (licenziare) to fire
manda'rino sm mandarin (orange); (cinese) mandarin
man'data sf (quantità) lot, batch; (di chiave) turn; **chiudere a doppia ~** to double-lock
man'dato sm (incarico) commission; (Dir: provvedimento) warrant; (di deputato ecc) mandate; (ordine di pagamento) postal o money order; **mandato d'arresto** warrant for arrest
man'dibola sf mandible, jaw
'mandorla sf almond; **'mandorlo** sm almond tree
'mandria sf herd
maneggi'are [maned'dʒare] vt (creta, cera) to mould, work, fashion; (arnesi, utensili) to handle; (: adoperare) to use; (fig: persone, denaro) to handle, deal with; **ma'neggio** sm moulding; handling; use; (intrigo) plot, scheme; (per cavalli) riding school
ma'nesco, -a, -schi, -sche ag free with one's fists
ma'nette sfpl handcuffs
manga'nello sm club
mangi'are [man'dʒare] vt to eat; (intaccare) to eat into o away; (Carte, Scacchi ecc) to take ▶ vi to eat ▶ sm eating; (cibo) food; (cucina) cooking; **possiamo ~ qualcosa?** can we have

something to eat?; **mangiarsi le parole** to mumble; **mangiarsi le unghie** to bite one's nails
man'gime [man'dʒime] sm fodder
'mango, -ghi sm mango
ma'nia sf (Psic) mania; (fig) obsession, craze; (Geo): **la M~** the (English) Channel; **essere di ~ larga/stretta** to be easy-going/ strict; **manica a vento** (Aer) wind sock
ma'niaco, -a, -ci, -che ag suffering from a mania; **maniaco (di)** obsessed (by), crazy (about)
'manica sf sleeve; (fig: gruppo) gang, bunch; (Geo): **la M~, il Canale della M~** the (English) Channel; **essere di ~ larga/stretta** to be easy-going/ strict; **manica a vento** (Aer) wind sock
mani'chino [mani'kino] sm (di sarto, vetrina) dummy
'manico, -ci sm handle; (Mus) neck
mani'comio sm mental hospital; (fig) madhouse
mani'cure sm o f inv manicure ▶ sf inv manicurist
mani'era sf way, manner; (stile) style, manner; **maniere** sfpl (comportamento) manners; **in ~ che** so that; **in ~ da** so as to; **in tutte le maniere** at all costs
manifes'tare vt to show, display; (esprimere) to express; (rivelare) to reveal, disclose ▶ vi to demonstrate; **manifestazi'one** sf show, display; expression; (sintomo) sign, symptom; (dimostrazione pubblica) demonstration; (cerimonia) event
mani'festo, -a ag obvious, evident ▶ sm poster, bill; (scritto ideologico) manifesto
ma'niglia [ma'niʎʎa] sf handle; (sostegno: negli autobus ecc) strap
manipo'lare vt to manipulate; (alterare: vino) to adulterate
man'naro: **lupo ~** sm werewolf
'mano, -i sf hand; (strato: di vernice ecc) coat; **di prima ~** (notizia) first-hand; **di seconda ~** second-hand; **man ~**

little by little, gradually; **man ~ che** as; **darsi** o **stringersi la ~** to shake hands; **mettere le mani avanti** (fig) to safeguard o.s.; **restare a mani vuote** to be left empty-handed; **venire alle mani** to come to blows; **a ~** by hand; **mani in alto!** hands up!

mano'dopera sf labour

ma'nometro sm gauge, manometer

mano'mettere vt (alterare) to tamper with; (aprire indebitamente) to break open illegally

ma'nopola sf (dell'armatura) gauntlet; (guanto) mitt; (di impugnatura) hand-grip; (pomello) knob

manos'critto, -a ag handwritten ▶ sm manuscript

mano'vale sm labourer

mano'vella sf handle; (Tecn) crank

ma'novra sf manoeuvre (BRIT), maneuver (US); (Ferr) shunting

man'sarda sf attic

mansi'one sf task, duty, job

mansu'eto, -a ag gentle, docile

man'tello sm cloak; (fig: di neve ecc) blanket, mantle; (Zool) coat

mante'nere vt to maintain; (adempiere: promesse) to keep, abide by; (provvedere a) to support, maintain; **mantenersi** vpr **mantenersi calmo/giovane** to stay calm/young

'Mantova sf Mantua

manu'ale ag manual ▶ sm (testo) manual, handbook

ma'nubrio sm handle; (di bicicletta ecc) handlebars pl; (Sport) dumbbell

manutenzi'one [manuten'tsjone] sf maintenance, upkeep; (d'impianti) maintenance, servicing

'manzo ['mandzo] sm (Zool) steer; (carne) beef

'mappa sf (Geo) map; **mappa'mondo** sm map of the world; (globo girevole) globe

mara'tona sf marathon

'marca, -che sf (Comm: di prodotti) brand; (contrassegno, scontrino) ticket, check; **prodotto di ~** (di buona qualità) high-class product; **marca da bollo** official stamp

mar'care vt (munire di contrassegno) to mark; (a fuoco) to brand; (Sport: gol) to score; (: avversario) to mark; (accentuare) to stress; **~ visita** (Mil) to report sick

marcherò ecc [marke'rɔ] vb vedi **marcare**

mar'chese, -a [mar'keze] sm/f marquis o marquess/marchioness

marchi'are [mar'kjare] vt to brand

'marcia, -ce ['martʃa] sf (anche Mus, Mil) march; (funzionamento) running; (il camminare) walking; (Aut) gear; **mettere in ~** to start; **mettersi in ~** to get moving; **far ~ indietro** (Aut) to reverse; (fig) to back-pedal

marciapi'ede [martʃa'pjɛde] sm (di strada) pavement (BRIT), sidewalk (US); (Ferr) platform

marci'are [mar'tʃare] vi to march; (andare: treno, macchina) to go; (funzionare) to run, work

'marcio, -a, -ci, -ce ['martʃo] ag (frutta, legno) rotten, bad; (Med) festering; (fig) corrupt, rotten

mar'cire [mar'tʃire] vi (andare a male) to go bad, rot; (suppurare) to fester; (fig) to rot, waste away

'marco, -chi sm (unità monetaria) mark

'mare sm sea; **in ~** at sea; **andare al ~** (in vacanza ecc) to go to the seaside; **il M~ del Nord** the North Sea

ma'rea sf tide; **alta/bassa ~** high/low tide

mareggi'ata [mared'dʒata] sf heavy sea

mare'moto sm seaquake

maresci'allo [mareʃ'ʃallo] sm (Mil) marshal; (: sottufficiale) warrant officer

marga'rina *sf* margarine
marghe'rita [marge'rita] *sf* (ox-eye) daisy, marguerite; (*di stampante*) daisy wheel
'**margine** ['mardʒine] *sm* margin; (*di bosco, via*) edge, border
mariju'ana [mæri'wa:nə] *sf* marijuana
ma'rina *sf* navy; (*costa*) coast; (*quadro*) seascape; **marina mercantile/militare** navy/merchant navy (BRIT) o marine (US)
mari'naio *sm* sailor
mari'nare *vt* (Cuc) to marinate; **~ la scuola** to play truant
ma'rino, -a *ag* sea *cpd*, marine
mario'netta *sf* puppet
ma'rito *sm* husband
ma'rittimo, -a *ag* maritime, sea *cpd*
marmel'lata *sf* jam; (*di agrumi*) marmalade
mar'mitta *sf* (*recipiente*) pot; (Aut) silencer; **marmitta catalitica** catalytic converter
'**marmo** *sm* marble
mar'motta *sf* (Zool) marmot
maroc'chino, -a [marok'kino] *ag, sm/f* Moroccan
Ma'rocco *sm* **il ~** Morocco
mar'rone *ag inv* brown ▶ *sm* (Bot) chestnut

> Attenzione! In inglese esiste la parola *maroon*, che però indica un altro colore, il rosso bordeaux.

mar'supio *sm* pouch; (*per denaro*) bum bag; (*per neonato*) sling
martedì *sm inv* Tuesday; **di** o **il ~** on Tuesdays; **martedì grasso** Shrove Tuesday
martel'lare *vt* to hammer ▶ *vi* (*pulsare*) to throb; (: *cuore*) to thump
mar'tello *sm* hammer; (: *di uscio*) knocker; **martello pneumatico** pneumatic drill
'**martire** *sm/f* martyr

mar'xista, -i, -e *ag, sm/f* Marxist
marza'pane [martsa'pane] *sm* marzipan
'**marzo** ['martso] *sm* March
mascal'zone [maskal'tsone] *sm* rascal, scoundrel
mas'cara *sm inv* mascara
ma'scella [maʃ'ʃɛlla] *sf* (Anat) jaw
'**maschera** ['maskera] *sf* mask; (*travestimento*) disguise; (: *per un ballo ecc*) fancy dress; (Teatro, Cinema) usher/usherette; (*personaggio del teatro*) stock character; **masche'rare** *vt* to mask; (*travestire*) to disguise; to dress up; (*fig: celare*) to hide, conceal; (Mil) to camouflage; **mascherarsi da** to disguise o.s. as; to dress up as; (*fig*) to masquerade as
mas'chile [mas'kile] *ag* masculine; (*sesso, popolazione*) male; (*abiti*) men's; (*per ragazzi: scuola*) boys'
mas'chilista, -i, -e *ag, sm/f* (*uomo*) (male) chauvinist, sexist; (*donna*) sexist
'**maschio, -a** ['maskjo] *ag* (Biol) male; (*virile*) manly ▶ *sm* (*anche Zool, Tecn*) male; (*uomo*) man; (*ragazzo*) boy; (*figlio*) son
masco'lino, -a *ag* masculine
'**massa** *sf* mass; (*di errori ecc*): **una ~ di** heaps of, masses of; (*di gente*) mass, multitude; (Elettr) earth; **in ~** (Comm) in bulk; (*tutti insieme*) en masse; **adunata in ~** mass meeting; **di ~** (*cultura, manifestazione*) mass *cpd*
mas'sacro *sm* massacre, slaughter; (*fig*) mess, disaster
massaggi'are [massad'dʒare] *vt* to massage
mas'saggio [mas'saddʒo] *sm* massage; **massaggio cardiaco** cardiac massage
mas'saia *sf* housewife
massaia [masse'rittsje] *sfpl* (household) furnishings

m

mas'siccio, -a, -ci, -ce [mas'sittʃo]
ag (oro, legno) solid; *(palazzo)* massive;
(corporatura) stout ▶ *sm (Geo)* massif
'massima *sf (sentenza, regola)* maxim;
(Meteor) maximum temperature; **in
linea di ~** generally speaking; *vedi*
massimo
massi'male *sm* maximum
'massimo, -a *ag, sm* maximum; **al ~**
at (the) most
'masso *sm* rock, boulder
masteriz'zare [masterid'dzare] *vt*
(CD, DVD) to burn
masterizza'tore [masteriddza'tore]
sm CD burner *o* writer
masti'care *vt* to chew
'mastice ['mastitʃe] *sm* mastic; *(per
vetri)* putty
mas'tino *sm* mastiff
ma'tassa *sf* skein
mate'matica *sf* mathematics *sg*
mate'matico, -a, -ci, -che *ag*
mathematical ▶ *sm/f* mathematician
materas'sino *sm* mat; **materassino
gonfiabile** air bed
mate'rasso *sm* mattress; **materasso
a molle** spring *o* interior-sprung
mattress
ma'teria *sf (Fisica)* matter; *(Tecn,
Comm)* material, matter *no pl*;
(disciplina) subject; *(argomento)*
subject matter, material; **in ~ di** *(per
quanto concerne)* on the subject of;
materie prime raw materials
materi'ale *ag* material; *(fig:
grossolano)* rough, rude ▶ *sm* material;
(insieme di strumenti ecc) equipment *no
pl*, materials *pl*
maternità *sf* motherhood,
maternity; *(reparto)* maternity ward
ma'terno, -a *ag (amore, cura ecc)*
maternal, motherly; *(nonno)*
maternal; *(lingua, terra)* mother *cpd*
ma'tita *sf* pencil; **matite colorate**
coloured pencils; **matita per gli**

occhi eyeliner (pencil)
ma'tricola *sf (registro)* register;
(numero) registration number;
(nell'università) freshman, fresher
ma'trigna [ma'triɲɲa] *sf* stepmother
matrimoni'ale *ag* matrimonial,
marriage *cpd*
matri'monio *sm* marriage,
matrimony; *(durata)* marriage,
married life; *(cerimonia)* wedding
mat'tina *sf* morning
'matto, -a *ag* mad, crazy; *(fig: falso)*
false, imitation ▶ *sm/f* madman/
woman; **avere una voglia matta di
qc** to be dying for sth
mat'tone *sm* brick; *(fig)*: **questo
libro/film è un ~** this book/film is
heavy going
matto'nella *sf* tile
matu'rare *vi (anche:* **maturarsi:** *frutta,
grano)* to ripen; *(ascesso)* to come
to a head; *(fig: persona, idea, Econ)*
to mature ▶ *vt* to ripen, to (make)
mature
maturità *sf* maturity; *(di frutta)*
ripeness, maturity; *(Ins)* school-
leaving examination; ≈ GCE A-levels
(BRIT)
ma'turo, -a *ag* mature; *(frutto)* ripe,
mature
max. *abbr (= massimo)* max
maxischermo [maxis'kermo] *sm*
giant screen
'mazza ['mattsa] *sf (bastone)* club;
(martello) sledge-hammer; *(Sport: da
golf)* club; *(: da baseball, cricket)* bat
maz'zata [mat'tsata] *sf (anche fig)*
heavy blow
'mazzo ['mattso] *sm (di fiori, chiavi ecc)*
bunch; *(di carte da gioco)* pack
me *pron* me; **me stesso(a)** myself; **sei
bravo quanto me** you are as clever as
I (am) *o* as me
mec'canico, -a, -ci, -che *ag*
mechanical ▶ *sm* mechanic; **può**

mandare un ~? can you send a mechanic?

mecca'nismo sm mechanism

me'daglia [me'daʎʎa] sf medal

me'desimo, -a ag same; (in persona): **io ~** I myself

'media sf average; (Mat) mean; (Ins: voto) end-of-term average; **le medie** sfpl = **scuola media**; **in ~** on average; vedi anche **medio**

medi'ante prep by means of

media'tore, -'trice sm/f mediator; (Comm) middle man, agent

medi'care vt to treat; (ferita) to dress

medi'cina [medi'tʃina] sf medicine; **medicina legale** forensic medicine

'medico, -a, -ci, -che ag medical ▶ sm doctor; **chiamate un ~** call a doctor; **medico generico** general practitioner, GP

medie'vale ag medieval

'medio, -a ag average; (punto, ceto) middle; (altezza, statura) medium ▶ sm (dito) middle finger; **licenza media** leaving certificate awarded at the end of 3 years of secondary education; **scuola media** first 3 years of secondary school

medi'ocre ag mediocre, poor

medi'tare vt to ponder over, meditate on; (progettare) to plan, think out ▶ vi to meditate

mediter'raneo, -a ag Mediterranean; **il (mare) M~** the Mediterranean (Sea)

me'dusa sf (Zool) jellyfish

mega'byte sm inv (Comput) megabyte

me'gafono sm megaphone

'meglio ['mεʎʎo] av, ag inv better; (con senso superlativo) best ▶ sm (la cosa migliore): **il ~** the best (thing); **faresti ~ ad andartene** you had better leave; **alla ~** as best one can; **andar di bene in ~** to get better and better; **fare del proprio ~** to do one's best; **per il ~** for the best; **aver la ~ su qn** to get the better of sb

'mela sf apple; **mela cotogna** quince

mela'grana sf pomegranate

melan'zana [melan'dzana] sf aubergine (BRIT), eggplant (US)

melato'nina sf melatonin

'melma sf mud, mire

'melo sm apple tree

melo'dia sf melody

me'lone sm (musk)melon

'membro sm member (pl(f) **membra**) (arto) limb

memo'randum sm inv memorandum

me'moria sf memory; **memorie** sfpl (opera autobiografica) memoirs; **a ~** (imparare, sapere) by heart; **a ~ d'uomo** within living memory

mendi'cante sm/f beggar

'meno
av

1 (in minore misura) less; **dovresti mangiare meno** you should eat less, you shouldn't eat so much

2 (comparativo): **meno ... di** not as ... as, less ... than; **sono meno alto di te** I'm not as tall as you (are), I'm less tall than you (are); **meno ... che** not as ... as, less ... than; **meno che mai** less than ever; **è meno intelligente che ricco** he's more rich than intelligent; **meno fumo più mangio** the less I smoke the more I eat

3 (superlativo) least; **il meno dotato degli studenti** the least gifted of the students; **è quello che compro meno spesso** it's the one I buy least often

4 (Mat) minus; **8 meno 5** 8 minus 5, 8 take away 5; **sono le 8 meno un quarto** it's a quarter to 8; **meno 5 gradi** 5 degrees below zero, minus 5 degrees; **1 euro in meno** 1 euro less

5 (fraseologia): **quanto meno poteva telefonare** he could at least have phoned; **non so se accettare o meno** I don't know whether to accept or not;

fare a meno di qc/qn to do without sth/sb; **non potevo fare a meno di ridere** I couldn't help laughing; **meno male!** thank goodness!; **meno male che sei arrivato** it's a good job that you've come
▶*ag inv (tempo, denaro)* less; *(errori, persone)* fewer; **ha fatto meno errori di tutti** he made fewer mistakes than anyone, he made the fewest mistakes of all
▶*sm inv*
1: **il meno** *(il minimo)* the least; **parlare del più e del meno** to talk about this and that
2 *(Mat)* minus
▶*prep (eccetto)* except (for), apart from; **a meno che, a meno di** unless; **a meno che non piova** unless it rains; **non posso, a meno di prendere ferie** I can't, unless I take some leave
meno'pausa *sf* menopause
'**mensa** *sf (locale)* canteen; (: *Mil)* mess; (: *nelle università)* refectory
men'sile *ag* monthly ▶ *sm (periodico)* monthly (magazine); *(stipendio)* monthly salary
'**mensola** *sf* bracket; *(ripiano)* shelf; *(Archit)* corbel
'**menta** *sf* mint; *(anche: ~ piperita)* peppermint; *(bibita)* peppermint cordial; *(caramella)* mint, peppermint
men'tale *ag* mental; **mentalità** *sf inv* mentality
'**mente** *sf* mind; **imparare/sapere qc a ~** to learn/know sth by heart; **avere in ~ qc** to have sth in mind; **passare di ~ a qn** to slip sb's mind
men'tire *vi* to lie
'**mento** *sm* chin
'**mentre** *cong (temporale)* while; *(avversativo)* whereas
menù *sm inv* menu; **ci può portare il ~?** could we see the menu?; **menù turistico** set menu

menzio'nare [mentsjo'nare] *vt* to mention
men'zogna [men'tsɔɲɲa] *sf* lie
mera'viglia [mera'viʎʎa] *sf* amazement, wonder; *(persona, cosa)* marvel, wonder; **a ~** perfectly, wonderfully; **meravigli'are** *vt* to amaze, astonish; **meravigliarsi (di)** to marvel (at); *(stupirsi)* to be amazed (at), be astonished (at); **meravigli'oso, -a** *ag* wonderful, marvellous
mer'cante *sm* merchant; **mercante d'arte** art dealer
merca'tino *sm (rionale)* local street market; *(Econ)* unofficial stock market
mer'cato *sm* market; **mercato dei cambi** exchange market; **mercato nero** black market
'**merce** ['mɛrtʃe] *sf* goods *pl*, merchandise
mercé [mer'tʃe] *sf* mercy
merce'ria [mertʃe'ria] *sf (articoli)* haberdashery *(BRIT)*, notions *pl (US)*; *(bottega)* haberdasher's shop *(BRIT)*, notions store *(US)*
mercoledì *sm inv* Wednesday; **di** o **il ~** on Wednesdays; **mercoledì delle Ceneri** Ash Wednesday
mer'curio *sm* mercury
'**merda** *(fam!)* *sf* shit (!)
me'renda *sf* afternoon snack
meren'dina *sf* snack
meridi'ana *sf (orologio)* sundial
meridi'ano, -a *ag* meridian; midday *cpd*, noonday ▶ *sm* meridian
meridio'nale *ag* southern ▶ *sm/f* southerner
meridi'one *sm* south
me'ringa, -ghe *sf (Cuc)* meringue
meri'tare *vt* to deserve, merit ▶ *vb impers* **merita andare** it's worth going
meri'tevole *ag* worthy
'**merito** *sm* merit; *(valore)* worth; **in ~**

a with regard to; **dare ~ a qn di** to give sb credit for; **finire a pari ~** to finish joint first (o second ecc); to tie

mer'letto sm lace

'**merlo** sm (Zool) blackbird; (Archit) battlement

mer'luzzo [mer'luttso] sm (Zool) cod

mes'chino, -a [mes'kino] ag wretched; (scarso) scanty, poor; (persona: gretta) mean; (: limitata) narrow-minded, petty

mesco'lare vt to mix; (vini, colori) to blend; (mettere in disordine) to mix up, muddle up; (carte) to shuffle

'**mese** sm month

'**messa** sf (Rel) mass; (il mettere): **messa in moto** starting; **messa in piega** set; **messa a punto** (Tecn) adjustment; (Aut) tuning; (fig) clarification

messag'gero [messad'dʒero] sm messenger

messaggi'arsi [messad'dʒarsi] vi to text

messaggino [messad'dʒino] sm (di telefonino) text (message)

mes'saggio [mes'saddʒo] sm message; **posso lasciare un ~?** can I leave a message?; **ci sono messaggi per me?** are there any messages for me?; **messaggio di posta elettronica** e-mail message

messag'gistica [messad'dʒistica] sf **~ immediata** (Inform) instant messaging; **programma di ~ immediata** instant messenger

mes'sale sm (Rel) missal

messi'cano, -a ag, sm/f Mexican

'**Messico** sm **il ~** Mexico

messin'scena [messin'ʃɛna] sf (Teatro) production

'**messo, -a** pp di **mettere** ▶ sm messenger

mesti'ere sm (professione) job; (: manuale) trade; (: artigianale) craft;

(fig: abilità nel lavoro) skill, technique

'**mestolo** sm (Cuc) ladle

mestruazi'one [mestruat'tsjone] sf menstruation

'**meta** sf destination; (fig) aim, goal

metà sf inv half; (punto di mezzo) middle; **dividere qc a o per ~** to divide sth in half; **fare a ~ (di qc con qn)** to go halves (with sb in sth); **a ~ prezzo** at half price; **a ~ strada** halfway

meta'done sm methadone

me'tafora sf metaphor

me'tallico, -a, -ci, -che ag (di metallo) metal cpd; (splendore, rumore ecc) metallic

me'tallo sm metal

metalmec'canico, -a, -ci, -che ag engineering cpd ▶ sm engineering worker

me'tano sm methane

meteoro'logico, -a, -ci, -che [meteoro'lɔdʒiko] ag meteorological, weather cpd

me'ticcio, -a, -ci, -ce [me'tittʃo] sm/f half-caste, half-breed

me'todico, -a, -ci, -che ag methodical

'**metodo** sm method

'**metro** sm metre; (nastro) tape measure; (asta) (metre) rule

metropoli'tana sf underground, subway

'**mettere** vt to put; (abito) to put on; (: portare) to wear; (installare: telefono) to put in; (fig: provocare): **~ fame/allegria a qn** to make sb hungry/happy; (supporre): **mettiamo che ...** let's suppose o say that ...; **mettersi** vpr (persona) to put o.s.; (oggetto) to go; (disporsi: faccenda) to turn out; **mettersi a sedere** to sit down; **mettersi a letto** to get into bed; (per malattia) to take to one's bed; **mettersi il cappello** to put on one's hat; **mettersi a** (cominciare) to begin to, start to; **mettersi al lavoro** to set to work; **mettersi con qn** (*in società*) to team up with sb; (*in coppia*) to start going out with sb; **metterci: metterci molta cura/molto tempo** to take a lot of care/a lot of time; **ci ho messo 3 ore per venire** it's taken me 3 hours to get here; **mettercela tutta** to do one's best; **~ a tacere qn/qc** to keep sb/sth quiet; **~ su casa** to set up house; **~ su un negozio** to start a shop; **~ via** to put away

mezza'notte [meddza'nɔtte] *sf* midnight

'mezzo, -a ['mɛddzo] *ag* half; **un ~ litro/panino** half a litre/roll ▶ *av* half-; **~ morto** half-dead ▶ *sm* (*metà*) half; (*parte centrale: di strada ecc*) middle; (*per raggiungere un fine*) means *sg*; (*veicolo*) vehicle; (*nell'indicare l'ora*): **le nove e ~** half past nine; **~ giorno e ~** half past twelve; **mezzi** *smpl* (*possibilità economiche*) means; **di mezza età** middle-aged; **un soprabito di mezza stagione** a spring (*o* autumn) coat; **di ~** middle, in the middle; **andarci di ~** (*patir danno*) to suffer; **levarsi** *o* **togliersi di ~** to get out of the way; **in ~ a** in the middle of; **per** *o* **a ~ di** by means of; **mezzi di comunicazione di massa** mass media *pl*; **mezzi pubblici** public transport *sg*; **mezzi di trasporto** means of transport

mezzogi'orno [meddzo'dʒorno] *sm* midday, noon; **a ~** at 12 (o'clock) *o* midday *o* noon; **il ~ d'Italia** southern Italy

mi (*dav lo, la, li, le, ne diventa* **me**) *pron* (*oggetto*) me; (*complemento di termine*) to me; (*riflessivo*) myself ▶ *sm* (*Mus*) E; (: *solfeggiando la scala*) mi

miago'lare *vi* to miaow, mew

'mica *av* (*fam*): **non ... ~** not ... at all; **non sono ~ stanco** I'm not a bit tired;

non sarà ~ partito? he wouldn't have left, would he?; **~ male** not bad

'miccia, -ce ['mittʃa] *sf* fuse

micidi'ale [mitʃi'djale] *ag* fatal; (*dannosissimo*) deadly

micro'fibra *sf* microfibre

mi'crofono *sm* microphone

micros'copio *sm* microscope

mi'dollo (*pl(f)* midolla) *sm* (*Anat*) marrow; **midollo osseo** bone marrow

mi'ele *sm* honey

'miglia ['miʎʎa] *sfpl di* miglio

migli'aio [miʎ'ʎajo] ((*pl*)*f* migliaia) *sm* thousand; **un ~ (di)** about a thousand; **a migliaia** by the thousand, in thousands

'miglio ['miʎʎo] *sm* (*Bot*) millet (*pl(f)* miglia) (*unità di misura*) mile; **~ marino** *o* **nautico** nautical mile

migliora'mento [miʎʎora'mento] *sm* improvement

miglio'rare [miʎʎo'rare] *vt, vi* to improve

migli'ore [miʎ'ʎore] *ag* (*comparativo*) better; (*superlativo*) best ▶ *sm* **il ~** the best (thing) ▶ *sm/f* **il(la) ~** the best (person); **il miglior vino di questa regione** the best wine in this area

'mignolo ['miɲɲolo] *sm* (*Anat*) little finger, pinkie; (: *dito del piede*) little toe

Mi'lano *sf* Milan

miliar'dario, -a *sm/f* millionaire

mili'ardo *sm* thousand million, billion (*US*)

mili'one *sm* million; **mille euro** one thousand euros

mili'tante *ag, sm/f* militant

mili'tare *vi* (*Mil*) to be a soldier, serve; (*fig: in un partito*) to be a militant ▶ *ag* military ▶ *sm* serviceman; **fare il ~** to do one's military service

'mille (*pl* mila) *num* a *o* one thousand; **dieci mila** ten thousand

mil'lennio *sm* millennium

millepi'edi sm inv centipede

mil'lesimo, -a ag, sm thousandth

milli'grammo sm milligram(me)

mil'limetro sm millimetre

'milza ['miltsa] sf (Anat) spleen

mimetiz'zare [mimetid'dzare] vt to camouflage; **mimetizzarsi** vpr to camouflage o.s.

'mimo sm (attore, componimento) mime

mi'mosa sf mimosa

min. abbr (= minuto, minimo) min.

'mina sf (esplosiva) mine; (di matita) lead

mi'naccia, -ce [mi'nattʃa] sf threat; **minacci'are** vt to threaten; **minacciare qn di morte** to threaten to kill sb; **minacciare di fare qc** to threaten to do sth

mi'nare vt (Mil) to mine; (fig) to undermine

mina'tore sm miner

mine'rale ag, sm mineral

mine'rario, -a ag (delle miniere) mining; (dei minerali) ore cpd

mi'nestra sf soup; **minestra in brodo** noodle soup; **minestra di verdure** vegetable soup

minia'tura sf miniature

mini'bar sm inv minibar

mini'era sf mine

mini'gonna sf miniskirt

'minimo, -a ag minimum, least, slightest; (piccolissimo) very small, slight; (il più basso) lowest, minimum ▶ sm minimum; **al ~** at least; **girare al ~** (Aut) to idle

minis'tero sm (Pol, Rel) ministry; (governo) government; **M~ delle Finanze** Ministry of Finance, ≈ Treasury

mi'nistro sm (Pol, Rel) minister

mino'ranza [mino'rantsa] sf minority

mi'nore ag (comparativo) less; (più piccolo) smaller; (numero) lower; (inferiore) lower, inferior; (meno importante) minor; (più giovane) younger; (superlativo) least; smallest; lowest; youngest ▶ sm/f = **minorenne**

mino'renne ag under age ▶ sm/f minor, person under age

mi'nuscolo, -a ag (scrittura, carattere) small; (piccolissimo) tiny ▶ sf small letter

mi'nuto, -a ag tiny, minute; (pioggia) fine; (corporatura) delicate, fine ▶ sm (unità di misura) minute; **al ~** (Comm) retail

'mio (f'mia, pl mi'ei or 'mie) det il ~, la mia ecc my ▶ pron il ~, la mia ecc mine; **i miei** my family; **un ~ amico** a friend of mine

'miope ag short-sighted

'mira sf (anche fig) aim; **prendere la ~** to take aim; **prendere di ~ qn** (fig) to pick on sb

mi'racolo sm miracle

mi'raggio [mi'raddʒo] sm mirage

mi'rare vi ~ **a** to aim at

mi'rino sm (Tecn) sight; (Fot) viewer, viewfinder

mir'tillo sm bilberry (BRIT), blueberry (US), whortleberry

mi'scela [miʃʃela] sf mixture; (di caffè) blend

'mischia ['miskja] sf scuffle; (Rugby) scrum, scrummage

mis'cuglio [mis'kuʎʎo] sm mixture, hotchpotch, jumble

'mise vb vedi **mettere**

mise'rabile ag (infelice) miserable, wretched; (povero) poverty-stricken; (di scarso valore) miserable

mi'seria sf extreme poverty; (infelicità) misery

miseri'cordia sf mercy, pity

'misero, -a ag miserable, wretched; (povero) poverty-stricken; (insufficiente) miserable

'misi vb vedi **mettere**

mi'sogino [mi'zɔdʒino] *sm* misogynist

'missile *sm* missile

missio'nario, -a *ag, sm/f* missionary

missi'one *sf* mission

misteri'oso, -a *ag* mysterious

mis'tero *sm* mystery

'misto, -a *ag* mixed; (*scuola*) mixed, coeducational ▶ *sm* mixture

mis'tura *sf* mixture

mi'sura *sf* measure; (*misurazione, dimensione*) measurement; (*taglia*) size; (*provvedimento*) measure, step; (*moderazione*) moderation; (*Mus*) time; (: *divisione*) bar; (*fig: limite*) bounds *pl*, limit; **nella ~ in cui** inasmuch as, insofar as; **(fatto) su ~** made to measure

misu'rare *vt* (*ambiente, stoffa*) to measure; (*terreno*) to survey; (*abito*) to try on; (*pesare*) to weigh; (*fig: parole ecc*) to weigh up; (: *spese, cibo*) to limit ▶ *vi* to measure; **misurarsi** *vpr* **misurarsi con qn** to have a confrontation with sb; to compete with sb

'mite *ag* mild

'mitico, -a, ci, che *ag* mythical

'mito *sm* myth; **mitolo'gia, -'gie** *sf* mythology

'mitra *sf* (*Rel*) mitre ▶ *sm inv* (*arma*) sub-machine gun

mit'tente *sm/f* sender

mm *abbr* (= *millimetro*) mm

'mobile *ag* mobile; (*parte di macchina*) moving; (*Dir: bene*) movable, personal ▶ *sm* (*arredamento*) piece of furniture; **mobili** *smpl* (*mobilia*) furniture *sg*

mocas'sino *sm* moccasin

'moda *sf* fashion; **alla ~, di ~** fashionable, in fashion

modalità *sf inv* formality

mo'della *sf* model

mo'dello *sm* model; (*stampo*) mould ▶ *ag inv* model *cpd*

'modem *sm inv* modem

modera'tore, -'trice *sm/f* moderator

mo'derno, -a *ag* modern

mo'desto, -a *ag* modest

'modico, -a, -ci, -che *ag* reasonable, moderate

mo'difica, -che *sf* modification

modifi'care *vt* to modify, alter

'modo *sm* way, manner; (*mezzo*) means, way; (*occasione*) opportunity; (*Ling*) mood; (*Mus*) mode; **modi** *smpl* (*comportamento*) manners; **a suo ~, a ~ suo** in his own way; **ad o in ogni ~** anyway; **di o in ~ che** so that; **in ~ da** so as to; **in tutti i modi** at all costs; (*comunque sia*) anyway; (*in ogni caso*) in any case; **in qualche ~** somehow or other; **per ~ di dire** so to speak; **modo di dire** turn of phrase

'modulo *sm* (*modello*) form; (*Archit, lunare, di comando*) module

'mogano *sm* mahogany

'mogio, -a, -gi, -gie ['mɔdʒo] *ag* down in the dumps, dejected

'moglie ['moʎʎe] *sf* wife

mo'ine *sfpl* cajolery *sg*; (*leziosità*) affectation *sg*

mo'lare *sm* (*dente*) molar

'mole *sf* mass; (*dimensioni*) size; (*edificio grandioso*) massive structure

moles'tare *vt* to bother, annoy; **mo'lestia** *sf* annoyance, bother; **recar molestia a qn** to bother sb; **molestie sessuali** sexual harassment *sg*

'molla *sf* spring; **molle** *sfpl* (*per camino*) tongs

mol'lare *vt* to release, let go; (*Naut*) to ease; (*fig: ceffone*) to give ▶ *vi* (*cedere*) to give in

'molle *ag* soft; (*muscoli*) flabby

mol'letta *sf* (*per capelli*) hairgrip; (*per panni stesi*) clothes peg

'mollica, -che *sf* crumb, soft part

mol'lusco, -schi *sm* mollusc
'molo *sm* mole, breakwater; jetty
moltipli'care *vt* to multiply;
  moltiplicarsi *vpr* to multiply;
  to increase in number;
  moltiplicazi'one *sf* multiplication
○ **'molto, -a**
  det (*quantità*) a lot of, much;
(*numero*) a lot of, many; **molto pane/
carbone** a lot of bread/coal; **molta
gente** a lot of people, many people;
molti libri a lot of books, many books;
non ho molto tempo I haven't got
much time; **per molto (tempo)** for a
long time
▶*av*
1 a lot, (very) much; **viaggia molto**
he travels a lot; **non viaggia molto** he
doesn't travel much *o* a lot
2 (*intensivo: con aggettivi, avverbi*)
very; (*: con participio passato*) (very)
much; **molto buono** very good; **molto
migliore, molto meglio** much *o* a
lot better
▶*pron* much, a lot
momentanea'mente *av* at the
  moment, at present
momen'taneo, -a *ag* momentary,
  fleeting
mo'mento *sm* moment; **da
un ~ all'altro** at any moment;
(*all'improvviso*) suddenly; **al ~ di fare**
just as I was (*o* you were *o* he was *ecc*)
doing; **per il ~** for the time being;
dal ~ che ever since; (*dato che*) since;
a momenti (*da un momento all'altro*)
any time *o* moment now; (*quasi*)
nearly
'monaca, -che *sf* nun
'Monaco *sf* Monaco; **Monaco (di
Baviera)** Munich
'monaco, -ci *sm* monk
monar'chia *sf* monarchy
monas'tero *sm* (*di monaci*)
  monastery; (*di monache*) convent

mon'dano, -a *ag* (*anche fig*) worldly;
(*anche: dell'alta società*) society *cpd*;
fashionable
mondi'ale *ag* (*campionato,
popolazione*) world *cpd*; (*influenza*)
world-wide
'mondo *sm* world; (*grande quantità*):
un ~ di lots of, a host of; **il bel ~** high
society
mo'nello, -a *sm/f* street urchin;
(*ragazzo vivace*) scamp, imp
mo'neta *sf* coin; (*Econ: valuta*)
currency; (*denaro spicciolo*) (small)
change; **moneta estera** foreign
currency; **moneta legale** legal
tender
mongol'fiera *sf* hot-air balloon
'monitor *sm inv* (*Tecn, TV*) monitor
monolo'cale *sm* studio flat
mono'polio *sm* monopoly
mo'notono, -a *ag* monotonous
monovo'lume *ag inv, sf inv
(automobile) ~** people carrier, MPV
mon'sone *sm* monsoon
monta'carichi [monta'kariki] *sm inv*
hoist, goods lift
mon'taggio [mon'taddʒo] *sm* (*Tecn*)
assembly; (*Cinema*) editing
mon'tagna [mon'taɲɲa] *sf*
mountain; (*zona montuosa*): **la ~** the
mountains *pl*; **andare in ~** to go to the
mountains; **montagne russe** roller
coaster *sg*, big dipper *sg* (BRIT)
monta'naro, -a *ag* mountain *cpd*
▶ *sm/f* mountain dweller
mon'tano, -a *ag* mountain *cpd*;
alpine
mon'tare *vt* to go (*o* come) up;
(*cavallo*) to ride; (*apparecchiatura*) to
set up, assemble; (*Cuc*) to whip; (*Zool*)
to cover; (*incastonare*) to mount, set;
(*Cinema*) to edit; (*Fot*) to mount ▶ *vi*
to go (*o* come) up; (*a cavallo*): **~ bene/
male** to ride well/badly; (*aumentare di
livello, volume*) to rise

monta'tura sf assembling no pl;
(di occhiali) frames pl; (di gioiello)
mounting, setting; (fig): **montatura
pubblicitaria** publicity stunt

'**monte** sm mountain; **a ~** upstream;
mandare a ~ qc to upset sth, cause
sth to fail; **il M~ Bianco** Mont Blanc;
monte di pietà pawnshop; **monte
premi** prize

mon'tone sm (Zool) ram; **carne di
~** mutton

montu'oso, -a ag mountainous

monu'mento sm monument

mo'quette [mɔ'kɛt] sf inv fitted
carpet

'**mora** sf (del rovo) blackberry; (del
gelso) mulberry; (Dir) delay; (: somma)
arrears pl

mo'rale ag moral ▶ sf (scienza) ethics
sg, moral philosophy; (complesso di
norme) moral standards pl, morality;
(condotta) morals pl; (insegnamento
morale) moral ▶ sm morale; **essere giù
di ~** to be feeling down

'**morbido, -a** ag soft; (pelle) soft,
smooth

> Attenzione! In inglese esiste la
> parola morbid, che però significa
> morboso.

mor'billo sm (Med) measles sg

'**morbo** sm disease

mor'boso, -a ag (fig) morbid

'**mordere** vt to bite; (addentare) to
bite into

mor'fina sf morphine

mori'bondo, -a ag dying, moribund

mo'rire vi to die; (abitudine, civiltà) to
die out; **~ di fame** to die of hunger;
(fig) to be starving; **~ di noia/paura** to
be bored/scared to death; **fa un caldo
da ~** it's terribly hot

mormo'rare vi to murmur;
(brontolare) to grumble

'**moro, -a** ag dark(-haired),
dark(-complexioned)

'**morsa** sf (Tecn) vice; (fig: stretta) grip

morsi'care vt to nibble (at), gnaw
(at); (insetto) to bite

'**morso, -a** pp di **mordere** ▶ sm bite;
(di insetto) sting; (parte della briglia) bit;
morsi della fame pangs of hunger

morta'della sf (Cuc) mortadella (type
of salted pork meat)

mor'taio sm mortar

mor'tale ag, sm mortal

'**morte** sf death

'**morto, -a** pp di **morire** ▶ ag dead
▶ sm/f dead man/woman; **i morti** the
dead; **fare il ~** (nell'acqua) to float on
one's back; **il Mar M~** the Dead Sea

mo'saico, -ci sm mosaic

'**Mosca** sf Moscow

'**mosca, -sche** sf fly; **mosca cieca**
blind-man's-buff

mosce'rino [moʃʃe'rino] sm midge

mos'chea [mos'kɛa] sf mosque

'**moscio, -a, -sci, -sce** ['mɔʃʃo] ag
(fig) lifeless

mos'cone sm (Zool) bluebottle; (barca)
pedalo; (: a remi) kind of pedalo with oars

'**mossa** sf movement; (nel gioco) move

'**mossi** ecc vb vedi **muovere**

'**mosso, -a** pp di **muovere** ▶ ag (mare)
rough; (capelli) wavy; (Fot) blurred

mos'tarda sf mustard; **mostarda di
Cremona** pickled fruit with mustard

'**mostra** sf exhibition, show;
(ostentazione) show; **in ~** on show; **far
~ di** (fingere) to pretend; **far ~ di sé** to
show off

mos'trare vt to show; **può
mostrarmi dov'è, per favore?** can
you show me where it is, please?

'**mostro** sm monster; **mostru'oso, -a**
ag monstrous

mo'tel sm inv motel

moti'vare vt (causare) to cause;
(giustificare) to justify, account for

mo'tivo sm (causa) reason, cause;
(movente) motive; (letterario) (central)

theme; (*disegno*) motif, design, pattern; (*Mus*) motif; **per quale ~?** why?, for what reason?

'moto *sm* (*anche Fisica*) motion; (*movimento, gesto*) movement; (*esercizio fisico*) exercise; (*sommossa*) rising, revolt; (*commozione*) feeling, impulse ▶ *sf inv* (*motocicletta*) motorbike; **mettere in ~** to set in motion; (*Aut*) to start up

motoci'cletta *sf* motorcycle

motoci'clista, -i, -e *sm/f* motorcyclist

mo'tore, -'trice *ag* motor; (*Tecn*) driving ▶ *sm* engine, motor; **a ~** motor *cpd*, power-driven; **~ a combustione interna/a reazione** internal combustion/jet engine; **motore di ricerca** (*Inform*) search engine; **moto'rino** *sm* moped; **motorino di avviamento** (*Aut*) starter

motos'cafo *sm* motorboat

'motto *sm* (*battuta scherzosa*) witty remark; (*frase emblematica*) motto

'mouse ['maus] *sm inv* (*Inform*) mouse

mo'vente *sm* motive

movi'mento *sm* movement; (*fig*) activity, hustle and bustle; (*Mus*) tempo, movement

mozi'one [mot'tsjone] *sf* (*Pol*) motion

mozza'rella [mottsa'rɛlla] *sf* mozzarella, *a moist Neapolitan curd cheese*

mozzi'cone [mottsi'kone] *sm* stub, butt, end; (*anche:* **~ di sigaretta**) cigarette end

'mucca, -che *sf* cow; **mucca pazza** mad cow disease

'mucchio ['mukkjo] *sm* pile, heap; (*fig*): **un ~ di** lots of, heaps of

'muco, -chi *sm* mucus

'muffa *sf* mould, mildew

mug'gire [mud'dʒire] *vi* (*vacca*) to low, moo; (*toro*) to bellow; (*fig*) to roar

mu'ghetto [mu'getto] *sm* lily of the valley

mu'lino *sm* mill; **mulino a vento** windmill

'mulo *sm* mule

'multa *sf* fine

multi'etnico, -a, -ci, -che *ag* multiethnic

multirazziale [multirat'tsjale] *ag* multiracial

multi'sala *ag inv* multiscreen

multivitami'nico, -a, -ci, -che *ag* **complesso ~** multivitamin

'mummia *sf* mummy

'mungere ['mundʒere] *vt* (*anche fig*) to milk

munici'pale [munitʃi'pale] *ag* municipal; town *cpd*

muni'cipio [muni'tʃipjo] *sm* town council, corporation; (*edificio*) town hall

munizi'oni [munit'tsjoni] *sfpl* (*Mil*) ammunition *sg*

'munsi *ecc vb vedi* **mungere**

mu'oio *ecc vb vedi* **morire**

mu'overe *vt* to move; (*ruota, macchina*) to drive; (*sollevare: questione, obiezione*) to raise, bring up; (: *accusa*) to make, bring forward; **muoversi** *vpr* to move; **muoviti!** hurry up!, get a move on!

'mura *sfpl vedi* **muro**

mu'rale *ag* wall *cpd*; mural

mura'tore *sm* mason; bricklayer

'muro *sm* wall

'muschio ['muskjo] *sm* (*Zool*) musk; (*Bot*) moss

musco'lare *ag* muscular, muscle *cpd*

'muscolo *sm* (*Anat*) muscle

mu'seo *sm* museum

museru'ola *sf* muzzle

'musica *sf* music; **musica da ballo/ camera** dance/chamber music; **musi'cale** *ag* musical; **musi'cista, -i, -e** *sm/f* musician

'müsli ['mysli] *sm* muesli

'muso sm muzzle; (di auto, aereo) nose;
tenere il ~ to sulk

mussul'mano, -a ag, sm/f Muslim,
Moslem

'muta sf (di animali) moulting; (di
serpenti) sloughing; (per immersioni
subacquee) diving suit; (gruppo di
cani) pack

mu'tande sfpl (da uomo) (under)pants

'muto, -a ag (Med) dumb; (emozione,
dolore, Cinema) silent; (Ling) silent,
mute; (carta geografica) blank; **~
per lo stupore** ecc speechless with
amazement ecc

'mutuo, -a ag (reciproco) mutual ▶ sm
(Econ) (long-term) loan

n

N abbr (= nord) N

n. abbr (= numero) no.

'nafta sf naphtha; (per motori diesel)
diesel oil

nafta'lina sf (Chim) naphthalene;
(tarmicida) mothballs pl

'naia sf (Mil) slang term for national
service

na'ïf [na'if] ag inv naïve

'nanna sf (linguaggio infantile): **andare
a ~** to go to beddy-byes

'nano, -a ag, sm/f dwarf

napole'tano, -a ag, sm/f
Neapolitan

'Napoli sf Naples

nar'ciso [nar'tʃizo] sm narcissus

nar'cotico, -ci sm narcotic

na'rice [na'ritʃe] sf nostril

nar'rare vt to tell the story of,
recount; **narra'tiva** sf (branca
letteraria) fiction

na'sale ag nasal

'nascere ['naʃʃere] vi (bambino) to be
born; (pianta) to come o spring up;
(fiume) to rise, have its source; (sole)
to rise; (dente) to come through; (fig:
derivare, conseguire): **~ da** to arise from,
be born out of; **è nata nel 1952** she
was born in 1952; **'nascita** sf birth

nas'condere vt to hide, conceal;
nascondersi vpr to hide;
nascon'diglio sm hiding place;
nascon'dino sm (gioco) hide-and-
seek; **nas'cosi** ecc vb vedi **nascondere**;
nas'costo, -a pp di **nascondere** ▶ ag
hidden; **di nascosto** secretly

na'sello sm (Zool) hake

'naso sm nose

'nastro sm ribbon; (magnetico, isolante,
Sport) tape; **nastro adesivo** adhesive
tape; **nastro trasportatore**
conveyor belt

nas'turzio [nas'turtsjo] sm
nasturtium

na'tale ag of one's birth ▶ sm (Rel):
N~ Christmas; (giorno della nascita)
birthday; **nata'lizio, -a** ag (del Natale)
Christmas cpd

'natica, -che sf (Anat) buttock

'nato, -a pp di **nascere** ▶ ag **un attore
~** a born actor; **nata Pieri** née Pieri

na'tura sf nature; **pagare in ~** to pay
in kind; **natura morta** still life

natu'rale ag natural

natural'mente av naturally;
(certamente, sì) of course

natu'rista, -i, e ag, sm/f naturist,
nudist

naufra'gare vi (nave) to be wrecked;

(persona) to be shipwrecked; (fig) to fall through; **'naufrago, -ghi** sm castaway, shipwreck victim

'nausea sf nausea; **nause'ante** ag (odore) nauseating; (sapore) disgusting; (fig) sickening

'nautico, -a, -ci, -che ag nautical

na'vale ag naval

na'vata sf (anche: ~ **centrale**) nave; (anche: ~ **laterale**) aisle

'nave sf ship, vessel; **nave cisterna** tanker; **nave da guerra** warship; **nave passeggeri** passenger ship

na'vetta sf shuttle; (servizio di collegamento) shuttle (service)

navi'cella [navi'tʃɛlla] sf (di aerostato) gondola; **navicella spaziale** spaceship

navi'gare vi to sail; ~ **in Internet** to surf the Net; **navigazi'one** sf navigation

nazio'nale [nattsjo'nale] ag national ▶ sf (Sport) national team; **nazionalità** sf inv nationality

nazi'one [nat'tsjone] sf nation

naziskin ['nɑːtsiskin] sm inv Nazi skinhead

NB abbr (= nota bene) NB

O ne
pron

1 (di lui, lei, loro) of him/her/them; about him/her/them; **ne riconosco la voce** I recognize his (o her) voice

2 (di questa, quella cosa) of it; about it; **ne voglio ancora** I want some more (of it o them); **non parliamone più!** let's not talk about it any more!

3 (con valore partitivo): **hai dei libri? — sì, ne ho** have you any books? — yes, I have (some); **hai del pane? — no, non ne ho** have you any bread? — no, I haven't any; **quanti anni hai? — ne ho 17** how old are you? — I'm 17

▶ av (moto da luogo: da lì) from there; **ne vengo ora** I've just come from there

né cong **né ... né** neither ... nor; **né l'uno né l'altro lo vuole** neither of them wants it; **non parla né l'italiano né il tedesco** he speaks neither Italian nor German, he doesn't speak either Italian or German; **non piove né nevica** it isn't raining or snowing

ne'anche [ne'anke] av, cong not even; **non ... ~** not even; **~ se volesse potrebbe venire** he couldn't come even if he wanted to; **non l'ho visto — ~ io** I didn't see him — neither did I o I didn't either; **~ per idea** o **sogno!** not on your life!

'nebbia sf fog; (foschia) mist

necessaria'mente [netʃessarjamente] av necessarily

neces'sario, -a [netʃes'sarjo] ag necessary

necessità [netʃessi'ta] sf inv necessity; (povertà) need, poverty

necro'logio [nekro'lɔdʒo] sm obituary notice

ne'gare vt to deny; (rifiutare) to deny, refuse; ~ **di aver fatto/che** to deny having done/that; **nega'tivo, -a** ag, sf, sm negative

negherò ecc [nege'rɔ] vb vedi **negare**

negli'gente [negli'dʒɛnte] ag negligent, careless

negozi'ante [negot'tsjante] sm/f trader, dealer; (bottegaio) shopkeeper (BRIT), storekeeper (US)

negozi'are [negot'tsjare] vt to negotiate ▶ vi ~ **in** to trade o deal in; **negozi'ato** sm negotiation

ne'gozio [ne'gɔttsjo] sm (locale) shop (BRIT), store (US)

'negro, -a ag, sm/f Negro

ne'mico, -a, -ci, -che ag hostile; (Mil) enemy cpd ▶ sm/f enemy; **essere ~ di** to be strongly averse o opposed to

nem'meno av, cong = **neanche**

'neo sm mole; (fig) (slight) flaw

'neon sm (Chim) neon

neo'nato, -a *ag* newborn ▶ *sm/f* newborn baby

neozelan'dese [neoddzelan'dese] *ag* New Zealand *cpd* ▶ *sm/f* New Zealander

'**Nepal** *sm* il ~ Nepal

nep'pure *av*, *cong* = **neanche**

'**nero, -a** *ag* black; (*scuro*) dark ▶ *sm* black; **il Mar N~** the Black Sea

'**nervo** *sm* (*Anat*) nerve; (*Bot*) vein; **avere i nervi** to be on edge; **dare sui nervi a qn** to get on sb's nerves; **ner'voso, -a** *ag* nervous; (*irritabile*) irritable ▶ *sm* (*fam*): **far venire il nervoso a qn** to get on sb's nerves

'**nespola** *sf* (*Bot*) medlar; (*fig*) blow, punch

'**nesso** *sm* connection, link

○ **nes'suno, -a**
(*det: dav sm* **nessun** +*C, V*, **nessuno** +*s impura, gn, pn, ps, x, z; dav sf* **nessuna** +*C*, **nessun'** +*V*) *det*

1 (*non uno*) no; (, *espressione negativa* +) any; **non c'è nessun libro** there isn't any book, there is no book; **nessun altro** no one else, nobody else; **nessun'altra cosa** nothing else; **in nessun luogo** nowhere

2 (*qualche*) any; **hai nessuna obiezione?** do you have any objections?
▶*pron*

1 (*non uno*) no one, nobody; (, *espressione negativa* +) any(one); (: *cosa*) none; (, *espressione negativa* +) any; **nessuno è venuto, non è venuto nessuno** nobody came

2 (*qualcuno*) anyone, anybody; **ha telefonato nessuno?** did anyone phone?

net'tare *vt* to clean

net'tezza [net'tettsa] *sf* cleanness, cleanliness; **nettezza urbana** cleansing department

'**netto, -a** *ag* (*pulito*) clean; (*chiaro*)

clear, clear-cut; (*deciso*) definite; (*Econ*) net

nettur'bino *sm* dustman (*BRIT*), garbage collector (*US*)

neu'trale *ag* neutral

'**neutro, -a** *ag* neutral; (*Ling*) neuter ▶ *sm* (*Ling*) neuter

'**neve** *sf* snow; **nevi'care** *vb impers* to snow; **nevi'cata** *sf* snowfall

ne'vischio [ne'viskjo] *sm* sleet

ne'voso, -a *ag* snowy; snow-covered

nevral'gia [nevral'dʒia] *sf* neuralgia

nevras'tenico, -a, -ci, -che *ag* (*Med*) neurasthenic; (*fig*) hot-tempered

ne'vrosi *sf* neurosis

ne'vrotico, -a, ci, che *ag, sm/f* (*anche fig*) neurotic

'**nicchia** ['nikkja] *sf* niche; (*naturale*) cavity, hollow; **nicchia di mercato** (*Comm*) niche market

nicchi'are [nik'kjare] *vi* to shilly-shally, hesitate

'**nichel** ['nikel] *sm* nickel

nico'tina *sf* nicotine

'**nido** *sm* nest; **a ~ d'ape** (*tessuto ecc*) honeycomb *cpd*

○ **ni'ente**
pron

1 (*nessuna cosa*) nothing; **niente può fermarlo** nothing can stop him; **niente di niente** absolutely nothing; **nient'altro** nothing else; **nient'altro che** nothing but, just, only; **niente affatto** not at all, not in the least; **come se niente fosse** as if nothing had happened; **cose da niente** trivial matters; **per niente** (*gratis, invano*) for nothing

2 (*qualcosa*): **hai bisogno di niente?** do you need anything?

3: **non ... niente** nothing; (*espressione negativa* +) anything; **non ho visto niente** I saw nothing, I didn't see anything; **non ho niente da dire** I have nothing *o* haven't anything to say

▶*sm* nothing; **un bel niente** absolutely nothing; **basta un niente per farla piangere** the slightest thing is enough to make her cry

▶*av* (*in nessuna misura*): **non ... niente** not ... at all; **non è (per) niente buono** it isn't good at all

Ni'geria [ni'dʒɛrja] *sf* **la ~** Nigeria

'ninfa *sf* nymph

nin'fea *sf* water lily

ninna-'nanna *sf* lullaby

'ninnolo *sm* (*gingillo*) knick-knack

ni'pote *sm/f* (*di zii*) nephew/niece; (*di nonni*) grandson/daughter, grandchild

'nitido, -a *ag* clear; (*specchio*) bright

ni'trire *vi* to neigh

ni'trito *sm* (*di cavallo*) neighing *no pl*; neigh; (*Chim*) nitrite

nitroglice'rina [nitroglitʃe'rina] *sf* nitroglycerine

no *av* (*risposta*) no; **vieni o no?** are you coming or not?; **perché no?** why not?; **lo conosciamo? — tu no ma io sì** do we know him? — you don't but I do; **verrai, no?** you'll come, won't you?

'nobile *ag* noble ▶ *sm/f* noble, nobleman/woman

'nocca, -che *sf* (*Anat*) knuckle

'noccio *ecc* ['nɔttʃo] *vb vedi* **nuocere**

nocci'ola [not'tʃɔla] *ag inv* (*colore*) hazel, light brown ▶ *sf* hazelnut

noccio'lina [nottʃo'lina] *sf*; **nocciolina americana** peanut

'nocciolo ['nɔttʃolo] *sm* (*di frutto*) stone; (*fig*) heart, core

'noce ['nɔtʃe] *sm* (*albero*) walnut tree ▶ *sf* (*frutto*) walnut; **noce di cocco** coconut; **noce moscata** nutmeg

no'cevo *ecc* [no'tʃevo] *vb vedi* **nuocere**

no'civo, -a [no'tʃivo] *ag* harmful, noxious

'nocqui *ecc vb vedi* **nuocere**

'nodo *sm* (*di cravatta, legname, Naut*) knot; (*Aut, Ferr*) junction; (*Med, Astr,* *Bot*) node; (*fig: legame*) bond, tie; (*: punto centrale*) heart, crux; **avere un ~ alla gola** to have a lump in one's throat

no-'global *sm/f* anti-globalization protester ▶ *ag* (*movimento, manifestazione*) anti-globalization

'noi *pron* (*soggetto*) we; (*oggetto: per dare rilievo, con preposizione*) us; **~ stessi(e)** we ourselves; (*oggetto*) ourselves

'noia *sf* boredom; (*disturbo, impaccio*) bother *no pl*; trouble *no pl*; **avere qn/qc a ~** not to like sb/sth; **mi è venuto a ~** I'm tired of it; **dare ~ a** to annoy; **avere delle noie con qn** to have trouble with sb

noi'oso, -a *ag* boring; (*fastidioso*) annoying, troublesome

> Attenzione! In inglese esiste la parola *noisy*, che però significa *rumoroso*.

noleggi'are [noled'dʒare] *vt* (*prendere a noleggio*) to hire (*BRIT*), rent; (*dare a noleggio*) to hire out (*BRIT*), rent (out); (*aereo, nave*) to charter; **no'leggio** *sm* hire (*BRIT*), rental; charter

'nomade *ag* nomadic ▶ *sm/f* nomad

'nome *sm* name; (*Ling*) noun; **in/a ~ di** in the name of; **di o per ~** (*chiamato*) called, named; **conoscere qn di ~** to know sb by name; **nome d'arte** stage name; **nome di battesimo** Christian name; **nome di famiglia** surname; **nome utente** login

no'mignolo [no'miɲɲolo] *sm* nickname

'nomina *sf* appointment

nomi'nale *ag* nominal; (*Ling*) noun *cpd*

nomi'nare *vt* to name; (*eleggere*) to appoint; (*citare*) to mention

nomina'tivo, -a *ag* (*Ling*) nominative; (*Econ*) registered ▶ *sm* (*Ling: anche: caso ~*) nominative (case); (*Amm*) name

non *av* not ▸ *prefisso* non-; *vedi* **affatto**; **appena** *ecc*

nonché [non'ke] *cong* (*tanto più, tanto meno*) let alone; (*e inoltre*) as well as

noncu'rante *ag* ~ **(di)** careless (of), indifferent (to)

'**nonno, -a** *sm/f* grandfather/ mother; (*in senso più familiare*) grandma/grandpa; **i nonni** *smpl* the grandparents

non'nulla *sm inv* **un** ~ nothing, a trifle

'**nono, -a** *ag, sm* ninth

nonos'tante *prep* in spite of, notwithstanding ▸ *cong* although, even though

nontiscordardimé *sm inv* (*Bot*) forget-me-not

nord *sm* North ▸ *ag inv* north; northern; **il Mare del N~** the North Sea; **nor'dest** *sm* north-east; **nor'dovest** *sm* north-west

'**norma** *sf* (*principio*) norm; (*regola*) regulation, rule; (*consuetudine*) custom, rule; **a ~ di legge** according to law, as laid down by law; **norme per l'uso** instructions for use; **norme di sicurezza** safety regulations

nor'male *ag* normal; standard *cpd*

normal'mente *av* normally

norve'gese [norve'dʒese] *ag, sm/f, sm* Norwegian

Nor'vegia [nor'vedʒa] *sf* **la ~** Norway

nostal'gia [nostal'dʒia] *sf* (*di casa, paese*) homesickness; (*del passato*) nostalgia

nos'trano, -a *ag* local; national; home-produced

'**nostro, -a** *det* **il (la) ~(-a)** *ecc* our ▸ *pron* **il (la) ~(-a)** *ecc* ours ▸ *sm* **il ~** our money; our belongings; **i nostri** our family; our own people; **è dei nostri** he's one of us

'**nota** *sf* (*segno*) mark; (*comunicazione scritta, Mus*) note; (*fattura*) bill; (*elenco*) list; **degno di** ~ noteworthy, worthy of note

no'taio *sm* notary

no'tare *vt* (*segnare: errori*) to mark; (*registrare*) to note (down), write down; (*rilevare, osservare*) to note, notice; **farsi** ~ to get o.s. noticed

no'tevole *ag* (*talento*) notable, remarkable; (*peso*) considerable

no'tifica, -che *sf* notification

no'tizia [no'tittsja] *sf* (*piece of*) news *sg*; (*informazione*) piece of information; **notizi'ario** *sm* (*Radio, TV, Stampa*) news *sg*

'**noto, -a** *ag* (well-)known

notorietà *sf* fame; notoriety

no'torio, -a *ag* well-known; (*peg*) notorious

not'tambulo, -a *sm/f* night-bird; (*fig*)

not'tata *sf* night

'**notte** *sf* night; **di** ~ at night; (*durante la notte*) in the night, during the night; **notte bianca** sleepless night

not'turno, -a *ag* nocturnal; (*servizio, guardiano*) night *cpd*

no'vanta *num* ninety; **novan'tesimo, -a** *num* ninetieth

'**nove** *num* nine

nove'cento [nove'tʃɛnto] *num* nine hundred ▸ *sm* **il N~** the twentieth century

no'vella *sf* (*Letteratura*) short story

no'vello, -a *ag* (*piante, patate*) new; (*insalata, verdura*) early; (*sposo*) newly-married

no'vembre *sm* November

novità *sf inv* novelty; (*innovazione*) innovation; (*cosa originale, insolita*) something new; (*notizia*) (piece of) news *sg*; **le ~ della moda** the latest fashions

nozi'one [not'tsjone] *sf* notion, idea

'**nozze** ['nɔttse] *sfpl* wedding *sg*, marriage *sg*; **nozze d'argento/d'oro** silver/golden wedding *sg*

'nubile ag (donna) unmarried, single

'nuca sf nape of the neck

nucle'are ag nuclear

'nucleo sm nucleus; (gruppo) team, unit, group; (Mil, Polizia) squad; **nucleo familiare** family unit

nu'dista, -i, -e sm/f nudist

'nudo, -a ag (persona) bare, naked, nude; (membra) bare, naked; (montagna) bare ▶ sm (Arte) nude

'nulla pron, av = **niente** ▶ sm = **il nulla** nothing

nullità sf inv nullity; (persona) nonentity

'nullo, -a ag useless, worthless; (Dir) null (and void); (Sport): **incontro ~** draw

nume'rale ag, sm numeral

nume'rare vt to number

nu'merico, -a, -ci, -che ag numerical

'numero sm number; (romano, arabo) numeral; (di spettacolo) act, turn; **numero civico** house number; **numero di scarpe** shoe size; **numero di telefono** telephone number; **nume'roso, -a** ag numerous, many; (con sostantivo sg) large

nu'occio ecc ['nwɔtʃo] vb vedi **nuocere**

nu'ocere ['nwɔtʃere] vi ~ **a** to harm, damage

nu'ora sf daughter-in-law

nuo'tare vi to swim; (galleggiare: oggetti) to float; **nuota'tore, -'trice** sm/f swimmer; **nu'oto** sm swimming

nu'ova sf (notizia) (piece of) news sg; vedi anche **nuovo**

nuova'mente av again

Nu'ova Ze'landa [-dze'landa] sf **la ~** New Zealand

nu'ovo, -a ag new; **di ~** again; **~ fiammante** o **di zecca** brand-new

nutri'ente ag nutritious, nourishing

nutri'mento sm food, nourishment

nu'trire vt to feed; (fig: sentimenti) to harbour, nurse; **nutrirsi** vpr **nutrirsi di** to feed on, to eat

'nuvola sf cloud; **nuvo'loso, -a** ag cloudy

nuzi'ale [nut'tsjale] ag nuptial; wedding cpd

'nylon ['nailən] sm nylon

O

o (dav V spesso **od**) cong or; **o ... o** either ... or; **o l'uno o l'altro** either (of them)

O abbr (= ovest) W

'oasi sf inv oasis

obbedi'ente ecc = **ubbidiente** ecc

obbli'gare vt (costringere): ~ **qn a fare** to force o oblige sb to do; (Dir) to bind; **obbliga'torio, -a** ag compulsory, obligatory; **'obbligo, -ghi** sm obligation; (dovere) duty; **avere l'obbligo di fare** to be obliged to do; **essere d'obbligo** (discorso, applauso) to be called for

o'beso, -a ag obese

obiet'tare vt ~ **che** to object that; ~ **su qc** to object to sth, raise objections concerning sth

obiet'tivo, -a ag objective ▶ sm (Ottica, Fot) lens sg, objective; (Mil, fig) objective

obiet'tore sm objector; **obiettore di coscienza** conscientious objector

obiezi'one [objet'tsjone] sf objection

obi'torio *sm* morgue, mortuary

o'bliquo, -a *ag* oblique; (*inclinato*) slanting; (*fig*) devious, underhand

oblite'rare *vt* (*biglietto*) to stamp; (*francobollo*) to cancel

oblò *sm inv* porthole

'oboe *sm* (*Mus*) oboe

'oca (*pl* **'oche**) *sf* goose

occasi'one *sf* (*caso favorevole*) opportunity; (*causa, motivo, circostanza*) occasion; (*Comm*) bargain: **d'~** (*a buon prezzo*) bargain *cpd*; (*usato*) secondhand

occhi'aia [ok'kjaja] *sf* **avere le occhiaie** to have shadows under one's eyes

occhi'ali [ok'kjali] *smpl* glasses, spectacles; **occhiali da sole/da vista** sunglasses/(prescription) glasses

occhi'ata [ok'kjata] *sf* look, glance; **dare un'~ a** to have a look at

occhi'ello [ok'kjɛllo] *sm* buttonhole; (*asola*) eyelet

'occhio ['ɔkkjo] *sm* eye; **~!** careful!, watch out!; **a ~ nudo** with the naked eye; **a quattr'occhi** privately, tête-à-tête; **dare all'~ o nell'~ a qn** to catch sb's eye; **fare l'~ a qc** to get used to sth; **tenere d'~ qn** to keep an eye on sb; **vedere di buon/mal ~ qc** to look favourably/unfavourably on sth

occhio'lino [okkjo'lino] *sm* **fare l'~ a qn** to wink at sb

occiden'tale [ottʃiden'tale] *ag* western ▶ *sm/f* Westerner

occi'dente [ottʃi'dɛnte] *sm* west; (*Pol*): **l'O~** the West; **a ~** in the west

occor'rente *ag* necessary ▶ *sm* all that is necessary

occor'renza [okkor'rɛntsa] *sf* necessity, need; **all'~** in case of need

oc'correre *vi* to be needed, be required ▶ *vb impers* **occorre farlo** it must be done; **occorre che tu parta** you must leave, you'll have to leave;

mi occorrono i soldi I need the money

> Attenzione! In inglese esiste il verbo *to occur*, che però significa *succedere*.

oc'culto, -a *ag* hidden, concealed; (*scienze, forze*) occult

occu'pare *vt* to occupy; (*manodopera*) to employ; (*ingombrare*) to occupy, take up; **occuparsi** *vpr* to occupy o.s., keep o.s. busy; (*impiegarsi*) to get a job; **occuparsi di** (*interessarsi*) to take an interest in; (*prendersi cura di*) to look after, take care of;

occu'pato, -a *ag* (*Mil, Pol*) occupied; (*persona: affaccendato*) busy; (*posto, sedia*) taken; (*toilette, Tel*) engaged; **la linea è occupata** the line's engaged; **è occupato questo posto?** is this seat taken?; **occupazi'one** *sf* occupation; (*impiego, lavoro*) job; (*Econ*) employment

o'ceano [o'tʃeano] *sm* ocean

'ocra *sf* ochre

'OCSE *sigla f* (= *Organizzazione per la Cooperazione e lo Sviluppo Economico*) OECD (*Organization for Economic Cooperation and Development*)

ocu'lare *ag* ocular, eye *cpd*; **testimone ~** eye witness

ocu'lato, -a *ag* (*attento*) cautious, prudent; (*accorto*) shrewd

ocu'lista, -i, -e *sm/f* eye specialist, oculist

odi'are *vt* to hate, detest

odi'erno, -a *ag* today's, of today; (*attuale*) present

'odio *sm* hatred; **avere in ~ qc/qn** to hate *o* detest sth/sb; **odi'oso, -a** *ag* hateful, odious

odo'rare *vt* (*annusare*) to smell; (*profumare*) to perfume, scent ▶ *vi* **~ (di)** to smell (of)

o'dore *sm* smell; **odori** *smpl* (*Cuc*) (aromatic) herbs

of'fendere vt to offend; (violare) to break, violate; (insultare) to insult; (ferire) to hurt; **offendersi** vpr (con senso reciproco) to insult one another; (risentirsi): **offendersi (di)** to take offence (at), be offended (by)

offe'rente sm (in aste): **al maggior ~** to the highest bidder

of'ferta sf offer; (donazione, anche Rel) offering; (in gara d'appalto) tender; (in aste) bid; (Econ) supply; **fare un'~** to make an offer; to tender; to bid; **"offerte d'impiego"** "situations vacant"; **offerta speciale** special offer

of'fesa sf insult, affront; (Mil) attack; (Dir) offence; vedi anche **offeso**

of'feso, -a pp di **offendere** ▶ ag offended; (fisicamente) hurt, injured ▶ sm/f offended party; **essere ~ con qn** to be annoyed with sb; **parte offesa** (Dir) plaintiff

offi'cina [offi'tʃina] sf workshop

of'frire vt to offer; **offrirsi** vpr (proporsi) to offer (o.s.), volunteer; (occasione) to present itself; (esporsi): **offrirsi a** to expose o.s. to; **ti offro da bere** I'll buy you a drink

offus'care vt to obscure, darken; (fig: intelletto) to dim, cloud; (: fama) to obscure, overshadow; **offuscarsi** vpr to grow dark; to cloud, grow dim; to be obscured

ogget'tivo, -a [oddʒet'tivo] ag objective

og'getto [od'dʒɛtto] sm object; (materia, argomento) subject (matter); **oggetti smarriti** lost property sg

'oggi ['ɔddʒi] av, sm today; **~ a otto** a week today; **oggigi'orno** av nowadays

OGM sigla m (= organismo geneticamente modificato) GMO

'ogni ['oɲɲi] det every, each; (tutti) all; (con valore distributivo) every; **~ uomo** è mortale all men are mortal; **viene ~ due giorni** he comes every two days; **~ cosa** everything; **ad ~ costo** at all costs, at any price; **in ~ luogo** everywhere; **~ tanto** every so often; **~ volta che** every time that

Ognis'santi [oɲɲis'santi] sm All Saints' Day

o'gnuno [oɲ'ɲuno] pron everyone, everybody

O'landa sf l'~ Holland; **olan'dese** ag Dutch ▶ sm (Ling) Dutch ▶ sm/f Dutchman/woman; **gli Olandesi** the Dutch

ole'andro sm oleander

oleo'dotto sm oil pipeline

ole'oso, -a ag oily; (che contiene olio) oil-yielding

ol'fatto sm sense of smell

oli'are vt to oil

oli'era sf oil cruet

Olim'piadi sfpl Olympic games; **o'limpico, -a, -ci, -che** ag Olympic

'olio sm oil; **sott'~** (Cuc) in oil; **~ di fegato di merluzzo** cod liver oil; **olio d'oliva** olive oil; **olio di semi** vegetable oil

o'liva sf olive; **o'livo** sm olive tree

'olmo sm elm

OLP sigla f (= Organizzazione per la Liberazione della Palestina) PLO

ol'traggio [ol'traddʒo] sm outrage; offence, insult; **~ a pubblico ufficiale** (Dir) insulting a public official; **oltraggio al pudore** (Dir) indecent behaviour

ol'tranza [ol'trantsa] sf **a ~** to the last, to the bitter end

'oltre av (più in là) further; (di più: aspettare) longer, more ▶ prep (di là da) beyond, over, on the other side of; (più di) more than, over; (in aggiunta a) besides; (eccetto): **~ a** except, apart from; **oltrepas'sare** vt to go beyond, exceed

o'maggio [o'maddʒo] *sm* (*dono*) gift; (*segno di rispetto*) homage, tribute; **omaggi** *smpl* (*complimenti*) respects; **rendere ~ a** to pay homage *o* tribute to; **in ~** (*copia, biglietto*) complimentary

ombe'lico, -chi *sm* navel

'ombra *sf* (*zona non assolata, fantasma*) shade; (*sagoma scura*) shadow; **sedere all'~** to sit in the shade; **restare nell'~** (*fig*) to remain in obscurity

om'brello *sm* umbrella; **ombrel'lone** *sm* beach umbrella

om'bretto *sm* eye shadow

O.M.C. *sigla f* (= *Organizzazione Mondiale del Commercio*) WTO

ome'lette [ɔmə'lɛt] *sf inv* omelet(te)

ome'lia *sf* (*Rel*) homily, sermon

omeopa'tia *sf* homoeopathy

omertà *sf* conspiracy of silence

o'mettere *vt* to omit, leave out; **~ di fare** to omit *o* fail to do

omi'cida, -i, -e [omi'tʃida] *ag* homicidal, murderous ▶ *sm/f* murderer/eress

omi'cidio [omi'tʃidjo] *sm* murder; **omicidio colposo** culpable homicide

o'misi *ecc vb vedi* **omettere**

omissi'one *sf* omission; **omissione di soccorso** (*Dir*) failure to stop and give assistance

omogeneiz'zato [omodʒeneid'dzato] *sm* baby food

omo'geneo, -a [omo'dʒɛneo] *ag* homogeneous

o'monimo, -a *sm/f* namesake ▶ *sm* (*Ling*) homonym

omosessu'ale *ag, sm/f* homosexual

O.M.S. *sigla f* (= *Organizzazione Mondiale della Sanità*) WHO

On. *abbr* (*Pol*) = **onorevole**

'onda *sf* wave; **mettere** *o* **mandare in ~** (*Radio, TV*) to broadcast; **andare in ~** (*Radio, TV*) to go on the air; **onde corte/lunghe/medie** short/long/medium wave

'onere *sm* burden; **oneri fiscali** taxes

onestà *sf* honesty

o'nesto, -a *ag* (*probo, retto*) honest; (*giusto*) fair; (*casto*) chaste, virtuous

ONG *sigla f inv* **Organizzazione Non Governativa** NGO

onnipo'tente *ag* omnipotent

ono'mastico, -ci *sm* name-day

ono'rare *vt* to honour; (*far onore a*) to do credit to

ono'rario, -a *ag* honorary ▶ *sm* fee

o'nore *sm* honour; **in ~ di** in honour of; **fare gli onori di casa** to play host (*o* hostess); **fare ~ a** to honour; (*pranzo*) to do justice to; (*famiglia*) to be a credit to; **farsi ~** to distinguish o.s.; **ono'revole** *ag* honourable ▶ *sm/f* (*Pol*) ≈ Member of Parliament (*BRIT*), ≈ Congressman/woman (*US*)

on'tano *sm* (*Bot*) alder

'O.N.U. ['ɔnu] *sigla f* (= *Organizzazione delle Nazioni Unite*) UN, UNO

o'paco, -a, -chi, -che *ag* (*vetro*) opaque; (*metallo*) dull, matt

o'pale *sm o f* opal

'opera *sf* work; (*azione rilevante*) action, deed, work; (*Mus*) work; opus; (: *melodramma*) opera; (: *teatro*) opera house; (*ente*) institution, organization; **opere pubbliche** public works; **opera d'arte** work of art; **opera lirica** (grand) opera

ope'raio, -a *ag* working-class; workers' ▶ *sm/f* worker; **classe operaia** working class

ope'rare *vt* to carry out, make; (*Med*) to operate on ▶ *vi* to operate, work; (*rimedio*) to act, work; (*Med*) to operate; **operarsi** *vpr* (*Med*) to have an operation; **operarsi d'appendicite** to have one's appendix out; **operazi'one** *sf* operation

ope'retta *sf* (*Mus*) operetta, light opera

opini'one sf opinion; **opinione pubblica** public opinion

'oppio sm opium

op'pongo ecc vb vedi **opporre**

op'porre vt to oppose; **opporsi** vpr **opporsi (a qc)** to oppose (sth); to object (to sth); ~ **resistenza/un rifiuto** to offer resistance/refuse

opportu'nista, -i, -e sm/f opportunist

opportunità sf inv opportunity; (convenienza) opportuneness, timeliness

oppor'tuno, -a ag timely, opportune

op'posi ecc vb vedi **opporre**

opposizi'one [oppozit'tsjone] sf opposition; (Dir) objection

op'posto, -a pp di **opporre** ▶ ag opposite; (opinioni) conflicting ▶ sm opposite, contrary; **all'~** on the contrary

oppressi'one sf oppression

oppri'mente ag (caldo, noia) oppressive; (persona) tiresome; (deprimente) depressing

op'primere vt (premere, gravare) to weigh down; (estenuare: caldo) to suffocate, oppress; (tiranneggiare: popolo) to oppress

op'pure cong or (else)

op'tare vi ~ **per** to opt for

o'puscolo sm booklet, pamphlet

opzi'one [op'tsjone] sf option

'ora sf (60 minuti) hour; (momento) time; **che - è?, che ore sono?** what time is it?; **a che ~ apre il museo/negozio?** what time does the museum/shop open?; **non veder l'~ di fare** to long to do, look forward to doing; **di buon'~** early; **alla buon'~!** at last!; **~ legale** o **estiva** summer time (BRIT), daylight saving time (US); **ora di cena** dinner time; **ora locale** local time; **ora di pranzo** lunchtime; **ora di punta** (Aut) rush hour

o'racolo sm oracle

o'rale ag, sm oral

o'rario, -a ag hourly; (fuso, segnale) time cpd; (velocità) per hour ▶ sm timetable, schedule; (di ufficio, visite ecc) hours pl, time(s pl); **in ~** on time

o'rata sf (Zool) sea bream

ora'tore, -'trice sm/f speaker; orator

'orbita sf (Astr, Fisica) orbit; (Anat) (eye-)socket

or'chestra [or'kɛstra] sf orchestra

orchi'dea [orki'dɛa] sf orchid

or'digno [or'diɲɲo] sm (esplosivo) explosive device

ordi'nale ag, sm ordinal

ordi'nare vt (mettere in ordine) to arrange, organize; (Comm) to order; (prescrivere: medicina) to prescribe; (comandare): **posso ~ per favore?** can I order now please?; **~ a qn di fare qc** to order o command sb to do sth; (Rel) to ordain

ordi'nario, -a ag (comune) ordinary; everyday; standard; (grossolano) coarse, common ▶ sm ordinary; (Ins: di università) full professor

ordi'nato, -a ag tidy, orderly

ordinazi'one [ordinat'tsjone] sf (Comm) order; (Rel) ordination; **eseguire qc su ~** to make sth to order

'ordine sm order; (carattere): **d'~ pratico** of a practical nature; **all'~** (Comm: assegno) to order; **di prim'~** first-class; **fino a nuovo ~** until further notice; **essere in ~** (documenti) to be in order; (stanza, persona) to be tidy; **mettere in ~** to put in order, tidy (up); **l'~ pubblico** law and order; **ordini (sacri)** (Rel) holy orders; **ordine del giorno** (di seduta) agenda; (Mil) order of the day; **ordine di pagamento** (Comm) order for payment

orec'chino [orek'kino] sm earring

o'recchio [o'rekkjo] (pl(f) **o'recchie**) sm (Anat) ear

orecchi'oni [orek'kjoni] smpl (Med) mumps sg

o'refice [o'rɛfitʃe] sm goldsmith; jeweller; **orefice'ria** sf (arte) goldsmith's art; (negozio) jeweller's (shop)

'orfano, -a ag orphan(ed) ▸ sm/f orphan; **~ di padre/madre** fatherless/motherless

orga'netto sm barrel organ; (fam: armonica a bocca) mouth organ; (: fisarmonica) accordion

or'ganico, -a, -ci, -che ag organic ▸ sm personnel, staff

organi'gramma, -i sm organization chart

orga'nismo sm (Biol) organism; (corpo umano) body; (Amm) body, organism

organiz'zare [organid'dzare] vt to organize; **organizzarsi** vpr to get organized; **organizzazi'one** sf organization

'organo sm organ; (di congegno) part; (portavoce) spokesman, mouthpiece

'orgia, -ge ['ɔrdʒa] sf orgy

or'goglio [or'gɔʎʎo] sm pride; **orgogli'oso, -a** ag proud

orien'tale ag oriental; eastern; east

orienta'mento sm positioning; orientation; direction; **senso di ~** sense of direction; **perdere l'~** to lose one's bearings; **orientamento professionale** careers guidance

orientarsi vpr to find one's bearings; (fig: tendere) to tend, lean; (: indirizzarsi): **~ verso** to take up, go in for

ori'ente sm east; **l'O~** the East, the Orient; **a ~** in the east

o'rigano sm oregano

origi'nale [oridʒi'nale] ag original; (bizzarro) eccentric ▸ sm original

origi'nario, -a [oridʒi'narjo] ag original; **essere ~ di** to be a native of; (provenire da) to originate from; to be native to

o'rigine [o'ridʒine] sf origin; **all'~** originally; **d'~ inglese** of English origin; **dare ~ a** to give rise to

origli'are [oriʎ'ʎare] vi **~ (a)** to eavesdrop (on)

o'rina sf urine

ori'nare vi to urinate ▸ vt to pass

orizzon'tale [oriddzon'tale] ag horizontal

oriz'zonte [orid'dzonte] sm horizon

'orlo sm edge, border; (di recipiente) rim, brim; (di vestito ecc) hem

'orma sf (di persona) footprint; (di animale) track; (impronta, traccia) mark, trace

or'mai av by now, by this time; (adesso) now; (quasi) almost, nearly

ormeggi'are [ormed'dʒare] vt (Naut) to moor

or'mone sm hormone

ornamen'tale ag ornamental, decorative

or'nare vt to adorn, decorate; **ornarsi** vpr **ornarsi (di)** to deck o.s. (out) (with)

ornitolo'gia [ornitolo'dʒia] sf ornithology

'oro sm gold; **d'~, in ~** gold cpd; **d'~** (colore, occasione) golden; (persona) marvellous

oro'logio [oro'lɔdʒo] sm clock; (da tasca, da polso) watch; **orologio al quarzo** quartz watch; **orologio da polso** wristwatch

o'roscopo sm horoscope

or'rendo, -a ag (spaventoso) horrible, awful; (bruttissimo) hideous

or'ribile ag horrible

or'rore sm horror; **avere in ~ qn/qc** to loathe o detest sb/sth; **mi fanno ~** I loathe o detest them

orsacchi'otto [orsak'kjɔtto] sm teddy bear

'orso *sm* bear; **orso bruno/bianco** brown/polar bear

or'taggio [or'taddʒo] *sm* vegetable

or'tensia *sf* hydrangea

or'tica, -che *sf* (stinging) nettle

orti'caria *sf* nettle rash

'orto *sm* vegetable garden, kitchen garden; (*Agr*) market garden (*BRIT*), truck farm (*US*); **orto botanico** botanical garden(s) (*pl*)

orto'dosso, -a *ag* orthodox

ortogra'fia *sf* spelling

orto'pedico, -a, -ci, -che *ag* orthopaedic ▶ *sm* orthopaedic specialist

orzai'olo [ordza'jɔlo] *sm* (*Med*) stye

'orzo ['ordzo] *sm* barley

o'sare *vt, vi* to dare; **~ fare** to dare (to) do

oscenità [oʃʃeni'ta] *sf inv* obscenity

o'sceno, -a [oʃʃeno] *ag* obscene; (*ripugnante*) ghastly

oscil'lare [oʃʃil'lare] *vi* (*pendolo*) to swing; (*dondolare: al vento ecc*) to rock; (*variare*) to fluctuate; (*Tecn*) to oscillate; (*fig*): **~ fra** to waver *o* hesitate between

oscu'rare *vt* to darken, obscure; (*fig*) to obscure; **oscurarsi** *vpr* (*cielo*) to darken, cloud over; (*persona*): **si oscurò in volto** his face clouded over

oscurità *sf* (*vedi ag*) darkness; obscurity

os'curo, -a *ag* dark; (*fig*) obscure; humble, lowly ▶ *sm* **all'~** in the dark; **tenere qn all'~ di qc** to keep sb in the dark about sth

ospe'dale *sm* hospital; **dov'è l'~ più vicino?** where's the nearest hospital?

ospi'tale *ag* hospitable

ospi'tare *vt* to give hospitality to; (*albergo*) to accommodate

'ospite *sm/f* (*persona che ospita*) host/hostess; (*persona ospitata*) guest

os'pizio [os'pittsjo] *sm* (*per vecchi ecc*) home

osser'vare *vt* to observe, watch; (*esaminare*) to examine; (*notare, rilevare*) to notice, observe; (*Dir: la legge*) to observe, respect; (*mantenere: silenzio*) to keep, observe; **far ~ qc a qn** to point sth out to sb; **osservazi'one** *sf* observation; (*di legge ecc*) observance; (*considerazione critica*) observation, remark; (*rimprovero*) reproof; **in osservazione** under observation

ossessio'nare *vt* to obsess, haunt; (*tormentare*) to torment, harass

ossessi'one *sf* obsession

os'sia *cong* that is, to be precise

'ossido *sm* oxide; **ossido di carbonio** carbon monoxide

ossige'nare [ossidʒe'nare] *vt* to oxygenate; (*decolorare*) to bleach; **acqua ossigenata** hydrogen peroxide

os'sigeno *sm* oxygen

'osso (*pl(f)* **ossa**) (*nel senso Anat*) *sm* bone; **d'~** (*bottone ecc*) of bone, bone *cpd*; **osso di seppia** cuttlebone

ostaco'lare *vt* to block, obstruct

os'tacolo *sm* obstacle; (*Equitazione*) hurdle, jump

os'taggio [os'taddʒo] *sm* hostage

os'tello *sm*; **ostello della gioventù** youth hostel

osten'tare *vt* to make a show of, flaunt

oste'ria *sf* inn

os'tetrico, -a, -ci, -che *ag* obstetric ▶ *sm* obstetrician

'ostia *sf* (*Rel*) host; (*per medicinali*) wafer

'ostico, -a, -ci, -che *ag* (*fig*) harsh; hard, difficult; unpleasant

os'tile *ag* hostile

osti'narsi *vpr* to insist, dig one's heels in; **~ a fare** to persist (obstinately) in doing; **osti'nato, -a** *ag* (*caparbio*) obstinate; (*tenace*) persistent, determined

'ostrica, -che sf oyster
Attenzione! In inglese esiste la parola *ostrich*, che però significa *struzzo*.
ostru'ire vt to obstruct, block
o'tite sf ear infection
ot'tanta num eighty
ot'tavo, -a num eighth
otte'nere vt to obtain, get; (*risultato*) to achieve, obtain
'ottica sf (*scienza*) optics sg; (*Fot: lenti, prismi ecc*) optics pl
'ottico, -a, -ci, -che ag (*della vista: nervo*) optic; (*dell'ottica*) optical ▶ sm optician
ottima'mente av excellently, very well
otti'mismo sm optimism;
otti'mista, -i, -e sm/f optimist
'ottimo, -a ag excellent, very good
'otto num eight
ot'tobre sm October
otto'cento [otto'tʃɛnto] num eight hundred ▶ sm l'O~ the nineteenth century
ot'tone sm brass; **gli ottoni** (*Mus*) the brass
ottu'rare vt to close (up); (*dente*) to fill; **il lavandino è otturato** the sink is blocked; **otturarsi** vpr to become o get blocked up; **otturazi'one** sf closing (up); (*dentaria*) filling
ot'tuso, -a ag (*Mat, fig*) obtuse; (*suono*) dull
o'vaia sf (*Anat*) ovary
o'vale ag, sm oval
o'vatta sf cotton wool; (*per imbottire*) padding, wadding
'ovest sm west
o'vile sm pen, enclosure
ovulazi'one [ovulat'tsjone] sf ovulation
'ovulo sm (*Fisiol*) ovum
o'vunque av = **dovunque**
ovvi'are vi ~ **a** to obviate
'ovvio, -a ag obvious

ozi'are [ot'tsjare] vi to laze, idle
'ozio ['ɔttsjo] sm idleness; (*tempo libero*) leisure; **ore d'~** leisure time; **stare in ~** to be idle
o'zono [o'dzɔno] sm ozone

p

P abbr (= *parcheggio*) P; (*Aut: = principiante*) L
p. abbr (= *pagina*) p.
pac'chetto [pak'ketto] sm packet; **pacchetto azionario** (*Comm*) shareholding
'pacco, -chi sm parcel; (*involto*) bundle; **pacco postale** parcel
'pace ['patʃe] sf peace; **darsi ~** to resign o.s.; **fare la ~ con** to make it up with
pa'cifico, -a, -ci, -che [pa'tʃi:fiko] ag (*persona*) peaceable; (*vita*) peaceful; (*fig: indiscusso*) indisputable; (: *ovvio*) obvious, clear ▶ sm **il P~, l'Oceano P~** the Pacific (Ocean)
paci'fista, -i, -e [patʃi'fista] sm/f pacifist
pa'della sf frying pan; (*per infermi*) bedpan
padigli'one [padiʎ'ʎone] sm pavilion
'Padova sf Padua
'padre sm father
pa'drino sm godfather
padro'nanza [padro'nantsa] sf command, mastery

pa'drone, -a sm/f master/mistress; (proprietario) owner; (datore di lavoro) employer; **essere ~ di sé** to be in control of o.s.; **padrone(a) di casa** master/mistress of the house; (per gli inquilini) landlord/lady

pae'saggio [pae'zaddʒo] sm landscape

pa'ese sm (nazione) country, nation; (terra) country, land; (villaggio) village, (small) town; **i Paesi Bassi** the Netherlands; **paese di provenienza** country of origin

'paga, -ghe sf pay, wages pl

paga'mento sm payment

pa'gare vt to pay; (acquisto, fig: colpa) to pay for; (contraccambiare) to repay, pay back ▶ vi to pay; **quanto l'hai pagato?** how much did you pay for it?; **posso ~ con la carta di credito?** can I pay by credit card?; **~ in contanti** to pay cash

pa'gella [pa'dʒɛlla] sf (Ins) report card

pagherò [page'rɔ] sm inv acknowledgement of a debt, IOU

'pagina ['padʒina] sf page; **pagine bianche** phone book, telephone directory; **pagine gialle** Yellow Pages

'paglia ['paʎʎa] sf straw

pagli'accio [paʎ'ʎattʃo] sm clown

pagli'etta [paʎ'ʎetta] sf (cappello per uomo) (straw) boater; (per tegami ecc) steel wool

pa'gnotta [paɲ'ɲɔtta] sf round loaf

'paio (pl(f) **'paia**) sm pair; **un ~ di** (alcuni) a couple of

'Pakistan sm **il ~** Pakistan

'pala sf shovel; (di remo, ventilatore, elica) blade; (di ruota) paddle

pa'lato sm palate

pa'lazzo [pa'lattso] sm (reggia) palace; (edificio) building; **palazzo di giustizia** courthouse; **palazzo dello sport** sports stadium

'palco, -chi sm (Teatro) box; (tavolato) platform, stand; (ripiano) layer

palco'scenico, -ci [palkoʃ'ʃeniko] sm (Teatro) stage

pa'lese ag clear, evident

Pales'tina sf **la ~** Palestine

palesti'nese ag, sm/f Palestinian

pa'lestra sf gymnasium; (esercizio atletico) exercise, training; (fig) training ground, school

pa'letta sf spade; (per il focolare) shovel; (del capostazione) signalling disc

pa'letto sm stake, peg; (spranga) bolt

'palio sm (gara): **il P~** horse race run at Siena; **mettere qc in ~** to offer sth as a prize

- **palio**
- The **palio** is a horse race which takes
- place in a number of Italian towns,
- the most famous being the one in
- Siena. This is usually held twice a
- year on July 2nd and August 16th
- in the Piazza del Campo in Siena.
- 10 of the 17 **contrade** or districts
- take part, each represented by a
- horse and rider. The winner is the
- first horse to complete the course,
- whether it has a rider or not.

'palla sf ball; (pallottola) bullet; **palla di neve** snowball; **palla ovale** rugby ball; **palla'canestro** sf basketball; **palla'mano** sf handball; **pallanu'oto** sf water polo; **palla'volo** sf volleyball

palleggi'are [palled'dʒare] vi (Calcio) to practise with the ball; (Tennis) to knock up

pallia'tivo sm palliative; (fig) stopgap measure

'pallido, -a ag pale

pal'lina sf (bilia) marble

pallon'cino [pallon'tʃino] sm balloon; (lampioncino) Chinese lantern

pal'lone sm (palla) ball; (Calcio) football; (aerostato) balloon; **gioco del ~** football

p

pal'lottola sf pellet; (proiettile) bullet

'**palma** sf (Anat) = **palmo**; (Bot, simbolo) palm; **palma da datteri** date palm

'**palmo** sm (Anat) palm; **restare con un ~ di naso** to be badly disappointed

'**palo** sm (legno appuntito) stake; (sostegno) pole; **fare da o il ~** (fig) to act as look-out

palom'baro sm diver

pal'pare vt to feel, finger

'**palpebra** sf eyelid

pa'lude sf marsh, swamp

pancarrè sm sliced bread

pan'cetta [pan'tʃetta] sf (Cuc) bacon

pan'china [pan'kina] sf garden seat; (di giardino pubblico) (park) bench

'**pancia, -ce** ['pantʃa] sf belly, stomach; **mettere o fare ~** to be getting a paunch; **avere mal di ~** to have stomachache o a sore stomach

panci'otto [pan'tʃɔtto] sm waistcoat

'**pancreas** sm inv pancreas

'**panda** sm inv panda

'**pane** sm bread; (pagnotta) loaf (of bread); (forma): **un ~ di burro** a pat of butter; **guadagnarsi il ~** to earn one's living; **pane a cassetta** sliced bread; **pane di Spagna** sponge cake; **pane integrale** wholemeal bread; **pane tostato** toast

panette'ria sf (forno) bakery; (negozio) baker's (shop), bakery

panetti'ere, -a sm/f baker

panet'tone sm a kind of spiced brioche with sultanas, eaten at Christmas

pangrat'tato sm breadcrumbs pl

'**panico, -a, -ci, -che** ag, sm panic

pani'ere sm basket

pani'ficio [pani'fitʃo] sm = **panetteria**

pa'nino sm roll; **panino caldo** toasted sandwich; **panino imbottito** filled roll; sandwich; **panino'teca, -che** sf sandwich bar

'**panna** sf (Cuc) cream; (Tecn) = **panne**; **panna da cucina** cooking cream;

panna montata whipped cream

'**panne** sf inv **essere in ~** (Aut) to have broken down

pan'nello sm panel; **pannello solare** solar panel

'**panno** sm cloth; **panni** smpl (abiti) clothes; **mettiti nei miei panni** (fig) put yourself in my shoes

pan'nocchia [pan'nɔkkja] sf (di mais ecc) ear

panno'lino sm (per bambini) nappy (BRIT), diaper (US)

pano'rama, -i sm panorama

panta'loni smpl trousers (BRIT), pants (US), pair sg of trousers o pants

pan'tano sm bog

pan'tera sf panther

pan'tofola sf slipper

'**Papa, -i** sm pope

papà sm inv dad(dy)

pa'pavero sm poppy

'**pappa** sf baby cereal; **pappa reale** royal jelly

pappa'gallo sm parrot; (fig: uomo) Romeo, wolf

pa'rabola sf (Mat) parabola; (Rel) parable

para'bolico, -a, ci, che ag (Mat) parabolic; vedi anche **antenna**

para'brezza [para'breddza] sm inv (Aut) windscreen (BRIT), windshield (US)

paraca'dute sm inv parachute

para'diso sm paradise

parados'sale ag paradoxical

para'fulmine sm lightning conductor

pa'raggi [pa'raddʒi] smpl **nei ~** in the vicinity, in the neighbourhood

parago'nare vt **~ con/a** to compare with/to

para'gone sm comparison; (esempio analogo) analogy, parallel

pa'ragrafo sm paragraph

pa'ralisi sf paralysis

paral'lelo, -a ag parallel ▶ sm (Geo)

parallel; (*comparazione*): **fare un ~ tra** to draw a parallel between

para'lume sm lampshade

pa'rametro sm parameter

para'noia sf paranoia; **para'noico, -a, -ci, -che** ag, sm/f paranoid

para'occhi [para'ɔkki] smpl blinkers

para'petto sm balustrade

pa'rare vt (*addobbare*) to adorn, deck; (*proteggere*) to shield, protect; (*scansare: colpo*) to parry; (*Calcio*) to save ▶ vi **dove vuole andare a ~?** what are you driving at?

pa'rata sf (*Sport*) save; (*Mil*) review, parade

para'urti sm inv (*Aut*) bumper

para'vento sm folding screen; **fare da ~ a qn** (*fig*) to shield sb

par'cella [par'tʃɛlla] sf account, fee (*of lawyer etc*)

parcheggi'are [parked'dʒare] vt to park; **posso ~ qui?** can I park here?; **parcheggiatore, -trice** [parkeddʒa'tore] sm/f (*Aut*) parking attendant

par'cheggio sm parking no pl; (*luogo*) car park; (*singolo posto*) parking space

par'chimetro [par'kimetro] sm parking meter

'parco, -chi sm park; (*spazio per deposito*) depot; (*complesso di veicoli*) fleet

par'cometro sm (pay-and-display) ticket machine

pa'recchio, -a [pa'rekkjo] det quite a lot of; (*tempo*) quite a lot of, a long

pareggi'are [pared'dʒare] vt to make equal; (*terreno*) to level, make level; (*bilancio, conti*) to balance ▶ vi (*Sport*) to draw; **pa'reggio** sm (*Econ*) balance; (*Sport*) draw

pa'rente sm/f relative, relation
Attenzione! In inglese esiste la parola *parent*, che però significa *genitore*.

paren'tela sf (*vincolo di sangue, fig*) relationship

pa'rentesi sf (*segno grafico*) bracket, parenthesis; (*frase incisa*) parenthesis; (*digressione*) parenthesis, digression

pa'rere sm (*opinione*) opinion; (*consiglio*) advice, opinion; **a mio ~** in my opinion ▶ vi to seem, appear ▶ vb impers **pare che** it seems o appears that, they say that; **mi pare che** it seems to me that; **mi pare di sì** I think so; **fai come ti pare** do as you like; **che ti pare del mio libro?** what do you think of my book?

pa'rete sf wall

'pari ag inv (*uguale*) equal, same; (*in giochi*) equal; drawn, tied; (*Mat*) even ▶ sm inv (*Pol: di Gran Bretagna*) peer ▶ sm/f inv peer, equal; **copiato ~ ~** copied word for word; **alla ~** on the same level; **ragazza alla ~** au pair girl; **mettersi alla ~ con** to place o.s. on the same level as; **mettersi in ~ con** to catch up with; **andare di ~ passo con qn** to keep pace with sb

Pa'rigi [pa'ridʒi] sf Paris

pari'gino, -a [pari'dʒino] ag, sm/f Parisian

parità sf parity, equality; (*Sport*) draw, tie

parlamen'tare ag parliamentary ▶ sm/f ≈ Member of Parliament (*BRIT*), ≈ Congressman/woman (*US*) ▶ vi to negotiate, parley

parla'mento sm parliament

- **parlamento**
- The Italian **Parlamento** is made
- up of two chambers, the **Camera**
- **dei deputati** and the **Senato**.
- Parliamentary elections are held
- every 5 years.

parlan'tina (*fam*) sf talkativeness; **avere ~** to have the gift of the gab

par'lare vi to speak, talk; (*confidare cose segrete*) to talk ▶ vt to speak;

p

~ (a qn) di to speak o talk (to sb) about; **posso ~ con…?** can I speak to …?; **parla italiano?** do you speak italian?; **non parlo inglese** I don't speak English

parmigi'ano [parmi'dʒano] sm (grana) Parmesan (cheese)

pa'rola sf word; (facoltà) speech; **parole** sfpl (chiacchiere) talk sg; **chiedere la ~** to ask permission to speak; **prendere la ~** to take the floor; **parola d'onore** word of honour; **parola d'ordine** (Mil) password; **parole incrociate** crossword (puzzle) sg; **paro'laccia, -ce** sf bad word, swearword

parrò ecc vb vedi **parere**

par'rocchia [par'rɔkkja] sf parish; parish church

par'rucca, -che sf wig

parrucchi'ere, -a [parruk'kjɛre] sm/f hairdresser ▶ sm barber

'parte sf part; (lato) side; (quota spettante a ciascuno) share; (direzione) direction; (Pol) party; (Dir) faction; party; **a ~** ag separate ▶ av separately; **scherzi a ~** joking aside; **a ~ ciò** apart from that; **da ~ di** (in disparte) to one side, aside; **d'altra ~** on the other hand; **da ~ di** (per conto di) on behalf of; **da ~ mia** as far as I'm concerned, as for me; **da ~ a ~** right through; **da ogni ~** on all sides, everywhere; (moto da luogo) from all sides; **da nessuna ~** nowhere; **da questa ~** (in questa direzione) this way; **prendere ~ a qc** to take part in sth; **mettere da ~** to put aside; **mettere qn a ~ di** to inform sb of

parteci'pare [partetʃi'pare] vi **~ a** to take part in, participate in; (utili ecc) to share in; (spese ecc) to contribute to; (dolore, successo di qn) to share (in)

parteggi'are [parted'dʒare] vi **~ per** to side with, be on the side of

par'tenza [par'tɛntsa] sf departure; (Sport) start; **essere in ~** to be about to leave, be leaving

parti'cipio [parti'tʃipjo] sm participle

partico'lare ag (specifico) particular; (proprio) personal, private; (speciale) special, particular; (caratteristico) distinctive, characteristic; (fuori dal comune) peculiar ▶ sm detail, particular; **in ~** in particular, particularly

par'tire vi to go, leave; (allontanarsi) to go (o drive ecc) away o off; (petardo, colpo) to go off; (fig: avere inizio, Sport) to start; **sono partita da Roma alle 7** I left Rome at 7; **a che ora parte il treno/l'autobus?** what time does the train/bus leave?; **il volo parte da Ciampino** the flight leaves from Ciampino; **a ~ da** from

par'tita sf (Comm) lot, consignment; (Econ: registrazione) entry, item; (Carte, Sport: gioco) game; (: competizione) match, game; **partita di caccia** hunting party; **partita IVA** VAT registration number

par'tito sm (Pol) party; (decisione) decision, resolution; (persona da maritare) match

'parto sm (Med) delivery, (child)birth; labour

'parvi ecc vb vedi **parere**

parzi'ale [par'tsjale] ag (limitato) partial; (non obiettivo) biased, partial

pasco'lare vt, vi to graze

'pascolo sm pasture

'Pasqua sf Easter; **Pas'quetta** sf Easter Monday

pas'sabile ag fairly good, passable

pas'saggio [pas'saddʒo] sm passing no pl, passage; (traversata) crossing no pl, passage; (luogo, prezzo della traversata, brano di libro ecc) passage; (su veicolo altrui) lift (BRIT), ride; (Sport) pass; **di ~** (persona) passing through;

può darmi un ~ fino alla stazione? can you give me a lift to the station?; **passaggio a livello** level (BRIT) o grade (US) crossing; **passaggio pedonale** pedestrian crossing

passamon'tagna [passamon'taɲɲa] sm inv balaclava

pas'sante sm/f passer-by ▶ sm loop

passa'porto sm passport

pas'sare vi (andare) to go; (veicolo, pedone) to pass (by), go by; (fare una breve sosta: postino ecc) to come, call; (: amico: per fare una visita) to call o drop in; (sole, aria, luce) to get through; (trascorrere: giorni, tempo) to pass, go by; (fig: proposta di legge) to be passed; (: dolore) to pass, go away; (Carte) to pass ▶ vt (attraversare) to cross; (trasmettere: messaggio): **~ qc a qn** to pass sth on to sb; (dare): **~ qc a qn** to pass sth to sb, give sb sth; (trascorrere: tempo) to spend; (superare: esame) to pass; (triturare: verdura) to strain; (approvare) to pass, approve; (oltrepassare, sorpassare: anche fig) to go beyond, pass; (fig: subire) to go through; **mi passa il sale/l'olio per favore?** could you pass the salt/oil please?; **~ da ... a** to pass from ... to; **~ di padre in figlio** to be handed down o to pass from father to son; **~ per** (anche fig) to go through; **~ per stupido/un genio** to be taken for a fool/a genius; **~ sopra** (anche fig) to pass over; **~ attraverso** (anche fig) to go through; **~ alla storia** to pass into history; **~ a un esame** to go up (to the next class) after an exam; **~ inosservato** to go unnoticed; **~ di moda** to go out of fashion; **le passo il Signor X** (al telefono) here is Mr X; I'm putting you through to Mr X; **lasciar ~ qn/qc** to let sb/sth through; **come te la passi?** how are you getting on?

passa'tempo sm pastime, hobby

pas'sato, -a ag past; (sfiorito) faded ▶ sm past; (Ling) past (tense); **passato prossimo/remoto** (Ling) present perfect/past historic; **passato di verdura** (Cuc) vegetable purée

passeg'gero, -a [passed'dʒero] ag passing ▶ sm/f passenger

passeggi'are [passed'dʒare] vi to go for a walk; (in veicolo) to go for a drive; **passeggi'ata** sf walk; drive; (luogo) promenade; **fare una passeggiata** to go for a walk (o drive); **passeg'gino** sm pushchair (BRIT), stroller (US)

passe'rella sf footbridge; (di nave, aereo) gangway; (pedana) catwalk

'passero sm sparrow

passi'one sf passion

pas'sivo, -a ag passive ▶ sm (Ling) passive; (Econ) debit; (: complesso dei debiti) liabilities pl

'passo sm step; (andatura) pace; (rumore) (foot)step; (orma) footprint; (passaggio, fig: brano) passage; (valico) pass; **a ~ d'uomo** at walking pace; **~ (a)** step by step; **fare due o quattro passi** to go for a walk o a stroll; **di questo ~** at this rate; **"passo carraio"** "vehicle entrance — keep clear"

'pasta sf (Cuc) dough; (: impasto per dolce) pastry; (: anche: **~ alimentare**) pasta; (massa molle di materia) paste; (fig: indole) nature; **paste** sfpl (pasticcini) pastries; **pasta in brodo** noodle soup; **pasta sfoglia** puff pastry o paste (US)

pastasci'utta [pastaʃʃutta] sf pasta

pas'tella sf batter

pas'tello sm pastel

pas'ticca, -che sf = pastiglia

pasticce'ria [pastittʃe'ria] sf (pasticcini) pastries pl, cakes pl; (negozio) cake shop; (arte) confectionery

pasticci'ere, -a [pastit'tʃere] sm/f pastrycook; confectioner

pastic'cino [pastit'tʃino] sm petit four
pas'ticcio [pas'tittʃo] sm (Cuc) pie;
(lavoro disordinato, imbroglio) mess;
trovarsi nei pasticci to get into
trouble
pas'tiglia [pas'tiʎʎa] sf pastille
pas'tina sf small pasta shapes used
in soup
'pasto sm meal
pas'tore sm shepherd; (Rel) pastor,
minister; (anche: **cane ~**) sheepdog;
pastore tedesco (Zool) Alsatian,
German shepherd
pa'tata sf potato; **patate fritte** chips
(BRIT), French fries; **pata'tine** sfpl
(potato) crisps; **patatine fritte** chips
pa'té sm inv pâté
pa'tente sf licence; **patente di guida**
driving licence (BRIT), driver's license
(US); **patente a punti** driving licence
with penalty points

Attenzione! In inglese esiste la
parola patent, che però significa
brevetto.

paternità sf paternity, fatherhood
pa'tetico, -a, -ci, -che ag pathetic;
(commovente) moving, touching
pa'tibolo sm gallows sg, scaffold
'patina sf (su rame ecc) patina; (sulla
lingua) fur, coating
pa'tire vt, vi to suffer
pa'tito, -a sm/f enthusiast, fan, lover
patolo'gia [patolo'dʒia] sf pathology
'patria sf homeland
pa'trigno [pa'triɲɲo] sm stepfather
patri'monio sm estate, property;
(fig) heritage
pa'trono sm (Rel) patron saint; (socio
di patronato) patron; (Dir) counsel
patteggi'are [patted'dʒare] vt, vi to
negotiate; (Dir) to plea-bargain
patti'naggio [patti'naddʒo] sm
skating; **pattinaggio a rotelle/sul
ghiaccio** roller-/ice-skating
patti'nare vi to skate; **~ sul ghiaccio**

to ice-skate; **pattina'tore, -'trice**
sm/f skater; **'pattino** sm skate; (di
slitta) runner; (Aer) skid; (Tecn) sliding
block; **pattini in linea** Rollerblades®;
pattini da ghiaccio/a rotelle
ice/roller skates
'patto sm (accordo) pact, agreement;
(condizione) term, condition; **a ~ che**
on condition that
pat'tuglia [pat'tuʎʎa] sf (Mil) patrol
pattu'ire vt to reach an agreement on
pattumi'era sf (dust)bin (BRIT),
ashcan (US)
pa'ura sf fear; **aver ~ di/di fare/che**
to be frightened o afraid of/of doing/
that; **far ~ a** to frighten; **per ~ di/che**
for fear of/that; **pau'roso, -a** ag (che
fa paura) frightening; (che ha paura)
fearful, timorous
'pausa sf (sosta) break; (nel parlare,
Mus) pause
pavi'mento sm floor

Attenzione! In inglese esiste la
parola pavement, che però significa
marciapiede.

pa'vone sm peacock
pazien'tare [pattsjen'tare] vi to be
patient
pazi'ente [pat'tsjɛnte] ag, sm/f
patient; **pazi'enza** sf patience
paz'zesco, -a, -schi, -sche
[pat'tsesko] ag mad, crazy
paz'zia [pat'tsia] sf (Med) madness,
insanity; (azione) folly; (di azione,
decisione) madness, folly
'pazzo, -a ['pattso] ag (Med) mad,
insane; (strano) wild, mad ▶ sm/f
madman/woman; **~ di** (gioia, amore
ecc) mad o crazy with; **~ per qc/qn**
mad o crazy about sth/sb
PC [pit'tʃi] sigla m inv (= personal
computer) PC; **PC portatile** laptop
pec'care vi to sin; (fig) to err
pec'cato sm sin; **è un ~ che** it's a pity
that; **che ~!** what a shame o pity!

peccherò *ecc* [pekke'rɔ] *vb vedi* **peccare**

'pece ['petʃe] *sf* pitch

Pe'chino [pe'kino] *sf* Beijing

'pecora *sf* sheep; **peco'rino** *sm* sheep's milk cheese

pe'daggio [pe'daddʒo] *sm* toll

pedago'gia [pedago'dʒia] *sf* pedagogy, educational methods *pl*

peda'lare *vi* to pedal; (*andare in bicicletta*) to cycle

pe'dale *sm* pedal

pe'dana *sf* footboard; (*Sport: nel salto*) springboard; (: *nella scherma*) piste

pe'dante *ag* pedantic ▶ *sm/f* pedant

pe'data *sf* (*impronta*) footprint; (*colpo*) kick; **prendere a pedate qn/qc** to kick sb/sth

pedi'atra, -i, -e *sm/f* paediatrician

pedi'cure *sm/f inv* chiropodist

pe'dina *sf* (*della dama*) draughtsman (*BRIT*), draftsman (*US*); (*fig*) pawn

pedi'nare *vt* to shadow, tail

pe'dofilo, -a *ag, sm/f* paedophile

pedo'nale *ag* pedestrian

pe'done, -a *sm/f* pedestrian ▶ *sm* (*Scacchi*) pawn

'peggio ['pɛddʒo] *av, ag inv* worse ▶ *sm o f il o la ~* the worst; **alla ~** at worst, if the worst comes to the worst; **peggio'rare** *vt* to make worse, worsen ▶ *vi* to grow worse, worsen; **peggi'ore** *ag* (*comparativo*) worse; (*superlativo*) worst ▶ *sm/f* **il(la) peggiore** the worst (person)

'pegno ['peɲɲo] *sm* (*Dir*) security, pledge; (*nei giochi di società*) forfeit; (*fig*) pledge, token; **dare in ~ qc** to pawn sth

pe'lare *vt* (*spennare*) to pluck; (*spellare*) to skin; (*sbucciare*) to peel; (*fig*) to make pay through the nose

pe'lato, -a *ag* **pomodori pelati** tinned tomatoes

'pelle *sf* skin; (*di animale*) skin, hide; (*cuoio*) leather; **avere la ~ d'oca** to have goose pimples *o* goose flesh

pellegri'naggio [pellegri'naddʒo] *sm* pilgrimage

pelle'rossa (*pl* **pelli'rosse**) *sm/f* Red Indian

pelli'cano *sm* pelican

pel'liccia, -ce [pel'littʃa] *sf* (*mantello di animale*) coat, fur; (*indumento*) fur coat; **pelliccia ecologica** fake fur

pel'licola *sf* (*membrana sottile*) film, layer; (*Fot, Cinema*) film

'pelo *sm* hair; (*pelame*) coat, hair; (*pelliccia*) fur; (*di tappeto*) pile; (*di liquido*) surface; **per un ~: per un ~ non ho perduto il treno** I very nearly missed the train; **c'è mancato un ~ che affogasse** he escaped drowning by the skin of his teeth; **pe'loso, -a** *ag* hairy

'peltro *sm* pewter

pe'luche [pə'lyʃ] *sm* plush; **giocattoli di ~** soft toys

pe'luria *sf* down

'pena *sf* (*Dir*) sentence; (*punizione*) punishment; (*sofferenza*) sadness *no pl*, sorrow; (*fatica*) trouble *no pl*, effort; (*difficoltà*) difficulty; **far ~** to be pitiful; **mi fai ~** I feel sorry for you; **prendersi** *o* **darsi la ~ di fare** to go to the trouble of doing; **pena di morte** death sentence; **pena pecuniaria** fine; **pe'nale** *ag* penal

pen'dente *ag* hanging; leaning ▶ *sm* (*ciondolo*) pendant; (*orecchino*) drop earring

'pendere *vi* (*essere appeso*) **~ da** to hang from; (*essere inclinato*) to lean; (*fig: incombere*) **~ su** to hang over

pen'dio, -'dii *sm* slope, slant; (*luogo in pendenza*) slope

'pendola *sf* pendulum clock

pendo'lare *sm/f* commuter

pendo'lino *sm* high-speed train

pene'trante *ag* piercing, penetrating

pene'trare *vi* to come *o* get in ▶ *vt* to penetrate; **~ in** to enter; (*proiettile*) to penetrate; (: *acqua, aria*) to go *o* come into

penicil'lina [penitʃil'lina] *sf* penicillin

pe'nisola *sf* peninsula

penitenzi'ario [peniten'tsjarjo] *sm* prison

'penna *sf* (*di uccello*) feather; (*per scrivere*) pen; **penne** *sfpl* (*Cuc*) quills (*type of pasta*); **penna a sfera** ballpoint pen; **penna stilografica** fountain pen

penna'rello *sm* felt(-tip) pen

pen'nello *sm* brush; (*per dipingere*) (paint)brush; **a ~** (*perfettamente*) to perfection, perfectly; **pennello per la barba** shaving brush

pe'nombra *sf* half-light, dim light

pen'sare *vi* to think ▶ *vt* to think; (*inventare, escogitare*) to think out; **~ a** to think of; (*amico, vacanze*) to think of *o* about; (*problema*) to think about; **~ di fare qc** to think of doing sth; **ci penso io** I'll see to *o* take care of it

pensi'ero *sm* thought; (*modo di pensare, dottrina*) thinking *no pl*; (*preoccupazione*) worry, care, trouble; **stare in ~ per qn** to be worried about sb; **pensie'roso, -a** *ag* thoughtful

'pensile *ag* hanging ▶ *sm* (*in cucina*) wall cupboard

pensio'nato, -a *sm/f* pensioner

pensi'one *sf* (*al prestatore di lavoro*) pension; (*vitto e alloggio*) board and lodging; (*albergo*) boarding house; **andare in ~** to retire; **mezza ~** half board; **pensione completa** full board

pen'tirsi *vpr* **~ di** to repent of; (*rammaricarsi*) to regret, be sorry for

'pentola *sf* pot; **pentola a pressione** pressure cooker

pe'nultimo, -a *ag* last but one (*BRIT*), next to last, penultimate

penzo'lare [pendzo'lare] *vi* to dangle

'pepe *sm* pepper; **pepe in grani/ macinato** whole/ground pepper

peperon'cino [peperon'tʃino] *sm* chilli pepper

pepe'rone *sm* pepper, capsicum; (*piccante*) chili

pe'pita *sf* nugget

O per
prep

1 (*moto attraverso luogo*) through; **i ladri sono passati per la finestra** the thieves got in (*o* out) through the window; **l'ho cercato per tutta la casa** I've searched the whole house *o* all over the house for it

2 (*moto a luogo*) for, to; **partire per la Germania/il mare** to leave for Germany/the sea; **il treno per Roma** the Rome train, the train for *o* to Rome

3 (*stato in luogo*): **seduto/sdraiato per terra** sitting/lying on the ground

4 (*tempo*) for; **per anni/lungo tempo** for years/a long time; **per tutta l'estate** throughout the summer, all summer long; **lo rividi per Natale** I saw him again at Christmas; **lo faccio per lunedì** I'll do it for Monday

5 (*mezzo, maniera*) by; **per lettera/via aerea/ferrovia** by letter/airmail/rail; **prendere qn per un braccio** to take sb by the arm

6 (*causa, scopo*) for; **assente per malattia** absent because of *o* through *o* owing to illness; **ottimo per il mal di gola** excellent for sore throats

7 (*limitazione*) for; **è troppo difficile per lui** it's too difficult for him; **per quel che mi riguarda** as far as I'm concerned; **per poco che sia** however little it may be; **per questa volta ti perdono** I'll forgive you this time

8 (*prezzo, misura*) for; (*distributivo*) a, per; **venduto per 3 milioni** sold for 3 million; **1 euro per persona** 1 euro a *o* per person; **uno per volta** one at a time; **uno per uno** one by one; **5 per cento** 5 per cent; **3 per 4 fa 12** 3 times 4 equals 12; **dividere/moltiplicare 12 per 4** to divide/multiply 12 by 4 **9** (*in qualità di*) as; (*al posto di*) for; **avere qn per professore** to have sb as a teacher; **ti ho preso per Mario** I mistook you for Mario, I thought you were Mario; **dare per morto qn** to give sb up for dead **10** (*seguito da vb: finale*): **per fare qc** so as to do sth, in order to do sth; (*: causale*): **per aver fatto qc** for having done sth; (*: consecutivo*): **è abbastanza grande per andarci da solo** he's big enough to go on his own

'pera *sf* pear

per'bene *ag inv* respectable, decent ▶ *av* (*con cura*) properly, well

percentu'ale [pertʃentu'ale] *sf* percentage

perce'pire [pertʃe'pire] *vt* (*sentire*) to perceive; (*ricevere*) to receive

○ **perché** ['per'ke] *av* why; **perché no?** why not?; **perché non vuoi andarci?** why don't you want to go?; **spiegami perché l'hai fatto** tell me why you did it
▶ *cong*
1 (*causale*) because; **non posso uscire perché ho da fare** I can't go out because *o* as I've a lot to do
2 (*finale*) in order that, so that; **te lo do perché tu lo legga** I'm giving it to you so (that) you can read it
3 (*consecutivo*): **è troppo forte perché si possa batterlo** he's too strong to be beaten
▶ *sm inv* reason; **il perché di** the reason for

perciò [per'tʃɔ] *cong* so, for this (*o* that) reason

per'correre *vt* (*luogo*) to go all over; (*: paese*) to travel up and down, go all over; (*distanza*) to cover

per'corso, -a *pp di* **percorrere** ▶ *sm* (*tragitto*) journey; (*tratto*) route

percu'otere *vt* to hit, strike

percussi'one *sf* percussion; **strumenti a ~** (*Mus*) percussion instruments

'perdere *vt* to lose; (*lasciarsi sfuggire*) to miss; (*sprecare: tempo, denaro*) to waste ▶ *vi* to lose; (*serbatoio ecc*) to leak; **perdersi** *vpr* (*smarrirsi*) to get lost; (*svanire*) to disappear, vanish; **mi sono perso** I'm lost; **ho perso il portafoglio/passaporto** I've lost my wallet/passport; **abbiamo perso il treno** we missed our train; **saper ~** to be a good loser; **lascia ~!** forget it!, never mind!

perdigi'orno [perdi'dʒorno] *sm/f inv* idler, waster

'perdita *sf* loss; (*spreco*) waste; (*fuoriuscita*) leak; **siamo in ~** (*Comm*) we are running at a loss; **a ~ d'occhio** as far as the eye can see

perdo'nare *vt* to pardon, forgive; (*scusare*) to excuse, pardon

per'dono *sm* forgiveness; (*Dir*) pardon

perduta'mente *av* desperately, passionately

pe'renne *ag* eternal, perpetual, perennial; (*Bot*) perennial

perfetta'mente *av* perfectly; **sai ~ che ...** you know perfectly well that ...

per'fetto, -a *ag* perfect ▶ *sm* (*Ling*) perfect (tense)

perfeziona'mento [perfettsjona'mento] *sm* **~ (di)** improvement (in), perfection (of); **corso di ~** proficiency course

perfezio'nare [perfettsjo'nare] *vt* to improve, perfect; **perfezionarsi** *vpr* to improve

perfezi'one [perfet'tsjone] *sf* perfection

per'fino *av* even

perfo'rare vt to perforate, to punch a hole (o holes) in; (banda, schede) to punch; (trivellare) to drill

perga'mena sf parchment

perico'lante ag precarious

pe'ricolo sm danger; **mettere in ~** to endanger, put in danger; **perico'loso, -a** ag dangerous

perife'ria sf (di città) outskirts pl

pe'rifrasi sf circumlocution

pe'rimetro sm perimeter

peri'odico, -a, -ci, -che ag periodic(al); (Mat) recurring ▶ sm periodical

pe'riodo sm period

peripe'zie [peripet'tsie] sfpl ups and downs, vicissitudes

pe'rito, -a ag expert, skilled ▶ sm/f expert; (agronomo, navale) surveyor; **perito chimico** qualified chemist

peri'zoma, -i [peri'dzoma] sm G-string

'perla sf pearl; **per'lina** sf bead

perlus'trare vt to patrol

perma'loso, -a ag touchy

perma'nente ag permanent ▶ sf permanent wave, perm; **perma'nenza** sf permanence; (soggiorno) stay

perme'are vt to permeate

per'messo, -a pp di **permettere** ▶ sm (autorizzazione) permission, leave; (dato a militare, impiegato) leave; (licenza) licence, permit; (Mil: foglio) pass; **~?, è ~?** (posso entrare?) may I come in?; (posso passare?) excuse me; **permesso di lavoro/pesca** work/fishing permit; **permesso di soggiorno** residence permit

per'mettere vt to allow, permit; **~ a qn qc/di fare qc** to allow sb sth/to do sth; **permettersi qc/di fare qc** to allow o.s. sth/to do sth; (avere la possibilità) to afford sth/to do sth

per'misi ecc vb vedi **permettere**

per'nacchia [per'nakkja] (fam) sf **fare una ~** to blow a raspberry

per'nice [per'nitʃe] sf partridge

'perno sm pivot

pernot'tare vi to spend the night, stay overnight

'pero sm pear tree

però cong (ma) but; (tuttavia) however, nevertheless

perpendico'lare ag, sf perpendicular

per'plesso, -a ag perplexed; uncertain, undecided

perqui'sire vt to search; **perquisizi'one** sf (police) search

'perse ecc vb vedi **perdere**

persecuzi'one [persekut'tsjone] sf persecution

persegui'tare vt to persecute

perseve'rante ag persevering

'persi ecc vb vedi **perdere**

persi'ana sf shutter; **persiana avvolgibile** roller shutter

per'sino av = **perfino**

persis'tente ag persistent

'perso, -a pp di **perdere**

per'sona sf person; (qualcuno): **una ~** someone, somebody; (espressione interrogativa +) anyone o anybody

perso'naggio [perso'naddʒo] sm (persona ragguardevole) personality, figure; (tipo) character, individual; (Letteratura) character

perso'nale ag personal ▶ sm staff; personnel; (figura fisica) build

personalità sf inv personality

perspi'cace [perspi'katʃe] ag shrewd, discerning

persu'adere vt ~ **qn (di qc/a fare)** to persuade sb (of sth/to do)

per'tanto cong (quindi) so, therefore

'pertica, -che sf pole

perti'nente ag ~ **(a)** relevant (to), pertinent (to)

per'tosse sf whooping cough

perturbazi'one [perturbat'tsjone]

sf disruption; perturbation;
perturbazione atmosferica
atmospheric disturbance
per'vadere *vt* to pervade
per'verso, -a *ag* depraved; perverse
perver'tito, -a *sm/f* pervert
p.es. *abbr* (= *per esempio*) e.g.
pe'sante *ag* heavy; **è troppo ~** it's
too heavy
pe'sare *vt* to weigh ▶ *vi* (*avere un
peso*) to weigh; (*essere pesante*) to
be heavy; (*fig*) to carry weight; **~ su**
(*fig*) to lie heavy on; to influence; to
hang over; **pesarsi** *vpr* to weigh o.s.;
~ le parole to weigh one's words;
~ sulla coscienza to weigh on sb's
conscience; **mi pesa ammetterlo**
I don't like admitting it; **tutta la
responsabilità pesa su di lui** all the
responsibility rests on him; **è una
situazione che mi pesa** I find the
situation difficult; **il suo parere pesa
molto** his opinion counts for a lot
'pesca (*pl* **pesche**) (: *frutto*) *sf* peach;
(*il pescare*) fishing; **andare a ~** to go
fishing; **~ con la lenza** angling;
pesca di beneficenza (*lotteria*)
lucky dip
pes'care *vt* (*pesce*) to fish for; to catch;
(*qc nell'acqua*) to fish out; (*fig: trovare*)
to get hold of, find; **andare a ~** to
go fishing
pesca'tore *sm* fisherman; angler
'pesce ['peʃʃe] *sm* fish *gen inv*; **Pesci**
(*dello zodiaco*) Pisces; **pesce d'aprile!**
April Fool!; **pesce rosso** goldfish;
pesce spada swordfish; **pesce'cane**
sm shark
pesche'reccio [peske'rettʃo] *sm*
fishing boat
pesche'ria [peske'ria] *sf* fishmonger's
(shop) (*BRIT*), fish store (*US*)
pescherò *ecc* [peske'rɔ] *vb vedi*
pescare
'peso *sm* weight; (*Sport*) shot; **rubare**

sul ~ to give short weight; **essere di
~ a qn** (*fig*) to be a burden to sb; **peso
lordo/netto** gross/net weight;
peso massimo/medio (*Pugilato*)
heavy/middleweight
pessi'mismo *sm* pessimism;
pessi'mista, -i, -e *ag* pessimistic
▶ *sm/f* pessimist
'pessimo, -a *ag* very bad, awful
pes'tare *vt* to tread on, trample on;
(*sale, pepe*) to grind; (*uva, aglio*) to
crush; (*fig: picchiare*): **~ qn** to beat
sb up
'peste *sf* plague; (*persona*) nuisance,
pest
pes'tello *sm* pestle
'petalo *sm* (*Bot*) petal
pe'tardo *sm* firecracker, banger (*BRIT*)
petizi'one [petit'tsjone] *sf* petition
petroli'era *sf* (*nave*) oil tanker
pe'trolio *sm* oil, petroleum; (*per
lampada, fornello*) paraffin

> Attenzione! In inglese esiste la
> parola **petrol** che però significa
> *benzina*.

pettego'lare *vi* to gossip
pettego'lezzo [pettego'leddzo] *sm*
gossip *no pl*; **fare pettegolezzi** to
gossip
pet'tegolo, -a *ag* gossipy ▶ *sm/f*
gossip
petti'nare *vt* to comb (the hair
of); **pettinarsi** *vpr* to comb one's
hair; **pettina'tura** *sf* (*acconciatura*)
hairstyle
'pettine *sm* comb; (*Zool*) scallop
petti'rosso *sm* robin
'petto *sm* chest; (*seno*) breast, bust;
(*Cuc: di carne bovina*) brisket; (: *di pollo
ecc*) breast; **a doppio ~** (*abito*) double-
breasted
petu'lante *ag* insolent
'pezza ['pɛttsa] *sf* piece of cloth;
(*toppa*) patch; (*cencio*) rag, cloth
pez'zente [pet'tsɛnte] *sm/f* beggar

p

'pezzo ['pɛttso] *sm* (*gen*) piece; (*brandello, frammento*) piece, bit; (*di macchina, arnese ecc*) part; (*Stampa*) article; (*di tempo*): **aspettare un ~** to wait quite a while *o* some time; **in** *o* **a pezzi** in pieces; **andare in pezzi** to break into pieces; **un bel ~ d'uomo** a fine figure of a man; **abito a due pezzi** two-piece suit; **pezzo di cronaca** (*Stampa*) report; **pezzo grosso** (*fig*) bigwig; **pezzo di ricambio** spare part
pi'accio *ecc* ['pjattʃo] *vb vedi* **piacere**
pia'cente [pja'tʃɛnte] *ag* attractive
pia'cere [pja'tʃere] *vi* to please; **una ragazza che piace** a likeable girl; an attractive girl; **~ a: mi piace** I like it; **quei ragazzi non mi piacciono** I don't like those boys; **gli ~bbe andare al cinema** he would like to go to the cinema ▶ *sm* pleasure; (*favore*) favour; **"~!"** (*nelle presentazioni*) "pleased to meet you!"; **~ (di conoscerla)** nice to meet you; **con ~** certainly; **per ~!** please; **fare un ~ a qn** to do sb a favour; **pia'cevole** *ag* pleasant, agreeable
pi'acqui *ecc vb vedi* **piacere**
pi'aga, -ghe *sf* (*lesione*) sore; (*ferita: anche fig*) wound; (*fig: flagello*) scourge, curse; (: *persona*) pest, nuisance
piagnuco'lare [pjaɲɲuko'lare] *vi* to whimper
pianeggi'ante [pjaned'dʒante] *ag* flat, level
piane'rottolo *sm* landing
pia'neta *sm* (*Astr*) planet
pi'angere ['pjandʒere] *vi* to cry, weep; (*occhi*) to water ▶ *vt* to cry, weep; (*lamentare*) to bewail, lament; **~ la morte di qn** to mourn sb's death
pianifi'care *vt* to plan
pia'nista, -i, -e *sm/f* pianist
pi'ano, -a *ag* (*piatto*) flat, level; (*Mat*) plane; (*chiaro*) clear, plain ▶ *av* (*adagio*) slowly; (*a bassa voce*)

softly; (*con cautela*) slowly, carefully ▶ *sm* (*Mat*) plane; (*Geo*) plain; (*livello*) level, plane; (*di edificio*) floor; (*programma*) plan; (*Mus*) piano; **a che ~ si trova?** what floor is it on?; **pian ~** very slowly; (*poco a poco*) little by little; **in primo/secondo ~** in the foreground/background; **di primo ~** (*fig*) prominent, high-ranking
piano'forte *sm* piano, pianoforte
piano'terra *sm inv* ground floor
pi'ansi *ecc vb vedi* **piangere**
pi'anta *sf* (*Bot*) plant; (*Anat: anche: ~ del piede*) sole (of the foot); (*grafico*) plan; (*topografica*) map; **in ~ stabile** on the permanent staff; **pian'tare** *vt* to plant; (*conficcare*) to drive *o* hammer in; (*tenda*) to put up, pitch; (*fig: lasciare*) to leave, desert; **piantarsi** *vpr* **piantarsi davanti a qn** to plant o.s. in front of sb; **piantala!** (*fam*) cut it out!
pianter'reno *sm* = **pianoterra**
pian'tina *sf* map
pia'nura *sf* plain
pi'astra *sf* plate; (*di pietra*) slab; (*di fornello*) hotplate; **panino alla ~** ≈ toasted sandwich; **piastra di registrazione** tape deck
pias'trella *sf* tile
pias'trina *sf* (*Mil*) identity disc
piatta'forma *sf* (*anche fig*) platform
piat'tino *sm* saucer
pi'atto, -a *ag* flat; (*fig: scialbo*) dull ▶ *sm* (*recipiente, vivanda*) dish; (*portata*) course; (*parte piana*) flat (part); **piatti** *smpl* (*Mus*) cymbals; **piatto fondo** soup dish; **piatto forte** main course; **piatto del giorno** dish of the day, plat du jour; **piatto del giradischi** turntable; **piatto piano** dinner plate
pi'azza ['pjattsa] *sf* square; (*Comm*) market; **far ~ pulita** to make a clean sweep; **piazza d'armi** (*Mil*) parade ground; **piaz'zale** *sm* (large) square

piaz'zola [pjat'tsɔla] *sf* (*Aut*) lay-by; (*di tenda*) pitch

pic'cante *ag* hot, pungent; (*fig*) racy; biting

pic'chetto [pik'ketto] *sm* (*Mil*, *di scioperanti*) picket; (*di tenda*) peg

picchi'are [pik'kjare] *vt* (*persona*: *colpire*) to hit, strike; (: *prendere a botte*) to beat (up); (*battere*) to beat; (*sbattere*) to bang ▶ *vi* (*bussare*) to knock; (: *con forza*) to bang; (*colpire*) to hit, strike; (*sole*) to beat down; **picchi'ata** *sf* (*Aer*) dive

'picchio ['pikkjo] *sm* woodpecker

pic'cino, -a [pit'tʃino] *ag* tiny, very small

picci'one [pit'tʃone] *sm* pigeon

'picco, -chi *sm* peak; **a ~** vertically

'piccolo, -a *ag* small; (*oggetto, mano, di età: bambino*) small, little; (*dav sostantivo: di breve durata: viaggio*) short; (*fig*) mean, petty ▶ *sm/f* child, little one

pic'cone *sm* pick(-axe)

pic'cozza [pik'kɔttsa] *sf* ice-axe

pic'nic *sm inv* picnic

pi'docchio [pi'dɔkkjo] *sm* louse

pi'ede *sm* foot; (*di mobile*) leg; **in piedi** standing; **a piedi** on foot; **a piedi nudi** barefoot; **su due piedi** (*fig*) at once; **prendere ~** (*fig*) to gain ground, catch on; **sul ~ di guerra** (*Mil*) ready for action; **piede di porco** crowbar

pi'ega, -ghe *sf* (*piegatura, Geo*) fold; (*di gonna*) pleat; (*di pantaloni*) crease; (*grinza*) wrinkle, crease; **prendere una brutta ~** (*fig*) to take a turn for the worse

pie'gare *vt* to fold; (*braccia, gambe, testa*) to bend ▶ *vi* to bend; **piegarsi** *vpr* to bend; (*fig*): **piegarsi (a)** to yield (to), submit (to)

piegherò *ecc* [pjege'rɔ] *vb vedi* **piegare**

pie'ghevole *ag* pliable, flexible; (*porta*) folding

Pie'monte *sm* **il ~** Piedmont

pi'ena *sf* (*di fiume*) flood, spate

pi'eno, -a *ag* full; (*muro, mattone*) solid ▶ *sm* (*colmo*) height, peak; (*carico*) full load; **~ di** full of; **in ~ giorno** in broad daylight; **il ~, per favore** (*Aut*) fill it up, please

piercing ['pirsing] *sm* piercing; **farsi il ~ all'ombelico** to have one's navel pierced

pietà *sf* pity; (*Rel*) piety; **senza ~** pitiless, merciless; **avere ~ di** (*compassione*) to pity, feel sorry for; (*misericordia*) to have pity o mercy on

pie'tanza [pje'tantsa] *sf* dish, course

pie'toso, -a *ag* (*compassionevole*) pitying, compassionate; (*che desta pietà*) pitiful

pi'etra *sf* stone; **pietra preziosa** precious stone, gem

'piffero *sm* (*Mus*) pipe

pigi'ama, -i [pi'dʒama] *sm* pyjamas *pl*

pigli'are [piʎ'ʎare] *vt* to take, grab; (*afferrare*) to catch

'pigna ['pinɲa] *sf* pine cone

pi'gnolo, -a [piɲ'nɔlo] *ag* pernickety

pi'grizia [pi'grittsja] *sf* laziness

'pigro, -a *ag* lazy

PIL *sigla m* (= *prodotto interno lordo*) GDP

'pila *sf* (*catasta, di ponte*) pile; (*Elettr*) battery; (*torcia*) torch (*BRIT*), flashlight

pi'lastro *sm* pillar

'pile ['pail] *sm inv* fleece

'pillola *sf* pill; **prendere la ~** to be on the pill

pi'lone *sm* (*di ponte*) pier; (*di linea elettrica*) pylon

pi'lota, -i, -e *sm/f* pilot; (*Aut*) driver ▶ *ag inv* pilot *cpd*; **pilota automatico** automatic pilot

pinaco'teca, -che *sf* art gallery

pi'neta *sf* pinewood

ping-'pong [pin'pɔn] *sm* table tennis

pingu'ino *sm* (*Zool*) penguin

'pinna sf (di pesce) fin; (di cetaceo, per nuotare) flipper

'pino sm pine (tree); **pi'nolo** sm pine kernel

'pinza ['pintsa] sf pliers pl; (Med) forceps pl; (Zool) pincer

pinzette [pin'tsette] sfpl tweezers

pi'oggia, -ge ['pjɔddʒa] sf rain; **pioggia acida** acid rain

pi'olo sm peg; (di scala) rung

piom'bare vi to fall heavily; (gettarsi con impeto): **~ su** to fall upon, assail ▶ vt (dente) to fill; **piomba'tura** sf (di dente) filling

piom'bino sm (sigillo) (lead) seal; (del filo a piombo) plummet; (Pesca) sinker

pi'ombo sm (Chim) lead; **a ~** (cadere) straight down; **senza ~** (benzina) unleaded

pionie're, -a sm/f pioneer

pi'oppo sm poplar

pi'overe vb impers to rain ▶ vi (fig: scendere dall'alto) to rain down; (lettere, regali) to pour into; **pioviggi'nare** vb impers to drizzle; **pio'voso, -a** ag rainy

pi'ovra sf octopus

pi'ovve ecc vb vedi **piovere**

'pipa sf pipe

pipì (fam) sf **fare ~** to have a wee (wee)

pipis'trello sm (Zool) bat

pi'ramide sf pyramid

pi'rata, -i sm pirate; **pirata della strada** hit-and-run driver; **pirata informatica** hacker

Pire'nei smpl **i ~** the Pyrenees

pi'romane sm/f pyromaniac; arsonist

pi'roscafo sm steamer, steamship

pisci'are [piʃʃare] (fam!) vi to piss (!), pee (!)

pi'scina [piʃʃina] sf (swimming) pool; (stabilimento) (swimming) baths pl

pi'sello sm pea

piso'lino sm nap

'pista sf (traccia) track, trail; (di stadio) track; (di pattinaggio) rink; (da sci) run; (Aer) runway; (di circo) ring; **pista da ballo** dance floor

pis'tacchio [pis'takkjo] sm pistachio (tree); pistachio (nut)

pis'tola sf pistol, gun

pis'tone sm piston

pi'tone sm python

pit'tore, -'trice sm/f painter; **pitto'resco, -a, -schi, -sche** ag picturesque

pit'tura sf painting; **pittu'rare** vt to paint

più
av

1 (in maggiore quantità) more; **più del solito** more than usual; **in più, di più** more; **ne voglio di più** I want some more; **ci sono 3 persone in o di più** there are 3 more o extra people; **più o meno** more or less; **per di più** (inoltre) what's more, moreover

2 (comparativo) more; (aggettivo corto +) ...er; **più ... di/che** more ... than; **lavoro più di te/Paola** I work harder than you/Paola; **è più intelligente che ricco** he's more intelligent than rich

3 (superlativo) most; (aggettivo corto +) ...est; **il più grande/intelligente** the biggest/most intelligent; **è quello che compro più spesso** that's the one I buy most often; **al più presto** as soon as possible; **al più tardi** at the latest

4 (negazione): **non ... più** no more, no longer; **non ho più soldi** I've got no more money, I don't have any more money; **non lavoro più** I'm no longer working, I don't work any more; **a più non posso** (gridare) at the top of one's voice; (correre) as fast as one can

5 (Mat) plus; **4 più 5 fa 9** 4 plus 5 equals 9; **più 5 gradi** 5 degrees above freezing, plus 5

▶prep plus

▶ag inv

1: **più ... (di)** more ... (than); **più denaro/tempo** more money/time; **più persone di quante ci aspettassimo** more people than we expected
2 (*numerosi, diversi*) several; **l'aspettai per più giorni** I waited for it for several days
▶*sm*
1 (*la maggior parte*): **il più è fatto** most of it is done
2 (*Mat*) plus (sign)
3: **i più** the majority

pi'uma *sf* feather; **piu'mino** *sm* (eider)down; (*per letto*) eiderdown; (: *tipo danese*) duvet, continental quilt; (*giacca*) quilted jacket (*with goose-feather padding*); (*per cipria*) powder puff; (*per spolverare*) feather duster
piut'tosto *av* rather; **~ che** (*anziché*) rather than
'pizza ['pittsa] *sf* pizza; **pizze'ria** *sf* place where pizzas are made, sold or eaten
pizzi'care [pittsi'kare] *vt* (*stringere*) to nip, pinch; (*pungere*) to sting; to bite; (*Mus*) to pluck ▶*vi* (*prudere*) to itch, be itchy; (*cibo*) to be hot o spicy
'pizzico, -chi ['pittsiko] *sm* (*pizzicotto*) pinch, nip; (*piccola quantità*) pinch, dash; (*d'insetto*) sting; bite
pizzi'cotto [pittsi'kotto] *sm* pinch, nip
'pizzo ['pittso] *sm* (*merletto*) lace; (*barbetta*) goatee beard
plagi'are [pla'dʒare] *vt* (*copiare*) to plagiarize
plaid [plɛd] *sm inv* (travelling) rug (*BRIT*), lap robe (*US*)
pla'nare *vi* (*Aer*) to glide
'plasma *sm* plasma
plas'mare *vt* to mould, shape
'plastica, -che *sf* (*arte*) plastic arts *pl*; (*Med*) plastic surgery; (*sostanza*) plastic; **plastica facciale** face lift
'platano *sm* plane tree
pla'tea *sf* (*Teatro*) stalls *pl*
'platino *sm* platinum

plau'sibile *ag* plausible
pleni'lunio *sm* full moon
'plettro *sm* plectrum
pleu'rite *sf* pleurisy
'plico, -chi *sm* (*pacco*) parcel; **in ~ a parte** (*Comm*) under separate cover
plo'tone *sm* (*Mil*) platoon; **plotone d'esecuzione** firing squad
plu'rale *ag, sm* plural
PM *abbr* (*Pol*) = **Pubblico Ministero**; (= Polizia Militare) MP (Military Police)
pneu'matico, -a, -ci, -che *ag* inflatable; pneumatic ▶*sm* (*Aut*) tyre (*BRIT*), tire (*US*)
po' *av, sm vedi* **poco**

○ **'poco, -a, -chi, -che**
ag (*quantità*) little, not much; (*numero*) few, not many; **poco pane/denaro/spazio** little o not much bread/money/space; **poche persone/ idee** few o not many people/ideas; **ci vediamo tra poco** (*sottinteso: tempo*) see you soon
▶*av*
1 (*in piccola quantità*) little, not much; (*numero limitato*) few, not many; **guadagna poco** he doesn't earn much, he earns little
2 (*con ag, av*) (a) little, not very; **sta poco bene** he isn't very well; **è poco più vecchia di lui** she's a little o slightly older than him
3 (*tempo*): **poco dopo/prima** shortly afterwards/before; **il film dura poco** the film doesn't last very long; **ci vediamo molto poco** we don't see each other very often, we hardly ever see each other
4: **un po'** a little, a bit; **è un po' corto** it's a little o a bit short; **arriverà fra un po'** he'll arrive shortly o in a little while
5: **a dir poco** to say the least; **a poco a poco** little by little; **per poco non cadevo** I nearly fell; **è una cosa da poco** it's nothing, it's of no importance; **una**

persona da poco a worthless person
▶*pron* (a) little
'**podcast** ['pɔdkast] *sm* podcast
po'dere *sm* (*Agr*) farm
'**podio** *sm* dais, platform; (*Mus*)
podium
po'dismo *sm* (*Sport*) track events *pl*
poe'sia *sf* (*arte*) poetry; (*componimento*)
poem
po'eta, -'essa *sm/f* poet/poetess
poggi'are [pod'dʒare] *vt* to lean, rest;
(*posare*) to lay, place; **poggia'testa** *sm*
inv (*Aut*) headrest
'**poggio** ['pɔddʒo] *sm* hillock, knoll
'**poi** *av* then; (*alla fine*) finally, at last;
e ~ (*inoltre*) and besides; **questa ~ (è
bella)!** (*ironico*) that's a good one!
poiché [poi'ke] *cong* since, as
'**poker** *sm* poker
po'lacco, -a, -chi, -che *ag* Polish
▶ *sm/f* Pole
po'lare *ag* polar
po'lemica, -che *sf* controversy
po'lemico, -a, -ci, -che *ag*
polemic(al), controversial
po'lenta *sf* (*Cuc*) sort of thick porridge
made with maize flour
'**polio(mie'lite)** *sf* polio(myelitis)
'**polipo** *sm* polyp
polisti'rolo *sm* polystyrene
po'litica, -che *sf* politics *sg*; (*linea di
condotta*) policy; **politica'mente** *av*
politically; **politicamente corretto**
politically correct
po'litico, -a, -ci, -che *ag* political
▶ *sm/f* politician
poli'zia [polit'tsia] *sf* police; **polizia
giudiziaria** ≈ Criminal Investigation
Department (*BRIT*), ≈ Federal
Bureau of Investigation (*US*); **polizia
stradale** traffic police; **polizi'esco,
-a, -schi, -sche** *ag* police *cpd*; (*film,
romanzo*) detective *cpd*; **polizi'otto**
sm policeman; **cane poliziotto** police
dog; **donna poliziotto** policewoman;

poliziotto di quartiere local police
officer
● **polizia di stato**
● The function of the **polizia di stato**
● is to maintain public order, to
● uphold the law and prevent and
● investigate crime. They are a civil
● body, reporting to the Minister of
● the Interior.
'**polizza** ['pɔlittsa] *sf* (*Comm*) bill; **~
di assicurazione** insurance policy;
polizza di carico bill of lading
pol'laio *sm* henhouse
'**pollice** ['pɔllitʃe] *sm* thumb
'**polline** *sm* pollen
'**pollo** *sm* chicken
pol'mone *sm* lung; **polmone
d'acciaio** (*Med*) iron lung;
polmo'nite *sf* pneumonia;
polmonite atipica SARS
'**polo** *sm* (*Geo, Fisica*) pole; (*gioco*) polo;
polo nord/sud North/South Pole
Po'lonia *sf* **la ~** Poland
'**polpa** *sf* flesh, pulp; (*carne*) lean meat
pol'paccio [pol'pattʃo] *sm* (*Anat*) calf
polpas'trello *sm* fingertip
pol'petta *sf* (*Cuc*) meatball
'**polpo** *sm* octopus
pol'sino *sm* cuff
'**polso** *sm* (*Anat*) wrist; (*pulsazione*)
pulse; (*fig: forza*) drive, vigour
pol'trire *vi* to laze about
pol'trona *sf* armchair; (*Teatro: posto*)
seat in the front stalls (*BRIT*) o
orchestra (*US*)
'**polvere** *sf* dust; (*sostanza ridotta
minutissima*) powder, dust; **latte in
~** dried o powdered milk; **caffè in
~** instant coffee; **sapone in ~** soap
powder; **polvere da sparo/pirica**
gunpowder
po'mata *sf* ointment, cream
po'mello *sm* knob
pome'riggio [pome'riddʒo] *sm*
afternoon

'pomice ['pɔmitʃe] *sf* pumice
'pomo *sm* (*mela*) apple; (*ornamentale*) knob; (*di sella*) pommel; **pomo d'Adamo** (*Anat*) Adam's apple
pomo'doro *sm* tomato; **pomodori pelati** skinned tomatoes
'pompa *sf* pump; (*sfarzo*) pomp (and ceremony); **pompe funebri** undertaker's *sg*; **pompa di benzina** petrol (*BRIT*) *o* gas (*US*) pump; (*distributore*) filling *o* gas (*US*) station; **pom'pare** *vt* to pump; (*trarre*) to pump out; (*gonfiare d'aria*) to pump up
pom'pelmo *sm* grapefruit
pompi'ere *sm* fireman
po'nente *sm* west
pongo, poni *ecc vb vedi* **porre**
'ponte *sm* bridge; (*di nave*) deck; (: *anche:* ~ **di comando**) bridge; (*impalcatura*) scaffold; **fare il** ~ (*fig*) to take the extra day off (*between 2 public holidays*); **governo** ~ interim government; **ponte aereo** airlift; **ponte levatoio** drawbridge; **ponte sospeso** suspension bridge
pon'tefice [pon'tɛfitʃe] *sm* (*Rel*) pontiff
'popcorn ['pɔpkɔːn] *sm inv* popcorn
popo'lare *ag* popular; (*quartiere, clientela*) working-class ▶ *vt* (*rendere abitato*) to populate; **popolarsi** *vpr* to fill with people, get crowded; **popolazi'one** *sf* population
'popolo *sm* people
'poppa *sf* (*di nave*) stern; (*seno*) breast
porcel'lana [portʃel'lana] *sf* porcelain, china; piece of china
porcel'lino, -a [portʃel'lino] *sm/f* piglet; **porcellino d'India** guinea pig
porche'ria [porke'ria] *sf* filth, muck; (*fig: oscenità*) obscenity; (: *azione disonesta*) dirty trick; (: *cosa mal fatta*) rubbish
por'cile [por'tʃile] *sm* pigsty
por'cino, -a [por'tʃino] *ag* of pigs,

pork *cpd* ▶ *sm* (*fungo*) type of edible mushroom
'porco, -ci *sm* pig; (*carne*) pork
porcos'pino *sm* porcupine
'porgere ['pɔrdʒere] *vt* to hand, give; (*tendere*) to hold out
pornogra'fia *sf* pornography; **porno'grafico, -a, -ci, -che** *ag* pornographic
'poro *sm* pore
'porpora *sf* purple
'porre *vt* (*mettere*) to put; (*collocare*) to place; (*posare*) to lay (down), put (down); (*fig: supporre*): **poniamo (il caso) che ...** let's suppose that ...
'porro *sm* (*Bot*) leek; (*Med*) wart
'porsi *ecc vb vedi* **porgere**
'porta *sf* door; (*Sport*) goal; **portaba'gagli** *sm inv* (*facchino*) porter; (*Aut, Ferr*) luggage rack; **porta-CD** [portatʃi'di] *sm inv* (*mobile*) CD rack; (*astuccio*) CD holder; **porta'cenere** *sm inv* ashtray; **portachi'avi** *sm inv* keyring; **porta'erei** *sf inv* (*nave*) aircraft carrier; **portafi'nestra** (*pl* **portefi'nestre**) *sf* French window; **porta'foglio** *sm* wallet; (*Pol, Borsa*) portfolio; **non trovo il portafoglio** I can't find my wallet; **portafor'tuna** *sm inv* lucky charm; mascot
por'tale *sm* (*di chiesa, Inform*) portal
porta'mento *sm* carriage, bearing
portamo'nete *sm inv* purse
por'tante *ag* (*muro ecc*) supporting
portan'tina *sf* sedan chair; (*per ammalati*) stretcher
portaom'brelli *sm inv* umbrella stand
porta'pacchi [porta'pakki] *sm inv* (*di moto, bicicletta*) luggage rack
porta'penne [porta'penne] *sm inv* pen holder; (*astuccio*) pencil case
por'tare *vt* (*sostenere, sorreggere: peso, bambino, pacco*) to carry; (*indossare: abito, occhiali*) to wear; (: *capelli*

P

lunghi) to have; (*avere: nome, titolo*) to have, bear; (*recare*): **~ qc a qn** to take (o bring) sth to sb; (*fig: sentimenti*) to bear

portasiga'rette *sm inv* cigarette case

por'tata *sf* (*vivanda*) course; (*Aut*) carrying (o loading) capacity; (*di arma*) range; (*volume d'acqua*) (rate of) flow; (*fig: limite*) scope, capability; (: *importanza*) impact, import; **alla ~ di tutti** (*conoscenza*) within everybody's capabilities; (*prezzo*) within everybody's means; **a/fuori ~ (di)** within/out of reach (of); **a ~ di mano** within (arm's) reach

por'tatile *ag* portable

por'tato, -a *ag* (*incline*): **~ a** inclined o apt to

portau'ovo *sm inv* eggcup

porta'voce [porta'votʃe] *sm/f inv* spokesman/woman

por'tento *sm* wonder, marvel

porti'era *sf* (*Aut*) door

porti'ere *sm* (*portinaio*) concierge, caretaker; (*di hotel*) porter; (*nel calcio*) goalkeeper

porti'naio, -a *sm/f* concierge, caretaker

portine'ria *sf* caretaker's lodge

'porto, -a *pp di* **porgere** ▶ *sm* (*Naut*) harbour, port ▶ *sm inv* port (wine); **porto d'armi** (*documento*) gun licence

Porto'gallo *sm* **il ~** Portugal; **porto'ghese** *ag, sm/f, sm* Portuguese *inv*

por'tone *sm* main entrance, main door

portu'ale *ag* harbour *cpd*, port *cpd* ▶ *sm* dock worker

porzi'one [por'tsjone] *sf* portion, share; (*di cibo*) portion, helping

'posa *sf* (*Fot*) exposure; (*atteggiamento, di modello*) pose

po'sare *vt* to put (down), lay (down)

▶ *vi* (*ponte, edificio, teoria*): **~ su** to rest on; (*Fot: atteggiarsi*) to pose; **posarsi** *vpr* (*aereo*) to land; (*uccello*) to alight; (*sguardo*) to settle

po'sata *sf* piece of cutlery

pos'critto *sm* postscript

'posi *ecc vb vedi* **porre**

posi'tivo, -a *ag* positive

posizi'one [pozit'tsjone] *sf* position; **prendere ~** (*fig*) to take a stand; **luci di ~** (*Aut*) sidelights

pos'porre *vt* to place after; (*differire*) to postpone, defer

posse'dere *vt* to own, possess; (*qualità, virtù*) to have, possess

posses'sivo, -a *ag* possessive

pos'sesso *sm* ownership *no pl*; possession

posses'sore *sm* owner

pos'sibile *ag* possible ▶ *sm* **fare tutto il ~** to do everything possible; **nei limiti del ~** as far as possible; **al più tardi ~** as late as possible; **possibilità** *sf inv* possibility ▶ *sfpl* (*mezzi*) means; **aver la possibilità di fare** to be in a position to do; to have the opportunity to do

possi'dente *sm/f* landowner

possi'edo *ecc vb vedi* **possedere**

'posso *ecc vb vedi* **potere**

'posta *sf* (*servizio*) post, postal service; (*corrispondenza*) post, mail; (*ufficio postale*) post office; (*nei giochi d'azzardo*) stake; **Poste** *sfpl* (*amministrazione*) post office; **c'è ~ per me?** are there any letters for me?; **ministro delle Poste e Telecomunicazioni** Postmaster General; **posta aerea** airmail; **posta elettronica** E-mail, e-mail, electronic mail; **posta ordinaria** ≈ second-class mail; **posta prioritaria** ≈ first-class post; **pos'tale** *ag* postal, post office *cpd*

posteggi'are [posted'dʒare] *vt, vi* to

park; **pos'teggio** sm car park (BRIT), parking lot (US); (di taxi) rank (BRIT), stand (US)

'poster sm inv poster

posteri'ore ag (dietro) back; (dopo) later ▶ sm (fam: sedere) behind

postici'pare [postitʃi'pare] vt to defer, postpone

pos'tino sm postman (BRIT), mailman (US)

'posto, -a pp di **porre** ▶ sm (sito, posizione) place; (impiego) job; (spazio libero) room, space; (di parcheggio) space; (sedile: al teatro, in treno ecc) seat; (Mil) post; **a ~** (in ordine) in place, tidy; (fig) settled; (: persona) reliable; **vorrei prenotare due posti** I'd like to book two seats; **al ~ di** in place of; **sul ~** on the spot; **mettere a ~** to tidy (up), put in order; (faccende) to straighten out; **posto di blocco** roadblock; **posto di lavoro** job; **posti in piedi** (in teatro, in autobus) standing room; **posto di polizia** police station

po'tabile ag drinkable; **acqua ~** drinking water

po'tare vt to prune

po'tassio sm potassium

po'tente ag (nazione) strong, powerful; (veleno, farmaco) potent, strong; **po'tenza** sf power; (forza) strength

potenzi'ale [poten'tsjale] ag, sm potential

po'tere

sm power; **al potere** (partito ecc) in power; **potere d'acquisto** purchasing power

▶vb aus

1 (essere in grado di) can, be able to; **non ha potuto ripararlo** he couldn't o he wasn't able to repair it; **non è potuto venire** he couldn't o he wasn't able to come; **spiacente di non poter aiutare** sorry not to be able to help

2 (avere il permesso) can, may, be allowed to; **posso entrare?** can o may I come in?; **si può sapere dove sei stato?** where on earth have you been?

3 (eventualità) may, might, could; **potrebbe essere vero** it might o could be true; **può aver avuto un incidente** he may o might o could have had an accident; **può darsi** perhaps; **può darsi o essere che non venga** he may o might not come

4 (augurio): **potessi almeno parlargli!** if only I could speak to him!

5 (suggerimento): **potresti almeno scusarti!** you could at least apologize! ▶vt can, be able to; **può molto per noi** he can do a lot for us; **non ne posso più** (per stanchezza) I'm exhausted; (per rabbia) I can't take any more

potrò ecc vb vedi **potere**

'povero, -a ag poor; (disadorno) plain, bare ▶ sm/f poor man/woman; **i poveri** the poor; **~ di** lacking in, having little; **povertà** sf poverty

poz'zanghera [pot'tsangera] sf puddle

'pozzo ['pottso] sm well; (cava: di carbone) pit; (di miniera) shaft; **pozzo petrolifero** oil well

P.R.A. [pra] sigla m (= Pubblico Registro Automobilistico) ≈ DVLA

pran'zare [pran'dzare] vi to dine, have dinner; to lunch, have lunch

'pranzo ['prandzo] sm dinner; (a mezzogiorno) lunch

'prassi sf usual procedure

'pratica, -che sf practice; (esperienza) experience; (conoscenza) knowledge, familiarity; (tirocinio) training, practice; (Amm: affare) matter, case; (: incartamento) file, dossier; **in ~** (praticamente) in practice; **mettere in ~** to put into practice

prati'cabile ag (progetto) practicable, feasible; (luogo) passable, practicable

pratica'mente av (*in modo pratico*) in a practical way, practically; (*quasi*) practically, almost

prati'care vt to practise; (*Sport: tennis ecc*) to play; (*: nuoto, scherma ecc*) to go in for; (*eseguire: apertura, buco*) to make; **~ uno sconto** to give a discount

'**pratico, -a, -ci, -che** ag practical; **~ di** (*esperto*) experienced o skilled in; (*familiare*) familiar with

'**prato** sm meadow; (*di giardino*) lawn

preav'viso sm notice; **telefonata con ~** personal o person to person call

pre'cario, -a ag precarious; (*Ins*) temporary

precauzi'one [prekaut'tsjone] sf caution, care; (*misura*) precaution

prece'dente [pretʃe'dɛnte] ag previous ▶ sm precedent; **il discorso/ film ~** the previous o preceding speech/film; **senza precedenti** unprecedented; **precedenti penali** criminal record sg; **prece'denza** sf priority, precedence; (*Aut*) right of way

pre'cedere [pre'tʃɛdere] vt to precede, go (o come) before

precipi'tare [pretʃipi'tare] vi (*cadere*) to fall headlong; (*fig: situazione*) to get out of control ▶ vt (*gettare dall'alto in basso*) to hurl, fling; (*fig: affrettare*) to rush; **precipitarsi** vpr (*gettarsi*) to hurl o fling o.s.; (*affrettarsi*) to rush; **precipi'toso, -a** ag (*caduta, fuga*) headlong; (*fig: avventato*) rash, reckless; (*: affrettato*) hasty, rushed

preci'pizio [pretʃi'pittsjo] sm precipice; **a ~** (*fig: correre*) headlong

precisa'mente [pretʃiza'mente] av (*gen*) precisely; (*con esattezza*) exactly

preci'sare [pretʃi'zare] vt to state, specify; (*spiegare*) to explain (in detail)

precisi'one [pretʃi'zjone] sf precision; accuracy

pre'ciso, -a [pre'tʃizo] ag (*esatto*) precise; (*accurato*) accurate, precise; (*deciso: idee*) precise, definite; (*uguale*): **2 vestiti precisi** 2 dresses exactly the same; **sono le 9 precise** it's exactly 9 o'clock

pre'cludere vt to block, obstruct

pre'coce [pre'kɔtʃe] ag early; (*bambino*) precocious; (*vecchiaia*) premature

precon'cetto [prekon'tʃɛtto] sm preconceived idea, prejudice

precur'sore sm forerunner, precursor

'**preda** sf (*bottino*) booty; (*animale, fig*) prey; **essere ~ di** to fall prey to; **essere in ~ a** to be prey to

'**predica, -che** sf sermon; (*fig*) lecture, talking-to

predi'care vt, vi to preach

predi'cato sm (*Ling*) predicate

predi'letto, -a pp di **prediligere** ▶ ag, sm/f favourite

predi'ligere [predi'lidʒere] vt to prefer, have a preference for

pre'dire vt to foretell, predict

predis'porre vt to get ready, prepare; **~ qn a qc** to predispose sb to sth

predizi'one [predit'tsjone] sf prediction

prefazi'one [prefat'tsjone] sf preface, foreword

prefe'renza [prefe'rɛntsa] sf preference

prefe'rire vt to prefer, like better; **~ il caffè al tè** to prefer coffee to tea, like coffee better than tea

pre'figgersi [pre'fiddʒersi] vpr **~ uno scopo** to set o.s. a goal

pre'fisso, -a pp di **prefiggere** ▶ sm (*Ling*) prefix; (*Tel*) dialling (*BRIT*) o dial (*US*) code; **qual è il ~ telefonico di Londra?** what is the dialling code for London?

pre'gare vi to pray ▶ vt (*Rel*) to pray to; (*implorare*) to beg; (*chiedere*): **~ qn**

di fare to ask sb to do; **farsi ~** to need coaxing *o* persuading

pre'gevole [pre'dʒevole] *ag* valuable

pregherò *ecc* [prege'rɔ] *vb vedi* **pregare**

preghi'era [pre'gjɛra] *sf* (*Rel*) prayer; (*domanda*) request

pregi'ato, -a [pre'dʒato] *ag* (*di valore*) valuable; **vino ~** vintage wine

'pregio ['predʒo] *sm* (*stima*) esteem, regard; (*qualità*) (good) quality, merit; (*valore*) value, worth

pregiudi'care [predʒudi'kare] *vt* to prejudice, harm, be detrimental to

pregiu'dizio [predʒu'dittsjo] *sm* (*idea errata*) prejudice; (*danno*) harm *no pl*

'prego *escl* (*a chi ringrazia*) don't mention it!; (*invitando qn ad accomodarsi*) please sit down!; (*invitando qn ad andare prima*) after you!

pregus'tare *vt* to look forward to

prele'vare *vt* (*denaro*) to withdraw; (*campione*) to take; (*polizia*) to take, capture

preli'evo *sm* (*di denaro*) withdrawal; (*Med*): **fare un ~ (di)** to take a sample (of); **prelievo di sangue**; **fare un ~ di sangue** to take a blood sample

prelimi'nare *ag* preliminary

'premere *vt* to press ▶ *vi* **~ su** to press down on; (*fig*) to put pressure on; **~ a** (*fig: importare*) to matter to

pre'mettere *vt* to put before; (*dire prima*) to start by saying, state first

premi'are *vt* to give a prize to; (*fig: merito, onestà*) to reward

premiazi'one [premjat'tsjone] *sf* prize giving

'premio *sm* prize; (*ricompensa*) reward; (*Comm*) premium; (*Amm: indennità*) bonus

pre'misi *ecc vb vedi* **premettere**

premu'nirsi *vpr* **~ di** to provide o.s. with; **~ contro** to protect o.s. from, guard o.s. against

pre'mura *sf* (*fretta*) haste, hurry; (*riguardo*) attention, care; **premure** *sfpl* (*attenzioni, cure*) care *sg*; **aver ~** to be in a hurry; **far ~ a qn** to hurry sb; **usare ogni ~ nei riguardi di qn** to be very attentive to sb; **premu'roso, -a** *ag* thoughtful, considerate

'prendere *vt* to take; (*andare a prendere*) to get, fetch; (*ottenere*) to get; (*guadagnare*) to get, earn; (*catturare: ladro, pesce*) to catch; (*collaboratore, dipendente*) to take on; (*passeggero*) to pick up; (*chiedere: somma, prezzo*) to charge, ask; (*trattare: persona*) to handle ▶ *vi* (*colla, cemento*) to set; (*pianta*) to take; (*fuoco: nel camino*) to catch; (*voltare*): **~ a destra** to turn (to the) right; **prendersi** *vpr* (*azzuffarsi*): **prendersi a pugni** to come to blows; **dove si prende il traghetto per...** where do we get the ferry to ...; **prendi qualcosa?** (*da bere, da mangiare*) would you like something to eat (*o* drink)?; **prendo un caffè** I'll have a coffee; **~ qn/qc per** (*scambiare*) to take sb/sth for; **~ fuoco** to catch fire; **~ parte a** to take part in; **prendersi cura di qn/qc** to look after sb/sth; **prendersela** (*adirarsi*) to get annoyed; (*preoccuparsi*) to get upset, worry

preno'tare *vt* to book, reserve; **vorrei ~ una camera doppia** I'd like to book a double room; **ho prenotato un tavolo al nome di ...** I booked a table in the name of ...; **prenotazi'one** *sf* booking, reservation; **ho confermato la prenotazione per fax/e-mail** I confirmed my booking by fax/e-mail

preoccu'pare *vt* to worry; to preoccupy; **preoccuparsi** *vpr* **preoccuparsi di qn/qc** to worry about sb/sth; **preoccuparsi per qn** to be anxious for sb; **preoccupazi'one** *sf* worry, anxiety

prepa'rare vt to prepare; (esame, concorso) to prepare for; **prepararsi** vpr (vestirsi) to get ready; **prepararsi a qc/a fare** to get ready o prepare (o.s.) for sth/to do; **~ da mangiare** to prepare a meal; **prepara'tivi** smpl preparations

preposizi'one [prepozit'tsjone] sf (Ling) preposition

prepo'tente ag (persona) domineering, arrogant; (bisogno, desiderio) overwhelming, pressing ▶ sm/f bully

'presa sf taking no pl; catching no pl; (di città) capture; (indurimento: di cemento) setting; (appiglio, Sport) hold; (di acqua, gas) (supply) point; (piccola quantità: di sale ecc) pinch; (Carte) trick; **far ~** (colla) to set; **far ~ sul pubblico** to catch the public's imagination; **essere alle prese con** (fig) to be struggling with; **presa d'aria** air inlet; **presa (di corrente) (Elettr)** socket; (: al muro) point

pre'sagio [pre'zadʒo] sm omen

'presbite ag long-sighted

pres'crivere vt to prescribe

'prese ecc vb vedi **prendere**

presen'tare vt to present; (far conoscere): **~ qn (a)** to introduce sb (to); (Amm: inoltrare) to submit; **presentarsi** vpr (recarsi, farsi vedere) to present o.s., appear; (farsi conoscere) to introduce o.s.; (occasione) to arise; **presentarsi come candidato** (Pol) to stand as a candidate; **presentarsi bene/male** to have a good/poor appearance

pre'sente ag present; (questo) this ▶ sm present; **i presenti** those present; **aver ~ qc/qn** to remember sth/sb; **presenti** (persone) people present; **aver ~ qc/qn** to remember sth/sb; **tenere ~ qn/qc** to keep sth/sb in mind

presenti'mento sm premonition

pre'senza [pre'zentsa] sf presence; (aspetto esteriore) appearance; **presenza di spirito** presence of mind

pre'sepio, pre'sepe sm crib

preser'vare vt to protect; to save; **preserva'tivo** sm sheath, condom

'presi ecc vb vedi **prendere**

'preside sm/f (Ins) head (teacher) (BRIT), principal (US); (di facoltà universitaria) dean; **preside di facoltà** (Univ) dean of faculty

presi'dente sm (Pol) president; (di assemblea, Comm) chairman; **presidente del consiglio** prime minister

presi'edere vt to preside over ▶ vi **~ a** to direct, be in charge of

pressap'poco av about, roughly

pres'sare vt to press

pressi'one sf pressure; **far ~ su qn** to put pressure on sb; **pressione sanguigna** blood pressure; **pressione atmosferica** atmospheric pressure

'presso av (vicino) nearby, close at hand ▶ prep (vicino a) near; (accanto a) beside, next to; (in casa di): **~ qn** at sb's home; (nelle lettere) care of, c/o; (alle dipendenze di): **lavora ~ di noi** he works for o with us ▶ smpl **nei pressi di** near, in the vicinity of

pres'tante ag good-looking

pres'tare vt **~ (qc a qn)** to lend (sb sth o sth to sb); **prestarsi** vpr (offrirsi): **prestarsi a fare** to offer to do; (essere adatto): **prestarsi a** to lend itself to, be suitable for; **mi può ~ dei soldi?** can you lend me some money?; **~ aiuto** to lend a hand; **~ attenzione** to pay attention; **~ fede a qc/qn** to give credence to sth/sb; **~ orecchio** to listen; **prestazi'one** sf (Tecn, Sport) performance

prestigia'tore, -'trice
[prestidʒa'tore] sm/f conjurer
pres'tigio [pres'tidʒo] sm (fama)
prestige; (illusione): **gioco di ~**
conjuring trick
'**prestito** sm lending no pl; loan; **dar in**
~ to lend; **prendere in ~** to borrow
'**presto** av (tra poco) soon; (in fretta)
quickly; (di buon'ora) early; **a ~** see you
soon; **fare ~ a fare qc** to hurry up and
do sth; (non costare fatica) to have no
trouble doing sth; **si fa ~ a criticare**
it's easy to criticize
pre'sumere vt to presume, assume
pre'sunsi ecc vb vedi **presumere**
presuntu'oso, -a ag presumptuous
presunzi'one [prezun'tsjone] sf
presumption
'**prete** sm priest
preten'dente sm/f pretender ▸ sm
(corteggiatore) suitor
pre'tendere vt (esigere) to demand,
require; (sostenere): **~ che** to claim
that; **pretende di aver sempre**
ragione he thinks he's always right
  Attenzione! In inglese esiste il
  verbo to pretend, che però significa
  far finta.
pre'tesa sf (esigenza) claim, demand;
(presunzione, sfarzo) pretentiousness;
senza pretese unpretentious
pre'testo sm pretext, excuse
preva'lere vi to prevail
preve'dere vt (indovinare) to foresee;
(presagire) to foretell; (considerare) to
make provision for
preve'nire vt (anticipare) to forestall;
to anticipate; (evitare) to avoid,
prevent
preven'tivo, -a ag preventive ▸ sm
(Comm) estimate
prevenzi'one [preven'tsjone] sf
prevention; (preconcetto) prejudice
previ'dente ag showing foresight;
prudent; **previ'denza** sf foresight;

istituto di previdenza provident
institution; **previdenza sociale**
social security (BRIT), welfare (US)
pre'vidi ecc vb vedi **prevedere**
previsi'one sf forecast, prediction;
previsioni meteorologiche weather
forecast sg; **previsioni del tempo**
weather forecast sg
pre'visto, -a pp di **prevedere** ▸ sm
più/meno del ~ more/less than
expected
prezi'oso, -a [pret'tsjoso] ag precious;
invaluable ▸ sm jewel; valuable
prez'zemolo [pret'tsemolo] sm
parsley
'**prezzo** ['prɛttso] sm price; **prezzo**
d'acquisto/di vendita buying/
selling price
prigi'one [pri'dʒone] sf prison;
prigioni'ero, -a ag captive ▸ sm/f
prisoner
'**prima** sf (Teatro) first night; (Cinema)
première; (Aut) first gear; vedi anche
primo ▸ av before; (in anticipo) in
advance, beforehand; (per l'addietro)
at one time, formerly; (più presto)
sooner, earlier; (in primo luogo) first
▸ cong **~ di fare/che parta** before
doing/he leaves; **~ di** before; **~ o poi**
sooner or later
pri'mario, -a ag primary; (principale)
chief, leading, primary ▸ sm (Med)
chief physician
prima'tista, -i, e sm/f (Sport) record
holder
pri'mato sm supremacy; (Sport) record
prima'vera sf spring
primi'tivo, -a ag primitive; original
pri'mizie [pri'mittsje] sfpl early
produce sg
'**primo, -a** ag first; (fig) initial; basic;
prime ▸ sm/f first (one) ▸ sm (Cuc) first
course; (in date): **il ~ luglio** the first
of July; **le prime ore del mattino** the
early hours of the morning; **ai primi**

di maggio at the beginning of May;
viaggiare in prima to travel first-class; **in ~ luogo** first of all, in the first place; **di prim'ordine** o **prima qualità** first-class, first-rate; **in un ~ tempo** at first; **prima donna** leading lady; (*di opera lirica*) prima donna
primordi'ale *ag* primordial
'primula *sf* primrose
princi'pale [printʃi'pale] *ag* main, principal ▶ *sm* manager, boss
principal'mente [printʃipal'mente] *av* mainly, principally
'principe ['printʃipe] *sm* prince; **principe ereditario** crown prince; **princi'pessa** *sf* princess
principi'ante [printʃi'pjante] *sm/f* beginner
prin'cipio [prin'tʃipjo] *sm* (*inizio*) beginning, start; (*origine*) origin, cause; (*concetto, norma*) principle; **al** o **in ~** at first; **per ~** on principle; **principi** *smpl* (*concetti fondamentali*) principles; **una questione di ~** a matter of principle
priorità *sf* priority
priori'tario, -a *ag* having priority, of utmost importance
pri'vare *vt* **~ qn di** to deprive sb of; **privarsi di** to go o do without
pri'vato, -a *ag* private ▶ *sm/f* private citizen; **in ~** in private
privilegi'are [privile'dʒare] *vt* to grant a privilege to
privilegi'ato, -a [privile'dʒato] *ag* (*individuo, classe*) privileged; (*trattamento, Comm: credito*) preferential; **azioni ~e** preference shares (*BRIT*), preferred stock (*US*)
privi'legio [privi'lɛdʒo] *sm* privilege
'privo, -a *ag* **~ di** without, lacking
pro *prep* for, on behalf of ▶ *sm inv* (*utilità*) advantage, benefit; **a che ~?** what's the use?; **il ~ e il contro** the pros and cons

pro'babile *ag* probable, likely; **probabilità** *sf inv* probability
probabil'mente *av* probably
pro'blema, -i *sm* problem
pro'boscide [pro'bɔʃʃide] *sf* (*di elefante*) trunk
pro'cedere [pro'tʃedere] *vi* to proceed; (*comportarsi*) to behave; (*iniziare*): **~ a** to start; **~ contro** (*Dir*) to start legal proceedings against; **proce'dura** *sf* (*Dir*) procedure
proces'sare [protʃes'sare] *vt* (*Dir*) to try
processi'one [protʃes'sjone] *sf* procession
pro'cesso [pro'tʃesso] *sm* (*Dir*) trial; proceedings *pl*; (*metodo*) process
pro'cinto [pro'tʃinto] *sm* **in ~ di fare** about to do, on the point of doing
procla'mare *vt* to proclaim
procre'are *vt* to procreate
procu'rare *vt* **~ qc a qn** (*fornire*) to get o obtain sth for sb; (*causare: noie ecc*) to bring o give sb sth
pro'digio [pro'didʒo] *sm* marvel, wonder; (*persona*) prodigy
pro'dotto, -a *pp di* **produrre** ▶ *sm* product; **prodotti agricoli** farm produce *sg*
pro'duco *ecc vb vedi* **produrre**
pro'durre *vt* to produce
pro'dussi *ecc vb vedi* **produrre**
produzi'one *sf* production; (*rendimento*) output
Prof. *abbr* (= *professore*) Prof.
profa'nare *vt* to desecrate
profes'sare *vt* to profess; (*medicina ecc*) to practise
professio'nale *ag* professional
professi'one *sf* profession; **professio'nista, -i, -e** *sm/f* professional
profes'sore, -'essa *sm/f* (*Ins*) teacher; (*: di università*) lecturer; (*: titolare di cattedra*) professor

pro'filo sm profile; (breve descrizione) sketch, outline; **di ~** in profile

pro'fitto sm advantage, profit, benefit; (fig: progresso) progress; (Comm) profit

profondità sf inv depth

pro'fondo, -a ag deep; (rancore, meditazione) profound ▶ sm depth(s pl), bottom; **quanto è profonda l'acqua?** how deep is the water?; **~ 8 metri** 8 metres deep

'profugo, -a, -ghi, -ghe sm/f refugee

profu'mare vt to perfume ▶ vi to be fragrant; **profumarsi** vpr to put on perfume o scent

profu'mato, -a ag (fiore, aria) fragrant; (fazzoletto, saponetta) scented; (pelle) sweet-smelling; (persona) with perfume on

profume'ria sf perfumery; (negozio) perfume shop

pro'fumo sm (prodotto) perfume, scent; (fragranza) scent, fragrance

proget'tare [prodʒet'tare] vt to plan; (edificio) to plan, design; **pro'getto** sm plan; (idea) plan, project; **progetto di legge** bill

pro'gramma, -i sm programme; (TV, Radio) programmes pl; (Ins) syllabus, curriculum; (Inform) program; **program'mare** vt (TV, Radio) to put on; (Inform) to program; (Econ) to plan; **programma'tore, -'trice** sm/f (Inform) computer programmer

progre'dire vi to progress, make progress

pro'gresso sm progress no pl; **fare progressi** to make progress

proi'bire vt to forbid, prohibit

proiet'tare vt (gen, Geom, Cinema) to project; (: presentare) to show, screen; (luce, ombra) to throw, cast, project; **proi'ettile** sm projectile, bullet (o shell ecc); **proiet'tore** sm (Cinema) projector; (Aut) headlamp; (Mil) searchlight; **proiezi'one** sf (Cinema) projection; showing

prolife'rare vi (fig) to proliferate

pro'lunga, -ghe sf (di cavo ecc) extension

prolun'gare vt (discorso, attesa) to prolong; (linea, termine) to extend

prome'moria sm inv memorandum

pro'messa sf promise

pro'mettere vt to promise ▶ vi to be o look promising; **~ a qn di fare** to promise sb that one will do

promi'nente ag prominent

pro'misi ecc vb vedi **promettere**

promon'torio sm promontory, headland

promozi'one [promot'tsjone] sf promotion

promu'overe vt to promote

proni'pote sm/f (di nonni) great-grandchild, great-grandson/ granddaughter; (di zii) great-nephew/ niece

pro'nome sm (Ling) pronoun

pron'tezza [pron'tettsa] sf readiness; quickness, promptness

'pronto, -a ag ready; (rapido) fast, quick, prompt; **quando saranno pronte le mie foto?** when will my photos be ready?; **~!** (Tel) hello!; **~ all'ira** quick-tempered; **pronto soccorso** (cure) first aid; (reparto) A&E (BRIT), ER (US)

prontu'ario sm manual, handbook

pro'nuncia [pro'nuntʃa] sf pronunciation

pronunci'are [pronun'tʃare] vt (parola, sentenza) to pronounce; (dire) to utter; (discorso) to deliver; **come si pronuncia?** how do you pronounce it?

propa'ganda sf propaganda

pro'pendere vi **~ per** to favour, lean towards

propi'nare vt to administer

pro'porre vt (suggerire): ~ qc (a qn) to suggest sth (to sb); (candidato) to put forward; (legge, brindisi) to propose; ~ **di fare** to suggest o propose doing; **proporsi di fare** to propose o intend to do; **proporsi una meta** to set o.s. a goal

proporzio'nale [proportsjo'nale] ag proportional

proporzi'one [propor'tsjone] sf proportion; **in ~ a** in proportion to; **proporzioni** sfpl (dimensioni) proportions; **di vaste proporzioni** huge

pro'posito sm (intenzione) intention, aim; (argomento) subject, matter; **a ~ di** regarding, with regard to; **di ~** (apposta) deliberately, on purpose; **a ~** by the way; **capitare a ~** (cosa, persona) to turn up at the right time

proposizi'one [propozit'tsjone] sf (Ling) clause; (: periodo) sentence

pro'posta sf proposal; (suggerimento) suggestion; **proposta di legge** bill

proprietà sf inv (ciò che si possiede) property gen no pl, estate; (caratteristica) property; (correttezza) correctness; **proprietà privata** private property; **proprie'tario, -a** sm/f owner; (di albergo ecc) proprietor, owner; (per l'inquilino) landlord/lady

'proprio, -a ag (possessivo) own; (: impersonale) one's; (esatto) exact, correct, proper; (senso, significato) literal; (Ling: nome) proper; (particolare): ~ **di** characteristic of, peculiar to ▶ av (precisamente) just, exactly; (davvero) really; (affatto): **non ... ~** not ... at all; **l'ha visto con i (suoi) propri occhi** he saw it with his own eyes

proro'gare vt to extend; (differire) to postpone, defer

'prosa sf prose

pro'sciogliere [proʃ'ʃɔʎʎere] vt to release; (Dir) to acquit

prosciu'gare [proʃʃu'gare] vt (terreni) to drain, reclaim; **prosciugarsi** vpr to dry up

prosci'utto [proʃ'ʃutto] sm ham; **prosciutto cotto/crudo** cooked/cured ham

prosegui'mento sm continuation; **buon ~!** all the best!; (a chi viaggia) enjoy the rest of your journey!

prosegu'ire vt to carry on with, continue ▶ vi to carry on, go on

prospe'rare vi to thrive

prospet'tare vt (esporre) to point out, show; **prospettarsi** vpr to look, appear

prospet'tiva sf (Arte) perspective; (veduta) view; (fig: previsione, possibilità) prospect

pros'petto sm (Disegno) elevation; (veduta) view, prospect; (facciata) façade, front; (tabella) table; (sommario) summary; **prospetto informativo** prospectus

prossimità sf nearness, proximity; **in ~ di** near (to), close to

'prossimo, -a ag (vicino): ~ **a** near (to), close to; (che viene subito dopo) next; (parente) close ▶ sm neighbour, fellow man

prostitu'irsi vpr to prostitute o.s.

prosti'tuta sf prostitute

protago'nista, -i, -e sm/f protagonist

pro'teggere [pro'tɛddʒere] vt to protect

prote'ina sf protein

pro'tendere vt to stretch out

pro'testa sf protest

protes'tante ag, sm/f Protestant

protes'tare vt, vi to protest

pro'tetto, -a pp di **proteggere**

protezi'one [protet'tsjone] sf protection; (patrocinio) patronage

pro'totipo sm prototype

pro'trarre vt (prolungare) to prolong; **protrarsi** vpr to go on, continue

protube'ranza [protube'rantsa] *sf*
protuberance, bulge

'prova *sf* (*esperimento, cimento*) test,
trial; (*tentativo*) attempt, try; (*Mat,
testimonianza, documento ecc*) proof;
(*Dir*) evidence *no pl*, proof; (*Ins*) exam,
test; (*Teatro*) rehearsal; (*di abito*)
fitting; **a ~ di** (*in testimonianza di*) as
proof of; **a ~ di fuoco** fireproof; **fino a ~
contraria** until it is proved otherwise;
mettere alla ~ to put to the test; **giro
di ~** test *o* trial run; **prova generale**
(*Teatro*) dress rehearsal

pro'vare *vt* (*sperimentare*) to test;
(*tentare*) to try, attempt; (*assaggiare*)
to try, taste; (*sperimentare in sé*) to
experience; (*sentire*) to feel; (*cimentare*)
to put to the test; (*dimostrare*) to
prove; (*abito*) to try on; **~ a fare** to try *o*
attempt to do

proveni'enza [prove'njentsa] *sf*
origin, source

prove'nire *vi* **~ da** to come from

pro'venti *smpl* revenue *sg*

pro'verbio *sm* proverb

pro'vetta *sf* test tube; **bambino in ~**
test-tube baby

pro'vider [pro'vaider] *sm inv* (*Inform*)
service provider

pro'vincia, -ce *o* **cie** [pro'vintʃa] *sf*
province

pro'vino *sm* (*Cinema*) screen test;
(*campione*) specimen

provo'cante *ag* (*attraente*) provocative

provo'care *vt* (*causare*) to cause,
bring about; (*eccitare: riso, pietà*) to
arouse; (*irritare, sfidare*) to provoke;
provocazi'one *sf* provocation

provve'dere *vi* (*disporre*): **~ (a)**
to provide (for); (*prendere un
provvedimento*) to take steps, act;
provvedi'mento *sm* measure; (*di
previdenza*) precaution

provvi'denza [provvi'dɛntsa] *sf* **la ~**
providence

provvigi'one [provvi'dʒone] *sf*
(*Comm*) commission

provvi'sorio, -a *ag* temporary

prov'viste *sfpl* supplies

'prua *sf* (*Naut*) bow(s) (*pl*), prow

pru'dente *ag* cautious, prudent;
(*assennato*) sensible, wise; **pru'denza**
sf prudence, caution; wisdom

'prudere *vi* to itch, be itchy

'prugna ['pruɲɲa] *sf* plum; **prugna
secca** prune

pru'rito *sm* itchiness *no pl*; itch

P.S. *abbr* (= *postscriptum*) P.S.; (*Polizia*)
= **Pubblica Sicurezza**

pseu'donimo *sm* pseudonym

psica'nalisi *sf* psychoanalysis

psicana'lista, -i, -e *sm/f*
psychoanalyst

'psiche ['psike] *sf* (*Psic*) psyche

psichi'atra, -i, -e [psi'kjatra] *sm/f*
psychiatrist; **psichi'atrico, -a, -ci,
-che** *ag* psychiatric

psicolo'gia [psikolo'dʒia] *sf*
psychology; **psico'logico, -a, -ci,
-che** *ag* psychological; **psi'cologo, -a,
-gi, -ghe** *sm/f* psychologist

psico'patico, -a, -ci, -che *ag*
psychopathic ▶ *sm/f* psychopath

pubbli'care *vt* to publish

pubblicazi'one [pubblikat'tsjone] *sf*
publication

pubblicità [pubblitʃi'ta] *sf* (*diffusione*)
publicity; (*attività*) advertising;
(*annunci nei giornali*) advertisements *pl*

'pubblico, -a, -ci, -che *ag* public;
(*statale: scuola ecc*) state *cpd* ▶ *sm*
public; (*spettatori*) audience; **in
~** in public; **P~ Ministero** Public
Prosecutor's Office; **la Pubblica
Sicurezza** the police; **pubblico
funzionario** civil servant

'pube *sm* (*Anat*) pubis

pubertà *sf* puberty

'pudico, -a, -ci, -che *ag* modest

pu'dore *sm* modesty

pue'rile ag childish
pugi'lato [pudʒi'lato] sm boxing
'pugile ['pudʒile] sm boxer
pugna'lare [puɲɲa'lare] vt to stab
pu'gnale [puɲ'ɲale] sm dagger
'pugno ['puɲɲo] sm fist; (colpo) punch;
  (quantità) fistful
'pulce ['pultʃe] sf flea
pul'cino [pul'tʃino] sm chick
pu'lire vt to clean; (lucidare) to polish;
  pu'lito, -a ag (anche fig) clean;
  (ordinato) neat, tidy; **puli'tura** sf
  cleaning; **pulitura a secco** dry
  cleaning; **puli'zia** sf cleaning;
  cleanness; **fare le pulizie** to do the
  cleaning o the housework; **pulizia
  etnica** ethnic cleansing
'pullman sm inv coach
pul'lover sm inv pullover, jumper
pullu'lare vi to swarm, teem
pul'mino sm minibus
'pulpito sm pulpit
pul'sante sm (push-)button
pul'sare vi to pulsate, beat
pul'viscolo sm fine dust; **pulviscolo
  atmosferico** specks pl of dust
'puma sm inv puma
pun'gente [pun'dʒɛnte] ag prickly;
  stinging; (anche fig) biting
'pungere ['pundʒere] vt to prick;
  (insetto, ortica) to sting; (: freddo)
  to bite
pungigli'one [pundʒiʎ'ʎone] sm sting
pu'nire vt to punish; **punizi'one** sf
  punishment; (Sport) penalty
'punsi ecc vb vedi **pungere**
'punta sf point; (parte terminale)
  tip, end; (di monte) peak; (di costa)
  promontory; (minima parte) touch,
  trace; **in ~ di piedi** on tip-toe; **ore di
  ~** peak hours; **uomo di ~** front-rank o
  leading man
pun'tare vt (piedi a terra, gomiti sul
  tavolo) to plant; (dirigere: pistola)
  to point; (scommettere) to bet ▶ vi

(mirare): **~ a** to aim at; **~ su** (dirigersi)
  to head o make for; (fig: contare) to
  count o rely on
pun'tata sf (gita) short trip;
  (scommessa) bet; (parte di opera)
  instalment; **romanzo a puntate**
  serial
puntaggia'tura [puntedʒa'tura] sf
  (Ling) punctuation
pun'teggio [pun'teddʒo] sm score
puntel'lare vt to support
pun'tello sm prop, support
pun'tina sf; **puntina da disegno**
  drawing pin
pun'tino sm dot; **fare qc a ~** to do sth
  properly
'punto, -a pp di **pungere** ▶ sm (segno,
  macchiolina) dot; (Ling) full stop; (di
  indirizzo e-mail) dot; (Mat, momento,
  di punteggio: fig: argomento) point;
  (posto) spot; (a scuola) mark; (nel
  cucire, nella maglia, Med) stitch ▶ av
  non ... ~ not at all; **punto cardinale**
  point of the compass, cardinal point;
  punto debole weak point; **punto
  esclamativo** exclamation mark;
  punto interrogativo question mark;
  punto nero (comedone) blackhead;
  punto di partenza (anche fig)
  starting point; **punto di riferimento**
  landmark; (fig) point of reference;
  punto (di) vendita retail outlet;
  punto e virgola semicolon; **punto di
  vista** (fig) point of view
puntu'ale ag punctual
pun'tura sf (di ago) prick; (Med)
  puncture; (: iniezione) injection;
  (dolore) sharp pain; **puntura
  d'insetto** sting, bite

  Attenzione! In inglese esiste la
  parola *puncture*, che si usa per
  indicare la foratura di una gomma.

punzecchi'are [puntsek'kjare] vt to
  prick; (fig) to tease
può ecc, **-pu'oi** vb vedi **potere**

pu'pazzo [pu'pattso] *sm* puppet
pu'pilla *sf (Anat)* pupil
purché [pur'ke] *cong* provided that, on condition that
'**pure** *cong (tuttavia)* and yet, nevertheless; *(anche se)* even if ▸ *av (anche)* too, also; **pur di** *(al fine di)* just to; **faccia ~!** go ahead!, please do!
purè *sm (Cuc)* purée; *(: di patate)* mashed potatoes
pu'rezza [pu'rettsa] *sf* purity
pur'gante *sm (Med)* purgative, purge
purga'torio *sm* purgatory
purifi'care *vt* to purify; *(metallo)* to refine
'**puro, -a** *ag* pure; *(acqua)* clear, limpid; *(vino)* undiluted; **puro'sangue** *sm/f inv* thoroughbred
pur'troppo *av* unfortunately
pus *sm* pus
'**pustola** *sf* pimple
puti'ferio *sm* rumpus, row
putre'fatto, -a *pp di* **putrefare**
put'tana *(fam!) sf* whore (!)
puz'zare [put'tsare] *vi* to stink
'**puzzo** ['puttso] *sm* stink, foul smell
'**puzzola** ['puttsola] *sf* polecat
puzzo'lente [puttso'lɛnte] *ag* stinking
pvc [pivi'tʃi] *sigla m (= polyvinyl chloride)* PVC

q

q *abbr (= quintale)* q.
qua *av* here; **in ~** *(verso questa parte)* this way; **da un anno in ~** for a year now; **da ~ndo in ~?** since when?; **per di ~** *(passare)* this way; **al di ~ di** *(fiume, strada)* on this side of; **~ dentro/fuori** *ecc* in/out here *ecc*; *vedi anche* **questo**
qua'derno *sm* notebook; *(per scuola)* exercise book
qua'drante *sm* quadrant; *(di orologio)* face
qua'drare *vi (bilancio)* to balance, tally; *(descrizione)* to correspond ▸ *vt (Mat)* to square; **non mi quadra** I don't like it; **qua'drato, -a** *ag* square; *(fig: equilibrato)* level-headed, sensible; *(: peg)* square ▸ *sm (Mat)* square; *(Pugilato)* ring; **5 al quadrato** 5 squared
quadri'foglio [kwadri'fɔʎʎo] *sm* four-leaf clover
quadri'mestre *sm (periodo)* four-month period; *(Ins)* term
'**quadro** *sm (pittura)* painting, picture; *(quadrato)* square; *(tabella)* table, chart; *(Tecn)* board, panel; *(Teatro)* scene; *(fig: scena, spettacolo)* sight; *(: descrizione)* outline, description; **quadri** *smpl (Pol)* party organizers; *(Mil)* cadres; *(Comm)* managerial staff; *(Carte)* diamonds
'**quadruplo, -a** *ag, sm* quadruple
quaggiù [kwad'dʒu] *av* down here
'**quaglia** ['kwaʎʎa] *sf* quail

○ **'qualche**
['kwalke] *det*

1 some, a few; (*in interrogative*) any; **ho comprato qualche libro** I've bought some *o* a few books; **qualche volta** sometimes; **hai qualche sigaretta?** have you any cigarettes?

2 (*uno*): **c'è qualche medico?** is there a doctor?; **in qualche modo** somehow

3 (*un certo, parecchio*) some; **un personaggio di qualche rilievo** a figure of some importance

4: **qualche cosa = qualcosa**

qual'cosa *pron* something; (*in espressioni interrogative*) anything; **qualcos'altro** something else; **~ di nuovo** something new; anything new; **~ da mangiare** something to eat; anything to eat; **c'è ~ che non va?** is there something *o* anything wrong?

qual'cuno *pron* (*persona*) someone, somebody; (: *in espressioni interrogative*) anyone, anybody; (*alcuni*) some; **~ è favorevole a noi** some are on our side; **qualcun altro** someone *o* somebody else; anyone *o* anybody else

○ **'quale**
(*spesso troncato in* **qual**) *det*

1 (*interrogativo*) what; (: *scegliendo tra due o più cose o persone*) which; **quale uomo/denaro?** what man/money?, which man/money?; **quali sono i tuoi programmi?** what are your plans?; **quale stanza preferisci?** which room do you prefer?

2 (*relativo: come*): **il risultato fu quale ci si aspettava** the result was as expected

3 (*esclamativo*) what; **quale disgrazia!** what bad luck!

▶*pron*

1 (*interrogativo*) which; **quale dei due scegli?** which of the two do you want?

2 (*relativo*): **il (la) quale** (*persona: soggetto*) who; (: *oggetto, con preposizione*) whom; (*cosa*) which; (*possessivo*) whose; **suo padre, il quale è avvocato, ...** his father, who is a lawyer, ...; **il signore con il quale parlavo** the gentleman to whom I was speaking; **l'albergo al quale ci siamo fermati** the hotel where we stayed *o* which we stayed at; **la signora della quale ammiriamo la bellezza** the lady whose beauty we admire

3 (*relativo: in elenchi*) such as, like; **piante quali l'edera** plants like *o* such as ivy; **quale sindaco di questa città** as mayor of this town

qua'lifica, -che *sf* qualification; (*titolo*) title

qualifi'cato, -a *ag* (*dotato di qualifica*) qualified; (*esperto, abile*) skilled; **non mi ritengo ~ per questo lavoro** I don't think I'm qualified for this job; **è un medico molto ~** he is a very distinguished doctor

qualificazi'one *sf* **gara di ~** (*Sport*) qualifying event

qualità *sf inv* quality; **in ~ di** in one's capacity as

qua'lora *cong* in case, if

qual'siasi *det inv* = **qualunque**

qua'lunque *det inv* any; (*quale che sia*) whatever; (*discriminativo*) whichever; (*posposto: mediocre*) poor, indifferent; ordinary; **mettiti un vestito ~** put on any old dress; **~ cosa** anything; **~ cosa accada** whatever happens; **a ~ costo** at any cost, whatever the cost; **l'uomo ~** the man in the street; **~ persona** anyone, anybody

○ **'quando** *cong, av* when; **~ sarò ricco** when I'm rich; **da ~** (*dacché*) since; (*interrogativo*): **da ~ sei qui?** how long have you been here?; **quand'anche** even if

quantità *sf inv* quantity; (*gran*

numero): **una ~ di** a great deal of; a lot of; **in grande ~** in large quantities

'quanto, -a *det*

1 (*interrogativo: quantità*) how much; (*: numero*) how many; **quanto pane/denaro?** how much bread/money?; **quanti libri/ragazzi?** how many books/boys?; **quanto tempo?** how long?; **quanti anni hai?** how old are you? **2** (*esclamativo*): **quante storie!** what a lot of nonsense!; **quanto tempo sprecato!** what a waste of time! **3** (*relativo: quantità*) as much ... as; (*: numero*) as many ... as; **ho quanto denaro mi occorre** I have as much money as I need; **prendi quanti libri vuoi** take as many books as you like ▶*pron*

1 (*interrogativo: quantità*) how much; (*: numero*) how many; (*: tempo*) how long; **quanto mi dai?** how much will you give me?; **quanti me ne hai portati?** how many did you bring me?; **da quanto sei qui?** how long have you been here?; **quanti ne abbiamo oggi?** what's the date today? **2** (*relativo: quantità*) as much as; (*: numero*) as many as; **farò quanto posso** I'll do as much as I can; **possono venire quanti sono stati invitati** all those who have been invited can come ▶*av*

1 (*interrogativo: con ag, av*) how; (*: con vb*) how much; **quanto stanco ti sembrava?** how tired did he seem to you?; **quanto corre la tua moto?** how fast can your motorbike go?; **quanto costa?** how much does it cost?; **quant'è?** how much is it? **2** (*esclamativo: con ag, av*) how; (*: con vb*) how much; **quanto sono felice!** how happy I am!; **sapessi quanto abbiamo camminato!** if you knew how far we've walked!; **studierò quanto posso** I'll

study as much as *o* all I can; **quanto prima** as soon as possible

3: **in quanto** (*in qualità di*) as; (*perché, per il fatto che*) as, since; **(in) quanto a** (*per ciò che riguarda*) as for, as regards **4**: **per quanto** (*nonostante, anche se*) however; **per quanto si sforzi, non ce la farà** try as he may, he won't manage it; **per quanto sia brava, fa degli errori** however good she may be, she makes mistakes; **per quanto io sappia** as far as I know

qua'ranta *num* forty

quaran'tena *sf* quarantine

quaran'tesimo, -a *num* fortieth

quaran'tina *sf* **una ~ (di)** about forty

'quarta *sf* (*Aut*) fourth (gear); *vedi anche* **quarto**

quar'tetto *sm* quartet(te)

quarti'ere *sm* district, area; (*Mil*) quarters *pl*; **quartier generale** headquarters *pl*

'quarto, -a *ag* fourth ▶ *sm* fourth; (*quarta parte*) quarter; **le 6 e un ~** a quarter past six; **quarti di finale** quarter final; **quarto d'ora** quarter of an hour

'quarzo ['kwartso] *sm* quartz

'quasi *av* almost, nearly ▶ *cong* (*anche:* **~ che**) as if; **(non) ... ~ mai** hardly ever; **~ ~ me ne andrei** I've half a mind to leave

quas'sù *av* up here

quat'tordici [kwat'torditʃi] *num* fourteen

quat'trini *smpl* money *sg*, cash *sg*

'quattro *num* four; **in ~ e quattr'otto** in less than no time; **quattro'cento** *num* four hundred ▶ *sm* **il Quattrocento** the fifteenth century

'quello, -a
(*dav sm* **quel** + *C*, **quell'** + *V*, **quello** + *s impura, gn, pn, ps, x, z; pl* **quei** + *C*, **quegli** + *V o s impura, gn, pn, ps, x, z; dav sf* **quella** + *C*, **quell'** + *V; pl* **quelle**) *det*

q

that; those *pl*; **quella casa** that house; **quegli uomini** those men; **voglio quella camicia (lì o là)** I want that shirt ▶*pron*

1 (*dimostrativo*) that (one), those (ones) *pl*; (*ciò*) that; **conosci quella?** do you know that woman?; **prendo quello bianco** I'll take the white one; **chi è quello?** who's that?; **prendi quello (lì o là)** take that one (there)

2 (*relativo*) **quello(a) che** (*persona*) the one (who); (*cosa*) the one (which), the one (that); **quelli(e) che** (*persone*) those who; (*cose*) those which; **è lui quello che non voleva venire** he's the one who didn't want to come; **ho fatto quello che potevo** I did what I could

'quercia, -ce ['kwɛrtʃa] *sf* oak (tree); (*legno*) oak

que'rela *sf* (*Dir*) (legal) action

que'sito *sm* question, query; problem

questio'nario *sm* questionnaire

questi'one *sf* problem, question; (*controversia*) issue; (*litigio*) quarrel; **in ~** in question; **è ~ di tempo** it's a matter *o* question of time

○ **'questo, -a**
    det

1 (*dimostrativo*) this; these *pl*; **questo libro (qui o qua)** this book; **io prendo questo cappotto, tu quello** I'll take this coat, you take that one; **quest'oggi** today; **questa sera** this evening

2 (*enfatico*): **non fatemi più prendere di queste paure** don't frighten me like that again

▶*pron* (*dimostrativo*) this (one); these (ones) *pl*; (*ciò*) this; **prendo questo (qui o qua)** I'll take this one; **preferisci questi o quelli?** do you prefer these (ones) or those (ones)?; **questo intendevo io** this is what I meant; **vengono Paolo e Luca: questo da Roma, quello da Palermo** Paolo and Luca are coming: the former from Palermo, the latter from Rome

ques'tura *sf* police headquarters *pl*

qui *av* here; **da** *o* **di ~** from here; **di ~ in avanti** from now on; **di ~ a poco/una settimana** in a little while/a week's time; **~ dentro/sopra/vicino** in/up/near here; *vedi anche* **questo**

quie'tanza [kwje'tantsa] *sf* receipt

qui'ete *sf* quiet, quietness; calmness; stillness; peace

qui'eto, -a *ag* quiet; (*notte*) calm, still; (*mare*) calm

'quindi *av* then ▶ *cong* therefore, so

'quindici ['kwinditʃi] *num* fifteen; **~ giorni** a fortnight (*BRIT*), two weeks

quindi'cina [kwindi'tʃina] *sf* (*serie*): **una ~ (di)** about fifteen; **fra una ~ di giorni** in a fortnight

quinta *sf vedi* **quinto**

quin'tale *sm* quintal (100 kg)

'quinto, -a *num* fifth

quiz [kwidz] *sm inv* (*domanda*) question; (*anche*): **gioco a ~** quiz game

'quota *sf* (*parte*) quota, share; (*Aer*) height, altitude; (*Ippica*) odds *pl*; **prendere/perdere ~** (*Aer*) to gain/lose height *o* altitude; **quota d'iscrizione** enrolment fee; (*a club*) membership fee

quotidi'ano, -a *ag* daily; (*banale*) everyday ▶ *sm* (*giornale*) daily (paper)

quozi'ente [kwot'tsjɛnte] *sm* (*Mat*) quotient; **quoziente d'intelligenza** intelligence quotient, IQ

r

R, r ['ɛrre] *sf o m (lettera)* R, r; **R come Roma** ≈ R for Robert (*BRIT*), R for Roger (*US*)

'rabbia *sf (ira)* anger, rage; *(accanimento, furia)* fury; *(Med: idrofobia)* rabies *sg*

rab'bino *sm* rabbi

rabbi'oso, -a *ag* angry, furious; *(facile all'ira)* quick-tempered; *(forze, acqua ecc)* furious, raging; *(Med)* rabid, mad

rabbo'nire *vt* to calm down

rabbrivi'dire *vi* to shudder, shiver

raccapez'zarsi [rakkapet'tsarsi] *vpr* **non ~** to be at a loss

raccapricci'ante [rakkaprit'tʃante] *ag* horrifying

raccatta'palle *sm inv (Sport)* ballboy

raccat'tare *vt* to pick up

rac'chetta [rak'ketta] *sf (per tennis)* racket; *(per ping-pong)* bat; **racchetta da neve** snowshoe; **racchetta da sci** ski stick

racchi'udere [rak'kjudere] *vt* to contain

rac'cogliere [rak'kɔʎʎere] *vt* to collect; *(raccattare)* to pick up; *(frutti, fiori)* to pick, pluck; *(Agr)* to harvest; *(approvazione, voti)* to win

raccogli'tore [rakkoʎʎi'tore] *sm* *(cartella)* folder, binder

rac'colta *sf* collecting *no pl*; collection; *(Agr)* harvesting *no pl*, harvest, crop; *(adunata)* gathering; **raccolta differenziata** *(dei rifiuti)* separate collection of different kinds of household waste

rac'colto, -a *pp di* **raccogliere** ▶ *ag* *(persona: pensoso)* thoughtful; *(luogo: appartato)* secluded, quiet ▶ *sm (Agr)* crop, harvest

raccoman'dabile *ag* (highly) commendable; **è un tipo poco ~** he is not to be trusted

raccoman'dare *vt* to recommend; *(affidare)* to entrust; *(esortare)*: **~ a qn di non fare** to tell *o* warn sb not to do; **raccoman'data** *sf (anche:* **lettera raccomandata***)* recorded-delivery letter

raccon'tare *vt* **~ (a qn)** *(dire)* to tell (sb); *(narrare)* to relate (to sb), tell (sb) about; **rac'conto** *sm* telling *no pl*; *(fatto raccontato)* story, tale; **racconti per bambini** children's stories

rac'cordo *sm (Tecn: giunto)* connection, joint; *(Aut)*: **raccordo anulare** *(Aut)* ring road *(BRIT)*, beltway *(US)*; **raccordo autostradale** slip road *(BRIT)*, entrance *(o exit)* ramp *(US)*; **raccordo ferroviario** siding; **raccordo stradale** link road

racimo'lare [ratʃimo'lare] *vt (fig)* to scrape together, glean

'rada *sf (natural)* harbour

'radar *sm* radar

raddoppi'are *vt, vi* to double

raddriz'zare [raddrit'tsare] *vt* to straighten; *(fig: correggere)* to put straight, correct

'radere *vt (barba)* to shave off; *(mento)* to shave; *(fig: rasentare)* to graze; to skim; **radersi** *vpr* to shave (o.s.); **~ al suolo** to raze to the ground

radi'are *vt* to strike off

radia'tore *sm* radiator

radiazi'one [radjat'tsjone] *sf (Fisica)* radiation; *(cancellazione)* striking off

radi'cale *ag* radical ▶ *sm (Ling)* root

ra'dicchio [ra'dikkjo] *sm* chicory
ra'dice [ra'ditʃe] *sf* root
'radio *sf inv* radio ▶ *sm* (*Chim*) radium;
  radioat'tivo, -a *ag* radioactive;
  radio'cronaca, -che *sf* radio
  commentary; **radiogra'fia** *sf*
  radiography; (*foto*) X-ray photograph
radi'oso, -a *ag* radiant
radios'veglia [radjoz'veʎʎa] *sf* radio
  alarm
'rado, -a *ag* (*capelli*) sparse, thin;
  (*visite*) infrequent; **di ~** rarely
radu'nare *vt* to gather, assemble;
  radunarsi *vpr* to gather, assemble
ra'dura *sf* clearing
raf'fermo, -a *ag* stale
'raffica, -che *sf* (*Meteor*) gust (of
  wind); (*di colpi: scarica*) burst of gunfire
raffigu'rare *vt* to represent
raffi'nato, -a *ag* refined
raffor'zare [raffor'tsare] *vt* to
  reinforce
raffredda'mento *sm* cooling
raffred'dare *vt* to cool; (*fig*) to
  dampen, have a cooling effect on;
  raffreddarsi *vpr* to grow cool *o* cold;
  (*prendere un raffreddore*) to catch a cold;
  (*fig*) to cool (off)
raffred'dato, -a *ag* (*Med*): **essere ~** to
  have a cold
raffred'dore *sm* (*Med*) cold
raf'fronto *sm* comparison
'rafia *sf* (*fibra*) raffia
rafting ['rafting] *sm* white-water
  rafting
ra'gazza [ra'gattsa] *sf* girl; (*fam:
  fidanzato*) girlfriend; **nome da ~**
  maiden name; **ragazza madre**
  unmarried mother
ra'gazzo [ra'gattso] *sm* boy; (*fam:
  fidanzato*) boyfriend; **ragazzi** *smpl*
  (*figli*) kids; **ciao ragazzi!** (*gruppo*)
  hi guys!
raggi'ante [rad'dʒante] *ag* radiant,
  shining

'raggio ['raddʒo] *sm* (*di sole ecc*) ray;
  (*Mat, distanza*) radius; (*di ruota ecc*)
  spoke; **raggio d'azione** range; **raggi
  X** X-rays
raggi'rare [raddʒi'rare] *vt* to take
  in, trick
raggi'ungere [rad'dʒundʒere] *vt* to
  reach; (*persona: riprendere*) to catch
  up (with); (*bersaglio*) to hit; (*fig: meta*)
  to achieve
raggomito'larsi *vpr* to curl up
raggranel'lare *vt* to scrape together
raggrup'pare *vt* to group (together)
ragiona'mento [radʒona'mento]
  sm reasoning *no pl*; arguing *no pl*;
  argument
ragio'nare [radʒo'nare] *vi* to reason; **~
  di** (*discorrere*) to talk about
ragi'one [ra'dʒone] *sf* reason;
  (*dimostrazione, prova*) argument,
  reason; (*diritto*) right; **aver ~** to be
  right; **aver ~ di qn** to get the better
  of sb; **dare ~ a qn** to agree with sb;
  to prove sb right; **perdere la ~** to
  become insane; (*fig*) to take leave of
  one's senses; **in ~ di** at the rate of; to
  the amount of; according to; **a o con
  ~** rightly, justly; **a ragion veduta** after
  due consideration; **ragione sociale**
  (*Comm*) corporate name
ragione'ria [radʒone'ria] *sf*
  accountancy; accounts department
ragio'nevole [radʒo'nevole] *ag*
  reasonable
ragioni'ere, -a [radʒo'njɛre] *sm/f*
  accountant
ragli'are [raʎ'ʎare] *vi* to bray
ragna'tela [raɲɲa'tela] *sf* cobweb,
  spider's web
'ragno ['raɲɲo] *sm* spider
ragù *sm inv* (*Cuc*) meat sauce; stew
RAI-TV [raiti'vu] *sigla f* = **Radio
  televisione italiana**
ralle'grare *vt* to cheer up; **rallegrarsi**
  vpr to cheer up; (*provare allegrezza*)

to rejoice; **rallegrarsi con qn** to congratulate sb

rallen'tare vt to slow down; (fig) to lessen, slacken ▶ vi to slow down

rallenta'tore sm (Cinema) slow-motion camera; **al ~** (anche fig) in slow motion

raman'zina [raman'dzina] sf lecture, telling-off

'rame sm (Chim) copper

rammari'carsi vpr **~ (di)** (rincrescersi) to be sorry (about), regret; (lamentarsi) to complain (about)

rammen'dare vt to mend; (calza) to darn

'ramo sm branch

ramo'scello [ramoʃʃɛllo] sm twig

'rampa sf flight (of stairs); **rampa di lancio** launching pad

rampi'cante ag (Bot) climbing

'rana sf frog

'rancido, -a ['rantʃido] ag rancid

ran'core sm rancour, resentment

ran'dagio, -a, -gi, -gie o **ge** [ran'dadʒo] ag (gatto, cane) stray

ran'dello sm club, cudgel

'rango, -ghi sm (condizione sociale, Mil, riga) rank

rannicchi'arsi [rannik'kjarsi] vpr to crouch, huddle

rannuvo'larsi vpr to cloud over, become overcast

'rapa sf (Bot) turnip

ra'pace [ra'patʃe] ag (animale) predatory; (fig) rapacious, grasping ▶ sm bird of prey

ra'pare vt (capelli) to crop, cut very short

rapida'mente av quickly, rapidly

rapidità sf speed

'rapido, -a ag fast; (esame, occhiata) quick, rapid ▶ sm (Ferr) express (train)

rapi'mento sm kidnapping; (fig) rapture

ra'pina sf robbery; **rapina in banca** bank robbery; **rapina a mano armata** armed robbery; **rapi'nare** vt to rob; **rapina'tore, -'trice** sm/f robber

ra'pire vt (cose) to steal; (persone) to kidnap; (fig) to enrapture, delight; **rapi'tore, -'trice** sm/f kidnapper

rap'porto sm (resoconto) report; (legame) relationship; (Mat, Tecn) ratio; **rapporti sessuali** sexual intercourse sg

rappre'saglia [rappre'saʎʎa] sf reprisal, retaliation

rappresen'tante sm/f representative

rappresen'tare vt to represent; (Teatro) to perform; **rappresentazi'one** sf representation; performing no pl; (spettacolo) performance

rara'mente av seldom, rarely

rare'fatto, -a ag rarefied

'raro, -a ag rare

ra'sare vt (barba ecc) to shave off; (siepi, erba) to trim, cut; **rasarsi** vpr to shave (o.s.)

raschi'are [ras'kjare] vt to scrape; (macchia, fango) to scrape off ▶ vi to clear one's throat

ra'sente prep **~ (a)** close to, very near

'raso, -a pp di **radere** ▶ ag (barba) shaved; (capelli) cropped; (con misure di capacità) level; (pieno: bicchiere) full to the brim ▶ sm (tessuto) satin; **un cucchiaio ~** a level spoonful; **raso terra** close to the ground

ra'soio sm razor; **rasoio elettrico** electric shaver o razor

ras'segna [ras'seɲɲa] sf (Mil) inspection, review; (esame) inspection; (resoconto) review, survey; (pubblicazione letteraria ecc) review; (mostra) exhibition, show; **passare in ~** (Mil, fig) to review

rassegnarsi vpr (accettare): **~ (a qc/a fare)** to resign o.s. (to sth/to doing)

rassicu'rare *vt* to reassure
rasso'dare *vt* to harden, stiffen;
　rassodarsi *vpr* to harden, strengthen
rassomigli'anza [rassomiʎ'ʎantsa]
　sf resemblance
rassomigli'are [rassomiʎ'ʎare] *vi* ~ **a**
　to resemble, look like
rastrel'lare *vt* to rake; (*fig: perlustrare*)
　to comb
ras'trello *sm* rake
'rata *sf* (*quota*) instalment; **pagare a**
　rate to pay by instalments *o* on hire
　purchase (*BRIT*)
ratifi'care *vt* (*Dir*) to ratify
'ratto *sm* (*Dir*) abduction; (*Zool*) rat
rattop'pare *vt* to patch
rattris'tare *vt* to sadden; **rattristarsi**
　vpr to become sad
'rauco, -a, -chi, -che *ag* hoarse
rava'nello *sm* radish
ravi'oli *smpl* ravioli *sg*
ravvi'vare *vt* to revive; (*fig*) to
　brighten up, enliven
razio'nale [rattsjo'nale] *ag* rational
razio'nare [rattsjo'nare] *vt* to ration
razi'one [rat'tsjone] *sf* ration;
　(*porzione*) portion, share
'razza ['rattsa] *sf* race; (*Zool*) breed;
　(*discendenza, stirpe*) stock, race; (*sorta*)
　sort, kind
razzi'ale [rat'tsjale] *ag* racial
raz'zismo [rat'tsizmo] *sm* racism
raz'zista, -i, -e [rat'tsista] *ag, sm/f*
　racist
'razzo ['raddzo] *sm* rocket
R.C. *sigla m* (= *partito della Rifondazione
　Comunista*) left-wing Italian political
　party
re *sm inv* king; (*Mus*) D; (: *solfeggiando*)
　re; **i Re Magi** the Three Wise Men,
　the Magi
rea'gire [rea'dʒire] *vi* to react
re'ale *ag* real; (*di, da re*) royal ▶ *sm* **il**
　~ reality
realiz'zare [realid'dzare] *vt* (*progetto*

ecc) to realize, carry out; (*sogno,
　desiderio*) to realize, fulfil; (*scopo*) to
　achieve; (*Comm: titoli ecc*) to realize;
　(*Calcio ecc*) to score; **realizzarsi** *vpr* to
　be realized
real'mente *av* really, actually
realtà *sf inv* reality
re'ato *sm* offence
reat'tore *sm* (*Fisica*) reactor; (*Aer:
　aereo*) jet; (: *motore*) jet engine
reazio'nario, -a [reattsjo'narjo] *ag*
　(*Pol*) reactionary
reazi'one [reat'tsjone] *sf* reaction
'rebus *sm inv* rebus; (*fig*) puzzle
recapi'tare *vt* to deliver
re'capito *sm* (*indirizzo*) address;
　(*consegna*) delivery; **recapito a
　domicilio** home delivery (service);
　recapito telefonico phone number
re'carsi *vpr* ~ **in città/a scuola** to go
　into town/to school
re'cedere [re'tʃɛdere] *vi* to withdraw
recensi'one [retʃen'sjone] *sf* review
re'cente [re'tʃɛnte] *ag* recent; **di** ~
　recently; **recente'mente** *av* recently
re'cidere [re'tʃidere] *vt* to cut off
recin'tare [retʃin'tare] *vt* to enclose,
　fence off
re'cinto [re'tʃinto] *sm* enclosure; (*ciò
　che recinge*) fence; surrounding wall
recipi'ente [retʃi'pjɛnte] *sm* container
re'ciproco, -a, -ci, -che [re'tʃiproko]
　ag reciprocal
'recita ['rɛtʃita] *sf* performance
reci'tare [retʃi'tare] *vt* (*poesia, lezione*)
　to recite; (*dramma*) to perform; (*ruolo*)
　to play *o* act (the part of)
recla'mare *vi* to complain ▶ *vt*
　(*richiedere*) to demand
re'clamo *sm* complaint
recli'nabile *ag* (*sedile*) reclining
reclusi'one *sf* (*Dir*) imprisonment
'recluta *sf* recruit
re'condito, -a *ag* secluded; (*fig*)
　secret, hidden

'record ag inv record cpd ▶ sm inv record; **in tempo ~, a tempo di ~** in record time; **detenere il ~ di** to hold the record for; **record mondiale** world record

recriminazi'one [rekriminat'tsjone] sf recrimination

recupe'rare vt (rientrare in possesso di) to recover, get back; (tempo perduto) to make up for; (Naut) to salvage; (: naufraghi) to rescue; (delinquente) to rehabilitate; **~ lo svantaggio** (Sport) to close the gap

redargu'ire vt to rebuke

re'dassi ecc vb vedi **redigere**

reddi'tizio, -a [reddi'tittsjo] ag profitable

'reddito sm income; (dello Stato) revenue; (di un capitale) yield

re'digere [re'didʒere] vt to write; (contratto) to draw up

'redini sfpl reins

'reduce ['rɛdutʃe] ag **~ da** returning from, back from ▶ sm/f survivor

refe'rendum sm inv referendum

refe'renze [refe'rɛntse] sfpl references

re'ferto sm medical report

rega'lare vt to give (as a present), make a present of

re'galo sm gift, present

re'gata sf regatta

'reggere ['rɛddʒere] vt (tenere) to hold; (sostenere) to support, bear, hold up; (portare) to carry, bear; (resistere) to withstand; (dirigere: impresa) to manage, run; (governare) to rule, govern; (Ling) to take, be followed by ▶ vi (resistere): **~ a** to stand up to, hold out against; (sopportare): **~ a** to stand; (durare) to last; (fig: teoria ecc) to hold water; **reggersi** vpr (stare ritto) to stand

'reggia, -ge ['rɛddʒa] sf royal palace

reggi'calze [rɛddʒi'kaltse] sm inv suspender belt

reggi'mento [rɛddʒi'mento] sm (Mil) regiment

reggi'seno [rɛddʒi'seno] sm bra

re'gia, -'gie [re'dʒia] sf (TV, Cinema ecc) direction

re'gime [re'dʒime] sm (Pol) regime; (Dir: aureo, patrimoniale ecc) system; (Med) diet; (Tecn) (engine) speed

re'gina [re'dʒina] sf queen

regio'nale [redʒo'nale] ag regional ▶ sm local train (stopping frequently)

regi'one [re'dʒone] sf region; (territorio) region, district, area

re'gista, -i, -e [re'dʒista] sm/f (TV, Cinema ecc) director

regis'trare [redʒis'trare] vt (Amm) to register; (Comm) to enter; (notare) to note, take note of; (canzone, conversazione: strumento di misura) to record; (mettere a punto) to adjust, regulate; (bagagli) to check in;

registra'tore sm (strumento) recorder, register; (magnetofono) tape recorder; **registratore di cassa** cash register; **registratore a cassette** cassette recorder

re'gistro [re'dʒistro] sm (libro, Mus, Tech) register; ledger; logbook; (Dir) registry

re'gnare [reɲ'ɲare] vi to reign, rule

'regno ['reɲɲo] sm kingdom; (periodo) reign; (fig) realm; **il R~ Unito** the United Kingdom; **regno animale/ vegetale** animal/vegetable kingdom

'regola sf rule; **a ~ d'arte** duly; perfectly; **in ~** in order

rego'labile ag adjustable

regola'mento sm (complesso di norme) regulations pl; (di debito) settlement; **regolamento di conti** (fig) settling of scores

rego'lare ag regular; (in regola: domanda) in order, lawful ▶ vt to regulate, control; (apparecchio) to adjust, regulate; (questione, conto,

debito) to settle; **regolarsi** *vpr*
(*moderarsi*): **regolarsi nel bere/nello
spendere** to control one's drinking/
spending; (*comportarsi*) to behave,
act

rela'tivo, -a *ag* relative

relazi'one [relat'tsjone] *sf* (*fra cose,
persone*) relation(ship); (*resoconto*)
report, account

rele'gare *vt* to banish; (*fig*) to relegate

religi'one [reli'dʒone] *sf* religion

religi'oso, a [reli'dʒoso] *ag* religious

re'liquia *sf* relic

re'litto *sm* wreck; (*fig*) down-and-out

re'mare *vi* to row

remini'scenze [reminiʃʃentse] *sfpl*
reminiscences

remis'sivo, -a *ag* submissive

'remo *sm* oar

re'moto, -a *ag* remote

'rendere *vt* (*ridare*) to return, give
back; (: *saluto ecc*) to return; (*produrre*)
to yield, bring in; (*esprimere, tradurre*)
to render; **rendersi** *vpr* **rendersi utile**
to make o.s. useful; **rendersi conto
di qc** to realize sth; ~ **qc possibile** to
make sth possible; ~ **grazie a qn** give
thanks to sb; ~ **omaggio a qn** to pay
homage to sb; ~ **un servizio a qn** to
do sb a service; ~ **una testimonianza**
to give evidence; **non so se rendo
l'idea** I don't know if I'm making
myself clear

rendi'mento *sm* (*reddito*) yield; (*di
manodopera, Tecn*) efficiency; (*capacità
di produrre*) output; (*di studenti*)
performance

'rendita *sf* (*di individuo*) private *o*
unearned income; (*Comm*) revenue;
rendita annua annuity

'rene *sm* kidney

'renna *sf* reindeer *inv*

re'parto *sm* department, section;
(*Mil*) detachment

repel'lente *ag* repulsive

repen'taglio [repen'taʎʎo] *sm*
mettere a ~ to jeopardize, risk

repen'tino, -a *ag* sudden, unexpected

reper'torio *sm* (*Teatro*) repertory;
(*elenco*) index, (alphabetical) list

'replica, -che *sf* repetition; reply,
answer; (*obiezione*) objection; (*Teatro,
Cinema*) repeat performance; (*copia*)
replica

repli'care *vt* (*ripetere*) to repeat;
(*rispondere*) to answer, reply

repressi'one *sf* repression

re'presso, -a *pp di* **reprimere**

re'primere *vt* to suppress, repress

re'pubblica, -che *sf* republic

reputazi'one [reputat'tsjone] *sf*
reputation

requi'sire *vt* to requisition

requi'sito *sm* requirement

'resa *sf* (*l'arrendersi*) surrender;
(*restituzione, rendimento*) return; **resa
dei conti** rendering of accounts; (*fig*)
day of reckoning

'resi *ecc vb vedi* **rendere**

resi'dente *ag* resident; **residenzi'ale**
ag residential

re'siduo, -a *ag* residual, remaining
▶ *sm* remainder; (*Chim*) residue

'resina *sf* resin

resis'tente *ag* (*che resiste*): ~ **a**
resistant to; (*forte*) strong; (*duraturo*)
long-lasting, durable; ~ **al caldo** heat-
resistant; **resis'tenza** *sf* resistance;
(*di persona: fisica*) stamina, endurance;
(: *mentale*) endurance, resistance

● **Resistenza**

● The **Resistenza** in Italy fought
● against the Nazis and the Fascists
● during the Second World War.
● Members of the **Resistenza**
● spanned a wide political spectrum
● and played a vital role in the
● Liberation and in the formation of
● the new democratic government at
● the end of the war.

re'sistere vi to resist; **~ a** (assalto, tentazioni) to resist; (dolore: pianta) to withstand; (non patir danno) to be resistant to

reso'conto sm report, account

res'pingere [res'pindʒere] vt to drive back, repel; (rifiutare) to reject; (Ins: bocciare) to fail

respi'rare vi to breathe; (fig) to get one's breath; to breathe again ▶ vt to breathe (in), inhale; **respirazi'one** sf breathing; **respirazione artificiale** artificial respiration; **res'piro** sm breathing no pl; (singolo atto) breath; (fig) respite, rest; **mandare un respiro di sollievo** to give a sigh of relief

respon'sabile ag responsible ▶ sm/f person responsible; (capo) person in charge; **~ di** responsible for; (Dir) liable for; **responsabilità** sf inv responsibility; (legale) liability

res'ponso sm answer

'ressa sf crowd, throng

'ressi ecc vb vedi **reggere**

res'tare vi (rimanere) to remain, stay; (avanzare) to be left, remain; **~ orfano/cieco** to become o be left an orphan/become blind; **~ d'accordo** to agree; **non resta più niente** there's nothing left; **restano pochi giorni** there are only a few days left

restau'rare vt to restore

res'tio, -a, -'tii, -'tie ag **~ a** reluctant to

restitu'ire vt to return, give back; (energie, forze) to restore

'resto sm remainder, rest; (denaro) change; (Mat) remainder; **resti** smpl (di cibo) leftovers; (di città) remains; **del ~** moreover, besides; **tenga pure il ~** keep the change; **resti mortali** (mortal) remains

res'tringere [res'trindʒere] vt to reduce; (vestito) to take in; (stoffa) to shrink; (fig) to restrict, limit;

restringersi vpr (strada) to narrow; (stoffa) to shrink

'rete sf net; (fig) trap, snare; (di recinzione) wire netting; (Aut, Ferr, di spionaggio ecc) network; **segnare una ~** (Calcio) to score a goal; **la R~** the Web; **rete ferroviaria** railway network; **rete del letto** (sprung) bed base; **rete social** social network; **rete stradale** road network; **rete (televisiva)** (sistema) network; (canale) channel

reti'cente [reti'tʃente] ag reticent

retico'lato sm grid; (rete) wire netting; (di filo spinato) barbed wire (fence)

re'tina sf (Anat) retina

re'torico, -a, -ci, -che ag rhetorical

retribu'ire vt to pay

'retro sm inv back ▶ av (dietro): **vedi ~** see over(leaf)

retro'cedere [retro'tʃedere] vi to withdraw ▶ vt (Calcio) to relegate; (Mil) to degrade

retro'grado, -a ag (fig) reactionary, backward-looking

retro'marcia [retro'martʃa] sf (Aut) reverse; (: dispositivo) reverse gear

retro'scena [retroʃʃena] sm inv (Teatro) backstage; **i ~** (fig) the behind-the-scenes activities

retrovi'sore sm (Aut) (rear-view) mirror

'retta sf (Mat) straight line; (di convitto) charge for bed and board; (fig: ascolto): **dar ~ a** to listen to, pay attention to

rettango'lare ag rectangular

ret'tangolo, -a ag right-angled ▶ sm rectangle

ret'tifica, -che sf correction

ret'tile sm reptile

retti'lineo, -a ag rectilinear

'retto, -a pp di **reggere** ▶ ag straight; (Mat): **angolo ~** right angle; (onesto) honest, upright; (giusto, esatto) correct, proper, right

r

ret'tore sm (Rel) rector; (di università) ≈ chancellor

reuma'tismo sm rheumatism

revisi'one sf auditing no pl; audit; servicing no pl; overhaul; review; revision; **revisione di bozze** proofreading

revi'sore sm; **revisore di bozze** proofreader; **revisore di conti** auditor

revival [ri'vaivəl] sm inv revival

'revoca sf revocation

revo'care vt to revoke

re'volver sm inv revolver

ri'abbia ecc vb vedi **riavere**

riabili'tare vt to rehabilitate

riabilitazi'one [riabilitat'tsjone] sf rehabilitation

rianimazi'one [rianimat'tsjone] sf (Med) resuscitation; **centro di ~** intensive care unit

ria'prire vt to reopen, open again; **riaprirsi** vpr to reopen, open again

ri'armo sm (Mil) rearmament

rias'sumere vt (riprendere) to resume; (impiegare di nuovo) to re-employ; (sintetizzare) to summarize; **rias'sunto, -a** pp di **riassumere** ▸ sm summary

riattac'care vt (attaccare di nuovo): **~ (a)** (manifesto, francobollo) to stick back (on); (bottone) to sew back (on); (quadro, chiavi) to hang back up (on); **~ (il telefono)** to hang up (the phone)

ria'vere vt to have again; (avere indietro) to get back; (riacquistare) to recover; **riaversi** vpr to recover

riba'dire vt (fig) to confirm

ri'balta sf flap; (Teatro: proscenio) front of the stage; (fig) limelight; **luci della ~** footlights pl

ribal'tabile ag (sedile) tip-up

ribal'tare vt, vi (anche: **ribaltarsi**) to turn over, tip over

ribas'sare vt to lower, bring down ▸ vi to come down, fall

ri'battere vt to return; (confutare) to refute; **~ che** to retort that

ribel'larsi vpr **~ (a)** to rebel (against); **ri'belle** ag (soldati) rebel; (ragazzo) rebellious ▸ sm/f rebel

'ribes sm inv currant; **ribes nero** blackcurrant; **ribes rosso** redcurrant

ri'brezzo [ri'breddzo] sm disgust, loathing; **far ~ a** to disgust

ributante ag disgusting, revolting

rica'dere vi to fall again; (scendere a terra: fig: nel peccato ecc) to fall back; (vestiti, capelli ecc) to hang (down); (riversarsi: fatiche, colpe): **~ su** to fall on; **rica'duta** sf (Med) relapse

rica'mare vt to embroider

ricambi'are vt to change again; (contraccambiare) to repay, return; **ri'cambio** sm exchange, return; (Fisiol) metabolism

ri'camo sm embroidery

ricapito'lare vt to recapitulate, sum up

ricari'care vt (arma, macchina fotografica) to reload; (pipa) to refill; (orologio) to rewind; (batteria) to recharge

ricat'tare vt to blackmail; **ri'catto** sm blackmail

rica'vare vt (estrarre) to draw out, extract; (ottenere) to obtain, gain

ric'chezza [rik'kettsa] sf wealth; (fig) richness

'riccio, -a ['rittʃo] ag curly ▸ sm (Zool) hedgehog; **riccio di mare** sea urchin; **'ricciolo** sm curl

'ricco, -a, -chi, -che ag rich; (persona, paese) rich, wealthy ▸ sm/f rich man/woman; **i ricchi** the rich; **~ di** full of; rich in

ri'cerca, -che [ri'tʃerka] sf search; (indagine) investigation, inquiry; (studio): **la ~** research; **una ~** piece of research; **ricerca di mercato** market research

ricer'care [ritʃer'kare] vt (motivi, cause) to look for; (successo, piacere) to pursue; (onore, gloria) to seek; **ricer'cato, -a** ag (apprezzato) much sought-after; (affettato) affected ▶ sm/f (Polizia) wanted man/woman

ricerca'tore, -'trice [ritʃerka'tore] sm/f (Ins) researcher

ri'cetta [ri'tʃetta] sf (Med) prescription; (Cuc) recipe; **mi può fare una ~ medica?** could you write me a prescription?

ricettazi'one [ritʃettat'tsjone] sf (Dir) receiving (stolen goods)

ri'cevere [ri'tʃevere] vt to receive; (stipendio, lettera) to get, receive; (accogliere: ospite) to welcome; (vedere: cliente, rappresentante ecc) to see; **ricevi'mento** sm receiving no pl; (festa) reception; **ricevi'tore** sm (Tecn) receiver; **rice'vuta** sf receipt; **posso avere una ricevuta, per favore?** can I have a receipt, please?; **ricevuta fiscale** receipt for tax purposes; **ricevuta di ritorno** (Posta) advice of receipt

richia'mare [rikja'mare] vt (chiamare indietro, ritelefonare) to call back; (ambasciatore, truppe) to recall; (rimproverare) to reprimand; (attirare) to attract, draw; **può ~ più tardi?** can you call back later?; **richiamarsi a** (riferirsi a) to refer to

richi'edere [ri'kjɛdere] vt to ask again for; (chiedere indietro): **~ qc** to ask for sth back; (chiedere: per sapere) to ask; (: per avere) to ask for; (Amm: documenti) to apply for; (esigere) to need, require; **richi'esta** sf (domanda) request; (Amm) application, request; (esigenza) demand, request; **a richiesta** on request

rici'claggio [ritʃi'kladdʒo] sm recycling

rici'clare [ritʃi'klare] vt to recycle

'ricino ['ritʃino] sm **olio di ~** castor oil

ricognizi'one [rikoɲɲit'tsjone] sf (Mil) reconnaissance; (Dir) recognition, acknowledgement

ricominci'are [rikomin'tʃare] vt, vi to start again, begin again

ricom'pensa sf reward

ricompen'sare vt to reward

riconciliarsi vpr to be reconciled

ricono'scente [rikonoʃʃente] ag grateful

rico'noscere [riko'noʃʃere] vt to recognize; (Dir: figlio, debito) to acknowledge; (ammettere: errore) to admit, acknowledge

rico'perto, -a pp di **ricoprire**

ricopi'are vt to copy

rico'prire vt (coprire) to cover; (occupare: carica) to hold

ricor'dare vt to remember, recall; (richiamare alla memoria): **~ qc a qn** to remind sb of sth; **ricordarsi** vpr **ricordarsi (di)** to remember; **ricordarsi di qc/di aver fatto** to remember sth/having done

ri'cordo sm memory; (regalo) keepsake, souvenir; (di viaggio) souvenir

ricor'rente ag recurrent, recurring; **ricor'renza** sf recurrence; (festività) anniversary

ri'correre vi (ripetersi) to recur; **~ a** (rivolgersi) to turn to; (: Dir) to appeal to; (servirsi di) to have recourse to

ricostitu'ente ag (Med): **cura ~** tonic

ricostru'ire vt (casa) to rebuild; (fatti) to reconstruct

ri'cotta sf soft white unsalted cheese made from sheep's milk

ricove'rare vt to give shelter to; **~ qn in ospedale** to admit sb to hospital

ri'covero sm shelter, refuge; (Mil) shelter; (Med) admission (to hospital)

ricreazi'one [rikreat'tsjone] sf recreation, entertainment; (Ins) break

ri'credersi *vpr* to change one's mind

ridacchi'are [ridak'kjare] *vi* to snigger

ri'dare *vt* to return, give back

'ridere *vi* to laugh; (*deridere, beffare*): ~ **di** to laugh at, make fun of

ri'dicolo, -a *ag* ridiculous, absurd

ridimensio'nare *vt* to reorganize; (*fig*) to see in the right perspective

ri'dire *vt* to repeat; (*criticare*) to find fault with; to object to; **trova sempre qualcosa da ~** he always manages to find fault

ridon'dante *ag* redundant

ri'dotto, -a *pp di* **ridurre** ▶ *ag* (*biglietto*) reduced; (*formato*) small

ri'duco *ecc vb vedi* **ridurre**

ri'durre *vt* (*anche Chim, Mat*) to reduce; (*prezzo, spese*) to cut, reduce; (*accorciare: opera letteraria*) to abridge; (*: Radio, TV*) to adapt; **ridursi** *vpr* (*diminuirsi*) to be reduced, shrink; **ridursi a** to be reduced to; **ridursi pelle e ossa** to be reduced to skin and bone; **ri'dussi** *ecc vb vedi* **ridurre**; **ridut'tore** *sm* (*Elec*) adaptor; **riduzi'one** *sf* reduction; abridgement; adaptation; **ci sono riduzioni per i bambini/gli studenti?** is there a reduction for children/students?

ri'ebbi *ecc vb vedi* **riavere**

riem'pire *vt* to fill (up); (*modulo*) to fill in *o* out; **riempirsi** *vpr* to fill (up); ~ **qc di** to fill sth (up) with

rien'tranza [rien'trantsa] *sf* recess; indentation

rien'trare *vi* (*entrare di nuovo*) to go (*o come*) back in; (*tornare*) to return; (*fare una rientranza*) to go in, curve inwards; to be indented; (*riguardare*): ~ **in** to be included among, form part of

riepilo'gare *vt* to summarize ▶ *vi* to recapitulate

ri'esco *ecc vb vedi* **riuscire**

ri'fare *vt* to do again; (*ricostruire*) to make again; (*nodo*) to tie again, do up again; (*imitare*) to imitate, copy; **rifarsi** *vpr* (*risarcirsi*): **rifarsi di** to make up for; (*vendicarsi*): **rifarsi di qc su qn** to get one's own back on sb for sth; (*riferirsi*): **rifarsi a** to go back to; to follow; ~ **il letto** to make the bed; **rifarsi una vita** to make a new life for o.s.

riferi'mento *sm* reference; **in** *o* **con ~ a** with reference to

rife'rire *vt* (*riportare*) to report ▶ *vi* to do a report; **riferirsi** *vpr* **riferirsi a** to refer to

rifi'nire *vt* to finish off, put the finishing touches to

rifiu'tare *vt* to refuse; ~ **di fare** to refuse to do; **rifi'uto** *sm* refusal; **rifiuti** *smpl* (*spazzatura*) rubbish *sg*, refuse *sg*

rifles'sione *sf* (*Fisica, meditazione*) reflection; (*il pensare*) thought, reflection; (*osservazione*) remark

rifles'sivo, -a *ag* (*persona*) thoughtful, reflective; (*Ling*) reflexive

ri'flesso, -a *pp di* **riflettere** ▶ *sm* (*di luce, allo specchio*) reflection; (*Fisiol*) reflex; **di** *o* **per ~** indirectly

riflessologia [riflessolo'dʒia] *sf* reflexology

ri'flettere *vt* to reflect ▶ *vi* to think; **riflettersi** *vpr* to be reflected; ~ **su** to think over

riflet'tore *sm* reflector; (*proiettore*) floodlight; searchlight

ri'flusso *sm* flowing back; (*della marea*) ebb; **un'epoca di ~** an era of nostalgia

ri'forma *sf* reform; **la R~** (*Rel*) the Reformation

riforma'torio *sm* (*Dir*) community home (*BRIT*), reformatory (*US*)

riforni'mento *sm* supplying, providing; restocking; **rifornimenti** *smpl* (*provviste*) supplies, provisions

rifor'nire vt (provvedere): ~ **di** to supply o provide with; (fornire di nuovo: casa ecc) to restock; **rifornirsi** vpr **rifornirsi di qc** to stock up on sth

rifugi'arsi [rifu'dʒarsi] vpr to take refuge; **rifugi'ato, -a** sm/f refugee

ri'fugio [ri'fudʒo] sm refuge, shelter; (in montagna) shelter; **rifugio antiaereo** air-raid shelter

'riga, -ghe sf line; (striscia) stripe; (di persone, cose) line, row; (regolo) ruler; (scriminatura) parting; **mettersi in ~** to line up; **a righe** (foglio) lined; (vestito) striped

ri'gare vt (foglio) to rule ▶ vi ~ **diritto** (fig) to toe the line

rigatti'ere sm junk dealer

ri'ghello [ri'gɛllo] sm ruler

righerò ecc [rige'rɔ] vb vedi **rigare**

'rigido, -a ['ridʒido] ag rigid, stiff; (membra ecc: indurite) stiff; (Meteor) harsh, severe; (fig) strict

rigogli'oso, -a [rigoʎ'ʎoso] ag (pianta) luxuriant; (fig: commercio, sviluppo) thriving

ri'gore sm (Meteor) harshness, rigours pl; (fig) severity, strictness; (anche: **calcio di ~**) penalty; **di ~** compulsory; **a rigor di termini** strictly speaking

riguar'dare vt to look at again; (considerare) to regard, consider; (concernere) to regard, concern; **riguardarsi** vpr (aver cura di sé) to look after o.s.

rigu'ardo sm (attenzione) care; (considerazione) regard, respect; **~ a** concerning, with regard to; **non aver riguardi nell'agire/nel parlare** to act/speak freely

rilasci'are [rilaʃ'ʃare] vt (rimettere in libertà) to release; (Amm: documenti) to issue

rilassarsi vpr to relax; (fig: disciplina) to become slack

rile'gare vt (libro) to bind

ri'leggere [ri'lɛddʒere] vt to reread, read again; (rivedere) to read over

ri'lento: a ~ av slowly

rile'vante ag considerable; important

rile'vare vt (ricavare) to find; (notare) to notice; (mettere in evidenza) to point out; (venire a conoscere: notizia) to learn; (raccogliere: dati) to gather, collect; (Topografia) to survey; (Mil) to relieve; (Comm) to take over

rili'evo sm (Arte, Geo) relief; (fig: rilevanza) importance; (Topografia) survey; **dar ~ a** o **mettere in ~ qc** (fig) to bring sth out, highlight sth

rilut'tante ag reluctant

'rima sf rhyme; (verso) verse

riman'dare vt to send again; (restituire, rinviare) to send back, return; (differire): **~ qc (a)** to postpone sth o put sth off (till); (fare riferimento): **~ qn a** to refer sb to; **essere rimandato** (Ins) to have to repeat one's exams

ri'mando sm (rinvio) return; (dilazione) postponement; (riferimento) cross-reference

rima'nente ag remaining ▶ sm rest, remainder; **i rimanenti** (persone) the rest of them, the others

rima'nere vi (restare) to remain, stay; (avanzare) to be left, remain; (restare stupito) to be amazed; (restare, mancare): **rimangono poche settimane a Pasqua** there are only a few weeks left till Easter; **rimane da vedere se** it remains to be seen whether; (diventare): **~ vedovo** to be left a widower; (trovarsi): **~ sorpreso** to be surprised

rimangi'are [riman'dʒare] vt to eat again; **~rsi la parola** (fig) to go back on one's word

ri'mango ecc vb vedi **rimanere**

rimargi'narsi vpr to heal

rimbal'zare [rimbal'tsare] *vi* to bounce back, rebound; (*proiettile*) to ricochet

rimbam'bito, -a *ag* senile, in one's dotage

rimboc'care *vt* (*coperta*) to tuck in; (*maniche, pantaloni*) to turn *o* roll up

rimbom'bare *vi* to resound

rimbor'sare *vt* to pay back, repay

rimedi'are *vi* **~ a** to remedy ▶ *vt* (*fam: procurarsi*) to get *o* scrape together

ri'medio *sm* (*medicina*) medicine; (*cura, fig*) remedy, cure

ri'mettere *vt* (*mettere di nuovo*) to put back; (*indossare di nuovo*): **~ qc** to put sth back on, put sth on again; (*affidare*) to entrust; (: *decisione*) to refer; (*condonare*) to remit; (*Comm: merci*) to deliver; (: *denaro*) to remit; (*vomitare*) to bring up; (*perdere: anche*: **rimetterci**) to lose; **rimettersi al bello** (*tempo*) to clear up; **rimettersi in salute** to get better, recover one's health

ri'misi *ecc vb vedi* **rimettere**

'rimmel® *sm inv* mascara

rimoder'nare *vt* to modernize

rimorchi'are [rimor'kjare] *vt* to tow; (*fig: ragazza*) to pick up

ri'morchio [ri'mɔrkjo] *sm* tow; (*veicolo*) trailer

ri'morso *sm* remorse

rimozi'one [rimot'tsjone] *sf* removal; (*da un impiego*) dismissal; (*Psic*) repression

rimpatri'are *vi* to return home ▶ *vt* to repatriate

rimpi'angere [rim'pjandʒere] *vt* to regret; (*persona*) to miss; **rimpi'anto, -a** *pp di* **rimpiangere** ▶ *sm* regret

rimpiaz'zare [rimpjat'tsare] *vt* to replace

rimpiccio'lire [rimpittʃo'lire] *vt* to make smaller ▶ *vi* (*anche*: **rimpicciolirsi**) to become smaller

rimpinzarsi [rimpin'tsarsi] *vpr* **~ (di qc)** to stuff o.s. (with sth)

rimprove'rare *vt* to rebuke, reprimand

rimu'overe *vt* to remove; (*destituire*) to dismiss

Rinasci'mento [rinaʃʃi'mento] *sm* **il ~** the Renaissance

ri'nascita [ri'naʃʃita] *sf* rebirth, revival

rinca'rare *vt* to increase the price of ▶ *vi* to go up, become more expensive

rinca'sare *vi* to go home

rinchi'udere [rin'kjudere] *vt* to shut (*o* lock) up; **rinchiudersi** *vpr* **rinchiudersi in** to shut o.s. up in; **rinchiudersi in se stesso** to withdraw into o.s.

rin'correre *vt* to chase, run after; **rin'corsa** *sf* short run

rin'crescere [rin'kreʃʃere] *vb impers* **mi rincresce che/di non poter fare** I'm sorry that/I can't do, I regret that/being unable to do

rinfacci'are [rinfat'tʃare] *vt* (*fig*): **~ qc a qn** to throw sth in sb's face

rinfor'zare [rinfor'tsare] *vt* to reinforce, strengthen ▶ *vi* (*anche*: **rinforzarsi**) to grow stronger

rinfres'care *vt* (*atmosfera, temperatura*) to cool (down); (*abito, pareti*) to freshen up ▶ *vi* (*tempo*) to grow cooler; **rinfrescarsi** *vpr* (*ristorarsi*) to refresh o.s.; (*lavarsi*) to freshen up; **rin'fresco, -schi** *sm* (*festa*) party; **rinfreschi** *smpl* refreshments

rin'fusa *sf* **alla ~** in confusion, higgledy-piggledy

ringhi'are [rin'gjare] *vi* to growl, snarl

ringhi'era [rin'gjɛra] *sf* railing; (*delle scale*) banister(s) (*pl*)

ringiova'nire [rindʒova'nire] *vt* (*vestito, acconciatura ecc*): **~ qn** to make sb look younger; (: *vacanze ecc*) to rejuvenate ▶ *vi* (*anche*: **ringiovanirsi**) to become (*o* look) younger

ringrazia'mento
[ringrattsja'mento] *sm* thanks *pl*
ringrazi'are [ringrat'tsjare] *vt* to
thank; **~ qn di qc** to thank sb for sth
rinne'gare *vt* (*fede*) to renounce;
(*figlio*) to disown, repudiate
rinno'vabile *ag* (*contratto, energia*)
renewable
rinnova'mento *sm* renewal;
(*economico*) revival
rinno'vare *vt* to renew; (*ripetere*) to
repeat, renew
rinoce'ronte [rinotʃe'ronte] *sm*
rhinoceros
rino'mato, -a *ag* renowned,
celebrated
rintracci'are [rintrat'tʃare] *vt* to
track down
rintro'nare *vi* to boom, roar ▶ *vt*
(*assordare*) to deafen; (*stordire*) to stun
rinunci'are [rinun'tʃare] *vi* **~ a** to give
up, renounce; **~ a fare qc** to give up
doing sth
rinvi'are *vt* (*rimandare indietro*) to
send back, return; (*differire*): **~ qc (a)**
to postpone sth *o* put sth off (till); to
adjourn sth (till); (*fare un rimando*): **~
qn a** to refer sb to
rin'vio, -'vii *sm* (*rimando*) return;
(*differimento*) postponement; (: *di
seduta*) adjournment; (*in un testo*)
cross-reference; **rinvio a giudizio**
(*Dir*) indictment
riò *ecc vb vedi* **riavere**
ri'one *sm* district, quarter
riordi'nare *vt* (*rimettere in ordine*) to
tidy; (*riorganizzare*) to reorganize
riorganiz'zare [riorganid'dzare] *vt*
to reorganize
ripa'gare *vt* to repay
ripa'rare *vt* (*proteggere*) to protect,
defend; (*correggere: male, torto*) to
make up for; (: *errore*) to put right;
(*aggiustare*) to repair ▶ *vi* (*mettere
rimedio*): **~ a** to make up for; **ripararsi**
vpr (*rifugiarsi*) to take refuge *o* shelter;
dove lo posso far ~? where can I get
this repaired?; **riparazi'one** *sf* (*di un
torto*) reparation; (*di guasto, scarpe*)
repairing *no pl*; repair; (*risarcimento*)
compensation
ri'paro *sm* (*protezione*) shelter,
protection; (*rimedio*) remedy
ripar'tire *vt* (*dividere*) to divide up;
(*distribuire*) to share out ▶ *vi* to set off
again; to leave again
ripas'sare *vi* to come (*o* go) back ▶ *vt*
(*scritto, lezione*) to go over (again)
ripen'sare *vi* to think; (*cambiare
pensiero*) to change one's mind;
(*tornare col pensiero*): **~ a** to recall
ripercu'otersi *vpr* **~ su** (*fig*) to have
repercussions on
ripercussi'one *sf* (*fig*): **avere una
~** *o* **delle ripercussioni su** to have
repercussions on
ripes'care *vt* (*pesce*) to catch again;
(*persona, cosa*) to fish out; (*fig:
ritrovare*) to dig out
ri'petere *vt* to repeat; (*ripassare*) to
go over; **può ~ per favore?** can you
repeat that please?; **ripetizi'one**
sf repetition; (*di lezione*) revision;
ripetizioni *sfpl* private tutoring *sg*
ripi'ano *sm* (*di mobile*) shelf
ri'picca *sf* **per ~** out of spite
'ripido, -a *ag* steep
ripie'gare *vt* to refold; (*piegare più
volte*) to fold (up) ▶ *vi* (*Mil*) to retreat,
fall back; (*fig: accontentarsi*): **~ su** to
make do with
ripi'eno, -a *ag* full; (*Cuc*) stuffed;
(: *panino*) filled ▶ *sm* (*Cuc*) stuffing
ri'pone, ri'pongo *ecc vb vedi* **riporre**
ri'porre *vt* (*porre al suo posto*) to put
back, replace; (*mettere via*) to put
away; (*fiducia, speranza*): **~ qc in qn** to
place *o* put sth in sb
ripor'tare *vt* (*portare indietro*) to bring
(*o* take) back; (*riferire*) to report;

(*citare*) to quote; (*vittoria*) to gain; (*successo*) to have; (*Mat*) to carry; **riportarsi a** (*anche fig*) to go back to; (*riferirsi a*) to refer to; **~ danni** to suffer damage

ripo'sare *vt, vi* to rest; **riposarsi** *vpr* to rest

ri'posi *ecc vb vedi* **riporre**

ri'poso *sm* rest; (*Mil*): **~!** at ease!; **a ~** (*in pensione*) retired; **giorno di ~** day off

ripos'tiglio [ripos'tiʎʎo] *sm* lumber-room

ri'prendere *vt* (*prigioniero, fortezza*) to recapture; (*prendere indietro*) to take back; (*ricominciare: lavoro*) to resume; (*andare a prendere*) to fetch, come back for; (*riassumere: impiegati*) to take on again, re-employ; (*rimproverare*) to tell off; (*restringere: abito*) to take in; (*Cinema*) to shoot; **riprendersi** *vpr* to recover; (*correggersi*) to correct o.s.; **ri'presa** *sf* recapture; resumption; (*economica, da malattia, emozione*) recovery; (*Aut*) acceleration *no pl*; (*Teatro, Cinema*) rerun; (*Cinema: presa*) shooting *no pl*; shot; (*Sport*) second half; (*: Pugilato*) round; **a più riprese** several times; **ripresa cinematografica** shot

ripristi'nare *vt* to restore

ripro'durre *vt* to reproduce; **riprodursi** *vpr* (*Biol*) to reproduce; (*riformarsi*) to form again

ripro'vare *vt* (*provare di nuovo: gen*) to try again; (*vestito*) to try on again; (*: sensazione*) to experience again ▶ *vi* (*tentare*): **~ (a fare qc)** to try (to do sth) again; **riproverò più tardi** I'll try again later

ripudi'are *vt* to repudiate, disown

ripu'gnante [ripuɲ'ɲante] *ag* disgusting, repulsive

ri'quadro *sm* square; (*Archit*) panel

ri'saia *sf* paddy field

risa'lire *vi* (*ritornare in su*) to go back

up; **~ a** (*ritornare con la mente*) to go back to; (*datare da*) to date back to, go back to

risal'tare *vi* (*fig: distinguersi*) to stand out; (*Archit*) to project, jut out

risa'puto, -a *ag* **è ~ che ...** everyone knows that ..., it is common knowledge that ...

risarci'mento [risartʃi'mento] *sm* **~ (di)** compensation (for); **risarcimento danni** damages

risar'cire [risar'tʃire] *vt* (*cose*) to pay compensation for; (*persona*): **~ qn di qc** to compensate sb for sth

ri'sata *sf* laugh

riscalda'mento *sm* heating; **riscaldamento centrale** central heating

riscal'dare *vt* (*scaldare*) to heat; (*: mani, persona*) to warm; (*minestra*) to reheat; **riscaldarsi** *vpr* to warm up

ris'catto *sm* ransom; redemption

rischia'rare [riskja'rare] *vt* (*illuminare*) to light up; (*colore*) to make lighter; **rischiararsi** *vpr* (*tempo*) to clear up; (*cielo*) to clear; (*fig: volto*) to brighten up; **rischiararsi la voce** to clear one's throat

rischi'are [ris'kjare] *vt* to risk ▶ *vi* **~ di fare qc** to risk o run the risk of doing sth

'rischio ['riskjo] *sm* risk; **rischi'oso, -a** *ag* risky, dangerous

riscia'cquare [riʃʃa'kware] *vt* to rinse

riscon'trare *vt* (*rilevare*) to find

riscri'vibile *ag* (*CD, DVD*) rewritable

ris'cuotere *vt* (*ritirare: somma*) to collect; (*: stipendio*) to draw, collect; (*assegno*) to cash; (*fig: successo ecc*) to win, earn

'rise *ecc vb vedi* **ridere**

risenti'mento *sm* resentment

risen'tire *vt* to hear again; (*provare*) to feel ▶ *vi* **~ di** to feel (o show) the effects of; **risentirsi** *vpr* **risentirsi di** o **per** to take offence at, resent; **risen'tito, -a** *ag* resentful

ri'serbo *sm* reserve

ri'serva *sf* reserve; (*di caccia, pesca*) preserve; (*restrizione, di indigeni*) reservation; **di ~** (*provviste ecc*) in reserve

riser'vare *vt* (*tenere in serbo*) to keep, put aside; (*prenotare*) to book, reserve; **ho riservato un tavolo a nome...** I booked a table in the name of ...; **riser'vato, -a** *ag* (*prenotato: fig: persona*) reserved; (*confidenziale*) confidential

'risi *ecc vb vedi* **ridere**

risi'edere *vi ~ a o in* to reside in

'risma *sf* (*di carta*) ream; (*fig*) kind, sort

'riso (*pl(f)* **risa**) (: *il ridere*) *sm* **il ~** laughter; (*pianta*) rice ▸ *pp di* **ridere**

riso'lino *sm* snigger

ri'solsi *ecc vb vedi* **risolvere**

ri'solto, -a *pp di* **risolvere**

riso'luto, -a *ag* determined, resolute

risoluzi'one [risolut'tsjone] *sf* solving *no pl*; (*Mat*) solution; (*decisione, di schermo, immagine*) resolution

ri'solvere *vt* (*difficoltà, controversia*) to resolve; (*problema*) to solve; (*decidere*): **~ di fare** to resolve to do; **risolversi** *vpr* (*decidersi*): **risolversi a fare** to make up one's mind to do; (*andare a finire*): **risolversi in** to end up, turn out; **risolversi in nulla** to come to nothing

riso'nanza [riso'nantsa] *sf* resonance; **aver vasta ~** (*fig: fatto ecc*) to be known far and wide

ri'sorgere [ri'sordʒere] *vi* to rise again; **risorgi'mento** *sm* revival; **il Risorgimento** (*Storia*) the Risorgimento

- **Risorgimento**
- The **Risorgimento** was the
- political movement which led to
- the proclamation of the Kingdom
- of Italy in 1861, and eventually to
- unification in 1871.

ri'sorsa *sf* expedient, resort; **risorse umane** human resources

ri'sorsi *ecc vb vedi* **risorgere**

ri'sotto *sm* (*Cuc*) risotto

risparmi'are *vt* to save; (*non uccidere*) to spare ▸ *vi* to save; **~ qc a qn** to spare sb sth

ris'parmio *sm* saving *no pl*; (*denaro*) savings *pl*; **risparmi** *smpl* (*denaro*) savings

rispec'chiare [rispek'kjare] *vt* to reflect

rispet'tabile *ag* respectable

rispet'tare *vt* to respect; **farsi ~** to command respect

rispet'tivo, -a *ag* respective

ris'petto *sm* respect; **rispetti** *smpl* (*saluti*) respects, regards; **~ a** (*in paragone a*) compared to; (*in relazione a*) as regards, as for

ris'pondere *vi* to answer, reply; (*freni*) to respond; **~ a** (*domanda*) to answer, reply to; (*persona*) to answer; (*invito*) to reply to; (*provocazione: veicolo, apparecchio*) to respond to; (*corrispondere a*) to correspond to; (: *speranze, bisogno*) to answer for; **~ di** to answer for; **ris'posta** *sf* answer, reply; **in risposta a** in reply to

'rissa *sf* brawl

ris'tampa *sf* reprinting *no pl*; reprint

risto'rante *sm* restaurant; **mi può consigliare un buon ~?** can you recommend a good restaurant?

ris'tretto, -a *pp di* **restringere** ▸ *ag* (*racchiuso*) enclosed, hemmed in; (*angusto*) narrow; (*limitato*): **~ (a)** restricted o limited (to); (*Cuc: brodo*) thick; (: *caffè*) extra strong

ristruttu'rare *vt* (*azienda*) to reorganize; (*edificio*) to restore; (*appartamento*) to alter; (*crema, balsamo*) to repair

risucchi'are [risuk'kjare] vt to suck in

risul'tare vi (dimostrarsi) to prove (to be), turn out (to be); (riuscire): ~ **vincitore** to emerge as the winner; ~ **da** (provenire) to result from, be the result of; **mi risulta che ...** I understand that ...; **non mi risulta** not as far as I know; **risul'tato** sm result

risuo'nare vi (rimbombare) to resound

risurrezi'one [risurret'tsjone] sf (Rel) resurrection

risusci'tare [risuʃʃi'tare] vt to resuscitate, restore to life; (fig) to revive, bring back ▶ vi to rise (from the dead)

ris'veglio [riz'veʎʎo] sm waking up; (fig) revival

ris'volto sm (di giacca) lapel; (di pantaloni) turn-up; (di manica) cuff; (di tasca) flap; (di libro) inside flap; (fig) implication

ritagli'are [ritaʎ'ʎare] vt (tagliar via) to cut out

ritar'dare vi (persona, treno) to be late; (orologio) to be slow ▶ vt (rallentare) to slow down; (impedire) to delay, hold up; (differire) to postpone, delay

ri'tardo sm delay; (di persona aspettata) lateness no pl; (fig: mentale) backwardness; **in** ~ late; **il volo ha due ore di** ~ the flight is two hours late; **scusi il** ~ sorry I'm late

ri'tegno [ri'teɲɲo] sm restraint

rite'nere vt (trattenere) to hold back; (: somma) to deduct; (giudicare) to consider, believe

ri'tengo, ri'tenni ecc vb vedi **ritenere**

riterrò, ritiene ecc vb vedi **ritenere**

riti'rare vt to withdraw; (Pol: richiamare) to recall; (andare a prendere: pacco ecc) to collect, pick up; **ritirarsi** vpr to withdraw; (da un'attività) to retire; (stoffa) to shrink; (marea) to recede

'ritmo sm rhythm; (fig) rate; (: della vita) pace, tempo

'rito sm rite; **di** ~ usual, customary

ritoc'care vt (disegno, fotografia) to touch up; (testo) to alter

ritor'nare vi to return, go (o come) back, to get back; (ripresentarsi) to recur; (ridiventare): ~ **ricco** to become rich again ▶ vt (restituire) to return, give back; **quando ritorniamo?** when do we get back?

ritor'nello sm refrain

ri'torno sm return; **essere di** ~ to be back; **avere un** ~ **di fiamma** (Aut) to backfire; (fig: persona) to be back in love again

ri'trarre vt (trarre indietro, via) to withdraw; (distogliere: sguardo) to turn away; (rappresentare) to portray, depict; (ricavare) to get, obtain

ritrat'tare vt (disdire) to retract, take back; (trattare nuovamente) to deal with again

ri'tratto, -a pp di **ritrarre** ▶ sm portrait

ritro'vare vt to find; (salute) to regain; (persona) to find; to meet again; **ritrovarsi** vpr (essere, capitare) to find o.s.; (raccapezzarsi) to find one's way; (con senso reciproco) to meet (again)

'ritto, -a ag (in piedi) standing, on one's feet; (levato in alto) erect, raised; (: capelli) standing on end; (posto verticalmente) upright

ritu'ale ag, sm ritual

riuni'one sf (adunanza) meeting; (riconciliazione) reunion

riu'nire vt (ricongiungere) to join (together); (riconciliare) to reunite, bring together (again); **riunirsi** vpr (adunarsi) to meet; (tornare insieme) to be reunited

riu'scire [riuʃ'ʃire] vi (uscire di nuovo) to go out again, go back out;

(aver esito: fatti, azioni) to go, turn out; (aver successo) to succeed, be successful; (essere, apparire) to be, prove; (raggiungere il fine) to manage, succeed; **~ a fare qc** to manage to do o succeed in doing o be able to do sth

'riva sf (di fiume) bank; (di lago, mare) shore

ri'vale sm/f rival; **rivalità** sf rivalry

rivalu'tare vt (Econ) to revalue

rive'dere vt to see again; (ripassare) to revise; (verificare) to check

rivedrò ecc vb vedi **rivedere**

rive'lare vt to reveal; (divulgare) to reveal, disclose; (dare indizio) to reveal, show; **rivelarsi** vpr (manifestarsi) to be revealed; **rivelarsi onesto** ecc to prove to be honest ecc; **rivelazi'one** sf revelation

rivendi'care vt to claim, demand

rivendi'tore, -'trice sm/f retailer; **rivenditore autorizzato** (Comm) authorized dealer

ri'verbero sm (di luce, calore) reflection; (di suono) reverberation

rivesti'mento sm covering; coating

rives'tire vt to dress again; (ricoprire) to cover; to coat; (fig: carica) to hold

ri'vidi ecc vb vedi **rivedere**

ri'vincita [ri'vintʃita] sf (Sport) return match; (fig) revenge

ri'vista sf review; (periodico) magazine, review; (Teatro) revue; variety show

ri'volgere [ri'vɔldʒere] vt (attenzione, sguardo) to turn, direct; (parole) to address; **rivolgersi** vpr to turn round; (fig: dirigersi per informazioni): **rivolgersi a** to go and see, go and speak to; (: ufficio) to enquire at

ri'volsi ecc vb vedi **rivolgere**

ri'volta sf revolt, rebellion

rivol'tella sf revolver

rivoluzio'nare [rivoluttsjo'nare] vt to revolutionize

rivoluzio'nario, -a [rivoluttsjo'narjo] ag, sm/f revolutionary

rivoluzi'one [rivolut'tsjone] sf revolution

riz'zare [rit'tsare] vt to raise, erect; **rizzarsi** vpr to stand up; (capelli) to stand on end

'roba sf stuff, things pl; (possessi, beni) belongings pl, things pl, possessions pl; **~ da mangiare** things pl to eat, food; **~ da matti** sheer madness o lunacy

'robot sm inv robot

ro'busto, -a ag robust, sturdy; (solido: catena) strong

roc'chetto [rok'ketto] sm reel, spool

'roccia, -ce ['rɔttʃa] sf rock; **fare ~** (Sport) to go rock climbing

'roco, -a, chi, che ag hoarse

ro'daggio [ro'daddʒo] sm running (BRIT) o breaking (US) in; **in ~** running (BRIT) o breaking (US) in

rodi'tore sm (Zool) rodent

rodo'dendro sm rhododendron

ro'gnone [roɲ'ɲone] sm (Cuc) kidney

'rogo, -ghi sm (per cadaveri) (funeral) pyre; (supplizio): **il ~** the stake

rol'lio sm roll(ing)

'Roma sf Rome

Roma'nia sf **la ~** Romania

ro'manico, -a, -ci, -che ag Romanesque

ro'mano, -a ag, sm/f Roman

ro'mantico, -a, -ci, -che ag romantic

romanzi'ere [roman'dzjɛre] sm novelist

ro'manzo, -a [ro'mandzo] ag (Ling) romance cpd ▶ sm novel; **romanzo d'appendice** serial (story); **romanzo giallo/poliziesco** detective story; **romanzo rosa** romantic novel

'rombo sm rumble, thunder, roar; (Mat) rhombus; (Zool) turbot; brill

'rompere vt to break; (fidanzamento) to break off ▶ vi to break; **rompersi** vpr to break; **mi rompe le scatole** (fam) he (o she) is a pain in the neck; **rompersi un braccio** to break an arm; **mi si è rotta la macchina** my car has broken down; **rompis'catole** (fam) sm/f inv pest, pain in the neck

'rondine sf (Zool) swallow

ron'zare [ron'dzare] vi to buzz, hum

ron'zio [ron'dzio] sm buzzing

'rosa sf rose ▶ ag inv, sm pink; **ro'sato, -a** ag pink, rosy ▶ sm (vino) rosé (wine)

rosicchi'are [rosik'kjare] vt to gnaw (at); (mangiucchiare) to nibble (at)

rosma'rino sm rosemary

roso'lare vt (Cuc) to brown

roso'lia sf (Med) German measles sg, rubella

ro'sone sm rosette; (vetrata) rose window

'rospo sm (Zool) toad

ros'setto sm (per labbra) lipstick

'rosso, -a ag, sm, sm/f red; **il mar R~** the Red Sea; **rosso d'uovo** egg yolk

rosticce'ria [rostittʃe'ria] sf shop selling roast meat and other cooked food

ro'taia sf rut, track; (Ferr) rail

ro'tella sf small wheel; (di mobile) castor

roto'lare vt, vi to roll; **rotolarsi** vpr to roll (about)

'rotolo sm roll; **andare a rotoli** (fig) to go to rack and ruin

ro'tondo, -a ag round

'rotta sf (Aer, Naut) course, route; (Mil) rout; **a ~ di collo** at breakneck speed; **essere in ~ con qn** to be on bad terms with sb

rotta'mare vt to scrap

rottamazione [rottama'tsjone] sf (come incentivo) the scrapping of old vehicles in return for incentives

rot'tame sm fragment, scrap, broken bit; **rottami** smpl (di nave, aereo ecc) wreckage sg

'rotto, -a pp di **rompere** ▶ ag broken; (calzoni) torn, split; **per il ~ della cuffia** by the skin of one's teeth

rot'tura sf breaking no pl; break; breaking off; (Med) fracture, break

rou'lotte [ru'lɔt] sf caravan

ro'vente ag red-hot

'rovere sm oak

ro'vescia [ro'veʃʃa] sf **alla ~** upside-down; inside-out; **oggi mi va tutto alla ~** everything is going wrong (for me) today

rovesci'are [roveʃ'ʃare] vt (versare in giù) to pour; (: accidentalmente) to spill; (capovolgere) to turn upside down; (gettare a terra) to knock down; (: fig: governo) to overthrow; (piegare all'indietro: testa) to throw back; **rovesciarsi** vpr (sedia, macchina) to overturn; (barca) to capsize; (liquido) to spill; (fig: situazione) to be reversed

ro'vescio, -sci [ro'veʃʃo] sm other side, wrong side; (della mano) back; (di moneta) reverse; (pioggia) sudden downpour; (fig) setback; (Maglia: anche: **punto ~**) purl (stitch); (Tennis) backhand (stroke); **a ~** upside-down; inside-out; **capire qc a ~** to misunderstand sth

ro'vina sf ruin; **andare in ~** (andare a pezzi) to collapse; (fig) to go to rack and ruin; **rovine** sfpl (ruderi) ruins; **mandare in ~** to ruin

rovi'nare vi to collapse, fall down ▶ vt (danneggiare: fig) to ruin; **rovinarsi** vpr (persona) to ruin o.s.; (oggetto, vestito) to be ruined

rovis'tare vt (casa) to ransack; (tasche) to rummage in

'rovo sm (Bot) blackberry bush, bramble bush

'rozzo, -a ['roddzo] ag rough, coarse

ru'bare vt to steal; **~ qc a qn** to steal sth from sb; **mi hanno rubato il portafoglio** my wallet has been stolen

rubi'netto sm tap, faucet (US)

ru'bino sm ruby

ru'brica, -che sf (Stampa) column; (quadernetto) index book; address book; **rubrica d'indirizzi** address book; **rubrica telefonica** list of telephone numbers

'rudere sm (rovina) ruins pl

rudimen'tale ag rudimentary, basic

rudi'menti smpl rudiments; basic principles; basic knowledge sg

ruffi'ano sm pimp

'ruga, -ghe sf wrinkle

'ruggine ['ruddʒine] sf rust

rug'gire [rud'dʒire] vi to roar

rugi'ada [ru'dʒada] sf dew

ru'goso, -a ag wrinkled

rul'lino sm (Fot) spool; (: pellicola) film; **vorrei un ~ da 36 pose** I'd like a 36-exposure film

'rullo sm (di tamburi) roll; (arnese cilindrico, Tip) roller; **rullo compressore** steam roller; **rullo di pellicola** roll of film

rum sm rum

ru'meno, -a ag, sm/f, sm Romanian

rumi'nare vt (Zool) to ruminate

ru'more sm **un ~** a noise, a sound; **il ~** noise; **non riesco a dormire a causa del ~** I can't sleep for the noise; **rumo'roso, -a** ag noisy

> Attenzione! In inglese esiste la parola *rumour*, che però significa *voce* nel senso di *diceria*.

ru'olo sm (Teatro: fig) role, part; (elenco) roll, register, list; **di ~** permanent, on the permanent staff

ru'ota sf wheel; **ruota anteriore/posteriore** front/back wheel; **ruota di scorta** spare wheel

ruo'tare vt, vi to rotate

'rupe sf cliff

'ruppi ecc vb vedi **rompere**

ru'rale ag rural, country cpd

ru'scello [ruʃʃɛllo] sm stream

'ruspa sf excavator

rus'sare vi to snore

'Russia sf **la ~** Russia; **'russo, -a** ag, sm/f, sm Russian

'rustico, -a, -ci, -che ag rustic; (fig) rough, unrefined

rut'tare vi to belch; **'rutto** sm belch

'ruvido, -a ag rough, coarse

S

S. abbr (= sud) S; (= santo) St

sa vb vedi **sapere**

'sabato sm Saturday; **di** o **il ~** on Saturdays

'sabbia sf sand; **sabbie mobili** quicksand(s); **sabbi'oso, -a** ag sandy

'sacca, -che sf bag; (bisaccia) haversack; **sacca da viaggio** travelling bag

sacca'rina sf saccharin(e)

saccheggi'are [sakked'dʒare] vt to sack, plunder

sac'chetto [sak'ketto] sm (small) bag, (small) sack; **sacchetto di carta/di plastica** paper/plastic bag

'sacco, -chi sm bag; (per carbone ecc) sack; (Anat, Biol) sac; (tela) sacking; (saccheggio) sack(ing); (fig: grande quantità): **un ~ di** lots of, heaps of; **sacco a pelo** sleeping bag; **sacco per i rifiuti** bin bag

sacer'dote [satʃer'dɔte] sm priest

sacrifi'care vt to sacrifice;
  sacrificarsi vpr to sacrifice o.s.;
  (privarsi di qc) to make sacrifices
sacri'ficio [sakri'fitʃo] sm sacrifice
'sacro, -a ag sacred
'sadico, -a, -ci, -che ag sadistic
  ▶ sm/f sadist
sa'etta sf arrow; (fulmine)
  thunderbolt; flash of lightning
sa'fari sm inv safari
sag'gezza [sad'dʒettsa] sf wisdom
'saggio, -a, -gi, -ge ['saddʒo] ag wise
  ▶ sm (persona) sage; (esperimento) test;
  (fig: prova) proof; (campione) sample;
  (scritto) essay
Sagit'tario [sadʒit'tarjo] sm
  Sagittarius
'sagoma sf (profilo) outline, profile;
  (forma) form, shape; (Tecn) template;
  (bersaglio) target; (fig: persona)
  character
'sagra sf festival
sagres'tano sm sacristan; sexton
sagres'tia sf sacristy
Sa'hara [sa'ara] sm **il (deserto del) ~**
  the Sahara (Desert)
'sai vb vedi **sapere**
'sala sf hall; (stanza) room; (Cinema:
  Yyy: di proiezione) cinema; **sala
  d'aspetto** waiting room; **sala
  da ballo** ballroom; **sala giochi**
  amusement arcade; **sala operatoria**
  operating theatre; **sala da pranzo**
  dining room; **sala per concerti**
  concert hall
sa'lame sm salami no pl, salami
  sausage
sala'moia sf (Cuc) brine
sa'lato, -a ag (sapore) salty; (Cuc)
  salted, salt cpd; (fig: prezzo) steep, stiff
sal'dare vt (congiungere) to join,
  bind; (parti metalliche) to solder; (: con
  saldatura autogena) to weld; (conto) to
  settle, pay
'saldo, -a ag (resistente, forte) strong,

firm; (fermo) firm, steady, stable; (fig)
  firm, steadfast ▶ sm (svendita) sale;
  (di conto) settlement; (Econ) balance;
  saldi smpl (Comm) sales; **essere ~
  nella propria fede** (fig) to stick to
  one's guns
'sale sm salt; (fig): **ha poco ~ in zucca**
  he doesn't have much sense; **sale fino**
  table salt; **sale grosso** cooking salt
'salgo ecc vb vedi **salire**
'salice ['salitʃe] sm willow; **salice
  piangente** weeping willow
sali'ente ag (fig) salient, main
sali'era sf salt cellar
sa'lire vi to go (o come) up; (aereo ecc)
  to climb, go up; (passeggero) to get
  on; (sentiero, prezzi, livello) to go up,
  rise ▶ vt (scale, gradini) to go (o come)
  up; **~ su** to climb (up); **~ sul treno/
  sull'autobus** to board the train/the
  bus; **~ in macchina** to get into the
  car; **sa'lita** sf climb, ascent; (erta) hill,
  slope; **in salita** ag, av uphill
sa'liva sf saliva
'salma sf corpse
'salmo sm psalm
sal'mone sm salmon
sa'lone sm (stanza) sitting room,
  lounge; (in albergo) lounge; (su nave)
  lounge, saloon; (mostra) show,
  exhibition; **salone di bellezza**
  beauty salon
sa'lotto sm lounge, sitting room;
  (mobilio) lounge suite
sal'pare vi (Naut) to set sail; (anche: ~
  l'ancora) to weigh anchor
'salsa sf (Cuc) sauce; **salsa di
  pomodoro** tomato sauce
sal'siccia, -ce [sal'sittʃa] sf pork
  sausage
sal'tare vi to jump, leap; (esplodere) to
  blow up, explode; (: valvola) to blow;
  (venir via) to pop off; (non aver luogo:
  corso ecc) to be cancelled ▶ vt to jump
  (over), leap (over); (fig: pranzo, capitolo)

to skip, miss (out); (*Cuc*) to sauté; **far ~** to blow up; to burst open; **~ fuori** (*fig: apparire all'improvviso*) to turn up

saltel'lare *vi* to skip; to hop

'**salto** *sm* jump; (*Sport*) jumping; **fare un ~ a** to jump, leap; **fare un ~ da qn** to pop over to sb's (place); **salto in alto/ lungo** high/long jump; **salto con l'asta** pole vaulting; **salto mortale** somersault

saltu'ario, -a *ag* occasional, irregular

sa'lubre *ag* healthy, salubrious

salume'ria *sf* delicatessen

sa'lumi *smpl* salted pork meats

salu'tare *ag* healthy; (*fig*) salutary, beneficial ▶ *vt* (*incontrandosi*) to greet; (*congedandosi*) to say goodbye to; (*Mil*) to salute

sa'lute *sf* health; **~!** (*a chi starnutisce*) bless you!; (*nei brindisi*) cheers!; **bere alla ~ di qn** to drink (to) sb's health

sa'luto *sm* (*gesto*) wave; (*parola*) greeting; (*Mil*) salute

salvada'naio *sm* money box, piggy bank

salva'gente [salva'dʒɛnte] *sm* (*Naut*) lifebuoy; (*ciambella*) life belt; (*giubbotto*) life jacket; (*stradale*) traffic island

salvaguar'dare *vt* to safeguard

sal'vare *vt* to save; (*trarre da un pericolo*) to rescue; (*proteggere*) to protect; **salvarsi** *vpr* to save o.s.; to escape; **salvaschermo** [salvas'kermo] *sm* (*Inform*) screen saver; **salvaslip** [salva'zlip] *sm inv* panty liner; **salva'taggio** *sm* rescue

'**salve** (*fam*) *escl* hi!

'**salvia** *sf* (*Bot*) sage

salvi'etta *sf* napkin; **salvietta umidificata** baby wipe

'**salvo, -a** *ag* safe, unhurt, unharmed; (*fuori pericolo*) safe, out of danger ▶ *sm* **in ~** safe ▶ *prep* (*eccetto*) except; **mettere qc in ~** to put sth in a safe place; **~ che** (*a meno che*) unless; (*eccetto che*) except (that); **~ imprevisti** barring accidents

sam'buco *sm* elder (tree)

'**sandalo** *sm* (*Bot*) sandalwood; (*calzatura*) sandal

'**sangue** *sm* blood; **farsi cattivo ~** to fret, get in a state; **sangue freddo** (*fig*) sang-froid, calm; **a ~ freddo** in cold blood; **sangui'nare** *vi* to bleed

sanità *sf* health; (*salubrità*) healthiness; **Ministero della S~** Department of Health; **sanità mentale** sanity

sani'tario, -a *ag* health *cpd*; (*condizioni*) sanitary ▶ *sm* (*Amm*) doctor; **sanitari** *smpl* (*impianti*) bathroom *o* sanitary fittings

'**sanno** *vb vedi* **sapere**

'**sano, -a** *ag* healthy; (*denti, costituzione*) healthy, sound; (*integro*) whole; (*fig: politica, consigli*) sound; **~ di mente** sane; **di sana pianta** completely, entirely; **~ e salvo** safe and sound

San Sil'vestro *sm* (*giorno*) New Year's Eve

'**santo, -a** *ag* holy; (*fig*) saintly; (*seguito da nome proprio*) saint ▶ *sm/f* saint; **la Santa Sede** the Holy See

santu'ario *sm* sanctuary

sanzi'one [san'tsjone] *sf* sanction; (*penale, civile*) sanction, penalty

sa'pere *vt* to know; (*essere capace di*): **so nuotare** I know how to swim, I can swim ▶ *vi* **~ di** (*aver sapore*) to taste of; (*aver odore*) to smell of ▶ *sm* knowledge; **far ~ qc a qn** to let sb know sth; **mi sa che non sia vero** I don't think that's true; **non lo so** I don't know; **non so l'inglese** I don't speak English; **sa dove posso…?** do you know where I can …?

sa'pone *sm* soap; **sapone da bucato** washing soap

sa'pore sm taste, flavour; **sapo'rito, -a** ag tasty

sappi'amo vb vedi **sapere**

saprò ecc vb vedi **sapere**

sarà ecc vb vedi **essere**

saraci'nesca [saratʃi'neska] sf (serranda) rolling shutter

sar'castico, -a, ci, che ag sarcastic

Sar'degna [sar'deɲɲa] sf **la ~** Sardinia

sar'dina sf sardine

'sardo, -a ag, sm/f Sardinian

sa'rei ecc vb vedi **essere**

SARS sigla f (Med: = severe acute respiratory syndrome) SARS

'sarta sf vedi **sarto**

'sarto, -a sm/f tailor/dressmaker

'sasso sm stone; (ciottolo) pebble; (masso) rock

sas'sofono sm saxophone

sas'soso, -a ag stony; pebbly

'Satana sm Satan

sa'tellite sm, ag satellite

'satira sf satire

'sauna sf sauna

sazi'are [sat'tsjare] vt to satisfy, satiate; **saziarsi** vpr **saziarsi (di)** to eat one's fill (of); (fig): **saziarsi di** to grow tired o weary of

'sazio, -a ['sattsjo] ag **~ (di)** sated (with), full (of); (fig: stufo) fed up (with), sick (of); **sono ~** I'm full (up)

sba'dato, -a ag careless, inattentive

sbadigli'are [zbadiʎ'ʎare] vi to yawn; **sba'diglio** sm yawn

sbagli'are [zbaʎ'ʎare] vt to make a mistake in, get wrong ▶ vi to make a mistake, be mistaken, be wrong; (operare in modo non giusto) to err; **sbagliarsi** vpr to make a mistake, be wrong; **~ strada/la mira** to take the wrong road/miss one's aim

sbagli'ato, -a [zbaʎ'ʎato] ag (gen) wrong; (compito) full of mistakes; (conclusione) erroneous

'sbaglio sm mistake, error; (morale) error; **fare uno ~** to make a mistake

sbalor'dire vt to stun, amaze ▶ vi to be stunned, be amazed

sbal'zare [zbal'tsare] vt to throw, hurl ▶ vi (balzare) to bounce; (saltare) to leap, bound

sban'dare vi (Naut) to list; (Aer) to bank; (Aut) to skid

sba'raglio [zba'raʎʎo] sm rout; defeat; **gettarsi allo ~** to risk everything

sbaraz'zarsi [zbarat'tsarsi] vpr **~ di** to get rid of, rid o.s. of

sbar'care vt (passeggeri) to disembark; (merci) to unload ▶ vi to disembark

'sbarra sf bar; (di passaggio a livello) barrier; (Dir): **presentarsi alla ~** to appear before the court

sbar'rare vt (strada ecc) to block, bar; (assegno) to cross; **~ il passo** to bar the way; **~ gli occhi** to open one's eyes wide

'sbattere vt (porta) to slam, bang; (tappeti, ali, Cuc) to beat; (urtare) to knock, hit ▶ vi (porta, finestra) to bang; (agitarsi: ali, vele ecc) to flap; **me ne sbatto!** (fam) I don't give a damn!

sba'vare vi to dribble; (colore) to smear, smudge

'sberla sf slap

sbia'dire vi, vt to fade; **sbia'dito, -a** ag faded, (fig) colourless, dull

sbian'care vt to whiten; (tessuto) to bleach ▶ vi (impallidire) to grow pale o white

sbirci'ata [zbir'tʃata] sf **dare una ~ a qc** to glance at sth, have a look at sth

sbloc'care vt to unblock, free; (freno) to release; (prezzi, affitti) to decontrol; **sbloccarsi** vpr (gen) to become unblocked; (passaggio, strada) to clear, become unblocked

sboc'care vi **~ in** (fiume) to flow into; (strada) to lead into; (persona) to come (out) into; (fig: concludersi) to end (up) in

sboc'cato, -a *ag* (*persona*) foul-mouthed; (*linguaggio*) foul

sbocci'are [zbot'tʃare] *vi* (*fiore*) to bloom, open (out)

sbol'lire *vi* (*fig*) to cool down, calm down

'sbornia (*fam*) *sf* **prendersi una ~** to get plastered

sbor'sare *vt* (*denaro*) to pay out

sbot'tare *vi* **~ in una risata/per la collera** to burst out laughing/explode with anger

sbotto'nare *vt* to unbutton, undo

sbrai'tare *vi* to yell, bawl

sbra'nare *vt* to tear to pieces

sbricio'lare [zbritʃo'lare] *vt* to crumble; **sbriciolarsi** *vpr* to crumble

sbri'gare *vt* to deal with; **sbrigarsi** *vpr* to hurry (up)

'sbronza ['zbrontsa] (*fam*) *sf* (*ubriaco*): **prendersi una ~** to get plastered

sbron'zarsi [zbron'tsarsi] *vpr* (*fam*) to get sozzled

'sbronzo, -a ['zbrontso] (*fam*) *ag* plastered

sbruf'fone, -a *sm/f* boaster

sbu'care *vi* to come out, emerge; (*improvvisamente*) to pop out (*o* up)

sbucci'are [zbut'tʃare] *vt* (*arancia, patata*) to peel; (*piselli*) to shell; **sbucciarsi un ginocchio** to graze one's knee

sbucherò *ecc* [zbuke'rɔ] *vb vedi* **sbucare**

sbuf'fare *vi* (*persona, cavallo*) to snort; (*ansimare*) to puff, pant; (*treno*) to puff

sca'broso, -a *ag* (*fig: difficile*) difficult, thorny; (: *imbarazzante*) embarrassing; (: *sconcio*) indecent

scacchi *smpl* (*gioco*) chess *sg*; **a ~** (*tessuto*) check(ed)

scacchi'era [skak'kjɛra] *sf* chessboard

scacci'are [skat'tʃare] *vt* to chase away *o* out, drive away *o* out

'scaddi *ecc vb vedi* **scadere**

sca'dente *ag* shoddy, of poor quality

sca'denza [ska'dɛntsa] *sf* (*di cambiale, contratto*) maturity; (*di passaporto*) expiry date; **a breve/lunga ~** short-/long-term; **data di ~** expiry date

sca'dere *vi* (*contratto ecc*) to expire; (*debito*) to fall due; (*valore, forze, peso*) to decline, go down

sca'fandro *sm* (*di palombaro*) diving suit; (*di astronauta*) space-suit

scaf'fale *sm* shelf; (*mobile*) set of shelves

'scafo *sm* (*Naut, Aer*) hull

scagio'nare [skadʒo'nare] *vt* to exonerate, free from blame

'scaglia ['skaʎʎa] *sf* (*Zool*) scale; (*scheggia*) chip, flake

scagli'are [skaʎ'ʎare] *vt* (*lanciare: anche fig*) to hurl, fling; **scagliarsi** (*anche:* **vr**): **scagliarsi su** *o* **contro** to hurl *o* fling o.s. at; (*fig*) to rail at

'scala *sf* (*a gradini ecc*) staircase, stairs *pl*; (*a pioli, di corda*) ladder; (*Mus, Geo, di colori, valori, fig*) scale; **scale** *sfpl* (*scalinata*) stairs; **su vasta ~/~ ridotta** on a large/small scale; **~ mobile (dei salari)** index-linked pay scale; **scala a libretto** stepladder; **scala mobile** escalator; (*Econ*) sliding scale

● **Scala**
● Milan's world-famous **la Scala**
● theatre first opened its doors in
● 1778 with a performance of Salieri's
● opera, "L'Europa riconosciuta".
● It suffered serious damage in the
● bombing of Milan in 1943 and
● reopened in 1946 with a concert
● conducted by Toscanini. It also has
● a famous classical dance school.

sca'lare *vt* (*Alpinismo, muro*) to climb, scale; (*debito*) to scale down, reduce

scalda'bagno [skalda'baɲɲo] *sm* water-heater

scal'dare vt to heat; **scaldarsi** vpr to warm up, heat up; (al fuoco, al sole) to warm o.s.; (fig) to get excited

scal'fire vt to scratch

scali'nata sf staircase

sca'lino sm (anche fig) step; (di scala a pioli) rung

'scalo sm (Naut) slipway; (: porto d'approdo) port of call; (Aer) stopover; **fare ~ (a)** (Naut) to call (at), put in (at); (Aer) to land (at), make a stop (at); **scalo merci** (Ferr) goods (BRIT) o freight yard

scalop'pina sf (Cuc) escalope

scal'pello sm chisel

scal'pore sm noise, row; **far ~** (notizia) to cause a sensation o a stir

'scaltro, -a ag cunning, shrewd

'scalzo, -a ['skaltso] ag barefoot

scambi'are vt to exchange; (confondere): **~ qn/qc per** to take o mistake sb/sth for; **mi hanno scambiato il cappello** they've given me the wrong hat; **scambiarsi** vpr (auguri, confidenze, visite) to exchange; **~ qn/qc per** (confondere) to mistake sth/sb for

'scambio sm exchange; (Ferr) points pl; **fare (uno) ~** to make a swap

scampa'gnata [skampaɲˈɲata] sf trip to the country

scam'pare vt (salvare) to rescue, save; (evitare: morte, prigione) to escape ▶ vi **~ (a qc)** to survive (sth), escape (sth); **scamparla bella** to have a narrow escape

'scampo sm (salvezza) escape; (Zool) prawn; **cercare ~ nella fuga** to seek safety in flight

'scampolo sm remnant

scanala'tura sf (incavo) channel, groove

scandagli'are [skandaʎˈʎare] vt (Naut) to sound; (fig) to sound out; to probe

scandaliz'zare [skandalidˈdzare] vt to shock, scandalize; **scandalizzarsi** vpr to be shocked

'scandalo sm scandal

Scandi'navia sf **la ~** Scandinavia; **scandi'navo, -a** ag, sm/f Scandinavian

scanner ['skanner] sm inv (Inform) scanner

scansafa'tiche [skansafaˈtike] sm/f inv idler, loafer

scan'sare vt (rimuovere) to move (aside), shift; (schivare: schiaffo) to dodge; (sfuggire) to avoid; **scansarsi** vpr to move aside

scan'sia sf shelves pl; (per libri) bookcase

'scanso sm **a ~ di** in order to avoid, as a precaution against

scanti'nato sm basement

scapacci'one [skapatˈtʃone] sm clout

scapes'trato, -a ag dissolute

'scapola sf shoulder blade

'scapolo sm bachelor

scappa'mento sm (Aut) exhaust

scap'pare vi (fuggire) to escape; (andare via in fretta) to rush off; **lasciarsi ~ un'occasione** to let an opportunity go by; **~ di prigione** to escape from prison; **~ di mano** (oggetto) to slip out of one's hands; **~ di mente a qn** to slip sb's mind; **mi scappò detto** I let it slip; **scappa'toia** sf way out

scara'beo sm beetle

scarabocchi'are [skarabokˈkjare] vt to scribble, scrawl; **scara'bocchio** sm scribble, scrawl

scara'faggio [skaraˈfaddʒo] sm cockroach

scaraman'zia [skaramanˈtsia] sf **per ~** for luck

scaraven'tare vt to fling, hurl; **scaraventarsi** vpr to fling o.s.

scarce'rare [skartʃeˈrare] vt to release (from prison)

scardi'nare vt ~ **una porta** to take a door off its hinges

scari'care vt (merci, camion ecc) to unload; (passeggeri) to set down, put off; (arma) to unload; (: sparare, Elettr) to discharge; (corso d'acqua) to empty, pour; (fig: liberare da un peso) to unburden, relieve; (da Internet) to download; **scaricarsi** vpr (orologio) to run o wind down; (batteria, accumulatore) to go flat o dead; (fig: rilassarsi) to unwind; (: sfogarsi) to let off steam

'**scarico, -a, -chi, -che** ag unloaded; (orologio) run down; (accumulatore) dead, flat ▶ sm (di merci, materiali) unloading; (di immondizie) dumping, tipping (BRIT); (Tecn: deflusso) draining; (: dispositivo) drain; (Aut) exhaust

scarlat'tina sf scarlet fever

scar'latto, -a ag scarlet

'**scarpa** sf shoe; **scarpe da ginnastica/tennis** gym/tennis shoes

scar'pata sf escarpment

scarpi'era sf shoe rack

scar'pone sm boot; **scarponi da montagna** climbing boots; **scarponi da sci** ski-boots

scarseggi'are vi to be scarce; ~ **di** to be short of, lack

'**scarso, -a** ag (insufficiente) insufficient, meagre; (povero: annata) poor, lean; (Ins: voto) poor; ~ **di** lacking in; **3 chili scarsi** just under 3 kilos, barely 3 kilos

scar'tare vt (pacco) to unwrap; (idea) to reject; (Mil) to declare unfit for military service; (carte da gioco) to discard; (Calcio) to dodge (past) ▶ vi to swerve

'**scarto** sm (cosa scartata: anche Comm) reject; (di veicolo) swerve; (differenza) gap, difference

scassi'nare vt to break, force

scate'nare vt (fig) to incite, stir up; **scatenarsi** vpr (temporale) to break; (rivolta) to break out; (persona: infuriarsi) to rage

'**scatola** sf box; (di latta) tin (BRIT), can; **cibi in ~** tinned (BRIT) o canned foods; **scatola cranica** cranium; **scato'lone** sm (big) box

scat'tare vt (fotografia) to take ▶ vi (congegno, molla ecc) to be released; (balzare) to spring up; (Sport) to put on a spurt; (fig: per l'ira) to fly into a rage; ~ **in piedi** to spring to one's feet

'**scatto** sm (dispositivo) release; (: di arma da fuoco) trigger mechanism; (rumore) click; (balzo) jump, start; (Sport) spurt; (fig: di ira ecc) fit; (: di stipendio) increment; **di ~** suddenly

scaval'care vt (ostacolo) to pass (o climb) over; (fig) to get ahead of, overtake

sca'vare vt (terreno) to dig; (legno) to hollow out; (pozzo, galleria) to bore; (città sepolta ecc) to excavate

'**scavo** sm excavating no pl; excavation

'**scegliere** ['ʃeʎʎere] vt to choose, select

sce'icco, -chi [ʃe'ikko] sm sheik

'**scelgo** ecc ['ʃelgo] vb vedi **scegliere**

scel'lino [ʃel'lino] sm shilling

'**scelta** ['ʃelta] sf choice; selection; **di prima ~** top grade o quality; **frutta o formaggi a ~** choice of fruit or cheese

'**scelto, -a** ['ʃelto] pp di **scegliere** ▶ ag (gruppo) carefully selected; (frutta, verdura) choice, top quality; (Mil: specializzato) crack cpd, highly skilled

'**scemo, -a** ['ʃemo] ag stupid, silly

'**scena** ['ʃena] sf (gen) scene; (palcoscenico) stage; **le scene** (fig: teatro) the stage; **fare una ~** to make a scene; **andare in ~** to be staged o put on o performed; **mettere in ~** to stage

sce'nario [ʃe'narjo] sm scenery; (di film) scenario

sce'nata [ʃe'nata] *sf* row, scene

'scendere ['ʃendere] *vi* to go (*o come*) down; (*strada, sole*) to go down; (*notte*) to fall; (*passeggero: fermarsi*) to get out, alight; (*fig: temperatura, prezzi*) to go *o* come down, fall, drop ▶ *vt* (*scale, pendio*) to go (*o come*) down; ~ **dalle scale** to go (*o come*) down the stairs; ~ **dal treno** to get off *o* out of the train; **dove devo ~?** where do I get off?; ~ **dalla macchina** to get out of the car; ~ **da cavallo** to dismount, get off one's horse

scenegi'ato [ʃened'dʒato] *sm* television drama

'scettico, -a, -ci, -che ['ʃettiko] *ag* sceptical

'scettro ['ʃettro] *sm* sceptre

'scheda ['skɛda] *sf* (index) card; **scheda elettorale** ballot paper; **scheda ricaricabile** (*Tel*) top-up card; **scheda telefonica** phone card; **sche'dario** *sm* file; (*mobile*) filing cabinet

sche'dina [ske'dina] *sf* ≈ pools coupon (*BRIT*)

'scheggia, -ge ['skeddʒa] *sf* splinter, sliver

'scheletro ['skɛletro] *sm* skeleton

'schema, -i ['skɛma] *sm* (*diagramma*) diagram, sketch; (*progetto, abbozzo*) outline, plan

'scherma ['skerma] *sf* fencing

scher'maglia [sker'maʎʎa] *sf* (*fig*) skirmish

'schermo ['skermo] *sm* shield, screen; (*Cinema, TV*) screen

scher'nire [sker'nire] *vt* to mock, sneer at

scher'zare [sker'tsare] *vi* to joke

'scherzo ['skertso] *sm* joke; (*tiro*) trick; (*Mus*) scherzo; **è uno ~!** (*una cosa facile*) it's child's play!, it's easy!; **per ~** in jest; for a joke *o* a laugh; **fare un brutto ~ a qn** to play a nasty trick on sb

schiaccia'noci [skjattʃa'notʃi] *sm inv* nutcracker

schiacci'are [skjat'tʃare] *vt* (*dito*) to crush; (*noci*) to crack; ~ **un pisolino** to have a nap; **schiacciarsi** *vpr* (*appiattirsi*) to get squashed; (*frantumarsi*) to get crushed

schiaffeggi'are [skjaffed'dʒare] *vt* to slap

schi'affo ['skjaffo] *sm* slap

schiantarsi *vpr* to break (up), shatter

schia'rire [skja'rire] *vt* to lighten, make lighter; **schiarirsi** *vpr* to grow lighter; (*tornar sereno*) to clear, brighten up; **schiarirsi la voce** to clear one's throat

schiavitù [skjavi'tu] *sf* slavery

schi'avo, -a ['skjavo] *sm/f* slave

schi'ena ['skjɛna] *sf* (*Anat*) back; **schie'nale** *sm* (*di sedia*) back

schi'era ['skjɛra] *sf* (*Mil*) rank; (*gruppo*) group, band

schiera'mento [skjera'mento] *sm* (*Mil, Sport*) formation; (*fig*) alliance

schie'rare [skje'rare] *vt* (*esercito*) to line up, draw up, marshal; **schierarsi** *vpr* to line up; (*fig*): **schierarsi con** *o* **dalla parte di/contro qn** to side with/oppose sb

'schifo ['skifo] *sm* disgust; **fare ~** (*essere fatto male, dare pessimi risultati*) to be awful; **mi fa ~** it makes me sick, it's disgusting; **quel libro è uno ~** that book's rotten; **schi'foso, -a** *ag* disgusting, revolting; (*molto scadente*) rotten, lousy

schioc'care [skjok'kare] *vt* (*frusta*) to crack; (*dita*) to snap; (*lingua*) to click; ~ **le labbra** to smack one's lips

schiudersi *vpr* to open

schi'uma ['skjuma] *sf* foam; (*di sapone*) lather; (*di latte*) froth; (*fig: feccia*) scum

schi'vare [ski'vare] *vt* to dodge, avoid

'schivo, -a ['skivo] *ag* (*ritroso*) standoffish, reserved; (*timido*) shy

schiz'zare [skit'tsare] *vt* (*spruzzare*) to spurt, squirt; (*sporcare*) to splash, spatter; (*fig: abbozzare*) to sketch ▶ *vi* to spurt, squirt; (*saltar fuori*) to dart up (*o olif ecc*)

schizzi'noso, -a [skittsi'noso] *ag* fussy, finicky

'schizzo ['skittso] *sm* (*di liquido*) spurt; splash, spatter; (*abbozzo*) sketch

sci [ʃi] *sm* (*attrezzo*) ski; (*attività*) skiing; **sci d'acqua** water-skiing; **sci di fondo** cross-country skiing, ski touring (*US*); **sci nautico** water-skiing

'scia ['ʃia] (*pl* **scie**) *sf* (*di imbarcazione*) wake; (*di profumo*) trail

scià [ʃa] *sm inv* shah

sci'abola ['ʃabola] *sf* sabre

scia'callo [ʃa'kallo] *sm* jackal

sciac'quare [ʃak'kware] *vt* to rinse

scia'gura [ʃa'gura] *sf* disaster, calamity; misfortune

scialac'quare [ʃalak'kware] *vt* to squander

sci'albo, -a ['ʃalbo] *ag* pale, dull; (*fig*) dull, colourless

sci'alle ['ʃalle] *sm* shawl

scia'luppa [ʃa'luppa] *sf*; **scialuppa di salvataggio** lifeboat

sci'ame ['ʃame] *sm* swarm

sci'are [ʃi'are] *vi* to ski

sci'arpa ['ʃarpa] *sf* scarf; (*fascia*) sash

scia'tore, -'trice [ʃia'tore] *sm/f* skier

sci'atto, -a ['ʃatto] *ag* (*persona*) slovenly, unkempt

scien'tifico, -a, -ci, -che [ʃen'tifiko] *ag* scientific

sci'enza ['ʃentsa] *sf* science; (*sapere*) knowledge; **scienze** *sfpl* (*Ins*) science *sg*; **scienze naturali** natural sciences; **scienzi'ato, -a** *sm/f* scientist

'scimmia ['ʃimmja] *sf* monkey

scimpanzé [ʃimpan'tse] *sm inv* chimpanzee

scin'tilla [ʃin'tilla] *sf* spark; **scintil'lare** *vi* to spark; (*acqua, occhi*) to sparkle

scioc'chezza [ʃok'kettsa] *sf* stupidity *no pl*; stupid *o* foolish thing; **dire sciocchezze** to talk nonsense

sci'occo, -a, -chi, -che ['ʃɔkko] *ag* stupid, foolish

sci'ogliere ['ʃɔʎʎere] *vt* (*nodo*) to untie; (*capelli*) to loosen; (*persona, animale*) to untie, release; (*fig: persona*): ~ **da** to release from; (*neve*) to melt; (*nell'acqua: zucchero ecc*) to dissolve; (*fig: mistero*) to solve; (*porre fine a: contratto*) to cancel; (*: società, matrimonio*) to dissolve; (*: riunione*) to bring to an end; **sciogliersi** *vpr* to loosen, come untied; to melt; to dissolve; (*assemblea ecc*) to break up; ~ **i muscoli** to limber up; **scioglilingua** [ʃoʎʎi'lingwa] *sm inv* tongue-twister

sci'olgo *ecc* ['ʃɔlgo] *vb vedi* **sciogliere**

sci'olto, -a ['ʃɔlto] *pp di* **sciogliere** ▶ *ag* loose; (*agile*) agile, nimble; supple; (*disinvolto*) free and easy; **versi sciolti** (*Poesia*) blank verse

sciope'rare [ʃope'rare] *vi* to strike, go on strike

sci'opero ['ʃopero] *sm* strike; **fare ~** to strike; **sciopero bianco** work-to-rule (*BRIT*), slowdown (*US*); **sciopero selvaggio** wildcat strike; **sciopero a singhiozzo** on-off strike

scio'via [ʃio'via] *sf* ski lift

scip'pare [ʃip'pare] *vt* ~ **qn** to snatch sb's bag; **mi hanno scippato** they snatched my bag

sci'rocco [ʃi'rɔkko] *sm* sirocco

sci'roppo [ʃi'roppo] *sm* syrup

'scisma, -i ['ʃizma] *sm* (*Rel*) schism

scissi'one [ʃis'sjone] *sf* (*anche fig*) split, division; (*Fisica*) fission

sciu'pare [ʃu'pare] *vt* (*abito, libro, appetito*) to spoil, ruin; (*tempo, denaro*) to waste

scivo'lare [ʃivo'lare] *vi* to slide *o* glide along; (*involontariamente*) to slip, slide; **'scivolo** *sm* slide; (*Tecn*) chute; **scivo'loso, -a** *ag* slippery

scle'rosi *sf* sclerosis

scoc'care *vt* (*freccia*) to shoot ▶ *vi* (*guizzare*) to shoot up; (*battere: ora*) to strike

scoccherò *ecc* [skokke'rɔ] *vb vedi* **scoccare**

scocci'are [skot'tʃare] (*fam*) *vt* to bother, annoy; **scocciarsi** *vpr* to be bothered *o* annoyed

sco'della *sf* bowl

scodinzo'lare [skodintso'lare] *vi* to wag its tail

scogli'era [skoʎ'ʎɛra] *sf* reef; cliff

'scoglio ['skoʎʎo] *sm* (*al mare*) rock

scoi'attolo *sm* squirrel

scola'pasta *sm inv* colander

scolapi'atti *sm inv* drainer (*for plates*)

sco'lare *ag* **età scolare** school age ▶ *vt* to drain ▶ *vi* to drip

scola'resca *sf* schoolchildren *pl*, pupils *pl*

sco'laro, -a *sm/f* pupil, schoolboy/girl

Attenzione! In inglese esiste la parola *scholar*, che però significa *studioso*.

sco'lastico, -a, -ci, -che *ag* school *cpd*; scholastic

scol'lato, -a *ag* (*vestito*) low-cut, low-necked; (*donna*) wearing a low-cut dress (*o blouse ecc*)

scolla'tura *sf* neckline

scolle'gare *vt* (*fili, apparecchi*) to disconnect

'scolo *sm* drainage

scolo'rire *vt* to fade; to discolour; **scolorirsi** *vpr* to fade; to become discoloured; (*impallidire*) to turn pale

scol'pire *vt* to carve, sculpt

scombusso'lare *vt* to upset

scom'messa *sf* bet, wager

scom'mettere *vt, vi* to bet

scomo'dare *vt* to trouble, bother; to disturb; **scomodarsi** *vpr* to put o.s. out; **scomodarsi a fare** to go to the bother *o* trouble of doing

'scomodo, -a *ag* uncomfortable; (*sistemazione, posto*) awkward, inconvenient

scompa'rire *vi* (*sparire*) to disappear, vanish; (*fig*) to be insignificant

scomparti'mento *sm* compartment; **uno ~ per non-fumatori** a non-smoking compartment

scompigli'are [skompiʎ'ʎare] *vt* (*cassetto, capelli*) to mess up, disarrange; (*fig: piani*) to upset

scomuni'care *vt* to excommunicate

'sconcio, -a, -ci, -ce ['skontʃo] *ag* (*osceno*) indecent, obscene ▶ *sm* disgrace

scon'figgere [skon'fiddʒere] *vt* to defeat, overcome

sconfi'nare *vi* to cross the border; (*in proprietà privata*) to trespass; (*fig*): **~ da** to stray *o* digress from

scon'fitta *sf* defeat

scon'forto *sm* despondency

sconge'lare [skondʒe'lare] *vt* to defrost

scongiu'rare [skondʒu'rare] *vt* (*implorare*) to entreat, beseech, implore; (*eludere: pericolo*) to ward off, avert; **scongi'uro** *sm* entreaty; (*esorcismo*) exorcism; **fare gli scongiuri** to touch wood (*BRIT*), knock on wood (*US*)

scon'nesso, -a *ag* incoherent

sconosci'uto, -a [skonoʃʃuto] *ag* unknown; new, strange ▶ *sm/f* stranger; unknown person

sconsigli'are [skonsiʎ'ʎare] *vt* **~ qc a qn** to advise sb against sth; **~ qn dal fare qc** to advise sb not to do *o* against doing sth

sconso'lato, -a *ag* inconsolable; desolate

scon'tare vt (Comm: detrarre) to deduct; (: debito) to pay off; (: cambiale) to discount; (pena) to serve; (colpa, errori) to pay for, suffer for

scon'tato, -a ag (previsto) foreseen, taken for granted; **dare per ~ che** to take it for granted that

scon'tento, -a ag ~ **(di)** dissatisfied (with) ▶ sm dissatisfaction

'sconto sm discount; **fare uno ~** to give a discount; **ci sono sconti per studenti?** are there discounts for students?

scon'trarsi vpr (treni ecc) to crash, collide; (venire ad uno scontro, fig) to clash; **~ con** to crash into, collide with

scon'trino sm ticket; (di cassa) receipt; **potrei avere lo ~ per favore?** can I have a receipt, please?

'scontro sm clash, encounter; crash, collision

scon'troso, -a ag sullen, surly; (permaloso) touchy

sconveni'ente ag unseemly, improper

scon'volgere [skon'vɔldʒere] vt to throw into confusion, upset; (turbare) to shake, disturb, upset; **scon'volto, -a** pp di **sconvolgere**

scooter ['skuter] sm inv scooter

'scopa sf broom; (Carte) Italian card game; **sco'pare** vt to sweep

sco'perta sf discovery

sco'perto, -a pp di **scoprire** ▶ ag uncovered; (capo) uncovered, bare; (macchina) open; (Mil) exposed, without cover; (conto) overdrawn

'scopo sm aim, purpose; **a che ~?** what for?

scoppi'are vi (spaccarsi) to burst; (esplodere) to explode; (fig) to break out; **~ in pianto** o **a piangere** to burst out crying; **~ dalle risa** o **dal ridere** to split one's sides laughing

scoppiet'tare vi to crackle

'scoppio sm explosion; (di tuono, arma ecc) crash, bang; (fig: di risa, ira) fit, outburst; (: di guerra) outbreak; **a ~ ritardato** delayed-action

sco'prire vt to discover; (liberare da ciò che copre) to uncover; (: monumento) to unveil; **scoprirsi** vpr to put on lighter clothes; (fig) to give o.s. away

scoraggi'are [skorad'dʒare] vt to discourage; **scoraggiarsi** vpr to become discouraged, lose heart

scorcia'toia [skortʃa'toja] sf short cut

'scorcio ['skortʃo] sm (Arte) foreshortening; (di secolo, periodo) end, close; **scorcio panoramico** vista

scor'dare vt to forget; **scordarsi** vpr **scordarsi di qc/di fare** to forget sth/to do

'scorgere ['skɔrdʒere] vt to make out, distinguish, see

scorpacci'ata [skorpat'tʃata] sf **fare una ~ (di)** to stuff o.s. (with), eat one's fill (of)

scorpi'one sm scorpion; (dello zodiaco): **S~** Scorpio

'scorrere vt (giornale, lettera) to run o skim through ▶ vi (liquido, fiume) to run, flow; (fune) to run; (cassetto, porta) to slide easily; (tempo) to pass (by)

scor'retto, -a ag incorrect; (sgarbato) impolite; (sconveniente) improper

scor'revole ag (porta) sliding; (fig: stile) fluent, flowing

'scorsi ecc vb vedi **scorgere**

'scorso, -a pp di **scorrere** ▶ ag last

scor'soio, -a ag **nodo ~** noose

'scorta sf (di personalità, convoglio) escort; (provvista) supply, stock

scor'tese ag discourteous, rude

'scorza ['skɔrdza] sf (di albero) bark; (di agrumi) peel, skin

sco'sceso, -a [skoʃ'ʃeso] ag steep

'scossa sf jerk, jolt, shake; (Elettr: fig) shock; **scossa di terremoto** earth tremor

S

'**scosso, -a** pp di **scuotere** ▶ ag (turbato) shaken, upset

scos'tante ag (fig) off-putting (BRIT), unpleasant

scotch [skɔtʃ] sm inv (whisky) Scotch; (nastro adesivo) Scotch tape®, Sellotape®

scot'tare vt (ustionare) to burn; (: con liquido bollente) to scald ▶ vi to burn; (caffè) to be too hot; **scottarsi** vpr to burn/scald o.s.; (fig) to have one's fingers burnt; **scotta'tura** sf burn; scald

'**scotto, -a** ag overcooked ▶ sm (fig): **pagare lo ~ (di)** to pay the penalty (for)

sco'vare vt to drive out, flush out; (fig) to discover

'**Scozia** ['skɔttsja] sf la ~ Scotland; **scoz'zese** ag Scottish ▶ sm/f Scot

scredi'tare vt to discredit

screen saver ['skriːn'sɛɪvər] sm inv (Inform) screen saver

scre'mato, -a ag skimmed; **parzialmente ~** semi-skimmed

screpo'lato, -a ag (labbra) chapped; (muro) cracked

'**screzio** ['skrɛttsjo] sm disagreement

scricchio'lare [skrikkjo'lare] vi to creak, squeak

'**scrigno** ['skriɲɲo] sm casket

scrimina'tura sf parting

'**scrissi** ecc vb vedi **scrivere**

'**scritta** sf inscription

'**scritto, -a** pp di **scrivere** ▶ ag written ▶ sm writing; (lettera) letter, note

scrit'toio sm writing desk

scrit'tore, -'trice sm/f writer

scrit'tura sf writing; (Comm) entry; (contratto) contract; (Rel): **la Sacra S~** the Scriptures pl

scrittu'rare vt (Teatro, Cinema) to sign up, engage; (Comm) to enter

scriva'nia sf desk

'**scrivere** vt to write; **come si scrive?** how is it spelt?, how do you write it?

scroc'cone, -a sm/f scrounger

'**scrofa** sf (Zool) sow

scrol'lare vt to shake; **scrollarsi** vpr (anche fig) to give o.s. a shake; (anche: **~ le spalle/il capo**) to shrug one's shoulders/shake one's head

'**scrupolo** sm scruple; (meticolosità) care, conscientiousness

scrupo'loso, -a ag scrupulous; conscientious

scru'tare vt to scrutinize; (intenzioni, causa) to examine, scrutinize

scu'cire [sku'tʃire] vt (orlo ecc) to unpick, undo; **scucirsi** vpr to come unstitched

scude'ria sf stable

scu'detto sm (Sport) (championship) shield; (distintivo) badge

'**scudo** sm shield

sculacci'are [skulat'tʃare] vt to spank

scul'tore, -'trice sm/f sculptor

scul'tura sf sculpture

scu'ola sf school; **scuola elementare/materna** primary (BRIT) o grade (US) /nursery school; **scuola guida** driving school; **scuola media** secondary (BRIT) o high (US) school; **scuola dell'obbligo** compulsory education; **scuola tecnica** technical college; **scuole serali** evening classes, night school sg

scu'otere vt to shake

'**scure** sf axe

'**scuro, -a** ag dark; (fig: espressione) grim ▶ sm darkness; dark colour; (imposta) (window) shutter; **verde/rosso** ecc **~** dark green/red ecc

'**scusa** sf apology; (pretesto) excuse; **chiedere ~ a qn (per)** to apologize to sb (for); **chiedo ~** I'm sorry; (disturbando ecc) excuse me

scu'sare vt to excuse; **scusarsi** vpr **scusarsi (di)** to apologize (for); **(mi) scusi** I'm sorry; (per richiamare l'attenzione) excuse me

sde'gnato, -a [zdeɲ'ɲato] *ag* indignant, angry

'sdegno ['zdeɲɲo] *sm* scorn, disdain

sdolci'nato, -a [zdoltʃi'nato] *ag* mawkish, oversentimental

sdrai'arsi *vpr* to stretch out, lie down

'sdraio *sm* **sedia a ~** deck chair

sdruccio'levole [zdruttʃo'levole] *ag* slippery

se
   pron vedi **si**

▶*cong*

1 (*condizionale, ipotetica*) if; **se nevica non vengo** I won't come if it snows; **sarei rimasto se me l'avessero chiesto** I would have stayed if they'd asked me; **non puoi fare altro se non telefonare** all you can do is phone; **se mai** if, if ever; **siamo noi se mai che le siamo grati** it is we who should be grateful to you; **se no** (*altrimenti*) or (*else*), otherwise

2 (*in frasi dubitative, interrogative indirette*) if, whether; **non so se scrivere o telefonare** I don't know whether o if I should write or phone

sé *pron* (*gen*) oneself; (*esso, essa, lui, lei, loro*) itself; himself; herself; themselves; **sé stesso(a)** *pron* oneself; itself; himself; herself

seb'bene *cong* although, though

sec. *abbr* (= *secolo*) c.

'secca *sf* (*del mare*) shallows *pl*; *vedi anche* **secco**

sec'care *vt* to dry; (*prosciugare*) to dry up; (*fig: importunare*) to annoy, bother ▶ *vi* to dry; to dry up; **seccarsi** *vpr* to dry; to dry up; (*fig*) to grow annoyed

sec'cato, -a *ag* (*fig: infastidito*) bothered, annoyed; (: *stufo*) fed up

secca'tura *sf* (*fig*) bother *no pl*, trouble *no pl*

seccherò *ecc* [sekke'rɔ] *vb vedi* **seccare**

secchi'ello *sm* bucket; **secchiello del ghiaccio** ice bucket

'secchio ['sekkjo] *sm* bucket, pail

'secco, -a, -chi, -che *ag* dry; (*fichi, pesce*) dried; (*foglie, ramo*) withered; (*magro: persona*) thin, skinny; (*fig: risposta, modo di fare*) curt, abrupt; (: *colpo*) clean, sharp ▶ *sm* (*siccità*) drought; **restarci ~** (*fig: morire sul colpo*) to drop dead; **mettere in ~** (*barca*) to beach; **rimanere a ~** (*fig*) to be left in the lurch

seco'lare *ag* age-old, centuries-old; (*laico, mondano*) secular

'secolo *sm* century; (*epoca*) age

se'conda *sf* (*Aut*) second (gear); **viaggiare in ~** to travel second-class; *vedi anche* **secondo**; **seconda colazione** lunch

secon'dario, -a *ag* secondary

se'condo, -a *ag* second ▶ *sm* second; (*di pranzo*) main course ▶ *prep* according to; (*nel modo prescritto*) in accordance with; **~ me** in my opinion, to my mind; **di seconda mano** second-hand; **a seconda di** according to; in accordance with; **seconda classe** second-class

'sedano *sm* celery

seda'tivo, -a *ag, sm* sedative

'sede *sf* seat; (*di ditta*) head office; (*di organizzazione*) headquarters *pl*; **sede centrale** head office; **sede sociale** registered office

seden'tario, -a *ag* sedentary

se'dere *vi* to sit, be seated

'sedia *sf* chair; **sedia elettrica** electric chair; **sedia a rotelle** wheelchair

'sedici ['seditʃi] *num* sixteen

se'dile *sm* seat; (*panchina*) bench

sedu'cente [sedu'tʃɛnte] *ag* seductive; (*proposta*) very attractive

se'durre *vt* to seduce

se'duta *sf* session, sitting; (*riunione*) meeting; **seduta spiritica** séance; **seduta stante** (*fig*) immediately

seduzi'one [sedut'tsjone] *sf* seduction; (*fascino*) charm, appeal

SEeO *abbr* (= *salvo errori e omissioni*) E and OE

'sega, -ghe *sf* saw

'segale *sf* rye

se'gare *vt* to saw; (*recidere*) to saw off

'seggio ['sɛddʒo] *sm* seat; **seggio elettorale** polling station

'seggiola ['sɛddʒola] *sf* chair; **seggio'lone** *sm* (*per bambini*) highchair

seggio'via [seddʒo'via] *sf* chairlift

segherò *ecc* [sege'rɔ] *vb vedi* **segare**

segna'lare [seɲɲa'lare] *vt* (*manovra ecc*) to signal; to indicate; (*annunciare*) to announce; to report; (*fig: far conoscere*) to point out; (: *persona*) to single out

se'gnale [seɲ'ɲale] *sm* signal; (*cartello*): **segnale acustico** acoustic *o* sound signal; **segnale d'allarme** alarm; (*Ferr*) communication cord; **segnale orario** (*Radio*) time signal; **segnale stradale** road sign

segna'libro [seɲɲa'libro] *sm* (*anche Inform*) bookmark

se'gnare [seɲ'ɲare] *vt* to mark; (*prendere nota*) to note; (*indicare*) to indicate, mark; (*Sport: goal*) to score

'segno ['seɲɲo] *sm* sign; (*impronta, contrassegno*) mark; (*limite*) limit, bounds *pl*; (*bersaglio*) target; **fare ~ di sì/no** to nod (one's head)/shake one's head; **fare ~ a qn di fermarsi** to motion (to) sb to stop; **cogliere** *o* **colpire nel ~** (*fig*) to hit the mark; **segno zodiacale** star sign

segre'tario, -a *sm/f* secretary; **segretario comunale** town clerk; **Segretario di Stato** Secretary of State

segrete'ria *sf* (*di ditta, scuola*) (secretary's) office; (*d'organizzazione internazionale*) secretariat; (*Pol ecc*: *carica*) office of Secretary; **segreteria telefonica** answering service

se'greto, -a *ag* secret ▶ *sm* secret; secrecy *no pl*; **in ~** in secret, secretly

segu'ace [se'gwatʃe] *sm/f* follower, disciple

segu'ente *ag* following, next

segu'ire *vt* to follow; (*frequentare: corso*) to attend ▶ *vi* to follow; (*continuare: testo*) to continue

segui'tare *vt* to continue, carry on with ▶ *vi* to continue, carry on

'seguito *sm* (*scorta*) suite, retinue; (*discepoli*) followers *pl*; (*favore*) following; (*continuazione*) continuation; (*conseguenza*) result; **di ~** at a stretch, on end; **in ~** later on; **in ~ a, a ~ di** following; (*a causa di*) as a result of, owing to

'sei *vb vedi* **essere** ▶ *num* six

sei'cento [sei'tʃɛnto] *num* six hundred ▶ *sm* **il S~** the seventeenth century

selci'ato [sel'tʃato] *sm* cobbled surface

selezio'nare [selettsjo'nare] *vt* to select

selezi'one [selet'tsjone] *sf* selection

'sella *sf* saddle

sel'lino *sm* saddle

selvag'gina [selvad'dʒina] *sf* (*animali*) game

sel'vaggio, -a, -gi, -ge [sel'vaddʒo] *ag* wild; (*tribù*) savage, uncivilized; (*fig*) savage, brutal ▶ *sm/f* savage

sel'vatico, -a, -ci, -che *ag* wild

se'maforo *sm* (*Aut*) traffic lights *pl*

sem'brare *vi* to seem ▶ *vb impers*: **sembra che** it seems that; **mi sembra che** it seems to me that, I think (that); **~ di essere** to seem to be

'seme *sm* seed; (*sperma*) semen; (*Carte*) suit

se'mestre *sm* half-year, six-month period

semifi'nale *sf* semifinal

semi'freddo *sm* ice-cream cake

semi'nare vt to sow

semi'nario sm seminar; (Rel) seminary

seminter'rato sm basement; (appartamento) basement flat

'**semola** sf; **semola di grano duro** durum wheat

semo'lino sm semolina

'**semplice** ['semplitʃe] ag simple; (di un solo elemento) single

'**sempre** av always; (ancora) still; **posso ~ tentare** I can always o still try; **da ~** always; **per ~** forever; **una volta per ~** once and for all; **~ che** provided (that); **~ più** more and more; **~ meno** less and less

sempre'verde ag, sm o f (Bot) evergreen

'**senape** sf (Cuc) mustard

se'nato sm senate; **sena'tore, -'trice** sm/f senator

'**senno** sm judgment, (common) sense; **col ~ di poi** with hindsight

'**seno** sm (Anat: petto, mammella) breast; (: grembo, fig) womb; (: cavità) sinus

sen'sato, -a ag sensible

sensazio'nale [sensattsjo'nale] ag sensational

sensazi'one [sensat'tsjone] sf feeling, sensation; **avere la ~ che** to have a feeling that; **fare ~** to cause a sensation, create a stir

sen'sibile ag sensitive; (ai sensi) perceptible; (rilevante, notevole) appreciable, noticeable; **~ a** sensitive to

> Attenzione! In inglese esiste la parola sensible, che però significa ragionevole.

sensibiliz'zare [sensibilid'dzare] vt (fig) to make aware, awaken

'**senso** sm (Fisiol, istinto) sense; (impressione, sensazione) feeling, sensation; (significato) meaning, sense; (direzione) direction; **sensi** smpl (coscienza) consciousness sg; (sensualità) senses; **ciò non ha ~** that doesn't make sense; **fare ~ a** (ripugnare) to disgust, repel; **in ~ orario/antiorario** clockwise/anticlockwise; **senso di colpa** sense of guilt; **senso comune** common sense; **senso unico** (strada) one-way; **senso vietato** (Aut) no entry

sensu'ale ag sensual; sensuous

sen'tenza [sen'tentsa] sf (Dir) sentence; (massima) maxim

senti'ero sm path

sentimen'tale ag sentimental; (vita, avventura) love cpd

senti'mento sm feeling

senti'nella sf sentry

sen'tire vt (percepire al tatto, fig) to feel; (udire) to hear; (ascoltare) to listen to; (odore) to smell; (avvertire con il gusto, assaggiare) to taste ▶ vi **~ di** (avere sapore) to taste of; (avere odore) to smell of; **sentirsi** vpr (uso reciproco) to be in touch; **sentirsi bene/male** to feel well/unwell o ill; **non mi sento bene** I don't feel well; **sentirsi di fare qc** (essere disposto) to feel like doing sth

sen'tito, -a ag (sincero) sincere, warm; **per ~ dire** by hearsay

'**senza** ['sentsa] prep, cong without; **~ dir nulla** without saying a word; **fare ~ qc** to do without sth; **~ di me** without me; **~ che io lo sapessi** without me o my knowing; **senz'altro** of course, certainly; **~ dubbio** no doubt; **~ scrupoli** unscrupulous; **~ amici** friendless

sepa'rare vt to separate; (dividere) to divide; (tenere distinto) to distinguish; **separarsi** vpr (coniugi) to separate, part; (amici) to part, leave each other; **separarsi da** (coniuge) to separate o part from; (amico, socio) to part company with; (*oggetto*) to part with; **sepa'rato, -a** *ag* (*letti, conto ecc*) separate; (*coniugi*) separated

seppel'lire *vt* to bury

'seppi *ecc vb vedi* **sapere**

'seppia *sf* cuttlefish ▶ *ag inv* sepia

se'quenza [se'kwentsa] *sf* sequence

seques'trare *vt* (*Dir*) to impound; (*rapire*) to kidnap; **se'questro** *sm* (*Dir*) impoundment; **sequestro di persona** kidnapping

'sera *sf* evening; **di ~** in the evening; **domani ~** tomorrow evening, tomorrow night; **se'rale** *ag* evening *cpd*; **se'rata** *sf* evening; (*ricevimento*) party

ser'bare *vt* to keep; (*mettere da parte*) to put aside; **~ rancore/odio verso qn** to bear sb a grudge/hate sb

serba'toio *sm* tank; (*cisterna*) cistern

'Serbia *sf* la **~** Serbia

'serbo *ag* Serbian ▶ *sm/f* Serbian, Serb ▶ *sm* (*Ling*) Serbian; (*il serbare*): **mettere/tenere** *o* **avere in ~ qc** to put/keep sth aside

se'reno, -a *ag* (*tempo, cielo*) clear; (*fig*) serene, calm

ser'gente [ser'dʒɛnte] *sm* (*Mil*) sergeant

'serie *sf inv* (*successione*) series *inv*; (*gruppo, collezione*) set; (*Sport*) division; league; (*Comm*): **modello di ~/fuori ~** standard/custom-built model; **in ~** in quick succession; (*Comm*) mass *cpd*

serietà *sf* seriousness; reliability

'serio, -a *ag* serious; (*impiegato*) responsible, reliable; (*ditta, cliente*) reliable, dependable; **sul ~** (*davvero*) really, truly; (*seriamente*) seriously, in earnest

ser'pente *sm* snake; **serpente a sonagli** rattlesnake

'serra *sf* greenhouse; hothouse

ser'randa *sf* roller shutter

serra'tura *sf* lock

server ['sɛrvɛr] *sm inv* (*Inform*) server

ser'vire *vt* to serve; (*clienti: al ristorante*) to wait on; (: *al negozio*) to serve, attend to; (*fig: giovare*) to aid, help; (*Carte*) to deal ▶ *vi* (*Tennis*) to serve; (*essere utile*): **~ a qn** to be of use to sb; **~ a qc/a fare** (*utensile ecc*) to be used for sth/for doing; **~ (a qn) da** to serve as (for sb); **servirsi** *vpr* (*usare*): **servirsi di** to use; (*prendere: cibo*): **servirsi di** to help o.s. (to); **serviti pure!** help yourself!; (*essere cliente abituale*): **servirsi da** to be a regular customer at, go to

servizi'evole [servit'tsjevole] *ag* obliging, willing to help

ser'vizio [ser'vittsjo] *sm* service; (*al ristorante: sul conto*) service (charge); (*Stampa, TV, Radio*) report; (*da tè, caffè ecc*) set, service; **servizi** *smpl* (*di casa*) kitchen and bathroom; (*Econ*) services; **essere di ~** to be on duty; **fuori ~** (*telefono ecc*) out of order; **~ compreso** service included; **servizio militare** military service; **servizio di posate** set of cutlery; **servizi segreti** secret service *sg*; **servizio da tè** tea set

ses'santa *num* sixty; **sessan'tesimo, -a** *num* sixtieth

sessi'one *sf* session

'sesso *sm* sex; **sessu'ale** *ag* sexual, sex *cpd*

ses'tante *sm* sextant

'sesto, -a *ag, sm* sixth

'seta *sf* silk

'sete *sf* thirst; **avere ~** to be thirsty

'setola *sf* bristle

'setta *sf* sect

set'tanta *num* seventy; **settan'tesimo, -a** *num* seventieth

set'tare *vt* (*Inform*) to set up

'sette *num* seven

sette'cento [sette'tʃɛnto] *num* seven hundred ▶ *sm* **il S~** the eighteenth century

set'tembre sm September

settentrio'nale ag northern

settentri'one sm north

setti'mana sf week; **settima'nale** ag, sm weekly

- settimana bianca
- **Settimana bianca** is the name
- given to a week-long winter-sports
- holiday taken by many Italians some
- time in the skiing season.

'settimo, -a ag, sm seventh

set'tore sm sector

severità sf severity

se'vero, -a ag severe

sevizi'are [sevit'tsjare] vt to torture

sezio'nare [settsjo'nare] vt to divide into sections; (Med) to dissect

sezi'one [set'tsjone] sf section

sfacchi'nata [sfakki'nata] sf (fam) chore, drudgery no pl

sfacci'ato, -a [sfat't∫ato] ag (maleducato) cheeky, impudent; (vistoso) gaudy

sfa'mare vt to feed; (cibo) to fill; **sfamarsi** vpr to satisfy one's hunger, fill o.s. up

sfasci'are [sfa∫'∫are] vt (ferita) to unbandage; (distruggere) to smash, shatter; **sfasciarsi** vpr (rompersi) to smash, shatter

sfavo'revole ag unfavourable

'sfera sf sphere

sfer'rare vt (fig: colpo) to land, deal; (: attacco) to launch

'sfida sf challenge

sfi'dare vt to challenge; (fig) to defy, brave

sfi'ducia [sfi'dut∫a] sf distrust, mistrust

sfi'gato, -a (fam) ag (sfortunato) unlucky

sfigu'rare vt (persona) to disfigure; (quadro, statua) to deface ▶ vi (far cattiva figura) to make a bad impression

sfi'lare vt (ago) to unthread; (abito, scarpe) to slip off ▶ vi (truppe) to march past; (atleti) to parade; **sfilarsi** vpr (perle ecc) to come unstrung; (orlo, tessuto) to fray; (calza) to run, ladder; **sfi'lata** sf march past; parade; **sfilata di moda** fashion show

'sfinge ['sfindʒe] sf sphinx

sfi'nito, -a ag exhausted

sfio'rare vt to brush (against); (argomento) to touch upon

sfio'rire vi to wither, fade

sfo'cato, -a ag (Fot) out of focus

sfoci'are [sfo't∫are] vi ~ **in** to flow into; (fig: malcontento) to develop into

sfode'rato, -a ag (vestito) unlined

sfogarsi vpr (sfogare la propria rabbia) to give vent to one's anger; (confidarsi): ~ **(con)** to pour out one's feelings (to); **non sfogarti su di me!** don't take your bad temper out on me!

sfoggi'are [sfod'dʒare] vt, vi to show off

'sfoglia ['sfoʎʎa] sf sheet of pasta dough; **pasta ~** (Cuc) puff pastry

sfogli'are [sfoʎ'ʎare] vt (libro) to leaf through

'sfogo, -ghi sm (eruzione cutanea) rash; (fig) outburst; **dare ~ a** (fig) to give vent to

sfon'dare vt (porta) to break down; (scarpe) to wear a hole in; (cesto, scatola) to burst, knock the bottom out of; (Mil) to break through ▶ vi (riuscire) to make a name for o.s.

'sfondo sm background

sfor'mato sm (Cuc) type of soufflé

sfor'tuna sf misfortune, ill luck no pl; **avere ~** to be unlucky; **sfortu'nato, -a** ag unlucky; (impresa, film) unsuccessful

sforzarsi vpr ~ **di** o **a** o **per fare** to try hard to do

'sforzo ['sfortso] sm effort; (tensione eccessiva, Tecn) strain; **fare uno ~** to make an effort

sfrat'tare vt to evict; **'sfratto** sm eviction

sfrecci'are [sfret'tʃare] vi to shoot o flash past

sfre'gare vt (strofinare) to rub; (graffiare) to scratch; **sfregarsi le mani** to rub one's hands; **~ un fiammifero** to strike a match

sfregi'are [sfre'dʒare] vt to slash, gash; (persona) to disfigure; (quadro) to deface

sfre'nato, -a ag (fig) unrestrained, unbridled

sfron'tato, -a ag shameless

sfrutta'mento sm exploitation

sfrut'tare vt (terreno) to overwork, exhaust; (miniera) to exploit, work; (fig: operai, occasione, potere) to exploit

sfug'gire [sfud'dʒire] vi to escape; **~ a** (custode) to escape (from); (morte) to escape; **~ a qn** (dettaglio, nome) to escape sb; **~ di mano a qn** to slip out of sb's hand (o hands)

sfu'mare vt (colori, contorni) to soften, shade off ▶ vi to shade (off), fade; (fig: svanire) to vanish, disappear; (: speranze) to come to nothing

sfuma'tura sf shading off no pl; (tonalità) shade, tone; (fig) touch, hint

sfuri'ata sf (scatto di collera) fit of anger; (rimprovero) sharp rebuke

sga'bello sm stool

sgabuz'zino [sgabud'dzino] sm lumber room

sgambet'tare vi to kick one's legs about

sgam'betto sm **far lo ~ a qn** to trip sb up; (fig) to oust sb

sganci'are [zgan'tʃare] vt to unhook; (Ferr) to uncouple; (bombe: da aereo) to release, drop; (fig: fam: soldi) to fork out; **sganciarsi** vpr (fig): **sganciarsi (da)** to get away (from)

sganghe'rato, -a [zgange'rato] ag (porta) off its hinges; (auto) ramshackle; (risata) wild, boisterous

sgar'bato, -a ag rude, impolite

'sgarbo sm **fare uno ~ a qn** to be rude to sb

sgargi'ante [zgar'dʒante] ag gaudy, showy

sgattaio'lare vi to sneak away o off

sge'lare [zdʒe'lare] vi, vt to thaw

sghignaz'zare [zgiɲɲat'tsare] vi to laugh scornfully

sgob'bare (fam) vi (scolaro) to swot; (operaio) to slog

sgombe'rare vt (tavolo, stanza) to clear; (piazza, città) to evacuate ▶ vi to move

'sgombro, -a ag **~ (di)** clear (of), free (from) ▶ sm (Zool) mackerel; (anche: **sgombero**) clearing; vacating; evacuation; (: trasloco) removal

sgonfi'are vt to let down, deflate; **sgonfiarsi** vpr to go down

'sgonfio, -a ag (pneumatico, pallone) flat

'sgorbio sm blot; scribble

sgra'devole ag unpleasant, disagreeable

sgra'dito, -a ag unpleasant, unwelcome

sgra'nare vt (piselli) to shell; **~ gli occhi** to open one's eyes wide

sgranchire [zgran'kire] vt (anche: **sgranchirsi**) to stretch; **~ le gambe** to stretch one's legs

sgranocchi'are [zgranok'kjare] vt to munch

'sgravio sm **~ fiscale** tax relief

sgrazi'ato, -a [zgrat'tsjato] ag clumsy, ungainly

sgri'dare vt to scold

sgual'cire [zgwal'tʃire] vt to crumple (up), crease

sgual'drina (peg) sf slut

sgu'ardo sm (occhiata) look, glance; (espressione) look (in one's eye)

sguaz'zare [zgwat'tsare] vi (nell'acqua) to splash about; (nella melma) to wallow; ~ **nell'oro** to be rolling in money

sguinzagli'are [zgwintsaʎ'ʎare] vt to let off the leash; (fig: persona): ~ **qn dietro a qn** to set sb on sb

sgusci'are [zguʃʃare] vt to shell ▶ vi (sfuggire di mano) to slip; ~ **via** to slip o slink away

'shampoo ['ʃampo] sm inv shampoo

shiatzu [ʃi'atstsu] sm inv shiatsu

shock [ʃɔk] sm inv shock

si
(dav lo, la, li, le, ne diventa **se**) pron
1 (riflessivo: maschile) himself; (: femminile) herself; (: neutro) itself; (: impersonale) oneself; (: pl) themselves; **lavarsi** to wash (oneself); **si è tagliato** he has cut himself; **si credono importanti** they think a lot of themselves
2 (riflessivo: con complemento oggetto): **lavarsi le mani** to wash one's hands; **si sta lavando i capelli** he (o she) is washing his (o her) hair
3 (reciproco) one another, each other; **si amano** they love one another o each other
4 (passivo): **si ripara facilmente** it is easily repaired
5 (impersonale): **si dice che ...** they o people say that ...; **si vede che è vecchio** one o you can see that it's old
6 (noi) we; **tra poco si parte** we're leaving soon

sì av yes; **un giorno sì e uno no** every other day

'sia cong ~ **...** ~ (o ... o): ~ **che lavori, ~ che non lavori** whether he works or not; (tanto ... quanto): **verranno ~ Luigi ~ suo fratello** both Luigi and his brother will be coming

si'amo vb vedi **essere**

si'cario sm hired killer

sicché [sik'ke] cong (perciò) so (that), therefore; (e quindi) (and) so

siccità [sittʃi'ta] sf drought

sic'come cong since, as

Si'cilia [si'tʃilja] sf **la ~** Sicily; **sicili'ano, a** [sitʃi'ljano] ag, sm/f Sicilian

si'cura sf safety catch; (Aut) safety lock

sicu'rezza [siku'rettsa] sf safety; security; (fiducia) confidence; (certezza) certainty; **di ~** safety cpd; **la ~ stradale** road safety

si'curo, -a ag safe; (ben difeso) secure; (fiducioso) confident; (certo) sure, certain; (notizia, amico) reliable; (esperto) skilled ▶ av (anche: **di ~**) certainly; **essere/mettere al ~** to be safe/put in a safe place; ~ **di sé** self-confident, sure of o.s.; **sentirsi ~** to feel safe o secure

si'edo ecc vb vedi **sedere**

si'epe sf hedge

si'ero sm (Med) serum; **sieronega'tivo, -a** ag HIV-negative; **sieroposi'tivo, -a** ag HIV-positive

si'ete vb vedi **essere**

si'filide sf syphilis

Sig. abbr (= signore) Mr

siga'retta sf cigarette

'sigaro sm cigar

Sigg. abbr (= signori) Messrs

sigil'lare [sidʒil'lare] vt to seal

si'gillo [si'dʒillo] sm seal

'sigla sf initials pl; acronym, abbreviation; **sigla musicale** signature tune

Sig.na abbr (= signorina) Miss

signifi'care [siɲɲifi'kare] vt to mean; **signifi'cato** sm meaning

si'gnora [siɲ'ɲora] sf lady; **la ~ X** Mrs X; **buon giorno S~/Signore/ Signorina** good morning; (deferente) good morning Madam/Sir/Madam; (quando si conosce il nome) good morning Mrs/Mr/Miss X; **Gentile**

S~/Signore/Signorina (*in una lettera*) Dear Madam/Sir/Madam; **il signor Rossi e ~** Mr Rossi and his wife; **signore e signori** ladies and gentlemen

si'gnore [siɲ'ɲore] *sm* gentleman; (*padrone*) lord, master; (*Rel*) **il S~** the Lord; **il signor X** Mr X; **i signori Bianchi** (*coniugi*) Mr and Mrs Bianchi; *vedi anche* **signora**

signo'rile [siɲɲo'rile] *ag* refined

signo'rina [siɲɲo'rina] *sf* young lady; **la ~ X** Miss X; *vedi anche* **signora**

Sig.ra *abbr* (= *signora*) Mrs

silenzia'tore [silentsja'tore] *sm* silencer

si'lenzio [si'lɛntsjo] *sm* silence; **fare ~** to be quiet, stop talking; **silenzi'oso, -a** *ag* silent, quiet

si'licio [si'litʃo] *sm* silicon

sili'cone *sm* silicone

'sillaba *sf* syllable

si'luro *sm* torpedo

SIM [sim] *sigla f inv* (*Tel*) **~ card** SIM card

simboleggi'are [simboled'dʒare] *vt* to symbolize

'simbolo *sm* symbol

'simile *ag* (*analogo*) similar; (*di questo tipo*): **un uomo ~** such a man, a man like this; **libri simili** such books; **~ a** similar to; **i suoi simili** one's fellow men; one's peers

simme'tria *sf* symmetry

simpa'tia *sf* (*qualità*) pleasantness; (*inclinazione*) liking; **avere ~ per qn** to like sb, have a liking for sb; **sim'patico, -a, -ci, -che** *ag* (*persona*) nice, pleasant, likeable; (*casa, albergo ecc*) nice, pleasant

> Attenzione! In inglese esiste la parola *sympathetic*, che però significa *comprensivo*.

simpatiz'zare [simpatid'dzare] *vi* **~ con** to take a liking to

simu'lare *vt* to sham, simulate; (*Tecn*) to simulate

simul'taneo, -a *ag* simultaneous

sina'goga, -ghe *sf* synagogue

sincerità [sintʃeri'ta] *sf* sincerity

sin'cero, -a [sin'tʃero] *ag* sincere; genuine; heartfelt

sinda'cale *ag* (trade-)union *cpd*

sinda'cato *sm* (*di lavoratori*) (trade) union; (*Amm, Econ, Dir*) syndicate, trust, pool

'sindaco, -ci *sm* mayor

sinfo'nia *sf* (*Mus*) symphony

singhioz'zare [singjot'tsare] *vi* to sob; to hiccup

singhi'ozzo [sin'gjottso] *sm* sob; (*Med*) hiccup; **avere il ~** to have the hiccups; **a ~** (*fig*) by fits and starts

single ['singol] *ag inv, sm/f inv* single

singo'lare *ag* (*insolito*) remarkable, singular; (*Ling*) singular ▶ *sm* (*Ling*) singular; (*Tennis*): **~ maschile/femminile** men's/women's singles

'singolo, -a *ag* single, individual ▶ *sm* (*persona*) individual; (*Tennis*) = **singolare**

si'nistra *sf* (*Pol*) left (wing); **a ~** on the left; (*direzione*) to the left

si'nistro, -a *ag* left, left-hand; (*fig*) sinister ▶ *sm* (*incidente*) accident

si'nonimo *sm* synonym; **~ di** synonymous with

sin'tassi *sf* syntax

'sintesi *sf* synthesis; (*riassunto*) summary, résumé

sin'tetico, -a, -ci, -che *ag* synthetic

sintetiz'zare [sintetid'dzare] *vt* to synthesize; (*riassumere*) to summarize

sinto'matico, -a, -ci, -che *ag* symptomatic

'sintomo *sm* symptom

sintonizzarsi *vpr* **~ su** to tune in to

si'pario *sm* (*Teatro*) curtain

si'rena *sf* (*apparecchio*) siren; (*nella mitologia, fig*) siren, mermaid

'Siria *sf* la ~ Syria
si'ringa, -ghe *sf* syringe
'sismico, -a, -ci, -che *ag* seismic
sis'tema, -i *sm* system; method, way; **sistema nervoso** nervous system; **sistema operativo** (*Inform*) operating system; **sistema solare** solar system
siste'mare *vt* (*mettere a posto*) to tidy, put in order; (*risolvere: questione*) to sort out, settle; (*procurare un lavoro a*) to find a job for; (*dare un alloggio a*) to settle, find accommodation for; **sistemarsi** *vpr* (*problema*) to be settled; (*persona: trovare alloggio*) to find accommodation; (: *trovarsi un lavoro*) to get fixed up with a job; **ti sistemo io!** I'll soon sort you out!
siste'matico, -a, -ci, -che *ag* systematic
sistemazi'one [sistemat'tsjone] *sf* arrangement, order; settlement; employment; accommodation (*BRIT*), accommodations (*US*)
'sito *sm* ~ **Internet** website
situ'ato, -a *ag* ~ **a/su** situated at/on
situazi'one [situat'tsjone] *sf* situation
ski-lift ['ski:lift] *sm inv* ski tow
slacci'are [zlat'tʃare] *vt* to undo, unfasten
slanci'ato, -a [zlan'tʃato] *ag* slender
'slancio *sm* dash, leap; (*fig*) surge; **di ~** impetuously
'slavo, -a *ag* Slav(onic), Slavic
sle'ale *ag* disloyal; (*concorrenza ecc*) unfair
sle'gare *vt* to untie
slip [zlip] *sm inv* briefs *pl*
'slitta *sf* sledge; (*trainata*) sleigh
slit'tare *vi* to slip, slide; (*Aut*) to skid
s.l.m. *abbr* (= *sul livello del mare*) a.s.l.
slo'gare *vt* (*Med*) to dislocate
sloggi'are [zlod'dʒare] *vt* (*inquilino*) to turn out ▶ *vi* to move out
Slo'vacchia [zlo'vakkja] *sf* Slovakia

slo'vacco, -a, -chi, -che *ag, sm/f* Slovak
Slovenia [zlo'vɛnja] *sf* Slovenia
slo'veno, -a *ag, sm/f* Slovene, Slovenian ▶ *sm* (*Ling*) Slovene
smacchi'are [zmak'kjare] *vt* to remove stains from; **smacchia'tore** *sm* stain remover
'smacco, -chi *sm* humiliating defeat
smagli'ante [zmaʎ'ʎante] *ag* brilliant, dazzling
smaglia'tura [zmaʎʎa'tura] *sf* (*su maglia, calza*) ladder; (*della pelle*) stretch mark
smalizi'ato, -a [smalit'tsjato] *ag* shrewd, cunning
smalti'mento *sm* (*di rifiuti*) disposal
smal'tire *vt* (*merce*) to sell off; (*rifiuti*) to dispose of; (*cibo*) to digest; (*peso*) to lose; (*rabbia*) to get over; ~ **la sbornia** to sober up
'smalto *sm* (*anche*: **di denti**) enamel; (*per ceramica*) glaze; **smalto per unghie** nail varnish
smantel'lare *vt* to dismantle
smarri'mento *sm* loss; (*fig*) bewilderment; dismay
smar'rire *vt* to lose; (*non riuscire a trovare*) to mislay; **smarrirsi** *vpr* (*perdersi*) to lose one's way, get lost; (: *oggetto*) to go astray
smasche'rare [zmaske'rare] *vt* to unmask
SME *sigla m* (= *Sistema Monetario Europeo*) EMS (*European Monetary System*)
smen'tire *vt* (*negare*) to deny; (*testimonianza*) to refute; **smentirsi** *vpr* to be inconsistent
sme'raldo *sm* emerald
'smesso, -a *pp di* **smettere**
'smettere *vt* to stop; (*vestiti*) to stop wearing ▶ *vi* to stop, cease; ~ **di fare** to stop doing
'smilzo, -a ['zmiltso] *ag* thin, lean

S

sminu'ire vt to diminish, lessen; (fig) to belittle

sminuz'zare [zminut'tsare] vt to break into small pieces; to crumble

'smisi ecc vb vedi **smettere**

smis'tare vt (pacchi ecc) to sort; (Ferr) to shunt

smisu'rato, -a ag boundless, immeasurable; (grandissimo) immense, enormous

smoking ['sməukıŋ] sm inv dinner jacket

smon'tare vt (mobile, macchina ecc) to take to pieces, dismantle; (fig: scoraggiare) to dishearten ▶ vi (scendere: da cavallo) to dismount; (: da treno) to get off; (terminare il lavoro) to stop (work); **smontarsi** vpr to lose heart; to lose one's enthusiasm

'smorfia sf grimace; (atteggiamento lezioso) simpering; **fare smorfie** to make faces; to simper

'smorto, -a ag (viso) pale; (colore) dull

smor'zare [zmor'tsare] vt (suoni) to deaden; (colori) to tone down; (luce) to dim; (sete) to quench; (entusiasmo) to dampen; **smorzarsi** vpr (suono, luce) to fade; (entusiasmo) to dampen

SMS sigla m inv (= short message service) text (message)

smu'overe vt to move, shift; (fig: commuovere) to move; (: dall'inerzia) to rouse, stir

snatu'rato, -a ag inhuman, heartless

'snello, -a ag (agile) agile; (svelto) slim

sner'vante ag (attesa, lavoro) exasperating

snif'fare [znif'fare] vt (fam: cocaina) to snort

snob'bare vt to snub

sno'dare vt (rendere agile, mobile) to loosen; **snodarsi** vpr to come loose; (articolarsi) to bend; (strada) to wind

sno'dato, -a ag (articolazione, persona) flexible; (fune ecc) undone

so vb vedi **sapere**

sobbar'carsi vpr ~ **a** to take on, undertake

'sobrio, -a ag sober

socchi'udere [sok'kjudere] vt (porta) to leave ajar; (occhi) to half-close; **socchi'uso, -a** pp di **socchiudere**

soc'correre vt to help, assist

soccorri'tore, -'trice sm/f rescuer

soc'corso, -a pp di **soccorrere** ▶ sm help, aid, assistance; **soccorso stradale** breakdown service

soci'ale [so'tʃale] ag social; (di associazione) club cpd, association cpd

socia'lismo [sotʃa'lizmo] sm socialism; **socia'lista, -i, -e** ag, sm/f socialist; **socializ'zare** [sotʃalid'dzare] vi to socialize

società [sotʃe'ta] sf inv society; (sportiva) club; (Comm) company; ~ **a responsabilità limitata** type of limited liability company; **società per azioni** limited (BRIT) o incorporated (US) company

soci'evole [so'tʃevole] ag sociable

'socio ['sɔtʃo] sm (Dir, Comm) partner; (membro di associazione) member

'soda sf (Chim) soda; (bibita) soda (water)

soddisfa'cente [soddisfa'tʃɛnte] ag satisfactory

soddis'fare vt, vi ~ **a** to satisfy; (impegno) to fulfil; (debito) to pay off; (richiesta) to meet, comply with; **soddis'fatto, -a** pp di **soddisfare** ▶ ag satisfied; **soddisfatto di** happy o satisfied with; pleased with; **soddisfazi'one** sf satisfaction

'sodo, -a ag firm, hard; (uovo) hard-boiled ▶ av (picchiare, lavorare) hard; (dormire) soundly

sofà sm inv sofa

soffe'renza [soffe'rɛntsa] sf suffering

sof'ferto, -a pp di **soffrire**

soffi'are vt to blow; (notizia, segreto)

to whisper ▶ vi to blow; (*sbuffare*) to puff (and blow); **soffiarsi il naso** to blow one's nose; **~ qc/qn a qn** (*fig*) to pinch o steal sth/sb from sb; **~ via qc** to blow sth away

soffi'ata *sf* (*fam*) tip-off; **fare una ~ alla polizia** to tip off the police

'soffice ['soffitʃe] *ag* soft

'soffio *sm* (*di vento*) breath; **soffio al cuore** heart murmur

sof'fitta *sf* attic

sof'fitto *sm* ceiling

soffo'cante *ag* suffocating, stifling

soffo'care *vi* (*anche:* **soffocarsi**) to suffocate, choke ▶ *vt* to suffocate, choke; (*fig*) to stifle, suppress

sof'frire *vt* to suffer, endure; (*sopportare*) to bear, stand ▶ *vi* to suffer; to be in pain; **~ (di) qc** (*Med*) to suffer from sth

sof'fritto, -a *pp di* **soffriggere** ▶ *sm* (*Cuc*) fried mixture of herbs, bacon and onions

sofisti'cato, -a *ag* sophisticated; (*vino*) adulterated

'software ['softwɛə] *sm* **~ applicativo** applications package

sogget'tivo, -a [soddʒet'tivo] *ag* subjective

sog'getto, -a [sod'dʒetto] *ag* **~ a** (*sottomesso*) subject to; (*esposto: a variazioni, danni ecc*) subject o liable to ▶ *sm* subject

soggezi'one [soddʒet'tsjone] *sf* subjection; (*timidezza*) awe; **avere ~ di qn** to stand in awe of sb; to be ill at ease in sb's presence

soggi'orno *sm* (*invernale, marino*) stay; (*stanza*) living room

'soglia ['sɔʎʎa] *sf* doorstep; (*anche fig*) threshold

'sogliola ['sɔʎʎola] *sf* (*Zool*) sole

so'gnare [soɲ'ɲare] *vt, vi* to dream; **~ a occhi aperti** to daydream

'sogno ['soɲɲo] *sm* dream

'soia *sf* (*Bot*) soya

sol *sm* (*Mus*) G; (: *solfeggiando*) so(h)

so'laio *sm* (*soffitta*) attic

sola'mente *av* only, just

so'lare *ag* solar, sun *cpd*

'solco, -chi *sm* (*scavo, fig: ruga*) furrow; (*incavo*) rut, track; (*di disco*) groove

sol'dato *sm* soldier; **soldato semplice** private

soldi *smpl* (*denaro*) money *sg*; **non ho ~** I haven't got any money

'sole *sm* sun; (*luce*) sun(light); (*tempo assolato*) sun(shine); **prendere il ~** to sunbathe

soleggi'ato, -a [soled'dʒato] *ag* sunny

so'lenne *ag* solemn

soli'dale *ag* **essere ~ (con)** to be in agreement (with)

solidarietà *sf* solidarity

'solido, -a *ag* solid; (*forte, robusto*) sturdy, solid; (*fig: ditta*) sound, solid ▶ *sm* (*Mat*) solid

so'lista, -i, -e *ag* solo ▶ *sm/f* soloist

solita'mente *av* usually, as a rule

soli'tario, -a *ag* (*senza compagnia*) solitary, lonely; (*solo, isolato*) solitary, lone; (*deserto*) lonely ▶ *sm* (*gioiello, gioco*) solitaire

'solito, -a *ag* usual; **essere ~ fare** to be in the habit of doing; **di ~** usually; **più tardi del ~** later than usual; **come al ~** as usual

soli'tudine *sf* solitude

sol'letico *sm* tickling; **soffrire il ~** to be ticklish

solleva'mento *sm* raising; lifting; revolt; **sollevamento pesi** (*Sport*) weight-lifting

solle'vare *vt* to lift, raise; (*fig: persona: alleggerire*): **~ (da)** to relieve (of); (: *dar conforto*) to comfort, relieve; (: *questione*) to raise; (: *far insorgere*) to stir (to revolt); **sollevarsi** *vpr* to rise; (*fig: riprendersi*) to recover; (: *ribellarsi*) to rise up

solli'evo sm relief; (conforto) comfort

'solo, -a ag alone; (in senso spirituale: isolato) lonely; (unico): **un ~ libro** only one book, a single book; (con ag numerale): **veniamo noi tre soli** just o only the three of us are coming ▶ av (soltanto) only, just; **non ~ ... ma anche** not only ... but also; **fare qc da ~** to do sth (all) by oneself

sol'tanto av only

so'lubile ag (sostanza) soluble

soluzi'one [solut'tsjone] sf solution

sol'vente ag, sm solvent

so'maro sm ass, donkey

somigli'anza [somiʎ'ʎantsa] sf resemblance

somigli'are [somiʎ'ʎare] vi **~ a** to be like, resemble; (nell'aspetto fisico) to look like; **somigliarsi** vpr to be (o look) alike

'somma sf (Mat) sum; (di denaro) sum (of money)

som'mare vt to add up; (aggiungere) to add; **tutto sommato** all things considered

som'mario, -a ag (racconto, indagine) brief; (giustizia) summary ▶ sm summary

sommer'gibile [sommer'dʒibile] sm submarine

som'merso, -a pp di **sommergere**

sommità sf inv summit, top; (fig) height

som'mossa sf uprising

'sonda sf (Med, Meteor, Aer) probe; (Mineralogia) drill ▶ ag inv **pallone** m **~** weather balloon

son'daggio [son'daddʒo] sm sounding; probe; boring, drilling; (indagine) survey; **sondaggio d'opinioni** opinion poll

son'dare vt (Naut) to sound; (atmosfera, piaga) to probe; (Mineralogia) to bore, drill; (fig: opinione ecc) to survey, poll

so'netto sm sonnet

son'nambulo, -a sm/f sleepwalker

sonnel'lino sm nap

son'nifero sm sleeping drug (o pill)

'sonno sm sleep; **prendere ~** to fall asleep; **aver ~** to be sleepy

'sono vb vedi **essere**

so'noro, -a ag (ambiente) resonant; (voce) sonorous, ringing; (onde, film) sound cpd

sontu'oso, -a ag sumptuous; lavish

sop'palco, -chi sm mezzanine

soppor'tare vt (subire: perdita, spese) to bear, sustain; (soffrire: dolore) to bear, endure; (cosa: freddo) to withstand; (persona: freddo, vino) to take; (tollerare) to put up with, tolerate

Attenzione! In inglese esiste il verbo to support, che però non significa sopportare.

sop'primere vt (carica, privilegi, testimone) to do away with; (pubblicazione) to suppress; (parola, frase) to delete

'sopra prep (gen) on; (al di sopra di, più in alto di) above; over; (riguardo a) on, about ▶ av on top; (attaccato, scritto) on it; (al di sopra) above; (al piano superiore) upstairs; **donne ~ i 30 anni** women over 30 (years of age); **abito di ~** I live upstairs; **dormirci ~** (fig) to sleep on it

so'prabito sm overcoat

soprac'ciglio [soprat'tʃiʎʎo] (pl(f) **sopracciglia**) sm eyebrow

sopraf'fare vt to overcome, overwhelm

sopral'luogo, -ghi sm (di esperti) inspection; (di polizia) on-the-spot investigation

sopram'mobile sm ornament

soprannatu'rale ag supernatural

sopran'nome sm nickname

so'prano, -a sm/f (persona) soprano ▶ sm (voce) soprano

soprappensi'ero *av* lost in thought

sopras'salto *sm* **di ~** with a start; suddenly

soprasse'dere *vi* **a** to delay, put off

soprat'tutto *av* (*anzitutto*) above all; (*specialmente*) especially

sopravvalu'tare *vt* to overestimate

soprav'vento *sm* **avere/prendere il ~ su** to have/get the upper hand over

sopravvis'suto, -a *pp di* **sopravvivere**

soprav'vivere *vi* to survive; (*continuare a vivere*): **~ (in)** to live on (in); **~ a** (*incidente ecc*) to survive; (*persona*) to outlive

so'pruso *sm* abuse of power; **subire un ~** to be abused

soq'quadro *sm* **mettere a ~** to turn upside-down

sor'betto *sm* sorbet, water ice

sor'dina *sf* **in ~** softly; (*fig*) on the sly

'sordo, -a *ag* deaf; (*rumore*) muffled; (*dolore*) dull; (*odio, rancore*) veiled ▶ *sm/f* deaf person; **sordo'muto, -a** *ag* deaf-and-dumb ▶ *sm/f* deaf-mute

so'rella *sf* sister; **sorel'lastra** *sf* stepsister; (*con genitore in comune*) half-sister

sor'gente [sor'dʒɛnte] *sf* (*d'acqua*) spring; (*di fiume, Fisica, fig*) source

'sorgere ['sordʒere] *vi* to rise; (*scaturire*) to spring, rise; (*fig: difficoltà*) to arise

sorni'one, -a *ag* sly

sorpas'sare *vt* (*Aut*) to overtake; (*fig*) to surpass; (: *eccedere*) to exceed, go beyond; **~ in altezza** to be higher than; (*persona*) to be taller than

sorpren'dente *ag* surprising

sor'prendere *vt* (*cogliere: in flagrante ecc*) to catch; (*stupire*) to surprise; **sorprendersi** *vpr* **sorprendersi (di)** to be surprised (at); **sor'presa** *sf* surprise; **fare una sorpresa a qn** to give sb a surprise; **sor'preso, -a** *pp di* **sorprendere**

sor'reggere [sor'rɛddʒere] *vt* to support, hold up; (*fig*) to sustain; **sorreggersi** *vpr* (*tenersi ritto*) to stay upright

sor'ridere *vi* to smile; **sor'riso, -a** *pp di* **sorridere** ▶ *sm* smile

'sorsi *ecc vb vedi* **sorgere**

'sorso *sm* sip

'sorta *sf* sort, kind; **di ~** whatever, of any kind, at all

'sorte *sf* (*fato*) fate, destiny; (*evento fortuito*) chance; **tirare a ~** to draw lots

sor'teggio [sor'teddʒo] *sm* draw

sorvegli'ante [sorveʎ'ʎante] *sm/f* (*di carcere*) guard, warder (BRIT); (*di fabbrica ecc*) supervisor

sorvegli'anza [sorveʎ'ʎantsa] *sf* watch; supervision; (*Polizia, Mil*) surveillance

sorvegli'are [sorveʎ'ʎare] *vt* (*bambino, bagagli, prigioniero*) to watch, keep an eye on; (*malato*) to watch over; (*territorio, casa*) to watch o keep watch over; (*lavori*) to supervise

sorvo'lare *vt* (*territorio*) to fly over ▶ *vi* **~ su** (*fig*) to skim over

S.O.S. *sigla m* mayday, SOS

'sosia *sm inv* double

sos'pendere *vt* (*appendere*) to hang (up); (*interrompere, privare di una carica*) to suspend; (*rimandare*) to defer; (*appendere*) to hang

sospet'tare *vt* to suspect ▶ *vi* **~ di** to suspect; (*diffidare*) to be suspicious of

sos'petto, -a *ag* suspicious ▶ *sm* suspicion; **sospet'toso, -a** *ag* suspicious

sospi'rare *vi* to sigh ▶ *vt* to long for, yearn for; **sos'piro** *sm* sigh

'sosta *sf* (*fermata*) stop, halt; (*pausa*) pause, break; **senza ~** non-stop, without a break

sostan'tivo *sm* noun, substantive

sos'tanza [sos'tantsa] *sf* substance; **sostanze** *sfpl* (*ricchezze*) wealth *sg*, possessions; **in ~** in short, to sum up

sos'tare *vi* (*fermarsi*) to stop (for a while), stay; (*fare una pausa*) to take a break

sos'tegno [sos'teɲɲo] *sm* support

soste'nere *vt* to support; (*prendere su di sé*) to take on, bear; (*resistere*) to withstand, stand up to; (*affermare*): **~ che** to maintain that; **sostenersi** *vpr* to hold o.s. up, support o.s.; (*fig*) to keep up one's strength; **~ gli esami** to sit exams

sosten'tamento *sm* maintenance, support

sostitu'ire *vt* (*mettere al posto di*): **~ qn/qc a** to substitute sb/sth for; (*prendere il posto di: persona*) to substitute for; (: *cosa*) to take the place of

sosti'tuto, -a *sm/f* substitute

sostituzi'one [sostitut'tsjone] *sf* substitution; **in ~ di** as a substitute for, in place of

sotta'ceti [sotta'tʃeti] *smpl* pickles

sot'tana *sf* (*sottoveste*) underskirt; (*gonna*) skirt; (*Rel*) soutane, cassock

sotter'fugio [sotter'fudʒo] *sm* subterfuge

sotter'raneo, -a *ag* underground ▶ *sm* cellar

sotter'rare *vt* to bury

sot'tile *ag* thin; (*figura, caviglia*) thin, slim, slender; (*fine: polvere, capelli*) fine; (*fig: leggero*) light; (: *vista*) sharp, keen; (: *olfatto*) fine, discriminating; (: *mente*) subtle; shrewd ▶ *sm* **non andare per il ~** not to mince matters

sottin'teso, -a *pp di* **sottintendere** ▶ *sm* allusion; **parlare senza sottintesi** to speak plainly

'sotto *prep* (*gen*) under; (*più in basso di*) below ▶ *av* underneath, beneath; below; **(al piano) di ~** downstairs; **~ forma di** in the form of; **~ il monte** at the foot of the mountain; **siamo ~ Natale** it's nearly Christmas; **~ la pioggia/il sole** in the rain/sun(shine); **~ terra** underground; **chiuso ~ vuoto** vacuum-packed

sotto'fondo *sm* background; **sottofondo musicale** background music

sottoline'are *vt* to underline; (*fig*) to emphasize, stress

sottoma'rino, -a *ag* (*flora*) submarine; (*cavo, navigazione*) underwater ▶ *sm* (*Naut*) submarine

sottopas'saggio [sottopas'saddʒo] *sm* (*Aut*) underpass; (*pedonale*) subway, underpass

sotto'porre *vt* (*costringere*) to subject; (*fig: presentare*) to submit; **sottoporsi** *vpr* to submit; **sottoporsi a** (*subire*) to undergo

sottos'critto, -a *pp di* **sottoscrivere**

sotto'sopra *av* upside-down

sotto'terra *av* underground

sotto'titolo *sm* subtitle

sottovalu'tare *vt* to underestimate

sotto'veste *sf* underskirt

sotto'voce [sotto'votʃe] *av* in a low voice

sottovu'oto *av* **confezionare ~** to vacuum-pack ▶ *ag* **confezione f ~** vacuum packed

sot'trarre *vt* (*Mat*) to subtract, take away; **~ qn/qc a** (*togliere*) to remove sb/sth from; (*salvare*) to save o rescue sb/sth from; **~ qc a qn** (*rubare*) to steal sth from sb; **sottrarsi** *vpr* **sottrarsi a** (*sfuggire*) to escape; (*evitare*) to avoid; **sottrazi'one** *sf* subtraction; removal

souve'nir [suv(ə)'nir] *sm inv* souvenir

sovi'etico, -a, -ci, -che *ag* Soviet ▶ *sm/f* Soviet citizen

sovrac'carico, -a, chi, che *ag* **~ (di)** overloaded (with) ▶ *sm* excess load; **~ di lavoro** extra work

sovraffol'lato, -a *ag* overcrowded

sovrannatu'rale *ag*
= **soprannatu'rale**

so'vrano, -a *ag* sovereign; (*fig: sommo*) supreme ▶ *sm/f* sovereign, monarch

sovrap'porre *vt* to place on top of, put on top of

sovvenzi'one [sovven'tsjone] *sf* subsidy, grant

'sozzo, -a ['sottso] *ag* filthy, dirty

S.P.A. *abbr* = **società per azioni**

spac'care *vt* to split, break; (*legna*) to chop; **spaccarsi** *vpr* to split, break; **spacca'tura** *sf* split

spaccherò *ecc* [spakke'rɔ] *vb vedi* **spaccare**

spacci'are [spat'tʃare] *vt* (*vendere*) to sell (off); (*mettere in circolazione*) to circulate; (*droga*) to peddle, push; **spacciarsi** *vpr* **spacciarsi per** (*farsi credere*) to pass o.s. off as, pretend to be; **spaccia'tore, -'trice** *sm/f* (*di droga*) pusher; (*di denaro falso*) dealer; **'spaccio** *sm* (*di merce rubata, droga*): **spaccio (di)** trafficking (in); **spaccio (di)** passing (of); (*vendita*) sale; (*bottega*) shop

'spacco, -chi *sm* (*fenditura*) split, crack; (*strappo*) tear; (*di gonna*) slit

spac'cone *sm/f* boaster, braggart

'spada *sf* sword

spae'sato, -a *ag* disorientated, lost

spa'ghetti [spa'getti] *smpl* (*Cuc*) spaghetti *sg*

'Spagna ['spaɲɲa] *sf* **la ~** Spain; **spa'gnolo, -a** *ag* Spanish ▶ *sm/f* Spaniard ▶ *sm* (*Ling*) Spanish; **gli Spagnoli** the Spanish

'spago, -ghi *sm* string, twine

spai'ato, -a *ag* (*calza, guanto*) odd

spalan'care *vt* to open wide; **spalancarsi** *vpr* to open wide

spa'lare *vt* to shovel

'spalla *sf* shoulder; (*fig: Teatro*) stooge; **spalle** *sfpl* (*dorso*) back

spalli'era *sf* (*di sedia ecc*) back; (*di letto: da capo*) head(board); (: *da piedi*) foot(board); (*Ginnastica*) wall bars *pl*

spal'lina *sf* (*bretella*) strap; (*imbottitura*) shoulder pad

spal'mare *vt* to spread

'spalti *smpl* (*di stadio*) terracing

'spamming ['spammiŋ] *sm* (*in Internet*) spam

'spandere *vt* to spread; (*versare*) to pour (out)

spa'rare *vt* to fire ▶ *vi* (*far fuoco*) to fire; (*tirare*) to shoot; **spara'toria** *sf* exchange of shots

sparecchi'are [sparek'kjare] *vt* **~ (la tavola)** to clear the table

spa'reggio [spa'reddʒo] *sm* (*Sport*) play-off

'spargere ['spardʒere] *vt* (*sparpagliare*) to scatter; (*versare: vino*) to spill; (: *lacrime, sangue*) to shed; (*diffondere*) to spread; (*emanare*) to give off (*o* out); **spargersi** *vpr* to spread

spa'rire *vi* to disappear, vanish

spar'lare *vi* **~ di** to speak ill of

'sparo *sm* shot

spar'tire *vt* (*eredità, bottino*) to share out; (*avversari*) to separate

spar'tito *sm* (*Mus*) score

sparti'traffico *sm inv* (*Aut*) central reservation (*BRIT*), median (strip) (*US*)

sparvi'ero *sm* (*Zool*) sparrowhawk

spasi'mante *sm* suitor

spassio'nato, -a *ag* impartial

'spasso *sm* (*divertimento*) amusement, enjoyment; **andare a ~** to go out for a walk; **essere a ~** (*fig*) to be out of work; **mandare qn a ~** (*fig*) to give sb the sack

'spatola *sf* spatula; (*di muratore*) trowel

spa'valdo, -a *ag* arrogant, bold

spaventa'passeri *sm inv* scarecrow

spaven'tare *vt* to frighten, scare; **spaventarsi** *vpr* to be frightened, be scared; to get a fright; **spa'vento** sm fear, fright; **far spavento a qn** to give sb a fright; **spaven'toso, -a** ag frightening, terrible; (fig: fam) tremendous, fantastic

spazientirsi [spattsjen'tirsi] vpr to lose one's patience

'spazio ['spattsjo] sm space; **spazio aereo** airspace; **spazi'oso, -a** ag spacious

spazzaca'mino [spattsaka'mino] sm chimney sweep

spazza'neve [spattsa'neve] sm inv snowplough

spaz'zare [spat'tsare] vt to sweep; (foglie ecc) to sweep up; (cacciare) to sweep away; **spazza'tura** sf sweepings pl; (immondizia) rubbish; **spaz'zino** sm street sweeper

'spazzola ['spattsola] sf brush; **spazzola da capelli** hairbrush; **spazzola per abiti** clothesbrush; **spazzo'lare** vt to brush; **spazzo'lino** sm (small) brush; **spazzolino da denti** toothbrush

specchi'arsi [spek'kjarsi] vpr to look at o.s. in a mirror; (riflettersi) to be mirrored, be reflected

specchi'etto [spek'kjetto] sm (tabella) table, chart; **specchietto da borsetta** pocket mirror; **specchietto retrovisore** (Aut) rear-view mirror

'specchio ['spɛkkjo] sm mirror

speci'ale [spe'tʃale] ag special; **specia'lista, -i, -e** sm/f specialist; **specialità** sf inv speciality; (branca di studio) special field, speciality; **vorrei assaggiare una specialità del posto** I'd like to try a local speciality; **specializzazi'one** sf specialization; **special'mente** av especially

'specie ['spɛtʃe] sf inv (Biol, Bot, Zool) species inv; (tipo) kind, sort ▶ av especially, particularly; **una ~ di** a kind of; **fare ~ a qn** to surprise sb; **la ~**

umana mankind

specifi'care [spetʃifi'kare] vt to specify, state

spe'cifico, -a, -ci, -che [spe'tʃifiko] ag specific

specu'lare vi ~ **su** (Comm) to speculate in; (sfruttare) to exploit; (meditare) to speculate on; **speculazi'one** sf speculation

spe'dire vt to send

'spegnere ['spɛɲɲere] vt (fuoco, sigaretta) to put out, extinguish; (apparecchio elettrico) to turn o switch off; (gas) to turn off; (fig: suoni, passioni) to stifle; (debito) to extinguish; **spegnersi** vpr to go out; to go off; (morire) to pass away; **puoi ~ la luce?** could you switch off the light?; **non riesco a ~ il riscaldamento** I can't turn the heating off

spellarsi vpr to peel

'spendere vt to spend

'spengo ecc vb vedi **spegnere**

'spensi ecc vb vedi **spegnere**

spensie'rato, -a ag carefree

'spento, -a pp di **spegnere** ▶ ag (suono) muffled; (colore) dull; (sigaretta) out; (civiltà, vulcano) extinct

spe'ranza [spe'rantsa] sf hope

spe'rare vt to hope for ▶ vi ~ **in** to trust in; ~ **che/di fare** to hope that/to do; **lo spero, spero di sì** I hope so

sper'duto, -a ag (isolato) out-of-the-way; (persona: smarrita, a disagio) lost

sperimen'tale ag experimental

sperimen'tare vt to experiment with, test; (fig) to test, put to the test

'sperma, -i sm sperm

spe'rone sm spur

sperpe'rare vt to squander

'spesa sf (somma di denaro) expense; (costo) cost; (acquisto) purchase; (fam: acquisto del cibo quotidiano) shopping; **spese postali** postage sg; **spese di viaggio** travelling expenses

'spesso, -a ag (fitto) thick; (frequente) frequent ▶ av often; **spesse volte** frequently, often

spes'sore sm thickness

Spett. abbr vedi **spettabile**

spet'tabile (abbr: **Spett.**: in lettere) ag **~ Ditta X** Messrs X and Co.

spet'tacolo sm (rappresentazione) performance, show; (vista, scena) sight; **dare ~ di sé** to make an exhibition o a spectacle of o.s.

spet'tare vi **~ a** (decisione) to be up to; (stipendio) to be due to; **spetta a te decidere** it's up to you to decide

spetta'tore, -'trice sm/f (Cinema, Teatro) member of the audience; (di avvenimento) onlooker, witness

spettego'lare vi to gossip

spetti'nato, -a ag dishevelled

'spettro sm (fantasma) spectre; (Fisica) spectrum

'spezie ['spɛttsje] sfpl (Cuc) spices

spez'zare [spet'tsare] vt (rompere) to break; (fig: interrompere) to break up; **spezzarsi** vpr to break

spezza'tino [spettsa'tino] sm (Cuc) stew

spezzet'tare [spettset'tare] vt to break up (o chop) into small pieces

'spia sf spy; (confidente della polizia) informer; (Elettr) indicating light; warning light; (fessura) peep-hole; (fig: sintomo) sign, indication

spia'cente [spja'tʃɛnte] ag sorry; **essere ~ di qc/di fare qc** to be sorry about sth/for doing sth

spia'cevole [spja'tʃevole] ag unpleasant

spi'aggia, -ge ['spjaddʒa] sf beach; **spiaggia libera** public beach

spia'nare vt (terreno) to level, make level; (edificio) to raze to the ground; (pasta) to roll out; (rendere liscio) to smooth (out)

spi'are vt to spy on

spi'azzo ['spjattso] sm open space; (radura) clearing

'spicchio ['spikkjo] sm (di agrumi) segment; (di aglio) clove; (parte) piece, slice

spicciarsi vpr to hurry up

spiccioli smpl (small) change; **mi dispiace, non ho ~** sorry, I don't have any change

'spicco, -chi sm **di ~** outstanding; (tema) main, principal; **fare ~ to** stand out

spie'dino sm (utensile) skewer; (pietanza) kebab

spi'edo sm (Cuc) spit

spie'gare vt (far capire) to explain; (tovaglia) to unfold; (vele) to unfurl; **spiegarsi** vpr to explain o.s., make o.s. clear; **~ qc a qn** to explain sth to sb; **spiegazi'one** sf explanation

spiegherò ecc [spjege'rɔ] vb vedi **spiegare**

spie'tato, -a ag ruthless, pitiless

spiffe'rare (fam) vt to blurt out, blab

'spiffero sm draught (BRIT), draft (US)

'spiga, -ghe sf (Bot) ear

spigli'ato, -a [spiʎ'ʎato] ag self-possessed, self-confident

'spigolo sm corner; (Mat) edge

'spilla sf brooch; (da cravatta, cappello) pin; **~ di sicurezza** o **da balia** safety pin

'spillo sm pin; **spillo da balia** o **di sicurezza** safety pin

spi'lorcio, -a, -ci, -ce [spi'lortʃo] ag mean, stingy

'spina sf (Bot) thorn; (Zool) spine, prickle; (di pesce) bone; (Elettr) plug; (di botte) bunghole; **birra alla ~** draught beer; **spina dorsale** (Anat) backbone

spinaci [spi'natʃi] smpl spinach sg

spi'nello sm (Droga: gergo) joint

'spingere ['spindʒere] vt to push; (condurre: anche fig) to drive; (stimolare) **~ qn a fare** to urge o press sb to do

spi'noso, -a ag thorny, prickly

'spinsi ecc vb vedi **spingere**

'spinta sf (urto) push; (Fisica) thrust; (fig: stimolo) incentive, spur; (: appoggio) string-pulling no pl; **dare una ~ a qn** (fig) to pull strings for sb

'spinto, -a pp di **spingere**

spio'naggio [spio'naddʒo] sm espionage, spying

spion'cino [spion'tʃino] sm peephole

spi'raglio [spi'raʎʎo] sm (fessura) chink, narrow opening; (raggio di luce, fig) glimmer, gleam

spi'rale sf spiral; (contraccettivo) coil; **a ~** spiral(-shaped)

spiri'tato, -a ag possessed; (fig: persona, espressione) wild

spiri'tismo sm spiritualism

'spirito sm (Rel, Chim, disposizione d'animo, di legge ecc, fantasma) spirit; (pensieri, intelletto) mind; (arguzia) wit; (umorismo) humour, wit; **lo S~ Santo** the Holy Spirit o Ghost

spirito'saggine [spirito'saddʒine] sf witticism; (peg) wisecrack

spiri'toso, -a ag witty

spiritu'ale ag spiritual

'splendere vi to shine

'splendido, -a ag splendid; (splendente) shining; (sfarzoso) magnificent, splendid

splen'dore sm splendour; (luce intensa) brilliance, brightness

spogli'are [spoʎ'ʎare] vt (svestire) to undress; (privare, fig: depredare): **~ qn di qc** to deprive sb of sth; (togliere ornamenti: anche fig): **~ qn/qc di** to strip sb/sth of; **spogliarsi** vpr to undress, strip; **spogliarsi di** (ricchezze ecc) to deprive o.s. of, give up; (pregiudizi) to rid o.s. of; **spoglia'rello** [spoʎʎa'rɛllo] sm striptease; **spoglia'toio** sm dressing room; (di scuola ecc) cloakroom; (Sport) changing room

'spola sf (bobina di filo) cop; **fare la ~ (fra)** to go to and fro o shuttle (between)

spolve'rare vt (anche Cuc) to dust; (con spazzola) to brush; (con battipanni) to beat; (fig) to polish off ▶ vi to dust

spon'taneo, -a ag spontaneous; (persona) unaffected, natural

spor'care vt to dirty, make dirty; (fig) to sully, soil; **sporcarsi** vpr to get dirty

spor'cizia [spor'tʃittsja] sf (stato) dirtiness; (sudiciume) dirt, filth; (cosa sporca) dirt no pl, something dirty

'sporco, -a, -chi, -che ag dirty, filthy

spor'genza [spor'dʒɛntsa] sf projection

'sporgere ['spordʒere] vt to put out, stretch out ▶ vi (venire in fuori) to stick out; **sporgersi** vpr to lean out; **~ querela contro qn** (Dir) to take legal action against sb

'sporsi ecc vb vedi **sporgere**

sport sm inv sport

spor'tello sm (di treno, auto ecc) door; (di banca, ufficio) window, counter; **sportello automatico** (Banca) cash dispenser, automated telling machine

spor'tivo, -a ag (gara, giornale, centro) sports cpd; (persona) sporty; (abito) casual; (spirito, atteggiamento) sporting

'sposa sf bride; (moglie) wife

sposa'lizio [spoza'littsjo] sm wedding

spo'sare vt to marry; (fig: idea, fede) to espouse; **sposarsi** vpr to get married, marry; **sposarsi con qn** to marry sb, get married to sb; **spo'sato, -a** ag married

'sposo sm (bride)groom; (marito) husband

spos'sato, -a ag exhausted, weary

spos'tare vt to move, shift; (cambiare: orario) to change; **spostarsi** vpr to move; **può ~ la macchina, per favore?** can you move your car please?

'spranga, -ghe *sf* (*sbarra*) bar

spre'care *vt* to waste

spre'gevole [spre'dʒevole] *ag* contemptible, despicable

'spremere *vt* to squeeze

spremia'grumi *sm inv* lemon squeezer

spre'muta *sf* fresh juice; **spremuta d'arancia** fresh orange juice

sprez'zante [spret'tsante] *ag* scornful, contemptuous

sprofon'dare *vi* to sink; (*casa*) to collapse; (*suolo*) to give way, subside

spro'nare *vt* to spur (on)

sproporzio'nato, -a [sproportsjo'nato] *ag* disproportionate, out of all proportion

sproporzi'one [spropor'tsjone] *sf* disproportion

spro'posito *sm* blunder; **a ~** at the wrong time; (*rispondere, parlare*) irrelevantly

sprovve'duto, -a *ag* inexperienced, naïve

sprov'visto, -a *ag* (*mancante*): **~ di** lacking in, without; **alla sprovvista** unawares

spruz'zare [sprut'tsare] *vt* (*a nebulizzazione*) to spray; (*aspergere*) to sprinkle; (*inzaccherare*) to splash

'spugna ['spuɲɲa] *sf* (*Zool*) sponge; (*tessuto*) towelling

'spuma *sf* (*schiuma*) foam; (*bibita*) fizzy drink

spu'mante *sm* sparkling wine

spun'tare *vt* (*coltello*) to break the point of; (*capelli*) to trim ▶ *vi* (*uscire: germogli*) to sprout; (: *capelli*) to begin to grow; (: *denti*) to come through; (*apparire*) to appear (suddenly)

spun'tino *sm* snack

'spunto *sm* (*Teatro, Mus*) cue; (*fig*) starting point; **dare lo ~ a** (*fig*) to give rise to

spu'tare *vt* to spit out; (*fig*) to belch (out) ▶ *vi* to spit

'squadra *sf* (*strumento*) (set) square; (*gruppo*) team, squad; (*di operai*) gang, squad; (*Mil*) squad; (: *Aer, Naut*) squadron; (*Sport*) team; **lavoro a squadre** teamwork

squagli'arsi [skwaʎ'ʎarsi] *vpr* to melt; (*fig*) to sneak off

squa'lifica *sf* disqualification

squalifi'care *vt* to disqualify

'squallido, -a *ag* wretched, bleak

'squalo *sm* shark

'squama *sf* scale

squarcia'gola [skwartʃa'gola]: **a ~** *av* at the top of one's voice

squattri'nato, -a *ag* penniless

squili'brato, -a *ag* (*Psic*) unbalanced

squil'lante *ag* shrill, sharp

squil'lare *vi* (*campanello, telefono*) to ring (out); (*tromba*) to blare; **'squillo** *sm* ring, ringing *no pl*; blare; **ragazza f squillo** *inv* call girl

squi'sito, -a *ag* exquisite; (*cibo*) delicious; (*persona*) delightful

squit'tire *vi* (*uccello*) to squawk; (*topo*) to squeak

sradi'care *vt* to uproot; (*fig*) to eradicate

srego'lato, -a *ag* (*senza ordine: vita*) disorderly; (*smodato*) immoderate; (*dissoluto*) dissolute

S.r.l. *abbr* = **società a responsabilità limitata**

sroto'lare *vt*, **sroto'larsi** ▶ *vpr* to unroll

SS *sigla* = **strada statale**

S.S.N. *abbr* (= *Servizio Sanitario Nazionale*) ≈ NHS

sta *ecc vb vedi* **stare**

'stabile *ag* stable, steady; (*tempo: non variabile*) settled; (*Teatro: compagnia*) resident ▶ *sm* (*edificio*) building

stabili'mento sm (edificio) establishment; (fabbrica) plant, factory

stabi'lire vt to establish; (fissare: prezzi, data) to fix; (decidere) to decide; **stabilirsi** vpr (prendere dimora) to settle

stac'care vt (levare) to detach, remove; (separare: anche fig) to separate, divide; (strappare) to tear off (o out); (scandire: parole) to pronounce clearly; (Sport) to leave behind; **staccarsi** vpr (bottone ecc) to come off; (scostarsi): **staccarsi (da)** to move away (from); (fig: separarsi): **staccarsi da** to leave; **non ~ gli occhi da qn** not to take one's eyes off sb

'stadio sm (Sport) stadium; (periodo, fase) phase, stage

'staffa sf (di sella, Tecn) stirrup; **perdere le staffe** (fig) to fly off the handle

staf'fetta sf (messo) dispatch rider; (Sport) relay race

stagio'nale [stadʒo'nale] ag seasonal

stagio'nato, -a [stadʒo'nato] ag (vedi vb) seasoned; matured; (scherzoso: attempato) getting on in years

stagi'one [sta'dʒone] sf season; **alta/bassa ~** high/low season

stagista, -i, -e [sta'dʒista] sm/f trainee, intern (US)

'stagno, -a ['stappo] ag watertight; (a tenuta d'aria) airtight ▸ sm (acquitrino) pond; (Chim) tin

sta'gnola [staɲ'ɲɔla] sf tinfoil

'stalla sf (per bovini) cowshed; (per cavalli) stable

stal'lone sm stallion

stamat'tina av this morning

stam'becco, -chi sm ibex

'stampa sf (Tip, Fot: tecnica) printing; (impressione, copia fotografica) print; (insieme di quotidiani, giornalisti ecc) press

stam'pante sf (Inform) printer

stam'pare vt to print; (pubblicare) to publish; (coniare) to strike, coin; (imprimere: anche fig) to impress

stampa'tello sm block letters pl

stam'pella sf crutch

'stampo sm mould; (fig: indole) type, kind, sort

sta'nare vt to drive out

stan'care vt to tire, make tired; (annoiare) to bore; (infastidire) to annoy; **stancarsi** vpr to get tired, tire o.s. out; **stancarsi (di)** to grow weary (of), grow tired (of)

stan'chezza [stan'kettsa] sf tiredness, fatigue

'stanco, -a, -chi, -che ag tired; **~ di** tired of, fed up with

stan'ghetta [stan'getta] sf (di occhiali) leg; (Mus, di scrittura) bar

'stanno vb vedi **stare**

sta'notte av tonight; (notte passata) last night

'stante prep a sé ~ (appartamento, casa) independent, separate

stan'tio, -a, -'tii, -'tie ag stale; (burro) rancid; (fig) old

stan'tuffo sm piston

'stanza ['stantsa] sf room; (Poesia) stanza; **stanza da bagno** bathroom; **stanza da letto** bedroom

stap'pare vt to uncork; to uncap

'stare vi (restare in un luogo) to stay, remain; (abitare) to stay, live; (essere situato) to be, be situated; (anche: ~ **in piedi**) to be, stand; (essere, trovarsi) to be; (dipendere): **se stesse in me** if it were up to me, if it depended on me; (seguito da gerundio): **sta studiando** he's studying; **starci** (esserci spazio): **nel baule non ci sta più niente** there's no more room in the boot; (accettare) to accept; **ci stai?** is that okay with you?; **~ a** (attenersi a) to follow, stick to; (seguito dall'infinito): **stiamo a discutere** we're talking; (toccare *a*): **sta a te giocare** it's your turn to play; **~ per fare qc** to be about to do sth; **come sta?** how are you?; **io sto bene/male** I'm very well/not very well; **~ a qn** (*abiti ecc*) to fit sb; **queste scarpe mi stanno strette** these shoes are tight for me; **il rosso ti sta bene** red suits you

starnu'tire *vi* to sneeze; **star'nuto** *sm* sneeze

sta'sera *av* this evening, tonight

sta'tale *ag* state *cpd*; government *cpd* ▶ *sm/f* state employee, local authority employee; (*nell'amministrazione*) ≈ civil servant; **strada statale** ≈ trunk (*BRIT*) *o* main road

sta'tista, -i *sm* statesman

sta'tistica *sf* statistics *sg*

'stato, -a *pp di* **essere**; **stare** ▶ *sm* (*condizione*) state, condition; (*Pol*) state; (*Dir*) status; **essere in ~ d'accusa** (*Dir*) to be committed for trial; **~ d'assedio/d'emergenza** state of siege/emergency; **~ civile** (*Amm*) marital status; **gli Stati Uniti (d'America)** the United States (of America); **stato d'animo** mood; **stato maggiore** (*Mil*) staff

'statua *sf* statue

statuni'tense *ag* United States *cpd*, of the United States

sta'tura *sf* (*Anat*) height, stature; (*fig*) stature

sta'tuto *sm* (*Dir*) statute; constitution

sta'volta *av* this time

stazio'nario, -a [stattsjo'narjo] *ag* stationary; (*fig*) unchanged

stazi'one [stat'tsjone] *sf* station; (*balneare, termale*) resort; **stazione degli autobus** bus station; **stazione balneare** seaside resort; **stazione ferroviaria** railway (*BRIT*) *o* railroad (*US*) station; **stazione invernale** winter sports resort; **stazione di polizia** police station (*in small town*);

stazione di servizio service *o* petrol (*BRIT*) *o* filling station

'stecca, -che *sf* stick; (*di ombrello*) rib; (*di sigarette*) carton; (*Med*) splint; (*stonatura*): **fare una ~** to sing (*o* play) a wrong note

stec'cato *sm* fence

'stella *sf* star; **stella alpina** (*Bot*) edelweiss; **stella cadente** shooting star; **stella di mare** (*Zool*) starfish

'stelo *sm* stem; (*asta*) rod; **lampada a ~** standard lamp

'stemma, -i *sm* coat of arms

'stemmo *vb vedi* **stare**

stempi'ato, -a *ag* with a receding hairline

'stendere *vt* (*braccia, gambe*) to stretch (out); (*tovaglia*) to spread (out); (*bucato*) to hang out; (*mettere a giacere*) to lay (down); (*spalmare: colore*) to spread; (*mettere per iscritto*) to draw up; **stendersi** *vpr* (*coricarsi*) to stretch out, lie down; (*estendersi*) to extend, stretch

stenogra'fia *sf* shorthand

sten'tare *vi* **~ a fare** to find it hard to do, have difficulty doing

'stento *sm* (*fatica*) difficulty; **stenti** *smpl* (*privazioni*) hardship *sg*, privation *sg*; **a ~** with difficulty, barely

'sterco *sm* dung

stereo ['stereo] *ag inv* stereo ▶ *sm inv* (*impianto*) stereo

'sterile *ag* sterile; (*terra*) barren; (*fig*) futile, fruitless

steriliz'zare [sterilid'dzare] *vt* to sterilize

ster'lina *sf* pound (sterling)

stermi'nare *vt* to exterminate, wipe out

stermi'nato, -a *ag* immense; endless

ster'minio *sm* extermination, destruction

'sterno *sm* (*Anat*) breastbone

ste'roide *sm* steroid

ster'zare [ster'tsare] vt, vi (Aut) to steer; **'sterzo** sm steering; (volante) steering wheel

'stessi ecc vb vedi **stare**

'stesso, -a ag same; (rafforzativo: in persona, proprio): **il re ~** the king himself o in person ▶ pron **lo(la) ~(a)** the same (one); **i suoi stessi avversari lo ammirano** even his enemies admire him; **fa lo ~** it doesn't matter; **per me è lo ~** it's all the same to me, it doesn't matter to me; vedi **io**; **tu** ecc

ste'sura sf drafting no pl, drawing up no pl; draft

'stetti ecc vb vedi **stare**

'stia ecc vb vedi **stare**

sti'lare vt to draw up, draft

'stile sm style; **stile libero** freestyle; **sti'lista, -i** sm designer

stilo'grafica, -che sf (anche: **penna ~**) fountain pen

'stima sf esteem; valuation; assessment, estimate

sti'mare vt (persona) to esteem, hold in high regard; (terreno, casa ecc) to value; (stabilire in misura approssimativa) to estimate, assess; (ritenere): **~ che** to consider that; **stimarsi fortunato** to consider o.s. (to be) lucky

stimo'lare vt to stimulate; (incitare): **~ qn (a fare)** to spur sb on (to do)

'stimolo sm (anche fig) stimulus

'stingere ['stindʒere] vt, vi (anche: **stingersi**) to fade; **'stinto, -a** pp di **stingere**

sti'pare vt to cram, pack; **stiparsi** vpr (accalcarsi) to crowd, throng

sti'pendio sm salary

'stipite sm (di porta, finestra) jamb

stipu'lare vt (redigere) to draw up

sti'rare vt (abito) to iron; (distendere) to stretch; (strappare: muscolo) to strain; **stirarsi** vpr to stretch (o.s.)

stiti'chezza [stiti'kettsa] sf constipation

'stitico, -a, -ci, -che ag constipated

'stiva sf (di nave) hold

sti'vale sm boot

'stizza ['stittsa] sf anger, vexation

'stoffa sf material, fabric; (fig): **aver la ~ di** to have the makings of

'stomaco, -chi sm stomach; **dare di ~** to vomit, be sick

sto'nato, -a ag (persona) off-key; (strumento) off-key, out of tune

stop sm inv (Tel) stop; (Aut: cartello) stop sign; (: fanalino d'arresto) brake-light

'storcere ['stɔrtʃere] vt to twist; **storcersi** vpr to writhe, twist; **~ il naso** (fig) to turn up one's nose; **storcersi la caviglia** to twist one's ankle

stor'dire vt (intontire) to stun, daze; **stor'dito, -a** ag stunned

'storia sf (scienza, avvenimenti) history; (racconto, bugia) story; (faccenda, questione) business no pl; (pretesto) excuse, pretext; **storie** sfpl (smancerie) fuss sg; **'storico, -a, -ci, -che** ag historic(al) ▶ sm historian

stori'one sm (Zool) sturgeon

'stormo sm (di uccelli) flock

'storpio, -a ag crippled, maimed

'storsi ecc vb vedi **storcere**

'storta sf (distorsione) sprain, twist

'storto, -a pp di **storcere** ▶ ag (chiodo) twisted, bent; (gamba, quadro) crooked

sto'viglie [sto'viʎʎe] sfpl dishes pl, crockery

'strabico, -a, -ci, -che ag squint-eyed; (occhi) squint

strac'chino [strak'kino] sm type of soft cheese

stracci'are [strat'tʃare] vt to tear; **stracciarsi** vpr to tear

'straccio, -a, -ci, -ce ['strattʃo] ag **carta straccia** waste paper ▶ sm rag;

(*per pulire*) cloth, duster; **stracci** smpl (*peg: indumenti*) rags; **si è ridotto a uno ~** he's worn himself out; **non ha uno ~ di lavoro** he's not got a job of any sort

'**strada** sf road; (*di città*) street; (*cammino, via, fig*) way; **che ~ devo prendere per andare a …?** which road do I take for …?; **farsi ~** (*fig*) to do well for o.s.; **essere fuori ~** (*fig*) to be on the wrong track; **~ facendo** on the way; **strada senza uscita** dead end; **stra'dale** ag road cpd

strafalci'one [strafal'tʃone] sm blunder, howler

stra'fare vi to overdo it

strafot'tente ag **è ~** he doesn't give a damn, he couldn't care less

'**strage** ['stradʒe] sf massacre, slaughter

stralu'nato, -a ag (*occhi*) rolling; (*persona*) beside o.s., very upset

'**strambo, -a** ag strange, queer

strampa'lato, -a ag odd, eccentric

stra'nezza [stra'nettsa] sf strangeness

strango'lare vt to strangle

strani'ero, -a ag foreign ▶ sm/f foreigner

> Attenzione! In inglese esiste la parola *stranger*, che però significa *sconosciuto* oppure *estraneo*.

'**strano, -a** ag strange, odd

straordi'nario, -a ag extraordinary; (*treno ecc*) special ▶ sm (*lavoro*) overtime

strapi'ombo sm overhanging rock; **a ~** overhanging

strap'pare vt (*gen*) to tear, rip; (*pagina ecc*) to tear off, tear out; (*sradicare*) to pull up; (*togliere*): **~ qc a qn** to snatch sth from sb; (*fig*) to wrest sth from sb; **strapparsi** vpr (*lacerarsi*) to rip, tear; (*rompersi*) to break; **strapparsi un muscolo** to tear a muscle;

'**strappo** sm pull, tug; tear, rip; **fare uno strappo alla regola** to make an exception to the rule; **strappo muscolare** torn muscle

strari'pare vi to overflow

'**strascico, -chi** ['straʃʃiko] sm (*di abito*) train; (*conseguenza*) after-effect

strata'gemma, -i [strata'dʒemma] sm stratagem

strate'gia, -'gie [strate'dʒia] sf strategy; **stra'tegico, -a, -ci, -che** ag strategic

'**strato** sm layer; (*rivestimento*) coat, coating; (*Geo, fig*) stratum; (*Meteor*) stratus; **strato d'ozono** ozone layer

strat'tone sm tug, jerk; **dare uno ~ a qc** to tug o jerk sth, give sth a tug o jerk

strava'gante ag odd, eccentric

stra'volto, -a pp di **stravolgere**

'**strazio** sm torture; (*fig: cosa fatta male*): **essere uno ~** to be appalling

'**strega, -ghe** sf witch

stre'gare vt to bewitch

stre'gone sm (*mago*) wizard; (*di tribù*) witch doctor

strepi'toso, -a ag clamorous, deafening; (*fig: successo*) resounding

stres'sante ag stressful

stres'sato, -a ag under stress

stretch [stretʃ] ag inv stretch

'**stretta** sf (*di mano*) grasp; (*finanziaria*) squeeze; (*fig: dolore, turbamento*) pang; **una ~ di mano** a handshake; **essere alle strette** to have one's back to the wall; *vedi anche* **stretto**

stretta'mente av tightly; (*rigorosamente*) strictly

'**stretto, -a** pp di **stringere** ▶ ag (*corridoio, limiti*) narrow; (*gonna, scarpe, nodo, curva*) tight; (*intimo: parente, amico*) close; (*rigoroso: osservanza*) strict; (*preciso: significato*) precise, exact ▶ sm (*braccio di mare*) strait; **a denti stretti** with clenched teeth;

lo ~ **necessario** the bare minimum;
stret'toia sf bottleneck; (fig) tricky situation

stri'ato, -a ag streaked

'stridulo, -a ag shrill

stril'lare vt, vi to scream, shriek; **'strillo** sm scream, shriek

strimin'zito, -a [strimin'tsito] ag (misero) shabby; (molto magro) skinny

strimpel'lare vt (Mus) to strum

'stringa, -ghe sf lace

strin'gato, -a ag (fig) concise

'stringere ['strindʒere] vt (avvicinare due cose) to press (together), squeeze (together); (tenere stretto) to hold tight, clasp, clutch; (pugno, mascella, denti) to clench; (labbra) to compress; (avvitare) to tighten; (abito) to take in; (scarpe) to pinch, be tight for; (fig: concludere: patto) to make; (: accelerare: passo, tempo) to quicken ▶ vi (essere stretto) to be tight; (tempo: incalzare) to be pressing

'strinsi ecc vb vedi **stringere**

'striscia, -sce ['striʃʃa] sf (di carta, tessuto ecc) strip; (riga) stripe; **strisce (pedonali)** zebra crossing sg

strisci'are [striʃ'ʃare] vt (piedi) to drag; (muro, macchina) to graze ▶ vi to crawl, creep

'striscio ['striʃʃo] sm graze; (Med) smear; **colpire di ~** to graze

strisci'one [striʃ'ʃone] sm banner

strito'lare vt to grind

striz'zare [strit'tsare] vt (panni) to wring (out); **~ l'occhio** to wink

'strofa sf strophe

strofi'naccio [strofi'nattʃo] sm duster, cloth; (per piatti) dishcloth; (per pavimenti) floorcloth

strofi'nare vt to rub

stron'care vt to break off; (fig: ribellione) to suppress, put down; (: film, libro) to tear to pieces

'stronzo ['strontso] sm (sterco) turd; (fig fam!: persona) shit (!)

stroz'zare [strot'tsare] vt (soffocare) to choke, strangle

struccarsi vpr to remove one's make-up

strumen'tale ag (Mus) instrumental

strumentaliz'zare [strumentalid'dzare] vt to exploit, use to one's own ends

stru'mento sm (arnese, fig) instrument, tool; (Mus) instrument; **~ a corda** o **ad arco/a fiato** stringed/wind instrument

'strutto sm lard

strut'tura sf structure

'struzzo ['struttso] sm ostrich

stuc'care vt (muro) to plaster; (vetro) to putty; (decorare con stucchi) to stucco

'stucco, -chi sm plaster; (da vetri) putty; (ornamentale) stucco; **rimanere di ~** (fig) to be dumbfounded

stu'dente, -'essa sm/f student; (scolaro) pupil, schoolboy/girl

studi'are vt to study

'studio sm studying; (ricerca, saggio, stanza) study; (di professionista) office; (di artista, Cinema, TV, Radio) studio; **studi** smpl (Ins) studies; **studio medico** doctor's surgery (BRIT) o office (US)

studi'oso, -a ag studious, hard-working ▶ sm/f scholar

'stufa sf stove; **stufa elettrica** electric fire o heater

stu'fare vt (Cuc) to stew; (fig: fam) to bore; **stufarsi** vpr (fam): **stufarsi (di)** (fig) to get fed up (with); **'stufo, -a** (fam) ag **essere stufo di** to be fed up with, be sick and tired of

stu'oia sf mat

stupefa'cente [stupefa'tʃɛnte] ag stunning, astounding ▶ sm drug, narcotic

stupe'fatto, -a pp di **stupefare**

stu'pendo, -a *ag* marvellous, wonderful

stupi'daggine [stupi'daddʒine] *sf* stupid thing (to do o say)

stupidità *sf* stupidity

'stupido, -a *ag* stupid

stu'pire *vt* to amaze, stun ▶ *vi* **stupirsi**; **~ (di)** to be amazed (at), be stunned (by)

stu'pore *sm* amazement, astonishment

stu'prare *vt* to rape

'stupro *sm* rape

stu'rare *vt* (*lavandino*) to clear

stuzzica'denti [stuttsika'dɛnti] *sm* toothpick

stuzzi'care [stuttsi'kare] *vt* (*ferita ecc*) to poke (at), prod (at); (*fig*) to tease; (: *appetito*) to whet; (: *curiosità*) to stimulate; **~ i denti** to pick one's teeth

⊙ **su**

(*su +il* = **sul**, *su +lo* = **sullo**, *su +l'* = **sull'**, *su +la* = **sulla**, *su +i* = **sui**, *su +gli* = **sugli**, *su +le* = **sulle**) *prep*

1 (*gen*) on; (*moto*) on(to); (*in cima a*) on (top of); **mettilo sul tavolo** put it on the table; **un paesino sul mare** a village by the sea

2 (*argomento*) about, on; **un libro su Cesare** a book on o about Caesar

3 (*circa*) about; **costerà sui 3 milioni** it will cost about 3 million; **una ragazza sui 17 anni** a girl of about 17 (years of age)

4: **su misura** made to measure; **su richiesta** on request; **3 casi su dieci** 3 cases out of 10

▶ *av*

1 (*in alto, verso l'alto*) up; **vieni su** come on up; **guarda su** look up; **su le mani!** hands up!; **in su** (*verso l'alto*) up(wards); (*in poi*) onwards; **dai 20 anni in su** from the age of 20 onwards

2 (*addosso*) on; **cos'hai su?** what have you got on?

▶ *escl* come on!; **su coraggio!** come on, cheer up!

su'bacqueo, -a *ag* underwater ▶ *sm* skin-diver

sub'buglio [sub'buʎʎo] *sm* confusion, turmoil

'subdolo, -a *ag* underhand, sneaky

suben'trare *vi* **~ a qn in qc** to take over sth from sb

su'bire *vt* to suffer, endure

'subito *av* immediately, at once, straight away

subodo'rare *vt* (*insidia ecc*) to smell, suspect

subordi'nato, -a *ag* subordinate; (*dipendente*): **~ a** dependent on, subject to

suc'cedere [sut'tʃɛdere] *vi* (*prendere il posto di qn*): **~ a** to succeed; (*venire dopo*): **~ a** to follow; (*accadere*) to happen; **cos'è successo?** what happened?; **succes'sivo, -a** *ag* successive; **suc'cesso, -a** *pp di* **succedere** ▶ *sm* (*esito*) outcome; (*buona riuscita*) success; **di successo** (*libro, personaggio*) successful

succhi'are [suk'kjare] *vt* to suck (up); **succhi'otto** *sm* (*per bambino*) dummy

succhi'otto [suk'kjotto] *sm* dummy (BRIT), pacifier (US), comforter (US)

suc'cinto, -a [sut'tʃinto] *ag* (*discorso*) succinct; (*abito*) brief

'succo, -chi *sm* juice; (*fig*) essence, gist; **succo di frutta/pomodoro** fruit/tomato juice

succur'sale *sf* branch (office)

sud *sm* south ▶ *ag inv* south; (*lato*) south, southern

Su'dafrica *sm* **il ~** South Africa; **sudafri'cano, -a** *ag, sm/f* South African

Suda'merica *sm* **il ~** South America

su'dare *vi* to perspire, sweat; **~ freddo** to come out in a cold sweat

su'dato, -a *ag* (*persona, mani*) sweaty; (*fig: denaro*) hard-earned ▶ *sf* (*anche* *fig*) sweat; **una vittoria sudata** a hard-won victory; **ho fatto una bella sudata per finirlo in tempo** it was a real sweat to get it finished in time

suddi'videre *vt* to subdivide

su'dest *sm* south-east

'sudicio, -a, -ci, -ce ['suditʃo] *ag* dirty, filthy

su'dore *sm* perspiration, sweat

su'dovest *sm* south-west

suffici'ente [suffi'tʃɛnte] *ag* enough, sufficient; (*borioso*) self-important; (*Ins*) satisfactory; **suffici'enza** *sf* self-importance; pass mark; **a sufficienza** enough; **ne ho avuto a sufficienza!** I've had enough of this!

suf'fisso *sm* (*Ling*) suffix

suggeri'mento [suddʒeri'mento] *sm* suggestion; (*consiglio*) piece of advice, advice *no pl*

sugge'rire [suddʒe'rire] *vt* (*risposta*) to tell; (*consigliare*) to advise; (*proporre*) to suggest; (*Teatro*) to prompt

suggestio'nare [suddʒestjo'nare] *vt* to influence

sugges'tivo, -a [suddʒes'tivo] *ag* (*paesaggio*) evocative; (*teoria*) interesting, attractive

'sughero ['sugero] *sm* cork

'sugo, -ghi *sm* (*succo*) juice; (*di carne*) gravy; (*condimento*) sauce; (*fig*) gist, essence

sui'cida, -i, -e [sui'tʃida] *ag* suicidal ▸ *sm/f* suicide

suici'darsi [suitʃi'darsi] *vpr* to commit suicide

sui'cidio [sui'tʃidjo] *sm* suicide

su'ino, -a *ag* **carne suina** pork ▸ *sm* pig

sul'tano, -a *sm/f* sultan/sultana

'suo (f'**sua**, *pl*'**sue, su'oi**) *det* **il ~, la sua** *ecc* (*di lui*) his; (*di lei*) her; (*di esso*) its; (*con valore indefinito*) one's, his/her; (*anche*: **S~**: *forma di cortesia*) your ▸ *pron* **il ~, la sua** *ecc* his; hers; yours; **i ~ i** his

(*o her o* one's *o* your) family

su'ocero, -a ['swɔtʃero] *sm/f* father/mother-in-law

su'ola *sf* (*di scarpa*) sole

su'olo *sm* (*terreno*) ground; (*terra*) soil

suo'nare *vt* (*Mus*) to play; (*campana*) to ring; (*ore*) to strike; (*clacson, allarme*) to sound ▸ *vi* to play; (*telefono, campana*) to ring; (*ore*) to strike; (*clacson, fig: parole*) to sound

suone'ria *sf* alarm

su'ono *sm* sound

su'ora *sf* (*Rel*) sister

'super *sf* (*anche*: **benzina ~**) ≈ four-star (petrol) (*BRIT*), premium (*US*)

supe'rare *vt* (*oltrepassare: limite*) to exceed, surpass; (*percorrere*) to cover; (*attraversare: fiume*) to cross; (*sorpassare: veicolo*) to overtake; (*fig: essere più bravo di*) to surpass, outdo; (: *difficoltà*) to overcome; (: *esame*) to get through; **~ qn in altezza/peso** to be taller/heavier than sb; **ha superato la cinquantina** he's over fifty (years of age)

su'perbia *sf* pride; **su'perbo, -a** *ag* proud; (*fig*) magnificent, superb

superfici'ale [superfi'tʃale] *ag* superficial

super'ficie, -ci [super'fitʃe] *sf* surface

su'perfluo, -a *ag* superfluous

superi'ore *ag* (*piano, arto, classi*) upper; (*più elevato: temperatura, livello*): **~ (a)** higher (than); (*migliore*): **~ (a)** superior (to)

superla'tivo, -a *ag, sm* superlative

supermer'cato *sm* supermarket

su'perstite *ag* surviving ▸ *sm/f* survivor

superstizi'one [superstit'tsjone] *sf* superstition; **superstizi'oso, -a** *ag* superstitious

super'strada *sf* ≈ (toll-free) motorway

su'pino, -a *ag* supine

supplemen'tare ag extra; (treno) relief cpd; (entrate) additional

supple'mento sm supplement

sup'plente sm/f temporary member of staff, supply (o substitute) teacher

'supplica, -che sf (preghiera) plea; (domanda scritta) petition, request

suppli'care vt to implore, beseech

sup'plizio [sup'plittsjo] sm torture

sup'pongo, sup'poni ecc vb vedi **supporre**

sup'porre vt to suppose

sup'porto sm (sostegno) support

sup'posta sf (Med) suppository

su'premo, -a ag supreme

surge'lare [surdʒe'lare] vt to (deep-)freeze

surge'lato, -a [surdʒe'lato] ag (deep-)frozen ▸ smpl **i surgelati** frozen food sg

sur'plus sm inv (Econ) surplus

surriscal'dare vt to overheat

suscet'tibile [suʃʃet'tibile] ag (sensibile) touchy, sensitive

susci'tare [suʃʃi'tare] vt to provoke, arouse

su'sina sf plum

susseguirsi vpr to follow one another

sus'sidio sm subsidy; **sussidi didattici** teaching aids

sussul'tare vi to shudder

sussur'rare vt, vi to whisper, murmur; **sus'surro** sm whisper, murmur

svagarsi vpr to amuse o.s.; to enjoy o.s.

'svago, -ghi sm (riposo) relaxation; (ricreazione) amusement; (passatempo) pastime

svaligi'are [zvali'dʒare] vt to rob, burgle (BRIT), burglarize (US)

svalutarsi vpr (Econ) to be devalued

svalutazi'one sf devaluation

sva'nire vi to disappear, vanish

svantaggi'ato, -a [zvantad'dʒato] ag at a disadvantage

svan'taggio [zvan'taddʒo] sm disadvantage; (inconveniente) drawback, disadvantage

svari'ato, -a ag varied; various

'svastica sf swastika

sve'dese ag Swedish ▸ sm/f Swede ▸ sm (Ling) Swedish

'sveglia ['zveʎʎa] sf waking up; (orologio) alarm (clock); **sveglia telefonica** alarm call

svegli'are [zveʎ'ʎare] vt to wake up; (fig) to awaken, arouse; **svegliarsi** vpr to wake up; (fig) to be revived, reawaken; **vorrei essere svegliato alle 7, per favore** could I have an alarm call at 7 am, please?

'sveglio, -a ['zveʎʎo] ag awake; (fig) quick-witted

sve'lare vt to reveal

'svelto, -a ag (passo) quick; (mente) quick, alert; **alla svelta** quickly

'svendere vt to sell off, clear

'svendita sf (Comm) (clearance) sale

'svengo ecc vb vedi **svenire**

sveni'mento sm fainting fit, faint

sve'nire vi to faint

sven'tare vt to foil, thwart

sven'tato, -a ag (distratto) scatterbrained; (imprudente) rash

svento'lare vt, vi to wave, flutter

sven'tura sf misfortune

sverrò ecc vb vedi **svenire**

sves'tire vt to undress; **svestirsi** vpr to get undressed

'Svezia ['zvɛttsja] sf **la ~** Sweden

svi'are vt to divert; (fig) to lead astray

svi'gnarsela [zviɲ'ɲarsela] vpr to slip away, sneak off

svilup'pare vt to develop; **svilupparsi** vpr to develop; **può ~ questo rullino?** can you develop this film?

svi'luppo sm development

'svincolo sm (stradale) motorway (BRIT) o expressway (US) intersection

'svista sf oversight

svi'tare vt to unscrew

'Svizzera ['zvittsera] sf la ~ Switzerland

'svizzero, -a ['zvittsero] ag, sm/f Swiss

svogli'ato, -a [zvoʎ'ʎato] ag listless; (pigro) lazy

'svolgere ['zvɔldʒere] vt to unwind; (srotolare) to unroll; (fig: argomento) to develop; (: piano, programma) to carry out; **svolgersi** vpr to unwind; to unroll; (fig: aver luogo) to take place; (: procedere) to go on

'svolsi ecc vb vedi **svolgere**

'svolta sf (atto) turning no pl; (curva) turn, bend; (fig) turning-point

svol'tare vi to turn

svuo'tare vt to empty (out)

t

T, t [ti] sf o m inv (lettera) T, t; **T come Taranto** ≈ T for Tommy

t abbr = **tonnellata**

tabacche'ria [tabakke'ria] sf tobacconist's (shop)

- **tabaccheria**
- **Tabaccherie** sell cigarettes and
- tobacco and can easily be identified
- by their sign, a large white "T" on
- a black background. You can buy
- postage stamps and bus tickets at
- a **tabaccheria** and some also sell
- newspapers.

ta'bacco, -chi sm tobacco

ta'bella sf (tavola) table; (elenco) list

tabel'lone sm (pubblicitario) billboard; (con orario) timetable board

TAC sigla f (Med: = Tomografia Assiale Computerizzata) CAT

tac'chino [tak'kino] sm turkey

'tacco, -chi sm heel; **tacchi a spillo** stiletto heels

taccu'ino sm notebook

ta'cere [ta'tʃere] vi to be silent o quiet; (smettere di parlare) to fall silent ▶ vt to keep to oneself, say nothing about; **far ~ qn** to make sb be quiet; (fig) to silence sb

ta'chimetro [ta'kimetro] sm speedometer

'tacqui ecc vb vedi **tacere**

ta'fano sm horsefly

'taglia ['taʎʎa] sf (statura) height; (misura) size; (riscatto) ransom; (ricompensa) reward; **taglia forte** (di abito) large size

taglia'carte [taʎʎa'karte] sm inv paperknife

tagli'ando [taʎ'ʎando] sm coupon

tagli'are [taʎ'ʎare] vt to cut; (recidere, interrompere) to cut off; (intersecare) to cut across, intersect; (carne) to carve; (vini) to blend ▶ vi to cut; (prendere una scorciatoia) to take a short-cut; **tagliarsi** vpr to cut o.s.; **mi sono tagliato** I've cut myself; **~ corto** (fig) to cut short; **~ la corda** (fig) to sneak off; **~ i ponti (con)** (fig) to break off relations (with); **~ la strada a qn** to cut across sb; **mi sono tagliato** I've cut myself

taglia'telle [taʎʎa'tɛlle] sfpl tagliatelle pl

taglia'unghie [taʎʎa'ungje] sm inv nail clippers pl

tagli'ente [taʎˈʎɛnte] *ag* sharp

'taglio [ˈtaʎʎo] *sm* cutting *no pl*; cut; (*parte tagliente*) cutting edge; (*di abito*) cut, style; (*di stoffa: lunghezza*) length; (*di vini*) blending; **di ~** on edge, edgeways; **banconote di piccolo/grosso ~** notes of small/large denomination; **taglio cesareo** Caesarean section

tailan'dese *ag, sm/f, sm* Thai

Tai'landia *sf* **la ~** Thailand

'talco *sm* talcum powder

O **'tale**
det

1 (*simile, così grande*) such; **un(a) tale … ** such (a) …; **non accetto tali discorsi** I won't allow such talk; **è di una tale arroganza** he is so arrogant; **fa una tale confusione!** he makes such a mess!

2 (*persona o cosa indeterminata*) such-and-such; **il giorno tale all'ora tale** on such-and-such a day at such-and-such a time; **la tal persona** that person; **ha telefonato una tale Giovanna** somebody called Giovanna phoned

3 (*nelle similitudini*): **tale … tale** like … like; **tale padre tale figlio** like father, like son; **hai il vestito tale quale il mio** your dress is just *o* exactly like mine

▶*pron* (*indefinito: persona*): **un(a) tale** someone; **quel (*o* quella) tale** that person, that man (*o* woman); **il tal dei tali** what's-his-name

tale'bano *sm* Taliban

ta'lento *sm* talent

talis'mano *sm* talisman

tallon'cino [tallonˈtʃino] *sm* counterfoil

tal'lone *sm* heel

tal'mente *av* so

'talpa *sf* (*Zool*) mole

tal'volta *av* sometimes, at times

tambu'rello *sm* tambourine

tam'buro *sm* drum

Ta'migi [taˈmidʒi] *sm* **il ~** the Thames

tampo'nare *vt* (*otturare*) to plug; (*urtare: macchina*) to crash *o* ram into

tam'pone *sm* (*Med*) wad, pad; (*per timbri*) ink-pad; (*respingente*) buffer; **tampone assorbente** tampon

'tana *sf* lair, den

'tanga *sm inv* G-string

tan'gente [tanˈdʒɛnte] *ag* (*Mat*): **~ a** tangential to ▶ *sf* tangent; (*quota*) share

tangenzi'ale [tandʒenˈtsjale] *sf* (*Aut*) bypass

'tanica *sf* (*contenitore*) jerry can

O **'tanto, -a**
det

1 (*molto: quantità*) a lot of, much; (*: numero*) a lot of, many; (*così tanto: quantità*) so much, such a lot of; (*: numero*) so many, such a lot of; **tante volte** so many times, so often; **tanti auguri!** all the best!; **tante grazie** many thanks; **tanto tempo** so long, such a long time; **ogni tanti chilometri** every so many kilometres

2: **tanto … quanto** (*quantità*) as much … as; (*numero*) as many … as; **ho tanta pazienza quanta ne hai tu** I have as much patience as you have *o* as you; **ha tanti amici quanti nemici** he has as many friends as he has enemies

3 (*rafforzativo*) such; **ho aspettato per tanto tempo** I waited so long *o* for such a long time

▶*pron*

1 (*molto*) much, a lot; (*così tanto*) so much, such a lot; **tanti, e** many, a lot; so many, such a lot; **credevo ce ne fosse tanto** I thought there was (such) a lot, I thought there was plenty

2: **tanto quanto** (*denaro*) as much as; (*cioccolatini*) as many as; **ne ho tanto quanto basta** I have as much as I need; **due volte tanto** twice as much

3 (*indeterminato*) so much; **tanto per**

l'affitto, tanto per il gas so much for the rent, so much for the gas; **costa un tanto al metro** it costs so much per metre; **di tanto in tanto, ogni tanto** every so often; **tanto vale che ...** I (o we ecc) may as well ...; **tanto meglio!** so much the better!; **tanto peggio per lui!** so much the worse for him!

▶av

1 (molto) very; **vengo tanto volentieri** I'd be very glad to come; **non ci vuole tanto a capirlo** it doesn't take much to understand it

2 (così tanto: con ag, av) so; (: con vb) so much, such a lot; **è tanto bella!** she's so beautiful!; **non urlare tanto** don't shout so much; **sto tanto meglio adesso** I'm so much better now; **tanto ... che** so ... (that); **tanto ... da** so ... as

3 : **tanto ... quanto** as ... as; **conosco tanto Carlo quanto suo padre** I know both Carlo and his father; **non è poi tanto complicato quanto sembri** it's not as difficult as it seems; **tanto più insisti, tanto più non mollerà** the more you insist, the more stubborn he'll be; **quanto più ... tanto meno** the more ... the less

4 (solamente) just; **tanto per cambiare/ scherzare** just for a change/a joke; **una volta tanto** for once

5 (a lungo) (for) long

▶cong after all

'tappa sf (luogo di sosta, fermata) stop, halt; (parte di un percorso) stage, leg; (Sport) lap; **a tappe** in stages

tap'pare vt to plug, stop up; (bottiglia) to cork; **tapparsi** vpr **tapparsi in casa** to shut o.s. up at home; **tapparsi la bocca** to shut up; **tapparsi le orecchie** to turn a deaf ear

tappa'rella sf rolling shutter

tappe'tino sm (per auto) car mat; **tappetino antiscivolo** (da bagno) non-slip mat

tap'peto sm carpet; (anche: **tappetino**) rug; (Sport): **andare al ~** to go down for the count; **mettere sul ~** (fig) to bring up for discussion

tappez'zare [tappet'tsare] vt (con carta) to paper; (rivestire): **~ qc (di)** to cover sth (with); **tappezze'ria** sf (tessuto) tapestry; (carta da parati) wallpaper; (arte) upholstery; **far da tappezzeria** (fig) to be a wallflower

'tappo sm stopper; (in sughero) cork

tar'dare vi to be late ▶vt to delay; **~ a fare** to delay doing

'tardi av late; **più ~** later (on); **al più ~** at the latest; **sul ~** (verso sera) late in the day; **far ~** to be late; (restare alzato) to stay up late; **è troppo ~** it's too late

'targa, -ghe sf plate; (Aut) number (BRIT) o license (US) plate; **tar'ghetta** sf (su bagaglio) name tag; (su porta) nameplate

ta'riffa sf (gen) rate, tariff; (di trasporti) fare; (elenco) price list; tariff

'tarlo sm woodworm

'tarma sf moth

tarocchi smpl (gioco) tarot sg

tarta'ruga, -ghe sf tortoise; (di mare) turtle; (materiale) tortoiseshell

tar'tina sf canapé

tar'tufo sm (Bot) truffle

'tasca, -sche sf pocket; **tas'cabile** ag (libro) pocket cpd

'tassa sf (imposta) tax; (doganale) duty; (per iscrizione: a scuola ecc) fee; **tassa di circolazione** road tax; **tassa di soggiorno** tourist tax

tas'sare vt to tax; to levy a duty on

tas'sello sm plug; wedge

tassì sm inv = **taxi**; **tas'sista, -i, -e** sm/f taxi driver

'tasso sm (di natalità, d'interesse ecc) rate; (Bot) yew; (Zool) badger; **tasso di cambio/d'interesse** rate of exchange/interest

tas'tare vt to feel; **~ il terreno** (fig) to see how the land lies

tasti'era sf keyboard

'tasto sm key; (tatto) touch, feel

tas'toni av **procedere (a) ~** to grope one's way forward

'tatto sm (senso) touch; (fig) tact; **duro al ~** hard to the touch; **aver ~** to be tactful, have tact

tatu'aggio [tatu'addʒo] sm tattooing; (disegno) tattoo

tatu'are vt to tattoo

'tavola sf table; (asse) plank, board; (lastra) tablet; (quadro) panel (painting); (illustrazione) plate; **tavola calda** snack bar; **tavola rotonda** (fig) round table; **tavola a vela** windsurfer

tavo'letta sf tablet, bar; **a ~** (Aut) flat out

tavo'lino sm small table; (scrivania) desk

'tavolo sm table; **un ~ per 4 per favore** a table for 4, please

'taxi sm inv taxi; **può chiamarmi un ~ per favore?** can you call me a taxi, please?

'tazza ['tattsa] sf cup; **una ~ di caffè/tè** a cup of coffee/tea; **tazza da tè/caffè** tea/coffee cup

TBC abbr f (= tubercolosi) TB

te pron (soggetto: in forme comparative, oggetto) you

tè sm inv tea; (trattenimento) tea party

tea'trale ag theatrical

te'atro sm theatre

techno ['tɛkno] ag inv (musica) techno

'tecnica, -che sf technique; (tecnologia) technology

'tecnico, -a, -ci, -che ag technical ▶ sm/f technician

tecnolo'gia [teknolo'dʒia] sf technology

te'desco, -a, -schi, -sche ag, sm/f, sm German

te'game sm (Cuc) pan

'tegola sf tile

tei'era sf teapot

tel. abbr (= telefono) tel.

'tela sf (tessuto) cloth; (per vele, quadri) canvas; (dipinto) canvas, painting; **di ~** (calzoni) (heavy) cotton cpd; (scarpe, borsa) canvas cpd; **tela cerata** oilcloth

te'laio sm (apparecchio) loom; (struttura) frame

tele'camera sf television camera

teleco'mando sm remote control

tele'cronaca sf television report

telefo'nare vi to telephone, ring; to make a phone call ▶ vt to telephone; **~ a** to phone up, ring up, call up

telefo'nata sf (telephone) call; **~ a carico del destinatario** reverse-charge (BRIT) o collect (US) call

tele'fonico, -a, -ci, -che ag (tele)phone cpd

telefon'ino sm mobile phone

te'lefono sm telephone; **telefono a gettoni** ≈ pay phone

telegior'nale [teledʒor'nale] sm television news (programme)

tele'gramma, -i sm telegram

telela'voro sm teleworking

teleno'vela sf soap opera

Tele'pass® sm inv automatic payment card for use on Italian motorways

telepa'tia sf telepathy

teles'copio sm telescope

teleselezi'one [teleselet'tsjone] sf direct dialling

telespetta'tore, -'trice sm/f (television) viewer

tele'vendita sf teleshopping

televisi'one sf television

televi'sore sm television set

'tema, -i sm theme; (Ins) essay

te'mere vt to fear, be afraid of; (essere sensibile a: freddo, calore) to be sensitive to ▶ vi to be afraid; (essere *preoccupato)*: ~ **per** to worry about, fear for; ~ **di/che** to be afraid of/that

temperama'tite *sm inv* pencil sharpener

tempera'mento *sm* temperament

tempera'tura *sf* temperature

tempe'rino *sm* penknife

tem'pesta *sf* storm; **tempesta di sabbia/neve** sand/snowstorm

'**tempia** *sf (Anat)* temple

'**tempio** *sm (edificio)* temple

'**tempo** *sm (Meteor)* weather; *(cronologico)* time; *(epoca)* time, times *pl*; *(di film, gioco: parte)* part; *(Mus)* time; *(: battuta)* beat; *(Ling)* tense; **che ~ fa?** what's the weather like?; **un ~** once; **~ fa** some time ago; **al ~ stesso** *o* **a un ~** at the same time; **per ~** early; **ha fatto il suo ~** it has had its day; **primo/secondo ~** *(Teatro)* first/second part; *(Sport)* first/second half; **in ~ utile** in due time *o* course; **a ~ pieno** full-time; **tempo libero** free time

tempo'rale *ag* temporal ▶ *sm (Meteor)* (thunder)storm

tempo'raneo, -a *ag* temporary

te'nace [te'natʃe] *ag* strong, tough; *(fig)* tenacious

te'naglie [te'naʎʎe] *sfpl* pincers *pl*

'**tenda** *sf (riparo)* awning; *(di finestra)* curtain; *(per campeggio ecc)* tent

ten'denza [ten'dɛntsa] *sf* tendency; *(orientamento)* trend; **avere ~ a** *o* **per qc** to have a bent for sth

'**tendere** *vt (allungare al massimo)* to stretch, draw tight; *(porgere: mano)* to hold out; *(fig: trappola)* to lay, set ▶ *vi* **~ a qc/a fare** to tend towards sth/to do; **~ l'orecchio** to prick up one's ears; **il tempo tende al caldo** the weather is getting hot; **un blu che tende al verde** a greenish blue

'**tendine** *sm* tendon, sinew

ten'done *sm (da circo)* tent

'**tenebre** *sfpl* darkness *sg*

te'nente *sm* lieutenant

te'nere *vt* to hold; *(conservare, mantenere)* to keep; *(ritenere, considerare)* to consider; *(spazio: occupare)* to take up, occupy; *(seguire: strada)* to keep to ▶ *vi* to hold; *(colori)* to be fast; *(dare importanza)*: **~ a** to care about; **~ a fare** to want to do, be keen to do; **tenersi** *vpr (stare in una determinata posizione)* to stand; *(stimarsi)* to consider o.s.; *(aggrapparsi)*: **tenersi a** to hold on to; *(attenersi)*: **tenersi a** to stick to; **~ una conferenza** to give a lecture; **~ conto di qc** to take sth into consideration; **~ presente qc** to bear sth in mind

'**tenero, -a** *ag* tender; *(pietra, cera, colore)* soft; *(fig)* tender, loving

'**tengo** *ecc vb vedi* **tenere**

'**tenni** *ecc vb vedi* **tenere**

'**tennis** *sm* tennis

ten'nista, -i, e *sm/f* tennis player

te'nore *sm (tono)* tone; *(Mus)* tenor; **tenore di vita** *(livello)* standard of living

tensi'one *sf* tension

ten'tare *vt (indurre)* to tempt; *(provare)*: **~ qc/di fare** to attempt *o* try sth/to do; **tenta'tivo** *sm* attempt; **tentazi'one** *sf* temptation

tenten'nare *vi* to shake, be unsteady; *(fig)* to hesitate, waver

ten'toni *av* **andare a ~** *(anche fig)* to grope one's way

'**tenue** *ag (sottile)* fine; *(colore)* soft; *(fig)* slender, slight

te'nuta *sf (capacità)* capacity; *(divisa)* uniform; *(abito)* dress; *(Agr)* estate; **a ~ d'aria** airtight; **tenuta di strada** roadholding power

teolo'gia [teolo'dʒia] *sf* theology

teo'ria *sf* theory

te'pore *sm* warmth

tep'pista, -i *sm* hooligan

tera'pia *sf* therapy; **terapia intensiva** intensive care

tergicris'tallo [terdʒikris'tallo] *sm* windscreen (*BRIT*) *o* windshield (*US*) wiper

tergiver'sare [terdʒiver'sare] *vi* to shilly-shally

ter'male *ag* thermal; **stazione** *sf* ~ spa

'terme *sfpl* thermal baths

termi'nale *ag*, *sm* terminal

termi'nare *vt* to end; (*lavoro*) to finish ▶ *vi* to end

'termine *sm* term; (*fine, estremità*) end; (*di territorio*) boundary, limit; **contratto a** ~ (*Comm*) forward contract; **a breve/lungo** ~ short-/long-term; **parlare senza mezzi termini** to talk frankly, not to mince one's words

ter'mometro *sm* thermometer

'termos *sm inv* = **thermos**®

termosi'fone *sm* radiator

ter'mostato *sm* thermostat

'terra *sf* (*gen, Elettr*) earth; (*sostanza*) soil, earth; (*opposto al mare*) land *no pl*; (*regione, paese*) land; (*argilla*) clay; **terre** *sfpl* (*possedimento*) lands, land *sg*; **a** *o* **per** ~ (*stato*) on the ground (*o* floor); (*moto*) to the ground, down; **mettere a** ~ (*Elettr*) to earth

terra'cotta *sf* terracotta; **vasellame** *sm* **di** ~ earthenware

terra'ferma *sf* dry land, terra firma; (*continente*) mainland

ter'razza [ter'rattsa] *sf* terrace

ter'razzo [ter'rattso] *sm* = **terrazza**

terre'moto *sm* earthquake

ter'reno, -a *ag* (*vita, beni*) earthly ▶ *sm* (*suolo, fig*) ground; (*Comm*) land *no pl*, plot (*of land*); site; (*Sport, Mil*) field

ter'restre *ag* (*superficie*) of the earth, earth's; (*di terra: battaglia, animale*) land *cpd*; (*Rel*) earthly, worldly

ter'ribile *ag* terrible, dreadful

terrifi'cante *ag* terrifying

ter'rina *sf* tureen

territori'ale *ag* territorial

terri'torio *sm* territory

ter'rore *sm* terror; **terro'rismo** *sm* terrorism; **terro'rista, -i, -e** *sm/f* terrorist

terroriz'zare [terrorid'dzare] *vt* to terrorize

terza ['tertsa] *sf* (*Scol: elementare*) ≈ third year at primary school; (: *media*) ≈ second year at secondary school; (: *superiore*) ≈ fifth year at secondary school; (*Aut*) third gear

ter'zino [ter'tsino] *sm* (*Calcio*) fullback, back

'terzo, -a ['tertso] *ag* third ▶ *sm* (*frazione*) third; (*Dir*) third party; **terza pagina** (*Stampa*) Arts page; **terzi** *smpl* (*altri*) others, other people

'teschio ['teskjo] *sm* skull

'tesi¹ *sf* thesis; **tesi di laurea** degree thesis

'tesi *ecc² vb vedi* **tendere**

'teso, -a *pp di* **tendere** ▶ *ag* (*tirato*) taut, tight; (*fig*) tense

te'soro *sm* treasure; **il Ministero del T** ~ the Treasury

'tessera *sf* (*documento*) card

tes'suto *sm* fabric, material; (*Biol*) tissue

test ['tɛst] *sm inv* test

'testa *sf* head; (*di cose: estremità, parte anteriore*) head, front; **di** ~ (*vettura ecc*) front; **tenere** ~ **a qn** (*nemico ecc*) to stand up to sb; **fare di** ~ **propria** to go one's own way; **in** ~ (*Sport*) in the lead; ~ **o croce?** heads or tails?; **avere la** ~ **dura** to be stubborn; **testa d'aglio** bulb of garlic; **testa di serie** (*Tennis*) seed, seeded player

testa'mento *sm* (*atto*) will; **l'Antico/il Nuovo T** ~ (*Rel*) the Old/New Testament

tes'tardo, -a *ag* stubborn, pig-headed

tes'tata sf (parte anteriore) head; (intestazione) heading

tes'ticolo sm testicle

testi'mone sm/f (Dir) witness; **testimone oculare** eye witness

testimoni'are vt to testify; (fig) to bear witness to, testify to ▶ vi to give evidence, testify

'testo sm text; **fare ~** (opera, autore) to be authoritative; **questo libro non fa ~** this book is not essential reading

tes'tuggine [tes'tuddʒine] sf tortoise; (di mare) turtle

'tetano sm (Med) tetanus

'tetto sm roof; **tet'toia** sf roofing; canopy

tettuccio [tet'tuttʃo] sm **~ apribile** (Aut) sunroof

'Tevere sm **il ~** the Tiber

TG, Tg abbr = **telegiornale**

'thermos® ['tɛrmos] sm inv vacuum o Thermos® flask

ti pron (dav lo, la, li, le, ne diventa **te**) ▶ pron (oggetto) you; (complemento di termine) (to) you; (riflessivo) yourself

'Tibet sm **il ~** Tibet

'tibia sf tibia, shinbone

tic sm inv tic, (nervous) twitch; (fig) mannerism

ticchet'tio [tikket'tio] sm (di macchina da scrivere) clatter; (di orologio) ticking; (della pioggia) patter

'ticket sm inv (su farmaci) prescription charge

ti'ene ecc vb vedi **tenere**

ti'epido, -a ag lukewarm, tepid

'tifo sm (Med) typhus; (fig): **fare il ~ per** to be a fan of

ti'fone sm typhoon

ti'foso, -a sm/f (Sport ecc) fan

tigì [ti'dʒi] sm inv TV news

'tiglio ['tiʎʎo] sm lime (tree), linden (tree)

'tigre sf tiger

tim'brare vt to stamp; (annullare: francobolli) to postmark; **~ il cartellino** to clock in

'timbro sm stamp; (Mus) timbre, tone

'timido, -a ag shy; timid

'timo sm thyme

ti'mone sm (Naut) rudder

ti'more sm (paura) fear; (rispetto) awe

'timpano sm (Anat) eardrum; (Mus)

'tingere ['tindʒere] vt to dye

'tinsi ecc vb vedi **tingere**

'tinta sf (materia colorante) dye; (colore) colour, shade

tintin'nare vi to tinkle

tinto'ria sf (lavasecco) dry cleaner's (shop)

tin'tura sf (operazione) dyeing; (colorante) dye; **tintura di iodio** tincture of iodine

'tipico, -a, -ci, -che ag typical

'tipo sm type; (genere) kind, type; (fam) chap, fellow; **che ~ di...?** what kind of...?

tipogra'fia sf typography; (procedimento) letterpress (printing); (officina) printing house

TIR sigla m (= Transports Internationaux Routiers) International Heavy Goods Vehicle

ti'rare vt (gen) to pull; (estrarre): **~ qc da** to take o pull sth out of; to get sth out of; to extract sth from; (chiudere: tenda ecc) to draw, pull; (tracciare, disegnare) to draw, trace; (lanciare: sasso, palla) to throw; (stampare) to print; (pistola, freccia) to fire ▶ vi (pipa, camino) to draw; (vento) to blow; (abito) to be tight; (fare fuoco) to fire; (fare del tiro, Calcio) to shoot; **tirarsi** vpr **tirarsi indietro** to draw back; (fig) to back out; **~ avanti** to struggle on; to keep going; **~ fuori** (estrarre) to take out, pull out; **~ giù** (abbassare) to bring down, to lower; (da scaffale ecc.) to take down; **~ su** to pull up; (capelli) to put up; (fig: bambino) to bring up;

~ a indovinare to take a guess; **~ sul prezzo** to bargain; **tirar dritto** to keep right on going; **tirati su!** (*fig*) cheer up!; **~ via** (*togliere*) to take off

tira'tura *sf* (*azione*) printing; (*di libro*) (print) run; (*di giornale*) circulation

'tirchio, -a ['tirkjo] *ag* mean, stingy

'tiro *sm* shooting *no pl*, firing *no pl*; (*colpo, sparo*) shot; (*di palla: lancio*) throwing *no pl*; throw; (*fig*) trick; **cavallo da ~** draught (*BRIT*) o draft (*US*) horse; **tiro a segno** target shooting; (*luogo*) shooting range; **tiro con l'arco** archery

tiro'cinio [tiro'tʃinjo] *sm* apprenticeship; (*professionale*) training

ti'roide *sf* thyroid (gland)

Tir'reno *sm* **il (mar) ~** the Tyrrhenian Sea

ti'sana *sf* herb tea

tito'lare *sm/f* incumbent; (*proprietario*) owner; (*Calcio*) regular player

'titolo *sm* title; (*di giornale*) headline; (*diploma*) qualification; (*Comm*) security; (: *azione*) share; **a che ~?** for what reason?; **a ~ di amicizia** out of friendship; **a ~ di premio** as a prize; **titolo di credito** share; **titoli di stato** government securities; **titoli di testa** (*Cinema*) credits

titu'bante *ag* hesitant, irresolute

toast [toust] *sm inv* toasted sandwich (*generally with ham and cheese*)

toc'cante *ag* touching

toc'care *vt* to touch; (*tastare*) to feel; (*fig: riguardare*) to concern; (: *commuovere*) to touch, move; (: *pungere*) to hurt, wound; (: *far cenno a: argomento*) to touch on, mention ▶ *vi* **~ a** (*accadere*) to happen to; (*spettare*) to be up to; **~ (il fondo)** (*in acqua*) to touch the bottom; **tocca a te difenderci** it's up to you to defend

us; **a chi tocca?** whose turn is it?; **mi toccò pagare** I had to pay

tocche'rò *ecc* [tokke'rɔ] *vb vedi* **toccare**

'togliere ['tɔʎʎere] *vt* (*rimuovere*) to take away (*o off*), remove; (*riprendere, non concedere più*) to take away, remove; (*Mat*) to take away, subtract; **~ qc a qn** to take sth (away) from sb; **ciò non toglie che** nevertheless, be that as it may; **togliersi il cappello** to take off one's hat

toi'lette [twa'lɛt] *sf inv* toilet; (*mobile*) dressing table; **dov'è la ~?** where's the toilet?

'Tokyo *sf* Tokyo

'tolgo *ecc vb vedi* **togliere**

tolle'rare *vt* to tolerate

'tolsi *ecc vb vedi* **togliere**

'tomba *sf* tomb

tom'bino *sm* manhole cover

'tombola *sf* (*gioco*) tombola; (*ruzzolone*) tumble

'tondo, -a *ag* round

'tonfo *sm* splash; (*rumore sordo*) thud; (*caduta*): **fare un ~** to take a tumble

tonifi'care *vt* (*muscoli, pelle*) to tone up; (*irrobustire*) to invigorate, brace

tonnel'lata *sf* ton

'tonno *sm* tuna (fish)

'tono *sm* (*gen*) tone; (*Mus: di pezzo*) key; (*di colore*) shade, tone

ton'silla *sf* tonsil

'tonto, -a *ag* dull, stupid

to'pazio [to'pattsjo] *sm* topaz

'topo *sm* mouse

'toppa *sf* (*serratura*) keyhole; (*pezza*) patch

to'race [to'ratʃe] *sm* chest

'torba *sf* peat

'torcere ['tɔrtʃere] *vt* to twist; **torcersi** *vpr* to twist, writhe

'torcia, -ce ['tɔrtʃa] *sf* torch; **torcia elettrica** torch (*BRIT*), flashlight (*US*)

torci'collo [tortʃi'kɔllo] *sm* stiff neck

'tordo sm thrush
To'rino sf Turin
tor'menta sf snowstorm
tormen'tare vt to torment;
  tormentarsi vpr to fret, worry o.s.
tor'nado sm tornado
tor'nante sm hairpin bend
tor'nare vi to return, go (o come)
  back; (ridiventare: anche fig) to become
  (again); (riuscire giusto, esatto: conto)
  to work out; (risultare) to turn out (to
  be), prove (to be); **~ utile** to prove o
  turn out (to be) useful; **~ a casa** to go
  (o come) home; **torno a casa martedì**
  I'm going home on Tuesday
tor'neo sm tournament
'tornio sm lathe
'toro sm bull; (dello zodiaco): **T~** Taurus
'torre sf tower; (Scacchi) rook, castle;
  torre di controllo (Aer) control tower
tor'rente sm torrent
torri'one sm keep
tor'rone sm nougat
'torsi ecc vb vedi **torcere**
torsi'one sf twisting; torsion
'torso sm torso, trunk; (Arte) torso
'torsolo sm (di cavolo ecc) stump; (di
  frutta) core
'torta sf cake
tortel'lini smpl (Cuc) tortellini
'torto, -a pp di **torcere** ▶ ag (ritorto)
  twisted; (storto) twisted, crooked
  ▶ sm (ingiustizia) wrong; (colpa) fault; **a
  ~** wrongly; **aver ~** to be wrong
'tortora sf turtle dove
tor'tura sf torture; **tortu'rare** vt to
  torture
to'sare vt (pecora) to shear; (siepe)
  to clip
Tos'cana sf **la ~** Tuscany
'tosse sf cough; **ho la ~** I've got a
  cough
'tossico, -a, -ci, -che ag toxic
tossicodipen'dente sm/f drug
  addict

tos'sire vi to cough
tosta'pane sm inv toaster
to'tale ag, sm total
toto'calcio [toto'kaltʃo] sm gambling
  pool betting on football results,
  ≈ (football) pools pl (BRIT)
to'vaglia [to'vaʎʎa] sf tablecloth;
  tovagli'olo sm napkin
tra prep (di due persone, cose) between;
  (di più persone, cose) among(st);
  (tempo: entro) within, in; **~ 5 giorni** in
  5 days' time; **sia detto ~ noi ...**
  between you and me ...; **litigano ~
  (di loro)** they're fighting amongst
  themselves; **~ breve** soon; **~ sé e sé**
  (parlare ecc) to oneself
traboc'care vi to overflow
traboc'chetto [trabok'ketto] sm
  (fig) trap
'traccia, -ce ['trattʃa] sf (segno, striscia)
  trail, track; (orma) tracks pl; (residuo,
  testimonianza) trace, sign; (abbozzo)
  outline
tracci'are [trat'tʃare] vt to trace,
  mark (out); (disegnare) to draw; (fig:
  abbozzare) to outline
tra'chea [tra'kɛa] sf windpipe
tra'colla sf shoulder strap; **borsa a ~**
  shoulder bag
tradi'mento sm betrayal; (Dir, Mil)
  treason
tra'dire vt to betray; (coniuge) to be
  unfaithful to; (doveri: mancare) to
  fail in; (rivelare) to give away, reveal;
  tradirsi vpr to give o.s. away
tradizio'nale [tradittsjo'nale] ag
  traditional
tradizi'one [tradit'tsjone] sf tradition
tra'durre vt to translate; (spiegare) to
  render, convey; **me lo può ~?** can you
  translate this for me?; **tradut'tore,
  -trice** sm/f translator; **traduzi'one** sf
  translation
'trae vb vedi **trarre**
traffi'cante sm/f dealer; (peg) trafficker

traffi'care vi (commerciare): **~ (in)** to trade (in), deal (in); (affaccendarsi) to busy o.s. ▶ vt (peg) to traffic in

'traffico, -ci sm traffic; (commercio) trade, traffic; **traffico di armi/droga** arms/drug trafficking

tra'gedia [tra'dʒɛdja] sf tragedy

'traggo ecc vb vedi **trarre**

tra'ghetto [tra'getto] sm ferry(boat)

'tragico, -a, -ci, -che ['tradʒiko] ag tragic

tra'gitto [tra'dʒitto] sm (passaggio) crossing; (viaggio) journey

tragu'ardo sm (Sport) finishing line; (fig) goal, aim

'trai ecc vb vedi **trarre**

traiet'toria sf trajectory

trai'nare vt to drag, haul; (rimorchiare) to tow

tralasci'are [tralaʃʃare] vt (studi) to neglect; (dettagli) to leave out, omit

tra'liccio [tra'littʃo] sm (Elettr) pylon

tram sm inv tram

'trama sf (filo) weft, woof; (fig: argomento, maneggio) plot

traman'dare vt to pass on, hand down

tram'busto sm turmoil

tramez'zino [tramed'dzino] sm sandwich

'tramite prep through

tramon'tare vi to set, go down; **tra'monto** sm setting; (del sole) sunset

trampo'lino sm (per tuffi) springboard, diving board; (per lo sci) ski-jump

tra'nello sm trap

'tranne prep except (for), but (for); **~ che** unless

tranquil'lante sm (Med) tranquillizer

tranquillità sf calm, stillness; quietness; peace of mind

tranquilliz'zare [trankwillid'dzare] vt to reassure

| Attenzione! In inglese esiste il verbo to tranquillize, che però significa "calmare con un tranquillante".

tran'quillo, -a ag calm, quiet; (bambino, scolaro) quiet; (sereno) with one's mind at rest; **sta' ~** don't worry

transazi'one [transat'tsjone] sf compromise; (Dir) settlement; (Comm) transaction, deal

tran'senna sf barrier

transgenico, -a, -ci, -che [trans'dʒɛniko] ag genetically modified

tran'sigere [tran'sidʒere] vi (venire a patti) to compromise, come to an agreement

transi'tabile ag passable

transi'tare vi to pass

transi'tivo, -a ag transitive

'transito sm transit; **di ~** (merci) in transit; (stazione) transit cpd; **"divieto di ~"** "no entry"

'trapano sm (utensile) drill; (Med) trepan

trape'lare vi to leak, drip; (fig) to leak out

tra'pezio [tra'pɛttsjo] sm (Mat) trapezium; (attrezzo ginnico) trapeze

trapian'tare vt to transplant; **trapi'anto** sm transplanting; (Med) transplant; **trapianto cardiaco** heart transplant

'trappola sf trap

tra'punta sf quilt

'trarre vt to draw, pull; (portare) to take; (prendere, tirare fuori) to take (out), draw; (derivare) to obtain; **~ origine da qc** to have its origins o originate in sth

trasa'lire vi to start, jump

trasan'dato, -a ag shabby

trasci'nare [traʃʃi'nare] vt to drag; **trascinarsi** vpr to drag o.s. along; (fig) to drag on

tras'correre vt (tempo) to spend, pass ▶ vi to pass

tras'crivere vt to transcribe

trascu'rare vt to neglect; (non considerare) to disregard

trasferi'mento sm transfer; (trasloco) removal, move; **trasferimento di chiamata** (Tel) call forwarding

trasfe'rire vt to transfer; **trasferirsi** vpr to move; **tras'ferta** sf transfer; (indennità) travelling expenses pl; (Sport) away game

trasfor'mare vt to transform, change; **trasformarsi** vpr to be transformed; **trasformarsi in qc** to turn into sth; **trasforma'tore** sm (Elec) transformer

trasfusi'one sf (Med) transfusion

trasgre'dire vt to disobey, contravene

traslo'care vt to move, transfer; **tras'loco, -chi** sm removal

tras'mettere vt (passare): ~ **qc a qn** to pass sth on to sb; (mandare) to send; (Tecn, Tel, Med) to transmit; (TV, Radio) to broadcast; **trasmissi'one** sf (gen, Fisica, Tecn) transmission; (passaggio) transmission, passing on; (TV, Radio) broadcast

traspa'rente ag transparent

traspor'tare vt to carry, move; (merce) to transport, convey; **lasciarsi ~ (da qc)** (fig) to let o.s. be carried away (by sth); **tras'porto** sm transport

'trassi ecc vb vedi **trarre**

trasver'sale ag transverse, cross(-); running at right angles

'tratta sf (Econ) draft; (di persone): **la ~ delle bianche** the white slave trade

tratta'mento sm treatment; (servizio) service

trat'tare vt (gen) to treat; (commerciare) to deal in; (svolgere: argomento) to discuss, deal with;

(negoziare) to negotiate ▶ vi ~ **di** to deal with; ~ **con** (persona) to deal with; **si tratta di ...** it's about ...

tratte'nere vt (far rimanere: persona) to detain; (intrattenere: ospiti) to entertain; (tenere, frenare, reprimere) to hold back, keep back; (astenersi dal consegnare) to hold, keep; (detrarre: somma) to deduct; **trattenersi** vpr (astenersi) to restrain o.s., stop o.s.; (soffermarsi) to stay, remain

trat'tino sm dash; (in parole composte) hyphen

'tratto, -a pp di **trarre** ▶ sm (di penna, matita) stroke; (parte) part, piece; (di strada) stretch; (di mare, cielo) expanse; (di tempo) period (of time)

trat'tore sm tractor

tratto'ria sf restaurant

'trauma, -i sm trauma

tra'vaglio [tra'vaλλo] sm (angoscia) pain, suffering; (Med) pains pl

trava'sare vt to decant

tra'versa sf (trave) crosspiece; (via) side street; (Ferr) sleeper (BRIT), (railroad) tie (US); (Calcio) crossbar

traver'sata sf crossing; (Aer) flight, trip; **quanto dura la ~?** how long does the crossing take?

traver'sie sfpl mishaps, misfortunes

tra'verso, -a ag oblique; **di ~** ag askew ▶ av sideways; **andare di ~** (cibo) to go down the wrong way; **guardare di ~** to look askance at

travesti'mento sm disguise

travestirsi vpr to disguise o.s.

tra'volgere [tra'voldʒere] vt to sweep away, carry away; (fig) to overwhelm

tre num three

'treccia, -ce ['trettʃa] sf plait, braid

tre'cento [tre'tʃɛnto] num three hundred ▶ sm **il T~** the fourteenth century

'tredici ['treditʃi] num thirteen

'tregua sf truce; (fig) respite

tre'mare vi ~ **di** (freddo ecc) to shiver o tremble with; (paura, rabbia) to shake o tremble with

tre'mendo, -a ag terrible, awful

> Attenzione! In inglese esiste la parola tremendous, che però significa enorme oppure fantastico, strepitoso.

'tremito sm trembling no pl; shaking no pl; shivering no pl

'treno sm train; **è questo il ~ per...?** is this the train for ...?; **treno di gomme** set of tyres (BRIT) o tires (US); **treno merci** goods (BRIT) o freight train; **treno viaggiatori** passenger train

- **treni**
- There are various types of train in
- Italy. For short journeys there are
- the "Regionali" (R), which generally
- operate within a particular region,
- and the "Interregionali" (IR),
- which operate beyond regional
- boundaries. Medium- and long-
- distance passenger journeys are
- carried out by "Intercity" (I) and
- "Eurocity" (EC) trains. The "Eurostar"
- service (ES) offers fast connections
- between the major Italian cities.
- Night services are operated by
- "Intercity Notte" (ICN), "Euronight"
- (EN) and by "Espressi" (EXP).

'trenta num thirty; **tren'tesimo, -a** num thirtieth; **tren'tina** sf **una trentina (di)** thirty or so, about thirty

'trepidante ag anxious

triango'lare ag triangular

tri'angolo sm triangle

tribù sf inv tribe

tri'buna sf (podio) platform; (in aule ecc) gallery; (di stadio) stand

tribu'nale sm court

tri'ciclo [tri'tʃiklo] sm tricycle

tri'foglio [tri'fɔʎʎo] sm clover

'triglia ['triʎʎa] sf red mullet

tri'mestre sm period of three months;

(Ins) term, quarter (US); (Comm) quarter

trin'cea [trin'tʃɛa] sf trench

trion'fare vi to triumph; ~ **su** to triumph over; **tri'onfo** sm triumph

tripli'care vt to triple

'triplo, -a ag triple; treble ▶ sm il ~ **(di)** three times as much (as); **la spesa è tripla** it costs three times as much

'trippa sf (Cuc) tripe

'triste ag sad; (luogo) dreary, gloomy

tri'tare vt to mince, grind (US)

trivi'ale ag vulgar, low

tro'feo sm trophy

'tromba sf (Mus) trumpet; (Aut) horn; **tromba d'aria** whirlwind; **tromba delle scale** stairwell

trom'bone sm trombone

trom'bosi sf thrombosis

tron'care vt to cut off; (spezzare) to break off

'tronco, -a, -chi, -che ag cut off; broken off; (Ling) truncated; (fig) cut short ▶ sm (Bot, Anat) trunk; (fig: tratto) section; **licenziare qn in ~** to fire sb on the spot

'trono sm throne

tropi'cale ag tropical

'troppo, -a det (in eccesso: quantità) too much; (: numero) too many; **c'era troppa gente** there were too many people; **fa troppo caldo** it's too hot ▶ pron (in eccesso: quantità) too much; (: numero) too many; **ne hai messo troppo** you've put in too much; **meglio troppi che pochi** better too many than too few ▶ av (eccessivamente: con ag, av) too; (: con vb) too much; **troppo amaro/tardi** too bitter/late; **lavora troppo** he works too much; **costa troppo** it costs too much; **di troppo** too much; too many; **qualche tazza di troppo** a few cups too many; **2 euro di troppo** 2 euros too much; **essere di troppo** to be in the way

'trota sf trout

'trottola sf spinning top

tro'vare vt to find; (giudicare): **trovo che** I find o think that; **trovarsi** vpr (reciproco: incontrarsi) to meet; (essere, stare) to be; (arrivare, capitare) to find o.s.; **non trovo più il portafoglio** I can't find my wallet; **andare a ~ qn** to go and see sb; **~ qn colpevole** to find sb guilty; **trovarsi bene** (in un luogo, con qn) to get on well

truc'care vt (falsare): (attore ecc) to make up; (travestire) to disguise; (Sport) to fix; (Aut) to soup up; **truccarsi** vpr to make up (one's face)

'trucco, -chi sm trick; (cosmesi) make-up

'truffa sf fraud, swindle; **truf'fare** vt to swindle, cheat

truffa'tore, -'trice sm/f swindler, cheat

'truppa sf troop

tu pron you; **tu stesso(a)** you yourself; **dare del tu a qn** to address sb as "tu"

'tubo sm tube; pipe; **tubo digerente** (Anat) alimentary canal, digestive tract; **tubo di scappamento** (Aut) exhaust pipe

tuffarsi vpr to plunge, dive

'tuffo sm dive; (breve bagno) dip

tuli'pano sm tulip

tu'more sm (Med) tumour

Tuni'sia sf la ~ Tunisia

'tuo (f'**tua**, pl **tu'oi, 'tue**) det il ~, la tua ecc your ▶ pron il ~, la tua ecc yours

tuo'nare vi to thunder; **tuona** it is thundering, there's some thunder

tu'ono sm thunder

tu'orlo sm yolk

tur'bante sm turban

tur'bare vt to disturb, trouble

tur'bato, -a ag upset; (preoccupato, ansioso) anxious

turbo'lenza [turbo'lɛntsa] sf turbulence

tur'chese [tur'kese] sf turquoise

Tur'chia [tur'kia] sf la ~ Turkey

'turco, -a, -chi, -che ag Turkish ▶ sm/f Turk/Turkish woman ▶ sm (Ling) Turkish; **parlare ~** (fig) to talk double-dutch

tu'rismo sm tourism; tourist industry; **tu'rista, -i, -e** sm/f tourist; **turismo sessuale** sex tourism; **tu'ristico, -a, -ci, -che** ag tourist cpd

'turno sm turn; (di lavoro) shift; **di ~** (soldato, medico, custode) on duty; **a ~** (rispondere) in turn; (lavorare) in shifts; **fare a ~ a fare qc** to take turns to do sth; **è il suo ~** it's your (o his ecc turn)

'turpe ag filthy, vile

'tuta sf overalls pl; (Sport) tracksuit

tu'tela sf (Dir: di minore) guardianship; (: protezione) protection; (difesa) defence

tutta'via cong nevertheless, yet

○ **'tutto, -a**
det

1 (intero) all; **tutto il latte** all the milk; **tutta la notte** all night, the whole night; **tutto il libro** the whole book; **tutta una bottiglia** a whole bottle

2 (pl, collettivo) all; every; **tutti i libri** all the books; **tutte le notti** every night; **tutti i venerdì** every Friday; **tutti gli uomini** all the men; (collettivo) all men; **tutto l'anno** all year long; **tutti e due** both o each of us (o them o you); **tutti e cinque** all five of us (o them o you)

3 (completamente): **era tutta sporca** she was all dirty; **tremava tutto** he was trembling all over; **è tutta sua madre** she's just o exactly like her mother

4: **a tutt'oggi** so far, up till now; **a tutta velocità** at full o top speed

▶*pron*

1 (*ogni cosa*) everything, all; (*qualsiasi cosa*) anything; **ha mangiato tutto** he's eaten everything; **tutto considerato** all things considered; **in tutto: 5 euro in tutto** 5 euros in all; **in tutto eravamo 50** there were 50 of us in all

2: **tutti, e** (*ognuno*) all, everybody; **vengono tutti** they are all coming, everybody's coming; **tutti quanti** all and sundry

▶*av* (*completamente*) entirely, quite; **è tutto il contrario** it's quite *o* exactly the opposite; **tutt'al più: saranno stati tutt'al più una cinquantina** there were about fifty of them at (the very) most; **tutt'al più possiamo prendere un treno** if the worst comes to the worst we can take a train; **tutt'altro** on the contrary; **è tutt'altro che felice** he's anything but happy; **tutt'a un tratto** suddenly

▶*sm* **il tutto** the whole lot, all of it

tut'tora *av* still

TV [ti'vu] *sf inv* (= *televisione*) TV ▶ *sigla* = Treviso

u

ubbidi'ente *ag* obedient
ubbi'dire *vi* to obey; **~ a** to obey; (*veicolo, macchina*) to respond to

ubria'care *vt* **~ qn** to get sb drunk; (*alcool*) to make sb drunk; (*fig*) to make sb's head spin *o* reel; **ubriacarsi** *vpr* to get drunk; **ubriacarsi di** (*fig*) to become intoxicated with

ubri'aco, -a, -chi, -che *ag, sm/f* drunk

uc'cello [ut'tʃɛllo] *sm* bird

uc'cidere [ut'tʃidere] *vt* to kill; **uccidersi** *vpr* (*suicidarsi*) to kill o.s.; (*perdere la vita*) to be killed

u'dito *sm* (sense of) hearing

UE *sigla f* (= *Unione Europea*) EU

UEM *sigla f* (= *Unione economica e monetaria*) EMU

'uffa *escl* tut!

uffici'ale [uffi'tʃale] *ag* official ▶ *sm* (*Amm*) official, officer; (*Mil*) officer; **~ di stato civile** registrar

uf'ficio [uf'fitʃo] *sm* (*gen*) office; (*dovere*) duty; (*mansione*) task, function, job; (*agenzia*) agency, bureau; (*Rel*) service; **d'~** *ag* office *cpd*; official ▶ *av* officially; **ufficio di collocamento** employment office; **ufficio informazioni** information bureau; **ufficio oggetti smarriti** lost property office (*BRIT*), lost and found (*US*); **ufficio (del) personale** personnel department; **ufficio postale** post office

uffici'oso, -a [uffi'tʃoso] *ag* unofficial

uguagli'anza [ugwaʎ'ʎantsa] *sf* equality

uguagli'are [ugwaʎ'ʎare] *vt* to make equal; (*essere uguale*) to equal, be equal to; (*livellare*) to level; **uguagliarsi a** *o* **con qn** (*paragonarsi*) to compare o.s. to sb

ugu'ale *ag* equal; (*identico*) identical, the same; (*uniforme*) level, even ▶ *av* **costano ~** they cost the same; **sono bravi ~** they're equally good

UIL *sigla f* (= *Unione Italiana del Lavoro*) trade union federation

'ulcera ['ultʃera] *sf* ulcer
U'livo *sm* **l'~** centre-left Italian political grouping
u'livo = **olivo**
ulteri'ore *ag* further
ultima'mente *av* lately, of late
ulti'mare *vt* to finish, complete
'ultimo, -a *ag* (*finale*) last; (*estremo*) farthest, utmost; (*recente: notizia, moda*) latest; (*fig: sommo, fondamentale*) ultimate ▶ *sm/f* last (one); **fino all'~** to the last, until the end; **da ~, in ~** in the end; **abitare all'~ piano** to live on the top floor; **per ~** (*entrare, arrivare*) last
ultravio'letto, -a *ag* ultraviolet
ulu'lare *vi* to howl
umanità *sf* humanity
u'mano, -a *ag* human; (*comprensivo*) humane
umidità *sf* dampness; humidity
'umido, -a *ag* damp; (*mano, occhi*) moist; (*clima*) humid ▶ *sm* dampness, damp; **carne in ~** stew
'umile *ag* humble
umili'are *vt* to humiliate; **umiliarsi** *vpr* to humble o.s.
u'more *sm* (*disposizione d'animo*) mood; (*carattere*) temper; **di buon/cattivo ~** in a good/bad mood
umo'rismo *sm* humour; **avere il senso dell'~** to have a sense of humour; **umo'ristico, -a, -ci, -che** *ag* humorous, funny
u'nanime *ag* unanimous
unci'netto [untʃi'netto] *sm* crochet hook
un'cino [un'tʃino] *sm* hook
undi'cenne [undi'tʃɛnne] *ag, sm/f* eleven-year-old
undi'cesimo, -a [undi'tʃɛzimo] *num* eleventh
'undici ['unditʃi] *num* eleven
'ungere ['undʒere] *vt* to grease, oil; (*Rel*) to anoint; (*fig*) to flatter

unghe'rese [unge'rese] *ag, sm/f, sm* Hungarian
Unghe'ria [unge'ria] *sf* **l'~** Hungary
'unghia ['ungja] *sf* (*Anat*) nail; (*di animale*) claw; (*di rapace*) talon; (*di cavallo*) hoof
ungu'ento *sm* ointment
'unico, -a, -ci, -che *ag* (*solo*) only; (*ineguagliabile*) unique; (*singolo: binario*) single; **figlio(a) ~(a)** only son/daughter, only child
unifi'care *vt* to unite, unify; (*sistemi*) to standardize; **unificazi'one** *sf* uniting; unification; standardization
uni'forme *ag* uniform; (*superficie*) even ▶ *sf* (*divisa*) uniform
uni'one *sf* union; (*fig: concordia*) unity, harmony; **Unione europea** European Union; **ex Unione Sovietica** former Soviet Union
u'nire *vt* to unite; (*congiungere*) to join, connect; (*: ingredienti, colori*) to combine; (*in matrimonio*) to unite, join together; **unirsi** *vpr* to unite; (*in matrimonio*) to be joined together; **~ qc a** to unite sth with; to join *o* connect sth with; to combine sth with; **unirsi a** (*gruppo, società*) to join
unità *sf inv* (*unione, concordia*) unity; (*Mat, Mil, Comm, di misura*) unit; **unità di misura** unit of measurement
u'nito, -a *ag* (*paese*) united; (*amici, famiglia*) close; **in tinta unita** plain, self-coloured
univer'sale *ag* universal; general
università *sf inv* university
uni'verso *sm* universe

○ **'uno, -a**
   (*dav sm* **un** + C, V, **uno** + *s impura, gn, pn, ps, x, z; dav sf* **un'** + V, **una** + C) *art indef*
1 a; (*dav vocale*) an; **un bambino** a child; **una strada** a street; **uno zingaro** a gypsy
2 (*intensivo*): **ho avuto una paura!** I got such a fright!

▶*pron*

1 one; **prendine uno** take one (of them); **l'uno o l'altro** either (of them); **l'uno e l'altro** both (of them); **aiutarsi l'un l'altro** to help one another *o* each other; **sono entrati l'uno dopo l'altro** they came in one after the other

2 (*un tale*) someone, somebody

3 (*con valore impersonale*) one, you; **se uno vuole** if one wants, if you want

▶*num* one; **una mela e due pere** one apple and two pears; **uno più uno fa due** one plus one equals two, one and one are two

▶*sf* **è l'una** it's one (o'clock)

'**unsi** *ecc vb vedi* **ungere**

'**unto, -a** *pp di* **ungere** ▶ *ag* greasy, oily ▶ *sm* grease

u'omo (*pl* **u'omini**) *sm* man; **da ~** (*abito, scarpe*) men's, for men; **uomo d'affari** businessman; **uomo di paglia** stooge; **uomo politico** politician; **uomo rana** frogman

u'ovo (*pl(f)* **u'ova**) *sm* egg; **uovo affogato/alla coque** poached/boiled egg; **uovo bazzotto/sodo** soft-/hard-boiled egg; **uovo di Pasqua** Easter egg; **uovo in camicia** poached egg; **uova strapazzate/al tegame** scrambled/fried eggs

ura'gano *sm* hurricane

urba'nistica *sf* town planning

ur'bano, -a *ag* urban, city *cpd*, town *cpd*; (*Tel: chiamata*) local; (*fig*) urbane

ur'gente [ur'dʒɛnte] *ag* urgent; **ur'genza** *sf* urgency; **in caso d'urgenza** in (case of) an emergency; **d'urgenza** *ag* emergency ▶ *av* urgently, as a matter of urgency

ur'lare *vi* (*persona*) to scream, yell; (*animale, vento*) to howl ▶ *vt* to scream, yell

'**urlo** (*pl(m)* '**urli**, *pl(f)* '**urla**) *sm* scream, yell; howl

urrà *escl* hurrah!

U.R.S.S. *abbr f* **l'U.R.S.S.** the USSR

ur'tare *vt* to bump into, knock against; (*fig: irritare*) to annoy ▶ *vi* **~ contro** *o* **in** to bump into, knock against, crash into; (*fig: imbattersi*) to come up against; **urtarsi** *vpr* (*reciproco: scontrarsi*) to collide; (: *fig*) to clash; (*irritarsi*) to get annoyed

'**U.S.A.** ['uza] *smpl* **gli U.S.A.** the USA

u'sanza [u'zantsa] *sf* custom; (*moda*) fashion

u'sare *vt* to use, employ ▶ *vi* (*servirsi*): **~ di** to use; (: *diritto*) to exercise; (*essere di moda*) to be fashionable; (*essere solito*): **~ fare** to be in the habit of doing, be accustomed to doing ▶ *vb impers* **qui usa così** it's the custom round here; **u'sato, -a** *ag* used; (*consumato*) worn; (*di seconda mano*) used, second-hand ▶ *sm* second-hand goods *pl*

u'scire [uʃʃire] *vi* (*gen*) to come out; (*partire, andare a passeggio, a uno spettacolo ecc*) to go out; (*essere sorteggiato: numero*) to come up; **~ da** (*gen*) to leave; (*posto*) to go (*o* come) out of, leave; (*solco, vasca ecc*) to come out of; (*muro*) to stick out of; (*competenza ecc*) to be outside; (*infanzia, adolescenza*) to leave behind; (*famiglia nobile ecc*) to come from; **~ da** *o* **di casa** to go out; (*fig*) to leave home; **~ in automobile** to go out in the car, go for a drive; **~ di strada** (*Aut*) to go off *o* leave the road

u'scita [uʃʃita] *sf* (*passaggio, varco*) exit, way out; (*per divertimento*) outing; (*Econ: somma*) expenditure; (*Teatro*) entrance; (*fig: battuta*) witty remark; **dov'è l'~?** where's the exit?; **uscita di sicurezza** emergency exit

usi'gnolo [uziɲ'ɲɔlo] *sm* nightingale

'**uso** *sm* (*utilizzazione*) use; (*esercizio*) practice; (*abitudine*) custom; **a ~ di** for (the use of); **d'~** (*corrente*) in use; **fuori ~**

out of use: **per ~ esterno** for external use only
usti'one *sf* burn
usu'ale *ag* common, everyday
u'sura *sf* usury; (*logoramento*) wear (and tear)
uten'sile *sm* tool, implement; **utensili da cucina** kitchen utensils
u'tente *sm/f* user
'utero *sm* uterus
'utile *ag* useful ▶ *sm* (*vantaggio*) advantage, benefit; (*Econ: profitto*) profit
utiliz'zare [utilid'dzare] *vt* to use, make use of, utilize
'uva *sf* grapes *pl*; **uva passa** raisins *pl*; **uva spina** gooseberry
UVA *abbr* (= *ultravioletto prossimo*) UVA
UVB *abbr* (= *ultravioletto remoto*) UVB

V

v. *abbr* (= *vedi*) v
va, va' *vb vedi* **andare**
va'cante *ag* vacant
va'canza [va'kantsa] *sf* (*riposo, ferie*) holiday(s) *pl* (BRIT), vacation (US); (*giorno di permesso*) day off, holiday; **vacanze** *sfpl* (*periodo di ferie*) holidays (BRIT), vacation *sg* (US); **essere/andare in ~** to be/go on holiday *o* vacation; **sono qui in ~** I'm on holiday here; **vacanze estive** summer holiday(s) *o* vacation; **vacanze natalizie** Christmas holidays *o* vacation

> Attenzione! In inglese esiste la parola *vacancy* che però indica un posto vacante o una camera disponibile.

'vacca, -che *sf* cow
vacci'nare [vattʃi'nare] *vt* to vaccinate
vac'cino [vat'tʃino] *sm* (*Med*) vaccine
vacil'lare [vatʃil'lare] *vi* to sway, wobble; (*luce*) to flicker; (*fig: memoria, coraggio*) to be failing, falter
'vacuo, -a *ag* (*fig*) empty, vacuous
'vado *ecc vb vedi* **andare**
vaga'bondo, -a *sm/f* tramp, vagrant
va'gare *vi* to wander
vagherò *ecc* [vage'rɔ] *vb vedi* **vagare**
va'gina [va'dʒina] *sf* vagina
'vaglia ['vaʎʎa] *sm inv* money order; **vaglia postale** postal order
vagli'are [vaʎ'ʎare] *vt* to sift; (*fig*) to weigh up
'vago, -a, -ghi, -ghe *ag* vague
va'gone *sm* (*Ferr: per passeggeri*) coach; (: *per merci*) truck, wagon; **vagone letto** sleeper, sleeping car; **vagone ristorante** dining *o* restaurant car
'vai *vb vedi* **andare**
vai'olo *sm* smallpox
va'langa, -ghe *sf* avalanche
va'lere *vi* (*avere forza, potenza*) to have influence; (*essere valido*) to be valid; (*avere vigore, autorità*) to hold, apply; (*essere capace: poeta, studente*) to be good, be able ▶ *vt* (*prezzo, sforzo*) to be worth; (*corrispondere*) to correspond to; (*procurare*): **~ qc a qn** to earn sb sth; **valersi di** to make use of, take advantage of; **far ~** (*autorità ecc*) to assert; **vale a dire** that is to say; **~ la pena** to be worth the effort *o* worth it
'valgo *ecc vb vedi* **valere**

vali'care *vt* to cross

'valico, -chi *sm* (*passo*) pass

'valido, -a *ag* valid; (*rimedio*) effective; (*aiuto*) real; (*persona*) worthwhile

vali'getta [vali'dʒetta] *sf* briefcase; **valigetta ventiquattrore** overnight bag *o* case

va'ligia, -gie *o* **ge** [va'lidʒa] *sf* (suit)case; **fare le valigie** to pack (up)

'valle *sf* valley; **a ~** (*di fiume*) downstream; **scendere a ~** to go downhill

va'lore *sm* (*gen*) value; (*merito*) merit, worth; (*coraggio*) valour, courage; (*Comm: titolo*) security; **valori** *smpl* (*oggetti preziosi*) valuables

valoriz'zare [valorid'dzare] *vt* (*terreno*) to develop; (*fig*) to make the most of

va'luta *sf* currency, money; (*Banca*): **~ 15 gennaio** interest to run from January 15th

valu'tare *vt* (*casa, gioiello, fig*) to value; (*stabilire: peso, entrate, fig*) to estimate

'valvola *sf* (*Tecn, Anat*) valve; (*Elettr*) fuse

'valzer ['valtser] *sm inv* waltz

vam'pata *sf* (*di fiamma*) blaze; (*di calore*) blast; (: *al viso*) flush

vam'piro *sm* vampire

vanda'lismo *sm* vandalism

'vandalo *sm* vandal

vaneggi'are [vaned'dʒare] *vi* to rave

'vanga, -ghe *sf* spade

van'gelo [van'dʒɛlo] *sm* gospel

va'niglia [va'niʎʎa] *sf* vanilla

vanità *sf* vanity; (*di promessa*) emptiness; (*di sforzo*) futility; **vani'toso, -a** *ag* vain, conceited

'vanno *vb vedi* **andare**

'vano, -a *ag* vain ▶ *sm* (*spazio*) space; (*apertura*) opening; (*stanza*) room

van'taggio [van'taddʒo] *sm* advantage; **essere/portarsi in ~** (*Sport*) to be in/take the lead;

vantaggi'oso, -a *ag* advantageous; favourable

vantarsi *vpr* **~ (di/di aver fatto)** to boast *o* brag (about/about having done)

'vanvera *sf* **a ~** haphazardly; **parlare a ~** to talk nonsense

va'pore *sm* vapour; (*anche:* **~ acqueo**) steam; (*nave*) steamer; **a ~** (*turbina ecc*) steam *cpd*; **al ~** (*Cuc*) steamed

va'rare *vt* (*Naut, fig*) to launch; (*Dir*) to pass

var'care *vt* to cross

'varco, -chi *sm* passage; **aprirsi un ~ tra la folla** to push one's way through the crowd

vare'china [vare'kina] *sf* bleach

vari'abile *ag* variable; (*tempo, umore*) changeable, variable ▶ *sf* (*Mat*) variable

vari'cella [vari'tʃɛlla] *sf* chickenpox

vari'coso, -a *ag* varicose

varietà *sf inv* variety ▶ *sm inv* variety show

'vario, -a *ag* varied; (*parecchi: col sostantivo al pl*) various; (*mutevole: umore*) changeable

'varo *sm* (*Naut: fig*) launch; (*di leggi*) passing

varrò *ecc vb vedi* **valere**

Var'savia *sf* Warsaw

va'saio *sm* potter

'vasca, -sche *sf* basin; **vasca da bagno** bathtub, bath

vas'chetta [vas'ketta] *sf* (*per gelato*) tub; (*per sviluppare fotografie*) dish

vase'lina *sf* Vaseline®

'vaso *sm* (*recipiente*) pot; (: *barattolo*) jar; (: *decorativo*) vase; (*Anat*) vessel; **vaso da fiori** vase; (*per piante*) flowerpot

vas'soio *sm* tray

'vasto, -a *ag* vast, immense

Vati'cano *sm* **il ~** the Vatican

ve *pron, av vedi* **vi**

vecchi'aia [vek'kjaja] *sf* old age
'vecchio, -a ['vɛkkjo] *ag* old ▸ *sm/f* old man/woman; **i vecchii** the old
ve'dere *vt, vi* to see; **vedersi** *vpr* to meet, see one another; **avere a che ~ con** to have something to do with; **far ~ qc a qn** to show sb sth; **farsi ~** to show o.s.; *(farsi vivo)* to show one's face; **vedi di non farlo** make sure *o* see you don't do it; **non (ci) si vede** *(è buio ecc)* you can't see a thing; **non lo posso ~** *(fig)* I can't stand him
ve'detta *sf (sentinella, posto)* look-out; *(Naut)* patrol boat
'vedovo, -a *sm/f* widower/widow
vedrò *ecc vb vedi* **vedere**
ve'duta *sf* view; **vedute** *sfpl (fig: opinioni)* views; **di larghe** *o* **ampie vedute** broad-minded; **di vedute limitate** narrow-minded
vege'tale [vedʒe'tale] *ag, sm* vegetable
vegetari'ano, -a [vedʒeta'rjano] *ag, sm/f* vegetarian; **avete piatti vegetariani?** do you have any vegetarian dishes?
vegetazi'one [vedʒetat'tsjone] *sf* vegetation
'vegeto, -a ['vɛdʒeto] *ag (pianta)* thriving; *(persona)* strong, vigorous
'veglia ['veʎʎa] *sf* wakefulness; *(sorveglianza)* watch; *(trattenimento)* evening gathering; **fare la ~ a un malato** to watch over a sick person
vegli'one [veʎ'ʎone] *sm* ball, dance; **veglione di Capodanno** New Year's Eve party
ve'icolo *sm* vehicle
'vela *sf (Naut: tela)* sail; *(Sport)* sailing
ve'leno *sm* poison; **vele'noso, -a** *ag* poisonous
veli'ero *sm* sailing ship
vel'luto *sm* velvet; **velluto a coste** cord
'velo *sm* veil; *(tessuto)* voile

ve'loce [ve'lotʃe] *ag* fast, quick ▸ *av* fast, quickly; **velocità** *sf* speed; **a forte velocità** at high speed; **velocità di crociera** cruising speed
'vena *sf (gen)* vein; *(filone)* vein, seam; *(fig: ispirazione)* inspiration; *(: umore)* mood; **essere in ~ di qc** to be in the mood for sth
ve'nale *ag (prezzo, valore)* market *cpd*; *(fig)* venal; mercenary
ven'demmia *sf (raccolta)* grape harvest; *(quantità d'uva)* grape crop, grapes *pl*; *(vino ottenuto)* vintage
'vendere *vt* to sell; **"vendesi"** "for sale"
ven'detta *sf* revenge
vendicarsi *vpr* **~ (di)** to avenge o.s. (for); *(per rancore)* to take one's revenge (for); **~ su qn** to revenge o.s. on sb
'vendita *sf* sale; **la ~** *(attività)* selling; *(smercio)* sales *pl*; **in ~** on sale; **vendita all'asta** sale by auction; **vendita per telefono** telesales *sg*
vene'rare *vt* to venerate
venerdì *sm inv* Friday; **di** *o* **il ~** on Fridays; **V~ Santo** Good Friday
ve'nereo, -a *ag* venereal
Ve'nezia [ve'nɛttsja] *sf* Venice
'vengo *ecc vb vedi* **venire**
veni'ale *ag* venial
ve'nire *vi* to come; *(riuscire: dolce, fotografia)* to turn out; *(come ausiliare: essere)*: **viene ammirato da tutti** he is admired by everyone; **~ da** to come from; **quanto viene?** how much does it cost?; **far ~** *(mandare a chiamare)* to send for; **~ giù** to come down; **~ meno** *(svenire)* to faint; **~ meno a qc** not to fulfil sth; **~ su** to come up; **~ a trovare qn** to come and see sb; **~ via** to come away
'venni *ecc vb vedi* **venire**
ven'taglio [ven'taʎʎo] *sm* fan
ven'tata *sf* gust (of wind)

ven'tenne *ag* **una ragazza ~** a twenty-year-old girl, a girl of twenty

ven'tesimo, -a *num* twentieth

'venti *num* twenty

venti'lare *vt* (*stanza*) to air, ventilate; (*fig: idea, proposta*) to air; **ventila'tore** *sm* ventilator, fan

ven'tina *sf* **una ~ (di)** around twenty, twenty or so

'vento *sm* wind

'ventola *sf* (*Aut, Tecn*) fan

ven'tosa *sf* (*Zool*) sucker; (*di gomma*) suction pad

ven'toso, -a *ag* windy

'ventre *sm* stomach

'vera *sf* wedding ring

vera'mente *av* really

ve'randa *sf* veranda(h)

ver'bale *ag* verbal ▶ *sm* (*di riunione*) minutes *pl*

'verbo *sm* (*Ling*) verb; (*parola*) word; (*Rel*): **il V~** the Word

'verde *ag, sm* green; **essere al ~** to be broke; **verde bottiglia/oliva** bottle/olive green

ver'detto *sm* verdict

ver'dura *sf* vegetables *pl*

'vergine ['vɛrdʒine] *sf* virgin; (*dello zodiaco*): **V~** Virgo ▶ *ag* virgin; (*ragazza*): **essere ~** to be a virgin

ver'gogna [ver'goɲɲa] *sf* shame; (*timidezza*) shyness, embarrassment; **vergo'gnarsi** *vpr* **vergognarsi (di)** to be o feel ashamed (of); to be shy (about); to be embarrassed (about); **vergo'gnoso, -a** *ag* ashamed; (*timido*) shy, embarrassed; (*causa di vergogna: azione*) shameful

ve'rifica, -che *sf* checking *no pl*, check

verifi'care *vt* (*controllare*) to check; (*confermare*) to confirm, bear out

verità *sf inv* truth

'verme *sm* worm

ver'miglio [ver'miʎʎo] *sm* vermilion, scarlet

ver'nice [ver'nitʃe] *sf* (*colorazione*) paint; (*trasparente*) varnish; (*pelle*) patent leather; **"~ fresca"** "wet paint"; **vernici'are** *vt* to paint; to varnish

'vero, -a *ag* (*veridico: fatti, testimonianza*) true; (*autentico*) real ▶ *sm* (*verità*) truth; (*realtà*) (real) life; **un ~ e proprio delinquente** a real criminal, an out-and-out criminal

vero'simile *ag* likely, probable

verrò *ecc vb vedi* **venire**

ver'ruca, -che *sf* wart

versa'mento *sm* (*pagamento*) payment; (*deposito di denaro*) deposit

ver'sante *sm* slopes *pl*, side

ver'sare *vt* (*fare uscire: vino, farina*) to pour (out); (*spargere: lacrime, sangue*) to shed; (*rovesciare*) to spill; (*Econ*) to pay; (: *depositare*) to deposit, pay in

versa'tile *ag* versatile

versi'one *sf* version; (*traduzione*) translation

'verso *sm* (*di poesia*) verse, line; (*di animale, uccello*) cry; (*direzione*) direction; (*modo*) way; (*di foglio di carta*) verso; (*di moneta*) reverse; **versi** *smpl* (*poesia*) verse *sg*; **non c'è ~ di persuaderlo** there's no way of persuading him, he can't be persuaded *prep* (*in direzione di*) toward(s); (*nei pressi di*) near, around (about); (*in senso temporale*) about, around; (*nei confronti di*) for; **~ di me** towards me; **~ sera** towards evening

'vertebra *sf* vertebra

verte'brale *ag* vertebral; **colonna ~** spinal column, spine

verti'cale *ag, sf* vertical

'vertice ['vɛrtitʃe] *sm* summit, top; (*Mat*) vertex; **conferenza al ~** (*Pol*) summit conference

ver'tigine [ver'tidʒine] *sf* dizziness *no pl*; dizzy spell; (*Med*) vertigo; **avere le vertigini** to feel dizzy

ve'scica, -che [veʃˈʃika] sf (Anat)
bladder; (Med) blister

'**vescovo** sm bishop

'**vespa** sf wasp

ves'taglia [vesˈtaʎʎa] sf dressing gown

ves'tire vt (bambino, malato) to dress;
(avere indosso) to have on, wear;
vestirsi vpr to dress, get dressed;
ves'tito, -a ag dressed ▶ sm garment;
(da donna) dress; (da uomo) suit;
vestiti smpl (indumenti) clothes;
vestito di bianco dressed in white

veteri'nario, -a ag veterinary
▶ sm veterinary surgeon (BRIT),
veterinarian (US), vet

'**veto** sm inv veto

ve'traio sm glassmaker; glazier

ve'trata sf glass door (o window); (di
chiesa) stained glass window

ve'trato, -a ag (porta, finestra)
glazed; (che contiene vetro) glass cpd
▶ sf glass door (o window); (di chiesa)
stained glass window; **carta vetrata**
sandpaper

ve'trina sf (di negozio) (shop) window;
(armadio) display cabinet; **vetri'nista,
-i, -e** sm/f window dresser

'**vetro** sm glass; (per finestra, porta)
pane (of glass)

'**vetta** sf peak, summit, top

vet'tura sf (carrozza) carriage; (Ferr)
carriage (BRIT), car (US); (auto) car
(BRIT), automobile (US)

vezzeggia'tivo [vettseddʒaˈtivo] sm
(Ling) term of endearment

vi (dav lo, la, li, le, ne diventa **ve**) pron
(oggetto) you; (complemento di termine)
(to) you; (riflessivo) yourselves;
(reciproco) each other ▶ av (lì) there;
(qui) here; (per questo/quel luogo)
through here/there; **vi è/sono** there
is/are

'**via** sf (gen) way; (strada) street;
(sentiero, pista) path, track; (Amm:
procedimento) channels pl ▶ prep
(passando per) via, by way of ▶ av away
▶ escl go away!; (suvvia) come on!;
(Sport) go! ▶ sm (Sport) starting signal;
in ~ di guarigione on the road to
recovery; **per ~ di** (a causa di) because
of, on account of; **in** o **per ~** on the
way; **per ~ aerea** by air; (lettere) by
airmail; **andare/essere ~** to go/be
away; **~ ~ che** (a mano a mano) as;
dare il ~ (Sport) to give the starting
signal; **dare il ~ a** (fig) to start; **in ~
provvisoria** provisionally; **Via lattea**
(Astr) Milky Way; **via di mezzo** middle
course; **via d'uscita** (fig) way out

via'dotto sm viaduct

viaggi'are [viadˈdʒare] vi to travel;
viaggia'tore, -'trice ag travelling
▶ sm traveller; (passeggero) passenger

vi'aggio [ˈvjaddʒo] sm travel(ling);
(tragitto) journey, trip; **buon ~!** have
a good trip!; **com'è andato il ~?** how
was your journey?; **il ~ dura due ore**
the journey takes two hours; **viaggio
di nozze** honeymoon; **siamo in ~ di
nozze** we're on honeymoon

vi'ale sm avenue

via'vai sm coming and going, bustle

vi'brare vi to vibrate

'**vice** [ˈvitʃe] sm/f deputy ▶ prefisso

vi'cenda [viˈtʃenda] sf event; **a ~**
in turn

vice'versa [vitʃeˈvɛrsa] av vice versa;
da Roma a Pisa e ~ from Rome to Pisa
and back

vici'nanza [vitʃiˈnantsa] sf nearness,
closeness

vi'cino, -a [viˈtʃino] ag (gen) near;
(nello spazio) near, nearby; (accanto)
next; (nel tempo) near, close at hand
▶ sm/f neighbour ▶ av near, close; **da**
(guardare) close up; (esaminare, seguire)
closely; (conoscere) well, intimately; **~
a** near (to), close to; (accanto a) beside;
c'è una banca qui ~? is there a bank
nearby?; **~ di casa** neighbour

'**vicolo** sm alley; **vicolo cieco** blind alley

'**video** sm inv (TV: schermo) screen; **video'camera** sf camcorder; **videocas'setta** sf videocassette; **videoclip** [video'klip] sm inv videoclip; **videogi'oco, -chi** [video'dʒɔko] sm video game; **videoregistra'tore** sm video (recorder); **videote'lefono** sm videophone

'**vidi** ecc vb vedi **vedere**

vie'tare vt to forbid; (Amm) to prohibit; **~ a qn di fare** to forbid sb to do; to prohibit sb from doing; "**vietato fumare/l'ingresso**" "no smoking/admittance"

vie'tato, -a ag (vedi vb) forbidden; prohibited; banned; "**~ fumare/ l'ingresso**" "no smoking/ admittance"; **~ ai minori di 14/18 anni** prohibited to children under 14/18; "**senso ~**" (Aut) "no entry"; "**sosta vietata**" (Aut) "no parking"

Viet'nam sm il **~** Vietnam; **vietna'mita, -i, -e** ag, sm/f, sm Vietnamese inv

vi'gente [vi'dʒɛnte] ag in force

'**vigile** ['vidʒile] ag watchful ▶ sm (anche: **~ urbano**) policeman (in towns); **vigile del fuoco** fireman

vi'gilia [vi'dʒilja] sf (giorno antecedente) eve; **la ~ di Natale** Christmas Eve

vigli'acco, -a, -chi, -che [viʎ'ʎakko] ag cowardly ▶ sm/f coward

vi'gneto [vin'ɲeto] sm vineyard

vi'gnetta [vin'ɲetta] sf cartoon

vi'gore sm vigour; (Dir): **essere/ entrare in ~** to be in/come into force

'**vile** ag (spregevole) low, mean, base; (codardo) cowardly

'**villa** sf villa

vil'laggio [vil'laddʒo] sm village; **villaggio turistico** holiday village

vil'lano, -a ag rude, ill-mannered

villeggia'tura [villeddʒa'tura] sf holiday(s) pl (BRIT), vacation (US)

vil'letta sf, **vil'lino** ▶ sm small house (with a garden), cottage

'**vimini** smpl **di ~** wicker

'**vincere** ['vintʃere] vt (in guerra, al gioco, a una gara) to defeat, beat; (premio, guerra, partita) to win; (fig) to overcome, conquer ▶ vi to win; **~ qn in bellezza** to be better-looking than sb; **vinci'tore** sm winner; (Mil) victor

vi'nicolo, -a ag wine cpd

'**vino** sm wine; **vino bianco/rosato/ rosso** white/rosé/red wine; **vino da pasto** table wine

'**vinsi** ecc vb vedi **vincere**

vi'ola sf (Bot) violet; (Mus) viola ▶ ag, sm inv (colore) purple

vio'lare vt (chiesa) to desecrate, violate; (giuramento, legge) to violate

violen'tare vt to use violence on; (donna) to rape

vio'lento, -a ag violent; **vio'lenza** sf violence; **violenza carnale** rape

vio'letta sf (Bot) violet

vio'letto, -a ag, sm (colore) violet

violi'nista, -i, -e sm/f violinist

vio'lino sm violin

violon'cello [violon'tʃɛllo] sm cello

vi'ottolo sm path, track

vip [vip] sigla m (= very important person) VIP

'**vipera** sf viper, adder

vi'rare vi (Naut, Aer) to turn; (Fot) to tone; **~ di bordo** (Naut) to tack

'**virgola** sf (Ling) comma; (Mat) point; **virgo'lette** sfpl inverted commas, quotation marks

vi'rile ag (proprio dell'uomo) masculine; (non puerile, da uomo) manly, virile

virtù sf inv virtue; **in o per ~ di** by virtue of, by

virtu'ale ag virtual

'**virus** sm inv (anche Inform) virus

'viscere [ˈviʃʃere] *sfpl* (*di animale*) entrails *pl*; (*fig*) bowels *pl*

'vischio [ˈviskjo] *sm* (*Bot*) mistletoe; (*pania*) birdlime

'viscido, -a [ˈviʃʃido] *ag* slimy

vi'sibile *ag* visible

visibilità *sf* visibility

visi'era *sf* (*di elmo*) visor; (*di berretto*) peak

visi'one *sf* vision; **prendere ~ di qc** to examine sth, look sth over; **prima/ seconda ~** (*Cinema*) first/second showing

'visita *sf* visit; (*Med*) visit, call; (: *esame*) examination; **visita guidata** guided tour; **a che ora comincia la ~ guidata?** what time does the guided tour start?; **visita medica** medical examination; **visi'tare** *vt* to visit; (*Med*) to visit, call on; (: *esaminare*) to examine; **visita'tore, -'trice** *sm/f* visitor

vi'sivo, -a *ag* visual

'viso *sm* face

vi'sone *sm* mink

'vispo, -a *ag* quick, lively

'vissi *ecc vb vedi* **vivere**

'vista *sf* (*facoltà*) (eye)sight; (*fatto di vedere*): **la ~ di** the sight of; (*veduta*) view; **sparare a ~** to shoot on sight; **in ~** in sight; **perdere qn di ~** to lose sight of sb; (*fig*) to lose touch with sb; **a ~ d'occhio** as far as the eye can see; (*fig*) before one's very eyes; **far ~ di fare** to pretend to do

'visto, -a *pp di* **vedere** ▶ *sm* visa; **~ che** seeing (that)

vis'toso, -a *ag* gaudy, garish; (*ingente*) considerable

visu'ale *ag* visual

'vita *sf* life; (*Anat*) waist; **a ~** for life

vi'tale *ag* vital

vita'mina *sf* vitamin

'vite *sf* (*Bot*) vine; (*Tecn*) screw

vi'tello *sm* (*Zool*) calf; (*carne*) veal; (*pelle*) calfskin

'vittima *sf* victim

'vitto *sm* food; (*in un albergo ecc*) board; **vitto e alloggio** board and lodging

vit'toria *sf* victory

'viva *escl* **~ il re!** long live the king!

vi'vace [viˈvatʃe] *ag* (*vivo, animato*) lively; (: *mente*) lively, sharp; (*colore*) bright

vi'vaio *sm* (*di pesci*) hatchery; (*Agr*) nursery

vivavoce [vivaˈvotʃe] *sm inv* (*dispositivo*) loudspeaker; **mettere il ~** to switch on the loudspeaker

vi'vente *ag* living, alive; **i viventi** the living

'vivere *vi* to live ▶ *vt* to live; (*passare: brutto momento*) to live through, go through; (*sentire: gioie, pene di qn*) to share ▶ *sm* life; (*anche*: **modo di ~**) way of life; **viveri** *smpl* (*cibo*) food *sg*, provisions; **~ di** to live on

'vivido, -a *ag* (*colore*) vivid, bright

vivisezi'one [viviseˈtsjone] *sf* vivisection

'vivo, -a *ag* (*vivente*) alive, living; (: *animale*) live; (*fig*) lively; (: *colore*) bright, brilliant; **i vivi** the living; **~ e vegeto** hale and hearty; **farsi ~** to show one's face; to be heard from; **ritrarre dal ~** to paint from life; **pungere qn nel ~** (*fig*) to cut sb to the quick

vivrò *ecc vb vedi* **vivere**

vizi'are [vitˈtsjare] *vt* (*bambino*) to spoil; (*corrompere moralmente*) to corrupt; **vizi'ato, -a** *ag* spoilt; (*aria, acqua*) polluted

'vizio [ˈvittsjo] *sm* (*morale*) vice; (*cattiva abitudine*) bad habit; (*imperfezione*) flaw, defect; (*errore*) fault, mistake

V.le *abbr* = **viale**

vocabo'lario *sm* (*dizionario*) dictionary; (*lessico*) vocabulary

vo'cabolo *sm* word

vo'cale *ag* vocal ▶ *sf* vowel

vocazi'one [vokat'tsjone] *sf* vocation; (*fig*) natural bent

'voce ['votʃe] *sf* voice; (*diceria*) rumour; (*di un elenco, in bilancio*) item; **aver ~ in capitolo** (*fig*) to have a say in the matter

'voga *sf* (*Naut*) rowing; (*usanza*): **essere in ~** to be in fashion *o* in vogue

vo'gare *vi* to row

vogherò *ecc* [voge'rɔ] *vb vedi* **vogare**

'voglia ['vɔʎʎa] *sf* desire, wish; (*macchia*) birthmark; **aver ~ di qc/di fare** to feel like sth/like doing; (*più forte*) to want sth/to do

'voglio *ecc* ['vɔʎʎo] *vb vedi* **volere**

'voi *pron* you; **voi'altri** *pron* you

vo'lante *ag* flying ▶ *sm* (steering) wheel

volan'tino *sm* leaflet

vo'lare *vi* (*uccello, aereo, fig*) to fly; (*cappello*) to blow away *o* off, fly away *o* off; **~ via** to fly away *o* off

vo'latile *ag* (*Chim*) volatile ▶ *sm* (*Zool*) bird

volente'roso, -a *ag* willing

volenti'eri *av* willingly; "**~**" "with pleasure", "I'd be glad to"

⭕ **vo'lere**

   sm will, wish(es); **contro il volere di** against the wishes of; **per volere di qn** in obedience to sb's will *o* wishes ▶ *vt*

1 (*esigere, desiderare*) to want; **voler fare/che qn faccia** to want to do/sb to do; **volete del caffè?** would you like *o* do you want some coffee?; **vorrei questo/fare** I would *o* I'd like this/to do; **come vuoi** as you like; **senza volere** (*inavvertitamente*) unintentionally

2 (*consentire*): **vogliate attendere, per piacere** please wait; **vogliamo andare?** shall we go?; **vuole essere così gentile da …?** would you be so kind as to …?; **non ha voluto ricevermi** he wouldn't see me

3: **volerci** (*essere necessario: materiale, attenzione*) to need; (: *tempo*) to take; **quanta farina ci vuole per questa torta?** how much flour do you need for this cake?; **ci vuole un'ora per arrivare a Venezia** it takes an hour to get to Venice

4: **voler bene a qn** (*amore*) to love sb; (*affetto*) to be fond of sb; **voler male a qn** to dislike sb; **volerne a qn** to bear sb a grudge; **voler dire** to mean

vol'gare *ag* vulgar

voli'era *sf* aviary

voli'tivo, -a *ag* strong-willed

'volli *ecc vb vedi* **volere**

'volo *sm* flight; **al ~: colpire qc al ~** to hit sth as it flies past; **capire al ~** to understand straight away; **volo charter** charter flight; **volo di linea** scheduled flight

volontà *sf* will; **a ~** (*mangiare, bere*) as much as one likes; **buona/cattiva ~** goodwill/lack of goodwill

volontari'ato *sm* (*lavoro*) voluntary work

volon'tario, -a *ag* voluntary ▶ *sm* (*Mil*) volunteer

'volpe *sf* fox

'volta *sf* (*momento, circostanza*) time; (*turno, giro*) turn; (*curva*) turn, bend; (*Archit*) vault; (*direzione*): **partire alla ~ di** to set off for; **a mia** (*o* **tua** *ecc*) **~** in turn; **una ~** once; **una ~ sola** only once; **due volte** twice; **una cosa per ~** one thing at a time; **una ~ per tutte** once and for all; **a volte** at times, sometimes; **una ~ che** (*temporale*) once; (*causale*) since; **3 volte 4** 3 times 4

volta'faccia [volta'fattʃa] *sm inv* (*fig*) volte-face

vol'taggio [vol'taddʒo] *sm* (*Elettr*) voltage

vol'tare *vt* to turn; (*girare: moneta*) to turn over; (*rigirare*) to turn round ▶ *vi* to turn; **voltarsi** *vpr* to turn; to turn over; to turn round

voltas'tomaco *sm* nausea; (*fig*) disgust

'**volto, -a** *pp di* **volgere** ▶ *sm* face

vo'lubile *ag* changeable, fickle

vo'lume *sm* volume

vomi'tare *vt, vi* to vomit; '**vomito** *sm* vomiting *no pl*; vomit

'**vongola** *sf* clam

vo'race [vo'ratʃe] *ag* voracious, greedy

vo'ragine [vo'radʒine] *sf* abyss, chasm

vorrò *ecc vb vedi* **volere**

'**vortice** ['vɔrtitʃe] *sm* whirlwind; whirlpool; (*fig*) whirl

'**vostro, -a** *det* **il(la) ~(a)** *ecc* your ▶ *pron* **il(la) ~(a)** *ecc* yours

vo'tante *sm/f* voter

vo'tare *vi* to vote ▶ *vt* (*sottoporre a votazione*) to take a vote on; (*approvare*) to vote for; (*Rel*): **~ qc a** to dedicate sth to

'**voto** *sm* (*Pol*) vote; (*Ins*) mark; (*Rel*) vow; (: *offerta*) votive offering; **aver voti belli/brutti** (*Ins*) to get good/bad marks

vs. *abbr* (*Comm*) = **vostro**

vul'cano *sm* volcano

vulne'rabile *ag* vulnerable

vu'oi, vu'ole *vb vedi* **volere**

vuo'tare *vt* to empty; **vuotarsi** *vpr* to empty

vu'oto, -a *ag* empty; (*fig: privo*): **~ di** (*senso ecc*) devoid of ▶ *sm* empty space, gap; (*spazio in bianco*) blank; (*Fisica*) vacuum; (*fig: mancanza*) gap, void; **a mani vuote** empty-handed; **vuoto d'aria** air pocket; **vuoto a rendere** returnable bottle

'**wafer** ['vafer] *sm inv* (*Cuc, Elettr*) wafer

'**water** ['wɔːtəʳ] *sm inv* toilet

watt [vat] *sm inv* watt

W.C. *sm inv* WC

web [ueb] *sm* **il ~** the Web; **cercare nel ~** to search the Web ▶ *ag inv* **pagina ~** web page; **web'cam** [web'kam] *sf inv* (*Comput*) webcam

'**weekend** ['wiːkend] *sm inv* weekend

'**western** ['wɛstern] *ag* (*Cinema*) cowboy *cpd* ▶ *sm inv* western, cowboy film; **western all'italiana** spaghetti western

'**whisky** ['wiski] *sm inv* whisky

Wi-Fi [uai'fai] *ag inv* (*Comput*) Wi-Fi

'**windsurf** ['windsəːf] *sm inv* (*tavola*) windsurfer; (*sport*) windsurfing

'**würstel** ['vyrstəl] *sm inv* frankfurter

X

Y

Z

xe'nofobo, -a [ksenɔfobo] *ag* xenophobic ▶ *sm/f* xenophobe
xi'lofono [ksiˈlɔfono] *sm* xylophone

yacht [jɔt] *sm inv* yacht
'yoga [ˈjɔga] *ag inv, sm* yoga (*cpd*)
yogurt [ˈjɔgurt] *sm inv* yog(h)urt

zabai'one [dzabaˈjone] *sm dessert made of egg yolks, sugar and marsala*
zaf'fata [tsafˈfata] *sf (tanfo)* stench
zaffe'rano [dzaffeˈrano] *sm* saffron
zaf'firo [dzafˈfiro] *sm* sapphire
zai'netto [zaiˈnetto] *sm* (small) rucksack
'zaino [ˈdzaino] *sm* rucksack
'zampa [ˈtsampa] *sf (di animale: gamba)* leg; (: *piede*) paw; **a quattro zampe** on all fours
zampil'lare [tsampilˈlare] *vi* to gush, spurt
zan'zara [dzanˈdzara] *sf* mosquito; **zanzari'era** *sf* mosquito net
'zappa [ˈtsappa] *sf* hoe
'zapping [ˈtsapiŋ] *sm* (*TV*) channel-hopping
zar, za'rina [tsar, tsaˈrina] *sm/f* tsar/tsarina
'zattera [ˈdzattera] *sf* raft
'zebra [ˈdzɛbra] *sf* zebra; **zebre** *sfpl* (*Aut*) zebra crossing *sg* (*BRIT*), crosswalk *sg* (*US*)
'zecca, -che [ˈtsekka] *sf* (*Zool*) tick; (*officina di monete*) mint
'zelo [ˈdzɛlo] *sm* zeal
'zenzero [ˈdzendzero] *sm* ginger
'zeppa [ˈtseppa] *sf* wedge
'zeppo, -a [ˈtseppo] *ag* **~ di** crammed *o* packed with
zer'bino [dzerˈbino] *sm* doormat
'zero [ˈdzɛro] *sm* zero, nought; **vincere per tre a ~** (*Sport*) to win three-nil

z

'zia ['tsia] *sf* aunt

zibel'lino [dzibel'lino] *sm* sable

'zigomo ['dzigomo] *sm* cheekbone

zig'zag [dzig'dzag] *sm inv* zigzag; **andare a ~** to zigzag

Zimbabwe [tsim'babwe] *sm* **lo ~** Zimbabwe

'zinco ['dzinko] *sm* zinc

'zingaro, -a ['dzingaro] *sm/f* gipsy

'zio ['tsio] (*pl* **'zii**) *sm* uncle

zip'pare *vt* (*Inform: file*) to zip

zi'tella [dzi'tɛlla] *sf* spinster; (*peg*) old maid

'zitto, -a ['tsitto] *ag* quiet, silent; **sta' ~!** be quiet!

'zoccolo ['tsɔkkolo] *sm* (*calzatura*) clog; (*di cavallo ecc*) hoof; (*basamento*) base; plinth

zodia'cale [dzodia'kale] *ag* zodiac *cpd*; **segno ~** sign of the zodiac

zo'diaco [dzo'diako] *sm* zodiac

'zolfo ['tsolfo] *sm* sulphur

'zolla ['dzɔlla] *sf* clod (of earth)

zol'letta [dzol'letta] *sf* sugar lump

'zona ['dzɔna] *sf* zone, area; **zona di depressione** (*Meteor*) trough of low pressure; **zona disco** (*Aut*) ≈ meter zone; **zona industriale** industrial estate; **zona pedonale** pedestrian precinct; **zona verde** (*di abitato*) green area

'zonzo ['dzondzo]: **a ~** *av*, **andare a ~** to wander about, stroll about

zoo ['dzɔo] *sm inv* zoo

zoolo'gia [dzoolo'dʒia] *sf* zoology

zoppi'care [tsoppi'kare] *vi* to limp; to be shaky, rickety

'zoppo, -a ['tsɔppo] *ag* lame; (*fig: mobile*) shaky, rickety

Z.T.L. *sigla f* (= *Zona a Traffico Limitato*) *controlled traffic zone*

'zucca, -che ['tsukka] *sf* (*Bot*) marrow; pumpkin

zucche'rare [tsukke'rare] *vt* to put sugar in; **zucche'rato, -a** *ag* sweet, sweetened

zuccheri'era [tsukke'rjɛra] *sf* sugar bowl

'zucchero ['tsukkero] *sm* sugar; **zucchero di canna** cane sugar; **zucchero filato** candy floss, cotton candy (*US*)

zuc'china [tsuk'kina] *sf* courgette (*BRIT*), zucchini (*US*)

'zuffa ['tsuffa] *sf* brawl

'zuppa ['tsuppa] *sf* soup; (*fig*) mixture, muddle; **zuppa inglese** (*Cuc*) dessert *made with sponge cake, custard and chocolate,* ≈ trifle (*BRIT*)

'zuppo, -a ['tsuppo] *ag* **~ (di)** drenched (with), soaked (with)

Italian in focus

Introduction

Italian in focus gives you an introduction to various aspects of Italy and the Italian language. The following pages help you get to know the country where the language is spoken and the people who speak it.

Practical language tips and helpful notes on common translation difficulties will enable you to become a more confident Italian speaker. A useful correspondence section gives you all the information you need to be able to communicate effectively.

We've also included a number of links to useful websites, which will give you the opportunity to read more about Italy and the Italian language.

We hope you will enjoy using your *Italian in focus* supplement. We are sure it will help you find out more about Italy and Italians and become more confident in writing and speaking Italian.

Cominciamo!

Italy and its regions

©Collins Bartholomew Ltd 2006

Italy's neighbours
Italian is an official language in two Swiss cantons – Ticino and Grigioni, in the republic of San Marino and in Vatican City. Italian is also spoken in Malta, part of Croatia, and part of Slovenia.

Italy and its regions

The six biggest Italian cities

City	Name of inhabitants	Population
Roma	i romani	2,542,003
Milano	i milanesi	1,272,898
Napoli	i napoletani	1,000,449
Torino	i torinesi	867,857
Palermo	i palermitani	679,430
Genova	i genovesi	601,338

Italy consists of the mainland and two large islands, Sardegna and Sicilia, together with smaller islands such as Elba and Capri.

There are 20 administrative regions, five of which are *regioni autonome*, which have more decision-making powers than the others. Three of the 'autonomous regions' are in the north – Valle d'Aosta, Friuli-Venezia Giulia and Trentino-Alto Adige. The other two are the islands of Sardegna and Sicilia. Central government retains jurisdiction for matters such as defence, foreign affairs and the legal system, which affect the country as a whole.

Italy has only been a unified country since 1870. Before then parts of the peninsula were under the control of various countries, such as Spain, Austria and France. There was, and still is, a strong regional identity, with many people speaking one of the diverse local dialects. Nowadays everyone learns standard Italian at school; however many people speak *dialetto* with neighbours, friends and family.

As is often the case in areas bordering other countries, there are some bilingual communities. For example, in the Trentino-Alto Adige area in the far north of Italy, the majority language is German.

A snapshot of Italy

- In area, Italy (301, 323 km²) is somewhat bigger than the UK (244,110 km²).

- The Po (652 km) is Italy's longest river. It rises in the Alps and flows into the Adriatic near Venice.

- The population of Italy is about 58.4 million, which is slightly less than that of the UK. The birth rate is very low (1.2 children per woman). Deaths outnumber births.

- The Italian economy is the fourth biggest in the EU and seventh biggest in the world.

- Italy is the world's biggest wine-producing country.

- Gran Paradiso (4061) is Italy's highest peak.

- About 37 million tourists visit Italy every year, making it the 5th most popular tourist destination in the world.

- Italy has four active volcanoes: Etna, Vesuvius, Stromboli and Vulcano. Etna erupts frequently and is Europe's most active volcano.

Some useful links are:
www.governo.it
Website of the Italian government.
www.istat.it
The Italian statistics office.
www.enit.it
Italian state tourist board.

The Italian-speaking world

PAÍSES O REGIONES DONDE EL ITALIANO ES LA LENGUA MATERNA O UNA LENGUA OFICIAL

Países con una cantidad importante de italoparlantes

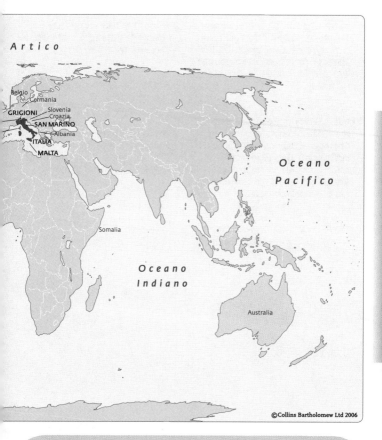

Artico

Belgio
Germania
Slovenia
GRIGIONI
Croazia
SAN MARINO
Albania
ITALIA
MALTA

Somalia

Oceano
Pacifico

Oceano
Indiano

Australia

©Collins Bartholomew Ltd 2006

Many Italians went to the Americas – particularly to the US and Argentina – and to Australia. There are 1 ½ million Italian speakers in Argentina and nearly a milion in the US. Italian has had a major influence on the way Spanish is spoken in Argentina

The Italian State

- Italy has dozens of political parties. The two main political groupings are the centre-right and the centre-left. The government tends to be formed by a coalition consisting of several parties.

- Italy has two houses of parliament: the Senate (*il Senato*) and the Chamber of Deputies (*la Camera dei Deputati*). The President of the Republic (*il Presidente della Repubblica*), who is the head of state, has a tenure of seven years.

- The Prime Minister (*il Presidente del Consiglio*) is the head of government.

- Inside Italy there are two tiny independent states: San Marino and Vatican City.

- San Marino is the smallest republic in Europe.

- Vatican City is the spiritual and administrative centre of the Roman Catholic Church. It has two official languages, Italian and Latin.

Italian words that have travelled the world

An important part of the language Italians took to foreign countries was to do with food – many immigrants opened cafés and restaurants. These days people all over the world drink cappuccinos and espressos, and eat ciabatta, spaghetti, minestrone and pizza.

While everyone is familiar with these food items, they may not realize that the Italian words themselves have interesting, highly descriptive meanings. Here are just a few:

- cappuccino
  This comes from the word capuchin. Capuchins are friars whose habits are brown – the colour of cappuccino coffee.

- ciabatta
  This means 'slipper'. The bread has this name because of its shape.

- macchiato
  macchiato means 'stained' and describes the look of a dark coffee with a little spot of milk on it .

- spaghetti
  spago means 'string' – so *spaghetti* are 'little strings'. There's another pasta called *orecchiette*. If you bear in mind that *un orecchio* is an ear, you can probably guess what this pasta looks like.

- tiramisù
  This word doesn't describe the appearance of the dessert, but the effect it has, as it means 'pick-me-up' (a reference to the stimulating effect of the coffee it contains).

- vermicelli
  This kind of pasta is very, very thin, and its name means 'little worms'.

Italian words used in English

Apart from lots of words to do with food, there are other Italian words that are very often used in English. Here are a few interesting examples:

• solo
This means 'alone' in Italian and was originally borrowed as a musical term – but it's now used in all kinds of contexts.

• fiasco
English has borrowed only one of this word's two senses: the other one is 'wine bottle'!

• piano
This is the Italian for 'soft'. When the pianoforte was invented it was so called because it could be played either soft (*piano*), or loud (*forte*), unlike its predecessor, the harpsichord.

• prima donna
This word for leading lady means 'first woman'. This is another musical term which has come to be used more generally.

• bimbo
Unlike in English, in Italian this is not a derogatory word for a woman – it just means 'little boy'. *Una bimba* is a little girl.

• al fresco
In Italian this doesn't mean 'outside' but 'in the cool', and in a figurative sense, 'in jail'.

English words used in Italian

Italians have as great an appetite for English words as other people have for Italian food. Words from every conceivable field are borrowed; daily life, popular culture, science, computing, sport, business and so on.

- Countless words are borrowed in their original form:

lo stress	*la privacy*
lo shopping	*il gay*
il fast food	*il blues*
il jazz	*lo show*
il talk show	*il computer*
il mouse	*il golf*
lo sport	*il supporter,*
il record	*il training*
il manager	*il target.*

In the plural, these words get a plural article (*i*, *gli* or *le*) but no final 's':

Singular	Plural
il talk show	*i talk show*
lo sport	*gli sport*
la star	*le star*

- Other words are Italianized, but still recognizably English:

chattare	to chat
craccare	to crack
dribblare	to dribble
sprintare	to sprint
scrollare	to scroll
standardizzare	to standardize
interfaccia	interface
reality	reality show

- Some words look English, but have taken on a different meaning:

un box	a garage
un golf	a cardigan (it also means the sport)
un ticket	a prescription charge
uno smoking	a dinner jacket
uno spot	a tv or radio advert

Improving your pronunciation

Italian sounds

Vowels

Each English vowel can be pronounced in several quite different ways – think of the sound the letter i has, for example, in the words milk, kind and circus. Italian vowels vary much less in their pronunciation:

a – is like the *a* in father
e – is like the *e* in set
i – is like the *ee* in sheep OR is pronounced like *y* in yard
o – is like the *o* in orange
u – is like the *oo* in soon

Avoid saying Italian words like their English lookalikes: the *i* in *Milano* and in *aprile*, for example is the long ee sound, not the short i used in Milan and April.

Unlike English, Italian is pronounced exactly as it is written, so *interessante*, for example, has five syllables, with a clearly pronounced vowel in each one: *in-te-res-san-te*.

- Italian vowels never disappear as they do in English words like interesting (int-res-ting) and camera (cam-ra). Always pronounce them fully.

- Italian vowels never have the indistinct 'uh' sound to be heard at the end of many English words, for example, hostel, hospital and circus. Always pronounce Italian vowels clearly.

- When *i* is pronounced *y*, make sure that it's *y* as in yard, not *y* as in very:

andiamo	an-dya-mo
	(not an-dy-a-mo)
ravioli	rav-yo-lee
	(not ra-vee-o-lee)
stazione	sta-zyo-ne
	(not sta-zee-o-ne)

Improving your pronunciation

Consonants

- The presence of a double consonant in Italian makes the consonant sound longer: *cat-ti-vo*, *inte-res-san-te*, *An-na*.

- *c* followed by *e* or *i*, is pronounced **tch** as in *centro* and *facile*.

- *ch* is pronounced **k**, as in *fuochi* and *chiuso*.

- *g* followed by *e* and *i* is pronounced *j* as in *leggero* and *giardino*.

- *gh* is pronounced like *g* in get, as in *lunghi* and *spaghetti*.

- *gl* followed by *e* and *i* is normally pronounced like the **lli** in million, for example *luglio*, *bagagli*.

- *gn* is pronounced **ny**, for example *gnocchi*, *giugno*.

- *sc* followed by *e* and *i* is pronounced **sh**, as in *lasciare* and *sciare*.

Stress

- Italian words are usually stressed on the next to the last syllable, for example *cucina*, *studente*, *straniero*, *diciassette*, *parlare*, *avere*.

- If a word is spelled with an accent on the last vowel, for example, *fedeltà*, *università*, *però*, *così*, *caffè*, put the stress on this vowel.

- Some words are stressed on other syllables; the 'they' form of verbs, for example, usually stresses the second to last syllable: *capiscono* (= they understand); *parlano* (= they speak).

- Other words, such as *subito*, *macchina*, *vendere* and *camera* stress the first syllable. Be aware that words aren't always stressed as you'd expect and when in doubt look in the dictionary: you'll see that in each headword there's a mark that looks like an apostrophe. The syllable immediately following this apostrophe is the one you stress.

A useful link is:
www.accademiadellacrusca.it
National language academy of Italy.

Improving your fluency

Conversational words and phrases

In English we insert lots of words and phrases, such as *so*, *then*, *by the way*, into our conversation, to give our thoughts a structure and often to show our attitude. The Italian words below do the same thing. If you use them you'll sound more fluent and natural.

- *allora*
  Allora, che facciamo stasera? (= so)

- *va bene*
  Va bene, ho capito. (= okay)

- *ecco*
  Ecco perché non sono venuti.
  (= that's)
  Ecco Mario! (= here's)
  Eccolo! (= there ... is)

- *forse*
  Sì, ma **forse** hanno ragione.
  (= maybe)

- *certo*
  Certo che puoi. (= of course)

- *dunque*
  Dunque, come dicevo ... (= well)
  Dunque ha ragione lui. (= so)

- *può darsi*
  Sì, lo so, ma **può darsi** che ...
  (= perhaps)

- *purtroppo*
  Sì, **purtroppo**. (= unfortunately)

- *sinceramente*
  Sinceramente, non m'importa niente.
  (= really)

- *comunque*
  Comunque, non è sempre così.
  (= however)

- *senz'altro*
  Mi scriverai? – **Senz'altro**!
  (= of course)
  È **senz'altro** meglio lui. (= definitely)

- *davvero*
  Ha pagato lui. – **Davvero**? (= really)

Improving your fluency

Varying the words you use to get your message across will also make you sound more fluent in Italian. For example, instead of *Mi piace molto il calcio*, you could say *Il calcio è la mia passione*. Here are some other suggestions.

Saying what you like or dislike

Adoro le ciliege.
Mi è piaciuto molto il tuo regalo.
Non mi piace il tennis.
Il suo ultimo film *non mi piace per niente*.
Detesto mentire.

I love …
I (really) liked …
I don't like …
I don't like … (at all).
I hate …

Expressing your opinion

Credo che sia giusto.
Penso che costino di più.
Sono sicuro/sicura che ti piacerà.
Secondo me è stato un errore.
A mio parere vincerà lui.
A me sembra che qualche volta …

I think …
I think …
I'm sure …
In my opinion …
In my opinion …
It seems to me …

Agreeing or disagreeing

Ha ragione.
Giusto!
(Non) sono d'accordo.
Non direi.
Certo!

You're right.
Quite right!
I (don't) agree.
I wouldn't say so.
Of course!

Correspondence

The following section on correspondence has been designed to help you communicate confidently in written as well as spoken Italian. Sample letters, e-mails and sections on text messaging and making telephone calls will ensure that you have all the vocabulary you need to correspond successfully.

Text messaging

un sms (*esse emme esse*) = text message
mandare un sms a qualcuno = to text somebody

Abbreviation	Italian	English
+ tardi	*più tardi*	later
+o-	*più o meno*	more or less
ba	*bacio*	kiss
bn	*bene*	well
C6?	*ci sei?*	are you there?
cs	*cosa*	what
c ved	*ci vediamo*	see you soon
dv	*dove*	where
k6?	*chi sei?*	who are you?
ke cs?	*che cosa?*	what?
tu6	*tu sei*	you are
k	*che*	that, what
qd	*quando*	when
nn	*non*	not
k fai?	*che fai?*	what are you doing?
qnd	*quando*	when
TVB	*ti voglio bene*	I love you
TVTB	*ti voglio tanto bene*	I love you so much
x	*per*	for
xke	*perché*	because
xke?	*perché?*	why?
TAT	*ti amo tanto*	love you loads

Writing an email

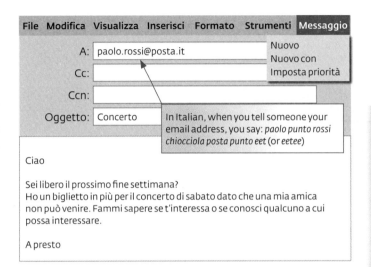

| File | Modifica | Visualizza | Inserisci | Formato | Strumenti | **Messaggio** |

> Nuovo
> Nuovo con
> Imposta priorità

A: paolo.rossi@posta.it

Cc:

Ccn:

Oggetto: Concerto

> In Italian, when you tell someone your email address, you say: *paolo punto rossi chiocciola posta punto eet* (or *eetee*)

Ciao

Sei libero il prossimo fine settimana?
Ho un biglietto in più per il concerto di sabato dato che una mia amica non può venire. Fammi sapere se t'interessa o se conosci qualcuno a cui possa interessare.

A presto

file	file	*rispondi al mittente*	reply to sender
modifica	edit	*rispondi a tutti*	reply to all
visualizza	view	*inoltrare*	to forward
formato	format	*allega*	attachment
inserisci	insert	*A*	to
?	help	*Cc (copia carbone)*	cc (carbon copy)
strumenti	tools	*Ccn (copia carbone nascosta)*	bcc (blind carbon copy)
scrivere	to compose	*oggetto*	subject
help	help	*da*	from
invia	send	*dat*	sent
crea messaggio	new message		

Here is some additional useful Internet vocabulary:

ADSL	broadband	*Internet*	the Internet
avanti	forward	*la Rete*	the (World-Wide) Web
cartella	folder	*motore di recerca*	search engine
cercare	to search	*navigare in Internet*	to surf the Net
cliccare	to click	*pagina iniziale*	home page
collegamenti	links	*pagina web*	web page
collegarsi	to log on	*prefereti*	favorites
copiare	to copy	*programma*	program
cronologia	history	*provider*	Internet Service Provider
domande frequenti	FAQs	*salvare*	to save
fare doppio click	to double-click	*scaricare*	to download
finestra	window	*scollegarsi*	to log off
foglio di calcolo	spreadsheet	*sito Internet*	website
icona	icon	*stampare*	print
impostazioni	settings	*tagliare*	to cut
incollare	to paste	*tartiera*	keyboard
indietro	back	*visualizzare*	to view

Writing a personal letter

→ *Siena, 5 giugno 2010*

Cara Maria,

ti ringrazio moltissimo del biglietto che mi hai mandato per il mio compleanno, che è arrivato proprio il giorno della mia festa!

Mi dispiace che tu non sia potuta venire a Milano per il mio compleanno e spero che ti sia ripresa dopo l'influenza. Mi piacerebbe poterti incontrare presto perché ho molte novità da raccontarti. Forse tra due settimane verrò a Torino con degli amici. Pensi di essere libera il giorno 12? Ti telefono la prossima settimana, così ci mettiamo d'accordo.

Baci,

Anna

Writing a personal letter

Other ways of starting a personal letter	Other ways of ending a personal letter
Carissima Maria *Mia cara Maria* *Cari Luigi e Silvia*	*Un abbraccio* *Bacioni* *Con affetto* *A presto*

Some useful phrases

Ti ringrazio per la tua lettera.	Thank you for your letter.
Mi ha fatto piacere ricevere tue notizie.	It was lovely to hear from you.
Scusami se non ti ho scritto prima.	I'm sorry I didn't reply sooner.
Salutami tanto Lucia.	Give my love to Lucia.
Tanti saluti anche da Paolo.	Paolo sends his best wishes.
Scrivi presto!	Write soon!

Writing a formal letter

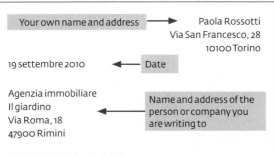

Your own name and address ➡ Paola Rossotti
Via San Francesco, 28
10100 Torino

19 settembre 2010 ⬅ Date

Agenzia immobiliare
Il giardino
Via Roma, 18 ⬅ Name and address of the person or company you are writing to
47900 Rimini

OGGETTO: Richiesta di rimborso

Egr. signori,
vi scrivo per presentare reclamo in merito all'appartamento
che ho affittato nel condominio Le Torri per il periodo 5-12
agosto. Avevo espressamente richiesto un appartamento
con due camere e invece mi è stato assegnato un
appartamento con una camera sola; mancava inoltre
il condizionatore d'aria di cui il contratto di locazione fa
specifica menzione.
Chiedo quindi un rimborso di 1000 euro comprensivo
della differenza tra la tariffa che ho pagato per un
appartamento con due camere e aria condizionata e quella
per un appartamento con una camera sola senza aria
condizionata, e di un risarcimento per i disagi subiti.

Allego fotocopia del contratto di locazione.

Distinti saluti

Paola Rossotti

Writing a formal letter

Other ways of starting a formal letter	Other ways of ending a formal letter
Egregio signore, *Gentile signora,* *Egregio Signor Paolozzo,* *Gentile Signora Paolozzo,* *Spett. Ditta,* (when writing to a firm)	*Distinti saluti* *La prego di accettare i miei più distinti saluti* *Cordiali saluti*

Some useful phrases

La ringrazio della sua lettera del …	Thank you for your letter of …
In riferimento a …	With reference to …
Vi prego di inviarmi …	Please send me …
In attesa di una sua risposta la ringrazio per l'attenzione.	I look forward to hearing from you.
La ringrazio in anticipo per …	Thank you in advance for …

Agenzia immobiliare
Il giardino
Via Roma, 18
47900 Rimini

The house number comes after the street name, and the postcode comes before the name of the town.

Making a call

Asking for information

Qual è il prefisso di Livorno?	What's the code for Livorno?
Cosa devo fare per ottenere la linea esterna?	How do I get an outside line?
Può darmi il numero dell'interno della Signora Busi?	Could you give me Ms Busi's extension number?

When your number answers

Buongiorno, c'è Andrea?	Hello! Is Andrea there?
Potrei parlare con Lucia, per favore?	Could I speak to Lucia, please?
Parla la signora de Maggio?	Is that Mrs de Maggio?
Può chiedergli/chiederle di richiamarmi?	Could you ask him/her to call me back?
Richiamo fra mezz'ora.	I'll call back in half an hour.
Posso lasciare un messaggio, per favore?	Could I leave a message, please?

When you answer the telephone

Pronto!	Hello!
Chi parla?	Who's speaking?
Sono Marco.	It's Marco speaking.
Sì, sono io.	Speaking.
Vuole lasciare un messaggio?	Would you like to leave a message?

What you may hear

Chi devo dire?	Who shall I say is calling?
Le passo la comunicazione.	I'm putting you through now.
Attenda in linea.	Please hold.
Non risponde nessuno.	There's no reply.
La linea è occupata.	The line is engaged (Brit)/busy (US).
Vuole lasciare un messaggio?	Would you like to leave a message?

If you have a problem

Scusi, ho sbagliato numero.	Sorry, I dialled the wrong number.
La linea è molto disturbata.	This is a very bad line.
Qui non c'è campo.	There's no signal here.
Ho la batteria quasi scarica.	My battery's low.
Non ti sento.	I can't hear you.

Italian phrases and sayings

In Italian, as in many languages, people use vivid expressions based on images from their experience of real life. We've grouped the common expressions below according to the type of image they use. For fun, we have given you the word-for-word translation as well as the English equivalent.

Food and drink

dire pane al pane e vino al vino → to call a spade a spade
word for word: *to call bread bread and wine wine*

Se non è zuppa è pan bagnato. → It's much of a muchness.
word for word: *if it's not soup it's wet bread*

rendere pan per focaccia → to give as good as you get
word for word: *to give bread for focaccia*

avere le mani in pasta → to have a finger in the pie
word for word: *to have your hands in the dough*

lavorare per la pagnotta → to earn your living
word for word: *to work for your loaf*

Ormai la frittata è fatta. → The damage is done.
word for word: *the omelette is made now*

Weather

fare il bello e il cattivo tempo → to do as one pleases
word for word: *to make the good and bad weather*

una tempesta in un bicchier d'acqua → a storm in a teacup
word for word: *a storm in a glass of water*

sposa bagnata sposa fortunata → rain on your wedding day is lucky
word for word: *wet bride, lucky bride*

Italian phrases and sayings

prendere due piccioni con una fava → to kill two birds with one stone
    word for word: *to get two pigeons with one broad bean*

Quando il gatto non c'è i topi ballano. → When the cat's away the mice will play.
    word for word: *when the cat's not there the mice dance*

Chi dorme non piglia pesci. → The early bird catches the worm.
    word for word: *if you're asleep you don't catch any fish*

In bocca al lupo! → Break a leg!
    word for word: *into the wolf's mouth!*

Meglio un uovo oggi che una gallina domani. → A bird in the hand is worth two in the bush.
    word for word: *better an egg today than a hen tomorrow*

L'ospite è come il pesce, dopo tre giorni puzza. → It's nice when they come and it's nice when they go.
    word for word: *guests are like fish – after three days they start to smell*

Parts of the body

essere un pugno in un occhio → to be an eyesore
    word for word: *to be a punch in the eye*

Chi non ha testa ha gambe. → Use your head to save your legs.
    word for word: *people who have no head have legs*

rimanere a bocca aperta → to be amazed
    word for word: *to be left open-mouthed*

avere le mani bucate → to spend money like water
    word for word: *to have holes in your hands*

Italian phrases and sayings

Clothes

nascere con la camicia
word for word:

→ to be born with a silver spoon in your mouth
to be born with with a shirt on

sudare sette camicie
word for word:

→ to work like a dog
to sweat seven shirts

tirare qualcuno per la giacca
word for word:

→ to twist someone's arm
to pull someone by the coat

Plants

Se sono rose fioriranno.
word for word:

→ The proof of the pudding is in the eating.
if they're roses they'll bloom

fare di ogni erba un fascio
word for word:

→ to lump everything together
to put all the grasses into one bundle

Non sono tutte rose e fiori.
word for word:

→ It's not all a bed of roses.
it's not all roses and flowers

Colours

Rosso di sera, bel tempo si spera.
word for word:

→ Red sky at night, shepherd's delight.
(if the sky's) red at night you can hope for good weather

vedere tutto nero
word for word:

→ to look on the black side
to see everything as black

Al buio tutti i gatti sono neri.
word for word:

→ At night all cats are grey.
in the dark all cats are black

Some common translation difficulties

On the following pages we have shown some of the translation difficulties you are most likely to come across. We hope that the tips we have given will help you to avoid these common pitfalls when writing or speaking Italian.

How to say 'you' in Italian

There are three ways of saying *you* in Italian: **tu** and **lei** are used to speak to one person, and **voi** is used to speak to more than one person.

- Use **tu** when you are speaking to a person you know well, or to a child. If you are a student you can call another student **tu**.

> And how old are you, Roberto? → *E **tu**, Roberto, quanti anni hai?*

- Use **lei** when speaking to strangers, or anyone you're not on familiar terms with. As you get to know someone better they may suggest that you call each other **tu** instead of **lei**. In shops, hotels and restaurants customers are always addressed as **lei**.

> Would you like a coffee too, madam? → *Vuole un caffè anche **lei**, signora?*

It may seem potentially confusing that **lei** also means 'she', but in practice it's quite obvious that if someone speaks directly to you using **lei**, the meaning is *you*.

- Use **voi** when you are speaking to more than one person.

> Where are you boys from? → ***Voi** ragazzi, di dove siete?*

'You' has to go with the verb in English, but in Italian you often use the verb alone:

> How old are you? → *Quanti anni hai?*
> You speak good Italian, madam. → *Parla bene l'italiano, signora.*
> You're young. → *Siete giovani.*

Some common translation difficulties

You use the words **tu**, **lei** and **voi** to attract someone's attention, or for the sake of emphasis.

> *Tu cosa pensi?* → What do <u>you</u> think?
> *Lei quale preferisce?* → Which one do <u>you</u> prefer?

Showing possession

In English -'s is a common way of showing who or what something belongs to. In Italian you have to use **di**:

> my brother**'s** car → *la macchina **di** mio fratello*
> Maria**'s** house → *la casa **di** Maria*

Translating 'to like'

There are two ways of saying you like something, depending whether it is singular or plural:

> I like Italy. → **Mi piace** *l'Italia.*
> word-for-word meaning of Italian: **to me is pleasing Italy**

> I like dogs. → **Mi piacciono** *i cani.*
> word-for-word meaning of Italian: **to me are pleasing dogs**

If you bear in mind the word-for-word meaning of the Italian you'll have no trouble deciding whether to use **piace** or **piacciono**.

To say 'we like', change **mi** to **ci**.

> We like the sea. → **Ci piace** *il mare.*
> We like his films. → **Ci piacciono** *i suoi film.*

Some common translation difficulties

If you want to ask someone if they like something:

• Use **ti** when asking someone you know well.

> Do you like my shoes?   →   **Ti piacciono** le mie scarpe?

• Use **le** when speaking politely

> Do you like Italian food, madam?   →   **Le piace** la cucina italiana, signora?

• Use **vi** when talking to more than one person.

> Do you like football, boys?   →   **Vi piace** il calcio, ragazzi?

Translating -ing

The English -*ing* form is used to talk about something you are doing or were doing. This can be translated into Italian by using the Italian present continuous tense (the verb form that ends -**ando** or -**endo**).

> They were gett**ing** bored.   →   *Si stavano annoiando.*
> He's read**ing** the paper.   →   *Sta leggendo il giornale.*
> She's talk**ing** to Mum.   →   *Sta parlando con la mamma.*

It is, however, just as common to translate the –*ing* form in English with the present simple tense in Italian.

> He's read**ing** the paper.   →   ***Legge*** il giornale.
> She's talk**ing** to Mum.   →   ***Parla*** con la mamma.

In other cases the Italian infinitive (the verb form that ends in -**are**, -**ere**, or -**ire**) is often used where the -*ing* form is used in English.

• Use the infinitive when talking about activities:

> I love **reading**.   →   *Mi piace moltissimo **leggere**.*
> We don't like **walking**.   →   *Non ci piace **camminare**.*
> **Smoking** is bad for you.   →   ***Fumare** fa male.*

Some common translation difficulties

Use the infinitive to translate prepositions such as without + -ing (**senza** + infinitive), before + -ing (**prima di** + infinitive), after + -ing (**dopo aver** + past participle).

He went away **without saying** anything.	➜ *È andato via **senza dire** niente.*
Before opening the packet, read the instructions.	➜ ***Prima di aprire** il pacchetto, leggi le istruzioni.*
After making a phone call she went out.	➜ ***Dopo aver** telefonato è uscita.*

More on prepositions

Sentences that have no preposition in English may contain a preposition in Italian. The dictionary can help you with these. For example:

They started **laughing**.	➜ *Hanno cominciato **a ridere**.*
Have you finished **eating**?	➜ *Hai finito **di mangiare**?*
When did you stop **smoking**?	➜ *Quando hai smesso **di fumare**?*

Saying Sorry

• To apologize about something, use **scusi** to someone you're on formal terms with, and **scusa** to a friend. Use **scusate** to more than one person.

Sorry.	➜ ***Scusi.***
Sorry I'm late.	➜ ***Scusi** il ritardo.*
Sorry, Paola, I've got to go.	➜ ***Scusa**, Paola, devo andare.*
Sorry to disturb you.	➜ ***Scusate** il disturbo.*

• **Scusi** is also used to mean '*excuse me*' when you stop somebody to ask something.

Excuse me, where is the station?	➜ ***Scusi**, dov'è la stazione?*

Some common translation difficulties

When you haven't heard what someone said, say **come, scusi**?

• To express regret use **mi dispiace**:

My grandfather has died. – Oh, **I'm sorry**.	→ *È morto mio nonno. – Oh, **mi dispiace**.*
I haven't got time, **sorry**.	→ *Non ho tempo, **mi dispiace**.*
I'm sorry but I can't come.	→ ***Mi dispiace** ma non posso venire.*
I'm sorry for them.	→ ***Mi dispiace** per loro.*

Translating 'to be'

'To be' usually corresponds to **essere**, but remember:

• In phrases describing how you feel, use **avere**:

I **am** hot/cold	→ **ho** *caldo/freddo*
they **are** hungry/thirsty	→ **hanno** *fame/sete*
he **is** scared	→ **ha** *paura*

• To describe the weather, use **fare**:

It**'s** nice weather today.	→ ***Fa** bel tempo oggi.*

• To say your age, use **avere**:

I**'m** fifteen.	→ ***Ho** guindici anni.*

• To talk about your health, use **stare**:

I**'m** fine, thanks.	→ ***Sto** bene, grazie*

Some common translation difficulties

'Have' or 'have got' usually correspond to **avere**:

I've **got** two brothers.	→ **Ho** due fratelli.
Have you **got** a bike?	→ **Hai** una bici?
I**'ve** spent a lot of money.	→ **Ho** speso molti soldi.
What **have** you done?	→ Cos' **hai** fatto?

Remember, though that 'have' and 'has' are translated by **essere**.

• In the perfect tense of some common verbs such as to go (*andare*), to come (*venire*) and to arrive (*arrivare*):

Where **have** they gone?	→ Dove **sono** andati?
She **has** come too.	→ **È** venuta anche lei.
We**'ve** arrived.	→ **Siamo** arrivati.

• In the perfect tense of all reflexive verbs:

I**'ve** hurt myself.	→ Mi **sono** fatto male.
Has she had a good time?	→ Si **è** divertita?

a

A [eɪ] n (Mus) la m

a
[ə] (before vowel or silent h **an**)
indef art

1 un (uno + s impure, gn, pn, ps, x, z), una
f (un' + vowel); **a book** un libro; **a mirror**
uno specchio; **an apple** una mela;
she's a doctor è medico

2 (instead of the number "one") un(o),
f una; **a year ago** un anno fa; **a
hundred/thousand** etc **pounds** cento/
mille etc sterline

3 (in expressing ratios, prices etc) a, per; **3
a day/week** 3 al giorno/alla settimana;
10 km an hour 10 km all'ora; **£5 a
person** 5 sterline a persona or per
persona

A.A. n abbr (= Alcoholics Anonymous)
AA; (BRIT: = Automobile Association)
≈ A.C.I. m

A.A.A. (US) n abbr (= American
Automobile Association) ≈ A.C.I. m

aback [ə'bæk] adv **to be taken ~** essere
sbalordito(-a)

abandon [ə'bændən] vt abbandonare
▶ n **with ~** sfrenatamente,
spensieratamente

abattoir ['æbətwɑːʳ] (BRIT) n
mattatoio

abbey ['æbɪ] n abbazia, badia

abbreviation [əbriːvɪ'eɪʃən] n
abbreviazione f

abdomen ['æbdəmən] n addome m

abduct [æb'dʌkt] vt rapire

abide [ə'baɪd] vt **I can't ~ it/him** non lo
posso soffrire or sopportare ▷ **abide
by** vt fus conformarsi a

ability [ə'bɪlɪtɪ] n abilità f inv

able ['eɪbl] adj capace; **to be ~ to do sth**
essere capace di fare qc, poter fare qc

abnormal [æb'nɔːməl] adj anormale

aboard [ə'bɔːd] adv a bordo ▶ prep a
bordo di

abolish [ə'bɔlɪʃ] vt abolire

abolition [æbəu'lɪʃən] n abolizione f

abort [ə'bɔːt] vt abortire; **abortion**
[ə'bɔːʃən] n aborto; **to have an
abortion** abortire

about
[ə'baut] adv

1 (approximately) circa, quasi; **about a
hundred/thousand** etc un centinaio/
migliaio etc, circa cento/mille etc; **it
takes about 10 hours** ci vogliono circa
10 ore; **at about 2 o'clock** verso le 2; **I've
just about finished** ho quasi finito

2 (referring to place) qua e là, in giro; **to
leave things lying about** lasciare delle
cose in giro; **to run about** correre qua e
là; **to walk about** camminare

3: **to be about to do sth** stare per
fare qc

▶ prep

1 (relating to) su, di; **a book about
London** un libro su Londra; **what is it
about?** di che si tratta?; (book, film etc)
di cosa tratta?; **we talked about it** ne
abbiamo parlato; **what or how about
doing this?** che ne dici di fare questo?

2 (referring to place): **to walk about
the town** camminare per la città; **her
clothes were scattered about the
room** i suoi vestiti erano sparsi or in
giro per tutta la stanza

above [ə'bʌv] adv, prep sopra;
mentioned ~ suddetto; **~ all**
soprattutto

abroad [ə'brɔːd] adv all'estero

abrupt [ə'brʌpt] adj (sudden)

improvviso(-a); (*gruff, blunt*) brusco(-a)

abscess ['æbsɪs] *n* ascesso

absence ['æbsəns] *n* assenza

absent ['æbsənt] *adj* assente; **absent-minded** *adj* distratto(-a)

absolute ['æbsəlu:t] *adj* assoluto(-a); **absolutely** [-'lu:tlɪ] *adv* assolutamente

absorb [əb'zɔ:b] *vt* assorbire; **to be ~ed in a book** essere immerso in un libro; **absorbent cotton** [əb'zɔ:bənt-] (*US*) *n* cotone *m* idrofilo; **absorbing** *adj* avvincente, molto interessante

abstain [əb'steɪn] *vi* **to ~ (from)** astenersi (da)

abstract ['æbstrækt] *adj* astratto(-a)

absurd [əb'sə:d] *adj* assurdo(-a)

abundance [ə'bʌndəns] *n* abbondanza

abundant [ə'bʌndənt] *adj* abbondante

abuse [*n* ə'bju:s, *vb* ə'bju:z] *n* abuso; (*insults*) ingiurie *fpl* ▶ *vt* abusare di; **abusive** *adj* ingiurioso(-a)

abysmal [ə'bɪzməl] *adj* spaventoso(-a)

academic [ækə'dɛmɪk] *adj* accademico(-a); (*pej: issue*) puramente formale ▶ *n* universitario(-a); **academic year** *n* anno accademico

academy [ə'kædəmɪ] *n* (*learned body*) accademia; (*school*) scuola privata; **academy of music** *n* conservatorio

accelerate [æk'sɛlərert] *vt*, *vi* accelerare; **acceleration** *n* accelerazione *f*; **accelerator** *n* acceleratore *m*

accent ['æksɛnt] *n* accento

accept [ək'sɛpt] *vt* accettare; **acceptable** *adj* accettabile; **acceptance** *n* accettazione *f*

access ['æksɛs] *n* accesso; **accessible** [æk'sɛsəbl] *adj* accessibile

accessory [æk'sɛsərɪ] *n* accessorio;

(*Law*): **~ to** complice *m/f* di

accident ['æksɪdənt] *n* incidente *m*; (*chance*) caso; **I've had an ~** ho avuto un incidente; **by ~** per caso; **accidental** [-'dɛntl] *adj* accidentale; **accidentally** [-'dɛntəlɪ] *adv* per caso; **Accident and Emergency Department** *n* (*BRIT*) pronto soccorso; **accident insurance** *n* assicurazione *f* contro gli infortuni

acclaim [ə'kleɪm] *n* acclamazione *f*

accommodate [ə'kɒmədeɪt] *vt* alloggiare; (*oblige, help*) favorire

accommodation [əkɒmə'deɪʃən] (*US* **accommodations**) *n* alloggio

accompaniment [ə'kʌmpənɪmənt] *n* accompagnamento

accompany [ə'kʌmpənɪ] *vt* accompagnare

accomplice [ə'kʌmplɪs] *n* complice *m/f*

accomplish [ə'kʌmplɪʃ] *vt* compiere; (*goal*) raggiungere; **accomplishment** *n* compimento; realizzazione *f*

accord [ə'kɔ:d] *n* accordo ▶ *vt* accordare; **of his own ~** di propria iniziativa; **accordance** *n* **in accordance with** in conformità con; **according**: **according to** *prep* secondo; **accordingly** *adv* in conformità

account [ə'kaunt] *n* (*Comm*) conto; (*report*) descrizione *f*; **~s** *npl* (*Comm*) conti *mpl*; **of no ~** di nessuna importanza; **on ~** in acconto; **on no ~** per nessun motivo; **on ~ of** a causa di; **to take into ~, take ~ of** tener conto di ▶ **account for** *vt fus* spiegare; giustificare; **accountable** *adj* **accountable (to)** responsabile (verso); **accountant** [ə'kauntənt] *n* ragioniere(-a); **account number** *n* numero di conto

accumulate [ə'kju:mjuleɪt] *vt*

accumulare ► *vi* accumularsi

accuracy ['ækjurəsɪ] *n* precisione *f*

accurate ['ækjurɪt] *adj* preciso(-a); **accurately** *adv* precisamente

accusation [ækju'zeɪʃən] *n* accusa

accuse [ə'kju:z] *vt* accusare; **accused** *n* accusato(-a)

accustomed [ə'kʌstəmd] *adj* ~ **to** abituato(-a) a

ace [eɪs] *n* asso

ache [eɪk] *n* male *m*, dolore *m* ► *vi* (be sore) far male, dolere; **my head** ~**s** mi fa male la testa

achieve [ə'tʃi:v] *vt* (aim) raggiungere; (victory, success) ottenere; **achievement** *n* compimento; successo

acid ['æsɪd] *adj* acido(-a) ► *n* acido

acknowledge [ək'nɔlɪdʒ] *vt* (letter: also: ~ **receipt of**) confermare la ricevuta di; (fact) riconoscere; **acknowledgement** *n* conferma; riconoscimento

acne ['æknɪ] *n* acne *f*

acorn ['eɪkɔ:n] *n* ghianda

acoustic [ə'ku:stɪk] *adj* acustico(-a)

acquaintance [ə'kweɪntəns] *n* conoscenza; (person) conoscente *m/f*

acquire [ə'kwaɪə'] *vt* acquistare; **acquisition** [ækwɪ'zɪʃən] *n* acquisto

acquit [ə'kwɪt] *vt* assolvere; **to ~ o.s. well** comportarsi bene

acre ['eɪkə'] *n* acro, ≈ 4047 m²

acronym ['ækrənɪm] *n* acronimo

across [ə'krɔs] *prep* (on the other side) attraverso ► *adv* dall'altra parte di; (crosswise) attraverso ► *adv* dall'altra parte; in larghezza; **to run/swim** ~ attraversare di corsa/a nuoto; ~ **from** di fronte a

acrylic [ə'krɪlɪk] *adj* acrilico(-a)

act [ækt] *n* atto; (in music-hall etc) numero; (Law) decreto ► *vi* agire; (Theatre) recitare; (pretend) fingere ► *vt* (part) recitare; **to ~ as** agire da ▷ **act**

up (inf) *vi* (person) comportarsi male; (knee, back, injury) fare male; (machine) non funzionare; **acting** *adj* che fa le funzioni di ► *n* (of actor) recitazione *f*; (activity): **to do some acting** fare del teatro (or del cinema)

action ['ækʃən] *n* azione *f*; (Mil) combattimento; (Law) processo; **out of** ~ fuori combattimento; fuori servizio; **to take** ~ agire; **action replay** *n* (TV) replay *m inv*

activate ['æktɪveɪt] *vt* (mechanism) attivare

active ['æktɪv] *adj* attivo(-a); **actively** *adv* (participate) attivamente; (discourage, dislike) vivamente

activist ['æktɪvɪst] *n* attivista *m/f*

activity [æk'tɪvɪtɪ] *n* attività *f inv*; **activity holiday** *n* vacanza organizzata con attività ricreative per ragazzi

actor ['æktə'] *n* attore *m*

actress ['æktrɪs] *n* attrice *f*

actual ['æktjuəl] *adj* reale, effettivo(-a)

| Be careful not to translate **actual** by the Italian word **attuale**.

actually ['æktjuəlɪ] *adv* veramente; (even) addirittura

| Be careful not to translate **actually** by the Italian word **attualmente**.

acupuncture ['ækjupʌŋktʃə'] *n* agopuntura

acute [ə'kju:t] *adj* acuto(-a); (mind, person) perspicace

ad [æd] *n abbr* = **advertisement**

A.D. *adv abbr* (= Anno Domini) d.C.

adamant ['ædəmənt] *adj* irremovibile

adapt [ə'dæpt] *vt* adattare ► *vi* **to** ~ **(to)** adattarsi (a); **adapter, adaptor** *n* (Elec) adattatore *m*

add [æd] *vt* aggiungere ► *vi* **to** ~ **to** (increase) aumentare ▷ **add up** *vt* (figures) addizionare ► *vi* (fig): **it doesn't** ~ **up** non ha senso ▷ **add up to** *vt fus* (Math) ammontare a; (fig:

mean) significare; **it doesn't ~ up to much** non è un granché

addict ['ædɪkt] n tossicomane m/f; (*fig*) fanatico(-a); **addicted** [ə'dɪktɪd] *adj* **to be addicted to** (*drink etc*) essere dedito(-a) a; (*fig: football etc*) essere tifoso(-a) di; **addiction** [ə'dɪkʃən] n (*Med*) tossicodipendenza; **addictive** [ə'dɪktɪv] *adj* che dà assuefazione

addition [ə'dɪʃən] n addizione f; (*thing added*) aggiunta; **in ~** inoltre; **in ~ to** oltre; **additional** *adj* supplementare

additive ['ædɪtɪv] n additivo

address [ə'drɛs] n indirizzo; (*talk*) discorso ▷ vt indirizzare; (*speak to*) fare un discorso a; (*issue*) affrontare; **address book** n rubrica

adequate ['ædɪkwɪt] *adj* adeguato(-a), sufficiente

adhere [əd'hɪəʳ] vi **to ~ to** aderire a; (*fig: rule, decision*) seguire

adhesive [əd'hiːzɪv] n adesivo; **adhesive tape** n (*BRIT: for parcels etc*) nastro adesivo; (*US Med*) cerotto adesivo

adjacent [ə'dʒeɪsənt] *adj* adiacente; **~ to** accanto a

adjective ['ædʒɛktɪv] n aggettivo

adjoining [ə'dʒɔɪnɪŋ] *adj* accanto *inv*, adiacente

adjourn [ə'dʒəːn] vt rimandare ▷ vi essere aggiornato(-a)

adjust [ə'dʒʌst] vt aggiustare; (*change*) rettificare ▷ vi **to ~ (to)** adattarsi (a); **adjustable** *adj* regolabile; **adjustment** n (*Psych*) adattamento; (*of machine*) regolazione f; (*of prices, wages*) modifica

administer [əd'mɪnɪstəʳ] vt amministrare; (*justice, drug*) somministrare; **administration** [ədmɪnɪs'treɪʃən] n amministrazione f; **administrative** [əd'mɪnɪstrətɪv] *adj* amministrativo(-a)

administrator [əd'mɪnɪstreɪtəʳ] n

amministratore(-trice)

admiral ['ædmərəl] n ammiraglio

admiration [ædmə'reɪʃən] n ammirazione f

admire [əd'maɪəʳ] vt ammirare; **admirer** n ammiratore(-trice)

admission [əd'mɪʃən] n ammissione f; (*to exhibition, nightclub etc*) ingresso; (*confession*) confessione f

admit [əd'mɪt] vt ammettere; far entrare; (*agree*) riconoscere ▷ **admit to** vt fus riconoscere; **admittance** n ingresso; **admittedly** *adv* bisogna pur riconoscere (che)

adolescent [ædəu'lɛsnt] *adj*, n adolescente m/f

adopt [ə'dɔpt] vt adottare; **adopted** *adj* adottivo(-a); **adoption** [ə'dɔpʃən] n adozione f

adore [ə'dɔːʳ] vt adorare

adorn [ə'dɔːn] vt ornare

Adriatic [eɪdrɪ'ætɪk] n **the ~ (Sea)** il mare Adriatico, l'Adriatico

adrift [ə'drɪft] *adv* alla deriva

ADSL n *abbr* (= *asymmetric digital subscriber line*) ADSL m

adult ['ædʌlt] *adj* adulto(-a); (*work, education*) per adulti ▷ n adulto(-a); **adult education** n scuola per adulti

adultery [ə'dʌltərɪ] n adulterio

advance [əd'vɑːns] n avanzamento; (*money*) anticipo ▷ *adj* (*booking etc*) in anticipo ▷ vt (*money*) anticipare ▷ vi avanzare; **in ~** in anticipo; **advanced** *adj* avanzato(-a); (*Scol: studies*) superiore

advantage [əd'vɑːntɪdʒ] n (*also Tennis*) vantaggio; **to take ~ of** approfittarsi di

advent ['ædvənt] n avvento; (*Rel*): **A~** Avvento

adventure [əd'vɛntʃəʳ] n avventura; **adventurous** [əd'vɛntʃərəs] *adj* avventuroso(-a)

adverb ['ædvəːb] n avverbio

adversary ['ædvəsərɪ] n avversario(-a)

adverse ['ædvəːs] adj avverso(-a)

advert ['ædvəːt] (BRIT) n abbr = **advertisement**

advertise ['ædvətaɪz] vi, vt fare pubblicità or réclame (a); fare un'inserzione (per vendere); **to ~ for** (staff) mettere un annuncio sul giornale per trovare; **advertisement** [əd'vəːtɪsmənt] n (Comm) réclame f inv, pubblicità f inv; (in classified ads) inserzione f; **advertiser** n azienda che reclamizza un prodotto; (in newspaper) inserzionista m/f; **advertising** ['ædvətaɪzɪŋ] n pubblicità

advice [əd'vaɪs] n consigli mpl; **piece of ~** consiglio; **to take legal ~** consultare un avvocato

advisable [əd'vaɪzəbl] adj consigliabile

advise [əd'vaɪz] vt consigliare; **to ~ sb of sth** informare qn di qc; **to ~ sb against sth/doing sth** sconsigliare qc a qn/a qn di fare qc; **adviser** n consigliere(-a); (in business) consulente m/f, consigliere(-a); **advisory** [-ərɪ] adj consultivo(-a)

advocate [n 'ædvəkət, vb 'ædvəkeɪt] n (upholder) sostenitore(-trice); (Law) avvocato (difensore) ▶ vt propugnare

Aegean [ɪ'dʒɪːən] n **the ~ (Sea)** il mar Egeo, l'Egeo

aerial ['ɛərɪəl] n antenna ▶ adj aereo(-a)

aerobics [ɛə'rəubɪks] n aerobica

aeroplane ['ɛərəpleɪn] (BRIT) n aeroplano

aerosol ['ɛərəsɔl] (BRIT) n aerosol m inv

affair [ə'fɛər] n affare m; (also: **love ~**) relazione f amorosa; **~s** (business) affari

affect [ə'fɛkt] vt toccare; (influence) influire su, incidere su; (feign) fingere;

affected adj affettato(-a); **affection** [ə'fɛkʃən] n affezione f; **affectionate** adj affettuoso(-a)

afflict [ə'flɪkt] vt affliggere

affluent ['æfluənt] adj ricco(-a); **the ~ society** la società del benessere

afford [ə'fɔːd] vt permettersi; (provide) fornire; **affordable** adj (che ha un prezzo) abbordabile

Afghanistan [æf'gænɪstaːn] n Afganistan m

afraid [ə'freɪd] adj impaurito(-a); **to be ~ of** or **to/that** aver paura di/che; **I am ~ so/not** ho paura di sì/no

Africa ['æfrɪkə] n Africa; **African** adj, n africano(-a); **African-American** adj, n afroamericano(-a)

after ['aːftər] prep, adv dopo ▶ conj dopo che; **what/who are you ~?** che/chi cerca?; **~ he left/having done** dopo che se ne fu andato/dopo aver fatto; **to name sb ~ sb** dare a qn il nome di qn; **it's twenty ~ eight** (US) sono le otto e venti; **to ask ~ sb** chiedere di qn; **~ all** dopo tutto; **~ you!** dopo di lei!; **after-effects** npl conseguenze fpl; (of illness) postumi mpl; **aftermath** n conseguenze fpl; **in the aftermath of** nel periodo dopo; **afternoon** n pomeriggio; **after-shave (lotion)** ['aːftəʃeɪv-] n dopobarba m inv; **aftersun (lotion/cream)** n doposole m inv; **afterwards** (US **afterward**) adv dopo

again [ə'gɛn] adv di nuovo; **to begin/see ~** ricominciare/rivedere; **not ... ~** non ... più; **~ and ~** ripetutamente

against [ə'gɛnst] prep contro

age [eɪdʒ] n età f inv ▶ vt, vi invecchiare; **it's been ~s since** sono secoli che; **he is 20 years of ~** ha 20 anni; **to come of ~** diventare maggiorenne; **~d 10** di 10 anni; **the ~d** ['eɪdʒɪd] gli anziani; **age group** n generazione f; **age limit** n limite m d'età

agency ['eɪdʒənsɪ] n agenzia
agenda [ə'dʒendə] n ordine m del giorno
agent ['eɪdʒənt] n agente m
aggravate ['ægrəveɪt] vt aggravare; (person) irritare
aggression [ə'grɛʃən] n aggressione f
aggressive [ə'grɛsɪv] adj aggressivo(-a)
agile ['ædʒaɪl] adj agile
agitated ['ædʒɪteɪtɪd] adj agitato(-a), turbato(-a)
AGM n abbr = **annual general meeting**
ago [ə'gəʊ] adv **2 days ~** 2 giorni fa; **not long ~** poco tempo fa; **how long ~?** quanto tempo fa?
agony ['ægənɪ] n dolore m atroce; **to be in ~** avere dolori atroci
agree [ə'griː] vt (price) pattuire ▶ vi **to ~ (with)** essere d'accordo (con); (Ling) concordare (con); **to ~ to sth/to do sth** accettare qc/di fare qc; **to ~ that** (admit) ammettere che; **to ~ on sth** accordarsi su qc; **garlic doesn't ~ with me** l'aglio non mi va; **agreeable** adj gradevole; (willing) disposto(-a); **agreed** adj (time, place) stabilito(-a); **agreement** n accordo; **in agreement** d'accordo
agricultural [ægrɪ'kʌltʃərəl] adj agricolo(-a)
agriculture ['ægrɪkʌltʃəʳ] n agricoltura
ahead [ə'hɛd] adv avanti; davanti; **~ of** davanti a; (fig: schedule etc) in anticipo su; **~ of time** in anticipo; **go right** or **straight ~** tiri diritto
aid [eɪd] n aiuto ▶ vt aiutare; **in ~ of** a favore di
aide [eɪd] n (person) aiutante m/f
AIDS [eɪdz] n abbr (= acquired immune deficiency syndrome) AIDS f
ailing ['eɪlɪŋ] adj sofferente; (fig: economy, industry etc) in difficoltà

ailment ['eɪlmənt] n indisposizione f
aim [eɪm] vt **to ~ sth at** (such as gun) mirare qc a, puntare qc a; (camera) rivolgere qc a; (missile) lanciare qc contro ▶ vi (also: **to take ~**) prendere la mira ▶ n mira; **to ~ at** mirare; **to ~ to do** aver l'intenzione di fare
ain't [eɪnt] (inf) = **am not**; **aren't**; **isn't**
air [ɛəʳ] n aria ▶ vt (room) arieggiare; (clothes) far prendere aria a; (grievances, ideas) esprimere pubblicamente ▶ cpd (currents) d'aria; (attack) aereo(-a); **to throw sth into the ~** lanciare qc in aria; **by ~** (travel) in aereo; **on the ~** (Radio, TV) in onda; **airbag** n airbag m inv; **airbed** (BRIT) n materassino; **airborne** ['ɛəbɔːn] adj (plane) in volo; (troops) aerotrasportato(-a); **as soon as the plane was airborne** appena l'aereo ebbe decollato; **air-conditioned** adj con or ad aria condizionata; **air conditioning** n condizionamento d'aria; **aircraft** n inv apparecchio; **airfield** n campo d'aviazione; **Air Force** n aviazione f militare; **air hostess** (BRIT) n hostess f inv; **airing cupboard** ['ɛərɪŋ-] n armadio riscaldato per asciugare panni.; **airlift** n ponte m aereo; **airline** n linea aerea; **airliner** n aereo di linea; **airmail** n **by airmail** per via aerea; **airplane** (US) n aeroplano; **airport** n aeroporto; **air raid** n incursione f aerea; **airsick** adj **to be airsick** soffrire di mal d'aria; **airspace** n spazio aereo; **airstrip** n pista d'atterraggio; **air terminal** n air-terminal m inv; **airtight** adj ermetico(-a); **air-traffic controller** n controllore m del traffico aereo; **airy** adj arioso(-a); (manners) noncurante
aisle [aɪl] n (of church) navata laterale; navata centrale; (of plane) corridoio; **aisle seat** n (on plane) posto sul corridoio

ajar [ə'dʒɑːʳ] *adj* socchiuso(-a)

à la carte [ɑːlɑː'kɑːt] *adv* alla carta

alarm [ə'lɑːm] *n* allarme *m* ▶ *vt* allarmare; **alarm call** *n* (*in hotel etc*) sveglia; **could I have an alarm call at 7 am, please?** vorrei essere svegliato alle 7, per favore; **alarm clock** *n* sveglia; **alarmed** *adj* (*person*) allarmato(-a); (*house, car etc*) dotato(-a) di allarme; **alarming** *adj* allarmante, preoccupante

Albania [æl'beɪnɪə] *n* Albania

albeit [ɔːl'biːɪt] *conj* sebbene + *sub*, benché + *sub*

album ['ælbəm] *n* album *m inv*

alcohol ['ælkəhɔl] *n* alcool *m*; **alcohol-free** *adj* analcolico(-a); **alcoholic** [-'hɔlɪk] *adj* alcolico(-a) ▶ *n* alcolizzato(-a)

alcove ['ælkəuv] *n* alcova

ale [eɪl] *n* birra

alert [ə'ləːt] *adj* vigile ▶ *n* allarme *m* ▶ *vt* avvertire; mettere in guardia; **on the ~** all'erta

algebra ['ældʒɪbrə] *n* algebra

Algeria [æl'dʒɪərɪə] *n* Algeria

alias ['eɪlɪəs] *adv* alias ▶ *n* pseudonimo, falso nome *m*

alibi ['ælɪbaɪ] *n* alibi *m inv*

alien ['eɪlɪən] *n* straniero(-a); (*extraterrestrial*) alieno(-a) ▶ *adj* **~ (to)** estraneo(-a) (a); **alienate** *vt* alienare

alight [ə'laɪt] *adj* acceso(-a) ▶ *vi* scendere; (*bird*) posarsi

align [ə'laɪn] *vt* allineare

alike [ə'laɪk] *adj* simile ▶ *adv* sia ... sia; **to look ~** assomigliarsi

alive [ə'laɪv] *adj* vivo(-a); (*lively*) vivace

⭕ **all**
[ɔːl] *adj* tutto(-a); **all day** tutto il giorno; **all night** tutta la notte; **all men** tutti gli uomini; **all five came** sono venuti tutti e cinque; **all the books** tutti i libri; **all the food** tutto il cibo; **all the time** sempre; tutto il tempo; **all his**

life tutta la vita

▶ *pron*

1 tutto(-a); **I ate it all, I ate all of it** l'ho mangiato tutto; **all of us went** tutti noi siamo andati; **all of the boys went** tutti i ragazzi sono andati

2 (*in phrases*): **above all** soprattutto; **after all** dopotutto; **at all: not at all** (*in answer to question*) niente affatto; (*in answer to thanks*) prego!, di niente!, s'immagini!; **I'm not at all tired** non sono affatto stanco(-a); **anything at all will do** andrà bene qualsiasi cosa; **all in all** tutto sommato

▶ *adv* **all alone** tutto(-a) solo(-a); **it's not as hard as all that** non è poi così difficile; **all the more/the better** tanto più/meglio; **all but** quasi; **the score is two all** il punteggio è di due a due

Allah ['ælə] *n* Allah *m*

allegation [ælɪ'geɪʃən] *n* asserzione *f*

alleged [ə'lɛdʒd] *adj* presunto(-a); **allegedly** [ə'lɛdʒɪdlɪ] *adv* secondo quanto si asserisce

allegiance [ə'liːdʒəns] *n* fedeltà

allergic [ə'ləːdʒɪk] *adj* **~ to** allergico(-a) a; **I'm ~ to penicillin** sono allergico alla penicillina

allergy ['ælədʒɪ] *n* allergia

alleviate [ə'liːvɪeɪt] *vt* sollevare

alley ['ælɪ] *n* vicolo

alliance [ə'laɪəns] *n* alleanza

allied ['ælaɪd] *adj* alleato(-a)

alligator ['ælɪgeɪtəʳ] *n* alligatore *m*

all-in ['ɔːlɪn] *adj* (BRIT: *also adv: charge*) tutto compreso

allocate ['æləkeɪt] *vt* assegnare

allot [ə'lɔt] *vt* assegnare

all-out ['ɔːlaut] *adj* (*effort etc*) totale ▶ *adv* **to go all out for** mettercela tutta per

allow [ə'lau] *vt* (*practice, behaviour*) permettere; (*sum to spend etc*) accordare; (*sum, time estimated*) dare; (*concede*): **to ~ that** ammettere che; **to**

~ sb to do permettere a qn di fare; **he is ~ed to** lo può fare ▷ **allow for** vt fus tener conto di; **allowance** n (money received) assegno; indennità f inv; (Tax) detrazione f di imposta; **to make allowances for** tener conto di

all right adv (feel, work) bene; (as answer) va bene

ally ['ælaɪ] n alleato

almighty [ɔːl'maɪtɪ] adj onnipotente; (row etc) colossale

almond ['ɑːmənd] n mandorla

almost ['ɔːlməust] adv quasi

alone [ə'ləun] adj, adv solo(-a); **to leave sb ~** lasciare qn in pace; **to leave sth ~** lasciare stare qc; **let ~ ...** figuriamoci poi ..., tanto meno ...

along [ə'lɒŋ] prep lungo ▷ adv **is he coming ~?** viene con noi?; **he was limping ~** veniva zoppicando; **~ with** insieme con; **all ~** (all the time) sempre, fin dall'inizio; **alongside** prep accanto a; lungo ▷ adv accanto

aloof [ə'luːf] adj distaccato(-a) ▷ adv **to stand ~** tenersi a distanza or in disparte

aloud [ə'laud] adv ad alta voce

alphabet ['ælfəbɛt] n alfabeto

Alps [ælps] npl **the ~** le Alpi

already [ɔːl'rɛdɪ] adv già

alright ['ɔːl'raɪt] (BRIT) adv = **all right**

also ['ɔːlsəu] adv anche

altar ['ɔltər] n altare m

alter ['ɔltər] vt, vi alterare; **alteration** [ɔltə'reɪʃən] n modificazione f, alterazione f; **alterations** (Sewing, Archit) modifiche fpl; **timetable subject to alteration** orario soggetto a variazioni

alternate [adj ɔl'təːnɪt, vb 'ɔltəːneɪt] adj alterno(-a); (US: plan etc) alternativo(-a) ▷ vi **to ~ (with)** alternarsi (a); **on ~ days** ogni due giorni

alternative [ɔl'təːnətɪv] adj

alternativo(-a) ▶ n (choice) alternativa; **alternatively** adv **alternatively one could ...** come alternativa si potrebbe ...

although [ɔːl'ðəu] conj benché + sub, sebbene + sub

altitude ['æltɪtjuːd] n altitudine f

altogether [ɔːltə'gɛðər] adv del tutto, completamente; (on the whole) tutto considerato; (in all) in tutto

aluminium [ælju'mɪnɪəm] (BRIT), **aluminum** [ə'luːmɪnəm] (US) n alluminio

always ['ɔːlweɪz] adv sempre

Alzheimer's (disease) ['æltshaɪməz-] n (malattia di) Alzheimer

am [æm] vb see **be**

amalgamate [ə'mælgəmeɪt] vt amalgamare ▶ vi amalgamarsi

amass [ə'mæs] vt ammassare

amateur ['æmətər] n dilettante m/f ▶ adj (Sport) dilettante

amaze [ə'meɪz] vt stupire; **amazed** adj sbalordito(-a); **to be amazed (at)** essere sbalordito (da); **amazement** n stupore m; **amazing** adj sorprendente, sbalorditivo(-a)

Amazon ['æməzən] n (Mythology) Amazzone f; (river): **the ~** il Rio delle Amazzoni ▶ cpd (basin, jungle) amazzonico(-a)

ambassador [æm'bæsədər] n ambasciatore(-trice)

amber ['æmbər] n ambra; **at ~** (BRIT Aut) giallo

ambiguous [æm'bɪgjuəs] adj ambiguo(-a)

ambition [æm'bɪʃən] n ambizione f; **ambitious** adj ambizioso(-a)

ambulance ['æmbjuləns] n ambulanza; **call an ~!** chiamate un'ambulanza!

ambush ['æmbuʃ] n imboscata

amen ['ɑː'mɛn] excl così sia, amen

amend [əˈmɛnd] *vt* (*law*) emendare; (*text*) correggere; **to make ~s** fare ammenda; **amendment** *n* emendamento; correzione *f*

amenities [əˈmiːnɪtɪz] *npl* attrezzature *fpl* ricreative e culturali

America [əˈmɛrɪkə] *n* America; **American** *adj*, *n* americano(-a); **American football** *n* (*BRIT*) football *m* americano

amicable [ˈæmɪkəbl] *adj* amichevole

amid(st) [əˈmɪd(st)] *prep* in mezzo a

ammunition [æmjuˈnɪʃən] *n* munizioni *fpl*

amnesty [ˈæmnɪstɪ] *n* amnistia; **to grant an ~ to** concedere l'amnistia a, amnistiare

among(st) [əˈmʌŋ(st)] *prep* fra, tra, in mezzo a

amount [əˈmaunt] *n* somma; ammontare *m*; quantità *f inv* ▶ *vi* **to ~ to** (*total*) ammontare a; (*be same as*) essere come

amp(ère) [ˈæmp(ɛər)] *n* ampère *m inv*

ample [ˈæmpl] *adj* ampio(-a); spazioso(-a); (*enough*): **this is ~** questo è più che sufficiente

amplifier [ˈæmplɪfaɪər] *n* amplificatore *m*

amputate [ˈæmpjuteɪt] *vt* amputare

Amtrak [ˈæmtræk] (*US*) *n* società ferroviaria americana

amuse [əˈmjuːz] *vt* divertire; **amusement** *n* divertimento; **amusement arcade** *n* sala giochi; **amusement park** *n* luna park *m inv*

amusing [əˈmjuːzɪŋ] *adj* divertente

an [æn] *indef art see* **a**

anaemia [əˈniːmɪə] (*US* **anemia**) *n* anemia

anaemic [əˈniːmɪk] (*US* **anemic**) *adj* anemico(-a)

anaesthetic [ænɪsˈθɛtɪk] (*US* **anesthetic**) *adj* anestetico(-a) ▶ *n* anestetico

analog(ue) [ˈænəlɔg] *adj* (*watch*, *computer*) analogico(-a)

analogy [əˈnælədʒɪ] *n* analogia; **to draw an ~ between** fare un'analogia tra

analyse [ˈænəlaɪz] (*US* **analyze**) *vt* analizzare; **analysis** [əˈnæləsɪs] (*pl* **analyses**) *n* analisi *f inv*; **analyst** [ˈænəlɪst] *n* (*Pol etc*) analista *m/f*; (*US*) (psic)analista *m/f*

analyze [ˈænəlaɪz] (*US*) *vt* = **analyse**

anarchy [ˈænəkɪ] *n* anarchia

anatomy [əˈnætəmɪ] *n* anatomia

ancestor [ˈænsɪstər] *n* antenato(-a)

anchor [ˈæŋkər] *n* ancora ▶ *vi* (*also:* **to drop ~**) gettare l'ancora ▶ *vt* ancorare; **to weigh ~** salpare *or* levare l'ancora

anchovy [ˈæntʃəvɪ] *n* acciuga

ancient [ˈeɪnʃənt] *adj* antico(-a); (*person, car*) vecchissimo(-a)

and [ænd] *conj* e; (*often ed before vowel*): **~ so on** e così via; **try ~ come** cerca di venire; **he talked ~ talked** non la finiva di parlare; **better ~ better** sempre meglio

Andes [ˈændiːz] *npl* **the ~** le Ande

anemia *etc* [əˈniːmɪə] (*US*) = **anaemia** *etc*

anesthetic [ænɪsˈθɛtɪk] (*US*) *adj*, *n* = **anaesthetic**

angel [ˈeɪndʒəl] *n* angelo

anger [ˈæŋgər] *n* rabbia

angina [ænˈdʒaɪnə] *n* angina pectoris

angle [ˈæŋgl] *n* angolo; **from their ~** dal loro punto di vista

angler [ˈæŋglər] *n* pescatore *m* con la lenza

Anglican [ˈæŋglɪkən] *adj*, *n* anglicano(-a)

angling [ˈæŋglɪŋ] *n* pesca con la lenza

angrily [ˈæŋgrɪlɪ] *adv* con rabbia

angry [ˈæŋgrɪ] *adj* arrabbiato(-a), furioso(-a); (*wound*) infiammato(-a); **to be ~ with sb/at sth** essere in collera con qn/per qc; **to get ~**

arrabbiarsi; **to make sb ~** fare arrabbiare qn

anguish ['æŋgwɪʃ] n angoscia

animal ['ænɪməl] adj animale ▶ n animale m

animated ['ænɪmeɪtɪd] adj animato(-a)

animation [ænɪ'meɪʃən] n animazione f

aniseed ['ænɪsiːd] n semi mpl di anice

ankle ['æŋkl] n caviglia

annex [n 'æneks, vb ə'neks] n (BRIT: also: ~**e**) (edificio) annesso ▶ vt annettere

anniversary [ænɪ'vəːsərɪ] n anniversario

announce [ə'nauns] vt annunciare; **announcement** n annuncio; (letter, card) partecipazione f; **announcer** n (Radio, TV: between programmes) annunciatore(-trice); (: in a programme) presentatore(-trice)

annoy [ə'nɔɪ] vt dare fastidio a; **don't get ~ed!** non irritarti!; **annoying** adj noioso(-a)

annual ['ænjuəl] adj annuale ▶ n (Bot) pianta annua; (book) annuario; **annually** adv annualmente

annum ['ænəm] n see **per**

anonymous [ə'nɔnɪməs] adj anonimo(-a)

anorak ['ænəræk] n giacca a vento

anorexia [ænə'reksɪə] n (Med: also: ~ **nervosa**) anoressia

anorexic [ænə'reksɪk] adj, n anoressico(-a)

another [ə'nʌðəʳ] adj ~ **book** (one more) un altro libro, ancora un libro; (a different one) un altro libro ▶ pron un altro(un'altra), ancora uno(-a); see also **one**

answer ['ɑːnsəʳ] n risposta; soluzione f ▶ vi rispondere ▶ vt (reply to) rispondere a; (problem) risolvere; (prayer) esaudire; **in ~ to your letter**

in risposta alla sua lettera; **to ~ the phone** rispondere (al telefono); **to ~ the bell** rispondere al campanello; **to ~ the door** aprire la porta ▷ **answer back** vi ribattere; **answerphone** n (esp BRIT) segreteria telefonica

ant [ænt] n formica

Antarctic [ænt'ɑːktɪk] n **the ~** l'Antartide f

antelope ['æntɪləup] n antilope f

antenatal ['æntɪ'neɪtl] adj prenatale

antenna [æn'tenə, -niː] (pl **antennae**) n antenna

anthem ['ænθəm] n **national ~** inno nazionale

anthology [æn'θɔlədʒɪ] n antologia

anthrax ['ænθræks] n antrace m

anthropology [ænθrə'pɔlədʒɪ] n antropologia

anti [æntɪ] prefix anti; **antibiotic** ['æntɪbaɪ'ɔtɪk] n antibiotico; **antibody** ['æntɪbɔdɪ] n anticorpo

anticipate [æn'tɪsɪpeɪt] vt prevedere; pregustare; (wishes, request) prevenire; **anticipation** [æntɪsɪ'peɪʃən] n anticipazione f; (expectation) aspettative fpl

anticlimax ['æntɪ'klaɪmæks] n **it was an ~** fu una completa delusione

anticlockwise ['æntɪ'klɔkwaɪz] adj, adv in senso antiorario

antics ['æntɪks] npl buffonerie fpl

anti: **antidote** ['æntɪdəut] n antidoto; **antifreeze** ['æntɪ'friːz] n anticongelante m; **anti-globalization** [æntɪgləubəlaɪ'zeɪʃən] n antiglobalizzazione f; **antihistamine** [æntɪ'hɪstəmɪn] n antistaminico; **antiperspirant** ['æntɪ'pəːspərənt] adj antitraspirante

antique [æn'tiːk] n antichità f inv ▶ adj antico(-a); **antique shop** n negozio d'antichità

antiseptic [æntɪ'septɪk] n antisettico

antisocial ['æntɪ'səuʃəl] adj asociale

antivirus [æntɪ'vaɪrəs] *adj* (*Comput*) antivirus *inv*; **antivirus software** *n* antivirus *m inv*

antlers ['æntləz] *npl* palchi *mpl*

anxiety [æŋ'zaɪətɪ] *n* ansia; (*keenness*): ~ **to do** smania di fare

anxious ['æŋkʃəs] *adj* ansioso(-a), inquieto(-a); (*worrying*) angosciante; (*keen*): ~ **to do/that** impaziente di fare/che + *sub*

⭕ **any**
['ɛnɪ] *adj*

1 (*in questions etc*): **have you any butter?** hai del burro?, hai un po' di burro?; **have you any children?** hai bambini?; **if there are any tickets left** se ci sono ancora (dei) biglietti, se c'è ancora qualche biglietto

2 (*with negative*): **I haven't any money/books** non ho soldi/libri

3 (*no matter which*) qualsiasi, qualunque; **choose any book you like** scegli un libro qualsiasi

4 (*in phrases*): **in any case** in ogni caso; **any day now** da un giorno all'altro; **at any moment** in qualsiasi momento, da un momento all'altro; **at any rate** ad ogni modo

▶*pron*

1 (*in questions, with negative*): **have you got any?** ne hai?; **can any of you sing?** qualcuno di voi sa cantare?; **I haven't any (of them)** non ne ho

2 (*no matter which one(s)*): **take any of those books (you like)** prendi uno qualsiasi di quei libri

▶*adv*

1 (*in questions etc*): **do you want any more soup/sandwiches?** vuoi ancora un po' di minestra/degli altri panini?; **are you feeling any better?** ti senti meglio?

2 (*with negative*): **I can't hear him any more** non lo sento più; **don't wait any longer** non aspettare più

any: **anybody** ['ɛnɪbɔdɪ] *pron* (*in questions etc*) qualcuno, nessuno; (*with negative*) nessuno; (*no matter who*) chiunque; **can you see anybody?** vedi qualcuno or nessuno?; **I can't see anybody** non vedo nessuno; **anybody could do it** chiunque potrebbe farlo; **anyhow** ['ɛnɪhau] *adv* (*at any rate*) ad ogni modo, comunque; (*haphazard*): **do it anyhow you like** fallo come ti pare; **I shall go anyhow** ci andrò lo stesso or comunque; **she leaves things just anyhow** lascia tutto come capita; **anyone** ['ɛnɪwʌn] *pron* = **anybody**; **anything** ['ɛnɪθɪŋ] *pron* (*in question etc*) qualcosa, niente; (*with negative*) niente; (*no matter what*): **you can say anything you like** puoi dire quello che ti pare; **can you see anything?** vedi niente or qualcosa?; **I can't see anything** non vedo niente; **anything will do** va bene qualsiasi cosa or tutto; **anytime** *adv* in qualunque momento; quando vuole; **anyway** ['ɛnɪweɪ] *adv* (*at any rate*) ad ogni modo, comunque; (*besides*) ad ogni modo; **anywhere** ['ɛnɪwɛər] *adv* (*in questions etc*) da qualche parte; (*with negative*) da nessuna parte; (*no matter where*) da qualsiasi or qualunque parte, dovunque; **can you see him anywhere?** lo vedi da qualche parte?; **I can't see him anywhere** non lo vedo da nessuna parte; **anywhere in the world** dovunque nel mondo

apart [ə'pɑːt] *adv* (*to one side*) a parte; (*separately*) separatamente; **with one's legs** ~ con le gambe divaricate; **10 miles** ~ a 10 miglia di distanza (l'uno dall'altro); **to take** ~ smontare; ~ **from** a parte, eccetto

apartment [ə'pɑːtmənt] (*US*) *n* appartamento; (*room*) locale *m*; **apartment building** (*US*) *n* stabile *m*, caseggiato

apathy ['æpəθɪ] n apatia

ape [eɪp] n scimmia ▶ vt scimmiottare

aperitif [ə'pɛrɪtiːf] n aperitivo

aperture ['æpətʃjuəʳ] n apertura

APEX n abbr (= advance purchase excursion) APEX m inv

apologize [ə'pɒlədʒaɪz] vi **to ~ (for sth to sb)** scusarsi (di qc a qn), chiedere scusa (a qn per qc)

apology [ə'pɒlədʒɪ] n scuse fpl

apostrophe [ə'pɒstrəfɪ] n (sign) apostrofo

appal [ə'pɔːl] (US **appall**) vt scioccare; **appalling** adj spaventoso(-a)

apparatus [æpə'reɪtəs] n apparato; (in gymnasium) attrezzatura

apparent [ə'pærənt] adj evidente; **apparently** adv evidentemente

appeal [ə'piːl] vi (Law) appellarsi alla legge ▶ n (Law) appello; (request) richiesta; (charm) attrattiva; **to ~ for** chiedere (con insistenza); **to ~ to** (person) appellarsi a; (thing) piacere a; **it doesn't ~ to me** mi dice poco; **appealing** adj (nice) attraente

appear [ə'pɪəʳ] vi apparire; (Law) comparire; (publication) essere pubblicato(-a); (seem) sembrare; **it would ~ that** sembra che; **appearance** n apparizione f; apparenza; (look, aspect) aspetto

appendicitis [əpɛndɪ'saɪtɪs] n appendicite f

appendix [ə'pɛndɪks] (pl **appendices**) n appendice f

appetite ['æpɪtaɪt] n appetito

appetizer ['æpɪtaɪzəʳ] n stuzzichino

applaud [ə'plɔːd] vt, vi applaudire

applause [ə'plɔːz] n applauso

apple ['æpl] n mela; **apple pie** n torta di mele

appliance [ə'plaɪəns] n apparecchio

applicable [ə'plɪkəbl] adj applicabile; **to be ~ to** essere valido per; **the law**

is ~ from January la legge entrerà in vigore in gennaio

applicant ['æplɪkənt] n candidato(-a)

application [æplɪ'keɪʃən] n applicazione f; (for a job, a grant etc) domanda; **application form** n modulo per la domanda

apply [ə'plaɪ] vt **to ~ (to)** (paint, ointment) dare (a); (theory, technique) applicare (a) ▶ vi **to ~ to** (ask) rivolgersi a; (be suitable for, relevant to) riguardare, riferirsi a; **to ~ (for)** (permit, grant, job) fare domanda (per); **to ~ o.s. to** dedicarsi a

appoint [ə'pɔɪnt] vt nominare; **appointment** n nomina; (arrangement to meet) appuntamento; **I have an appointment (with) ...** ho un appuntamento (con) ...; **I'd like to make an appointment (with)** vorrei prendere un appuntamento (con)

appraisal [ə'preɪzl] n valutazione f

appreciate [ə'priːʃɪeɪt] vt (like) apprezzare; (be grateful for) essere riconoscente di; (be aware of) rendersi conto di ▶ vi (Finance) aumentare; **I'd ~ your help** ti sono grato per l'aiuto; **appreciation** [əpriːʃɪ'eɪʃən] n apprezzamento; (Finance) aumento del valore

apprehension [æprɪ'hɛnʃən] n (fear) inquietudine f

apprehensive [æprɪ'hɛnsɪv] adj apprensivo(-a)

apprentice [ə'prɛntɪs] n apprendista m/f

approach [ə'prəʊtʃ] vi avvicinarsi ▶ vt (come near) avvicinarsi a; (ask, apply to) rivolgersi a; (subject, passer-by) avvicinare ▶ n approccio; accesso; (to problem) modo di affrontare

appropriate [adj ə'prəʊprɪɪt, vb ə'prəʊprɪeɪt] adj appropriato(-a), adatto(-a) ▶ vt (take) appropriarsi

approval [ə'pruːvəl] n approvazione f;

on **~** (Comm) in prova, in esame
approve [ə'pruːv] vt, vi approvare
▷ **approve of** vt fus approvare
approximate [ə'prɔksımıt] adj
approssimativo(-a); **approximately**
adv circa
Apr. abbr (= April) apr.
apricot ['eıprıkɔt] n albicocca
April ['eıprəl] n aprile m; **~ fool!** pesce
d'aprile!; **April Fools' Day** n vedi nota

- **April Fool's Day**
- **April Fool's Day** è il primo aprile, il
- giorno degli scherzi e delle burle. Il
- nome deriva dal fatto che, se una
- persona cade nella trappola che gli è
- stata tesa, fa la figura del "fool", cioè
- dello sciocco. Tradizionalmente,
- gli scherzi vengono fatti entro
- mezzogiorno.

apron ['eıprən] n grembiule m
apt [æpt] adj (suitable) adatto(-a);
(able) capace; (likely): **to be ~ to do**
avere tendenza a fare
aquarium [ə'kwɛərıəm] n acquario
Aquarius [ə'kwɛərıəs] n Acquario
Arab ['ærəb] adj, n arabo(-a)
Arabia [ə'reıbıə] n Arabia; **Arabian**
[ə'reıbıən] adj arabo(-a); **Arabic**
['ærəbık] adj arabico(-a), arabo(-a)
▷ n arabo; **Arabic numerals** npl
numeri mpl arabi, numerazione f
araba
arbitrary ['ɑːbıtrərı] adj arbitrario(-a)
arbitration [ɑːbı'treıʃən] n (Law)
arbitrato; (Industry) arbitraggio
arc [ɑːk] n arco
arcade [ɑː'keıd] n portico; (passage
with shops) galleria
arch [ɑːtʃ] n arco; (of foot) arco plantare
▷ vt inarcare
archaeology [ɑːkı'ɔlədʒı] (US
archeology) n archeologia
archbishop [ɑːtʃ'bıʃəp] n arcivescovo
archeology etc [ɑːkı'ɔlədʒı] (US)
= **archaeology** etc

architect ['ɑːkıtɛkt] n architetto;
architectural [ɑːkı'tɛktʃərəl] adj
architettonico(-a); **architecture**
['ɑːkıtɛktʃəʳ] n architettura
archive ['ɑːkaıv] n (often pl: also
Comput) archivio
Arctic ['ɑːktık] adj artico(-a) ▶ n **the**
~ l'Artico
are [ɑːʳ] vb see **be**
area ['ɛərıə] n (Geom) area; (zone) zona;
(: smaller) settore m; **area code** (US)
(Tel) prefisso
arena [ə'riːnə] n arena
aren't [ɑːnt] = **are not**
Argentina [ɑːdʒən'tiːnə] n Argentina;
Argentinian [-'tınıən] adj, n
argentino(-a)
arguably ['ɑːgjuəblı] adv **it is ~ ...** si
può sostenere che sia ...
argue ['ɑːgjuː] vi (quarrel) litigare;
(reason) ragionare; **to ~ that** sostenere
che
argument ['ɑːgjumənt] n (reasons)
argomento; (quarrel) lite f
Aries ['ɛərız] n Ariete m
arise [ə'raız] (pt **arose**, pp **arisen**) vi
(opportunity, problem) presentarsi
arithmetic [ə'rıθmətık] n aritmetica
arm [ɑːm] n braccio ▶ vt armare; **~s** npl
(weapons) armi fpl; **~ in ~** a braccetto;
armchair n poltrona
armed [ɑːmd] adj armato(-a); **armed**
robbery n rapina a mano armata
armour ['ɑːməʳ] (US **armor**) n
armatura; (Mil: tanks) mezzi mpl
blindati
armpit ['ɑːmpıt] n ascella
armrest ['ɑːmrɛst] n bracciolo
army ['ɑːmı] n esercito
A road n strada statale
aroma [ə'rəumə] n aroma;
aromatherapy n aromaterapia
arose [ə'rəuz] pt of **arise**
around [ə'raund] adv attorno, intorno
▶ prep intorno a; (fig: about): **~ £5/3**

o'clock circa 5 sterline/le 3; **is he ~?** è in giro?

arouse [ə'rauz] vt (*sleeper*) svegliare; (*curiosity*, *passions*) suscitare

arrange [ə'reɪndʒ] vt sistemare; (*programme*) preparare; **to ~ to do sth** mettersi d'accordo per fare qc; **arrangement** n sistemazione f; (*agreement*) accordo; **arrangements** npl (*plans*) progetti mpl, piani mpl

array [ə'reɪ] n **~ of** fila di

arrears [ə'rɪəz] npl arretrati mpl; **to be in ~ with one's rent** essere in arretrato con l'affitto

arrest [ə'rɛst] vt arrestare; (*sb's attention*) attirare ▶ n arresto; **under ~** in arresto

arrival [ə'raɪvəl] n arrivo; (*person*) arrivato(-a); **a new ~** un nuovo venuto; (*baby*) un neonato

arrive [ə'raɪv] vi arrivare; **what time does the train from Rome ~?** a che ora arriva il treno da Roma? ▷ **arrive at** vt fus arrivare a

arrogance ['ærəgəns] n arroganza

arrogant ['ærəgənt] adj arrogante

arrow ['ærəu] n freccia

arse [ɑːs] (*inf!*) n culo (!)

arson ['ɑːsn] n incendio doloso

art [ɑːt] n arte f; (*craft*) mestiere m; **art college** n scuola di belle arti

artery ['ɑːtərɪ] n arteria

art gallery n galleria d'arte

arthritis [ɑː'θraɪtɪs] n artrite f

artichoke ['ɑːtɪtʃəuk] n carciofo; **Jerusalem ~** topinambur m inv

article ['ɑːtɪkl] n articolo

articulate [adj ɑː'tɪkjulɪt, vb ɑː'tɪkjuleɪt] adj (*person*) che si esprime forbitamente; (*speech*) articolato(-a) ▶ vi articolare

artificial [ɑːtɪ'fɪʃəl] adj artificiale

artist ['ɑːtɪst] n artista m/f; **artistic** [ɑː'tɪstɪk] adj artistico(-a)

art school n scuola d'arte

as

[æz] conj

1 (*referring to time*) mentre; **as the years went by** col passare degli anni; **he came in as I was leaving** arrivò mentre stavo uscendo; **as from tomorrow** da domani

2 (*in comparisons*): **as big as** grande come; **twice as big as** due volte più grande di; **as much/many as** tanto quanto/tanti quanti; **as soon as possible** prima possibile

3 (*since, because*) dal momento che, siccome

4 (*referring to manner, way*) come; **do as you wish** fa' come vuoi; **as she said** come ha detto lei

5 (*concerning*): **as for** or **to that** per quanto riguarda or quanto a quello

6: **as if** or **as though** come se; **he looked as if he was ill** sembrava stare male; *see also* **long**; **such**; **well**

▶ prep **he works as a driver** fa l'autista; **as chairman of the company he …** come presidente della compagnia lui …; **he gave me it as a present** me lo ha regalato

a.s.a.p. abbr = **as soon as possible**

asbestos [æz'bɛstəs] n asbesto, amianto

ascent [ə'sɛnt] n salita

ash [æʃ] n (*dust*) cenere f; (*wood, tree*) frassino

ashamed [ə'ʃeɪmd] adj vergognoso(-a); **to be ~ of** vergognarsi di

ashore [ə'ʃɔː] adv a terra

ashtray ['æʃtreɪ] n portacenere m

Ash Wednesday n mercoledì m inv delle Ceneri

Asia ['eɪʃə] n Asia; **Asian** adj, n asiatico(-a)

aside [ə'saɪd] adv da parte ▶ n a parte m

ask [ɑːsk] vt (*question*) domandare; (*invite*) invitare; **to ~ sb sth/sb to**

do sth chiedere qc a qn/a qn di fare qc; **to ~ sb about sth** chiedere a qn di qc; **to ~ (sb) a question** fare una domanda (a qn); **to ~ sb out to dinner** invitare qn a mangiare fuori ▷ **ask for** vt fus chiedere; (trouble etc) cercare

asleep [ə'sli:p] adj addormentato(-a); **to be ~** dormire; **to fall ~** addormentarsi

asparagus [əs'pærəgəs] n asparagi mpl

aspect ['æspɛkt] n aspetto

aspirations [æspə'reɪʃənz] npl aspirazioni fpl

aspire [əs'paɪər] vi **to ~ to** aspirare a

aspirin ['æsprɪn] n aspirina

ass [æs] n asino; (inf) scemo(-a); (US: inf!) culo (!)

assassin [ə'sæsɪn] n assassino; **assassinate** [ə'sæsɪneɪt] vt assassinare

assault [ə'sɔ:lt] n (Mil) assalto; (gen: attack) aggressione f ▶ vt assaltare; aggredire; (sexually) violentare

assemble [ə'sɛmbl] vt riunire; (Tech) montare ▶ vi riunirsi

assembly [ə'sɛmblɪ] n (meeting) assemblea; (construction) montaggio

assert [ə'sə:t] vt asserire; (insist on) far valere; **assertion** [ə'sə:ʃən] n asserzione f

assess [ə'sɛs] vt valutare; **assessment** n valutazione f

asset ['æsɛt] n vantaggio; **~s** npl (Finance: of individual) beni mpl; (: of company) attivo

assign [ə'saɪn] vt **to ~ (to)** (task) assegnare (a); (resources) riservare (a); (cause, meaning) attribuire (a); **to ~ a date to sth** fissare la data di qc; **assignment** n compito

assist [ə'sɪst] vt assistere, aiutare; **assistance** n assistenza, aiuto; **assistant** n assistente m/f; (BRIT: also: **shop assistant**) commesso(-a)

associate [adj, n ə'səʊʃɪɪt, vb ə'sə uʃɪeɪt] adj associato(-a); (member) aggiunto(-a) ▶ n collega m/f ▶ vt associare ▶ vi **to ~ with sb** frequentare qn

association [əsəʊsɪ'eɪʃən] n associazione f

assorted [ə'sɔ:tɪd] adj assortito(-a)

assortment [ə'sɔ:tmənt] n assortimento

assume [ə'sju:m] vt supporre; (responsibilities etc) assumere; (attitude, name) prendere

assumption [ə'sʌmpʃən] n supposizione f, ipotesi f inv; (of power) assunzione f

assurance [ə'ʃʊərəns] n assicurazione f; (self-confidence) fiducia in se stesso

assure [ə'ʃʊər] vt assicurare

asterisk ['æstərɪsk] n asterisco

asthma ['æsmə] n asma

astonish [ə'stɒnɪʃ] vt stupire; **astonished** adj stupito(-a), sorpreso(-a); **to be astonished (at)** essere stupito(-a) (da); **astonishing** adj sorprendente, stupefacente; **I find it astonishing that ...** mi stupisce che ...; **astonishment** n stupore m

astound [ə'staund] vt sbalordire

astray [ə'streɪ] adv **to go ~** smarrirsi; **to lead ~** portare sulla cattiva strada

astrology [əs'trɒlədʒɪ] n astrologia

astronaut ['æstrənɔ:t] n astronauta m/f

astronomer [əs'trɒnəmər] n astronomo(-a)

astronomical [æstrə'nɒmɪkl] adj astronomico(-a)

astronomy [əs'trɒnəmɪ] n astronomia

astute [əs'tju:t] adj astuto(-a)

asylum [ə'saɪləm] n (politico) asilo; (per malati) manicomio

at
[æt] prep

1 (*referring to position, direction*) a; **at the top** in cima; **at the desk** al banco, alla scrivania; **at home/school** a casa/scuola; **at the baker's** dal panettiere; **to look at sth** guardare qc; **to throw sth at sb** lanciare qc a qn

2 (*referring to time*) a; **at 4 o'clock** alle 4; **at night** di notte; **at Christmas** a Natale; **at times** a volte

3 (*referring to rates, speed etc*) a; **at £1 a kilo** a 1 sterlina al chilo; **two at a time** due alla volta, due per volta; **at 50 km/h** a 50 km/h

4 (*referring to manner*): **at a stroke** d'un solo colpo; **at peace** in pace

5 (*referring to activity*): **to be at work** essere al lavoro; **to play at cowboys** giocare ai cowboy; **to be good at sth/doing sth** essere bravo in qc/fare qc

6 (*referring to cause*): **shocked/surprised/annoyed at sth** colpito da/sorpreso da/arrabbiato per qc; **I went at his suggestion** ci sono andato dietro suo consiglio

7 (*@ symbol*) chiocciola

ate [eɪt] *pt of* **eat**
atheist ['eɪθɪɪst] *n* ateo(-a)
Athens ['æθɪnz] *n* Atene *f*
athlete ['æθliːt] *n* atleta *m/f*
athletic [æθ'lɛtɪk] *adj* atletico(-a); **athletics** *n* atletica
Atlantic [ət'læntɪk] *adj* atlantico(-a) ▸ *n* **the ~ (Ocean)** l'Atlantico, l'Oceano Atlantico
atlas ['ætləs] *n* atlante *m*
A.T.M. *n abbr* (= *automated telling machine*) cassa automatica prelievi, sportello automatico
atmosphere ['ætməsfɪəʳ] *n* atmosfera
atom ['ætəm] *n* atomo; **atomic** [ə'tɒmɪk] *adj* atomico(-a); **atom(ic) bomb** *n* bomba atomica

A to Z® *n* (*map*) stradario
atrocity [ə'trɒsɪtɪ] *n* atrocità *f inv*
attach [ə'tætʃ] *vt* attaccare; (*document, letter*) allegare; (*importance etc*) attribuire; **to be ~ed to sb/sth** (*to like*) essere affezionato(-a) a qn/qc; **attachment** [ə'tætʃmənt] *n* (*tool*) accessorio; (*love*): **attachment (to)** affetto (per)
attack [ə'tæk] *vt* attaccare; (*person*) aggredire; (*task etc*) iniziare; (*problem*) affrontare ▸ *n* attacco; **heart ~** infarto; **attacker** *n* aggressore *m*
attain [ə'teɪn] *vt* (*also*: **to ~ to**) arrivare a, raggiungere
attempt [ə'tɛmpt] *n* tentativo ▸ *vt* tentare; **to make an ~ on sb's life** attentare alla vita di qn
attend [ə'tɛnd] *vt* frequentare; (*meeting, talk*) andare a; (*patient*) assistere ▷ **attend to** *vt fus* (*needs, affairs etc*) prendersi cura di; (*customer*) occuparsi di; **attendance** *n* (*being present*) presenza; (*people present*) gente *f* presente; **attendant** *n* custode *m/f*; persona di servizio ▸ *adj* concomitante

> Be careful not to translate **attend** by the Italian word **attendere**.

attention [ə'tɛnʃən] *n* attenzione *f* ▸ *excl* (*Mil*) attenti!; **for the ~ of** (*Admin*) per l'attenzione di
attic ['ætɪk] *n* soffitta
attitude ['ætɪtjuːd] *n* atteggiamento
attorney [ə'tɜːnɪ] *n* (*lawyer*) avvocato; (*having proxy*) mandatario; **Attorney General** *n* (*BRIT*) Procuratore *m* Generale; (*US*) Ministro della Giustizia
attract [ə'trækt] *vt* attirare; **attraction** [ə'trækʃən] *n* (*gen pl: pleasant things*) attrattiva; (*Physics, fig: towards sth*) attrazione *f*; **attractive** *adj* attraente
attribute [*n* 'ætrɪbjuːt, *vb* ə'trɪbjuːt]

n attributo ▶ *vt* **to ~ sth to** attribuire qc a

aubergine ['əubəʒi:n] *n* melanzana

auburn ['ɔːbən] *adj* tizianesco(-a)

auction ['ɔːkʃən] *n* (*also:* **sale by ~**) asta ▶ *vt* (*also:* **to sell by ~**) vendere all'asta; (*also:* **to put up for ~**) mettere all'asta

audible ['ɔːdɪbl] *adj* udibile

audience ['ɔːdɪəns] *n* (*people*) pubblico; spettatori *mpl*; ascoltatori *mpl*; (*interview*) udienza

audit ['ɔːdɪt] *vt* rivedere, verificare

audition [ɔːˈdɪʃən] *n* audizione *f*

auditor ['ɔːdɪtəʳ] *n* revisore *m*

auditorium [ɔːdɪˈtɔːrɪəm] *n* sala, auditorio

Aug. *abbr* (= *August*) ago., ag.

August ['ɔːgəst] *n* agosto

aunt [ɑːnt] *n* zia; **auntie** *n* zietta; **aunty** *n* zietta

au pair ['əuˈpeəʳ] *n* (*also:* **~ girl**) (ragazza *f*) alla pari *inv*

aura ['ɔːrə] *n* aura

austerity [ɔsˈtɛrɪtɪ] *n* austerità *f inv*

Australia [ɔsˈtreɪlɪə] *n* Australia; **Australian** *adj*, *n* australiano(-a)

Austria ['ɔstrɪə] *n* Austria; **Austrian** *adj*, *n* austriaco(-a)

authentic [ɔːˈθɛntɪk] *adj* autentico(-a)

author ['ɔːθəʳ] *n* autore(-trice)

authority [ɔːˈθɔrɪtɪ] *n* autorità *f inv*; (*permission*) autorizzazione *f*; **the authorities** *npl* (*government etc*) le autorità

authorize ['ɔːθəraɪz] *vt* autorizzare

auto ['ɔːtəu] (*US*) *n* auto *f inv*; **autobiography** [ɔːtəbaɪˈɔgrəfɪ] *n* autobiografia; **autograph** ['ɔːtəgrɑːf] *n* autografo ▶ *vt* firmare; **automatic** [ɔːtəˈmætɪk] *adj* automatico(-a) ▶ *n* (*gun*) arma automatica; (*washing machine*) lavatrice *f* automatica; (*car*) automobile *f* con cambio automatico; **automatically** *adv*

automaticamente; **automobile** ['ɔːtəməbiːl] (*US*) *n* automobile *f*; **autonomous** [ɔːˈtɔnəməs] *adj* autonomo(-a); **autonomy** [ɔːˈtɔnəmɪ] *n* autonomia

autumn ['ɔːtəm] *n* autunno

auxiliary [ɔːgˈzɪlɪərɪ] *adj* ausiliario(-a) ▶ *n* ausiliare *m/f*

avail [əˈveɪl] *vt* **to ~ o.s. of** servirsi di; approfittarsi di ▶ *n* **to no ~** inutilmente

availability [əveɪləˈbɪlɪtɪ] *n* disponibilità

available [əˈveɪləbl] *adj* disponibile

avalanche ['ævəlɑːnʃ] *n* valanga

Ave. *abbr* = **avenue**

avenue ['ævənjuː] *n* viale *m*; (*fig*) strada, via

average ['ævərɪdʒ] *n* media ▶ *adj* medio(-a) ▶ *vt* (*a certain figure*) fare di *or* in media; **on ~** in media

avert [əˈvəːt] *vt* evitare, prevenire; (*one's eyes*) distogliere

avid ['ævɪd] *adj* (*supporter etc*) accanito(-a)

avocado [ævəˈkɑːdəu] *n* (*BRIT: also:* **~ pear**) avocado *m inv*

avoid [əˈvɔɪd] *vt* evitare

await [əˈweɪt] *vt* aspettare

awake [əˈweɪk] (*pt* **awoke**, *pp* **awoken, awaked**) *adj* sveglio(-a) ▶ *vt* svegliare ▶ *vi* svegliarsi

award [əˈwɔːd] *n* premio; (*Law*) risarcimento ▶ *vt* assegnare; (*Law: damages*) accordare

aware [əˈwɛəʳ] *adj* **~ of** (*conscious*) conscio(-a) di; (*informed*) informato(-a) di; **to become ~ of** accorgersi di; **awareness** *n* consapevolezza

away [əˈweɪ] *adj*, *adv* via; lontano(-a); **two kilometres ~** a due chilometri di distanza; **two hours ~ by car** a due ore di distanza in macchina; **the holiday was two weeks ~** mancavano due settimane alle vacanze; **he's ~ for a week** è andato via per una settimana; **to take ~** togliere; **he was working/pedalling** etc **~** (la particella indica la continuità e l'energia dell'azione) lavorava/pedalava etc più che poteva; **to fade/wither** etc **~** (la particella rinforza l'idea della diminuzione)

awe [ɔː] n timore m; **awesome** adj imponente

awful ['ɔːfəl] adj terribile; **an ~ lot of** un mucchio di; **awfully** adv (very) terribilmente

awkward ['ɔːkwəd] adj (clumsy) goffo(-a); (inconvenient) scomodo(-a); (embarrassing) imbarazzante

awoke [ə'wəuk] pt of **awake**

awoken [ə'wəukn] pp of **awake**

axe [æks] (US **ax**) n scure f ▶ vt (project etc) abolire; (jobs) sopprimere

axle ['æksl] n (also: **~-tree**) asse m

ay(e) [aɪ] excl (yes) sì

azalea [ə'zeɪlɪə] n azalea

b

B [biː] n (Mus) si m

B.A. n abbr = **Bachelor of Arts**

baby ['beɪbɪ] n bambino(-a); **baby carriage** (US) n carrozzina; **baby-sit** vi fare il (o la) baby-sitter; **baby-sitter** n baby-sitter m/f inv; **baby wipe** n salvietta umidificata

bachelor ['bætʃələʳ] n scapolo; **B~ of Arts/Science** ≈ laureato(-a) in lettere/scienze

back [bæk] n (of person, horse) dorso, schiena; (as opposed to front) dietro; (of hand) dorso; (of train) coda; (of chair) schienale m; (of page) rovescio; (of book) retro; (Football) difensore m ▶ vt (candidate) appoggiare; (horse: at races) puntare su; (car) guidare a marcia indietro ▶ vi indietreggiare; (car etc) fare marcia indietro ▶ cpd posteriore, di dietro; (Aut: seat, wheels) posteriore ▶ adv (not forward) indietro; (returned): **he's ~** è tornato; **he ran ~** tornò indietro di corsa; (restitution): **throw the ball ~** ritira la palla; **can I have it ~?** posso riaverlo?; (again): **he called ~** ha richiamato ▷ **back down** vi fare marcia indietro ▷ **back out** vi (of promise) tirarsi indietro ▷ **back up** vt (support) appoggiare, sostenere; (Comput) fare una copia di riserva di; **backache** n mal m di schiena; **backbencher** (BRIT) n membro del Parlamento senza potere amministrativo; **backbone** n spina dorsale; **back door** n porta sul retro; **backfire** vi (Aut) dar ritorni di fiamma; (plans) fallire; **backgammon** n tavola reale; **background** n sfondo; (of events) background m inv; (basic knowledge) base f; (experience) esperienza; **family background** ambiente m familiare; **backing** n (fig) appoggio; **backlog** n **backlog of work** lavoro arretrato; **backpack** n zaino; **backpacker** n chi viaggia con zaino e sacco a pelo; **backslash** n backslash m inv, barra obliqua inversa; **backstage** adv nel retroscena; **backstroke** n nuoto sul dorso; **backup** adj (train, plane) supplementare; (Comput) di riserva ▶ n (support) appoggio, sostegno; (also: **backup file**) file m inv di riserva; **backward** adj (movement) indietro inv; (person) tardivo(-a); (country) arretrato(-a); **backwards** adv indietro; (fall, walk) all'indietro; **backyard** n cortile m dietro la casa

bacon ['beɪkən] n pancetta

bacteria [bæk'tɪərɪə] npl batteri mpl

bad [bæd] adj cattivo(-a); (accident, injury) brutto(-a); (meat, food) andato(-a) a male; **his ~ leg** la sua gamba malata; **to go ~** andare a male

badge [bædʒ] n insegna; (of policeman) stemma m

badger ['bædʒəʳ] n tasso

badly ['bædlɪ] adv (work, dress etc) male; **~ wounded** gravemente ferito; **he needs it ~** ne ha un gran bisogno

bad-mannered [bæd'mænəd] adj maleducato(-a), sgarbato(-a)

badminton ['bædmɪntən] n badminton m

bad-tempered ['bæd'tɛmpəd] adj irritabile; di malumore

bag [bæg] n sacco; (handbag etc) borsa; **~s of** (inf: lots of) un sacco di; **baggage** n bagagli mpl; **baggage allowance** n franchigia f bagaglio inv; **baggage reclaim** n ritiro m bagagli inv; **baggy** adj largo(-a), sformato(-a); **bagpipes** npl cornamusa

bail [beɪl] n cauzione f ▶ vt (prisoner: also: **grant ~ to**) concedere la libertà provvisoria su cauzione a; (boat: also: **~ out**) aggottare; **on ~** in libertà provvisoria su cauzione

bait [beɪt] n esca ▶ vt (hook) innescare; (trap) munire di esca; (fig) tormentare

bake [beɪk] vt cuocere al forno ▶ vi cuocersi al forno; **baked beans** [-bi:nz] npl fagioli mpl in salsa di pomodoro; **baked potato** n patata cotta al forno con la buccia; **baker** n fornaio(-a), panettiere(-a); **bakery** n panetteria; **baking** n cottura (al forno); **baking powder** n lievito in polvere

balance ['bæləns] n equilibrio; (Comm: sum) bilancio; (remainder) resto; (scales) bilancia ▶ vt tenere in equilibrio; (budget) far quadrare; (account) pareggiare; (compensate) contrappesare; **~ of trade/payments** bilancia commerciale/dei pagamenti; **balanced** adj (personality, diet) equilibrato(-a); **balance sheet** n bilancio

balcony ['bælkənɪ] n balcone m; (in theatre) balconata; **do you have a room with a ~?** avete una camera con balcone?

bald [bɔːld] adj calvo(-a); (tyre) liscio(-a)

Balearics [bælɪ'ærɪks] npl **the ~** le Baleari fpl

ball [bɔːl] n palla; (football) pallone m; (for golf) pallina; (of wool, string) gomitolo; (dance) ballo; **to play ~** (fig) stare al gioco

ballerina [bælə'riːnə] n ballerina

ballet ['bæleɪ] n balletto; **ballet dancer** n ballerino(-a) classico(-a)

balloon [bə'luːn] n pallone m

ballot ['bælət] n scrutinio

ballpoint (pen) ['bɔːlpɔɪnt(-)] n penna a sfera

ballroom ['bɔːlrum] n sala da ballo

Baltic ['bɔːltɪk] adj, n **the ~ Sea** il (mar) Baltico

bamboo [bæm'buː] n bambù m

ban [bæn] n interdizione f ▶ vt interdire

banana [bə'nɑːnə] n banana

band [bænd] n banda; (at a dance) orchestra; (Mil) fanfara

bandage ['bændɪdʒ] n benda, fascia

Band-Aid® ['bændeɪd] (US) n cerotto

B. & B. n abbr = **bed and breakfast**

bandit ['bændɪt] n bandito

bang [bæŋ] n (of door) lo sbattere; (of gun, blow) colpo ▶ vt battere (violentemente); (*door*) sbattere ▶ *vi* scoppiare; sbattere

Bangladesh [bɑːŋgləˈdɛʃ] *n* Bangladesh *m*

bangle [ˈbæŋgl] *n* braccialetto

bangs [bæŋz] (*US*) *npl* (*fringe*) frangia, frangetta

banish [ˈbænɪʃ] *vt* bandire

banister(s) [ˈbænɪstə(z)] *n(pl)* ringhiera

banjo [ˈbændʒəu] (*pl* **banjoes** *or* **banjos**) *n* banjo *m inv*

bank [bæŋk] *n* banca, banco; (*of river, lake*) riva, sponda; (*of earth*) banco ▶ *vi* (*Aviat*) inclinarsi in virata ▷ **bank on** *vt fus* contare su; **bank account** *n* conto in banca; **bank balance** *n* saldo; **a healthy bank balance** un solido conto in banca; **bank card** *n* carta *f* assegni *inv*; **bank charges** *npl* (*BRIT*) spese *fpl* bancarie; **banker** *n* banchiere *m*; **bank holiday** (*BRIT*) *n* giorno di festa; *vedi nota*; **banking** *n* attività bancaria; professione *f* di banchiere; **bank manager** *n* direttore *m* di banca; **banknote** *n* banconota

● **bank holiday**
● Una **bank holiday**, in Gran
● Bretagna, è una giornata in cui
● banche e molti negozi sono chiusi.
● Generalmente le **bank holidays**
● cadono di lunedì e molti ne
● approfittano per fare una breve
● vacanza fuori città.

bankrupt [ˈbæŋkrʌpt] *adj* fallito(-a); **to go ~** fallire; **bankruptcy** *n* fallimento

bank statement *n* estratto conto

banner [ˈbænəʳ] *n* striscione *m*

bannister(s) [ˈbænɪstə(z)] *n(pl) see* **banister(s)**

banquet [ˈbæŋkwɪt] *n* banchetto

baptism [ˈbæptɪzəm] *n* battesimo

baptize [bæpˈtaɪz] *vt* battezzare

bar [bɑːʳ] *n* (*place*) bar *m inv*; (*counter*) banco; (*rod*) barra; (*of window etc*) sbarra; (*of chocolate*) tavoletta; (*fig*) ostacolo; restrizione *f*; (*Mus*) battuta ▶ *vt* (*road, window*) sbarrare; (*person*) escludere; (*activity*) interdire; **~ of soap** saponetta; **the B~** (*Law*) l'Ordine *m* degli avvocati; **behind ~s** (*prisoner*) dietro le sbarre; **~ none** senza eccezione

barbaric [bɑːˈbærɪk] *adj* barbarico(-a)

barbecue [ˈbɑːbɪkjuː] *n* barbecue *m inv*

barbed wire [ˈbɑːbd-] *n* filo spinato

barber [ˈbɑːbəʳ] *n* barbiere *m*; **barber's (shop)** (*US* **barber (shop)**) *n* barbiere *m*

bar code *n* (*on goods*) codice *m* a barre

bare [bɛəʳ] *adj* nudo(-a) ▶ *vt* scoprire, denudare; (*teeth*) mostrare; **the ~ necessities** lo stretto necessario; **barefoot** *adj*, *adv* scalzo(-a); **barely** *adv* appena

bargain [ˈbɑːgɪn] *n* (*transaction*) contratto; (*good buy*) affare *m* ▶ *vi* trattare; **into the ~** per giunta ▷ **bargain for** *vt fus* **he got more than he ~ed for** gli è andata peggio di quel che si aspettasse

barge [bɑːdʒ] *n* chiatta ▷ **barge in** *vi* (*walk in*) piombare dentro; (*interrupt talk*) intromettersi a sproposito

bark [bɑːk] *n* (*of tree*) corteccia; (*of dog*) abbaio ▶ *vi* abbaiare

barley [ˈbɑːlɪ] *n* orzo

barmaid [ˈbɑːmeɪd] *n* cameriera al banco

barman [ˈbɑːmən] (*irreg*) *n* barista *m*

barn [bɑːn] *n* granaio

barometer [bəˈrɔmɪtəʳ] *n* barometro

baron [ˈbærən] *n* barone *m*; **baroness** *n* baronessa

barracks [ˈbærəks] *npl* caserma

barrage [ˈbærɑːʒ] *n* (*Mil*, *dam*) sbarramento; (*fig*) fiume *m*

barrel [ˈbærəl] *n* barile *m*; (*of gun*)

canna

barren ['bærən] *adj* sterile; *(soil)* arido(-a)

barrette [bə'rɛt] *(US) n* fermaglio per capelli

barricade [bærɪ'keɪd] *n* barricata

barrier ['bærɪəʳ] *n* barriera

barring ['bɑːrɪŋ] *prep* salvo

barrister ['bærɪstəʳ] *(BRIT) n* avvocato(-essa) *(con diritto di parlare davanti a tutte le corti)*

barrow ['bærəu] *n (cart)* carriola

bartender ['bɑːtɛndəʳ] *(US) n* barista *m*

base [beɪs] *n* base *f* ▸ *vt* **to ~ sth on** basare qc su ▸ *adj* vile

baseball ['beɪsbɔːl] *n* baseball *m*; **baseball cap** *n* berretto da baseball

basement ['beɪsmənt] *n* seminterrato; *(of shop)* interrato

bases¹ ['beɪsiːz] *npl of* **basis**

bases² ['beɪsɪz] *npl of* **base**

bash [bæʃ] *(inf) vt* picchiare

basic ['beɪsɪk] *adj* rudimentale; essenziale; **basically** [-lɪ] *adv* fondamentalmente; sostanzialmente; **basics** *npl* **the basics** l'essenziale *m*

basil ['bæzl] *n* basilico

basin ['beɪsn] *n (vessel: also Geo)* bacino; *(also: wash~)* lavabo

basis ['beɪsɪs] *(pl bases) n* base *f*; **on a part-time ~** part-time; **on a trial ~** in prova

basket ['bɑːskɪt] *n* cesta; *(smaller)* cestino; *(with handle)* paniere *m*; **basketball** *n* pallacanestro *f*

bass [beɪs] *n (Mus)* basso

bastard ['bɑːstəd] *n* bastardo(-a); *(inf!)* stronzo *(!)*

bat [bæt] *n* pipistrello; *(for baseball etc)* mazza; *(BRIT: for table tennis)* racchetta ▸ *vt* **he didn't ~ an eyelid** non battè ciglio

batch [bætʃ] *n (of bread)* infornata; *(of papers)* cumulo

bath [bɑːθ] *n* bagno; *(bathtub)* vasca da bagno ▸ *vt* far fare il bagno a; **to have a ~** fare un bagno; *see also* **baths**

bathe [beɪð] *vi* fare il bagno ▸ *vt (wound)* lavare

bathing ['beɪðɪŋ] *n* bagni *mpl*; **bathing costume** *(US* **bathing suit)** *n* costume *m* da bagno

bath: bathrobe ['bɑːθrəub] *n* accappatoio; **bathroom** ['bɑːθrum] *n* stanza da bagno; **baths** [bɑːðz] *npl* bagni *mpl* pubblici; **bath towel** *n* asciugamano da bagno; **bathtub** *n (vasca da)* bagno

baton ['bætən] *n (Mus)* bacchetta; *(Athletics)* testimone *m*; *(club)* manganello

batter ['bætəʳ] *vt* battere ▸ *n* pastetta; **battered** *adj (hat)* sformato(-a); *(pan)* ammaccato(-a)

battery ['bætərɪ] *n* batteria; *(of torch)* pila; **battery farming** *n* allevamento in batteria

battle ['bætl] *n* battaglia ▸ *vi* battagliare, lottare; **battlefield** *n* campo di battaglia

bay [beɪ] *n (of sea)* baia; **to hold sb at ~** tenere qn a bada

bazaar [bə'zɑːʳ] *n* bazar *m inv*; vendita di beneficenza

BBC *n abbr (= British Broadcasting Corporation)* rete nazionale di radiotelevisione in Gran Bretagna

- **BBC**
- La **BBC** è l'azienda statale che
- fornisce il servizio radiofonico
- e televisivo in Gran Bretagna.
- Ha due reti televisive terrestri
- (BBC1 e BBC2), e cinque stazioni
- radiofoniche nazionali. Oggi la BBC
- ha anche diverse stazioni digitali
- radiofoniche e televisive. Da molti
- anni fornisce inoltre un servizio di
- intrattenimento e informazione

- internazionale, il "BBC World
- Service", trasmesso in tutto il
- mondo.

B.C. *adv abbr* (= *before Christ*) a.C.

be
[biː] (*pt* **was, were**, *pp* **been**)
aux vb

1 (*with present participle: forming continuous tenses*): **what are you doing?** che fa?, che sta facendo?; **they're coming tomorrow** vengono domani; **I've been waiting for her for hours** sono ore che l'aspetto

2 (*with pp: forming passives*) essere; **to be killed** essere *or* venire ucciso(-a); **the box had been opened** la scatola era stata aperta; **the thief was nowhere to be seen** il ladro non si trovava da nessuna parte

3 (*in tag questions*): **it was fun, wasn't it?** è stato divertente, no?; **he's good-looking, isn't he?** è un bell'uomo, vero?; **she's back, is she?** così è tornata, eh?

4 (+ *to* + *infinitive*): **the house is to be sold** abbiamo *or* hanno *etc* intenzione di vendere casa; **you're to be congratulated for all your work** dovremo farvi i complimenti per tutto il vostro lavoro; **he's not to open it** non deve aprirlo

▸*vb + complement*

1 (*gen*) essere; **I'm English** sono inglese; **I'm tired** sono stanco(-a); **I'm hot/cold** ho caldo/freddo; **he's a doctor** è medico; **2 and 2 are 4** 2 più 2 fa 4; **be careful!** sta attento(-a)!; **be good** sii buono(-a)

2 (*of health*) stare; **how are you?** come sta?; **he's very ill** sta molto male

3 (*of age*): **how old are you?** quanti anni hai?; **I'm sixteen (years old)** ho sedici anni

4 (*cost*) costare; **how much was the meal?** quant'era *or* quanto costava

il pranzo?; **that'll be £5, please** (fa) 5 sterline, per favore

▸*vi*

1 (*exist, occur etc*) essere, esistere; **the best singer that ever was** il migliore cantante mai esistito *or* di tutti i tempi; **be that as it may** comunque sia, sia come sia; **so be it** sia pure, e sia

2 (*referring to place*) essere, trovarsi; **I won't be here tomorrow** non ci sarò domani; **Edinburgh is in Scotland** Edimburgo si trova in Scozia

3 (*referring to movement*): **where have you been?** dov'è stato?; **I've been to China** sono stato in Cina

▸*impers vb*

1 (*referring to time, distance*) essere; **it's 5 o'clock** sono le 5; **it's the 28th of April** è il 28 aprile; **it's 10 km to the village** di qui al paese sono 10 km

2 (*referring to the weather*) fare; **it's too hot/cold** fa troppo caldo/freddo; **it's windy** c'è vento

3 (*emphatic*): **it's me** sono io; **it was Maria who paid the bill** è stata Maria che ha pagato il conto

beach [biːtʃ] *n* spiaggia ▸ *vt* tirare in secco

beacon ['biːkən] *n* (*lighthouse*) faro; (*marker*) segnale *m*

bead [biːd] *n* perlina; **~s** *npl* (*necklace*) collana

beak [biːk] *n* becco

beam [biːm] *n* trave *f*; (*of light*) raggio ▸ *vi* brillare

bean [biːn] *n* fagiolo; (*of coffee*) chicco; **runner ~** fagiolino; **beansprouts** *npl* germogli *mpl* di soia

bear [bɛəʳ] (*pt* **bore**, *pp* **borne**) *n* orso ▸ *vt* portare; (*endure*) sopportare; (*produce*) generare ▸ *vi* **to ~ right/left** piegare a destra/sinistra

beard [bɪəd] *n* barba

bearer ['bɛərəʳ] *n* portatore *m*

bearing ['bɛərɪŋ] *n* portamento;

(*connection*) rapporto

beast [biːst] *n* bestia

beat [biːt] (*pt* **beat**, *pp* **beaten**) *n* colpo; (*of heart*) battito; (*Mus*) tempo; battuta; (*of policeman*) giro ▶ *vt* battere; (*eggs, cream*) sbattere ▶ *vi* battere; **off the ~ en track** fuori mano; **~ it!** (*inf*) fila!, fuori dai piedi! ▷ **beat up** *vt* (*person*) picchiare; (*eggs*) sbattere; **beating** *n* bastonata

beautiful ['bjuːtɪful] *adj* bello(-a); **beautifully** *adv* splendidamente

beauty ['bjuːtɪ] *n* bellezza; **beauty parlour** [-'pɑːləʳ] (*US* **beauty parlor**) *n* salone *m* di bellezza; **beauty salon** *n* istituto di bellezza; **beauty spot** (*BRIT*) *n* (*Tourism*) luogo pittoresco

beaver ['biːvəʳ] *n* castoro

became [bɪ'keɪm] *pt of* **become**

because [bɪ'kɔz] *conj* perché; **~ of** a causa di

beckon ['bɛkən] *vt* (*also*: **~ to**) chiamare con un cenno

become [bɪ'kʌm] (*irreg: like* **come**) *vt* diventare; **to ~ fat/thin** ingrassarsi/ dimagrire

bed [bɛd] *n* letto; (*of flowers*) aiuola; (*of coal, clay*) strato; **single/double ~** letto a una piazza/a due piazze *or* matrimoniale; **bed and breakfast** *n* (*place*) ≈ pensione *f* familiare; (*terms*) camera con colazione; *vedi nota*; **bedclothes** ['bɛdkləuðz] *npl* biancheria e coperte *fpl* da letto; **bedding** *n* coperte e lenzuola *fpl*; **bed linen** *n* biancheria da letto; **bedroom** *n* camera da letto; **bedside** *n* **at sb's bedside** al capezzale di qn; **bedside lamp** *n* lampada da comodino; **bedside table** *n* comodino; **bedsit(ter)** (*BRIT*) *n* monolocale *m*; **bedspread** *n* copriletto; **bedtime** *n* **it's bedtime** è ora di andare a letto

● **bed and breakfast**

● I **bed and breakfasts**, anche B & Bs,

● sono piccole pensioni a conduzione

● familiare, più economiche rispetto

● agli alberghi, dove al mattino viene

● servita la tradizionale colazione

● all'inglese.

bee [biː] *n* ape *f*

beech [biːtʃ] *n* faggio

beef [biːf] *n* manzo; **roast ~** arrosto di manzo; **beefburger** *n* hamburger *m inv*; **Beefeater** *n* guardia della Torre di Londra

been [biːn] *pp of* **be**

beer [bɪəʳ] *n* birra; **beer garden** *n* (*BRIT*) giardino (*di pub*)

beet [biːt] (*US*) *n* (*also*: **red ~**) barbabietola rossa

beetle ['biːtl] *n* scarafaggio; coleottero

beetroot ['biːtruːt] (*BRIT*) *n* barbabietola

before [bɪ'fɔːʳ] *prep* (*in time*) prima di; (*in space*) davanti a ▶ *conj* prima che + *sub*; prima di ▶ *adv* prima; **~ going** prima di andare; **~ she goes** prima che vada; **the week ~** la settimana prima; **I've seen it ~** l'ho già visto; **I've never seen it ~** è la prima volta che lo vedo; **beforehand** *adv* in anticipo

beg [bɛg] *vi* chiedere l'elemosina ▶ *vt* (*also*: **~ for**) chiedere in elemosina; (*favour*) chiedere; **to ~ sb to do** pregare qn di fare

began [bɪ'gæn] *pt of* **begin**

beggar ['bɛgəʳ] *n* mendicante *m/f*

begin [bɪ'gɪn] (*pt* **began**, *pp* **begun**) *vt, vi* cominciare; **to ~ doing** *or* **to do sth** incominciare *or* iniziare a fare qc; **beginner** *n* principiante *m/f*; **beginning** *n* inizio, principio

begun [bɪ'gʌn] *pp of* **begin**

behalf [bɪ'hɑːf] *n* **on ~ of** per conto di; a nome di

behave [bɪ'heɪv] *vi* comportarsi; (*well: also*: **~ o.s.**) comportarsi bene; **behaviour** [bɪ'heɪvjəʳ] (*US* **behavior**) *n* comportamento, condotta

behind [bɪ'haɪnd] *prep* dietro; (*followed by pronoun*) dietro di; (*time*) in ritardo con ▶ *adv* dietro; (*leave, stay*) indietro ▶ *n* didietro; **to be ~ (schedule)** essere in ritardo rispetto al programma; **~ the scenes** (*fig*) dietro le quinte

beige [beɪʒ] *adj* beige *inv*

Beijing ['beɪ'dʒɪŋ] *n* Pechino *f*

being ['biːɪŋ] *n* essere *m*

belated [bɪ'leɪtɪd] *adj* tardo(-a)

belch [bɛltʃ] *vi* ruttare ▶ *vt* (*gen: belch out: smoke etc*) eruttare

Belgian ['bɛldʒən] *adj, n* belga *m/f*

Belgium ['bɛldʒəm] *n* Belgio *m*

belief [bɪ'liːf] *n* (*opinion*) opinione *f*, convinzione *f*; (*trust, faith*) fede *f*

believe [bɪ'liːv] *vt, vi* credere; **to ~ in** (*God*) credere in; (*ghosts*) credere a; (*method*) avere fiducia in; **believer** *n* (*Rel*) credente *m/f*; (*in idea, activity*): **to be a believer in** credere in

bell [bɛl] *n* campana; (*small, on door, electric*) campanello

bellboy ['bɛlbɔɪ], (*US*) **bellhop** ['bɛlhɔp] *n* ragazzo d'albergo, fattorino d'albergo

bellow ['bɛləʊ] *vi* muggire

bell pepper (*esp US*) *n* peperone *m*

belly ['bɛlɪ] *n* pancia; **belly button** *n* ombelico

belong [bɪ'lɔŋ] *vi* **to ~ to** appartenere a; (*club etc*) essere socio di; **this book ~s here** questo libro va qui; **belongings** *npl* cose *fpl*, roba

beloved [bɪ'lʌvɪd] *adj* adorato(-a)

below [bɪ'ləʊ] *prep* sotto, al di sotto di ▶ *adv* sotto, di sotto; giù; **see ~** vedi sotto *or* oltre

belt [bɛlt] *n* cintura; (*Tech*) cinghia ▶ *vt* (*thrash*) picchiare ▶ *vi* (*inf*) filarsela; **beltway** (*US*) *n* (*Aut: ring road*) circonvallazione *f*; (: *motorway*) autostrada

bemused [bɪ'mjuːzd] *adj*

perplesso(-a), stupito(-a)

bench [bɛntʃ] *n* panca; (*in workshop, Pol*) banco; **the B~** (*Law*) la Corte

bend [bɛnd] (*pt, pp* **bent**) *vt* curvare; (*leg, arm*) piegare ▶ *vi* curvarsi; piegarsi ▶ *n* (*BRIT: in road*) curva; (*in pipe, river*) gomito ▷ **bend down** *vi* chinarsi ▷ **bend over** *vi* piegarsi

beneath [bɪ'niːθ] *prep* sotto, al di sotto di; (*unworthy of*) indegno(-a) di ▶ *adv* sotto, di sotto

beneficial [bɛnɪ'fɪʃəl] *adj* che fa bene; vantaggioso(-a)

benefit ['bɛnɪfɪt] *n* beneficio, vantaggio; (*allowance of money*) indennità *f inv* ▶ *vt* far bene a ▶ *vi* **he'll ~ from it** ne trarrà beneficio *or* profitto

benign [bɪ'naɪn] *adj* (*person, smile*) benevolo(-a); (*Med*) benigno(-a)

bent [bɛnt] *pt, pp of* **bend** ▶ *n* inclinazione *f* ▶ *adj* (*inf: dishonest*) losco(-a); **to be ~ on** essere deciso(-a) a

bereaved [bɪ'riːvd] *n* **the ~** i familiari in lutto

beret ['bɛreɪ] *n* berretto

Berlin [bəː'lɪn] *n* Berlino *f*

Bermuda [bəː'mjuːdə] *n* le Bermude

berry ['bɛrɪ] *n* bacca

berth [bəːθ] *n* (*bed*) cuccetta; (*for ship*) ormeggio ▶ *vi* (*in harbour*) entrare in porto; (*at anchor*) gettare l'ancora

beside [bɪ'saɪd] *prep* accanto a; **to be ~ o.s. (with anger)** essere fuori di sé (dalla rabbia); **that's ~ the point** non c'entra; **besides** [bɪ'saɪdz] *adv* inoltre, per di più ▶ *prep* oltre a; a parte

best [bɛst] *adj* migliore ▶ *adv* meglio; **the ~ part of** (*quantity*) la maggior parte di; **at ~** tutt'al più; **to make the ~ of sth** cavare il meglio possibile da qc; **to do one's ~** fare del proprio meglio; **to the ~ of my knowledge** per quel che ne so; **to the ~ of my ability**

al massimo delle mie capacità;
best-before date n scadenza; **best man** (irreg) n testimone m dello sposo; **bestseller** n bestseller m inv

bet [bɛt] (pt, pp **bet** or **betted**) n scommessa ▶ vt, vi scommettere; **to ~ sb sth** scommettere qc con qn

betray [bɪ'treɪ] vt tradire

better ['bɛtə'] adj migliore ▶ adv meglio ▶ vt migliorare ▶ n **to get the ~ of** avere la meglio su; **you had ~ do it** è meglio che lo faccia; **he thought ~ of it** cambiò idea; **to get ~** migliorare

betting ['bɛtɪŋ] n scommesse fpl; **betting shop** (BRIT) n ufficio dell'allibratore

between [bɪ'twiːn] prep tra ▶ adv in mezzo, nel mezzo

beverage ['bɛvərɪdʒ] n bevanda

beware [bɪ'wɛə'] vt, vi **to ~ (of)** stare attento(-a) (a); **"~ of the dog"** "attenti al cane"

bewildered [bɪ'wɪldəd] adj sconcertato(-a), confuso(-a)

beyond [bɪ'jɔnd] prep (in space) oltre; (exceeding) al di sopra di ▶ adv di là; **~ doubt** senza dubbio; **~ repair** irreparabile

bias ['baɪəs] n (prejudice) pregiudizio; (preference) preferenza; **bias(s)ed** adj parziale

bib [bɪb] n bavaglino

Bible ['baɪbl] n Bibbia

bicarbonate of soda [baɪ'kɑːbənɪt-] n bicarbonato (di sodio)

biceps ['baɪsɛps] n bicipite m

bicycle ['baɪsɪkl] n bicicletta; **bicycle pump** n pompa della bicicletta

bid [bɪd] (pt **bade** or **bid**, pp **bidden** or **bid**) n offerta; (attempt) tentativo ▶ vi fare un'offerta ▶ vt fare un'offerta di; **to ~ sb good day** dire buon giorno a qn; **bidder** n **the highest bidder** il maggior offerente

bidet ['biːdeɪ] n bidè m inv

big [bɪg] adj grande; grosso(-a); **Big Apple** n vedi nota; **bigheaded** ['bɪg'hɛdɪd] adj presuntuoso(-a); **big toe** n alluce m

● **Big Apple**

● Tutti sanno che **The Big Apple**, la Grande Mela, è New York ("apple" in gergo significa grande città) ma sicuramente i soprannomi di altre città americane non sono così conosciuti. Chicago è soprannominata "the Windy City" perché è ventosa, New Orleans si chiama "the Big Easy" per il modo di vivere tranquillo e rilassato dei suoi abitanti, e l'industria automobilistica ha fatto sì che Detroit fosse soprannominata "Motown".

bike [baɪk] n bici f inv; **bike lane** n pista ciclabile

bikini [bɪ'kiːnɪ] n bikini m inv

bilateral [baɪ'lætərl] adj bilaterale

bilingual [baɪ'lɪŋgwəl] adj bilingue

bill [bɪl] n conto; (Pol) atto; (US: banknote) banconota; (of bird) becco; (of show) locandina; **can I have the ~, please** il conto, per favore; **put it on my ~** lo metta sul mio conto; **"post no ~s"** "divieto di affissione"; **to fit** or **fill the ~** (fig) fare al caso; **billboard** n tabellone m; **billfold** ['bɪlfəuld] (US) n portafoglio

billiards ['bɪljədz] n biliardo

billion ['bɪljən] num (BRIT) bilione m; (US) miliardo

bin [bɪn] n (for coal, rubbish) bidone m; (for bread) cassetta; (dustbin) pattumiera; (litter bin) cestino

bind [baɪnd] (pt, pp **bound**) vt legare; (oblige) obbligare ▶ n (inf) scocciatura

binge [bɪndʒ] (inf) n **to go on a ~** fare baldoria

bingo ['bɪŋgəu] n gioco simile alla tombola

binoculars [bɪ'nɔkjuləz] *npl* binocolo
bio... [baɪə'...] *prefix*; **biochemistry**
n biochimica; **biodegradable**
adj biodegradabile; **biography**
[baɪ'ɔgrəfɪ] *n* biografia; **biological**
adj biologico(-a); **biology** [baɪ'ɔlədʒɪ]
n biologia
birch [bə:tʃ] *n* betulla
bird [bə:d] *n* uccello; (*BRIT: inf: girl*)
bambola; **bird flu** *n* influenza aviaria;
bird of prey *n* (uccello) rapace *m*;
birdwatching *n* birdwatching *m*
Biro® ['baɪrəu] *n* biro® *f inv*
birth [bə:θ] *n* nascita; **to give ~**
to partorire; **birth certificate**
n certificato di nascita; **birth**
control *n* controllo delle nascite;
contraccezione *f*; **birthday** *n*
compleanno ▶ *cpd* di compleanno;
birthmark *n* voglia; **birthplace** *n*
luogo di nascita
biscuit ['bɪskɪt] (*BRIT*) *n* biscotto
bishop ['bɪʃəp] *n* vescovo
bistro ['bi:strəu] *n* bistrò *m inv*
bit [bɪt] *pt of* **bite** ▶ *n* pezzo; (*Comput*)
bit *m inv*; (*of horse*) morso; **a ~ of** un
po' di; **a ~ mad** un po' matto; **~ by ~** a
poco a poco
bitch [bɪtʃ] *n* (*dog*) cagna; (*inf!*) vacca
bite [baɪt] (*pt, pp* **bit, bitten**) *vt, vi*
mordere; (*insect*) pungere ▶ *n* morso;
(*insect bite*) puntura; (*mouthful*)
boccone *m*; **let's have a ~ to eat**
mangiamo un boccone; **to ~ one's**
nails mangiarsi le unghie
bitten ['bɪtn] *pp of* **bite**
bitter ['bɪtə'] *adj* amaro(-a); (*wind,*
criticism) pungente ▶ *n* (*BRIT: beer*)
birra amara
bizarre [bɪ'zɑ:'] *adj* bizzarro(-a)
black [blæk] *adj* nero(-a) ▶ *n* nero;
(*person*): **B~** negro(-a) ▶ *vt* (*BRIT*
Industry) boicottare; **to give sb a ~**
eye fare un occhio nero a qn; **in the**
~ (*bank account*) in attivo ▷ **black out**

vi (*faint*) svenire; **blackberry** *n* mora;
blackbird *n* merlo; **blackboard** *n*
lavagna; **black coffee** *n* caffè *m inv*
nero; **blackcurrant** *n* ribes *m inv*;
black ice *n* strato trasparente di
ghiaccio; **blackmail** *n* ricatto ▶ *vt*
ricattare; **black market** *n* mercato
nero; **blackout** *n* oscuramento;
(*TV, Radio*) interruzione *f* delle
trasmissioni; (*fainting*) svenimento;
black pepper *n* pepe *m* nero; **black**
pudding *n* sanguinaccio; **Black Sea** *n*
the Black Sea il Mar Nero
bladder ['blædə'] *n* vescica
blade [bleɪd] *n* lama; (*of oar*) pala; **~ of**
grass filo d'erba
blame [bleɪm] *n* colpa ▶ *vt* **to ~ sb/sth**
for sth dare la colpa di qc a qn/qc;
who's to ~? chi è colpevole?
bland [blænd] *adj* mite; (*taste*)
blando(-a)
blank [blæŋk] *adj* bianco(-a); (*look*)
distratto(-a) ▶ *n* spazio vuoto;
(*cartridge*) cartuccia a salve
blanket ['blæŋkɪt] *n* coperta
blast [blɑ:st] *n* (*of wind*) raffica; (*of*
bomb etc) esplosione *f* ▶ *vt* far saltare
blatant ['bleɪtənt] *adj* flagrante
blaze [bleɪz] *n* (*fire*) incendio; (*fig*)
vampata; splendore *m* ▶ *vi* (*fire*)
ardere, fiammeggiare; (*guns*) sparare
senza sosta; (*fig: eyes*) ardere ▶ *vt* **to ~**
a trail (*fig*) tracciare una via nuova; **in**
a ~ of publicity circondato da grande
pubblicità
blazer ['bleɪzə'] *n* blazer *m inv*
bleach [bli:tʃ] *n* varechina ▶ *vt*
(*material*) candeggiare; **bleachers**
(*US*) *npl* (*Sport*) posti *mpl* di gradinata
bleak [bli:k] *adj* tetro(-a)
bled [blɛd] *pt, pp of* **bleed**
bleed [bli:d] (*pt, pp* **bled**) *vi*
sanguinare; **my nose is ~ing** mi viene
fuori sangue dal naso
blemish ['blɛmɪʃ] *n* macchia

blend [blɛnd] n miscela ▶ vt mescolare ▶ vi (colours etc: also: ~ **in**) armonizzare; **blender** n (Culin) frullatore m

bless [blɛs] (pt, pp **blessed** or **blest**) vt benedire; ~ **you!** (after sneeze) salute!; **blessing** n benedizione f; fortuna

blew [blu:] pt of **blow**

blight [blaɪt] vt (hopes etc) deludere; (life) rovinare

blind [blaɪnd] adj cieco(-a) ▶ n (for window) avvolgibile m; (Venetian blind) veneziana ▶ vt accecare; **the ~** npl i ciechi; **blind alley** n vicolo cieco; **blindfold** n benda ▶ adj, adv bendato(-a) ▶ vt bendare gli occhi a

blink [blɪŋk] vi battere gli occhi; (light) lampeggiare

bliss [blɪs] n estasi f

blister ['blɪstər] n (on skin) vescica; (on paintwork) bolla

blizzard ['blɪzəd] n bufera di neve

bloated ['bləʊtɪd] adj gonfio(-a)

blob [blɒb] n (drop) goccia; (stain, spot) macchia

block [blɒk] n blocco; (in pipes) ingombro; (toy) cubo; (of buildings) isolato ▶ vt bloccare; **the sink is ~ed** il lavandino è otturato ▷ **block up** vt bloccare; (pipe) ingorgare, intasare; **blockade** [-'keɪd] n blocco; **blockage** n ostacolo; **blockbuster** n (film, book) grande successo; **block capitals** npl stampatello; **block letters** npl stampatello

blog [blɒg] n blog m ▶ vi scrivere blog

bloke [bləʊk] (BRIT: inf) n tizio

blond(e) [blɒnd] adj, n biondo(-a)

blood [blʌd] n sangue m; **blood donor** n donatore(-trice) di sangue; **blood group** n gruppo sanguigno; **blood poisoning** n setticemia; **blood pressure** n pressione f sanguigna; **bloodshed** n spargimento di sangue; **bloodshot** adj **bloodshot eyes** occhi iniettati di sangue; **bloodstream** n

flusso del sangue; **blood test** n analisi f inv del sangue; **blood transfusion** n trasfusione f di sangue; **blood type** n gruppo sanguigno; **blood vessel** n vaso sanguigno; **bloody** adj (fight) sanguinoso(-a); (nose) sanguinante; (BRIT: inf!): **this bloody ...** questo maledetto ...; **bloody awful/good** (inf!) veramente terribile/forte

bloom [blu:m] n fiore m ▶ vi (tree) essere in fiore; (flower) aprirsi

blossom ['blɒsəm] n fiore m; (with pl sense) fiori mpl ▶ vi essere in fiore

blot [blɒt] n macchia ▶ vt macchiare

blouse [blauz] n camicetta

blow [bləʊ] (pt **blew**, pp **blown**) n colpo ▶ vi soffiare ▶ vt (fuse) far saltare; (wind) spingere; (instrument) suonare; **to ~ one's nose** soffiarsi il naso; **to ~ a whistle** fischiare ▷ **blow away** vt portare via ▷ **blow out** vi scoppiare ▷ **blow up** vi saltare in aria ▶ vt far saltare in aria; (tyre) gonfiare; (Phot) ingrandire; **blow-dry** n messa in piega a föhn

blown [bləʊn] pp of **blow**

blue [blu:] adj azzurro(-a); (depressed) giù inv; ~ **film/joke** film/barzelletta pornografico(-a); **out of the ~** (fig) all'improvviso; **bluebell** n giacinto dei boschi; **blueberry** n mirtillo; **blue cheese** n formaggio tipo gorgonzola; **blues** npl **the blues** (Mus) il blues; **to have the blues** (inf: feeling) essere a terra; **bluetit** n cinciarella

bluff [blʌf] vi bluffare ▶ n bluff m inv ▶ adj (person) brusco(-a); **to call sb's ~** mettere alla prova il bluff di qn

blunder ['blʌndər] n abbaglio ▶ vi prendere un abbaglio

blunt [blʌnt] adj smussato(-a); spuntato(-a); (person) brusco(-a)

blur [bləːr] n forma indistinta ▶ vt offuscare; **blurred** adj (photo) mosso(-a); (TV) sfuocato(-a)

blush [blʌʃ] *vi* arrossire ▶ *n* rossore *m*;
blusher *n* fard *m inv*
board [bɔːd] *n* tavola; (*on wall*)
tabellone *m*; (*committee*) consiglio,
comitato; (*in firm*) consiglio
d'amministrazione; (*Naut, Aviat*):
on ~ a bordo ▶ *vt* (*ship*) salire a bordo
di; (*train*) salire su; **full ~** (*BRIT*)
pensione completa; **half ~** (*BRIT*)
mezza pensione; **~ and lodging**
vitto e alloggio; **which goes by the ~**
(*fig*) che viene abbandonato; **board
game** *n* gioco da tavolo; **boarding
card** *n* = **boarding pass**; **boarding
pass** *n* (*Aviat, Naut*) carta d'imbarco;
boarding school *n* collegio; **board
room** *n* sala del consiglio
boast [bəʊst] *vi* **to ~ (about** *or* **of)**
vantarsi (di)
boat [bəʊt] *n* nave *f*; (*small*) barca
bob [bɔb] *vi* (*boat, cork on water: also: ~
up and down*) andare su e giù
bobby pin ['bɔbɪ-] (*US*) *n* fermaglio
per capelli
body ['bɔdɪ] *n* corpo; (*of car*)
carrozzeria; (*of plane*) fusoliera;
(*fig: group*) gruppo; (: *organization*)
organizzazione *f*; (: *quantity*) quantità
f inv; **body-building** *n* culturismo;
bodyguard *n* guardia del corpo;
bodywork *n* carrozzeria
bog [bɔg] *n* palude *f* ▶ *vt* **to get ~ged
down** (*fig*) impantanarsi
bogus ['bəʊgəs] *adj* falso(-a); finto(-a)
boil [bɔɪl] *vt, vi* bollire ▶ *n* (*Med*)
foruncolo; **to come to the** (*BRIT*) *or*
a (*US*) **~** raggiungere l'ebollizione
▷ **boil over** *vi* traboccare (bollendo);
boiled egg *n* uovo alla coque; **boiled
potatoes** *npl* patate *fpl* bollite *or*
lesse; **boiler** *n* caldaia; **boiling** *adj*
bollente; **I'm boiling (hot)** (*inf*) sto
morendo di caldo; **boiling point** *n*
punto di ebollizione
bold [bəʊld] *adj* audace; (*child*)

impudente; (*colour*) deciso(-a)
Bolivia [bə'lɪvɪə] *n* Bolivia
Bolivian [bə'lɪvɪən] *adj, n* boliviano(-a)
bollard ['bɔləd] (*BRIT*) *n* (*Aut*)
colonnina luminosa
bolt [bəʊlt] *n* chiavistello; (*with nut*)
bullone *m* ▶ *adv* **~ upright** diritto(-a)
come un fuso ▶ *vt* serrare; (*also:
~ together*) imbullonare; (*food*)
mangiare in fretta ▶ *vi* scappare via
bomb [bɔm] *n* bomba ▶ *vt*
bombardare; **bombard** [bɔm'bɑːd]
vt bombardare; **bomber** *n* (*Aviat*)
bombardiere *m*; **bomb scare** *n* stato
di allarme (*per sospetta presenza di
una bomba*)
bond [bɔnd] *n* legame *m*; (*binding
promise, Finance*) obbligazione
f; (*Comm*): **in ~** in attesa di
sdoganamento
bone [bəʊn] *n* osso; (*of fish*) spina, lisca
▶ *vt* disossare; togliere le spine a
bonfire ['bɔnfaɪə'] *n* falò *m inv*
bonnet ['bɔnɪt] *n* cuffia; (*BRIT: of car*)
cofano
bonus ['bəʊnəs] *n* premio; (*fig*)
sovrappiù *m inv*
boo [buː] *excl* ba! ▶ *vt* fischiare
book [buk] *n* libro; (*of stamps etc*)
blocchetto ▶ *vt* (*ticket, seat, room*)
prenotare; (*driver*) multare; (*football
player*) ammonire; **~s** *npl* (*Comm*) conti
mpl; **I'd like to ~ a double room** vorrei
prenotare una camera doppia; **I ~ed a
table in the name of …** ho prenotato
un tavolo al nome di… ▷ **book in** *vi*
(*BRIT: at hotel*) prendere una camera
▷ **book up** *vt* riservare, prenotare;
the hotel is ~ed up l'albergo è al
completo; **all seats are ~ed up** è
tutto esaurito; **bookcase** *n* scaffale
m; **booking** *n* (*BRIT*) prenotazione
f; **I confirmed my booking by
fax/e-mail** ho confermato la mia
prenotazione tramite fax/e-mail;

booking office (BRIT) n (Rail) biglietteria; (Theatre) botteghino; **book-keeping** n contabilità; **booklet** n libricino; **bookmaker** n allibratore m; **bookmark** (also Comput) n segnalibro ▶ vt (Comput) mettere un segnalibro a; (Internet Explorer) aggiungere a "Preferiti"; **bookseller** n libraio; **bookshelf** n mensola (per libri); **bookshop, bookstore** n libreria

boom [bu:m] n (noise) rimbombo; (in prices etc) boom m inv ▶ vi rimbombare; andare a gonfie vele

boost [bu:st] n spinta ▶ vt spingere

boot [bu:t] n stivale m; (for hiking) scarpone m da montagna; (for football etc) scarpa; (BRIT: of car) portabagagli m inv ▶ vt (Comput) inizializzare; **to ~** (in addition) per giunta, in più

booth [bu:ð] n cabina; (at fair) baraccone m

booze [bu:z] (inf) n alcool m

border ['bɔ:dəʳ] n orlo; margine m; (of a country) frontiera; (for flowers) aiuola (laterale) ▶ vt (road) costeggiare; (another country: also: ~ **on**) confinare con; **the B~s** la zona di confine tra l'Inghilterra e la Scozia; **borderline** n (fig): **on the borderline** incerto(-a)

bore [bɔ:ʳ] pt of **bear** ▶ vt (hole etc) scavare; (person) annoiare ▶ n (person) seccatore(-trice); (of gun) calibro; **bored** adj annoiato(-a); **to be bored** annoiarsi; **he's bored to tears** or **to death** or **stiff** è annoiato a morte; **boredom** n noia

boring ['bɔ:rɪŋ] adj noioso(-a)

born [bɔ:n] adj **to be ~** nascere; **I was ~ in 1960** sono nato nel 1960

borne [bɔ:n] pp of **bear**

borough ['bʌrə] n comune m

borrow ['bɔrəu] vt **to ~ sth (from sb)** prendere in prestito qc (da qn)

Bosnia(-Herzegovina) ['bɔznɪə(hɛrzə'gəuvi:nə)] n Bosnia-Erzegovina; **Bosnian** ['bɔznɪən] n, adj bosniaco(-a) m/f

bosom ['buzəm] n petto; (fig) seno

boss [bɔs] n capo ▶ vt comandare; **bossy** adj prepotente

both [bəuθ] adj entrambi(-e), tutt'e due ▶ pron ~ **of them** entrambi(-e); ~ **of us went, we ~ went** ci siamo andati tutt'e due ▶ adv **they sell ~ meat and poultry** vendono insieme la carne ed il pollame

bother ['bɔðəʳ] vt (worry) preoccupare; (annoy) infastidire ▶ vi (also: ~ **o.s.**) preoccuparsi ▶ n it is a ~ **to have to do** è una seccatura dover fare; **it was no ~** non c'era problema; **to ~ doing sth** darsi la pena di fare qc

bottle ['bɔtl] n bottiglia; (baby's) biberon m inv ▶ vt imbottigliare; **bottle bank** n contenitore m per la raccolta del vetro; **bottle-opener** n apribottiglie m inv

bottom ['bɔtəm] n fondo; (buttocks) sedere m ▶ adj più basso(-a); ultimo(-a); **at the ~ of** in fondo a

bought [bɔ:t] pt, pp of **buy**

boulder ['bəuldəʳ] n masso (tondeggiante)

bounce [bauns] vi (ball) rimbalzare; (cheque) essere restituito(-a) ▶ vt far rimbalzare ▶ n (rebound) rimbalzo; **bouncer** (inf) n buttafuori m inv

bound [baund] pt, pp of **bind** ▶ n (gen pl) limite m; (leap) salto ▶ vi saltare ▶ vt (limit) delimitare ▶ adj ~ **by law** obbligato(-a) per legge; **to be ~ to do sth** (obliged) essere costretto(-a) a fare qc; **he's ~ to fail** (likely) fallirà di certo; ~ **for** diretto(-a) a; **out of ~s** il cui accesso è vietato

boundary ['baundrɪ] n confine m

bouquet ['bukeɪ] n bouquet m inv

bourbon ['buəbən] (US) n (also: ~ **whiskey**) bourbon m inv

bout [baut] n periodo; (of malaria etc) attacco; (Boxing etc) incontro

boutique [buː'tiːk] n boutique f inv

bow¹ [bəu] n nodo; (weapon) arco; (Mus) archetto

bow² [bau] n (with body) inchino; (Naut: also: **~s**) prua ▶ vi inchinarsi; (yield): **to ~ to** or **before** sottomettersi a

bowels ['bauəlz] npl intestini mpl; (fig) viscere fpl

bowl [bəul] n (for eating) scodella; (for washing) bacino; (ball) boccia ▶ vi (Cricket) servire (la palla); **bowler** ['bəulər] n (Cricket, Baseball) lanciatore m; (BRIT: also: **bowler hat**) bombetta; **bowling** ['bəuliŋ] n (game) gioco delle bocce; **bowling alley** n pista da bowling; **bowling green** n campo di bocce; **bowls** [bəulz] n gioco delle bocce

bow tie n cravatta a farfalla

box [bɔks] n scatola; (also: **cardboard ~**) cartone m; (Theatre) palco ▶ vt inscatolare ▶ vi fare del pugilato; **boxer** n (person) pugile m; **boxer shorts** ['bɔksəʃɔːts] pl n boxer; **a pair of boxer shorts** un paio di boxer; **boxing** n (Sport) pugilato; **Boxing Day** (BRIT) n ≈ Santo Stefano; vedi nota; **boxing gloves** npl guantoni mpl da pugile; **boxing ring** n ring m inv; **box office** n biglietteria

- **Boxing Day**
- Il **Boxing Day** è un giorno di festa
- e cade in genere il 26 dicembre.
- Prende il nome dalla tradizionale
- usanza di donare pacchi regalo
- natalizi, chiamati "Christmas
- boxes", per i fornitori e dipendenti.

boy [bɔɪ] n ragazzo

boycott ['bɔɪkɔt] n boicottaggio ▶ vt boicottare

boyfriend ['bɔɪfrɛnd] n ragazzo

bra [brɑː] n reggipetto, reggiseno

brace [breɪs] n (on teeth) apparecchio correttore; (tool) trapano ▶ vt rinforzare, sostenere; **~s** (BRIT) npl (Dress) bretelle fpl; **to ~ o.s.** (also fig) tenersi forte

bracelet ['breɪslɪt] n braccialetto

bracket ['brækɪt] n (Tech) mensola; (group) gruppo; (Typ) parentesi f inv ▶ vt mettere fra parentesi

brag [bræg] vi vantarsi

braid [breɪd] n (trimming) passamano; (of hair) treccia

brain [breɪn] n cervello; **~s** npl (intelligence) cervella fpl; **he's got ~s** è intelligente

braise [breɪz] vt brasare

brake [breɪk] n (on vehicle) freno ▶ vi frenare; **brake light** n (fanalino dello) stop m inv

bran [bræn] n crusca

branch [brɑːntʃ] n ramo; (Comm) succursale f ▷ **branch off** vi diramarsi ▷ **branch out** vi (fig) intraprendere una nuova attività

brand [brænd] n marca; (fig) tipo ▶ vt (cattle) marcare (a ferro rovente); **brand name** n marca; **brand-new** adj nuovo(-a) di zecca

brandy ['brændɪ] n brandy m inv

brash [bræʃ] adj sfacciato(-a)

brass [brɑːs] n ottone m; **the ~** (Mus) gli ottoni; **brass band** n fanfara

brat [bræt] n (pej) marmocchio, monello(-a)

brave [breɪv] adj coraggioso(-a) ▶ vt affrontare; **bravery** n coraggio

brawl [brɔːl] n rissa

Brazil [brə'zɪl] n Brasile m; **Brazilian** adj, n brasiliano(-a)

breach [briːtʃ] vt aprire una breccia in ▶ n (gap) breccia, varco; (breaking): **~ of contract** rottura di contratto; **~ of the peace** violazione f dell'ordine pubblico

bread [brɛd] n pane m; **breadbin** n cassetta f portapane inv; **breadbox**

(US) n cassetta f portapane inv;
breadcrumbs npl briciole fpl; (Culin)
pangrattato
breadth [brɛtθ] n larghezza; (fig: of
knowledge etc) ampiezza
break [breɪk] (pt **broke**, pp **broken**) vt
rompere; (law) violare; (record) battere
▶ vi rompersi; (storm) scoppiare;
(weather) cambiare; (dawn) spuntare;
(news) saltare fuori ▶ n (gap) breccia;
(fracture) rottura; (rest, also Scol)
intervallo; (: short) pausa; (chance)
possibilità f inv; **to ~ one's leg** etc
rompersi la gamba ecc; **to ~ the news
to sb** comunicare per primo la notizia
a qn; **to ~ even** coprire le spese; **to
~ free** or **loose** spezzare i legami; **to
~ open** (door etc) sfondare ▷ **break
down** vt (figures, data) analizzare
▶ vi (person) avere un esaurimento
(nervoso); (Aut) guastarsi; **my car
has broken down** mi si è rotta la
macchina ▷ **break in** vt (horse etc)
domare ▶ vi (burglar) fare irruzione;
(interrupt) interrompere ▷ **break into**
vt fus (house) fare irruzione in ▷ **break
off** vi (speaker) interrompersi; (branch)
troncarsi ▷ **break out** vi evadere;
(war, fight) scoppiare; **to ~ out in
spots** coprirsi di macchie ▷ **break
up** vi (ship) sfondarsi; (meeting)
sciogliersi; (crowd) disperdersi;
(marriage) andare a pezzi; (Scol)
chiudere ▶ vt fare a pezzi, spaccare;
(fight etc) interrompere, far cessare;
breakdown n (Aut) guasto; (in
communications) interruzione f; (of
marriage) rottura; (Med: also: **nervous
breakdown**) esaurimento nervoso;
(of statistics) resoconto; **breakdown
truck, breakdown van** n carro m
attrezzi inv
breakfast ['brɛkfəst] n colazione f;
what time is ~? a che ora è servita la
colazione?

break: **break-in** n irruzione f;
breakthrough n (fig) passo avanti
breast [brɛst] n (of woman) seno;
(chest, Culin) petto; **breast-feed** (irreg:
like **feed**) vt, vi allattare (al seno);
breast-stroke n nuoto a rana
breath [brɛθ] n respiro; **out of ~**
senza fiato
Breathalyser® ['brɛθəlaɪzəʳ] (BRIT) n
alcoltest m inv
breathe [bri:ð] vt, vi respirare
▷ **breathe in** vt respirare ▶ vi inspirare
▷ **breathe out** vt, vi espirare;
breathing n respiro, respirazione f
breath: **breathless** ['brɛθlɪs] adj senza
fiato; **breathtaking** ['brɛθteɪkɪŋ] adj
mozzafiato inv; **breath test** n ≈ prova
del palloncino
bred [brɛd] pt, pp of **breed**
breed [bri:d] (pt, pp **bred**) vt allevare
▶ vi riprodursi ▶ n razza; (type, class)
varietà f inv
breeze [bri:z] n brezza
breezy ['bri:zɪ] adj allegro(-a),
ventilato(-a)
brew [bru:] vt (tea) fare un infuso
di; (beer) fare ▶ vi (storm, fig: trouble
etc) prepararsi; **brewery** n fabbrica
di birra
bribe [braɪb] n bustarella ▶ vt
comprare; **bribery** n corruzione f
bric-a-brac ['brɪkəbræk] n bric-a-
brac m
brick [brɪk] n mattone m; **bricklayer**
n muratore m
bride [braɪd] n sposa; **bridegroom**
n sposo; **bridesmaid** n damigella
d'onore
bridge [brɪdʒ] n ponte m; (Naut) ponte
di comando; (of nose) dorso; (Cards)
bridge m inv ▶ vt (fig: gap) colmare
bridle ['braɪdl] n briglia
brief [bri:f] adj breve ▶ n (Law)
comparsa; (gen) istruzioni fpl ▶ vt
mettere al corrente; **~s** npl (underwear)

mutande *fpl*; **briefcase** *n* cartella;
briefing *n* briefing *m inv*; **briefly**
adv (*glance*) di sfuggita; (*explain, say*)
brevemente
brigadier [brɪgə'dɪə^r] *n* generale *m*
di brigata
bright [braɪt] *adj* luminoso(-a); (*clever*)
sveglio(-a); (*lively*) vivace
brilliant ['brɪljənt] *adj* brillante; (*light,
smile*) radioso(-a); (*inf*) splendido(-a)
brim [brɪm] *n* orlo
brine [braɪn] *n* (*Culin*) salamoia
bring [brɪŋ] (*pt, pp* brought) *vt* portare
▷ **bring about** *vt* causare ▷ **bring
back** *vt* riportare ▷ **bring down** *vt*
portare giù; abbattere ▷ **bring in** *vt*
(*person*) fare entrare; (*object*) portare;
(*Pol: bill*) presentare; (: *legislation*)
introdurre; (*Law: verdict*) emettere;
(*produce: income*) rendere ▷ **bring on**
vt (*illness, attack*) causare, provocare;
(*player, substitute*) far scendere in
campo ▷ **bring out** *vt* tirar fuori;
(*meaning*) mettere in evidenza;
(*book, album*) far uscire ▷ **bring up** *vt*
(*carry up*) portare su; (*child*) allevare;
(*question*) introdurre; (*food: vomit*)
rimettere, rigurgitare
brink [brɪŋk] *n* orlo
brisk [brɪsk] *adj* (*manner*) spiccio(-a);
(*trade*) vivace; (*pace*) svelto(-a)
bristle ['brɪsl] *n* setola ▶ *vi* rizzarsi;
bristling with irto(-a) di
Brit [brɪt] *n abbr* (*inf*: = British person)
britannico(-a)
Britain ['brɪtən] *n* (*also*: **Great ~**) Gran
Bretagna
British ['brɪtɪʃ] *adj* britannico(-a);
British Isles *npl* Isole Britanniche
Briton ['brɪtən] *n* britannico(-a)
brittle ['brɪtl] *adj* fragile
broad [brɔːd] *adj* largo(-a); (*distinction*)
generale; (*accent*) spiccato(-a);
in ~ daylight in pieno giorno;
broadband *adj* (*Comput*) a banda

larga ▶ *n* banda larga; **broad bean** *n*
fava; **broadcast** (*pt, pp* **broadcast**)
n trasmissione *f* ▶ *vt* trasmettere
per radio (*or* per televisione) ▶ *vi*
fare una trasmissione; **broaden** *vt*
allargare ▶ *vi* allargarsi; **broadly** *adv*
(*fig*) in generale; **broad-minded** *adj* di
mente aperta
broccoli ['brɔkəlɪ] *n* broccoli *mpl*
brochure ['brəʊʃjʊə^r] *n* dépliant *m inv*
broil [brɔɪl] *vt* cuocere a fuoco vivo
broiler ['brɔɪlə^r] (*US*) *n* (*grill*) griglia
broke [brəʊk] *pt of* **break** ▶ *adj* (*inf*)
squattrinato(-a)
broken ['brəʊkn] *pp of* **break** ▶ *adj*
rotto(-a); **a ~ leg** una gamba rotta; **in
~ English** in un inglese stentato
broker ['brəʊkə^r] *n* agente *m*
bronchitis [brɔn'kaɪtɪs] *n* bronchite *f*
bronze [brɔnz] *n* bronzo
brooch [brəʊtʃ] *n* spilla
brood [bruːd] *n* covata ▶ *vi* (*person*)
rimuginare
broom [brum] *n* scopa; (*Bot*) ginestra
Bros. *abbr* (= *Brothers*) F.lli
broth [brɔθ] *n* brodo
brothel ['brɔθl] *n* bordello
brother ['brʌðə^r] *n* fratello; **brother-
in-law** *n* cognato
brought [brɔːt] *pt, pp of* **bring**
brow [braʊ] *n* fronte *f*; (*rare, gen*:
eyebrow) sopracciglio; (*of hill*) cima
brown [braʊn] *adj* bruno(-a),
marrone; (*tanned*) abbronzato(-a) ▶ *n*
(*colour*) color *m* bruno *or* marrone ▶ *vt*
(*Culin*) rosolare; **brown bread** *n* pane
m integrale, pane nero
Brownie ['braʊnɪ] *n* giovane
esploratrice *f*
brown rice *n* riso greggio
brown sugar *n* zucchero greggio
browse [braʊz] *vi* (*among books*)
curiosare fra i libri; **to ~ through a
book** sfogliare un libro; **browser** *n*
(*Comput*) browser *m inv*

bruise [bruːz] n (on person) livido ▶ vt farsi un livido a

brunette [bruːˈnɛt] n bruna

brush [brʌʃ] n spazzola; (for painting, shaving) pennello; (quarrel) schermaglia ▶ vt spazzolare; (also: ~ against) sfiorare

Brussels [ˈbrʌslz] n Bruxelles f

Brussels sprout [spraut] n cavolo di Bruxelles

brutal [ˈbruːtl] adj brutale

B.Sc. n abbr (Univ) = **Bachelor of Science**

BSE n abbr (= bovine spongiform encephalopathy) encefalite f bovina spongiforme

bubble [ˈbʌbl] n bolla ▶ vi ribollire; (sparkle: fig) essere effervescente; **bubble bath** n bagnoschiuma m inv; **bubble gum** n gomma americana

buck [bʌk] n maschio (di camoscio, caprone, coniglio ecc); (US: inf) dollaro ▶ vi sgroppare; **to pass the ~ to sb** scaricare (su di qn) la propria responsabilità

bucket [ˈbʌkɪt] n secchio

buckle [ˈbʌkl] n fibbia ▶ vt allacciare ▶ vi (wheel etc) piegarsi

bud [bʌd] n gemma; (of flower) bocciolo ▶ vi germogliare; (flower) sbocciare

Buddhism [ˈbudɪzəm] n buddismo

Buddhist [ˈbudɪst] adj, n buddista (m/f)

buddy [ˈbʌdɪ] (US) n compagno

budge [bʌdʒ] vt scostare; (fig) smuovere ▶ vi spostarsi; smuoversi

budgerigar [ˈbʌdʒərɪgɑːʳ] n pappagallino

budget [ˈbʌdʒɪt] n bilancio preventivo ▶ vi to ~ **for sth** fare il bilancio per qc

budgie [ˈbʌdʒɪ] n = **budgerigar**

buff [bʌf] adj color camoscio ▶ n (inf: enthusiast) appassionato(-a)

buffalo [ˈbʌfələu] n (pl **buffalo** or **buffaloes**) n bufalo; (US) bisonte m

buffer [ˈbʌfəʳ] n respingente m; (Comput) memoria tampone, buffer m inv

buffet[1] [ˈbʌfɪt] vt sferzare

buffet[2] [ˈbufeɪ] n (food, BRIT: bar) buffet m inv; **buffet car** (BRIT) n (Rail) ≈ servizio ristoro

bug [bʌg] n (esp US: insect) insetto; (Comput, fig: germ) virus m inv; (spy device) microfono spia ▶ vt mettere sotto controllo; (inf: annoy) scocciare

buggy [ˈbʌgɪ] n (baby buggy) passeggino

build [bɪld] (pt, pp **built**) n (of person) corporatura ▶ vt costruire ▷ **build up** vt accumulare; aumentare; **builder** n costruttore m; **building** n costruzione f; edificio; (industry) edilizia; **building site** n cantiere m di costruzione; **building society** (BRIT) n società f inv immobiliare

built [bɪlt] pt, pp of **build**; **built-in** adj (cupboard) a muro; (device) incorporato(-a); **built-up** adj **built-up area** abitato

bulb [bʌlb] n (Bot) bulbo; (Elec) lampadina

Bulgaria [bʌlˈgɛərɪə] n Bulgaria; **Bulgarian** adj bulgaro(-a) ▶ n bulgaro(-a); (Ling) bulgaro

bulge [bʌldʒ] n rigonfiamento ▶ vi essere protuberante or rigonfio(-a); **to be bulging with** essere pieno(-a) or zeppo(-a) di

bulimia [bəˈlɪmɪə] n bulimia

bulimic [bjuːˈlɪmɪk] adj, n bulimico(-a)

bulk [bʌlk] n massa, volume m; **in ~** a pacchi or cassette etc; (Comm) all'ingrosso; **the ~ of** il grosso di; **bulky** adj grosso(-a), voluminoso(-a)

bull [bul] n toro; (male elephant, whale) maschio

bulldozer [ˈbuldəuzəʳ] n bulldozer m inv

bullet [ˈbulɪt] n pallottola

bulletin ['bulItIn] n bollettino;
bulletin board n (Comput) bulletin
board m inv
bullfight ['bulfaIt] n corrida;
bullfighter n torero; **bullfighting** n
tauromachia
bully ['bulI] n prepotente m ▶ vt
angariare; (frighten) intimidire
bum [bʌm] (inf) n (backside) culo;
(tramp) vagabondo(-a)
bumblebee ['bʌmblbi:] n bombo
bump [bʌmp] n (in car) piccolo
tamponamento; (jolt) scossa; (on
road etc) protuberanza; (on head)
bernoccolo ▶ vt battere ▷ **bump
into** vt fus scontrarsi con; (person)
imbattersi in; **bumper** n paraurti m
inv ▶ adj **bumper harvest** raccolto
eccezionale; **bumpy** ['bʌmpI] adj
(road) dissestato(-a)
bun [bʌn] n focaccia; (of hair) crocchia
bunch [bʌntʃ] n (of flowers, keys)
mazzo; (of bananas) casco; (of people)
gruppo; ~ **of grapes** grappolo d'uva;
~**es** npl (in hair) codine fpl
bundle ['bʌndl] n fascio ▶ vt (also: ~ **up**)
legare in un fascio; (put): **to ~ sth/sb
into** spingere qc/qn in
bungalow ['bʌŋgələu] n bungalow
m inv
bungee jumping ['bʌndʒi:'dʒʌmpIŋ]
n salto nel vuoto da ponti, grattacieli etc
con un cavo fissato alla caviglia
bunion ['bʌnjən] n callo (al piede)
bunk [bʌŋk] n cuccetta; **bunk beds** npl
letti mpl a castello
bunker ['bʌŋkəʳ] n (coal store)
ripostiglio per il carbone; (Mil, Golf)
bunker m inv
bunny ['bʌnI] n (also: ~ **rabbit**)
coniglietto
buoy [bɔI] n boa; **buoyant** adj
galleggiante; (fig) vivace
burden ['bə:dn] n carico, fardello ▶ vt
to ~ sb with caricare qn di

bureau [bjuə'rəu] (pl **bureaux**) n (BRIT:
writing desk) scrivania; (US: chest of
drawers) cassettone m; (office) ufficio,
agenzia
bureaucracy [bjuə'rɔkrəsI] n
burocrazia
bureaucrat ['bjuərəkræt] n burocrate
m/f
bureau de change [-də'ʃɑ̃ʒ] (pl
bureaux de change) n cambiavalute
m inv
bureaux [bjuə'rəuz] npl of **bureau**
burger ['bə:gəʳ] n hamburger m inv
burglar ['bə:gləʳ] n scassinatore
m; **burglar alarm** n campanello
antifurto; **burglary** n furto con scasso
burial ['berIəl] n sepoltura
burn [bə:n] (pt, pp **burned** or **burnt**) vt,
vi bruciare ▶ n bruciatura, scottatura
▷ **burn down** vt distruggere col fuoco
▷ **burn out** vt (writer etc): **to ~ o.s. out**
esaurirsi; **burning** adj in fiamme;
(sand) che scotta; (ambition) bruciante
Burns Night n vedi nota
● **Burns Night**
●
● **Burns Night** è la festa celebrata il 25
● gennaio per commemorare il poeta
● scozzese Robert Burns (1759-1796).
● Gli scozzesi festeggiano questa data
● con una cena, la "Burns supper", a
● base di "haggis", piatto tradizionale
● scozzese, e whisky.
burnt [bə:nt] pt, pp of **burn**
burp [bə:p] (inf) n rutto ▶ vi ruttare
burrow ['bʌrəu] n tana ▶ vt scavare
burst [bə:st] (pt, pp **burst**) vt far
scoppiare ▶ vi esplodere; (tyre)
scoppiare ▶ n scoppio; (also: ~ **pipe**)
rottura nel tubo, perdita; **a ~ of
speed** uno scatto di velocità; **to
~ into flames/tears** scoppiare in
fiamme/lacrime; **to ~ out laughing**
scoppiare a ridere; **to be ~ing with**
scoppiare di ▷ **burst into** vt fus (room
etc) irrompere in

bury ['bɛrɪ] vt seppellire

bus [bʌs] (pl **buses**) n autobus m inv; **bus conductor** n autista m/f (dell'autobus)

bush [buʃ] n cespuglio; (scrub land) macchia; **to beat about the ~** menare il cane per l'aia

business ['bɪznɪs] n (matter) affare m; (trading) affari mpl; (firm) azienda; (job, duty) lavoro; **to be away on ~** essere andato via per affari; **it's none of my ~** questo non mi riguarda; **he means ~** non scherza; **business class** n (Aer) business class f; **businesslike** adj serio(-a), efficiente; **businessman** (irreg) n uomo d'affari; **business trip** n viaggio d'affari; **businesswoman** (irreg) n donna d'affari

busker ['bʌskəʳ] (BRIT) n suonatore(-trice) ambulante

bus: **bus pass** n tessera dell'autobus; **bus shelter** n pensilina (alla fermata dell'autobus); **bus station** n stazione f delle corriere, autostazione f; **bus-stop** n fermata d'autobus

bust [bʌst] n busto; (Anat) seno ▶ adj (inf: broken) rotto(-a); **to go ~** fallire

bustling ['bʌslɪŋ] adj movimentato(-a)

busy ['bɪzɪ] adj occupato(-a); (shop, street) molto frequentato(-a) ▶ vt **to ~ o.s.** darsi da fare; **busy signal** (US) n (Tel) segnale m di occupato

O but
[bʌt] conj ma; **I'd love to come, but I'm busy** vorrei tanto venire, ma ho da fare

▶prep (apart from, except) eccetto, tranne, meno; **he was nothing but trouble** non dava altro che guai; **no-one but him can do it** nessuno può farlo tranne lui; **but for you/your help** se non fosse per te/per il tuo aiuto; **anything but that** tutto ma non questo

▶adv (just, only) solo, soltanto; **she's but a child** è solo una bambina; **had I but known** se solo avessi saputo; **I can but try** tentar non nuoce; **all but finished** quasi finito

butcher ['butʃəʳ] n macellaio ▶ vt macellare; **butcher's (shop)** n macelleria

butler ['bʌtləʳ] n maggiordomo

butt [bʌt] n (cask) grossa botte f; (of gun) calcio; (of cigarette) mozzicone m; (BRIT: fig: target) oggetto ▶ vt cozzare

butter ['bʌtəʳ] n burro ▶ vt imburrare; **buttercup** n ranuncolo

butterfly ['bʌtəflaɪ] n farfalla; (Swimming: also: ~ **stroke**) (nuoto a) farfalla

buttocks ['bʌtəks] npl natiche fpl

button ['bʌtn] n bottone m; (US: badge) distintivo ▶ vt (also: ~ **up**) abbottonare ▶ vi abbottonarsi

buy [baɪ] (pt, pp **bought**) vt comprare ▶ n acquisto; **where can I ~ some postcards?** dove posso comprare delle cartoline?; **to ~ sb sth/sth from sb** comprare qc per qn/qc da qn; **to ~ sb a drink** offrire da bere a qn ▷ **buy out** vt (business) rilevare ▷ **buy up** vt accaparrarsi; **buyer** n compratore(-trice)

buzz [bʌz] n ronzio; (inf: phone call) colpo di telefono ▶ vi ronzare; **buzzer** ['bʌzəʳ] n cicalino

O by
[baɪ] prep

1 (referring to cause, agent) da; **killed by lightning** ucciso da un fulmine; **surrounded by a fence** circondato da uno steccato; **a painting by Picasso** un quadro di Picasso

2 (referring to method, manner, means): **by bus/car/train** in autobus/ macchina/treno, con l'autobus/la macchina/il treno; **to pay by cheque** pagare con (un) assegno; **by**

moonlight al chiaro di luna; **by saving hard, he …** risparmiando molto, lui …
3 (*via, through*) per; **we came by Dover** siamo venuti via Dover
4 (*close to, past*) accanto a; **the house by the river** la casa sul fiume; **a holiday by the sea** una vacanza al mare; **she sat by his bed** si sedette accanto al suo letto; **she rushed by me** mi è passata accanto correndo; **I go by the post office every day** passo davanti all'ufficio postale ogni giorno
5 (*not later than*) per, entro; **by 4 o'clock** per *or* entro le 4; **by this time tomorrow** domani a quest'ora; **by the time I got here it was too late** quando sono arrivato era ormai troppo tardi
6 (*during*): **by day/night** di giorno/notte
7 (*amount*) a; **by the kilo/metre** a chili/metri; **paid by the hour** pagato all'ora; **one by one** uno per uno; **little by little** a poco a poco
8 (*Math, measure*): **to divide/multiply by 3** dividere/moltiplicare per 3; **it's broader by a metre** è un metro più largo, è più largo di un metro
9 (*according to*) per; **to play by the rules** attenersi alle regole; **it's all right by me** per me va bene
10: **(all) by oneself** *etc* (tutto(-a)) solo(-a); **he did it (all) by himself** lo ha fatto (tutto) da solo
11: **by the way** a proposito; **this wasn't my idea by the way** tra l'altro l'idea non è stata mia
▶*adv*
1 *see* **go**; **pass** *etc*
2: **by and by** (*in past*) poco dopo; (*in future*) fra breve; **by and large** nel complesso
bye(-bye) ['baɪ('baɪ)] *excl* ciao!, arrivederci!
by-election ['baɪɪlɛkʃən] (*BRIT*) *n* elezione *f* straordinaria

bypass ['baɪpɑːs] *n* circonvallazione *f*; (*Med*) by-pass *m inv* ▶*vt* fare una deviazione intorno a
byte [baɪt] *n* (*Comput*) byte *m inv*, bicarattere *m*

C

C [siː] *n* (*Mus*) do
cab [kæb] *n* taxi *m inv*; (*of train, truck*) cabina
cabaret ['kæbəreɪ] *n* cabaret *m inv*
cabbage ['kæbɪdʒ] *n* cavolo
cabin ['kæbɪn] *n* capanna; (*on ship*) cabina; **cabin crew** *n* equipaggio
cabinet ['kæbɪnɪt] *n* (*Pol*) consiglio dei ministri; (*furniture*) armadietto; (*also:* **display ~**) vetrinetta; **cabinet minister** *n* ministro (*membro del Consiglio*)
cable ['keɪbl] *n* cavo; fune *f*; (*Tel*) cablogramma *m* ▶*vt* telegrafare; **cable car** *n* funivia; **cable television** *n* televisione *f* via cavo
cactus ['kæktəs] (*pl* **cacti**) *n* cactus *m inv*
café ['kæfeɪ] *n* caffè *m inv*
cafeteria [kæfɪ'tɪərɪə] *n* self-service *m inv*
caffein(e) ['kæfiːn] *n* caffeina
cage [keɪdʒ] *n* gabbia
cagoule [kə'ɡuːl] *n* K-way® *m inv*
cake [keɪk] *n* (*large*) torta; (*small*)

pasticcio; **cake of soap** n saponetta
calcium ['kælsɪəm] n calcio
calculate ['kælkjuleɪt] vt calcolare;
calculation [-'leɪʃən] n calcolo;
calculator n calcolatrice f
calendar ['kæləndər] n calendario
calf [kɑːf] (pl **calves**) n (of cow) vitello;
(of other animals) piccolo; (also: **~skin**)
(pelle f di) vitello; (Anat) polpaccio
calibre ['kælɪbər] (US **caliber**) n calibro
call [kɔːl] vt (gen: also Tel) chiamare;
(meeting) indire ▶ vi chiamare; (visit:
also: **~ in, ~ round**) passare ▶ n (shout)
grido, urlo; (Tel) telefonata; **to be
~ed** (person, object) chiamarsi; **can
you ~ back later?** può richiamare
più tardi?; **can I make a ~ from here?**
posso telefonare da qui?; **to be on ~**
essere a disposizione ▷ **call back** vi
(return) ritornare; (Tel) ritelefonare,
richiamare ▷ **call for** vt fus richiedere;
(fetch) passare a prendere ▷ **call in**
vt (doctor, expert, police) chiamare,
far venire ▷ **call off** vt disdire ▷ **call
on** vt fus (visit) passare da; (appeal
to) chiedere a ▷ **call out** vi (in pain)
urlare; (to person) chiamare ▷ **call up**
vt (Mil) richiamare; (Tel) telefonare
a; **callbox** (BRIT) n cabina telefonica;
call centre (US **call center**) n
centro informazioni telefoniche;
caller n persona che chiama,
visitatore(-trice)
callous ['kæləs] adj indurito(-a),
insensibile
calm [kɑːm] adj calmo(-a) ▶ n calma
▶ vt calmare ▷ **calm down** vi calmarsi
▶ vt calmare; **calmly** adv con calma
Calor gas® ['kælər-] n butano
calorie ['kælərɪ] n caloria
calves [kɑːvz] npl of **calf**
camcorder ['kæmkɔːdər] n camcorder
f inv
came [keɪm] pt of **come**
camel ['kæməl] n cammello

camera ['kæmərə] n macchina
fotografica; (Cinema, TV) cinepresa; **in
~** a porte chiuse; **cameraman** (irreg) n
cameraman m inv
camouflage ['kæməflɑːʒ] n (Mil, Zool)
mimetizzazione f ▶ vt mimetizzare
camp [kæmp] n campeggio;
(Mil) campo ▶ vi accamparsi ▶ adj
effeminato(-a)
campaign [kæm'peɪn] n (Mil, Pol
etc) campagna ▶ vi (also fig) fare
una campagna; **campaigner** n
campaigner for fautore(-trice)
di; **campaigner against**
oppositore(-trice) di
camp: **campbed** n (BRIT)
brandina; **camper** ['kæmpər] n
campeggiatore(-trice); (vehicle)
camper m inv; **campground** (US) n
campeggio; **camping** ['kæmpɪŋ] n
campeggio; **to go camping** andare in
campeggio; **campsite** ['kæmpsaɪt] n
campeggio
campus ['kæmpəs] n campus m inv
can¹ [kæn] n (of milk) scatola; (of oil)
bidone m; (of water) tanica; (tin)
scatola ▶ vt mettere in scatola

○ **can²**
[kæn] (negative **cannot, can't**,
conditional and pt **could**) aux vb
1 (be able to) potere; **I can't go any
further** non posso andare oltre; **you
can do it if you try** sei in grado di farlo
— basta provarci; **I'll help you all I can**
ti aiuterò come potrò; **I can't see you**
non ti vedo
2 (know how to) sapere, essere capace
di; **I can swim** so nuotare; **can you
speak French?** parla francese?
3 (may) potere; **could I have a word
with you?** posso parlarle un momento?
4 (expressing disbelief, puzzlement etc):
it can't be true! non può essere vero!;
what can he want? cosa può mai
volere?

5 (*expressing possibility, suggestion etc*): **he could be in the library** può darsi che sia in biblioteca; **she could have been delayed** può aver avuto un contrattempo

Canada ['kænədə] *n* Canada *m*; **Canadian** [kə'neɪdɪən] *adj, n* canadese *m/f*

canal [kə'næl] *n* canale *m*

canary [kə'nɛərɪ] *n* canarino

Canary Islands, Canaries [kə'nɛərɪz] *npl* **the ~** le (isole) Canarie

cancel ['kænsəl] *vt* annullare; (*train*) sopprimere; (*cross out*) cancellare; **I want to ~ my booking** vorrei disdire la mia prenotazione; **cancellation** [-'leɪʃən] *n* annullamento; soppressione *f*; cancellazione *f*; (*Tourism*) prenotazione *f* annullata

cancer ['kænsər] *n* cancro

Cancer ['kænsər] *n* (*sign*) Cancro

candidate ['kændɪdeɪt] *n* candidato(-a)

candle ['kændl] *n* candela; (*in church*) cero; **candlestick** *n* bugia; (*bigger, ornate*) candeliere *m*

candy ['kændɪ] *n* zucchero candito; (*US*) caramella; caramelle *fpl*; **candy bar** (*US*) *n* lungo biscotto, in genere ricoperto di cioccolata; **candyfloss** ['kændɪflɒs] *n* (*BRIT*) zucchero filato

cane [keɪn] *n* canna; (*for furniture*) bambù *m*; (*stick*) verga ▶ *vt* (*BRIT Scol*) punire a colpi di verga

canister ['kænɪstər] *n* scatola metallica

cannabis ['kænəbɪs] *n* canapa indiana

canned ['kænd] *adj* (*food*) in scatola

cannon ['kænən] (*pl* **cannon** *or* **cannons**) *n* (*gun*) cannone *m*

cannot ['kænɒt] = **can not**

canoe [kə'nuː] *n* canoa; **canoeing** *n* canottaggio

canon ['kænən] *n* (*clergyman*) canonico; (*standard*) canone *m*

can-opener ['kænəʊpnər] *n* apriscatole *m inv*

can't [kænt] = **can not**

canteen [kæn'tiːn] *n* mensa; (*BRIT: of cutlery*) portaposate *m inv*

▎ Be careful not to translate **canteen** by the Italian word *cantina*.

canter ['kæntər] *vi* andare al piccolo galoppo

canvas ['kænvəs] *n* tela

canvass ['kænvəs] *vi* (*Pol*): **to ~ for** raccogliere voti per ▶ *vt* fare un sondaggio di

canyon ['kænjən] *n* canyon *m inv*

cap [kæp] *n* (*hat*) berretto; (*of pen*) coperchio; (*of bottle, toy gun*) tappo; (*contraceptive*) diaframma *m* ▶ *vt* (*outdo*) superare; (*limit*) fissare un tetto (a)

capability [keɪpə'bɪlɪtɪ] *n* capacità *f inv*, abilità *f inv*

capable ['keɪpəbl] *adj* capace

capacity [kə'pæsɪtɪ] *n* capacità *f inv*; (*of lift etc*) capienza

cape [keɪp] *n* (*garment*) cappa; (*Geo*) capo

caper ['keɪpər] *n* (*Culin*) cappero; (*prank*) scherzetto

capital ['kæpɪtl] *n* (*also*: **~ city**) capitale *f*; (*money*) capitale *m*; (*also*: **~ letter**) (lettera) maiuscola; **capitalism** *n* capitalismo; **capitalist** *adj, n* capitalista *m/f*; **capital punishment** *n* pena capitale

Capitol ['kæpɪtl] *n* **the ~** il Campidoglio

Capricorn ['kæprɪkɔːn] *n* Capricorno

capsize [kæp'saɪz] *vt* capovolgere ▶ *vi* capovolgersi

capsule ['kæpsjuːl] *n* capsula

captain ['kæptɪn] *n* capitano

caption ['kæpʃən] *n* leggenda

captivity [kæp'tɪvɪtɪ] *n* cattività

capture ['kæptʃər] *vt* catturare; (*Com*

put) registrare ▶ *n* cattura; (*data*) registrazione *f* or rilevazione *f* di dati

car [kɑːʳ] *n* (*Aut*) macchina, automobile *f*; (*Rail*) vagone *m*

carafe [kəˈræf] *n* caraffa

caramel [ˈkærəməl] *n* caramello

carat [ˈkærət] *n* carato; **18 ~ gold** oro a 18 carati

caravan [ˈkærəvæn] *n* (*BRIT*) roulotte *f inv*; (*of camels*) carovana; **caravan site** (*BRIT*) *n* campeggio per roulotte

carbohydrate [kɑːbəuˈhaɪdreɪt] *n* carboidrato

carbon [ˈkɑːbən] *n* carbonio; **carbon dioxide** [-daɪˈɒksaɪd] *n* diossido di carbonio; **carbon footprint** *n* impronta ecologica; **carbon monoxide** [-mɔˈnɒksaɪd] *n* monossido di carbonio

car boot sale *n vedi nota*

- **car boot sale**
- Il **car boot sale** è un mercatino
- dell'usato molto popolare in Gran
- Bretagna. Normalmente ha luogo
- in un parcheggio o in un grande
- spiazzo, e la merce viene in genere
- esposta nei bagagliai, in inglese
- appunto "boots", aperti delle
- macchine.

carburettor [kɑːbjuˈrɛtəʳ] (*US* **carburetor**) *n* carburatore *m*

card [kɑːd] *n* carta; (*visiting card etc*) biglietto; (*Christmas card etc*) cartolina; **cardboard** *n* cartone *m*; **card game** *n* gioco di carte

cardigan [ˈkɑːdɪgən] *n* cardigan *m inv*

cardinal [ˈkɑːdɪnl] *adj* cardinale ▶ *n* cardinale *m*

cardphone [ˈkɑːdfəun] *n* telefono a scheda

care [kɛəʳ] *n* cura, attenzione *f*; (*worry*) preoccupazione *f* ▶ *vi* **to ~ about** curarsi di; (*thing, idea*) interessarsi di; **~ of** presso; **in sb's ~** alle cure di qn; **to take ~ (to do)** fare attenzione

(a fare); **to take ~ of** curarsi di; (*bill, problem*) occuparsi di; **I don't ~** non me ne importa; **I couldn't ~ less** non m'interessa affatto ▷ **care for** *vt fus* aver cura di; (*like*) volere bene a

career [kəˈrɪəʳ] *n* carriera ▶ *vi* (*also: ~ along*) andare di (gran) carriera

care: carefree [ˈkɛəfriː] *adj* sgombro(-a) di preoccupazioni; **careful** [ˈkɛəful] *adj* attento(-a); (*cautious*) cauto(-a); **(be) careful!** attenzione!; **carefully** *adv* con cura; cautamente; **caregiver** (*US*) *n* (*professional*) badante *m/f*; (*unpaid*) persona che si prende cura di un parente malato o anziano; **careless** [ˈkɛəlɪs] *adj* negligente; (*heedless*) spensierato(-a); **carelessness** *n* negligenza; mancanza di tatto; **carer** [ˈkɛərəʳ] *n* assistente *m/f* (*di persone malata o handicappata*); **caretaker** [ˈkɛəteɪkəʳ] *n* custode *m*

car-ferry [ˈkɑːfɛrɪ] *n* traghetto

cargo [ˈkɑːgəu] (*pl* **cargoes**) *n* carico

car hire *n* autonoleggio

Caribbean [kærɪˈbiːən] *adj* **the ~ Sea** il Mar dei Caraibi

caring [ˈkɛərɪŋ] *adj* (*person*) premuroso(-a); (*society, organization*) umanitario(-a)

carnation [kɑːˈneɪʃən] *n* garofano

carnival [ˈkɑːnɪvəl] *n* (*public celebration*) carnevale *m*; (*US: funfair*) luna park *m inv*

carol [ˈkærəl] *n* **Christmas ~** canto di Natale

carousel [kærəˈsɛl] (*US*) *n* giostra

car park (*BRIT*) *n* parcheggio

carpenter [ˈkɑːpɪntəʳ] *n* carpentiere *m*

carpet [ˈkɑːpɪt] *n* tappeto ▶ *vt* coprire con tappeto

car rental (*US*) *n* autonoleggio

carriage [ˈkærɪdʒ] *n* vettura; (*of goods*) trasporto; **carriageway** (*BRIT*) *n* (*part of road*) carreggiata

carrier ['kærɪəʳ] n (of disease) portatore(-trice); (Comm) impresa di trasporti; **carrier bag** (BRIT) n sacchetto

carrot ['kærət] n carota

carry ['kærɪ] vt (person) portare; (: vehicle) trasportare; (involve: responsibilities etc) comportare; (Med) essere portatore(-trice) di ▶ vi (sound) farsi sentire; **to be** or **get carried away** (fig) entusiasmarsi ▷ **carry on** vi **to ~ on with sth/doing** continuare qc/a fare ▶ vt mandare avanti ▷ **carry out** vt (orders) eseguire; (investigation) svolgere

cart [kɑːt] n carro ▶ vt (inf) trascinare

carton ['kɑːtən] n (box) scatola di cartone; (of yogurt) cartone m; (of cigarettes) stecca

cartoon [kɑːˈtuːn] n (Press) disegno umoristico; (comic strip) fumetto; (Cinema) disegno animato

cartridge ['kɑːtrɪdʒ] n (for gun, pen) cartuccia; (music tape) cassetta

carve [kɑːv] vt (meat) trinciare; (wood, stone) intagliare; **carving** n (in wood etc) scultura

car wash n lavaggio auto

case [keɪs] n caso; (Law) causa, processo; (box) scatola; (BRIT: also: **suit~**) valigia; **in ~ of** in caso di; **in ~ he** caso mai lui; **in any ~** in ogni caso; **just in ~** in caso di bisogno

cash [kæʃ] n denaro; (coins, notes) denaro liquido ▶ vt incassare; **I haven't got any ~** non ho contanti; **to pay (in) ~** pagare in contanti; **~ on delivery** pagamento alla consegna; **cashback** (discount) sconto; (at supermarket etc) anticipo di contanti ottenuto presso la cassa di un negozio tramite una carta di debito; **cash card** (BRIT) n tesserino di prelievo; **cash desk** (BRIT) n cassa; **cash dispenser** (BRIT) n sportello automatico

cashew [kæˈʃuː] n (also: **~ nut**) anacardio

cashier [kæˈʃɪəʳ] n cassiere(-a)

cashmere ['kæʃmɪəʳ] n cachemire m

cash point n sportello bancario automatico, Bancomat® m inv

cash register n registratore m di cassa

casino [kəˈsiːnəu] n casinò m inv

casket ['kɑːskɪt] n cofanetto; (US: coffin) bara

casserole ['kæsərəul] n casseruola; (food): **chicken ~** pollo in casseruola

cassette [kæˈsɛt] n cassetta; **cassette player** n riproduttore m a cassette

cast [kɑːst] (pt, pp **cast**) vt (throw) gettare; (metal) gettare, fondere; (Theatre): **to ~ sb as Hamlet** scegliere qn per la parte di Amleto ▶ n (Theatre) cast m inv; (also: **plaster ~**) ingessatura; **to ~ one's vote** votare, dare il voto ▷ **cast off** vi (Naut) salpare; (Knitting) calare

castanets [kæstəˈnɛts] npl castagnette fpl

caster sugar ['kɑːstəʳ-] (BRIT) n zucchero semolato

cast-iron ['kɑːstaɪən] adj (lit) di ghisa; (fig: case) di ferro

castle ['kɑːsl] n castello

casual ['kæʒjul] adj (chance) casuale, fortuito(-a); (: work etc) avventizio(-a); (unconcerned) noncurante, indifferente; **~ wear** casual m

casualty ['kæʒjultɪ] n ferito(-a); (dead) morto(-a), vittima; (Med: department) pronto soccorso

cat [kæt] n gatto

catalogue ['kætəlɔg] (US **catalog**) n catalogo ▶ vt catalogare

catalytic converter [kætəlɪtɪk-] n marmitta catalitica, catalizzatore m

cataract ['kætərækt] n (also Med) cateratta

catarrh [kəˈtɑːʳ] n catarro

catastrophe [kə'tæstrəfɪ] n
catastrofe f

catch [kætʃ] (pt, pp **caught**) vt
prendere; (ball) afferrare; (surprise:
person) sorprendere; (attention)
attirare; (comment, whisper) cogliere;
(person) raggiungere ▸ vi (fire)
prendere ▸ n (fish etc caught) retata;
(of ball) presa; (trick) inganno; (Tech)
gancio; (game) catch m inv; **to ~
fire** prendere fuoco; **to ~ sight of**
scorgere ▷ **catch up** vi mettersi in
pari ▸ vt (also: ~ **up with**) raggiungere;
catching ['kætʃɪŋ] adj (Med)
contagioso(-a)

category ['kætɪgərɪ] n categoria

cater ['keɪtər] vi ~ **for** (BRIT: needs)
provvedere a; (: readers, consumers)
incontrare i gusti di; (Comm: provide
food) provvedere alla ristorazione di

caterpillar ['kætəpɪlər] n bruco

cathedral [kə'θiːdrəl] n cattedrale
f, duomo

Catholic ['kæθəlɪk] adj, n (Rel)
cattolico(-a)

Catseye® [kæts'aɪ] (BRIT) n (Aut)
catarifrangente m

cattle ['kætl] npl bestiame m,
bestie fpl

catwalk ['kætwɔːk] n passerella

caught [kɔːt] pt, pp of **catch**

cauliflower ['kɔlɪflauər] n
cavolfiore m

cause [kɔːz] n causa ▸ vt causare

caution ['kɔːʃən] n prudenza;
(warning) avvertimento ▸ vt avvertire;
ammonire; **cautious** ['kɔːʃəs] adj
cauto(-a), prudente

cave [keɪv] n caverna, grotta ▷ **cave in**
vi (roof etc) crollare

caviar(e) ['kævɪɑːr] n caviale m

cavity ['kævɪtɪ] n cavità f inv

cc abbr = **cubic centimetres**; **carbon
copy**

CCTV n abbr (= closed-circuit television)

televisione f a circuito chiuso

CD abbr (disc) CD m inv; (player) lettore
m CD inv; **CD player** n lettore m CD;
CD-ROM [-rɔm] n abbr CD-ROM m inv

cease [siːs] vt, vi cessare; **ceasefire** n
cessate il fuoco m inv

cedar ['siːdər] n cedro

ceilidh ['keɪlɪ] n festa con musiche e
danze popolari scozzesi o irlandesi

ceiling ['siːlɪŋ] n soffitto; (on wages
etc) tetto

celebrate ['sɛlɪbreɪt] vt, vi
celebrare; **celebration** [-'breɪʃən] n
celebrazione f

celebrity [sɪ'lɛbrɪtɪ] n celebrità f inv

celery ['sɛlərɪ] n sedano

cell [sɛl] n cella; (of revolutionaries, Biol)
cellula; (Elec) elemento (di batteria)

cellar ['sɛlər] n sottosuolo; cantina

cello ['tʃɛləu] n violoncello

Cellophane® ['sɛləfeɪn] n
cellophane® m

cellphone ['sɛləfeɪn] n cellulare m

Celsius ['sɛlsɪəs] adj Celsius inv

Celtic ['kɛltɪk, 'sɛltɪk] adj celtico(-a)

cement [sə'mɛnt] n cemento

cemetery ['sɛmɪtrɪ] n cimitero

censor ['sɛnsər] n censore m ▸ vt
censurare; **censorship** n censura

census ['sɛnsəs] n censimento

cent [sɛnt] n (US: coin) centesimo
(=1.100 di un dollaro); (unit of euro)
centesimo; see also **per**

centenary [sɛn'tiːnərɪ] n centenario

centennial [sɛn'tɛnɪəl] (US) n
centenario

center ['sɛntər] (US) n, vt = **centre**

centi... [sɛntɪ] prefix: **centigrade**
['sɛntɪgreɪd] adj centigrado(-a);
centimetre ['sɛntɪmiːtər] (US
centimeter) n centimetro;
centipede ['sɛntɪpiːd] n centopiedi
m inv

central ['sɛntrəl] adj centrale; **Central
America** n America centrale; **central**

heating n riscaldamento centrale;
central reservation n (BRITAut)
banchina f spartitraffico inv
centre ['sɛntər] (US **center**) n centro
▶ vt centrare; **centre-forward** n
(Sport) centroavanti m inv; **centre-
half** n (Sport) centromediano
century ['sɛntjurɪ] n secolo;
twentieth ~ ventesimo secolo
CEO n abbr = **chief executive officer**
ceramic [sɪ'ræmɪk] adj ceramico(-a)
cereal ['siːrɪəl] n cereale m
ceremony ['sɛrɪmənɪ] n cerimonia; **to
stand on ~** fare complimenti
certain ['səːtən] adj certo(-a); **to make
~ of** assicurarsi di; **for ~** per certo, di
sicuro; **certainly** adv certamente,
certo; **certainty** n certezza
certificate [sə'tɪfɪkɪt] n certificato;
diploma m
certify ['səːtɪfaɪ] vt certificare; (award
diploma to) conferire un diploma a;
(declare insane) dichiarare pazzo(-a)
cf. abbr (= compare) cfr.
CFC n (= chlorofluorocarbon) CFC m inv
chain [tʃeɪn] n catena ▶ vt (also: ~ **up**)
incatenare; **chain-smoke** vi fumare
una sigaretta dopo l'altra
chair [tʃɛər] n sedia; (armchair)
poltrona; (of university) cattedra; (of
meeting) presidenza ▶ vt (meeting)
presiedere; **chairlift** n seggiovia;
chairman (irreg) n presidente m;
chairperson n presidente(-essa);
chairwoman (irreg) n presidentessa
chalet ['ʃæleɪ] n chalet m inv
chalk [tʃɔːk] n gesso; **chalkboard** (US)
n lavagna
challenge ['tʃælɪndʒ] n sfida ▶ vt
sfidare; (statement, right) mettere
in dubbio; **to ~ sb to do** sfidare
qn a fare; **challenging** adj (task)
impegnativo(-a); (look) di sfida
chamber ['tʃeɪmbər] n camera;
chambermaid n cameriera

champagne [ʃæm'peɪn] n
champagne m inv
champion ['tʃæmpɪən] n
campione(-essa); **championship** n
campionato
chance [tʃɑːns] n caso; (opportunity)
occasione f; (likelihood) possibilità f
inv ▶ vt **to ~ it** rischiare, provarci ▶ adj
fortuito(-a); **to take a ~** rischiare; **by
~** per caso
chancellor ['tʃɑːnsələr] n cancelliere
m; **Chancellor of the Exchequer**
[-ɪks'tʃɛkər] (BRIT) n Cancelliere dello
Scacchiere
chandelier [ʃændə'lɪər] n lampadario
change [tʃeɪndʒ] vt cambiare;
(transform): **to ~ sb into** trasformare
qn in ▶ vi cambiare; (change one's
clothes) cambiarsi; (be transformed):
to ~ into trasformarsi in ▶ n
cambiamento; (of clothes) cambio;
(money returned) resto; (coins) spiccioli;
where can I ~ some money? dove
posso cambiare dei soldi?; **to ~ one's
mind** cambiare idea; **keep the ~!**
tenga pure il resto!; **sorry, I don't
have any ~** mi dispiace, non ho
spiccioli; **for a ~** tanto per cambiare
▷ **change over** vi (from sth to sth)
passare; (players etc) scambiarsi
(di posto o di campo) ▶ vt cambiare;
changeable adj (weather) variabile;
change machine n distributore
automatico di monete; **changing
room** n (BRIT: in shop) camerino;
(: Sport) spogliatoio
channel ['tʃænl] n canale m; (of river,
sea) alveo ▶ vt canalizzare; **Channel
Tunnel** n the Channel Tunnel il
tunnel sotto la Manica
chant [tʃɑːnt] n canto; salmodia ▶ vt
cantare; salmodiare
chaos ['keɪɔs] n caos m
chaotic [keɪ'ɔtɪk] adj caotico(-a)
chap [tʃæp] (BRIT: inf) n (man) tipo

chapel ['tʃæpəl] n cappella
chapped [tʃæpt] adj (skin, lips) screpolato(-a)
chapter ['tʃæptəʳ] n capitolo
character ['kærɪktəʳ] n carattere m; (in novel, film) personaggio; **characteristic** [-'rɪstɪk] adj caratteristico(-a) ▶ n caratteristica; **characterize** ['kærɪktəraɪz] vt caratterizzare; (describe): **to characterize (as)** descrivere (come)
charcoal ['tʃɑːkəul] n carbone m di legna
charge [tʃɑːdʒ] n accusa; (cost) prezzo; (responsibility) responsabilità ▶ vt (gun, battery, Mil: enemy) caricare; (customer) fare pagare a; (sum) fare pagare; (Law): **to ~ sb (with)** accusare qn (di) ▶ vi lanciarsi; **charge card** n carta f clienti inv; **charger** n (also: **battery charger**) caricabatterie m inv
charismatic [kærɪz'mætɪk] adj carismatico(-a)
charity ['tʃærɪtɪ] n carità; (organization) opera pia; **charity shop** n (BRIT) negozi che vendono articoli di seconda mano e devolvono il ricavato in beneficenza
charm [tʃɑːm] n fascino; (on bracelet) ciondolo ▶ vt affascinare, incantare; **charming** adj affascinante
chart [tʃɑːt] n tabella; grafico; (map) carta nautica ▶ vt fare una carta nautica di; **~s** npl (Mus) hit parade f
charter ['tʃɑːtəʳ] vt (plane) noleggiare ▶ n (document) carta; **chartered accountant** ['tʃɑːtəd-] (BRIT) n ragioniere(-a) professionista; **charter flight** n volo m charter inv
chase [tʃeɪs] vt inseguire; (also: ~ **away**) cacciare ▶ n caccia
chat [tʃæt] vi chiacchierare; (on Internet) chattare ▶ n chiacchierata; (on Internet) chat f inv ▷ **chat up** vt (BRIT inf: girl) abbordare; **chat room** n

(Internet) chat room f inv; **chat show** (BRIT) n talk show m inv
chatter ['tʃætəʳ] vi (person) ciarlare; (bird) cinguettare; (teeth) battere ▶ n ciarle fpl; cinguettio
chauffeur ['ʃəufəʳ] n autista m
chauvinist ['ʃəuvɪnɪst] n (male chauvinist) maschilista m; (nationalist) sciovinista m/f
cheap [tʃiːp] adj economico(-a); (joke) grossolano(-a); (poor quality) di cattiva qualità ▶ adv a buon mercato; **can you recommend a ~ hotel/restaurant, please?** potrebbe indicarmi un albergo/ristorante non troppo caro?; **cheap day return** n biglietto ridotto di andata e ritorno valido in giornata; **cheaply** adv a buon prezzo, a buon mercato
cheat [tʃiːt] vi imbrogliare; (at school) copiare ▶ vt ingannare ▶ n imbroglione m; **to ~ sb out of sth** defraudare qn di qc ▷ **cheat on** vt fus (husband, wife) tradire
Chechnya [tʃɪtʃ'njɑː] n Cecenia
check [tʃɛk] vt verificare; (passport, ticket) controllare; (halt) fermare; (restrain) contenere ▶ n verifica; controllo; (curb) freno; (US: bill) conto; (pattern: gen pl) quadretti mpl; (US) = **cheque** ▶ adj (pattern, cloth) a quadretti ▷ **check in** vi (in hotel) registrare; (at airport) presentarsi all'accettazione ▶ vt (luggage) depositare ▷ **check off** vt segnare ▷ **check out** vi (in hotel) saldare il conto ▷ **check up** vi **to ~ up (on sth)** investigare (qc); **to ~ up on sb** informarsi sul conto di qn; **checkbook** (US) n = **chequebook**; **checked** adj a quadretti; **checkers** (US) n dama; **check-in** n (also: **check-in desk**: at airport) check-in m inv, accettazione f (bagagli inv); **checking account** (US) n conto corrente;

checklist n lista di controllo;
checkmate n scaccomatto;
checkout n (*in supermarket*) cassa;
checkpoint n posto di blocco;
checkroom (*US*) n deposito m bagagli *inv*; **checkup** n (*Med*) controllo medico
cheddar ['tʃedə'] n formaggio duro di latte di mucca di colore bianco o arancione
cheek [tʃi:k] n guancia; (*impudence*) faccia tosta; **cheekbone** n zigomo; **cheeky** adj sfacciato(-a)
cheer [tʃɪə'] vt applaudire; (*gladden*) rallegrare ▸ vi applaudire ▸ n grido (di incoraggiamento) ▷ **cheer up** vi rallegrarsi, farsi animo ▸ vt rallegrare; **cheerful** adj allegro(-a)
cheerio ['tʃɪərɪ'əu] (*BRIT*) excl ciao!
cheerleader ['tʃɪəli:də'] n cheerleader f inv
cheese [tʃi:z] n formaggio; **cheeseburger** n cheeseburger m inv; **cheesecake** n specie di torta di ricotta, a volte con frutta
chef [ʃef] n capocuoco
chemical ['kemɪkəl] adj chimico(-a) ▸ n prodotto chimico
chemist ['kemɪst] n (*BRIT: pharmacist*) farmacista m/f; (*scientist*) chimico(-a); **chemistry** n chimica; **chemist's (shop)** (*BRIT*) n farmacia
cheque [tʃek] (*US* **check**) n assegno; **chequebook** n libretto degli assegni; **cheque card** n carta f assegni inv
cherry ['tʃerɪ] n ciliegia; (*also:* **~ tree**) ciliegio
chess [tʃes] n scacchi mpl
chest [tʃest] n petto; (*box*) cassa
chestnut ['tʃesnʌt] n castagna; (*also:* **~ tree**) castagno
chest of drawers n cassettone m
chew [tʃu:] vt masticare; **chewing gum** n chewing gum m
chic [ʃi:k] adj elegante
chick [tʃɪk] n pulcino; (*inf*) pollastrella
chicken ['tʃɪkɪn] n pollo; (*inf: coward*)

coniglio ▷ **chicken out** (*inf*) vi avere fifa; **chickenpox** n varicella
chickpea ['tʃɪkpi:] n cece m
chief [tʃi:f] n capo ▸ adj principale; **chief executive (officer)** n direttore m generale; **chiefly** adv per lo più, soprattutto
child [tʃaɪld] (*pl* **children**) n bambino(-a); **child abuse** n molestie fpl a minori; **child benefit** n (*BRIT*) ≈ assegni mpl familiari; **childbirth** n parto; **child-care** n il badare ai bambini; **childhood** n infanzia; **childish** adj puerile; **child minder** [-'maɪndə'] n (*BRIT*) bambinaia; **children** ['tʃɪldrən] npl of **child**
Chile ['tʃɪlɪ] n Cile m
Chilean ['tʃɪlɪən] adj, n cileno(-a)
chill [tʃɪl] n freddo; (*Med*) infreddatura ▸ vt raffreddare ▷ **chill out** (*esp US*) vi (*inf*) darsi una calmata
chil(l)i ['tʃɪlɪ] n peperoncino
chilly ['tʃɪlɪ] adj freddo(-a), fresco(-a); **to feel ~** sentirsi infreddolito(-a)
chimney ['tʃɪmnɪ] n camino
chimpanzee [tʃɪmpæn'zi:] n scimpanzé m inv
chin [tʃɪn] n mento
China ['tʃaɪnə] n Cina
china ['tʃaɪnə] n porcellana
Chinese [tʃaɪ'ni:z] adj cinese ▸ n inv cinese m/f; (*Ling*) cinese m
chip [tʃɪp] n (*gen pl: Culin*) patatina fritta; (: *US: also:* **potato ~**) patatina; (*of wood, glass, stone*) scheggia; (*also:* **micro~**) chip m inv ▸ vt (*cup, plate*) scheggiare; **chip shop** n (*BRIT*) vedi nota

● **chip shop**
● I **chip shops**, anche chiamati "fish
● and chip shops", sono friggitorie che
● vendono principalmente filetti di
● pesce impanati e patatine fritte.

chiropodist [kɪ'rɔpədɪst] (*BRIT*) n pedicure m/f inv

chisel ['tʃɪzl] n cesello

chives [tʃaɪvz] npl erba cipollina

chlorine ['klɔ:ri:n] n cloro

choc-ice ['tʃɔkaɪs] n (BRIT) gelato ricoperto al cioccolato

chocolate ['tʃɔklɪt] ▶ n (substance) cioccolato, cioccolata; (drink) cioccolata; (a sweet) cioccolatino

choice [tʃɔɪs] n scelta ▶ adj scelto(-a)

choir ['kwaɪəʳ] n coro

choke [tʃəuk] vi soffocare ▶ vt soffocare; (block): **to be ~d with** essere intasato(-a) di ▶ n (Aut) valvola dell'aria

cholesterol [kə'lɛstərɔl] n colesterolo

choose [tʃu:z] (pt **chose**,, pp **chosen**) vt scegliere; **to ~ to do** decidere di fare; preferire fare

chop [tʃɔp] vt (wood) spaccare; (Culin: also: ~ **up**) tritare ▶ n (Culin) costoletta ▷ **chop down** vt (tree) abbattere ▷ **chop off** vt tagliare; **chopsticks** ['tʃɔpstɪks] npl bastoncini mpl cinesi

chord [kɔ:d] n (Mus) accordo

chore [tʃɔ:ʳ] n faccenda; **household ~s** faccende fpl domestiche

chorus ['kɔ:rəs] n coro; (repeated part of song: also fig) ritornello

chose [tʃəuz] pt of **choose**

chosen ['tʃəuzn] pp of **choose**

Christ [kraɪst] n Cristo

christen ['krɪsn] vt battezzare; **christening** n battesimo

Christian ['krɪstɪən] adj, n cristiano(-a); **Christianity** [-'ænɪtɪ] n cristianesimo; **Christian name** n nome m (di battesimo)

Christmas ['krɪsməs] n Natale m; **Merry ~!** Buon Natale!; **Christmas card** n cartolina di Natale; **Christmas carol** n canto natalizio; **Christmas Day** n il giorno di Natale; **Christmas Eve** n la vigilia di Natale; **Christmas pudding** n (esp BRIT) specie di budino con frutta secca, spezie e brandy;

Christmas tree n albero di Natale

chrome [krəum] n cromo

chronic ['krɔnɪk] adj cronico(-a)

chrysanthemum [krɪ'sænθəməm] n crisantemo

chubby ['tʃʌbɪ] adj paffuto(-a)

chuck [tʃʌk] (inf) vt buttare, gettare; (BRIT: also: ~ **up**) piantare ▷ **chuck out** vt buttar fuori

chuckle ['tʃʌkl] vi ridere sommessamente

chum [tʃʌm] n compagno(-a)

chunk [tʃʌŋk] n pezzo

church [tʃə:tʃ] n chiesa; **churchyard** n sagrato

churn [tʃə:n] n (for butter) zangola; (for milk) bidone m

chute [ʃu:t] n (also: **rubbish ~**) canale m di scarico; (BRIT: children's slide) scivolo

chutney ['tʃʌtnɪ] n salsa piccante (di frutta, zucchero e spezie)

CIA (US) n abbr (= Central Intelligence Agency) CIA f

CID (BRIT) n abbr (= Criminal Investigation Department) ≈ polizia giudiziaria

cider ['saɪdəʳ] n sidro

cigar [sɪ'gɑ:ʳ] n sigaro

cigarette [sɪgə'rɛt] n sigaretta; **cigarette lighter** n accendino

cinema ['sɪnəmə] n cinema m inv

cinnamon ['sɪnəmən] n cannella

circle ['sə:kl] n cerchio; (of friends etc) circolo; (in cinema) galleria ▶ vi girare in circolo ▶ vt (surround) circondare; (move round) girare intorno a

circuit ['sə:kɪt] n circuito

circular ['sə:kjuləʳ] adj circolare ▶ n circolare f

circulate ['sə:kjuleɪt] vi circolare ▶ vt far circolare; **circulation** [-'leɪʃən] n circolazione f; (of newspaper) tiratura

circumstances ['sə:kəmstənsɪz] npl circostanze fpl; (financial condition)

condizioni *fpl* finanziarie
circus ['sə:kəs] *n* circo
cite [saɪt] *vt* citare
citizen ['sɪtɪzn] *n* (*of country*)
cittadino(-a); (*of town*) abitante *m/f*;
citizenship *n* cittadinanza
citrus fruits ['sɪtrəs-] *npl* agrumi *mpl*
city ['sɪtɪ] *n* città *f inv*; **the C~** la Città
di Londra (*centro commerciale*);
city centre *n* centro della città;
city technology college *n* (*BRIT*)
istituto tecnico superiore (*finanziato
dall'industria*)
civic ['sɪvɪk] *adj* civico(-a)
civil ['sɪvɪl] *adj* civile; **civilian** [sɪ'vɪlɪə
n] *adj, n* borghese *m/f*
civilization [sɪvɪlaɪ'zeɪʃən] *n* civiltà
f inv
civilized ['sɪvɪlaɪzd] *adj* civilizzato(-a);
(*fig*) cortese
civil: **civil law** *n* codice *m*, civile;
(*study*) diritto civile; **civil rights**
npl diritti *mpl* civili; **civil servant** *n*
impiegato(-a) statale; **Civil Service** *n*
amministrazione *f* statale; **civil war**
n guerra civile
CJD *abbr* (= *Creutzfeld Jacob disease*)
malattia di Creutzfeldt-Jacob
claim [kleɪm] *vt* (*assert*): **to ~ (that)/to
be** sostenere (che)/di essere; (*credit,
rights etc*) rivendicare; (*damages*)
richiedere ▶ *vi* (*for insurance*) fare una
domanda d'indennizzo ▶ *n* pretesa;
rivendicazione *f*; richiesta; **claim
form** *n* (*gen*) modulo di richiesta; (*for
expenses*) modulo di rimborso spese
clam [klæm] *n* vongola
clamp [klæmp] *n* pinza; morsa ▶ *vt*
stringere con una morsa; (*Aut*: *wheel*)
applicare i ceppi bloccaruote a
clan [klæn] *n* clan *m inv*
clap [klæp] *vi* applaudire
claret ['klærət] *n* vino di Bordeaux
clarify ['klærɪfaɪ] *vt* chiarificare,
chiarire

clarinet [klærɪ'nɛt] *n* clarinetto
clarity ['klærɪtɪ] *n* clarità
clash [klæʃ] *n* frastuono; (*fig*) scontro
▶ *vi* scontrarsi; cozzare
clasp [klɑ:sp] *n* (*hold*) stretta; (*of
necklace, bag*) fermaglio, fibbia ▶ *vt*
stringere
class [klɑ:s] *n* classe *f* ▶ *vt* classificare
classic ['klæsɪk] *adj* classico(-a) ▶ *n*
classico; **classical** *adj* classico(-a)
classification [klæsɪfɪ'keɪʃən] *n*
classificazione *f*
classify ['klæsɪfaɪ] *vt* classificare
classmate ['klɑ:smeɪt] *n*
compagno(-a) di classe
classroom ['klɑ:srʊm] *n* aula
classy ['klɑ:sɪ] *adj* (*inf*) chic *inv*,
elegante
clatter ['klætə'] *n* tintinnio; scalpitio
▶ *vi* tintinnare; scalpitare
clause [klɔ:z] *n* clausola; (*Ling*)
proposizione *f*
claustrophobic [klɔ:strə'fəubɪk] *adj*
claustrofobico(-a)
claw [klɔ:] *n* (*of bird of prey*) artiglio; (*of
lobster*) pinza
clay [kleɪ] *n* argilla
clean [kli:n] *adj* pulito(-a); (*clear,
smooth*) liscio(-a) ▶ *vt* pulire ▷ **clean
up** *vt* (*also fig*) ripulire; **cleaner** *n*
(*person*) donna delle pulizie; **cleaner's**
n (*also*: **dry cleaner's**) tintoria;
cleaning *n* pulizia
cleanser ['klɛnzə'] *n* detergente *m*
clear [klɪə'] *adj* chiaro(-a); (*glass etc*)
trasparente; (*road, way*) libero(-a);
(*conscience*) pulito(-a) ▶ *vt* sgombrare;
liberare; (*table*) sparecchiare;
(*cheque*) fare la compensazione di;
(*Law*: *suspect*) discolpare; (*obstacle*)
superare ▶ *vi* (*weather*) rasserenarsi;
(*fog*) andarsene ▶ *adv* ~ **of** distante
da ▷ **clear away** *vt* (*things, clothes
etc*) mettere a posto; **to ~ away the
dishes** sparecchiare la tavola ▷ **clear**

up vt mettere in ordine; (mystery) risolvere; **clearance** n (removal) sgombro; (permission) autorizzazione f, permesso; **clear-cut** adj ben delineato(-a), distinto(-a); **clearing** n radura; **clearly** adv chiaramente; **clearway** (BRIT) n strada con divieto di sosta

clench [klɛntʃ] vt stringere

clergy ['klə:dʒɪ] n clero

clerk [klɑːk, (US) klə:rk] n (BRIT) impiegato(-a); (US) commesso(-a)

clever ['klɛvəʳ] adj (mentally) intelligente; (deft, skilful) abile; (device, arrangement) ingegnoso(-a)

cliché ['kliːʃeɪ] n cliché m inv

click [klɪk] vi scattare ▸ vt (heels etc) battere; (tongue) far schioccare

client ['klaɪənt] n cliente m/f

cliff [klɪf] n scogliera scoscesa, rupe f

climate ['klaɪmɪt] n clima m

climax ['klaɪmæks] n culmine m; (sexual) orgasmo

climb [klaɪm] vi salire; (clamber) arrampicarsi ▸ vt salire; (Climbing) scalare ▸ n salita; arrampicata; scalata ▹ **climb down** vi scendere; (BRIT fig) far marcia indietro; **climber** n rocciatore(-trice); alpinista m/f; **climbing** n alpinismo

clinch [klɪntʃ] vt (deal) concludere

cling [klɪŋ] (pt, pp **clung**) vi **to ~ (to)** aggrapparsi (a); (of clothes) aderire strettamente (a)

Clingfilm® ['klɪŋfɪlm] n pellicola trasparente (per alimenti)

clinic ['klɪnɪk] n clinica

clip [klɪp] n (for hair) forcina; (also: **paper ~**) graffetta; (TV, Cinema) sequenza ▸ vt attaccare insieme; (hair, nails) tagliare; (hedge) tosare; **clipping** n (from newspaper) ritaglio

cloak [kləuk] n mantello ▸ vt avvolgere; **cloakroom** n (for coats etc) guardaroba m inv; (BRIT: W.C.) gabinetti mpl

clock [klɔk] n orologio ▹ **clock in** or **on** vi timbrare il cartellino (all'entrata) ▹ **clock off** or **out** vi timbrare il cartellino (all'uscita); **clockwise** adv in senso orario; **clockwork** n movimento or meccanismo a orologeria ▸ adj a molla

clog [klɔg] n zoccolo ▸ vt intasare ▸ vi (also: **~ up**) intasarsi, bloccarsi

clone [kləun] n clone m

close¹ [kləus] adj **~ (to)** vicino(-a) (a); (watch, link, relative) stretto(-a); (examination) attento(-a); (contest) combattuto(-a); (weather) afoso(-a) ▸ adv vicino, dappresso; **~ to** vicino a; **~ by**, **~ at hand** a portata di mano; **a ~ friend** un amico intimo; **to have a ~ shave** (fig) scamparla bella

close² [kləuz] vt chiudere ▸ vi (shop etc) chiudere; (lid, door etc) chiudersi; (end) finire ▸ n (end) fine f; **what time do you ~?** a che ora chiudete? ▹ **close down** vi cessare (definitivamente); **closed** adj chiuso(-a)

closely ['kləuslɪ] adv (examine, watch) da vicino; (related) strettamente

closet ['klɔzɪt] n (cupboard) armadio

close-up ['kləusʌp] n primo piano

closing time n orario di chiusura

closure ['kləuʒəʳ] n chiusura

clot [klɔt] n (also: **blood ~**) coagulo; (inf: idiot) scemo(-a) ▸ vi coagularsi

cloth [klɔθ] n (material) tessuto, stoffa; (rag) strofinaccio

clothes [kləuðz] npl abiti mpl, vestiti mpl; **clothes line** n corda (per stendere il bucato); **clothes peg** (US **clothes pin**) n molletta

clothing ['kləuðɪŋ] n = **clothes**

cloud [klaud] n nuvola ▹ **cloud over** vi rannuvolarsi; (fig) offuscarsi; **cloudy** adj nuvoloso(-a); (liquid) torbido(-a)

clove [kləuv] n chiodo di garofano; **clove of garlic** n spicchio d'aglio

clown [klaun] n pagliaccio ▶ vi (also: ~ **about, ~ around**) fare il pagliaccio

club [klʌb] n (society) club m inv, circolo; (weapon, Golf) mazza ▶ vt bastonare ▶ vi **to ~ together** associarsi; **~s** npl (Cards) fiori mpl; **club class** n (Aviat) classe f club inv

clue [klu:] n indizio; (in crosswords) definizione f; **I haven't a ~** non ho la minima idea

clump [klʌmp] n (of flowers, trees) gruppo; (of grass) ciuffo

clumsy ['klʌmzɪ] adj goffo(-a)

clung [klʌŋ] pt, pp of **cling**

cluster ['klʌstər] n gruppo ▶ vi raggrupparsi

clutch [klʌtʃ] n (grip, grasp) presa, stretta; (Aut) frizione f ▶ vt afferrare, stringere forte

cm abbr (= centimetre) cm

Co. abbr = **county; company**

c/o abbr (= care of) presso

coach [kəutʃ] n (bus) pullman m inv; (horse-drawn, of train) carrozza; (Sport) allenatore(-trice); (tutor) chi dà ripetizioni ▶ vt allenare; dare ripetizioni a; **coach station** (BRIT) n stazione f delle corriere; **coach trip** n viaggio in pullman

coal [kəul] n carbone m

coalition [kəuə'lɪʃən] n coalizione f

coarse [kɔ:s] adj (salt, sand etc) grosso(-a); (cloth, person) rozzo(-a)

coast [kəust] n costa ▶ vi (with cycle etc) scendere a ruota libera; **coastal** adj costiero(-a); **coastguard** n guardia costiera; **coastline** n linea costiera

coat [kəut] n cappotto; (of animal) pelo; (of paint) mano f ▶ vt coprire; **coat hanger** n attaccapanni m inv; **coating** n rivestimento

coax [kəuks] vt indurre (con moine)

cob [kɔb] n see **corn**

cobbled ['kɔbld] adj ~ **street** strada pavimentata a ciottoli

cobweb ['kɔbwɛb] n ragnatela

cocaine [kə'keɪn] n cocaina

cock [kɔk] n (rooster) gallo; (male bird) maschio ▶ vt (gun) armare; **cockerel** n galletto

cockney ['kɔknɪ] n cockney m/f inv (abitante dei quartieri popolari dell'East End di Londra)

cockpit ['kɔkpɪt] n abitacolo

cockroach ['kɔkrəutʃ] n blatta

cocktail ['kɔkteɪl] n cocktail m inv

cocoa ['kəukəu] n cacao

coconut ['kəukənʌt] n noce f di cocco

cod [kɔd] n merluzzo

C.O.D. abbr = **cash on delivery**

code [kəud] n codice m

coeducational ['kəuɛdju'keɪʃənl] adj misto(-a)

coffee ['kɔfɪ] n caffè m inv; **coffee bar** (BRIT) n caffè m inv; **coffee bean** n grano or chicco di caffè; **coffee break** n pausa per il caffè; **coffee maker** n bollitore m per il caffè; **coffeepot** n caffettiera; **coffee shop** n ≈ caffè m inv; **coffee table** n tavolino

coffin ['kɔfɪn] n bara

cog [kɔg] n dente m

cognac ['kɔnjæk] n cognac m inv

coherent [kəu'hɪərənt] adj coerente

coil [kɔɪl] n rotolo; (Elec) bobina; (contraceptive) spirale f ▶ vt avvolgere

coin [kɔɪn] n moneta ▶ vt (word) coniare

coincide [kəuɪn'saɪd] vi coincidere; **coincidence** [kəu'ɪnsɪdəns] n combinazione f

Coke® [kəuk] n coca

coke [kəuk] n coke m

colander ['kɔləndər] n colino

cold [kəuld] adj freddo(-a) ▶ n freddo; (Med) raffreddore m; **it's ~** fa freddo; **to be ~** (person) aver freddo; (object) essere freddo(-a); **to catch ~** prendere freddo; **to catch a ~** prendere un raffreddore; **in ~ blood** a sangue freddo; **cold sore** n erpete m

coleslaw ['kəʊlslɔ:] n insalata di cavolo bianco

colic ['kɒlɪk] n colica

collaborate [kə'læbəreɪt] vi collaborare

collapse [kə'læps] vi crollare ▶ n crollo; (Med) collasso

collar ['kɒlə'] n (of coat, shirt) colletto; (of dog, cat) collare m; **collarbone** n clavicola

colleague ['kɒli:g] n collega m/f

collect [kə'lɛkt] vt (gen) raccogliere; (as a hobby) fare collezione di; (BRIT: call and pick up) prendere; (money owed, pension) riscuotere; (donations, subscriptions) fare una colletta di ▶ vi adunarsi, riunirsi; ammucchiarsi; **to call ~** (US Tel) fare una chiamata a carico del destinatario; **collection** [kə'lɛkʃən] n raccolta; collezione f; (for money) colletta; **collective** adj collettivo(-a) ▶ n collettivo; **collector** [kə'lɛktə'] n collezionista m/f

college ['kɒlɪdʒ] n college m inv; (of technology etc) istituto superiore

collide [kə'laɪd] vi **to ~ with** scontrarsi (con)

collision [kə'lɪʒən] n collisione f, scontro

cologne [kə'ləʊn] n (also: **eau de ~**) acqua di colonia

Colombia [kə'lɒmbɪə] n Colombia; **Colombian** adj, n colombiano(-a)

colon ['kəʊlən] n (sign) due punti mpl; (Med) colon m inv

colonel ['kɜ:nl] n colonnello

colonial [kə'ləʊnɪəl] adj coloniale

colony ['kɒlənɪ] n colonia

colour etc ['kʌlə'] (US **color**) n colore m ▶ vt colorare; (tint, dye) tingere; (fig: affect) influenzare ▶ vi (blush) arrossire ▷ **colour in** vt colorare; **colour-blind** adj daltonico(-a); **coloured** adj (photo) a colori; (person) di colore; **colour**

film n (for camera) pellicola a colori; **colourful** adj pieno(-a) di colore, a vivaci colori; (personality) colorato(-a); **colouring** n (substance) colorante m; (complexion) colorito; **colour television** n televisione f a colori

column ['kɒləm] n colonna

coma ['kəʊmə] n coma m inv

comb [kəʊm] n pettine m ▶ vt (hair) pettinare; (area) battere a tappeto

combat ['kɒmbæt] n combattimento ▶ vt combattere, lottare contro

combination [kɒmbɪ'neɪʃən] n combinazione f

combine [vb kəm'baɪn, n 'kɒmbaɪn] vt **to ~ (with)** combinare (con); (one quality with another) unire (a) ▶ vi unirsi; (Chem) combinarsi ▶ n (Econ) associazione f

come [kʌm] (pt **came**, pp **come**) vi venire; arrivare; **to ~ to** (decision etc) raggiungere; **I've ~ to like him** ha cominciato a piacermi; **to ~ undone** slacciarsi; **to ~ loose** allentarsi ▷ **come across** vt fus trovare per caso ▷ **come along** vi (pupil, work) fare progressi; **~ along!** avanti!, andiamo!, forza! ▷ **come back** vi ritornare ▷ **come down** vi scendere; (prices) calare; (buildings) essere demolito(-a) ▷ **come from** vt fus venire da; provenire da ▷ **come in** vi entrare ▷ **come off** vi (button) staccarsi; (stain) andar via; (attempt) riuscire ▷ **come on** vi (pupil, work, project) fare progressi; (lights) accendersi; (electricity) entrare in funzione; **~ on!** avanti!, andiamo!, forza! ▷ **come out** vi uscire; (stain) andare via ▷ **come round** vi (after faint, operation) riprendere conoscenza, rinvenire ▷ **come to** vi rinvenire ▷ **come up** vi (sun) salire; (problem) sorgere; (event) essere in arrivo; (in conversation) saltar fuori ▷ **come up with** vt fus he

came up with an idea venne fuori con un'idea

comeback [ˈkʌmbæk] n ritorno

comedian [kəˈmiːdɪən] n comico

comedy [ˈkɒmɪdɪ] n commedia

comet [ˈkɒmɪt] n cometa

comfort [ˈkʌmfət] n comodità f inv, benessere m; (relief) consolazione f, conforto ▶ vt consolare, confortare; **comfortable** adj comodo(-a); (financially) agiato(-a); **comfort station** (US) n gabinetti mpl

comic [ˈkɒmɪk] adj (also: ~al) comico(-a) ▶ n comico; (BRIT: magazine) giornaletto; **comic book** (US) n giornalino (a fumetti); **comic strip** n fumetto

comma [ˈkɒmə] n virgola

command [kəˈmɑːnd] n ordine m, comando; (Mil: authority) comando; (mastery) padronanza ▶ vt comandare; **to ~ sb to do** ordinare a qn di fare; **commander** n capo; (Mil) comandante m

commemorate [kəˈmɛməreɪt] vt commemorare

commence [kəˈmɛns] vt, vi cominciare; **commencement** (US) n (Univ) cerimonia di consegna dei diplomi

commend [kəˈmɛnd] vt lodare; raccomandare

comment [ˈkɒmɛnt] n commento ▶ vi **to ~ (on)** fare commenti (su); **commentary** [ˈkɒməntərɪ] n commentario; (Sport) radiocronaca; telecronaca; **commentator** [ˈkɒmənteɪtəʳ] n commentatore(-trice); radiocronista m/f; telecronista m/f

commerce [ˈkɒməːs] n commercio

commercial [kəˈməːʃəl] adj commerciale ▶ n (TV, Radio: advertisement) pubblicità f inv; **commercial break** n intervallo

pubblicitario

commission [kəˈmɪʃən] n commissione f ▶ vt (work of art) commissionare; **out of ~** (Naut) in disarmo; **commissioner** n (Police) questore m

commit [kəˈmɪt] vt (act) commettere; (to sb's care) affidare; **to ~ o.s. to do** impegnarsi (a fare); **to ~ suicide** suicidarsi; **commitment** n impegno; promessa

committee [kəˈmɪtɪ] n comitato

commodity [kəˈmɒdɪtɪ] n prodotto, articolo

common [ˈkɒmən] adj comune; (pej) volgare; (usual) normale ▶ n terreno comune; **the C~s** (BRIT) ▶ npl la Camera dei Comuni; **in ~** in comune; **commonly** adv comunemente, usualmente; **commonplace** adj banale, ordinario(-a); **Commons** npl (BRIT Pol): **the (House of) Commons** la Camera dei Comuni; **common sense** n buon senso; **Commonwealth** n **the Commonwealth** il Commonwealth

- **Commonwealth**
- Il **Commonwealth** è
- un'associazione di stati sovrani
- indipendenti e di alcuni territori
- annessi che facevano parte
- dell'antico Impero Britannico.
- Nel 1931 questi assunsero il nome
- di "Commonwealth of Nations",
- denominazione successivamente
- semplificata in "Commonwealth".
- Attualmente gli stati del
- "Commonwealth" riconoscono
- ancora il proprio capo di stato.

communal [ˈkɒmjuːnl] adj (for common use) pubblico(-a)

commune [n ˈkɒmjuːn, vb kəˈmjuːn] n (group) comune f ▶ vi **to ~ with** mettersi in comunione con

communicate [kəˈmjuːnɪkeɪt] vt

comunicare, trasmettere ▶ vi **to ~ with** comunicare (con)

communication [kəmju:nɪ'keɪʃən] n comunicazione f

communion [kə'mju:nɪən] n (also: **Holy C~**) comunione f

communism ['kɔmjunɪzəm] n comunismo; **communist** adj, n comunista m/f

community [kə'mju:nɪtɪ] n comunità f inv; **community centre** (US **community center**) n circolo ricreativo; **community service** n (BRIT) ≈ lavoro sostitutivo

commute [kə'mju:t] vi fare il pendolare ▶ vt (Law) commutare; **commuter** n pendolare m/f

compact [adj kəm'pækt, n 'kɔmpækt] adj compatto(-a) ▶ n (also: **powder ~**) portacipria m inv; **compact disc** n compact disc m inv; **compact disc player** n lettore m CD inv

companion [kəm'pænɪən] n compagno(-a)

company ['kʌmpənɪ] n (also Comm, Mil, Theatre) compagnia; **to keep sb ~** tenere compagnia a qn; **company car** n macchina (di proprietà) della ditta; **company director** n amministratore m, consigliere m di amministrazione

comparable ['kɔmpərəbl] adj simile

comparative [kəm'pærətɪv] adj relativo(-a); (adjective etc) comparativo(-a); **comparatively** adv relativamente

compare [kəm'pɛəʳ] vt **to ~ sth/sb with/to** confrontare qc/qn con/a ▶ vi **to ~ (with)** reggere il confronto (con); **comparison** [-'pærɪsn] n confronto; **in comparison (with)** in confronto (a)

compartment [kəm'pɑ:tmənt] n compartimento; (Rail) scompartimento; **a non-smoking**

~ uno scompartimento per non-fumatori

compass ['kʌmpəs] n bussola; **~es** npl (Math) compasso

compassion [kəm'pæʃən] n compassione f

compatible [kəm'pætɪbl] adj compatibile

compel [kəm'pɛl] vt costringere, obbligare; **compelling** adj (fig: argument) irresistibile

compensate ['kɔmpənseɪt] vt risarcire ▶ vi **to ~ for** compensare; **compensation** [-'seɪʃən] n compensazione f; (money) risarcimento

compete [kəm'pi:t] vi (take part) concorrere; (vie): **to ~ with** fare concorrenza (a)

competent ['kɔmpɪtənt] adj competente

competition [kɔmpɪ'tɪʃən] n gara; concorso; (Econ) concorrenza

competitive [kəm'pɛtɪtɪv] adj (Econ) concorrenziale; (sport) agonistico(-a); (person) che ha spirito di competizione; che ha spirito agonistico

competitor [kəm'pɛtɪtəʳ] n concorrente m/f

complacent [kəm'pleɪsnt] adj compiaciuto(-a) di sé

complain [kəm'pleɪn] vi lagnarsi, lamentarsi; **complaint** n lamento; (in shop etc) reclamo; (Med) malattia

complement [n 'kɔmplɪmənt, vb 'kɔmplɪment] n complemento; (especially of ship's crew etc) effettivo ▶ vt (enhance) accompagnarsi bene a; **complementary** [kɔmplɪ'mentərɪ] adj complementare

complete [kəm'pli:t] adj completo(-a) ▶ vt completare; (a form) riempire; **completely** adv completamente; **completion** n completamento

complex ['kɔmplɛks] *adj*
complesso(-a) ▶ *n* (*Psych, of buildings etc*) complesso
complexion [kəm'plɛkʃən] *n* (*of face*) carnagione *f*
compliance [kəm'plaɪəns] *n*
acquiescenza; **in ~ with** (*orders, wishes etc*) in conformità con
complicate ['kɔmplɪkeɪt] *vt*
complicare; **complicated** *adj*
complicato(-a); **complication** [-'keɪʃən] *n* complicazione *f*
compliment [*n* 'kɔmplɪmənt, *vb* 'kɔmplɪmɛnt] *n* complimento ▶ *vt* fare un complimento a; **complimentary** [-'mɛntərɪ] *adj* complimentoso(-a), elogiativo(-a); (*free*) in omaggio
comply [kəm'plaɪ] *vi* **to ~ with**
assentire a; conformarsi a
component [kəm'pəunənt] *adj*
componente ▶ *n* componente *m*
compose [kəm'pəuz] *vt* (*form*):
to be ~d of essere composto di;
(*music, poem etc*) comporre; **to ~ o.s.** ricomporsi; **composer** *n* (*Mus*) compositore(-trice); **composition** [kɔmpə'zɪʃən] *n* composizione *f*
composure [kəm'pəuʒəʳ] *n* calma
compound ['kɔmpaund] *n* (*Chem, Ling*) composto; (*enclosure*) recinto ▶ *adj* composto(-a)
comprehension [kɔmprɪ'hɛnʃən] *n*
comprensione *f*
comprehensive [kɔmprɪ'hɛnsɪv]
adj completo(-a); **comprehensive (school)** (*BRIT*) *n* scuola secondaria aperta a tutti

> Be careful not to translate **comprehensive** by the Italian word *comprensivo*.

compress [*vb* kəm'prɛs, *n* 'kɔmprɛs] *vt*
comprimere ▶ *n* (*Med*) compressa
comprise [kəm'praɪz] *vt* (*also:* **be ~d**)
comprendere
compromise ['kɔmprəmaɪz] *n*

compromesso ▶ *vt* compromettere
▶ *vi* venire a un compromesso
compulsive [kəm'pʌlsɪv] *adj* (*liar, gambler*) che non riesce a controllarsi;
(*viewing, reading*) cui non si può fare a meno
compulsory [kəm'pʌlsərɪ] *adj*
obbligatorio(-a)
computer [kəm'pju:təʳ] *n* computer *m inv*, elaboratore *m* elettronico;
computer game *n* gioco per computer; **computer-generated** *adj* realizzato(-a) al computer;
computerize *vt* computerizzare;
computer programmer *n*
programmatore(-trice); **computer programming** *n* programmazione *f* di computer; **computer science** *n* informatica; **computer studies** *npl* informatica; **computing** *n* informatica
con [kɔn] (*inf*) *vt* truffare ▶ *n* truffa
conceal [kən'si:l] *vt* nascondere
concede [kən'si:d] *vt* ammettere
conceited [kən'si:tɪd] *adj*
presuntuoso(-a), vanitoso(-a)
conceive [kən'si:v] *vt* concepire ▶ *vi*
concepire un bambino
concentrate ['kɔnsəntreɪt] *vi*
concentrarsi ▶ *vt* concentrare
concentration [kɔnsən'treɪʃən] *n*
concentrazione *f*
concept ['kɔnsɛpt] *n* concetto
concern [kən'sə:n] *n* affare *m*;
(*Comm*) azienda, ditta; (*anxiety*)
preoccupazione *f* ▶ *vt* riguardare; **to be ~ed (about)** preoccuparsi (di);
concerning *prep* riguardo a, circa
concert ['kɔnsət] *n* concerto; **concert hall** *n* sala da concerti
concerto [kən'tʃə:təu] *n* concerto
concession [kən'sɛʃən] *n*
concessione *f*
concise [kən'saɪs] *adj* conciso(-a)
conclude [kən'klu:d] *vt* concludere;

conclusion [-'klu:ʒən] n conclusione f

concrete ['kɔŋkri:t] n calcestruzzo ▶ adj concreto(-a), di calcestruzzo

concussion [kən'kʌʃən] n commozione f cerebrale

condemn [kən'dɛm] vt condannare; (building) dichiarare pericoloso(-a)

condensation [kɔndɛn'seɪʃən] n condensazione f

condense [kən'dɛns] vi condensarsi ▶ vt condensare

condition [kən'dɪʃən] n condizione f; (Med) malattia ▶ vt condizionare; **on ~ that** a condizione che + sub, a condizione di; **conditional** adj condizionale; **to be conditional upon** dipendere da; **conditioner** n (for hair) balsamo; (for fabrics) ammorbidente m

condo ['kɔndəu] (US) n abbr (inf) = **condominium**

condom ['kɔndəm] n preservativo

condominium [kɔndə'mɪnɪəm] (US) n condominio

condone [kən'dəun] vt condonare

conduct [n 'kɔndʌkt, vb kən'dʌkt] n condotta ▶ vt condurre; (manage) dirigere; amministrare; (Mus) dirigere; **to ~ o.s.** comportarsi; **conducted tour** [kən'dʌktɪd-] n gita accompagnata; **conductor** n (of orchestra) direttore m d'orchestra; (on bus) bigliettaio; (US: on train) controllore m; (Elec) conduttore m

cone [kəun] n cono; (Bot) pigna; (traffic cone) birillo

confectionery [kən'fɛkʃənrɪ] n dolciumi mpl

confer [kən'fə:ʳ] vt **to ~ sth on** conferire qc a ▶ vi conferire

conference ['kɔnfərns] n congresso

confess [kən'fɛs] vt confessare, ammettere ▶ vi confessare; **confession** [kən'fɛʃən] n confessione f

confide [kən'faɪd] vi **to ~ in** confidarsi con

confidence ['kɔnfɪdns] n confidenza; (trust) fiducia; (self-assurance) sicurezza di sé; **in ~** (speak, write) in confidenza, confidenzialmente; **confident** adj sicuro(-a), sicuro(-a) di sé; **confidential** [kɔnfɪ'dɛnʃəl] adj riservato(-a), confidenziale

confine [kən'faɪn] vt limitare; (shut up) rinchiudere; **confined** adj (space) ristretto(-a)

confirm [kən'fə:m] vt confermare; **confirmation** [kɔnfə'meɪʃən] n conferma; (Rel) cresima

confiscate ['kɔnfɪskeɪt] vt confiscare

conflict [n 'kɔnflɪkt, vb kən'flɪkt] n conflitto ▶ vi essere in conflitto

conform [kən'fɔ:m] vi **to ~ to** conformarsi (a

confront [kən'frʌnt] vt (enemy, danger) affrontare; **confrontation** [kɔnfrən'teɪʃən] n scontro

confuse [kən'fju:z] vt (one thing with another) confondere; **confused** adj confuso(-a); **confusing** adj che fa confondere; **confusion** [-'fju:ʒən] n confusione f

congestion [kən'dʒɛstʃən] n congestione f

congratulate [kən'grætjuleɪt] vt **to ~ sb (on)** congratularsi con qn (per or di); **congratulations** [-'leɪʃənz] npl auguri mpl; (on success) complimenti mpl, congratulazioni fpl

congregation [kɔŋgrɪ'geɪʃən] n congregazione f

congress ['kɔŋgrɛs] n congresso; **congressman** (irreg: US) n membro del Congresso; **congresswoman** (irreg: US) n (donna) membro del Congresso

conifer ['kɔnɪfəʳ] n conifero

conjugate ['kɔndʒugeɪt] vt coniugare

conjugation [kɔndʒə'geɪʃən] n coniugazione f

conjunction [kənˈdʒʌŋkʃən] *n* congiunzione *f*

conjure [ˈkʌndʒəʳ] *vi* fare giochi di prestigio

connect [kəˈnɛkt] *vt* connettere, collegare; (*Elec, Tel*) collegare; (*fig*) associare ▸ *vi* (*train*): **to ~ with** essere in coincidenza con; **to be ~ed with** (*associated*) aver rapporti con; **connecting flight** *n* volo in coincidenza; **connection** [-ʃən] ▸ *n* relazione *f*, rapporto; (*Elec*) connessione *f*; (*train, plane*) coincidenza; (*Tel*) collegamento

conquer [ˈkɒŋkəʳ] *vt* conquistare; (*feelings*) vincere

conquest [ˈkɒŋkwɛst] *n* conquista

cons [kɒnz] *npl see* **convenience**; **pro**

conscience [ˈkɒnʃəns] *n* coscienza

conscientious [kɒnʃɪˈɛnʃəs] *adj* coscienzioso(-a)

conscious [ˈkɒnʃəs] *adj* consapevole; (*Med*) cosciente; **consciousness** *n* consapevolezza; coscienza

consecutive [kənˈsɛkjutɪv] *adj* consecutivo(-a); **on 3 ~ occasions** 3 volte di fila

consensus [kənˈsɛnsəs] *n* consenso; **the ~ of opinion** l'opinione *f* unanime *or* comune

consent [kənˈsɛnt] *n* consenso ▸ *vi* **to ~ (to)** acconsentire (a)

consequence [ˈkɒnsɪkwəns] *n* conseguenza, risultato; importanza

consequently [ˈkɒnsɪkwəntlɪ] *adv* di conseguenza, dunque

conservation [kɒnsəˈveɪʃən] *n* conservazione *f*

conservative [kənˈsəːvətɪv] *adj* conservatore(-trice); (*cautious*) cauto(-a); **Conservative** (*BRIT*) *adj, n* (*Pol*) conservatore(-trice)

conservatory [kənˈsəːvə trɪ] *n* (*greenhouse*) serra; (*Mus*) conservatorio

consider [kənˈsɪdəʳ] *vt* considerare; (*take into account*) tener conto di; **to ~ doing sth** considerare la possibilità di fare qc; **considerable** [kənˈsɪdə rəbl] *adj* considerevole, notevole; **considerably** *adv* notevolmente, decisamente; **considerate** [kənˈsɪdə rɪt] *adj* premuroso(-a); **consideration** [kənsɪdəˈreɪʃən] *n* considerazione *f*; **considering** [kənˈsɪdərɪŋ] *prep* in considerazione di

consignment [kənˈsaɪnmənt] *n* (*of goods*) consegna; spedizione *f*

consist [kənˈsɪst] *vi* **to ~ of** constare di, essere composto(-a) di

consistency [kənˈsɪstənsɪ] *n* consistenza; (*fig*) coerenza

consistent [kənˈsɪstənt] *adj* coerente

consolation [kɒnsəˈleɪʃən] *n* consolazione *f*

console¹ [kənˈsəul] *vt* consolare

console² [ˈkɒnsəul] *n* quadro di comando

consonant [ˈkɒnsənənt] *n* consonante *f*

conspicuous [kənˈspɪkjuəs] *adj* cospicuo(-a)

conspiracy [kənˈspɪrəsɪ] *n* congiura, cospirazione *f*

constable [ˈkʌnstəbl] (*BRIT*) *n* ≈ poliziotto, agente *m* di polizia; **chief ~** ≈ questore *m*

constant [ˈkɒnstənt] *adj* costante, continuo(-a); **constantly** *adv* costantemente; continuamente

constipated [ˈkɒnstɪpeɪtɪd] *adj* stitico(-a); **constipation** [kɒnstɪˈpeɪʃən] *n* stitichezza

constituency [kənˈstɪtjuənsɪ] *n* collegio elettorale

constitute [ˈkɒnstɪtjuːt] *vt* costituire

constitution [kɒnstɪˈtjuːʃən] *n* costituzione *f*

constraint [kənˈstreɪnt] *n* costrizione *f*

construct [kən'strʌkt] vt costruire;
construction [-ʃən] n costruzione f;
constructive adj costruttivo(-a)
consul ['kɔnsl] n console m;
consulate ['kɔnsjulɪt] n consolato
consult [kən'sʌlt] vt consultare;
consultant n (Med) consulente m
medico; (other specialist) consulente;
consultation [-'teɪʃən] n (Med)
consulto; (discussion) consultazione f;
consulting room [kən'sʌltɪŋ-] (BRIT)
n ambulatorio
consume [kən'sjuːm] vt consumare;
consumer n consumatore(-trice)
consumption [kən'sʌmpʃən] n
consumo
cont. abbr = **continued**
contact ['kɔntækt] n contatto;
(person) conoscenza ▶ vt mettersi in
contatto con; **contact lenses** npl
lenti fpl a contatto
contagious [kən'teɪdʒəs] adj (also fig)
contagioso(-a)
contain [kən'teɪn] vt contenere;
to ~ o.s. contenersi; **container**
n recipiente m; (for shipping etc)
container m inv
contaminate [kən'tæmɪneɪt] vt
contaminare
cont'd abbr = **continued**
contemplate ['kɔntəmpleɪt] vt
contemplare; (consider) pensare a
(or di)
contemporary [kən'tempərərɪ] adj, n
contemporaneo(-a)
contempt [kən'tempt] n disprezzo; **~
of court** (Law) oltraggio alla Corte
contend [kən'tend] vt **to ~ that**
sostenere che ▶ vi **to ~ with** lottare
contro
content¹ ['kɔntent] n contenuto; **~s**
npl (of box, case etc) contenuto; **(table
of) ~s** indice m
content² [kən'tent] adj contento(-a),
soddisfatto(-a) ▶ vt contentare,

soddisfare; **contented** adj
contento(-a), soddisfatto(-a)
contest [n 'kɔntest, vb kən'test] n
lotta; (competition) gara, concorso ▶ vt
contestare; impugnare; (compete for)
essere in lizza per; **contestant** [kə
n'testənt] n concorrente m/f; (in fight)
avversario(-a)
context ['kɔntekst] n contesto
continent ['kɔntɪnənt] n
continente m; **the C~** (BRIT) l'Europa
continentale; **continental** [-'nentl]
adj continentale; **continental
breakfast** n colazione f all'europea
(senza piatti caldi); **continental quilt**
(BRIT) n piumino
continual [kən'tɪnjuəl] adj
continuo(-a); **continually** adv di
continuo
continue [kən'tɪnjuː] vi continuare
▶ vt continuare; (start again) riprendere
continuity [kɔntɪ'njuːɪtɪ] n
continuità; (TV, Cinema) (ordine m
della) sceneggiatura
continuous [kən'tɪnjuəs] adj
continuo(-a), ininterrotto(-a);
continuous assessment n
(BRIT) valutazione f continua;
continuously adv (repeatedly)
continuamente; (uninterruptedly)
ininterrottamente
contour ['kɔntuə'] n contorno,
profilo; (also: **~ line**) curva di livello
contraception [kɔntrə'sepʃən] n
contraccezione f
contraceptive [kɔntrə'septɪv] adj
contraccettivo(-a) ▶ n contraccettivo
contract [n 'kɔntrækt, vb kən'trækt]
n contratto ▶ vi (become smaller)
contrarsi; (Comm): **to ~ to do sth**
fare un contratto per fare qc ▶ vt
(illness) contrarre; **contractor** n
imprenditore m
contradict [kɔntrə'dɪkt] vt
contraddire; **contradiction**

[kɔntrə'dɪkʃən] n contraddizione f; **to be in contradiction with** discordare con

contrary[1] ['kɔntrərɪ] adj contrario(-a); (unfavourable) avverso(-a), contrario(-a) ▶ n contrario; **on the ~** al contrario; **unless you hear to the ~** salvo contrordine

contrary[2] [kən'trɛərɪ] adj (perverse) bisbetico(-a)

contrast [n 'kɔntrɑːst, vb kən'trɑːst] n contrasto ▶ vt mettere in contrasto; **in ~ to** contrariamente a

contribute [kən'trɪbjuːt] vi contribuire ▶ vt **to ~ £10/an article to** dare 10 sterline/un articolo a; **to ~ to** contribuire a; (newspaper) scrivere per; **contribution** [kɔntrɪ'bjuːʃə n] n contributo; **contributor** n (to newspaper) collaboratore(-trice)

control [kən'trəul] vt controllare; (firm, operation etc) dirigere ▶ n controllo; **~s** npl (of vehicle etc) comandi mpl; (governmental) controlli mpl; **under ~** sotto controllo; **to be in ~ of** avere il controllo di; **to go out of ~** (car) non rispondere ai comandi; (situation) sfuggire di mano; **control tower** n (Aviat) torre f di controllo

controversial [kɔntrə'vəːʃl] adj controverso(-a), polemico(-a)

controversy ['kɔntrəvəːsɪ] n controversia, polemica

convenience [kən'viːnɪəns] n comodità f inv; **at your ~** a suo comodo; **all modern ~s** (BRIT), **all mod cons** tutte le comodità moderne

convenient [kən'viːnɪənt] adj comodo(-a)

Be careful not to translate **convenient** by the Italian word conveniente.

convent ['kɔnvənt] n convento

convention [kən'vɛnʃən] n convenzione f; (meeting) convegno;

conventional adj convenzionale

conversation [kɔnvə'seɪʃən] n conversazione f

conversely [kɔn'vəːslɪ] adv al contrario, per contro

conversion [kən'vəːʃən] n conversione f; (BRIT: of house) trasformazione f, rimodernamento

convert [vb kən'vəːt, n 'kɔnvəːt] vt (Comm, Rel) convertire; (alter) trasformare ▶ n convertito(-a); **convertible** n macchina decappottabile

convey [kən'veɪ] vt trasportare; (thanks) comunicare; (idea) dare; **conveyor belt** [kən'veɪəʳ-] n nastro trasportatore

convict [vb kən'vɪkt, n 'kɔnvɪkt] vt dichiarare colpevole ▶ n carcerato(-a); **conviction** [-ʃən] n condanna; (belief) convinzione f

convince [kən'vɪns] vt convincere, persuadere; **convinced** adj **convinced of/that** convinto(-a) di/ che; **convincing** adj convincente

convoy ['kɔnvɔɪ] n convoglio

cook [kuk] vt cucinare, cuocere ▶ vi cuocere; (person) cucinare ▶ n cuoco(-a); **cook book** n libro di cucina; **cooker** n fornello, cucina; **cookery** n cucina; **cookery book** (BRIT) n = **cook book**; **cookie** (US) n biscotto; **cooking** n cucina

cool [kuːl] adj fresco(-a); (not afraid, calm) calmo(-a); (unfriendly) freddo(-a) ▶ vt raffreddare; (room) rinfrescare ▶ vi (water) raffreddarsi; (air) rinfrescarsi ▷ **cool down** vi raffreddarsi; (fig: person, situation) calmarsi ▷ **cool off** vi (become calmer) calmarsi; (lose enthusiasm) perdere interesse

cop [kɔp] (inf) n sbirro

cope [kəup] vi **to ~ with** (problems) far fronte a

copper ['kɔpəʳ] n rame m; (inf:

policeman) sbirro

copy ['kɔpɪ] *n* copia ▶ *vt* copiare; **copyright** *n* diritto d'autore

coral ['kɔrəl] *n* corallo

cord [kɔːd] *n* corda; (*Elec*) filo; **~s** *npl* (*trousers*) calzoni *mpl* (di velluto) a coste; **cordless** *adj* senza cavo

corduroy ['kɔːdərɔɪ] *n* fustagno

core [kɔːr] *n* (*of fruit*) torsolo; (*of organization etc*) cuore *m* ▶ *vt* estrarre il torsolo da

coriander [kɔrɪ'ændər] *n* coriandolo

cork [kɔːk] *n* sughero; (*of bottle*) tappo; **corkscrew** *n* cavatappi *m inv*

corn [kɔːn] *n* (*BRIT: wheat*) grano; (*US: maize*) granturco; (*on foot*) callo; **~ on the cob** (*Culin*) pannocchia cotta

corned beef ['kɔːnd-] *n* carne *f* di manzo in scatola

corner ['kɔːnər] *n* angolo; (*Aut*) curva ▶ *vt* intrappolare; mettere con le spalle al muro; (*Comm: market*) accaparrare ▶ *vi* prendere una curva

corner shop (*BRIT*) piccolo negozio di generi alimentari

cornflakes ['kɔːnfleɪks] *npl* fiocchi *mpl* di granturco

cornflour ['kɔːnflauər] (*BRIT*) *n* farina finissima di granturco

cornstarch ['kɔːnstɑːtʃ] (*US*) *n* = **cornflour**

Cornwall ['kɔːnwəl] *n* Cornovaglia

coronary ['kɔrənərɪ] *n* **~ (thrombosis)** trombosi *f* coronaria

coronation [kɔrə'neɪʃən] *n* incoronazione *f*

coroner ['kɔrənər] *n* magistrato incaricato di indagare la causa di morte in circostanze sospette

corporal ['kɔːpərl] *n* caporalmaggiore *m* ▶ *adj* **~ punishment** pena corporale

corporate ['kɔːpərɪt] *adj* costituito(-a) (in corporazione), comune

corporation [kɔːpə'reɪʃən] *n* (*of town*) consiglio comunale; (*Comm*) ente *m*

corps [kɔː, *pl* kɔːz] *n inv* corpo

corpse [kɔːps] *n* cadavere *m*

correct [kə'rɛkt] *adj* (*accurate*) corretto(-a), esatto(-a); (*proper*) corretto(-a) ▶ *vt* correggere; **correction** [-ʃən] *n* correzione *f*

correspond [kɔrɪs'pɔnd] *vi* corrispondere; **correspondence** *n* corrispondenza; **correspondent** *n* corrispondente *m/f*; **corresponding** *adj* corrispondente

corridor ['kɔrɪdɔːr] *n* corridoio

corrode [kə'rəud] *vt* corrodere ▶ *vi* corrodersi

corrupt [kə'rʌpt] *adj* corrotto(-a); (*Comput*) alterato(-a) ▶ *vt* corrompere; **corruption** *n* corruzione *f*

Corsica ['kɔːsɪkə] *n* Corsica

cosmetic [kɔz'mɛtɪk] *n* cosmetico ▶ *adj* (*fig: measure etc*) superficiale; **cosmetic surgery** *n* chirurgia plastica

cosmopolitan [kɔzmə'pɔlɪtn] *adj* cosmopolita

cost [kɔst] (*pt, pp* **cost**) *n* costo ▶ *vt* costare; (*find out the cost of*) stabilire il prezzo di; **~s** *npl* (*Comm, Law*) spese *fpl*; **how much does it ~?** quanto costa?; **at all ~s** a ogni costo

co-star ['kəustɑːr] *n* attore/trice della stessa importanza del protagonista

Costa Rica ['kɔstə'riːkə] *n* Costa Rica

costly ['kɔstlɪ] *adj* costoso(-a), caro(-a)

cost of living *adj* **~ allowance** indennità *f inv* di contingenza

costume ['kɔstjuːm] *n* costume *m*; (*lady's suit*) tailleur *m inv*; (*BRIT: also:* **swimming ~**) costume *m* da bagno

cosy ['kəuzɪ] (*US* **cozy**) *adj* intimo(-a); **I'm very ~ here** sto proprio bene qui

cot [kɔt] *n* (*BRIT: child's*) lettino; (*US: campbed*) brandina

cottage ['kɔtɪdʒ] *n* cottage *m inv*; **cottage cheese** *n* fiocchi *mpl* di latte magro

cotton ['kɔtn] n cotone m ▷ **cotton on**
vi (inf): **to ~ on (to sth)** afferrare (qc);
cotton bud n (BRIT) cotton fioc® m
inv; **cotton candy** (US) n zucchero
filato; **cotton wool** (BRIT) n cotone
idrofilo

couch [kautʃ] n sofà m inv

cough [kɔf] vi tossire ▶ n tosse f; **I've
got a ~** ho la tosse; **cough mixture,
cough syrup** n sciroppo per la tosse

could [kud] pt of **can²**

couldn't = **could not**

council ['kaunsl] n consiglio; **city or
town ~** consiglio comunale; **council
estate** (BRIT) n quartiere m di case
popolari; **council house** (BRIT) n casa
popolare; **councillor** (US **councilor**)
n consigliere(-a); **council tax** n (BRIT)
tassa comunale sulla proprietà

counsel ['kaunsl] n avvocato;
consultazione f ▶ vt consigliare;
counselling (US **counseling**) n
(Psych) assistenza psicologica;
counsellor (US **counselor**) n
consigliere(-a); (US) avvocato

count [kaunt] vt, vi contare ▶ n (of
votes etc) conteggio; (of pollen etc)
livello; (nobleman) conte m ▷ **count
in** (inf) vt includere; **~ me in** ci sto
anch'io ▷ **count on** vt fus contare su;
countdown n conto alla rovescia

counter ['kauntə'] n banco ▶ vt
opporsi a ▶ adv **~ to** contro; in
opposizione a; **counter clockwise**
[-'klɔkwaɪz] (US) adv in senso
antiorario

counterfeit ['kauntəfit] n
contraffazione f, falso ▶ vt
contraffare, falsificare ▶ adj falso(-a)

counterpart ['kauntəpɑːt] n (of
document etc) copia; (of person)
corrispondente m/f

countess ['kauntɪs] n contessa

countless ['kauntlɪs] adj
innumerevole

country ['kʌntrɪ] n paese m; (native
land) patria; (as opposed to town)
campagna; (region) regione f;
country and western (music) n
musica country e western, country m;
country house n villa in campagna;
countryside n campagna

county ['kauntɪ] n contea

coup [kuː] (pl **coups**) n colpo; (also: **~
d'état**) colpo di Stato

couple ['kʌpl] n coppia; **a ~ of** un
paio di

coupon ['kuːpɔn] n buono; (detachable
form) coupon m inv

courage ['kʌrɪdʒ] n coraggio;
courageous adj coraggioso(-a)

courgette [kuə'ʒɛt] (BRIT) n zucchina

courier ['kurɪə'] n corriere m; (for
tourists) guida

course [kɔːs] n corso; (of ship) rotta;
(for golf) campo; (part of meal) piatto;
of ~ senz'altro, naturalmente; **~
of ~ of action** modo d'agire; **a ~ of
treatment** (Med) una cura

court [kɔːt] n corte f; (Tennis) campo
▶ vt (woman) fare la corte a; **to take to
~** citare in tribunale

courtesy ['kɜːtəsɪ] n cortesia; **(by) ~ of**
per gentile concessione di; **courtesy
bus, courtesy coach** n autobus m inv
gratuito (di hotel, aeroporto)

court: **court-house** (US) n palazzo di
giustizia; **courtroom** n tribunale m;
courtyard n cortile m

cousin ['kʌzn] n cugino(-a); **first ~**
cugino di primo grado

cover ['kʌvə'] vt coprire; (book, table)
rivestire; (include) comprendere;
(Press) fare un servizio su ▶ n (of pan)
coperchio; (over furniture) fodera; (of
bed) copriletto; (of book) copertina;
(shelter) riparo; (Comm, Insurance, of
spy) copertura; **~s** npl (on bed) lenzuola
fpl e coperte fpl; **to take ~** (shelter)
ripararsi; **under ~** al riparo; **under ~**

of darkness protetto dall'oscurità; **under separate ~** (*Comm*) a parte, in plico separato ▷ **cover up** *vi* **to ~ up for sb** coprire qn; **coverage** *n* (*Press, Radio, TV*): **to give full coverage to sth** fare un ampio servizio su qc; **cover charge** *n* coperto; **cover-up** *n* occultamento (di informazioni)

cow [kaʊ] *n* vacca ▷ *vt* (*person*) intimidire

coward ['kaʊəd] *n* vigliacco(-a); **cowardly** *adj* vigliacco(-a)

cowboy ['kaʊbɔɪ] *n* cow-boy *m inv*

cozy ['kəʊzɪ] (*US*) *adj* = **cosy**

crab [kræb] *n* granchio

crack [kræk] *n* fessura, crepa; incrinatura; (*noise*) schiocco; (*: of gun*) scoppio; (*drug*) crack *m inv* ▷ *vt* spaccare; incrinare; (*whip*) schioccare; (*nut*) schiacciare; (*problem*) risolvere; (*code*) decifrare ▷ *adj* (*troops*) fuori classe; **to ~ a joke** fare una battuta ▷ **crack down on** *vt fus* porre freno a; **cracked** *adj* (*inf*) matto(-a); **cracker** *n* cracker *m inv*; petardo

crackle ['krækl] *vi* crepitare

cradle ['kreɪdl] *n* culla

craft [krɑːft] *n* mestiere *m*; (*cunning*) astuzia; (*boat*) naviglio; **craftsman** (*irreg*) *n* artigiano; **craftsmanship** *n* abilità

cram [kræm] *vt* (*fill*): **to ~ sth with** riempire qc di; (*put*): **to ~ sth into** stipare qc in ▷ *vi* (*for exams*) prepararsi (in gran fretta)

cramp [kræmp] *n* crampo; **I've got ~ in my leg** ho un crampo alla gamba; **cramped** *adj* ristretto(-a)

cranberry ['krænbərɪ] *n* mirtillo

crane [kreɪn] *n* gru *f inv*

crap [kræp] *n* (*inf!*) fesserie *fpl*; **to have a ~** cacare (*!*)

crash [kræʃ] *n* fragore *m*; (*of car*) incidente *m*; (*of plane*) caduta; (*of business etc*) crollo ▷ *vt* fracassare ▷ *vi* (*plane*) fracassarsi; (*car*) avere un incidente; (*two cars*) scontrarsi; (*business etc*) fallire, andare in rovina; **crash course** *n* corso intensivo; **crash helmet** *n* casco

crate [kreɪt] *n* cassa

crave [kreɪv] *vt, vi* **to ~ (for)** desiderare ardentemente

crawl [krɔːl] *vi* strisciare carponi; (*vehicle*) avanzare lentamente ▷ *n* (*Swimming*) crawl *m*

crayfish ['kreɪfɪʃ] *n inv* (*freshwater*) gambero (d'acqua dolce); (*saltwater*) gambero

crayon ['kreɪən] *n* matita colorata

craze [kreɪz] *n* mania

crazy ['kreɪzɪ] *adj* matto(-a); (*inf: keen*): **~ about sb** pazzo(-a) di qn; **~ about sth** matto(-a) per qc

creak [kriːk] *vi* cigolare, scricchiolare

cream [kriːm] *n* crema; (*fresh*) panna ▷ *adj* (*colour*) color crema *inv*; **cream cheese** *n* formaggio fresco; **creamy** *adj* cremoso(-a)

crease [kriːs] *n* grinza; (*deliberate*) piega ▷ *vt* sgualcire ▷ *vi* sgualcirsi

create [kriː'eɪt] *vt* creare; **creation** [-ʃən] *n* creazione *f*; **creative** *adj* creativo(-a); **creator** *n* creatore(-trice)

creature ['kriːtʃə^r] *n* creatura

crèche [krɛʃ] *n* asilo infantile

credentials [krɪ'dɛnʃlz] *npl* credenziali *fpl*

credibility [krɛdɪ'bɪlɪtɪ] *n* credibilità

credible ['krɛdɪbl] *adj* credibile; (*witness, source*) attendibile

credit ['krɛdɪt] *n* credito; onore *m* ▷ *vt* (*Comm*) accreditare; (*believe: also:* **give ~ to**) credere, prestar fede a; **~s** *npl* (*Cinema*) titoli *mpl*; **to ~ sb with** (*fig*) attribuire a qn; **to be in ~** (*person*) essere creditore(-trice); (*bank account*) essere coperto(-a); **credit card** *n* carta di credito; **credit crunch** n improvvisa stretta di credito

creek [kri:k] n insenatura; (US) piccolo fiume m

creep [kri:p] (pt, pp crept) vi avanzare furtivamente (or pian piano)

cremate [krɪ'meɪt] vt cremare

crematorium [kremə'tɔ:rɪəm] (pl **crematoria**) n forno crematorio

crept [krɛpt] pt, pp of **creep**

crescent ['krɛsnt] n (shape) mezzaluna; (street) strada semicircolare

cress [krɛs] n crescione m

crest [krɛst] n cresta; (of coat of arms) cimiero

crew [kru:] n equipaggio; **crew-neck** n girocollo

crib [krɪb] n culla ▶ vt (inf) copiare

cricket ['krɪkɪt] n (insect) grillo; (game) cricket m; **cricketer** n giocatore m di cricket

crime [kraɪm] n crimine m; **criminal** ['krɪmɪnl] adj, n criminale m/f

crimson ['krɪmzn] adj color cremisi inv

cringe [krɪndʒ] vi acquattarsi; (in embarrassment) sentirsi sprofondare

cripple ['krɪpl] n zoppo(-a) ▶ vt azzoppare

crisis ['kraɪsɪs] (pl **crises**) n crisi f inv

crisp [krɪsp] adj croccante; (fig) frizzante; vivace; deciso(-a); **crispy** adj croccante

criterion [kraɪ'tɪərɪən] (pl **criteria**) n criterio

critic ['krɪtɪk] n critico; **critical** adj critico(-a); **criticism** ['krɪtɪsɪzm] n critica; **criticize** ['krɪtɪsaɪz] vt criticare

Croat ['krəuæt] adj, n = **Croatian**

Croatia [krəu'eɪʃə] n Croazia; **Croatian** adj croato(-a) ▶ n croato(-a); (Ling) croato

crockery ['krɔkərɪ] n vasellame m

crocodile ['krɔkədaɪl] n coccodrillo

crocus ['krəukəs] n croco

croissant ['krwasã] n brioche f inv, croissant m inv

crook [kruk] n truffatore m; (of shepherd) bastone m; **crooked** ['krukɪd] adj curvo(-a), storto(-a); (action) disonesto(-a)

crop [krɔp] n (produce) coltivazione f; (amount produced) raccolto; (riding crop) frustino ▶ vt (hair) rapare ▷ **crop up** vi presentarsi

cross [krɔs] n croce f; (Biol) incrocio ▶ vt (street etc) attraversare; (arms, legs, Biol) incrociare; (cheque) sbarrare ▶ adj di cattivo umore ▷ **cross off** vt cancellare (tirando una riga con la penna) ▷ **cross out** vt cancellare ▷ **cross over** vi attraversare; **cross-Channel ferry** ['krɔs'tʃænl-] n traghetto che attraversa la Manica; **crosscountry (race)** n cross-country m inv; **crossing** n incrocio; (sea passage) traversata; (also: **pedestrian crossing**) passaggio pedonale; **how long does the crossing take?** quanto dura la traversata?; **crossing guard** (US) n dipendente comunale che aiuta i bambini ad attraversare la strada; **crossroads** n incrocio; **crosswalk** (US) n strisce fpl pedonali, passaggio pedonale; **crossword** n cruciverba m inv

crotch [krɔtʃ] n (Anat) inforcatura; (of garment) pattina

crouch [krautʃ] vi acquattarsi; rannicchiarsi

crouton ['kru:tɔn] n crostino

crow [krəu] n (bird) cornacchia; (of cock) canto del gallo ▶ vi (cock) cantare

crowd [kraud] n folla ▶ vt affollare, stipare ▶ vi **to ~ round/in** affollarsi intorno a/in; **crowded** adj affollato(-a); **crowded with** stipato(-a) di

crown [kraun] n corona; (of head) calotta cranica; (of hat) cocuzzolo; (of hill) cima ▶ vt incoronare; (fig: career) coronare; **crown jewels** npl gioielli mpl della Corona

crucial ['kru:ʃl] adj cruciale, decisivo(-a)

crucifix ['kru:sɪfɪks] n crocifisso

crude [kru:d] adj (materials) greggio(-a), non raffinato(-a); (fig: basic) crudo(-a), primitivo(-a); (: vulgar) rozzo(-a), grossolano(-a); **crude (oil)** n (petrolio) greggio

cruel ['kruəl] adj crudele; **cruelty** n crudeltà f inv

cruise [kru:z] n crociera ▶ vi andare a velocità di crociera; (taxi) circolare

crumb [krʌm] n briciola

crumble ['krʌmbl] vt sbriciolare ▶ vi sbriciolarsi; (plaster etc) sgretolarsi; (land, earth) franare; (building, fig) crollare

crumpet ['krʌmpɪt] n specie di frittella

crumple ['krʌmpl] vt raggrinzare, spiegazzare

crunch [krʌntʃ] vt sgranocchiare; (underfoot) scricchiolare ▶ n (fig) punto or momento cruciale; **crunchy** adj croccante

crush [krʌʃ] n folla; (love): **to have a ~ on sb** avere una cotta per qn; (drink): **lemon ~** spremuta di limone ▶ vt schiacciare; (crumple) sgualcire

crust [krʌst] n crosta; **crusty** adj (bread) croccante; (person) brontolone(-a); (remark) brusco(-a)

crutch [krʌtʃ] n gruccia

cry [kraɪ] vi piangere; (shout) urlare ▶ n urlo, grido ▷ **cry out** vi, vt gridare

crystal ['krɪstl] n cristallo

cub [kʌb] n cucciolo; (also: ~ **scout**) lupetto

Cuba ['kju:bə] n Cuba

Cuban ['kju:bən] adj, n cubano(-a)

cube [kju:b] n cubo ▶ vt (Math) elevare al cubo; **cubic** adj cubico(-a); (metre, foot) cubo(-a)

cubicle ['kju:bɪkl] n scompartimento separato; cabina

cuckoo ['kuku:] n cucù m inv

cucumber ['kju:kʌmbər] n cetriolo

cuddle ['kʌdl] vt abbracciare, coccolare ▶ vi abbracciarsi

cue [kju:] n (snooker cue) stecca; (Theatre etc) segnale m

cuff [kʌf] n (BRIT: of shirt, coat etc) polsino; (US: of trousers) risvolto; **off the ~** improvvisando; **cufflinks** npl gemelli mpl

cuisine [kwɪ'zi:n] n cucina

cul-de-sac ['kʌldəsæk] n vicolo cieco

cull [kʌl] vt (ideas etc) scegliere ▶ n (of animals) abbattimento selettivo

culminate ['kʌlmɪneɪt] vi **to ~ in** culminare con

culprit ['kʌlprɪt] n colpevole m/f

cult [kʌlt] n culto

cultivate ['kʌltɪveɪt] vt (also fig) coltivare

cultural ['kʌltʃərəl] adj culturale

culture ['kʌltʃər] n (also fig) cultura

cumin ['kʌmɪn] n (spice) cumino

cunning ['kʌnɪŋ] n astuzia, furberia ▶ adj astuto(-a), furbo(-a)

cup [kʌp] n tazza; (prize, of bra) coppa

cupboard ['kʌbəd] n armadio

cup final n (BRIT Football) finale f di coppa

curator [kjuə'reɪtər] n direttore m (di museo ecc)

curb [kə:b] vt tenere a freno ▶ n freno; (US) bordo del marciapiede

curdle ['kə:dl] vi cagliare

cure [kjuər] vt guarire; (Culin) trattare; affumicare; essiccare ▶ n rimedio

curfew ['kə:fju:] n coprifuoco

curiosity [kjuərɪ'ɒsɪtɪ] n curiosità

curious ['kjuərɪəs] adj curioso(-a)

curl [kə:l] n riccio ▶ vt ondulare; (tightly) arricciare ▶ vi arricciarsi ▷ **curl up** vi rannicchiarsi; **curler** n bigodino; **curly** ['kə:lɪ] adj ricciuto(-a)

currant ['kʌrnt] n (dried) sultanina; (bush, fruit) ribes m inv

currency ['kʌrnsɪ] n moneta; **to gain ~** (fig) acquistare larga diffusione

current ['kʌrnt] adj corrente ▶ n corrente f; **current account** (BRIT) n conto corrente; **current affairs** npl attualità fpl; **currently** adv attualmente

curriculum [kə'rɪkjuləm] (pl **curriculums** or **curricula**) n curriculum m inv; **curriculum vitae** [-'viːtaɪ] n curriculum vitae m inv

curry ['kʌrɪ] n curry m inv ▶ vt **to ~ favour with** cercare di attirarsi i favori di; **curry powder** n curry m

curse [kəːs] vt maledire ▶ vi bestemmiare ▶ n maledizione f; bestemmia

cursor ['kəːsəʳ] n (Comput) cursore m

curt [kəːt] adj secco(-a)

curtain ['kəːtn] n tenda; (Theatre) sipario

curve [kəːv] n curva ▶ vi curvarsi; **curved** adj curvo(-a)

cushion ['kuʃən] n cuscino ▶ vt (shock) fare da cuscinetto a

custard ['kʌstəd] n (for pouring) crema

custody ['kʌstədɪ] n (of child) tutela; **to take into ~** (suspect) mettere in detenzione preventiva

custom ['kʌstəm] n costume m, consuetudine f; (Comm) clientela

customer ['kʌstəməʳ] n cliente m/f

customized ['kʌstəmaɪzd] adj (car etc) fuoriserie inv

customs ['kʌstəmz] npl dogana; **customs officer** n doganiere m

cut [kʌt] (pt, pp **cut**) vt tagliare; (shape, make) intagliare; (reduce) ridurre ▶ vi tagliare ▶ n taglio; (in salary etc) riduzione f; **I've ~ myself** mi sono tagliato; **to ~ a tooth** mettere un dente ▷ **cut back** vt (plants) tagliare; (production, expenditure) ridurre ▷ **cut**

down vt (tree etc) abbattere ▶ vt fus (also: **~ down on**) ridurre ▷ **cut off** vt tagliare; (fig) isolare ▷ **cut out** vt tagliare fuori; eliminare; ritagliare ▷ **cut up** vt tagliare a pezzi; **cutback** n riduzione f

cute [kjuːt] adj (sweet) carino(-a)

cutlery ['kʌtlərɪ] n posate fpl

cutlet ['kʌtlɪt] n costoletta; (nut etc cutlet) cotoletta vegetariana

cut: **cut-price** (BRIT) adj a prezzo ridotto; **cut-rate** (US) adj = **cut-price**; **cutting** ['kʌtɪŋ] adj tagliente ▶ n (from newspaper) ritaglio (di giornale); (from plant) talea

CV n abbr = **curriculum vitae**

cwt abbr = **hundredweight(s)**

cybercafé ['saɪbəkaefeɪ] n cybercaffè m inv

cyberspace ['saɪbəspeɪs] n ciberspazio

cycle ['saɪkl] n ciclo; (bicycle) bicicletta ▶ vi andare in bicicletta; **cycle hire** n noleggio m biciclette inv; **cycle lane** n pista ciclabile; **cycle path** n pista ciclabile; **cycling** ['saɪklɪŋ] n ciclismo; **cyclist** ['saɪklɪst] n ciclista m/f

cyclone ['saɪkləun] n ciclone m

cylinder ['sɪlɪndəʳ] n cilindro

cymbal ['sɪmbl] n piatto

cynical ['sɪnɪkl] adj cinico(-a)

Cypriot ['sɪprɪət] adj, n cipriota (m/f)

Cyprus ['saɪprəs] n Cipro

cyst [sɪst] n cisti f inv; **cystitis** [sɪs'taɪtɪs] n cistite f

czar [zɑːʳ] n zar m inv

Czech [tʃɛk] adj ceco(-a) ▶ n ceco(-a); (Ling) ceco; **Czech Republic** n **the Czech Republic** la Repubblica Ceca

d

D [diː] n (Mus) re m

dab [dæb] vt (eyes, wound) tamponare; (paint, cream) applicare (con leggeri colpetti)

dad, daddy [dæd, 'dædɪ] n babbo, papà m inv

daffodil ['dæfədɪl] n trombone m, giunchiglia

daft [dɑːft] adj sciocco(-a)

dagger ['dægəʳ] n pugnale m

daily ['deɪlɪ] adj quotidiano(-a), giornaliero(-a) ▶ n quotidiano ▶ adv tutti i giorni

dairy ['dɛərɪ] n (BRIT: shop) latteria; (on farm) caseificio ▶ adj caseario(-a); **dairy produce** npl latticini mpl

daisy ['deɪzɪ] n margherita

dam [dæm] n diga ▶ vt sbarrare; costruire dighe su

damage ['dæmɪdʒ] n danno, danni mpl; (fig) danno ▶ vt danneggiare; **~s** npl (Law) danni

damn [dæm] vt condannare; (curse) maledire ▶ n (inf): **I don't give a ~** non me ne frega niente ▶ adj (inf: also: **~ed**): **this ~ ...** questo maledetto ...; **~ it!** accidenti!

damp [dæmp] adj umido(-a) ▶ n umidità, umido ▶ vt (also: **~en**: cloth, rag) inumidire, bagnare; (: enthusiasm etc) spegnere

dance [dɑːns] n danza, ballo; (ball) ballo ▶ vi ballare; **dance floor** n pista da ballo; **dancer** n danzatore(-trice); (professional) ballerino(-a); **dancing** ['dɑːnsɪŋ] n danza, ballo

dandelion ['dændɪlaɪən] n dente m di leone

dandruff ['dændrəf] n forfora

Dane [deɪn] n danese m/f

danger ['deɪndʒəʳ] n pericolo; **there is a ~ of fire** c'è pericolo di incendio; **in ~** in pericolo; **he was in ~ of falling** rischiava di cadere; **dangerous** adj pericoloso(-a)

dangle ['dæŋgl] vt dondolare; (fig) far balenare ▶ vi pendolare

Danish ['deɪnɪʃ] adj danese ▶ n (Ling) danese m

dare [dɛəʳ] vt **to ~ sb to do** sfidare qn a fare ▶ vi **to ~ to do sth** osare fare qc; **I ~ say** (I suppose) immagino (che); **daring** adj audace, ardito(-a) ▶ n audacia

dark [dɑːk] adj (night, room) buio(-a), scuro(-a); (colour, complexion) scuro(-a); (fig) cupo(-a), tetro(-a), nero(-a) ▶ n **in the ~** al buio; **in the ~ about** (fig) all'oscuro di; **after ~** a notte fatta; **darken** vt (colour) scurire ▶ vi (sky, room) oscurarsi; **darkness** n oscurità, buio; **darkroom** n camera oscura

darling ['dɑːlɪŋ] adj caro(-a) ▶ n tesoro

dart [dɑːt] n freccetta; (Sewing) pince f inv ▶ vi **to ~ towards** precipitarsi verso; **to ~ away/along** sfrecciare via/lungo; **dartboard** n bersaglio (per freccette); **darts** n tiro al bersaglio (con freccette)

dash [dæʃ] n (sign) lineetta; (small quantity) punta ▶ vt (missile) gettare; (hopes) infrangere ▶ vi **to ~ towards** precipitarsi verso

dashboard ['dæʃbɔːd] n (Aut) cruscotto

data ['deɪtə] npl dati mpl; **database** n base f di dati, data base m inv; **data processing** n elaborazione f (elettronica) dei dati

date [deɪt] n data; appuntamento; (*fruit*) dattero ▶ vt datare; (*person*) uscire con; **what's the ~ today?** quanti ne abbiamo oggi?; **~ of birth** data di nascita; **to ~** (*until now*) fino a oggi; **dated** adj passato(-a) di moda

daughter ['dɔːtər] n figlia; **daughter-in-law** n nuora

daunting ['dɔːntɪŋ] adj non invidiabile

dawn [dɔːn] n alba ▶ vi (*day*) spuntare; (*fig*): **it ~ed on him that ...** gli è venuto in mente che ...

day [deɪ] n giorno; (*as duration*) giornata; (*period of time, age*) tempo, epoca; **the ~ before** il giorno avanti or prima; **the ~ after, the following ~** il giorno dopo or seguente; **the ~ after tomorrow** dopodomani; **the ~ before yesterday** l'altroieri; **by ~** di giorno; **day-care centre** n scuola materna; **daydream** vi sognare a occhi aperti; **daylight** n luce f del giorno; **day return** (*BRIT*) n biglietto giornaliero di andata e ritorno; **daytime** n giorno; **day-to-day** adj (*life, organization*) quotidiano(-a); **day trip** n gita (di un giorno)

dazed [deɪzd] adj stordito(-a)

dazzle ['dæzl] vt abbagliare; **dazzling** adj (*light*) abbagliante; (*colour*) violento(-a); (*smile*) smagliante

DC abbr (= direct current) c.c.

dead [dɛd] adj morto(-a); (*numb*) intirizzito(-a); (*telephone*) muto(-a); (*battery*) scarico(-a) ▶ adv assolutamente ▶ npl **the ~** i morti; **he was shot ~** fu colpito a morte; **~ tired** stanco(-a) morto(-a); **to stop ~** fermarsi di colpo; **dead end** n vicolo cieco; **deadline** n scadenza; **deadly** adj mortale; (*weapon, poison*) micidiale; **Dead Sea** n **the Dead Sea** il mar Morto

deaf [dɛf] adj sordo(-a); **deafen** vt assordare; **deafening** adj fragoroso(-a), assordante

deal [diːl] (*pt, pp* **dealt**) n accordo; (*business deal*) affare m ▶ vt (*blow, cards*) dare; **a great ~ (of)** molto(-a) ▷ **deal with** vt fus (*Comm*) fare affari con, trattare con; (*handle*) occuparsi di; (*be about: book etc*) trattare di; **dealer** n commerciante m/f; **dealings** npl (*Comm*) relazioni fpl; (*relations*) rapporti mpl

dealt [dɛlt] pt, pp of **deal**

dean [diːn] n (*Rel*) decano; (*Scol*) preside m di facoltà (or di collegio)

dear [dɪər] adj caro(-a) ▶ n **my ~** caro mio/cara mia ▶ excl **~ me!** Dio mio!; **D~ Sir/Madam** (*in letter*) Egregio Signore/Egregia Signora; **D~ Mr/Mrs X** Gentile Signor/Signora X; **dearly** adv (*love*) moltissimo; (*pay*) a caro prezzo

death [dɛθ] n morte f; (*Admin*) decesso; **death penalty** n pena di morte; **death sentence** n condanna a morte

debate [dɪ'beɪt] n dibattito ▶ vt dibattere; discutere

debit ['dɛbɪt] n debito ▶ vt **to ~ a sum to sb** addebitare una somma a qn; **debit card** n carta di debito

debris ['dɛbriː] n detriti mpl

debt [dɛt] n debito; **to be in ~** essere indebitato(-a)

debug [diː'bʌg] vt (*Comput*) localizzare e rimuovere errori in

debut ['deɪbjuː] n debutto

Dec. abbr (= December) di c.

decade ['dɛkeɪd] n decennio

decaffeinated [dɪ'kæfɪneɪtɪd] adj decaffeinato(-a)

decay [dɪ'keɪ] n decadimento; (*also:* **tooth ~**) carie f ▶ vi (*rot*) imputridire

deceased [dɪ'siːst] n defunto(-a)

deceit [dɪ'siːt] n inganno; **deceive** [dɪ'siːv] vt ingannare

December [dɪ'sɛmbə^r] *n* dicembre *m*

decency ['di:sənsɪ] *n* decenza

decent ['di:sənt] *adj* decente; (*respectable*) per bene; (*kind*) gentile

deception [dɪ'sɛpʃən] *n* inganno

deceptive [dɪ'sɛptɪv] *adj* ingannevole

decide [dɪ'saɪd] *vt* (*person*) far prendere una decisione a; (*question, argument*) risolvere, decidere ▶ *vi* decidere, decidersi; **to ~ to do/that** decidere di fare/che; **to ~ on** decidere per

decimal ['dɛsɪməl] *adj* decimale ▶ *n* decimale *m*

decision [dɪ'sɪʒən] *n* decisione *f*

decisive [dɪ'saɪsɪv] *adj* decisivo(-a); (*person*) deciso(-a)

deck [dɛk] *n* (*Naut*) ponte *m*; (*of bus*): **top ~** imperiale *m*; (*record deck*) piatto; (*of cards*) mazzo; **deckchair** *n* sedia a sdraio

declaration [dɛklə'reɪʃən] *n* dichiarazione *f*

declare [dɪ'klɛə^r] *vt* dichiarare

decline [dɪ'klaɪn] *n* (*decay*) declino; (*lessening*) ribasso ▶ *vt* declinare; rifiutare ▶ *vi* declinare; diminuire

decorate ['dɛkəreɪt] *vt* (*adorn, give a medal to*) decorare; (*paint and paper*) tinteggiare e tappezzare; **decoration** [-'reɪʃən] *n* (*medal etc, adornment*) decorazione *f*; **decorator** *n* decoratore *m*

decrease [*n* 'di:kri:s, *vb* di:'kri:s] *n* diminuzione *f* ▶ *vt, vi* diminuire

decree [dɪ'kri:] *n* decreto

dedicate ['dɛdɪkeɪt] *vt* consacrare; (*book etc*) dedicare; **dedicated** *adj* coscienzioso(-a); (*Comput*) specializzato(-a), dedicato(-a); **dedication** [dɛdɪ'keɪʃən] *n* (*devotion*) dedizione *f*; (*in book etc*) dedica

deduce [dɪ'dju:s] *vt* dedurre

deduct [dɪ'dʌkt] *vt* **to ~ sth from** dedurre qc (da); **deduction** [dɪ'dʌkʃən] *n* deduzione *f*

deed [di:d] *n* azione *f*, atto; (*Law*) atto

deem [di:m] *vt* (*formal*) giudicare, ritenere; **to ~ it wise to do** ritenere prudente fare

deep [di:p] *adj* profondo(-a); **4 metres ~** profondo(-a) 4 metri ▶ *adv* **spectators stood 20 ~** c'erano 20 file di spettatori; **how ~ is the water?** quanto è profonda l'acqua?; **deep-fry** *vt* friggere in olio abbondante; **deeply** *adv* profondamente

deer [dɪə^r] *n inv* **the ~** i cervidi; **(red) ~** cervo; **(fallow) ~** daino; **roe ~** capriolo

default [dɪ'fɔ:lt] *n* (*Comput: also: ~ value*) default *m inv*; **by ~** (*Sport*) per abbandono

defeat [dɪ'fi:t] *n* sconfitta ▶ *vt* (*team, opponents*) sconfiggere

defect [*n* 'di:fɛkt, *vb* dɪ'fɛkt] *n* difetto ▶ *vi* **to ~ to the enemy** passare al nemico; **defective** [dɪ'fɛktɪv] *adj* difettoso(-a)

defence [dɪ'fɛns] (*US* **defense**) *n* difesa

defend [dɪ'fɛnd] *vt* difendere; **defendant** *n* imputato(-a); **defender** *n* difensore(-a)

defense [dɪ'fɛns] (*US*) *n* = **defence**

defensive [dɪ'fɛnsɪv] *adj* difensivo(-a) ▶ *n* **on the ~** sulla difensiva

defer [dɪ'fə:^r] *vt* (*postpone*) differire, rinviare

defiance [dɪ'faɪəns] *n* sfida; **in ~ of** a dispetto di; **defiant** [dɪ'faɪənt] *adj* (*attitude*) di sfida; (*person*) ribelle

deficiency [dɪ'fɪʃənsɪ] *n* deficienza; carenza; **deficient** *adj* deficiente; insufficiente; **to be deficient in** mancare di

deficit ['dɛfɪsɪt] *n* deficit *m inv*

define [dɪ'faɪn] *vt* definire

definite ['dɛfɪnɪt] *adj* (*fixed*) definito(-a), preciso(-a); (*clear, obvious*) ben definito(-a), esatto(-a); (*Ling*) determinativo(-a); **he was ~**

about it ne era sicuro; **definitely** adv indubbiamente

definition [dɛfɪ'nɪʃən] n definizione f

deflate [diː'fleɪt] vt sgonfiare

deflect [dɪ'flɛkt] vt deflettere, deviare

defraud [dɪ'frɔːd] vt defraudare

defrost [diː'frɔst] vt (fridge) disgelare

defuse [diː'fjuːz] vt disinnescare; (fig) distendere

defy [dɪ'faɪ] vt sfidare; (efforts etc) resistere a; **it defies description** supera ogni descrizione

degree [dɪ'griː] n grado; (Scol) laurea (universitaria); **a first ~ in maths** una laurea in matematica; **by ~s** (gradually) gradualmente, a poco a poco; **to some ~** fino a un certo punto, in certa misura

dehydrated [diːhaɪ'dreɪtɪd] adj disidratato(-a); (milk, eggs) in polvere

de-icer [diː'aɪsəʳ] n sbrinatore m

delay [dɪ'leɪ] vt ritardare ▶ vi **to ~ (in doing sth)** ritardare (a fare qc) ▶ n ritardo; **to be ~ed** subire un ritardo; (person) essere trattenuto(-a)

delegate [n 'dɛlɪgɪt, vb 'dɛlɪgeɪt] n delegato(-a) ▶ vt delegare

delete [dɪ'liːt] vt cancellare

deli ['dɛlɪ] n = **delicatessen**

deliberate [adj dɪ'lɪbərɪt, vb dɪ'lɪbəreɪt] adj (intentional) intenzionale; (slow) misurato(-a) ▶ vi deliberare, riflettere; **deliberately** adv (on purpose) deliberatamente

delicacy ['dɛlɪkəsɪ] n delicatezza

delicate ['dɛlɪkɪt] adj delicato(-a)

delicatessen [dɛlɪkə'tɛsn] n ≈ salumeria

delicious [dɪ'lɪʃəs] adj delizioso(-a), squisito(-a)

delight [dɪ'laɪt] n delizia, gran piacere m ▶ vt dilettare; **to take (a) ~ in** dilettarsi in; **delighted** adj **delighted (at or with)** contentissimo(-a) (di), felice (di); **delighted to do** felice di

fare; **delightful** adj delizioso(-a), incantevole

delinquent [dɪ'lɪŋkwənt] adj, n delinquente m/f

deliver [dɪ'lɪvəʳ] vt (mail) distribuire; (goods) consegnare; (speech) pronunciare; (Med) far partorire; **delivery** n distribuzione f; consegna; (of speaker) dizione f; (Med) parto

delusion [dɪ'luːʒən] n illusione f

de luxe [də'lʌks] adj di lusso

delve [dɛlv] vi **to ~ into** frugare in; (subject) far ricerche in

demand [dɪ'mɑːnd] vt richiedere; (rights) rivendicare ▶ n domanda; (claim) rivendicazione f; **in ~** ricercato(-a), richiesto(-a); **on ~** a richiesta; **demanding** adj (boss) esigente; (work) impegnativo(-a)

demise [dɪ'maɪz] n decesso

demo ['dɛməu] (inf) n abbr (= demonstration) manifestazione f

democracy [dɪ'mɔkrəsɪ] n democrazia; **democrat** ['dɛməkræt] n democratico(-a); **democratic** [dɛmə'krætɪk] adj democratico(-a)

demolish [dɪ'mɔlɪʃ] vt demolire

demolition [dɛmə'lɪʃən] n demolizione f

demon ['diːmən] n (also fig) demonio ▶ cpd **a ~ squash player** un mago dello squash; **a ~ driver** un guidatore folle

demonstrate ['dɛmənstreɪt] vt dimostrare, provare ▶ vi dimostrare, manifestare; **demonstration** [-'streɪʃən] n dimostrazione f; (Pol) dimostrazione, manifestazione f; **demonstrator** n (Pol) dimostrante m/f; (Comm) dimostratore(-trice)

demote [dɪ'məut] vt far retrocedere

den [dɛn] n tana, covo; (room) buco

denial [dɪ'naɪəl] n diniego; rifiuto

denim ['dɛnɪm] n tessuto di cotone ritorto; **~s** npl (jeans) blue jeans mpl

Denmark ['dɛnmɑːk] n Danimarca

denomination [dɪnɔmɪˈneɪʃən] n (money) valore m; (Rel) confessione f

denounce [dɪˈnauns] vt denunciare

dense [dɛns] adj fitto(-a); (smoke) denso(-a); (inf: person) ottuso(-a), duro(-a)

density [ˈdɛnsɪtɪ] n densità f inv

dent [dɛnt] n ammaccatura ▶ vt (also: **make a ~ in**) ammaccare

dental [ˈdɛntl] adj dentale; **dental floss** [-flɔs] n filo interdentale; **dental surgery** n ambulatorio del dentista

dentist [ˈdɛntɪst] n dentista m/f

dentures [ˈdɛntʃəz] npl dentiera

deny [dɪˈnaɪ] vt negare; (refuse) rifiutare

deodorant [diːˈəudərənt] n deodorante m

depart [dɪˈpɑːt] vi partire; **to ~ from** (fig) deviare da

department [dɪˈpɑːtmənt] n (Comm) reparto; (Scol) sezione f, dipartimento; (Pol) ministero; **department store** n grande magazzino

departure [dɪˈpɑːtʃər] n partenza; (fig): **~ from** deviazione f da; **a new ~** una svolta (decisiva); **departure lounge** n (at airport) sala d'attesa

depend [dɪˈpɛnd] vi **to ~ on** dipendere da; (rely on) contare su; **it ~s** dipende; **~ing on the result …** a seconda del risultato …; **dependant** n persona a carico; **dependent** adj **to be dependent on** dipendere da; (child, relative) essere a carico di ▶ n = **dependant**

depict [dɪˈpɪkt] vt (in picture) dipingere; (in words) descrivere

deport [dɪˈpɔːt] vt deportare; espellere

deposit [dɪˈpɔzɪt] n (Comm, Geo) deposito; (of ore, oil) giacimento; (Chem) sedimento; (part payment) acconto; (for hired goods etc) cauzione

f ▶ vt depositare; dare in acconto; mettere or lasciare in deposito; **deposit account** n conto vincolato

depot [ˈdɛpəu] n deposito; (US) stazione f ferroviaria

depreciate [dɪˈpriːʃɪeɪt] vi svalutarsi

depress [dɪˈprɛs] vt deprimere; (price, wages) abbassare; (press down) premere; **depressed** adj (person) depresso(-a), abbattuto(-a); (price) in ribasso; (industry) in crisi; **depressing** adj deprimente; **depression** [dɪˈprɛʃən] n depressione f

deprive [dɪˈpraɪv] vt **to ~ sb of** privare qn di; **deprived** adj disgraziato(-a)

dept. abbr = **department**

depth [dɛpθ] n profondità f inv; **in the ~s of** nel profondo di; nel cuore di; **out of one's ~** (in water) dove non si tocca; (fig) a disagio

deputy [ˈdɛpjutɪ] adj **~ head** (BRIT Scol) vicepreside m/f ▶ n (assistant) vice m/f inv; (US: also: **~ sheriff**) vice-sceriffo

derail [dɪˈreɪl] vt **to be ~ed** deragliare

derelict [ˈdɛrɪlɪkt] adj abbandonato(-a)

derive [dɪˈraɪv] vt **to ~ sth from** derivare qc da; trarre qc da ▶ vi **to ~ from** derivare da

descend [dɪˈsɛnd] vt, vi discendere, scendere; **to ~ from** discendere da; **to ~ to** (lying, begging) abbassarsi a; **descendant** n discendente m/f; **descent** [dɪˈsɛnt] n discesa; (origin) discendenza, famiglia

describe [dɪsˈkraɪb] vt descrivere; **description** [-ˈkrɪpʃən] n descrizione f; (sort) genere m, specie f

desert [n ˈdɛzət, vb dɪˈzəːt] n deserto ▶ vt lasciare, abbandonare ▶ vi (Mil) disertare; **deserted** [dɪˈzəːtɪd] adj deserto(-a)

deserve [dɪˈzəːv] vt meritare

design [dɪˈzaɪn] n (art, sketch) disegno; (layout, shape) linea; (pattern) fantasia;

(*intention*) intenzione f ▶ vt disegnare; progettare

designate [vb 'dɛzɪgneɪt, adj 'dɛzɪgnɪt] vt designare ▶ adj designato(-a)

designer [dɪ'zaɪnə'] n (Art, Tech) disegnatore(-trice); (of fashion) modellista m/f

desirable [dɪ'zaɪərəbl] adj desiderabile; **it is ~ that** è opportuno che + sub

desire [dɪ'zaɪə'] n desiderio, voglia ▶ vt desiderare, volere

desk [dɛsk] n (in office) scrivania; (for pupil) banco; (BRIT: in shop, restaurant) cassa; (in hotel) ricevimento; (at airport) accettazione f; **desk-top publishing** n desktop publishing m

despair [dɪs'pɛə'] n disperazione f ▶ vi **to ~ of** disperare di

despatch [dɪs'pætʃ] n, vt = **dispatch**

desperate ['dɛspərɪt] adj disperato(-a); (fugitive) capace di tutto; **to be ~ for sth/to do** volere disperatamente qc/fare; **desperately** adv disperatamente; (very) terribilmente, estremamente; **desperation** [dɛspə'reɪʃən] n disperazione f

despise [dɪs'paɪz] vt disprezzare, sdegnare

despite [dɪs'paɪt] prep malgrado, a dispetto di, nonostante

dessert [dɪ'zə:t] n dolce m; frutta; **dessertspoon** n cucchiaio da dolci

destination [dɛstɪ'neɪʃən] n destinazione f

destined ['dɛstɪnd] adj **to be ~ to do/ for** essere destinato(-a) a fare/per

destiny ['dɛstɪnɪ] n destino

destroy [dɪs'trɔɪ] vt distruggere

destruction [dɪs'trʌkʃən] n distruzione f

destructive [dɪs'trʌktɪv] adj distruttivo(-a)

detach [dɪ'tætʃ] vt staccare, distaccare; **detached** adj (attitude) distante; **detached house** n villa

detail ['di:teɪl] n particolare m, dettaglio m ▶ vt dettagliare, particolareggiare; **in ~** nei particolari; **detailed** adj particolareggiato(-a)

detain [dɪ'teɪn] vt trattenere; (in captivity) detenere

detect [dɪ'tɛkt] vt scoprire, scorgere; (Med, Police, Radar etc) individuare; **detection** [dɪ'tɛkʃən] n scoperta; individuazione f; **detective** n investigatore(-trice); **detective story** n giallo

detention [dɪ'tɛnʃən] n detenzione f; (Scol) permanenza forzata per punizione

deter [dɪ'tə:'] vt dissuadere

detergent [dɪ'tə:dʒənt] n detersivo

deteriorate [dɪ'tɪərɪəreɪt] vi deteriorarsi

determination [dɪtə:mɪ'neɪʃən] n determinazione f

determine [dɪ'tə:mɪn] vt determinare; **determined** adj (person) risoluto(-a), deciso(-a); **determined to do** deciso(-a) a fare

deterrent [dɪ'tɛrənt] n deterrente m; **to act as a ~** fungere da deterrente

detest [dɪ'tɛst] vt detestare

detour ['di:tuə'] n deviazione f

detract [dɪ'trækt] vi **to ~ from** detrarre da

detrimental [dɛtrɪ'mɛntl] adj **~ to** dannoso(-a) a, nocivo(-a) a

devastating ['dɛvəsteɪtɪŋ] adj devastatore(-trice), sconvolgente

develop [dɪ'vɛləp] vt sviluppare; (habit) prendere (gradualmente) ▶ vi svilupparsi; (facts, symptoms: appear) manifestarsi, rivelarsi; **can you ~ this film?** può sviluppare questo rullino?; **developing country** n paese m in via di sviluppo; **development** n sviluppo

device [dɪ'vaɪs] n (apparatus) congegno

devil ['dɛvl] *n* diavolo; demonio

devious ['di:vɪəs] *adj* (*person*) subdolo(-a)

devise [dɪ'vaɪz] *vt* escogitare, concepire

devote [dɪ'vəut] *vt* **to ~ sth to** dedicare qc a; **devoted** *adj* devoto(-a); **to be devoted to sb** essere molto affezionato(-a) a qn; **devotion** [dɪ'və uʃən] *n* devozione *f*, attaccamento; (*Rel*) atto di devozione, preghiera

devour [dɪ'vauər] *vt* divorare

devout [dɪ'vaut] *adj* pio(-a), devoto(-a)

dew [dju:] *n* rugiada

diabetes [daɪə'bi:ti:z] *n* diabete *m*

diabetic [daɪə'bɛtɪk] *adj, n* diabetico(-a)

diagnose [daɪəg'nəuz] *vt* diagnosticare

diagnosis [daɪəg'nəusɪs] (*pl* **diagnoses**) *n* diagnosi *f inv*

diagonal [daɪ'ægənl] *adj* diagonale ▶ *n* diagonale *f*

diagram ['daɪəgræm] *n* diagramma *m*

dial ['daɪəl] *n* quadrante *m*; (*on radio*) lancetta; (*on telephone*) disco combinatore ▶ *vt* (*number*) fare

dialect ['daɪəlɛkt] *n* dialetto

dialling code (*US* **area code**) *n* prefisso; **what's the ~ for Paris?** qual è il prefisso telefonico di Parigi?

dialling tone (*US* **dial tone**) *n* segnale *m* di linea libera

dialogue ['daɪəlɔg] (*US* **dialog**) *n* dialogo

diameter [daɪ'æmɪtər] *n* diametro

diamond ['daɪəmənd] *n* diamante *m*; (*shape*) rombo; **~s** *npl* (*Cards*) quadri *mpl*

diaper ['daɪəpər] (*US*) *n* pannolino

diarrhoea [daɪə'ri:ə] (*US* **diarrhea**) *n* diarrea

diary ['daɪərɪ] *n* (*daily account*) diario; (*book*) agenda

dice [daɪs] *n inv* dado ▶ *vt* (*Culin*) tagliare a dadini

dictate [dɪk'teɪt] *vt* dettare; **dictation** [dɪk'teɪʃən] *n* dettatura; (*Scol*) dettato

dictator [dɪk'teɪtər] *n* dittatore *m*

dictionary ['dɪkʃənrɪ] *n* dizionario

did [dɪd] *pt of* **do**

didn't [dɪdnt] = **did not**

die [daɪ] *vi* morire; **to be dying for sth/to do sth** morire dalla voglia di qc/di fare qc ▷ **die down** *vi* abbassarsi ▷ **die out** *vi* estinguersi

diesel ['di:zəl] *n* (*vehicle*) diesel *m inv*

diet ['daɪət] *n* alimentazione *f*; (*restricted food*) dieta ▶ *vi* (*also*: **be on a ~**) stare a dieta

differ ['dɪfər] *vi* **to ~ from sth** differire da qc, essere diverso(-a) da qc; **to ~ from sb over sth** essere in disaccordo con qn su qc; **difference** *n* differenza; (*disagreement*) screzio; **different** *adj* diverso(-a); **differentiate** [-'rɛnʃɪeɪt] *vi* **to differentiate between** discriminare *or* fare differenza fra; **differently** *adv* diversamente

difficult ['dɪfɪkəlt] *adj* difficile; **difficulty** *n* difficoltà *f inv*

dig [dɪg] (*pt, pp* **dug**) *vt* (*hole*) scavare; (*garden*) vangare ▶ *n* (*prod*) gomitata; (*archaeological*) scavo; (*fig*) frecciata ▷ **dig up** *vt* (*tree etc*) sradicare; (*information*) scavare fuori

digest [*vb* daɪ'dʒɛst, *n* 'daɪdʒɛst] *vt* digerire ▶ *n* compendio; **digestion** [dɪ'dʒɛstʃən] *n* digestione *f*

digit ['dɪdʒɪt] *n* cifra; (*finger*) dito; **digital** *adj* digitale; **digital camera** *n* macchina fotografica digitale; **digital TV** *n* televisione *f* digitale

dignified ['dɪgnɪfaɪd] *adj* dignitoso(-a)

dignity ['dɪgnɪtɪ] *n* dignità

digs [dɪgz] (*BRIT*: *inf*) *npl* camera ammobiliata

dilemma [daɪˈlɛmə] n dilemma m
dill [dɪl] n aneto
dilute [daɪˈluːt] vt diluire; (with water) annacquare
dim [dɪm] adj (light) debole; (shape etc) vago(-a); (room) in penombra; (inf: person) tonto(-a) ▶ vt (light) abbassare
dime [daɪm] (US) n =10 cents
dimension [daɪˈmɛnʃən] n dimensione f
diminish [dɪˈmɪnɪʃ] vt, vi diminuire
din [dɪn] n chiasso, fracasso
dine [daɪn] vi pranzare; **diner** n (person) cliente m/f; (US: place) tavola calda
dinghy [ˈdɪŋɡɪ] n battello pneumatico; (also: **rubber ~**) gommone m
dingy [ˈdɪndʒɪ] adj grigio(-a)
dining car [ˈdaɪnɪŋ-] (BRIT) n vagone m ristorante
dining room n sala da pranzo
dining table n tavolo da pranzo
dinner [ˈdɪnəʳ] n (lunch) pranzo; (evening meal) cena; (public) banchetto; **dinner jacket** n smoking m inv; **dinner party** n cena; **dinner time** n ora di pranzo (or cena)
dinosaur [ˈdaɪnəsɔːʳ] n dinosauro
dip [dɪp] n discesa; (in sea) bagno; (Culin) salsetta ▶ vt immergere; bagnare; (BRIT Aut: lights) abbassare ▶ vi abbassarsi
diploma [dɪˈpləumə] n diploma m
diplomacy [dɪˈpləuməsɪ] n diplomazia
diplomat [ˈdɪpləmæt] n diplomatico; **diplomatic** [dɪpləˈmætɪk] adj diplomatico(-a)
dipstick [ˈdɪpstɪk] n (Aut) indicatore m di livello dell'olio
dire [daɪəʳ] adj terribile; estremo(-a)
direct [daɪˈrɛkt] adj diretto(-a) ▶ vt dirigere; (order): **to ~ sb to do sth** dare direttive a qn di fare qc ▶ adv direttamente; **can you ~ me to ...?** mi

può indicare la strada per ...?; **direct debit** n (Banking) addebito effettuato per ordine di un cliente di banca
direction [dɪˈrɛkʃən] n direzione f; **~s** npl (advice) chiarimenti mpl; **sense of ~** senso dell'orientamento; **~s for use** istruzioni fpl
directly [dɪˈrɛktlɪ] adv (in straight line) direttamente; (at once) subito
director [dɪˈrɛktəʳ] n direttore(-trice), amministratore(-trice); (Theatre, Cinema) regista m/f
directory [dɪˈrɛktərɪ] n elenco; **directory enquiries** (US **directory assistance**) n informazioni fpl elenco abbonati inv
dirt [dəːt] n sporcizia; immondizia; (earth) terra; **dirty** adj sporco(-a) ▶ vt sporcare
disability [dɪsəˈbɪlɪtɪ] n invalidità f inv; (Law) incapacità f inv
disabled [dɪsˈeɪbld] adj invalido(-a); (mentally) ritardato(-a) ▶ npl **the ~** gli invalidi
disadvantage [dɪsədˈvɑːntɪdʒ] n svantaggio
disagree [dɪsəˈɡriː] vi (differ) discordare; (be against, think otherwise): **to ~ (with)** essere in disaccordo (con), dissentire (da); **disagreeable** adj sgradevole; (person) antipatico(-a); **disagreement** n disaccordo; (argument) dissapore m
disappear [dɪsəˈpɪəʳ] vi scomparire; **disappearance** n scomparsa
disappoint [dɪsəˈpɔɪnt] vt deludere; **disappointed** adj deluso(-a); **disappointing** adj deludente; **disappointment** n delusione f
disapproval [dɪsəˈpruːvəl] n disapprovazione f
disapprove [dɪsəˈpruːv] vi **to ~ of** disapprovare
disarm [dɪsˈɑːm] vt disarmare; **disarmament** n disarmo

disaster [dɪ'zɑ:stə^r] n disastro; **disastrous** [dɪ'zɑ:strəs] adj disastroso(-a)

disbelief ['dɪsbə'li:f] n incredulità

disc [dɪsk] n disco; (Comput) = **disk**

discard [dɪs'kɑ:d] vt (old things) scartare; (fig) abbandonare

discharge [vb dɪs'tʃɑ:dʒ, n 'dɪstʃɑ:dʒ] vt (duties) compiere; (Elec, waste etc) scaricare; (Med) emettere; (patient) dimettere; (employee) licenziare; (soldier) congedare; (defendant) liberare ▶ n (Elec) scarica; (Med) emissione f; (dismissal) licenziamento; congedo; liberazione f

discipline ['dɪsɪplɪn] n disciplina ▶ vt disciplinare; (punish) punire

disc jockey n disc jockey m inv

disclose [dɪs'kləuz] vt rivelare, svelare

disco ['dɪskəu] n abbr discoteca

discoloured [dɪs'kʌləd] (US **discolored**) adj scolorito(-a), ingiallito(-a)

discomfort [dɪs'kʌmfət] n disagio; (lack of comfort) scomodità f inv

disconnect [dɪskə'nɛkt] vt sconnettere, staccare; (Elec, Radio) staccare; (gas, water) chiudere

discontent [dɪskən'tɛnt] n scontentezza

discontinue [dɪskən'tɪnju:] vt smettere, cessare; **"~d"** (Comm) "fuori produzione"

discount [n 'dɪskaunt, vb dɪs'kaunt] n sconto ▶ vt scontare; (idea) non badare a; **are there ~s for students?** ci sono sconti per studenti?

discourage [dɪs'kʌrɪdʒ] vt scoraggiare

discover [dɪs'kʌvə^r] vt scoprire; **discovery** n scoperta

discredit [dɪs'krɛdɪt] vt screditare; mettere in dubbio

discreet [dɪ'skri:t] adj discreto(-a)

discrepancy [dɪ'skrɛpənsɪ] n discrepanza

discretion [dɪ'skrɛʃən] n discrezione f; **use your own ~** giudichi lei

discriminate [dɪ'skrɪmɪneɪt] vi **to ~ between** distinguere tra; **to ~ against** discriminare contro; **discrimination** ['-neɪʃən] n discriminazione f; (judgment) discernimento

discuss [dɪ'skʌs] vt discutere; (debate) dibattere; **discussion** [dɪ'skʌʃən] n discussione f

disease [dɪ'zi:z] n malattia

disembark [dɪsɪm'bɑ:k] vt, vi sbarcare

disgrace [dɪs'greɪs] n vergogna; (disfavour) disgrazia ▶ vt disonorare, far cadere in disgrazia; **disgraceful** adj scandaloso(-a), vergognoso(-a)

disgruntled [dɪs'grʌntld] adj scontento(-a), di cattivo umore

disguise [dɪs'gaɪz] n travestimento ▶ vt **to ~ (as)** travestire (da); **in ~** travestito(-a)

disgust [dɪs'gʌst] n disgusto, nausea ▶ vt disgustare, far schifo a; **disgusted** [dɪs'gʌstɪd] adj indignato(-a); **disgusting** [dɪs'gʌstɪŋ] adj disgustoso(-a), ripugnante

dish [dɪʃ] n piatto; **to do or wash the ~es** fare i piatti; **dishcloth** n strofinaccio

dishonest [dɪs'ɔnɪst] adj disonesto(-a)

dishtowel ['dɪʃtauəl] (US) n strofinaccio dei piatti

dishwasher ['dɪʃwɔʃə^r] n lavastoviglie f inv

disillusion [dɪsɪ'lu:ʒən] vt disilludere, disingannare

disinfectant [dɪsɪn'fɛktənt] n disinfettante m

disintegrate [dɪs'ɪntɪgreɪt] vi disintegrarsi

disk [dɪsk] n (Comput) disco; **single-/double-sided ~** disco a facciata

singola/doppia; **disk drive** n lettore
m; **diskette** (US) n = **disk**
dislike [dɪs'laɪk] n antipatia,
avversione f; (gen pl) cosa che non
piace ▶ vt he **~s it** non gli piace
dislocate ['dɪsləkeɪt] vt slogare
disloyal [dɪs'lɔɪəl] adj sleale
dismal ['dɪzml] adj triste, cupo(-a)
dismantle [dɪs'mæntl] vt (machine)
smontare
dismay [dɪs'meɪ] n costernazione f
▶ vt sgomentare
dismiss [dɪs'mɪs] vt congedare;
(employee) licenziare; (idea) scacciare;
(Law) respingere; **dismissal** n
congedo; licenziamento
disobedient [dɪsə'biːdɪənt] adj
disubbidiente
disobey [dɪsə'beɪ] vt disubbidire a
disorder [dɪs'ɔːdə] n disordine m;
(rioting) tumulto; (Med) disturbo
disorganized [dɪs'ɔːgənaɪzd] adj
(person, life) disorganizzato(-a);
(system, meeting) male organizzato(-a)
disown [dɪs'əun] vt rinnegare
dispatch [dɪs'pætʃ] vt spedire, inviare
▶ n spedizione f, invio; (Mil, Press)
dispaccio
dispel [dɪs'pɛl] vt dissipare, scacciare
dispense [dɪs'pɛns] vt distribuire,
amministrare ▷ **dispense with** vt fus
fare a meno di; **dispenser** n (container)
distributore m
disperse [dɪs'pəːs] vt disperdere;
(knowledge) disseminare ▶ vi
disperdersi
display [dɪs'pleɪ] n esposizione f; (of
feeling etc) manifestazione f; (screen)
schermo ▶ vt mostrare; (goods)
esporre; (pej) ostentare
displease [dɪs'pliːz] vt dispiacere a,
scontentare; **~d with** scontento di
disposable [dɪs'pəuzəbl] adj (pack etc)
a perdere; (income) disponibile
disposal [dɪs'pəuzl] n eliminazione f;

(of property) cessione f; **at one's ~** alla
sua disposizione
dispose [dɪs'pəuz] vi **~ of** sbarazzarsi
di; **disposition** [-'zɪʃən] n
disposizione f; (temperament)
carattere m
disproportionate [dɪsprə'pɔːʃənət]
adj sproporzionato(-a)
dispute [dɪs'pjuːt] n disputa; (also:
industrial ~) controversia (sindacale)
▶ vt contestare; (matter) discutere;
(victory) disputare
disqualify [dɪs'kwɔlɪfaɪ] vt (Sport)
squalificare; **to ~ sb from sth/from
doing** rendere qn incapace a qc/a
fare; squalificare qn da qc/da fare; **to
~ sb from driving** ritirare la patente
a qn
disregard [dɪsrɪ'gɑːd] vt non far caso
a, non badare a
disrupt [dɪs'rʌpt] vt disturbare; creare
scompiglio in; **disruption**
[dɪs'rʌpʃən] n disordine m;
interruzione f
dissatisfaction [dɪssætɪs'fækʃən] n
scontentezza, insoddisfazione f
dissatisfied [dɪs'sætɪsfaɪd]
adj **~ (with)** scontento(a) or
insoddisfatto(a) (di)
dissect [dɪ'sɛkt] vt sezionare
dissent [dɪ'sɛnt] n dissenso
dissertation [dɪsə'teɪʃən] n tesi f inv,
dissertazione f
dissolve [dɪ'zɔlv] vt dissolvere,
sciogliere; (Pol, marriage etc) sciogliere
▶ vi dissolversi, sciogliersi
distance ['dɪstns] n distanza; **in the ~**
in lontananza
distant ['dɪstnt] adj lontano(-a),
distante; (manner) riservato(-a)
distil [dɪs'tɪl] (US **distill**) vt distillare;
distillery n distilleria
distinct [dɪs'tɪŋkt] adj distinto(-a);
as ~ from a differenza di; **distinction**
[dɪs'tɪŋkʃən] n distinzione f; (in exam)

lode f; **distinctive** adj distintivo(-a)
distinguish [dɪsˈtɪŋgwɪʃ]
vt distinguere; discernere;
distinguished adj (eminent) eminente
distort [dɪsˈtɔːt] vt distorcere; (Tech)
deformare
distract [dɪsˈtrækt] vt distrarre;
distracted adj distratto(-a);
distraction [dɪsˈtrækʃən] n
distrazione f
distraught [dɪsˈtrɔːt] adj stravolto(-a)
distress [dɪsˈtrɛs] n angoscia
▶ vt affliggere; **distressing** adj
doloroso(-a)
distribute [dɪsˈtrɪbjuːt] vt distribuire;
distribution [-ˈbjuːʃən] n
distribuzione f; **distributor** n
distributore m
district [ˈdɪstrɪkt] n (of country)
regione f; (of town) quartiere m;
(Admin) distretto; **district attorney**
(US) n ≈ sostituto procuratore m della
Repubblica
distrust [dɪsˈtrʌst] n diffidenza,
sfiducia ▶ vt non aver fiducia in
disturb [dɪsˈtəːb] vt disturbare;
disturbance n disturbo; (political etc)
disordini mpl; **disturbed** adj (worried,
upset) turbato(-a); **emotionally
disturbed** con turbe emotive;
disturbing adj sconvolgente
ditch [dɪtʃ] n fossa ▶ vt (inf) piantare
in asso
ditto [ˈdɪtəu] adv idem
dive [daɪv] n tuffo; (of submarine)
immersione f ▶ vi tuffarsi;
immergersi; **diver** n tuffatore(-trice),
palombaro
diverse [daɪˈvəːs] adj vario(-a)
diversion [daɪˈvəːʃən] n (BRIT
Aut) deviazione f; (distraction)
divertimento
diversity [daɪˈvəːsɪtɪ] n diversità f inv,
varietà f inv
divert [daɪˈvəːt] vt deviare

divide [dɪˈvaɪd] vt dividere; (separate)
separare ▶ vi dividersi; **divided
highway** (US) n strada a doppia
carreggiata
divine [dɪˈvaɪn] adj divino(-a)
diving [ˈdaɪvɪŋ] n tuffo; **diving board**
n trampolino
division [dɪˈvɪʒən] n divisione f;
separazione f; (esp Football) serie f
divorce [dɪˈvɔːs] n divorzio ▶ vt
divorziare da; (dissociate) separare;
divorced adj divorziato(-a); **divorcee**
[-ˈsiː] n divorziato(-a)
D.I.Y. (BRIT) n abbr = **do-it-yourself**
dizzy [ˈdɪzɪ] adj **to feel ~** avere il
capogiro
DJ n abbr = **disc jockey**
DNA n abbr (= deoxyribonucleic acid) DNA
m; **DNA test** n test m inv del DNA

do
[duː] (pt **did**, pp **done**) n (inf:
party etc) festa; **it was rather a grand
do** è stato un ricevimento piuttosto
importante

▶ vb

1 (in negative constructions: non tradotto):
I don't understand non capisco
2 (to form questions: non tradotto):
didn't you know? non lo sapevi?;
why didn't you come? perché non
sei venuto?
3 (for emphasis, in polite expressions):
she does seem rather late sembra
essere piuttosto in ritardo; **do sit
down** si accomodi la prego, prego si
sieda; **do take care!** mi raccomando,
sta attento!
4 (used to avoid repeating vb): **she swims
better than I do** lei nuota meglio di
me; **do you agree? — yes, I do/no, I
don't** sei d'accordo? — sì/no; **she lives
in Glasgow — so do I** lei vive a Glasgow
— anch'io; **he asked me to help him
and I did** mi ha chiesto di aiutarlo ed
io l'ho fatto

5 (in question tags): **you like him, don't you?** ti piace, vero?; **I don't know him, do I?** non lo conosco, vero?
▶vt (gen, carry out, perform etc) fare; **what are you doing tonight?** che fa stasera?; **to do the cooking** cucinare; **to do the washing-up** fare i piatti; **to do one's teeth** lavarsi i denti; **to do one's hair/nails** farsi i capelli/le unghie; **the car was doing 100** la macchina faceva i 100 all'ora
▶vi
1 (act, behave) fare; **do as I do** faccia come me, faccia come faccio io
2 (get on, fare) andare; **he's doing well/badly at school** va bene/male a scuola; **how do you do?** piacere!
3 (suit) andare bene; **this room will do** questa stanza va bene
4 (be sufficient) bastare; **will £10 do?** basteranno 10 sterline?; **that'll do** basta così; **that'll do!** (in annoyance) ora basta!; **to make do (with)** arrangiarsi (con)
▷ **do away with** vt fus (kill) far fuori; (abolish) abolire
▷ **do up** vt (laces) allacciare; (dress, buttons) abbottonare; (renovate: room, house) rimettere a nuovo, rifare
▷ **do with** vt fus (need) aver bisogno di; (be connected): **what has it got to do with you?** e tu che c'entri?; **I won't have anything to do with it** non voglio avere niente a che farci; **it has to do with money** si tratta di soldi
▷ **do without** vi fare senza ▶ vt fus fare a meno di

dock [dɔk] n (Naut) bacino; (Law) banco degli imputati ▶ vi entrare in bacino; (Space) agganciarsi; **~s** npl (Naut) dock m inv

doctor ['dɔktər] n medico(-a); (Ph. D. etc) dottore(-essa) ▶ vt (drink etc) adulterare; **call a ~!** chiamate un dottore!; **Doctor of Philosophy** n

dottorato di ricerca; (person) titolare m/f di un dottorato di ricerca

document ['dɔkjumənt] n documento; **documentary** [-'mɛntəri] adj (evidence) documentato(-a) ▶ n documentario; **documentation** [dɔkjumən'teɪʃən] n documentazione f

dodge [dɔdʒ] n trucco; schivata ▶ vt schivare, eludere

dodgy ['dɔdʒi] adj (inf: uncertain) rischioso(-a); (untrustworthy) sospetto(-a)

does [dʌz] vb see **do**

doesn't ['dʌznt] = **does not**

dog [dɔg] n cane m ▶ vt (follow closely) pedinare; (fig: memory etc) perseguitare; **doggy bag** n sacchetto per gli avanzi (da portare a casa)

do-it-yourself ['duːɪtjɔː'sɛlf] n il far da sé

dole [dəul] n (BRIT) sussidio di disoccupazione; **to be on the ~** vivere del sussidio

doll [dɔl] n bambola

dollar ['dɔlər] n dollaro

dolphin ['dɔlfin] n delfino

dome [dəum] n cupola

domestic [də'mɛstik] adj (duty, happiness, animal) domestico(-a); (policy, affairs, flights) nazionale; **domestic appliance** n elettrodomestico

dominant ['dɔminənt] adj dominante

dominate ['dɔmineit] vt dominare

domino ['dɔminəu] (pl **dominoes**) n domino; **dominoes** n (game) gioco del domino

donate [də'neit] vt donare; **donation** [də'neiʃən] n donazione f

done [dʌn] pp of **do**

donkey ['dɔŋki] n asino

donor ['dəunər] n donatore(-trice); **donor card** n tessera di donatore di organi

don't [dəunt] = **do not**

donut ['dəunʌt] (US) n = **doughnut**

doodle ['du:dl] vi scarabocchiare

doom [du:m] n destino; rovina ▶ vt **to be ~ed (to failure)** essere predestinato(-a) (a fallire)

door [dɔ:ʳ] n porta; **doorbell** n campanello; **door handle** n maniglia; **doorknob** ['dɔ:nɒb] n pomello, maniglia; **doorstep** n gradino della porta; **doorway** n porta

dope [dəup] n (inf: drugs) roba ▶ vt (horse etc) drogare

dormitory ['dɔ:mɪtrɪ] n dormitorio; (US) casa dello studente

DOS [dɒs] n abbr (= disk operating system) DOS m

dosage ['dəusɪdʒ] n posologia

dose [dəus] n dose f; (bout) attacco

dot [dɒt] n punto; macchiolina ▶ vt **~ted with** punteggiato(-a) di; **on the ~** in punto; **dotted line** ['dɒtɪd-] n linea punteggiata

double ['dʌbl] adj doppio(-a) ▶ adv (twice): **to cost ~ sth** costare il doppio (di qc) ▶ n sosia m inv ▶ vt raddoppiare; (fold) piegare doppio or in due ▶ vi raddoppiarsi; **at the ~** (BRIT), **on the ~** a passo di corsa ▷ **double back** vi (person) tornare sui propri passi; **double bass** n contrabbasso; **double bed** n letto matrimoniale; **double-check** vt, vi ricontrollare; **double-click** vi (Comput) fare doppio click; **double-cross** vt fare il doppio gioco con; **doubledecker** n autobus m inv a due piani; **double glazing** (BRIT) n doppi vetri mpl; **double room** n camera matrimoniale; **doubles** n (Tennis) doppio; **double yellow lines** npl (BRIT: Aut) linea gialla doppia continua che segnala il divieto di sosta

doubt [daut] n dubbio ▶ vt dubitare di; **to ~ that** dubitare che + sub; **doubtful** adj dubbioso(-a), incerto(-a); (person) equivoco(-a); **doubtless** adv indubbiamente

dough [dəu] n pasta, impasto; **doughnut** (US **donut**) n bombolone m

dove [dʌv] n colombo(-a)

down [daun] n piume fpl ▶ adv giù, di sotto ▶ prep giù per ▶ vt (inf: drink) scolarsi; **~ with X!** abbasso X!; **down-and-out** n barbone m; **downfall** n caduta; rovina; **downhill** adv **to go downhill** andare in discesa; (fig) lasciarsi andare; andare a rotoli

Downing Street ['daunɪŋ-] n **10 ~** residenza del primo ministro inglese

 ● **Downing Street**
 ● Al numero 10 di **Downing Street**, nel
 ● quartiere di Westminster a Londra,
 ● si trova la residenza del primo
 ● ministro inglese, al numero 11 quella
 ● del **Chancellor of the Exchequer**.

down: **download** vt (Comput) scaricare; **downloadable** adj (Comput) scaricabile; **downright** adj franco(-a); (refusal) assoluto(-a)

Down's syndrome n sindrome f di Down

down: **downstairs** adv di sotto; al piano inferiore; **down-to-earth** adj pratico(-a); **downtown** adv in città; **down under** adv (Australia etc) agli antipodi; **downward** ['daunwəd] adj, adv in giù, in discesa; **downwards** ['daunwədz] adv = **downward**

doz. abbr = **dozen**

doze [dəuz] vi sonnecchiare

dozen ['dʌzn] n dozzina; **a ~ books** una dozzina di libri; **~s of** decine fpl di

Dr. abbr (= doctor) dott.; (in street names) = **drive**

drab [dræb] adj tetro(-a), grigio(-a)

draft [drɑ:ft] n abbozzo; (Pol) bozza; (Comm) tratta; (US: call-up) leva ▶ vt abbozzare; see also **draught**

drag [dræg] vt trascinare; (river) dragare ▶ vi trascinarsi ▶ n (inf)

noioso(-a); noia, fatica; (*women's clothing*): **in ~** travestito (da donna)
dragon ['drægən] n drago
dragonfly ['drægənflaɪ] n libellula
drain [dreɪn] n (*for sewage*) fogna; (*on resources*) salasso ▶ vt (*land, marshes*) prosciugare; (*vegetables*) scolare ▶ vi (*water*) defluire (via); **drainage** n prosciugamento; fognatura; **drainpipe** n tubo di scarico
drama ['drɑːmə] n (*art*) dramma m, teatro; (*play*) commedia; (*event*) dramma; **dramatic** [drə'mætɪk] adj drammatico(-a)
drank [dræŋk] pt of **drink**
drape [dreɪp] vt drappeggiare; **~s** (*US*) npl (*curtains*) tende fpl
drastic ['dræstɪk] adj drastico(-a)
draught [drɑːft] (*US* **draft**) n corrente f d'aria; (*Naut*) pescaggio; **on ~** (*beer*) alla spina; **draught beer** n birra alla spina; **draughts** (*BRIT*) n (gioco della) dama
draw [drɔː] (*pt* **drew**, *pp* **drawn**) vt tirare; (*take out*) estrarre; (*attract*) attirare; (*picture*) disegnare; (*line, circle*) tracciare; (*money*) ritirare ▶ vi (*Sport*) pareggiare ▶ n pareggio; (*in lottery*) estrazione f; **to ~ near** avvicinarsi ▷ **draw out** vi (*lengthen*) allungarsi ▶ vt (*money*) ritirare ▷ **draw up** vi (*stop*) arrestarsi, fermarsi ▶ vt (*chair*) avvicinare; (*document*) compilare; **drawback** n svantaggio, inconveniente m
drawer [drɔːʳ] n cassetto
drawing ['drɔːɪŋ] n disegno; **drawing pin** (*BRIT*) n puntina da disegno; **drawing room** n salotto
drawn [drɔːn] pp of **draw**
dread [drɛd] n terrore m ▶ vt tremare all'idea di; **dreadful** adj terribile
dream [driːm] (*pt, pp* **dreamed** or **dreamt**) n sogno ▶ vt, vi sognare; **dreamer** n sognatore(-trice)

dreamt [drɛmt] pt, pp of **dream**
dreary ['drɪərɪ] adj tetro(-a); monotono(-a)
drench [drɛntʃ] vt inzuppare
dress [drɛs] n vestito; (*no pl: clothing*) abbigliamento ▶ vt vestire; (*wound*) fasciare ▶ vi vestirsi; **to get ~ed** vestirsi ▷ **dress up** vi vestirsi a festa; (*in fancy dress*) vestirsi in costume; **dress circle** (*BRIT*) n prima galleria; **dresser** n (*BRIT: cupboard*) credenza; (*US*) cassettone m; **dressing** n (*Med*) benda; (*Culin*) condimento; **dressing gown** (*BRIT*) n vestaglia; **dressing room** n (*Theatre*) camerino; (*Sport*) spogliatoio; **dressing table** n toilette f inv; **dressmaker** n sarta
drew [druː] pt of **draw**
dribble ['drɪbl] vi (*baby*) sbavare ▶ vt (*ball*) dribblare
dried [draɪd] adj (*fruit, beans*) secco(-a); (*eggs, milk*) in polvere
drier ['draɪəʳ] n = **dryer**
drift [drɪft] n (*of current etc*) direzione f; forza; (*of snow*) cumulo; turbine m; (*general meaning*) senso ▶ vi (*boat*) essere trasportato(-a) dalla corrente; (*sand, snow*) ammucchiarsi
drill [drɪl] n trapano; (*Mil*) esercitazione f ▶ vt trapanare; (*troops*) addestrare ▶ vi (*for oil*) fare trivellazioni
drink [drɪŋk] (*pt* **drank**, *pp* **drunk**) n bevanda, bibita; (*alcoholic drink*) bicchierino; (*sip*) sorso ▶ vt, vi bere; **to have a ~** bere qualcosa; **would you like a ~?** vuoi qualcosa da bere?; **a ~ of water** un po' d'acqua; **drink-driving** n guida in stato di ebbrezza; **drinker** n bevitore(-trice); **drinking water** n acqua potabile
drip [drɪp] n goccia; gocciolamento; (*Med*) fleboclisi f inv ▶ vi gocciolare; (*tap*) sgocciolare
drive [draɪv] (*pt* **drove**, *pp* **driven**)

n passeggiata *or* giro in macchina; (*also*: **~way**) viale *m* d'accesso; (*energy*) energia; (*campaign*) campagna; (*also*: **disk ~**) lettore *m* ▶ *vt* guidare; (*nail*) piantare; (*push*) cacciare, spingere; (*Tech: motor*) azionare; far funzionare ▶ *vi* (*Aut: at controls*) guidare; (: *travel*) andare in macchina; **left-/right-hand ~** guida a sinistra/destra; **to ~ sb mad** far impazzire qn ▷ **drive out** *vt* (*force out*) cacciare, mandare via; **drive-in** (*esp US*) *adj, n* drive-in (*m inv*)

driven ['drɪvn] *pp of* **drive**

driver ['draɪvə'] *n* conducente *m/f*; (*of taxi*) tassista *m*; (*chauffeur: of bus*) autista *m/f*; **driver's license** (*US*) *n* patente *f* di guida

driveway ['draɪvweɪ] *n* viale *m* d'accesso

driving ['draɪvɪŋ] *n* guida; **driving instructor** *n* istruttore(-trice) di scuola guida; **driving lesson** *n* lezione *f* di guida; **driving licence** (*BRIT*) *n* patente *f* di guida; **driving test** *n* esame *m* di guida

drizzle ['drɪzl] *n* pioggerella

droop [druːp] *vi* (*flower*) appassire; (*head, shoulders*) chinarsi

drop [drɔp] *n* (*of water*) goccia; (*lessening*) diminuzione *f*; (*fall*) caduta ▶ *vt* lasciare cadere; (*voice, eyes, price*) abbassare; (*set down from car*) far scendere; (*name from list*) lasciare fuori ▶ *vi* cascare; (*wind*) abbassarsi ▷ **drop in** *vi* (*inf: visit*): **to ~ in (on)** fare un salto (da), passare (da) ▷ **drop off** *vi* (*sleep*) addormentarsi ▶ *vt* (*passenger*) far scendere ▷ **drop out** *vi* (*withdraw*) ritirarsi; (*student etc*) smettere di studiare

drought [draʊt] *n* siccità *f inv*

drove [drəʊv] *pt of* **drive**

drown [draʊn] *vt* affogare; (*fig: noise*) soffocare ▶ *vi* affogare

drowsy ['draʊzɪ] *adj* sonnolento(-a),

assonnato(-a)

drug [drʌg] *n* farmaco; (*narcotic*) droga ▶ *vt* drogare; **to be on ~s** drogarsi; (*Med*) prendere medicinali; **hard/soft ~s** droghe pesanti/leggere; **drug addict** *n* tossicomane *m/f*; **drug dealer** *n* trafficante *m/f* di droga; **druggist** (*US*) *n* persona che gestisce un *drugstore*; **drugstore** (*US*) *n* drugstore *m inv*

drum [drʌm] *n* tamburo; (*for oil, petrol*) fusto ▶ *vi* tamburellare; **~s** *npl* (*set of drums*) batteria; **drummer** *n* batterista *m/f*

drunk [drʌŋk] *pp of* **drink** ▶ *adj* ubriaco(-a); ebbro(-a) ▶ *n* (*also*: **~ard**) ubriacone(-a); **drunken** *adj* ubriaco(-a); da ubriaco

dry [draɪ] *adj* secco(-a); (*day, clothes*) asciutto(-a) ▶ *vt* seccare; (*clothes, hair, hands*) asciugare ▶ *vi* asciugarsi ▷ **dry off** *vi* asciugarsi ▶ *vt* asciugare ▷ **dry up** *vi* seccarsi; **dry-cleaner's** *n* lavasecco *m inv*; **dry-cleaning** *n* pulitura a secco; **dryer** *n* (*for hair*) föhn *m inv*, asciugacapelli *m inv*; (*for clothes*) asciugabiancheria; (*US: spin-dryer*) centrifuga

DSS *n abbr* (= *Department of Social Security*) ministero della Previdenza sociale

DTP *n abbr* (= *desk-top publishing*) desktop publishing *m inv*

dual ['djuəl] *adj* doppio(-a); **dual carriageway** (*BRIT*) *n* strada a doppia carreggiata

dubious ['djuːbɪəs] *adj* dubbio(-a)

Dublin ['dʌblɪn] *n* Dublino *f*

duck [dʌk] *n* anatra ▶ *vi* abbassare la testa

due [djuː] *adj* dovuto(-a); (*expected*) atteso(-a); (*fitting*) giusto(-a) ▶ *n* dovuto ▶ *adv* **~ north** diritto verso nord

duel ['djuəl] *n* duello

duet [djuː'ɛt] n duetto

dug [dʌg] pt, pp of **dig**

duke [djuːk] n duca m

dull [dʌl] adj (light) debole; (boring) noioso(-a); (slow-witted) ottuso(-a); (sound, pain) sordo(-a); (weather, day) fosco(-a), scuro(-a) ▶ vt (pain, grief) attutire; (mind, senses) intorpidire

dumb [dʌm] adj muto(-a); (pej) stupido(-a)

dummy ['dʌmɪ] n (tailor's model) manichino; (Tech, Comm) riproduzione f; (BRIT: for baby) tettarella ▶ adj falso(-a), finto(-a)

dump [dʌmp] n (also: **rubbish ~**) discarica di rifiuti; (inf: place) buco ▶ vt (put down) scaricare; mettere giù; (get rid of) buttar via

dumpling ['dʌmplɪŋ] n specie di gnocco

dune [djuːn] n duna

dungarees [dʌŋgə'riːz] npl tuta

dungeon ['dʌndʒən] n prigione f sotterranea

duplex ['djuːplɛks] (US) n (house) casa con muro divisorio in comune con un'altra; (apartment) appartamento su due piani

duplicate [n 'djuːplɪkət, vb 'djuːplɪkeɪt] n doppio ▶ vt duplicare; **in ~** in doppia copia

durable ['djuərəbl] adj durevole; (clothes, metal) resistente

duration [djuə'reɪʃən] n durata

during ['djuərɪŋ] prep durante, nel corso di

dusk [dʌsk] n crepuscolo

dust [dʌst] n polvere f ▶ vt (furniture) spolverare; (cake etc): **to ~ with** cospargere con; **dustbin** (BRIT) n pattumiera; **duster** n straccio per la polvere; **dustman** (irreg: BRIT) n netturbino; **dustpan** n pattumiera; **dusty** adj polveroso(-a)

Dutch [dʌtʃ] adj olandese ▶ n (Ling) olandese m; **the ~** npl gli Olandesi;

to go ~ (inf) fare alla romana; **Dutchman, Dutchwoman** (irreg) n olandese m/f

duty ['djuːtɪ] n dovere m; (tax) dazio, tassa; **on ~** di servizio; **off ~** libero(-a), fuori servizio; **duty-free** adj esente da dazio

duvet ['duːveɪ] (BRIT) n piumino, piumone m

DVD n abbr (= digital versatile or video disk) DVD m inv; **DVD player** n lettore m DVD

dwarf [dwɔːf] n nano(-a) ▶ vt far apparire piccolo

dwell [dwɛl] (pt, pp **dwelt**) vi dimorare ▷ **dwell on** vt fus indugiare su

dwelt [dwɛlt] pt, pp of **dwell**

dwindle ['dwɪndl] vi diminuire

dye [daɪ] n tinta ▶ vt tingere

dying ['daɪɪŋ] adj morente, moribondo(-a)

dynamic [daɪ'næmɪk] adj dinamico(-a)

dynamite ['daɪnəmaɪt] n dinamite f

dyslexia [dɪs'lɛksɪə] n dislessia

dyslexic [dɪs'lɛksɪk] adj, n dislessico(-a)

e

E [i:] n (Mus) mi m

E111 n abbr (also: **form ~**) E111 (modulo CEE per rimborso spese mediche)

each [i:tʃ] adj ogni, ciascuno(-a) ▶ pron ciascuno(-a), ognuno(-a); **~ one** ognuno(-a); **~ other** si o ci etc; **they hate ~ other** si odiano (l'uno l'altro); **you are jealous of ~ other** siete gelosi l'uno dell'altro; **they have 2 books ~** hanno 2 libri ciascuno

eager ['i:gəʳ] adj impaziente, desideroso(-a); ardente; **to be ~ for** essere desideroso di, aver gran voglia di

eagle ['i:gl] n aquila

ear [ɪəʳ] n orecchio; (of corn) pannocchia; **earache** n mal m d'orecchi; **eardrum** n timpano

earl [ə:l] (BRIT) n conte m

earlier ['ə:lɪəʳ] adj precedente ▶ adv prima

early ['ə:lɪ] adv presto, di buon'ora; (ahead of time) in anticipo ▶ adj (near the beginning) primo(-a); (sooner than expected) prematuro(-a); (quick: reply) veloce; **at an ~ hour** di buon'ora; **to have an ~ night** andare a letto presto; **in the ~ or ~ in the spring/19th century** all'inizio della primavera/dell'Ottocento; **early retirement** n ritiro anticipato

earmark ['ɪəmɑːk] vt **to ~ sth for** destinare qc a

earn [ə:n] vt guadagnare; (rest, reward) meritare

earnest ['ə:nɪst] adj serio(-a); **in ~** sul serio

earnings ['ə:nɪŋz] npl guadagni mpl; (salary) stipendio

ear: **earphones** ['ɪəfəunz] npl cuffia; **earplugs** npl tappi mpl per le orecchie; **earring** ['ɪərɪŋ] n orecchino

earth [ə:θ] n terra ▶ vt (BRIT Elec) mettere a terra; **earthquake** n terremoto

ease [i:z] n agio, comodo ▶ vt (soothe) calmare; (loosen) allentare; **to ~ sth out/in** tirare fuori/infilare qc con delicatezza; facilitare l'uscita/l'entrata di qc; **at ~** a proprio agio; (Mil) a riposo

easily ['i:zɪlɪ] adv facilmente

east [i:st] n est m ▶ adj dell'est ▶ adv a oriente; **the E~** l'Oriente m; (Pol) l'Est; **eastbound** ['i:stbaund] adj (traffic) diretto(-a) a est; (carriageway) che porta a est

Easter ['i:stəʳ] n Pasqua; **Easter egg** n uovo di Pasqua

eastern ['i:stən] adj orientale, d'oriente; dell'est

Easter Sunday n domenica di Pasqua

easy ['i:zɪ] adj facile; (manner) disinvolto(-a) ▶ adv **to take it** or **things ~** prendersela con calma; **easy-going** adj accomodante

eat [i:t] (pt **ate**, pp **eaten**) vt, vi mangiare; **can we have something to ~?** possiamo mangiare qualcosa? ▷ **eat out** vi mangiare fuori

eavesdrop ['i:vzdrɔp] vi **to ~ (on a conversation)** origliare (una conversazione)

e-book ['i:buk] n libro elettronico

e-business ['i:bɪznɪs] n (company) azienda che opera in Internet; (commerce) commercio elettronico

EC n abbr (= European Community) CE f

eccentric [ɪk'sɛntrɪk] adj, n

eccentrico(-a)

echo ['ɛkəʊ] (pl **echoes**) n eco m or f ▶ vt
ripetere; fare eco a ▶ vi echeggiare;
dare un eco

eclipse [ɪ'klɪps] n eclissi f inv

eco-friendly [i:kəʊ'frɛndlɪ] adj
ecologico(-a)

ecological [i:kə'lɒdʒɪkəl] adj
ecologico(-a)

ecology [ɪ'kɒlədʒɪ] n ecologia

e-commerce [i:kɔmə:s] n commercio
elettronico

economic [i:kə'nɒmɪk] adj
economico(-a); **economical** adj
economico(-a); (person) economo(-a);
economics n economia ▶ npl lato
finanziario

economist [ɪ'kɒnəmɪst] n
economista m/f

economize [ɪ'kɒnəmaɪz] vi
risparmiare, fare economia

economy [ɪ'kɒnəmɪ] n economia;
economy class n (Aviat) classe f
turistica; **economy class syndrome**
n sindrome f della classe economica

ecstasy ['ɛkstəsɪ] n estasi f inv;
ecstatic [ɛks'tætɪk] adj estatico(-a),
in estasi

eczema ['ɛksɪmə] n eczema m

edge [ɛdʒ] n margine m; (of table,
plate, cup) orlo; (of knife etc) taglio ▶ vt
bordare; **on ~** (fig) = **edgy**; **to edge
away from** sgattaiolare da

edgy ['ɛdʒɪ] adj nervoso(-a)

edible ['ɛdɪbl] adj commestibile; (meal)
mangiabile

Edinburgh ['ɛdɪnbərə] n Edimburgo f

edit ['ɛdɪt] vt curare; **edition** [ɪ'dɪʃən]
n edizione f; **editor** n (in newspaper)
redattore(-trice), redattore(-trice)
capo; (of sb's work) curatore(-trice);
editorial [-'tɔ:rɪəl] adj redazionale,
editoriale ▶ n editoriale m

▌ Be careful not to translate **editor**
by the Italian word **editore**.

educate ['ɛdjʊkeɪt] vt istruire;
educare; **educated** adj istruito(-a)

education [ɛdjʊ'keɪʃən] n educazione
f; (schooling) istruzione f; **educational**
adj pedagogico(-a); scolastico(-a);
istruttivo(-a)

eel [i:l] n anguilla

eerie ['ɪərɪ] adj che fa accapponare
la pelle

effect [ɪ'fɛkt] n effetto ▶ vt effettuare;
to take ~ (law) entrare in vigore; (drug)
fare effetto; **in ~** effettivamente;
~s npl (Theat) effetti mpl scenici;
(property) effetti mpl; **effective**
adj efficace; (actual) effettivo(-a);
effectively adv efficacemente;
effettivamente

efficiency [ɪ'fɪʃənsɪ] n efficienza;
rendimento effettivo

efficient [ɪ'fɪʃənt] adj efficiente;
efficiently adv efficientemente;
efficacemente

effort ['ɛfət] n sforzo; **effortless** adj
senza sforzo, facile

e.g. adv abbr (= exempli gratia) per
esempio, p.es.

egg [ɛg] n uovo; **hard-boiled/soft-
boiled ~** uovo sodo/alla coque;
eggcup n portauovo m inv; **eggplant**
(esp US) n melanzana; **eggshell** n
guscio d'uovo; **egg white** n albume
m, bianco d'uovo; **egg yolk** n tuorlo,
rosso (d'uovo)

ego ['i:gəʊ] n ego m inv

Egypt ['i:dʒɪpt] n Egitto; **Egyptian**
[ɪ'dʒɪpʃən] adj, n egiziano(-a)

eight [eɪt] num otto; **eighteen**
num diciotto; **eighteenth** num
diciottesimo(-a); **eighth** [eɪtθ] num
ottavo(-a); **eightieth** ['eɪtɪɪθ] num
ottantesimo(-a); **eighty** num ottanta

Eire ['ɛərə] n Repubblica d'Irlanda

either ['aɪðər] adj l'uno(-a) o l'altro(-a);
(both, each) ciascuno(-a) ▶ pron **~ (of
them)** (o) l'uno(-a) o l'altro(-a) ▶ adv

neanche ▶ *conj* ~ **good or bad** o buono
o cattivo; **on ~ side** su ciascun lato; **I
don't like ~** non mi piace né l'uno né
l'altro; **no, I don't ~** no, neanch'io
eject [ɪ'dʒɛkt] *vt* espellere; lanciare
elaborate [*adj* ɪ'læbərɪt, *vb* ɪ'læbəreɪt]
adj elaborato(-a), minuzioso(-a) ▶ *vt*
elaborare ▶ *vi* fornire i particolari
elastic [ɪ'læstɪk] *adj* elastico(-a)
▶ *n* elastico; **elastic band** (*BRIT*) *n*
elastico
elbow ['ɛlbəʊ] *n* gomito
elder ['ɛldə'] *adj* maggiore, più
vecchio(-a) ▶ *n* (*tree*) sambuco;
one's ~s i più anziani; **elderly** *adj*
anziano(-a) ▶ *npl* **the elderly** gli
anziani
eldest ['ɛldɪst] *adj, n* **the ~ (child)** il(la)
maggiore (dei bambini)
elect [ɪ'lɛkt] *vt* eleggere ▶ *adj* **the
president ~** il presidente designato;
to ~ to do decidere di fare; **election**
[ɪ'lɛkʃən] *n* elezione *f*; **electoral**
[ɪ'lɛktərəl] *adj* elettorale; **electorate**
n elettorato
electric [ɪ'lɛktrɪk] *adj* elettrico(-a);
electrical *adj* elettrico(-a); **electric
blanket** *n* coperta elettrica; **electric
fire** *n* stufa elettrica; **electrician**
[ɪlɛk'trɪʃən] *n* elettricista *m*;
electricity [ɪlɛk'trɪsɪtɪ] *n* elettricità;
electric shock *n* scossa (elettrica);
electrify [ɪ'lɛktrɪfaɪ] *vt* (*Rail*)
elettrificare; (*audience*) elettrizzare
electronic [ɪlɛk'trɔnɪk] *adj*
elettronico(-a); **electronic mail**
n posta elettronica; **electronics** *n*
elettronica
elegance ['ɛlɪgəns] *n* eleganza
elegant ['ɛlɪgənt] *adj* elegante
element ['ɛlɪmənt] *n* elemento; (*of
heater, kettle etc*) resistenza
elementary [ɛlɪ'mɛntərɪ] *adj*
elementare; **elementary school** (*US*)
n scuola elementare

elephant ['ɛlɪfənt] *n* elefante(-essa)
elevate ['ɛlɪveɪt] *vt* elevare
elevator ['ɛlɪveɪtə'] *n* elevatore *m*; (*US:
lift*) ascensore *m*
eleven [ɪ'lɛvn] *num* undici; **eleventh**
adj undicesimo(-a)
eligible ['ɛlɪdʒəbl] *adj* eleggibile; (*for
membership*) che ha i requisiti
eliminate [ɪ'lɪmɪneɪt] *vt* eliminare
elm [ɛlm] *n* olmo
eloquent ['ɛləkwənt] *adj* eloquente
else [ɛls] *adv* altro; **something ~**
qualcos'altro; **somewhere ~** altrove;
everywhere ~ in qualsiasi altro
luogo; **nobody ~** nessun altro; **where
~?** in quale altro luogo?; **little ~** poco
altro; **elsewhere** *adv* altrove
elusive [ɪ'luːsɪv] *adj* elusivo(-a)
e-mail *n abbr* (= *electronic mail*)
posta elettronica ▶ *vt* mandare un
messaggio di posta elettronica a;
e-mail address *n* indirizzo di posta
elettronica
embankment [ɪm'bæŋkmənt] *n* (*of
road, railway*) terrapieno
embargo [ɪm'bɑːgəʊ] *n* (*pl
embargoes*) (*Comm, Naut*) embargo
▶ *vt* mettere l'embargo su; **to put an ~
on sth** mettere l'embargo su qc
embark [ɪm'bɑːk] *vi* **to ~ (on)**
imbarcarsi (su) ▶ *vt* imbarcare; **to ~ on**
(*fig*) imbarcarsi in
embarrass [ɪm'bærəs] *vt*
imbarazzare; **embarrassed** *adj*
imbarazzato(-a); **embarrassing** *adj*
imbarazzante; **embarrassment** *n*
imbarazzo
embassy ['ɛmbəsɪ] *n* ambasciata
embrace [ɪm'breɪs] *vt* abbracciare ▶ *vi*
abbracciarsi ▶ *n* abbraccio
embroider [ɪm'brɔɪdə'] *vt* ricamare;
embroidery *n* ricamo
embryo ['ɛmbrɪəʊ] *n* embrione *m*
emerald ['ɛmərəld] *n* smeraldo
emerge [ɪ'məːdʒ] *vi* emergere

emergency [ɪˈməːdʒənsɪ] n
emergenza; **in an ~** in caso di
emergenza; **emergency brake** (US)
n freno a mano; **emergency exit**
n uscita di sicurezza; **emergency
landing** n atterraggio forzato;
emergency room (US: Med) n pronto
soccorso; **emergency services** npl
(fire, police, ambulance) servizi mpl di
pronto intervento

emigrate [ˈɛmɪgreɪt] vi emigrare;
emigration [ɛmɪˈgreɪʃən] n
emigrazione f

eminent [ˈɛmɪnənt] adj eminente

emissions [ɪˈmɪʃənz] npl emissioni fpl

emit [ɪˈmɪt] vt emettere

emoticon [ɪˈməutɪkən] n (Comput)
faccina

emotion [ɪˈməuʃən] n emozione f;
emotional adj (person) emotivo(-a);
(scene) commovente; (tone, speech)
carico(-a) d'emozione

emperor [ˈɛmpərər] n imperatore m

emphasis [ˈɛmfəsɪs] (pl -ases) n enfasi
f inv; importanza

emphasize [ˈɛmfəsaɪz] vt (word,
point) sottolineare; (feature) mettere
in evidenza

empire [ˈɛmpaɪər] n impero

employ [ɪmˈplɔɪ] vt impiegare;
employee [-ˈiː] n impiegato(-a);
employer n principale m/f, datore m
di lavoro; **employment** n impiego;
employment agency n agenzia di
collocamento

empower [ɪmˈpauər] vt **to ~ sb to do**
concedere autorità a qn di fare

empress [ˈɛmprɪs] n imperatrice f

emptiness [ˈɛmptɪnɪs] n vuoto

empty [ˈɛmptɪ] adj vuoto(-a); (threat,
promise) vano(-a) ▶ vt vuotare ▶ vi
vuotarsi; (liquid) scaricarsi; **empty-
handed** adj a mani vuote

EMU n abbr (= economic and monetary
union) unione f economica e monetaria

emulsion [ɪˈmʌlʃən] n emulsione f

enable [ɪˈneɪbl] vt **to ~ sb to do**
permettere a qn di fare

enamel [ɪˈnæməl] n smalto; (also: ~
paint) vernice f a smalto

enchanting [ɪnˈtʃɑːntɪŋ] adj
incantevole, affascinante

encl. abbr (= enclosed) all.

enclose [ɪnˈkləuz] vt (land) circondare,
recingere; (letter etc): **to ~ (with)**
allegare (con); **please find ~d** trovi
qui accluso

enclosure [ɪnˈkləuʒər] n recinto

encore [ɔŋˈkɔːʳ] excl bis ▶ n bis m inv

encounter [ɪnˈkauntər] n incontro
▶ vt incontrare

encourage [ɪnˈkʌrɪdʒ] vt
incoraggiare; **encouragement** n
incoraggiamento

encouraging [ɪnˈkʌrɪdʒɪŋ] adj
incoraggiante

encyclop(a)edia [ɛnsaɪkləuˈpiːdɪə] n
enciclopedia

end [ɛnd] n fine f; (aim) fine m; (of table)
bordo estremo; (of pointed object)
punta ▶ vt finire; (also: **bring to an ~,
put an ~ to**) mettere fine a ▶ vi finire;
in the ~ alla fine; **on ~** (object) ritto(-a);
to stand on ~ (hair) rizzarsi; **for hours
on ~** per ore ed ore ▷ **end up** vi **to ~ up
in** finire in

endanger [ɪnˈdeɪndʒər] vt mettere
in pericolo

endearing [ɪnˈdɪərɪŋ] adj accattivante

endeavour [ɪnˈdɛvər] (US **endeavor**)
n sforzo, tentativo ▶ vi **to ~ to do**
cercare or sforzarsi di fare

ending [ˈɛndɪŋ] n fine f, conclusione f;
(Ling) desinenza

endless [ˈɛndlɪs] adj senza fine

endorse [ɪnˈdɔːs] vt (cheque) girare;
(approve) approvare, appoggiare;
endorsement n approvazione f

endurance [ɪnˈdjuərəns] n
resistenza; pazienza

endure [ɪn'djuər] vt sopportare, resistere a ▸ vi durare

enemy ['ɛnəmɪ] adj, n nemico(-a)

energetic [ɛnə'dʒɛtɪk] adj energico(-a), attivo(-a)

energy ['ɛnədʒɪ] n energia

enforce [ɪn'fɔːs] vt (Law) applicare, far osservare

engaged [ɪn'geɪdʒd] adj (BRIT: busy, in use) occupato(-a); (betrothed) fidanzato(-a); **the line's ~** la linea è occupata; **to get ~** fidanzarsi; **engaged tone** (BRIT) n (Tel) segnale m di occupato

engagement [ɪn'geɪdʒmənt] n impegno, obbligo; appuntamento; (to marry) fidanzamento; **engagement ring** n anello di fidanzamento

engaging [ɪn'geɪdʒɪŋ] adj attraente

engine ['ɛndʒɪn] n (Aut) motore m; (Rail) locomotiva

engineer [ɛndʒɪ'nɪər] n ingegnere m; (BRIT: for repairs) tecnico; (on ship: US: Rail) macchinista m; **engineering** n ingegneria

England ['ɪŋglənd] n Inghilterra

English ['ɪŋglɪʃ] adj inglese ▸ n (Ling) inglese m; **the ~** npl gli Inglesi; **English Channel** n **the English Channel** la Manica; **Englishman** (irreg) n inglese m; **Englishwoman** (irreg) n inglese f

engrave [ɪn'greɪv] vt incidere

engraving [ɪn'greɪvɪŋ] n incisione f

enhance [ɪn'hɑːns] vt accrescere

enjoy [ɪn'dʒɔɪ] vt godere; (have: success, fortune) avere; **to ~ o.s.** godersela, divertirsi; **enjoyable** adj piacevole; **enjoyment** n piacere m, godimento

enlarge [ɪn'lɑːdʒ] vt ingrandire ▸ vi **to ~ on** (subject) dilungarsi su; **enlargement** n (Phot) ingrandimento

enlist [ɪn'lɪst] vt arruolare; (support) procurare ▸ vi arruolarsi

enormous [ɪ'nɔːməs] adj enorme

enough [ɪ'nʌf] adj, n ~ **time/books** assai tempo/libri; **have you got ~?** ne ha abbastanza or a sufficienza? ▸ adv **big ~** abbastanza grande; **he has not worked ~** non ha lavorato abbastanza; **~!** basta!; **that's ~, thanks** basta così, grazie; **I've had ~ of him** ne ho abbastanza di lui; **...which, funnily** or **oddly ~** ... che, strano a dirsi

enquire [ɪn'kwaɪər] vt, vi (esp BRIT) = **inquire**

enquiry [ɪn'kwaɪrɪ] n (esp BRIT) = **inquiry**

enrage [ɪn'reɪdʒ] vt fare arrabbiare

enrich [ɪn'rɪtʃ] vt arricchire

enrol [ɪn'rəul] (US **enroll**) vt iscrivere ▸ vi iscriversi; **enrolment** (US **enrollment**) n iscrizione f

en route [ɔn'ruːt] adv ~ **for/from/to** in viaggio per/da/a

en suite [ɔn'swiːt] adj **room with ~ bathroom** camera con bagno

ensure [ɪn'ʃuər] vt assicurare; garantire

entail [ɪn'teɪl] vt comportare

enter ['ɛntər] vt entrare in; (army) arruolarsi in; (competition) partecipare a; (sb for a competition) iscrivere; (write down) registrare; (Comput) inserire ▸ vi entrare

enterprise ['ɛntəpraɪz] n (undertaking, company) impresa; (spirit) iniziativa; **free ~** liberalismo economico; **private ~** iniziativa privata; **enterprising** ['ɛntəpraɪzɪŋ] adj intraprendente

entertain [ɛntə'teɪn] vt divertire; (invite) ricevere; (idea, plan) nutrire; **entertainer** n comico(-a); **entertaining** adj divertente; **entertainment** n (amusement) divertimento; (show) spettacolo

enthusiasm [ɪn'θuːzɪæzəm] n entusiasmo

enthusiast [ɪnˈθuːzɪæst] n entusiasta m/f; **enthusiastic** [-ˈæstɪk] adj entusiasta, entusiastico(-a); **to be enthusiastic about sth/sb** essere appassionato(-a) di qc/entusiasta di qn

entire [ɪnˈtaɪəʳ] adj intero(-a); **entirely** adv completamente, interamente

entitle [ɪnˈtaɪtl] vt (give right): **to ~ sb to sth/to do** dare diritto a qn a qc/a fare; **entitled** adj (book) che si intitola; **to be entitled to do** avere il diritto di fare

entrance [n ˈɛntrns, vb ɪnˈtrɑːns] n entrata, ingresso; (of person) entrata ▶vt incantare, rapire; **where's the ~?** dov'è l'entrata?; **to gain ~ to** (university etc) essere ammesso a; **entrance examination** n esame m di ammissione; **entrance fee** n tassa d'iscrizione; (to museum etc) prezzo d'ingresso; **entrance ramp** (US) n (Aut) rampa di accesso; **entrant** n partecipante m/f; concorrente m/f

entrepreneur [ɔntrəprəˈnəːʳ] n imprenditore m

entrust [ɪnˈtrʌst] vt **to ~ sth to** affidare qc a

entry [ˈɛntrɪ] n entrata; (way in) entrata, ingresso; (item: on list) iscrizione f; (in dictionary) voce f; **no ~** vietato l'ingresso; (Aut) divieto di accesso; **entry phone** n citofono

envelope [ˈɛnvələup] n busta

envious [ˈɛnvɪəs] adj invidioso(-a)

environment [ɪnˈvaɪərnmənt] n ambiente m; **environmental** [-ˈmɛntl] adj ecologico(-a); ambientale; **environmentally** [ɪnvaɪərənˈmɛntəlɪ] adv **environmentally sound/friendly** che rispetta l'ambiente

envisage [ɪnˈvɪzɪdʒ] vt immaginare; prevedere

envoy [ˈɛnvɔɪ] n inviato(-a)

envy [ˈɛnvɪ] n invidia ▶vt invidiare; **to ~ sb sth** invidiare qn per qc

epic [ˈɛpɪk] n poema m epico ▶adj epico(-a)

epidemic [ɛpɪˈdɛmɪk] n epidemia

epilepsy [ˈɛpɪlɛpsɪ] n epilessia

epileptic [ɛpɪˈlɛptɪk] adj, n epilettico(-a); **epileptic fit** n attacco epilettico

episode [ˈɛpɪsəud] n episodio

equal [ˈiːkwl] adj uguale ▶n pari m/f inv ▶vt uguagliare; **~ to** (task) all'altezza di; **equality** [iːˈkwɔlɪtɪ] n uguaglianza; **equalize** vi pareggiare; **equally** adv ugualmente

equation [ɪˈkweɪʃən] n (Math) equazione f

equator [ɪˈkweɪtəʳ] n equatore m

equip [ɪˈkwɪp] vt equipaggiare, attrezzare; **to ~ sb/sth with** fornire qn/qc di; **to be well ~ped** (office etc) essere ben attrezzato(-a); **he is well ~ped for the job** ha i requisiti necessari per quel lavoro; **equipment** n attrezzatura; (electrical etc) apparecchiatura

equivalent [ɪˈkwɪvələnt] adj equivalente ▶n equivalente m; **to be ~ to** equivalere a

ER abbr (BRIT) = **Elizabeth Regina**; (US: Med) = **emergency room**

era [ˈɪərə] n era, età f inv

erase [ɪˈreɪz] vt cancellare; **eraser** n gomma

erect [ɪˈrɛkt] adj eretto(-a) ▶vt costruire; (assemble) montare; **erection** [ɪˈrɛkʃən] n costruzione f; montaggio; (Physiol) erezione f

ERM n (= Exchange Rate Mechanism) ERM m

erode [ɪˈrəud] vt erodere; (metal) corrodere

erosion [ɪˈrəuʒən] n erosione f

erotic [ɪˈrɔtɪk] adj erotico(-a)

errand [ˈɛrnd] n commissione f

erratic [ɪˈrætɪk] *adj* imprevedibile; (*person, mood*) incostante

error [ˈɛrəʳ] *n* errore *m*

erupt [ɪˈrʌpt] *vi* (*volcano*) mettersi (*or* essere) in eruzione; (*war, crisis*) scoppiare; **eruption** [ɪˈrʌpʃən] *n* eruzione *f*; scoppio

escalate [ˈɛskəleɪt] *vi* intensificarsi

escalator [ˈɛskəleɪtəʳ] *n* scala mobile

escape [ɪˈskeɪp] *n* evasione *f*; fuga; (*of gas etc*) fuga, fuoriuscita ▶ *vi* fuggire; (*from jail*) evadere, scappare; (*leak*) uscire ▶ *vt* sfuggire a; **to ~ from** (*place*) fuggire da; (*person*) sfuggire a

escort [*n* ˈɛskɔːt, *vb* ɪˈskɔːt] *n* scorta; (*male companion*) cavaliere *m* ▶ *vt* scortare; accompagnare

especially [ɪˈspɛʃlɪ] *adv* specialmente; soprattutto; espressamente

espionage [ˈɛspɪənɑːʒ] *n* spionaggio

essay [ˈɛseɪ] *n* (*Scol*) composizione *f*

essence [ˈɛsns] *n* essenza

essential [ɪˈsɛnʃl] *adj* essenziale ▶ *n* elemento essenziale; **essentially** *adv* essenzialmente; **essentials** *npl* **the essentials** l'essenziale *msg*

establish [ɪˈstæblɪʃ] *vt* stabilire; (*business*) mettere su; (*one's power etc*) affermare; **establishment** *n* stabilimento; **the Establishment** la classe dirigente, l'establishment *m*

estate [ɪˈsteɪt] *n* proprietà *f inv*; beni *mpl*, patrimonio; (*BRIT: also:* **housing ~**) complesso edilizio; **estate agent** (*BRIT*) *n* agente *m* immobiliare

estimate [*n* ˈɛstɪmət, *vb* ˈɛstɪmeɪt] *n* stima; (*Comm*) preventivo ▶ *vt* stimare, valutare

etc *abbr* (= *et cetera*) etc., ecc.

eternal [ɪˈtəːnl] *adj* eterno(-a)

eternity [ɪˈtəːnɪtɪ] *n* eternità

ethical [ˈɛθɪkl] *adj* etico(-a), morale; **ethics** [ˈɛθɪks] *n* etica ▶ *npl* morale *f*

Ethiopia [iːθɪˈəupɪə] *n* Etiopia

ethnic [ˈɛθnɪk] *adj* etnico(-a); **ethnic**

minority *n* minoranza etnica

e-ticket [ˈiːtɪkɪt] *n* biglietto elettronico

etiquette [ˈɛtɪkɛt] *n* etichetta

EU *n abbr* (= *European Union*) UE *f*

euro [ˈjuərəu] *n* (*currency*) euro *m inv*

Europe [ˈjuərəp] *n* Europa; **European** [-ˈpiːən] *adj, n* europeo(-a); **European Community** *n* Comunità Europea; **European Union** *n* Unione *f* europea

Eurostar® [ˈjuərəustɑːʳ] *n* Eurostar® *m inv*

evacuate [ɪˈvækjueɪt] *vt* evacuare

evade [ɪˈveɪd] *vt* (*tax*) evadere; (*duties etc*) sottrarsi a; (*person*) schivare

evaluate [ɪˈvæljueɪt] *vt* valutare

evaporate [ɪˈvæpəreɪt] *vi* evaporare

eve [iːv] *n* **on the ~ of** alla vigilia di

even [ˈiːvn] *adj* regolare; (*number*) pari *inv* ▶ *adv* anche, perfino; **~ if, ~ though** anche se; **~ more** ancora di più; **~ so** ciò nonostante; **not ~** nemmeno; **to get ~ with sb** dare la pari a qn

evening [ˈiːvnɪŋ] *n* sera; (*as duration, event*) serata; **in the ~** la sera; **evening class** *n* corso serale; **evening dress** *n* (*woman's*) abito da sera; **in evening dress** (*man*) in abito scuro; (*woman*) in abito lungo

event [ɪˈvɛnt] *n* avvenimento; (*Sport*) gara; **in the ~ of** in caso di; **eventful** *adj* denso(-a) di eventi

eventual [ɪˈvɛntʃuəl] *adj* finale

> Be careful not to translate **eventual** by the Italian word *eventuale*.

eventually [ɪˈvɛntʃuəlɪ] *adv* alla fine

> Be careful not to translate **eventually** by the Italian word *eventualmente*.

ever [ˈɛvəʳ] *adv* mai; (*at all times*) sempre; **the best ~** il migliore che ci sia mai stato; **have you ~ seen it?** l'ha mai visto?; **~ since** *adv* da allora ▶ *conj* sin da quando; **~ so pretty** così

bello(-a); **evergreen** n sempreverde m
every ['εvrɪ] adj ogni; **~ day** tutti i
giorni, ogni giorno; **~ other/third day**
ogni due/tre giorni; **~ other car** una
macchina su due; **~ now and then**
ogni tanto, di quando in quando;
everybody pron = **everyone**;
everyday adj quotidiano(-a); di ogni
giorno; **everyone** pron ognuno, tutti
pl; **everything** pron tutto, ogni cosa;
everywhere adv (gen) dappertutto;
(wherever) ovunque
evict [ɪ'vɪkt] vt sfrattare
evidence ['εvɪdns] n (proof) prova;
(of witness) testimonianza; (sign):
to show ~ of dare segni di; **to give**
~ deporre
evident ['εvɪdnt] adj evidente;
evidently adv evidentemente
evil ['iːvl] adj cattivo(-a), maligno(-a)
▶ n male m
evoke [ɪ'vəuk] vt evocare
evolution [iːvə'luːʃən] n evoluzione f
evolve [ɪ'vɔlv] vt elaborare ▶ vi
svilupparsi, evolversi
ewe [juː] n pecora
ex (inf) [eks] n **my ex** il (la) mio(-a) ex
ex- [εks] prefix ex
exact [ɪg'zækt] adj esatto(-a) ▶ vt **to ~**
sth (from) estorcere qc (da); esigere
qc (da); **exactly** adv esattamente
exaggerate [ɪg'zædʒəreɪt] vt, vi
esagerare; **exaggeration** [-'reɪʃən] n
esagerazione f
exam [ɪg'zæm] n abbr (Scol)
= **examination**
examination [ɪgzæmɪ'neɪʃən] n (Scol)
esame m; (Med) controllo
examine [ɪg'zæmɪn] vt esaminare;
examiner n esaminatore(-trice)
example [ɪg'zɑːmpl] n esempio; **for ~**
ad or per esempio
exasperated [ɪg'zɑːspəreɪtɪd] adj
esasperato(-a)
excavate ['εkskəveɪt] vt scavare

exceed [ɪk'siːd] vt superare; (one's
powers, time limit) oltrepassare;
exceedingly adv eccessivamente
excel [ɪk'sεl] vi eccellere ▶ vt
sorpassare; **to ~ o.s** (BRIT) superare
se stesso
excellence ['εksələns] n eccellenza
excellent ['εksələnt] adj eccellente
except [ɪk'sεpt] prep (also: **~ for,**
~ing) salvo, all'infuori di, eccetto
▶ vt escludere; **~ if/when** salvo
se/quando; **~ that** salvo che;
exception [ɪk'sεpʃən] n eccezione
f; **to take exception to** trovare a
ridire su; **exceptional** [ɪk'sεpʃənl] adj
eccezionale; **exceptionally**
[ɪk'sεpʃənəlɪ] adv eccezionalmente
excerpt ['εksəːpt] n estratto
excess [ɪk'sεs] n eccesso; **excess**
baggage n bagaglio in eccedenza;
excessive adj eccessivo(-a)
exchange [ɪks'tʃeɪndʒ] n scambio;
(also: **telephone ~**) centralino ▶ vt **to**
~ (for) scambiare (con); **could I ~ this,**
please? posso cambiarlo, per favore?;
exchange rate n tasso di cambio
excite [ɪk'saɪt] vt eccitare; **to get ~d**
eccitarsi; **excited** adj **to get excited**
essere elettrizzato(-a); **excitement**
n eccitazione f; agitazione f; **exciting**
adj avventuroso(-a); (film, book)
appassionante
exclaim [ɪk'skleɪm] vi esclamare;
exclamation [εksklə'meɪʃən] n
esclamazione f; **exclamation mark**
(US **exclamation point**) n punto
esclamativo
exclude [ɪk'skluːd] vt escludere
excluding [ɪk'skluːdɪŋ] prep **~ VAT**
IVA esclusa
exclusion [ɪk'skluːʒən] n esclusione f;
to the ~ of escludendo
exclusive [ɪk'skluːsɪv] adj
esclusivo(-a); **~ of VAT** I.V.A. esclusa;
exclusively adv esclusivamente

excruciating [ɪkˈskruːʃieɪtɪŋ] *adj*
straziante, atroce

excursion [ɪkˈskəːʃən] *n* escursione
f, gita

excuse [*n* ɪkˈskjuːs, *vb* ɪkˈskjuːz]
n scusa ▶ *vt* scusare; **to ~ sb from**
(*activity*) dispensare qn da; **~ me!** mi
scusi!; **now, if you will ~ me ...** ora, mi
scusi ma ...

ex-directory [ˈɛksdɪˈrɛktərɪ] (*BRIT*) *adj*
(*Tel*): **to be ~** non essere sull'elenco

execute [ˈɛksɪkjuːt] *vt* (*prisoner*)
giustiziare; (*plan etc*) eseguire;
execution [ɛksɪˈkjuːʃən] *n*
esecuzione *f*

executive [ɪgˈzɛkjutɪv] *n* (*Comm*)
dirigente *m*; (*Pol*) esecutivo ▶ *adj*
esecutivo(-a)

exempt [ɪgˈzɛmpt] *adj* esentato(-a)
▶ *vt* **to ~ sb from** esentare qn da

exercise [ˈɛksəsaɪz] *n* (*keep fit*) moto;
(*Scol, Mil etc*) esercizio ▶ *vt* esercitare;
(*patience*) usare; (*dog*) portar fuori ▶ *vi*
(*also*: **take ~**) fare del moto; **exercise
book** *n* quaderno

exert [ɪgˈzəːt] *vt* esercitare; **to ~ o.s.**
sforzarsi; **exertion** [-ʃən] *n* sforzo

exhale [ɛksˈheɪl] *vt*, *vi* espirare

exhaust [ɪgˈzɔːst] *n* (*also*: **~ fumes**)
scappamento; (*also*: **~ pipe**) tubo
di scappamento ▶ *vt* esaurire;
exhausted *adj* esaurito(-a);
exhaustion [ɪgˈzɔːstʃən] *n*
esaurimento; **nervous exhaustion**
sovraffaticamento mentale

exhibit [ɪgˈzɪbɪt] *n* (*Art*) oggetto
esposto; (*Law*) documento *or* oggetto
esibito ▶ *vt* esporre; (*courage, skill*)
dimostrare; **exhibition** [ɛksɪˈbɪʃən] *n*
mostra, esposizione *f*

exhilarating [ɪgˈzɪləreɪtɪŋ] *adj*
esilarante; stimolante

exile [ˈɛksaɪl] *n* esilio; (*person*)
esiliato(-a) ▶ *vt* esiliare

exist [ɪgˈzɪst] *vi* esistere; **existence** *n*

esistenza; **existing** *adj* esistente

exit [ˈɛksɪt] *n* uscita ▶ *vi* (*Theatre,
Comput*) uscire; **where's the ~?** dov'è
l'uscita?; **exit ramp** (*US*) *n* (*Aut*) rampa
di uscita

exotic [ɪgˈzɔtɪk] *adj* esotico(-a)

expand [ɪkˈspænd] *vt* espandere;
estendere; allargare ▶ *vi* (*business, gas*)
espandersi; (*metal*) dilatarsi

expansion [ɪkˈspænʃən] *n* (*gen*)
espansione *f*; (*of town, economy*)
sviluppo; (*of metal*) dilatazione *f*

expect [ɪkˈspɛkt] *vt* (*anticipate*)
prevedere, aspettarsi, prevedere
or aspettarsi che + *sub*; (*require*)
richiedere, esigere; (*suppose*)
supporre; (*await, also baby*) aspettare
▶ *vi* **to be ~ing** essere in stato
interessante; **to ~ sb to do** aspettarsi
che qn faccia; **expectation**
[ɛkspɛkˈteɪʃən] *n* aspettativa,
speranza

expedition [ɛkspəˈdɪʃən] *n* spedizione
f

expel [ɪkˈspɛl] *vt* espellere

expenditure [ɪkˈspɛndɪtʃəʳ] *n* spesa

expense [ɪkˈspɛns] *n* spesa; (*high
cost*) costo; **~s** *npl* (*Comm*) spese *fpl*,
indennità *fpl*; **at the ~ of** a spese di;
expense account *n* conto *m* spese *inv*

expensive [ɪkˈspɛnsɪv] *adj* caro(-a),
costoso(-a); **it's too ~** è troppo caro

experience [ɪkˈspɪərɪəns] *n*
esperienza ▶ *vt* (*pleasure*) provare;
(*hardship*) soffrire; **experienced** *adj*
esperto(-a)

experiment [*n* ɪkˈspɛrɪmənt, *vb*
ɪkˈspɛrɪmɛnt] *n* esperimento,
esperienza ▶ *vi* **to ~ (with/on)** fare
esperimenti (con/su); **experimental**
[ɪkspɛrɪˈmɛntl] *adj* sperimentale;
at the experimental stage in via di
sperimentazione

expert [ˈɛkspəːt] *adj*, *n* esperto(-a);
expertise [-ˈtiːz] *n* competenza

expire [ɪk'spaɪəʳ] vi (period of time, licence) scadere; **expiry** n scadenza; **expiry date** n (of medicine, food item) data di scadenza

explain [ɪk'spleɪn] vt spiegare; **explanation** [ɛksplə'neɪʃən] n spiegazione f

explicit [ɪk'splɪsɪt] adj esplicito(-a)

explode [ɪk'spləud] vi esplodere

exploit [n 'ɛksplɔɪt, vb ɪk'splɔɪt] n impresa ▶ vt sfruttare; **exploitation** [-'teɪʃən] n sfruttamento

explore [ɪk'splɔːʳ] vt esplorare; (possibilities) esaminare; **explorer** n esploratore(-trice)

explosion [ɪk'spləuʒən] n esplosione f; **explosive** [ɪk'spləusɪv] adj esplosivo(-a) ▶ n esplosivo

export [vb ɛk'spɔːt, n 'ɛkspɔːt] vt esportare ▶ n esportazione f; articolo di esportazione; ▶ cpd d'esportazione; **exporter** n esportatore m

expose [ɪk'spəuz] vt esporre; (unmask) smascherare; **exposed** adj (position) esposto(-a); **exposure** [ɪk'spəuʒəʳ] n esposizione f; (Phot) posa; (Med) assideramento

express [ɪk'sprɛs] adj (definite) chiaro(-a), espresso(-a); (BRIT: letter etc) espresso inv ▶ n (train) espresso ▶ vt esprimere; **expression** [ɪk'sprɛʃən] n espressione f; **expressway** (US) n (urban motorway) autostrada che attraversa la città

exquisite [ɛk'skwɪzɪt] adj squisito(-a)

extend [ɪk'stɛnd] vt (visit) protrarre; (road, deadline) prolungare; (building) ampliare; (offer) offrire, porgere ▶ vi (land, period) estendersi; **extension** [ɪk'stɛnʃən] n (of road, term) prolungamento; (of contract, deadline) proroga; (building) annesso; (to wire, table) prolunga; (telephone) interno; (: in private house) apparecchio supplementare; **extension lead** n

prolunga

extensive [ɪk'stɛnsɪv] adj esteso(-a), ampio(-a); (damage) su larga scala; (coverage, discussion) esauriente; (use) grande

extent [ɪk'stɛnt] n estensione f; **to some ~** fino a un certo punto; **to such an ~ that ...** a un tal punto che ...; **to what ~?** fino a che punto?; **to the ~ of ...** fino al punto di ...

exterior [ɛk'stɪərɪəʳ] adj esteriore, esterno(-a) ▶ n esteriore m, esterno; aspetto (esteriore)

external [ɛk'stə:nl] adj esterno(-a), esteriore

extinct [ɪk'stɪŋkt] adj estinto(-a); **extinction** [ɪk'stɪŋkʃən] n estinzione f

extinguish [ɪk'stɪŋgwɪʃ] vt estinguere

extra ['ɛkstrə] adj extra inv, supplementare ▶ adv (in addition) di più ▶ n extra m inv; (surcharge) supplemento; (Cinema, Theatre) comparsa

extract [vb ɪk'strækt, n 'ɛkstrækt] vt estrarre; (money, promise) strappare ▶ n estratto; (passage) brano

extradite ['ɛkstrədaɪt] vt estradare

extraordinary [ɪk'strɔːdnrɪ] adj straordinario(-a)

extravagance [ɪk'strævəgəns] n sperpero, stravaganza

extravagant [ɪk'strævəgənt] adj (lavish) prodigo(-a); (wasteful) dispendioso(-a)

▌ Be careful not to translate **extravagant** by the Italian word *stravagante*.

extreme [ɪk'striːm] adj estremo(-a) ▶ n estremo; **extremely** adv estremamente

extremist [ɪk'striːmɪst] adj, n estremista (m/f)

extrovert ['ɛkstrəvəːt] n estroverso(-a)

eye [aɪ] n occhio; (of needle) cruna ▶ vt

osservare; **to keep an ~ on** tenere d'occhio; **eyeball** n globo dell'occhio; **eyebrow** n sopracciglio; **eyedrops** npl gocce fpl oculari, collirio; **eyelash** n ciglio; **eyelid** n palpebra; **eyeliner** n eye-liner m inv; **eyeshadow** n ombretto; **eyesight** n vista; **eye witness** n testimone m/f oculare

F [ɛf] n (Mus) fa m
fabric ['fæbrɪk] n stoffa, tessuto
fabulous ['fæbjuləs] adj favoloso(-a); (super) favoloso(-a), fantastico(-a)
face [feɪs] n faccia, viso, volto; (expression) faccia; (of clock) quadrante m; (of building) facciata ▶ vt essere di fronte a; (facts, situation) affrontare; **~ down** a faccia in giù; **to make or pull a ~** fare una smorfia; **in the ~ of** (difficulties etc) di fronte a; **on the ~ of it** a prima vista; **~ to ~** faccia a faccia ▷ **face up to** vt fus affrontare, far fronte a; **face cloth** (BRIT) n guanto di spugna; **face pack** n (BRIT) maschera di bellezza
facial ['feɪʃəl] adj del viso
facilitate [fə'sɪlɪteɪt] vt facilitare
facilities [fə'sɪlɪtɪz] npl attrezzature fpl; **credit ~** facilitazioni fpl di credito
fact [fækt] n fatto; **in ~** in effetti
faction ['fækʃən] n fazione f

factor ['fæktə'] n fattore m; **I'd like a ~ 15 suntan lotion** vorrei una crema solare con fattore di protezione 15
factory ['fæktərɪ] n fabbrica, stabilimento

⬛ Be careful not to translate **factory** by the Italian word *fattoria*.

factual ['fæktjuəl] adj che si attiene ai fatti
faculty ['fækəltɪ] n facoltà f inv; (US) corpo insegnante
fad [fæd] n mania; capriccio
fade [feɪd] vi sbiadire, sbiadirsi; (light, sound, hope) attenuarsi, affievolirsi; (flower) appassire ▷ **fade away** vi (sound) affievolirsi
fag [fæg] (BRIT: inf) n (cigarette) cicca
Fahrenheit ['fɑːrənhaɪt] n Fahrenheit m inv
fail [feɪl] vt (exam) non superare; (candidate) bocciare; (courage, memory) mancare a ▶ vi fallire; (student) essere respinto(-a); (eyesight, health, light) venire a mancare; **to ~ to do sth** (neglect) mancare di fare qc; (be unable) non riuscire a fare qc; **without ~** senza fallo; certamente; **failing** n difetto ▶ prep in mancanza di; **failure** ['feɪljə'] n fallimento; (person) fallito(-a); (mechanical etc) guasto
faint [feɪnt] adj debole; (recollection) vago(-a); (mark) indistinto(-a) ▶ n (Med) svenimento ▶ vi svenire; **to feel ~** sentirsi svenire; **faintest** adj **I haven't the faintest idea** non ho la più pallida idea; **faintly** adv debolmente; vagamente
fair [fɛə'] adj (person, decision) giusto(-a), equo(-a); (quite large, quite good) discreto(-a); (hair etc) biondo(-a); (skin, complexion) chiaro(-a); (weather) bello(-a), clemente ▶ adv (play) lealmente ▶ n fiera; (BRIT: funfair) luna park m inv; **fairground** n luna park m inv;

fair-haired [fɛə'hɛəd] *adj* (*person*) biondo(-a); **fairly** *adv* equamente; (*quite*) abbastanza; **fairway** *n* (*Golf*) fairway *m inv*

fairy ['fɛərɪ] *n* fata; **fairy tale** *n* fiaba

faith [feɪθ] *n* fede *f*; (*trust*) fiducia; (*sect*) religione *f*, fede *f*; **faithful** *adj* fedele; **faithfully** *adv* fedelmente; **yours faithfully** (BRIT: *in letters*) distinti saluti

fake [feɪk] *n* imitazione *f*; (*picture*) falso; (*person*) impostore(-a) ▸ *adj* falso(-a) ▸ *vt* (*accounts*) falsificare; (*illness*) fingere; (*painting*) contraffare

falcon ['fɔːlkən] *n* falco, falcone *m*

fall [fɔːl] (*pt* fell, *pp* fallen) *n* caduta; (*in temperature*) abbassamento; (*in price*) ribasso; (*US: autumn*) autunno ▸ *vi* cadere; (*temperature, price, night*) scendere; **~s** *npl* (*waterfall*) cascate *fpl*; **to ~ flat** (*on one's face*) cadere bocconi; (*joke*) fare cilecca; (*plan*) fallire ▷ **fall apart** *vi* cadere a pezzi ▷ **fall down** *vi* (*person*) cadere; (*building*) crollare ▷ **fall for** *vt fus* (*person*) prendere una cotta per; **to ~ for a trick** (*or a story etc*) cascarci ▷ **fall off** *vi* cadere; (*diminish*) diminuire, abbassarsi ▷ **fall out** *vi* (*hair, teeth*) cadere; (*friends etc*) litigare ▷ **fall over** *vi* cadere ▷ **fall through** *vi* (*plan, project*) fallire

fallen ['fɔːlən] *pp of* **fall**

fallout ['fɔːlaut] *n* fall-out *m*

false [fɔːls] *adj* falso(-a); **under ~ pretences** con l'inganno; **false alarm** *n* falso allarme *m*; **false teeth** (BRIT) *npl* denti *mpl* finti

fame [feɪm] *n* fama, celebrità

familiar [fə'mɪlɪəʳ] *adj* familiare; (*close*) intimo(-a); **to be ~ with** (*subject*) conoscere; **familiarize** [fə'mɪlɪəraɪz] *vt* **to familiarize o.s. with** familiarizzare con

family ['fæmɪlɪ] *n* famiglia; **family doctor** *n* medico di famiglia; **family**

planning *n* pianificazione *f* familiare

famine ['fæmɪn] *n* carestia

famous ['feɪməs] *adj* famoso(-a)

fan [fæn] *n* (*folding*) ventaglio; (*Elec*) ventilatore *m*; (*person*) ammiratore(-trice), tifoso(-a) ▸ *vt* far vento a; (*fire, quarrel*) alimentare

fanatic [fə'nætɪk] *n* fanatico(-a)

fan belt *n* cinghia del ventilatore

fan club *n* fan club *m inv*

fancy ['fænsɪ] *n* immaginazione *f*, fantasia; (*whim*) capriccio ▸ *adj* (*hat*) stravagante; (*hotel, food*) speciale ▸ *vt* (*feel like, want*) aver voglia di; (*imagine, think*) immaginare; **to take a ~ to** incapricciarsi di; **he fancies her** (*inf*) gli piace; **fancy dress** *n* costume *m* (per maschera)

fan heater *n* (BRIT) stufa ad aria calda

fantasize ['fæntəsaɪz] *vi* fantasticare, sognare

fantastic [fæn'tæstɪk] *adj* fantastico(-a)

fantasy ['fæntəsɪ] *n* fantasia, immaginazione *f*; fantasticheria; chimera

fanzine ['fænziːn] *n* rivista specialistica (per appassionati)

FAQs *abbr* (= *frequently asked questions*) FAQ *fpl*

far [fɑːʳ] *adj* lontano(-a) ▸ *adv* lontano; (*much, greatly*) molto; **is it ~ from here?** è molto lontano da qui?; **how ~?** quanto lontano?; (*referring to activity etc*) fino a dove?; **how ~ is the town centre?** quanto dista il centro da qui?; **~ away, ~ off** lontano, distante; **~ better** assai migliore; **~ from** lontano da; **by ~** di gran lunga; **go as ~ as the farm** vada fino alla fattoria; **as ~ as I know** per quel che so

farce [fɑːs] *n* farsa

fare [fɛəʳ] *n* (*on trains, buses*) tariffa; (*in taxi*) prezzo della corsa; (*food*) vitto, cibo; **half ~** metà tariffa; **full ~**

tariffa intera

Far East n **the ~** l'Estremo Oriente m

farewell [fɛə'wɛl] excl, n addio

farm [fɑːm] n fattoria, podere m ▶ vt coltivare; **farmer** n coltivatore(-trice), agricoltore(-trice); **farmhouse** n fattoria; **farming** n (gen) agricoltura; (of crops) coltivazione f; (of animals) allevamento; **farmyard** n aia

far-reaching [fɑː'riːtʃɪŋ] adj di vasta portata

fart [fɑːt] (inf!) vi scoreggiare (!)

farther ['fɑːðə'] adv più lontano ▶ adj più lontano(-a)

farthest ['fɑːðɪst] superl of **far**

fascinate ['fæsɪneɪt] vt affascinare; **fascinated** adj affascinato(-a); **fascinating** adj affascinante; **fascination** [-'neɪʃən] n fascino

fascist ['fæʃɪst] adj, n fascista (m/f)

fashion ['fæʃən] n moda; (manner) maniera, modo ▶ vt foggiare, formare; **in ~** alla moda; **out of ~** passato(-a) di moda; **fashionable** adj alla moda, di moda; **fashion show** n sfilata di moda

fast [fɑːst] adj rapido(-a), svelto(-a), veloce; (clock): **to be ~** andare avanti; (dye, colour) solido(-a) ▶ adv rapidamente; (stuck, held) saldamente ▶ n digiuno ▶ vi digiunare; **~ asleep** profondamente addormentato

fasten ['fɑːsn] vt chiudere, fissare; (coat) abbottonare, allacciare ▶ vi chiudersi, fissarsi; abbottonarsi, allacciarsi

fast food n fast food m

fat [fæt] adj grasso(-a); (book, profit etc) grosso(-a) ▶ n grasso

fatal ['feɪtl] adj fatale; mortale; disastroso(-a); **fatality** [fə'tælɪtɪ] n (road death etc) morto(-a), vittima; **fatally** adv a morte

fate [feɪt] n destino; (of person) sorte f

father ['fɑːðə'] n padre m; **Father Christmas** n Babbo Natale; **father-in-law** n suocero

fatigue [fə'tiːg] n stanchezza

fattening ['fætnɪŋ] adj (food) che fa ingrassare

fatty ['fætɪ] adj (food) grasso(-a) ▶ n (inf) ciccione(-a)

faucet ['fɔːsɪt] (US) n rubinetto

fault [fɔːlt] n colpa; (Tennis) fallo; (defect) difetto; (Geo) faglia ▶ vt criticare; **it's my ~** è colpa mia; **to find ~ with** trovare da ridire su; **at ~** in fallo; **faulty** adj difettoso(-a)

fauna ['fɔːnə] n fauna

favour etc ['feɪvə'] (US **favor**) n favore m ▶ vt (proposition) favorire, essere favorevole a; (pupil etc) favorire; (team, horse) dare per vincente; **to do sb a ~** fare un favore or una cortesia a qn; **to find ~ with** (person) entrare nelle buone grazie di; (: suggestion) avere l'approvazione di; **in ~ of** in favore di; **favourable** adj favorevole; **favourite** [-rɪt] adj, n favorito(-a)

fawn [fɔːn] n daino ▶ adj (also: ~-coloured) marrone chiaro inv ▶ vi **to ~ (up)on** adulare servilmente

fax [fæks] n (document) facsimile m inv, telecopia; (machine) telecopiatrice f ▶ vt telecopiare, trasmettere in facsimile

FBI (US) n abbr (= Federal Bureau of Investigation) F.B.I. f

fear [fɪə'] n paura, timore m ▶ vt aver paura di, temere; **for ~ of** per paura di; **fearful** adj pauroso(-a); (sight, noise) terribile, spaventoso(-a); **fearless** adj intrepido(-a), senza paura

feasible ['fiːzəbl] adj possibile, realizzabile

feast [fiːst] n festa, banchetto; (Rel: also: **~ day**) festa ▶ vi banchettare

feat [fiːt] n impresa, fatto insigne

feather ['fɛðə'] n penna

feature ['fi:tʃəʳ] n caratteristica; (*Press*, *TV*) articolo ▶ vt (*film*) avere come protagonista ▶ vi figurare; **~s** npl (*of face*) fisionomia; **feature film** n film m inv principale

Feb. [fɛb] abbr (= *February*) feb

February ['fɛbruərɪ] n febbraio

fed [fɛd] pt, pp of **feed**

federal ['fɛdərəl] adj federale

federation [fɛdə'reɪʃən] n federazione f

fed up adj **to be ~** essere stufo(-a)

fee [fi:] n pagamento; (*of doctor*, *lawyer*) onorario; (*for examination*) tassa d'esame; **school ~s** tasse fpl scolastiche

feeble ['fi:bl] adj debole

feed [fi:d] (pt, pp **fed**) n (*of baby*) pappa; (*of animal*) mangime m; (*on printer*) meccanismo di alimentazione ▶ vt nutrire; (*baby*) allattare; (*horse etc*) dare da mangiare a; (*fire*, *machine*) alimentare; (*data*, *information*): **to ~ into** inserire in; **feedback** n feed-back m

feel [fi:l] (pt, pp **felt**) n consistenza; (*sense of touch*) tatto ▶ vt toccare; palpare; tastare; (*cold*, *pain*, *anger*) sentire; (*think*, *believe*): **to ~ (that)** pensare che; **to ~ hungry/cold** aver fame/freddo; **to ~ lonely/better** sentirsi solo/meglio; **I don't ~ well** non mi sento bene; **it ~s soft** è morbido al tatto; **to ~ like** (*want*) aver voglia di; **to ~ about or around for** cercare a tastoni; **feeling** n sensazione f; (*emotion*) sentimento

feet [fi:t] npl of **foot**

fell [fɛl] pt of **fall** ▶ vt (*tree*) abbattere

fellow ['fɛləu] n individuo, tipo; compagno; (*of learned society*) membro cpd; **fellow citizen** n concittadino(-a); **fellow countryman** (*irreg*) n compatriota m; **fellow men** npl simili mpl; **fellowship** n associazione f;

compagnia; specie di borsa di studio universitaria

felony ['fɛlənɪ] n reato, crimine m

felt [fɛlt] pt, pp of **feel** ▶ n feltro

female ['fi:meɪl] n (*Zool*) femmina; (*pej: woman*) donna, femmina ▶ adj (*Biol*, *Elec*) femmina inv; (*sex*, *character*) femminile; (*vote etc*) di donne

feminine ['fɛmɪnɪn] adj femminile

feminist ['fɛmɪnɪst] n femminista m/f

fence [fɛns] n recinto ▶ vt (*also*: **~ in**) recingere ▶ vi (*Sport*) tirare di scherma; **fencing** n (*Sport*) scherma

fend [fɛnd] vi **to ~ for o.s.** arrangiarsi ▷ **fend off** vt (*attack*, *questions*) respingere, difendersi da

fender ['fɛndəʳ] n parafuoco; (*on boat*) parabordo; (*US*) parafango; paraurti m inv

fennel ['fɛnl] n finocchio

ferment [vb fə'mɛnt, n 'fə:mɛnt] vi fermentare ▶ n (*fig*) agitazione f, eccitazione f

fern [fə:n] n felce f

ferocious [fə'rəuʃəs] adj feroce

ferret ['fɛrɪt] n furetto

ferry ['fɛrɪ] n (*small*) traghetto; (*large*: *also*: **~boat**) nave f traghetto inv ▶ vt traghettare

fertile ['fə:taɪl] adj fertile; (*Biol*) fecondo(-a); **fertilize** ['fə:tɪlaɪz] vt fertilizzare; fecondare; **fertilizer** ['fə:tɪlaɪzəʳ] n fertilizzante m

festival ['fɛstɪvəl] n (*Rel*) festa; (*Art*, *Mus*) festival m inv

festive ['fɛstɪv] adj di festa; **the ~ season** (*BRIT*: *Christmas*) il periodo delle feste

fetch [fɛtʃ] vt andare a prendere; (*sell for*) essere venduto(-a) per

fête [feɪt] n festa

fetus ['fi:təs] (*US*) n = **foetus**

feud [fju:d] n contesa, lotta

fever ['fi:vəʳ] n febbre f; **feverish** adj febbrile

few [fju:] *adj* pochi(-e); **a ~** *adj* qualche *inv* ▶ *pron* alcuni(-e); **fewer** *adj* meno *inv*, meno numerosi(-e); **fewest** *adj* il minor numero di

fiancé [fɪ'ɑ̃:ŋseɪ] *n* fidanzato; **fiancée** *n* fidanzata

fiasco [fɪ'æskəu] *n* fiasco

fib [fɪb] *n* piccola bugia

fibre ['faɪbə'] (US **fiber**) *n* fibra; **Fibreglass®** ['faɪbəglɑ:s] (US **fiberglass**) *n* fibra di vetro

fickle ['fɪkl] *adj* incostante, capriccioso(-a)

fiction ['fɪkʃən] *n* narrativa, romanzi *mpl*; (*sth made up*) finzione *f*; **fictional** *adj* immaginario(-a)

fiddle ['fɪdl] *n* (*Mus*) violino; (*cheating*) imbroglio; truffa ▶ *vt* (*BRIT: accounts*) falsificare, falsare ▷ **fiddle with** *vt fus* gingillarsi con

fidelity [fɪ'dɛlɪtɪ] *n* fedeltà; (*accuracy*) esattezza

field [fi:ld] *n* campo; **field marshal** *n* feldmaresciallo

fierce [fɪəs] *adj* (*animal, person, fighting*) feroce; (*loyalty*) assoluto(-a); (*wind*) furioso(-a); (*heat*) intenso(-a)

fifteen [fɪf'ti:n] *num* quindici; **fifteenth** *num* quindicesimo(-a)

fifth [fɪfθ] *num* quinto(-a)

fiftieth ['fɪftɪɪθ] *num* cinquantesimo(-a)

fifty ['fɪftɪ] *num* cinquanta; **fifty-fifty** *adj* **a fifty-fifty chance** una possibilità su due ▶ *adv* fifty-fifty, metà per ciascuno

fig [fɪg] *n* fico

fight [faɪt] (*pt, pp* **fought**) *n* zuffa, rissa; (*Mil*) battaglia, combattimento; (*against cancer etc*) lotta ▶ *vt* (*person*) azzuffarsi con; (*enemy: also Mil*) combattere; (*cancer, alcoholism, emotion*) lottare contro, combattere; (*election*) partecipare a ▶ *vi* combattere ▷ **fight back**

vi difendersi; (*Sport, after illness*) riprendersi ▶ *vt* (*tears*) ricacciare ▷ **fight off** *vt* (*attack, attacker*) respingere; (*disease, sleep, urge*) lottare contro; **fighting** *n* combattimento

figure ['fɪgə'] *n* figura; (*number, cipher*) cifra ▶ *vt* (*think: esp US*) pensare ▶ *vi* (*appear*) figurare ▷ **figure out** *vt* riuscire a capire; calcolare

file [faɪl] *n* (*tool*) lima; (*dossier*) incartamento; (*folder*) cartellina; (*Comput*) archivio; (*row*) fila ▶ *vt* (*nails, wood*) limare; (*papers*) archiviare; (*Law: claim*) presentare; passare agli atti; **filing cabinet** ['faɪlɪŋ-] *n* casellario

Filipino [fɪlɪ'pi:nəu] *n* filippino(-a); (*Ling*) tagal *m*

fill [fɪl] *vt* riempire; (*job*) coprire ▶ *n* **to eat one's ~** mangiare a sazietà ▷ **fill in** *vt* (*hole*) riempire; (*form*) compilare ▷ **fill out** *vt* (*form, receipt*) riempire ▷ **fill up** *vt* riempire; **~ it up, please** (*Aut*) il pieno, per favore

fillet ['fɪlɪt] *n* filetto; **fillet steak** *n* bistecca di filetto

filling ['fɪlɪŋ] *n* (*Culin*) impasto, ripieno; (*for tooth*) otturazione *f*; **filling station** *n* stazione *f* di rifornimento

film [fɪlm] *n* (*Cinema*) film *m inv*; (*Phot*) pellicola, rullino; (*of powder, liquid*) sottile strato ▶ *vt, vi* girare; **I'd like a 36-exposure ~** vorrei un rullino da 36 pose; **film star** *n* divo(-a) dello schermo

filter ['fɪltə'] *n* filtro ▶ *vt* filtrare; **filter lane** (*BRIT*) *n* (*Aut*) corsia di svincolo

filth [fɪlθ] *n* sporcizia; **filthy** *adj* lordo(-a), sozzo(-a); (*language*) osceno(-a)

fin [fɪn] *n* (*of fish*) pinna

final ['faɪnl] *adj* finale, ultimo(-a); definitivo(-a) ▶ *n* (*Sport*) finale *f*; **~s** *npl* (*Scol*) esami *mpl* finali; **finale** [fɪ'nɑ:lɪ] *n* finale *m*; **finalist** ['faɪnəlɪst] *n* (*Sport*) finalista *m/f*; **finalize** ['faɪnəlaɪz] *vt* mettere a punto; **finally** ['faɪnə lɪ] *adv* (*lastly*) alla fine; (*eventually*) finalmente

finance [faɪ'næns] *n* finanza; (*capital*) capitale *m* ▶ *vt* finanziare; **~s** *npl* (*funds*) finanze *fpl*; **financial** [faɪ'nænʃəl] *adj* finanziario(-a); **financial year** *n* anno finanziario, esercizio finanziario

find [faɪnd] (*pt, pp* **found**) *vt* trovare; (*lost object*) ritrovare ▶ *n* trovata, scoperta; **to ~ sb guilty** (*Law*) giudicare qn colpevole ▷ **find out** *vt* (*truth, secret*) scoprire; (*person*) cogliere in fallo; **to ~ out about** informarsi su; (*by chance*) scoprire; **findings** *npl* (*Law*) sentenza, conclusioni *fpl*; (*of report*) conclusioni

fine [faɪn] *adj* bello(-a); ottimo(-a); (*thin, subtle*) fine ▶ *adv* (*well*) molto bene ▶ *n* (*Law*) multa ▶ *vt* (*Law*) multare; **to be ~** (*person*) stare bene; (*weather*) far bello; **fine arts** *npl* belle arti *fpl*

finger ['fɪŋgəʳ] *n* dito ▶ *vt* toccare, tastare; **little/index ~** mignolo/(dito) indice *m*; **fingernail** *n* unghia; **fingerprint** *n* impronta digitale; **fingertip** *n* punta del dito

finish ['fɪnɪʃ] *n* fine *f*; (*polish etc*) finitura ▶ *vt, vi* finire; **when does the show ~?** quando finisce lo spettacolo?; **to ~ doing sth** finire di fare qc; **to ~ third** arrivare terzo(-a) ▷ **finish off** *vt* compiere; (*kill*) uccidere ▷ **finish up** *vi, vt* finire

Finland ['fɪnlənd] *n* Finlandia; **Finn** [fɪn] *n* finlandese *m/f*; **Finnish** *adj* finlandese ▶ *n* (*Ling*) finlandese *m*

fir [fəːʳ] *n* abete *m*

fire [faɪəʳ] *n* fuoco; (*destructive*) incendio; (*gas fire, electric fire*) stufa ▶ *vt* (*gun*) far fuoco con; (*arrow*)

sparare; (*fig*) infiammare; (*inf: dismiss*) licenziare ▶ *vi* sparare, far fuoco; **~!** al fuoco!; **on ~** in fiamme; **fire alarm** *n* allarme *m* d'incendio; **firearm** *n* arma da fuoco; **fire brigade** [-brɪ'geɪd] (*US* **fire department**) *n* (*corpo dei*) pompieri *mpl*; **fire engine** *n* autopompa; **fire escape** *n* scala di sicurezza; **fire exit** *n* uscita di sicurezza; **fire extinguisher** [-ɪk'stɪŋgwɪʃəʳ] *n* estintore *m*; **fireman** (*irreg*) *n* pompiere *m*; **fireplace** *n* focolare *m*; **fire station** *n* caserma dei pompieri; **firetruck** (*US*) *n* = **fire engine**; **firewall** *n* (*Internet*) firewall *m inv*; **firewood** *n* legna; **fireworks** *npl* fuochi *mpl* d'artificio

firm [fəːm] *adj* fermo(-a) ▶ *n* ditta, azienda; **firmly** *adv* fermamente

first [fəːst] *adj* primo(-a) ▶ *adv* (*before others*) il primo, la prima; (*before other things*) per primo; (*when listing reasons etc*) per prima cosa ▶ *n* (*person: in race*) primo(-a); (*BRIT Scol*) laurea con lode; (*Aut*) prima; **at ~** dapprima, all'inizio; **~ of all** prima di tutto; **first aid** *n* pronto soccorso; **first-aid kit** *n* cassetta pronto soccorso; **first-class** *adj* di prima classe; **first-hand** *adj* di prima mano; **first lady** (*US*) *n* moglie *f* del presidente; **firstly** *adv* in primo luogo; **first name** *n* prenome *m*; **first-rate** *adj* di prima qualità, ottimo(-a)

fiscal ['fɪskəl] *adj* fiscale; **fiscal year** *n* anno fiscale

fish [fɪʃ] *n inv* pesce *m* ▶ *vt* (*river, area*) pescare in ▶ *vi* pescare; **to go ~ing** andare a pesca; **fish and chip shop** *n see* **chip shop**; **fisherman** (*irreg*) *n* pescatore *m*; **fish fingers** (*BRIT*) *npl* bastoncini *mpl* di pesce (*surgelati*); **fishing** *n* pesca; **fishing boat** *n* barca da pesca; **fishing line** *n* lenza; **fishmonger** *n* pescivendolo; **fishmonger's (shop)** *n* pescheria;

fish sticks (US) npl = **fish fingers**; **fishy** (inf) adj (tale, story) sospetto(-a)
fist [fɪst] n pugno
fit [fɪt] adj (Med, Sport) in forma; (proper) adatto(-a), appropriato(-a); conveniente ▶ vt (clothes) stare bene a; (put in, attach) mettere; installare; (equip) fornire, equipaggiare ▶ vi (clothes) stare bene; (parts) andare bene, adattarsi; (in space, gap) entrare ▶ n (Med) accesso, attacco; **~ to** in grado di; **~ for** adatto(-a) a, degno(-a) di; **a ~ of anger** un accesso d'ira; **this dress is a good ~** questo vestito sta bene; **by ~s and starts** a sbalzi ▷ **fit in** vi accordarsi; adattarsi; **fitness** n (Med) forma fisica; **fitted** adj **fitted cupboards** armadi mpl a muro; **fitted carpet** moquette f inv; **fitted kitchen** (BRIT) cucina componibile; **fitting** adj appropriato(-a) ▶ n (of dress) prova; (of piece of equipment) montaggio, aggiustaggio; **fitting room** n camerino; **fittings** npl (in building) impianti mpl
five [faɪv] num cinque; **fiver** (inf) n (BRIT) biglietto da cinque sterline; (US) biglietto da cinque dollari
fix [fɪks] vt fissare; (mend) riparare; (meal, drink) preparare ▶ n **to be in a ~** essere nei guai ▷ **fix up** vt (meeting) fissare; **to ~ sb up with sth** procurare qc a qn; **fixed** [fɪkst] adj (prices etc) fisso(-a); **fixture** ['fɪkstʃə^r] n impianto (fisso); (Sport) incontro (del calendario sportivo)
fizzy ['fɪzɪ] adj frizzante; gassato(-a)
flag [flæg] n bandiera; (also: **~stone**) pietra da lastricare ▶ vi stancarsi; affievolirsi; **flagpole** ['flægpəʊl] n albero
flair [flɛə^r] n (for business etc) fiuto; (for languages etc) facilità; (style) stile m
flak [flæk] n (Mil) fuoco d'artiglieria; (inf: criticism) critiche fpl

flake [fleɪk] n (of rust, paint) scaglia; (of snow, soap powder) fiocco ▶ vi (also: **~ off**) sfaldarsi
flamboyant [flæm'bɔɪənt] adj sgargiante
flame [fleɪm] n fiamma
flamingo [flə'mɪŋgəʊ] n fenicottero, fiammingo
flammable ['flæməbl] adj infiammabile
flan [flæn] (BRIT) n flan m inv
flank [flæŋk] n fianco ▶ vt fiancheggiare
flannel ['flænl] n (BRIT: also: **face ~**) guanto di spugna; (fabric) flanella
flap [flæp] n (of pocket) patta; (of envelope) lembo ▶ vt (wings) battere ▶ vi (sail, flag) sbattere; (inf: also: **be in a ~**) essere in agitazione
flare [flɛə^r] n razzo; (in skirt etc) svasatura; **~s** (trousers) pantaloni mpl a zampa d'elefante ▷ **flare up** vi andare in fiamme; (fig: person) infiammarsi di rabbia; (: revolt) scoppiare
flash [flæʃ] n vampata; (also: **news ~**) notizia f lampo inv; (Phot) flash m inv ▶ vt accendere e spegnere; (send: message) trasmettere; (: look, smile) lanciare ▶ vi brillare; (light on ambulance, eyes etc) lampeggiare; **in a ~** in un lampo; **to ~ one's headlights** lampeggiare; **he ~ed by or past** ci passò davanti come un lampo; **flashback** n flashback m inv; **flashbulb** n cubo m flash inv; **flashlight** n lampadina tascabile
flask [flɑːsk] n fiasco; (also: **vacuum ~**) Thermos® m inv
flat [flæt] adj piatto(-a); (tyre) sgonfio(-a), a terra; (battery) scarico(-a); (beer) svampito(-a); (denial) netto(-a); (Mus) bemolle inv; (: voice) stonato(-a); (rate, fee) unico(-a) ▶ n (BRIT: rooms)

appartamento; (*Aut*) pneumatico sgonfio; (*Mus*) bemolle *m*; **to work ~ out** lavorare a più non posso; **flatten** *vt* (*also:* **flatten out**) appiattire; (*building, city*) spianare

flatter ['flætəʳ] *vt* lusingare; **flattering** *adj* lusinghiero(-a); (*dress*) che dona

flaunt [flɔ:nt] *vt* fare mostra di

flavour *etc* ['fleɪvəʳ] (*US* **flavor**) *n* gusto ▶ *vt* insaporire, aggiungere sapore a; **what ~s do you have?** che gusti avete?; **strawberry-~ed** al gusto di fragola; **flavouring** *n* essenza (artificiale)

flaw [flɔ:] *n* difetto; **flawless** *adj* senza difetti

flea [fli:] *n* pulce *f*; **flea market** *n* mercato delle pulci

flee [fli:] (*pt, pp* **fled**) *vt* fuggire da ▶ *vi* fuggire, scappare

fleece [fli:s] *n* vello ▶ *vt* (*inf*) pelare

fleet [fli:t] *n* flotta; (*of lorries etc*) convoglio; parco

fleeting ['fli:tɪŋ] *adj* fugace, fuggitivo(-a); (*visit*) volante

Flemish ['flɛmɪʃ] *adj* fiammingo(-a)

flesh [flɛʃ] *n* carne *f*; (*of fruit*) polpa

flew [flu:] *pt of* **fly**

flex [flɛks] *n* filo (flessibile) ▶ *vt* flettere; (*muscles*) contrarre; **flexibility** *n* flessibilità; **flexible** *adj* flessibile; **flexitime** ['flɛksɪtaɪm] *n* orario flessibile

flick [flɪk] *n* colpetto; scarto ▶ *vt* dare un colpetto a ▷ **flick through** *vt fus* sfogliare

flicker ['flɪkəʳ] *vi* tremolare

flies [flaɪz] *npl of* **fly**

flight [flaɪt] *n* volo; (*escape*) fuga; (*also:* **~ of steps**) scalinata; **flight attendant** (*US*) *n* steward *m inv*, hostess *f inv*

flimsy ['flɪmzɪ] *adj* (*shoes, clothes*) leggero(-a); (*building*) poco solido(-a);

(*excuse*) che non regge

flinch [flɪntʃ] *vi* ritirarsi; **to ~ from** tirarsi indietro di fronte a

fling [flɪŋ] (*pt, pp* **flung**) *vt* lanciare, gettare

flint [flɪnt] *n* selce *f*; (*in lighter*) pietrina

flip [flɪp] *vt* (*switch*) far scattare; (*coin*) lanciare in aria

flip-flops ['flɪpflɔps] *npl* (*esp BRIT: sandals*) infradito *mpl*

flipper ['flɪpəʳ] *n* pinna

flirt [flə:t] *vi* flirtare ▶ *n* civetta

float [fləut] *n* galleggiante *m*; (*in procession*) carro; (*money*) somma ▶ *vi* galleggiare

flock [flɔk] *n* (*of sheep, Rel*) gregge *m*; (*of birds*) stormo ▶ *vi* **to ~ to** accorrere in massa a

flood [flʌd] *n* alluvione *m*; (*of letters etc*) marea ▶ *vt* allagare; (*people*) invadere ▶ *vi* (*place*) allagarsi; (*people*): **to ~ into** riversarsi in; **flooding** *n* inondazione *f*; **floodlight** *n* riflettore *m* ▶ *vt* illuminare a giorno

floor [flɔ:ʳ] *n* pavimento; (*storey*) piano; (*of sea, valley*) fondo ▶ *vt* (*blow*) atterrare; (: *question*) ridurre al silenzio; **which ~ is it on?** a che piano si trova?; **ground ~** (*BRIT*), **first ~** (*US*) pianterreno; **first ~** (*BRIT*), **second ~** (*US*) primo piano; **floorboard** *n* tavellone *m* di legno; **flooring** *n* (*floor*) pavimento; (*material*) materiale *m* per pavimentazioni; **floor show** *n* spettacolo di varietà

flop [flɔp] *n* fiasco ▶ *vi* far fiasco; (*fall*) lasciarsi cadere; **floppy** ['flɔpɪ] *adj* floscio(-a), molle

floral ['flɔ:rl] *adj* floreale

Florence ['flɔrəns] *n* Firenze *f*

Florentine ['flɔrəntaɪn] *adj* fiorentino(-a)

florist ['flɔrɪst] *n* fioraio(-a); **florist's (shop)** *n* fioraio(-a)

flotation [fləu'teɪʃən] *n* (*Comm*) lancio

flour ['flauə^r] n farina
flourish ['flʌrɪʃ] vi fiorire ▶ n (bold gesture): **with a ~** con ostentazione
flow [fləu] n flusso; circolazione f ▶ vi fluire; (traffic, blood in veins) circolare; (hair) scendere
flower ['flauə^r] n fiore m ▶ vi fiorire; **flower bed** n aiuola; **flowerpot** n vaso da fiori
flown [fləun] pp of **fly**
fl. oz. abbr = **fluid ounce**
flu [flu:] n influenza
fluctuate ['flʌktjueɪt] vi fluttuare, oscillare
fluent ['flu:ənt] adj (speech) facile, sciolto(-a); corrente; **he speaks ~ Italian, he's ~ in Italian** parla l'italiano correntemente
fluff [flʌf] n lanugine f; **fluffy** adj lanuginoso(-a); (toy) di peluche
fluid ['flu:ɪd] adj fluido(-a) ▶ n fluido; **fluid ounce** n (BRIT) = 0.028 l; 0.05 pints
fluke [flu:k] (inf) n colpo di fortuna
flung [flʌŋ] pt, pp of **fling**
fluorescent [fluə'rɛsnt] adj fluorescente
fluoride ['fluəraɪd] n fluoruro
flurry ['flʌrɪ] n (of snow) tempesta; **a ~ of activity** uno scoppio di attività
flush [flʌʃ] n rossore m; (fig: of youth, beauty etc) rigoglio, pieno vigore ▶ vt ripulire con un getto d'acqua ▶ vi arrossire ▶ adj **~ with** a livello di, pari a; **to ~ the toilet** tirare l'acqua
flute [flu:t] n flauto
flutter ['flʌtə^r] n agitazione f; (of wings) battito ▶ vi (bird) battere le ali
fly [flaɪ] (pt **flew**, pp **flown**) n (insect) mosca; (on trousers: also: **flies**) chiusura ▶ vt pilotare; (passengers, cargo) trasportare (in aereo); (distances) percorrere ▶ vi volare; (passengers) andare in aereo; (escape) fuggire; (flag) sventolare ▷ **fly away** vi volar via; **fly-drive** n fly-drive **holiday** fly and drive m inv; **flying** n (activity) aviazione f; (action) volo ▶ adj **flying visit** visita volante; **with flying colours** con risultati brillanti; **flying saucer** n disco volante; **flyover** (BRIT) n (bridge) cavalcavia m inv
FM abbr (= frequency modulation) FM
foal [fəul] n puledro
foam [fəum] n schiuma; (also: **~ rubber**) gommapiuma® ▶ vi schiumare; (soapy water) fare la schiuma
focus ['fəukəs] (pl **focuses**) n fuoco; (of interest) centro ▶ vt (field glasses etc) mettere a fuoco ▶ vi **to ~ on** (with camera) mettere a fuoco; (person) fissare lo sguardo su; **in ~** a fuoco; **out of ~** sfocato(-a)
foetus ['fi:təs] (US **fetus**) n feto
fog [fɔg] n nebbia; **foggy** adj **it's foggy** c'è nebbia; **fog lamp** (US **fog light**) n (Aut) faro m antinebbia inv
foil [fɔɪl] vt confondere, frustrare ▶ n lamina di metallo; (kitchen foil) foglio di alluminio; (Fencing) fioretto; **to act as a ~ to** (fig) far risaltare
fold [fəuld] n (bend, crease) piega; (Agr) ovile m; (fig) gregge m ▶ vt piegare; (arms) incrociare ▷ **fold up** vi (map, bed, table) piegarsi; (business) crollare ▶ vt (map etc) piegare, ripiegare; **folder** n (for papers) cartella; cartellina; **folding** adj (chair, bed) pieghevole
foliage ['fəulɪɪdʒ] n fogliame m
folk [fəuk] npl gente f ▶ adj popolare; **~s** npl (family) famiglia; **folklore** ['fəuklɔ:^r] n folclore m; **folk music** n musica folk inv; **folk song** n canto popolare
follow ['fɔləu] vt seguire ▶ vi seguire; (result) conseguire, risultare; **to ~ suit** fare lo stesso ▷ **follow up** vt (letter, offer) fare seguito a; (case)

seguire; **follower** n seguace m/f, discepolo(-a); **following** adj seguente ▸ n seguito, discepoli mpl; **follow-up** n seguito

fond [fɒnd] adj (memory, look) tenero(-a), affettuoso(-a); **to be ~ of sb** volere bene a qn; **he's ~ of walking** gli piace fare camminate

food [fuːd] n cibo; **food mixer** n frullatore m; **food poisoning** n intossicazione f; **food processor** [-'prəʊsɛsə] n tritatutto m inv elettrico; **food stamp** (US) n buono alimentare dato agli indigenti

fool [fuːl] n sciocco(-a); (Culin) frullato ▸ vt ingannare ▸ vi (gen: fool around) fare lo sciocco ▷ **fool about, fool around** vi (waste time) perdere tempo; **foolish** adj scemo(-a), stupido(-a); imprudente; **foolproof** adj (plan etc) sicurissimo(-a)

foot [fʊt] (pl **feet**) n piede m; (measure) piede (=304 mm; 12 inches); (of animal) zampa ▸ vt (bill) pagare; **on ~** a piedi; **footage** n (Cinema: length) ≈ metraggio m; (: material) sequenza; **foot-and-mouth (disease)** [fʊtə nd'maʊθ-] n afta epizootica; **football** n pallone m; (sport: BRIT) calcio; (: US) football m americano; **footballer** n (BRIT) = football player; **football match** n (BRIT) partita di calcio; **football player** n (BRIT: also: **footballer**) calciatore m; (US) giocatore m di football americano; **footbridge** n passerella; **foothills** npl contrafforti fpl; **foothold** n punto d'appoggio; **footing** n (fig) posizione f; **to lose one's footing** mettere un piede in fallo; **footnote** n nota (a piè di pagina); **footpath** n sentiero; (in street) marciapiede m; **footprint** n orma, impronta; **footstep** n passo; (footprint) orma, impronta; **footwear** n calzatura

for
[fɔːʳ] prep
1 (indicating destination, intention, purpose) per; **the train for London** il treno per Londra; **he went for the paper** è andato a prendere il giornale; **it's time for lunch** è ora di pranzo; **what's it for?** a che serve?; **what for?** (why) perché?
2 (on behalf of, representing) per; **to work for sb/sth** lavorare per qn/qc; **I'll ask him for you** glielo chiederò a nome tuo; **G for George** G come George
3 (because of) per, a causa di; **for this reason** per questo motivo
4 (with regard to) per; **it's cold for July** è freddo per luglio; **for everyone who voted yes, 50 voted no** per ogni voto a favore ce n'erano 50 contro
5 (in exchange for) per; **I sold it for £5** l'ho venduto per 5 sterline
6 (in favour of) per, a favore di; **are you for or against us?** è con noi o contro di noi?; **I'm all for it** sono completamente a favore
7 (referring to distance, time) per; **there are roadworks for 5 km** ci sono lavori in corso per 5 km; **he was away for 2 years** è stato via per 2 anni; **she will be away for a month** starà via un mese; **it hasn't rained for 3 weeks** non piove da 3 settimane; **can you do it for tomorrow?** può farlo per domani?
8 (with infinitive clauses): **it is not for me to decide** non sta a me decidere; **it would be best for you to leave** sarebbe meglio che lei se ne andasse; **there is still time for you to do it** ha ancora tempo per farlo; **for this to be possible ...** perché ciò sia possibile ...
9 (in spite of) nonostante; **for all his complaints, he's very fond of her** nonostante tutte le sue lamentele, le vuole molto bene
▸conj (since, as: rather formal) dal momento che, poiché

forbid [fəˈbɪd] (*pt* **forbad(e)**, *pp* **forbidden**) *vt* vietare, interdire; **to ~ sb to do sth** proibire a qn di fare qc; **forbidden** *pt of* **forbid** ▶ *adj* (*food*) proibito(-a); (*area*, *territory*) vietato(-a); (*word*, *subject*) tabù *inv*

force [fɔːs] *n* forza ▶ *vt* forzare; **forced** *adj* forzato(-a); **forceful** *adj* forte, vigoroso(-a)

ford [fɔːd] *n* guado

fore [fɔːʳ] *n* **to come to the ~** mettersi in evidenza; **forearm** [ˈfɔːrɑːm] *n* avambraccio; **forecast** [ˈfɔːkɑːst] (*irreg*: *like* **cast**) *n* previsione *f* ▶ *vt* prevedere; **forecourt** [ˈfɔːkɔːt] *n* (*of garage*) corte *f* esterna; **forefinger** [ˈfɔːfɪŋgəʳ] *n* (dito) indice *m*; **forefront** [ˈfɔːfrʌnt] *n* **in the forefront of** all'avanguardia in; **foreground** [ˈfɔːgraund] *n* primo piano; **forehead** [ˈfɔrɪd] *n* fronte *f*

foreign [ˈfɔrɪn] *adj* straniero(-a); (*trade*) estero(-a); (*object*, *matter*) estraneo(-a); **foreign currency** *n* valuta estera; **foreigner** *n* straniero(-a); **foreign exchange** *n* cambio con l'estero; (*currency*) valuta estera; **Foreign Office** (*BRIT*) *n* Ministero degli Esteri; **Foreign Secretary** (*BRIT*) *n* ministro degli Affari esteri

fore: **foreman** [ˈfɔːmən] (*irreg*) *n* caposquadra *m*; **foremost** *adj* principale; più in vista ▶ *adv* **first and foremost** innanzitutto; **forename** *n* nome *m* di battesimo

forensic [fəˈrɛnsɪk] *adj* **~ medicine** medicina legale

foresee [fɔːˈsiː] (*irreg*: *like* **see**) *vt* prevedere; **foreseeable** *adj* prevedibile

forest [ˈfɔrɪst] *n* foresta; **forestry** [ˈfɔrɪstrɪ] *n* silvicoltura

forever [fəˈrɛvəʳ] *adv* per sempre; (*endlessly*) sempre, di continuo

foreword [ˈfɔːwəːd] *n* prefazione *f*

forfeit [ˈfɔːfɪt] *vt* perdere; (*one's happiness*, *health*) giocarsi

forgave [fəˈgeɪv] *pt of* **forgive**

forge [fɔːdʒ] *n* fucina ▶ *vt* (*signature*, *money*) contraffare, falsificare; (*wrought iron*) fucinare, foggiare; **forger** *n* contraffattore *m*; **forgery** *n* falso; (*activity*) contraffazione *f*

forget [fəˈgɛt] (*pt* **forgot**, *pp* **forgotten**) *vt*, *vi* dimenticare; **I've forgotten my key/passport** ho dimenticato la chiave/il passaporto; **forgetful** *adj* di corta memoria; **forgetful of** dimentico(-a) di

forgive [fəˈgɪv] (*pt* **forgave**, *pp* **forgiven**) *vt* perdonare; **to ~ sb for sth** perdonare qc a qn

forgot [fəˈgɔt] *pt of* **forget**

forgotten [fəˈgɔtn] *pp of* **forget**

fork [fɔːk] *n* (*for eating*) forchetta; (*for gardening*) forca; (*of roads*, *rivers*, *railways*) biforcazione *f* ▶ *vi* (*road etc*) biforcarsi

forlorn [fəˈlɔːn] *adj* (*person*) sconsolato(-a); (*place*) abbandonato(-a); (*attempt*) disperato(-a); (*hope*) vano(-a)

form [fɔːm] *n* forma; (*Scol*) classe *f*; (*questionnaire*) scheda ▶ *vt* formare; **in top ~** in gran forma

formal [ˈfɔːməl] *adj* formale; (*gardens*) simmetrico(-a), regolare; **formality** [fɔːˈmælɪtɪ] *n* formalità *f inv*

format [ˈfɔːmæt] *n* formato ▶ *vt* (*Comput*) formattare

formation [fɔːˈmeɪʃən] *n* formazione *f*

former [ˈfɔːməʳ] *adj* vecchio(-a); (*before n*) ex *inv* (*before n*); **the ~ ... the latter** quello ... questo; **formerly** *adv* in passato

formidable [ˈfɔːmɪdəbl] *adj* formidabile

formula [ˈfɔːmjulə] *n* formula

fort [fɔːt] *n* forte *m*

forthcoming [fɔːˈθkʌmɪŋ]
adj (*event*) prossimo(-a); (*help*)
disponibile; (*character*) aperto(-a),
comunicativo(-a)

fortieth [ˈfɔːtɪɪθ] *num*
quarantesimo(-a)

fortify [ˈfɔːtɪfaɪ] *vt* (*city*) fortificare;
(*person*) armare

fortnight [ˈfɔːtnaɪt] (*BRIT*) *n* quindici
giorni *mpl*, due settimane *fpl*;
fortnightly *adj* bimensile ▶ *adv* ogni
quindici giorni

fortress [ˈfɔːtrɪs] *n* fortezza, rocca

fortunate [ˈfɔːtʃənɪt] *adj*
fortunato(-a); **it is ~ that** è una
fortuna che; **fortunately** *adv*
fortunatamente

fortune [ˈfɔːtʃən] *n* fortuna; **fortune-
teller** *n* indovino(-a)

forty [ˈfɔːtɪ] *num* quaranta

forum [ˈfɔːrəm] *n* foro

forward [ˈfɔːwəd] *adj* (*ahead of
schedule*) in anticipo; (*movement,
position*) in avanti; (*not shy*) aperto(-a),
diretto(-a) ▶ *n* (*Sport*) avanti *m inv*
▶ *vt* (*letter*) inoltrare; (*parcel, goods*)
spedire; (*career, plans*) promuovere,
appoggiare; **to move ~** avanzare;
forwarding address *n* nuovo recapito
cui spedire la posta; **forward(s)** *adv*
avanti; **forward slash** *n* barra obliqua

fossil [ˈfɔsl] *adj* fossile ▶ *n* fossile *m*

foster [ˈfɔstər] *vt* incoraggiare,
nutrire; (*child*) avere in affidamento;
foster child *n* bambino(-a) preso(-a)
in affidamento; **foster mother** *n*
madre *f* affidataria

fought [fɔːt] *pt, pp of* **fight**

foul [faul] *adj* (*smell, food, temper etc*)
cattivo(-a); (*weather*) brutto(-a);
(*language*) osceno(-a) ▶ *n* (*Sport*) fallo
▶ *vt* sporcare; **foul play** *n* (*Law*): **the
police suspect foul play** la polizia
sospetta un atto criminale

found [faund] *pt, pp of* **find** ▶ *vt*

(*establish*) fondare; **foundation**
[-ˈdeɪʃən] *n* (*act*) fondazione *f*; (*base*)
base *f*; (*also:* **foundation cream**)
fondo tinta; **foundations** *npl* (*of
building*) fondamenta *fpl*

founder [ˈfaundər] *n* fondatore(-trice)
▶ *vi* affondare

fountain [ˈfauntɪn] *n* fontana;
fountain pen *n* penna stilografica

four [fɔːr] *num* quattro; **on all ~s** a
carponi; **four-letter word**
[ˈfɔːlɛtə-] *n* parolaccia; **four-poster**
n (*also:* **four-poster bed**) letto a
quattro colonne; **fourteen** *num*
quattordici; **fourteenth** *num*
quattordicesimo(-a); **fourth** *num*
quarto(-a); **four-wheel drive**
[ˈfɔːwiːl-] *n* (*Aut*): **with four-wheel
drive** con quattro ruote motrici

fowl [faul] *n* pollame *m*; volatile *m*

fox [fɔks] *n* volpe *f* ▶ *vt* confondere

foyer [ˈfɔɪeɪ] *n* atrio; (*Theatre*) ridotto

fraction [ˈfrækʃən] *n* frazione *f*

fracture [ˈfræktʃər] *n* frattura

fragile [ˈfrædʒaɪl] *adj* fragile

fragment [ˈfrægmənt] *n* frammento

fragrance [ˈfreɪɡrəns] *n* fragranza,
profumo

frail [freɪl] *adj* debole, delicato(-a)

frame [freɪm] *n* (*of building*) armatura;
(*of human, animal*) ossatura, corpo;
(*of picture*) cornice *f*; (*of door, window*)
telaio; (*of spectacles: also:* **~s**)
montatura ▶ *vt* (*picture*) incorniciare;
framework *n* struttura

France [frɑːns] *n* Francia

franchise [ˈfræntʃaɪz] *n* (*Pol*) diritto di
voto; (*Comm*) concessione *f*

frank [fræŋk] *adj* franco(-a),
aperto(-a) ▶ *vt* (*letter*) affrancare;
frankly *adv* francamente,
sinceramente

frantic [ˈfræntɪk] *adj* frenetico(-a)

fraud [frɔːd] *n* truffa; (*Law*) frode *f*;
(*person*) impostore(-a)

fraught [frɔːt] adj ~ **with** pieno(-a) di, intriso(-a) da

fray [freɪ] vt logorare ▶ vi logorarsi

freak [friːk] n fenomeno, mostro

freckle ['frɛkl] n lentiggine f

free [friː] adj libero(-a); (gratis) gratuito(-a) ▶ vt (prisoner, jammed person) liberare; (jammed object) districare; **is this seat ~?** è libero questo posto?; **~ of charge, for ~** gratuitamente; **freedom** ['friːdəm] n libertà; **Freefone**® n numero verde; **free gift** n regalo, omaggio; **free kick** n calcio libero; **freelance** adj indipendente; **freely** adv liberamente; (liberally) liberalmente; **Freepost**® n affrancatura a carico del destinatario; **free-range** adj (hen) ruspante; (eggs) di gallina ruspante; **freeway** (US) n superstrada; **free will** n libero arbitrio; **of one's own free will** di spontanea volontà

freeze [friːz] (pt **froze**, pp **frozen**) vi gelare ▶ vt gelare; (food) congelare; (prices, salaries) bloccare ▶ n gelo; blocco; **freezer** n congelatore m; **freezing** ['friːzɪŋ] adj (wind, weather) gelido(-a); **freezing point** n punto di congelamento; **3 degrees below freezing point** 3 gradi sotto zero

freight [freɪt] n (goods) merce f, merci fpl; (money charged) spese fpl di trasporto; **freight train** (US) n treno m merci inv

French [frɛntʃ] adj francese ▶ n (Ling) francese m; **the ~** npl i Francesi; **French bean** n fagiolino; **French bread** n baguette f inv; **French dressing** n (Culin) condimento per insalata; **French fried potatoes** (US **French fries**) npl patate fpl fritte; **Frenchman** (irreg) n francese m; **French stick** n baguette f inv; **French window** n portafinestra; **Frenchwoman** (irreg) n francese f

frenzy ['frɛnzɪ] n frenesia

frequency ['friːkwənsɪ] n frequenza

frequent [adj 'friːkwənt, vb frɪ'kwɛnt] adj frequente ▶ vt frequentare; **frequently** adv frequentemente, spesso

fresh [frɛʃ] adj fresco(-a); (new) nuovo(-a); (cheeky) sfacciato(-a); **freshen** vi (wind, air) rinfrescare ▶ **freshen up** vi rinfrescarsi; **fresher** (BRIT: inf) n (Scol) matricola; **freshly** adv di recente, di fresco; **freshman** (irreg: US) n = **fresher**; **freshwater** adj (fish) d'acqua dolce

fret [frɛt] vi agitarsi, affliggersi

Fri. abbr (= Friday) ven.

friction ['frɪkʃən] n frizione f, attrito

Friday ['fraɪdɪ] n venerdì m inv

fridge [frɪdʒ] n frigo, frigorifero

fried [fraɪd] pt, pp of **fry** ▶ adj fritto(-a)

friend [frɛnd] n amico(-a); **friendly** adj amichevole; **friendship** n amicizia

fries [fraɪz] (esp US) npl patate fpl fritte

frigate ['frɪgɪt] n (Naut: modern) fregata

fright [fraɪt] n paura, spavento; **to take ~** spaventarsi; **frighten** vt spaventare, far paura a; **frightened** adj spaventato(-a); **frightening** adj spaventoso(-a), pauroso(-a); **frightful** adj orribile

frill [frɪl] n balza

fringe [frɪndʒ] n (decoration: BRIT: of hair) frangia; (edge: of forest etc) margine m

Frisbee® ['frɪzbɪ] n frisbee® m inv

fritter ['frɪtər] n frittella

frivolous ['frɪvələs] adj frivolo(-a)

fro [frəu] see **to**

frock [frɔk] n vestito

frog [frɔg] n rana; **frogman** (irreg) n uomo m rana inv

from

[frɔm] prep

1 (*indicating starting place, origin etc*) da; **where do you come from?, where are you from?** da dove viene?, di dov'è?; **from London to Glasgow** da Londra a Glasgow; **a letter from my sister** una lettera da mia sorella; **tell him from me that …** gli dica da parte mia che …

2 (*indicating time*) da; **from one o'clock to** *or* **until** *or* **till two** dall'una alle due; **from January (on)** da gennaio, a partire da gennaio

3 (*indicating distance*) da; **the hotel is 1 km from the beach** l'albergo è a 1 km dalla spiaggia

4 (*indicating price, number etc*) da; **prices range from £10 to £50** i prezzi vanno dalle 10 alle 50 sterline

5 (*indicating difference*) da; **he can't tell red from green** non sa distinguere il rosso dal verde

6 (*because of, on the basis of*): **from what he says** da quanto dice lui; **weak from hunger** debole per la fame

front [frʌnt] n (*of house, dress*) davanti m inv; (*of train*) testa; (*of book*) copertina; (*promenade: also:* **sea ~**) lungomare m; (*Mil, Pol, Meteor*) fronte m; (*fig: appearances*) fronte f ▶ adj primo(-a); anteriore, davanti inv; **in ~ of** davanti a; **front door** n porta d'entrata; (*of car*) sportello anteriore; **frontier** n frontiera; **front page** n prima pagina; **front-wheel drive** n trasmissione f anteriore

frost [frɔst] n gelo; (*also:* **hoar~**) brina; **frostbite** n congelamento; **frosting** (*US*) n (*on cake*) glassa; **frosty** adj (*weather, look*) gelido(-a)

froth ['frɔθ] n spuma; schiuma

frown [fraun] vi accigliarsi

froze [frəuz] pt of **freeze**

frozen ['frəuzn] pp of **freeze**

fruit [fru:t] n inv (*also fig*) frutto; (*collectively*) frutta; **fruit juice** n succo di frutta; **fruit machine** (*BRIT*) n macchina f mangiasoldi inv; **fruit salad** n macedonia

frustrate [frʌs'treɪt] vt frustrare; **frustrated** adj frustrato(-a)

fry [fraɪ] (*pt, pp* **fried**) vt friggere; *see also* **small**; **frying pan** n padella

ft. abbr = **foot**; **feet**

fudge [fʌdʒ] n (*Culin*) specie di caramella a base di latte, burro e zucchero

fuel [fjuəl] n (*for heating*) combustibile m; (*for propelling*) carburante m; **fuel tank** n deposito m nafta inv; (*on vehicle*) serbatoio (della benzina)

fulfil [ful'fɪl] vt (*function*) compiere; (*order*) eseguire; (*wish, desire*) soddisfare, appagare

full [ful] adj pieno(-a); (*details, skirt*) ampio(-a) ▶ adv **to know ~ well that** sapere benissimo che; **I'm ~ (up)** sono sazio; **a ~ two hours** due ore intere; **at ~ speed** a tutta velocità; **in ~** per intero; **full-length** adj (*film*) a lungometraggio; (*coat, novel*) lungo(-a); (*portrait*) in piedi; **full moon** n luna piena; **full-scale** adj (*attack, war*) su larga scala; (*model*) in grandezza naturale; **full stop** n punto; **full-time** adj, adv (*work*) a tempo pieno; **fully** adv interamente, pienamente, completamente; (*at least*) almeno

fumble ['fʌmbl] vi **to ~ with sth** armeggiare con qc

fume [fju:m] vi essere furioso(-a); **fumes** npl esalazioni fpl, vapori mpl

fun [fʌn] n divertimento, spasso; **to have ~** divertirsi; **for ~** per scherzo; **to make ~ of** prendersi gioco di

function ['fʌŋkʃən] n funzione f; cerimonia ▶ vi funzionare

fund [fʌnd] n fondo, cassa; (*source*) fondo; (*store*) riserva; **~s** npl (*money*) fondi mpl

fundamental [fʌndə'mɛntl] *adj* fondamentale

funeral ['fjuːnərəl] *n* funerale *m*; **funeral director** *n* impresario di pompe funebri; **funeral parlour** [-'pɑːləʳ] *n* impresa di pompe funebri

funfair ['fʌnfɛəʳ] *n* luna park *m inv*

fungus ['fʌŋɡəs] (*pl* **fungi**) *n* fungo; (*mould*) muffa

funnel ['fʌnl] *n* imbuto; (*of ship*) ciminiera

funny ['fʌnɪ] *adj* divertente, buffo(-a); (*strange*) strano(-a), bizzarro(-a)

fur [fəːʳ] *n* pelo; pelliccia; (*BRIT: in kettle etc*) deposito calcare; **fur coat** *n* pelliccia

furious ['fjuərɪəs] *adj* furioso(-a); (*effort*) accanito(-a)

furnish ['fəːnɪʃ] *vt* ammobiliare; (*supply*) fornire; **furnishings** *npl* mobili *mpl*, mobilia

furniture ['fəːnɪtʃəʳ] *n* mobili *mpl*; **piece of ~** mobile *m*

furry ['fəːrɪ] *adj* (*animal*) peloso(-a)

further ['fəːðəʳ] *adj* supplementare, altro(-a); nuovo(-a); più lontano(-a) ▶ *adv* più lontano; (*more*) di più; (*moreover*) inoltre ▶ *vt* favorire, promuovere; **further education** *n* ≈ corsi *mpl* di formazione; **college of further education** *istituto statale con corsi specializzati (di formazione professionale, aggiornamento professionale ecc)*; **furthermore** [fəːðə'mɔːʳ] *adv* inoltre, per di più

furthest ['fəːðɪst] *superl of* **far**

fury ['fjuərɪ] *n* furore *m*

fuse [fjuːz] (*US* **fuse**) *n* fusibile *m*; (*for bomb etc*) miccia, spoletta ▶ *vt* fondere ▶ *vi* fondersi; **to ~ the lights** (*BRIT Elec*) far saltare i fusibili; **fuse box** *n* cassetta dei fusibili

fusion ['fjuːʒən] *n* fusione *f*

fuss [fʌs] *n* agitazione *f*; (*complaining*) storie *fpl*; **to make a ~** fare delle storie;

fussy *adj* (*person*) puntiglioso(-a), esigente; che fa le storie; (*dress*) carico(-a) di fronzoli; (*style*) elaborato(-a)

future ['fjuːtʃəʳ] *adj* futuro(-a) ▶ *n* futuro, avvenire *m*; (*Ling*) futuro; **in ~** in futuro; **~s** *npl* (*Comm*) operazioni *fpl* a termine

fuze [fjuːz] (*US*) = **fuse**

fuzzy ['fʌzɪ] *adj* (*Phot*) indistinto(-a), sfocato(-a); (*hair*) crespo(-a)

g

G [dʒiː] *n* (*Mus*) sol *m*

g. *abbr* (= *gram, gravity*) g.

gadget ['gædʒɪt] *n* aggeggio

Gaelic ['geɪlɪk] *adj* gaelico(-a) ▶ *n* (*Ling*) gaelico

gag [gæg] *n* bavaglio; (*joke*) facezia, scherzo ▶ *vt* imbavagliare

gain [geɪn] *n* guadagno, profitto ▶ *vt* guadagnare ▶ *vi* (*clock, watch*) andare avanti; (*benefit*): **to ~ (from)** trarre beneficio (da); **to ~ 3lbs (in weight)** aumentare di 3 libbre; **to ~ on sb** (*in race etc*) guadagnare su qn

gal. *abbr* = **gallon**

gala ['gɑːlə] *n* gala; **swimming ~** manifestazione *f* di nuoto

galaxy ['gæləksɪ] *n* galassia

gale [geɪl] *n* vento forte; burrasca

gall bladder ['gɔːl-] *n* cistifellea

gallery ['gæləri] n galleria
gallon ['gælən] n gallone m (= 8 pints;
  BRIT = 4.543l; US = 3.785l)
gallop ['gæləp] n galoppo ▶ vi
  galoppare
gallstone ['gɔːlstəun] n calcolo biliare
gamble ['gæmbl] n azzardo,
  rischio calcolato ▶ vt, vi giocare;
  to ~ on (fig) giocare su; **gambler**
  n giocatore(-trice) d'azzardo;
  gambling n gioco d'azzardo
game [geɪm] n gioco; (event) partita;
  (Tennis) game m inv; (Culin, Hunting)
  selvaggina ▶ adj (ready): **to be ~ (for**
  sth/to do) essere pronto(-a) (a
  qc/a fare); **big ~** selvaggina grossa;
  ~s npl (Scol) attività fpl sportive;
  big ~ selvaggina grossa; **games**
  console [geɪmz-] n console f inv dei
  videogame; **game show** ['geɪmʃəu] n
  gioco a premi
gammon ['gæmən] n (bacon)
  quarto di maiale; (ham) prosciutto
  affumicato
gang [gæŋ] n banda, squadra ▶ vi **to ~**
  up on sb far combutta contro qn
gangster ['gæŋstəʳ] n gangster m inv
gap [gæp] n (space) buco; (in time)
  intervallo; (difference): **~ (between)**
  divario (tra)
gape [geɪp] vi (person) restare a
  bocca aperta; (shirt, hole) essere
  spalancato(-a)
gap year n (Scol) anno di pausa durante il
  quale gli studenti viaggiano o lavorano
garage ['gærɑːʒ] n garage m inv;
  garage sale n vendita di oggetti usati
  nel garage di un privato
garbage ['gɑːbɪdʒ] (US) n immondizie
  fpl, rifiuti mpl; (inf) sciocchezze fpl;
  garbage can (US) n bidone m della
  spazzatura; **garbage collector** (US) n
  spazzino(-a)
garden ['gɑːdn] n giardino; **~s**
  npl (public park) giardini pubblici;

garden centre n vivaio; **gardener**
  n giardiniere(-a); **gardening** n
  giardinaggio
garlic ['gɑːlɪk] n aglio
garment ['gɑːmənt] n indumento
garnish ['gɑːnɪʃ] vt (food) guarnire
garrison ['gærɪsn] n guarnigione f
gas [gæs] n gas m inv; (US: gasoline)
  benzina ▶ vt asfissiare con il gas; **I**
  can smell ~ sento odore di gas; **gas**
  cooker (BRIT) n cucina a gas; **gas**
  cylinder n bombola del gas; **gas fire**
  (BRIT) n radiatore m a gas
gasket ['gæskɪt] n (Aut) guarnizione f
gasoline ['gæsəliːn] (US) n benzina
gasp [gɑːsp] n respiro affannoso,
  ansito ▶ vi ansare, ansimare; (in
  surprise) restare senza fiato
gas: **gas pedal** (esp US) n pedale m
  dell'acceleratore; **gas station** (US) n
  distributore m di benzina; **gas tank**
  (US) n (Aut) serbatoio (di benzina)
gate [geɪt] n cancello; (at airport)
  uscita
gateau ['gætəu, -z] (pl **gateaux**)
  n torta
gatecrash ['geɪtkræʃ] (BRIT) vt
  partecipare senza invito a
gateway ['geɪtweɪ] n porta
gather ['gæðəʳ] vt (flowers, fruit)
  cogliere; (pick up) raccogliere;
  (assemble) radunare; raccogliere;
  (understand) capire; (Sewing)
  increspare ▶ vi (assemble) radunarsi;
  to ~ speed acquistare velocità;
  gathering n adunanza
gauge [geɪdʒ] n (instrument) indicatore
  m ▶ vt misurare; (fig) valutare
gave [geɪv] pt of **give**
gay [geɪ] adj (homosexual)
  omosessuale; (cheerful) gaio(-a),
  allegro(-a); (colour) vivace, vivo(-a)
gaze [geɪz] n sguardo fisso ▶ vi **to ~ at**
  guardare fisso
GB abbr = **Great Britain**

GCSE (*BRIT*) *n abbr General Certificate of Secondary Education*

gear [gɪə^r] *n* attrezzi *mpl*, equipaggiamento; (*Tech*) ingranaggio; (*Aut*) marcia ▶ *vt* (*fig: adapt*): **to ~ sth to** adattare qc a; **in top** *or* (*US*) **high/low ~** in quarta (*or* quinta)/seconda; **in ~** in marcia ▷ **gear up** *vi* **to ~ up (to do)** prepararsi (a fare); **gear box** *n* scatola del cambio; **gear lever** *n* leva del cambio; **gear shift** (*US*), **gear stick** (*BRIT*) *n* = **gear lever**

geese [giːs] *npl of* **goose**

gel [dʒɛl] *n* gel *m inv*

gem [dʒɛm] *n* gemma

Gemini [ˈdʒɛmɪnaɪ] *n* Gemelli *mpl*

gender [ˈdʒɛndə^r] *n* genere *m*

gene [dʒiːn] *n* (*Biol*) gene *m*

general [ˈdʒɛnərl] *n* generale *m* ▶ *adj* generale; **in ~** in genere; **general anaesthetic** (*US* **general anesthetic**) *n* anestesia totale; **general election** *n* elezioni *fpl* generali; **generalize** *vi* generalizzare; **generally** *adv* generalmente; **general practitioner** *n* medico generico; **general store** *n* emporio

generate [ˈdʒɛnəreɪt] *vt* generare

generation [dʒɛnəˈreɪʃən] *n* generazione *f*

generator [ˈdʒɛnəreɪtə^r] *n* generatore *m*

generosity [dʒɛnəˈrɔsɪtɪ] *n* generosità

generous [ˈdʒɛnərəs] *adj* generoso(-a); (*copious*) abbondante

genetic [dʒɪˈnɛtɪk] *adj* genetico(-a); **~ engineering** ingegneria genetica; **genetically modified** *adj* geneticamente modificato(-a), transgenico(-a); **genetics** *n* genetica

Geneva [dʒɪˈniːvə] *n* Ginevra

genitals [ˈdʒɛnɪtlz] *npl* genitali *mpl*

genius [ˈdʒiːnɪəs] *n* genio

Genoa [ˈdʒɛnəuə] *n* Genova

gent [dʒɛnt] *n abbr* = **gentleman**

gentle [ˈdʒɛntl] *adj* delicato(-a); (*person*) dolce

📖 Be careful not to translate **gentle** by the Italian word *gentile*.

gentleman [ˈdʒɛntlmən] (*irreg*) *n* signore *m*; (*well-bred man*) gentiluomo

gently [ˈdʒɛntlɪ] *adv* delicatamente

gents [dʒɛnts] *n* W.C. *m* (per signori)

genuine [ˈdʒɛnjuɪn] *adj* autentico(-a); sincero(-a); **genuinely** *adv* genuinamente

geographic(al) [dʒɪəˈɡræfɪk(l)] *adj* geografico(-a)

geography [dʒɪˈɔɡrəfɪ] *n* geografia

geology [dʒɪˈɔlədʒɪ] *n* geologia

geometry [dʒɪˈɔmətrɪ] *n* geometria

geranium [dʒɪˈreɪnjəm] *n* geranio

geriatric [dʒɛrɪˈætrɪk] *adj* geriatrico(-a)

germ [dʒəːm] *n* (*Med*) microbo; (*Biol*, *fig*) germe *m*

German [ˈdʒəːmən] *adj* tedesco(-a) ▶ *n* tedesco(-a); (*Ling*) tedesco; **German measles** (*BRIT*) *n* rosolia

Germany [ˈdʒəːmənɪ] *n* Germania

gesture [ˈdʒɛstjə^r] *n* gesto

⭕ **get**
[ɡɛt] (*pt*, *pp* **got**, (*US*) *pp* **gotten**) *vi*
🔳 (*become, be*) diventare, farsi; **to get old** invecchiare; **to get tired** stancarsi; **to get drunk** ubriacarsi; **to get killed** venire *or* rimanere ucciso(-a); **when do I get paid?** quando mi pagate?; **it's getting late** si sta facendo tardi
🔳 (*go*): **to get to/from** andare a/da; **to get home** arrivare *or* tornare a casa; **how did you get here?** come sei venuto?
🔳 (*begin*) mettersi a, cominciare a; **to get to know sb** incominciare a conoscere qn; **let's get going** *or* **started** muoviamoci

4 (*modal aux vb*): **you've got to do it** devi farlo

▶*vt*

1: **to get sth done** (*do*) fare qc; (*have done*) far fare qc; **to get one's hair cut** farsi tagliare i capelli; **to get sb to do sth** far fare qc a qn

2 (*obtain: money, permission, results*) ottenere; (*find: job, flat*) trovare; (*fetch: person, doctor*) chiamare; (: *object*) prendere; **to get sth for sb** prendere or procurare qc a qn; **get me Mr Jones, please** (*Tel*) mi passi il signor Jones, per favore; **can I get you a drink?** le posso offrire da bere?

3 (*receive: present, letter, prize*) ricevere; (*acquire: reputation*) farsi; **how much did you get for the painting?** quanto le hanno dato per il quadro?

4 (*catch*) prendere; (*hit: target etc*) colpire; **to get sb by the arm/throat** afferrare qn per un braccio/alla gola; **get him!** prendetelo!

5 (*take, move*) portare; **to get sth to sb** far avere qc a qn; **do you think we'll get it through the door?** pensi che riusciremo a farlo passare per la porta?

6 (*catch, take: plane, bus etc*) prendere; **where do we get the ferry to …?** dove si prende il traghetto per …?

7 (*understand*) afferrare; (*hear*) sentire; **I've got it!** ci sono arrivato!, ci sono!; **I'm sorry, I didn't get your name** scusi, non ho capito (*or* sentito) il suo nome

8 (*have, possess*): **to have got** avere; **how many have you got?** quanti ne ha?

▷ **get along** *vi* (*agree*) andare d'accordo; (*depart*) andarsene; (*manage*) = **get by**

▷ **get at** *vt fus* (*attack*) prendersela con; (*reach*) raggiungere, arrivare a

▷ **get away** *vi* partire, andarsene; (*escape*) scappare

▷ **get away with** *vt fus* cavarsela; farla franca

▷ **get back** *vi* (*return*) ritornare, tornare

▶ *vt* riottenere, riavere; **when do we get back?** quando ritorniamo?

▷ **get by** *vi* (*pass*) passare; (*manage*) farcela

▷ **get down** *vi*, *vt fus* scendere ▶ *vt* far scendere; (*depress*) buttare giù

▷ **get down to** *vt fus* (*work*) mettersi a (fare)

▷ **get in** *vi* entrare; (*train*) arrivare; (*arrive home*) ritornare, tornare

▷ **get into** *vt fus* entrare in; **to get into a rage** incavolarsi

▷ **get off** *vi* (*from train etc*) scendere; (*depart: person, car*) andare via; (*escape*) cavarsela ▶ *vt* (*remove: clothes, stain*) levare ▶ *vt fus* (*train, bus*) scendere da; **where do I get off?** dove devo scendere?

▷ **get on** *vi* (*at exam etc*) andare; (*agree*): **to get on (with)** andare d'accordo (con) ▶ *vt fus* montare in; (*horse*) montare su

▷ **get out** *vi* uscire; (*of vehicle*) scendere ▶ *vt* tirar fuori, far uscire

▷ **get out of** *vt fus* uscire da; (*duty etc*) evitare

▷ **get over** *vt fus* (*illness*) riaversi da

▷ **get round** *vt fus* aggirare; (*fig: person*) rigirare

▷ **get through** *vi* (*Tel*) avere la linea

▷ **get through to** *vt fus* (*Tel*) parlare a

▷ **get together** *vi* riunirsi ▶ *vt* raccogliere; (*people*) adunare

▷ **get up** *vi* (*rise*) alzarsi ▶ *vt fus* salire su per

▷ **get up to** *vt fus* (*reach*) raggiungere; (*prank etc*) fare

getaway ['gɛtəweɪ] *n* fuga

Ghana ['gɑːnə] *n* Ghana *m*

ghastly ['gɑːstlɪ] *adj* orribile, orrendo(-a); (*pale*) spettrale

ghetto ['gɛtəʊ] *n* ghetto

ghost [gəʊst] *n* fantasma *m*, spettro

giant ['dʒaɪənt] *n* gigante *m* ▶ *adj* gigantesco(-a), enorme

gift [gɪft] n regalo; (donation, ability) dono; **gifted** adj dotato(-a); **gift shop** (US **gift store**) n negozio di souvenir

gift token, gift voucher n buono m omaggio inv

gig [gɪg] n (inf: of musician) serata

gigabyte [giːgəbaɪt] n gigabyte m inv

gigantic [dʒaɪˈɡæntɪk] adj gigantesco(-a)

giggle [ˈɡɪɡl] vi ridere scioccamente

gills [ɡɪlz] npl (of fish) branchie fpl

gilt [ɡɪlt] n doratura ▶ adj dorato(-a)

gimmick [ˈɡɪmɪk] n trucco

gin [dʒɪn] n (liquor) gin m inv

ginger [ˈdʒɪndʒəʳ] n zenzero

gipsy [ˈdʒɪpsɪ] n zingaro(-a)

giraffe [dʒɪˈrɑːf] n giraffa

girl [ɡəːl] n ragazza; (young unmarried woman) signorina; (daughter) figlia, figliola; **girlfriend** n (of girl) amica, (of boy) ragazza; **Girl Scout** (US) n Giovane Esploratrice f

gist [dʒɪst] n succo

give [ɡɪv] (pt **gave**, pp **given**) vt dare ▶ vi cedere; **to ~ sb sth, ~ sth to sb** dare qc a qn; **I'll ~ you £5 for it** te lo pago 5 sterline; **to ~ a cry/sigh** emettere un grido/sospiro; **to ~ a speech** fare un discorso ▷ **give away** vt dare via; (disclose) rivelare; (bride) condurre all'altare ▷ **give back** vt rendere ▷ **give in** vi cedere ▶ vt consegnare ▷ **give out** vt distribuire; annunciare ▷ **give up** vi rinunciare ▶ vt rinunciare a; **to ~ up smoking** smettere di fumare; **to ~ o.s. up** arrendersi

given [ˈɡɪvn] pp of **give** ▶ adj (fixed: time, amount) dato(-a), determinato(-a) ▶ conj **~ (that) ...** dato che ...; **~ the circumstances ...** date le circostanze ...

glacier [ˈɡlæsɪəʳ] n ghiacciaio

glad [ɡlæd] adj lieto(-a), contento(-a); **gladly** [ˈɡlædlɪ] adv volentieri

glamorous [ˈɡlæmərəs] adj affascinante, seducente

glamour [ˈɡlæməʳ] (US **glamor**) n fascino

glance [ɡlɑːns] n occhiata, sguardo ▶ vi **to ~ at** dare un'occhiata a; **to ~ off** (bullet) rimbalzare su

gland [ɡlænd] n ghiandola

glare [ɡlɛəʳ] n (of anger) sguardo furioso; (of light) riverbero, luce f abbagliante; (of publicity) chiasso ▶ vi abbagliare; **to ~ at** guardare male; **glaring** adj (mistake) madornale

glass [ɡlɑːs] n (substance) vetro; (tumbler) bicchiere m; **~es** npl (spectacles) occhiali mpl

glaze [ɡleɪz] vt (door) fornire di vetri; (pottery) smaltare ▶ n smalto

gleam [ɡliːm] vi luccicare

glen [ɡlɛn] n valletta

glide [ɡlaɪd] vi scivolare; (Aviat, birds) planare; **glider** n (Aviat) aliante m

glimmer [ˈɡlɪməʳ] n barlume m

glimpse [ɡlɪmps] n impressione f fugace ▶ vt vedere al volo

glint [ɡlɪnt] vi luccicare

glisten [ˈɡlɪsn] vi luccicare

glitter [ˈɡlɪtəʳ] vi scintillare

global [ˈɡləubl] adj globale; **global warming** n effetto m serra inv

globe [ɡləub] n globo, sfera

gloom [ɡluːm] n oscurità, buio; (sadness) tristezza, malinconia; **gloomy** adj scuro(-a), fosco(-a), triste

glorious [ˈɡlɔːrɪəs] adj glorioso(-a), magnifico(-a)

glory [ˈɡlɔːrɪ] n gloria; splendore m

gloss [ɡlɔs] n (shine) lucentezza; (also: **~ paint**) vernice f a olio

glossary [ˈɡlɔsərɪ] n glossario

glossy [ˈɡlɔsɪ] adj lucente

glove [ɡlʌv] n guanto; **glove compartment** n (Aut) vano portaoggetti

glow [ɡləu] vi ardere; (face) essere luminoso(-a)

glucose ['glu:kəus] *n* glucosio
glue [glu:] *n* colla ▸ *vt* incollare
GM *adj abbr* (= *genetically modified*)
geneticamente modificato(-a)
gm *abbr* = **gram**
GMO *n abbr* (= *genetically modified organism*) OGM *m inv*
GMT *abbr* (= *Greenwich Mean Time*) T.M.G.
gnaw [nɔ:] *vt* rodere
go [gəu] (*pt* went, *pp* gone) (*pl* goes) *vi*
andare; (*depart*) partire, andarsene;
(*work*) funzionare; (*time*) passare;
(*break etc*) rompersi; (*be sold*): **to go for £10** essere venduto per 10 sterline;
(*fit, suit*): **to go with** andare bene
con; (*become*): **to go pale** diventare
pallido(-a); **to go mouldy** ammuffire
▸ *n* **to have a go (at)** provare; **to be on the go** essere in moto; **whose go is it?** a chi tocca?; **he's going to do** sta per fare; **to go for a walk**
andare a fare una passeggiata; **to go dancing/shopping** andare a
ballare/fare la spesa; **just then the bell went** proprio allora suonò il
campanello; **how did it go?** com'è
andato?; **to go round the back/by the shop** passare da dietro/davanti al
negozio ▷ **go ahead** *vi* andare avanti
▷ **go away** *vi* partire, andarsene ▷ **go back** *vi* tornare, ritornare ▷ **go by** *vi*
(*years, time*) scorrere ▸ *vt fus* attenersi
a, seguire (alla lettera); prestar
fede a ▷ **go down** *vi* scendere; (*ship*)
affondare; (*sun*) tramontare ▸ *vt fus*
scendere ▷ **go for** *vt fus* (*fetch*) andare
a prendere; (*like*) andar matto(-a) per;
(*attack*) attaccare; saltare addosso
a ▷ **go in** *vi* entrare ▷ **go into** *vt fus*
entrare in; (*investigate*) indagare,
esaminare; (*embark on*) lanciarsi
in ▷ **go off** *vi* partire, andar via;
(*food*) guastarsi; (*explode*) esplodere,
scoppiare; (*event*) passare ▸ *vt fus*
I've ~ne off chocolate la cioccolata

non mi piace più; **the gun went off** il
fucile si scaricò ▷ **go on** *vi* continuare;
(*happen*) succedere; **to ~ on doing**
continuare a fare ▷ **go out** *vi* uscire;
(*couple*): **they went out for 3 years**
sono stati insieme per 3 anni; (*fire, light*) spegnersi ▷ **go over** *vi* (*ship*)
ribaltarsi ▸ *vt fus* (*check*) esaminare
▷ **go past** *vi* passare ▸ *vt fus* passare
davanti a ▷ **go round** *vi* (*circulate: news, rumour*) circolare; (*revolve*)
girare; (*visit*): **to ~ round (to sb's)**
passare (da qn); (*make a detour*): **to ~ round (by)** passare (per); (*suffice*)
bastare (per tutti) ▷ **go through** *vt fus*
(*town etc*) attraversare; (*files, papers*)
passare in rassegna; (*examine: list etc*) leggere da cima a fondo ▷ **go up**
vi salire ▷ **go with** *vt fus* (*accompany*)
accompagnare ▷ **go without** *vt fus*
fare a meno di
go-ahead ['gəuəhɛd] *adj*
intraprendente ▸ *n* via *m*
goal [gəul] *n* (*Sport*) gol *m*, rete *f*;
(: *place*) porta; (*fig: aim*) fine *m*, scopo;
goalkeeper *n* portiere *m*; **goal-post** *n*
palo (della porta)
goat [gəut] *n* capra
gobble ['gɔbl] *vt* (*also: ~ down, ~ up*)
ingoiare
god [gɔd] *n* dio; **G~** Dio; **godchild**
n figlioccio(-a); **goddaughter** *n*
figlioccia; **goddess** *n* dea; **godfather**
n padrino; **godmother** *n* madrina;
godson *n* figlioccio
goggles ['gɔglz] *npl* occhiali *mpl* (di
protezione)
going ['gəuɪŋ] *n* (*conditions*) andare
m, stato del terreno ▸ *adj* **the ~ rate** la
tariffa in vigore
gold [gəuld] *n* oro ▸ *adj* d'oro; **golden**
adj (*made of gold*) d'oro; (*gold in colour*)
dorato(-a); **goldfish** *n* pesce *m* dorato
or rosso; **goldmine** *n* (*also fig*) miniera
d'oro; **gold-plated** *adj* placcato(-a)

oro *inv*

golf [gɔlf] *n* golf *m*; **golf ball** *n* (*for game*) pallina da golf; (*on typewriter*) pallina; **golf club** *n* circolo di golf; (*stick*) bastone *m* or mazza da golf; **golf course** *n* campo di golf; **golfer** *n* giocatore(-trice) di golf

gone [gɔn] *pp of* **go** ▶ *adj* partito(-a)

gong [gɔŋ] *n* gong *m inv*

good [gud] *adj* buono(-a); (*kind*) buono(-a), gentile; (*child*) bravo(-a) ▶ *n* bene *m*; **~s** *npl* (*Comm etc*) beni *mpl*; merci *fpl*; **~!** bene!, ottimo!; **to be ~ at** essere bravo(-a) in; **to be ~ for** andare bene per; **it's ~ for you** fa bene; **would you be ~ enough to …?** avrebbe la gentilezza di …?; **a ~ deal (of)** molto(-a), una buona quantità (di); **a ~ many** molti(-e); **to make ~** (*loss, damage*) compensare; **it's no ~ complaining** brontolare non serve a niente; **for ~** per sempre, definitivamente; **~ morning!** buon giorno!; **~ afternoon/evening!** buona sera!; **~ night!** buona notte!; **goodbye** *excl* arrivederci!; **Good Friday** *n* Venerdì Santo; **good-looking** *adj* bello(-a); **good-natured** *adj* affabile; **goodness** *n* (*of person*) bontà; **for goodness sake!** per amor di Dio!; **goodness gracious!** santo cielo!, mamma mia!; **goods train** (*BRIT*) *n* treno *m* merci *inv*; **goodwill** *n* amicizia, benevolenza

goose [gu:s] (*pl* **geese**) *n* oca

gooseberry ['guzbərɪ] *n* uva spina; **to play ~** (*BRIT*) tenere la candela

goose bumps, goose pimples *npl* pelle *f* d'oca

gorge [gɔ:dʒ] *n* gola ▶ *vt* **to ~ o.s. (on)** ingozzarsi (di)

gorgeous ['gɔ:dʒəs] *adj* magnifico(-a)

gorilla [gə'rɪlə] *n* gorilla *m inv*

gosh (*inf*) [gɔʃ] *excl* perdinci!

gospel ['gɔspl] *n* vangelo

gossip ['gɔsɪp] *n* chiacchiere *fpl*; pettegolezzi *mpl*; (*person*) pettegolo(-a) ▶ *vi* chiacchierare; **gossip column** *n* cronaca mondana

got [gɔt] *pt, pp of* **get**

gotten ['gɔtn] (*US*) *pp of* **get**

gourmet ['guəmeɪ] *n* buongustaio(-a)

govern ['gʌvən] *vt* governare; **government** ['gʌvnmənt] *n* governo; **governor** ['gʌvənəʳ] *n* (*of state, bank*) governatore *m*; (*of school, hospital*) amministratore *m*; (*BRIT: of prison*) direttore(-trice)

gown [gaun] *n* vestito lungo; (*of teacher, BRIT: of judge*) toga

G.P. *n abbr* = **general practitioner**

grab [græb] *vt* afferrare, arraffare; (*property, power*) impadronirsi di ▶ *vi* **to ~ at** cercare di afferrare

grace [greɪs] *n* grazia ▶ *vt* onorare; **5 days' ~** dilazione *f* di 5 giorni; **graceful** *adj* elegante, aggraziato(-a); **gracious** ['greɪʃəs] *adj* grazioso(-a), misericordioso(-a)

grade [greɪd] *n* (*Comm*) qualità *f inv*; classe *f*; categoria; (*in hierarchy*) grado; (*Scol: mark*) voto; (*US: school class*) classe ▶ *vt* classificare; ordinare; graduare; **grade crossing** (*US*) *n* passaggio a livello; **grade school** (*US*) *n* scuola elementare

gradient ['greɪdɪənt] *n* pendenza, inclinazione *f*

gradual ['grædjuəl] *adj* graduale; **gradually** *adv* man mano, a poco a poco

graduate [*n* 'grædjuɪt, *vb* 'grædjueɪt] *n* (*of university*) laureato(-a); (*US: of high school*) diplomato(-a) ▶ *vi* laurearsi; diplomarsi; **graduation** [-'eɪʃən] *n* (*ceremony*) consegna delle lauree (*or* dei diplomi)

graffiti [grə'fi:tɪ] *npl* graffiti *mpl*

graft [grɑ:ft] *n* (*Agr, Med*) innesto; (*bribery*) corruzione *f*; (*BRIT: hard*

work): **it's hard ~** è un lavoraccio ▶ *vt*
innestare

grain [greɪn] *n* grano; (*of sand*)
granello; (*of wood*) venatura

gram [græm] *n* grammo

grammar ['græmər] *n* grammatica;
grammar school (*BRIT*) *n* ≈ liceo

gramme [græm] *n* = **gram**

gran (*inf*) [græn] *n* (*BRIT*) nonna

grand [grænd] *adj* grande,
magnifico(-a); grandioso(-a);
grandad (*inf*) *n* = **granddad**;
grandchild (*pl* **-children**) *n* nipote
m; **granddad** (*inf*) *n* nonno;
granddaughter *n* nipote *f*;
grandfather *n* nonno; **grandma**
(*inf*) *n* nonna; **grandmother** *n*
nonna; **grandpa** (*inf*) *n* = **granddad**;
grandparents *npl* nonni *mpl*;
grand piano *n* pianoforte *m* a coda;
Grand Prix ['grɑ̃:'pri:] *n* (*Aut*) Gran
Premio, Grand Prix *m inv*; **grandson**
n nipote *m*

granite ['grænɪt] *n* granito

granny ['grænɪ] (*inf*) *n* nonna

grant [grɑːnt] *vt* accordare; (*a request*)
accogliere; (*admit*) ammettere,
concedere ▶ *n* (*Scol*) borsa; (*Admin*)
sussidio, sovvenzione *f*; **to take**
sth for ~ed dare qc per scontato; **to**
take sb for ~ed dare per scontata la
presenza di qn

grape [greɪp] *n* chicco d'uva, acino

grapefruit ['greɪpfruːt] *n* pompelmo

graph [grɑːf] *n* grafico; **graphic**
adj grafico(-a); (*vivid*) vivido(-a);
graphics *n* grafica ▶ *npl* illustrazioni
fpl

grasp [grɑːsp] *vt* afferrare ▶ *n* (*grip*)
presa; (*fig*) potere *m*; comprensione *f*

grass [grɑːs] *n* erba; **grasshopper** *n*
cavalletta

grate [greɪt] *n* graticola (del focolare)
▶ *vi* cigolare, stridere ▶ *vt* (*Culin*)
grattugiare

grateful ['greɪtful] *adj* grato(-a),
riconoscente

grater ['greɪtər] *n* grattugia

gratitude ['grætɪtjuːd] *n* gratitudine *f*

grave [greɪv] *n* tomba ▶ *adj* grave,
serio(-a)

gravel ['grævl] *n* ghiaia

gravestone ['greɪvstəun] *n* pietra
tombale

graveyard ['greɪvjɑːd] *n* cimitero

gravity ['grævɪtɪ] *n* (*Physics*) gravità;
pesantezza; (*seriousness*) gravità,
serietà

gravy ['greɪvɪ] *n* intingolo della
carne; salsa

gray [greɪ] *adj* = **grey**

graze [greɪz] *vi* pascolare, pascere
▶ *vt* (*touch lightly*) sfiorare; (*scrape*)
escoriare ▶ *n* (*Med*) escoriazione *f*

grease [griːs] *n* (*fat*) grasso; (*lubricant*)
lubrificante *m* ▶ *vt* ingrassare;
lubrificare; **greasy** *adj* grasso(-a),
untuoso(-a)

great [greɪt] *adj* grande; (*inf*)
magnifico(-a), meraviglioso(-a);
Great Britain *n* Gran Bretagna;
great-grandfather *n* bisnonno;
great-grandmother *n* bisnonna;
greatly *adv* molto

Greece [griːs] *n* Grecia

greed [griːd] *n* (*also*: **~iness**) avarizia;
(*for food*) golosità, ghiottoneria;
greedy *adj* avido(-a); goloso(-a),
ghiotto(-a)

Greek [griːk] *adj* greco(-a) ▶ *n*
greco(-a); (*Ling*) greco

green [griːn] *adj* verde; (*inexperienced*)
inesperto(-a), ingenuo(-a) ▶ *n* verde
m; (*stretch of grass*) prato; (*on golf*
course) green *m inv*; **~s** *npl* (*vegetables*)
verdura; **green card** *n* (*BRIT Aut*) carta
verde; (*US Admin*) permesso di soggiorno
e di lavoro; **greengage** ['griːngeɪdʒ] *n*
susina Regina Claudia; **greengrocer**
(*BRIT*) *n* fruttivendolo(-a),

erbivendolo(-a); **greenhouse** n serra; **greenhouse effect** n effetto serra

Greenland ['gri:nlənd] n Groenlandia

green salad n insalata verde

greet [gri:t] vt salutare; **greeting** n saluto; **greeting(s) card** n cartolina d'auguri

grew [gru:] pt of **grow**

grey [greɪ] (US **gray**) adj grigio(-a); **grey-haired** adj dai capelli grigi; **greyhound** n levriere m

grid [grɪd] n grata; (Elec) rete f; **gridlock** ['grɪdlʊk] n (traffic jam) paralisi f inv del traffico; **gridlocked** adj paralizzato(-a) dal traffico; (talks etc) in fase di stallo

grief [gri:f] n dolore m

grievance ['gri:vəns] n lagnanza

grieve [gri:v] vi addolorarsi; rattristarsi ▶ vt addolorare; **to ~ for sb** (dead person) piangere qn

grill [grɪl] n (on cooker) griglia; (also: **mixed ~**) grigliata mista ▶ vt (BRIT) cuocere ai ferri; (inf: question) interrogare senza sosta

grille [grɪl] n grata; (Aut) griglia

grim [grɪm] adj sinistro(-a), brutto(-a)

grime [graɪm] n sudiciume m

grin [grɪn] n sorriso smagliante ▶ vi fare un gran sorriso

grind [graɪnd] (pt, pp **ground**) vt macinare; (make sharp) arrotare ▶ n (work) sgobbata

grip [grɪp] n impugnatura; presa; (holdall) borsa da viaggio ▶ vt (object) afferrare; (attention) catturare; **to come to ~s with** affrontare; cercare di risolvere; **gripping** ['grɪpɪŋ] adj avvincente

grit [grɪt] n ghiaia; (courage) fegato ▶ vt (road) coprire di sabbia; **to ~ one's teeth** stringere i denti

grits [grɪts] (US) npl macinato grosso (di avena etc)

groan [grəun] n gemito ▶ vi gemere

grocer ['grəusəʳ] n negoziante m di generi alimentari; **groceries** npl provviste fpl; **grocer's (shop)** n negozio di (generi) alimentari

grocery ['grəusərɪ] n (shop) (negozio di) alimentari

groin [grɔɪn] n inguine m

groom [gru:m] n palafreniere m; (also: **bride~**) sposo ▶ vt (horse) strigliare; (fig): **to ~ sb for** avviare qn a; **well-~ed** (person) curato(-a)

groove [gru:v] n scanalatura, solco

grope [grəup] vi **to ~ for** cercare a tastoni

gross [grəus] adj grossolano(-a); (Comm) lordo(-a); **grossly** adv (greatly) molto

grotesque [grəu'tɛsk] adj grottesco(-a)

ground [graund] pt, pp of **grind** ▶ n suolo, terra; (land) terreno; (Sport) campo; (reason: gen pl) ragione f; (US: also: **~ wire**) terra ▶ vt (plane) tenere a terra; (US Elec) mettere la presa a terra a; **~s** npl (of coffee etc) fondi mpl; (gardens etc) terreno, giardini mpl; **on/to the ~** per/a terra; **to gain/lose ~** guadagnare/perdere terreno; **ground floor** n pianterreno; **groundsheet** (BRIT) n telone m impermeabile; **groundwork** n preparazione f

group [gru:p] n gruppo ▶ vt (also: **~ together**) raggruppare ▶ vi (also: **~ together**) raggrupparsi

grouse [graus] n inv (bird) tetraone m ▶ vi (complain) brontolare

grovel ['grɔvl] vi (fig): **to ~ (before)** strisciare (di fronte a)

grow [grəu] (pt **grew,**, pp **grown**) vi crescere; (increase) aumentare; (develop) svilupparsi; (become): **to ~ rich/weak** arricchirsi/indebolirsi ▶ vt coltivare, far crescere ▷ **grow on** vt fus **that painting is ~ing on me** quel

quadro più lo guardo più mi piace
▷ **grow up** vi farsi grande, crescere
growl [graul] vi ringhiare
grown [grəun] pp of **grow**; **grown-up**
n adulto(-a), grande m/f
growth [grəuθ] n crescita, sviluppo;
(what has grown) crescita; (Med)
escrescenza, tumore m
grub [grʌb] n larva; (inf: food) roba (da
mangiare)
grubby ['grʌbɪ] adj sporco(-a)
grudge [grʌdʒ] n rancore m ▶ vt **to**
~ sb sth dare qc a qn di malavoglia;
invidiare qc a qn; **to bear sb a ~ (for)**
serbar rancore a qn (per)
gruelling ['gruəlɪŋ] (US **grueling**) adj
estenuante
gruesome ['gru:səm] adj orribile
grumble ['grʌmbl] vi brontolare,
lagnarsi
grumpy ['grʌmpɪ] adj scorbutico(-a)
grunt [grʌnt] vi grugnire
guarantee [gærən'ti:] n garanzia ▶ vt
garantire
guard [gɑ:d] n guardia; (one man)
guardia, sentinella; (BRIT Rail)
capotreno; (on machine) schermo
protettivo; (also: **fire~**) parafuoco
▶ vt fare la guardia a; (protect): **to ~**
(against) proteggere (da); **to be on**
one's ~ stare in guardia; **guardian** n
custode m; (of minor) tutore(-trice)
guerrilla [gə'rɪlə] n guerrigliero
guess [gɛs] vi indovinare ▶ vt
indovinare; (US) credere, pensare
▶ n **to take** or **have a ~** provare a
indovinare
guest [gɛst] n ospite m/f; (in hotel)
cliente m/f; **guest house** n pensione
f; **guest room** n camera degli ospiti
guidance ['gaɪdəns] n guida,
direzione f
guide [gaɪd] n (person, book etc) guida;
(BRIT: also: **girl ~**) giovane esploratrice
f ▶ vt guidare; **is there an English-**

speaking ~? c'è una guida che parla
inglese?; **guidebook** n guida; **do you**
have a guidebook in English? avete
una guida in inglese?; **guide dog** n
cane m guida inv; **guided tour** n visita
guidata; **what time does the guided**
tour start? a che ora comincia la
visita guidata?; **guidelines** npl (fig)
indicazioni fpl, linee fpl direttive
guild [gɪld] n arte f, corporazione f;
associazione f
guilt [gɪlt] n colpevolezza; **guilty** adj
colpevole
guinea pig ['gɪnɪ-] n cavia
guitar [gɪ'tɑ:ʳ] n chitarra; **guitarist** n
chitarrista m/f
gulf [gʌlf] n golfo; (abyss) abisso
gull [gʌl] n gabbiano
gulp [gʌlp] vi deglutire; (from emotion)
avere il nodo in gola ▶ vt (also: **~**
down) tracannare, inghiottire
gum [gʌm] n (Anat) gengiva; (glue)
colla; (also: **~drop**) caramella
gommosa; (also: **chewing ~**)
chewing-gum m inv ▶ vt **to ~**
(together) incollare
gun [gʌn] n fucile m; (small) pistola,
rivoltella; (rifle) carabina; (shotgun)
fucile da caccia; (cannon) cannone m;
gunfire n spari mpl; **gunman** (irreg)
n bandito armato; **gunpoint** n **at**
gunpoint sotto minaccia di fucile;
gunpowder n polvere f da sparo;
gunshot n sparo
gush [gʌʃ] vi sgorgare; (fig)
abbandonarsi a effusioni
gust [gʌst] n (of wind) raffica; (of smoke)
buffata
gut [gʌt] n intestino, budello; **~s** npl
(Anat) interiora fpl; (courage) fegato
gutter ['gʌtəʳ] n (of roof) grondaia; (in
street) cunetta
guy [gaɪ] n (inf: man) tipo, elemento;
(also: **~rope**) cavo or corda di
fissaggio; (figure) effigie di Guy Fawkes

Guy Fawkes Night [-'fɔːks-] *n* (*BRIT*)
vedi nota

- **Guy Fawkes Night**
- La sera del 5 novembre, in occasione
- della **Guy Fawkes Night**, altrimenti
- chiamata **Bonfire Night**, viene
- commemorato con falò e fuochi
- d'artificio il fallimento della
- Congiura delle Polveri contro
- Giacomo I nel 1605. La festa prende
- il nome dal principale congiurato
- della cospirazione, Guy Fawkes, la
- cui effigie viene bruciata durante i
- festeggiamenti.

gym [dʒɪm] *n* (*also:* **~nasium**)
palestra; (*also:* **~nastics**) ginnastica;
gymnasium [dʒɪm'neɪzɪəm] *n*
palestra; **gymnast** ['dʒɪmnæst] *n*
ginnasta *m/f*; **gymnastics** [-'næstɪks]
n, *npl* ginnastica; **gym shoes** *npl*
scarpe *fpl* da ginnastica
gynaecologist [gaɪnɪ'kɔlədʒɪst] (*US*
gynecologist) *n* ginecologo(-a)
gypsy ['dʒɪpsɪ] *n* = **gipsy**

h

haberdashery ['hæbə'dæʃərɪ] (*BRIT*)
n merceria
habit ['hæbɪt] *n* abitudine *f*; (*costume*)
abito; (*Rel*) tonaca
habitat ['hæbɪtæt] *n* habitat *m inv*
hack [hæk] *vt* tagliare, fare a pezzi

▶ *n* (*pej: writer*) scribacchino(-a);
hacker ['hækər] *n* (*Comput*) pirata *m*
informatico
had [hæd] *pt*, *pp of* **have**
haddock ['hædək] (*pl* **haddock** *or*
haddocks) *n* eglefino
hadn't ['hædnt] = **had not**
haemorrhage ['hɛmərɪdʒ] (*US*
hemorrhage) *n* emorragia
haemorrhoids ['hɛmərɔɪdz] (*US*
hemorrhoids) *npl* emorroidi *fpl*
haggle ['hægl] *vi* mercanteggiare
Hague [heɪg] *n* **The ~** L'Aia
hail [heɪl] *n* grandine *f*; (*of criticism
etc*) pioggia ▶ *vt* (*call*) chiamare; (*flag
down: taxi*) fermare; (*greet*) salutare
▶ *vi* grandinare; **hailstone** *n* chicco
di grandine
hair [hɛər] *n* capelli *mpl*; (*single hair:
on head*) capello; (: *on body*) pelo; **to
do one's ~** pettinarsi; **hairband**
['hɛəbænd] *n* (*elastic*) fascia per i
capelli; (*rigid*) cerchietto; **hairbrush**
n spazzola per capelli; **haircut**
n taglio di capelli; **hairdo** ['hɛə
duː] *n* acconciatura, pettinatura;
hairdresser *n* parrucchiere(-a);
hairdresser's *n* parrucchiere(-a);
hair dryer *n* asciugacapelli *m inv*;
hair gel *n* gel *m inv* per capelli; **hair
spray** *n* lacca per capelli; **hairstyle** *n*
pettinatura, acconciatura; **hairy** *adj*
irsuto(-a), peloso(-a); (*inf: frightening*)
spaventoso(-a)
hake [heɪk] (*pl* **hake** *or* **hakes**) *n*
nasello
half [hɑːf] (*pl* **halves**) *n* mezzo, metà
f inv ▶ *adj* mezzo(-a) ▶ *adv* a mezzo, a
metà; **~ an hour** mezz'ora; **~ a dozen**
mezza dozzina; **~ a pound** mezza
libbra; **two and a ~** due e mezzo; **a
week and a ~** una settimana e mezza;
~ (of it) la metà; **~ (of)** la metà di;
to cut sth in ~ tagliare qc in due; **~
asleep** mezzo(-a) addormentato(-a);

half board (*BRIT*) n mezza pensione;
half-brother n fratellastro; **half day**
n mezza giornata; **half fare** n tariffa
a metà prezzo; **half-hearted** adj
tiepido(-a); **half-hour** n mezz'ora;
half-price adj, adv a metà prezzo; **half
term** (*BRIT*) n (*Scol*) vacanza a or di
metà trimestre; **half-time** n (*Sport*)
intervallo; **halfway** adv a metà strada
hall [hɔːl] n sala, salone m; (*entrance
way*) entrata
hallmark ['hɔːlmɑːk] n marchio di
garanzia; (*fig*) caratteristica
hallo [hə'ləʊ] excl = **hello**
hall of residence (*BRIT*) n casa dello
studente
Halloween [hæləʊ'iːn] n vigilia
d'Ognissanti
- **Halloween**
- Negli Stati Uniti e in Gran Bretagna
- il 31 ottobre si festeggia **Halloween**,
- la notte delle streghe e dei fantasmi.
- I bambini, travestiti da fantasmi,
- streghe o mostri, bussano alle porte
- e ricevono dolci e piccoli doni.
hallucination [həluːsɪ'neɪʃən] n
allucinazione f
hallway ['hɔːlweɪ] n corridoio;
(*entrance*) ingresso
halo ['heɪləʊ] n (*of saint etc*) aureola
halt [hɔːlt] n fermata ▸ vt fermare ▸ vi
fermarsi
halve [hɑːv] vt (*apple etc*) dividere a
metà; (*expense*) ridurre di metà
halves [hɑːvz] npl of **half**
ham [hæm] n prosciutto
hamburger ['hæmbəːgəʳ] n
hamburger m inv
hamlet ['hæmlɪt] n paesetto
hammer ['hæməʳ] n martello ▸ vt
martellare ▸ vi to ~ on or at the door
picchiare alla porta
hammock ['hæmək] n amaca
hamper ['hæmpəʳ] vt impedire ▸ n
cesta

hamster ['hæmstəʳ] n criceto
hamstring ['hæmstrɪŋ] n (*Anat*)
tendine m del ginocchio
hand [hænd] n mano f; (*of clock*)
lancetta; (*handwriting*) scrittura; (*at
cards*) mano; (: *game*) partita; (*worker*)
operaio(-a) ▸ vt dare, passare; **to
give sb a ~** dare una mano a qn; **at ~** a
portata di mano; **in ~** a disposizione;
(*work*) in corso; **on ~** (*person*)
disponibile; (*services*) pronto(-a) a
intervenire; **to ~** (*information etc*) a
portata di mano; **on the one ~ ...**, **on
the other ~** da un lato ..., dall'altro
▸ **hand down** vt passare giù;
(*tradition, heirloom*) tramandare; (*US:
sentence, verdict*) emettere ▸ **hand in** vt
consegnare ▸ **hand out** vt distribuire
▸ **hand over** vt passare; cedere;
handbag n borsetta; **hand baggage**
n bagaglio a mano; **handbook** n
manuale m; **handbrake** n freno a
mano; **handcuffs** npl manette fpl;
handful n manciata, pugno
handicap ['hændɪkæp] n
handicap m inv ▸ vt handicappare;
to be physically ~ped essere
handicappato(-a); **to be mentally
~ped** essere un(a) handicappato(-a)
mentale
handkerchief ['hæŋkətʃɪf] n
fazzoletto
handle ['hændl] n (*of door etc*)
maniglia; (*of cup etc*) ansa; (*of knife etc*)
impugnatura; (*of saucepan*) manico;
(*for winding*) manovella ▸ vt toccare,
maneggiare; (*deal with*) occuparsi
di; (*treat: people*) trattare; **"~ with
care"** "fragile"; **to fly off the ~** (*fig*)
perdere le staffe, uscire dai gangheri;
handlebar(s) n(pl) manubrio
hand: **hand luggage** n bagagli mpl
a mano; **handmade** adj fatto(-a)
a mano; **handout** n (*money, food*)
elemosina; (*leaflet*) volantino; (*at

lecture) prospetto

handsome ['hænsəm] *adj* bello(-a); (*profit, fortune*) considerevole

handwriting ['hændraɪtɪŋ] *n* scrittura

handy ['hændɪ] *adj* (*person*) bravo(-a); (*close at hand*) a portata di mano; (*convenient*) comodo(-a)

hang [hæŋ] (*pt, pp* **hung**) *vt* appendere; (*criminal: pt, pp* **hanged**) impiccare ▶ *vi* (*painting*) essere appeso(-a); (*hair*) scendere; (*drapery*) cadere; **to get the ~ of sth** (*inf*) capire come qc funziona ▶ **hang about** *or* **around** *vi* bighellonare, ciondolare ▷ **hang down** *vi* ricadere ▷ **hang on** *vi* (*wait*) aspettare ▷ **hang out** *vt* (*washing*) stendere (fuori); (*inf: live*) stare ▶ *vi* penzolare, pendere ▷ **hang round** *vi* = **hang around** ▷ **hang up** *vi* (*Tel*) riattaccare ▶ *vt* appendere

hanger ['hæŋə^r] *n* gruccia

hang-gliding ['-glaɪdɪŋ] *n* volo col deltaplano

hangover ['hæŋəʊvə^r] *n* (*after drinking*) postumi *mpl* di sbornia

hankie ['hæŋkɪ] *n abbr* = **handkerchief**

happen ['hæpən] *vi* accadere, succedere; (*chance*): **to ~ to do sth** fare qc per caso; **what ~ed?** cos'è successo?; **as it ~s** guarda caso

happily ['hæpɪlɪ] *adv* felicemente; fortunatamente

happiness ['hæpɪnɪs] *n* felicità, contentezza

happy ['hæpɪ] *adj* felice, contento(-a); **~ with** (*arrangements etc*) soddisfatto(-a) di; **to be ~ to do** (*willing*) fare volentieri; **~ birthday!** buon compleanno!

harass ['hærəs] *vt* molestare; **harassment** *n* molestia

harbour ['hɑːbə^r] (*US* **harbor**) *n* porto ▶ *vt* (*hope, fear*) nutrire; (*criminal*) dare rifugio a

hard [hɑːd] *adj* duro(-a) ▶ *adv* (*work*) sodo; (*think, try*) bene; **to look ~ at** guardare fissamente; esaminare attentamente; **no ~ feelings!** senza rancore!; **to be ~ of hearing** essere duro(-a) d'orecchio; **to be ~ done by** essere trattato(-a) ingiustamente; **hardback** *n* libro rilegato; **hardboard** *n* legno precompresso; **hard disk** *n* (*Comput*) disco rigido; **harden** *vt, vi* indurire

hardly ['hɑːdlɪ] *adv* (*scarcely*) appena; **it's ~ the case** non è proprio il caso; **~ anyone/anywhere** quasi nessuno/da nessuna parte; **~ ever** quasi mai

hard: **hardship** ['hɑːdʃɪp] *n* avversità *f inv*; privazioni *fpl*; **hard shoulder** (*BRIT*) *n* (*Aut*) corsia d'emergenza; **hard-up** (*inf*) *adj* al verde; **hardware** ['hɑːdwɛə^r] *n* ferramenta *fpl*; (*Comput*) hardware *m*; (*Mil*) armamenti *mpl*; **hardware shop** (*US* **hardware store**) *n* (negozio di) ferramenta *fpl*; **hard-working** [-'wɜːkɪŋ] *adj* lavoratore(-trice)

hardy ['hɑːdɪ] *adj* robusto(-a); (*plant*) resistente al gelo

hare [hɛə^r] *n* lepre *f*

harm [hɑːm] *n* male *m*; (*wrong*) danno ▶ *vt* (*person*) fare male a; (*thing*) danneggiare; **out of ~'s way** al sicuro; **harmful** *adj* dannoso(-a); **harmless** *adj* innocuo(-a), inoffensivo(-a)

harmony ['hɑːmənɪ] *n* armonia

harness ['hɑːnɪs] *n* (*for horse*) bardatura, finimenti *mpl*; (*for child*) briglie *fpl*; (*safety harness*) imbracatura ▶ *vt* (*horse*) bardare; (*resources*) sfruttare

harp [hɑːp] *n* arpa ▶ *vi* **to ~ on about** insistere tediosamente su

harsh [hɑːʃ] *adj* (*life, winter*) duro(-a); (*judge, criticism*) severo(-a); (*sound*) rauco(-a); (*light*) violento(-a)

harvest [ˈhɑːvɪst] n raccolto; (of grapes) vendemmia ▶ vt fare il raccolto di, raccogliere; vendemmiare

has [hæz] vb see **have**

hasn't [ˈhæznt] = **has not**

hassle [ˈhæsl] (inf) n sacco di problemi

haste [heɪst] n fretta; precipitazione f; **hasten** [ˈheɪsn] vt affrettare ▶ vi to **hasten (to)** affrettarsi (a); **hastily** adv in fretta; precipitosamente; **hasty** adj affrettato(-a), precipitoso(-a)

hat [hæt] n cappello

hatch [hætʃ] n (Naut: also: ~way) boccaporto; (also: **service ~**) portello di servizio ▶ vi (bird) uscire dal guscio; (egg) schiudersi

hatchback [ˈhætʃbæk] n (Aut) tre (or cinque) porte f inv

hate [heɪt] vt odiare, detestare ▶ n odio; **hatred** [ˈheɪtrɪd] n odio

haul [hɔːl] vt trascinare, tirare ▶ n (of fish) pescata; (of stolen goods etc) bottino

haunt [hɔːnt] vt (fear) pervadere; (person) frequentare ▶ n rifugio; **this house is ~ed** questa casa è abitata da un fantasma; **haunted** adj (castle etc) abitato(-a) dai fantasmi or dagli spiriti; (look) ossessionato(-a), tormentato(-a)

have
[hæv] (pt, pp **had**) aux vb
1 (gen) avere; essere; **to have arrived/ gone** essere arrivato(-a)/andato(-a); **to have eaten/slept** avere mangiato/ dormito; **he has been kind/promoted** è stato gentile/promosso; **having finished** or **when he had finished, he left** dopo aver finito, se n'è andato
2 (in tag questions): **you've done it, haven't you?** l'ha fatto, (non è) vero?; **he hasn't done it, has he?** non l'ha fatto, vero?
3 (in short answers and questions): **you've made a mistake — no I haven't/so I have** ha fatto un errore

— ma no, niente affatto/sì, è vero; **we haven't paid — yes we have!** non abbiamo pagato — ma sì che abbiamo pagato!; **I've been there before, have you?** ci sono già stato, e lei?
▶ modal aux vb (be obliged): **to have (got) to do sth** dover fare qc; **I haven't got** or **I don't have to wear glasses** non ho bisogno di portare gli occhiali
▶ vt
1 (possess, obtain) avere; **he has (got) blue eyes/dark hair** ha gli occhi azzurri/i capelli scuri; **do you have** or **have you got a car/phone?** ha la macchina/il telefono?; **may I have your address?** potrebbe darmi il suo indirizzo?; **you can have it for £5** te lo lascio per 5 sterline
2 (+ noun: take, hold etc): **to have breakfast/a swim/a bath** fare colazione/una nuotata/un bagno; **to have lunch** pranzare; **to have dinner** cenare; **to have a drink** bere qualcosa; **to have a cigarette** fumare una sigaretta
3: **to have sth done** far fare qc; **to have one's hair cut** farsi tagliare i capelli; **to have sb do sth** far fare qc a qn
4 (experience, suffer) avere; **to have a cold/flu** avere il raffreddore/ l'influenza; **she had her bag stolen** le hanno rubato la borsa
5 (inf: dupe): **you've been had!** ci sei cascato!
▷ **have out** vt **to have it out with sb** (settle a problem etc) mettere le cose in chiaro con qn

haven [ˈheɪvn] n porto; (fig) rifugio

haven't [ˈhævnt] = **have not**

havoc [ˈhævək] n caos m

Hawaii [həˈwaɪ] n le Hawaii

hawk [hɔːk] n falco

hawthorn [ˈhɔːθɔːn] n biancospino

hay [heɪ] n fieno; **hay fever** n febbre f da fieno; **haystack** n pagliaio

hazard ['hæzəd] n azzardo, ventura; pericolo, rischio ▶ vt (guess etc) azzardare; **hazardous** adj pericoloso(-a); **hazard warning lights** npl (Aut) luci fpl di emergenza

haze [heɪz] n foschia

hazel ['heɪzl] n (tree) nocciolo ▶ adj (eyes) (color) nocciola inv; **hazelnut** ['heɪzlnʌt] n nocciola

hazy ['heɪzɪ] adj fosco(-a); (idea) vago(-a)

he [hiː] pron lui, egli; **it is he who ...** è lui che ...

head [hɛd] n testa; (leader) capo; (of school) preside m/f ▶ vt (list) essere in testa a; (group) essere a capo di; **~s or tails** testa (o croce), pari (o dispari); **~ first** a capofitto, di testa; **~ over heels in love** pazzamente innamorato(-a); **to ~ the ball** colpire una palla di testa ▷ **head for** vt fus dirigersi verso ▷ **head off** vt (threat, danger) sventare; **headache** n mal m di testa; **heading** n titolo; intestazione f; **headlamp** (BRIT) n = **headlight**; **headlight** n fanale m; **headline** n titolo; **head office** n sede f (centrale); **headphones** npl cuffia; **headquarters** npl ufficio centrale; (Mil) quartiere m generale; **headroom** n (in car) altezza dell'abitacolo; (under bridge) altezza limite; **headscarf** n foulard m inv; **headset** n = **headphones**; **headteacher** n (of primary school) direttore(-trice); (of secondary school) preside; **head waiter** n capocameriere m

heal [hiːl] vt, vi guarire

health [hɛlθ] n salute f; **health care** n assistenza sanitaria; **health centre** (BRIT) n poliambulatorio; **health food** n cibo macrobiotico; **Health Service** (BRIT) n **the Health Service** ≈ il Servizio Sanitario Statale;

healthy adj (person) sano(-a), in buona salute; (climate) salubre; (appetite, economy etc) sano(-a)

heap [hiːp] n mucchio ▶ vt (stones, sand): **to ~ (up)** ammucchiare; (plate, sink): **to ~ sth with** riempire qc di; **~s of** (inf) un mucchio di

hear [hɪər] (pt, pp heard) vt sentire; (news) ascoltare ▶ vi sentire; **to ~ about** avere notizie di; sentire parlare di; **to ~ from sb** ricevere notizie da qn

hearing ['hɪərɪŋ] n (sense) udito; (of witnesses) audizione f; (of a case) udienza; **hearing aid** n apparecchio acustico

hearse [həːs] n carro funebre

heart [hɑːt] n cuore m; **~s** npl (Cards) cuori mpl; **to lose ~** scoraggiarsi; **to take ~** farsi coraggio; **at ~** in fondo; **by ~** (learn, know) a memoria; **heart attack** n attacco di cuore; **heartbeat** n battito del cuore; **heartbroken** adj **to be heartbroken** avere il cuore spezzato; **heartburn** n bruciore m di stomaco; **heart disease** n malattia di cuore

hearth [hɑːθ] n focolare m

heartless ['hɑːtlɪs] adj senza cuore

hearty ['hɑːtɪ] adj caloroso(-a); robusto(-a), sano(-a); vigoroso(-a)

heat [hiːt] n calore m; (fig) ardore m; fuoco; (Sport: also: **qualifying ~**) prova eliminatoria; **at ~** vt scaldare ▷ **heat up** vi (liquids) scaldarsi; (room) riscaldarsi ▶ vt riscaldare; **heated** adj riscaldato(-a); (argument) acceso(-a); **heater** n radiatore m; (stove) stufa

heather ['hɛðər] n erica

heating ['hiːtɪŋ] n riscaldamento

heatwave ['hiːtweɪv] n ondata di caldo

heaven ['hɛvn] n paradiso, cielo; **heavenly** adj divino(-a), celeste

heavily ['hɛvɪlɪ] adv pesantemente; (drink, smoke) molto

heavy ['hɛvɪ] adj pesante; (sea) grosso(-a); (rain, blow) forte; (weather) afoso(-a); (drinker, smoker) gran (before noun); **it's too ~** è troppo pesante

Hebrew ['hi:bru:] adj ebreo(-a) ▶ n (Ling) ebraico

hectare ['hɛktɑ:'] n (BRIT) ettaro

hectic ['hɛktɪk] adj movimentato(-a)

he'd [hi:d] = **he would; he had**

hedge [hɛdʒ] n siepe f ▶ vi essere elusivo(-a); **to ~ one's bets** (fig) coprirsi dai rischi

hedgehog ['hɛdʒhɔg] n riccio

heed [hi:d] vt (also: **take ~ of**) badare a, far conto di

heel [hi:l] n (Anat) calcagno; (of shoe) tacco ▶ vt (shoe) rifare i tacchi a

hefty ['hɛftɪ] adj (person) robusto(-a); (parcel) pesante; (profit) grosso(-a)

height [haɪt] n altezza; (high ground) altura; (fig: of glory) apice m; (: of stupidity) colmo; **heighten** vt (fig) accrescere

heir [ɛə'] n erede m; **heiress** n erede f

held [hɛld] pt, pp of **hold**

helicopter ['hɛlɪkɔptə'] n elicottero

hell [hɛl] n inferno; **~!** (inf) porca miseria!, accidenti!

he'll [hi:l] = **he will; he shall**

hello [hə'ləu] excl buon giorno!; ciao! (to sb one addresses as "tu"); (surprise) ma guarda!

helmet ['hɛlmɪt] n casco

help [hɛlp] n aiuto; (charwoman) donna di servizio ▶ vt aiutare; **~!** aiuto!; **can you ~ me?** può aiutarmi?; **~ yourself (to bread)** si serva (del pane); **he can't ~ it** non ci può far niente ▷ **help out** vi aiutare ▶ vt **to ~ sb out** aiutare qn; **helper** n aiutante m/f, assistente m/f; **helpful** adj di grande aiuto; (useful) utile; **helping** n porzione f; **helpless** adj impotente; debole; **helpline** n ≈ telefono amico; (Comm) servizio m informazioni inv (a pagamento)

hem [hɛm] n orlo ▶ vt fare l'orlo a

hemisphere ['hɛmɪsfɪə'] n emisfero

hemorrhage ['hɛmərɪdʒ] (US) n = **haemorrhage**

hemorrhoids ['hɛmərɔɪdz] (US) npl = **haemorrhoids**

hen [hɛn] n gallina; (female bird) femmina

hence [hɛns] adv (therefore) dunque; **2 years ~** di qui a 2 anni

hen night n (inf) addio al nubilato

hepatitis [hɛpə'taɪtɪs] n epatite f

her [hə:'] pron (direct) la, l' + vowel; (indirect) le; (stressed, after prep) lei ▶ adj il (la) suo(-a), i (le) suoi (sue); see also **me; my**

herb [hə:b] n erba; **herbal** adj di erbe; **herbal tea** n tisana

herd [hə:d] n mandria

here [hɪə'] adv qui, qua ▶ excl ehi!; **~!** (at roll call) presente!; **~ is/are** ecco; **~ he/she is** eccolo/eccola

hereditary [hɪ'rɛdɪtrɪ] adj ereditario(-a)

heritage ['hɛrɪtɪdʒ] n eredità; (fig) retaggio

hernia ['hə:nɪə] n ernia

hero ['hɪərəu] (pl **heroes**) n eroe m; **heroic** [hɪ'rəuɪk] adj eroico(-a)

heroin ['hɛrəuɪn] n eroina

heroine ['hɛrəuɪn] n eroina

heron ['hɛrən] n airone m

herring ['hɛrɪŋ] n aringa

hers [hə:z] pron il (la) suo(-a), i (le) suoi (sue); see also **mine**[1]

herself [hə:'sɛlf] pron (reflexive) si; (emphatic) lei stessa; (after prep) se stessa, sé; see also **oneself**

he's [hi:z] = **he is; he has**

hesitant ['hɛzɪtənt] adj esitante, indeciso(-a)

hesitate ['hɛzɪteɪt] vi **to ~ (about/to do)** esitare (su/a fare); **hesitation** [-'teɪʃən] n esitazione f

heterosexual ['hɛtərəu'sɛksjuəl] adj,

n eterosessuale *m/f*
hexagon [ˈhɛksəgən] *n* esagono
hey [heɪ] *excl* ehi!
heyday [ˈheɪdeɪ] *n* **the ~ of** i bei giorni di, l'età d'oro di
HGV *n abbr* = **heavy goods vehicle**
hi [haɪ] *excl* ciao!
hibernate [ˈhaɪbəneɪt] *vi* ibernare
hiccough [ˈhɪkʌp] *vi* singhiozzare
hiccup [ˈhɪkʌp] = **hiccough**
hid [hɪd] *pt of* **hide**
hidden [ˈhɪdn] *pp of* **hide**
hide [haɪd] (*pt* **hid**, *pp* **hidden**) *n* (*skin*) pelle *f* ▸ *vt* **to ~ sth (from sb)** nascondere qc (a qn) ▸ *vi* **to ~ (from sb)** nascondersi (da qn)
hideous [ˈhɪdɪəs] *adj* laido(-a); orribile
hiding [ˈhaɪdɪŋ] *n* (*beating*) bastonata; **to be in ~** (*concealed*) tenersi nascosto(-a)
hi-fi [ˈhaɪfaɪ] *n* stereo ▸ *adj* ad alta fedeltà, hi-fi *inv*
high [haɪ] *adj* alto(-a); (*speed, respect, number*) grande; (*wind*) forte; (*voice*) acuto(-a) ▸ *adv* alto, in alto; **20m ~** alto(-a) 20m; **highchair** *n* seggiolone *m*; **high-class** *adj* (*neighbourhood*) elegante; (*hotel*) di prim'ordine; (*person*) di gran classe; (*food*) raffinato(-a); **higher education** *n* studi *mpl* superiori; **high heels** *npl* (*heels*) tacchi *mpl* alti; (*shoes*) scarpe *fpl* con i tacchi alti; **high jump** *n* (*Sport*) salto in alto; **highlands** *npl* zona montuosa; **the Highlands** le Highlands scozzesi; **highlight** *n* (*fig: of event*) momento culminante; (*in hair*) colpo di sole ▸ *vt* mettere in evidenza; **highlights** *npl* (*in hair*) colpi *mpl* di sole; **highlighter** *n* (*pen*) evidenziatore *m*; **highly** *adv* molto; **to speak highly of** parlare molto bene di; **highness** *n* **Her Highness** Sua Altezza; **high-rise** *n* (*also:* **high-rise block, high-rise building**) palazzone

m; **high school** *n* scuola secondaria; (*US*) istituto superiore d'istruzione; **high season** (*BRIT*) *n* alta stagione; **high street** (*BRIT*) *n* strada principale; **high-tech** (*inf*) *adj* high-tech *inv*; **highway** [ˈhaɪweɪ] *n* strada maestra; **Highway Code** (*BRIT*) *n* codice *m* della strada
hijack [ˈhaɪdʒæk] *vt* dirottare; **hijacker** *n* dirottatore(-trice)
hike [haɪk] *vi* fare un'escursione a piedi ▸ *n* escursione *f* a piedi; **hiker** *n* escursionista *m/f*; **hiking** *n* escursioni *fpl* a piedi
hilarious [hɪˈlɛərɪəs] *adj* (*behaviour, event*) spassosissimo(-a)
hill [hɪl] *n* collina, colle *m*; (*fairly high*) montagna; (*on road*) salita; **hillside** *n* fianco della collina; **hill walking** *n* escursioni *fpl* in collina; **hilly** *adj* collinoso(-a); montagnoso(-a)
him [hɪm] *pron* (*direct*) lo, l' + *vowel*; (*indirect*) gli; (*stressed, after prep*) lui; *see also* **me**; **himself** *pron* (*reflexive*) si; (*emphatic*) lui stesso; (*after prep*) se stesso, sé; *see also* **oneself**
hind [haɪnd] *adj* posteriore ▸ *n* cerva
hinder [ˈhɪndəʳ] *vt* ostacolare
hindsight [ˈhaɪndsaɪt] *n* **with ~** con il senno di poi
Hindu [ˈhɪnduː] *n* indù *m/f inv*; **Hinduism** *n* (*Rel*) induismo
hinge [hɪndʒ] *n* cardine *m* ▸ *vi*: **to ~ on** dipendere da
hint [hɪnt] *n* (*suggestion*) allusione *f*; (*advice*) consiglio; (*sign*) accenno ▸ *vt* **to ~ that** lasciar capire che ▸ *vi* **to ~ at** alludere a
hip [hɪp] *n* anca, fianco
hippie [ˈhɪpɪ] *n* hippy *m/f inv*
hippo [ˈhɪpəu] *n* (*pl* **hippos**) ippopotamo
hippopotamus [hɪpəˈpɔtəməs] (*pl* **hippopotamuses** *or* **hippopotami**) *n* ippopotamo

hippy ['hɪpɪ] n = **hippie**
hire ['haɪəʳ] vt (BRIT: car, equipment) noleggiare; (worker) assumere, dare lavoro a ▶ n nolo, noleggio; **for ~** da nolo; (taxi) libero(-a); **I'd like to ~ a car** vorrei noleggiare una macchina; **hire(d) car** (BRIT) n macchina a nolo; **hire purchase** (BRIT) n acquisto (or vendita) rateale
his [hɪz] adj, pron il (la) suo (sua), i (le) suoi (sue); see also **my**; **mine**[1]
Hispanic [hɪs'pænɪk] adj ispanico(-a)
hiss [hɪs] vi fischiare; (cat, snake) sibilare
historian [hɪ'stɔ:rɪən] n storico(-a)
historic(al) [hɪ'stɔrɪk(l)] adj storico(-a)
history ['hɪstərɪ] n storia
hit [hɪt] (pt, pp **hit**) vt colpire, picchiare; (knock against) battere; (reach: target) raggiungere; (collide with: car) urtare contro; (fig: affect) colpire; (find: problem etc) incontrare ▶ n colpo; (success, song) successo; **to ~ it off with sb** andare molto d'accordo con qn ▷ **hit back** vi **to ~ back at sb** restituire il colpo a qn
hitch [hɪtʃ] vt (fasten) attaccare; (also: ~ **up**) tirare su ▶ n (difficulty) intoppo, difficoltà f inv; **to ~ a lift** fare l'autostop; **hitch-hike** vi fare l'autostop; **hitch-hiker** n autostoppista m/f; **hitch-hiking** n autostop m
hi-tech ['haɪtɛk] adj high-tech inv
hitman ['hɪtmæn] (irreg) n (inf) sicario
HIV abbr **~-negative/-positive** adj sieronegativo(-a)/sieropositivo(-a)
hive [haɪv] n alveare m
hoard [hɔ:d] n (of food) provviste fpl; (of money) gruzzolo ▶ vt ammassare
hoarse [hɔ:s] adj rauco(-a)
hoax [həuks] n scherzo; falso allarme m
hob [hɔb] n piastra (con fornelli)
hobble ['hɔbl] vi zoppicare

hobby ['hɔbɪ] n hobby m inv, passatempo
hobo ['həubəu] (US) n vagabondo
hockey ['hɔkɪ] n hockey m; **hockey stick** n bastone m da hockey
hog [hɔg] n maiale m ▶ vt (fig) arraffare; **to go the whole ~** farlo fino in fondo
Hogmanay [hɔgmə'neɪ] n (Scottish) ≈ San Silvestro
hoist [hɔɪst] n paranco ▶ vt issare
hold [həuld] (pt, pp **held**) vt tenere; (contain) contenere; (keep back) trattenere; (believe) mantenere; considerare; (possess) avere, possedere; detenere ▶ vi (withstand pressure) tenere; (be valid) essere valido(-a) ▶ n presa; (control): **to have a ~ over** avere controllo su; (Naut) stiva; **~ the line!** (Tel) resti in linea!; **to ~ one's own** (fig) difendersi bene; **to catch** or **get (a) ~ of** afferrare ▷ **hold back** vt trattenere; (secret) tenere celato(-a) ▷ **hold on** vi tener fermo; (wait) aspettare; **~ on!** (Tel) resti in linea! ▷ **hold out** vt offrire ▶ vi (resist) resistere ▷ **hold up** vt (raise) alzare; (support) sostenere; (delay) ritardare; (rob) assaltare;
holdall (BRIT) n borsone m; **holder** n (container) contenitore m; (of ticket, title) possessore/posseditrice; (of office etc) incaricato(-a); (of record) detentore(-trice)
hole [həul] n buco, buca
holiday ['hɔlədɪ] n vacanza; (day off) giorno di vacanza; (public) giorno festivo; **on ~** in vacanza; **I'm on ~ here** sono qui in vacanza; **holiday camp** (BRIT) n (also: **holiday centre**) ≈ villaggio (di vacanze); **holiday job** n (BRIT) ≈ lavoro estivo; **holiday-maker** (BRIT) n villeggiante m/f; **holiday resort** n luogo di villeggiatura
Holland ['hɔlənd] n Olanda

hollow ['hɔləu] *adj* cavo(-a); (*container, claim*) vuoto(-a); (*laugh, sound*) cupo(-a) ▶ *n* cavità *f inv*; (*in land*) valletta, depressione *f* ▶ *vt* **to ~ out** scavare

holly ['hɔlɪ] *n* agrifoglio

Hollywood ['hɔlɪwud] *n* Hollywood *f*

holocaust ['hɔləkɔ:st] *n* olocausto

holy ['həulɪ] *adj* santo(-a); (*bread, ground*) benedetto(-a), consacrato(-a)

home [həum] *n* casa; (*country*) patria; (*institution*) casa, ricovero ▶ *cpd* familiare; (*cooking etc*) casalingo(-a); (*Econ, Pol*) nazionale, interno(-a); (*Sport*) di casa ▶ *adv* a casa; in patria; (*right in: nail etc*) fino in fondo; **at ~** a casa; (*in situation*) a proprio agio; **to go** *or* **come ~** tornare a casa (*or* in patria); **make yourself at ~** si metta a suo agio; **home address** *n* indirizzo di casa; **homeland** *n* patria; **homeless** *adj* senza tetto; spatriato(-a); **homely** *adj* semplice, alla buona; accogliente; **home-made** *adj* casalingo(-a); **home match** *n* partita in casa; **Home Office** (*BRIT*) *n* ministero degli Interni; **home owner** *n* proprietario(-a) di casa; **home page** *n* (*Comput*) home page *f inv*; **Home Secretary** (*BRIT*) *n* ministro degli Interni; **homesick** *adj* **to be homesick** avere la nostalgia; **home town** *n* città *f inv* natale; **homework** *n* compiti *mpl* (per casa)

homicide ['hɔmɪsaɪd] (*US*) *n* omicidio

homoeopathic [həumɪə'pæθɪk] (*US* **homeopathic**) *adj* omeopatico(-a)

homoeopathy [həumɪ'ɔpəθɪ] (*US* **homeopathy**) *n* omeopatia

homosexual [hɔməu'sɛksjuəl] *adj, n* omosessuale *m/f*

honest ['ɔnɪst] *adj* onesto(-a); sincero(-a); **honestly** *adv* onestamente; sinceramente; **honesty** *n* onestà

honey ['hʌnɪ] *n* miele *m*; **honeymoon** *n* luna di miele, viaggio di nozze; **we're on honeymoon** siamo in luna di miele; **honeysuckle** *n* (*Bot*) caprifoglio

Hong Kong ['hɔŋ'kɔŋ] *n* Hong Kong *f*

honorary ['ɔnərərɪ] *adj* onorario(-a); (*duty, title*) onorifico(-a)

honour ['ɔnə*r*] (*US* **honor**) *vt* onorare ▶ *n* onore *m*; **honourable** (*US* **honorable**) *adj* onorevole; **honours degree** *n* (*Scol*) laurea specializzata

hood [hud] *n* cappuccio; (*on cooker*) cappa; (*BRIT Aut*) capote *f*; (*US Aut*) cofano

hoof [hu:f] (*pl* **hooves**) *n* zoccolo

hook [huk] *n* gancio; (*for fishing*) amo ▶ *vt* uncinare; (*dress*) agganciare

hooligan ['hu:lɪgən] *n* giovinastro, teppista *m*

hoop [hu:p] *n* cerchio

hooray [hu:'reɪ] *excl* = **hurray**

hoot [hu:t] *vi* (*Aut*) suonare il clacson; (*siren*) ululare; (*owl*) gufare

Hoover® ['hu:və*r*] (*BRIT*) *n* aspirapolvere *m inv* ▶ *vt* **hoover** pulire con l'aspirapolvere

hooves [hu:vz] *npl of* **hoof**

hop [hɔp] *vi* saltellare, saltare; (*on one foot*) saltare su una gamba

hope [həup] *vt* **to ~ that/to do** sperare che/di fare ▶ *vi* sperare ▶ *n* speranza; **I ~ so/not** spero di sì/no; **hopeful** *adj* (*person*) pieno(-a) di speranza; (*situation*) promettente; **hopefully** *adv* con speranza; **hopefully he will recover** speriamo che si riprenda; **hopeless** *adj* senza speranza, disperato(-a); (*useless*) inutile

hops [hɔps] *npl* luppoli *mpl*

horizon [hə'raɪzn] *n* orizzonte *m*; **horizontal** [hɔrɪ'zɔntl] *adj* orizzontale

hormone ['hɔ:məun] *n* ormone *m*

horn [hɔ:n] *n* (*Zool, Mus*) corno; (*Aut*) clacson *m inv*

horoscope ['hɔrəskəup] n oroscopo

horrendous [hə'rɛndəs] adj
orrendo(-a)

horrible ['hɔrɪbl] adj orribile,
tremendo(-a)

horrid ['hɔrɪd] adj orrido(-a); (person)
odioso(-a)

horrific [hɔ'rɪfɪk] adj (accident)
spaventoso(-a); (film) orripilante

horrifying ['hɔrɪfaɪɪŋ] adj terrificante

horror ['hɔrəʳ] n orrore m; **horror film**
n film m inv dell'orrore

hors d'œuvre [ɔː'dəːvrə] n antipasto

horse [hɔːs] n cavallo; **horseback**:
on horseback adj, adv a cavallo;
horse chestnut n ippocastano;
horsepower n cavallo (vapore);
horse-racing n ippica; **horseradish**
n rafano; **horse riding** n (BRIT)
equitazione f

hose [həuz] n (also: **~pipe**) tubo; (also:
garden~) tubo per annaffiare

hospital ['hɔspɪtl] n ospedale m

hospitality [hɔspɪ'tælɪtɪ] n ospitalità

host [həust] n ospite m; (Rel) ostia;
(large number): **a ~ of** una schiera di

hostage ['hɔstɪdʒ] n ostaggio(-a)

hostel ['hɔstl] n ostello; (also: **youth ~**)
ostello della gioventù

hostess ['həustɪs] n ospite f; (BRIT: air
hostess) hostess f inv

hostile ['hɔstaɪl] adj ostile

hostility [hɔ'stɪlɪtɪ] n ostilità f inv

hot [hɔt] adj caldo(-a); (as opposed to
only warm) molto caldo(-a); (spicy)
piccante; (fig) accanito(-a); ardente;
violento(-a), focoso(-a); **to be ~**
(person) aver caldo; (object) essere
caldo(-a); (weather) far caldo; **hot dog**
n hot dog m inv

hotel [həu'tɛl] n albergo

hotspot ['hɔtspɔt] n (Comput: also
wireless hotspot) hotspot m inv Wi-Fi

hot-water bottle [hɔt'wɔːtə-] n
borsa dell'acqua calda

hound [haund] vt perseguitare ▶ n
segugio

hour ['auəʳ] n ora; **hourly** adj all'ora

house [n haus, pl 'hauzɪz] [vb hauz]
n (also: **firm**) casa; (Pol) camera;
(Theatre) sala; pubblico; spettacolo;
(dynasty) casata ▶ vt (person) ospitare,
alloggiare; **on the ~** (fig) offerto(-a)
dalla casa; **household** n famiglia;
casa; **householder** n padrone(-a)
di casa; (head of house) capofamiglia
m/f; **housekeeper** n governante f;
housekeeping n (work) governo della
casa; (money) soldi mpl per le spese di
casa; **housewife** (irreg) n massaia,
casalinga; **house wine** n vino della
casa; **housework** n faccende fpl
domestiche

housing ['hauzɪŋ] n alloggio;
housing development (BRIT),
housing estate n zona residenziale con
case popolari e/o private

hover ['hɔvəʳ] vi (bird) librarsi;
hovercraft n hovercraft m inv

how [hau] adv come; **~ are you?** come
sta?; **~ do you do?** piacere!; **~ far is
it to the river?** quanto è lontano il
fiume?; **~ long have you been here?**
da quando è qui?; **~ lovely!/awful!**
che bello!/orrore!; **~ many?**
quanti(-e)?; **~ much?** quanto(-a)?; **~
much milk?** quanto latte?; **~ many
people?** quante persone?; **~ old are
you?** quanti anni ha?

however [hau'ɛvəʳ] adv in qualsiasi
modo or maniera che; (+ adjective) per
quanto + sub; (in questions) come ▶ conj
comunque, però

howl [haul] vi ululare

H.P. abbr = **hire purchase**;
horsepower

h.p. n abbr = **H.P**

HQ n, abbr = **headquarters**

hr(s) abbr (= hour(s)) h

HTML abbr (= hypertext markup

language) HTML *m inv*
hubcap ['hʌbkæp] *n* coprimozzo
huddle ['hʌdl] *vi* **to ~ together**
rannicchiarsi l'uno contro l'altro
huff [hʌf] *n* **in a ~** stizzito(-a)
hug [hʌg] *vt* abbracciare; (*shore, kerb*)
stringere
huge [hjuːdʒ] *adj* enorme,
immenso(-a)
hull [hʌl] *n* (*of ship*) scafo
hum [hʌm] *vt* (*tune*) canticchiare ▸ *vi*
canticchiare; (*insect*) ronzare
human ['hjuːmən] (*irreg*) *adj*
umano(-a) ▸ *n* essere *m* umano
humane [hjuːˈmeɪn] *adj*
umanitario(-a)
humanitarian [hjuːmænɪˈtɛərɪən]
adj umanitario(-a)
humanity [hjuːˈmænɪtɪ] *n* umanità
human rights *npl* diritti *mpl*
dell'uomo
humble ['hʌmbl] *adj* umile,
modesto(-a) ▸ *vt* umiliare
humid ['hjuːmɪd] *adj* umido(-a);
humidity [hjuːˈmɪdɪtɪ] *n* umidità
humiliate [hjuːˈmɪlɪeɪt] *vt* umiliare;
humiliating *adj* umiliante;
humiliation [-ˈeɪʃən] *n* umiliazione *f*
hummus ['huməs] *n* purè di ceci
humorous ['hjuːmərəs] *adj*
umoristico(-a); (*person*) buffo(-a)
humour ['hjuːmə*] (*US* **humor**) *n*
umore *m* ▸ *vt* accontentare
hump [hʌmp] *n* gobba
hunch [hʌntʃ] *n* intuizione *f*
hundred ['hʌndrəd] *num* cento; **~s**
of centinaia *fpl* di; **hundredth** [-ɪdθ]
num centesimo(-a)
hung [hʌŋ] *pt, pp of* **hang**
Hungarian [hʌŋˈgɛərɪən] *adj*
ungherese ▸ *n* ungherese *m/f*; (*Ling*)
ungherese *m*
Hungary ['hʌŋgərɪ] *n* Ungheria
hunger ['hʌŋgə*] *n* fame *f* ▸ *vi* **to ~ for**
desiderare ardentemente

hungry ['hʌŋgrɪ] *adj* affamato(-a); **to**
be ~ aver fame
hunt [hʌnt] *vt* (*seek*) cercare; (*Sport*)
cacciare ▸ *vi* **to ~ (for)** andare a caccia
(di) ▸ *n* caccia; **hunter** *n* cacciatore *m*;
hunting *n* caccia
hurdle ['həːdl] *n* (*Sport, fig*) ostacolo
hurl [həːl] *vt* lanciare con violenza
hurrah [huˈrɑː] *excl* = **hurray**
hurray [huˈreɪ] *excl* urra!, evviva!
hurricane ['hʌrɪkən] *n* uragano
hurry ['hʌrɪ] *n* fretta ▸ *vi* (*also:* **~ up**)
affrettarsi ▸ *vt* (*also:* **~ up**: *person*)
affrettare; (*work*) far in fretta; **to be in**
a ~ aver fretta ▸ **hurry up** *vi* sbrigarsi
hurt [həːt] (*pt, pp* **hurt**) *vt* (*cause pain*
to) far male a; (*injure, fig*) ferire ▸ *vi*
far male
husband ['hʌzbənd] *n* marito
hush [hʌʃ] *n* silenzio, calma ▸ *vt* zittire
husky ['hʌskɪ] *adj* roco(-a) ▸ *n* cane *m*
eschimese
hut [hʌt] *n* rifugio; (*shed*) ripostiglio
hyacinth ['haɪəsɪnθ] *n* giacinto
hydrangea [haɪˈdreɪnʒə] *n* ortensia
hydrofoil ['haɪdrəʊfɔɪl] *n* aliscafo
hydrogen ['haɪdrədʒən] *n* idrogeno
hygiene ['haɪdʒiːn] *n* igiene *f*;
hygienic [haɪˈdʒiːnɪk] *adj* igienico(-a)
hymn [hɪm] *n* inno; cantica
hype [haɪp] (*inf*) *n* campagna
pubblicitaria
hyperlink ['haɪpəlɪŋk] *n* link *m inv*
ipertestuale
hyphen ['haɪfn] *n* trattino
hypnotize ['hɪpnətaɪz] *vt* ipnotizzare
hypocrite ['hɪpəkrɪt] *n* ipocrita *m/f*
hypocritical [hɪpəˈkrɪtɪkl] *adj*
ipocrita
hypothesis [haɪˈpɒθɪsɪs] (*pl*
hypotheses) *n* ipotesi *f inv*
hysterical [hɪˈstɛrɪkl] *adj* isterico(-a)
hysterics [hɪˈstɛrɪks] *npl* accesso di
isteria; (*laughter*) attacco di riso

♦

I

I [aɪ] *pron* io
ice [aɪs] *n* ghiaccio; (*on road*) gelo; (*ice cream*) gelato ▶ *vt* (*cake*) glassare ▶ *vi* (*also*: ~ **over**) ghiacciare; (*also*: ~ **up**) gelare; **iceberg** *n* iceberg *m inv*; **ice cream** *n* gelato; **ice cube** *n* cubetto di ghiaccio; **ice hockey** *n* hockey *m* su ghiaccio
Iceland ['aɪslənd] *n* Islanda; **Icelander** *n* islandese *m/f*; **Icelandic** [aɪs'lændɪk] *adj* islandese ▶ *n* (*Ling*) islandese *m*
ice: **ice lolly** (*BRIT*) *n* ghiacciolo; **ice rink** *n* pista di pattinaggio; **ice skating** *n* pattinaggio sul ghiaccio
icing ['aɪsɪŋ] *n* (*Culin*) glassa; **icing sugar** (*BRIT*) *n* zucchero a velo
icon ['aɪkɔn] *n* icona
icy ['aɪsɪ] *adj* ghiacciato(-a); (*weather, temperature*) gelido(-a)
I'd [aɪd] = **I would**; **I had**
ID card *n* = **identity card**
idea [aɪ'dɪə] *n* idea
ideal [aɪ'dɪəl] *adj* ideale ▶ *n* ideale *m*; **ideally** [aɪ'dɪəlɪ] *adv* perfettamente, assolutamente; **ideally the book should have ...** l'ideale sarebbe che il libro avesse ...
identical [aɪ'dɛntɪkl] *adj* identico(-a)
identification [aɪdɛntɪfɪ'keɪʃən] *n* identificazione *f*; **(means of)** ~ carta d'identità
identify [aɪ'dɛntɪfaɪ] *vt* identificare
identity [aɪ'dɛntɪtɪ] *n* identità *f inv*;

identity card *n* carta d'identità
ideology [aɪdɪ'ɔlədʒɪ] *n* ideologia
idiom ['ɪdɪəm] *n* idioma *m*; (*phrase*) espressione *f* idiomatica
idiot ['ɪdɪət] *n* idiota *m/f*
idle ['aɪdl] *adj* inattivo(-a); (*lazy*) pigro(-a), ozioso(-a); (*unemployed*) disoccupato(-a); (*question, pleasures*) ozioso(-a) ▶ *vi* (*engine*) girare al minimo
idol ['aɪdl] *n* idolo
idyllic [ɪ'dɪlɪk] *adj* idillico(-a)
i.e. *adv abbr* (= *that is*) cioè
if [ɪf] *conj* se; **if I were you ...** se fossi in te ..., io al tuo posto ...; **if so** se è così; **if not** se no; **if only** se solo *or* soltanto
ignite [ɪg'naɪt] *vt* accendere ▶ *vi* accendersi
ignition [ɪg'nɪʃən] *n* (*Aut*) accensione *f*; **to switch on/off the ~** accendere/spegnere il motore
ignorance ['ɪgnərəns] *n* ignoranza; **to keep sb in ~ of sth** tenere qn all'oscuro di qc
ignorant ['ɪgnərənt] *adj* ignorante; **to be ~ of** (*subject*) essere ignorante in; (*events*) essere ignaro(-a) di
ignore [ɪg'nɔː'] *vt* non tener conto di; (*person, fact*) ignorare
I'll [aɪl] = **I will**; **I shall**
ill [ɪl] *adj* (*sick*) malato(-a); (*bad*) cattivo(-a) ▶ *n* male *m* ▶ *adv* **to speak** *etc* ~ **of sb** parlare *etc* male di qn; **to take** *or* **be taken ~** ammalarsi
illegal [ɪ'liːgl] *adj* illegale
illegible [ɪ'lɛdʒɪbl] *adj* illeggibile
illegitimate [ɪlɪ'dʒɪtɪmət] *adj* illegittimo(-a)
ill health *n* problemi *mpl* di salute
illiterate [ɪ'lɪtərət] *adj* analfabeta, illetterato(-a); (*letter*) scorretto(-a)
illness ['ɪlnɪs] *n* malattia
illuminate [ɪ'luːmɪneɪt] *vt* illuminare
illusion [ɪ'luːʒən] *n* illusione *f*

illustrate ['ɪləstreɪt] vt illustrare
illustration [ɪlə'streɪʃən] n illustrazione f
I'm [aɪm] = **I am**
image ['ɪmɪdʒ] n immagine f; (public face) immagine (pubblica)
imaginary [ɪ'mædʒɪnərɪ] adj immaginario(-a)
imagination [ɪmædʒɪ'neɪʃən] n immaginazione f, fantasia
imaginative [ɪ'mædʒɪnətɪv] adj immaginoso(-a)
imagine [ɪ'mædʒɪn] vt immaginare
imbalance [ɪm'bæləns] n squilibrio
imitate ['ɪmɪteɪt] vt imitare; **imitation** [-'teɪʃən] n imitazione f
immaculate [ɪ'mækjulət] adj immacolato(-a); (dress, appearance) impeccabile
immature [ɪmə'tjuər] adj immaturo(-a)
immediate [ɪ'miːdɪət] adj immediato(-a); **immediately** adv (at once) subito, immediatamente; **immediately next to** proprio accanto a
immense [ɪ'mɛns] adj immenso(-a); enorme; **immensely** adv immensamente
immerse [ɪ'məːs] vt immergere
immigrant ['ɪmɪgrənt] n immigrante m/f; immigrato(-a); **immigration** [ɪmɪ'greɪʃən] n immigrazione f
imminent ['ɪmɪnənt] adj imminente
immoral [ɪ'mɔrl] adj immorale
immortal [ɪ'mɔːtl] adj, n immortale m/f
immune [ɪ'mjuːn] adj **~ (to)** immune (da); **immune system** n sistema m immunitario
immunize ['ɪmjunaɪz] vt immunizzare
impact ['ɪmpækt] n impatto
impair [ɪm'pɛər] vt danneggiare
impartial [ɪm'pɑːʃl] adj imparziale

impatience [ɪm'peɪʃəns] n impazienza
impatient [ɪm'peɪʃənt] adj impaziente; **to get** or **grow ~** perdere la pazienza
impeccable [ɪm'pɛkəbl] adj impeccabile
impending [ɪm'pɛndɪŋ] adj imminente
imperative [ɪm'pɛrətɪv] adj imperativo(-a); necessario(-a), urgente; (voice) imperioso(-a)
imperfect [ɪm'pəːfɪkt] adj imperfetto(-a); (goods etc) difettoso(-a) ▶ n (Ling: also: **~ tense**) imperfetto
imperial [ɪm'pɪərɪəl] adj imperiale; (measure) legale
impersonal [ɪm'pəːsənl] adj impersonale
impersonate [ɪm'pəːsəneɪt] vt impersonare; (Theatre) fare la mimica di
impetus ['ɪmpətəs] n impeto
implant [ɪm'plɑːnt] vt (Med) innestare; (fig: idea, principle) inculcare
implement [n 'ɪmplɪmənt, vb 'ɪmplɪmɛnt] n attrezzo; (for cooking) utensile m ▶ vt effettuare
implicate ['ɪmplɪkeɪt] vt implicare
implication [ɪmplɪ'keɪʃən] n implicazione f; **by ~** implicitamente
implicit [ɪm'plɪsɪt] adj implicito(-a); (complete) completo(-a)
imply [ɪm'plaɪ] vt insinuare; suggerire
impolite [ɪmpə'laɪt] adj scortese
import [vb ɪm'pɔːt, n 'ɪmpɔːt] vt importare ▶ n (Comm) importazione f
importance [ɪm'pɔːtns] n importanza
important [ɪm'pɔːtnt] adj importante; **it's not ~** non ha importanza
importer [ɪm'pɔːtər] n importatore(-trice)

impose [ɪm'pəuz] vt imporre ▶ vi
to ~ on sb sfruttare la bontà di qn;
imposing [ɪm'pəuzɪŋ] adj
imponente
impossible [ɪm'pɔsɪbl] adj
impossibile
impotent ['ɪmpətnt] adj impotente
impoverished [ɪm'pɔvərɪʃt] adj
impoverito(-a)
impractical [ɪm'præktɪkl] adj non
pratico(-a)
impress [ɪm'prɛs] vt impressionare;
(mark) imprimere, stampare; **to ~ sth
on sb** far capire qc a qn
impression [ɪm'prɛʃən] n
impressione f; **to be under the ~ that**
avere l'impressione che
impressive [ɪm'prɛsɪv] adj notevole
imprison [ɪm'prɪzn] vt imprigionare;
imprisonment n imprigionamento
improbable [ɪm'prɔbəbl] adj
improbabile; (excuse) inverosimile
improper [ɪm'prɔpər] adj
scorretto(-a); (unsuitable)
inadatto(-a), improprio(-a),
sconveniente, indecente
improve [ɪm'pruːv] vt migliorare ▶ vi
migliorare; (pupil etc) fare progressi;
improvement n miglioramento;
progresso
improvise ['ɪmprəvaɪz] vt, vi
improvvisare
impulse ['ɪmpʌls] n impulso; **on
~** d'impulso, impulsivamente;
impulsive [ɪm'pʌlsɪv] adj
impulsivo(-a)

○ **in**
[ɪn] prep
1 (indicating place, position) in; **in the
house/garden** in casa/giardino; **in
the box** nella scatola; **in the fridge**
nel frigorifero; **I have it in my hand** ce
l'ho in mano; **in town/the country** in
città/campagna; **in school** a scuola; **in
here/there** qui/lì dentro

2 (with place names: of town, region,
country): **in London** a Londra; **in
England** in Inghilterra; **in the United
States** negli Stati Uniti; **in Yorkshire**
nello Yorkshire
3 (indicating time: during, in the
space of) in; **in spring/summer** in
primavera/estate; **in 1988** nel 1988; **in
May** in or a maggio; **I'll see you in July**
ci vediamo a luglio; **in the afternoon**
nel pomeriggio; **at 4 o'clock in the
afternoon** alle 4 del pomeriggio; **I
did it in 3 hours/days** l'ho fatto in
3 ore/giorni; **I'll see you in 2 weeks**
or **in 2 weeks' time** ci vediamo tra 2
settimane
4 (indicating manner etc) a; **in a
loud/soft voice** a voce alta/bassa; **in
pencil** a matita; **in English/French** in
inglese/francese; **the boy in the blue
shirt** il ragazzo con la camicia blu
5 (indicating circumstances): **in the sun**
al sole; **in the shade** all'ombra; **in the
rain** sotto la pioggia; **a rise in prices** un
aumento dei prezzi
6 (indicating mood, state): **in tears**
in lacrime; **in anger** per la rabbia;
in despair disperato(-a); **in good
condition** in buono stato, in buone
condizioni; **to live in luxury** vivere
nel lusso
7 (with ratios, numbers): **1 in 10** 1 su
10; **20 pence in the pound** 20 pence
per sterlina; **they lined up in twos** si
misero in fila a due a due
8 (referring to people, works) in; **the
disease is common in children** la
malattia è comune nei bambini; **in
(the works of) Dickens** in Dickens
9 (indicating profession etc) in; **to be in
teaching** fare l'insegnante, insegnare;
to be in publishing essere nell'editoria
10 (after superlative) di; **the best in the
class** il migliore della classe
11 (with present participle): **in saying this**

dicendo questo, nel dire questo
▶*adv* **to be in** (*person: at home, work*)
esserci; (*train, ship, plane*) essere
arrivato(-a); (*in fashion*) essere di moda;
to ask sb in invitare qn ad entrare;
to run/limp *etc* **in** entrare di corsa/
zoppicando *etc*
▶*n* **the ins and outs of the problem**
tutti i particolari del problema
inability [ɪnəˈbɪlɪtɪ] *n* **~ (to do)**
incapacità (di fare)
inaccurate [ɪnˈækjurət] *adj*
inesatto(-a), impreciso(-a)
inadequate [ɪnˈædɪkwət] *adj*
insufficiente
inadvertently [ɪnədˈvəːtntlɪ] *adv*
senza volerlo
inappropriate [ɪnəˈprəuprɪət] *adj*
non adatto(-a); (*word, expression*)
improprio(-a)
inaugurate [ɪˈnɔːgjureɪt] *vt*
inaugurare; (*president, official*)
insediare
Inc. (*US*) *abbr* (= *incorporated*) S.A.
incapable [ɪnˈkeɪpəbl] *adj* incapace
incense [*n* ˈɪnsɛns, *vb* ɪnˈsɛns] *n*
incenso ▶*vt* (*anger*) infuriare
incentive [ɪnˈsɛntɪv] *n* incentivo
inch [ɪntʃ] *n* pollice *m* (25 *mm*, 12 *in a*
foot); **within an ~ of** a un pelo da; **he**
didn't give an ~ non ha ceduto di un
millimetro
incidence [ˈɪnsɪdns] *n* (*of crime,*
disease) incidenza
incident [ˈɪnsɪdnt] *n* incidente *m*; (*in*
book) episodio
incidentally [ɪnsɪˈdɛntəlɪ] *adv* (*by the*
way) a proposito
inclination [ɪnklɪˈneɪʃən] *n*
inclinazione *f*
incline [*n* ˈɪnklaɪn, *vb* ɪnˈklaɪn] *n*
pendenza, pendio ▶*vt* inclinare
▶*vi* (*surface*) essere inclinato(-a); **to**
be ~d to do tendere a fare; essere
propenso(-a) a fare

include [ɪnˈkluːd] *vt* includere,
comprendere; **is service ~d?** il
servizio è compreso?; **including**
prep compreso(-a), incluso(-a);
inclusion [ɪnˈkluːʒən] *n* inclusione *f*;
inclusive [ɪnˈkluːsɪv] *adj* incluso(-a),
compreso(-a); **inclusive of tax** *etc*
tasse *etc* comprese
income [ˈɪnkʌm] *n* reddito; **income**
support *n* (*BRIT*) sussidio di
indigenza *or* povertà; **income tax** *n*
imposta sul reddito
incoming [ˈɪnkʌmɪŋ] *adj* (*flight, mail*)
in arrivo; (*government*) subentrante;
(*tide*) montante
incompatible [ɪnkəmˈpætɪbl] *adj*
incompatibile
incompetence [ɪnˈkɔmpɪtns] *n*
incompetenza, incapacità
incompetent [ɪnˈkɔmpɪtnt] *adj*
incompetente, incapace
incomplete [ɪnkəmˈpliːt] *adj*
incompleto(-a)
inconsistent [ɪnkənˈsɪstənt] *adj*
incoerente; **~ with** non coerente con
inconvenience [ɪnkənˈviːnjəns] *n*
inconveniente *m*; (*trouble*) disturbo
▶*vt* disturbare
inconvenient [ɪnkənˈviːnjənt] *adj*
scomodo(-a)
incorporate [ɪnˈkɔːpəreɪt] *vt*
incorporare; (*contain*) contenere
incorrect [ɪnkəˈrɛkt] *adj* scorretto(-a);
(*statement*) inesatto(-a)
increase [*n* ˈɪnkriːs, *vb* ɪnˈkriːs]
n aumento ▶*vi, vt* aumentare;
increasingly *adv* sempre più
incredible [ɪnˈkrɛdɪbl] *adj* incredibile;
incredibly *adv* incredibilmente
incur [ɪnˈkəːʳ] *vt* (*expenses*) incorrere;
(*anger, risk*) esporsi a; (*debt*) contrarre;
(*loss*) subire
indecent [ɪnˈdiːsnt] *adj* indecente
indeed [ɪnˈdiːd] *adv* infatti;
veramente; **yes ~!** certamente!

indefinitely [ɪnˈdɛfɪnɪtlɪ] *adv* (*wait*) indefinitamente

independence [ɪndɪˈpɛndns] *n* indipendenza; **Independence Day** (*US*) *n vedi nota*

● **Independence Day**
● Negli Stati Uniti il 4 luglio si
● festeggia **l'Independence Day**,
● giorno in cui, nel 1776, 13 colonie
● britanniche proclamarono la propria
● indipendenza dalla Gran Bretagna
● ed entrarono ufficialmente a far
● parte degli Stati Uniti d'America.

independent [ɪndɪˈpɛndnt] *adj* indipendente; **independent school** *n* (*BRIT*) *istituto scolastico indipendente che si autofinanzia*

index [ˈɪndɛks] (*pl* **indexes**) *n* (*in book*) indice *m*; (: *in library etc*) catalogo; (*pl* *indices: ratio, sign*) indice *m*

India [ˈɪndɪə] *n* India; **Indian** *adj*, *n* indiano(-a)

indicate [ˈɪndɪkeɪt] *vt* indicare; **indication** [-ˈkeɪʃən] *n* indicazione *f*, segno; **indicative** [ɪnˈdɪkətɪv] *adj* **indicative of** indicativo(-a) di; **indicator** [ˈɪndɪkeɪtər] *n* indicatore *m*; (*Aut*) freccia

indices [ˈɪndɪsiːz] *npl of* **index**

indict [ɪnˈdaɪt] *vt* accusare; **indictment** [ɪnˈdaɪtmənt] *n* accusa

indifference [ɪnˈdɪfrəns] *n* indifferenza

indifferent [ɪnˈdɪfrənt] *adj* indifferente; (*poor*) mediocre

indigenous [ɪnˈdɪdʒɪnəs] *adj* indigeno(-a)

indigestion [ɪndɪˈdʒɛstʃən] *n* indigestione *f*

indignant [ɪnˈdɪgnənt] *adj* ~ **(at sth/with sb)** indignato(-a) (per qc/contro qn)

indirect [ɪndɪˈrɛkt] *adj* indiretto(-a)

indispensable [ɪndɪˈspɛnsəbl] *adj* indispensabile

individual [ɪndɪˈvɪdjuəl] *n* individuo ▶ *adj* individuale; (*characteristic*) particolare, originale; **individually** *adv* singolarmente, uno(-a) per uno(-a)

Indonesia [ɪndəˈniːzɪə] *n* Indonesia

indoor [ˈɪndɔːʳ] *adj* da interno; (*plant*) d'appartamento; (*swimming pool*) coperto(-a); (*sport*, *games*) fatto(-a) al coperto; **indoors** [ɪnˈdɔːz] *adv* all'interno

induce [ɪnˈdjuːs] *vt* persuadere; (*bring about, Med*) provocare

indulge [ɪnˈdʌldʒ] *vt* (*whim*) compiacere, soddisfare; (*child*) viziare ▶ *vi* **to ~ in sth** concedersi qc; abbandonarsi a qc; **indulgent** *adj* indulgente

industrial [ɪnˈdʌstrɪəl] *adj* industriale; (*injury*) sul lavoro; **industrial estate** (*BRIT*) *n* zona industriale; **industrialist** *n* industriale *m*; **industrial park** (*US*) *n* = **industrial estate**

industry [ˈɪndəstrɪ] *n* industria; (*diligence*) operosità

inefficient [ɪnɪˈfɪʃənt] *adj* inefficiente

inequality [ɪnɪˈkwɔlɪtɪ] *n* ineguaglianza

inevitable [ɪnˈevɪtəbl] *adj* inevitabile; **inevitably** *adv* inevitabilmente

inexpensive [ɪnɪkˈspɛnsɪv] *adj* poco costoso(-a)

inexperienced [ɪnɪksˈpɪərɪənst] *adj* inesperto(-a), senza esperienza

inexplicable [ɪnɪkˈsplɪkəbl] *adj* inesplicabile

infamous [ˈɪnfəməs] *adj* infame

infant [ˈɪnfənt] *n* bambino(-a)

infantry [ˈɪnfəntrɪ] *n* fanteria

infant school *n* (*BRIT*) scuola elementare (*per bambini dall'età di 5 a 7 anni*)

infect [ɪnˈfɛkt] *vt* infettare; **infection**

[ɪnˈfɛkʃən] n infezione f; **infectious**
[ɪnˈfɛkʃəs] adj (disease) infettivo(-a),
contagioso(-a); (person: fig:
enthusiasm) contagioso(-a)
infer [ɪnˈfəːʳ] vt inferire, dedurre
inferior [ɪnˈfɪərɪəʳ] adj inferiore;
(goods) di qualità scadente ▶ n
inferiore m/f; (in rank) subalterno(-a)
infertile [ɪnˈfəːtaɪl] adj sterile
infertility [ɪnfəˈtɪlɪtɪ] n sterilità
infested [ɪnˈfɛstɪd] adj ~ **(with)**
infestato(-a) (di)
infinite [ˈɪnfɪnɪt] adj infinito(-a);
infinitely adv infinitamente
infirmary [ɪnˈfəːmərɪ] n ospedale m;
(in school, factory) infermeria
inflamed [ɪnˈfleɪmd] adj
infiammato(-a)
inflammation [ɪnfləˈmeɪʃən] n
infiammazione f
inflatable [ɪnˈfleɪtəbl] adj gonfiabile
inflate [ɪnˈfleɪt] vt (tyre, balloon)
gonfiare; (fig) esagerare; gonfiare;
inflation [ɪnˈfleɪʃən] n (Econ)
inflazione f
inflexible [ɪnˈflɛksɪbl] adj inflessibile,
rigido(-a)
inflict [ɪnˈflɪkt] vt **to ~ on** infliggere a
influence [ˈɪnfluəns] n influenza ▶ vt
influenzare; **under the ~ of alcohol**
sotto l'effetto dell'alcool; **influential**
[ɪnfluˈɛnʃl] adj influente
influx [ˈɪnflʌks] n afflusso
info (inf) [ˈɪnfəu] n = **information**
inform [ɪnˈfɔːm] vt **to ~ sb (of)**
informare qn (di) ▶ vi **to ~ on sb**
denunciare qn
informal [ɪnˈfɔːml] adj informale;
(announcement, invitation) non ufficiale
information [ɪnfəˈmeɪʃən] n
informazioni fpl; particolari mpl;
a piece of ~ un'informazione;
information office n ufficio m
informazioni inv; **information
technology** n informatica

informative [ɪnˈfɔːmətɪv] adj
istruttivo(-a)
infra-red [ɪnfrəˈrɛd] adj infrarosso(-a)
infrastructure [ˈɪnfrəstrʌktʃəʳ] n
infrastruttura
infrequent [ɪnˈfriːkwənt] adj
infrequente, raro(-a)
infuriate [ɪnˈfjuərɪeɪt] vt rendere
furioso(-a)
infuriating [ɪnˈfjuərɪeɪtɪŋ] adj molto
irritante
ingenious [ɪnˈdʒiːnjəs] adj
ingegnoso(-a)
ingredient [ɪnˈɡriːdɪənt] n
ingrediente m; elemento
inhabit [ɪnˈhæbɪt] vt abitare;
inhabitant [ɪnˈhæbɪtnt] n abitante
m/f
inhale [ɪnˈheɪl] vt inalare ▶ vi
(in smoking) aspirare; **inhaler** n
inalatore m
inherent [ɪnˈhɪərənt] adj ~ **(in or to)**
inerente (a)
inherit [ɪnˈhɛrɪt] vt ereditare;
inheritance n eredità
inhibit [ɪnˈhɪbɪt] vt (Psych) inibire;
inhibition [-ˈbɪʃən] n inibizione f
initial [ɪˈnɪʃl] adj iniziale ▶ n iniziale
f ▶ vt siglare; **~s** npl (of name) iniziali
fpl; (as signature) sigla; **initially** adv
inizialmente, all'inizio
initiate [ɪˈnɪʃɪeɪt] vt (start) avviare;
intraprendere; iniziare; (person)
iniziare; **to ~ sb into a secret**
mettere qn a parte di un segreto;
to ~ proceedings against sb (Law)
intentare causa contro qn
initiative [ɪˈnɪʃətɪv] n iniziativa
inject [ɪnˈdʒɛkt] vt (liquid) iniettare;
(patient): **to ~ sb with sth** fare a qn
un'iniezione di qc; (funds) immettere;
injection [ɪnˈdʒɛkʃən] n iniezione
f, puntura
injure [ˈɪndʒəʳ] vt ferire; (damage:
reputation etc) nuocere a; **injured** adj

ferito(-a); **injury** ['ɪndʒərɪ] n ferita

injustice [ɪn'dʒʌstɪs] n ingiustizia

ink [ɪŋk] n inchiostro; **ink-jet printer** ['ɪŋkdʒɛt-] n stampante f a getto d'inchiostro

inland [adj 'ɪnlənd, adv ɪn'lænd] adj interno(-a) ▶ adv all'interno; **Inland Revenue** (BRIT) n Fisco

in-laws ['ɪnlɔːz] npl suoceri mpl; famiglia del marito (or della moglie)

inmate ['ɪnmeɪt] n (in prison) carcerato(-a); (in asylum) ricoverato(-a)

inn [ɪn] n locanda

inner ['ɪnə'] adj interno(-a), interiore; **inner-city** n centro di una zona urbana

inning ['ɪnɪŋ] n (US: Baseball) ripresa; **~s** (Cricket) turno di battuta

innocence ['ɪnəsns] n innocenza

innocent ['ɪnəsnt] adj innocente

innovation [ɪnəu'veɪʃən] n innovazione f

innovative ['ɪnəu'veɪtɪv] adj innovativo(-a)

in-patient ['ɪnpeɪʃənt] n ricoverato(-a)

input ['ɪnput] n input m

inquest ['ɪnkwɛst] n inchiesta

inquire [ɪn'kwaɪə'] vi informarsi ▶ vt domandare, informarsi su; **inquiry** n domanda; (Law) indagine f, investigazione f; **"inquiries"** "informazioni"

ins. abbr = **inches**

insane [ɪn'seɪn] adj matto(-a), pazzo(-a); (Med) alienato(-a)

insanity [ɪn'sænɪtɪ] n follia; (Med) alienazione f mentale

insect ['ɪnsɛkt] n insetto; **insect repellent** n insettifugo

insecure [ɪnsɪ'kjuə'] adj malsicuro(-a); (person) insicuro(-a)

insecurity [ɪnsɪ'kjuərɪtɪ] n mancanza di sicurezza

insensitive [ɪn'sɛnsɪtɪv] adj insensibile

insert [ɪn'səːt] vt inserire, introdurre

inside ['ɪn'saɪd] n interno, parte f interiore ▶ adj interno(-a), interiore ▶ adv dentro, all'interno ▶ prep dentro, all'interno di; (of time): **~ 10 minutes** entro 10 minuti; **inside lane** n (Aut) corsia di marcia; **inside out** adv (turn) a rovescio; (know) in fondo

insight ['ɪnsaɪt] n acume m, perspicacia; (glimpse, idea) percezione f

insignificant [ɪnsɪg'nɪfɪknt] adj insignificante

insincere [ɪnsɪn'sɪə'] adj insincero(-a)

insist [ɪn'sɪst] vi insistere; **to ~ on doing** insistere per fare; **to ~ that** insistere perché + sub; (claim) sostenere che; **insistent** adj insistente

insomnia [ɪn'sɔmnɪə] n insonnia

inspect [ɪn'spɛkt] vt ispezionare; (BRIT: ticket) controllare; **inspection** [ɪn'spɛkʃən] n ispezione f; controllo; **inspector** n ispettore(-trice); (BRIT: on buses, trains) controllore m

inspiration [ɪnspə'reɪʃən] n ispirazione f; **inspire** [ɪn'spaɪə'] vt ispirare; **inspiring** adj stimolante

instability [ɪnstə'bɪlɪtɪ] n instabilità

install [ɪn'stɔːl] (US instal) vt installare; **installation** [ɪnstə'leɪʃən] n installazione f

instalment [ɪn'stɔːlmənt] (US **installment**) n rata; (of TV serial etc) puntata; **in ~s** (pay) a rate; (receive) una parte per volta; (: publication) a fascicoli

instance ['ɪnstəns] n esempio, caso; **for ~** per or ad esempio; **in the first ~** in primo luogo

instant ['ɪnstənt] n istante m, attimo ▶ adj immediato(-a); urgente; (coffee, food) in polvere; **instantly** adv immediatamente, subito

instead [ɪnˈstɛd] *adv* invece; **~ of** invece di

instinct [ˈɪnstɪŋkt] *n* istinto; **instinctive** *adj* istintivo(-a)

institute [ˈɪnstɪtjuːt] *n* istituto ▶ *vt* istituire, stabilire; (*inquiry*) avviare; (*proceedings*) iniziare

institution [ɪnstɪˈtjuːʃən] *n* istituzione *f*; (*educational institution*, *mental institution*) istituto

instruct [ɪnˈstrʌkt] *vt* **to ~ sb in sth** insegnare qc a qn; **to ~ sb to do** dare ordini a qn di fare; **instruction** [ɪnˈstrʌkʃən] *n* istruzione *f*; **instructions (for use)** istruzioni per l'uso; **instructor** *n* istruttore(-trice); (*for skiing*) maestro(-a)

instrument [ˈɪnstrəmənt] *n* strumento; **instrumental** [-ˈmɛntl] *adj* (*Mus*) strumentale; **to be instrumental in** essere d'aiuto in

insufficient [ɪnsəˈfɪʃənt] *adj* insufficiente

insulate [ˈɪnsjuleɪt] *vt* isolare; **insulation** [-ˈleɪʃən] *n* isolamento

insulin [ˈɪnsjulɪn] *n* insulina

insult [*n* ˈɪnsʌlt, *vb* ɪnˈsʌlt] *n* insulto, affronto ▶ *vt* insultare; **insulting** *adj* offensivo(-a), ingiurioso(-a)

insurance [ɪnˈʃuərəns] *n* assicurazione *f*; **fire/life ~** assicurazione contro gli incendi/ sulla vita; **insurance company** *n* società di assicurazioni; **insurance policy** *n* polizza d'assicurazione

insure [ɪnˈʃuəʳ] *vt* assicurare

intact [ɪnˈtækt] *adj* intatto(-a)

intake [ˈɪnteɪk] *n* (*Tech*) immissione *f*; (*of food*) consumo; (*BRIT: of pupils etc*) afflusso

integral [ˈɪntɪɡrəl] *adj* integrale; (*part*) integrante

integrate [ˈɪntɪɡreɪt] *vt* integrare ▶ *vi* integrarsi

integrity [ɪnˈtɛɡrɪtɪ] *n* integrità

intellect [ˈɪntəlɛkt] *n* intelletto; **intellectual** [-ˈlɛktjuəl] *adj*, *n* intellettuale *m/f*

intelligence [ɪnˈtɛlɪdʒəns] *n* intelligenza; (*Mil etc*) informazioni *fpl*

intelligent [ɪnˈtɛlɪdʒənt] *adj* intelligente

intend [ɪnˈtɛnd] *vt* (*gift etc*): **to ~ sth for** destinare qc a; **to ~ to do** aver l'intenzione di fare

intense [ɪnˈtɛns] *adj* intenso(-a); (*person*) di forti sentimenti

intensify [ɪnˈtɛnsɪfaɪ] *vt* intensificare

intensity [ɪnˈtɛnsɪtɪ] *n* intensità

intensive [ɪnˈtɛnsɪv] *adj* intensivo(-a); **intensive care** *n* terapia intensiva; **intensive care unit** *n* reparto terapia intensiva

intent [ɪnˈtɛnt] *n* intenzione *f* ▶ *adj* **~ (on)** intento(-a) (a), immerso(-a) (in); **to all ~s and purposes** a tutti gli effetti; **to be ~ on doing sth** essere deciso a fare qc

intention [ɪnˈtɛnʃən] *n* intenzione *f*; **intentional** *adj* intenzionale, deliberato(-a)

interact [ɪntərˈækt] *vi* interagire; **interaction** [ɪntərˈækʃən] *n* azione *f* reciproca, interazione *f*; **interactive** *adj* (*Comput*) interattivo(-a)

intercept [ɪntəˈsɛpt] *vt* intercettare; (*person*) fermare

interchange [ˈɪntətʃeɪndʒ] *n* (*exchange*) scambio; (*on motorway*) incrocio pluridirezionale

intercourse [ˈɪntəkɔːs] *n* rapporti *mpl*

interest [ˈɪntrɪst] *n* interesse *m*; (*Comm: stake, share*) interessi *mpl* ▶ *vt* interessare; **interested** *adj* interessato(-a); **to be interested in** interessarsi di; **interesting** *adj* interessante; **interest rate** *n* tasso di interesse

interface ['ɪntəfeɪs] n (Comput)
interfaccia
interfere [ɪntə'fɪəʳ] vi **to ~ in** (quarrel,
other people's business) immischiarsi
in; **to ~ with** (object) toccare; (plans,
duty) interferire con; **interference**
[ɪntə'fɪərəns] n interferenza
interim ['ɪntərɪm] adj provvisorio(-a)
▶ n **in the ~** nel frattempo
interior [ɪn'tɪərɪəʳ] n interno; (of
country) entroterra ▶ adj interno(-a);
(minister) degli Interni; **interior
design** n architettura d'interni
intermediate [ɪntə'miːdɪət] adj
intermedio(-a)
intermission [ɪntə'mɪʃən] n pausa;
(Theatre, Cinema) intermissione f,
intervallo
intern [vb ɪn'təːn, n 'ɪntəːn] vt
internare ▶ n (US) medico interno
internal [ɪn'təːnl] adj interno(-a);
Internal Revenue Service (US)
n Fisco
international [ɪntə'næʃənl] adj
internazionale ▶ n (BRIT Sport)
incontro internazionale
Internet ['ɪntənɛt] n **the ~** Internet
f; **Internet café** n cybercaffè m inv;
Internet Service Provider n Provider
m inv; **Internet user** n utente m/f
Internet
interpret [ɪn'təːprɪt] vt
interpretare ▶ vi fare da interprete;
interpretation [ɪntəːprɪ'teɪʃən]
n interpretazione f; **interpreter** n
interprete m/f; **could you act as an
interpreter for us?** ci potrebbe fare da
interprete?
interrogate [ɪn'tɛrəugeɪt] vt
interrogare; **interrogation** [-'geɪʃən]
n interrogazione f; (of suspect etc)
interrogatorio
interrogative [ɪntə'rɔgətɪv]
adj interrogativo(-a) ▶ n (Ling)
interrogativo

interrupt [ɪntə'rʌpt] vt, vi
interrompere; **interruption**
[-'rʌpʃən] n interruzione f
intersection [ɪntə'sɛkʃən] n
intersezione f; (of roads) incrocio
interstate ['ɪntəsteɪt] (US) n fra stati
interval ['ɪntəvl] n intervallo; **at ~s**
a intervalli
intervene [ɪntə'viːn] vi (time)
intercorrere; (event, person)
intervenire
interview ['ɪntəvjuː] n (Radio, TV etc)
intervista; (for job) colloquio ▶ vt
intervistare; avere un colloquio con;
interviewer n intervistatore(-trice)
intimate [adj 'ɪntɪmət, vb 'ɪntɪmeɪt]
adj intimo(-a); (knowledge)
profondo(-a) ▶ vt lasciar capire
intimidate [ɪn'tɪmɪdeɪt] vt intimidire,
intimorire
intimidating [ɪn'tɪmɪdeɪtɪŋ] adj
(sight) spaventoso(-a); (appearance,
figure) minaccioso(-a)
into ['ɪntuː] prep dentro, in; **come ~ the
house** entra in casa; **he worked late ~
the night** lavorò fino a tarda notte; **~
Italian** in italiano
intolerant [ɪn'tɔlərnt] adj **~ of**
intollerante di
intranet ['ɪntrənɛt] n intranet f
intransitive [ɪn'trænsɪtɪv] adj
intransitivo(-a)
intricate ['ɪntrɪkət] adj intricato(-a),
complicato(-a)
intrigue [ɪn'triːg] n intrigo ▶ vt
affascinare; **intriguing** adj
affascinante
introduce [ɪntrə'djuːs] vt introdurre;
to ~ sb (to sb) presentare qn (a qn);
to ~ sb to (pastime, technique) iniziare
qn a; **introduction** [-'dʌkʃən]
n introduzione f; (of person)
presentazione f; (to new experience)
iniziazione f; **introductory** adj
introduttivo(-a)

intrude [ɪn'truːd] *vi (person)*: **to ~ (on)** intromettersi (in); **intruder** *n* intruso(-a)

intuition [ɪntjuː'ɪʃən] *n* intuizione *f*

inundate ['ɪnʌndeɪt] *vt* **to ~ with** inondare di

invade [ɪn'veɪd] *vt* invadere

invalid [*n* 'ɪnvəlɪd, *adj* ɪn'vælɪd] *n* malato(-a); *(with disability)* invalido(-a) ▶ *adj (not valid)* invalido(-a), non valido(-a)

invaluable [ɪn'væljuəbl] *adj* prezioso(-a); inestimabile

invariably [ɪn'vɛərɪəblɪ] *adv* invariabilmente; sempre

invasion [ɪn'veɪʒən] *n* invasione *f*

invent [ɪn'vɛnt] *vt* inventare; **invention** [ɪn'vɛnʃən] *n* invenzione *f*; **inventor** *n* inventore *m*

inventory ['ɪnvəntrɪ] *n* inventario

inverted commas [ɪn'vəːtɪd-] *(BRIT) npl* virgolette *fpl*

invest [ɪn'vɛst] *vt* investire ▶ *vi* **to ~ (in)** investire (in)

investigate [ɪn'vɛstɪgeɪt] *vt* investigare, indagare; *(crime)* fare indagini su; **investigation** [-'geɪʃən] *n* investigazione *f*; *(of crime)* indagine *f*

investigator [ɪn'vɛstɪgeɪtəʳ] *n* investigatore(-trice); **a private ~** un investigatore privato, un detective

investment [ɪn'vɛstmənt] *n* investimento

investor [ɪn'vɛstəʳ] *n* investitore(-trice); azionista *m/f*

invisible [ɪn'vɪzɪbl] *adj* invisibile

invitation [ɪnvɪ'teɪʃən] *n* invito

invite [ɪn'vaɪt] *vt* invitare; *(opinions etc)* sollecitare; **inviting** *adj* invitante

invoice ['ɪnvɔɪs] *n* fattura ▶ *vt* fatturare

involve [ɪn'vɔlv] *vt (entail)* richiedere, comportare; *(associate)*: **to ~ sb (in)** implicare qn (in); coinvolgere qn (in); **involved** *adj*

involuto(-a), complesso(-a); **to be involved in** essere coinvolto(-a) in; **involvement** *n* implicazione *f*; coinvolgimento

inward ['ɪnwəd] *adj (movement)* verso l'interno; *(thought, feeling)* interiore, intimo(-a); **inward(s)** *adv* verso l'interno

iPod® ['aɪpɔd] *n* iPod® *m inv*

IQ *n abbr (= intelligence quotient)* quoziente *m* d'intelligenza

IRA *n abbr (= Irish Republican Army)* IRA *f*

Iran [ɪ'rɑːn] *n* Iran *m*; **Iranian** *adj, n* iraniano(-a)

Iraq [ɪ'rɑːk] *n* Iraq *m*; **Iraqi** *adj, n* iracheno(-a)

Ireland ['aɪələnd] *n* Irlanda

iris ['aɪrɪs] *(pl irises) n* iride *f*; *(Bot)* giaggiolo, iride

Irish ['aɪrɪʃ] *adj* irlandese ▶ *npl* **the ~** gli Irlandesi; **Irishman** *(irreg) n* irlandese *m*; **Irish Sea** *n* Mar *m* d'Irlanda; **Irishwoman** *(irreg) n* irlandese *f*

iron ['aɪən] *n* ferro; *(for clothes)* ferro da stiro ▶ *adj* di or in ferro ▶ *vt (clothes)* stirare

ironic(al) [aɪ'rɔnɪk(l)] *adj* ironico(-a); **ironically** *adv* ironicamente

ironing ['aɪənɪŋ] *n (act)* stirare *m*; *(clothes)* roba da stirare; **ironing board** *n* asse *f* da stiro

irony ['aɪrənɪ] *n* ironia

irrational [ɪ'ræʃənl] *adj* irrazionale

irregular [ɪ'rɛgjuləʳ] *adj* irregolare

irrelevant [ɪ'rɛləvənt] *adj* non pertinente

irresistible [ɪrɪ'zɪstɪbl] *adj* irresistibile

irresponsible [ɪrɪ'spɔnsɪbl] *adj* irresponsabile

irrigation [ɪrɪ'geɪʃən] *n* irrigazione *f*

irritable ['ɪrɪtəbl] *adj* irritabile

irritate ['ɪrɪteɪt] *vt* irritare; **irritating** *adj (person, sound etc)* irritante; **irritation** [-'teɪʃən] *n* irritazione *f*

IRS (US) n abbr = **Internal Revenue Service**

is [ɪz] vb see **be**

ISDN n abbr (= Integrated Services Digital Network) I.S.D.N. f

Islam ['ɪzlɑːm] n Islam m; **Islamic** [ɪz'læmɪk] adj islamico(-a)

island ['aɪlənd] n isola; **islander** n isolano(-a)

isle [aɪl] n isola

isn't ['ɪznt] = **is not**

isolated ['aɪsəleɪtɪd] adj isolato(-a)

isolation [aɪsə'leɪʃən] n isolamento

ISP n abbr (= Internet Service Provider) provider m inv

Israel ['ɪzreɪl] n Israele m; **Israeli** [ɪz'reɪlɪ] adj, n israeliano(-a)

issue ['ɪʃjuː] n questione f, problema m; (of banknotes etc) emissione f; (of newspaper etc) numero ▶ vt (statement) rilasciare; (rations, equipment) distribuire; (book) pubblicare; (banknotes, cheques, stamps) emettere; **at** ~ in gioco, in discussione; **to take ~ with sb (over sth)** prendere posizione contro qn (riguardo a qc); **to make an ~ of sth** fare un problema di qc

it

[ɪt] pron

1 (specific: subject) esso(-a); (: direct object) lo (la), l'; (: indirect object) gli (le); **where's my book? — it's on the table** dov'è il mio libro? — è sulla tavola; **I can't find it** non lo (or la) trovo; **give it to me** dammelo (or dammela); **about/from/of it** ne; **I spoke to him about it** gliene ho parlato; **what did you learn from it?** quale insegnamento ne hai tratto?; **I'm proud of it** ne sono fiero; **did you go to it?** ci sei andato?; **put the book in it** mettici il libro

2 (impers): **it's raining** piove; **it's Friday tomorrow** domani è venerdì; **it's 6 o'clock** sono le 6; **who is it? — it's me** chi è? — sono io

IT n abbr see **information technology**

Italian [ɪ'tæljən] adj italiano(-a) ▶ n italiano(-a); (Ling) italiano; **the ~s** gli Italiani; **what's the ~ (word) for ...?** come si dice in italiano ...?

italics [ɪ'tælɪks] npl corsivo

Italy ['ɪtəlɪ] n Italia

itch [ɪtʃ] n prurito ▶ vi (person) avere il prurito; (part of body) prudere; **to ~ to do sth** aver una gran voglia di fare qc; **itchy** adj che prude; **to be itchy** = **to itch**

it'd ['ɪtd] = **it would**; **it had**

item ['aɪtəm] n articolo; (on agenda) punto; (also: **news ~**) notizia

itinerary [aɪ'tɪnərərɪ] n itinerario

it'll ['ɪtl] = **it will**; **it shall**

its [ɪts] adj il (la) suo(-a), i (le) suoi (sue)

it's [ɪts] = **it is**; **it has**

itself [ɪt'sɛlf] pron (emphatic) esso(-a) stesso(-a); (reflexive) si

ITV (BRIT) n abbr (= Independent Television) rete televisiva in concorrenza con la BBC

I've [aɪv] = **I have**

ivory ['aɪvərɪ] n avorio

ivy ['aɪvɪ] n edera

j

jab [dʒæb] *vt* dare colpetti a ▶ *n* (*Med: inf*) puntura; **to ~ sth into** affondare *or* piantare qc dentro

jack [dʒæk] *n* (*Aut*) cricco; (*Cards*) fante *m*

jacket ['dʒækɪt] *n* giacca; (*of book*) copertura; **jacket potato** *n* patata cotta al forno con la buccia

jackpot ['dʒækpɔt] *n* primo premio (in denaro)

Jacuzzi® [dʒə'kuːzɪ] *n* vasca per idromassaggio Jacuzzi®

jagged ['dʒægɪd] *adj* seghettato(-a); (*cliffs etc*) frastagliato(-a)

jail [dʒeɪl] *n* prigione *f* ▶ *vt* mandare in prigione; **jail sentence** *n* condanna al carcere

jam [dʒæm] *n* marmellata; (*also:* **traffic ~**) ingorgo; (*inf*) pasticcio ▶ *vt* (*passage etc*) ingombrare, ostacolare; (*mechanism, drawer etc*) bloccare; (*Radio*) disturbare con interferenze ▶ *vi* incepparsi; **to ~ sth into** forzare qc dentro; infilare qc a forza dentro

Jamaica [dʒə'meɪkə] *n* Giamaica

jammed [dʒæmd] *adj* (*door*) bloccato(-a); (*rifle, printer*) inceppato(-a)

Jan. *abbr* (= *January*) gen., genn.

janitor ['dʒænɪtə'] *n* (*caretaker*) portiere *m*; (: *Scol*) bidello

January ['dʒænjuərɪ] *n* gennaio

Japan [dʒə'pæn] *n* Giappone *m*; **Japanese** [dʒæpə'niːz] *adj*

giapponese ▶ *n inv* giapponese *m/f*; (*Ling*) giapponese *m*

jar [dʒɑː'] *n* (*glass*) barattolo, vasetto ▶ *vi* (*sound*) stridere; (*colours etc*) stonare

jargon ['dʒɑːgən] *n* gergo

javelin ['dʒævlɪn] *n* giavellotto

jaw [dʒɔː] *n* mascella

jazz [dʒæz] *n* jazz *m*

jealous ['dʒɛləs] *adj* geloso(-a); **jealousy** *n* gelosia

jeans [dʒiːnz] *npl* (blue-)jeans *mpl*

Jello® ['dʒɛləʊ] (*US*) *n* gelatina di frutta

jelly ['dʒɛlɪ] *n* gelatina; **jellyfish** *n* medusa

jeopardize ['dʒɛpədaɪz] *vt* mettere in pericolo

jerk [dʒəːk] *n* sobbalzo, scossa; sussulto; (*inf: idiot*) tonto(-a) ▶ *vt* dare una scossa a ▶ *vi* (*vehicles*) sobbalzare

Jersey ['dʒəːzɪ] *n* Jersey *m*

jersey ['dʒəːzɪ] *n* maglia; (*fabric*) jersey *m*

Jesus ['dʒiːzəs] *n* Gesù *m*

jet [dʒɛt] *n* (*of gas, liquid*) getto; (*Aviat*) aviogetto; **jet lag** *n* (problemi *mpl* dovuti allo) sbalzo dei fusi orari; **jet-ski** *vi* acquascooter *m inv*

jetty ['dʒɛtɪ] *n* molo

Jew [dʒuː] *n* ebreo

jewel ['dʒuːəl] *n* gioiello; **jeweller** (*US* **jeweler**) *n* orefice *m*, gioielliere(-a); **jeweller's (shop)** (*US* **jewelry store**) *n* oreficeria, gioielleria; **jewellery** (*US* **jewelry**) *n* gioielli *mpl*

Jewish ['dʒuːɪʃ] *adj* ebreo(-a), ebraico(-a)

jigsaw ['dʒɪgsɔː] *n* (*also:* **~ puzzle**) puzzle *m inv*

job [dʒɔb] *n* lavoro; (*employment*) impiego, posto; **it's not my ~** (*duty*) non è compito mio; **it's a good ~ that ...** meno male che ...; **just the ~!** proprio quello che ci vuole; **job centre** (BRIT) n ufficio di collocamento; **jobless** adj senza lavoro, disoccupato(-a)

jockey ['dʒɔkɪ] n fantino, jockey m inv ▶ vi **to ~ for position** manovrare per una posizione di vantaggio

jog [dʒɔg] vt urtare ▶ vi (Sport) fare footing, fare jogging; **to ~ sb's memory** rinfrescare la memoria a qn; **to ~ along** trottare; (fig) andare avanti piano piano; **jogging** n footing m, jogging m

join [dʒɔɪn] vt unire, congiungere; (become member of) iscriversi a; (meet) raggiungere; riunirsi a ▶ vi (roads, rivers) confluire ▶ n giuntura ▷ **join in** vi partecipare ▶ vt fus unirsi a ▷ **join up** vi incontrarsi; (Mil) arruolarsi

joiner ['dʒɔɪnər] (BRIT) n falegname m

joint [dʒɔɪnt] n (Tech) giuntura; giunto; (Anat) articolazione f, giuntura; (BRIT Culin) arrosto; (inf: place) locale m; (: of cannabis) spinello ▶ adj comune; **joint account** n (at bank etc) conto in partecipazione, conto comune; **jointly** adv in comune, insieme

joke [dʒəuk] n scherzo; (funny story) barzelletta; (also: **practical ~**) beffa ▶ vi scherzare; **to play a ~ on sb** fare uno scherzo a qn; **joker** n (Cards) matta, jolly m inv

jolly ['dʒɔlɪ] adj allegro(-a), gioioso(-a) ▶ adv (BRIT: inf) veramente, proprio

jolt [dʒəult] n scossa, sobbalzo ▶ vt urtare

Jordan ['dʒɔːdən] n (country) Giordania; (river) Giordano

journal ['dʒɜːnl] n giornale m; rivista; diario; **journalism** n giornalismo; **journalist** n giornalista m/f

journey ['dʒɜːnɪ] n viaggio; (distance covered) tragitto; **how was your ~?** com'è andato il viaggio?; **the ~ takes two hours** il viaggio dura due ore

joy [dʒɔɪ] n gioia; **joyrider** n chi ruba un'auto per farvi un giro; **joy stick** n (Aviat) barra di comando; (Comput) joystick m inv

Jr abbr = **junior**

judge [dʒʌdʒ] n giudice m/f ▶ vt giudicare

judo ['dʒuːdəu] n judo

jug [dʒʌg] n brocca, bricco

juggle ['dʒʌgl] vi fare giochi di destrezza; **juggler** n giocoliere(-a)

juice [dʒuːs] n succo; **juicy** ['dʒuːsɪ] adj succoso(-a)

Jul. abbr (= July) lug., lu.

July [dʒuː'laɪ] n luglio

jumble ['dʒʌmbl] n miscuglio ▶ vt (also: **~ up**) mischiare; **jumble sale** (BRIT) n vendita di beneficenza

- **jumble sale**
- Una **jumble sale** è un mercatino
- di oggetti di seconda mano
- organizzati in chiese, scuole o
- in circoli ricreativi, i cui proventi
- vengono devoluti in beneficenza.

jumbo ['dʒʌmbəu] adj **~ jet** jumbo-jet m inv; **~ size** formato gigante

jump [dʒʌmp] vi saltare, balzare; (start) sobbalzare; (increase) rincarare ▶ vt saltare ▶ n salto, balzo; sobbalzo

jumper ['dʒʌmpər] n (BRIT: pullover) maglione m, pullover m inv; (US: dress) scamiciato

jumper cables (US) npl = **jump leads**

jump leads (BRIT) npl cavi mpl per batteria

Jun. abbr = **junior**

junction ['dʒʌŋkʃən] n (BRIT: of roads) incrocio; (of rails) nodo ferroviario

June [dʒuːn] n giugno

jungle ['dʒʌŋgl] n giungla

junior ['dʒuːnɪər] adj, n **he's ~ to me by 2 years, he's my ~ by 2 years** è più giovane di me (di 2 anni); **he's ~ to me** (seniority) è al di sotto di me, ho più anzianità di lui; **junior high**

school (*US*) *n* scuola media (*da 12 a 15 anni*); **junior school** (*BRIT*) *n* scuola elementare (*da 8 a 11 anni*)

junk [dʒʌŋk] *n* cianfrusaglie *fpl*; (*cheap goods*) robaccia; **junk food** *n* porcherie *fpl*

junkie ['dʒʌŋkɪ] (*inf*) *n* drogato(-a)

junk mail *n* stampe *fpl* pubblicitarie

Jupiter ['dʒuːpɪtəʳ] *n* (*planet*) Giove *m*

jurisdiction [dʒuərɪs'dɪkʃən] *n* giurisdizione *f*; **it falls** *or* **comes within/outside our ~** è/non è di nostra competenza

jury ['dʒuərɪ] *n* giuria

just [dʒʌst] *adj* giusto(-a) ▶ *adv* **he's ~ done it/left** lo ha appena fatto/è appena partito; **~ right** proprio giusto; **~ 2 o'clock** le 2 precise; **she's ~ as clever as you** è in gamba proprio quanto te; **it's ~ as well that …** meno male che …; **~ as I arrived** proprio mentre arrivavo; **it was ~ before/enough/here** era poco prima/appena abbastanza/proprio qui; **it's ~ me** sono solo io; **~ missed/caught** appena perso/preso; **~ listen to this!** senta un po' questo!

justice ['dʒʌstɪs] *n* giustizia

justification [dʒʌstɪfɪ'keɪʃən] *n* giustificazione *f*; (*Typ*) giustezza

justify ['dʒʌstɪfaɪ] *vt* giustificare

jut [dʒʌt] *vi* (*also*: **~ out**) sporgersi

juvenile ['dʒuːvənaɪl] *adj* giovane, giovanile; (*court*) dei minorenni; (*books*) per ragazzi ▶ *n* giovane *m/f*, minorenne *m/f*

K *abbr* (= *one thousand*) mille; (= *kilobyte*) K

kangaroo [kæŋgə'ruː] *n* canguro

karaoke [kɑːrə'əʊkɪ] *n* karaoke *m inv*

karate [kə'rɑːtɪ] *n* karatè *m*

kebab [kə'bæb] *n* spiedino

keel [kiːl] *n* chiglia; **on an even ~** (*fig*) in uno stato normale

keen [kiːn] *adj* (*interest, desire*) vivo(-a); (*eye, intelligence*) acuto(-a); (*competition*) serrato(-a); (*edge*) affilato(-a); (*eager*) entusiasta; **to be ~ to do** *or* **on doing sth** avere una gran voglia di fare qc; **to be ~ on sth** essere appassionato(-a) di qc; **to be ~ on sb** avere un debole per qn

keep [kiːp] (*pt, pp* **kept**) *vt* tenere; (*hold back*) trattenere; (*feed: one's family etc*) mantenere, sostentare; (*a promise*) mantenere; (*chickens, bees, pigs etc*) allevare ▶ *vi* (*food*) mantenersi; (*remain: in a certain state or place*) restare ▶ *n* (*of castle*) maschio; (*food etc*): **enough for his ~** abbastanza per vitto e alloggio; (*inf*): **for ~s** per sempre; **to ~ doing sth** continuare a fare qc; fare qc di continuo; **to ~ sb from doing** impedire a qn di fare; **to ~ sb busy/a place tidy** tenere qn occupato(-a)/un luogo in ordine; **to ~ sth to o.s.** tenere qc per sé; **to ~ sth (back) from sb** celare qc a qn; **to ~ time** (*clock*) andar bene ▶ **keep away** *vt* **to ~ sth/sb away from sb** tenere qc/qn lontano da qn ▶ *vi* **to**

k

~ away (from) stare lontano (da) ▷ **keep back** vt (crowds, tears, money) trattenere ▶ vi tenersi indietro ▷ **keep off** vt (dog, person) tenere lontano da ▶ vi stare alla larga; **~ your hands off!** non toccare!, giù le mani!; **"~ off the grass"** "non calpestare l'erba" ▷ **keep on** vi **to ~ on doing** continuare a fare; **to ~ on (about sth)** continuare a insistere (su qc) ▷ **keep out** vt tener fuori; **"~ out"** "vietato l'accesso" ▷ **keep up** vt continuare, mantenere ▶ vi **to ~ up with** tener dietro a, andare di pari passo con; (work etc) farcela a seguire; **keeper** n custode m/f, guardiano(-a); **keeping** n (care) custodia; **in keeping with** in armonia con; in accordo con

kennel ['kɛnl] n canile m; **~s** npl canile m; **to put a dog in ~s** mettere un cane al canile

Kenya ['kɛnjə] n Kenia m

kept [kɛpt] pt, pp of **keep**

kerb [kəːb] n (BRIT) n orlo del marciapiede

kerosene ['kɛrəsiːn] n cherosene m

ketchup ['kɛtʃəp] n ketchup m inv

kettle ['kɛtl] n bollitore m

key [kiː] n (gen, Mus) chiave f; (of piano, typewriter) tasto ▶ adj chiave inv ▶ vt (also: **~ in**) digitare; **can I have my ~?** posso avere la mia chiave?; **keyboard** n tastiera; **keyhole** n buco della serratura; **keyring** n portachiavi m inv

kg abbr (= kilogram) Kg

khaki ['kɑːkɪ] adj cachi ▶ n cachi m

kick [kɪk] vt calciare, dare calci a; (inf: habit etc) liberarsi di ▶ vi (horse) tirar calci ▶ n calcio; (thrill): **he does it for ~s** lo fa giusto per il piacere di farlo ▷ **kick off** vi (Sport) dare il primo calcio; **kick-off** n (Sport) calcio d'inizio

kid [kɪd] n (inf: child) ragazzino(-a); (animal, leather) capretto ▶ vi (inf) scherzare

kidnap ['kɪdnæp] vt rapire, sequestrare; **kidnapping** n sequestro (di persona)

kidney ['kɪdnɪ] n (Anat) rene m; (Culin) rognone m; **kidney bean** n fagiolo borlotto

kill [kɪl] vt uccidere, ammazzare ▶ n uccisione f; **killer** n uccisore m, killer m inv; assassino(-a); **killing** n assassinio; **to make a killing** (inf) fare un bel colpo

kiln [kɪln] n forno

kilo ['kiːləu] n chilo; **kilobyte** n (Comput) kilobyte m inv; **kilogram(me)** ['kɪləugræm] n chilogrammo; **kilometre** ['kɪləmiːtə'] (US **kilometer**) n chilometro; **kilowatt** ['kɪləuwɔt] n chilowatt m inv

kilt [kɪlt] n gonnellino scozzese

kin [kɪn] n see **next**; **kith**

kind [kaɪnd] adj gentile, buono(-a) ▶ n sorta, specie f; (species) genere m; **what ~ of …?** che tipo di …?; **to be two of a ~** essere molto simili; **in ~** (Comm) in natura

kindergarten ['kɪndəgɑːtn] n giardino d'infanzia

kindly ['kaɪndlɪ] adj pieno(-a) di bontà, benevolo(-a) ▶ adv con bontà, gentilmente; **will you ~ …** vuole … per favore

kindness ['kaɪndnɪs] n bontà, gentilezza

king [kɪŋ] n re m inv; **kingdom** n regno, reame m; **kingfisher** n martin m inv pescatore; **king-size(d) bed** n letto king-size

kiosk ['kiːɔsk] n edicola, chiosco; (BRIT Tel) cabina (telefonica)

kipper ['kɪpə'] n aringa affumicata

kiss [kɪs] n bacio ▶ vt baciare; **to ~ (each other)** baciarsi; **kiss of life** n respirazione f bocca a bocca

kit [kɪt] n equipaggiamento, corredo; (set of tools etc) attrezzi mpl; (for

assembly) scatola di montaggio
kitchen ['kɪtʃɪn] *n* cucina
kite [kaɪt] *n* (*toy*) aquilone *m*
kitten ['kɪtn] *n* gattino(-a), micino(-a)
kiwi ['ki:wi:] *n* (*also*: **~ fruit**) kiwi *m inv*
km *abbr* (= *kilometre*) km
km/h *abbr* (= *kilometres per hour*) km/h
knack [næk] *n* **to have the ~ of** avere
l'abilità di
knee [ni:] *n* ginocchio; **kneecap** *n*
rotula
kneel [ni:l] (*pt, pp* **knelt**) *vi* (*also*: **~
down**) inginocchiarsi
knelt [nɛlt] *pt, pp of* **kneel**
knew [nju:] *pt of* **know**
knickers ['nɪkəz] (*BRIT*) *npl*
mutandine *fpl*
knife [naɪf] (*pl* **knives**) *n* coltello ▶ *vt*
accoltellare, dare una coltellata a
knight [naɪt] *n* cavaliere *m*; (*Chess*)
cavallo
knit [nɪt] *vt* fare a maglia ▶ *vi* lavorare
a maglia; (*broken bones*) saldarsi;
to ~ one's brows aggrottare le
sopracciglia; **knitting** *n* lavoro a
maglia; **knitting needle** *n* ferro (da
calza); **knitwear** *n* maglieria
knives [naɪvz] *npl of* **knife**
knob [nɔb] *n* bottone *m*; manopola
knock [nɔk] *vt* colpire; urtare; (*fig: inf*)
criticare ▶ *vi* (*at door etc*): **to ~ at/on**
bussare a ▶ *n* bussata; colpo, botta
▷ **knock down** *vt* abbattere ▷ **knock
off** *vi* (*inf: finish*) smettere (di lavorare)
▶ *vt* (*from price*) far abbassare; (*inf:
steal*) sgraffignare ▷ **knock out** *vt*
stendere; (*Boxing*) mettere K.O.;
(*defeat*) battere ▷ **knock over** *vt*
(*person*) investire; (*object*) far cadere;
knockout *n* (*Boxing*) knock out *m inv*
▶ *cpd* a eliminazione
knot [nɔt] *n* nodo ▶ *vt* annodare
know [nəu] (*pt* **knew**, *pp* **known**)
vt sapere; (*person, author, place*)
conoscere; **I don't ~** non lo so; **do**

you ~ where I can …? sa dove posso
…?; **to ~ how to do** sapere fare; **to ~
about** *or* **of sth/sb** conoscere qc/qn;
know-all *n* sapientone(-a); **know-
how** *n* tecnica; pratica; **knowing**
adj (*look etc*) d'intesa; **knowingly** *adv*
(*purposely*) consapevolmente; (*smile,
look*) con aria d'intesa; **know-it-all**
(*US*) *n* = **know-all**
knowledge ['nɔlɪdʒ] *n*
consapevolezza; (*learning*)
conoscenza, sapere *m*;
knowledgeable *adj* ben
informato(-a)
known [nəun] *pp of* **know**
knuckle ['nʌkl] *n* nocca
koala [kəu'ɑ:lə] *n* (*also*: **~ bear**) koala
m inv
Koran [kɔ'rɑ:n] *n* Corano
Korea [kə'rɪə] *n* Corea; **Korean** *adj, n*
coreano(-a)
kosher ['kəuʃəʳ] *adj* kasher *inv*
Kosovar, Kosovan ['kɔsəvaʳ,
'kɔsəvən] *adj* kosovaro(-a)
Kosovo ['kusəvəu] *n* Kosovo
Kremlin ['krɛmlɪn] *n* **the ~** il Cremlino
Kuwait [ku'weɪt] *n* Kuwait *m*

L (*BRIT*) *abbr* = **learner driver**

l. *abbr* (= *litre*) l

lab [læb] *n abbr* (= *laboratory*) laboratorio

label ['leɪbl] *n* etichetta, cartellino; (*brand: of record*) casa ▶ *vt* etichettare

labor *etc* ['leɪbə'] (*US*) = **labour** *etc*

laboratory [lə'bɔrətərɪ] *n* laboratorio

Labor Day (*US*) *n* festa del lavoro

● **Labor Day**

● Negli Stati Uniti e nel Canada

● il **Labor Day**, la festa del lavoro,

● cade il primo lunedì di settembre,

● contrariamente a quanto accade

● nella maggior parte dei paesi

● europei dove tale celebrazione ha

● luogo il primo maggio.

labor union (*US*) *n* sindacato

labour ['leɪbə'] (*US* **labor**) *n* (*task*) lavoro; (*workmen*) manodopera; (*Med*): **to be in ~** avere le doglie ▶ *vi* **to ~ (at)** lavorare duro (a); **L~, the L~ party** (*BRIT*) il partito laburista, i laburisti; **hard ~** lavori *mpl* forzati; **labourer** *n* manovale *m*; **farm labourer** lavoratore *m* agricolo

lace [leɪs] *n* merletto, pizzo; (*of shoe etc*) laccio ▶ *vt* (*shoe: also:* **~ up**) allacciare

lack [læk] *n* mancanza ▶ *vt* mancare di; **through** *or* **for ~ of** per mancanza di; **to be ~ing** mancare; **to be ~ing in** mancare di

lacquer ['lækə'] *n* lacca

lacy ['leɪsɪ] *adj* (*like lace*) che sembra un pizzo

lad [læd] *n* ragazzo, giovanotto

ladder ['lædə'] *n* scala; (*BRIT: in tights*) smagliatura

ladle ['leɪdl] *n* mestolo

lady ['leɪdɪ] *n* signora; dama; **L~ Smith** lady Smith; **the ladies' (room)** i gabinetti per signore; **ladybird** (*US* **ladybug**) *n* coccinella

lag [læg] *n* (*of time*) lasso, intervallo ▶ *vi* (*also:* **~ behind**) trascinarsi ▶ *vt* (*pipes*) rivestire di materiale isolante

lager ['lɑːgə'] *n* lager *m inv*

lagoon [lə'guːn] *n* laguna

laid [leɪd] *pt, pp of* **lay; laid back** (*inf*) *adj* rilassato(-a), tranquillo(-a)

lain [leɪn] *pp of* **lie**

lake [leɪk] *n* lago

lamb [læm] *n* agnello

lame [leɪm] *adj* zoppo(-a); (*excuse etc*) zoppicante

lament [lə'mɛnt] *n* lamento ▶ *vt* lamentare, piangere

lamp [læmp] *n* lampada; **lamppost** ['læmppəust] (*BRIT*) *n* lampione *m*; **lampshade** ['læmpʃeɪd] *n* paralume *m*

land [lænd] *n* (*as opposed to sea*) terra (ferma); (*country*) paese *m*; (*soil*) terreno; suolo; (*estate*) terreni *mpl*, terre *fpl* ▶ *vi* (*from ship*) sbarcare; (*Aviat*) atterrare; (*fig: fall*) cadere ▶ *vt* (*passengers*) sbarcare; (*goods*) scaricare; **to ~ sb with sth** affibbiare qc a qn; **landing** *n* atterraggio; (*of staircase*) pianerottolo; **landing card** *n* carta di sbarco; **landlady** *n* padrona *or* proprietaria di casa; **landlord** *n* padrone *m or* proprietario di casa; (*of pub etc*) padrone *m*; **landmark** *n* punto di riferimento; (*fig*) pietra miliare; **landowner** *n* proprietario(-a) terriero(-a); **landscape** *n* paesaggio; **landslide** *n* (*Geo*) frana; (*fig: Pol*) valanga

lane [leɪn] n stradina; (Aut, in race) corsia; **"get in ~"** "immettersi in corsia"

language ['læŋgwɪdʒ] n lingua; (way one speaks) linguaggio; **what ~s do you speak?** che lingue parla?; **bad ~** linguaggio volgare; **language laboratory** n laboratorio linguistico

lantern ['læntn] n lanterna

lap [læp] n (of track) giro; (of body): **in** or **on one's ~** in grembo ▶ vt (also: **~ up**) papparsi, leccare ▶ vi (waves) sciabordare

lapel [lə'pɛl] n risvolto

lapse [læps] n lapsus m inv; (longer) caduta ▶ vi (law) cadere; (membership, contract) scadere; **to ~ into bad habits** pigliare cattive abitudini; **~ of time** spazio di tempo

laptop (computer) ['læptɔp-] n laptop m inv

lard [lɑːd] n lardo

larder ['lɑːdər] n dispensa

large [lɑːdʒ] adj grande; (person, animal) grosso(-a); **at ~** (free) in libertà; (generally) in generale; nell'insieme; **largely** adv in gran parte; **large-scale** adj (map, drawing etc) in grande scala; (reforms, business activities) su vasta scala

lark [lɑːk] n (bird) allodola; (joke) scherzo, gioco

laryngitis [lærɪn'dʒaɪtɪs] n laringite f

lasagne [lə'zænjə] n lasagne fpl

laser ['leɪzər] n laser m; **laser printer** n stampante f laser inv

lash [læʃ] n frustata; (also: **eye~**) ciglio ▶ vt frustare; (tie): **to ~ to/together** legare a insieme ▶ **lash out** vi **to ~ out (at** or **against sb)** attaccare violentemente (qn)

lass [læs] n ragazza

last [lɑːst] adj ultimo(-a); (week, month, year) scorso(-a), passato(-a) ▶ adv per ultimo ▶ vi durare; **~ week** la settimana scorsa; **~ night** ieri sera, la notte scorsa; **at ~** finalmente, alla fine; **~ but one** penultimo(-a); **lastly** adv infine, per finire; **last-minute** adj fatto(-a) (or preso(-a) etc) all'ultimo momento

latch [lætʃ] n chiavistello ▶ **latch onto** vt fus (cling to: person) attaccarsi a, appiccicarsi a; (: idea) afferrare, capire

late [leɪt] adj (not on time) in ritardo; (far on in day etc) tardi inv; tardo(-a); (former) ex; (dead) defunto(-a) ▶ adv tardi; (behind time, schedule) in ritardo; **sorry I'm ~** scusi il ritardo; **the flight is two hours ~** il volo ha due ore di ritardo; **it's too ~** è troppo tardi; **of ~** di recente; **in the ~ afternoon** nel tardo pomeriggio; **in ~ May** verso la fine di maggio; **latecomer** n ritardatario(-a); **lately** adv recentemente; **later** ['leɪtər] adj (date etc) posteriore; (version etc) successivo(-a) ▶ adv più tardi; **later on** più avanti; **latest** ['leɪtɪst] adj ultimo(-a), più recente; **at the latest** al più tardi

lather ['lɑːðər] n schiuma di sapone ▶ vt insaponare

Latin ['lætɪn] n latino ▶ adj latino(-a); **Latin America** n America Latina; **Latin American** adj sudamericano(-a)

latitude ['lætɪtjuːd] n latitudine f; (fig) libertà d'azione

latter ['lætər] adj secondo(-a), più recente ▶ n **the ~** quest'ultimo, il secondo

laugh [lɑːf] n risata ▶ vi ridere ▶ **laugh at** vt fus (misfortune etc) ridere di; **laughter** n riso; risate fpl

launch [lɔːntʃ] n (of rocket, Comm) lancio; (of new ship) varo; (also: **motor ~**) lancia ▶ vt (rocket, Comm) lanciare; (ship, plan) varare ▶ **launch into** vt fus lanciarsi in

launder ['lɔːndər] vt lavare e stirare
Launderette® [lɔːn'drɛt] (BRIT) n
lavanderia (automatica)
Laundromat® ['lɔːndrəmæt] (US) n
lavanderia automatica
laundry ['lɔːndrɪ] n lavanderia;
(clothes) biancheria; (: dirty) panni
mpl da lavare
lava ['lɑːvə] n lava
lavatory ['lævətərɪ] n gabinetto
lavender ['lævəndər] n lavanda
lavish ['lævɪʃ] adj copioso(-a),
abbondante; (giving freely): ~ with
prodigo(-a) di, largo(-a) in ▶ vt to ~ sth
on sb colmare qn di qc
law [lɔː] n legge f; **civil/criminal ~**
diritto civile/penale; **lawful** adj
legale, lecito(-a); **lawless** adj che non
conosce nessuna legge
lawn [lɔːn] n tappeto erboso;
lawnmower n tosaerba m or f inv
lawsuit ['lɔːsuːt] n processo, causa
lawyer ['lɔːjər] n (for sales, wills
etc) ≈ notaio; (partner, in court)
≈ avvocato(-essa)
lax [læks] adj rilassato(-a), negligente
laxative ['læksətɪv] n lassativo
lay [leɪ] (pt, pp **laid**) pt of **lie** ▶ adj
laico(-a); (not expert) profano(-a) ▶ vt
posare, mettere; (eggs) fare; (trap)
tendere; (plans) fare, elaborare; **to
~ the table** apparecchiare la tavola
▷ **lay down** vt mettere giù; (rules etc)
formulare, fissare; **to ~ down the law**
dettar legge; **to ~ down one's life** dare
la propria vita ▷ **lay off** vt (workers)
licenziare ▷ **lay on** vt (provide) fornire
▷ **lay out** vt (display) presentare,
disporre; **lay-by** (BRIT) n piazzola
(di sosta)
layer ['leɪər] n strato
layman ['leɪmən] (irreg) n laico;
profano
layout ['leɪaʊt] n lay-out m inv,
disposizione f; (Press)
impaginazione f
lazy ['leɪzɪ] adj pigro(-a)
lb. abbr = **pound** (weight)
lead¹ [liːd] (pt, pp **led**) n (front position)
posizione f di testa; (distance, time
ahead) vantaggio; (clue) indizio; (Elec)
filo (elettrico); (for dog) guinzaglio;
(Theatre) parte f principale ▶ vt
guidare, condurre; (induce) indurre;
(be leader of) essere a capo di ▶ vi
condurre; (Sport) essere in testa; **in
the ~** in testa; **to ~ the way** fare strada
▷ **lead up to** vt fus portare a
lead² [lɛd] n (metal) piombo; (in pencil)
mina
leader ['liːdər] n capo; leader m inv; (in
newspaper) articolo di fondo; (Sport)
chi è in testa; **leadership** n direzione
f; capacità di comando
lead-free ['lɛdfriː] adj senza piombo
leading ['liːdɪŋ] adj primo(-a),
principale
lead singer n cantante alla testa di
un gruppo
leaf [liːf] (pl **leaves**) n foglia ▶ vi to ~
through sth sfogliare qc; **to turn over
a new ~** cambiar vita
leaflet ['liːflɪt] n dépliant m inv; (Pol,
Rel) volantino
league [liːg] n lega; (Football)
campionato; **to be in ~ with** essere
in lega con
leak [liːk] n (out) fuga; (in) infiltrazione
f; (security leak) fuga d'informazioni
▶ vi (roof, bucket) perdere; (liquid)
uscire; (shoes) lasciar passare l'acqua
▶ vt (information) divulgare
lean [liːn] (pt, pp **leaned** or **leant**)
adj magro(-a) ▶ vt to ~ **sth on sth**
appoggiare qc su qc ▶ vi (slope)
pendere; (rest): **to ~ against**
appoggiarsi contro; essere
appoggiato(-a) a; **to ~ on** appoggiarsi
a ▷ **lean forward** vi sporgersi in
avanti ▷ **lean over** vi inclinarsi;

leaning n leaning (towards)
propensione f (per)
leant [lɛnt] pt, pp of **lean**
leap [li:p] (pt, pp **leaped** or **leapt**) n
salto, balzo ▶ vi saltare, balzare
leapt [lɛpt] pt, pp of **leap**
leap year n anno bisestile
learn [ləːn] (pt, pp **learned** or **learnt**)
vt, vi imparare; **to ~ about sth**
(hear, read) apprendere qc; **to ~ to
do sth** imparare a fare qc; **learner**
n principiante m/f; apprendista
m/f; (BRIT: also: **learner driver**)
guidatore(-a) principiante; **learning**
n erudizione f, sapienza
learnt [ləːnt] pt, pp of **learn**
lease [li:s] n contratto d'affitto ▶ vt
affittare
leash [li:ʃ] n guinzaglio
least [li:st] adj **the ~** (+ noun) il (la)
più piccolo(-a), il (la) minimo(-a);
(smallest amount of) il (la) meno ▶ adv
(+ verb) meno; **the ~** (+ adjective): **the ~
beautiful girl** la ragazza meno bella;
the ~ possible effort il minimo sforzo
possibile; **I have the ~ money** ho
meno denaro di tutti; **at ~** almeno;
not in the ~ affatto, per nulla
leather ['lɛðər] n cuoio
leave [li:v] (pt, pp **left**) vt lasciare; (go
away from) partire da ▶ vi partire,
andarsene; (bus, train) partire ▶ n (time
off) congedo; (Mil, consent) licenza;
what time does the train/bus ~? a
che ora parte il treno/l'autobus?; **to
be left** rimanere; **there's some milk
left over** c'è rimasto del latte; **on ~** in
congedo ▷ **leave behind** vt (person,
object) lasciare; (: forget) dimenticare
▷ **leave out** vt omettere, tralasciare
leaves [li:vz] npl of **leaf**
Lebanon ['lɛbənən] n Libano
lecture ['lɛktʃər] n conferenza; (Scol)
lezione f ▶ vi fare conferenze; fare
lezioni ▶ vt (scold): **to ~ sb on** or

about sth rimproverare qn or fare
una ramanzina a qn per qc; **to give
a ~ on** tenere una conferenza su;
lecture hall n aula magna; **lecturer**
['lɛktʃərər] (BRIT) n (at university)
professore(-essa), docente m/f;
lecture theatre n = **lecture hall**
led [lɛd] pt, pp of **lead**
ledge [lɛdʒ] n (of window) davanzale m;
(on wall etc) sporgenza; (of mountain)
cornice f, cengia
leek [li:k] n porro
left [lɛft] pt, pp of **leave** ▶ adj
sinistro(-a) ▶ adv a sinistra ▶ n
sinistra; **on the ~, to the ~** a sinistra;
the L~ (Pol) la sinistra; **left-hand** adj
the left-hand side il lato sinistro;
left-hand drive adj guida a sinistra;
left-handed adj mancino(-a);
left-luggage locker n armadietto
per deposito bagagli; **left-luggage
(office)** (BRIT) n deposito m bagagli
inv; **left-overs** npl avanzi mpl, resti
mpl; **left-wing** adj (Pol) di sinistra
leg [lɛg] n gamba; (of animal) zampa;
(of furniture) piede m; (Culin: of chicken)
coscia; (of journey) tappa; **1st/2nd ~**
(Sport) partita di andata/ritorno
legacy ['lɛgəsɪ] n eredità f inv
legal ['li:gl] adj legale; **legal holiday**
(US) n giorno festivo, festa nazionale;
legalize vt legalizzare; **legally**
adv legalmente; **legally binding**
legalmente vincolante
legend ['lɛdʒənd] n leggenda;
legendary ['lɛdʒəndərɪ] adj
leggendario(-a)
leggings ['lɛgɪŋz] npl ghette fpl
legible ['lɛdʒəbl] adj leggibile
legislation [lɛdʒɪs'leɪʃən] n
legislazione f
legislative ['lɛdʒɪslətɪv] adj
legislativo(-a)
legitimate [lɪ'dʒɪtɪmət] adj
legittimo(-a)

leisure ['lɛʒəʳ] n agio, tempo libero; ricreazioni fpl; **at ~** con comodo; **leisure centre** n centro di ricreazione; **leisurely** adj tranquillo(-a), fatto(-a) con comodo or senza fretta

lemon ['lɛmən] n limone m; **lemonade** [-'neɪd] n limonata; **lemon tea** n tè m inv al limone

lend [lɛnd] (pt, pp **lent**) vt **to ~ sth (to sb)** prestare qc (a qn); **could you ~ me some money?** mi può prestare dei soldi?

length [lɛŋθ] n lunghezza; (distance) distanza; (section: of road, pipe etc) pezzo, tratto; (of time) periodo; **at ~** (at last) finalmente, alla fine; (lengthily) a lungo; **lengthen** vt allungare, prolungare ▶ vi allungarsi; **lengthways** adv per il lungo; **lengthy** adj molto lungo(-a)

lens [lɛnz] n lente f; (of camera) obiettivo

Lent [lɛnt] n Quaresima

lent [lɛnt] pt, pp of **lend**

lentil ['lɛntl] n lenticchia

Leo ['liːəu] n Leone m

leopard ['lɛpəd] n leopardo

leotard ['liːətɑːd] n calzamaglia

leprosy ['lɛprəsɪ] n lebbra

lesbian ['lɛzbɪən] n lesbica

less [lɛs] adj, pron, adv meno ▶ prep ~ **tax/10% discount** meno tasse/il 10% di sconto; ~ **than ever** meno che mai; ~ **than half** meno della metà; ~ **and** ~ sempre meno; **the** ~ **he works ...** meno lavora ...; **lessen** ['lɛsn] vi diminuire, attenuarsi ▶ vt diminuire, ridurre; **lesser** ['lɛsəʳ] adj minore, più piccolo(-a); **to a lesser extent** in grado or misura minore

lesson ['lɛsn] n lezione f; **to teach sb a** ~ dare una lezione a qn

let [lɛt] (pt, pp **let**) vt lasciare; (BRIT: lease) dare in affitto; **to ~ sb do sth** lasciar fare qc a qn, lasciare che qn faccia qc; **to ~ sb know sth** far sapere qc a qn; ~**'s go** andiamo; ~ **him come** lo lasci venire; **"to ~"** "affittasi" ▷ **let down** vt (lower) abbassare; (dress) allungare; (hair) sciogliere; (tyre) sgonfiare; (disappoint) deludere ▷ **let in** vt lasciare entrare; (visitor etc) far entrare ▷ **let off** vt (allow to go) lasciare andare; (firework etc) far partire ▷ **let out** vt lasciare uscire; (scream) emettere

lethal ['liːθl] adj letale, mortale

letter ['lɛtəʳ] n lettera; **letterbox** (BRIT) n buca delle lettere

lettuce ['lɛtɪs] n lattuga, insalata

leukaemia [luː'kiːmɪə] (US **leukemia**) n leucemia

level ['lɛvl] adj piatto(-a), piano(-a); orizzontale ▶ adv **to draw ~ with** mettersi alla pari di ▶ n livello ▶ vt livellare, spianare; **to be ~ with** essere alla pari di; **level crossing** (BRIT) n passaggio a livello

lever ['liːvəʳ] n leva; **leverage** n **leverage (on** or **with)** forza (su); (fig) ascendente m (su)

levy ['lɛvɪ] n tassa, imposta ▶ vt imporre

liability [laɪə'bɪlətɪ] n responsabilità f inv; (handicap) peso

liable ['laɪəbl] adj (subject): ~ **to** soggetto(-a) a; passibile di; (responsible): ~ **for** responsabile (di); (likely): ~ **to do** propenso(-a) a fare

liaise [liː'eɪz] vi **to ~ (with)** mantenere i contatti (con)

liar ['laɪəʳ] n bugiardo(-a)

liberal ['lɪbərl] adj liberale; (generous): **to be ~ with** distribuire liberalmente; **Liberal Democrat** n liberaldemocratico(-a)

liberate ['lɪbəreɪt] vt liberare

liberation [lɪbə'reɪʃən] n liberazione f

liberty ['lɪbətɪ] n libertà f inv; **at**

~ (criminal) in libertà; **at ~ to do**
libero(-a) di fare
Libra ['liːbrə] n Bilancia
librarian [laɪ'brɛərɪən] n
bibliotecario(-a)
library ['laɪbrərɪ] n biblioteca
Libya ['lɪbɪə] n Libia
lice [laɪs] npl of **louse**
licence ['laɪsns] (US **license**) n
autorizzazione f, permesso; (Comm)
licenza; (Radio, TV) canone m,
abbonamento; (also: **driving ~**: US:
also: **driver's license**) patente f di
guida; (excessive freedom) licenza
license ['laɪsns] n (US) = **licence** ▶ vt
dare una licenza a; **licensed** adj (for
alcohol) che ha la licenza di vendere
bibite alcoliche; **license plate** (esp
US) n (Aut) targa (automobilistica);
licensing hours (BRIT) npl orario
d'apertura (di un pub)
lick [lɪk] vt leccare; (inf: defeat)
stracciare; **to ~ one's lips** (fig) leccarsi
i baffi
lid [lɪd] n coperchio; (eyelid) palpebra
lie [laɪ] (pt **lay**, pp **lain**) vi (rest) giacere,
star disteso(-a); (of object: be situated)
trovarsi, essere; (tell lies: pt, pp **lied**)
mentire, dire bugie ▶ n bugia,
menzogna; **to ~ low** (fig) latitare ▷ **lie
about** or **around** vi (things) essere in
giro; (person) bighellonare ▷ **lie down**
vi stendersi, sdraiarsi
Liechtenstein ['lɪktənstaɪn] n
Liechtenstein m
lie-in ['laɪɪn] (BRIT) n **to have a ~**
rimanere a letto
lieutenant [lɛf'tɛnənt, (US) luː'tɛnə
nt] n tenente m
life [laɪf] (pl **lives**) n vita ▶ cpd di
vita; della vita; a vita; **to come to ~**
rianimarsi; **life assurance** (BRIT) n
= **life insurance**; **lifeboat** n scialuppa
di salvataggio; **lifeguard** n bagnino;
life insurance n assicurazione f

sulla vita; **life jacket** n giubbotto di
salvataggio; **lifelike** adj verosimile;
rassomigliante; **life preserver**
[-prɪ'zəːvəʳ] (US) n salvagente m;
giubbotto di salvataggio; **life
sentence** n ergastolo; **lifestyle** n stile
m di vita; **lifetime** n **in his lifetime**
durante la sua vita; **once in a lifetime**
una volta nella vita
lift [lɪft] vt sollevare; (ban, rule) levare
▶ vi (fog) alzarsi ▶ n (BRIT: elevator)
ascensore m; **to give sb a ~** (BRIT)
dare un passaggio a qn; **can you give
me a ~ to the station?** può darmi un
passaggio fino alla stazione? ▷ **lift up**
vt sollevare, alzare; **lift-off** n decollo
light [laɪt] (pt, pp **lighted** or **lit**) n luce
f, lume m; (daylight) luce f, giorno;
(lamp) lampada; (Aut: rear light) luce
f di posizione; (: headlamp) fanale
m; (for cigarette etc) **have you got
a ~?** ha da accendere?; **~s** npl (Aut:
traffic lights) semaforo vt (candle,
cigarette, fire) accendere; (room): **to
be lit by** essere illuminato(-a) da adj
(room, colour) chiaro(-a); (not heavy,
also fig) leggero(-a); **to come to ~**
venire alla luce, emergere ▷ **light
up** vi illuminarsi ▶ vt illuminare;
light bulb n lampadina; **lighten** vt
(make less heavy) alleggerire; **lighter**
n (also: **cigarette lighter**) accendino;
light-hearted adj gioioso(-a),
gaio(-a); **lighthouse** n faro;
lighting n illuminazione f; **lightly**
adv leggermente; **to get off lightly**
cavarsela a buon mercato
lightning ['laɪtnɪŋ] n lampo,
fulmine m
lightweight ['laɪtweɪt] adj (suit)
leggero(-a) ▶ n (Boxing) peso leggero
like [laɪk] vt (person) volere bene a;
(activity, object, food): **I ~ swimming/
that book/chocolate** mi piace
nuotare/quel libro/il cioccolato

▶ *prep* come ▶ *adj* simile, uguale ▶ *n*
the ~ uno(-a) uguale; **his ~s and
dis~s** i suoi gusti; **I would ~, I'd ~**
mi piacerebbe, vorrei; **would you
~ a coffee?** gradirebbe un caffè?;
to be/look ~ sb/sth somigliare a
qn/qc; **what does it look/taste ~?**
che aspetto/gusto ha?; **what does it
sound ~?** come fa?; **that's just ~ him** è
proprio da lui; **do it ~ this** fallo così; **it
is nothing ~ ...** non è affatto come ...;
likeable *adj* simpatico(-a)
likelihood ['laɪklɪhud] *n* probabilità
likely ['laɪklɪ] *adj* probabile; plausibile;
he's ~ to leave probabilmente partirà,
è probabile che parta; **not ~!** neanche
per sogno!
likewise ['laɪkwaɪz] *adv* similmente,
nello stesso modo
liking ['laɪkɪŋ] *n* **~ (for)** debole *m* (per);
to be to sb's ~ piacere a qn
lilac ['laɪlək] *n* lilla *m inv*
Lilo® ['laɪləu] *n* materassino
gonfiabile
lily ['lɪlɪ] *n* giglio
limb [lɪm] *n* arto
limbo ['lɪmbəu] *n* **to be in ~** (*fig*) essere
lasciato(-a) nel dimenticatoio
lime [laɪm] *n* (*tree*) tiglio; (*fruit*)
limetta; (*Geo*) calce *f*
limelight ['laɪmlaɪt] *n* **in the ~** (*fig*) alla
ribalta, in vista
limestone ['laɪmstəun] *n* pietra
calcarea; (*Geo*) calcare *m*
limit ['lɪmɪt] *n* limite *m* ▶ *vt* limitare;
limited *adj* limitato(-a), ristretto(-a);
to be limited to limitarsi a
limousine ['lɪməzi:n] *n* limousine *f inv*
limp [lɪmp] *n* **to have a ~** zoppicare
▶ *vi* zoppicare ▶ *adj* floscio(-a),
flaccido(-a)
line [laɪn] *n* linea; (*rope*) corda; (*for
fishing*) lenza; (*wire*) filo; (*of poem*)
verso; (*row, series*) fila, riga; coda; (*on
face*) ruga ▶ *vt* (*clothes*): **to ~ (with)**

foderare (di); (*box*): **to ~ (with)**
rivestire *or* foderare (di); (*trees, crowd*)
fiancheggiare; **~ of business** settore
m or ramo d'attività; **in ~ with** in linea
con ▷ **line up** *vi* allinearsi, mettersi
in fila ▶ *vt* mettere in fila; (*event,
celebration*) preparare
linear ['lɪnɪə'] *adj* lineare
linen ['lɪnɪn] *n* biancheria, panni *mpl*;
(*cloth*) tela di lino
liner ['laɪnə'] *n* nave *f* di linea; (*for bin*)
sacchetto
line-up ['laɪnʌp] *n* allineamento, fila;
(*Sport*) formazione *f* di gioco
linger ['lɪŋgə'] *vi* attardarsi; indugiare;
(*smell, tradition*) persistere
lingerie ['lænʒəri:] *n* biancheria
intima femminile
linguist ['lɪŋgwɪst] *n* linguista
m/f; poliglotta *m/f*; **linguistic** *adj*
linguistico(-a)
lining ['laɪnɪŋ] *n* fodera
link [lɪŋk] *n* (*of a chain*) anello;
(*relationship*) legame *m*; (*connection*)
collegamento ▶ *vt* collegare, unire,
congiungere; (*associate*): **to ~ with**
or **to** collegare a; **~s** *npl* (*Golf*) pista *or*
terreno da golf ▷ **link up** *vt* collegare,
unire ▶ *vi* riunirsi; associarsi
lion ['laɪən] *n* leone *m*; **lioness** *n*
leonessa
lip [lɪp] *n* labbro; (*of cup etc*) orlo; **lip-
read** *vi* leggere sulle labbra; **lip salve**
[-sælv] *n* burro di cacao; **lipstick** *n*
rossetto
liqueur [lɪˈkjuə'] *n* liquore *m*
liquid ['lɪkwɪd] *n* liquido ▶ *adj*
liquido(-a); **liquidizer** *n* frullatore *m*
(a brocca)
liquor ['lɪkə'] *n* alcool *m*; **liquor store**
(*US*) *n* negozio di liquori
Lisbon ['lɪzbən] *n* Lisbona
lisp [lɪsp] *n* pronuncia blesa della "s"
list [lɪst] *n* lista, elenco ▶ *vt* (*write down*)
mettere in lista; fare una lista di;

(*enumerate*) elencare
listen ['lɪsn] *vi* ascoltare; **to
~ to** ascoltare; **listener** *n*
ascoltatore(-trice)
lit [lɪt] *pt, pp of* **light**
liter ['liːtər] (*US*) *n* = **litre**
literacy ['lɪtərəsɪ] *n* il sapere leggere
e scrivere
literal ['lɪtərl] *adj* letterale; **literally**
adv alla lettera, letteralmente
literary ['lɪtərərɪ] *adj* letterario(-a)
literate ['lɪtərət] *adj* che sa leggere
e scrivere
literature ['lɪtərɪtʃər] *n* letteratura;
(*brochures etc*) materiale *m*
litre ['liːtər] (*US* **liter**) *n* litro
litter ['lɪtər] *n* (*rubbish*) rifiuti *mpl*;
(*young animals*) figliata; **litter bin**
(*BRIT*) *n* cestino per rifiuti; **littered** *adj*
littered with coperto(-a) di
little ['lɪtl] *adj* (*small*) piccolo(-a); (*not
much*) poco(-a) ▶ *adv* poco; **a ~** un po'
(di); **a ~ bit** un pochino; **~ by ~** a poco a
poco; **little finger** *n* mignolo
live¹ [lɪv] *vi* vivere; (*reside*) vivere,
abitare; **where do you ~?** dove abita?
▷ **live together** *vi* vivere insieme,
convivere ▷ **live up to** *vt fus* tener fede
a, non venir meno a
live² [laɪv] *adj* (*animal*) vivo(-a); (*wire*)
sotto tensione; (*bullet, missile*)
inesploso(-a); (*broadcast*) diretto(-a);
(*performance*) dal vivo
livelihood ['laɪvlɪhud] *n* mezzi *mpl* di
sostentamento
lively ['laɪvlɪ] *adj* vivace, vivo(-a)
liven up ['laɪvn ʌp] *vt* (*discussion,
evening*) animare ▶ *vi* ravvivarsi
liver ['lɪvər] *n* fegato
lives [laɪvz] *npl of* **life**
livestock ['laɪvstɔk] *n* bestiame *m*
living ['lɪvɪŋ] *adj* vivo(-a), vivente ▶ *n*
to earn *or* **make a ~** guadagnarsi la
vita; **living room** *n* soggiorno
lizard ['lɪzəd] *n* lucertola

load [ləud] *n* (*weight*) peso; (*thing
carried*) carico ▶ *vt* (*also*: **~ up**): **to ~
(with)** (*lorry, ship*) caricare (di); (*gun,
camera, Comput*) caricare (con); **a ~
of, ~s of** (*fig*) un sacco di; **loaded** *adj*
(*vehicle*): **loaded (with)** carico(-a)
(di); (*question*) capzioso(-a); (*inf: rich*)
carico(-a) di soldi
loaf [ləuf] (*pl* **loaves**) *n* pane *m*,
pagnotta
loan [ləun] *n* prestito ▶ *vt* dare in
prestito; **on ~** in prestito
loathe [ləuð] *vt* detestare, aborrire
loaves [ləuvz] *npl of* **loaf**
lobby ['lɔbɪ] *n* atrio, vestibolo; (*Pol:
pressure group*) gruppo di pressione
▶ *vt* fare pressione su
lobster ['lɔbstər] *n* aragosta
local ['ləukl] *adj* locale ▶ *n* (*BRIT: pub*)
≈ bar *m inv* all'angolo; **the ~s** *npl* (*local
inhabitants*) la gente della zona; **local
anaesthetic** *n* anestesia locale; **local
authority** *n* ente *m* locale; **local
government** *n* amministrazione *f*
locale; **locally** ['ləukəlɪ] *adv* da queste
parti; nel vicinato
locate [ləu'keɪt] *vt* (*find*) trovare;
(*situate*) collocare; situare
location [ləu'keɪʃən] *n* posizione *f*; **on
~** (*Cinema*) all'esterno
loch [lɔx] *n* lago
lock [lɔk] *n* (*of door, box*) serratura; (*of
canal*) chiusa; (*of hair*) ciocca, riccio
▶ *vt* (*with key*) chiudere a chiave ▶ *vi*
(*door etc*) chiudersi; (*wheels*) bloccarsi,
incepparsi ▷ **lock in** *vt* chiudere
dentro (a chiave) ▷ **lock out** *vt*
chiudere fuori ▷ **lock up** *vt* (*criminal,
mental patient*) rinchiudere; (*house*)
chiudere (a chiave) ▶ *vi* chiudere tutto
(a chiave)
locker ['lɔkər] *n* armadietto; **locker-
room** (*US*) *n* spogliatoio
locksmith ['lɔksmɪθ] *n* magnano
locomotive [ləukə'məutɪv] *n*

locomotiva
lodge [lɔdʒ] n casetta, portineria;
(*hunting lodge*) casino di caccia ▶ vi
(*person*): **to ~ (with)** essere a pensione
(presso or da); (*bullet etc*) conficcarsi
▶ vt (*appeal etc*) presentare, fare;
lodger n affittuario(-a); (*with room and
meals*) pensionante m/f
lodging [ˈlɔdʒɪŋ] n alloggio; *see also*
board
loft [lɔft] n solaio, soffitta
log [lɔg] n (*of wood*) ceppo; (*also:* **~book**:
Naut, Aviat) diario di bordo; (*Aut*)
libretto di circolazione ▶ vt registrare
▷ **log in** vi (*Comput*) aprire una
sessione (*con codice di riconoscimento*)
▷ **log off** vi (*Comput*) terminare una
sessione
logic [ˈlɔdʒɪk] n logica; **logical** adj
logico(-a)
login [ˈlɔgɪn] n (*Comput*) nome m
utente *inv*
logo [ˈləʊgəʊ] n logo m inv
lollipop [ˈlɔlɪpɔp] n lecca lecca m inv
lolly [ˈlɔlɪ] (*inf*) n lecca lecca m inv; (*also:*
ice ~) ghiacciolo; (*money*) grana
London [ˈlʌndən] n Londra; **Londoner**
n londinese m/f
lone [ləʊn] adj solitario(-a)
loneliness [ˈləʊnlɪnɪs] n solitudine f,
isolamento
lonely [ˈləʊnlɪ] adj solo(-a);
solitario(-a), isolato(-a)
long [lɔŋ] adj lungo(-a) ▶ adv a lungo,
per molto tempo ▶ vi **to ~ for sth/to
do** desiderare qc/di fare, non veder
l'ora di aver qc/di fare; **so** or **as ~ as**
(*while*) finché; (*provided that*) sempre
che + *sub*; **don't be ~!** fai presto!; **how
~ is this river/course?** quanto è lungo
questo fiume/corso?; **6 metres ~**
lungo 6 metri; **6 months ~** che dura
6 mesi, di 6 mesi; **all night ~** tutta la
notte; **he no ~er comes** non viene
più; **~ before** molto tempo prima;

before ~ (+*future*) presto, fra poco;
(+*past*) poco tempo dopo; **at ~ last**
finalmente; **long-distance** adj (*race*)
di fondo; (*call*) interurbano(-a); **long-
haul** [ˈlɔŋhɔːl] adj (*flight*) a lunga
percorrenza inv; **longing** n desiderio
longitude [ˈlɔŋgɪtjuːd] n longitudine f
long: **long jump** n salto in lungo;
long-life adj (*milk*) a lunga
conservazione; (*batteries*) di lunga
durata; **long-sighted** adj presbite;
long-standing adj di vecchia data;
long-term adj a lungo termine
loo [luː] (*BRIT: inf*) n W.C. m inv, cesso
look [luk] vi guardare; (*seem*)
sembrare, parere; (*building etc*): **to ~
south/on to the sea** dare a sud/sul
mare ▶ n sguardo; (*appearance*)
aspetto, aria; **~s** npl (*good looks*)
bellezza ▷ **look after** vt fus occuparsi
di, prendere cura di; (*keep an eye on*)
guardare, badare a ▷ **look around**
vi guardarsi intorno ▷ **look at** vt fus
guardare ▷ **look back** vi (*on*) ▷ **look at** vt fus
(*event etc*) ripensare a ▷ **look down
on** vt fus (*fig*) guardare dall'alto,
disprezzare ▷ **look for** vt fus cercare;
we're ~ing for a hotel/restaurant
stiamo cercando un albergo/
ristorante ▷ **look forward to** vt fus
non veder l'ora di; (*in letters*): **we ~
forward to hearing from you** in
attesa di una vostra gentile risposta
▷ **look into** vt fus esaminare ▷ **look
out** vi (*beware*): **to ~ out (for)** stare
in guardia (per) ▷ **look out for** vt fus
cercare ▷ **look round** vi (*turn*) girarsi,
voltarsi; (*in shop*) dare un'occhiata
▷ **look through** vt fus (*papers,
book*) scorrere; (*telescope*) guardare
attraverso ▷ **look up** vi alzare gli
occhi; (*improve*) migliorare ▶ vt (*word*)
cercare; (*friend*) andare a trovare
▷ **look up to** vt fus avere rispetto per;
lookout n posto d'osservazione;

guardia; **to be on the lookout (for)** stare in guardia (per)

loom [lu:m] n telaio ▶ vi (also: **~ up**) apparire minaccioso(-a); (event) essere imminente

loony ['lu:nɪ] (inf) n pazzo(-a)

loop [lu:p] n cappio ▶ vt **to ~ sth round sth** passare qc intorno a qc; **loophole** n via d'uscita; scappatoia

loose [lu:s] adj (knot) sciolto(-a); (screw) allentato(-a); (stone) cadente; (clothes) ampio(-a), largo(-a); (animal) in libertà, scappato(-a); (life, morals) dissoluto(-a) ▶ n **to be on the ~** essere in libertà; **loosely** adv senza stringere; approssimativamente; **loosen** vt sciogliere; (belt etc) allentare

loot [lu:t] n bottino ▶ vt saccheggiare

lop-sided ['lɔp'saɪdɪd] adj non equilibrato(-a), asimmetrico(-a)

lord [lɔ:d] n signore m; **L~ Smith** lord Smith; **the L~** il Signore; **good L~!** buon Dio!; **the (House of) L~s** (BRIT) la Camera dei Lord

lorry ['lɔrɪ] (BRIT) n camion m inv; **lorry driver** (BRIT) n camionista m

lose [lu:z] (pt, pp **lost**) vt perdere ▶ vi perdere; **I've lost my wallet/passport** ho perso il portafoglio/passaporto; **to ~ (time)** (clock) ritardare ▷ **lose out** vi rimetterci; **loser** n perdente m/f

loss [lɔs] n perdita; **to be at a ~** essere perplesso(-a)

lost [lɔst] pt, pp of **lose** ▶ adj perduto(-a); **I'm ~** mi sono perso; **lost property** (US **lost and found**) n oggetti mpl smarriti

lot [lɔt] n (at auctions) lotto; (destiny) destino, sorte f; **the ~** tutto(-a) quanto(-a); tutti(-e) quanti(-e); **a ~** molto; **a ~ of** una gran quantità di, un sacco di; **~s of** molto(-a); **to draw ~s (for sth)** tirare a sorte (per qc)

lotion ['ləʊʃən] n lozione f

lottery ['lɔtərɪ] n lotteria

loud [laud] adj forte, alto(-a); (gaudy) vistoso(-a), sgargiante ▶ adv (speak etc) forte; **out ~** (read etc) ad alta voce; **loudly** adv fortemente, ad alta voce; **loudspeaker** n altoparlante m

lounge [laundʒ] n salotto, soggiorno; (at airport, station) sala d'attesa; (BRIT: also: **~ bar**) bar m inv con servizio a tavolino ▶ vi oziare

louse [laus] (pl **lice**) n pidocchio

lousy ['lauzɪ] (inf) adj orrendo(-a), schifoso(-a); **to feel ~** stare da cani

love [lʌv] n amore m ▶ vt amare; voler bene a; **to ~ to do: I ~ to do** mi piace fare; **to be/fall in ~ with** essere innamorato(-a)/innamorarsi di; **to make ~** fare l'amore; **"15 ~"** (Tennis) "15 a zero"; **love affair** n relazione f; **love life** n vita sentimentale

lovely ['lʌvlɪ] adj bello(-a); (delicious: smell, meal) buono(-a)

lover ['lʌvə^r] n amante m/f; (person in love) innamorato(-a); (amateur): **a ~ of** un(-un') amante di; un(-un') appassionato(-a) di

loving ['lʌvɪŋ] adj affettuoso(-a)

low [ləʊ] adj basso(-a) ▶ adv in basso ▶ n (Meteor) depressione f; **to be ~ on** (supplies etc) avere scarsità di; **to feel ~** sentirsi giù; **low-alcohol** adj a basso contenuto alcolico; **low-calorie** adj a basso contenuto calorico

lower ['ləʊə^r] adj (bottom: of 2 things) più basso; (less important) meno importante ▶ vt calare; (prices, eyes, voice) abbassare

low-fat ['ləʊ'fæt] adj magro(-a)

loyal ['lɔɪəl] adj fedele, leale; **loyalty** n fedeltà, lealtà; **loyalty card** n carta che offre sconti a clienti abituali

L.P. n abbr = **long-playing record**

L-plates ['ɛlpleɪts] (BRIT) npl contrassegno P principiante

Lt abbr (= lieutenant) Ten.

Ltd *abbr* (= *limited*) ≈ S.r.l.

luck [lʌk] *n* fortuna, sorte *f*; **bad ~** sfortuna, mala sorte; **good ~!** buona fortuna!; **luckily** *adv* fortunatamente, per fortuna; **lucky** *adj* fortunato(-a); (*number etc*) che porta fortuna

lucrative ['luːkrətɪv] *adj* lucrativo(-a), lucroso(-a), profittevole

ludicrous ['luːdɪkrəs] *adj* ridicolo(-a)

luggage ['lʌgɪdʒ] *n* bagagli *mpl*; **our ~ hasn't arrived** i nostri bagagli non sono arrivati; **luggage rack** *n* portabagagli *m inv*

lukewarm ['luːkwɔːm] *adj* tiepido(-a)

lull [lʌl] *n* intervallo di calma ▶ *vt* **to ~ sb to sleep** cullare qn finché si addormenta

lullaby ['lʌləbaɪ] *n* ninnananna

lumber ['lʌmbəʳ] *n* (*wood*) legname *m*; (*junk*) roba vecchia

luminous ['luːmɪnəs] *adj* luminoso(-a)

lump [lʌmp] *n* pezzo; (*in sauce*) grumo; (*swelling*) gonfiore *m*; (*also*: **sugar ~**) zolletta ▶ *vt* (*also*: **~ together**) riunire, mettere insieme; **lump sum** *n* somma globale; **lumpy** *adj* (*sauce*) pieno(-a) di grumi; (*bed*) bitorzoluto(-a)

lunatic ['luːnətɪk] *adj* pazzo(-a), matto(-a)

lunch [lʌntʃ] *n* pranzo, colazione *f*; **lunch break** *n* intervallo del pranzo; **lunch time** *n* ora di pranzo

lung [lʌŋ] *n* polmone *m*

lure [luəʳ] *n* richiamo; lusinga ▶ *vt* attirare (con l'inganno)

lurk [ləːk] *vi* stare in agguato

lush [lʌʃ] *adj* lussureggiante

lust [lʌst] *n* lussuria; cupidigia; desiderio; (*fig*): **~ for** sete *f* di

Luxembourg ['lʌksəmbəːg] *n* (*state*) Lussemburgo *m*; (*city*) Lussemburgo *f*

luxurious [lʌg'zjuəriəs] *adj* sontuoso(-a), di lusso

luxury ['lʌkʃəri] *n* lusso ▶ *cpd* di lusso

Be careful not to translate **luxury** by the Italian word *lussuria*.

Lycra® ['laɪkrə] *n* lycra® *f inv*

lying ['laɪɪŋ] *n* bugie *fpl*, menzogne *fpl* ▶ *adj* bugiardo(-a)

lyrics ['lɪrɪks] *npl* (*of song*) parole *fpl*

m

m. *abbr* = **metre**; **mile**; **million**

M.A. *abbr* = **Master of Arts**

ma (*inf*) [mɑː] *n* mamma

mac [mæk] (*BRIT*) *n* impermeabile *m*

macaroni [mækə'rəʊni] *n* maccheroni *mpl*

Macedonia [mæsɪ'dəʊniə] *n* Macedonia; **Macedonian** [mæsɪ'dəʊniən] *adj* macedone ▶ *n* macedone *m/f*; (*Ling*) macedone *m*

machine [mə'ʃiːn] *n* macchina ▶ *vt* (*Tech*) lavorare a macchina; (*dress etc*) cucire a macchina; **machine gun** *n* mitragliatrice *f*; **machinery** *n* macchinario, macchine *fpl*; (*fig*) macchina; **machine washable** *adj* lavabile in lavatrice

macho ['mætʃəʊ] *adj* macho *inv*

mackerel ['mækrl] *n inv* sgombro

mackintosh ['mækɪntəʃ] (*BRIT*) *n* impermeabile *m*

mad [mæd] *adj* matto(-a), pazzo(-a); (*foolish*) sciocco(-a); (*angry*) furioso(-a); **to be ~ about** (*keen*) andare pazzo(-a) per

Madagascar [mædə'gæskər] *n* Madagascar *m*

madam ['mædəm] *n* signora

mad cow disease *n* encefalite *f* bovina spongiforme

made [meɪd] *pt, pp of* **make**; **made-to-measure** (*BRIT*) *adj* fatto(-a) su misura; **made-up** ['meɪdʌp] *adj* (*story*) inventato(-a)

madly ['mædlɪ] *adv* follemente

madman ['mædmən] (*irreg*) *n* pazzo, alienato

madness ['mædnɪs] *n* pazzia

Madrid [mə'drɪd] *n* Madrid *f*

Mafia ['mæfɪə] *n* mafia *f*

mag [mæg] *n abbr* (*BRIT inf*) = **magazine** (*Press*)

magazine [mægə'ziːn] *n* (*Press*) rivista; (*Radio, TV*) rubrica

> Be careful not to translate **magazine** by the Italian word *magazzino*.

maggot ['mægət] *n* baco, verme *m*

magic ['mædʒɪk] *n* magia ▶ *adj* magico(-a); **magical** *adj* magico(-a); **magician** [mə'dʒɪʃən] *n* mago(-a)

magistrate ['mædʒɪstreɪt] *n* magistrato; giudice *m/f*

magnet ['mægnɪt] *n* magnete *m*, calamita; **magnetic** [-'nɛtɪk] *adj* magnetico(-a)

magnificent [mæg'nɪfɪsnt] *adj* magnifico(-a)

magnify ['mægnɪfaɪ] *vt* ingrandire; **magnifying glass** *n* lente *f* d'ingrandimento

magpie ['mægpaɪ] *n* gazza

mahogany [mə'hɔgənɪ] *n* mogano

maid [meɪd] *n* domestica; (*in hotel*) cameriera

maiden name ['meɪdn-] *n* nome *m* da nubile *or* da ragazza

mail [meɪl] *n* posta ▶ *vt* spedire (per posta); **mailbox** (*US*) *n* cassetta delle lettere; **mailing list** *n* elenco d'indirizzi; **mailman** (*irreg*: *US*) *n* portalettere *m inv*, postino; **mail-order** *n* vendita (*or* acquisto) per corrispondenza

main [meɪn] *adj* principale ▶ *n* (*pipe*) conduttura principale; **main course** *n* (*Culin*) piatto principale, piatto forte; **mainland** *n* continente *m*; **mainly** *adv* principalmente, soprattutto; **main road** *n* strada principale; **mainstream** *n* (*fig*) corrente *f* principale; **main street** *n* strada principale

maintain [meɪn'teɪn] *vt* mantenere; (*affirm*) sostenere; **maintenance** ['meɪntənəns] *n* manutenzione *f*; (*alimony*) alimenti *mpl*

maisonette [meɪzə'nɛt] *n* (*BRIT*) appartamento a due piani

maize [meɪz] *n* granturco, mais *m*

majesty ['mædʒɪstɪ] *n* maestà *f inv*

major ['meɪdʒər] *n* (*Mil*) maggiore *m* ▶ *adj* (*greater, Mus*) maggiore; (*in importance*) principale, importante

Majorca [mə'jɔːkə] *n* Maiorca

majority [mə'dʒɔrɪtɪ] *n* maggioranza

make [meɪk] (*pt, pp* **made**) *vt* fare; (*manufacture*) fare, fabbricare; (*cause to be*): **to ~ sb sad** *etc* rendere qn triste *etc*; (*force*): **to ~ sb do sth** costringere qn a fare qc, far fare qc a qn; (*equal*): **2 and 2 ~ 4** 2 più 2 fa 4 ▶ *n* fabbricazione *f*; (*brand*) marca; **to ~ a fool of sb** far fare a qn la figura dello scemo; **to ~ a profit** realizzare un profitto; **to ~ a loss** subire una perdita; **to ~ it** (*arrive*) arrivare; (*achieve sth*) farcela; **what time do you ~ it?** che ora fai?; **to ~ do with** arrangiarsi con ▷ **make off** *vi* svignarsela ▷ **make out** *vt* (*write out*) scrivere; (: *cheque*) emettere; (*understand*) capire; (*see*) distinguere; (: *numbers*) decifrare ▷ **make up**

vt (*constitute*) formare; (*invent*) inventare; (*parcel*) fare ▶ *vi* conciliarsi; (*with cosmetics*) truccarsi ▷ **make up for** *vt fus* compensare; ricuperare; **makeover** ['meɪkəʊvəˤ] *n* (*change of image*) cambiamento di immagine; (*of room, house*) trasformazione *f*; **maker** *n* (*of programme etc*) creatore(-trice); (*manufacturer*) fabbricante *m*; **makeshift** *adj* improvvisato(-a); **make-up** *n* trucco

making ['meɪkɪŋ] *n* (*fig*): **in the ~** in formazione; **to have the ~s of** (*actor, athlete etc*) avere la stoffa di

malaria [mə'lɛərɪə] *n* malaria

Malaysia [mə'leɪzɪə] *n* Malaysia

male [meɪl] *n* (*Biol*) maschio ▶ *adj* maschile; maschio(-a)

malicious [mə'lɪʃəs] *adj* malevolo(-a); (*Law*) doloso(-a)

malignant [mə'lɪgnənt] *adj* (*Med*) maligno(-a)

mall [mɔːl] *n* (*also*: **shopping ~**) centro commerciale

mallet ['mælɪt] *n* maglio

malnutrition [mælnjuː'trɪʃən] *n* denutrizione *f*

malpractice [mæl'præktɪs] *n* prevaricazione *f*; negligenza

malt [mɔːlt] *n* malto

Malta ['mɔːltə] *n* Malta; **Maltese** [mɔːl'tiːz] *adj*, *n* (*pl inv*) maltese (*m/f*); (*Ling*) maltese *m*

mammal ['mæml] *n* mammifero

mammoth ['mæməθ] *adj* enorme, gigantesco(-a)

man [mæn] (*pl* **men**) *n* uomo ▶ *vt* fornire d'uomini; stare a; **an old ~** un vecchio; **~ and wife** marito e moglie

manage ['mænɪdʒ] *vi* farcela ▶ *vt* (*be in charge of*) occuparsi di; gestire; **to ~ to do sth** riuscire a far qc; **manageable** *adj* maneggevole; fattibile; **management** *n* amministrazione *f*, direzione *f*; **manager** *n* direttore

m; (*of shop, restaurant*) gerente *m*; (*of artist, Sport*) manager *m inv*; **manageress** [-ə'rɛs] *n* direttrice *f*; gerente *f*; **managerial** [-ə'dʒɪərɪəl] *adj* dirigenziale; **managing director** *n* amministratore *m* delegato

mandarin ['mændərɪn] *n* (*person, fruit*) mandarino

mandate ['mændeɪt] *n* mandato

mandatory ['mændətərɪ] *adj* obbligatorio(-a), ingiuntivo(-a)

mane [meɪn] *n* criniera

mangetout ['mɒnʒ'tuː] *n* pisello dolce, taccola

mango ['mæŋgəʊ] (*pl* **mangoes**) *n* mango

man: manhole ['mænhəʊl] *n* botola stradale; **manhood** ['mænhud] *n* età virile; virilità

mania ['meɪnɪə] *n* mania; **maniac** ['meɪnɪæk] *n* maniaco(-a)

manic ['mænɪk] *adj* (*behaviour, activity*) maniacale

manicure ['mænɪkjuəˤ] *n* manicure *f inv*

manifest ['mænɪfɛst] *vt* manifestare ▶ *adj* manifesto(-a), palese

manifesto [mænɪ'fɛstəʊ] *n* manifesto

manipulate [mə'nɪpjuleɪt] *vt* manipolare

man: mankind [mæn'kaɪnd] *n* umanità, genere *m* umano; **manly** ['mænlɪ] *adj* virile; coraggioso(-a); **man-made** *adj* sintetico(-a); artificiale

manner ['mænəˤ] *n* maniera, modo; (*behaviour*) modo di fare; (*type, sort*): **all ~ of things** ogni genere di cosa; **~s** *npl* (*conduct*) maniere *fpl*; **bad ~s** maleducazione *f*

manoeuvre [mə'nuːvəˤ] (*US* **maneuver**) *vt* manovrare ▶ *vi* far manovre ▶ *n* manovra

manpower ['mænpauəˤ] *n* manodopera

mansion ['mænʃən] *n* casa signorile

manslaughter ['mænslɔːtəʳ] *n* omicidio preterintenzionale

mantelpiece ['mæntlpiːs] *n* mensola del caminetto

manual ['mænjuəl] *adj* manuale ▸ *n* manuale *m*

manufacture [mænjuˈfæktʃəʳ] *vt* fabbricare ▸ *n* fabbricazione *f*, manifattura; **manufacturer** *n* fabbricante *m*

manure [məˈnjuəʳ] *n* concime *m*

manuscript ['mænjuskrɪpt] *n* manoscritto

many ['mɛnɪ] *adj* molti(-e) ▸ *pron* molti(-e); **a great ~** moltissimi(-e), un gran numero (di); **~ a time** molte volte

map [mæp] *n* carta (geografica); (*of city*) cartina; **can you show it to me on the ~?** può indicarmelo sulla cartina?

maple ['meɪpl] *n* acero

mar [mɑːʳ] *vt* sciupare

Mar. *abbr* (= *March*) mar.

marathon ['mærəθən] *n* maratona

marble ['mɑːbl] *n* marmo; (*toy*) pallina, bilia

March [mɑːtʃ] *n* marzo

march [mɑːtʃ] *vi* marciare; sfilare ▸ *n* marcia

mare [mɛəʳ] *n* giumenta

margarine [mɑːdʒəˈriːn] *n* margarina

margin ['mɑːdʒɪn] *n* margine *m*; **marginal** *adj* marginale; **marginal seat** (*Pol*) seggio elettorale ottenuto con una stretta maggioranza; **marginally** *adv* (*bigger, better*) lievemente, di poco; (*different*) un po'

marigold ['mærɪɡəuld] *n* calendola

marijuana [mærɪˈwɑːnə] *n* marijuana

marina [məˈriːnə] *n* marina

marinade *n* [mærɪˈneɪd] marinata ▸ *vt* ['mærɪneɪd] = **marinate**

marinate ['mærɪneɪt] *vt* marinare

marine [məˈriːn] *adj* (*animal, plant*) marino(-a); (*forces, engineering*) marittimo(-a) ▸ *n* (*BRIT*) fante *m* di marina; (*US*) marine *m inv*

marital ['mærɪtl] *adj* maritale, coniugale; **marital status** *n* stato civile

maritime ['mærɪtaɪm] *adj* marittimo(-a)

marjoram ['mɑːdʒərəm] *n* maggiorana

mark [mɑːk] *n* segno; (*stain*) macchia; (*of skid etc*) traccia; (*BRIT Scol*) voto; (*Sport*) bersaglio; (*currency*) marco ▸ *vt* segnare; (*stain*) macchiare; (*indicate*) indicare; (*BRIT Scol*) dare un voto a; correggere; **to ~ time** segnare il passo; **marked** *adj* spiccato(-a), chiaro(-a); **marker** *n* (*sign*) segno; (*bookmark*) segnalibro

market ['mɑːkɪt] *n* mercato ▸ *vt* (*Comm*) mettere in vendita; **marketing** *n* marketing *m*; **marketplace** *n* (piazza del) mercato; (*world of trade*) piazza, mercato; **market research** *n* indagine *f* or ricerca di mercato

marmalade ['mɑːməleɪd] *n* marmellata d'arance

maroon [məˈruːn] *vt* (*also fig*): **to be ~ed (in** *or* **at)** essere abbandonato(-a) (in) ▸ *adj* bordeaux *inv*

marquee [mɑːˈkiː] *n* padiglione *m*

marriage ['mærɪdʒ] *n* matrimonio; **marriage certificate** *n* certificato di matrimonio

married ['mærɪd] *adj* sposato(-a); (*life, love*) coniugale, matrimoniale

marrow ['mærəu] *n* midollo; (*vegetable*) zucca

marry ['mærɪ] *vt* sposare, sposarsi con; (*vicar, priest etc*) dare in matrimonio ▸ *vi* (*also*: **get married**) sposarsi

Mars [mɑːz] *n* (*planet*) Marte *m*

marsh [mɑːʃ] *n* palude *f*

marshal ['mɑ:ʃl] n maresciallo; (US: fire) capo; (: police) capitano ▶ vt (thoughts, support) ordinare; (soldiers) adunare

martyr ['mɑ:tər] n martire m/f

marvel ['mɑ:vl] n meraviglia ▶ vi to ~ (at) meravigliarsi (di); **marvellous** (US **marvelous**) adj meraviglioso(-a)

Marxism ['mɑ:ksɪzəm] n marxismo

Marxist ['mɑ:ksɪst] adj, n marxista m/f

marzipan ['mɑ:zɪpæn] n marzapane m

mascara [mæs'kɑ:rə] n mascara m

mascot ['mæskət] n mascotte f inv

masculine ['mæskjulɪn] adj maschile; (woman) mascolino(-a)

mash [mæʃ] vt passare, schiacciare; **mashed potatoes** npl purè m di patate

mask [mɑ:sk] n maschera ▶ vt mascherare

mason ['meɪsn] n (also: **stone~**) scalpellino; (also: **free~**) massone m; **masonry** n muratura

mass [mæs] n moltitudine f, massa; (Physics) massa; (Rel) messa ▶ cpd di massa ▶ vi ammassarsi; **the ~es** npl (ordinary people) le masse; **~es of** (inf) una montagna di

massacre ['mæsəkər] n massacro

massage ['mæsɑ:ʒ] n massaggio

massive ['mæsɪv] adj enorme, massiccio(-a)

mass media npl mass media mpl

mass-produce ['mæsprə'dju:s] vt produrre in serie

mast [mɑ:st] n albero

master ['mɑ:stər] n padrone m; (Art etc, teacher: in primary school) maestro; (: in secondary school) professore m; (title for boys): **M~ X** Signorino X ▶ vt domare; (learn) imparare a fondo; (understand) conoscere a fondo; **mastermind** n mente f superiore ▶ vt essere il cervello di; **Master**

of Arts/Science n Master m inv in lettere/scienze; **masterpiece** n capolavoro

masturbate ['mæstəbeɪt] vi masturbare

mat [mæt] n stuoia; (also: **door~**) stoino, zerbino; (also: **table~**) sottopiatto ▶ adj = **matt**

match [mætʃ] n fiammifero; (game) partita, incontro; (fig) uguale m/f; matrimonio; partito ▶ vt intonare; (go well with) andare benissimo con; (equal) uguagliare; (correspond to) corrispondere a; (pair: also: **~ up**) accoppiare ▶ vi combaciare; **to be a good ~** andare bene; **matchbox** n scatola per fiammiferi; **matching** adj ben assortito(-a)

mate [meɪt] n compagno(-a) di lavoro; (inf: friend) amico(-a); (animal) compagno(-a); (in merchant navy) secondo ▶ vi accoppiarsi

material [mə'tɪərɪəl] n (substance) materiale m, materia; (cloth) stoffa ▶ adj materiale; **~s** npl (equipment) materiali mpl

materialize [mə'tɪərɪəlaɪz] vi materializzarsi, realizzarsi

maternal [mə'tə:nl] adj materno(-a)

maternity [mə'tə:nɪtɪ] n maternità; **maternity hospital** n ≈ clinica ostetrica; **maternity leave** n congedo di maternità

math [mæθ] (US) n = **maths**

mathematical [mæθə'mætɪkl] adj matematico(-a)

mathematician [mæθəmə'tɪʃən] n matematico(-a)

mathematics [mæθə'mætɪks] n matematica

maths [mæθs] (US **math**) n matematica

matinée ['mætɪneɪ] n matinée f inv

matron ['meɪtrən] n (in hospital) capoinfermiera; (in school) infermiera

matt [mæt] *adj* opaco(-a)

matter ['mætə^r] *n* questione *f*; (*Physics*) materia, sostanza; (*content*) contenuto; (*Med: pus*) pus *m* ▶ *vi* importare; **it doesn't ~** non importa; (*I don't mind*) non fa niente; **what's the ~?** che cosa c'è?; **no ~ what** qualsiasi cosa accada; **as a ~ of course** come cosa naturale; **as a ~ of fact** in verità; **~s** *npl* (*affairs*) questioni

mattress ['mætrıs] *n* materasso

mature [mə'tjuə^r] *adj* maturo(-a); (*cheese*) stagionato(-a) ▶ *vi* maturare; stagionare; **mature student** *n* studente universitario che ha più di 25 anni; **maturity** *n* maturità

maul [mɔːl] *vt* lacerare

mauve [məuv] *adj* malva *inv*

max *abbr* = **maximum**

maximize ['mæksımaız] *vt* (*profits etc*) massimizzare; (*chances*) aumentare al massimo

maximum ['mæksıməm] (*pl* **maxima**) *adj* massimo(-a) ▶ *n* massimo

May [meı] *n* maggio

may [meı] (*conditional* **might**) *vi* (*indicating possibility*): **he ~ come** può darsi che venga; (*be allowed to*): **~ I smoke?** posso fumare?; (*wishes*): **~ God bless you!** Dio la benedica!; **you ~ as well go** tanto vale che tu te ne vada

maybe ['meıbiː] *adv* forse, può darsi; **~ he'll ...** può darsi che lui ... + *sub*, forse lui ...

May Day *n* il primo maggio

mayhem ['meıhɛm] *n* cagnara

mayonnaise [meıə'neız] *n* maionese *f*

mayor [mɛə^r] *n* sindaco; **mayoress** *n* sindaco (*donna*); moglie *f* del sindaco

maze [meız] *n* labirinto, dedalo

MD *n abbr* (= *Doctor of Medicine*) titolo di studio; (*Comm*) see **managing director**

me [miː] *pron* mi, m' + *vowel or silent "h"*; (*stressed, after prep*) me; **he heard me** mi ha *or* m'ha sentito; **give me a book** dammi (*or* mi dia) un libro; **it's me** sono io; **with me** con me; **without me** senza di me

meadow ['mɛdəu] *n* prato

meagre ['miːgə^r] (*US* **meager**) *adj* magro(-a)

meal [miːl] *n* pasto; (*flour*) farina; **mealtime** *n* l'ora di mangiare

mean [miːn] (*pt, pp* **meant**) *adj* (*with money*) avaro(-a), gretto(-a); (*unkind*) meschino(-a), maligno(-a); (*shabby*) misero(-a); (*average*) medio(-a) ▶ *vt* (*signify*) significare, voler dire; (*intend*): **to ~ to do** aver l'intenzione di fare ▶ *n* mezzo; (*Math*) media; **~s** *npl* (*way, money*) mezzi *mpl*; **by ~s of** per mezzo di; **by all ~s** ma certo, prego; **to be ~t for** essere destinato(-a) a; **do you ~ it?** dice sul serio?; **what do you ~?** che cosa vuol dire?

meaning ['miːnıŋ] *n* significato, senso; **meaningful** *adj* significativo(-a); **meaningless** *adj* senza senso

meant [mɛnt] *pt, pp of* **mean**

meantime ['miːntaım] *adv* (*also:* **in the ~**) nel frattempo

meanwhile ['miːnwaıl] *adv* nel frattempo

measles ['miːzlz] *n* morbillo

measure ['mɛʒə^r] *vt, vi* misurare ▶ *n* misura; (*also:* **tape ~**) metro

measurement ['mɛʒəmənt] *n* (*act*) misurazione *f*; (*measure*) misura; **chest/hip ~** giro petto/fianchi; **to take sb's ~s** prendere le misure di qn

meat [miːt] *n* carne *f*; **I don't eat ~** non mangio carne; **cold ~** affettato; **meatball** *n* polpetta di carne

Mecca ['mɛkə] *n* (*also fig*) la Mecca

mechanic [mı'kænık] *n* meccanico; **can you send a ~?** può mandare un meccanico?; **mechanical** adj meccanico(-a)

mechanism ['mɛkənɪzəm] n meccanismo

medal ['mɛdl] n medaglia; **medallist** (US **medalist**) n (Sport): **to be a gold medallist** essere medaglia d'oro

meddle ['mɛdl] vi **to ~ in** immischiarsi in, mettere le mani in; **to ~ with** toccare

media ['mi:dɪə] npl media mpl

mediaeval [mɛdɪ'i:vl] adj = **medieval**

mediate ['mi:dɪeɪt] vi fare da mediatore(-trice)

medical ['mɛdɪkl] adj medico(-a) ▶ n visita medica; **medical certificate** n certificato medico

medicated ['mɛdɪkeɪtɪd] adj medicato(-a)

medication [mɛdɪ'keɪʃən] n medicinali mpl, farmaci mpl

medicine ['mɛdsɪn] n medicina

medieval [mɛdɪ'i:vl] adj medievale

mediocre [mi:dɪ'əukəʳ] adj mediocre

meditate ['mɛdɪteɪt] vi **to ~ (on)** meditare (su)

meditation [mɛdɪ'teɪʃən] n meditazione f

Mediterranean [mɛdɪtə'reɪnɪən] adj mediterraneo(-a); **the ~ (Sea)** il (mare) Mediterraneo

medium ['mi:dɪəm] (pl **media**) adj medio(-a) ▶ n (means) mezzo; (pl **mediums**: person) medium m inv; **medium-sized** adj (tin etc) di grandezza media; (clothes) di taglia media; **medium wave** n onde fpl medie

meek [mi:k] adj dolce, umile

meet [mi:t] (pt, pp **met**) vt incontrare; (for the first time) fare la conoscenza di; (go and fetch) andare a prendere; (fig) affrontare; soddisfare; raggiungere ▶ vi incontrarsi; (in session) riunirsi; (join: objects) unirsi; **nice to ~ you**

piacere (di conoscerla) ▷ **meet up** vi **to ~ up with sb** incontrare qn ▷ **meet with** vt fus incontrare; **meeting** n incontro; (session: of club etc) riunione f; (interview) intervista; **she's at a meeting** (Comm) è in riunione; **meeting place** n luogo d'incontro

megabyte ['mɛgəbaɪt] n (Comput) megabyte m inv

megaphone ['mɛgəfəun] n megafono

melancholy ['mɛlənkəlɪ] n malinconia ▶ adj malinconico(-a)

melody ['mɛlədɪ] n melodia

melon ['mɛlən] n melone m

melt [mɛlt] vi (gen) sciogliersi, struggersi; (metals) fondersi ▶ vt sciogliere, struggere; fondere

member ['mɛmbəʳ] n membro; **Member of Congress** (US) n membro del Congresso; **Member of Parliament** (BRIT) n deputato(-a); **Member of the European Parliament** (BRIT) n eurodeputato(-a); **Member of the Scottish Parliament** (BRIT) n deputato(-a) del Parlamento scozzese; **membership** n iscrizione f, (numero d')iscritti mpl, membri mpl; **membership card** n tessera (di iscrizione)

memento [mə'mɛntəu] n ricordo, souvenir m inv

memo ['mɛməu] n appunto; (Comm etc) comunicazione f di servizio

memorable ['mɛmərəbl] adj memorabile

memorandum [mɛmə'rændəm] (pl **memoranda**) n appunto; (Comm etc) comunicazione f di servizio

memorial [mɪ'mɔ:rɪəl] n monumento commemorativo ▶ adj commemorativo(-a)

memorize ['mɛməraɪz] vt memorizzare

memory ['mɛmərɪ] n (also Comput) memoria; (recollection) ricordo; **memory stick** n (Comput) stick m inv di memoria

men [mɛn] npl of **man**

menace ['mɛnəs] n minaccia ▸ vt minacciare

mend [mɛnd] vt aggiustare, riparare; (darn) rammendare ▸ n **on the ~** in via di guarigione

meningitis [mɛnɪn'dʒaɪtɪs] n meningite f

menopause ['mɛnəupɔːz] n menopausa

men's room n **the men's room** (esp US) la toilette degli uomini

menstruation [mɛnstru'eɪʃən] n mestruazione f

menswear ['mɛnzwɛəʳ] n abbigliamento maschile

mental ['mɛntl] adj mentale; **mental hospital** n ospedale m psichiatrico; **mentality** [mɛn'tælɪtɪ] n mentalità f inv; **mentally** adv **to be mentally handicapped** essere minorato psichico

menthol ['mɛnθɔl] n mentolo

mention ['mɛnʃən] n menzione f ▸ vt menzionare, far menzione di; **don't ~ it!** non c'è di che!, prego!

menu ['mɛnjuː] n (set menu, Comput) menù m inv; (printed) carta; **could we see the ~?** ci può portare il menù?

MEP n abbr = **Member of the European Parliament**

mercenary ['məːsɪnərɪ] adj venale ▸ n mercenario

merchandise ['məːtʃəndaɪz] n merci fpl

merchant ['məːtʃənt] n mercante m, commerciante m; **merchant navy** n marina mercantile

merciless ['məːsɪlɪs] adj spietato(-a)

mercury ['məːkjurɪ] n mercurio

mercy ['məːsɪ] n pietà; (Rel) misericordia; **at the ~ of** alla mercè di

mere [mɪəʳ] adj semplice; **by a ~ chance** per mero caso; **merely** adv semplicemente, non … che

merge [məːdʒ] vt unire ▸ vi fondersi, unirsi; (Comm) fondersi; **merger** n (Comm) fusione f

meringue [mə'ræŋ] n meringa

merit ['mɛrɪt] n merito, valore m ▸ vt meritare

mermaid ['məːmeɪd] n sirena

merry ['mɛrɪ] adj gaio(-a), allegro(-a); **M~ Christmas!** Buon Natale!; **merry-go-round** n carosello

mesh [mɛʃ] n maglia; rete f

mess [mɛs] n confusione f, disordine m; (fig) pasticcio; (dirt) sporcizia; (Mil) mensa ▸ **mess about** or **around** (inf) vi trastullarsi ▸ **mess with** (inf) vt fus (challenge) litigare con; (drugs) abusare di ▸ **mess up** vt sporcare; fare un pasticcio di; rovinare

message ['mɛsɪdʒ] n messaggio; **can I leave a ~?** posso lasciare un messaggio?; **are there any ~s for me?** ci sono messaggi per me?

messenger ['mɛsɪndʒəʳ] n messaggero(-a)

Messrs ['mɛsəz] abbr (on letters) Spett.

messy ['mɛsɪ] adj sporco(-a), disordinato(-a)

met [mɛt] pt, pp of **meet**

metabolism [mɛ'tæbəlɪzəm] n metabolismo

metal ['mɛtl] n metallo; **metallic** [-'tælɪk] adj metallico(-a)

metaphor ['mɛtəfəʳ] n metafora

meteor ['miːtɪəʳ] n meteora; **meteorite** ['miːtɪəraɪt] n meteorite m

meteorology [miːtɪə'rɔlədʒɪ] n meteorologia

meter ['miːtəʳ] n (instrument) contatore m; (parking meter) parchimetro; (US: unit) = **metre**

method ['mɛθəd] n metodo;

m

methodical [mɪ'θɒdɪkl] *adj*
metodico(-a)
meths [mɛθs] (*BRIT*) *n* alcool *m*
denaturato
meticulous [mɛ'tɪkjuləs] *adj*
meticoloso(-a)
metre ['miːtə^r] (*US* **meter**) *n* metro
metric ['mɛtrɪk] *adj* metrico(-a)
metro ['mɛtrəu] *n* metro *m inv*
metropolitan [mɛtrə'pɒlɪtən] *adj*
metropolitano(-a)
Mexican ['mɛksɪkən] *adj, n*
messicano(-a)
Mexico ['mɛksɪkəu] *n* Messico
mg *abbr* (= *milligram*) mg
mice [maɪs] *npl of* **mouse**
micro... ['maɪkrəu] *prefix* micro...;
microchip *n* microcircuito
integrato; **microphone** *n* microfono;
microscope *n* microscopio;
microwave *n* (*also*: **microwave oven**)
forno a microonde
mid [mɪd] *adj* ~ **May** metà maggio; ~
afternoon metà pomeriggio; **in ~ air**
a mezz'aria; **midday** *n* mezzogiorno
middle ['mɪdl] *n* mezzo; centro;
(*waist*) vita ▶ *adj* di mezzo; **in the
~ of the night** nel bel mezzo della
notte; **middle-aged** *adj* di mezza
età; **Middle Ages** *npl* **the Middle
Ages** il Medioevo; **middle-class** *adj*
≈ borghese; **Middle East** *n* Medio
Oriente *m*; **middle name** *n* secondo
nome *m*; **middle school** *n* (*US*) scuola
media per ragazzi dagli 11 ai 14 anni; (*BRIT*)
scuola media per ragazzi dagli 8 o 9 ai
12 o 13 anni
midge [mɪdʒ] *n* moscerino
midget ['mɪdʒɪt] *n* nano(-a)
midnight ['mɪdnaɪt] *n* mezzanotte *f*
midst [mɪdst] *n* **in the ~ of** in mezzo a
midsummer [mɪd'sʌmə^r] *n* mezza or
piena estate *f*
midway [mɪd'weɪ] *adj, adv* ~
(between) a mezza strada (fra); ~

(through) a metà (di)
midweek [mɪd'wiːk] *adv* a metà
settimana
midwife ['mɪdwaɪf] (*pl* **midwives**) *n*
levatrice *f*
midwinter [mɪd'wɪntə^r] *n* pieno
inverno
might [maɪt] *vb see* **may** ▶ *n* potere *m*,
forza; **mighty** *adj* forte, potente
migraine ['miːgreɪn] *n* emicrania
migrant ['maɪgrənt] *adj* (*bird*)
migratore(-trice); (*worker*)
emigrato(-a)
migrate [maɪ'greɪt] *vi* (*bird*) migrare;
(*person*) emigrare
migration [maɪ'greɪʃən] *n*
migrazione *f*
mike [maɪk] *n abbr* (= *microphone*)
microfono
Milan [mɪ'læn] *n* Milano *f*
mild [maɪld] *adj* mite; (*person, voice*)
dolce; (*flavour*) delicato(-a); (*illness*)
leggero(-a); (*interest*) blando(-a) ▶ *n*
(*beer*) birra leggera; **mildly** ['maɪldlɪ]
adv mitemente; dolcemente;
delicatamente; leggermente;
blandamente; **to put it mildly** a
dire poco
mile [maɪl] *n* miglio; **mileage** *n*
distanza in miglia, ≈ chilometraggio;
mileometer [maɪ'lɒmɪtə^r] *n*
≈ contachilometri *m inv*; **milestone**
['maɪlstəun] *n* pietra miliare
military ['mɪlɪtərɪ] *adj* militare
militia [mɪ'lɪʃə] *n* milizia
milk [mɪlk] *n* latte *m* ▶ *vt* (*cow*)
mungere; (*fig*) sfruttare; **milk
chocolate** *n* cioccolato al latte;
milkman (*irreg*) *n* lattaio; **milky** *adj*
lattiginoso(-a); (*colour*) latteo(-a)
mill [mɪl] *n* mulino; (*small: for coffee,
pepper etc*) macinino; (*factory*)
fabbrica; (*spinning mill*) filatura ▶ *vt*
macinare ▶ *vi* (*also*: ~ **about**) brulicare
millennium [mɪ'lɛnɪəm] (*pl*

millenniums or **millennia**) n millennio

milli... ['mɪlɪ] prefix: **milligram(me)** n milligrammo; **millilitre** ['mɪlɪliːtəʳ] (US **milliliter**) n millilitro; **millimetre** (US **millimeter**) n millimetro

million ['mɪljən] num milione m; **millionaire** n milionario, ≈ miliardario; **millionth** num milionesimo(-a)

milometer [maɪ'lɔmɪtəʳ] n = **mileometer**

mime [maɪm] n mimo ▶ vt, vi mimare

mimic ['mɪmɪk] n imitatore(-trice) ▶ vt fare la mimica di

min. abbr = **minute(s)**; **minimum**

mince [mɪns] vt tritare, macinare ▶ n (BRIT Culin) carne f tritata or macinata; **mincemeat** n frutta secca tritata per uso in pasticceria; (US) carne f tritata or macinata; **mince pie** n specie di torta con frutta secca

mind [maɪnd] n mente f ▶ vt (attend to, look after) badare a, occuparsi di; (be careful) fare attenzione a, stare attento(-a) a; (object to): **I don't ~ the noise** il rumore non mi dà alcun fastidio; **I don't ~** non m'importa; **do you ~ if ...?** le dispiace se...?; **it is on my ~** mi preoccupa; (Rel) pastore m secondo me, a mio parere; **to be out of one's ~** essere uscito(-a) di mente; **to keep** or **bear sth in ~** non dimenticare qc; **to make up one's ~** decidersi; **you, ...** sì, però va detto che ...; **never ~** non importa, non fa niente; (don't worry) non preoccuparti; **"~ the step"** "attenzione allo scalino"; **mindless** adj idiota

mine¹ [maɪn] pron il (la) mio(-a); (pl) i (le) miei (mei); **that book is ~** quel libro è mio; **yours is red, ~ is green** il tuo è rosso, il mio è verde; **a friend of ~** un mio amico

mine² [maɪn] n miniera; (explosive)

mina ▶ vt (coal) estrarre; (ship, beach) minare; **minefield** n (also fig) campo minato; **miner** ['maɪnəʳ] n minatore m

mineral ['mɪnərəl] adj minerale ▶ n minerale m; **mineral water** n acqua minerale

mingle ['mɪŋgl] vi **to ~ with** mescolarsi a, mischiarsi con

miniature ['mɪnətʃəʳ] adj in miniatura ▶ n miniatura

minibar ['mɪnɪbɑːʳ] n minibar m inv

minibus ['mɪnɪbʌs] n minibus m inv

minicab ['mɪnɪkæb] n (BRIT) ≈ taxi m inv

minimal ['mɪnɪml] adj minimo(-a)

minimize ['mɪnɪmaɪz] vt minimizzare

minimum ['mɪnɪməm] (pl **minima**) n minimo ▶ adj minimo(-a)

mining ['maɪnɪŋ] n industria mineraria

miniskirt ['mɪnɪskəːt] n minigonna

minister ['mɪnɪstəʳ] n (BRIT Pol) ministro; (Rel) pastore m

ministry ['mɪnɪstrɪ] n ministero

minor ['maɪnəʳ] adj minore, di poca importanza; (Mus) minore ▶ n (Law) minorenne m/f

Minorca [mɪ'nɔːkə] n Minorca

minority [maɪ'nɔrɪtɪ] n minoranza

mint [mɪnt] n (plant) menta; (sweet) pasticca di menta ▶ vt (coins) battere; **the (Royal) M~** (BRIT), **the (US) M~** (US) la Zecca; **in ~ condition** come nuovo(-a) di zecca

minus ['maɪnəs] n (also: **~ sign**) segno meno ▶ prep meno

minute [adj maɪ'njuːt, n 'mɪnɪt] adj minuscolo(-a); (detail) minuzioso(-a) ▶ n minuto; **~s** npl (of meeting) verbale m

miracle ['mɪrəkl] n miracolo

miraculous [mɪ'rækjuləs] adj miracoloso(-a)

mirage ['mɪrɑːʒ] n miraggio

mirror ['mɪrəʳ] n specchio; (in car) specchietto

misbehave [mɪsbɪ'heɪv] vi comportarsi male

misc. abbr = **miscellaneous**

miscarriage ['mɪskærɪdʒ] n (Med) aborto spontaneo; **miscarriage of justice** errore m giudiziario

miscellaneous [mɪsɪ'leɪnɪəs] adj (items) vario(-a); (selection) misto(-a)

mischief ['mɪstʃɪf] n (naughtiness) birichineria; (maliciousness) malizia; **mischievous** adj birichino(-a)

misconception ['mɪskən'sɛpʃən] n idea sbagliata

misconduct [mɪs'kɒndʌkt] n cattiva condotta; **professional ~** reato professionale

miser ['maɪzəʳ] n avaro

miserable ['mɪzərəbl] adj infelice; (wretched) miserabile; (weather) deprimente; (offer, failure) misero(-a)

misery ['mɪzərɪ] n (unhappiness) tristezza; (wretchedness) miseria

misfortune [mɪs'fɔːtʃən] n sfortuna

misgiving [mɪs'gɪvɪŋ] n apprensione f; **to have ~s about** avere dei dubbi per quanto riguarda

misguided [mɪs'gaɪdɪd] adj sbagliato(-a), poco giudizioso(-a)

mishap ['mɪshæp] n disgrazia

misinterpret [mɪsɪn'təːprɪt] vt interpretare male

misjudge [mɪs'dʒʌdʒ] vt giudicare male

mislay [mɪs'leɪ] (irreg) vt smarrire

mislead [mɪs'liːd] (irreg) vt sviare; **misleading** adj ingannevole

misplace [mɪs'pleɪs] vt smarrire

misprint ['mɪsprɪnt] n errore m di stampa

misrepresent [mɪsrɛprɪ'zɛnt] vt travisare

Miss [mɪs] n Signorina

miss [mɪs] vt (fail to get) perdere; (fail to hit) mancare; (fail to see): **you can't**

~ it non puoi non vederlo; (regret the absence of): **I ~ him** sento la sua mancanza ▶ vi mancare ▶ n (shot) colpo mancato; **we ~ed our train** abbiamo perso il treno ▷ **miss out** (BRIT) vt omettere ▷ **miss out on** vt fus (fun, party) perdersi; (chance, bargain) lasciarsi sfuggire

missile ['mɪsaɪl] n (Mil) missile m; (object thrown) proiettile m

missing ['mɪsɪŋ] adj perso(-a), smarrito(-a); (person) scomparso(-a); (: after disaster, Mil) disperso(-a); (removed) mancante; **to be ~** mancare

mission ['mɪʃən] n missione f; **missionary** n missionario(-a)

misspell [mɪs'spɛl] vt (irreg: like **spell**) sbagliare l'ortografia di

mist [mɪst] n nebbia, foschia ▶ vi (also: **~ over**, **~ up**) annebbiarsi; (: BRIT: windows) appannarsi

mistake [mɪs'teɪk] (irreg: like **take**) n sbaglio, errore m ▶ vt sbagliarsi di; fraintendere; **to make a ~** fare uno sbaglio, sbagliare; **there must be some ~** ci dev'essere un errore; **by ~** per sbaglio; **to ~ for** prendere per; **mistaken** pp of **mistake** ▶ adj (idea etc) sbagliato(-a); **to be mistaken** sbagliarsi

mister ['mɪstəʳ] (inf) n signore m; see **Mr**

mistletoe ['mɪsltəu] n vischio

mistook [mɪs'tuk] pt of **mistake**

mistress ['mɪstrɪs] n padrona; (lover) amante f; (BRIT Scol) insegnante f

mistrust [mɪs'trʌst] vt diffidare di

misty ['mɪstɪ] adj nebbioso(-a), brumoso(-a)

misunderstand [mɪsʌndə'stænd] (irreg) vt, vi capire male, fraintendere; **misunderstanding** n malinteso, equivoco; **there's been a misunderstanding** c'è stato un malinteso

misunderstood [mɪsʌndəˈstud] *pt, pp of* **misunderstand**

misuse [*n* mɪsˈjuːs, *vb* mɪsˈjuːz] *n* cattivo uso; (*of power*) abuso ▸ *vt* far cattivo uso di; abusare di

mitt(en) [ˈmɪt(n)] *n* mezzo guanto; manopola

mix [mɪks] *vt* mescolare ▸ *vi* (*people*): **to ~ with** avere a che fare con ▸ *n* mescolanza; preparato ▸ **mix up** *vt* mescolare; (*confuse*) confondere; **mixed** *adj* misto(-a); **mixed grill** *n* (*BRIT*) misto alla griglia; **mixed salad** *n* insalata mista; **mixed-up** *adj* (*confused*) confuso(-a); **mixer** *n* (*for food: electric*) frullatore *m*; (: *hand*) frullino; (*person*): **he is a good mixer** è molto socievole; **mixture** *n* mescolanza; (*blend: of tobacco etc*) miscela; (*Med*) sciroppo; **mix-up** *n* confusione *f*

ml *abbr* (= *millilitre(s)*) ml

mm *abbr* (= *millimetre*) mm

moan [məun] *n* gemito ▸ *vi* (*inf: complain*) lamentarsi (di)

moat [məut] *n* fossato

mob [mɔb] *n* calca ▸ *vt* accalcarsi intorno a

mobile [ˈməubaɪl] *adj* mobile ▸ *n* (*decoration*) mobile *m*; **mobile home** *n* grande roulotte *f inv* (utilizzata come domicilio); **mobile phone** *n* telefono portatile, telefonino

mobility [məuˈbɪlɪtɪ] *n* mobilità; (*of applicant*) disponibilità a viaggiare

mobilize [ˈməubɪlaɪz] *vt* mobilitare ▸ *vi* mobilitarsi

mock [mɔk] *vt* deridere, burlarsi di ▸ *adj* falso(-a); **~s** *npl* (*BRIT: Scol: inf*) simulazione *f* degli esami; **mockery** *n* derisione *f*; **to make a mockery of** burlarsi di; (*exam*) rendere una farsa

mod cons [ˈmɔdˈkɔnz] *npl abbr* (*BRIT*) = **modern conveniences**; *see* **convenience**

mode [məud] *n* modo

model [ˈmɔdl] *n* modello; (*person: for fashion*) indossatore(-trice); (: *for artist*) modello(-a) ▸ *adj* (*small-scale: railway etc*) in miniatura; (*child, factory*) modello *inv* ▸ *vt* modellare ▸ *vi* fare l'indossatore (*or* l'indossatrice); **to ~ clothes** presentare degli abiti

modem [ˈməudɛm] *n* modem *m inv*

moderate [*adj* ˈmɔdərət, *vb* ˈmɔdəreɪt] *adj* moderato(-a) ▸ *vi* moderarsi, placarsi ▸ *vt* moderare

moderation [mɔdəˈreɪʃən] *n* moderazione *f*, misura; **in ~** in quantità moderata, con moderazione

modern [ˈmɔdən] *adj* moderno(-a); **mod cons** comodità *fpl* moderne; **modernize** *vt* modernizzare; **modern languages** *npl* lingue *fpl* moderne

modest [ˈmɔdɪst] *adj* modesto(-a); **modesty** *n* modestia

modification [mɔdɪfɪˈkeɪʃən] *n* modificazione *f*; **to make ~s** fare *or* apportare delle modifiche

modify [ˈmɔdɪfaɪ] *vt* modificare

module [ˈmɔdjuːl] *n* modulo

mohair [ˈməuhɛəʳ] *n* mohair *m*

Mohammed [məuˈhæmɪd] *n* Maometto

moist [mɔɪst] *adj* umido(-a); **moisture** [ˈmɔɪstʃəʳ] *n* umidità; (*on glass*) goccioline *fpl* di vapore; **moisturizer** [ˈmɔɪstʃəraɪzəʳ] *n* idratante *f*

mold *etc* [məuld] (*US*) *n, vt* = **mould**

mole [məul] *n* (*animal, fig*) talpa; (*spot*) neo

molecule [ˈmɔlɪkjuːl] *n* molecola

molest [məuˈlɛst] *vt* molestare

molten [ˈməultən] *adj* fuso(-a)

mom [mɔm] (*US*) *n* = **mum**

moment [ˈməumənt] *n* momento, istante *m*; **at that ~** in quel momento; **at the ~** al momento, in questo

momento; **momentarily** ['məumə
ntərɪlɪ] *adv* per un momento; (*US:
very soon*) da un momento all'altro;
momentary *adj* momentaneo(-a),
passeggero(-a); **momentous** [-
'mentəs] *adj* di grande importanza

momentum [məu'mentəm] *n*
(*Physics*) momento; (*fig*) impeto; **to
gather ~** aumentare di velocità

mommy ['mɔmɪ] (*US*) *n* = **mummy**

Mon. *abbr* (= *Monday*) lun.

Monaco ['mɔnəkəu] *n* Principato di
Monaco

monarch ['mɔnək] *n* monarca *m*;
monarchy *n* monarchia

monastery ['mɔnəstərɪ] *n* monastero

Monday ['mʌndɪ] *n* lunedì *m inv*

monetary ['mʌnɪtərɪ] *adj*
monetario(-a)

money ['mʌnɪ] *n* denaro, soldi *mpl*;
I haven't got any ~ non ho soldi;
money belt *n* marsupio (*per soldi*);
money order *n* vaglia *m inv*

mongrel ['mʌŋgrəl] *n* (*dog*) cane *m*
bastardo

monitor ['mɔnɪtə'] *n* (*TV, Comput*)
monitor *m inv* ▶ *vt* controllare

monk [mʌŋk] *n* monaco

monkey ['mʌŋkɪ] *n* scimmia

monologue ['mɔnəlɔg] *n* monologo

monopoly [mə'nɔpəlɪ] *n* monopolio

monosodium glutamate
[mɔnə'səudiəm'gluːtəmeɪt] *n*
glutammato di sodio

monotonous [mə'nɔtənəs] *adj*
monotono(-a)

monsoon [mɔn'suːn] *n* monsone *m*

monster ['mɔnstə'] *n* mostro

month [mʌnθ] *n* mese *m*; **monthly** *adj*
mensile ▶ *adv* al mese; ogni mese

monument ['mɔnjumənt] *n*
monumento

mood [muːd] *n* umore *m*; **to be in a
good/bad ~** essere di buon/cattivo
umore; **moody** *adj* (*variable*)

capriccioso(-a), lunatico(-a); (*sullen*)
imbronciato(-a)

moon [muːn] *n* luna; **moonlight** *n*
chiaro di luna

moor [muə'] *n* brughiera ▶ *vt* (*ship*)
ormeggiare ▶ *vi* ormeggiarsi

moose [muːs] *n inv* alce *m*

mop [mɔp] *n* lavapavimenti *m inv*;
(*also: ~ of hair*) zazzera ▶ *vt* lavare con
lo straccio; (*face*) asciugare ▷ **mop up**
vt asciugare con uno straccio

mope [məup] *vi* fare il broncio

moped ['məupɛd] *n* (*BRIT*)
ciclomotore *m*

moral ['mɔrl] *adj* morale ▶ *n* morale *f*;
~s *npl* (*principles*) moralità

morale [mɔ'rɑːl] *n* morale *m*

morality [mə'rælɪtɪ] *n* moralità

morbid ['mɔːbɪd] *adj* morboso(-a)

more
[mɔː'] *adj*

1 (*greater in number etc*) più; **more
people/letters than we expected**
più persone/lettere di quante ne
aspettavamo; **I have more wine/
money than you** ho più vino/soldi di
te; **I have more wine than beer** ho più
vino che birra

2 (*additional*) altro(-a), ancora; **do you
want (some) more tea?** vuole dell'altro
tè?, vuole ancora del tè?; **I have no** *or* **I
don't have any more money** non ho
più soldi

▶*pron*

1 (*greater amount*) più; **more than
10** più di 10; **it cost more than we
expected** ha costato più di quanto ci
aspettavamo

2 (*further or additional amount*) ancora;
is there any more? ce n'è ancora?;
there's no more non ce n'è più; **a little
more** ancora un po'; **many/much
more** molti(-e)/molto(-a) di più

▶*adv* **more dangerous/easily (than)**
più pericoloso/facilmente (di); **more**

and more sempre di più; **more and more difficult** sempre più difficile; **more or less** più o meno; **more than ever** più che mai

moreover [mɔːˈrəuvəʳ] *adv* inoltre, di più

morgue [mɔːg] *n* obitorio

morning [ˈmɔːnɪŋ] *n* mattina, mattino; *(duration)* mattinata ▶ *cpd* del mattino; **in the ~** la mattina; **7 o'clock in the ~** le 7 di *or* della mattina; **morning sickness** *n* nausee *fpl* mattutine

Moroccan [məˈrɔkən] *adj, n* marocchino(-a)

Morocco [məˈrɔkəu] *n* Marocco

moron [ˈmɔːrɔn] *(inf) n* deficiente *m/f*

morphine [ˈmɔːfiːn] *n* morfina

morris dancing *n vedi nota*

- **morris dancing**
- Il **morris dancing** è una
- danza folcloristica inglese
- tradizionalmente riservata agli
- uomini. Vestiti di bianco e con dei
- campanelli attaccati alle caviglie,
- i ballerini eseguono una danza
- tenendo in mano dei fazzoletti
- bianchi e lunghi bastoni. Questa
- danza è molto popolare nelle feste
- paesane.

Morse [mɔːs] *n (also: ~ code)* alfabeto Morse

mortal [ˈmɔːtl] *adj* mortale ▶ *n* mortale *m*

mortar [ˈmɔːtəʳ] *n (Constr)* malta; *(dish)* mortaio

mortgage [ˈmɔːgɪdʒ] *n* ipoteca; *(loan)* prestito ipotecario ▶ *vt* ipotecare

mortician [mɔːˈtɪʃən] *(US) n* impresario di pompe funebri

mortified [ˈmɔːtɪfaɪd] *adj* umiliato(-a)

mortuary [ˈmɔːtjuərɪ] *n* camera mortuaria; obitorio

mosaic [məuˈzeɪɪk] *n* mosaico

Moscow [ˈmɔskəu] *n* Mosca

Moslem [ˈmɔzləm] *adj, n* = **Muslim**

mosque [mɔsk] *n* moschea

mosquito [mɔsˈkiːtəu] *(pl* **mosquitoes)** *n* zanzara

moss [mɔs] *n* muschio

most [məust] *adj (almost all)* la maggior parte di; *(largest, greatest)*: **who has (the) ~ money?** chi ha più soldi di tutti? ▶ *pron* la maggior parte ▶ *adv* più; *(work, sleep etc)* di più; *(very)* molto, estremamente; **the ~** *(also:* **+ adjective)** il(-la) più; **~ of** la maggior parte di; **~ of them** quasi tutti; **I saw (the) ~** ho visto più io; **at the (very) ~** al massimo; **to make the ~ of** trarre il massimo vantaggio da; **a ~ interesting book** un libro estremamente interessante; **mostly** *adv* per lo più

MOT *(BRIT) n abbr* = **Ministry of Transport; the ~ (test)** *revisione annuale obbligatoria degli autoveicoli*

motel [məuˈtɛl] *n* motel *m inv*

moth [mɔθ] *n* farfalla notturna; tarma

mother [ˈmʌðəʳ] *n* madre *f* ▶ *vt (care for)* fare da madre a; **motherhood** *n* maternità; **mother-in-law** *n* suocera; **mother-of-pearl** [mʌðərəvˈpəːl] *n* madreperla; **Mother's Day** *n* la festa della mamma; **mother-to-be** [mʌðətəˈbiː] *n* futura mamma; **mother tongue** *n* madrelingua

motif [məuˈtiːf] *n* motivo

motion [ˈməuʃən] *n* movimento, moto; *(gesture)* gesto; *(at meeting)* mozione *f* ▶ *vt, vi* **to ~ (to) sb to do** fare cenno a qn di fare; **motionless** *adj* immobile; **motion picture** *n* film *m inv*

motivate [ˈməutɪveɪt] *vt (act, decision)* dare origine a, motivare; *(person)* spingere

motivation [məutɪˈveɪʃən] *n* motivazione *f*

motive ['məʊtɪv] n motivo
motor ['məʊtəʳ] n motore m;
(BRIT: inf: vehicle) macchina ▶ cpd
automobilistico(-a); **motorbike** n
moto f inv; **motorboat** n motoscafo;
motorcar (BRIT) n automobile
f; **motorcycle** n motocicletta;
motorcyclist n motociclista
m/f; **motoring** (BRIT) n turismo
automobilistico; **motorist** n
automobilista m/f; **motor racing**
(BRIT) n corse fpl automobilistiche;
motorway (BRIT) n autostrada
motto ['mɒtəʊ] (pl **mottoes**) n motto
mould [məʊld] (US **mold**) n forma,
stampo; (mildew) muffa ▶ vt
formare; (fig) foggiare; **mouldy** adj
ammuffito(-a); (smell) di muffa
mound [maʊnd] n rialzo, collinetta;
(heap) mucchio
mount [maʊnt] n (Geo) monte m
▶ vt montare; (horse) montare a ▶ vi
(increase) aumentare ▷ **mount up** vi
(build up) accumularsi
mountain ['maʊntɪn] n montagna
▶ cpd di montagna; **mountain
bike** n mountain bike f inv;
mountaineer [-'nɪəʳ] n alpinista
m/f; **mountaineering** [-'nɪərɪŋ]
n alpinismo; **mountainous** adj
montagnoso(-a); **mountain range** n
catena montuosa
mourn [mɔːn] vt piangere, lamentare
▶ vi **to ~ (for sb)** piangere (la morte
di qn); **mourner** n parente m/f or
amico(-a) del defunto; **mourning** n
lutto; **in mourning** in lutto
mouse [maʊs] (pl **mice**) n topo;
(Comput) mouse m inv; **mouse mat,
mouse pad** n (Comput) tappetino
del mouse
moussaka [muːˈsɑːkə] n moussaka
mousse [muːs] n mousse f inv
moustache [məsˈtɑːʃ] (US **mustache**)
n baffi mpl

mouth [maʊθ, pl maʊðz] n bocca; (of
river) bocca, foce f; (opening) orifizio;
mouthful n boccata; **mouth organ**
n armonica; **mouthpiece** n (Mus)
imboccatura, bocchino; (spokesman)
portavoce m/f inv; **mouthwash** n
collutorio
move [muːv] n (movement)
movimento; (in game) mossa;
(: turn to play) turno; (change: of house)
trasloco; (: of job) cambiamento
▶ vt muovere; (change position of)
spostare; (emotionally) commuovere;
(Pol: resolution etc) proporre ▶ vi (gen)
muoversi, spostarsi; (also: ~ **house**)
cambiar casa, traslocare; **to get a
~ on** affrettarsi, sbrigarsi; **can you
~ your car, please?** può spostare la
macchina, per favore?; **to ~ sb to do
sth** indurre or spingere qn a fare qc;
to ~ towards andare verso ▷ **move
back** vi (return) ritornare ▷ **move in**
vi (to a house) entrare (in una nuova
casa); (police etc) intervenire ▷ **move
off** vi partire ▷ **move on** vi riprendere
la strada ▷ **move out** vi (of house)
sgomberare ▷ **move over** vi spostarsi
▷ **move up** vi avanzare; **movement**
['muːvmənt] n (gen) movimento;
(gesture) gesto; (of stars, water,
physical) moto
movie ['muːvɪ] n film m inv; **the ~s**
il cinema; **movie theater** (US) n
cinema m inv
moving ['muːvɪŋ] adj mobile; (causing
emotion) commovente
mow [məʊ] (pt **mowed**, pp **mowed**
or **mown**) vt (grass) tagliare; (corn)
mietere; **mower** n (also: **lawnmower**)
tagliaerba m inv
Mozambique [məʊzəmˈbiːk] n
Mozambico
MP n abbr = **Member of Parliament**
MP3 n abbr M3; **MP3 player** n lettore
m MP3

mpg *n abbr* = **miles per gallon** (30 mpg = 9.4 l. per 100 km)

m.p.h. *n abbr* = **miles per hour** (60 m.p.h = 96 km/h)

Mr ['mɪstə'] (*US* **Mr.**) *n* **Mr X** Signor X, Sig. X

Mrs ['mɪsɪz] (*US* **Mrs.**) *n* **Mrs X** Signora X, Sig.ra X

Ms [mɪz] (*US* **Ms.**) *n* = **Miss or Mrs**; **Ms X** ≈ Signora X, ≈ Sig.ra X

- **Ms**
- In inglese si usa **Ms** al posto di "Mrs"
- (Signora) o "Miss" (Signorina) per
- evitare la distinzione tradizionale
- tra le donne sposate e quelle nubili.

MSP *n abbr* = **Member of the Scottish Parliament**

Mt *abbr* (*Geo*: = **mount**) M.

○ **much**
[mʌtʃ] *adj, pron* molto(-a); **he's done so much work** ha lavorato così tanto; **I have as much money as you** ho tanti soldi quanti ne hai tu; **how much is it?** quant'è?; **it costs too much** costa troppo; **as much as you want** quanto vuoi

▶*adv*

1 (*greatly*) molto, tanto; **thank you very much** molte grazie; **he's very much the gentleman** è il vero gentiluomo; **I read as much as I can** leggo quanto posso; **as much as you** tanto quanto te

2 (*by far*) molto; **it's much the biggest company in Europe** è di gran lunga la più grossa società in Europa

3 (*almost*) grossomodo, praticamente; **they're much the same** sono praticamente uguali

muck [mʌk] *n* (*dirt*) sporcizia ▷ **muck up** (*inf*) *vt* (*ruin*) rovinare; **mucky** *adj* (*dirty*) sporco(-a), lordo(-a)

mucus ['mju:kəs] *n* muco

mud [mʌd] *n* fango

muddle ['mʌdl] *n* confusione f,

disordine *m*; pasticcio ▶*vt* (*also*: **~ up**) confondere

muddy ['mʌdɪ] *adj* fangoso(-a)

mudguard ['mʌdɡɑːd] *n* parafango

muesli ['mju:zlɪ] *n* muesli *m*

muffin ['mʌfɪn] *n* specie di pasticcino soffice da tè

muffled ['mʌfld] *adj* smorzato(-a), attutito(-a)

muffler ['mʌflə'] (*US*) *n* (*Aut*) marmitta; (: *on motorbike*) silenziatore *m*

mug [mʌɡ] *n* (*cup*) tazzone *m*; (*for beer*) boccale *m*; (*inf*: *face*) muso; (: *fool*) scemo(-a) ▶ *vt* (*assault*) assalire; **mugger** ['mʌɡə'] *n* aggressore *m*; **mugging** *n* assalto

muggy ['mʌɡɪ] *adj* afoso(-a)

mule [mju:l] *n* mulo

multicoloured ['mʌltɪkʌləd] (*US* **multicolored**) *adj* multicolore, variopinto(-a)

multimedia ['mʌltɪ'mi:dɪə] *adj* multimedia *inv*

multinational [mʌltɪ'næʃənl] *adj, n* multinazionale (*f*)

multiple ['mʌltɪpl] *adj* multiplo(-a), molteplice ▶ *n* multiplo; **multiple choice (test)** *n* esercizi *mpl* a scelta multipla; **multiple sclerosis** [-sklɪ'rəusɪs] *n* sclerosi *f* a placche

multiplex cinema ['mʌltɪplɛks-] *n* cinema *m inv* multisala *inv*

multiplication [mʌltɪplɪ'keɪʃən] *n* moltiplicazione *f*

multiply ['mʌltɪplaɪ] *vt* moltiplicare ▶ *vi* moltiplicarsi

multistorey ['mʌltɪ'stɔːrɪ] (*BRIT*) *adj* (*building, car park*) a più piani

mum [mʌm] (*BRIT*: *inf*) *n* mamma ▶ *adj* **to keep ~** non aprire bocca

mumble ['mʌmbl] *vt, vi* borbottare

mummy ['mʌmɪ] *n* (*BRIT*: *mother*) mamma; (*embalmed*) mummia

mumps [mʌmps] *n* orecchioni *mpl*

m

munch [mʌntʃ] vt, vi sgranocchiare
municipal [mjuːˈnɪsɪpl] adj municipale
mural [ˈmjuərl] n dipinto murale
murder [ˈməːdəʳ] n assassinio, omicidio ▶ vt assassinare; **murderer** n omicida m, assassino
murky [ˈməːkɪ] adj tenebroso(-a)
murmur [ˈməːməʳ] n mormorio ▶ vt, vi mormorare
muscle [ˈmʌsl] n muscolo; (fig) forza; **muscular** [ˈmʌskjuləʳ] adj muscolare; (person, arm) muscoloso(-a)
museum [mjuːˈzɪəm] n museo
mushroom [ˈmʌʃrum] n fungo ▶ vi crescere in fretta
music [ˈmjuːzɪk] n musica; **musical** adj musicale; (person) portato(-a) per la musica ▶ n (show) commedia musicale; **musical instrument** n strumento musicale; **musician** [-ˈzɪʃən] n musicista m/f
Muslim [ˈmʌzlɪm] adj, n musulmano(-a)
muslin [ˈmʌzlɪn] n mussola
mussel [ˈmʌsl] n cozza
must [mʌst] aux vb (obligation): **I ~ do it** devo farlo; (probability): **he ~ be there by now** dovrebbe essere arrivato ormai; **I ~ have made a mistake** devo essermi sbagliato ▶ n **it's a ~** è d'obbligo
mustache [ˈmʌstæʃ] (US) n = **moustache**
mustard [ˈmʌstəd] n senape f, mostarda
mustn't [ˈmʌsnt] = **must not**
mute [mjuːt] adj, n muto(-a)
mutilate [ˈmjuːtɪleɪt] vt mutilare
mutiny [ˈmjuːtɪnɪ] n ammutinamento
mutter [ˈmʌtəʳ] vt, vi borbottare, brontolare
mutton [ˈmʌtn] n carne f di montone
mutual [ˈmjuːtʃuəl] adj mutuo(-a), reciproco(-a)

muzzle [ˈmʌzl] n muso; (protective device) museruola; (of gun) bocca ▶ vt mettere la museruola a
my [maɪ] adj il (la) mio(-a); (pl) i (le) miei (mie); **my house** la mia casa; **my books** i miei libri; **my brother** mio fratello; **I've washed my hair/cut my finger** mi sono lavato i capelli/tagliato il dito
myself [maɪˈsɛlf] pron (reflexive) mi; (emphatic) io stesso(-a); (after prep) me; see also **oneself**
mysterious [mɪsˈtɪərɪəs] adj misterioso(-a)
mystery [ˈmɪstərɪ] n mistero
mystical [ˈmɪstɪkəl] adj mistico(-a)
mystify [ˈmɪstɪfaɪ] vt mistificare; (puzzle) confondere
myth [mɪθ] n mito; **mythology** [mɪˈθɒlədʒɪ] n mitologia

n

n/a abbr = **not applicable**
nag [næg] vt tormentare ▶ vi brontolare in continuazione
nail [neɪl] n (human) unghia; (metal) chiodo ▶ vt inchiodare; **to ~ sb down to (doing) sth** costringere qn a (fare) qc; **nailbrush** n spazzolino da or per unghie; **nailfile** n lima da or per unghie; **nail polish** n smalto da or per unghie; **nail polish remover** n

acetone *m*, solvente *m*; **nail scissors** *npl* forbici *fpl* da or per unghie; **nail varnish** (*BRIT*) *n* = **nail polish**

naïve [nar'i:v] *adj* ingenuo(-a)

naked ['neɪkɪd] *adj* nudo(-a)

name [neɪm] *n* nome *m*; (*reputation*) nome, reputazione *f* ▶ *vt* (*baby etc*) chiamare; (*plant, illness*) nominare; (*person, object*) identificare; (*price, date*) fissare; **what's your ~?** come si chiama?; **by ~** di nome; **she knows them all by ~** li conosce tutti per nome; **namely** *adv* cioè

nanny ['nænɪ] *n* bambinaia

nap [næp] *n* (*sleep*) pisolino; (*of cloth*) peluria; **to be caught ~ping** essere preso alla sprovvista

napkin ['næpkɪn] *n* (*also*: **table~**) tovagliolo

nappy ['næpɪ] (*BRIT*) *n* pannolino

narcotics [nɑː'kɔtɪkz] *npl* (*drugs*) narcotici, stupefacenti *mpl*

narrative ['nærətɪv] *n* narrativa

narrator [nə'reɪtə˞] *n* narratore(-trice)

narrow ['nærəʊ] *adj* stretto(-a); (*fig*) limitato(-a), ristretto(-a) ▶ *vi* restringersi; **to have a ~ escape** farcela per un pelo ▷ **narrow down** *vt* (*search, investigation, possibilities*) restringere; (*list*) ridurre; **narrowly** *adv* per un pelo; (*time*) per poco; **narrow-minded** *adj* meschino(-a)

nasal ['neɪzl] *adj* nasale

nasty ['nɑːstɪ] *adj* (*person, remark*: *unpleasant*) cattivo(-a); (: *rude*) villano(-a); (*smell, wound, situation*) brutto(-a)

nation ['neɪʃən] *n* nazione *f*

national ['næʃənl] *adj* nazionale ▶ *n* cittadino(-a); **national anthem** *n* inno nazionale; **national dress** *n* costume *m* nazionale; **National Health Service** (*BRIT*) *n* servizio nazionale di assistenza sanitaria,

≈ S.S.N. *m*; **National Insurance** (*BRIT*) *n* ≈ Previdenza Sociale;

nationalist *adj*, *n* nazionalista (*m/f*);

nationality [-'nælɪtɪ] *n* nazionalità *f inv*; **nationalize** *vt* nazionalizzare;

national park *n* parco nazionale;

National Trust *n* sovrintendenza ai beni culturali e ambientali

- **National Trust**
- Fondato nel 1895, il **National Trust**
- è un'organizzazione che si occupa
- della tutela e della salvaguardia
- di luoghi di interesse storico o
- ambientale nel Regno Unito.

nationwide ['neɪʃənwaɪd] *adj* diffuso(-a) in tutto il paese ▶ *adv* in tutto il paese

native ['neɪtɪv] *n* abitante *m/f* del paese ▶ *adj* indigeno(-a); (*country*) natio(-a); (*ability*) innato(-a); **a ~ of Russia** un nativo della Russia; **a ~ speaker of French** una persona di madrelingua francese; **Native American** *n* discendente di tribù dell'America settentrionale

NATO ['neɪtəʊ] *n abbr* (= *North Atlantic Treaty Organization*) N.A.T.O. *f*

natural ['nætʃrəl] *adj* naturale; (*ability*) innato(-a); (*manner*) semplice; **natural gas** *n* gas *m* metano; **natural history** *n* storia naturale; **naturally** *adv* naturalmente; (*by nature: gifted*) di natura; **natural resources** *npl* risorse *fpl* naturali

nature ['neɪtʃə˞] *n* natura; (*character*) natura, indole *f*; **by ~** di natura; **nature reserve** *n* (*BRIT*) parco naturale

naughty ['nɔːtɪ] *adj* (*child*) birichino(-a), cattivello(-a); (*story, film*) spinto(-a)

nausea ['nɔːsɪə] *n* (*Med*) nausea; (*fig: disgust*) schifo

naval ['neɪvl] *adj* navale

navel ['neɪvl] *n* ombelico

navigate ['nævɪɡeɪt] vt percorrere navigando ▶ vi navigare; (Aut) fare da navigatore; **navigation** [-'ɡeɪʃən] n navigazione f

navy ['neɪvɪ] n marina

Nazi ['nɑːtsɪ] n nazista m/f

NB abbr (= nota bene) N.B.

near [nɪəʳ] adj vicino(-a); (relation) prossimo(-a) ▶ adv vicino ▶ prep (also: ~ to) vicino a, presso; (: time) verso ▶ vt avvicinarsi a; **nearby** [nɪə'baɪ] adj vicino(-a) ▶ adv vicino; **is there a bank nearby?** c'è una banca qui vicino?; **nearly** adv quasi; **I nearly fell** per poco non sono caduto; **near-sighted** [nɪə'saɪtɪd] adj miope

neat [niːt] adj (person, room) ordinato(-a); (work) pulito(-a); (solution, plan) ben indovinato(-a), azzeccato(-a); (spirits) liscio(-a); **neatly** adv con ordine; (skilfully) abilmente

necessarily ['nɛsɪsrɪlɪ] adv necessariamente

necessary ['nɛsɪsrɪ] adj necessario(-a)

necessity [nɪ'sɛsɪtɪ] n necessità f inv

neck [nɛk] n collo; (of garment) colletto ▶ vi (inf) pomiciare, sbaciucchiarsi; **~ and ~** testa a testa; **necklace** ['nɛklɪs] n collana; **necktie** ['nɛktaɪ] n cravatta

nectarine ['nɛktərɪn] n nocepesca

need [niːd] n bisogno ▶ vt aver bisogno di; **do you ~ anything?** ha bisogno di qualcosa?; **to ~ to do** dover fare; aver bisogno di fare; **you don't ~ to go** non devi andare, non c'è bisogno che tu vada

needle ['niːdl] n ago; (on record player) puntina ▶ vt punzecchiare

needless ['niːdlɪs] adj inutile

needlework ['niːdlwəːk] n cucito

needn't ['niːdnt] = **need not**

needy ['niːdɪ] adj bisognoso(-a)

negative ['nɛɡətɪv] n (Ling) negazione f; (Phot) negativo ▶ adj negativo(-a)

neglect [nɪ'ɡlɛkt] vt trascurare ▶ n (of person, duty) negligenza; (of child, house etc) scarsa cura; **state of ~** stato di abbandono

negotiate [nɪ'ɡəʊʃɪeɪt] vi **to ~ (with)** negoziare (con) ▶ vt (Comm) negoziare; (obstacle) superare; **negotiations** [nɪɡəʊʃɪ'eɪʃənz] pl n trattative fpl, negoziati mpl

negotiator [nɪ'ɡəʊʃɪeɪtəʳ] n negoziatore(-trice)

neighbour ['neɪbəʳ] (US **neighbor**) n vicino(-a); **neighbourhood** n vicinato; **neighbouring** adj vicino(-a)

neither ['naɪðəʳ] adj, pron né l'uno(-a), nessuno(-a) dei (delle) due ▶ conj neanche, nemmeno, neppure ▶ adv **~ good nor bad** né buono né cattivo; **I didn't move and ~ did Claude** io non mi mossi e nemmeno Claude; **..., ~ did I refuse** ..., ma non ho nemmeno rifiutato

neon ['niːɔn] n neon m

Nepal [nɪ'pɔːl] n Nepal m

nephew ['nɛvjuː] n nipote m

nerve [nəːv] n nervo; (fig) coraggio; (impudence) faccia tosta; **~s** (nervousness) nervoso; **a fit of ~s** una crisi di nervi

nervous ['nəːvəs] adj nervoso(-a); (anxious) agitato(-a), in apprensione; **nervous breakdown** n esaurimento nervoso

nest [nɛst] n nido ▶ vi fare il nido, nidificare

net [nɛt] n rete f ▶ adj netto(-a) ▶ vt (fish etc) prendere con la rete; (profit) ricavare un utile netto di; **the N~** (Internet) Internet f; **netball** n specie di pallacanestro

Netherlands ['nɛðələndz] npl **the ~** i Paesi Bassi

nett [nɛt] adj = **net**

nettle ['nɛtl] n ortica

network ['nɛtwəːk] n rete f

neurotic [njuəˈrɔtɪk] *adj, n* nevrotico(-a)

neuter [ˈnjuːtəʳ] *adj* neutro(-a) ▶ *vt (cat etc)* castrare

neutral [ˈnjuːtrəl] *adj* neutro(-a); *(person, nation)* neutrale ▶ *n (Aut):* **in ~** in folle

never [ˈnɛvəʳ] *adv* (non...) mai; **I've ~ been to Spain** non sono mai stato in Spagna; **~ again** mai più; **I'll ~ go there again** non ci vado più; **~ in my life** mai in vita mia; *see also* **mind**; **never-ending** *adj* interminabile; **nevertheless** [nɛvəðəˈlɛs] *adv* tuttavia, ciò nonostante, ciò nondimeno

new [njuː] *adj* nuovo(-a); *(brand new)* nuovo(-a) di zecca; **New Age** *n* New Age *f inv;* **newborn** *adj* neonato(-a); **newcomer** [ˈnjuːkʌməʳ] *n* nuovo(-a) venuto(-a); **newly** *adv* di recente

news [njuːz] *n* notizie *fpl;* (Radio) giornale *m* radio; *(TV)* telegiornale *m;* **a piece of ~** una notizia; **news agency** *n* agenzia di stampa; **newsagent** *(BRIT) n* giornalaio; **newscaster** *n (Radio, TV)* annunciatore(-trice); **news dealer** *(US) n* = **newsagent**; **newsletter** *n* bollettino; **newspaper** *n* giornale *m;* **newsreader** *n* = **newscaster**

newt [njuːt] *n* tritone *m*

New Year *n* Anno Nuovo; **New Year's Day** *n* il Capodanno; **New Year's Eve** *n* la vigilia di Capodanno

New York [-ˈjɔːk] *n* New York *f*

New Zealand [-ˈziːlənd] *n* Nuova Zelanda; **New Zealander** *n* neozelandese *m/f*

next [nɛkst] *adj* prossimo(-a) ▶ *adv* accanto; *(in time)* dopo; **the ~ day** il giorno dopo, l'indomani; **~ time** la prossima volta; **~ year** l'anno prossimo; **when do we meet ~?** quando ci rincontriamo?; **~ to**

accanto a; **~ to nothing** quasi niente; **~ please!** (avanti) il prossimo!; **next door** *adv, adj* accanto *inv;* **next-of-kin** *n* parente *m/f* prossimo(-a)

NHS *n abbr* = **National Health Service**

nibble [ˈnɪbl] *vt* mordicchiare

nice [naɪs] *adj (holiday, trip)* piacevole; *(flat, picture)* bello(-a); *(person)* simpatico(-a), gentile; **nicely** *adv* bene

niche [niːʃ] *n (Archit)* nicchia

nick [nɪk] *n* taglietto; tacca ▶ *vt (inf)* rubare; **in the ~ of time** appena in tempo

nickel [ˈnɪkl] *n* nichel *m;* (US) *moneta da cinque centesimi di dollaro*

nickname [ˈnɪkneɪm] *n* soprannome *m*

nicotine [ˈnɪkətiːn] *n* nicotina

niece [niːs] *n* nipote *f*

Nigeria [naɪˈdʒɪərɪə] *n* Nigeria

night [naɪt] *n* notte *f;* (evening) sera; **at ~** la sera; **by ~** di notte; **the ~ before last** l'altro ieri notte (or sera); **night club** *n* locale *m* notturno; **nightdress** *n* camicia da notte; **nightie** [ˈnaɪtɪ] *n* = **nightdress**; **nightlife** [ˈnaɪtlaɪf] *n* vita notturna; **nightly** [ˈnaɪtlɪ] *adj* di ogni notte or sera; (by night) notturno(-a) ▶ *adv* ogni notte or sera; **nightmare** [ˈnaɪtmɛəʳ] *n* incubo

night: **night school** *n* scuola serale; **night shift** *n* turno di notte; **night-time** *n* notte *f*

nil [nɪl] *n* nulla *m;* (BRIT Sport) zero

nine [naɪn] *num* nove; **nineteen** *num* diciannove; **nineteenth** [naɪnˈtiːnθ] *num* diciannovesimo(-a); **ninetieth** [ˈnaɪntɪɪθ] *num* novantesimo(-a); **ninety** *num* novanta; **ninth** [naɪnθ] *num* nono(-a)

nip [nɪp] *vt* pizzicare; *(bite)* mordere

nipple [ˈnɪpl] *n (Anat)* capezzolo

nitrogen [ˈnaɪtrədʒən] *n* azoto

no
[nəu] (pl **noes**) adv (opposite of
"yes") no; **are you coming? — no (I'm
not)** viene? — no (non vengo); **would
you like some more? — no thank you**
ne vuole ancora un po'? — no, grazie
▶adj (not any) nessuno(-a); **I have no
money/time/books** non ho soldi/
tempo/libri; **no student would have
done it** nessuno studente lo avrebbe
fatto; **"no parking"** "divieto di sosta";
"no smoking" "vietato fumare"
▶n no m inv

nobility [nəuˈbɪlɪtɪ] n nobiltà
noble [ˈnəubl] adj nobile
nobody [ˈnəubədɪ] pron nessuno
nod [nɔd] vi accennare col capo, fare
un cenno; (in agreement) annuire
con un cenno del capo; (sleep)
sonnecchiare ▶vt **to ~ one's head**
fare di sì col capo ▶n cenno ▷ **nod off**
vi assopirsi
noise [nɔɪz] n rumore m; (din, racket)
chiasso; **I can't sleep for the ~** non
riesco a dormire a causa del rumore;
noisy adj (street, car) rumoroso(-a);
(person) chiassoso(-a)
nominal [ˈnɔmɪnl] adj nominale;
(rent) simbolico(-a)
nominate [ˈnɔmɪneɪt] vt (propose)
proporre come candidato; (elect)
nominare; **nomination**
[nɔmɪˈneɪʃən] n nomina; candidatura;
nominee [nɔmɪˈniː] n persona
nominata, candidato(-a)
none [nʌn] pron (not one thing) niente;
(not one person) nessuno(-a); **~ of you**
nessuno(-a) di voi; **I've ~ left** non ne
ho più; **he's ~ the worse for it** non ne
ha risentito
nonetheless [nʌnðəˈlɛs] adv
nondimeno
non-fiction [nɔnˈfɪkʃən] n saggistica
nonsense [ˈnɔnsəns] n sciocchezze fpl
non: **non-smoker** n non

fumatore(-trice); **non-smoking** adj
(person) che non fuma; (area, section)
per non fumatori; **non-stick** adj
antiaderente, antiadesivo(-a)
noodles [ˈnuːdlz] npl taglierini mpl
noon [nuːn] n mezzogiorno
no-one [ˈnəuwʌn] pron = **nobody**
nor [nɔːʳ] conj = **neither** ▶ adv see
neither
norm [nɔːm] n norma
normal [ˈnɔːml] adj normale;
normally adv normalmente
north [nɔːθ] n nord m, settentrione m
▶ adj nord inv, del nord, settentrionale
▶ adv verso nord; **North America**
n America del Nord; **North
American** adj, n nordamericano(-a);
northbound [ˈnɔːθbaund] adj (traffic)
diretto(-a) a nord; (carriageway)
nord inv; **north-east** n nord-est m;
northeastern adj nordorientale;
northern [ˈnɔːðən] adj del nord,
settentrionale; **Northern Ireland**
n Irlanda del Nord; **North Korea**
n Corea del Nord; **North Pole** n
Polo Nord; **North Sea** n Mare m del
Nord; **north-west** n nord-ovest m;
northwestern adj nordoccidentale
Norway [ˈnɔːweɪ] n Norvegia;
Norwegian [nɔːˈwiːdʒən] adj
norvegese ▶ n norvegese m/f; (Ling)
norvegese m
nose [nəuz] n naso; (of animal) muso
▶ vi **to ~ about** aggirarsi; **nosebleed**
n emorragia nasale; **nosey** (inf) adj
= **nosy**
nostalgia [nɔsˈtældʒɪə] n nostalgia
nostalgic [nɔsˈtældʒɪk] adj
nostalgico(-a)
nostril [ˈnɔstrɪl] n narice f; (of horse)
frogia
nosy [ˈnəuzɪ] (inf) adj curioso(-a)
not [nɔt] adv non; **he is ~** or **isn't here**
non è qui, non c'è; **you must ~** or
you mustn't do that non devi fare

quello; **it's too late, isn't it** or **is it ~?** è troppo tardi, vero?; **~ that I don't like him** non che (lui) non mi piaccia; **~ yet/now** non ancora/ora; see also **all**; **only**

notable ['nəutəbl] adj notevole; **notably** ['nəutəblɪ] adv (markedly) notevolmente; (particularly) in particolare

notch [nɔtʃ] n tacca; (in saw) dente m

note [nəut] n nota; (letter, banknote) biglietto ▶ vt (also: **~ down**) prendere nota di; **to take ~s** prendere appunti; **notebook** n taccuino; **noted** ['nəutɪd] adj celebre; **notepad** n bloc-notes m inv; **notepaper** n carta da lettere

nothing ['nʌθɪŋ] n nulla m, niente m; (zero) zero; **he does ~** non fa niente; **~ new/much** etc niente di nuovo/ speciale etc; **for ~** per niente

notice ['nəutɪs] n avviso; (of leaving) preavviso ▶ vt notare, accorgersi di; **to take ~ of** fare attenzione a; **to bring sth to sb's ~** far notare qc a qn; **at short ~** con un breve preavviso; **until further ~** fino a nuovo avviso; **to hand in one's ~** licenziarsi; **noticeable** adj evidente

notify ['nəutɪfaɪ] vt **to ~ sth to sb** far sapere qc a qn; **to ~ sb of sth** avvisare qn di qc

notion ['nəuʃən] n idea; (concept) nozione f; **~s** npl (US: haberdashery) merceria

notorious [nəu'tɔ:rɪəs] adj famigerato(-a)

notwithstanding [nɔtwɪθ'stændɪŋ] adv nondimeno ▶ prep nonostante, malgrado

nought [nɔ:t] n zero

noun [naun] n nome m, sostantivo

nourish ['nʌrɪʃ] vt nutrire; **nourishment** n nutrimento

Nov. abbr (= November) nov

novel ['nɔvl] n romanzo ▶ adj nuovo(-a); **novelist** n romanziere(-a); **novelty** n novità f inv

November [nəu'vɛmbər] n novembre m

novice ['nɔvɪs] n principiante m/f; (Rel) novizio(-a)

now [nau] adv ora, adesso ▶ conj **~ (that)** adesso che, ora che; **by ~** ormai; **just ~** proprio ora; **right ~** subito, immediatamente; **~ and then, ~ and again** ogni tanto; **from ~ on** da ora in poi; **nowadays** ['nauə deɪz] adv oggidì

nowhere ['nəuwɛər] adv in nessun luogo, da nessuna parte

nozzle ['nɔzl] n (of hose etc) boccaglio; (of fire extinguisher) lancia

nr abbr (BRIT) = **near**

nuclear ['nju:klɪər] adj nucleare

nucleus ['nju:klɪəs] (pl nuclei) n nucleo

nude [nju:d] adj nudo(-a) ▶ n (Art) nudo; **in the ~** tutto(-a) nudo(-a)

nudge [nʌdʒ] vt dare una gomitata a

nudist ['nju:dɪst] n nudista m/f

nudity ['nju:dɪtɪ] n nudità

nuisance ['nju:sns] n **it's a ~** è una seccatura; **he's a ~** è uno scocciatore

numb [nʌm] adj **~ (with)** intorpidito(-a) (da); (with fear) impietrito(-a) (da); **~ with cold** intirizzito(-a) (dal freddo)

number ['nʌmbər] n numero ▶ vt numerare; (include) contare; **a ~ of** un certo numero di; **to be ~ed among** venire annoverato(-a) tra; **they were 10 in ~** erano in tutto 10; **number plate** (BRIT) n (Aut) targa; **Number Ten** n (BRIT: = 10 Downing Street) residenza del Primo Ministro del Regno Unito

numerical [nju:'mɛrɪkl] adj numerico(-a)

numerous ['nju:mərəs] adj numeroso(-a)

nun [nʌn] n suora, monaca
nurse [nəːs] n infermiere(-a); (also:
~maid) bambinaia ▶ vt (patient, cold)
curare; (baby: BRIT) cullare; (: US)
allattare, dare il latte a
nursery ['nəːsərɪ] n (room) camera dei
bambini; (institution) asilo; (for plants)
vivaio; **nursery rhyme** n filastrocca;
nursery school n scuola materna;
nursery slope (BRIT) n (Ski) pista per
principianti
nursing ['nəːsɪŋ] n (profession)
professione f di infermiere (or di
infermiera); (care) cura; **nursing
home** n casa di cura
nurture ['nəːtʃəʳ] vt allevare; nutrire
nut [nʌt] n (of metal) dado; (fruit) noce f
nutmeg ['nʌtmɛg] n noce f moscata
nutrient ['njuːtrɪənt] adj nutriente ▶ n
sostanza nutritiva
nutrition [njuːˈtrɪʃən] n nutrizione f
nutritious [njuːˈtrɪʃəs] adj nutriente
nuts [nʌts] (inf) adj matto(-a)
NVQ n abbr (BRIT) = **National
Vocational Qualification**
nylon ['naɪlɔn] n nailon m ▶ adj di
nailon

O

oak [əuk] n quercia ▶ adj di quercia
O.A.P. (BRIT) n, abbr = **old age
pensioner**
oar [ɔːʳ] n remo
oasis [əuˈeɪsɪs] (pl oases) n oasi f inv
oath [əuθ] n giuramento; (swear word)
bestemmia
oatmeal ['əutmiːl] n farina d'avena
oats [əuts] npl avena
obedience [əˈbiːdɪəns] n ubbidienza
obedient [əˈbiːdɪənt] adj ubbidiente
obese [əuˈbiːs] adj obeso(-a)
obesity [əuˈbiːsɪtɪ] n obesità
obey [əˈbeɪ] vt ubbidire a; (instructions,
regulations) osservare
obituary [əˈbɪtjuərɪ] n necrologia
object [n ˈɔbdʒɪkt, vb əbˈdʒɛkt] n
oggetto; (purpose) scopo, intento;
(Ling) complemento oggetto ▶ vi **to ~
to** (attitude) disapprovare; (proposal)
protestare contro, sollevare delle
obiezioni contro; **expense is no ~** non
si bada a spese; **to ~ that** obiettare
che; **objection** [əbˈdʒɛkʃən] n
obiezione f; **objective** n obiettivo
obligation [ɔblɪˈgeɪʃən] n obbligo,
dovere m; **without ~** senza impegno
obligatory [əˈblɪgətərɪ] adj
obbligatorio(-a)
oblige [əˈblaɪdʒ] vt (force): **to ~ sb to do**
costringere qn a fare; (do a favour) fare
una cortesia a; **to be ~d to sb for sth**
essere grato a qn per qc
oblique [əˈbliːk] adj obliquo(-a);

(allusion) indiretto(-a)

obliterate [ə'blɪtəreɪt] vt cancellare

oblivious [ə'blɪvɪəs] adj ~ **of** incurante di; inconscio(-a) di

oblong ['ɔblɔŋ] adj oblungo(-a) ▶ n rettangolo

obnoxious [əb'nɔkʃəs] adj odioso(-a); (smell) disgustoso(-a), ripugnante

oboe ['əubəu] n oboe m

obscene [əb'siːn] adj osceno(-a)

obscure [əb'skjuə^r] adj oscuro(-a) ▶ vt oscurare; (hide: sun) nascondere

observant [əb'zəːvnt] adj attento(-a)

Be careful not to translate **observant** by the Italian word **osservante**.

observation [ɔbzə'veɪʃən] n osservazione f; (by police etc) sorveglianza

observatory [əb'zəːvətrɪ] n osservatorio

observe [əb'zəːv] vt osservare; (remark) fare osservare; **observer** n osservatore(-trice)

obsess [əb'sɛs] vt ossessionare; **obsession** [əb'sɛʃən] n ossessione f; **obsessive** adj ossessivo(-a)

obsolete ['ɔbsəliːt] adj obsoleto(-a)

obstacle ['ɔbstəkl] n ostacolo

obstinate ['ɔbstɪnɪt] adj ostinato(-a)

obstruct [əb'strʌkt] vt (block) ostruire, ostacolare; (halt) fermare; (hinder) impedire; **obstruction** [əb'strʌkʃən] n ostruzione f; ostacolo

obtain [əb'teɪn] vt ottenere

obvious ['ɔbvɪəs] adj ovvio(-a), evidente; **obviously** adv ovviamente; certo

occasion [ə'keɪʒən] n occasione f; (event) avvenimento; **occasional** adj occasionale; **occasionally** adv ogni tanto

occult [ɔ'kʌlt] adj occulto(-a) ▶ n the ~ l'occulto

occupant ['ɔkjupənt] n occupante

m/f; (of boat, car etc) persona a bordo

occupation [ɔkju'peɪʃən] n occupazione f; (job) mestiere m, professione f

occupy ['ɔkjupaɪ] vt occupare; **to ~ o.s. in doing** occuparsi a fare

occur [ə'kəː^r] vi succedere, capitare; **to ~ to sb** venire in mente a qn; **occurrence** n caso, fatto; presenza

Be careful not to translate **occur** by the Italian word **occorrere**.

ocean ['əuʃən] n oceano

o'clock [ə'klɔk] adv **it is 5 o'clock** sono le 5

Oct. abbr (= October) ott.

October [ɔk'təubə^r] n ottobre m

octopus ['ɔktəpəs] n polpo, piovra

odd [ɔd] adj (strange) strano(-a), bizzarro(-a); (number) dispari inv; (not of a set) spaiato(-a); **60-~** 60 e oltre; **at ~ times** di tanto in tanto; **the ~ one out** l'eccezione f; **oddly** adv stranamente; **odds** npl (in betting) quota

odometer [ɔ'dɔmɪtə^r] n odometro

odour ['əudə^r] (US **odor**) n odore m; (unpleasant) cattivo odore

O of
[ɔv, əv] prep

1 (gen) di; **a boy of 10** un ragazzo di 10 anni; **a friend of ours** un nostro amico; **that was kind of you** è stato molto gentile da parte sua

2 (expressing quantity, amount, dates etc) di; **a kilo of flour** un chilo di farina; **how much of this do you need?** quanto gliene serve?; **there were 3 of them** (people) erano in 3; (objects) ce n'erano 3; **3 of us went** 3 di noi sono andati; **the 5th of July** il 5 luglio

3 (from, out of) di, in; of **made of wood** (fatto) di or in legno

O off
[ɔf] adv

1 (distance, time): **it's a long way off**

è lontano; **the game is 3 days off** la partita è tra 3 giorni

2 (*departure, removal*) via; **to go off to Paris** andarsene a Parigi; **I must be off** devo andare via; **to take off one's coat** togliersi il cappotto; **the button came off** il bottone è venuto via *or* si è staccato; **10% off** con lo sconto del 10%

3 (*not at work*): **to have a day off** avere un giorno libero; **to be off sick** essere assente per malattia

▶*adj* (*engine*) spento(-a); (*tap*) chiuso(-a); (*cancelled*) sospeso(-a); (*BRIT: food*) andato(-a) a male; **on the off chance** nel caso; **to have an off day** non essere in forma

▶*prep*

1 (*motion, removal etc*) da; (*distant from*) a poca distanza da; **a street off the square** una strada che parte dalla piazza

2: **to be off meat** non mangiare più la carne

offence [ə'fɛns] (*US* **offense**) *n* (*Law*) contravvenzione *f*; (*: more serious*) reato; **to take ~ at** offendersi per

offend [ə'fɛnd] *vt* (*person*) offendere; **offender** *n* delinquente *m/f*; (*against regulations*) contravventore(-trice)

offense [ə'fɛns] (*US*) *n* = **offence**

offensive [ə'fɛnsɪv] *adj* offensivo(-a); (*smell etc*) sgradevole, ripugnante ▶*n* (*Mil*) offensiva

offer ['ɔfə'] *n* offerta, proposta ▶*vt* offrire; **"on ~"** (*Comm*) "in offerta speciale"

offhand [ɔf'hænd] *adj* disinvolto(-a), noncurante ▶*adv* su due piedi

office ['ɔfɪs] *n* (*place*) ufficio; (*position*) carica; **doctor's ~** (*US*) studio; **to take ~** entrare in carica; **office block** (*US* **office building**) *n* complesso di uffici; **office hours** *npl* orario d'ufficio; (*US Med*) orario di visite

officer ['ɔfɪsə'] *n* (*Mil etc*) ufficiale *m*;

(*also:* **police ~**) agente *m* di polizia; (*of organization*) funzionario

office worker *n* impiegato(-a) d'ufficio

official [ə'fɪʃl] *adj* (*authorized*) ufficiale ▶*n* ufficiale *m*; (*civil servant*) impiegato statale; funzionario

off: **off-licence** (*BRIT*) *n* (*shop*) spaccio di bevande alcoliche; **off-line** *adj, adv* (*Comput*) off-line *inv*, fuori linea; (*: switched off*) spento(-a); **off-peak** *adj* (*ticket, heating etc*) a tariffa ridotta; (*time*) non di punta; **off-putting** (*BRIT*) *adj* sgradevole, antipatico(-a); **off-season** *adj, adv* fuori stagione; **offset** ['ɔfsɛt] (*irreg*) *vt* (*counteract*) controbilanciare, compensare; **offshore** [ɔf'ʃɔ:'] *adj* (*breeze*) di terra; (*island*) vicino alla costa; (*fishing*) costiero(-a); **offside** ['ɔf'saɪd] *adj* (*Sport*) fuori gioco; (*Aut: in Britain*) destro(-a); (*: in Italy etc*) sinistro(-a); **offspring** ['ɔfsprɪŋ] *n inv* prole *f*, discendenza

often ['ɔfn] *adv* spesso; **how ~ do you go?** quanto spesso ci vai?

oh [əu] *excl* oh!

oil [ɔɪl] *n* olio; (*petroleum*) petrolio; (*for central heating*) nafta ▶*vt* (*machine*) lubrificare; **oil filter** *n* (*Aut*) filtro dell'olio; **oil painting** *n* quadro a olio; **oil refinery** *n* raffineria di petrolio; **oil rig** *n* derrick *m inv*; (*at sea*) piattaforma per trivellazioni subacquee; **oil slick** *n* chiazza d'olio; **oil tanker** *n* (*ship*) petroliera; (*truck*) autocisterna per petrolio; **oil well** *n* pozzo petrolifero; **oily** *adj* unto(-a), oleoso(-a); (*food*) grasso(-a)

ointment ['ɔɪntmənt] *n* unguento

O.K. ['əu'keɪ] *excl* d'accordo! ▶*adj* non male *inv* ▶*vt* approvare; **is it O.K.?, are you O.K.?** tutto bene?

old [əuld] *adj* vecchio(-a); (*ancient*) antico(-a), vecchio(-a); (*person*) vecchio(-a), anziano(-a); **how ~ are you?** quanti anni ha?; **he's 10 years ~** ha 10 anni; **~er brother** fratello maggiore; **old age** n vecchiaia; **old-age pension** ['əuldeɪdʒ-] n (BRIT) pensione f di vecchiaia; **old-age pensioner** (BRIT) n pensionato(-a); **old-fashioned** adj antiquato(-a), fuori moda; (person) all'antica; **old people's home** n ricovero per anziani

olive ['ɔlɪv] n (fruit) oliva; (tree) olivo ▶ adj (also: ~-green) verde oliva inv; **olive oil** n olio d'oliva

Olympic [əu'lɪmpɪk] adj olimpico(-a); **the ~ Games, the ~s** i giochi olimpici, le Olimpiadi

omelet(te) ['ɔmlɪt] n omelette f inv

omen ['əumən] n presagio, augurio

ominous ['ɔmɪnəs] adj minaccioso(-a); (event) di malaugurio

omit [əu'mɪt] vt omettere

on
[ɔn] prep

1 (indicating position) su; **on the wall** sulla parete; **on the left** a or sulla sinistra

2 (indicating means, method, condition etc): **on foot** a piedi; **on the train/plane** in treno/aereo; **on the telephone** al telefono; **on the radio/ television** alla radio/televisione; **to be on drugs** drogarsi; **on holiday** in vacanza

3 (of time): **on Friday** venerdì; **on Fridays** il or di venerdì; **on June 20th** il 20 giugno; **on Friday, June 20th** venerdì, 20 giugno; **a week on Friday** venerdì a otto; **on his arrival** al suo arrivo; **on seeing this** vedendo ciò

4 (about, concerning) su, di; **information on train services** informazioni sui collegamenti ferroviari; **a book on Goldoni/physics** un libro su Goldoni/di or sulla fisica

▶ adv

1 (referring to dress, covering): **to have one's coat on** avere indosso il cappotto; **to put one's coat on** mettersi il cappotto; **what's she got on?** cosa indossa?; **she put her boots/ gloves/hat on** si mise gli stivali/i guanti/il cappello; **screw the lid on tightly** avvita bene il coperchio

2 (further, continuously): **to walk on, go on** etc continuare, proseguire etc; **to read on** continuare a leggere; **on and off** ogni tanto

▶ adj

1 (in operation: machine, TV, light) acceso(-a); (: tap) aperto(-a); (: brake) inserito(-a); **is the meeting still on?** (in progress) la riunione è ancora in corso?; (not cancelled) è confermato l'incontro?; **there's a good film on at the cinema** danno un buon film al cinema

2 (inf): **that's not on!** (not acceptable) non si fa così!; (not possible) non se ne parla neanche!

once [wʌns] adv una volta ▶ conj non appena, quando; **~ he had left/it was done** dopo che se n'era andato/fu fatto; **at ~** subito; (simultaneously) a un tempo; **~ a week** una volta per settimana; **~ more** ancora una volta; **~ and for all** una volta per sempre; **~ upon a time** c'era una volta

oncoming ['ɔnkʌmɪŋ] adj (traffic) che viene in senso opposto

one
[wʌn] num uno(-a); **one hundred and fifty** centocinquanta; **one day** un giorno

▶ adj

1 (sole) unico(-a); **the one book which** l'unico libro che; **the one man who** l'unico che

2 (same) stesso(-a); **they came in the one car** sono venuti nella stessa macchina

▶*pron*

1: this one questo(-a); that one quello(-a); **I've already got one/a red one** ne ho già uno/uno rosso; **one by one** uno per uno

2: one another l'un l'altro; to look at one another guardarsi; to help one another auitarsi l'un l'altro *or* a vicenda

3 (*impersonal*) si; one never knows non si sa mai; to cut one's finger tagliarsi un dito; one needs to eat bisogna mangiare

one: **one-off** (*BRIT: inf*) *n* fatto eccezionale

oneself [wʌn'sɛlf] *pron* (*reflexive*) si; (*after prep*) se stesso(-a), sé; **to do sth (by) ~** fare qc da sé; **to hurt ~** farsi male; **to keep sth for ~** tenere qc per sé; **to talk to ~** parlare da solo

one: **one-shot** [wʌn'ʃɔt] (*US*) *n* = **one-off**; **one-sided** *adj* (*argument*) unilaterale; **one-to-one** *adj* (*relationship*) univoco(-a); **one-way** *adj* (*street, traffic*) a senso unico

ongoing ['ɔngəuɪŋ] *adj* in corso; in attuazione

onion ['ʌnjən] *n* cipolla

on-line ['ɔnlaɪn] *adj, adv* (*Comput*) on-line *inv*

onlooker ['ɔnlukəʳ] *n* spettatore(-trice)

only ['əunlɪ] *adv* solo, soltanto ▶ *adj* solo(-a), unico(-a) ▶ *conj* solo che, ma; **an ~ child** un figlio unico; **not ~ ... but also** non solo ... ma anche

on-screen [ɔn'skri:n] *adj* sullo schermo *inv*

onset ['ɔnsɛt] *n* inizio

onto ['ɔntu] *prep* = **on to**

onward(s) ['ɔnwəd(z)] *adv* (*move*) in avanti; **from that time onward(s)** da quella volta in poi

oops [ups] *excl* ops! (*esprime rincrescimento per un piccolo contrattempo*); **~-a-daisy!** oplà!

ooze [u:z] *vi* stillare

opaque [əu'peɪk] *adj* opaco(-a)

open ['əupn] *adj* aperto(-a); (*road*) libero(-a); (*meeting*) pubblico(-a) ▶ *vt* aprire ▶ *vi* (*eyes, door, debate*) aprirsi; (*flower*) sbocciare; (*shop, bank, museum*) aprire; (*book etc: commence*) cominciare; **is it ~ to the public?** è aperto al pubblico?; **in the ~ (air)** all'aperto; **what time do you ~?** a che ora aprite? ▷ **open up** *vt* aprire; (*blocked road*) sgombrare ▶ *vi* (*shop, business*) aprire; **open-air** *adj* all'aperto; **opening** *adj* (*speech*) di apertura ▶ *n* apertura; (*opportunity*) occasione *f*, opportunità *f inv*; sbocco; **opening hours** *npl* orario d'apertura; **open learning** *n* sistema educativo secondo il quale lo studente ha maggior controllo e gestione delle modalità di apprendimento; **openly** *adv* apertamente; **open-minded** *adj* che ha la mente aperta; **open-necked** *adj* col collo slacciato; **open-plan** *adj* senza pareti divisorie; **Open University** *n* (*BRIT*) vedi nota

● **Open University**
● La **Open University**, fondata in Gran
● Bretagna nel 1969, organizza corsi
● di laurea per corrispondenza o via
● Internet. Alcune lezioni possono
● venir seguite per radio o alla
● televisione e vengono organizzati
● regolari corsi estivi.

opera ['ɔpərə] *n* opera; **opera house** *n* opera; **opera singer** *n* cantante *m/f* d'opera *or* lirico(-a)

operate ['ɔpəreɪt] *vt* (*machine*) azionare, far funzionare; (*system*) usare ▶ *vi* funzionare; (*drug*) essere efficace; **to ~ on sb (for)** (*Med*) operare qn (di)

operating room (*US*) *n* = **operating theatre**

operating theatre *n* (*Med*) sala operatoria

operation [ɔpəˈreɪʃən] n operazione f; **to be in ~** (machine) essere in azione or funzionamento; (system) essere in vigore; **to have an ~** (Med) subire un'operazione; **operational** adj in funzione; d'esercizio

operative [ˈɔpərətɪv] adj (measure) operativo(-a)

operator [ˈɔpəreɪtər] n (of machine) operatore(-trice); (Tel) centralinista m/f

opinion [əˈpɪnɪən] n opinione f, parere m; **in my ~** secondo me, a mio avviso; **opinion poll** n sondaggio di opinioni

opponent [əˈpəunənt] n avversario(-a)

opportunity [ɔpəˈtjuːnɪtɪ] n opportunità f inv, occasione f; **to take the ~ of doing** cogliere l'occasione per fare

oppose [əˈpəuz] vt opporsi a; **~d to** contrario(-a) a; **as ~d to** in contrasto con

opposite [ˈɔpəzɪt] adj opposto(-a); (house etc) di fronte ▶ adv di fronte, dirimpetto ▶ prep di fronte a ▶ n **the ~** il contrario, l'opposto; **the ~ sex** l'altro sesso

opposition [ɔpəˈzɪʃən] n opposizione f

oppress [əˈprɛs] vt opprimere

opt [ɔpt] vi **to ~ for** optare per; **to ~ to do** scegliere di fare ▷ **opt out** vi **to ~ out of** ritirarsi da

optician [ɔpˈtɪʃən] n ottico

optimism [ˈɔptɪmɪzəm] n ottimismo

optimist [ˈɔptɪmɪst] n ottimista m/f; **optimistic** [-ˈmɪstɪk] adj ottimistico(-a)

optimum [ˈɔptɪməm] adj ottimale

option [ˈɔpʃən] n scelta; (Scol) materia facoltativa; (Comm) opzione f; **optional** adj facoltativo(-a); (Comm) a scelta

or [ɔːr] conj o, oppure; (with negative):

he hasn't seen or heard anything non ha visto né sentito niente; **or else** se no, altrimenti; oppure

oral [ˈɔːrəl] adj orale ▶ n esame m orale

orange [ˈɔrɪndʒ] n (fruit) arancia ▶ adj arancione; **orange juice** n succo d'arancia; **orange squash** n succo d'arancia (da diluire con l'acqua)

orbit [ˈɔːbɪt] n orbita ▶ vt orbitare intorno a

orchard [ˈɔːtʃəd] n frutteto

orchestra [ˈɔːkɪstrə] n orchestra; (US: seating) platea

orchid [ˈɔːkɪd] n orchidea

ordeal [ɔːˈdiːl] n prova, travaglio

order [ˈɔːdər] n ordine m; (Comm) ordinazione f ▶ vt ordinare; **can I ~ now, please?** posso ordinare, per favore?; **in ~** in ordine; (of document) in regola; **in (working) ~** funzionante; **in ~ to do** per fare; **in ~ that** affinché + sub; **on ~** (Comm) in ordinazione; **out of ~** non in ordine; (not working) guasto; **to ~ sb to do** ordinare a qn di fare; **order form** n modulo d'ordinazione; **orderly** n (Mil) attendente m; (Med) inserviente m ▶ adj (room) in ordine; (mind) metodico(-a); (person) ordinato(-a), metodico(-a)

ordinary [ˈɔːdnrɪ] adj normale, comune; (pej) mediocre; **out of the ~** diverso dal solito, fuori dell'ordinario

ore [ɔːr] n minerale m grezzo

oregano [ɔrɪˈgɑːnəu] n origano

organ [ˈɔːgən] n organo; **organic** [ɔːˈgænɪk] adj organico(-a); (of food) biologico(-a); **organism** n organismo

organization [ɔːgənaɪˈzeɪʃən] n organizzazione f

organize [ˈɔːgənaɪz] vt organizzare; **to get ~d** organizzarsi; **organized** [ˈɔːgənaɪzd] adj organizzato(-a); **organizer** n organizzatore(-trice)

orgasm [ˈɔːgæzəm] n orgasmo

orgy ['ɔːdʒɪ] n orgia
oriental [ɔːrɪ'entl] adj, n orientale m/f
orientation [ɔːrɪen'teɪʃən] n
orientamento
origin ['ɒrɪdʒɪn] n origine f
original [ə'rɪdʒɪnl] adj originale;
(earliest) originario(-a) ▶ n originale
m; **originally** adv (at first) all'inizio
originate [ə'rɪdʒɪneɪt] vi **to ~ from**
essere originario(-a) di; (suggestion)
provenire da; **to ~ in** avere origine in
Orkneys ['ɔːknɪz] npl **the ~** (also: **the
Orkney Islands**) le Orcadi
ornament ['ɔːnəmənt] n ornamento;
(trinket) ninnolo; **ornamental**
[-'mentl] adj ornamentale
ornate [ɔː'neɪt] adj molto ornato(-a)
orphan ['ɔːfn] n orfano(-a)
orthodox ['ɔːθədɒks] adj
ortodosso(-a)
orthopaedic [ɔːθə'piːdɪk] (US
orthopedic) adj ortopedico(-a)
osteopath ['ɒstɪəpæθ] n specialista
m/f di osteopatia
ostrich ['ɒstrɪtʃ] n struzzo
other ['ʌðəʳ] adj altro(-a) ▶ pron **the
~ (one)** l'altro(-a); **~s** (other people)
altri mpl; **~ than** altro che; a parte;
otherwise adv, conj altrimenti
otter ['ɒtəʳ] n lontra
ouch [autʃ] excl ohi!, ahi!
ought [ɔːt] (pt **ought**) aux vb **I ~ to do
it** dovrei farlo; **this ~ to have been
corrected** questo avrebbe dovuto
essere corretto; **he ~ to win** dovrebbe
vincere
ounce [auns] n oncia (=28.35 g, 16 in
a pound)
our ['auəʳ] adj il (la) nostro(-a); (pl) i (le)
nostri(-e); see also **my**; **ours** pron il (la)
nostro(-a); (pl) i (le) nostri(-e); see also
mine; **ourselves** pron pl (reflexive) ci;
(after preposition) noi; (emphatic) noi
stessi(-e); see also **oneself**
oust [aust] vt cacciare, espellere

out [aut] adv (gen) fuori; **~ here/there**
qui/là fuori; **to speak ~ loud** parlare
forte; **to have a night ~** uscire una
sera; **the boat was 10 km ~** la barca
era a 10 km dalla costa; **3 days ~ from
Plym~h** a 3 giorni da Plymouth; **~ of**
(outside) fuori di; (because of) per; **~ of
10** su 10; **~ of petrol** senza benzina;
outback ['autbæk] n (in Australia)
interno, entroterra; **outbound** adj
outbound (for or **from)** in partenza
(per or da); **outbreak** ['autbreɪk] n
scoppio; epidemia; **outburst**
['autbəːst] n scoppio; **outcast**
['autkɑːst] n esule m/f; (socially)
paria m inv; **outcome** ['autkʌm] n
esito, risultato; **outcry** ['autkraɪ]
n protesta, clamore m; **outdated**
[aut'deɪtɪd] adj (custom, clothes) fuori
moda; (idea) sorpassato(-a); **outdoor**
[aut'dɔːʳ] adj all'aperto; **outdoors** adv
fuori; all'aria aperta
outer ['autəʳ] adj esteriore; **outer
space** n spazio cosmico
outfit ['autfɪt] n (clothes) completo;
(: for sport) tenuta
out: **outgoing** ['autgəuɪŋ] adj
(character) socievole; **outgoings**
(BRIT) npl (expenses) spese fpl,
uscite fpl; **outhouse** ['authaus] n
costruzione f annessa
outing ['autɪŋ] n gita; escursione f
out: **outlaw** ['autlɔː] n fuorilegge
m/f ▶ vt bandire; **outlay** ['autleɪ] n
spese fpl; (investment) sborsa, spesa;
outlet ['autlɛt] n (for liquid etc) sbocco,
scarico; (US Elec) presa di corrente;
(also: **retail outlet**) punto di vendita;
outline ['autlaɪn] n contorno, profilo;
(summary) abbozzo, grandi linee fpl
▶ vt (fig) descrivere a grandi linee;
outlook ['autluk] n prospettiva,
vista; **outnumber** [aut'nʌmbəʳ] vt
superare in numero; **out-of-date** adj
(passport) scaduto(-a); (clothes) fuori

moda *inv*; **out-of-doors** [autəv'dɔːz] *adv* all'aperto; **out-of-the-way** *adj* (*place*) fuori mano *inv*; **out-of-town** [autəv'taun] *adj* (*shopping centre etc*) fuori città; **outpatient** ['autpeɪʃənt] *n* paziente *m/f* esterno(-a); **outpost** ['autpəust] *n* avamposto; **output** ['autput] *n* produzione f; (*Comput*) output *m inv*

outrage ['autreɪdʒ] *n* oltraggio; scandalo ▶ *vt* oltraggiare; **outrageous** [-'reɪdʒəs] *adj* oltraggioso(-a), scandaloso(-a)

outright [*adv* aut'raɪt, *adj* 'autraɪt] *adv* completamente; schiettamente; apertamente; sul colpo ▶ *adj* completo(-a), schietto(-a) e netto(-a)

outset ['autset] *n* inizio

outside [aut'saɪd] *n* esterno, esteriore *m* ▶ *adj* esterno(-a), esteriore ▶ *adv* fuori, all'esterno ▶ *prep* fuori di, all'esterno di; **at the ~** (*fig*) al massimo; **outside lane** *n* (*Aut*) corsia di sorpasso; **outside line** *n* (*Tel*) linea esterna; **outsider** *n* (*in race etc*) outsider *m inv*; (*stranger*) estraneo(-a)

out: **outsize** ['autsaɪz] *adj* (*clothes*) per taglie forti; **outskirts** ['autskə:ts] *npl* sobborghi *mpl*; **outspoken** [aut'spəukən] *adj* molto franco(-a); **outstanding** [aut'stændɪŋ] *adj* eccezionale, di rilievo; (*unfinished*) non completo(-a); non evaso(-a); non regolato(-a)

outward ['autwəd] *adj* (*sign*, *appearances*) esteriore; (*journey*) d'andata; **outwards** ['autwədz] *adv* (*esp BRIT*) = **outward**

outweigh [aut'weɪ] *vt* avere maggior peso di

oval ['əuvl] *adj* ovale ▶ *n* ovale *m*

ovary ['əuvərɪ] *n* ovaia

oven ['ʌvn] *n* forno; **oven glove** *n* guanto da forno; **ovenproof** *adj* da forno; **oven-ready** *adj* pronto(-a) da infornare

over ['əuvə'] *adv* al di sopra ▶ *adj* (*or adv*) (*finished*) finito(-a), terminato(-a); (*too*) troppo; (*remaining*) che avanza ▶ *prep* su; sopra; (*above*) al di sopra di; (*on the other side of*) di là di; (*more than*) più di; (*during*) durante; **~ here** qui; **~ there** là; **all ~** (*everywhere*) dappertutto; (*finished*) tutto(-a) finito(-a); **~ and ~ (again)** più e più volte; **~ and above** oltre (a); **to ask sb ~** invitare qn (a passare)

overall [*adj*, *n* 'əuvərɔːl, *adv* əuvər'ɔːl] *adj* totale ▶ *n* (*BRIT*) grembiule *m* ▶ *adv* nell'insieme, complessivamente; **~s** *npl* (*worker's overalls*) tuta (da lavoro)

overboard ['əuvəbɔːd] *adv* (*Naut*) fuori bordo, in mare

overcame [əuvə'keɪm] *pt of* **overcome**

overcast ['əuvəkɑːst] *adj* (*sky*) coperto(-a)

overcharge [əuvə'tʃɑːdʒ] *vt* **to ~ sb for sth** far pagare troppo caro a qn per qc

overcoat ['əuvəkəut] *n* soprabito, cappotto

overcome [əuvə'kʌm] (*irreg*) *vt* superare; sopraffare

over: **overcrowded** [əuvə'kraudɪd] *adj* sovraffollato(-a); **overdo** [əuvə'duː] (*irreg*) *vt* esagerare; (*overcook*) cuocere troppo; **overdone** [əuvə'dʌn] *adj* troppo cotto(-a); **overdose** ['əuvədəus] *n* dose f eccessiva; **overdraft** ['əuvədrɑːft] *n* scoperto (di conto); **overdrawn** [əuvə'drɔːn] *adj* (*account*) scoperto(-a); **overdue** [əuvə'djuː] *adj* in ritardo; **overestimate** [əuvər'estɪmeɪt] *vt* sopravvalutare

overflow [*vb* əuvə'fləu, *n* 'əuvəfləu] *vi* traboccare ▶ *n* (*also*: **~ pipe**) troppopieno

overgrown [əuvə'grəun] *adj* (*garden*)

ricoperto(-a) di vegetazione
overhaul [vb əuvə'hɔːl, n 'əuvəhɔːl] vt
revisionare ▶ n revisione f
overhead [adv əuvə'hɛd, adj,
n 'əuvəhɛd] adv di sopra ▶ adj
aereo(-a); (lighting) verticale ▶ n (US)
= **overheads**; **overhead projector**
n lavagna luminosa; **overheads** npl
spese fpl generali
over: **overhear** [əuvə'hɪəʳ] (irreg) vt
sentire (per caso); **overheat** [əuvə'hiːt]
vi (engine) surriscaldare; **overland** adj,
adv per via di terra; **overlap** [əuvə'læp]
vi sovrapporsi; **overleaf** [əuvə'liːf] adv
a tergo; **overload** [əuvə'ləud] vt
sovraccaricare; **overlook** [əuvə'luk]
vt (have view of) dare su; (miss)
trascurare; (forgive) passare sopra a
overnight [əuvə'naɪt] adv (happen)
durante la notte; (fig) tutto ad un
tratto ▶ adj di notte; **he stayed there
~** ci ha passato la notte; **overnight
bag** n borsa da viaggio
overpass ['əuvəpɑːs] n cavalcavia
m inv
overpower [əuvə'pauəʳ] vt sopraffare;
overpowering adj irresistibile; (heat,
stench) soffocante
over: **overreact** [əuvəriː'ækt] vi
reagire in modo esagerato; **overrule**
[əuvə'ruːl] vt (decision) annullare;
(claim) respingere; **overrun** [ə
uvə'rʌn] (irreg: like **run**) vt (country)
invadere; (time limit) superare
overseas [əuvə'siːz] adv oltremare;
(abroad) all'estero ▶ adj (trade)
estero(-a); (visitor) straniero(-a)
oversee [əuvə'siː] vt irreg sorvegliare
overshadow [əuvə'ʃædəu] vt far
ombra su; (fig) eclissare
oversight ['əuvəsaɪt] n omissione
f, svista
oversleep [əuvə'sliːp] (irreg) vt
dormire troppo a lungo
overspend [əuvə'spɛnd] vi irreg

spendere troppo; **we have overspent
by 5000 dollars** abbiamo speso 5000
dollari di troppo
overt [əu'vɜːt] adj palese
overtake [əuvə'teɪk] (irreg) vt
sorpassare
over: **overthrow** [əuvə'θrəu] (irreg) vt
(government) rovesciare; **overtime**
['əuvətaɪm] n (lavoro) straordinario
overtook [əuvə'tuk] pt of **overtake**
over: **overturn** [əuvə'tɜːn]
vt rovesciare ▶ vi rovesciarsi;
overweight [əuvə'weɪt] adj (person)
troppo grasso(-a); **overwhelm** [ə
uvə'wɛlm] vt sopraffare; sommergere;
schiacciare; **overwhelming** adj
(victory, defeat) schiacciante; (heat,
desire) intenso(-a)
ow [əu] excl ahi!
owe [əu] vt **to ~ sb sth, to ~ sth to
sb** dovere qc a qn; **how much do I ~
you?** quanto le devo?; **owing to** prep
a causa di
owl [aul] n gufo
own [əun] vt possedere ▶ adj
proprio(-a); **a room of my ~** la mia
propria camera; **to get one's ~ back**
vendicarsi; **on one's ~** tutto(-a)
solo(-a) ▷ **own up** vi confessare;
owner n proprietario(-a); **ownership**
n possesso
ox [ɔks] (pl **oxen**) n bue m
Oxbridge ['ɔksbrɪdʒ] n le università di
Oxford e/o Cambridge
oxen ['ɔksn] npl of **ox**
oxygen ['ɔksɪdʒən] n ossigeno
oyster ['ɔɪstəʳ] n ostrica
oz. abbr = **ounce(s)**
ozone ['əuzəun] n ozono; **ozone
friendly** adj che non danneggia
l'ozono; **ozone layer** n fascia d'ozono

p

p [piː] *abbr* = **penny**; **pence**

P.A. *n abbr* = **personal assistant**; **public address system**

p.a. *abbr* = **per annum**

pace [peɪs] *n* passo; (*speed*) passo; velocità ▶ *vi* **to ~ up and down** camminare su e giù; **to keep ~ with** camminare di pari passo a; (*events*) tenersi al corrente di; **pacemaker** *n* (*Med*) segnapasso; (*Sport: also:* **pace setter**) battistrada *m inv*

Pacific [pə'sɪfɪk] *n* **the ~** (*Ocean*) il Pacifico, l'Oceano Pacifico

pacifier ['pæsɪfaɪə^r] (*US*) *n* (*dummy*) succhiotto, ciuccio (*col*)

pack [pæk] *n* pacco; (*US: of cigarettes*) pacchetto; (*backpack*) zaino; (*of hounds*) muta; (*of thieves etc*) banda; (*of cards*) mazzo ▶ *vt* (*in suitcase etc*) mettere; (*box*) riempire; (*cram*) stipare, pigiare; **to ~ (one's bags)** fare la valigia; **to ~ sb off** spedire via qn; **~ it in!** (*inf*) dacci un taglio! ▷ **pack in** (*BRIT inf*) *vi* (*watch, car*) guastarsi ▶ *vt* mollare, piantare; **~ it in!** piantala! ▷ **pack up** *vi* (*BRIT inf: machine*) guastarsi; (: *person*) far fagotto ▶ *vt* (*belongings, clothes*) mettere in una valigia; (*goods, presents*) imballare

package ['pækɪdʒ] *n* pacco; balla; (*also:* **~ deal**) pacchetto; forfait *m inv*; **package holiday** *n* vacanza organizzata; **package tour** *n* viaggio organizzato

packaging ['pækɪdʒɪŋ] *n* confezione *f*, imballo

packed [pækt] *adj* (*crowded*) affollato(-a); **packed lunch** *n* pranzo al sacco

packet ['pækɪt] *n* pacchetto

packing ['pækɪŋ] *n* imballaggio

pact [pækt] *n* patto, accordo; trattato

pad [pæd] *n* blocco; (*to prevent friction*) cuscinetto; (*inf: flat*) appartamentino ▶ *vt* imbottire; **padded** *adj* imbottito(-a)

paddle ['pædl] *n* (*oar*) pagaia; (*US: for table tennis*) racchetta da ping-pong ▶ *vi* sguazzare ▶ *vt* **to ~ a canoe** *etc* vogare con la pagaia; **paddling pool** (*BRIT*) *n* piscina per bambini

paddock ['pædək] *n* prato recintato; (*at racecourse*) paddock *m inv*

padlock ['pædlɔk] *n* lucchetto

paedophile ['piːdəufaɪl] (*US* **pedophile**) *adj, n* pedofilo(-a)

page [peɪdʒ] *n* pagina; (*also:* **~ boy**) paggio ▶ *vt* (*in hotel etc*) (far) chiamare

pager ['peɪdʒə^r] *n* (*Tel*) cercapersone *m inv*

paid [peɪd] *pt, pp of* **pay** ▶ *adj* (*work, official*) rimunerato(-a); **to put ~ to** (*BRIT*) mettere fine a

pain [peɪn] *n* dolore *m*; **to be in ~** soffrire, aver male; **to take ~s to do** mettercela tutta per fare; **painful** *adj* doloroso(-a), che fa male; difficile, penoso(-a); **painkiller** *n* antalgico, antidolorifico; **painstaking** ['peɪnzteɪkɪŋ] *adj* (*person*) sollecito(-a); (*work*) accurato(-a)

paint [peɪnt] *n* vernice *f*, colore *m* ▶ *vt* dipingere; (*walls, door etc*) verniciare; **to ~ the door blue** verniciare la porta di azzurro; **paintbrush** *n* pennello; **painter** *n* (*artist*) pittore *m*; (*decorator*) imbianchino; **painting** *n* pittura; (*picture*) dipinto, quadro

pair [pɛə^r] *n* (*of shoes, gloves etc*) paio;

(*of people*) coppia; duo *m inv*; **a ~ of scissors/trousers** un paio di forbici/pantaloni

pajamas [pɪˈdʒɑːməz] (*US*) *npl* pigiama *m*

Pakistan [pɑːkɪˈstɑːn] *n* Pakistan *m*; **Pakistani** *adj, n* pakistano(-a)

pal [pæl] (*inf*) *n* amico(-a), compagno(-a)

palace [ˈpæləs] *n* palazzo

pale [peɪl] *adj* pallido(-a) ▶ *n* **to be beyond the ~** aver oltrepassato ogni limite

Palestine [ˈpælɪstaɪn] *n* Palestina; **Palestinian** [-ˈtɪnɪən] *adj, n* palestinese *m/f*

palm [pɑːm] *n* (*Anat*) palma, palmo; (*also:* **~ tree**) palma ▶ *vt* **to ~ sth off on sb** (*inf*) rifilare qc a qn

pamper [ˈpæmpəʳ] *vt* viziare, coccolare

pamphlet [ˈpæmflət] *n* dépliant *m inv*

pan [pæn] *n* (*also:* **sauce~**) casseruola; (*also:* **frying ~**) padella

pancake [ˈpænkeɪk] *n* frittella

panda [ˈpændə] *n* panda *m inv*

pane [peɪn] *n* vetro

panel [ˈpænl] *n* (*of wood, cloth etc*) pannello; (*Radio, TV*) giuria

panhandler [ˈpænhændləʳ] (*US*) *n* (*inf*) accattone(-a)

panic [ˈpænɪk] *n* panico ▶ *vi* perdere il sangue freddo

panorama [pænəˈrɑːmə] *n* panorama *m*

pansy [ˈpænzɪ] *n* (*Bot*) viola del pensiero, pensée *f inv*; (*inf: pej*) femminuccia

pant [pænt] *vi* ansare

panther [ˈpænθəʳ] *n* pantera

panties [ˈpæntɪz] *npl* slip *m*, mutandine *fpl*

pantomime [ˈpæntəmaɪm] (*BRIT*) *n* pantomima

- **pantomime**
- In Gran Bretagna la **pantomime** è

- una sorta di libera interpretazione
- delle favole più conosciute, che
- vengono messe in scena a teatro
- durante il periodo natalizio. È uno
- spettacolo per tutta la famiglia
- che prevede la partecipazione del
- pubblico.

pants [pænts] *npl* mutande *fpl*; slip *m*; (*US: trousers*) pantaloni *mpl*

paper [ˈpeɪpəʳ] *n* carta; (*also:* **wall~**) carta da parati, tappezzeria; (*also:* **news~**) giornale *m*; (*study, article*) saggio; (*exam*) prova scritta ▶ *adj* di carta ▶ *vt* tappezzare; **~s** *npl* (*also:* **identity ~s**) carte *fpl*, documenti *mpl*; **paperback** *n* tascabile *m*; edizione *f* economica; **paper bag** *n* sacchetto di carta; **paper clip** *n* graffetta, clip *f inv*; **paper shop** *n* (*BRIT*) giornalaio (*negozio*); **paperwork** *n* lavoro amministrativo

paprika [ˈpæprɪkə] *n* paprica

par [pɑːʳ] *n* parità, pari *f*; (*Golf*) norma; **on a ~ with** alla pari con

paracetamol [pærəˈsiːtəmɔl] (*BRIT*) *n* paracetamolo

parachute [ˈpærəʃuːt] *n* paracadute *m inv*

parade [pəˈreɪd] *n* parata ▶ *vt* (*fig*) fare sfoggio di ▶ *vi* sfilare in parata

paradise [ˈpærədaɪs] *n* paradiso

paradox [ˈpærədɔks] *n* paradosso

paraffin [ˈpærəfɪn] (*BRIT*) *n* **~ (oil)** paraffina

paragraph [ˈpærəgrɑːf] *n* paragrafo

parallel [ˈpærəlɛl] *adj* parallelo(-a); (*fig*) analogo(-a) ▶ *n* (*line*) parallela; (*fig, Geo*) parallelo

paralysed [ˈpærəlaɪzd] *adj* paralizzato(-a)

paralysis [pəˈrælɪsɪs] *n* paralisi *f inv*

paramedic [pærəˈmɛdɪk] *n* paramedico

paranoid [ˈpærənɔɪd] *adj* paranoico(-a)

parasite ['pærəsaɪt] n parassita m
parcel ['pɑːsl] n pacco, pacchetto ▶ vt (also: ~ up) impaccare
pardon ['pɑːdn] n perdono; grazia ▶ vt perdonare; (Law) graziare; ~ me! mi scusi!; I beg your ~! scusi!; I beg your ~? (BRIT), ~ me? (US) prego?
parent ['pɛərənt] n genitore m; ~s npl (mother and father) genitori mpl; **parental** [pə'rɛntl] adj dei genitori
▌ Be careful not to translate **parent** by the Italian word **parente**.
Paris ['pærɪs] n Parigi f
parish ['pærɪʃ] n parrocchia; (BRIT: civil) ≈ municipio
Parisian [pə'rɪzɪən] adj, n parigino(-a)
park [pɑːk] n parco ▶ vt, vi parcheggiare; **can I ~ here?** posso parcheggiare qui?
parking ['pɑːkɪŋ] n parcheggio; "**no ~**" "sosta vietata"; **parking lot** (US) n posteggio, parcheggio; **parking meter** n parchimetro; **parking ticket** n multa per sosta vietata
parkway ['pɑːkweɪ] (US) n viale m
parliament ['pɑːləmənt] n parlamento; **parliamentary** [pɑːlə'mɛntərɪ] adj parlamentare
Parmesan [pɑːmɪ'zæn] n (also: ~ cheese) parmigiano
parole [pə'rəʊl] n on ~ in libertà per buona condotta
parrot ['pærət] n pappagallo
parsley ['pɑːslɪ] n prezzemolo
parsnip ['pɑːsnɪp] n pastinaca
parson ['pɑːsn] n prete m; (Church of England) parroco
part [pɑːt] n parte f; (of machine) pezzo; (US: in hair) scriminatura ▶ adj in parte ▶ adv = **partly** ▶ vt separare ▶ vi (people) separarsi; **to take ~ in** prendere parte a; **for my ~** per parte mia; **to take sth in good ~** prendere bene qc; **to take sb's ~** parteggiare per or prendere le parti di qn; **for the**

most ~ in generale; nella maggior parte dei casi ▷ **part with** vt fus separarsi da; rinunciare a
partial ['pɑːʃl] adj parziale; **to be ~ to** avere un debole per
participant [pɑː'tɪsɪpənt] n ~ (in) partecipante m/f (a)
participate [pɑː'tɪsɪpeɪt] vi to ~ (in) prendere parte (a), partecipare (a)
particle ['pɑːtɪkl] n particella
particular [pə'tɪkjʊləʳ] adj particolare; speciale; (fussy) difficile; meticoloso(-a); **in ~** in particolare, particolarmente; **particularly** adv particolarmente; in particolare; **particulars** npl particolari mpl, dettagli mpl; (information) informazioni fpl
parting ['pɑːtɪŋ] n separazione f; (BRIT: in hair) scriminatura ▶ adj d'addio
partition [pɑː'tɪʃən] n (Pol) partizione f; (wall) tramezzo
partly ['pɑːtlɪ] adv parzialmente; in parte
partner ['pɑːtnəʳ] n (Comm) socio(-a); (wife, husband etc, Sport) compagno(-a); (at dance) cavaliere/ dama; **partnership** n associazione f; (Comm) società f inv
part of speech n parte f del discorso
partridge ['pɑːtrɪdʒ] n pernice f
part-time ['pɑːt'taɪm] adj, adv a orario ridotto
party ['pɑːtɪ] n (Pol) partito; (group) gruppo; (Law) parte f; (celebration) ricevimento; serata; festa ▶ cpd (Pol) del partito, di partito
pass [pɑːs] vt (gen) passare; (place) passare davanti a; (exam) passare, superare; (candidate) promuovere; (overtake, surpass) sorpassare, superare; (approve) approvare ▶ vi passare ▶ n (permit) lasciapassare m inv; permesso; (in mountains) passo,

gola; (*Sport*) passaggio; (*Scol*): **to get a ~** prendere la sufficienza; **could you ~ the salt/oil, please?** mi passa il sale/l'olio, per favore?; **to ~ sth through a hole** *etc* far passare qc attraverso un buco *etc*; **to make a ~ at sb** (*inf*) fare delle proposte *or* delle avances a qn ▷ **pass away** *vi* morire ▷ **pass by** *vi* passare ▶ *vt* trascurare ▷ **pass on** *vt* passare ▷ **pass out** *vi* svenire ▷ **pass over** *vi* (*die*) spirare ▶ *vt* lasciare da parte ▷ **pass up** *vt* (*opportunity*) lasciarsi sfuggire, perdere; **passable** *adj* (*road*) praticabile; (*work*) accettabile

passage ['pæsɪdʒ] *n* (*gen*) passaggio; (*also:* **~way**) corridoio; (*in book*) brano, passo; (*by boat*) traversata

passenger ['pæsɪndʒəʳ] *n* passeggero(-a)

passer-by [pɑːsə'baɪ] *n* passante *m/f*

passing place *n* (*Aut*) piazzola di sosta

passion ['pæʃən] *n* passione *f*; amore *m*; **passionate** *adj* appassionato(-a); **passion fruit** *n* frutto della passione

passive ['pæsɪv] *adj* (*also Ling*) passivo(-a)

passport ['pɑːspɔːt] *n* passaporto; **passport control** *n* controllo *m* passaporti *inv*; **passport office** *n* ufficio *m*, passaporti *inv*

password ['pɑːswəːd] *n* parola d'ordine

past [pɑːst] *prep* (*further than*) oltre, di là di; dopo; (*later than*) dopo ▶ *adj* passato(-a); (*president etc*) ex *inv* ▶ *n* passato; **he's ~ forty** ha più di quarant'anni; **ten ~ eight** le otto e dieci; **for the ~ few days** da qualche giorno; in questi ultimi giorni; **to run ~** passare di corsa

pasta ['pæstə] *n* pasta

paste [peɪst] *n* (*glue*) colla; (*Culin*) pâté *m inv*; pasta ▶ *vt* collare

pastel ['pæstl] *adj* pastello *inv*

pasteurized ['pæstəraɪzd] *adj* pastorizzato(-a)

pastime ['pɑːstaɪm] *n* passatempo

pastor ['pɑːstəʳ] *n* pastore *m*

past participle [-'pɑːtɪsɪpl] *n* (*Ling*) participio passato

pastry ['peɪstrɪ] *n* pasta

pasture ['pɑːstʃəʳ] *n* pascolo

pasty¹ ['pæstɪ] *n* pasticcio di carne

pasty² ['peɪstɪ] *adj* (*face etc*) smorto(-a)

pat [pæt] *vt* accarezzare, dare un colpetto (affettuoso) a

patch [pætʃ] *n* (*of material, on tyre*) toppa; (*eye patch*) benda; (*spot*) macchia ▶ *vt* (*clothes*) rattoppare; **(to go through) a bad ~** (attraversare) un brutto periodo; **patchy** *adj* irregolare

pâté ['pæteɪ] *n* pâté *m inv*

patent ['peɪtnt] *n* brevetto ▶ *vt* brevettare ▶ *adj* patente, manifesto(-a)

paternal [pə'təːnl] *adj* paterno(-a)

paternity leave [pə'təːnɪtɪ-] *n* congedo di paternità

path [pɑːθ] *n* sentiero, viottolo; viale *m*; (*fig*) via, strada; (*of planet, missile*) traiettoria

pathetic [pə'θɛtɪk] *adj* (*pitiful*) patetico(-a); (*very bad*) penoso(-a)

pathway ['pɑːθweɪ] *n* sentiero

patience ['peɪʃns] *n* pazienza; (*BRIT Cards*) solitario

patient ['peɪʃnt] *n* paziente *m/f*, malato(-a) ▶ *adj* paziente

patio ['pætɪəʊ] *n* terrazza

patriotic [pætrɪ'ɔtɪk] *adj* patriottico(-a)

patrol [pə'trəʊl] *n* pattuglia ▶ *vt* pattugliare; **patrol car** *n* autoradio *f inv* (della polizia)

patron ['peɪtrən] *n* (*in shop*) cliente *m/f*; (*of charity*) benefattore(-trice); **~ of the arts** mecenate *m/f*

patronizing ['pætrənaɪzɪŋ] *adj*

condiscendente

pattern ['pætən] n modello; (design) disegno, motivo; **patterned** adj a disegni, a motivi; (material) fantasia inv

pause [pɔːz] n pausa ▶ vi fare una pausa, arrestarsi

pave [peɪv] vt pavimentare; **to ~ the way for** aprire la via a

pavement ['peɪvmənt] (BRIT) n marciapiede m

> Be careful not to translate **pavement** by the Italian word pavimento.

pavilion [pə'vɪlɪən] n (Sport) edificio annesso a campo sportivo

paving ['peɪvɪŋ] n pavimentazione f

paw [pɔː] n zampa

pawn [pɔːn] n (Chess) pedone m; (fig) pedina ▶ vt dare in pegno; **pawn broker** n prestatore m su pegno

pay [peɪ] (pt, pp **paid**) n stipendio; paga ▶ vt pagare ▶ vi (be profitable) rendere; **can I ~ by credit card?** posso pagare con la carta di credito?; **to ~ attention (to)** fare attenzione (a); **to ~ sb a visit** far visita a qn; **to ~ one's respects to sb** porgere i propri rispetti a qn ▷ **pay back** vt rimborsare ▷ **pay for** vt fus pagare ▷ **pay in** vt versare ▷ **pay off** vt (debt) saldare; (person) pagare; (employee) pagare e licenziare ▶ vi (scheme, decision) dare dei frutti ▷ **pay out** vt (money) sborsare, tirar fuori; (rope) far allentare ▷ **pay up** vt saldare; **payable** adj pagabile; **pay day** n giorno di paga; **pay envelope** (US) n = **pay packet**; **payment** n pagamento; versamento; saldo; **payout** n pagamento; (in competition) premio; **pay packet** (BRIT) n busta f paga inv; **pay phone** n cabina telefonica; **payroll** n ruolo (organico); **pay slip** n foglio m paga inv; **pay television** n televisione f a

pagamento, pay-tv f inv

PC n abbr = **personal computer** ▶ adv abbr = **politically correct**

p.c. abbr = **per cent**

PDA n abbr (= personal digital assistant) PDA m inv

PE n abbr (= physical education) ed. fisica

pea [piː] n pisello

peace [piːs] n pace f; **peaceful** adj pacifico(-a), calmo(-a)

peach [piːtʃ] n pesca

peacock ['piːkɔk] n pavone m

peak [piːk] n (of mountain) cima, vetta; (mountain itself) picco; (of cap) visiera; (fig) apice m, culmine m; **peak hours** npl ore fpl di punta

peanut ['piːnʌt] n arachide f, nocciolina americana; **peanut butter** n burro di arachidi

pear [pɛəʳ] n pera

pearl [pəːl] n perla

peasant ['pɛznt] n contadino(-a)

peat [piːt] n torba

pebble ['pɛbl] n ciottolo

peck [pɛk] vt (also: ~ **at**) beccare ▶ n colpo di becco; (kiss) bacetto; **peckish** (BRIT: inf) adj **I feel peckish** ho un languorino

peculiar [pɪ'kjuːlɪəʳ] adj strano(-a), bizzarro(-a); peculiare; ~ **to** peculiare di

pedal ['pɛdl] n pedale m ▶ vi pedalare

pedalo ['pɛdələu] n pedalò m inv

pedestal ['pɛdəstl] n piedestallo

pedestrian [pɪ'dɛstrɪən] n pedone(-a) ▶ adj pedonale; (fig) prosaico(-a), pedestre; **pedestrian crossing** (BRIT) n passaggio pedonale; **pedestrianized** adj **a pedestrianized street** una zona pedonalizzata; **pedestrian precinct** (BRIT: US **pedestrian zone**) n zona pedonale

pedigree ['pɛdɪgriː] n (of animal) pedigree m inv; (fig) background m inv ▶ cpd (animal) di razza

pedophile ['pi:dəufaɪl] (US) n
= **paedophile**

pee [pi:] (inf) vi pisciare

peek [pi:k] vi guardare furtivamente

peel [pi:l] n buccia; (of orange, lemon)
scorza ▶ vt sbucciare ▶ vi (paint etc)
staccarsi

peep [pi:p] n (BRIT: look) sguardo
furtivo, sbirciata; (sound) pigolio ▶ vi
(BRIT) guardare furtivamente

peer [pɪəʳ] vi **to ~ at** scrutare ▶ n
(noble) pari m inv; (equal) pari
m/f inv, uguale m/f; (contemporary)
contemporaneo(-a)

peg [pɛg] n caviglia; (for coat etc)
attaccapanni m inv; (BRIT: also:
clothes ~) molletta

pelican ['pɛlɪkən] n pellicano; **pelican
crossing** (BRIT) n (Aut) attraversamento
pedonale con semaforo a controllo
manuale

pelt [pɛlt] vt **to ~ sb (with)**
bombardare qn (con) ▶ vi (rain)
piovere a dirotto; (inf: run) filare
▶ n pelle f

pelvis ['pɛlvɪs] n pelvi f inv, bacino

pen [pɛn] n penna; (for sheep) recinto

penalty ['pɛnltɪ] n penalità f inv;
sanzione f penale; (fine) ammenda;
(Sport) penalizzazione f

pence [pɛns] (BRIT) npl of **penny**

pencil ['pɛnsl] n matita ▶ **pencil in**
vt scrivere a matita; **pencil case**
n astuccio per matite; **pencil
sharpener** n temperamatite m inv

pendant ['pɛndnt] n pendaglio

pending ['pɛndɪŋ] prep in attesa di
▶ adj in sospeso

penetrate ['pɛnɪtreɪt] vt penetrare

penfriend ['pɛnfrɛnd] (BRIT) n
corrispondente m/f

penguin ['pɛŋgwɪn] n pinguino

penicillin [pɛnɪ'sɪlɪn] n penicillina

peninsula [pə'nɪnsjulə] n penisola

penis ['pi:nɪs] n pene m

penitentiary [pɛnɪ'tɛnʃərɪ] (US) n
carcere m

penknife ['pɛnnaɪf] n temperino

penniless ['pɛnɪlɪs] adj senza un soldo

penny ['pɛnɪ] (pl **pennies** or **pence**)
(BRIT) n penny m; (US) centesimo

penpal ['pɛnpæl] n
corrispondente m/f

pension ['pɛnʃən] n pensione f;
pensioner (BRIT) n pensionato(-a)

pentagon ['pɛntəgən] n pentagono;
the P~ (US Pol) il Pentagono

penthouse ['pɛnthaus] n
appartamento (di lusso) nell'attico

penultimate [pɪ'nʌltɪmət] adj
penultimo(-a)

people ['pi:pl] npl gente f; persone
fpl; (citizens) popolo ▶ n (nation,
race) popolo; **4/several ~ came**
4/parecchie persone sono venute;
~ say that ... si dice che ...

pepper ['pɛpəʳ] n pepe m; (vegetable)
peperone m ▶ vt (fig): **to ~ with**
spruzzare di; **peppermint** n (sweet)
pasticca di menta

per [pə:ʳ] prep per; a; **~ hour** all'ora;
~ kilo etc il chilo etc; **~ day** al giorno

perceive [pə'si:v] vt percepire; (notice)
accorgersi di

per cent adv per cento

percentage [pə'sɛntɪdʒ] n
percentuale f

perception [pə'sɛpʃən] n percezione f;
sensibilità; perspicacia

perch [pə:tʃ] n (fish) pesce m persico; (for
bird) sostegno, ramo ▶ vi appollaiarsi

percussion [pə'kʌʃən] n percussione
f; (Mus) strumenti mpl a percussione

perfect [adj, n 'pə:fɪkt, vb pə'fɛkt]
adj perfetto(-a) ▶ n (also: **~ tense**)
perfetto, passato prossimo ▶ vt
perfezionare; mettere a punto;
perfection [pə'fɛkʃən] n perfezione
f; **perfectly** adv perfettamente, alla
perfezione

perform [pə'fɔ:m] vt (carry out)
eseguire, fare; (symphony etc) suonare;
(play, ballet) dare; (opera) fare ▶ vi
suonare; recitare; **performance**
n esecuzione f; (at theatre etc)
rappresentazione f, spettacolo; (of an artist) interpretazione f; (of
player etc) performance f; (of car,
engine) prestazione f; **performer** n
artista m/f

perfume ['pə:fju:m] n profumo

perhaps [pə'hæps] adv forse

perimeter [pə'rımıtə'] n perimetro

period ['pıərıəd] n periodo; (History)
epoca; (Scol) lezione f; (full stop)
punto; (Med) mestruazioni fpl
▶ adj (costume, furniture) d'epoca;
periodical [-'ɔdıkl] n periodico;
periodically adv periodicamente

perish ['pɛrıʃ] vi perire, morire; (decay)
deteriorarsi

perjury ['pə:dʒərı] n spergiuro

perk [pə:k] (inf) n vantaggio

perm [pə:m] n (for hair) permanente f

permanent ['pə:mənənt] adj
permanente; **permanently** adv
definitivamente

permission [pə'mıʃən] n permesso

permit [n 'pə:mıt, vb pə'mıt] n
permesso ▶ vt permettere; **to ~ sb to
do** permettere a qn di fare

perplex [pə'plɛks] vt lasciare
perplesso(-a)

persecute ['pə:sıkju:t] vt
perseguitare

persecution [pə:sı'kju:ʃən] n
persecuzione f

persevere [pə:sı'vıə'] vi perseverare

Persian ['pə:ʃən] adj persiano(-a) ▶ n
(Ling) persiano; **the (~) Gulf** n il Golfo
Persico

persist [pə'sıst] vi **to ~ (in doing)**
persistere (nel fare); ostinarsi (a fare);
persistent adj persistente

person ['pə:sn] n persona; **in ~** di or In

persona, personalmente; **personal**
adj personale; individuale; **personal
assistant** n segretaria personale;
personal computer n personal
computer m inv; **personality**
[-'nælıtı] n personalità f inv;
personally adv personalmente;
to take sth personally prendere qc
come una critica personale;
personal organizer n (Filofax®)
Fulltime®; (electronic) agenda
elettronica; **personal stereo** n
Walkman® m inv

personnel [pə:sə'nɛl] n personale m

perspective [pə'spɛktıv] n
prospettiva

perspiration [pə:spı'reıʃən] n
traspirazione f, sudore m

persuade [pə'sweıd] vt **to ~ sb to do
sth** persuadere qn a fare qc

persuasion [pə'sweıʒən] n
persuasione f; (creed) convinzione
f, credo

persuasive [pə'sweısıv] adj
persuasivo(-a)

perverse [pə'və:s] adj perverso(-a)

pervert [n 'pə:və:t, vb pə'və:t] n
pervertito(-a) ▶ vt pervertire

pessimism ['pɛsımızəm] n
pessimismo

pessimist ['pɛsımıst] n pessimista
m/f; **pessimistic** [-'mıstık] adj
pessimistico(-a)

pest [pɛst] n animale m (or insetto)
pestifero; (fig) peste f

pester ['pɛstə'] vt tormentare,
molestare

pesticide ['pɛstısaıd] n pesticida m

pet [pɛt] n animale m domestico
▶ cpd favorito(-a) ▶ vt accarezzare;
teacher's ~ favorito(-a) del maestro

petal ['pɛtl] n petalo

petite [pə'ti:t] adj piccolo(-a) e
aggraziato(-a)

petition [pə'tıʃən] n petizione f

petrified ['pɛtrɪfaɪd] adj (fig) morto(-a) di paura

petrol ['pɛtrəl] (BRIT) n benzina; **two/four-star ~** ≈ benzina normale/super; **I've run out of ~** sono rimasto senza benzina

▌ Be careful not to translate **petrol** by the Italian word **petrolio**.

petroleum [pə'trəʊlɪəm] n petrolio

petrol: **petrol pump** (BRIT) n (in car, at garage) pompa di benzina; **petrol station** (BRIT) n stazione f di rifornimento; **petrol tank** (BRIT) n serbatoio della benzina

petticoat ['pɛtɪkəʊt] n sottana

petty ['pɛtɪ] adj (mean) meschino(-a); (unimportant) insignificante

pew [pju:] n panca (di chiesa)

pewter ['pju:təʳ] n peltro

phantom ['fæntəm] n fantasma m

pharmacist ['fɑ:məsɪst] n farmacista m/f

pharmacy ['fɑ:məsɪ] n farmacia

phase [feɪz] n fase f, periodo ▷ **phase in** vt introdurre gradualmente ▷ **phase out** vt (machinery) eliminare gradualmente; (product) ritirare gradualmente; (job, subsidy) abolire gradualmente

Ph.D. n abbr = **Doctor of Philosophy**

pheasant ['fɛznt] n fagiano

phenomena [fə'nɔmɪnə] npl of **phenomenon**

phenomenal [fɪ'nɔmɪnl] adj fenomenale

phenomenon [fə'nɔmɪnən] (pl **phenomena**) n fenomeno

Philippines ['fɪlɪpi:nz] npl **the ~** le Filippine

philosopher [fɪ'lɔsəfəʳ] n filosofo(-a)

philosophical [fɪlə'sɔfɪkl] adj filosofico(-a)

philosophy [fɪ'lɔsəfɪ] n filosofia

phlegm [flɛm] n flemma

phobia ['fəʊbjə] n fobia

phone [fəʊn] n telefono ▶ vt telefonare; **to be on the ~** avere il telefono; (be calling) essere al telefono ▷ **phone back** vt, vi richiamare ▷ **phone up** vt telefonare a ▶ vi telefonare; **phone book** n guida del telefono, elenco telefonico; **phone booth** n = **phone box**; **phone box** n cabina telefonica; **phone call** n telefonata; **phonecard** n scheda telefonica; **phone number** n numero di telefono

phonetics [fə'nɛtɪks] n fonetica

phoney ['fəʊnɪ] adj falso(-a), fasullo(-a)

photo ['fəʊtəʊ] n foto f inv

photo... ['fəʊtəʊ] prefix: **photo album** n (new) album m inv per fotografie; (containing photos) album m inv delle fotografie; **photocopier** n fotocopiatrice f; **photocopy** n fotocopia ▶ vt fotocopiare

photograph ['fəʊtəgræf] n fotografia ▶ vt fotografare; **photographer** [fə'tɔgrəfəʳ] n fotografo; **photography** [fə'tɔgrəfɪ] n fotografia

phrase [freɪz] n espressione f; (Ling) locuzione f; (Mus) frase f ▶ vt esprimere; **phrase book** n vocabolarietto

physical ['fɪzɪkl] adj fisico(-a); **physical education** n educazione f fisica; **physically** adv fisicamente

physician [fɪ'zɪʃən] n medico

physicist ['fɪzɪsɪst] n fisico

physics ['fɪzɪks] n fisica

physiotherapist [fɪzɪəʊ'θɛrəpɪst] n fisioterapista m/f

physiotherapy [fɪzɪəʊ'θɛrəpɪ] n fisioterapia

physique [fɪ'zi:k] n fisico; costituzione f

pianist ['pi:ənɪst] n pianista m/f

piano [pɪ'ænəʊ] n pianoforte m

pick [pɪk] n (tool: also: **~-axe**) piccone

m ▶ vt scegliere; (gather) cogliere; (remove) togliere; (lock) far scattare; **take your ~** scelga; **the ~ of** il fior fiore di; **to ~ one's nose** mettersi le dita nel naso; **to ~ one's teeth** pulirsi i denti con lo stuzzicadenti; **to ~ a quarrel** attaccar briga ▷ **pick on** vt fus (person) avercela con ▷ **pick out** vt scegliere; (distinguish) distinguere ▷ **pick up** vi (improve) migliorarsi ▶ vt raccogliere; (Police, Radio) prendere; (collect) passare a prendere; (Aut: give lift to) far salire; (person: for sexual encounter) rimorchiare; (learn) imparare; **to ~ up speed** acquistare velocità; **to ~ o.s. up** rialzarsi

pickle ['pɪkl] n (also: ~**s**: as condiment) sottaceti mpl; (fig: mess) pasticcio ▶ vt mettere sottaceto; mettere in salamoia

pickpocket ['pɪkpɔkɪt] n borsaiolo

pick-up ['pɪkʌp] n (BRIT: on record player) pick-up m inv; (small truck: also: ~ **truck**, ~ **van**) camioncino

picnic ['pɪknɪk] n picnic m inv; **picnic area** n area per il picnic

picture ['pɪktʃər] n quadro; (painting) pittura; (photograph) foto(grafia); (drawing) disegno; (film) film m inv ▶ vt raffigurarsi; ~**s** (BRIT) npl cinema; **the ~s** il cinema; **would you take a ~ of us, please?** può farci una foto, per favore?; **picture frame** n cornice m inv; **picture messaging** n picture messaging m, invio di messaggini con disegni

picturesque [pɪktʃə'rɛsk] adj pittoresco(-a)

pie [paɪ] n torta; (of meat) pasticcio

piece [piːs] n pezzo; (of land) appezzamento; (item): **a ~ of furniture/advice** un mobile/consiglio ▶ vt **to ~ together** mettere insieme; **to take to ~s** smontare

pie chart n grafico a torta

pier [pɪər] n molo; (of bridge etc) pila

pierce [pɪəs] vt forare; (with arrow etc) trafiggere; **pierced** adj **I've got pierced ears** ho i buchi per gli orecchini

pig [pɪg] n maiale m, porco

pigeon ['pɪdʒən] n piccione m

piggy bank ['pɪgɪ-] n salvadanaro

pigsty ['pɪgstaɪ] n porcile m

pigtail ['pɪgteɪl] n treccina

pike [paɪk] n (fish) luccio

pilchard ['pɪltʃəd] n specie di sardina

pile [paɪl] n (pillar, of books) pila; (heap) mucchio; (of carpet) pelo; **to ~ into** (car) stiparsi or ammucchiarsi in ▷ **pile up** vt ammucchiare ▶ vi ammucchiarsi; **piles** [paɪlz] npl emorroidi fpl; **pile-up** ['paɪlʌp] n (Aut) tamponamento a catena

pilgrimage ['pɪlgrɪmɪdʒ] n pellegrinaggio

pill [pɪl] n pillola; **the ~** la pillola

pillar ['pɪlər] n colonna

pillow ['pɪləu] n guanciale m; **pillowcase** n federa

pilot ['paɪlət] n pilota m/f ▷ cpd (scheme etc) pilota inv ▶ vt pilotare; **pilot light** n fiamma pilota

pimple ['pɪmpl] n foruncolo

pin [pɪn] n spillo; (Tech) perno ▶ vt attaccare con uno spillo; ~**s and needles** formicolio; **to ~ sb down** (fig) obbligare qn a pronunziarsi; **to ~ sth on sb** (fig) addossare la colpa di qc a qn

PIN n abbr (= personal identification number) codice m segreto

pinafore ['pɪnəfɔːr] n (also: ~ **dress**) grembiule m (senza maniche)

pinch [pɪntʃ] n pizzicotto, pizzico ▶ vt pizzicare; (inf: steal) grattare; **at a ~** in caso di bisogno

pine [paɪn] n (also: ~ **tree**) pino ▶ vi **to ~ for** struggersi dal desiderio di

pineapple ['paɪnæpl] n ananas m inv

ping [pɪŋ] n (noise) tintinnio; **ping-pong®** n ping-pong® m

pink [pɪŋk] adj rosa inv ▸ n (colour) rosa m inv; (Bot) garofano

pinpoint ['pɪnpɔɪnt] vt indicare con precisione

pint [paɪnt] n pinta (BRIT = 0.57l; US = 0.47l); (BRIT: inf) ≈ birra da mezzo

pioneer [paɪə'nɪəʳ] n pioniere(-a)

pious ['paɪəs] adj pio(-a)

pip [pɪp] n (seed) seme m; (BRIT: time signal on radio) segnale m orario

pipe [paɪp] n tubo; (for smoking) pipa ▸ vt portare per mezzo di tubazione; **pipeline** n conduttura; (for oil) oleodotto; **piper** n piffero; suonatore(-trice) di cornamusa

pirate ['paɪərət] n pirata m ▸ vt riprodurre abusivamente

Pisces ['paɪsiːz] n Pesci mpl

piss [pɪs] (inf) vi pisciare; **pissed** (inf) adj (drunk) ubriaco(-a) fradicio(-a)

pistol ['pɪstl] n pistola

piston ['pɪstən] n pistone m

pit [pɪt] n buca, fossa; (also: **coal ~**) miniera; (quarry) cava ▸ vt **to ~ sb against sb** opporre qn a qn

pitch [pɪtʃ] n (BRIT Sport) campo; (Mus) tono; (tar) pece f; (fig) grado, punto ▸ vt (throw) lanciare ▸ vi (fall) cascare; **to ~ a tent** piantare una tenda; **pitch-black** adj nero(-a) come la pece

pitfall ['pɪtfɔːl] n trappola

pith [pɪθ] n (of plant) midollo; (of orange) parte f interna della scorza; (fig) essenza, succo; vigore m

pitiful ['pɪtɪful] adj (touching) pietoso(-a)

pity ['pɪtɪ] n pietà ▸ vt aver pietà di; **what a ~!** che peccato!

pizza ['piːtsə] n pizza

placard ['plækɑːd] n affisso

place [pleɪs] n posto, luogo; (proper position, rank, seat) posto; (house) casa, alloggio; (home): **at/to his ~** a casa sua ▸ vt (object) posare, mettere; (identify)

riconoscere; individuare; **to take ~** aver luogo; succedere; **to change ~s with sb** scambiare il posto con qn; **out of ~** (not suitable) inopportuno(-a); **in the first ~** in primo luogo; **to ~ an order** dare un'ordinazione; **to be ~d** (in race, exam) classificarsi; **place mat** n sottopiatto; (in linen etc) tovaglietta; **placement** n collocamento; (job) lavoro

placid ['plæsɪd] adj placido(-a), calmo(-a)

plague [pleɪg] n peste f ▸ vt tormentare

plaice [pleɪs] n inv pianuzza

plain [pleɪn] adj (clear) chiaro(-a), palese; (simple) semplice; (frank) franco(-a), aperto(-a); (not handsome) bruttino(-a); (without seasoning etc) scondito(-a); naturale; (in one colour) tinta unita inv ▸ adv francamente, chiaramente ▸ n pianura; **plain chocolate** n cioccolato fondente; **plainly** adv chiaramente; (frankly) francamente

plaintiff ['pleɪntɪf] n attore(-trice)

plait [plæt] n treccia

plan [plæn] n pianta; (scheme) progetto, piano ▸ vt (think in advance) progettare; (prepare) organizzare ▸ vi far piani or progetti; **to ~ to do** progettare di fare

plane [pleɪn] n (Aviat) aereo; (tree) platano; (tool) pialla; (Art, Math etc) piano ▸ adj piano(-a), piatto(-a) ▸ vt (with tool) piallare

planet ['plænɪt] n pianeta m

plank [plæŋk] n tavola, asse f

planning ['plænɪŋ] n progettazione f; **family ~** pianificazione f delle nascite

plant [plɑːnt] n pianta; (machinery) impianto; (factory) fabbrica ▸ vt piantare; (bomb) mettere

plantation [plæn'teɪʃən] n piantagione f

plaque [plæk] n placca

plaster ['plɑːstə^r] n intonaco; (also: ~ of Paris) gesso; (BRIT: also: **sticking ~**) cerotto ▶ vt intonacare; ingessare; (cover): **to ~ with** coprire di; **plaster cast** n (Med) ingessatura, gesso; (model, statue) modello in gesso

plastic ['plæstɪk] n plastica ▶ adj (made of plastic) di or in plastica; **plastic bag** n sacchetto di plastica; **plastic surgery** n chirurgia plastica

plate [pleɪt] n (dish) piatto; (in book) tavola; (dental plate) dentiera; **gold/silver ~** vasellame m d'oro/d'argento

plateau ['plætəu] (pl **plateaus** or **plateaux**) n altipiano

platform ['plætfɔːm] n (stage, at meeting) palco; (Rail) marciapiede m; (BRIT: of bus) piattaforma; **which ~ does the train for Rome go from?** da che binario parte il treno per Roma?

platinum ['plætɪnəm] n platino

platoon [plə'tuːn] n plotone m

platter ['plætə^r] n piatto

plausible ['plɔːzɪbl] adj plausibile, credibile; (person) convincente

play [pleɪ] n gioco; (Theatre) commedia ▶ vt (game) giocare a; (team, opponent) giocare contro; (instrument, piece of music) suonare; (record, tape) ascoltare; (role, part) interpretare ▶ vi giocare; suonare; recitare; **to ~ safe** giocare sul sicuro ▷ **play back** vt riascoltare, risentire ▷ **play up** vi (cause trouble) fare i capricci; **player** n giocatore(-trice); (Theatre) attore(-trice); (Mus) musicista m/f; **playful** adj giocoso(-a); **playground** n (in school) cortile m per la ricreazione; (in park) parco m giochi inv; **playgroup** n giardino d'infanzia; **playing card** n carta da gioco; **playing field** n campo sportivo; **playschool** n = **playgroup**; **playtime** n (Scol) ricreazione f; **playwright** n

drammaturgo(-a)

plc abbr (= public limited company) società per azioni a responsabilità limitata quotata in borsa

plea [pliː] n (request) preghiera, domanda; (Law) (argomento di) difesa

plead [pliːd] vt patrocinare; (give as excuse) addurre a pretesto ▶ vi (Law) perorare la causa; (beg): **to ~ with sb** implorare qn

pleasant ['plɛznt] adj piacevole, gradevole

please [pliːz] excl per piacere!, per favore!; (acceptance): **yes, ~** sì, grazie ▶ vt piacere a ▶ vi piacere; (think fit): **do as you ~** faccia come le pare; **~ yourself!** come ti (or le) pare!; **pleased** adj pleased (with) contento(-a) (di); **pleased to meet you!** piacere!

pleasure ['plɛʒə^r] n piacere m; **"it's a ~"** "prego"

pleat [pliːt] n piega

pledge [plɛdʒ] n pegno; (promise) promessa ▶ vt impegnare; promettere

plentiful ['plɛntɪful] adj abbondante, copioso(-a)

plenty ['plɛntɪ] n **~ of** tanto(-a), molto(-a); un'abbondanza di

pliers ['plaɪəz] npl pinza

plight [plaɪt] n situazione f critica

plod [plɔd] vi camminare a stento; (fig) sgobbare

plonk [plɔŋk] (inf) n (BRIT: wine) vino da poco ▶ vt **to ~ sth down** buttare giù qc bruscamente

plot [plɔt] n congiura, cospirazione f; (of story, play) trama; (of land) lotto ▶ vt (mark out) segnare la pianta di; rilevare; (: diagram etc) tracciare; (conspire) congiurare, cospirare ▶ vi congiurare

plough [plau] (US **plow**) n aratro ▶ vt (earth) arare; **to ~ money into** (company etc) investire danaro in;

ploughman's lunch ['plaumənz-] (BRIT) n pasto a base di pane, formaggio e birra

plow [plau] (US) = **plough**

ploy [plɔɪ] n stratagemma m

pluck [plʌk] vt (fruit) cogliere; (musical instrument) pizzicare; (bird) spennare; (hairs) togliere ▶ n coraggio, fegato; **to ~ up courage** farsi coraggio

plug [plʌg] n tappo; (Elec) spina; (Aut: also: **spark(ing) ~**) candela ▶ vt (hole) tappare; (inf: advertise) spingere ▷ **plug in** vt (Elec) attaccare a una presa; **plughole** n (BRIT) scarico

plum [plʌm] n (fruit) susina

plumber ['plʌməʳ] n idraulico

plumbing ['plʌmɪŋ] n (trade) lavoro di idraulico; (piping) tubature fpl

plummet ['plʌmɪt] vi **to ~ (down)** cadere a piombo

plump [plʌmp] adj grassoccio(-a) ▶ vi **to ~ for** (inf: choose) decidersi per

plunge [plʌndʒ] n tuffo; (fig) caduta ▶ vt immergere ▶ vi (fall) cadere, precipitare; (dive) tuffarsi; **to take the ~** saltare il fosso

plural ['pluərl] adj plurale ▶ n plurale m

plus [plʌs] n (also: **~ sign**) segno più ▶ prep più; **ten ~** più di dieci

ply [plaɪ] n (a trade) esercitare ▶ vi (ship) fare il servizio ▶ n (of wool, rope) capo; **to ~ sb with drink** dare di bere continuamente a qn; **plywood** n legno compensato

P.M. n abbr = **prime minister**

p.m. adv abbr (= post meridiem) del pomeriggio

PMS n abbr (= premenstrual syndrome) sindrome f premestruale

PMT n abbr (= premenstrual tension) sindrome f premestruale

pneumatic drill [njuː'mætɪk-] n martello pneumatico

pneumonia [njuː'məunɪə] n polmonite f

poach [pəutʃ] vt (cook: egg) affogare; (: fish) cuocere in bianco; (steal) cacciare (or pescare) di frodo ▶ vi fare il bracconiere; **poached** adj (egg) affogato(-a)

P.O. Box n abbr = **Post Office Box**

pocket ['pɔkɪt] n tasca ▶ vt intascare; **to be out of ~** (BRIT) rimetterci; **pocketbook** (US) n (wallet) portafoglio; **pocket money** n paghetta, settimana

pod [pɔd] n guscio

podcast ['pɔdkɑːst] n podcast m

podiatrist [pɔ'diːətrɪst] (US) n callista m/f, pedicure m/f

podium ['pəudɪəm] n podio

poem ['pəuɪm] n poesia

poet ['pəuɪt] n poeta/essa; **poetic** [-'ɛtɪk] adj poetico(-a); **poetry** n poesia

poignant ['pɔɪnjənt] adj struggente

point [pɔɪnt] n (gen) punto; (tip: of needle etc) punta; (in time) punto, momento; (Scol) voto; (main idea, important part) nocciolo; (Elec) presa (di corrente); (also: **decimal ~**): **2 ~ 3 (2.3)** 2 virgola 3 (2,3) ▶ vt (show) indicare; (gun etc): **to ~ sth at** puntare qc contro ▶ vi **to ~ at** mostrare a dito; **~s** npl (Aut) puntine fpl; (Rail) scambio; **to be on the ~ of doing sth** essere sul punto di or stare per fare qc; **to make a ~** fare un'osservazione; **to get/miss the ~** capire/non capire; **to come to the ~** venire al fatto; **there's no ~ in doing** è inutile (fare) ▷ **point out** vt far notare; **point-blank** adv (also: **at point-blank range**) a bruciapelo; (fig) categoricamente; **pointed** adj (shape) aguzzo(-a), appuntito(-a); (remark) specifico(-a); **pointer** n (needle) lancetta; (fig) indicazione f, consiglio; **pointless** adj inutile, vano(-a); **point of view** n punto di vista

poison ['pɔɪzn] n veleno ▶ vt avvelenare; **poisonous** adj velenoso(-a)

poke [pəʊk] vt (fire) attizzare; (jab with finger, stick etc) punzecchiare; (put): **to ~ sth in(to)** spingere qc dentro ▷ **poke about** or **around** vi frugare ▷ **poke out** vi (stick out) sporger fuori

poker ['pəʊkə'] n attizzatoio; (Cards) poker m

Poland ['pəʊlənd] n Polonia

polar ['pəʊlə'] adj polare; **polar bear** n orso bianco

Pole [pəʊl] n polacco(-a)

pole [pəʊl] n (of wood) palo; (Elec, Geo) polo; **pole bean** (US) n (runner bean) fagiolino; **pole vault** n salto con l'asta

police [pə'liːs] n polizia ▷ vt mantenere l'ordine in; **police car** n macchina della polizia; **police constable** (BRIT) n agente m di polizia; **police force** n corpo di polizia, polizia; **policeman** (irreg) n poliziotto, agente m di polizia; **police officer** n = **police constable**; **police station** n posto di polizia; **policewoman** (irreg) n donna f poliziotto inv

policy ['pɒlɪsɪ] n politica; (also: **insurance ~**) polizza (d'assicurazione)

polio ['pəʊlɪəʊ] n polio f

Polish ['pəʊlɪʃ] adj polacco(-a) ▶ n (Ling) polacco

polish ['pɒlɪʃ] n (for shoes) lucido; (for floor) cera; (for nails) smalto; (shine) lucentezza, lustro; (fig: refinement) raffinatezza ▶ vt lucidare; (fig: improve) raffinare ▷ **polish off** vt (food) mangiarsi; **polished** adj (fig) raffinato(-a)

polite [pə'laɪt] adj cortese; **politeness** n cortesia

political [pə'lɪtɪkl] adj politico(-a); **politically** adv politicamente; **politically correct** politicamente corretto(-a)

politician [pɒlɪ'tɪʃən] n politico

politics ['pɒlɪtɪks] n politica ▶ npl (views, policies) idee fpl politiche

poll [pəʊl] n scrutinio; (votes cast) voti mpl; (also: **opinion ~**) sondaggio (d'opinioni) ▶ vt ottenere

pollen ['pɒlən] n polline m

polling station ['pəʊlɪŋ-] (BRIT) n sezione f elettorale

pollute [pə'luːt] vt inquinare

pollution [pə'luːʃən] n inquinamento

polo ['pəʊləʊ] n polo; **polo-neck** n collo alto; (also: **polo-neck sweater**) dolcevita ▶ adj a collo alto; **polo shirt** n polo f inv

polyester [pɒlɪ'ɛstə'] n poliestere m

polystyrene [pɒlɪ'staɪriːn] n polistirolo

polythene ['pɒlɪθiːn] n politene m; **polythene bag** n sacco di plastica

pomegranate ['pɒmɪɡrænɪt] n melagrana

pompous ['pɒmpəs] adj pomposo(-a)

pond [pɒnd] n pozza; stagno

ponder ['pɒndə'] vt ponderare, riflettere su

pony ['pəʊnɪ] n pony m inv; **ponytail** n coda di cavallo; **pony trekking** [-trɛkɪŋ] (BRIT) n escursione f a cavallo

poodle ['puːdl] n barboncino, barbone m

pool [puːl] n (puddle) pozza; (pond) stagno; (also: **swimming ~**) piscina; (fig: of light) cerchio; (billiards) specie di biliardo a buca ▶ vt mettere in comune; **~s** npl (football pools) ≈ totocalcio; **typing ~** servizio comune di dattilografia

poor [pʊə'] adj povero(-a); (mediocre) mediocre, cattivo(-a) ▶ npl **the ~** i poveri; **~ in** povero(-a) di; **poorly** adv poveramente; male ▶ adj indisposto(-a), malato(-a)

pop [pɒp] n (noise) schiocco; (Mus) musica pop; (drink) bibita gasata; (US: inf: father) babbo ▶ vt (put) mettere (in fretta) ▶ vi scoppiare; (cork) schioccare ▷ **pop in** vi passare ▷ **pop**

out vi fare un salto fuori; **popcorn** n pop-corn m

poplar ['pɒplər] n pioppo

popper ['pɒpər] n bottone m a pressione

poppy ['pɒpɪ] n papavero

Popsicle® ['pɒpsɪkl] (US) n (ice lolly) ghiacciolo

pop star n pop star f inv

popular ['pɒpjulər] adj popolare; (fashionable) in voga; **popularity** [-'lærɪtɪ] n popolarità

population [pɒpju'leɪʃən] n popolazione f

porcelain ['pɔːslɪn] n porcellana

porch [pɔːtʃ] n veranda

pore [pɔːr] n poro ▶ vi to ~ over essere immerso(-a) in

pork [pɔːk] n carne f di maiale; **pork chop** n braciola or costoletta di maiale; **pork pie** n (BRIT: Culin) pasticcio di maiale in crosta

porn [pɔːn] (inf) n pornografia ▶ adj porno inv; **pornographic** [pɔːnə'græfɪk] adj pornografico(-a); **pornography** [pɔː'nɒgrəfɪ] n pornografia

porridge ['pɒrɪdʒ] n porridge m

port [pɔːt] n (gen, wine) porto; (Naut: left side) babordo

portable ['pɔːtəbl] adj portatile

porter ['pɔːtər] n (for luggage) facchino, portabagagli m inv; (doorkeeper) portiere m, portinaio

portfolio [pɔːt'fəulɪəu] n (case) cartella; (Pol, Finance) portafoglio; (of artist) raccolta dei propri lavori

portion ['pɔːʃən] n porzione f

port of call n (porto di) scalo

portrait ['pɔːtreɪt] n ritratto

portray [pɔː'treɪ] vt fare il ritratto di; (character on stage) rappresentare; (in writing) ritrarre

Portugal ['pɔːtjugl] n Portogallo

Portuguese [pɔːtju'giːz] adj

portoghese ▶ n inv portoghese m/f; (Ling) portoghese m

pose [pəuz] n posa ▶ vi posare; (pretend): **to ~ as** atteggiarsi a, posare a ▶ vt porre

posh [pɒʃ] (inf) adj elegante; (family) per bene

position [pə'zɪʃən] n posizione f; (job) posto ▶ vt sistemare

positive ['pɒzɪtɪv] adj positivo(-a); (certain) sicuro(-a), certo(-a); (definite) preciso(-a), definitivo(-a); **positively** adv (affirmatively, enthusiastically) positivamente; (decisively) decisamente; (really) assolutamente

possess [pə'zɛs] vt possedere; **possession** [pə'zɛʃən] n possesso; **possessions** npl (belongings) beni mpl; **possessive** adj possessivo(-a)

possibility [pɒsɪ'bɪlɪtɪ] n possibilità f inv

possible ['pɒsɪbl] adj possibile; **as big as ~** il più grande possibile; **possibly** ['pɒsɪblɪ] adv (perhaps) forse; **if you possibly can** se le è possibile; **I cannot possibly come** proprio non posso venire

post [pəust] n (BRIT) posta; (: collection) levata; (job, situation) posto; (Mil) postazione f; (pole) palo ▶ vt (BRIT: send by post) imbucare; (: appoint): **to ~ to** assegnare a; **where can I ~ these cards?** dove posso imbucare queste cartoline?; **postage** n affrancatura; **postal** adj postale; **postal order** n vaglia m inv postale; **postbox** (BRIT) n cassetta postale; **postcard** n cartolina; **postcode** n (BRIT) codice m (di avviamento) postale

poster ['pəustər] n manifesto, affisso

postgraduate ['pəust'grædjuət] n laureato/a che continua gli studi

postman ['pəustmən] n (irreg) postino

postmark ['pəustmɑːk] n bollo or timbro postale

post-mortem [-'mɔːtəm] n autopsia
post office n (building) ufficio postale; (organization): **the Post Office** ≈ le Poste e Telecomunicazioni
postpone [pəs'pəun] vt rinviare
posture ['pɒstʃər] n portamento; (pose) posa, atteggiamento
postwoman ['pəustwumən] (BRIT: irreg) n postina
pot [pɒt] n (for cooking) pentola; casseruola; (teapot) teiera; (coffeepot) caffettiera; (for plants, jam) vaso; (inf: marijuana) erba ▶ vt (plant) piantare in vaso; **a ~ of tea for two** tè per due; **to go to ~** (inf: work, performance) andare in malora
potato [pə'teɪtəu] (pl potatoes) n patata; **potato peeler** n sbucciapatate m inv
potent ['pəutnt] adj potente, forte
potential [pə'tɛnʃl] adj potenziale ▶ n possibilità fpl
pothole ['pɒthəul] n (in road) buca; (BRIT: underground) caverna
pot plant n pianta in vaso
potter ['pɒtər] n vasaio ▶ vi **to ~ around, ~ about** (BRIT) lavoracchiare; **pottery** n ceramiche fpl; (factory) fabbrica di ceramiche
potty ['pɒtɪ] adj (inf: mad) tocco(-a) ▶ n (child's) vasino
pouch [pautʃ] n borsa; (Zool) marsupio
poultry ['pəultrɪ] n pollame m
pounce [pauns] vi **to ~ (on)** piombare (su)
pound [paund] n (weight) libbra; (money) (lira) sterlina ▶ vt (beat) battere; (crush) pestare, polverizzare ▶ vi (beat) battere, martellare; **pound sterling** n sterlina (inglese)
pour [pɔːr] vt versare ▶ vi riversarsi; (rain) piovere a dirotto ▷ **pour in** vi affluire in gran quantità ▷ **pour out** vi (people) uscire a fiumi ▶ vt vuotare;

versare; (fig) sfogare; **pouring** adj
pouring rain pioggia torrenziale
pout [paut] vi sporgere le labbra; fare il broncio
poverty ['pɒvətɪ] n povertà, miseria
powder ['paudər] n polvere f ▶ vt **to ~ one's face** incipriarsi il viso; **powdered milk** n latte m in polvere
power ['pauər] n (strength) potenza, forza; (ability, Pol: of party, leader) potere m; (Elec) corrente f; **to be in ~** (Pol etc) essere al potere; **power cut** (BRIT) n interruzione f or mancanza di corrente; **power failure** n interruzione f della corrente elettrica; **powerful** adj potente, forte; **powerless** adj impotente; **powerless to do** impossibilitato(-a) a fare; **power point** (BRIT) n presa di corrente; **power station** n centrale f elettrica
p.p. abbr = per procurationem; **p.p.J. Smith** per J. Smith; (= pages) p.p.
PR abbr = public relations
practical ['præktɪkl] adj pratico(-a); **practical joke** n beffa; **practically** adv praticamente
practice ['præktɪs] n pratica; (of profession) esercizio; (at football etc) allenamento; (business) gabinetto; clientela ▶ vt, vi (US) = **practise**; **in ~** (in reality) in pratica; **out of ~** fuori esercizio
practise ['præktɪs] (US **practice**) vt (work at: piano, one's backhand etc) esercitarsi a; (train for: skiing, running etc) allenarsi a; (a sport, religion) praticare; (method) usare; (profession) esercitare ▶ vi esercitarsi; (train) allenarsi; (lawyer, doctor) esercitare; **practising** adj (Christian etc) praticante; (lawyer) che esercita la professione
practitioner [præk'tɪʃənər] n professionista m/f

p

pragmatic [præg'mætɪk] *adj* pragmatico(-a)

prairie ['prɛərɪ] *n* prateria

praise [preɪz] *n* elogio, lode *f* ▶ *vt* elogiare, lodare

pram [præm] (*BRIT*) *n* carrozzina

prank [præŋk] *n* burla

prawn [prɔːn] *n* gamberetto; **prawn cocktail** *n* cocktail *m inv* di gamberetti

pray [preɪ] *vi* pregare; **prayer** [prɛəʳ] *n* preghiera

preach [priːtʃ] *vt, vi* predicare; **preacher** *n* predicatore(-trice); (*US: minister*) pastore *m*

precarious [prɪ'kɛərɪəs] *adj* precario(-a)

precaution [prɪ'kɔːʃən] *n* precauzione *f*

precede [prɪ'siːd] *vt* precedere; **precedent** ['prɛsɪdənt] *n* precedente *m*; **preceding** [prɪ'siːdɪŋ] *adj* precedente

precinct ['priːsɪŋkt] (*US*) *n* circoscrizione *f*

precious ['prɛʃəs] *adj* prezioso(-a)

precise [prɪ'saɪs] *adj* preciso(-a); **precisely** *adv* precisamente

precision [prɪ'sɪʒən] *n* precisione *f*

predator ['prɛdətəʳ] *n* predatore *m*

predecessor ['priːdɪsɛsəʳ] *n* predecessore(-a)

predicament [prɪ'dɪkəmənt] *n* situazione *f* difficile

predict [prɪ'dɪkt] *vt* predire; **predictable** *adj* prevedibile; **prediction** [prɪ'dɪkʃən] *n* predizione *f*

predominantly [prɪ'dɔmɪnəntlɪ] *adv* in maggior parte; soprattutto

preface ['prɛfəs] *n* prefazione *f*

prefect ['priːfɛkt] *n* (*BRIT: in school*) studente(-essa) con funzioni disciplinari; (*French etc, Admin*) prefetto

prefer [prɪ'fəːʳ] *vt* preferire; **to ~ doing** *or* **to do** preferire fare; **preferable**

['prɛfrəbl] *adj* preferibile; **preferably** ['prɛfrəblɪ] *adv* preferibilmente; **preference** ['prɛfrəns] *n* preferenza

prefix ['priːfɪks] *n* prefisso

pregnancy ['prɛgnənsɪ] *n* gravidanza

pregnant ['prɛgnənt] *adj* incinta *ag*

prehistoric ['priːhɪs'tɔrɪk] *adj* preistorico(-a)

prejudice ['prɛdʒudɪs] *n* pregiudizio; (*harm*) torto, danno; **prejudiced** *adj* **prejudiced (against)** prevenuto(-a) (contro); **prejudiced (in favour of)** ben disposto(-a) (verso)

preliminary [prɪ'lɪmɪnərɪ] *adj* preliminare

prelude ['prɛljuːd] *n* preludio

premature ['prɛmətʃuəʳ] *adj* prematuro(-a)

premier ['prɛmɪəʳ] *adj* primo(-a) ▶ *n* (*Pol*) primo ministro

première ['prɛmɪɛəʳ] *n* prima

Premier League *n* ≈ serie A

premises ['prɛmɪsɪz] *npl* locale *m*; **on the ~** sul posto; **business ~** locali commerciali

premium ['priːmɪəm] *n* premio; **to be at a ~** essere ricercatissimo

premonition [prɛmə'nɪʃən] *n* premonizione *f*

preoccupied [priː'ɔkjupaɪd] *adj* preoccupato(-a)

prepaid [priː'peɪd] *adj* pagato(-a) in anticipo

preparation [prɛpə'reɪʃən] *n* preparazione *f*; **~s** *npl* (*for trip, war*) preparativi *mpl*

preparatory school [prɪ'pærətərɪ-] *n* scuola elementare privata

prepare [prɪ'pɛəʳ] *vt* preparare ▶ *vi* **to ~ for** prepararsi a; **~d to** pronto(-a) a

preposition [prɛpə'zɪʃən] *n* preposizione *f*

prep school *n* = **preparatory school**

prerequisite [priː'rɛkwɪzɪt] *n* requisito indispensabile

preschool ['pri:'sku:l] adj (age) prescolastico(-a); (child) in età prescolastica

prescribe [pri'skraib] vt (Med) prescrivere

prescription [pri'skripʃən] n prescrizione f; (Med) ricetta; **could you write me a ~?** mi può fare una ricetta medica?

presence ['prɛzns] n presenza; **~ of mind** presenza di spirito

present [adj, n 'prɛznt, vb pri'zɛnt] adj presente; (wife, residence, job) attuale ▶ n (actuality): **the ~** il presente; (gift) regalo ▶ vt presentare; (give): **to ~ sb with sth** offrire qc a qn; **to give sb a ~** fare un regalo a qn; **at ~** al momento; **presentable** [pri'zɛntəbl] adj presentabile; **presentation** [-'teiʃən] n presentazione f; (ceremony) consegna ufficiale; **present-day** adj attuale, d'oggigiorno; **presenter** n (Radio, TV) presentatore(-trice); **presently** adv (soon) fra poco, presto; (at present) al momento; **present participle** n participio presente

preservation [prɛzə'veiʃən] n preservazione f, conservazione f

preservative [pri'zə:vətiv] n conservante m

preserve [pri'zə:v] vt (keep safe) preservare, proteggere; (maintain) conservare; (food) mettere in conserva ▶ n (often pl: jam) marmellata; (: fruit) frutta sciroppata

preside [pri'zaid] vi **to ~ (over)** presiedere (a)

president ['prɛzidənt] n presidente m; **presidential** [-'dɛnʃl] adj presidenziale

press [prɛs] n (newspapers etc): **the P~** la stampa; (tool, machine) pressa; (for wine) torchio ▶ vt (push) premere, pigiare; (squeeze) spremere; (: hand) stringere; (clothes: iron) stirare; (pursue) incalzare; (insist): **to ~ sth on sb** far accettare qc da qn ▶ vi premere; accalcare; **we are ~ed for time** ci manca il tempo; **to ~ for sth** insistere per avere qc; **press conference** n conferenza f stampa inv; **pressing** adj urgente; **press stud** (BRIT) n bottone m a pressione; **press-up** (BRIT) n flessione f sulle braccia

pressure ['prɛʃə'] n pressione f; **to put ~ on sb (to do)** mettere qn sotto pressione (affinché faccia); **pressure cooker** n pentola a pressione; **pressure group** n gruppo di pressione

prestige [prɛs'ti:ʒ] n prestigio

prestigious [prɛs'tidʒəs] adj prestigioso(-a)

presumably [pri'zju:məbli] adv presumibilmente

presume [pri'zju:m] vt supporre

pretence [pri'tɛns] (US **pretense**) n (claim) pretesa; **to make a ~ of doing** far finta di fare; **under false ~s** con l'inganno

pretend [pri'tɛnd] vt (feign) fingere ▶ vi far finta; **to ~ to do** far finta di fare

pretense [pri'tɛns] (US) n = **pretence**

pretentious [pri'tɛnʃəs] adj pretenzioso(-a)

pretext ['pri:tɛkst] n pretesto

pretty ['priti] adj grazioso(-a), carino(-a) ▶ adv abbastanza, assai

prevail [pri'veil] vi (win, be usual) prevalere; (persuade): **to ~ (up)on sb to do** persuadere qn a fare; **prevailing** adj dominante

prevalent ['prɛvələnt] adj (belief) predominante; (customs) diffuso(-a); (fashion) corrente; (disease) comune

prevent [pri'vɛnt] vt **to ~ sb from doing** impedire a qn di fare; **to ~ sth from happening** impedire che qc succeda; **prevention** [-'vɛnʃən] n prevenzione f; **preventive** adj preventivo(-a)

p

preview ['pri:vju:] n (of film) anteprima

previous ['pri:vɪəs] adj precedente; anteriore; **previously** adv prima

prey [preɪ] n preda ▶ vi **to ~ on** far preda di; **it was ~ing on his mind** lo stava ossessionando

price [praɪs] n prezzo ▶ vt (goods) fissare il prezzo di; valutare; **priceless** adj inapprezzabile; **price list** n listino (dei) prezzi

prick [prɪk] n puntura ▶ vt pungere; **to ~ up one's ears** drizzare gli orecchi

prickly ['prɪklɪ] adj spinoso(-a)

pride [praɪd] n orgoglio; superbia ▶ vt **to ~ o.s. on** essere orgoglioso(-a) di, vantarsi di

priest [pri:st] n prete m, sacerdote m

primarily ['praɪmərɪlɪ] adv principalmente, essenzialmente

primary ['praɪmərɪ] adj primario(-a); (first in importance) primo(-a) ▶ n (US: election) primarie fpl; **primary school** (BRIT) n scuola elementare

prime [praɪm] adj primario(-a), fondamentale; (excellent) di prima qualità ▶ vt (wood) preparare; (fig) mettere al corrente ▶ n **in the ~ of life** nel fiore della vita; **Prime Minister** n primo ministro

primitive ['prɪmɪtɪv] adj primitivo(-a)

primrose ['prɪmrəʊz] n primavera

prince [prɪns] n principe m

princess [prɪn'sɛs] n principessa

principal ['prɪnsɪpl] adj principale ▶ n (headmaster) preside m; **principally** adv principalmente

principle ['prɪnsɪpl] n principio; **in ~** in linea di principio; **on ~** per principio

print [prɪnt] n (mark) impronta; (letters) caratteri mpl; (fabric) tessuto stampato; (Art, Phot) stampa ▶ vt imprimere; (publish) stampare, pubblicare; (write in capitals) scrivere in stampatello; **out of ~** esaurito(-a)

▷ **print out** vt (Comput) stampare; **printer** n tipografo; (machine) stampante f; **printout** n tabulato

prior ['praɪəʳ] adj precedente; (claim etc) più importante; **~ to doing** prima di fare

priority [praɪ'ɒrɪtɪ] n priorità f inv; precedenza

prison ['prɪzn] n prigione f ▶ cpd (system) carcerario(-a); (conditions, food) nelle or delle prigioni; **prisoner** n prigioniero(-a); **prisoner-of-war** n prigioniero(-a) di guerra

pristine ['prɪsti:n] adj immacolato(-a)

privacy ['prɪvəsɪ] n solitudine f, intimità

private ['praɪvɪt] adj privato(-a); personale ▶ n soldato semplice; **"~"** (on envelope) "riservata"; (on door) "privato"; **in ~** in privato; **privately** adv in privato; (within oneself) dentro di sé; **private property** n proprietà privata; **private school** n scuola privata

privatize ['praɪvɪtaɪz] vt privatizzare

privilege ['prɪvɪlɪdʒ] n privilegio

prize [praɪz] n premio ▶ adj (example, idiot) perfetto(-a); (bull, novel) premiato(-a) ▶ vt apprezzare, pregiare; **prize-giving** n premiazione f; **prizewinner** n premiato(-a)

pro [prəʊ] n (Sport) professionista m/f ▶ prep pro; **the ~s and cons** il pro e il contro

probability [prɒbə'bɪlɪtɪ] n probabilità f inv; **in all ~** con tutta probabilità

probable ['prɒbəbl] adj probabile

probably ['prɒbəblɪ] adv probabilmente

probation [prə'beɪʃən] n **on ~** (employee) in prova; (Law) in libertà vigilata

probe [prəʊb] n (Med, Space) sonda; (enquiry) indagine f, investigazione f

▶ *vt* sondare, esplorare; indagare

problem ['prɔbləm] *n* problema *m*

procedure [prə'si:dʒər] *n* (*Admin*, *Law*) procedura; (*method*) metodo, procedimento

proceed [prə'si:d] *vi* (*go forward*) avanzare, andare avanti; (*go about it*) procedere; (*continue*): **to ~ (with)** continuare; **to ~ to** andare a; passare a; **to ~ to do** mettersi a fare; **proceedings** *npl* misure *fpl*; (*Law*) procedimento; (*meeting*) riunione *f*; (*records*) rendiconti *mpl*; atti *mpl*; **proceeds** ['prəusi:dz] *npl* profitto, incasso

process ['prəusɛs] *n* processo; (*method*) metodo, sistema *m* ▶ *vt* trattare; (*information*) elaborare

procession [prə'sɛʃən] *n* processione *f*, corteo; **funeral ~** corteo funebre

proclaim [prə'kleɪm] *vt* proclamare, dichiarare

prod [prɔd] *vt* dare un colpetto a; pungolare ▶ *n* colpetto

produce [*n* 'prɔdju:s, *vb* prə'dju:s] *n* (*Agr*) prodotto, prodotti *mpl* ▶ *vt* produrre; (*show*) esibire, mostrare; (*cause*) cagionare, causare; **producer** *n* (*Theatre*) regista *m/f*; (*Agr*, *Cinema*) produttore *m*

product ['prɔdʌkt] *n* prodotto; **production** [prə'dʌkʃən] *n* produzione *f*; **productive** [prə'dʌktɪv] *adj* produttivo(-a); **productivity** [prɔdʌk'tɪvɪtɪ] *n* produttività

Prof. *abbr* (= *professor*) Prof.

profession [prə'fɛʃən] *n* professione *f*; **professional** *n* professionista *m/f* ▶ *adj* professionale; (*work*) da professionista

professor [prə'fɛsər] *n* professore *m* (*titolare di una cattedra*); (*US*) professore(-essa)

profile ['prəufaɪl] *n* profilo

profit ['prɔfɪt] *n* profitto; beneficio ▶ *vi* **to ~ (by** *or* **from)** approfittare (di); **profitable** *adj* redditizio(-a)

profound [prə'faund] *adj* profondo(-a)

programme ['prəugræm] (*US* **program**) *n* programma *m* ▶ *vt* programmare; **programmer** (*US* **programer**) *n* programmatore(-trice); **programming** (*US* **programing**) *n* programmazione *f*

progress [*n* 'prəugrɛs, *vb* prə'grɛs] *n* progresso ▶ *vi* avanzare, procedere; **in ~** in corso; **to make ~** far progressi; **progressive** [-'grɛsɪv] *adj* progressivo(-a); (*person*) progressista

prohibit [prə'hɪbɪt] *vt* proibire, vietare

project [*n* 'prɔdʒɛkt, *vb* prə'dʒɛkt] *n* (*plan*) piano; (*venture*) progetto; (*Scol*) studio ▶ *vt* proiettare ▶ *vi* (*stick out*) sporgere; **projection** [prə'dʒɛkʃən] *n* proiezione *f*; sporgenza; **projector** [prə'dʒɛktər] *n* proiettore *m*

prolific [prə'lɪfɪk] *adj* (*artist etc*) fecondo(-a)

prolong [prə'lɔŋ] *vt* prolungare

prom [prɔm] *n abbr* = **promenade**; (*US*: *ball*) ballo studentesco

- **Prom**
- In Gran Bretagna i **Proms**, o
- "promenade concerts", sono
- concerti di musica classica, i più
- noti dei quali sono eseguiti nella
- prestigiosa **Royal Albert Hall** a
- Londra. Si chiamano così perché
- un tempo il pubblico seguiva i
- concerti in piedi, passeggiando
- (in inglese "promenade" voleva
- dire, appunto, passeggiata). Negli
- Stati Uniti, invece, con **prom**, si
- intende l'annuale ballo studentesco
- di un'università o di una scuola
- secondaria.

promenade [prɔmə'nɑːd] *n* (*by sea*) lungomare *m*

prominent ['prɒmɪnənt] *adj* (*standing out*) prominente; (*important*) importante

promiscuous [prə'mɪskjuəs] *adj* (*sexually*) di facili costumi

promise ['prɒmɪs] *n* promessa ▶ *vt, vi* promettere; **to ~ sb sth, ~ sth to sb** promettere qc a qn; **to ~ (sb) that/to do sth** promettere (a qn) che/di fare qc; **promising** *adj* promettente

promote [prə'məut] *vt* promuovere; (*venture, event*) organizzare; **promotion** [-'məuʃən] *n* promozione *f*

prompt [prɒmpt] *adj* rapido(-a), svelto(-a); puntuale; (*reply*) sollecito(-a) ▶ *adv* (*punctually*) in punto ▶ *n* (*Comput*) prompt *m* ▶ *vt* incitare; provocare; (*Theatre*) suggerire a; **to ~ sb to do** incitare qn a fare; **promptly** *adv* prontamente; puntualmente

prone [prəun] *adj* (*lying*) prono(-a); **~ to** propenso(-a) a, incline a

prong [prɒŋ] *n* rebbio, punta

pronoun ['prəunaun] *n* pronome *m*

pronounce [prə'nauns] *vt* pronunciare; **how do you ~ it?** come si pronuncia?

pronunciation [prənʌnsɪ'eɪʃən] *n* pronuncia

proof [pruːf] *n* prova; (*of book*) bozza; (*Phot*) provino ▶ *adj* **~ against** a prova di

prop [prɒp] *n* sostegno, appoggio ▶ *vt* (*also*: **~ up**) sostenere, appoggiare; (*lean*): **to ~ sth against** appoggiare qc contro *or* a; **~s** *oggetti m inv* di scena ▷ **prop up** *vt* sostenere, appoggiare

propaganda [prɒpə'gændə] *n* propaganda

propeller [prə'pɛləʳ] *n* elica

proper ['prɒpəʳ] *adj* (*suited, right*) adatto(-a), appropriato(-a); (*seemly*) decente; (*authentic*) vero(-a); (*inf: real: noun*) + vero(-a) e proprio(-a);

properly ['prɒpəlɪ] *adv* (*eat, study*) bene; (*behave*) come si deve; **proper noun** *n* nome *m* proprio

property ['prɒpətɪ] *n* (*things owned*) beni *mpl*; (*land, building*) proprietà *f inv*; (*Chem etc: quality*) proprietà

prophecy ['prɒfɪsɪ] *n* profezia

prophet ['prɒfɪt] *n* profeta *m*

proportion [prə'pɔːʃən] *n* proporzione *f*; (*share*) parte *f*; **~s** *npl* (*size*) proporzioni *fpl*; **proportional** *adj* proporzionale

proposal [prə'pəuzl] *n* proposta; (*plan*) progetto; (*of marriage*) proposta di matrimonio

propose [prə'pəuz] *vt* proporre, suggerire ▶ *vi* fare una proposta di matrimonio; **to ~ to do** proporsi di fare, aver l'intenzione di fare

proposition [prɒpə'zɪʃən] *n* proposizione *f*; (*offer*) proposta

proprietor [prə'praɪətəʳ] *n* proprietario(-a)

prose [prəuz] *n* prosa

prosecute ['prɒsɪkjuːt] *vt* processare; **prosecution** [-'kjuːʃən] *n* processo; (*accusing side*) accusa; **prosecutor** *n* (*also*: **public prosecutor**) ≈ procuratore *m* della Repubblica

prospect [*n* 'prɒspɛkt, *vb* prə'spɛkt] *n* prospettiva; (*hope*) speranza ▶ *vi* **to ~ for** cercare; **~s** *npl* (*for work etc*) prospettive *fpl*; **prospective** [-'spɛktɪv] *adj* possibile; futuro(-a)

prospectus [prə'spɛktəs] *n* prospetto, programma *m*

prosper ['prɒspəʳ] *vi* prosperare; **prosperity** [prɒ'spɛrɪtɪ] *n* prosperità; **prosperous** *adj* prospero(-a)

prostitute ['prɒstɪtjuːt] *n* prostituta; **male ~** uomo che si prostituisce

protect [prə'tɛkt] *vt* proteggere, salvaguardare; **protection** *n* protezione *f*; **protective** *adj* protettivo(-a)

protein ['prəuti:n] n proteina

protest [n 'prəutest, vb prə'test] n protesta ▶ vt, vi protestare

Protestant ['prɔtɪstənt] adj, n protestante m/f

protester [prə'testə'] n dimostrante m/f

protractor [prə'træktə'] n (Geom) goniometro

proud [praud] adj fiero(-a), orgoglioso(-a); (pej) superbo(-a)

prove [pru:v] vt provare, dimostrare ▶ vi to ~ (to be) correct etc risultare vero(-a) etc; to ~ o.s. mostrare le proprie capacità

proverb ['prɔvə:b] n proverbio

provide [prə'vaɪd] vt fornire, provvedere; to ~ sb with sth fornire or provvedere qn di qc ▷ **provide for** vt fus provvedere a; (future event) prevedere; **provided** conj **provided (that)** purché + sub, a condizione che + sub; **providing** [prə'vaɪdɪŋ] conj purché +sub, a condizione che +sub

province ['prɔvɪns] n provincia; **provincial** [prə'vɪnʃəl] adj provinciale

provision [prə'vɪʒən] n (supply) riserva; (supplying) provvista; rifornimento; (stipulation) condizione f; ~s npl (food) provviste fpl; **provisional** adj provvisorio(-a)

provocative [prə'vɔkətɪv] adj (aggressive) provocatorio(-a); (thought-provoking) stimolante; (seductive) provocante

provoke [prə'vəuk] vt provocare; incitare

prowl [praul] vi (also: ~ **about, ~ around**) aggirarsi ▶ n **to be on the ~** aggirarsi

proximity [prɔk'sɪmɪtɪ] n prossimità

proxy ['prɔksɪ] n **by ~** per procura

prudent ['pru:dnt] adj prudente

prune [pru:n] n prugna secca ▶ vt potare

pry [praɪ] vi **to ~ into** ficcare il naso in

PS abbr (= postscript) P.S.

pseudonym ['sju:dənɪm] n pseudonimo

psychiatric [saɪkɪ'ætrɪk] adj psichiatrico(-a)

psychiatrist [saɪ'kaɪətrɪst] n psichiatra m/f

psychic ['saɪkɪk] adj (also: ~**al**) psichico(-a); (person) dotato(-a) di qualità telepatiche

psychoanalysis [saɪkəuə'nælɪsɪs, -si:z] (pl -ses) n psicanalisi f inv

psychological [saɪkə'lɔdʒɪkl] adj psicologico(-a)

psychologist [saɪ'kɔlədʒɪst] n psicologo(-a)

psychology [saɪ'kɔlədʒɪ] n psicologia

psychotherapy [saɪkəu'θerəpɪ] n psicoterapia

pt abbr (= pint; point) pt.

PTO abbr (= please turn over) v.r.

pub [pʌb] n abbr (= public house) pub m inv

puberty ['pju:bətɪ] n pubertà

public ['pʌblɪk] adj pubblico(-a) ▶ n pubblico; **in ~** in pubblico

publication [pʌblɪ'keɪʃən] n pubblicazione f

public: **public company** n società f inv per azioni (costituita tramite pubblica sottoscrizione); **public convenience** (BRIT) n gabinetti mpl; **public holiday** n giorno festivo, festa nazionale; **public house** (BRIT) n pub m inv

publicity [pʌb'lɪsɪtɪ] n pubblicità

publicize ['pʌblɪsaɪz] vt rendere pubblico(-a)

public: **public limited company** n ≈ società per azioni a responsabilità limitata (quotata in Borsa); **publicly** ['pʌblɪklɪ] adv pubblicamente; **public opinion** n opinione f pubblica; **public relations** n pubbliche relazioni fpl; **public school** n (BRIT) scuola privata;

p

(US) scuola statale; **public transport** n mezzi mpl pubblici

publish ['pʌblɪʃ] vt pubblicare; **publisher** n editore m; **publishing** n (industry) editoria; (of a book) pubblicazione f

pub lunch n pranzo semplice ed economico servito nei pub

pudding ['pudɪŋ] n budino; (BRIT: dessert) dolce m; **black ~**, (US) **blood ~** sanguinaccio

puddle ['pʌdl] n pozza, pozzanghera

Puerto Rico ['pwə:təu'ri:kəu] n Portorico

puff [pʌf] n sbuffo ▶ vt **to ~ one's pipe** tirare sboccate di fumo ▶ vi (pant) ansare; **puff pastry** n pasta sfoglia

pull [pul] n (tug): **to give sth a ~** tirare su qc ▶ vt tirare; (muscle) strappare; (trigger) premere ▶ vi tirare; **to ~ to pieces** fare a pezzi; **to ~ one's punches** (Boxing) risparmiare l'avversario; **to ~ one's weight** dare il proprio contributo; **to ~ o.s. together** ricomporsi, riprendersi; **to ~ sb's leg** prendere in giro qn ▷ **pull apart** vt (break) fare a pezzi ▷ **pull away** vi (move off: vehicle) muoversi, partire; (boat) staccarsi dal molo, salpare; (draw back: person) indietreggiare ▷ **pull back** vt (lever etc) tirare indietro; (curtains) aprire ▶ vi (from confrontation etc) tirarsi indietro; (Mil: withdraw) ritirarsi ▷ **pull down** vt (house) demolire; (tree) abbattere ▷ **pull in** vi (Aut: at the kerb) accostarsi; (Rail) entrare in stazione ▷ **pull off** vt (clothes) togliere; (deal etc) portare a compimento ▷ **pull out** vi partire; (Aut: come out of line) spostarsi sulla mezzeria ▶ vt staccare; far uscire (withdraw) ritirare ▷ **pull over** vi (Aut) accostare ▷ **pull up** vi (stop) fermarsi ▶ vt (raise) sollevare; (uproot) sradicare

pulley ['pulɪ] n puleggia, carrucola

pullover ['puləuvəʳ] n pullover m inv

pulp [pʌlp] n (of fruit) polpa

pulpit ['pulpɪt] n pulpito

pulse [pʌls] n polso; (Bot) legume m; **~s** npl (Culin) legumi mpl

puma ['pju:mə] n puma m inv

pump [pʌmp] n pompa; (shoe) scarpetta ▶ vt pompare ▷ **pump up** vt gonfiare

pumpkin ['pʌmpkɪn] n zucca

pun [pʌn] n gioco di parole

punch [pʌntʃ] n (blow) pugno; (tool) punzone m; (drink) ponce m ▶ vt (hit): **to ~ sb/sth** dare un pugno a qn/qc; **punch-up** (BRIT: inf) n rissa

punctual ['pʌŋktjuəl] adj puntuale

punctuation [pʌŋktju'eɪʃən] n interpunzione f, punteggiatura

puncture ['pʌŋktʃəʳ] n foratura ▶ vt forare

> Be careful not to translate **puncture** by the Italian word *puntura*.

punish ['pʌnɪʃ] vt punire; **punishment** n punizione f

punk [pʌŋk] n (also: **~ rocker**) punk m/f inv; (also: **~ rock**) musica punk, punk rock m; (US: inf: hoodlum) teppista m

pup [pʌp] n cucciolo(-a)

pupil ['pju:pl] n allievo(-a); (Anat) pupilla

puppet ['pʌpɪt] n burattino

puppy ['pʌpɪ] n cucciolo(-a), cagnolino(-a)

purchase ['pə:tʃɪs] n acquisto, compera ▶ vt comprare

pure [pjuəʳ] adj puro(-a); **purely** ['pjuəlɪ] adv puramente

purify ['pjuərɪfaɪ] vt purificare

purity ['pjuərɪtɪ] n purezza

purple ['pə:pl] adj di porpora; viola inv

purpose ['pə:pəs] n intenzione f, scopo; **on ~** apposta

purr [pə:ʳ] vi fare le fusa

purse [pə:s] n (BRIT) borsellino; (US)

borsetta ▶ vt contrarre
pursue [pə'sjuː] vt inseguire; (fig:
activity etc) continuare con; (: aim etc)
perseguire
pursuit [pə'sjuːt] n inseguimento;
(fig) ricerca; (pastime) passatempo
pus [pʌs] n pus m
push [puʃ] n spinta; (effort) grande
sforzo; (drive) energia ▶ vt spingere;
(button) premere; (thrust): **to ~
sth (into)** ficcare qc (in); (fig)
fare pubblicità a ▶ vi spingere;
premere; **to ~ for** (fig) insistere
per ▷ **push in** vi introdursi a forza
▷ **push off** (inf) vi filare ▷ **push on** vi
(continue) continuare ▷ **push over**
vt far cadere ▷ **push through** vi
farsi largo spingendo ▶ vt (measure)
far approvare; **pushchair** (BRIT) n
passeggino; **pusher** n (drug pusher)
spacciatore(-trice); **push-up** (US) n
(press-up) flessione f sulle braccia
pussy(-cat) ['pusi(-)] (inf) n micio
put [put] (pt, pp **put**) vt mettere, porre;
(say) dire, esprimere; (a question)
fare; (estimate) stimare ▷ **put away**
vt (return) mettere a posto ▷ **put
back** vt (replace) rimettere (a posto);
(postpone) rinviare; (delay) ritardare
▷ **put by** vt (money) mettere da parte
▷ **put down** vt (parcel etc) posare,
mettere giù; (pay) versare; (in writing)
mettere per iscritto; (revolt, animal)
sopprimere; (attribute) attribuire
▷ **put forward** vt (ideas) avanzare,
proporre ▷ **put in** vt (application,
complaint) presentare; (time, effort)
mettere ▷ **put off** vt (postpone)
rimandare, rinviare; (discourage)
dissuadere ▷ **put on** vt (clothes, lipstick
etc) mettere; (light etc) accendere;
(play etc) mettere in scena; (food,
meal) mettere su; (brake) mettere; **to
~ on weight** ingrassare; **to ~ on airs**
darsi delle arie ▷ **put out** vt mettere

fuori; (one's hand) porgere; (light etc)
spegnere; (person: inconvenience)
scomodare ▷ **put through** vt (Tel:
call) passare; (: person) mettere in
comunicazione; (plan) far approvare
▷ **put up** vt (raise) sollevare, alzare;
(: umbrella) aprire; (: tent) montare;
(pin up) affiggere; (hang) appendere;
(build) costruire, erigere; (increase)
aumentare; (accommodate) alloggiare
▷ **put aside** vt (lay down: book etc)
mettere da una parte, posare; (save)
mettere da parte; (in shop) tenere
da parte ▷ **put together** vt mettere
insieme, riunire; (assemble: furniture)
montare; (: meal) improvvisare ▷ **put
up with** vt fus sopportare
putt [pʌt] n colpo leggero; **putting
green** n green m inv; campo da
putting
puzzle ['pʌzl] n enigma m, mistero;
(jigsaw) puzzle m; (also: **crossword ~**)
parole fpl incrociate, cruciverba m inv
▶ vt confondere, rendere perplesso(-a)
▶ vi scervellarsi; **puzzled** adj
perplesso(-a); **puzzling** adj (question)
poco chiaro(-a); (attitude, set of
instructions) incomprensibile
pyjamas [pɪ'dʒɑːməz] (BRIT) npl
pigiama m
pylon ['paɪlən] n pilone m
pyramid ['pɪrəmɪd] n piramide f
Pyrenees [pɪrɪ'niːz] npl **the ~** i Pirenei

p

q

quack [kwæk] n (of duck) qua qua m inv; (pej: doctor) dottoruccio(-a)

quadruple [kwɔ'drupl] vt quadruplicare ▶ vi quadruplicarsi

quail [kweɪl] n (Zool) quaglia ▶ vi (person): **to ~ at** or **before** perdersi d'animo davanti a

quaint [kweɪnt] adj bizzarro(-a); (old-fashioned) antiquato(-a); grazioso(-a), pittoresco(-a)

quake [kweɪk] vi tremare ▶ n abbr = **earthquake**

qualification [kwɔlɪfɪ'keɪʃən] n (degree etc) qualifica, titolo; (ability) competenza, qualificazione f; (limitation) riserva, restrizione f

qualified ['kwɔlɪfaɪd] adj qualificato(-a); (able): **~ to** competente in, qualificato(-a) a; (limited) condizionato(-a)

qualify ['kwɔlɪfaɪ] vt abilitare; (limit: statement) modificare, precisare ▶ vi **to ~ (as)** qualificarsi (come); **to ~ (for)** acquistare i requisiti necessari (per); (Sport) qualificarsi (per or a)

quality ['kwɔlɪtɪ] n qualità f inv

qualm [kwɑːm] n dubbio; scrupolo

quantify ['kwɔntɪfaɪ] vt quantificare

quantity ['kwɔntɪtɪ] n quantità f inv

quarantine ['kwɔrntiːn] n quarantena

quarrel ['kwɔrl] n lite f, disputa ▶ vi litigare

quarry ['kwɔrɪ] n (for stone) cava; (animal) preda

quart [kwɔːt] n ≈ litro

quarter ['kwɔːtəʳ] n quarto; (US: coin) quarto di dollaro; (of year) trimestre m; (district) quartiere m ▶ vt dividere in quattro; (Mil) alloggiare; **~s** npl (living quarters) alloggio; (Mil) alloggi mpl, quadrato; **a ~ of an hour** un quarto d'ora; **quarter final** n quarto di finale; **quarterly** adj trimestrale ▶ adv trimestralmente

quartet(te) [kwɔː'tɛt] n quartetto

quartz [kwɔːts] n quarzo

quay [kiː] n (also: **~side**) banchina

queasy ['kwiːzɪ] adj (stomach) delicato(-a); **to feel ~** aver la nausea

queen [kwiːn] n (gen) regina, donna; (Cards etc) regina, donna

queer [kwɪəʳ] adj strano(-a), curioso(-a) ▶ n (inf) finocchio

quench [kwɛntʃ] vt **to ~ one's thirst** dissetarsi

query ['kwɪərɪ] n domanda, questione f ▶ vt mettere in questione

quest [kwɛst] n cerca, ricerca

question ['kwɛstʃən] n domanda, questione f ▶ vt (person) interrogare; (plan, idea) mettere in questione or in dubbio; **it's a ~ of doing** si tratta di fare; **beyond ~** fuori di dubbio; **out of the ~** fuori discussione, impossibile; **questionable** adj discutibile; **question mark** n punto interrogativo; **questionnaire** [kwɛstʃə'nɛəʳ] n questionario

queue [kjuː] n (BRIT) coda, fila ▶ vi fare la coda

quiche [kiːʃ] n torta salata a base di uova, formaggio, prosciutto o altro

quick [kwɪk] adj rapido(-a), veloce; (reply) pronto(-a); (mind) pronto(-a), acuto(-a) ▶ n **cut to the ~** (fig) toccato(-a) sul vivo; **be ~!** fa presto!; **quickly** adv rapidamente, velocemente

r

quid [kwɪd] (*BRIT: inf*) *n inv* sterlina
quiet ['kwaɪət] *adj* tranquillo(-a),
quieto(-a); (*ceremony*) semplice
▶ *n* tranquillità, calma ▶ *vt, vi* (*US*)
= **quieten**; **keep ~!** sta zitto!; **quieten**
(*also:* **quieten down**) *vi* calmarsi,
chetarsi ▶ *vt* calmare, chetare;
quietly *adv* tranquillamente,
calmamente; sommessamente
quilt [kwɪlt] *n* trapunta; (*continental
quilt*) piumino
quirky ['kwə:kɪ] *adj* stravagante
quit [kwɪt] (*pt, pp* **quit** *or* **quitted**) *vt*
mollare; (*premises*) lasciare, partire
da ▶ *vi* (*give up*) mollare; (*resign*)
dimettersi
quite [kwaɪt] *adv* (*rather*) assai;
(*entirely*) completamente, del tutto; **I
~ understand** capisco perfettamente;
that's not ~ big enough non è proprio
sufficiente; **~ a few of them** non pochi
di loro; **~ (so)!** esatto!
quits [kwɪts] *adj* **~ (with)** pari (con);
let's call it ~ adesso siamo pari
quiver ['kwɪvə'] *vi* tremare, fremere
quiz [kwɪz] *n* (*game*) quiz *m inv*;
indovinello ▶ *vt* interrogare
quota ['kwəʊtə] *n* quota
quotation [kwəʊ'teɪʃən] *n* citazione
f; (*of shares etc*) quotazione *f*; (*estimate*)
preventivo; **quotation marks** *npl*
virgolette *fpl*
quote [kwəʊt] *n* citazione *f* ▶ *vt*
(*sentence*) citare; (*price*) dare, fissare;
(*shares*) quotare ▶ *vi* **to ~ from** citare;
~s *npl* = **quotation marks**

rabbi ['ræbaɪ] *n* rabbino
rabbit ['ræbɪt] *n* coniglio
rabies ['reɪbi:z] *n* rabbia
RAC (*BRIT*) *n abbr* = **Royal Automobile
Club**
rac(c)oon [rə'ku:n] *n* procione *m*
race [reɪs] *n* razza; (*competition, rush*)
corsa ▶ *vt* (*horse*) far correre ▶ *vi*
correre; (*engine*) imballarsi; **race
car** (*US*) *n* = **racing car**; **racecourse**
n campo di corse, ippodromo;
racehorse *n* cavallo da corsa;
racetrack *n* pista
racial ['reɪʃl] *adj* razziale
racing ['reɪsɪŋ] *n* corsa; **racing
car** (*BRIT*) *n* macchina da corsa;
racing driver (*BRIT*) *n* corridore *m*
automobilista
racism ['reɪsɪzəm] *n* razzismo; **racist**
adj, n razzista *m/f*
rack [ræk] *n* rastrelliera; (*also:* **luggage
~**) rete *f*, portabagagli *m inv*; (*also:* **roof
~**) portabagagli; (*dish rack*) scolapiatti
m inv ▶ *vt* **~ed by** torturato(-a) da; **to ~
one's brains** scervellarsi
racket ['rækɪt] *n* (*for tennis*) racchetta;
(*noise*) fracasso; baccano; (*swindle*)
imbroglio, truffa; (*organized crime*)
racket *m inv*
racquet ['rækɪt] *n* racchetta
radar ['reɪdɑ:'] *n* radar *m*
radiation [reɪdɪ'eɪʃən] *n*
irradiamento; (*radioactive*)
radiazione *f*

radiator ['reɪdɪeɪtə'] n radiatore m
radical ['rædɪkl] adj radicale
radio ['reɪdɪəu] n radio f inv; **on the ~** alla radio; **radioactive** [reɪdɪəu'æktɪv] adj radioattivo(-a); **radio station** n stazione f radio inv
radish ['rædɪʃ] n ravanello
RAF n abbr = **Royal Air Force**
raffle ['ræfl] n lotteria
raft [rɑːft] n zattera; (also: **life ~**) zattera di salvataggio
rag [ræg] n straccio, cencio; (pej: newspaper) giornalaccio, bandiera; (for charity) iniziativa studentesca a scopo benefico; **~s** npl (torn clothes) stracci mpl, brandelli mpl
rage [reɪdʒ] n (fury) collera, furia ▶ vi (person) andare su tutte le furie; (storm) infuriare; **it's all the ~** fa furore
ragged ['rægɪd] adj (edge) irregolare; (clothes) logoro(-a); (appearance) pezzente
raid [reɪd] n (Mil) incursione f; (criminal) rapina; (by police) irruzione f ▶ vt fare un'incursione in; rapinare; fare irruzione in
rail [reɪl] n (on stair) ringhiera; (on bridge, balcony) parapetto; (of ship) battagliola; **railcard** n (BRIT) tessera di riduzione ferroviaria; **railing(s)** n(pl) ringhiere fpl; **railroad** (US) n = **railway; railway** (BRIT: irreg) n ferrovia; **railway line** (BRIT) n linea ferroviaria; **railway station** (BRIT) n stazione f ferroviaria
rain [reɪn] n pioggia ▶ vi piovere; **in the ~** sotto la pioggia; **it's ~ing** piove; **rainbow** n arcobaleno; **raincoat** n impermeabile m; **raindrop** n goccia di pioggia; **rainfall** n pioggia; (measurement) piovosità; **rainforest** n foresta pluviale; **rainy** adj piovoso(-a)
raise [reɪz] n aumento ▶ vt (lift) alzare; sollevare; (increase) aumentare; (a protest, doubt, question) sollevare;

(cattle, family) allevare; (crop) coltivare; (army, funds) raccogliere; (loan) ottenere; **to ~ one's voice** alzare la voce
raisin ['reɪzn] n uva secca
rake [reɪk] n (tool) rastrello ▶ vt (garden) rastrellare
rally ['rælɪ] n (Pol etc) riunione f; (Aut) rally m inv; (Tennis) scambio ▶ vt riunire, radunare ▶ vi (sick person, Stock Exchange) riprendersi
RAM [ræm] n abbr (= random access memory) memoria ad accesso casuale
ram [ræm] n montone m, ariete m ▶ vt conficcare; (crash into) cozzare, sbattere contro; percuotere; speronare
Ramadan [ræmə'dæn] n Ramadan m inv
ramble ['ræmbl] n escursione f ▶ vi (pej: also: **~ on**) divagare; **rambler** n escursionista m/f; (Bot) rosa rampicante; **rambling** adj (speech) sconnesso(-a); (house) tutto(-a) a nicchie e corridoi; (Bot) rampicante
ramp [ræmp] n rampa; **on/off ~** (US Aut) raccordo di entrata/uscita
rampage [ræm'peɪdʒ] n **to go on the ~** scatenarsi in modo violento
ran [ræn] pt of **run**
ranch [rɑːntʃ] n ranch m inv
random ['rændəm] adj fatto(-a) or detto(-a) per caso; (Comput, Math) casuale ▶ n **at ~** a casaccio
rang [ræŋ] pt of **ring**
range [reɪndʒ] n (of mountains) catena; (of missile, voice) portata; (of proposals, products) gamma; (Mil: also: **shooting ~**) campo di tiro; (also: **kitchen ~**) fornello, cucina economica ▶ vt disporre ▶ vi **to ~ over** coprire; **to ~ from … to** andare da … a
ranger ['reɪndʒə'] n guardia forestale
rank [ræŋk] n fila; (status, Mil) grado; (BRIT: also: **taxi ~**) posteggio di

taxi ▶ *vi* **to ~ among** essere tra ▶ *adj* puzzolente; vero(-a) e proprio(-a); **the ~ and file** (*fig*) la gran massa

ransom ['rænsəm] *n* riscatto; **to hold sb to ~** (*fig*) esercitare pressione su qn

rant [rænt] *vi* vociare

rap [ræp] *vt* bussare a; picchiare su ▶ *n* (*music*) rap *m inv*

rape [reɪp] *n* violenza carnale, stupro; (*Bot*) ravizzone *m* ▶ *vt* violentare

rapid ['ræpɪd] *adj* rapido(-a); **rapidly** *adv* rapidamente; **rapids** *npl* (*Geo*) rapida

rapist ['reɪpɪst] *n* violentatore *m*

rapport [ræ'pɔːʳ] *n* rapporto

rare [rɛəʳ] *adj* raro(-a); (*Culin: steak*) al sangue; **rarely** ['rɛəlɪ] *adv* raramente

rash [ræʃ] *adj* imprudente, sconsiderato(-a) ▶ *n* (*Med*) eruzione *f*; (*of events etc*) scoppio

rasher ['ræʃəʳ] *n* fetta sottile (di lardo *or* prosciutto)

raspberry ['rɑːzbərɪ] *n* lampone *m*

rat [ræt] *n* ratto

rate [reɪt] *n* (*proportion*) tasso, percentuale *f*; (*speed*) velocità *f inv*; (*price*) tariffa ▶ *vt* giudicare; stimare; **~s** *npl* (*BRIT: property tax*) imposte *fpl* comunali; (*fees*) tariffe *fpl*; **to ~ sb/sth as** valutare qn/qc come

rather ['rɑːðəʳ] *adv* piuttosto; **it's ~ expensive** è piuttosto caro; (*too*) è un po' caro; **there's ~ a lot** ce n'è parecchio; **I would** *or* **I'd ~ go** preferirei andare

rating ['reɪtɪŋ] *n* (*assessment*) valutazione *f*; (*score*) punteggio di merito; **~s** *npl* (*Radio, TV*) indice *m* di ascolto

ratio ['reɪʃɪəu] *n* proporzione *f*, rapporto

ration ['ræʃən] *n* (*gen pl*) razioni *fpl* ▶ *vt* razionare; **~s** *npl* razioni *fpl*

rational ['ræʃənl] *adj* razionale, ragionevole; (*solution, reasoning*) logico(-a)

rattle ['rætl] *n* tintinnio; (*louder*) strepito; (*for baby*) sonaglino ▶ *vi* risuonare, tintinnare; fare un rumore di ferraglia ▶ *vt* scuotere (con strepito)

rave [reɪv] *vi* (*in anger*) infuriarsi; (*with enthusiasm*) andare in estasi; (*Med*) delirare ▶ *n* (*BRIT: inf: party*) rave *m inv*

raven ['reɪvn] *n* corvo

ravine [rə'viːn] *n* burrone *m*

raw [rɔː] *adj* (*uncooked*) crudo(-a); (*not processed*) greggio(-a); (*sore*) vivo(-a); (*inexperienced*) inesperto(-a); (*weather, day*) gelido(-a)

ray [reɪ] *n* raggio; **a ~ of hope** un barlume di speranza

razor ['reɪzəʳ] *n* rasoio; **razor blade** *n* lama di rasoio

Rd *abbr* = **road**

re [riː] *prep* con riferimento a

RE *n abbr* (*BRIT Mil*: = *Royal Engineers*) ≈ G.M. (*Genio Militare*); (*BRIT*) = **religious education**

reach [riːtʃ] *n* portata; (*of river etc*) tratto ▶ *vt* raggiungere; arrivare a ▶ *vi* stendersi; **out of/within ~** fuori/a portata di mano; **within ~ of the shops/station** vicino ai negozi/alla stazione ▷ **reach out** *vt* (*hand*) allungare ▶ *vi* **to ~ out for** stendere la mano per prendere

react [riː'ækt] *vi* reagire; **reaction** [-'ækʃən] *n* reazione *f*; **reactor** [riː'æktəʳ] *n* reattore *m*

read [riːd, *pt, pp* rɛd] (*pt, pp* **read**) *vi* leggere ▶ *vt* leggere; (*understand*) intendere, interpretare; (*study*) studiare ▷ **read out** *vt* leggere ad alta voce; **reader** *n* lettore(-trice); (*BRIT: at university*) professore con funzioni preminenti di ricerca

readily ['rɛdɪlɪ] *adv* volentieri; (*easily*) facilmente; (*quickly*) prontamente

reading ['riːdɪŋ] *n* lettura;

r

(*understanding*) interpretazione f; (*on instrument*) indicazione f

ready ['rɛdɪ] *adj* pronto(-a); (*willing*) pronto(-a), disposto(-a); (*available*) disponibile ▶ *n* **at the ~** (*Mil*) pronto a sparare; **when will my photos be ~?** quando saranno pronte le mie foto?; **to get ~** *vi* prepararsi ▶ *vt* preparare; **ready-made** *adj* prefabbricato(-a); (*clothes*) confezionato(-a)

real [rɪəl] *adj* reale; vero(-a); **in ~ terms** in realtà; **real ale** *n* birra ad effervescenza naturale; **real estate** *n* beni *mpl* immobili; **realistic** [-'lɪstɪk] *adj* realistico(-a); **reality** [ri:'ælɪtɪ] *n* realtà *f inv*; **reality TV** *n* reality TV *f*

realization [rɪəlaɪ'zeɪʃən] *n* presa di coscienza; realizzazione f

realize ['rɪəlaɪz] *vt* (*understand*) rendersi conto di

really ['rɪəlɪ] *adv* veramente, davvero; **~!** (*indicating annoyance*) oh, insomma!

realm [rɛlm] *n* reame *m*, regno

Realtor® ['rɪəltɔːʳ] (*US*) *n* agente *m* immobiliare

reappear [ri:ə'pɪəʳ] *vi* ricomparire, riapparire

rear [rɪəʳ] *adj* di dietro; (*Aut: wheel etc*) posteriore ▶ *n* di dietro, parte f posteriore ▶ *vt* (*cattle, family*) allevare ▶ *vi* (*also: ~ up: animal*) impennarsi

rearrange [ri:ə'reɪndʒ] *vt* riordinare

rear: rear-view mirror ['rɪəvju:-] *n* (*Aut*) specchio retrovisore; **rear-wheel drive** *n* trazione *fpl* posteriore

reason ['ri:zn] *n* ragione f; (*cause, motive*) ragione, motivo ▶ *vi* **to ~ with sb** far ragionare qn; **it stands to ~ that** è ovvio che; **reasonable** *adj* ragionevole; (*not bad*) accettabile; **reasonably** *adv* ragionevolmente; **reasoning** *n* ragionamento

reassurance [ri:ə'ʃuərəns] *n* rassicurazione f

reassure [ri:ə'ʃuəʳ] *vt* rassicurare; **to ~ sb of** rassicurare qn di or su

rebate ['ri:beɪt] *n* (*on tax etc*) sgravio

rebel [*n* 'rɛbl, *vb* rɪ'bɛl] *n* ribelle *m/f* ▶ *vi* ribellarsi; **rebellion** *n* ribellione f; **rebellious** *adj* ribelle

rebuild [ri:'bɪld] *vt irreg* ricostruire

recall [rɪ'kɔ:l] *vt* richiamare; (*remember*) ricordare, richiamare alla mente ▶ *n* richiamo

rec'd *abbr* = **received**

receipt [rɪ'si:t] *n* (*document*) ricevuta; (*act of receiving*) ricevimento; **~s** *npl* (*Comm*) introiti *mpl*; **can I have a ~, please?** posso avere una ricevuta, per favore?

receive [rɪ'si:v] *vt* ricevere; (*guest*) ricevere, accogliere; **receiver** [rɪ'si:vəʳ] *n* (*Tel*) ricevitore *m*; (*Radio, TV*) apparecchio ricevente; (*of stolen goods*) ricettatore(-trice); (*Comm*) curatore *m* fallimentare

recent ['ri:snt] *adj* recente; **recently** *adv* recentemente

reception [rɪ'sɛpʃən] *n* ricevimento; (*welcome*) accoglienza; (*TV etc*) ricezione f; **reception desk** *n* (*in hotel*) reception *f inv*; (*in hospital, at doctor's*) accettazione f; (*in offices etc*) portineria; **receptionist** *n* receptionist *m/f inv*

recession [rɪ'sɛʃən] *n* recessione f

recharge [ri:'tʃɑ:dʒ] *vt* (*battery*) ricaricare

recipe ['rɛsɪpɪ] *n* ricetta

recipient [rɪ'sɪpɪənt] *n* beneficiario(-a); (*of letter*) destinatario(-a)

recital [rɪ'saɪtl] *n* recital *m inv*

recite [rɪ'saɪt] *vt* (*poem*) recitare

reckless ['rɛkləs] *adj* (*driver etc*) spericolato(-a); (*spending*) folle

reckon ['rɛkən] *vt* (*count*) calcolare; (*think*): **I ~ that ...** penso che ...

reclaim [rɪ'kleɪm] *vt* (*demand back*) richiedere, reclamare; (*land*)

bonificare; (*materials*) recuperare
recline [rɪ'klaɪn] *vi* stare sdraiato(-a)
recognition [rɛkəg'nɪʃən] *n*
  riconoscimento; **transformed
  beyond ~** irriconoscibile
recognize ['rɛkəgnaɪz] *vt* **to ~ (by/as)**
  riconoscere (a *or* da/come)
recollection [rɛkə'lɛkʃən] *n* ricordo
recommend [rɛkə'mɛnd] *vt*
  raccomandare; (*advise*) consigliare;
  can you ~ a good restaurant? mi
  può consigliare un buon ristorante?;
  recommendation [rɛkəmɛn'deɪʃən]
  n raccomandazione *f*; consiglio
reconcile ['rɛkənsaɪl] *vt* (*two people*)
  riconciliare; (*two facts*) conciliare,
  quadrare; **to ~ o.s. to** rassegnarsi a
reconsider [ri:kən'sɪdər] *vt*
  riconsiderare
reconstruct [ri:kən'strʌkt] *vt*
  ricostruire
record [*n* 'rɛkɔːd, *vb* rɪ'kɔːd] *n* ricordo,
  documento; (*of meeting etc*) nota,
  verbale *m*; (*register*) registro; (*file*)
  pratica, dossier *m inv*; (*Comput*) record
  m inv; (*also*: **criminal ~**) fedina penale
  sporca; (*Mus: disc*) disco; (*Sport*) record
  m inv, primato ▶ *vt* (*set down*) prendere
  nota di, registrare; (*Mus: song etc*)
  registrare; **in ~ time** a tempo di
  record; **off the ~** *adj* ufficioso(-a) ▶ *adv*
  ufficiosamente; **recorded delivery**
  (*BRIT*) *n* (*Post*): **recorded delivery
  letter** *etc* lettera *etc* raccomandata;
  recorder *n* (*Mus*) flauto diritto;
  recording *n* (*Mus*) registrazione *f*;
  record player *n* giradischi *m inv*
recount [rɪ'kaunt] *vt* raccontare,
  narrare
recover [rɪ'kʌvər] *vt* ricuperare ▶ *vi* **to
  ~ (from)** riprendersi (da); **recovery**
  [rɪ'kʌvərɪ] *n* ricupero; ristabilimento;
  ripresa

  Be careful not to translate **recover**
  by the Italian word *ricoverare*.

recreate [ri:krɪ'eɪt] *vt* ricreare
recreation [rɛkrɪ'eɪʃən] *n* ricreazione
  f; svago; **recreational drug**
  [rɛkrɪ'eɪʃənl-] *n sostanza stupefacente
  usata a scopo ricreativo*; **recreational
  vehicle** (*US*) *n* camper *m inv*
recruit [rɪ'kru:t] *n* recluta; (*in company*)
  nuovo(-a) assunto(-a) ▶ *vt* reclutare;
  recruitment *n* reclutamento
rectangle ['rɛktæŋgl] *n* rettangolo;
  rectangular [-'tæŋgjulər] *adj*
  rettangolare
rectify ['rɛktɪfaɪ] *vt* (*error*) rettificare;
  (*omission*) riparare
rector ['rɛktər] *n* (*Rel*) parroco
  (*anglicano*)
recur [rɪ'kəːr] *vi* riaccadere; (*symptoms*)
  ripresentarsi; **recurring** *adj* (*Math*)
  periodico(-a)
recyclable [ri:'saɪkləbl] *adj* riciclabile
recycle [ri:'saɪkl] *vt* riciclare
recycling [ri:'saɪklɪŋ] *n* riciclaggio
red [rɛd] *n* rosso; (*Pol: pej*) rosso(-a)
  ▶ *adj* rosso(-a); **in the ~** (*account*)
  scoperto; (*business*) in deficit; **Red
  Cross** *n* Croce *f* Rossa; **redcurrant** *n*
  ribes *m inv*
redeem [rɪ'di:m] *vt* (*debt*) riscattare;
  (*sth in pawn*) ritirare; (*fig, also Rel*)
  redimere
red: **red-haired** [-'hɛəd] *adj* dai capelli
  rossi; **redhead** ['rɛdhɛd] *n* rosso(-a);
  red-hot *adj* arroventato(-a); **red
  light** *n* **to go through a red light** (*Aut*)
  passare col rosso; **red-light district**
  ['rɛdlaɪt-] *n* quartiere *m* a luci rosse;
  red meat *n* carne *f* rossa
reduce [rɪ'dju:s] *vt* ridurre; (*lower*)
  ridurre, abbassare; **"~ speed now"**
  (*Aut*) "rallentare"; **at a ~d price**
  scontato(-a); **reduced** *adj* (*decreased*)
  ridotto(-a); **at a reduced price** a
  prezzo ribassato *or* ridotto; **"greatly
  reduced prices"** "grandi ribassi";
  reduction [rɪ'dʌkʃən] *n* riduzione *f*;

r

(*of price*) ribasso; (*discount*) sconto; **is there a reduction for children/ students?** ci sono riduzioni per i bambini/gli studenti?

redundancy [rɪ'dʌndənsɪ] *n* licenziamento

redundant [rɪ'dʌndnt] *adj* (*worker*) licenziato(-a); (*detail, object*) superfluo(-a); **to be made ~** essere licenziato (per eccesso di personale)

reed [ri:d] *n* (*Bot*) canna; (*Mus: of clarinet etc*) ancia

reef [ri:f] *n* (*at sea*) scogliera

reel [ri:l] *n* bobina, rocchetto; (*Fishing*) mulinello; (*Cinema*) rotolo; (*dance*) *danza veloce scozzese* ▶ *vi* (*sway*) barcollare

ref [rɛf] (*inf*) *n abbr* (= *referee*) arbitro

refectory [rɪ'fɛktərɪ] *n* refettorio

refer [rɪ'fə:ʳ] *vt* **to ~ sth to** (*dispute, decision*) deferire qc a; **to ~ sb to** (*inquirer, Med: patient*) indirizzare qn a; (*reader: to text*) rimandare qn a ▶ *vi* **~ to** (*allude to*) accennare a; (*consult*) rivolgersi a

referee [rɛfə'ri:] *n* arbitro; (*BRIT: for job application*) referenza ▶ *vt* arbitrare

reference ['rɛfrəns] *n* riferimento; (*mention*) menzione *f*, allusione *f*; (*for job application*) referenza; **with ~ to** (*Comm: in letter*) in or con riferimento a; **reference number** *n* numero di riferimento

refill [*vb* ri:'fɪl, *n* 'ri:fɪl] *vt* riempire di nuovo; (*pen, lighter etc*) ricaricare ▶ *n* (*for pen etc*) ricambio

refine [rɪ'faɪn] *vt* raffinare; **refined** *adj* (*person, taste*) raffinato(-a); **refinery** *n* raffineria

reflect [rɪ'flɛkt] *vt* (*light, image*) riflettere; (*fig*) rispecchiare ▶ *vi* (*think*) riflettere, considerare; **it ~s badly/ well on him** si ripercuote su di lui in senso negativo/positivo; **reflection** [-'flɛkʃən] *n* riflessione *f*; (*image*)

riflesso; (*criticism*): **reflection on** giudizio su; attacco a; **on reflection** pensandoci sopra

reflex ['ri:flɛks] *adj* riflesso(-a) ▶ *n* riflesso

reform [rɪ'fɔ:m] *n* (*of sinner etc*) correzione *f*; (*of law etc*) riforma ▶ *vt* correggere; riformare

refrain [rɪ'freɪn] *vi* **to ~ from doing** trattenersi dal fare ▶ *n* ritornello

refresh [rɪ'frɛʃ] *vt* rinfrescare; (*food, sleep*) ristorare; **refreshing** *adj* (*drink*) rinfrescante; (*sleep*) riposante, ristoratore(-trice); **refreshments** *npl* rinfreschi *mpl*

refrigerator [rɪ'frɪdʒəreɪtəʳ] *n* frigorifero

refuel [ri:'fjuəl] *vi* far rifornimento (di carburante)

refuge ['rɛfjuːdʒ] *n* rifugio; **to take ~ in** rifugiarsi in; **refugee** [rɛfju'dʒi:] *n* rifugiato(-a), profugo(-a)

refund [*n* 'ri:fʌnd, *vb* rɪ'fʌnd] *n* rimborso ▶ *vt* rimborsare

refurbish [ri:'fə:bɪʃ] *vt* rimettere a nuovo

refusal [rɪ'fju:zəl] *n* rifiuto; **to have first ~ on** avere il diritto d'opzione su

refuse [*n* 'rɛfju:s, *vb* rɪ'fju:z] *n* rifiuti *mpl* ▶ *vt, vi* rifiutare; **to ~ to do** rifiutare di fare

regain [rɪ'geɪn] *vt* riguadagnare; riacquistare, ricuperare

regard [rɪ'gɑ:d] *n* riguardo, stima ▶ *vt* considerare, stimare; **to give one's ~s to** porgere i suoi saluti a; **"with kindest ~s"** "cordiali saluti"; **regarding** *prep* riguardo a, per quanto riguarda; **regardless** *adv* lo stesso; **regardless of** a dispetto di, nonostante

regenerate [rɪ'dʒɛnəreɪt] *vt* rigenerare

reggae ['rɛgeɪ] *n* reggae *m*

regiment ['rɛdʒɪmənt] *n* reggimento

region ['riːdʒən] n regione f; **in the ~ of** (fig) all'incirca di; **regional** adj regionale

register ['redʒɪstər] n registro; (also: **electoral ~**) lista elettorale ▶ vt registrare; (vehicle) immatricolare; (letter) assicurare; (instrument) segnare ▶ vi iscriversi; (at hotel) firmare il registro; (make impression) entrare in testa; **registered** (BRIT) adj (letter) assicurato(-a)

registrar ['redʒɪstrɑːʳ] n ufficiale m di stato civile; segretario

registration [redʒɪs'treɪʃən] n (act) registrazione f; iscrizione f; (Aut: also: **~ number**) numero di targa

registry office (BRIT) n anagrafe f; **to get married in a ~** ≈ sposarsi in municipio

regret [rɪ'gret] n rimpianto, rincrescimento ▶ vt rimpiangere; **regrettable** adj deplorevole

regular ['regjulər] adj regolare; (usual) abituale, normale; (soldier) dell'esercito regolare ▶ n (client etc) cliente m/f abituale; **regularly** adv regolarmente

regulate ['regjuleɪt] vt regolare; **regulation** [-'leɪʃən] n regolazione f; (rule) regola, regolamento

rehabilitation ['riːhəbɪlɪ'teɪʃən] n (of offender) riabilitazione f; (of disabled) riadattamento

rehearsal [rɪ'həːsəl] n prova

rehearse [rɪ'həːs] vt provare

reign [reɪn] n regno ▶ vi regnare

reimburse [riːɪm'bəːs] vt rimborsare

rein [reɪn] n (for horse) briglia

reincarnation [riːɪnkɑːˈneɪʃən] n reincarnazione f

reindeer ['reɪndɪəʳ] n inv renna

reinforce [riːɪn'fɔːs] vt rinforzare; **reinforcements** npl (Mil) rinforzi mpl

reinstate [riːɪn'steɪt] vt reintegrare

reject [n 'riːdʒɛkt, vb rɪ'dʒɛkt] n (Comm) scarto ▶ vt rifiutare, respingere; (Comm: goods) scartare; **rejection** [rɪ'dʒɛkʃən] n rifiuto

rejoice [rɪ'dʒɔɪs] vi **to ~ (at or over)** provare diletto in

relate [rɪ'leɪt] vt (tell) raccontare; (connect) collegare ▶ vi **to ~ to** (connect) riferirsi a; (get on with) stabilire un rapporto con; **relating to** che riguarda, rispetto a; **related** adj **related (to)** imparentato(-a) (con); collegato(-a) or connesso(-a) (a)

relation [rɪ'leɪʃən] n (person) parente m/f; (link) rapporto, relazione f; **~s** npl (relatives) parenti mpl; **relationship** n rapporto; (personal ties) rapporti mpl, relazioni fpl; (also: **family relationship**) legami mpl di parentela

relative ['relətɪv] n parente m/f ▶ adj relativo(-a); (respective) rispettivo(-a); **relatively** adv relativamente; (fairly, rather) abbastanza

relax [rɪ'læks] vi rilasciarsi; (person: unwind) rilassarsi ▶ vt rilasciare; (mind, person) rilassare; **relaxation** [riːlæk'seɪʃən] n rilasciamento, rilassamento; (entertainment) ricreazione f, svago; **relaxed** adj rilassato(-a); **relaxing** adj rilassante

relay ['riːleɪ] n (Sport) corsa a staffetta ▶ vt (message) trasmettere

release [rɪ'liːs] n (from prison) rilascio; (from obligation) liberazione f; (of gas etc) emissione f; (of film etc) distribuzione f; (record) disco; (device) disinnesto ▶ vt (prisoner) rilasciare; (from obligation, wreckage etc) liberare; (book, film) fare uscire; (news) rendere pubblico(-a); (gas etc) emettere; (Tech: catch, spring etc) disinnestare

relegate ['relədʒeɪt] vt relegare; (BRIT Sport): **to be ~d** essere retrocesso(-a)

relent [rɪ'lent] vi cedere; **relentless** adj implacabile

relevant ['relevent] adj pertinente;

(*chapter*) in questione; **~ to** pertinente a

■ Be careful not to translate **relevant** by the Italian word *rilevante*.

reliable [rɪˈlaɪəbl] *adj* (*person, firm*) fidato(-a), che dà affidamento; (*method*) sicuro(-a); (*machine*) affidabile

relic [ˈrɛlɪk] *n* (*Rel*) reliquia; (*of the past*) resto

relief [rɪˈliːf] *n* (*from pain, anxiety*) sollievo; (*help, supplies*) soccorsi *mpl*; (*Art, Geo*) rilievo

relieve [rɪˈliːv] *vt* (*pain, patient*) sollevare; (*bring help*) soccorrere; (*take over from: gen*) sostituire; (: *guard*) rilevare; **to ~ sb of sth** (*load*) alleggerire qn di qc; **to ~ o.s.** fare i propri bisogni; **relieved** *adj* sollevato(-a); **to be relieved that ...** essere sollevato(-a) (dal fatto) che ...; **I'm relieved to hear it** mi hai tolto un peso con questa notizia

religion [rɪˈlɪdʒən] *n* religione *f*

religious [rɪˈlɪdʒəs] *adj* religioso(-a); **religious education** *n* religione *f*

relish [ˈrɛlɪʃ] *n* (*Culin*) condimento; (*enjoyment*) gran piacere *m* ▶ *vt* (*food etc*) godere; **to ~ doing** adorare fare

relocate [ˈriːləuˈkeɪt] *vt* trasferire ▶ *vi* trasferirsi

reluctance [rɪˈlʌktəns] *n* riluttanza

reluctant [rɪˈlʌktənt] *adj* riluttante, mal disposto(-a); **reluctantly** *adv* di mala voglia, a malincuore

rely [rɪˈlaɪ]: **to ~ on** *vt fus* contare su; (*be dependent*) dipendere da

remain [rɪˈmeɪn] *vi* restare, rimanere; **remainder** *n* resto; (*Comm*) rimanenza; **remaining** *adj* che rimane; **remains** *npl* resti *mpl*

remand [rɪˈmɑːnd] *n* **on ~** in detenzione preventiva ▶ *vt* **to ~ in custody** rinviare in carcere; trattenere a disposizione della legge

remark [rɪˈmɑːk] *n* osservazione *f* ▶ *vt* osservare, dire; **remarkable** *adj* notevole; eccezionale

remarry [riːˈmærɪ] *vi* risposarsi

remedy [ˈrɛmədɪ] *n* **~ (for)** rimedio (per) ▶ *vt* rimediare a

remember [rɪˈmɛmbər] *vt* ricordare, ricordarsi di; **~ me to him** salutalo da parte mia; **Remembrance Day** [rɪˈmɛmbrəns-] *n* 11 novembre, giorno della commemorazione dei caduti in guerra

● **Remembrance Day**
● In Gran Bretagna, il
● **Remembrance Day** è un giorno
● di commemorazione dei caduti
● in guerra. Si celebra ogni anno
● la domenica più vicina all'11
● novembre, anniversario della firma
● dell'armistizio con la Germania
● nel 1918.

remind [rɪˈmaɪnd] *vt* **to ~ sb of sth** ricordare qc a qn; **to ~ sb to do** ricordare a qn di fare; **reminder** *n* richiamo; (*note etc*) promemoria *m inv*

reminiscent [rɛmɪˈnɪsnt] *adj* **~ of** che fa pensare a, che richiama

remnant [ˈrɛmnənt] *n* resto, avanzo

remorse [rɪˈmɔːs] *n* rimorso

remote [rɪˈməut] *adj* remoto(-a), lontano(-a); (*person*) distaccato(-a); **remote control** *n* telecomando; **remotely** *adv* remotamente; (*slightly*) vagamente

removal [rɪˈmuːvəl] *n* (*taking away*) rimozione *f*; soppressione *f*; (*BRIT: from house*) trasloco; (*from office: dismissal*) destituzione *f*; (*Med*) ablazione *f*; **removal man** (*irreg*) *n* (*BRIT*) addetto ai traslochi; **removal van** (*BRIT*) *n* furgone *m* per traslochi

remove [rɪˈmuːv] *vt* togliere, rimuovere; (*employee*) destituire; (*stain*) far sparire; (*doubt, abuse*) sopprimere, eliminare

Renaissance [rɪˈneɪsɑ̃:ns] n **the ~** il Rinascimento

rename [ri:ˈneɪm] vt ribattezzare

render [ˈrɛndəʳ] vt rendere

rendezvous [ˈrɒndɪvu:] n appuntamento; (place) luogo d'incontro; (meeting) incontro

renew [rɪˈnju:] vt rinnovare; (negotiations) riprendere; **renewable** adj (contract, energy) rinnovabile

renovate [ˈrɛnəveɪt] vt rinnovare

renowned [rɪˈnaund] adj rinomato(-a)

rent [rɛnt] n affitto ▶ vt (take for rent) prendere in affitto; (also: **~ out**) dare in affitto; **rental** n (for car etc) fitto

reorganize [ri:ˈɔ:gənaɪz] vt riorganizzare

rep [rɛp] n abbr (Comm: = representative) rappresentante m/f; (Theatre: = repertory) teatro di repertorio

repair [rɪˈpeəʳ] n riparazione f ▶ vt riparare; **in good/bad ~** in buone/cattive condizioni; **where can I get this ~ed?** dove lo posso far riparare?; **repair kit** n corredo per riparazioni

repay [ri:ˈpeɪ] (irreg) vt (money, creditor) rimborsare, ripagare; (sb's efforts) ricompensare; (favour) ricambiare; **repayment** n pagamento; rimborso

repeat [rɪˈpi:t] n (Radio, TV) replica ▶ vt ripetere; (pattern) riprodurre; (promise, attack, also Comm: order) rinnovare ▶ vi ripetere; **can you ~ that, please?** può ripetere, per favore?; **repeatedly** adv ripetutamente, spesso; **repeat prescription** n (BRIT) ricetta ripetibile

repellent [rɪˈpɛlənt] adj repellente ▶ n **insect ~** prodotto m anti-insetti inv

repercussions [ri:pəˈkʌʃənz] npl ripercussioni fpl

repetition [rɛpɪˈtɪʃən] n ripetizione f

repetitive [rɪˈpɛtɪtɪv] adj (movement) che si ripete; (work) monotono(-a);

(speech) pieno(-a) di ripetizioni

replace [rɪˈpleɪs] vt (put back) rimettere a posto; (take the place of) sostituire; **replacement** n rimessa; sostituzione f; (person) sostituto(-a)

replay [ˈri:pleɪ] n (of match) partita ripetuta; (of tape, film) replay m inv

replica [ˈrɛplɪkə] n replica, copia

reply [rɪˈplaɪ] n risposta ▶ vi rispondere

report [rɪˈpɔ:t] n rapporto; (Press etc) cronaca; (BRIT: also: **school ~**) pagella; (of gun) sparo ▶ vt riportare; (Press etc) fare una cronaca su; (bring to notice: occurrence) segnalare; (: person) denunciare ▶ vi (make a report) fare un rapporto (or una cronaca); (present o.s.): **to ~ (to sb)** presentarsi (a qn); **I'd like to ~ a theft** vorrei denunciare un furto; **report card** n (US, SCOTTISH) n pagella; **reportedly** adv stando a quanto si dice; **he reportedly told them to ...** avrebbe detto loro di ...; **reporter** n reporter m inv

represent [rɛprɪˈzɛnt] vt rappresentare; **representation** [-ˈteɪʃən] n rappresentazione f; (petition) rappresentanza; **representative** n rappresentante m/f; (US Pol) deputato(-a) ▶ adj rappresentativo(-a)

repress [rɪˈprɛs] vt reprimere; **repression** [-ˈprɛʃən] n repressione f

reprimand [ˈrɛprɪmɑ:nd] n rimprovero ▶ vt rimproverare

reproduce [ri:prəˈdju:s] vt riprodurre ▶ vi riprodursi; **reproduction** [-ˈdʌkʃən] n riproduzione f

reptile [ˈrɛptaɪl] n rettile m

republic [rɪˈpʌblɪk] n repubblica; **republican** adj, n repubblicano(-a)

reputable [ˈrɛpjutəbl] adj di buona reputazione; (occupation) rispettabile

reputation [rɛpjuˈteɪʃən] n reputazione f

request [rɪ'kwɛst] n domanda; (formal) richiesta ▶ vt **to ~ (of** or **from sb)** chiedere (a qn); **request stop** (BRIT) n (for bus) fermata facoltativa or a richiesta

require [rɪ'kwaɪə^r] vt (need: person) aver bisogno di; (: thing, situation) richiedere; (want) volere; esigere; (order): **to ~ sb to do sth** ordinare a qn di fare qc; **requirement** n esigenza; bisogno; requisito

resat [riː'sæt] pt, pp of **resit**

rescue ['rɛskjuː] n salvataggio; (help) soccorso ▶ vt salvare

research [rɪ'sɜːtʃ] n ricerca, ricerche fpl ▶ vt fare ricerche su

resemblance [rɪ'zɛmbləns] n somiglianza

resemble [rɪ'zɛmbl] vt assomigliare a

resent [rɪ'zɛnt] vt risentirsi di; **resentful** adj pieno(-a) di risentimento; **resentment** n risentimento

reservation [rɛzə'veɪʃən] n (booking) prenotazione f; (doubt) dubbio; (protected area) riserva; (BRIT: on road: also: **central ~**) spartitraffico m inv; **reservation desk** (US) n (in hotel) reception f inv

reserve [rɪ'zɜːv] n riserva ▶ vt (seats etc) prenotare; **reserved** adj (shy) riservato(-a)

reservoir ['rɛzəvwɑː^r] n serbatoio

residence ['rɛzɪdəns] n residenza; **residence permit** (BRIT) n permesso di soggiorno

resident ['rɛzɪdənt] n residente m/f; (in hotel) cliente m/f fisso(-a) ▶ adj residente; (doctor) fisso(-a); (course, college) a tempo pieno con pernottamento; **residential** [-'dɛnʃəl] adj di residenza; (area) residenziale

residue ['rɛzɪdjuː] n resto; (Chem, Physics) residuo

resign [rɪ'zaɪn] vt (one's post)

dimettersi da ▶ vi dimettersi; **to ~ o.s. to** rassegnarsi a; **resignation** [rɛzɪg'neɪʃən] n dimissioni fpl; rassegnazione f

resin ['rɛzɪn] n resina

resist [rɪ'zɪst] vt resistere a; **resistance** n resistenza

resit ['riːsɪt] (BRIT) (pt, pp **resat**) vt (exam) ripresentarsi a; (subject) ridare l'esame di ▶ n **he's got his French ~ on Friday** deve ridare l'esame di francese venerdì

resolution [rɛzə'luːʃən] n risoluzione f

resolve [rɪ'zɔlv] n risoluzione f ▶ vi (decide): **to ~ to do** decidere di fare ▶ vt (problem) risolvere

resort [rɪ'zɔːt] n (town) stazione f; (recourse) ricorso ▶ vi **to ~ to** aver ricorso a; **in the last ~** come ultima risorsa

resource [rɪ'sɔːs] n risorsa; **resourceful** adj pieno(-a) di risorse, intraprendente

respect [rɪs'pɛkt] n rispetto ▶ vt rispettare; **respectable** adj rispettabile; **respectful** adj rispettoso(-a); **respective** [rɪs'pɛktɪv] adj rispettivo(-a); **respectively** adv rispettivamente

respite ['rɛspaɪt] n respiro, tregua

respond [rɪs'pɔnd] vi rispondere; **response** [rɪs'pɔns] n risposta

responsibility [rɪspɔnsɪ'bɪlɪtɪ] n responsabilità f inv

responsible [rɪs'pɔnsɪbl] adj (trustworthy) fidato(-a); (job) di (grande) responsabilità; **~ (for)** responsabile (di); **responsibly** adv responsabilmente

responsive [rɪs'pɔnsɪv] adj che reagisce

rest [rɛst] n riposo; (stop) sosta, pausa; (Mus) pausa; (object: to support sth) appoggio, sostegno; (remainder) resto, avanzi mpl ▶ vi riposarsi;

(*remain*) rimanere, restare; (*be supported*): **to ~ on** appoggiarsi su ▶ *vt* (*far*) riposare; (*lean*): **to ~ sth on/against** appoggiare qc su/contro; **the ~ of them** gli altri; **it ~s with him to decide** sta a lui decidere

restaurant ['rɛstərɔn] *n* ristorante *m*; **restaurant car** (*BRIT*) *n* vagone *m* ristorante

restless ['rɛstlɪs] *adj* agitato(-a), irrequieto(-a)

restoration [rɛstə'reɪʃən] *n* restauro, restituzione *f*

restore [rɪ'stɔːʳ] *vt* (*building, to power*) restaurare; (*sth stolen*) restituire; (*peace, health*) ristorare

restrain [rɪs'treɪn] *vt* (*feeling, growth*) contenere, frenare; (*person*): **to ~ (from doing)** trattenere (dal fare); **restraint** *n* (*restriction*) limitazione *f*; (*moderation*) ritegno; (*of style*) contenutezza

restrict [rɪs'trɪkt] *vt* restringere, limitare; **restriction** [-kʃən] *n* **restriction (on)** restrizione *f* (di), limitazione *f*

rest room (*US*) *n* toletta

restructure [riː'strʌktʃəʳ] *vt* ristrutturare

result [rɪ'zʌlt] *n* risultato ▶ *vi* **to ~ in** avere per risultato; **as a ~ of** in or di conseguenza a, in seguito a

resume [rɪ'zjuːm] *vt, vi* (*work, journey*) riprendere

résumé ['reɪzjuːmeɪ] *n* riassunto; (*US*) curriculum *m inv* vitae

resuscitate [rɪ'sʌsɪteɪt] *vt* (*Med*) risuscitare

retail ['riːteɪl] *adj, adv* al minuto ▶ *vt* vendere al minuto; **retailer** *n* commerciante *m/f* al minuto, dettagliante *m/f*

retain [rɪ'teɪn] *vt* (*keep*) tenere, serbare

retaliation [rɪtælɪ'eɪʃən] *n* rappresaglie *fpl*

retarded [rɪ'tɑːdɪd] *adj* ritardato(-a)

retire [rɪ'taɪəʳ] *vi* (*give up work*) andare in pensione; (*withdraw*) ritirarsi, andarsene; (*go to bed*) andare a letto, ritirarsi; **retired** *adj* (*person*) pensionato(-a); **retirement** *n* pensione *f*; (*act*) pensionamento

retort [rɪ'tɔːt] *vi* rimbeccare

retreat [rɪ'triːt] *n* ritirata; (*place*) rifugio ▶ *vi* battere in ritirata

retrieve [rɪ'triːv] *vt* (*sth lost*) ricuperare, ritrovare; (*situation, honour*) salvare; (*error, loss*) rimediare a

retrospect ['rɛtrəspɛkt] *n* **in ~** guardando indietro; **retrospective** [-'spɛktɪv] *adj* retrospettivo(-a); (*law*) retroattivo(-a)

return [rɪ'təːn] *n* (*going or coming back*) ritorno; (*of sth stolen etc*) restituzione *f*; (*Finance: from land, shares*) profitto, reddito ▶ *cpd* (*journey, match*) di ritorno; (*BRIT: ticket*) di andata e ritorno ▶ *vi* tornare, ritornare ▶ *vt* rendere, restituire; (*bring back*) riportare; (*send back*) mandare indietro; (*put back*) rimettere; (*Pol: candidate*) eleggere; **~s** *npl* (*Comm*) incassi *mpl*; profitti *mpl*; **in ~ (for)** in cambio (di); **by ~ of post** a stretto giro di posta; **many happy ~s (of the day)!** cento di questi giorni!; **return ticket** *n* (*esp BRIT*) biglietto di andata e ritorno

reunion [riː'juːnɪən] *n* riunione *f*

reunite [riːjuː'naɪt] *vt* riunire

revamp ['riː'væmp] *vt* (*firm*) riorganizzare

reveal [rɪ'viːl] *vt* (*make known*) rivelare, svelare; (*display*) rivelare, mostrare; **revealing** *adj* rivelatore(-trice); (*dress*) scollato(-a)

revel ['rɛvl] *vi* **to ~ in sth/in doing** dilettarsi di qc/a fare

revelation [rɛvə'leɪʃən] *n* rivelazione *f*

revenge [rɪ'vɛndʒ] *n* vendetta ▶ *vt*

r

vendicare; **to take ~ on** vendicarsi di
revenue ['rɛvənjuː] n reddito
Reverend ['rɛvərənd] adj (in titles)
reverendo(-a)
reversal [rɪ'vəːsl] n capovolgimento
reverse [rɪ'vəːs] n contrario, opposto;
(back, defeat) rovescio; (Aut: also: ~
gear) marcia indietro ▸ adj (order,
direction) contrario(-a), opposto(-a)
▸ vt (turn) invertire, rivoltare; (change)
capovolgere, rovesciare; (Law:
judgment) cassare; (car) fare marcia
indietro con ▸ vi (BRITAut, person etc)
fare marcia indietro; **reverse-charge
call** [rɪ'vəːstʃɑːdʒ-] (BRIT) n (Tel)
telefonata con addebito al ricevente;
reversing lights (BRIT) npl (Aut) luci
fpl per la retromarcia
revert [rɪ'vəːt] vi to ~ **to** tornare a
review [rɪ'vjuː] n rivista; (of book, film)
recensione f; (of situation) esame
m ▸ vt passare in rivista; fare la
recensione di; fare il punto di
revise [rɪ'vaɪz] vt (manuscript) rivedere,
correggere; (opinion) modificare;
(study: subject) ripassare; **revision**
[rɪ'vɪʒən] n revisione f; ripasso
revival [rɪ'vaɪvəl] n ripresa;
ristabilimento; (of faith) risveglio
revive [rɪ'vaɪv] vt (person) rianimare;
(custom) far rivivere; (hope, courage,
economy) ravvivare; (play, fashion)
riesumare ▸ vi (person) rianimarsi;
(hope) ravvivarsi; (activity) riprendersi
revolt [rɪ'vəult] n rivolta, ribellione
f ▸ vi rivoltarsi, ribellarsi ▸ vt (far)
rivoltare; **revolting** adj ripugnante
revolution [rɛvə'luːʃən] n rivoluzione
f; (of wheel etc) rivoluzione,
giro; **revolutionary** adj, n
rivoluzionario(-a)
revolve [rɪ'vɔlv] vi girare
revolver [rɪ'vɔlvə^r] n rivoltella
reward [rɪ'wɔːd] n ricompensa,
premio ▸ vt to ~ **(for)** ricompensare

(per); **rewarding** adj (fig) gratificante
rewind [riː'waɪnd] (irreg) vt (watch)
ricaricare; (ribbon etc) riavvolgere
rewritable [riː'raɪtəbl] adj (CD, DVD)
riscrivibile
rewrite [riː'raɪt] vt irreg riscrivere
rheumatism ['ruːmətɪzəm] n
reumatismo
rhinoceros [raɪ'nɔsərəs] n
rinoceronte m
rhubarb ['ruːbɑːb] n rabarbaro
rhyme [raɪm] n rima; (verse) poesia
rhythm ['rɪðm] n ritmo
rib [rɪb] n (Anat) costola
ribbon ['rɪbən] n nastro; **in ~s** (torn)
a brandelli
rice [raɪs] n riso; **rice pudding** n
budino di riso
rich [rɪtʃ] adj ricco(-a); (clothes)
sontuoso(-a); (abundant): **~ in**
ricco(-a) di
rid [rɪd] (pt, pp rid) vt to ~ **sb of**
sbarazzare or liberare qn di; **to get ~ of**
sbarazzarsi di
riddle ['rɪdl] n (puzzle) indovinello
▸ vt to be **~d with** (holes) essere
crivellato(-a) di; (doubts) essere
pieno(-a) di
ride [raɪd] (pt rode, pp ridden) n (on
horse) cavalcata; (outing) passeggiata;
(distance covered) cavalcata; corsa ▸ vi
(as sport) cavalcare; (go somewhere:
on horse, bicycle) andare (a cavallo or
in bicicletta etc); (journey: on bicycle,
motorcycle, bus) andare, viaggiare
▸ vt (a horse) montare, cavalcare;
to take sb for a ~ (fig) prendere in
giro qn; fregare qn; **to ~ a horse/
bicycle/camel** montare a cavallo/in
bicicletta/in groppa a un cammello;
rider n cavalcatore(-trice); (in race)
fantino; (on bicycle) ciclista m/f; (on
motorcycle) motociclista m/f
ridge [rɪdʒ] n (of hill) cresta; (of roof)
colmo; (on object) riga (in rilievo)

ridicule ['rɪdɪkjuːl] n ridicolo; scherno ▶ vt mettere in ridicolo; **ridiculous** [rɪ'dɪkjʊləs] adj ridicolo(-a)
riding ['raɪdɪŋ] n equitazione f; **riding school** n scuola d'equitazione
rife [raɪf] adj diffuso(-a); **to be ~ with** abbondare di
rifle ['raɪfl] n carabina ▶ vt vuotare
rift [rɪft] n fessura, crepatura; (fig: disagreement) incrinatura, disaccordo
rig [rɪg] n (also: **oil ~**: on land) derrick m inv; (: at sea) piattaforma di trivellazione ▶ vt (election etc) truccare
right [raɪt] adj giusto(-a); (suitable) appropriato(-a); (not left) destro(-a) ▶ n giusto; (title, claim); (not left) destra ▶ adv (answer) correttamente; (not on the left) a destra ▶ vt raddrizzare; (fig) riparare ▶ excl bene!; **to be ~** (person) aver ragione; (answer) essere giusto(-a) or corretto(-a); **by ~s** di diritto; **on the ~** a destra; **to be in the ~** aver ragione, essere nel giusto; **~ now** proprio adesso; subito; **~ away** subito; **right angle** n angolo retto; **rightful** adj (heir) legittimo(-a); **right-hand** adj **right-hand drive** guida a destra; **the right-hand side** il lato destro; **right-handed** adj (person) che adopera la mano destra; **rightly** adv bene, correttamente; (with reason) a ragione; **right of way** n diritto di passaggio; (Aut) precedenza; **right-wing** adj (Pol) di destra
rigid ['rɪdʒɪd] adj rigido(-a); (principle) rigoroso(-a)
rigorous ['rɪgərəs] adj rigoroso(-a)
rim [rɪm] n orlo; (of spectacles) montatura; (of wheel) cerchione m
rind [raɪnd] n (of bacon) cotenna; (of lemon etc) scorza
ring [rɪŋ] (pt **rang**, pp **rung**) n anello; (of people, objects) cerchio; (of spies) giro; (of smoke etc) spirale m; (arena) pista, arena; (for boxing) ring m inv;

(sound of bell) scampanio ▶ vi (person, bell, telephone) suonare; (also: ~ **out**: voice, words) risuonare; (Tel) telefonare; (ears) fischiare ▶ vt (BRIT Tel) telefonare a; (: bell, doorbell) suonare; **to give sb a ~** (BRIT Tel) dare un colpo di telefono a qn ▷ **ring back** vt, vi (Tel) richiamare ▷ **ring off** (BRIT) vi (Tel) mettere giù, riattaccare ▷ **ring up** (BRIT) vt (Tel) telefonare a; **ringing tone** (BRIT) n (Tel) segnale m di libero; **ringleader** n (of gang) capobanda m; **ring road** (BRIT) n raccordo anulare
ring tone n suoneria
rink [rɪŋk] n (also: **ice ~**) pista di pattinaggio
rinse [rɪns] n risciacquatura; (hair tint) cachet m inv ▶ vt sciacquare
riot ['raɪət] n sommossa, tumulto; (of colours) orgia ▶ vi tumultuare; **to run ~** creare disordine
rip [rɪp] n strappo ▶ vt strappare ▶ vi strapparsi ▷ **rip off** vt (inf: cheat) fregare ▷ **rip up** vt stracciare
ripe [raɪp] adj (fruit, grain) maturo(-a); (cheese) stagionato(-a)
rip-off ['rɪpɔf] n (inf): **it's a ~!** è un furto!
ripple ['rɪpl] n increspamento, ondulazione f; mormorio ▶ vi incresparsi
rise [raɪz] (pt **rose**, pp **risen**) n (slope) salita, pendio; (hill) altura; (increase: in wages: BRIT) aumento; (: in prices, temperature) rialzo, aumento; (fig: to power etc) ascesa ▶ vi alzarsi, levarsi; (prices) aumentare; (waters, river) crescere; (sun, wind, person: from chair, bed) levarsi; (also: ~ **up**: building) ergersi; (: rebel) insorgere; ribellarsi; (in rank) salire; **to give ~ to** provocare, dare origine a; **to ~ to the occasion** essere all'altezza; **risen** ['rɪzn] pp of **rise**; **rising** adj (increasing: number) sempre crescente; (: prices) in

aumento; (*tide*) montante; (*sun, moon*) nascente, che sorge

risk [rɪsk] *n* rischio; pericolo ▶ *vt* rischiare; **to take** *or* **run the ~ of doing** correre il rischio di fare; **at ~** in pericolo; **at one's own ~** a proprio rischio e pericolo; **risky** *adj* rischioso(-a)

rite [raɪt] *n* rito; **last ~s** l'estrema unzione

ritual ['rɪtjuəl] *adj* rituale ▶ *n* rituale *m*

rival ['raɪvl] *n* rivale *m/f*; (*in business*) concorrente *m/f* ▶ *adj* rivale; che fa concorrenza ▶ *vt* essere in concorrenza con; **to ~ sb/sth in** competere con qn/qc in; **rivalry** *n* rivalità; concorrenza

river ['rɪvəʳ] *n* fiume *m* ▶ *cpd* (*port, traffic*) fluviale; **up/down ~** a monte/valle

riverbank *n* argine *m*

rivet ['rɪvɪt] *n* ribattino, rivetto ▶ *vt* (*fig*) concentrare, fissare

Riviera [rɪvɪ'ɛərə] *n* **the (French) ~** la Costa Azzurra; **the Italian ~** la Riviera

road [rəud] *n* strada; (*small*) cammino; (*in town*) via ▶ *cpd* stradale; **major/minor ~** strada con/senza diritto di precedenza; **which ~ do I take for ...?** che strada devo prendere per andare a...?; **roadblock** *n* blocco stradale; **road map** *n* carta stradale; **road rage** *n comportamento aggressivo al volante*; **road safety** *n* sicurezza sulle strade; **roadside** *n* margine *m* della strada; **roadsign** *n* cartello stradale; **road tax** *n* (*BRIT*) tassa di circolazione; **roadworks** *npl* lavori *mpl* stradali

roam [rəum] *vi* errare, vagabondare

roar [rɔːʳ] *n* ruggito; (*of crowd*) tumulto; (*of thunder, storm*) muggito; (*of laughter*) scoppio ▶ *vi* ruggire; tumultuare; muggire; **to ~ with laughter** scoppiare dalle risa; **to do a ~ing trade** fare affari d'oro

roast [rəust] *n* arrosto ▶ *vt* arrostire;

(*coffee*) tostare, torrefare; **roast beef** *n* arrosto di manzo

rob [rɔb] *vt* (*person*) rubare; (*bank*) svaligiare; **to ~ sb of sth** derubare qn di qc; (*fig: deprive*) privare qn di qc; **robber** *n* ladro; (*armed*) rapinatore *m*; **robbery** *n* furto; rapina

robe [rəub] *n* (*for ceremony etc*) abito; (*also: bath ~*) accappatoio; (*US: also: lap ~*) coperta

robin ['rɔbɪn] *n* pettirosso

robot ['rəubɔt] *n* robot *m inv*

robust [rəu'bʌst] *adj* robusto(-a); (*economy*) solido(-a)

rock [rɔk] *n* (*substance*) roccia; (*boulder*) masso; roccia; (*in sea*) scoglio; (*US: pebble*) ciottolo; (*BRIT: sweet*) zucchero candito ▶ *vt* (*swing gently: cradle*) dondolare; (*: child*) cullare; (*shake*) scrollare, far tremare ▶ *vi* dondolarsi; scrollarsi, tremare; **on the ~s** (*drink*) col ghiaccio; (*marriage etc*) in crisi; **rock and roll** *n* rock and roll *m*; **rock climbing** *n* roccia

rocket ['rɔkɪt] *n* razzo

rocking chair *n* sedia a dondolo

rocky ['rɔkɪ] *adj* (*hill*) roccioso(-a); (*path*) sassoso(-a); (*marriage etc*) instabile

rod [rɔd] *n* (*metallic, Tech*) asta; (*wooden*) bacchetta; (*also: fishing ~*) canna da pesca

rode [rəud] *pt of* **ride**

rodent ['rəudnt] *n* roditore *m*

rogue [rəug] *n* mascalzone *m*

role [rəul] *n* ruolo; **role-model** *n* modello (di comportamento)

roll [rəul] *n* rotolo; (*of banknotes*) mazzo; (*also: bread ~*) panino; (*register*) lista; (*sound: of drums etc*) rullo ▶ *vt* rotolare; (*also: ~ up: string*) aggomitolare; (*: sleeves*) rimboccare; (*cigarettes*) arrotolare; (*eyes*) roteare; (*also: ~ out: pastry*) stendere; (*lawn, road etc*) spianare ▶ *vi* rotolare; (*wheel*) girare; (*drum*) rullare; (*vehicle: also:* ~ **along**) avanzare; (*ship*) rollare ▷ **roll over** *vi* rivoltarsi ▷ **roll up** (*inf*) *vi* (*arrive*) arrivare ▶ *vt* (*carpet*) arrotolare; **roller** *n* rullo; (*wheel*) rotella; (*for hair*) bigodino; **Rollerblades®** *npl* pattini *mpl* in linea; **roller coaster** [-'kəustər] *n* montagne *fpl* russe; **roller skates** *npl* pattini *mpl* a rotelle; **roller-skating** *n* pattinaggio a rotelle; **to go roller-skating** andare a pattinare (*con i pattini a rotelle*); **rolling pin** *n* matterello

ROM [rɔm] *n abbr* (= read only memory) memoria di sola lettura

Roman ['rəumən] *adj*, *n* romano(-a); **Roman Catholic** *adj*, *n* cattolico(-a)

romance [rə'mæns] *n* storia (*or* avventura *or* film *m inv*) romantico(-a); (*charm*) poesia; (*love affair*) idillio

Romania [rəu'meɪnɪə] *n* Romania

Romanian [rəu'meɪnɪən] *adj* romeno(-a) ▶ *n* romeno; (*Ling*) romeno

Roman numeral *n* numero romano

romantic [rə'mæntɪk] *adj* romantico(-a); sentimentale

Rome [rəum] *n* Roma

roof [ru:f] *n* tetto; (*of tunnel, cave*) volta ▶ *vt* coprire (con un tetto); ~ **of the mouth** palato; **roof rack** *n* (*Aut*) portabagagli *m inv*

rook [ruk] *n* (*bird*) corvo nero; (*Chess*) torre *f*

room [ru:m] *n* (*in house*) stanza; (*bedroom, in hotel*) camera; (*in school etc*) sala; (*space*) posto, spazio; **roommate** *n* compagno(-a) di stanza; **room service** *n* servizio da camera; **roomy** *adj* spazioso(-a); (*garment*) ampio(-a)

rooster ['ru:stər] *n* gallo

root [ru:t] *n* radice *f* ▶ *vi* (*plant, belief*) attechire

rope [rəup] *n* corda, fune *f*; (*Naut*) cavo ▶ *vt* (*box*) legare; (*climbers*) legare in cordata; (*area: also:* ~ **off**) isolare cingendo con cordoni; **to know the ~s** (*fig*) conoscere i trucchi del mestiere

rose [rəuz] *pt of* **rise** ▶ *n* rosa; (*also:* ~ **bush**) rosaio; (*on watering can*) rosetta

rosé ['rəuzeɪ] *n* vino rosato

rosemary ['rəuzmərɪ] *n* rosmarino

rosy ['rəuzɪ] *adj* roseo(-a)

rot [rɔt] *n* (*decay*) putrefazione *f*; (*inf: nonsense*) stupidaggini *fpl* ▶ *vt*, *vi* imputridire, marcire

rota ['rəutə] *n* tabella dei turni

rotate [rəu'teɪt] *vt* (*revolve*) far girare; (*change round: jobs*) fare a turno ▶ *vi* (*revolve*) girare

rotten ['rɔtn] *adj* (*decayed*) putrido(-a), marcio(-a); (*dishonest*) corrotto(-a); (*inf: bad*) brutto(-a); (: *action*) vigliacco(-a); **to feel ~** (*ill*) sentirsi da cani

rough [rʌf] *adj* (*skin, surface*) ruvido(-a); (*terrain, road*) accidentato(-a); (*voice*) rauco(-a); (*person, manner: coarse*) rozzo(-a), aspro(-a); (: *violent*) brutale; (*district*) malfamato(-a); (*weather*) cattivo(-a); (*sea*) mosso(-a); (*plan*) abbozzato(-a); (*guess*) approssimativo(-a) ▶ *n* (*Golf*) macchia; **to ~ it** far vita dura; **to sleep ~** (BRIT) dormire all'addiaccio; **roughly** *adv* (*handle*) rudemente, brutalmente; (*make*) grossolanamente; (*speak*) bruscamente; (*approximately*) approssimativamente

roulette [ru:'lɛt] *n* roulette *f*

round [raund] *adj* rotondo(-a); (*figures*) tondo(-a) ▶ *n* (BRIT: *of toast*) fetta; (*duty: of policeman, milkman etc*) giro; (: *of doctor*) visite *fpl*; (*game: of cards, golf, in competition*) partita; (*of ammunition*) cartuccia; (*Boxing*) round *m inv*; (*of talks*) serie *f inv* ▶ *vt* (*corner*)

girare; (bend) prendere ▶ prep intorno
a ▶ adv all ~ tutt'attorno; **to go the
long way** ~ fare il giro più lungo; **all
the year** ~ tutto l'anno; **it's just** ~
the corner (also fig) è dietro l'angolo;
~ **the clock** ininterrottamente; **to
go** ~ **to sb's house** andare da qn; **go
~ the back** passi dietro; **enough
to go** ~ abbastanza per tutti; ~ **of
applause** applausi mpl; ~ **of drinks**
giro di bibite; ~ **of sandwiches**
sandwich m inv ▷ **round off** vt (speech
etc) finire ▷ **round up** vt radunare;
(criminals) fare una retata di; (prices)
arrotondare; **roundabout** n (BRIT
Aut) rotatoria; (: at fair) giostra ▶ adj
(route, means) indiretto(-a); **round
trip** n (viaggio di) andata e ritorno;
roundup n raduno; (of criminals)
retata

rouse [rauz] vt (wake up) svegliare; (stir
up) destare; provocare; risvegliare

route [ru:t] n itinerario; (of bus)
percorso

routine [ru:'ti:n] adj (work) corrente,
abituale; (procedure) solito(-a) ▶ n
(pej) routine f, tran tran m; (Theatre)
numero

row¹ [rəu] n (line) riga, fila; (Knitting)
ferro; (behind one another: of cars,
people) fila; (in boat) remata ▶ vi (in
boat) remare; (as sport) vogare ▶ vt
(boat) manovrare a remi; **in a** ~ (fig)
di fila

row² [rau] n (racket) baccano, chiasso;
(dispute) lite f; (scolding) sgridata ▶ vi
(argue) litigare

rowboat ['rəubəut] (US) n barca
a remi

rowing ['rəuɪŋ] n canottaggio;
rowing boat (BRIT) n barca a remi

royal ['rɔɪəl] adj reale; **royalty**
['rɔɪəltɪ] n (royal persons) (membri
mpl della) famiglia reale; (payment: to
author) diritti mpl d'autore

rpm abbr (= revolutions per minute)
giri/min.

R.S.V.P. abbr (= répondez s'il vous plaît)
R.S.V.P.

Rt. Hon. (BRIT) abbr (= Right
Honourable) ≈ Onorevole

rub [rʌb] n **to give sth a** ~ strofinare
qc; (sore place) massaggiare qc ▶ vt
strofinare; massaggiare; (hands: also:
~ **together**) sfregarsi; **to** ~ **sb up** (BRIT)
or ~ **sb the wrong way** (US) lisciare
qn contro pelo ▷ **rub in** vt (ointment)
far penetrare (massaggiando or
frizionando) ▷ **rub off** vi andare via
▷ **rub out** vt cancellare

rubber ['rʌbə'] n gomma; **rubber
band** n elastico; **rubber gloves** npl
guanti mpl di gomma

rubbish ['rʌbɪʃ] n (from household)
immondizie fpl, rifiuti mpl; (fig,
pej) cose fpl senza valore; robaccia;
sciocchezze fpl; **rubbish bin** (BRIT)
n pattumiera; **rubbish dump** n (in
town) immondezzaio

rubble ['rʌbl] n macerie fpl; (smaller)
pietrisco

ruby ['ru:bɪ] n rubino

rucksack ['rʌksæk] n zaino

rudder ['rʌdə'] n timone m

rude [ru:d] adj (impolite: person)
scortese, rozzo(-a); (: word, manners)
grossolano(-a), rozzo(-a); (shocking)
indecente

ruffle ['rʌfl] vt (hair) scompigliare;
(clothes, water) increspare; (fig: person)
turbare

rug [rʌg] n tappeto; (BRIT: for knees)
coperta

rugby ['rʌgbɪ] n (also: ~ **football**)
rugby m

rugged ['rʌgɪd] adj (landscape)
aspro(-a); (features, determination)
duro(-a); (character) brusco(-a)

ruin ['ru:ɪn] n rovina ▶ vt rovinare; ~**s**
npl (of building, castle etc) rovine fpl,

ruderi *mpl*

rule [ruːl] *n* regola; (*regulation*) regolamento, regola; (*government*) governo; (*ruler*) riga ▶ *vt* (*country*) governare; (*person*) dominare ▶ *vi* regnare; decidere; (*Law*) dichiarare; **as a ~** normalmente ▷ **rule out** *vt* escludere; **ruler** *n* (*sovereign*) sovrano(-a); (*for measuring*) regolo, riga; **ruling** *adj* (*party*) al potere; (*class*) dirigente ▶ *n* (*Law*) decisione *f*

rum [rʌm] *n* rum *m*

Rumania *etc* [ruːˈmeɪnɪə] *n* = **Romania** *etc*

rumble [ˈrʌmbl] *n* rimbombo; brontolio ▶ *vi* rimbombare; (*stomach, pipe*) brontolare

rumour [ˈruːməʳ] (*US* **rumor**) *n* voce *f* ▶ *vt* **it is ~ed that** corre voce che

⬛ Be careful not to translate **rumour** by the Italian word *rumore*.

rump steak [rʌmp-] *n* bistecca di girello

run [rʌn] (*pt* **ran**, *pp* **run**) *n* corsa; (*outing*) gita (in macchina); (*distance travelled*) percorso, tragitto; (*Ski*) pista; (*Cricket, Baseball*) meta; (*series*) serie *f*; (*Theatre*) periodo di rappresentazione; (*in tights, stockings*) smagliatura ▶ *vt* (*distance*) correre; (*operate: business*) gestire, dirigere; (*: competition, course*) organizzare; (*: hotel*) gestire; (*: house*) governare; (*Comput*) eseguire; (*water, bath*) far scorrere; (*force through: rope, pipe*): **to ~ sth through** far passare qc attraverso; (*pass: hand, finger*): **to ~ sth over** passare qc su; (*Press: feature*) presentare ▶ *vi* correre; (*flee*) scappare; (*pass: road etc*) passare; (*work: machine, factory*) funzionare, andare; (*bus, train: operate*) far servizio; (*: travel*) circolare; (*continue: play, contract*) durare; (*slide: drawer; flow: river, bath*) scorrere; (*colours, washing*) stemperarsi; (*in*

election) presentarsi candidato; (*nose*) colare; **there was a ~ on ...** c'era una corsa a ...; **in the long ~** a lungo andare; **on the ~** in fuga; **to ~ a race** partecipare a una gara; **I'll ~ you to the station** la porto alla stazione; **to ~ a risk** correre un rischio ▷ **run after** *vt fus* (*to catch up*) rincorrere; (*chase*) correre dietro a ▷ **run away** *vi* fuggire ▷ **run down** *vt* (*production*) ridurre gradualmente; (*factory*) rallentare l'attività di; (*Aut*) investire; (*criticize*) criticare; **to be ~ down** (*person: tired*) essere esausto(-a) ▷ **run into** *vt fus* (*meet: person*) incontrare per caso; (*: trouble*) incontrare, trovare; (*collide with*) andare a sbattere contro ▷ **run off** *vi* fuggire ▶ *vt* (*water*) far scolare; (*copies*) fare ▷ **run out** *vi* (*person*) uscire di corsa; (*liquid*) colare; (*lease*) scadere; (*money*) esaurirsi ▷ **run out of** *vt fus* rimanere a corto di ▷ **run over** *vt* (*Aut*) investire, mettere sotto ▶ *vt fus* (*revise*) rivedere ▷ **run through** *vt fus* (*instructions*) dare una scorsa a; (*rehearse: play*) riprovare, ripetere ▷ **run up** *vt* (*debt*) lasciar accumulare; **to ~ up against** (*difficulties*) incontrare; **runaway** *adj* (*person*) fuggiasco(-a); (*horse*) in libertà; (*truck*) fuori controllo

rung [rʌŋ] *pp of* **ring** ▶ *n* (*of ladder*) piolo

runner [ˈrʌnəʳ] *n* (*in race*) corridore *m*; (*: horse*) partente *m/f*; (*on sledge*) pattino; (*for drawer etc*) guida; **runner bean** (*BRIT*) *n* fagiolo rampicante; **runner-up** *n* secondo(-a) arrivato(-a)

running [ˈrʌnɪŋ] *n* corsa; direzione *f*; organizzazione *f*; funzionamento ▶ *adj* (*water*) corrente; (*commentary*) simultaneo(-a); **to be in/out of the ~ for sth** essere/non essere più in lizza per qc; **6 days ~** 6 giorni di seguito

runny [ˈrʌnɪ] *adj* che cola

run-up [ˈrʌnʌp] *n* **~ to** (*election etc*)

r

periodo che precede

runway ['rʌnweɪ] n (Aviat) pista (di
decollo)

rupture ['rʌptʃəˀ] n (Med) ernia

rural ['rʊərəl] adj rurale

rush [rʌʃ] n corsa precipitosa; (hurry)
furia, fretta; (sudden demand): ~ for
corsa a; (current) flusso; (of emotion)
impeto; (Bot) giunco ▶ vt mandare
or spedire velocemente; (attack:
town etc) prendere d'assalto ▶ vi
precipitarsi; **rush hour** n ora di punta

Russia ['rʌʃə] n Russia; **Russian** adj
russo(-a) ▶ n russo(-a); (Ling) russo

rust [rʌst] n ruggine f ▶ vi arrugginirsi

rusty ['rʌstɪ] adj arrugginito(-a)

ruthless ['ruːθlɪs] adj spietato(-a)

RV abbr (= revised version) versione
riveduta della Bibbia ▶ n abbr (US) see
recreational vehicle

rye [raɪ] n segale f

S

Sabbath ['sæbəθ] n (Jewish) sabato;
(Christian) domenica

sabotage ['sæbətɑːʒ] n sabotaggio
▶ vt sabotare

saccharin(e) ['sækərɪn] n saccarina

sachet ['sæʃeɪ] n bustina

sack [sæk] n (bag) sacco ▶ vt (dismiss)
licenziare, mandare a spasso;
(plunder) saccheggiare; **to get the ~**

essere mandato a spasso

sacred ['seɪkrɪd] adj sacro(-a)

sacrifice ['sækrɪfaɪs] n sacrificio ▶ vt
sacrificare

sad [sæd] adj triste

saddle ['sædl] n sella ▶ vt (horse)
sellare; **to be ~d with sth** (inf) avere qc
sulle spalle

sadistic [sə'dɪstɪk] adj sadico(-a)

sadly ['sædlɪ] adv tristemente;
(regrettably) sfortunatamente; ~
lacking in penosamente privo di

sadness ['sædnɪs] n tristezza

s.a.e. n abbr (= stamped addressed
envelope) busta affrancata e con indirizzo

safari [sə'fɑːrɪ] n safari m inv

safe [seɪf] adj sicuro(-a); (out of
danger) salvo(-a), al sicuro; (cautious)
prudente ▶ n cassaforte f; ~ **from** al
sicuro da; ~ **and sound** sano(-a) e
salvo(-a); **(just) to be on the ~ side**
per non correre rischi; **could you
put this in the ~, please?** lo potrebbe
mettere nella cassaforte, per favore?;
safely adv sicuramente; sano(-a) e
salvo(-a); prudentemente; **safe sex** n
sesso sicuro

safety ['seɪftɪ] n sicurezza; **safety belt**
n cintura di sicurezza; **safety pin** n
spilla di sicurezza

saffron ['sæfrən] n zafferano

sag [sæg] vi incurvarsi; afflosciarsi

sage [seɪdʒ] n (herb) salvia; (man)
saggio

Sagittarius [sædʒɪ'tɛərɪəs] n
Sagittario

Sahara [sə'hɑːrə] n the ~ (Desert) il
(deserto del) Sahara

said [sɛd] pt, pp of **say**

sail [seɪl] n (on boat) vela; (trip): **to go
for a ~** fare un giro in barca a vela ▶ vt
(boat) condurre, governare ▶ vi (travel:
ship) navigare; (: passenger) viaggiare
per mare; (set off) salpare; (sport)
fare della vela; **they ~ed into Genoa**

entrarono nel porto di Genova; **sailboat** (US) n barca a vela; **sailing** n (sport) vela; **to go sailing** fare della vela; **sailing boat** n barca a vela; **sailor** n marinaio

saint [seɪnt] n santo(-a)

sake [seɪk] n **for the ~ of** per, per amore di

salad ['sæləd] n insalata; **salad cream** (BRIT) n (tipo di) maionese f; **salad dressing** n condimento per insalata

salami [sə'lɑ:mɪ] n salame m

salary ['sælərɪ] n stipendio

sale [seɪl] n vendita; (at reduced prices) svendita, liquidazione f; (auction) vendita all'asta; **"for ~"** "in vendita"; **on ~** in vendita; **on ~ or return** da vendere o rimandare; **~s** npl (total amount sold) vendite fpl; **sales assistant** (US **sales clerk**) n commesso(-a); **salesman/woman** (irreg) n commesso(-a); (representative) rappresentante m/f; **salesperson** (irreg) n (in shop) commesso; (representative) rappresentante m/f di commercio; **sales rep** n rappresentante m/f di commercio

saline ['seɪlaɪn] adj salino(-a)

saliva [sə'laɪvə] n saliva

salmon ['sæmən] n inv salmone m

salon ['sælɔn] n (hairdressing salon) parrucchiere(-a); (beauty salon) salone m di bellezza

saloon [sə'lu:n] n (US) saloon m inv, bar m inv; (BRIT: Aut) berlina; (ship's lounge) salone m

salt [sɔlt] n sale m ▶ vt salare; **saltwater** adj di mare; **salty** adj salato(-a)

salute [sə'lu:t] n saluto ▶ vt salutare

salvage ['sælvɪdʒ] n (saving) salvataggio; (things saved) beni mpl salvati or recuperati ▶ vt salvare, mettere in salvo

Salvation Army [sæl'veɪʃən-] n Esercito della Salvezza

same [seɪm] adj stesso(-a), medesimo(-a) ▶ pron **the ~** lo (la) stesso(-a), gli (le) stessi(-e); **the ~ book as** lo stesso libro di (o che); **at the ~ time** allo stesso tempo; **all** or **just the ~** tuttavia; **to do the ~ as sb** fare come qn; **the ~ to you!** altrettanto a te!

sample ['sɑ:mpl] n campione m ▶ vt (food) assaggiare; (wine) degustare

sanction ['sæŋkʃən] n sanzione f ▶ vt sancire, sanzionare; **~s** npl (Pol) sanzioni fpl

sanctuary ['sæŋktjuərɪ] n (holy place) santuario; (refuge) rifugio; (for wildlife) riserva

sand [sænd] n sabbia ▶ vt (also: ~ down) cartavetrare

sandal ['sændl] n sandalo

sand: sandbox ['sændbɔks] (US) n = **sandpit**; **sandcastle** ['sændkɑ:sl] n castello di sabbia; **sand dune** n duna di sabbia; **sandpaper** ['sændpeɪpər] n carta vetrata; **sandpit** ['sændpɪt] n (for children) buca di sabbia; **sands** npl spiaggia; **sandstone** ['sændstəun] n arenaria

sandwich ['sændwɪtʃ] n tramezzino, panino, sandwich m inv ▶ vt **~ed between** incastrato(-a) fra; **cheese/ham ~** sandwich al formaggio/prosciutto

sandy ['sændɪ] adj sabbioso(-a); (colour) color sabbia inv, biondo(-a) rossiccio(-a)

sane [seɪn] adj (person) sano(-a) di mente; (outlook) sensato(-a)

sang [sæŋ] pt of **sing**

sanitary towel ['sænɪtərɪ-] (US **sanitary napkin**) n assorbente m (igienico)

sanity ['sænɪtɪ] n sanità mentale; (common sense) buon senso

sank [sæŋk] pt of **sink**

S

Santa Claus [sæntə'klɔːz] *n* Babbo Natale

sap [sæp] *n (of plants)* linfa ▶ *vt (strength)* fiaccare

sapphire ['sæfaɪər] *n* zaffiro

sarcasm ['sɑːkæzm] *n* sarcasmo

sarcastic [sɑː'kæstɪk] *adj* sarcastico(-a); **to be ~** fare del sarcasmo

sardine [sɑː'diːn] *n* sardina

Sardinia [sɑː'dɪnɪə] *n* Sardegna

SASE *(US) n abbr (= self-addressed stamped envelope)* busta affrancata e con indirizzo

sat [sæt] *pt, pp of* **sit**

Sat. *abbr (= Saturday)* sab.

satchel ['sætʃl] *n* cartella

satellite ['sætəlaɪt] *adj* satellite ▶ *n* satellite *m*; **satellite dish** *n* antenna parabolica; **satellite television** *n* televisione *f* via satellite

satin ['sætɪn] *n* raso ▶ *adj* di raso

satire ['sætaɪər] *n* satira

satisfaction [sætɪs'fækʃən] *n* soddisfazione *f*

satisfactory [sætɪs'fæktərɪ] *adj* soddisfacente

satisfied ['sætɪsfaɪd] *adj (customer)* soddisfatto(-a); **to be ~ (with sth)** essere soddisfatto(-a) (di qc)

satisfy ['sætɪsfaɪ] *vt* soddisfare; *(convince)* convincere

Saturday ['sætədɪ] *n* sabato

sauce [sɔːs] *n* salsa; *(containing meat, fish)* sugo; **saucepan** *n* casseruola

saucer ['sɔːsər] *n* sottocoppa *m*, piattino

Saudi Arabia ['saʊdɪ-] *n* Arabia Saudita

sauna ['sɔːnə] *n* sauna

sausage ['sɔsɪdʒ] *n* salsiccia; **sausage roll** *n* rotolo di pasta sfoglia ripieno di salsiccia

sautéed ['səʊteɪd] *adj* saltato(-a)

savage ['sævɪdʒ] *adj (cruel, fierce)* selvaggio(-a), feroce; *(primitive)* primitivo(-a) ▶ *n* selvaggio(-a) ▶ *vt* attaccare selvaggiamente

save [seɪv] *vt (person, belongings, Comput)* salvare; *(money)* risparmiare, mettere da parte; *(time)* risparmiare; *(food)* conservare; *(avoid: trouble)* evitare; *(Sport)* parare ▶ *vi (also: ~ up)* economizzare ▶ *n (Sport)* parata ▶ *prep* salvo, a eccezione di

savings ['seɪvɪŋz] *npl (money)* risparmi *mpl*; **savings account** *n* libretto di risparmio; **savings and loan association** *(US) n* ≈ società di credito immobiliare

savoury ['seɪvərɪ] *(US* **savory**) *adj (dish: not sweet)* salato(-a)

saw [sɔː] *(pt* **sawed**, *pp* **sawed** *or* **sawn**) *pt of* **see** ▶ *n (tool)* sega ▶ *vt* segare; **sawdust** *n* segatura

sawn [sɔːn] *pp of* **saw**

saxophone ['sæksəfəʊn] *n* sassofono

say [seɪ] *(pt, pp* **said**) *n* **to have one's ~** fare sentire il proprio parere; **to have a** *or* **some ~** avere voce in capitolo ▶ *vt* dire; **could you ~ that again?** potrebbe ripeterlo?; **that goes without ~ing** va da sé; **saying** *n* proverbio, detto

scab [skæb] *n* crosta; *(pej)* crumiro(-a)

scaffolding ['skæfəldɪŋ] *n* impalcatura

scald [skɔːld] *n* scottatura ▶ *vt* scottare

scale [skeɪl] *n* scala; *(of fish)* squama ▶ *vt (mountain)* scalare; **~s** *npl (for weighing)* bilancia; **on a large ~** su vasta scala; **~ of charges** tariffa

scallion ['skæljən] *n* cipolla; *(US: shallot)* scalogna; *(: leek)* porro

scallop ['skɔləp] *n (Zool)* pettine *m*; *(Sewing)* smerlo

scalp [skælp] *n* cuoio capelluto ▶ *vt* scotennare

scalpel ['skælpl] *n* bisturi *m inv*

scam [skæm] n (inf) truffa

scampi ['skæmpɪ] npl scampi mpl

scan [skæn] vt scrutare; (glance at quickly) scorrere, dare un'occhiata a; (TV) analizzare; (Radar) esplorare ▶ n (Med) ecografia

scandal ['skændl] n scandalo; (gossip) pettegolezzi mpl

Scandinavia [skændɪ'neɪvɪə] n Scandinavia; **Scandinavian** adj, n scandinavo(-a)

scanner ['skænər] n (Radar, Med) scanner m inv

scapegoat ['skeɪpgəʊt] n capro espiatorio

scar [skɑ:] n cicatrice f ▶ vt sfregiare

scarce [skɛəs] adj scarso(-a); (copy, edition) raro(-a); **to make o.s. ~** (inf) squagliarsela; **scarcely** adv appena

scare [skɛər] n spavento; panico ▶ vt spaventare, atterrire; **there was a bomb ~ at the bank** hanno evacuato la banca per paura di un attentato dinamitardo; **to ~ sb stiff** spaventare a morte qn; **scarecrow** n spaventapasseri m inv; **scared** adj **to be scared** aver paura

scarf [skɑ:f] (pl **scarves** or **scarfs**) n (long) sciarpa; (square) fazzoletto da testa, foulard m inv

scarlet ['skɑ:lɪt] adj scarlatto(-a)

scarves [skɑ:vz] npl of **scarf**

scary ['skɛərɪ] adj che spaventa

scatter ['skætər] vt spargere; (crowd) disperdere ▶ vi disperdersi

scenario [sɪ'nɑ:rɪəʊ] n (Theatre, Cinema) copione m; (fig) situazione f

scene [si:n] n (Theatre, fig etc) scena; (of crime, accident) scena, luogo; (sight, view) vista, veduta; **scenery** n (Theatre) scenario; (landscape) panorama m; **scenic** adj scenico(-a); panoramico(-a)

scent [sɛnt] n profumo; (sense of smell) olfatto, odorato; (fig: track) pista

sceptical ['skɛptɪkəl] (US **skeptical**) adj scettico(-a)

schedule ['ʃɛdju:l, (US) 'skɛdju:l] n programma m, piano; (of trains) orario; (of prices etc) lista, tabella ▶ vt fissare; **on ~** in orario; **to be ahead of/behind ~** essere in anticipo/ ritardo sul previsto; **scheduled flight** n volo di linea

scheme [ski:m] n piano, progetto; (method) sistema m; (dishonest plan, plot) intrigo, trama; (arrangement) disposizione f, sistemazione f; (pension scheme etc) programma m ▶ vi fare progetti; (intrigue) complottare

schizophrenic [skɪtsə'frɛnɪk] adj, n schizofrenico(-a)

scholar ['skɒlər] n (expert) studioso(-a); **scholarship** n erudizione f; (grant) borsa di studio

school [sku:l] n (primary, secondary) scuola; (university: US) università f inv ▶ cpd scolare, scolastico(-a) ▶ vt (animal) addestrare; **schoolbook** n libro scolastico; **schoolboy** n scolaro; **school children** npl scolari mpl; **schoolgirl** n scolara; **schooling** n istruzione f; **schoolteacher** n insegnante m/f, docente m/f; (primary) maestro(-a)

science ['saɪəns] n scienza; **science fiction** n fantascienza; **scientific** [-'tɪfɪk] adj scientifico(-a); **scientist** n scienziato(-a)

sci-fi ['saɪfaɪ] n abbr (inf) = **science fiction**

scissors ['sɪzəz] npl forbici fpl

scold [skəʊld] vt rimproverare

scone [skɒn] n focaccina da tè

scoop [sku:p] n mestolo; (for ice cream) cucchiaio dosatore; (Press) colpo giornalistico, notizia (in) esclusiva

scooter ['sku:tər] n (motor cycle) motoretta, scooter m inv; (toy) monopattino

S

scope [skəup] n (*capacity: of plan, undertaking*) portata; (: *of person*) capacità fpl; (*opportunity*) possibilità fpl

scorching ['skɔːtʃɪŋ] adj cocente, scottante

score [skɔːʳ] n punti mpl, punteggio; (*Mus*) partitura, spartito; (*twenty*) venti ▶ vt (*goal, point*) segnare, fare; (*success*) ottenere ▶ vi segnare; (*Football*) segnare un goal; (*keep score*) segnare i punti; ~**s of** (*very many*) un sacco di; **on that** ~ a questo riguardo; **to** ~ **6 out of 10** prendere 6 su 10 ▷ **score out** vt cancellare con un segno; **scoreboard** n tabellone m segnapunti; **scorer** n marcatore(-trice); (*keeping score*) segnapunti m inv

scorn [skɔːn] n disprezzo ▶ vt disprezzare

Scorpio ['skɔːpɪəu] n Scorpione m

scorpion ['skɔːpɪən] n scorpione m

Scot [skɔt] n scozzese m/f

Scotch tape® n scotch® m

Scotland ['skɔtlənd] n Scozia

Scots [skɔts] adj scozzese; **Scotsman** (*irreg*) n scozzese m; **Scotswoman** (*irreg*) n scozzese f; **Scottish** ['skɔtɪʃ] adj scozzese; **Scottish Parliament** n Parlamento scozzese

scout [skaut] n (*Mil*) esploratore m; (*also: boy* ~) giovane esploratore, scout m inv

scowl [skaul] vi accigliarsi, aggrottare le sopracciglia; **to** ~ **at** guardare torvo

scramble ['skræmbl] n arrampicata ▶ vi inerpicarsi; **to** ~ **out** etc uscire etc in fretta; **to** ~ **for** azzuffarsi per; **scrambled eggs** npl uova fpl strapazzate

scrap [skræp] n pezzo, pezzetto; (*fight*) zuffa; (*also:* ~ **iron**) rottami mpl di ferro, ferraglia ▶ vt demolire; (*fig*) scartare ▶ vi **to** ~ (**with sb**) fare a botte (con qn); ~**s** npl (*waste*) scarti mpl; **scrapbook** n album m inv di ritagli

scrape [skreɪp] vt, vi raschiare, grattare ▶ n **to get into a** ~ cacciarsi in un guaio

scrap paper n cartaccia

scratch [skrætʃ] n graffio ▶ cpd ~ **team** squadra raccogliticcia ▶ vt graffiare, rigare ▶ vi grattare; (*paint, car*) graffiare; **to start from** ~ cominciare or partire da zero; **to be up to** ~ essere all'altezza; **scratch card** n (*BRIT*) cartolina f gratta e vinci

scream [skriːm] n grido, urlo ▶ vi urlare, gridare

screen [skriːn] n schermo; (*fig*) muro, cortina, velo ▶ vt schermare, fare schermo a; (*from the wind etc*) riparare; (*film*) proiettare; (*book*) adattare per lo schermo; (*candidates etc*) selezionare; **screening** n (*Med*) dépistage m inv; **screenplay** n sceneggiatura; **screen saver** n (*Comput*) screen saver m inv

screw [skruː] n vite f ▶ vt avvitare ▷ **screw up** vt (*paper etc*) spiegazzare; (*inf: ruin*) rovinare; **to** ~ **up one's eyes** strizzare gli occhi; **screwdriver** n cacciavite m

scribble ['skrɪbl] n scarabocchio ▶ vt scribacchiare in fretta ▶ vi scarabocchiare

script [skrɪpt] n (*Cinema etc*) copione m; (*in exam*) elaborato or compito d'esame

scroll [skrəul] n rotolo di carta

scrub [skrʌb] n (*land*) boscaglia ▶ vt pulire strofinando; (*reject*) annullare

scruffy ['skrʌfɪ] adj sciatto(-a)

scrum(mage) ['skrʌm(ɪdʒ)] n mischia

scrutiny ['skruːtɪnɪ] n esame m accurato

scuba diving ['skuːbə-] n immersioni fpl subacquee

sculptor ['skʌlptəʳ] n scultore m

sculpture ['skʌlptʃə^r] n scultura

scum [skʌm] n schiuma; (pej: people) feccia

scurry ['skʌrɪ] vi sgambare, affrettarsi

sea [si:] n mare m ▶ cpd marino(-a), del mare; (bird, fish) di mare; (route, transport) marittimo(-a); **by ~** (travel) per mare; **on the ~** (boat) in mare; (town) di mare; **to be all at ~** (fig) non sapere che pesci pigliare; **out to ~** al largo; (**out) at ~** in mare; **seafood** n frutti mpl di mare; **sea front** n lungomare m; **seagull** n gabbiano

seal [si:l] n (animal) foca; (stamp) sigillo; (impression) impronta del sigillo ▶ vt sigillare ▷ **seal off** vt (close) sigillare; (forbid entry to) bloccare l'accesso a

sea level n livello del mare

seam [si:m] n cucitura; (of coal) filone m

search [sə:tʃ] n ricerca; (Law: at sb's home) perquisizione f ▶ vt frugare ▶ vi **to ~ for** ricercare; **in ~ of** alla ricerca di; **search engine** n (Comput) motore m di ricerca; **search party** n squadra di soccorso

sea: seashore ['si:ʃɔ:^r] n spiaggia; **seasick** ['si:sɪk] adj che soffre il mal di mare; **seaside** ['si:saɪd] n spiaggia; **seaside resort** n stazione f balneare

season ['si:zn] n stagione f ▶ vt condire, insaporire; **seasonal** adj stagionale; **seasoning** n condimento; **season ticket** n abbonamento

seat [si:t] n sedile m; (in bus, train: place) posto; (Parliament) seggio; (buttocks) didietro; (of trousers) fondo ▶ vt far sedere; (have room for) avere or essere fornito(-a) di posti a sedere per; **I'd like to book two ~s** vorrei prenotare due posti; **to be ~ed** essere seduto(-a); **seat belt** n cintura di sicurezza; **seating** n posti mpl a sedere

sea: sea water n acqua di mare; **seaweed** ['si:wi:d] n alghe fpl

sec. abbr = **second(s)**

secluded [sɪ'klu:dɪd] adj isolato(-a), appartato(-a)

second ['sɛkənd] num secondo(-a) ▶ adv (in race etc) al secondo posto ▶ n (unit of time) secondo; (Aut: also: **~ gear**) seconda; (Comm: imperfect) scarto; (BRIT: Scol: degree) laurea con punteggio discreto ▶ vt (motion) appoggiare; **secondary** adj secondario(-a); **secondary school** n scuola secondaria; **second-class** adj di seconda classe ▶ adv in seconda classe; **secondhand** adj di seconda mano, usato(-a); **secondly** adv in secondo luogo; **second-rate** adj scadente; **second thoughts** npl ripensamenti mpl; **on second thoughts** (BRIT) or **thought** (US) ripensandoci bene

secrecy ['si:krəsɪ] n segretezza

secret ['si:krɪt] adj segreto(-a) ▶ n segreto; **in ~** in segreto

secretary ['sɛkrətrɪ] n segretario(-a); **S~ of State (for)** (BRIT: Pol) ministro (di)

secretive ['si:krətɪv] adj riservato(-a)

secret service n servizi mpl segreti

sect [sɛkt] n setta

section ['sɛkʃən] n sezione f

sector ['sɛktə^r] n settore m

secular ['sɛkjulə^r] adj secolare

secure [sɪ'kjuə^r] adj sicuro(-a); (firmly fixed) assicurato(-a), ben fermato(-a); (in safe place) al sicuro ▶ vt (fix) fissare, assicurare; (get) ottenere, assicurarsi; **securities** npl (Stock Exchange) titoli mpl

security [sɪ'kjuərɪtɪ] n sicurezza; (for loan) garanzia; **security guard** n guardia giurata

sedan [sə'dæn] (US) n (Aut) berlina

S

sedate [sɪ'deɪt] *adj* posato(-a), calmo(-a) ▶ *vt* calmare
sedative ['sɛdɪtɪv] *n* sedativo, calmante *m*
seduce [sɪ'djuːs] *vt* sedurre; **seductive** [-'dʌktɪv] *adj* seducente
see [siː] (*pt* **saw**, *pp* **seen**) *vt* vedere; (*accompany*): **to ~ sb to the door** accompagnare qn alla porta ▶ *vi* vedere; (*understand*) capire ▶ *n* sede *f* vescovile; **to ~ that** (*ensure*) badare che + *sub*, fare in modo che + *sub*; **~ you soon!** a presto! ▷ **see off** *vt* salutare alla partenza ▷ **see out** *vt* (*take to the door*) accompagnare alla porta ▷ **see through** *vt* portare a termine ▶ *vt fus* non lasciarsi ingannare da ▷ **see to** *vt fus* occuparsi di
seed [siːd] *n* seme *m*; (*fig*) germe *m*; (*Tennis etc*) testa di serie; **to go to ~** fare seme; (*fig*) scadere
seeing ['siːɪŋ] *conj* **~ (that)** visto che
seek [siːk] (*pt*, *pp* **sought**) *vt* cercare
seem [siːm] *vi* sembrare, parere; **there ~s to be ...** sembra che ci sia ...; **seemingly** *adv* apparentemente
seen [siːn] *pp of* **see**
seesaw ['siːsɔː] *n* altalena a bilico
segment ['sɛgmənt] *n* segmento
segregate ['sɛgrɪgeɪt] *vt* segregare, isolare
seize [siːz] *vt* (*grasp*) afferrare; (*take possession of*) impadronirsi di; (*Law*) sequestrare
seizure ['siːʒəʳ] *n* (*Med*) attacco; (*Law*) confisca, sequestro
seldom ['sɛldəm] *adv* raramente
select [sɪ'lɛkt] *adj* scelto(-a) ▶ *vt* scegliere, selezionare; **selection** [-'lɛkʃən] *n* selezione *f*, scelta; **selective** *adj* selettivo(-a)
self [sɛlf] *n* **the ~** l'io *m* ▶ *prefix* auto...; **self-assured** *adj* sicuro(-a) di sé; **self-catering** (*BRIT*) *adj* in cui ci si cucina da sé; **self-centred** (*US* **self-centered**) *adj* egocentrico(-a); **self-confidence** *n* sicurezza di sé; **self-confident** *adj* sicuro(-a) di sé; **self-conscious** *adj* timido(-a); **self-contained** (*BRIT*) *adj* (*flat*) indipendente; **self-control** *n* autocontrollo; **self-defence** (*US* **self-defense**) *n* autodifesa; (*Law*) legittima difesa; **self-drive** *adj* (*BRIT*: *rented car*) senza autista; **self-employed** *adj* che lavora in proprio; **self-esteem** *n* amor proprio *m*; **self-indulgent** *adj* indulgente verso se stesso(-a); **self-interest** *n* interesse *m* personale; **selfish** *adj* egoista; **self-pity** *n* autocommiserazione *f*; **self-raising** (*US* **self-rising**) *adj* **self-raising flour** miscela di farina e lievito; **self-respect** *n* rispetto di sé, amor proprio; **self-service** *n* autoservizio, self-service *m*
sell [sɛl] (*pt*, *pp* **sold**) *vt* vendere ▶ *vi* vendersi; **to ~ at** *or* **for 1000 euros** essere in vendita a 1000 euro ▷ **sell off** *vt* svendere, liquidare ▷ **sell out** *vi* **to ~ out (of sth)** esaurire (qc); **the tickets are all sold out** i biglietti sono esauriti; **sell-by date** ['sɛlbaɪ-] *n* data di scadenza; **seller** *n* venditore(-trice)
Sellotape® ['sɛləuteɪp] (*BRIT*) *n* nastro adesivo, scotch® *m*
selves [sɛlvz] *npl of* **self**
semester [sɪ'mɛstəʳ] (*US*) *n* semestre *m*
semi... ['sɛmɪ] *prefix* semi...; **semicircle** *n* semicerchio; **semidetached (house)** [sɛmɪdɪ'tætʃt-] (*BRIT*) *n* casa gemella; **semi-final** *n* semifinale *f*
seminar ['sɛminɑːʳ] *n* seminario
semi-skimmed ['sɛmɪ'skɪmd] *adj* (*milk*) parzialmente scremato(-a)
senate ['sɛnɪt] *n* senato; **senator** *n* senatore(-trice)
send [sɛnd] (*pt*, *pp* **sent**) *vt* mandare

▷ **send back** vt rimandare ▷ **send for** vt fus mandare a chiamare, far venire ▷ **send in** vt (report, application, resignation) presentare ▷ **send off** vt (goods) spedire; (BRIT: Sport: player) espellere ▷ **send on** vt (BRIT: letter) inoltrare; (luggage etc: in advance) spedire in anticipo ▷ **send out** vt (invitation) diramare ▷ **send up** vt (person, price) far salire; (BRIT: parody) mettere in ridicolo; **sender** n mittente m/f; **send-off** n **to give sb a good send-off** festeggiare la partenza di qn

senile ['siːnaɪl] adj senile

senior ['siːnɪər] adj (older) più vecchio(-a); (of higher rank) di grado più elevato; **senior citizen** n persona anziana; **senior high school** (US) n ≈ liceo

sensation [sɛnˈseɪʃən] n sensazione f; **sensational** adj sensazionale; (marvellous) eccezionale

sense [sɛns] n senso; (feeling) sensazione f, senso; (meaning) senso, significato; (wisdom) buonsenso ▶ vt sentire, percepire; **it makes ~** ha senso; **senseless** adj sciocco(-a); (unconscious) privo(-a) di sensi; **sense of humour** (BRIT) n senso dell'umorismo

sensible ['sɛnsɪbl] adj sensato(-a), ragionevole

■ Be careful not to translate **sensible** by the Italian word **sensibile**.

sensitive ['sɛnsɪtɪv] adj sensibile; (skin, question) delicato(-a)

sensual ['sɛnsjuəl] adj sensuale

sensuous ['sɛnsjuəs] adj sensuale

sent [sɛnt] pt, pp of **send**

sentence ['sɛntns] n (Ling) frase f; (Law: judgment) sentenza; (: punishment) condanna ▶ vt **to ~ sb to death/to 5 years** condannare qn a morte/a 5 anni

sentiment ['sɛntɪmənt] n sentimento; (opinion) opinione f; **sentimental** [-ˈmɛntl] adj sentimentale

Sep. abbr (= September) Sett.

separate [adj ˈsɛprɪt, vb ˈsɛpəreɪt] adj separato(-a) ▶ vt separare ▶ vi separarsi; **separately** adv separatamente; **separates** npl (clothes) coordinati mpl; **separation** [-ˈreɪʃən] n separazione f

September [sɛpˈtɛmbər] n settembre m

septic ['sɛptɪk] adj settico(-a); (wound) infettato(-a); **septic tank** n fossa settica

sequel ['siːkwl] n conseguenza; (of story) seguito; (of film) sequenza

sequence ['siːkwəns] n (series) serie f; (order) ordine m

sequin ['siːkwɪn] n lustrino, paillette f inv

Serb [səːb] adj, n = **Serbian**

Serbia ['səːbɪə] n Serbia

Serbian ['səːbɪən] adj serbo(-a) ▶ n serbo(-a); (Ling) serbo

sergeant ['sɑːdʒənt] n sergente m; (Police) brigadiere m

serial ['sɪərɪəl] n (Press) romanzo a puntate; (Radio, TV) trasmissione f a puntate, serial m inv; **serial killer** n serial-killer m/f inv; **serial number** n numero di serie

series ['sɪəriːz] n inv serie f inv; (Publishing) collana

serious ['sɪərɪəs] adj serio(-a), grave; **seriously** adv seriamente

sermon ['səːmən] n sermone m

servant ['səːvənt] n domestico(-a)

serve [səːv] vt (employer etc) servire, essere a servizio di; (purpose) servire a; (customer, food, meal) servire; (apprenticeship) fare; (prison term) scontare ▶ vi (also Tennis) servire; (be useful): **to ~ as/for/to do** servire da/

per/per fare ▶ n (*Tennis*) servizio; **it ~s him right** ben gli sta, se l'è meritata; **server** n (*Comput*) server m inv

service ['sə:vɪs] n servizio; (*Aut: maintenance*) assistenza, revisione f ▶ vt (*car, washing machine*) revisionare; **to be of ~ to sb** essere d'aiuto a qn; **~ included/not included** servizio compreso/escluso; **~s** (*BRIT: on motorway*) stazione f di servizio; (*Mil*): **the S~s** le Forze Armate; **service area** n (*on motorway*) area di servizio; **service charge** (*BRIT*) n servizio; **serviceman** (*irreg*) n militare m; **service station** n stazione f di servizio

serviette [sə:vɪ'ɛt] (*BRIT*) n tovagliolo

session ['sɛʃən] n (*sitting*) seduta, sessione f; (*Scol*) anno scolastico (*or* accademico)

set [sɛt] (*pt, pp* **set**) n serie f inv; (*of cutlery etc*) servizio; (*Radio, TV*) apparecchio; (*Tennis*) set m inv; (*group of people*) mondo, ambiente m; (*Cinema*) scenario; (*Theatre: stage*) scene fpl; (: *scenery*) scenario; (*Math*) insieme m; (*Hairdressing*) messa in piega ▶ adj (*fixed*) stabilito(-a), determinato(-a); (*ready*) pronto(-a) ▶ vt (*place*) posare, mettere; (*arrange*) sistemare; (*fix*) fissare; (*adjust*) regolare; (*decide: rules etc*) stabilire, fissare ▶ vi (*sun*) tramontare; (*jam, jelly*) rapprendersi; (*concrete*) fare presa; **to be ~ on doing** essere deciso a fare; **to ~ to music** mettere in musica; **to ~ on fire** dare fuoco a; **to ~ free** liberare; **to ~ sth going** mettere in moto qc; **to ~ sail** prendere il mare ▷ **set aside** vt mettere da parte ▷ **set down** vt (*bus, train*) lasciare ▷ **set in** vi (*infection*) svilupparsi; (*complications*) intervenire; **the rain has ~ in for the day** ormai pioverà tutto il giorno ▷ **set off** vi partire ▶ vt (*bomb*) far

scoppiare; (*cause to start*) mettere in moto; (*show up well*) dare risalto a ▷ **set out** vi partire ▶ vt (*arrange*) disporre; (*state*) esporre, presentare; **to ~ out to do** proporsi di fare ▷ **set up** vt (*organization*) fondare, costituire; **setback** n (*hitch*) contrattempo, inconveniente m; **set menu** n menù m inv fisso

settee [sɛ'ti:] n divano, sofà m inv

setting ['sɛtɪŋ] n (*background*) ambiente m; (*of controls*) posizione f; (*of sun*) tramonto; (*of jewel*) montatura

settle ['sɛtl] vt (*argument, matter*) appianare; (*accounts*) regolare; (*Med: calm*) calmare ▶ vi (*bird, dust etc*) posarsi; (*sediment*) depositarsi; **to ~ for sth** accontentarsi di qc; **to ~ on sth** decidersi per qc ▷ **settle down** vi (*get comfortable*) sistemarsi; (*calm down*) calmarsi; (*get back to normal: situation*) tornare alla normalità ▷ **settle in** vi sistemarsi ▷ **settle up** vi **to ~ up with sb** regolare i conti con qn; **settlement** n (*payment*) pagamento, saldo; (*agreement*) accordo; (*colony*) colonia; (*village etc*) villaggio, comunità f inv

setup ['sɛtʌp] n (*arrangement*) sistemazione f; (*situation*) situazione f

seven ['sɛvn] num sette; **seventeen** num diciassette; **seventeenth** [sɛvn'ti:nθ] num diciassettesimo(-a); **seventh** num settimo(-a); **seventieth** ['sɛvntɪɪθ] num settantesimo(-a); **seventy** num settanta

sever ['sɛvər] vt recidere, tagliare; (*relations*) troncare

several ['sɛvərl] adj, pron alcuni(-e), diversi(-e); **~ of us** alcuni di noi

severe [sɪ'vɪər] adj severo(-a); (*serious*) serio(-a), grave; (*hard*) duro(-a); (*plain*) semplice, sobrio(-a)

sew [səu] (pt **sewed**, pp **sewn**) vt, vi cucire

sewage ['suːɪdʒ] n acque fpl di scolo

sewer ['suːəʳ] n fogna

sewing ['səuɪŋ] n cucitura; cucito; **sewing machine** n macchina da cucire

sewn [səun] pp of **sew**

sex [sɛks] n sesso; **to have ~ with** avere rapporti sessuali con; **sexism** ['sɛksɪzəm] n sessismo; **sexist** adj, n sessista m/f; **sexual** ['sɛksjuəl] adj sessuale; **sexual intercourse** n rapporti mpl sessuali; **sexuality** [sɛksju'ælɪtɪ] n sessualità; **sexy** ['sɛksɪ] adj provocante, sexy inv

shabby ['ʃæbɪ] adj malandato(-a); (behaviour) vergognoso(-a)

shack [ʃæk] n baracca, capanna

shade [ʃeɪd] n ombra; (for lamp) paralume m; (of colour) tonalità f inv; (small quantity): **a ~ (more/too large)** un po' (di più/troppo grande) ▶ vt ombreggiare, fare ombra a; **in the ~** all'ombra; **~s** (US) npl (sunglasses) occhiali mpl da sole

shadow ['ʃædəu] n ombra ▶ vt (follow) pedinare; **shadow cabinet** (BRIT) n (Pol) governo m ombra inv

shady ['ʃeɪdɪ] adj ombroso(-a); (fig: dishonest) losco(-a), equivoco(-a)

shaft [ʃɑːft] n (of arrow, spear) asta; (Aut, Tech) albero; (of mine) pozzo; (of lift) tromba; (of light) raggio

shake [ʃeɪk] (pt **shook**, pp **shaken**) vt scuotere; (bottle, cocktail) agitare ▶ vi tremare; **to ~ one's head** (in refusal, dismay) scuotere la testa; **to ~ hands with sb** stringere or dare la mano a qn ▷ **shake off** vt scrollare (via); (fig) sbarazzarsi di ▷ **shake up** vt scuotere; **shaky** adj (hand, voice) tremante; (building) traballante

shall [ʃæl] aux vb **I ~ go** andrò; **~ I open the door?** apro io la porta?; **I'll get**

some, **~ I?** ne prendo un po', va bene?

shallow ['ʃæləu] adj poco profondo(-a); (fig) superficiale

sham [ʃæm] n finzione f, messinscena; (jewellery, furniture) imitazione f

shambles ['ʃæmblz] n confusione f, baraonda, scompiglio

shame [ʃeɪm] n vergogna ▶ vt far vergognare; **it is a ~ (that/to do)** è un peccato (che + sub/fare); **what a ~!** che peccato!; **shameful** adj vergognoso(-a); **shameless** adj sfrontato(-a); (immodest) spudorato(-a)

shampoo [ʃæm'puː] n shampoo m inv ▶ vt fare lo shampoo a

shandy ['ʃændɪ] n birra con gassosa

shan't [ʃɑːnt] = **shall not**

shape [ʃeɪp] n forma ▶ vt formare; (statement) formulare; (sb's ideas) condizionare; **to take ~** prendere forma

share [ʃɛəʳ] n (thing received, contribution) parte f; (Comm) azione f ▶ vt dividere; (have in common) condividere, avere in comune; **shareholder** n azionista m/f

shark [ʃɑːk] n squalo, pescecane m

sharp [ʃɑːp] adj (razor, knife) affilato(-a); (point) acuto(-a), acuminato(-a); (nose, chin) aguzzo(-a); (outline, contrast) netto(-a); (cold, pain) pungente; (voice) stridulo(-a); (person: quick-witted) sveglio(-a); (: unscrupulous) disonesto(-a); (Mus): **C ~** do diesis ▶ n (Mus) diesis m inv ▶ adv **at 2 o'clock ~** alle due in punto; **sharpen** vt affilare; (pencil) fare la punta a; (fig) acuire; **sharpener** n (also: **pencil sharpener**) temperamatite m inv; **sharply** adv (turn, stop) bruscamente; (stand out, contrast) nettamente; (criticize, retort) duramente, aspramente

shatter ['ʃætəʳ] vt mandare in

frantumi, frantumare; (fig: upset)
distruggere; (: ruin) rovinare ▶ vi
frantumarsi, andare in pezzi;
shattered adj (grief-stricken)
sconvolto(-a); (exhausted) a pezzi,
distrutto(-a)

shave [ʃeɪv] vt radere, rasare ▶ vi
radersi, farsi la barba ▶ n **to have a ~**
farsi la barba; **shaver** n (also: **electric
shaver**) rasoio elettrico

shaving cream n crema da barba

shaving foam n = **shaving cream**

shavings ['ʃeɪvɪŋz] npl (of wood etc)
trucioli mpl

shawl [ʃɔːl] n scialle m

she [ʃiː] pron ella, lei; **~-cat** gatta;
~-elephant elefantessa

sheath [ʃiːθ] n fodero, guaina;
(contraceptive) preservativo

shed [ʃɛd] (pt, pp **shed**) n capannone
m ▶ vt (leaves, fur etc) perdere; (tears,
blood) versare; (workers) liberarsi di

she'd [ʃiːd] = **she had**; **she would**

sheep [ʃiːp] n inv pecora; **sheepdog** n
cane m da pastore; **sheepskin** n pelle
f di pecora

sheer [ʃɪəʳ] adj (utter) vero(-a)
(e proprio(-a)); (steep) a picco,
perpendicolare; (almost transparent)
sottile ▶ adv a picco

sheet [ʃiːt] n (on bed) lenzuolo; (of
paper) foglio; (of glass, ice) lastra; (of
metal) foglio, lamina

sheik(h) [ʃeɪk] n sceicco

shelf [ʃɛlf] (pl **shelves**) n scaffale m,
mensola

shell [ʃɛl] n (on beach) conchiglia;
(of egg, nut etc) guscio; (explosive)
granata; (of building) scheletro ▶ vt
(peas) sgranare; (Mil) bombardare

she'll [ʃiːl] = **she will**; **she shall**

shellfish ['ʃɛlfɪʃ] n inv (crab etc)
crostaceo; (scallop etc) mollusco; (as
food) crostacei; molluschi

shelter ['ʃɛltəʳ] n riparo, rifugio ▶ vt

riparare, proteggere; (give lodging to)
dare rifugio or asilo a ▶ vi ripararsi,
mettersi al riparo; **sheltered** adj
riparato(-a)

shelves ['ʃɛlvz] npl of **shelf**

shelving ['ʃɛlvɪŋ] n scaffalature fpl

shepherd ['ʃɛpəd] n pastore m ▶ vt
(guide) guidare; **shepherd's pie**
(BRIT) n timballo di carne macinata e
purè di patate

sheriff ['ʃɛrɪf] (US) n sceriffo

sherry ['ʃɛrɪ] n sherry m inv

she's [ʃiːz] = **she is**; **she has**

Shetland ['ʃɛtlənd] n (also: **the ~s, the
~ Isles**) le isole Shetland, le Shetland

shield [ʃiːld] n scudo; (trophy)
scudetto; (protection) schermo ▶ vt
to ~ (from) riparare (da), proteggere
(da or contro)

shift [ʃɪft] n (change) cambiamento; (of
workers) turno ▶ vt spostare, muovere;
(remove) rimuovere ▶ vi spostarsi,
muoversi

shin [ʃɪn] n tibia

shine [ʃaɪn] (pt, pp **shone**) n splendore
m, lucentezza ▶ vi (ri)splendere,
brillare ▶ vt far brillare, far
risplendere; (torch): **to ~ sth on**
puntare qc verso

shingles ['ʃɪŋglz] n (Med) herpes
zoster m

shiny ['ʃaɪnɪ] adj lucente, lucido(-a)

ship [ʃɪp] n nave f ▶ vt trasportare
(via mare); (send) spedire (via mare);
shipment n carico; **shipping** n (ships)
naviglio; (traffic) navigazione f;
shipwreck n relitto; (event) naufragio
▶ vt **to be shipwrecked** naufragare,
fare naufragio; **shipyard** n cantiere
m navale

shirt [ʃəːt] n camicia; **in ~ sleeves** in
maniche di camicia

shit [ʃɪt] (inf!) excl merda (!)

shiver ['ʃɪvəʳ] n brivido ▶ vi
rabbrividire, tremare

shock [ʃɔk] n (impact) urto, colpo; (Elec) scossa; (emotional) colpo, shock m inv; (Med) shock ▶ vt colpire, scioccare; scandalizzare; **shocking** adj scioccante, traumatizzante; scandaloso(-a)

shoe [ʃuː] (pt, pp **shod**) n scarpa; (also: **horse~**) ferro di cavallo ▶ vt (horse) ferrare; **shoelace** n stringa; **shoe polish** n lucido per scarpe; **shoeshop** n calzoleria

shone [ʃɔn] pt, pp of **shine**

shook [ʃuk] pt of **shake**

shoot [ʃuːt] (pt, pp **shot**) n (on branch, seedling) germoglio ▶ vt (game) cacciare, andare a caccia di; (person) sparare a; (execute) fucilare; (film) girare ▶ vi (with gun): **to ~ (at)** sparare (a), fare fuoco (su); (with bow): **to ~ (at)** tirare (su); (Football) sparare, tirare (forte) ▶ **shoot down** vt (plane) abbattere ▷ **shoot up** vi (fig) salire alle stelle; **shooting** n (shots) sparatoria; (Hunting) caccia

shop [ʃɔp] n negozio; (workshop) officina ▶ vi (also: **go ~ping**) fare spese; **shop assistant** (BRIT) n commesso(-a); **shopkeeper** n negoziante m/f, bottegaio(-a); **shoplifting** n taccheggio; **shopping** n (goods) spesa, acquisti mpl; **shopping bag** n borsa per la spesa; **shopping centre** (US **shopping center**) n centro commerciale; **shopping mall** n centro commerciale; **shopping trolley** n (BRIT) carrello del supermercato; **shop window** n vetrina

shore [ʃɔːʳ] n (of sea) riva, spiaggia; (of lake) riva ▶ vt **to ~ (up)** puntellare; **on ~** a riva

short [ʃɔːt] adj (not long) corto(-a); (soon finished) breve; (person) basso(-a); (curt) brusco(-a), secco(-a); (insufficient) insufficiente ▶ n (also: ~

film) cortometraggio; **to be ~ of sth** essere a corto di or mancare di qc; **in ~** in breve; **~ of doing** a meno che non si faccia; **everything ~ of** tutto fuorché; **it is ~ for** è l'abbreviazione or il diminutivo di; **to cut ~** (speech, visit) accorciare, abbreviare; **to fall ~ of** venir meno a; non soddisfare; **to run ~ of** rimanere senza; **to stop ~** fermarsi di colpo; **to stop ~ of** non arrivare fino a; **shortage** n scarsezza, carenza; **shortbread** n biscotto di pasta frolla; **shortcoming** n difetto; **short(crust) pastry** (BRIT) n pasta frolla; **shortcut** n scorciatoia; **shorten** vt accorciare, ridurre; **shortfall** n deficit m; **shorthand** (BRIT) n stenografia; **short-lived** adj di breve durata; **shortly** adv fra poco; **shorts** npl (also: **a pair of shorts**) i calzoncini; **short-sighted** (BRIT) adj miope; **short-sleeved** [ˈʃɔːtsliːvd] adj a maniche corte; **short story** n racconto, novella; **short-tempered** adj irascibile; **short-term** adj (effect) di or a breve durata; (borrowing) a breve scadenza

shot [ʃɔt] pt, pp of **shoot** ▶ n sparo, colpo; (try) prova; (Football) tiro; (injection) iniezione f; (Phot) foto f inv; **like a ~** come un razzo; (very readily) immediatamente; **shotgun** n fucile m da caccia

should [ʃud] aux vb **I ~ go now** dovrei andare ora; **he ~ be there now** dovrebbe essere arrivato ora; **I ~ go if I were you** se fossi in te andrei; **I ~ like to** mi piacerebbe

shoulder [ˈʃəuldəʳ] n spalla; (BRIT: of road): **hard ~** banchina ▶ vt (fig) addossarsi, prendere sulle proprie spalle; **shoulder blade** n scapola

shouldn't [ˈʃudnt] = **should not**

shout [ʃaut] n urlo, grido ▶ vt gridare ▶ vi (also: ~ **out**) urlare, gridare

shove [ʃʌv] vt spingere; (inf: put): **to ~ sth in** ficcare qc in

shovel [ˈʃʌvl] n pala ▸ vt spalare

show [ʃəu] (pt **showed**, pp **shown**) n (of emotion) dimostrazione f, manifestazione f; (semblance) apparenza; (exhibition) mostra, esposizione f; (Theatre, Cinema) spettacolo ▸ vt far vedere, mostrare; (courage etc) dimostrare, dar prova di; (exhibit) esporre ▸ vi vedersi, essere visibile; **for ~** per fare scena; **on ~** (exhibits etc) esposto(-a); **can you ~ me where it is, please?** può mostrarmi dov'è, per favore? ▸ **show in** vt (person) far entrare ▸ **show off** vi (pej) esibirsi, mettersi in mostra ▸ vt (display) mettere in risalto; (pej) mettere in mostra ▸ **show out** vt (person) accompagnare alla porta ▸ **show up** vi (stand out) essere ben visibile; (inf: turn up) farsi vedere ▸ vt mettere in risalto; **show business** n industria dello spettacolo

shower [ˈʃauəʳ] n (rain) acquazzone m; (of stones etc) pioggia; (also: ~bath) doccia ▸ vi fare la doccia ▸ vt **to ~ sb with** (gifts, abuse etc) coprire qn di; (missiles) lanciare contro qn una pioggia di; **to have a ~** fare la doccia; **shower cap** n cuffia da doccia; **shower gel** n gel m doccia inv

showing [ˈʃəuɪŋ] n (of film) proiezione f

show jumping n concorso ippico (di salto ad ostacoli)

shown [ʃəun] pp of **show**

show: **show-off** (inf) n (person) esibizionista m/f; **showroom** n sala d'esposizione

shrank [ʃræŋk] pt of **shrink**

shred [ʃred] n (gen pl) brandello ▸ vt fare a brandelli; (Culin) sminuzzare, tagliuzzare

shrewd [ʃruːd] adj astuto(-a), scaltro(-a)

shriek [ʃriːk] n strillo ▸ vi strillare

shrimp [ʃrɪmp] n gamberetto

shrine [ʃraɪn] n reliquario; (place) santuario

shrink [ʃrɪŋk] (pt **shrank**, pp **shrunk**) vi restringersi; (fig) ridursi; (also: ~ away) ritrarsi ▸ vt (wool) far restringere ▸ n (inf: pej) psicanalista m/f; **to ~ from doing sth** rifuggire dal fare qc

shrivel [ˈʃrɪvl] (also: ~ up) vt raggrinzare, avvizzire ▸ vi raggrinzirsi, avvizzire

shroud [ʃraud] n lenzuolo funebre ▸ vt **~ed in mystery** avvolto(-a) nel mistero

Shrove Tuesday [ˈʃrəuv-] n martedì m grasso

shrub [ʃrʌb] n arbusto

shrug [ʃrʌg] n scrollata di spalle ▸ vt, vi **to ~ (one's shoulders)** alzare le spalle, fare spallucce ▸ **shrug off** vt passare sopra a

shrunk [ʃrʌŋk] pp of **shrink**

shudder [ˈʃʌdəʳ] n brivido ▸ vi rabbrividire

shuffle [ˈʃʌfl] vt (cards) mescolare; **to ~ (one's feet)** strascicare i piedi

shun [ʃʌn] vt sfuggire, evitare

shut [ʃʌt] (pt, pp **shut**) vt chiudere ▸ vi chiudersi, chiudere ▸ **shut down** vt, vi chiudere definitivamente ▸ **shut up** vi (inf: keep quiet) stare zitto(-a), fare silenzio ▸ vt (close) chiudere; (silence) far tacere; **shutter** n imposta; (Phot) otturatore m

shuttle [ˈʃʌtl] n spola, navetta; (space shuttle) navetta (spaziale); (also: ~ service) servizio m navetta inv; **shuttlecock** [ˈʃʌtlkɔk] n volano

shy [ʃaɪ] adj timido(-a)

sibling [ˈsɪblɪŋ] n (formal) fratello/ sorella

Sicily [ˈsɪsɪlɪ] n Sicilia

sick [sɪk] adj (ill) malato(-a);

(*vomiting*): **to be ~** vomitare; (*humour*) macabro(-a); **to feel ~** avere la nausea; **to be ~ of** (*fig*) averne abbastanza di; **sickening** *adj* (*fig*) disgustoso(-a), rivoltante; **sick leave** *n* congedo per malattia; **sickly** *adj* malaticcio(-a); (*causing nausea*) nauseante; **sickness** *n* malattia; (*vomiting*) vomito

side [saɪd] *n* lato; (*of lake*) riva; (*team*) squadra ▶ *cpd* (*door, entrance*) laterale ▶ *vi* **to ~ with sb** parteggiare per qn, prendere le parti di qn; **by the ~ of** a fianco di; (*road*) sul ciglio di; **~ by ~** fianco a fianco; **from ~ to ~** da una parte all'altra; **to take ~s (with)** schierarsi (con); **sideboard** *n* credenza; **sideburns** ['saɪdbə:nz] *npl* basette *fpl*; **sidelight** *n* (*Aut*) luce *f* di posizione; **sideline** *n* (*Sport*) linea laterale; (*fig*) attività secondaria; **side order** *n* contorno (*pietanza*); **side road** *n* strada secondaria; **side street** *n* traversa; **sidetrack** *vt* (*fig*) distrarre; **sidewalk** (*US*) *n* marciapiede *m*; **sideways** *adv* (*move*) di lato, di fianco

siege [si:dʒ] *n* assedio

sieve [sɪv] *n* setaccio ▶ *vt* setacciare

sift [sɪft] *vt* passare al crivello; (*fig*) vagliare

sigh [saɪ] *n* sospiro ▶ *vi* sospirare

sight [saɪt] *n* (*faculty*) vista; (*spectacle*) spettacolo; (*on gun*) mira ▶ *vt* avvistare; **in ~** in vista; **on ~** a vista; **out of ~** non visibile; **sightseeing** *n* giro turistico; **to go sightseeing** visitare una località

sign [saɪn] *n* segno; (*with hand etc*) segno, gesto; (*notice*) insegna, cartello ▶ *vt* firmare; (*player*) ingaggiare; **where do I ~?** dove devo firmare? ▷ **sign for** *vt fus* (*item*) firmare per l'accettazione di ▷ **sign in** *vi* firmare il registro (all'arrivo) ▷ **sign on** *vi* (*Mil*) arruolarsi; (*as unemployed*) iscriversi sulla lista (dell'ufficio di

collocamento) ▶ *vt* (*Mil*) arruolare; (*employee*) assumere ▷ **sign up** *vi* (*Mil*) arruolarsi; (*for course*) iscriversi ▶ *vt* (*player*) ingaggiare; (*recruits*) reclutare

signal ['sɪgnl] *n* segnale *m* ▶ *vi* (*Aut*) segnalare, mettere la freccia ▶ *vt* (*person*) fare segno a; (*message*) comunicare per mezzo di segnali

signature ['sɪgnətʃə^r] *n* firma

significance [sɪg'nɪfɪkəns] *n* significato; importanza

significant [sɪg'nɪfɪkənt] *adj* significativo(-a)

signify ['sɪgnɪfaɪ] *vt* significare

sign language *n* linguaggio dei muti

signpost ['saɪnpəust] *n* cartello indicatore

Sikh [si:k] *adj, n* sikh (*m/f*) *inv*

silence ['saɪlns] *n* silenzio ▶ *vt* far tacere, ridurre al silenzio

silent ['saɪlnt] *adj* silenzioso(-a); (*film*) muto(-a); **to remain ~** tacere, stare zitto

silhouette [sɪlu:'ɛt] *n* silhouette *f inv*

silicon chip ['sɪlɪkən-] *n* piastrina di silicio

silk [sɪlk] *n* seta ▶ *adj* di seta

silly ['sɪlɪ] *adj* stupido(-a), sciocco(-a)

silver ['sɪlvə^r] *n* argento; (*money*) *monete da 5, 10, 20 or 50 pence*; (*also:* **~ware**) argenteria ▶ *adj* d'argento; **silver-plated** *adj* argentato(-a)

SIM card ['sɪm-] *n* (*Tel*) SIM card *f inv*

similar ['sɪmɪlə^r] *adj* **~ (to)** simile (a); **similarity** [sɪmɪ'lærɪtɪ] *n* somiglianza, rassomiglianza; **similarly** *adv* allo stesso modo; così pure

simmer ['sɪmə^r] *vi* cuocere a fuoco lento

simple ['sɪmpl] *adj* semplice; **simplicity** [-'plɪsɪtɪ] *n* semplicità; **simplify** *vt* semplificare; **simply** *adv* semplicemente

simulate ['sɪmjuleɪt] *vt* fingere,

simulare

simultaneous [siməl'teiniəs] *adj* simultaneo(-a); **simultaneously** *adv* simultaneamente, contemporaneamente

sin [sin] *n* peccato ▶ *vi* peccare

since [sins] *adv* da allora ▶ *prep* da ▶ *conj* (*time*) da quando; (*because*) poiché, dato che; **~ then, ever ~** da allora

sincere [sin'siə'] *adj* sincero(-a); **sincerely** *adv* **yours sincerely** (*in letters*) distinti saluti

sing [sin] (*pt* **sang**, *pp* **sung**) *vt, vi* cantare

Singapore [siŋgə'pɔ:'] *n* Singapore *f*

singer ['siŋə'] *n* cantante *m/f*

singing ['siŋiŋ] *n* canto

single ['siŋgl] *adj* solo(-a), unico(-a); (*unmarried: man*) celibe; (: *woman*) nubile; (*not double*) semplice ▶ *n* (*BRIT: also:* **~ ticket**) biglietto di (sola) andata; (*record*) 45 giri *m*; **~s** *n* (*Tennis*) singolo ▷ **single out** *vt* scegliere; (*distinguish*) distinguere; **single bed** *n* letto singolo; **single file** *n* **in single file** in fila indiana; **single-handed** *adv* senza aiuto, da solo(-a); **single-minded** *adj* tenace, risoluto(-a); **single parent** *n* (*mother*) ragazza *f* madre *inv*; (*father*) ragazzo *m* padre *inv*; **single-parent family** famiglia monoparentale; **single room** *n* camera singola

singular ['siŋgjulə'] *adj* (*exceptional, Ling*) singolare ▶ *n* (*Ling*) singolare *m*

sinister ['sinistə'] *adj* sinistro(-a)

sink [siŋk] (*pt* **sank**, *pp* **sunk**) *n* lavandino, acquaio ▶ *vt* (*ship*) (fare) affondare, colare a picco; (*foundations*) scavare; (*piles etc*): **to ~ sth into** conficcare qc in ▶ *vi* affondare, andare a fondo; (*ground etc*) cedere, avvallarsi; **my heart sank** mi sentii venir meno ▷ **sink in** *vi* penetrare

sinus ['sainəs] *n* (*Anat*) seno

sip [sip] *n* sorso ▶ *vt* sorseggiare

sir [sə'] *n* signore *m*; **S~ John Smith** Sir John Smith; **yes ~** sì, signore

siren ['saiərn] *n* sirena

sirloin ['sə:lɔin] *n* controfiletto

sister ['sistə'] *n* sorella; (*nun*) suora; (*BRIT: nurse*) infermiera *f* caposala *inv*; **sister-in-law** *n* cognata

sit [sit] (*pt, pp* **sat**) *vi* sedere, sedersi; (*assembly*) essere in seduta; (*for painter*) posare ▶ *vt* (*exam*) sostenere, dare ▷ **sit back** *vi* (*in seat*) appoggiarsi allo schienale ▷ **sit down** *vi* sedersi ▷ **sit on** *vt fus* (*jury, committee*) far parte di ▷ **sit up** *vi* tirarsi su a sedere; (*not go to bed*) stare alzato(-a) fino a tardi

sitcom ['sitkɔm] *n abbr* (= *situation comedy*) commedia di situazione; (*TV*) telefilm *m inv* comico d'interni

site [sait] *n* posto; (*also:* **building ~**) cantiere *m* ▶ *vt* situare

sitting ['sitiŋ] *n* (*of assembly etc*) seduta; (*in canteen*) turno; **sitting room** *n* soggiorno

situated ['sitjueitid] *adj* situato(-a)

situation [sitju'eiʃən] *n* situazione *f*; (*job*) lavoro; (*location*) posizione *f*; **"~s vacant"** (*BRIT*) "offerte *fpl* di impiego"

six [siks] *num* sei; **sixteen** *num* sedici; **sixteenth** [siks'ti:nθ] *num* sedicesimo(-a); **sixth** *num* sesto(-a); **sixth form** *n* (*BRIT*) ultimo biennio delle scuole superiori; **sixth-form college** *n* istituto che offre corsi di preparazione all'esame di maturità per ragazzi dai 16 ai 18 anni; **sixtieth** ['sikstiiθ] *num* sessantesimo(-a) ▶ *pron* (*in series*) sessantesimo(-a) ▷ (*fraction*) sessantesimo; **sixty** *num* sessanta

size [saiz] *n* dimensioni *fpl*; (*of clothing*) taglia, misura; (*of shoes*) numero; (*glue*) colla; **sizeable** *adj* considerevole

sizzle ['sɪzl] vi sfrigolare

skate [skeɪt] n pattino; (fish: pl inv) razza ▶ vi pattinare; **skateboard** n skateboard m inv; **skateboarding** n skateboard m inv; **skater** n pattinatore(-trice); **skating** n pattinaggio; **skating rink** n pista di pattinaggio

skeleton ['skɛlɪtn] n scheletro

skeptical ['skɛptɪkl] (US) adj = **sceptical**

sketch [skɛtʃ] n (drawing) schizzo, abbozzo; (Theatre) scenetta comica, sketch m inv ▶ vt abbozzare, schizzare

skewer ['skju:ər] n spiedo

ski [ski:] n sci m inv ▶ vi sciare; **ski boot** n scarpone m da sci

skid [skɪd] n slittamento ▶ vi slittare

ski: skier ['ski:ər] n sciatore(-trice); **skiing** ['ski:ɪŋ] n sci m

skilful ['skɪlful] (US **skillful**) adj abile

ski lift n sciovia

skill [skɪl] n abilità f inv, capacità f inv; **skilled** adj esperto(-a); (worker) qualificato(-a), specializzato(-a)

skim [skɪm] vt (milk) scremare; (glide over) sfiorare ▶ vi **to ~ through** (fig) scorrere, dare una scorsa a; **skimmed milk** (US **skim milk**) n latte m scremato

skin [skɪn] n pelle f ▶ vt (fruit etc) sbucciare; (animal) scuoiare, spellare; **skinhead** n skinhead m/f inv; **skinny** adj molto magro(-a), pelle e ossa inv

skip [skɪp] n saltello, balzo; (BRIT: container) benna ▶ vi saltare; (with rope) saltare la corda ▶ vt saltare

ski: ski pass n ski pass m; **ski pole** n racchetta (da sci)

skipper ['skɪpər] n (Naut, Sport) capitano

skipping rope ['skɪpɪŋ-] (US **skip rope**) n corda per saltare

skirt [skə:t] n gonna, sottana ▶ vt fiancheggiare, costeggiare

skirting board (BRIT) n zoccolo

ski slope n pista da sci

ski suit n tuta da sci

skull [skʌl] n cranio, teschio

skunk [skʌŋk] n moffetta

sky [skaɪ] n cielo; **skyscraper** n grattacielo

slab [slæb] n lastra; (of cake, cheese) fetta

slack [slæk] adj (loose) allentato(-a); (slow) lento(-a); (careless) negligente; **slacks** npl (trousers) pantaloni mpl

slain [sleɪn] pp of **slay**

slam [slæm] vt (door) sbattere; (throw) scaraventare; (criticize) stroncare ▶ vi sbattere

slander ['slɑ:ndər] n calunnia; diffamazione f

slang [slæŋ] n gergo, slang m

slant [slɑ:nt] n pendenza, inclinazione f; (fig) angolazione f, punto di vista

slap [slæp] n manata, pacca; (on face) schiaffo ▶ vt dare una manata a; schiaffeggiare ▶ adv (directly) in pieno; **~ a coat of paint on it** dagli una mano di vernice

slash [slæʃ] vt tagliare; (face) sfregiare; (fig: prices) ridurre drasticamente, tagliare

slate [sleɪt] n ardesia; (piece) lastra di ardesia ▶ vt (fig: criticize) stroncare, distruggere

slaughter ['slɔ:tər] n strage f, massacro ▶ vt (animal) macellare; (people) trucidare, massacrare; **slaughterhouse** n macello, mattatoio

Slav [slɑ:v] adj, n slavo(-a)

slave [sleɪv] n schiavo(-a) ▶ vi (also: ~ away) lavorare come uno schiavo; **slavery** n schiavitù f

slay [sleɪ] (pt **slew**, pp **slain**) vt (formal) uccidere

sleazy ['sli:zɪ] adj trasandato(-a)

sled [slɛd] (US) = **sledge**
sledge [slɛdʒ] n slitta
sleek [sliːk] adj (hair, fur) lucido(-a), lucente; (car, boat) slanciato(-a), affusolato(-a)
sleep [sliːp] (pt, pp **slept**) n sonno ▶ vi dormire; **to go to ~** addormentarsi ▷ **sleep in** vi (oversleep) dormire fino a tardi ▷ **sleep together** vi (have sex) andare a letto insieme; **sleeper** (BRIT) n (Rail: on track) traversina; (: train) treno di vagoni letto; **sleeping bag** n sacco a pelo; **sleeping car** n vagone m letto inv, carrozza f letto inv; **sleeping pill** n sonnifero; **sleepover** n notte f che un ragazzino passa da amici; **sleepwalk** vi camminare nel sonno; (as a habit) essere sonnambulo(-a); **sleepy** adj assonnato(-a), sonnolento(-a); (fig) addormentato(-a)
sleet [sliːt] n nevischio
sleeve [sliːv] n manica; (of record) copertina; **sleeveless** adj (garment) senza maniche
sleigh [sleɪ] n slitta
slender ['slɛndəʳ] adj snello(-a), sottile; (not enough) scarso(-a), esiguo(-a)
slept [slɛpt] pt, pp of **sleep**
slew [sluː] pt of **slay** ▶ vi (BRIT) girare
slice [slaɪs] n fetta ▶ vt affettare, tagliare a fette
slick [slɪk] adj (skilful) brillante; (clever) furbo(-a) ▶ n (also: **oil ~**) chiazza di petrolio
slide [slaɪd] (pt, pp **slid**) n scivolone m; (in playground) scivolo; (Phot) diapositiva; (BRIT: also: **hair ~**) fermaglio (per capelli) ▶ vt far scivolare ▶ vi scivolare; **sliding** adj (door) scorrevole
slight [slaɪt] adj (slim) snello(-a), sottile; (frail) delicato(-a), fragile; (trivial) insignificante; (small)

piccolo(-a) ▶ n offesa, affronto; **not in the ~est** affatto, neppure per sogno; **slightly** adv lievemente, un po'
slim [slɪm] adj magro(-a), snello(-a) ▶ vi dimagrire; fare (or seguire) una dieta dimagrante; **slimming** ['slɪmɪŋ] adj (diet) dimagrante; (food) ipocalorico(-a)
slimy ['slaɪmɪ] adj (also fig: person) viscido(-a); (covered with mud) melmoso(-a)
sling [slɪŋ] (pt, pp **slung**) n (Med) fascia al collo; (for baby) marsupio ▶ vt lanciare, tirare
slip [slɪp] n scivolata, scivolone m; (mistake) errore m, sbaglio; (underskirt) sottoveste f; (of paper) striscia di carta; tagliando, scontrino ▶ vt (slide) far scivolare ▶ vi (slide) scivolare; (move smoothly): **to ~ into/out of** scivolare in/fuori da; (decline) declinare; **to ~ sth on/off** infilarsi/togliersi qc; **to give sb the ~** sfuggire qn; **a ~ of the tongue** un lapsus linguae ▷ **slip up** vi sbagliarsi
slipper ['slɪpəʳ] n pantofola
slippery ['slɪpərɪ] adj scivoloso(-a)
slip road (BRIT) n (to motorway) rampa di accesso
slit [slɪt] (pt, pp **slit**) n fessura, fenditura; (cut) taglio ▶ vt fendere; tagliare
slog [slɔg] (BRIT) n faticata ▶ vi lavorare con accanimento, sgobbare
slogan ['sləugən] n motto, slogan m inv
slope [sləup] n pendio; (side of mountain) versante m; (ski slope) pista; (of roof) pendenza; (of floor) inclinazione f ▶ vi **to ~ down** declinare; **to ~ up** essere in salita; **sloping** adj inclinato(-a)
sloppy ['slɔpɪ] adj (work) tirato(-a) via; (appearance) sciatto(-a)
slot [slɔt] n fessura ▶ vt **to ~ sth**

into infilare qc in; **slot machine** n (BRIT: vending machine) distributore m automatico; (for gambling) slot-machine f inv

Slovakia [sləʊˈvækɪə] n Slovacchia

Slovene [ˈsləʊviːn] adj sloveno(-a) ▶ n sloveno(-a); (Ling) sloveno

Slovenia [sləʊˈviːnɪə] n Slovenia; **Slovenian** adj, n = **Slovene**

slow [sləʊ] adj lento(-a); (watch): **to be ~** essere indietro ▶ adv lentamente ▶ vt, vi (also: **~ down, ~ up**) rallentare; **"~"** (road sign) "rallentare" ▷ **slow down** vi rallentare; **slowly** adv lentamente; **slow motion** n **in slow motion** al rallentatore

slug [slʌg] n lumaca; (bullet) pallottola; **sluggish** adj lento(-a); (trading) stagnante

slum [slʌm] n catapecchia

slump [slʌmp] n crollo, caduta; (economic) depressione f, crisi f inv ▶ vi crollare

slung [slʌŋ] pt, pp of **sling**

slur [sləːʳ] n (fig): **~ (on)** calunnia (su) ▶ vt pronunciare in modo indistinto

sly [slaɪ] adj (smile, remark) sornione(-a); (person) furbo(-a)

smack [smæk] n (slap) pacca; (on face) schiaffo ▶ vt schiaffeggiare; (child) picchiare ▶ vi **to ~ of** puzzare di

small [smɔːl] adj piccolo(-a); **small ads** (BRIT) npl piccola pubblicità; **small change** n moneta, spiccioli mpl

smart [smɑːt] adj elegante; (fashionable) alla moda; (clever) intelligente; (quick) sveglio(-a) ▶ vi bruciare; **smartcard** [ˈsmɑːtkɑːd] n smartcard f inv, carta intelligente

smash [smæʃ] n (also: **~-up**) scontro, collisione f; (smash hit) successone m ▶ vt frantumare, fracassare; (Sport: record) battere ▶ vi frantumarsi, andare in pezzi; **smashing** (inf) adj favoloso(-a), formidabile

smear [smɪəʳ] n macchia; (Med) striscio ▶ vt spalmare; (make dirty) sporcare; **smear test** n (BRIT Med) Pap-test m inv

smell [smɛl] (pt **smelt** or **smelled**) n odore m; (sense) olfatto, odorato ▶ vt sentire (l')odore di ▶ vi (food etc): **to ~ (of)** avere odore (di); (pej) puzzare, avere un cattivo odore; **smelly** adj puzzolente

smelt [smɛlt] pt, pp of **smell** ▶ vt (ore) fondere

smile [smaɪl] n sorriso ▶ vi sorridere

smirk [sməːk] n sorriso furbo; sorriso compiaciuto

smog [smɔg] n smog m

smoke [sməʊk] n fumo ▶ vt, vi fumare; **do you mind if I ~?** le dà fastidio se fumo?; **smoke alarm** n rivelatore f di fumo; **smoked** adj (bacon, glass) affumicato(-a); **smoker** n (person) fumatore(-trice); (Rail) carrozza per fumatori; **smoking** n fumo; **"no smoking"** (sign) "vietato fumare"; **smoky** adj fumoso(-a); (taste) affumicato(-a)

smooth [smuːð] adj liscio(-a); (sauce) omogeneo(-a); (flavour, whisky) amabile; (movement) regolare; (person) mellifluo(-a) ▶ vt (also: **~ out**) lisciare, spianare; (: difficulties) appianare

smother [ˈsmʌðəʳ] vt soffocare

SMS abbr (= short message service) SMS; **SMS message** n SMS m inv, messaggino

smudge [smʌdʒ] n macchia; sbavatura ▶ vt imbrattare, sporcare

smug [smʌg] adj soddisfatto(-a), compiaciuto(-a)

smuggle [ˈsmʌgl] vt contrabbandare; **smuggling** n contrabbando

snack [snæk] n spuntino; **snack bar** n tavola calda, snack bar m inv

snag [snæg] n intoppo, ostacolo imprevisto

S

snail [sneɪl] n chiocciola

snake [sneɪk] n serpente m

snap [snæp] n (sound) schianto, colpo secco; (photograph) istantanea ▸ adj improvviso(-a) ▸ vt (far) schioccare; (break) spezzare di netto ▸ vi spezzarsi con un rumore secco; (fig: person) parlare con tono secco; **to ~ shut** chiudersi di scatto ▷ **snap at** vt fus (dog) cercare di mordere ▷ **snap up** vt afferrare; **snapshot** n istantanea

snarl [snɑ:l] vi ringhiare

snatch [snætʃ] n (small amount) frammento ▸ vt strappare (con violenza); (fig) rubare

sneak [sni:k] (pt US **snuck**) vi **to ~ in/out** entrare/uscire di nascosto ▸ n spione(-a); **to ~ up on sb** avvicinarsi quatto quatto a qn; **sneakers** npl scarpe fpl da ginnastica

sneer [snɪə^r] vi sogghignare; **to ~ at** farsi beffe di

sneeze [sni:z] n starnuto ▸ vi starnutire

sniff [snɪf] n fiutata, annusata ▸ vi tirare su col naso ▸ vt fiutare, annusare

snigger ['snɪgə^r] vi ridacchiare, ridere sotto i baffi

snip [snɪp] n pezzetto; (bargain) (buon) affare m, occasione f ▸ vt tagliare

sniper ['snaɪpə^r] n (marksman) franco tiratore m, cecchino

snob [snɔb] n snob m/f inv

snooker ['snu:kə^r] n tipo di gioco del biliardo

snoop ['snu:p] vi **to ~ about** curiosare

snooze [snu:z] n sonnellino, pisolino ▸ vi fare un sonnellino

snore [snɔ:^r] vi russare

snorkel ['snɔ:kl] n (of swimmer) respiratore m a tubo

snort [snɔ:t] n sbuffo ▸ vi sbuffare

snow [snəʊ] n neve f ▸ vi nevicare; **snowball** n palla di neve ▸ vi (fig)

crescere a vista d'occhio; **snowstorm** n tormenta

snub [snʌb] vt snobbare ▸ n offesa, affronto

snug [snʌg] adj comodo(-a); (room, house) accogliente, comodo(-a)

so

[səʊ] adv

1 (thus, likewise) così; **if so** se è così, quand'è così; **I didn't do it — you did so!** non l'ho fatto io — sì che l'hai fatto!; **so do I, so am I** etc anch'io; **it's 5 o'clock — so it is!** sono le 5 — davvero!; **I hope so** lo spero; **I think so** penso di sì; **so far** finora, fin qui; (in past) fino ad allora

2 (in comparisons etc: to such a degree) così; **so big (that)** così grande (che); **she's not so clever as her brother** lei non è (così) intelligente come suo fratello

3: **so much** adj tanto(-a) ▸adv tanto; **I've got so much work/ money** ho tanto lavoro/tanti soldi; **I love you so much** ti amo tanto; **so many** tanti(-e)

4 (phrases): **10 or so** circa 10; **so long!** (inf: goodbye) ciao!, ci vediamo! ▸conj

1 (expressing purpose): **so as to do** in modo or così da fare; **we hurried so as not to be late** ci affrettammo per non fare tardi; **so (that)** affinché + sub, perché + sub

2 (expressing result): **he didn't arrive so I left** non è venuto così me ne sono andata; **so you see, I could have gone** vedi, sarei potuto andare

soak [səʊk] vt inzuppare; (clothes) mettere a mollo ▸ vi (clothes etc) essere a mollo ▷ **soak up** vt assorbire; **soaking** adj (also: **soaking wet**) fradicio(-a)

so-and-so ['səʊənsəʊ] n (somebody) un tale; **Mr/Mrs ~** signor/signora tal dei tali

soap [səup] n sapone m; **soap opera** n soap opera f inv; **soap powder** n detersivo

soar [sɔːʳ] vi volare in alto; (price etc) salire alle stelle; (building) ergersi

sob [sɔb] n singhiozzo ▸ vi singhiozzare

sober ['səubəʳ] adj sobrio(-a); (not drunk) non ubriaco(-a); (moderate) moderato(-a) ▷ **sober up** vt far passare la sbornia a ▸ vi farsi passare la sbornia

so-called ['səu'kɔːld] adj cosiddetto(-a)

soccer ['sɔkəʳ] n calcio

sociable ['səuʃəbl] adj socievole

social ['səuʃl] adj sociale ▸ n festa, serata; **socialism** n socialismo; **socialist** adj, n socialista m/f; **socialize** vi to socialize (with) socializzare (con); **social life** n vita sociale; **socially** adv socialmente, in società; **social networking** n il comunicare tramite una rete sociale; **social security** (BRIT) n previdenza sociale; **social services** npl servizi mpl sociali; **social work** n servizio sociale; **social worker** n assistente m/f sociale

society [sə'saɪətɪ] n società f inv; (club) società, associazione f; (also: **high ~**) alta società

sociology [səusɪ'ɔlədʒɪ] n sociologia

sock [sɔk] n calzino

socket ['sɔkɪt] n cavità f inv; (of eye) orbita; (BRIT: Elec: also: **wall ~**) presa di corrente

soda ['səudə] n (Chem) soda; (also: **~ water**) acqua di seltz; (US: also: **~ pop**) gassosa

sodium ['səudɪəm] n sodio

sofa ['səufə] n sofà m inv; **sofa bed** n divano m letto inv

soft [sɔft] adj (not rough) morbido(-a); (not hard) soffice;

(not loud) sommesso(-a); (not bright) tenue; (kind) gentile; **soft drink** n analcolico; **soft drugs** npl droghe fpl leggere; **soften** ['sɔfn] vt ammorbidire; addolcire; attenuare ▸ vi ammorbidirsi; addolcirsi; attenuarsi; **softly** adv dolcemente; morbidamente; **software** ['sɔftwɛəʳ] n (Comput) software m

soggy ['sɔgɪ] adj inzuppato(-a)

soil [sɔɪl] n terreno ▸ vt sporcare

solar ['səuləʳ] adj solare; **solar power** n energie solare; **solar system** n sistema m solare

sold [səuld] pt, pp of **sell**

soldier ['səuldʒəʳ] n soldato, militare m

sold out adj (Comm) esaurito(-a)

sole [səul] n (of foot) pianta (del piede); (of shoe) suola; (fish: pl inv) sogliola ▸ adj solo(-a), unico(-a); **solely** adv solamente, unicamente

solemn ['sɔləm] adj solenne

solicitor [sə'lɪsɪtəʳ] (BRIT) n (for wills etc) ≈ notaio; (in court) ≈ avvocato

solid ['sɔlɪd] adj solido(-a); (not hollow) pieno(-a); (meal) sostanzioso(-a) ▸ n solido

solitary ['sɔlɪtərɪ] adj solitario(-a)

solitude ['sɔlɪtjuːd] n solitudine f

solo ['səuləu] n assolo; **soloist** n solista m/f

soluble ['sɔljubl] adj solubile

solution [sə'luːʃən] n soluzione f

solve [sɔlv] vt risolvere

solvent ['sɔlvənt] adj (Comm) solvibile ▸ n (Chem) solvente m

sombre ['sɔmbəʳ] (US **somber**) adj scuro(-a); (mood, person) triste

○ **some**
[sʌm] adj

1 (a certain amount or number of): **some tea/water/cream** del tè/dell'acqua/della panna; **some children/apples** dei bambini/delle mele

S

2 (*certain: in contrasts*) certo(-a); **some people say that ...** alcuni dicono che ..., certa gente dice che ...

3 (*unspecified*) un(a) certo(-a), qualche; **some woman was asking for you** una tale chiedeva di lei; **some day** un giorno; **some day next week** un giorno della prossima settimana

▶*pron*

1 (*a certain number*) alcuni(-e), certi(-e); **I've got some** (*books etc*) ne ho alcuni; **some (of them) have been sold** alcuni sono stati venduti

2 (*a certain amount*) un po'; **I've got some** (*money, milk*) ne ho un po'; **I've read some of the book** ho letto parte del libro

▶*adv* **some 10 people** circa 10 persone

some: somebody ['sʌmbədɪ] *pron* = **someone; somehow** ['sʌmhau] *adv* in un modo o nell'altro, in qualche modo; (*for some reason*) per qualche ragione; **someone** ['sʌmwʌn] *pron* qualcuno; **someplace** ['sʌmpleɪs] (*US*) *adv* = **somewhere; something** ['sʌmθɪŋ] *pron* qualcosa, qualche cosa; **something nice** qualcosa di bello; **something to do** qualcosa da fare; **sometime** ['sʌmtaɪm] *adv* (*in future*) una volta o l'altra; (*in past*): **sometime last month** durante il mese scorso; **sometimes** ['sʌmtaɪmz] *adv* qualche volta; **somewhat** ['sʌmwɔt] *adv* piuttosto; **somewhere** ['sʌmwɛə^r] *adv* in *or* da qualche parte

son [sʌn] *n* figlio

song [sɔŋ] *n* canzone *f*

son-in-law ['sʌnɪnlɔː] *n* genero

soon [suːn] *adv* presto, fra poco; (*early, a short time after*) presto; **~ afterwards** poco dopo; *see also* **as; sooner** *adv* (*time*) prima; (*preference*): **I would sooner do** preferirei fare; **sooner or later** prima o poi

soothe [suːð] *vt* calmare

sophisticated [sə'fɪstɪkeɪtɪd] *adj* sofisticato(-a); raffinato(-a); complesso(-a)

sophomore ['sɔfəmɔː^r] (*US*) *n* studente(-essa) del secondo anno

soprano [sə'prɑːnəu] *n* (*voice*) soprano *m*; (*singer*) soprano *m/f*

sorbet ['sɔːbeɪ] *n* sorbetto

sordid ['sɔːdɪd] *adj* sordido(-a)

sore [sɔː^r] *adj* (*painful*) dolorante ▶ *n* piaga

sorrow ['sɔrəu] *n* dolore *m*

sorry ['sɔrɪ] *adj* spiacente; (*condition, excuse*) misero(-a); **~!** scusa! (*or* scusi! *or* scusate!); **to feel ~ for sb** rincrescersi per qn

sort [sɔːt] *n* specie *f*, genere *m* ▷ **sort out** *vt* (*papers*) classificare; ordinare; (: *letters etc*) smistare; (: *problems*) risolvere; (*Comput*) ordinare

SOS *n abbr* (= *save our souls*) S.O.S. *m inv*

so-so ['səusəu] *adv* così così

sought [sɔːt] *pt, pp of* **seek**

soul [səul] *n* anima

sound [saund] *adj* (*healthy*) sano(-a); (*safe, not damaged*) solido(-a), in buono stato; (*reliable, not superficial*) solido(-a); (*sensible*) giudizioso(-a), di buon senso ▶ *adv* **~ asleep** profondamente addormentato ▶ *n* suono; (*noise*) rumore *m*; (*Geo*) stretto ▶ *vt* (*alarm*) suonare ▶ *vi* suonare; (*fig: seem*) sembrare; **to ~ like** rassomigliare a; **soundtrack** *n* (*of film*) colonna sonora

soup [suːp] *n* minestra; brodo; zuppa

sour ['sauə^r] *adj* aspro(-a); (*fruit*) acerbo(-a); (*milk*) acido(-a); (*fig*) arcigno(-a); acido(-a); **it's ~ grapes** è soltanto invidia

source [sɔːs] *n* fonte *f*, sorgente *f*; (*fig*) fonte

south [sauθ] *n* sud *m*, meridione *m*, mezzogiorno ▶ *adj* del sud, sud

inv, meridionale ▶ *adv* verso sud;
South Africa *n* Sudafrica *m*; **South African** *adj*, *n* sudafricano(-a); **South America** *n* Sudamerica *m*, America del sud; **South American** *adj*, *n* sudamericano(-a); **southbound** ['sauθbaund] *adj* (*gen*) diretto(-a) a sud; (*carriageway*) sud *inv*;
southeastern [sauθ'i:stən] *adj* sudorientale; **southern** ['sʌðən] *adj* del sud, meridionale; esposto(-a) a sud; **South Korea** *n* Corea *f* del Sud; **South Pole** *n* Polo Sud; **southward(s)** *adv* verso sud; **southwest** *n* sud-ovest *m*; **southwestern** [sauθ'westən] *adj* sudoccidentale
souvenir [su:və'nɪər] *n* ricordo, souvenir *m inv*
sovereign ['sɔvrɪn] *adj*, *n* sovrano(-a)
sow¹ [səu] (*pt* **sowed**, *pp* **sown**) *vt* seminare
sow² [sau] *n* scrofa
soya ['sɔɪə] (*US* **soy**) *n* ~ **bean** *n* seme *m* di soia; **soya sauce** *n* salsa di soia
spa [spɑː] *n* (*resort*) stazione *f* termale; (*US: also:* **health ~**) centro di cure estetiche
space [speɪs] *n* spazio; (*room*) posto; spazio; (*length of time*) intervallo ▶ *cpd* spaziale ▶ *vt* (*also:* **~ out**) distanziare; **spacecraft** *n inv* veicolo spaziale; **spaceship** *n* = **spacecraft**
spacious ['speɪʃəs] *adj* spazioso(-a), ampio(-a)
spade [speɪd] *n* (*tool*) vanga; pala; (*child's*) paletta; **~s** *npl* (*Cards*) picche *fpl*
spaghetti [spə'gɛtɪ] *n* spaghetti *mpl*
Spain [speɪn] *n* Spagna
spam [spæm] (*Comput*) *n* spamming ▶ *vt* **to ~ sb** inviare a qn messaggi pubblicitari non richiesti via email
span [spæn] *n* (*of bird, plane*) apertura alare; (*of arch*) campata; (*in time*) periodo; durata ▶ *vt* attraversare; (*fig*)

abbracciare
Spaniard ['spænjəd] *n* spagnolo(-a)
Spanish ['spænɪʃ] *adj* spagnolo(-a) ▶ *n* (*Ling*) spagnolo; **the ~** *npl* gli Spagnoli
spank [spæŋk] *vt* sculacciare
spanner ['spænər] (*BRIT*) *n* chiave *f* inglese
spare [spɛər] *adj* di riserva, di scorta; (*surplus*) in più, d'avanzo ▶ *n* (*part*) pezzo di ricambio ▶ *vt* (*do without*) fare a meno di; (*afford to give*) concedere; (*refrain from hurting, using*) risparmiare; **to ~** (*surplus*) d'avanzo; **spare part** *n* pezzo di ricambio; **spare room** *n* stanza degli ospiti; **spare time** *n* tempo libero; **spare tyre** (*US* **spare tire**) *n* (*Aut*) gomma di scorta; **spare wheel** *n* (*Aut*) ruota di scorta
spark [spɑːk] *n* scintilla; **spark(ing) plug** *n* candela
sparkle ['spɑːkl] *n* scintillio, sfavillio ▶ *vi* scintillare, sfavillare
sparrow ['spærəu] *n* passero
sparse [spɑːs] *adj* sparso(-a), rado(-a)
spasm ['spæzəm] *n* (*Med*) spasmo; (*fig*) accesso, attacco
spat [spæt] *pt, pp of* **spit**
spate [speɪt] *n* (*fig*): ~ **of** diluvio *or* fiume *m* di
spatula ['spætjulə] *n* spatola
speak [spiːk] (*pt* **spoke**, *pp* **spoken**) *vt* (*language*) parlare; (*truth*) dire ▶ *vi* parlare; **I don't ~ Italian** non parlo italiano; **do you ~ English?** parla inglese?; **to ~ to sb/of** *or* **about sth** parlare a qn/di qc; **can I ~ to ...?** posso parlare con...?; **~ up!** parla più forte!; **speaker** *n* (*in public*) oratore(-trice); (*also:* **loudspeaker**) altoparlante *m*; (*Pol*): **the Speaker** *il presidente della Camera dei Comuni* (*BRIT*) *or dei Rappresentanti* (*US*)
spear [spɪər] *n* lancia ▶ *vt* infilzare
special ['spɛʃl] *adj* speciale; **special**

S

delivery n (Post): **by special delivery** per espresso; **special effects** npl (Cine) effetti mpl speciali; **specialist** n specialista m/f; **speciality** [spɛʃɪˈælɪtɪ] n specialità f inv; **I'd like to try a local speciality** vorrei assaggiare una specialità del posto; **specialize** vi **to specialize (in)** specializzarsi (in); **specially** adv specialmente, particolarmente; **special needs** adj **special needs children** bambini mpl con difficoltà di apprendimento; **special offer** n (Comm) offerta speciale; **special school** n (BRIT) scuola speciale (per portatori di handicap); **specialty** (US) n = **speciality**

species [ˈspiːʃiːz] n inv specie f inv

specific [spəˈsɪfɪk] adj specifico(-a); preciso(-a); **specifically** adv esplicitamente; (especially) appositamente

specify [ˈspɛsɪfaɪ] vt specificare, precisare; **unless otherwise specified** salvo indicazioni contrarie

specimen [ˈspɛsɪmən] n esemplare m, modello; (Med) campione m

speck [spɛk] n puntino, macchiolina; (particle) granello

spectacle [ˈspɛktəkl] n spettacolo; **~s** npl (glasses) occhiali mpl; **spectacular** [-ˈtækjuləʳ] adj spettacolare

spectator [spɛkˈteɪtəʳ] n spettatore m

spectrum [ˈspɛktrəm] (pl **spectra**) n spettro

speculate [ˈspɛkjuleɪt] vi speculare; (try to guess): **to ~ about** fare ipotesi su

sped [spɛd] pt, pp of **speed**

speech [spiːtʃ] n (faculty) parola; (talk, Theatre) discorso; (manner of speaking) parlata; **speechless** adj ammutolito(-a), muto(-a)

speed [spiːd] n velocità f inv; (promptness) prontezza; **at full** or **top ~** a tutta velocità ▷ **speed up** vi, vt

accelerare; **speedboat** n motoscafo; **speeding** n (Aut) eccesso di velocità; **speed limit** n limite m di velocità; **speedometer** [spɪˈdɔmɪtəʳ] n tachimetro; **speedy** adj veloce, rapido(-a); pronto(-a)

spell [spɛl] (pt, pp **spelt** (BRIT) or **spelled**) n (also: **magic ~**) incantesimo; (period of time) (breve) periodo ▷ vt (in writing) scrivere (lettera per lettera); (aloud) dire lettera per lettera; (fig) significare; **to cast a ~ on sb** fare un incantesimo a qn; **he can't ~** fa errori di ortografia ▷ **spell out** vt (letter by letter) dettare lettera per lettera; (explain): **to ~ sth out for sb** spiegare qc a qn per filo e per segno; **spellchecker** [ˈspɛltʃɛkəʳ] n correttore m ortografico; **spelling** n ortografia

spelt [spɛlt] (BRIT) pt, pp of **spell**

spend [spɛnd] (pt, pp **spent**) vt (money) spendere; (time, life) passare; **spending** n **government spending** spesa pubblica

spent [spɛnt] pt, pp of **spend**

sperm [spəːm] n sperma m

sphere [sfɪəʳ] n sfera

spice [spaɪs] n spezia ▷ vt aromatizzare

spicy [ˈspaɪsɪ] adj piccante

spider [ˈspaɪdəʳ] n ragno

spike [spaɪk] n punta

spill [spɪl] (pt, pp **spilt** or **spilled**) vt versare, rovesciare ▷ vi versarsi, rovesciarsi

spin [spɪn] (pt, pp **spun**) n (revolution of wheel) rotazione f; (Aviat) avvitamento; (trip in car) giretto ▷ vt (wool etc) filare; (wheel) far girare ▷ vi girare

spinach [ˈspɪnɪtʃ] n spinacio; (as food) spinaci mpl

spinal [ˈspaɪnl] adj spinale

spin doctor (inf) n esperto di

comunicazioni responsabile dell'immagine di un partito politico

spin-dryer [spɪn'draɪəʳ] (BRIT) n centrifuga

spine [spaɪn] n spina dorsale; (thorn) spina

spiral ['spaɪərl] n spirale f ▶ vi (fig) salire a spirale

spire ['spaɪəʳ] n guglia

spirit ['spɪrɪt] n spirito; (ghost) spirito, fantasma m; (mood) stato d'animo, umore m; (courage) coraggio; **~s** npl (drink) alcolici mpl; **in good ~s** di buon umore

spiritual ['spɪrɪtjuəl] adj spirituale

spit [spɪt] n (pt, pp **spat**) n (for roasting) spiedo; (saliva) sputo; saliva ▶ vi sputare; (fire, fat) scoppiettare

spite [spaɪt] n dispetto ▶ vt contrariare, far dispetto a; **in ~ of** nonostante, malgrado; **spiteful** adj dispettoso(-a)

splash [splæʃ] n spruzzo; (sound) splash m inv; (of colour) schizzo ▶ vt spruzzare ▶ vi (also: **~ about**) sguazzare ▷ **splash out** (inf) vi (BRIT) fare spese folli

splendid ['splɛndɪd] adj splendido(-a), magnifico(-a)

splinter ['splɪntəʳ] n scheggia ▶ vi scheggiarsi

split [splɪt] (pt, pp **split**) n spaccatura; (fig: division, quarrel) scissione f ▶ vt spaccare; (party) dividere; (work, profits) spartire, ripartire ▶ vi (divide) dividersi ▷ **split up** vi (couple) separarsi, rompere; (meeting) sciogliersi

spoil [spɔɪl] (pt, pp **spoilt** or **spoiled**) vt (damage) rovinare, guastare; (mar) sciupare; (child) viziare

spoilt [spɔɪlt] pt, pp of **spoil**

spoke [spəuk] pt of **speak** ▶ n raggio

spoken ['spəukn] pp of **speak**

spokesman ['spəuksmən] (irreg) n

portavoce m inv

spokesperson ['spəukspə:sn] n portavoce m/f

spokeswoman ['spəukswumən] (irreg) n portavoce f inv

sponge [spʌndʒ] n spugna; (also: **~ cake**) pan m di spagna ▶ vt spugnare, pulire con una spugna ▶ vi **to ~ off** or **on** scroccare a; **sponge bag** (BRIT) n nécessaire m inv

sponsor ['spɒnsəʳ] n (Radio, TV, Sport etc) sponsor m inv; (Pol: of bill) promotore(-trice) ▶ vt sponsorizzare; (bill) presentare; **sponsorship** n sponsorizzazione f

spontaneous [spɒn'teɪnɪəs] adj spontaneo(-a)

spooky ['spu:kɪ] (inf) adj che fa accapponare la pelle

spoon [spu:n] n cucchiaio; **spoonful** n cucchiaiata

sport [spɔ:t] n sport m inv; (person) persona di spirito ▶ vt sfoggiare; **sport jacket** (US) n = **sports jacket**; **sports car** n automobile f sportiva; **sports centre** (BRIT) n centro sportivo; **sports jacket** (BRIT) n giacca sportiva; **sportsman** (irreg) n sportivo; **sportswear** n abiti mpl sportivi; **sportswoman** (irreg) n sportiva; **sporty** adj sportivo(-a)

spot [spɒt] n punto; (mark) macchia; (dot: on pattern) pallino; (pimple) foruncolo; (place) posto; (Radio, TV) spot m inv; (small amount): **a ~ of** un po' di ▶ vt (notice) individuare, distinguere; **on the ~** sul posto; (immediately) su due piedi; (in difficulty) nei guai; **spotless** adj immacolato(-a); **spotlight** n proiettore m; (Aut) faro ausiliario

spouse [spauz] n sposo(-a)

sprain [spreɪn] n storta, distorsione f ▶ vt **to ~ one's ankle** storcersi una caviglia

sprang [spræŋ] *pt of* **spring**

sprawl [sprɔ:l] *vi* sdraiarsi (in modo scomposto); (*place*) estendersi (disordinatamente)

spray [spreɪ] *n* spruzzo; (*container*) nebulizzatore *m*, spray *m inv*; (*of flowers*) mazzetto ▶ *vt* spruzzare; (*crops*) irrorare

spread [sprɛd] (*pt, pp* **spread**) *n* diffusione *f*; (*distribution*) distribuzione *f*; (*Culin*) pasta (da spalmare); (*inf: food*) banchetto ▶ *vt* (*cloth*) stendere, distendere; (*butter etc*) spalmare; (*disease, knowledge*) propagare, diffondere ▶ *vi* stendersi, distendersi; spalmarsi; propagarsi, diffondersi ▷ **spread out** *vi* (*move apart*) separarsi; **spreadsheet** *n* foglio elettronico ad espansione

spree [spri:] *n* **to go on a ~** fare baldoria

spring [sprɪŋ] (*pt* **sprang**, *pp* **sprung**) *n* (*leap*) salto, balzo; (*coiled metal*) molla; (*season*) primavera; (*of water*) sorgente *f* ▶ *vi* saltare, balzare ▷ **spring up** *vi* (*problem*) presentarsi; **spring onion** *n* (*BRIT*) cipollina

sprinkle [ˈsprɪŋkl] *vt* spruzzare; spargere; **to ~ water** *etc* **on, ~ with water** *etc* spruzzare dell'acqua *etc* su

sprint [sprɪnt] *n* scatto ▶ *vi* scattare

sprung [sprʌŋ] *pp of* **spring**

spun [spʌn] *pt, pp of* **spin**

spur [spə:ʳ] *n* sperone *m*; (*fig*) sprone *m*, incentivo ▶ *vt* (*also*: **~ on**) spronare; **on the ~ of the moment** lì per lì

spurt [spə:t] *n* (*of water*) getto; (*of energy*) scatto ▶ *vi* sgorgare

spy [spaɪ] *n* spia ▶ *vi* **to ~ on** spiare ▶ *vt* (*see*) scorgere

sq. *abbr* = **square**

squabble [ˈskwɔbl] *vi* bisticciarsi

squad [skwɔd] *n* (*Mil*) plotone *m*; (*Police*) squadra

squadron [ˈskwɔdrn] *n* (*Mil*)

squadrone *m*; (*Aviat, Naut*) squadriglia

squander [ˈskwɔndəʳ] *vt* dissipare

square [skwɛəʳ] *n* quadrato; (*in town*) piazza ▶ *adj* quadrato(-a); (*inf: ideas, person*) di vecchio stampo ▶ *vt* (*arrange*) regolare; (*Math*) elevare al quadrato; (*reconcile*) conciliare; **all ~** pari; **a ~ meal** un pasto abbondante; **2 metres ~** di 2 metri per 2; **1 ~ metre** 1 metro quadrato; **square root** *n* radice *f* quadrata

squash [skwɔʃ] *n* (*Sport*) squash *m*; (*BRIT: drink*): **lemon/orange ~** sciroppo di limone/arancia; (*US*) zucca; (*Sport*) squash *m* ▶ *vt* schiacciare

squat [skwɔt] *adj* tarchiato(-a), tozzo(-a) ▶ *vi* (*also*: **~ down**) accovacciarsi; **squatter** *n* occupante *m/f* abusivo(-a)

squeak [skwi:k] *vi* squittire

squeal [skwi:l] *vi* strillare

squeeze [skwi:z] *n* pressione *f*; (*also Econ*) stretta ▶ *vt* premere; (*hand, arm*) stringere

squid [skwɪd] *n* calamaro

squint [skwɪnt] *vi* essere strabico(-a) ▶ *n* **he has a ~** è strabico

squirm [skwə:m] *vi* contorcersi

squirrel [ˈskwɪrəl] *n* scoiattolo

squirt [skwə:t] *vi* schizzare; zampillare ▶ *vt* spruzzare

Sr *abbr* = **senior**

Sri Lanka [srɪˈlæŋkə] *n* Sri Lanka *m*

St *abbr* = **saint**; **street**

stab [stæb] *n* (*with knife etc*) pugnalata; (*of pain*) fitta; (*inf: try*): **to have a ~ at (doing) sth** provare (a fare) qc ▶ *vt* pugnalare

stability [stəˈbɪlɪtɪ] *n* stabilità

stable [ˈsteɪbl] *n* (*for horses*) scuderia; (*for cattle*) stalla ▶ *adj* stabile

stack [stæk] *n* catasta, pila ▶ *vt* accatastare, ammucchiare

stadium [ˈsteɪdɪəm] *n* stadio

staff [stɑːf] n (work force: gen)
personale m; (: BRIT: Scol) personale
insegnante ▶ vt fornire di personale

stag [stæg] n cervo

stage [steɪdʒ] n palcoscenico;
(profession): **the ~** il teatro, la scena;
(point) punto; (platform) palco ▶ vt
(play) allestire, mettere in scena;
(demonstration) organizzare; **in ~s** per
gradi; a tappe

stagger ['stægər] vi barcollare ▶ vt
(person) sbalordire; (hours, holidays)
scaglionare; **staggering** adj (amazing)
sbalorditivo(-a)

stagnant ['stægnənt] adj stagnante

stag night, stag party n festa di
addio al celibato

stain [steɪn] n macchia; (colouring)
colorante m ▶ vt macchiare; (wood)
tingere; **stained glass** [steɪnd'glɑːs]
n vetro colorato; **stainless steel** n
acciaio inossidabile

staircase ['stɛəkeɪs] n scale fpl, scala

stairs [stɛəz] npl (flight of stairs) scale
fpl, scala

stairway ['stɛəweɪ] n = **staircase**

stake [steɪk] n palo, piolo; (Comm)
interesse m; (Betting) puntata,
scommessa ▶ vt (bet) scommettere;
(risk) rischiare; **to be at ~** essere in
gioco

stale [steɪl] adj (bread) raffermo(-a);
(food) stantio(-a); (air) viziato(-a);
(beer) svaporato(-a); (smell) di chiuso

stalk [stɔːk] n gambo, stelo ▶ vt
inseguire

stall [stɔːl] n bancarella; (in stable) box
m inv di stalla ▶ vt (Aut) far spegnere;
(fig) bloccare ▶ vi (Aut) spegnersi,
fermarsi; (fig) temporeggiare

stamina ['stæmɪnə] n vigore m,
resistenza

stammer ['stæmər] n balbuzie f ▶ vi
balbettare

stamp [stæmp] n (postage stamp)
francobollo; (implement) timbro;
(mark, also fig) marchio, impronta;
(on document) bollo; timbro ▶ vi (also:
~ one's foot) battere il piede ▶ vt
battere; (letter) affrancare; (mark with
a stamp) timbrare ▷ **stamp out** vt
(fire) estinguere; (crime) eliminare;
(opposition) soffocare; **stamped
addressed envelope** n (BRIT) busta
affrancata e indirizzata

⬛ Be careful not to translate **stamp**
the Italian word by **stampa**.

stampede [stæm'piːd] n fuggi fuggi
m inv

stance [stæns] n posizione f

stand [stænd] (pt, pp **stood**) n
(position) posizione f; (for taxis)
posteggio; (structure) supporto,
sostegno; (at exhibition) stand m inv;
(in shop) banco; (at market) bancarella;
(booth) chiosco; (Sport) tribuna
▶ vi stare in piedi; (rise) alzarsi in
piedi; (be placed) trovarsi ▶ vt (place)
mettere, porre; (tolerate, withstand)
resistere, sopportare; (treat) offrire;
to make a ~ prendere posizione; **to
~ for parliament** (BRIT) presentarsi
come candidato (per il parlamento)
▷ **stand back** vi prendere le
distanze ▷ **stand by** vi (be ready)
tenersi pronto(-a) ▶ vt fus (opinion)
sostenere ▷ **stand down** vi (withdraw)
ritirarsi ▷ **stand for** vt fus (signify)
rappresentare, significare; (tolerate)
sopportare, tollerare ▷ **stand in for**
vt fus sostituire ▷ **stand out** vi (be
prominent) spiccare ▷ **stand up** vi (rise)
alzarsi in piedi ▷ **stand up for** vt fus
difendere ▷ **stand up to** vt fus tener
testa a, resistere a

standard ['stændəd] n modello,
standard m inv; (level) livello; (flag)
stendardo ▶ adj (size etc) normale,
standard inv; **~s** npl (morals) principi
mpl, valori mpl; **standard of living** n

S

livello di vita

stand-by ['stændbaɪ] n riserva, sostituto; **to be on ~** (gen) tenersi pronto(-a); (doctor) essere di guardia; **stand-by ticket** n (Aviat) biglietto senza garanzia

standing ['stændɪŋ] adj diritto(-a), in piedi; (permanent) permanente ▶ n rango, condizione f, posizione f; **of many years' ~** che esiste da molti anni; **standing order** (BRIT) n (at bank) ordine m di pagamento (permanente)

stand: **standpoint** ['stændpɔɪnt] n punto di vista; **standstill** ['stændstɪl] n **at a standstill** fermo(-a); (fig) a un punto morto; **to come to a standstill** fermarsi; giungere a un punto morto

stank [stæŋk] pt of **stink**

staple ['steɪpl] n (for papers) graffetta ▶ adj (food etc) di base ▶ vt cucire

star [stɑː'] n stella; (celebrity) divo(-a) ▶ vi **to ~ (in)** essere il (or la) protagonista (di) ▶ vt (Cinema) essere interpretato(-a) da; **the ~s** npl (Astrology) le stelle

starboard ['stɑːbəd] n dritta

starch [stɑːtʃ] n amido

stardom ['stɑːdəm] n celebrità

stare [stɛə'] n sguardo fisso ▶ vi **to ~ at** fissare

stark [stɑːk] adj (bleak) desolato(-a) ▶ adv **~ naked** completamente nudo(-a)

start [stɑːt] n inizio; (of race) partenza; (sudden movement) sobbalzo; (advantage) vantaggio ▶ vt cominciare, iniziare; (car) mettere in moto ▶ vi cominciare; (on journey) partire, mettersi in viaggio; (jump) sobbalzare; **when does the film ~?** a che ora comincia il film?; **to ~ doing** or **to do sth** (in)cominciare a fare qc ▷ **start off** vi cominciare; (leave) partire ▷ **start out** vi (begin)

cominciare; (set out) partire ▷ **start up** vi cominciare; (car) avviarsi ▶ vt iniziare; (car) avviare; **starter** n (Aut) motorino d'avviamento; (Sport: official) starter m inv; (BRIT: Culin) primo piatto; **starting point** n punto di partenza

startle ['stɑːtl] vt far trasalire; **startling** adj sorprendente

starvation [stɑː'veɪʃən] n fame f, inedia

starve [stɑːv] vi morire di fame; soffrire la fame ▶ vt far morire di fame, affamare

state [steɪt] n stato ▶ vt dichiarare, affermare; annunciare; **the S~s** (USA) gli Stati Uniti; **to be in a ~** essere agitato(-a); **statement** n dichiarazione f; **state school** n scuola statale; **statesman** (irreg) n statista m

static ['stætɪk] n (Radio) scariche fpl ▶ adj statico(-a)

station ['steɪʃən] n stazione f ▶ vt collocare, disporre

stationary ['steɪʃənərɪ] adj fermo(-a), immobile

stationer's (shop) n cartoleria

stationery ['steɪʃnərɪ] n articoli mpl di cancelleria

station wagon (US) n giardinetta

statistic [stə'tɪstɪk] n statistica; **statistics** n (science) statistica

statue ['stætjuː] n statua

stature ['stætʃə'] n statura

status ['steɪtəs] n posizione f, condizione f sociale; prestigio; stato; **status quo** [-'kwəʊ] n **the status quo** lo statu quo

statutory ['stætjutrɪ] adj stabilito(-a) dalla legge, statutario(-a)

staunch [stɔːntʃ] adj fidato(-a), leale

stay [steɪ] n (period of time) soggiorno, permanenza ▶ vi rimanere; (reside) alloggiare, stare; (spend some time) trattenersi, soggiornare; **to ~ put** non muoversi; **to ~ the night** fermarsi per la notte ▷ **stay away** vi (from person, building) stare lontano (from event) non andare ▷ **stay behind** vi restare indietro ▷ **stay in** vi (at home) stare in casa ▷ **stay on** vi restare, rimanere ▷ **stay out** vi (of house) rimanere fuori (di casa) ▷ **stay up** vi (at night) rimanere alzato(-a)

steadily ['stɛdɪlɪ] adv (firmly) saldamente; (constantly) continuamente; (fixedly) fisso; (walk) con passo sicuro

steady ['stɛdɪ] adj (not wobbling) fermo(-a); (regular) costante; (person, character) serio(-a); (: calm) calmo(-a), tranquillo(-a) ▶ vt stabilizzare; calmare

steak [steɪk] n (meat) bistecca; (fish) trancia

steal [stiːl] (pt **stole**, pp **stolen**) vt rubare ▶ vi rubare; (move) muoversi furtivamente; **my wallet has been stolen** mi hanno rubato il portafoglio

steam [stiːm] n vapore m ▶ vt (Culin) cuocere a vapore ▶ vi fumare ▷ **steam up** vi (window) appannarsi; **to get ~ed up about sth** (fig) andare in bestia per qc; **steamy** adj (room) pieno(-a) di vapore; (window) appannato(-a)

steel [stiːl] n acciaio ▶ adj di acciaio

steep [stiːp] adj ripido(-a), scosceso(-a); (price) eccessivo(-a) ▶ vt inzuppare; (washing) mettere a mollo

steeple ['stiːpl] n campanile m

steer [stɪəʳ] vt guidare ▶ vi (Naut: person) governare; (car) guidarsi; **steering** n (Aut) sterzo; **steering wheel** n volante m

stem [stɛm] n (of flower, plant) stelo; (of tree) fusto; (of glass) gambo; (of fruit, leaf) picciolo ▶ vt contenere, arginare

step [stɛp] n passo; (stair) gradino, scalino; (action) mossa, azione f ▶ vi to **~ forward/back** fare un passo avanti/

indietro; **~s** npl (BRIT) = **stepladder**; **to be in/out of ~ (with)** stare/non stare al passo (con) ▷ **step down** vi (fig) ritirarsi ▷ **step in** vi fare il proprio ingresso ▷ **step up** vt aumentare; intensificare; **stepbrother** n fratellastro; **stepchild** n figliastro(-a); **stepdaughter** n figliastra; **stepfather** n patrigno; **stepladder** n scala a libretto; **stepmother** n matrigna; **stepsister** n sorellastra; **stepson** n figliastro

stereo ['stɛrɪəu] n (system) sistema m stereofonico; (record player) stereo m inv ▶ adj (also: **~phonic**) stereofonico(-a)

stereotype ['stɪərɪətaɪp] n stereotipo

sterile ['stɛraɪl] adj sterile; **sterilize** ['stɛrɪlaɪz] vt sterilizzare

sterling ['stəːlɪŋ] adj (gold, silver) di buona lega ▶ n (Econ) (lira) sterlina; **a pound ~** una lira sterlina

stern [stəːn] adj severo(-a) ▶ n (Naut) poppa

steroid ['stɛrɔɪd] n steroide m

stew [stjuː] n stufato ▶ vt cuocere in umido

steward ['stjuːəd] n (Aviat, Naut, Rail) steward m inv; (in club etc) dispensiere m; **stewardess** n assistente f di volo, hostess f inv

stick [stɪk] (pt, pp **stuck**) n bastone m; (of rhubarb, celery) gambo; (of dynamite) candelotto ▶ vt (glue) attaccare; (thrust): **to ~ sth into** conficcare or piantare or infiggere qc in; (inf: put) ficcare; (inf: tolerate) sopportare ▶ vi attaccarsi; (remain) restare, rimanere ▷ **stick out** vi sporgere, spuntare ▷ **stick up** vi sporgere, spuntare ▷ **stick up for** vt fus difendere; **sticker** n cartellino adesivo; **sticking plaster** n cerotto adesivo; **stick shift** (US) n (Aut) cambio manuale

sticky ['stɪkɪ] adj attaccaticcio(-a),

vischioso(-a); (*label*) adesivo(-a); (*fig: situation*) difficile

stiff [stɪf] *adj* rigido(-a), duro(-a); (*muscle*) legato(-a), indolenzito(-a); (*difficult*) difficile, arduo(-a); (*cold*) freddo(-a), formale; (*strong*) forte; (*high: price*) molto alto(-a) ▶ *adv* **bored ~** annoiato(-a) a morte

stifling ['staɪflɪŋ] *adj* (*heat*) soffocante

stigma ['stɪgmə] *n* (*fig*) stigma *m*

stiletto [stɪ'lɛtəu] (*BRIT*) *n* (*also:* **~ heel**) tacco a spillo

still [stɪl] *adj* fermo(-a); silenzioso(-a) ▶ *adv* (*up to this time, even*) ancora; (*nonetheless*) tuttavia, ciò nonostante

stimulate ['stɪmjuleɪt] *vt* stimolare

stimulus ['stɪmjuləs] (*pl* **stimuli**) *n* stimolo

sting [stɪŋ] (*pt, pp* **stung**) *n* puntura; (*organ*) pungiglione *m* ▶ *vt* pungere

stink [stɪŋk] (*pt* **stank**, *pp* **stunk**) *n* fetore *m*, puzzo ▶ *vi* puzzare

stir [stə:ʳ] *n* agitazione *f*, clamore *m* ▶ *vt* mescolare; (*fig*) risvegliare ▶ *vi* muoversi ▷ **stir up** *vt* provocare, suscitare; **stir-fry** *vt* saltare in padella ▶ *n* pietanza al salto

stitch [stɪtʃ] *n* (*Sewing*) punto; (*Knitting*) maglia; (*Med*) punto (di sutura); (*pain*) fitta ▶ *vt* cucire, attaccare; suturare

stock [stɔk] *n* riserva, provvista; (*Comm*) giacenza, stock *m inv*; (*Agr*) bestiame *m*; (*Culin*) brodo; (*descent*) stirpe *f*; (*Finance*) titoli *mpl*; azioni *fpl* ▶ *adj* (*fig: reply etc*) consueto(-a); classico(-a) ▶ *vt* (*have in stock*) avere, vendere; **~s and shares** valori *mpl* di borsa; **in ~** in magazzino; **out of ~** esaurito(-a); **stockbroker** ['stɔkbrəukəʳ] *n* agente *m* di cambio; **stock cube** (*BRIT*) *n* dado; **stock exchange** *n* Borsa (valori); **stockholder** ['stɔkhəuldəʳ] *n* (*Finance*) azionista *m/f*

stocking ['stɔkɪŋ] *n* calza

stock market *n* Borsa, mercato finanziario

stole [stəul] *pt of* **steal** ▶ *n* stola

stolen ['stəuln] *pp of* **steal**

stomach ['stʌmək] *n* stomaco; (*belly*) pancia ▶ *vt* sopportare, digerire; **stomachache** *n* mal *m* di stomaco

stone [stəun] *n* pietra; (*pebble*) sasso, ciottolo; (*in fruit*) nocciolo; (*Med*) calcolo; (*BRIT: weight*) = 6.348 *kg*; 14 *libbre* ▶ *adj* di pietra ▶ *vt* lapidare; (*fruit*) togliere il nocciolo a

stood [stud] *pt, pp of* **stand**

stool [stu:l] *n* sgabello

stoop [stu:p] *vi* (*also:* **have a ~**) avere una curvatura; (*also:* **~ down**) chinarsi, curvarsi

stop [stɔp] *n* arresto; (*stopping place*) fermata; (*in punctuation*) punto ▶ *vt* arrestare, fermare; (*break off*) interrompere; (*also:* **put a ~ to**) porre fine a ▶ *vi* fermarsi; (*rain, noise etc*) cessare, finire; **to ~ doing sth** cessare *or* finire di fare qc; **could you ~ here/at the corner?** può fermarsi qui/all'angolo?; **to ~ dead** fermarsi di colpo ▷ **stop by** *vi* passare, fare un salto ▷ **stop off** *vi* sostare brevemente; **stopover** *n* breve sosta; (*Aviat*) scalo; **stoppage** ['stɔpɪdʒ] *n* arresto, fermata; (*of pay*) trattenuta; (*strike*) interruzione *f* del lavoro

storage ['stɔ:rɪdʒ] *n* immagazzinamento

store [stɔ:ʳ] *n* provvista, riserva; (*depot*) deposito; (*BRIT: department store*) grande magazzino; (*US: shop*) negozio ▶ *vt* immagazzinare; **~s** *npl* (*provisions*) rifornimenti *mpl*, scorte *fpl*; **in ~** di riserva; in serbo; **storekeeper** (*US*) *n* negoziante *m/f*

storey ['stɔ:rɪ] (*US* **story**) *n* piano

storm [stɔ:m] *n* tempesta, temporale *m*, burrasca; uragano ▶ *vi* (*fig*)

infuriarsi ▶ vt prendere d'assalto;
stormy adj tempestoso(-a),
burrascoso(-a)

story ['stɔːrɪ] n storia; favola;
racconto; (US) = **storey**

stout [staut] adj solido(-a),
robusto(-a); (friend, supporter) tenace;
(fat), grasso(-a) ▶ n birra scura

stove [stəuv] n (for cooking) fornello;
(: small) fornelletto; (for heating) stufa

straight [streɪt] adj dritto(-a); (frank)
onesto(-a), franco(-a); (simple)
semplice ▶ adv direttamente; (drink) liscio;
to put or **get ~** mettere in ordine,
mettere ordine in; **~ away, ~ off** (at
once) immediatamente; **straighten**
vt (also: **straighten out**) raddrizzare;
straightforward adj semplice;
onesto(-a), franco(-a)

strain [streɪn] n (Tech) sollecitazione
f; (physical) sforzo; (mental) tensione
f; (Med) strappo; distorsione f;
(streak, trace) tendenza; elemento
▶ vt tendere; (muscle) sforzare; (ankle)
storcere; (resources) pesare su; (food)
colare; passare; **strained** adj (muscle)
stirato(-a); (laugh etc) forzato(-a);
(relations) teso(-a); **strainer** n
passino, colino

strait [streɪt] n (Geo) stretto; **~s** npl **to
be in dire ~s** (fig) essere nei guai

strand [strænd] n (of thread) filo;
stranded adj nei guai; senza mezzi
di trasporto

strange [streɪndʒ] adj (not
known) sconosciuto(-a); (odd)
strano(-a), bizzarro(-a); **strangely**
adv stranamente; **stranger** n
sconosciuto(-a); estraneo(-a)

strangle ['stræŋgl] vt strangolare

strap [stræp] n cinghia; (of slip, dress)
spallina, bretella

strategic [strə'tiːdʒɪk] adj
strategico(-a)

strategy ['strætɪdʒɪ] n strategia

straw [strɔː] n paglia; (drinking straw)
cannuccia; **that's the last ~!** è la
goccia che fa traboccare il vaso!

strawberry ['strɔːbərɪ] n fragola

stray [streɪ] adj (animal) randagio(-a);
(bullet) vagante; (scattered) sparso(-a)
▶ vi perdersi

streak [striːk] n striscia; (of hair)
mèche f inv ▶ vt striare, screziare ▶ vi
to ~ past passare come un fulmine

stream [striːm] n ruscello; corrente f;
(of people, smoke etc) fiume m ▶ vt (Scol)
dividere in livelli di rendimento ▶ vi
scorrere; **to ~ in/out** entrare/uscire
a fiotti

street [striːt] n strada, via; **streetcar**
(US) n tram m inv; **street light** n
lampione m; **street map** n pianta
(di una città); **street plan** n pianta
(di una città)

strength [strɛŋθ] n forza;
strengthen vt rinforzare; fortificare;
consolidare

strenuous ['strɛnjuəs] adj
vigoroso(-a), energico(-a); (tiring)
duro(-a), pesante

stress [strɛs] n (force, pressure)
pressione f; (mental strain) tensione
f; (accent) accento ▶ vt insistere su,
sottolineare; accentare; **stressed**
adj (tense: person) stressato(-a);
(Ling, Poetry: syllable) accentato(-a);
stressful adj (job) difficile, stressante

stretch [strɛtʃ] n (of sand etc) distesa
▶ vi stirarsi; (extend): **to ~ to** or **as far
as** estendersi fino a ▶ vt tendere,
allungare; (spread) distendere; (fig)
spingere (al massimo); ▷ **stretch out**
vi allungarsi, estendersi ▶ vt (arm
etc) allungare, tendere; (to spread)
distendere

stretcher ['strɛtʃəʳ] n barella, lettiga

strict [strɪkt] adj (severe) rigido(-a),
severo(-a); (precise) preciso(-a),
stretto(-a); **strictly** adv severamente;

S

rigorosamente; strettamente

stride [straɪd] (*pt* **strode**, *pp* **stridden**) *n* passo lungo ▶ *vi* camminare a grandi passi

strike [straɪk] (*pt*, *pp* **struck**) *n* sciopero; (*of oil etc*) scoperta; (*attack*) attacco ▶ *vt* colpire; (*oil etc*) scoprire, trovare; (*bargain*) fare; (*fig*): **the thought** *or* **it ~s me that ...** mi viene in mente che ... ▶ *vi* scioperare; (*attack*) attaccare; (*clock*) suonare; **on ~** (*workers*) in sciopero; **to ~ a match** accendere un fiammifero; **striker** *n* scioperante *m/f*; (*Sport*) attaccante *m*; **striking** *adj* che colpisce

string [strɪŋ] (*pt*, *pp* **strung**) *n* spago; (*row*) fila; sequenza; catena; (*Mus*) corda ▶ *vt* **to ~ out** disporre di fianco; **to ~ together** (*words, ideas*) mettere insieme; **the ~s** *npl* (*Mus*) gli archi; **to pull ~s for sb** (*fig*) raccomandare qn

strip [strɪp] *n* striscia ▶ *vt* spogliare; (*paint*) togliere; (*also*: **~ down**: *machine*) smontare ▶ *vi* spogliarsi ▷ **strip off** *vt* (*paint etc*) staccare ▶ *vi* (*person*) spogliarsi

stripe [straɪp] *n* striscia, riga; (*Mil, Police*) gallone *m*; **striped** *adj* a strisce *or* righe

stripper ['strɪpər] *n* spogliarellista *m/f*

strip-search ['strɪpsəːtʃ] *vt* **to ~ sb** perquisire qn facendolo(-a) spogliare ▶ *n* perquisizione (*facendo spogliare il perquisito*)

strive [straɪv] (*pt* **strove**, *pp* **striven**) *vi* **to ~ to do** sforzarsi di fare

strode [strəud] *pt of* **stride**

stroke [strəuk] *n* colpo; (*Swimming*) bracciata; (: *style*) stile *m*; (*Med*) colpo apoplettico ▶ *vt* accarezzare; **at a ~** in un attimo

stroll [strəul] *n* giretto, passeggiatina ▶ *vi* andare a spasso; **stroller** (*US*) *n* passeggino

strong [strɔŋ] *adj* (*gen*) forte; (*sturdy:*

table, fabric etc) robusto(-a); **they are 50 ~** sono in 50; **stronghold** *n* (*also fig*) roccaforte *f*; **strongly** *adv* fortemente, con forza; energicamente; vivamente

strove [strəuv] *pt of* **strive**

struck [strʌk] *pt*, *pp of* **strike**

structure ['strʌktʃər] *n* struttura; (*building*) costruzione *f*, fabbricato

struggle ['strʌgl] *n* lotta ▶ *vi* lottare

strung [strʌŋ] *pt*, *pp of* **string**

stub [stʌb] *n* mozzicone *m*; (*of ticket etc*) matrice *f*, tall/oncino ▶ *vt* **to ~ one's toe** urtare o sbattere il dito del piede ▷ **stub out** *vt* schiacciare

stubble ['stʌbl] *n* stoppia; (*on chin*) barba ispida

stubborn ['stʌbən] *adj* testardo(-a), ostinato(-a)

stuck [stʌk] *pt*, *pp of* **stick** ▶ *adj* (*jammed*) bloccato(-a)

stud [stʌd] *n* bottoncino; borchia; (*also*: **~ earring**) orecchino a pressione; (*also*: **~ farm**) scuderia, allevamento di cavalli; (*also*: **~ horse**) stallone *m* ▶ *vt* (*fig*): **~ded with** tempestato(-a) di

student ['stjuːdənt] *n* studente(-essa) ▶ *cpd* studentesco(-a); universitario(-a); degli studenti; **student driver** (*US*) *n* conducente *m/f* principiante; **students' union** *n* (*BRIT*: *association*) circolo universitario; (: *building*) sede *f* del circolo universitario

studio ['stjuːdɪəu] *n* studio; **studio flat** (*US* **studio apartment**) *n* monolocale *m*

study ['stʌdɪ] *n* studio ▶ *vt* studiare; esaminare ▶ *vi* studiare

stuff [stʌf] *n* roba; (*substance*) sostanza, materiale *m* ▶ *vt* imbottire; (*Culin*) farcire; (*dead animal*) impagliare; (*inf: push*) ficcare; **stuffing** *n* imbottitura;

(Culin) ripieno; **stuffy** adj (room) mal ventilato(-a), senz'aria; (ideas) antiquato(-a)

stumble ['stʌmbl] vi inciampare; **to ~ across** (fig) imbattersi in

stump [stʌmp] n ceppo; (of limb) moncone m ▸ vt **to be ~ed** essere sconcertato(-a)

stun [stʌn] vt stordire; (amaze) sbalordire

stung [stʌŋ] pt, pp of **sting**

stunk [stʌŋk] pp of **stink**

stunned [stʌnd] adj (from blow) stordito(-a); (amazed, shocked) sbalordito(-a)

stunning ['stʌnɪŋ] adj sbalorditivo(-a); (girl etc) fantastico(-a)

stunt [stʌnt] n bravata; trucco pubblicitario

stupid ['stjuːpɪd] adj stupido(-a); **stupidity** [-'pɪdɪtɪ] n stupidità f inv, stupidaggine f

sturdy ['stɜːdɪ] adj robusto(-a), vigoroso(-a); solido(-a)

stutter ['stʌtəʳ] n balbuzie f ▸ vi balbettare

style [staɪl] n stile m; (distinction) eleganza, classe f; **stylish** adj elegante; **stylist** n **hair stylist** parrucchiere(-a)

sub... [sʌb] prefix sub..., sotto...; **subconscious** adj subcosciente ▸ n subcosciente m

subdued [səb'djuːd] adj pacato(-a); (light) attenuato(-a)

subject [n 'sʌbdʒɪkt, vb səb'dʒɛkt] n soggetto; (citizen etc) cittadino(-a); (Scol) materia ▸ vt **to ~ to** sottomettere a; esporre a; **to be ~ to** (law) essere sottomesso(-a) a; (disease) essere soggetto(-a) a; **subjective** [-'dʒɛktɪv] adj soggettivo(-a); **subject matter** n argomento; contenuto

subjunctive [səb'dʒʌŋktɪv] adj congiuntivo(-a) ▸ n congiuntivo

submarine [sʌbmə'riːn] n sommergibile m

submission [səb'mɪʃən] n sottomissione f; (claim) richiesta

submit [səb'mɪt] vt sottomettere ▸ vi sottomettersi

subordinate [sə'bɔːdɪnət] adj, n subordinato(-a)

subscribe [səb'skraɪb] vi contribuire; **to ~ to** (opinion) approvare, condividere; (fund) sottoscrivere a; (newspaper) abbonarsi a; essere abbonato(-a) a

subscription [səb'skrɪpʃən] n sottoscrizione f; abbonamento

subsequent ['sʌbsɪkwənt] adj successivo(-a), seguente; conseguente; **subsequently** adv in seguito, successivamente

subside [səb'saɪd] vi cedere, abbassarsi; (flood) decrescere; (wind) calmarsi

subsidiary [səb'sɪdɪərɪ] adj sussidiario(-a); accessorio(-a) ▸ n filiale f

subsidize ['sʌbsɪdaɪz] vt sovvenzionare

subsidy ['sʌbsɪdɪ] n sovvenzione f

substance ['sʌbstəns] n sostanza

substantial [səb'stænʃl] adj solido(-a); (amount, progress etc) notevole; (meal) sostanzioso(-a)

substitute ['sʌbstɪtjuːt] n (person) sostituto(-a); (thing) succedaneo, surrogato ▸ vt **to ~ sth/sb for** sostituire qc/qn a; **substitution** [sʌbstɪ'tjuːʃən] n sostituzione f

subtle ['sʌtl] adj sottile

subtract [səb'trækt] vt sottrarre

suburb ['sʌbəːb] n sobborgo; **the ~s** la periferia; **suburban** [sə'bəːbən] adj suburbano(-a)

subway ['sʌbweɪ] n (US: underground) metropolitana; (BRIT: underpass) sottopassaggio

succeed [sək'siːd] *vi* riuscire; avere
successo ▶ *vt* succedere a; **to ~ in
doing** riuscire a fare

success [sək'sɛs] *n* successo;
successful *adj* (*venture*) coronato(-a)
da successo, riuscito(-a); **to be
successful (in doing)** riuscire (a fare);
successfully *adv* con successo

succession [sək'sɛʃən] *n* successione *f*

successive [sək'sɛsɪv] *adj*
successivo(-a); consecutivo(-a)

successor [sək'sɛsə^r] *n* successore *m*

succumb [sə'kʌm] *vi* soccombere

such [sʌtʃ] *adj* tale; (*of that kind*): **~ a
book** un tale libro, un libro del genere;
(*so much*): **~ courage** tanto coraggio
▶ *adv* talmente, così; **~ a long trip** un
viaggio così lungo; **~ a lot of** talmente
or così tanto(-a); **~ as** (*like*) come; **as
~** come *or* in quanto tale; **such-and-
such** *adj* tale (*after noun*)

suck [sʌk] *vt* succhiare; (*breast, bottle*)
poppare

Sudan [suː'dɑːn] *n* Sudan *m*

sudden ['sʌdn] *adj* improvviso(-a);
all of a ~ improvvisamente,
all'improvviso; **suddenly** *adv*
bruscamente, improvvisamente,
di colpo

sudoku [su'dəukuː] *n* sudoku *m inv*

sue [suː] *vt* citare in giudizio

suede [sweɪd] *n* pelle *f* scamosciata

suffer ['sʌfə^r] *vt* soffrire, patire; (*bear*)
sopportare, tollerare ▶ *vi* soffrire;
to ~ from soffrire di; **suffering** *n*
sofferenza

suffice [sə'faɪs] *vi* essere sufficiente,
bastare

sufficient [sə'fɪʃənt] *adj* sufficiente; **~
money** abbastanza soldi

suffocate ['sʌfəkeɪt] *vi* (*have difficulty
breathing*) soffocare; (*die through lack of
air*) asfissiare

sugar ['ʃugə^r] *n* zucchero ▶ *vt*
zuccherare

suggest [sə'dʒɛst] *vt* proporre,
suggerire; indicare; **suggestion**
[-'dʒɛstʃən] *n* suggerimento,
proposta; indicazione *f*

suicide ['suɪsaɪd] *n* (*person*) suicida
m/f; (*act*) suicidio; *see also* **commit**;
suicide bombing *n* attentato suicida

suit [suːt] *n* (*man's*) vestito; (*woman's*)
completo, tailleur *m inv*; (*Law*) causa;
(*Cards*) seme *m*, colore *m* ▶ *vt* andar
bene a *or* per; essere adatto(-a) a *or*
per; (*adapt*): **to ~ sth to** adattare qc a;
well ~ed ben assortito(-a); **suitable**
adj adatto(-a); appropriato(-a);
suitcase ['suːtkeɪs] *n* valigia

suite [swiːt] *n* (*of rooms*)
appartamento; (*Mus*) suite *f inv*;
(*furniture*): **bedroom/dining room
~** arredo *or* mobilia per la camera da
letto/sala da pranzo

sulfur ['sʌlfə^r] (*US*) *n* = **sulphur**

sulk [sʌlk] *vi* fare il broncio

sulphur ['sʌlfə^r] (*US* **sulfur**) *n* zolfo

sultana [sʌl'tɑːnə] *n* (*fruit*) uva (secca)
sultanina

sum [sʌm] *n* somma; (*Scol etc*)
addizione *f* ▶ **sum up** *vt*, *vi* riassumere

summarize ['sʌməraɪz] *vt*
riassumere, riepilogare

summary ['sʌmərɪ] *n* riassunto

summer ['sʌmə^r] *n* estate *f* ▶ *cpd*
d'estate, estivo(-a); **summer
holidays** *npl* vacanze *fpl* estive;
summertime *n* (*season*) estate *f*

summit ['sʌmɪt] *n* cima, sommità;
(*Pol*) vertice *m*

summon ['sʌmən] *vt* chiamare,
convocare

Sun. *abbr* (= *Sunday*) dom.

sun [sʌn] *n* sole *m*; **sunbathe** *vi*
prendere un bagno di sole; **sunbed** *n*
lettino solare; **sunblock** *n* protezione
f solare totale; **sunburn** *n* (*painful*)
scottatura; **sunburned, sunburnt**
adj abbronzato(-a); (*painfully*)

scottato(-a)

Sunday ['sʌndɪ] n domenica

Sunday paper n giornale m della
  domenica

- **Sunday paper**
- I **Sunday papers** sono i giornali
- che escono di domenica. Sono
- generalmente corredati da
- supplementi e riviste di argomento
- culturale, sportivo e di attualità.

sunflower ['sʌnflaʊəʳ] n girasole m

sung [sʌŋ] pp of **sing**

sunglasses ['sʌnglɑ:sɪz] npl occhiali
  mpl da sole

sunk [sʌŋk] pp of **sink**

sun: **sunlight** n (luce f del) sole m;
  sun lounger n sedia a sdraio; **sunny**
  adj assolato(-a), soleggiato(-a); (fig)
  allegro(-a), felice; **sunrise** n levata
  del sole, alba; **sun roof** n (Aut) tetto
  apribile; **sunscreen** n (cream) crema
  solare protettiva; **sunset** n tramonto;
  sunshade n parasole m; **sunshine**
  n luce f (del) sole m; **sunstroke** n
  insolazione f, colpo di sole; **suntan**
  n abbronzatura; **suntan lotion** n
  lozione f solare; **suntan oil** n olio
  solare

super ['su:pəʳ] (inf) adj fantastico(-a)

superb [su:'pə:b] adj magnifico(-a)

superficial [su:pə'fɪʃəl] adj
  superficiale

superintendent [su:pərɪn'tendə
  nt] n direttore(-trice); (Police)
  ≈ commissario (capo)

superior [su'pɪərɪəʳ] adj, n superiore
  m/f

superlative [su'pə:lətɪv] adj
  superlativo(-a), supremo(-a) ▶ n (Ling)
  superlativo

supermarket ['su:pəmɑ:kɪt] n
  supermercato

supernatural [su:pə'nætʃərəl] adj
  soprannaturale ▶ n soprannaturale m

superpower ['su:pəpaʊəʳ] n (Pol)

superpotenza

superstition [su:pə'stɪʃən] n
  superstizione f

superstitious [su:pə'stɪʃəs] adj
  superstizioso(-a)

superstore ['su:pəstɔ:ʳ] n (BRIT)
  grande supermercato

supervise ['su:pəvaɪz] vt (person
  etc) sorvegliare; (organization)
  soprintendere a; **supervision**
  [-'vɪʒən] n sorveglianza; supervisione
  f; **supervisor** n sorvegliante
  m/f; soprintendente m/f; (in shop)
  capocommesso(-a)

supper ['sʌpəʳ] n cena

supple ['sʌpl] adj flessibile; agile

supplement [n 'sʌplɪmənt, vb
  sʌplɪ'mənt] n supplemento ▶ vt
  completare, integrare

supplier [sə'plaɪəʳ] n fornitore m

supply [sə'plaɪ] vt (provide) fornire;
  (equip): **to ~ (with)** approvvigionare
  (di), attrezzare (con) ▶ n
  riserva, provvista; (supplying)
  approvvigionamento; (Tech)
  alimentazione f; **supplies** npl (food)
  viveri mpl; (Mil) sussistenza

support [sə'pɔ:t] n (moral, financial
  etc) sostegno, appoggio; (Tech)
  supporto ▶ vt sostenere; (financially)
  mantenere; (uphold) sostenere,
  difendere; **supporter** n (Pol etc)
  sostenitore(-trice), fautore(-trice);
  (Sport) tifoso(-a)

> ┃ Be careful not to translate **support**
> by the Italian word *sopportare*.

suppose [sə'pəʊz] vt supporre;
  immaginare; **to be ~d to do** essere
  tenuto(-a) a fare; **supposedly**
  [sə'pəʊzɪdlɪ] adv presumibilmente;
  supposing conj se, ammesso che + sub

suppress [sə'prɛs] vt reprimere;
  sopprimere; occultare

supreme [su'pri:m] adj supremo(-a)

surcharge ['sə:tʃɑ:dʒ] n supplemento

sure [ʃuə^r] *adj* sicuro(-a); (*definite, convinced*) sicuro(-a), certo(-a); **~!** (*of course*) senz'altro!, certo!; **~ enough** infatti; **to make ~ of sth/that** assicurarsi di qc/che; **surely** *adv* sicuramente; certamente

surf [sə:f] *n* (*waves*) cavalloni *mpl*; (*foam*) spuma

surface ['sə:fɪs] *n* superficie *f* ▶ *vt* (*road*) asfaltare ▶ *vi* risalire alla superficie; (*fig: news, feeling*) venire a galla

surfboard ['sə:fbɔ:d] *n* tavola per surfing

surfing ['sə:fɪŋ] *n* surfing *m*

surge [sə:dʒ] *n* (*strong movement*) ondata; (*of feeling*) impeto ▶ *vi* gonfiarsi; (*people*) riversarsi

surgeon ['sə:dʒən] *n* chirurgo

surgery ['sə:dʒərɪ] *n* chirurgia; (*BRIT: room*) studio *or* gabinetto medico, ambulatorio; (: *also:* **~ hours**) orario delle visite *or* di consultazione; **to undergo ~** subire un intervento chirurgico

surname ['sə:neɪm] *n* cognome *m*

surpass [sə:'pɑ:s] *vt* superare

surplus ['sə:pləs] *n* eccedenza; (*Econ*) surplus *m inv* ▶ *adj* eccedente

surprise [sə'praɪz] *n* sorpresa; (*astonishment*) stupore *m* ▶ *vt* sorprendere; stupire; **surprised** [sə'praɪzd] *adj* (*look, smile*) sorpreso(-a); **to be surprised** essere sorpreso, sorprendersi; **surprising** *adj* sorprendente, stupefacente; **surprisingly** *adv* (*easy, helpful*) sorprendentemente

surrender [sə'rɛndə^r] *n* resa, capitolazione *f* ▶ *vi* arrendersi

surround [sə'raund] *vt* circondare; (*Mil etc*) accerchiare; **surrounding** *adj* circostante; **surroundings** *npl* dintorni *mpl*; (*fig*) ambiente *m*

surveillance [sə:'veɪləns] *n* sorveglianza, controllo

survey [*n* 'sə:veɪ, *vb* sə:'veɪ] *n* quadro generale; (*study*) esame *m*; (*in housebuying etc*) perizia; (*of land*) rilevamento, rilievo topografico ▶ *vt* osservare; esaminare; valutare; rilevare; **surveyor** *n* perito; geometra *m*; (*of land*) agrimensore *m*

survival [sə'vaɪvl] *n* sopravvivenza

survive [sə'vaɪv] *vi* sopravvivere ▶ *vt* sopravvivere a; **survivor** *n* superstite *m/f*, sopravvissuto(-a)

suspect [*adj, n* 'sʌspɛkt, *vb* səs'pɛkt] *adj* sospetto(-a) ▶ *n* persona sospetta ▶ *vt* sospettare; (*think likely*) supporre; (*doubt*) dubitare

suspend [səs'pɛnd] *vt* sospendere; **suspended sentence** *n* condanna con la condizionale; **suspenders** *npl* (*BRIT*) giarrettiere *fpl*; (*US*) bretelle *fpl*

suspense [səs'pɛns] *n* apprensione *f*; (*in film etc*) suspense *m*; **to keep sb in ~** tenere qn in sospeso

suspension [səs'pɛnʃən] *n* (*gen Aut*) sospensione *f*; (*of driving licence*) ritiro temporaneo; **suspension bridge** *n* ponte *m* sospeso

suspicion [səs'pɪʃən] *n* sospetto; **suspicious** [səs'pɪʃəs] *adj* (*suspecting*) sospettoso(-a); (*causing suspicion*) sospetto(-a)

sustain [səs'teɪn] *vt* sostenere; sopportare; (*Law: charge*) confermare; (*suffer*) subire

SUV *n abbr* (= sport utility vehicle) SUV *m inv*

swallow ['swɔləu] *n* (*bird*) rondine *f* ▶ *vt* inghiottire; (*fig: story*) bere

swam [swæm] *pt of* **swim**

swamp [swɔmp] *n* palude *f* ▶ *vt* sommergere

swan [swɔn] *n* cigno

swap [swɔp] *vt* **to ~ (for)** scambiare (con)

swarm [swɔ:m] *n* sciame *m* ▶ *vi* (*bees*)

sciamare; (*people*) brulicare; (*place*): **to be ~ing with** brulicare di

sway [sweɪ] *vi* (*tree*) ondeggiare; (*person*) barcollare ▶ *vt* (*influence*) influenzare, dominare

swear [swɛəʳ] (*pt* **swore**, *pp* **sworn**) *vi* (*curse*) bestemmiare, imprecare ▶ *vt* (*promise*) giurare ▷ **swear in** *vt* prestare giuramento a; **swearword** *n* parolaccia

sweat [swɛt] *n* sudore *m*, traspirazione *f* ▶ *vi* sudare

sweater ['swɛtəʳ] *n* maglione *m*

sweatshirt ['swɛtʃəːt] *n* felpa

sweaty ['swɛtɪ] *adj* sudato(-a), bagnato(-a) di sudore

Swede [swiːd] *n* svedese *m/f*

swede [swiːd] (*BRIT*) *n* rapa svedese

Sweden ['swiːdn] *n* Svezia; **Swedish** ['swiːdɪʃ] *adj* svedese ▶ *n* (*Ling*) svedese *m*

sweep [swiːp] (*pt*, *pp* **swept**) *n* spazzata; (*also*: **chimney ~**) spazzacamino ▶ *vt* spazzare, scopare; (*current*) spazzare ▶ *vi* (*hand*) muoversi con gesto ampio; (*wind*) infuriare

sweet [swiːt] *n* (*BRIT*: *pudding*) dolce *m*; (*candy*) caramella ▶ *adj* dolce; (*fresh*) fresco(-a); (*fig*) piacevole; delicato(-a), grazioso(-a); gentile; **sweetcorn** *n* granturco dolce; **sweetener** ['swiːtnəʳ] *n* (*Culin*) dolcificante *m*; **sweetheart** *n* innamorato(-a); **sweetshop** *n* (*BRIT*) ≈ pasticceria

swell [swɛl] (*pt* **swelled**, *pp* **swollen**, **swelled**) *n* (*of sea*) mare *m* lungo ▶ *adj* (*US*: *inf*: *excellent*) favoloso(-a) ▶ *vt* gonfiare, ingrossare; aumentare ▶ *vi* gonfiarsi, ingrossarsi; (*sound*) crescere; (*also*: **~ up**) gonfiarsi; **swelling** *n* (*Med*) tumefazione *f*, gonfiore *m*

swept [swɛpt] *pt*, *pp of* **sweep**

swerve [swəːv] *vi* deviare; (*driver*) sterzare; (*boxer*) scartare

swift [swɪft] *n* (*bird*) rondone *m* ▶ *adj* rapido(-a), veloce

swim [swɪm] (*pt* **swam**, *pp* **swum**) *n* **to go for a ~** andare a fare una nuotata ▶ *vi* nuotare; (*Sport*) fare del nuoto; (*head*, *room*) girare ▶ *vt* (*river*, *channel*) attraversare *or* percorrere a nuoto; (*length*) nuotare; **swimmer** *n* nuotatore(-trice); **swimming** *n* nuoto; **swimming costume** (*BRIT*) *n* costume *m* da bagno; **swimming pool** *n* piscina; **swimming trunks** *npl* costume *m* da bagno (da uomo); **swimsuit** *n* costume *m* da bagno

swing [swɪŋ] (*pt*, *pp* **swung**) *n* altalena; (*movement*) oscillazione *f*; (*Mus*) ritmo; swing *m* ▶ *vt* dondolare, far oscillare; (*also*: **~ round**) far girare ▶ *vi* oscillare, dondolare; (*also*: **~ round**: *object*) roteare; (: *person*) girarsi, voltarsi; **to be in full ~** (*activity*) essere in piena attività; (*party etc*) essere nel pieno

swipe card *n* tessera magnetica

swirl [swəːl] *vi* turbinare, far mulinello

Swiss [swɪs] *adj*, *n inv* svizzero(-a)

switch [swɪtʃ] *n* (*for light*, *radio etc*) interruttore *m*; (*change*) cambiamento ▶ *vt* (*change*) cambiare; scambiare ▷ **switch off** *vt* spegnere; **could you ~ off the light?** puoi spegnere la luce? ▷ **switch on** *vt* accendere; (*engine*, *machine*) mettere in moto, avviare; **switchboard** *n* (*Tel*) centralino

Switzerland ['swɪtsələnd] *n* Svizzera

swivel ['swɪvl] *vi* (*also*: **~ round**) girare

swollen ['swəulən] *pp of* **swell**

swoop [swuːp] *n* incursione *f* ▶ *vi* (*also*: **~ down**) scendere in picchiata, piombare

swop [swɔp] *n*, *vt* = **swap**

sword [sɔːd] *n* spada; **swordfish** *n* pesce *m* spada *inv*

swore [swɔːʳ] *pt of* **swear**

S

sworn [swɔ:n] *pp of* **swear** ▶ *adj*
giurato(-a)

swum [swʌm] *pp of* **swim**

swung [swʌŋ] *pt, pp of* **swing**

syllable ['sɪləbl] *n* sillaba

syllabus ['sɪləbəs] *n* programma *m*

symbol ['sɪmbl] *n* simbolo;
symbolic(al) [sɪm'bɔlɪk(l)] *adj*
simbolico(-a); **to be symbolic(al) of
sth** simboleggiare qc

symmetrical [sɪ'mɛtrɪkl] *adj*
simmetrico(-a)

symmetry ['sɪmɪtrɪ] *n* simmetria

sympathetic [sɪmpə'θɛtɪk] *adj*
(*showing pity*) compassionevole; (*kind*)
comprensivo(-a); **~ towards** ben
disposto(-a) verso

> Be careful not to translate
> **sympathetic** by the Italian word
> *simpatico*.

sympathize ['sɪmpəθaɪz] *vi* **to ~ with**
(*person*) compatire; partecipare al
dolore di; (*cause*) simpatizzare per

sympathy ['sɪmpəθɪ] *n* compassione *f*

symphony ['sɪmfənɪ] *n* sinfonia

symptom ['sɪmptəm] *n* sintomo;
indizio

synagogue ['sɪnəgɔg] *n* sinagoga

syndicate ['sɪndɪkɪt] *n* sindacato

syndrome ['sɪndrəum] *n* sindrome *f*

synonym ['sɪnənɪm] *n* sinonimo

synthetic [sɪn'θɛtɪk] *adj* sintetico(-a)

Syria ['sɪrɪə] *n* Siria

syringe [sɪ'rɪndʒ] *n* siringa

syrup ['sɪrəp] *n* sciroppo; (*also:* **golden
~**) melassa raffinata

system ['sɪstəm] *n* sistema *m*;
(*order*) metodo; (*Anat*) organismo;
systematic [-'mætɪk] *adj*
sistematico(-a); metodico(-a);
systems analyst *n* analista *m* di
sistemi

t

ta [tɑ:] (*BRIT: inf*) *excl* grazie!

tab [tæb] *n* (*loop on coat etc*) laccetto;
(*label*) etichetta; **to keep ~s on** (*fig*)
tenere d'occhio

table ['teɪbl] *n* tavolo, tavola; (*Math,
Chem etc*) tavola ▶ *vt* (*BRIT: motion
etc*) presentare; **a ~ for 4, please** un
tavolo per 4, per favore; **to lay** *or* **set
the ~** apparecchiare *or* preparare
la tavola; **tablecloth** *n* tovaglia;
table d'hôte [tɑ:bl'dəut] *adj* (*meal*) a
prezzo fisso; **table lamp** *n* lampada
da tavolo; **tablemat** *n* sottopiatto;
tablespoon *n* cucchiaio da tavola;
(*also:* **tablespoonful**: *as measurement*)
cucchiaiata

tablet ['tæblɪt] *n* (*Med*) compressa; (*of
stone*) targa

table tennis *n* tennis *m* da tavolo,
ping-pong® *m*

tabloid ['tæblɔɪd] *n* (*newspaper*)
tabloid *m inv* (*giornale illustrato di
formato ridotto*); **the ~s, the ~ press** i
giornali popolari

taboo [tə'bu:] *adj, n* tabù *m inv*

tack [tæk] *n* (*nail*) bulletta; (*fig*)
approccio ▶ *vt* imbullettare;
imbastire ▶ *vi* bordeggiare

tackle ['tækl] *n* attrezzatura,
equipaggiamento; (*for lifting*)
paranco; (*Football*) contrasto; (*Rugby*)
placcaggio ▶ *vt* (*difficulty*) affrontare;
(*Football*) contrastare; (*Rugby*)
placcare

tacky ['tækɪ] *adj* appiccicaticcio(-a); (*pej*) scadente

tact [tækt] *n* tatto; **tactful** *adj* delicato(-a), discreto(-a)

tactics ['tæktɪks] *n*, *npl* tattica

tactless ['tæktlɪs] *adj* che manca di tatto

tadpole ['tædpəul] *n* girino

taffy ['tæfɪ] (*US*) *n* caramella *f* mou *inv*

tag [tæg] *n* etichetta

tail [teɪl] *n* coda; (*of shirt*) falda ▶ *vt* (*follow*) seguire, pedinare; **~s** *npl* (*formal suit*) frac *m inv*

tailor ['teɪlə^r] *n* sarto

Taiwan [taɪ'wɑːn] *n* Taiwan *m*; **Taiwanese** [taɪwə'niːz] *adj*, *n* taiwanese

take [teɪk] (*pt* **took**, *pp* **taken**) *vt* prendere; (*gain: prize*) ottenere, vincere; (*require: effort, courage*) occorrere, volerci; (*tolerate*) accettare, sopportare; (*hold: passengers etc*) contenere; (*accompany*) accompagnare; (*bring, carry*) portare; (*exam*) sostenere, presentarsi a; **to ~ a photo/a shower** fare una fotografia/una doccia; **I ~ it that** suppongo che ▷ **take after** *vt fus* assomigliare a ▷ **take apart** *vt* smontare ▷ **take away** *vt* portare via; togliere ▷ **take back** *vt* (*return*) restituire; riportare; (*one's words*) ritirare ▷ **take down** *vt* (*building*) demolire; (*letter etc*) scrivere ▷ **take in** *vt* (*deceive*) imbrogliare, abbindolare; (*understand*) capire; (*include*) comprendere, includere; (*lodger*) prendere, ospitare ▷ **take off** *vi* (*Aviat*) decollare; (*go away*) andarsene ▶ *vt* (*remove*) togliere ▷ **take on** *vt* (*work*) accettare, intraprendere; (*employee*) assumere; (*opponent*) sfidare, affrontare ▷ **take out** *vt* portare fuori; (*remove*) togliere; (*licence*) prendere, ottenere; **to ~ sth out of sth** (*drawer, pocket etc*)

tirare qc fuori da qc; estrarre qc da qc ▷ **take over** *vt* (*business*) rilevare ▶ *vi* **to ~ over from sb** prendere le consegne *or* il controllo da qn ▷ **take up** *vt* (*dress*) accorciare; (*occupy: time, space*) occupare; (*engage in: hobby etc*) mettersi a; **to ~ sb up on sth** accettare qc da qn; **takeaway** (*BRIT*) *n* (*shop etc*) ≈ rosticceria; (*food*) pasto per asporto; **taken** *pp of* **take**; **takeoff** *n* (*Aviat*) decollo; **takeout** (*US*) *n* = **takeaway**; **takeover** *n* (*Comm*) assorbimento; **takings** ['teɪkɪnz] *npl* (*Comm*) incasso

talc [tælk] *n* (*also:* **~um powder**) talco

tale [teɪl] *n* racconto, storia; **to tell ~s** (*fig: to teacher, parent etc*) fare la spia

talent ['tælnt] *n* talento; **talented** *adj* di talento

talk [tɔːk] *n* discorso; (*gossip*) chiacchiere *fpl*; (*conversation*) conversazione *f*; (*interview*) discussione *f* ▶ *vi* parlare; **~s** *npl* (*Pol etc*) colloqui *mpl*; **to ~ about** parlare di; **to ~ sb out of/into doing** dissuadere qn da/convincere qn a fare; **to ~ shop** parlare di lavoro *or* di affari ▷ **talk over** *vt* discutere; **talk show** *n* conversazione *f* televisiva, talk show *m inv*

tall [tɔːl] *adj* alto(-a); **to be 6 feet ~** ≈ essere alto 1 metro e 80

tambourine [tæmbə'riːn] *n* tamburello

tame [teɪm] *adj* addomesticato(-a); (*fig: story, style*) insipido(-a), scialbo(-a)

tamper ['tæmpə^r] *vi* **to ~ with** manomettere

tampon ['tæmpɔn] *n* tampone *m*

tan [tæn] *n* (*also:* **sun~**) abbronzatura ▶ *vi* abbronzarsi ▶ *adj* (*colour*) marrone rossiccio *inv*

tandem ['tændəm] *n* tandem *m inv*

tangerine [tændʒə'riːn] *n* mandarino

tangle ['tæŋgl] n groviglio; **to get into a** ~ aggrovigliarsi; (fig) combinare un pasticcio

tank [tæŋk] n serbatoio; (for fish) acquario; (Mil) carro armato

tanker ['tæŋkə'] n (ship) nave f cisterna inv; (truck) autobotte f, autocisterna

tanned [tænd] adj abbronzato(-a)

tantrum ['tæntrəm] n accesso di collera

Tanzania [tænzə'nɪə] n Tanzania

tap [tæp] n (on sink etc) rubinetto; (gentle blow) colpetto ▶ vt dare un colpetto a; (resources) sfruttare, utilizzare; (telephone) mettere sotto controllo; **on** ~ (fig: resources) a disposizione; **tap dancing** n tip tap m

tape [teɪp] n nastro; (also: **magnetic** ~) nastro (magnetico); (sticky tape) nastro adesivo ▶ vt (record) registrare (su nastro); (stick) attaccare con nastro adesivo; **tape measure** n metro a nastro; **tape recorder** n registratore m (a nastro)

tapestry ['tæpɪstrɪ] n arazzo; tappezzeria

tar [tɑː'] n catrame m

target ['tɑːgɪt] n bersaglio; (fig: objective) obiettivo

tariff ['tærɪf] n tariffa

tarmac ['tɑːmæk] n (BRIT: on road) macadam m al catrame; (Aviat) pista di decollo

tarpaulin [tɑː'pɔːlɪn] n tela incatramata

tarragon ['tærəgən] n dragoncello

tart [tɑːt] n (Culin) crostata; (BRIT: inf: pej: woman) sgualdrina ▶ adj (flavour) aspro(-a), agro(-a)

tartan ['tɑːtn] n tartan m inv

tartar(e) sauce n salsa tartara

task [tɑːsk] n compito; **to take to** ~ rimproverare

taste [teɪst] n gusto; (flavour) sapore m, gusto; (sample) assaggio; (fig: glimpse, idea) idea ▶ vt gustare; (sample) assaggiare ▶ vi **to** ~ **of** or **like** (fish etc) sapere or avere sapore di; **in good/bad** ~ di buon/cattivo gusto; **can I have a** ~? posso assaggiarlo?; **you can** ~ **the garlic (in it)** (ci) si sente il sapore dell'aglio; **tasteful** adj di buon gusto; **tasteless** adj (food) insipido(-a); (remark) di cattivo gusto; **tasty** adj saporito(-a), gustoso(-a)

tatters ['tætəz] npl **in** ~ a brandelli

tattoo [tə'tuː] n tatuaggio; (spectacle) parata militare ▶ vt tatuare

taught [tɔːt] pt, pp of **teach**

taunt [tɔːnt] n scherno ▶ vt schernire

Taurus ['tɔːrəs] n Toro

taut [tɔːt] adj teso(-a)

tax [tæks] n (on goods) imposta; (on services) tassa; (on income) imposte fpl, tasse fpl ▶ vt tassare; (fig: strain: patience etc) mettere alla prova; **tax-free** adj esente da imposte

taxi ['tæksɪ] n taxi m inv ▶ vi (Aviat) rullare; **can you call me a** ~, **please?** può chiamarmi un taxi, per favore?; **taxi driver** n tassista m/f; **taxi rank** (BRIT) n = **taxi stand**; **taxi stand** n posteggio dei taxi

tax payer n contribuente m/f

TB n abbr = **tuberculosis**

tea [tiː] n tè m inv; (BRIT: snack: for children) merenda; **high** ~ (BRIT) cena leggera (presa nel tardo pomeriggio); **tea bag** n bustina di tè; **tea break** (BRIT) n intervallo per il tè

teach [tiːtʃ] (pt, pp **taught**) vt **to** ~ **sb sth**, ~ **sth to sb** insegnare qc a qn ▶ vi insegnare; **teacher** n insegnante m/f; (in secondary school) professore(-essa); (in primary school) maestro(-a); **teaching** n insegnamento

tea: **tea cloth** n (for dishes) strofinaccio; (BRIT: for trolley) tovaglietta da tè; **teacup** ['tiːkʌp] n tazza da tè

tea leaves npl foglie fpl di tè
team [ti:m] n squadra; (of animals) tiro
▷ **team up** vi **to ~ up (with)** mettersi insieme (a)
teapot ['ti:pɔt] n teiera
tear¹ [tɛəʳ] (pt **tore**, pp **torn**) n strappo
▶ vt strappare ▶ vi strapparsi ▷ **tear apart** vt (also fig) distruggere
▷ **tear down** vt +adv (building, statue) demolire; (poster, flag) tirare giù ▷ **tear off** vt (sheet of paper etc) strappare; (one's clothes) togliersi di dosso ▷ **tear up** vt (sheet of paper etc) strappare
tear² [tɪəʳ] n lacrima; **in ~s** in lacrime; **tearful** ['tɪəful] adj piangente, lacrimoso(-a); **tear gas** n gas m lacrimogeno
tearoom ['ti:ru:m] n sala da tè
tease [ti:z] vt canzonare; (unkindly) tormentare
tea: **teaspoon** n cucchiaino da tè; (also: **teaspoonful**: as measurement) cucchiaino; **teatime** n ora del tè; **tea towel** (BRIT) n strofinaccio (per i piatti)
technical ['tɛknɪkl] adj tecnico(-a)
technician [tɛk'nɪʃən] n tecnico(-a)
technique [tɛk'ni:k] n tecnica
technology [tɛk'nɔlədʒɪ] n tecnologia
teddy (bear) ['tɛdɪ-] n orsacchiotto
tedious ['ti:dɪəs] adj noioso(-a), tedioso(-a)
tee [ti:] n (Golf) tee m inv
teen [ti:n] adj = **teenage** ▶ n (US) = **teenager**
teenage ['ti:neɪdʒ] adj (fashions etc) per giovani, per adolescenti; **teenager** n adolescente m/f
teens [ti:nz] npl **to be in one's ~** essere adolescente
teeth [ti:θ] npl of **tooth**
teetotal ['ti:'təutl] adj astemio(-a)
telecommunications
['tɛlɪkəmju:nɪ'keɪʃənz] n telecomunicazioni fpl
telegram ['tɛlɪgræm] n telegramma m
telegraph pole n palo del telegrafo
telephone ['tɛlɪfəun] n telefono
▶ vt (person) telefonare a; (message) comunicare per telefono; **telephone book** n elenco telefonico; **telephone booth** (BRIT), **telephone box** n cabina telefonica; **telephone call** n telefonata; **telephone directory** n elenco telefonico; **telephone number** n numero di telefono
telesales ['tɛlɪseɪlz] n vendita per telefono
telescope ['tɛlɪskəup] n telescopio
televise ['tɛlɪvaɪz] vt teletrasmettere
television ['tɛlɪvɪʒən] n televisione f; **on ~** alla televisione; **television programme** n programma m televisivo
tell [tɛl] (pt, pp **told**) vt dire; (relate: story) raccontare; (distinguish): **to ~ sth from** distinguere qc da ▶ vi (talk): **to ~ (of)** parlare (di); (have effect) farsi sentire, avere effetto; **to ~ sb to do** dire a qn di fare ▷ **tell off** vt rimproverare, sgridare; **teller** n (in bank) cassiere(-a)
telly ['tɛlɪ] (BRIT: inf) n abbr (= television) tivù f inv
temp [tɛmp] n abbr (= temporary) segretaria temporanea
temper ['tɛmpəʳ] n (nature) carattere m; (mood) umore m; (fit of anger) collera
▶ vt (moderate) moderare; **to be in a ~** essere in collera; **to lose one's ~** andare in collera
temperament ['tɛmprəmənt] n (nature) temperamento; **temperamental** [-'mɛntl] adj capriccioso(-a)
temperature ['tɛmprətʃəʳ] n temperatura; **to have or run a ~** avere la febbre

t

temple ['tɛmpl] n (building) tempio;
(Anat) tempia

temporary ['tɛmpərərɪ] adj
temporaneo(-a); (job, worker)
avventizio(-a), temporaneo(-a)

tempt [tɛmpt] vt tentare; **to ~ sb into
doing** indurre qn a fare; **temptation**
[-'teɪʃən] n tentazione f; **tempting**
adj allettante

ten [tɛn] num dieci

tenant ['tɛnənt] n inquilino(-a)

tend [tɛnd] vt badare a, occuparsi
di ▶ vi **to ~ to do** tendere a fare;
tendency ['tɛndənsɪ] n tendenza

tender ['tɛndə'] adj tenero(-a); (sore)
dolorante ▶ n (Comm: offer) offerta;
(money): **legal ~** moneta in corso
legale ▶ vt offrire

tendon ['tɛndən] n tendine m

tenner ['tɛnə'] n (BRIT inf) (banconota
da) dieci sterline fpl

tennis ['tɛnɪs] n tennis m; **tennis
ball** n palla da tennis; **tennis court**
n campo da tennis; **tennis match**
n partita da tennis; **tennis player**
n tennista m/f; **tennis racket** n
racchetta da tennis

tenor ['tɛnə'] n (Mus) tenore m

tenpin bowling ['tɛnpɪn-] n
bowling m

tense [tɛns] adj teso(-a) ▶ n (Ling)
tempo

tension ['tɛnʃən] n tensione f

tent [tɛnt] n tenda

tentative ['tɛntətɪv] adj
esitante, incerto(-a); (conclusion)
provvisorio(-a)

tenth [tɛnθ] num decimo(-a)

tent: tent peg n picchetto da
tenda; **tent pole** n palo da tenda,
montante m

tepid ['tɛpɪd] adj tiepido(-a)

term [tə:m] n termine m; (Scol)
trimestre m; (Law) sessione f ▶ vt
chiamare, definire; **~s** npl (conditions)
condizioni fpl; (Comm) prezzi mpl,
tariffe fpl; **in the short/long ~** a
breve/lunga scadenza; **to be on good
~s with sb** essere in buoni rapporti
con qn; **to come to ~s with** (problem)
affrontare

terminal ['tə:mɪnl] adj finale,
terminale; (disease) terminale ▶ n
(Elec) morsetto; (Comput) terminale
m; (Aviat, for oil, ore etc) terminal m inv;
(BRIT: also: **coach ~**) capolinea m

terminate ['tə:mɪneɪt] vt mettere
fine a

termini ['tə:mɪnaɪ] npl of **terminus**

terminology [tə:mɪ'nɔlədʒɪ] n
terminologia

terminus ['tə:mɪnəs] (pl **termini**)
n (for buses) capolinea m; (for trains)
stazione f terminale

terrace ['tɛrəs] n terrazza; (BRIT: row of
houses) fila di case a schiera; **terraced**
adj (garden) a terrazze

terrain [tɛ'reɪn] n terreno

terrestrial [tɪ'rɛstrɪəl] adj (life)
terrestre; (BRIT: channel) terrestre

terrible ['tɛrɪbl] adj terribile; **terribly**
adv terribilmente; (very badly)
malissimo

terrier ['tɛrɪə'] n terrier m inv

terrific [tə'rɪfɪk] adj incredibile,
fantastico(-a); (wonderful)
formidabile, eccezionale

terrified ['tɛrɪfaɪd] adj atterrito(-a)

terrify ['tɛrɪfaɪ] vt terrorizzare;
terrifying adj terrificante

territorial [tɛrɪ'tɔ:rɪəl] adj territoriale

territory ['tɛrɪtərɪ] n territorio

terror ['tɛrə'] n terrore m; **terrorism** n
terrorismo; **terrorist** n terrorista m/f

test [tɛst] n (trial, check: of courage etc)
prova; (Med) esame m; (Chem) analisi
f inv; (exam: of intelligence etc) test m
inv; (: in school) compito in classe;
(also: **driving ~**) esame m di guida
▶ vt provare; esaminare; analizzare;

sottoporre ad esame; **to ~ sb in history** esaminare qn in storia

testicle ['tɛstɪkl] n testicolo

testify ['tɛstɪfaɪ] vi (Law) testimoniare, deporre; **to ~ to sth** (Law) testimoniare qc; (gen) comprovare or dimostrare qc

testimony ['tɛstɪmənɪ] n (Law) testimonianza, deposizione f

test: **test match** n (Cricket, Rugby) partita internazionale; **test tube** n provetta

tetanus ['tɛtənəs] n tetano

text [tɛkst] n testo; (on mobile phone) SMS m inv, messaggino ▶vt **to ~ sb** (inf) mandare un SMS a qn ▶vi messaggiarsi; **textbook** n libro di testo

textile ['tɛkstaɪl] n tessile m

text message n (Tel) SMS m inv, messaggino

text messaging [-'mɛsɪdʒɪŋ] n il mandarsi SMS

texture ['tɛkstʃəʳ] n tessitura; (of skin, paper etc) struttura

Thai [taɪ] adj tailandese ▶n tailandese m/f; (Ling) tailandese m

Thailand ['taɪlænd] n Tailandia

Thames [tɛmz] n **the ~** il Tamigi

than [ðæn, ðən] conj (in comparisons) che; (with numerals, pronouns, proper names) di; **more ~ 10/once** più di 10/una volta; **I have more/less ~ you** ne ho più/meno di te; **I have more pens ~ pencils** ho più penne che matite; **she is older ~ you think** è più vecchia di quanto tu (non) pensi

thank [θæŋk] vt ringraziare; **~ you (very much)** grazie (tante); **~s** npl ringraziamenti mpl, grazie fpl excl grazie!; **~s to** grazie a; **thankfully** adv con riconoscenza; con sollievo; **thankfully there were few victims** grazie al cielo ci sono state poche vittime; **Thanksgiving (Day)** n

giorno del ringraziamento
Thanksgiving (Day)
Negli Stati Uniti il quarto giovedì di
novembre ricorre il **Thanksgiving
(Day)**, festa che rievoca la
celebrazione con cui i Padri
Pellegrini, fondatori della colonia
di Plymouth in Massachusetts,
ringraziarono Dio del buon raccolto
del 1621.

that [ðæt] (pl **those**) adj (demonstrative) quel (quell', quello) m; quella (quell') f; **that man/woman/book** quell'uomo/quella donna/quel libro; (not "this") quell'uomo/quella donna/quel libro là; **that one** quello(-a) là
▶pron
1 (demonstrative) ciò; (not "this one") quello(-a); **who's that?** chi è?; **what's that?** cos'è quello?; **is that you?** sei tu?; **I prefer this to that** preferisco questo a quello; **that's what he said** questo è ciò che ha detto; **what happened after that?** che è successo dopo?; **that is (to say)** cioè
2 (relative: direct) che; (: indirect) cui; **the book (that) I read** il libro che ho letto; **the box (that) I put it in** la scatola in cui l'ho messo; **the people (that) I spoke to** le persone con cui or con le quali ho parlato
3 (relative: of time) in cui; **the day (that) he came** il giorno in cui è venuto
▶conj che; **he thought that I was ill** pensava che io fossi malato
▶adv (demonstrative) così; **I can't work that much** non posso lavorare (così) tanto; **that high** così alto; **the wall's about that high and that thick** il muro è alto circa così e spesso circa così

thatched [θætʃt] adj (roof) di paglia

thaw [θɔ:] n disgelo ▶vi (ice)

sciogliersi; (*food*) scongelarsi ▶ *vt*
(*food: also:* ~ **out**) (fare) scongelare

the
[ði:, ðə] *def art*

1 (*gen*) il (lo, l') *m*; la (l') *f*; i (gli) *mpl*;
le *fpl*; **the boy/girl/ink** il ragazzo/la
ragazza/l'inchiostro; **the books/
pencils** i libri/le matite; **the history
of the world** la storia del mondo; **give
it to the postman** dallo al postino;
I haven't the time/money non ho
tempo/soldi; **the rich and the poor** i
ricchi e i poveri

2 (*in titles*): **Elizabeth the First**
Elisabetta prima; **Peter the Great**
Pietro il grande

3 (*in comparisons*): **the more he works,
the more he earns** più lavora più
guadagna

theatre ['θɪətər] (*US* **theater**) *n* teatro;
(*also:* **lecture** ~) aula magna; (*also:*
operating ~) sala operatoria

theft [θɛft] *n* furto

their [ðɛər] *adj* il (la) loro; (*pl*) i (le) loro;
theirs *pron* il (la) loro; (*pl*) i (le) loro; *see
also* **my**; **mine**

them [ðɛm, ðəm] *pron* (*direct*) li (le);
(*indirect*) gli (loro (*after vb*)); (*stressed,
after prep: people*) loro; (: *people, things*)
essi(-e); *see also* **me**

theme [θi:m] *n* tema *m*; **theme park**
n parco di divertimenti (*intorno a un
tema centrale*)

themselves [ðəm'sɛlvz] *pl pron*
(*reflexive*) si; (*emphatic*) loro stessi(-e);
(*after prep*) se stessi(-e)

then [ðɛn] *adv* (*at that time*) allora;
(*next*) poi, dopo; (*and also*) e poi ▶ *conj*
(*therefore*) perciò, dunque, quindi ▶ *adj*
the ~ **president** il presidente di allora;
by ~ allora; **from** ~ **on** da allora in poi

theology [θɪ'ɔlədʒɪ] *n* teologia

theory ['θɪərɪ] *n* teoria

therapist ['θɛrəpɪst] *n* terapista *m/f*

therapy ['θɛrəpɪ] *n* terapia

there
[ðɛər] *adv*

1: **there is, there are** c'è, ci sono; **there
are 3 of them** (*people*) sono in 3; (*things*)
ce ne sono 3; **there is no-one here** non
c'è nessuno qui; **there has been an
accident** c'è stato un incidente

2 (*referring to place*) là, lì; **up/in/down
there** lassù/là dentro/laggiù; **he went
there on Friday** ci è andato venerdì; **I
want that book there** voglio quel libro
là *or* lì; **there he is!** eccolo!

3: **there, there** (*esp to child*) su, su

there: **thereabouts** [ðɛərə'bauts]
adv (*place*) nei pressi, da quelle
parti; (*amount*) giù di lì, all'incirca;
thereafter [ðɛər'ɑ:ftər] *adv* da allora
in poi; **thereby** [ðɛə'baɪ] *adv* con ciò;
therefore ['ðɛəfɔ:r] *adv* perciò, quindi;
there's [ðɛəz] = **there is**; **there has**

thermal ['θə:ml] *adj* termico(-a)

thermometer [θə'mɔmɪtər] *n*
termometro

thermostat ['θə:məstæt] *n*
termostato

these [ði:z] *pl pron, adj* questi(-e)

thesis ['θi:sɪs] (*pl* **theses**) *n* tesi *f inv*

they [ðeɪ] *pl pron* essi (esse); (*people
only*) loro; ~ **say that ...** (*it is said
that*) si dice che ...; **they'd** = **they
had**; **they would**; **they'll** = **they
shall**; **they will**; **they're** = **they are**;
they've = **they have**

thick [θɪk] *adj* spesso(-a); (*crowd*)
compatto(-a); (*stupid*) ottuso(-a),
lento(-a) ▶ *n* **in the** ~ **of** nel folto di;
it's 20 cm ~ ha uno spessore di 20
cm; **thicken** *vi* ispessire ▶ *vt* (*sauce
etc*) ispessire, rendere più denso(-a);
thickness *n* spessore *m*

thief [θi:f] (*pl* **thieves**) *n* ladro(-a)

thigh [θaɪ] *n* coscia

thin [θɪn] *adj* sottile; (*person*)
magro(-a); (*soup*) poco denso(-a) ▶ *vt*
to ~ **(down)** (*sauce, paint*) diluire

thing [θɪŋ] *n* cosa; (*object*) oggetto; (*mania*): **to have a ~ about** essere fissato(-a) con; **~s** *npl* (*belongings*) cose *fpl*; **poor ~** poverino(-a); **the best ~ would be to** la cosa migliore sarebbe di; **how are ~s?** come va?

think [θɪŋk] (*pt, pp* **thought**) *vi* pensare, riflettere ▶ *vt* pensare, credere; (*imagine*) immaginare; **to ~ of** pensare a; **what did you ~ of them?** cosa ne ha pensato?; **to ~ about sth/sb** pensare a qc/qn; **I'll ~ about it** ci penserò; **to ~ of doing** pensare di fare; **I ~ so/not** penso di sì/no; **to ~ well of** avere una buona opinione di ▷ **think over** *vt* riflettere su ▷ **think up** *vt* ideare

third [θəːd] *num* terzo(-a) ▶ *n* terzo(-a); (*fraction*) terzo, terza parte *f*; (*Aut*) terza; (*BRIT: Scol: degree*) laurea col minimo dei voti; **thirdly** *adv* in terzo luogo; **third party insurance** (*BRIT*) *n* assicurazione *f* contro terzi; **Third World** *n* **the Third World** il Terzo Mondo

thirst [θəːst] *n* sete *f*; **thirsty** *adj* (*person*) assetato(-a), che ha sete

thirteen [θəːˈtiːn] *num* tredici; **thirteenth** [-ˈtiːnθ] *num* tredicesimo(-a)

thirtieth [ˈθəːtɪɪθ] *num* trentesimo(-a)

thirty [ˈθəːtɪ] *num* trenta

this [ðɪs] (*pl* **these**) *adj* (*demonstrative*) questo(-a); **this man/woman/book** quest'uomo/questa donna/questo libro; (*not "that"*) quest'uomo/questa donna/questo libro qui; **this one** questo(-a) qui
▶ *pron* (*demonstrative*) questo(-a); (*not "that one"*) questo(-a) qui; **who/what is this?** chi è/che cos'è questo?; **I prefer this to that** preferisco questo a quello; **this is where I live** io abito qui; **this is what he said** questo è ciò che ha detto;

this is Mr Brown (*in introductions, photo*) questo è il signor Brown; (*on telephone*) sono il signor Brown
▶ *adv* (*demonstrative*): **this high/long** *etc* alto/lungo *etc* così; **I didn't know things were this bad** non sapevo andasse così male

thistle [ˈθɪsl] *n* cardo

thorn [θɔːn] *n* spina

thorough [ˈθʌrə] *adj* (*search*) minuzioso(-a); (*knowledge, research*) approfondito(-a), profondo(-a); (*person*) coscienzioso(-a); (*cleaning*) a fondo; **thoroughly** *adv* (*search*) minuziosamente; (*wash, study*) a fondo; (*very*) assolutamente

those [ðəuz] *pl pron* quelli(-e) ▶ *pl adj* quei (quegli) *mpl*; quelle *fpl*

though [ðəu] *conj* benché, sebbene
▶ *adv* comunque

thought [θɔːt] *pt, pp of* **think** ▶ *n* pensiero; (*opinion*) opinione *f*; **thoughtful** *adj* pensieroso(-a), pensoso(-a); (*considerate*) premuroso(-a); **thoughtless** *adj* sconsiderato(-a); (*behaviour*) scortese

thousand [ˈθauzənd] *num* mille; **one ~** mille; **~s of** migliaia di; **thousandth** *num* millesimo(-a)

thrash [θræʃ] *vt* picchiare; bastonare; (*defeat*) battere

thread [θrɛd] *n* filo; (*of screw*) filetto
▶ *vt* (*needle*) infilare

threat [θrɛt] *n* minaccia; **threaten** *vi* (*storm*) minacciare ▶ *vt* **to threaten sb with/to do** minacciare qn con/di fare; **threatening** *adj* minaccioso(-a)

three [θriː] *num* tre; **three-dimensional** *adj* tridimensionale; (*film*) stereoscopico(-a); **three-piece suite** [ˈθriːpiːs-] *n* salotto comprendente un divano e due poltrone; **three-quarters** *npl* tre quarti *mpl*; **three-quarters full** pieno per tre quarti

threshold ['θrɛʃhəuld] n soglia
threw [θruː] pt of **throw**
thrill [θrɪl] n brivido ▶ vt (audience) elettrizzare; **to be ~ed** (with gift etc) essere elettrizzato(-a); **thrilled** adj **I was thrilled to get your letter** la tua lettera mi ha fatto veramente piacere; **thriller** n thriller m inv; **thrilling** adj (book) pieno(-a) di suspense; (news, discovery) elettrizzante
thriving ['θraɪvɪŋ] adj fiorente
throat [θrəut] n gola; **to have a sore ~** avere (un or il) mal di gola
throb [θrɔb] vi palpitare; pulsare; vibrare
throne [θrəun] n trono
through [θruː] prep attraverso; (time) per, durante; (by means of) per mezzo di; (owing to) a causa di ▶ adj (ticket, train, passage) diretto(-a) ▶ adv attraverso; **to put sb ~ to sb** (Tel) passare qn a qn; **to be ~** (Tel) ottenere la comunicazione; (have finished) essere finito(-a); **"no ~ road"** (BRIT) "strada senza sbocco"; **throughout** prep (place) dappertutto in; (time) per or durante tutto(-a) ▶ adv dappertutto; sempre
throw [θrəu] (pt **threw**, pp **thrown**) n (Sport) lancio, tiro ▶ vt tirare, gettare; (Sport) lanciare, tirare; (rider) disarcionare; (fig) confondere; **to ~ a party** dare una festa ▷ **throw away** vt gettare or buttare via ▷ **throw in** vt (Sport: ball) rimettere in gioco; (include) aggiungere ▷ **throw off** vt sbarazzarsi di ▷ **throw out** vt buttare fuori; (reject) respingere ▷ **throw up** vi vomitare
thru [θruː] (US) prep, adj, adv = **through**
thrush [θrʌʃ] n tordo
thrust [θrʌst] (pt, pp **thrust**) vt spingere con forza; (push in) conficcare

thud [θʌd] n tonfo
thug [θʌg] n delinquente m
thumb [θʌm] n (Anat) pollice m; **to ~ a lift** fare l'autostop; **thumbtack** (US) n puntina da disegno
thump [θʌmp] n colpo forte; (sound) tonfo ▶ vt (person) picchiare; (object) battere su ▶ vi picchiare; battere
thunder ['θʌndər] n tuono ▶ vi tuonare; (train etc): **to ~ past** passare con un rombo; **thunderstorm** n temporale m
Thur(s). abbr (= Thursday) gio.
Thursday ['θəːzdɪ] n giovedì m inv
thus [ðʌs] adv così
thwart [θwɔːt] vt contrastare
thyme [taɪm] n timo
Tiber ['taɪbər] n **the ~** il Tevere
Tibet [tɪ'bɛt] n Tibet m
tick [tɪk] n (sound: of clock) tic tac m inv; (mark) segno; spunta; (Zool) zecca; (BRIT: inf): **in a ~** in un attimo ▶ vi fare tic tac ▶ vt spuntare ▷ **tick off** vt spuntare; (person) sgridare
ticket ['tɪkɪt] n biglietto; (in shop: on goods) etichetta; (parking ticket) multa; (for library) scheda; **a single/return ~ to …** un biglietto di sola andata/di andata e ritorno per…; **ticket barrier** n (BRIT: Rail) cancelletto d'ingresso; **ticket collector** n bigliettaio; **ticket inspector** n controllore m; **ticket machine** n distributore m di biglietti; **ticket office** n biglietteria
tickle ['tɪkl] vt fare il solletico a; (fig) solleticare ▶ vi **it ~s** mi (or gli etc) fa il solletico; **ticklish** [-lɪʃ] adj che soffre il solletico; (problem) delicato(-a)
tide [taɪd] n marea; (fig: of events) corso; **high/low ~** alta/bassa marea
tidy ['taɪdɪ] adj (room) ordinato(-a), lindo(-a); (dress, work) curato(-a), in ordine; (person) ordinato(-a) ▶ vt (also: **~ up**) riordinare, mettere in ordine
tie [taɪ] n (string etc) legaccio; (BRIT:

also: **neck~**) cravatta; (*fig*: *link*) legame *m*; (*Sport*: *draw*) pareggio ▶ *vt* (*parcel*) legare; (*ribbon*) annodare ▶ *vi* (*Sport*) pareggiare; **to ~ sth in a bow** annodare qc; **to ~ a knot in sth** fare un nodo a qc ▷ **tie down** *vt* legare; (*to price etc*) costringere ad accettare ▷ **tie up** *vt* (*parcel, dog*) legare; (*boat*) ormeggiare; (*arrangements*) concludere; **to be ~d up** (*busy*) essere occupato(-a) *or* preso(-a)

tier [tɪəʳ] *n* fila; (*of cake*) piano, strato

tiger ['taɪgəʳ] *n* tigre *f*

tight [taɪt] *adj* (*rope*) teso(-a), tirato(-a); (*money*) poco(-a); (*clothes, budget, bend etc*) stretto(-a); (*control*) severo(-a), fermo(-a); (*inf*: *drunk*) sbronzo(-a) ▶ *adv* (*squeeze*) fortemente; (*shut*) ermeticamente; **tighten** *vt* (*rope*) tendere; (*screw*) stringere; (*control*) rinforzare ▶ *vi* tendersi; stringersi; **tightly** *adv* (*grasp*) bene, saldamente; **tights** (*BRIT*) *npl* collant *m inv*

tile [taɪl] *n* (*on roof*) tegola; (*on wall or floor*) piastrella, mattonella

till [tɪl] *n* registratore *m* di cassa ▶ *vt* (*land*) coltivare ▶ *prep, conj* = **until**

tilt [tɪlt] *vt* inclinare, far pendere ▶ *vi* inclinarsi, pendere

timber [tɪmbəʳ] *n* (*material*) legname *m*

time [taɪm] *n* tempo; (*epoch: often pl*) epoca, tempo; (*by clock*) ora; (*moment*) momento; (*occasion*) volta; (*Mus*) tempo ▶ *vt* (*race*) cronometrare; (*programme*) calcolare la durata di; (*fix moment for*) programmare; (*remark etc*) dire (*or* fare) al momento giusto; **a long ~** molto tempo; **what ~ does the museum/shop open?** a che ora apre il museo/negozio?; **for the ~ being** per il momento; **4 at a ~** 4 per *or* alla volta; **from ~ to ~** ogni tanto; **at ~s** a volte; **in ~** (*soon enough*) in tempo; (*after some time*) col tempo; (*Mus*) a tempo; **in a week's ~** fra una settimana; **in no ~** in un attimo; **any ~** in qualsiasi momento; **on ~** puntualmente; **5 ~s 5** 5 volte 5, 5 per 5; **what ~ is it?** che ora è?, che ore sono?; **to have a good ~** divertirsi; **time limit** *n* limite *m* di tempo; **timely** *adj* opportuno(-a); **timer** *n* (*time switch*) temporizzatore *m*; (*in kitchen*) contaminuti *m inv*; **time-share** *adj* **time-share apartment/villa** appartamento/villa in multiproprietà; **timetable** *n* orario; **time zone** *n* fuso orario

timid ['tɪmɪd] *adj* timido(-a); (*easily scared*) pauroso(-a)

timing ['taɪmɪŋ] *n* (*Sport*) cronometraggio; (*fig*) scelta del momento opportuno

tin [tɪn] *n* stagno; (*also*: **~ plate**) latta; (*container*) scatola; (*BRIT*: *can*) barattolo (di latta), lattina; **tinfoil** *n* stagnola

tingle ['tɪŋgl] *vi* pizzicare

tinker ['tɪŋkəʳ]: **~ with** *vt fus* armeggiare intorno a; cercare di riparare

tinned [tɪnd] (*BRIT*) *adj* (*food*) in scatola

tin opener ['-əupnəʳ] (*BRIT*) *n* apriscatole *m inv*

tint [tɪnt] *n* tinta; **tinted** *adj* (*hair*) tinto(-a); (*spectacles, glass*) colorato(-a)

tiny ['taɪnɪ] *adj* minuscolo(-a)

tip [tɪp] *n* (*end*) punta; (*gratuity*) mancia; (*BRIT*: *for rubbish*) immondezzaio; (*advice*) suggerimento ▶ *vt* (*waiter*) dare la mancia a; (*tilt*) inclinare; (*overturn*: *also*: **~ over**) capovolgere; (*empty*: *also*: **~ out**) scaricare; **how much should I ~?** quanto devo lasciare di mancia? ▷ **tip off** *vt* fare una soffiata a

tiptoe ['tɪptəu] *n* **on ~** in punta di piedi

tire ['taɪəʳ] n (US) = **tyre** ▸ vt stancare
▸ vi stancarsi; **tired** adj stanco(-a); **to
be tired of** essere stanco or stufo di;
tire pressure (US) = **tyre pressure**;
tiring adj faticoso(-a)

tissue ['tɪʃuː] n tessuto; (paper
handkerchief) fazzoletto di carta;
tissue paper n carta velina

tit [tɪt] n (bird) cinciallegra; **to give ~
for tat** rendere pan per focaccia

title ['taɪtl] n titolo

T-junction ['tiːˈdʒʌŋkʃən] n incrocio
a T

TM abbr = **trademark**

to [tuː, tə] prep

1 (direction) a; **to go to France/
London/school** andare in Francia/a
Londra/a scuola; **to go to Paul's/the
doctor's** andare da Paul/dal dottore;
the road to Edinburgh la strada
per Edimburgo; **to the left/right** a
sinistra/destra

2 (as far as) (fino) a; **from here to
London** da qui a Londra; **to count to 10**
contare fino a 10; **from 40 to 50 people**
da 40 a 50 persone

3 (with expressions of time): **a quarter to
5** le 5 meno un quarto; **it's twenty to 3**
sono le 3 meno venti

4 (for, of): **the key to the front door** la
chiave della porta d'ingresso; **a letter
to his wife** una lettera per la moglie

5 (expressing indirect object) a; **to give
sth to sb** dare qc a qn; **to talk to sb**
parlare a qn; **to be a danger to sb/sth**
rappresentare un pericolo per qn/qc

6 (in relation to) a; **3 goals to 2** 3 goal a
2; **30 miles to the gallon** ≈ 11 chilometri
con un litro

7 (purpose, result): **to come to sb's aid**
venire in aiuto a qn; **to sentence sb to
death** condannare a morte qn; **to my
surprise** con mia sorpresa
▸ with vb

1 (simple infinitive): **to go/eat** etc
andare/mangiare etc

2 (following another vb): **to want/
try/start to do** volere/cercare
di/cominciare a fare

3 (with vb omitted): **I don't want to** non
voglio (farlo); **you ought to** devi (farlo)

4 (purpose, result) per; **I did it to help
you** l'ho fatto per aiutarti

5 (equivalent to relative clause): **I have
things to do** ho da fare; **the main
thing is to try** la cosa più importante
è provare

6 (after adjective etc): **ready to go**
pronto a partire; **too old/young to ...**
troppo vecchio/giovane per ...
▸ adv **to push the door to** accostare
la porta

toad [təud] n rospo; **toadstool** n
fungo (velenoso)

toast [təust] n (Culin) pane m tostato;
(drink, speech) brindisi m inv ▸ vt (Culin)
tostare; (drink to) brindare a; **a piece
or slice of ~** una fetta di pane tostato;
toaster n tostapane m inv

tobacco [təˈbækəu] n tabacco

toboggan [təˈbɒgən] n toboga m inv

today [təˈdeɪ] adv oggi ▸ n (also fig)
oggi m

toddler ['tɒdləʳ] n bambino(-a) che
impara a camminare

toe [təu] n dito del piede; (of shoe)
punta; **to ~ the line** (fig) stare in
riga, conformarsi; **toenail** n unghia
del piede

toffee ['tɒfɪ] n caramella

together [təˈgeðəʳ] adv insieme; (at
same time) allo stesso tempo; **~ with**
insieme a

toilet ['tɔɪlət] n (BRIT: lavatory)
gabinetto ▸ cpd (bag, soap etc) da
toletta; **where's the ~?** dov'è il
bagno?; **toilet bag** n (BRIT) nécessaire
m inv da toilette; **toilet paper** n carta
igienica; **toiletries** npl articoli mpl

da toletta; **toilet roll** n rotolo di carta igienica

token ['təukən] n (sign) segno; (substitute coin) gettone m; **book/ record/gift ~** (BRIT) buono-libro/ disco/regalo

Tokyo ['təukjəu] n Tokyo f

told [təuld] pt, pp of **tell**

tolerant ['tɔlərnt] adj **~ (of)** tollerante (nei confronti di)

tolerate ['tɔləreɪt] vt sopportare; (Med, Tech) tollerare

toll [təul] n (tax, charge) pedaggio ▶ vi (bell) suonare; **the accident ~ on the roads** il numero delle vittime della strada; **toll call** (US) n (Tel) (telefonata) interurbana; **toll-free** (US) adj senza addebito, gratuito(-a) ▶ adv gratuitamente; **toll-free number** ≈ numero verde

tomato [tə'mɑːtəu] (pl **tomatoes**) n pomodoro; **tomato sauce** n salsa di pomodoro

tomb [tuːm] n tomba; **tombstone** ['tuːmstəun] n pietra tombale

tomorrow [tə'mɔrəu] adv domani ▶ n (also fig) domani m inv; **the day after ~** dopodomani; **~ morning** domani mattina

ton [tʌn] n tonnellata; (BRIT: 1016 kg: US: 907 kg: metric 1000 kg): **~s of** (inf) un mucchio or sacco di

tone [təun] n tono ▶ vi (also: **~ in**) intonarsi ▷ **tone down** vt (colour, criticism, sound) attenuare

tongs [tɔŋz] npl tenaglie fpl; (for coal) molle fpl; (for hair) arricciacapelli m inv

tongue [tʌŋ] n lingua; **~ in cheek** (say, speak) ironicamente

tonic ['tɔnɪk] n (Med) tonico; (also: **~ water**) acqua tonica

tonight [tə'naɪt] adv stanotte; (this evening) stasera ▶ n questa notte; questa sera

tonne [tʌn] n (BRIT: metric ton)

tonnellata

tonsil ['tɔnsl] n tonsilla; **tonsillitis** [-'laɪtɪs] n tonsillite f

too [tuː] adv (excessively) troppo; (also) anche; (also: **~ much**) ▶ adv troppo ▶ adj troppo(-a); **~ many** troppi(-e)

took [tuk] pt of **take**

tool [tuːl] n utensile m, attrezzo; **tool box** n cassetta f portautensili; **tool kit** n cassetta di attrezzi

tooth [tuːθ] (pl **teeth**) n (Anat, Tech) dente m; **toothache** n mal m di denti; **toothbrush** n spazzolino da denti; **toothpaste** n dentifricio; **toothpick** n stuzzicadenti m inv

top [tɔp] n (of mountain, page, ladder) cima; (of box, cupboard, table) sopra m inv, parte f superiore; (lid: of box, jar) coperchio; (: of bottle) tappo; (blouse etc) sopra m inv; (toy) trottola ▶ adj più alto(-a); (in rank) primo(-a); (best) migliore ▶ vt (exceed) superare; (be first in) essere in testa a; **on ~ of** sopra, in cima a; (in addition to) oltre a; **from ~ to bottom** da cima a fondo ▷ **top up** (US **top off**) vt riempire; (salary) integrare; **top floor** n ultimo piano; **top hat** n cilindro

topic ['tɔpɪk] n argomento; **topical** adj d'attualità

topless ['tɔplɪs] adj (bather etc) col seno scoperto

topping ['tɔpɪŋ] n (Culin) guarnizione f

topple ['tɔpl] vt rovesciare, far cadere ▶ vi cadere; traballare

torch [tɔːtʃ] n torcia; (BRIT: electric) lampadina tascabile

tore [tɔːʳ] pt of **tear¹**

torment [n 'tɔːmɛnt, vb tɔː'mɛnt] n tormento ▶ vt tormentare

torn [tɔːn] pp of **tear¹**

tornado [tɔː'neɪdəu] (pl **tornadoes**) n tornado

torpedo [tɔː'piːdəu] (pl **torpedoes**) n siluro

t

torrent ['tɔrnt] *n* torrente *m*;
torrential [tɔ'rɛnʃl] *adj* torrenziale
tortoise ['tɔːtəs] *n* tartaruga
torture ['tɔːtʃəʳ] *n* tortura ▶ *vt*
torturare
Tory ['tɔːrɪ] (*BRIT*: *Pol*) *adj* dei tories,
conservatore(-trice) ▶ *n* tory *m/f inv*,
conservatore(-trice)
toss [tɔs] *vt* gettare, lanciare; (*one's
head*) scuotere; **to ~ a coin** fare a testa
o croce; **to ~ up for sth** fare a testa
o croce per qc; **to ~ and turn** (*in bed*)
girarsi e rigirarsi
total ['təutl] *adj* totale ▶ *n* totale *m*
▶ *vt* (*add up*) sommare; (*amount to*)
ammontare a
totalitarian [təutælɪ'tɛərɪən] *adj*
totalitario(-a)
totally ['təutəlɪ] *adv* completamente
touch [tʌtʃ] *n* tocco; (*sense*) tatto;
(*contact*) contatto ▶ *vt* toccare; **a ~
of** (*fig*) un tocco di; un pizzico di; **to
get in ~ with** mettersi in contatto
con; **to lose ~** (*friends*) perdersi di
vista ▷ **touch down** *vi* (*on land*)
atterrare; **touchdown** *n* atterraggio;
(*on sea*) ammaraggio; (*US: Football*)
meta; **touched** *adj* commosso(-a);
touching *adj* commovente;
touchline *n* (*Sport*) linea laterale;
touch-sensitive *adj* sensibile al tatto
tough [tʌf] *adj* duro(-a); (*resistant*)
resistente
tour ['tuəʳ] *n* viaggio; (*also:* **package
~**) viaggio organizzato *or* tutto
compreso; (*of town, museum*) visita;
(*by artist*) tournée *f inv* ▶ *vt* visitare;
tour guide *n* guida turistica
tourism ['tuərɪzəm] *n* turismo
tourist ['tuərɪst] *n* turista *m/f* ▶ *adv*
(*travel*) in classe turistica ▶ *cpd*
turistico(-a); **tourist office** *n* pro
loco *f inv*
tournament ['tuənəmənt] *n* torneo
tour operator *n* (*BRIT*) operatore *m*

turistico
tow [təu] *vt* rimorchiare; **"on ~"** (*BRIT*),
"in ~" (*US*) "veicolo rimorchiato"
▷ **tow away** *vt* rimorchiare
toward(s) [tə'wɔːd(z)] *prep* verso;
(*of attitude*) nei confronti di; (*of
purpose*) per
towel ['tauəl] *n* asciugamano; (*also:*
tea ~) strofinaccio; **towelling** *n*
(*fabric*) spugna
tower ['tauəʳ] *n* torre *f*; **tower block**
(*BRIT*) *n* palazzone *m*
town [taun] *n* città *f inv*; **to go to ~**
andare in città; (*fig*) mettercela tutta;
town centre *n* centro (città); **town
hall** *n* ≈ municipio
tow truck (*US*) *n* carro *m*, attrezzi *inv*
toxic ['tɔksɪk] *adj* tossico(-a)
toy [tɔɪ] *n* giocattolo ▷ **toy with** *vt
fus* giocare con; (*idea*) accarezzare,
trastullarsi con; **toyshop** *n* negozio
di giocattoli
trace [treɪs] *n* traccia ▶ *vt* (*draw*)
tracciare; (*follow*) seguire; (*locate*)
rintracciare
track [træk] *n* (*of person, animal*)
traccia; (*on tape, Sport, path: gen*) pista;
(*: of bullet etc*) traiettoria;
(*: of suspect, animal*) pista, tracce *fpl*;
(*Rail*) binario, rotaie *fpl* ▶ *vt* seguire le
tracce di; **to keep ~ of** seguire ▷ **track
down** *vt* (*prey*) scovare; snidare; (*sth
lost*) rintracciare; **tracksuit** *n* tuta
sportiva
tractor ['træktəʳ] *n* trattore *m*
trade [treɪd] *n* commercio; (*skill, job*)
mestiere *m* ▶ *vi* commerciare ▶ *vt* **to
~ sth (for sth)** barattare qc (con qc);
to ~ with/in commerciare con/in
▷ **trade in** *vt* (*old car etc*) dare come
pagamento parziale; **trademark**
n marchio di fabbrica; **trader** *n*
commerciante *m/f*; **tradesman** (*irreg*)
n fornitore *m*; (*shopkeeper*) negoziante
m; **trade union** *n* sindacato

trading ['treɪdɪŋ] n commercio
tradition [trə'dɪʃən] n tradizione f;
  traditional adj tradizionale
traffic ['træfɪk] n traffico ▶ vi **to ~
  in** (pej: liquor, drugs) trafficare in;
  traffic circle (US) n isola rotatoria;
  traffic island n salvagente m, isola
  f, spartitraffico inv; **traffic jam** n
  ingorgo (del traffico); **traffic lights**
  npl semaforo; **traffic warden** n
  addetto(-a) al controllo del traffico e
  del parcheggio
tragedy ['trædʒədɪ] n tragedia
tragic ['trædʒɪk] adj tragico(-a)
trail [treɪl] n (tracks) tracce fpl,
  pista; (path) sentiero; (of smoke etc)
  scia ▶ vt trascinare, strascicare;
  (follow) seguire ▶ vi essere al
  traino; (dress etc) strusciare; (plant)
  arrampicarsi; strisciare; (in game)
  essere in svantaggio; **trailer** n (Aut)
  rimorchio; (US) roulotte f inv; (Cinema)
  prossimamente m inv
train [treɪn] n treno; (of dress) coda,
  strascico ▶ vt (apprentice, doctor etc)
  formare; (sportsman) allenare; (dog)
  addestrare; (memory) esercitare;
  (point: gun etc): **to ~ sth on** puntare
  qc contro ▶ vi formarsi; allenarsi;
  **what time does the ~ from Rome
  get in?** a che ora arriva il treno da
  Roma?; **is this the ~ for ...?** è questo
  il treno per...?; **one's ~ of thought**
  il filo dei propri pensieri; **trainee**
  [treɪ'niː] n (in trade) apprendista m/f;
  trainer n (Sport) allenatore(-trice);
  (: shoe) scarpa da ginnastica; (of
  dogs etc) addestratore(-trice);
  trainers npl (shoes) scarpe fpl da
  ginnastica; **training** n formazione
  f; allenamento; addestramento;
  in training (Sport) in allenamento;
  training course n corso di
  formazione professionale; **training
  shoes** npl scarpe fpl da ginnastica

trait [treɪt] n tratto
traitor ['treɪtər] n traditore m
tram [træm] (BRIT) n (also: **~car**)
  tram m inv
tramp [træmp] n (person)
  vagabondo(-a); (inf: pej: woman)
  sgualdrina
trample ['træmpl] vt **to ~ (underfoot)**
  calpestare
trampoline ['træmpəliːn] n
  trampolino
tranquil ['træŋkwɪl] adj
  tranquillo(-a); **tranquillizer** (US
  tranquilizer) n (Med) tranquillante m
transaction [træn'zækʃən] n
  transazione f
transatlantic ['trænzət'læntɪk] adj
  transatlantico(-a)
transcript ['trænskrɪpt] n
  trascrizione f
transfer [n 'trænsfər, vb træns'fə
  r] n (gen: also Sport) trasferimento;
  (Pol: of power) passaggio; (picture,
  design) decalcomania; (: stick-on)
  autoadesivo ▶ vt trasferire; passare;
  to ~ the charges (BRIT: Tel) fare una
  chiamata a carico del destinatario
transform [træns'fɔːm] vt
  trasformare; **transformation** n
  trasformazione f
transfusion [træns'fjuːʒən] n
  trasfusione f
transit ['trænzɪt] n **in ~** in transito
transition [træn'zɪʃən] n passaggio,
  transizione f
transitive ['trænzɪtɪv] adj (Ling)
  transitivo(-a)
translate [trænz'leɪt] vt tradurre;
  can you ~ for me? me lo può
  tradurre?; **translation** [-'leɪʃən] n
  traduzione f; **translator** n
  traduttore(-trice)
transmission [trænz'mɪʃən] n
  trasmissione f
transmit [trænz'mɪt] vt trasmettere;

transmitter n trasmettitore m
transparent [træns'pærnt] adj
trasparente
transplant [vb træns'plɑːnt, n
'trænsplɑːnt] vt trapiantare ▶ n (Med)
trapianto
transport [n 'trænspɔːt, vb
træns'pɔːt] n trasporto ▶ vt
trasportare; **transportation**
[-'teɪʃən] n (mezzo di) trasporto
transvestite [trænz'vɛstaɪt] n
travestito(-a)
trap [træp] n (snare, trick) trappola;
(carriage) calesse m ▶ vt prendere in
trappola, intrappolare
trash [træʃ] (pej) n (goods) ciarpame m;
(nonsense) sciocchezze fpl; **trash can**
(US) n secchio della spazzatura
trauma ['trɔːmə] n trauma
m; **traumatic** [-'mætɪk] adj
traumatico(-a)
travel ['trævl] n viaggio; viaggi mpl ▶ vi
viaggiare ▶ vt (distance) percorrere;
travel agency n agenzia (di) viaggi;
travel agent n agente m di viaggio;
travel insurance n assicurazione f
di viaggio; **traveller** (US **traveler**)
n viaggiatore(-trice); **traveller's
cheque** (US **traveler's check**) n
assegno turistico; **travelling** (US
traveling) n viaggi mpl; **travel-sick**
adj **to get travel-sick** (in vehicle)
soffrire di mal d'auto; (in aeroplane)
soffrire di mal d'aria; (in boat) soffrire
di mal di mare; **travel sickness** n mal
m d'auto (or di mare or d'aria)
tray [treɪ] n (for carrying) vassoio; (on
desk) vaschetta
treacherous ['trɛtʃərəs] adj infido(-a)
treacle ['triːkl] n melassa
tread [trɛd] (pt **trod**, pp **trodden**) n
passo; (sound) rumore m di passi; (of
stairs) pedata; (of tyre) battistrada m
inv ▶ vi camminare ▷ **tread on** vt fus
calpestare

treasure ['trɛʒər] n tesoro ▶ vt (value)
tenere in gran conto, apprezzare
molto; (store) custodire gelosamente;
treasurer ['trɛʒərər] n tesoriere(-a)
treasury ['trɛʒərɪ] n **the T~** (BRIT),
the T~ Department (US) il ministero
del Tesoro
treat [triːt] n regalo ▶ vt trattare;
(Med) curare; **to ~ sb to sth** offrire
qc a qn; **treatment** ['triːtmənt] n
trattamento
treaty ['triːtɪ] n patto, trattato
treble ['trɛbl] adj triplo(-a), triplice ▶ vt
triplicare ▶ vi triplicarsi
tree [triː] n albero
trek [trɛk] n escursione f a piedi;
escursione f in macchina; (tiring walk)
camminata sfiancante ▶ vi (as holiday)
fare dell'escursionismo
tremble ['trɛmbl] vi tremare
tremendous [trɪ'mɛndəs] adj
(enormous) enorme; (excellent)
fantastico(-a), strepitoso(-a)

> Be careful not to translate
> **tremendous** by the Italian word
> **tremendo**.

trench [trɛntʃ] n trincea
trend [trɛnd] n (tendency) tendenza; (of
events) corso; (fashion) moda; **trendy**
adj (idea) di moda; (clothes) all'ultima
moda
trespass ['trɛspəs] vi **to ~ on**
entrare abusivamente in; **"no ~ing"**
"proprietà privata", "vietato l'accesso"
trial ['traɪəl] n (Law) processo; (test:
of machine etc) collaudo; **on ~** (Law)
sotto processo; **trial period** n periodo
di prova
triangle ['traɪæŋgl] n (Math, Mus)
triangolo
triangular [traɪ'æŋgjʊlər] adj
triangolare
tribe [traɪb] n tribù f inv
tribunal [traɪ'bjuːnl] n tribunale m
tribute ['trɪbjuːt] n tributo, omaggio;

to pay ~ to rendere omaggio a
trick [trɪk] n trucco; (joke) tiro; (Cards) presa ▶ vt imbrogliare, ingannare; **to play a ~ on sb** giocare un tiro a qn; **that should do the ~** vedrai che funziona

trickle ['trɪkl] n (of water etc) rivolo; gocciolio ▶ vi gocciolare

tricky ['trɪkɪ] adj difficile, delicato(-a)

tricycle ['traɪsɪkl] n triciclo

trifle ['traɪfl] n sciocchezza; (BRIT: Culin) ≈ zuppa inglese ▶ adv **a ~ long** un po' lungo

trigger ['trɪgə[r]] n (of gun) grilletto

trim [trɪm] adj (house, garden) ben tenuto(-a); (figure) snello(-a) ▶ n (haircut etc) spuntata, regolata; (embellishment) finiture fpl; (on car) guarnizioni fpl ▶ vt spuntare; (decorate): **to ~ (with)** decorare (con); (Naut: a sail) orientare

trio ['tri:əu] n trio

trip [trɪp] n viaggio; (excursion) gita, escursione f; (stumble) passo falso ▶ vi inciampare; (go lightly) camminare con passo leggero; **on a ~** in viaggio ▷ **trip up** vi inciampare ▶ vt fare lo sgambetto a

triple ['trɪpl] adj triplo(-a)

triplets ['trɪplɪts] npl bambini(-e) trigemini(-e)

tripod ['traɪpɔd] n treppiede m

triumph ['traɪʌmf] n trionfo ▶ vi **to ~ (over)** trionfare (su); **triumphant** [traɪ'ʌmfənt] adj trionfante

trivial ['trɪvɪəl] adj insignificante; (commonplace) banale

▌ Be careful not to translate **trivial** by the Italian word **triviale**.

trod [trɔd] pt of **tread**
trodden [trɔdn] pp of **tread**
trolley ['trɔlɪ] n carrello
trombone [trɔm'bəun] n trombone m
troop [tru:p] n gruppo; (Mil) squadrone m; **~s** npl (Mil) truppe fpl

trophy ['trəufɪ] n trofeo
tropical ['trɔpɪkl] adj tropicale
trot [trɔt] n trotto ▶ vi trottare; **on the ~** (BRIT: fig) di fila, uno(-a) dopo l'altro(-a)

trouble ['trʌbl] n difficoltà f inv, problema m; difficoltà fpl, problemi; (worry) preoccupazione f; (bother, effort) sforzo; (Pol) conflitti mpl, disordine m; (Med): **stomach** etc **~** disturbi mpl gastrici etc ▶ vt disturbare; (worry) preoccupare ▶ vi **to ~ to do** disturbarsi a fare; **~s** npl (Pol etc) disordini mpl; **to be in ~** avere dei problemi; **it's no ~!** di niente!; **what's the ~?** cosa c'è che non va?; **I'm sorry to ~ you** scusi il disturbo; **troubled** adj (person) preoccupato(-a), inquieto(-a); (epoch, life) agitato(-a), difficile; **troublemaker** n elemento disturbatore, agitatore(-trice); (child) disloco(-a); **troublesome** adj fastidioso(-a), seccante

trough [trɔf] n (drinking trough) abbeveratoio; (also: **feeding ~**) trogolo, mangiatoia; (channel) canale m

trousers ['trauzəz] npl pantaloni mpl, calzoni mpl; **short ~** calzoncini mpl

trout [traut] n inv trota

trowel ['trauəl] n cazzuola

truant ['truənt] (BRIT) n **to play ~** marinare la scuola

truce [tru:s] n tregua

truck [trʌk] n autocarro, camion m inv; (Rail) carro merci aperto; (for luggage) carrello m portabagagli inv; **truck driver** n camionista m/f

true [tru:] adj vero(-a); (accurate) accurato(-a), esatto(-a); (genuine) reale; (faithful) fedele; **to come ~** avverarsi

truly ['tru:lɪ] adv veramente; (truthfully) sinceramente; (faithfully): **yours ~** (in letter) distinti saluti

trumpet ['trʌmpɪt] n tromba

trunk [trʌŋk] n (of tree, person) tronco; (of elephant) proboscide f; (case) baule m; (US: Aut) bagagliaio; **~s** (also: **swimming ~s**) calzoncini mpl da bagno

trust [trʌst] n fiducia; (Law) amministrazione f fiduciaria; (Comm) trust m inv ▶ vt (rely on) contare su; (hope) sperare; (entrust): **to ~ sth to sb** affidare qc a qn; **trusted** adj fidato(-a); **trustworthy** adj fidato(-a), degno(-a) di fiducia

truth [truːθ, pl truːðz] n verità f inv; **truthful** adj (person) sincero(-a); (description) veritiero(-a), esatto(-a)

try [traɪ] n prova, tentativo; (Rugby) meta ▶ vt (Law) giudicare; (test: also: **~ out**) provare; (strain) mettere alla prova ▶ vi provare; **to have a ~** fare un tentativo; **to ~ to do** (seek) cercare di fare ▷ **try on** vt (clothes) provare; **trying** adj (day, experience) logorante, pesante; (child) difficile, insopportabile

T-shirt ['tiːʃəːt] n maglietta

tub [tʌb] n tinozza; mastello; (bath) bagno

tube [tjuːb] n tubo; (BRIT: underground) metropolitana, metrò m inv; (for tyre) camera d'aria

tuberculosis [tjubəːkjuˈləusɪs] n tubercolosi f inv

tube station (BRIT) n stazione f della metropolitana

tuck [tʌk] vt (put) mettere ▷ **tuck away** vt riporre; (building): **to be ~ed away** essere in un luogo isolato ▷ **tuck in** vt mettere dentro; (child) rimboccare ▶ vi (eat) mangiare di buon appetito; abbuffarsi; **tuck shop** n negozio di pasticceria (in una scuola)

Tue(s). abbr (= Tuesday) mar.

Tuesday ['tjuːzdɪ] n martedì m inv

tug [tʌg] n (ship) rimorchiatore m ▶ vt tirare con forza

tuition [tjuːˈɪʃən] n (BRIT) lezioni fpl; (: private tuition) lezioni fpl private; (US: school fees) tasse fpl scolastiche

tulip ['tjuːlɪp] n tulipano

tumble ['tʌmbl] n (fall) capitombolo ▶ vi capitombolare, ruzzolare; **to ~ to sth** (inf) realizzare qc; **tumble dryer** (BRIT) n asciugatrice f

tumbler ['tʌmblər] n bicchiere m (senza stelo)

tummy ['tʌmɪ] (inf) n pancia

tumour ['tjuːmər] (US **tumor**) n tumore m

tuna ['tjuːnə] n inv (also: **~ fish**) tonno

tune [tjuːn] n (melody) melodia, aria ▶ vt (Mus) accordare; (Radio, TV, Aut) regolare, mettere a punto; **to be in/out of ~** (instrument) essere accordato(-a)/scordato(-a); (singer) essere intonato(-a)/stonato(-a) ▷ **tune in** vi **to ~ in (to)** (Radio, TV) sintonizzarsi (su) ▷ **tune up** vi (musician) accordare lo strumento

tunic ['tjuːnɪk] n tunica

Tunisia [tjuːˈnɪzɪə] n Tunisia

tunnel ['tʌnl] n galleria ▶ vi scavare una galleria

turbulence ['təːbjuləns] n (Aviat) turbolenza

turf [təːf] n terreno erboso; (clod) zolla ▶ vt coprire di zolle erbose

Turin [tjuəˈrɪn] n Torino f

Turk [təːk] n turco(-a)

Turkey ['təːkɪ] n Turchia

turkey ['təːkɪ] n tacchino

Turkish ['təːkɪʃ] adj turco(-a) ▶ n (Ling) turco

turmoil ['təːmɔɪl] n confusione f, tumulto

turn [təːn] n giro; (change) cambiamento; (in road) curva; (tendency: of mind, events) tendenza; (performance) numero; (chance) turno; (Med) crisi f inv, attacco ▶ vt girare, voltare; (*change*): **to ~ sth into** trasformare qc in ▶ *vi* girare; (*person: look back*) girarsi, voltarsi; (*reverse direction*) girare; (*change*) cambiare; (*milk*) andare a male; (*become*) diventare; **a good ~** un buon servizio; **it gave me quite a ~** mi ha fatto prendere un bello spavento; **"no left ~"** (*Aut*) "divieto di svolta a sinistra"; **it's your ~** tocca a lei; **in ~** a sua volta; a turno; **to take ~s (at sth)** fare (qc) a turno; **~ left/right at the next junction** al prossimo incrocio, giri a sinistra/destra ▷ **turn around** *vi* (*person*) girarsi; (*rotate*) girare ▶ *vt* (*object*) girare ▷ **turn away** *vi* girarsi (dall'altra parte) ▶ *vt* mandare via ▷ **turn back** *vi* ritornare, tornare indietro ▶ *vt* far tornare indietro; (*clock*) spostare indietro ▷ **turn down** *vt* (*refuse*) rifiutare; (*reduce*) abbassare; (*fold*) ripiegare ▷ **turn in** *vi* (*inf: go to bed*) andare a letto ▶ *vt* (*fold*) voltare in dentro ▷ **turn off** *vi* (*from road*) girare, voltare ▶ *vt* (*light, radio, engine etc*) spegnere; **I can't ~ the heating off** non riesco a spegnere il riscaldamento ▷ **turn on** *vt* (*light, radio etc*) accendere; **I can't ~ the heating on** non riesco ad accendere il riscaldamento ▷ **turn out** *vt* (*light, gas*) chiudere; spegnere ▶ *vi* (*voters*) presentarsi; **to ~ out to be ...** rivelarsi ..., risultare ... ▷ **turn over** *vi* (*person*) girarsi ▶ *vt* girare ▷ **turn round** *vi* girarsi ▶ *vt* girare ▷ **turn to** *vt fus* **to ~ to sb** girarsi verso qn; **to ~ to sb for help** rivolgersi a qn per aiuto ▷ **turn up** *vi* (*person*) arrivare, presentarsi; (*lost object*) saltar fuori ▶ *vt* (*collar, sound*) alzare; **turning** *n* (*in road*) curva; **turning point** *n* (*fig*) svolta decisiva

turnip ['tə:nɪp] *n* rapa

turn: **turnout** ['tə:naʊt] *n* presenza,

affluenza; **turnover** ['tə:nəʊvə^r] *n* (*Comm*) turnover *m inv*; (*Culin*): **apple** *etc* **turnover** sfogliatella alle mele ecc; **turnstile** ['tə:nstaɪl] *n* tornella; **turn-up** (*BRIT*) *n* (*on trousers*) risvolto

turquoise ['tə:kwɔɪz] *n* turchese *m* ▶ *adj* turchese

turtle ['tə:tl] *n* testuggine *f*; **turtleneck (sweater)** ['tə:tlnɛk-] *n* maglione *m* con il collo alto

Tuscany ['tʌskənɪ] *n* Toscana

tusk [tʌsk] *n* zanna

tutor ['tju:tə^r] *n* (*in college*) docente *m/f* (*responsabile di un gruppo di studenti*); (*private teacher*) precettore *m*; **tutorial** [-'tɔ:rɪəl] *n* (*Scol*) lezione *f* con discussione (*a un gruppo limitato*)

tuxedo [tʌk'si:dəʊ] (*US*) *n* smoking *m inv*

TV [ti:'vi:] *n abbr* (= *television*) tivù *f inv*

tweed [twi:d] *n* tweed *m inv*

tweezers ['twi:zəz] *npl* pinzette *fpl*

twelfth [twɛlfθ] *num* dodicesimo(-a)

twelve [twɛlv] *num* dodici; **at ~ o'clock** alle dodici, a mezzogiorno; (*midnight*) a mezzanotte

twentieth ['twɛntɪɪθ] *num* ventesimo(-a)

twenty ['twɛntɪ] *num* venti

twice [twaɪs] *adv* due volte; **~ as much** due volte tanto; **~ a week** due volte alla settimana

twig [twɪg] *n* ramoscello ▶ *vt, vi* (*inf*) capire

twilight ['twaɪlaɪt] *n* crepuscolo

twin [twɪn] *adj, n* gemello(-a) ▶ *vt* **to ~ one town with another** fare il gemellaggio di una città con un'altra; **twin(-bedded) room** *n* stanza con letti gemelli; **twin beds** *npl* letti *mpl* gemelli

twinkle ['twɪŋkl] *vi* scintillare; (*eyes*) brillare

twist [twɪst] *n* torsione *f*; (*in wire, flex*) piega; (*in road*) curva; (*in story*) colpo di scena ▸vt attorcigliare; (*ankle*) slogare; (*weave*) intrecciare; (*roll around*) arrotolare; (*fig*) distorcere ▸vi (*road*) serpeggiare

twit [twɪt] (*inf*) n cretino(-a)

twitch [twɪtʃ] n tiratina; (*nervous*) tic m inv ▸vi contrarsi

two [tuː] num due; **to put ~ and ~ together** (*fig*) fare uno più uno

type [taɪp] n (*category*) genere m; (*model*) modello; (*example*) tipo; (*Typ*) tipo, carattere m ▸vt (*letter etc*) battere (a macchina), dattilografare; **typewriter** n macchina da scrivere

typhoid ['taɪfɔɪd] n tifoidea

typhoon [taɪ'fuːn] n tifone m

typical ['tɪpɪkl] adj tipico(-a); **typically** adv tipicamente; **typically, he arrived late** come al solito è arrivato tardi

typing ['taɪpɪŋ] n dattilografia

typist ['taɪpɪst] n dattilografo(-a)

tyre ['taɪəʳ] (*US* **tire**) n pneumatico, gomma; **I've got a flat ~** ho una gomma a terra; **tyre pressure** n pressione f (delle gomme)

u

UFO ['juːfəu] n abbr (= unidentified flying object) UFO m inv

Uganda [juː'gændə] n Uganda

ugly ['ʌɡlɪ] adj brutto(-a)

UHT abbr (= ultra heat treated) UHT inv, a lunga conservazione

UK n abbr = **United Kingdom**

ulcer ['ʌlsəʳ] n ulcera; (*also:* **mouth ~**) afta

ultimate ['ʌltɪmət] adj ultimo(-a), finale; (*authority*) massimo(-a), supremo(-a); **ultimately** adv alla fine, in definitiva, in fin dei conti

ultimatum [ʌltɪ'meɪtəm, -tə] (*pl* **ultimatums** *or* **ultimata**) n ultimatum m inv

ultrasound [ʌltrə'saund] n (*Med*) ultrasuono

ultraviolet ['ʌltrə'vaɪəlɪt] adj ultravioletto(-a)

umbrella [ʌm'brɛlə] n ombrello

umpire ['ʌmpaɪəʳ] n arbitro

UN n abbr (= United Nations) ONU f

unable [ʌn'eɪbl] adj **to be ~ to** non potere, essere nell'impossibilità di; essere incapace di

unacceptable [ʌnək'sɛptəbl] adj (*proposal, behaviour*) inaccettabile; (*price*) impossibile

unanimous [juː'nænɪməs] adj unanime

unarmed [ʌn'ɑːmd] adj (*without a weapon*) disarmato(-a); (*combat*) senz'armi

unattended [ʌnə'tɛndɪd] adj (*car, child, luggage*) incustodito(-a)

unattractive [ʌnə'træktɪv] adj poco attraente

unavailable [ʌnə'veɪləbl] adj (*article, room, book*) non disponibile; (*person*) impegnato(-a)

unavoidable [ʌnə'vɔɪdəbl] adj inevitabile

unaware [ʌnə'wɛəʳ] adj **to be ~ of** non sapere, ignorare; **unawares** adv di sorpresa, alla sprovvista

unbearable [ʌn'bɛərəbl] adj insopportabile

unbeatable [ʌn'biːtəbl] adj imbattibile

unbelievable [ʌnbɪˈliːvəbl] *adj* incredibile

unborn [ʌnˈbɔːn] *adj* non ancora nato(-a)

unbutton [ʌnˈbʌtn] *vt* sbottonare

uncalled-for [ʌnˈkɔːldfɔːʳ] *adj* (*remark*) fuori luogo *inv*; (*action*) ingiustificato(-a)

uncanny [ʌnˈkænɪ] *adj* misterioso(-a), strano(-a)

uncertain [ʌnˈsəːtn] *adj* incerto(-a); dubbio(-a); **uncertainty** *n* incertezza

unchanged [ʌnˈtʃeɪndʒd] *adj* invariato(-a)

uncle [ˈʌŋkl] *n* zio

unclear [ʌnˈklɪəʳ] *adj* non chiaro(-a); **I'm still ~ about what I'm supposed to do** non ho ancora ben capito cosa dovrei fare

uncomfortable [ʌnˈkʌmfətəbl] *adj* scomodo(-a); (*uneasy*) a disagio, agitato(-a); (*unpleasant*) fastidioso(-a)

uncommon [ʌnˈkɔmən] *adj* raro(-a), insolito(-a), non comune

unconditional [ʌnkənˈdɪʃənl] *adj* incondizionato(-a), senza condizioni

unconscious [ʌnˈkɔnʃəs] *adj* privo(-a) di sensi, svenuto(-a); (*unaware*) inconsapevole, inconscio(-a) ▶ *n* **the ~** l'inconscio

uncontrollable [ʌnkənˈtrəuləbl] *adj* incontrollabile; indisciplinato(-a)

unconventional [ʌnkənˈvɛnʃənl] *adj* poco convenzionale

uncover [ʌnˈkʌvəʳ] *vt* scoprire

undecided [ʌndɪˈsaɪdɪd] *adj* indeciso(-a)

undeniable [ʌndɪˈnaɪəbl] *adj* innegabile, indiscutibile

under [ˈʌndəʳ] *prep* sotto; (*less than*) meno di; al disotto di; (*according to*) secondo, in conformità a ▶ *adv* (al) disotto; **~ there** là sotto; **~ repair** in riparazione; **undercover** *adj* segreto(-a), clandestino(-a);

underdone *adj* (*Culin*) al sangue; (*pej*) poco cotto(-a); **underestimate** *vt* sottovalutare; **undergo** *vt* (*irreg*) subire; (*treatment*) sottoporsi a; **undergraduate** *n* studente(-essa) universitario(-a); **underground** *n* (BRIT: *railway*) metropolitana; (*Pol*) movimento clandestino ▶ *adj* sotterraneo(-a); (*fig*) clandestino(-a) ▶ *adv* sotterra; **to go underground** (*fig*) darsi alla macchia; **undergrowth** *n* sottobosco; **underline** *vt* sottolineare; **undermine** *vt* minare; **underneath** [ʌndəˈniːθ] *adv* sotto, disotto ▶ *prep* sotto, al di sotto di; **underpants** *npl* mutande *fpl*, slip *m inv*; **underpass** (BRIT) *n* sottopassaggio; **underprivileged** *adj* non abbiente; meno favorito(-a); **underscore** *vt* sottolineare; **undershirt** (US) *n* maglietta; **underskirt** (BRIT) *n* sottoveste *f*

understand [ʌndəˈstænd] (*irreg: like* **stand**) *vt, vi* capire, comprendere; **I don't ~** non capisco; **I ~ that ...** sento che ...; credo di capire che ...; **understandable** *adj* comprensibile; **understanding** *adj* comprensivo(-a) ▶ *n* comprensione *f*; (*agreement*) accordo

understatement [ʌndəˈsteɪtmənt] *n* **that's an ~!** a dire poco!

understood [ʌndəˈstud] *pt, pp of* **understand** ▶ *adj* inteso(-a); (*implied*) sottinteso(-a)

undertake [ʌndəˈteɪk] (*irreg: like* **take**) *vt* intraprendere; **to ~ to do sth** impegnarsi a fare qc

undertaker [ˈʌndəteɪkəʳ] *n* impresario di pompe funebri

undertaking [ʌndəˈteɪkɪŋ] *n* impresa; (*promise*) promessa

under: **underwater** [ʌndəˈwɔːtəʳ] *adv* sott'acqua ▶ *adj* subacqueo(-a);

u

underway [ˌʌndəˈweɪ] *adj* **to be underway** essere in corso;
underwear [ˈʌndəwɛəʳ] *n* biancheria (intima); **underwent** [ˌʌndəˈwɛnt] *vb see* **undergo**; **underworld** [ˈʌndəwəːld] *n* (*of crime*) malavita

undesirable [ˌʌndɪˈzaɪərəbl] *adj* sgradevole

undisputed [ˌʌndɪsˈpjuːtɪd] *adj* indiscusso(-a)

undo [ʌnˈduː] *vt* (*irreg*) disfare

undone [ʌnˈdʌn] *pp of* **undo**; **to come ~** slacciarsi

undoubtedly [ʌnˈdautɪdlɪ] *adv* senza alcun dubbio

undress [ʌnˈdrɛs] *vi* spogliarsi

unearth [ʌnˈəːθ] *vt* dissotterrare; (*fig*) scoprire

uneasy [ʌnˈiːzɪ] *adj* a disagio; (*worried*) preoccupato(-a); (*peace*) precario(-a)

unemployed [ˌʌnɪmˈplɔɪd] *adj* disoccupato(-a) ▶ *npl* **the ~** i disoccupati

unemployment [ˌʌnɪmˈplɔɪmənt] *n* disoccupazione *f*; **unemployment benefit** (*US* **unemployment compensation**) *n* sussidio di disoccupazione

unequal [ʌnˈiːkwəl] *adj* (*length, objects*) disuguale; (*amounts*) diverso(-a); (*division of labour*) ineguale

uneven [ʌnˈiːvn] *adj* ineguale; irregolare

unexpected [ˌʌnɪkˈspɛktɪd] *adj* inatteso(-a), imprevisto(-a); **unexpectedly** *adv* inaspettatamente

unfair [ʌnˈfɛəʳ] *adj* **~ (to)** ingiusto(-a) (nei confronti di)

unfaithful [ʌnˈfeɪθful] *adj* infedele

unfamiliar [ˌʌnfəˈmɪlɪəʳ] *adj* sconosciuto(-a), strano(-a); **to be ~ with** non avere familiarità con

unfashionable [ʌnˈfæʃnəbl] *adj* (*clothes*) fuori moda; (*district*) non alla moda

unfasten [ʌnˈfɑːsn] *vt* slacciare; sciogliere

unfavourable [ʌnˈfeɪvərəbl] (*US* **unfavorable**) *adj* sfavorevole

unfinished [ʌnˈfɪnɪʃt] *adj* incompleto(-a)

unfit [ʌnˈfɪt] *adj* (*ill*) malato(-a), in cattiva salute; (*incompetent*): **~ (for)** incompetente (in); (: *work, Mil*) inabile (a)

unfold [ʌnˈfəuld] *vt* spiegare ▶ *vi* (*story, plot*) svelarsi

unforgettable [ˌʌnfəˈgɛtəbl] *adj* indimenticabile

unfortunate [ʌnˈfɔːtʃnət] *adj* sfortunato(-a); (*event, remark*) infelice; **unfortunately** *adv* sfortunatamente, purtroppo

unfriendly [ʌnˈfrɛndlɪ] *adj* poco amichevole, freddo(-a)

unfurnished [ʌnˈfəːnɪʃt] *adj* non ammobiliato(-a)

unhappiness [ʌnˈhæpɪnɪs] *n* infelicità

unhappy [ʌnˈhæpɪ] *adj* infelice; **~ about/with** (*arrangements etc*) insoddisfatto(-a) di

unhealthy [ʌnˈhɛlθɪ] *adj* (*gen*) malsano(-a); (*person*) malaticcio(-a)

unheard-of [ʌnˈhəːdɔv] *adj* inaudito(-a), senza precedenti

unhelpful [ʌnˈhɛlpful] *adj* poco disponibile

unhurt [ʌnˈhəːt] *adj* illeso(-a)

unidentified [ˌʌnaɪˈdɛntɪfaɪd] *adj* non identificato(-a)

uniform [ˈjuːnɪfɔːm] *n* uniforme *f*, divisa ▶ *adj* uniforme

unify [ˈjuːnɪfaɪ] *vt* unificare

unimportant [ˌʌnɪmˈpɔːtənt] *adj* senza importanza, di scarsa importanza

uninhabited [ˌʌnɪnˈhæbɪtɪd] *adj* disabitato(-a)

unintentional [ˌʌnɪnˈtɛnʃənəl] *adj*

involontario(-a)

union ['ju:njən] *n* unione *f*; (*also:* **trade ~**) sindacato ▶ *cpd* sindacale, dei sindacati; **Union Jack** *n* bandiera *nazionale britannica*

unique [ju:'ni:k] *adj* unico(-a)

unisex ['ju:nɪsɛks] *adj* unisex *inv*

unit ['ju:nɪt] *n* unità *f inv*; (*section: of furniture etc*) elemento; (*team, squad*) reparto, squadra

unite [ju:'naɪt] *vt* unire ▶ *vi* unirsi; **united** *adj* unito(-a); unificato(-a); (*efforts*) congiunto(-a); **United Kingdom** *n* Regno Unito; **United Nations (Organization)** *n* (Organizzazione *f* delle) Nazioni Unite; **United States (of America)** *n* Stati *mpl* Uniti (d'America)

unity ['ju:nɪtɪ] *n* unità

universal [ju:nɪ'və:sl] *adj* universale

universe ['ju:nɪvə:s] *n* universo

university [ju:nɪ'və:sɪtɪ] *n* università *f inv*

unjust [ʌn'dʒʌst] *adj* ingiusto(-a)

unkind [ʌn'kaɪnd] *adj* scortese; crudele

unknown [ʌn'nəun] *adj* sconosciuto(-a)

unlawful [ʌn'lɔ:ful] *adj* illecito(-a), illegale

unleaded [ʌn'lɛdɪd] *adj* (*petrol, fuel*) verde, senza piombo

unleash [ʌn'li:ʃ] *vt* (*fig*) scatenare

unless [ʌn'lɛs] *conj* a meno che (non) + *sub*

unlike [ʌn'laɪk] *adj* diverso(-a) ▶ *prep* a differenza di, contrariamente a

unlikely [ʌn'laɪklɪ] *adj* improbabile

unlimited [ʌn'lɪmɪtɪd] *adj* illimitato(-a)

unlisted [ʌn'lɪstɪd] (*US*) *adj* (*Tel*): **to be ~** non essere sull'elenco

unload [ʌn'ləud] *vt* scaricare

unlock [ʌn'lɔk] *vt* aprire

unlucky [ʌn'lʌkɪ] *adj* sfortunato(-a);

(*object, number*) che porta sfortuna

unmarried [ʌn'mærɪd] *adj* non sposato(-a); (*man only*) scapolo, celibe; (*woman only*) nubile

unmistak(e)able [ʌnmɪs'teɪkəbl] *adj* inconfondibile

unnatural [ʌn'nætʃrəl] *adj* innaturale; contro natura

unnecessary [ʌn'nɛsəsərɪ] *adj* inutile, superfluo(-a)

UNO ['ju:nəu] *n abbr* (= *United Nations Organization*) ONU *f*

unofficial [ʌnə'fɪʃl] *adj* non ufficiale; (*strike*) non dichiarato(-a) dal sindacato

unpack [ʌn'pæk] *vi* disfare la valigia (*or* le valigie) ▶ *vt* disfare

unpaid [ʌn'peɪd] *adj* (*holiday*) non pagato(-a); (*work*) non retribuito(-a); (*bill, debt*) da pagare

unpleasant [ʌn'plɛznt] *adj* spiacevole

unplug [ʌn'plʌg] *vt* staccare

unpopular [ʌn'pɔpjulər] *adj* impopolare

unprecedented [ʌn'prɛsɪdəntɪd] *adj* senza precedenti

unpredictable [ʌnprɪ'dɪktəbl] *adj* imprevedibile

unprotected ['ʌnprə'tɛktɪd] *adj* (*sex*) non protetto(-a)

unqualified [ʌn'kwɔlɪfaɪd] *adj* (*teacher*) non abilitato(-a); (*success*) assoluto(-a), senza riserve

unravel [ʌn'rævl] *vt* dipanare, districare

unreal [ʌn'rɪəl] *adj* irreale

unrealistic [ʌnrɪə'lɪstɪk] *adj* non realistico(-a)

unreasonable [ʌn'ri:znəbl] *adj* irragionevole

unrelated [ʌnrɪ'leɪtɪd] *adj* **~ (to)** senza rapporto (con); non imparentato(-a) (con)

unreliable [ʌnrɪ'laɪəbl] *adj* (*person, machine*) che non dà affidamento;

(news, source of information)
inattendibile

unrest [ʌnˈrɛst] n agitazione f

unroll [ʌnˈrəul] vt srotolare

unruly [ʌnˈruːlɪ] adj indisciplinato(-a)

unsafe [ʌnˈseɪf] adj pericoloso(-a), rischioso(-a)

unsatisfactory [ˈʌnsætɪsˈfæktərɪ] adj che lascia a desiderare, insufficiente

unscrew [ʌnˈskruː] vt svitare

unsettled [ʌnˈsɛtld] adj (person) turbato(-a); indeciso(-a); (weather) instabile

unsettling [ʌnˈsɛtlɪŋ] adj inquietante

unsightly [ʌnˈsaɪtlɪ] adj brutto(-a), sgradevole a vedersi

unskilled [ʌnˈskɪld] adj non specializzato(-a)

unspoiled [ˈʌnˈspɔɪld], **unspoilt** [ˈʌnˈspɔɪlt] adj (place) non deturpato(-a)

unstable [ʌnˈsteɪbl] adj (gen) instabile; (mentally) squilibrato(-a)

unsteady [ʌnˈstɛdɪ] adj instabile, malsicuro(-a)

unsuccessful [ʌnsəkˈsɛsful] adj (writer, proposal) che non ha successo; (marriage, attempt) mal riuscito(-a), fallito(-a); **to be ~** (in attempting sth) non avere successo

unsuitable [ʌnˈsuːtəbl] adj inadatto(-a); inopportuno(-a); sconveniente

unsure [ʌnˈʃuə] adj incerto(-a); **to be ~ of o.s** essere insicuro(-a)

untidy [ʌnˈtaɪdɪ] adj (room) in disordine; (appearance) trascurato(-a); (person) disordinato(-a)

untie [ʌnˈtaɪ] vt (knot, parcel) disfare; (prisoner, dog) slegare

until [ʌnˈtɪl] prep fino a; (after negative) prima di ▸ conj finché, fino a quando; (in past, after negative) prima che + sub, prima di + infinitive; **~ he comes** finché or fino a quando non arriva; **~ now**

finora; **~ then** fino ad allora

untrue [ʌnˈtruː] adj (statement) falso(-a), non vero(-a)

unused [ʌnˈjuːzd] adj nuovo(-a)

unusual [ʌnˈjuːʒuəl] adj insolito(-a), eccezionale, raro(-a); **unusually** adv insolitamente

unveil [ʌnˈveɪl] vt scoprire; svelare

unwanted [ʌnˈwɔntɪd] adj (clothing) smesso(-a); (child) non desiderato(-a)

unwell [ʌnˈwɛl] adj indisposto(-a); **to feel ~** non sentirsi bene

unwilling [ʌnˈwɪlɪŋ] adj **to be ~ to do** non voler fare

unwind [ʌnˈwaɪnd] (irreg: like **wind**¹) vt svolgere, srotolare ▸ vi (relax) rilassarsi

unwise [ʌnˈwaɪz] adj poco saggio(-a)

unwittingly [ʌnˈwɪtɪŋlɪ] adv senza volerlo

unwrap [ʌnˈræp] vt disfare; aprire

unzip [ʌnˈzɪp] vt aprire (la chiusura lampo di); (Comput) dezippare

○ up
[ʌp] prep **he went up the stairs/ the hill** è salito su per le scale/sulla collina; **the cat was up a tree** il gatto era su un albero; **they live further up the street** vivono un po' più su nella stessa strada
▸adv
1 (upwards, higher) su, in alto; **up in the sky/the mountains** su nel cielo/in montagna; **up there** lassù; **up above** su in alto
2: **to be up** (out of bed) essere alzato(-a); (prices, level) essere salito(-a)
3: **up to** (as far as) fino a; **up to now** finora
4: **to be up to** (depending on): **it's up to you** sta a lei, dipende da lei; (equal to): **he's not up to it** (job, task etc) non ne è all'altezza; (inf: be doing): **what is he up to?** cosa sta combinando?
▸n **ups and downs** alti e bassi mpl

up-and-coming [ˈʌpəndˈkʌmɪŋ] *adj* pieno(-a) di promesse, promettente

upbringing [ˈʌpbrɪŋɪŋ] *n* educazione *f*

update [ʌpˈdeɪt] *vt* aggiornare

upfront [ʌpˈfrʌnt] *adj* (*inf*) franco(-a), aperto(-a) ▸ *adv* (*pay*) subito

upgrade [ʌpˈgreɪd] *vt* (*house, job*) migliorare; (*employee*) avanzare di grado

upheaval [ʌpˈhiːvl] *n* sconvolgimento; tumulto

uphill [ʌpˈhɪl] *adj* in salita; (*fig: task*) difficile ▸ *adv* **to go ~** andare in salita, salire

upholstery [ʌpˈhəulstərɪ] *n* tappezzeria

upmarket [ʌpˈmɑːkɪt] *adj* (*product*) che si rivolge ad una fascia di mercato superiore

upon [əˈpɔn] *prep* su

upper [ˈʌpəʳ] *adj* superiore ▸ *n* (*of shoe*) tomaia; **upper-class** *adj* dell'alta borghesia

upright [ˈʌpraɪt] *adj* diritto(-a); verticale; (*fig*) diritto(-a), onesto(-a)

uprising [ˈʌpraɪzɪŋ] *n* insurrezione *f*

uproar [ˈʌprɔːʳ] *n* tumulto, clamore *m*

upset [*n* ˈʌpsɛt, *vb, adj* ʌpˈsɛt] (*irreg: like set*) *n* (*to plan etc*) contrattempo; (*stomach upset*) disturbo ▸ *vt* (*glass etc*) rovesciare; (*plan, stomach*) scombussolare; (*person: offend*) contrariare; (*: grieve*) addolorare; sconvolgere ▸ *adj* contrariato(-a), addolorato(-a); (*stomach*) scombussolato(-a)

upside-down [ʌpsaɪdˈdaun] *adv* sottosopra

upstairs [ʌpˈstɛəz] *adv, adj* di sopra, al piano superiore ▸ *n* piano di sopra

up-to-date [ˈʌptəˈdeɪt] *adj* moderno(-a); aggiornato(-a)

uptown [ˈʌptaun] (*US*) *adv* verso i quartieri residenziali ▸ *adj* dei quartieri residenziali

upward [ˈʌpwəd] *adj* ascendente; verso l'alto; **upward(s)** *adv* in su, verso l'alto

uranium [juəˈreɪnɪəm] *n* uranio

Uranus [juəˈreɪnəs] *n* (*planet*) Urano

urban [ˈəːbən] *adj* urbano(-a)

urge [əːdʒ] *n* impulso; stimolo; forte desiderio ▸ *vt* **to ~ sb to do** esortare qn a fare, spingere qn a fare; raccomandare a qn di fare

urgency [ˈəːdʒənsɪ] *n* urgenza; (*of tone*) insistenza

urgent [ˈəːdʒənt] *adj* urgente; (*voice*) insistente

urinal [ˈjuərɪnl] *n* (*BRIT: building*) vespasiano; (*: vessel*) orinale *m*

urinate [ˈjuərɪneɪt] *vi* orinare

urine [ˈjuərɪn] *n* orina

URL *n abbr* (= uniform resource locator) URL *m inv*

us [ʌs] *pron* ci; (*stressed, after prep*) noi; *see also* **me**

US(A) *n abbr* (= United States (of America)) USA *mpl*

use [*n* juːs, *vb* juːz] *n* uso; impiego, utilizzazione *f* ▸ *vt* usare, utilizzare, servirsi di; **in ~** in uso; **out of ~** fuori uso; **to be of ~** essere utile, servire; **it's no ~** non serve, è inutile; **she ~d to do it** lo faceva (una volta), era solita farlo; **to be ~d to** avere l'abitudine di ▸ **use up** *vt* consumare; esaurire; **used** *adj* (*object, car*) usato(-a); **useful** *adj* utile; **useless** *adj* inutile; (*person*) inetto(-a); **user** *n* utente *m/f*; **user-friendly** *adj* (*computer*) di facile uso

usual [ˈjuːʒuəl] *adj* solito(-a); **as ~** come al solito, come d'abitudine; **usually** *adv* di solito

utensil [juːˈtɛnsl] *n* utensile *m*; **kitchen ~s** utensili da cucina

utility [juːˈtɪlɪtɪ] *n* utilità; (*also*: **public ~**) servizio pubblico

utilize [ˈjuːtɪlaɪz] *vt* utilizzare; sfruttare

u

utmost ['ʌtməust] *adj* estremo(-a)
▸ *n* **to do one's ~** fare il possibile *or*
di tutto
utter ['ʌtər] *adj* assoluto(-a), totale
▸ *vt* pronunciare, proferire; emettere;
utterly *adv* completamente, del tutto
U-turn ['juː'təːn] *n* inversione *f* a U

V

v. *abbr* = **verse**; **versus**; **volt**; (= *vide*)
vedi, vedere
vacancy ['veɪkənsɪ] *n* (*BRIT: job*)
posto libero; (*room*) stanza libera; **"no
vacancies"** "completo"

▌ Be careful not to translate **vacancy**
by the Italian word *vacanza*.

vacant ['veɪkənt] *adj* (*job, seat etc*)
libero(-a); (*expression*) assente
vacate [və'keɪt] *vt* lasciare libero(-a)
vacation [və'keɪʃən] (*esp US*)
n vacanze *fpl*; **vacationer** (*US*
vacationist) *n* vacanziere(-a)
vaccination [væksɪ'neɪʃən] *n*
vaccinazione *f*
vaccine ['væksiːn] *n* vaccino
vacuum ['vækjum] *n* vuoto; **vacuum
cleaner** *n* aspirapolvere *m inv*
vagina [və'dʒaɪnə] *n* vagina
vague [veɪg] *adj* vago(-a); (*blurred:
photo, memory*) sfocato(-a)
vain [veɪn] *adj* (*useless*) inutile,
vano(-a); (*conceited*) vanitoso(-a); **in ~**

inutilmente, invano
Valentine's Day ['væləntaɪnzdeɪ] *n*
San Valentino *m*
valid ['vælɪd] *adj* valido(-a), valevole;
(*excuse*) valido(-a)
valley ['vælɪ] *n* valle *f*
valuable ['væljuəbl] *adj* (*jewel*)
di (grande) valore; (*time, help*)
prezioso(-a); **valuables** *npl* oggetti
mpl di valore
value ['væljuː] *n* valore *m* ▸ *vt* (*fix price*)
valutare, dare un prezzo a; (*cherish*)
apprezzare, tenere a; **~s** *npl* (*principles*)
valori *mpl*
valve [vælv] *n* valvola
vampire ['væmpaɪər] *n* vampiro
van [væn] *n* (*Aut*) furgone *m*; (*BRIT:
Rail*) vagone *m*
vandal ['vændl] *n* vandalo(-a);
vandalism *n* vandalismo; **vandalize**
vt vandalizzare
vanilla [və'nɪlə] *n* vaniglia ▸ *cpd* (*ice
cream*) alla vaniglia
vanish ['vænɪʃ] *vi* svanire, scomparire
vanity ['vænɪtɪ] *n* vanità
vapour ['veɪpər] (*US* **vapor**) *n* vapore *m*
variable ['vɛərɪəbl] *adj* variabile;
(*mood*) mutevole
variant ['vɛərɪənt] *n* variante *f*
variation [vɛərɪ'eɪʃən] *n* variazione *f*;
(*in opinion*) cambiamento
varied ['vɛərɪd] *adj* vario(-a),
diverso(-a)
variety [və'raɪətɪ] *n* varietà *f inv*;
(*quantity*) quantità, numero
various ['vɛərɪəs] *adj* vario(-a),
diverso(-a); (*several*) parecchi(-e),
molti(-e)
varnish ['vɑːnɪʃ] *n* vernice *f*; (*nail
varnish*) smalto ▸ *vt* verniciare;
mettere lo smalto su
vary ['vɛərɪ] *vt, vi* variare, mutare
vase [vɑːz] *n* vaso
Vaseline® ['væsiliːn] *n* vaselina
vast [vɑːst] *adj* vasto(-a); (*amount,*

success) enorme

VAT [væt] *n abbr* (= *value added tax*) I.V.A. *f*

Vatican ['vætɪkən] *n* **the ~** ilVaticano

vault [vɔ:lt] *n* (*of roof*) volta; (*tomb*) tomba; (*in bank*) camera blindata ▶ *vt* (*also:* **~ over**) saltare (d'un balzo)

VCR *n abbr* = **video cassette recorder**

VDU *n abbr* = **visual display unit**

veal [vi:l] *n* vitello

veer [vɪəʳ] *vi* girare; virare

vegan ['vi:gən] *n* vegetaliano(-a)

vegetable ['vɛdʒtəbl] *n* verdura, ortaggio ▶ *adj* vegetale

vegetarian [vɛdʒɪ'tɛərɪən] *adj, n* vegetariano(-a); **do you have any ~ dishes?** avete piatti vegetariani?

vegetation [vɛdʒɪ'teɪʃən] *n* vegetazione *f*

vehicle ['vi:ɪkl] *n* veicolo

veil [veɪl] *n* velo

vein [veɪn] *n* vena; (*on leaf*) nervatura

Velcro® ['vɛlkrəu] *n* velcro® *m inv*

velvet ['vɛlvɪt] *n* velluto ▶ *adj* di velluto

vending machine ['vɛndɪŋ-] *n* distributore *m* automatico

vendor ['vɛndəʳ] *n* venditore(-trice)

vengeance ['vɛndʒəns] *n* vendetta; **with a ~** (*fig*) davvero; furiosamente

Venice ['vɛnɪs] *n* Venezia

venison ['vɛnɪsn] *n* carne *f* di cervo

venom ['vɛnəm] *n* veleno

vent [vɛnt] *n* foro, apertura; (*in dress, jacket*) spacco ▶ *vt* (*fig: one's feelings*) sfogare, dare sfogo a

ventilation [vɛntɪ'leɪʃən] *n* ventilazione *f*

venture ['vɛntʃəʳ] *n* impresa (rischiosa) ▶ *vt* rischiare, azzardare ▶ *vi* avventurarsi; **business ~** iniziativa commerciale

venue ['vɛnju:] *n* luogo (designato) per l'incontro

Venus ['vi:nəs] *n* (*planet*) Venere *m*

verb [və:b] *n* verbo; **verbal** *adj* verbale; (*translation*) orale

verdict ['və:dɪkt] *n* verdetto

verge [və:dʒ] (*BRIT*) *n* bordo, orlo; **"soft ~s"** (*BRIT: Aut*) banchine *fpl* cedevoli; **on the ~ of doing** sul punto di fare

verify ['vɛrɪfaɪ] *vt* verificare; (*prove the truth of*) confermare

versatile ['və:sətaɪl] *adj* (*person*) versatile; (*machine, tool etc*) (che si presta) a molti usi

verse [və:s] *n* versi *mpl*; (*stanza*) stanza, strofa; (*in bible*) versetto

version ['və:ʃən] *n* versione *f*

versus ['və:səs] *prep* contro

vertical ['və:tɪkl] *adj* verticale ▶ *n* verticale *m*

very ['vɛrɪ] *adv* molto ▶ *adj* **the ~ book which** proprio il libro che; **the ~ last** proprio l'ultimo; **at the ~ least** almeno; **~ much** moltissimo

vessel ['vɛsl] *n* (*Anat*) vaso; (*Naut*) nave *f*; (*container*) recipiente *m*

vest [vɛst] *n* (*BRIT*) maglia; (: *sleeveless*) canottiera; (*US: waistcoat*) gilè *m inv*

vet [vɛt] *n abbr* (*BRIT*: = *veterinary surgeon*) veterinario ▶ *vt* esaminare minuziosamente

veteran ['vɛtərn] *n* (*also:* **war ~**) veterano

veterinary surgeon ['vɛtrɪnərɪ-] (*US* **veterinarian**) *n* veterinario

veto ['vi:təu] (*pl* **vetoes**) *n* veto ▶ *vt* opporre il veto a

via ['vaɪə] *prep* (*by way of*) via; (*by means of*) tramite

viable ['vaɪəbl] *adj* attuabile; vitale

vibrate [vaɪ'breɪt] *vi* **to ~ (with)** vibrare (di); (*resound*) risonare (di)

vibration [vaɪ'breɪʃən] *n* vibrazione *f*

vicar ['vɪkəʳ] *n* pastore *m*

vice [vaɪs] *n* (*evil*) vizio; (*Tech*) morsa; **vice-chairman** (*irreg*) *n* vicepresidente *m*

vice versa ['vaɪsɪ'və:sə] *adv* viceversa

vicinity [vɪ'sɪnɪtɪ] *n* vicinanze *fpl*

V

vicious ['vɪʃəs] adj (remark, dog) cattivo(-a); (blow) violento(-a)

victim ['vɪktɪm] n vittima

victor ['vɪktər] n vincitore m

Victorian [vɪk'tɔːrɪən] adj vittoriano(-a)

victorious [vɪk'tɔːrɪəs] adj vittorioso(-a)

victory ['vɪktərɪ] n vittoria

video ['vɪdɪəu] cpd video... ▶ n (video film) video m inv; (also: ~ **cassette**) videocassetta; (also: ~ **cassette recorder**) videoregistratore m; **video camera** n videocamera; **video (cassette) recorder** n videoregistratore m; **video game** n videogioco; **videophone** n videotelefono; **video shop** n videonoleggio; **video tape** n videotape m inv; **video wall** n schermo m multivideo inv

vie [vaɪ] vi to ~ with competere con, rivaleggiare con

Vienna [vɪ'ɛnə] n Vienna

Vietnam [vjɛt'næm] n Vietnam m; **Vietnamese** adj, n inv vietnamita m/f

view [vjuː] n vista, veduta; (opinion) opinione f ▶ vt (look at: also fig) considerare; (house) visitare; **on ~** (in museum etc) esposto(-a); **in full ~ of** sotto gli occhi di; **in ~ of the weather/the fact that** considerato il tempo/che; **in my ~** a mio parere; **viewer** n spettatore(-trice); **viewpoint** n punto di vista; (place) posizione f

vigilant ['vɪdʒɪlənt] adj vigile

vigorous ['vɪgərəs] adj vigoroso(-a)

vile [vaɪl] adj (action) vile; (smell) disgustoso(-a), nauseante; (temper) pessimo(-a)

villa ['vɪlə] n villa

village ['vɪlɪdʒ] n villaggio; **villager** n abitante m/f di villaggio

villain ['vɪlən] n (scoundrel) canaglia; (BRIT: criminal) criminale m; (in novel etc) cattivo

vinaigrette [vɪneɪ'grɛt] n vinaigrette f inv

vine [vaɪn] n vite f

vinegar ['vɪnɪgər] n aceto

vineyard ['vɪnjɑːd] n vigna, vigneto

vintage ['vɪntɪdʒ] n (year) annata, produzione f ▶ cpd d'annata

vinyl ['vaɪnl] n vinile m

viola [vɪ'əulə] n viola

violate ['vaɪəleɪt] vt violare

violation [vaɪə'leɪʃən] n violazione f; **in ~ of sth** violando qc

violence ['vaɪələns] n violenza

violent ['vaɪələnt] adj violento(-a)

violet ['vaɪələt] adj (colour) viola inv, violetto(-a) ▶ n (plant) violetta; (colour) violetto

violin [vaɪə'lɪn] n violino

VIP n abbr (= very important person) V.I.P. m/f inv

virgin ['vəːdʒɪn] n vergine f ▶ adj vergine inv

Virgo ['vəːgəu] n (sign) Vergine f

virtual ['vəːtjuəl] adj effettivo(-a), vero(-a); (Comput, Physics) virtuale; (in effect): **it's a ~ impossibility** è praticamente impossibile; **the ~ leader** il capo all'atto pratico; **virtually** ['vəːtjuəlɪ] adv (almost) praticamente; **virtual reality** n (Comput) realtà virtuale

virtue ['vəːtjuː] n virtù f inv; (advantage) pregio, vantaggio; **by ~ of** grazie a

virus ['vaɪərəs] n (also Comput) virus m inv

visa ['viːzə] n visto

vise [vaɪs] (US) n (Tech) = **vice**

visibility [vɪzɪ'bɪlɪtɪ] n visibilità

visible ['vɪzəbl] adj visibile

vision ['vɪʒən] n (sight) vista; (foresight, in dream) visione f

visit ['vɪzɪt] n visita; (stay) soggiorno ▶ vt (person: US: also: ~ **with**) andare a trovare; (place) visitare; **visiting**

hours npl (in hospital etc) orario delle visite; **visitor** n visitatore(-trice); (guest) ospite m/f; **visitor centre** (US **visitor center**) n centro informazioni per visitatori di museo, zoo, parco ecc

visual ['vɪzjuəl] adj visivo(-a); visuale; ottico(-a); **visualize** ['vɪzjuəlaɪz] vt immaginare, figurarsi; (foresee) prevedere

vital ['vaɪtl] adj vitale

vitality [vaɪ'tælɪtɪ] n vitalità

vitamin ['vɪtəmɪn] n vitamina

vivid ['vɪvɪd] adj vivido(-a)

V-neck ['viːnɛk] n maglione m con lo scollo a V

vocabulary [vəu'kæbjulərɪ] n vocabolario

vocal ['vəukl] adj (Mus) vocale; (communication) verbale

vocational [vəu'keɪʃənl] adj professionale

vodka ['vɔdkə] n vodka f inv

vogue [vəug] n moda; (popularity) popolarità, voga

voice [vɔɪs] n voce f ▶ vt (opinion) esprimere; **voice mail** n servizio di segreteria telefonica

void [vɔɪd] n vuoto ▶ adj (invalid) nullo(-a); (empty): ~ **of** privo(-a) di

volatile ['vɔlətaɪl] adj volatile; (fig) volubile

volcano [vɔl'keɪnəu] (pl **volcanoes**) n vulcano

volleyball ['vɔlɪbɔːl] n pallavolo f

volt [vəult] n volt m inv; **voltage** n tensione f, voltaggio

volume ['vɔljuːm] n volume m

voluntarily ['vɔləntrɪlɪ] adv volontariamente; gratuitamente

voluntary ['vɔləntərɪ] adj volontario(-a); (unpaid) gratuito(-a), non retribuito(-a)

volunteer [vɔlən'tɪə^r] n volontario(-a) ▶ vt offrire volontariamente ▶ vi (Mil) arruolarsi volontario; **to ~ to do**

offrire (volontariamente) di fare

vomit ['vɔmɪt] n vomito ▶ vt, vi vomitare

vote [vəut] n voto, suffragio; (cast) voto; (franchise) diritto di voto ▶ vt **to be ~d chairman** etc venir eletto presidente etc; (propose): **to ~ that** approvare la proposta che ▶ vi votare; **~ of thanks** discorso di ringraziamento; **voter** n elettore(-trice); **voting** n scrutinio

voucher ['vautʃə^r] n (for meal, petrol etc) buono

vow [vau] n voto, promessa solenne ▶ vt **to ~ to do/that** giurare di fare/che

vowel ['vauəl] n vocale f

voyage ['vɔɪɪdʒ] n viaggio per mare, traversata

vulgar ['vʌlgə^r] adj volgare

vulnerable ['vʌlnərəbl] adj vulnerabile

vulture ['vʌltʃə^r] n avvoltoio

W

waddle ['wɔdl] vi camminare come una papera

wade [weɪd] vi **to ~ through** camminare a stento in; (fig: book) leggere con fatica

wafer ['weɪfə^r] n (Culin) cialda

waffle ['wɔfl] n (Culin) cialda; (inf)

ciance *fpl* ▶ *vi* cianciare

wag [wæg] *vt* agitare, muovere ▶ *vi* agitarsi

wage [weɪdʒ] *n* (*also*: **~s**) salario, paga ▶ *vt* **to ~ war** fare la guerra

wag(g)on ['wægən] *n* (*horse-drawn*) carro; (*BRIT: Rail*) vagone *m* (merci)

wail [weɪl] *n* gemito; (*of siren*) urlo ▶ *vi* gemere; urlare

waist [weɪst] *n* vita, cintola; **waistcoat** (*BRIT*) *n* panciotto, gilè *m inv*

wait [weɪt] *n* attesa ▶ *vi* aspettare, attendere; **to lie in ~ for** stare in agguato a; **to ~ for** aspettare; **~ for me, please** aspettami, per favore; **I can't ~ to** (*fig*) non vedo l'ora di ▷ **wait on** *vt fus* servire; **waiter** *n* cameriere *m*; **waiting list** *n* lista di attesa; **waiting room** *n* sala d'aspetto *or* d'attesa; **waitress** *n* cameriera

waive [weɪv] *vt* rinunciare a, abbandonare

wake [weɪk] (*pt* **woke, waked**, *pp* **woken, waked**) *vt* (*also*: **~ up**) svegliare ▶ *vi* (*also*: **~ up**) svegliarsi ▶ *n* (*for dead person*) veglia funebre; (*Naut*) scia

Wales [weɪlz] *n* Galles *m*

walk [wɔːk] *n* passeggiata; (*short*) giretto; (*gait*) passo, andatura; (*path*) sentiero; (*in park etc*) sentiero, vialetto ▶ *vi* camminare; (*for pleasure, exercise*) passeggiare ▶ *vt* (*distance*) fare *or* percorrere a piedi; (*dog*) accompagnare, portare a passeggiare; **10 minutes' ~ from** 10 minuti di cammino *or* a piedi da; **from all ~s of life** di tutte le condizioni sociali ▷ **walk out** *vi* (*audience*) andarsene; (*workers*) scendere in sciopero; **walker** *n* (*person*) camminatore(-trice); **walkie-talkie** ['wɔːkɪ'tɔːkɪ] *n* walkie-talkie *m inv*; **walking** *n* camminare

m; **walking shoes** *npl* pedule *fpl*; **walking stick** *n* bastone *m* da passeggio; **Walkman®** ['wɔːkmən] *n* Walkman® *m inv*; **walkway** *n* passaggio pedonale

wall [wɔːl] *n* muro; (*internal, of tunnel, cave*) parete *f*

wallet ['wɒlɪt] *n* portafoglio; **I can't find my ~** non trovo il portafoglio

wallpaper ['wɔːlpeɪpər] *n* carta da parati ▶ *vt* (*room*) mettere la carta da parati in

walnut ['wɔːlnʌt] *n* noce *f*; (*tree, wood*) noce *m*

walrus ['wɔːlrəs] (*pl* **walrus** *or* **walruses**) *n* tricheco

waltz [wɔːlts] *n* valzer *m inv* ▶ *vi* ballare il valzer

wand [wɒnd] *n* (*also*: **magic ~**) bacchetta (magica)

wander ['wɒndər] *vi* (*person*) girare senza meta, girovagare; (*thoughts*) vagare ▶ *vt* girovagare per

want [wɒnt] *vt* volere; (*need*) aver bisogno di ▶ *n* **for ~ of** per mancanza di; **wanted** *adj* (*criminal*) ricercato(-a); **"wanted"** (*in adverts*) "cercasi"

war [wɔːr] *n* guerra; **to make ~ (on)** far guerra (a)

ward [wɔːd] *n* (*in hospital: room*) corsia; (*: section*) reparto; (*Pol*) circoscrizione *f*; (*Law: child: also*: **~ of court**) pupillo(-a)

warden ['wɔːdn] *n* (*of park, game reserve, youth hostel*) guardiano(-a); (*BRIT: of institution*) direttore(-trice); (*BRIT: also*: **traffic ~**) addetto(-a) al controllo del traffico e del parcheggio

wardrobe ['wɔːdrəub] *n* (*cupboard*) guardaroba *m inv*, armadio; (*clothes*) guardaroba; (*Cinema, Theatre*) costumi *mpl*

warehouse ['wɛəhaus] *n* magazzino

warfare ['wɔːfɛər] *n* guerra

warhead ['wɔːhɛd] *n* (*Mil*) testata

warm [wɔːm] *adj* caldo(-a); (*thanks, welcome, applause*) caloroso(-a); (*person*) cordiale; **it's ~** fa caldo; **I'm ~** ho caldo ▷ **warm up** *vi* scaldarsi, riscaldarsi ▶ *vt* scaldare, riscaldare; (*engine*) far scaldare; **warmly** *adv* (*applaud, welcome*) calorosamente; (*dress*) con abiti pesanti; **warmth** *n* calore *m*

warn [wɔːn] *vt* **to ~ sb that/(not) to do/of** avvertire *or* avvisare qn che/di (non) fare/di; **warning** *n* avvertimento; (*notice*) avviso; (*signal*) segnalazione *f*; **warning light** *n* spia luminosa

warrant ['wɔrnt] *n* (*voucher*) buono; (*Law: to arrest*) mandato di cattura; (*: to search*) mandato di perquisizione

warranty ['wɔrəntɪ] *n* garanzia

warrior ['wɔrɪəʳ] *n* guerriero(-a)

Warsaw ['wɔːsɔː] *n* Varsavia

warship ['wɔːʃɪp] *n* nave *f* da guerra

wart [wɔːt] *n* verruca

wartime ['wɔːtaɪm] *n* **in ~** in tempo di guerra

wary ['wɛərɪ] *adj* prudente

was [wɔz] *pt of* **be**

wash [wɔʃ] *vt* lavare ▶ *vi* lavarsi; (*sea*): **to ~ over/against sth** infrangersi su/contro qc ▶ *n* lavaggio; (*of ship*) scia; **to give sth a ~** lavare qc, dare una lavata a qc; **to have a ~** lavarsi ▷ **wash up** *vi* (*BRIT*) lavare i piatti; (*US*) darsi una lavata; **washbasin** (*US* **washbowl**) *n* lavabo; **wash cloth** (*US*) *n* pezzuola (per lavarsi); **washer** *n* (*Tech*) rondella; **washing** *n* (*linen etc*) bucato; **washing line** *n* (*BRIT*) corda del bucato; **washing machine** *n* lavatrice *f*; **washing powder** (*BRIT*) *n* detersivo (in polvere)

Washington ['wɔʃɪŋtən] *n* Washington *f*

wash: **washing-up** *n* rigovernatura, lavatura dei piatti; **washing-up**

liquid *n* detersivo liquido (per stoviglie); **washroom** *n* gabinetto

wasn't ['wɔznt] = **was not**

wasp [wɔsp] *n* vespa

waste [weɪst] *n* spreco; (*of time*) perdita; (*rubbish*) rifiuti *mpl*; (*also:* **household ~**) immondizie *fpl* ▶ *adj* (*material*) di scarto; (*food*) avanzato(-a); (*land*) incolto(-a) ▶ *vt* sprecare; **waste ground** (*BRIT*) *n* terreno incolto *or* abbandonato; **wastepaper basket** ['weɪstpeɪpə-] *n* cestino per la carta straccia

watch [wɔtʃ] *n* (*also:* **wrist ~**) orologio (da polso); (*act of watching, vigilance*) sorveglianza; (*guard: Mil, Naut*) guardia; (*Naut: spell of duty*) quarto ▶ *vt* (*look at*) osservare; (*: match, programme*) guardare; (*spy on, guard*) sorvegliare, tenere d'occhio; (*be careful of*) fare attenzione a ▶ *vi* osservare, guardare; (*keep guard*) fare *or* montare la guardia ▷ **watch out** *vi* fare attenzione; **watchdog** *n* (*also fig*) cane *m* da guardia; **watch strap** *n* cinturino da orologio

water ['wɔːtəʳ] *n* acqua ▶ *vt* (*plant*) annaffiare ▶ *vi* (*eyes*) lacrimare; (*mouth*): **to make sb's mouth ~** far venire l'acquolina in bocca a qn; **in British ~s** nelle acque territoriali britanniche ▷ **water down** *vt* (*milk*) diluire; (*fig: story*) edulcorare; **watercolour** (*US* **watercolor**) *n* acquerello; **watercress** *n* crescione *m*; **waterfall** *n* cascata; **watering can** *n* annaffiatoio; **watermelon** *n* anguria, cocomero; **waterproof** *adj* impermeabile; **water-skiing** *n* sci *m* acquatico

watt [wɔt] *n* watt *m inv*

wave [weɪv] *n* onda; (*of hand*) gesto, segno; (*in hair*) ondulazione *f*; (*fig: surge*) ondata ▶ *vi* fare un cenno con la mano; (*branches, grass*) ondeggiare;

(*flag*) sventolare ▶ *vt* (*hand*) fare un gesto con; (*handkerchief*) sventolare; (*stick*) brandire; **wavelength** *n* lunghezza d'onda

waver ['weɪvə'] *vi* esitare; (*voice*) tremolare

wavy ['weɪvɪ] *adj* ondulato(-a); ondeggiante

wax [wæks] *n* cera ▶ *vt* dare la cera a; (*car*) lucidare ▶ *vi* (*moon*) crescere

way [weɪ] *n* via, strada; (*path, access*) passaggio *m*; (*distance*) distanza; (*direction*) parte *f*, direzione *f*; (*manner*) modo, stile *m*; (*habit*) abitudine *f*; **which ~? — this ~** da che parte *or* in quale direzione? — da questa parte *or* per di qua; **on the ~** (*en route*) per strada; **to be on one's ~** essere in cammino *or* sulla strada; **to be in the ~** bloccare il passaggio; (*fig*) essere tra i piedi *or* d'impiccio; **to go out of one's ~ to do** (*fig*) mettercela tutta *or* fare di tutto per fare; **under ~** (*project*) in corso; **to lose one's ~** perdere la strada; **in a ~** in un certo senso; **in some ~s** sotto certi aspetti; **no ~!** (*inf*) neanche per idea!; **by the ~ ...** a proposito ...; **"~ in"** (*BRIT*) "entrata", "ingresso"; **"~ out"** (*BRIT*) "uscita"; **the ~ back** la strada del ritorno; **"give ~"** (*BRIT: Aut*) "dare la precedenza"

W.C. ['dʌblju:'si:] (*BRIT*) *n* W.C. *m inv*, gabinetto

we [wi:] *pl pron* noi

weak [wi:k] *adj* debole; (*health*) precario(-a); (*beam etc*) fragile; (*tea*) leggero(-a); **weaken** *vi* indebolirsi ▶ *vt* indebolire; **weakness** *n* debolezza; (*fault*) punto debole, difetto; **to have a weakness for** avere un debole per

wealth [wɛlθ] *n* (*money, resources*) ricchezza, ricchezze *fpl*; (*of details*) abbondanza, profusione *f*; **wealthy** *adj* ricco(-a)

weapon ['wɛpən] *n* arma; **~s of mass destruction** armi *mpl* di distruzione di massa

wear [wɛə'] (*pt* **wore**, *pp* **worn**) *n* (*use*) uso; (*damage through use*) logorio, usura; (*clothing*): **sports/baby ~** abbigliamento sportivo/per neonati ▶ *vt* (*clothes*) portare; (*put on*) mettersi; (*damage: through use*) consumare ▶ *vi* (*last*) durare; (*rub etc through*) consumarsi; **evening ~** abiti *mpl* *or* tenuta da sera ▷ **wear off** *vi* sparire lentamente ▷ **wear out** *vt* consumare; (*person, strength*) esaurire

weary ['wɪərɪ] *adj* stanco(-a) ▶ *vi* **to ~ of** stancarsi di

weasel ['wi:zl] *n* (*Zool*) donnola

weather ['wɛðə'] *n* tempo ▶ *vt* (*storm, crisis*) superare; **What's the ~ like?** che tempo fa?; **under the ~** (*fig: ill*) poco bene; **weather forecast** *n* previsioni *fpl* del tempo

weave [wi:v] (*pt* **wove**, *pp* **woven**) *vt* (*cloth*) tessere; (*basket*) intrecciare

web [wɛb] *n* (*of spider*) ragnatela; (*on foot*) palma; (*fabric, also fig*) tessuto; **the (World Wide) W~** la Rete; **webcam** *n* webcam *f inv*; **web page** *n* (*Comput*) pagina *f* web *inv*; **website** *n* (*Comput*) sito (Internet)

wed [wɛd] (*pt*, *pp* **wedded**) *vt* sposare ▶ *vi* sposarsi

we'd [wi:d] = **we had**; **we would**

Wed. *abbr* (= *Wednesday*) mer.

wedding ['wɛdɪŋ] *n* matrimonio; **wedding anniversary** *n* anniversario di matrimonio; **wedding day** *n* giorno delle nozze *or* del matrimonio; **wedding dress** *n* abito nuziale; **wedding ring** *n* fede *f*

wedge [wɛdʒ] *n* (*of wood etc*) zeppa; (*of cake*) fetta ▶ *vt* (*fix*) fissare con zeppe; (*pack tightly*) incastrare

Wednesday ['wɛdnzdɪ] *n* mercoledì *m inv*

wee [wi:] (*SCOTTISH*) *adj* piccolo(-a)

weed [wiːd] n erbaccia ▶ vt diserbare; **weedkiller** n diserbante m

week [wiːk] n settimana; **a ~ today/on Friday** oggi/venerdì a otto; **weekday** n giorno feriale; (Comm) giornata lavorativa; **weekend** n fine settimana m or f inv, weekend m inv; **weekly** adv ogni settimana, settimanalmente ▶ adj settimanale ▶ n settimanale m

weep [wiːp] (pt, pp **wept**) vi (person) piangere

weigh [weɪ] vt, vi pesare; **to ~ anchor** salpare l'ancora ▷ **weigh up** vt valutare

weight [weɪt] n peso; **to lose/put on ~** dimagrire/ingrassare; **weightlifting** n sollevamento pesi

weir [wɪər] n diga

weird [wɪəd] adj strano(-a), bizzarro(-a); (eerie) soprannaturale

welcome ['wɛlkəm] adj benvenuto(-a) ▶ n accoglienza, benvenuto ▶ vt dare il benvenuto a; (be glad of) rallegrarsi di; **thank you — you're ~!** grazie — prego!

weld [wɛld] n saldatura ▶ vt saldare

welfare ['wɛlfɛər] n benessere m; **welfare state** n stato assistenziale

well [wɛl] n pozzo ▶ adv bene ▶ adj **to be ~** (person) stare bene ▶ excl allora!; ma!; ebbene!; **as ~** anche; **as ~ as** così come; oltre a; **~ done!** bravo(-a)!; **get ~ soon!** guarisci presto!; **to do ~** andare bene

we'll [wiːl] = we will; we shall

well: **well-behaved** adj ubbidiente; **well-built** adj (person) ben fatto(-a); **well-dressed** adj ben vestito(-a), vestito(-a) bene

wellies ['wɛlɪz] (inf) npl (BRIT) stivali mpl di gomma

well: **well-known** adj noto(-a), famoso(-a); **well-off** adj benestante, danaroso(-a); **well-paid** [wɛl'peɪd] adj ben pagato(-a)

Welsh [wɛlʃ] adj gallese ▶ n (Ling) gallese m; **Welshman** (irreg) n gallese m; **Welshwoman** (irreg) n gallese f

went [wɛnt] pt of go

wept [wɛpt] pt, pp of weep

were [wəːr] pt of be

we're [wɪər] = we are

weren't [wəːnt] = were not

west [wɛst] n ovest m, occidente m, ponente m ▶ adj (a) ovest inv, occidentale ▶ adv verso ovest; **the W~** l'Occidente m; **westbound** ['wɛstbaʊnd] adj (traffic) diretto(-a) a ovest; (carriageway) ovest inv; **western** adj occidentale, dell'ovest ▶ n (Cinema) western m inv; **West Indian** adj delle Indie Occidentali ▶ n abitante m/f delle Indie Occidentali; **West Indies** [-'ɪndɪz] npl Indie fpl Occidentali

wet [wɛt] adj umido(-a), bagnato(-a); (soaked) fradicio(-a); (rainy) piovoso(-a) ▶ n (BRIT: Pol) politico moderato; **to get ~** bagnarsi; **"~ paint"** "vernice fresca"; **wetsuit** n tuta da sub

we've [wiːv] = we have

whack [wæk] vt picchiare, battere

whale [weɪl] n (Zool) balena

wharf [wɔːf] (pl **wharves**) n banchina

○ **what**
[wɒt] adj

1 (in direct/indirect questions) che; quale; **what size is it?** che taglia è?; **what colour is it?** di che colore è?; **what books do you want?** quali or che libri vuole?

2 (in exclamations) che; **what a mess!** che disordine!

▶ pron

1 (interrogative) che cosa, cosa, che; **what are you doing?** che or (che) cosa fai?; **what are you talking about?** di che cosa parli?; **what is it called?** come si chiama?; **what about me?**

w

e io?; **what about doing ...?** e se facessimo ...?

2 (*relative*) ciò che, quello che; **I saw what you did/was on the table** ho visto quello che hai fatto/quello che era sul tavolo

3 (*indirect use*) (che) cosa; **he asked me what she had said** mi ha chiesto che cosa avesse detto; **tell me what you're thinking about** dimmi a cosa stai pensando

▸*excl* (*disbelieving*) cosa!, come!

whatever [wɔt'ɛvə] *adj* ~ **book** qualunque *or* qualsiasi libro + *sub* ▸ *pron* **do ~ is necessary/you want** faccia qualunque *or* qualsiasi cosa sia necessaria/lei voglia; ~ **happens** qualunque cosa accada; **no reason ~** *or* **whatsoever** nessuna ragione affatto *or* al mondo; **nothing ~** proprio niente

whatsoever [wɔtsəu'ɛvə] *adj* = **whatever**

wheat [wiːt] *n* grano, frumento

wheel [wiːl] *n* ruota; (*Aut: also:* **steering ~**) volante *m*; (*Naut*) (ruota del) timone *m* ▸ *vt* spingere ▸ *vi* (*birds*) roteare; (*also:* ~ **round**) girare; **wheelbarrow** *n* carriola; **wheelchair** *n* sedia a rotelle; **wheel clamp** *n* (*Aut*) morsa che blocca la ruota di una vettura in sosta vietata

wheeze [wiːz] *vi* ansimare

when
[wɛn] *adv* quando; **when did it happen?** quando è successo?
▸*conj*
1 (*at, during, after the time that*) quando; **she was reading when I came in** quando sono entrato lei leggeva; **that was when I needed you** era allora che avevo bisogno di te
2 (*on, at which*): **on the day when I met him** il giorno in cui l'ho incontrato; **one day when it was raining** un giorno che pioveva
3 (*whereas*) quando, mentre; **you said I was wrong when in fact I was right** mi hai detto che avevo torto, quando in realtà avevo ragione

whenever [wɛn'ɛvə] *adv* quando mai ▸ *conj* quando; (*every time that*) ogni volta che

where [wɛər] *adv*, *conj* dove; **this is ~** è qui che; **whereabouts** *adv* dove ▸ *n* **sb's whereabouts** luogo dove qn si trova; **whereas** *conj* mentre; **whereby** *pron* per cui; **wherever** [-'ɛvər] *conj* dovunque + *sub*; (*interrogative*) dove mai

whether ['wɛðər] *conj* se; **I don't know ~ to accept or not** non so se accettare o no; **it's doubtful ~** è poco probabile che; ~ **you go or not** che lei vada o no

which
[wɪtʃ] *adj*
1 (*interrogative: direct, indirect*) quale; **which picture do you want?** quale quadro vuole?; **which one?** quale?; **which one of you did it?** chi di voi lo ha fatto?
2: **in which case** nel qual caso
▸*pron*
1 (*interrogative*) quale; **which (of these) are yours?** quali di questi sono suoi?; **which of you are coming?** chi di voi viene?
2 (*relative*) che; (: *indirect*) cui, il (la) quale; **the apple which you ate/which is on the table** la mela che hai mangiato/che è sul tavolo; **the chair on which you are sitting** la sedia sulla quale *or* su cui sei seduto; **he said he knew, which is true** ha detto che lo sapeva, il che è vero; **after which** dopo di che

whichever [wɪtʃ'ɛvə] *adj* **take ~ book you prefer** prenda qualsiasi libro che preferisce; ~ **book you take** qualsiasi libro prenda

while [waɪl] n momento ▶ conj
mentre; (as long as) finché; (although)
sebbene + sub; per quanto + sub; **for a
~** per un po'

whilst [waɪlst] conj = **while**

whim [wɪm] n capriccio

whine [waɪn] n gemito ▶ vi gemere;
uggiolare; piagnucolare

whip [wɪp] n frusta; (for riding)
frustino; (Pol: person) capogruppo (che
sovrintende alla disciplina dei colleghi
di partito) ▶ vt frustare; (cream, eggs)
sbattere; **whipped cream** n panna
montata

whirl [wəːl] vt (far) girare
rapidamente, (far) turbinare ▶ vi
(dancers) volteggiare; (leaves, water)
sollevarsi in vortice

whisk [wɪsk] n (Culin) frusta; frullino
▶ vt sbattere, frullare; **to ~ sb away** or
off portar via qn a tutta velocità

whiskers ['wɪskəz] npl (of animal) baffi
mpl; (of man) favoriti mpl

whisky ['wɪskɪ] (US, Ireland **whiskey**)
n whisky m inv

whisper ['wɪspəʳ] n sussurro ▶ vt, vi
sussurrare

whistle ['wɪsl] n (sound) fischio;
(object) fischietto ▶ vi fischiare

white [waɪt] adj bianco(-a); (with
fear) pallido(-a) ▶ n bianco; (person)
bianco(-a); **White House** n Casa
Bianca; **whitewash** n (paint) bianco
di calce ▶ vt imbiancare; (fig) coprire

whiting ['waɪtɪŋ] n inv (fish) merlango

Whitsun ['wɪtsn] n Pentecoste f

whittle ['wɪtl] vt **to ~ away**, **~ down**
ridurre, tagliare

whizz [wɪz] vi **to ~ past** or **by** passare
sfrecciando

⊙ **who**
  [huː] pron

1 (interrogative) chi; **who is it?**, **who's
there?** chi è?

2 (relative) che; **the man who spoke**

to me l'uomo che ha parlato con me;
those who can swim quelli che sanno
nuotare

whoever [huːˈɛvə] pron **~ finds it**
chiunque lo trovi; **ask ~ you like**
lo chieda a chiunque vuole; **~ she
marries** chiunque sposerà, non
importa chi sposerà; **~ told you that?**
chi mai gliel'ha detto?

whole [həul] adj (complete) tutto(-a),
completo(-a); (not broken) intero(-a),
intatto(-a) ▶ n (all): **the ~ of** tutto(-a)
il (la); (entire unit) tutto; (not broken)
tutto; **the ~ of the town** tutta la
città, la città intera; **on the ~, as
a ~** nel complesso, nell'insieme;
wholefood(s) n(pl) cibo integrale;
wholeheartedly [həulˈhɑːtɪdlɪ]
adv sentitamente, di tutto cuore;
wholemeal adj (bread, flour) integrale;
wholesale n commercio or vendita
all'ingrosso ▶ adj all'ingrosso;
(destruction) totale; **wholewheat**
adj = **wholemeal**; **wholly** adv
completamente, del tutto

⊙ **whom**
  [huːm] pron

1 (interrogative) chi; **whom did you
see?** chi hai visto?; **to whom did you
give it?** a chi lo hai dato?

2 (relative) che, prep + il (la) quale (check
syntax of Italian verb used); **the man
whom I saw/to whom I spoke** l'uomo
che ho visto/al quale ho parlato

whore [hɔː] (inf: pej) n puttana

⊙ **whose**
  [huːz] adj

1 (possessive: interrogative) di chi;
whose book is this?, **whose is this
book?** di chi è questo libro?; **whose
daughter are you?** di chi sei figlia?

2 (possessive: relative): **the man whose
son you rescued** l'uomo il cui figlio
hai salvato; **the girl whose sister you
were speaking to** la ragazza alla cui

w

sorella stavi parlando
▶*pron* di chi; **whose is this?** di chi è
questo?; **I know whose it is** so di chi è

◯ **why**
[waɪ] *adv* perché; **why not?**
perché no?; **why not do it now?** perché
non farlo adesso?
▶*conj* **I wonder why he said that** mi
chiedo perché l'abbia detto; **that's not
why I'm here** non è questo il motivo
per cui sono qui; **the reason why** il
motivo per cui
▶*excl* (*surprise*) ma guarda un po'!;
(*remonstrating*) ma (via)!; (*explaining*)
ebbene!

wicked ['wɪkɪd] *adj* cattivo(-a),
malvagio(-a); maligno(-a); perfido(-a)
wicket ['wɪkɪt] *n* (*Cricket*) porta
wide [waɪd] *adj* largo(-a); (*area,
knowledge*) vasto(-a); (*choice*)
ampio(-a) ▶ *adv* **to open ~** spalancare;
to shoot ~ tirare a vuoto *or* fuori
bersaglio; **widely** *adv* (*differing*) molto,
completamente; (*travelled, spaced*)
molto; (*believed*) generalmente;
widen *vt* allargare, ampliare; **wide
open** *adj* spalancato(-a); **widescreen
TV** *n* TV a schermo panoramico;
widespread *adj* (*belief etc*) molto *or*
assai diffuso(-a)
widow ['wɪdəu] *n* vedova; **widower**
n vedovo
width [wɪdθ] *n* larghezza
wield [wiːld] *vt* (*sword*) maneggiare;
(*power*) esercitare
wife [waɪf] (*pl* **wives**) *n* moglie *f*
Wi-Fi ['waɪfaɪ] *n* Wi-Fi *m*
wig [wɪg] *n* parrucca
wild [waɪld] *adj* selvatico(-a);
selvaggio(-a); (*sea, weather*)
tempestoso(-a); (*idea, life*) folle;
stravagante; (*applause*) frenetico(-a);
wilderness ['wɪldənɪs] *n* deserto;
wildlife *n* natura; **wildly** *adv*
selvaggiamente; (*applaud*)

freneticamente; (*hit, guess*) a
casaccio; (*happy*) follemente

◯ **will**
[wɪl] (*pt, pp* **willed**) *aux vb*
1 (*forming future tense*): **I will finish it
tomorrow** lo finirò domani; **I will have
finished it by tomorrow** lo finirò entro
domani; **will you do it? — yes I will/no
I won't** lo farai? — sì (lo farò)/no (non
lo farò)
2 (*in conjectures, predictions*): **he will** *or*
he'll be there by now dovrebbe essere
arrivato ora; **that will be the postman**
sarà il postino
3 (*in commands, requests, offers*): **will
you be quiet!** vuoi stare zitto?; **will you
help me?** mi aiuti?, mi puoi aiutare?;
will you have a cup of tea? vorrebbe
una tazza di tè?; **I won't put up with it!**
non lo accetterò!
▶*vt* **to will sb to do** volere che qn faccia;
he willed himself to go on continuò
grazie a un grande sforzo di volontà
▶*n* volontà; testamento
willing ['wɪlɪŋ] *adj* volenteroso(-a); **~
to do** disposto(-a) a fare; **willingly**
adv volentieri
willow ['wɪləu] *n* salice *m*
willpower ['wɪlpauəʳ] *n* forza di
volontà
wilt [wɪlt] *vi* appassire
win [wɪn] (*pt, pp* **won**) *n* (*in sports
etc*) vittoria ▶ *vt* (*battle, prize, money*)
vincere; (*popularity*) conquistare ▶ *vi*
vincere ▷ **win over** *vt* convincere
wince [wɪns] *vi* trasalire
wind¹ [waɪnd] (*pt, pp* **wound**) *vt*
attorcigliare; (*wrap*) avvolgere;
(*clock, toy*) caricare ▶ *vi* (*road, river*)
serpeggiare ▷ **wind down** *vt* (*car
window*) abbassare; (*fig: production,
business*) diminuire ▷ **wind up** *vt*
(*clock*) caricare; (*debate*) concludere
wind² [wɪnd] *n* vento; (*Med*)
flatulenza; (*breath*) respiro, fiato ▶ *vt*

(*take breath away*) far restare senza fiato; **~ power** energia eolica
windfall ['wɪndfɔ:l] *n* (*money*) guadagno insperato
wind farm *n* centrale *f* eolica
winding ['waɪndɪŋ] *adj* (*road*) serpeggiante; (*staircase*) a chiocciola
windmill ['wɪndmɪl] *n* mulino a vento
window ['wɪndəu] *n* finestra; (*in car, train, plane*) finestrino; (*in shop etc*) vetrina; (*also:* **~ pane**) vetro; **I'd like a ~ seat** vorrei un posto vicino al finestrino; **window box** *n* cassetta da fiori; **window cleaner** *n* (*person*) pulitore *m* di finestre; **window pane** *n* vetro; **window seat** *n* posto finestrino; **windowsill** *n* davanzale *m*
windscreen ['wɪndskri:n] (*US* **windshield**) *n* parabrezza *m inv*; **windscreen wiper** (*US* **windshield wiper**) *n* tergicristallo
windsurfing ['wɪndsə:fɪŋ] *n* windsurf *m inv*
windy ['wɪndɪ] *adj* ventoso(-a); **it's ~** c'è vento
wine [waɪn] *n* vino; **wine bar** *n* enoteca; **wine glass** *n* bicchiere *m* da vino; **wine list** *n* lista dei vini; **wine tasting** *n* degustazione *f* dei vini
wing [wɪŋ] *n* ala; (*Aut*) fiancata; **wing mirror** *n* (*BRIT*) specchietto retrovisore esterno
wink [wɪŋk] *n* ammiccamento ▶ *vi* ammiccare, fare l'occhiolino; (*light*) baluginare
winner ['wɪnə'] *n* vincitore(-trice)
winning ['wɪnɪŋ] *adj* (*team, goal*) vincente; (*smile*) affascinante
winter ['wɪntə'] *n* inverno; **winter sports** *npl* sport *mpl* invernali; **wintertime** *n* inverno, stagione *f* invernale
wipe [waɪp] *n* pulita, passata ▶ *vt* pulire (strofinando); (*erase: tape*) cancellare ▷ **wipe out** *vt*

(*debt*) pagare, liquidare; (*memory*) cancellare; (*destroy*) annientare
▷ **wipe up** *vt* asciugare
wire ['waɪə'] *n* filo; (*Elec*) filo elettrico; (*Tel*) telegramma *m* ▶ *vt* (*house*) fare l'impianto elettrico di; (*also:* **~ up**) collegare, allacciare; (*person*) telegrafare a
wiring ['waɪərɪŋ] *n* impianto elettrico
wisdom ['wɪzdəm] *n* saggezza; (*of action*) prudenza; **wisdom tooth** *n* dente *m* del giudizio
wise [waɪz] *adj* saggio(-a); prudente; giudizioso(-a)
wish [wɪʃ] *n* (*desire*) desiderio; (*specific desire*) richiesta ▶ *vt* desiderare, volere; **best ~es** (*on birthday etc*) i migliori auguri; **with best ~es** (*in letter*) cordiali saluti, con i migliori saluti; **to ~ sb goodbye** dire arrivederci a qn; **he ~ed me well** mi augurò di riuscire; **to ~ to do/sb to do** desiderare *or* volere fare/che qn faccia; **to ~ for** desiderare
wistful ['wɪstful] *adj* malinconico(-a)
wit [wɪt] *n* (*also:* **~s**) intelligenza; presenza di spirito; (*wittiness*) spirito, arguzia; (*person*) bello spirito
witch [wɪtʃ] *n* strega

with
[wɪð, wɪθ] *prep*
1 (*in the company of*) con; **I was with him** ero con lui; **we stayed with friends** siamo stati da amici; **I'll be with you in a minute** vengo subito
2 (*descriptive*) con; **a room with a view** una stanza con vista sul mare (*or* sulle montagne *etc*); **the man with the grey hat/blue eyes** l'uomo con il cappello grigio/gli occhi blu
3 (*indicating manner, means, cause*): **with tears in her eyes** con le lacrime agli occhi; **red with anger** rosso dalla rabbia; **to shake with fear** tremare di paura

W

4: **I'm with you** (*I understand*) la seguo; **to be with it** (*inf: up-to-date*) essere alla moda; (: *alert*) essere sveglio(-a)

withdraw [wɪθ'drɔː] (*irreg: like draw*) *vt* ritirare; (*money from bank*) ritirare; prelevare ▶ *vi* ritirarsi; **withdrawal** *n* ritiro; prelievo; (*of army*) ritirata; **withdrawal symptoms** *n* (*Med*) crisi *f* di astinenza; **withdrawn** *adj* (*person*) distaccato(-a)

withdrew [wɪθ'druː] *pt of* **withdraw**

wither ['wɪðəʳ] *vi* appassire

withhold [wɪθ'həuld] (*irreg: like hold*) *vt* (*money*) trattenere; (*permission*): **to ~ (from)** rifiutare (a); (*information*): **to ~ (from)** nascondere (a)

within [wɪð'ɪn] *prep* all'interno; (*in time, distances*) entro ▶ *adv* all'interno, dentro; **~ reach (of)** alla portata (di); **~ sight (of)** in vista (di); **~ a mile of** entro un miglio da; **~ the week** prima della fine della settimana

without [wɪð'aut] *prep* senza; **to go ~ sth** fare a meno di qc

withstand [wɪθ'stænd] (*irreg: like stand*) *vt* resistere a

witness ['wɪtnɪs] *n* (*person, also Law*) testimone *m/f* ▶ *vt* (*event*) essere testimone di; (*document*) attestare l'autenticità di

witty ['wɪtɪ] *adj* spiritoso(-a)

wives [waɪvz] *npl of* **wife**

wizard ['wɪzəd] *n* mago

wk *abbr* = **week**

wobble ['wɔbl] *vi* tremare; (*chair*) traballare

woe [wəu] *n* dolore *m*; disgrazia

woke [wəuk] *pt of* **wake**

woken ['wəukn] *pp of* **wake**

wolf [wulf] (*pl* **wolves**) *n* lupo

woman ['wumən] (*pl* **women**) *n* donna

womb [wuːm] *n* (*Anat*) utero

women ['wɪmɪn] *npl of* **woman**

won [wʌn] *pt, pp of* **win**

wonder ['wʌndəʳ] *n* meraviglia ▶ *vi* **to ~ whether/why** domandarsi se/perché; **to ~ at** essere sorpreso(-a) di; meravigliarsi di; **to ~ about** domandarsi di; pensare a; **it's no ~ that** c'è poco or non c'è da meravigliarsi che + *sub*; **wonderful** *adj* meraviglioso(-a)

won't [wəunt] = **will not**

wood [wud] *n* legno; (*timber*) legname *m*; (*forest*) bosco; **wooden** *adj* di legno; (*fig*) rigido(-a); inespressivo(-a); **woodwind** *npl* (*Mus*): **the woodwind** i legni; **woodwork** *n* (*craft, subject*) falegnameria

wool [wul] *n* lana; **to pull the ~ over sb's eyes** (*fig*) imbrogliare qn; **woollen** (*US* **woolen**) *adj* di lana; (*industry*) laniero(-a); **woolly** (*US* **wooly**) *adj* di lana; (*fig: ideas*) confuso(-a)

word [wəːd] *n* parola; (*news*) notizie *fpl* ▶ *vt* esprimere, formulare; **in other ~s** in altre parole; **to break/keep one's ~** non mantenere/mantenere la propria parola; **to have ~s with sb** avere un diverbio con qn; **wording** *n* formulazione *f*; **word processing** *n* elaborazione *f* di testi, word processing *m*; **word processor** *n* word processor *m inv*

wore [wɔːʳ] *pt of* **wear**

work [wəːk] *n* lavoro; (*Art, Literature*) opera ▶ *vi* lavorare; (*mechanism, plan etc*) funzionare; (*medicine*) essere efficace ▶ *vt* (*clay, wood etc*) lavorare; (*mine etc*) sfruttare; (*machine*) far funzionare; (*cause: effect, miracle*) fare; **to be out of ~** essere disoccupato(-a); **~s** *n* (*BRIT: factory*) fabbrica *npl* (*of clock, machine*) meccanismo; **how does this ~?** come funziona?; **the TV isn't ~ing** la TV non funziona; **to ~ loose** allentarsi ▷ **work out** *vi* (*plans etc*) riuscire, andare bene ▶ *vt* (*problem*) risolvere; (*plan*) elaborare; **it ~s out at £100** fa 100 sterline; **worker** n lavoratore(-trice), operaio(-a); **work experience** n (*previous jobs*) esperienze fpl lavorative; (*student training placement*) tirocinio; **workforce** n forza lavoro; **working class** n classe f operaia; **working week** n settimana lavorativa; **workman** (*irreg*) n operaio; **work of art** n opera d'arte; **workout** n (*Sport*) allenamento; **work permit** n permesso di lavoro; **workplace** n posto di lavoro; **workshop** n officina; (*practical session*) gruppo di lavoro; **work station** n stazione f da lavoro; **work surface** n piano di lavoro; **worktop** n piano di lavoro

world [wə:ld] n mondo ▶ cpd (*champion*) del mondo; (*power, war*) mondiale; **to think the ~ of sb** (*fig*) pensare un gran bene di qn; **World Cup** n (*Football*) Coppa del Mondo; **world-wide** adj universale; **World-Wide Web** n World Wide Web m

worm [wə:m] n (*also:* **earth~**) verme m

worn [wɔ:n] pp of **wear** ▶ adj usato(-a); **worn-out** adj (*object*) consumato(-a), logoro(-a); (*person*) sfinito(-a)

worried ['wʌrɪd] adj preoccupato(-a)

worry ['wʌrɪ] n preoccupazione f ▶ vt preoccupare ▶ vi preoccuparsi; **worrying** adj preoccupante

worse [wə:s] adj peggiore ▶ adv, n peggio; **a change for the ~** un peggioramento; **worsen** vt, vi peggiorare; **worse off** adj in condizioni (economiche) peggiori

worship ['wə:ʃɪp] n culto ▶ vt (*God*) adorare, venerare; (*person*) adorare; **Your W~** (*BRIT: to mayor*) signor sindaco; (: *to judge*) signor giudice

worst [wə:st] adj il (la) peggiore ▶ adv, n peggio; **at ~** al peggio, per male che vada

worth [wə:θ] n valore m ▶ adj **to be ~** valere; **it's ~ it** ne vale la pena; **it is ~ one's while (to do)** vale la pena (fare); **worthless** adj di nessun valore; **worthwhile** adj (*activity*) utile; (*cause*) lodevole

worthy ['wə:ðɪ] adj (*person*) degno(-a); (*motive*) lodevole; **~ of** degno di

⊙ **would**
[wʊd] aux vb

1 (*conditional tense*): **if you asked him he would do it** se glielo chiedesse lo farebbe; **if you had asked him he would have done it** se glielo avesse chiesto lo avrebbe fatto

2 (*in offers, invitations, requests*): **would you like a biscuit?** vorrebbe or vuole un biscotto?; **would you ask him to come in?** lo faccia entrare, per cortesia; **would you open the window please?** apra la finestra, per favore

3 (*in indirect speech*): **I said I would do it** ho detto che l'avrei fatto

4 (*emphatic*): **it WOULD have to snow today!** doveva proprio nevicare oggi!

5 (*insistence*): **she wouldn't do it** non ha voluto farlo

6 (*conjecture*): **it would have been midnight** sarà stato mezzanotte; **it would seem so** sembrerebbe proprio di sì

7 (*indicating habit*): **he would go there on Mondays** andava lì ogni lunedì

wouldn't ['wʊdnt] = **would not**

wound[1] [waʊnd] pt, pp of **wind**[1]

wound[2] [wu:nd] n ferita ▶ vt ferire

wove [wəʊv] pt of **weave**

woven ['wəʊvn] pp of **weave**

wrap [ræp] vt avvolgere; (*pack: also:* **~ up**) incartare; **wrapper** n (*on chocolate*) carta; (*BRIT: of book*) copertina; **wrapping** ['ræpɪŋ] n carta; **wrapping paper** n carta da pacchi; (*for gift*) carta da regali

wreath [ri:θ, pl ri:ðz] n corona

wreck [rɛk] n (sea disaster) naufragio; (ship) relitto; (pej: person) rottame m ▶ vt demolire; (ship) far naufragare; (fig) rovinare; **wreckage** n rottami mpl; (of building) macerie fpl; (of ship) relitti mpl

wren [rɛn] n (Zool) scricciolo

wrench [rɛntʃ] n (Tech) chiave f; (tug) torsione f brusca; (fig) strazio ▶ vt strappare; storcere; **to ~ sth from** strappare qc a or da

wrestle ['rɛsl] vi **to ~ (with sb)** lottare (con qn); **wrestler** n lottatore(-trice); **wrestling** n lotta

wretched ['rɛtʃɪd] adj disgraziato(-a); (inf: weather, holiday) orrendo(-a), orribile; (: child, dog) pestifero(-a)

wriggle ['rɪgl] vi (also: **~ about**) dimenarsi; (: snake, worm) serpeggiare, muoversi serpeggiando

wring [rɪŋ] (pt, pp **wrung**) vt torcere; (wet clothes) strizzare; (fig): **to ~ sth out of** strappare qc a

wrinkle ['rɪŋkl] n (on skin) ruga; (on paper etc) grinza ▶ vt (nose) torcere; (forehead) corrugare ▶ vi (skin, paint) raggrinzirsi

wrist [rɪst] n polso

write [raɪt] (pt **wrote**, pp **written**) vt, vi scrivere ▷ **write down** vt annotare; (put in writing) mettere per iscritto ▷ **write off** vt (debt, plan) cancellare ▷ **write out** vt mettere per iscritto; (cheque, receipt) scrivere; **write-off** n perdita completa; **writer** n autore(-trice), scrittore(-trice)

writing ['raɪtɪŋ] n scrittura; (of author) scritto, opera; **in ~** per iscritto; **writing paper** n carta da lettere

written ['rɪtn] pp of **write**

wrong [rɔŋ] adj sbagliato(-a); (not suitable) inadatto(-a); (wicked) cattivo(-a); (unfair) ingiusto(-a) ▶ adv in modo sbagliato, erroneamente ▶ n (injustice) torto ▶ vt fare torto a; I

took a ~ turning ho sbagliato strada; **you are ~ to do it** ha torto a farlo; **you are ~ about that, you've got it ~** si sbaglia; **to be in the ~** avere torto; **what's ~?** cosa c'è che non va?; **to go ~** (person) sbagliarsi; (plan) fallire, non riuscire; (machine) guastarsi; **wrongly** adv (incorrectly, by mistake) in modo sbagliato; **wrong number** n (Tel): **you've got the wrong number** ha sbagliato numero

wrote [rəut] pt of **write**

wrung [rʌŋ] pt, pp of **wring**

WWW n abbr = World Wide Web; **the ~** la Rete

XL abbr = **extra large**

Xmas ['ɛksməs] n abbr = **Christmas**

X-ray ['ɛksreɪ] n raggio X; (photograph) radiografia ▶ vt radiografare

xylophone ['zaɪləfəun] n xilofono

y

yacht [jɔt] n panfilo, yacht m inv;
yachting n yachting m, sport m
della vela

yard [jɑːd] n (of house etc) cortile m;
(measure) iarda (= 914 mm; 3 feet); **yard
sale** n (US) n vendita di oggetti usati nel
cortile di una casa privata

yarn [jɑːn] n filato; (tale) lunga storia

yawn [jɔːn] n sbadiglio ▶ vi sbadigliare

yd. abbr = **yard(s)**

yeah [jɛə] (inf) adv sì

year [jɪər] n anno; (referring to harvest,
wine etc) annata; **he is 8 ~s old** ha
8 anni; **an eight-~-old child** un(a)
bambino(-a) di otto anni; **yearly** adj
annuale ▶ adv annualmente

yearn [jəːn] vi to ~ **for sth/to do**
desiderare ardentemente qc/di fare

yeast [jiːst] n lievito

yell [jɛl] n urlo ▶ vi urlare

yellow ['jɛləu] adj giallo(-a); **Yellow
Pages®** npl pagine fpl gialle

yes [jɛs] adv sì ▶ n sì m inv; **to say/
answer ~** dire/rispondere di sì

yesterday ['jɛstədɪ] adv ieri ▶ n
ieri m inv; **~ morning/evening** ieri
mattina/sera; **all day ~** ieri per tutta
la giornata

yet [jɛt] adv ancora; già ▶ conj ma,
tuttavia; **it is not finished ~** non è
ancora finito; **the best ~** finora il
migliore; **as ~** finora

yew [juː] n tasso (albero)

Yiddish ['jɪdɪʃ] n yiddish m

yield [jiːld] n produzione f, resa;
reddito ▶ vt produrre, rendere;
(surrender) cedere ▶ vi cedere; (US: Aut)
dare la precedenza

yob(bo) ['jɔb(əu)] n (BRIT inf) bullo

yoga ['jəugə] n yoga m

yog(h)urt ['jəugət] n iogurt m inv

yolk [jəuk] n tuorlo, rosso d'uovo

you
[juː] pron
1 (subject) tu; (: polite form) lei; (: pl) voi;
(: very formal) loro; **you Italians enjoy
your food** a voi Italiani piace mangiare
bene; **you and I will go** tu ed io or lei ed
io andiamo
2 (object: direct) ti; la; vi; loro (after vb);
(: indirect) ti; le; vi; loro (after vb); **I know
you** ti or la or vi conosco; **I gave it to
you** te l'ho dato; gliel'ho dato; ve l'ho
dato; l'ho dato loro
3 (stressed, after prep, in comparisons) te;
lei; voi; loro; **I told you to do it** ho detto
a TE (or a LEI etc) di farlo; **she's younger
than you** è più giovane di te (or lei etc)
4 (impers: one) si; **fresh air does you
good** l'aria fresca fa bene; **you never
know** non si sa mai

you'd [juːd] = **you had; you would**

you'll [juːl] = **you will; you shall**

young [jʌŋ] adj giovane ▶ npl (of
animal) piccoli mpl; (people): **the ~**
i giovani, la gioventù; **youngster**
n giovanotto, ragazzo; (child)
bambino(-a)

your [jɔːr] adj il (la) tuo(-a) pl, i (le)
tuoi (tue); il (la) suo(-a); (pl) i (le)
suoi (sue); il (la) vostro(-a); (pl) i (le)
vostri(-e); il (la) loro; (pl) i (le) loro;
see also **my**

you're [juər] = **you are**

yours [jɔːz] pron il (la) tuo(-a); (pl)
i (le) tuoi (tue); (polite form) il (la)
suo(-a); (pl) i (le) suoi (sue) il (la)
vostro(-a); (pl) i (le) vostri(-e); (: very
formal) il (la) loro; (pl) i (le) loro; see also

mine; faithfully; sincerely
yourself [jɔː'sɛlf] *pron (reflexive)* ti;
si; *(after prep)* te; sé; *(emphatic)* tu
stesso(-a); lei stesso(-a); **yourselves**
pl pron (reflexive) vi; si; *(after prep)* voi;
loro; *(emphatic)* voi stessi(-e); loro
stessi(-e); *see also* **oneself**
youth [juːθ, *pl* juːðz] *n* gioventù *f*;
(young man) giovane *m*, ragazzo;
youth club *n* centro giovanile;
youthful *adj* giovane; da giovane;
giovanile; **youth hostel** *n* ostello
della gioventù
you've [juːv] = **you have**
Yugoslavia ['juːgəu'slaːvɪə] *n (Hist)*
Jugoslavia

zero ['zɪərəu] *n* zero
zest [zɛst] *n* gusto; *(Culin)* buccia
zigzag ['zɪgzæg] *n* zigzag *m inv* ▶ *vi*
zigzagare
Zimbabwe [zɪm'baːbwɪ] *n*
Zimbabwe *m*
zinc [zɪŋk] *n* zinco
zip [zɪp] *n (also:* ~ **fastener**) chiusura *f*
or cerniera *f* lampo *inv* ▶ *vt (also:* ~ **up**)
chiudere con una cerniera lampo; **zip
code** *(US) n* codice *m* di avviamento
postale; **zipper** *(US) n* cerniera *f*
lampo *inv*
zit [zɪt] *n* brufolo
zodiac ['zəudɪæk] *n* zodiaco
zone [zəun] *n (also Mil)* zona
zoo [zuː] *n* zoo *m inv*
zoology [zuː'ɔlədʒɪ] *n* zoologia
zoom [zuːm] *vi* **to ~ past** sfrecciare;
zoom lens *n* zoom *m inv*, obiettivo a
focale variabile
zucchini [zuː'kiːnɪ] *(US) npl (courgettes)*
zucchine *fpl*

Z

zeal [ziːl] *n* zelo; entusiasmo
zebra ['ziːbrə] *n* zebra; **zebra crossing**
(BRIT) n (passaggio pedonale a)
strisce *fpl*, zebre *fpl*

VERB TABLES

Introduction

The **Verb Tables** in the following section contain 32 tables of the most common Italian verbs (some regular and some irregular) in alphabetical order. Each table shows you the following forms: **Present**, **Perfect**, **Imperfect**, **Future**, **Conditional**, **Present Subjunctive**, **Imperative** and the **Past Participle** and **Gerund**.

In order to help you use the verbs shown in Verb Tables correctly, there are also a number of example phrases at the bottom of each page to show the verb as it is used in context.

In Italian there are **regular** verbs (their forms follow the regular patterns of -are, -ere or -ire verbs), and **irregular** verbs (their forms do not follow the normal rules). Examples of regular verbs in these tables are:

> **parlare** (regular **-are** verb, Verb Table 16)
> **credere** (regular **-ere** verb, Verb Table 7)
> **capire** (regular **-ire** verb, Verb Table 6)

Some irregular verbs are irregular in most of their forms, while others may only have a couple of irregular forms.

▶ **addormentarsi** (to go to sleep)

PRESENT		**FUTURE**	
(io)	mi addormento	(io)	mi addormenterò
(tu)	ti addormenti	(tu)	ti addormenterai
(lui/lei) (lei/Lei)	si addormenta	(lui/lei) (lei/Lei)	si addormenterà
(noi)	ci addormentiamo	(noi)	ci addormenteremo
(voi)	vi addormentate	(voi)	vi addormenterete
(loro)	si addormentano	(loro)	si addormenteranno

PERFECT		**CONDITIONAL**	
(io)	mi sono addormentato/a	(io)	mi addormenterei
(tu)	ti sei addormentato/a	(tu)	ti addormenteresti
(lui/lei) (lei/Lei)	si è addormentato/a	(lui/lei) (lei/Lei)	si addormenterebbe
(noi)	ci siamo addormentati/e	(noi)	ci addormenteremmo
(voi)	vi siete addormentati/e	(voi)	vi addormentereste
(loro)	si sono addormentati/e	(loro)	si addormenterebbero

IMPERFECT		**PRESENT SUBJUNCTIVE**	
(io)	mi addormentavo	(io)	mi addormenti
(tu)	ti addormentavi	(tu)	ti addormenti
(lui/lei) (lei/Lei)	si addormentava	(lui/lei) (lei/Lei)	si addormenti
(noi)	ci addormentavamo	(noi)	ci addormentiamo
(voi)	vi addormentavate	(voi)	vi addormentiate
(loro)	si addormentavano	(loro)	si addormentino

IMPERATIVE
addormentati
addormentiamoci
addormentatevi

PAST PARTICIPLE
addormentato

GERUND
addormentando

EXAMPLE PHRASES

Non voleva **addormentarsi**. *He didn't want to go to sleep.*
Mi si **è addormentato** un piede. *My foot has gone to sleep.*
Sono stanco: stasera **mi addormenterò** subito. *I'm tired: I'll go to sleep immediately tonight.*

Italic letters in Italian words show where stress does not follow the usual rules.

▶ andare (to go)

PRESENT

(io)	vado
(tu)	vai
(lui/lei) (lei/Lei)	va
(noi)	andiamo
(voi)	andate
(loro)	vanno

FUTURE

(io)	andrò
(tu)	andrai
(lui/lei) (lei/Lei)	andrà
(noi)	andremo
(voi)	andrete
(loro)	andranno

PERFECT

(io)	sono andato/a
(tu)	sei andato/a
(lui/lei) (lei/Lei)	è andato/a
(noi)	siamo andati/e
(voi)	siete andati/e
(loro)	sono andati/e

CONDITIONAL

(io)	andrei
(tu)	andresti
(lui/lei) (lei/Lei)	andrebbe
(noi)	andremmo
(voi)	andreste
(loro)	andrebbero

IMPERFECT

(io)	andavo
(tu)	andavi
(lui/lei) (lei/Lei)	andava
(noi)	andavamo
(voi)	andavate
(loro)	andavano

PRESENT SUBJUNCTIVE

(io)	vada
(tu)	vada
(lui/lei) (lei/Lei)	vada
(noi)	andiamo
(voi)	andiate
(loro)	vadano

IMPERATIVE

vai
andiamo
andate

PAST PARTICIPLE

andato

GERUND

andando

EXAMPLE PHRASES

Andremo in Grecia quest'estate. *We're going to Greece this summer.*
Su, **andiamo**! *Come on, let's go!*
Com'è **andata**? *How did it go?*
Come **va**? – bene, grazie! *How are you? – fine thanks!*
Stasera **andrei** volentieri al ristorante. *I'd like to go to a restaurant this evening.*

Remember that subject pronouns are not used very often in Italian.

▶ **avere** (to have)

PRESENT			FUTURE	
(io)	ho		(io)	avrò
(tu)	hai		(tu)	avrai
(lui/lei) (lei/Lei)	ha		(lui/lei) (lei/Lei)	avrà
(noi)	abbiamo		(noi)	avremo
(voi)	avete		(voi)	avrete
(loro)	hanno		(loro)	avranno

PERFECT			CONDITIONAL	
(io)	ho avuto		(io)	avrei
(tu)	hai avuto		(tu)	avresti
(lui/lei) (lei/Lei)	ha avuto		(lui/lei) (lei/Lei)	avrebbe
(noi)	abbiamo avuto		(noi)	avremmo
(voi)	avete avuto		(voi)	avreste
(loro)	hanno avuto		(loro)	avrebbero

IMPERFECT			PRESENT SUBJUNCTIVE	
(io)	avevo		(io)	abbia
(tu)	avevi		(tu)	abbia
(lui/lei) (lei/Lei)	aveva		(lui/lei) (lei/Lei)	abbia
(noi)	avevamo		(noi)	abbiamo
(voi)	avevate		(voi)	abbiate
(loro)	avevano		(loro)	abbiano

IMPERATIVE

abbi
abbiamo
abbiate

PAST PARTICIPLE

avuto

GERUND

avendo

EXAMPLE PHRASES

All'inizio **ha avuto** un sacco di problemi. *He had a lot of problems at first.*
Ho già **mangiato**. *I've already eaten.*
Ha la macchina nuova. *She's got a new car.*
Aveva la mia età. *He was the same age as me.*
Quanti ne **abbiamo** oggi? *What's the date today?*

Italic letters in Italian words show where stress does not follow the usual rules.

▶ **bere** (to drink)

PRESENT

(io)	bevo
(tu)	bevi
(lui/lei) (lei/Lei)	beve
(noi)	beviamo
(voi)	bevete
(loro)	bevono

FUTURE

(io)	berrò
(tu)	berrai
(lui/lei) (lei/Lei)	berrà
(noi)	berremo
(voi)	berrete
(loro)	berranno

PERFECT

(io)	ho bevuto
(tu)	hai bevuto
(lui/lei) (lei/Lei)	ha bevuto
(noi)	abbiamo bevuto
(voi)	avete bevuto
(loro)	hanno bevuto

CONDITIONAL

(io)	berrei
(tu)	berresti
(lui/lei) (lei/Lei)	berrebbe
(noi)	berremmo
(voi)	berreste
(loro)	berrebbero

IMPERFECT

(io)	bevevo
(tu)	bevevi
(lui/lei) (lei/Lei)	beveva
(noi)	bevevamo
(voi)	bevevate
(loro)	bevevano

PRESENT SUBJUNCTIVE

(io)	beva
(tu)	beva
(lui/lei) (lei/Lei)	beva
(noi)	beviamo
(voi)	beviate
(loro)	bevano

IMPERATIVE

bevi
beviamo
bevete

PAST PARTICIPLE

bevuto

GERUND

bevendo

EXAMPLE PHRASES

Vuoi **bere** qualcosa? *Would you like something to drink?*
Berrei volentieri un bicchiere di vino bianco. *I'd love a glass of white wine.*
Beveva sei caffè al giorno, ma ora ha smesso. *He used to drink six cups of coffee a day, but he's stopped now.*

Remember that subject pronouns are not used very often in Italian.

▶ cadere (to fall)

PRESENT		FUTURE	
(io)	cado	(io)	cadrò
(tu)	cadi	(tu)	cadrai
(lui/lei) (lei/Lei)	cade	(lui/lei) (lei/Lei)	cadrà
(noi)	cadiamo	(noi)	cadremo
(voi)	cadete	(voi)	cadrete
(loro)	*cadono*	(loro)	cadranno

PERFECT		CONDITIONAL	
(io)	sono caduto/a	(io)	cadrei
(tu)	sei caduto/a	(tu)	cadresti
(lui/lei) (lei/Lei)	è caduto/a	(lui/lei) (lei/Lei)	cadrebbe
(noi)	siamo caduti/e	(noi)	cadremmo
(voi)	siete caduti/e	(voi)	cadreste
(loro)	sono caduti/e	(loro)	cadrebbero

IMPERFECT		PRESENT SUBJUNCTIVE	
(io)	cadevo	(io)	cada
(tu)	cadevi	(tu)	cada
(lui/lei) (lei/Lei)	cadeva	(lui/lei) (lei/Lei)	cada
(noi)	cadevamo	(noi)	cadiamo
(voi)	cadevate	(voi)	cadiate
(loro)	cadevano	(loro)	*cadano*

IMPERATIVE
cadi
cadiamo
cadete

PAST PARTICIPLE
caduto

GERUND
cadendo

EXAMPLE PHRASES

Ho inciampato e **sono caduta**. *I tripped and fell.*
Il mio compleanno **cade** di lunedì. *My birthday is on a Monday.*
Ti **è caduta** la sciarpa. *You've dropped your scarf.*
Attento che fai **cadere** il bicchiere. *Mind you don't knock over your glass.*

Italic letters in Italian words show where stress does not follow the usual rules.

▶ capire (to understand)

PRESENT

(io)	capisco
(tu)	capisci
(lui/lei) (lei/Lei)	capisce
(noi)	capiamo
(voi)	capite
(loro)	capiscono

FUTURE

(io)	capirò
(tu)	capirai
(lui/lei) (lei/Lei)	capirà
(noi)	capiremo
(voi)	capirete
(loro)	capiranno

PERFECT

(io)	ho capito
(tu)	hai capito
(lui/lei) (lei/Lei)	ha capito
(noi)	abbiamo capito
(voi)	avete capito
(loro)	hanno capito

CONDITIONAL

(io)	capirei
(tu)	capiresti
(lui/lei) (lei/Lei)	capirebbe
(noi)	capiremmo
(voi)	capireste
(loro)	capirebbero

IMPERFECT

(io)	capivo
(tu)	capivi
(lui/lei) (lei/Lei)	capiva
(noi)	capivamo
(voi)	capivate
(loro)	capivano

PRESENT SUBJUNCTIVE

(io)	capisca
(tu)	capisca
(lui/lei) (lei/Lei)	capisca
(noi)	capiamo
(voi)	capiate
(loro)	capíscano

IMPERATIVE

capisci
capiamo
capite

PAST PARTICIPLE

capito

GERUND

capendo

EXAMPLE PHRASES

Va bene, **capisco**. *OK, I understand.*
Non **ho capito** una parola. *I didn't understand a word.*
Fammi **capire**... *Let me get this straight...*
Non ti **capirò** mai. *I'll never understand you.*

Italic letters in Italian words show where stress does not follow the usual rules.

▶ credere (to believe)

PRESENT

(io)	credo
(tu)	credi
(lui/lei) (lei/Lei)	crede
(noi)	crediamo
(voi)	credete
(loro)	credono

FUTURE

(io)	crederò
(tu)	crederai
(lui/lei) (lei/Lei)	crederà
(noi)	crederemo
(voi)	crederete
(loro)	crederanno

PERFECT

(io)	ho creduto
(tu)	hai creduto
(lui/lei) (lei/Lei)	ha creduto
(noi)	abbiamo creduto
(voi)	avete creduto
(loro)	hanno creduto

CONDITIONAL

(io)	crederei
(tu)	crederesti
(lui/lei) (lei/Lei)	crederebbe
(noi)	crederemmo
(voi)	credereste
(loro)	crederebbero

IMPERFECT

(io)	credevo
(tu)	credevi
(lui/lei) (lei/Lei)	credeva
(noi)	credevamo
(voi)	credevate
(loro)	credevano

PRESENT SUBJUNCTIVE

(io)	creda
(tu)	creda
(lui/lei) (lei/Lei)	creda
(noi)	crediamo
(voi)	crediate
(loro)	credano

IMPERATIVE

credi
crediamo
credete

PAST PARTICIPLE

creduto

GERUND

credendo

EXAMPLE PHRASES

Non dirmi che **credi** ai fantasmi! *Don't tell me you believe in ghosts!*
Non **credeva** ai suoi occhi. *She couldn't believe her eyes.*
Non ti **crederò** mai. *I'll never believe you.*

Remember that subject pronouns are not used very often in Italian.

▶ **dare** (to give)

PRESENT

(io)	do
(tu)	dai
(lui/lei) (lei/Lei)	dà
(noi)	diamo
(voi)	date
(loro)	danno

FUTURE

(io)	darò
(tu)	darai
(lui/lei) (lei/Lei)	darà
(noi)	daremo
(voi)	darete
(loro)	daranno

PERFECT

(io)	ho dato
(tu)	hai dato
(lui/lei) (lei/Lei)	ha dato
(noi)	abbiamo dato
(voi)	avete dato
(loro)	hanno dato

CONDITIONAL

(io)	darei
(tu)	daresti
(lui/lei) (lei/Lei)	darebbe
(noi)	daremmo
(voi)	dareste
(loro)	darebbero

IMPERFECT

(io)	davo
(tu)	davi
(lui/lei) (lei/Lei)	dava
(noi)	davamo
(voi)	davate
(loro)	davano

PRESENT SUBJUNCTIVE

(io)	dia
(tu)	dia
(lui/lei) (lei/Lei)	dia
(noi)	diamo
(voi)	diate
(loro)	diano

IMPERATIVE
dai
diamo
date

PAST PARTICIPLE
dato

GERUND
dando

EXAMPLE PHRASES

Gli **ho dato** un libro. *I gave him a book.*
Dammelo. *Give it to me.*
La mia finestra **dà** sul giardino. *My window looks onto the garden.*
Domani sera **daranno** un bel film in tv. *There's a good film on TV tomorrow evening.*
Dandoti da fare, potresti ottenere molto di più. *If you exerted yourself you could achieve a lot more.*

Remember that subject pronouns are not used very often in Italian.

▶ dire (to say)

PRESENT

(io)	dico
(tu)	dici
(lui/lei)(lei/Lei)	dice
(noi)	diciamo
(voi)	dite
(loro)	dicono

PERFECT

(io)	ho detto
(tu)	hai detto
(lui/lei)(lei/Lei)	ha detto
(noi)	abbiamo detto
(voi)	avete detto
(loro)	hanno detto

IMPERFECT

(io)	dicevo
(tu)	dicevi
(lui/lei)(lei/Lei)	diceva
(noi)	dicevamo
(voi)	dicevate
(loro)	dicevano

IMPERATIVE

di'
diciamo
dite

FUTURE

(io)	dirò
(tu)	dirai
(lui/lei)(lei/Lei)	dirà
(noi)	diremo
(voi)	direte
(loro)	diranno

CONDITIONAL

(io)	direi
(tu)	diresti
(lui/lei)(lei/Lei)	direbbe
(noi)	diremmo
(voi)	direste
(loro)	direbbero

PRESENT SUBJUNCTIVE

(io)	dica
(tu)	dica
(lui/lei)(lei/Lei)	dica
(noi)	diciamo
(voi)	diciate
(loro)	dicano

PAST PARTICIPLE

detto

GERUND

dicendo

EXAMPLE PHRASES

Ha detto che verrà. *He said he'll come.*
Come si **dice** "quadro" in inglese? *How do you say "quadro" in English?*
Che ne **diresti** di andarcene? *Shall we leave?*
Ti **dirò** un segreto. *I'll tell you a secret.*
Dimmi dov'è. *Tell me where it is.*

Italic letters in Italian words show where stress does not follow the usual rules.

▶ dormire (to sleep)

PRESENT

(io)	dormo
(tu)	dormi
(lui/lei) (lei/Lei)	dorme
(noi)	dormiamo
(voi)	dormite
(loro)	dormono

PERFECT

(io)	ho dormito
(tu)	hai dormito
(lui/lei) (lei/Lei)	ha dormito
(noi)	abbiamo dormito
(voi)	avete dormito
(loro)	hanno dormito

IMPERFECT

(io)	dormivo
(tu)	dormivi
(lui/lei) (lei/Lei)	dormiva
(noi)	dormivamo
(voi)	dormivate
(loro)	dormivano

IMPERATIVE

dormi
dormiamo
dormite

FUTURE

(io)	dormirò
(tu)	dormirai
(lui/lei) (lei/Lei)	dormirà
(noi)	dormiremo
(voi)	dormirete
(loro)	dormiranno

CONDITIONAL

(io)	dormirei
(tu)	dormiresti
(lui/lei) (lei/Lei)	dormirebbe
(noi)	dormiremmo
(voi)	dormireste
(loro)	dormirebbero

PRESENT SUBJUNCTIVE

(io)	dorma
(tu)	dorma
(lui/lei) (lei/Lei)	dorma
(noi)	dormiamo
(voi)	dormiate
(loro)	dormano

PAST PARTICIPLE

dormito

GERUND

dormendo

EXAMPLE PHRASES

Sta dormendo. *She's sleeping.*
Vado a **dormire**. *I'm going to bed.*
Stanotte **dormirò** come un ghiro. *I'll sleep like a log tonight.*

Italic letters in Italian words show where stress does not follow the usual rules.

▶ **dovere** (to have to)

PRESENT

(io)	devo
(tu)	devi
(lui/lei) (lei/Lei)	deve
(noi)	dobbiamo
(voi)	dovete
(loro)	devono

PERFECT

(io)	ho dovuto
(tu)	hai dovuto
(lui/lei) (lei/Lei)	ha dovuto
(noi)	abbiamo dovuto
(voi)	avete dovuto
(loro)	hanno dovuto

IMPERFECT

(io)	dovevo
(tu)	dovevi
(lui/lei) (lei/Lei)	doveva
(noi)	dovevamo
(voi)	dovevate
(loro)	dovevano

IMPERATIVE

–

FUTURE

(io)	dovrò
(tu)	dovrai
(lui/lei) (lei/Lei)	dovrà
(noi)	dovremo
(voi)	dovrete
(loro)	dovranno

CONDITIONAL

(io)	dovrei
(tu)	dovresti
(lui/lei) (lei/Lei)	dovrebbe
(noi)	dovremmo
(voi)	dovreste
(loro)	dovrebbero

PRESENT SUBJUNCTIVE

(io)	debba
(tu)	debba
(lui/lei) (lei/Lei)	debba
(noi)	dobbiamo
(voi)	dobbiate
(loro)	debbano

PAST PARTICIPLE

dovuto

GERUND

dovendo

EXAMPLE PHRASES

È **dovuto** partire. *He had to leave.*
Devi finire i compiti prima di uscire. *You must finish your homework before you go out.*
Dev'essere tardi. *It must be late.*
Dovrebbe arrivare alle dieci. *He should arrive at ten.*
Gli **dovevo** 30 euro e così l'ho invitato a cena. *I owed him 30 euros so I took him out to dinner.*

Remember that subject pronouns are not used very often in Italian.

▶ *essere* (to be)

PRESENT

(io)	sono
(tu)	sei
(lui/lei) (lei/Lei)	è
(noi)	siamo
(voi)	siete
(loro)	sono

PERFECT

(io)	sono stato/a
(tu)	sei stato/a
(lui/lei) (lei/Lei)	è stato/a
(noi)	siamo stati/e
(voi)	siete stati/e
(loro)	sono stati/e

IMPERFECT

(io)	ero
(tu)	eri
(lui/lei) (lei/Lei)	era
(noi)	eravamo
(voi)	eravate
(loro)	erano

IMPERATIVE

sii
siamo
siate

FUTURE

(io)	sarò
(tu)	sarai
(lui/lei) (lei/Lei)	sarà
(noi)	saremo
(voi)	sarete
(loro)	saranno

CONDITIONAL

(io)	sarei
(tu)	saresti
(lui/lei) (lei/Lei)	sarebbe
(noi)	saremmo
(voi)	sareste
(loro)	sarebbero

PRESENT SUBJUNCTIVE

(io)	sia
(tu)	sia
(lui/lei) (lei/Lei)	sia
(noi)	siamo
(voi)	siate
(loro)	siano

PAST PARTICIPLE

stato

GERUND

essendo

EXAMPLE PHRASES

Sono italiana. *I'm Italian.*
Mario **è** appena partito. *Mario has just left.*
Siete mai **stati** in Africa? *Have you ever been to Africa?*
Quando **è** arrivato erano le quattro in punto. *It was exactly four o'clock when he arrived.*
Alla festa ci **saranno** tutti i miei amici. *All my friends will be at the party.*

Italic letters in Italian words show where stress does not follow the usual rules.

▶ **fare** (to do; make)

PRESENT

(io)	faccio
(tu)	fai
(lui/lei) (lei/Lei)	fa
(noi)	facciamo
(voi)	fate
(loro)	fanno

FUTURE

(io)	farò
(tu)	farai
(lui/lei) (lei/Lei)	farà
(noi)	faremo
(voi)	farete
(loro)	faranno

PERFECT

(io)	ho fatto
(tu)	hai fatto
(lui/lei) (lei/Lei)	ha fatto
(noi)	abbiamo fatto
(voi)	avete fatto
(loro)	hanno fatto

CONDITIONAL

(io)	farei
(tu)	faresti
(lui/lei) (lei/Lei)	farebbe
(noi)	faremmo
(voi)	fareste
(loro)	farebbero

IMPERFECT

(io)	facevo
(tu)	facevi
(lui/lei) (lei/Lei)	faceva
(noi)	facevamo
(voi)	facevate
(loro)	facevano

PRESENT SUBJUNCTIVE

(io)	faccia
(tu)	faccia
(lui/lei) (lei/Lei)	faccia
(noi)	facciamo
(voi)	facciate
(loro)	facciano

IMPERATIVE
fai
facciamo
fate

PAST PARTICIPLE
fatto

GERUND
facendo

EXAMPLE PHRASES

Ho fatto un errore. *I made a mistake.*
Due più due **fa** quattro. *Two and two makes four.*
Cosa **stai facendo**? *What are you doing?*
Fa il medico. *He is a doctor.*
Fa caldo. *It's hot.*

Remember that subject pronouns are not used very often in Italian.

▶ **mettere** (to put)

PRESENT

(io)	metto
(tu)	metti
(lui/lei) (lei/Lei)	mette
(noi)	mettiamo
(voi)	mettete
(loro)	mettono

PERFECT

(io)	ho messo
(tu)	hai messo
(lui/lei) (lei/Lei)	ha messo
(noi)	abbiamo messo
(voi)	avete messo
(loro)	hanno messo

IMPERFECT

(io)	mettevo
(tu)	mettevi
(lui/lei) (lei/Lei)	metteva
(noi)	mettevamo
(voi)	mettevate
(loro)	mettevano

IMPERATIVE

metti
mettiamo
mettete

FUTURE

(io)	metterò
(tu)	metterai
(lui/lei) (lei/Lei)	metterà
(noi)	metteremo
(voi)	metterete
(loro)	metteranno

CONDITIONAL

(io)	metterei
(tu)	metteresti
(lui/lei) (lei/Lei)	metterebbe
(noi)	metteremmo
(voi)	mettereste
(loro)	metterebbero

PRESENT SUBJUNCTIVE

(io)	metta
(tu)	metta
(lui/lei) (lei/Lei)	metta
(noi)	mettiamo
(voi)	mettiate
(loro)	mettano

PAST PARTICIPLE

messo

GERUND

mettendo

EXAMPLE PHRASES

Hai messo i bambini a letto? *Have you put the children to bed?*
Metterò un annuncio sul giornale. *I'll put an advert in the paper.*
Mettiti là e aspetta. *Wait there.*
Quanto tempo ci **hai messo**? *How long did it take you?*
Non **metto** più quelle scarpe. *I don't wear those shoes any more.*

Remember that subject pronouns are not used very often in Italian.

▶ **parere** (to appear)

PRESENT

(io)	p*a*io
(tu)	pari
(lui/lei) (lei/Lei)	pare
(noi)	pariamo
(voi)	parete
(loro)	p*a*iono

FUTURE

(io)	parrò
(tu)	parrai
(lui/lei) (lei/Lei)	parr*à*
(noi)	parremo
(voi)	parrete
(loro)	parranno

PERFECT

(io)	sono parso/a
(tu)	sei parso/a
(lui/lei) (lei/Lei)	è parso/a
(noi)	siamo parsi/e
(voi)	siete parsi/e
(loro)	sono parsi/e

CONDITIONAL

(io)	parrei
(tu)	parresti
(lui/lei) (lei/Lei)	parrebbe
(noi)	parremmo
(voi)	parreste
(loro)	parrebbero

IMPERFECT

(io)	parevo
(tu)	parevi
(lui/lei) (lei/Lei)	pareva
(noi)	parevamo
(voi)	parevate
(loro)	parevano

PRESENT SUBJUNCTIVE

(io)	p*a*ia
(tu)	p*a*ia
(lui/lei) (lei/Lei)	p*a*ia
(noi)	paiamo
(voi)	paiate
(loro)	p*a*iano

IMPERATIVE

pari
pariamo
parete

PAST PARTICIPLE

parso

GERUND

parendo

EXAMPLE PHRASES

Mi **pare** che sia già arrivato. *I think he's already here.*
Ci **è parso** che foste stanchi. *We thought you were tired.*
Faceva solo ciò che gli **pareva**. *He did just what he wanted.*

Italic letters in Italian words show where stress does not follow the usual rules.

▶ parlare (to speak)

PRESENT

(io)	parlo
(tu)	parli
(lui/lei) (lei/Lei)	parla
(noi)	parliamo
(voi)	parlate
(loro)	parlano

PERFECT

(io)	ho parlato
(tu)	hai parlato
(lui/lei) (lei/Lei)	ha parlato
(noi)	abbiamo parlato
(voi)	avete parlato
(loro)	hanno parlato

IMPERFECT

(io)	parlavo
(tu)	parlavi
(lui/lei) (lei/Lei)	parlava
(noi)	parlavamo
(voi)	parlavate
(loro)	parlavano

IMPERATIVE

parla
parliamo
parlate

FUTURE

(io)	parlerò
(tu)	parlerai
(lui/lei) (lei/Lei)	parlerà
(noi)	parleremo
(voi)	parlerete
(loro)	parleranno

CONDITIONAL

(io)	parlerei
(tu)	parleresti
(lui/lei) (lei/Lei)	parlerebbe
(noi)	parleremmo
(voi)	parlereste
(loro)	parlerebbero

PRESENT SUBJUNCTIVE

(io)	parli
(tu)	parli
(lui/lei) (lei/Lei)	parli
(noi)	parliamo
(voi)	parliate
(loro)	parlino

PAST PARTICIPLE

parlato

GERUND

parlando

EXAMPLE PHRASES

Pronto, chi **parla**? *Hello, who's speaking?*
Non **parliamone** più. *Let's just forget about it.*
Abbiamo parlato per ore. *We talked for hours.*
Gli **parlerò** di te. *I'll talk to him about you.*
Di cosa **parla** quel libro? *What is that book about?*

Remember that subject pronouns are not used very often in Italian.

▶ piacere (to be pleasing)

PRESENT

(io)	piaccio
(tu)	piaci
(lui/lei) (lei/Lei)	piace
(noi)	piacciamo
(voi)	piacete
(loro)	piacciono

PERFECT

(io)	sono piaciuto/a
(tu)	sei piaciuto/a
(lui/lei) (lei/Lei)	è piaciuto/a
(noi)	siamo piaciuti/e
(voi)	siete piaciuti/e
(loro)	sono piaciuti/e

IMPERFECT

(io)	piacevo
(tu)	piacevi
(lui/lei) (lei/Lei)	piaceva
(noi)	piacevamo
(voi)	piacevate
(loro)	piacevano

IMPERATIVE

piaci
piacciamo
piacciate

FUTURE

(io)	piacerò
(tu)	piacerai
(lui/lei) (lei/Lei)	piacerà
(noi)	piaceremo
(voi)	piacerete
(loro)	piaceranno

CONDITIONAL

(io)	piacerei
(tu)	piaceresti
(lui/lei) (lei/Lei)	piacerebbe
(noi)	piaceremmo
(voi)	piacereste
(loro)	piacerebbero

PRESENT SUBJUNCTIVE

(io)	piaccia
(tu)	piaccia
(lui/lei) (lei/Lei)	piaccia
(noi)	piacciamo
(voi)	piacciate
(loro)	piacciano

PAST PARTICIPLE

piaciuto

GERUND

piacendo

EXAMPLE PHRASES

Questa musica non **mi piace**. *I don't like this music.*
Cosa **ti piacerebbe** fare? *What would you like to do?*
Da piccola non **mi piacevano** i ragni. *When I was little I didn't like spiders.*

Remember that subject pronouns are not used very often in Italian.

▶ **potere** (to be able)

PRESENT

(io)	posso
(tu)	puoi
(lui/lei)(lei/Lei)	può
(noi)	possiamo
(voi)	potete
(loro)	possono

PERFECT

(io)	ho potuto
(tu)	hai potuto
(lui/lei)(lei/Lei)	ha potuto
(noi)	abbiamo potuto
(voi)	avete potuto
(loro)	hanno potuto

IMPERFECT

(io)	potevo
(tu)	potevi
(lui/lei)(lei/Lei)	poteva
(noi)	potevamo
(voi)	potevate
(loro)	potevano

IMPERATIVE

–

FUTURE

(io)	potrò
(tu)	potrai
(lui/lei)(lei/Lei)	potrà
(noi)	potremo
(voi)	potrete
(loro)	potranno

CONDITIONAL

(io)	potrei
(tu)	potresti
(lui/lei)(lei/Lei)	potrebbe
(noi)	potremmo
(voi)	potreste
(loro)	potrebbero

PRESENT SUBJUNCTIVE

(io)	possa
(tu)	possa
(lui/lei)(lei/Lei)	possa
(noi)	possiamo
(voi)	possiate
(loro)	possano

PAST PARTICIPLE

potuto

GERUND

potendo

EXAMPLE PHRASES

Si **può** visitare il castello tutti i giorni dell'anno. *You can visit the castle any day of the year.*

Non **è potuto** venire. *He couldn't come.*

Non **potrò** venire domani. *I won't be able to come tomorrow.*

Può aver avuto un incidente. *He may have had an accident.*

Potrebbe essere vero. *It could be true.*

Remember that subject pronouns are not used very often in Italian.

▶ **prendere** (to take)

PRESENT

(io)	prendo
(tu)	prendi
(lui/lei) (lei/Lei)	prende
(noi)	prendiamo
(voi)	prendete
(loro)	prendono

FUTURE

(io)	prenderò
(tu)	prenderai
(lui/lei) (lei/Lei)	prenderà
(noi)	prenderemo
(voi)	prenderete
(loro)	prenderanno

PERFECT

(io)	ho preso
(tu)	hai preso
(lui/lei) (lei/Lei)	ha preso
(noi)	abbiamo preso
(voi)	avete preso
(loro)	hanno preso

CONDITIONAL

(io)	prenderei
(tu)	prenderesti
(lui/lei) (lei/Lei)	prenderebbe
(noi)	prenderemmo
(voi)	prendereste
(loro)	prenderebbero

IMPERFECT

(io)	prendevo
(tu)	prendevi
(lui/lei) (lei/Lei)	prendeva
(noi)	prendevamo
(voi)	prendevate
(loro)	prendevano

PRESENT SUBJUNCTIVE

(io)	prenda
(tu)	prenda
(lui/lei) (lei/Lei)	prenda
(noi)	prendiamo
(voi)	prendiate
(loro)	prendano

IMPERATIVE

prendi
prendiamo
prendete

PAST PARTICIPLE

preso

GERUND

prendendo

EXAMPLE PHRASES

Prendi quella borsa. *Take that bag.*
Ho preso un bel voto. *I got a good mark.*
Prende qualcosa da bere? *Would you like something to drink?*
Per chi mi **prendi**? *Who do you think I am?*

Italic letters in Italian words show where stress does not follow the usual rules.

▶ rimanere (to stay)

PRESENT

(io)	rimango
(tu)	rimani
(lui/lei) (lei/Lei)	rimane
(noi)	rimaniamo
(voi)	rimanete
(loro)	rimangono

FUTURE

(io)	rimarrò
(tu)	rimarrai
(lui/lei) (lei/Lei)	rimarrà
(noi)	rimarremo
(voi)	rimarrete
(loro)	rimarranno

PERFECT

(io)	sono rimasto/a
(tu)	sei rimasto/a
(lui/lei) (lei/Lei)	è rimasto/a
(noi)	siamo rimasti/e
(voi)	siete rimasti/e
(loro)	sono rimasti/e

CONDITIONAL

(io)	rimarrei
(tu)	rimarresti
(lui/lei) (lei/Lei)	rimarrebbe
(noi)	rimarremmo
(voi)	rimarreste
(loro)	rimarrebbero

IMPERFECT

(io)	rimanevo
(tu)	rimanevi
(lui/lei) (lei/Lei)	rimaneva
(noi)	rimanevamo
(voi)	rimanevate
(loro)	rimanevano

PRESENT SUBJUNCTIVE

(io)	rimanga
(tu)	rimanga
(lui/lei) (lei/Lei)	rimanga
(noi)	rimaniamo
(voi)	rimaniate
(loro)	rimangano

IMPERATIVE

rimani
rimaniamo
rimanete

PAST PARTICIPLE

rimasto

GERUND

rimanendo

EXAMPLE PHRASES

Sono rimasto a casa tutto il giorno. *I stayed at home all day.*
Mi piacerebbe **rimanere** qualche altro giorno. *I'd like to stay a few more days.*
Ci **rimarrebbero** molto male. *They'd be very upset.*

Italic letters in Italian words show where stress does not follow the usual rules.

▶ **sapere** (to know)

PRESENT

(io)	so
(tu)	sai
(lui/lei) (lei/Lei)	sa
(noi)	sappiamo
(voi)	sapete
(loro)	sanno

PERFECT

(io)	hai saputo
(tu)	ha saputo
(lui/lei) (lei/Lei)	abbiamo saputo
(noi)	avete saputo
(voi)	hanno saputo
(loro)	ho saputo

IMPERFECT

(io)	sapevo
(tu)	sapevi
(lui/lei) (lei/Lei)	sapeva
(noi)	sapevamo
(voi)	sapevate
(loro)	sapevano

IMPERATIVE

sappi
sappiamo
sappiate

FUTURE

(io)	saprò
(tu)	saprai
(lui/lei) (lei/Lei)	saprà
(noi)	sapremo
(voi)	saprete
(loro)	sapranno

CONDITIONAL

(io)	saprei
(tu)	sapresti
(lui/lei) (lei/Lei)	saprebbe
(noi)	sapremmo
(voi)	sapreste
(loro)	saprebbero

PRESENT SUBJUNCTIVE

(io)	sappia
(tu)	sappia
(lui/lei) (lei/Lei)	sappia
(noi)	sappiamo
(voi)	sappiate
(loro)	sappiano

PAST PARTICIPLE

saputo

GERUND

sapendo

EXAMPLE PHRASES

Sai dove abita? *Do you know where he lives?*
Non **sapeva** andare in bicicletta. *He couldn't ride a bike.*
Sa di fragola. *It tastes of strawberries.*

Remember that subject pronouns are not used very often in Italian.

▶ scegliere (to choose)

PRESENT		FUTURE	
(io)	scelgo	(io)	sceglierò
(tu)	scegli	(tu)	sceglierai
(lui/lei) (lei/Lei)	sceglie	(lui/lei) (lei/Lei)	sceglierà
(noi)	scegliamo	(noi)	sceglieremo
(voi)	scegliete	(voi)	sceglierete
(loro)	scelgono	(loro)	sceglieranno

PERFECT		CONDITIONAL	
(io)	ho scelto	(io)	sceglierei
(tu)	hai scelto	(tu)	sceglieresti
(lui/lei) (lei/Lei)	ha scelto	(lui/lei) (lei/Lei)	sceglierebbe
(noi)	abbiamo scelto	(noi)	sceglieremmo
(voi)	avete scelto	(voi)	scegliereste
(loro)	hanno scelto	(loro)	sceglierebbero

IMPERFECT		PRESENT SUBJUNCTIVE	
(io)	sceglievo	(io)	scelga
(tu)	sceglievi	(tu)	scelga
(lui/lei) (lei/Lei)	sceglieva	(lui/lei) (lei/Lei)	scelga
(noi)	sceglievamo	(noi)	scegliamo
(voi)	sceglievate	(voi)	scegliate
(loro)	sceglievano	(loro)	scelgano

IMPERATIVE
scegli
scegliamo
scegliete

PAST PARTICIPLE
scelto

GERUND
scegliendo

EXAMPLE PHRASES

Chi **sceglie** il vino? *Who's going to choose the wine?*
Hai scelto il regalo per lei? *Have you chosen her present?*
Sceglievano sempre il vino più costoso. *They always chose the most expensive wine.*
Scegli la pizza che vuoi. *Choose which pizza you want.*
Non sa ancora quale abito **sceglierà**. *She hasn't decided yet which dress she'll choose.*
Stavo **scegliendo** le pesche più mature. *I was choosing the ripest peaches.*

Remember that subject pronouns are not used very often in Italian.

▶ **sedere** (to sit)

PRESENT

(io)	siedo
(tu)	siedi
(lui/lei) (lei/Lei)	siede
(noi)	sediamo
(voi)	sedete
(loro)	siedono

FUTURE

(io)	sederò
(tu)	sederai
(lui/lei) (lei/Lei)	sederà
(noi)	sederemo
(voi)	sederete
(loro)	sederanno

PERFECT

(io)	sono seduto/a
(tu)	sei seduto/a
(lui/lei) (lei/Lei)	è seduto/a
(noi)	siamo seduti/e
(voi)	siete seduti/e
(loro)	sono seduti/e

CONDITIONAL

(io)	sederei
(tu)	sederei
(lui/lei) (lei/Lei)	sederesti
(noi)	sederebbe
(voi)	sederemmo
(loro)	sedereste

IMPERFECT

(io)	sedevo
(tu)	sedevi
(lui/lei) (lei/Lei)	sedeva
(noi)	sedevamo
(voi)	sedevate
(loro)	sedevano

PRESENT SUBJUNCTIVE

(io)	sieda
(tu)	sieda
(lui/lei) (lei/Lei)	sieda
(noi)	sediamo
(voi)	sediate
(loro)	siedano

IMPERATIVE

siedi
sediamo
sedete

PAST PARTICIPLE

seduto

GERUND

sedendo

EXAMPLE PHRASES

Era seduta accanto a me. *She was sitting beside me.*
Si **è seduto** per terra. *He sat on the floor.*
Siediti qui! *Sit here!*

Italic letters in Italian words show where stress does not follow the usual rules.

▶ spegnere (to put out)

PRESENT

(io)	spengo
(tu)	spegni
(lui/lei)(lei/Lei)	spegne
(noi)	spegniamo
(voi)	spegnete
(loro)	spengono

FUTURE

(io)	spegnerò
(tu)	spegnerai
(lui/lei)(lei/Lei)	spegnerà
(noi)	spegneremo
(voi)	spegnerete
(loro)	spegneranno

PERFECT

(io)	ho spento
(tu)	hai spento
(lui/lei)(lei/Lei)	ha spento
(noi)	abbiamo spento
(voi)	avete spento
(loro)	hanno spento

CONDITIONAL

(io)	spegnerei
(tu)	spegneresti
(lui/lei)(lei/Lei)	spegnerebbe
(noi)	spegneremmo
(voi)	spegnereste
(loro)	spegnerebbero

IMPERFECT

(io)	spegnevo
(tu)	spegnevi
(lui/lei)(lei/Lei)	spegneva
(noi)	spegnevamo
(voi)	spegnevate
(loro)	spegnevano

PRESENT SUBJUNCTIVE

(io)	spenga
(tu)	spenga
(lui/lei)(lei/Lei)	spenga
(noi)	spegniamo
(voi)	spegniate
(loro)	spengano

IMPERATIVE

spegni
spegniamo
spegnete

PAST PARTICIPLE

spento

GERUND

spegnendo

EXAMPLE PHRASES

Hai spento la sigaretta? *Have you put your cigarette out?*
Spegnete le luci che guardiamo il film. *Turn off the lights and we'll watch the film.*
La luce si **è spenta** all'improvviso. *The light went off suddenly.*

Italic letters in Italian words show where stress does not follow the usual rules.

▶ **stare** (to be)

PRESENT

(io)	sto
(tu)	stai
(lui/lei) (lei/Lei)	sta
(noi)	stiamo
(voi)	state
(loro)	stanno

FUTURE

(io)	starò
(tu)	starai
(lui/lei) (lei/Lei)	starà
(noi)	staremo
(voi)	starete
(loro)	staranno

PERFECT

(io)	sono stato/a
(tu)	sei stato/a
(lui/lei) (lei/Lei)	è stato/a
(noi)	siamo stati/e
(voi)	siete stati/e
(loro)	sono stati/e

CONDITIONAL

(io)	starei
(tu)	staresti
(lui/lei) (lei/Lei)	starebbe
(noi)	staremmo
(voi)	stareste
(loro)	starebbero

IMPERFECT

(io)	stavo
(tu)	stavi
(lui/lei) (lei/Lei)	stava
(noi)	stavamo
(voi)	stavate
(loro)	stavano

PRESENT SUBJUNCTIVE

(io)	stia
(tu)	stia
(lui/lei) (lei/Lei)	stia
(noi)	stiamo
(voi)	stiate
(loro)	stiano

IMPERATIVE

stai
stiamo
state

PAST PARTICIPLE

stato

GERUND

stando

EXAMPLE PHRASES

Sei mai **stato** in Francia? *Have you ever been to France?*
Come **stai**? *How are you?*
Stavo andando a casa. *I was going home.*
A Londra **starò** da amici. *I'll be staying with friends in London.*
Stavo per uscire quando ha squillato il telefono. *I was about to go out when the phone rang.*

Italic letters in Italian words show where stress does not follow the usual rules.

▶ tenere (to hold)

PRESENT

(io)	tengo
(tu)	tieni
(lui/lei) (lei/Lei)	tiene
(noi)	teniamo
(voi)	tenete
(loro)	tengono

FUTURE

(io)	terrò
(tu)	terrai
(lui/lei) (lei/Lei)	terrà
(noi)	terremo
(voi)	terrete
(loro)	terranno

PERFECT

(io)	ho tenuto
(tu)	hai tenuto
(lui/lei) (lei/Lei)	ha tenuto
(noi)	abbiamo tenuto
(voi)	avete tenuto
(loro)	hanno tenuto

CONDITIONAL

(io)	terrei
(tu)	terresti
(lui/lei) (lei/Lei)	terrebbe
(noi)	terremmo
(voi)	terreste
(loro)	terrebbero

IMPERFECT

(io)	tenevo
(tu)	tenevi
(lui/lei) (lei/Lei)	teneva
(noi)	tenevamo
(voi)	tenevate
(loro)	tenevano

PRESENT SUBJUNCTIVE

(io)	tenga
(tu)	tenga
(lui/lei) (lei/Lei)	tenga
(noi)	teniamo
(voi)	teniate
(loro)	tengano

IMPERATIVE

tieni
teniamo
tenete

PAST PARTICIPLE

tenuto

GERUND

tenendo

EXAMPLE PHRASES

Tiene la racchetta con la sinistra. *He holds the racket with his left hand.*
Tieniti forte! *Hold on tight!*
Si **tenevano** per mano. *They were holding hands.*
Tieniti pronta per le cinque. *Be ready by five.*
Tieni, questo è per te. *Here, this is for you*

Remember that subject pronouns are not used very often in Italian.

▶ **togliere** (to take off)

PRESENT

(io)	tolgo
(tu)	togli
(lui/lei) (lei/Lei)	toglie
(noi)	togliamo
(voi)	togliete
(loro)	tolgono

FUTURE

(io)	toglierò
(tu)	toglierai
(lui/lei) (lei/Lei)	toglierà
(noi)	toglieremo
(voi)	toglierete
(loro)	toglieranno

PERFECT

(io)	ho tolto
(tu)	hai tolto
(lui/lei) (lei/Lei)	ha tolto
(noi)	abbiamo tolto
(voi)	avete tolto
(loro)	hanno tolto

CONDITIONAL

(io)	toglierei
(tu)	toglieresti
(lui/lei) (lei/Lei)	toglierebbe
(noi)	toglieremmo
(voi)	togliereste
(loro)	toglier*e*bbero

IMPERFECT

(io)	toglievo
(tu)	toglievi
(lui/lei) (lei/Lei)	toglieva
(noi)	toglievamo
(voi)	toglievate
(loro)	toglievano

PRESENT SUBJUNCTIVE

(io)	tolga
(tu)	tolga
(lui/lei) (lei/Lei)	tolga
(noi)	togliamo
(voi)	togliate
(loro)	tolgano

IMPERATIVE

togli
togliamo
togliete

PAST PARTICIPLE

tolto

GERUND

togliendo

EXAMPLE PHRASES

Togliti il cappotto. *Take off your coat.*
Ho tolto il poster dalla parete. *I took the poster off the wall.*
Mi **toglieranno** due denti. *I'm going to have two teeth out.*

Italic letters in Italian words show where stress does not follow the usual rules.

▶ uscire (to go out)

PRESENT

(io)	esco
(tu)	esci
(lui/lei) (lei/Lei)	esce
(noi)	usciamo
(voi)	uscite
(loro)	escono

FUTURE

(io)	uscirò
(tu)	uscirai
(lui/lei) (lei/Lei)	uscirà
(noi)	usciremo
(voi)	uscirete
(loro)	usciranno

PERFECT

(io)	sono uscito/a
(tu)	sei uscito/a
(lui/lei) (lei/Lei)	è uscito/a
(noi)	siamo usciti/e
(voi)	siete usciti/e
(loro)	sono usciti/e

CONDITIONAL

(io)	uscirei
(tu)	usciresti
(lui/lei) (lei/Lei)	uscirebbe
(noi)	usciremmo
(voi)	uscireste
(loro)	uscirebbero

IMPERFECT

(io)	uscivo
(tu)	uscivi
(lui/lei) (lei/Lei)	usciva
(noi)	uscivamo
(voi)	uscivate
(loro)	uscivano

PRESENT SUBJUNCTIVE

(io)	esca
(tu)	esca
(lui/lei) (lei/Lei)	esca
(noi)	usciamo
(voi)	usciate
(loro)	escano

IMPERATIVE

esci
usciamo
uscite

PAST PARTICIPLE

uscito

GERUND

uscendo

EXAMPLE PHRASES

È uscita a comprare il giornale. *She's gone out to buy a newspaper.*
Uscirà dall'ospedale domani. *He's coming out of hospital tomorrow.*
L'ho incontrata che **usciva** dalla farmacia. *I met her coming out of the chemist's.*
La rivista **esce** di lunedì. *The magazine comes out on Mondays.*

Italic letters in Italian words show where stress does not follow the usual rules.

▶ **valere** (to be worth)

PRESENT

(io)	valgo
(tu)	vali
(lui/lei) (lei/Lei)	vale
(noi)	valiamo
(voi)	valete
(loro)	valgono

PERFECT

(io)	sono valso/a
(tu)	sei valso/a
(lui/lei) (lei/Lei)	è valso/a
(noi)	siamo valsi/e
(voi)	siete valsi/e
(loro)	sono valsi/e

IMPERFECT

(io)	valevo
(tu)	valevi
(lui/lei) (lei/Lei)	valeva
(noi)	valevamo
(voi)	valevate
(loro)	valevano

IMPERATIVE

vali
valiamo
valete

FUTURE

(io)	varrò
(tu)	varrai
(lui/lei) (lei/Lei)	varrà
(noi)	varremo
(voi)	varrete
(loro)	varranno

CONDITIONAL

(io)	varrei
(tu)	varresti
(lui/lei) (lei/Lei)	varrebbe
(noi)	varremmo
(voi)	varreste
(loro)	varrebbero

PRESENT SUBJUNCTIVE

(io)	valga
(tu)	valga
(lui/lei) (lei/Lei)	valga
(noi)	valiamo
(voi)	valiate
(loro)	valgano

PAST PARTICIPLE

valso

GERUND

valendo

EXAMPLE PHRASES

L'auto **vale** tremila euro. *The car is worth three thousand euros.*
Non ne **vale** la pena. *It's not worth it.*
Senza il giardino, la casa non **varrebbe** niente. *Without the garden the house wouldn't be worth anything.*

Remember that subject pronouns are not used very often in Italian.

▶ vedere (to see)

PRESENT

(io)	vedo
(tu)	vedi
(lui/lei) (lei/Lei)	vede
(noi)	vediamo
(voi)	vedete
(loro)	vedono

PERFECT

(io)	ho visto
(tu)	hai visto
(lui/lei) (lei/Lei)	ha visto
(noi)	abbiamo visto
(voi)	avete visto
(loro)	hanno visto

IMPERFECT

(io)	vedevo
(tu)	vedevi
(lui/lei) (lei/Lei)	vedeva
(noi)	vedevamo
(voi)	vedevate
(loro)	vedevano

IMPERATIVE

vedi
vediamo
vedete

FUTURE

(io)	vedrò
(tu)	vedrai
(lui/lei) (lei/Lei)	vedrà
(noi)	vedremo
(voi)	vedrete
(loro)	vedranno

CONDITIONAL

(io)	vedrei
(tu)	vedresti
(lui/lei) (lei/Lei)	vedrebbe
(noi)	vedremmo
(voi)	vedreste
(loro)	vedrebbero

PRESENT SUBJUNCTIVE

(io)	veda
(tu)	veda
(lui/lei) (lei/Lei)	veda
(noi)	vediamo
(voi)	vediate
(loro)	vedano

PAST PARTICIPLE

visto

GERUND

vedendo

EXAMPLE PHRASES

Non ci **vedo** senza occhiali. *I can't see without my glasses.*
Ci **vediamo** domani! *See you tomorrow!*
Non **vedevo** l'ora di conoscerlo. *I couldn't wait to meet him.*

Italic letters in Italian words show where stress does not follow the usual rules.

▶ **venire** (to come)

PRESENT

(io)	vengo
(tu)	vieni
(lui/lei) (lei/Lei)	viene
(noi)	veniamo
(voi)	venite
(loro)	vengono

FUTURE

(io)	verrò
(tu)	verrai
(lui/lei) (lei/Lei)	verrà
(noi)	verremo
(voi)	verrete
(loro)	verranno

PERFECT

(io)	sono venuto/a
(tu)	sei venuto/a
(lui/lei) (lei/Lei)	è venuto/a
(noi)	siamo venuti/e
(voi)	siete venuti/e
(loro)	sono venuti/e

CONDITIONAL

(io)	verrei
(tu)	verresti
(lui/lei) (lei/Lei)	verrebbe
(noi)	verremmo
(voi)	verreste
(loro)	verrebbero

IMPERFECT

(io)	venivo
(tu)	venivi
(lui/lei) (lei/Lei)	veniva
(noi)	venivamo
(voi)	venivate
(loro)	venívano

PRESENT SUBJUNCTIVE

(io)	venga
(tu)	venga
(lui/lei) (lei/Lei)	venga
(noi)	veniamo
(voi)	veniate
(loro)	vengano

IMPERATIVE

vieni
veniamo
venite

PAST PARTICIPLE

venuto

GERUND

venendo

EXAMPLE PHRASES

È venuto in macchina. *He came by car.*
Da dove **vieni**? *Where do you come from?*
Vieni a trovarci. *Come and see us!*
Quanto **viene**? *How much is it?*

Remember that subject pronouns are not used very often in Italian.

▶ **volere** (to want)

PRESENT

(io)	voglio
(tu)	vuoi
(lui/lei) (lei/Lei)	vuole
(noi)	vogliamo
(voi)	volete
(loro)	vogliono

FUTURE

(io)	vorrò
(tu)	vorrai
(lui/lei) (lei/Lei)	vorrà
(noi)	vorremo
(voi)	vorrete
(loro)	vorranno

PERFECT

(io)	ho voluto
(tu)	hai voluto
(lui/lei) (lei/Lei)	ha voluto
(noi)	abbiamo voluto
(voi)	avete voluto
(loro)	hanno voluto

CONDITIONAL

(io)	vorrei
(tu)	vorresti
(lui/lei) (lei/Lei)	vorrebbe
(noi)	vorremmo
(voi)	vorreste
(loro)	vorrebbero

IMPERFECT

(io)	volevo
(tu)	volevi
(lui/lei) (lei/Lei)	voleva
(noi)	volevamo
(voi)	volevate
(loro)	volevano

PRESENT SUBJUNCTIVE

(io)	voglia
(tu)	voglia
(lui/lei) (lei/Lei)	voglia
(noi)	vogliamo
(voi)	vogliate
(loro)	vogliano

IMPERATIVE

–

PAST PARTICIPLE

voluto

GERUND

volendo

EXAMPLE PHRASES

Voglio comprare una macchina nuova. *I want to buy a new car.*

Devo pagare subito o posso pagare domani? – Come **vuole**. *Do I have to pay now or can I pay tomorrow? – As you prefer.*

Quanto ci **vorrà** prima che finiate? *How long will it take you to finish?*

La campanella **voleva** dire che la lezione era finita. *The bell meant that the lesson was over.*

Anche **volendo** non posso invitarti: la festa è sua. *I'd like to, but I can't invite you: it's his party.*

Italic letters in Italian words show where stress does not follow the usual rules.

WORLD SHIPPING

An Economic Geography of Ports

and Seaborne Trade

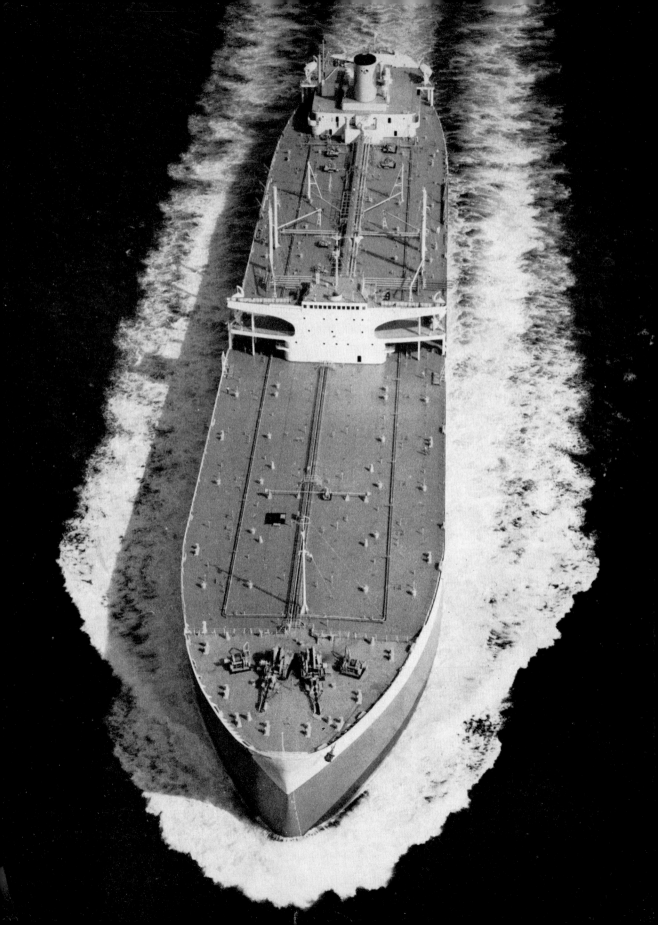

GUNNAR ALEXANDERSSON

GÖRAN NORSTRÖM

World Shipping

An Economic Geography
of Ports and Seaborne Trade

Almqvist & Wiksell
STOCKHOLM / GÖTEBORG / UPPSALA
John Wiley & Sons
NEW YORK / LONDON

Maps and diagrams: Lillemor Ahlström, Anita Hedlund

Editing and research assistance: Susan Snodgrass

Research financed by

The Axel and Margaret Ax:son Johnson Foundation

The Swedish Council for Social Science Research

Design: Dick Hallström

Typeface: Times new roman

Paper: Lessebo machine coated

Line cuts: AB Grohmann & Eichelberg, Stockholm

Halftones: AB Centralkliché, Uppsala

Printed in Sweden by Almqvist & Wiksells Boktryckeri AB, Uppsala 1963

In Memory of

IVAR HÖGBOM

Preface

We have written this book with a double purpose in mind. Firstly, it might serve as a textbook or work of reference for students and teachers of economic geography, the economics of transportation and related fields. A world survey of this type did not exist in English before. Secondly, it should serve a wider public, including not only that abstract person, the interested layman, who reads all books, but also port authorities, shipping companies, etc., who undoubtedly know more about port traffic and shipping than we do but nonetheless might find reference material in this volume not so readily available elsewhere. We would be most pleased if the men who sail the ships and work the cargo found something of value in these pages.

When reading the book it may be useful to have a good college atlas at hand for such basic geographic facts as topography, climate, vegetation, distribution of population, road and railroad patterns, etc.

Many of our maps are based on data for 1956. That was the latest year for which data were available when we started but world events have helped to make it a representative year for the late 1950s even seen in retrospect and with newer material available. In 1957 the Suez Crisis caused some deviations in the flow of waterborne trade, in 1958 the United States and some other countries had a recession, in 1959 there was a prolonged steel strike in the United States and data for 1960 will only be available when this book has gone to press. It has been possible to include data for later years in the text and in many diagrams and tables.

As a rule no maps, diagrams or tables are based on data that can be found in any one copy of such basic sources as the *Statistical Yearbook,* the *Yearbook of International Trade Statistics* or the *Monthly Bulletin of Statistics* published by the United Nations. Photographs have been included not for their esthetic qualities but as the most efficient way of conveying some types of information.

We have expressed weight in metric tons throughout the book except in a few cases which are clearly indicated.

We are aware that the minimum limit for ports included on our maps is very low. But small ports are also part of a pattern, in some areas of the world a very important part. For example, much of Sweden's exports move through small timber and pulp shipping ports, and many of the small ports in Africa or Latin America serve a large population. We had the choice of not naming the small ports or giving the names in small type. We chose the latter alternative knowing that it is easier to use a magnifying glass, if necessary, than to get hold of the national port statistics and large-scale maps. Some of the ports could be located only after consulting maps on the scale 1: 100,000 or similar. Some ports are new and could be located only with the help of recent newspaper and magazine articles, pamphlets, etc.

Acknowledgments

This book is the offspring of Ivar Högbom's monograph on world shipping published in Swedish in 1934. Högbom's book was written by a man, originally trained as a geologist, who after many and long journeys in various capacities, primarily in Latin America and Egypt, had become interested in economic geography and particularly shipping. The book was a success both with university students and with the shipping world.

The authors, as young students at the Stockholm School of Economics, became interested in world shipping stimulated by Ivar Högbom's book and lectures. Many years later we suggested to our colleague Ivar Högbom that he should write a new edition of his *Världssjöfarten* in English. But by that time Högbom knew that his failing health would not allow him to undertake such a project. It was agreed that we should write the book together. This was in 1958. And now, five years later, we have finished a volume that is much larger than originally planned.

Ivar Högbom died on June 15, 1962, about half a year before the manuscript was completed. He followed the work with great interest when he was out of hospital and his health permitted short visits to the department. We have used basically the same outline for our book as Ivar Högbom used for his and we have drawn heavily on the large collection of diagrams that Högbom made during his long period as Dean of the Stockholm School of Economics (1936–1957), when time did not permit him to publish more than occasional papers on shipping problems.

Ivar Högbom asked us a few days before his death, when he seemed to be in better health than for years, not to list him as an author. He had participated in the planning of the book, we had used his material but he had had no chance of working with the text. Our hopes that he would be able to follow this book to its conclusion as senior author did not come true.

In writing this book the authors have drawn heavily on the works of many geographers and economists. We have used hundreds of official statistical publications, as a rule borrowed from the libraries of the Stockholm School of Economics and the Central Bureau of Statistics in Stockholm. In both libraries we have received excellent service, although at times our demands on their resources have been out of the ordinary. The librarians have devoted many hours to source hunting for this book, with many intercity loans and loans from abroad. We have been in correspondence with a large number of port authorities and business concerns all over the world who have supplied us with information and with photographs, of which a selection is included in the book. The number of persons and organizations to whom the authors are grateful is staggering and only a general acknowledgment is therefore possible. We are fully aware that credit given in the footnotes and in the picture texts is by no means complete.

But to many we owe more personal acknowledgment. Professor Knut Rodhe, Dean of the Stockholm School of Economics, and Professor W. William-Olsson, Chairman of the Department of Geography, have helped us in many ways. We have discussed shipping and related problems with Johannes Humlum, Aarhus, Arnljot Strømme Svendsen and Tore Ouren, Bergen, Harold M. Mayer, Chicago, William Wonders, Edmonton, Eiler Alkjaer, København, James Bird, London, I. V. Nikol'skij, Moskva, James B. Kenyon, New York, Birger Nossum, Oslo, Hilgard O'Reilly Sternberg, Rio de Janeiro, Toshio Noh and Ryoji Moriwaki, Sendai, Thomas Thorburn and Ingemar Dalgård, Stockholm, and Donald Patton, Washington.

We also thank our collaborators and those who financed our research as well as those who ventured to publish this volume. They are all mentioned in a more prominent place, deserved by their contribution.

We wish to stress that this book is the result of teamwork, with the authors and their collaborators working in daily contact. For the benefit of those who want to know who wrote what we have listed in the contents the author mainly responsible for each section. We should highly appreciate comments that will make it possible for us to improve the text. For those mistakes which escaped us and which will be glaring to our readers in Japan, Argentina, East Africa, Australia, etc. the authors alone are responsible.

Department of Geography,
The Stockholm School of Economics,
January, 1963.

Gunnar Alexandersson
Göran Norström

Contents

A General Survey

International Trade and Shipping

The volume of cargo moved by sea increases rapidly. Statistical data are not at hand to show the development of seaborne cargo traffic since, say, the time of the Great Discoveries or from the beginning of the Industrial Revolution, but there can be no doubt that the increase has been tremendous. But even in shorter perspective the increase has been impressive as evidenced by the diagrams found elsewhere in this book showing production developments in the past century. Of cane sugar for instance, for centuries probably the leading commodity in transoceanic trade but now far surpassed by many commodities, more than twenty times as much was produced in 1960 as a hundred years earlier.

Data on seaborne trade are still quite incomplete for most countries and many statements in this book must therefore be based on more or less crude estimates. International trade is better covered than domestic and the United Nations' statistics of cargo loaded and unloaded may provide a good indication of the development of seaborne transports in the last few decades. The tonnage of cargo handled in international trade has doubled in the short span of ten years according to the United Nations.

Seen from the different angle of the total exchange of commodities and services between nations, seaborne cargo movements account for a declining share for two reasons: (a) an ever increasing share of the commodity flow has been transported across land boundaries by rail, road and pipeline since the revolution in land transportation started in the middle of last century, (b) services account for an increasing share of the total exchange between countries. The trend in the most advanced countries towards more rapid development of service production than of commodity production also has another effect. As services are not so readily transferable across national boundaries foreign trade will account for a declining share of the gross national product. In long distance transportation air traffic rather than shipping seems to gain from the increasing importance of service production. In most cases a transfer of people is involved, business men, tourists, students, etc. or material for the press, radio, television, movies, etc. and this is just the type of transports in which air traffic has been most successful. On some international routes air passengers already far exceed sea passengers. For mass tourism in distant places no means of transportation can compete with chartered flights. Air transportation has already taken over much transocean express cargo that was earlier a monopoly of ships and very likely this is just a small beginning. Rapidly increasing quantities of freight will move by plane.[1] It seems that the airplane, the most flexible carrier in long-distance transport but also the most expensive per ton-mile, will in the future be a more serious competitor for shipping than trucks or trains, which are limited to the one-fourth of the earth that is land. Land transport in many

[1] Vehicle ferry service by air between Britain and the Continent can be taken as one example. It commenced in 1948 and accounted for 138,000 cars, 419,000 passengers and 21,000 tons of freight on 32,000 round-trips in 1962. Eleven places on the Continent (and the Channel Islands) were served from three airports in Britain. Geneva, Basel, Strasbourg are among the places served by British United Air Ferries.

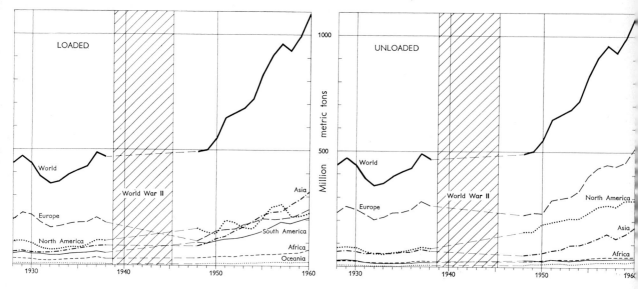

International seaborne cargo 1928–1960.
Data from United Nations, *Statistical Yearbook,*
and *Monthly Bulletin of Statistics.*

cases is not a competitor of but a complement to sea transport.

But for the foreseeable future ships will carry the greater part of the cargo sent between countries separated by water and also most of the low-value cargo sent coastwise, especially commodities transported in bulk. A description of world trade measured in value may therefore serve as a substitute for synoptic pictures of international seaborne traffic measured in tons which cannot yet be drawn.

International Trade Maps

There is a great disparity between the units participating in international trade. The smallest units reporting their foreign trade to the United Nations export a few shiploads of cargo a year worth a few million dollars. The United States and the United Kingdom at the other extreme each import over a hundred million tons of seaborne cargo per annum, worth 10 billion dollars or more. The United States, the United Kingdom and the other large trading

nations are likely to rank high as trade partners of any country, the minute trading units at the other extreme are likely to rank low.[1]

In order to describe international trade patterns both in survey and detail most of the available space has been devoted to a series of maps on which have been inserted two indexes to facilitate comparison. The world map was based on the United Nations *Yearbook of International Trade Statistics* and the country maps on official trade statistics from respective countries as the breakdown in the Yearbook is not sufficiently detailed.

THE PER CAPITA TRADE INDEX. The following statements hold true, other things being equal:

(a) countries with a high standard of living (e.g. measured as gross national product per inhabitant) have a larger foreign trade per capita than those with a low standard of living;

[1] The number of units reporting their foreign trade to the United Nations plus those which do not report but which are entitled to do so amounts to 148, most of which can be classified as countries or nations. This means that there are theoretically 10,878 country pairs to account for in a detailed description of world trade and twice as many if imports and exports are treated separately.

THE WORLD

Imports Exports

20 '000 million U. S. $
10
5   + 25 - 50 million U. S. $
        ~ 10 - 25
1   .. 0 - 10
0,3   () estimated value
0,0   N no data   For index numbers see text

Symbols show total imports and exports of respective countries.

(b) small nations have a greater foreign trade per capita than large nations.

From these statements it follows that large, poor countries (China, India, Pakistan) will have the smallest foreign trade per capita and small, rich countries (New Zealand, Switzerland, Sweden) will have the largest per capita foreign trade.

This is clearly brought out on the map of world trade. The numbers at the trade symbols represent an index of foreign trade per capita. The number 100 means that a country has the same share of the world's total international trade as of its total population, the number 700 indicates a seven times larger proportion of trade than of population and the number 10 means that the share of trade is only one-tenth as large as the share of population.

THE TRADE DISTRIBUTION INDEX. The observation, repeated for country after country, that the United States and the United Kingdom are large trade partners, is not a good starting point for a description of foreign trade patterns. Nor is it interesting to know that Laos or Malta are small trading partners for most countries. Some simple mathematical construction that can serve as a bench mark would make the description more meaningful. Such a construction need not be economically realistic to be useful, but it should be conceptually and mathematically simple.

The trade distribution index, used on the country maps and in the text, shows in numerical form deviations from a hypothetical situation in which each country in the world has the same percentage of the foreign trade of any other country as it has of the total international trade. Expressed in terms of distribution maps this hypothetical situation occurs when each country has a foreign trade pattern that exactly agrees with the map of the total world trade, with only the scales of value being different. The world map (page 20) can thus serve as the bench mark with which the actual distribution patterns are being compared. By making the sum of symbol surfaces the same on all maps a quick comparison is facilitated. The index value only serves to underline in numerical form what can be seen by comparing each of the country maps in turn with the world map. If a country map completely agrees with the world map each trade relation[2] would be given the index value 100. The index value 700 means that the actual trade is seven times larger than the hypothetical trade, the value 10 means that it is only one-tenth of the hypothetical value.

Mathematically the formula of the index can be written in the following way:

$$I = \frac{\dfrac{T_{1-2}}{T_1}}{\dfrac{T_2}{T_w}} \cdot 100 = \frac{T_{1-2} \cdot T_w}{T_1 \cdot T_2} \cdot 100$$

where I is the index value, T_{1-2} is the total trade between country 1 and country 2, T_1 is the total foreign trade of country 1, T_2 is the total foreign trade of country 2 and T_w is the sum of all imports and all exports in the world.

Meaningful comparisons can be made not only between index values on the same map but also between values on different maps. Reference is always made to the same bench mark, the hypothetical case where each trade relation has the index value 100 and whose pattern is represented by the map of world trade. From the formula it is evident that the index value for country 2 on the map of country 1 should be the same as the index value for country 1 on the map of country 2.

In practice there may be deviations, however. Foreign trade statistics are not always precision tools.[3] Exports are measured in f.o.b. prices and imports in c.i.f. prices and this may also lead to differences if freight costs in one direction make up a larger percentage of the c.i.f. prices than in the opposite direction. The United States and a few other countries report both imports and exports in f.o.b. prices, which may also influence the index values of those countries and which will systematically give them a higher value on their trade partners' maps.

No systematic analysis of the deviations from the hypothetical distribution has been attempted. Some factors causing deviations are obvious. (a) Distance definitely influences foreign trade as well as other forms of trade. Neighbor countries should, other things being equal, have more trade than countries separated by long distances. The distance factor is relatively simple and could have been taken into consideration to make the hypothetical model economically more realistic but then the mathematical construction would have become more complicated. (b) Differences in the equipment with natural, human and financial resources, and (c) the economies of scale are among the main factors making foreign trade profitable. They cannot be expected to create foreign trade patterns that agree with the hypothetical distribution.

Foreign trade patterns are influenced not only by *homo oeconomicus* but also by *homo politicus*. National security, political ideology and the interests of domestic pressure groups

[2] One trade relation includes both imports and exports.

[3] For instance in 1958 Japanese exports to Liberia according to Japanese statistics amounted to 236.7 million U.S. dollars and Liberian imports from Japan according to Liberian statistics amounted to 1.1 million U.S. dollars. Vessels built in Japan and sold to American shipowners in New York to sail under the Liberian flag of convenience were registered by the Japanese authorities as sold to Liberia but they were never seen by any Liberian customs officer.

influence foreign trade patterns more than is usually acknowledged in textbooks on foreign trade. This is seen especially on the maps of the Soviet Union and the United States but also on those of the United Kingdom and France.[4] The latter two countries were until recently the centers of large empires and the large British and French trade with distant former colonies may be seen as the legacy of the past. The smallness of trade between these two neighbor countries is quite abnormal.

THE UNITED KINGDOM, center of the most widespread empire the world has ever known, now transformed into a more loose association, has a foreign trade pattern that is the reverse of patterns observed for other countries. Britain's trade with her neighbors on the Continent—France, Belgium and West Germany—has exceedingly low index values (50–60) and with her antipodes, Australia and New Zealand, it has extremely high values (400–600). Britain's index values are high for most of her former colonies with the United States as a notable exception. Britain does not have higher index values for her American trade than other countries in western Europe. This situation was different a hundred years ago and even at the turn of the century when America's trade was much more concentrated on Europe, especially the United Kingdom. The British trade with Canada is represented by a relatively low index value, although much higher than for the Canadian trade of other European countries. The Canadian economy has become more and more oriented towards the American.

The low index values for trade between countries on both sides of the North Atlantic may be somewhat deceptive. Many firms establish subsidiary plants on the other side of the Atlantic when trade reaches a large volume and this leads to a decline and even a complete

cessation of the commodity flow from those firms. Personnel travel back and forth over the Atlantic between the mother company and her subsidiary plant, and profits, patent and license fees, etc. flow through the banks but there is little or no commodity flow. The economic ties may therefore be very strong between countries with relatively low index values for their commodity exchange.

Until the Second World War the United Kingdom was the leading foreign trade nation in the world. Its commodity trade surpassed that of the United States. After the war the American trade has surpassed the British by a wide margin and in 1960 West German trade was on a par with the British.

As a response to the creation of the European Economic Community on the continent, including Belgium-Luxembourg, France, West Germany, Italy and the Netherlands, Britain in 1959 formed the European Free Trade Area with Denmark, Norway, Sweden, Austria, Switzerland, and Portugal. This organization was thought of as an instrument that would enable its members to join the Common Market, thus creating a large free trade area encompassing the whole of Western Europe. EFTA represents a total foreign trade which is about two-thirds that of the EEC. Early in 1963 France, after long negotiations, vetoed a British application for membership of the Common Market, which at least temporarily halted the large-scale integration of the West European economies. As a result Western Europe remained divided into two trade blocs.

THE UNITED STATES, the leading nation in international trade in the postwar period, has a remarkably well developed exchange of commodities with most countries in the western hemisphere but also with Japan and the former American colony, the Philippines, in East Asia. The intensity of the American trade with these nations is similar to that between the United Kingdom and the former members of

---

[4] The map of French trade is not included.

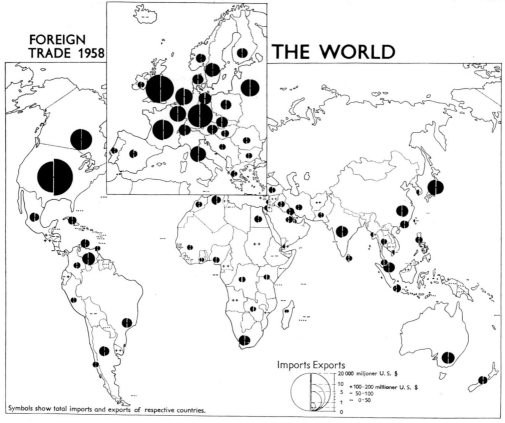

FOREIGN TRADE 1958

THE WORLD

Imports Exports

20 000 miljoner U. S. $
+ 100–200 millioner U. S. $
– 50–100
·· 0–50

Symbols show total imports and exports of respective countries.

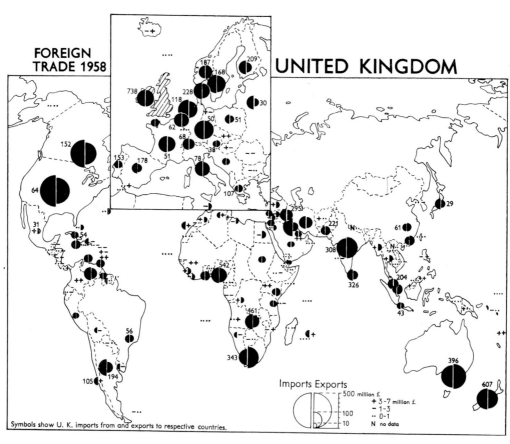

FOREIGN TRADE 1958

UNITED KINGDOM

Imports Exports

500 million £
+ 3–7 million £
– 1–3
·· 0–1
N no data

Symbols show U. K. imports from and exports to respective countries.

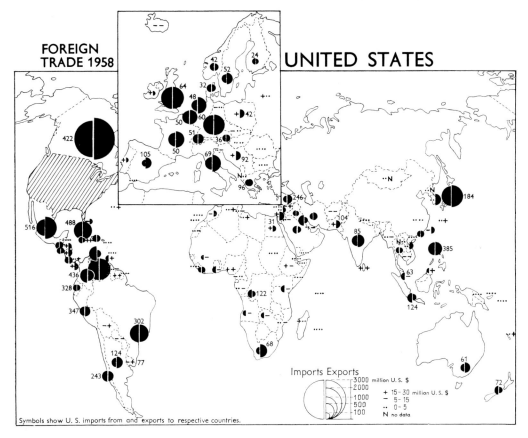

FOREIGN TRADE 1958

UNITED STATES

Symbols show U. S. imports from and exports to respective countries.

Imports Exports

3000 million U. S. $
2000
1000
500
100

\+ 15 – 30 million U. S. $
\- 5 – 15
∴ 0 – 5
N no data

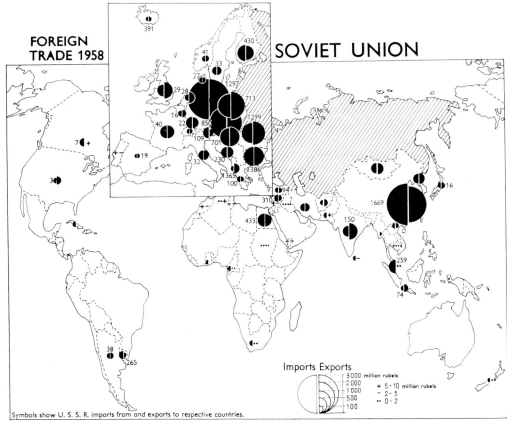

FOREIGN TRADE 1958

SOVIET UNION

Symbols show U. S. S. R. imports from and exports to respective countries.

Imports Exports

3000 million rubels
2000
1000
500
100

\+ 5 – 10 million rubels
\- 2 – 5
∴ 0 – 2

the British Empire, most of whom are now members of the Commonwealth. As the United States accounted for 14 per cent of the sum of the world's imports and exports in 1958 the index value 500 for a given country means that the United States had 70 per cent of its total foreign trade. Such reliance on one trade partner involves a great risk of political friction, however profitable the trade may be to both partners. Groups in the small country will feel that they are dominated by their big trade partner. The American dominance in Latin America was strengthened by the two world wars which cut off these countries from trade with Europe for long periods. It is likely that this dominance will become less pronounced and that Western Europe and Japan will expand their trade with Latin America.

Only two countries, Canada and Mexico, have land boundaries with the United States and most of their American trade moves by rail, road or pipeline.

The United States has low index values for countries in northwestern Europe. They are remarkably low for Finland and Denmark. The relatively high values for Spain, Italy, Yugoslavia, Greece and, particularly, Turkey, but also for many countries in southern and eastern Asia (Pakistan, India, Thailand and Indonesia) support the thesis that political geography may be as influential as economics in shaping trade patterns.

THE SOVIET UNION. The foreign trade of the Soviet Union has a remarkable distribution. About 75 per cent is trade with countries of the Communist Bloc, most of which have land boundaries with the U.S.S.R. Many of these trade relations are reflected in extremely high index values, only exceptionally found elsewhere. But as the Soviet Union had only 3.9 per cent of the world's imports and exports in 1958 the index values of about 1300 for East Germany and Rumania correspond to a Soviet share of 51 per cent in the foreign trade of

these two countries. The East European nations are dominated by a political and economic giant with little foreign trade—it ranks between Canada and the Netherlands—and much of their remaining trade is with other East European countries within the framework of the COMECON. The large Soviet trade with China has been drastically reduced since 1958.

The most remarkable feature of Soviet trade with the non-communist world is the complete absence of trade with a large number of countries outside the Eurasian continent. Trade with Finland, Iceland, Egypt, Syria, Iran, Afghanistan, Uruguay and Malaya show high index values. Most of the few countries outside the Communist Bloc with which the Soviet Union has a well developed trade are neighbors. As foreign trade plays a subordinate role in the Soviet economy—the Soviet Union has less than one-third of the international trade of the United States—even limited Soviet commitments to build airfields, ports, hospitals, etc. in underdeveloped countries will show up in high index values. By and large, however, the Soviet foreign trade pattern seems to be fairly stable. The Soviet trade with underdeveloped countries in Africa and Latin America is limited indeed. The most noteworthy changes between 1958 and 1960 were the increased trade with the Common Market (Finland is no longer the only important Soviet trade partner in Western Europe), the decrease in trade with China and the appearance of Cuba as a medium-sized trade partner. Trade with the United States and Canada remains insignificant.

WEST GERMANY. The last year typical of *l'ancien régime* in the foreign trade of Continental Western Europe was 1958 which still showed a low index value for the trade between the two neighbors West Germany and France. Two years later, when the effects of the EEC agreement had begun to show up in the trade statistics, that trade had doubled. The choice

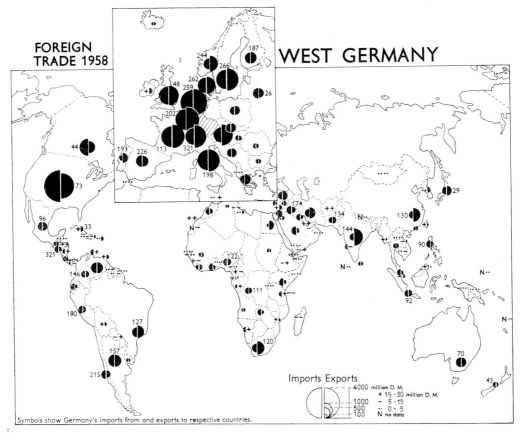

FOREIGN TRADE 1958

WEST GERMANY

Symbols show Germany's imports from and exports to respective countries.

Imports Exports	
4000 million D.M.	+ 15−30 million D.M.
1000	− 5 − 15
500	∴ 0 − 5
100	N no data

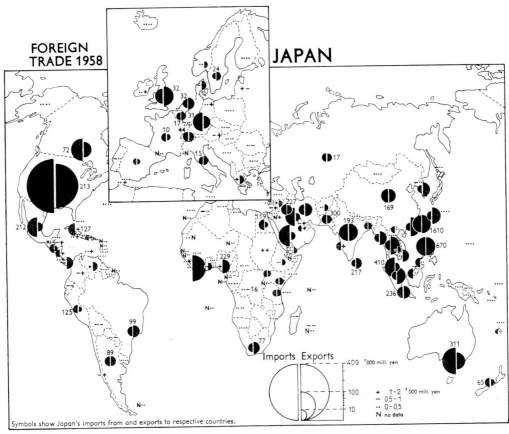

FOREIGN TRADE 1958

JAPAN

Symbols show Japan's imports from and exports to respective countries.

Imports Exports	
400 '000 mill. yen	+ 1−2 '000 mill. yen
100	− 0,5 − 1
10	∴ 0 − 0,5
	N no data

of the year 1958 for our trade maps might therefore be justified although it was a year of recession for the United States and some other countries. A later year would have shown a Europe in rapid transition and would not have been typical of any longer period.

West Germany has a foreign trade pattern which radically differs from that of the former colonial powers Britain and France. The German index values are rather high for the countries of non-communist Europe except Britain and France and for Austria and Switzerland even very high. But West Germany also has a well developed trade with Latin America, Africa and southern Asia, including Mainland China. The small trade with Japan is a striking exception. No country has a trade pattern that more closely resembles the world distribution of total international trade.

JAPAN is more isolated than any other of the economically advanced countries. In addition to isolation by long distances from the two poles of the world economy, Europe and Anglo-America on either side of the North Atlantic, it is also separated by having a cultural and linguistic background different from the dominating European. Australia and New Zealand are also isolated geographically, but the language dominating in international trade is theirs. The necessity of teaching hundreds of thousands of young Japanese enough of the European languages, primarily English, to enable them to participate in international business, read scientific and technical journals, etc., is a serious handicap. The design of goods for export has to be adapted to the taste of New York or Paris even if the domestic design should be far superior. The average American or European business man would be staggered by the thought of doing business in Japanese and of adapting the design of his products according to the taste of Kyoto or Tokyo.

In the postwar period Japanese foreign trade has been mainly directed towards North America, primarily the United States. That country alone accounted for 35 per cent of Japan's imports and 32 per cent of her exports in 1958 if the large exports of ships to Liberia (8 per cent) are included as exports to the United States. Trade with North America exceeded trade with Asia in 1958. In comparison with these two continents Europe is of little importance as a Japanese trade partner.

The large and diversified trade between Japan and the United States was promoted by the Cold War and the obvious American strategic and political interest in favorable economic developments in Japan. Machinery tops the list of Japanese imports from the United States with 23 per cent, but then follows a long list of raw materials (raw cotton, soybeans, wheat, coal, petroleum, scrap, barley, corn) which together account for 47 per cent. The export list is even more diversified but almost all of the leading items on this list can be characterized as labor-intensive manufactured products. Japan thus imports primarily raw materials from the world's leading industrial nation and exports almost exclusively manufactured products of a wide variety.

The intense Japanese trade with the United States is not merely a postwar phenomenon. In the late 1920s when raw silk made up almost 40 per cent of the Japanese export value the United States was by far the leading silk consuming country in the world and the Japan-to-United States flow of raw silk was one of the leading commodity flows in international trade measured by value. We must go back to the turn of the century to find Europe on a par with the United States as a Japanese trade partner.

Japan's trade with Asia apart from the Soviet Union is well developed. Trade with Mainland China has fluctuated widely in recent years. Even if closer commercial relations should in the future be established between Japan and China the potentials for Chinese

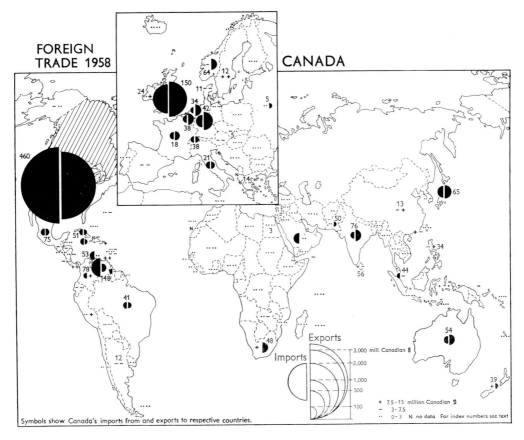

FOREIGN TRADE 1958

CANADA

Symbols show Canada's imports from and exports to respective countries.

Exports
Imports

3,000 mill. Canadian $
2,000
1,000
500
100

+ 7.5 - 15 million Canadian $
- 3 - 7.5
·· 0 - 3 N no data For index numbers see text

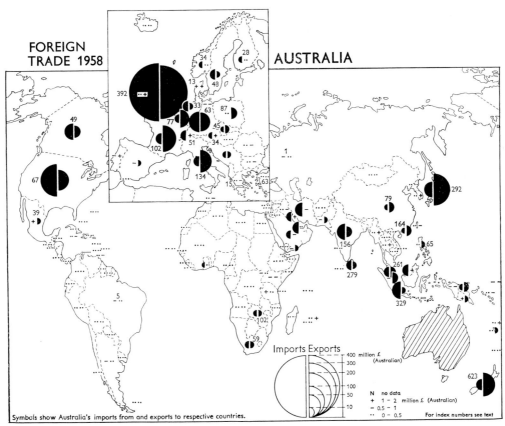

FOREIGN TRADE 1958

AUSTRALIA

Symbols show Australia's imports from and exports to respective countries.

Imports Exports
400 million £ (Australian)
300
200
100
50
10

N no data
+ 1 - 2 million £ (Australian)
- 0.5 - 1
·· 0 - 0.5   For index numbers see text

trade should not be exaggerated. China's total foreign trade is small and cannot be expected to increase drastically. However, political friction with the Soviet Union might lead China to turn to Japan for increased trade, which would lead to the re-establishment of some of the interwar trade patterns with Chinese coal, iron ore, other mineral products and soybeans moving to Japan and Japanese manufactured products moving in the opposite direction. The last few years have seen a rapid increase in trade between Japan and the Soviet Union, a reflection of Soviet efforts to increase trade between Japan and the Communist Bloc. The Japanese trade with Australia and New Zealand has increased substantially since 1958 and trade with Australia had become somewhat better balanced by 1960.

Europe is an almost unexploited continent for the Japanese foreign trade, largely due to European discrimination against Japanese products.

CANADA AND AUSTRALIA are good illustrations of the thesis that politics has a great influence on foreign trade patterns. Canada with almost all her eggs in the American basket has, compared to Australia, a relatively small trade with the United Kingdom, their common mother country. This is in spite of shorter distances to England from Canada than from Australia. The reasons for the different foreign trade patterns of these two countries with a similar historic background are primarily a matter of political geography.

About two-thirds of Canada's population live within a hundred-mile discontinuous zone along the American border, a border that cuts through several natural economic regions. Her neighbor to the south, with a population about ten times as large and a somewhat higher standard of living, has the same language as the majority in bi-lingual Canada. Culturally the two countries are similar. It has been natural for American companies to move

across the border and make investments in Canada and for Canadians to make investments in the United States. In spite of a certain fear expressed from time to time that Canada will be economically swallowed up by her big neighbor the relations between the two countries have been good; their common boundary is one of the least marked in the world. Thanks to her great trade with the United States Canada ranks as one of the big ten in international trade. As the Canadian economy is closely tied to the American it is very sensitive to fluctuations in American business and the Canadian standard of living closely follows the American.

Canadian trade with European countries, apart from the United Kingdom, is small. The index value for France is noticeably low. The French-speaking minority in Canada is almost one-third of the population but the linguistic and cultural ties in this case do not seem to have created much trade. The relatively high value for Norway is a result of Canadian exports of alumina to the Norwegian electro-metallurgical industry. In contrast to her southern neighbor Canada has not engaged much in trade with Latin America. Only for Venezuela (petroleum), Jamaica (bauxite) and British Guiana (bauxite and sugar) is the index value above 100. In her trade with Japan Canada has a higher index value than the European countries but considerably lower than the United States.

Australia in contrast to Canada has no great power as a closely related neighbor. New Zealand is smaller than Australia and does not qualify. Japan is the closest economic great power but relations between Australia and Japan have been far from ideal. Twenty years ago the two nations were at war and before that Australia was in a defensive position against expansive Japan. But with Japan closely tied to the Western democracies foreign trade between the two countries can be expected to increase considerably. The index

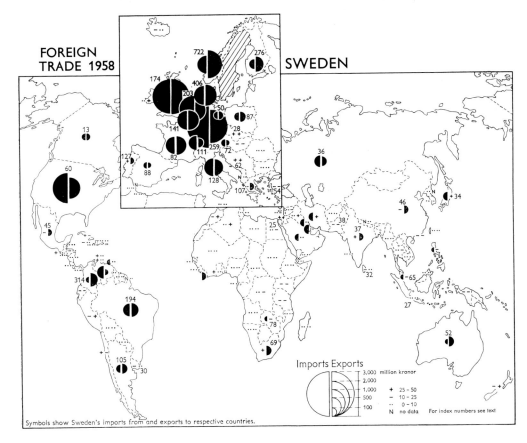

FOREIGN
TRADE 1958

SWEDEN

Symbols show Sweden's imports from and exports to respective countries.

Imports Exports

3,000 million kronor
2,000
1,000   + 25 – 50
500   – 10 – 25
100   ·· 0 – 10
         N no data   For index numbers see text

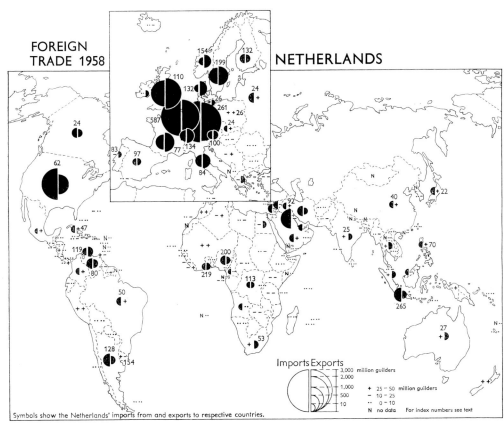

FOREIGN
TRADE 1958

NETHERLANDS

Symbols show the Netherlands' imports from and exports to respective countries.

Imports Exports

3,000 million guilders
2,000
1,000   + 25 – 50 million guilders
500   – 10 – 25
10   ·· 0 – 10
         N no data   For index numbers see text

value approached 300 in 1958 thanks to large exports of raw materials from Australia to Japan. If Australia increases her imports of Japanese manufactures total trade will expand and become more balanced like the trade that the United States, partly for strategic reasons, has developed with Japan. A democratic Japan, with a sound economy, is of primary interest to the United States and Australia. But it can be expected that Australia's trade with most countries in East and South Asia will increase, especially if the United Kingdom joins the European market and becomes involved in developing her underdeveloped trade with the Continent.

Australia has high index values for the countries along the sea route to Great Britain. Most of the trade with the Persian Gulf area, Indonesia and North Borneo is petroleum imports, which engage special tonnage. But for the trade with Singapore, Malaya, Ceylon, India, Aden, Italy, France, Belgium, West Germany and Poland, which all have unexpectedly high index values, the excellent connections by cargo liners between Northwest Europe and Australia should be of great importance. The old problem of the chicken and the egg can probably be solved in its liner shipping or foreign trade version by giving liner shipping the priority. At least this seems to hold true for underdeveloped countries along the main shipping routes. Trade between Ceylon and Australia would not have been so well developed had European cargo liners not called at Ceylon on their way to or from Australia.[1] The lack of such connections goes a long way to explain Australia's underdeveloped trade with Latin America and Africa.

SWEDEN AND THE NETHERLANDS, like Canada, have their foreign trade strongly concentrated to the neighboring markets. But the two European states in contrast to Canada have many neighbor countries speaking different languages and having different customs, marketing patterns, etc. Canada, being a well-developed neighbor of the world's largest homogeneous free trade area, represents the unique case, and the two European countries conform to the normal world pattern.

Sweden has well developed trade with her three Nordic neighbors and with the countries around the North Sea, West Germany, the Netherlands, Belgium and Great Britain. The neighbors behind the Iron Curtain are exceptions. For the Soviet Union, East Germany and Poland the index values are below 100. The value for trade with Norway is exceptionally high, higher than the Sweden–Denmark and the Norway–Denmark relations, both of which are a little over 400. The large Swedish exports of ships to Norway explain the excess over this value. The high index values for trade between the Nordic countries and especially between Sweden, Norway and Denmark have very few counterparts in Western Europe.

Sweden's trade with transoceanic countries is on the whole little developed. Exceptions are Brazil, Argentina and Colombia in Latin America and South Africa and Liberia in Africa. The Swedish exports to Colombia were exceptionally large in 1958. Normally this index value is about 100. In Swedish trade with South Africa and Liberia the exports dominate. The exports to Liberia doubled between 1958 and 1960 as a result of the Lamco project.

The Netherlands has a very high index value for trade with Belgium and about the same as Sweden for trade with West Germany. Both countries have a low value for their French trade. The Netherlands is the only country on the Continent with a value above 100 for trade with the United Kingdom. The large Dutch trade with the Middle East and the Guinea Coast reflect the importance of the

---

[1] The same observation can be made for trade between countries in Latin America, page 318.

Dutch oil refineries and the chocolate industry. Trade with Indonesia has declined considerably since this former Dutch colony gained independence, but the index value is still five to ten times larger than "normal" for countries separated by such distances.

Norden and Benelux should be ardent adherents of close economic cooperation in Western Europe. They should be anxious to defend and build out an already well developed trade with their neighbors. But the United Kingdom and France should have the most to gain from such cooperation. An increase of their trade with some countries to "normal" neighbor level would mean a doubling (France–Germany) and in some cases a fourfold increase (France–United Kingdom, United Kingdom–Germany) of present trade volumes.

The Shipping Industry

The World Merchant Fleet

At the beginning of the present century the gross tonnage of the world merchant fleet of steamers was less than 23 million tons. It doubled in the fourteen years up to World War I and continued to grow in the inter-war period with the exception of 1924 and the depression years of the early thirties. During World War II many vessels were lost,[1] but the newbuildings, especially in the United States, more than compensated for the losses.

[1] "Nearly 7,000 merchant vessels of 1,000 gross tons and over, totalling almost 34,000,000 gross tons, were lost during World War II from war causes alone." *Encyclopedia Britannica*, 1956 ed., Vol. 20. P. 557.

[2]

	Percentage of World Merchant Fleet (Tonnage)		
	1914	1939	1961
Coal-burning steamships	96.6	45.3	4.1
Oil-burning steamships	2.9	30.0	50.5
Motorships	0.5	24.7	45.4

Steam turbine machinery is used in very large vessels and in those requiring high speed, but in recent years new types of diesel engines have also been gaining favor in super carriers. (Lloyd's Register of Shipping, *Annual Report*, 1961.)

After a short period of reduction immediately after the war the fleet again resumed a rapid increase and in 1961 there were 130 million gross tons of steamers and motorships.

In addition to the steamer fleet of less than 23 million gross tons in 1900 there were sailing ships and barges totaling 6.5 million net tons. Although the sailing ships were far less efficient than the steamers they still accounted for a significant part of all sea transport, even in some trans-oceanic trades, e.g. the Australian wheat trade and the Chilean nitrate trade. Most of the large sailing ships disappeared in the early years of the century. The first diesel-engined ocean-going ship, the *Selandia*, was built in 1912 and the share of motor ships in the total fleet has been on the increase ever since. Very few steamships with reciprocating engines are now being built but steam turbines propel a rapidly expanding tonnage and the total tonnage of steamships has been slowly increasing.[2]

The age composition of the world fleet in the early sixties has been determined, firstly, by the rapidly increasing new-building activity in the post-war period, making the newest age groups relatively large, and, secondly, by the intense ship-building activity (primarily dry cargo vessels) during the war, especially in the

World Merchant Fleet 1900-1960

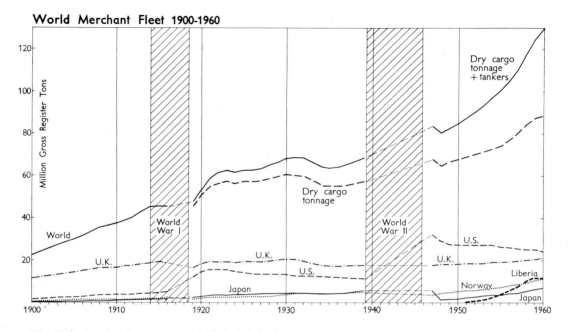

The United States' Reserve Fleet is included in the U.S. total and the World total. The Reserve Fleet on June 30, 1950, totaled 21,853,000 deadweight tons (or approximately 15.8 million gross register tons), and on June 30, 1960, 18,279,000 deadweight tons (approximately 13.2 million gross register tons).

Data from *Lloyd's Register of Shipping*. (U.S. Reserve Fleet 1950 according to *Statistical Abstract of the United States;* 1960 according to *Statistik der Schiffahrt.*)

United States. In 1961, no less than 43 per cent of the tanker tonnage and 24 per cent of the dry cargo tonnage was less than five years old. Of the tankers, only 14 per cent of the

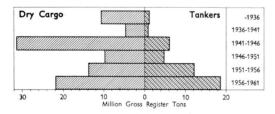

Age composition of the world merchant fleet, June 30, 1961. Age groups refer to year of construction July 1–June 30.
Data from *Lloyd's Register of Shipping.*

tonnage belonged to the age group 15–20 years (built during or immediately after the war), while the corresponding percentage for dry cargo vessels was 34. The proportion of tonnage in the active fleet built during the war is smaller than would appear from this analysis. The American reserve fleet of 13.5 million gross tons consists mainly of wartime buildings, and old ships make up a large proportion of the laid-up tonnage.[3] Considering the continued high ship-building activity, despite the prolonged slump in the freight markets, it seems unlikely that many of the inactive ships, built before or during World War II, will ever be brought into service again.

In recent years vessels in the largest tonnage categories have made up an increasingly greater part of the world fleet. While in 1939 ships of less than 6,000 gross register tons accounted for 57 per cent of the total tonnage, the corresponding figure in 1961 was only 23 per cent. The 4,000–5,999 ton group shrank from 26 to 7 per cent of the total gross registered tons in the period 1939–1961, and the following

[3] Cf. page 32.

30

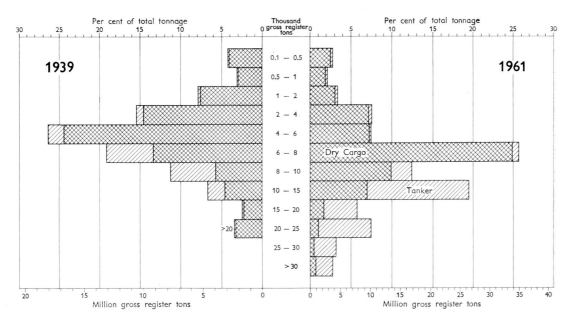

Size composition of the world merchant fleet, June 30, 1939 and June 30, 1961.
Data from *Lloyd's Register of Shipping.*

group now contains more tonnage than any other. Among the largest ships, the growing importance of large tankers is very obvious. In 1939 most tankers fell in the 6,000–9,999 ton groups, and there were very few of over 15,000 tons. (Most of these were actually whaling vessels.) In 1961 on the other hand, most of the tanker tonnage consisted of vessels of over 10,000 tons, and most of the tonnage in these size groups consisted of tankers.[4]

The rapid growth of the fleet must be seen against the background of expanding seaborne trade.[5] Total international seaborne trade in 1929 was 470 million tons; falling during the depression to a low of 350 million tons it was not until 1937 that it surpassed the 1929 level. After the war trade increased very rapidly and in 1960 reached close to 1,100 million tons. Between 1929 and 1960 seaborne international trade increased 2.3 times by weight,

[4] Note that the world fleet practically doubled in the period 1939–1961.
[5] The development in a few important commodities is treated on pages 55–110.
[6] Cf. page 85.

whereas the world merchant fleet not quite doubled. In the ten-year period 1950–1960 trade practically doubled, while the fleet increased only by 53 per cent. There are several factors that help to explain these differences in rates of growth. Modern ships are faster and more efficient and can produce more ton-miles per year than older ships. The share of tanker cargoes has increased: 21 per cent in 1937, 48 per cent in 1960. This is likely to increase the average hauling capacity of the fleet due to the large cargoes and short turn round time of tankers. The same is true of some important dry bulk cargoes, e.g. iron ore.[6] The average length of haul also affects the ratio of goods tonnage loaded to shipping tonnage needed. The long hauls of petroleum and iron ore and the emergence of the United States as the major coal exporter seem likely to have lengthened the average haul. If this is true, it has tended to lessen the difference in growth rates between trade and fleet. The opposite is true, however, of switches from domestic to

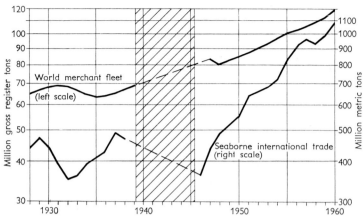

World merchant fleet and seaborne international trade 1928–1960.
Data from *Lloyd's Register of Shipping;* and United Nations *Statistical Yearbook*.

international trade, e.g. American oil imports from Venezuela instead of further increases in the shipments from Gulf ports to the North Atlantic Seaboard, even if the distances are of the same magnitude.

At the beginning of the present century the United Kingdom had more than half the merchant tonnage of the world. Although the British fleet continued to grow until 1915, its share dropped below 50 per cent already in 1902, and in 1914 was 42 per cent. The war losses were regained by 1921, but after that year the British fleet increased but little and actually decreased in the thirties. In 1947 the tonnage was about the same as it had been at the outbreak of World War II—and smaller than at the outbreak of World War I. In the 1950s there was again a moderate increase in the British fleet.

The United States fleet (including the Great Lakes fleet) at the beginning of the century totaled 1.45 million gross register tons of steamers, less than a seventh of the British, yet was the third largest after that of Germany (2.16 million tons). A rapid increase took place during and immediately after World War I, but the decrease begun in the early twenties lasted until World War II. This again brought with it a rapid increase of the American fleet, which surpassed that of the United Kingdom

and in 1947 was 32.4 million tons or 41 per cent of the world fleet. Many ships were sold abroad in the post-war years and the American fleet has been continually declining since. Due to the high cost of running American-flag ships, particularly the wartime buildings, which soon proved uncompetitive in the post-war world, a large part of the fleet has had to be inactivated, now forming the reserve fleet, which in 1961 was about 13.5 million tons or more than half the American-registered tonnage.

The Norwegian fleet at the beginning of the century consisted of 0.76 million gross tons of steamers and 0.88 million net tons of sailing ships. The steamer tonnage grew but suffered great losses during World War I. The development during the inter-war period was more favorable than for the British and American fleets and in 1939 Norway had nearly five million tons of steamers and motorships. World War II again brought heavy losses, but already in 1949 the fleet reached a new high and in 1961 the Norwegian fleet of 12 million tons was the world's third largest. More than half the tonnage consisted of tankers.

The Japanese fleet has enjoyed substantial support from the government. Its development during this century up to World War II is similar to that of Norway's, but Japan came

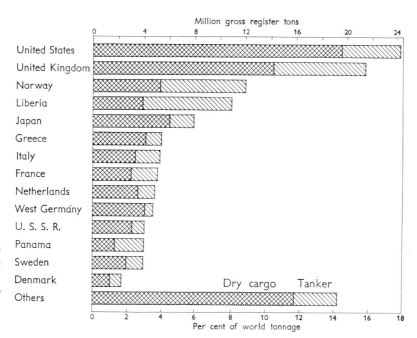

Flag distribution of the world merchant fleet, June 30, 1961.
Data from *Lloyd's Register of Shipping.*

out of World War I with a fleet larger than before the war and had surpassed Norway. World War II brought the Japanese fleet down to one-fifth of its prewar size, but reconstruction has been rapid, and with almost eight million tons in 1961 it was the world's fifth largest.

A spectacular and much-discussed phenomenon in the years since the end of World War II has been the fleets under the so-called *flags of convenience,* primarily those of Liberia and Panama and to a less extent of Honduras and Costa Rica. These fleets are owned by interests in other countries, primarily the United States and Greece. There are several reasons why ship-owners have placed their vessels on the registers of these countries. To a certain extent old ships with crew quarters and working conditions regarded as unsatisfactory have been transferred to Panamanian or Liberian registry, and it is particularly this fact which has caused violent opposition by seamen's unions, leading to threats of boycotts, etc. The greater part of the fleets flying flags

of convenience, however, are large, modern vessels, in every respect comparable to those under the national flags of their owners. The reasons for registering them under flags of convenience are two, high wages and high taxes. The first is of particular importance to American owners, who pay three to four times as high wages as European shipowners. The only way in which the Americans have been able to compete with the Europeans has been by Government subsidy or by registering their ships abroad and manning them with European seamen. To these shipowners tax evasion is a secondary problem and if the revenue is brought back to the American mother company it will be taxed. But there are also many shipowners for whom the virtual freedom from taxation is of primary importance. As long as freight rates were high, it was a great advantage to be able to use the revenue for writing off the value of the ships and to reinvest money in newbuildings. It was especially Greek shipowners who for this reason registered their ships abroad. In a long period of very low

33

freight rates, such as the one that has prevailed since 1957, hitting the tanker freight market especially hard, this reason loses its validity, and in the last few years many ships have been transferred from Liberian to Greek registry. In 1959 the Liberian fleet was 11.9 million gross tons, 7.1 million tons of which were tankers. In 1961 the fleet was down to 10.9 million tons, the tankers to 7.0 million tons, despite many large new ships having been registered in Liberia. In the two years the Greek fleet increased from 2.2 million tons to 5.4 million tons, the tanker fleet from 0.3 to 1.3 million tons. That the flags of convenience do not protect from the effect of a depressed freight market is illustrated by the fact that out of a total of 189 tankers of 1.9 million tons laid up in November, 1961, 65 totaling 0.74 million tons were registered in Liberia and Panama.[7]

With 4 million gross tons in 1961 the Soviet merchant marine was the eleventh largest. It is expected to grow rapidly in the next few years; the 1959–1965 seven-year plan calls for a doubling of the tonnage.

In 1961 there were 14 countries with a merchant fleet in excess of two million gross tons (page 33). Between them they had 83 per cent of the dry cargo fleet, 92 per cent of the tankers and 86 per cent of the total fleet. Liberia, Panama and Norway have more than half their tonnage in tankers, West Germany only 14 per cent and the United States 19 per cent.

Tramps, Liners and Industrial Carriers

According to the manner in which they are employed merchant vessels are described as tramps, liners or industrial carriers. It should be made clear from the outset that the divisions between these categories are not well defined.

There are several definitions of a tramp ship. One source states in general terms that the tramp is "a freight vessel that does not run in any regular line but takes cargo wherever the shippers desire".[1] The ship is hired either on trip charter for one voyage or several consecutive voyages or on time charter for a certain period. The conditions are set down in the *charter party,* for which there are many standardized forms for different trades. A ship in liner service has scheduled sailings from a given port or group of ports to one or more other ports. Its main purpose is the carrying of general cargo, often comprising a wide variety of goods, from many shippers to many receivers. A cargo liner may also take as many as twelve passengers; if more are to be taken the ship has to be licensed as a passenger liner or a combined passenger-cargo liner. The document regulating the conditions under which the shipment takes place is a *bill of lading.* The industrial carrier is a vessel owned by a manufacturing or business firm for the transport of its raw materials or products. Important examples are the tanker fleets of the big international oil companies and ore carriers owned by ore importing steel companies or exporting mining companies.

Historically the industrial carrier may be considered as the oldest of these three categories of ships. In the old days, say before the middle of the nineteenth century, the ships were small sailing vessels, and no telegraph communications enabled a ship-owner to know where his ship was and where a cargo could be picked up, nor could he give instructions to the master. Trade and shipping were parts of the same business; the master, who often owned part or all of the ship, had to decide on the buying and selling of goods in distant ports. In some ways the activities of the merchant-trader were similar to those of tramps. They did not follow fixed routes or time

[7] Roger Comoy, "Les transports maritimes pétroliers", *Transports,* No. 48, June 1960; *Lloyd's Register of Shipping; Statistik der Schiffahrt,* December, 1961.
[1] René de Kerchove, *International Maritime Dictionary.* Second Ed. New York, 1961. P. 853.

schedules and sought cargoes wherever they might find them. The increasing trade of the nineteenth century created the need for larger vessels, especially for the carrying of grain and cotton and later on for coal and other commodities. The functions of shipping and merchandising were separated, a development facilitated by the invention of the telegraph. The world tramp fleet grew with the growth in trade and an increasing share of it consisted of steamers, although large sailing ships were built even after the turn of the century. The estimates of the total world tramp fleet that have been made at different times vary in definitions and figures are not strictly comparable. Tank ships are not generally included, even if some of them perform services of the same character as the dry cargo tramps. It should be noted, however, that most tankers which are not owned by the oil companies are chartered by them on long-term contracts, and are closer to industrial carriers than to tramps as far as the general economic character of their employment is concerned. An estimate for 1914 put the tramp tonnage at 23 million gross tons or 46 per cent of the world fleet. The growing importance of liners, and to some extent of industrial carriers, caused a stagnation in the growth of the tramp fleet and a marked decline in its relative importance. In 1933 the tonnage was 22 million and the percentage 33.[2] The low figure of 10.4 million tons for 1935[3] is probably due both to a real

reduction of the tonnage and differences in definitions. It would correspond to 16 per cent of the world tonnage. The total tonnage of tramp ships over 1,000 gross tons in 1951 is given as 10.3 million tons, 16 per cent of the world fleet.[4] In the 1950s the tramps seem to have increased again, not only in tonnage but also in percentage of the world fleet. For 1957 an estimate of 19 per cent or 20 million tons has been published.[5]

There are several reasons for the decline of tramp shipping. These may be classed under four headings: (1) the absolute decline of some cargo movements; (2) the expansion of liner trade; (3) the accentuated development of specialized shipping (some of which, however, must be counted as tramp shipping in the wide sense of the term applied here); (4) the introduction of industry-owned tonnage by large-scale shippers (industrial carriers proper).[6] The decline of some cargo movements is due to technical and economic developments. The increasing use of synthetic nitrates instead of saltpeter from the Chilean desert meant a loss of an important tramp trade,[7] as did the drastic reduction in British coal exports in the interwar period and especially during and after World War II.[8] The market for British coal was partly taken over by oil, leading to a change from the services of the general tramp to those of specialized carriers, whether these be industrial carriers proper or not. The increase of the liner fleet at the expense of tramps has various reasons. The main purpose of tramps is the carrying of whole shiploads of bulk cargo, that of the liner the carrying of general cargo—manufactured goods but also raw materials and foodstuffs in less than shipload lots, usually in bags, bales, etc. But there is no fixed borderline between the two categories. Some bulk cargoes are available more or less at all times in large ports, served by liners, and rather than having to sail with part of their capacity unutilized the liners take part loads of them, e.g. grains or coal, carrying

[2] Franz Lohse, *Die Entwicklung der Trampschiff-fahrt in der Nachkriegszeit,* 1934 and *Report of the United States Maritime Commission on Tramp Shipping Service of 17 February 1938,* both quoted from Osborne Mance, *International Sea Transport.* London, 1945. P. 68.

[3] International Labour Office, quoted from Frank M. Fisser, *Trampschiffahrt—Tramp Shipping.* Bremen, 1957. P. 20.

[4] Kjeld B016akhus, *Trampskipsfartens fremtid.* Oslo, 1955. Pp. 17 ff.

[5] *Bremer Jahrbuch der Weltschiffahrt 1956/57,* quoted from Fisser, *op. cit.* P. 20.

[6] Fisser, *op. cit.* P. 23.

[7] Cf. page 365.

[8] Cf. page 77.

them at rates much lower than those prevailing for general cargo. Many commodities, which might technically be carried by tramps in shipload lots, are seldom bought in large enough quantities to make the chartering of a ship an economical proposition and are consequently shipped as parcels by liners. Cotton, wool, coffee, tobacco, tropical hardwoods all belong to this group. Sometimes the higher speed[9] and often better loading and unloading facilities, ventilation, etc. of a liner are decisive. By adjusting their conditions accordingly liner conferences[10] may discourage shippers, for whom it would otherwise pay to ship partly by tramps, partly by liners, from using the former possibility.

Some industrial carriers, e.g. ferry boats and other ships run by railroad companies, perform services of a liner character. Others transport large quantities of bulk cargoes, a service that would otherwise have been left to tramps. This is the case when specialized vessels are necessary, such as tankers or refrigerated ships, or desirable for their large capacity or equipment for rapid loading and unloading, such as large ore carriers and other bulk carriers. A large part of this specialized shipping is owned by commercial and industrial firms, other ships are time-chartered for long periods, often on bareboat charter, i.e. the charterer hires the crew, pays for bunkers and supplies, etc. Other ships are chartered for shorter periods or on voyage charter, and thus actually belong to the tramp fleet in a wide sense. The industrial carrier has become more and more important with the rapid increase in the world's tanker fleet, since a large part of the tankers belong to this category. Of the tanker fleet at the end of 1959, oil companies owned 37 per cent, tramp companies 57 per cent, governments 5 per cent, and others less than 1 per cent.[11]

Bulk carriers are dry cargo single-deck vessels with wide hatches, built to facilitate rapid loading and unloading of bulk cargoes. They are commonly grouped into ore carriers and

other bulk carriers, but ore carriers may occasionally carry other bulk commodities and many other bulk carriers may also be used in the ore trades. The large boats on the Great Lakes carrying iron ore, coal, limestone and grains[12] were the first large vessels in this category, but in ocean-borne trade they were rare until the 1950s, and those that existed were small, compared to the lakeboats and to the large bulk carriers of the last decade. In the mid-fifties the fleet of large bulk carriers began to grow very rapidly, and at the beginning of 1962 there were 611 ships of more than 10,000 deadweight tons, totaling over 11.5 million deadweight tons. Less than half the number of ships but slightly more than half the tonnage was ore carriers. The rapid increase results in a very young fleet; 72 per cent of the tonnage was less than 6 years old and newbuildings on order totaled no less than over seven million deadweight tons, of which less than a fourth was ore carriers.[13] Over half the seaborne trade in ores is now carried by bulk carriers, and they are becoming increasingly important in shipments of coal, grains and other bulk cargo commodities.[14]

The Freight Market

The freight rates, the prices paid for the services of the shipping industry, are determined by

[9] Older tramps, including Liberty and other warbuilt ships, have speeds of 10–11 knots. New large tramps often attain about 15 knots. Modern cargo liners commonly have speeds in the 16–18 knot range, often more. Subsidized American liners of over 21 knots are now in service.

[10] Cf. page 53.

[11] John I. Jacobs Company Limited, quoted from *Statistik der Schiffahrt*, April, 1960.

[12] Cf. page 261.

[13] Of the existing fleet Liberia accounted for 21 per cent, Norway 17, the United Kingdom 11, and Sweden 8. Liberia has the lead in ore carriers, Norway in other bulk carriers. Norway topped the list of vessels on order with 27 per cent, Liberia 15, Panama and Italy 9 each. Fearnley & Egers Chartering Co. Ltd., *World Bulk Carriers*. January, 1962.

[14] Fearnley & Egers Chartering Co. Ltd., *Shipments by Bulk Carriers 1961*. March, 1962. Cf. pages 85, 103.

supply and demand. On the supply side, "a ship-owner has a vessel with a definite cargo capacity, and has a choice of allowing it to perform transports over different distances". On the demand side, on the other hand, "a ware-owner generally needs transport between two definite harbours, and can choose between large and small consignments at a time. Thus the ship-owner is interested in freight rates over different transport distances for a certain ship, the ware-owner in freight rates over the same distance for vessels of different sizes."[1]

A characteristic feature of the tramp market is the possibility of employing the same vessel for shipments of different cargoes and over different routes. Although each individual ship is not interchangeable with every other ship, there are enough ships having a range of use overlapping that of other ships for the freight rates on different trades to follow one another closely. Until recently there was for most purposes very little interdependence between the markets for dry cargo ships and tankers. In the last few years grain shipments by tankers have become common,[2] and the two fields have become more closely connected. The time charter market and the trip charter market are also connected by the possibility for both ship-owner and shipper to turn from one to the other if more favorable terms should be obtainable there.

Most fixtures in the tramp and tanker market are made through brokers. The most important market is the Baltic Exchange in London. Information is generally made available immediately, and the situation can be followed day by day all over the world. The *Daily Freight Register,* the newspapers and business and shipping periodicals contain information of vessels fixed and the freight rates agreed on. To give an overall picture of the freight market several authorities, business organisations and trade journals calculate freight indices. These may have world-wide coverage or relate to freights in limited sectors of the market. The development of the *Norwegian Shipping News'* dry cargo indices (page 38) is taken as an expression of the general freight level for dry cargo tonnage fixed on trip charter and time charter 1947–1961. The laid-up tonnage is indicated by the curve for shipping laid up in British and Irish ports for all reasons.[3]

When tonnage available is in excess of demand freight rates are low. It pays for the shipowner to keep his ship in operation as long as the freight revenue covers variable costs, i.e. costs for fuel, crew, etc., which only accrue if the vessel is in operation. Should the freight rates fall below this level the ship is laid up. A further fall in rates will cause more ships to be laid up, thus restricting the supply and acting as a brake on the downward movement of rates. An increase in demand, on the other hand, will re-activate the most economic of the laid-up ships, increasing supply and preventing a further rise in the rate level. Under these circumstances the supply of tonnage is very elastic, i.e. small changes in the rate level cause large changes in the supply of tonnage. The general state of the freight market is not reflected so much by changes in the freight indices as by changes in laid-up tonnage. An increasing demand for tonnage

[1] Thomas Thorburn, *Supply and Demand of Water Transport.* Stockholm, 1960. P. 188. This work, subtitled "Studies in cost and revenue structures of ships, ports and transport buyers with respect to their effects on supply and demand of water transport of goods", discusses theoretically the mechanism of price determination in water transport. In this chapter only a few important points which help to explain the variations in the over-all rate fluctuations are discussed. Liner freights are discussed in a following chapter (page 54), and we limit ourselves here to voyage and time charter rates for dry cargo and tanker tonnage.

[2] Cf. page 103.

[3] These data are readily available for the whole period, whereas data on total laid-up tonnage in the world for other reasons than repair are available only for the later part of it. They would otherwise have shown a closer relationship between freight rates and inactive tonnage. It can be shown, however, that both curves vary in considerable agreement with one another.

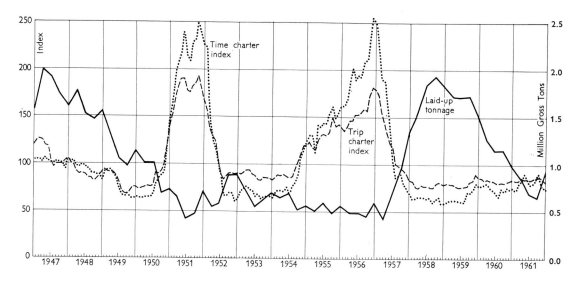

Laid-up tonnage in British and Irish ports and Norwegian Shipping News Freight Indices 1947–1961.
Data from Chamber of Shipping of the United Kingdom, *Annual Report;* and *Norwegian Shipping News.*

causes more and more ships to be taken out of lay-up until a stage is reached, where only ships undergoing repair or inspection remain and now supply becomes very inelastic; even very large increases in freight rates produce but little increase in the supply of tonnage. Should demand continue to be in excess of supply very rapid increases in freight rates will occur. Only a limited part of the freight market is affected by competition from other means of transport: some coastwise shipments may be taken over by over-land routes. For most commodities the freight constitutes only a small part of the price at which the goods are sold. If the freight makes up 10 per cent of the c.i.f. price of grains, a 20 per cent increase in freight rates will raise the price of grains by 2 per cent, a very small amount in comparison to other variations in grain prices.[4]

In 1947–1950 there was a considerable amount of tonnage laid up. Freight rates were low and falling. In 1950 demand increased as

a result of the Korean War, both for military shipments and increased civilian demand during the armament boom. Freight rates more than doubled in less than a year. Laid-up tonnage was very small. But the shipping boom did not last long. By mid-1952 freights were back almost at their previous level and a little tonnage was again laid up. In 1954 the increasing world trade had again created a demand large enough to reduce the laying-up and freight rates started to rise. This development was accentuated by the Suez Crisis in 1956, although dry cargo freights were not affected to the same degree as tanker freights. During the shipping boom many new ships had been ordered, and when conditions returned to a more normal state after the Suez incident tonnage supply exceeded demand, resulting in rapidly falling rates and increased laying-up. Since 1958 growing trade has again reduced the laid-up tonnage in spite of the rapidly expanding fleet, but not enough to substantially raise the freight rates. One factor contributing

[4] Ivar Högbom, *Världssjöfarten.* Göteborg, 1934. Pp. 286 ff; T. Koopmans, *Tanker Freight Rates and Tankship Building.* Haarlem 1939. P. 39; Thorburn, *op. cit.* Pp. 196 ff.

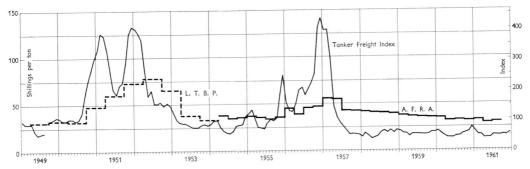

Comparison between Tanker Freight Index and "Award Rates" 1949–1961.
Norwegian Shipping News Tank Freight Index MOT/Scale = 100.
L.T.B.P. and A.F.R.A. Shillings per ton Aruba/Curaçao–United Kingdom.
Scales of graph: Index 100 = 35s 6d = MOT/Scale.
Break in curve August–September 1949 due to devaluation of pound.
Data from *Norwegian Shipping News; World Petroleum*, April, 1958, p. 43; Fearnley & Egers Chartering Co. Ltd.

to the persistently low tramp freight rates has been the inroads made by tankers in the grain trades.[5]

In times of low freights time charter rates tend to be relatively lower than trip charter rates. When rates go up, time charter rates rise more quickly and in boom periods are higher than trip charter rates. Harbor charges and fuel are paid for by the charterer in the case of time charter and by the shipowner in the case of trip charter. These cost items are relatively unaffected by the state of affairs in the freight market. In a situation of surplus tonnage the charterer will therefore have to see time charter rates reduced to a level lower than that of trip charter rates, otherwise it would be more economical to charter the ship on a trip charter basis. In times of very high rates he will, for the same reason, be willing to pay relatively more for a time chartered vessel, since part of his cost for the shipment will not be affected by the high cost level for transport.[6]

The main features of the development of rates in the tanker market in the 1947–1961 period were the same as those in the market for dry cargo tonnage. The tanker curve had a very high peak in the winter of 1947–1948, for which there was no counterpart in the dry cargo curve. Another difference is the amplitude of the variations. The trip charter index

for dry cargo tonnage never reached three times the lowest value recorded in the period, whereas the tanker index fell to one-tenth of the peak value from December 1956 to January 1958.

Even if industrial carriers and vessels on long term charter are important, voyage charter is the normal form of employment for most dry cargo vessels outside the liner services. In the tanker trades, however, industrial carriers and vessels on long term charter to the oil companies account for the bulk of the fleet, and the average cost of transport is only to a limited degree influenced by the rates paid for voyage chartered vessels and consequently fluctuates much less violently. The variations in the cost of transport for the 1949–1954 period are shown on the graph above by the London Tanker Broker Panel Award Rates (L.T.B.P.) and from 1954 by the Average Freight Rate Assessment (A.F.R.A.). The L.T.B.P. rates were calculated on the cost of two-year time charters, the A.F.R.A. rates are calculated as

[5] Cf. page 103.
[6] Thorburn, *op. cit.* Pp. 111 f., 197 f.

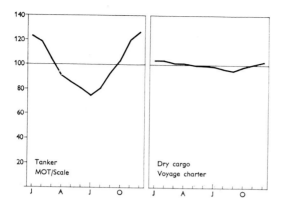

Norwegian Shipping News Freight Indices: Average seasonal variations 1947–1961.
Calculated from data in *Norwegian Shipping News.*

weighted averages for trip charter, short and long time charter and the cost of the company-owned tankers. The A.F.R.A. rates are used by the oil companies in determining prices.

Freight rates in the tanker market are generally determined as percentages of constant price scales, and freight indices and L.T.B.P. and A.F.R.A. rates are quoted in the same way. These scales were first established during World War II by the United States Maritime Commission and the British Ministry of Transport and are referred to as U.S.M.C. and M.O.T. The M.O.T. scale has later been modified to the London Market Tanker Nominal Freight Scale, and further to Scale Nos. 2 and 3, and in 1962 it was succeeded by the Intascale of the International Nominal Freight Scale Association, Ltd. The U.S.M.C. has been replaced by the American Tanker Rate Schedule, A.T.R.S. The index curve on page 39 is based on fixtures in sterling and given as percentages of M.O.T. and Scale. After the devaluation of the pound in 1949 it became necessary to differentiate between dollar freights in percentage of U.S.M.C. rates and sterling freights in percentage of M.O.T. and, later, Scale rates.

The tanker freight rate curve (page 39) shows considerable seasonal variations with winter maximum and summer minimum. When averaged to a seasonal index for the 1949–1961 period, the December maximum is 126 per cent of the annual average, while the July minimum is only 75 per cent. The seasonal variations in the dry cargo tramp freight index are much smaller. The average varies only between a February maximum of 103 per cent and a September minimum of 96 per cent of the yearly average, but a statistical analysis indicates a clear seasonal component in the variations (see left). The seasonal variations of the freight rates are a result of variations in demand for tonnage, caused by the seasonal character of many important trades. In the case of dry cargo shipments, the commodities which contribute most to the seasonality are grains, iron ore and lumber.[7] Of these grains has its annual maximum tonnage demand in May, while iron ore and lumber have theirs later in the summer. Some index series of tramp freight rates are published not only for the tramp freight market as a whole but also for individual commodities.[8] A comparison between the variations in estimated tonnage employment for a commodity and the corresponding freight index generally shows a certain agreement between the two series. This agreement is far from perfect and there is a time-lag. Freight rates usually reach maxima and minima one to three months earlier, since many ships are chartered well ahead of the actual trip. The seasonal maximum in freight rates in the late northern winter corresponds with the seasonal peak of grain shipments in the spring, while the late summer maximum of iron ore and lumber shipments have little effect on the ore and lumber freight indices, in the former case probably due to the large

[7] Göran Norström, "Seasonal Variations in the Employment of Bulk Cargo Tonnage", *Tijdschrift voor Economische en Sociale Geografie,* 1961. P. 119.

[8] E.g. the tramp freight index of the Chamber of Shipping of the United Kingdom, the weekly freight index of Maritime Research Inc., the Netherlands index of Joh. den Braber.

share of industrial carriers in the ore trades.[9] The high state of the freight index in the fall and early winter, in spite of the seasonally low demand, is to be seen against the background of the seasonally high laying-up of tonnage in the winter (page 38).

The seasonal patterns of the freight rates differ not only between commodities but also between trade routes for the same commodity. Particularly on long routes, e.g. the Australia—Europe grain trade, the seasonal variations may be very different from those in world averages.

An important factor influencing the freight rates in a particular trade is the return cargo position. If the goods flow over a certain route is predominantly unidirectional many ships have to proceed in ballast to the port of loading, and for these ships it will pay to accept a cargo at a very low rate, as long as it covers the extra costs incurred for the loading and unloading of the return cargo and possible

[9] Cf. page 85.

[10] It can be shown that theoretically the difference between freights in the two directions may be expected to be twice the cost per dwt ton of a trip of the empty ship over the route. Thus the difference increases with growing transport distance, not only absolutely, but also relatively in relation to the freight rates. Thorburn, *op. cit.* P. 180.

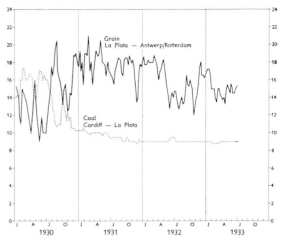

Freight market fixtures 1930–1933. Freight rates in shillings per ton.
Source: Ivar Högbom, *Världssjöfarten,* Göteborg, 1934. P. 296.

costs under way in excess of sailing in ballast. In this way the freight rates in the light direction (i.e. the direction of the ballast trips) will be lower than in the opposite direction.[10] The most striking example of this was the freights paid in the La Plata—Europe trades before World War II. While the grain freights in the heavy direction from the River Plate to Europe

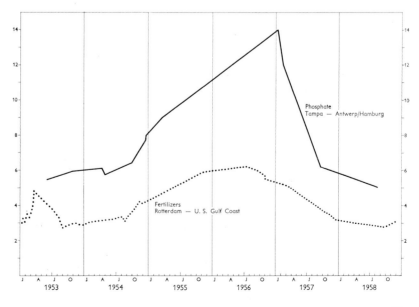

Freight market fixtures 1953–1958. Freight rates in U.S. dollars per ton. Data from *Daily Freight Register.*

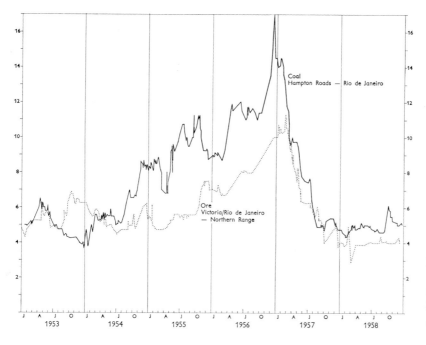

Freight market fixtures 1953–1958. Freight rates in U.S. dollars per ton. Data from *Daily Freight Register*.

varied over a rather wide range, coal freights in the light direction from Europe to the River Plate were constant over long periods, rising considerably only when a crop failure in Argentina reduced grain shipments to approximately the same quantities as those of coal shipments in 1930 (page 41). A similar difference between freights in the heavy direction from the United States and those in the light direction from Europe and Brazil can be shown in the post-war years (page 41 and above), even if the lower curves here fluctuate much more than in the 1930s.[11]

Shipbuilding activity varies with the state of the freight market. Generally a shortage of tonnage tending to raise the level of freight rates also stimulates shipbuilding, but due to the time required before the intention of shipowners to increase their fleets results in orders to the shipyards there is a time-lag, and the peak in construction in hand and on order is reached some time after the peak in freight rates has passed. For instance, the high freight level in 1951 was followed by a peak in building activity in early 1952 and the maxi-

mum of orders on the books of the yards in 1957 was not reached until after the collapse of the freight market early in that year (page 43).

A thorough German study of the influence of freight rates on shipbuilding[12] shows that this general dependence of shipbuilding on the level of freight rates is far from universal and varies between different countries. After World War II there has been a tendency towards less pronounced variations in newbuildings than previously. This has been particularly noticeable in the building of dry cargo ships for British owners, while many of the orders causing the shipbuilding boom beginning in 1950 came from American and Japanese

[11] The smoothness of the curves for fertilizer freights (page 41) is due to the small number of fixtures reported as compared with the coal and ore curves above.

[12] Jörg Schneider, *Empirische Untersuchungen über den Einfluß von Frachtraten, Frachteinnahmen und Schiffbaupreisen auf den Bau von seegehenden Güterschiffen 1900–1958*. Verkehrswissenschaftliche Forschungen. Schriftenreihe des Verkehrswissenschaftlichen Seminars der Universität Hamburg. Band 6. Berlin, 1961.

owners; those of 1954–1957 came from Norwegians and Dutch and from owners registering their vessels in Panama and Liberia. The
building of tankers for the oil companies has
been rather less variable, while Norwegian
tankers seem to have been ordered in periods
of low freight rates. In several cases the rise
in the number of new orders started before the
rise in the freight level, and could therefore
not be considered as a result of an influence
from the freight market.[13] On the other hand
not all periods of high freights were followed
by a corresponding increase in construction.
The German study stresses the fact that the
ship-owners as investors are more directly
concerned with the revenue and the possibility
of acquiring capital for investment than with
the temporary freight level. After a period of
low freights many owners lack even the capital
necessary for reinvestment to replace obsolete
tonnage. Only after a period of better freight
earnings do they have the means to order new
vessels, sometimes assisted by credits from the
shipyards, which are anxious to see their
orderbooks replenished.[14]

In times of rapid technical and economic
changes the shipbuilding activity tends to be
stimulated, even if the total tonnage afloat
is more than necessary to carry out all
transportation required by contemporary trade.
The increasing importance of very large vessels,
operating more economically than older,
smaller ones in the late 1950s and early 1960s[15]
has meant much to stimulate the ordering of
new tonnage in spite of the depressed freight
rates and much tonnage being laid up.

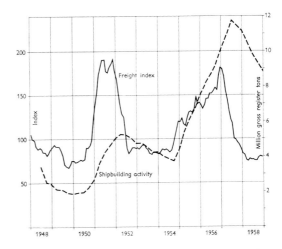

Shipbuilding activity (construction in hand and on
order) and freight rates 1948–1958.
Data from Shipbuilding Council of America, quoted
in Jörg Schneider, *Empirische Untersuchungen
über den Einfluß von Frachtraten, Frachteinnahmen und Schiffbaupreisen auf den Bau von
seegehenden Güterschiffen 1900–1958.* Berlin, 1961;
Norwegian Shipping News (Dry cargo trip charter
index).

Legislation and Government Subsidy

The demand and supply of water transport is
influenced not only by the free market forces
and by conferences and other agreements between shipowners but also by the institutional
framework within which they operate. Taxation and general economic legislation pertain-
ing to shipping and other industries alike will
not be treated here, nor technical regulations
regarding safety at sea, etc.

Most countries protect their shipping industry by reserving coastal shipping for ships
flying the national flag. Among the exceptions
are the United Kingdom and the Nordic
countries.[1] Trade between a mother country
and its colonies and dependencies often follows
the same rules. The United States, for instance,
reserves not only trade between ports on the
same seaboard but also intercoastal traffic and

---

[13] Large, financially well consolidated companies
are in a position to plan their newbuildings on a
long term basis more rationally than one or two-
vessel companies.
[14] Schneider, *op. cit.* Pp. 128, 144 f.
[15] Cf. page 36.
[1] However, until 1958 Sweden discriminated against
Norwegian vessels in coastal trade and Norway likewise against Swedish vessels, by mutual agreement of
1905.

traffic with Hawaii and Puerto Rico for American vessels.

While coastal shipping as a rule is restricted to ships of national registry international shipping is generally in principle open to ships of any nationality, and exceptions to this rule are considered as flag discrimination and energetically opposed by those who consider their rights infringed upon. Historically, however, the rule of flag equality is rather recent. Before the middle of the nineteenth century the maritime powers legislated to protect the interests of their merchant marines in international trade. An English law enacted in 1381 stated that "none of the King's liege people should from henceforth ship any merchandise in going out or coming within the realm of England but only in the ships of the King's liegeance, on penalty of forfeiture of vessel and cargo".[2] This law was a forerunner of later English legislation, particularly Cromwell's Navigation Act, which protected the English merchant fleet against competition, particularly from the Dutch, in the period when England developed into the world's leading seafaring nation. Similar measures were taken in France and other countries. Along with laws restricting the participation of foreign ships in the import and export trade went subsidies to shipping and fishing. They often were designed to ensure the recruitment of trained sailors for the navy. The shipbuilding industry was also stimulated in various ways. In the United States, for instance, only American-built ships could be registered from 1792 to 1914.[3]

The British Navigation Act was repealed in 1849 and the freedom of the seas gradually was accepted. Government support to the shipping industry lessened and generally took the form of subsidies. Conditions changed during the two world wars, and since the end of World War II flag discrimination has become a problem of increasing importance to the old maritime powers. The most common form

has been bilateral agreements between the parties to trade agreements that commodities exchanged should be carried in ships registered in one of the countries concerned. A particular arrangement of quantitatively great importance is the American rule that 50 per cent of all goods paid for by the U.S. Government as military and economic assistance to other countries must be shipped in American bottoms. Other discriminatory practices include currency control measures, import and export licences restraining the choice of the flag, discriminatory taxes and port charges. These practices have been fought by the old shipping nations. The Convention for European Economic Cooperation of 1948 contains rules preventing flag discrimination. Although they do not have the legal force of law binding on states they are being followed by the great majority of the seventeen OEEC member countries.[4] British shipping, with its world-wide services, has found the discriminatory practices particularly damaging. "Of the 64 countries to which British ships traded in 1957 no fewer than 40 have, during the past five years, practised flag discrimination in one form or another... Trade treaties known to include discriminatory shipping clauses were concluded by no fewer than 35 countries with the Argentine, Brazil, Egypt and India well to the fore in the number of such treaties to which they are parties."[5]

Multilateral and unilateral action by states has sometimes proved successful,[6] but unless

[2] David A. Wells, *Our Merchant Marine*. Here quoted from Edwin M. Bacon, *Manual of Ship Subsidies*. Chicago, 1911. P. 11.

[3] Grosvenor M. Jones, *Government Aid to Merchant Shipping*. Department of Commerce, Bureau of Foreign and Domestic Commerce. Special Agents Series No. 119. Revised ed. Washington, 1925. P. 11.

[4] Hans Georg Röhreke, *The Formal and the Material Concept of Flag Equality*. Göteborg, 1961. Pp. 12 f.

[5] Chamber of Shipping of the United Kingdom, *Annual Report 1958–59*. Pp. 58 f.

[6] When for instance Ecuador charged consular fees at a rate one per cent higher when goods were imported in non-Ecuadorian ships, the United States

an international agreement is reached different forms of flag discrimination will remain an important factor affecting the supply and demand of shipping tonnage and thereby the freight market.

Although the payment of bounties had sometimes formed part of the mercantile system supporting shipping like other industries, it was with the advent of the steam liners shortly before the middle of the last century that the modern forms of government subsidies were first used. The earliest of these forms is the mail subsidy system: the government pays a fixed amount to a liner company which undertakes to operate a regular service with a given frequency of sailings and to carry mails. The first contract of this type was signed in 1837 by the British Admiralty and the Peninsular Company, later the Peninsular and Oriental Steam Navigation Company, for a weekly service between England and Spain and Portugal.[7] The first contract for a transatlantic service was concluded between the Admiralty and Samuel Cunard in 1839, effective from June 1, 1840.[8] The mail subsidies soon developed into a normal practice in most countries and have remained so up to the present. They

have been instrumental in developing fast, regular trans-oceanic liner services. There are also examples of lines that have been able to operate without subsidies from the beginning,[9] and many mail contracts are no more than normal business contracts involving no government bounty.

Besides mail subsidies there are other forms of payments by the government for services performed, which might include a subsidy, if the payment is more than the additional cost to the shipowner. A common form is payments for extra equipment, strength or speed to enable the ship to be used as a naval auxiliary or troop transport in wartime. An early example of this was the stipulation in the contract of 1837 between the British Admiralty and the Peninsular Company that each vessel in the service should be fitted with armament consisting of six, nine or twelve pound guns, 20 muskets, 20 pistols, 20 swords and 30 rounds of powder and ball and that on each ship a naval officer should be carried.[10] The American Merchant Marine Act stipulates that a ship, in order to qualify for construction-differential subsidies,[11] should meet certain specifications with regard to Navy requirements for rapid conversion as a military or naval auxiliary.[12]

Shipbuilding subsidies, paid by the governments of many countries, are designed to help both the shipbuilding industries and the merchant fleets. The forms they take decide whether the former or latter gain most. They may consist of the government outright paying for part of the construction cost. Often they consist of loans to the shipowners, and then only the difference between normal market interest and the interest demanded by the government is a real subsidy. An early example of a government loan fund in aid of shipping and shipbuilding was given by an act of the Swedish parliament in 1903.[13] In many other countries similar funds were established during World War I or during the inter-war

threatened to levy a one per cent equalising fee on all exports shipped in Ecuadorian vessels from the United States to Ecuador. Ecuador abolished the discriminatory fees. Chamber of Shipping of the United Kingdom, *Annual Report 1959–60.* P. 58.

[7] Jones, *op. cit.* P. 53.

[8] Jesse E. Saugstad, *Shipping and Shipbuilding Subsidies.* U. S. Department of Commerce, Bureau of Foreign and Domestic Commerce. Trade Promotion Series No. 129. Washington, 1932. Pp. 233 f.

[9] The Hamburg–America Line had considered an unsubsidized steamer service to North America as impossible in 1853, but threatening competition to their sailing packet service from a steam line from Bremen and Antwerp caused them to put two unsubsidized steamers in service in 1855. Erich Murken, *Die großen transatlantischen Linienreederei-Verbände, Pools und Interessengemeinschaften.* Jena, 1922. P. 11.

[10] Saugstad, *op. cit.* P. 219.

[11] *Cf. inf.,* page 46.

[12] Carl E. McDowell and Helen M. Gibbs, *Ocean Transportation.* New York, 1954. P. 260.

[13] Saugstad, *op. cit.* P. 565.

depression years. Sometimes these credit facilities are given to particular ships, considered to be of special national interest. In 1960 the British Government announced that it was willing to grant the Cunard Line a loan of nearly £15 million in addition to a direct grant of over £3 million to replace the *Queen Mary*.[14] In spite of this the line decided not to build a new liner of this size in view of the changing conditions in the North Atlantic passenger service.

Most of the early shipping subsidy programs were designed to stimulate the creation of rapid and frequent liner services. During the long periods of depressed freight rates after World War I more and more countries found it necessary to subsidize tramp shipping too. The British Shipping (Assistance) Act of 1935 was designed to help tramp shipping during the depression by direct subsidies as well as by encouraging scrapping of old vessels and modernization of the fleet.[15]

Of the major maritime nations the United States has the most comprehensive subsidy scheme. It operates according to the principles laid down in the Merchant Marine Act of 1936 with later amendments. This legislation recognized the importance of American participation in international shipping (domestic traffic was already reserved for American-flag ships) and of the existence of an American ship-building industry. Since the cost of American-built ships was higher than that of equivalent foreign-built ships construction-differential subsidies were paid for vessels built for use on certain defined foreign trade routes that were deemed essential to American foreign trade. Many of the vessels built are of standardized types: before World War II C1, C2 and C3 and after the war the Mariner Class. Not only are shipbuilding costs higher in the United States than elsewhere; operating costs are also higher, particularly manning costs. To off-set this disadvantage operation-differential subsidies are paid. These are restricted in the same way as the construction-differential subsidies, the regulations being designed to ensure that only modern ships receive the subsidy for service on essential trade routes. The operators have to undertake not to compete with other subsidized operators and not to engage in protected coastal shipping.[16]

Passenger Traffic

Passenger transport by scheduled liners began early in the nineteenth century simultaneously with cargo liner traffic.[1] When steamers first began to carry passengers they quickly became an important means of travel, competing successfully with stage-coaches and still slower and less comfortable land transport. But the further development of waterborne passenger transport took place under conditions different from those of goods transport.

The cargo carrying fleet increased as a result of the development of production and trade in an industrial economy. The great economies of sea transport placed it in a strong competitive position for heavy cargoes, even if the greater speed and the obviating of transship-

[14] *The New York Times,* November 4, 1960.

[15] Osborne Mance, *International Sea Transport.* London, 1945. P. 122.

[16] McDowell and Gibbs, *op. cit.* Pp. 268 ff.

[1] Among the first regular trans-oceanic passenger lines were the Cunard Line (Liverpool) 1840, Norddeutscher Lloyd (Bremen) 1857, White Star Line (Liverpool) 1869. (Erich Murken, *Die großen transatlantischen Linienreederei-Verbände, Pools und Interessengemeinschaften.* Jena, 1922. Pp. 11 f.)

ment in many cases favored rail and road where available. The railroads also brought competition to passenger shipping, taking over much traffic from coastwise, lake, river and canal shipping, and in many areas only pleasure traffic remained. The premium on speed made waterborne passenger traffic more vulnerable than the cargo traffic. In recent years air transport has taken over shipments of some cargoes, either of high value per unit of weight or of a perishable character, but tonnagewise air transport is quite insignificant in comparison to sea transport. Over routes where no overland transport existed the passenger liners had no competition until after World War I when the airlines began to carry passengers and mail and after World War II they also became serious competitors for large numbers of passengers on the longest runs.

From the mid-nineteenth century up to World War I the carrying of emigrants was the most important task of trans-oceanic passenger lines, especially on the North Atlantic run. The ships took a large number of passengers in crowded quarters as a cheap passage was a necessary condition. The passenger traffic from overseas areas to Europe, on the other hand, was comparatively insignificant and corresponded to out-bound passages by better paying passengers on shorter visits. After World War I transatlantic passenger traffic changed character. The number of emigrants dwindled with the restrictive American immigration laws, the number of passengers in the higher classes increased, and traffic in the two directions became more balanced. The liners were increasingly used for pleasure cruises in the off season. The depression years in the early 1930s saw a drastic reduction in the number of transatlantic passengers reported by the lines in the Atlantic Passenger Steamship Conference

[2] The average annual flow of emigrants in 1840–1850 was 150,000, increased to 500,000 in 1890–1900 and to 1,000,000 in the prewar years of this century. Högbom, *Världssjöfarten, op. cit.,* p. 258. M. Benoist and F. Pettier, *Les transports maritimes.* Paris, 1961.

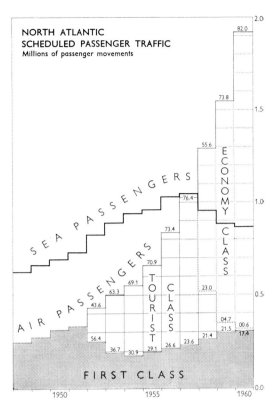

NORTH ATLANTIC
SCHEDULED PASSENGER TRAFFIC
Millions of passenger movements

Figures on columns refer to percentage of air passengers in each class. In 1961 sea passenger traffic declined for the fourth consecutive year (785,000) and the number of air passengers continued to increase (2,170,000). The airlines thus carried 73 per cent of North Atlantic travelers.
Sources: ICAO *Annual Report of the Council to the Assembly for 1960.* Montreal, 1961; Sea passenger statistics provided by Mr. R. M. L. Duffy of the Atlantic Passenger Steamship Conference.

from 1.1 million in 1929 to 0.5 million in 1933.[2] Until World War II sea traffic accounted for virtually all the traffic, as experimental passenger flights over the Atlantic were undertaken only immediately before the war. Due to the development of aircraft and the experience won during the war the situation had changed when peaceful conditions were restored. The airlines took over a growing share of the rapidly increasing passenger traffic over the North Atlantic as

47

Passenger Movements to and from the United Kingdom by Sea and Air

	1950		1960	
	Thousand Passengers Sea and Air	Per cent Air	Thousand Passengers Sea and Air	Per cent Air
Continental Europe	3477	23	8852	48
Non-European Countries	842	30	1731	66
Republic of Ireland	1482	14	2187	33
Channel Islands	528	30	897	72
Total	6329	23	13666	48

Data from *Board of Trade Journal*.

Percentage Air Passengers in Passenger Traffic between the United Kingdom and Selected Overseas Countries

	1952	1953	1954	1955	1956	1957	1958	1959	1960
South Africa				11	13	13	19	19	24
Australia	4	5	5	5	7	9	9	10	12
Canada	25	29	29	31	32	41	46	50	64
United States	38	39	40	47	50	58	63	70	76
Central and South America	29	25	13	7	9	10	20	40	60

Data from *Board of Trade Journal*.

well as over other long distance routes. In 1958 more passengers flew than sailed over the Atlantic, and in that year a decline in absolute numbers of seaborne passengers started.

The importance of air transport varies very much from route to route according to the character of the traffic, services provided by shipping lines and airlines, etc. Of the two short runs from the United Kingdom to Ireland and to the Channel Islands the one to Ireland had a quite low percentage of air passengers in 1960, while that to the Channel Islands had a very high percentage. Among the passengers going between Britain and Australia in 1960, only 12 per cent chose to go by air as against 76 per cent in traffic with the United States. The length of the journey thus does not seem to decide the strength of the competition that shipping has to face from air transport. Emigration still plays a role on some routes: the number of passengers going to Australia is larger than that of people returning, and the percentage of air passengers is lower on out-bound voyages. The seemingly high relative importance of sea travel to Latin America in the years 1954–1958 is due to the fact that the British Overseas Airways Corporation did not operate services to South America

in the period April 1954–October 1958.[3] Air passengers between Britain and Latin America are likely to have flown via continental airports, since the number of sea passengers was virtually constant 1952–1957.

In ports where large numbers of passengers embark and disembark special facilities have to be provided for customs inspection, immigration control, baggage handling, rail and road transport terminals, etc. While bulk cargo ports are chosen in such a way that the goods are brought as close to their destination as possible in order to minimize the costlier land transport and large general cargo ports are mostly located in great cities, speed is more important in the choice of passenger and mail ports. It was even more vital formerly, when sea traffic had to cater for passengers and mail demanding rapid transport, now provided by the airlines. Southampton, not London, is the terminal of the British transatlantic lines, with Cherbourg on the peninsula of Normandy as a port of call on the French side of the Channel. In the same way Southampton is a port of call for ships bound for continental ports. In southern Europe Brindisi in southeast Italy was important for rapid traffic to the eastern Mediterranean and beyond Suez; Vigo and La Coruña in north-west Spain are

[3] Information provided by Mr. H. A. E. Geiser, Sales Development Officer, B.O.A.C., July 25, 1962.

served by liners from northern Europe to the South Atlantic. In some instances estuary ports have outports at the outer end of the estuary to serve the rapid traffic: Tilbury on the Thames, Bremerhaven on the Weser and Cuxhaven on the Elbe are all of this type.

The total passenger capacity of the world merchant fleet in 1961 was reported to be 305,000, ferries and excursion ships excluded.[4] The United Kingdom alone accounted for 70,000 or 23 per cent of the total, followed by Italy, France, the United States and the Netherlands. These five leading nations had 57 per cent of the passenger carrying capacity, but no information is available on its utilization.

In order to make better use of the capacity, passenger lines employ their vessels for cruises, particularly in the off season. Most cruises go from the United States, others from Europe. The Caribbean area is a very popular destination, but Europe, the Far East and other parts of the world are also frequented, sometimes on round-the-world trips. Cruises from Europe often go to North Africa, including Madeira and the Canary Islands.

Not only cruises but also the regular services appeal to those who travel for pleasure or have the time to spare to combine a business trip with a few days or weeks in the floating first class hotel that is a modern passenger liner. The lines stress this in their advertising and also cooperate with the air lines to facilitate combined tours: air one way and sea the other.

A special category of passengers are the pilgrims. Mecca, Rome and Jerusalem receive every year hundreds of thousands of worshipers by land, sea and air. As early as 1912 about 100,000 people came to Mecca by sea (Jidda on the Red Sea is Mecca's port), as against 200,000 overland.[5] Here, too, air transport now offers keen competition, but still in 1956 out of a registered total of 221,000 pilgrims 126,000 arrived by sea.[6]

General Cargo Traffic

Cargo Lines

The first liners antedate steamships in transoceanic service. As early as 1816, the American Black Ball Line operated four swift sailing packets between New York and Liverpool. The packets carried passengers as well as express-type freight. The first steamships in transoceanic liner service were operated by the Royal Mail Steam Packet Company to the Caribbean in 1839. The sailing packets gradually lost out to the steamers, and by 1865 Europe was connected with every continent by steam liner service.[1]

Over routes with a considerable passenger traffic special passenger liners were developed. Although their main purpose is the carrying of passengers, they also carry some cargo. Over routes where the number of passengers is insufficient to support special passenger liner service either combined passenger-cargo liners or cargo liners with accomodation for a few passengers are employed.[2] Their ports of call, sailing schedules, etc. are largely determined by the needs for cargo service, the more so the less important the passenger service.

[4] Statistik der Schiffahrt, December, 1961.

[5] C. Rathjens, Die Pilgerfahrt nach Mekka, Hamburg, 1948, quoted from Erich Otremba, Allgemeine Geographie des Welthandels und des Weltverkehrs. Erde und Weltwirtschaft, Volume 4. Stuttgart, 1957.

[6] The New York Times, June 28, 1957.

[1] Carl E. McDowell and Helen M. Gibbs, Ocean Transportation. New York, 1954. P. 48.

[2] Cf. page 34.

There is no clearcut division between ships used as general tramps and liners, many ships being used in both types of service at different times. However, the main purpose of the liner is the carrying of general cargo. Since this is usually low density cargo, liners are built with a large cubic capacity in relation to dead-weight capacity. Many are equipped for the carrying of refrigerated cargo—frozen meat, vegetables and fruits. If the complete cargo space is refrigerated the ship is a refrigerated vessel or *reefer*. Vegetable oils and other liquid cargo are often carried in deep tanks. High speed is more necessary for the valuable and perishable general cargo than for the raw materials and staple foodstuffs carried by the tramps.[3] Quick and easy loading and unloading of small shipments is desirable, as many liners call at a number of different ports. Facilities for rapid loading and unloading of bulk cargo, necessary for tramps and specialized bulk carriers, are less essential, even if it is customary for liners to take parcel lots of grains and other bulk commodities in order to utilize space and carrying capacity not taken up by general cargo.[4]

While it is possible to get a fairly good idea of the quantities involved in seaborne trade in the important bulk commodities,[5] and to estimate the tonnage employed from these data and from transport distances, loading and unloading times, etc., it is impossible to make a similar quantitative description of the trade in the commodities making up the typical liner cargoes. Steel and other metals, machinery of all kinds, including vehicles, make up a large part. Wool, cotton, textiles, foodstuffs, chemicals, pulp and paper are also carried in large quantities. Manufactured articles are naturally most important in the trade between the industrialized countries in North America, Europe and Japan and from these areas to other parts of the world, while raw materials and foodstuffs are carried to the industrialized countries. Trade between distant non-indus-trialized countries is comparatively insignificant.

Goods to be shipped by liners are brought to the port by road and rail and sometimes by small vessels in *feeder* service. These ships may either be owned by the liner company or by other companies operating in co-operation. Many liner companies own much terminal operating gear, piers and sheds, tenders, lighters and tugs.[6]

General Cargo Handling

The amount and quality of cargo handling equipment provided in general ports varies greatly. Cargo liners are regularly equipped to load and unload from and to quays or lighters using their own gear exclusively, but in many cases more rapid handling is assured by quay cranes. In Europe ports are well equipped with cranes, while in some other parts of the world, including the large American ports, ships have to rely on their own facilities.[1] It has been claimed[2] that many European ports have gone too far, insisting on providing this service whether it is economically advantageous or not.

Even in modern and rationally equipped ports the cost of loading and unloading general cargo is high. Rising labor costs are an incentive to adopt new cargo handling methods, reducing the number of manual handling operations between the original shipper and the ultimate receiver of the goods. This can be achieved by the use of more mechanical equipment, e.g. fork lift trucks both on the quays and in the holds of the ships. The ships should

[3] McDowell and Gibbs, *op. cit.* Pp. 114 ff., 163.
[4] Cf. pages 102 f.
[5] Cf. page 55–110.
[6] Steward R. Bross, *Ocean Shipping*. Cambridge, Maryland, 1956. P. 94.
[1] Cf. the many port photographs in Part II.
[2] M. Markussen, "Moderne stykkgodsfart og rasjo-nell godsbehandling", *Norwegian Shipping News*, 1962. No. 12 C. P. 3.

A typical cargo-working scene in the Port of Los Angeles. Boxes on pallets are brought to the side of the ship by fork lift trucks and loaded by the ship's booms. (Port of Los Angeles)

be designed to make the best possible use of this equipment.

To minimize manual handling of the goods one tries to avoid break of bulk by keeping shipments together in unit loads, sized to permit mechanical handling. This can be done by *palletization* or *containerization*. The greatest economies are realized if the pallets or containers can be handled as units all the way from the shipper to the receiver of the goods, but even if the units are kept together only part of the way, loading and unloading operations may be sufficiently facilitated to warrant their use. Pallets and containers should be of standardized sizes, chosen to permit easy handling and the best possible use of the cubic capacity of the ships' holds.[3] Containers for

sea transport are often very large, carrying as much as 20 tons.[4] They are owned either by the shippers of the goods, by forwarding firms or by the shipowners. The greatest gains to be made by reduced turn round time are over shorter routes where terminal costs make up a larger share of total costs. The reduction in utilized carrying capacity, through the lower stowage factor for containerized goods, also tends to be a greater disadvantage the longer the transport distance and the time spent at sea. But containers have advantages other than ease of handling; the risk of breakage and pilferage is reduced and perishable foodstuffs can be kept continuously refrigerated in reefer containers. These added advantages can also make containerization economical over very long transport distances, e.g. between the Pacific coast of North America and Hawaii and the Far East. The handling of large containers necessitates special cranes, either on board ship or—if the ship calls at only a few ports—on the quay.

[3] Markussen, *op. cit.*, See also F. S. Macomber, "Cargo Handling Savings Short of Full Containerization", *Research Techniques in Maritime Transportation*, National Academy of Sciences—National Research Council, Publication 720, Washington, D.C., 1959. P. 89.

[4] See pages 52 and 53.

51

An aluminum container with steel undercarriage and a loading capacity of 23 tons shipped between Minneapolis and Rotterdam. Transportation in containers is only in its infancy but is catching on fast. Standardization of equipment is the major problem to be solved before the full advantages of containers in international trade can be realized. (Container Transport International, Inc.)

The containers are transported overland by trucks or on railroad flatcars. Sometimes the container consists of an entire truck trailer. The carrying of trailers aboard specially designed trailer ships is particularly important in the United States, where it is known as *fishyback,* a counterpart of *piggy-back,* the carrying of truck trailers on railroad cars. The *Seatrain* service operating between New York and Gulf ports since before World War II ships loaded railcars.[5] The ships best suited for the carriage of loaded trucks or trailers are the ferry-like so-called *roll-on, roll-off ships,* developed from military landing craft. They are also used to carry automobiles, a very large item on the export and import lists of the countries of Western Europe and North America.

An increasing use of containerization will tend to increase further the advantages of the large general cargo ports, since only they will have frequent services to many destinations. The rapid loading and unloading of a containership means that its optimum size for a given trade is larger than that of an ordinary general cargo liner, and this will also tend to con-

centrate traffic to a few large ports. At the same time an increasing cargo flow would tend to increase the number of points generating enough traffic to warrant the establishment of general cargo services. As trucks, with costs rapidly increasing with distance, account for more and more of the overland hauls, the customers are anxious to ship and receive the goods through the nearest port, and this also counteracts the concentrating forces. Which of these two tendencies will prove to be the stronger in the long run is difficult to foretell.

Shipping Conferences and Liner Freight Rates

Since a large proportion of the total costs in liner shipping are fixed costs unlimited price competition is likely to lead to freight rates far below average costs, which, however, should be covered in the long run. The shipping industry has therefore developed means of

[5] Benjamin Chinitz, *Freight and the Metropolis.* Cambridge, Mass., 1960. Pp. 85 f., 159 ff.

The American President Lines operates four container vessels between the American west coast ports of San Francisco, Los Angeles and San Diego and the Orient. Two of these vessels, the largest and fastest cargo liners sailing under any flag, were especially designed for the container service. The 23,000-ton *President Lincoln* has one hold exclusively for containers and another may easily be converted in the future. A 25-ton gantry crane rides above the container hatch where six containers can be stacked on top of each other. This vessel and its sister ship the *President Taylor* have a capacity of 126 containers. The service across the Pacific has been planned on a basis of 80 cargo-vans per vessel and the company has purchased 420 containers of $2.4 \times 2.4 \times 6.1$ meters dimensions. These "fishyback" containers, made from aluminum and steel, weigh almost two tons. Each container can hold approximately 20 tons. (American President Lines, 1962)

avoiding this cut-throat competition between competing lines. It is reduced partly by a concentration through mergers and amalgamations, partly by agreements reducing competition, either informal gentlemen's agreements or formal *shipping conferences*. The methods employed by the conferences to regulate competition among conference members are manifold. They could be summarized under the following headings, although few conferences, if any, employ all of them: (1) rate agreements, (2) control of sailing schedules, (3) pooling, and (4) "good faith" or performance bonds.

The costs, particularly the fixed costs, of liner shipping are higher than those of tramp shipping. The speed and comfort called for by passengers and general cargo require more powerful machinery, more space, larger crews and more costly administration. The liner has to sail according to schedule whether it is fully loaded or not, more ports are called at, etc. The high costs of liner shipping, reflected in the freight rates determined by the conference members, sometimes make possible competition from tramps, and therefore the liner companies desire an assurance of the loyalty of the shippers. The conferences try to minimize the competition from outsiders by: (1) agreements, (2) the use of "fighting ships", and (3) tying arrangements with shippers.[1]

---

[1] Lauge Stetting, *Råvarepriser og søfragtrater*. Mimeographed, København, 1960. Pp. 154 ff; Daniel Marx, Jr., *International Shipping Cartels*. Princeton, 1953. P. 53.

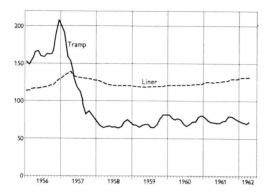

German Freight Index 1956–1962.
Data from Bundesverkehrsministerium, quoted from *Statistik der Schiffahrt*.

Rate agreements provide for either fixed rates or minimum rates, sometimes for differential rates, lower for slower services. The rates vary with different commodities, bulk cargoes often being excluded. The *control of sailing schedules* limits the number of sailings, fixes the dates of sailing or restricts the ports served by each member. *Pooling arrangements* provide for the pooling of available traffic, gross or net earnings. *"Good faith" agreements* stipulate the deposition of a sum of money to be forfeited in part or entirely for violations of the agreement. *Agreements to minimize competition from non-members* may be concluded with outside interests or other conferences, equalizing rates or stabilizing agreed rate differentials. A *"fighting ship"* is operated by a conference at below-normal rates to compete with outsiders, the loss to be distributed over the members of the conference. *Tying arrangements* of different kinds exist, but the most common is the deferred rebate system. Under this system a shipper who undertakes to confine his shipments exclusively to the members of the conference receives a rebate, usually 5 or 10 per cent, on the fixed rates. If he fails to fulfill the agreement, he loses his right to the rebate not only for goods shipped during the current period but also on goods shipped during the previous period. The original rebate period may be three, six or twelve months, the deferment period another three or six months. The Shipping Act of 1916 made both the "fighting ship" and the deferred rebate illegal in the United States, but the deferred rebate is still employed in the rest of the world.[2]

The conferences regulate conditions for members operating services over the same trade route. Since the competitive situation is different on outward and homeward trades, most conference agreements refer only to trade in one direction. Although outward and homeward conferences may comprise the same lines, conditions agreed on differ.[3] In the early 1950s about 200 conferences were in existence, the largest group being outward conferences from Europe.[4]

The conferences have succeeded in preventing much cut-throat competition in the liner industry, but like other restrictive practices they have also been criticized, and several commissions have been formed in various countries to study their effects.[5]

The restriction of competition in the liner trades results in freight rates which are stable in comparison with the tramp freight rates. It is often difficult for the members of a conference to reach an agreement on changes in the rates as a reaction to changes in demand for transport. If changes are called for by

---

[2] Marx, *op. cit.* Pp. 53 ff.

[3] Stetting, *op. cit.* P. 156.

[4] *Bremer Jahrbuch der Weltschiffahrt 1952/53.* P. 167.

[5] For a study of the early history of shipping conferences, see Erich Murken, *Die großen transatlantischen Linienreederei-Verbände, Pools und Interessengemeinschaften.* Jena 1922; Marx, *op. cit.* contains chapters on investigations of shipping conferences, actions of British Dominions and other countries and U.S. regulation of overseas shipping. A discussion of shipping conferences with a bibliography is found in Edmond Langer, *Les Conférences Maritimes.* Dissertation, Université de Liége 1954–1955. Mimeographed.

increases or decreases in costs, more or less equal for different members, rate adjustments are more easily brought about. Liner rates are thus less strongly influenced by changes in demand than tramp rates, while changes in cost affect them more.

Bulk Cargo Traffic

A few bulk cargo commodities, liquid and dry, make up a large part of the total sea-borne cargo tonnage. Petroleum alone accounts for almost half. Other liquid cargoes are vegetable and animal fats and wine. The most important classes of dry cargo are grains, coal, ore, sugar, lumber, and fertilizers. They are all to a great extent carried in tramp ships, but some of them are also important liner cargoes. Special bulk carriers have recently taken over some of the cargoes which previously were mostly carried by tramps, particularly iron ore. There are many other commodities entering sea-borne trade in large quantities, but for different reasons seldom by the shipload, e.g. wool, cotton, coffee, and fruit. These are generally carried by cargo liners, many of which are equipped for special trades, such as chilled or frozen meat from Australia, New Zealand and the Plata region to Europe and bananas from the Caribbean to the United States and Europe.

In order to appreciate the relative importance to shipping of different commodities entering world trade it is necessary to know not only the quantities shipped but also the shipping tonnage employed. In the case of oil transports this is relatively easy, since the total tonnage of oil tankers is known with a fair degree of accuracy. In recent years a good many tankers have been used for carrying grains, since the oil trade has not been able to employ the whole tanker fleet at remunerative rates. The grain-carrying tankers have, however, been relatively few, so that it has been possible to assess the tanker tonnage employed.[1]

For dry cargoes the situation is totally different. Many commodities are as a rule carried in small lots by liners, and even if many large bulk commodities are generally carried by tramp ships, these ships may carry coal on one trip, wheat or scrap on the next, etc. In addition, some cargoes are partly carried in liners (e.g. grains) or in specialized bulk carriers (e.g. ore). The only possible way of estimating the tonnage employed for the transport of dry commodities is therefore to resort to official trade statistics, making some approximations about average distances from the ports of the country of origin to those of the country of destination. If distances and average speeds are known the time under way can easily be calculated. To this should be added the average time spent in port.

Our calculations are based on estimates, which must evidently be fairly rough. Another factor which makes the results approximate is the role played by return cargoes. Sometimes the commodity moves in the *light* direction, i.e. more ships have carried cargo to the port of loading than are needed to carry cargo from it. Since these ships have to take the cargo offered or proceed in ballast only their time in port has been taken to represent tonnage employment. Should the cargo move in the *heavy* direction, requiring more ships than those available by imports to the port of loading, time under way includes the time needed

---

[1] Cf. page 103.

by the ships to reach this port, regardless of whether they arrive loaded or in ballast.

These factors have all been taken into account in making the estimates of the tonnage employment of the commodities treated in the following pages. It is clear, though, that the margins of error must be fairly wide; we have no means of knowing the situation in the specific exporting ports at the time of the chartering of vessels, nor is it possible to allow for the specialization of ships in some trades, and, above all, tramp ships are not limited to moving back and forth between two ports or groups of ports but make triangular and still more complicated journeys too.

Petroleum: The Leading Bulk Cargo

In the century since 1859 when the first well was drilled in Pennsylvania,[1] world production of petroleum has increased at an even rate, faster than that of almost all other mineral products(see graph).[2] Due to their high calorific value and to the ease of handling liquid fuels once the necessary facilities are provided,

petroleum products have become vital to the functioning of the industrial economy, competing in many areas where coal and other solid fuels are locally available. Since the turn

[1] Petroleum seepages had been known since prehistoric days, and petroleum and asphalt had been used in small quantities for several purposes. However, "Colonel" Edwin L. Drake's discovery of oil by drilling near Titusville, Pennsylvania on August 27, 1859, is generally taken as the beginning of the petroleum industry. At about the same time oil wells were also drilled in Ontario, Rumania, Austria–Hungary and Russia.

[2] The rate of increase of world production of industrial raw materials has been remarkably constant (although differing for various commodities) since the beginning of the industrial era. This "law" was demonstrated about 1930 by several authors working independently.

(Percy E. Barbour, "Copper", *The Mineral Industry during 1930*. New York, 1931, Pp. 118 f.

Carl Snyder, "Overproduction and Business Cycles", *Proceedings of the Academy of Political Science*, 1931. Pp. 350 ff.

Ivar Högbom, *Mineral Production*. Ingeniörsvetenskapsakademiens Handlingar Nr 117. Stockholm, 1932.)

Although the development in individual countries may show a retardation of growth (cf. Simon S. Kuznets, *Secular Movements in Production and Prices*. Boston, 1930) new producers have appeared and world production has continued to grow, materially affected only by the world wars and to some extent by the world depression in the early thirties. (Cf. Ivar Högbom, "Development of World Production of Raw Materials", League of Nations, *Report of the Committee for the Study of the Problem of Raw Materials*, Annex I. Geneva, 1937. P. 41.)

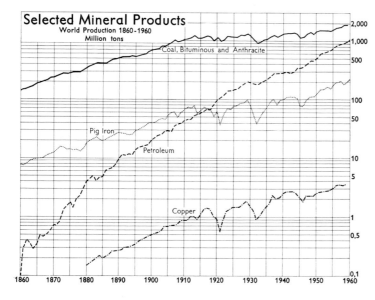

Selected Mineral Products
World Production 1860-1960
Million tons

Coal, Bituminous and Anthracite

Pig Iron

Petroleum

Copper

Data from *The Mineral Industry; Minerals Yearbook; Weltmontanstatistik;* United Nations, *Statistical Yearbook;* United Nations, *Monthly Bulletin of Statistics.*

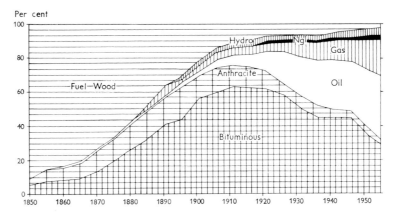

Energy sources as percentages of aggregate energy consumption in the United States, five-year intervals, 1850–1955. (Ngl = natural gas liquids.) For 1960 the corresponding percentages were bituminous 22.1, anthracite 1.0, petroleum 41.5, natural gas (dry and liquids) 31.5, and hydroelectricity 3.9. *(Statistical Abstract of the United States 1961)*
Source: Sam H. Schurr and Bruce C. Netschert, *Energy in the American Economy 1850–1975.* Baltimore, 1960. P. 37.

The U.S.S.R. Fuel Balance of Consumed Energy Resources

Type of Fuel	1913	1932	1940	1950	1958	1965 (planned)
Coal	54.7	59.4	69.4	75.9	73.9	49.2
Oil	14.1	17.0	8.3	7.1	10.3	17.8
Natural Gas	—	—	1.9	2.4	6.5	24.8
Peat	1.0	3.7	6.0	5.0	4.1	3.6
Oil Shale	—	—	0.3	0.5	0.8	1.1
Wood	30.2	19.9	14.1	9.1	4.4	3.5

Source: Jordan A. Hodgkins, *Soviet Power: Energy Resources, Production and Potentials.* Englewood Cliffs, 1961. P. 102.

of the century the development of land, sea and air transport has provided a rapidly expanding market for petroleum products.[3] Petroleum has taken an increasing share of the world's rapidly growing consumption of energy and is the raw material for the rapidly expanding petro-chemical industry.

[3] Lenoir's internal-combustion engine 1860. Diesel engine designed 1892, applied 1897. First experiments with Lenoir's engine in road vehicle 1862, Benz's automobile 1884, Ford's Model T 1908. First seagoing vessels powered by internal-combustion engines 1910, first oceangoing diesel ship 1912. Wright Brothers' first powered flight 1903.

An analysis of the distribution of petroleum resources and the main consuming regions reveals a pattern of deficit and surplus areas. Crude oil and refined products are by far the most important maritime cargoes. Petroleum is less ubiquitous than coal, which is found in large quantites in all continents and within most important fuel-consuming regions. In 1959 "interregional" trade alone moved 396 million tons of petroleum and products of a total world production of 1,050 million tons. Virtually all of this was seaborne, and in addition vast quantities of crude and products were carried in tankers in "intraregional" trade, e.g. between the Gulf of Mexico and the northeastern seaboard in the United States and within Western Europe.

In the early years of the petroleum industry the United States and Russia were the two outstanding producers. After the turn of the century Russian production stagnated and from that time until the early 1950s the United States produced each year more than half the world production, often considerably more. In the late 1920s Venezuela rapidly began to acquire a position as an oil producer of worldwide importance. After World War II Middle East production began to soar and in the 1950s Soviet production increased sharply. At the rate of increase of the last five years the Soviet

Interregional Trade in Petroleum and Petroleum Products 1959
Million metric tons

From:	Canada	Mexico	U.S.	Vene-zuela	OLA	Europe	Africa	Middle East	Far East	Com-munist Bloc	World Total
To:											
Canada	—	—	2.1	12.8	0.5	—	—	5.2	—	—	20.6
Mexico	—	—	1.2	—	—	—	—	—	—	—	1.2
United States	4.9	1.8	—	56.6	5.7	0.2	—	16.7	3.3	—	89.2
Venezuela/Neth.Ant.	—	—	0.3	—	1.6	—	—	—	—	—	1.9
Other Latin America	—	—	0.8	29.4	—	—	—	3.8	—	1.1	35.1
Europe	—	—	2.5	24.9	5.4	—	4.0	131.1	0.5	12.1	180.5
Africa	—	—	0.6	4.1	0.3	5.7	—	9.9	—	2.0	22.6
Middle East	—	—	0.2	—	—	1.5	—	—	—	—	1.7
Far East	—	—	3.0	0.1	—	0.1	—	39.3	—	0.1	42.6
Communist Bloc	—	—	—	—	—	1.0	—	—	—	—	1.0
Word Total	4.9	1.8	10.6	127.8	13.4	8.4	4.0	206.0	3.8	15.3	396.0

Source: *World Petroleum,* September, 1960. Statistics were converted from barrels per day to metric tons per year using the conversion factor 50.

Union would again vie with the United States for the position as the number one oil producer by the end of the 1960s. In 1953 the United States still produced 49 per cent of the world total. In the late fifties the American production ceased to expand, and by 1960 its share of world production had dropped to 34 per cent. In that year the combined production of the Middle East states was 26 per cent, that of the Soviet Union, the world's second largest producer, 14 per cent, and that of Venezuela 13 per cent. Between them these countries had 87 per cent of the total crude oil output of the world (page 59). The world trade in petroleum, summarized in the table above, is a function of the distribution of production just outlined and that of consumption discussed below.

Western Europe has never had any substantial oil production, and has to rely on imports for most of her rapidly increasing needs. The demand for oil rose from 100 million tons in 1955 to 150 million tons in 1959, raising the share of oil in total energy consumption from 21 to 30 per cent. A forecast for 1965 puts the demand at 200–240 million tons.[4]

Domestic production in the OEEC area has in recent years been a little less than 10 per cent and in view of the expected rapid increase in consumption this percentage is not likely to rise although European crude production is on the increase. The gross imports of crude and products into the OEEC area in 1959 came from the following sources:

Source Region	Million tons	Per cent
Western Hemisphere	33.8	20.0
Middle East	118.8	70.4
Africa	3.0	1.8
U.S.S.R. and Eastern Europe	10.2	6.0
Other	2.9	1.8
Total	168.7	100

Data from O.E.E.C., *Oil: Recent Developments in the O.E.E.C. Area, 1960.* Paris, 1961. P. 50.

The Middle East, by far the most important source of Europe's crude oil supplies, is ex-

[4] O.E.E.C., *Oil: Recent Developments in the O.E.E.C. Area, 1960.* Paris, 1961. P. 13.

pected to remain the main source. But three new sources could have a significant impact on the relative share of Middle East oil: North Africa, West Africa and the U.S.S.R. Important discoveries have been made in Algeria and Libya and the new fields now have access to the European markets by the opening of the pipelines from Hassi Messaoud to Bougie (1959), from the Edjeleh—Zarzaitine—Tiguentourine area to La Skhirra in Tunisia (1960), from Zelten to Marsa el Brega (1961) and from Dahra to Sirte (1962). The rapidly increasing output will surpass 40 million tons in 1963. This oil, however, is light and not particularly suitable for European requirements, which are in general for heavy oils mainly for use as industrial fuel oil. It is therefore possible that an exchange of Saharan oil or refined products derived from Saharan crude may take place between Western Europe and markets more suitable for the light Saharan oil like the United States. This would promote long-distance ocean transport of petroleum.[5] The most important producer in West Africa is Nigeria. Since 1956, when Shell-BP struck oil at Oloibiri in the Niger delta, several fields have been discovered as many European and American companies rushed to the area.

Data for 1860–1950 from *World Oil*, Vol. 137, No. 3, 1953; for 1950–1960 from United Nations, *Monthly Bulletin of Statistics*.

In 1962 production surpassed three million tons. Pipelines connect the fields with the new oil port at Bonny. The reserves are very large and Nigeria seems likely to become a major producer. Gabon's production in the Port Gentil area has amounted to about 0.8 million tons annually since 1959. The West European imports of Soviet oil, which had been very small for many years, have been rapidly increasing since the late 1950s. The expanding Soviet petroleum industry has reached an output larger than the effective demand within the U.S.S.R. and the Communist countries and by competitive pric-

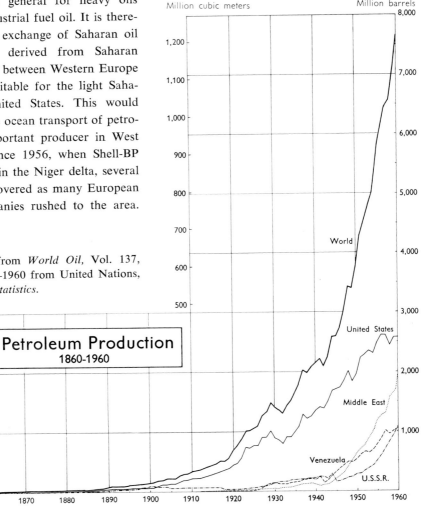

Petroleum Production
1860-1960

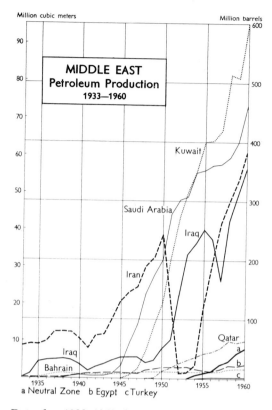

Million cubic meters

Million barrels

MIDDLE EAST
Petroleum Production
1933—1960

Kuwait

Saudi Arabia

Iraq

Iran

Iraq

Qatar
a

Bahrain

b

c

a Neutral Zone b Egypt c Turkey

Data for 1933–1950 from *World Oil,* Vol. 137, No. 3, 1953; for 1950–1960 from United Nations, *Monthly Bulletin of Statistics.*

ing it has been possible to find an outlet in other countries, above all in Western Europe, the largest potential market for petroleum. In 1960 Western Europe imported 12 million tons of oil, the larger part of which was products, from Communist countries, primarily the Soviet Union. About 90 per cent of the Soviet exports are shipped from Black Sea ports, 5 per cent from Klaipeda on the Baltic and the remaining 5 per cent overland, mainly to West Germany and Austria.[6] The largest buyers were Italy, West Germany, Finland, Sweden and France.[7] The Soviet petroleum exports to Western Europe are likely to continue to increase and even to make up a larger share of consumption. Their importance to the shipping industry, however, will be affected

by the construction of long-distance pipe lines from the Soviet oil fields in the Caucasus area and the Volga-Ural fields to Poland, East Germany, Czechoslovakia and Hungary, as well as to Klaipeda and Ventspils for export to northern Europe.

Although the United States has remained the largest oil producer in the world and Canada has developed an important production in the 1950s, North America has become second to Western Europe as an import area for petroleum. United States exports have declined as Canada has become a major oil producer and Europe has come to rely heavily on cheap Middle East oil. Exports of crude have almost ceased. The years 1956 and 1957 were exceptional, as European countries were cut off from their normal source of supply by the blockade of the Suez Canal. Since oil can be produced more cheaply in Venezuela and the Middle East than in most fields in the United States American imports of crude and residual fuel oil increased and by 1948 petroleum imports exceeded the volume of exports. Ten years later the American net imports of petroleum approached 100 million tons. Those American oil producers who did not take part in foreign operations sought protection from the competition of imported lowcost petroleum and they had the political support of pressure groups representing the oil and coal producing states as well as the coal and natural gas industries. Since a heavy reliance on foreign oil was deemed a strategical risk, should the United States be cut off from overseas supplies, restrictions on the import of oil could always count on the support of the Pentagon. A voluntary program, limiting the imports of crude oil for the area east of the

[5] O.E.E.C., *op. cit.* Pp. 51 f.
O.E.C.D., *Pipelines and Tankers.* Paris, 1961. Pp. 17 f.
[6] O.E.C.D., *op. cit.* P. 24.
[7] O.E.E.C., *op. cit.* P. 53, which does not include Finland, not a member of O.E.E.C.

Pipelines in Europe and the Mediterranean

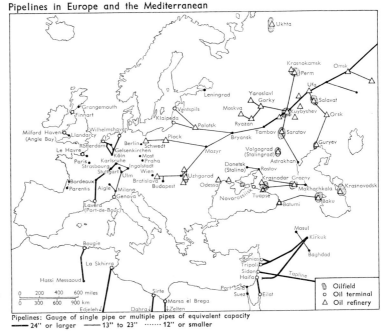

Crude petroleum pipelines supplying Western Europe, existing or under construction at the end of 1962. The few product lines are not shown. For the Soviet Union and its export pipelines oil refineries have also been indicated. For map of oil refineries in Western Europe, see page 65.

Rocky Mountains to 12 per cent of the domestic production, came into effect on July 1, 1957. By December, 1957, it was extended to the West Coast states, Alaska, and Hawaii, and in March, 1959, the rules were made mandatory. Imports from Canada and Mexico by pipe line were exempt. Since the curbs were imposed, American oil imports have grown more slowly, and ship owners, who had ordered tankers in the expectation of rapidly growing imports were reported to have had to cancel the contracts.[8]

The most important supplier is Venezuela, which in 1960 accounted for 68 per cent of U.S.-Canadian imports, while other Latin American countries, mainly Colombia, accounted for 6 per cent and the Middle East for 21 per

cent.[9] Since the distance from Venezuela to American East Coast ports is the same as that from the Gulf ports, it is of small importance to the shipping industry whether oil is brought in from the Mid-Continent fields or from Venezuela.[10]

From 1958 the growth of Venezuelan production has stagnated. The American import restrictions contributed, but more important

[8] *The New York Times,* September 22, 1957; January 29, March 1, September 11, 1958; March 11, 1959; *Minerals Yearbook* 1959, Vol. II. P. 450.

[9] Page 58, United Nations, Statistical Papers, Series D, *Commodity Trade Statistics.*

[10] To the individual shipowner the fact that American coastwise shipping is reserved for American vessels is important.

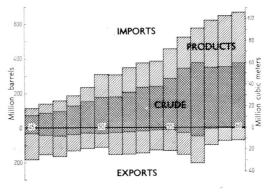

United States foreign trade in petroleum 1945–1960.

Data from *Minerals Yearbook.*

Comparative Prices of Crude Oil Delivered in New York, December 1959

Dollars per barrel

	Long Term Charter Rate		Single Voyage Spot Rate	
	From Kuwait	From Cardón	From Kuwait	From Cardón
Posted Price	1.67	2.55	1.67	2.55
Freight	1.19	0.31	0.46	0.10
Delivered Price	2.86	2.86	2.13	2.65

Sources: *Petroleum Press Service* and *Petroleum Week,* quoted from *The Economic Development of Venezuela, op. cit.*

was the changed competitive position of Venezuelan oil in comparison with that of other producers, particularly in the Middle East. Production costs in Venezuela are considerably higher than in the Middle East, but when tanker freights are high, Venezuelan oil has a freight cost advantage in North American ports over more distant producers. When tanker freights dropped to very low levels in 1957 after the Suez crisis, much of this advantage was lost as is shown by the comparison in the table above.[11]

A great part of the Venezuelan crude is refined in the large refineries on Curaçao and Aruba in the Netherlands Antilles. The other Latin American countries get the bulk of their oil supply from this area. Some of them, however, produce petroleum themselves. Mexico, which in the early 1920s was one of the world's leading producers (page 320) has revived her production in recent years. In 1960 it exceeded 14 million tons and Mexico was a net exporter. Argentina, Colombia, Trinidad, Brazil, Peru and Chile are the other Latin American producers. Although Latin America with the exception of Venezuela is a net importing region it also exports to North America and Europe and in small quantities to other parts of the world. A special case is Cuba, which

for political reasons has turned to the Soviet Union for her supply of crude oil since 1960.

Africa was still unimportant both as an exporter and an importer of petroleum in 1960, but this situation is already changing as a result of the developments in the Sahara and West Africa. The Middle East was the leading exporter of oil to Africa, followed by Europe and Venezuela. Since the African refinery capacity is very small, the imports consist mainly of products, which explains Europe's important position.

The interregional petroleum trade of the Middle East is dominated by its position as the leading supplier of Western Europe. The second most important customer is the Far East, dominated by Japan. The shipments of Middle East oil to North America are also significant both by volume and by the long transport distances, although the volume is small in comparison with Middle East shipments to Europe or North American imports from Venezuela. The rising trend in U.S. imports of Middle East oil was broken by the import restrictions in 1957.

The Far East has some petroleum production of its own, in Indonesia and North Borneo, most of which is consumed within the region, while small quantities are exported to America and Europe. The dominating importer is Japan, and Japanese imports from the Middle East are of paramount importance in the interregional petroleum trade of the Far East, while imports from Indonesia and North Borneo account for a large part of the intraregional trade. Japan is also a market for a considerable part of the American petroleum export (mainly products) and has recently bought Soviet oil (mainly crude).

[11] *The Economic Development of Venezuela.* Report of a Mission Organized by the International Bank for Reconstruction and Development at the Request of the Government of Venezuela. Baltimore, 1961. Pp. 125 ff. See also Alexander Melamid, "Geography of the World Petroleum Price Structure", *Economic Geography,* 1962. P. 283.

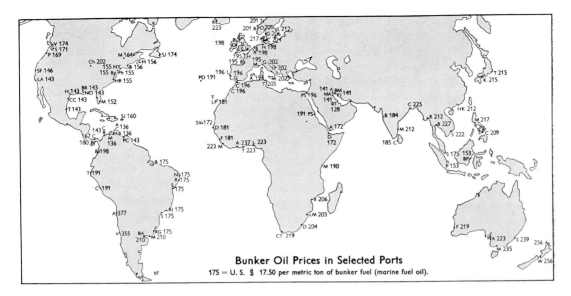

Bunker Oil Prices in Selected Ports
175 = U. S. $ 17.50 per metric ton of bunker fuel (marine fuel oil).

Bunker oil prices are lowest at large oil shipping ports with refineries (U.S. Gulf, Caribbean, Persian Gulf, Indonesia). They are higher all over Europe than in the United States, an apparent paradox as Europe gets most of her crude petroleum from the Persian Gulf whose posted oil prices are considerably lower than the Caribbean and the U.S. Gulf prices. Persian Gulf prices are low enough to make that oil cheaper in New York than Caribbean and U.S. Gulf oil. Fuel oil bunkers sell slightly below the price of crude oil in areas where natural gas or coal effectively compete with fuel oil. In Europe there is no such competition and there bunkers sell at a premium. This is particularly evident in Italy which is so short of local energy supplies. Bunkers are frequently handled by independents which helps to increase competition at the large ports of call on the main shipping routes. Discounts are frequent and the difference between actual prices paid at, say, Hamburg and Las Palmas may be smaller than indicated by the map and no large enough to warrant an extra call at Las Palmas.

Tankers usually bunker at the oil shipping terminals. Mina al Ahmadi in Kuwait in 1960 shipped 76 million tons of crude oil in 2,766 tankers which also took on 3.1 million tons of bunker fuel. Other important oil bunkering stations are old coaling stations and ports of call like Aden (3.3 million tons of bunker fuel in 1959) and Singapore on the Europe–Suez–Far East run and Las Palmas, São Vicente and Dakar on the Europe–South Atlantic routes. The terminal ports of transoceanic routes concentrated in Western Europe and the Atlantic seaboard of northeastern United States and Canada are important bunker stations in spite of higher list prices for bunker fuel. Some of the most important shipping routes in the world do not come close to low-price bunkering stations.

Price data from Esso, *Current Prices,* 18th September 1961; Shell, *Oil Fuel Spot Prices,* 1st September 1961; BP *International Bunkering,* No. 107. Professor Alexander Melamid kindly provided comments on the price map.

Refineries and Oil Transport

To the tanker owner, it is not without importance whether his ship carries clean or dirty cargoes, i.e. light refined products or residual fuel oil and crude. Clean oil is a more valuable cargo and pays higher rates, but its corrosive effect is higher, reducing the time the tanks can be used. Also the loss through evaporation is higher for clean products. The tendency in recent years to build very large tankers to reduce the transport costs has strengthened the cost advantage of the market oriented refinery, since hardly any customers other than oil

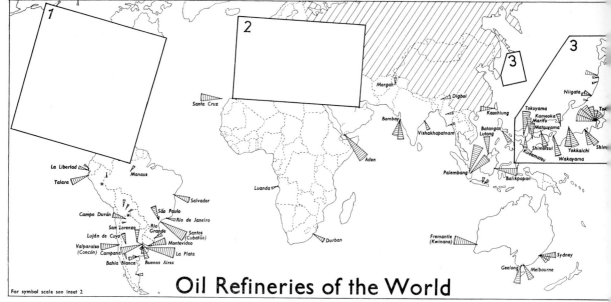

Oil Refineries of the World

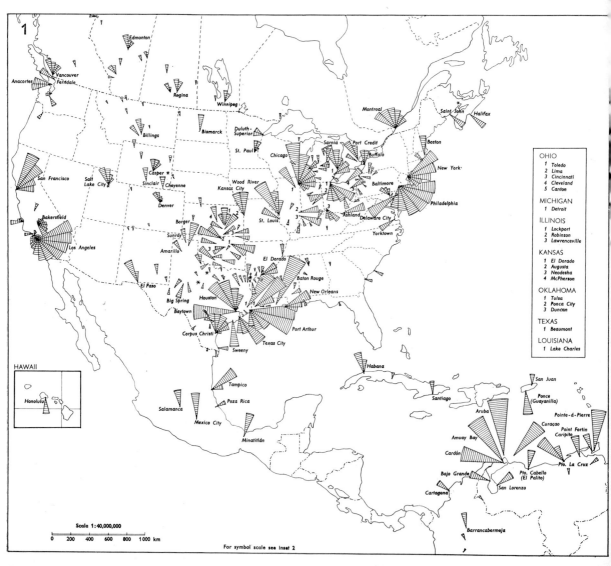

OHIO
1 Toledo
2 Lima
3 Cincinnati
4 Cleveland
5 Canton

MICHIGAN
1 Detroit

ILLINOIS
1 Lockport
2 Robinson
3 Lawrenceville

KANSAS
1 El Dorado
2 Augusta
3 Neodesha
4 McPherson

OKLAHOMA
1 Tulsa
2 Ponca City
3 Duncan

TEXAS
1 Beaumont

LOUISIANA
1 Lake Charles

HAWAII

Scala 1:40,000,000
0 200 400 600 800 1000 km

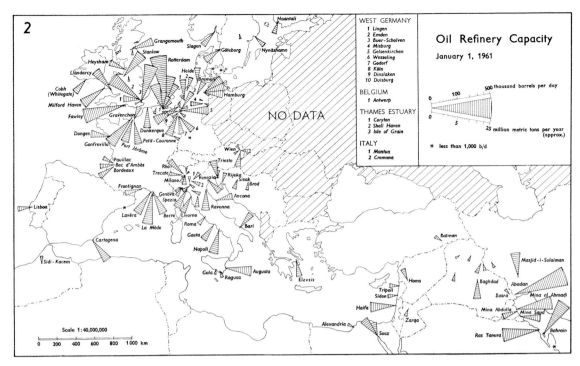

Data from *The Petroleum Times,* January 30, 1961.

refineries are large enough to buy a full load at a time. The rapidly growing consumption of petroleum products has also made more market areas large enough consumers to buy all or most of the output of large, efficient refineries. Therefore a large part of all seaborne petroleum trade is in crude, destined for refineries in the market areas, generally located on tidewater. There are also inland refining centers, located in market areas and supplied by crude oil pipe lines from ocean ports.

Not all markets can be supplied from local refineries, and few refineries have local markets providing an outlet for all their products in the proportions produced, even if these proportions can be varied within certain limits. If refined products are to be shipped in dif-

[1] Erich W. Zimmermann, *World Resources and Industries.* Rev. Ed. New York, 1951. P. 542.

Data from *The Oil and Gas Journal,* April 3, 1961; and *The Petroleum Times,* January 30, 1961.

ferent directions, refineries located at crude shipping ports may have the lowest total transport costs, as much back-hauling is eliminated. Many oil-exporting countries have required a certain part of the production to be refined within the country, and this too has helped the crude export ports to acquire a large share of the total refining capacity.

A third type of oil refinery location is along the transport routes. The best known examples are Aruba and Curaçao in the Netherlands Antilles. When the refineries were built only shallow-draft craft could reach the producing area on Lake Maracaibo, and the two islands were obvious transshipment points. In addition, "there may have been a time when the Dutch flag waving from the flagpole of a $100 million investment looked better than the flag of a country whose government seemed far less stable than that of the Netherlands".[1]

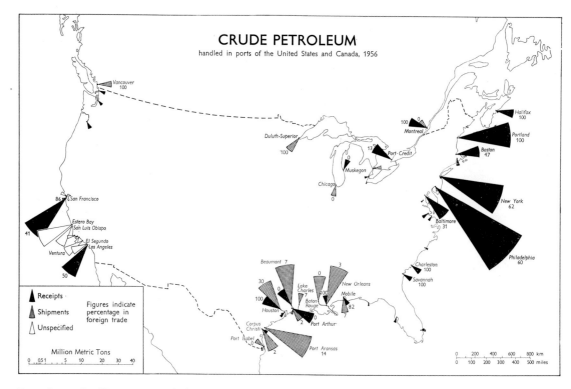

CRUDE PETROLEUM

handled in ports of the United States and Canada, 1956

Data from the Department of the Army, Corps of Engineers, *Waterborne Commerce of the United States,* 1956 and Dominion Bureau of Statistics, *Shipping Report,* 1956.

Refineries mainly intended for the supply of marine fuel oil to ocean shipping also belong to this category.

Finally there are refineries located on or close to inland oil fields. These are generally small and serve a local market and are of no direct interest to the shipping industry.

The oil refinery map of North America shows examples of all the types of locations described. Philadelphia and New York on the North Atlantic seaboard supply the eastern part of the Manufacturing Belt with petroleum products refined from crude brought by tankers. Montreal, Canada's largest refining center, before the opening of the extended St. Lawrence Seaway in 1959 was at the head of navigation on the St. Lawrence River, but the bulk of its crude is brought by pipe line from

Portland, Maine. This pipe line gives Montreal access to an ice-free port, while its own port is frozen. At the same time the long trip around Nova Scotia and the Gaspé Peninsula is obviated, which shortens the tanker routes, especially from the Caribbean area. The large refineries in the inland part of the Manufacturing Belt are also market located, but are supplied by pipe lines and tanker barges. On the Pacific coast, Los Angeles and San Francisco are large refining centers, combining the locational advantages of large markets, proximity to oil fields and, at least in earlier times, of crude shipping ports. The refineries in the Pacific Northwest are more clearly market located, the crude coming in by tanker, as well as by pipe line from the fields east of the Canadian Rockies. The many large refineries at the Gulf ports, which ship crude from the Midcontinent and Gulf Coast fields are primarily examples of the attraction to crude

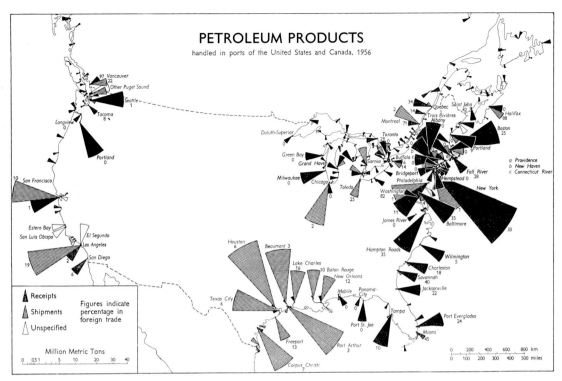

PETROLEUM PRODUCTS
handled in ports of the United States and Canada, 1956

Data from the Department of the Army, Corps of Engineers, Waterborne Commerce of the United States, 1956 and Dominion Bureau of Statistics, Shipping Report, 1956.

shipping ports, although they of course now also cater for a large local market, including a large part of the American petro-chemical industry. The many small refineries that dot the map in the Great Plains—Rocky Mountains area from Texas to Alberta are mainly oil field located, catering for local markets, which due to the high per capita consumption are rather large, despite the relatively low population density.

The location of the refineries to a large extent determines the petroleum traffic through the ports of Anglo-America. The refinery map shows the refinery capacity at the beginning of 1960, whereas the port map shows the quantities loaded and unloaded in 1956, but the main features of the maps have remained constant in recent years.

The most important flow of crude oil within North America goes from a number of ports on the Gulf of Mexico to the east coast, where

Philadelphia and New York dominate. These ports also import large quantities of crude oil from abroad, while only a small portion of the shipments from the Gulf ports is bound for foreign countries. The two large crude-receiving ports in California, San Francisco and Los Angeles, also import from foreign countries a large part of the oil, but some comes from the ports shown as "unspecified" on the map, which are located close to the oil fields. There is little traffic in crude oil on the Great Lakes. The most important in 1956 was that from the Superior terminal of the pipe line from the Canadian prairie provinces (now extended to Sarnia) to Port Credit on Lake Ontario.

Petroleum products are shipped through many more ports than is crude oil, and the total quantity is larger too. The most important shipping area for products is again the Gulf Coast, while the North Atlantic seaboard is the largest receiving area. The north-eastern ports also import products, although the share of domestic traffic is higher than for crude. The differences between the crude map and the products map are striking. The number of ports on all seaboard sectors, the Great Lakes and the St. Lawrence River where petroleum products are unloaded is much larger than the number of ports receiving crude. The reason is obvious. There are many more coastal oil depots than tidewater located oil refineries.

The products map shows that many ports both ship and receive petroleum products. There are always several oil companies in a given market and one may ship petroleum products from its refinery while another receives products for its depot and a third has entrepôt trade.

Among the oil refineries in Europe and the Middle East we find examples of the same types of locations as in North America and the Caribbean. A great number of large refineries are located at ports in the industrialized countries in north-western Europe, most of which are estuary ports: the Rhine (Rotterdam), the Seine (Gonfreville, Port-Jérôme, Petit-Couronne), the Thames (Shellhaven, Isle of Grain), the Elbe (Hamburg). The increasing size of the tankers bringing in the crude has necessitated the deepening of fairways and the extension of port areas to reach deep water.[2] The Southampton waters are to be dredged to enable the Fawley jetties to accomodate tankers of up to 65,000 tons.[3] Rotterdam's new "Europoort" will accomodate tankers of up to 100,000 tons and forward the oil by pipe line to refineries farther inland. Milford Haven in Wales is situated far from any major concentration of population but was chosen as a refinery site due to its facilities for receiving large vessels. It is also the ocean terminal of a pipe line to Llandarcy, another refinery in Wales. Llandarcy is also served by

Refinery Capacity for Selected West European Countries

Million metric tons
December 31 in respective years

	1950	1955	1960	1963 (planned)
Italy	6.5	26.0	39.0	54.6
United Kingdom	9.8	30.7	50.5	52.5
France	13.0	29.9	40.4	48.3
West Germany	4.7	14.7	40.5	48.2
Netherlands	3.9	13.7	23.3	24.8
Belgium	0.8	5.9	8.8	12.8
Sweden	1.3	1.8	3.6	3.6
Austria	1.3	2.3	3.3	3.3
Norway	0.05	0.1	2.1	2.1
Switzerland	—	—	—	2.0

Source: Esso A. G., Düsseldorf, here quoted from O. von Kries, "Rohölleitungen nach Süddeutschland", *Raumforschung und Raumordnung,* 1961, H. 2, p. 89.

the Swansea Docks, which, however, cannot handle tankers of more than 32,000 tons. A similar pipe line from Finnart on Loch Long on the west coast of Scotland to Grangemouth on the Firth of Forth shortens the transport route and enables the refinery to receive crude by 100,000 ton tankers, whereas the jetties at Grangemouth are limited to ships of 14,000 tons.[4]

[2] *Examples of Tankship Dimensions*

Dead-weight, Tons	Length over all, Meters	Beam, Meters	Draft, Meters	Speed, Knots
16,550	159.6	20.8	9.8	15.9
33,600	207.0	26.3	10.5	17.0
47,000	236.1	29.0	11.9	16.0
65,000	259.0	35.1	12.8	16.0
84,700	259.5	38.1	14.0	15.5
131,000	291.0	43.0	16.5	16.0

Sources: 16,550–84,700 ton ships: Permanent International Organisation of Navigation Congresses, here quoted from E. Schouten, "De havenuitbreiding te Rotterdam", *Polytechnisch Tijdschrift,* B, 1957. P. 666 b. The dimensions of the 131,000 ton ship are those of the *Nissho Maru,* launched in July, 1962.
[3] J. R. James, Sheila F. Scott and E. C. Willatts, "Land Use and the Changing Power Industry in England and Wales", *Geographical Journal,* 1961. P. 306.
[4] James, Scott and Willatts, *op. cit.*
O.E.C.D., *op. cit.* P. 17.
David Semple, "The Growth of Grangemouth: A

In the last few years several other pipe lines have been built and projected in Europe, which have influenced the distribution of refining and the pattern of oil transport or will do so in the near future (page 61).[5] The Rhine-Ruhr industrial region is linked with Rotterdam and Wilhelmshaven. This region is a natural location for refineries, since it has a large and concentrated market, but its refinery capacity exceeds the purely local demand, so a surplus will be available for sale outside the area. The same is true of the less concentrated Strasbourg–Karlsruhe–Stuttgart area, which is to be connected with the Mediterranean through pipe lines from Lavéra near Marseille and Genova, the latter line also serving northern Italy, Switzerland and western Austria. The great importance of these pipe lines is in shortening the route for Middle East and North African oil to the inland refineries of France and southern Germany by about 3,500

Note", *Scottish Geographical Magazine,* September 1958. P. 84.
[5] In addition, product pipe lines for military purposes exist both in Britain and in continental Europe.
[6] O.E.C.D., *op. cit.* P. 16.

nautical miles per round trip as against the voyage to a North Sea port.[6]

Since Western Europe has so small a production of crude, we have no examples of refineries located at crude shipping ports, while the oil field located plants are few and small, for instance in northern Germany and eastern Austria. In East Europe and the Soviet Union, for which no data have been available to permit mapping, there are more and larger oil fields having a considerable refining capacity. The large refineries in the Middle East are mainly located at crude shipping ports, but Aden has its refinery thanks to its position as a bunker port and is thus transport located. Ships' bunkers are also an important outlet for other refineries, both for those located at the crude shipping ports, e.g. in the Persian Gulf, and for those located at the major seaports in the market area, e.g. Rotterdam.

The refineries in Asia and Australia also provide many examples of market locations: the Japanese refineries are in the industrial regions of the Kanto plain and northern Kyushu, most Australian refineries in the

Capital Cost for Tankers and Pipe Lines

	Investment Million $		Investment per million ton-miles of transport capacity per year, $	
	Built in U.S.	Built outside U.S.	Built in U.S.	Built outside U.S.
30,000 tons dwt tanker	9.25	6.20	4,590	3,070
45,000 tons dwt tanker	13.25	9.20	4,500	3,140
100,000 tons dwt tanker		16.00		2,740
1,000 mile pipe line 8-inch diameter	30		23,100	
1,000 mile pipe line 12-inch diameter	40		10,250	
1,000 mile pipe line 16-inch diameter	55		8,450	
1,000 mile pipe line 24-inch diameter	80		4,100	

Source: Paper presented by Mr. H. N. Emerson to the annual meeting of the American Petroleum Institute, November, 1957. Quoted from O.E.C.D., *Pipelines and Tankers.* Paris, 1961. P. 13.

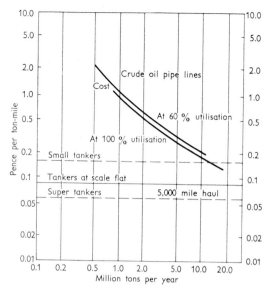

Pipe line and tanker transport: costs and charges in relation to annual tonnage transported.
Source: O.E.C.D. *Pipelines and Tankers,* Paris, 1961. P. 43.

populated south-eastern part of the country (even if the largest—Kwinana in Western Australia—has a capacity in excess of local demand and ships products to other parts of the country). The refineries in Sumatra and Borneo are located at oil ports.

Tankers and Overland Transport

In general the cost of tanker transport is lower than that of any other means of transport.[1] As a rule, therefore, overland transport is complementary to and not competitive with tanker transport. Pipe lines are large investments and financial charges make up 70–80 per cent of their total annual costs.[2] Thus they can only be built where a steady flow of oil, large enough to keep the line operating at or near capacity, is assured over a long period. The larger the diameter of the line, the lower the cost per ton-mile at the same degree of utilisation. If the overland route is considerably shorter than the tanker haul, a large-diameter pipe line may compete with tanker transport.

The Tapline across the Arabian peninsula from the Persian Gulf to the Mediterranean is competitive with the longer tanker route around the peninsula and through the Suez Canal, and also in this case the oil on the land route has the additional advantage of not being subject to canal dues. In the last few years tanker freights have been very low, and at least transport by supertankers has been less costly than by the Tapline, which consequently has had to operate below capacity. In 1960 it carried about 12.5 million tons as against a full capacity of 23.5 million tons.[3] The new Soviet pipe lines under construction to Eastern Europe and the Baltic in a similar way will be competitive with tanker transport from Black Sea ports to the Baltic. The Big Inch and Little Big Inch lines, built during World War II to carry oil from the Gulf Coast to north-eastern United States were possible only due to the necessity of avoiding sending tankers through waters infested with enemy submarines and were converted to gas pipe lines after the war. A 36-inch pipe line to carry products from the Gulf refineries to the south-eastern states and the New York area is scheduled for completion late in 1963.[4]

Tanker and pipe line transport have different cost structures, an important factor in assessing their potentialities in competition

[1] The relative costs of different means of transportation are not constant, but the general relationship may be gotten from the average cost of moving a barrel of oil over 100 miles in the United States in 1954.

	Cents
Tanker	1.5–1.8
Barge	1.75
Pipe line (16-inch)	1.9
Rail	11.0–16.0
Road	80

(R. J. Lindsey, *The Location of Oil Refining in the United States.* Unpublished Ph.D. Thesis. Harvard University, 1954. Quoted from Gerald Manners, "The Pipeline Revolution", *Geography,* 1962. P. 156.)

[2] A. Lascaud, "L'Economie des pipelines", *L'Industrie de pétrole,* January 1960, quoted from O.E.C.D., *op. cit.* P. 13.

[3] O.E.C.D., *op. cit.* P. 19.

[4] *The New York Times,* April 21, 1962.

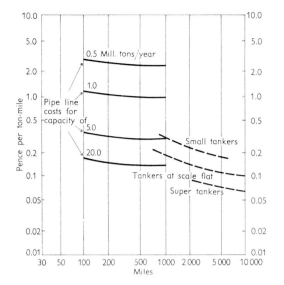

Pipe line and tanker transport: costs and charges in relation to distance.
Source: O.E.C.D. *Pipelines and Tankers*, Paris, 1961. P. 44.

with one another. As shown in the graphs, the cost per ton-mile of transport by tanker is independent of the total volume carried, but decreases with distance. In the case of transport by pipe line, the larger the capacity of the line, the lower the ton-mile cost, but this cost is hardly affected by distance.[5] At the freight levels shown, a pipe line with a capacity of about 12 million tons annually or more could compete successfully with small tankers for a 5,000 mile haul, but not with supertankers. If the quantity to be transported were only 5

[5] O.E.C.D., *op. cit.* P. 44.

[1] At first oil was transported in barrels, but already by 1863 a sailing vessel was equipped with tanks for oil in bulk in addition to a cargo of oil barrels. In 1879 iron vessels with built-in tanks were used on the Baku-Volga route by the Nobel company. The first ocean-going tanker along modern lines, with the hull divided into tanks, machinery aft and pumping equipment for the cargo, was the *Glückauf*, built for a German owner by a British yard in 1886. She had a carrying capacity of 3,000 tons deadweight and a speed of $10^{1}/_{2}$ knots.

[2] For growth of world fleet, age and size of vessels etc. see pages 29–34.

[3] *Lloyd's Register of Shipping*, Statistical Tables 1961.

million tons per year, the pipe line could compete at a distance of 1,000 miles, but not for greater distances.

The World Tanker Fleet

Seaborne trade in petroleum started in the early years of the petroleum industry,[1] but it was not until the First World War that the tanker fleet made up any significant part of the world tonnage. The growth of the tanker fleet has been quicker than that of the total world fleet and tankers have subsequently made up an increasing share of the merchant fleet of the world.[2] In 1961, out of a total of 136 million gross register tons 44 million tons or 32 per cent were tanker tonnage.[3] The development of the world tanker fleet has run parallel with the growth of petroleum production. It is of course to be expected that the growth of oil production would lead to an increasing demand for tanker tonnage. The close co-variation is nevertheless striking, considering the changes in the relative importance among the producing and consuming areas (e.g. the United States changing from net exporter to net importer and Europe's increasing dependence on Middle East oil) and the growing efficiency of tankers in the 40-year period covered by the graph (page 72).

Liquefied Petroleum Gases

Natural gas occurs together with oil and alone in gas fields. In the United States particularly, gas has developed into a major resource (page 57), and is piped over long distances. In many other areas, e.g. Canada, Italy, France and the Soviet Union, the use of natural gas is rapidly expanding, and long pipe lines for natural gas have been built. Along with the development of the North African oil fields have gone plans for the construction of a gas pipe line beneath the Mediterranean Sea and through Spanish territory to southern France. In places without

The Japanese 131,000-ton tanker *Nissho Maru,* built at the Sasebo shipyard for the Idemitsu Kosan Company, Japan's largest independent oil operation, was delivered in October, 1962. The ship is 291 meters long, has a 43-meter beam, a draft of 16.5 meters and a service speed of 16 knots.

access to natural gas by pipe bottled gas under high pressure has long been used, but this is a high cost fuel with rather restricted use. If it were possible to transport liquefied gas from areas without any large domestic market to areas with a great demand for gas, a switch from oil, coal or gas made from coal to imported natural gas might prove economical.

Methane, the main component of natural gas, has to be cooled to about $-125°C$ ($-260°F$) to become liquid. Propane and butane liquefy under pressure at normal temperatures.[1] They are found in natural gas but commercial production is from refinery gases. By liquefied petroleum gases (LPG) is generally understood propane and butane. The first full-scale installations for bulk delivery of LPG by tanker are at Ras Tanura in Saudi Arabia and Mina al Ahmadi in Kuwait.

In 1959 the *Methane Pioneer,* a rebuilt dry cargo ship, started moving methane, cooled to a liquefied state, from Louisiana to Thameshaven. The ship, owned jointly by the British Gas Council and the American company Constock International Methane, has a carrying capacity of 2,000 tons of liquefied gas.[2] In 1961 a fifteen-year contract was signed between Algeria and the British Gas Council for the delivery of liquefied methane. The gas

WORLD PETROLEUM PRODUCTION AND TANKER TONNAGE 1919-1961

Petroleum Production

Tanker Tonnage

World War II

Data for petroleum production 1919–1950 from *World Oil,* Vol. 137, No. 3, 1953; for petroleum production 1950–1961 from United Nations, *Monthly Bulletin of Statistics;* for tanker tonnage from *Lloyd's Register of Shipping.*

[1] Propane at about 8 kg/cm² (110 lbs/sq in), butane at about 1.8 kg/cm² (26 lbs/sq in) at a temperature of 16°C (60°F). These two gases liquefy under atmospheric pressure at temperatures much higher than those required for methane; propane at just under 0°C (32°F) and butane at about $-40°C$ ($-40°F$).

[2] *Norwegian Shipping News,* 1959, pp. 895 ff., and 1260 ff. and 1962, pp. 108 ff.

will be moved by pipeline from Hassi R'Mel in the Sahara to Port Arzew near Oran and from the liquefying plant there to a terminal at Canvey Island near London. From the gasification plant at the terminal it will be distributed by pipeline to Leeds and through branch lines to eight other cities.[3] Large tank-ships have been built equipped with tanks for liquefied gas in addition to the tanks for crude oil, and the LPG tanker fleet is increasing. There have also been plans to combine the installations for gasification with cool storage facilities. Since these developments are at an experimental stage, it is still too early to predict their future importance, but if they prove economical they will affect not only the new gas trades but also coal transport.

Coal

At the end of the 1950s world production of coal was about twice that of petroleum and it has for a long time been about ten times that of wheat or rice, the most important foodstuffs. Coal is also a major commodity in sea-borne trade, although only a rather small part of the coal produced is transported by sea and in recent decades other fuels have gained in importance at the expense of coal.

The graph on page 56 shows the production of a few essential industrial minerals during the past century. Unlike petroleum coal was already of great importance a hundred years ago. The production of coal, similar to that of many other industrial raw materials, expanded at a rapidly and evenly increasing rate. This trend was broken by World War I, and the post-war depression years. The early thirties saw production figures drop to the same level as at the beginning of the century. The armament boom before and during World War II caused a resumed increase in coal production

[3] *The New York Times,* December 12, 1962.

and after a setback in the immediate post-war years the increase has continued.

The relative importance of the major coal producing countries has changed considerably. The United Kingdom—the first country to develop its coal resources on an industrial scale—accounted for more than half the production in 1860 and the British production continued to increase until 1913, when it reached a level unattained since. The American production, only a quarter of that of the United Kingdom in 1860, grew at a faster rate, especially after 1880, and surpassed the British production before the turn of the century to reach a maximum of over 600 million tons in 1918. The increasing use of oil and natural gas and the severe curtailment of industrial production during the Depression kept American production down, and not until World War II did it again reach the 1918 level. During the fifties the American output has again decreased considerably. Germany's production has followed a pattern similar to that of the United Kingdom. The abrupt decline in British output in 1921 and 1926, caused by prolonged strikes, have no counter-parts in the German curve, which on the other hand was more affected by the economic crisis in 1923. Germany's production was continuously high before and during World War II only to be drastically reduced in 1945.

Before the Revolution Russia had a quite small production in comparison with the United States, the United Kingdom and Germany; the destruction and disorganisation caused by the civil war reduced it to almost nothing around 1920. The industrialisation of the Soviet Union with its emphasis on heavy metallurgical industries necessitated a rapid increase in the production of coal. The increase was temporarily halted by World War II, but the latter part of the forties and the fifties have witnessed a rapid growth of Soviet coal production, comparable to that in the United States from 1890 to World War I.

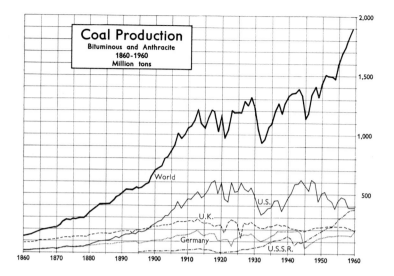

Coal Production
Bituminous and Anthracite
1860-1960
Million tons

Data from *The Mineral Industry; Minerals Yearbook; Weltmontanstatistik;* Emil Müssig, *Eisen- und Kohlen-Konjunkturen seit 1870.* Third Edition, Augsburg, 1925; United Nations *Statistical Yearbook;* United Nations, *Monthly Bulletin of Statistics; Historical Statistics of the United States 1789–1945,* Washington, 1949; *Statistical Abstract of the United States; Narodnoe Chozjajstvo SSSR.*

While the coal production of the older industrial nations has stagnated and even decreased in recent years, Soviet output has soared to surpass that of the United States. (If lignite is included—particularly important to Germany and the U.S.S.R.—the Soviet Union overtook the United States in coal production by 1958.) In addition to the four most important producers shown, many others contribute to the world's coal supply. The rapid increase of coal production in the Soviet Union alone cannot account for the increase in the world total. Increases in production in China, Poland, India, Japan and other countries in the 1950s have helped to offset the decrease in the United States, the United Kingdom and Germany.

UNITED STATES. The American coal reserves in 1953 were estimated at 860,000 million metric tons, 54 per cent of which were in the large deposits in the Great Plains, Rocky Mountains and the Pacific states (mainly sub-bituminous and lignite).[1] However, the production in these areas is small—only 3 per cent of the total production in 1958. The leading states in 1954–58 were West Virginia (30 per cent of total production of bituminous coal and lignite), Pennsylvania (18), Kentucky (15), Illinois (10) and Ohio (8 per cent). The production of anthracite, previously a substantial part of the American coal production, is confined to eastern Pennsylvania.

The development of American coal production has already been described. Coal consumption has decreased because the chief customers (railroads, etc.) have switched to other fuels. The chief remaining consumers are the thermo-electric plants and the steel industry. The thermo-electric plants, despite their improved fuel efficiency, consume increasing quantities and are now the leading customers (46 per cent in 1960). The coke ovens of the steel industry will continue to use large quantities of coal, about 1 ton per ton of steel. Thus despite its relative decline at the expense of other forms of primary energy coal is likely to remain one of the fundamental industrial commodities.

The dominating means of transportation for coal shipments in the United States is the railroad. Of all bituminous coal and lignite mined

---

[1] Paul Averitt, Louise R. Berryhill, and Dorothy A. Taylor, *Coal resources of the United States*: Geol. Survey Circ. 293, 1954, P. 5, quoted from *Minerals Yearbook.*

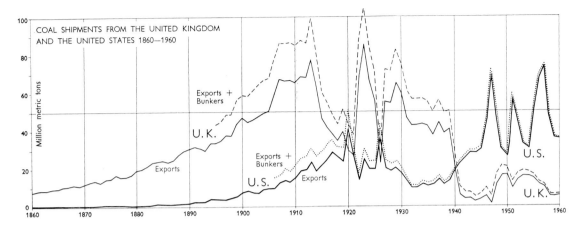

COAL SHIPMENTS FROM THE UNITED KINGDOM AND THE UNITED STATES 1860—1960

Data from *Statistical Abstract of the United Kingdom; Annual Abstract of Statistics; Annual Statement of the Trade of the United Kingdom with British Countries and Foreign Countries; Statistical Abstract of the United States; Minerals Yearbook.*

in 1954–58 no less than 77 per cent left the mines by rail or by truck to be transferred to rail. Trucked to final destination accounted for 11 per cent. Only 10 per cent was shipped by water or trucked to water. Shipments by rail have tended to decrease while truck and water shipments have increased. The importance of water transportation is, however, greater than these figures indicate. Of the total production of bituminous coal and lignite in 1958, only 47 per cent reached their destinations after an all-rail haul. River shipments (entirely or in part) accounted for 16 per cent, the Great Lakes for 11, tidewater for 6, and overseas exports for 9 per cent.[2] The transport of crushed coal mixed with water by pipeline seems likely to become important in the future, but has not, so far, shown up in transport statistics.

Practically all the river transport of coal in the United States takes place on the Mississippi river system, particularly the Ohio and its tributaries. The Pittsburgh area dominates the

total coal tonnage hauled on American inland waterways, but hauls are short. The Monongahela River, which after its confluence with the Alleghany at Pittsburgh forms the Ohio River, carried a total of 26 million metric tons of coal in 1956. Of this total, 52 per cent was carried on the Monongahela alone, most of it downstream. The Ohio River/Pittsburgh District received 41 per cent and the Ohio River/Huntingdon District, immediately downstream from the Pittsburgh District, 5 per cent. Another 5 per cent were brought to the Monongahela from the upper Ohio River. The Pittsburgh area also received shipments from the Alleghany and the Kanawha. Outside the Ohio and its tributaries coal barges are important only on the Illinois. The port of Chicago received over 4.5 million tons of coal by river in 1956, more than four times the lakewise receipts.[3] There is also some coal transported on the Gulf Intracoastal Waterway. Coal trade on the Great Lakes consists mainly of shipments from Toledo and other ports on the southern shore of Lake Erie to a large number of ports on the Lakes and the St. Lawrence. (For a discussion of this trade see page 264.)

[2] *Minerals Yearbook*, 1958, Vol. II, Pp. 25 ff.
[3] Department of the Army, Corps of Engineers, *Waterborne Commerce of the United States, Calendar Year 1956, Domestic Inland Traffic: Areas of Origin and Destinations of Principal Commodities* (Supplement to Part 5, National Summaries).
See also Donald Patton, "The Traffic Pattern on American Inland Waterways", *Economic Geography*, 1956. P. 29.

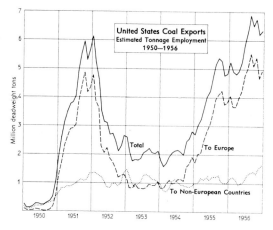

United States Coal Exports
Estimated Tonnage Employment
1950–1956

Total

To Europe

To Non-European Countries

Data from Göran Norström, *Säsongväxlingar i tonnagesysselsättningen i internationell handel med massgodsvaror,* mimeographed, Stockholm, 1959.

The tidewater shipments of American coal are dominated by Norfolk and Newport News on Hampton Roads. Most of the coal is exported (82 per cent in 1956). Smaller quantities are shipped through a few other ports on the east coast. The coastwise shipments go to a number of ports to the north, from Philadelphia to Maine. Practically no coal is shipped through ports on the southern Atlantic seaboard, the Gulf or the Pacific coasts. An estimate of the fleet carrying American export coal and coke in 1950–56[4] shows that on an average 3.2 million deadweight tons were so employed, of which 2.2 million tons for exports to Europe alone. The variations were great, especially in shipments to Europe. When the exports were exceptionally large—in 1951 and 1956 they employed over 6 million tons— they greatly influenced total demand for bulk cargo tonnage and thereby the tramp rates.

UNITED KINGDOM. Great Britain is still one of the world's leading producers of coal, although she was long ago surpassed by the United States and more recently by the Soviet Union. Without petroleum resources of her own, she still relies heavily on her coal as a source of primary energy.[5]

Great Britain has several coal fields, and except in southeast England and northern Scotland no place is more than 100 kilometers from a major coal field.[6] The distribution of the coal fields has greatly influenced the distribution of industry and population in Britain. London is the only major concentration of population outside the immediate vicinity of the coal fields, and the transportation of coal to London has been an important task of British coastwise trade for centuries.[7]

The decline of coal production and coal exports has been paralleled by a gradual change in the relative importance of individual fields. A comparison of production in 1958 with that in 1938 shows that the inland fields generally have gained, particularly the East Midlands region (Derbyshire, Nottinghamshire and Leicestershire), the only region where production actually increased. The coastal fields have experienced a reduction, not only in physical output, but in most cases also in their share of the total production. Exports have been drastically reduced; electricity production relies increasingly on power stations on inland coal fields rather than on market oriented stations.[8] The plan for 1965 does not foresee any

[4] Summarized in Göran Norström, "Seasonal Variations in the Employment of Bulk Cargo Tonnage", *Tijdschrift voor Economische en Sociale Geografie,* 1961. Pp. 119–128. The estimate was made according to the principles discussed on page 55.

[5] In 1958 solid fuels accounted for 82 per cent of total energy consumption (excluding fuel wood) in the United Kingdom, more than in any other major industrial country except Germany (87 per cent). In the United States the corresponding percentage was 26. In nations without substantial fuel resources of their own it was still lower; Italy covered 23 per cent of her energy needs with solid fuels, Sweden 15 and Brazil 14 per cent. Statistical Office of the United Nations, Statistical Papers, Series J, No. 3, *World Energy Supplies 1955–1958.* New York, 1960.

[6] E. M. Rawstron, "Grundzüge der Geographie der Brenn- und Energiestoffe in Großbritannien", *Geographische Rundschau,* 1958. Pp. 419 ff.

[7] J. U. Nef, *The Rise of the British Coal Industry,* London, 1932. E.g. Vol. I. P. 124. See also N. R. Elliott, "Tyneside, A Study in the Development of an Industrial Seaport", *Tijdschrift voor Economische en Sociale Geografie,* 1962. Pp. 225 ff.

[8] Rawstron, *op. cit.* Pp. 421 ff.

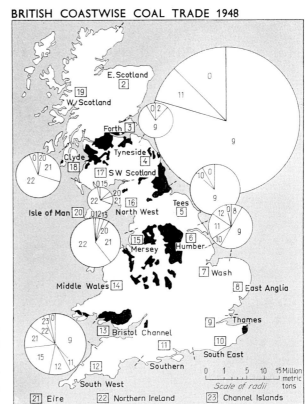

BRITISH COASTWISE COAL TRADE 1948

Circles are proportionate to quantities shipped. Figures in circle sectors refer to areas of unloading. O = Other areas.
Data from P. Ford and J. A. Bound, *Coastwise Shipping and the Small Ports*. Oxford, 1951. P. 17.

major changes in the quantities produced in the different regions.[9]

The British shipping statistics do not give a detailed picture of the coastwise shipping. A study of the coasting trade in 1948[10] shows that tramps of over 100 G.R.T. carried 30 million tons of cargo, 84 per cent of which was coal. Tyneside dominated as an area of origin while the Thames was the most important receiving area. The Tyne—Thames traffic alone accounted for 47 per cent of the total coastwise coal trade (including exports to the Irish Republic). There is no similar breakdown for subsequent years. The following table shows that changes in total tonnage between 1948 and 1959 were not very great.

[9] National Coal Board, *Revised Plan for Coal*. Oct. 1959. P. 12.
[10] P. Ford and J. A. Bound, *Coastwise Shipping and the Small Ports*. Oxford, 1951. Pp. 16 ff.

Coastwise Shipments of Coal and Coke

Million metric tons

1948	25.0	1954	29.5
1949	26.4	1955	25.9
1950	27.7	1956	30.4
1951	29.8	1957	30.5
1952	29.7	1958	27.2
1953	30.8	1959	22.8

Source: National Coal Board.

The decline in British coal exports has been striking. In the peak year 1923 the United Kingdom exported 86 million tons of coal, coke and manufactured fuel (bunker coals excluded); in 1956 the quantity had dropped to 11 million tons. Imports of coal, virtually non-existent before World War II, were 5.5 million tons in 1956. Major coal import ports were London (over two million tons), South-

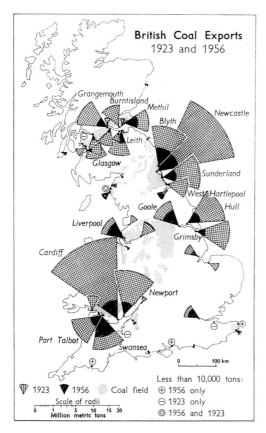

British Coal Exports
1923 and 1956

Less than 10,000 tons:
⊕ 1956 only
⊖ 1923 only
◎ 1956 and 1923

☗ 1923   ▼ 1956   Coal field
Scale of radii
0 1 5 10 15 20
Million metric tons

Data from *Annual Statement of the Trade of the United Kingdom.*

ampton, Manchester and Poole. Several coal export ports imported coal, besides Manchester e.g. Cardiff, Hull, Liverpool.

The table shows the change in the distribution of British coal exports among groups of ports. (On the map the large absolute reductions overshadow these relative changes.) The relative importance of the inland fields has increased considerably. The increase in "other areas" is due partly to the relative increase in coke exports through London and other ports in southern England, and partly to increased exports from the coastal fields in north-west England.

Before World War II British coal exports employed a significant part of the world's tramp fleet. An estimate for 1929,[11] when the

Coal Exports by Port Groups

Ports serving	Percentage of U.K. coal exports		Change
	1923	1956	
South Yorkshire, East Midlands and Other Inland Fields	15	30	+ 15
South Wales	37	29	− 8
Northumberland-Durham	32	25	− 7
Scotland	14	10	− 4
Other areas	2	6	+ 4

Sources: *Annual Statement of The Trade of the United Kingdom with Foreign Countries and British Possessions, 1923. Vol. IV. Annual Statement of The Trade of the United Kingdom with Commonwealth Countries and Foreign Countries, 1956. Vol. IV, Supplement.*

United Kingdom exported 65 million tons of coal (excluding bunkers) shows an average tonnage employment of 2.5 million tons, although much of the long distance shipments, particularly to South America, were return cargoes where only the extra time in port counted. In the period from 1950 to 1956 the average can be estimated at less than 0.4 million tons and the maximum at less than 0.7 million tons.

GERMANY. The most important coal producing country in continental Europe (outside the Soviet Union) is Germany (page 74). In addition, Germany has more than half the world production of lignite, and with only very limited petroleum production she has come to rely very heavily on solid fuels.

Germany's and Europe's most important coal field is the Ruhr, where much of the German heavy industry is concentrated. The defeat of Germany in two world wars caused disruptions in the Ruhr coal production, but never caused the fields to be severed from

[11] Ivar Högbom, *Världssjöfarten.* Göteborg, 1934. Pp. 203 ff.

German territory. The Saar on the other hand, was placed under international control after World War I and formed an autonomous state after World War II—in both cases under French economic influence—only to be returned to Germany in 1935 and 1957 respectively. Most of the Silesian coal fields were ceded to the restored Poland after World War I and the remainder was lost as a result of World War II. These territorial changes should be kept in mind when studying German coal production. Another important political factor is the division of Germany into the German Federal Republic, formed by the American, British, and French zones of occupation in West Germany and the German Democratic Republic in the Soviet zone in East Germany. The coal production is almost entirely in West Germany, while East Germany has more than half the lignite production.

Unlike Great Britain, Germany does not have any coalfields close to the sea, even if the Ruhr area has access to cheap inland water transportation on the Rhine and on the northwestern German canals. This is probably one reason why she has never developed an overseas coal export trade comparable to that of Britain before World War II. Another advantage that Britain had, but which was not present to the same degree in Germany was the favorable return cargo position in relation to overseas countries exporting food and raw materials.

In 1956 West Germany exported 25 million tons of coal, coke and briquettes, somewhat less than a third by inland waterways, less than a sixth through sea ports, primarily Emden and Bremen, and more than half by rail. The imports in the same year were 23 million tons, of which the inland waterways and seagoing ships each accounted for approximately a third and the railroads for the remainder. Coal leaving or entering Germany by barge on inland waterways was partly transshipped to or from ocean going ships in the Dutch and Belgian ports at the Rhine and Scheldt estuaries. Since much of the imports came from the United States West German coal imports were more important to the shipping industry than her coal exports. In 1956 Germany, like other European countries, had an abnormally high coal import. In 1960 exports were 30 million tons while imports had dropped to 12 million tons. It was still imports that dominated Germany's maritime coal trade, however. Almost half the imports came through seaports, most of it from the United States, while only one-tenth of the exports passed through German seaports, most of it for European destinations.

According to an estimate for the 1950–56 period, founded on export statistics[12] the West German exports of coal and coke employed on the average 0.43 million deadweight tons of shipping.

POLAND. The bulk of the Polish coal production comes from the Upper Silesian coal field. Before the reconstitution of Poland after World War I the larger part of this field was within the German border, while the southernmost part was in Austria. After the war Poland was in possession of the larger part, with Czechoslovakia and Germany holding smaller shares in the south and the west. In the interwar period Poland expanded her coal production rapidly and became an important coal exporter. Her overseas exports passed through the ports of the free city of Danzig (Gdańsk) and the new Polish port of Gdynia. A new railroad, completed in 1933, was built from Silesia to Gdynia. Freight rates were set very low which made it possible for Polish coal to compete successfully in the Baltic with British coal from the coastal coal fields.[13] In the 1920s and 1930s Poland exported 10–15 million tons of coal annually.

[12] Cf. page 76, footnote 4.
[13] Ivar Högbom, *Världssjöfarten*. Göteborg 1934. Pp. 71, 212.

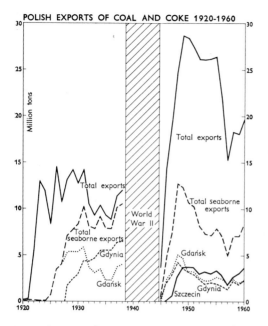

POLISH EXPORTS OF COAL AND COKE 1920-1960

Data from *Weltmontanstatistik I–IV;* Polish Export Statistics; Czesław Wojewódka, *Structural Changes in the Traffic of Polish Seaports 1945–1960.* Part 2. Transactions of the Maritime Institute at Gdańsk, Series III. Gdańsk, 1961. (In Polish with English summary.)

During World War II, when the coal fields were occupied by the Germans, production was increased and this increase has continued after the war. Also exports increased, and in the mid-fifties Poland exported about 25 million tons per annum. About two-thirds of the exports went to the Soviet Union and East European countries, largely by over-land routes. The remaining third went mainly to Western Europe by sea.[14] The port of Stettin was taken over by Poland at the end of the war, and Szczecin, as it is called in Polish, has overtaken Gdańsk and Gdynia as a coal shipping port. A fourth Polish port, Kołobrzeg, was reopened to international traffic in 1960 and is intended to serve the coal export.[15] The short distances of Polish sea-borne coal exports make the shipping tonnage employed rather moderate. An estimate for the 1950–56 period[16] puts it

at 0.20 million deadweight tons, the monthly averages varying between 0.07 and 0.39 million.

Ores

Ores constitute one of the most important commodity groups in seaborne trade. Of the dry cargoes only grains and coal employ as much or more shipping tonnage. Most important by far is iron ore. The world production of iron ore has grown at approximately the same rate as that of pig iron (page 56). From an estimated 18 million tons in 1860, it grew to 88 million in 1900 and 177 million tons in 1913, or about tenfold in 53 years. During the same period pig iron production increased from 7.6 to 78 million tons. Ore production dropped during World War I and the resumed upward trend was interrupted by the Depression in the early thirties, and not until 1937 was the 200-million mark passed. World War II brought with it another set-back, and only in 1948 did the annual production again surpass 200 million tons. Since then the increase has been rapid, and by 1960 the production was close to 450 million tons.[1]

Iron ores vary greatly in composition; the presence of other metals, phosphorus and sulphur affects the smelting properties of the ore and determines the smelting and steelmaking processes in which it can be used. Low-grade ores were formally used only close to the mine, while much high-grade ore was transported over long distances. As, however, many low-grade ores can now be economically beneficiated at the mine to a cocentrate with

[14] United Nations Economic Commission for Europe, *Economic Survey of Europe 1957.*
[15] Arnljot Strømme Svendsen, "Shipping in the Countries of the Eastern Bloc", *Norwegian Shipping News,* 1962. P. 57.
[16] Cf. page 76, footnote 4.
[1] *Weltmontanstatistik* (Stuttgart), I–IV, *Minerals Yearbook.*

International Seaborne Iron Ore Trade over Major Trade Routes 1960

Million tons

Exporting Countries	Importing Countries			
	E.E.C.	U.K.	U.S.	Japan
Sweden + Norway	13.6	5.1	0.1	—
Spain + Portugal	1.5	1.1	—	—
North Africa	2.5	3.7	—	—
West Africa	3.0	1.7	1.0	—
India + Goa	3.0	0.0	0.1	4.5
Malaya	0.1	—	—	5.3
Philippines	—	—	—	1.2
Canada	1.8	3.3	10.6	1.1
United States	—	—	—	0.8
Venezuela	2.7	1.6	14.6	0.0
Brazil	1.8	0.6	1.5	0.4
Chile	0.5	—	3.9	0.3
Peru	1.5	—	2.8	0.6

Sources: Fearnley & Egers Chartering Co., Ltd., *World Trade and Bulk Carriers*. Oslo, 1961, p. 3. "World Iron Ore Trade in 1960", *Westinform Shipping Report*, No. 182, 1961. United Nations, Statistical Papers, Ser. D. *Commodity Trade Statistics*. Vol. X, No. 4.

a high iron content even low-grade deposits may be of interest to the ore trade. Ore concentrates make up a large and increasing proportion of the iron ore consumption.

International sea-borne trade in ore in 1960 is summarized in the table and the ports of loading and unloading are shown on the maps. The main importing areas are the highly industrialised countries—the United States, Western Europe, particularly West Germany and the United Kingdom, and Japan. The Soviet Union, the world's second largest steel producer, covers her needs from domestic ore fields and also supplies the East European countries with the bulk of their ore imports, but both transport within the Soviet Union and exports are predominantly overland and are of no direct importance to world shipping. The same is true of another major iron ore

[2] *Minerals Yearbook*, 1960, Vol. 3. P. 535.

exporter, France. The French low-grade *minette* ores are shipped by rail and inland waterways to Belgium, Luxembourg and Germany.

The United States traditionally produces most of her iron ore needs from the fields near Lake Superior (page 262) and the Great Lakes form the world's most important shipping lane for iron ore. Most of the United States ore export is destined for Canada and moves by lake boats. In the last decade the ore imports have increased rapidly. A major reason for this has been the dwindling reserves in the Lake Superior fields, which have made it necessary to turn to foreign sources if their complete depletion is to be avoided. This increased use of imported ore has so far contributed more than the use of concentrates from the low-grade taconite ores of the Lake Superior fields, although this resource is gaining in importance. In 1960 Minnesota plants shipped 11 million tons of taconite pellets.[2]

The American iron ore imports in 1950 were 8.4 million tons or less than 8 per cent of a total consumption of 108 million tons. In 1960 the imports made up 32 per cent of the consumption, or 35 million out of 110 million tons. The largest suppliers were Venezuela and Canada, but other South American countries, West Africa, India and Sweden also exported iron ore to the United States in 1960. Several of these countries have supplied a marginal part of U.S. ore needs for decades. The large increase in American ore imports has considerably enhanced the share of ore shipments in world shipping. Baltimore and Philadelphia are the principal tidewater ore receiving ports (page 262). Some ore from the Labrador peninsula reaches the Great Lakes through the St. Lawrence Seaway (page 264).

The large steel producing countries in Western Europe have iron ore resources of their own, but these are mainly of a low grade. While the French iron industry is based mainly on domestic low-grade ore, Britain, Belgium, Luxembourg and Germany get most of the ore

Iron Ore Ports

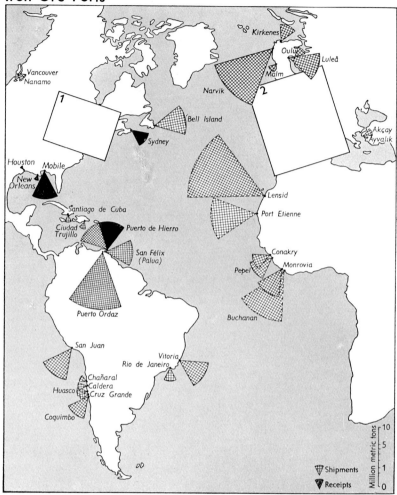

For inset 1 see page 262.

from abroad. Part of it (particularly in Belgium and Luxembourg) is French low-grade *minette* ore brought over short distances by rail or barge, part is high-grade ore brought from more distant sources. The largest supplier is Sweden, whose ore exports are shipped mainly through Narvik in Norway and Luleå on the Gulf of Bothnia while smaller quantities from the ore fields of South Sweden are shipped through a number of smaller ports. Other sources of some importance within or near

Europe are Norway, Spain, Portugal, Morocco, Algeria, and Tunisia. But also Canadian, South American, West African and other ores are smelted in Western Europe.

The third major deficit area for iron ore, Japan, has also increased her imports very rapidly. In 1950, when the Japanese steel industry had not yet recovered from World War II, less than 2 million tons were imported, while in 1960 imports exceeded 14 million tons. Malaya, India, Goa and the Philippines

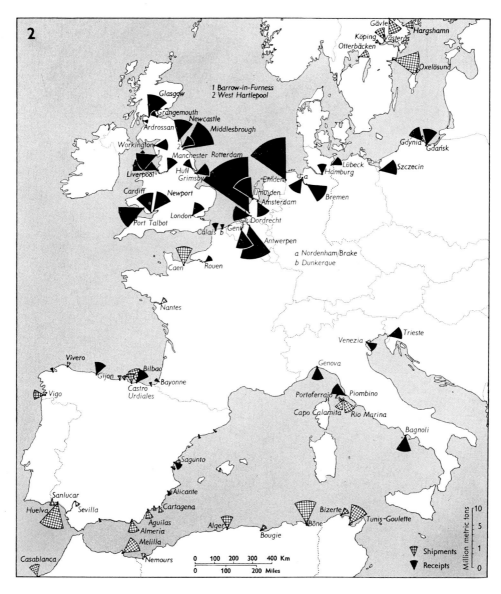

2

1 Barrow-in-Furness
2 West Hartlepool

a Nordenham/Brake
b Dunkerque

Shipments
Receipts

Million metric tons

were the largest suppliers, but Japan also bought iron ore from Canada and the United States (shipped through Pacific ports) and South America.

The ore shipments clearly show seasonal variations. These are largely caused by variations in exports from Sweden and Canada. The freezing of ore ports and shipping lanes that handle the exports of these countries

results in a pronounced winter minimum—summer maximum pattern despite the fact that about 60 per cent of the Swedish ore is shipped via ice-free Narvik in Norway.

Many iron ores contain a little manganese, and iron ores containing 5–10 per cent manganese are classed as manganiferous iron ores, 10–35 per cent as ferruginous manganese ores and over 35 per cent as manganese ores. The world production of manganese ores in 1959 was estimated at 13 million tons.[3] The largest

[3] *Minerals Yearbook,* 1959, Vol. 1. P. 743.

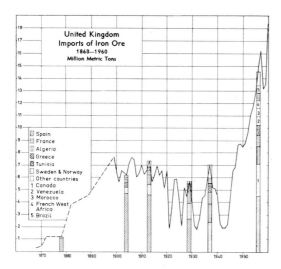

United Kingdom
Imports of Iron Ore
1868—1960
Million Metric Tons

Spain
France
Algeria
Greece
Tunisia
Sweden & Norway
Other countries
1 Canada
2 Venezuela
3 Morocco
4 French West Africa
5 Brazil

Data from T. B. Roddy, "The Development of Iron Ore Imports", *Steel Review*, 9, 1958.

producers are the Soviet Union, India, China, South Africa, and Brazil. The United States and Western Europe have to import most of their requirements, consequently much of the production enters international trade, most of it sea-borne. The largest exporters are India (including Goa), the Soviet Union, Brazil, Ghana, the Congo, and South Africa.

Bauxite, the only important aluminum ore, is second to iron ore as a cargo for the ore-carrying fleet. World production of bauxite has increased very rapidly. In 1960 it was about 25 million tons, three times as much as a decade earlier. The production of aluminum from bauxite takes place in three stages: the beneficiation of the ore; the production of alumina (aluminum oxide); and the electrolytic reduction of alumina to metallic aluminum. Most bauxite is beneficiated before shipment by crushing, washing and drying. Since it takes about four tons of bauxite to produce two tons of alumina, which yields one ton of aluminum, transport cost considerations would tend to locate the aluminum industry near the bauxite deposits. Since the cost of electricity is a large part of the production cost (20,000

kilowatt hours are needed for the production of one ton of aluminum) the reduction plants have to be located where cheap electric power is available. The alumina plants are often located in places far from the smelters. Some have been built near the bauxite deposits, e.g. in Jamaica (Alumina Jamaica Ltd., ALJAM) and Guinea. Most bauxite, however, is shipped to alumina plants in the industrialised countries in North America and Europe.

The largest bauxite exporters are Jamaica, Surinam, and British Guiana. In 1960 they accounted for two-thirds of world exports.[4] All of the Jamaican bauxite exports goes to alumina plants on the American Gulf coast, while alumina is shipped to Canada (Kitimat, British Colombia) and Norway. The bauxite shipping ports are Port Kaiser at Little Pedro (Kaiser Bauxite Co.) and Ocho Rios (Reynolds Jamaica Mines Ltd.). The receiving ports are Baton Rouge, Louisiana and La Quinta at Corpus Christi, Texas. From the Kaiser alumina plant at Baton Rouge alumina is sent for reduction at Chalmette, Louisiana, Mead, Washington, and Tacoma, Washington. The La Quinta plant belongs to the Reynolds Metals Co., which has reduction plants in Texas, Washington, Oregon, and New York in addition to the bauxite producing states of Arkansas and Alabama.[5] Port Esquivel ships alumina from the ALJAM reduction plants at Kirkvine and Ewarton.

Whereas the bauxite shipments from Jamaica started in the 1950s, the Guianas have been important exporters since about 1920. The ALCOA subsidiary SURALCO is the largest producer in Surinam and most of the shipments go to the United States, some to Canada, Germany and other countries. The bauxite is shipped from Moengo on the Cottica River and Paranam and Smalkalden on the Surinam

[4] "The Minor Ore Trades: Bauxite", *Westinform Shipping Report*, No. 194, 1961.
[5] *Westinform Shipping Report*, op. cit. Minerals Yearbook, 1959.

River. These ports can only be reached by shallow-draft vessels. Much of the bauxite is therefore transshipped in Trinidad, where the ore is brought by smaller vessels from the river ports. Some bauxite is also shipped through Paramaribo. In British Guiana Canadian interests dominate (The Demerara Bauxite Co., DEMBA, is an ALCAN subsidiary), and most of the exports go to Canada. The ore comes from deposits on the Demerara and Berbice Rivers. The Demerara ore is railed to Mackenzie, where there is a beneficiation plant and where some of the ore is turned into alumina. From Mackenzie the ore is shipped in shallow-draft vessels, some of it to be transshipped in Trinidad,[6] as the Demerara River is closed to larger vessels by the Georgetown bar. Since the receiving port, Port Alfred, Quebec, on the Saguenay River, is closed by ice in the winter, shipments are concentrated in the period when it can be reached and stockpiles are built up to last through the winter. Bauxite from the Berbice deposits is shipped by barge from the drying plant at Kwakani to Everton at the mouth of the river, where it is transshipped to ocean-going vessels.

In the Caribbean area the Dominican Republic and Haiti have appeared as bauxite exporters in the 1950s. Other minor exporters are Greece, Yugoslavia, France, Ghana, Guinea, Malaya, Sarawak and India. The European exports are mainly directed to France, Germany and the Soviet Union. Most of the South East Asian exports are directed to Japan and some to Australia.

ORE CARRIERS. Ores have traditionally been an important commodity group in the trade of the general tramp ship. Quite early, however, specially built ocean-going ore carriers were developed. They were used particularly for the carrying of ore from Scandinavia and between Chile and the United States. The rapid increase in international ore trade, particularly long distance iron ore trade, has concurred with a still more rapid increase in the world's bulk carrier fleet, and now a large share of the ore shipments is carried in special ore carriers, oil/ ore carriers and general bulk carriers. According to one estimate, "bulk carriers transported 56 million tons of iron and manganese ore in 1960, slightly more than half of the total sea-borne ore trade in tons. Measured in ton-miles nearly two-thirds of the total ore trade was shipped by bulk carriers."[7]

The largest quantities carried by bulk carriers were those from Venezuela to the United States (all of the trade on this route being shipped by bulk carriers) and from Scandinavia to the Continent (54 per cent in bulk carriers). Also very important for bulk carriers were the routes from Canada to the United Kingdom (100 per cent bulk carriers) and from Peru and Chile to the United States (70 per cent bulk carriers), because of the long distances over which large quantities were carried. The share of bulk carrier shipments in the exports of Spain and Portugal, North Africa, India and Malaya is small.

Grain

During most of the post-war period grains have employed more tonnage than any other dry cargo commodity group. The only occasional exception has been coal and coke. The table summarizes world production and international trade in grains for a number of years. Some international trade is carried overland or by lake vessels and does not employ seagoing ships, but on the other hand some grain is also carried in coastwise trade, and the quantities entering international trade give an idea of the importance of grain transports to the shipping industry.

---

[6] Total transshipments of bauxite in Trinidad exceed 3 million tons annually.

[7] Fearnley & Egers Chartering Co. Ltd., *World Trade and Bulk Carriers*. Oslo, 1961. P. 7.

Cereals Production and Trade

Million metric tons

	Production			Exports	
	Average 1934–38	Average 1948–52	1960	Average 1934–38	1960
Wheat	167.5	169.6	243.7	17.3[a]	40.0[a]
Rye	46.5	37.7	37.2	1.0	1.3
Barley	52.1	59.0	93.0	2.7	5.3
Oats	65.2	62.1	60.4	0.9	1.3
Corn	114.9	146.0	224.2	10.2	11.8
Millet and sorghum	52.4	46.5	71.6	0.6	3.1
Rice[b]	151.5	164.7	239.5	9.6	6.5
Total cereals	650.2	685.6	969.6	42.3	69.3

[a] Includes flour in wheat equivalent.
[b] Production: paddy; exports: milled.
    The statistics are not complete; e.g. the production of Mainland China of grains other than wheat and rice are not included. Sources: *FAO Production Yearbook, FAO Trade Yearbook.*

The production of rice, wheat and corn (maize) are roughly equal and each is about three times the production of barley, the fourth most important grain. In international trade, however, wheat is by far the most important grain, while only a small fraction of the rice crop is exported. Since a large part of the rice trade takes place within southeast Asia and the wheat trade is to a great extent transoceanic, the position of wheat in sea-borne trade is still more prominent. The international corn trade has lost in relative importance in recent years, and the United States has taken the place of Argentina as the foremost supplier of corn to Europe which has led to a further reduction of the shipping engaged in the corn trade. Among the feed grains, barley and particularly sorghum have gained.

Wheat

Both world production and exports of wheat have roughly doubled in fifty years. A large part of this increase has taken place since

Wheat Production

Average Crop Years 1957/58–1959/60

	Million metric tons	Per cent
Europe	*53.8*	*22.2*
France	10.7	4.4
Germany (E.,W., Saar)	5.4	2.2
Italy	8.9	3.7
Spain	4.7	1.9
U.S.S.R.	*67.9*	*28.0*
North and Central America	*44.1*	*18.2*
Canada	10.6	4.4
United States	32.1	13.2
South America	*8.8*	*3.6*
Argentina	6.1	2.5
Asia	*57.8*	*23.8*
China, Mainland	28.0	11.5
India	9.1	3.7
Turkey	8.4	3.4
Africa	*5.3*	*2.2*
Oceania	*4.8*	*2.0*
Australia	4.6	1.9
World Total	*242.4*	*100.0*

Source: *FAO Production Yearbook* 1960.

World War II. Most wheat is produced in northern temperate lands, but also subtropical areas in both hemispheres are important producers. The countries that grow the largest quantities are not necessarily those which are the most significant in international trade. The three largest producers are the Soviet Union, the United States and China. Of these only the United States has been a major exporter, usually ranking first, for many years. Canada, Argentina and Australia, the remaining major exporters, rank considerably lower as producers, but their population is so much smaller that they have a large surplus in excess of their own needs.

In the years immediately before World War I Russia was the leading wheat exporting country, followed by the United States, Ar-

Wheat Exports

Average 1958–60

	Million metric tons	Per cent
Europe	*3.83*	*10.6*
France	1.30	3.6
Germany (E.,W.)	0.75	2.1
Italy	0.63	1.7
U.S.S.R.	*5.19*	*14.3*
North and Central America	*21.38*	*59.0*
Canada	8.03	22.2
United States	13.29	36.7
South America	*2.47*	*6.8*
Argentina	2.36	6.5
Asia	*0.46*	*1.3*
Africa	*0.34*	*0.9*
Oceania	*2.57*	*7.1*
Australia	2.57	7.1
World Total	*36.24*	*100.0*

Wheat flour converted to grain equivalent included.
Source: *FAO Trade Yearbook* 1961.

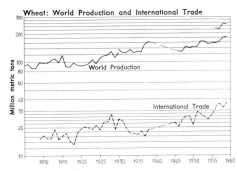

Wheat: World Production and International Trade

World production for 1905–1938 excluding China; for 1946–1959 excluding U.S.S.R. (lower curve); for 1956–1959 including U.S.S.R. (upper curve).
Sources: (1) production: 1905–1930 "World Wheat Crops, 1885–1932", *Wheat Studies of the Food Research Institute,* Vol. IX, No. 7; 1930–1938 *Bulletin mensuel de statistique agricole;* 1946–1959 *FAO Production Yearbook.*

(2) exports: 1909–1923 J. A. LeClerc, *International Trade in Wheat and Wheat Flour,* Washington, 1925; 1924–1938 *Bulletin mensuel de statistique agricole;* 1945–1959 *FAO Trade Yearbook.* After 1956 the trade figures are more comprehensive.

gentina, Canada, India, Rumania and Australia (wheat flour included).[1] During the interwar period and the years following World War II only four of these seven countries remained as major exporters. Towards the end of the 1950s the Soviet Union again appeared in the wheat export market. Since the larger part of Soviet wheat exports goes to European countries,[2] this trade is of less importance to shipping than the largely transoceanic exports of the "Big Four".

UNITED STATES. With the exception of 1953 and 1954, the United States has been the

[1] J. A. LeClerc, *International Trade in Wheat and Wheat Flour.* Department of Commerce Trade Promotion Series No. 10. Washington, 1925.

[2] Of 6 million tons exported in 1959, 4.3 million tons went to Eastern Europe, and 1.3 million tons to Western Europe. (Alexander N. Sakoff, "Agricultural Commodities in the Foreign Trade of the U.S.S.R.", *Monthly Bulletin of Agricultural Economics and Statistics,* June 1961.)

world's foremost wheat exporter in every year since World War II. Some wheat is produced in almost every state, but the bulk of the production comes from four areas: an eastern winter wheat region from Illinois to Pennsylvania and Maryland, a winter wheat area in the southern Great Plains centered on Kansas, a spring wheat area in the northern Great Plains with North Dakota as the leading producer (this area extends north and northwest into Canada) and the Palouse area in south-eastern Washington, growing mainly winter wheat in the southern part and spring wheat farther north, predominantly soft varieties.

The direction of the American wheat exports, some of which is in the form of economic aid, varies considerably from year to year. Europe, the most important market for wheat, buys a large share of the American exports. The major wheat purchaser on the world market, the United Kingdom, imports

Wheat Imports

Average 1958–60

	Million metric tons	Per cent
Europe	*16.32*	*48.0*
Belgium-Luxembourg	0.46	1.4
Czechoslovakia	1.04	3.1
France	0.51	1.5
Germany (E.,W.)	3.64	10.7
Italy	0.27	0.8
Netherlands	1.08	3.2
Poland	1.23	3.6
Switzerland	0.36	1.1
United Kingdom	4.89	14.4
Yugoslavia	0.69	2.0
U.S.S.R.	*0.22*	*0.6*
North and Central America	*1.03*	*3.0*
South America	*3.00*	*8.8*
Brazil	1.80	5.3
Asia	*10.29*	*30.2*
India	3.53	10.4
Japan	2.55	7.5
Pakistan	0.85	2.5
Africa	*2.91*	*8.6*
U.A.R.: Egypt	1.31	3.8
Oceania	*0.27*	*0.8*
Word Total	*34.03*	*100.0*

Wheat flour converted to grain equivalent included.
Source: *FAO Trade Yearbook* 1961.

primarily from the Commonwealth countries Canada and Australia, and the American share in the British wheat supply is generally small. On the other hand many countries in Asia, particularly Japan and India, have taken increasing quantities of wheat from the United States. The United States also exports wheat, often in the form of flour, to many countries in Africa and Central and South America. The exports to South America have been quite large in some years, when crop failures in Argentina have made it impossible for Brazil to cover her needs from there. Of the 13.3 million tons of wheat exported yearly 1958–60,

no less than 2.5 million tons were exported in the form of flour (1.8 million tons). It is mainly tropical countries that import much wheat as flour. The largest customer was Egypt, which bought 15 per cent of the exports. Other large buyers were Italy (7 per cent), the Philippines (6 per cent), Ceylon, the Netherlands and Cuba.

The American wheat is exported through a number of ports in three areas: the Atlantic seaboard (from Portland, Maine to Hampton Roads), the Gulf Coast, and the Pacific Northwest.[3] Since the opening of the deepened St. Lawrence Seaway in 1959 some changes have taken place, but it is still too early to predict with certainty the future pattern of shipments. Before the opening of the Seaway it was believed that little grain would be carried by oceangoing ships from ports on Lake Superior, whereas there would be a substantial increase in exports by cargo liners from Lake Michigan ports. The low operating costs per cargo ton of the specially constructed Lake boats would make it more economical to ship the wheat to Lower St. Lawrence ports for transshipment to ocean-going vessels. Regardless of transshipment, the Seaway would take over a large part of the grain shipments from a large tributary area in the Midwest.[4] The first years of the Seaway have witnessed a large increase in wheat exports from lake ports, and owing to the low ocean freight rates many oceangoing vessels have loaded there, rather than picking up the cargo at Lower St. Lawrence transshipment points. Whether this situation will continue remains to be seen.[5] As a result,

[3] Very little of the soft wheat exports of the Pacific Northwest goes to Europe. This is in marked contrast to the Canadian hard wheat exports from the West Coast, of which roughly half is bound for Europe.

[4] Harold M. Mayer, *The Port of Chicago and the St. Lawrence Seaway*, University of Chicago, Department of Geography, Research Paper No. 49. Chicago, 1957; Joseph R. Hartley, *The Effects of the St. Lawrence Seaway on Grain Movements*, Indiana Business Report Number 24. Bloomington, 1957.

[5] The Seaway allows ocean vessels of about 10 thousand tons and lake boats of over 20 thousand

WHEAT EXPORTS OF THE UNITED STATES AND CANADA

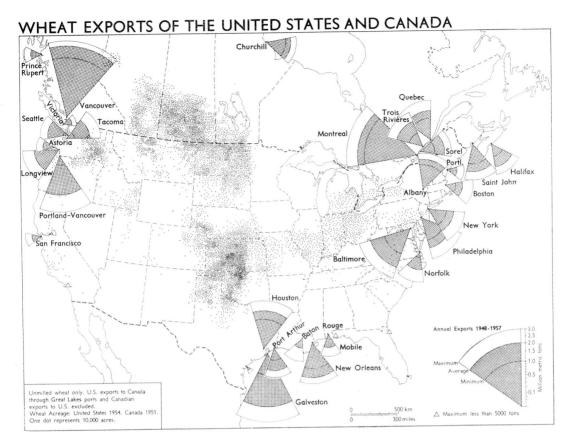

Unmilled wheat only. U.S. exports to Canada through Great Lakes ports and Canadian exports to U.S. excluded.
Wheat Acreage: United States 1954, Canada 1951.
One dot represents 10,000 acres.

Annual Exports 1948-1957

Maximum / Average / Minimum

△ Maximum less than 5000 tons

Atlantic ports, with the exception of Norfolk, have decreased in relative importance among United States wheat exporting ports. The Gulf ports, on the other hand, have continued to increase, a development which was under way before the opening of the Seaway.[6]

The bulk of the wheat moves by rail from the interior to the export ports, but a substantial

Since the opening of the Seaway in 1959 much wheat has been exported overseas direct from Great Lakes ports (pp. 88, 267–269).

Sources: Exports by ports: Department of the Army, Corps of Engineers, *Waterborne Commerce of the United States.* Information provided by the Dominion Bureau of Statistics.

Wheat Acreage: Bureau of the Census, *National Atlas of the United States. Atlas of Canada,* Ottawa, 1957.

amount of export grain from the Midwest moves to the Gulf coast by barge. The freight rate structure of the railroads is important for the ports as well as for the competition among the railroads and between rail, truck and barge.[7]

The American wheat exports employ a large but varying amount of shipping tonnage. Since liners carry virtually all the flour and much of the grain the tramp fixtures do not give an ade-

---

tons. Hybrid forms of ocean vessels with a capacity of 16–17 thousand tons, suited to the dimensions of the Seaway locks, have been launched or are under construction.

[6] *Impact of the St. Lawrence Seaway on the Location of Grain Export Facilities,* U.S. Department of Agriculture, Marketing Research Report No. 442. Washington, 1960.

The St. Lawrence Seaway and its Impact on the Freight Market, Westinform Shipping Report, No. 176, 1961.

[7] U.S. Department of Agriculture, *op. cit.* Pp. 21 f.

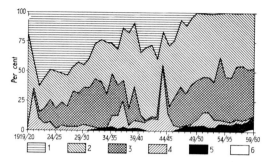

Canadian Wheat Exports 1919–1960

1. Via U.S. Atlantic Seabord ports
2. Via Canadian St. Lawrence-Atlantic Seaboard ports
3. Via Canadian Pacific Seaboard ports
4. U.S. imports
5. Via Churchill
6. Fort William-Port Arthur direct

Sources: George J. Miller, Almon E. Parkins,
Bert Hudgins, *Geography of North America,* Third
Edition, New York, 1954. P. 564 (data from
Canadian Board of Grain Commissioners); Do-
minion Bureau of Statistics, *Grain Trade of Ca-
nada.*

quate picture of the total tonnage employment.
An estimate for the 1948–56 period[8] showed
the fleet carrying American export wheat to
vary between 0.6 and 2.6 million deadweight
tons, averaging 1.5 million tons. The great
variations were caused partly by changes in
exported quantities from year to year but also
by seasonal variations in exports. An average
seasonal index of tonnage employment for
1948–56 shows January–June above the twelve-
month average and July–December below. A
maximum of about 120 per cent of the average
occurred in March and a minimum of about
80 per cent in November. This may seem
strange, since the larger part of the American
wheat production comes from the winter wheat
areas, where it is harvested in June and July
and will be ready for shipment during the
summer and fall. The maximum would therefore be expected to occur in the latter half of
the year and the minimum in the spring, and
such was in fact the case before World War

II. The reversal of the earlier pattern is in all
likelihood a result of the large American wheat
surplus. When the exporting country at the
end of a crop year has quantities corresponding
to several years' exports in stock there is clearly
no need to let the harvesting season influence
the shipping seasons and other market considerations become decisive.

CANADA. Canada is usually second only to the
United States as a wheat exporter. Before
World War II it was often the largest exporter,
and this happened again in 1953 and 1954.
Most of the crop comes from the Prairie
Provinces, Saskatchewan, Alberta and Mani-
toba. The Canadian export wheat is hard
spring wheat.

Canada exports her wheat all over the
world, but has the United Kingdom as her
foremost customer (33 per cent in 1958–60).
The wheat exports in 1958–60 averaged 8.0
million tons, 1.0 million being the wheat equivalent of 0.75 million tons of flour. The countries buying the largest quantities of Canadian
wheat flour were the United Kingdom, (36
per cent), the Philippines (10), and Ceylon (5
per cent). Most of the wheat is loaded in the
Lower St. Lawrence ports, where Montreal
has the largest shipments. The largest single
port, however, is Vancouver (with New Westminster) on the Pacific. In winter when the St.
Lawrence is ice-bound, much wheat is shipped
through St. John and Halifax on the Atlantic,[9]
and during a few months in the late summer
and early fall Churchill on Hudson Bay ships
several hundred thousand tons. Prior to 1950
much Canadian wheat was shipped through
United States east coast ports, but these shipments have now ceased almost completely.

The Pacific ports and Churchill receive the

[8] Cf. page 76, footnote 4.
[9] For a study of these shipments, see Donald J.
Patton, "Railroad Rate Structures, Ocean Trade Routes
and the Hinterland Relations of Halifax and Saint
John", *Tijdschrift voor Economische en Sociale Geografie,* 1961. Pp. 2–13.

wheat by rail. The large increase in the wheat flow through Canadian Pacific ports has taken place after changes in the railroad rates in 1925.[10] The Atlantic and Lower St. Lawrence ports, on the other hand, rely heavily on lake shipments combined with rail haulage. The wheat is brought to Fort William—Port Arthur on Lake Superior by rail. Before the opening of the extended St. Lawrence Seaway it was shipped by lake freighters either to Georgian Bay and other Lake Huron ports for transshipment by rail to one of the St. Lawrence or Atlantic ports, or to Erie or Ontario ports for transshipment to the St. Lawrence either by rail or by "canaller", the small freighters that could pass the old locks in the St. Lawrence. The opening of the new Seaway enabled the lake boats to reach the St. Lawrence ports, thereby obviating the necessity of the latter transshipment. At the same time it made it possible for ocean-going vessels to pick up their cargo at the elevators at Fort William—Port Arthur, and this has also been common in the last few years.[11]

According to an estimate for 1948–56, the deadweight tonnage of the fleet carrying Canadian export wheat varied between 0.7 and 2.5 million tons, averaging 1.2 million tons. The freezing of the St. Lawrence ports makes the seasonal component of the variations strong. The average pattern for the 1948–56 period was a January minimum of 78 per cent of the twelve month average, high figures particularly in May and June (130 per cent), a decrease to 97 per cent in September, and after the new harvest a new, lower maximum of 105 per cent in November. Like the seasonal pattern of the United States wheat exports, that of Canadian ports has changed considerably since

Wheat exports of Argentina 1949–1957 and wheat acreage 1950.

The shaded area of the port sectors represents a nine year average; the outer arc marks the maximum and the inner arc the minimum. Most ports did not export any wheat in 1952 (crop failure). One dot represents 2,000 hectares sown area.

Sources: Export data for 1949–1950 from *Anuario Estadístico de la República Argentina*. Data for 1951–1957 provided by the Dirección Nacional de Estadística y Censos. Acreage data according to Ministerio del Agricultura mapped in *La Argentina: Suma de geografía*, Tomo IV, Buenos Aires, 1959, Figs. 147 and 152.

pre-war years. The fall maximum was then by far the higher and the spring maximum less pronounced.

ARGENTINA. Since Argentina first gained importance as a wheat exporter towards the end of the last century,[12] she has maintained a position as one of the principal countries shipping

---

[10] T. L. Hills, *The St. Lawrence Seaway*. New York, 1959. P. 45.

[11] The effect of the prevailing freight rates on the choice of loading port for the ocean transport was discussed for the United States wheat shipments, page 88.

[12] Cf. page 361.

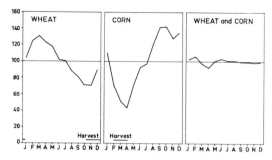

Average seasonal variations in estimated tonnage employed by Argentine grain exports 1948–1956. Data from Göran Norström, *Säsongväxlingar i tonnagesysselsättningen i internationell handel med massgodsvaror,* mimeographed, Stockholm, 1959. For calculation of index, see Göran Norström, "Seasonal Variations in the Employment of Bulk Cargo Tonnage", *Tijdschrift voor Economische en Sociale Geografie,* 1961. Pp. 119–128.

grain cargoes, exporting also corn and linseed. The quantities have varied much, though, and sometimes crop failures have caused an almost complete termination of wheat exports. Last time this happened was in 1952. The bulk of the wheat comes from the provinces of Buenos Aires, Córdoba and Santa Fe, i.e. from the Pampas region except the north-eastern part, which is rather too humid for wheat cultivation.

The exports from Argentina are directed mainly to Europe and Brazil. Countries outside Europe and South America buy only insignificant quantities. The wheat is exported as grain, and the flour export is limited to a few per cent of the wheat export. It is possible to ship the wheat from ports within or very close to the wheat producing areas. Río Paraná and Río Uruguay are navigable through the eastern Pampas region and the wheat lands reach the coast between Bahía Blanca and Mar del Plata. The navigation on the Río Paraná is impeded by sand bars, and at low water it is often necessary to take only a part load at the up-river ports. The balance is picked up at a down-river port, Buenos Aires or La Plata. The Pampas region is unique in South America

in having a dense railroad net, which facilitates the transport from areas farther from the ports.

The estimated deadweight tonnage of the fleet moving Argentine wheat exports in the 1948–56 period varied from nil (during much of 1952) to 0.7 million tons. The average was 0.4 million tons.[13] The Argentine wheat trade in this period consequently never employed much more tonnage than that of the United States or Canada at their lowest points. The variations have a clearly seasonal component with March as the peak month and a November minimum. This pattern has remained unchanged since before World War II, although the range of the seasonal variations has been considerably reduced. The variations in tonnage employment are somewhat more pronounced than those in export quantities. Exports to Europe, a long haul, constitute a large part of Argentine shipments in the early months of the year, whereas the exports to Brazil, a short haul, are most important during the rest of the year.

AUSTRALIA. Australia has been a large-scale exporter of wheat since the beginning of the twentieth century. Her position resembles that of Canada and Argentina: a country with vast areas of grassland, opened for settlement in the nineteenth century, with a population that is still small enough to leave a large part of the production for the export market. There are two major wheat producing areas in Australia. In the east a crescent-shaped belt follows the western slopes of the Great Dividing Range and reaches the coast in South Australia. A second belt is in the south-western corner of the continent.

The direction of Australian wheat exports is determined by her close economic relations with Britain and her position as the nearest

[13] A similar estimate for 1924–32 indicated an average of 0.7 million tons. Ivar Högbom, *Världssjöfarten.* Göteborg, 1934. P. 249.

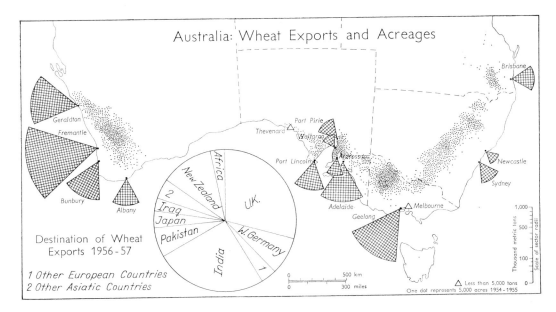

Australia: Wheat Exports and Acreages

Destination of Wheat Exports 1956-57

1 Other European Countries
2 Other Asiatic Countries

One dot represents 5,000 acres 1954-1955

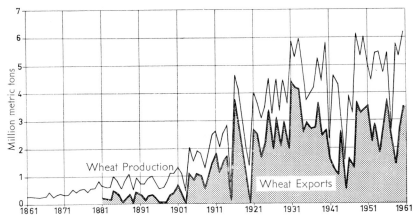

Sources: Graph and wheat acreage from the *Yearbook of the Commonwealth of Australia, 1957*; information on exports by ports provided by the Commonwealth Bureau of Census and Statistics; destination of exports from Commonwealth Bureau of Census and Statistics, *Oversea Trade and Customs and Excise Revenue, 1956–57*.

surplus wheat producer to the wheat-importing countries of eastern and southern Asia. The dominance of tropical countries as importers of wheat flour is as clear in Australian exports as in those of the United States and Canada. Flour is also more important in the wheat exports of Australia than is the case for any other major exporter. In 1958–60, when the average export was 2.6 million tons, no less than 25

per cent or 0.64 million tons constituted the wheat equivalent of 0.46 million tons of flour.

The wheat is shipped through a number of ports close to the areas of production. Western Australia had an unusually large share of the shipments in 1956–57, the year on which the map is based. Most of the flour is shipped from the two big city ports in the east, Sydney and Melbourne. In 1948–56 the Australian wheat exports employed a fleet of 0.2–0.9 million deadweight tons, the average being about 0.5 million tons. Due to the long transport distances[14] the seasonal index of tonnage employ-

[14] Wheat from Australia moves in the heavy direction and ship employment thus includes voyages in two directions from the importing countries. Shipments to Europe thus employ a wheat carrier for more than three months.

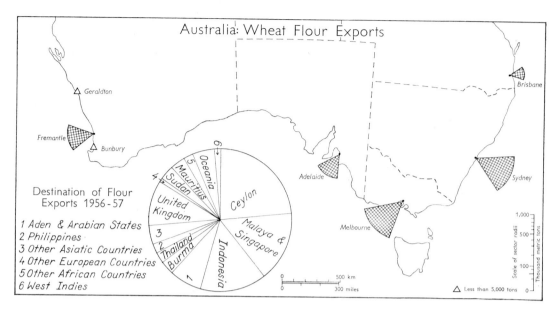

Australia: Wheat Flour Exports

Destination of Flour
Exports 1956-57

1 Aden & Arabian States
2 Philippines
3 Other Asiatic Countries
4 Other European Countries
5 Other African Countries
6 West Indies

For sources see page 93.

ment is rather evened out in comparison with the variations in exported quantities. The tonnage rises steadily from January to a flat maximum of about 120 per cent of the twelve-month average in June, after which it sinks to a low of about 80 per cent in December. In Australia like the other major exporting countries the seasonal variations in wheat shipments have been considerably reduced as compared to prewar conditions. This is at least partly attributed to the expansion of wheat storage facilities in the exporting ports.

MINOR WHEAT EXPORTERS. In 1948–56 the combined wheat exports of the Soviet Union, France, Sweden, Turkey, Morocco, Tunisia, and Uruguay employed on the average an estimated fleet of 0.18 million dead weight tons, the extremes being 0.09 and 0.38 million tons. This should be compared with an average for the "Big Four" of 3.7 million tons.

TOTAL TONNAGE EMPLOYMENT IN THE WHEAT TRADES. The total estimated tonnage employ-

ment for wheat shipments in 1948–56 averaged 3.8 million deadweight tons, varying between a minimum of 2.4 in October, 1955 and a maximum of 5.9 million tons in June, 1956. A seasonal component is clearly discernible in the variations. The maximum tonnage employment occurred in May. No single exporting country reached its maximum tonnage employment during that month, but the United States and Argentina were still on a high level after having passed their maxima, while Canada and Australia were approaching theirs.

It has been customary to regard the opposite pattern of the seasons in the northern and the southern hemispheres as exercising a leveling effect upon the seasonal fluctuations of world trade in grains. But since the seasonal pattern of United States and Canadian wheat exports have changed to spring maximum with a fall or late summer minimum the variations tend to reinforce rather than to offset one another. At the same time, however, the amplitude of the variations in the exports of the individual countries has tended to decrease.

94

Barley Production

Average Crop Years 1957/58–1959/60

	Million metric tons	Per cent
Europe	*23.8*	*28.9*
Denmark	2.5	3.0
France	4.2	5.0
Germany (E.,W., Saar)	3.5	4.3
Spain	1.9	2.3
United Kingdom	3.4	4.2
U.S.S.R.	*10.5*	*12.8*
North and Central America	*14.8*	*18.0*
Canada	5.0	6.1
United States	9.7	11.8
South America	*1.6*	*2.0*
Asia	*27.6*	*33.5*
China, Mainland	15.4	18.7
India	2.6	3.2
Japan	2.2	2.7
Turkey	3.5	4.3
Africa	*2.9*	*3.5*
Oceania	*1.0*	*1.2*
World Total	*82.3*	*100.0*

Source: *FAO Production Yearbook* 1960.

Barley

The production of barley has increased rapidly during the twentieth century. At the turn of the century the world crop (excluding China) was 25 million tons per annum,[1] in the years immediately before World War I it was 40 million tons,[2] and in the 1930s 50 million tons. At the end of the 1950s the annual crop was 82 million tons (including the Chinese production of 15 million). The proportion of the crop that enters international trade has gone up after World War II, from 5.2 per cent in 1934–38 to 7.6 per cent in 1958–60. At the same time the exported share of the world's corn

[1] Gustav Sundbärg, *Aperçus statistiques internationaux*, Dixième année. Stockholm, 1906.
[2] *Annuaire international de statistique agricole.*

Barley Exports

Average 1958–60

	Million metric tons	Per cent
Europe	*0.90*	*14.4*
Denmark	0.22	3.5
France	0.25	4.0
U.S.S.R.	*0.24*	*3.8*
North and Central America	*3.71*	*59.5*
Canada	1.38	22.1
United States	2.37	38.0
South America	*0.32*	*5.1*
Argentina	0.31	5.0
Asia	*0.31*	*5.0*
Africa	*0.22*	*3.5*
Oceania	*0.53*	*8.5*
Australia	0.53	8.5
World Total	*6.24*	*100.0*

Source: *FAO Trade Yearbook* 1961.

and rice crops has gone down, and only wheat has now a larger share of the total crop exported. Although the corn and rice crops are both more than twice the barley crop, more barley than corn or rice has been exported during many years in the 1950s.

Most barley is used either for feed grain or for malting, but in some countries it is also an important foodstuff. Different qualities are used for different purposes, which explains why the same country can appear both as a large exporter and importer of barley, e.g. the United States and Denmark.

Europe dominates the import trade in barley, in 1958–60 buying 81 per cent of the total. Of this a considerable part was intra-European trade since European countries exported 14 per cent of the world total. Most of the remainder came from the United States and Canada. The remaining major wheat exporters, Argentina, Australia, and the Soviet Union, are also exporters of barley. The international

Barley Imports

Average 1958–60

	Million metric tons	Per cent
Europe	*5.02*	*81.1*
Belgium-Luxembourg	0.36	5.8
Denmark	0.44	7.1
Germany (E.,W.)	1.43	23.1
Italy	0.26	4.2
Netherlands	0.47	7.6
Switzerland	0.21	3.4
United Kingdom	1.02	16.5
U.S.S.R.	*0.07*	*1.1*
North and Central America	*0.33*	*5.3*
United States	0.29	4.7
South America	*0.04*	*0.6*
Asia	*0.69*	*11.1*
Japan	0.40	6.5
Africa	*0.04*	*0.6*
World Total	*6.19*	*100.0*

Source: *FAO Trade Yearbook* 1961.

Corn Production

Average Crop Years 1957/58–1959/60

	Million metric tons	Per cent
Europe	*23.0*	*11.4*
Hungary	3.2	1.6
Italy	3.7	1.8
Rumania	5.2	2.6
Yugoslavia	5.4	2.7
U.S.S.R.	*11.9*	*5.9*
North and Central America	*105.5*	*52.6*
Mexico	5.1	2.5
United States	98.1	48.9
South America	*14.3*	*7.1*
Argentina	4.6	2.3
Brazil	7.6	3.8
Asia	*35.0*	*17.5*
China, Mainland	25.1	12.5
India	3.4	1.7
Africa	*10.8*	*5.4*
Union of South Africa	3.6	1.8
Oceania	*0.2*	*0.1*
World Total	*200.7*	*100.0*

Source: *FAO Production Yearbook* 1960.

barley trade is a large tonnage employer, as much of it is transoceanic. For the 1948–56 period it was estimated that on an average 0.6 million deadweight tons of shipping was moving the barley of the twelve most important exporters. The minimum was less than 0.3 million tons and the maximum over 1.1 million. The most important grain, wheat, thus employed a fleet about six times as large as that moving barley in international trade.

Corn (Maize)

The world production of corn at the beginning of this century was 75 million tons[1] and before World War I it had risen to 115 million tons. In 1934–38 it was still about 115 million tons, but from the late 1930s the world crop has increased rapidly and at the end of the 1950s it surpassed 200 million tons. This increase is mainly a result of the introduction of high-yield hybrid corn, rather than a great expansion of corn acreages. In the United States, for instance, the acreage under corn was substantially reduced. The international trade in corn has not experienced the same rapid growth. In the years before World War I eight million tons were exported annually, and although there were considerable variations from year to year, the trend has been one of stagnation, and at the end of the 1950s the international corn trade was still about 10 million tons.

The western hemisphere is the most important corn producer, with the United States harvesting about half the world crop. Before World War II Argentina exported about two-thirds of all corn in international trade, but

[1] Sundbärg, *op. cit.*

96

Corn Exports

Average 1958–60

	Million metric tons	Per cent
Europe	*0.96*	*9.1*
Rumania	0.26	2.5
Yugoslavia	0.47	4.4
U.S.S.R.	*0.17*	*1.6*
North and Central America	*5.47*	*51.6*
United States	5.25	49.5
South America	*2.33*	*22.0*
Argentina	2.31	21.8
Asia	*0.59*	*5.6*
Thailand	0.31	2.9
Africa	*1.09*	*10.3*
Union of South Africa	0.69	6.5
World Total	*10.60*	*100.0*

Source: *FAO Trade Yearbook* 1961.

Corn Imports

Average 1958–60

	Million metric tons	Per cent
Europe	*8.06*	*77.2*
Austria	0.38	3.6
Belgium-Luxembourg	0.52	5.0
France	0.23	2.2
Germany (E.,W.)	0.98	9.4
Italy	1.15	11.0
Netherlands	1.13	10.8
United Kingdom	2.82	27.0
U.S.S.R.	*0.13*	*1.2*
North and Central America	*0.75*	*7.2*
Canada	0.34	3.3
Mexico	0.28	2.7
South America	*0.02*	*0.2*
Asia	*1.33*	*12.7*
Japan	0.98	9.4
Africa	*0.14*	*1.3*
World Total	*10.44*	*100.0*

Source: *FAO Trade Yearbook* 1961.

after the War the United States has been the most important exporter with about half the world export. On the import side Europe has consistently bought most of the corn to supplement her own large production of feed-stuffs.

UNITED STATES. In the post-war period the United States has retained the position of the world's leading corn exporter. Prior to the War the American exports were very variable, and in some years of small harvests the United States even had a large net import. The increased production, resulting in a large surplus, has made it possible to sell as much as half the world exports, even though only a small fraction of the American crop is exported, (in 1958–60 5.4 per cent and earlier considerably less). Dent corn, the type of corn most common in the United States, is less suited for storage and long distance trade than flint corn, largely grown for export in Argentina.

The bulk of the corn production comes from the Corn Belt south and south-west of the Great Lakes. Iowa and Illinois are the leading corn producing states. Most of the exports is shipped through ports on the Atlantic seaboard, above all Baltimore, Norfolk and Philadelphia. New Orleans has large export shipments of corn, and some other Gulf ports ship small quantities. In 1959 Chicago and Toledo also became major corn exporters.

The United States exports half and Europe imports three-quarters of all corn in international trade and European countries are the buyers of most of the American corn export. The United Kingdom, the Benelux countries and Germany are all large importers of corn. Canada and Mexico also import much American corn, while exports to other continents are small. The shipping tonnage employed by the American corn export in 1948–56 can be estimated at 0.33 million deadweight tons,

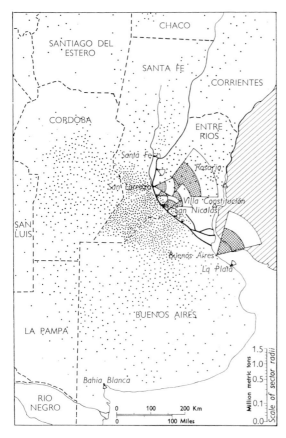

Corn exports of Argentina 1949–1957 and corn acreage 1950.
For legend and sources see page 91. Triangles represent ports with less than 5,000 tons maximum annual exports.

varying between nil during most of 1948 and 0.91 million in the peak month, December 1952. The variations are highly seasonal, with December and January, a few months after the harvest, having the largest exports, and the yearly minimum occurring in the late summer. This is not quite the same pattern as that of total American corn exports, which are influenced by lake shipments to Canada, interrupted by ice in the winter months.

ARGENTINA. Argentina has been an important corn exporter since the end of the nineteenth century (page 361). For a long time corn ex-

ports were larger than wheat exports, and Argentina had a dominating position in world trade in corn. The corn, which is flint corn, well suited for storage and transportation, is largely grown for the export market. In 1934–38, when Argentine corn exports were 64 per cent of the world total, no less than 83 per cent of the crop was exported. In 1958–60 the percentage had dropped to 50. A larger share was for domestic use and although the production had fallen from 7.9 to 4.6 million tons more corn was used as a feedstuff in Argentina than was the case in the days of the largest crops.

The major corn growing region is west of River Paraná in the Rosario area east of the region with the largest wheat acreage. Nine-tenths of the crop is harvested in the provinces of Santa Fe, Buenos Aires, and Córdoba. Unlike the too humid lands in Entre Ríos and the eastern part of Buenos Aires province, the major corn region is also well suited for wheat production. But two major reasons account for the dominance of corn rather than wheat. The low costs of transportation to the river ports on the Paraná mean that corn can be profitably grown for export only here, while wheat can stand the transportation cost from the drier areas farther west, where wheat but not corn finds a suitable climate.[2] Secondly there is the large supply of labor available in the Paraná area essential for the little mechanized Argentine corn culture. The falling off of Argentine corn production is explained by the migration of farm labor to the cities.[3]

In addition to Rosario Buenos Aires has large shipments of corn, and some is also shipped through a number of up-river ports. These are also wheat ports. The large wheat ports in southern Buenos Aires province, Bahía Blanca, Necochea and Mar del Plata, on the

[2] Hendrikus Vredenrijk Hogerzeil. *Argentinië*. Leiden, 1945. P. 74.
[3] Juan L. Tenembaum, "Cultivos", *La Argentina, Suma de geografía*. Tomo IV, Capitulo V. Buenos Aires, 1959. Pp. 527 f.

other hand, have no corn shipments. Most of the Argentine corn export goes to countries in Western Europe and only occasionally do other countries buy significant quantities.

In the inter-war period, when Argentine grains were more important in the world market than today, the corn shipments employed 0.9 million tons (average 1924–32).[4] In 1948–56 Argentine corn only gave employment to an average of 0.2 million deadweight tons, but in a peak month like January, 1948, close to one million tons of shipping were moving Argentine corn. The variations have a very marked seasonal character. The corn crop is harvested in March and April, and these months have small export shipments. After the harvest export shipments increase, but in this period the maximum was not reached until October, and tonnage employment remained above the twelve-month average until February. The difference in timing between corn and wheat exports tended to even out the seasonal variations in tonnage employment in the Plata grain trade (page 92).

MINOR CORN EXPORTERS. In the 1948–56 period the United States and Argentina combined exported annually between 60 and 86 per cent of the world export of corn. The most important minor exporter in recent years has been the Republic of South Africa. Other African corn exporting countries are Rhodesia, Angola, Morocco, and Kenya. In Europe Hungary, Italy, Rumania and Yugoslavia regularly export corn and so do the Soviet Union, China, Cambodia, and Thailand.

An estimate of the tonnage engaged in carrying corn from eight of these countries[5] in 1948–56 shows an average of 0.14 million deadweight tons, but the range of variations is from 0.03 to 0.27 million tons. The corn exports of the eight countries employed a fleet

[4] Högbom, *op. cit.* P. 251.
[5] U.S.S.R., Rumania, Yugoslavia, China, Indochina, Angola, Kenya and the Union of South Africa.

which was one quarter the size of that employed in corn shipments from the United States and Argentina.

Rice

In 1925 the rice production of the world was estimated at 120–130 million tons. This quantity had approximately doubled by 1959. Rice is the staple food of hundreds of millions of people in southern and eastern Asia, and Asiatic countries produce over 90 per cent of the world's rice crop. The two largest producers, China and India, between them produce 60 per cent.

While the rice crop is of the same magnitude as the wheat crop international trade in rice is much smaller than that in wheat, and since much of it is intra-Asiatic its importance to world shipping is even relatively smaller. It

Rice Production

Paddy, Average Crop Years 1957/58–1959/60

	Million metric tons	Per cent
Europe	*1.6*	*0.7*
U.S.S.R.	*0.2*	*0.1*
North and Central America	*3.0*	*1.3*
South America	*5.6*	*2.3*
Brazil	4.1	1.7
Asia	*226.1*	*93.8*
Burma	6.2	2.6
China, Mainland	104.8	43.5
India	43.0	17.8
Indonesia	11.9	5.0
Japan	15.0	6.2
Pakistan	13.1	5.4
Thailand	6.7	2.8
Viet-Nam (N., S.)	8.9	3.7
Africa	*4.5*	*1.8*
Oceania	*0.1*	*0.1*
World Total	*241.1*	*100.0*

Source: *FAO Production Yearbook* 1960.

Rice Exports

Milled Equivalent, Average 1958–60

	Million metric tons	Per cent
Europe	0.37	5.5
U.S.S.R.	0.07	1.0
North and Central America	0.77	11.4
United States	0.71	10.5
South America	0.14	2.1
Asia	5.06	74.9
Burma	1.65	24.4
China, Mainland	1.36	20.1
Thailand	1.15	17.0
Africa	0.30	4.4
Oceania	0.06	0.9
World Total	6.76	100.0

Source: *FAO Trade Yearbook* 1961.

Rice Imports

Milled Equivalent, Average 1958–60

	Million metric tons	Per cent
Europe	0.94	14.9
U.S.S.R.	0.56	8.9
North and Central America	0.28	4.4
South America	0.07	1.1
Asia	3.91	62.0
Ceylon	0.53	8.4
Fed. Malaya-Singapore	0.61	9.7
Hong Kong	0.36	5.7
India	0.46	7.3
Indonesia	0.75	11.9
Japan	0.32	5.1
Pakistan	0.26	4.1
Africa	0.49	7.8
Oceania	0.04	0.6
World Total	6.31	100.0

Source: *FAO Trade Yearbook* 1961.

has decreased in comparison with pre-war conditions, while the trade in wheat has increased.

The largest rice producers have a very large domestic consumption. India is regularly an importer of rice to supplement her own production. China's position in the rice market varies considerably from year to year with the size of her crop. In the late 1950s China exported considerable quantities, which were, however, only about 1 per cent of her total production. The Indochinese states had lost most of their pre-war importance with the persistent guerilla warfare. Some countries outside Asia are important rice exporters, although their production is quite small compared to that of Asiatic states. To this category belong the United States, Italy and Brazil. Most of the needs of the large importers are covered from the surplus countries in south-east Asia, but part comes from other continents, notably from the United States. Europe and the Soviet Union, areas of large population and very limited possibilites for rice cultivation, also represent important deficit areas, although their per capita consumption of rice is very much smaller than that of Monsoon Asia.

Much rice is exported in the form of paddy, or rough rice, i.e. the hull or husk of the rice grain has not been removed. The figures for rice production are generally given for paddy rice. If the hull but not the outer bran layer and germ have been removed the rice is called brown rice. Brown rice is not traded internationally to any significant degree. Milled rice has had the outer bran layer and germ removed and is the most common form in long distance trade. Export and import statistics are generally given in the equivalent of milled rice. A further removal of the inner bran layer and polishing gives polished, or white rice, which can be further manufactured into coated rice.[1]

[1] William Van Royen, *The Agricultural Resources of the World*. Atlas of the World's Resources, Vol. I. New York, 1954. P. 84.

BURMA. In most years after World War II, as in the inter-war period, Burma has been the largest rice exporter, although exported quantities have shrunk. The most important rice-growing area is the valleys of the Irrawaddy and Sittang Rivers and their common delta. It is also here that Rangoon, the world's foremost rice port, is situated. Most of the Burmese rice is exported to countries in southern and eastern Asia, and Europe and Africa buy only small quantities. In 1948–56 the average fleet moving Burmese exports of rice could be estimated at 0.13 million deadweight tons, varying between 0.03 and 0.27 million tons. The variations are highly seasonal. Most of the rice is harvested in November and is ready for shipment early in the following year. March is the peak month of the average seasonal curve; shipments remain above the annual average during the spring and summer and drop in the fall and winter. This seasonal pattern has remained fairly stable for many years.[2]

THAILAND. Thailand is normally the second most important rice exporter. Bangkok, the chief export port, is situated within the rice growing region in the alluvial valley of the Menam. Large vessels cannot proceed to the city port and previously had to anchor further downstream and load from lighters. A new port has been constructed at Klongtoi, which can accomodate vessels of 27 foot draft.[3] Most of the Thai rice export is to Malaya, Japan, China and Korea. In 1948–56 it employed an estimated average tonnage of 0.10 million, varying from 0.03 to 0.18 million deadweight tons.

UNITED STATES. The largest rice producer outside Monsoon Asia is Brazil, but the United States ranks higher as an exporter. The American production, which has more than doubled since the 1930s, is confined to the Gulf coast and the Mississippi Valley (Texas, Louisiana and Arkansas) and Californa. The leading rice ports are Houston, New Orleans and Lake Charles on or near the Gulf of Mexico and Stockton, San Francisco and Oakland in California. Most of the rice export goes to Asia, above all India, Indonesia and Pakistan, and to Cuba. The exports to Cuba have been cut off for political reasons in the last few years. Smaller quantities go to Europe and Africa. The estimated rice-carrying fleet in 1948–56 averaged 0.08 million tons, the minimum being 0.01 and the maximum 0.24 million. The variations in shipments were rather irregular, but there was a seasonal maximum in October–December, immediately following the harvest. The shipping season varied with the destination. It was particularly shipments to Cuba that took place in the fall, while shipments to Asia were largest in the spring and early summer. The rice harvest in Japan, which was then the most important buyer, takes place in September–November, and the American shipments seem to be timed to reach their destination towards the end of the crop year, when domestic supplies dwindle.

OTHER RICE EXPORTERS. In 1958–60 Burma, Thailand and the United States accounted for slightly more than 50 per cent of world rice exports, and Mainland China for another 20 per cent. The remainder was exported from a large number of countries in all continents, among them Taiwan, Viet-Nam, Cambodia, Italy, Spain, British Guiana and Brazil. The combined tonnage employed by the rice exports of Viet-Nam, Cambodia, China including Taiwan, Italy, Spain and Brazil in 1948–56 is estimated at 0.09 million deadweight tons on the average, less than a third of that employed by the rice exports of Burma, Thailand, and the United States.

[2] V. D. Wickizer and M. K. Bennett, *The Rice Economy of Monsoon Asia*. Stanford, 1941. Pp. 88 f.
[3] V. D. Wickizer and M. K. Bennett, *loc. cit.* E. G. Godfrey and K. Macdonald, eds., *Ports, Dues and Charges on Shipping throughout the World*. 21st Ed. London, 1959. P. 424.

Rye, Oats, Millet and Sorghum

The international trade in grain is dominated by wheat, barley, corn and rice. The much smaller role played by rye, oats and the group of grains generally referred to as millet and sorghum is partly explained by the smaller production and partly by the fact that so much of the international trade in these grains takes place between neighboring countries. Against world exports in 1958 of 55 million tons of wheat, barley, corn and rice stood 5.4 million tons of rye, oats, millet and sorghum.

Rye is primarily a European crop. Europe and the Soviet Union account for about 95 per cent of the world production. Much of the international trade in rye is intra-European and of small importance to the shipping industry. The largest producers outside Europe are the United States, Canada, and Argentina. These countries often export a large share of the crop to Europe, and the transatlantic rye shipments sometimes offer employment to a considerable amount of shipping tonnage. In the 1948–56 period the tonnage required for the combined rye exports of Sweden, Turkey, the United States, Canada and Argentina averaged an estimated 0.09 million tons, varying between 0.01 million and as much as 0.39 million in the beginning of 1954, when Argentine shipments were unusually high.

Oats are also particularly important in Europe, but in addition the United States and Canada produce large quantities. These two countries and Argentina and Australia export a considerable part of the oats entering international trade. Much of the Canadian export goes to the United States and does not employ ocean-going vessels, but all four countries sell oats to Europe. The export shipments from them in 1948–56 employed on the average 0.13 million deadweight tons. The variations were smaller than those in the rye carrying fleet, from a minimum of 0.06 million to a maximum of 0.26 million.

Oats and certain light qualities of barley are *light grains,* i.e. the relation between their volume and weight is such that an ordinary cargo ship fully loaded is not down to her marks. Since oats and barley are mostly shipped from ports also handling heavy grain, it is often possible to take a combined cargo of light and heavy grains, balanced so that the ship is *full and down,* utilizing both the carrying and the cubic capacity.

Millet and sorghum are a group of grains grown particularly in Northern China, India and tropical Africa for food, and in the southern Great Plains of the United States for feed. Only a small part of the production enters sea-borne trade, but the quantities have increased in recent years. The only large-scale international trade is that in grain sorghum from the United States to Europe, where the United Kingdom, Belgium and West Germany are the largest importers. The export shipments go through ports on the Gulf of Mexico. The shipping carrying American sorghum in the period from 1948–56 can be estimated at 0.21 million deadweight tons, fluctuating between nil and 0.53 million. The variations were irregular, but the largest quantities were generally shipped during the second and third quarters of the year.

Grain Carriers

Most grain is carried in tramp ships. In order to prevent the cargo from shifting and upsetting the stability of the ship, the holds have to be provided with loose bulkheads and the hatches with feeders. Sometimes bagged grain is placed on top of the bulk cargo for the same purpose. Grain is a semi-liquid cargo which can be loaded and unloaded at grain elevators by gravity or suction. In some ports floating elevators are available for transfer to lighters, barges or coasters.

Grain also constitutes an important cargo for liners. In the large grain ports grains are usually available and can be taken on as a bottoming cargo, which reduces the risk of the liner having to sail with unutilized capacity. The availability of grain cargoes serves as an inducement for regular liner services and thereby increases the number of scheduled sailings from the grain ports.[1]

The multi-purpose bulk carriers, which make up a rapidly increasing part of the world's merchant fleet, are well suited for grain shipments. Another type of bulk carrier that has found widespread use as a grain transporter in recent years is the oil tanker. This use of a type of vessel constructed exclusively for the carrying of liquid cargo for a dry cargo is possible thanks to the semi-liquid quality of grains. It has become economical through the changed relations between freight rates for tankers and dry cargo vessels. This change has been brought about by the rapid increase in tanker tonnage, more rapid than the increase in demand for oil transportation. It has lasted since the mid-1950s, the Suez Crisis excepted. The cleaning and fitting of a tanker for the grain trades is a fairly easy affair. The freights that a tanker can earn carrying grain are lower than those paid for a dry cargo vessel of the same carrying capacity, due to the longer turn round time. The tanker has a more restricted market; the United Kingdom does not accept grain cargoes carried in tankers and some other countries only accept tanker transport for feed grains. In spite of the extra cost and the discount in freight rates, the carrying of grain has seemed to be a better proposition to the ship-owners than to lay up the vessel, the alternative when no freights can be found in the regular tanker market. By carrying

grains and oil alternatively, one can also obviate the necessity of long ballast voyages, otherwise so characteristic of the tanker trades. Here it is the relations between tanker freight rates, grain freight rates, and the cost of cleaning and fitting the vessel that determines whether it is profitable to carry a grain cargo. The most common example of the mixed oil-grain trade has been the triangular run United States—India (grain); India—Persian Gulf (ballast); Persian Gulf—United States (oil). Another pattern is United States—India (grain); India—Persian Gulf (ballast); Persian Gulf—Far East (oil); Far East—Canadian West Coast (ballast); Canadian West Coast—Atlantic (grain). The total tonnage of the grain-carrying tanker fleet is difficult to determine, but the reported tonnage fixed for loading grain in November, 1959, was as much as 0.89 million tons and in June, 1960 0.59 million tons.[2] To what extent tankers will remain an important part of the grain-carrying fleet depends upon the future relationship between dry cargo and tanker freight rates, determined by the supply and demand of the respective kind of transportation. It seems likely, however, that some tankers will always prefer to take grains to making very long ballast voyages, as long as the freight offered pays for the cleaning of the tanks and the time needed for loading and unloading.

Sugar

The bulk of the world's sugar is produced from sugar cane and sugar beet. Total production in 1921/22 was estimated at 18.5 million tons, of which almost three-quarters was cane sugar.[3] In 1948/49 production had grown to 32 million tons, 68 per cent from cane. The 1959/60 production was 57.7 million tons, cane sugar accounting for 65 per cent.[4] Over four-fifths of the beet sugar production takes place in Europe and the Soviet Union, one-tenth in the United States. Most of it is for protected

[1] Harold M. Mayer, *The Port of Chicago and the St. Lawrence Seaway*. Chicago, 1957. P. 97.
[2] *Westinform Shipping Report*, No. 162, 1960.
[3] International Institute of Agriculture. Quoted from *Annuaire Statistique de la Société des Nations*.
[4] *FAO Production Yearbook*. In all figures cane sugar comprises centrifugal as well as non-centrifugal sugar.

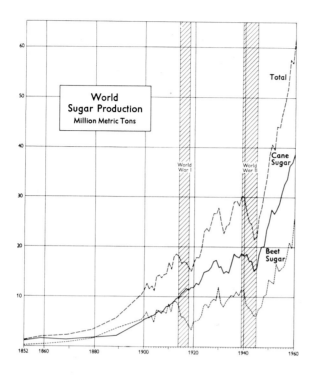

World
Sugar Production
Million Metric Tons

Total

Cane
Sugar

Beet
Sugar

World
War I

World
War II

Sources: 1852–1899: Schmidt and Heise, *Welt-handelsatlas,* Berlin-Lichterfelde, 1927; 1900–1948: H. Riegraf, *Geographie der Rohstoffe-wirtschaft der Erde,* 2nd ed., Potsdam, 1957; both quoted from Walther Schmidt, *Wirt-schaftsgüter der Erde,* Gotha, 1962; 1949–1960: *FAO Production Yearbook.*

domestic markets, and the intra-European beet sugar trade is of small importance to world shipping. Sugar cane is grown mostly in tropical areas and to some extent in climatically suited subtropical areas. About two-fifths of the world production of centrifugal cane sugar enters international trade (the large shipments from Hawaii and Puerto Rico to Continental United States not included).

The Caribbean area is the leading sugar producing region. Cuba alone produced 5.9 million tons of sugar in 1959, 20 per cent of all centrifugal cane sugar. Mexico, the Dominican Republic, Puerto Rico and Jamaica are also large producers, and the sugar cane growing of Continental United States (much smaller than sugar beet production) is concentrated in the Gulf coast states. In spite of the large American sugar production, most of the sugar consumed in Continental United States has to be imported. Four sugar producers have had a favored position on the American sugar market since the turn of the century: nearby

Cuba and Puerto Rico, faraway Hawaii and the Philippines. Since political events cut off Cuba from the American market in 1960, Cuban sugar has been exported in larger quantities to other countries, e.g. the Soviet Union and China, and the United States has increased her purchases from other sources. Several South American countries are also important sugar exporters. The largest quantities come from Brazil and Peru. In Asia the largest producers are India and China. Much of the output, particularly in India, is non-centrifugal sugar, e.g. Indian *gur.* The largest exporters are the Philippines and Taiwan. Before World War II Indonesia was a major exporter (over one million tons average 1934–38). After a postwar maximum of 0.15 million tons in 1951 exports again dropped to 35,000 tons in 1960.

The largest sugar importer outside Europe and the United States is Japan. Taiwan's sugar exports were developed at a time when this island was a Japanese colony, and it still is a

Production, Exports and Imports of Sugar 1959

Million tons raw sugar equivalent

	Production	Exports	Imports
Europe (Beet)	*10.5*	*2.5*	*4.7*
Czechoslovakia	0.8	0.4	
France	1.1	0.4	0.6
East Germany	0.6	0.4	
Poland	1.0	0.3	
United Kingdom	0.9	0.6	2.5
U.S.S.R. (Beet)	*6.5*	*0.2*	*0.3*
North and Central America (85 % Cane)	*15.0*	*6.7*	*4.9*
Cuba	5.9	4.9	
Dominican Republic	1.1	0.7	
Hawaii	0.8	(0.9)[a]	
Mexico	1.6	0.2	
Puerto Rico	0.9	(0.9)[a]	
United States (Cont.)	2.7		5.9[b]
Jamaica	0.4	0.3	
South America (Cane)	*7.2*	*1.4*	*0.3*
Argentina	1.0		
Brazil	3.5	0.6	
Peru	0.8	0.5	
Asia (92 % Cane)	*14.4*	*1.8*	*2.8*
China, Mainland	2.7		
Taiwan	0.8	0.7	
India	6.5		
Indonesia	1.0		
Japan	0.2		1.2
Pakistan	1.1		
Philippines	1.5	0.9	
Africa (Cane)	*2.6*	*1.1*	*1.3*
Mauritius	0.6	0.5	
Union of South Africa	0.9	0.2	
Oceania (Cane)	*1.6*	*0.8*	*0.1*
Australia	1.3	0.7	
World Total	*57.7*	*14.6*	*14.5*

[a] Exports to Continental United States, not included in continental total.

[b] Including imports from Hawaii and Puerto Rico 1.8 million tons, not included in continental total.

Sources: *FAO Production Yearbook* and *FAO Trade Yearbook*, 1960.

[5] Cf. page 76, footnote 4.

very important supplier of sugar to Japan. Central and South America, the Philippines and Australia are others. The largest African producers are the Republic of South Africa, Mauritius and Egypt, of which the little island of Mauritius, like its neighbor Réunion, has an agriculture based on sugar and is a leading exporter. Australia produces enough sugar to export about half the crop, making her a major supplier of the United Kingdom and Japan and dominating the imports of New Zealand.

The import trade of the United States and Japan has already been described. The sugar imports of the most important West European countries in 1959 is summarized in the following table:

Thousand tons

Exporting Countries	Importing Countries			
	U.K. and Ireland	E.E.C.	Nordic Countries	Yugoslavia and Greece
Western Europe	52	177	117	9
Eastern Europe	75	77	251	100
Anglo-America	131	42	1	0
Central America	1329	536	66	68
South America	356	117	—	0
Africa	682	220	1	22
Asia	66	2	7	2
Oceania	382	—	—	—
Total Imports	3072	1171	444	202

(U.K.-Ireland, intra-E.E.C., intra-Nordic and Yugoslav-Greek trade shown as imports from West Europe.)

Source: United Nations, Statistical Papers, Ser. D., *Commodity Trade Statistics*.

According to an estimate,[5] the total shipping tonnage engaged in international trade (excluding shipments from Hawaii and Puerto Rico to the United States) in sugar in 1956 was 1.7 million tons. Since then sugar exports have increased but little, but the shift of Cuban exports to more distant destinations and American imports from more distant sources have tended to increase the tonnage requirements. Due to the effect of the harvest seasons the variations in sugar shipments have a clearly seasonal component. The large shipments from the West Indies determine the variations in total tonnage engagement, which is highest during March–May, later decreasing to low values during September–November.

Sugar is an important tramp cargo shipped in bags or in bulk. In recent years sugar has been carried in specially built bulk carriers, smaller than the new large general-purpose bulk-carriers.

Lumber and Pulp

Lumber is one of the major cargoes in world shipping, carried in bulk by tramps and also increasingly as general cargo by liners. Pulp belongs to the category of general cargo, but will be treated here with lumber, since export and to some extent import areas coincide and the two have much in common.

Most of the world's forests grow in two discontinuous belts: the coniferous forest belt in the northern subpolar and cold temperate lands and the tropical belt of deciduous rain forests. In the southern hemisphere the ocean covers the areas where otherwise a southern circumpolar forest belt would occur. Commercial production is most important in the northern area, although much of this is economically inaccessible. Large scale operations take place mainly in parts of Canada and the United States, Scandinavia and the north-western Soviet Union, while parts of Canada and most of the Soviet Union in Asia have forests of little commercial value. Much of the forest in lower temperate latitudes has been removed and large agricultural areas in central Europe (including Russia) and the United States are found in areas previously covered by mixed and broadleaf (hardwood) forests. Thanks to their location near densely inhabited market areas and a tree growth more rapid than in the more northerly areas the forests remaining in this belt (e.g. in mountainous areas in Central Europe) are economically important, but are of little significance to shipping. The utilization of the tropical forests is hampered by the

Interregional Trade of Major Exporters in Coniferous Sawnwood 1960

Thousand standards. (1 standard = 4.67 cubic meters)

	Importing Regions						
Exporting Regions	United Kingdom and Ireland	Continental Europe excl. Norden	Central America[a]	South America	Africa	Asia	Pacific Area[b]
Finland, Norway, Sweden	997	953	—	—	55	40	8
U.S.S.R.	385	559	2	—	60	30	0
Austria, West Germany, France, Czechoslovakia, Poland, Yugoslavia	112		—	1	93	17	—
Canada, United States	356	67	76	19	101	63	138

[a] Continent Mexico–Panama, West Indies.
[b] Australia, Australian New Guinea, New Zealand, Fiji, French Polynesia, etc.

Data from *FAO Yearbook of Forest Products Statistics* 1961 and *Vnešnjaja Torgovlja SSSR* 1960.

Interregional Trade of Major Exporters in Hardwood Sawlogs and Veneer Logs 1960

Thousand cubic meters (solid volume of roundwood)

Exporting Regions	Importing Regions				
	Europe	North America	Japan	Others	Total
Ghana, Nigeria, Gabon, Ivory Coast	3,489	66	3	124[a]	3,680
Philippines, British North Borneo, Sarawak, Indonesia, Thailand	184	45	4,323	211[b]	4,762

[a] African countries excluded.
[b] Asiatic countries excluded.

Data from *FAO Yearbook of Forest Products Statistics 1961*.

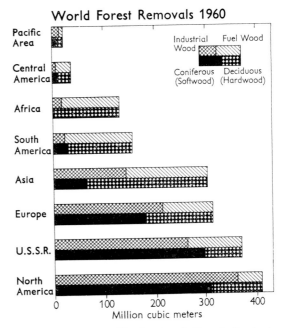

World Forest Removals 1960

Data from *FAO Yearbook of Forest Products Statistics 1961*.

variety of species, of which only a few are commercially important. In many areas they have a great importance as fuel, either as fuelwood or charcoal.

Lumber in many forms, as sawlogs, sawn and planed goods, veneer etc., is an important commodity group in international trade, as is pulp, paper, hardboard and other forest products. The largest groups in international trade are coniferous sawnwood, deciduous sawlogs and pulp. Total international trade is dominated by intra-European and Canadian-American trade. By dividing Europe outside the Soviet Union into three regions, it has been possible to give an idea of intra-European trade relying on sea transport. In total tonnage shipped short hauls dominate trade in forest products; but due to the long distances much tonnage is also employed in carrying softwood from the northern forest belt to tropical and southern hemisphere temperate lands and tropical hardwoods from Africa to Europe and from southeast Asia to Japan. In the short trades small tramp ships account for most of the lumber trade, while pulp, board etc. are generally

liner cargoes. Much of the lumber in intercontinental trade is also liner cargo. Since lumber is a light commodity it is customary for the ships to carry it as deck cargo.

In certain regions of the world most of the port traffic is made up of forest products, e.g. in the Soviet Arctic, the Baltic and parts of West Africa. Since most of the imports is to densely populated industrially developed countries, no such dominance exists on the receiving side, even if individual ports may rely heavily on the import of forest products.

Of all major commodities in sea-borne trade, lumber shows the most pronounced seasonal variations in shipments and tonnage engagement. This is due primarily to the freezing of Finnish, Swedish and Soviet harbors for many months of the year. Exports are very small in January–March, and maximum shipments generally take place in June, but it is not until December that a great drop occurs.

Much of Canada's export moves through ice-free Pacific ports and it is therefore not

Interregional Trade of Major Exporters in Wood Pulp, All Grades, 1960
Thousand tons air dry weight

Exporting Regions	Importing Regions							
	United Kingdom and Ireland	Continental Europe excl. Norden	U.S.S.R.	North and Central America[a]	South America	Africa	Asia	Pacific Area[b]
Finland, Norway, Sweden	2,057	2,306	69	326	171	39	129	83
United States, Canada	516	496	—	68[c]	137	7	245	57

[a] Central America: Continent Mexico–Panama, West Indies.
[b] Australia, Australian New Guinea, New Zealand, Fiji, French Polynesia, etc.

[c] Exports to Central America.

Data from *FAO Yearbook of Forest Products Statistics* 1961.

as seasonal in character as that of the Baltic countries. The Canadian maximum is usually during the summer and the minimum during the first months of the year. An estimate for 1950–56 of the tonnage employed by the seaborne lumber exports of Finland, Sweden, the Soviet Union, Canada and the United States[1] puts the 1956 average at 1.25 million deadweight tons. In most cases the difference between the maximum and minimum of a single year was greater than one million tons. The amplitude of the seasonal variation measured in deadweight tons was thus as high as that in the grain trades, employing three times as much tonnage.

Fertilizers

The use of mineral fertilizers is increasing rapidly, both in countries where it has been practiced for a long time (mostly in Europe) and elsewhere. There are many types of fertilizers, but they serve mainly to replace three elements that are removed from the soil in large quantities with each crop, potassium, phosphorus and nitrogen. Both crude and manufactured fertilizers are important in seaborne trade. Most important is phosphate rock, the bulk of which goes to the manufacture of superphosphate. Since the manufactured product is heavier than the phosphate rock, manufacturing usually takes place in the consuming area. Other crude fertilizers are guano, Chilean nitrate and potash salts. Among the manufactured fertilizers are, in addition to superphosphate, Thomas slag, synthetic nitrogen compounds, nitrogenous coke oven by-products and manufactured potash fertilizers.

At the turn of the century world production of phosphate rock was about four million tons per annum with the United States and Belgium as leading producers. In 1937 production was close to 13 million tons. The United States was still the leading producer, followed by the Soviet Union, Tunisia and Algeria.[2] In 1959 world production was 37 million tons.

Although most of the American production is used domestically, enough is exported to make the United States one of the major exporters of phosphate rock (3.3 million tons in 1959). Florida accounts for the bulk of the exports and Tampa is the main phosphate port. The Soviet Union also retains most of her production for domestic use. North Africa and the phosphate islands of the Indian Ocean and

[1] Cf. page 76, footnote 4.
[2] *Weltmontanstatistik* I: 2 (Stuttgart, 1925), P. 277; IV (Stuttgart, 1939), P. 349.

Phosphate Rock Production 1959

	Million tons	Per cent
North America	16.2	44
United States	16.1	43
South America	0.4	1
Europe	0.3	1
U.S.S.R.	6.0	16
Asia	1.5	4
China	0.5	1
Christmas Island	0.4	1
Africa	10.7	29
Morocco (S. Zone)	7.2	19
Tunisia	2.2	6
Algeria	0.5	1
Egypt	0.5	1
Oceania	1.9	5
Nauru	1.2	3
Ocean Island	0.3	1
World Total	37.1	100

Source: *Minerals Yearbook,* 1959, Vol. I. P. 847.

the Pacific on the other hand produce mainly for export. The major phosphate ports of North Africa are Casablanca and Safi in Morocco and Sfax in Tunisia.

Most nitrogenous and potash fertilizers appear in the trade only as manufactured fertilizers. Saltpeter, Chilean nitrate, used to account for most of the production of nitrogen compounds, but the increasing use since World War I of synthetic nitrates based on nitrogen from the air, together with by-products from coke ovens and other sources, have reduced it to a minor position. The quantities shipped are still substantial, however, and the distances between the producing area and the main consuming regions, the United States and Europe, are great.

The table shows the importance of commercial fertilizers to European agriculture. The quantities used in South America, Asia and Africa are rapidly increasing, but they are still small in comparison with those in Europe,

Seaborne Trade in Crude Fertilizers over Major Trade Routes 1959

Thousand tons

Exporting Country	Importing Countries		
	E.E.C.	U.K.	Japan
United States	626	181	1,125
North Africa	4,543	720	391
U.S.S.R.	222[a]		
Nauru/Ocean Island		180	
French Oceania			186
Chile	203		16
	5,594	1,081	1,718

[a] Sea and land transport.

Source: "Shipping Report for the Fertiliser Trade", *Westinform Shipping Report,* No. 170, 1960.

North America and the Soviet Union. The most important surplus area is Europe (for nitrogenous and potash fertilizers); the most important deficit area is Asia (particularly for potash). Total interregional trade is small compared with total production.

The largest exporters of manufactured fertilizers in Europe are West Germany, Belgium, France, the Netherlands and Norway.

Production and Consumption of Commercial Fertilizers 1959/60

	Nitrogenous Nitrogen content, Per cent		Phosphorous Phosphoric acid content, Per cent		Potash Potash content, Per cent	
	Prod.	Cons.	Prod.	Cons.	Prod.	Cons.
Europe	49	43	46	46	61	53
U.S.S.R.	8	8	9	9	11	9
North America	29	31	28	27	27	26
South America	2	2	1	1	0	1
Asia	11	14	6	8	1	8
Africa	1	3	3	2	0	1
Oceania	0	0	8	8	0	1

Source: *FAO Production Yearbook* 1960.

Most of the exports stay within Europe and engage little or no shipping tonnage. Shipments to the Far East and Southeast Asia are by far the most important overseas exports, but considerable quantities go to the Americas and other areas.[3] Japanese exports of manufactured fertilizers, which have expanded rapidly in recent years, go almost entirely to the Far East and Southeast Asia.

According to an estimate for 1956,[4] the fertilizer-carrying fleet averaged 1.28 million deadweight tons. Since the number of ton-miles required for the combined exports of crude and manufactured fertilizers from the major exporters increased from 69,000 million to 83,000 million[5] between 1956 and 1959 the fleet in 1959 should be about 1.5 million deadweight tons.

Shipbuilding and Ship Repair

The Glasgow Herald in its annual *Trade Review* contains a list of shipyards in the world, specifying ships of 100 tons or more launched in the preceeding year, with data on the gross tonnage of the vessels and also listing the flag under which the ship will be sailed.

The map, based on the Glasgow Herald data on launchings in 1959, shows a concentration of shipbuilding[1] in the same areas which are active in the shipping industry: Europe, especially the countries around the North Sea, Japan and Anglo-America. Outside these regions—on the world map represented by insets A, B and C—construction yards are rare. Data were not available for the Soviet Union and Mainland China. The former country has some medium-sized or large shipyards, two in Leningrad and one at Kherson, but although its production, especially of tankers, seems to be rapidly increasing, the U.S.S.R. does not yet rank among the leading shipbuilding nations.

The economically advanced countries are the most fruitful milieu for a competitive shipbuilding industry.[2] A ship is a highly composite product. The shipyards get plates and shapes —the construction material proper—from the steelworks, machinery, instruments, etc. from the engineering industry, furniture, woodwork, paints, fabrics and a long list of other products

from various industries. Thus the cost advantage lies with the shipbuilders in countries with a highly diversified economy. As shipbuilding is a capital intensive industry wealthy countries are in a better position than underdeveloped nations. Shipping is basically an international industry and so is shipbuilding. Shipowners normally place their orders for new vessels where they get the best conditions. A large mercantile marine is however, other things being equal, an advantage to the shipbuilding industry of any nation. The same may be said with even more emphasis of a navy; naval vessels are almost exclusively built at domestic yards, often at commercial yards. A large merchant fleet and a substantial navy, a diversified industrial base and a good supply of capital are characteristic of economically advanced nations. Construction of modern

[3] Of the combined shipments of West Germany, Belgium, France and Italy in 1959 totaling 5.1 million tons 40 per cent went to the Far East and Southeast Asia, 13 per cent each to Anglo-America and Latin America. (*Westinform, op. cit.*)

[4] Cf. page 76, footnote 4.

[5] *Westinform, op. cit.*

[1] Each shipyard is represented by a sector of a circle. Some shipbuilding centers, like Sunderland, Glasgow or Hamburg, with many yards thus show up on the map with a fanlike symbol.

[2] The United States is a remarkable exception.

Shipyards of the World
Tonnage Launched
Each sector represents one yard launching more than 100 tons in 1959

1

St. Middlesbrough
Glasgow — Aberdeen
Dumbarton — Dundee
Greenock — Blyth
Port Glasgow — Walker — Wallsend
Clydebank — South Shields
Belfast — Hebburn — West Hartlepool
Barrow — Haverton — Sunderland
Birkenhead — Rotterdam
Schiedam
Amsterdam
Vlissingen — Heusden
Alblasserdam
Dunkerque — Tamise — Hoboken

0 100 200 KM

2

Bergona
Oslo
Stockholm
Fredrikstad
Stavanger
Uddevalla
Göteborg
Oskarshamn
Kiel — Helsingor
Landskrona
Malmö
Flensburg — Lübeck
Bremerhaven — Rendsburg — Gdansk
Emden — Wismar — Szczecin
Bremen — Hamburg

K København
L Lervik
W Warnemünde
O Odense

0 100 200 KM

A

Collingwood — Quebec
Quincy
River Rouge — Port Weller — Camden
Sparrows Point — Chester
San Francisco — Newport News
Pascagoula

0 500 1000 KM

B

2
Rauma — Turku
Helsinki

1

Le Trait
St. Nazaire — Nantes
Monfalcone
Muggiano — Rijeka
Bordeaux — Genova
El Ferrol — Port-de-Bouc — Pula
Bilbao — Split
La Ciotat — Livorno
La Seyne — Napoli
Cadiz — Palermo

Thousand Gross
Register Tons

500
200
100
50
10
0.1

0 200 400 600 KM

C

Hakodate
Kawasaki (Tsurumi)
Maizuru — Kobe — Tokyo
Innoshima
Hiroshima — Nagoya
Yokohama
Osaka
Yokosuka
Sasebo — Nagasaki — Aioi
Kure — Uno (Tamano)
Sakurajima

0 100 200 KM

Keelung
Hong Kong
Whyalla

0 2500 5000 KM

Data from the Glasgow Herald Trade Review, January 1960

steel ships in an underdeveloped country would be possible only at high cost and with large government subsidy. This explains why modern shipyards are almost entirely missing in Latin America, Africa and southern Asia.

Northwestern Europe, for centuries dominating the shipbuilding industry of the world, has experienced considerable postwar changes in the location of the industry. The United Kingdom, for about a century having launched more tonnage than any other country, has declined in relative importance and Scandinavia and continental Europe (West Germany, the Netherlands, and France) have expanded.

The British shipyards are strongly concentrated in two areas, the North-East Coast and the Clyde Valley. The northeastern district comprises Blyth, the lower Tyne with Wallsend, Walker, Hebburn and South Shields as leading centers, Sunderland on the lower Wear with no less than six medium-sized yards and the lower Tees and adjacent coast with yards at Haverton Hill, Middlesbrough and West Hartlepool. At the turn of the century about half of the British tonnage and almost one-third of the world tonnage was launched in this concentrated district.[3] In 1959 the northeastern area launched 45 per cent of the British tonnage or about the same share as in the late 1920s. During the Depression it was surpassed by the Clyde district. The North-East Coast was the leading shipbuilding district in the world in 1959 followed by Hamburg, the Clyde Valley and Göteborg.

The other large shipyard district in Great Britain, the Clyde Valley downstream from central Glasgow, has developed with the iron and steel vessels whereas the North-East Coast district was already a leading shipbuilding center when ships were built of wood. The Clyde has long been known as the leading shipyard river in the world but at the end of the 1950s about the same tonnages were launched on the Elbe, the Göta älv and the Rhine. Many of the famous British passenger liners, such as the *Queen Mary* and the *Queen Elizabeth,* were built on the Clyde.

In addition to the two dominating British shipyard districts there are large yards at Belfast, Birkenhead near Liverpool and Barrow-in-Furness. But the Thames Valley has no construction yards of any importance. Before the days of iron and steel ships the lower Thames was a leading shipbuilding district. Also ships of the new type were built here, among those the *Great Eastern,* a most remarkable vessel for its time, a passenger ship planned for 4,000 passengers, with a length of 693 feet and a displacement of 22,500 tons. This gigantic ship was launched in 1858 at Millwall. Large ships at this time measured some hundred tons and the largest ship in the world less than 4,000 tons. The *Great Eastern* was a flop; time was not yet ripe for such large vessels. The Thames estuary declined as a shipbuilding center in the latter half of the nineteenth century. The North-East district and the Clyde Valley, centers of heavy manufacturing, especially steelworks, based on local coal fields, had great advantages at a time when heavy ship plates, machinery etc. could not be transported as easily as now.

In the 1950s Great Britain never launched over 1.5 million tons a year. World production in 1959 was 8.7 million tons. In the peak years 1913 and 1920 British yards accounted for about 2 million tons. Already in the 1890s they had produced about 1 million tons but then world production was only 1.2 million tons.

The British stagnation stands in sharp contrast to the rapid development in other European countries. Sweden launched less than 10,000 tons at the turn of the century but 857,000 tons in 1959. Most of this expansion has occurred in the post-war period. The Swedish curve for launched tonnage shows a

[3] L. Dudley Stamp and Stanley H. Beaver, *The British Isles.* London, 1941. P. 382 ff.

rather even growth rate from about 1910 with dips for the two inter-war depressions and a stagnation during World War II. Swedish yards have specialized in tankers and bulk carriers with the large Norwegian merchant fleet as the leading foreign customer. The Danish shipbuilding industry, of about the same size as the Swedish in the inter-war period, grew relatively slowly in the 1950s whereas the Norwegian industry expanded rapidly and now is larger than the Danish. Both the Danish and the Norwegian yards, but especially the latter, have the advantage of a large domestic merchant fleet but the disadvantage of smaller and less diversified base industries than the Swedish yards.

The German yards compete with the British for the second largest output in the world after Japan. The German expansion to 1.2 million tons in 1959 occurred after 1949 when German yards were again allowed to build ships. Compared with the 0.4 million tons produced in the peak years of the inter-war period, the German expansion stands out as smaller than the Swedish and much smaller than the Japanese. Other European countries with a rapidly expanding shipbuilding industry at the end of the 1950s were the Netherlands, France, Italy and Yugoslavia.

The tremendous increase in shipbuilding in European countries other than the United Kingdom—evident in the inter-war period but accentuated after World War II—is basically a result of Great Britain having lost the monopoly created by an early start in the new techniques of steel making and in the construction of steel ships. Behind this development is a complex of factors which are difficult to separate and assess. A certain con-

servatism may have prevented the British yards from accepting innovations which for her competitors led to lower production costs. Swedish yards for instance were quicker than the British to accept techniques developed in the United States during the war: to weld instead of rivet the hulls and to subassemble sections. These techniques considerably shorten the time a ship occupies a slipway. Swedish and some continental yards early started to offer standard vessels which are made in series with as a result lower costs. The British labor market with trade unions organized according to occupation or craft rather than industry has not functioned as smoothly as its Swedish counterpart.[4] The British industry is divided between a large number of medium-sized yards which must also have adverse effects on costs. The new distribution pattern of the world's steel industry which shows considerably reduced dependence on coal and increased attraction to coastal locations, has altered the premise of the shipbuilding industry. It has reduced the great advantage that the two British shipyard districts had at the beginning of this century. Steelworks making ship plates have been built in coastal locations at other points in Europe and the low shipping rates sometimes make it advantageous to import plates from the United States or Japan.

Japan in the feudal period had a lively coastwise traffic by small vessels, but ocean-going ships were outlawed in the interest of the Japanese seclusion policy. After the restoration in 1868 the Government made efforts to build up both an engineering industry and a mercantile marine. Some Government yards taken over from the Shogunate were transferred to private ownership in the early 1880s and new private yards were established.[5] The first steel ship was built in the 1890s and in 1896 the Government started to subsidize builders of steel vessels of over 700 gross tons. However, the shipbuilding industry expanded slowly: almost all construction material had to be

[4] As Sweden has the highest wage level of the major shipbuilding nations competing on the world market, Swedish shipyards have to be on the alert for new techniques and organizational innovations which may lower costs and thus compensate for the higher wages.

[5] G. C. Allen, *A Short Economic History of Modern Japan*. London, 1946.

imported and the Japanese engineers lacked experience. In 1901 the first modern steel mill went into operation at Yahata and at the outbreak of war considerable experience in shipbuilding had been gained. Launched steamship tonnage increased from less than 10,000 gross tons a year at the end of the 1890s to over 50,000 tons in the period 1909–13. World War I was a great boom period for Japanese industry including the shipyards. Launched tonnage increased from 85,000 tons in 1914 to 650,000 tons in 1919. The following depression and competition from abroad soon turned these achievements into a thing of the past—the Japanese cost level was still high. In the boom year 1929 only 165,000 tons were launched; it was not until the end of the 1930s that production surpassed 400,000 tons. The tremendous Japanese expansion in shipbuilding, which in 1956 placed Japan ahead of all other nations, is thus a postwar phenomenon. Several factors contributed to this development. Surprisingly much was left after the American bombings of Japanese military and civilian yards during the war. The shipyards were soon concentrated on civilian production.

Most regions in the world, but especially Anglo-America and Europe, in the 1950s had a rapidly rising curve for imports of bulk cargo, particularly oil. American (and Greek) shipowners increased their tonnage rapidly, especially of tankers, and registered their vessels under flags of convenience, primarily in Liberia. The Japanese shipyards were in a favorable position to compete for these orders, although their costs were not especially low. They could deliver ships within a short time when European yards were booked for several years. The rapid expansion of the Japanese shipyard capacity was possible because of a good supply of ship building engineers from civilian and military yards, a large pool of labor and rapidly expanding base industries, especially steelworks geared to the needs of the shipyards. The Cold War made it in the strategic interest of the United States to support the economic development in Japan. The Japanese-American cooperation has been very close. For instance, the Imperial Japanese navy yard at Kure is operated on a lease by the New York company National Bulk Carriers, Inc., owned by the shipping tycoon Daniel K. Ludwig.

The Japanese shipyards also have a large domestic market. In 1941 Japan had a merchant fleet of 6.1 million tons, the third largest in the world. At the end of the war this fleet was on the bottom of the Pacific; only 750,000 tons were left. The Japanese mercantile marine was rapidly being rebuilt in the 1950s; in 1961 it was the fifth largest in the world with 8.0 million tons. The demand for maritime transports will increase substantially in Japan in the next few decades. The demand for petroleum alone is expected to increase from 25 million tons in 1959 to about 70 million in 1970 and 130 million tons in 1980 according to the Japanese long term plan.[6] The long distances from the Middle East from where most of the oil will probably come means that much tonnage will be employed in this transport. Japanese refinery interests placed orders for two 130,000 ton tankers at Japanese yards in 1960, so far the largest ships anywhere in the world.

A large percentage of the Japanese (and Swedish and German) launched tonnage is accounted for by super tankers, that are cheaper per ton than the dry cargo liners which are the mainstay of the British yards. Measured by value the British decline and the Japanese expansion in shipbuilding would be less drastic.

The United States, from the beginning of the nineteenth century to the Civil War (1861–65) the leading shipbuilding nation in the world,[7] has a rather small construction of

[6] *Prospects of Japan's Economy in 1980.* Economic Planning Agency. Tokyo, 1960. Here quoted from Saburo Okita, "Japan's Economic Prospects", *Foreign Affairs*, October 1960, p. 129.

[7] E. B. Alderfer and H. E. Michl, *Economics of American Industry.* 3rd ed., New York, 1957.

merchant ships which in peacetime is kept alive by large government subsidies. In the heyday of American shipbuilding, when yankee clippers were among the finest ships on the seven seas, shipping was an important American industry, especially in New England. As long as wooden hulls were in use the American Atlantic seaboard had abundant raw materials for shipbuilding. Since the colonial period ships had been built for export as well.

Two basic changes are responsible for the weak position of the American shipbuilding industry after the Civil War. In Great Britain ships were increasingly built of iron and later of steel. The new technique was rapidly adopted in the 1850s and 1860s. Britain was several decades ahead of the United States in the iron and steel industry. In 1880 wood accounted for only 4 per cent of the tonnage launched in Great Britain.[8] In the United States the change to steel ships did not occur on a large scale until the turn of the century. Throughout this period maritime activity was on the decline in America. Investment of domestic and European capital was concentrated on railroad construction and on the development of mining and manufacturing. The United States turned its back on the sea and concentrated on the development of the tremendous resources of the North American continent. Shipbuilding was neglected. At the outbreak of the First World War 90 per cent of America's foreign trade was carried in foreign ships.

The American manufacturing industry has been highly competitive in the world market in mass production of machinery, durable consumer goods, etc. The United States has often produced about 70 per cent of the

world's automobiles but normally less than 5 per cent of the tonnage launched. Cars are mass produced while ships are custom-built. During World War I and to an even higher degree during World War II conditions were also favorable for mass production of ships. The increased demand for tonnage had to be met as quickly as possible and ships lost in the war had to be replaced. The American mass production technique was mobilized and in a short time remarkable results were achieved. Shipbuilding even temporarily became the second largest American industry after airplane manufacturing. In the peak year 1943 no less than 11.6 million gross tons were launched which should be compared with 75,000 tons twelve years later, the lowest figure for the postwar period.

In peacetime American shipbuilding and shipping are not competitive in the world market. The high American wage level does not reflect a correspondingly high efficiency in these two industries. The Merchant Marine Act of 1936 instituted Federal government subsidies amounting to from one-third to one-half the cost of construction of new ships built according to some standard patterns at American shipyards. American ship operators receive other types of subsidies as well.[9]

The five largest American shipyards are located on the Atlantic seaboard, one in Boston (Quincy), two in Philadelphia on the Delaware River (Chester and Camden), one in Baltimore (Sparrows Point) and one at Hampton Roads (Newport News).

The American shipbuilding industry is larger than reflected by the yearly launchings of merchant vessels. The civilian yards participate in the construction of naval vessels of all kinds and their repairing activity is very substantial. Measured in "value added" repairs exceed construction in the United States. The ranking of countries according to the value of ship repairs differs drastically from the ranking by newbuildings, as exemplified by the following

[8] Stamp and Beaver, *The British Isles, op. cit.,* p. 383.
[9] For more details on Government support to American shipbuilding and shipping see H. Gerrish Smith, "The Shipbuilding, Ship Repairing, and Shipping Industries". In *The Development of American Industries* (J. G. Glover and W. B. Cornell, editors), 3rd edition. New York, 1951.

selection: United States 435 million dollars, United Kingdom 210 million, the Netherlands 112 million, West Germany 100 million, Japan 93 million, Belgium 40 million, and Sweden 29 million dollars.[10]

The repair docks have a distribution pattern different from that of the construction docks. They are scattered along the main shipping routes of the world but there is a strong concentration of dry docks and floating docks[11] in northwestern Europe, northeastern United States and Japan, the main terminals of shipping lines as well as bulk transportation. Rot-

terdam, Hamburg, Antwerp, Newcastle, London, Liverpool and New York have many repair docks. Wherever possible the shipyards combine construction and repair work and repairs often account for a considerable share of the total income of a shipyard. As operating costs are high ships usually go to ports on their routes for repairs. Shipyards in big ports are therefore in a better position than those of smaller ports to attract ships for repair. Uddevalla, Sweden, has much less repairs than the three yards at Göteborg to mention one example.

Ports and Shipping

Cargo Flow and Port Traffic

Flow cartograms showing the movement of goods and passengers over oceans and coastwise might seem the most logical approach to the problem of quantitative mapping of world shipping. Maps of this type have been constructed for total international seaborne trade, for individual commodities, and for the international trade of individual countries.[1] As data for origins and destinations are available only

by country, as a rule not by individual ports, and as information on coastal shipping is usually scanty, even the best global map arrived at by this method is rough, although it may have great value as a synoptic picture.[2] It is not possible to see from a world map of this type how much of the goods originating in, say, Brazil are destined for, say, Norway or vice versa. This limitation, inherent in the flow map technique and not in the data, can be

---

[10] The figures refer to one year around 1957. They were taken from different sources and are not strictly comparable but should give a rough idea of the magnitudes.

[11] *Lloyds Register of Shipping* lists these docks. For world maps based on these lists see Gunnar Alexandersson, Jan Lindén and Anders Segerdahl, "Världens varvsindustri", *Svenska Stadsförbundets Tidskrift,* 1961. Pp. 184–185.

[1] See for instance: *The International Seaborne Traffic.* Institut für Schiffahrtsforschung. Bremen, (wall map); *Oxford Economic Atlas of the World.* London, 1959. Pp. 102–103. (Liner sailings only; in addition data on number and tonnage of ships entering the largest ports of the world); Olof Jonasson, *Atlas of World Commodities,* Göteborg, 1961; Johannes Humlum, *Oversøiske transportproblemer.* København, 1943 (Commodity maps of the world); Edward L. Ullman, *Flow Maps of United States Oceanborne Foreign Trade.* Office of Naval Research, Report No. 4., Cambridge, 1951, and reprinted in Edward L. Ullman,

"Transportation Geography", *American Geography: Inventory and Prospect* (P. E. James and C. F. Jones, eds.). Syracuse, 1954; Olof Jonasson, *Den svenska världssjöfarten.* Göteborg, 1943, (wall map).

Flow maps are routine tools for showing shipping and other means of transportation on a local, a regional or a national basis. Examples of national railway maps of this type are: Aage Aagesen, *Geografiske studier over jernbanene i Danmark.* København, 1949. Pp. 134–135; I. V. Nikol'skij, *Geografija transporta SSSR.* Moskva, 1960. P. 157; H. Haufe, *Die geographische Struktur des deutschen Eisenbahnverkehrs.* Berlin, 1931; W. William-Olsson, *Ekonomiskgeografisk karta över Sverige* (text appendix). Stockholm, 1946. P. 48; Edward L. Ullman, "The Role of Transportation and the Bases for Interaction", *Man's Role in Changing the Face of the Earth* (W. L. Thomas, Jr., ed.). Chicago, 1956. P. 874.

[2] Maps of this type can be found in school atlases, encyclopedias, etc., and they euphemistically have been referred to as "informed guesses".

avoided by constructing a series of maps, one for each country in the world showing the origins and destinations of its foreign trade, and these may be constructed either as flow maps or as distribution maps.[3]

A special case of the flow map would be the position map showing the location of all vessels in the world at a given time.[4]

In this study the cargo flow is seen from the point of view of the ports and measured there. The service conducted by the shipping industry consists of two parts: (a) the loading and unloading of goods in ports, and (b) the carrying of goods between ports. The flow map illustrates the second operation. In terms of costs the first operation is very important, however. Terminal costs often make up 50 to 75 per cent of total costs in liner shipping.[5] To the geographer the terminal installations are the most interesting in all forms of transportation and should be so especially in shipping with its notoriously high terminal costs.

Definition of a Seaport

Seaports are points where the physical equipment for the transfer of goods from water to land transportation or vice versa and from large ocean-going ships to small coastal vessels or river barges is installed, where almost all economic activities directly connected with shipping are located, where heavy manufacturing industries dependent on cheap transportation of bulky raw materials or products tend to locate, where most ships are being built and repaired and where most sailors have their homes and families. This description will probably satisfy many readers as a definition of a seaport. It embraces the main characteristics of a contemporary large seaport. A definition that also includes small ports and ports of other ages should be confined to one or a few of the most crucial characteristics of a port.

A transfer between land and water is not essential to constitute a seaport. Rotterdam, Hamburg, Singapore and Hong Kong are generally accepted as ports although at some time much of their cargo traffic was a transfer from one type of water carrier to another, and not between land and water. The cargo traffic was directed by merchants living in these port cities and there were many installations both on land and in the sea but theoretically all cargo could have been transshipped in the river or in the roads in direct traffic with ports of their tributary trade area without much change in the physical and economic characteristics of these seaports.

Transfer points like Puerto de Hierro in Venezuela, where iron ore is transferred from small vessels to large and Chaguaramas and Point Templadora in Trinidad, where bauxite is transferred, do not have the complex of merchants and services found for instance in Singapore, only some technicians in charge of the local equipment. Although handling large quantities of cargo they may be such small places that they do not occur even on large scale maps. Are they ports? For the shipping industry these ephemeral phenomena do not differ from the more familiar ports.

---

[3] See pages 20–27. The foreign trade of the World and selected countries is expressed in value on these distribution maps but could just as well have been in tonnage. Ullman has made a series of maps showing interstate railway traffic in the United States using this method. Edward L. Ullman, *American Commodity Flow*, Seattle, 1957.

[4] A map showing the position of British vessels on November 24, 1937, is printed in André Siegfried, *Suez, Panama et les routes maritimes mondiales* (Paris, 1940; pp. 124–25), and another with the location of Norwegian vessels on August 1, 1939, in Hans W:son Ahlmann, *Norge, natur och näringsliv* (Stockholm, 1943; p. 272).
Life International, January 28, 1963, carries two maps prepared with the help of W. G. Weston, Ltd., London, showing the approximate location of cargo liners and tramps in intercontinental trade on June 30, 1962, and tanker trades with somewhat greater detail.

[5] Thomas Thorburn, *Supply and Demand of Water Transport.* Stockholm, 1960. For tankers and other bulk carriers this percentage should be considerably lower, for a large tanker probably not more than 20 per cent.

But if in the future it becomes common to transfer oil, ore or other cargo commercially from super-carriers to coastal carriers in the open sea, how would the transfer points then be considered? The location of such transfer points would not be fixed by any installations outside of the vessels engaged and there seems to be little justification for using the term seaport for such transfer points.

The definition has now been trimmed down to two elements: shipping routes and coastal points. *A seaport is a coastal point acting as a focus of one or more shipping lanes.* Almost always it is also the focus of one or more inland routes: highway, railroad, pipeline, and inland waterway.

Classification and Delimitation of Ports

For a comparative description of ports it is useful to group and classify them according to types. In terms of form ports vary between tremendous collections of docks, piers, wharves, quays and warehouses, like London and New York, and simple roadsteads where passengers and goods are unloaded offshore into small boats. In terms of location ports may be classified as estuary ports, lake ports, river ports, etc.

A classification according to size and function is obviously what primarily interests the economist. How should the size of a port be measured? (a) By the number and tonnage of ships calling at the port? This was used earlier as the information was easily available but it has obvious disadvantages. It is a very crude instrument for measuring trade flows. Ferries in shuttle traffic will inflate the figures of shipping tonnage; even if ferry traffic is exempted the relation between cargo flow and shipping tonnage is far from perfect. (b) By the capacity, which is a function of quay length and cargo handling facilities? Even if it were possible to calculate port capacity it would be difficult to find a close correlation between capacity and actual cargo flow. By (c) value or (d) tonnage of the cargo actually handled at the port? It has often been pointed out that no single measure tells the whole story of a port and its functions. However, there seems to be a consensus that the tonnage of cargo handled is the most satisfactory single measure of the size of a port.

But by which categories of cargo turnover should the size of a port be gauged? By waterborne foreign trade? Then five-kilometer hauls across the Sound between Denmark and Sweden would be included but not the 23,500-kilometer hauls between Leningrad and Vladivostok, or the 9,800-kilometer hauls between New York and San Francisco, or the 3,500-kilometer hauls between the western Gulf Coast and the Delaware River—New York area, one of the heaviest long-distance flows of cargo ever established. By total oceanborne trade? Then short distance hauls of petroleum products, coal, sand, etc. along the coast would be included but not similar hauls by barge on an inland waterway system. After much hesitation it was decided that the total waterborne cargo turnover should be used as the gauge of port size. A strong case can be made for using only seaborne trade but foreign trade for reasons given above is quite unsatisfactory.

The size of a port is measured by tonnage of cargo handled just as naturally as the size of a city is measured by the number of its inhabitants. The value of cargo handled provides complementary information to that of goods tonnage handled and is of special importance when analyzing the economic significance and ranking of the ports of a region. High-value cargo tends to concentrate to a few metropolitan ports which provide special services.

The problem of comparing ports when measured by tonnage of cargo turnover has complications other than the obvious one of incomplete statistical coverage. What criteria should be used when grouping port installations together as one port? One reasonable principle would be to see the urbanized area of a city as one functional unit and group all port installations within such an area as one port irrespective of the official groupings.

The twin ports of Los Angeles and Long Beach would then with some minor ports in the Los Angeles urbanized area be grouped as the port of Los Angeles. Similar groupings would be made for San Francisco and Chicago, etc. New York and London are more complicated cases. In these two cities there have existed for decades port authorities whose statistics cover almost all port installations within the urbanized area of the city (New York) or include some installations outside the built-up area (London). As official statistics are presented it would be easy to add some installations for New York but it would be impossible to deduct any for London. Is it justified to make minor adjustments in the total figures for New York and London to adhere to our main principle? If the ports on Long Island within the urbanized area of New York were added to the port of New York the cargo turnover of the port would paradoxically decline. Almost all the cargo handled in these ports is sand, petroleum products and coal, classified as coastwise traffic in the statistics. Almost all of it would be regrouped as intra-port traffic and thus excluded which means that the total cargo turnover of New York would decline.[1] If Vlaardingen and Schiedam, closer to central Rotterdam than the new

Europoort and located within Rotterdam's urbanized area, are included in the port of Rotterdam all cargo reported for the two ports will be added as all is foreign trade.

Theoretically there is no lower limit to the size of a seaport. In this study the limit has arbitrarily been put as low as 10,000 metric tons of cargo handled in a year, a limit imposed by the map and symbol scales chosen. The small ports are part of the geographic pattern and although many ports of more than 10,000 cargo-tons a year have been excluded due to incomplete breakdown in available statistical sources it has seemed worth-while to aim at complete coverage. Many ports with an unknown cargo turnover estimated to be more than 10,000 tons have been marked on the maps with a dot and a name.

The measurement of size is only the first step in quantitative description. The next step in classifying a port will be to analyze the structure of its traffic.

A point could be made for separating petroleum and dry cargo as they move in different types of vessels and require radically different handling facilities. This division has not been made because (a) all metropolitan and big city ports are dominated by petroleum, which often makes up 50–75 per cent of cargo handled; tankers are an integrated part of the traffic in such ports, often motivating the dredging of entrances to the port, which also benefits other traffic, and sharing in the costs of operating the port and its accesses; and (b) ports constructed to serve the oil industry by their existence attract other industries and other types of shipping. Even if the oil port may often be physically separated from the dry cargo port, functionally the two ports are closely integrated and should not be treated as separate entities. From the point of view of shipping the cleavage between the types of carriers is no longer so sharp; there are combined oil/ore carriers and sometimes grains are transported in tankers.

---

[1] Sand shipped from Hempstead, or Northport, Long Island, to a wharf within the boundary of the New York Port Authority area is now classified as coastwise receipts for New York and coastwise shipments for Hempstead or Northport. It would become intra-port traffic for both ports if Hempstead and Northport were included in New York. The cargo turnover would thus be reduced not only for Hempstead but also for the Port Authority area. The net effect would be that New York's total cargo turnover, defined as the sum of foreign, coastwise and inland waterborne cargo, but not including intra-port traffic, would decline.

General Ports

It is possible to distinguish two major groups of ports, *general ports* and *special ports,* although often the distinction is not very sharp. In the general port goods from several shippers are dispatched and goods for many receivers unloaded. In the large general ports a substantial part of the turnover consists of general cargo. But in addition both large and small general ports handle a variety of cargoes in bulk and these often make up as much as three-fourths of the total cargo turnover. Typical special ports, on the other hand, exclusively handle one or a few bulk commodities or serve a single industrial plant.

All large, coastal cities are general ports and the growth of port and city has often been closely associated.[1] The manufacturing industries and wholesale firms of the city generate much of the port traffic. In addition the ports have a large, often rather undefined hinterland. Since only a large port can provide all the services of foreign trade specialists and frequent sailings to and from all parts of the world one or a few large ports often account for a large share of a nation's or a region's general cargo traffic, often serving customers in remote places. For many purposes the port of New York may include all of the United States in its general cargo hinterland and ports like Antwerp and Hamburg most of Western and Northern Europe.

The type of port administration varies widely from country to country and sometimes within one country. National governments are generally responsible for building canals, dredging channels, providing pilotage and icebreaker service, lighting and other navigational aids, etc. In some countries they also own ports. Much more common than national ownership is some form of local port authority, public or private. Some ports, especially in the former colonies, have been constructed by commercial interests: trading companies, railroads, etc. But most general ports are owned in one form or another by local governments or autonomous port authorities. Sometimes the local port authority runs the whole port, builds docks, piers and wharves, provides cranes and other goods handling equipment, sheds and warehouses. In other cases they restrict themselves to the dredging of channels, providing navigational aids, etc. within the port, but leave the rest to private enterprise. The piers in New York, for instance, are owned partly by the Port of New York Authority and by the City of New York, partly by railroads and other private groups.[2]

The increasing use of truck transport to and from the ports leads to demands for large areas for parking, turning, etc., often a difficult problem in ports constructed to handle primarily railborne goods. The difficulties in old ports are further accentuated by containerization, which necessitates space for container parks and lifting gear. The sites of new port installations are chosen to meet these demands, e.g. Port Newark and Port Elizabeth in the Port of New York. But the problem is common to most general cargo ports. At Göteborg a container and automobile port will be built on the island of Tjörn forty-five kilometers from the center of the city.

[1] The most noticeable exceptions may be found on the Great Lakes in North America where the large cities are special ports. Tel Aviv is a large coastal city with a very small port and Los Angeles was a large city before it built its port.

The statement may also be reversed: large general ports are also large cities. Very few special ports are large cities, and a few large cities and general ports originated as special ports (Houston).

The term commercial port is often used in a similar sense as general port, emphasizing the role of the commercial establishments of the city in the development of such a port. The opposite is the industrial port, built to handle traffic for one or more industrial plants. Such ports are here included under special ports.

[2] Benjamin Chinitz, *Freight and the Metropolis.* Cambridge, Mass., 1960. Pp. 39, 82.

Special Ports

A special port, e.g. an oil shipping port like Umm Sa'id, ships one commodity from one distinct area—the Dukhan oil field in Qatar— or handles the cargo of one manufacturing unit, a steelworks, an oil refinery, a pulp mill, etc. In its main function it does not compete with other ports, but there are many examples of special ports that have attracted secondary port activities. The deepwater channels of the American Gulf Coast, constructed to provide an outlet for oil, have attracted petrochemical industries, steelworks, alumina plants, grain elevators, etc. and some have also become general ports. Houston, for instance, starting as an oil port, may now be considered as a general port. Buchanan in Liberia, built as an outlet for the Nimba iron ore deposits, will also have some general cargo facilities.

Industrial ports do not only handle bulk cargoes. Steel mills and pulp mills rank among the most important shippers of liner cargo. In the Baltic area it is common that even trans-oceanic liners call at several pulp mills and sawmills before starting their outward trip.

The special ports are often owned by industrial concerns even if they are built near the municipal general cargo terminals of a metropolitan city. Such ports are usually considered as part of the general port. Passenger terminals are also often part of the general port but some special passenger ports exist.

Low-value bulk cargo moves by the shortest route to a port equipped with bulk handling facilities and increasingly is moved by special bulk carriers to bulk receiving ports located as close as possible to the receiver. Whereas transportation costs usually make up a small fraction of the c.i.f. value of general cargo and such cargo therefore can be routed through distant ports offering special services and frequent sailings, transportation costs are of great importance for bulk cargo. For example, 36.5 per cent of the c.i.f. value of 108.6 million tons of iron ore imported to Britain by the British Iron and Steel Corporation (Ore) Limited in 1946–1956 was freight.[1]

[1] T. B. Roddy, "The Development of Iron Ore Imports", *Steel Review*, 9, January 1958. P. 19.

A Regional Survey

ATLANTIC EUROPE

Europe west of the Soviet Union has easier access to the sea than any other continent. No place is more than about 700 kilometers from the coast and more than half the population live within a distance of 100 kilometers from the sea.[1]

The peoples of Atlantic Europe have depended upon the sea as a highway for trade within the continent and with overseas countries. It was from Atlantic Europe that for the first time trade routes were extended to encompass the whole globe, and it was from here that new continents were settled and maintained and here originated the scientific and technical revolution which has so profoundly transformed the conditions of human life. For centuries people in Atlantic Europe have been among the leading seafaring nations and today not only has most of the world's shipping tonnage been built in Europe, but also half the active merchant marine flies a West European flag.

Nature has endowed this coast with many advantages. Even in northernmost Norway the ice-free waters permit navigation throughout the year; only the Baltic and its approaches are troubled by ice. The rise and fall of the tide helped to scour the lower reaches of the rivers in the densely populated North Sea lowlands region and the estuaries thus formed have provided protected harbors far inland, a great advantage when land transportation was still undeveloped. When vessels grew in size man could increase the scouring effect and deepen the channels by rather simple engineering works. In addition he was provided with ample space for industrial development, of great importance in the postwar period when the economy of bulk transportation of raw materials by super carriers has strongly influenced the location of such heavy industries as oil refineries, petro-chemical works, steel mills, etc.

If the postwar trend towards economic unity continues and the EEC and EFTA merge into a United Europe, this would finally allow Europe to take full advantage of her singularly favorable configuration and location.

The table of trade index values for the EEC countries in 1958, the last year typical of l'ancien régime in European trade, indicates

Trade Distribution Index for EEC Countries 1958

Country	West Germany	Netherlands	Belgium	France	Italy
West Germany	—	261	196	150	176
Netherlands	259	—	583	73	75
Belgium-Luxembourg	202	587	—	208	75
France	155[a]	77	228	—	101
Italy	198	84	84	107	—
Switzerland	321	134	171	195	349
Austria	410	100	63	65	424
United Kingdom	48	110	76	49	70
Spain	226	97	98	230	87
Portugal	193	83	211	159	149
Denmark	262	132	89	56	127
Norway	244	154	107	79	74
Sweden	266	199	141	84	112
Finland	187	132	121	122	56
United States	73	62	69	58	96
Japan	29	22	23	10	14
U.S.S.R.	26	24	18	40	31

[1] Ivar Högbom, *Världssjöfarten.* Göteborg, 1934. Pp. 34 ff.

[a] Including Saar.

For description of index, see page 18.

that there is plenty of room for the expansion of trade within Europe. Already in their first few years the EEC agreements seem to have drastically changed the situation depicted in the table. The greatest gains in European trade would be made if the United Kingdom joined the Common Market and her index values for trade with France, Germany, etc. were brought up to the level typical of highly industrialized neighbor countries.

Norden

The Nordic countries have a large foreign trade per capita and for many products the Scandinavian market ranks not far behind the leading countries in Europe, the United Kingdom and West Germany, and on a par with France and Italy. In spite of great similarities in natural resources between Norway, Sweden and Finland the inter-Nordic trade is surprisingly well developed. The index values for trade between Denmark, Norway[1] and Sweden are approximately 400. The trade between Finland and the other Nordic countries is also large. There is no other group of four neighbor countries in the Western world with higher average intensity in their inter-country trade. The eco-nomic integration of the Nordic countries has been a gradual evolution without fanfare. Inter-country trade within the EEC will have to increase considerably before it reaches the level already attained within the Nordic countries. The inter-Nordic trade intensity is on a par with the American-Canadian trade but falls far short of the trade intensity between the Soviet Union and the countries of the Communist Bloc.

Apart from trade within Norden the Scandinavian countries trade primarily with north-western Europe. For West Germany, the United Kingdom, the Netherlands and Belgium-Luxembourg the index values are well above 100, in some cases above 200. For Germany, Sweden alone is as important as France as a trade partner and for the United Kingdom Sweden is more important than France.

Much cargo in inter-Nordic trade is carried by ferries and combined passenger and cargo vessels moving in shuttle traffic between two ports. Where traffic is intense and the dividing waters narrow it becomes profitable to build bridges or tunnels. Within Denmark the Little Belt was bridged in the 1930s and the bridging of the Great Belt between Sjælland and Fyn is one of the great national projects which has long been debated in Denmark. This bridge

Trade Distribution Index for the Nordic Countries 1958

Trade Partners	Norway	Sweden	Finland	Denmark
Norway	—	722	100	442
Sweden	675	—	272	428
Finland	92	276	—	226
Denmark	416	406	218	—
Germany, Fed.Rep.	244	259	185	268
United Kingdom	195	174	204	278
United States	55	60	37	65
U.S.S.R.	42	36	445	29
Japan	15	34	6	32

For index construction, see page 18. Iceland, the fifth Nordic country, was not included.

[1] The exceptionally high index value for the trade between Norway and Sweden is mainly due to the large deliveries of ships from Swedish shipyards to Norwegian shipowners.

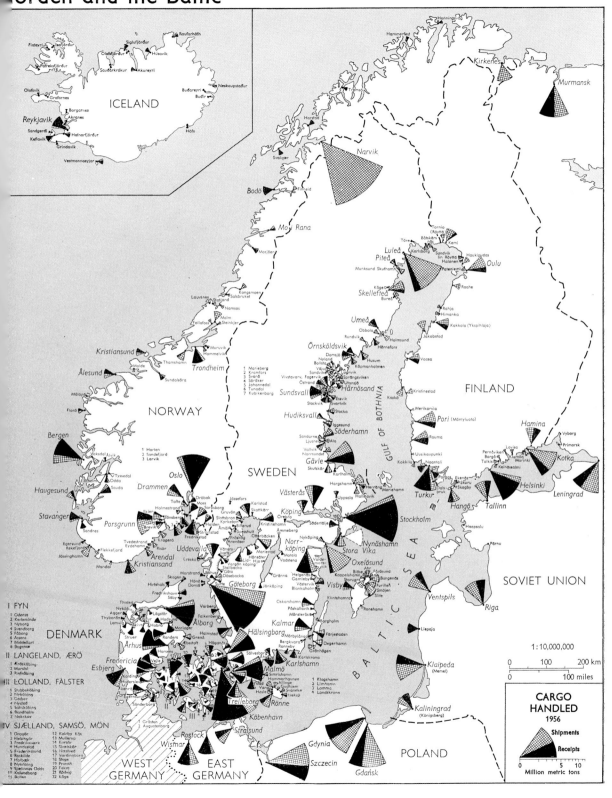

will probably be built within the next decade. Bridges across the Sound are planned, one at Hälsingborg–Helsingør, which will be especially favorable for railroad traffic, and one at Malmö–København, which will connect the two largest cities. Both will probably be built eventually. Construction of the northern bridge may be started within the next few years, but necessary decisions have not yet been made.

When the Scandinavian Peninsula is united with the European continent by bridges, traffic by truck and rail should be further stimulated and the great ports of northwestern Europe (especially Hamburg) with their frequent sailings may become more competitive in Denmark and southern Sweden for high value general cargo.

Norway

No country in the world is as dependent on its shipping industry as Norway. The net earnings of Norway's mercantile marine in 1957 paid for 37 per cent of her imports. Only one-tenth of her tonnage—but one-fifth of her ships— call at Norwegian ports in a normal year.[1] To supply the world market with shipping service is one of the chief export industries of Norway. The annual investment in ships in recent years has been larger than the total investment in the manufacturing industries. As an employer the shipping industry is of less importance, however. In 1957 only 70,000 people were employed in Norwegian vessels engaged in foreign trade.[2] In terms of employment several other industries, including fishing, are more important than shipping. Paying higher wages than most other shipping nations the Norwegians can be competitive in the world market only by constantly renewing their fleet of first class vessels and by closely watching the market for new opportunities. The remarkable expansion of Norway's fleet of bulk carriers after 1955 offers a good example of daring initiative

made possible by the know-how accumulated in the Norwegian shipping companies.

Norway is much less prominent on a port map of the world than in the world's shipping industry. The leading Norwegian port by tonnage, Narvik, ships iron ore from the Swedish mines at Kiruna! But the Norwegian ports are small because they serve a small population. Except for rather insignificant quantities of cargo passing over the long Swedish border by train or truck all of Norway's foreign trade moves through her ports.[3] Mountainous Norway is one of the few areas in the world where coastal cargo and passenger liners still operate on a large scale, where coastal shipping accounts for more transportation work than railroads. The main coastal service is *hurtigruten* between Bergen and Kirkenes. With daily sailings its express liners cover the 2,000 kilometer distance in five and a half days. Since its inauguration in 1893 it has been the only regular means of surface transportation be-

[1] Tore Sund, "Norway", *The Geography of Norden* (Axel Sømme, ed.). Oslo, 1960. Pp. 235–291.
[2] This means that 2 per cent of Norway's population pay "sailor's tax". Using the tax returns Sund has mapped the distribution of sailors in Norwegian communities. Along the southern and western coast they almost everywhere made up more than 2 per cent, in Oslo and large parts of eastern Norway less than 2 per cent. In two towns (Haugesund and Arendal) and six rural districts they constituted more than 5 per cent. Sund, *op. cit.* P. 282.
[3] Norwegian port statistics are scanty. Coastal traffic by liners (2.4 million tons in 1960) and tramps, including combined fishing and tramp vessels (4.3 million tons in 1957), is given as a total for the country, not for individual ports. Transports by company vessels is not accounted for at all. They are important in some trades (petroleum, limestone, sand and gravel, etc.). See Tore Ouren, *The Port Traffic of the Oslofjord Region* (Bergen, 1958), p. 16. Tonnage data on foreign trade by customs districts, which often coincide with ports but may include several ports, have been published only since 1959. The total seaborne foreign trade of Norway in 1959 was: imports 8.1 million tons, exports 16.2 million tons. If shipment of 9.9 million tons of Swedish iron ore through Narvik is deducted the Norwegian exports amount to 6.3 million tons. For our map we have obtained complete data, foreign trade and coastwise traffic, for Oslo (1956) and an estimate for Bergen. For other ports the map shows only foreign trade as of 1959. Dr. Tore Ouren helped us obtain these data in manuscript form before they were published.

tween southern and northern Norway. It serves the large tourist traffic which means a passenger peak in July of four or five times as many passengers as in February. In addition to over half a million passengers *hurtigruten* carries mail and about 100,000 tons of cargo, chiefly fresh fish. Many settlements on the west coast, which has an extremely long coast line due to the many fiords, are entirely dependent on sea routes for their contacts with the outside world.

The geographic pattern of Norway's foreign trade is rather simple. The Oslofjord is the seafront of *Østlandet* with more than half of Norway's population. A core region centered on Oslo has one-third of her population on five per cent of her land area. Oslo handles about half of the imports by value and the other Oslofjord ports another ten per cent. The rest of the Norwegian imports are handled by Bergen, Trondheim and a few other ports. As in most countries exports are more widely scattered. They can be arranged into four groups: products in which cheap electric power is an important cost element, fish, forest products and other commodities. The first three groups obviously draw on Norway's natural resources. The electro-chemical and electro-metallurgical industries have expanded rapidly and account for about one-third of Norway's export value, the forest industries and the fisheries each for about one-fifth. By value Porsgrunn[4] and Kristiansand are the leading ports for the power oriented export industries, almost all of the remainder being on the west coast with its large power potential. Bergen and Ålesund lead in the exports of fish products. Drammen, Sarpsborg and other Oslofjord ports dominate shipments of forest products. Oslo is by far the leading port in the exports of other goods.[5]

[4] The port of Norsk Hydro's large Rjukan works, the world's first establishment for extracting nitrogen from the air.

[5] For maps of Norway's exports divided between these four categories, see Sund, *op. cit.,* p. 280.

The Norwegian Merchant Fleet by Port of Registration

December 31, 1961

Port	Vessels	Million GRT
Oslo	669	5.18
Bergen	380	1.50
Tønsberg	100	0.79
Sandefjord	62	0.65
Haugesund	169	0.61
Stavanger	105	0.60
Kristiansand	66	0.50
Arendal	30	0.29
Farsund	35	0.27
Moss	19	0.20
Others	594	1.10
Total	2229	11.69

Source: *Statistisk Årbok for Norge 1962.* P. 152.

The two largest cities, Oslo and Bergen, are also the leading home ports of Norwegian vessels. With modern telecommunications ships can be directed from almost any place in an advanced country, but the major cities offer great advantages as headquarters of the large shipping companies. It is therefore rather astonishing that so many small towns, but great names in the history of Norwegian shipping, still rank high on the list of home-ports for Norwegian vessels.

Since the turn of the century the Norwegians have taken a leading part in the whaling operations in Antarctic waters. Until the middle of the 1920s they operated from bases on British controlled islands but later large factory ships made them independent of land bases. The small town of Sandefjord at the mouth of the Oslofjord has been the chief home town for the floating whaling factories of which many have been sold in recent years, chiefly to Japanese interests. By the 1880s Sandefjord was a leading port in southern Norway for Arctic seal and whale hunting.

Of the Norwegian islands in the Arctic Svalbard (Spitsbergen) has some production of coal.

One mine at Longyearbyen, originally established by American interests in 1900, ships some 300 to 400 thousand tons a year. Another mine at Ny-Ålesund has an annual production of 60 to 80 thousand tons. The Soviet Union leases some coal mines from which probably 300,000 tons are shipped.

Sweden

A characteristic feature of the Swedish port pattern are the many small ports, especially along the Gulf of Bothnia, with heavy concentrations in the Sundsvall and Härnösand districts. These ports serve the forest industries,

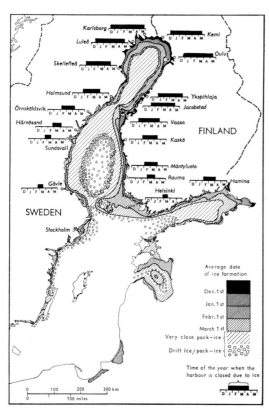

Average extension of ice in the Baltic at different dates during the winter. At selected harbors the mean date of closing and opening are indicated. Source: Bertil Rodhe, map in C. C. Wallén, "Climate", *A Geography of Norden, op. cit.* P. 51.

which for decades have accounted for 35–45 per cent of Swedish exports by value. As a rule each pulp mill or saw mill has its own wharves, from which the products are sent direct to foreign destinations and to which fuel oil, limestone, sulphur and other materials are brought. Most pulp and much lumber is shipped by cargo liners which normally call at several of the Gulf of Bothnia ports before leaving for European or transoceanic destinations.[1] With the help of modern icebreakers it is possible to keep much traffic going in the winter but in a normal year all Gulf of Bothnia ports are closed for four to twenty-four weeks depending on latitude. In that period the pulpmills send consignments which cannot wait for the new shipping season by rail to the ports of Göteborg, Uddevalla, and Stock-

---

[1] The large trans-oceanic liners of 7,000–10,000 deadweight tons usually do not call at more than one port in each district. Consignments from other mills are assembled by barge. Smaller liners of 1,000–3,000 tons employed in shuttle traffic with North Sea and English Channel ports, the chief markets of the Nordic forest industries, have lower overhead costs and are therefore more flexible. They may call at several ports in the same district. As hand-to-mouth buying has become more and more common among customers of the forest industries the tramp vessels of 1,000 tons or larger have been squeezed out of the market.

The wooden sailing vessels, which fifty years ago carried much of the Gulf of Bothnia products, were later converted to motor sailers, but in the postwar period they have failed to compete with new steel coasters of about 500 gross tons flying the German or Dutch flag. New Swedish vessels of this size, known as "paragraph ships" because they are limited to less than 500 gross tons in order to evade the stricter rules of manning, etc. applying to vessels over this tonnage, have not been in a position to compete with continental vessels paying lower wages and having a different social legislation.

The ten northernmost coastal customs districts are named according to the administrative center (in large print on the map), which is not necessarily the largest port in each district. Although some of these towns are quite small they are trade centers of wide areas in sparsely populated Norrland. The forest industry plants are located outside the towns and around each plant has grown a small factory town. This arrangement of the many small urban places along the Gulf of Bothnia coast is clearly brought out on W. William-Olsson's *Ekonomisk-geografisk karta över Sverige* (Stockholm, 1945). On this map urban places are shown with spheres proportionate to population and colored according to economic functions.

Cargo liners loading from covered lighters in the lumber port of Holmsund, Sweden, on the Gulf of Bothnia. In the foreground the timber pond of the sawmill. Most sawmills and pulp mills on this coast have their own port facilities. (Svenska Cellulosa AB, Arkivet)

holm. This is a time when Swedish railroads work at capacity.

Lumber shipments from the Gulf of Bothnia ports increased rapidly from about 1850, when steam mills were introduced, to the turn of the century. For a long time sawmills were the leading manufacturing industry of the country and lumber the leading export.[2] The first three decades of this century saw a stagnation in the production and exports of lumber and in the

[2] For a detailed geographic treatment of the Gulf of Bothnia lumber industry, see Harald Wik, *Norra Sveriges sågverksindustri* (Stockholm, 1950). *Sveriges industri*, published by Sveriges Industriförbund (The Federation of Swedish Industries) is the best general survey of all manufacturing industries. It contains distribution maps for various industries as well as diagrams on production, exports, etc. The last two editions were published in 1948 and 1961.

[3] The floating pattern has changed with the increased use of motor vehicles. Within a rather wide radius of the mill logs and pulpwood are hauled direct by truck or tractor and in the inland areas the small tributaries are no longer used for floating but the trucks carry their loads to the main rivers. There is considerable rafting along the coast from one river district to another, especially from the northernmost rivers to the Härnösand and Sundsvall districts. In 1959 sea-rafted timber amounted to 3.3 million cubic meters. An additional 0.1 million cubic meters of rafted timber was imported from Finland. These quantities are not included in the port statistics.

1930s and 1940s there was an actual decline. In the postwar period the upward trend was resumed, and by 1957 lumber exports amounted to 5 million cubic meters, or roughly the same as in the early years of this century. The wood pulp industry which represents a more advanced processing of the wood, or in economic terms, a higher value added by manufacturing, is now by far the most important of the forest industries. Its remarkable expansion started about 1890. In the late 1950s over 4 million tons of wood pulp were produced in Sweden of which 2.5 million were exported. The bulk of pulp exports originate in the Gulf of Bothnia ports where integrated pulp and saw mills, often combined with other wood processing units, including chemical plants utilizing by-products, are located at the mouths of rivers on which logs and pulp wood are floated down to the coast from the interior.[3] A second large con-

131

centration of forest industries is found along the north and west shores of Lake Vänern and along the Göta älv.

Shipments of forest products are not limited to the Gulf of Bothnia and Lake Vänern ports, however. Such shipments have always bulked large in the traffic of the Småland ports. Pitprops for Britain and the Continent, fuel wood for Öland and Gotland used to be important along with lumber for various foreign destinations. In recent decades the farmer-owned forests of south Sweden have improved considerably and through a more rational silviculture it should be possible to increase the yearly cut even further as the growth rate is much higher than further north. Three coastal pulp mills primarily designed for exports have recently been opened at Mönsterås, Karlshamn and Sölvesborg.

Another major Swedish export, iron ore, also originates chiefly in Norrland. The large deposits of magnetite ore at Kiruna and Gällivare, containing 60–70 per cent iron and a generally high percentage of phosphorus, had to await the introduction of the Thomas-Gilchrist process, patented in 1879, before a market was created. Shipments from Gällivare started in 1892 when the railway to Luleå was completed and from Kiruna in 1902 when the extension through Kiruna to Narvik on the icefree Norwegian coast had been opened.[4] The mines at Kiruna and Gällivare, located north of the Arctic Circle, were a joint state-private venture with an option for the government to buy the shares held by the private Grängesberg company. The railway between Luleå and Narvik, like most of the Swedish trunk routes, was built by the government. At the beginning of World War II, the government built a small steelworks at Luleå, which was later enlarged. In 1957 the government bought out its private partner in the Lapland mines and the Grängesberg company invested most of the money received in a new steel mill at Oxelösund, the third largest export terminal for Swedish iron

ore. Oxelösund has been the ore port of the Grängesberg mine, containing a high-phosphorus ore similar to that of the Lapland fields, since about 1880. Grängesberg is located in the Bergslagen district north-west of Stockholm. This district for centuries has been the chief center of the Swedish iron and steel industry, based on a large number of small deposits of low-phosphorus ores. Small quantities of this type of ore are exported.

The Bergslagen district of Sweden and the Ural district of Russia, both highly mineralized areas in the *taiga* region of northern Europe, were leading exporters of iron on the world market, i.e. Britain and north-western Europe, until the advent of the puddling process made it possible to use coal instead of charcoal in iron making. In the densely populated parts of Europe the limited supply of charcoal restricted iron production. The modern Swedish steel industry, which for some high-quality types of steel ranks as one of the leading producers in the world but is a minor producer of tonnage steel, has developed out of this centuries old industry. The Bergslagen district is characterized by a large number of steel mills which are small measured in tonnage but quite large measured in value added.

In recent years the forest industries have been surpassed by the engineering industries as contributors to Swedish exports.[5] They are located in the three largest cities, Stockholm, Göteborg and Malmö, but also in a large number of medium and small-sized towns, primarily in a wide belt stretching from Norrköping, Stockholm and Gävle on the Baltic to Göteborg on the west coast and including the

---

[4] The shipping capacity of the ore ports at Narvik and Luleå will be increased considerably, from 13 million tons to 15 million at Narvik and from 5 million to 9–12 million at Luleå, when a new investment program has been completed by 1965.

[5] In 1960 the engineering industries, defined in a broad sense as industries manufacturing iron and steel into a wide variety of products, accounted for 35 per cent, the forest industries for 34, and iron ore for 8 per cent of the export value.

old Bergslagen district. On the west coast it stretches from Uddevalla in the north to Malmö in the south. The high-value products exported from these industries are shipped through the large general ports, Göteborg, Stockholm and Malmö, but also to some extent through such smaller ports as Gävle, Norrköping and Uddevalla.

STOCKHOLM. Stockholm and Göteborg are Sweden's two dominating general ports. They are also by far the leading centers of wholesale trade and banking. The present importance of these two cities can only be understood against a historical background. Stockholm was founded in the thirteenth century when the postglacial rise of land relative to sea level, amounting to 44 centimeters a century at Stockholm,[6] had turned the Mälaren from a bay of the Baltic into a lake. About 1200 A.D. seagoing vessels could no longer enter Lake Mälaren and Stockholm became a transshipment point for seaborne cargo to and from the Swedish heartland.[7] A fortress was built to protect this strategic point and, later, the king made this settlement the capital of Sweden by taking up residence in the fortified castle. For centuries Stockholm had a central location as the capital of a realm extending on both sides of the Baltic. Legal restrictions on how and where trade could be conducted favored the merchants of Stockholm who had a virtual monopoly of the important iron exports from the Bergslagen district.[8] Central administration and wholesale trade have remained the pillars of Stockholm's economy throughout its

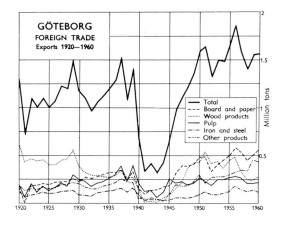

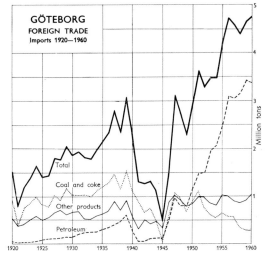

Redrawn from diagrams provided by the Port Director, Göteborg.

history. Until the beginning of this century most of the port traffic was concentrated at Skeppsbron in the Old City and at nearby Stadsgården. Recently the functions and the layout of the port of Stockholm have changed considerably and it is now a typical metropolitan port.[9] The opening of the Hammarby Canal in the south of Stockholm (1929) and the deepening of the hundred year old Södertälje Canal (1924) made Lake Mälaren directly accessible for seagoing vessels. The Free Port, opened in 1919, provided Stockholm with a good general cargo port which could handle the large liners in the transoceanic and

---

[6] Erik Fromm, "Nedisning och landhöjning under kvartärtiden", *Atlas över Sverige*. Sheet 19–20.

[7] W. William-Olsson, *Stockholm: Structure and Development*. Stockholm, 1960. Pp. 9 ff. Ivar Högbom, *Världssjöfarten*. Göteborg, 1934. Pp. 50 ff.

[8] H. Eneborg, "Om Stockholms hamn", *Ymer*, 1930. Pp. 350 ff.

[9] For detailed studies of Stockholm's cargo hinterland in recent decades, see O. Jonasson, *Stockholms varuutbyte med in- och utlandet* (Stockholm, 1934) and Olof Hölcke, *Varutrafiken över Stockholms hamn* (Stockholm, 1952).

The Port of Göteborg looking downstream with the Fish Harbor (Sweden's largest) in the foreground and the Eriksberg shipyard on the opposite bank of the Göta älv. The largest cargo vessel built in Europe, the 95,000-ton tanker *Mobil Brilliant* was launched in April, 1963, after only 22 weeks on the slip in the unusual dry construction dock of this shipyard. The width of the river does not permit the launching of such large vessels from ordinary slipways.

Mediterranean trades. Oil ports have been built east of the city on the long approach through the archipelago, partly outside the port area proper. As a result of these changes very little of the port activities, except for the passenger liners along Skeppsbron and the near-European traffic at Stadsgården, can be seen from the center of the city.

GÖTEBORG was founded in the early seventeenth century as the Swedish "gateway to the Atlantic" in the narrow corridor between the Danish Halland and the Norwegian Bohuslän. When these two provinces after a few decades had become parts of Sweden Göteborg retained, in addition to its royal trade privileges, the advantage of a location on the Göta älv. This river and Lake Vänern extended Göteborg's hinterland far inland to include the western part of the Bergslagen district. Cargo, which included increasing amounts of Bergslagen iron, had to by-pass the Trollhättan Falls by wagon until a canal was completed in 1800. Many British merchants settled in Göteborg in the heyday of Swedish iron exports which were primarily directed to the British market. By

the middle of last century Göteborg had surpassed Stockholm as an outlet for Swedish iron. The Göteborg merchants were actively participating in the development of manufacturing industries in its vast hinterland. In the last hundred years the towns and ports of the Swedish west coast have grown faster than those of the east coast as a result of the changed economic and political geography of Europe, although Stockholm has been able to hold its own as a port thanks to its size. Of vital importance for Stockholm and other east coast ports in the competition with ports on the west coast has been the Kiel Canal, which considerably shortens the routes between eastern Sweden and West European destinations.

Göteborg is now the leading port of Norden closely followed by København and Stockholm. As the port is concentrated in the narrow Göta älv, which is also one of the world's busiest shipbuilding rivers, the shipping and shipbuilding activities completely dominate the urban landscape of Göteborg. To the eye it is one of the most impressive ports although the tonnage handled is far surpassed by many ports in the world.

The Port of Göteborg looking up-stream towards the central business district (right) and the Lindholmen and Götaverken shipyards (left). The latter has facilities for building vessels of any size at Arendal further down the estuary. Göte-borg's general cargo facilities are a series of basins (including the Free Port) on the far bank and the river berths along the near bank. The two pictures were taken from the same point. (G.A., September 1962)

Finland

Finland in a sense has a more northerly loca-tion than either Sweden or Norway. No part of the country reaches as far south as Stock-holm. It is well served with ports both on the Gulf of Finland in the south and on the Gulf of Bothnia in the west. These two gulfs of the Baltic are covered by ice for one to five months in an average winter whereas the wider part of the sea south of the Åland Islands is open with only some ice near the coast. Since water-borne trade with other countries in western Europe is far more important than rail trans-ported trade across the Soviet border or across the Swedish border in the north, Finland is more completely isolated in the winter than any other country in Europe. However, the Finns have been pioneers in the development of an icebreaker service and since the 1890s they have been able to keep the two ports of Hangö and Turku open for winter traffic. With

more powerful icebreakers it is now possible to prolong the shipping season in all ports and five to seven ports in the southwest and south are kept open in normal winters.

The cold season is a busy period for the Finnish railroads; exports carried swell to three or four times the normal tonnage as mills located in the northern and eastern ports send their consignments by rail to Hangö and Turku. The whole of Finland is part of Hangö's and Turku's winter hinterland.

Traditionally forest products have dominated Finland's exchange with the outside world. Until about 1835 tar was the leading export. For over two hundred years it was Finland's great commodity on the world market.[1] Mo-dern forest industries were established some-what later in Finland than in Norway and Sweden. Steam sawmills were built at the river mouths in the 1860s and lumber, which had already passed tar in the export statistics in the 1830s, became the mainstay of Finnish ex-ports. The pulp industry is essentially a crea-tion of this century and mainly of the period since 1920. Up to 1955 the sawmills consumed more wood than did the pulpmills.[2]

[1] Jorma Pohjanpalo, "Mercantile Shipping of Fin-land", *Geographical Studies* 1. Kauppakorkeakoulun julkaisuja. Helsinki, 1949.
[2] Helmer Smeds, "Finland", *A Geography of Nor-den, op. cit.* Pp. 181 ff.

135

Today there is no country in the world more dependent on its forest industries than Finland, where they have long accounted for 80 per cent of the export value. Detailed statistical comparisons with the interwar period are made difficult by Finland's heavy territorial losses after the last world war, which included Viborg at the mouth of the Saimaa Canal, second only to Helsinki among Finnish ports. Viborg, together with Kotka, was the leading outlet for the Finnish forest industries. However, despite the losses of forest areas and of manufacturing plants the annual cut has been restored to prewar levels and the manufacturing capacity for most products far exceeds prewar quantities. With improved silviculture it should be possible to increase the annual cut substantially and by substituting petroleum products for fuel wood it should be possible to make very large quantities of wood available for the mills. Finland thus has the raw material base for a continued increase in the output of its traditional export industries.

About 60 per cent of Finland's timber is floated, 25 is sent by truck and 15 by rail. Truck transport is replacing floating in small rivers where floating costs are high. Owing to the flatness of the country timber has to be towed in rafts across the lakes and also considerable distances on the rivers. The large lake system of southeastern Finland has the disadvantage of a natural outlet, the Vuoksi River, flowing into Lake Ladoga (now in the Soviet Union). This difficulty was early overcome by the construction of wood processing plants on the southern shores of Lake Saimaa and by the cutting of the Saimaa Canal to Viborg (1855). In the interwar period this canal with its many locks could not compete with the Kymi River. This was reflected in a declining share of Finnish export tonnages for Viborg and an increasing share for Kotka at the mouth of the Kymi River. The companies on the Kymi River now haul substantial quantities of timber from Lake Saimaa over the low

Percentage of Finland's Exports by Sea

Port	1926–27	1938–39
Viborg	19.2	17.5
Kotka	16.3	24.0

Source: Pohjanpalo, *op. cit.*

watershed to the Kymi River. In the postwar period, after the loss of Viborg, Hamina has developed into a complementary port to Kotka. Both serve the two leading Finnish wood processing districts, the Kymi River and the south Saimaa shore area.[3]

The leading centers of forest manufacturing on the Gulf of Bothnia are Pori, Oulu and Kemi, the latter two cities located on the northernmost part of the Gulf.[4] In Finland wood processing industries are not so strongly concentrated at the river mouths as in Sweden and Norway. Most of the many inland mills send their export products by rail to ports on the south coast.[5] Although there is a clear trend in Finland, as in the other Nordic countries, towards a higher degree of processing in the forest industries the Finnish exports of pulpwood, pitprops and other unprocessed wood are still quite substantial.[6]

Finland's leading general ports are Helsinki and Turku, the present and the former capital

[3] R. A. Helin, *Economic-Geographic Reorientation in Western Finnish Karelia.* Washington, D.C., 1961.
[4] Many of the old Finnish cities on the Gulf of Bothnia which in the last century became centers of forest manufacturing have developed outports where most of the cargo is handled. Examples are Pori (Mäntyluoto, Reposaari), Vaasa (Vaskiluoto), Jakobstad (Leppäluoto), Kokkola (Ykspihlaja), Oulu (Toppila) and Tornio (Röyttä).
[5] For an interesting cartographic description of the seasonal variation in the destination of railway transports from selected inland points as well as winter shipments by rail of pulp and paper from northern and eastern ports, see Auvo A. Säntti, "Railway Traffic in Finland from Centres of Population to Export Ports in 1948", *Publicationes Instituti Geographici Universitatis Turkuensis*, No. 25. Turku, 1952.
[6] In 1956 exports of pulpwood were 2.1 million cubic meters, pitprops 1.4 and other unsawn wood 0.3 million.

city. In addition to being the two largest cities in the country and thus generating much traffic of their own they serve Finland's economic core area in the south, the outer margin of which may be marked by Pori–Tampere–Lahti–Kotka.[7] Both cities participate in the passenger traffic with Stockholm. Finland's fastest surface connection for passengers and mail with western Europe and America is by way of Stockholm and Göteborg. In Stockholm the many vessels in traffic with Finland, docking at Skeppsbron in the heart of the city, are a characteristic feature of the urban landscape and a reminder that Finland by economic, cultural and historical ties is an integral part of Norden.

Denmark

For centuries Denmark controlled the entrances to the Baltic. When vessels became large enough to sail direct between ports on the North Sea and the Baltic round the stormy northern point of the Jylland peninsula the Sound provided the shortest route; the old isthmian portage route[1] was virtually discontinued. The Danish king collected dues from ships passing through the Sound from 1429 to 1857, which at times caused friction with other maritime powers interested in the Baltic trade. The records of the Sound dues provide one of the main sources for the history of

international trade and shipping, as they were made during centuries when the Baltic trade was of greater relative importance than in the last hundred years.

The growth from the thirteenth century of Denmark's dominating city on the Sound was influenced not only by the primacy of that strait as a sailing route. One of the most important commercial industries of medieval northern Europe, the herring fisheries in the Sound, had its main base at Skanör–Falsterbo in the then Danish province of Skåne, and København had a strategic position at the crossroads of the land route from Jylland to the great Skåne markets and the sea route through the Sound. For centuries København had a more central location in Denmark than it has today; parts of southern Sweden and all of Norway were within the realm.

Coastwise shipping has always been of great importance in Denmark as most of the provincial towns and trade centers are located on the long, indented coastline on the Jylland peninsula or one of the one hundred inhabited islands.[2] København is the dominating center in the network of coastal express services for passengers and cargo. Competition from railroads and trucks has led to a decline in coastwise shipping and some of the smaller lines have been discontinued but on the larger, like those to Århus and Ålborg, competition has been met by more efficient cargo handling, including container service according to the roll-on, roll-off principle.[3] On these longer routes nightly passenger services have to compete not only with sleeper service on the trains but also with air traffic. Coastwise shipping is much more important for cargo than for passengers. In 1960 almost 3 million tons were carried coastwise. But this was only one-third of the quantity carried by the railroads.

Denmark is a small kingdom of islands, a disadvantage for modern short-distance domestic transport as it necessitates costly bridges or slow and expensive ferry services, but an

---

[7] The dominance of this area can be seen from a series of maps in Ilmari Hustich's *Finlands råvarutillgångar* (Helsinki, 1953), or from maps in *Atlas of Finland* (Helsinki, 1960).

[1] This route was first at Schleswig (Haithabu, Hedeby), which was then under Danish control, and later, during the Hanseatic period, it connected Lübeck and Hamburg. Some passenger and cargo traffic followed this route until the 1890s when the Kiel Canal was constructed, which again made the isthmian route a major traffic artery between the North Sea and the Baltic.

[2] Axel Schou and Kristian Antonsen, "Denmark", *A Geography of Norden, op. cit.* Pp. 87 ff.

[3] Aa. Hendrup, "Rute- og paketfarten på Københavns havn", *J. P. Trap, Danmark* (Niels Nielsen and others, editors), 5th ed. København, 1959. P. 648.

advantage in foreign trade as bulk cargo can be transported to its final destination by water. Denmark has a very large number of small ports. Almost 85 per cent of Denmark's 25 million tons of foreign trade in 1961 were seaborne.[4] Coal, coke and petroleum made up 11.0 million tons of the imports. The 1961 foreign trade is shown in the following table (million metric tons).

	Sea	Rail	Road	Total
Imports	17.5	1.2	0.4	19.1
Exports	3.5	0.5	1.6	5.7

Source: *Danmarks vareindførsel og -udførsel 1961.*

KØBENHAVN. København was for centuries the leading general port of Norden and the Baltic. The construction of the Kiel Canal made Hamburg a serious competitor for the Baltic transit trade and the political developments in the Baltic area, brought about by the First World War, were detrimental to the growth of the great port on the Sound. In the postwar period København has lost her primacy among the Nordic ports to Göteborg at the same time as she has become the undisputed center of air traffic in all of northern Europe. The disparity between the rates of growth of air and sea traffic reveals interesting traits in København's geographic location. Most of Norden's international contacts are with countries to the south of København, which makes the largest metropolis in Norden the natural focus of international air routes originating or ending in other Nordic cities.[5] But the international shipping routes from Norden and the Baltic do not naturally converge on København. It is a detour to call at that port not only for liners from Göteborg or Oslo but also from Stockholm and Helsinki. Liners from Baltic ports normally pass through the Kiel Canal. The general cargo traffic of Jylland and Fyn flows through Hamburg rather than København if it is not shipped through Århus, Odense, or Esbjerg. The cargo liners calling at København usually also call at Hamburg, which is thus several days closer to most trade partners; in addition Hamburg offers more frequent sailings than København. The latter port has a restricted undisputed hinterland for general cargo. Even København concerns may route their cargo through Hamburg in order to save time. With the completion of faster truck connections with the Continent the competition from Hamburg will also be felt in southern Sweden.

The main reason for the stagnation of København's cargo turnover must be sought in the development of her bulk cargo traffic, which dominates any large port.[6] For this type of traffic København has two great disadvantages. Firstly, the sea aproaches are not deep enough; from the north vessels with a 33-foot draft are the maximum and from the south vessels of 25-foot draft. The largest vessels that can proceed through the Sound fully laden are 8,000-tonners. Larger vessels must pass through the Great Belt which allows ships of 45,000 tons. Secondly, there is little land available in the København region for heavy industries and the port is hemmed in by the city. As a result København did not get any of the several oil refineries built or planned by the large international oil companies in the late 1950s and early 1960s near the København–Göteborg–Oslo population axis, which had a high market potential for refined products but which had earlier been supplied with oil prod-

---

[4] All port statistics in Denmark exclude traffic by ferries. In 1960 ferries on international routes carried 1.5 million tons of cargo and those on domestic routes 3.7 million tons.

[5] København's position as a stepping stone on trans-arctic flights between Europe and North America or East Asia is also of importance for the total traffic volume.

[6] København's cargo turnover was 3.6 million tons in 1900 and 8.4 million in 1956; Göteborg reported 7.1 million tons in 1956 to which should be added 1.5 million tons of estimated coastwise shipments not covered by statistics.

ucts from the oil refineries in western Europe.[7] Three oil companies chose locations in Denmark—two on the Sjælland-side of the Great Belt (Kalundborg and Stigsnæs south of Korsør) and one on the Little Belt (Fredericia)—one chose Oslo and one Göteborg (decision not yet final). In addition one international company acquired a Göteborg refinery that had been built by Swedish interests. Göteborg could offer a suitable site for a 5-million ton refinery and could easily provide facilities to accomodate 100,000-ton tankers. Göteborg is therefore likely to remain the leading general port in Norden measured by cargo turnover.

OTHER DANISH PORTS. Århus and Ålborg on the east coast of Jylland are the two leading provincial ports. Århus in October, 1962, was acknowledged by the 18 shipping companies of the Far Eastern Freight Conference as a basic port for shipments to the Far East. This event broke the monopoly of København as the only Danish basic port for cargo liners and it was hoped that Århus would in the future be in a better position to compete with Hamburg for the general cargo of Jylland and Fyn. The Great Belt will probably be the divide between the two Danish basic ports. The divide between Hamburg and Århus should be less clearly defined, but much closer to the new basic port than to the old continental metropolis.[8]

The large cargo turnover of Ålborg, which is a smaller city than Århus, is primarily generated by three of Denmark's five cement works. The concern F. L. Smidth & Co., which owns most of the Danish cement industry, has pioneered cement making machinery which is now used all over the world. Nørresundby is here included in Ålborg.

Odense on Fyn, Denmark's leading manufacturing center after København, also ranks among the largest of the medium-sized Danish ports. Ports serving medium-sized cities and very restricted hinterlands are Kalundborg, Fredericia, Vejle, Kolding and Åbenrå. They receive coal for the local gasworks and possibly also for a thermo-electric plant, petroleum products, lumber, fertilizers and feedstuffs and they usually ship some agricultural products.

Esbjerg, the only significant port on the west coast of the Jylland peninsula, is unique in Denmark. It is less than a hundred years old, built after a decision by the Danish *Rigsdag* in 1868 to create a west coast port in response to the rapid development of Denmark as a major supplier of bacon, dairy products and eggs to the British market. Esbjerg, which in 1960 had 58,000 inhabitants, became a railroad focus and it offered fast connections with British ports. As an outlet for Danish agricultural products it serves almost all of Jylland and Fyn but its hinterland for imported cargo is much more restricted.[9] Before the war Esbjerg shipped two-thirds of Denmark's bacon exports and almost half of her exports of butter and eggs. After the war these percentages have been considerably lower as Britain's share of Denmark's agricultural exports has declined. With its large shipments of high-value products Esbjerg ranks higher among Danish ports if measured by value rather than by tonnage. Before the war Esbjerg shipped one-seventh of Denmark's exports by tonnage but one-third by value.

Esbjerg is the leading fish harbor in Denmark measured by the value of fish landed and the number of fishermen. It is the home-port of a large merchant fleet.

[7] The establishment of these refineries followed a pattern familiar from the United States and other parts of the world. When one of the Big Few decides to locate producing facilities within a market area that has earlier been supplied from outside, the other concerns will follow in rapid succession.

[8] Johannes Humlum, "Aarhus havn har et naturligt opland—men det kræver en stærk udbygning", *Jyllands-Posten*, November 13, 1962. Special Issue.

[9] Aage Aagesen, "Geographical Studies on Esbjerg, the Port of Western Denmark", *Comptes Rendus du Congrès International de Géographie, Lisbonne 1949.* Tome III. Lisbon, 1951. Pp. 509 ff. Also Aagesen, *Geografiske studier over jernbanerne i Danmark.* København, 1949.

The Soviet Union

The Soviet Union has a longer coast line than any other nation in the world, more than 47,000 kilometers which far exceeds the great circle distance around the earth.[1] But, due to many factors, the U.S.S.R. is not one of the world's leading maritime nations. (a) Originating as a landlocked state around Moscow, Russia rather late in its history reached out to its various seaboards and thus lacks the maritime traditions of England, Northwestern Europe and the United States. (b) The Soviet Union is a landmass of continental dimensions with most of its large rivers running north into an iceblocked ocean. The Soviet rivers are thus of little significance in the transportation pattern of the country. The main exceptions are the Volga, one of the most important inland waterways in the world, and the Neva. (c) The icebound Arctic Ocean, which under more favorable climatic conditions might have served as an all-Soviet trunk route, is hostile to transportation. (d) Population and economic activities for climatic reasons are concentrated in the southern parts of the Union; the Trans-Siberian Railroad, about 2,000 kilometers south of the Arctic coast, serves as the backbone of the transportation system in the Asiatic part of the Soviet Union.[2] In large parts of the U.S.S.R. the flow of traffic has an east-west tendency, while the rivers generally flow in a north-south direction. In contrast to North America the Soviet Union has no Great Lakes to serve as an east-west waterway. (e) The configuration of the U.S.S.R. and the adjacent countries is such that railroad distances in the Soviet Union are much shorter than ocean routes; major cabotage[3] is not an attractive alternative to rail transport. (f) The autarkical policy of the Soviet Government has favored the development of heavy manufacturing in the Urals, in central Siberia and in other inland areas, where railroads are the only means of

transportation, and not in coastal locations where one or more imported raw materials might have been used to advantage.[4]

The relative importance of the various means of transportation is shown in the table below.

Type of Transport	1913	1940	1950	1958	1965 (plan)
	Per cent of ton-kilometers				
Railroads	57.4	85.1	84.4	81.2	73.3
Maritime shipping	17.4	4.9	5.6	6.6	9.3
Inland waterways	24.8	7.4	6.5	5.3	5.5
Trucks	0.1	1.8	2.8	4.8	4.6
Pipelines	0.3	0.8	0.7	2.1	7.3
	100.0	100.0	100.0	100.0	100.0
	Billions of ton-kilometers				
Total	114.5	487.6	713.3	1604.8	

Source: *Narodnoe Chozjajstvo SSSR v 1958 godu.* P. 540. Plan figures from T. S. Chačaturov, *Ėkonomika transporta,* Moskva, 1959. P. 142.

The most striking feature of the Soviet transportation structure is the complete dominance of the railroads. In Czarist Russia they played a less significant role; inland waterways and coastal shipping had a larger relative importance. In 1913 Russian ports handled 41 million tons of cargo, of which 11.9 million was minor cabotage and 0.6 million was major

[1] I. V. Nikol'skij, *Geografija transporta SSSR.* Moskva, 1960. P. 30.

[2] Nikol'skij, *op. cit.,* maps, pp. 153 and 157.

[3] Coastwise shipping in the U.S.S.R. is divided into major cabotage, navigation between domestic ports located on different seas, and minor cabotage, navigation between domestic ports on the same sea.

[4] Before World War I Russia imported 2 to 3 million tons of British coal per annum to St. Petersburg. Now the Soviet Union hauls large quantities of coal to Leningrad by rail from distant Vorkuta. The advantage that St. Petersburg had for heavy manufacturing because of its coastal location has been lost for the modern city of Leningrad as a result of the change in economic philosophy.

Sea Basin	Tonnage transported in 1956 Per cent	Number of vessels Jan. 1, 1957 Per cent	Capacity of vessels Jan. 1, 1957 Per cent
Arctic Ocean	7	14	9
Baltic Sea	9	12	12
Black Sea — Azov Sea	35	21	28
Caspian Sea	36	23	20
Far East	13	30	31
	100	100	100

Source: V. G. Bakaev, *Morskoj transport SSSR za 40 let.* Moskva, 1957. P. 64. Here quoted from Nikol'skij, *op. cit.* P. 220.

cabotage. About 70 per cent was foreign trade, 19.3 million tons exports and 9.3 million imports. The seaports were Russia's chief points of contact with the outside world; 71 per cent of the exports and 61 per cent of the imports passed through Russian ports.[5] The Russian mercantile marine, of which about 70 per cent were sailing vessels, transported 15.1 million tons. Most of the seaborne foreign trade was carried in foreign vessels; 92 per cent of the exports and 86 per cent of the imports.

The distribution by sea basins of the Soviet mercantile marine on January 1, 1957, and the percentage of the total tonnage transported by these vessels in 1956 is given in the table above. The Soviet mercantile marine in 1956 transported 57.7 million tons of cargo. Most of this was minor cabotage of bulk cargoes in the Caspian Sea and the Black Sea, primarily oil but also coal, ore, mineral construction materials, lumber and grains.[6] The long dis-

[5] Nikol'skij, *op. cit.* P. 216. Of the remainder about one-third was shipped through the German Baltic ports of Königsberg, Danzig and Memel. For a detailed and carefully documented account of cargo turnover in Baltic ports just before World War I and around 1930, see Peter-Heinz Seraphim, *Die Ostseehäfen und der Ostseeverkehr.* Berlin, 1937.

[6] Dry cargo in minor cabotage accounted for 22.0 million tons in the U.S.S.R. in 1956 (coal 5.3, ore 5.0, mineral construction materials 4.4, lumber and fuel wood 2.1, grains 1.3, metals 0.4, salt 0.3, and fish and fish products 0.2 million metric tons).

tances between ports in the Far East means that this area accounts for a much larger percentage of vessels and vessel capacity than of tons transported.

The cargo turnover by sea basins in selected years is listed below.

Sea Basin	1913[a]	1939	1956
Arctic Ocean	4.4	11.3	7.0
Baltic Sea	16.5	3.3	9.0
Black Sea — Azov Sea	45.7	34.3	35.0
Caspian Sea	29.0	45.0	36.0
Far East	4.4	6.2	13.0
	100.0	100.0	100.0

[a] T. S. Chačaturov, *Rasmeščenie transporta v kapitalističeskich stranach i v SSSR.* Moskva, 1939. P. 489.
Figures in the table quoted from Nikol'skij, *op. cit.* Pp. 215 ff.

The Distribution of Soviet Seaborne Traffic by Sea Basin, 1960

Sea Basin	Interregional and Intraregional Domestic Traffic Per Cent		Foreign Trade Per Cent	
	Tons	Ton-miles	Tons	Ton-miles
Arctic Ocean	4.2	7.1	9.8	6.3
Baltic Sea	5.3	4.8	23.3	15.1
Black Sea — Azov Sea	38.9	35.6	57.0	69.8
Caspian Sea	36.0	23.6	0.6	0.1
Far East	15.6	28.9	9.3	8.7
	100.0	100.0	100.0	100.0

Source: V. G. Bakaev and S. M. Baev (eds.), *Transport SSSR: Morskoj Transport.* Moskva, 1961. P. 38.

Soviet Ports on the Arctic and the Baltic

Despite a tremendous coastline and vast land areas facing the Arctic Ocean, this ocean accounts for only a small share of the Soviet sea-

141

Main Seaports of the Soviet Union

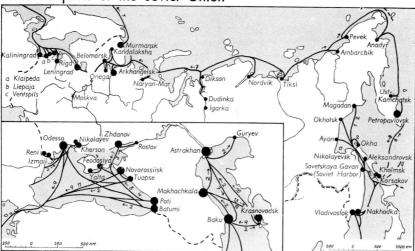

Size of symbols varies with cargo handled in the port. Figures refer to main commodities shipped on respective routes.
1. Coal 2. Petroleum 3. Ore 4. Manganese 5. Apatite 6. Salt 7. Timber 8. Fish 9. Grain 10. Cotton 11. Cement 12. Machinery 13. Chemicals. Map adapted from I. V. Nikol'skij, *Geografija transporta SSSR, op. cit.,* p. 219 (no date given) and N. N. Baransky, *Economic Geography of the U.S.S.R.,* Moscow, 1956. P. 91.

borne trade. Most of the traffic is concentrated in the extreme western part of the coast, the Barents Sea and White Sea areas. Forest products make up more than half of the freight traffic while coal and apatite have significant shares. Two ports are outstanding—Arkhangelsk at the mouth of the Northern Dvina River[1] and Murmansk on a deep and narrow fiord of the Barents Sea. The two ports have almost equal cargo turnover; Arkhangelsk primarily lumber and Murmansk apatite and coal.[2] Arkhangelsk is an old port, founded in 1583. It was the only Russian seaport, prior to the founding of St. Petersburg in 1703, and the gateway for Moscow's trade with England. Its normal navigation season (from May to October) is somewhat shorter than that of northern ports in the Baltic, but it can be kept

open by icebreakers. Arkhangelsk is one of two large seaports in the Soviet belt of coniferous forests, Leningrad being the other. It is predominantly a town of sawmills and lumber shipping. Lumber traditionally ranks as one of the major exports[3] of the Soviet Union and Arkhangelsk is the chief outlet.[4]

Murmansk is a new city, founded as the northern terminal of the Murmansk Railroad, which was built hurriedly by the Russian Government between 1914 and 1916 to secure supplies from the Allies. It has grown rapidly and in 1959 had 222,000 inhabitants, by far the largest city north of the Arctic Circle. Its

---

[1] Arkhangelsk is located at the head of the delta, 40 kilometers from the White Sea. It has an outport, Severodvinsk, on the White Sea, just west of the delta.

[2] I. V. Nikol'skij, *Geografija Transporta SSSR.* Moskva, 1960. Pp. 220 ff.

[3] In 1958 the Soviet Union exported 3.6 million cubic meters of coniferous lumber accounting for 3.2 per cent of the total export value. Almost two-thirds went to Western Europe, primarily the United Kingdom. *Vnešnjaja Torgovlja SSSR za 1958 god.*

[4] The Leningrad region is primarily a center of pulp and paper manufacturing. Through the port of Leningrad are shipped large quantities of pulpwood, partly to Soviet pulp and paper manufacturing centers on the Baltic. For the coastal trade sea barges are used.

raison d'être is the ice-free port, kept open by a branch of the Gulf Stream; its chief disadvantage is the long overland distance from the densely populated parts of the Soviet Union. Murmansk is the natural outlet for the large Khibiny apatite deposits on the Kola Peninsula.[5] It also ships some lumber and fish and receives coal from Spitsbergen and Pechora. Murmansk is the base of a rapidly expanding trawler fleet and has a large fish processing industry.

In addition to Arkhangelsk there are several timber ports on the White Sea: Onega, Belomorsk, Kem and Kandalaksha and Naryan-Mar on the lower Pechora which is also a coal port, shipping coal from the Vorkuta field.

Regular shipping in the Arctic Ocean outside the Barents Sea—White Sea area had to await the advent of powerful icebreakers. The first voyage from the Atlantic Ocean to the Pacific along the north coast of Siberia was made at the end of last century (Nordenskiöld, 1878–79) but it was not until 1932 that a Soviet icebreaker made the trip in one season. Regular sailings from Arkhangelsk to Vladivostok started in 1935. Navigation on the

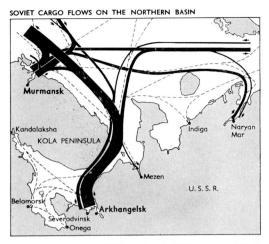

SOVIET CARGO FLOWS ON THE NORTHERN BASIN

Source: *Transport SSSR, Morskoj Transport* (V. G. Bakaev and S. M. Baev, eds.). Moskva, 1961.

---

[5] In 1958 the Soviet Union exported 1.5 million tons of apatite concentrates, two-thirds to Eastern Europe and one-third to Western Europe.

[6] In 1954 three icebreakers, taking a pay load of 4 to 5 thousand tons, operated on this route. They made a speed of 15 knots. The construction of three new icebreakers was started in 1954–56.
The first icebreaker in the world to be propelled by atomic power went into operation on the Soviet Arctic route in 1959. This vessel, the *Lenin*, has a displacement of 16,000 tons and her turbo-electric engines develop 44,000 horsepower, almost twice as much as the largest conventional icebreakers. The captain of the *Lenin* claims that his ship can reach any point in the Arctic Ocean at any time of the year. It is expected that future Soviet icebreakers will be atomic.
M. I. Belov, *Severnyj morskoj put'*. Leningrad, 1957; H. W. Bowker, "Nuclear Populsion of Ships", *Norwegian Shipping News*, 1959. Pp. 1215–1223; *The New York Times*, June 2, 1962.

[7] T. E. Armstrong, "The Soviet Northern Sea Route", *Geographical Journal*, 1955. Pp. 136–146.
T. E. Armstrong, *The Northern Sea Route: Soviet Exploitation of the North East Passage*. Cambridge, 1952.

Siberian coast is possible for 70 to 120 days from June to October. Ice conditions become successively more difficult towards the east. Thick, almost continuous ice is found in the Chuckchee Sea. Ships on the northern route are built for traveling through ice but only cargo-carrying icebreakers can make the full trip.[6] Usually vessels operating on the Siberian coast steam in convoys, preceded by icebreakers.

Ports on the Kara Sea chiefly ship lumber, which makes up about 70 per cent of the cargo. Leading ports are Igarka and Dudinka on the lower Yenisei. Igarka draws lumber from a wide area, including the shores of the Angara. Dudinka is a coal port, connected by a short railroad to Norilsk, a mining center with deposits of coal and a large number of metals.

In the Laptev Sea ice conditions are unfavorable both in the east and the west and the navigation season is short. Nordvik and Tiksi are the chief ports. Ports on the East Siberian and Chuckchee Seas have very little traffic.[7]

LENINGRAD, formerly St. Petersburg, for two centuries the Russian capital, is the second largest city in the Soviet Union and the leading

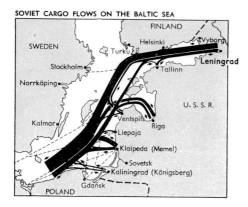

Source: *Transport SSSR, Morskoj Transport* (V. G. Bakaev and S. M. Baev, eds.). Moskva, 1961.

Soviet port on the Baltic. It is second only to Odessa as a general port measured by value of its foreign trade. Leningrad is known as the leading center of the engineering industry and as one of the major manufacturing districts in the Soviet Union. It is an important rail hub; the line to Moscow is all-electric since 1962. By inland waterways it is connected with the White Sea, the Black Sea and the Caspian Sea.

The Port of Leningrad

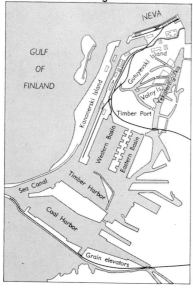

Source: I. V. Nikol'skij, *Geografija transporta SSSR*. Moskva, 1960. P. 32.

The Leningrad Region

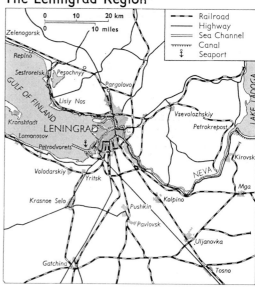

Source: I. V. Nikol'skij, *Geografija transporta SSSR*. Moskva, 1960. P. 277.

From its foundation in 1703 in territory conquered from Sweden Peter the Great and succeeding Russian czars favored the development of St. Petersburg, Russia's "window looking on Europe", and the short trade route it offered between Moscow and the North Sea countries compared to the old route by way of Arkhangelsk. Before the Revolution St. Petersburg was the largest and best equipped port in Russia. In 1913 it handled 7.2 million tons, more than any other port on the Baltic. Exports accounted for 2.6 million tons, imports for 4.0 million and cabotage for 0.5 million tons. British coal made up 70 per cent of the imports.[8] As an outlet for Russian exports St. Petersburg was surpassed by Riga among the Baltic ports.[9]

Forest products traditionally bulk large in the traffic of the port. Leningrad is a natural outlet for the large coniferous forest region

---

[8] Nikol'skij, *op. cit.* Pp. 215 f.

[9] Riga handled 18 per cent by value of the Russian exports as an average for 1912–13 and St. Petersburg 8–10 per cent. Sten De Geer and Helmer Eneborg, *Östersjöhamnarna*. Stockholm, 1927. P. 88.

making up its hinterland, which is extended inland by the Neva River and the Ladoga-Onega lake system. This system in combination with the Volga River was also important for the transportation of grain before the Revolution. Much of the large Russian grain exports were then handled by the Baltic ports.[10] The railway pattern was much influenced by the grain exports. The line from Siberia to St. Petersburg by way of Vologda, completed in 1906, was explicitly built to tap the Siberian grain regions.[11] Another railroad serving the same purpose had been constructed seven years earlier to Arkhangelsk by way of Perm and Kotlas, but proved to be less successful due to the shorter navigation season on the White Sea.[12] Leningrad's present status as a grain

port should be less important as most of the Soviet grain exports are now directed towards European countries bordering on the Soviet Union and thus probably sent all the way by rail.[13]

Klaipeda, before World War I the northernmost German port (Memel), as a major Soviet port on the Baltic ships chiefly petroleum and receives Polish coal. Recently Ventspils became the second oil terminal. Ice is normally no problem for these ports, whereas Leningrad is frozen for 180 days and Riga for 80–90 days. Riga ships grain and lumber and receives coal but both Riga and Königsberg (now Kaliningrad), well-known ports in the history of Baltic shipping, have declined in relative importance.

Poland and Germany

Poland

In the interwar period Poland had only a short seacoast on the Baltic between Germany and the German exclave of East Prussia. In part because of the strained political and commercial relations between Poland and her neighbors most of the Polish foreign trade was at the end of the period funneled through two ports in the Polish Corridor, the old Hanseatic city of Gdańsk at the mouth of the Vistula River,

which under the Treaty of Versailles became the Free City of Danzig included in Polish customs territory, and the newly-built port of Gdynia, constructed from 1921 only 20 kilometers north of Gdańsk, in order to diminish Polish dependence on the old German city at the mouth of the Polish river. Over 70 per cent of Poland's foreign trade was shipped through these ports before World War II. The great importance of seaborne trade was a result of a deliberate Polish policy inaugurated in 1926.

[10] A detailed flow map of grain shipments on railroads and waterways in 1884 made by S. V. Bernštejn-Kogan and reprinted by Nikol'skij (*op. cit.,* p. 89) strikingly shows the dominance of St. Petersburg as a destination both for railborne grains and grains shipped on the inland waterways. In comparison, the railroad flows to Liepaja, Riga and German ports on the Baltic as well as those to Odessa, were rather small. At the end of the century the Azov Sea–Black Sea ports, close to the new grain regions of southern Russia, got a larger share of the grain shipments. They accounted for two-thirds of the total Russian grain exports in 1913. (Nikol'skij, *op. cit.* P. 215.)

[11] Nikol'skij, *op. cit.* P. 273.

[12] Grain exports still had a pronounced peak just after the harvest; a few weeks longer navigation season in the fall was a great advantage. Before the Revolution Tallinn was used as an outport of St. Petersburg in the winter and the small port of Paldiski (Baltischport) was built to serve as an outport of Tallinn.

[13] In 1958 Soviet grain exports were 5.1 million tons of which more than 70 per cent went to communist countries in Eastern Europe, primarily East Germany and Czechoslovakia. Coastwise shipments accounted for 1.4 million tons, which should be compared with 71.5 million tons sent by railroad and 6.9 million tons on inland waterways. Nikol'skij, *op. cit.* P. 177. *Vnešnjaja torgovlja SSSR za 1958 god.*

Development of Cargo Traffic in Polish Ports

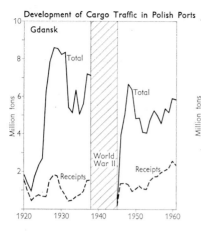
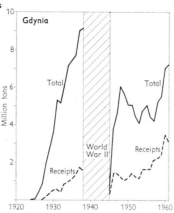
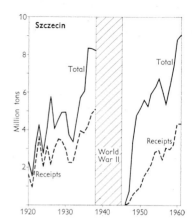

Data from Czesław Wojewódka, *Structural Changes in the Traffic of Polish Seaports 1945–1960*. Part 2. Transactions of the Maritime Institute at Gdańsk, Series III. Gdańsk, 1961. Tables 3, 9, 15, 23–25. (In Polish with English summary.)

Most of the trade was outgoing coal from the fields of Upper Silesia with smaller quantities of iron ore and scrap moving in the opposite direction to the coalfield-oriented steel mills.[1]

Since World War II a reduced Poland, which had ceded a large area to the Soviet Union but had gained from Germany a territory more than half the size of the ceded area, controls a long coast on the Baltic, including the old German port of Stettin at the mouth of the Oder River and the former Free City of Danzig. The tonnage of the Polish foreign trade has increased considerably, from 19 million tons in 1938 to nearly 50 million in 1960. As a result of the postwar reorientation of Eastern Europe's economy Poland's foreign trade is now dominated by exchange with other countries in the Communist Bloc,[2] especially the Soviet Union, and most of the cargo—even bulk cargo such as iron ore, coal and petroleum—moves across the land borders. Total maritime trade of the three Polish ports reached a postwar peak of 17 million tons in 1949, was 14 to 15 million tons in the period 1950 to 1957 and then expanded to almost 22 million tons in 1960. This quantity is less than the combined prewar cargo turnover of the three ports.[3]

Transit traffic, which in prewar Poland was quite insignificant, now accounts for about 20 per cent of the total seaborne cargo. It is especially important in Szczecin, where it accounts for 35 per cent. Polish ports handle over 50 per cent of Czechoslovakia's international seaborne trade and sizable quantities of East Germany's and Hungary's seaborne cargo.[4] Szczecin handles more than two-thirds of the transit traffic in Polish ports which increased from 2.6 million tons in 1954 to 4.2 million in 1960.

[1] Peter-Heinz Seraphim, *Die Ostseehäfen und der Ostseeverkehr*. Berlin, 1937. Pp. 99 ff.

[2] The Communist countries of Europe in 1949 formed a Council for Mutual Economic Aid, usually referred to as COMECON.

[3] Czesław Wojewódka, *Structural Changes in the Traffic of Polish Seaports 1945–1960*. Transactions of the Maritime Institute at Gdańsk. Series III. Economics and Law Problems of Sea Transport. No. 17. Gdańsk, 1961. In Polish with English Summary.

Werner Gumpel, "Die Seeverkehrspolitik des CO-MECON und ihre Bedeutung für Hamburg", *Geographische Rundschau*, 1962. Pp. 45 ff.

[4] The COMECON countries are attempting to increase their mercantile marine and to expand their port capacity and thereby make themselves less dependent on West European shipping services, which in Western Europe is primarily felt in Hamburg.

Seaborne Transit Cargo of Czechoslovakia, Hungary and East Germany by Ports

Port	1956	1958	1960
	Million tons		
Czechoslovakia			
Polish ports	1.5	1.8	2.7
Hamburg	1.5	1.0	0.9
Rijeka	0.3	0.4	0.4
Trieste	0.1	0.0	0.2
Hungary			
Polish ports	0.17	0.19	0.25
Hamburg	0.09	0.06	0.09
Rijeka	0.22	0.19	0.22
Trieste	0.05	0.04	0.05
East Germany			
Polish ports	0.4	0.6	1.1
Hamburg	1.8	1.0	1.8

Source: Wojewódka, *op. cit.*, Part 2. Table 30.

Another striking change in the trade structure of the Polish ports is the increased importance of general cargo which in 1960 accounted for 20 per cent of total goods traffic as against 10 to 15 per cent before the war. Gdynia is the most pronounced general cargo port (30–35 per cent). Gdańsk (15–20) and Szczecin (10–15 per cent) have smaller proportions of general cargo.

Coal was still the leading cargo in 1960 accounting for almost 40 per cent of the total cargo turnover in Polish ports but this proportion was 70 per cent ten years earlier. The chief destinations for the 8 million tons of seaborne coal were Finland and Denmark. Szczecin was the leading coal shipping port.[5] About 60 per cent of Poland's declining coal exports were sent across the land borders, chiefly to the Soviet Union, East Germany and Czechoslovakia.

In 1960 Poland imported 7.3 million tons of iron ore of which about 75 per cent came across the land border from the Soviet Union.

[5] See page 80.

Polish receipts of Soviet iron ore exceeded coal shipments in the opposite direction by one million tons. Seaborne ore receipts amounted to 3.6 million tons in 1960 of which almost half was in transit. Ore receipts in Polish ports increased at a slower rate in the 1950s than the total Polish imports of iron ore. Also for iron ore Szczecin was the leading port.

Grain receipts, which were handled primarily at Gdynia and Gdańsk, in 1960 amounted to 2.1 million tons.

As a result of the growing importance of general cargo in Polish ports, the tonnage of vessels calling in recent years has increased more rapidly than the tonnage of cargo handled. Gdynia, the leading liner port, accounts for a larger vessel tonnage than Szczecin, the leading cargo port. On the other hand the number of vessels calling at Szczecin is twice as high as for Gdańsk or Gdynia. All three ports in 1960 had a good balance between imports and exports for the first time in recent history. From 1926 to the middle 1950s coal shipments completely dominated the traffic of Gdynia and Gdańsk. Prewar Stettin was primarily a bulk cargo receiving port for Berlin and the population centers of eastern Germany. The trade structure of postwar Szczecin is radically changed. In comparison with ports of western Europe and most other parts of the world the almost complete absence of petroleum and petroleum products from the Polish ports is conspicuous.

East Germany

The old Hanseatic cities on the coast of Mecklenburg and Pomerania—Wismar, Rostock (with its outport Warnemünde) and Stralsund —were small ports in prewar Germany, located in the traffic shadow of the two great Baltic ports, Stettin at the mouth of the Oder and the isthmus port of Lübeck. Lübeck, the smaller of these two ports, had a cargo turnover about four times as large as that of Rostock

The Port of Rostock

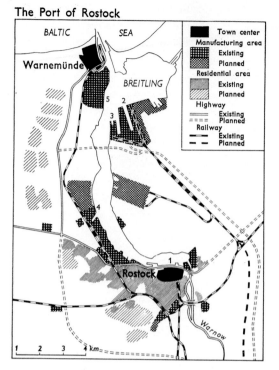

1. Old port 2. New port 3. Passenger port 4. Fish quay 5. Shipyard

Source: M. Léger, "Rostock: notes d'excursion", *Annales de Géographie,* 1960. P. 15.

and Wismar combined. The tremendous superiority of Hamburg prevented these ports from extending their hinterland, which was restricted to a sparsely populated agricultural region.

The radically changed political and commercial relations after the war for East Germany have altered the premises for its transportation geography. An East German state has been created *de facto* out of the German territory occupied by the Soviet Union. Both Stettin and Lübeck are just outside this new state. The Soviet Union is by far the most important trade partner of East Germany which includes some of the leading manufacturing regions of prewar Germany. The long overland distances between the Soviet Union and East Germany make sea transportation attractive. This does not explain, however, the

very large investments being made in the development of national ports at Wismar, Rostock and Stralsund. The Polish port of Szczecin is well located to serve the East German—Soviet traffic within the Baltic. The plans for a cargo turnover of 6 million tons at Rostock in 1965 and 16 million in 1970[1] indicate a nationalist tendency within the COMECON. Overland hauls from Berlin and other production centers in East Germany are considerably longer to Rostock than to Szczecin.

The already accomplished postwar expansion of East German seaport traffic is impressive. In 1959 Wismar was the leading port handling 2.1 million tons of cargo or exactly ten times as much as in 1936. Petroleum and petroleum products, lumber and grains are leading receipts; potash and general cargo top the export list. The harbor has been deepened from 6.5 meters to 9.5 meters. Rostock–Warnemünde, which has been selected to become the great port of East Germany, was second in 1959 with 1.0 million tons and Stralsund third with 0.7 million tons.

The ferry traffic between Gedser (Denmark) and Warnemünde, and between Trelleborg (Sweden) and Sassnitz is much reduced compared to prewar conditions. The main ferry traffic from Gedser now moves through the West German port of Grossenbrode.[2] There is also a ferry connection between Trelleborg and Lübeck's outport Travemünde. This is, however, of less importance than the Trelleborg–Sassnitz line which carries railroad cargo between Scandinavia and Eastern and Southern Europe.

[1] Total seaborne trade of East Germany in 1957 was 5.7 million tons of which 3.4 million were handled at East German ports. For a discussion of the new port plans see "Rostock: notes d'excursion" (eleven authors). *Annales de géographie,* 1960. Pp. 15 ff.
Also Paul Olbrich, *Die Schiffahrt in der sowjetischen Besatzungszone.* Bonn, 1958.
[2] A new, more direct route between København and Hamburg is scheduled for completion in May, 1963. Ferries will run between Rødbyhavn on Lolland and Puttgarden on Fehmarn. The Gedser-Grossenbrode service will then be discontinued.

Lübeck and the Kiel Canal

Lübeck, the leading city of the Hanseatic League, was by 1500 the largest city in Germanic Europe. For centuries it dominated the important Baltic trade under the leadership of a powerful merchant aristocracy. A canal built in the 1390s, the first artificial waterway in Germany, made possible the large-scale exports of salt from Lüneburg, an important item in medieval commerce. The canal connected Lübeck to the Elbe and made Hamburg an outport on the North Sea.

Lübeck's entrepôt function declined with the emergence of powerful national states on the Baltic, competition from the Dutch, and the failure of its efforts to participate in the Atlantic trade. Present-day Lübeck is the leading German port on the Baltic, a natural gateway for West German trade with the Nordic countries. Most of the 1961 cargo turnover (3.3 million tons), the largest in the history of the port, was generated by the industries along the Trave River. Leading cargo receipts were coal, timber, ore and pyrite residue, pulp and paper and leading shipments salt, coke, and motor vehicles.

The Kiel Canal, constructed for military purposes between 1887 and 1895, also served commercial traffic. But instead of bringing Lübeck and the other Baltic ports to the North Sea it brought the Baltic to Hamburg. The time saved on a voyage between Hamburg and Baltic ports was more than twice that saved on the voyage between London and the Baltic.

The 99-kilometer canal is 11.3 meters deep. In recent years almost 30 million tons of cargo has been transported in each direction with timber, general cargo, ore, coal and pulp the leading westbound commodities and petroleum, general cargo, coal and ores the most important eastbound items.

Northwest Europe

West Germany

Hamburg

Hamburg was founded by the year 825 but its rise to the position as Germany's leading port and at times the leading port on the European continent came at a much later date. During the Viking period Haithabu near present Schleswig on the Schlei was the center of long distance trade between the Baltic region and Western Europe. During the Hanseatic period Lübeck became the hub of commercial activity and Hamburg slowly developed as Lübeck's outport on the North Sea. High value cargo was transported overland between Lübeck and Hamburg. The decline of the Hanseatic League did not mean a decline for Hamburg, however. The framework of European trade widened; the Baltic Sea and Flanders were no longer the only centers of trade. Hamburg's Elbe hinterland in Bohemia and Silesia came into greater prominence and Hamburg developed commercial ties stretching from Russia (Arkhangelsk) and Iceland in the north to the Mediterranean in the south. Trade was especially well developed with England and Holland. From 1567 the Merchant Adventurers were represented in the city and after 1600 many Dutch merchants settled there.[1]

The discovery of new continents was of

[1] Claus Lafrenz, *Der Hafen Hamburg: Tatsachen, Daten und Zahlen.* Hamburg, 1962.

Hamburg: Cargo Turnover by Coastal Area

Coastal Area	1936	1961
	Per cent of tonnage	
Germany	13.4	5.5
Other Europe	42.8	26.1
America	24.6	32.2
Africa	6.2	7.5
Asia	12.4	27.4
Australia	0.4	1.3
	Million tons	
Total cargo	22.1	29.9
General cargo	10.8	10.7
Bulk cargo	11.3	19.2

Source: Lafrenz, *op. cit.* P. 24.

little direct benefit to Hamburg until the end of the eighteenth century. The colonial powers reserved the trade with the colonies for their own vessels. The creation of the United States and, a few decades later, the emancipation of the Spanish and Portuguese colonies broke the old trade monopolies and was a great stimulus to Hamburg (and Bremen). The nineteenth century was a period of tremendous expansion for Hamburg. More and more overseas nations were opened for direct trade and through the political developments in Europe Hamburg became the chief port and trade center of a great power with ambitions to build a colonial empire and eager to further the economic interests of her main port through preferential railroad tariffs, etc. The decades before World War I were Hamburg's "Golden Age". Population doubled from 1885 to 1913, when Hamburg had one million inhabitants. With a seaborne cargo turnover of 25.5 million tons in 1913 Hamburg was the fourth largest port in the world after New York, London and Rotterdam. Germany's "Gate to the World" was competing with Rotterdam for the position as continental Europe's leading port by tonnage. By value Hamburg led by a wide margin as general cargo made up a much higher percentage than at the Rhine port.

Hamburg: Selected General Cargo Commodities 1961

Commodity	Thousand tons
Fruit	867
Coffee	197
Cocoa	149
Tobacco	67
Hides and skins	122
Vehicles	239

Source: Lafrenz, *op. cit.* P. 23.

To meet the demands of the increased port traffic a large number of tidal basins were constructed in Hamburg, the first in 1862–1866 (Sandtorhafen). Before this time cargo was loaded and unloaded from ships berthed at dolphins in the river. This system is still common in Hamburg and Rotterdam where much of the transit traffic has traditionally been handled by barges or coasters. Floating cranes and floating elevators loading and unloading to barges and coasters on both sides of an ocean vessel are a common sight in these ports. Some of the basins were also made wide enough to allow dolphin berths. In addition, a combination of the old and the new system was common—working barges or coasters on the outside of vessels at the quays.

In 1871 Hamburg joined the German *Reich* but remained outside the German customs area. The whole city was a free port. The status was changed in 1888 when a special area in the harbor was marked off as a free port and the rest of the city was incorporated into the German customs area. The Kiel Canal, opened in 1895, strengthened Hamburg's position as a sea transit port for Scandinavia and the Baltic region.[2]

The great political changes in Europe as a

[2] The contemporary establishment of direct overseas lines from København, Göteborg, Stockholm and Oslo worked in the opposite direction, however. But most of the new lines from the Nordic ports called at Hamburg and thus strengthened its position as a liner port.

Kaiser-Wilhelm-Hafen in Hamburg with a floating grain elevator and a floating crane for heavy lifts. Note the many barges and the forest of cranes on the dockside. (G. Werbeck, Hamburger Hafen- und Lagerhaus-Aktiengesellschaft)

consequence of World War II have afflicted Hamburg more than any other large North Sea port. The Iron Curtain, economically the most important boundary in Europe, cuts off Hamburg from its Elbe hinterland about 45 kilometers upstream from the city center. But all the changes in Hamburg's trade structure should not be referred to the changed political map of Europe. Some are common for most large seaports in industrialized areas. The postwar expansion of petroleum refineries and some other heavy industries in these ports has led to an increased share of bulk cargo in their total turnover. Hamburg before the war was a pronounced general cargo port with a 50 : 50 ratio between general cargo and bulk cargo. In 1961 this ratio had changed to 36 : 64. The postwar expansion of port-oriented

Hamburg: Selected Bulk Cargo Commodities

Commodity	1936	1961
	Million tons	
Petroleum	3.9	10.7
Coal	3.1	3.0
Grain	0.9	2.2
Ore	0.5	0.8
Oil seed	1.2	0.9
Fertilizer	0.4	0.8

Source: Lafrenz, *op. cit.* P. 24.

Hamburg: Cargo Turnover by Hinterland

Area	1936	1956	1961
	Million tons		
West Germany	13.3	21.4	24.6
Hamburg	*5.5*	*13.8*	*17.1*
East Germany	4.1	1.9	1.2
Land Transit (Czechoslovakia, Austria etc.)	2.3	2.4	1.9
Sea Transit (Nordic Countries, etc.)	2.4	1.9	2.2
Total	22.1	27.5	29.9

Source: Lafrenz, *op. cit.* P. 24.

industries also means, in Hamburg as in other ports, that the city itself accounts for an increasing share of the cargo handled. Before the war only 25 per cent of the cargo originated in or was destined for Hamburg. In 1961 this ratio was 57 per cent. The greatest loss to the port of Hamburg has been the decline in traffic with the area now included in East Germany. Before the war this region, embracing some of the most important manufacturing districts of Germany, accounted for 19 per cent of Hamburg's cargo turnover but in 1961 for only 4 per cent. For reasons just mentioned this share would have been lower than the prewar figure even without an Iron Curtain.

151

Shell Europoort in 1962 received 2.5 million tons of crude oil at its 250 meters long jetty. (Shell, January 1962)

eighteenth century and in 1950 it was transformed into a fresh-water basin, Brielse Meer, through the construction of a dam downstream from Brielle.

A great change in Rotterdam's development came with the Industrial Revolution in Germany which started about 1850 and which gradually turned the Rhine into the main "manufacturing river" in Europe. The legal basis for the freedom of shipping on this international river had been laid by the Treaty of Mainz (1832) followed by the Mannheim Treaty (1867). The abolition of the tolls and the improvement of the waterways enabled Rhine shipping to assume very large propor-

Grain being unloaded by floating elevators from a tanker in the Waal Basin, Rotterdam. Note the river barges to the left and the Dutch coaster to the right, typical of the North Sea and the Baltic. (Havenbedrijf der Gemeente Rotterdam)

tions.[3] Rotterdam's response to Germany's industrialization was the cutting of the New Waterway through the Hoek van Holland sand dunes between 1866 and 1872. The New Waterway provided Rotterdam with a direct channel to the sea. At first it was only ten feet deep and until 1884 large vessels had to use the longer alternative routes. But it has been enlarged several times and can now be negotiated

[3] "The Largest Port of Europe Builds for its Future", *Rotterdamsche Bank N.V.*, May 1959, No. 19.

The oil port for supertankers in Europoort is now accessible for tankers of 85,000 deadweight tons. In the near future it will be able to receive vessels of 100,000 tons and more. From bottom to top are the Dutch 67,000-ton tanker *Sepia,* the Italian 50,000-ton tanker *Antonietta Fassio* and the Dutch tanker *Caltex Madrid.* (Copyright Aero-Camera, Rotterdam, 1962)

The 1st Petroleum Basin at Pernis in the port of Rotterdam with the Dutch tanker *Ondina.* (Shell Pernis)

by vessels drawing up to thirty-three feet. The New Waterway also provided land on both banks for the expansion of port facilities and of port oriented industries.

The enormous growth of port traffic in Rotterdam after the opening of the New Waterway has led to the construction of one port basin after the other and this expansion is still going on. First came Rijnhaven (1894), Maashaven (1905), Waalhaven (1912, first part) on the left bank of the Maas and smaller general cargo basins on the right bank. Merwehaven was completed in 1932. Rotterdam's chief function as the meeting point of river and sea traffic meant that cargo overwhelmingly was transferred between seagoing vessels and river barges. The basins had to be wide to accomodate steamers loading and unloading on both sides, either at a quay with barges on the outside or at a dolphin berth with barges on both sides. The basins were wider than at such 'railroad ports' as Antwerp or Bremen where the most common transfer of cargo was between steamer and rail car or truck.

Rotterdam is at the crossroads of two main waterways, the Rhine River with its heavy barge traffic and the sea route through the North Sea, the world's most heavily trafficked sea lane. The Rhine was most important in the beginning of Rotterdam's modern development. Rotterdam became one of the world's leading ports as the transshipment point for cargo between ocean vessels and river barges. This function could well be performed about 30 kilometers inland as long as sufficient depth for ocean vessels was provided in the New Waterway. But in the last three decades a second function has become more and more important and now accounts for most of the cargo traffic. This is the development of heavy manufacturing industries which is more related to Rotterdam's being a deep seaport with a superb location than to its river port function. Products of the heavy manufacturing plants in Rotterdam (as in Antwerp, Dunkerque and IJmuiden) can be carried by coasters up and down the coast, by liners to trans-ocean destinations, and by barges, pipelines, railroads and trucks to inland points. These ports are also the points of lowest assembly costs for raw materials. Their position is rapidly being improved with the increase in the size of bulk carriers which bring raw materials from more and more distant sources. At the same time the coal fields have lost much of their attraction for heavy manufacturing industries. Industrial inertia rather than coal is the chief locational factor in the old manufacturing districts. Rotterdam used to serve the Ruhr area as a seaport. Now, while still performing this function, it has become a major competitor of the Ruhr as a location for heavy industry.

The petroleum industry was first to acknowledge Rotterdam's advantages of superb location. Royal Dutch chose Rotterdam as their distributing center for Western Europe already in 1901 and even built a small refinery where the entrance to the Waalhaven is now situated. But the modern petroleum industry in Rotterdam only dates back to the 1930s. To provide space for this expanding industry the village of Pernis was annexed by Rotterdam and a petroleum basin was constructed between 1929 and 1933. Work on a second petroleum basin was started just before World War II. In the meantime the Royal Dutch/Shell Group had built a modern refinery at Pernis, completed

Distillation Capacity of Oil Refineries in Selected Northwest European Ports

Port	1938	1952	1961
	Million tons per year		
Antwerp	0.3	2.8	8.6
Rotterdam	0.7	6.5	22.8
Amsterdam	—	—	—
Bremen	0.3	0.6	1.4
Hamburg	1.8	2.1	8.1

Source: "Refineries in the Eastern Hemisphere", *The Petroleum Times*, January 13, 1961. Pp. 6 ff.

Seaborne Cargo Traffic in Rotterdam in Selected Years

Commodity	1929			1938			1950			1956			1960		
	In	Out	Total	In	Out	Total	In	Out	Total	In	Out	Total	In	Out	Total
	Million metric tons														
Coal	1.6	9.2	10.8	0.8	10.2	11.0	0.9	4.8	5.7	11.2	4.8	16.0	2.2	3.1	5.3
Ore	10.4	—	10.4	11.0	0.1	11.1	3.0	—	3.0	9.4	0.0	9.4	12.7	0.0	12.7
Timber	1.8	0.0	1.8	1.1	0.0	1.1	0.6	0.1	0.7	0.8	0.0	0.8	1.2	0.1	1.3
Grain	3.6	0.1	3.7	3.6	0.2	3.9	1.7	—	1.7	4.2	0.1	4.3	5.1	0.3	5.4
Other bulk cargo	0.9	0.4	1.3	1.1	1.4	2.5	0.8	0.8	1.6	1.7	0.3	2.0	2.2	1.9	4.1
Total dry bulk cargo	18.3	9.7	28.0	17.6	12.0	29.5	7.0	5.7	12.7	27.3	5.2	32.5	23.5	5.4	28.9
General cargo	3.7	4.0	7.6	4.2	3.6	7.8	3.7	3.7	7.4	5.6	5.4	11.0	9.3	5.0	14.3
Total dry cargo	22.0	13.6	35.6	21.8	15.5	37.3	10.6	9.4	20.0	32.9	10.6	43.5	32.8	10.4	43.2
Petroleum	1.1	0.0	1.1	2.7	0.2	2.9	6.9	2.1	9.0	20.1	6.8	26.9	28.7	9.4	38.1
Total cargo	23.1	13.6	36.7	24.5	15.7	40.2	17.5	11.5	29.0	53.0	17.4	70.4	61.6	19.8	81.4

Sources: E. Schouten, "De havenuitbreiding te Rotterdam", *Polytechnisch Tijdschrift*, B, 1957. P. 668 B; *Statistisch zakboek 1961.* P. 97; Port of Rotterdam, *Statistical Review*, No. 13. P. 7.

in 1936. It had an initial capacity of 0.7 million tons a year. In 1938 the oil traffic in Rotterdam amounted to 2.9 million tons.

The most remarkable development of Rotterdam as a manufacturing center has taken place after World War II. According to the 1930 census Rotterdam had a lower ratio than the nation for manufacturing employment. Now it is a highly industrialized region and the most important manufacturing center in the Netherlands. Industries located in the port area account for an increasing share of the cargo turnover. Given the physical circumstances in the Rhine-Maas delta industrial development must go hand in hand with large-scale planning of waterways, port facilities and sites. Two long-term projects command special attention, the Botlek Plan and the Europoort Plan.

The Botlek plan was conceived during the war and published in 1947. The Botlek, a small river branch connecting the Nieuwe Maas and the Brielse Maas, was converted into a harbor basin and additional basins were dredged in

[4] After Aruba, Abadan, Baton Rouge and Amuay Bay.

adjacent land areas. One of the Botlek basins was made into Rotterdam's third oil harbor to accomodate super tankers. It can receive vessels of 50,000 tons deadweight. Work on this project was started in 1952 and most of the plan, which is almost as extensive as the Europoort plan, was realized in the 1950s.

The postwar expansion of Rotterdam's refinery capacity has been striking. The Shell refinery at Pernis has become the largest in Europe and the fifth largest in the world,[4] with a capacity of 15 million tons a year. About two-thirds of the output is exported. Caltex after the war realized its plans from 1939 to build a refinery at the second oil basin at Pernis. After expansion it has a capacity of 2.8 million tons a year. Construction work for a 5 million ton refinery for Esso in the Botlek area was begun in 1958 and completed in 1960.

The execution of the Europoort plan, the logical sequel to the Botlek plan, was started in 1958. According to the official definition "the plan is to construct a series of basins for very big vessels at the head of the island of Rozenburg opposite the Hoek van Holland". Rotter-

Ocean Shipping in Rotterdam in Selected Years

A = number of vessels
B = aggregate tonnage of vessels, million N.R.T.
C = cargo handled, million metric tons

Year	A	B	C
1929	12,739	21.50	36.65
1938	15,360	24.72	40.25
1950	12,883	20.43	29.00
1956	21,239	43.27	70.36
1960	24,344	56.91	81.35
Index 1960 (1929 = 100)	*191*	*265*	*222*

Data from Schouten, *op. cit.,* and Port of Rotterdam, *Statistical Review, op. cit.*

dam's fourth oil basin in the Europoort area, which has already been completed, is accessible for 85,000 ton tankers. In the future even larger vessels can be accomodated. Both Shell and Caltex have piers in the new oil harbor which is connected with Pernis by pipeline. It is continued from Pernis to the German Rhineland (Godorf and Wesseling near Cologne) by a 24-inch pipeline with a capacity of 6.5 million tons a year.

AMSTERDAM. In the Middle Ages several important centers for commerce, shipping and fishing grew up on the coast of the shallow Zuider Zee. Of these only one, Amsterdam, has been able to maintain and even improve its standing. Others, like Enkhuizen, Edam, Hoorn and Medemblik, are little if any larger than they were before the Industrial Revolution and they function as local trade centers of agricultural regions. Amsterdam, as the constitutional capital of the Netherlands, has attracted many administrative functions while others are in The Hague, the nation's *de facto* capital. Being the seat of most large commercial, industrial, banking and insurance companies as well as of an important stock exchange Amsterdam is the undisputed economic metropolis of the Netherlands.

An important event in Amsterdam's modern history was the opening in 1876 of the North Sea Canal by which the city turned its back on the Zuider Zee and looked towards the North Sea.[5] The increased size of vessels made this move necessary. Amsterdam was the almost exclusive market place of the products from the Dutch colonies in the East and West Indies.[6] This position could be maintained only if Amsterdam provided port facilities for the ever larger cargo liners. The new canal was 24 kilometers long, 125 meters wide and 9.6 meters deep.

The port is well connected with the extensive inland waterway system but Amsterdam played a minor role in the dominating Rhine traffic until the opening in 1952 of the Amsterdam—Rhine Canal. The total international barge traffic in the port increased from 1.6 million tons in 1951 to 6.2 million in 1958. Of this, 81 per cent was Rhine traffic, mainly ore, petroleum and coal moving upstream. Traffic on the new canal is expected to increase even more with the widening of sluices which have acted as a bottle-neck.

Total international cargo traffic in Amsterdam's port was 8.3 million tons in 1951 or just above the pre-war level (8.1 million in 1938). In 1956 it was 14.0 million and in 1958 no less than 18.0 million.[7] This rapid increase in cargo turnover is a result of Amsterdam's changed port functions. It is becoming a major Rhine estuary port with excellent equipment for handling both dry bulk cargo and petroleum products. Large tracts of polder land are being converted into new dock basins and industrial sites. The North Sea Canal is being widened to 250 yards at the bottom and deep-

[5] F. J. Monkhouse, *A Regional Geography of Western Europe.* London, 1959. P. 59.

[6] Kurt Wiedenfeld, *Die nordwesteuropäischen Welthäfen.* Berlin, 1903. P. 277; W. E. Boerman, "Wirtschaftsgeographische Probleme der Rheinhäfen und ihres Hinterlandes", *Tijdschrift voor Economische en Sociale Geografie,* 1957. Pp. 102 ff.

[7] F. W. Adriaanse, "The Port of Amsterdam in 1958", *Wyt's Digest of Dutch Shipping and Shipbuilding 1959.* Pp. 305 ff.

Port of IJmuiden

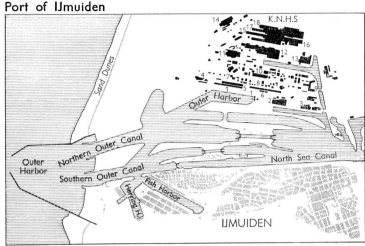

1. Ore yard, 2. Coal yard, 3. Cement works, 4. Ore sintering plant, 5. Blast furnaces, 6. Coke ovens, 7. Power station, 8. By-products plant, 9. Head office, 10. Nitrogenous fertilizer plant, 11. Open-hearth steelworks, 12. Heavy plate mill, 13. Old sheet mill, 14. Oxygen steelworks, 15. Slabbing mill, 16. Hot strip mill, 17. Cold strip mill, 18. Tinning plant.

K.N.H.S Royal Netherlands Blast Furnaces and Steelworks

ened to 48 feet, so that in 1965 the port will be accessible for vessels of 100,000 tons dwt, a large increase from the earlier 30,000 tons (34-foot draft). The widened Canal permits two 65,000 ton vessels to pass each other.

The North Sea Canal has greatly influenced the location of industries in the Netherlands. In the 1890s a harbor was built at the North Sea entrance of the Canal, IJmuiden. This has become the main Dutch fishing port[8] and in the early 1920s two blast furnaces were com-

pleted here. A third blast furnace, a fertilizer plant and a cement works were built by 1930. By 1939 the output of pig iron was 280,000 tons, of which only a tiny quantity was used in the small open-hearth furnace, which had been put into operation in the year before. The Netherlands was one of the world's largest pig-iron exporters. The tremendous postwar market for steel created a favorable boom atmosphere for this excellently located steel plant which through successive expansion has become one of the largest integrated steel mills in Europe.[9]

The IJmuiden steel works, originally planned as an integrated plant but for financial reasons limited to a pig-iron department during the first two decades of its existence, is the pioneer of a new trend in continental Europe. Several large, integrated steel works with tidewater locations have recently been built or are now in the planning stage (Bremen, Dunkerque, Gent-Terneuzen Canal, Europoort). The Depression in the 1930s, World War II and the postwar construction boom[10] apparently delayed this trend for several decades.

There are many manufacturing plants in addition to the IJmuiden steel works and its by-product plants along the North Sea Canal,

[8] The famous Dutch herring fisheries of the Middle Ages and later operated from the Zuider Zee ports. These fisheries have been considered as a nursery for the mercantile marine, on which the Dutch based their position as one of the leading mercantile nations.

[9] It will have a capacity of 2.5 million tons of crude steel when present expansion programs have been completed in 1964. In 1960 the steel company's port received 2.4 million tons of iron ore in 258 vessels, 0.4 million tons of coal in 36 vessels and shipped 333,000 tons of rolled products in 613 vessels and 38,000 tons of pig iron in 52 vessels. In addition it received 158,000 tons of miscellaneous products and shipped 104,000 tons.

[10] During the reconstruction boom the long-term cost situation was of little relevance. The important matter was to increase steel production rapidly and this could best be done by rebuilding the steel mills in their old locations. This was also the cheapest way in the short run. The great advantages of the tidewater location increased with the development of iron ore mines in Labrador, Venezuela and Africa and the construction of huge ore carriers in the late 1950s and early 1960s.

Good railroad connections have been a characteristic of this great seaport from the beginning of its modern expansion period. The famous railroad to Cologne, the "Iron Rhine" was built already in 1843. But in the postwar period rail traffic has lost in importance while barge and truck traffic have made noticeable gains. The modernization of the inland waterways, and primarily the completion of the Albert Canal,[4] the motorization of the barges and the increased competitiveness of highway transport also for long hauls explain this development.

In 1957 barges accounted for 23.5 million tons of cargo in the port of Antwerp and railroads for 9.4 million. Truck traffic is more difficult to assess but estimates indicate an increase from 5 per cent of the port cargo in 1953 to 20 per cent in 1958.[5]

Thirty per cent, or 6.9 million tons, of the total tonnage handled by barges in the port of Antwerp in 1957 was Rhine traffic, a decrease since the prewar period, when the corresponding figures were 44 per cent or 8.1 million tons (1937). The Belgians, looking for improved waterway connections with the Rhine, would like to build a canal from Zandvliet at the northern end of the large basin canal now under construction (map, page 169), to Moerdijk

[4] The Albert Canal, one of Europe's busiest inland waterways, provides a direct connection between Belgium's leading center of heavy manufacturing at Liége on the Meuse and the nation's dominating port. The fall of 55 meters between Liége and Antwerp is negotiated by six groups of triple locks, of which the two largest can accomodate 2,000-ton Rhine barges. An older canal between the two cities, completed in 1844, could only handle 600-ton barges and required much more time for the voyage. In 1957 no less than 76,000 journeys by laden barges were made through the Albert Canal. The amount of freight was 24.7 million tons. For a short survey of the Albert Canal and the Dutch Juliana Canal—the lateral canal along the right bank of the Maas between Maastricht and Maasbracht, opened in 1936 and built entirely in Dutch territory after the Belgians had proved unwilling to undertake any joint navigation improvement scheme in the border river—see F. J. Monkhouse, "Albert and Juliana: Two Great Waterways", *Scottish Geographical Magazine*, 1956. Pp. 163 ff.

[5] Paul Wagret, *op. cit.* P. 103.

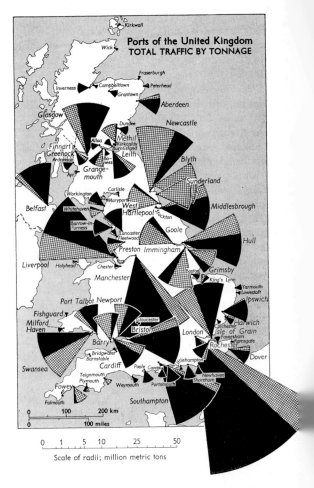

Estimates calculated from data in *Annual Statement of the Trade of the United Kingdom,* Vol. IV: Supplement, 1955–57; P. Ford and J. A. Bound, *Coastwise Shipping and Small Ports.* Oxford, 1951.

To make traffic in French ports commensurable with other ports in northwestern Europe and the United States, river traffic handled in the seaports was added. Data were obtained from *Atlas de France (Métropole),* (Comité National de Géographie, Paris), and it is shown as a white margin on some port symbols.

Western Europe

*For ports of the United Kingdom
see map on same scale on opposite page.*

NORTH SEA

IRISH SEA

REPUBLIC OF IRELAND

Sligo
Dundalk · Drogheda
Dublin
Dun Laoghaire
Galway
Kilrush · Limerick
Foynes
Fenit
Cork
New Ross
Waterford
Wexford
Rosslare

Flensburg
Kappeln
Grossenbrode
Kiel
Neustadt
Rendsburg
Itzehoe
Lübeck
Helgo-Brunsbüttel-Koog
Cuxhaven
Emshorn
Uetersen
Emden
Bremerhaven
Norderney
Borkum
Calffrum
Leer
Nordenham
Hamburg
Zaandam
Brake
Bremen
IJmuiden
Amsterdam

BENELUX

1 Dordrecht (incl. Zwijndrecht)
2 Terneuzen
3 Zelzate
4 Brugge
5 Oostende

Groningen
Harlingen
Delfzijl

Hoek van Holland
Vlissingen
Zeebrugge
Rotterdam
(incl. Vlaardingen
and Schiedam)

Dunkerque
Gravelines
Calais
Boulogne
Gent
Saint-Valery
Abbeville
Le Tréport
Le Havre
Fécamp
Dieppe
Cherbourg
Gonfreville
Duclair
ENGLISH
Honfleur
Caen
Petit-Couronne
Rouen
Port-Jerome
Antwerpen

CHANNEL

Brest
Roscoff · Tréguier · Paimpol
Morlaix
L'Aberwrach
Le Légué
Saint-Malo
Douarnenez
Quimper
Loctudy
Concarneau
Vannes
Lorient
Quiberon
Saint Nazaire
Paimbœuf
Port-Joinville
Donges
Basse-Indre
Nantes
Granville

FRANCE

Les Sables d'Olonne
La Rochelle
Rochefort
La Pallice
Tonnay-Charente
Pauillac
Blaye
Ambès
Libourne
Arcachon
Bordeaux
Bayonne
Le Boucau

BAY OF BISCAY

1 : 10,000,000

0   100   200   300 km
0   100   200 miles

Saint-Louis-du-Rhone
Port-de-Bouc
Nice
Antibes
Saint Raphaël
Sète
La Ciotat
La Seyne
Toulon
La Nouvelle
Marseille
Port-Vendres
Ile-Rousse
Bastia
Ajaccio
Propriano
Porto-Vecchio

MEDITERRANEAN SEA

CARGO HANDLED 1956

Million Metric Tons

100
50
10
5
1
0

Shipments
Receipts

Cargo liners at the Scheldt quays and a general view of downtown Antwerp. Though port activity is concentrated mainly in the docks, the 5.5 kilometer quays along the Scheldt remain important. (The City of Antwerp)

on Hollandsch Diep through the Dutch province of Noord-Brabant. This would shorten the Scheldt-Rhine/Maas route by 40 kilometers and provide calm water for the Rhine barges. This program meets Dutch opposition as the proposed canal would cut through a densely populated part of the Netherlands. The Dutch propose instead that a solution be found within the framework of the large Delta Plan, which envisages coastal dikes sealing off all delta waters from the sea, except the two entrances to Rotterdam and Antwerp. When in the future the Zeeland waters are protected from the tide a natural waterway could be found west of Noord-Brabant to the Rhine and this waterway could serve Gent as well.[6] The Belgians have a further alternative

of improving the Rhine connections by extending the Albert Canal to the Rhine near Cologne (the Ventdebout Canal).[7] A clause was inserted in the Versailles Treaty giving the Belgians the right to construct a canal between the Rhine (Ruhrort) and the Meuse. The distance Antwerp–Ruhrort would be reduced from 330 kilometers to 183 kilometers or less than the distance Ruhrort–Rotterdam (215 km). The Dutch successfully blocked this plan.[8]

Antwerp's barge traffic on the Albert Canal and the Scheldt was 7.0 and 5.7 million tons respectively in 1957.

Belgium–Luxembourg is one of the leading

[6] W. E. Boerman, "Wirtschaftsgeographische Probleme der Rheinhäfen und ihres Hinterlandes", *Tijdschrift voor Economische en Sociale Geografie*, 1957. Pp. 111–112; J. De Keuster, *La concurrence entre les trois grands ports nord-européens: Hambourg, Rotterdam, Anvers*. Anvers, 1930. P. 163.

[7] Paul Wagret, *op. cit.*, p. 103.

[8] J. De Keuster, *op. cit.* Pp. 163–164.

exporters of steel products on the world market. For many steel exporters in the neighboring countries France and Germany, Antwerp is closer than any national port. The frequent sailings and the special steel handling facilities and services available make Antwerp the port *par excellence* of the European Coal and Steel Community.[9] This goes a long way to explain why there is so much general cargo to pick up at Antwerp and why Antwerp has become the leading general cargo port on the European continent.

The British Isles

The United Kingdom was before World War II the small mother country of a global empire, located in the center of the land hemisphere, and the leading nation in international trade. Coastwise shipping was also important and many British ports ranked among the largest in the world. Great Britain was comfortably separated from the most densely populated and economically most advanced part of continental Europe which had tremendous economic potentials but too often engaged in devastating military and economic warfare. Britain's location and history have made her a rather detached member of the European community which is most clearly reflected in the map of her foreign trade (page 20). In spite of an increase in her foreign trade by tonnage Britain after the war has been surpassed by the United States, which is now the dominating nation on the map of origins and destinations of world shipping. The United States waterborne foreign trade totaled 95 million metric tons in 1938 when the United Kingdom trade reached 117 million tons. In 1961 the situation had been reversed with United States trade at 300 million tons and United Kingdom trade 156 million.

The major ports of Britain have a long and complicated history. In the early days ports were normally located at the head of an estuary where goods could be brought as far inland as possible and shelter was available. As the size of vessels increased it was often possible to deepen the access waterways by embankments and other construction works in the river to increase the tidal scour. Docks were built somewhat downstream from the old port but still near the city center, wet docks where the tidal range was great, tidal basins where it was small and both types of docks in many ports. By and large British ports were pioneers in modern port construction and now have to pay the price of pioneering—too small docks, too narrow dock gates, poor road access, etc. A comparison of London and a late-comer like Antwerp shows striking differences. Just to take one example: in Antwerp 125 dry cargo berths, out of a total of 249 with over 15 feet of water have a depth exceeding 35 feet; in London only 19 berths of 207 are so deep.[1] In Antwerp large port construction projects have been going on almost continuously since the modern expansion period started in the 1860s and in 1956 a tremendous 10-year program was enacted. In London no important additions to the dry cargo facilities have been made since the 1920s.

The greatest change in the British ports from the interwar to the postwar period is the decline of coal and the rise of petroleum. Coal

[9] Of a total steel export of 12 million tons in 1957 Antwerp handled 6 million tons.

[1] *Report of the Committee of Inquiry into the Major Ports of Great Britain* (Rochdale Report). Her Majesty's Stationery Office. London, 1962. P. 250.

exports went down from a peak in 1923 of 84 million tons to 38 million in 1938 and 7 million in 1961. A large amount of coal is still carried coastwise, 21 million tons in 1961 out of a total dry cargo coastal trade of 29 million tons, while coastwise tanker traffic amounted to more than 20 million tons. But this coastal coal flow, directed chiefly to power stations on navigable water (12.5 million tons to London alone in 1961), has also declined. The drastic reduction in coal shipments has created redundancies in the old coal ports in spite of vigorous efforts to provide them with new business. They are often badly located and are ill-equipped to fit the needs of other trades.

Petroleum imports more than trebled between 1948 and 1961, when they totaled 62 million tons. The increase reflects both an absolute expansion of the British energy needs and a shift from coal to oil. As a secondary effect petroleum now exceeds coal in the British export list too (7.7 million tons in 1961). Depths required by modern mammoth tankers are available at several places along the British coasts. Some oil terminals are within the boundaries of great general ports (London, Southampton, Liverpool and Manchester), others are in ports which revolve almost entirely around the oil trade (Isle of Grain, Milford Haven, Finnart). Even where the oil terminals are located in a general port they are often physically and operationally remote from the rest of the port (Thameshaven, Shellhaven and Coryton in London).

Import of ore, especially iron ore, is another expanding trade in which there has been a tremendous increase in vessel size since the early 1950s. Ore now accounts for 25 per cent of the British dry cargo imports and this commodity group is expected to double between 1961 and 1970, reaching 30 million tons in the latter year. The ore trade is a great problem for the British ports. To reap full advantage of the large, specially constructed ore carriers the integrated steelworks must be

Average Size of Ore Carriers Discharging in Certain Areas, Year Ended June 30, 1961

Area	Tons dwt
British ports	13,500
Continental ports	17,100
Japanese ports	20,200
U.S. East Coast north of Cape Hatteras	32,800

Source: *Westinform Report*, No. 189.

served by a deep-water port. But only one British ore quay can take 35,000-tonners (Newcastle). Such important ore terminals as Port Talbot in South Wales and Newport are limited to vessels of 10,000 and 23,000 tons respectively. Newport thus is in almost the same situation as the Great Lakes ports but inferior to many ports on the European continent, in Japan and on the Atlantic and Gulf coasts of the United States. One solution,

Foreign Trade of the United Kingdom
Estimated Tonnage

	1938	1961
	Million metric tons	
Imports	*65.6*	*124.4*
Dry cargo	53.8	62.4
Cereals	10.2	9.1
Sugar	3.0	2.7
Timber, plywood, etc.	9.9	6.8
Pulp, paper and board	3.0	4.2
Crude fertilizers	0.8	3.6
Ores and scrap	7.3	17.1
Petroleum	11.8	62.0
Exports	*51*	*32.2*
Dry cargo	50	24.5
Coal and coke[a]	39	7.2
Petroleum	1	7.7

[a] In 1923 British exports of coal and coke amounted to 85.8 million tons; in addition 18.5 million tons were sold as bunkers to ships engaged in foreign trade. Bunkers in 1938 were 10.7 million tons and in 1961 only 0.1 million tons.

Source: *Report of the Committee of Inquiry into the Major Ports of Great Britain.* Cmnd. 1824. September, 1962.

United Kingdom: Percentage of Foreign Seaborne
Trade Handled by Leading Ports (Value)

Port	1913	1926–30	1948	1957
London	29.3	34.5	31.8	35.6
Liverpool	26.4	23.3	27.3	26.6
Hull	6.3	5.3	5.3	5.5
Manchester	4.0	4.7	5.6	5.5
Southampton	3.8	4.5	3.0	4.2
Glasgow	3.9	4.0	4.4	4.2
Bristol	1.5	1.8	2.9	2.3
Swansea	0.9	1.2	0.9	1.6
Tyne Ports	1.7	1.9	1.5	1.6
Dover and Folkestone	2.5	1.8	1.1	1.5
Middlesbrough	1.0	0.7	0.8	1.2
Harwich	2.4	2.5	0.7	1.2
Grimsby	2.7	1.7	1.0	0.9
Goole	1.3	1.3	0.8	0.9
Leith	1.6	1.3	0.8	0.8
Grangemouth	0.6	0.5	0.5	0.7
Newport, Mon.	0.6	0.6	0.7	0.7
Cardiff	1.7	1.1	0.8	0.6
Holyhead	—[a]	0.9	0.7	0.4
Newhaven	1.5	0.7	0.4	0.4
Other Ports, Gr. Britain	4.9	4.4	8.2	2.6
Ports of Northern Ireland	1.4	1.3	1.3	1.0
	100	100	100	100

[a] No data.
Data for 1913, 1926–30 and 1948 from Stamp and Beaver, *The British Isles*. London 1954; for 1957 from *Annual Statement of the Trade of the United Kingdom*, Vol. IV: Supplement. 1955–57.
Trade handled by airports amounted to 3.8 per cent of total seaborne trade in 1957; trade across the land boundary between Northern Ireland and the Irish Republic to 0.6 per cent.

transshipping the ore from very large ore carriers at Milford Haven to smaller ships for the South Wales ports, has been investigated but does not seem to be financially attractive.

[2] A vivid picture of the urban concentration in this rectangle is provided by W. William-Olsson's *Economic Map of Europe*, Stockholm, 1952, which shows all cities of 10,000 or more inhabitants with spheres proportionate to their population.
[3] M. J. Wise, "The Role of London in the Industrial Geography of Great Britain", *Geography*, 1956; R. C. Estall and J. E. Martin, "Industry in Greater London", *Town Planning Review*, 1958.

The alternative is to construct deep-water facilities at existing ore ports.

London and Liverpool remain the two dominating British liner ports. The four estuaries of the Thames, Mersey, Bristol Channel and Humber handle over two-thirds of Britain's foreign trade by value. They are in the four corners of a rectangle whose diagonals intersect roughly in the Midlands industrial area centered on Birmingham. A large part of Britain's population and manufacturing capacity is also concentrated in this rectangle.[2] The greatest expansion of employment and population in recent decades has been in the southeastern quarter of this region centered on Greater London. The most expansive industries in the British economy (electronics, administration, etc.) are highly concentrated in the capital region.[3] This has of course favored the Port of London but also Bristol and Southampton.

Recent cost developments in truck transportation have extended the rayon of this flexible carrier. With the growing size of cargo liners, many of which will carry containers, it will become necessary to provide more deep-water dry cargo berths and space for container parks. This can obviously not be done in the old dock systems of London and the Rochdale Report recommends major developments in the port of Southampton and that the major development of the port of London should take place at Tilbury. The port of Southampton is already well served by railroads.

The Port of London

London was an important settlement in Roman times. For the Romans roads were more important than seaways. Their chief line of entry from the Continent of Europe was via Dover; the River Thames acted as a barrier to easy movement north, not because of its width but because of its marshy flood plain, which remained unsettled until modern techniques made possible first the excavation of wet docks

175

The Port of London

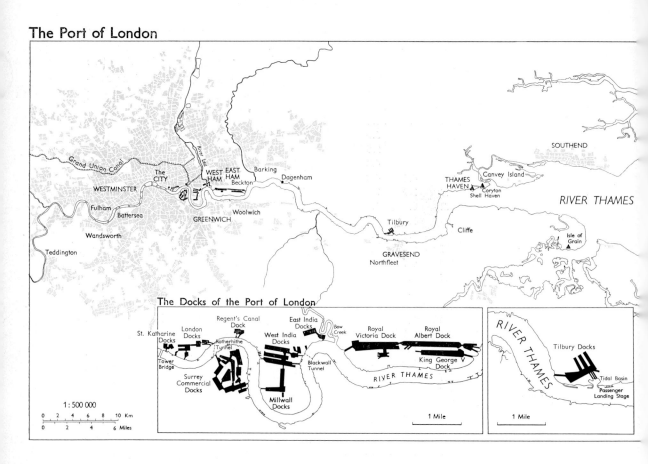

The Docks of the Port of London

1 : 500 000

The London and St. Katharine Docks in the foreground and the River Thames, known in this stretch as the Pool of London, in the background. The river is lined with general wharves. Note the many barges in the river and the docks. The Tower and Tower Bridge are in the upper right corner adjacent to the St. Katharine Docks. (Port of London Authority)

176

The Pool of London and the Surrey Commercial Docks. (Port of London Authority)

The L-shaped Millwall Docks in the foreground connected to the three parallel West India Docks. The East India Docks can be seen in the upper right corner. (Port of London Authority)

The Royal Victoria, Albert and King George V Docks, the largest dock system in the Port of London. (Port of London Authority)

and later the construction of heavy manufacturing plants. Most authorities agree that the site chosen for the Roman settlement, which coincides with the present City of London, was the place furthest downstream where the Romans could conveniently cross the river. Here the bluffs come close to the river on both sides. It is almost certain that the Romans built a bridge at the site later occupied by the old London Bridge, completed in 1209, which for centuries marked the head of ocean navigation on the river.

In mediaeval London foreign merchants played important roles; the Lombards in banking and the Hansards in shipping. The Hanseatic League had a depot and privileges in London as early as the twelfth century and for a time they were the chief merchants of the port. Gradually English merchants took over more and more of the trade and in 1597 Elizabeth I expelled the Hansards from London. Foreign competition was also reduced through the destruction of the Spanish Armada, Spain's occupation of the southern Low Countries, the sack of Antwerp in 1576 and the capture of this city in 1585. Antwerp was the center of European trade until these disasters; now London became the commercial and financial metropolis of the world. Many interacting factors were responsible for this pre-eminence. Before the Industrial Revolution most of England's population was on the fertile land in the southeast where London had

The Tilbury Docks with the Floating Landing Stage in the foreground. These docks in contrast to the systems upstream are transit docks. (Port of London Authority)

a focal position, being the point farthest inland accessible to ocean vessels. It had a circular hinterland, an advantage enjoyed by few ports. The estuary of the Thames faced the Low Countries, the economic heartland of the Continent, with which England for centuries had strong commercial ties. London was the capital of an emerging world power which benefited from its location off the coast of Europe's heartland, so often troubled by warfare. After the great discoveries the North Sea—English Channel region was in the center of the land hemisphere—not on the periphery of the known world, as it had been in the earlier centuries.

From the sixteenth century onward the Thames played an increasingly important role in the expansion of the city. Coastal shipping was vital at a time when roads were few and notoriously bad. The ebb and flow of the tide helped vessels in and out of the port independent of wind direction; it helped to scour the channel and prevent silting. But the Thames was not only a local highway of a capital city; it was the home port of most of the great trading monopolies of Elizabethan times, which laid the foundations of commerce on Russia's Arctic coast (1555), in the Baltic (1579), in the Levant (1581), in the East Indies (1600), in Virginia (1606) and in Hudson Bay (1670). Until the middle of the nineteenth century the fully armed ships of the East India Company

179

were the largest vessels using the port. All ships were moored in the river, almost all below London Bridge which was the great obstruction to upstream traffic. A large number of lighters, a typical feature of London's port from early days, carried the cargo to the many specialized quays that lined the river.

Wool, wine, timber, salt, hay, etc., all had their appropriate quays, many of them west of the bridge. In the eighteenth century London handled 70–80 per cent of England's imports and 55–75 per cent of her exports by value. All other ports in England were referred to as 'outports'. The congestion in the river became extremely serious with the increased coastal and foreign trade. The annual receipts of coal, to take the bulkiest cargo, increased from 380,000 tons in 1726–32 to 720,000 tons in 1796, brought by 4,000 colliers.[1] Often 90 of these colliers would be discharged simultaneously, each unloading into a dozen barges. Thus about 1,100 craft would be laden with coal at one time. Under the disorganized conditions in the river plundering and smuggling assumed huge proportions.

A Parliamentary Committee was set up in 1796 and it reported in favor of the construction of enclosed dock-basins equipped with warehouses. Such docks were no novelty; it was possible to point to successful examples at Liverpool and Le Havre. Even London had two small docks, originally built for repair and outfitting and often used as 'parking places' for ships, but they had no warehouses. The vast land areas needed for docks could be acquired cheaply away from the river frontage. Few of the land areas chosen for dock excavations were used for anything but pasture.[2] The marshlands along the river, about 2 miles wide at Gravesend and even 4 miles at Woolwich, were unhealthy because of the dampness. Malaria occurred in the estuary marshes until late in the nineteenth century.

The West India Docks, opened in 1802, were granted a 21-year monopoly to deal with all ships in the port arriving from and departing to the West Indies. These docks, enlarged and modernized, still retain connections with the West Indies, receiving large quantities of sugar, citrus fruits, bananas, rum and hardwoods. In addition come bananas from the Canary Islands and hardwoods from West Africa. The West India Docks are the center of London's hardwood trade.

In 1805 the London Docks were opened and in 1828 the adjoining St. Katharine Docks. These docks are closer to the City than their cousins farther downstream but they are much smaller. The London Docks were granted the monopoly of the tobacco, rice, wine, and brandy traffic (with the exception of products from the East and West Indies). The link with the wine trade still remains. The lock entrances restrict the trade of the docks in the system to barges and small vessels in coastwise and continental trade. In their warehouses are stored casks of wine and spirits from every liquor producing land. Here are also stored the wool cargoes of the port, which chiefly arrive at the Royal Docks. Though far from Leeds and Bradford London is the chief wool port of the country; its wool auctions used to completely dominate the world market. However, improved shipping services between the wool-producing and the wool-consuming countries have contributed to the decline in London's wool turnover during this century. There was for instance a considerable saving in freight rates on the Australia–Japan route when London was by-passed. After the Second World War the United States emerged as a major wool importer and similar considerations applied to the American wool imports. The auctions in the wool-producing countries have

[1] L. Rodwell Jones, *The Geography of the London River*. London, 1931.
[2] James Bird, *The Geography of the Port of London*. London, 1957. P. 45. This section on the port of London draws heavily on this illuminating little book and on the work by Henry Rees, *British Ports and Shipping*. London, 1958.

taken over more and more of the wool trade. In 1960 Liverpool, much closer to the textile mills, accounted for somewhat larger wool imports than London.

The chief characteristics of the London and St. Katharine Docks are the wide range of warehouse accomodation available; half the cargoes arrive by barge, chiefly from the larger docks downstream.[3]

South of the river lie the Surrey Commercial Docks, consisting of twelve basins which are now connected, but which were constructed independently by four separate companies. In this dock system is the oldest dock in London, the Greenland Dock, which got its name in 1763 when it was the port of the whaling fleet. It was completed already in 1703 but has subsequently been enlarged and improved several times. The Greenland Dock handles general cargo but the other docks in the group are dominated by the softwood trade, trading chiefly with Scandinavia and the Soviet Union. Facing the Surrey Commercial Docks, on the north side of the river, is the small Regent's Canal Dock, the only dock not directly controlled by the Port of London Authority. It stems from the early nineteenth century and now trades with near Continental ports.

The East India Docks, opened in 1806, were constructed furthest downstream of the old docks. They used to consist of an Import and an Export Dock but the latter has been filled in and is now the site of a power station. The former is used mainly by coastal lines with regular services between London and other British ports.

The East India trade is today carried on by larger vessels which use the Royal Docks. These docks were built after steamers and railroads had become an indispensable part of the British transportation system. The Royal Docks therefore got much larger dimensions and

[3] The Rochdale Report (*op. cit.,* p. 179) recommends that these docks be filled in and the land used for other purposes.

better land connections than the older docks upstream. The Royal Victoria Dock was the first (1855), later joined by the Royal Albert Dock (1880) and the King George V Dock (1921). The three docks are linked by deepwater cuttings to form one huge dock, the world's largest, with about ten miles of quays. No less than 53 of the 117 deep-sea berths in the five docks systems of the Port of London are to be found here. No legal restrictions as to types of cargo to be handled were enforced on these docks but a natural differentiation has taken place, as in all large ports, motivated by the highly specialized types of handling facilities (including warehouses) required by many types of cargo. To mention a few examples: tobacco is stored in the upper stories of many warehouses on the north side of the Victoria Dock and the King George V Dock, grain cargoes are unloaded at four large flour mills on the south side of the Victoria Dock, chilled or frozen meat is loaded direct into refrigerated trucks or railroad cars but much is also temporarily kept in cold store of which the largest is in the north-east corner of the Albert Dock.

The Millwall Docks, which are now connected with the West India Docks to the north, were also built in the latter half of last century (1868). Since their early days the Millwall Docks have concentrated on the grain trade. They house the Central Granary, with a capacity of 24,000 tons, and other storage served by floating elevators as well as fixed installations.

The Tilbury Docks (1886), 45 kilometers from central London, were built by the East and West India Docks Company to meet competition from the Royal Albert Dock (1880), owned by the rival concern, the London and St. Katharine Docks Company. Due to the unfavorable site with deeper alluvium than in the other dock areas upstream construction costs were higher than expected and for a time the docks were a costly failure. The Tilbury

Docks were designed for rail transit and the dock company leased warehousing facilities in London. Even today there are no multi-storied warehouses at Tilbury. Such buildings would be expensive to erect on the spongy alluvium and in addition Tilbury is too far from the market to serve as a general storehouse. After World War II traffic at Tilbury has increased very much and most of the cargo to and from the port is now hauled by road. When the docks were opened there were no roads to London and railway traffic continued to dominate until 1939. Tilbury is well known as the passenger terminal of London. Passengers arriving in the port may be landed at the Floating Landing Stage, opened in 1930, where ships may come alongside at any state of the tide. Special boat trains meet the passenger liners at Tilbury.

The first serious crisis in the history of London's port, the congestion in the river at the end of the eighteenth century, was met by the construction of wet docks. The second crisis, which occurred at the beginning of this century when the river could not offer sufficient depth for vessels wishing to reach the port, was met by the setting up of the Port of London Authority (P.L.A.) in 1909. The five distinct dock systems, built by eight private dock companies, which at the beginning of the century had been amalgamated into three companies, were taken over by the P.L.A. In addition, the new organization was charged with the maintenance and efficiency of the river highway, which in the new situation meant the construction of deeper channels aligned to take advantage of the tidal scour. This had been too large a task for the private dock companies but was apparently in the interest of all in the port.

It should be remembered that the port of London has never been synonymous with its docks. In the year ending March 31, 1956, when London handled 54.8 million metric tons, 10.4 million tons were received in the docks and no less than 30.6 million tons in the river (chiefly by power-stations, gasworks, oil refineries, and other heavy manufacturing plants with their own wharves and jetties), 4.8 million tons were shipped from the docks and 4.9 million from the river, 2.6 million tons were transshipped in the docks and 1.5 million in the river. More than twice as much cargo was thus handled outside the docks as inside.[4] Cargoes are handled in the river from Hammersmith Bridge downstream to Canvey Island —a distance of about 65 kilometers. Large colliers of 800–1,000 N.R.T. with flat superstructure and collapsible funnels can negotiate the many low bridges across the Thames to the gasworks at Fulham and Wandsworth and the Fulham and Battersea power-stations. Even if this up-river traffic is large in volume most of the river cargo is handled below London Bridge. Heavy manufacturing plants line the river for a long distance. Modern construction techniques have made possible the erection of heavy buildings on marshland. To mention just a few of the most important traffic generators there is the world's largest gasworks at Beckton; the Ford Motor Works at Dagenham, integrated from blast furnace to assembly line like Ford's home plant at River Rouge, Detroit; the thermo-electric plants at Barking and Littlebrook on opposite sides of Barking Creek; the large cement works at Cliffe; and Britain's two largest newsprint mills at Northfleet.

The port installations on the lower Thames below Tilbury account for an increasing share of London's cargo turnover. In addition to the petroleum installations at Thames Haven, a new terminal on Canvey Island, opened in 1963, will receive about 700,000 tons of Saharan methane gas per annum. The gas is sent by pipeline from the re-gasification plant at Canvey to several gas consuming districts in-

[4] In the year ending March, 1961, the port handled 59.8 million metric tons, of which 42.7 million in the river and 17.1 in the docks.

cluding London, Manchester, Liverpool, Birmingham, and Sheffield. Two special vessels corresponding in size to 28,000-ton tankers, but costing more than twice as much to build, carry 12,000-ton loads of liquefied gas from Port Arzew in Algeria at the rate of one vessel per week. The gas originates in the Hassi R'Mel field. It is expected to reduce the price of gas in England by 25 per cent.

But river traffic has not been confined to bulk cargo. When the wet docks were planned they were opposed by the vested interests of the wharfingers (the owners of public wharves and warehouses along the river) and the owners of the river craft. A clause was inserted in every dock act granting free access to the docks for the large barge fleet and this free water concession was not omitted when the P.L.A. was incepted. The free water clause has permitted private wharfingers to compete with the dock companies and later with the P.L.A. London's large fleet of tugs (336 in 1961) and barges (6,340) have a larger transportation capacity than before the war.

Like most metropolitan ports London has a large excess of imports over exports both measured by tonnage and value. London's share of the total imports of the United Kingdom was somewhat higher in the mid-1950s than in 1913 and somewhat lower than in the interwar period. By value London handled almost twice as much imports as Liverpool, the second largest port. As a gateway for British exports London used to be second to Liverpool—by a wide margin before World War I and in the 1920s, by a narrow margin in the 1930s and immediately after World War II—but in the mid-1950s London's exports exceeded Liverpool's. The remarkable increase in London's share of British exports which is now almost equal to her share of British imports, reflects important changes in the economic geography of the United Kingdom. In the days when most industries were tied to the coal fields London was out of the way for

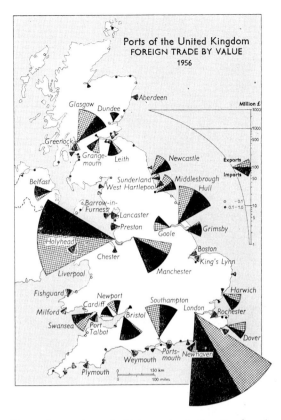

Data from *Annual Statement of the Trade of the United Kingdom,* 1955–57. Vol. IV: Supplement.

much of Britain's exports. Recent decades have seen the London region, dominated by light industries, expand more rapidly than other manufacturing areas in the United Kingdom, which naturally has favored the exports through the port of London.

With its frequent sailings to all destinations London has the United Kingdom as its hinterland for many commodities. Before the Industrial Revolution London's share of British foreign trade was much larger than now; in this century, however, London has kept its place among British ports and even strengthened it. Seen in a global perspective London, once the undisputed leader among the world's ports, has lost relative to New York, Rotterdam and Antwerp, which reflects Britain's decline in world trade relative to the United States and the European Common Market. If nationalist policies, which in the past have played an important role in the establishment of trade flows in northwestern Europe, are allowed less leeway, Rotterdam and Antwerp should in the future grow faster than London. The natural hinterland of these two ports has a population several times as large as that of Britain.

Liverpool and the Merseyside-Manchester Port Complex

The port of Liverpool here includes all docks on Merseyside under the administration of the Mersey Docks and Harbour Board plus the now state-owned Garston Docks and the private docks at Bromborough (Port Sunlight). The port of Manchester is the 55-kilometer Ship Canal, which stretches from Eastham on the western shore of the Mersey estuary ten kilometers from Birkenhead to the heart of the city of Manchester. The Canal is a port throughout its length but the main installations are at each end with the Manchester Docks almost in the center of the city and the Queen Elizabeth II Oil Dock at the seaward end, much closer to Liverpool than to Manchester. A large part of the petroleum traffic in this part of England until recently was concentrated in the Ship Canal which means that Manchester in recent years has handled a larger tonnage than Liverpool but measured by value Liverpool is by far the most important of the two ports.

The geographic location of these two ports suggests that they should be treated as one port complex although they are separately listed in official statistics and usually are seen as two ports by British geographers.

LIVERPOOL. Whereas London has been a great port for two thousand years the history of Liverpool as a leading port covers little more

than two hundred years. Two locational factors have worked in favor of Liverpool during that period. The port faces west, a great advantage when the trade with North America was expanding rapidly. This advantage, however, was not fully realized until after the construction of railroads which made Liverpool a gateway to North America both for passengers and high-value cargo, not only from Liverpool's immediate hinterland but from the whole of Britain and from other European countries. Liverpool was one of the leading emigrant ports in Europe. But the American trade alone cannot account for the dominance of the port of Liverpool, for other ports, like Bristol, shared the advantage of a position on the west coast and participated in the North American trade. The basic fact behind Liverpool's rapid rise was the tremendous industrial developments taking place during the last two centuries in areas which naturally would look to a point near present Liverpool as an outlet to the overseas markets.

A few miles east of Liverpool there is the Lancashire coal field. At about the same distance to the southeast occur the large salt deposits of the Cheshire plain which have been worked from pre-Roman times and have enabled Britain to become one of the world's leading salt producers. Both salt and coal have been shipped through the port of Liverpool in considerable quantities but they have been of even greater importance as the raw material base of large manufacturing industries which have used Liverpool as their port. The mid-Mersey region and the Cheshire salt field have the largest concentration of chemical industries in Britain.

In the first half of the eighteenth century when Liverpool's expansion began white salt was an important export item. It was sent to Newfoundland and traded for cod which was carried to the West Indies and exchanged for sugar and coffee or to the Mediterranean and traded for wine and fruit. So started the con-

nections with the Caribbean which have remained important in the trade of Liverpool. In the latter half of the eighteenth century Liverpool shipping was dominated by another trade triangle, the notorious slave-trade in which Bristol and Liverpool were the British participants. Cheap manufactured goods were traded in West Africa with local slave-traders or "kings" who made slave raids into the interior. The same ships loaded with negroes then sailed to the West Indies and returned to Liverpool with cargoes of molasses, tobacco and cotton.

The enterprising citizens of Liverpool completed the first British dock planned with warehouses in 1715 and by 1800, when dock building got under way in London, there were four docks in a row along the Mersey shore. In the new century port traffic in Liverpool

Liverpool's Alexandra and Gladstone Docks in the northern dock system, which together with the southern system serve most of the overseas trade. Closed docks stretch for more than 10 km along the right bank of the Mersey which has a tidal range of up to 31 feet. The older docks in the central system have been downgraded to handle coasters. (Mersey Docks and Harbour Board)

became more and more dominated by the expanding Lancashire cotton industry. The imports of raw cotton increased rapidly and Liverpool became Europe's leading cotton market. Besides raw cotton, grains soon ranked high in the list of imports and Liverpool became the leading British grain port and one of the world's largest milling centers. Cotton manufactures ranked as the leading export item by value. With the rapid growth of the Lancashire, Yorkshire and Midland manufacturing regions Liverpool's share of British exports expanded and became larger than that

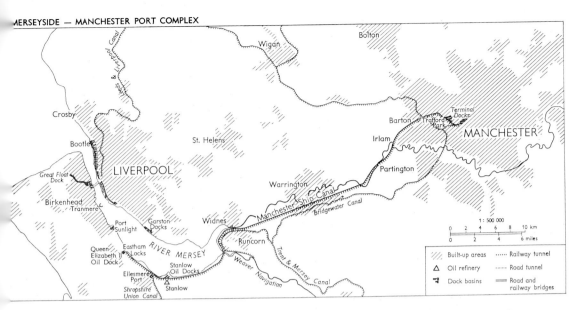

The Terminal Docks, Manchester's general cargo port, are dominated by the large No. 9 Dock with the grain elevator at the head. The seven other docks are much smaller. All berths are rail connected. (Manchester Ship Canal Company)

Since 1922 Stanlow on the Manchester Ship Canal has become one of the major centers of the petroleum industry in Britain. Pipelines under the Canal connect the docks to the right with the refineries and tank farms on the opposite bank. One tanker is berthed in the lay-bye adjacent to the tank farm. (Manchester Ship Canal Company)

Close-up view of the No. 9 Dock, looking towards the city center. The grain elevator at the head of the dock has a capacity of 40,000 tons. (Manchester Ship Canal Company)

The Queen Elizabeth II Dock, with four tankers discharging simultaneously, is Britain's largest oil dock. It is adjacent to Eastham Locks, which give access to the Manchester Ship Canal. (Manchester Ship Canal Company)

187

of London. Measured by value Liverpool was primarily a port of exports, London one of imports. London was a metropolitan port, Liverpool a port serving the British industrial heartland.

In the first half of last century port installations were also established on the other side of the Mersey at Birkenhead. The largest dock on Merseyside, the Great Float, was opened here in 1860. The early dock construction was carried out by private companies as in London, but Merseyside got a unifying authority for its port areas much earlier than London. The Mersey Docks and Harbour Board was set up in 1858. It now controls all docks on both sides of the river except the Garston docks which were built by a railroad company and are now nationalized and the private docks at Bromborough.

Liverpool or Merseyside for a long time has been second only to London among the British ports. It is one of the leading liner ports in the world. As a transoceanic passenger port it is surpassed only by Southampton.

Cotton has declined in importance in the traffic of Liverpool in recent decades. Still in the early 1920s textiles represented about half of Liverpool's export value; in 1960 more than 60 per cent consisted of cars and other vehicles, machinery, tools, chemicals and related products. This reflects the decline of the cotton industry in Lancashire as a result of lost markets, especially in tropical areas, where local cotton industries have been established in the last fifty years. Several of the former markets have become large exporters of cotton textiles, starting with Japan, followed by India, Hong Kong and Egypt. Raw cotton receipts have also declined and in 1956 cotton ranked ninth on the list by tonnage.

Leading traffic generators in the highly diversified trade of Merseyside are the iron and steel industry with an iron ore terminal in the Great Float, the coal tips at Garston which ship over a million tons of coal and coke a

year to Ireland, the Unilever Factories which dominate the industrial estate of Bromborough Port and the cattle-landing wharves of Birkenhead which receive large quantities of Irish cattle (about 22,000 head a month in 1956). The construction of a new oil terminal at Tranmere serving Shell's Stanlow refinery has suddenly changed the cargo turnover relations between Liverpool and Manchester. Liverpool's foreign petroleum imports rose from 0.5 million tons in 1959 to 6.4 million tons in 1961. The new terminal can accept 65,000-ton tankers whereas the Queen Elizabeth II Dock in the Manchester Ship Canal, completed in 1953, cannot take tankers much larger than 30,000 tons dwt.

MANCHESTER. The Manchester Ship Canal was opened in 1894. It is 28 feet deep, below Stanlow 30 feet, and provides more actual and potential industrial sites fronting a deep waterway independent of tides than any other port in Britain. Nowhere else in Britain is there such close connection between industry and shipping. The Manchester Ship Canal offers striking similarities in this respect with the waterways built to the oil ports on the American Gulf coast a few decades later. But it is not as deep as the ship canals of Texas and Louisiana and it is burdened by immense dredging costs. The cost of dredging per ton of cargo handled is higher at Manchester than at any other major British port.

Only two years after the opening of the canal a company developed an industrial estate close to the terminal docks, the first of its kind and still the largest in the country. Today 200 firms in Trafford Park employ about 50,000 people. Many use bulky raw materials and have a wharf fronting the Ship Canal. Half a mile nearer the terminal docks is the Irwell Park Wharf, the chief depot for bulk cargoes such as sulphur, iron ore, and phosphates. The approach to the terminal docks is lined with wharves and jetties of factories and storage depots. The Manchester Docks differ from those of most other British ports. They were planned as a group from the beginning. Only one has been added later.

Along the Ship Canal are other large ports. At Runcorn, where the canal has recently been spanned by a bridge, raw materials for the Potteries of Staffordshire have been received for the last 200 years. The Runcorn-Widnes area has become a center of chemical manufacturing. By the Weaver Navigation canal it is connected to the mid-Cheshire salt field and the chemical works of Northwich and Winsford. This small waterway carries a heavy traffic in coal, chemicals and salt and is used by coasters and barges up to a capacity of 400 gross tons.

Stanlow has one of the largest oil refineries in Britain and several oil depots. Nearby Ellesmere Port has a large granary, flour-mills, chemical industries, metal works and a coal quay. Between Ellesmere Port and Eastham Locks, the entrance to the Canal, is a large paper mill.

The port of Manchester or the Manchester Ship Canal has made great strides since 1894. In its first year it handled 926,000 tons and in 1900 three million tons. The pre-war peak of 5.8 million in 1913 was surpassed in the 1920s. In 1948 eight million tons of seaborne traffic was handled and each of the following years broke the record. No less than 18.6 million tons were accounted for in 1955. But in 1961 the cargo turnover had declined to 15.1 million tons as a result of Shell's transfer of its main importing terminal down the Mersey to Tranmere. Petroleum, crude and products, is still by far the leading item in the port. It heads the list of receipts as well as shipments, both foreign and coastwise. But for petroleum as well as almost all other cargoes Liverpool handles larger quantities than Manchester.

[1] In most other countries fish landings are not included in the port statistics.

The Humber Ports

The four Humber ports, Hull, Grimsby, Goole and Immingham Dock, have a location on England's east coast similar to Merseyside's and Manchester's on the west cost. The deepwater estuary of the Humber, collecting the waters of several river systems, is the natural outlet for the greater part of the Yorkshire, Derbyshire and Nottinghamshire coal field. The industrial complex on this coal field provides the Humber ports with a hinterland analogous to Liverpool's in Lancashire. But the Humber ports have not become national ports comparable with Merseyside. Hull normally ranks a poor third among British ports measured by value of goods handled.

Hull and Grimsby compete for the position as Britain's leading fishing port with Hull usually in the lead if measured by landed tonnage but with Grimsby leading if tallied by value. Although of great importance in the economy of the two cities and in port space requirements, fish accounts for only 2–3 per cent of the cargo handled in Hull and for 10 per cent in Grimsby (Immingham Dock excluded).[1]

Hull is a mediaeval port which has been able to adapt itself to modern conditions and retain its position among British ports through the centuries. It has the advantage of being close to the deepwater channel. Before it became a leading fishing port after 1850 Hull was for long recognized as the world center of whaling. Crews trained in whaling transferred to fishing vessels. Adaptation to a period of larger vessels started early in Hull. The first docks were built at the end of the eighteenth century and the beginning of the nineteenth century on the site of the old wall and moat. In the traffic of the modern port rapidly expanding receipts of petroleum products and declining shipments of coal are followed by receipts of grain and lumber. Hull is one of the leading milling centers in Britain and in the lumber trade it has long been second only to London.

It is the only British port which can be compared with London as a lighterage port. Barges operate on the Humber, the Ouse and the Trent.

Grimsby is the nearest port to the rich fishing grounds of the Dogger Bank. The mediaeval port stagnated as the result of silting and not until the end of the nineteenth century was there any serious attempt at harbor improvement. The docks were built about 1850. Grimsby's modern development was made possible by the construction of railroads. It has fast connections with all parts of Britain but especially with London and the South. Grimsby distributes fresh fish to some 3,000 railway stations throughout the country.[2] The installations for the handling of fish dominate the port but by tonnage more than half of the traffic is accounted for by coal from Nottinghamshire and south Yorkshire, especially the Doncaster area, carried by a fleet of colliers to the power stations in the London area. General trade is chiefly with Scandinavia and the Baltic countries, imports of lumber, pulp and dairy produce.

Immingham Dock, opened in 1912, was built by a railroad company to relieve growing congestion at Grimsby. It is located eight kilometers to the north and the two ports share a common labor pool; Immingham is a port without a town. At Immingham the deep channel comes close to the southern shore and large vessels may enter or leave at any state of the tide. The new dock was built to deal with the increasing coal exports which were expected to result from the expansion of mining in Nottinghamshire and south Yorkshire. The dock is clearly designed to deal with bulk cargoes. It handles twice as much coal as Grimsby. It has an iron ore wharf which receives imported ore and other raw materials for the growing iron and steel industry at Scunthorpe only 37 kilometers

away. Petroleum is unloaded at two deepwater jetties outside the dock itself.

Goole, the most inland of all British seaports, began in 1826 as the eastern terminus of an extensive canal system. It was built and owned—until nationalized—by the canal company. A depth of twenty feet is maintained in the docks of Goole, which means that small coasters and vessels in near-Continental trade handle the traffic, of which coal shipments account for five-sixths.

Bristol Channel Ports

BRISTOL. In the first centuries after the great discoveries Bristol was a miniature London. It became the port for the whole of the Severn basin and the West Country. Being a west-facing port Bristol developed a flourishing trade, first across the Irish Sea and later across the Atlantic. John Cabot, who discovered the coast of North America in 1497, was a naturalized Venetian of Genoese birth, who had settled in Bristol as a merchant. Although London had monopolized much of the trade with America, the merchants of Bristol were very active and competed with those of London. Bristol ranked as Britain's second port. It took a leading part in the slave trade with the West Indies even before Jamaica had been taken from Spain in 1655. The wealth accrued from the American trade and the slave trade made Bristol a prosperous city. To keep pace with the growing traffic a monumental harbor project was completed in 1809. The Avon was diverted to a more southerly course (the New Cut) and almost two miles of its old channel were sealed off by locks to form a single wet dock, the Floating Harbor, in the heart of the city. With increasing size of vessels the City Docks proved to be of insufficient depth and

[2] K. C. Edwards, "Grimsby and Immingham: A Port Study", *Preliminary Report of the Commission on Industrial Ports.* International Geographical Congress, Washington, 1952. P. 41.

at the end of the century deeper docks were built at the mouth of the river, 11 kilometers downstream from the city center. The greater part of the cargo is now dealt with at Avonmouth Docks. The great tidal range in the Severn estuary made it imperative to construct enclosed basins. Only the Bay of Fundy, Nova Scotia, has a greater range than Avonmouth.

During the Industrial Revolution and the era of railway construction Bristol declined in relative importance and Liverpool, much better located with respect to the new manufacturing regions, went far ahead. In recent decades, however, as a result of the rapid economic expansion of southern England, Bristol has improved its position among British ports.

Petroleum ranks first both in receipts and in shipments and represents nearly two-thirds of the total tonnage. Bristol has no refinery but it has become a distributing center for the West Country. With the expansion of Britain's refining capacity in the 1950s there was a sudden change from overseas imports to coastwise receipts. In 1949 ten times as much petroleum products came from overseas refineries as from British. By 1953 coastwise receipts had overtaken foreign traffic. The grain trade is second only to petroleum; before World War II grain was the leading cargo in the port. Almost a million tons of wheat, barley and corn are imported in a normal year.

The cargo list of Bristol is very diversified as befits a trading center with Bristol's traditions. Feedstuffs, fertilizers, pulp, lumber, metals (zinc, aluminum, steel), oilseeds, bananas, and tobacco account for sizable quantities. Bristol's overseas trade is extremely unbalanced. Its overseas exports are negligible. Shipments from the port are coastwise—mainly petroleum and grain.

THE SOUTH WALES PORTS. The peak production of the South Wales coal field was reached in

1913, when 57 million tons were raised and 39 million shipped mainly from Newport, Cardiff, Barry and Swansea. In 1938 about 20 million tons were sent out, but by 1954 production was down to 25 million and shipments to 7 million. In 1956 shipments had fallen still further to 6 million and in 1961 to 3 million tons. The ports of South Wales have suffered heavily from this decline since their docks were designed chiefly for the shipment of coal. The coal field contains all types of coal, from soft house-coal in the east, through steam, gas and coking coals in the central area, to anthracite in the west. Newport and Cardiff have been known for their almost smokeless steam coals, Swansea for its anthracite.

The modern coal traffic in South Wales did not start until the beginning of last century when the canals and their tributary tramways, and later the railways, made possible the transport of increasing quantities of coal from the mining valleys to the ports. Of special importance to the South Wales coal field was the gradual transition from sailing ships to steamers. Cardiff coal gained a reputation as the ideal bunker-coal. It was supplied to coaling stations on all the shipping routes of the world.[1]

In the postwar period the ports of South Wales have undergone a remarkable transformation. The British Transport Commission has made vigorous efforts to find new business to offset the decline in coal trade. Iron ore and petroleum now play a more important role in the port traffic than coal. However, the South Wales ports remain seriously underemployed.

Newport, the earliest of the coal ports, is in England but has always been closely linked with the South Wales coal field. Newport is the outlet for some large pits in Ebbw Vale and in one of its tributary valleys. Coal is still the dominant outward cargo, but inward bound iron ore accounts for similar quantities. This ore goes to the integrated steel mill in Ebbw

[1] Henry Rees, *British Ports and Shipping*. London, 1958. Pp. 176 ff.

Vale, which was sited at this controversial inland location in the 1930s, chiefly for social reasons. With the completion in 1962 of the same company's Spencer Works at Llanwern just outside Newport, iron ore will establish itself as the leading cargo handled in the port. With an initial capacity of 1.4 million tons this is one of the largest steel plants ever built on a green field site. Newport was chosen because it offers a deepwater anchorage which can take ore carriers of up to 24,000 tons and eventually, after harbor improvements which are now being considered, it should be able to take even larger vessels. Deepwater anchorages are one of Britain's scarcest industrial resources, but in addition other factors clearly favor Newport: an adequate supply of local coking coal, limestone and water, a population with a tradition of steel-making and, not the least, excellent rail communications with London and the Midlands, the two main home markets for thin sheet steel for automobiles and consumer durables.[2]

Newport to a certain degree competes with the Thames and the Mersey for the Midland traffic. The general cargo facilities of the port have recently been improved and it may in the future be in a better position to take advantage of its excellent location with regard to Britain's industrial heartland.

Coal shipments from Cardiff passed the 2-million-ton mark in 1860, rising steadily to about 10 million tons at the turn of the century and reaching a maximum of 26 million tons in 1913. Cardiff was then the greatest coal port in the world. By 1956 the coal traffic at Cardiff and Barry had shrunk to 2.4 million tons. The decline in coal traffic at the Cardiff docks, from 5 million tons in 1938 to 0.6 million tons in 1956, was to some extent offset by an increase in the imports of iron ore from 0.5 million tons to 1.0 million tons and by expansion in the petroleum traffic. Nevertheless, the total tonnage handled in 1956 was well below half that of 1938. At Barry the coal

situation is even more gloomy. Coal represented more than 90 per cent of the prewar traffic. In 1956 only about a third of the 1938 volume was handled. Through the efforts of the Transport Commission Barry has handled bananas since 1959.

Iron ore thus accounts for larger quantities than coal in the traffic of Cardiff. The iron and steel works in the dock estate, transferred from an inland location in 1930, provide an example of the recent tendency for the iron and steel industry to move to the coast, where imported ores may be unloaded at the works.

At Port Talbot iron ore accounts for two-thirds of the tonnage handled in the port. The large postwar expansion in the steel industry has more than compensated for the decrease in coal traffic and Port Talbot now handles a much larger tonnage than it did in 1938. Port Talbot is the home of the Steel Company of Wales formed in 1947, which has done much to achieve concentration in the world-famous tinplate industry of Wales. In 1945 there were over 300 handmills of the tinplate industry in operation in South Wales; in 1956 they had been reduced to 100, most of them in west South Wales and by the end of 1958 there were hardly any left.[3] The gradual closing of these mills had been expected since the construction of the Ebbw Vale works in 1938 and the installation of an electrolytic tinning line there in 1947. When the Steel Company of Wales built an 80-inch hot strip mill at Port Talbot and two cold-reduction and electrolytic tinning plants inland at Trostre and Velindre, the fate of the handmills was sealed. The siting of the two cold-reduction plants away from the strip mill is another example of a controversial decision on industrial location based on social rather than on economic factors. With an ingot capacity of 3 million

[2] J. E. Hartshorn, "Steelworks in the Making", *Steel Review* 23, 1961. Pp. 18 f.
[3] G. Manners, "The Tinplate and Steel Industries in West South Wales", *Geography,* 1959. Pp. 38 ff.

Angle Bay on Milford Haven, oil terminal of the British Petroleum Company, with two 35,000-ton tankers discharging crude for the Llandarcy refinery. (British Petroleum Company)

tons the iron and steel complex at Port Talbot is the largest steel works in Western Europe. The ore dock cannot take ships larger than 10,000 tons dwt. A major scheme for the construction of a new tidal harbor outside the existing dock is under consideration. This would allow the steelworks to benefit from the low freight rates made possible by large ore carriers.

Swansea, the most westerly of the old coal ports of South Wales, handles the greatest tonnage and its trade shows the greatest expansion since 1938. This port is chiefly associated with petroleum, anthracite and tinplate. The Swansea area got the first major oil refinery in Britain in 1922 at Llandarcy 10 kilometers northeast of the city. Swansea's prospects of becoming a major British oil port have been dimmed recently by the construction of a pipeline from Milford Haven to Llandarcy. Swansea is the chief outlet of anthracite, but these shipments have decreased

considerably compared with prewar quantities. The two new tinplate works at Trostre and Velindre are located northwest and north of Swansea, in an area where the South Wales tinplate industry has been located for almost a century. Virtually all British tinplate originates in South Wales. Until the 1880s Swansea was the chief copper smelting area in the world but this industry has migrated to the ore producing lands. Some production of copper plates and sheets remains in the region. Several of the copper smelting works were converted to the smelting of zinc and the Swansea area is one of the leading zinc smelting districts in Britain. In addition it has the largest nickel refinery in the country.

The potentialities of the great natural harbor of Milford Haven are just beginning to be

193

Sea Passenger Traffic at United Kingdom Ports and Traffic by Air[a]

Thousands of passenger movements

	1938	1956	1961
Total by sea	4716	5850	7063
Total by air	179	2979	7017
By sea:			
London	212	211	205
Southampton	380	458	472
Bristol	5	2	2
Liverpool	304	469	372
Glasgow	97	65	57
Tyne Ports	57	127	139
Hull	32	15	25
Dover	1117	1791	2794
Folkestone	535	564	840
Newhaven	383	365	340
Plymouth	29	25	8
Harwich	399	609	652
Holyhead	560	850	844
Fishguard	165	257	270
Other ports	442	42	43

[a] Excludes passengers to and from the Channel Islands, amounting to 254,000 by sea and 642,000 by air in 1960. Sea passengers used the ports of Southampton and Weymouth.

Source: *Board of Trade Journal.*

utilised. The waterway is a drowned outlet of several rivers with at least 60 feet of water everywhere, except for a small part of the entrance where there is 50 feet at low tide. The largest tankers can thus enter at any state of the tide. A large oil refinery has recently been completed by Esso on Milford Haven and an oil terminal has been built at Angle Bay for the pipeline carrying crude petroleum to the BP refinery at Llandarcy.

Passenger Ports

SOUTHAMPTON. Southampton is a major European passenger terminal. It handles more transoceanic passengers than any other port in Europe, catering for more than fifty per cent of all ocean-going travelers to and from the United Kingdom. It is the chief general port on the south coast of England, specializing in express goods and perishable cargo like fruits and vegetables, which require speed in handling and distribution. It is Britain's principal port for trade with South Africa. With the construction of the large oil refinery at Fawley in 1951 Southampton's traffic in petroleum has increased rapidly. It is also becoming a center of petrochemical manufacturing but on the whole Southampton's immediate hinterland has been of little significance to the modern port.

There has been a major seaport in the vicinity of Southampton since Roman times. After the Norman Conquest it became the port for Winchester, then capital of England. Southampton's great natural advantages and favorable location have been fully appreciated in modern times. The port is located on a sheltered estuary with the Isle of Wight acting as a natural breakwater at the entrance. The approaches to the docks are deep, but the advent of big ocean liners has made dredging necessary. The tide at Southampton has four remarkable characteristics: an unusually low range of only 13 feet, a pause on the rising tide, a double high tide, and a short ebb. It has not been possible to find a satisfactory explanation for this combination of phenomena but they are of great economic importance as they make closed docks unnecessary.

To the unique natural advantages of Southampton's sea approach should be added its favorable location both with respect to continental ports and with respect to its hinterland, especially London, for which Southampton acts as an outport. For the French ocean liners with their terminal at Le Havre it is not much of a detour to call at Southampton, nor is it for Dutch or German liners passing through the English Channel. For the British liners, having their terminal at Southampton, the French port of Cherbourg is not much off their route.

The development of the modern port coin-

cides with the period of railroad construction. The first dock was opened in 1842 and from 1892 the Southampton Docks were owned by a railway company until nationalized after World War II. From the start the Southampton Docks have been dealing with the world's largest liners.[1] Railroads and docks were by coincidence planned by the same engineers. The docks were laid out in such a way that passengers and express cargo to and from London and other inland points could be dealt with quickly and smoothly. In 1955 no less than 165,000 passenger movements were re-

[1] In the beginning the docks were used by the P & O Line and by the Royal Mail Line. In 1893 the American Line transferred their service from Liverpool to Southampton, followed by the White Star Line 1907 and the Cunard Line 1919. L. E. Tavener, "The Port of Southampton", *Economic Geography*, 1950. Pp. 260 ff.

General view of the port installations at Southampton with the Old Docks, forming a triangle, in the foreground. In addition to the river quays they comprise three large tidal basins (year of construction given in parenthesis): Ocean Dock (1911), Empress Dock (1890) and Outer Dock (1842). The Ocean Dock accomodates the largest liners on the North Atlantic route. Above the Old Docks on the picture are the New Docks, a straight line of 2.5 kilometers of deep-water quay, constructed after 1923. Behind the quays are over 1.6 square kilometers of reclaimed marshland. At the upper end is the King George V Graving Dock, which accomodates vessels of up to 100,000 tons.

Three of the world's four largest passenger liners are at berth simultaneously on the picture. The *Queen Elizabeth* is at the Ocean Terminal, the two-storied building completed in 1950 which occupies almost the entire length of the Ocean Dock near the center of the picture. The two giant liners at the New Docks are the *Queen Mary* (nearest) and the *United States*. (British Transport Commission)

corded for the traffic with the United States, 37,000 for Canada, 49,000 for South Africa, and 32,000 for Australia and New Zealand.

OTHER INTERNATIONAL PASSENGER PORTS. As a populous island separated by narrow seas from the heartland of north-west Europe Britain has developed an intensively used network of international sea routes and passenger ports. London and Paris, Europe's two largest metropolises, are located at a relatively short distance from each other on opposite sides of the English Channel. If artificial obstacles are not introduced the exchange of passengers and high value cargo should be very large between two neighboring cities of such magnitude. In the west the small Republic of Ireland is economically closely tied to Britain and the passenger traffic is very intense.

Dover's pre-eminence in the cross-channel passenger traffic has not been challenged since the Middle Ages.[2] The Dover area commands the shortest sea passage across the Channel and the site of the town is in the only break in the chalk cliffs which fringe the coast of Kent between Folkestone and Deal. Calais, Dover's continental counterpart since the late fourteenth century, remained an English possession until 1558. From 1227 Dover enjoyed a legal monopoly of passenger traffic across the Channel.

Today Dover has one of the largest artificial harbors in the world, constructed mainly for naval purposes. It is by far the busiest passenger port in Britain. Since 1936 a train-ferry service has been maintained between Dover and Dunkerque. Through-coaches run between London and Paris. The passenger train-ferry is normally a night service while during the daytime the same vessels are used to carry freight cars. In this way high value cargo is handled—fruit, vegetables, flowers and wine imported into the United Kingdom, and machinery and vehicles traveling in both directions.

International Sea Passenger Traffic by Ports 1961
Thousands of passenger movements

	To and from U. K.
European Continent:	
All Ports	5030
Southampton	143
Newhaven	340
Folkestone	840
Dover	2794
London	82
Harwich	653
Hull	25
Tyne Ports	139
Other Ports	14
Non-European Countries:	
All Ports	569
Glasgow	2
Liverpool	88
Bristol	2
Plymouth	8
Southampton	328
London	123
Other Ports	19
Republic of Ireland:	
All Ports	1464
Glasgow	56
Liverpool	284
Holyhead	844
Fishguard	270
Other Ports	10

Source: *Board of Trade Journal*, Vol. 183, August 1962.

In 1962 over a million tons of cargo passed through the port.

After World War II special auto ferries have been introduced linking Dover with Calais, Boulogne and Ostend. Before 1936 all cars shipped to the Continent were handled by crane; with the inauguration of the train-ferry a limited number of cars could be driven

[2] J. H. Andrews, "The Development of the Passenger Ports of South-East England", *Geography*, 1950. Pp. 239 ff.

196

aboard the ferry-boat. The auto ferry service has seen a remarkable expansion in recent years. In 1939 31,000 accompanied cars used the harbor and in 1956 no less than 190,000. In 1961 the number had risen to 373,000 and in 1962 to 440,000.

Out of at least ten other packet stations on the English side of the Channel two have survived to the present day but none of them has played a continuous part in the history of cross-channel passenger transport like Dover. The Folkestone to Boulogne service handles about twice as many passengers as the New-haven to Dieppe service which is farther down the English Channel and thus involves a much longer sea passage. Southampton, still further to the west, takes some part in the cross-channel passenger traffic with services to Le Havre, Cherbourg and St. Malo, but South-ampton is primarily a passenger port serving transoceanic passengers. It used to have pas-senger services to the Channel Islands, but these were concentrated at Weymouth in 1961. They involve longer distances than most of the cross-channel lines but are classified as do-mestic traffic. The total number of passengers using the docks at Southampton is less than one-fifth of the corresponding number at Dover. By number of passenger movements Dover is followed by Holyhead—the dominat-ing passenger port in the traffic with the Re-public of Ireland—Folkestone, and Harwich—with services to Hoek van Holland, Esbjerg and Zeebrugge.

The North-East Coast

Coal mining, steel making, shipbuilding and engineering—these four interrelated industries have decided the pattern of traffic in the ports of the North-East Coast.[1] The Northumber-land-Durham coal field, worked since mediae-val times, and the ironstone bands on the

[1] James Bird, *The Major Seaports of the United Kingdom*. London, 1963. Pp. 37 ff.

flanks of the Cleveland Hills, discovered about a century ago, were the raw materials upon which this heavy manufacturing district was based. It has outgrown this local source of ore but the coal production is sufficient for the largest coal shipments in Britain, now almost entirely coastwise. Five ports or groups of ports can be distinguished: Blyth, a specialised port shipping only coal; Newcastle (Tyneside), Britain's leading coal shipping area, which has a sizeable import of iron ore and petroleum products; Sunderland, also a coal port; the Hartlepools; and Middlesbrough (Tees-side), Britain's leading importer of iron ore.

The development of the Tyne, which by nature is not well endowed to serve modern shipping, has been closely associated with the expansion of the coal trade. The shipment of "sea-cole" to London had become well de-veloped by the fourteenth century, and this traffic led to the establishment of a ship-building industry at both ends of the sea route. The yards on the Tyne and in the other ports of the North-East Coast survived the introduc-tion of the new construction material steel and from the latter half of last century have provided a large local market for the rapidly growing steel industry. Coal shipments from the Tyne reached their maximum just before and after the First World War. In 1923 the Tyne shipped 22 million metric tons of coal of which 18 million was to foreign destinations. The coastwise traffic continues and has after World War II reached record figures but total shipments have declined to less than one-third of the 1923 quantities.

The Tyne is lined with manufacturing towns and port installations from Blaydon to the sea. The Iron Ore Quay can take 35,000-ton ore-carriers. In addition to coal, iron ore and petroleum products, Tyneside handles grain, lumber, cement, pit props and a long list of other cargoes destined for the large manu-facturing region. This has its focus in New-castle, which serves as a general port also for

Tees-side. Newcastle even has international passenger services (Bergen and Esbjerg).

Until 1953 iron ore for the steel mill at Consett was the chief import at Sunderland but this traffic has passed to Tyneside, where modern facilities for reception, storage and despatch of the ore have been constructed. The Consett steel mill is located on the coal field 38 kilometers from the new ore port. Sunderland still handles the scrap that is imported for the steel mill.

While Tyneside has concentrated on coal and shipbuilding, Tees-side has specialized in steel and chemicals. For some decades south Tees-side has been providing about one-fifth of the national output of steel. Much of this is consumed by the engineering, shipbuilding, and mining industries of the North-East Coast but large quantities are supplied to other parts of Britain or exported. As the Cleveland ore field nears exhaustion the dependence on foreign ore has increased. Ore production has fallen below 600,000 tons since 1956, compared with over 6 million tons per annum for thirty years before 1914.[2] Large quantities of fertilizers are produced as by-products of the intergrated steel mills. Chemical industries on a yet larger scale are represented by two plants of the Imperial Chemical Industries. One owes its origin to a government project in the First World War for the manufacture of synthetic nitrogen compounds on the basis of local coal and brine at Billingham opposite Middlesbrough. The second unit, built in the post-war period at Wilton south of the Tees, also lies on the salt field. It is concerned with the electrolysis of brine but its major activity is in the new field of petrochemicals. Although ranking far behind the steel industry as a traffic generator in the port the chemical industry accounts for sizeable quantities of imported raw materials and exported products.

Four new deep water berths for dry cargo vessels were completed at the end of 1962 at the Lackenby Dock near the mouth of the river on the south bank. These deep water facilities for general cargo at Teesport are the only ones started in Britain since the 1930s. There is scope for further development if trade justifies it.

Glasgow

The Clyde is no natural waterway although it has been the world's busiest shipbuilding river most of the time since ships of iron or steel were introduced. Like the Tyne, the Clyde below Glasgow is almost as artificial as the Suez Canal.[3] When the growth of industry and commerce at the end of the eighteenth century made it desirable to construct a deep waterway to Glasgow, a plan was drawn up for a series of locks to overcome the waterfalls and rapids in the river. But this was rejected in favor of constructions, which by narrowing the river increased its scour. In addition rocky barriers were blasted away and the river dredged. In this way the bed of the river has been lowered at least 24 feet, and in places more than 30 feet. But a reasonable depth in the narrow river can only be maintained by constant dredging.[4]

Glasgow is the major port of Scotland and it primarily serves the industrial central lowlands. The average tidal range is only about 12 feet and all the docks with one exception at Greenock are open, tidal docks. Almost all available sites along the river are occupied by shipyards which has prevented any great development of other riverside industry. The steel works are the greatest generators of traffic in the port. Originally both coal and coal measure iron ore were available in the immediate vicinity of Glasgow. For some time in the 1830s and 1840s the ironworks on the Lanarkshire coal

[2] A. E. Smailes, *North England.* London, 1960. P. 220.

[3] Henry Rees, *British Ports and Shipping.* London, 1958. P. 203.

[4] Dredging at Glasgow costs a shilling for every ton of cargo handled in the port. *Rochdale Report, op. cit.* P. 195.

field formed the chief iron-producing region in Britain, the basis for the shipbuilding and heavy engineering industries in Glasgow. The present iron works southeast and east of Glasgow have a less favorable situation regarding raw materials. They receive all their iron ore and some coking coal through docks on the Clyde. As a result of the poor raw material base the Scottish steel industry has in recent decades relied much more heavily on scrap than has the United Kingdom as a whole. The Scottish steelmakers have encouraged the development of ship-breaking. With the recent development of integrated works the proportion of scrap to pig iron has decreased but is still higher than the United Kingdom average.

Greenock on the lower Clyde is a separate port beyond the jurisdiction of the Clyde Navigation Trust. It imports large quantities of sugar. Transatlantic passenger liners (Canada) call at Greenock and passengers are embarked or disembarked with the help of tenders.[5] A new graving dock, the largest in the United Kingdom, is scheduled to be in use by the mid-sixties. It will be able to take the largest ships envisaged and its chief users are expected to be tankers calling at the B.P. Finnart oil terminal, which is capable of accomodating the largest tankers.

Port Glasgow, founded as the port for Glasgow in 1662 when the Clyde was not navigable for ships further upstream, lost the reason for its existence when the river was deepened to central Glasgow. Like Greenock, its neighbor and one-time competitor, it has remained an important ship-building center.

Eastern Scotland

The east coast of Scotland has no single dominating port like Glasgow on the west coast but several sizable ports. The east coast north of the Firth of Forth is followed by a narrow stretch of rather densely populated lowland whereas the wet and high west coast north of the Firth of Clyde has a very low population density. The east coast ports have obvious geographic advantages in the trade with Nordic, Baltic and near-Continental countries whereas Glasgow is better situated for the American trade. This has played a great role in their historic development and in the division of labor between Glasgow and the other Scottish ports.

Grangemouth, commanding a similar position as Glasgow with regard to the all-important central lowlands, has grown rapidly both as a port and as an industrial area, but it is still small compared with Glasgow. It grew up at the eastern entrance of the Forth and Clyde Canal, completed in 1790, which in its heyday saw as many as 3,000 vessels per year pass through its 39 locks. Now this small waterway across the narrow waist of Scotland is little used. The canal and the docks at Grangemouth were purchased in the 1860s by a railway company that owned much of the Lanarkshire coal field and wanted an east coast outlet for its Continental markets.[1] After the First World War Grangemouth was chosen as the location of a Scottish dye factory, which had become too crowded in its original location, and a refinery based on Scottish shale oil. These two plants have expanded considerably after the Second World War. Both have been incorporated into large British concerns, the refinery into the British Petroleum Company and the dyeworks into the Imperial Chemical Industries. A number of petrochemical factories have been attracted to Grangemouth by the oil refinery.

As the oil jetties at Grangemouth cannot accomodate vessels exceeding 14,000 tons it was necessary to find a new harbor for the super tankers of the postwar period. Finnart on Loch Long on the west coast of Scotland was chosen. Crude oil is pumped from there to

[5] Ian A. G. Kinniburgh, "Greenock: Growth and Change in the Harbours of the Town", *The Scottish Geographical Magazine*, 1960. Pp. 89 ff.

[1] David Semple, "The Growth of Grangemouth: A Note", *The Scottish Geographical Magazine*, 1958. Pp. 78 ff.

Finnart oil terminal, Loch Long, Scotland, with the 12,000-ton tanker *British Swordfish* at the jetty in the foreground and the 32,000-ton *British Glory* in the background. (British Petroleum Company)

the Grangemouth refinery through a 90-kilometer pipeline.

Located halfway between Glasgow and Edinburgh and within easy reach of all industrial Scotland by road and rail Grangemouth may well become the nucleus of a large industrial conurbation. The list of imports is headed by lumber, cement, iron ore and pulp and the export list by oil products, coal and coke, and iron and steel. Grangemouth has long been the chief Scottish lumber port.

Leith, the port of Edinburgh, is located within the city limits. It is a diversified port with large receipts of grain. With the completion of a road bridge across the Firth of Forth, parallel to the railway bridge, Leith's hinterland should be extended in the north. Close to Leith is the private port of Granton. Methil, on the northern shore of the Firth of Forth, is a coal port.

Dundee's economy is inextricably tied to the jute industry. The docks and wharves were built mainly for the jute traffic and 93 per cent of the United Kingdom's jute spindles are in the city. Dundee has a long tradition of textiles. First came the making of plaids from the wool of local sheep. The Union of the Parliaments in 1707 exposed this industry to competition from England with the result that there was a gradual shift to linen. A failure in the flax harvest led to experiments with the jute fiber in the 1830s. By chance it was discovered that if jute fibers were softened with whale oil they could be spun. From that time onward the jute and the whaling industries progressed hand in hand and Dundee became one of the leading whaling ports of Europe. Today more than 40 firms are engaged in the jute industry which employs 18,000 people or 20 per cent of Dundee's gainfully employed population. Jute accounts for one-fifth of the receipts by tonnage and for one-third of shipments in the port of Dundee. One cargo of raw jute per week arrives directly from the two loading ports, Chittagong and Chalna, both in East Pakistan. In addition to jute Dundee handles a long list of cargoes including flax from Belgium and the Soviet Union. The linen industry is still rather important.[2]

Aberdeen, Scotland's third city and first fishing port, has a central location on the east coast. Herrings from the North sea and Iceland form a large part of the Aberdeen landings. Fish from the northerly fishing grounds can be sent from Aberdeen by rail and arrive in London twenty hours earlier than if landed in Grimsby. This also means a quicker turn-round for the fishing vessel. Coal is by far the leading cargo handled at Aberdeen, both as receipts and shipments. Most of the inmoving coal moves out again in the form of bunkers for the fishing vessels and for coastal liners.

[2] Henry Rees, *op. cit.* Pp. 232 ff.

Irish Ports

Two ports are dominant in Ireland's external trade, Belfast in Northern Ireland and Dublin in the Republic. The greater part of Ireland's trade is with Great Britain across the Irish Sea and both these ports have the advantage of a position on the east coast. Industrialized Northern Ireland has about twice as much trade with the outside world as the agricultural Republic.[1] For more than a century there has been a large flow of coal from Great Britain to Ireland. In the 1950s the two Irelands were the chief recipients of British coal. In the opposite direction is the world's heaviest seaborne flow of live cattle and sheep. Passenger traffic between the two islands is considerable.

BELFAST. The concentration of Northern Ireland's population and economic activity in Belfast and its surroundings is striking. In 1960 two-thirds of Northern Ireland's seaborne tonnage passed through the Port of Belfast. And yet Belfast is the most artificial port in the United Kingdom. It has been carved out of the mudbanks of the Lagan River estuary. But Belfast's favorable geographic location on the east coast controlling the mouth of the river valley has made it the dominating port of Ulster in spite of an unfavorable site. The economy of the city is based on a few manufacturing industries, of which linen manufacturing is the most important in terms of employment followed by shipbuilding and airplane manufacturing.

The linen industry of the northeast was largely an eighteenth century growth, though its foundations were laid by Scottish pioneers who had settled there earlier and by various Huguenot refugees. A regular cargo service from Belfast to Liverpool was established in 1824 and the modern port began to take shape in the 1840s. Virtually the whole of the linen

[1] T. W. Freeman, *Ireland*. London, 1960. Pp. 208 and 224.

output is shipped through Belfast. The chief linen market, the United States, buys more than in prewar years. In the late 1950s handkerchiefs and other linen goods have been exported to Hong Kong where they are embroidered and then re-exported.

The crisis in the British shipbuilding industry in recent years has hit the large Harland and Wolff yard in Belfast hard. This shipyard, which came into production in 1863, has been topping world statistics of tonnage launched more than twenty times. It was one of the first large shipyards to be located away from a coastal steel producing region based on a coal field.

Coal accounts for one-third of total receipts in the port of Belfast. A fleet of colliers carry coal from South Wales, Merseyside, Preston, Ayr and Whitehaven. Grain and feedstuffs amount to almost one-fourth of the receipts, and petroleum products are handled in increasing quantities. Steel for the shipyards, lumber, building materials, fertilizers and flax for the linen industry (from Belgium and the Soviet Union) are received in sizable quantities. Total shipments amount only to one-sixth of total receipts. Leading shipments are potatoes and livestock. In 1961 Belfast shipped 271,000 head of cattle in roughly equal proportions to Liverpool, Glasgow and Heysham. In terms of value textiles head the list of shipments, accounting for twice as much as the second item, machinery.

Much of the cargo traffic between Belfast and the ports of Great Britain is handled by liners and ferries. Containers were used early on these routes. Specially designed vessels carry trucks and trailers according to the "roll-on-roll-off" principle, which further simplifies cargo handling in the terminals.

Work commenced in the beginning of 1962 on Northern Ireland's first oil refinery at Dufferin Dock at the entrance to the port of Belfast. The refinery is to have an initial capacity of 1.3 million tons per annum and is expected to start operation at the end of 1963. A jetty, dredged alongside to 37 feet, is being constructed.

DUBLIN. Dublin handles two-thirds of the Republic's imports by value and half of the exports. It is the focal point of the island's roads and railways, and of the canal system. The thousand year old city of Dublin has, however, had to create the modern port in the last two hundred years by confining the Liffey River between embankments to increase its scour and by dredging and carving out docks and basins. Receipts are dominated by petroleum products and coal; livestock and porter and stout from the famous Guinness brewery are the major shipments from the port. Three specially designed beer-carrying vessels serve Liverpool and Manchester with two sailings a week to each port. Shipments to Bristol and Glasgow form part of the general cargo traffic. The London region and eastern England are supplied from the large Guinness brewery in London. During 1956 more than a million live animals were shipped from the Republic and Northern Ireland: 785,000 cattle, 330,000 sheep, 23,000 horses, and 17,000 pigs. Belfast handles most of the pigs and sheep, Dublin the bulk of the cattle and horses.[2] In 1956 Birkenhead received 159,000 head of cattle from Dublin, Holyhead 127,000 and Glasgow 61,000. Only one-seventh of the cattle shipped from Dublin went to countries other than the United Kingdom, but a large proportion of the horses went to Belgium and the Netherlands.

Cork, a poor second among the ports of the Republic, comprises two distinct parts—the Lower Harbour, a commodious natural harbor where a large fleet can lie securely at anchor, and the Upper Harbour, an artificially created river port in the city proper. Through its location Cork has become a port-of-call for Atlantic shipping. Passengers and mail are embarked and disembarked by tender from transatlantic liners in the ocean approach to the Lower Harbour (Cobh).

Cork has almost all of the few large industries in the country not based on agriculture. To the steel mill, the Ford automobile factory, the Dunlop rubber plant and similar manufacturing plants working with imported raw materials was added the Republic's first oil refinery at Whitegate in 1959. A shipload of 36,000 tons of crude oil arrives at the Whitegate jetty every week and the refinery covers the requirements of the Republic for most petroleum products.[3] The withdrawal of the British naval dockyard from Cobh (Queenstown) was a serious economic loss to the region. The installations were acquired by a Dutch shipbuilding firm in 1959 and are now used for shipbuilding and repairs.

Drogheda on the east coast, comes third among the ports of the Republic.[4] Limerick, the largest west coast port, is fourth. In nearly all Irish ports coal ranks as the dominating cargo.

French and Iberian Ports on the Atlantic

The French ports on the English Channel have a more favorable location than those on the Bay of Biscay. They face Britain across a narrow sea and they are near the densely populated manufacturing regions of Western

[2] Henry Rees, British Ports and Shipping. London, 1958.
[3] Cork Harbour Commissioners, Year Book 1962. P. 26.
[4] During the year ending September 30, 1962, container service was opened at Drogheda. About 10,000 tons were shipped in each direction.

Europe which extend into France from Germany and Belgium; they lie on the nearest seaboard to the Paris metropolitan region and also near the great shipping routes through the English Channel. The main all-French traffic artery stretches from Le Havre, Rouen to Paris, Lyon and Marseille, leaving the Bay of Biscay ports in a dead corner of modern France. These ports have only a regional hinterland with a rather sparse, predominantly rural population and they cannot hope to derive much advantage from an economic integration of Europe, at least not in terms of transit traffic. The Channel ports and Marseille compete with each other and with the other ports serving the West European manufacturing belts and population clusters, primarily Antwerp and Rotterdam. Port authorities in Rouen, Le Havre and Dunkerque are much more concerned about developments in Antwerp, Rotterdam and Amsterdam than in Nantes or Bordeaux.

French North Sea and Channel Ports

The lower Seine has an interesting arrangement of ports. Paris, the hub of France's economic life, is located too far upstream to be a seaport. Instead this conurbation of seven million people is served by two ports, one, Rouen, located 106 kilometers from the mouth of the Seine and 120 kilometers from Paris; the other, Le Havre, situated on the north bank of the estuary. Theoretically the former should specialize in bulk cargo and the latter in passengers and high value cargo for which speed is a prime concern.

ROUEN was settled by the Romans but it was rather unimportant as a port, for most of the trade with Britain went through Boulogne. At Rouen the tide was strong enough to carry the vessels upstream from the Channel, which seems to have been the main reason for the choice of this site.[1] The Norman Conquest of Britain was the beginning of many centuries of active trade by the merchants of Rouen, especially after the Great Discoveries. In the peak period 1650–1750 Rouen ranked among the leading ports of Europe but the latter half of the eighteenth century saw a period of decline chiefly due to the increase in the size of vessels from less than 150 tons to as much as 500 tons, which meant that they were now unable to negotiate the approach to the port. In 1821 the port handled only 30,000 tons of cargo. Rouen was then chiefly a manufacturing town with textile mills and other industries located there during the heyday of its commerce. The local authorities (*Chambre de Commerce*) were concerned about the decline in the activity of the port, but it took about a century before the national government in 1846 made the decision to build dikes along the river and thus increase the tidal scour. The works were strikingly successful and depths in the lower Seine increased from 3.5 meters to 6.5 meters. A period of rapid expansion followed in the port of Rouen. Seaborne cargo increased from 0.5 million tons in 1869 to 5.6 million in 1913 and 8.3 million in 1923. Imports of coal, primarily from Great Britain, dominated, accounting for 6 to 7 million tons a year during the peak years of World War I. Receipts of wine in bulk from Algeria increased to 0.7 million tons in the 1930s and again in the 1950s. Other leading commodities are pulp, pulpwood and paper from the Baltic. Rouen is the leading paper producing center in France accounting for about 60 per cent of the French production of newsprint. Most of the vessels calling at Rouen, colliers from Britain and the Netherlands, ships carrying forest products from the Baltic and wine from Algeria, are engaged in short or medium runs and thus are of moderate size.

[1] Albert Demangeon, *Géographie économique et humaine de la France*. Paris, 1948. Pierre George and Pierre Randet, *La région parisienne*. Paris, 1959.

A project for increasing the depth of the Seine channel to allow vessels of eight meter draft to proceed to Rouen at any state of the tide was accepted by the French Parliament in 1932. Only preparatory works were carried out because of lack of pressure from the users of the port and because of the engineering difficulties encountered. The works were resumed in 1948 and now the situation had changed. The four petroleum refineries built between Rouen and Le Havre at Petit-Couronne (1928), Gravenchon (1933), Port-Jérôme (1934) and Gonfreville (1933) originally received crude oil by tanker at their own wharves but with the rapid increase in the size of tankers it became obvious that no program for deepening the Seine could make these refineries accessible for the largest vessels. The oil port of Le Havre was made the crude terminal for all four refineries. But the average size of dry cargo vessels had also increased and for the future development of the port of Rouen, in competition with the port of Le Havre, it became necessary to resume the original plan passed in 1932 for the deepening of the river channel. The new technique of experimenting on a laboratory working model made it possible to find an economic solution to the complicated engineering problems in the Seine estuary. A smoothly curved channel between two converging dikes, partly cut out of the alluvial plain between Berville and Honfleur, was opened to traffic in 1960. Increased tidal scour and dredging makes the channel deep enough to allow vessels of 27-foot draft to reach Rouen at any state of the tide. Vessels of 30–35 feet can proceed to Rouen at high tide.[2] Ore vessels and other bulk carriers can thus reach this industrial port located almost halfway to Paris.

The Seine is the only all-French inland waterway of any importance. It has a cargo traffic of about 10 million tons a year, most of which is handled at Rouen. Shipments by barge from Rouen reached a peak during World War I with 5.5 million tons, almost all of which was coal. In 1961 the corresponding figure was 3.7 million tons or about the same as in the late 1950s. Coal made up only 6 per cent[3] and petroleum products now accounted for 68 per cent. For the first time, except for a few years immediately after World War II, shipments by rail have somewhat exceeded river shipments since 1957. Receipts by barge have increased steadily at Rouen and in 1961 amounted to 2.2 million tons.[4] In addition 1.8 million tons passed Rouen en route from Le Havre and 0.6 million tons on its way to Le Havre. Paris is thus connected with its two outports by river, rail, highway and pipe line. The latter, a ten inch product line from Le Havre completed in 1953, is connected with the four refineries. A second pipeline between Le Havre and Paris is under construction.

LE HAVRE was founded as a naval port in the early sixteenth century and it retained its military functions until 1801 when it was succeeded by Cherbourg. It remained a small commercial port until the mid-nineteenth century. The period 1850–1913 saw a rapid expansion of the port traffic; the cargo turnover increased tenfold. It was 4.4 million tons in 1913 and 4.9 million as an average for 1929–1936.

Two factors favored the growth of Le Havre: the increase in the average size of vessels and the growing importance of liner traffic. Depths of sixteen to seventeen meters are found in a trough near the coast at Le Havre and since about 1880 it has been possible to increase the depth of the entrance channel with the help

[2] *La mer remonte à Rouen: le nouveau chenal dans l'estuaire de la Seine et son histoire.* La Chambre de Commerce et d'Industrie de Rouen. Rouen, 1961.

[3] From being one of the most specialized coal-receiving ports in the world at the time of World War I Rouen has become a diversified port in which coal accounts for less than 20 per cent of seaborne receipts.

[4] *Statistique du port de Rouen: Année 1961.* Direction du port de Rouen.

The Port of Rouen with the St-Gervais Basin in the foreground and the city center in the upper right corner. The near side of the basin handles fruit, especially bananas, and the far side is the chief wine port. The near bank of the river is lined with general cargo berths; the far bank and basin handle coal, timber, chemicals, etc. Before the war Rouen was the outport of Paris and received much more coal than any other French port (from Britain) and much more wine (from Algeria). In the postwar period the outport function has declined and Rouen's own industries generate more and more of the traffic. (Chambre de Commerce)

of large dredgers. Another favorable phenomenon at Le Havre is the prolonged high tide which gives vessels more time to enter or leave the port, just as at Southampton. In the beginning of this century the eleven wet docks of Le Havre with a depth of eight to nine meters proved to be insufficient for large passenger liners. A tidal basin covering 285 hectares, surrounded by enormous dikes, was constructed outside the wet docks (1909–1919). Facilities for the transatlantic passenger liners and for the ferry-steamers from Southampton were provided on the dockside of the *Bassin de Marée* and on the dikeside of the basin three petroleum basins have subsequently been added, the first one completed in 1925, and the third in 1955. Crude pipe lines run from this oil port to the four oil refineries along

the lower Seine and product lines to the large oil depots in the Paris agglomeration. The concentration of the seaborne petroleum receipts for the lower Seine refineries and the Paris region to Le Havre has swelled total cargo traffic and made Le Havre the second

205

Le Havre, looking east with the Seine estuary in the upper right corner and the Tancarville Canal connecting the city docks with the Seine. Plans for the future expansion of the port include new tidal basins towards the Seine estuary and a large industrial area on filled land on the seaward side of the new basins. A terminal for the receipt of liquefied gases will be completed in the oil port in 1964 and later part of the oil port will be deepened to receive tankers of up to 200,000 tons. (Port Autonome du Havre)

largest port in France after Marseille. Seaborne cargo turnover increased from 9.9 million tons in 1950 to 16.1 million in 1956 and 20.1 million in 1961.

Besides being the second largest oil port in France, and the leading transatlantic passenger terminal, Le Havre is second only to Marseille as a cargo liner port. There are several commodity exchanges in Le Havre: cotton, pepper, wool, copper, cocoa, etc. For these products and several others Le Havre is the chief gateway to the French market. For some products, like coffee, the port has some entrepôt trade.

In order to protect the Seine barges from the dangers of the estuary the Tancarville Canal was constructed in 1887. It leads direct to the docks at Le Havre. The canal handled 3.8 million tons in 1961, almost exclusively petroleum products.

DUNKERQUE, the chief city of maritime Flanders, was long contested by France, England and Spain before being finally attached to France in 1662.[5] It has an excellent geographic location on the North Sea approach to the English channel, and at the seaward extension of the manufacturing belt along France's northern border.[6] Seen in a wider, European perspective, Dunkerque has, however, one

[5] Raymond Guitonneau, "Dunkerque, grand port français des régions industrielles du Nord et de l'Est". *Revue de la Navigation Intérieure et Rhénane*. No. 11, June 1961. Pp. 465 ff. A concise discussion of past, present and expected cargo traffic in Dunkerque by the Director of the port.

[6] For a superb cartographic picture of Dunkerque and other European port cities in their relation to interior centers of population, see W. William-Olsson, *Economic Map of Europe*, Stockholm, 1952.

The Lower Seine

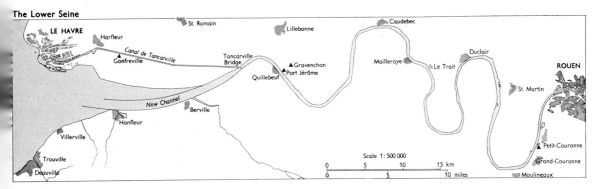

great drawback; it is in the traffic shadow of continental Europe's leading liner port, Antwerp. The competition between Antwerp and Dunkerque has been a leading theme throughout most of Dunkerque's history. In recent decades it has been especially keen for steel exports from northern France. Much of this has been funneled through Dunkerque thanks to favorable railway rates and to the monopoly for French vessels to carry cargo to French colonies.[7] But most of the seaborne French steel exports have been shipped through foreign ports, primarily Antwerp. This port, which ships more steel than any other port in the world, in the middle 1950s accounted for about twice as much of the French steel shipments as Dunkerque. In both ports steel products made up more than half of the general cargo shipments. Dunkerque's claim to the epithet "the French steel port" will be strengthened with the opening, in 1962, of the first stage of the large Usinor steel mill, which is expected to have an ingot capacity of 5–6 million tons a year 1970–75. It is located in the extended port area of Dunkerque and will have a capacity of 1.5 million tons in 1963. This steel mill will be one of the largest in Europe. It is another example of the world-wide tendency of locating new steel capacity at deepwater ports in areas of high market potential.

[7] Except Morocco and the Cameroons. See Alain Odouard, *Dunkerque et la compétition Dunkerque-Anvers.* Roubaix, 1958.

The new ore wharves in the port of Dunkerque can receive two 60,000 ton ore carriers simultaneously.

The cargo traffic of Dunkerque is diversified with the petroleum industry as the leading traffic generator but also with large imports of phosphates, vegetable oils, wool (almost the whole French imports), and wine and with exports of cement, sugar, and grains in addition to the leading steel products. Dunkerque's imports and exports of dry cargo are almost balanced. With the new steel mill and with expansion plans for the petroleum refinery Dunkerque's cargo traffic should at least double in the 1960s.

Dunkerque has been at a disadvantage compared to the major Dutch and Belgian ports as it lacks waterway connections of modern dimensions with its hinterland. The completion in the mid-1960s of the modernized canal from Valenciennes with an extension north to Lille, which is designed for 1,350-ton barges and replaces the obsolete system taking barges of only 280 tons, should improve Dunkerque's competitive position as a major North Sea port.

Dunkerque handles a large car-ferry traffic with Dover, but as a passenger port it comes far behind nearby Calais and Boulogne which have long been competing for the second place after Marseille among French passenger ports. The ferry also carries considerable quantities of cargo (*primeurs,* cars, etc.).

207

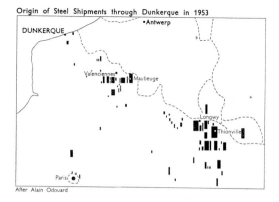

Origin of Steel Shipments through Dunkerque in 1953

After Alain Odouard

Metals (chiefly steel) is the leading outgoing commodity group through the port of Dunkerque, accounting for 300–600 thousand tons per annum in the period 1925–1940 and 700–900 thousand tons in the 1950s.

French Steel Exports through Dunkerque and Antwerp in 1953

Thousand tons

| Ports | French Steel Districts | | | |
	Est	*Nord*	Other Basins	Total
Dunkerque	521.0	233.3	33.2	787.5
Antwerp	1054.5	390.0	—	1444.5
received by:				
Rhine	482.5	—	—	482.5
Canal	125.0	133.0	—	258.0
Railroad	447.0	257.0	—	704.0

Source: Alain Odouard, *op. cit.*, p. 85.

OTHER CHANNEL PORTS. Calais, commanding the shortest sea-route to England, is primarily a ferry port. It was an English base on the continent between 1347 and 1558. In contrast to Dunkerque, where most of the port installations are in the form of wet docks for cargo vessels, the most vital part of the port of Calais is its *avant-port* where the fast channel ferries in shuttle traffic with Dover can enter or leave at any time of the day. There is also a wet dock for the cargo vessels and, as at Dunkerque, this is linked to the canal system.

Boulogne played a role as a cross-channel port before Calais. It is a harbor on a rocky coast whereas Calais and Dunkerque are on a dune coast. The Romans built a fortress at Boulogne and several roads converged on this center of Roman commerce and passenger traffic with Britain. In the mediaeval period Boulogne was surpassed by Calais in the traffic between England and Flanders. Boulogne then lived primarily from its fisheries. Today Boulogne is France's leading fish landing port, with fast freight service to the large urban centers, especially Paris; it is also a passenger port with cross-channel traffic, particularly with Folkestone, but also with some transatlantic traffic by Dutch and German liners. Thus as the emphasis is on express traffic tidal quays account for the largest part of the port installations. A local iron works generates most of the cargo traffic, receiving manganese and iron ore.

Dieppe is another port on the Channel coast which has played a leading role in the past, particularly during the sixteenth century, and has adapted its port installations for modern cross-channel traffic. Since World War I it has been the leading French banana port and it is second only to Marseille in the import of citrus fruit.

Since the turn of the century Caen has been the shipping port for the iron ore deposits of Basse-Normandie. From 1916 a steelworks at Caen has been using local iron ore. The first item in the shipments of the port is steel products, in which Caen rivals Dunkerque. Receipts are dominated by coal.

France's only naval port on the English Channel, Cherbourg, has only a small cargo turnover in spite of its excellent port installations created since the end of the eighteenth century. Cherbourg's immediate hinterland generates little seaborne traffic and other ports are better located to serve the Paris region. As a port-of-call for foreign transatlantic passenger liners Cherbourg ranks high, however. The configuration of the English Channel makes it natural for liners en route to or from Southampton to call at Cherbourg and for those to or from Le Havre to call at Southampton.

French Atlantic Ports

BREST-LORIENT. Brest, the only sizeable port of Brittany, is a naval port, older than Cherbourg. The site was chosen because of its splendid harbor and Vauban's fortifications were commenced in 1683. The port and city are dominated by its military function. The cargo turnover is small and diversified, smaller than in prewar years when coal imports were more important.

In Lorient the commercial function preceded the military. The port was established by the *Compagnie des Indes orientales* (1666) and took its name after the company. Lorient experienced a period of prosperity in the eighteenth century with the East India trade and with the construction of warships for the Government. After the virtual disappearance of the French empire in India and the dissolution of the company in 1769 the government took over the port and carried on the building and repair of naval vessels. Lorient's importance is now almost wholly as a fishing port; much of the arsenal has been closed after the war and its activities transferred to Brest. A modern tidal fishing port was constructed at Kéroman in the 1920s and Lorient is now second only to Boulogne in the quantity of fish landed.

NANTES. In the Loire estuary the port arrangement of the lower Seine is repeated: Nantes is the old city like Rouen, situated fifty kilometers upstream from its outport Saint-Nazaire, even newer than Le Havre, being only a little more than a hundred years old.

[1] Albert Demangeon, *op. cit.* P. 608.

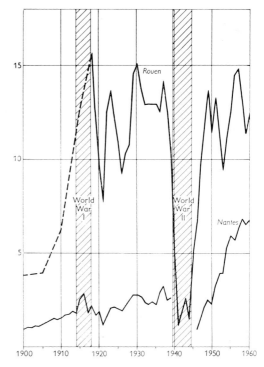

Maritime and fluvial cargo turnover in Rouen and Nantes. *Annexes* included.
Data from Max Canu, "Le Port de Rouen", *Transports*, 1959. P. 343; *Statistiques du Port de Nantes et Annexes*, 1960.

From Roman times Nantes was primarily a fortress guarding the entrance of the river Loire, which penetrates far into the heart of France. The river was used as a waterway in spite of serious physical handicaps, carrying a fleet of small barges. But barge traffic on the Loire was directed by the merchants of Orléans. After the great discoveries Nantes gradually played a greater role as a center of commerce and its golden age fell within the period 1720–1790 when its merchants took an active part in the slave triangle traffic. Nantes became a great entrepôt for cane sugar. Manufacturing industries processing imported colonial goods were established in the city, especially sugar refineries which were also built along the Loire all the way to Orléans.[1] But the loss of colonies, the devastation of war, the abolition of slavery, the expansion of sugar beet cultivation in northern France under government protection, the construction of railroads which successfully outstripped barge traffic on the Loire, and the insufficient depth in the Loire estuary for the ever larger sea vessels contributed to the stagnation of Nantes in the nineteenth century.

A solution to the problem of the shallow Loire estuary was sought in the construction of a wet dock near the mouth of the river at Saint-Nazaire in 1856. A second dock was opened in 1881. Almost from its beginning as an outport of Nantes, Saint-Nazaire was chosen as the terminal of a regular passenger line to the West Indies.[2] The shipping company was required to build at least half of its fleet in France. The company made an agreement with a Scottish firm to establish a shipyard at Saint-Nazaire. From this yard have come nearly all the great French liners and some of the most well-known warships. The shipyard and some ancillary industries are the mainstay of Saint-Nazaire's economy. But the outport never took over the functions of Nantes as a regional center of trade and shipping and it remains a small port. Just as in the case of Rouen the traffic of Nantes was saved by the creation of a deeper river.[3]

The city has become an important manufacturing center. Downstream several industrial towns, Basse-Indre, Couëron, Paimboeuf and Donges, form the *annexes* of Nantes. The *annexes* handle more cargo than the city port. The refinery at Donges generates most of the traffic.

LA ROCHELLE–LA PALLICE. Like Nantes and Bordeaux the old port city of La Rochelle reached a peak in the eighteenth century when it participated in the slave trade. The port comprises two parts, the old city port which got its first wet dock in 1808, and La Pallice, the *avant-port,* located 6 kilometers from the

city port, serving the larger vessels which can reach its tidal quay at any stage of the tide.

BORDEAUX is the fourth city of France after Paris, Marseille and Lyon. It is one of the oldest ports in the country, at one time the leading port of France. In Roman times Bordeaux was primarily the hub of an extensive road network, the market center of a viticultural region. But after 1152, when the Aquitaine Basin passed under English rule, the port became a vital part of the city. For three hundred years until 1453 the Bordeaux region could reach its capital, London, only by sea. Close and lasting commercial ties were established with England and other countries in northwestern Europe. The basis of trade was Bordeaux wine, or "claret" as it was known in England.[4] In 1717 Bordeaux was awarded the franchise for colonial trade with the West Indies, which marked the beginning of its second great period of prosperity. Bordeaux became the leading commercial center of France and one of the great ports of Europe. Some manufacturing and commercial industries concerned with "colonial" products (cane sugar, rum, coffee, etc.) which are important today originated then. For a variety of reasons, most of which had their roots in the changed population distribution within France caused by the Industrial Revolution, the autonomous port of Bordeaux[5] stagnated when such ports

[2] The *Compagnie Générale Transatlantique,* (the French Line), in 1861 created two transatlantic passenger and mail services: Le Havre–New York and Saint-Nazaire–West Indies.
[3] The river was deepened by four meters between 1900 and 1935. Vessels of eight meter draft can now proceed to Nantes at any stage of the tide. *Guide des ports de la Loire Maritime.* L'Union Maritime de la Basse-Loire, 1954.
[4] G. G. Weigend, "The Basis and Significance of Viticulture in Southwest France", *Annals of the Association of American Geographers,* 1954. Pp. 75–101.
G. G. Weigend, "Bordeaux: An Example of Changing Port Functions", *Geographical Review,* 1955. Pp. 217–243.
[5] There are three *ports autonomes* in France,

as Le Havre, Marseille, Rouen and Dunkerque rapidly increased their traffic. Today Bordeaux has relinquished its national functions to Marseille and Le Havre and has become a purely regional port. The principal shipments of the city port are forest products, cement and wine. Pit props and other forest products, chiefly from the Landes, have ranked high in the traffic of Bordeaux since the 1860s. The traffic in props, mainly to Britain, reached a peak of between 700 and 800 thousand tons before the British coal strike in 1926. In the postwar period shipments of forest products have been much smaller. The bulk of the import tonnage consists of raw materials for manufacturing plants in and near the port area. The next large industrial center inland, Toulouse, is situated where the hinterlands of Bordeaux, Marseille and Sète overlap.

An "inland" port in the center of an agricultural region and with no million-city in its immediate hinterland, located off the great shipping routes of the world, has little chance of becoming a great liner port. Outports are hardly a solution as they only offset one of the disadvantages. Bordeaux attempted to solve her problems with the construction of Pauillac-Trompeloup (1894), situated halfway between Bordeaux and the sea, and with Verdon (1933) at the mouth of the estuary. The *avant-port* of Verdon consisted of a liner pier with a 42-foot approach channel (at low water), linked to Bordeaux by means of an electrified railway.[6] The liner pier and other facilities were

destroyed by the Germans during the occupation and so far have not been reconstructed.

According to the general plan of refineries under the legislation of 1928 two refineries on the Gironde estuary should serve southwestern France. These two refineries and about half a dozen riverside oil-depots maintained by other oil companies now create most of the shipping activity in the *port autonome* of Bordeaux.

The Iberian Atlantic Coast

The Atlantic coast of the Iberian Peninsula holds a prominent position in the history of world shipping. The northern Atlantic seaboard of the two Iberian countries early had close contacts with the world's economic center round the North Sea and with the Newfoundland fishing grounds while ports on the southern Atlantic coast, Sevilla and Cádiz in Spain and Lagos and Lisboa in Portugal, had a monopoly of colonial trade. The wool of the Meseta was shipped through the Basque ports of Bilbao and Santander on its way to the Flemish weavers. A large number of iron ore deposits and dense forests providing charcoal early gave rise to a Basque iron industry which had a market in Britain. In Portugal British merchants took an active part in the development of the port wine industry. With the development of modern manufacturing from the end of last century the old commercial ties, particularly with Britain, were again strengthened.

From the southern Atlantic ports sailed the great discoverers who in a few decades around 1500 mapped much of the coastline of the unknown continents. For a long period the trade route from Sevilla[1] to the Caribbean carried more cargo than other transatlantic routes. But as time went on Spain's and Portugal's colonial empires shrank in size and their claim to the monopoly of trade with their remaining colonies became less and less of a reality. The

Bordeaux, Le Havre and the river port of Strasbourg. *Le port autonome* of Bordeaux includes the ports of the Gironde estuary. The other ports of France are under combined state and local administration. The local authorities (*Chambres de Commerce*) run the ports and contribute 50 per cent to the investments in the large ports and even more in the smaller ports.

[6] F. J. Monkhouse, *A Regional Geography of Western Europe*. London, 1959. P. 330.

[1] Sevilla held its monopoly of colonial trade until the middle of the eighteenth century when it was transferred to Cádiz. The abolishment of the monopoly in the 1770s gave all Spanish ports a chance to participate in this trade.

mother countries were small in population for the gigantic tasks. They were societies which placed land, the church, and crusading high on the list of values but put commerce and manual labor low.[2] Both Spain and Portugal have long held low rank among the European nations when measured by economic development and standards of living.

Spain

With much of her economic activity concentrated to widely separated zones near the coast of the peninsula coastal shipping (cabotage) has always been important in Spain. It accounted for about 60 per cent of the port traffic in 1959. But in the 1950s traffic in international trade was increasing much faster than cabotage in Spanish ports and with improved land transport trains and trucks will take over much cargo formerly carried by coasters.

In modern Spain the Cantabrian coast ranks with the Barcelona region as a dominating manufacturing area. Bilbao, which used to be the main outlet for the Spanish iron ore exports reaching their highest levels before the First World War with about 8 million tons a year,[3] has long been the dominating Spanish center for heavy manufacturing including iron and steel. Bilbao's port stretches for fifteen kilometers along the river estuary lined with factories, ore loading docks, coal receiving docks and shipyards. Bilbao receives more coal than any other Spanish port but this is now domestic coal. The trade in Basque iron ore in exchange for British coal, so important for Bilbao before the First World War, no longer exists. Bilbao surpasses Barcelona by a wide margin as a home port for Spanish vessels.

Pasajes is another important industrial port serving a small hinterland with many paper, textile and chemical plants. Santander has the best harbor on the north coast. In addition to local industries the port serves a wide hinterland in the interior of Spain.

The Asturian ports of Gijón, Avilés and San Esteban de Pravia, primarily serve Spain's leading coal district in the inland valleys of Oviedo province, which accounts for two-thirds of the national production. Productivity is low in the Spanish coal mines owing to unfavorable geological conditions and other factors: 725 kilograms per man-day,[4] which should be compared with 1100 kilograms in Belgium, lowest among the EEC-nations, and with 11,600 kilograms in the United States, highest in the world. In spite of this, total production has been increasing steadily and in recent years about five million tons per annum have been shipped coastwise through the Asturian coal ports. The collier fleet, about 100 larger vessels averaging 3000 tons and about the same number of smaller averaging 350 tons, is old and inefficient. More than half of the larger ships are more than 30 years old and as a rule their speed is less than 10 knots. It has been estimated that with efficient ports and modern vessels, a collier fleet of less than half the present deadweight tonnage might be able to handle the existing coal traffic.[5]

An old and inefficient iron and steel industry is located adjacent to the coal field with two mills outside Oviedo and one at Gijón. Together they accounted for 242,000 tons of pig iron (one-fourth of the national production) and 187,000 tons of steel ingots (14 per cent of production) in 1957. With the construction of a large, integrated steel mill at Avilés

[2] Herbert Heaton, *Economic History of Europe*. New York, 1948. P. 264.

[3] F. Cortada Reus, *Geografía Económica de España*. Barcelona, 1952. P. 242.

[4] Manuel Ferrer, "Asturias y el C. E. S. de Oviedo", *Geographica*, Vol. VII, 1960. Pp. 122 ff. Comments on a government report on the economic development in Asturias.

[5] *The Economic Development of Spain*. The International Bank for Reconstruction and Development. Baltimore, 1963. P. 238.

this situation has changed. In 1958, its first year of production, it accounted for 294,000 tons of steel, which was expected to increase to 1.39 million tons in 1962, on completion of the first stage of expansion, and eventually to 2.5 million tons. The steel mill will greatly influence the cargo traffic in the port of Avilés, which is already less dominated by coal than that of the other two ports.

Galicia has the prototype of a *ria*-coast and thus is favored with good harbors but it has a peripheral location within Spain and it has nothing that can compare with the large Cantabrian ports. Vigo and La Coruña are ports of call on international routes and the leading commercial ports in the region. Vigo in addition is the leading fishing port in Spain with many canneries. El Ferrol, the principal Spanish naval station, has little commercial traffic.

On the southern coast Huelva, with its large shipments of pyrites, copper and other minerals, accounts for the largest tonnages, but Sevilla, 110 kilometers from the sea, is the leading general port in this part of Spain. Main exports are wine, olives and cork. The port is accessible only for vessels of less than 21-foot draft. Cádiz in our time ranks low among Spanish ports in terms of tonnage. Near Cádiz is the American naval base Rota, which is also the sea terminal of the pipeline supplying the American air bases in Spain with fuel, pumped as far as Zaragoza, 780 kilometers away.

Portugal

The foreign trade of Portugal is dominated by the two large cities, Lisboa and Porto. Lisboa alone accounts for two-thirds of the imports and three-fifths of the exports by value. Leading exports to the world market are cork, canned sardines and wine and to the colonies manufactured products, primarily cotton fabrics. Lisboa's dominance in seaborne passenger traffic is even more striking than in freight traffic.

Lisboa on the estuary of the Tejo has one of the greatest harbors in Europe, an excellent site for a city that became the capital of a far-flung maritime empire and was, for some time, the leading entrepôt for colonial products in Europe. Two channels of about fifty feet cross the bar and the largest vessels can anchor in the river. Modern Lisboa, constructed on the ruins after the earthquake of 1755, is centered on the *Praça do Comercio,* a large square facing the Tejo. The close association of the business quarter and the waterfront is typical of the great trading capitals. The commercial and administrative function are most important in Lisboa but the city has also the largest concentration of manufacturing industries in Portugal. Barreiro on the other side of the Tejo is an industrial suburb. Setúbal, the third largest port in mainland Portugal, has a good harbor but is somewhat in the traffic shadow of Lisboa.

Porto is the economic focus of densely populated northern Portugal. The ancient castle Portucale, in a strategic location on the right bank of the Douro near its mouth, gave its name first to the region north of the river and later to the whole country. Porto and surrounding towns form one of the few manufacturing regions in the Iberian peninsula. Among other things cotton textiles are produced for Portugal and her colonies primarily from cotton grown in Portuguese Africa according to the pattern established by the European colonial powers last century. Porto is also the outlet for the wine district along the upper Douro. The wine firms have their warehouses on the left bank of the river in Vila Nova de Gaia. The wine is known in the world market as port wine. The wine trade was developed by British merchants in the second half of the seventeenth century and the Methuen Treaty of 1703, which gave Portuguese wines preferential treatment over French on the British market, consolidated this export.[1] The port wine industry has always been strictly regulated. The wine is made from grapes grown within a small area favored by geology, topography and climate. The wine barrels are transported by river boat—and now also by railroad—down to Porto.

A sand bar prevents vessels of more than 2000 tons from entering the Douro which has led to the construction of an artificial harbor at Leixões near Matozinhos. Porto-Leixões is the second largest port on the Portuguese mainland. The urbanized área of Porto includes both Leixões and Matozinhos. The latter is Portugal's leading fishing port with many sardine canneries.

The small ports of Algarve have some liner traffic which is attracted by the canneries, treating sardines at Olhão and Portimão and tuna at Vila Real. This province accounts for about one-third of the Portuguese cannery output. Lagos, famous in the history of Portugal as the harbor from which sailed most of the caravels sent out by Henry the Navigator, remained an important city even after Lisboa had taken over the role as the departure point for overseas expeditions. It was completely destroyed in the earthquake of 1755, from which it never recovered. Today it is a small town whose port is even unable to accomodate the large fishing boats which use nearby Portimão as their base.[2] The leading shipments from Vila Real are pyrites transported down the river by barge.

[1] Jorge Dias, *Minho, Trás-os-Montes, Haut-Douro.* Lisbon, 1949. Pp. 93 ff.
[2] Mariano Feio, *Le Bas Alentejo et l'Algarve.* Lisbon, 1949. Pp. 158 ff.

THE MEDITERRANEAN

The relative decline of the Mediterranean world from the position it once held and which is implied in its name has long been a matter of speculation. All essential economic indices show appreciably lower values for this area than for Northwestern Europe and Anglo-America. In many Mediterranean regions the living standards are even below those of the Soviet Union and Japan and the growth rate of the economy is much lower.

The discovery of new continents proved the North Sea to be the geographic center of the land hemisphere and after the impetus in exploration and colonization had passed from Spain and Portugal, the North Sea lowlands became commercial empires whose power and influence extended to all corners of the earth. The Industrial Revolution reinforced this pattern; the North Sea region was singularly well endowed by nature to become the technological cradle of the new world.

The Mediterranean, which had been a political unit in Antiquity, became a battlefield between the Christian world and the Mohammedan world. After centuries of brilliant history the Mohammedan world stagnated and seemed incapable of assimilating new ideas and techniques.[1] The economic development was particularly unfavorable in the Balkans, Asia Minor and North Africa, the areas where Mohammedan domination had persisted the longest. The Barbary pirates for long periods paralyzed maritime commerce.

The Suez Canal again turned the Mediterranean into a major through-route on the maritime map of the world, but it had only a limited influence on the economic development in the Mediterranean lands. The fabulous postwar expansion of the oil industry in regions bordering on the Mediterranean, the Middle East, northern Africa and the Soviet Union, has swelled the commodity flow through this sea until now it surpasses that of the North Atlantic in tonnage. Favorably located Mediterranean ports, like Marseille and Genova, will soon again rank among the leading ports of the world.

Mediterranean Europe

Spanish Mediterranean Ports

Barcelona was a great trade center in the late Middle Ages, shipping linen cloth all over the Mediterranean. But the discovery of America did not favor the city which declined in importance. From the beginning of the eighteenth century Barcelona was allowed to trade with the Antilles and in 1778 the monopoly of Cádiz was abolished. With the introduction of a modern textile industry based on cotton a new boom period was started, which made Barcelona the largest city on the Mediter-

---

[1] Pierre Birot and Jean Dresch, *La Méditerranée et le Moyen-Orient*. Tome Premier. Paris, 1953. P. 89.

ranean. After cotton followed mechanical and chemical industries but the Catalonian industrial complex centered on Barcelona works almost exclusively for the domestic and colonial market. Barcelona's relative importance was greater in the 1920s when it was the largest city in Spain. The cargo turnover in the port of Barcelona was somewhat larger in 1925 than in 1956, which is unique among the large ports of the world. About 70 kilometers northwest of Barcelona are the Spanish potash deposits. The other main Catalonian port, Tarragona, is primarily an outlet for the exports from the Ebro Valley. It serves as the port city of Reus, the commercial center of that region. Both Reus and Tarragona are located a long distance to the north of the Ebro delta.

Valencia is the leading port of Spain's largest irrigated fruit region stretching approximately from Gandía to Castellón. More than four-fifths of the oranges, the leading Spanish export by value, are grown in the irrigation districts or *huertas* of this region. The Spanish orange exports, which were about 25,000 tons a year in the 1850s and 100,000 tons in the 1880s, increased rapidly from the early 1890s and, after a setback during the First World War, reached one million tons in 1930.[1] After a long period of decline during the Civil War and the Second World War the exported quantities are again back at the level attained in the period 1925–35. Valencia, the third largest city in Spain and, since the Moorish period, a prosperous trade center of this rich agricultural area, has its port El Grao at the mouth of the Turia River five kilometers from the city center. The steel works at Sagunto helps to boost the cargo turnover of that port.

Alicante is the main port of a series of *huertas* of which the largest is centered on Murcia. The large cargo turnover of Cartagena is primarily derived from its large oil refinery, but it also ships minerals and fruit, like all

ports on this coast of Spain. It is the chief Spanish naval base on the Mediterranean.

Almería has exported large quantities of grapes since the end of last century.[2] A maximum was reached by 1907 when 2.5 million barrels (almost 60,000 tons) were shipped not only to the traditional markets in the United Kingdom (Liverpool and London) and Germany (Hamburg) but also to the United States (New York) especially after failures in the Californian grape crop. After a long break during the Civil War and World War II grapes from Almería have again appeared in their old markets in Europe but in the late 1950s this traditional Almería product met with increased competition from other Spanish vineyard districts. In recent years 20–25 thousand tons of grapes have been shipped through the port of Almería. Grapes rank first in value but only third in tonnage after iron ore and coal in the traffic of the port.

French Mediterranean Ports

The physical geography of France has destined the Rhône-Saône Valley to play a vital role in the European transportation network. It offers an easy route across the 'isthmus' of France between the Alps and the Massif Central connecting Mediterranean Europe with the Gallic, Germanic and Britannic worlds. But the great seaport controlling the trade of this valley is not located at the river mouth but about 50 kilometers to the east. The Rhône has been of limited importance as a waterway because of its irregular profile.[3] The heavy

---

[1] Cortada Reus, *op. cit.*, p. 168.

[2] Joaquín Bosque Maurel, "La Uva de Almería", *Geographica*, Vol. VII, 1960. Pp. 3 ff.

[3] About 1855 traffic on the Rhône amounted to 600,000 tons a year, exceeding that on the Rhine. With competition from the railroads the Rhône traffic declined to 200,000 tons in 1890 whereas traffic on the Rhine increased rapidly with the expansion of heavy industry in the Rhine Valley. By 1890 it already exceeded 8 million tons. In 1960 traffic on the natural waterway of the Rhine, penetrating almost 1,000 km

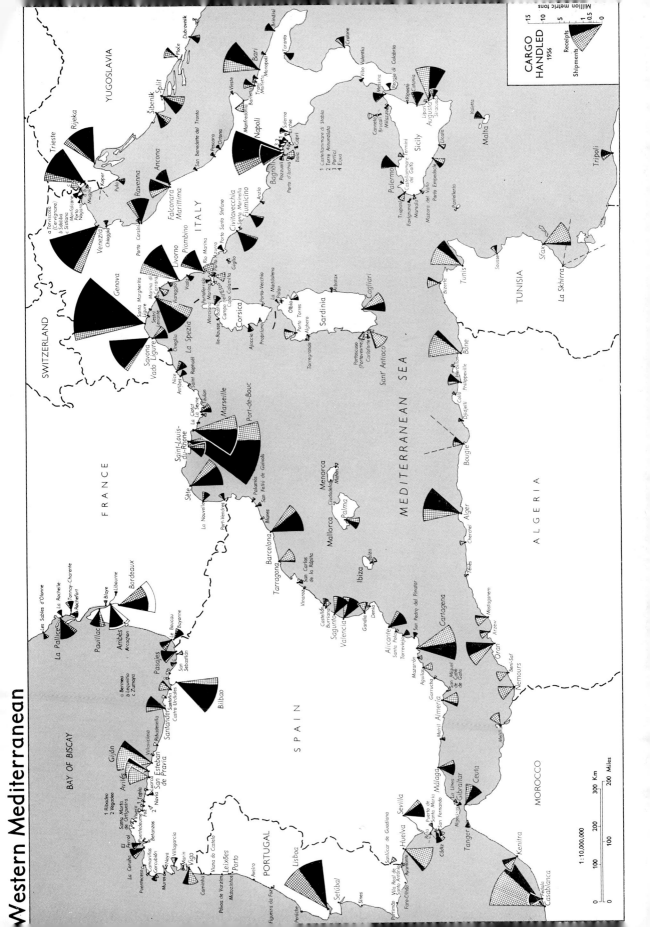

Western Mediterranean

YUGOSLAVIA

Dubrovnik
Ploče
Split
Šibenik
Rijeka
Trieste
Koper
Piran
Pula

Bari
Vieste
Trani
Molfetta
Monopoli
Barletta
Taranto
Brindisi

Manfredonia
San Benedetto del Tronto
Pescara
Ortona

Ancona
Ravenna
Falconara
Marittima

Venezia
a Torricella (Cervignano)
b Sdobba
c Sistiana
Monfalcone
Porto Nogaro
Chioggia
Porto Corsini

ITALY

Civitavecchia
Santa Marinella
Santa Severa
Porto Santo Stefano
Fiumicino
Anzio

Napoli
Pozzuoli
Torre Annunziata
Salerno
Torre del Greco
Baia Capri
Porto d'Ischia

1 Castellammare di Stabia
2 Torre Annunziata
3 Portici
4 Egua

Livorno
Piombino

Santa Margherita
Ligure
Marina di
Carrara
Viareggio
Marina di Pisa
Marciana Marina
Bagni
Campo nell'Elba
Rio Marina
Porto Azzurro
Giglio
Porto Santo Stefano
Giglio

Genova
Savona
Vado Ligure
La Spezia
Sestri Levante
Nervi
Oneglia
Nice
Antibes
Saint Raphaël
Toulon

SWITZERLAND

Corsica
Ile-Rousse
Ajaccio
Propriano
Bastia

Porto-Vecchio

Sardinia
Olbia
Porto Torres
Alghero
Cagliari
Arbatax
La Maddalena
Palau

Sant'Antioco
Carloforte
Portoscuso
(Portovesme)
Torregrande

FRANCE

Marseille
Port-de-Bouc
Saint-Louis-du-Rhône
La Ciotat
La Seyne
Sète

La Nouvelle
Port-Vendres
Biarritz

Menorca
Mahón
Ciudadela

Mallorca
Palma

MEDITERRANEAN SEA

Sicily
Palermo
Lipari
Milazzo
Messina
Catania
Augusta
Siracusa
Reggio di Calabria
Trapani
Marsala
Mazara del Vallo
Favignana
Porto Empedocle
Castellammare del Golfo
Licata
Pantelleria
Vibo Valentia
Crotone

Malta

Tripoli

Tunis
Bizerte
La Goulette

TUNISIA
Sfax
Sousse
La Skhirra

TUNISIA

Bône
La Calle
Herbillon
Philippeville
Collo
Djidjelli
Bougie

Alger
Cherchel
Tenès

ALGERIA

Oran
Arzew
Mostaganem
Beni-Saf
Nemours

Tarragona
Barcelona
Blanes
Palamós
San Feliú de Guíxols

Vinaroz
San Carlos de la Rápita
Castellón
Burriana
Sagunto
Valencia
Gandía
Denia

Ibiza

Alicante
Santa Pola
Torrevieja
San Pedro del Pinatar

Cartagena
Mazarrón
Aguilas
Garrucha
San Miguel
Cabo de Gata
Almería
Adra
Motril

SPAIN

Málaga
La Línea
Algeciras
San Fernando
Cádiz
Puerto de Santa María
Sanlúcar de Barrameda
Sevilla
Huelva
Ayamonte

Melilla
Ceuta
Gibraltar
Tanger

MOROCCO
Kenitra
Fedala
Casablanca

Les Sables d'Olonne
La Rochelle
Tonnay-Charente
Rochefort
La Pallice

BAY OF BISCAY

Pauillac
Blaye
Libourne
Bordeaux
Ambès
Arcachon
Le Boucau
Bayonne

a Bermeo
b Lequeitio
c Zumaya

Pasajes
San Sebastián
San Antón
San Esteban de Pravia
Santoña
Castro Urdiales
Santander
Requejada
Villaviciosa
Ribadesella

Bilbao

Gijón
Avilés

1 Ribadeo
2 Vegadeo

El Ferrol
Santa Marta
de Ortigueira
Cedeira
Pontedeume
Ares
Betanzos
La Coruña
Camariñas
Corcubión
Muros
Noya
Villagarcía
Carril
Marín
Pontevedra
Vigo
Bayona
La Guardia
Camiña

PORTUGAL
Viana do Castelo
Leixões
Porto
Aveiro
Figueira da Foz
Peniche
Lisboa
Setúbal
Sines

Vila Real de
Santo António
Faro-Olhão
Portimão

Sanlúcar de Guadiana

1:10,000,000

0   100   200   300 Km
0   100   200 Miles

silting in its delta closed such old ports as Arles and Aigues-Mortes.[4] It is thus not the Rhône river but the Rhône valley which is of interest for the European transportation map. This valley is the chief axis for long distance railroad and highway transportation in France and recently also a pipe line for crude petroleum was constructed here. The Rhône's limited importance is further illustrated by the following: in Marseille river transport contributes 0.3 per cent to the seaborne cargo turnover, at Le Havre 20 and at Rouen 62.

Marseille

Marseille, the oldest port serving western Europe, was founded by the Greeks in the year 600 B.C. and for five centuries *Massalia* dominated commerce in the western Mediterranean. The Romans, basing their empire on land rather than sea transport, built a road

Marseille, city and general cargo port. Note the finger piers stretching towards the breakwaters, which follow the coast line. The steep profile leaves little room for port construction by filling or by carving out basins. The entrance of the *Vieux-Port* can be seen in the upper right corner. (Cellard–CCIM)

through the heart of industrial Europe, amounted to 68 million tons (at the Dutch-German border), whereas traffic on the Rhône between Lyon and the sea was only 1.6 million tons, despite a sizeable increase in recent years.

Whereas barges of 3,000 tons can reach Duisburg on the Rhine and those of 2,000 tons can proceed all the way to Basel, the Rhône is navigable only for units of 280 tons and 350 tons throughout the year and for the larger international units of 1,350 tons for only 50 days a year. A large multi-purpose program for the Rhône, which accounts for almost one-forth of France's hydro-electric power potential, has been in operation since the 1920s. *Compagnie Nationale du Rhône*, in charge of this program, has completed several large dams and power plants in the river, but of the 12 locks between Lyon and the sea, which are included in the program and which will greatly improve navigation conditions, only four had been completed or were under construction in 1962.

Marseille on the Mediterranean and Rotterdam on the North Sea are the two gateways to the heart of Europe, one commanding the entrance of the Rhône-Saône Valley, the other the Rhine routeway. These two natural axes are gradually being united. Linked by road and rail, they were recently also connected by pipe line. The missing link in this trans-European trunk route is a waterway of modern standards, designed for barges of more than a thousand tons, connecting the Rhine with the upper Saône. Existing canals can only be used by vessels of less than 300 tons.

[4] Albert Demangeon, *Géographie économique et humaine de la France*. Paris, 1948. Pp. 638 ff.

Rhone Delta and Marseille Region

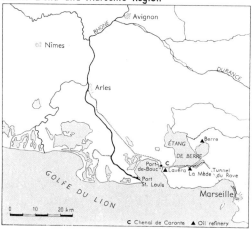

Annexes de Marseille. The oil port Lavéra (right) opposite Port-de-Bouc (left) at the entrance of Chenal de Caronte leading to Etang de Berre. Marseille is barely discernible in the upper right corner. (Cellard–CCIM)

Lavéra, the petroleum port built after the war in the *Annexes de Marseille* and now also the sea terminal of a pipeline to Strasbourg, Karlsruhe and Bavaria. (Cellard–CCIM)

219

Marseille, passenger liners on the North Africa route. (Rouard–CCIM)

through the Rhône Valley and made Arles the chief center of the region. During the invasions and the decline of the Roman Empire Arles was destroyed and Marseille gained in importance. In the following centuries up to modern times Marseille was a major center of trade, for long periods the leading entrepôt in the Mediterranean.

The modern period in Marseille started with the French conquest of Algeria in the 1830s and 40s; the establishment about 1840 of large-scale imports of peanuts and palm oil from West Africa for the soap and oil factories, which had old roots in the city; the construction of the Suez Canal 1859–1869, in which the Chambers of Commerce of Marseille and Lyon took an active part; and the development of a French colonial empire. Marseille's favorable location after railroads had been constructed made it the great colonial port both for cargo and passengers, normally handling almost 50 per cent of the colonial trade by value.

Together with the rapid increase of the volume of cargo and passengers went an expansion of port facilities. This, however, offered many problems as the city is hemmed in by hills and the depth of water increases rapidly seawards. One port basin after another was added along the coast north of the *Vieux-Port* but in the early part of this century it became obvious that the future expansion of space-demanding activities would have to take place at some distance from the city. Etang de Berre, the large body of salt water on the northern side of the Chaîne de l'Estaque— 6,000 hectares of a total 15,000 hectares having a natural depth of 8 meters—was a logical choice. It is surrounded by potential building land and connected with the sea by the Etang de Caronte. The decision to concentrate future space-demanding traffic in this area was made in 1919. In 1926 a canal was completed which connects the port basins of Marseille with the Etang de Berre and the Rhône. This canal goes in the 7-kilometer Rove Tunnel under the Chaîne de l'Estaque and its 4-meter depth allows traffic with barges of 1,500 tons.

An oil depot was completed at Lavéra in 1922 followed by a refinery in 1932. Two other oil companies built refineries at Berre (1931) and La Mède (1934).[1] A deep-water

[1] The San Remo Agreement in 1920 allotted 23.75 per cent of crude oil production in Iraq to France. Pipe lines from the Kirkuk field to the Levant coast were completed in 1934. A French law of 1928 made

channel was dredged in the Etang de Caronte, permitting large tankers to enter the Etang de Berre in 1932. After 1948 an oil port serving all three refineries by pipeline has been constructed at Lavéra opposite Port-de-Bouc at the entrance of the Chenal de Caronte.[2] It became impossible for each refinery to build out private facilities and long approaches to accomodate the ever larger tankers. The Lavéra oilport in 1962 also became the terminal of the 34-inch crude pipeline to new refineries at Strasbourg and Karlsruhe. A smaller line continues into Bavaria.

In 1961 the three Marseille refineries received 13.7 million tons of crude petroleum and shipped 5.4 million tons of refined products by tanker. Petroleum and petroleum products thus made up the bulk of the 26.4 million tons of cargo handled in Marseille and its *annexes* in 1961. This dominance will be even greater with the new pipeline on stream. Its initial flow will be 10 million tons with an expected increase to 25 million in 1965 and 30 million in 1970. The new pipeline will serve refineries that will not compete with those of the Etang de Berre region. Added to the rapidly increasing quantities handled by the Etang de Berre refineries these volumes will help to make Marseille and its *annexes* one of the largest ports in Europe measured by tonnage of cargo handled. The depth of the Port-de-Bouc entrance has been successively increased and in 1960 it was 13.25 meters permitting tankers of 39.5 foot draft to enter Lavéra. Tankers of about 60,000 tons thus can enter the port. In the future it will be possible for this maritime oilport to expand into the

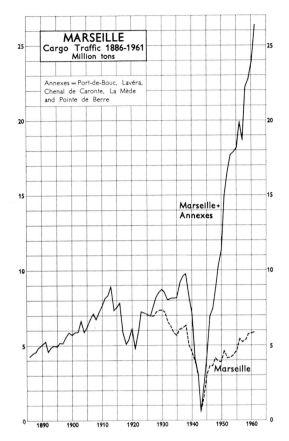

Data from Jean Couteaud, "Les Cinq Fonctions du Port de Marseille", *Transports,* No. 13, March, 1957. P. 112; *Trafic du Port de Marseille,* Principaux éléments statistiques, Années 1957, 1958, 1959, 1960, 1961. Chambre de Commerce de Marseille.

Golfe de Fos and thus make it possible to receive any size of tankers.

In the postwar period the oil refineries of the Etang de Berre have attracted a considerable petrochemical industry. Some preliminary investigations for a steel complex on the Golfe de Fos have been made. If this project and the plans for connecting the Rhône and Rhine waterways materialize a large bulk cargo port will develop on the Golfe de Fos proper.

In the city port the net tonnage of ships calling increased from 14.3 million tons in 1938 to 18.2 million in 1961 but the amount

it attractive for the international oil companies to build refineries on French territory. The lower Seine and the Etang de Berre area rapidly became the two dominating French refining centers in the early 1930s.

[2] Pierre Keller, "Le complexe pétrolier de Lavéra et de l'étang de Berre", *Transports,* January, 1957. Pp. 10 ff; Chambre de Commerce et d'Industrie de Marseille, "Le complexe pétrolier de Lavéra et de l'étang de Berre", *Note de Documentation,* No. 4. (Edition 1962: mimeographed.)

of cargo handled remained constant (5.8 million tons). The overseas passenger traffic increased from 24,000 in 1890, 566,000 in 1913, 830,000 in 1938 to 1,580,000 in 1961. The passenger routes to North Africa dominate but Marseille has regular sailings by French and foreign vessels to a large number of more distant destinations. Algeria alone accounted for 1,100,000 passengers in 1961, followed by Tunisia (79,000), Israel (44,000), Morocco (43,000) and Senegal (28,000). The entrepôt trade which used to be very important at various times in the history of the port is of little significance; the West European countries now have direct connections with the ports of the Levant. The port oriented industries which process imported raw materials (wheat, sugar, oilseed, phosphates, etc.) and ship out finished products, account for a large share in the diversified cargo turnover. The imports of vegetables and fruits, especially from North Africa, has been a rapidly growing trade in the postwar period. In 1951 Marseille got a fruit and vegetable exchange and it has become a gateway for North African *primeurs* not only for France but for much of western Europe.

In 1830, before the Industrial Revolution, Marseille was the leading port of Continental Europe but at the end of last century it was surpassed by three North Sea ports in turn: Hamburg in 1889, Antwerp in 1893, and Rotterdam in 1896.[3] These ports were closer to the manufacturing regions of continental Europe—to a large extent centered on the coal fields—and they had the advantage over Marseille of being served by a system of good inland waterways. The very rapid increase in cargo turnover, which now occurs at Marseille and which will probably bring Marseille and its *annexes* ahead of all continental ports but Rotterdam, is a result of the geological accident that Europe now is being supplied with petroleum from fields around the Mediterranean (the Middle East, the Sahara). Due to the shorter sea route Mediterranean oil can,

other things being equal, penetrate somewhat further into Europe from a Mediterranean port than from a North Sea port. Two of Marseille's chief functions may, however, rest on a rather shaky foundation: the passenger traffic to North Africa and the imports for the European market of *primeurs* from Algeria, Morocco and Tunisia. This traffic should increase rapidly with the economic integration of Europe and with rising standards of living, but both are prime targets for air competition.

OTHER MEDITERRANEAN PORTS. Most of the many small ports on the coast of Provence have a long history as seaports but their present importance is small. The pleasant winter climate of this coast, protected as it is from the *mistral*, has attracted a large number of foreign and French winter residents since the middle of last century and the old ports are now better known as fashionable resorts. Toulon is the chief French naval port and its commercial functions are completely overshadowed by its military. Bastia and Ajaccio are the largest cities and ports of Corsica.

The coast of Languedoc and Roussillon, between the Rhône delta and the Pyrenees, has no natural harbors. Deposits from the river have built up long, curved sand bars which block off lagoons or *étangs*. Sète, the only port of any consequence on this coast, is manmade. Very impressive works have been carried out during Sète's three hundred years of existence to make this the maritime trade center of Languedoc. The works include two canals, the Canal du Midi, which connects Sète with Toulouse, and another which leads to the Rhône at Beaucaire. Both have too small dimensions for modern barge traffic and play an insignificant role for the modern port. The fortunes of Sète have been closely associated with the wine trade. Before the ravages of the *phylloxera* in the 1880s it was the

[a] Demangeon, *op. cit.* P. 648.

great wine shipping port but the decline in French wine production led to large imports of wine from Spain, Italy and Algeria. Sète soon received much more wine than it had ever shipped. It has remained a leading port of entry for Algerian wines. The large volumes of cargo now handled at Sète are primarily associated with the petroleum refinery at Frontignan and with fertilizer and cement plants.

Port Vendres at the foot of the Pyrenees has a deep harbor but a limited cargo hinterland. It is the French port closest to North Africa and has regular passenger sailings to Algeria.

Italy

Ports and shipping have always been vital to Italy, a narrow peninsula where the relief has been an obstacle to land transportation.[1] Eighty per cent of Italy's foreign trade is handled by her ports in spite of a land border to her European neighbor countries; the mountain barrier of the Alps does not invite international bulk transport by rail.

The opening of the Suez Canal (1869), a few years after the unification of Italy (1861), turned the Mediterranean into the main route between Europe and the Orient. The new Italy was poor in raw materials for the developing industries, which were strongly concentrated

in the north, especially the regions centered on Milano and Torino. Coal imports increased from 0.25 million tons in 1861 to over 10 million in 1912 and 15 million just before World War II. Savona, Genova and Venezia were leading among the many coal ports.[2] The dependence on imported raw materials for the manufacturing industries[3] led to the development of industrial ports, although, due to the primacy of the Po Valley as an industrial region, this has not been so striking as in Japan with which Italy has many similarities. In addition to such old industrial ports as Portoferraio and Piombino, which became at the turn of the century centers of the iron and steel industry based on the Elba ore deposits, Italy got in the interwar period several specially designed industrial ports built to accomodate a variety of industries using bulk materials: oil refineries, chemical works, steel works, heavy engineering industries, etc. This development has continued at an accelerated tempo in the postwar period. Such industrial ports are often built on the periphery of large cities and are included in the port statistics of the old commercial port. Porto Marghera, established in the interwar period on a malaria-infested lagoon near Venezia, is one of the best examples. It helped to again make the old trading republic a major Italian port.

The development of port-oriented industries has not been concentrated to one or a few large ports but has been scattered along the coast, partly for physical reasons and partly as a result of a long-term policy. The Ligurian coast with a very high potential for this type of development has many industrial ports: Vado, Savona, Genova, La Spezia and Livorno; the mountainous coast does not invite a concentration of such space-demanding activities. The many large ports along the coasts of the economically underdeveloped South do not reflect a response to spontaneous transportation needs in this poor part of Italy but are a result of a government policy to develop the

---

[1] Giuseppe Barbieri, *I porti d'Italia.* Napoli, 1959. This volume, treating all the Italian ports, is the last in a long series of port studies published since 1936 by the Consiglio Nazionale delle ricerche. The opening volume by Ferdinando Milone on Napoli was a rewrite of an earlier volume published in 1927. Individual ports treated in this series are Napoli (F. Milone), Genova (G. Jaja), Trieste (G. Roletto), and Venezia (L. Candida). Regional studies cover Abruzzo and Puglia (U. Toschi), Marche and Emilia (G. Merlini), Sardegna (A. Mori and B. Spano), Toscana and Lazio (G. Barbieri), Riviere Liguri (L. Pedrini), and Campania, Calabria and Venezia (M. Bianchini, A. Pecora, and R. Albertini).

[2] Barbieri, *op. cit.* P. 66.

[3] In 1961 Italy imported 68 million tons of seaborne cargo and exported 12 million tons.

One of the two breakwaters, 4.5 and 5.5 kilometers long, which protect Genova's port and airport. The breakwaters are as a rule built at a depth of 15 to 20 meters. The airport has been laid out parellel to the coastline at a depth of 9–15 meters. On the landward side of the airport is the new petroleum port and the Ansaldo shipyards. (Consorzio Autonomo del Porto di Genova)

The circular harbor of Genova was the heart of the medieval maritime republic which had colonies and trading privileges from Spain to the Crimea and the Levant. The whole port with its permanent and temporary piers and its basins was confined to the *Porto Vecchio* Basin in the inner part of the present harbor. By 1905 the port of Genova was roughly what can be seen to the left of the 800 m pier covered by railroad tracks. Later the port has been extended 7 km to the west behind gigantic breakwaters. (Consorzio Autonomo del Porto di Genova)

Port and Airport of Genoa

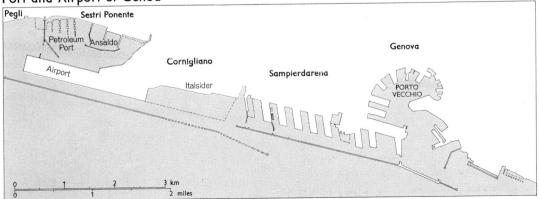

economy of the region. And this decentralization of cargo movements to many ports along the coasts of Italy is likely to continue in the future. Under the existing laws all state-owned industries in Italy, such as ENI (oil, gas, petrochemicals, fertilizers, rubber) and IRI (a tenth of the nation's industries, including shipbuilding and steel), must place forty per cent of their investments in the South.[4] IRI is building one of Europe's largest steelworks at Taranto, and ENI has put up a large petrochemical plant at Gela, Sicily, and is constructing another near Matera to exploit a vast deposit of natural gas. In addition new, large oil refineries will be built at Milazzo and Gela on Sicily and the capacity at Augusta will be more than doubled. Plans for two refineries in the five-million-ton class have been published for Sardinia. Italy is expected to have the largest oil refining capacity in Europe by the end of 1963.

Genova

Genova traditionally competes with Marseille for the position as the leading port in the Mediterranean. Both are pre-Roman ports and before the Industrial Revolution both were great maritime trade centers. Their hinterlands were of minor importance for their growth.

Modern Genova has a double function. After the construction of railroads in the middle of last century it became the logical port of the populous Po Valley and especially of the industrial triangle Milano–Torino–Bologna. As the Po Valley cities themselves are convergence points for important trans-Alpine routes Genova's hinterland extends beyond the national border. Genova has also become one of the leading manufacturing centers in the country.

But the physical geography has created serious problems for Genova. The Ligurian Appenines follow the coast and form an obstacle for transportation between Genova and its hinterland although there is a rather low

pass behind the city. Series of tunnels have been blasted through the mountains for three railroad lines and for a highway, the *auto-camionale,* built to accomodate the increasing truck traffic to and from the piers of Genova. The scale of railroad and truck traffic has been determined by the flow of cargo inland from the port, always much larger than the reverse outward flow. The mountains dive below the surface of the sea at a steep gradient leaving little flat land for port installations and industrial sites. Such land can be created only at tremendous cost. The engineering problems faced by the port constructors in Genova are diametrically opposed to those of Venezia, Genova's old competitor, and those of the North Sea ports, where sedimentation is the great problem and where the natural depth of the harbor was quite insufficient for a modern port. The expansion of the port of Genova has followed the coast westwards from the small notch in the even Ligurian coastline to which all port activities were confined until the beginning of this century. Man-made protection for this open port is provided by two tremendous breakwaters behind which finger piers have been built out from the coast. Genova has had no Etang de Berre for the development of heavy industries, but in spite of this its cargo turnover has kept pace with that of Marseille in recent years.

In Genova as in so many other large ports the rapid increase in port traffic after the war has been generated by petroleum and steel. In inbound bulk cargo there has been a striking substitution of petroleum for coal.[1] In 1961 no less than 9.5 million tons of petroleum were discharged at Genova. Almost two-thirds were piped to tank farms and refineries in the hinterland, 4.1 million tons to Val Polcevera

[4] Claire Sterling, "Transformation South of Rome", *The Reporter,* September 27, 1962. P. 34.
[1] Allan L. Rodgers, "The Port of Genova: External and Internal Relations", *Annals of the Association of American Geographers* 1958. Pp. 319–351.

near Genova and 2.1 million to Rho at Milano. When the pipeline now being built by the ENI from Genova to the refineries of Aigle (Switzerland) and Ingolstadt and Munich (Germany) has been completed, this quantity should increase substantially.

The bulk cargo pier of the Italsider steelworks at Cornigliano, completed in 1952, received 2.2 million tons in 1961 of which two-thirds were ore and one-third coal. At other piers large quantities of other materials, scrap, alloy metals, etc., were received for this steelworks.

Genova in 1961 accounted for 18.7 per cent of the cargo movement in Italian ports, followed by Napoli 10.8 per cent, Venezia 9.6 and Savona 5.0 per cent. Genova's transit trade is small, in recent years about 0.7 million tons of which 0.6 million was with Switzerland. Almost all of this is inward cargo, chiefly petroleum.[2]

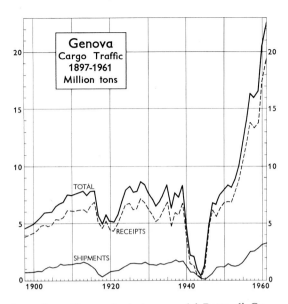

Data from Consorzio Autonomo del Porto di Genova; and Giuseppe Barbieri, *I Porti d'Italia*, Memorie di Geografia Economica, Vol. XX, Napoli, 1959. P. 229.

NAPOLI. Before the First World War Napoli was the great emigration port of Italy, followed by Genova. The two ports between them accounted for two-thirds of the Italian international passenger traffic by sea in 1913. Through Napoli went 377,000 passengers per annum 1911–13 and through Genova 255,000. The two ports at this time had a division of labor.[3] In Napoli the North American traffic accounted for four-fifths of the passengers and in Genova South and Central America accounted for almost two-thirds. Napoli and Genova have remained the leading passenger

ports but with a considerably smaller volume of traffic. Napoli has a favorable location, about halfway between Gibraltar and Port Said, and it is the port of call of many foreign passenger lines. In 1961 Napoli had 251,000 passengers in international traffic.[4]

Modern Napoli is an interesting example of an industrial port in the South. Total cargo turnover in the port oscillated between 2.1 and 3.2 million tons a year in the period 1923–1940, chiefly inmoving coal and grains. In the postwar period the cargo turnover increased rapidly from 1.6 million tons in 1948 to 13.3 million in 1961.[5] The industrial installations in the port account for most of the traffic, both of the imports and of the exports. In 1961 Napoli imported 4.1 million tons of crude petroleum (and 0.4 million tons of petroleum products) out of total imports amounting to 8.3 million tons. It exported 1.8 million tons of petroleum products out of total exports of 2.3 million tons. The steel industry was the second most important traffic

---

[2] Consorzio autonomo del porto di Genova, *Traffic in the Port of Genoa during 1961*. An unusually detailed account, which even lists Genova's trade relations by port, indicating the leading commodity or commodity type for each port.

[3] Ferdinando Milone, *Il Porto di Napoli*. Roma, 1936. Pp. 16 ff.

[4] North America 90,000, foreign ports in the Mediterranean 83,000, Central and South America 51,000, and Australia 19,000.

[5] Ente Autonomo del Porto di Napoli, *Il movimento del Porto di Napoli nel 1961*. This publication contains a detailed statistical analysis of the port traffic of Napoli.

generator with 1.3 million tons of iron ore imported; in addition it received most of the 1.1 million tons of coal unloaded in the port. On the export side more than 100,000 tons of steel products were exceeded by over 200,000 tons of fruits and vegetables, the most important exports based on the region's natural resources.

The direction of the petroleum exports from Napoli shifts much from year to year, but small countries in the Mediterranean and in Africa with insufficient or no refining capacity receive most of the exports. As all petroleum companies in the market do not have refineries in all the major ports there is also much cross-hauling of petroleum products between refinery ports.[6]

VENEZIA, for centuries the second largest port in Italy, remains a major port but has in recent years been overtaken by Napoli (including Bagnoli). The glorious maritime and commercial traditions of Venezia were the basis of the modern economic initiative which led to the creation of Porto Marghera which in 1926 accounted for 18 per cent of Venezia's total cargo turnover and in recent years for about three-quarters. Bulk cargoes, chiefly destined for the industries of Porto Marghera, make up 80 per cent of the receipts, petroleum alone for about half. In addition coal, ores and scrap, phosphates and grains are received in sizeable quantities. Total cargo turnover increased steadily, with interruptions for the two world wars, from half a million tons in 1880 to 10.9 million tons in 1961.

TRIESTE, as the only Austrian seaport and a natural outlet for Central Europe, grew rapidly from about 1800. The first parts of the modern port were built in the period 1867–83. The cargo turnover exceeded three million tons in the years before World War I, and Trieste was ahead of its Italian competitor Venezia. It was the major port of Austria–Hungary, a nation

of 52 million, with an expanding economy and good railroad connections with its port. The Vienna–Trieste railroad, completed in 1854, was the main rail artery between the Mediterranean and Central Europe. Trieste was a major European port in the trade with the Levant, Egypt and the Far East.

After the First World War and the disintegration of the Austro–Hungarian Empire Trieste, which had belonged to Austria since medieval times, was transferred to Italy and became the 'Trieste Problem'.[7] It was cut off from most of its hinterland by one or more national boundaries. It had an extremely eccentric location in Italy, which was already well served by ports. Genova and Venezia were firmly established as the ports of the densely populated Po Valley. Trieste's prewar cargo turnover was not again reached until 1938, and then the cargo structure was radically different with petroleum, coal, metals, construction materials, timber, grains and oil seed accounting for 90 per cent of the traffic. Trieste had, through the efforts of the Italian Government, become an industrial port but its commercial functions had contracted. After the Second World War Trieste's total cargo turnover has expanded and even exceeded five million tons but this is due to its growth as an industrial port. The high value commodities have continued to decline in quantity even compared with 1938. Coffee, one of the leading commodities by value in international trade and a prime indicator of ranking commercial ports, accounted for only 15,000 tons in 1957 as against 80,000 tons before the First World

---

[6] The exports from Napoli to Europe were 0.95 million tons in 1961 of which 0.81 million tons were petroleum products (Turkey 0.49 million, U.K. 0.10 and Greece 0.08 million tons). Asia received 0.47 million tons of which 0.40 million were petroleum products (Japan 0.14 million, Aden 0.10, Cyprus 0.07 and Lebanon 0.05) and Africa 0.60 million of which 0.53 million were petroleum products (Nigeria 0.15, Ghana 0.09, Guinea 0.06) and the Americas 0.28 million of which 0.10 million petroleum products (U.S. 0.09).

[7] Barbieri, *op. cit.* Pp. 260 ff.

War. The Iron Curtain has efficiently severed Trieste from large parts of its original hinterland for high-value cargo. But it still is the main port for Austria's seaborne trade.[8]

The Dalmatian Coast

The ports of the Dalmatian coast were for centuries protected by the natural barrier of the Dinaric Alps from the full force of the Turkish invasion and have retained a Latin urban life from the Roman period up to the present. But in modern times the same barrier has isolated the ports from the Danubian economic heartland of Yugoslavia. Except for its wine, bauxite and tourism the narrow Mediterranean fringe plays a subordinate role in the economy of the country.

Dubrovnik was in the sixteenth century one of the leading emporia in the Mediterranean, a semi-independent republic with a wealthy nobility of southern Slavs who had assimilated a Mediterranean way of life. It had a great merchant fleet. Now it is a small port connected by a narrow-gauge railroad with Sarajevo. Ploče is the outlet of the bauxite mines at Mostar. Šibenik and Split have a common standard gauge railroad to Zagreb and Danubian Yugoslavia and were in the interwar period the main domestic ports of the country. After the Second World War Rijeka, the former Italian Fiume, originally constructed to serve as an outlet for Hungary and thus a counterpart of the Austrian outlet of Trieste, has become Yugoslavia's chief port on the Mediterranean. The twin port of Susak, built by Yugoslavia in the interwar period on the Yugoslavian side of the border, is now part of the city. Like Trieste Rijeka has a considerable transit traffic, which in 1960 exceeded one-third of the total cargo turnover. The construction of a new dry cargo port at Koper near Trieste was started in the 1950s.

[8] Joachim Kuligowski, *Die Seehäfen des österreichischen Außenhandels.* Wien, 1957.

Greece

Modern Greece has two economic centers, the dominating Athens-Piraeus conurbation, the economic core of the nation with about two-thirds of its industrial output, and Salonica at the mouth of the Vardar Valley, which was formerly a major traffic artery of the Balkan Peninsula.

Athens was a small town at the time of the liberation of Greece from Turkish domination in 1829, but the magic of a glorious past and a location less exposed to earthquakes than Corinth made it the capital. Ancient Greece was maritime, with an empire extending its influence across the Mediterranean. Piraeus was the center of the entrepôt trade for the far-flung colonies. But modern Piraeus has no such function; it is a typical port of a capital city receiving raw materials for her manufacturing plants but also foodstuffs for the metropolitan region which approaches two million inhabitants. Piraeus is favorably located to serve as the hub of coastwise shipping, especially since the opening of the Corinth Canal in 1893, which brought the port in closer contact with the west coast. Elevsis, a few kilometers west of Piraeus, is the sea terminal of a new oil refinery.

International boundaries cut across Salonica's hinterland and have for decades prevented the city from taking advantage of its favorable geographic location. At times in the past Salonica was second only to Constantinople as a trade center in this part of the world. It is a manufacturing city and the outlet for Greece's tobacco exports.

The prominent ranking of Greece among the shipping nations results from the activity of a few shipowners operating in the international market. Before the Second World War the Greek merchant marine had a rather poor reputation for old, second-hand vessels. In the postwar period the Greek shipping tycoons have operated a modern fleet, but in 1957 an

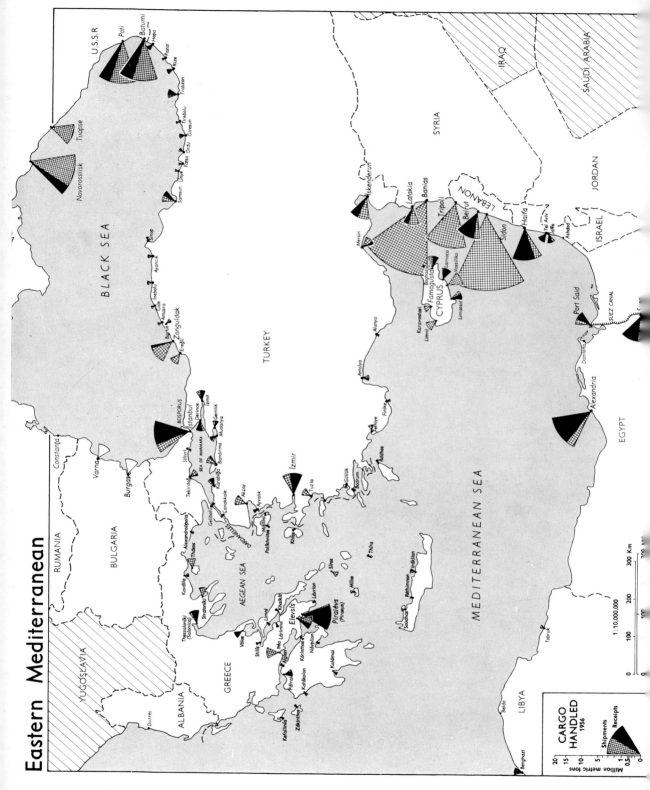

Eastern Mediterranean

YUGOSLAVIA

RUMANIA

BULGARIA

ALBANIA

GREECE

U.S.S.R.

BLACK SEA

Constanţa

Varna

Burgas

TURKEY

Poti
Batumi
Hopa
Pazar
Rize
Trabzon
Tirebolu
Giresun
Ordu
Fatsa
Ünye
Samsun
Sinop
Ayancık
İnebolu
Cide
Amasra
Bartın
Zonguldak
Ereğli
Tuapse
Novorossiisk

BOSPORUS
İstanbul
Derince
Gemlik
İzmit
Mudanya
Bandırma
Karabiğa
SEA OF MARMARA
Silivri
Tekirdağ

İzmir

SYRIA

İskenderun
Mersin
Latakia
Banias
Tripoli
Beirut
Sidon
Haifa
Tel Aviv
Jaffa
Ashdod

LEBANON

ISRAEL

JORDAN

IRAQ

SAUDI ARABIA

CYPRUS
Famagusta
Karavostasi
Limni
Larnaca
Vassiliko
Limassol

Boğaz

Port Said
SUEZ CANAL
Damietta
Alexandria

EGYPT

Alanya
Antalya
Finike
Fethiye
Gülük
Bodrum
Rodhos

MEDITERRANEAN SEA

Gallipoli
Çanakkale
Akçay
Ayvalık
DARDANELLES
Alexandroúpolis
Thásos
Kavála
Stratóni
Thessaloníki
(Salonica)
Vólos
Stilís
Néa Ephrate
Lávrion
Khálkis
Páloúkhrios
Míllina
Palaiokhóra
Pothia
Khíos
E Thíra
Míllos
Síros
Andíllion
Réthimnon
Sóudha

Eleusis
Piraiévs
(Piraeus)
Korí11thos
Návplion
Kalamai
Patrai
Kardamíla
Kefallinía
Zákinthos
Lávrion

AEGEAN SEA

Tabruk
Derna
Benghazi
LIBYA

1:10,000,000

0   100   200   300 Km

**CARGO
HANDLED**
1956

Million metric tons
20
15
10
5
1
0

Shipments
Receipts

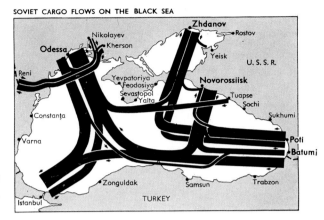

SOVIET CARGO FLOWS ON THE BLACK SEA

Source: *Transport SSSR, Morskoj Transport* (V. G. Bakaev and S. M. Baev, eds.). Moskva, 1961.

estimated 10.6 million GRT were sailed under foreign flags and the shipowners lived abroad. However, new legislation (1953) made possible the repatriation of many ships, starting with the freight depression in 1957.

Rumania and Bulgaria

The Lower Danube is accessible for ocean vessels of 7-meter draft (6000 dwt tons) from the mouth at Sulina to Braila. The two Danube ports of Braila and Galați have long been major outlets for Rumanian grain. The Danube is one of Europe's chief waterways, but it primarily serves domestic trade and trade between the riverine states. With the postwar reorientation of trade patterns in Eastern Europe the latter function has been strengthened. The Danube provides cheap water transport between the economically most important parts of the Communist countries. Both Braila and Galați, as well as the Soviet ports of Reni and Izmail, are transit points between ocean vessels and river barges but they also handle cargo transported by rail and pipeline. Galați

[1] Mibail Haseganu, *Wirtschaftsgeographie der Rumänischen Volksrepublik*. Berlin, 1962. Pp. 146 ff.
[2] R. P. Rochlin, *Die Wirtschaft Bulgariens seit 1945*. Berlin, 1957. P. 103.

ships timber (from the forests of the eastern Carpathians), petroleum and grain and transships ore, fertilizers and steel from the Soviet Union to Hungary and Czechoslovakia.[1] Braila has large elevators and is the chief grain shipping port.

Constanța on the Black Sea, the leading seaport of Rumania, is connected by pipeline to the Ploești oilfields, the oldest commercially exploited fields in the world. Other pipelines lead to Odessa in the Soviet Union and to the Danube ports. In addition to petroleum Constanța ships grain, timber and cement. In the interwar period Constanța developed into a rather important liner port favored by the decline of Constantinople and Odessa and by government efforts to attract foreign shipping. In addition to being the leading foreign trade port of Rumania Constanța handles some transit traffic for Hungary and Czechoslovakia.

For the small foreign trade of Bulgaria river transport on the Danube plays a greater role than ocean transport through the two seaports of Burgas and Varna on either side of the Balkan Mountains.[2] Bulgaria's leading river port Ruse was connected by a bridge in the 1950s with Giurgiu, the river port serving Bucharest. This is the only bridge between the two countries.

SOVIET CARGO FLOWS ON THE CASPIAN SEA

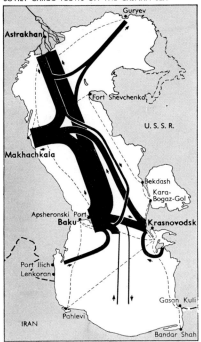

Source: *Transport SSSR, Morskoj Transport* (V. G. Bakaev and S. M. Baev, eds.). Moskva, 1961.

Soviet Ports on the Black Sea and the Caspian

The Black Sea, the main maritime face of the Soviet Union, accounts for about 55 per cent of its seaborne foreign trade and 40 per cent of its cabotage. Three bulk commodities—petroleum, ores and coal—together account for about 80 per cent of the cargo turnover of the Black Sea ports.[1]

The Russians did not gain access to this seaboard until the last years of the eighteenth century and the conquest of the Caucasus was not completed until 1878. The period of rapid economic development in the Ukraine began with the construction in the 1870s of railroads stretching from Moscow to the ports of the Black Sea. The southern steppes, which had been uninhabited or used as extensive grazing land, were planted with wheat for export through the Black Sea ports. French and Belgian capital and know-how were used for the development of a modern iron and steel industry based on the Donets coal and the iron ore of Krivoi Rog.[2] The small ironworks of the Urals, based on scattered deposits of iron ore and charcoal, which had been of great importance earlier, were soon eclipsed. By the beginning of this century the steel industry of the Ukraine was the chief concentration of heavy industry in Russia. The large petroleum reservoirs of the Apsheron Peninsula centered on Baku were developed after 1871 with the help of Swedish, Dutch and British capital. It is one of the oldest oil fields in the world that is still producing. The Ukrainian heavy industry and the petroleum production of the Caucasus region were further expanded after the Revolution and they are still the major generators of seaborne traffic in the Black Sea and the Caspian.

Odessa, the largest city on the Black Sea, is second only to Baku among the Soviet ports measured by tonnage of cargo handled. It is the leading foreign trade port in the Union.[3] In contrast to Leningrad Odessa is kept open for navigation throughout the year. Petroleum from the ports of the Caucasus region and coal from the Donets Basin dominate in the diversified cargo receipts of Odessa. Leading shipments are grain and lumber. After Odessa, Novorossiisk, Poti, Batumi and Tuapse are the leading ports of the Black Sea proper and Zhdanov (formerly Mariupol) of the Azov Sea. The petroleum port of Novorossiisk also handles large quantities of grain, coal and cement. Poti is the sea terminal of the railroad from the Chiatura manganese mine. Batumi, terminal of a pipeline from Baku, and

[1] V. G. Bakaev and S. M. Baev (eds.), *Transport SSSR: Morskoj Transport.* Moskva, 1961. P. 49.

[2] N. N. Baransky, *Economic Geography of the U.S.S.R.* Moscow, 1956. P. 289.

[3] I. V. Nikol'skij, *Geografija transporta SSSR.* Moskva, 1960. P. 225.

Tuapse are oil ports but Batumi also ships tea, citrus fruit, canned fruit, etc. Timber, grain, steel and machinery dominate the in-moving cargo through Batumi.

Other ports with more than one million tons of cargo turnover are Nikolayev, a grain terminal and the sea outlet for manganese from Nikopol and iron ore from Krivoi Rog, Kherson, at the mouth of the Dnepr, and Reni and Izmail on the lower Danube.

The Caspian was an enclosed sea until connected with the Black Sea by the Volga-Don Canal in 1952 but the two water systems were in close contact even earlier by pipelines and railroads. The large oil shipments have made Baku the leading Soviet port by tonnage.[4] Petroleum accounts for over 90 per cent of Baku's cargo turnover; in addition grains, fresh water and other cargoes are shipped across the lake to Krasnovodsk. The two cities are connected by train ferries.

From the beginning the Volga River was used for the transport of Baku oil to the central parts of Russia and small quantities reached as far as St. Petersburg.[5] Navigation on the Caspian has been impeded by the falling water level particularly in the northern part. An artificial island port, including storage sheds, repair shops and fish-processing plants, has been constructed in the Caspian 200 kilometers south of Astrakhan for the transfer of cargo between Caspian tankers of up to 32 foot draft and Volga river boats of 14 foot. The transfer point handles northbound petroleum, cotton and rice and southbound lumber, steel and manufactured products. A second large oil flow moves from Baku to Makhachkala from where a pipeline leads to the Donbass region by way of the oil fields north of the Caucasus—Grozny, Maikop and Ilskii. Over 85 per cent of the cargo handled in the Caspian Sea ports is petroleum.

Mediterranean Asia

Turkey

Asia Minor consists of an inner plateau hemmed in by mountain ranges that usually fall steeply to the sea. Land communications tend to run from west to east from the Aegean region rather than southwards from the steep and rocky Black Sea coast. The narrow coastal plains along the Black Sea have a rather high density of population.[1] Here is also the coal district at Zonguldak and Ereğli which promises to be the chief Turkish region of heavy industry. Coal is shipped to Istanbul and other port cities and some is also used in the local steel industry (Karabük). A new steel plant is under construction at Ereğli.

As inland transportation meets many obstacles coastal shipping has always been of great importance in the economic life of Turkey.

Istanbul is the dominating hub in Turkey's international and domestic shipping relations. This metropolis of 1.2 million inhabitants was the capital of a country almost three times as large as present Turkey during the Ottoman Empire. It remained the economic capital even

---

[4] Baku produced almost 8 million tons in 1913 and reached a peak of 22 million tons in 1940 when it accounted for more than two-thirds of the total Soviet petroleum production. In recent years the production has been only 16 million tons. This figure shows that Soviet ports are small in comparison to other world ports.

[5] Map by S. V. Bernštejn-Kogan of Russian oil transports in 1910 reprinted in Nikol'skij, *op. cit.,* p. 87.

[1] George B. Cressey, *Crossroads, Land and Life in Southwest Asia.* Chicago, 1960. P. 282.

The Suez Canal with a northbound convoy led by
the Italian 50,000-ton tanker *Agrigentum,* one of
the largest vessels that can pass through the
canal. (Suez Canal Authority)

Selected distances	Via Suez Canal	Via Cape of Good Hope	Via Panama Canal
London to:			
Bombay	6,260	10,700	—
Kuwait	6,500	11,300	—
Singapore	8,250	11,750	15,200
Hong Kong	9,690	13,020	14,100
Yokohama	11,150	14,470	12,520
Melbourne	11,060	11,900	12,950
Auckland	12,670	13,480	11,380
New York to:			
Bombay	8,150	11,400	11,340
Ras Tanura	8,400	11,900	—
Singapore	10,140	12,430	12,500
Hong Kong	11,580	13,700	11,340

Detailed traffic statistics are available since
the opening of the Suez Canal which makes
possible an analysis of much greater detail
than is practicable for any of the vague routes
over the oceans which are not tallied at specific
points. Around the turn of the century three
out of four vessels in transit were British; in
the thirties this proportion had declined to one
out of two. Since 1945 the proportion of
British tonnage passing through the Canal has
declined sharply, although tonnage under the
British flag actually doubled in the ten years
following the war. This was chiefly a result of
the tremendous increase in oil shipments. The
Norwegians specialize in tankers and so do

operated the Canal until it was nationalized by Egypt
in 1956 (the Suez Crisis) and transferred to the Egyptian Suez Canal Authority, was an international company with headquarters in Paris and Ismailia. Of the
32 board members 16 were French. The British
Government, working against the project until it was
completed, afterwards tried to gain control of the
Canal Company. In 1875 with the help of Rothschild
it acquired stock reserved for the Viceroy of Egypt,
after the French Government had refused to buy.

Thus Great Britain had ten members on the board.
After the British intervention in Egypt in 1882 and
subsequent agreements with France and Russia, Britain
had military control of the canal zone. With a chain
of bases it strengthened its control of the route
through the Canal—Cyprus, Perim, British Somaliland, Aden and Socotra.

According to the Constantinople Convention of
1888 the Canal should be open to all ships, in war
as well as in peace.

The Suez Canal

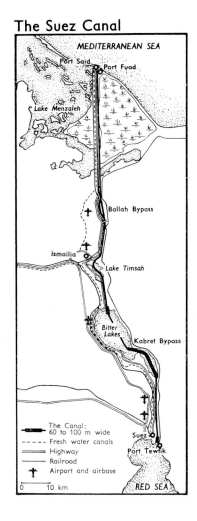

Suez Canal Traffic

Northbound

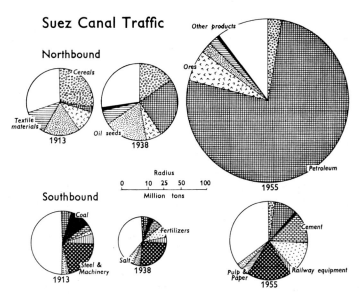

Southbound

Sources Alan B. Mountjoy, "The Suez Canal at Mid-Century", *Economic Geography*, 1958. P. 155.

Canal could only take 35,000-tonners. Plans exist for further deepening to allow 65,000-ton tankers. The largest tankers afloat will have to use other routes even after the Canal has been deepened.

The increases in dry cargo trade passing through the Canal have been moderate. Over half a million passengers a year passed through the Canal in the 1950s compared to a quarter of a million in the early 1930s. A large part of the increase may be attributed to the large postwar emigration from Europe to Australia and New Zealand.

Egypt

The truth of Herodotus' statement, made some 2,500 years ago, that Egypt is the gift of the Nile is clearly brought out by a modern population map. The 27 million Egyptians are concentrated in the narrow Nile Valley, the Nile Delta and a few desert oases, together making up less than four per cent of Egypt's land area. Since times immemorial the Nile has

American and Greek interests, primarily sailing under the flags of Liberia and Panama. Norway, Liberia and Panama accounted for 33.3 per cent of the 1959 tonnage,[3] and Great Britain for 21.6 per cent. With an authorized draft of 37 feet the Canal allows tankers of 45,000 tons dwt but larger tankers may 'top up' their load at pipe heads in the Mediterranean. Before the deepening program from 35 to 37 feet, carried through about 1960, the

[3] In 1955, the last complete year before the Suez Crisis, 115.8 million net register tons passed through the Canal and in 1959 no less than 163.4 million tons. In the late 1950s the tonnage of the Suez Canal surpassed that of the Soo Canals in the Great Lakes, making it the world's busiest man-made waterway.

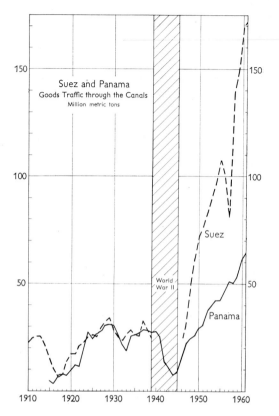

Suez and Panama
Goods Traffic through the Canals
Million metric tons

Data from *Suez Canal Report,* Suez Canal Authority, 1959; and Panama Canal Company, Canal Zone Government, *Annual Report,* 1951, 1961.

been the great traffic artery of the elongated oasis, which the river itself has created. River transportation is still important although railroads and highways have taken over almost all passengers and most of the cargo traffic. An estimated 15,000 small sailing vessels, *dahabiyas,* operate on the Nile.[1] They proceed upstream taking advantage of the prevailing north and north-east winds; on the return voyage they drift with the current, sails lowered. In addition to the *dahabiyas,* about 450 shallow draft steamers ply the river as far as Aswan. Statistics only cover the mechanized craft which handled one million tons of an estimated nine million tons carried on the river in the mid-1950s. River ports in the European sense hardly exist in Egypt; cargo is loaded and

unloaded almost anywhere along the river and the navigable channels.

Statistics are available for some important commodities which may help to illustrate the role of the three competing means of transportation. Since their beginning in the 1850s the railroads have been strongly favored by the government, at first in competition with river transportation, and since the early 1930s in competition with highway traffic. Transport by road accounts for a large proportion of the export cotton moved to the port of Alexandria. This is mainly short haul traffic since the delta is the chief cotton-producing area.

Type of transport	Cotton received at Alexandria 1953/54	Fuel oil transported 1954
	Thousand tons	
Railroad	57	922
Highway	133	941
River	32	249

More remarkable are the large quantities of fuel oil carried by trucks and the small quantities handled by river vessels. However, the two largest Egyptian refineries are located at Suez, and Cairo, the largest city in Africa, provides the leading oil market. The dominating oil traffic between these two cities moves by rail and road as the Ismailia canal is too small for petroleum barges.

Among Egypt's exports high-quality cotton has long been dominant. In the late 1950s cotton accounted for about 70 per cent of the export value. The concentration of the Egyptian economy on one export crop dates back to the American Civil War, when the textile industry of Lancashire was cut off from its normal supplies. Almost all Egyptian cotton is shipped through Alexandria.

Measured by weight phosphate is the leading

[1] Jacques Besançon, *L'homme et le Nil.* Paris, 1957. Pp. 312 ff.

export item, followed by cotton, rice and onions each accounting for between 150,000 tons and 500,000 tons. Among imports about two million tons of petroleum and petroleum products are followed by half a million tons of nitrogenous fertilizers and about 200,000 tons of steel products and lumber. Egypt's contribution to world trade thus is small, both in terms of value and volume. However, its geographical location on the world's most important canal which runs through Egyptian territory and which was nationalized by Egypt in 1956, twelve years before the expiration of the concession period, means that Egypt now commands a place in international commerce out of proportion to its own trade.

Alexandria, founded by Alexander the Great in 332 B.C., is the leading seaport of Egypt. The other large ports, Port Said and Suez, have special functions related to the canal and handle only a small share of Egypt's commerce. Alexandria is located at the extreme north-west of the delta outside the range of the silt-depositing Nile. In its early history Alexandria was a cosmopolitan rather than an Egyptian city;[2] apart from being a center of Hellenism it was for long the principal Jewish city of the Ancient world and later became a center of Christian learning under the Byzantine Empire. Alexandria flourished as an entrepôt in the trade between the Mediterranean and the coasts of Arabia and India. At times Alexandria had been the largest city in the Western world; when it fell to the Arabs in 642 it still had about 300,000 inhabitants. The Arabs made Cairo the capital of Egypt and Alexandria's decline continued, especially in the fourteenth century when the canal to the Nile was silted up. The discovery of the sea route to India in 1498 reduced the city to one

of local importance only. In the beginning of the last century it had a mere 4,000 inhabitants.

Mohammed Ali, the founder of modern Egypt, is to be accredited with restoring Alexandria's greatness. The construction of the Mahmudiya Canal in 1819 brought most of the Nile trade to Alexandria and made it possible to irrigate large areas in the delta. Since Mohammed Ali's days Alexandria has been the summer capital of Egypt; the heat at the coast is less oppressive than at Cairo.

Libya

Most of the long, arid coast between the Nile Valley and the coastal plains of Tunisia belongs to Libya, one of the most predominantly desert countries in Africa. Libya is a small country in terms of population with 1.25 million inhabitants. Until the recent developments of oil shipping from Port Brega and Ras el Sidra the two capitals, Tripoli and Benghazi, were the leading ports. Benghazi was developed as a naval port by the Italians before the Second World War but due to silting and the destruction of the outer mole the port has been limited to vessels of 14.5 foot draft or less in the postwar period. In stormy weather it has sometimes been inaccessible to shipping. As a result certain cargoes have been transshipped at Tripoli, Malta or other ports, which has added to the costs of Cyrenaica's imports.[3]

Port Brega made its first oil shipment in September 1961 and the second of the two extremely costly oil terminals completed on the Libyan coast, Ras el Sidra, was completed in 1962. The off-shore loading facilities at Port Brega can accomodate tankers of 77,000 tons dwt. Port Brega is connected with the Zelten and Raguba oil fields by a 30-inch pipeline with a capacity of about 18 million tons. Another 30-inch line from the Dahra, Waha and Samaha fields to Ras el Sidra provides a shipping capacity of 15 million tons per

---

[2] Walter Fitzgerald, *Africa*. 7th ed. London, 1950. Pp. 440 ff.

[3] *The Economic Development of Libya*. The International Bank for Reconstruction and Development. Baltimore, 1960.

most companies found it advantageous to make Chicago a terminal and thus establish connections with the western lines. Chicago soon became the largest railroad center in the world; no railroad passes through the city, which means that all passengers of the 27 railroads with terminals in Chicago have to change trains.[3] The railroads in the 1870s surpassed the waterway in amount of goods carried, but the all-water route provided an alternative and cheaper route, which influenced the freight rates of the railroads. Chicago and New York had freight advantages over competing cities, which helped to make the traffic flow between these two cities by far the most important of any comparable flows in North America. Chicago overtook St. Louis in population by the 1870s and has since been the undisputed economic capital of the Middle West. For the rapid change in relative importance between the Ohio—Mississippi cities of St. Louis, Cincinnati and Louisville on one hand and the Lake-shore cities of Chicago, Cleveland and Detroit on the other, the Civil War played a significant role. The northern cities were further away from the areas of warfare and gained more from the manufacturing boom caused by the war. In the post-war period the southern cities were left with part of their natural trade area devastated.

Some 90 per cent of Great Lakes shipping is handled by bulk-carrying lake boats, the rest by car ferries and ocean vessels. Car ferries are especially important on Lake Michigan, where they act as bridges connecting eastern and western railroads. All car ferry lines here are operated by eastern railroads, indicating an attempt to make connection with western railroads beyond the Chicago terminal district. Ludington is largest of the east shore terminals. On the west shore Milwaukee has about half the total traffic of over 5 million tons. The ferries are important links in the east-west movement of coal, grain, lumber, paper, newsprint, salt and a variety of manufactured goods.

Overseas Traffic of the Great Lakes Ports 1960
Thousand metric tons

	United States	Canada
Imports	821	1,073
Exports	3,564	1,262

Source: Saint Lawrence Seaway Development Corporation, *Annual Report 1960*.

Over 200,000 railroad cars are transported over the lake every year.

Overseas trade of American and Canadian ports on the Great Lakes was small before the opening of the St. Lawrence Seaway with the shipping season of 1959, averaging about two-thirds of a million tons. Four American ports (Chicago, Detroit, Milwaukee, Cleveland) and three Canadian (Toronto, Sarnia, Hamilton) handled four-fifths of this tonnage in 1956. The overseas trade handled by the Great Lakes ports jumped in 1959, and in 1960, the second year of the new Seaway, amounted to 6.7 million tons.

The first overseas sailing from a Great Lakes port occurred in 1856 when a cargo of wheat was lifted at Milwaukee for Liverpool.[4] Subsequent cargoes for European destinations left at irregular intervals; but by 1880 foreign sailings had practically disappeared from the Lakes. In 1933 the Norwegian Fjell Line pioneered regular liner service between the Great Lakes ports and Europe. Other European companies followed suit. Before 1959 only ships of about 2,500 dwt tons could proceed into the Lakes. The St. Lawrence Seaway opened the Great Lakes to ocean vessels of about 10,000 dwt tons or 80 per cent of the world's general cargo ships. As a result the number of shipping lines entering the Great Lakes rapidly increased to over 30 in 1959.

[3] Freight cars are switched from one railroad to another in the Chicago terminal district.
[4] Edward Hamming, *The Port of Milwaukee*. Chicago, 1952. P. 122.

a good location for the production of steel. Iron ore and limestone could be brought in cheaply by lake carriers, coal from the Appalachian field either by combined rail and lake transportation, or, more often, by direct rail haul. Chicago's position as a steel center has been gradually improved with innovations in fuel techniques requiring less and less coal in the iron and steel process. Now the world's leading steel center with a capacity of approximately 25 million tons, Chicago has in recent years kept pace with the national growth rate whereas the second and third American centers, Pittsburgh and Youngstown, have had lower increases.

The rapid development of a wide range of manufacturing industries in Chicago, of which only a few have been mentioned, have made the city the second largest American manufacturing center after New York. It is now the western cornerstone of the American Manufacturing Belt.

Great Lakes traffic contributes roughly four-fifths of the 60 million tons handled in the port of Chicago. About two million tons is foreign trade with Canada. Overseas traffic amounted to about 200,000 tons before the St. Lawrence Seaway was opened in 1959. In 1960 it had increased to 890,000 tons. Barges on the Illinois Lakes-to-Gulf Waterway contribute about one-fifth of the total port traffic.

The iron and steel industry is by far the most important generator of traffic. Iron ore accounts for about 25 million tons in a normal year. It is unloaded at private wharves of the steel companies at Calumet Harbor, along the Calumet River, at Indiana Harbor and at Gary. Virtually none of the ore is transferred to inland carriers. The second largest commodity received, limestone (8 million tons) from northern Michigan, is also primarily associated with the steel industry but considerable amounts are used in the cement industry and for other purposes. Of the coal receipts (6–8 million tons) only a small proportion is consumed by

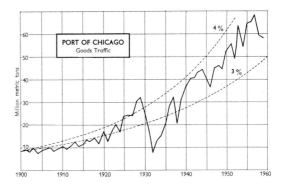

Source: U.S. Army Corps of Engineers, *Annual Report, Vol. 2, Commercial Statistics, 1900–1952;* U.S. Army Corps of Engineers, *Waterborne Commerce of the United States,* Part 3, 1953–1960, adapted from Harold M. Mayer, *The Port of Chicago and the St. Lawrence Seaway* (Chicago, 1957) for 1900–1955.
Intraport and local cargo, making up less than five per cent of total cargo turnover, are included on this diagram, but not on other maps and diagrams. Two curves show how the 1900 traffic would have developed with an annual increase of 3 and 4 per cent.

the iron and steel industry. Most of the lakewise receipts of coal originate in West Virginia and Kentucky and are shipped from Lake Erie ports, principally Toledo. The movement of coking coal via this route has been relatively small in recent years. Most of the coal from the Appalachian area moves by rail all the way. The lake boats find it more profitable to carry ore one way and return in ballast which allows more turn-arounds per season. Barge-transported coal from central Illinois, chiefly for thermo-electric plants along the canals, account for roughly half of the coal received. Coal shipments from the port have increased rapidly in recent years and are now of the same order as coal receipts. Other important commodities are petroleum products, chiefly shipments from Indiana Harbor, gypsum from Alabaster, sand and gravel dredged from the bed of Lake Michigan and from the upper Illinois Valley, newsprint from Canada, grain and soybeans. Nearly all of the newsprint used in Chicago is imported by water during the navigation season.

Both boat traffic on the Great Lakes and barge traffic on the canals are unbalanced. Lakewise receipts in 1956 were 40 million tons and shipments only 10 million; barge receipts were 10 million tons and shipments 2 million. In both cases shipments were more varied and of much higher value per ton.

Chicago Harbor, which includes the break-water-protected area at the mouth of Chicago River and about half a mile within the river entrance, is the original Port of Chicago. From a maximum traffic about 1890 it gradually declined to a low point in 1943 but has since increased slowly. Some of the terminal facilities for overseas commerce are located here. In the diversified traffic inbound Canadian newsprint is the largest item. Most of the traffic in the Chicago River and its North and South Branches consists of inbound coal, sand and gravel from the canal and cement from the Lakes.

The Chicago Sanitary and Ship Canal, opened in 1900 and designed primarily for the discharge of sewage, in 1933 became part of the Illinois Lakes-to-Gulf Waterway which was to serve modern barge traffic more adequately than the old Illinois and Michigan Canal (1848–1932). About 10 million tons of cargo are handled at port facilities along the canal, chiefly inbound petroleum products, coal, sand and gravel and outbound petroleum products. The canal has serious limitations for navigation. Inadequate width prevents the use of barge tows, common on the Illinois and the Mississippi rivers, where tows of up to 25 barges containing over 20,000 tons of cargo can navigate. They have to be broken up near Joliet into individual barges or groups of not more than two or three. Specially designed towboats with retractable pilot houses are used because of the many low bridges. These were constructed as movable bridges but are normally in a fixed position. Under special conditions the bridges can be opened with temporary machinery. During World War II small naval and merchant ships built in the Great Lakes, but exceeding the dimensions of the locks and canals then available on the St. Lawrence route, reached salt water through the Mississippi. During the Korean War ocean freighters were moved in the opposite direction and converted into iron ore carriers.

The Calumet Sag Channel, opened in 1922 as a sewage diversion route, connects the waterways of the Mississippi Basin with Lake Calumet and Calumet Harbor and River, the main parts of the port of Chicago. It was not designed for barge traffic and therefore has even more serious limitations than those of the Sanitary and Ship Canal. A Federal program for its enlargement, expected to be completed by 1963, will remove this bottleneck which prevents Chicago from taking full advantage of its location between the two largest waterways in North America. The same type of goods are handled as along the Sanitary and Ship Canal. Whereas land along the latter is intensively used by manufacturing, wholesale and railroad establishments, there is much land available for industrial expansion along the Calumet Sag route.

Most of the traffic of Lake Calumet, in contrast to other ports in Chicago, is with overseas countries. Comprehensive port terminal and industrial developments were undertaken in this area in the 1950s to make it the principal American terminal for direct traffic with ports overseas through the St. Lawrence Seaway.

Calumet Harbor and River, the leading port area in Chicago, handles 24 million tons, chiefly inbound iron ore, limestone, and coal, and outbound coal. The harbor consists of a large breakwater-protected area in Lake Michigan including private slips serving large steel plants. The six mile river is lined with large manufacturing plants and grain elevators. Coal shipments have increased substantially with the

establishment of new loading facilties on Calumet River in 1948—greatly enlarged in 1956 —and now by far exceed the receipts.

Almost half of Chicago's port traffic is handled in Indiana. The largest port east of the state line is Indiana Harbor, a bifurcated canal, not directly connected with the canals leading to the Mississippi. It is lined with large manufacturing plants, including two huge steel mills, oil refineries and oil terminals, and chemical plants. The harbor handles about 18 million tons, mainly inbound iron ore, limestone and coal, and outbound petroleum products. It is the largest port on the Great Lakes for the shipment of refined mineral oil.

Further east are two private harbors, Buffington, which receives about 1 million tons of limestone for a large cement plant, and

Indiana Harbor, Chicago. To the left of the Indiana Harbor Ship Canal is the steel works of Youngstown Sheet and Tube Company. On the near side of the canal and stretching far out into Lake Michigan is the works of the Inland Steel Company, the third largest steel plant in the United States. The shoreline to the extreme right in the picture remains unchanged. The railroad tracks running straight across the picture from this point mark the former shoreline. Both steel companies have added substantial areas by filling. Inland Steel has created a three kilometer "peninsula" into Lake Michigan. Another 1,200 meters of filling on the lakeward side has been authorized. (Inland Steel Company)

Gary, serving one of the worlds' largest steel mills. It handles over 7 million tons, virtually all inbound iron ore from Lake Superior and limestone from northern Michigan.

259

Other Metropolitan Ports

Besides Chicago there are five ports on the Great Lakes serving urbanized areas of about one million people or more: Milwaukee, Detroit, Cleveland, Buffalo and Toronto. In Detroit, Cleveland and Buffalo the iron and steel industry is the primary generator of traffic; Milwaukee and Toronto have no integrated iron and steel mills.

MILWAUKEE has had a remarkably stable waterborne commerce. Since 1910 it has averaged 6.3 million tons per year with the minimum 30 per cent below and the maximum 25 per cent above this figure. Milwaukee does not have the locational advantages of Chicago, but various efforts have been made in the past to overcome this. Just before the advent of the railroads a project was started to connect the Milwaukee River with the Mississippi by a canal, but only one mile of the proposed waterway was completed. The first railroad in Wisconsin was built from Milwaukee, reaching the Mississippi in 1857. The city had one of the most extensive public port facilities among the American lake ports and thus was well prepared to participate in the overseas trade when the St. Lawrence Seaway was opened in 1959.

Milwaukee is the largest rail ferry terminal on the west side of Lake Michigan. The car ferries account for one-third of the city's tonnage and one-fifth of its railroad traffic.

Coal has for many years been the leading cargo for other vessels; coal receipts have not been below one million tons since the 1890s. Unlike Chicago Milwaukee depends almost entirely on deliveries by water. On the average for 1946–50 bituminous coal constituted two-thirds of total receipts (4.6 million tons), followed by petroleum products, anthracite, cement and sand and gravel. In 1956 petroleum products had taken first place, almost one-half, closely followed by coal; of secondary importance were cement, limestone, and sand and gravel. All the petroleum products arrive from refineries in the Chicago area. Lakewise shipments are quite unimportant, totaling only 0.1 million tons.

Overseas trade, 75,000 tons in 1956, increased to 210,000 tons in 1960.

DETROIT. The port extends along the Detroit River and includes, in addition to Detroit itself, the facilities of the downriver industrial suburbs of River Rouge, Ecorse, Wyandotte, Riverview and Trenton. The principal general cargo terminal is located about two miles downstream from Detroit's central business district. A second terminal is near the mouth of the Rouge River. Coal receipts account for 9 of the 25 million tons handled in the port; iron ore and limestone come second with about 5 million tons each. Receipts of cement, steel, pig iron, oil products and gypsum all exceed 200,000 tons. In addition to the usual bulk commodities moving within the lakes, Detroit has a considerable traffic in new automobiles, moving in specially designed vessels.

Before 1959 Detroit was second only to Chicago among American Great Lakes ports in volume of overseas trade, but it handled less than 100,000 tons. In 1960, this trade had grown to 550,000 tons.

CLEVELAND. Cleveland on the southern shore of Lake Erie and in the center of the Detroit-to-Pittsburgh metal manufacturing belt is a major Great Lakes port, dominated by the traffic for the steelworks in the city and in the Pittsburgh-Youngstown areas. After 1959 Cleveland has become the dominating American destination for inbound bulk cargo (iron ore) through the Seaway, receiving over two million tons of such cargo in 1961. No other American port received more than half a million tons of bulk cargo through the Seaway. But most of Cleveland's iron ore receipts still originate at the Lake Superior ore ports. For overseas general cargo Cleveland is third among the American ports after Chicago and Detroit but in 1961 it handled only 200,000 tons.

BUFFALO at the east end of Lake Erie is the western terminus of the New York State Barge Canal, the successor of the historic Erie Canal. The completion of the first canal in 1825 laid the foundations for the rapid growth of Buffalo. There was no natural harbor at this strategic point but the canal made it necessary to provide a harbor and shelter.

Two industries today create almost all of the harbor traffic, steel and flour-milling. Iron ore, limestone, coal and grain dominate receipts and pig iron and steel are the two leading shipments. Being a major transshipment point for midwestern grain on its way to the markets on the Atlantic seaboard and abroad, Buffalo has become the leading flour-milling center of the world. It has been in a position to take advantage of the milling-in-bond privilege offered by the government. Canadian wheat is milled in transit to foreign markets. However, the flow of Canadian wheat through Buffalo (and New York) which used to be important has been diverted over other routes. Almost all of the American vessels used for grain storage in the winter are laid up in Buffalo, whereas the Canadian vessels are in the Georgian Bay ports, and in Goderich, Prescott and Toronto.

Measured by employment and harbor traffic the steel industry is much more important than flour-milling in Buffalo. General cargo traffic has increased after the opening of the Seaway but Buffalo shares its natural hinterland with New York and this type of cargo is likely to remain insignificant in the traffic of the port.

TORONTO. The first settlers to come to the Ontario Peninsula in considerable numbers were American colonists who remained loyal to the English crown during the Revolutionary War. The region has remained the core of British Canada with Toronto as its economic focus. With nearly two million inhabitants Toronto is Canada's second city.

Ample general cargo facilities near the downtown area serve not only overseas traffic but also, in contrast to the United States' Great Lakes ports, a considerable domestic traffic. But bulk cargoes dominate the total cargo turnover with coal, grains, petroleum the leading items. In Toronto's suburb Port Credit the petroleum trade completely dominates. Toronto is far surpassed by the steel center Hamilton as a generator of traffic through the St. Lawrence Seaway.

Bulk Cargoes on the Great Lakes

Iron Ore

Large-scale iron ore shipments on the Great Lakes have developed parallel with the modern steel industry in the United States. The flow of high-grade, cheap ore from the Lake Superior iron ranges to the iron and steel plants in the Manufacturing Belt south of the Lakes, along with the favorably located and easily mined coking coal, were the unique raw material basis for the United States' emergence as the world's leading manufacturing nation. The large waterbody of the Lakes has, economically speaking, placed the distant ore bodies of Minnesota, Wisconsin and Michigan on the doorsteps of the densely populated southern shores of the Lakes. This heavy flow of ore is unsurpassed elsewhere. Already before the opening of the St. Lawrence Seaway in 1959 a complementary but much smaller flow had started from the vast ore fields of Labrador–Quebec. Ore for the rapidly expanding, but still relatively small, Canadian iron and steel industry comes from both American and Canadian mines. Canadian steel companies are co-owners of American mines just as American steel interests participate in the exploitation of

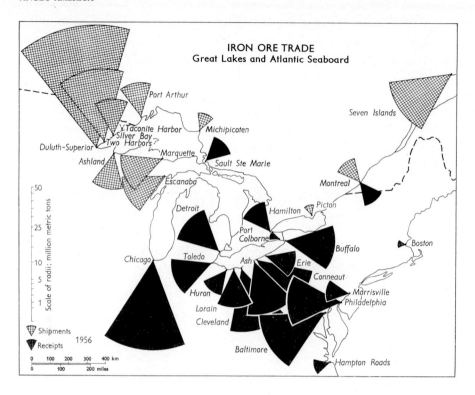

IRON ORE TRADE
Great Lakes and Atlantic Seaboard

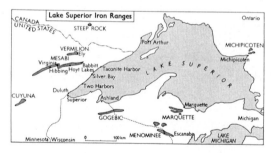

Lake Superior Iron Ranges

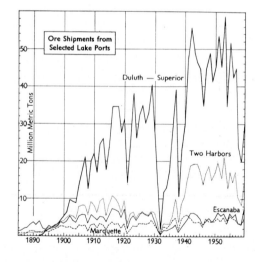

Ore Shipments from Selected Lake Ports

Canadian fields, which makes for movement of ore in both directions across the international boundary.

The first iron ore shipment on the Great Lakes antedates the modern steel industry and the construction of the "Soo" locks in the St. Mary's River between Lake Superior and Lake Huron. The first Bessemer converter in the United States was blown in 1864 but the first canal around the rapids in the St. Mary's River was opened in 1855 and some ore was shipped from Marquette in the early 1850s, unloaded at the river, hauled by wagon past the rapids, reloaded into vessels and transported to Cleveland. Regular shipments from the Marquette Range to lower Lake ports began in 1856, the birth-year of the Bessemer process. The Menominee Range, shipping through Escanaba, was opened next, in 1877. Then followed the Gogebic Range, with its port Ashland, and the

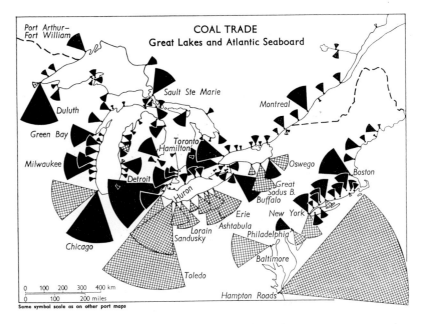

COAL TRADE
Great Lakes and Atlantic Seaboard

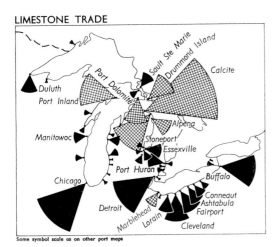

LIMESTONE TRADE

Same symbol scale as on other port maps

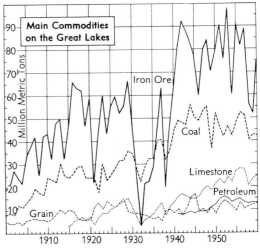

Main Commodities on the Great Lakes

Vermilion Range, with its port Two Harbors, both in 1884. The gigantic Mesabi Range, shipping through Duluth-Superior and Two Harbors, opened in 1892 and the Cuyuna Range, shipping through Superior, in 1911. More recent additions to the ore fields in the Lake Superior area are Helen Mine in Ontario,

shipping through Michipicoten (1939), and Steep Rock, shipping through Port Arthur (1944). The newest ore shipping ports in this old mining region are Silver Bay (1956), Taconite Harbor (1957), and Little Current (1958).[1] The latter accounts for less than 100,000 tons. Taconite Harbor in 1961 shipped 7.6 million tons of pellets from the Mesabi Range and Silver Bay 6.0 million.[2] Shipments through these two pellet ports have increased rapidly while the old ore ports on Lake Supe-

[1] Lake Carriers' Association, *Annual Report 1960*. P. 60.
[2] American Iron Ore Association, *Statistical Report*, December 13, 1961.

The steamer *Edward L. Ryerson,* one of the newest (1960) and largest (24,000 tons) bulk carriers on the Great Lakes at ore dock No. 4 at Superior, Wisconsin. Laden iron ore cars can be seen atop the near dock. Cars bottom-dump ore into "pockets" in the dock. Chutes, when lowered, gravity unload the pockets into the ship's hold. (Inland Steel Company)

rior account for decreasing quantities. Duluth-Superior was down to 20 million tons in 1961 and Two Harbors to less than 11 million.

Shipments from the huge ore deposits in Labrador started in 1954 via Seven Islands. Two million tons of this ore entered the Great Lakes in 1956, all of which was transshipped at Contrecoeur, Quebec. In the second season of the new Seaway 3.9 million tons of iron ore made up about 50 per cent of the upbound traffic. The Marmora Mine started to ship through Picton, Ontario, in 1955 and the new ore port of Depot Harbor (0.5 million tons) in Georgian Bay was opened in 1959.

Bituminous Coal

Almost all ports on the Great Lakes and the St. Lawrence River handle coal. It is the leading commodity at many ports. The coal trade was already important in the latter half of the last century when coal was carried in wooden

sailing vessels with capacities of 300–700 tons. For a long time anthracite from eastern Pennsylvania, shipped chiefly via Buffalo, was more important than bituminous coal. Buffalo was the first million-ton coal port on the Great Lakes, shipping this tonnage as early as 1883. Lake traffic in anthracite has decreased sharply since the early 1920s. The 1956 shipments were quite insignificant, about 0.5 million tons, moving mainly through Ashtabula.

The volume of bituminous coal handled by the Great Lakes ports has increased steadily despite the stagnation in American coal production after World War I. In 1956 no less than 11 per cent of the total United States production was shipped from ten ports on Lake Erie, three on Lake Ontario and one on Lake Michigan. The western ports have experienced the most rapid expansion. By 1920 Toledo was the largest coal shipping port on the Great Lakes and a few years later Sandusky emerged as the second largest.[1] Coal shipments from Chicago (Calumet River) were started during World War II; they have expanded rapidly in the postwar period.

[1] Albert G. Ballert, "The Coal Trade of the Great Lakes and the Port of Toledo", *Geographical Review,* 1948, pp. 194–205, and "Great Lakes Coal Trade: Present and Future", *Economic Geography,* 1953, pp. 48–59.

The westward migration of coal shipping facilities along the southern shores of the Great Lakes reflects the geographic changes of coal production in the Appalachian field. In 1917 about 37 per cent of the coal shipped on the Lakes originated in southern West Virginia and eastern Kentucky–Tennessee; in 1945 this percentage had risen to 65. While most of the coal came from the western Pennsylvanian fields, Cleveland, Ashtabula and other central and eastern Lake Erie ports were closer to the coal fields and had a dominating share of the shipments. For coal originating in the Middle Appalachian fields, Toledo, Sandusky and Chicago have a virtual monopoly. This is easily understood if topography, distances and location of lake-oriented markets are taken into consideration.

Toledo, in 1956 shipping 24.3 million tons or 46 per cent of the coal moving on the Great Lakes, has in several years been the world's largest coal shipping port. Its 1956 shipments slightly exceed the volumes shipped from the British ports of Cardiff and Newcastle during their peaks in 1913. The only coal port that has exceeded Toledo is another American port, Hampton Roads, which in 1956 shipped 47.1 million tons, of which 38.2 million tons were exports. Whereas coal shipments from Hampton Roads fluctuate considerably from year to year the traffic at Toledo is stable.

The destination of Lake Erie coal has changed greatly in recent years. In 1925 about 75 per cent went to ports on Lake Superior and Lake Michigan; in 1950 only 44 per cent had such destinations. This in turn is the result of changes in the demand for coal. The railroads, once the leading consumer, have rapidly changed to diesel locomotives after World War II. Domestic consumption has decreased due to the competition from fuel oil and natural gas. The iron and steel industry, still a large consumer despite coal saving innovations, prefers to have its coal sent direct without transshipment to avoid breakage. For example,

The steamer *Wilfred Sykes* at the Great Northern Dock No. 4 at Superior, Wisconsin. The chutes are in the up position. (Inland Steel Company)

the huge Gary Works in Chicago, one of the world's largest steel mills, gets all its coking coal by direct rail-haul from the Central Appalachian fields. The thermo-electric industry is now the largest—and an expanding—consumer of coal. Coal accounts for two-thirds of the United States steam-generated electricity. The steam-generating capacity is very large along the lower Lakes with its high density of population and manufacturing activity.

As a result of these changes in the demand for coal, ports on the lower Lakes, especially those in the Detroit–St. Clair district, receive a larger share of the coal. In the lower Lakes region the world's first pipeline for coal transportation was opened in 1959. Finely-ground coal, mixed half and half with water, was pumped 173 kilometers from Cadiz, Ohio, to an electric generating plant at Cleveland. The pipeline was reported to operate in excess of its rated capacity of 1.1 million tons per year, but early in 1963 it had to close down after the railroads had reorganized their coal traffic and had become more competitive.

The Chesapeake and Ohio Railway's docks at Toledo, in the center of the picture, are the largest coal docks on the Great Lakes. About 16 million tons of coal originating at mines on the C & O lines in Kentucky and West Virginia have been dumped here in one year by the three coal dumpers, each with a maximum capacity of 50 rail cars per hour. The third pier, in the foreground, has three ore unloaders which can unload a 13,000 ton cargo in eight hours.

In the lower left corner are the approaches to the coal loading facilities of the Baltimore & Ohio and the New York Central Railroads.

Coal vessels operate throughout the winter between Toledo and Detroit when the other lake ports are closed. (Toledo Chamber of Commerce)

Limestone

From 1918, when limestone for the first time exceeded grain shipments on the Great Lakes, these two commodities alternated as the third

most important bulk item after iron ore and coal until the rapid postwar expansion of limestone shipments firmly established limestone as the number three bulk cargo on the Lakes. It is quarried almost exclusively in northern Michigan where, under a thin overburden, are found extensive, thick, nearly pure deposits of limestone. The crushed stone is shipped from six large private harbors with highly mechanized loading equipment. Largest of these ports are Calcite near Rogers City, in operation since 1912, and Stoneport, opened in 1955.

The iron and steel industry, using limestone as a flux, is the largest consumer. Considerable quantities go to cement and chemical plants. Some cement mills are located near the quarries and ship finished cement (Alpena,

The *John G. Munson,* one of the largest self-unloaders on the Lakes with a cargo capacity of 20,000 tons, length of 203 meters and 22-meter beam. (Lake Carriers' Association)

Petoskey). The stone is used in the ports to which it is delivered; only small quantities of the cheap and almost ubiquitous raw material move to Youngstown or other inland points.[1]

Limestone is carried by ordinary lake boats or by self-unloaders. The latter, modified types of the common bulk freighters, were initially developed to handle limestone but they were soon found to be useful also in the coal trade. The first modern self-unloader was put into operation in 1908. The self-unloader is independent of the facilities in the receiving port and can usually unload in a few hours. It therefore has great advantages for the relatively short voyages which stone or coal usually make

[1] Paul Cross Morrison, "The Michigan Limestone Industry", *Economic Geography,* 1942, pp. 259–274, "Michigan Limestone in the Great Lakes Stone Trade", *Economic Geography,* 1942, pp. 413–427, and "Cement Production and Trade on the Great Lakes", *Economic Geography,* 1944, pp. 37–53.

as compared to grain and ore. The self-unloaders of the Great Lakes have few counterparts; some have been operating in the coal trade along the east coast of the United States.

Grain

Grain is the only important export commodity originating in the geographic center of the Anglo-American continent and it reaches the world market through ports on all four coasts. Traditionally the grain exporters have made good use of the Great Lakes for the transport of the bulky cargo from the grain elevators at the railroad stations in the prairie districts to the export elevators in the Atlantic ports and the large flour mills in the Manufacturing Belt,

General cargo terminal and grain elevators at Duluth-Superior. Several Great Lakes ports built general cargo facilities in connection with the opening of the St. Lawrence Seaway. Non-grain foreign cargoes at Duluth-Superior increased from 35,000 tons in 1959 to 215,000 tons in 1961. But total trade in the port dropped to half between 1956 and 1961 due to the decline in iron ore shipments. In spite of this Duluth-Superior remains the world's leading ore shipping port. (Seaway Port Authority of Duluth)

especially in Buffalo. Wheat accounts for over half of the grain shipments on the Great Lakes followed by barley, oats and corn.

Two grain heads on the Great Lakes dominate: the Canadian twin ports of Fort William–Port Arthur, which in 1960 accounted for 7.0 million metric tons of the 12.7 million tons of grain shipped on the Lakes, and the American twin ports of Duluth-Superior (3.9

million tons). Chicago (1.1 million tons) and Toledo (0.5 million) rank far behind and are dominated by corn and soybeans, reflecting their strategic location with regard to the Corn Belt. The chief grain destinations in Canada are the St. Lawrence River ports, ports on Georgian Bay, Port Colborne[2] and Toronto. Buffalo is by far the most important destination in the United States. With the opening of the St. Lawrence Seaway in 1959 direct

[2] Before the opening of the Welland Canal in 1932 the large lake boats unloaded their grain at Port Colborne, from where it was carried through the St. Lawrence by small canallers. The Welland Canal allowed the large lake boats to proceed all the way to the grain elevators at Prescott, from where the grain was brought by canaller to Montreal and other lower St. Lawrence ports. Much grain is also forwarded by rail from Georgian Bay ports, chiefly Midland, and Goderich to the lower St. Lawrence ports and (in the winter) Halifax and St. John.

Grain elevators in Port Colborne at the entrance to the Welland Canal. (National Harbours Board)

overseas shipments of grain to continental Europe and the United Kingdom became more common. In 1960 vessels from overseas picked up 463 cargoes of grain at the Great Lakes grain terminals, or 24 per cent of the available business, while Canadian vessels accounted for 60 per cent and American for the remaining 16 per cent.[3]

The Atlantic Seaboard

Canada: The St. Lawrence Valley and the Maritime Provinces

On a world map Canada stands out as a country of continental dimensions, but if only the *ecumene* or the inhabited area is considered, Canada shrinks and becomes a discontinuous strip of territory along the northern border of the United States. The pieces of this narrow strip are separated by wide stretches of uninhabited or sparsely settled land. The economies of these inhabited regions are closely linked with adjacent areas in the United States. Regionalism is further emphasized by differences in cultural background between the French-speaking Canadians, along the lower St. Lawrence River, and their English-speaking compatriots. The fundamental political problem in Canada has been to integrate seven economic regions into one nation.[1] There have been times in Canadian history when it seemed that the country would disintegrate and be swallowed by its big neighbor to the south.

The successful efforts to integrate the *ecumene* and thus attain national unity are reflected in the extension of the transportation system. Canals were constructed in the St. Lawrence River in the 1840s to compete with the seven-foot deep Erie Canal, completed in 1825, and thus prevent Montreal from being completely eclipsed by New York.[2] Plans for

[3] Lake Carriers' Association, *Annual Report* 1960. Pp. 88 ff.

[1] A. W. Currie, *Economic Geography of Canada.* Toronto, 1945.

[2] The St. Lawrence River may seem to be the natural outlet for the Anglo-American heartland, now the world's leading manufacturing belt and a century or more ago an important wheat-producing pioneer region with a promising future. (The St. Lawrence Valley is itself part of the Canadian heartland.) The many rapids formed when the river falls 68 meters from Lake Ontario to Montreal made it impossible to use the river, however, even after primitive canals had been constructed, except with unwieldy, flat-bottomed Durham boats carrying up to ten tons. By the end of the eighteenth century the St. Lawrence River had become the great Canadian freight route to the east on which wheat and lumber for Europe were shipped to the exporting ports, Montreal and Quebec.

such canals had existed almost as long as settlement in Canada but the tremendous boost given to New York by the Erie Canal precipitated construction. However, these nine-foot canals were rendered more or less obsolete in the 1850s by railroads. The Grand Trunk Railroad was built from Montreal through Toronto to Chicago with an extension to Portland, Maine, to be used especially in winter when Montreal was blocked by ice. After the Dominion had been formed in 1867 the Government decided to build a railroad from Montreal to Saint John and Halifax entirely through Canadian territory. Both cities are important regional centers whose ports are open the whole year round; from mid-December to mid-April, when Montreal is closed, they traditionally handle general cargo and passengers. The use of icebreakers on the lower St. Lawrence in recent years has opened up Quebec as a winter port and even ports further up-river have been accessible. This has adversely affected the winter traffic of Saint John and Halifax.

In the 1880s the Canadian Pacific Railway was generously subsidized to build a line from Ottawa to the Pacific and early in this century two more transcontinental railroads were built with the support of provincial and municipal governments. These two private lines were not complete at the outbreak of World War I and in 1917, after financial troubles, were taken over by the Dominion Government. The transcontinental railroads effectively integrated the Canadian *ecumene*. In the last decades air traffic has narrowed the time distance between the far-flung regions of Canada for passengers and high-value express cargo. The airplane has also integrated into the economy the scattered, small settlements in the huge wilderness to the north (mining camps, lake fishing centers, etc.). Gold, uranium, radium, fish and other products are flown out of the area and supplies are brought in by plane. Many postwar radar stations have been close enough to the Arctic coast to be supplied by ships which arrive in late summer when ice conditions are favorable.

The St. Lawrence Seaway

Railroad construction, however, did not detract attention from the obvious advantages of cheap water transportation through the Canadian heartland. The canals in the St. Lawrence River were deepened and by 1904 a fourteen-foot channel ran all the way from Montreal to Lake Erie. In 1932 the Welland Ship Canal was completed. It served ships of up to 25 foot draft and overcame the difference of 100 meters in the elevations of Lakes Erie and Ontario. Being of the same standard as other canals in the Great Lakes it made Lake Ontario accessible to the large lake carriers. The big *lakers* could now proceed with their grain from Port Arthur—Fort William all the way to the transshipment elevators at Prescott at the head of the St. Lawrence canals. From here it was taken to Montreal by *canallers*, carriers of about 2,500 tons, plying the St. Lawrence canals. It also became possible for ocean-going vessels carrying less than 2,000 tons to enter the Great Lakes. Within a few years several European lines established direct connections between Europe and Great Lakes ports.

With the Welland Canal completed, attention was again directed to the projected deep channel (27 feet) through the St. Lawrence River, considered by many to be long overdue. The United States Presidents from Wilson to Eisenhower strongly supported American participation but an anti-Seaway lobby (railroads, Atlantic ports, the coal-mining industry) controlled enough votes in Congress to hold up necessary legislation for several decades.[3]

Not until 1954 did work on the project get underway after Canada had decided, if necessary, to build the St. Lawrence Seaway alone.

[3] Lionel Chevrier, *The St. Lawrence Seaway*. New York, 1959. P. 33; T. L. Hills, *The St. Lawrence Seaway*. New York, 1959. P. 49.

With the 1959 shipping season the Seaway was opened to traffic, thus creating entirely new premises for transportation in the Anglo-American heartland. The Great Lakes, of tremendous importance in American transportation history, had now been connected with the ocean; a 3,800-kilometer deepwater route stretched from the Atlantic Ocean to mid-continent.

However, the St. Lawrence Seaway cannot be compared with the two great world canals, Suez and Panama, in cargo traffic and importance to international trade. Freight traffic through the St. Lawrence was 19 million metric tons as an average for the first three years of the new Seaway (1959–61), a sharp increase from the pre-Seaway average (1955–57) of 11 million tons. The St. Lawrence Seaway and the Great Lakes have controlling depths of 27 feet in the channels and canals and 30 feet over the sills in the locks.[4] The Suez Canal allows vessels with a thirty-seven-foot draft and plans provide for further work to enable the passage of 65,000-ton vessels with a forty-five-foot draft. Minimum depth of water in the Panama Canal locks is 40 feet. Neither the Suez nor the Panama can accomodate the largest vessels afloat.

The rapid development since about 1955 towards giant carriers in the oil and ore trades may have made the new Seaway somewhat obsolete almost before it was completed. The switch to ever larger carriers, favorable for western Europe and Japan with their long coastlines, should also be a boon to those American ocean ports which can provide sufficient depth.

As seen from the table, downbound traffic dominates with grain by far the most important commodity group. Upbound iron ore traffic has been remarkably small during the first years of the new Seaway. Bulk cargoes in 1961 comprised 91 per cent of the traffic. *Lakers*

[4] Saint Lawrence Seaway Development Corporation, *Annual Report 1960.* P. 4.

Commodities Moved Through the St. Lawrence River Section of the St. Lawrence Seaway 1961
Million metric tons

Commodity	Upbound	Down-bound
Agricultural products	*0.08*	*9.60*
Wheat	—	5.91
Corn	—	1.45
Barley	0.04	0.58
Soybeans	—	0.48
Oats	—	0.25
Mine products	*4.39*	*1.13*
Iron ore	3.45	0.19
Coal	0.51	0.54
Crude petroleum	0.10	—
Forest products	*0.18*	*0.01*
Pulpwood	0.16	—
Petroleum products	*1.10*	*0.19*
Fuel oil	0.93	0.07
Iron and steel	*0.41*	*1.55*
Scrap	—	1.21
Miscellaneous	*1.30*	*1.29*
Newsprint	0.26	0.01
Total	*7.47*	*13.77*

Source: *Traffic Report of the St. Lawrence Seaway 1961.* Prepared by The St. Lawrence Seaway Authority and the Saint Lawrence Seaway Development Corporation. Ottawa, 1962. P. 29.

accounted for two-thirds of the traffic and overseas vessels for one-third.

MONTREAL. The port map of the Great Lakes (page 253) depicts the situation in 1956, three years before the Seaway was opened to traffic. Montreal stands out as the dominating Atlantic port in Canada. It is located at the head of deepwater navigation on the St. Lawrence River, within sight of the first rapids. Montreal's position as Canada's principal gateway to the world market would stand out even more clearly if measured by value of goods handled. It is Canada's largest city and its chief economic center. Montreal itself with its diversified manufacturing district generates much port traffic. More important is its function as a wholesale center and a transshipment

Distance to Liverpool from selected North American Ports

	Nautical Miles
Montreal	2760
Halifax	2485
Churchill	2936
New York	3066
Philadelphia	3172
Baltimore	3328
Toledo	3300

Source: *Mercantile Marine Atlas,* London, 1956.

point for a large part of the Canadian *ecumene.* Montreal is one of the leading grain shipping ports although in the 1950s it has been surpassed by Vancouver. As most of the wheat arrives by ship from the Great Lakes these quantities figure twice in the total port statistics. Considerable quantities of grain arrive by rail from the Georgian Bay ports. Montreal's cargo turnover was temporarily increased in 1954–58 by the transshipment at Contrecoeur of iron ore from Seven Islands. In 1956 large ore carriers unloaded 2 million tons which were reloaded into small canallers and thus increased the turnover by 4 million tons. It should be noted that the port of Montreal receives very small quantities of petroleum for a city of its size. Most of the crude oil for its refineries moves by pipeline from Portland, Maine, the old winter-shipping port of Montreal in the days before Halifax and St. John were developed to fulfill this function. The deepwater channel to Montreal is 35 feet deep or the same as in the oil-shipping ports of the American Gulf Coast. Thus the chief reason for making Portland the outport for the Montreal refineries apparently was the yearly four month ice blockade of the latter port. This handicap is shared by all ports on the Great Lakes and the St. Lawrence. Montreal is the world's largest ice-bound ocean port. Were it not for the shortness of the shipping season, the St. Lawrence River, flowing roughly along the Great Circle route from the Great Lakes to Europe, would have played an even more important role in the economic history of North America. By the common shipping lanes Montreal is about 300 miles closer to Liverpool than is New York, which commands the other gateway to the Middle West, the Hudson–Mohawk Gap.

There has been much discussion in Canada about the possible influences of the St. Lawrence Seaway on the position of Montreal. Will Toronto capture some of its trade? Reference is often made to the fate of Quebec as a parallel; the city declined relatively each time the channel to Montreal was deepened. The size of present Montreal and its port makes such a development unlikely. It is safe to predict an increase in grain shipments through the St. Lawrence; transshipments will probably increase at Montreal despite the fact that many ocean vessels proceed to lakeheads (Fort William–Port Arthur, Duluth–Superior, and Chicago) for their grain cargo and many *lakers* go all the way to the newly built grain elevators at Seven Islands, much less troubled by ice. It is likely that Montreal will become an important center for heavy manufacturing; steel mills are planned or under construction. The expansion of industry is particularly marked in the Contrecoeur area on the southern shore of the St. Lawrence about 45 kilometers northeast of central Montreal. The recently completed pipeline for natural gas from Alberta is a great asset in this development.

OTHER LOWER ST. LAWRENCE PORTS. The other main ports on the lower St. Lawrence, Sorel, Trois Rivières, and Quebec, also have a large grain elevator capacity although much smaller than that of Montreal. Sorel in addition has a smelter. Trois Rivières, the leading pulp and paper center of the world, situated at the mouth of Quebec's "wood-pulp valley" receives almost a million tons of pulpwood from

domestic ports and a couple of hundred thousand tons of petroleum products and coal. It exports over one hundred thousand tons of newsprint per year. The total capacity of the seven mills in the St. Maurice River Valley is approximately one million tons; most of the production thus moves by railroad. The port trade structure of the provincial capital, Quebec, is as diversified as that of Montreal but the volume is smaller. Located "where the river narrows" (the meaning of the name in Algonquin), Quebec commands a strategic position at this entrance to the continent. For a short period after the union of Upper and Lower Canada (1841) and before the Federation in 1867 Quebec was the national capital. Now it is the second largest city in the second largest

Upper portion of Montreal Harbor, Canada's main Atlantic port and one of the leading grain ports of the world. In the center foreground is Windmill Point Basin with Bickerdike Pier on the right and Windmill Point Wharf on the left. Note the grain elevators and the coal heaps. Bituminous coal from Nova Scotia is one of the main cargoes handled in the port. In 1961 Montreal received 1.4 million tons of coal and shipped 0.5 million tons. In the upper left corner is downtown Montreal. The four finger piers on the left bank are followed by wharves stretching two miles downstream past the Jacques Cartier Bridge to three additional finger piers. There are three more elevators and a refrigerated warehouse along this stretch. (National Harbours Board)

province. It is less favorably located than Montreal which is in the heart of the St. Lawrence lowlands and closer to the densely

273

The aluminum smelter at Baie Comeau on the lower St. Lawrence, built by the British Aluminium Company after 1956. It has a capacity of 180,000 tons. Alumina and coke are transported by belt conveyors one kilometer to storage silos. Control of the British company was acquired by Canadian-American interests in 1959 and the production is earmarked for the British market. (British Aluminium Company)

populated parts of Ontario. Quebec, once a larger port than Montreal, still is a port of call for many passenger and cargo liners between Montreal and overseas destinations.[5] It is the chief outlet for the Thetford asbestos mines, which dominate world production of this mineral. Asbestos is one of the leading exports from Quebec.

The largest ports in the St. Lawrence estuary are Port Alfred and Seven Islands, both primarily ore ports. Port Alfred serves the world's largest aluminum plant at Arvida, built during World War II. The ore carriers with bauxite from Guiana and Jamaica dock within 30 kilometers of the Arvida plant. This aluminum mill and other Canadian metal smelters in the transition zone between the Laurentian Shield and the St. Lawrence lowlands were attracted by cheap hydro-electric power. Another large consumer of electricity are the many newsprint mills on both sides of the St. Lawrence River.

[5] This is in contrast to New York and Boston. Few of the liners from New York sailing to Europe call at Boston, once the leading American port and still a thriving metropolis. It is out of the way for ships sailing for European ports from New York.

Labrador Iron Ores

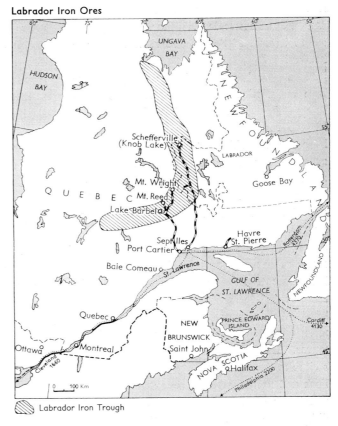

Labrador Iron Trough

Simplified orientation map after J. Küchler," Bergwirtschaft und Industrie in Labrador", *Geographische Rundschau, 1963.* P. 47. Distances are in kilometers.

Three major iron ore areas in Labrador are now being exploited and others are under investigation. From Schefferville unconcentrated ore is sent by single-track railway (trains of four diesel engines, 125 cars, carrying 10,000 tons) on the ten hour trip to Seven Islands. The port was built for 12 million tons a year, which could easily be expanded to 20 million. Twelve million tons were shipped during several years in the late 1950s. From 1962 the Wabush Lake area, halfway between Schefferville and Seven Islands, started to ship 65 per cent concentrate (capacity 7 million tons) derived from 38 per cent iron ore. Another concentration plant has been built on Lake Jeannine shipping through Port Cartier.

Several pulp and newsprint mills are served by Port Alfred. Chicoutimi, at the head of navigation on the Saguenay River, is the oil and coal receiving port.

Iron ore shipments from Seven Islands started in 1954, when the railroad to the mine at Schefferville (Knob Lake), 575 kilometers to the north, had been completed. In 1956 over 12 million tons of ore went through the port; the United States took 79 per cent (chiefly through Atlantic ports), the United Kingdom

[6] Port Cartier, capable of accomodating vessels of up to 100,000 tons, has an all-year shipping season. It has a capacity of 8 million tons, handling ore concentrates (65 per cent iron content) derived from low grade iron ore. The unconcentrated ore from Schefferville cannot be sent to Seven Islands in the winter because of its 14 per cent water content which makes it freeze. G. Humphreys, "The Montferré Mining Region Labrador-Ungava", *Scottish Geographical Magazine*, 1960. Pp. 38–45.

12 and Canada 6 per cent. The prospecting activities in Labrador, straddling the Quebec-Newfoundland boundary, have been intense in the 1950s and new areas are being opened up and exploited for their mineral wealth. Mines and concentration plants are under construction at Wabush Lake and in the Montferré area, a little more than halfway between Seven Islands and Schefferville. A new railroad parallel to the older one with ocean terminal at Port Cartier[6] west of Seven Islands was opened in 1961. Through Havre St. Pierre is shipped ilmenite, an oxide of iron and titanium, to the smelter at Sorel. The ilmenite deposits in Labrador are the largest known and it is expected that with increased use of titanium this production will expand. So far titanium is used only for the production of dyes. Several ore companies, representing a large number

of American, Canadian and European steel interests, are active in Labrador, which promises to be one of the world's richest iron ore districts.

Plans have been published for shipping ore from the northern part of the Labrador Iron Trough through a terminal on Ungava Bay. Due to the cold current along the coast of Labrador the shipping season is only four months. Four 72,000-ton Ludwig ore carriers will take the ore to Godthåb (Rype Island) on the ice-free coast of Greenland and thence ship it to German steel works during the remaining months.

HALIFAX AND SAINT JOHN. During approximately five months each year when access to the St. Lawrence is blocked by ice, Halifax and Saint John become the second and third ranking ports of Canada, surpassed only by Vancouver.[7] Halifax has a magnificent harbor. It is close to the Great Circle route between New York and northwestern Europe, a natural port of call for passenger and cargo liners on this all-important route. The greatest handicap of Halifax is its peripheral location within Canada.[8] Saint John, competing with Halifax as a winter port, is ice-free due to the high tides of the Bay of Fundy. A major export item from Halifax (a million tons a year) is gypsum from Nova Scotia deposits, exploited since 1770. Hantsport, purely a gypsum port, ships even larger quantities chiefly to the metropolitan cities of the American east coast.[9]

SYDNEY, on the north coast of Cape Breton Island, ships coal from the local field, primarily to domestic destinations. It also serves one of the largest steel mills in Canada. Assembly costs for raw materials are low at this mill; coal comes from company-owned pits a few miles from the mill, company ships transport iron ore from company-owned mines on Bell Island, Newfoundland, and limestone comes also by sea from a coastal quarry in New-

foundland. But distance to domestic markets, poor quality coking coal and lack of local supplies of scrap are serious disadvantages.[10] The hopes that the steel mill would attract secondary industries to Nova Scotia have failed to materialize just as for most other peripheral steel mills in the world.

NEWFOUNDLAND. Sparsely populated Newfoundland, the oldest British colony, became the tenth province of Canada in 1949. St. John's, the capital, has been a fishing harbor since the early sixteenth century and now is the chief commercial center of the island, dominating the import traffic. It also has some winter export shipments of paper. St. John's is the eastern terminus of a railroad running across the island to Port-aux-Basques, where steamers connect with Sydney, Nova Scotia. Two large paper mill centers, Grand Falls and Corner Brook, are on this railroad. Grand Falls is a company town begun in 1909 to house the employees of a large newsprint mill.[11] Pulp-

[7] Donald J. Patton, "Railroad Rate Structures, Ocean Trade Routes, and the Hinterland Relations of Halifax and Saint John", *Tijdschrift voor Economische en Sociale Geographie,* 1961. Pp. 2–13.

[8] In the days before regular transatlantic air service for passengers and express cargo, the combination of transcontinental railroad to Halifax and liner from there to Europe was the fastest connection between Canada and Europe. For high-value cargo, paying a premium for speed but not enough to justify air transport, Halifax retains this advantage, reflected in a rather large general cargo turnover in the port. An extension of this route was established at the end of the last century between England and the Far East by way of Montreal or Halifax and Vancouver. The old slogan of the Canadian Pacific Railway—"The C.P.R. spans the world"—is true. The railroad company has a liner service between Liverpool and Montreal (in winter Halifax) and between Vancouver and Yokohama—Hong Kong and between Vancouver and Auckland—Sydney.

[9] Gypsum ranks among the ten leading import commodities by weight in the Port of New York. It is used in the manufacture of plaster and plasterboard and as a retarder in cement. Nova Scotia accounts for 80 per cent of Canada's production.

[10] Donald Kerr, "The Geography of the Canadian Iron and Steel Industry", *Economic Geography,* 1959. Pp. 151–163.

[11] Donald F. Putnam (Editor), *Canadian Regions.* London, 1952.

wood is unloaded at Grand Falls but most of
its traffic is handled by its outport, Botwood,
which also ships over a hundred thousand tons
of lead and zinc concentrates. The large newsprint and pulp mill at Corner Brook was
established in 1925. Newfoundland's leading
port, measured by tonnage of shipments and
receipts, is the iron ore port on Bell Island, in
operation since 1895. Of 2.7 million tons shipped from the Wabana field in 1956, the United
Kingdom and Germany took 40 per cent each
and less than 20 per cent went to Sydney.

To the traditional resources of Newfoundland, fish, forests, waterpower, World War II
added another—geographical location. In addition to army camps and naval bases two large
airfields were built, one at Gander on the railroad near Grand Falls, and the other at Goose
Bay on the coast of Labrador. In the postwar
period they have served commercial airlines
on the North Atlantic run as alternative fueling
stations. Goose Bay has its own port through
which petroleum products and other supplies
for the air base are received.

CHURCHILL. North of Goose Bay Atlantic Canada has only one port of significance, at
Churchill on Hudson Bay. Its grain elevator
was built in the early 1930s; since 1929 it has
had a railroad to the Prairie Provinces. Being
on the Great Circle route between the Canadian wheat areas and northwestern Europe,
Churchill represents the shortest distance both
in land and in water transportation for Canada's great staple product. Nevertheless Churchill has been less of a success than anticipated

---

[1] The 200 kilometers from Amsterdam—IJmuiden
to Dunkerque, which includes Rotterdam, Antwerp
and Gent.
[2] Portland, Maine, has again become the outport
of Montreal which is icebound for four months a
year. It primarily handles the imports of crude
petroleum for the Montreal refineries. Pipelines connect the two cities.
[3] From Hamburg to the River Seine and including
Great Britain.

because of its great handicap—Hudson Bay
is ice-bound from late October to the end of
July.

United States: Atlantic Ports

The coast between Boston and Baltimore is the
ocean-front of the American Manufacturing
Belt. Boston has had a long relative decline as
a seaport because of its eccentric location. It
has more and more moved into the traffic
shadow of New York for general cargo and
passengers, whereas Philadelphia and Baltimore
have established keen competition with New
York, favored by rail rate differentials, by
shorter distance to most points in the Middle
West and by a less crowded waterfront which
has allowed the establishment of heavy, bulk
cargo consuming industries. The success of
Baltimore and Philadelphia has been most
striking for bulk cargo, primarily petroleum,
ore and grain. Only one coastal stretch in the
world[1] can show such a concentration of seaborne traffic as the 300 kilometers separating
New York and Baltimore. Together the ports
of New York, the Delaware River and Baltimore handle about 200 million tons of cargo,
of which 100 million tons are in foreign trade.

Seen in a wider perspective and including
Hampton Roads in the south and Portland,
Maine, in the north,[2] the North Atlantic coast
of the United States is second only to northwestern Europe[3] as a focus on the world map
of waterborne trade measured by tonnage. The
Persian Gulf, the American Gulf coast, Venezuela (including Aruba, Curaçao and Trinidad),
and the Japanese ports between Tokyo and
northern Kyushu come close in a group of
secondary focuses.

New York

New York's share of the United States foreign
trade by value increased from 6 per cent in
1790 to 37 per cent in 1830 and no less than

Selected Commodities Handled in the Five Major Ports on the Northeastern Seaboard of the United States in 1956

Thousand metric tons

Port	Foreign Trade		Coastwise		Internal		Total
	Receipts	Shipments	Receipts	Shipments	Receipts	Shipments	
Boston	4,970	1,000	10,900	990	—	—	17,860
Crude petroleum	1,000	—	1,120	—			2,120
Petroleum products	2,390	0	6,950	880			10,220
Coal	—	—	2,430	—			2,430
Iron ore	170	—	—	—			170
Other metals and ores	20	0	0	0			20
Sugar	430	—	0	—			430
Sand, gravel, crushed rock	0	—	—	0			0
Grain	0	510	0	0			510
New York	28,740	8,320	40,710	10,310	4,980	3,820	96,880
Crude petroleum	9,260	10	5,780	0	0	0	15,050
Petroleum products	10,800	520	22,600	7,100	50	3,580	44,650
Coal	0	0	940	1,750	—	0	2,690
Iron ore	0	0	—	0	—	—	0
Other metals and ores	1,300	170	30	50	—	—	1,550
Sugar	950	10	470	0	—	40	1,470
Sand, gravel, crushed rock	10	10	7,530	0	4,310	0	11,860
Grain	0	660	80	0	30	—	770
Delaware River	32,420	5,010	18,990	4,740	—	—	61,160
Crude petroleum	19,870	—	13,280	60			33,210
Petroleum products	690	330	3,120	3,810			7,950
Coal	—	430	1,080	150			1,660
Iron ore	9,400	0	—	0			9,400
Other metals and ores	660	20	20	0			700
Sugar	280	0	490	0			770
Sand, gravel, crushed rock	0	0	—	0			0
Grain	—	640	0	0			640
Baltimore	18,480	8,760	7,250	1,640	1,360	2,180	39,670
Crude petroleum	890	—	2,000	—	—	—	2,890
Petroleum products	2,080	20	3,980	360	1,050	1,350	8,840
Coal	—	4,350	—	—	—	10	4,360
Iron ore	11,140	0	—	—	0	0	11,140
Other metals and ores	2,770	40	0	10	50	0	2,870
Sugar	360	0	150	0	0	50	560
Sand, gravel, crushed rock	0	0	—	0	0	20	20
Grain	0	2,420	—	0	10	—	2,430
Hampton Roads[a]	4,560	40,100	4,790	8,850	2,790	3,410	64,500
Crude petroleum	50	—	—	—	—	—	50
Petroleum products	2,270	0	4,440	20	710	3,050	10,490
Coal	—	38,240	—	8,760	0	80	47,080
Iron ore	700	—	—	0	0	0	700
Other metals and ores	590	0	0	0	0	0	590
Sugar	0	—	0	—	40	0	40
Sand, gravel, crushed rock	0	—	—	0	1,320	0	1,320
Grain	—	980	—	0	0	—	980

[a] Includes Norfolk and Newport News.
Figures are rounded off to the nearest ten thousand tons. A zero stands for a quantity less than five thousand tons and a dash for no quantity reported.

Waterborne Foreign Trade of the United States by Selected Ports and Port Groups on the Atlantic and Gulf Coasts 1961

Ports and Port Groups	Tonnage (Million metric tons)			Tonnage (per cent)			Value (per cent)		
	Imports	Exports	Total	Imports	Exports	Total	Imports	Exports	Total
Boston	5.8	0.9	6.8	3.4	0.8	2.4	4.3	0.9	2.4
New York	31.2	5.9	37.1	18.3	5.1	13.0	40.0	34.9	37.1
Delaware River	36.7	3.1	39.7	21.5	2.6	13.9	9.9	2.7	5.9
Baltimore	13.8	4.1	17.9	8.1	3.5	6.2	5.1	4.3	4.6
Hampton Roads	5.5	23.2	28.9	3.2	20.1	10.0	2.7	5.8	4.4
Morehead City	0.2	0.1	0.2	0.1	0.1	0.1	0.0	0.5	0.3
Wilmington	0.5	0.2	0.7	0.3	0.2	0.2	0.4	0.3	0.3
Charleston	1.3	0.4	1.7	0.7	0.4	0.6	1.4	0.9	1.1
Savannah	1.6	0.6	2.2	1.0	0.5	0.8	0.9	0.8	0.9
Florida:									
Atlantic Ports	3.7	0.6	4.3	2.2	0.5	1.5	1.8	0.8	1.2
Gulf Ports	1.2	4.3	5.4	0.7	3.7	1.9	0.6	0.8	0.7
Mobile	4.8	1.3	6.1	2.8	1.1	2.1	1.0	0.9	1.0
New Orleans	3.1	8.4	11.6	1.8	7.3	4.0	4.9	9.3	7.4
Galveston	0.1	4.3	4.4	0.1	3.7	1.6	0.3	3.9	2.3
Houston	2.5	6.7	9.2	1.5	5.8	3.2	2.9	7.2	5.3
U.S. Total	171.1	115.8	286.8	100.0	100.0	100.0	100.0	100.0	100.0

Data from: *Tabular Summary of Foreign Waterborne Commerce of Virginia Ports,* see page 294.

57 per cent in 1870.[1] Since then the proportion has been decreasing but in spite of an almost century-long relative decline New York at the end of the 1950s handled 32 per cent of the United States foreign trade.[2] The story of New York's rapid rise to foreign trade dominance in the early part of last century is also the story of the city becoming the undisputed economic capital of the nation, and, in recent decades, of the world.

In colonial America foreign trade was channeled through many seaports, each little port serving only its immediate surroundings. In the southern colonies this area was often just a plantation on a river and the port a simple wharf at which occasional British ships discharged products from the home country and took on big tobacco hogsheads containing the main cash crop of the area. This pattern persisted even after the United States had been formed. The new nation, which had 5.3 million inhabitants at the beginning of the nineteenth century, much less than the 27.3 million of France and the 11.9 million of Great Britain, was concentrated on the Atlantic coast although settlers had begun to pour over the Appalachians and down the Ohio Valley.

The remarkable concentration of foreign trade to New York and a few other ports during the first half of last century was made possible by radical improvements of inland transportation: canals, surfaced roads and, after 1830, railroads. The increasing size of

[1] For a concise discussion of New York's role as the leading foreign trade port of the United States, see Benjamin Chinitz, *Freight and the Metropolis,* Cambridge, Mass., 1960. See also Jean Gottman, *Megalopolis,* New York, 1961. Both volumes contain bibliographies.

[2] New York handled 38 per cent of the ocean-borne foreign trade. No other port could claim more than 10 per cent.

THE PORT OF NEW YORK

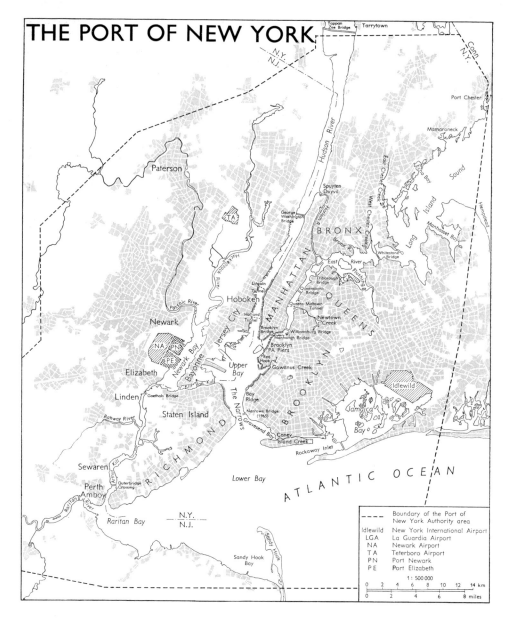

New York's general cargo, primarily carried in foreign trade, is handled at the many piers on either side of the Hudson River and the lower part of East River and in addition at the two new ports on Newark Bay, Port Newark and Port Elizabeth. The construction of these two ports marks a radical departure from the old system of handling general cargo at facilities close to the foreign trade merchants in Manhattan.

But by far the largest quantities of cargo are handled at the port installations along the channels from Raritan Bay to Upper Bay (Arthur Kill and Kill Van Kull), where New York's oil refineries, with only one exception, are located.

Large quantities of sand and gravel are received at outlying ports on Long Island Sound, the upper East River and at other peripheral port installations in the New York Port Authority area. Some of these ports also have oil depots but they usually receive oil from other installations within the port area. It is then classified as intraport traffic and is not included in our data.

vessels[3] also favored port concentration as did a number of commercial innovations.

In 1816 the three-masted *James Monroe* sailed from Manhattan inaugurating the Black Ball Line, the first regular transatlantic service, with monthly sailings from New York and Liverpool. These sail packets, larger and faster than ordinary merchant ships, specialized in high-grade freight and passenger traffic. Twenty years later steam ships were introduced on this line but the efficient sail packets remained in operation long after the steam ship became dominant. And today the frequency of sailings on regular lines is one of the yardsticks by

[3] The "Golden Age" of American shipping and shipbuilding in the early nineteenth century reached an apex in the beginning of the 1850s when the American tonnage came close to the British. The Yankee clippers, most of which were built in New England, reached tonnages over 1,000 tons. These, the fastest sailing ships ever built, sailed the Seven Seas and brought wealth and prosperity to New York and the other American seaports. In 1860 New York handled waterborne foreign commerce valued at 393 million dollars, followed by New Orleans with 129 million, Boston 58 million, Mobile 40 million, Philadelphia 19 million and Baltimore 18 million. Gottman, *op. cit.,* p. 144.

View of Manhattan and New York Harbor facing south from a point just below the George Washington Bridge. Only the central part of the world's largest conurbation can be seen in the picture. The mighty Hudson River provided an excellent harbor for the early New York. Manhattan, Brooklyn, Newark, Jersey City, and Hoboken were the main clusters of population in 1825 when the Erie Canal was completed. Each cluster was arranged around its waterfront to make the best use of its navigable water. With the coming of railroads and, much later, the cars and trucks, which made possible the spread of the urbanized area, the large water surfaces became formidable traffic barriers, but the tunnels and bridges built in recent decades as an integral part of an effective system of radial and circumferential highways are tying the far-flung parts of the metropolis together. Much of this remains to be completed. The Narrows Bridge linking Long Island to New Jersey by way of Staten Island promises to be a major part of such a circumferential system. It is scheduled for completion in 1965. (The Port of New York Authority, Sept. 1958)

which the general cargo port is measured, probably its most important selling point.

When the cost of inland transport had been reduced sufficiently, much could be gained by bringing buyers of foreign products together at one point. For example, British textiles, which made up about one-third of the United States imports in the period 1820–1850, were normally shipped to American agents. The buyers would come from all over the United States to choose from a wide assortment. The gathering of merchants and goods could obviously not be duplicated at many ports.

Most American producers and purchasers found it convenient to use the services of specialized middlemen, the foreign-trade merchants, for whom the port was the natural location. Before the first successful transatlantic cable was completed in 1866 it was imperative for the foreign trade merchant to be in close contact with the coming and going of ships to be informed on the world market situation. Foreign trade was more complex than domestic trade and the foreign trade merchants more in need of specialized services, such as those provided by banks and insurance companies, which therefore also tended to concentrate in the port city.

A large number of factors, of which only a few of the most important have been listed, thus favored a concentration of foreign trade to a national gateway on the Atlantic coast.[4] But why New York and not some other port?

The splendid harbor of New York compared favorably with the good harbors of Boston, Philadelphia and Baltimore. For the dominating trade with Europe Boston and New York had the advantage of being located on the sea whereas Philadelphia and Baltimore were far upstream on south-facing estuaries. Boston had the advantage of being closer to Europe than New York but it was eccentric to the interior of the continent. New York ranked as the number one port in the nation already by 1800 thanks to a densely populated hinterland. It was followed by Philadelphia, Boston and Baltimore.[5]

The aggressive merchants of New York were more successful than their competitors in capturing the cotton trade. More and more southern planters channeled their cotton exports through New York, and in this trade New York was favored by the configuration of the coastline. The invention of the cotton gin in 1793 made possible cotton exports in ever increasing quantities to northwestern Europe, primarily Lancashire, making cotton overwhelmingly the leading United States export, far exceeding such traditional exports as tobacco and wheat flour even as early as 1820.

Physical geography favored New York over its competitors also in relation to the trans-Appalachian world, which was becoming increasingly important in the early part of last century. The Erie Canal, opened to traffic in 1825, was built in the only water-level route through the mountains, the Mohawk Gap. It connected Lake Erie with the Hudson River and slashed the Buffalo to New York freight rate from 100 to 6 dollars per ton. For decades this canal made a tremendous impact on the flow of cargo and passengers and probably was the single most important factor in establishing New York as the nation's principal gateway for foreign trade and immigration. When major railroads were completed a couple of decades later from the Atlantic coast to Chicago and other points in the Middle West they chose New York and points south of it as their Atlantic terminals, but primarily New York.

[4] This may seem to be in contradiction to the contemporary development in Great Britain, where London had been much more dominating in earlier centuries, but Liverpool, Glasgow and a few other ports gained in relative importance as foreign trade centers in the early nineteenth century. It is no real contradiction, however. The economic forces tending towards concentration of foreign trade in Europe were also the same. Much of the early concentration in Great Britain and other European countries was based on royal privileges, which gradually were abolished.

The change in the economic geography of the European countries brought about by the Industrial Revolution led to the rise of some ports and the relative decline of others. In England the expansion of the Lancashire cotton industry favored the port of Liverpool which became a serious competitor of London as the leading foreign trade port of Britain.

[5] Ralph H. Brown, *Historical Geography of the United States*, New York, 1948. P. 129.

Boston was too far away; Baltimore and Philadelphia were somewhat closer to the Middle West but New York, thanks to its canal, already had a heavy flow of freight and passengers and it was far superior in its connections with Europe.[6]

After the Civil War[7] the foreign trade passing through New York continued to increase rapidly—but less rapidly than the total foreign trade of the United States. All other major seaports except Boston have been gaining on New York. Some simple explanations go a long way to explain New York's relative decline. The population near the Pacific coast or Gulf coast, which is definitely in the hinterland of other ports, has grown much faster than the national average. American foreign trade is no longer overwhelmingly with Europe but has a more global distribution, which means that shipment via New York more often than earlier will mean a detour. A significant and increasing amount of foreign trade does not pass through ocean ports (to Canada and Mexico). Bulk cargo is playing a greater role in foreign trade and bulk cargo follows the route that will minimize land transportation. The growing role of the truck makes shippers

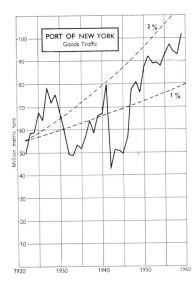

[6] The importance of the Mohawk Gap on the American transportation map is witnessed by the long string of cities between New York and Buffalo along the old Erie Canal. A larger canal along this route, the New York State Barge Canal, was completed in 1918.

The Mohawk Valley is still an outstanding route through the Appalachians into the interior followed by one of America's leading railroads (The New York Central), by a turnpike and by the New York State Barge Canal, which in the period 1950–1956 averaged only 4.6 million tons of cargo per annum, almost exclusively petroleum products.

[7] The War was a serious blow to New Orleans and helped to strengthen the east-west routes.

[8] New York has no steel industry and the oil refining industry has recently grown more slowly here than along the Delaware River. One oil company chose Delaware City for its new refinery after having existed in New York for many decades. The only land reserve in the New York area which corresponds to the alluvial plains downstream from the port cities listed would be the New Jersey Meadows, the marsh land along the Hackensack River which stands out on all New York maps as an "empty" area.

A port city with a large steel industry will have

more sensitive to small differences in distance, as truck rates climb much faster than rail rates; the nearest port becomes more attractive.

Although the total tonnage of goods has been more evenly distributed between several major seaports some services remain concentrated to New York. For example, New York still accounts for the bulk of foreign trade financing and New York foreign trade merchants negotiate much trade that is routed through other ports.

But New York's relative decline as a port especially since the 1920s remains a fact. Measured by the tonnage of its total cargo turnover, New York has grown more slowly than most of the large world ports. The location at the mouth of the Hudson River was a great asset when New York gained its dominance but in this century it has posed serious problems. New York does not have plenty of unoccupied flat land downstream for the construction of large oil refineries, steel mills and other heavy manufacturing plants, which has been characteristic of Philadelphia, Baltimore, New Orleans, Houston, London, Rotterdam and Antwerp. This means that the traffic in bulk cargo has increased only slowly.[8] The general cargo traffic which

New York's tidal range of only 4.5 feet has allowed an extensive use of finger piers instead of dock basins as in the large ports of northwestern Europe. The finger piers were of special advantage on the Manhattan side of the lower Hudson River, adding substantially to the water frontage near the heart of the New York business district where land was scarce. The piers are inadequate today for general cargo traffic, being too narrow to give convenient access for trucks, but with an expressway running along the waterfront passengers to and from the giant transatlantic liners can be assembled and dispersed within a reasonably short time. The two liners in the foreground are the French *Liberté* and the American *United States*. (The Port of New York Authority, July 18, 1956)

New York has no peer as a long-distance passenger port. Almost all transatlantic sea passengers to and from the United States pass through New York. There are also regular passenger lines to continents other than Europe. About eighty per cent of all passengers arriving in or departing from the United States by sea in recent years have passed through the port of New York. In 1950 sea passengers and air passengers bound to or from the United States totaled 1.1 million in each category; in 1959 air passengers had increased to 4.1 million and sea passengers to 1.4 million.

On August 16, 1962, a port record was set with 32,500 passengers arriving or departing in 43 vessels in a 24-hour period. Nine liners left for Europe with 10,039 travelers according to the *New York Times*. (The Port of New York Authority, July 10, 1958)

Most of the New York railroad terminals are concentrated opposite downtown Manhattan on the New Jersey side of the Hudson River. Until the Holland Tunnel was completed in 1927 cargo between railroad and vessel had to be carried by lighters or carfloats which made New York a port with high terminal costs. (The Port of New York Authority, Oct. 28, 1955)

Some of the more than 200 piers in the Port of New York belong to railroad and shipping companies, others were built by municipalities. The Port Authority has, by agreement, taken over a number of the latter terminals for reconstruction. The largest project is now in progress on the Brooklyn waterfront where the Port Authority has bought two miles of terminals stretching between Brooklyn Bridge and Atlantic Basin on Upper Bay. The contrast between the new Brooklyn P. A. Piers 1, 2 and 3 and the old, pre-truck piers nearby is striking. The experience with the new piers suggest that both time and cost of handling cargo will be considerably reduced in the Port of New York in the 1960s. (The Port of New York Authority, July 7, 1959)

In 1952 the Port Authority made an agreement with the City of Hoboken to rebuild two piers and improve a third on the New Jersey side of the Hudson. Port cranes, a typical feature of European general cargo ports, are absent on the new piers of New York. Cargo is handled by the ship's own equipment as in very small European ports. This difference between the large ports in Europe and America reflects basic differences in the ownership and administration of port facilities in the two continents. (The Port of New York Authority, Sept. 17, 1956)

Port Newark has been rebuilt since 1948 and made into a modern ocean port. Work on a similar port further south on Newark Bay was started in 1958. Together Port Newark and Port Elizabeth provide 63 ship berths with a total capacity of about 11 million tons of general cargo a year or about 40 per cent of the total general cargo capacity of the port of New York. The twin ports, which have been reclaimed from marsh land, have an extensive open storage area, which is indispensable in the handling of general cargo in the age of container-ships. They also have easy access to the express-way network enmeshing Greater New York. (The Port of New York Authority, Nov. 12, 1958)

traditionally is handled at piers in Manhattan and Brooklyn is handicapped by these piers being on the wrong side of the river. The lower New Jersey waterfront would have been the logical site of a general cargo port serving a huge hinterland to the west of the river had it not been pre-empted by the railroad terminals. When these terminals were built last century the general layout of the New York port complex, which had grown without any coordinating plan, had certain obvious advantages. Cargo was transferred between piers and railroad terminals by lighters or carfloats.[9] This system allowed great flexibility; freight could be transferred between any rail terminal on the New Jersey side and any pier on the New York side without switching the railcars. But the terminal costs to the railroads were higher than at other ports and this disparity widened as time went on. In recent decades trucks have played an increasing role both for the transfer of cargo between rail terminal and pier, for which purpose the Holland Tunnel is used, and for shipments directly between the foreign trade pier and inland points. In the late 1950s most of the general cargo of the New York hinterland was handled by truck. And the typical piers were not built to accomodate trucks! They were designed to save space on *terra firma,* not to speed up the transfer of freight between truck and vessel. As a result of the delays to the truckers, from time to time they imposed additional charges for pickup and delivery on the New York piers.

The problems caused by congestion and high terminal costs prompted a special study by a bi-state commission during World War I. The commission recommended the formation of the Port of New York Authority. It was created in 1921 by treaty between the states of New York and New Jersey with the dual task of promoting commerce and developing transport facilities. It played a prominent part during the inter-war period in the construction of the major bridges and tunnels to improve

road access between Manhattan and the peripheral parts of the port.[10] Among the Port Authority's most recent moves to counteract the increasing competition primarily from Baltimore and New Orleans has been the construction of two super-modern ports on reclaimed marsh land along Newark Bay, Port Newark and Port Elizabeth, of which the latter is still under construction. These facilities have been designed for the modern transport situation in which trucks dominate and in which container shipments are playing an increasing role. The Port Authority has also rebuilt piers at Hoboken and Brooklyn. The new piers are at least twice as wide as the old, and provide space for covered sheds within which there is a loop traffic lane. They also provide good road access.

The Holland-America Line in 1963 opened a modern pier on Manhattan. Pier 40 can accomodate 500 trucks of which those handling

bulk handling facilities which can also be used for transshipping ore to inland points (as at Baltimore and Philadelphia). But also the freight structure on the American railroads seems to have worked against New York as a bulk handling port. In 1877 the main east-west railroads, the trunk-lines, agreed on differential rates for freight between Midwest points and the large ports on the Atlantic seaboard. At the time of the agreement grain constituted over 70 per cent of the total tonnage carried by the trunk-lines to the principal Atlantic ports. Rates to Baltimore were made 3 cents per hundred pounds and those to Philadelphia 2 cents lower than the New York rates; rates to Boston should at no time be less than those to New York. The rail differentials were intended to offset the lower ocean freight rates charged at New York as compared to other North Atlantic ports. But for some decades now the ocean carriers have observed the same rates at all these ports and New York has been at a disadvantage in handling bulk cargo to and from inland points. The 1963 Supreme Court decision in favor of equalization of rail rates between the Midwest and North Atlantic ports improved New York's competitive position by eliminating what the Port Authority long had described as "archaic railroad rates".

For a short discussion of the seaboard differentials, see Stuart Dagget, *Principles of Inland Transportation,* 4th edition, New York, 1955. Pp. 374 ff.

[9] A carfloat is a lighter which has rails on it and carries the cars across the harbor.

[10] G. Joan Fuller, "Communications in the Port of New York", *Geography,* 1959. Pp. 128–130.

heavy freight can drive alongside the ships. Passengers are brought by taxi or automobile right up to the customs hall. The pier has parking and garaging facilities for 1,000 automobiles.

New York's share of the nation's oceanborne general cargo will probably continue to decline in spite of the remarkable modernization program for terminals and highways which will allow faster and cheaper transit for hinterland cargo. Several trends combine to bring about a continued decline. The construction and modernization of general cargo terminals at many ports along the Atlantic and Gulf coasts and on the Great Lakes by state and municipal authorities provide the physical equipment for a dispersion of general cargo traffic. The increased use of trucks for transports between inland points and piers will favor the "nearest port", as truck rates increase faster with distance than rail rates. General cargo is overwhelmingly carried by liners and keen competition prompts the liners to call at more ports in spite of increasing vessel size. All over the world the liner space offered is increasing faster than the tonnage of cargo handled. The table on the next page shows that New York has more sailings to various destinations than earlier but, and this is important, its margin over competing ports is narrowing. Since 1959 ports on the Great Lakes have to be included among New York's competitors.

[11] John L. Hazard, "The Seaway: A New Dimension for the Great Lakes Region and Mid-Continent Area", *Great Lakes Port Organization and Administration,* Proceedings of a Symposium Sponsored by the Great Lakes Commission, November 10, 1958.

[12] For an interesting study mapping the hinterlands of New York, Philadelphia, Baltimore and New Orleans, see Donald J. Patton, "General Cargo Hinterlands of New York, Philadelphia, Baltimore, and New Orleans", *Annals of the Association of American Geographers,* New York, 1958. Pp. 436–455. This study is based on waybills and does not include trucks which now dominate land traffic between the general cargo port and its hinterland. Patton's study should give a fairly good outline of the overlapping hinterlands of the four ports, however.

The final impact of the St. Lawrence Seaway on the flow of America's oceanborne general cargo is still difficult to assess. As the St. Lawrence River lies approximately on the Great Circle route between Lake Erie and Liverpool, the distances between ports on this lake and Liverpool are not much greater than the distance from New York (see page 272). General cargo vessels of 8,000 to 9,500 tons experience line-haul costs as low as 2 mills per ton-mile which is about 5 to 10 per cent of truck line-haul costs and only 20–25 per cent of railroad line-haul costs. These vessels have cost capabilities of reaching from Chicago to western Europe as economically as trucks reach from Chicago to Detroit or railroads from Chicago to New York.[11] The greatest drawback for direct seaborne trade between the Great Lakes and Europe is the annual four months closure of the waterway when traffic must pass through New York or other ice-free ports. New York is evidently loosing some of its Midwestern general cargo traffic as a result of the deepened St. Lawrence Seaway. The question is: how much?

Even if New York's share of the United States oceanborne foreign trade continues to decline its hinterland will still include most of the nation east of the Rocky Mountains and for transatlantic passengers most of North America. For high-value general cargo competition may come from the air carriers rather than from the competing ports. The only American port whose hinterland approaches New York's in size is New Orleans. Baltimore has a smaller hinterland and Philadelphia's is still more restricted.[12] New York will continue to be the first port of call for most incoming vessels and the last port of call for outgoing ships. Combined with an edge over other ports in number of sailings and unequalled foreign trade services this will help New York compete for high-value general cargo which pays a premium for speed.

Scheduled Sailings from New York, Baltimore, and New Orleans to Selected Foreign Ports during May 1923 and May 1957

Destination	1923			1957		
	New York	Balti-more	New Orleans	New York	Balti-more	New Orleans
London	19	7	1	11	9	9
Antwerp	10	6	1	35	20	18
Bremen	8	2	1	28	14	17
Copenhagen	9	2	1	24	11	5
Marseille	7	2	4	5	2	2
Naples	8	1	1	32	12	5
Alexandria	9	0	1	10	4	1
Havana	10	5	14	33	12	20
Rio de Janeiro	10	0	0	28	17	6
Buenos Aires	9	0	3	24	15	6
Yokohama	9	2	3	24	13	19
Hong Kong	7	2	0	16	14	2

Source: *Shipping Digest,* April 30, 1923; April 29 and May 20, 1957. Here quoted from Chinitz, *op. cit.* P. 35.

The New England Ports

Greater Boston of today includes three ports associated with the American trade with the Far East during the heyday of American shipping in the beginning of last century: Salem, Beverly and Boston. These and several other New England ports are great names in the history of American shipping. For more than two centuries New England looked to the sea for much of its economic activity—fishing, whaling, shipping and shipbuilding. In this there has been a great change in the last hundred and fifty years, however. From the beginning of the nineteenth century New England, especially its southern parts, went through a period of rapid industrialization based on the water resources of the region, later supplemented by coastwise received coal and, still later, petroleum. The New England industry to a large extent works for the American market as a whole. Exported products are of high value shipped in small amounts to any one destination. For this type of cargo New

York with its many sailings and unequalled services has become the natural gateway. New England is part of the New York hinterland for general cargo and passengers.[1] This to a large extent is true also of metropolitan Boston. Few liners call at Boston on their way to or from New York. The New England ports have been relegated to the role of handling bulk cargo only, mostly incoming petroleum products, coal, gypsum, etc.

Boston long retained the function of the leading American wool market. Now wool imports are routed through several ports. In 1956 New York imported somewhat more wool than Boston, which was rather closely followed by Philadelphia. Hampton Roads and

[1] In 1928 an extensive survey indicated that 65 per cent of New England's exports were shipped through New York and only 14 per cent through Boston. Twenty years later another study corroborated the earlier results: 81 per cent of the interviewed manufacturers shipped through New York and only 12 per cent by way of Boston. Howard L. Green, "Hinterland Boundaries of New York and Boston in Southern New England", *Economic Geography,* 1955. Pp. 283–300.

288

Charleston, serving the textile districts of the Piedmont, handled sizable quantities of wool. Boston is, however, still the leading leather market handling the largest imports of hides in the United States.

Portland, Maine, which served for 70 years after 1853 as a winter port for Montreal before the railroads to Halifax and St. John were completed and Canadian traffic was rerouted with the help of tariffs, has regained its earlier function as a short cut to the Canadian heartland with the construction of pipelines to Montreal. The first pipeline was built during the emergency conditions of the War with its serious tanker shortage. In 1950 an additional line was laid. Portland now primarily serves as an oil outport of the Canadian metropolis. A tanker depositing its cargo at Portland saves 2,000 miles per round trip.

Coal receipts at Portland, which reached a peak of two million tons in 1913 when five or six-masted schooners brought bituminous coal from Hampton Roads, were overtaken in

[2] *Ships and the Sea.* 1954, Summer. P. 22.

volume by petroleum in 1933 and are now far behind receipts of non-pipeline oil.[2]

The Delaware River Ports

The Delaware River provides a deep waterway 215 kilometers long from the sea to the head of navigation at Trenton, New Jersey. When the present dredging operations above Philadelphia have been completed in 1964 the depth of the river channel will be 40 feet all the way to Fairless, Pennsylvania. Since 1952 a Delaware River Port Authority has been active with mainly promotional tasks. It operates two bridges across the river at Philadelphia but does not own or operate any port facilities. Philadelphia, located 160 kilometers from the sea, is the main port. Upstream and downstream from the general cargo piers of downtown Philadelphia are many large manufacturing plants with their own piers, most of them located within the urbanized area. The Delaware River is pre-eminently a bulk handling port. In tonnage of foreign trade it is the largest port in the United States, handling

The gray tone indicates the approximate extension of the continuous built-up area, according to the 1960 census, for the great port cities of New York, Philadelphia and Baltimore. The urbanized areas of Washington, Wilmington, Trenton, etc. have been excluded. The 35-foot Chesapeake and Delaware Canal is a short cut between Baltimore and ports to the north.

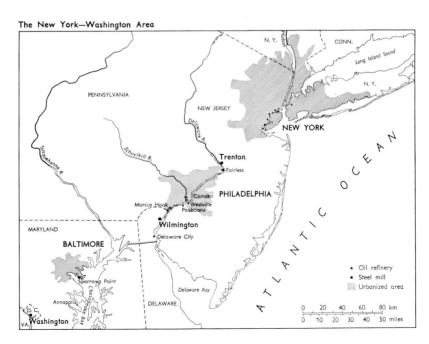

The New York—Washington Area

Looking north at the central harbor area in Philadelphia with the new Walt Whitman Bridge in the foreground. Camden, New Jersey, is to the right and Philadelphia's central business district to the left. (Delaware River Port Authority)

42.2 million metric tons in 1960 of which 39.7 were imports. No less than 62 per cent of the import tonnage was petroleum and 30 per cent ores.

The many large oil refineries on the Delaware River (at Delaware City, Claymont, Marcus Hook, Paulsboro, Westville and Philadelphia) import more crude petroleum than all other ports of the United States combined. Imports of petroleum to the Delaware River ports have grown faster than total oil receipts which reflects an increased American reliance on imported petroleum since the end of the 1940s. But also the ore imports have increased substantially. As a result the total imports of the Delaware River ports grew from 11.5 million tons in 1948 to 39.7 million in 1961.[1]

Chemical manufacturing is another major industry on the Delaware River. Brandywine Creek, a tributary of the Christina River which flows into the Delaware River at Wilmington, holds a prominent position in the history of American chemical manufacturing. It was here that the French emigrant family Du Pont in 1802 started a powder mill. The headquarters and the main experimental station of the Du Pont Company still remain at Wilmington. Several other large chemical companies are sited along the riverfront of the Delaware.

With the establishment of the United States Steel Corporation's integrated mill at Fairless the imports of iron ore, mainly from Venezuela, have increased. Large quantities of ore are also handled at Philadelphia for steel plants

[1] The total cargo turnover of the Delaware River ports increased at a more modest rate than foreign trade, from 51.7 million tons in 1948 to 90.6 million in 1959. Venezuela supplied no less than 20.8 million tons of the 1960 imports followed by Kuwait with 5.0 million. *Foreign Waterborne Commerce of the Delaware River Port* 1960. Delaware River Port Authority, 1961.

in eastern Pennsylvania and further inland. In addition to iron ore sizable quantities of alloy metals are received, primarily manganese and chrome. About one million tons of sugar are handled at the piers of two large sugar refineries.

The Delaware River has been known for its shipbuilding activities since Colonial times. The world's first nuclear powered merchant ship, the N. S. *Savannah,* was built at Camden. Another two large shipyards are located in greater Philadelphia. Like other American shipbuilding centers Philadelphia has depended on navy contracts and the construction of heavily subsidized merchant ships for the survival of this time-honored industry.

Baltimore

Baltimore by the end of the eighteenth century had become one of the leading American ports, well-known for its fast vessels, later called *Baltimore clippers.* It had locational advantages for the West Indian and South American trade. Like New York and Philadelphia it had large exports of wheat flour. The winter wheat grown in the Piedmont of Maryland, Virginia and Pennsylvania was the basis

The large integrated Fairless Works of the United States Steel Corporation at Morrisville on the Delaware River with an ocean-going ore carrier unloading at the ore yard in front of the blast furnaces. The steelworks has been in operation since 1952. (United States Steel Corporation)

291

of a high grade flour with good keeping qualities in the Tropics. Until the Civil War Baltimore's flour exports were second only to those of New York, a position held by virtue of Baltimore's trade with South America, primarily Brazil. From Brazil coffee was taken as a return cargo. Chilean copper was an important return cargo from South America's west coast until the 1869 Copper Act put a stop to this import.[1] Baltimore still is an important milling center and a large grain shipping port. It is also one of the chief copper refining centers in the world.

The fertilizer industry had its beginning in the guano trade in which Baltimore was prominent already in the 1850s, when Peruvian guano was the leading import from the west coast of South America.[2] In the 1930s Baltimore had become the largest fertilizer center in the world. Until the middle 1930s, when the new American farm policy made it profitable for farmers in the Middle West to put on more commercial fertilizers to compensate for reduced acreages, the south-eastern states accounted for most of the fertilizers consumed in the United States. Baltimore was in an advantageous position as a supply point for the South.

The most important traffic generator in the port of Baltimore is, however, the steel industry. The Bethlehem Steel plant at Sparrows Point receives large quantities of alloy ores as well as iron ores and ships steel products. But Baltimore is also a receiving and shipping port for inland steel works. For this traffic Baltimore's traditional freight differential was an advantage.

Baltimore is located 270 kilometers from the Capes. An attempt to overcome the disadvantage of Baltimore's distance from the sea for the trade with American ports to the north and with Europe was made already in 1829 when a 10-foot locked canal, the Chesapeake and Delaware Canal, was completed. The Federal Government acquired this private canal

Shortest Rail Distances in Miles

From	To		
	Balti-more	Phila-delphia	New York
Buffalo	404	406	390
Cleveland	444	490	562
Chicago	767	814	890
Pittsburgh	313	360	426
St. Louis	891	964	1,040

Data from Blood, *op. cit.* P. 196.

and in the 1930s improved it to a 27-foot sea-level waterway which after 1954 was deepened to 35 feet. The canal cuts a day off the sailing time between Baltimore and ports to the north.

Being far from the sea in Baltimore's case means being close to the interior. As can be seen from the table Baltimore is closer than New York and Philadelphia to most points in the Middle West. The agreement between the trunk railroads in 1877, after the great rate war, fixed the differentials for the three competitors so that Baltimore's rate on westbound traffic, until the recent Supreme Court decision in favor of equalization, was from three to eight cents per hundred pounds below New York's, while Philadelphia's was from two to six cents below; on eastbound traffic Baltimore's rate was three cents below New York's while Philadelphia's was two cents below.

Baltimore is the only Atlantic port whose general cargo hinterland stretches far enough inland to be a serious competitor of New York and New Orleans in the Middle West.

In the days of George Washington Alexandria on the Potomac was a prosperous trading center at which many small ocean vessels

[1] Pearle Blood, "Factors in the Economic Development of Baltimore, Maryland", *Economic Geography*, 1937. Pp. 187–208.

[2] There was a steady demand for the guano in Maryland and in the tobacco and cotton districts to the south where the soils were exposed to heavy precipitation.

The steel plant at Sparrows Point in Greater Baltimore was established in 1887, based on iron ore from Cuba and coal from the nearby Appalachian fields. The works was acquired by the Bethlehem Steel Company in 1915 and has subsequently been expanded several times until in 1960 it was listed with the largest steel ingot capacity in the United States (7.5 million metric tons per year). Ore is still imported, chiefly from Latin America. The mill is located in one of the leading canning regions of the United States, but the works also ships large quantities of steel products to the Pacific Coast. In addition to tinplate ship's plate is a major product. The mill is adjoined by a large shipyard (left). (Bethlehem Steel Company)

called.[3] Today it is a residential suburb of Washington, D.C., which itself was planned as a gateway for east-west trade. But Washington has become one of the most pronounced administrative cities the world has known and the only cargoes handled at its river quays are bulk commodities transported on interior waterways, petroleum products and sand and gravel. Richmond, Virginia, has had a similar history as a port, but it also has about half a million tons of foreign and coastwise trade, chiefly handled at the deepwater terminal seven kilometers below the city. Washington and Richmond are in the trade shadow of more favorably endowed ports, Baltimore and Hampton Roads.

Hampton Roads

The drowned mouth of the James River, which enters the lower Chesapeake Bay near the At-

[3] J. R. Smith, M. O. Phillips and T. R. Smith, *Industrial and Commercial Geography*. New York, 1955. P. 563.
[1] J. R. Smith & M. O. Phillips, *North America*. New York, 1942. Pp. 211–212.

lantic Ocean, is an excellent harbor, the best between New York and Rio de Janeiro.[1] The urban settlement on Hampton Roads, Greater Norfolk with the satellite towns of Portsmouth and Newport News, has remained rather small, at least in comparison with Boston, New York, Philadelphia and Baltimore. This must chiefly be explained by the great differences in historic background between the northern and southern colonies and the contrasting economies that developed in the northern and southern states.

Hampton Roads has long played a role as an ocean gateway of North Carolina, Virginia and West Virginia but became a large port when it was made the ocean outlet of the Pocahontas coal field. The railroads that connect Hampton Roads on the ocean and Toledo-Sandusky on Lake Erie with the central Appalachian coal fields in West Virginia and Virginia rank among the most heavily trafficked railroads in the United States.

Most of the coal coming through Hampton Roads used to be sent north in coasters, some was exported and, in the days of steamships, substantial quantities were used as bunker coal. The Pocahontas field is famous for its smokeless steam coals. After World War II the shipping pattern has changed. Coastwise shipments of coal have decreased but the United States has become the leading coal exporter in the world. Thanks to favorable geological conditions which permit open pit mining and a high degree of mechanization and thanks also to an efficient transport system American coals have competed successfully in a shrinking world market. Most of the American coal exports have been shipped from Hampton Roads, making this port one of the chief hubs on the world map of oceanborne dry cargo.

In addition to shipments of growing but widely fluctuating quantities of grain on the export side and ores and gypsum on the import side Hampton Roads also handles some general cargo. In 1961 the leading countries of destination for cargo shipped through Hampton Roads were Japan, Italy, West Germany and the Netherlands. These countries received 6.2–2.8 million metric tons. They were followed by six countries receiving between half and one million tons: United Kingdom, Brazil, Belgium, Sweden, France and Argentina.[2] Total exports amounted to 23.4 million tons of which coal was 20.6 million and grains 1.9 million.[3]

The excellent harbor at Hampton Roads in addition to its large bulk traffic has the major

east coast naval installations and a large shipbuilding and repair industry.[4]

Atlantic Ports South of Hampton Roads

The ports south of Hampton Roads fall into two groups. In the first group are those ports from Morehead, North Carolina, to Jacksonville, Florida, which serve the forest industries, mainly the pulp and paper industries located in the coastal cities, as well as the manufacturing areas in the Piedmont and the agricultural hinterland known for its heavy consumption of fertilizers. The high turpentine content of the southern pines makes turpentine and rosin important bi-products of the pulp and paper industry. Some of the turpentine is recovered by pine chipping-and-cupping, a process that accounted for almost all of the naval stores as late as 1930.[1] The steady climb in the volume of pine that is pulped should make increasing quantities of turpentine available in the world's leading naval stores producing area.

The second group of ports are those serving the residential areas of southeastern Florida where the subtropical climate is the chief prop of the economy and exportable products are almost entirely lacking.

Charleston, Savannah and Wilmington were important ports and trading centers in colonial days. At the first Federal Census in 1790

[2] *Tabular Summary of Foreign Waterborne Commerce of Virginia Ports Calendar Year and Fourth Quarter of 1961.* Prepared by Research Economist, Virginia State Ports Authority, Norfolk, Virginia, May 1962. VIII: 4.

[3] Total coal dumpings at Hampton Roads were 26.0 million tons.

[4] The Bureau of Population and Economic Research at the University of Virginia (Charlottesville) has published a series of reports on the impact of the Virginia ports (for all practical purposes = Hampton Roads) on the economy of Virginia. The latest is entitled *Measuring the Impact of the Waterborne Commerce of the Ports of Virginia on Employment, Wages, and Other Key Indices of the Virginian Economy 1953–1960.* December, 1961.

[1] Merle Prunty, Jr., "Recent Expansion in the Southern Pulp-Paper Industries", *Economic Geography,* 1956. P. 56.

Hampton Roads, the world's leading coal shipping port, has expanded its facilities for handling other bulk cargo and also general cargo. The new 5-berth general cargo pier under construction for the Virginia State Ports Authority at Norfolk will have wide aprons and gantry cranes that can be moved from one side of the pier to the other. The cargo hatches in the roof of the transit shed are designed for the largest anticipated containers. Note also the excellent access for railroad cars and trucks. Large open storage areas will be provided inshore for containerized cargo or other cargo not requiring covered storage. (Virginia State Ports Authority)

Charleston surpassed Baltimore, the only other large city in the South, and it was the southern center of culture and wealth. At the beginning of last century the Gulf coast and Florida became parts of the United States and New Orleans and Mobile soon overtook the Atlantic ports as gateways of the rapidly expanding Cotton Belt. After the Civil War the Atlantic ports became historic monuments of bygone days until they have recently seen a renaissance with the expansion of the southern forest industries. Each of the three ports is the main port of its state. But their promotional efforts are not limited to the southeastern states, which have had a rather expansive economy in recent decades. They also attempt to attract traffic from the Middle West for their modern state docks.

[2] *The Port of Jacksonville, Florida.* Port Series No. 15, Revised 1956. Corps of Engineers, U.S. Army and Maritime Administration, U.S. Department of Commerce. The reports in this series, compiled and published since 1946, have been consulted also for other United States ports. They give a detailed account of the physical port and harbor facilities and some general information on the trade relations of the port.

Jacksonville, on the St. Johns River in northeastern Florida, is the largest Atlantic port in the United States south of Hampton Roads. Many railroads and highways converge on the city making it one of the major trade and transportation hubs in the Southeast. Its principal items of waterborne commerce are petroleum products, as in all big cities, fertilizer and fertilizer materials, as in all ports of southeastern United States, gypsum, lumber and naval stores.[2]

The continuous urbanized area stretching about 150 kilometers from Coral Gables south of Miami to North Palm Beach has three ports. Port Everglades, on the city limits of Fort Lauderdale and Hollywood, handles the largest tonnages. This modern port is overwhelmingly a petroleum port but has also general cargo facilities. Both Port Everglades and Miami have a considerable passenger traffic. The proximity to Cuba and the Caribbean influences the passenger traffic but is very little reflected in the cargo structure of the three ports. Some sugar is imported to Palm Beach and molasses to Port Everglades.

The Gulf Coast

The Eastern Gulf Coast

TAMPA, the outstanding seaport on Florida's west coast, is known on the map of world trade for one cargo, phosphate. Deposits of this fertilizer mineral were discovered a short distance east of Tampa in 1882 and the first shipments were made in 1888. Phosphate shipments from the richest deposits in the world thus antedate the port of Tampa which goes back to 1908 when a twenty-foot canal was completed across the shallow Hillsborough Bay. This canal has later been deepened in stages to its present depth of 34 feet. In the early days most of the phosphate was sent out through an outport, Port Tampa, but today, with a deep channel leading to the city much phosphate is loaded in Tampa. In 1960 phosphate shipments amounted to 5.5 million tons or about 40 per cent of the 13.3 million tons handled in the port. Most of the phosphate is exported and most of the phosphate exports go to Japan.[1]

But Tampa since early days has also been the leading trade and transportation focus of Florida's west coast. This is reflected in large domestic receipts of petroleum products and imports of almost one million tons of various commodities including bananas, cement and steel products. Exports, other than phosphate, are small. They include steel scrap and citrus fruit. The cargo turnover of Tampa has trebled in the postwar period.

After World War II barge traffic has become important at Tampa, accounting for ten per cent of the cargo turnover in 1960. There are both deep sea barges, operating between Tampa and Texas and Louisiana ports, and the standard barge designed for nine-foot channels. The old project of connecting the Gulf Intracoastal Waterway, stretching from Brownsville, Texas, to St. Marks on the Florida panhandle, and the Atlantic Intracoastal Waterway, extending from New Jersey to Florida's east coast, by a canal across Florida is again under consideration. For Tampa the most important part of this project seems to be the "missing link" of the Gulf Intracoastal from St. Marks to Tampa which would give Tampa a sheltered barge canal all along the Gulf Coast and to the Midwest via the Mississippi Waterway.[2]

MOBILE. In antebellum days Mobile was one of the leading American ports. It was dominated by the cotton exports and cotton was overwhelmingly the leading item on the American export list. The Mobile Bay region was occupied by the Americans in 1813. Mobile became the natural gateway for the cotton grown in the Alabama-Tombigbee Basin which took in most of Alabama and a strip of eastern Mississippi; it was the economic focus of this vast region. Cotton from the northern part of the state was shipped down the Tennessee and eventually reached New Orleans, the number one cotton port.[3] Mobile was second only to New Orleans in cotton shipments which reached an all time peak in 1860 with 800,000 bales.

For many years after the war Mobile lay dormant like Charleston and Savannah; cotton shipments fluctuated around 300,000 bales a year. A new phase in Mobile's history began at the end of last century with the lumber industry, which had migrated from the cutover forests of the east to the Great Lakes and, somewhat later, to the South. In 1906, the first year for which complete data are avail-

[1] Charlotte south of Tampa is the second port serving the Florida phosphate industry.
[2] *Tampa Port*, April 1962. Published by Hillsborough County Port Authority.
[3] Edward L. Ullman, *Mobile: Industrial Seaport and Trade Center*. Chicago, 1943.

The phosphate terminal at Port Tampa. Twelve of the sixteen million tons of phosphate mined in the United States in 1960 came from the Tampa Bay area. Less than six million tons were shipped through Tampa's phosphate terminals, of which over half was exports. Much of the domestic deliveries are thus made by rail. (Hillsborough County Port Authority)

Barge loading phosphate at Seddon Island, Tampa. Barge traffic in the port began after World War II with large seagoing barges towed singly to Freeport, Texas, bringing sulphur as a return cargo. Later river barges, the standard "jumbo" barges carrying 1,100 to 1,300 tons and drawing 8.5 feet of water, were introduced. The latest development is "convertible" barges. Two of these and a river barge are towed down the Mississippi, all drawing 8.5 feet. At New Orleans the cargo on the river barge is transferred onto the two convertibles which now draw 12 feet each. The conversion is reversed at New Orleans on the return trip. (Hillsborough County Port Authority)

able on Mobile's ocean trade, cotton amounted to 60,000 tons of a total cargo turnover of 1.7 million tons. Forest products was the leading item (617,000 tons) followed by coal (335,000 tons, almost entirely bunker), grain (over 100,000 tons) and bananas (55,000 tons). Mobile also began to ship out iron and steel products from the rapidly developing Birmingham district. The United States Steel Corporation, which after 1907 dominated Birmingham, supplied their West Coast customers primarily from their Alabama mills, whereas the second largest steel concern, the Bethlehem Steel Company, shipped from their tidewater plant at Sparrows Point, Baltimore. The improvements of the Warrior River since 1920, providing barge connection with Birmingham, aided this trade. In the 1950s this has developed into a two-way traffic with imported iron ore and alloy ores moving to Birmingham and steel products moving downstream. From 1936 Mobile has also had increasing imports of bauxite.

The Western Gulf Coast

Most of the many large ports in the western part of the Gulf Coast exist because of one important fact of transport economics—it is cheaper to send oil by tanker than by pipe line from the Gulf Coast fields and the interior fields of Texas, Oklahoma and adjacent states to the huge markets on the Atlantic seaboard.[1] As a result petroleum and petroleum products from the oil ports on the Gulf Coast to the ports on the Atlantic seaboard move by tanker, making this one of the world's busiest trade routes.[2] As refineries are located both in shipping ports and the receiving ports the oil flow from the Gulf is made up of both crude and various refined products. Shipments of oil to foreign destinations have declined considerably in the post-war period and are quite unimportant in comparison with domestic shipments. The United States has become a large net importer of petroleum in the 1950s.

United States: Tidewater Located Refineries by Coastal Region

Percentage of total U.S. crude oil refinery capacity, January 1, in respective years.

Coastal Region	1931	1938	1950	1961
Atlantic Coast	14.5	14.3	16.0	14.7
Gulf Coast	15.0	23.2	29.8	29.9
Pacific Coast	18.6	16.9	12.6	14.5
Continental U.S.	48.1	54.4	58.4	59.1
Puerto Rico	—	—	—	0.9
Hawaii	—	—	—	0.1
Total on tidewater	48.1	54.4	58.4	60.1

Data from *The Oil and Gas Journal.*

Not only petroleum has attracted shipping to the Gulf Coast. Many manufacturing firms have made good use of the advantages offered by the region: (a) an abundance of natural gas for fuel and power; (b) large supplies of raw materials such as oil and gas, sulphur, salt, lime (sea shells), magnesium (from sea water), and forest products; (c) location both on tidewater and the inland waterway system, providing cheap freight rates for shipments of bulky manufactured products as well as receipts of ores from abroad and bulky semi-manufactured goods from the Manufacturing Belt. Some large plants were built on the Gulf Coast in the 1930s but the industrial boom started with World War II and has continued in the post-war period. In the post-war years the region from New Orleans-Baton Rouge to Brownsville, Texas, bordering the Gulf Intracoastal Waterway has been one of the most expansive in the United States. In addition to traffic generated by petroleum and various manufacturing industries several ports have shipments of agricultural products (cotton, wheat, corn, soybeans, rice, etc.).

[1] Erich W. Zimmermann, World Resources and Industries. New York, 1951. P. 531. See also O.E.C.D., *Pipelines and Tankers.* Paris, 1961. P. 22.
[2] A products pipeline from Texas to New York is scheduled for completion in 1963. Cf. page 70.

Inset 2: Ports on the American Gulf Coast

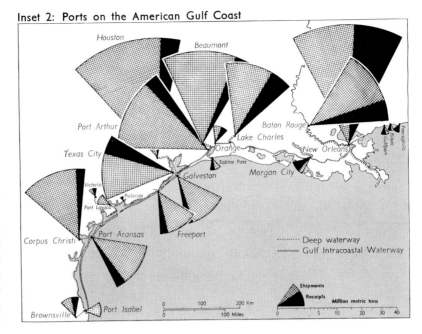

The concentration of large seaports in the western part of the American Gulf Coast necessitates the map scale 1 : 10,000,000. The same symbol scale is used on all port maps, irrespective of map scale.

Historically, the western Gulf Coast was important on the map of world trade even before the discovery of oil about the turn of the century.[3] However, shipping was largely confined to New Orleans on the Mississippi River, the natural traffic artery to the rich agricultural regions of the present Middle West. New Orleans was already a trade center during French and Spanish colonial times. Following the Louisiana Purchase in 1803 and the rise of steamboat traffic New Orleans grew rapidly and for several decades ranked as the fifth largest city in the United States, surpassed only by New York, Baltimore, Boston and Philadelphia. In 1850 it had over 100,000 inhabitants. But the flat, almost featureless coastal plain, only a few feet above sea level, suffering from poor drainage, with shallow salt water lagoons behind the offshore barrier reefs, did not provide natural harbors.[4] Before the Civil War wild cattle were hunted on the coastal plain for the hides; later some small cattle ports on the Texas coast shipped animals "on the hoof" to New Orleans, Havana and New York.[5] After the Civil War the cattle men turned their back on the ocean; the great cattle drives began, and they went north, not to the coast. With the coming of the railroads, the interior of Texas and the lower Rio Grande valley were settled. Galveston, the only coastal port of some significance, was still undeveloped.

The Mississippi Delta Ports

The Mississippi had a serious drawback as a trade route for the Middle West in the early

[3] The first commercial production of oil in Texas occurred in 1899 and two years later a well in the famous Spindletop field near Beaumont, the first of the rich salt domes in the Gulf Coast region, was drilled. (E. N. Tiratsoo, *Petroleum Geology*, London, 1951.) Texas became the leading oil producing state in the 1920s and Louisiana vies with California for the second place, having increased production much more rapidly than California. The two Gulf states produced 54 per cent of the United States total in 1956.

[4] Edwin J. Foscue, "The Ports of Texas and their Hinterlands", *Tijdschrift voor Economische en Sociale Geografie*, 1957. Pp. 1–14.

[5] C. Langdon White and Edwin J. Foscue, *A Regional Geography of Anglo-America*, New York, 1954. P. 184.

part of last century: it flows in the wrong direction. The demand was overwhelmingly for east-west traffic, for the Atlantic Seaboard and Europe were the important trade partners of the Middle West. United States foreign trade was primarily with Europe a hundred years ago; it has since gradually become more global in distribution,[1] favoring the Gulf Coast which has time and distance advantages over North Atlantic ports in trade between the central Middle West and Latin America and Australasia. The Erie Canal was a serious competitor of the Mississippi from 1825 and by the 1870s the east-west railroads had taken over most of the cargo between the Middle West and the Atlantic seaboard. At the end of the nineteenth century the Gulf ports, including New Orleans, were at a low ebb. Only exports of cotton to Europe were important.

In spite of the fact that the Mississippi barges now carry several times as much cargo as the steamboats did during their heyday, and that New Orleans in 1950 had six times as many inhabitants as a hundred years earlier, the role of the river traffic in the national traffic pattern, and of the city among American cities, is much less prominent. But in one important respect New Orleans is in a better position than ever before—as a foreign trade port for general cargo. This is because of its unique geographic location which gave the city an early start among Gulf ports and because of the increasing importance of the Gulf in American foreign trade.

New Orleans, like New York, acquired good railroad connections with the Middle West. The Illinois Central system especially, having New Orleans as its single port outlet, has acted as a powerful solicitor for traffic through New Orleans. Railroads and trucks now are the chief carriers of general cargo between the port and its wide hinterland, which in extent is only surpassed by that of New York. Two commodities imported in large quantities at New Orleans, bananas and coffee, reach north-

eastward into western Pennsylvania and western New York state and into the northern Great Plains. New Orleans gets more trade than New York in parts of the Middle West, west of a line from Chicago through Indianapolis and Cincinnati to Louisville.[2]

NEW ORLEANS. The port of New Orleans comprises both banks of the Mississippi from the mouth of the river to a point about 200 kilometers upstream. It lies at the pivot of the South's inland waterway system, the meeting point of the Mississippi River and the Gulf Intracoastal Waterway.[3] About half of New Orleans' traffic in 1956 was handled within the corporate city limits. Points above the city handled 40 per cent and points below 60 per cent of the remainder. Whereas traffic in the city increased but slightly in the preceeding decade, upstream traffic had almost doubled. Downstream seven times as much cargo was handled as ten years earlier. Among downstream wharves is Port Sulphur, about halfway between New Orleans and the mouth of the river. New Orleans has had its share of the postwar industrial expansion, which typically takes place on the deepwater channels away from the built-up areas.[4]

[1] *Historical Statistics of the United States 1789–1945. A Supplement to the Statistical Abstract of the United States.* Washington, D.C., 1949.

[2] Donald J. Patton, "General Cargo Hinterlands of New York, Philadelphia, Baltimore and New Orleans", *Annals of the Association of American Geographers,* 1958. Pp. 436–455.

[3] This waterway, extending for more than 1,750 kilometers from St. Marks, Florida, to Brownsville, Texas, annually handles almost 50 million metric tons of commerce. In the summer of 1942 Congress enacted legislation deepening the canal from nine to twelve feet and widening it from one hundred to one hundred and twenty five feet and extending it from Corpus Christi to Rio Grande. It was desirable for the protected interior waterway to take over more of the coastal traffic exposed to submarine attacks.

[4] Work on a new seaway channel, the Mississippi River Gulf Outlet, was begun in 1958 and it is scheduled for completion in 1963. It provides a 36-foot channel for the 110 kilometers between the 38-foot contour in the Gulf of Mexico and the Industrial Canal near the center of New Orleans. *New Orleans: Port Handbook and Manual.* P. 21.

Bulk cargo, primarily petroleum products, also makes up most of the traffic in New Orleans, which is one of the chief gateways to the interior of the North American continent, ranking second only to New York in the value of its foreign trade. The following commodities accounted for the largest tonnages in 1956: petroleum and petroleum products, sulphur, sea shells, sugar, rolled steel products, soybeans, corn and wheat.

New Orleans leads all other ports in the United States in the export of corn, cotton, soybeans, wheat flour, and farm machinery and it is one of the leading wheat exporters. It has the largest imports of bananas, sugar, and sisal and stands second in coffee.[5]

By value cotton is still the leading export commodity. The Cotton Exchange in New Orleans, organized in 1871, has played a prominent role in the economic life of the South.

The vigorous promotion of the port of New Orleans in the last decades has found expression in the International House, which was founded in 1943 and later has been followed by similar institutions in other American cities. It supplies visiting business men with a dining-room, lounge, private office space with bilingual secretarial service, a world trade reference library with a trained research staff and guidance by experts on foreign trade, who also provide trade contacts and information on purchasing, selling and shipping. New Orleans is one of four American ports having a foreign trade zone, corresponding to the free ports of Europe.[6]

Lake Pontchartrain, not included in the port of New Orleans, handled two million tons of sea shells and sand and gravel in 1956. This traffic is not shown on page 299.

[5] *New York Herald Tribune,* Special Supplement devoted to Ports of Louisiana. Paris, February, 1957.

[6] Richard S. Thoman, "Foreign Trade Zones of the United States", *Geographical Review,* 1952, and *Free Ports and Foreign Trade Zones,* Cambridge, Md., 1956.

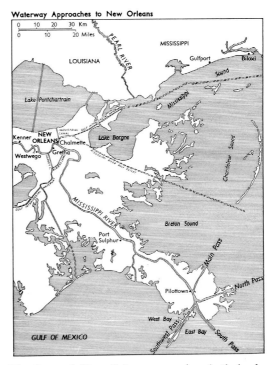

Waterway Approaches to New Orleans

The Port of New Orleans comprises both banks of the Mississippi River from a point 203 kilometers above the Head of Passes to the mouth of the Passes. The main part of the port is located about 175 kilometers from the Gulf of Mexico. Most of the general cargo terminals are situated along the left bank of the river within the city limits. Petroleum facilities are located chiefly along the right bank, and wharves for handling dry bulk cargo are generally confined to the Harvey and Industrial Canals.

Deep-draft vessels have traditionally entered the river through the Southwest or the South Pass. Work on a new sea-level route to the open Gulf of Mexico at the 38-foot contour was begun in early 1958. It will be opened for traffic in 1963. Miles of industrial sites adjacent to deep water will become available. The new Public Bulk Terminal and some industries have already been located on the Tidewater Channel.

BATON ROUGE, the northernmost deep-water port on the Mississippi, is located 370 kilometers from the Gulf of Mexico. The port includes both banks of the river for a distance of about 15 kilometers. Baton Rouge is a larger refining center than New Orleans and

Canal Street, the main thoroughfare of New Orleans, with the old French Quarter (*Vieux Carré*) to the right and the main parts of the central business district to the left. The old type of paddle wheel river boat at the Canal Street Wharf reminds the many tourists of ante-bellum days when the Mississippi was a main highway for river steamers carrying cargo and passengers.

The huge Public Grain Elevator at New Orleans. Note the barges at the receiving wharves in the foreground. About half of the grain and the soybeans arrives by barge down the Mississippi; the rest comes by rail. Because of its large shipments of soybeans and corn in addition to wheat New Orleans often ranks as one of the world's leading grain ports. (Board of Commissioners of the Port of New Orleans)

Bananas in plastic wrapping being unloaded by conveyor belts at the United Fruit terminal in the port of New Orleans. (United Fruit Company)

The general cargo wharves near downtown New Orleans. The Greater New Orleans Highway Bridge crosses the river to the right and in the background can be seen Lake Pontchartrain. (Board of Commissioners of the Port of New Orleans)

One of the most important post-war developments in American transportation has been the renaissance of traffic on inland waterways. In 1930 rivers and canals accounted for 1.8 per cent of the total freight ton-miles which should be compared with 75.2 per cent for the railroads. In 1959 the corresponding percentages were 8.8 and 46.1.

The perfection of barges and towboats, allowing tows of 25 barges containing about 25,000 tons of diverse cargoes, and the large federal investments in waterways since the early 1920s have made this possible. The low cost of inland water transport is derived from two main factors. The cargo is handled at the terminals by efficient bulk handling equipment. The motive power and the crew, the two most expensive elements of any vessel, are separated from the cargo container. The towboat can leave the barges to be loaded or unloaded and thus it spends little time at the terminals. For comparison it should be mentioned that a general cargo liner often spends more than half its time in port.

The broad impact on the American economy of the increased inland waterway traffic is a more rapid growth of industries using bulk cargo in areas adjacent to waterways than in areas served only by rail. As the American inland waterways are almost synonymous with the Mississippi River system, the Gulf Intracoastal Waterway and the Warrior River system the new trend must favor the Gulf ports. It should particularly favor New Orleans, the pivot point for the two leading waterways, the Mississippi and the Gulf Intracoastal Waterway.

The photograph shows a barge tow being pushed downstream on the Mississippi with 22 barges— 19 loads and 3 empties—carrying a total of 15,000 tons of steel, grain and merchandise. (Board of Commissioners of the Port of New Orleans)

petroleum and petroleum products make up a larger share of total port traffic. The leading dry cargo item is bauxite imported for the Kaiser alumina plant, which was built by the government at the beginning of the Second World War and sold to the private company after the war. Other commodities are grains, including soybeans, received by barge and exported by ocean vessels, sea shells also received by barge and industrial chemicals chiefly shipped coastwise.

As centers for chemical and other heavy fresh water consuming industries Baton Rouge and New Orleans have the advantage of an inexhaustible supply from the river. In some other manufacturing ports of the western Gulf Coast region the fresh water supply may very well in the future become a limiting factor for further industrial expansion.

The Canal Ports of Texas and Louisiana

Everywhere in the Gulf South port development has depended more on community initiative and drive than on natural advantages.[1] Most of the deep-water ports are largely manmade. Through the 1,100-kilometer Gulf Intracoastal Waterway from the Mississippi to the Mexican border all ports are connected to the Mississippi waterway system. The Gulf Coast petroleum region is one of the two major originating areas for barge traffic on the rivers and canals of the United States.[2] The other one

[1] James J. Parsons, "Recent Industrial Development in the Gulf South", *Geographical Review,* 1950. Pp. 67–83.
[2] Donald J. Patton, "The Traffic Pattern on American Inland Waterways", *Economic Geography,* 1956. Pp. 29–37.

is the Appalachian coal fields, especially along the Monongahela River.

Between the Mississippi and the Rio Grande six deep waterways (thirty to forty feet) have been dredged inland from the coast creating twelve deepwater ports with direct access to the Gulf of Mexico. These are Calcasieu (Lake Charles), Sabine-Neches (Port Arthur, Beaumont, Orange), Houston Ship Channel (Galveston, Texas City, Houston), Old Brazos River (Freeport), the Port Aransas—Corpus Christi Waterway (Corpus Christi, Port Aransas) and the Brownsville Channel (Brownsville, Port Isabel). Plans have been published for adding two deepwater ports by building a deep waterway to the shallow ports of Point Comfort and Port Lavaca some hundred kilometers northeast of Corpus Christi. The ports listed usually consist of many kilometers of deep waterway.

Many factories, removed from existing built-up areas, line the deep channels. Large plants commonly stand in the center of vast tracts of company-owned land. The industrial landscape developing on the Gulf Coast differs strikingly from the congested factory districts of the older manufacturing centers. The expansion has been particularly marked in petroleum refining and in heavy chemical manufacturing. The plants have been financed by the government (during World War II; especially synthetic rubber) and by already established national concerns, several of which have concentrated a large part of their postwar expansion along the Gulf Coast. As most of the plants built in this area represent a high ratio of capital investment to employment, the population increase, although one of the highest in the nation, does not match the increase in industrial capacity. Port statistics also fail to show the development of manufacturing in the oil ports of the Gulf Coast since most products are shipped by rail

or truck. Nevertheless, deep water was essential in attracting heavy industry.[3]

The deep water channels, dredged at high cost for the large tanker traffic, can of course also be utilized by dry cargo ships. The additional costs are limited to those of building quays, warehouses, etc., or costs that would be incurred in any natural harbor. Ports developing general cargo traffic as a "parasite" on oil traffic may eventually become important general cargo ports which they would never have been had the oil traffic not been there first. Almost all the large Gulf Coast ports have shared in this development, building grain elevators, warehouses, etc., but Houston is probably the outstanding example. New Orleans and Galveston are the only important dry cargo ports in their own right. The Gulf Coast ports have made themselves felt more and more in the Middle West, the zone of competition between the North Atlantic and the Gulf. The St. Lawrence Seaway introduces a new element into this competitive pattern.

LAKE CHARLES on the Calcasieu River was opened as a deep-water port in 1926. Petroleum and petroleum products dominate more than in the other two large Louisiana ports. Besides oil refineries Lake Charles has chemical plants which also generate traffic. It is a leading rice exporting port.

PORT ARTHUR—BEAUMONT—ORANGE. Port Arthur was established in 1897 by a railroad company as a shipping port for lumber and other wood products. In a short time, however, with the development of oil fields in the immediate hinterland, Port Arthur became a major oil port. The shipping canal was transferred to the government in 1906. Petroleum makes up more than 90 per cent of the cargo handled in the port. Three million tons of crude oil were received by coastal tankers and barges for the refineries in 1956 but most of the oil arrived

[3] Edwin J. Foscue, "The Industrial Port of Corpus Christi", *Proceedings, International Geographical Union*, Washington, D.C., 1952. P. 151.

The Norwegian bulk carrier *Gerwi* unloading 22,000 tons of Chilean iron ore at the new public bulk-handling facilities on the Houston Ship Channel, opened in 1961. Both in Houston and New Orleans public bulk ports have recently been completed. (Port of Houston)

by pipeline. Port Arthur also has considerable shipments of grain.

Beaumont, at the head of navigation on the Neches River, had some shallowdraft shipping of lumber from 1870. It became a major port after 1916 when the shipping district was reorganized, but it was the discovery of oil at Spindletop, about five kilometers from the present port, that was a major factor in the development of the port. Oil accounts for 95 per cent of the cargo handled in the 30 kilometer long waterway, which includes loading docks at Smith Bluff and Port Neches. Near Beaumont is a Bethlehem Steel shipyard specializing in offshore drilling rigs and river and seagoing craft for the oil industry.

In 1918 the port of Orange was opened to

ocean vessels. It is chiefly a barge port, shipping crude oil and chemicals and receiving rolled steel and sea shells. A section of the harbor is owned by the navy and has been used to store "moth-ball ships".

All three ports of Port Arthur, Beaumont and Orange have large chemical plants. Port Arthur–Beaumont is one of the leading oil refining districts in the United States and the hub of an extensive pipe line system.

HOUSTON–TEXAS CITY–GALVESTON. The oldest deep-water port on the Texas coast is Galveston which has been in service for ocean shipping since 1839. Few, if any, of the major ports in the world are more specialized on dry cargo; petroleum products make up less than two per cent of the total port traffic. The chief commodities handled in Galveston are sulphur, grain, cotton and sugar. Galveston is the world's largest sulphur shipping port. Much sulphur is shipped in molten form to sulphuric

The Turning Basin at the head of the 40-kilometer Houston Ship Channel lies about 8 kilometers from downtown Houston. Public wharves ring the Turning Basin and continue down the left side of the Channel. The public wharves provide 25 ship berths, four privately operated steamship terminals have a combined total of 19 berths and 32 private industrial wharves can handle 47 vessels. Note the Public Grain Elevator on the left bank and the many tank farms in the distance. (Port of Houston)

acid plants located close to the market. Terminals to receive molten sulphur are also being built in Europe (Rotterdam and Immingham) and the first deliveries are planned for 1964. In many years Galveston ships more wheat than any other port in the United States.

Texas City is primarily an oil port but it also has large chemical plants and the only American tin smelter. In 1947 the port suffered a major disaster when two ships exploded and destroyed most of the terminals and waterfront industrial plants. The Seatrain Wharf, handling railroad cars transported by ship between Texas City and New York, has few counterparts. A 125-ton electric hoist loads fifteen cars per hour.

The completion of the Houston Ship Channel in 1915 created the modern port of Houston. The port comprises the 40-kilometer long channel from Galveston Bay to the Turning Basin in Houston. It has berthing space for 91 ocean-going vessels and 50 barge docks. The present channel depth of 36 feet will be increased to 40 feet when works begun in 1960 have been completed. Petroleum products make up most of the cargo handled in the port. The leading dry cargo commodities in 1956

Source: Edwin J. Foscue, "The Ports of Texas and their Hinterlands", *Tijdschrift voor Economische en Sociale Geografie,* 1957. Pp. 1–14.

were sea shells, received by barge, rolled steel products, chiefly pipe, received by barge from domestic steel mills and by ocean vessels from abroad, and grains.

By value domestic trade and foreign trade were of roughly equal importance; shipments in both cases represented twice the value of receipts. Fuel oil and gasoline accounted for almost five-sevenths of the value of domestic shipments. Tubular products made up one-third of domestic receipts followed by automobiles and parts. The export list is more diversified with oil field equipment, cotton, wheat and sorghum at the top. Coffee is the leading import item.[4]

Houston, one of the fastest growing cities in the United States, now is the largest city in the South. As the undisputed metropolis of the Gulf Coast petroleum region it has expanded with the growth of petroleum production in this area. The diversity of Houston's port traffic is characteristic of any metropolitan port. Houston—Galveston are rather serious competitors of New Orleans, partly competing in the same trading area, but having distance advantages in the western part of the Middle West, from where several railroads focus on these ports.[5] The Houston–Baytown–Texas City area

is one of the leading oil refining districts in the United States.[6] The Houston Ship Channel is lined with manufacturing plants for much of the 40 kilometers from Houston to Galveston Bay. The petrochemical industry and a variety of other industries are represented.

FREEPORT. West of the Galveston Bay complex is Freeport Harbor, an interesting engineering achievement. In 1929 the Brazos River was cut off by a diversion dam 15 kilometers from its outlet in the Gulf of Mexico. The river, which carries a heavy load of silt, was sent in a new channel which had been dredged south of the old outlet. The old channel was then deepened and became the present deep-water harbor.

The town of Velasco on the north bank of the Brazos was one of the earliest and most important ports of Texas. With more and more silt deposited in the mouth of the river it became inaccessible even to shallow-draft vessels. Attention was again focused on the ports of the lower Brazos when extensive deposits of sulphur were discovered, which led to the dredging and modernization of the port. Sulphur shipments have later been discontinued, however, and Freeport is primarily an oil port with the chemical industry as a secondary traffic generator.

CORPUS CHRISTI–PORT ARANSAS. The port of Corpus Christi dates from 1926 when the 45 kilometer channel was completed. It is one of the newer deep-water harbors of the Gulf coast, and also one of the fastest growing ports. Petroleum products account for most of the cargo handled in Corpus Christi. Bauxite,

[4] Foscue, The Ports of Texas, *op. cit.* Pp. 8–9. For detailed statistics on the origin and destination of Houston's foreign trade, see *Port of Houston 1960: Foreign Trade Statistics,* Navigation & Canal Commissioners, Houston, 1961.
[5] Edward L. Ullman, "The Railroad Pattern of the United States", *Geographical Review,* 1949. Pp. 242 ff.
[6] Baytown is located on Galveston Bay at the entrance of the Houston Ship Channel and is included in the port of Houston although an urbanized area of its own.

The La Quinta alumina plant at Corpus Christi owned by the Reynolds Metals Company is an example of the large manufacturing plants which have been located on the deep waterways of the Gulf Coast. Bauxite from Ocho Rios, Jamaica, just arriving by the 32,000-ton ore carrier *Richard* will be unloaded at the pier by conveyor belts. In the background is the San Patricio reduction plant of the same company. (Reynolds Metals Company)

imported from Jamaica for the Reynolds alumina plant, is the chief dry cargo item, followed by imported grains, imported non-ferrous ores (lead, zinc, etc.) and industrial chemicals, shipped and received in trade with domestic ports.

Port Aransas, at the mouth of the channel, has a location similar to Galveston on the seaward side of Houston. In its functions it is quite different, however. It is purely an oil port, shipping crude petroleum coastwise and to foreign refineries.

BROWNSVILLE–PORT ISABEL. Brownsville, on the Rio Grande, got a port 10 kilometers northeast of the city in 1936. It was connected with the Gulf of Mexico through a 30 kilometer channel parallel to the river. In 1949 the southern link of the Intracoastal Waterway was extended to Brownsville. Through this newest Texas port a large region in southern Texas and northern Mexico is now in direct contact with the world market. Foreign and domestic trade are roughly equal in quantity. Receipts and shipments of

petroleum and petroleum products, chiefly in domestic trade, and exports of cotton are the leading traffic components, but the dry cargo list is quite diversified. The immediate trade area of Brownsville is the rich farm district of the lower Rio Grande valley on both sides of the river and the oil fields of the coastal plain. In addition, the port hinterland extends as far as California in handling shipments of cotton; it serves a large part of northern Mexico as an outlet for agricultural products and non-ferrous metals.

Port Isabel, one of the pioneer ports of Texas, in its rejuvenated form serves as a shipping port for the coastal oil fields. It has a refinery.

The Pacific Coast

The Pacific coast of Anglo-America is one of the most recently settled coastal areas in the world. The present political division only dates back to the middle of last century. Earlier the Spaniards, pushing up from the south, had established a few settlements in south California and in the north the Russians, with a firm footing in Alaska, had scattered posts along the coast down to present San Francisco Bay.[1] In Puget Sound and along the lower Columbia River they met competition from the British and the Americans. The southern boundary of Alaska was fixed in 1825, the present United States–Canada border was established in 1846, California was ceded by Mexico to the United States in 1848, and Alaska was bought by the Americans from Russia in 1867. The first great influx of people came with the discovery of gold near Sacramento in 1848 which led to the famous gold rush of 1849. San Francisco became the port of entry for gold-seekers arriving by sea and it soon developed into a trade and financial center not only for the gold fields but also for much of the American West.

The ports of the American and Canadian Pacific coast have much in common. They are separated from the economic heartland of the two nations by vast areas of semiarid or mountainous country. The transcontinental railroads, completed in the period 1870–1910, helped to bridge this wide gap. For towns chosen as terminals the arrival of the railroad is always listed as one of the outstanding events in their economic history. Another such event, common to all Pacific ports, was the opening of the Panama Canal in 1914. It offered a cheap waterway, bringing San Francisco and New York 7,800 nautical miles closer than by the Strait of Magellan route. It also had its effects on the railroad rates. For example, the rail rate for steel from the Ca-

nadian steel center Hamilton to the prairie metropolis Edmonton is about twice the rate from Hamilton to Vancouver.[2] The "Panama alternative" helped to press the railroad rates even where it did not have such powerful effects in favor of the coastal cities as in the example just mentioned.[3] The Canal thus is of much greater economic importance to the Pacific coast than is reflected in the relatively small flow of intercoastal waterborne cargo after World War II. The railroads have taken over much of the traffic handled by water in the 1920s.

The long distances from the main centers of production give a measure of protection from eastern competition for companies working for a regional market. For national companies with headquarters in the east it is often feasible to open branch plants on the Pacific coast to save on transportation costs. This has benefited all large cities on the Pacific but especially the largest city in each country, Los Angeles and Vancouver.

The Pacific ports of North America fulfill similar national functions as gateways to Hawaii and the Orient for passengers and express cargo as the Atlantic ports do as gateways to Europe. Any map of American port hinterlands will show large areas of influence

---

[1] The Spaniards, later the Mexicans, were ranchers, who exported hides and tallow to the United States and Europe by way of the Cape Horn route; the Europeans in the northwest were primarily interested in furs. The first Spanish explorer (Cabrillo) came to California already in 1542, but the first settlements were established in the last three decades of the 18th century. In 1835 R. H. Dana visited California on board a ship from Boston and in *Two Years Before the Mast,* an American classic, Dana describes life on this coast during its Mexican period. The competing fur companies in the northwest sold much of their products in China.

[2] P. D. McGovern, "Industrial Development in the Vancouver Area", *Economic Geography,* 1961. P. 191.

[3] For more details see Stuart Daggett, *Principles of Inland Transportation,* 4th edition, New York, 1955, and the many references cited there.

for the leading Pacific ports. But except for some alluvial plains near the coast and scattered irrigated districts in the interior the population densities are still very low in western Anglo-America. Half the population in four south-western states live in either the Los Angeles or the San Francisco urbanized area. Greater Los Angeles alone accounts for about half the value added by manufacturing in these four states.

The Californian Ports

San Francisco and Los Angeles

For many decades San Francisco was the un-disputed leader among the ports on the American Pacific coast. Its immediate hinterland, the Central Valley formed by the San Joaquin and Sacramento Rivers between the Sierra Nevada and the Coastal Ranges, became a grain producing area making San Francisco one of the world's important wheat and barley ports in the period 1870–1890. The transcontinental railroads, constructed in the last decades of the nineteenth century, opened the large eastern markets for fruit and vegetables from Califor-nia. With the help of irrigation it became possible to make full use of California's greatest natural resource, its Mediterranean climate. The Central Valley, largest of the alluvial plains in the entire West, gradually became a densely settled agricultural region based on irrigation. The ports of the San Francisco Bay area were the natural gateway for most of this region. Recently an ocean port was constructed at Stockton on the San Joaquin River, which ships almost one million tons of iron ore to Japan in addition to agricultural products, and in 1963 Sacramento became a seaport.

Greater San Francisco, which now forms an almost continuous urbanized area around the Bay,[1] is functionally a twin city. A small

[1] The San Francisco-Oakland urbanized area has 2.4 million inhabitants and San Jose 0.6 million.

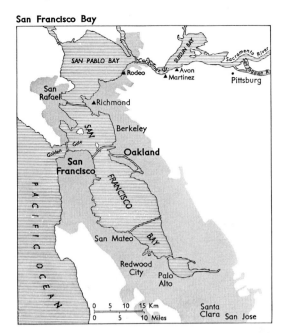

San Francisco Bay

Cargo handled at the ports of San Francisco Bay Calendar Year 1956

Thousand metric tons

Port Area	Foreign		Coastwise		Type of cargo
	Imports	Exports	Receipts	Shipments	
Carquinez Strait	1,464	44	1,580	1,903	Petroleum, sugar
Suisun Bay	816	203	847	965	Petroleum
San Pablo Bay	—	50	1,745	1,340	Petroleum
Richmond	1,471	785	4,652	3,482	Petroleum
Oakland	85	739	825	664	General cargo
Redwood City	18	83	—	812	Cement, gypsum
San Francisco	797	786	409	294	General cargo
Total	4,651	2,690	10,058	9,460	

Source: Department of the Army, Corps of En-gineers, *Waterborne Commerce of the United States.* Calendar Year 1956. Part 4. The gray tone on land shows approximately the continuous built up area (urbanized area) around San Fran-cisco Bay according to the 1960 census of popula-tion. Black triangles = oil refineries.

area of level land on the bay side of the hilly peninsula, which stretches between the Bay and the ocean northwards to the Golden Gate, is the original site[2] and the present core of the city with the business and financial districts centered on Market Street. A second downtown area developed at Oakland, the terminal of the railroads, of which the first transcontinental line, the Union Pacific, was completed in 1869. Several bridges carry traffic between the urban centers around the Bay. The famous Golden Gate and Bay bridges were opened in the mid-1930s.

The population of the Los Angeles conurbation surpassed that of Greater San Francisco in the early 1920s and now southern California is by far the most populous part of America's most populous state. Greater Los Angeles is more than twice as large as Greater San Francisco. The two conurbations between them have more than half of California's population. Their historical background is quite different, however. San Francisco is a real port city that became a metropolis because of its location on one of the world's finest natural harbors guarding the entrance to a rich agricultural region. Its downtown district is in close contact with the general cargo piers along the Embarcadero. Los Angeles, on the other hand, is an inland metropolis that built a harbor to take advantage of the new Panama Canal. It grew up around a central business district located about 35 kilometers from the small port of San Pedro. When Los Angeles needed a modern port it incorporated San Pedro, and a narrow strip of land leading to the port in 1909, and then constructed a completely manmade harbor.[3] The neighboring city of Long Beach, which with some forty other corporate cities is part of Greater Los Angeles, invested its oil profits in a modern harbor alongside the Los Angeles harbor.

Los Angeles is the world's fastest growing metropolis. It was little influenced by the influx of people during the Gold Rush and at the census of 1880 it had only 11,000 people. Seventy years later the urbanized area of Los Angeles had 4.0 million inhabitants and was the third largest city in the United States after New York (12.3 million) and Chicago (4.9 million). In the census of 1960 Los Angeles had a population of 6.5 million and has outgrown Chicago (6.0 million) but is still far behind New York (14.1). A series of booms can be distinguished in Los Angeles' short history, most of which can be attributed more or less directly to its Mediterranean climate. The completion of two competing transcontinental railroads and the introduction of refrigerated cars started a citrus boom in the 1880s. The discovery of rich oil fields within the present urbanized area of Los Angeles in 1899 started another boom which was strengthened by the opening of the Panama Canal in 1914 and the construction of the modern harbor. In 1925 no less than 70 per cent of the 12 million tons passing through the Canal originated at or was destined for Los Angeles.[4] The movie boom after 1910, later followed by radio and television, also helped to increase population as did the localization of various manufacturing industries to the city. Los Angeles early became one of the chief centers of the American aircraft industry.[5] The year-round flying weather and the possibility of working out of doors for twelve months were appreciated by early flying enthusiasts. In the postwar period tremendous government contracts have been placed with firms associated with the aircraft industry in the Los Angeles

[2] In the Spanish and Mexican period the settlement was called Yerba Buena.
[3] The dramatic developments leading to the choice of the San Pedro—Wilmington area for the construction of the Port of Los Angeles are summarized in Willis H. Miller, "Competition for the Ocean Trade of Los Angeles", *Economic Geography*, 1937. Pp. 325–333.
[4] Port of Los Angeles, *1960–1961 Annual Report*. P. 10.
[5] W. G. Cunningham, *The Aircraft Industry: A Study in Industrial Location*. Los Angeles, 1951. By 1928 California was second only to New York, ten years later it was the undisputed leader.

area, but gradually missiles and scientific instruments have made "electronics" a bigger employer than "aircraft". No region in the United States is economically more dependent on the armament race than is southern California.[6] Los Angeles is also the world's leading production center for commercial aircraft.

Another type of industries well represented in the diversified industrial structure of Los Angeles are branch plants for which the city was chosen because it is by far the largest center of the rapidly expanding western market. For example, Los Angeles is an important center for the assembly of automobiles and it

[6] California has about 209,000 workers in the air-craft-missile field, more than one-third of the national total, and most of them are in the Los Angeles area. *The New York Times,* May 29, 1962.

[7] On the map, page 252, Los Angeles includes all the port installations in the Greater Los Angeles area. The statistics quoted here only refer to the Port of Los Angeles and do not include Long Beach, El Segundo and Huntington Beach.

In 1909 the inland city of Los Angeles annexed the small settlements of San Pedro and Wilmington 35 kilometers to the south. The modern port of Los Angeles was created out of the roadstead of San Pedro and the mud flats of Wilmington in time to take advantage of the increase in waterborne trade following the opening of the Panama Canal. The twin port of Long Beach, for the purpose of this study included in the port of Los Angeles, starts on the extreme right of the picture. The long breakwater protecting the two adjacent ports is just out of view. (Board of Harbor Commissioners, Los Angeles)

is second only to Akron, Ohio, in rubber manufacturing. The market for these branch plants is all the Pacific Ocean area, including Hawaii, Alaska, New Zealand, etc., which are served through the port of Los Angeles.

The rapid expansion of the population and the economy in recent decades has not been reflected by an increased cargo turnover in the Port of Los Angeles.[7] The city port handled about two million tons a year in 1917–18

A recent addition to the Port of Los Angeles facilities is this container operation whose huge gantry automatically moves 23-ton cargo vans to and from Hawaii-bound freighters. The 18,000-ton container ship *Hawaiian Citizen* of the Matson Line has been converted to carry 436 containers of which 72 are refrigerated. The line also operates seven freighters carrying containers stacked on deck and conventional cargo in the holds. Note the petroleum pumps in the background. (Board of Harbor Commissioners, L. A.)

which rapidly increased to over 25 million tons in 1924. But in the 1950s the cargo turnover was the same as in the late 1920s or about 24–26 million tons a year. The importance of petroleum in the total tonnage had slightly increased and was about 20 million tons, of which over 3 million were bunkers. The direction and composition of the petroleum movements had changed considerably, however. In 1961 Los Angeles was a net importer of petroleum, receiving 3.6 million tons from abroad and shipping 1.8 million tons. Domestic movements along the Pacific coast accounted for 8 million tons, of which 5 million tons were shipped from Los Angeles. Intercoastal shipments, which were of great importance in the 1920s, amounted to less than one million tons in 1961. Lumber receipts from the Pacific Northwest declined to about one-third. The general cargo turnover was about the same in the late 1950s as in the late 1920s or approximately 4 million tons. The composition had changed, however; 25 per cent of the dry cargo traffic was in foreign trade in the 1920s, while in the late 1950s the proportion had increased to 75 per cent. This is just another example of the difficulties for American domestic shipping to compete with the railroads after World War II.

OTHER CALIFORNIAN PORTS. The remaining Californian ports are more specialized in function. Estero Bay and San Luis Obispo ship crude petroleum to the refineries in San Francisco and Los Angeles. San Diego, a major naval base, is in the traffic shadow of Los Angeles and too close to the Mexican border to have a sizeable hinterland. It serves the densely populated coastal strip and is close enough to Greater Los Angeles to serve as an alternative port.

The Northern Pacific Coast

The Pacific coast region from northern California to southern Alaska is one of the world's leading timber producing areas. Precipitation is high on the slopes of the coastal mountain ranges which are exposed to the moist air-masses moving in from the Pacific; the summer drought is not long enough to prevent the growth of dense stands of tall coniferous trees, while it creates a great fire hazard. A rather narrow belt along the coast accounts for almost half of the United States' timber production. The difficult terrain and the large size of trees complicates felling and transportation. Forest operations are highly mechanized and many mills are larger than is common in most other timber producing regions. Most of the large sawmills and pulp and paper mills have a tidewater location; timber and the many products made from it provide most of the cargo handled at many of the small ports but this commodity group is also important in the large ports.

There are many timber towns along the American coast from Eureka, California, served by Humboldt Harbor, to Aberdeen-Hoquiam on Grays Harbor, Washington. Small indentations in the coast provided harbors which attracted sawmills and later other timber processing industries. The lower Columbia River got many forest industries and the protected waters of Puget Sound were ideal for sawmill towns. The coast of British Columbia and Alaska also provides excellent harbors. All of the large cities in this region started out as sawmill towns, such as Portland, Tacoma, Seattle and Vancouver, and manufacturing industries based on timber still rank among the leading industries in these cities.[1]

The flow of timber products out of the American Northwest is mainly directed towards domestic markets, primarily the Manufacturing Belt and California. The railroads have taken over more and more of this traffic; only minor quantities move in coastal and inter-coastal trade. Some American ports on this coast account for larger receipts of timber (from British Columbia) than of shipments.

The north Pacific coast region is sparsely settled except for the eastern shore of Puget Sound, from Vancouver to Tacoma, and the Willamette Valley.

Portland and the Lower Columbia River Ports

Portland's position at a natural crossroads, the junction of the north-south route from California to Puget Sound and the only water-level passage from the Columbia basin to the coast, has made it the trade center and the port of the fertile Willamette Valley, one of the richest agricultural regions of the American West,[2] and the vast wheat growing and cattle raising lands east of the Cascades. It is the oldest city and throughout last century it was also the largest city of the Northwest but it is now surpassed in population by Seattle and Vancouver. Early growth was based primarily upon forest resources and these still are of major importance. Grain and lumber are leading commodities shipped from the port which includes facilities located in the suburb of Vancouver, Washington. Since the end of last century the lower Columbia has been greatly improved for navigation; the channel is now 35 feet deep. The major port installations are along the Willamette River. In comparison with the Puget Sound ports Portland has a more hazardous entrance from the ocean but it has also the advantage of an inland waterway system which brings wheat, paper, lumber, and crushed stone downstream and sends petroleum products in the opposite direction. Barge traffic on the Columbia is increasing considerably.

Other ports on the lower Columbia are Longview, which in contrast to most timber towns was laid out on a large scale as a company town in the early 1920s, and Astoria

---

[1] Rafted logs are significant in the traffic of many ports in this region but they were excluded from the statistics for the map, page 252.

[2] This valley was settled in the early 1840s by New England colonists who came overland via the Oregon Trail. It is thus the oldest American region on the west coast.

where the first white settlement in the North-west was established in 1811.[3]

Seattle and the Puget Sound Ports

After nearly half a century of moderate growth as a muddy sawmill and lumber shipping town Seattle had a boom period between 1898 and 1910 as a result of the Klondike gold rush. Seattle became the port and outfitting center and it still remains the continental gateway for seaborne trade with Alaska. In 1896 a Japanese steamship line, in conjunction with one of the transcontinental railroads, established the first direct service between Seattle and the Orient. In steaming time Seattle is two days closer to the Orient than San Francisco and Los Angeles and this was of special importance for high-value cargo in the days before air freight. Seattle became the chief American gateway for the imports of raw silk from Yokohama —one of the leading commodities on the American list of imports in the 1920s. In 1929 raw silk accounted for 69 per cent of the import value in the Washington Customs District.[1] Fast trains carried it to the silk manufacturing centers in the New York region. For raw silk New York was then in the hinterland of Seattle! World War II and the Korean War were busy periods for the Seattle Port of Embarkation through which military supplies were sent in large quantities. Seattle offered the same advantages for these shipments as for the civilian raw silk receipts.[2]

The other Puget Sound ports are dominated by forest products and petroleum, but Tacoma, once competing with Seattle for the hegemony among ports on the Puget Sound, has a diversified cargo traffic. Its large copper smelter is an important generator of seaborne traffic.

Vancouver

Vancouver, Canada's third largest city and its second port after Montreal, is situated on the south side of Burrard Inlet, one of the world's finest land-locked harbors. A second port of Greater Vancouver is located at New Westminster on the Fraser River. Settlement started with a sawmill (1862) but Vancouver's history as a port only dates back to 1886 when the Canadian Pacific Railway was completed. The inauguration in 1891 of the "White Empresses" of the Canadian Pacific Railway, in regular traffic between Vancouver and the Orient, was an early milestone in the history of the port. The Canadian transcontinental railway company provided a fast all-British service between the Orient and Liverpool, of importance especially for passengers and mail and such cargo as tea and raw silk. Forest products have played a great role in the traffic of the port from its beginnings. Grain, primarily wheat from Alberta, has been shipped in increasing quantities since World War I until Vancouver now ranks as the world's leading wheat port. The opening of the Panama Canal in 1914 was an event of lasting importance in Vancouver's history as much of the grain and lumber is shipped to ports in Europe. With grain and lumber looming large Vancouver is by far the leading dry cargo port on the west coast of the two American continents. This

[3] It was named for the famous New York fur merchant J. J. Astor, who sent out two parties, one overland and one by sea. The War of 1812 caused the Astorians to sell out to the Canadian North West Company which in 1821 was merged with the Hudson's Bay Company. This company built a new and larger post known as Fort Vancouver at the present city of Vancouver, Washington, now a suburb in greater Portland. In addition to this center of European enterprise in the Northwest some twenty secondary posts were established up the coast and in the interior. Few of the old fur-trading posts had locations favorable for modern railroads and highways but Vancouver survived the fur epoch. Greater Portland has a magnificent geographic location, whereas the forested hinterland of Astoria has a low density of population. Astoria had almost disappeared when it was revived as a sawmilling and fishing center.
[1] Frances M. Earle, "Foreign Trade of the Pacific Northwest", *The Pacific Northwest*, (O. W. Freeman and H. H. Martin, editors). New York. 1954.
[2] The short great-circle distance to the Orient has made the Seattle–Tacoma Airport an important terminal for trans-Pacific flights.

position was strengthened with the opening in 1960 of bulk loading facilities for coal, potash (from Saskatchewan) and sulphur (from Alberta and British Columbia). Physical geography and the low density of population on the coast of British Columbia favor coastwise shipping. Vancouver, the only metropolitan city on the Canadian west coast, is the natural supply and service center for the coastal settlements northward on Vancouver Island and the mainland coast.[4]

[4] J. L. Robinson, "The Canadian Ports", in *The Pacific Northwest* (O. W. Freeman and H. H. Martin, editors). New York, 1954.

LATIN AMERICA

It is customary to see Latin America as a relatively sparsely populated part of the world. This conception may, however, be misleading. On the effective national territory or the ecumene rural population densities are often as high as in northwestern Europe. The population of Latin America already exceeds that of Anglo-America and with a considerably higher natural increase the southern "cultural" continent will soon far surpass the northern. Latin America falls naturally into three parts, each with about seventy million inhabitants: (a) isthmian America and the West Indies made up chiefly of former Spanish colonies, (b) Spanish South America, and (c) Portuguese South America or Brazil.

Most countries in Latin America gained independence in the early part of last century making their history as independent states nearly as long as that of the United States and longer than that of Canada. But the economic development of Latin America has been less favorable. In almost all the Latin American countries about half the population is still engaged in agriculture and the only exportable products are derived from agriculture and mining. The economies of the Latin American states are thus exposed to the fluctuations of world market prices for raw materials.

South America has a "dead heart", the tremendous virtually uninhabited rain forest of the Amazon Valley. In all countries, except landlocked Bolivia and Paraguay, transport has traditionally been by sea, not only between individual countries but also between isolated population centers in the same country.

A characteristic feature of Latin America's trade relations is the dominance of the United States as a trade partner. The trade index values between the United States and the countries listed in the table become gradually lower as one proceeds southwards from the Rio Grande. Mexico tops the list with Argentina and Uruguay at the bottom. The dominance of the United States is of recent origin. Before the First World War European countries played a greater role in South American affairs. Europe is as close as the United States to the South American east coast and the "complementarity" between highly industrialized northwestern Europe and raw material producing South America was greater than between the United States and South America. However, the two world wars were disastrous breaks in the trade relations between Europe and her overseas trade partners. The shortage of shipping tonnage restricted the haulage of raw materials to Great Britain and much of the Continent was effectively cut off from her overseas trade connections.

Trade between Latin American states shows an irregular pattern, which can, however, be easily explained. Countries with insufficient domestic oil production have high index values for trade with Venezuela. Countries on the main shipping lanes from the United States and Europe, passing down the east coast to the La Plata or through the Panama Canal down the west coast to Chile, are provided with good and frequent shipping facilities by the many cargo lines sailing on these routes. Trade between Argentina, Uruguay and Brazil is very intense and so is trade between the west coast countries of Chile, Peru and Ecuador.[1] The former three countries also have

[1] The Pan American Highway, stretching along the west coast of South America, provides an alternative to ocean shipping for high value cargo in foreign trade.

Trade Distribution Index for Selected Latin American Countries, 1958

Country	Mexico	Colombia	Venezuela	Brazil	Uruguay	Argentina	Chile	Peru
Mexico	—	7	13	7	17	10	20	16
Colombia	13	—	28	1	81	3	20	114
Venezuela	15	21	—	316	661	282	10	4
Brazil	5	0	224	—	1039	776	122	24
Uruguay	29	41	361	934	—	89	92	414
Argentina	12	3	213	744	145	—	614	227
Chile	10	60	9	187	102	558	—	1404
Peru	18	112	17	28	305	247	843	—
Ecuador	25	474	0	2	21	61	498	472
United States	546	464	343	281	71	107	336	307
Canada	41	43	53	26	19	13	18	54
United Kingdom	31	33	77	43	123	176	118	98
West Germany	55	143	64	115	74	128	181	116
France	34	37	37	55	168	55	57	44
Italy	50	28	113	92	150	209	78	96
Japan	79	21	25	83	10	71	30	86
Netherlands	44	73	64	84	187	215	132	146
Sweden	55	136	56	175	59	100	61	86
Spain	101	55	121	137	361	51	328	27
Portugal	27	8	18	77	6	33	39	25

For construction and discussion of index, see pages 17 ff.

overland connections by rail and road as well as by river. But on the whole trade across land boundaries is small in Latin America as many of these borders cut through areas with a very low population density.

Of the countries listed in the table Mexico has an extremely small trade with other Latin American countries. It seems that Mexico is on a backwater for the regular shipping lanes between the United States and South America.

Many other country pairs have a low trade index: Argentina–Colombia, Peru–Venezuela, Ecuador–Uruguay, etc. However, the often repeated statement that the countries of Latin America have little trade with other countries in the same continent is only partly true. The statement describes an average of well developed trade between some countries in the continent and almost non-existent trade between others.

Mexico and Central America

Mexico and the six Central American republics are similar in terms of their significance to world shipping. Their foreign trade is small measured by value and even less impressive by volume. None of them produces a bulk cargo for export to be compared with the sugar of Cuba or the bauxite of Jamaica, not to mention the oil of Venezuela. In addition almost half of Mexico's foreign trade tonnage and more than half of the value is accounted for by rail and truck transports over the United States border. Between them all the ports of Mexico do not handle more foreign trade cargo than a medium-sized world port, say Göteborg, Boston or Rio de Janeiro. The Central American ports are even smaller than those of Mexico.

Mexico

Although facing two oceans Mexico's economy is that of a self-contained inland state. Its heartland is in the central highland plateau centered on Mexico City. The Mexican–United States boundary in the north, separating Latin America and Anglo-America, for the most part runs through empty territory. This is in contrast to the boundary between the two Anglo-American nations which cuts through the densely populated American Manufacturing Belt and other important economic regions. However, a series of railways and highways bridge the empty zone on both sides of the Mexican–United States border and the Mexican heartland has good land connections with various parts of the huge neighbor country to the north, which is the dominating trade partner of Mexico. Almost two-thirds of the Mexican import tonnage and close to one-third of the exports are shipped across this land border. The leading border stations (1956) are Nuevo Laredo, Ciudad Juarez, Matamoros (all handling more foreign trade cargo than Mexico's leading general cargo port, Veracruz), Mexicali, Piedras Negras, Tijuana, Nogales, Ojinago and Reinosa.

In Mexico, as in several other highland republics in Latin America, the lowlands remained undeveloped into the twentieth century. The coastal plain along the Gulf of Mexico for centuries was a region to be avoided. The tropical diseases (yellow fever, malaria, etc.) of the *tierra caliente* were powerful deterrents to settlement. The coast is inhospitable with mangrove swamps, offshore sand bars, lagoons and coral reefs. Veracruz, the logical port of the Mexican heartland, is located somewhat south of the original port, founded in 1520 after the first landing of Cortés. It was the terminus of the Spanish fleet's annual trading voyage to supply all its northern and trans-Pacific Empire. But it has had a poor reputation throughout the centuries as a hotbed of tropical diseases. The modern port, Mexico's largest for passengers and general foreign trade, must spend large amounts to prevent its harbor being silted up. In recent decades health conditions have improved radically. The coastal plain has become an important agricultural region and with modern techniques it could be transformed into one of the greatest zones of tropical agriculture in the Americas, especially in the areas with soils derived from volcanic material.[1]

The other major port on this coast, Tampico, is a creation of the present century. It developed as an oil port but has also become the port of northern Mexico with railroads and highways to the large mining and manufacturing centers of San Luis Potosí and Monterrey. Oil was struck near Tampico in 1901 and in twenty years the squalid little town grew to a city of 100,000 inhabitants. In 1921, the peak year of Mexican oil production (27.6 million tons), Tampico was the leading oil port in the world. Mexico was second only to the United States as an oil producer. With the subsequent decline of oil production, due to the exhaustion of producing wells and the lack of development of new fields, Tampico lost one-third of its population in a decade. The friction between the Mexican Government and the American and British oil companies in 1938 led to the

---

[1] Gilbert J. Butland, *Latin America*. London, 1960. P. 33.

expropriation of foreign property. Since 1949 the Mexican oil company has been able to undertake new exploratory drilling with the help of foreign oil companies working under contract. Production increased considerably, now chiefly from the Poza Rica field, and reached a new peak of 16.7 million tons in 1961.

The Mexican Government is encouraging the use of oil in industry and for domestic fuel to reduce deforestation for charcoal, which has produced so many problems of soil erosion and water conservation. The same is being done in other tropical areas by the international oil companies. As a result of this and other developments the domestic oil consumption has increased rapidly. Mexico no longer exports crude oil and the net exports of petroleum products only amount to about two million tons. In 1956 Mexico's total petroleum exports were 4 million tons and imports 1.6 million tons, chiefly from California to points on the Pacific coast. A new oil refinery was constructed at Minatitlán in 1956 to replace an old one on the Coatzacoalcos River with the main object of supplying the Pacific Coast with petroleum products through a pipeline across the Isthmus of Tehuantepec to Salina Cruz.[2] As a result Mexican oil imports have declined. Oil refineries have also been constructed on the inland plateau at Mexico City (1946) and Salamanca (1950). As they get their crude supply through pipelines the railroads and highways between coastal plain and high plateau have been greatly relieved.

Seondary ports on the Mexican Gulf coast are Tuxpan, an oil terminal near the Poza Rica field, Coatzacoalcos (Puerto México), and Progreso, the leading henequen port.

Mexico's long Pacific coast has few ports and little international trade. In southern Mexico the mountains descend steeply to the Pacific shore and the narrow coastal strip is an isolated part of the country. Manzanillo, the only southern port linked directly by rail with the Central Plateau, has the largest traffic. Acapulco, one of the oldest ports on the North American Pacific coast and for two hundred and fifty years the port of departure for the Manila galleons, has become a fashionable resort but is now only a minor port.

In the north the Sierra Madre Occidental runs further from the coast and thus leaves a wider coastal plain. The isolation of the region is relieved by a road and a railway running parallel to the coast and linking the region in the north to the United States and in the south to the central plateau via Guadalajara. The main ports on this coast are Mazatlán and Guaymas. On the barren Lower California Peninsula an American copper mine at Santa Rosalía and the salt works at Vizcaino generate most of the waterborne traffic. The latter, operated by Ludwig's National Bulk Carriers Corporation, produces solar evaporated salt at the unique Black Warrior Lagoon; production will eventually reach two million tons.[3]

The large and rapidly expanding economy of the American Pacific Coast may in the future stimulate the development of natural resources also on the less richly endowed Mexican side of the border and thus increase waterborne trade on Mexico's "backside".

Central America

Like Mexico five of the six Central American republics are centered on an interior core region, the economic and political heart of each country. Panama, newest of the republics, separating from Colombia at the time of the construction of the Panama Canal, is the exception. It is centered on a port city, the city of Panama. British Honduras, a small colony with less than 100,000 inhabitants, is confined to the Caribbean lowlands. Five of the six

---

[2] *World Petroleum*, July 15, 1958. Pp. 70–73.

[3] Lambert B. Halsema, "Exportadora de Sal: A Study in Developmental Economic Geography", *Annals of the Association of American Geographers*, 1958. P. 267.

Banana Exports by Selected Countries
Million stems of 50 pounds (22.5 kg)

Continent and Country	1935–1939	1958–1960
World	*103.7*	*169.2*
Middle America	*66.3*	*78.6*
Costa Rica	4.6	10.9
Dominican Republic	0.3	5.4
Guatemala	8.4	9.5
Honduras	11.7	19.3
Jamaica	13.0	5.8
Mexico	13.1	0.9
Panama	9.8	12.7
South America	*18.8*	*63.3*
Brazil	9.4	10.5
Colombia	7.5	9.6
Ecuador	1.9	43.2
Africa	*12.5*	*23.4*
Canary Islands	5.3	7.7
Guinea	1.9	2.8
Ivory Coast	0.5	2.5
Nigeria	2.3	3.3
Somalia	1.0	2.5
Asia	*5.6*	*2.5*
Taiwan	5.6	1.9
Oceania	*0.6*	*1.5*

Source: Richard A. Smith and A. Clinton Cook, *Bananas: World Production and Trade*. Foreign Agricultural Service, U.S. Department of Agriculture, April, 1962. FAS M-128. P. 11.

republics stretch from coast to coast, while the sixth, Salvador, only faces the Pacific.

Due to the isolation of one core region from the other[1] and due also to differences in history, each of the small republics has a distinct character of its own. However there are marked similarities in their economies. Most of them rely on two agricultural products for foreign exchange: coffee from the highlands, and bananas from foreign company-owned plantations in the lowlands.

The United States dominates the foreign trade of the Central American republics. The perishable nature of the banana necessitates well-organized transportation from producer to consumer: railroads from banana districts to banana ports where the fruit is loaded with special equipment into special fruit vessels within a matter of hours and transported to a few receiving ports equipped to handle bananas and despatch them to interior consumption centers in fruit wagons. Since 1960 increasing quantities have been boxed at the plantations before shipment, particularly in Honduras. In most countries the banana trade is in the hands of a few large companies. The leading banana firm in the United States, the United Fruit Company, which through subsidiaries also operates in the European market (Fyffes), has long been a business empire of its own in Latin America. It operates a fleet of banana ships, which have plenty of cargo space for other commodities like coffee, most of which is sent to market in these vessels. The "Great White Fleet" of the United Fruit Company also carries most of the imports of the Central American countries as well as passengers, the latter particularly in the winter cruising season.

Serious diseases have threatened the banana plantations of the Caribbean lowlands and in the 1930s many plantations and banana districts were wiped out by the *sigatoka* disease. The Company converted many of these plantations to other products and laid out new plantations in the Pacific lowlands. It also developed a chemical spray which allowed some banana districts on the Atlantic coast to be saved.

Guatemala's exports have been dominated by coffee for more than sixty years. Before the Second World War two-thirds of the coffee exports were accounted for by German colonists who settled in Guatemala in the 1860s. During the war their plantations were con-

[1] The only capitals linked by rail are San Salvador and Guatemala City. The new Pan American Highway and the recent increase in air traffic may somewhat have reduced the earlier isolation but trade between the Central American countries is still very small.

fiscated and are now run by the government (*fincas nacionales*). In recent years the German influence in Guatemala has recovered rapidly.

The United Fruit Company established its first banana plantation near Puerto Barrios in 1906. This port on Guatemala's Caribbean coast, which now handles 77 per cent of her exports and half of the imports, and 20 per cent of El Salvador's imports and 10 per cent of the exports, is connected by railroad and highway with the capital. When the banana plantations at Puerto Barrios were struck by disease in the 1930s the Company started to plant in the Pacific lowlands and rail bananas across the isthmus to Puerto Barrios. In 1934 no less than 88 per cent of the bananas were produced in the eastern lowlands but in 1939 the Pacific coast contributed 53 per cent.

In El Salvador, as in Guatemala, coffee accounts for more than two-thirds of the export value. In Honduras, the chief banana producing country in Central America, bananas account for two or three times the value of coffee, the second largest export product. Bananas are grown on the northern coastlands. Two American companies, United Fruit and Standard Fruit, control the industry. They run their own railways and shipping lines. United Fruit has two ports—Puerto Cortés, which handles over half of the Honduran trade, and Tela. Standard Fruit's banana port is La Ceiba.

Nicaragua has a more diversified production and exports than its neighbors. For some years during World War II gold accounted for a higher export value than all merchandise, but in the late 1950s gold was a poor third on the export list after coffee and cotton, which alternated in first place. Gold is produced by American and Canadian companies which send rough gold ingots by air to the United States and Britain for final refining. Corinto on the Pacific is the main port, handling about 60 per cent of Nicaragua's commerce. It is joined by rail to the three largest cities in the country.

Costa Rica was the first of the Central American republics to grow coffee, which was introduced in 1797 and from about 1850 the prosperity of the coffee industry began to influence the country profoundly.[2] It was also the first country to grow bananas for the United States market. A North American railroad builder established banana plantations in 1878 along the lower section of the San José—Limón railroad, which was built to bring Costa Rican coffee to market. In 1909 Costa Rica was the leading banana producer and its exports increased until 1913 when 11 million stems were shipped. But then the spread of banana disease reduced shipments to 4.3 million stems in 1933 (about the same as in 1902) and the dense Negro population brought in from Jamaica was almost stranded when the United Fruit Company shifted its operations elsewhere. The Company has withdrawn from banana cultivation in the Caribbean lowlands of Costa Rica, but it still operates cacao and abacá plantations and is experimenting with methods of eradicating the Panama disease, which if successful might again make it possible to establish a commercial banana region on this coast. In the western lowlands of Costa Rica United Fruit has, after the Second World War, created banana plantations equipped with overhead irrigation towers from which the banana plants are sprayed, partly to control diseases and partly to provide irrigation during the dry season. This district is served by the new banana port of Golfito.

Most of the coffee, which in recent years has accounted for half of Costa Rica's export value, is sent through Limón. Coffee exports amount to twice the value of bananas but to less than one-fifth in tonnage. Costa Rica is one of the most prosperous countries in Latin America with a low rate of illiteracy and a high per capita income.

Panama normally pays for most of her im-

[2] For concise descriptions of Costa Rica and other Latin American countries see *The South American Handbook* (annual).

The United Fruit Company's new banana port Golfito on the Pacific coast of Costa Rica. The company had fifty-five vessels in service in 1961 but of these only twenty, all built in the 1940s, sailed under the American flag. (United Fruit Company)

ports by invisible exports in the form of income derived from the Canal Zone. Merchandise exports before the war paid for one-fifth of the imports, during the war for less than one-tenth and in recent years for about one-third. Bananas, grown in the Pacific lowlands and shipped primarily through the port of Puerto Armuelles, account for two-thirds of the visible exports.

The Panama Canal

The Panama Canal, opened to traffic in the first days of World War I, has a long and dramatic history. It was the focus of political interest for long periods even before it existed.

In 1513 Balboa crossed the narrow isthmus of Panama and discovered the Pacific Ocean. Panama City was founded in 1519 and it was from here that Pizarro started five years later on his conquest of Peru. The fortified town became the emporium on which all of Spain's trade with her rich South American colonies on the Pacific was focused. The mule route across the isthmus from Panama to Nombre de Dios and later to Portobelo was immensely important and the terminal towns were classical targets of the buccaneers. In 1671 Panama was sacked by Morgan and his men but it was rebuilt in its present location two years later. Other trans-isthmian passages of less importance were organized at Nicaragua and Tehuantepec, which have always figured as alternatives to Panama. Spanish kings investigated the possibility of constructing a canal across the isthmus already in the middle of the sixteenth century but the task was too enormous for the engineering techniques of the time.

Two and a half centuries later the German geographer Humboldt again drew attention to a canal by suggesting nine alternative routes between Tehuantepec and Darién. Many American and European canal projects were put forward in the early nineteenth century but it was not until the United States had reached the Pacific (Oregon 1846, California 1848) that the canal became a matter of practical politics. In 1846 the governments of the United States and New Granada signed an agreement guaranteeing the Americans free transit across the isthmus of Panama. In 1849 a treaty was signed with Nicaragua giving the United States the exclusive rights of constructing a trans-isthmian canal in that country.

The need for a modern cross route had become pressing, especially in connection with the gold rush to California in 1849. Shipping lines were created between New York and Colón and between Panama and San Francisco, but for the short overland trip through the

malaria and yellow fever infested jungle there was only the old Spanish mule route (*Camino Real*). A railroad, built with United States capital, was completed in 1855 between Colón, which was then called Aspinwall after one of the railroad builders, and Panama. Tropical diseases took a heavy toll of the Chinese railroad gangs.

The French, stimulated by the tremendous success of the Suez Canal, were the first to get down to business with a canal project. A French company, with Ferdinand de Lesseps as its president, started work on a sea-level canal in 1881 after having bought the American railroad company and its concessions.[1] The French met with tremendous difficulties and, in spite of achievements worthy of the reputation of French civil engineering, the company went into liquidation in 1889.[2] A private American company began work on a canal through Nicaragua in 1890 but it also went bankrupt. The Nicaraguan route had a strong appeal to the Americans.

The war with Spain in 1898 gave the United States another lesson on the need for a canal. The new battleship *Oregon*, uselessly located at San Francisco, made the 13,000 nautical mile voyage around Cape Horn followed by the newspaper-reading public for two months before it could participate in the Santiago campaign. After several years of complicated political and economic negotiations during which the Nicaraguan alternative seemed to win, the United States in 1903 bought the New French Canal Company. In the same year the Colombian province of Panama declared its independence and leased in perpetuity a strip of land ten miles wide (the Canal Zone) to the United States. Actual construction work took seven years and was completed in 1914.[3] The canal was built by the United States Government as a strategic waterway but its commercial importance is obvious.

Plans for a new sea-level canal to be completed by 1980 have been published. It has

[1] André Siegfried, *Suez, Panama et les routes maritimes mondiales*. Paris, 1940.
[2] Ferdinand de Lesseps stubbornly stuck to his vision of a sea-level canal, whereas the Americans working a quarter of a century later under far more favorable conditions settled for the simpler alternative of a canal with locks. How malaria and yellow fever are transmitted was not known in the 1880s and therefore the death rate among the personnel working on the canal was shockingly high. When the Americans took over the Canal work the role of certain mosquitos as carriers of disease had just become known and both yellow fever and malaria could be eradicated through a tremendous pioneer campaign against the vector before serious construction works were started.
[3] The Canal is 82 km from deep water to deep water. In the dredged channel it has a minimum width of 300 feet and a minimum depth of 42 feet. A ship transiting the Canal is raised in three steps from sea level to the Gatun Lake, normally 85 feet above sea level, and subsequently lowered in three steps to sea level at the other side of the isthmus. The six lock systems are in duplicate. Average transit time in 1961 was 16.5 hours. The present Canal tolls, 90 cents per net vessel-ton of 100 cubic feet of actual earning capacity for loaded vessels and 72 cents for vessels in ballast, were imposed in 1938. They are lower than those charged from 1915 to 1938.

The Panama Canal

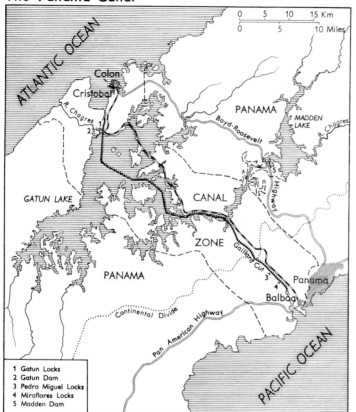

The Panama Canal traverses a mountainous area covered by tropical rain forest. It is fitted into a gap where one mountain chain ends and another begins. The isthmus at this point stretches north towards South America and south towards North America; the Atlantic entrance of the Canal is 25 kilometers west of the Pacific entrance. The artificial Gatun Lake, formed by the damming of the Rio Chagres about 10 kilometers from its outlet into the Atlantic Ocean, is 26 meters above sea level. Since 1935 the Madden Dam has helped to accumulate water in the rainy season to feed the Gatun Lake in the dry season.

been suggested that underground nuclear blasts should be used for the excavations of this canal.[4]

Trade through the Canal

The two world canals, Suez and Panama, are the only check points where important world trade flows are being measured regularly. The *Annual Report* of the Panama Canal Company is one of the most informative sources on recent changes in such cargo flows. Space only permits an analysis of some highlights of trade through the Canal.

For ten years the trade route between the east coast of the United States and Asia, primarily Japan, has ranked first in importance in terms of tonnage of cargo. The Asia-bound traffic accounted for the greater part—14.8 million tons in 1961, of which 12.9 million went to Japan. The five most important commodities on this route all went from the United States to Asia: coal and coke (5.4 million tons), scrap (3.0), phosphates (1.5), soybeans (1.4) and corn (0.7). The sustained growth of Japan's industrial production is largely responsible for the marked increases over the route. Since 1958 it is justifiable to talk about the period of Japanese influence in the Canal traffic. The total volume of cargo passing through the Canal destined for Japan increased from 8.6 million tons in 1958 to 14.4 million in 1961. The Korean conflict, the closing of

---

[4] W. N. Hess, "New Horizons in Resource Development: The Role of Nuclear Explosions", *Geographical Review*, 1962. Pp. 1–24.

The Gatun Locks on the Atlantic side of the Panama Canal raise and lower vessels 26 meters in three steps. They are in pairs which allow simultaneous lockage of ships in opposite directions. The greater part of the Canal channel is at the level of the Gatun Lake.

In the year ending June 30, 1961, records were established both for the number of transits (10,866) and for cargo movements (65.9 million metric tons). The average time spent in Canal zone waters was 16.5 hours in 1961 as compared with 19.3 hours in 1960. The Canal has a minimum width of 100 meters and a minimum depth of 42 feet. (Official Panama Canal Photograph, 1961)

The Dutch 32,000-ton tanker *Vivipara* being assisted into the one-step, 9.5-meter Pedro Miguel Locks on the Pacific side of the Panama Canal. In the background are the two-step, 16.5-meter Miraflores Locks, nearer the Pacific entrance.

In 1951 only 10 commercial vessels of 18,000 gross register tons or over transited the Canal; in 1961 there were 336. The increase in vessel size makes it more difficult to reach the optimum scheduling and dispatching of ships. (Official Panama Canal Photograph, 1960)

Panama Canal Traffic

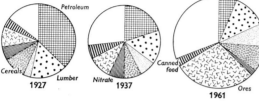

Atlantic to Pacific

1927 — Steel, Cotton

1937 — Other products, Scrap, Sugar, Phosphates

1961 — Coal

Radius
0   10 25 50   100
Million tons

Pacific to Atlantic

1927 — Petroleum, Cereals, Lumber

1937 — Nitrate, Canned food

1961 — Ores

Data from *Annual Report of the Governor of the Panama Canal,* 1930 and 1940; Panama Canal Company, Canal Zone Government, *Annual Report,* 1961.

the Suez Canal and Japan's economic expansion were main events leading to rapid increases in traffic on this route and in total canal traffic during the last decade.

Cargo Traffic through the Panama Canal 1961

Trade Route	Million metric tons
U.S. east coast–Asia	17.6
U.S. east cost–S.A.[a] west coast	8.0
Europe–S.A. west coast	6.5
Europe–U.S./Canada west coast	5.7
U.S. Intercoastal[b]	5.6
S.A. east coast–U.S. west coast	3.0
Europe–Oceania	2.4
West Indies–U.S. west coast	2.4
Subtotal	51.3
All other	13.4
Total	64.7

[a] South America.
[b] Including Alaska and Hawaii.
Source: Panama Canal Company, Canal Zone Government, *Annual Report.* Fiscal Year ended June 30, 1961, p. 10.

The second of the listed routes is predominantly a movement of raw materials from the west coast of South America to the east coast of the United States. Iron ore normally accounts for over half of the total flow. Bananas (0.6 million tons), primarily from Ecuador, account for many transits as they are shipped in small vessels. A German ship transporting bananas from Ecuadorian ports to Florida made 52 transits in 1961, the largest number that year. The flow of sugar from Peru (0.5 million tons in 1961) was more than five times the 1960 flow as a result of recent political developments in Cuba.

The third route on the list is also mainly raw materials moving from South America to Europe. Iron ore accounted for almost half of the total flow in 1961. The movement of fish-meal from Peru to Europe increased from 9,000 tons in 1955 to 470,000 tons in 1961, a reflection of the remarkable development of Peruvian fisheries in recent years.

The trade between the Pacific coast of Anglo-America and Europe is also dominated by a heavy flow of raw materials to Europe (lumber and wheat from Canada, barley from the United States).

The United States intercoastal traffic is now of much smaller importance than in the early decades of the canal's history when petroleum from California and lumber from the Pacific Northwest were shipped in large quantities. In 1961 traffic from the Pacific to the Atlantic still accounted for two-thirds of the total flow; petroleum products and lumber made up more than 75 per cent. Traffic in the opposite direction is dominated by petroleum products and steel manufactures.

The trade between Europe and Oceania is chiefly New Zealand's trade with Europe. Australia's European trade moves almost exclusively through the Suez Canal. French Oceania also accounts for sizable quantities in both directions.

The two cargo flows between the North

American west coast and the West Indies and South America's east coast are almost exclusively petroleum and petroleum products moving from the Caribbean (Venezuela and the Netherlands Antilles) to the Pacific coast of the United States.

The West Indies

The islands of the West Indies, extending for over 2500 kilometers in an east–west direction and more than 1500 kilometers north–south, were the first part of the Americas to be discovered and settled by Europeans and the Caribbean soon became the Mediterranean of the New World. The indigenous population was rapidly annihilated and replaced by Negroes, imported as slaves for the sugar plantations. Although the islands were first claimed by Spain, other European powers, chiefly Britain, France and the Netherlands, gained a foothold, and the islands are today a cultural mosaic in which the Spanish-speaking element is the largest.

Cuba and Puerto Rico were Spain's last American colonies. The Spanish-American War of 1898 was the end of four centuries of Spanish rule in the western hemisphere and the beginning of large scale United States intervention in Caribbean affairs.

Sugar, which later was to play a vital role in the history of the islands, was not an important crop in the first century of colonization. The few early Spanish settlers lived by a predominantly pastoral economy.[1] Only Hispaniola, with the best communications with Europe and an early start thanks to settlers from the Canary Islands, had an exportable surplus of sugar in the sixteenth century. From the 1530s smuggling, privateering and naval raids brought foreign ships to the Spanish West Indies, but the first British, Dutch and French colonies were not established until about 1630. The three powers cooperated in fighting Spain. The British and French were dependent on Dutch trade until Cromwell's Navigation Act of 1651 gave English ships exclusive rights to trade with the English colonies. It was also the Dutch who introduced sugar into the English and French colonies after having learned growing and processing techniques in north-eastern Brazil, where they held a large territory between 1624 and 1654. Sugar soon became predominant in many islands, grown with indentured white labor and with a rapidly expanding number of negro slaves, but in the Spanish colonies sugar continued to be one crop among many. Trade with the West Indies became very important for the mother countries; at the end of the seventeenth century the West Indies supplied nine per cent of England's imports and took more than four per cent of her exports, much larger shares than those of her colonies in North America.[2] Throughout the eighteenth century the British West Indies were Britain's leading trade partner. An important role was played by the triangular trade from England or France to West Africa with 'trade goods', to the sugar islands of the West Indies with slaves, and back to Europe with a return cargo, usually sugar. Even today Guadeloupe and Martinique are more important trade partners for France than is her European neighbor Norway.

---

[1] J. H. Parry and P. M. Sherlock, *A Short History of the West Indies*. London, 1957. Pp. 14 f.

[2] Parry and Sherlock, *op. cit.* P. 78; and E. B. Schumpeter, *English Overseas Trade Statistics 1697–1808*. Oxford, 1960.

International Passenger Traffic in the West Indies 1959

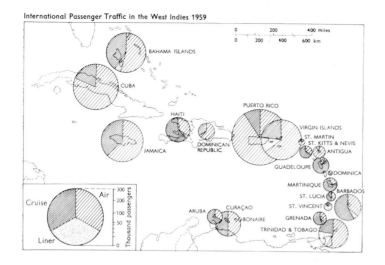

Although 62 per cent of the West Indian tourist traffic is by air, cruising vessels (34%) and passenger liners (4%) make significant contributions to the well-organized industry, which for some smaller islands is already the leading source of income.

Map adapted after Helmut Blume.

The West Indies, located on the doorstep of Anglo-America with its high standard of living, have developed into one of the major tourist areas in the tropics. The number of foreign visitors increased steadily from 45,000 in 1919 to 131,000 in 1929 and 190,000 in 1938. In the 1940s, when the American tourists were cut off from Europe by the war and its aftermath, the tourist industry in the West Indies mushroomed and this expansion continued in the 1950s. No less than 1.5 million foreign visitors were recorded in 1959.[3] Tourism ranks as a major export industry and for several islands it is on a par with agriculture as a source of foreign exchange. For many passenger lines on the North Atlantic route the winter cruises to the West Indies are of great economic importance as they permit the full employment of ships and crew even in the slack season.

The Greater Antilles

Cuba

At the turn of the century nearly half of the land under crops in Cuba was devoted to sugar cane and 60 years later this proportion was

over three-quarters, despite a large increase in arable land. In 1960 sugar accounted for 76 per cent of Cuba's exports by value, and 32 per cent of all sugar in international trade was Cuban. Tobacco and tobacco manufactures were second with 10 per cent of the exports in 1960.

A treaty of 1901 gave Cuban sugar a 20 per cent tariff reduction and a favored position in the American import quota system for sugar. Until 1960 the Cuban economy was closely linked with the American. Almost a billion dollars of American capital was invested in Cuba in 1929, but much was lost in the Depression. The value of direct American investment in 1949 was estimated at 650 million dollars, mostly in the sugar and tobacco industries and in public utilities and transportation.[4] In 1958 the United States accounted for two-thirds of Cuba's exports and for even more of her imports. But after the 1959 revolution and the ensuing American embargo on trade with Cuba following the seizure of American property, trade with the countries of

[3] Helmut Blume, "Westindien als Fremdenverkehrsgebiet", *Die Erde*, 1963. Pp. 48 ff. Many visitors went to more than one island and were thus counted more than once.
[4] *Report on Cuba.* International Bank for Reconstruction and Development. Baltimore, 1951. Pp. 732 f.

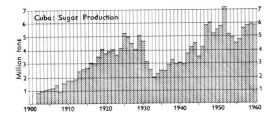

Sources: Gerardo Canet, *Atlas de Cuba,* Cambridge, Mass., 1949. P. 44; United Nations *Statistical Yearbook.*

the Communist Bloc has become increasingly important.

Sugar cultivation is well distributed over most of the island except the limestone area in the west and the rugged mountains in the southeast. The harvested cane must reach the grinding mills, the *centrales,* within a matter of hours and, although production is much more concentrated than earlier, there are still about 160 *centrales* scattered over the island.[5] Most of the sugar is exported in the form of raw sugar (92 per cent in 1960).

Cuba has many good harbors both on the northern and southern coasts and no sugar plantation is more than eighty kilometers from a port.[6] All except one of Cuba's nineteen ports on the map ship sugar. Nuevitas is the leading sugar port. Habana, the capital and economic center of the island, dominates Cuba's import trade. It has two oil refineries but it is also one of the most important sugar ports. Santiago de Cuba in the southeast has an oil refinery and is the largest ore port in the island, exporting manganese ore and until 1958 iron ore from nearby deposits. Cuba also exports small quantities of other ores, particularly chrome and nickel, through several ports.

    [5] Donald R. Dyer, "Sugar Regions of Cuba", *Economic Geography,* 1956. Pp. 177–184.
    [6] Preston E. James, *Latin America.* Third Ed., London, 1959. P. 761.
    [7] *Jamaica: Report for the year 1959.* Her Majesty's Stationery Office, London, 1962. P. 298.

Jamaica

Jamaica, British since 1655, is a large producer of sugar and bananas for export. Jamaica's position as a banana exporter is, however, much less prominent than some decades ago. From 1938 to 1959 the number of stems exported declined from 23.8 million to 10.3 million,[7] and Jamaica's share of world exports dropped from 12 per cent in 1936–39 to 3 per cent in 1958–60. Production and export of citrus fruit, on the other hand, are expanding and the fruit juice exports now bring in almost as much as the time-honored rum.

After the Second World War Jamaica has emerged as the world's largest bauxite exporter, and bauxite and alumina are by far the leading export items by weight. Together they account for almost half the export value.

Since 1952 Ocho Rios on the north coast has shipped bauxite from the Reynolds company deposits. The ore is transported ten kilometers from the drying plant to the storage facilities in the port by two aerial tramways. For the shipment to La Quinta near Corpus Christi, Texas, self-unloading ore carriers of up to 32,000 tons are used. Since 1953 Port Kaiser in the southwestern part of the island has shipped bauxite brought by a 22-kilometer railroad. Ore carriers of up to 37,500 tons move the ore to two alumina plants at Baton Rouge and Gramercy (halfway between New Orleans and Baton Rouge). Port Kaiser has been dredged to 45 feet. The Canadian-owned alumina plants at Kirkvine (operating since 1952) and Ewarton (1959) ship alumina through Port Esquivel to reduction plants in Canada and other countries.

Kingston, the capital, is Jamaica's leading general port. The land-locked harbor can accomodate ships of 36 foot draft and tidal movement is negligible. It is a port of call for liners and is visited by many cruises. Kingston's hotel capacity is surpassed by that of

Two gantry loaders on the Port Kaiser pier are capable of loading over 4,000 tons of bauxite per hour. (Kaiser Aluminum)

Montego Bay on the north coast, the leading tourist center in Jamaica.

Hispaniola

The political boundary between Haiti and the Dominican Republic is a real cultural border. Haiti's population is predominantly Negro and French-speaking whereas the Dominican Republic has a Mulatto majority (with a large white minority) and is Spanish in language and culture.

Haiti's leading exports are coffee and sisal. In the last few years it has also become a bauxite exporter. The bauxite from the Reynolds mine in the Salagnac Mountains is shipped through Miragoâne on the southern coast of the Gonaïves Gulf. The capital Port-au-Prince is the leading general port and a popular port of call for pleasure cruises.

Sugar and molasses account for over half of the Dominican Republic's exports both by tonnage and value. Coffee, cocoa and bananas follow if measured by value, but bauxite and iron ore by tonnage.

Santo Domingo, formerly Ciudad Trujillo, is the political and economic capital and the largest general port. It also handles the iron ore exports. Since 1959 bauxite has been shipped from the ALCOA mines at Cabo Rojo on the southern coast near the Haitian border.

Puerto Rico

The history of Puerto Rico before the end of last century is similar to that of other colonies in the West Indies, but although the immediate changes brought about by the American occupation in 1898 were not very great, they made possible a later development that has been considered as a model for the expansion of the economy and the raising of living standards in the tropics. Since 1952 Puerto Rico has been a self-governing Commonwealth associated with the United States.

Manufacturing is becoming increasingly important. Firms are induced to move to the island from the mainland by tax reductions and by low wages. The location is also favorable for industries producing goods that are shipped by water. Foreign firms are induced by these factors and by the advantages of getting inside the American customs barrier.

Although agriculture emphasizes sugar and coffee with 34 and 16 per cent of the crop land it is rather diversified. Livestock products, primarily milk, accounted for 35 per cent of the farm value of agricultural products in 1958–59.

The capital San Juan on the north coast handles most of the cargo traffic. It is a general port with large imports of crude and refined petroleum. This is the only commodity group brought in large quantities from sources other than the United States, the dominating trade partner with 83 per cent of the import value and no less than 97 per cent of the export value in 1959. Sugar made up 39 per cent of the cargo shipped in 1956, with petroleum and products second with 21 per cent.

The passenger traffic between the United States and Puerto Rico is very intense, with departures exceeding arrivals by tens of thousands each year. The Puerto Ricans are American citizens and, unhampered by immigration restrictions, they have moved in large numbers especially to New York. But passenger traffic with the United States and foreign countries is overwhelmingly by air— one per cent of the 1958–59 departures were by sea. Only the traffic with the neighboring Virgin Islands accounts for large numbers of sea passengers.

The Lesser Antilles

Sometimes the term the Lesser Antilles is used in a restricted sense to mean the chain of islands stretching from the Anegada Passage, east of the Virgin Islands, to Grenada, but it

is used here in its wider sense, including the Virgin Islands, Barbados, and the islands off the coast of Venezuela from Tobago and Trinidad to Curaçao and Aruba. Most of the islands are small; the largest, Trinidad, is little more than half the size of Puerto Rico, the smallest of the Greater Antilles.

The American Virgin Islands, bought from Denmark in 1917, grow some sugar cane and export bay rum, but tourism is the most important source of income. Charlotte Amalie on the island of St. Thomas has a well-protected harbor and was an important coaling station in the days of coal-burning steamers. It is a general port; cargo turnover is dominated by petroleum imports. The British Virgin Islands are economically dependent on the American neighbor islands, where the inhabitants more easily find employment, and where livestock products, the major exports, are sold. St. Thomas is the social and economic focus of the whole group and transships goods to and from the British islands.[1]

The British Leeward Islands have a few small ports. Basseterre on St. Kitts ships small quantities of sugar, molasses, cotton, and copra and receives general cargo. St. John's on Antigua also ships sugar and cotton and Plymouth on Montserrat cotton and fruit. The cargo traffic of the British Windward Islands farther south is similar.

As generators of seaborne traffic the three northerly islands of the Netherlands Antilles, St. Eustatius, Saba and St. Martin are insignificant.

The trade of Guadeloupe and Martinique is completely dominated by France. The twin islands of Guadeloupe have two ports, Pointe-à-Pitre on the eastern island and the smaller Basse-Terre, the capital, on the western island. The main exports are sugar and bananas. Petroleum, cement, fertilizers and consumer goods are imported.

Fort-de-France is the capital and the main port of Martinique. This island has had several

---

[1] *British Virgin Islands: Report for the years 1957 and 1958.* Her Majesty's Stationery Office, London, 1960; John P. Augelli, "The British Virgin Islands: A West Indian Anomaly", *Geographical Review*, 1956. Pp. 43–58.

volcanic eruptions in historic times; in 1902 Mt. Pelée erupted and destroyed St. Pierre, formerly a major port. Like the other islands in this part of the Antilles Martinique is often ravaged by hurricanes.[2] Sugar cane is the dominating crop, and sugar and rum are important exports. Bananas and other tropical crops are also produced.

The economy of the densely populated island of Barbados is based on sugar, and in 1960 sugar, molasses and rum accounted for 93 per cent of the export value. Food accounted for over one-fourth of the import value. The United Kingdom and Canada are the most important trade partners. The capital and main port, Bridgetown, is located in the southwestern part of the island. Only vessels of less than 200 foot length and 14.5 foot draft can be accomodated at wharves; sugar loading is usually from lighters.[3]

Trinidad is by far the largest of the islands here included among the Lesser Antilles, and its oil deposits and its location as a suitable transshipment point for bauxite from the Guianas have contributed to make its port traffic so much greater than that of the other islands, except Aruba and Curaçao. Trinidad is south of the tracks of hurricanes, which are a major hazard in the islands farther north.

While Barbados and the Windward and Leeward Islands have been British since the seventeenth century, Trinidad remained Spanish until 1797. The chief activity at that time was sugar growing, carried out by French planters with slave labor. The main sugar growing district was along the Gulf of Paria in the western part of the island, but after the British had introduced East Indian contract laborers in 1845 cane growing spread to other parts of the island and production increased rapidly. Sugar cane is still a major crop but it accounts for less than 10 per cent of the export value. Trinidad's major export is petroleum. The natural asphalt from La Brea in the southwest was known when Europeans first

visited the island, and it still contributes to Trinidad's trade. Petroleum and asphalt accounted for 84 per cent of the 1960 export value. Bunkers constitute an important outlet for Trinidad oil.

Port-of-Spain, the political and economic capital, is the major general port. It is a liner port and receives many cruise ships. The largest oil refinery is at Pointe-a-Pierre. Other oil ports are Brighton near the La Brea asphalt lake and Point Fortin. Trinidad has proved a suitable location for transshipment of bauxite brought by small, shallow-draft vessels, the only ones that can take a full load from the river ports in British Guiana and Surinam. These transshipment ports are located at Point Templadora at the old fishing port of Carenage west of Port-of-Spain and at Chaguaramas still further west. Shipments to Canada are concentrated in the part of the year when the receiving port, Port Alfred on the Saguenay River, is ice-free.

Two of the Netherlands Antilles, Aruba and Curaçao, have ports that rank among the largest in the world by tonnage. They offered few possibilities for agriculture but by the seventeenth century Curaçao developed a flourishing entrepôt trade with Venezuela. The Dutch could trade freely both with Europe and with the Spanish settlements in Venezuela and took part in the slave trade between Africa and America. The abolition of the Spanish trade monopoly and of the slave trade reduced the importance of the Dutch colonies. Curaçao remained a bunker and transit port for Dutch and foreign ships destined for the western Caribbean.

It was the oil industry that gave Curaçao renewed importance as a transshipment point for the Maracaibo area. Since only shallow-draft vessels could pass the sand banks in the

[2] Jean Pouquet, *Les Antilles françaises*. Paris, 1952. Pp. 38 f.
[3] E. G. Godfrey and K. Macdonald, eds., *Ports, Dues and Charges on Shipping Throughout the World*. 21st Ed., London, 1959. P. 538.

channel from Lake Maracaibo, and in addition neither climate nor political conditions favored the construction of refineries in Venezuela, Shell in 1917 decided to build a refinery on Curaçao and Standard Oil of New Jersey built one in 1928 on Aruba, originally planned to refine Mexican crude oil.[4] These two refineries now completely dominate the port traffic of the islands, receiving crude oil by lake tankers from Venezuela and shipping refined products. The construction of refineries in Venezuela and the deepening of the channel to Lake Maracaibo in the 1950s makes further expansion of the refinery capacity uncertain.

South America

Colombia

Although facing two oceans, Colombia is a classic example of a country with poor access to the great trade routes of the world. Colombia's largest population clusters and its leading economic centers are located far inland in the Andes, which in Colombia branch off into three parallel ranges, separated by two deep longitudinal troughs, the valleys of the Magdalena and the Cauca. These two north-south river valleys control all forms of surface transportation. Almost the whole population is concentrated in the one-third of the country occupied by the Andes and in the lowlands at the mouth of the Magdalena River. The rough terrain makes surface transport the most difficult economic problem of Colombia.

The largest population concentrations are in the Cordillera Oriental and in the Antioqueño Highland of the Cordillera Central. Bogotá, founded in 1538, Colombia's largest city and its political, intellectual and financial capital, is located in the former area; Medellín, founded in 1675, Colombia's second largest city and its leading manufacturing and economic center, is the focus of the latter. The rivalry between the two leading cities is similar to that between Rio de Janeiro and São Paulo in Brazil. Bogotá and Medellín have had quite different histories. When the Spaniards arrived the high basins of the eastern Cordillera, of which Bogotá became the leading urban center, had a rather dense population of Chibcha Indians who were sedentary farmers. The Spanish conquerors imposed their system of large estates on this region, using the Indians as laborers. Food production is still the major economic activity of the high Andes basins.

The Antioquía region in the central Cordillera was first penetrated by Europeans in search of gold. For permanent settlement this region, in contrast to the eastern region, was handicapped by a scanty Indian population. During the seventeenth century, however, a large group of immigrants arrived from Spain, made up of Basques and of converted Jews, *cristianos nuevos*. They sought an isolated and easily protected region.[1] The Antioqueños have

---

[4] Edgar Nordlohne, *De economisch-geografische structuur der Nederlandse Benedenwindse eilanden.* Haarlem, 1951. Pp. 92 ff.

[1] James J. Parsons, *Antioqueño Colonization in Western Colombia.* Berkeley, 1949. The rugged and deeply dissected country between Medellín and Cartagena is so difficult to cross that not until the 1950s was a road constructed. Most of the very small trade in and out of Medellín was carried on an oxcart road to Puerto Berrío on the Magdalena, crossing the Cordillera by a pass. The Cordillera was still crossed by oxcart or mule until a tunnel was blasted to connect the railroads. Another trail, used mostly by mule trains, connected Medellín with the Cauca Valley, from which connection was relatively easy with Buenaventura by way of Cali. Gold and silver were the chief exports from this region before the advent of coffee.

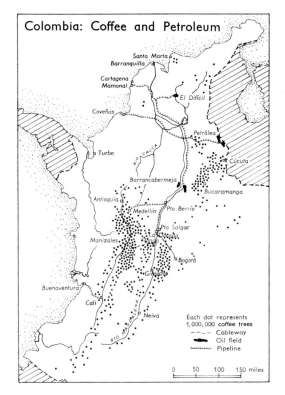

Colombia: Coffee and Petroleum

Each dot represents
1,000,000 coffee trees
--- Cableway
Oil field
······· Pipeline

0   50   100   150 miles

Source: G. J. Butland, *Latin America,* London,
1960. P. 166; see also Parsons, *op. cit.,* p. 143.

Colombia's Coffee Exports 1957

Port	Thousand tons	Per cent
Buenaventura	235.9	80.8
Barranquilla	36.7	12.6
Cartagena	17.5	6.0
Tumaco	1.6	0.6
Santa Marta	0.1	0.0
Cúcuta	0.1	0.0
Total	291.9	100.0

Country	Thousand tons	Per cent
United States	244.0	83.6
Germany	17.0	5.8
Sweden	7.5	2.6
Canada	6.2	2.1
Spain	3.7	1.3
Netherlands	3.6	1.2
Belgium	3.1	1.1
Italy	2.0	0.7
Finland	1.9	0.6
Other Countries	2.9	1.0
Total	291.9	100.0

Source: *Anuario de Comercio Exterior de 1957,*
Departamento Administrativo Nacional de Estadística.
Bogotá, 1958.

had an extraordinary birth rate, have been very
expansive and have remained almost unmixed.
They resisted the importation of Negro slaves
when their neighbors in the Cauca Valley became wealthy on slave labor. The rapid population increase was sufficient to sustain a large
expansion of settlement, chiefly towards the
south, beginning in the early nineteenth century. Coffee, which was grown in the Magdalena Valley about 1865 and entered the foreign
trade of Colombia in the early 1880s, has
radically changed the economy of the Antioqueños in this century. Earlier their agriculture
consisted of the shifting cultivation of food
crops for the local market. In the Antioqueño
region, accounting for half of Colombia's coffee
production, small owner-operated farms are the
rule. Just as in the Paulista capital of Brazil
the urban industries and especially the textile

factories of the Antioqueño capital grew rapidly
with the expansion of coffee cultivation. In a
short time Medellín emerged from obscurity to
become Colombia's chief economic center. The
isolation of the past was ended by the construction of roads and railroads.

In recent years coffee has accounted for
75–80 per cent of Colombia's export value.
Since 1920 Colombia has been the world's
leading source of mild, high grade coffee and
has been second only to Brazil in total exports.
Because of its excellent flavor this coffee is
much in demand in the world market for
blending with cheaper Brazilian varieties. Second in value among Colombia's export items
is crude petroleum (10–20%). In volume Co-

lombia's foreign trade is small. The 300–400 thousand tons of coffee rank far behind the 4–5 million tons of petroleum.

The Magdalena River, unsatisfactory as it is for navigation, has always been the traffic artery between the heart of Colombia and the Caribbean.[2] Three ports, Barranquilla, Cartagena and Santa Marta, are located on the swampy lowlands built by the Río Magdalena when it emerges from its valley between the Cordillera Oriental and the Cordillera Central. From early colonial times these ports have been competing for the trade moving to and from the interior of Colombia.[3]

During most of the colonial period Cartagena, founded in 1533, was the dominating port, one of the leading ports of Spanish America. The city was built on the shores of a harbor protected by a strong fortress, a key point in the Spanish defense system. Just south of Cartagena an entrance of the Magdalena, known as El Dique, was navigable for the small vessels of that period. However, the silting

of El Dique cut off Cartagena from the Magdalena trade more than a hundred years ago. In recent decades the port has increased in importance due chiefly to four factors: the construction of a railroad to Calamar on the Magdalena, the completion in 1926 of an oil terminal at Mamonal south of the city for a pipeline from the Barrancabermeja oil fields, the increase in population and economic activity in the immediate hinterland of Cartagena in the western part of the plain and the completion of a highway to Medellín and points further south.

Santa Marta on the eastern side of the lowlands, also located on a good harbor and with access to the Magdalena River for small, shallow-draft vessels, became the leading port for a short time after the silting of El Dique. In this century Santa Marta has been known as a leading banana port. The United Fruit Company has special banana loading docks and a plantation south of the port. Most of the bananas are grown by small farmers, chiefly negroes. After a temporary decline in the 1940s when banana disease struck the area, shipments are again increasing. Santa Marta has a restricted immediate hinterland but with the completion in 1961 of the railroad to Bogotá Santa Marta will be in a better position to compete for the foreign trade of the capital region.[4]

The third center of the Caribbean Lowlands, Barranquilla, has controlled the trade of the Magdalena Valley since the middle of last century when steamboats began to navigate the river as far as the Honda rapids. It has long been the leading port of Colombia, although now surpassed by Buenaventura on the Pacific Coast. The sand bars at the mouth of the river prohibited the entrance of ocean vessels but in 1862 a short railroad was built to a pier outside the bars and later an outport was established, Puerto Colombia. After dredging operations in the river mouth ocean vessels of 10,000 tons can now proceed to Barranquilla,

---

[2] About two million tons of cargo, 200,000 passengers and 100,000 head of cattle have been handled in recent years by steamboats (500 tons), usually pulling barges, and by barge trains of about 2,000 tons. The river valley has a low density of population, the many river ports being the chief settlements. They are linked by rail or road with the Cordilleran cities on both sides of the valley. The irregular flow of the river with shifting sand bars and the winter dry season are normal obstacles to navigation even below the Honda rapids about 1,100 km upstream from the estuary. Upstream from Honda the river is again navigable as far as Neiva. Much of the cargo carried on the Magdalena is domestic trade: cattle, sugar and cotton moving up the river from the Coastal Lowlands; grain and potatoes moving down from the high basins in the Cordilleras. The textile factories of Medellín get most of their cotton from the lowlands. Petroleum products from the refinery in the Barrancabermeja field move up and down the river.

[3] Preston E. James, *Latin America*. New York, 1950. Pp. 101 ff.

[4] Jean Labasse, "La vie de relation en Colombie", *Annales de Géographie*, 1957. P. 536. Map pp. 526–27.

A freight train will run from Santa Marta to Bogotá in 44 hours, an express train in 26 hours. This should be compared with 9 days for a barge from Barranquilla to La Dorada, the river port of Bogotá, or with 4 days for a truck from Barranquilla to Bogotá when the road has been completed and improved. *Op. cit.* P. 578.

South America

CARIBBEAN SEA

ST. MARTIN
ST. KITTS
ANTIGUA
GUADELOUPE
Basse-Terre   Pointe-à-Pitre
DOMINICA
Fort-de-France   MARTINIQUE
ST. LUCIA
ST. VINCENT
BARBADOS
Bridgetown

Inset Venezuela

Cartagena
Barranquilla
Coveñas   Santa Marta
Turbo

Buenaventura
Tumaco
Esmeraldas

COLOMBIA

ECUADOR
Guayaquil
Cabo Blanco   Puerto Bolivar
Mâncora   Iquitos
Lobitos
Talara   Paita
Pimentel   Pto Eten
Pto Chicama   Pacasmayo
Salaverry   Guañape
Chimbote   Samanco
Supe
Huacho
Callao
Asia   Cerro Azul
Chincha
Pisco
San Juan   La Vieja

Matarani   Ilo
Mollendo
Arica

Iquique
Punta de Lobos   Guanillos de Norte
Tocopilla   Mejillones

Antofagasta
Taltal
Chañaral
Caldera
Huasco
Cruz Grande

Coquimbo
Los Vilos
Valparaiso
San Antonio
Talcahuano   Tomé
Lota   Coronel
Lebu
Valdivia
Puerto Montt
Ancud
Castro

Puerto Aysén

Río Gallegos
Caleta Clarence
Punta Arenas
Port Stanley
FALKLAND ISLANDS

PERU

BOLIVIA

PARAGUAY

ARGENTINA

CHILE

VENEZUELA

Mackenzie   Georgetown   Paramaribo
New Amsterdam   Moengo
(Everton)   Nickerie
BRITISH   DUTCH   Cayenne
GUIANA   FRENCH
GUIANA

Macapá
Belém
São Luiz
Parnaiba   Camocim
Fortaleza
Macau
Areia Branca
Natal
Cabedelo
Recife
Maceió
Aracaju
Salvador
Ilhéus

Manaus

Iquitos

BRAZIL

Vitória

Angra dos Reis   Rio de Janeiro
Santos
Antonina
Paranaguá
São Francisco   Itajaí
Florianópolis   Laguna
Imbituba
Pôrto Alegre
Pelotas

Santa Fé   Sta Elena
San Lorenzo   Paraná
Rosario
San Nicolás   Rio Grande
Villa Constitución
Campana   Montevideo
URUGUAY
Buenos Aires   La Plata
Mar del Plata
Bahía Blanca
San Antonio Oeste   Quequén
(Necochea)

Puerto Ocampo

Comodoro Rivadavia

1 Diamante
2 Ramallo
3 San Pedro
4 Baradero
5 Zárate

PACIFIC OCEAN

ATLANTIC OCEAN

1:40,000,000

| 0 | 500 | 1,000 km |
| 0 | 200 | 400 | 600 miles |

CARGO HANDLED
1956
Million metric tons

Shipments

Receipts

0 0.5 1   5   10   15

Venezuela

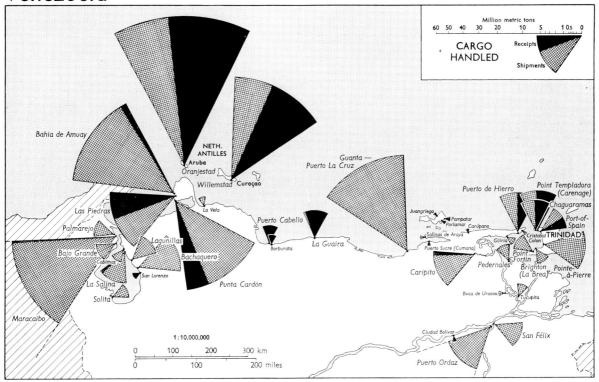

CARGO HANDLED

Million metric tons

60 50 40 30 20 10 5 1 0.5 0

Receipts

Shipments

1:10,000,000

0   100   200   300 km

0   100   200 miles

which is the fourth largest city of Colombia. Larger ships must dock at Puerto Colombia.

Since 1939 there is a fourth major port on the Caribbean, the oil terminal at Coveñas which receives oil from the fields in the Colombian part of the Maracaibo Basin. The capacity of the Coveñas pipeline is about 3.5 million tons a year and of the Mamonal pipeline 3.0 million tons.

Buenaventura on the sparsely populated Pacific coast has grown rapidly as a port since the opening of the Panama Canal and the railroad over the Cordillera Occidental to Cali in the Cauca Valley. Cali is the chief trade and transportation center of the valley in which sugar cane, grown on large estates with imported negro slaves, has been the leading crop since early colonial days. With a population (385,000) fifteen times as large as before

In recent years Venezuela's port map has been subject to major changes, which have been elaborated in the text and on map 343. The somewhat unbalanced trade of the Netherlands Antilles, which import crude oil and export petroleum products, is mainly the result of large receipts of fresh water (5 million tons).

World War I Cali is Colombia's third city. It has a wide range of industries. A railroad and a highway connect the city with Medellín, the economic capital of Colombia. Medellín is also served by a railroad to Puerto Berrío on the Magdalena River and by a highway to Cartagena. The Antioqueño capital is thus the chief point of competition between Buenaventura and the Atlantic ports. In recent years Buenaventura has handled more cargo than Barranquilla. Of the all-important coffee exports four-fifths move through Buenaventura. A distribution map of coffee trees gives a good indication of the coffee hinterlands of the two leading ports. Buenaventura is one of the few ports on the west coast of Latin America where ships can be berthed alongside wharves and where the use of lighters is therefore unnecessary.

Venezuela

Until World War I Venezuela was a small out-of-the-way republic with a primitive agro-pastoral economy. In the late 1950s, though still a small nation in terms of population, it had become by far the most important country of Latin America on the world shipping map, by a wide margin outstripping the Plata region at the peak of its grain shipping heyday. Venezuela in the late 1950s had the largest foreign trade of all the Latin American republics. In per capita foreign trade Venezuela ranked among the leading countries in the world, surpassed only by New Zealand, Canada, Hong Kong and a few small countries in Western Europe (page 17). Its petroleum production, second only to that of the United States,[1] accounted for over 90 per cent of its export value[2] and iron ore was a rapidly growing new export item.

The revenues from the foreign exploitation of Venezuela's rich natural resources have helped to build cities, ports, highways etc. and have greatly improved the finances of the state but have not profoundly changed the welfare of the majority of the Venezuelan population. Only 3 per cent of the gainfully employed people were engaged in the oil industry when the census was taken in 1950. No less than 44 per cent earned their living in agriculture.

In spite of the large percentage of people engaged in farming and ranching, Venezuela has a substantial net import of agricultural products. The differences in the ways of living between the urban and the rural population has widened and deepened in the last four decades of urban expansion, directly or indirectly associated with the tremendous development of Venezuela's oil production.

The Oil Industry

Asphalt from the seepages near the shore of Lake Maracaibo was used by the Indians in pre-Columbian days for calking their vessels. Later the Spanish *conquistadores* and English and French pirates used it for the same purpose. The first commercial oil field of any importance was Mene Grande, near Lake Maracaibo, discovered by a subsidiary of the Shell group in 1914. Three years later another Shell subsidiary discovered the Rosa field in the same region. The Venezuelan oil boom really got under way when, in December 1922, one La Rosa well started blowing wild for an estimated 100,000 b/d, which called the world's attention to the tremendous production potential of the Lake Maracaibo area.[3] An era of active prospecting was initiated both in the Lake Maracaibo region and in the *llanos* of eastern Venezuela.[4] Many companies participated in the search for oil but only three were really successful: Standard Oil of New Jersey (Creole), Shell, and Gulf (Mene Grande).

[1] In 1960 the Soviet Union passed Venezuela in the list of petroleum producers and became second to the United States, like Czarist Russia had been for several decades until World War I. The countries of the Middle East, taken as a group, have produced more oil than Venezuela since 1949. For further details see page 59.

[2] Oil in the late 1950s contributed about 20 per cent of Venezuela's Gross National Product and over 60 per cent of the government revenue. *The Economic Development of Venezuela.* International Bank for Reconstruction and Development. Baltimore, 1961. Pp. 410 and 414.

[3] Guillermo Zuloaga, "Venezuela", *World Geography of Petroleum* (Wallace E. Pratt and Dorothy Good, editors). Princeton University Press, 1950. Pp. 49 ff. Erich Otremba, "Entwicklung und Wandlung der venezolanischen Kulturlandschaft unter der Herrschaft des Erdöles", *Erdkunde,* 1954. Pp. 169 ff.

[4] In 1926 the Lagunillas field was discovered. It rapidly became the chief oil field in Venezuela and has maintained this position ever since. The Tía Juana field, discovered in 1923, is the second largest on the Lake.

Source of Crude Oil Output for Major Companies, 1957

(percentages)

Company	North America	Middle East	Venezuela	Other
Standard Oil (N.J.)	27	20	50	3
Royal Dutch/Shell	18	26	45	11
British Petroleum	1	99	—	—
Gulf	31	53	15	1
Texaco	42	37	14	7
Standard Oil (Cal.)	42	40	10	8
Standard Oil (N.Y.)	40	38	16	6
All companies	27	37	29	7

Note: These firms in 1957 produced 93% of Middle East oil and 92% of Venezuela's. In 1959 they produced 92% of Middle East oil and 88% of Venezuela's. Source: *The Economic Development of Venezuela*. The International Bank for Reconstruction and Development. Baltimore, 1961. P. 133. Data compiled from Corporate Annual Reports.

The Big Three have dominated Venezuelan oil production since the late 1920s and in 1956 accounted for 88 per cent of the crude output.[5]

Seventy per cent of Venezuela's 1956 production came from the fields in and around the shallow Lake Maracaibo. When Shell in 1917 developed the first large oil field in this region it was necessary to find a transshipment point outside the lake area as the shifting sandbanks at the entrance of the lake prevented the passage of ocean-going tankers. Willemstad on the adjacent island of Curaçao was chosen and a refinery was also built here. The choice was simplified as both the company and the island were Dutch. Points on the mainland must have seemed less attractive for large investments as Venezuela was known for its unstable governments. In 1928 Standard Oil of New Jersey chose another Dutch island, Aruba, as the site

[5] Warren L. Baker, "Venezuela Oil Enters Vastly Bigger Era", *World Oil*, August 15, 1957. Pp. 130 ff.
[6] *World Petroleum*, July, 1958. Pp. 60–61.
[7] *Petróleo y Minería de Venezuela*. October 1959. Pp. 56 ff.

of its refinery. Both refineries have later been enlarged and now rank among the largest in the world. In the postwar period the Lake Maracaibo area got two new deepwater outlets for its oil. In rapid succession Shell and Standard Oil completed large refineries on the west coast of the Paraguaná Peninsula at Puerto Cardón (1947) and Amuay Bay (1950). They receive their oil through pipelines. These large refineries were built after the Venezuelan Government had adopted measures to stimulate petroleum refining within its own borders. In 1956 Lake Maracaibo was opened to ocean-going tankers when a deepwater channel, built by the Government of Venezuela, was completed at the mouth of the lake. The channel has later been deepened to 43 feet and extended through the Straits of Maracaibo (95 kilometers). Before this channel was built crude oil was transported by shallow-draft tankers from a number of small terminals along the lake shore to the large refineries on Aruba and Curaçao. Now the loading will be concentrated to a few big lake terminals. Shell is building one on the east shore of the lake near its mouth (Puerto Miranda), which will take oil from the east shore districts, from the lake itself and from a field on the west side of the lake. It will be possible to accomodate tankers as large as 65,000 tons.[6] Standard Oil is constructing an off-shore terminal 1.5 kilometers from the coast at La Salina, where the company has most of its industrial installations. With a capacity of about 50 million tons a year this will be one of the largest oil terminals in the world.[7]

The second large oil district is found in the eastern and central *llanos* of the Orinoco basin. Numerous exploratory wells were drilled between 1918 and 1927 and in the following year oil was found near Caripito. As there are no oil seeps on the surface of the *llanos* the large-scale production of oil in this region had to await the development of the new science of geophysics (the torsion balance first, and later the seismograph and gravimeter). In 1937 Gulf found oil in the rich Oficina field thus initiating oil production in the central *llanos*. Oil from this area is sent by pipeline through the Barcelona gap in the Coastal Range to Puerto la Cruz which has developed into one of the major terminals. It is located adjacent to Guanta, the port of Barcelona. Smaller ports serving parts of this oil region are Caripito and Tucupita.

Since 1947 a new oil district has been developed in the western part of the *llanos* in the Barinas-Apure basin. A pipeline from this region has been constructed to the El Palito

refinery (1959), thirteen kilometers west of Puerto Cabello.

Iron ore

The Guiana highlands south of the Orinoco, covering almost half of the national territory, have experienced some mining booms in the past but have remained almost uninhabited. Large deposits of rich iron ore were investigated by United States Steel and Bethlehem Steel, the two leading American steel companies, in the 1930s and 1940s. Bethlehem Steel started regular shipments from its El Pao mine in 1951. About 2.5 million tons of ore a year is sent by rail to Palúa just west of San

Oil terminal and refinery at Amuay Bay, Venezuela. The refinery is one of the largest in the world. (Creole Petroleum Corporation)

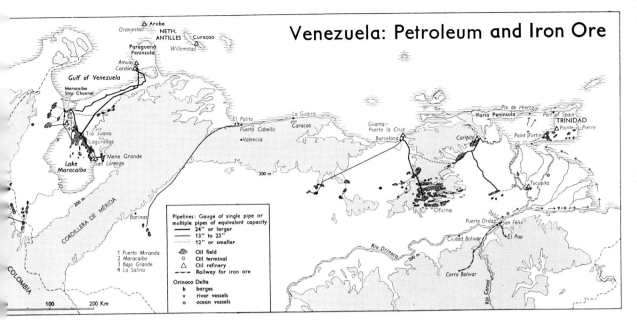

Venezuela: Petroleum and Iron Ore

Pipelines: Gauge of single pipe or multiple pipes of equivalent capacity
— 24" or larger
— 13" to 23"
····· 12" or smaller

⬡ Oil field
○ Oil terminal
△ Oil refinery
▬ Railway for iron ore

Orinoco Delta
b barges
v river vessels
o ocean vessels

1 Puerto Miranda
2 Maracaibo
3 Bajo Grande
4 La Salina

The crude petroleum pipelines are those existing or under construction in 1962.

Félix at the mouth of the Caroní River, a tributary of the Orinoco. From there it is taken by five 8,000-ton river carriers through the main distributary of the Orinoco, the Boca Grande, to the new ore port at Puerto de Hierro on the Gulf of Paria, which can accomodate the 22,000 and 40,000-ton ore vessels that carry the ore to the United States.[1] However, Bethlehem Steel has announced plans to move the ore direct from Palúa by ocean carriers.[2]

United States Steel obtained concessions for the Cerro Bolívar deposit where production was started in 1954. From the new mining town, Ciudad Piar, a railroad was built to Puerto Ordaz opposite Palúa at the mouth of the Caroní. From Puerto Ordaz to the Atlantic Ocean the Orinoco was dredged permitting ore carriers of 50,000 tons.[3] As an alternative to the canalization of the Orinoco a railroad was originally considered between Cerro Bolívar and Guanta-Puerto la Cruz.[4] Most of the ore from Puerto Ordaz moves to the United States but large quantities also to Europe.

In adjacent areas reserved by the government there are ore bodies of a magnitude exceeding those of Cerro Bolívar and El Pao combined.

The Venezuelan Government is pushing plans to develop a center of heavy manufacturing in the Guayana region. In addition to water power and iron ore the area has untapped resources of diamonds, gold, bauxite, vanadium, manganese, nickel, asbestos and natural gas. A 370,000-kilowatt hydro-electric power plant was completed in 1960–61 near the mouth of the Caroní River. The latest estimates of the power potential of this river give the total as 10 million kilowatts.[5] A steel

[1] *Venezuelan Iron Ore for Bethlehem Steel Company Furnaces.* Bethlehem Steel Company, Booklet 550.

[2] *Carta semanal* (Ministerio de minas e hidrocarburos) October 20, 1962. P. 14.

[3] For data on 1962 record loadings at Puerto Ordaz see *Carta semanal*, October 20, 1962. P. 16.

[4] Marco-Aurelio Vila, *Geografía de Venezuela.* 6th ed. Caracas, 1959. Pp. 203 ff.

[5] C. V. F.—*Boletín informativo de la corporación venezolana de fomento. No. 2 y 3, 1960.*

343

The new Puerto Miranda oil terminal on Lake Maracaibo, inaugurated in February, 1960, can receive 65,000-ton tankers. In its final form it will have a capacity of 40 million tons a year. (Shell)

mill, of 750,000 tons ingot capacity in its first stage, started production in 1961–62 at San Félix 15 kilometers from the power plant[6] and an aluminum plant will be built by the Reynolds Company. The steel mill will receive domestic coal from the Barcelona region[7] and may also get American coal as a return cargo. The plans for industrial development at the mouth of the Caroní River include the construction of a model city, Santo Tomé, which aims at 250,000 people by 1970 and eventually 600,000. Santo Tomé will encompass the present San Félix, the ore-loading ramp at Palúa and Puerto Ordaz.

General Ports

Most of the people of Venezuela live in highlands formed by the eastern branch of the Andes which swings northeastward into Venezuela as the Cordillera de Mérida and then runs along the Caribbean. The Central Highlands, with Caracas and Valencia as the leading urban centers, have always been the economic and political heartland of Venezuela. The basin of Valencia remains the chief agricultural area of the country. Sugar, coffee, cocoa, tobacco and indigo, chiefly from this region, were leading export products at various times in the past until completely eclipsed by the exports of oil in the 1920s. The Valencia area also provided fattening pastures for the lean cattle raised on the *llanos*. Valencia has several advantages of location compared to Caracas, which is separated from the rest of the country by rugged terrain. Valencia can be reached by relatively easy passes both from the Caribbean and from the *llanos*. The dominance of Caracas is the result of history rather than favorable location. The landowners of the disease-ridden estates around the Lake of Valencia left their sugar lands under the direction of overseers and made their homes in Caracas at a somewhat higher altitude. Once Caracas became the capital of Venezuela its pre-eminence in the economic and social life of the country was assured.[1] Since the oil boom started Caracas has undergone a remarkable development manifested by numerous large buildings of radical design.

The principal general ports of Venezuela are La Guaira, Maracaibo, Puerto Cabello and

[6] *The New York Times,* January 17, 1962.
[7] A 27-kilometer railroad is being constructed from the coal mines to the port of Guanta.
[1] Preston E. James, *Latin America.* New York, 1950. P. 56.

The new oil terminal La Salina on Lake Maracaibo. (Creole Petroleum Corporation)

Guanta, each serving an important section of the country.

Venezuela's economic heartland is served by La Guaira and Puerto Cabello, both having a trade structure typical of big city ports. A railroad from La Guaira to Caracas and one from Puerto Cabello to Valencia were built with British capital at the end of last century. A German-built railroad connects Caracas and Valencia. Because of the rugged terrain these railroads and the modern concrete highways, which were built between the same cities after Venezuela's oil prosperity had begun, were very expensive undertakings. Traffic on the railroads declined conspicuously in the 1950s and highways now dominate the inland surface transport.

The Guianas

The three Guiana colonies, located where the almost uninhabited zone between Spanish and Portuguese South America approaches the coast, have a combined population of only a little more than three quarters of a million. As in adjacent parts of Venezuela and Brazil the forest covered Guiana plateau is almost uninhabited. More than half a million live in the British colony and most of the remainder in Surinam. The population is concentrated in the narrow coastal plain. The Dutch did most to settle this plain in the seventeenth and eighteenth centuries. The present division was agreed upon in treaties following the Napoleonic Wars.

For more than three centuries the colonies depended on sugar exports; in British Guiana the shipment of 250–300 thousand tons of sugar a year still accounts for half the export value. When slavery was abolished last century indentured and free labor was brought from various countries. As a result the Guianas have a greater variety of ethnic groups than any other Latin American region. East Indians, Negroes and people of mixed races make up the largest groups, followed by Indonesians,

345

indigenous Indians and Europeans. For employment and the domestic economy rice is more important than sugar which in British Guiana is grown on the estates of two large companies.

For a long time Dutch and British Guiana have been the world's leading producers of aluminum ore. In recent years their combined shipment of about 5 million tons—3 million from Surinam and 2 million from British Guiana—has been challenged by the rapidly increasing shipments from Jamaica. The mining operations, dating back to 1914, are in the hands of two North American companies. The Aluminum Company of America (Alcoa) has bauxite mines on the Surinam River near Paramaribo and at Moengo on the Cottica River in Surinam. The Canadian Aluminum Company is working mines at Mackenzie on the Demerara in British Guiana. The bauxite is shipped to alumina plants in North America. Alcoa has, however, pledged itself to build the large hydro-electric plant at Affobakka near Brokopondo on the Surinam River about 100 kilometers upstream from Paramaribo. Construction of the Affobakka power plant, that will produce over one billion kilowatt-hours a year, started in 1960. The company will also build an alumina plant and an aluminum smelter of at least 40,000 tons in Surinam.[2]

Brazil

Almost all of Brazil's foreign trade moves through her ports; the quantities crossing the land borders are negligible. Many railroads and roads in Brazil were originally planned to channel raw materials to the ports for export and not to provide a national transportation system. Most of the traffic moving through Brazilian ports is foreign trade. Each port has a fanlike tributary network of rails and roads but few north-south links with other regions.[3] Each port or group of ports with its hinter-

land forms an isolated "island". Immediately behind the narrow coastal plain the Serra do Mar escarpment rises abruptly and most of the rivers either flow inland to the Paraná—Uruguay river system or, due to falls and rapids, are unnavigable the full distance to the sea. The coast has few natural routes to the interior. As alternative means of transport are lacking (or have been lacking until recently) for north-south hauls between the "islands", Brazil has remained more dependent upon coastal shipping in interstate commerce than most countries of continental dimensions. Cabotage accounted for 1.8 million tons in 1927 and 6.5 million in 1956, a sharp increase in a period when coastal shipping almost disappeared in Anglo-America and Europe.[4] Two government companies operate about three-quarters of the coastal fleet; most of their ships are, however, overage, operating with high fuel costs and spending about 20 per cent of available time for repairs.[5]

Coastal vessels are largely engaged in transporting bulk raw materials to the consuming and manufacturing centers of São Paulo and Rio, salt from the north and coal and lumber from the south, and transporting a smaller volume of cotton textiles, iron and steel products and other manufactured goods in the other direction. A second major flow is that of food stuffs: wheat flour and wheat, rice, manioc flour and charque (jerked beef) from the southern states to Santos—Rio and to the northern states, with sugar moving in the opposite direction. In summary, eight states in the north and south with over one-third of the Brazilian population depend upon coastal ship-

[2] *Facts and Figures about Surinam.* The Government Information Service. Paramaribo, 1960. See also pages 84 f.

[3] *Brazilian Technical Studies.* Prepared for the Joint Brazil-United States Economic Development Commission. Washington, D.C., 1955. Pp. 187 ff.

[4] Except for a few bulk commodities like the petroleum flow from the Gulf to the Atlantic seaboard in the United States.

[5] *Brazilian Technical Studies, op. cit.,* p. 188.

ping to carry three-fourths of their total interstate commerce. Their economies depend upon coastal trade between themselves and the other regions of Brazil.[6]

The Amazon Region

The tremendous drainage basin of the Amazon River, covered with tropical rain forest, occupies about half of Brazil's territory. The sparse population, about three million in the Brazilian Amazon, is concentrated to the banks of the rivers, the only transportation routes within the area.[1] The Amazon region, of which about 70 per cent is in Brazil, is one of the largest "population voids" in the world, a "green desert". The rubber boom from about 1875 to World War I caused an influx of people, especially from the drought-ridden north-eastern states. This boom came to an end when the rubber plantations in southeastern Asia started to put large quantities of rubber on the world market, which led to a sharp drop in prices and an economic crisis in the wild rubber collecting areas of the Amazon Basin. Wild rubber is still, however, a major export product from the region. Others are Brazil nuts, rose-wood oil and tropical hard woods. The collection of forest products supplies most of the income but the subsistence farming of manioc and some other crops on a shifting cultivation basis and cattle raising in some areas account for by far the most work-hours.

Belém, located 140 kilometers from the sea on the southernmost distributary of the Amazon, is the economic capital of the Amazon River Valley.[2] Its influence stretches beyond the national border into the Andean countries. Almost all of the exports and imports pass through Belém: about 90 per cent of the goods handled in the port are in transit.[3] Belém is in a situation analogous to that of New Orleans in the early nineteenth century: an ocean port connected to its vast zone of influence only by an excellent river network. In contrast to New Orleans it has a great handicap as a modern port due to the severe shoaling in the river. It has therefore been suggested that the port should be moved to a point 15 kilometers downstream where the physical conditions are more favorable for a deep seaport. Belém, founded in 1916,[4] grew rapidly during the rubber boom but has since experienced a moderate growth. Its future expansion is closely tied with the economic development in the Amazon Basin.

Manaus, the transportation center of the central and western Amazon Basin, has a position similar to St. Louis in the Mississippi Valley in the early nineteenth century. Located on the Rio Negro near its confluence with Rio Solimões, where they form the Amazon River, it commands a strategic location in the vast river network. Manaus grew from a small town to almost its present size in a short period during the rubber boom. In this wave of prosperity great private and public buildings were constructed, among them the famous *Teatro Amazonas*, where opera groups from Europe were sometimes heard. Because of the tremendous yearly fluctuations in the level of the Rio Negro[5] the port is equipped with

---

[6] *Brazilian Technical Studies, op. cit.,* p. 190.

[1] The Amazon River is navigable by any vessel for over two-thirds of its length, even during low water. Lucio de Castro Soares, *Excursion Guidebook No. 8, Amazônia.* Eighteenth International Geographical Congress. Rio de Janeiro, 1956. P. 55.

[2] The Belém commercial houses buy the products gathered from the forests and sell manufactured goods by means of agents scattered along the banks of the rivers. The agent is usually the local merchant, to whom the peasants are normally tied by debts. Each trading post is visited by the river steamer of its Belém wholesaler each month or so. Pierre Gourou, "Le pays de Belém (Brésil)". *Bulletin de la Société Belge d'Etudes Géographiques,* 1949. Pp. 19–36. See also Charles Wagley, *Amazon Town.* New York, 1953.

[3] *Brazilian Technical Studies.* Prepared for the Joint Brazil—United States Economic Development Commission. Washington, D.C., 1954. Pp. 216 ff.

[4] Aroldo de Azevedo, *Vilas e Cidades do Brasil Colonial.* São Paulo, 1956.

[5] The maximum variation recorded is 16 m. *Excursion Guidebook, op. cit.,* p. 151.

General view of Manaus, a city of 150,000, located on the Rio Negro in the middle of the tropical rain forest and with no surface transportation, other than by river, to the outside world. (Manchete)

floating wharves at which the medium depth varies from 12 to 24 meters.[6] The port of Manaus, built in 1907 by an English company, is a collecting and distributing center for an area several times the size of France. Some of the trade with overseas ports and Brazilian Atlantic ports is carried direct, but most by way of Belém.

A new ore port constructed in the early 1950s by ICOMI, a joint Brazilian–Bethlehem Steel venture, at Porto Macapá in the estuary of the Amazon River started to ship manganese ore from the Serra do Navio mines in the rain forests of Amapá in 1957. The mine, designed for an annual production of 0.6 million tons, may be increased to 1.0 million tons. A 195-kilometer railroad carries the ore to the river, where a floating dock 20 kilometers upstream from the town of Macapá offers a depth of 40 to 80 feet for oceangoing ore carriers.[7]

The Northeast

The northeastern states, from Maranhão to Bahia, are an economically depressed area of Brazil, with recurrent droughts, serious famines, heavy overpopulation, and a continous outflow of people to other parts of the country. The Northeast is also the oldest region. The first Portuguese settlement was established in 1502 at Salvador in the state of Bahia. The coast of Brazil was divided into *capitanias*,

[6] One of the wharves is constructed for transatlantic vessels. It is 200 m long and 26 m wide, supported by 30 rows of 4 drums, each drum 5 m long with a 2 m diameter. The wharf is connected with the warehouses ashore by three 150 m overhead cables. Another wharf of similar size is reserved for coastal shipping and river traffic. Aziz Nacib Ab'Saber, "A Cidade de Manaus". *Boletim Paulista de Geografia*, 1953. Pp. 18–45.

[7] ICOMI: *The Discovery and Development of Manganese Ore Resources in the Serra do Navio District, Federal Territory of Amapá, Brazil*. Bethlehem Steel Company, Booklet 490.

348

The pontoon bridge to one of the two floating wharves at Manaus in a raised position during a flood. (Hilgard O'Reilly Sternberg)

each under direction of a person selected by the Portuguese crown. The success of these colonies depended partly on the organizing capacity of their leaders. The chief settlement centers from which the Portuguese pushed the borders of Brazil far to the west of the demarcation line agreed upon at Tordesillas (1494), were São Paulo (São Vicente, 1532), Salvador, and Recife (Olinda, 1537). The last two are now the leading cities of the Northeast.

Throughout the colonial period and until about 1830 cane sugar was the dominating export of Brazil, sugar from the Northeast. Slaves were imported from Africa for the large sugar estates which makes the negro element in the Brazilian population large, especially in the northeastern region. In recent decades the high-

cost producers of this area have had difficulties in holding their own even in the domestic market. Competition from more efficient producers in São Paulo has been keen. Since 1933 the Federal Government has assigned production quotas to the various states, fixed prices and dumped surpluses abroad[1] in an effort to prevent the poor northeastern states from losing their most important exchange product.

The large sugar estates are confined to a narrow humid strip along the coast from Bahia to Rio Grande do Norte, exposed to the southeast trade winds. Precipitation declines sharply at the escarpment some 60 to 80 kilometers inland. This is the limit between two vegetation regions, the humid forest strip along the coast and the dry inland area, which in the north extends to the ocean. The north coast

[1] G. Wythe, R. A. Wight and H. M. Midkiff, *Brazil, An Expanding Economy*. New York, 1949. P. 78. Manuel Diégues Junion, *População e açúcar no Nordeste do Brasil*. Rio de Janeiro, 1953. Mário Lacerda de Melo, "Aspectos da geografia do açúcar no Brasil", *Revista Brasileira de Geografia,* 1954. Pp. 467 ff.

from Rio Grande do Norte to eastern Maranhão is semiarid in spite of its closeness to the Equator.

Recife, the capital of Pernambuco, is the leading port of the Northeast; in the days of the great sugar trade it was the largest port in Brazil. The first capital, Olinda, was located in hilly country 6 kilometers further to the north and Recife was used as an outport. But the Dutch, who occupied the area 1630–1654, moved the capital from Olinda to its port. The harbor became an integrated part of the new capital. With its islands, flatlands and river it was a site similar to that of several Dutch towns.[2] Sugar is still the leading outbound cargo. In the early 1950s it accounted for two-thirds of tonnage shipped. Shipments to other Brazilian ports were stable at about 300,000 tons a year whereas exports fluctuated between 14,000 and 190,000 tons. Most of the sugar was sent to Distrito Federal, São Paulo and Rio Grande do Sul.[3]

The other leading ports in the Northeast are also capitals and the largest cities of their states. They are focal points of a rudimentary transportation system, usually just one or two railroads and highways connecting the city with its hinterland.

Natal in Rio Grande do Norte, located at the eastern extreme of the bulge, became a point of great strategic importance during World War II. The air route from the Americas, including the United States and Canada, to North Africa, the Middle East, India and Southeast Asia converged on its large air base. For some time after the war, just as in the relatively few prewar flights, commercial airlines connecting Europe with South America crossed the Atlantic Ocean between Dakar or Bathurst and Natal. With longer-range planes metropolitan Recife took over this traffic. Natal ships cotton and some corn, sugar and salt. By far the leading commodity shipped from the state of Rio Grande do Norte is salt from the salinas on the northern coast. Macau and Areia Branca are in the center of the largest salinas in South America.[4]

Salvador, seat of the colonial government for two centuries before it was moved to Rio de Janeiro in 1763 and now capital of the state of Bahia, has an excellent harbor at the largest bay of the Brazilian coast, *Bahia de Todos os Santos*.[5] It is the commercial center of the *Recôncavo* region, one of the oldest and most densely settled agricultural areas of Brazil, since the earliest colonial days characterized by large sugar latifundias. Many of the exporting firms and other institutions associated with cacao and tobacco, two of the major exports of Brazil by value, have their headquarters in Salvador. The chief tobacco district is located in the *Recôncavo* but cacao is grown in a strip parallel to the coast in the southern part of the state with the largest concentration in the Itabuna-Ilhéus area. Most cacao used to be transshipped at Salvador but now only small quantities are handled that way. Since 1944 Ilhéus has been the principal cacao port of Brazil. This river port is shallow and the ships have to load from lighters off the coast.[6]

[2] Mário Lacerda de Melo, *Excursion Guidebook No. 7, Northeast.* Eighteenth International Geographical Congress, Rio de Janeiro, 1956. Pp. 36 ff.

[3] *Anuário Estatístico, Ano XV.* Estado de Pernambuco, Secretaria de Agricultura, Industria e Comercio. Recife, 1955.

[4] José Veríssimo da Costa Pereira, "Salinas". In *Tipos e Aspectos do Brasil.* Rio de Janeiro, 1956. P. 295.

The symbols for Macau and Areia Branca on the map, page 338, are rough estimates. Salt does not enter international trade; figures for cabotage are listed only by commodity or by state, not by port, in the statistical yearbook of Brazil. It was assumed that all salt in Brazilian (interstate) cabotage originates in Rio Grande do Norte which is strongly suggested by the cabotage figures for this and neighboring states. See also *Brazilian Technical Studies,* op. cit., p. 191.

[5] Present Salvador was founded in 1549 after an earlier Portuguese town had been destroyed by the Indians. It immediately became the capital of Brazil under the name of *Cidade de São Salvador da Bahia de Todos os Santos.* The official name is Salvador. The city used to be known as São Salvador or Bahia.

[6] Alfredo José Porto Domingues and Elza Coelho de Souza Keller, *Livret-Guide No. 6, Bahia.* XVIII Congrès International de Géographie, Rio de Janeiro, 1956. Pp. 60 ff.

The Economic Heartland

Brazil's exports have been dominated by coffee for more than a century. Without doubt coffee more than anything else was the economic basis for the spectacular expansion in population and industrial activity experienced by the state of São Paulo and adjacent states, Rio de Janeiro, Minas Gerais and Paraná, during the last hundred years. A small triangle on the vast surface of Brazil with the cities of São Paulo, Rio de Janeiro and Belo Horizonte at its corners is the economic heart of the country. It contains two of the largest cities in Latin America, São Paulo and Rio de Janeiro, of which the former is the leading manufactur-

[1] Pierre Monbeig, *La croissance de la ville de São Paulo*. Grenoble, 1953. P. 3.

Hundreds of *saveiros* arrive at the markets of the half-million city of Salvador every day, bringing manioc flour, fish, fruit and other food products, as well as fuel wood and charcoal from the many small ports of the Reconcâvo. They return with kerosene, wheat flour, cloth, household utensils, and other manufactured products. These small sailing vessels, usually carrying the name of a saint, are also used for fishing and for the transportation of passengers. (Jablonsky, C.N.G.)

ing center south of the Rio Grande. Both have over three million inhabitants. São Paulo is one of the fastest growing metropolises in the world, only exceeded by Los Angeles. It had 26,000 inhabitants in 1872 before it was definitely drawn into the coffee boom.[1] By any measure it is the economic capital of Brazil whereas Rio de Janeiro has derived its vitality

Brazilian Exports

Selected Commodities

Years	Coffee	Cotton	Cocoa	Rubber
Per cent of total exports by value				
1901–10	51.5	2.1	2.8	27.9
1921–30	69.6	2.4	3.2	2.5
1931–40	50.0	14.3	4.1	1.1
1951–57	59.8	7.7	5.6	0.1

Source: *Anuário Estatístico do Brasil.*

chiefly from its function as the administrative center of the federation. With the movement of the capital to Brasília in 1960 Rio de Janeiro's future looks uncertain. Much depends on how much of its chief economic base, the federal administration, is eventually moved to the new capital.

When Rio de Janeiro became the capital of Brazil in 1763 it was already a major port, the chief outlet for the gold fields of Minas Gerais.[2] From 1830 coffee became Brazil's principal export product; large-scale coffee cultivation originated in the immediate hinterland of Rio. The entire social and economic structure of Brazil was to be reorganized on a new basis. In the eighteenth century the owners of the sugar *engenhos* (chiefly in the Northeast) and the gold and diamond fields (in Minas Gerais) had directed the economic, social and political life of Brazil; now they were followed by the owners of the coffee *fazendas.*[3] The coffee frontier gradually advanced from the neighborhood of Rio de Janeiro through the Paraíba Valley to the plateau in the state of São Paulo and has now reached the Paraná River and into the northern part of the state of Paraná. Already in the 1880s two *Paulista* cities, Campinas and Ribeirão Prêto, were centers of coffee growing districts. Although outside the actual coffee area the city of São Paulo became its great trade and transportation center on which converged a railroad network, in Latin America second only to that

of the La Plata region. The railroads penetrated inland with the advancing coffee frontier on the interfluves, where soil and climatic conditions for coffee were more favorable than in the river valleys.[4] Most of the smaller *Paulista* cities are strung like pearls on a string along these railroads.[5] Most of them have at one time been terminuses of the railroads before they pushed further west. In recent years the "civilizing rail" has met with strong competition from highways. Where there are no hard-surface roads highway traffic meets with difficulties in the rainy season.

A very large portion of the 12 million inhabitants of the state of São Paulo originate from the large immigration started at the end of the 1880s,[6] organized by the coffee *fazendeiros,* who needed laborers on their *fazendas.* The majority of the immigrants, who came chiefly from Italy but also from Spain and Portugal, were funneled to the *fazendas* of São Paulo state by way of Santos and São Paulo. Each coffee *fazenda* has several hundred workers. The *fazendeiros* organized railway companies, made investments in textile mills and other forms of manufacturing, acquired interests in the new banks, etc. They could not stay all the year on their *fazendas* and many also had a residence in São Paulo, where most of these urban activities were located. São Paulo became the *capital dos fazendeiros.*[7]

Santos is the port of São Paulo; the two

[2] For about a hundred years Brazil was the world's greatest source of gold.

[3] Ary França, *Guide-Book of Excursion 3, The Coffee Trail and Pioneer Fringes.* XVIII International Geographical Congress, Rio de Janeiro, 1956.

[4] The standard work on the Brazilian coffee region of São Paulo and Paraná was written by Monbeig, a French geographer working in Brazil for many years. Pierre Monbeig, *Pionniers et planteurs de São Paulo.* Paris, 1952.

[5] See population maps, e.g. Ary França, *The Coffee Trail, op. cit.* p. 21. Gunnar Alexandersson, *Population Map of Brazil.* Stockholm, 1957. *Atlas do Brasil.* Conselho Nacional de Geografia. Rio de Janeiro, 1959. Pp. 110 ff.

[6] Slavery was abolished in 1888.

[7] Monbeig, *La croissance de São Paulo, op. cit.* P. 28.

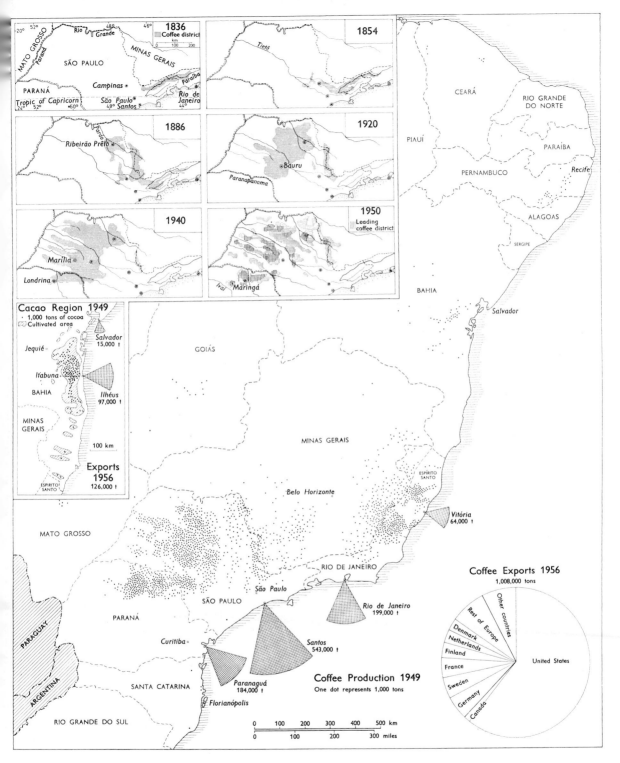

1836
Coffee district
km
0 100 200

MATO GROSSO
Paraná
Rio Grande
MINAS GERAIS
SÃO PAULO
Campinas
Paraíba
PARANÁ
Rio de Janeiro
Tropic of Capricorn
São Paulo
Santos

1854
Tietê

1886
Ribeirão Prêto

1920
Bauru
Paranapanema

1940
Marília
Londrina

1950
Leading coffee district
Ival Maringá

Cacao Region 1949
· 1,000 tons of cocoa
Cultivated area
Salvador 15,000 t
Jequié
Itabuna
BAHIA
Ilhéus 97,000 t
MINAS GERAIS
100 km
Exports 1956
126,000 t
ESPÍRITO SANTO

CEARÁ
RIO GRANDE DO NORTE
PIAUÍ
PARAÍBA
PERNAMBUCO
Recife
ALAGOAS
SERGIPE
BAHIA
Salvador

GOIÁS

MATO GROSSO

MINAS GERAIS
ESPÍRITO SANTO
Belo Horizonte
Vitória 64,000 t

PARAGUAY

PARANÁ
Curitiba
São Paulo
SÃO PAULO
RIO DE JANEIRO
Rio de Janeiro 199,000 t
Santos 543,000 t

Coffee Exports 1956
1,008,000 tons
Other countries
Rest of Europe
Denmark
Netherlands
Finland
France
Sweden
Germany
Canada
United States

ARGENTINA
SANTA CATARINA
Paranaguá 184,000 t
Florianópolis
RIO GRANDE DO SUL

Coffee Production 1949
One dot represents 1,000 tons

0 100 200 300 400 500 km
0 100 200 300 miles

Sources: Data on exports of coffee and cocoa are from the *Anuário Estatístico do Brasil* and on production from the *VI Recenseamento geral do Brasil,* 1950. Production dots were distributed on a map of *municípios,* the smallest Brazilian administrative units. The series of historic maps was adapted from Ary França, *The Coffee Trail, op. cit.*

353

Data from *Anuário Estatístico do Brasil* 1951, p. 243 (1910–1950); *Anuário Estatístico do Brasil,* various issues (1949–1960); *Comercio Internacional,* Boletim mensal do Banco do Brasil, Ano X, January–March 1961, Nos. 6, 7, 8. Rio de Janeiro, p. 43.

cities are connected by rail,[8] a 68 kilometer superhighway and a pipeline. New suburbs are growing up between the two cities, often around large manufacturing plants built by foreign or Brazilian interests, and eventually a conurbation will be formed. Manufacturing development is also considerable west of São Paulo in a triangle formed by São Paulo, Campinas and Sorocaba, and northeast of the city along the highway to Rio de Janeiro. For a long distance the highway and the railroad between the two metropolises run in the Paraíba Valley, the old coffee country of a hundred years ago, where partly demolished old coffee mansions in colonial style remind us of the past. In recent decades this transportation corridor between Brazil's two largest cities has experienced rapid industrialization. Among the largest plants is the steelworks at Volta Redonda.[9]

The most noteworthy of the installations between São Paulo and Santos are the huge hydro-electric power plant[10] and the oil refinery at Cubatão, at the foot of the 800-meter escarpment,[11] known under the misnomer Serra do Mar, which delimits the interior plateau. This escarpment has been a great obstacle for communications with the interior. Located about 750 meters above sea level São Paulo has a

[8] The famous São Paulo Railway, built by a British company and inaugurated in 1867, became the most profitable of South American railways. In 11 km it climbs over 700 m to the plateau. Originally, the route included four inclined planes with gradients of 10 per cent, up which trains were hauled by cables and stationary steam engines, burning British coal; later the maximum gradient has been reduced to 8 per cent. The railways on the plateau spread out from this trunk line. The great prosperity of the railroad was due to its virtual control of the coffee shipments. This railway was nationalized in 1946 and is now known as the *E. F. Santos a Jundiaí*. It handles more cargo than any Brazilian railroad but is surpassed by several in ton-kilometers. R. H. Whitbeck, *Economic Geography of South America.* New York, 1926. Pp. 369–370. *Brazilian Technical Studies, op. cit.* Pp. 63 and 95 ff.

[9] Built during World War II and partly financed by the Export-Import Bank, began operations in 1946, produced 0.47 million tons of steel ingots in 1952, 0.81 million in 1958 and 1.3 million in 1961 (capacity).

[10] The waters of the Tietê are reversed and pumped *eastward* to plunge 711 m down the slope of the Serra do Mar. Cheap hydro-electric power is one of the basic advantages of São Paulo.

[11] Brazil's second large steel mill is now under construction at Piaçaguera at the foot of the Serra do Mar near Cubatão (and Santos). The raw material will be assembled by ship: iron ore from Vitória (Itabira), coal from Imbituba and Laguna in Santa Catarina and from abroad (United States) and limestone from Iguapé on the southern coast of São Paulo state. Ingot production for 1963 is planned at 0.5 million tons and eventually the plant will produce 2.5 million tons. It is expected to become the largest plate and sheet metal plant in Latin America, producing raw material for ships, cars, trucks, buses, refrigerators and other household appliances, railroad cars etc. Plants for many of these products have already been established by a large number of European and American firms in the São Paulo region, originally as assembly plants but later, with strong government incentives, changed into producing units. The new plate and sheet plant will improve the raw material situation for these rapidly expanding industries. The port of Santos will increase considerably with the new steel mill. It is an interesting example of the tendency to locate new integrated steel mills in ports near metropolitan markets rather than oriented to the sources of raw materials.

The city of Santos, founded in 1536 on the island of São Vicente, remained in obscurity for three hundred and fifty years. The tremendous expansion of coffee cultivation on the plateau, for which Santos became the natural outlet, led to a startling increase in population from 9,000 in 1880 to 390,000 in 1960 (Greater Santos).

Coffee accounted for 485,000 tons in 1961 or 20 per cent of the shipments through Santos. The total cargo turnover was over twelve million tons. (Companhia Docas de Santos)

cooler and for work a more agreeable climate than Santos or Rio on the coastal plain. Before World War I Santos and Rio de Janeiro had a poor reputation for yellow fever and malaria; the plateau was then more healthy than the port cities. The combination of a large city on the plateau and a satellite port city below the escarpment is repeated further south in the state of Paraná, where the capital Curitiba has its port at Paranaguá.

Santos exceeds Rio de Janeiro as a port both in volume and value of its imports and exports. As cabotage ports the two are of about equal importance. In 1956 Santos handled 48 per cent of the national imports and 46 per cent of the exports by value.[12] It has been the world's leading coffee port since the end of last century. The world looks to Santos and New York for the price of coffee. This high-value commodity accounted for 56 per cent of the exports by tonnage in 1956 and for 81 per cent by value. Cotton, cultivated on a large scale in the western part of the state

since the coffee crisis in the 1930s, is normally one of the leading export items at Santos.

The port of Rio de Janeiro, located in one of the world's best natural harbors and with scenery more beautiful than that of any other large port in the world, serves a metropolis only slightly smaller than São Paulo and a large hinterland including Brazil's largest steel works at Volta Redonda and, traditionally, the state of Minas Gerais. Rio has remained the second largest coffee port of Brazil since it was surpassed by Santos last century, but in 1956 Paranaguá, the outlet favored by the state of Paraná for its rapidly expanding coffee district, had almost caught up with Rio. Among leading export items are also iron ore and

[12] Rio de Janeiro accounted for 30 and 14 per cent.

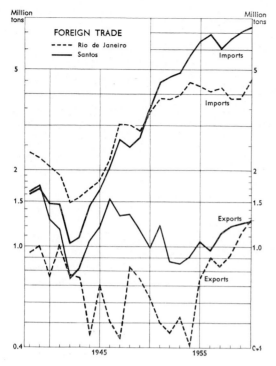

Data from *Anuário Estatístico do Brasil.*

manganese ore. The influence of Volta Redonda is reflected in large imports of American coal, which is mixed with Brazilian coal from Santa Catarina in the coke ovens of Volta Redonda. The iron ore for the steel-

Data from *Companhia Docas de Santos.*

works comes from Lafaiete in Minas Gerais by rail and does not pass through the port.

Vitória is primarily an iron ore port. A government company operates the iron mines at Itabira, the railroad through the Rio Doce Valley and the ore docks at Vitória. The very large Brazilian deposits of iron ore were known abroad by 1910 and in the years prior to World War I European financial groups were much interested in their development. Mass export of Brazilian iron ore with coal as a return cargo was a challenging proposition. After the war new negotiations were started by a group of American and European businessmen to secure a basis for large investments in railroad and port facilities to open up the iron ore mines in Minas Gerais. Agreements were not reached until 1928 and the Depression made it impossible to raise the necessary capital. Brazilian nationalist tendencies were strengthened and it was not possible to secure an inflow of foreign private capital. It was not until after World War II that a government company, through Export–Import Bank financing, started to export iron ore:[13] 150,000 tons in 1947, 1.5 million tons 1952, 2.3 million 1956 and about 6 million tons in 1961. For comparison it should be mentioned that a British plan of 1909 had called for exports of 3 million tons. This level was not reached until 1957. Brazil has taken a different view from that of Canada and Venezuela on foreign investment for the development of her natural resources, which undoubtedly has delayed economic progress.

Paranaguá, the leading port of Paraná, has had a rapidly growing export of coffee since 1947 and now this commodity dominates its exports. The large companies buying from the growers in northern Paraná[14] used to ship by

[13] *The Development of Brazil.* Report of Joint Brazil-United States Economic Development Commission. Washington, D.C., 1954.

[14] The coffee district of northern Paraná is the logical extension of the São Paulo coffee area, which at the end of the 1920s was running out of land in

356

way of Santos, but the government of Paraná made great efforts to direct that flow to Paranaguá. Both railroad and highway have been built to connect Paranaguá with the coffee district. About 80 per cent of the coffee grown in the state moves this way, by truck and by rail.[15]

The South

São Francisco and Itajaí in Santa Catarina ship lumber of Paraná pine (*Araucaria*) from sawmills on the plateau, sent to the ports by truck or rail. Pôrto Alegre ranks with these two as a lumber port. Small quantities are sent down the Paraná River. Most of the lumber is exported, chiefly to Argentina and the United Kingdom, but large quantities move to Santos and Rio de Janeiro. About one million tons a year of lumber was shipped 1955–1957 out of the southern ports. Southern Brazil is the leading source of softwood in the southern hemisphere.

The low grade coal of Santa Catarina makes good coking coal if mixed with purer imported coal: over half a million tons a year is shipped

this direction and spilled over into the neighbor state. The eastern part was settled by the end of the 1920s; the most striking development came after 1929, however, on 12,500 km² of land bought by a British colonizing company, which in 1944 was sold to Brazilian interests. Londrina, the first headquarters of the company, and Maringá, the present headquarters, are the leading urban centers. Almost one million people live on this land of rich purple soil, *terra roxa*, with yields twice as high as the average for São Paulo but exposed to the hazards of recurring frosts. In 1960 Paraná's coffee production for the first time exceeded that of São Paulo. In contrast to São Paulo most of the coffee comes from small holdings. The pioneer fringe is still pushing in a south-westerly direction and a new urban center is growing up at Cianorte, in the forest south of the Ivaí River. The railroad is being extended through the forest to Guaira on the Paraná River connecting Santos and Paranaguá with the transportation system of Paraguay. The highway distance from Maringá to Paranaguá is 580 km and to Santos 880 km.

[15] Orlando Valverde, *Excursion Guidebook No. 9: The Southern Plateau.* XVIII International Geographical Congress, Rio de Janeiro, 1956. P. 159.

Ary França, *op. cit.*

[1] *Brazilian Technical Studies, op. cit.* Pp. 226–227.

from Imbituba to Rio de Janeiro for the coke-ovens of the Volta Redonda steel mill. The ash-rich coal at São Jerônimo south of the Rio Jacuí has been a great asset for the industrial development of Pôrto Alegre. Transportation costs are low; there is a short rail haul to the river and barge transport to the wharves of Pôrto Alegre. But coal of such low grade could not compete with imported coal if Pôrto Alegre were not an inland port: fully loaded ocean vessels have to transship to lake boats or barges at Rio Grande. The cost of this operation has the same effect as a protective tariff.

Rio Grande is the outport for the two inland ports on the Lagoa dos Patos, Pôrto Alegre and Pelotas. It has a depth of 9 meters whereas the lake is only 6 meters. A barge fleet operates on the lake, where the conditions for barge traffic are ideal. Coal, petroleum products, rice, wheat and potatoes constitute the bulk of the cargo in the region. Of the tonnage handled in the port of Pôrto Alegre about 60 per cent is carried in barges and small lake vessels.[1] Pôrto Alegre has a direct foreign trade of somewhat less than half a million tons and Rio Grande handles close to a million, chiefly imports and primarily petroleum. A large percentage is goods in transit to or from Pôrto Alegre and Pelotas. Pôrto Alegre is the hub of railroads and highways to the interior of northern and central Rio Grande do Sul; Pelotas has a similar location in the southern part of the state. Rio Grande do Sul is the leading grain producing state in Brazil and an important cattle region which is reflected in the shipments from the three ports: wheat, rice, dried or frozen meat, leather and wool. Pôrto Alegre in addition ships lumber and wine. Brazil's leading wine district is located north of the city.

The Río de la Plata Region

By far the largest share of the foreign trade of Argentina, Uruguay and Paraguay is handled by ports on the Plata and the lower Paraná. The rivers flowing into the Plata form one of the three great river systems of South America, draining an area somewhat larger than the United States east of the Mississippi.[1] Modern barge traffic on the rivers in this system is small but may in the future increase in importance. The Paraná and the Paraguay traverse some of the most undeveloped areas of South America which, however, contain potentially rich agricultural land and mineral deposits (e.g. manganese at Corumbá). River transportation, a prerequisite for such long distance bulk hauls of agricultural and mineral products, has been slow to develop, partly because the rivers for large stretches are national boundaries which would require international cooperation for their development as inland waterways.

The long gulf, the Río de la Plata, that collects the waters of the Paraná-Paraguay and the Uruguay, has a well defined northern shore but the southern shore is very low and muddy. West of Montevideo the natural depth between the many large sandbanks is only 8–18 feet; seaward of Montevideo the water deepens rapidly. The main shipping channel, which follows the Uruguayan coast, as well as the channels to the ports have, since the end of last century, been kept open to ocean shipping only by expensive dredging operations. Oceangoing vessels can intermittently proceed up the Paraná beyond Rosario to the port of Santa Fe, but cannot leave this port fully laden. Some docks in Buenos Aires maintain a depth of 28 feet and in Rosario 24 feet.

The vast grass plains of the Plata region were long a remote and unimportant part of the Spanish Empire. The first permanent Spanish colony was founded at Asunción in 1537. It became the focus of early colonization in the Plata region. The colonists looked to the Spanish settlements of the high Andes (Peru and Upper Peru) for their only legal trade. By the road through Santa Fe, Córdoba,

Tucumán, Salta and Jujuy the Plata region supplied mules and some other commodities to the highland mining centers and to Peru. Another route led across the *pampa* to Chile. These were the most heavily traveled roads in the Plata region until the early nineteenth century.[2]

Within the Plata region the rivers served as the chief means of transportation. Large quantities of goods came to Buenos Aires and Montevideo from the river ports: firewood and construction woods, charcoal, fruits, cereals, vegetables, tobacco and *yerba mate*. Limited trade direct with the homeland had been allowed even before 1776, when the Viceroyalty of the Río de la Plata was created and a freer trade policy announced. Economic activity in the Plata region accelerated rapidly after 1776 and especially after independence was gained in 1810. Seagoing ships could not dock even in the large estuary ports and cargoes were transported to the anchorages in small boats. After 1860 large investments were made in the port of Buenos Aires, which had been the foreign trade market of the Plata estuary even before the improvement of the port. During the 1830s the dictator Juan Manuel de Rosas had concentrated the hide trade to the capital. After the fall of Rosas in 1852 foreign capital felt secure in Argentina. Between 1880 and 1886 the flow of British capital was especially strong. Most of the railroads in the densest rail net in Latin America were built by British companies, using British rolling stock and burning British coal.[3] The railroads converge on Buenos Aires with Rosario, Santa Fe and Bahía Blanca as secondary focal points.

The Humid Pampa had already before the advent of the railroads been divided into large

[1] Clifton B. Kroeber, *The Growth of the Shipping Industry in the Río de la Plata Region 1794–1860*. Madison, Wisconsin, 1957. P. 10.
[2] Kroeber, *op. cit*. P. 17.
[3] Preston E. James, *Latin America*. New York, 1950. P. 309.

estates but the land was used for extensive cattle and horse raising. A rapidly rising tide of immigrants from Europe started in the 1850s, reaching a peak in 1889 and again in 1913. About 80 per cent of the newcomers came from Italy and Spain. The immigrants brought agriculture to Argentina. The *estancieros* were primarily interested in improving the grazing capacity of their land. The most effective way to prepare the virgin land for alfalfa was to hand over the land to a *gringo* on condition that he return it after two or three years planted with alfalfa. In this *mediero* system the *gringo* usually planted flax on the virgin land, wheat the second year and alfalfa mixed with one of the other two crops the third year. Between 1852 and 1914 the tenant group transformed the Argentine Pampa into

one of the world's chief surplus grain and meat producing regions.[4,5]

The grain and flax producing area thus coincides with that of cattle raising, roughly delimited by latitude 30° and 40° south and longitude 57°30' and 65° west. Fine beef cattle strains such as Shorthorn, Aberdeen Angus and Hereford in this region substitute for *criollo* cows, descendents of the animals brought to the Plata region by the early Spaniards. *Criollos* dominate in most areas outside the Pampas and they were the only cows in Argentina until breeding with more purebred strains started on a large scale at the end of last century.[6]

The introduction of agriculture into the economy of the Plata region changed the composition of its exports. Until the 1880s ranching supplied almost the whole export: salted hides, salt meat and wool.[7] From then on agricultural products became more and more important and the two commodity groups have since alternated as the leading export group, together making up about 90 per cent or more of Argentina's export value. Salt meat gradually disappeared when modern packing plants, *frigoríficos*, were built, the first in 1883 but the large ones in the first years of this century.[8] The rapid increase in the Argentine exports of frozen meat to Europe coincided with a decline in American exports of fresh beef. The large American packers, like Armour and Swift, no longer able to supply the European market with United States beef, transferred their beef-exporting interests to newer grasslands, primarily Argentina and Paraguay, but also South Africa, Australia and New Zealand.[9] The large packing plants thus incorporate the techniques developed in Chicago and other packing centers. Argentina has about twenty *frigoríficos*, located on the seaboard and only a short rail haul from the cattle on the all-year open grazing range. During World War I chilled beef[10] became the leading export from the Argentine packing industry.

---

[4] Preston E. James, *op. cit.* Pp. 314 ff.

[5] The cultivated area of Argentina increased from 6.4 million hectares at the turn of the century to 22.2 million at the outbreak of World War I. Since then the cultivated area has remained rather stable. It reached a maximum in 1934/35 with 28.5 million hectares or 10 per cent of Argentina's land area. In 1950/51 grains and flax occupied 14.8 million hectares, fodder plants 7.4 million, industrial plants 2.9 million, and vegetables 0.4 million. *La Argentina, Suma de geografía.* Tomo IV. P. 494.

[6] *La Argentina, Suma de geografía.* Tomo IV. P. 353.

[7] The export of hides, about 1.5 million a year in the late 18th century, created a useless by-product: tremendous quantities of meat. The only economic way of preserving some of this meat was to salt it and pack it in barrels. There was a market for salt meat among slaves and ship crews. Exports of salt meat grew rapidly from the end of the 18th century. *La Argentina, Suma de geografía.* Tomo IV. Pp. 273–74.

[8] The first ship equipped to carry frozen meat arrived in Argentina from France in 1876. However, after two successful test shipments the French did not continue. The first British refrigerator ship arrived in 1880 and from the beginning British capital was involved in the development of the modern Argentine packing industry; Great Britain became by far the dominating market for the Argentine meat exports. In 1895 products from the *frigoríficos* represented 16 per cent of the meat export; in 1914 it represented no less than 87 per cent. *La Argentina, Suma de geografía.* Tomo IV. Pp. 250–51.

[9] Erich W. Zimmermann, *World Resources and Industries.* New York, 1951. P. 304.

[10] Chilled beef represents a higher quality. The carcasses are kept hanging in rooms with a temperature of 1–2 degrees centigrade below zero. The meat does

International Trade in Meat

Selected Countries 1000 tons

Exporting Country	Prewar	1956–58	Importing Country	Prewar	1956–58
Argentina	692	482	United Kingdom	1617	908
New Zealand	301	410	United States	119	101
Australia	259	227	Germany	83	174[a]
Denmark	215	120	Italy	61	128
Uruguay	150	32	France	27	57
United States	110	88	Belgium	16	23
Brazil	103	25	Netherlands	10	25
Canada	88	46	Spain	1	27

Prewar figures from FAO, *Livestock and Meat*. Commodity Series No. 12, May, 1949, Pp. 27–30. For Canada and the United States 1935–1939, Continental Europe 1935–1938 and for others 1934–1938.

Average 1956–1958 from *FAO Trade Yearbook*, 1959. Roma, 1960.
[a] West Germany.

The raising of beef cattle is the mainstay of the rural economy in the Humid Pampa, where 80 per cent of the Argentine exports originate and where two-thirds of the Argentine people live. Other rural activities are more or less subsidiary. Second in importance comes the commercial growing of wheat, corn and linseed. The number of cattle has increased by 50 per cent since the 1930s, the cultivation of forage crops, alfalfa in particular, has expanded, but the acreage devoted to commercial crops has been reduced. The Argentine pastoral-agricultural system is flexible. It is relatively easy, depending on price relations between crops and livestock products, to quickly convert large areas usually used for crops into pastures, and vice versa.[11]

Between five and eight million hectares are sown with wheat, producing as many tons depending on the weather, insect attacks, etc. Domestic consumption amounts to between three and three and a half million tons a year; the difference is exported, chiefly in the form of grains but some also as flour.

In Argentina corn is grown primarily for export, not for the local feeding of cattle and pigs as in the United States. Before the last war Argentina was the leading corn exporting country in the world but production and exports of corn have been drastically reduced. In the 1950s corn acreages were less than half those of the 1930s. The heavy dependence on migratory farm labor for the corn harvest—mechanized corn pickers are still rare in Argentina—has contributed to the decline in corn production; farm workers have moved to the cities with their higher wages[12] resulting in a labor shortage in the rural districts.[13]

Argentina was the world's leading linseed producer before World War II with a yearly production of 1.5 to 2 million tons as against 0.4 million tons for the United States in 1935, a peak year. During the war the American output of oil from domestic sources was increased

not freeze but keeps its physical characteristics. This way it can be kept for two months but preferably not more than 45 days. Frozen beef on the other hand is prepared in rooms with a temperature of 10–20 degrees below zero. The meat becomes frozen in 80–100 hours. It is then packed and stored at a temperature of 4–10 degrees below zero. This meat requires much less space in storage and transportation. Bruno A. Defelippe, *Geografía económica Argentina*. Buenos Aires, 1959. Pp. 111 ff.

[11] Gilbert J. Butland, *Latin America*. London, 1960. P. 271.

[12] Argentina is the most urbanized country in Latin America besides Uruguay. About 65 per cent of the population is urban.

[13] *La Argentina. Suma de Geografía*. Tomo IV. Pp. 527 ff.

and after the war the United States became an exporter of linseed oil seriously hitting the production of Argentina, which used to have the United States as its principal market. Argentina produced about 0.5 million tons a year in the 1950s, of which roughly one-third was exported.

Small grains other than wheat (rye, oats and barley) are grown primarily as winter feed for cattle. Less than half of the sown area is normally harvested. In the 1950s the combined export tonnage of these small grains often exceeded that of corn.

Argentina is one of the few countries in the world with a smaller foreign trade tonnage in the 1950s than in the interwar period. The decline in export volume, due to smaller grain shipments, is conspicuous. The volume of imports does not show the rapid rise in the 1950s typical of many countries as a result of increased petroleum consumption. Argentina's domestic production of petroleum has developed favorably and by 1960 the country was almost self-sufficient.

The long-term changes in the direction of Argentina's foreign trade are striking. During the rapid expansion of her economy before 1914 and in the interwar period, with a setback during World War I, the country was closely associated with Europe, especially the United Kingdom. Few independent states had a so typically "colonial" economy as Argentina. World War II hit the economy very hard. The general shortage of tonnage led to a reduced foreign trade for the distant republic. Food was preferably produced closer to the markets. After the war the old foreign markets of Argentine agriculture were at least partly lost; the United States emerged as a major surplus producer of wheat, corn and even linseed, Argentina's leading export products by volume. Changing world conditions made the United States Argentina's leading trade partner. The old "complementarity" of the British and the Argentine economies is not so

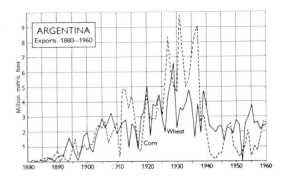

Data from *La Argentina: Suma de Geografía,* Tomo IV. Buenos Aires, 1959. P. 514; and *FAO Trade Yearbook.*

evident in the Argentine-American relations. The United States can supply manufactured products like the British, but with its agricultural surplus problems is not an ideal market for Argentine agricultural exports. However, enough wool, hides, canned meat, quebracho extracts, etc., are exported to make the United States the second most important market of Argentina.

Brazil accounts for a steadily increasing share of Argentina's foreign trade. The exchange with other Latin American republics is small.

Since the volume of Argentine foreign trade now is smaller than in the 1920s and 1930s, whereas global maritime transports have in-

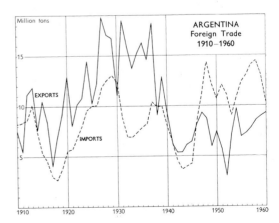

Data from *La Argentina: Suma de Geografía,* Tomo VI, Buenos Aires, 1960. P. 428.

EXPORTS   IMPORTS

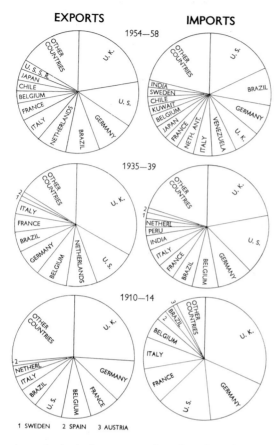

1954—58

1935—39

1910—14

1 SWEDEN   2 SPAIN   3 AUSTRIA

Argentina's trade partners in selected periods. Data from *La Argentina: Suma de geografía.* Tomo VI. Buenos Aires, 1960. P. 454.

creased considerably, the position of the Plata on the world trade map has declined. In the 1950s Brazil with more than three times Argentina's population forged ahead and wrested the economic leadership of Latin America from its southern neighbor. Santos, Rio de Janeiro and Vitória now handle about the same tonnage as the Plata ports. But the geographic location of the Plata makes it the natural terminal for most cargo and passenger lines to South America's east coast.

The port of Buenos Aires dominates the foreign trade of Argentina, accounting for 90 per cent of the imports by value and 80 per cent by volume; one-half of the exports by value and one-third by volume. Three-fourths of the meat and almost all of the hides and wool are shipped from Buenos Aires; but as a grain port it ranks behind Rosario and Bahía Blanca.

The estuary of the small Riachuelo was the original port of Buenos Aires; in the late nineteenth century new facilities were added at Madero about five kilometers to the north, which are now the main part of the port. Buenos Aires is a more artificial port than most metropolitan ports in the world. The site had little to recommend it but the location was favorable with about equal distances to the edge of the Humid Pampa in any direction. The rail and road systems, built to converge on Buenos Aires, strengthened its position as the commercial, industrial, financial, administrative and social center of the country. Greater Buenos Aires has about 5 million inhabitants, the largest city in Latin America and the Southern Hemisphere. La Plata, situated closer to deep water, acts as an outport of Buenos Aires. It is the second largest meat port and has Argentina's two largest oil refineries.

Both Rosario and Bahía Blanca are near the periphery of the Humid Pampa and both are leading wheat ports. Rosario in addition is in the center of Argentina's corn district and before the war shipped more corn than any other port in the world.

Coastwise shipping along Argentina's long coastline is small for the simple reason that two-thirds to three-quarters of the population, agricultural production and manufacturing capacity are located in the Humid Pampa between Bahía Blanca and Santa Fe. Patagonia and Tierra del Fuego have a low population density. The small settlements on the coast do not generate enough traffic to warrant cabotage on a commercial basis and their direct foreign trade is negligible. They are connected with the economic center of the republic by navy transports that call at long intervals. The two chief exceptions to the general rule are Comodoro Rivadavia and Río Gallegos. The former is the port of Argentina's earliest and still leading oil field, discovered in 1907. Almost all of the oil from Comodoro Rivadavia is sent by tanker to the refineries in or near Buenos Aires. In the late 1950s production approached 3 million tons. Natural gas from the same field is sent by a 1,600-kilometer pipeline to the national capital. Río Gallegos is the port of the Río Turbio coal field, the only important coal deposit in Argentina. Production is still very small, limited by the capacity of the 260-kilometer narrow gauge railroad which handles less than 1,000 tons a day. This could, however, relatively easily be increased to 6–8 thousand tons a day.

One of the largest steel mills in Latin America, with a planned ingot capacity of 3.5 million tons, is under construction at San Nicolás on the Paraná, and will be a major generator of traffic. This plant, with mixed government and private financing, will have a fleet of 10,000-ton bulk carriers to haul iron ore and coal, at first from abroad but later, it is hoped, from domestic sources. The largest iron ore deposits in Argentina, discovered in 1947, are located at Sierra Grande 125 kilometers south of the small port of San Antonio Oeste on the Gulf of San Matías. The ore contains 56 per cent iron.

Chile

With a length of 4,200 kilometers and an average breadth of only 180 kilometers Chile is the most elongated country on earth. It stretches from the humid and cool Tierra del Fuego in the south—on the same latitude as the southern tip of Sweden or Alaska—to the hot and extremely dry deserts in the north—reaching the latitude of Timbuktu or Puerto Rico. Climate rather than relief differentiate

[1] Gilbert J. Butland, *Latin America: A Regional Geography*. London, 1960. P. 224.

one economic region from the other. The main regions are: (1) the northern desert, (2) the Mediterranean area, and (3) the central and southern forests. About 90 per cent of the population live in the central third of Chile between Coquimbo and Puerto Montt. Chile's heartland, characterized by its Mediterranean climate, is even smaller, stretching from the Aconcagua Valley to the Bío-Bío Valley. The Vale of Chile and the Central Valley between Santiago and Concepción until a century ago were the only effective part of the nation and even today are the home of 65 per cent of its population.[1] The Bío-Bío Valley marks a sharp climatic and cultural boundary, the southern limit of the Mediterranean climate.

In large parts of Chile three structural regions can be distinguished: the high Andes, a central depression and a coastal plateau. The latter, usually about 100 meters above the central depression and up to 1,000 meters above sea level, plunges into the Pacific in a series of abrupt cliffs and steep, barren slopes. Good harbors are therefore rare, the best being Talcahuano, Chile's naval base, Caldera, Coquimbo, and Puerto Montt.

Before 1850 central Chile was a pastoral region with hides and tallow as the main export products. Chile was very similar to California in the corresponding location north of the Equator, but it was closer to Europe and the east coast of the United States. A radical change occurred as a result of the gold rushes in California and Australia, which opened up new markets for wheat from the Central Valley of Chile; grains became the mainstay of the agricultural economy. About 1873 Chile ran into a serious agricultural crisis. California and Australia after the gold rush became grain exporters themselves and other countries, like Argentina, well endowed to produce cheap grains, entered the market on a large scale. Chilean agriculture recovered gradually as the domestic market grew—the metropolitan market in central Chile and the mining camps in the northern deserts—and it became more diversified, producing the crops usually associated with agriculture in a Mediterranean climate. Early in the pastoral period Chile's agricultural land was divided into large estates (*haciendas*), which survived the cereal period and still are a characteristic feature of Chile's economic and social scene. In the last two decades Chile has imported wheat from Argentina. The outdated *hacienda* system does not encourage an intensive use of the land in the Central Valley, one of the richest agricultural areas in Latin America. The southern part of the Central Valley, between the Bío-Bío River and Puerto Montt has heavy precipitation throughout the year. This originally forest covered area has been settled in the last century by pioneering Chileans from further north and by German immigrants. It is a region of medium-sized farms, a sharp social contrast to the large estates of a landed aristrocracy north of the Bío-Bío in the lands of summer drought.

The forest covered southern third of Chile is potentially a rich pulp-producing region. Chile's pulp production has increased rapidly in the 1950s and it has already started to export pulp to the neighboring countries. Only about one per cent of Chile's population lives in this region of high winds, heavy rains and steep rocky slopes. In the extreme south the territory east of the Andes on both sides of Magellan's Strait belongs to Chile. This pastoral region yields high quality wool, Chile's fourth export item after copper, nitrate and iron ore. Punta Arenas is the economic capital of the far south. Chile's only oilfield is located in this area, south of the Strait.

The Chileans in recent years have been accustomed to look upon the copper market as a thermometer indicating the state of their economy. In 1958–60 copper accounted for 67 per cent of the export value, with nitrate second (8) and iron ore third (6). Copper has been an important export item for centuries.[2]

About 1870 Chile's share of the world market reached its maximum with 61 per cent.[3] One after the other the high-grade copper ores in northern Chile have been exhausted but new low-grade deposits have been exploited. For a long time almost all of Chile's copper has been produced by American interests at three large mines: Chuquicamata, Potrerillos and El Teniente, all in the Andes. The first two are controlled by the Anaconda Company and the last one by the Kennecott Copper Corporation.

Chuquicamata, once exploited by the Incas and since 1911 developed on a large scale, now employs about 10,000 people, which means a camp of 25,000. The copper is shipped through Antofagasta. Potrerillos, a smaller mine with a camp of 12,000 people, was producing between 1927 and 1959. Simultaneously with the closing down of this mine the Anaconda Company opened up a new deposit at El Salvador. The copper concentrates from El Salvador move to the smelter at Potrerillos from where they are hauled by rail to Barquito in the port of Chañaral for shipment to the refinery at Perth Amboy in the Port of New York.[4] The mine at El Teniente southeast of Santiago employs 8,000 people and has been in operation since 1906. It is served by the port of San Antonio. Chile's copper exports in 1960 were 530,000 tons.

Before the Depression of the 1930s the mining of nitrate in the deserts of northern Chile often accounted for over 50 per cent of the export value; the export tax on nitrate at times exceeded all other state revenues combined.[5] This industry goes back to 1830 when the first shipments were made to Europe. In the War of the Pacific (1879–1883), fought over the nitrate fields in the Atacama Desert, Chile took from

[2] *Outlook for Chile's Foreign Trade and Economic Growth 1959–1965.* Institute of Economic Research. University of Chile. Santiago, 1959.
[3] Andrés Javier García-Huidobro Guzmán, *Geografía de Chile.* Santiago, 1955. P. 112.
[4] *The New York Times,* April 12, 1959.
[5] R. H. Whitbeck, *Economic Geography of South America.* New York, 1926. Pp. 168 ff.

Bolivia its only strip of sea coast and from Peru some of its southern coast lands. In this area and south of it are the world's only deposits of sodium nitrate, Chile saltpeter. The nitrate is the cementing material of the sands and clays which fill the tectonic basins between the coast range and the main Andes from about latitude 19° to 27° south. It is preserved by the extreme dryness of the region, one of the driest on earth.[6] There are many theories about the origin of the nitrate. A large number of plants or *oficinas* were built to refine the *caliche* or the saline "ore". In the 1890s output exceeded one million tons and during World War I reached about three million. The long distance to Europe and southeastern United States round Cape Horn and the large quantities transported made the saltpeter trade one of the most important in international shipping before the First World War. Until about 1910 the only other form of nitrogen for the fertilizer and explosives industries was obtained as a by-product in the coking of coal. After the serious setback of the 1930s saltpeter production has been concentrated to a few *oficinas* of which the largest are Pedro de Valdivia and María Elena east of Tocopilla. The introduction of the Guggenheim system for refining the *caliche* has lowered production costs. In the 1950s saltpeter shipments accounted for a small percentage of the world's nitrogen consumption which is now dominated by synthetic nitrogen. Exports were strongly concentrated to the port of Tocopilla with Iquique, Taltal and Antofagasta shipping smaller quantities.

Exports of iron ore to Sparrows Point, Balti-

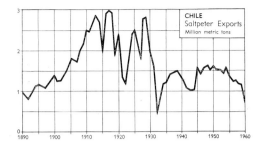

Data from Ivar Högbom, "Chile", *Ymer*, 1932. P. 99; and United Nations, *Yearbook of International Trade Statistics*.

more, from Bethlehem Steel Corporation's El Tofo mine started in 1921. Terminal facilities similar to those at the head of Lake Superior were built at Cruz Grande 10 kilometers from the mine. The loaded railroad cars generated electricity going down which was used to haul the empty cars back and special bulk carriers took the ore by way of the Panama Canal to the company's steelworks on the ocean front near Baltimore.[7] This was one of the first long distance hauls of iron ore, established at a time when the domestic American sources of rich ore were far from being exhausted. Shipments were suspended in World War II after German U-boats had sunk several of the ore carriers. The Tofo mine was about exhausted in the late 1950s but a new mine, El Romeral, began operation in 1955. New terminal facilities for this mine are located at Guayacán adjacent to Coquimbo.

With financial support from the Export-Import Bank Chile in 1945–1950 built a steel mill at Huachipato just south of the port of Talcahuano and close to Chile's most important coal fields. Huachipato is a suburb of Concepción, Chile's third largest city. Two-thirds of the coal comes from local mines and one-third (high-grade coking coal) is brought from the United States. Iron ore is obtained from the Romeral mine, owned jointly by the Chilean steel company and Bethlehem Steel. The Chilean steel company owns a large ore

[6] At Calama behind the coastal plateau no rain has ever been recorded. On the coast the relative humidity is high, 81 per cent on the average at Iquique, but it does not rain much. Out of twenty years fourteen were rainless at Iquique and in the remaining six only 26 mm were recorded. Preston E. James, *Latin America*. 3rd Ed., London, 1959. P. 256.

[7] Whitbeck, *op. cit.* P. 183. Ivar Högbom, "Chile", *Ymer*, 1932. P. 70.

Volume of Inland Freight Traffic in Chile, 1958

	Tons (millions)	Per cent	Ton-km (billions)	Per cent	Average distance (km)
Railways	15.12	33.6	2.56	32.0	170
Cabotage	2.58	5.7	3.41	42.5	1,320
Highways[a]	27.30	60.7	2.05	25.5	75
Airways[b]	.01	—	.01	—	—
Total	45.00	100.0	8.03	100.0	

[a] Preliminary estimates only indicating magnitude.
[b] Refers to 1957.
Source: *Movimiento de carga de cabotaje 1950–1958.* Instituto de Economía. Universidad de Chile. Santiago. 1959. P. 1.

deposit at El Algarrobo, 30 kilometers southeast of Huasco. The 600,000-ton ore consumption of 1956 was expected to reach 1.2 million tons in 1962.[8] Limestone is brought from the Punta Arenas area, 1,500 kilometers to the south, and dolomite of low silica content is imported from Uruguay.[9] Huachipato now covers all of Chile's need for basic steel and even allows some exports, chiefly to Argentina. Between 1959 and 1964 its capacity will increase from 430 to 650 thousand ingot tons.

After 1951 several mining companies have started operations in Chile and since 1955 they have produced more iron ore than Bethlehem Steel. Iron ore exports are expected to increase from the early 1950 level of two million tons a year to 10–12 million tons in 1965.[10] Chile's largest known iron ore deposit at El Laco is expected to start operations in 1963.

The leading general cargo port is Valparaiso, the second largest city of the country, located near the outlet of the rich Vale of Chile. It serves the capital Santiago, a metropolis of nearly two million inhabitants. Valparaiso is built on a north-facing bay sheltered from southerly winds. A breakwater now protects the bay from northerly winds, making it possible for ships to berth at wharves. Before

the 1920s lighterage was the rule in Valparaiso as in most of the other ports on the unprotected Chilean coast. Vessels always had to have steam up not to be surprised by sudden northerly storm winds.[11] The Panama Canal made Valparaiso a terminal port on the South American west coast. Before 1914 it was a port of call for almost all ships sailing between the American west coast and the Atlantic.

San Antonio is even closer to Santiago and now shares with Valparaiso the traffic generated by the capital. The manufacturing industries of Chile, which were stimulated during World War I and even more so during World War II, are strongly concentrated to four cities, Santiago, Valparaiso, Concepción and Valdivia. Since 1939 the Chilean Development Corporation, a Government agency, has sponsored the development of new industries by means of international loans. It is probably the most successful example of central economic planning in Latin America.

In a country of Chile's configuration coastwise shipping is bound to be important. The Chileans have never been a seafaring people, however, and much cargo has been carried in foreign ships. In the northern two-thirds of the country Chile has a fairly dense railroad net. A longitudinal railway runs all the way from Iquique to Puerto Montt. But most of the railways run to the numerous ports; many, especially in the north, were built by the mining companies. Both Antofagasta and Arica are connected with La Paz in Bolivia; they handle most of the small transoceanic traffic of this landlocked republic.

Coal from Lota and Coronel, primarily to

[8] *The New York Times*, January 8, 1958.
[9] C. Langdon White and Ronald H. Chilcote, "Chile's New Iron and Steel Industry", *Economic Geography*, 1961. Pp. 258–266.
[10] *Outlook for Chile's etc.*, *op. cit.* See also Mervin L. Bohan and Morton Pomeranz, *Investment in Chile.* U.S. Department of Commerce. Washington, D.C., 1960.
[11] Högbom, *op. cit.* P. 83.

Valparaiso and San Antonio, have long accounted for over half of the coastal cargo. From about one million tons in the middle of the 1950s the quantities dropped rapidly towards the end of the decade indicating a change to petroleum. Increasing quantities of iron ore have moved in the 1950s from Cruz Grande and Coquimbo to Talcahuano. Starting in 1957 crude oil has been shipped from Chile's only petroleum field in Tierra del Fuego to the Concón refinery near Valparaiso. The new oil port Caleta Clarence is located opposite Punta Arenas. By 1958 the oil flow exceeded the coal flow.

Peru

The Peruvian coast has many small ports, each serving a clearly defined hinterland.[1] The population of the arid coastal zone is concentrated in the irrigated valleys of the short rivers descending from the Andes. Each main valley or group of valleys, where they lie close together, has its own port. With the completion of the Pan American Highway in the late 1930s passengers and light goods could for the first time be carried easily by land from one part of the coast to another across the desert which stretches between each irrigated valley. As a result the earlier complete dependency on coastal shipping was reduced considerably and some of the smaller ports lost trade. The coast is the political and economic heart of Peru but only one-quarter of its population live in the oases of the coastal region. Almost two-thirds, chiefly Indians, live in the highlands and one-tenth in the forested Amazon Valley of eastern Peru.[2]

Callao, the port of Greater Lima, which has more than one-eighth of Peru's population,

almost half of its urban population and most of its manufacturing, accounts for 80 per cent of the Peruvian imports by value and somewhat less by volume. Callao became a leading port on the Pacific coast of South America as soon as the Spaniards founded the Viceroyalty of Peru. Lima, the capital, for a long time was the largest Spanish settlement in the continent. Most of western South America was under the dominance of Lima, and its influence was felt as far as the mouth of the La Plata in Argentina. For hundreds of years silver from the famous Cerro de Pasco mines was carried over a steep trail to Callao from whence ships with this valuable cargo were escorted to Panama, en route to Europe. Pirates frequently attacked the port, which was walled in 1683. The railway which now taps the mining region around Cerro de Pasco, where copper, lead and zinc have become the most important products, is one of the most remarkable mountain railroads in the world.

The only other port with a diversified trade is Mollendo, which since colonial days has been the port of Arequipa, the important trading center of the south. North of Mollendo, long distinguished by its exposed location which makes landing operations difficult, a port was completed during the War at Matarani in a sheltered natural harbor. Callao and Mollendo-Matarani are linked with the interior by the only important railroads of Peru and therefore serve a considerable part of the Andean region. Mollendo serves Cusco, the grazing area around Lake Titicaca and northern Bolivia, but the trade of the twin ports is limited compared with that of Callao.

The leading Peruvian port by tonnage is the recently constructed ore terminal in the natural harbor at San Juan, which started to ship iron ore from the Marcona field in 1953 and from the Acari field in 1959. The two neighboring ore fields were developed by American interests. The beneficiated ore is sent by trucks and trailers on a fifty-five-kilometer highway

[1] J. P. Cole, "Ports and Hinterlands in Peru", *Tijdschrift voor Economische en Sociale Geografie*, 1956, pp. 173–177.
[2] Preston E. James, *Latin America*. New York, 1950. P. 134.

to San Juan, which handles all iron ore mined in Peru. Small quantities move to the recently constructed steel mill at Chimbote,[3] in operation since 1958, but by far the largest quantities are exported, chiefly to the United States and Japan.

Other bulk ports are Talara and Cabo Blanco serving the oil fields in the north which date back to the end of last century. Talara has a refinery and ships refined products up and down the coast. Oil products make up most of the coastal trade.

The exports of cotton and cane sugar, which rank with copper, lead and zinc among the leading export items of Peru by value, but far behind iron ore and petroleum in volume, are handled by the many ports serving the irrigated areas of the coastal zone, each oasis and port as a rule specializing in one of these products. The hinterlands of the many small ports only extend a short distance inland and do not include the highlands.

Many Peruvian ports, including some of the larger ones, such as Callao and Talara, have fishing fleets. Fishing underwent a dramatic expansion in the 1950s and became a major industry. Peru's catch in 1961 was 5.2 million tons, which placed the nation second after Japan. Exports of fish meal increased from 5,000 tons in 1950 to 560,000 tons in 1960. Peru displaced Norway as the leading fish meal exporter. In 1959 this product accounted for about 10 per cent of Peru's export value.[4] The Peru Coastal Current is exceptionally rich in microscopic organisms which provide food for an amazing number of fish preyed upon by a tremendous bird population. The excrement of these birds, deposited on islands and promontories where they nest, and preserved in the arid climate, forms one of the most notable resources of the country, guano.

Eastern Peru can also be reached by small ocean-going vessels sailing up the Amazon River, but the volume of trade is small. Iquitos, the largest port, ships lumber to Callao by way of the Panama Canal. In the beginning of this century, during the rubber boom, Iquitos handled Peru's rubber exports.

Ecuador

Unlike the other Andean countries Ecuador lacks any significant mineral production. More than 80 per cent of its exports are made up of three agricultural products: bananas, coffee and cocoa. All of these are grown in the lowlands, chiefly the Guayas lowland. This is one of the truly fertile tropical areas.[5] The majority of the people, however, live in the interior basins of the Andes. Quito, the political capital, is located in one of these population clusters. The contrast is striking between the speculative commercial agriculture of the lowlands and the subsistence farming of the Indians in the highlands. Most of the commercial activity in Ecuador is centered in Guayaquil. The transportation routes converge on this city, which is somewhat larger than Quito. In 1908 the two cities were connected by a railroad and both are now also on the Pan American Highway.

Until the 1930s cocoa was the dominating export product. In some years it made up as much as 75 per cent of the export value. Ecuador was the leading cocoa producer in the world before World War I.[6] But since 1916 Ecuador's cacao plantations have been progressively ruined by plant diseases.[7] Almost all cocoa for export originates in the hinterland of Guayaquil. The beans are sent to the

[3] C. Langdon White and Gary Chenkin, "Peru Moves onto the Iron and Steel Map of the Western Hemisphere", *Journal of Inter-American Studies,* 1959. Pp. 377–386.

[4] *The New York Times,* November 25, 1960 and January 17, 1962. Also Ecuador is expanding its fishing industry. Both countries export tuna.

[5] E. V. Miller, "Agricultural Ecuador", *Geographical Review,* 1959. P. 205.

[6] R. H. Whitbeck, *Economic Geography of South America.* New York, 1926, P. 89.

[7] Preston E. James, *Latin America.* New York, 1950. P. 123.

city, where they are spread out to dry and ferment on certain side streets, giving a special odor to this town and port. Cocoa remained the leading export until 1941 followed by rice, which had a boom during World War II when shipments from southeast Asia were cut off.

In the post-war period there has been a banana boom in Ecuador, which has few parallels in tropical agriculture. Plant diseases, hurricanes, floods and labor unrest in some of the traditionally dominating banana areas in the West Indies and Central America with a consequent decline in production created a favorable market for Ecuador's banana growers. In a few years Ecuador grew from a rather insignificant position to be the leading banana exporter on the world market. Whereas cocoa always has been a plantation crop most of the new banana farms are small-holdings. Most of the fruit moves to foreign markets in specially designed banana boats but also liners handle bananas. None of the ports can accomodate ocean-going ships at a wharf or pier. Thus the fruit must be loaded from lighters. Before it reaches the port, long hauls and numerous transfers are often necessary and as a result quality suffers.[8]

In the peak year 1959 almost 35 million stems were exported, 23 million through

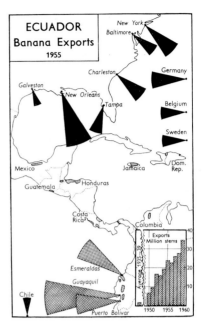

Source: James J. Parsons, "Bananas in Ecuador: A New Chapter in the History of Tropical Agriculture", *Economic Geography,* 1957. P. 201.

Guayaquil, 7 million through the new port in the south, Puerto Bolívar, in operation since 1949, and 4 million from Esmeraldas on the north coast, the only port showing a slight decrease from a peak in 1955.[9] Banana diseases have now also spread to Ecuador and they are a more serious problem than the diseases of cacao. However, on Ecuador's fertile soils both bananas and cacao yield in spite of these handicaps. New disease resistant plants give promise for the agricultural future of the two crops.[10]

[8] James J. Parsons, "Bananas in Ecuador: A New Chapter in the History of Tropical Agriculture", *Economic Geography,* 1957. Pp. 201–216.

[9] Banco Central del Ecuador, Departamento de Investigaciones Económicas. These figures should be compared with the 27 million stems exported in the peak year 1937 from Jamaica, then the world's leading exporter of bananas.

[10] E. V. Miller, *op. cit.* P. 206.

AFRICA SOUTH OF THE SAHARA

Transportation is a crucial problem in most parts of Africa south of the Sahara. The physical environment is hindering transportation in many ways. The interior is composed of plateaus, several hundred meters above sea level, and consequently all major rivers descend over falls and rapids, often located close to the coast. There are no large rivers penetrating deep into the continent at sea level, as in North and South America and Asia, to offset the long distances to the coast for the vast inland areas. Only segments of the rivers are navigable, e.g. the Congo. Some rivers only carry seasonal traffic, e.g. the Niger. The use of a combined river and rail system makes for high transportation costs to and from the interior of Africa.

The coast is inhospitable with very few good harbors. There is no railroad network except in the Republic of South Africa. Railroads serve as feeders to the ports, which are either artificial harbors, constructed and maintained at high cost, or open roadsteads. Truck traffic is increasing in importance; new all-weather roads are being constructed. But the railroads carry the bulk of the goods handled in the ports. As in other areas with poor surface transportation the airplane takes over more and more of the long distance passenger traffic and express service.

In each country the core of the modern economy is primary production for export, either minerals, timber or agricultural products.[1] The main infrastructure has been built to forward that trade; contact between territories is so slight that in some neighboring countries roads do not connect at frontiers and long-distance calls can be put through only via Paris or London.[2] Trade between African countries is very small.

West Africa

For more than two thousand kilometers between Agadir, the most southerly port of the Barbary Coast which is economically part of the Mediterranean region, and St. Louis, the most northerly port of *l'Afrique noire,* the west coast of Africa as yet has no cargo port. The Spanish Sahara and Mauritania have long coastlines, as a rule blocked by sand bars, but these desert areas have a small population and a negligible coastal trade. Mauritania has a good harbor only at the small fishing port of Port Étienne on the border to the Spanish Sahara. Several oil companies have been prospecting in the Spanish Sahara and Mauritania. In the 1950s an international consortium explored the rich iron ore deposits at Khédia d'Idjil in Mauritania. A 650-kilometer railway will take six million tons of ore a year from Fort Gouraud to the ore terminal at Port Étienne, which will be capable of berthing

[1] A detailed map of export production in Tropical Africa compiled by William A. Hance, Vincent Kotschar and Richard Peterec was included in *Geographical Review* 1961. The map, which accounts for 95 per cent of the 1957 export value, shows railroads, main ports and cities and the producing areas.
[2] B. W. Jackson, "Free Africa and the Common Market", *Foreign Affairs,* 1962. P. 420.

65,000 ton vessels.[1] Shipments should start in 1963–64 and reach full capacity by 1967. Another large seaport is planned at Lensid in the Spanish Sahara through which will be shipped iron ore from the Agracha deposits and possibly also petroleum and phosphates.[2]

The territories of West Africa are, for the exchange of goods, in contact with the outside world only through their ports. The volume of trade, although still very small, has expanded rapidly in the postwar period. Cabotage is of little importance in West Africa and there is little inter-territorial trade; the cargo liners call at most ports, keeping transshipment at a minimum.

The 3,800-kilometer coast from Cape Verde to Mount Cameroons presents peculiar difficulties in the establishment of ports.[3] There are only two really good natural harbors, the *Rade de Dakar* and the Sierra Leone River.

The rivers are generally small in volume and vary greatly from season to season. They fail to prevent the formation of formidable offshore bars by coastal drift. These bars may be several kilometers wide; they are shifting and unpredictable. Cargo-liners on the West African run are designed to give maximum size at a draft of 25 feet which is the controlling depth of the bars at Bathurst and Lagos. Much of the coast is continuously beaten by surf that can be negotiated only by special boats of small capacity, which require extremely skillful handling. This singularly inhospitable coast enjoys only one major natural advantage; serious storms of any duration and dangerous seas are both almost unknown. The anchorages of the surf ports are therefore safe. But the transfer of cargo by lighter or surf boat is expensive; bulk freight cannot be handled this way. Therefore artificial ports have been constructed at considerable cost. The capacity of these ports is often a restriction on the economic development of their hinterlands and congestion has at times been a serious problem.

The seaward approach to a port tells only half the story of its development. The landward connections and the resources of the hinterland must also be taken into account. Before the present century land transportation in West Africa was rudimentary. The numerous 'factories' served as distributing centers for goods landed across the surf from ships anchoring offshore and for the collection of exportable products brought in by canoe and porter. Where a nearby navigable river extended the hinterland, certain ports could gain some advantage over their rivals. But during the opening years of this century those ports selected as railroad termini gained permanent advantage over their neighbors. The trend thus started by the building of railroads has been reinforced by the development of a road system. The highways have been focused on the larger existing ports, whose supremacy had already been established by the railroad. In this way less than a dozen ports of West Africa have come to handle over ninety per cent of the overseas trade.

But even today the old conditions prevail in some areas, e.g. the 570-kilometer coastal stretch between Abidjan and Buchanan where no railway leads inland. Here are still numerous surf ports at which an occasional ship pauses for an hour or two to land a few cases of beer and textiles and take on some bags of palm kernels, copra or coffee. These ports handle a few hundred tons of cargo a year.

DAKAR, capital of Senegal, is the leading general port of West Africa. On the basis of shipping tonnage cleared, it was the third port of the former French Union, following Marseille and Le Havre and surpassing all other

[1] Michael Crowder, "Iron Ore from Mauritania", *Steel Review* 19, 1960. Pp. 39–43; Ch. Toupet, "Les grands traits de la République Islamique de Mauritanie", *L'Information Géographique*, 1962. Pp. 47 ff.

[2] *Norwegian Shipping News*, 1962. P. 1,268.

[3] This section leans heavily on H. P. White's excellent study "The Ports of West Africa", *Tijdschrift voor Economische en Sociale Geografie*, 1959. Pp. 1–8.

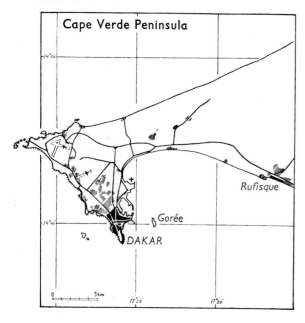

Cape Verde Peninsula

The Rade de Dakar is reputed to be the safest anchorage in West Africa; the surf breaks heavily only a few kilometers to the east. The old trading center of Rufisque is just another surf port. The port of Dakar has been constructed in the lee of the low basaltic plateau, connected to the mainland by a wide spit, thus forming a tombolo. The northwesterly trade winds blow permanently, giving a more pleasant climate to Dakar than is found anywhere else in West Africa.
Source: Ch. Toupet, "Dakar", *Tijdschrift voor Economische en Sociale Geografie,* 1958. P. 35.

400,000 inhabitants, some milestones may be pointed out: in 1898 the decision was taken to make Dakar into an important naval base; in 1902 it became the capital of French West Africa; World War I brought a great increase in shipping to Dakar; in 1923 the railway to Bamako on the Niger River was opened, making Dakar the main port for the French Sudan. A superb airport was built after 1943 with American lend-lease. In the postwar period Dakar with its strategic location has developed into an air traffic node of world significance. Its position at the most westerly point of Africa and at the nearest point to South America combined with its excellent harbor has helped develop Dakar into a leading port-of-call on South American, West and South African routes. Already at the end of last century it started to take the place of St. Vincent (Cape Verde Islands) and it is now competing with Las Palmas (Canary Islands) as a port-of-call on inter-continental sea routes. The calling port function explains Dakar's large figures for tonnage cleared.

In international trade Dakar is best known for its peanut exports. Although Kaolack, a river port southeast of Dakar, ships larger quantities, Dakar has benefited much from this trade and, especially in the postwar period, from the processing of peanut oil. Nearby Rufisque, antedating Dakar by several centuries, was for long the main exporter of peanuts until replaced by Dakar and Kaolack.

Much French capital has been invested since the war in commercial and manufacturing undertakings in the booming city of Dakar. For its 25,000 Europeans Dakar has the

overseas ports.[4] The first French settlement in West Africa was St. Louis located at the mouth of the Senegal River. This river does not provide a desirable port site or a convenient route of penetration into the interior, but it was the best available in pre-railroad days. In 1885 West Africa's first railway was opened between Dakar and St. Louis. The new railroad diverted most of the traffic to and from the Senegal Valley through Dakar, one of the very few natural harbors on this coast. As a result St. Louis declined as a port.

In the ensuing period of rapid development for Dakar, which is now a metropolis of

[4] Léon Coursin, "Dakar: Port Atlantique", *Les Cahiers d'Outre-Mer,* 1948; J. Dresch, "Les Villes d'Afrique Occidentale", *Les Cahiers d'Outre-Mer,* 1950; R. J. Harrison Church, *West Africa.* London, 1957; Benjamin E. Thomas, "Railways and Ports in French West Africa", *Economic Geography,* 1957. Pp. 1–15; Ch. Toupet, "Dakar", *Tijdschrift voor Economische en Sociale Geografie,* 1958. Pp. 35–39; Bernard Kayser and Jean Tricart, "Rail et route au Sénégal", *Annales de Géographie,* 1958. Pp. 328–350.

advantage of a more pleasant climate than any other part of West Africa.

THE GAMBIA, under British control since 1588, oldest and smallest of the British West African territories and the only one not to have gained independence, is a riverine enclave, averaging only some 12 kilometers in width extending for 470 kilometers along either bank of the river Gambia. It extends to the tidal limit of one of the finest navigable rivers of Africa. Its usefulness has been much reduced by the political boundary. Were it not for political considerations, the Gambia River would have acted as the natural focus of trade routes in the western Sudan and a major port would have developed on the river with rail connections into the interior.[5]

Government steamers call at thirty-three wharf towns on the Gambia River. The small town of Bathurst on the river estuary serves as an administrative and commercial center for the territory; it is a transfer point for peanut exports. Although the site was used as an anchorage for over three hundred years, it was not until 1952 that seagoing ships were able to load and unload at a deep-water wharf.[6]

PORTUGUESE GUINEA. The Portuguese enclave of Guinea is a reminder of the very early Portuguese explorations in West Africa. Fortified posts were established in this land of rivers and estuaries as early as 1446. The main trade, carried on through African intermediaries, was in slaves, gold and ivory, exchanged for European goods. The three main rivers are each navigable for about 150 kilometers. Cheap water transportation, supplemented by earth roads, has made the construction of a railroad less urgent. Bissau, the capital, is the main port. Peanuts, the main

[5] H. R. Jarrett, "The Port of Bathurst", *Proceedings, Seventeenth International Geographical Congress.* Washington, D.C., 1952. P. 160.
[6] George H. T. Kimble, *Tropical Africa, Land and Livelihood.* New York, 1960. P. 450.

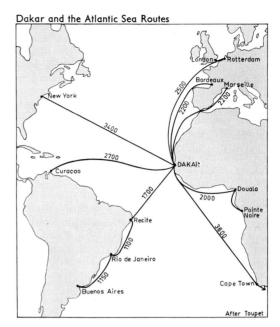

Dakar and the Atlantic Sea Routes

Dakar functions as a port-of-call and a strategic base. It is close to important world shipping routes. Distances on the map are in nautical miles.

export and the leading cash crop, together with oil palm produce and copra account for 90 per cent of the exports, mainly sent to a large company in Lisbon.

CONAKRY, the capital of Guinea, remained a minor port until 1952, despite natural advantages, largely because of the poverty of the territory. In 1910 it handled 60,000 tons which gradually rose to 184,000 tons in 1938. In 1952 the ore port for nearby iron and bauxite mines went into operation. Guinea's ore deposits are among the largest in tropical Africa. An international consortium exploits the bauxite at Fria where the largest alumina plant in Africa or Europe went into operation in 1960. The Fria Company, the largest economic unit in Guinea, built a 150-kilometer railroad between Fria and Conakry and doubled the capacity of the port. Conakry, which has a railroad to Kankan on the Niger, also handles bananas, citrus fruit and pineapples.

The only other true port in Guinea is Benty, accessible to banana boats of about 8,000 tons. Most bananas from the southern coastlands move through this port.

FREETOWN, capital of Sierra Leone, was founded in 1792 and settled with ex-slaves, among others a large group who had fought with the British in the American Revolutionary War. The British Navy used the port as its main base in suppressing the slave trade from West Africa. Over 30,000 slaves liberated at sea were resettled in and around Freetown. Descendants of ex-slaves, known as Creoles, often had higher standards of literacy than most Africans. During much of the nineteenth century, when Freetown, as the main naval base and the senior British settlement, was responsible for the government of other territories down the coast, Creoles were often engaged in this service. Others were in business and in education. The architecture of older parts of Freetown (and of Monrovia) is typical of the old American South.

Palm produce (almost exclusively kernels) is Sierra Leone's leading export, accounting for about half of the export value. The oil palm is most common along the branch railway from Freetown. The second largest export item by value and by far the largest by tonnage is iron ore from the Lunsar field.[7] Well over a million tons of ore is exported by an 83-kilometer railway to the ore port of Pepel, located upstream and on the other side of the estuary from Freetown. About half of the ore is shipped to Britain, and the United States and Germany take about 25 per cent each.

Liberia

Liberia, with an origin similar to that of the British Freetown settlement in Sierra Leone, received ex-slaves from the United States,

brought by private American societies. The first permanent settlement was in 1822 at Monrovia, named after the American president. In 1847 Liberia became an independent state. From the beginning the new nation had tremendous problems. It covers probably the most inhospitable part of West Africa, with the heaviest rainfall, leached soils, and a very difficult shoreline. The ex-slaves, who were partly supported by annual subsidies from the United States, encountered the hostility of the Africans and unfriendly attitudes from the European powers, especially France and Britain.

Until 1926 Liberia was chronically in debt. But in 1924–26 the Firestone Rubber Company secured a concession to plant rubber, in return for which the government was granted a large loan. Since 1942, when the Americans secured the right to land troops in Liberia, the economic development has been especially rapid. A deep-water port at Monrovia, and a first-class airport have been built with American financial assistance. The deep-water harbor, built in the face of great physical difficulties, can accomodate four ships of 28-foot draft. Monrovia is the only free port in West Africa.

Firestone exports of rubber began in 1933 and in 1945 accounted for 97 per cent of the total exports of Liberia. Despite an increase in exported rubber (48,000 tons in 1960) its share of the total value of exports has declined to about 47 per cent as a result of the development of iron ore exports. The largest of the two Firestone plantations is located some 50 kilometers east of Monrovia, and the rubber is brought to the port by diesel-powered lighters. The minor plantation, located on the

[7] H. Reginald Jarrett, "Lunsar: A Study of an Iron Ore Mining Center in Sierra Leone", *Economic Geography*, 1956. Pp. 153–161; H. Reginald Jarrett, "Recent Port and Harbour Developments at Freetown", *The Scottish Geographical Magazine*, 1955. Pp. 157–163; H. Reginald Jarrett, "The Port and Town of Freetown", *Geography*, 1955. Pp. 108–118.

The ore port at Lower Buchanan, Liberia, under construction. It is expected to start regular iron ore shipments in July, 1963. Rail, sleepers and other equipment for the railroad are received at the general cargo wharf during the construction period. A 2,000-meter breakwater will protect the ore quay. The port includes general cargo facilities built for the Liberian Government. (The Gränges-berg Company, August 1962)

border to the Ivory Coast, ships its rubber through Harper.

The Bomi Hills iron ore, some 50 kilometers north of Monrovia, exploited by the Republic Steel Corporation of the United States, is sent by rail to the port. The first ore was shipped in 1951; in 1960 almost three million tons were handled at Monrovia. The Mano River mines near the Sierra Leone border, exploited by the National Iron Ore Company Ltd., began shipments in 1961 and are expected to reach an annual production of 4 million tons by 1965. An even larger iron ore project is the Liberian American-Swedish Minerals Company (Lamco) in which participate the Swedish Grängesberg company and the American Bethlehem Steel. It will exploit a large iron ore deposit in the Nimba Mountains. A 270-kilometer railway has been constructed through the jungles to Buchanan. Facilities are being built for the shipment of 7 million tons. The first shipments are planned for 1963. Possibly even larger deposits of iron ore exist

[1] *The New York Times,* January 17, 1962.

on the Guinea side of the border. A West European banking group is working on plans for the exploitation of these ores, which would have to be shipped through Liberia (Buchanan or Monrovia). National routes would range up to 1,280 kilometers or more.[1]

THE IVORY COAST has no natural harbors. Along the coast there is heavy surf, dense forest, a sparse population and little or no gold. Thus the attention of Europeans seeking gold and slaves was directed to the favored Gold Coast. At Abidjan, the capital since 1934, a deep-water port was completed in 1950, which was an economic stimulus to the Ivory Coast and the Upper Volta. Traffic from the latter area is tapped through a 1,140-kilometer railway to Ouagadougou.

Abidjan is located on a 15 meter deep lagoon. The great Vridi Canal, started in 1936 and half finished when halted by World War II, was completed in 1950. It cuts through the sand bar fronting Abidjan and is 15 meters deep. Traffic at Abidjan increased immediately by over fifty per cent. The ultimate capacity is three times greater or some 850,000 tons. The deep-water port enables the railway to use imported diesel oil instead of wood fuel. The economic expansion of Abidjan is reflected in its population numbers: 25,000 in 1937, 125,000 in 1955.

Coffee accounts for about half of the total value of exports, cocoa for one-quarter. Before the great political changes in Africa in the late 1950s and early 1960s almost all of the exported coffee and most of the cocoa moved to protected markets in France and French North Africa. At least three-quarters of the coffee land is owned by native farmers and they produce almost all of the cocoa. In contrast bananas, first grown for export in 1931, are produced almost entirely by French planters. Output is considerably smaller than in French Guinea. Palm produce from mainly semi-wild oil palms is still exported, but as in other areas in West Africa it has ceded the high place it once held in foreign trade to more remunerative crops. Timber was one of the earliest exports and is still the most important by tonnage; improved handling facilities at Abidjan and Sassandra should help exports, though competition from Ghana and Nigeria is keen.

Ghana

Like several other coastal stretches in West Africa Ghana lacks natural harbors and coastwise shipping is unimportant. In 1928 an artificial deep-water port was opened at Takoradi. It handles ninety per cent of the exports and over half of the imports.[1] Takoradi super-

seded Sekondi,[2] which until then had been the largest port in the western part of the colony and the terminus of the railroad to Kumasi. Accra, capital and largest city, and until recently the second largest port, also has a railway to Kumasi. Accra has a small breakwater, providing shelter for lighters and surf boats. Cape Coast, Winneba and Keta are open surf ports, handling small quantities of overseas trade. At Accra and the other surf ports ocean-going vessels anchor about a mile out to sea and goods are loaded and unloaded by surf boats, specially constructed to ride the heavy surf near the shore. Passengers also travel by the same method if they go by cargo ships. The only real passenger liners, the fortnightly mail boats from Liverpool, since World War II have called only at Takoradi.

The construction of a modern port at Tema, 30 kilometers east of Accra, was started in 1954. It was prompted primarily by the special needs of the Volta River Project,[3] whose aluminum plant is planned at Kpong, 60 kilometers north of Tema. With its location near the capital, Tema after completion has rapidly superseded Accra as a port.

The principal exports of Ghana in order of value are: cocoa (50–75 per cent of total exports), gold, diamonds, manganese ore, and timber (all with less than 10 per cent). Ghana tops the list of cocoa producing countries. The Latin American cacao tree was introduced from the Spanish island of Fernando Póo in 1879; already by 1905 it was the leading cash crop in the country. Cacao is usually grown on small farms of from one to two acres. Al-

[1] Ghana has experienced an increase in the volume of trade handled by its ports. From annual averages of 469,000 tons for imports and 735,000 tons for exports in 1936–39, the volume has increased to 1.7 and 1.8 million tons respectively for 1957–61. Before 1957 Ghana was known as the Gold Coast.

[2] E. A. Boateng, *A Geography of Ghana*. Cambridge, 1959.

[3] H. P. White, "Port Developments in the Gold Coast", *The Scottish Geographical Magazine*, 1955. Pp. 170 ff.

though originally most important in the eastern parts of the forest zone the dominating cacao region is now the area from Accra to Kumasi and beyond. Ghana's main mineral deposits and chief timber region are located in the south-western part of the country in the immediate hinterland of Takoradi. From the large manganese mine at Nsuta, about 65 kilometers by rail from the port, shipments have averaged over 500,000 tons in recent years.

One of the most ambitious economic projects in West Africa at present is the damming of the Volta River some 100 kilometers from the coast.[4] A 320 kilometers long lake will be formed behind this dam, at which a power plant of 564 megawatts will be built.[5] Most of this power will, according to the plans, be used to produce 210,000 tons of aluminum at the Kpong plant. The bauxite will come by

The breakwater protected harbor of Takoradi, Ghana, was enlarged in the 1950s. It has facilities for loading manganese ore and bauxite in addition to transit sheds for general cargo. Inside the breakwater are floating logs awaiting shipment. Sheds and open accomodation for sawn timber and for logs too heavy to float are found on filled land in the inner harbor. (Taylor Woodrow Group)

rail from deposits west of Kumasi and the finished aluminum will be shipped through Tema.

TOGO, under French trusteeship until 1960, is the larger eastern part of former German Togoland. It includes all the coastline, the capital and the railways of the German pre-World-War-I colony. Lomé, the capital, is also the commercial center, railhead of three short lines and until recently the only port. The wharf at Lomé is rather unsatisfactory; traffic is small. Togo's main exports by value are cocoa, coffee, palm kernels and cotton. Since 1961 the new port of Kpeme about 20 kilometers east of Lomé has shipped phosphate rock brought by a new railroad from Akoumapé. Shipments of one million tons per year are planned.

DAHOMEY is the smallest territory of former French West Africa and the most easterly

[4] The Ghanaian Government signed a contract for preliminary work on the project with the Kaiser Industries Corporation in April, 1959. (*The New York Times*, April 16, 1959.)

[5] The dam project will require eighteen months for engineers and four years for construction to the point of the first delivery of power. In December, 1961 the United States decided to lend Ghana 133 million dollars for the construction of this hydroelectric project. *The New York Times*, December 15, 1961.

377

on the Guinea Coast. Porto-Novo, located on a shallow lagoon, is the capital and Cotonou is the port and commercial center. The waterway between Porto-Novo and Cotonou can be used only at intervals by small vessels. Cotonou is the port terminus of two railways, the longest running to Parakou, half way to the Niger Valley. Cotonou is the only coastal railhead in former French West Africa, where ocean-going vessels must still use an open roadstead.

Some 40 kilometers west of Cotonou is Ouidah, the former slave roadstead, for long probably the greatest slave exporter on the Gulf of Guinea. At the end of the seventeenth century 20,000 slaves were exported annually, but in the early nineteenth century the number had fallen to 10–12 thousand a year, chiefly because of increasing shortage of potential slaves in the interior. The last Portuguese slave ship left Ouidah in 1885.[6]

Oil palm plantations, laid out and cultivated by prisoners of local kings in the last century when the prisoners could no longer be sold as slaves, supply by far the most important export items.

Nigeria

Nigeria, the most populous country in Africa, has a dominating port in Lagos, which handles two-thirds of its total volume of seaborne traffic. Lagos was one of the last great centers of the illegal slave trade. In order to prevent this traffic, the British occupied Lagos in 1851 and again ten years later, after Portuguese merchants had restarted the trade. With the unification of Nigeria in 1914 Lagos became the capital and the main gateway of this huge country. In the decade before World War I the entrance to the Lagos Lagoon was deepened, breakwaters were built and the first ocean vessels entered in 1914. Previously passengers were transferred by 'mammy chairs' to surf boats while cargo was transshipped at

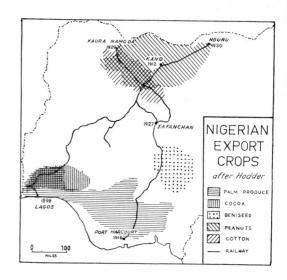

NIGERIAN EXPORT CROPS
after Hodder

PALM PRODUCE
COCOA
BENISEED
PEANUTS
COTTON
RAILWAY

Forcados to small 'branch boats' which could pass over the sand at Lagos. Lagos became a railhead in 1898. The railway reached Kano in 1912 and was extended to Nguru in 1930.

Lagos is the second largest city in Nigeria. Its immediate hinterland is the most densely populated part of the country and includes Ibadan, the largest city in tropical Africa.[1]

Second in importance to Lagos is Port Harcourt, the coastal terminus of the eastern railway. Originally intended to serve as the outlet for the Enugu coalfields (railroad 1916), the port now serves a much wider hinterland following the extension of the railway northwards.[2] The construction of the branch line to Jos deflected to Port Harcourt the tin ore from this field. The development of the lead—zinc deposits of the Eastern Provinces has increased mineral exports. The port also ships palm produce and peanuts and is the natural gateway for imported goods to the Eastern Region.

At one time there were numerous ports in

[6] R. J. Harrison Church, *West Africa*. London, 1957. P. Brasseur-Marion, "Cotonou, porte du Dahomey", *Les Cahiers d'Outre-Mer*, 1953.
[1] B. W. Hodder, "The Growth of Trade at Lagos (Nigeria)", *Tijdschrift voor Economische en Sociale Geografie*, 1959. Pp. 197–202.
[2] K. M. Buchanan and J. C. Pugh, *Land and People in Nigeria*. London, 1955.

the Niger Delta. Small ships could cross the bars and sail up the branches of the Niger. A hulk anchored in mid-stream made up the rudimentary port; all communications with the hinterland were by canoe. The constant changes in the profiles of the bars, difficult landward communications and the relative decline of the Niger as a routeway after the railway from Lagos to Kano had been opened, led to a decline in the importance of these delta ports. In addition to Port Harcourt, which is a special case, being a railhead, only three of them retain some importance, Sapele, Burutu and Warri. They are usually referred to as the Benin ports. Ocean vessels do not load to capacity in these ports but proceed to Lagos for a full cargo. Goods are also carried to Lagos in coastal vessels for transshipment. The Benin ports provide an outlet for timber exports; they also ship palm products and peanuts. Exports of crude petroleum from a new field northeast of Port Harcourt started in 1958. The ocean terminal is at the old slave port of Bonny on the outer edge of the Niger delta, thirty-five kilometers southeast of Port Harcourt. An oil refinery is under construction at the latter town. The petroleum reserves of Nigeria are proving to be very large.

Calabar, east of Port Harcourt, has a restricted hinterland but its trade volume is more than half that of the combined Benin

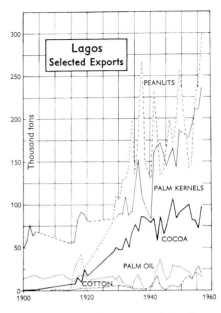

Source: B. W. Hodder, "The Growth of Trade at Lagos, Nigeria", *Tijdschrift voor Economische en Sociale Geografie,* 1959.

ports, chiefly exports of palm produce. Of the two ports of Cameroons Province, Tiko ships bananas from the local plantations and Victoria is a small general port. Tiko is visited once or twice a week by special fruit carriers running direct to the port of discharge in Europe; Victoria receives general cargo liners, which include the port as one of their ports-of-call on the West African coast.

Central Africa: Atlantic Coast

The 1,200-kilometer coastline from Cameroons Mountain to the mouth of the Congo River was under French administration till the end of the 1950s with the exception of two minor areas, the Spanish Rio Muni and the Cabinda enclave of Portuguese Angola. The French have built two deepwater harbors on this coast,

Douala and Pointe Noire. The former is the only port of importance in the Cameroons, shipping cocoa, coffee, aluminum, bananas and hardwood.

GABON. The two Gabon ports, Libreville and Port Gentil, account for considerable tonnages

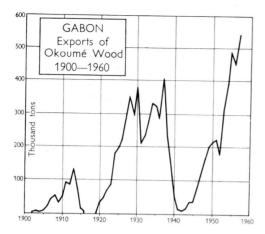

GABON
Exports of
Okoumé Wood
1900—1960

The okoumé (*Aucoumea klaineana*), common in the Gabon forests, is a tree of 30–45 meter height and a diameter of 1.0–1.5 meters carrying its first branches at about 30 meters. The trunks can be easily floated (density 0.45). In Europe it found a market from the beginning of this century in the furniture industry competing with aspen which it resembles. In the world market Gabon and okoumé have become synonymous.
Source: Guy Lasserre, *op. cit.*

because of their timber shipments. Libreville is an old colonial town—originally a French factory—and the administrative capital of Gabon; Port Gentil is a new port and manufacturing center. It emerged in 1910 as a timber port and until 1949 it was the first port of French Equatorial Africa by volume of traffic surpassing Pointe Noire, which was constructed in the thirties.

Both Libreville and Port Gentil command strategic locations at river mouths. *Okoumé* wood, the chief export of Gabon, is floated down the rivers to the coast. Port Gentil, with the larger tributary area of the two, has benefited most from the postwar investments in the Gabon wood industries, which include one of the world's largest plywood factories in addition to sawmills. Libreville has no manufacturing plants but most companies active in the exploitation of Gabon's forest resources have their headquarters in the city.[1]

The *okoumé* is loaded at several roadsteads

on the coast. Shipments from Equata, Owendo, Mondah and Mouny are included in the statistics of Libreville, those from Batanga and Gonoué are listed under Port Gentil, and those from Myanga, Mayumba, Banda Pointe, Conkouate, Noumbi and Bas Kouilou under Pointe Noire. Libreville is still a lighterage terminal. In recent years it only handled about 40,000 tons of imports and a few thousand tons of exports, which is a mere ten per cent of the cargo listed for the port. Owendo, Libreville's chief loading place for *okoumé* logs, is located about ten kilometers southeast of the port.

Both Owendo and Kango, at the head of the Gabon estuary, have been mentioned as the future ocean terminal of a railroad from the large iron ore deposits at Boka-Boka near Mekambo. Ore shipments of 10 million tons are planned for this undertaking, in which Bethlehem Steel is the leading participant. In 1957 Port Gentil started to ship crude petroleum (0.8 million tons in 1960) which has greatly increased its traffic volume.

POINTE NOIRE, with harbor installations begun in 1934 and completed after World War II, is the port of Brazzaville, the largest city of former French Equatorial Africa and the downstream limit of navigation on the Congo-Ubangi river system. Pointe Noire—Brazzaville on the former French side of the Congo River are a duplicate of Matadi— Leopoldville on the former Belgian side of the river. The first city-pair developed on the French national route to Equatorial Africa, the latter on the Belgian route. Both routes are primarily the result of political ambitions to keep as much traffic as possible within the national territory.

Pointe Noire will get a large increase in mineral shipments when the manganese mine

[1] For a detailed study of Libreville and its region see Guy Lasserre, *Libreville, la ville et sa région.* (Paris, 1958.) See also William A. Hance and Irene S. Van Dongen, "Gabon and its Main Gateways: Libreville and Port Gentil", *Tijdschrift voor Economische en Sociale Geografie,* 1961. Pp. 286–295.

380

at Moanda in the Franceville region of Gabon, one of the world's largest deposits, starts production. Initially 500,000 tons will be sent 80 kilometers by overhead cable cars to M'Binda from where a railroad has been constructed to Dolisie on the Brazzaville—Pointe Noire railway. Shipments are expected later to increase to a million tons.[2]

SPANISH GUINEA comprises Rio Muni on the mainland and some islands of which Fernando Póo is the largest. Rio Muni's economy is dominated by the forest industries. In recent years about 200,000 tons of *okoumé* wood have been exported through two or three roadsteads. Fernando Póo ships about 20,000 tons of cocoa and some coffee to Spain through Santa Isabel.

SÃO TOMÉ AND PRINCIPE. The two small islands, settled by the Portuguese since 1485, were long known for a prosperous sugar trade. Sugar was replaced early last century by coffee and cocoa and by 1905 the islands were the world's leading cocoa exporters. Cocoa still provides three-quarters of the total exports.

The Congo

The Congo is an almost landlocked country with only a narrow corridor to the ocean. The dominating port of the former Belgian Congo, Matadi, 130 kilometers up the estuary of the Congo River, is a political creation. The site has numerous deficiencies both in navigational approaches and for port construction, but it offered a national outlet accessible to ocean-going vessels and was easily connected with the rest of the Congo by rail through Belgian

[2] George H. T. Kimble, *Tropical Africa: Land and Livelihood.* New York, 1960. P. 308.
[1] William A. Hance and Irene S. Van Dongen, "Matadi, Focus of Belgian African Transport", *Annals of the Association of American Geographers,* 1958. Pp. 41–72.

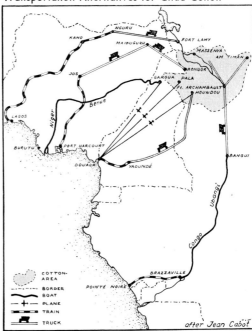

Transportation Alternatives for Chad Cotton

Some distances and freight rates for goods moving between Chad and the coast. After Jean Cabot.

1. Fort Lamy–Lagos (via Nguru-Kano):
   1980 km, open 9 months, takes 50 days.
2. Garoua–Burutu (on the Benue):
   1577 km, open 2 months, takes 4–10 months.
3. Federal road: Archambault–Bangui–Brazzaville–Pointe Noire:
   3048 km, open 8 months, takes 4–8 months.
4. Douala (by plane):
   1050 km, open 12 months, takes one day.

	Freight rate (U.S. dollars/ton)	
	Imports	Exports
1.	67–100	61–65
2.	74–110	65–83
3.	137–231	130–154
4.	257	200

Conversion factor: 1 franc C.F.A. = 0.5714 cent.

territory. Its position was fixed by the last of the series of thirty-two rapids in the Congo River. The establishment of any other ocean head down the estuary would have involved bridging the Congo or running a rail line through French territory.[1]

Commodity Flow of Belgian Africa through Various Sea Ports, 1955

Thousand Metric Tons

	Matadi	Lobito	Mombasa	Dar es Salaam	Beira	Durban	Port Elizabeth	Pointe Noire	Boma
Exports	677	399	5	23	87	—	—	22	125
Oils and fats	177	1	0	0	—	—	—	0	14
Lumber	89	0	—	—	—	—	—	—	65
Copper metal	90	45	—	—	70	—	—	21	—
Other minerals	83	348	0	1	16	—	—	—	—
Imports	1151	173	7	48	2	0	2	0	38
Petroleum and coal	459	84	2	15	—	—	—	—	3
Cement, construction materials	209	4	2	8	—	—	—	—	22
Metals, metal manufactures	193	35	1	10	1	—	0	0	3
Food, drink, tobacco	117	6	0	4	0	0	0	0	7

After Hance and Van Dongen.

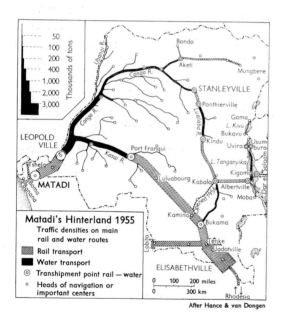

Matadi's Hinterland 1955
Traffic densities on main rail and water routes
▨ Rail transport
■ Water transport
◎ Transhipment point rail — water
○ Heads of navigation or important centers

After Hance & van Dongen

Matadi has practically no immediate hinterland; it is a transshipment point for the railroad to Leopoldville above the rapids. Petroleum products move to Leopoldville by two pipelines from the port annex of Ango Ango six kilometers downstream from the main port.

Leopoldville is the main river port for navigation on the Congo River system. Since 1926 it has been the capital and the most important commercial and manufacturing city of former Belgian Africa. Much of the imports thus have Leopoldville for their final destination.

Berthing accomodation suitable for deep-sea vessels was not completed at Matadi until 1933. The increase in cargo handled was particularly great after World War II leading to acute congestion. Shipping companies imposed freight surcharges of up to 30 per cent on goods booked for Matadi between 1948 and 1951. Despite a strong desire to employ the national route[2] it has always been necessary for the Congo to use foreign outlets. However, Matadi (including Ango Ango) handles over half of the exports and over four-fifths of the imports.

Whereas the flow through the extra-national

[2] Tariffs and rates have been manipulated to induce the traffic of Katanga to flow through Matadi, but the geographical advantages of Lobito make this route the shortest and fastest. It takes eight days for a shipment of machinery to reach Elisabethville from Lobito as against 24 days from Matadi.

General view of the port installations in Lobito harbor, Angola. (Serviços de Portos, Caminhos de Ferro e Transportes)

ports of Lobito and Beira is predominantly made up of minerals, Matadi ships chiefly agricultural and forestry products. These are drawn to Matadi not only because it is closest to most producing areas, but also because of a favorable rate structure and the low cost of transport over the vast interior waterway system converging on the Leopoldville–Matadi railroad.

The other ocean ports in the Congo are small. Boma on the northern shore of the Congo River, one of the oldest European trading settlements in central Africa and the capital of the Belgian Congo until 1926, only serves its immediate hinterland. It handles less than six per cent of the Congo's foreign trade. Banana, at the mouth of the river, has lost its earlier importance as a commercial port.

Angola

The Portuguese colony of Angola with its long coastline has a magnificent natural harbor, Lobito, located behind a sandspit, which forms a natural breakwater. Lobito is the ocean terminal of the 1,340-kilometer Benguela Rail-

The shipments of manganese ore from Katanga through Lobito have increased rapidly since 1948. The mine is close to the Benguela Railway. (Serviços de Portos, Caminhos de Ferro e Transportes)

way, which is connected with the Congo and the Rhodesia rail systems.[1] The port was opened to traffic in 1928; it grew rather slowly in the beginning and handled only 210,000 tons in 1938. From 475,000 tons in 1948 traffic grew rapidly in the 1950s, surpassing one million tons in 1954 and reaching 1.7 million in 1961. In this period of rapid growth for foreign trade in Central Africa some ports serving the area, especially Beira in Mozambique and Matadi in the Congo, were congested.[2] Lobito has hardly ever been fully utilized; its capacity can be more readily expanded than that of most other ports serving the same large hinterland. It has in recent years been enlarged to a capacity of 3.5 million tons, but it would be possible to enlarge the port still further to several times this tonnage, should the need arise. The Lobito route is the shortest and fastest connection for Katanga, but it was not until after World War II that the Congo decided to make use of this route on a substantial scale.

Of the 30,000 inhabitants in Lobito probably 90 per cent derive their livelihood directly or indirectly from activities connected with the operation of the port and the railway. The railway is the life line of the port. It serves the

coastal plain south of Lobito, the central Angolan plateau, which has an increasing export of cash crops, the Katanga Province of the Congo and, to a much lesser extent, the Copper Belt of Northern Rhodesia.[3] In the 1950s transit traffic exceeded Angolan traffic both for outgoing and incoming trade. Domestic exports through Lobito are primarily agricultural products (corn, sisal, manioc flour, etc.) and transit exports almost exclusively minerals (manganese ore, copper, zinc and cobalt). Since 1952 manganese ore has accounted for by far the largest quantities.

Luanda, capital and second port of Angola, ranks second by volume of Angolan foreign trade but because of the high value of its exports (coffee and cotton) it has consistently led Lobito by value.

[1] The aim of the Benguela Railway Company, constituted in 1902, was to provide access to mineral-rich Katanga and adjacent parts of Northern Rhodesia. It was financed by British capital. Work was begun in 1903 but the railroad did not reach the Congo border until 1928. It took another three years before the railway was connected with the Katanga lines.
[2] William A. Hance and Irene S. Van Dongen, "The Port of Lobito and the Benguela Railway", *Geographical Review*, 1956. Pp. 460–487.
[3] In 1961 Angola accounted for 950,000 tons, the Congo for 680,000 tons, and the Rhodesias for 31,000 tons of Lobito's cargo turnover.

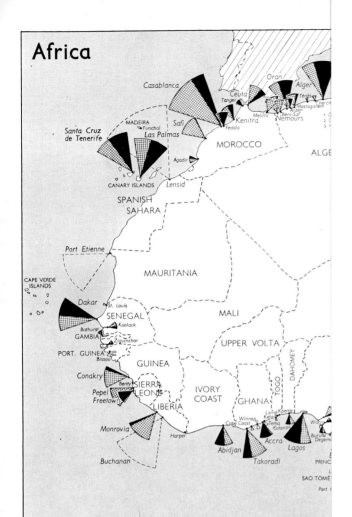

Africa

Casablanca
Oran
Alger
Ceuta
Tanger
Cherch...
Ténès
Mostaganem
Safi
Melilla
Arzen
Beni-Saf
Nemours
Santa Cruz
de Tenerife
MADEIRA
Funchal
Las Palmas
Kenitra
Fedala
MOROCCO
ALGE...
Agadir
Lensid
CANARY ISLANDS
SPANISH
SAHARA
Port Etienne
MAURITANIA
MALI
CAPE VERDE
ISLANDS
Dakar
St. Louis
SENEGAL
Kaolack
Bathurst
GAMBIA
Ziguinchor
PORT. GUINEA
Bissau
GUINEA
UPPER VOLTA
Conakry
Benty
SIERRA
LEONE
IVORY
COAST
GHANA
TOGO
DAHOMEY
Pepel
Freetown
LIBERIA
Monrovia
Harper
Winneba
Cape Coast
Loma
Keta
Kpeme
Lome
Tema
Cotonou
Wa...
Burutu
Degema
Abidjan
Accra
Lagos
Buchanan
Takoradi
PRINC...
SAO TOMÉ
Port ...

ATLANTIC
OCEAN

CARGO HANDLED

Shipments
Receipts

0 0.5 1   5   10   15
Million metric tons

1:40,000,000
0   500   1,000 K...
0   200   400   600 Mile...

Southern Africa

The ports of South Africa have been constructed by the South Africans to serve their expanding trade. There are no good natural harbors on this coast. For a long time Table Bay, Cape Town, was the only important anchorage but the bay offered little protection before the completion of the modern harbor works in the latter half of last century. The largest of the basins built at Cape Town, the Duncan Dock, was completed in 1939 and it includes the largest graving dock in the southern hemisphere, designed to provide repair facilities for the largest vessels afloat. Port Elizabeth, with its origin as the port of entry for the 1820 settlers, was little more than an open roadstead with three small jetties on Algoa Bay before the completion of a breakwater in 1927 and a modern quay in 1935, at which the large mailships could berth. Today the port is able to handle the largest ships engaged in the South African trade. East London is a river port which needs continuous dredging to maintain a sufficient depth for large cargo liners. The Bay of Natal formed the best natural harbor in the Union but it was the last to be utilised. It was not until the discovery of the Witwatersrand goldfields in 1886, an event which more than any other was to alter the population distribution in Southern Africa, that this harbor became important. A shipping channel was constructed to the marshy, almost landlocked bay then referred to as Port Natal, which was rapidly transformed into the modern well-equipped port of Durban.

When the Union of South Africa was formed in 1910 her exports were made up of a few items of small volume and high value— gold, diamonds, ostrich feathers—and almost all of the foreign trade cargo was incoming overseas traffic destined for the Witwatersrand. The Portuguese port of Lourenço Marques in Delagoa Bay received nearly two-thirds of the traffic. The desired dispersion of this traffic between the major ports could only be achieved by agreement between the Portuguese and South African governments and by manipulation of railway rates within the Union.[1] The greater distances from the South African ports to the new economic heartland of South Africa were obviously a great handicap. The Cape ports were allotted 15–20 per cent, Durban 30 per cent, and Lourenço Marques 50–55 per cent of the traffic. Adjustments were also made to secure for each port the import traffic for which it was best suited: Port Elizabeth—mailboat cargo; East London —flour and American cargoes; Durban—heavy machinery and general cargo; and Lourenço Marques—bulky cargo like cement, lumber and steel. The proportions of the Mozambique Convention (1909) were confirmed in 1928 but during the Depression the agreement was revised (1934) and Lourenço Marques' share of the seaborne traffic to the competitive area was reduced to 47.5 per cent.

The export traffic has been less subject to rate manipulation. Bulk commodities move to the nearest port and cargo requiring special handling facilities moves to the port which has specialized in that type of cargo. Gold and diamonds are now being sent by air. Until 1950 gold accounted for a larger export value than merchandise but in the 1950s it has been considerably less.

As a result of the old policy of regulating import trade through railway tariffs the four major South African ports and Lourenço Marques show relatively small differences in the volume of incoming cargo and a remarkably uniform cargo composition. The export trade

---

[1] This section draws heavily on Monica M. Cole's substantial and well-documented volume *South Africa* (London, 1961).

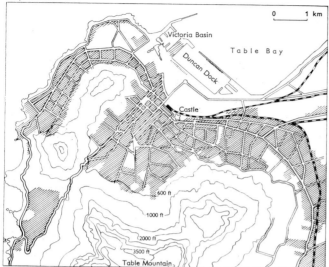

Cape Town

The construction of the Duncan Dock increased the capacity of the port tremendously and provided space for the future expansion of Cape Town's central business area. As a passenger port Table Bay is on a par with Durban; it leads in the number of passengers embarked but is surpassed by Durban in passengers landed. Bulk commodities account for an unusually low share of Cape Town's seaborne trade.

is different, however. It reveals more closely the character of the port's hinterland. The two northerly ports, Lourenço Marques and Durban, have a good balance between incoming and outgoing tonnage due to shipments of coal and ore, whereas the Cape ports mainly ship agricultural produce of relatively high value. They have a large excess of incoming cargo.

Lourenço Marques is the outlet for the rapidly expanding production of chrome ore and asbestos in eastern Transvaal, while Durban receives manganese ore railed from Postmasburg, where it has been mined since 1929. After a triangle deal in 1948[2] the bottleneck caused by an insufficient railway capacity on the 950-kilometer route between port and mine was removed and manganese production was stepped up considerably. In 1960 South African manganese exports amounted to 880,000 tons. Part of this came from a deposit in South West Africa, which has been mined since 1950, and which uses Walvis Bay as its outlet. Coal shipments through Lourenço Marques originate in eastern Transvaal whereas Durban is the natural outlet for the Natal coalfields. Coal production has expanded

rapidly in South Africa which is now a major coal producer, but exports and bunker account for less tonnage than in the 1920s when total production was one-third of the present output.[3]

Port Elizabeth and East London with their pastoral hinterlands are the main wool ports. The former port also ships citrus fruit and the latter pineapples. Cape Town is, however, the main fruit port in the Republic, handling a variety of deciduous fruits from the near hinterland and citrus fruit from the Transvaal. In addition it ships a great variety of agricultural produce from the whole of the Republic.

During the Second World War and to a lesser extent during the short Suez Crisis the Cape route regained the importance it had before the opening of the Suez Canal. A permanent revival of the Cape route seems unlikely, however. The Canal will probably be successively deepened to accomodate larger

[2] The United States supplied steel to Canada, Canada sent railroad cars to South Africa and South Africa shipped manganese ore to the United States.
[3] Through Durban 0.6 million tons of coal were shipped in 1961 and 1.8 million in 1910. Total shipments in the two years were 4.8 and 2.1 million tons.

Table Bay Harbour, Cape Town, with the Duncan Dock to the left and the adjoining Victoria Basin. On the land filled in after 1937 along with the construction of the Duncan Dock only a few tall buildings can be seen. (The Cape Argus)

The Victoria Basin at Cape Town with Table Mountain in the background. (The Cape Argus)

387

General view of Durban and harbor. The protected bay side of the Point, stretching towards the entrance of Durban Bay, is lined with ocean berths. Coal and petroleum are handled at berths in the foreground. (South African Railways)

vessels, and it is also possible that parallel canals may be built to increase the capacity. Nuclear underground blasts offer a technique for building canals of dimensions hitherto unheard of. Even if tankers too large for the Suez Canal take the Cape route this should have little influence on port traffic in South African ports as these vessels will take bunker for the return trip at the oil ports of the Persian Gulf, where prices are much lower than in South Africa. Thus traffic in the South African ports will be entirely dependent on the development in their potentially rich hinterlands.

Central Africa: East Coast

Mozambique

The Portuguese colony of Mozambique on the east coast of Africa has a strategic location with respect to the great mineral and industrial area of the Transvaal in South Africa and the rapidly developing but landlocked areas of the

The modern ocean terminal near the central business area in Durban. Elevated roadways give access to the new passenger terminal and parking areas, while goods are transferred to railroad cars and trucks on the lower level. (South African Railways)

Rhodesias and Nyasaland.[1] Its character as a transit area is evidenced by a cargo turnover of 6.7 million tons at Lourenço Marques and 3.3 million tons at Beira in 1961, while the foreign trade of the colony amounted to less than two million tons. Foreign investments have been heavy, notably in the two great ports and in the railways, including the great Zambezi Bridge, linking Beira with Nyasaland.[2]

LOURENÇO MARQUES, founded as a Portuguese trading post in 1544, has for centuries been regarded as the finest harbor on the east coast of Africa. Final agreements on territorial rights

in that part of the continent were reached by Portugal and Great Britain between 1870 and 1895; Lourenço Marques was made the capital of Portuguese East Africa. As one of the first ports in sub-Saharan Africa Lourenço Marques completed a deepwater wharf already in 1903. It is one of the few ports in Africa which has not suffered periodic congestion. The volume of cargo handled increased from 1.8 million tons in 1940 to 6.7 million in 1961. In addition to the downtown wharf there are petroleum and lumber wharves at Matola, six kilometers up the estuary.

A railroad was built from the port to Preto-

[1] William A. Hance and Irene S. Van Dongen, "Lourenço Marques in Delagoa Bay", *Economic Geography,* 1957. Pp. 232 ff.
[2] L. Dudley Stamp, *Africa: A Study in Tropical Development.* New York, 1953. P. 399.

389

ria via Ressano Garcia between 1886 and 1894. This line was designed to carry heavy traffic, in recent years petroleum products and timber moving inwards and ore, coal and citrus fruit moving out. Although single track it has an estimated annual capacity of over four million tons. Its capacity could quickly be doubled.

A second line, started in 1912 to connect Lourenço Marques with Johannesburg through Swaziland, was completed only as far as the Mozambique border. As Swaziland generates little traffic it is of limited importance.

In 1955 the domestic Limpopo line was connected with the Rhodesian Railways and thereby Lourenço Marques was able to join Beira as a seaport for the Rhodesias. It was expected that the new line in its tenth year would move 2.2 million tons. Beira previously handled 80 per cent of the total overseas trade of the Central African Federation but congestion at that port had at times been serious and in 1950–51 a 60 per cent surcharge was temporarily imposed by the East African Shipping Conference on freights booked for Beira.[3]

BEIRA has achieved prominence as a seaport despite a mediocre site. The modern port, established at the end of last century, is only a few miles north of the famous Sofala, center of early Arabic and Portuguese trade. The railroad to Rhodesia was built in the 1890s and the Boer War contributed to an early concentration on Beira as the chief outlet of the Rhodesias. Port traffic reached 200,000 tons by 1915, one million tons by 1929 and 3.3 million in 1961. Leading shipments from Beira are copper from the great mines of the Copper Belt and chrome ore from the Southern Rhodesian High Veld.

Several of the lines calling at Beira have made it their terminal point as the port is equidistant from northwestern Europe either via the Suez Canal or via the Cape of Good Hope.

NACALA. A third ocean terminal in Portuguese East Africa was opened in 1951 at the splendid natural harbor of Nacala north of Mozambique Island, the former capital, which for centuries epitomized the Portuguese strength along the African margins of the Indian Ocean, but which has remained unimportant as a center for modern trade.[4] A railway was built after 1924 from Lumbo on the mainland opposite the island. It has been extended inland to Porto Arroio on Lake Nyasa and a branch line has been constructed to Nacala. The new terminal had a capacity of half a million tons of cargo about 1960.

Madagascar

Madagascar was first opened for trade with the outside world by Arabs from Oman and Hadhramaut, who had trading posts on the east coast of Africa, from Zanzibar to Sofala, near present Beira. On Madagascar they favored the most accessible northwest coast.[1] From the beginning of the sixteenth century European vessels participated in this trade and later Yankee ships as well. Until the opening of the Suez Canal Madagascar was on a main trade route and many ships called for supplies. At times buccaneers used the island as a base. After 1850 French trade became dominant, profiting from the older French establishments on Réunion, Comoro Islands and the two islands off the coast of Madagascar, Nossi Bé and Sainte Marie. In 1956 France accounted for 62 per cent of Madagascar's exports and

[3] William A. Hance and Irene S. Van Dongen, "Beira, Mozambique Gateway to Central Africa", *Annals of the Association of American Geographers*, 1957. Pp. 307 ff.

[4] Irene S. Van Dongen, "Nacala: Newest Mozambique Gateway to Interior Africa", *Tijdschrift voor Economische en Sociale Geografie*, 1957. Pp. 65 ff.

[1] Charles Robequain, *Madagascar et les bases dispersées de l'Union française*. Paris, 1958; William A. Hance, "The Economic Geography of Madagascar", *Tijdschrift voor Economische en Sociale Geografie*, 1957. Pp. 161–172; William A. Hance, "Transportation in Madagascar", *Geographical Review*, 1958. Pp. 45 ff.

72 per cent of her imports. From the end of last century trade with France was strongly favored in Madagascar as in other French colonies.

The east coast of Madagascar is inhospitable with strong trade winds, high seas, occasional storms and no protected harbors. A series of lagoons lie behind a narrow sand bar which extends in a remarkably straight line with one or more coral reefs, usually submerged, immediately off much of the coast. Communications with the interior have always been difficult; the narrow coastal plain is backed by two high escarpments covered with tropical rain forest. The many rivers flowing off the escarpment are a great obstacle for north-south land transportation along the coast. Since the end of last century plans for a canal connecting the many lagoons on the east coast have been partly realized. Part of the *Canal des Pangalanes* has been built for barges of 40 tons; in other sections only boats of three to five tons may pass.

In spite of all handicaps Madagascar's dominating port, Tamatave, is located on the east coast. It is third in size among Madagascan cities. The port was seriously damaged when the city was hit by a cyclone in 1927 but is now protected by a dike. It can handle three ships of 8–9 meter draft at a time. The other ports on the east coast, except the old trade center of Port Dauphin, are open roadsteads. Since 1913 Tamatave has been connected by a 370-kilometer narrow-gauge railroad with the economic and political capital, Tananarive, located on the high plateau. The railroad climbs two escarpments of 900 and 500 meters by means of bridges, viaducts and tunnels.

Majunga, the other port serving the capital, is located in the western savanna area. It has only highway connections. As it is the first Madagascan port of call for ships coming through the Suez Canal, high value products are often sent this way to the capital, rather than via Tamatave. Majunga is the hub of coastal shipping. Many times as many ships call here as at Tamatave but the cargo tonnage handled is smaller. The *boutres* of 40–150 tons with their characteristic triangular sail handle much of the cabotage. Most of them are no longer owned by Arabs, but by Indians and Pakistanis. The *goélettes* of about the same size, often owned by Europeans and equipped with a motor, also participate in this trade.

Diego Suarez in the extreme north has one of the world's best harbors. It has a restricted hinterland, however, and is largely used as a transshipment port. The French have built a noted naval base here with dry docks and coal and oil depots; it was occupied by British troops during World War II. The three largest ports, all in the north, handle more than four-fifths of Madagascar's waterborne traffic.

Coffee for the French market is by far the most important export item; in the 1950s it accounted for over 40 per cent of the export value. Rice, tobacco, vanilla, cloves and a great number of other agricultural products add to the list of exports; of minerals exported only graphite and mica are worth mentioning.

Réunion and Mauritius

The volcanic island of Réunion, with peaks exceeding 2000 meters, is one of the oldest French possessions in Africa. From 1665 it was a base of the French East India Company supplying ships en route to and from Pondicherry with vegetables, fresh meat, etc. By calling at Bourbon, as the island was then called, the ships avoided the Mozambique Channel which had a poor reputation in the days of sailing ships. Large estates were established for the production of colonial products, primarily coffee and sugar, and slaves were imported from Madagascar. There was also large-scale immigration from India, especially after the abolition of slavery, and from other coasts around the Indian Ocean. Sugar production reached its peak in 1860–65 and again in the 1950s. The capital St. Denis, located on the north coast, is the largest city and Pointe des Galets the only port.

The neighboring island of Mauritius, British since the Napoleonic Wars, is less elevated than Réunion and has more cultivable land on rich volcanic soils. The small island has half a million inhabitants, chiefly of Indian origin. Like Réunion it is a sugar island. Port Louis is the principal town.

East Africa

Ocean shipping on this monsoon coast may antedate the mythical days of Solomon and Sheba, whose ships sailed this way to Sofala and the gold of Ophir. Phoenicians and Sabaean Arabs searched for precious metals and spices in East Africa long before the Christian era. Islamic Arabs first settled on the East African coast about 740. The Arabian, Persian and Indian colonies on the eastern littoral attained their highest prosperity in the period between 1100 and 1300. They were visited by the famous geographer Ibn Batuta in 1328.[1] When Vasco da Gama "discovered" them in 1498 towns like Sofala, Kilwa, Zanzibar, Mombasa and Malindi were thriving trade centers. Under Arab guidance Vasco da Gama learned to utilize the monsoons on his voyage to and from India. It took thirty years for the Portuguese to establish suzerainty over the east coast of Africa. They stayed for 200 years of continual bloodshed, fighting the Arabs but also the Turkish corsair Ali Bey and the strange Wasimba tribe. When the Portuguese went in 1730 they left a legacy of turmoil. They were ejected by Arabs of Oman, which was the beginning of close political connections between Oman and Zanzibar. The opening of the Suez Canal in 1869, the fight against the slave trade in eastern Africa with an entrepôt in Zanzibar, and the period of frantic empire building in the last quarter of the nineteenth

century again drew the attention of Europe to the East African littoral.

A ten mile strip of the mainland coast remained part of the Sultanate of Zanzibar; Germany, Britain and Italy acquired stretches of this strip from which they penetrated inland. In German East Africa, now Tanganyika, the construction of railroads was started from Tanga (1893) and Dar es Salaam (1905). The British started to build the Uganda Railway from Mombasa in 1895. Prior to the opening of the East African territories by railroads, seaports for European steamers were unknown along the coast although jetties to deal with the *dhow* traffic had existed for centuries.[2]

MOMBASA is the leading port in East Africa. Its railroad carries three to four times as much cargo as the line from Dar es Salaam. The railroads serving Tanga and Mtwara have only a small capacity.[3] The cosmopolitan city of Mombasa with 100,000 inhabitants is located on a five-kilometer island in a deep sea inlet. The Old Town on the eastern side of the island faces Mombasa Harbour, which is now used by *dhows* and coastal schooners. In addition to the large ocean-going *dhows*, which begin to arrive at the end of December or early in January and depart in April, there are smaller coastal *dhows*, mostly based on the Island of Lamu, which all the year ply up and down the coast.

The modern port, Kilindini, is on the western side of Mombasa Island. It is the terminus of the railroad to Nairobi, Kisumu on Lake Victoria and to Uganda. A short rail and road causeway connects the island with the mainland in the north. The excellent Kilindini

[1] Walter Fitzgerald, *Africa*. 7th ed. London, 1950. P. 79.
[2] This section draws heavily on three mimeographed pamphlets issued by the Public Relations Office, East African Railways and Harbours. History of Mombasa (November, 1961), Kilindini (November, 1961) and The Ports of East Africa (April, 1962).
[3] East African Railways and Harbours, *Annual Report 1961*. Map on inside cover.

Mombasa

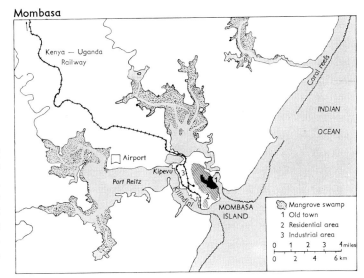

Mombasa is the ocean terminal of the Kenya-Uganda Railway, by far the most important rail route in East Africa. It runs through Nairobi and has major terminals at Kisumu and Kampala on Lake Victoria. Map adapted from L. Dudley Stamp, *Africa,* London, 1953. P. 412.

Harbour, the "place of deep water" in Swahili, has nine deep water berths for dry cargo and an oil jetty. Space for future expansion is available on the mainland as a direct continuation of the Kilindini port. Four new deep-water berths have been constructed at Kipevu of which two were brought into service in 1961 and the remaining will become operational when traffic warrants their equipment and use. An oil refinery with a new jetty in Port Reitz is scheduled for completion in 1963. The jetty is capable of accommodating 65,000-ton tankers. The main cargoes loaded at Mombasa are coffee, cotton, sisal, soda, and cement.

DAR ES SALAAM, the principal port of Tanganyika, handles transit traffic of the eastern Congo and Burundi and Rwanda. The railroad has termini both on Lake Tanganyika (Kigoma) and on Lake Victoria (Mwanza).[4] Cotton, coffee, oil seed and cake, and sisal are the main export commodities.

[4] Public cargo traffic on the inland waterways of East Africa is most important on Lake Victoria (240,000 tons 1961) followed by Lake Kioga (50,000 tons) Lake Albert (40,000 tons) and Lake Tanganyika (7,000 tons).

[5] *Modern Transport,* July 24, 1954.

TANGA, although initially important as an ocean terminus of a railroad, now appears on the port map chiefly because of the large sisal plantations in its immediate hinterland. Sisal was introduced from Yucatan in 1893 and is now easily the most important commercial plant of the littoral. It is grown on plantations owned by Europeans and Indians. Tanganyika has become the leading supplier of sisal to the world market.

MTWARA had its genesis in the Overseas Food Corporation's groundnut scheme and the construction of port facilities with an annual capacity of 400,000 tons of peanuts was started in 1948. Mtwara was chosen in preference to the existing port of Lindi, which was closer to the proposed peanut area, because of its physical advantages for the development of a major port.[5] With the failure of the peanut project Mtwara has attained only a small part of the traffic envisaged for it. Cassava flour and cashew nuts rank among the leading export commodities.

ZANZIBAR. The two islands of Zanzibar and Pemba lying some twenty-two miles off the

393

The old harbor of Mombasa at the height of the *dhow* season (above). Behind Mombasa's old town in the foreground are the modern office buildings along the Kilindini Road. The entrance to the modern port facilities at Kilindini and Kipevu can be seen behind Mombasa Island. The modern port is just out of view to the right.

In the *dhow* season sailors from Arabia, Persia and India sailing the same type of vessels as two thousand years ago, with the same type of cargo (in recent decades slaves excluded), following the same routes and the same seasonal rhythm, crowd the narrow streets of the bazaar.

The two deepwater berths at Kipevu (left) were added to the modern port of Mombasa in 1961. In addition to the travelling quay cranes provided by the harbor the cargo handling company is operating 22 fork-lift trucks and ten platform trucks, all electric battery driven.

394

An Arab *dhow* off the east coast of Africa
(right).

Kilindini Harbour (below), the modern port of
Mombasa, is one of the best harbors on the east
coast of Africa. The first berths were brought
into service in 1926 and the last of the nine
berths for which there was room in the Island
section of the port was completed in 1958. When
the photo was taken (February 6, 1960), the port
was working at capacity with six more vessels at
anchor in Port Reitz. The berths at Kipevu on the
mainland were then under construction.

Mombasa is a highly mechanized general port
serving as the ocean terminus of one of Africa's
major railways. Like the other modern seaports
of East Africa it is under the administration of
the East African Railways and Harbours, employing a staff of 2,000 persons in the port. The
Landing and Shipping Company, in charge of all
cargo handling operations ashore, and four private
stevedoring companies employ 6,000 men. (All
four photographs: E. A. R. & H.)

Tanganyika coast are part of the Sultanate of Zanzibar, a British protectorate. The islands produce 80 per cent of the world's supply of cloves and clove oil. Other exports are copra and coconut oil.

The port of Zanzibar lies on the sheltered western side of the island and has a good harbor, well-protected from the south-east monsoon. For centuries before railroads were constructed on the mainland this great Arab trading center held a focal position in the trade of East Africa. The typical Arab city still occupies the sea front. Much of the trade has passed into the hands of recent immigrant Indians. In addition the city has a small European quarter and a large, sprawling African city.[6]

SOMALIA. The Somali Republic, consisting of the former British Somaliland Protectorate and the former Italian Trust Territory of Somalia, occupies the Horn of Africa, with coasts on both the Indian Ocean and the Gulf of Aden. This long desert-backed coast is probably the most inhospitable in tropical Africa. There are no anchorages providing shelter during the summer monsoon, when the prevailing winds are onshore and a heavy swell is running. Only one port, Kismayu, at the mouth of the Juba River, offers a sheltered anchorage and a depth of 21 feet, but it has failed to exploit its advantage.

The main port is Mogadishu, the capital and the outlet for Somalia's only large cultivated area. It is an open roadstead with an exposed offshore anchorage and cargoes are discharged into lighters and small *dhows* which can unload at an inner breakwater. The modest exports are bananas and live animals and animal products, with imports of fuels and manufactured goods.

The only port of any significance on the Gulf of Aden is Berbera, which is occasionally visited by small ocean-going vessels and *dhows* in traffic with Aden.

Ethiopia and the Sudan

FRENCH SOMALILAND has only a little over 60,000 inhabitants of whom almost half live in the capital, Djibouti. The growth of Djibouti cannot be explained by the economic development in the territory; it is a port of call and the ocean-head of the railway to Addis Ababa. It is also a free port. Measured by tonnage cleared (5.2 million tons in 1955) Djibouti ranked fourth among French transoceanic ports, after Casablanca, Dakar and Alger. With the construction of the railway, authorized in 1894, reaching Harar in 1904 and Addis Ababa in 1917, Djibouti became the main gateway to Ethiopia. Like so many railways in Africa, this narrow-gauge, 785-kilometer railway, which reaches an altitude of 2,400 meters in Ethiopia, had to overcome great physical obstacles as well as financial difficulties. In the postwar period it has suffered competition from truck traffic on the highways from Addis Ababa to Assab[1] and Massawa on the coast of former Italian Eritrea, which is now federated with Ethiopia.

ETHIOPIA. Of Eritrea's two ports Massawa is the larger and better equipped, but Assab is closer to the capital and is likely to benefit most from the changed political situation of Eritrea. In 1957 a contract was signed with a Yugoslavian firm for the enlargement and modernization of the Assab harbor. This is one of the largest postwar investments in Ethiopia. Port movements at Massawa and Assab now greatly exceed Ethiopian transit traffic via Djibouti. The two ports are the largest in Africa supported only by highways.[2]

[6] L. Dudley Stamp, *Africa: A Study in Tropical Development.* New York, 1953. P. 419.
[1] Charles Robequain, *Madagascar, op. cit.*
[2] The railway from Massawa to Asmara and Agordat (306 km) has a very small traffic. See *Economic Handbook,* December 1958. Issued by the Imperial Ethiopian Government, Ministry of Commerce and Industry, Addis Ababa, 1958.

THE SUDAN. Until 1906, when the railroad to the Red Sea was opened, the Sudan's external trade was transited through Egypt, which led to almost prohibitive costs and long delays. Port Sudan was built as a sea terminus of the railroad, replacing the old Arab port and caravan terminus Suakin a short distance to the south. The harbor chosen for the new port offered approaches through the coral reef suitable for ocean vessels. The rail distance from Port Sudan to Khartoum, the capital and economic focus of the Sudan, is 790 km.

With the development after 1925 of the Gezira irrigation project in the vast triangle between the White and the Blue Nile south of Khartoum, cotton has come to dominate the exports of the Sudan, accounting for over half of the export value in recent years. An expansion program inaugurated in the early 1960s envisages almost doubling the irrigated area.

After a rapid increase in the exports of oilseeds (sesame, peanuts and cottonseed) the export value of this commodity group exceeds that of gum arabic, of which the Sudan supplies three-quarters of the world's consumption.

ASIA

The Persian Gulf and the Arabian Peninsula

The ports of the Persian Gulf are of three general types. (a) The oil terminals, with or without refineries, which are creations of the twentieth century petroleum exploitation. Most of them were built after World War II and they now rank high among the ports of the world by tonnage, making the Persian Gulf one of the most important generating areas for seaborne trade. (b) A few ports equipped to handle the limited trade in dry cargo carried by ordinary liners and tramps between the countries around the Persian Gulf and the rest of the world. Although still small this trade has increased very rapidly in recent decades and the deep-sea berthing facilities have been expanded. (c) Ports engaged in *dhow* traffic, usually open roadsteads. Many of these have been ports for thousands of years but are now losing out to the modern type of traffic. Their port activities are not covered by statistics. In most cases the traffic is probably quite small.

On the other coasts of the Arabian Peninsula *dhow* ports are the most common but the Yemen and the west coast of Saudi Arabia each have one modern liner port. Aden is in a category of its own. In its modern role it is a product of a strategic position created by the opening of the Suez Canal.

Iran

The tremendous petroleum developments in the countries bordering the Persian Gulf were initiated before World War I when oil was found in the western foothills of the Zagros Mountains in southwestern Iran. Oil and gas seeps were known here in Antiquity. The first unsuccessful holes were drilled in 1884 and the first oil was struck in 1908 near Masjid-i-Sulaiman by the Anglo-Persian Oil Company in which the British Government was a major stockholder. By 1913 roads and pipelines had been constructed to this inaccessible area from Abadan on the Shatt al Arab, where a refinery was completed in the same year. In the closing years of World War II this refinery was enlarged from a capacity of 12 million tons a year to 25 million tons and thus became the world's largest.[1]

Production in the Iranian fields increased steadily until 1951 when the Iranian Government canceled the concession of the Anglo-Iranian Oil Company, later known as the British Petroleum Company, and expropriated its holdings. For several years the oil facilities were almost idle but an agreement in 1954 provided for two international companies, one for oil production and the other for the Abadan refinery, to take over operations. The two consortia, controlled by seventeen companies in four countries, are incorporated in the Netherlands and 40 per cent of their capital is American.

In the 1950s the Agha Jari field was by far the leading producer followed by Haft Kel. With the opening in 1960 of the new oil terminal on Kharg Island will follow a substantial expansion of production at Gach Saran. Ex-

[1] Alexander Melamid, "The Geographical Pattern of Iranian Oil Development", *Economic Geography*, 1959. Pp. 199–218.

ploitation and discovery on the east coast of the Persian Gulf and offshore have further emphasized the southward shift of the Iranian oil activity. The fields of southeastern Iran and other Persian Gulf areas are notable for their large production per well. Such yields are almost unknown in other parts of the world and are made possible by the very large reserves and the unified control of each field which allows the optimum spacing of wells. A new large oil reservoir was discovered in 1957 at Qum Alborz south of Tehran. Large-scale production from this purely Iranian development must await the construction of a pipeline.

A large part of the Iranian oil is refined at Abadan which in recent years has been listed with a lower capacity than before the 1951 oil conflict but still is the world's second largest refinery (after Aruba). However most of Iran's oil is shipped as crude from Bandar Mashur or from the new oil terminal at Kharg Island. The port of Bandar Mashur, which can handle 40,000-ton tankers but not the largest supertankers, was opened in 1948 for the sole purpose of delivering Agha Jari crude oil received by gravity-flow pipeline. Iran's answer to the latest increase in tanker size was the expansion of production in the Gach Saran field, and the construction of a 35-kilometer submarine pipeline to a pier on Kharg Island where 100,000-ton tankers can load.

Access to Abadan is limited by sand bars in the Shatt al Arab to ships of up to 30 foot

PERSIAN GULF OIL FIELDS

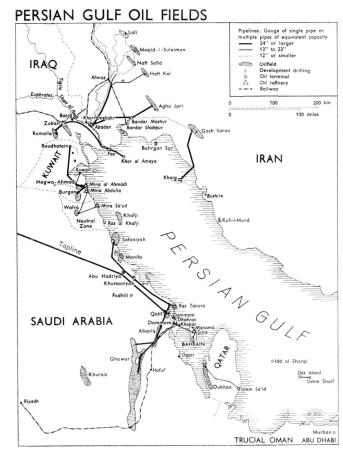

The crude petroleum pipelines are those existing or under construction in 1962.

draft; supertankers cannot enter the river. Abadan is now a city of probably 275,000 people, entirely dependent on its refinery. It can only handle oil but 18 kilometers upstream is the old port of Khorramshahr, Iran's leading foreign trade outlet. A modern port was built here in 1943 to handle American lend-lease to the Soviet Union. The small size of the port and town of Khorramshahr is an indication of Iran's restricted overseas trade. In the 1930s a new dry cargo port was built at Bandar Shahpur, intended as the Persian Gulf terminal of the Trans-Iranian Railroad, completed in 1938. When a branch line was constructed to Khorramshahr during the war the Trans-Iranian Railroad had two terminals which now have approximately the same cargo turnover.[2]

In 1962 the U.S. Government gave high priority to a foreign aid plan for developing in three years new facilities at the old port of Bandar Abbas in eastern Iran to expand the present insignificant cargo capacity to 500,000 tons a year. A highway will be built to Kerman and Zahedan and continued to Kabul so that the new port can also serve landlocked Afghanistan which has twice in recent years been politically isolated from its traditional sea outlet through Karachi.[3]

Iran's total foreign trade excluding petroleum exports only amounts to between one and two million tons, the greater part of which is imports. Imported sugar and steel products are the dominating cargoes. In addition to the two rail terminals at the head of the Persian Gulf, Iran has only half a dozen small general ports, often mere roadsteads, on its long coast. An arc of mountains runs through the western and southern parts of the country, enclosing the "dead heart" of Iran, the arid and sparsely populated high plateau, where very little traffic is generated. In addition to the Trans-Iranian Railroad only half a dozen roads cross the mountains; no highway parallels the coast. Bushire, the port of Shiraz,

is old and quite small. Iran's trade with the Soviet Union, its northern neighbor, only amounts to a few per cent of its total foreign trade. It is handled by two or three small ports on the Caspian Sea and by railroad. Bandar Shah, chosen by Riza Shah as the northern terminal of the Trans-Iranian Railroad, was extremely badly sited, and has been greatly affected by the shrinkage of the Caspian Sea. It was even less successful than the southern terminal at Bandar Shahpur, which has remained a rather small port and town. The harbor of Bandar Shah was silted up within one year of the opening of the railroad. After a temporary reopening during the war, the port is now abandoned.[4] Pahlevi is the chief Iranian port on the Caspian Sea.

Iraq

Oil concessions in modern Iraq date from the end of last century but the initial well in the rich Kirkuk field, 225 kilometers north of Baghdad, was drilled in 1927 and large-scale production did not start until 1934, having to await the completion of two 12-inch pipelines to the Mediterranean ports of Haifa and Tripoli.[1] After the war 16-inch lines were laid out parallel to these two lines but the second line to Haifa was only completed to the Israeli border owing to the Arab-Israeli conflict and the 12-inch line was closed down. The large Shell refinery at Haifa was thus cut off from its crude supply and has for many years operated at only a fraction of its capacity. A fifth pipeline from the Kirkuk field, 30/32 inches in diameter, was completed in 1952. It

[2] During World War II the Iranian railroad was operated by the Soviets and the British, the latter being replaced by the Americans. New lines were laid to connect the Trans-Iranian Railroad both to Khorramshahr and to Basra. The line to Basra was later abandoned.
[3] *The New York Times*, June 20, 1962.
[4] W. B. Fisher, *The Middle East*. London, 1956.
[1] Oil concessions in Iraq are owned jointly by British, French, American and Dutch interests.

follows the other two active lines almost to the coast but has its terminal at Banias, Syria.

In the postwar period two large oilfields came into operation at Zubair (1949) and Rumaila (1953), southwest of Basra. Oil from the Basra area is shipped from Fao on the lower Shatt al Arab and from a new deepwater terminal for supertankers about twenty kilometers offshore, Khor al Amaya.

Oil production in Iraq long increased as fast as pipeline capacity was made available. By 1962 the pipelines to the Mediterranean, after improvements, should have a capacity of 48 million tons a year and those in the Basra area 22 million tons.[2] However, actual production, which was 49 million tons in 1961, failed to increase in 1962 due to political unrest.

Almost all of Iraq's dry cargo trade is handled at Basra on the Shatt al Arab, 120 kilometers upstream from the Persian Gulf, at the head of navigation for ocean-going vessels. Basra was an important commercial center on the great trade routes between Europe and India by way of the Persian Gulf, trade routes that antedate the town of Basra founded in A.D. 636. Its modern port was begun during World War I by the British in the Mesopotamia campaign. The British also built a railroad to Baghdad, the largest city and the economic and political capital of Iraq. During World War II, when Basra handled large quantities of oil and military supplies for transshipment to the Soviet Union, the port and the railroads were improved, but the Basra–Baghdad line is still of meter gauge whereas the line from Baghdad through Mosul to the Syrian border, completed in 1940, is of standard gauge.[3]

[2] George B. Cressey, *Crossroads, Land and Life in Southwest Asia.* Chicago, 1960. P. 215.

[3] This railroad continues to Aleppo, Ankara, and Istanbul. A short section north from Baghdad was built before World War I by German engineers as part of the projected Berlin–Baghdad Railroad which was to have an ocean terminal at Kuwait. Pierre Birot and Jean Dresch, *La Méditerranée et le Moyen-Orient.* Tome second. Paris 1956. P. 336.

[1] Cressey, *op. cit.* Pp. 215–216.

Iraq's total foreign trade, other than petroleum and petroleum products, is usually less than one million tons a year, chiefly imports of sugar and steel products and exports of dates and barley, each group accounting for about 200,000 tons. Dates are the characteristic product of Iraq. Primarily a tree of the hot deserts, date palms are also typical of riverine areas in the desert regions. The heaviest yields of dates are obtained under irrigation. In the world's chief date-growing region on the banks of the Shatt al Arab the date groves are irrigated by the tide of the estuary. Iraq furnishes about three-quarters of the world trade in dates, which because of the high sugar content and good keeping qualities are an ideal staple food for the nomadic and semi-nomadic peoples around the Persian Gulf. However, barley in some years exceeds dates both in value and volume of exports.

In addition to the Basra gateway, providing a roundabout route for the dominating trade with Europe, Iraq has truck connections with the Mediterranean by way of a paved highway, which for a long stretch follows the pipeline to Haifa and ends at Beirut. Because of the long overland haul this route is used only for rather small quantities of high-value products.

Kuwait

The extraordinary petroleum developments in this small desert sheikdom are a postwar phenomenon. A concession was granted jointly to the British Anglo-Iranian Oil Company and the American Gulf Oil Company in 1934. The Burgan field was discovered in 1937 but the first shipments were made after the war in 1946. In addition to the fabulous Burgan field, probably the world's richest single oil reservoir, there are other fields at Magwa and Ahmadi north of Burgan and at Raudhatain in northern Kuwait.[1] The pipelines from these fields converge on Mina al Ahmadi, which is now the world's leading oil shipping port. Thirteen tankers can load simultaneously at the two piers which handle all of Kuwait's crude exports and can accomodate the largest tankers afloat. Depths range up to sixty feet. During the construction period seven sea-loading berths were in use. A large refinery at Mina al Ahmadi produces chiefly bunker oil for the tankers.[2] The other oil port in Kuwait, Mina Abdulla, serves the oilfield in the Neutral Zone.

About half of the Sheikdom's 200,000 inhabitants live in the city of Kuwait. Its good harbor has long been a transshipment point for goods from smaller ports on the Persian Gulf. It used to be known as a center of shipbuilding and pearl fishing. Many of the larger *dhows* and pearling craft of the Gulf were built there, from teak imported from Burma. Most of the trade until recently was with India.[3] In 1760 a German traveler noted that Kuwait had a fleet of 800 vessels operating as far as India and Africa. Fresh water used to be brought by barges from the mouth of the Shatt al Arab but now Kuwait City and

the oilfield towns get their water from large distillation plants in which natural gas is used to desalt sea water.

Almost all of Kuwait's foreign trade other than petroleum is handled at the capital port, primarily at the new four-berth Shuwaikh port opened in 1959. Statistics on the foreign trade of Kuwait are not available, but an estimate based on returns from Kuwait's trade partners indicates that Kuwait has a total foreign trade larger than that of Spain. Imports from all leading trade partners have increased rapidly in recent years. The tremendous oil revenues give Kuwait a per capita income on a par with that of the United States. They have allowed imports of a variety of manufactured goods as well as food. In addition, the oil companies bring in equipment for the oilfields and oil terminals. In 1959 the United States, the

[2] No less than 76.1 million tons of crude oil and products were loaded by 2,766 tankers at Mina al Ahmadi in 1960. The average cargo lifted increased from 15,000 tons in 1949 to 27,500 tons in 1960. The average time for turn around went down from 40 hours 49 minutes in 1949 to 24 hours 49 minutes in 1960. About 3.1 million tons of bunker oil were delivered to 2,766 ships.

[3] W. B. Fisher, *The Middle East*. London, 1956. Pp. 447–448.

The 108,000-ton tanker *Universe Daphne* at the North Pier, Mina al Ahmadi. At the opposite berth is the 28,000-ton *Eskfield*. (Kuwait Oil Company, March 31, 1961)

The South Pier and the oil refinery at Mina al Ahmadi, Kuwait. (Kuwait Oil Company, September, 1960)

Tankers loading at Mina al Ahmadi's South Pier. (Kuwait Oil Company)

United Kingdom, Japan and Germany were the leading suppliers of Kuwait's imports.[4]

THE NEUTRAL ZONE. In the Neutral Zone between Kuwait and Saudi Arabia, where petroleum was discovered in 1953, oil rights are held by two separate American concessionaires, representing a large number of companies which had not earlier operated in the international field. One got its concession from Kuwait, the other from Saudi Arabia. Oil from the rich Wafra field is shipped from Mina Abdulla in Kuwait and Mina Sa'ud in the Neutral Zone. Both oil terminals have medium-sized refineries. Oilfield operations are carried out jointly by the two companies but they have separate terminals and refineries.

In 1958 Japanese interests (Arabian Oil Co.) obtained offshore rights off the coast of the Neutral Zone and they seem to have found a major field at Khafji. The first shipments have been made from temporary installations. An eight million ton output is planned for 1963 and loading facilities are being constructed onshore at Ras al Khafji.

Saudi Arabia

Oil developments in Saudi Arabia got under way in the 1930s, but large-scale production belongs to the postwar period. All operations are in the hands of American interests. Four large American companies, Standard Oil of California, Texaco, Standard Oil of New Jersey and the Socony Mobil Oil, control the Arabian American Oil Company (Aramco), which holds all oil concessions in the country. The Dammam field, producing since 1938, was soon followed by a much larger field at Abqaiq (1940), the Qatif field (1945) and after 1948, by the giant Ghawar field, one of the most extensive fields in the world and one of the largest producers in the Middle East. In 1951 oil was also found offshore at Safaniya.

The tremendous oil developments have made a great impact on economic life in the Kingdom of Saudi Arabia, a gigantic country by area, but a small one by population. The effects have been especially noticeable in the Persian Gulf province of Hasa where all oilfields so far known are located. After 1938 Aramco built a modern company town for its Arabian headquarters at Dhahran, center of the first oilfield. Dhahran, with its supermarket, golf course and movie theater and its typical American homes surrounded by flowers and green lawns, along tree-lined residential streets, is "a bit of America dropped down in the desert".[1] Dhahran's airport is one of the major hubs in the Middle East. About ten commercial airlines call at Dhahran and Aramco's planes fly between here and the company's New York headquarters.

The barren costal plain of Hasa was almost uninhabited before the exploitation of Saudi Arabia's oil resources. The coast is shallow and ships cannot come closer to the shore than several kilometers. A most unusual deepwater general cargo port was constructed some 10 kilometers to the north of Dhahran at the ancient seaport of Dammam, starting in 1948. An eight kilometer rock fill causeway joins a three kilometer steel trestle. At the junction of the causeway and the trestle is a small-craft pier built to accomodate the local *dhows*. The steel trestle leads to a 225-meter two-berth pier. An unusual feature of the pier is the 18-meter cargo handling tower extending over the greater length of the pier. Each tackle on the tower can lift ten tons and the tower helps to speed up the transfer of cargo between ship and railroad car. This port became the sea terminal of the railroad to Hofuf and Riyadh, completed in 1951. Four additional general cargo berths were provided with the completion in 1961 of the new Abdul Aziz port at

[4] The United Kingdom, the United States, France, the Netherlands, Japan and Italy in 1959 received each in excess of 100 million U.S. dollars worth of Kuwaiti exports.

[1] Cressey, *Crossroads, op. cit.* P. 324.

Dammam. To accomodate traffic by rail and truck a long causeway has also been built to this port. The pier is equipped with eight electric portal cranes and provided with offices for port and customs authorities. The cargo turnover at the Dammam ports in the two years before July 1962 averaged 385,000 tons.[2] Dammam supplanted the small port of Oqair, a poor harbor that used to handle the traffic for the interior of Arabia via Hofuf and Riyadh.[3] A third new city, only a few kilometers from Dhahran is Khobar, which is rapidly becoming the commercial center for the Saudi Persian Gulf coast. The three towns of Dhahran, Dammam and Khobar taken together have a population exceeding 50,000.

Oil from the Saudi Arabian fields has three outlets, one domestic and two foreign. Ras Tanura has a large refinery and loading facilities for crude oil. A pipeline also leads to the large refinery and the crude loading facilties on nearby Bahrain Island. Through the longest pipeline in the Middle East, the Trans-Arabian Pipeline or the Tapline, completed in 1950, crude oil is pumped 1,200 kilometers from the Abqaiq field to offshore loading facilities at Sidon, Lebanon. This 30/31 inch line has a capacity in excess of 22 million tons a year.

The impact of the large oil revenues is also obvious in Riyadh, the capital of Saudi Arabia, where large buildings in modern western style are in striking contrast to the traditional Arabic architecture. Also Jidda on the Red Sea, the traditional sea gateway and now also the air gateway to Mecca, shares in the prosperity brought by the oil developments. Jidda is western Saudi Arabia's point of contact with the world. The Ministry of Foreign Affairs as well as all foreign legations are located in the city; the other ministries are in Riyadh.

[2] Data on the Dammam ports kindly provided by Mr. A. Alquraishi, General Manager, Saudi Government Railroad.
[3] Fisher, *The Middle East, op. cit.* P. 447.
[4] Birot and Dresch, *op. cit.* P. 427.

Modern piers for deep-sea vessels as well as a large airport have been constructed at Jidda, which has long been the economic capital of Saudi Arabia, handling over 90 per cent of the international pilgrim traffic. Before the tremendous increase in oil revenues the pilgrims supplied the greater part of Saudi Arabia's income. The special pilgrim tax was discontinued in 1952, but pilgrimage is still an important source of income for Saudi Arabia. Most of the population of Jidda and Mecca were recruited from the pilgrims, making these cities cosmopolitan in character. The majority of merchants and entrepreneurs are non-Arab in origin. Pilgrimage used to be associated with commercial operations and in the eighteenth century Mecca was the leading world market for coffee, which came from Asir and the Yemen, but this economic function is now on the decline.[4]

With improved transportation the number of pilgrims increases. Already before the First World War 60–80 thousand pilgrims arrived by sea, especially from Java. Of Mecca's half a million pilgrims in 1953 about 118,000 arrived by sea and 17,000 by air. No railroad exists in western Arabia; the Arabian part of the Pilgrim Railroad from Damascus to Medina has not been used since World War I but will now be rebuilt. Paved roads extend from Jidda to Mecca as well as north to Medina and its insignificant seaport, Yenbo.

Bahrain

The British-protected Sheikdom of Bahrain, after Iran and Iraq, is the oldest oil producer among countries bordering the Persian Gulf. After British interests were unsuccessful in the search for oil, an American company took over the concessions and found oil in 1932. Bahrain was the first area in the then largely British-dominated Persian Gulf region where American oil interests gained a foothold.

The oilfield in the center of Bahrain is

linked by pipeline with a large refinery near the island's northeastern shore and with a loading terminal on Sitra Island. However, the refinery and the loading terminal of Bahrain primarily serve as an outlet for Saudi Arabian oil. Bahrain's own reserves appear to be modest and production has remained rather small. In 1937 the one-million-ton level was exceeded and in 1958 production was greater than two million tons.

Bahrain has for centuries been one of the economically most active areas of the Persian Gulf. The outlying areas, especially in the north, are irrigated from artesian wells and covered by date groves.[1] Also citrus fruit, cereals, alfalfa and vegetables are grown. The artesian wells are characteristic of Bahrain but also occur in many parts of Hasa. There are even springs of drinking water on the sea bed. Bahrain has long been a center of pearl fishing, an industry which has declined greatly, partly due to competition from Japanese cultured pearls. It also is an important fishing center.

The principal dry cargo port is Manama, the capital of Bahrain, which like Kuwait has an important entrepôt trade. The new deep-sea facilities of Mina Sulman in the port of Manama provide free port storage.

QATAR. The Sheikdom of Qatar, like Bahrain and the many tiny sheikdoms along the Trucial Coast, is under British protection. In 1935 oil concessions were granted to the same interests that operate the oilfields in Iraq. Oil was found in 1939 in the Dukhan field near the west coast of the peninsula, probably the world's most desolate oil area. Production did not begin until 1949, but it increased rapidly and in 1958 exceeded eight million tons, four times as much as Bahrain's output. A pipeline runs across the peninsula to the terminal at Umm Sa'id.

TRUCIAL OMAN. The barren coast from the base of the Qatar Peninsula to Ras Musandum used

to be known as the Pirate Coast. It consists of seven trucial sheikdoms bound by treaties concluded with Great Britain in 1820, after a British expedition had ended the power of the pirates. Trucial Oman has no political unity and most internal and external boundaries are undefined, which has led to conflicts after oil exploration was begun in 1950.

Oil has been found in the Abu Dhabi Sheikdom, both offshore in the Umm Shaif field and onshore in the Murban field. The offshore reservoirs are connected by submarine pipeline with loading facilities on the small Das Island, where a town for a couple of thousand people has been built. Shipments started in 1962. The onshore field is scheduled to start production in 1964. It is expected that Abu Dhabi's oil production will exceed that of Qatar.

MUSCAT AND OMAN. The Sultanate of Muscat and Oman in southeast Arabia borders the Gulf of Oman and the Arabian Sea between Trucial Oman and the Aden Protectorate. The tip of the Oman Promontory is an exclave of the Sultanate. Because of its desert-backed location Muscat has primarily maritime interests, trading chiefly with India and Iraq. Most of the area is barren but there are a few oases. Muscat's small exports (dates, camels, fruit and dried fish) pass through the capital of Muscat and its commercial twin-town, Matrah, which is now the larger port. Matrah is a port of call for mail steamers between Bombay and Basra and the starting point for caravan routes into the interior.

Aden

Aden consists of two distinct parts—Aden Colony and Aden Protectorate. The latter comprises a group of independent Arab petty states in protective treaty relations with Great Britain. The chief port is Mukalla. Although

---

[1] Fisher, *The Middle East, op. cit.* Pp. 445 ff.

Oil terminal, tank farms and oil refinery at Little Aden. (Public Relations and Information Department, Aden)

Part of Aden Harbour with Tawahi Town in the foreground. The harbor has eighteen first class berths, the deepest permitting vessels drawing up to thirty-seven feet. The berthing system is based on the use of mooring buoys, which is particularly suitable for a port which needs only limited cargo handling facilities. At the oiling berths, the floating ends of submarine pipelines, oil can be pumped into a ship at an average rate of 400–500 tons an hour, which means that the normal stay of a ship taking 2,000 tons of bunkers seldom exceeds five hours. (Public Relations and Information Department, Aden)

Ships calling at Aden in 1961

	Number	Net Tonnage
Merchant vessels	5,942	28,167,000
Dhows	1,441	130,000

Data supplied by Public Relations and Information Department, Aden.

small, it is second only to Aden on the south coast of the Arabian Peninsula. Aden Colony comprises a small area around the city of Aden. Also included are some islands, among which Perim in the Bab el Mandeb was until 1936 the site of a coaling station.

Aden has been an important center of trade since ancient times. It flourished on the Europe–Asia trade route and was reported by Marco Polo to have a population of 80,000. The opening of the Cape of Good Hope route marked the beginning of its decline. Aden became a base for pirates, including Americans, and it was partly for this reason that Britain took possession in 1839. Aden then had only a few hundred inhabitants. The opening of the Suez Canal in 1869 and the revival of the Red Sea route, dominated by British trade, regained for the British port of Aden its old importance.[1] It has been a free port since 1850. Aden Colony in 1955 had 138,000 inhabitants, of which 106,000 were Arabs, 16,000 Indians, 11,000 Somalis, 4,400 Europeans and 800 Jews.[2] Of the estimated labor force 10 per cent are directly engaged in port activities.

Aden has two chief functions, both derived from its strategic location on one of the world's most important sea routes; to serve the passing ships with bunker and stores, and to serve as an entrepôt for large coastal areas of Asia and Africa. Transit trade with the Aden Protectorate and the Yemen amount to about 10 per cent of Aden's external trade. Both entrepôt and transit trade have been declining as a result of increased direct foreign trade by the other countries.

As a bunkering depot Aden claims to be first in the world. In 1954, three years after the Iranian Government had expropriated its refinery in Abadan, British Petroleum (B.P.) built a large refinery at Little Aden, across the bay from Aden harbor. It now has a capacity of six million tons a year. Other companies have petroleum depots in the port. In 1960 over four million tons of crude and almost two million tons of petroleum products were imported; over two million tons of petroleum products were exported and over three and a half million tons of bunker oil were sold to passing ships. By value petroleum and petroleum products accounted for one half of the imports and two-thirds of the exports. By weight petroleum had an even larger share— over 90 per cent of the tonnage handled in the port.

The entrepôt trade comprises a wide range of products, grains, cotton, fabrics, sugar and miscellaneous manufactured articles.

Salt, obtained from sea water through solar evaporation, is the only major product originating in Aden. Some 200,000 tons a year are shipped, chiefly to Japan. The former main customer, India, now produces nearly all the salt she needs and production in Aden has been declining.

The Yemen

The Yemen is the most humid country in Arabia; it has the highest population density and the richest agricultural resources but its mineral wealth is still largely unknown. It has

[1] A rapid increase in the number of ships calling at the port came in the early 1880s. Until then sailing vessels making the longer voyage around the Cape offered lower freight rates than steamers. The introduction in the 1880s of the economic triple-expansion steam engine changed this situation in favor of the steamers. R. Gavin, "The Port of Aden 1839–1959", *Port of Aden Annual*, 1961–1962. P. 36.
[2] *Aden 1957 and 1958*. Her Majesty's Stationery Office. London, 1961. P. 8.

remained one of the most isolated countries in the world in spite of its location close to one of the major sea routes.

Hodeida on the Red Sea has been the Yemen's chief port since the middle of last century. It supplanted Mocha that flourished in the Middle Ages as the export center of coffee from southern Arabia. Foreign consular and steamship offices are located in Hodeida. In 1961 a modern port was completed for this town, built by Soviet engineers under the Soviet Union's technical assistance program.

The port was named Ahmadi in honor of the Imam.[3] Before the new port was built, ships calling at Hodeida had to anchor off the coast as in many other small Arabian ports. Goods were transferred in small boats or by men carrying the cargo on their shoulders. For the new port a deep channel was dredged, a breakwater and a number of piers with modern loading cranes, warehouses and oil storage tanks were built. The capacity of the Ahmadi port has not been revealed; in 1960 more than 60,000 tons were unloaded there.

The Indian Subcontinent

The Indian Peninsula during the British era witnessed a notable concentration of trade to a few large ports. Economies usually associated with large undertakings and the increasing size of vessels favored a concentration, strengthened by the focusing effect of railways and by special freight rates quoted by railway companies with terminals at major ports. It is clear from the early records that rail transport was planned and geared essentially to meet the requirements of the ports,[1] so that the main lines converged on the three great port cities, Bombay, Calcutta and Madras. Bombay and Calcutta, competing for supremacy among Indian cities and ports, between them handle no less than 75 per cent of India's tonnage of foreign trade, and Cochin and Madras the bulk of the remainder.

The partition of India in 1947 has led to some adjustments of hinterlands and duplications of port facilities. This is especially true in the Ganges Delta where a national boundary was inserted between the jute producing areas of East Bengal and their customary outlet at Calcutta. After partition the Pakistan Government has made great efforts to develop Chittagong as one of the major ports of the east. A new port has been opened at Chalna on the Pussur River in East Pakistan. Meanwhile Calcutta has at times been congested due to the diversion of Assam tea exports from Chittagong.

In the west cotton shipments from Karachi to Bombay were reclassified as foreign trade and Karachi became the great entrepôt for Pakistan. It lost a considerable part of its hinterland in East Punjab. To serve this area and thereby relieve congestion at Bombay the West Coast Major Port Development Committee recommended to the Government of India that a major port should be built at Kandla. It will have an ultimate annual capacity of 3 million tons a year.

Bombay

Bombay is the leading port of India. Greater Bombay has an estimated 4.5 million in-

---

[3] *The New York Times,* March 27, 1961; *Pravda,* March 25 and April 12, 1961.

[1] William Kirk, "The Cotton and Jute Industries of India", *The Scottish Geographical Magazine,* 1956. Pp. 38 ff.

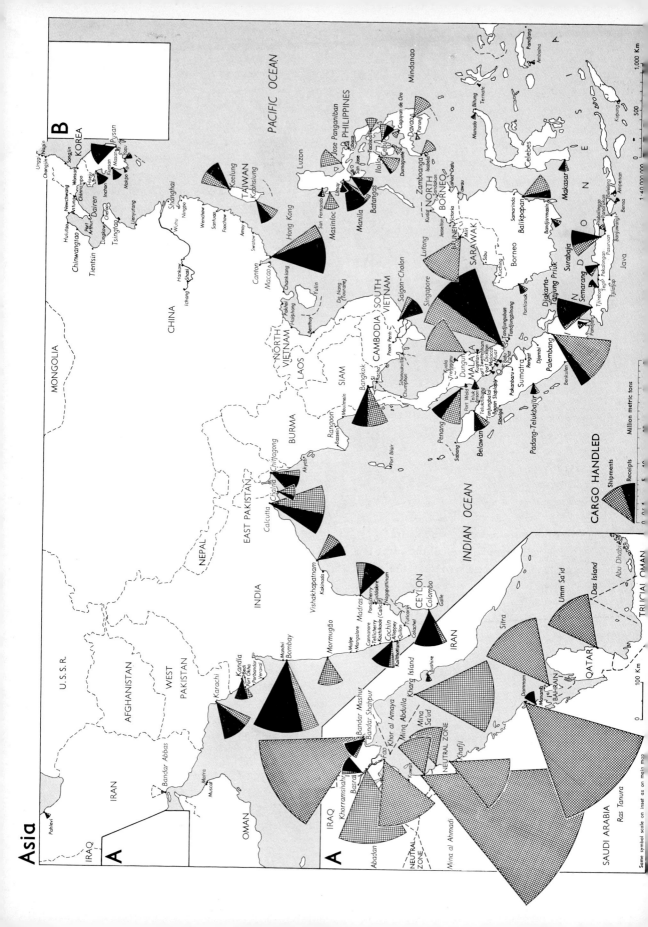

Asia

apan Total Cargo Turnover

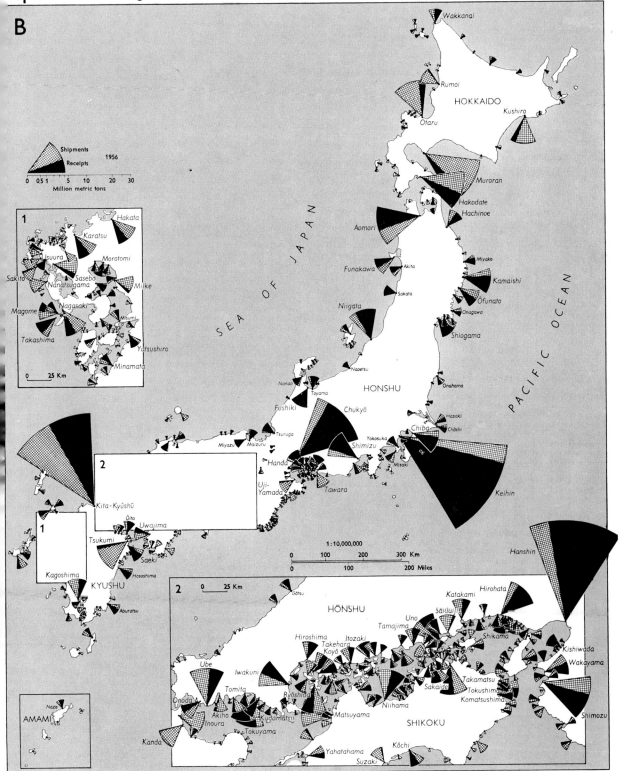

B

Shipments
Receipts 1956
0 0.5 1 5 10 20 30
Million metric tons

HOKKAIDO Wakkanai, Rumoi, Otaru, Kushiro, Muroran, Hakodate, Hachinoe

1 Hakata, Karatsu, Isuura, Morotomi, Sakito, Sasebo, Nanatsugama, Miike, Nagasaki, Magome, Misumi, Takashima, Yatsushiro, Minamata
0 25 Km

SEA OF JAPAN

PACIFIC OCEAN

Aomori, Funakawa, Akita, Sakata, Niigata, Miyako, Kamaishi, Ōfunato, Onagawa, Shiogama, Naoetsu, Onahama, Nanao, Toyama, Fushiki, Chukyō, Chiba, Hasaki, Chōshi, Tsuruga, Yokosuka, Shimizu, Miyazu, Maizuru, Handa, Misaki, Uji-Yamada, Tawara, Keihin

HONSHU

2 Kita-Kyūshū, Ōita, Uwajima, Tsukumi, Saeki, Hososhima, Aburatsu

1 Kagoshima

KYUSHU

Hanshin

1:10,000,000
0 100 200 300 Km
0 100 200 Miles

2 Gōtsu, Katakami, Hirohata, Saiduji, Uno, Tamajima, Shikama, Hiroshima, Itozaki, Takehara, Koyō, Kishiwada, Ube, Iwakuni, Tomita, Ryōshida, Takamatsu, Wakayama, Onoda, Akiho, Kudamatsu, Sakaide, Tokushima, Inoura, Tokuyama, Niihama, Komatsushima, Matsuyama, Shimozu, Kanda, Yahatahama, Kōchi, Suzaki
HONSHU **SHIKOKU**
0 25 Km

AMAMI Naze

Keihin Port Complex includes Tokyo, Yokohama and Kawasaki; Chukyo Port Complex includes Nagoya, Yokosuka, Yokkaichi, Kuwana, Tomisuhara; Hanshin Port Complex includes Osaka, Sakai, Kobe, Amagasaki, Nishinomiya, Naruo; and Kita-Kyushu Port Complex includes Shimonoseki, Moji, Kokura, Wakamatsu, Yahata and Tobata. Data assembled by Mr. Ryoji Moriwaki, Sendai.

habitants and its port now surpasses that of Calcutta. It handles more than one-third of India's foreign trade. The rise of Bombay is connected with British rule in India. The seven lava islets which are now joined to form Bombay Island were held by the Portuguese but they made little use of them. After Bombay had been ceded to England in 1661 it soon supplanted Surat as the chief English base on the west coast and for more than two and a half centuries this magnificent natural harbor has been the leading port on the Indian coast that faces Europe. This location became of great importance after the introduction of steamer services and especially after the opening of the Suez Canal. Steamer service via Suez for home mails and passengers put Bombay within 30 days of London by 1843.[1] Bombay rapidly developed into an Indian gateway to Europe. An improved road through the Western Ghats to Poona was opened in 1830 followed by a railroad in the early 1860s. Bombay soon developed good railroad connections with all parts of India.

The blockade of the South in the American Civil War led to a spectacular cotton boom followed by a catastrophic collapse in 1865. But meanwhile a modern textile industry had taken root. The first cotton mill in Bombay was constructed in 1854 and by 1885 there were almost 50 textile factories with over 30,000 workers. In cotton, India's leading manufacturing industry, Bombay Province is supreme with the largest concentration of looms and spindles in Bombay and Ahmedabad.[2] The Parsees occupy a key position in Bombay's economic development. Two-thirds of this small population group live in the city,[3] making up a minority of less than 100,000. The great Parsee house of Tata has had some share in almost all modern economic developments in India.

Bombay's port installations are on the east side of the island. Much of the foreign trade is handled in three wet docks, Prince's Dock

(1880), Victoria Dock (1888) and Alexandra Dock (1914), which provide 40 berths. There are also several deepwater open berths on the outer side of the docks. One of these, the Ballard Pier at the entrance lock of the Alexandra Dock, accomodates the large mail and passenger liners. For the two oil refineries recently built at Bombay a new marine oil terminal has been constructed at Butcher Island in the harbor. The large coastal traffic, primarily carried by a fleet of sailing vessels, is handled at the open wharves and basins along the harbor front, the *bunders*. The extensive timber ponds at Sewri covering over 60 acres form an important part of the *bunders*.

In the year ending March 31, 1961, 6.7 million tons of cargo were handled at the docks and 8.0 million tons at the *bunders*. Petroleum accounted for about half of both receipts and shipments. Almost five million tons of crude oil was received for the two refineries. Wheat was the only other commodity accounting for more than 10 per cent of total receipts. Construction materials, steel, machinery, rice, chemicals, cotton, and fertilizers each accounted for 2–6 per cent of the diversified receipts. Manganese ore, other ore and oil cake topped the list of shipments after the dominating petroleum products.

The cargo turnover of the port of Bombay has been detailed at some length to show that cotton, which has played a key role in the economic development of the city and the province, is not directly responsible for much cargo traffic. In 1961 about 241,000 tons of raw cotton were received (chiefly from West Pakistan) and 58,000 tons were shipped.

Calcutta

Among the factories founded in Bengal by early European traders (Portuguese, Dutch,

[1] O. H. K. Spate, *India and Pakistan*. 2nd ed., London, 1957. Pp. 611 ff.
[2] Kirk, *op. cit.*
[3] L. Dudley Stamp, *Asia*. 9th ed., London, 1957.

British, Danish, French and Austrian), who were buying fine textiles for the European markets from the flourishing Mogul cities on the Ganges Plain, the British settlement of Calcutta on the Hooghly River, established in the 1690s, was going to dwarf all others. The site of Calcutta, an unhealthy swamp, had little to recommend it and the river channel, one of the most capricious in the world, was difficult and dangerous in sailing days and today is made costly by constant dredging, maintenance and pilotage. Nonetheless Calcutta was the British capital of India from 1773 until 1912. In the hot season most government departments moved to Simla, 1,750 kilometers away.

In the nineteenth century Calcutta outstripped Madras and became the leading port of India. It was a transshipment point between ocean and river vessels in the most densely populated agricultural region, producing such early staple exports as opium, tea and indigo. When the Crimean War blocked the hemp supplies to Dundee the Scots found a substitute in the jute of Bengal. The first jute factory was established in 1855, the year after the first cotton factory in Bombay, and now mills are strung out along the Hooghly 50 kilometers upriver and 25 kilometers downriver from Calcutta. The Hooghlyside jute industry from the beginning was dominated by Scots but now most of the capital is Indian. The Hooghly has been the main axis of industrial development rather than the city itself. Calcutta proper is more commercial and ad-

ministrative than industrial. The factories are directly accessible for lighterage to ocean vessels and they receive fuel and raw jute by rail or water. By 1921 a third of India's factory workers were in the tremendous Hooghlyside conurbation. With the expansion of manufacturing in other parts of India this ratio has declined but Hooghlyside is still the leading manufacturing district. Jute dominates, 94 mills out of 105 reported for India in 1949, employing about 300,000 workers. By 1910 Dundee itself was outstripped as a jute manufacturing center[1] and jute manufactures for a long time have been India's leading export. Before partition, British India had a world monopoly of jute growing and also of low-priced burlap production. Partition saw 80 per cent of the jute acreage in Pakistan but almost all the jute factories on Hooghlyside. The effects of partition have been to divert raw jute exports to the ports of Chalna and Chittagong, to create jute mills in East Pakistan and to increase jute acreages in India. Calcutta still retains world leadership in jute manufactures. The jute industry, in addition to the postwar political complications, for decades has been plagued by the switch to bulk transport (wheat, sugar) and to other materials (paper sacks) which has narrowed the market.

The Hooghly is navigable to Calcutta for ocean vessels of 25 foot draft. Incoming ships used to discharge into lighters at the mooring buoys in the river or berth at the floating wharves near the central business district, but now both imports and exports are handled primarily in the large wet docks, five kilometers downstream, shut off from the river's tidal bores of 9 to 15 feet.[2] All ocean vessels are worked along the left bank of the river.[3] On the right bank, in the suburb Howrah opposite Calcutta, are coal jetties at which river vessels load rail transported coal from the Damodar coal field for the many factories on Hooghlyside. Besides raw jute, received chiefly from East Bengal up the river through

[1] The average jute factory on Hooghlyside is single-storied, almost three times as large as that in Dundee where multi-storied units on cramped urban sites are common. The banks of the Hooghly have provided ample space.

[2] Port improvement plans include the deepening of the navigable channel and the probable construction of a new tidal port at Haldia, 100 km downstream on the right bank of the Hooghly, with good access to India's leading coal fields and the principal heavy manufacturing district. Calcutta Metropolitan Planning Organisation, *First Report 1962.*

[3] Norton Ginsburg, ed., *The Pattern of Asia.* Englewood Cliffs, 1958. P. 562.

the estuary, coal has been the most important raw material for India's largest industrial district. North of the coal jetties in Howrah is the rail terminal of three main railroads from the Ganges Plain, central India and south India. The first of these lines was built already in the 1850s. Another railroad connects Calcutta with Darjeeling and Assam. It carries the bulk of India's tea exports.

Madras and Cochin

Madras, the third city of India, in contrast to Cochin does not have an advantageous site.[1] It is a matter of historic chance that Madras was chosen by the British as their chief trading station on the east coast of India, making it today a much larger city than the French Pondicherry further down the coast. The center of British power in India was moved to Calcutta in 1773, only 16 years after Plassey and the first important territorial acquisitions. Madras continued to grow as a commercial, cultural and administrative center and as a hub of communications for much of south India. Until the 1870s the port facilities were a jetty and a roadstead, from which passengers and goods were landed by surf-boats. The artificial harbor then built had an entrance facing east which was shifted to the northeast twenty years later to avoid shoaling. Today the port is too small with room for only twelve to fifteen large ships of which only seven can berth at the wharves. But large extensions are planned. Exports include peanuts, hides, raw and manufactured cotton; imports are miscellaneous as Madras is the large entrepôt for south India.

Cochin is the oldest European settlement in India (1500) but the development of a modern port was for long impeded by a curious political situation; the approaches and major port installations were in British territory, the inner harbor in the state of Cochin and much of the neighboring lagoon area in Travancore.

After a century of planning a 5-kilometer approach channel, 450 feet wide and 36 feet deep was dredged in the late 1920s so that the port is now accessible to any vessel that can pass Suez. Cargo turnover increased from 0.4 million tons a year in 1926 to 1.3 million in 1950.[2] As a port of call on the Far East and Australia routes the seaport of densely populated Kerala may rival Colombo; a call at Cochin adds only 40 miles to the Aden–Fremantle run.[3] Cochin is becoming a serious competitor of Madras as a port for south India.

Colombo

Nearly all the foreign trade of Ceylon passes through the port of Colombo, the dominating city. For several centuries Colombo was less important than Galle, which has a natural harbor with a treacherous entrance. The British, who captured the Dutch coastal possessions in the 1790s, annexed the whole island in 1815. They made Colombo the focus of their road and rail systems and the center of their investments. In 1885 an artificial harbor was completed. Colombo was equipped with coaling jetties and later with oil-fuel depots, a graving dock, etc., and became a port of call on the Far East and Australia runs; Galle was reduced to a commercial center of only local importance. The large oil powered cargo liners of today do not have to call at Colombo to refuel and the number of calls will depend on the availability of paying cargo. Most of Ceylon's foreign trade is made up of commodities transported as general cargo; its location near one of the great shipping lanes of the world is most fortunate both for its dominating ex-

[1] The small creek on which the fort was located could take the 50-ton ships of the 1630s (Madras was founded in 1639) but later in the same century the East Indiamen already ran up to 1,500 tons or more.
[2] Heinrich Gutersohn, "Malabar und der Hafen Cochin", *Geographica Helvetica*, 1952. Pp. 210 ff.
[3] Spate, *op. cit.* P. 637.

ports of tea, rubber and coconut products and for its miscellaneous imports. Like Belgium it can benefit from cheap sea transport of its foreign trade without possessing a national merchant marine of any importance.

Karachi

About one hundred years after the British conquest of Sind in the 1840s Karachi had been transformed from a mere local port of some 14,000 people to a million-city and the major port of South Asia west of Bombay. The first impetus to Karachi's export trade came when the American Civil War cut the South's cotton flow to Europe's textile districts. Steamer navigation on the Indus had just begun and the railroad tapping Indus traffic at Kotri opposite Hyderabad was completed in time for the postwar slump. The railroad was later extended to the Punjab. Karachi became a shipping port for agricultural products, especially cotton and wheat from the Punjab and Sind. The city itself is in a semidesert on a mangrove-fringed coast. Until World War II, when Karachi reached a population of 360,000, exports far exceeded imports, but this relationship changed when the city became the capital of a new country.[1] The influx of refugees from India swelled the population and in 1951 Karachi had more than a million inhabitants. Karachi is not only the port of West Pakistan and landlocked Afghanistan[2] but also an entre-

pôt for East Pakistan. It is a major airport in South Asia.

Other Ports in the Subcontinent

Mormugao in former Portuguese Goa, occupied by India in 1961, is the only modern deep-water port between Bombay and Cochin. It became a major iron ore port in the late 1950s.

Once flourishing ports on the Malabar Coast, such as Calicut, the first Indian port reached by Vasco da Gama in 1498, and Mangalore, now mainly have coastal traffic by small country craft. However, owing to its proximity to the plantations Mangalore handles most of India's coffee trade. The city is known throughout southern India for its tile works which have a large local market on this rain-swept coast and in addition supply markets from Karachi to Colombo and in East Africa by sailing vessels.

Vishakhapatnam was opened for ocean going vessels in 1933 with quays especially equipped to handle manganese ore. In 1949 a modern shipyard was located there.

CHITTAGONG, vigorously promoted by East Pakistan since partition, has an eccentric location as a national port. It was rather unimportant before the war, serving primarily as an outlet for the tea districts of Assam, for which it had a locational advantage over Calcutta. Four jetties were built at Chittagong in the two decades following 1890 by the Assam Bengal Railway. Cargo turnover has increased from 0.5 million tons at the time of partition to 1.5 million by 1956 and 2.9 million tons by 1962. Exports declined slightly between 1956 and 1962 from 0.54 to 0.44 million tons due to a decline in jute shipments. The imports of petroleum products, general cargo, cement and grain have all more than doubled between 1956 and 1962 and all account for larger quantities than the jute exports.[3]

---

[1] On August 2, 1960 an executive order proclaimed Rawalpindi as capital of Pakistan in place of Karachi which was in the future to be known as the Federal Territory of Karachi.

[2] An Afghan—Pakistani border dispute in 1955 led to a temporary stop in the Afghan transit trade through Karachi. This occurred again in August, 1961. The planned Iranian port of Bandar Abbas will serve as an alternative sea outlet for Afghanistan. However, much of Afghanistan's foreign trade moves across the land borders; about 70 per cent of her trade is with the Communist Bloc.

[3] *Yearbook of Information* 1962. Port of Chittagong, Pakistan. See also I. S. Maxwell, "The Development of the Ports of East Pakistan", *Geography*, 1957. Pp. 64–66.

Southeast Asia

Burma

The deltas of the three great rivers of the Indochinese peninsula, the Irrawaddy, Menam and Mekong, have had a similar importance for Monsoon Asia's rice-eating peoples as the prairie lands of North America, Argentina and Australia have had for the bread-eating Europeans. Contemporary with the plowing up of the prairie lands for wheat the deltas were adapted to extensive rice cultivation for export.[1] Burma in the beginning of last century was merely self-supporting in rice and the delta areas were covered with swamp forest. Pioneer farming on a large scale in the virgin swamps of Lower Burma (the deltas of the Irrawaddy, Sittang and Salween) began just before the middle of the century, later followed by similar developments in the deltas of the Menam and the Mekong. The migration of peasants from the Burmese heartland in the dry zone of the middle Irrawaddy with Mandalay as its cultural center reached a peak in the last two decades of the nineteenth century. Burma's close affiliation with India during British rule[2] led to an influx of permanent and seasonal Indian farm laborers, but also of traders, ricebrokers and moneylenders. Rangoon was said to be the largest immigration port in the world in the inter-war period. India was also the main market for the rice exports.

The average rice yield in Burma was about one-third of Japan's and about half of China's before World War II. But acreage of paddy land and tonnage of rice per farmer was high in Burma. Her rich delta lands have an extensive type of farming compared to the old and densely settled alluvial plains in Asia. Typical Burmese farms are eight to ten acres. Irrigation is unnecessary; the heavy rains in the delta supply the paddy water and the farmers face the problem of protecting their paddies against flooding from the rivers.

Burmese rice exports increased from 0.5 million tons in 1881 to 1.8 million in 1911 and 3.5 million in 1941. The postwar recovery of rice exports has been slow due to political instability and guerilla warfare. In 1960 they amounted to only 1.8 million metric tons. The rice is harvested in November–December. From mid-December to mid-January most of the crop moves from local collection points to milling centers in small country boats and barges or—on main streams—in river steamers. The Irrawaddy and its tributaries have always been the main highway of Burma;[3] in the delta region the network of waterways is dense. For Burma's position as one of the world's foremost low-cost rice producers this has been a great advantage.

The absence of sufficient storage space leads to a hurried post-harvest export which reaches a peak in March. About 70 per cent of the rice moves out through Rangoon and smaller quantities through Bassein, Akyab and Moulmein.

Teak is Burma's second great asset. It occurs over large areas and in the interwar period allowed a sustained annual yield of 450,000 tons of round logs. The industry requires careful planning. The logs are hauled by elephants to the waterside and floated downstream. Large teak rafts are assembled at several points along the rivers to be taken down to the chief commercial center, Rangoon, during the rainy season July–October. Most of

---

[1] E. H. G. Dobby, *Southeast Asia*. London, 1950. Pp. 172 ff.

[2] Burma was annexed piecemeal by the British in three Anglo-Burmese Wars, Lower Burma through the campaigns of 1824–26 and 1852 and Upper Burma in 1885. It was made a province of India in 1886 and in 1937 acquired a quasi-dominion status. In 1948 Burma became a sovereign republic, completely independent from Britain.

[3] The railways have supplemented the rivers rather than replaced them. Burma has no international rail connections.

the large sawmills are located at Rangoon and Moulmein.

Before the war three-quarters of the teak exports, 60 per cent of the rice, and almost all of the petroleum went to India. Burma was the great raw material supplier for the Indian subcontinent.

RANGOON developed to its present position as the capital of Burma and the world's greatest rice and teak port under British rule.[4] It was originally a fishing village. The city is located 30 kilometers from the coast at a point accessible by ocean-going vessels of 28-foot draft and connected by waterways, railroads and highways with the Irrawaddy and Sittang valleys. It even has a pipeline from the Yenang-yaung oil fields.[5]

Prewar Rangoon was a distinctly Indian city; more than half of its population was Indian and only one-third Burmese according to the 1941 census. It was the most westernized city in the country, the center for foreign financial interests. Rangoon handled over four-fifths of Burma's foreign trade and ranked next to Bombay and Calcutta among Asian ports on the Indian Ocean. Rice exports were rather stable at 2 million tons a year, petroleum at 800,000 tons, timber at 200,000 tons, bran at 200,000 tons and minerals at 170,000 tons. Passenger traffic to and from India totaled over half a million passengers annually.

The city of Rangoon and the commercialized agriculture in the delta areas suffered more from World War II than other parts of South-east Asia with the exception of Manila. In 1942 over 600,000 Indians trekked into Assam, an event of great impact on the postwar economic structure of Burma. Guerilla warfare by various insurgent groups has created a confused political situation in many parts of the country and caused an influx of refugees to Rangoon. The city now has an overwhelmingly Burmese population; Indians and Pakistanis probably make up one-fifth of the total.

The tremendous postwar increase in air travel has brought Rangoon in closer contact with the great cities of the world. It is off the great shipping routes but on the main air lane.

Thailand

Thailand in many ways resembles Burma. Both countries are centered on a single river system; in both rice and teak have long been leading export products; both are economically and politically dominated by a million city located near the coast on a wide delta plain which by and large has been settled in the last hundred years and therefore has a much lower density of population than other alluvial plains in Monsoon Asia. Both countries have former capital cities further upstream (Mandalay in Burma, Ayutthaya in Siam). But there are also great differences. Burma faces the Indian Ocean and has had much economic contact with India; Thailand faces the South China Sea and its economy is dominated by the Chinese. The Menam River system is not so navigable by steam launches as the Irrawaddy, which has meant a slower opening up of the Siamese interior. Thailand remained politically independent as a buffer state between French Indochina and British Malaya and Burma. This has meant that no colonial scholars have been working in Thailand, which is the least documented territory in Southeast Asia.

The delta plain of Lower Siam[1] is a one-

---

[4] O. H. K. Spate and L. W. Trueblood, "Rangoon: A Study in Urban Geography", *Geographical Review,* 1942. Pp. 56–73.

[5] The Yenangyaung petroleum has been known and worked in hand-dug wells for a couple of centuries and with modern methods since the 1880s. From 1909 to 1939 the annual production did not depart much from a million tons. The largest oil company sent the oil by pipeline; other companies used river barges. L. Dudley Stamp, *Asia.* London, 1957. P. 393.

[1] The chief river of Siam is conventionally referred to as the Menam. This word in Siamese means river

crop rice area. Precipitation is here too low for wet paddy and the rainfall deficiency is made up by floods from the rivers, whose spate is about a month after rains begin in the mountains to the north. The crop risks are very great as the flooding through the network of canals is uncontrollable. But a dam project at Yanhee on the Ping River 420 kilometers northwest of Bangkok, started in the late 1950s with financial support from the World Bank, is expected to reduce these risks. In addition to producing 560,000 kilowatts of electricity when completed it will help control floods and provide water for irrigation in the dry season.[2]

The area under paddy more than doubled between 1910 and 1950, rice production expanded from 1.9 million tons before the First World War to 7.8 million in 1960 and rice exports grew from 0.8 million tons to 1.2 million. No foreigners were brought in for the large-scale settlement of the Siamese delta land; the natural population increase has been unusually large for Southeast Asia outside Java. It has been so large that the exportable rice surplus has failed to keep pace with the increase in production.

The delta land is owned in large units and most of the export rice comes from estates farmed by migrating tenants. Tenancies are usually on a yearly basis and average 20 hectares. The rice moves through a complex middleman system, mostly run by Chinese, to the rice mills located along the major river channels near the one port, Bangkok. Most of the rice is exported to Singapore and Hong Kong. Ocean vessels of 27-foot draft may enter the new port of Klongtoi downstream from Bangkok and 20 kilometers from the sea. The Kohsichang anchorage outside the bar is little used after the completion of the channel through the bar. A new seaport is planned at Si Racha on the eastern side of the Bight of Bangkok to avoid the high dredging costs of the rapidly silting Menam delta.

Teak comes from the monsoon forests of northern Thailand. Before World War II over a million logs a year were cut by foreign firms and floated down to the coast. Three-quarters went by the Menam to Bangkok and small quantities by way of the Burmese rivers. Bangkok has many sawmills but some Siamese teak logs went to Singapore along with much Siamese rattan, for which Singapore was also an entrepôt. The timber trade has, however, been declining since the beginning of the century and now accounts for only 5 per cent of the export value.

The tin and rubber produced in the Kra Isthmus move by rail to Penang, Malaya. Rubber exports have expanded and in 1960 equaled rice exports by value (30 per cent).

Bangkok and Thailand are located on a backwater for international shipping lanes, whose natural focus in Southeast Asia is Singapore. But Bangkok has the best location among the non-communist metropolitan cities to serve as a focus of international air routes. The tremendous postwar increase in air travel has turned the formerly isolated Bangkok into a major crossroads in Southeast Asia, the Singapore of the air.[3]

Indochina

In the nineteenth century scramble for colonial empires France occupied the eastern portion of the Indochinese peninsula (1862–1907). The French were stimulated by the British advances in Burma towards the south China border; the French aim was as much to extend French

and the main distributary should be called the Menam Chao Praya. Dobby, *op. cit.* P. 263.

[2] *The New York Times,* September 13, 1957.

[3] Thailand has plans for building a deep canal across the Isthmus of Kra along the Burma-Thailand border, where a small canal used by barges and country craft exists. The Far East routes would be cut by 800 miles. The Thai government hope that the port of Chumphon on the planned canal will develop into a major competitor of Singapore. *The Observer,* February 4, 1962.

influence into southern China as it was to dominate Indochina itself.[1]

After World War II the French disengagement in Indochina was complicated by the Vietminh revolt, but the loosely integrated political-economic units of French Indochina acquired their independence from France by 1954. The communist domination of the Vietminh Nationalist Party in North Vietnam made the liberation of Vietnam an issue in the East-West balance of power. Elongated, bi-focal Vietnam, with major population clusters in the Tonkin delta centered on Hanoi and its port city Haiphong and in the lower Mekong delta centered on the twin cities of Saigon and Cholon, and connected by a narrow string of densely populated small river deltas and coastal plains, was divided into two countries along the 17th parallel, North Vietnam and South Vietnam. The two Viet have an estimated population of 15 and 14 million respectively. Laos and Cambodia are the other two countries which were included in French Indochina.

The prewar foreign trade of Indochina was primarily with France (53 per cent in 1938); rice, rubber and corn were the leading export items accounting for three-fourths of the export value.

CAMBODIA. The capital Phnom-Penh is located on the Mekong River and can be reached by small ocean-going vessels. By agreement with Vietnam the river is treated as an international waterway, but since it is only navigable for small vessels, Cambodia has built with French aid a new ocean port Sihanoukville at the entrance to Kompong Som Bay about 190

kilometers southwest of the capital.[2] The new port is connected to Phnom-Penh by a two-lane highway, built by the United States.[3] Foreign trade amounts to almost one million tons: exports of rice, corn, timber and rubber and imports of petroleum products and cement and other manufactured products.

SOUTH VIETNAM. The delta of the Mekong or Cochin China is the third of the three major rice producing regions in Southeast Asia which has a surplus for export. Rice cultivation is much less intensive than in the Tonkin delta in North Vietnam and the population density is much lower. Landholdings of over 50 hectares account for nearly half of the arable land in this recently settled area. The estates are cultivated by tenants who operate units of about 5 hectares or about the same size as the small farms. The rice is brought by barges to the great rice mills at Cholon, the twin city of Saigon. These mills are usually run by Chinese who act as middlemen over most of former French Indochina. Cholon, a Chinese city, was settled as early as 1778, whereas Saigon is new, built for the most part by the French after 1860. The agglomeration had 260,000 inhabitants in 1939 and about 1.5 million in 1951 after a large influx of refugees from North Vietnam. Saigon is an excellent port thanks to the Dong Nai distributary which carries little silt; but owing to its inland position off the main maritime routes and its undeveloped hinterland Saigon is not used extensively as a liner port. In 1936 the rice exports amounted to 1.7 million tons of which 160,000 tons originated in Cambodia.[4] The rice exports of South Vietnam in 1960 were 1.0 million tons.

NORTH VIETNAM. The heartland of the Vietnamese or Annamese people is the Tonkin delta and the many small deltas of Annam, especially its northern part.[5] During ten cen-

[1] Norton Ginsburg, editor, *The Pattern of Asia.* Englewood Cliffs, 1958. P. 414. See also Jules Sion, *Asie des Moussons.* Géographie Universelle, IX: 2. Paris, 1929.
[2] William A. Withington, "Cambodia", *Focus,* April 1962.
[3] Substantial foreign aid to neutral Cambodia has also been provided by the Soviet Union and China.
[4] Pierre Gourou, *L'Asie.* Paris, 1953. P. 326.
[5] Gourou, *op. cit.* P. 318.

turies of Chinese occupation the Vietnamese acquired the perfected techniques of cultivating the alluvial plains. The Tonkin or Red River delta has among the highest rural population densities in the world. In 1936 the delta had a population of 7.5 million with an average rural density of 450 persons per square kilometer; in large areas the density was three times the average. The average farm was less than one hectare. The agricultural landscape is similar to the Si-Kiang valley of southern China.

North Vietnam before the war was essentially an area of subsistence farming. Its participation in international trade was limited indeed. Hanoi in the delta was the capital of French Indochina between 1902 and the end of World War II. After 1874 a port developed at Haiphong, which also attracted some manufacturing industries. Haiphong is, however, seriously hampered by heavy silting.

A coal field along the northern rim of the Tonkin delta produced 2.5 million tons in 1940 of which 1.5 million tons were exported to Far Eastern markets through the ports of Hongay and Campha.

Malaysia

On July 31, 1962, an agreement was concluded in London to form the Federation of Malaysia by August, 1963. The federation would consist of Malaya, Singapore, Sarawak, Brunei and North Borneo. This would formally bring together the units of the old British Empire in Southeast Asia, economically centered on Singapore. The close economic relations within this area were already manifest by a common legal tender, the Malay Dollar, previously the Straits or Singapore Dollar. The new federation will have a population of 10 million with Singapore and the peninsula having among the highest standards of living in Asia.

The Federation of Malaya

Since the turn of the century rubber has become the most important crop in Malaya by area, by value and by number of people employed. The *Hevea brasiliensis,* introduced by the British as an experimental crop shortly before 1880, was well suited to Malaya's poor but well drained lateritic soils and equatorial climate, an environment resembling that of the Amazon basin. The new crop also introduced a new economic and social system. The heavy initial costs of jungle clearance and of waiting at least seven years for the tree to reach maturity required financial backing from outside. Rubber-growing was financed from Europe and organized into plantations averaging about 1,000 hectares, normally owned by companies with British management. Workers were brought from Southern India and China. About half of the workers on the rubber estates are Indian and a quarter Chinese. Gradually Chinese and Indians have acquired estates, usually under private ownership and smaller than the European plantations. Units of less than 50 hectares are classified as smallholdings. However, this demarcation by acreage may be confusing as several units of, say, 30–40 hectares owned by one Chinese or Indian owner and tapped by contract labor will be classified in the same group as a 2–3 hectare holding tapped by a resident Malay owner.

After the rapid expansion from 1905 to the early 1920s the industry was forced to restrict production and between the 1924 Stevenson restriction plan and the outbreak of World War II the smallholders of the Netherlands East Indies expanded their production so much that Malaya was displaced by Indonesia as the leading rubber producer. In Malaya smallholdings produce about 45 per cent of the rubber.

There are also large coconut and oil palm plantations along the coasts of Malaya but they are of much smaller importance for the economy than rubber.

Tin is the second pillar of the Malayan economy, antedating the rubber industry by several hundred years. The tin-bearing mineral (cassiterite, containing about 75 per cent tin) occurs mostly in alluvial deposits. It is extracted by dredging or gravel-pumping, which gives Malaya the lowest production costs of any major tin-producing country. The Chinese worked the tin deposits of Malaya as early as five hundred years ago and most of the workers in the modern mines are Chinese. Production has remained fairly constant since 1900, with large short-term fluctuations, but due to mechanization, a result of increased European participation in the industry, employment has fallen to less than 20 per cent. Three-fifths of the production is accounted for by Perak State with deposits in the Kinta Valley near Ipoh and Taiping. Mines near Kuala Lumpur account for most of the remainder. The cassiterite is sacked and sent in granular form to the large smelter at Butterworth on the mainland opposite Penang.

The mining of iron ore is also quite important in Malaya. By 1940 Japanese interests produced almost 2 million tons of hematite ore from mines primarily located on the east coast, where the ore carriers had to anchor offshore to load from barges. Shipments from the Bukit Besi mine through the port of Dungun were restarted in 1949, again destined for Japan. They increased rapidly with the remarkable postwar expansion of the Japanese steel industry, reaching 1.6 million tons in 1955 and 4.4 million in 1960. Penang shipped another 1.2 million tons of Malayan iron ore.

Coastwise shipping plays an important role in the transportation system of the peninsula although railroads, and recently also trucks,

offer competition. The small ports played a greater role around the turn of the century before the railways were completed.[1] Coastwise traffic is incompletely recorded, omitting such important cargoes as fish, firewood and timber moved in country craft of all kinds. Traffic focuses on Singapore, the overwhelming regional center. Singapore is the chief gateway for the Federation's foreign trade. As the west coast of Malaya faces the busy Strait of Malacca many liners call at Penang, the largest port in the Federation, and at Port Swettenham, the main port for central Malaya, located about an hour by train from Kuala Lumpur.

Penang is a natural harbor three kilometers wide between the Island of Penang and the mainland. The port facilities include a two-berth pier on the island, mooring buoys for vessels working in the Roads and wharves at Prai on the mainland, originally built by the railway company. Six deep-water berths with a capacity of one million tons are planned for Butterworth on the mainland. Exports from Penang include tin from the local smelter (over one-third of the world's production), rubber and increasing quantities of iron ore.

Singapore

Singapore and Hong Kong, the largest ports in Southeast and East Asia, in many ways resemble the mediaeval maritime trading republics of northern Italy, Genova and Venezia. They are large cities on limited territory and they have far-flung maritime trade connections but insignificant trade hinterlands served by inland transport. The state of Singapore consists of an island off the southern tip of the Malay Peninsula joined to the mainland by a causeway, carrying a road and a railway. Since 1959 Singapore has full internal self-government but the United Kingdom is responsible for defense and external affairs. It is the headquarters of the British armed forces in the Far East. Singapore's population in

[1] D. F. Allen, *Minor Ports of Malaya*. Government Printing Office, Singapore, 1953. The main line runs from Singapore to Prai opposite the island of Penang. Branch lines lead to the railway operated ports of Port Swettenham, Teluk Anson and Port Weld.

View towards the southeast over old Singapore with the winding Singapore River, the original port, in the center of the picture. The Outer Roads (behind the breakwaters) are used by trans-oceanic vessels loading and unloading by means of lighters or awaiting berths at the Harbor Board. The Inner Roads are used by coasters. Singapore's main port installations are in the southern part of the city just off the right margin of the picture. They are usually referred to as the "Harbor Board". (Straits Times)

1960 was estimated at 1.7 million, of which three-quarters are Chinese.

There is no obvious land route between the two Asiatic core areas, India and China. For centuries before the arrival of Europeans trade between the two areas had been by sea, through the Straits of Malacca. Singapore's predecessor Tumasek had been an important meeting point for traders from India and China. But modern

Singapore started from scratch in 1819, when Raffles signed a treaty with the Sultan of Johore, which allowed the East India Company to establish a trading station on the coast at the small Singapore River. The advantages of Singapore's location at a cross-roads of world trade routes were obvious, but also the site was favorable with good anchorage outside the river and surf-free unloading beaches inside. The new free port, to which traders from all quarters were invited without restriction, rapidly became the chief trading center of the region, surpassing Penang and Malacca. It became an important link in the chain of British bases protecting the shipping lanes from Gibraltar to the Far East. From 1824 to 1941 the entire region enjoyed the *Pax Britannica*.[1]

[1] Norton Ginsburg and Chester F. Roberts, Jr., *Malaya*. Seattle, 1958. Pp. 36 ff.

Cargo Turnover at Singapore in 1961

Million freight tons

	Receipts	Shipments
General cargo[a]	4.59	2.68
Petroleum	7.15	3.78
Vegetable oil	—	0.02
Bulk latex	—	0.03
Live animals	0.01	0.00
Total	11.75	6.51

[a] The S. H. B. Wharves accounted for 54 per cent of the receipts and 76 per cent of the shipments in 1961.

Singapore traditionally has offered a fine harbor with a free anchorage, a stable currency, a free-port organization, a commercial establishment equipped to handle trade matters in any of the oriental countries, political stability, and cultural and ethnic ties with the producers and traders within the region.[2]

In 1960 over ten thousand vessels with an aggregate net tonnage of 34 million cleared the port, making Singapore one of the ten largest ports in the world measured by the tonnage of vessels calling. Measured by cargo turnover Singapore occupies a more modest position among the ports of the world.

The commerce of early Singapore had been built around the river because it offered good facilities for lighterage. More than 600 of Singapore's 1,300 lighters still operate from the river which is lined with *godowns*. But more and more of the general cargo is handled at the wharves of the modern Keppel Harbour under the administration of the Singapore Harbour Board and less by lighters in the Roads.

Petroleum, which now dominates both receipts and shipments in the port, is handled primarily at oil installations controlled by Shell on Pulau Bukom Island 8 kilometers off the

[2] Norton Ginsburg, ed., *The Pattern of Asia*. New York, 1958. P. 385.

southwest coast of Singapore Island, and by Standard-Vacuum on nearby Pulau Sebarok Island. In addition Caltex has oil installations at Tandjung Uban in the Riouw Archipelago, Indonesia, 45 kilometers southeast of Singapore. Two oil refineries were built at Singapore in the early 1960s, one by Shell at their oil port and one by the Japanese Maruzen Toyo Oil Co.

About 40 per cent of the Federation's trade is with Singapore and the Federation accounts for over 20 per cent of Singapore's trade. Indonesia is Singapore's second largest trade partner accounting for 15 per cent of her trade in 1961 and for no less than one-fourth of her imports, primarily rubber and petroleum. Sarawak (4 per cent), Thailand (3 per cent) and North Borneo (1 per cent) are other important trade partners in Southeast Asia. Much of the produce of the Federation, Indonesia and the British territories on northern Borneo arrives in small coasters for processing, grading, packing and re-exporting to world markets. Among the products are rubber, copra, spices, coffee, tea, and timber. Manufactured goods of every description are imported in bulk to be broken up into smaller lots for distribution to the neighboring countries. Much of the entrepôt trade is in the hands of Chinese and Indian traders.

The rapid population increase in the small state calls for a high rate of economic expansion. Singapore has sought to attract manufacturing industries and the 1961–64 development plan envisages government investments to provide cheap power and water, to lay out industrial estates and to provide good communications and port facilities. However, Singapore's status as a free port and its complete dependence on international trade restrict the role of the government to providing the infrastructure for future industrialization. The government hopes that an iron and steelworks using ore from Malaya and coal from Indonesia will form the nucleus of the Jurong industrial area now under development in the southwestern corner of the island. Ship-building, ship-breaking and other heavy industries are planned for this completely new city that the government hopes will develop behind the deep-water berths.

BORNEO, one of the largest islands in the world and one of the most undeveloped areas in Southeast Asia, has only four million inhabitants, scattered along the various river systems. Three-quarters live in Kalimantan, former Dutch Borneo, now part of Indonesia; the rest in the three British possessions on the northwest coast: Sarawak, Brunei and North Borneo. The water courses serve as natural highways amidst forests, swamps and mountains for people with chiefly a subsistence economy.

Borneo was drawn into the world economy about 1900, when petroleum was discovered and *Hevea* rubber introduced. These are now by far the most important export items. Rubber is produced by smallholders in all parts of the island and collected by Chinese traders. Apart from direct bulk shipments of petroleum (Balikpapan, Tarakan and Lutong-Miri) and timber (Tanjong Mani at the Rajang mouth) for transoceanic delivery and some imports of rice from Thailand, the commerce of Borneo is subsidiary to Singapore, Hong Kong and the Java ports of Djakarta and Surabaja.[1] Connections with these overseas entrepôts are largely maintained by scheduled coasters of 1,500 to 2,500 GRT.

The lack of land transportation means that the hinterland of each port reaches as far inland as river boats and canoes can travel. Some of the major ports serve several river basins and act as an intermediary between the transoceanic entrepôt and the river port, e.g. Kuching for most of Sarawak and Bandjarmasin for southern Kalimantan.

The Seria oilfield in Brunei ships its oil via a pipe terminal at Lutong near Miri, Sarawak, where ocean tankers load at an open roadstead. The other large oil port, Balikpapan, is a fine natural harbor. Both oil ports have refineries.

Indonesia

Indonesia, a country of several thousand islands lying astride the equator and stretching for a distance equivalent to that between New York and San Francisco, is one of the world's largest nations with a population of 96 million according to the 1961 census.

Early in the Christian era, Indonesia came under the influence of Hindu traders and priests, followed by some permanent migrants. By the seventh century a strong empire based on Sumatra had been established, but by 1377 it was overthrown by another Indonesian-Hindu empire based on eastern Java. Islam came to Indonesia in the wake of Moslem Indian and Arab traders at the end of the Hindu period but no united Islamic empire was formed and the victory of Islam (1478) was not complete. Bali for instance kept a form of Hinduism. In 1511 the Portuguese captured the strategic commercial center of Malacca on the Malay Peninsula, and from there established trading posts in Indonesia. The Dutch followed in 1596 and the English at the turn of the century. After a series of Anglo-Dutch conflicts the Dutch East India Company, formed in 1602, expanded its control over the region, which was taken over by the Dutch Government in 1798 and became known as the Netherlands East Indies.

Java (with Madura) was the heart of the Indies; the remainder constituted for the Dutch the Outer Provinces. Java's population increased from an estimated 5 million in 1815 to an estimated 50 million in 1945 and 63 million in 1961, one of the most populous and

[1] Jan O. M. Broek, *The Ports of Borneo*. Office of Naval Research. Contract No. N onr 710(09). Technical Report No. 1, May 1957. Department of Geography, University of Minnesota, Minneapolis. (Mimeographed.)

highly developed regions in the Tropics. The Dutch maintained interior and exterior peace for two centuries, organized irrigation and introduced scientific methods in Java's agriculture. The botanical garden at Buitenzorg (now Bogor) is famous. After World War II Indonesian leaders declared the independence of the Indies and in 1949 the Dutch were forced to relinquish their hold over the territory with the exception of western New Guinea. An agreement for a gradual transfer of this territory to Indonesia was reached in 1962. Independence has been associated with chauvinistic discrimination against western business firms and Chinese middlemen and as a result the economic development of Indonesia has been retarded.

During the Dutch period interisland traffic was the virtual monopoly of the *Koninklijke Paketvaart Maatschappij,* one of the largest shipping companies active in Asia. The *KPM* called at three hundred ports in the archipelago, tying the outlying islands to Java and connecting them with the great entrepôts of Singapore and Penang. The Indonesians have bought and chartered many vessels since 1956 but have not yet been able to develop a modern merchant marine able to replace the *KPM*.

Java

Java, the core of Indonesia, for over three centuries was exposed to western influence. The great intensity and variety of Javanese agriculture is made possible by the variety of the environment and by the extremely favorable soil conditions. The many volcanoes in the mountainous backbone of the island provide material for fertile soil, either weathered *in situ* or deposited as river-transported alluvials and in many places the soil is fertilized by

ejecta from the volcanoes. By procuring exportable agricultural products from local farmers rather than from European plantations the Dutch introduced cash crops among the Javanese. Under the Culture System (introduced in 1834), which tied in with the pre-European economy, the farmers were compelled to grow certain export crops (sugar, coffee, indigo) to be sold in Europe for the benefit of the Dutch Government. The system was abandoned in 1870, but European planters continued to produce crops along the lines of the Culture System up to World War II. The Agrarian Law of 1870 forbade the alienation of land to non-natives. For example, sugar, grown on land suitable for rice, was produced on acreages rented by the European planter from local farmers, who worked for him for wages and devoted the rest of their land to the usual subsistence food crops. When sugar prices were unfavorable the farmer turned his land to other uses. Thus Javanese sugar production dropped from 2.9 million tons in 1930 to less than half a million in 1936. Before the war four-fifths of Java's agricultural exports were derived from estates, either on leased land in sparsely populated uplands (rubber, cinchona, tea and coffee) or on periodically rented land in irrigated areas (sugar, tobacco).[1]

The chief ports of Java are located on the extremely densely populated alluvial plain in the north, Jakarta, Semarang and Surabaja. Jakarta, the former Batavia, founded in 1619 and the original base for Dutch influence in the archipelago consists of two parts, Old Batavia with warehouses and business offices near the old river port and a residential suburb (Weltevreden) four kilometers to the south. As the river became inadequate for vessels of increasing size the Dutch completed a modern port ten kilometers to the east of the city, Tandjung Priuk.[2]

Surabaja's port, Tandjungperak, is located just north of the city proper, adjacent to Udjung, the chief naval base of Indonesia.

[1] Jan O. M. Broek, "Man and Resources in the Netherlands Indies", *The Far Eastern Quarterly,* 1946. Pp. 121 ff.
[2] Sion, *Asie des Moussons, op. cit.* Pp. 492–93.

Smaller ports are Tjilatjap, the only deep-water port on the south coast of Java, and Tjirebon, Pekalongan and Pasuruan on the north coast.

Sumatra

Sumatra (Andalas) consists of three parallel belts: a mountain backbone along the west coast with many volcanic peaks rising to over 3,000 meters with large areas covered by lavas, an intermediary piedmont and a very extensive, flat, alluvial lowland along most of the east coast. This forest-covered swamp gradually shelves into the shallow Malacca Strait. It is the largest equatorial swamp in Southeast Asia still beyond the control of human technology.[1] In spite of a very rapid population increase (15 million inhabitants in 1961) Sumatra still has a low population density, but accounts for much of Indonesia's exports. Traditionally a large part of Sumatra's foreign trade has passed through Singapore and Penang. The whole island came under Dutch control early in this century.

Major land, water and air routes converge on the two primary centers of the eastern plain, Medan in the northeast and Palembang in the southeast, both cities with populations of about half a million.[2] At Medan the piedmont lavas come near the coast and tobacco, rubber, coffee, tea, oil palm and sisal plantations support a rather dense population. The first European plantations (tobacco) were established in the 1860s upon basic lava soils in the sultanate of Deli inland from Medan. Large rubber plantations were established later and soon exceeded the tobacco plantations in importance.

As the river became too shallow for ocean-going vessels to reach Medan an outport was created at Belawan, now the leading dry cargo port on Sumatra.

Palembang, the outlet of Indonesia's leading oilfield, has two large oil refineries in the suburbs of Pladju and Sungei Gerong. These loading ports lie 70 kilometers from the mouth of the Musi River, accessible for large tankers.

The oil industry in Southeast Asia is old. A tobacco planter found oil seepages near his plantation at Medan in 1880 and in 1885 the first well was drilled. This first productive well in Indonesia led to the foundation of the "Royal Dutch Company for the Working of Petroleum Wells in the Netherlands Indies", later changed to "Royal Dutch Petroleum Company". It was the nucleus of the world-wide Royal Dutch/Shell Group.[3] Within fifteen years after the first oil had been struck in North Sumatra the basins in South Sumatra, East Java, eastern and northeastern Borneo were all producing. Since the early 1930s South Sumatra has held first place, surpassing eastern Borneo. The industry suffered great damage as a result of the war; the postwar political instability in Indonesia has hampered restoration. In 1940 Sumatra produced 5 million tons or 1.7 per cent of world production; in 1962 the corresponding figures were 21 million tons and 1.6 per cent. The old fields along the coast north of Medan have not been reopened after the war due to political unrest. A primitive refinery was built here already in 1892 (Pangkalan Brandan) and five years later a loading site was completed at Pangkalan Susu ten kilometers from the refinery. Both were in operation till World War II.

Both Palembang and Djambi serve as ocean ports for rubber plantations established inland from these two large and rather isolated cities on the marshy plain.

Fluctuating quantities of tin ore, about 35,000 tons as an average for 1956–1960, are produced in the east coast islands of Bangka,

[1] Dobby, *op. cit.* Pp. 198–199.
[2] William A. Withington, "The Cities of Sumatra", *Tijdschrift voor Economische en Sociale Geografie*, 1962. Pp. 242–246.
[3] I. Swemle, "Indonesia, British Borneo, and Burma", *World Geography of Petroleum* (Wallace E. Pratt and Dorothy Good, eds.). Princeton, 1950. Pp. 277–78.

Billiton and Singkep, making Indonesia the second largest tin producer in the world.

Padang, Sumatra's third largest city (144,000 inhabitants) and the leading center on the west coast, is served by an outport a short distance to the south, Teluk Bajur, formerly known as Emmahaven. Padang's own harbor is too shallow and unprotected for modern shipping. The Padang Highlands with fertile volcanic soils have the highest population density in Sumatra; they produce tobacco, coffee and coconuts. Coal is also produced near Padang.

The Philippines

In the Philippines, as in much of Southeast Asia and Oceania, transportation is traditionally by water. The daily life of the average Filipino has always been oriented towards the sea, since the republic comprises over 7,000 islands and islets. Sailing outriggers and a variety of small motor craft carry large quantities of cargo. The smallest vessels deliver locally produced commodities to the nearest port where some may be transshipped by ocean going vessels to larger ports in the Philippines or abroad. Manufactured products, imported or originating in the main cities, follow the same pattern in the opposite direction down through the hierarchy of lesser ports and roadsteads. Larger vessels make regular runs throughout the islands. There are hundreds of ports to handle coastwise and interisland commerce but most of them are restricted to domestic shipping service. Records of domestic transport are incomplete. Therefore it is impossible to describe in detail what happens to

the time-honored transport pattern as the road network on the islands is extended and improved. Logically there should be a concentration of traffic to fewer ports.

Prior to the arrival of the Spaniards overseas trade was in the hands of the Chinese. Under Spanish administration both domestic and foreign trade were strictly regulated; foreign trade was confined to Manila to facilitate control. Under pressure from other powers Spain in 1830 declared Manila an open port for foreign trade; by 1860 four other cities had been added to the list of open ports. Foreign trade was stimulated by the new policy which had far-reaching effects on agriculture and transportation, specially after the United States had acquired the islands in the Spanish–American War (1898).

Some areas specialized in export crops, e.g. sugar cane in central Luzon north of Manila and on northwestern Negros; coconuts[1] in southern Luzon (on the wetter east side, out of the tracks of the more damaging typhoons)[2] and in eastern Mindanao; abaca (the native perennial plant which supplies the Manila hemp) in southern Luzon and southern Mindanao near Davao; and tobacco in northern Luzon. Other regions specialized in producing food surpluses to feed the population growing export crops and the expanding cities. All this stimulated interisland transport.[3]

Manila and Cebu are the main centers in the complicated web of shipping connections that bind this archipelagic nation together. Cebu with its strategic location within the Archipelago has no peer in domestic trade measured by number and tonnage of vessels calling, amount of copra landed and number of passengers using the port. However, Manila handles about the same amount of domestic cargo and is by far the leading foreign trade port, dominating the import trade. In 1960 Manila accounted for 50 per cent of the imports by tonnage and for no less than 87 per cent by value. But bulky exports tend to by-

---

[1] Coconuts before World War II accounted for almost 30 per cent of the value of exports and employed more people than any other cash crop. The Philippines is the world's leading exporter of coconut products.

[2] E. H. G. Dobby, *Southeast Asia*, London, 1950. P. 335.

[3] Frederick L. Wernstedt, "Cebu: Focus of Philippine Interisland Trade", *Economic Geography*, 1956. Pp. 336 ff.

pass Manila, a pattern repeated in most other countries. They are shipped abroad direct from ports and coastal landings scattered throughout the islands, but some are handled through entrepôts, including Manila.[4] In 1960 Manila accounted for 9 per cent of the Filipino export by tonnage and 21 per cent by value.

Among the large ports other than Manila[5] are Batangas (with its oil refinery), Iloilo (sugar from Negros), Davao (iron ore, Manila hemp) and José Panganiban (iron ore, copra).

MANILA. Manila, with a population of 1.7 million, nearly ten times larger than Cebu, the next largest Philippine center, is a typical primate city, connected by international airlines with the capital cities of the world and by domestic lines with every large island and city in the archipelago. It was made the seat of Spanish government in 1571 and remained the capital till 1948 when Quezon City, a suburb of Manila, named for the first Filipino president, was officially designated. Manila's international trade connections have chiefly been trans-Pacific, in the Spanish time through the famous Manila galleons based on Acapulco in Mexico and later through the dominating trade with the United States. Manila's peripheral location with regard to main shipping lanes and large population clusters in Southeast Asia has prevented her from playing any important role as an entrepôt; Singapore and Hong Kong with their more favorable locations and freeport status have fulfilled this function.

East Asia

Hong Kong

The establishment of Hong Kong as a Crown Colony in 1841 provided British merchants with a base for their trade with South China. The island is located at the entrance of the Chu Kiang (or Pearl River), the main distributary of the Si Kiang (West River) and the natural line of entry to South China. The Portuguese settlement Macau, on the other side of Canton Bay, is much older. The Viceroy of Canton granted the Portuguese the use of Macau in 1557 after they had defeated a pirate fleet in a sea battle. Pirates have been part of shipping life in the South China Sea until recently and the battle against piracy was a serious concern of the British navy both in Singapore and Hong Kong.

The Portuguese were followed by Dutch, Spanish and English traders and still later by Americans in South China. But it was only towards the end of the seventeenth century that regular and substantial trade was begun. The basis of the trade was tea but in the middle of the eighteenth century the opium trade assumed tremendous importance. The East India Company had a monopoly of opium production in India and the carrying of opium in English ships, first openly and later illicitly, was a major factor in the settlement of Hong Kong as a British colony.[1]

[4] Edward L. Ullman, "Trade Centers and Tributary Areas of the Philippines", *Geographical Review*, 1960. Pp. 203 ff. Ullman's article contains a carefully documented division of the Philippines into socio-economic regions. Manila is seen as a national center and Cebu, Iloilo, Davao and Zamboanga as inter-regional centers.

[5] The place names listed in our source (*Foreign Trade Statistics 1960*, published by the Bureau of Census and Statistics in Manila) refer to customs districts rather than ports. For example, the sugar exported from Negros formerly was transferred through Iloilo, which has a deep protected harbor, but now most of the sugar is lightered to offshore ships on the coast of Negros. Ullman, *op. cit.* P. 212.

[1] S. G. Davis, *Hong Kong in its geographical setting*. London, 1949.

Opium-smoking became widespread and created a big demand for the drug in a society which had been highly self-sufficient and in which the merchants had been loath to do business with foreigners. When the importation of opium was made illegal smuggled opium went up in price which meant that China was being seriously drained of its silver. Finally the Chinese Government expelled all foreigners from Canton and banned trade relations. Foreign shipping had to stand out several miles from Canton, near Whampoa. Things came to a head in 1839 when the Chinese, determined to suppress the opium trade, impounded all foreign *godowns* and arrested all foreigners. The British sent a fleet to secure British interests in China, hostilities were proclaimed but little fighting took place. In 1841 an agreement was reached by which China ceded the Island and Harbor of Hong Kong to England. The agreement was ratified by the Treaty of Nanking in 1843.

Like Singapore before her, Hong Kong was from the start declared a free port. The early years saw merchants establish themselves in temporary premises on the island foreshore facing the harbor. Thousands of *tan ka,* or boat people, flocked to the new settlement, attracted by the prospects for lighterage and ferry work.[2] Already in 1845 a monthly steamship service from London was opened by the Peninsular and Oriental Steam Navigation Company. Passengers and mail were carried overland between Alexandria and Suez and the voyage usually took 48 days. The French Messageries Maritimes began a mail service in 1863, the first foreign company to open a regular service to Hong Kong.

The typhoon hazard soon made it necessary

[2] Modern American mining camps are not the first mushrooming settlements of mobile homes.

[3] E. G. Godfrey and K. Macdonald, eds., *Ports, Dues and Charges on Shipping Throughout the World,* ("*The Blue Book of Shipping*"). 21st Ed., London, 1959;
Hong Kong. Report for the Year 1960. Hong Kong, 1961.

to build permanent structures instead of the temporary wooden buildings. Bitter experience has taught the Colony that every precaution is necessary in the choice of sites and the construction of buildings. In one of Hong Kong's most disastrous typhoons in 1906 over 10,000 people were drowned, 2,400 junks and sampans were reported lost and 141 ocean going vessels were badly damaged.

The territory of the Colony has been extended twice, in 1861 when the Kowloon Peninsula was ceded by China and in 1898 when Hong Kong took over the New Territories on a 99 year lease.

Until recently Hong Kong was the port and the port was Hong Kong, but in the 1950s manufacturing became a more important industry than trade in Hong Kong's economy. In its early years the Colony existed purely as a free port where the manufactured goods of Europe were exchanged for the products of China. Throughout the nineteenth century the Colony's trade was almost exclusively concerned with her neighbor. But there has been a steady widening of the trade with Southeast Asia. The position of Great Britain as the principal manufacturing country selling through Hong Kong has been lost in this century and is now shared with Japan and the United States. Cotton textiles, which formed the bulk of the British trade in the last century, were later supplied by Japan and in the postwar period Hong Kong has herself become a major exporter of cotton goods selling on the British and American markets and competing with Japan in Southeast Asia.

The excellent harbor provided at Hong Kong for the sailing ships of the 1840s has also proved to be an outstanding port for modern ocean liners. Maximum draft at low water for vessels entering through the deeper, eastern channel is 36 feet and depths in the harbor area vary between 24 and 54 feet. The tidal range is only 6 to 9 feet.[3] The efficient commercial services and communications avail-

The Canton — Hong Kong Region

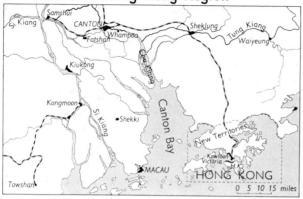

Note the triangular positions of Hong Kong, Canton and Macau relative to the Chu Kiang (Pearl River), the most important distributary of the Si Kiang and the natural line of entry to South China.

able in the British free port of Hong Kong have been of great value to China and Southeast Asia as evidenced by Hong Kong's large entrepôt trade.[4] With the large-scale development of manufacturing industries in Hong Kong after World War II, the Colony is gradually generating more and more of its own port traffic, a trend it has in common with most of the large ports in the world but for a different reason. Hong Kong has become noted for the price, quality and range of its light industries, especially textiles and garments, whereas European and American port cities have developed heavy industries. The large and rapidly growing population, 3.1 million according to the 1961 census, provide cheap and skilled labor in a territory that economically is part of the Western world. The imports of food and raw materials and the exports of Hong Kong-made products make up increasing shares of Hong Kong's trade.

China

The world's most populous country takes little part in international trade. No country has a lower trade per capita and the total trade of the 700-million nation is modest. China does not publish trade statistics but the best avail-

able estimates indicate a foreign trade on a par with that of Switzerland.

China's history is long, about thirty-five centuries since the rise of the Shang dynasty, but the hundred years prior to the Communist Revolution, a period of frequent contact with the technically and scientifically more advanced culture of the West, was characterized by a weak central government and slow economic progress. The Chinese were as reluctant as the Westerners were eager to open trade connections. In a series of treaties the Chinese government was forced to grant many concessions to foreign powers. An interesting sidelight on the attitude of the Chinese government to all foreigners is given by a clause inserted in the Treaty of Tientsin in 1858 where it was agreed that the Chinese character for barbarian should not be used about the British Government or British subjects in any official Chinese documents.[1] More important were the extraterritorial rights given to many

[4] The Colony's total trade dropped by one-third between 1951 and 1953 as a result of the Western world's abrupt embargo on trade with Communist China in connection with the Korean War. In the late 1950s Mainland China accounted for a mere five per cent of Hong Kong's exports but for one-fourth of her imports. Hong Kong has been of great importance to China in these years as a window on the Western world.

[1] Davis, *Hong Kong, op. cit.* P. 29.

430

General view of Hong Kong. Victoria on Hong Kong Island is the Colony's center of business and administration (foreground). The 1961 Census showed the population of the island to be just over one million, while the total population of the Colony was 3.1 million.

During the past 10 years Victoria has completely changed in appearance. Prewar buildings have been demolished to make way for "skyscrapers" of 20 stories and more. In the background is Kowloon. The twin cities are connected by frequent ferry services that carry 130 million passengers and two million vehicles a year. The principal wharves are in Kowloon where vessels with 230-meter length and 32-foot draft can be accomodated at 10 pier berths. Many vessels anchor in mid-stream loading and unloading with the help of lighters and junks. Of 1,800 such craft only 100 are mechanically propelled.

In the upper left corner is one of the typhoon shelters, built to safeguard fishing junks and boats of the *tan ka*. In the upper right corner are the long runways of the Kai Tak Airport, laid out on reclaimed land in the bay in 1932. The mountainous coast of South China has helped make the harbor of Hong Kong famous for its scenic beauty. (Hong Kong Government, Information Services, 1962)

Western powers in the Chinese ports, which gave China a semi-colonial status.[2]

The West was eager to purchase tea and silk which in 1842 accounted for 71 and 20 per cent respectively of China's exports. In 1891 these two items had 30 per cent each. British and American sailing vessels, especially the Yankee clippers, carried these products to Europe and the United States. But other countries were more eager than China to supply Europe and America, and soon Assam and Ceylon took over most of the tea trade and Japan became dominant as a supplier of raw silk. The British paid with opium from India which in 1867 made up 46 per cent of China's import value and the Americans and Russians sold fur from their Pacific coasts. But the end of last century saw a rapid change in the structure of China's import. Cotton goods, chiefly supplied from factories in India, made up an increasing share of the imports and so did kerosene and kerosene lamps imported from the United States. Western-type industries producing consumer goods were soon established in some of the leading treaty ports.

In this century agricultural products and minerals have been the dominant Chinese exports. By 1931, when Manchuria became a puppet state under Japanese control, soybeans was the leading export accounting for one-fifth of the total value. The loss of Manchuria and the war with Japan, which started in 1937, were great setbacks in China's economic development. These and later upheavals make a 'normal year' for international Chinese trade an illusion.

The treaty ports acted as Western bridge-heads on the coast of China from which Western ideas gradually penetrated inland. The manufacturing industries established in these ports greatly influenced the structure of China's foreign trade. In 1913 cotton goods and cotton yarn were the two leading import items accounting for 20 and 13 per cent, but in 1930 the two items had declined to 11 and 1 per cent and raw cotton had become a major import item (10 per cent). The cotton industry was a pioneer among the Western industries in China as in most other countries, and it soon could undersell the domestic product.[3] It was followed by other consumer goods industries. In the import statistics this was also reflected in the imports of machinery and spare parts. The rapid increase of industrial workers in the mushrooming coastal cities led to increased imports of foodstuffs, rice, sugar, wheat, etc.

Imports have usually exceeded exports. Much of the difference has been covered by remittances from overseas Chinese and by foreign credits.

Despite the beginnings of industrialization and the high priority given to railroad building by the Communist government, China is still characterized by a high degree of regional self-sufficiency.[4] The country is exceptionally favored by natural waterways, which in contrast to those of other continental states, the Soviet Union, the United States and Brazil, flow in the right direction and serve a major part of the ecumene. The two major systems are the Yangtze and the Si Kiang. By virtue of the Yangtze route Szechuan, although it lies two thousand kilometers from the sea, supplied more agricultural products for overseas export than any other Chinese province.[5]

[2] In 1943, when China became a member of the United Nations, it was agreed that all foreign powers would surrender their extraterritorial rights. The original five treaty ports established by the Treaty of Nanking in 1842—Amoy, Canton, Foochow, Ningpo and Shanghai—had then increased to 65 ports opened for foreign trade and 25 ports of call on the Yangtze and Si Kiang. Davis, *Hong Kong, op. cit.* P. 193.

[3] In the 1930s many Japanese industrialists moved their plants from Osaka to Shanghai or started branch plants in that city. Labor costs were lower in China than in Japan. By 1960 China again became a competitor of Japan in some southeast Asian markets but the most important postwar export drives from the 'three Chinas' have come from Hong Kong.

[4] Rhoads Murphey, "China's Transport Problem, and Communist Planning", *Economic Geography*, 1956. Pp. 17 ff.

[5] Murphey, *op. cit.* P. 19.

CANTON. In China proper the Canton region ranks next to those of Shanghai and Peking-Tientsin in economic importance. Canton had contacts with overseas countries earlier than the other parts of China. The first Arab vessels reached Canton around A.D. 300 and the Portuguese arrived in 1514. In the beginning of this century Canton was still the largest city in China but according to the 1953 census it ranked below Shanghai, Peking, Tientsin, Mukden and Chungking.[6] Canton had 1.6 million inhabitants in 1953. Prior to 1842 when Canton became a treaty port international business had to be transacted on board ships or in warehouses along the shore known as factories or *godowns*. Many of the overseas Chinese originate in Canton's hinterland. The Cantonese form an entrepreneurial elite around the China seas. But in spite of a glorious past as China's window on the world and in spite of an outward-looking population Canton is today a regional metropolis and not a world port. Some of its international trade is funneled through Hong Kong. Canton, at the head of the Pearl River estuary, has a poor site for a modern port. Depths alongside the wharves range from 2 to 13 feet which means that ocean-going vessels cannot proceed further than Whampoa where a deep-draft port has been constructed. The rock bed of the river makes it difficult to deepen the channel to Canton.

The Chinese government, in its efforts to bypass Hong Kong as the dominating seaport for South China, has also constructed a new port at Chankiang (Tsamkong) further down the coast on territory previously leased to France (1898–1946) and then known as Fort Bayard. Chankiang, like Canton, has rail connections with Hankow. The port was built with aid from the Soviet Union on a deep silt-free natural harbor. Five berths equipped with cranes can accomodate large ocean-going vessels.[7] The chief port on the nearby island of Hainan is Yulin in an excellent harbor on the south coast. Before the war several hundred thousand tons of high-grade iron ore were shipped through this port to Japan from large deposits in the northwest.

With the expansion of Whampoa and Chankiang Hong Kong's trade with China has declined. Mainland China in recent years has only accounted for about three per cent of Hong Kong's exports. In the colony's imports China plays a more important role with about 20 per cent, but this is chiefly foodstuffs for local consumption.

The other foreign port on the southern coast of China, the old Portuguese settlement of Macau, founded in 1557 and recognized as a Portuguese colony by the Chinese government in 1887, has remained a small port in the traffic shadow of Hong Kong, which has a superior harbor and is supported by the vast resources of a great maritime power.

PORTS ON THE SOUTHEAST COAST. Several ports on the southeastern coast between Shanghai and Hong Kong have played a prominent role in China's maritime history, not least during the nineteenth century when Yankee clippers loaded tea at Pagoda Anchorage in the port of Foochow. This region, with its drowned coastline, is more sea conscious than any other part of China. The percentage of arable land is very low and although farmed intensively the crops must be supplemented by seafood provided by China's leading sea fisheries and by the seaborne imports of rice, wheat and sugar from other regions and from abroad. The port cities have long carried on trade with the Philippines, Malaya and the South Seas by seagoing junks. Most of the twelve million Chinese abroad originate in the southeastern coastal region including Canton, China's major area of emigration.

The cities of Ningpo, Wenchow, Foochow,

[6] Theodore Shabad, "The Population of China's Cities", *Geographical Review*, 1959. Pp. 32 ff.
[7] *Pravda*, June 30, 1961.

Amoy and Swatow have between 200 and 600 thousand inhabitants. Like Hong Kong they all have a large population of *tan ka* or boat people who earn their living by carrying passengers and freight in the harbor and who have no home on land. Each port is at the mouth of a short river and the river valley is its sharply defined hinterland.

Shanghai and Hong Kong normally serve as entrepôts for these ports. The decline of China's tea trade in competition with Ceylon and Assam has reduced their attraction for foreign shipping.

Shanghai

Shanghai, surpassed in population only by New York, Tokyo and London and on a par with Moscow, Paris and Los Angeles, has a magnificent location at the mouth of the Yangtze, probably the world's busiest river. Statistics are lacking but both passenger and freight traffic below the Ichang gorges, the head of navigation for ocean-going vessels, and especially on the one thousand kilometers below Hankow, must be enormous.[1] During the century prior to World War II the Yangtze was opened to foreign shipping through treaty arrangements. Ocean-going vessels called at Hankow and the traffic by junks and river steamers was intense. Hankow was at the junction of China's chief traffic arteries, the Yangtze Kiang, navigable for small vessels for some 2400 kilometers, and the main railroads connecting Hankow with Peking, 1200 kilometers to the north, and Canton, 1100 kilometers to the south.[2] The westernized treaty port of Hankow[3] thus was in the center of China proper, about equal distances from the four major economic complexes, Shanghai and Chungking on the east-west axis, and Peking-Tientsin and Canton on the north-south axis. Before the creation of the People's Republic in 1949 China's foreign trade moved almost exclusively through her seaports and nearly half through Shanghai alone. This great entrepôt not only served the Yangtze Kiang basin with more than 200 million people but also had a large coastal trade.

Shanghai's international prominence dates from its opening as one of the original treaty ports by the Treaty of Nanking in 1842. The city lies 80 kilometers from the ocean on the Whangpoo, a river flowing into the Yangtze estuary. There is no good site for a metropolis at the mouth of the main river. The greatest obstacles to shipping are the Fairy Flats, a large sand bar area at the entrance to the Yangtze estuary. Large ocean vessels have to take advantage of the 15-foot tidal range to enter the river. The Whangpoo also has sand bars, but being a tributary tidal creek, it has less sedimentation. A depth of 37 feet is maintained in Shanghai's typhoon sheltered harbor, but the entrance channel has only 24 feet at low water.[4] The shifting banks in the main river have been a handicap for the development of such Yangtze ports as Chinkiang, at the confluence of the Yangtze and the Grand Canal, and Nanking.[5]

Shanghai offers striking contrast to the countryside around it, which is a typical Chinese rural landscape on an intensively cultivated and densely populated alluvial plain. This city, born out of Western commercial enterprise, was in effect superimposed on a peasant civilization.[6] The site of the city is a mud flat barely above sea level on the left bank of the Whangpoo River on which

[1] George B. Cressey, *Land of the 500 Million.* New York, 1955. P. 190.
[2] The two railroads were connected by a bridge across the Yangtze in the 1950s.
[3] Hankow is part of the Wuhan conurbation.
[4] Shanghai has an outport at the mouth of the Whangpoo, Woosung, at which larger ocean-going vessels call.
[5] The Grand Canal was started in the seventh century and completed in the thirteenth. It carried tribute rice from the Yangtze valley to the Imperial Court in Peking. Only parts of this narrow but long canal are now being used.
[6] Rhoads Murphey, *Shanghai, Key to Modern China.* Cambridge, 1953. P. 1.

434

Shanghai and the Yangtze Delta

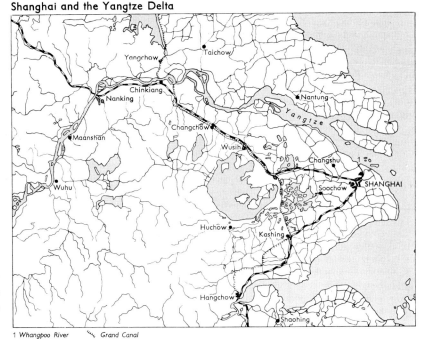

1 *Whangpoo River*   *Grand Canal*

Shanghai, the chief point of contact with the outside world for the secluded Chinese society, is a creation of the last hundred years of western influence. The city commands a strategic location near the main thoroughfare of China, the Yangtze River.

have been erected some of the tallest buildings in Asia. The British concessions of 1843–1848 and the American of 1862 were consolidated in 1863 into the International Settlement whereas the French concession of 1849, located north and west of the old walled city, remained a separate unit. The central business district is in the former International Settlement where some well-known thoroughfares, the Bund, Nanking Road and Bubbling Well Road, are lined with tall buildings (banks and other office buildings, hotels and department stores). The northeastern section of the former Settlement is studded with factories and warehouses along the Whangpoo. The former French concession is a residential district. Outside the old city and the concessions stretches the modern Chinese city with factories and dwellings for factory workers.

Shanghai ranks with Los Angeles and São Paulo among the fastest growing cities in the world. It had a quarter of a million inhabitants in 1870, one million in 1910, three million by 1930 and seven and a half million in 1958. This tremendous population increase cannot be accounted for solely by Shanghai's commercial functions. The city early became the leading manufacturing center of China with large cotton mills and a variety of factories primarily producing consumer goods. It was estimated that Shanghai before the Second World War had nearly half of China's western-type industries and over 40 per cent of the Chinese industrial labor force.

The abolition of the international concessions during the Second World War and the reorientation of China's economy after the Communist take-over in 1949 created new conditions for Shanghai. With the Soviet Union as China's dominating trade partner instead of the United States, Japan and Great Britain, Shanghai has lost some of its former prominence as the undisputed commercial, financial and industrial capital of China. But this relative decline has been less than expected and since 1958 the Peking government has again

435

decided to build out Shanghai's industrial potential.[7] The city still has one-third of China's textile industry and remains her largest commercial and industrial center.[8] The advantages of Shanghai's geographical location and the know-how of her population should be guarantees against drastic changes.

TIENTSIN, one of the two million-cities on the north China plain, was before the Revolution a cosmopolitan city. The old Chinese town was surrounded by westernized areas originally developed as Austrian, Belgian, British, French, German, Italian, Japanese and Russian concessions. As a port Tientsin serves the northern half of the plain, including the capital Peking and the new coal and steel center Tangshan. The loess plateau east of the Hwang Ho, including the steel center Paotow, and much of Mongolia are also within its hinterland. But Tientsin proper has a poor port site. Limited to vessels of 15-foot draft, it is now used only for coastal traffic. The construction of a modern outport at Tangku on the northern bank of the Hai Ho was started in 1938. One of the two wharves in the Tangku New Harbor is reserved for coal shipments. It is equipped with two belt conveyors. Even before the construction of this new port ocean vessels were worked at Taku and Tangku at the mouth of the river.

In 'normal' interwar years Tientsin was third after Shanghai and Dairen among the Chinese ports, but after the blockade of Shanghai it became China's chief port although with less trade than before World War II. It is one of China's major manufacturing centers.

OTHER PORTS IN NORTHERN CHINA. The marshy coast of the Yangtze and Hwang Ho deltas between Shanghai and Tientsin is poor in natural harbors. In contrast the Shantung Peninsula, which became an area of foreign penetration at the turn of the century, has a more inviting coast for port development.

Lienyunkang, north of the Hwang Ho's 1852 mouth, was constructed by the Chinese government in the 1930s as the sea terminus of the important 1600-kilometer east–west Lunghai Railway and especially planned as an outlet for Chinese coal exports. It was in poor condition after the war. An American consulting firm advised against reconstruction and further expansion but despite this it has been rebuilt.

Tsingtao's excellent harbor was made into a German naval base and commercial port. With good rail connections to the interior and superior port facilities Tsingtao is a port of more than local importance. Chefoo and the former British naval base at Weihaiwei are small ports on the northern coast of Shantung.

Chinwangtao, near the ocean end of the Great Wall, was built and operated by a British mining company, owner of the large Kailan mine northeast of Tientsin, China's second largest coal producer. Some of the coal from this mine was shipped through the company port to Shanghai. Chinwangtao has been competing with Tientsin-Tangku for general cargo as it can offer faster cargo handling.

Manchuria

Manchuria had been recognized as part of China even before the Manchus captured Peking in 1644 and set up the Manchu dynasty which reigned until 1911. But this section of China has had the most complex recent history. The fertile plain of Manchuria remained grassland, used only by nomads until the restrictions on migration were removed in the beginning of the present century and large numbers of Chinese farmers from the Yellow Plain moved into this rich area. In 1896 the Russians obtained concessions to build their

---

[7] Albert Kolb, *Ostasien*. Heidelberg, 1963. P. 280.
[8] According to *Pravda* (June 30, 1961) Shanghai in 1960 handled over 36 million tons of waterborne cargo after having doubled its cargo turnover in a short time.

Trans-Siberian Railway through northern Manchuria, but it was not until the First World War that the all-Russian route north of the Amur River was completed. At the turn of the century China's weakness became evident and it was generally thought that China would be divided between the European powers and Japan. Russia occupied parts of Manchuria in 1900 and built a branch railroad from Harbin to Port Arthur on the tip of the Liaotung Peninsula. But then the Japanese were alarmed by the Russian advances. After the victory in the Russo-Japanese war of 1904–1905 Japan took over the Russian concessions in southern Manchuria including the railroad from Dairen to Changchun. The Japanese built numerous railways in Manchuria especially after 1931 when the new puppet state of Manchoukuo was created. They invested a billion dollars in Manchuria in mines, manufacturing plants and railways. Many of the new railways were designed for military purposes. The Japanese activity resulted in Manchuria today having a denser network of railroads than other parts of China and being industrially the most advanced region, with large coal mines at Fushun, steelworks at Anshan, machine works in Mukden and diversified industry in Dairen.

Manchuria has four main seaports. Dairen is the outlet for most of the Manchurian Plain. Under Japanese administration it became one of the leading ports in China, specially serving the soybean trade. With the nearby smaller town of Port Arthur, built as a naval base by the Russians, it forms the million-conurbation Luta. The Japanese used Port Arthur as a commercial port but after the Second World War it became a joint Sino-Soviet naval base. Only Chinese and Soviet merchant vessels may call.[1] Yingkow (Newchwang), closer to Mukden and the Manchurian Plain than Dairen, is the historic port of Manchuria. It is hampered by silting and is ice-bound in winter.

The new port of Hulutao was planned by the Chinese government to compete with the Japanese Dairen. It was built in the late 1930s and is connected by a twelve kilometer branch line with the Peking-Mukden railroad. In the beginning of the 1950s it was the second largest port in Manchuria with a capacity of one million tons which was to be increased to four million. Antung near the mouth of the Yalu River on the border between Manchuria and Korea is chiefly a lumber port. Some ocean-vessels call at Antung but most call at the outport Tatungkow.

Two ports outside China provide ocean outlets for northern Manchuria, Vladivostok in the Soviet Union and Najin (Rashin) in North Korea.

Taiwan

Taiwan, also known by its Portuguese name Formosa, abbreviated from *Ilha Formosa* (the beautiful island), was a Japanese possession between 1895 and 1945 before it was returned to China. After the Communist take-over in 1949 Taiwan and some minor islands have been the only territories under the control of the Nationalist Government. The foreign trade of Taiwan was before the war dominated by Japan and this country remains the leading trade partner of the island accounting for over 40 per cent of both exports and imports. Keelung and Kaohsiung at the northern and southern ends of the longitudinal railway, the main transportation artery of the island, handle almost all of Taiwan's seaborne trade. Sugar (chiefly refined sugar) accounts for about half of Taiwan's export value and is also the leading item by tonnage, while fertilizers, raw cotton and petroleum top the import list ranked by value. The minor ports, essentially used as fishing ports and not suitable for oceangoing

[1] H. J. v. Lochow, "Chinas Seehäfen", *Internationales Archiv für Verkehrswesen*, 1951. P. 222.

vessels, were closed to trade with the outside world in 1950. Keelung is the port of the capital Taipeh.[1]

Korea

Korea, a Japanese colony between 1910 and 1945, underwent rapid economic expansion after 1931 when Japan took over Manchuria. The mineral and hydro-electric resources were developed, many cities mushroomed, a network of railroads was established to move export products to the ports and the ports were modernized. Most of the industrial development took place in northern Korea, where coal and iron deposits and hydro-electric power resources abound. The main railroad was the double-track line from Pusan through Seoul to Manchuria.

After World War II Korea became independent but was divided at the 38th parallel. In reality Korea became two countries with little or no interchange after a short initial period, which led to an extensive reorientation of the economy. Even greater catastrophes hit Korea with the outbreak of the Korean War in 1950.

Among the leading ports in North Korea are Chinnampo and Haeju on the Yellow Sea. Chinnampo serves Pyongyang, the capital of North Korea and an industrial center in a region with coal and iron ore deposits. The port has been reconstructed after the war with Soviet aid.[2] On the Sea of Japan the Japanese built ports at Wonsan, Songjin and Chongjin. Two modern ports were constructed in the extreme northeast, Najin and Unggi, to serve as outlets for the products of central and northern Manchuria.[3]

South Korea has more extensive plains than North Korea and much more cultivated land. Industries are of two types, those which produce light consumer goods and those which process agricultural products, particularly rice. The Japanese developed the ports of Inchon, Kunsan, Mokpo and Pusan as major rice ports.

In recent years South Korea's foreign trade has chiefly been imports for its 25 million inhabitants and it has been a net importer of grain. The value of exports is less than one-tenth the value of the commodity imports. South Korea has about three times as large a population as North Korea.

Japan

Sparsely populated mountains covered with forests make up 60 per cent of Japan's land area. By far the largest part of the population is crowded on small alluvial and coastal plains and inland basins. Arable land accounts for only 16 per cent of the land surface. The ratio of population per square kilometer of cultivated land (1,570) is among the highest in the world. The four main islands stretch in arc form from southwest to northeast for about 2,200 kilometers. From a global shipping point of view, however, Japan may be considered as a single focus; over 90 per cent of her foreign trade moves through ports in the 850 kilometer Tokyo-to-northern Kyushu belt. After a rapid postwar economic expansion Japan in 1960 accounted for 90 million tons of cargo imports or half of Asia's total international cargo receipts.

The coasts with their many indentations are often rocky and steep, and in many places it has been difficult to secure enough flat land for port and manufacturing installations. The sea is everywhere easily accessible; few countries have a higher ratio of coastline per square kilometer of land surface. Nature thus seems to have predestined the Japanese to become a seafaring people; coastal shipping

[1] Cheng-Siang Chen, "The Port of Keelung", *Tijdschrift voor Economische en Sociale Geografie*, 1957. Pp. 142 ff.; *China Handbook 1955–56*. Taipei, 1955. P. 486; Frederick Hung, "Notes on the Historical Geography of Taiwan", *The Oriental Geographer*, 1958. Pp. 47 ff.

[2] *Pravda*, August 9, 1960.

[3] Shannon McCune, *Korea's Heritage, A Regional and Social Geography*. Tokyo, 1956.

has always played an important role in the communications between the scattered population nuclei. The feudal government did not permit the building of ocean vessels because of its policy of seclusion, yet there was a considerable and well organised traffic between the chief ports, especially between Edo and Osaka. The first modern shipyard was built in 1891. From this time on the construction of steel vessels increased rapidly; in 1956 Japan launched a larger tonnage than any other nation in the world. Its merchant marine has grown simultaneously and now is surpassed only by those of the United Kingdom, the United States, Norway and Liberia.

In modern times the dense net of efficient railways has offered serious competition for coastal shipping. Japan is among the leading railway nations. Expressed in passenger-kilometers it is second only to the Soviet Union. Also goods traffic is very large. The small size of the country, about the same as Norway or California, means that average transportation distances are rather short which favors the railways in competition with coastal shipping. Roads are poor, an anomaly in a small, well-developed country. Hence trucks and cars are scarce outside the four main conurbations.

In almost all countries, except Japan, modern

shipping is part of an economic pattern imposed by European sea power. It shows great similarities from country to country. The Japanese economic development, although modeled on and influenced by the West, is essentially an indigenous feature. The present distribution and importance of maritime activities require some understanding of Japan's feudal background and its subsequent economic development.

Historical Background

Until the arrival in 1853 of a squadron of United States naval vessels under Commodore Perry rather little had been known in the outside world about the Japanese in their secluded country. The rise of Japan to the position of a great power in the fifty years following the Meiji Restoration in 1868 seemed astonishing to most Westerners. Penetrating studies by foreign and native scholars indicate, however, that the break between the old and the new Japan was less sharp than has been supposed in the West.[1] The energy and restless ambition of the Japanese were deeply rooted in the cultural patterns of the nation; even before 1868 these islanders had rapidly assimilated foreign modes and new ideas,[2] they had often shown boldness in executing large projects and, above all, they had a trained and frequently exercised capacity for organization.[3]

In feudal Japan four-fifths of the population lived from agriculture. The population had been stationary at about 30 million during the greater part of the Tokugawa Shogunate (1603–1867): abortions and infanticides were efficient checks on population growth in this period. Food production was the chief economic and social concern of the nation; life was centered on the growing of the staple product, rice. Population densities in different areas were in direct proportion to the amount of arable land; only a few, large cities drew on the resources of the whole nation.[4]

[1] G. C. Allen, *A Short Economic History of Modern Japan 1867–1937*. London, 1946.

[2] During the seclusion the Japanese intellectual classes had acquired knowledge of Western science through the medium of the Dutch language. Allen, *op. cit.* Pp. 18 ff.

[3] Trained on village, county and state level especially in connection with irrigation and reclamation projects.

[4] The small urban population was made up of the soldier class (*samurai*), merchants and craftsmen. The political power was in the hands of the *shogun*, who during the Tokugawa period resided in Edo (now Tokyo), which was in the beginning of the eighteenth century after Peking the world's largest city with about one million inhabitants and the chief consuming center in the country. The largest population group in the city were the *samurai*, retainers of the *shogun* who owned one-fifth to one-quarter of Japan's arable land. The prevailing *sankin kotai* system provided that all feudal lords, *daimyo*, must reside alternate years in Edo and leave their wives and children as hostages in that city. The emperor lived in seclusion in Kyoto,

After the Meiji Restoration the coastal belt between Tokyo and Northern Kyushu, which contained the largest cities and the most densely populated parts (i.e. the largest alluvial plains) of feudal Japan, became dominant. It developed into the Manufacturing Belt, including all the four leading manufacturing districts: Keihin on the Kanto plain (Tokyo, Kawasaki, Yokohama), Nagoya on the Nobi plain, Kinki with the three million-cities Osaka, Kobe and Kyoto and finally northern Kyushu, a conurbation of five cities with approximately one million inhabitants, dominated by heavy manufacturing based on Japan's chief coal-field. The population of the narrow coastal strip of the Manufacturing Belt continues to grow at a fast rate, while most of the rural areas, covering the greater part of Japan's surface, report population declines.[5]

Outside the Manufacturing Belt urbanization has been much less conspicuous; cities are chiefly of local or regional importance with a relatively small production for the national or international market. The two extremes of Old Japan, southern Kyushu and northern Honshu (Tohoku), are underdeveloped areas. A striking example of differences in relative growth is offered by the two cities Nagoya and Kanazawa. Both were castle towns of powerful *daimyo*; they were two out of five cities having more than 100,000 inhabitants at the end of the shogunate. Nagoya, located in the Manufacturing Belt, has grown from 125,000 inhabitants in 1873 to 1,337,000 in 1955; Kanazawa on the Sea of Japan in the same period grew from 109,000 to 277,000.

Population and Industry

The Japanese population, almost stationary at about 30 million for 150 years before the Restoration, has since tripled. Seen in the global perspective this increase is rather normal. The population employed in agriculture, four-fifths of the total in the beginning of the

Meiji period, has remained stable at 14–15 million with a temporary increase after World War II. In 1955 it was 41 per cent of the total and the ratio has since declined rapidly. It is now well below 40 per cent. But Japan, like the Soviet Union, is still to a large extent an agrarian country.

A stagnation and even a decline in the Japanese population can now be foreseen when it has reached somewhat over 100 million.[1] For continued urbanization and expansion of urban industries the large rural population offers a source of recruitment for some decades. Mechanization of farming operations has started. The use of small machines on the

capital since 793. The second largest city was Osaka, also located in the old core region of Japan, Kinki (= near the imperial court). Osaka was dominated by its commercial functions. It was the chief rice market, an important position in feudal Japan where most economic transactions were in terms of rice. *Daimyo* kept warehouses in Osaka, where they stored the rice received from their fiefs. The merchants of Osaka built up considerable influence from their position outside the feudal hierarchy. These merchant families played a leading part in the economic revolution that followed the restoration.

The 300 *daimyo* were scattered over the country, residing in their castle towns, inhabited chiefly by *samurai,* merchants and craftsmen. For the *sankin kotai* good roads for their time existed from Edo to all parts of the country, and along the main roads were many stage towns. When railroads were built they closely followed the old highways. (See R. B. Hall, "Tokaido: Road and Region", *Geographical Review,* 1937.) The best road, the famous Tokaido, connected Edo with Kyoto. Other roads continued along the Inland Sea to Nagasaki on Kyushu, Japan's window on the world, where the Chinese and the Dutch were allowed to carry on a strictly supervised trade even after the seclusion of the country in 1641. The Edo—Nagasaki roads connected the largest cities and the most densely populated parts of Japan and the Kyoto—Edo stretch was probably the most heavily trafficked road in the world.

[5] See for instance Peter Schöller, "Wandlungen der Industriestruktur Japans", *Deutscher Geographentag Köln,* 1961. Pp. 238 ff.

[1] The tremendous population increase in the years immediately following the last war, a consequence of exceptionally high birth rates and rapidly falling death rates, drastically pointed out over-population as one of the chief national problems. Through liberal abortion laws and active propaganda for the use of contraceptives the Japanese Government, first in the world, took steps to counteract the risks for pauperization of the people. The natural population increase, being 1.7 million in 1948, was reduced to 0.8 million in 1957.

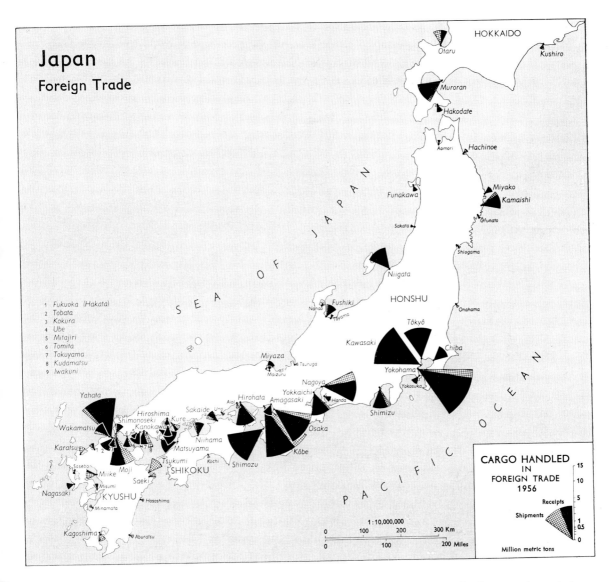

Japan
Foreign Trade

1 Fukuoka (Hakata)
2 Tobata
3 Kokura
4 Ube
5 Mitajiri
6 Tomita
7 Tokuyama
8 Kudamatsu
9 Iwakuni

SEA OF JAPAN

HOKKAIDO

HONSHU

PACIFIC OCEAN

KYUSHU

SHIKOKU

CARGO HANDLED
IN
FOREIGN TRADE
1956

Receipts

Shipments

Million metric tons

1:10,000,000

minute farms (0.7 hectares being the average size) is possible to a larger extent than is generally thought in the West. Rice production increased rapidly till the middle of the 1920s, chiefly thanks to the application of fertilizers and to some extent due to increased acreage. After a long period of stagnation at about 10 million tons a year—with increasing quantities being imported in the 1920s and 30s, chiefly from the Japanese dependencies Formosa and Korea—the rice-crop curve in the 1950s again showed a rising tendency. Of the other grains wheat and barley are imported in sizeable quantities. Both are grown in Japan chiefly as winter crops on the paddy fields. Rice is the preferred food even if wheat has been accepted in the form of *pasta,* etc. in the diet of city people. Barley is still the poor man's food; to a certain extent this is also true of imported rice. The imports of sugar and soybeans are considerable. Japan will continue to be dependent on the imports of marginal quantities of food but with the stagnation of population and larger domestic production of rice there should hardly be an increase. The government's efforts to promote a more diversified diet with an increased consumption of animal protein has met with success.

Food crops occupy 92 per cent of Japan's arable land. Of industrial crops only mulberry for the raw silk industry is of any importance.[2] Cocoon production is an integrated part of farming; for years it was after rice growing economically the most important activity for Japanese farmers. Silk-reeling, on the other hand, is a manufacturing industry.

First the Depression and then World War II brought tremendous changes to the silk industry; the introduction and expansion of new fibers (rayon, nylon, etc.) also contributed. The mulberry planted area in 1955 was only one-third of the 1934–36 area, silk raisers numbered less than half (1.9 and 0.8 million respectively), production of cocoons and raw silk was approximately one-third and exports were only 15 per cent. Two-thirds of the silk exports still go to the United States, the rest chiefly to France and Italy.

From the beginning raw silk was the chief export product of modern Japan; the United States was the leading silk weaving and silk consuming country. The trade reached its peak in the prosperous 1920s when silk shirts and silk dresses became symbols of wealth in the United States. Raw silk production was chiefly concentrated in the inland valleys of central Japan but it was represented in all of the three southern islands (Old Japan). The silk was exported chiefly through Yokohama by fast vessels to Seattle, the closest American port, from where it was sent by rapid trains to New York. The silk industry was located near this fashion center (in Paterson and in eastern Pennsylvania). In 1929 silk made up 37 per cent of the Japanese export value; this luxury export was hit very hard by the Depression and was soon surpassed by cotton goods on the export list. In the postwar years it has occupied a modest place among the export

items with only 1.3 per cent of the export value in 1960. Yokohama is still the leading silk port.

The postwar industrial expansion has been widely diversified, which is reflected by the export list. Two base industries, steel production and petroleum refining, are now by far the dominating generators of seaborne traffic, whereas food imports, contrary to common belief, play a rather subordinate role in tonnage as well as in value of imports.[3]

The rapidly increasing petroleum imports are primarily in the form of crude for the many Japanese oil refineries. Crude imports in 1960 approached 30 million tons and the imports of products were 5.8 million tons. According to the long-term plan[4] Japan is expected to import 70 million tons of petroleum in 1970 and 130 million tons by 1980.

The steel industry generates almost as large tonnages as the petroleum trade. Steel production increased from a prewar level of 6–7 million tons to 28 million tons in 1961 which placed Japan after the United States, the Soviet Union and West Germany among the steel nations. In 1960, when production amounted to 22.2 million tons, the Japanese steel mills consumed 15.9 million tons of iron ore of which only 1.3 million were supplied by domestic mines. Malaya (5.3 million), India (2.4), Goa (2.0), South America (1.3), the Philippines (1.2), Canada (1.1) and the United States (0.8) were the chief suppliers. The steel mills also consumed 13.5 million

[2] Mulberry is grown on the diluvial terraces which cannot be used for rice. Raw cotton was grown in feudal Japan but is now imported, until recently the leading import by value.

[3] Rice imports fluctuate somewhat but have in recent years not exceeded a few hundred thousand tons. To wheat imports of 2–3 million tons, sugar imports of 1.2 million tons and soybean imports of about one million tons come rapidly increasing imports of corn (1.4 million tons in 1960). By value the food imports do not exceed 15 per cent. They are of about the same order as petroleum imports.

[4] *Prospects of Japan's Economy in 1980.* Economic Planning Agency, (Seiichi Tobata, chairman). Tokyo, 1960.

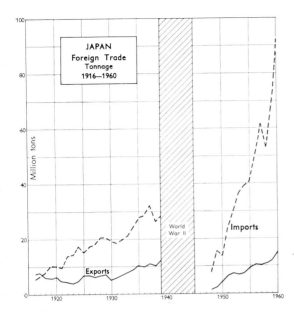

JAPAN
Foreign Trade
Tonnage
1916—1960

Million tons

World War II

Imports

Exports

Data from *Port Statistics of Japan,* Ministry of Transportation. (Published in Japanese and extracted for this diagram by Mr. Shozo Yamamoto of Tokyo Kyoiku University.)

tons of scrap most of which was home scrap (5.4 million tons) and domestic purchased scrap (3.7 million tons), but a sizeable quantity (4.4 million) was imported, primarily from the United States (3.0 million tons). The consumption of coking coal amounted to 17.9 million tons of which 10.9 million came from domestic mines and the rest was imported, chiefly from the United States (4.9 million) and Australia (1.2 million tons).[5]

The Japanese have pushed the development of their steel industry far beyond the demands of the home market in spite of higher production costs than the European and American mills. This made it possible to expand the

[5] Data on raw materials for Japan's steel industry from Brian Beedham, "Japan: Political Ally—Commercial Competitor", *Steel Review* 25, 1962. P. 31.

[1] The Tokyo–Yokohama area is often referred to as Keihin and the Osaka–Kobe area as Hanshin. Keihin in 1956 had a total cargo turnover of 34.5 million tons, of which 17.1 was in foreign trade and Hanshin had 28.2 million tons (11.6 million foreign trade). Intraport traffic has been deducted from these figures.

shipyard capacity and take advantage of the shipbuilding boom in the middle of the 1950s, when date of delivery was more important than price. In addition to ships Japan exports steel mill products (2.2 million tons in 1960) and a great variety of machinery. Products made of metal account for over one-third of the Japanese exports by value. Most of the raw materials for this industry are imported but so are the raw materials for the textile industry, which still accounts for over one-fifth of the export value. Cotton long topped the list of imports by value but is now surpassed by petroleum.

Ports

The two dominating ports, Yokohama and Kobe, show striking similarities. Both grew in a surprisingly short time from insignificant fishing harbors to world ports and the most cosmopolitan cities in the country; they are products of modern Japan. They serve the two most populous areas, the Kanto Plain (20 million inhabitants) and the Kinki region (15 million). They are located on deep water, close to the two largest cities, Tokyo and Osaka, which are situated on river deltas in the inner part of shallow bays, accessible for the vessels of the feudal period, but only after dredging for small and medium-sized ocean-going vessels. They serve not only as ports for Japan's two largest consuming centers and manufacturing districts but also as collecting and distributing points for the foreign trade of large areas of Nippon: Yokohama for the northeastern parts, including the Tohoku region on northern Honshu and the pioneer area of Hokkaido, and Kobe for the southwestern regions, including the manufacturing districts along the Inland Sea. Both Yokohama and Kobe have seen the adjacent metropolitan port being dredged and built out to accomodate fairly large ships; Tokyo—Yokohama and Kobe—Osaka[1] form large port complexes al-

THE PORTS OF GREATER TOKYO

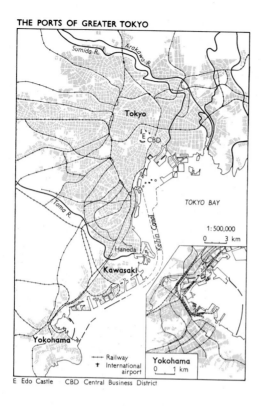

though not under unified port administrations. From the beginning of modern times, even before they were opened to foreign trade, Osaka and Tokyo had an intense lighter traffic.

TOKYO–KAWASAKI–YOKOHAMA (KEIHIN). The Kanto plain is Japan's largest area of relatively level land and it is also the leading manufacturing district accounting for almost 23 per cent of the manufacturing employment.[2] Greater Tokyo or Keihin, including the cities of Tokyo, Kawasaki and Yokohama, is the core of this region. Tokyo, the political, financial and modern cultural center, in recent decades has developed diversified heavy industry in addition to its traditional light industries. The Kawasaki and northern Yokohama waterfront is dominated by heavy manufacturing plants depending on waterborne raw materials. Many factories occupy filled-land sites. Port installations are concentrated on the

western shore of the bay but recently a steel mill was built at Chiba on the eastern shore. In the 1930s a channel was dredged from the deepwater port at Yokohama to Tokyo, allowing vessels of 23-foot draft to proceed all the way to the capital port, which had only been accessible for small coastal vessels and lighters.

Yokohama's trade has traditionally been across the Pacific with the United States to a much larger extent than is true of the other principal ports.[3] As much as 70 per cent of Japan's silk exports, most of which were produced in Yokohama's immediate hinterland, passed through the port and the United States was the dominating raw silk customer. The trans-Pacific liners normally call first at Yokohama on their way to the China seas and the Straits region of Southeast Asia. Kobe and Yokohama have been competing for the position as the ranking port of Japan measured by the value of their foreign trade. For fifteen years before the 1923 earthquake Yokohama was at the top, a position it regained in 1938. In the postwar period Kobe has been the number one port by a wide margin, but it is surpassed by Yokohama when measured by cargo tonnage. Before the war Yokohama was also Japan's main gateway for trans-Pacific passengers but this function has been taken over by the nearby Haneda airport.

SHIMIZU with a superb natural harbor has attracted oil refineries and shipyards. Cargo liners call at the port to pick up locally produced tea (May–September) and canned citrus fruit (November). Soybeans for a large oil mill rank high among the imports.

NAGOYA AND YOKKAICHI. The Nobi Plain, the second largest lowland in southern Honshu and the Chukyo manufacturing district, the

[2] John H. Thompson and Michihiro Miyazaki, "A Map of Japan's Manufacturing", *Geographical Review*, 1959. Pp. 1 ff.

[3] Glenn T. Trewartha, *Japan: A Physical, Cultural and Regional Geography*. Madison, 1945. Pp. 485 ff.

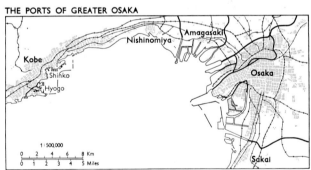

THE PORTS OF GREATER OSAKA

General view of the port of Kobe, Japan's leading foreign trade port by value. To the left are the two Hyogo piers and in the center the several Shinko piers. Plans exist for considerable extension of the port and industrial facilities on filled land to the right margin of the picture and beyond in the direction of Osaka.

Mount Rokko in the background hems in the city on the narrow coastal strip. (Port & Harbor Bureau, Kobe)

third largest in Japan with 13 per cent of Japan's manufacturing employment, center on Nagoya. None of the ports serving this region can be compared with Kobe or Yokohama. The Chukyo area is in the traffic shadow of the two leading general ports. Light industries (textiles, wood products, chinaware and food products) dominate and for the export of high-value cargo the two leading ports, particularly Kobe, with their frequent sailings, are superior to the local ports, Nagoya and Yokkaichi. However, the imports of raw materials, such as wool and pulp for the rayon industry, pass through the local ports. Much of the china is exported, primarily to the United States. This industry is based on local china clay and dates back far into the feudal period. Seto near Nagoya is closely associated with porcelain as

445

evidenced by the Japanese word for china, *setomono* (object from Seto). Nagoya has Japan's leading automobile factory started in the 1930s as part of a factory producing automatic looms.

OSAKA—KOBE (HANSHIN). Osaka's commercial and industrial preeminence is of long standing. The city straddles the large Yodogawa delta with its many distributaries. In the feudal period vessels were small and the shallow water did not prevent Osaka from being a busy port. The old port of Hyogo, before the Tokugawa shogunate the gateway for trade with China and Korea,[4] was used to some extent as an outport. After the Industrial Revolution, which turned Osaka into the commercial and industrial capital of Japan and soon gave the city the apt epithet "the Manchester of the Far East", large transoceanic vessels appeared and they had to use the booming new outport of Kobe located near the old port of Hyogo. The twelve and fifteen meter contours run close to Kobe but at Osaka the ten meter contour is seven kilometers from the city.[5]

In the 1890s Osaka started an extensive harbor improvement program. The main Yodo River was diverted to a new, shorter and straighter channel north of the downtown area, breakwaters were built and inside of these a fairly deep harbor was dredged and land for wharves and warehouses was created by filling. As the city area is criss-crossed with river distributaries and canals most of the large and medium-sized manufacturing plants have water frontage. Lighter traffic is intense and many factory sites are accessible for small ocean vessels.

With the improved port facilities went a rapid increase in direct foreign trade through Osaka. In 1929 Osaka was a poor third among the Japanese foreign trade ports (17 per cent by value) after Kobe (36 per cent) and Yokohama (31 per cent), but in 1939 Osaka accounted for 25 per cent, the same as Kobe

and only slightly less than Yokohama (29 per cent).

Raw cotton, traditionally Japan's leading import item by value, arrives at Kobe by large transoceanic liners, while the large exports of cotton goods of the 1930s were primarily directed to China and other nearby Asiatic countries and were shipped by small and medium-sized ocean vessels direct from Osaka. Kobe in 1960 handled almost three-quarters of Japan's raw cotton imports.

Just as the postwar Japanese exports have become extremely diversified as compared with the 1920s and 1930s so has the industrial structure of the Hanshin manufacturing region, the second largest in Japan, and the trade structure of Hanshin's two main ports.

The Wakayama oil refinery south of Osaka is served by the oil jetties in the excellent harbor of Shimozu.

KITA-KYUSHU. The conurbation of six cities at the western entrance of the Inland Sea, totaling over a million inhabitants, has no dominating city but Yahata (Yawata) is the largest and best known abroad because of its steelworks. Three cities are located around the small Dokai Bay, a natural harbor which with moderate improvements became the obvious exit of the Chikuho coal field: Wakamatsu, well-known as a coal-shipping port; Yahata, the site of the first modern iron and steel mill based on coal in Japan, built by the Government between 1896 and 1901; and Tobata with a branch plant of the Yahata steelworks. The combined capacities of the two steel plants make it the largest in Asia (6.1 million tons). The early development of the Yahata Iron and Steel Works triggered a striking chain reaction of satellite-plant growth in the conurbation, especially on Dokai Bay.[6]

[4] *Kinki Guidebook*, IGU Regional Conference in Japan 1957. Tokyo, 1957. P. 55.
[5] L. Mecking, *Japans Häfen*. Hamburg, 1931. P. 355.
[6] L. Mecking, *Japans Häfen* (Hamburg, 1931)

Steel Works of Japan 1960

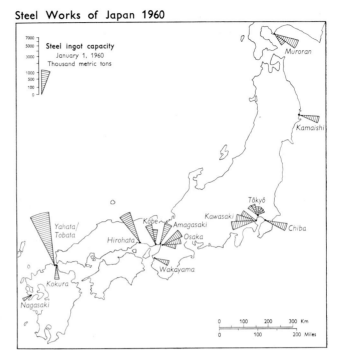

All Japanese steel mills have a tide-water location. Production is expected to double between 1960 and 1970 when it should be 48 million tons. Nearly four times as much coal will have to be imported and four times as much iron ore (45 million tons). The expected large increase in ore imports is partly a result of the emphasis on oxygen converters in the expansion plans. Converter steel will increase from 3 million tons to 25 million.

The steel industry will continue to be the chief generator of seaborne traffic after the petroleum trade.

Data from *Steel Review* 25, January, 1962. P. 27.

The coal shipped from Dokai Bay is almost exclusively sent coastwise, primarily to thermo-electric and industrial plants in the Manufacturing Belt. Most of Japan's electricity is generated in hydro-electric plants but for topographical reasons these are small and have an uneven production which necessitates a large stand-by thermo-electric capacity.

The two cities of Moji and Shimonoseki, separated by the 700 meter wide Shimonoseki Strait, were connected by a 3,600 meter tunnel in 1942. Moji has the best harbor in northern Kyushu and its location at the convergence of major land and sea routes makes

it a natural collecting and distributing center for general cargo. Many overseas shipping lines call at Moji on their way between Yokohama-Kobe and ports on the mainland of Asia.

HAKATA, Japan's oldest port, recorded in Chinese books from the third century, only allows shallow draft vessels. Hakata's twin city Fukuoka has, however, developed into the seventh largest city in Japan and the chief business center of northern Kyushu.[7]

NAGASAKI with its long history of foreign trading has played a subordinate role as a port in the postwar period. The loss of the trade with China has probably contributed to the decline. Nagasaki and the former naval base of Sasebo have large shipyards.

KAMAISHI. In feudal Japan iron was made from iron sand and charcoal and the many small works were located in the mountain areas of

contains a detailed discussion of all the main ports and port groups in Japan. Coal, the Yahata Steel Works and the forests of masts of the sailing vessels gave the character to Dokai Bay as described by Mecking in the 1920s. In 1927 no less than 47,000 calls by sailing vessels, engaged in coastal trade, and 4,600 by steamers were recorded at Dokai Bay. The small wooden sailing vessels are still common along the coasts of Japan but they are now motor-powered.

[7] Hikoichi Shimomura and Jiro Yonekura (editors), *Inland Sea and Kyushu: Guidebook*. IGU Regional Conference in Japan. Tokyo, 1957. P. 57.

southwestern Honshu (Chugoku) and northern Honshu (Tohoku). The large amounts of charcoal required forced the works to move from place to place. The first blast furnace of the western type was built by the government at Kamaishi in Tohoku in 1874, only twenty kilometers from an iron mine. Local charcoal was available and the pig iron could be shipped by coastal vessels.[8] However, the plant was not a success[9] but it was reopened under private management in 1887 and is now the oldest existing steel mill in Japan.

MURORAN from the 1890s developed into the principal port of the Ishikari coal fields. The coal is sent coastwise as far as Nagoya. Two steel mills, the first constructed in 1907, account for most of the industrial employment and generate much of the cargo traffic in the well-protected harbor. The steel works receive iron ore by rail from small deposits about 80 kilometers away, but additional quantities of iron ore and coking coal must be imported. Muroran also ships timber and newsprint coastwise.

Of the other Hokkaido ports Hakodate is the ferry port and Otaru the seaport of the interior capital of Sapporo. They serve the whole of Hokkaido for passengers and general cargo traffic respectively. Hakodate is also the chief fishing port of Hokkaido and one of the largest in Japan. Kushiro ships coal, newsprint and timber and is a base for deep-sea fishing.

Prospects

The prospects for continued rapid economic expansion in Japan in the 1960s seem bright.[1] The demographic situation is specially favorable in a transition period with an annual increase in total population of one per cent or less, while the gainfully employed population, due to the previous high birth rates, increases by two per cent. A continued transfer of people from agriculture and urban industries with hidden unemployment to the more efficient service and manufacturing industries is also likely to occur. As Japan is more dependent on seaborne raw materials than any of the other great industrial nations she will benefit most from the gradual shift to ever larger and more economic vessels, and also from low raw material prices on the world market. Japan's heavy manufacturing industry is already located on the coast, as a rule close to the great markets. In Western Europe and the United States steel works and other heavy industries were often built near interior coal fields without access to waterways or on waterways with insufficient capacity for modern barge transport. The European and American firms will have to face difficult decisions—expanding the old works on the coal fields (cheapest in the short run) or constructing new works on the coast. The Soviet Union and Eastern Europe in this respect are even worse off. In the Communist Bloc heavy manufacturing is almost entirely based on rail transport. The present trend of locating heavy manufacturing industries at deepwater seaports is especially favorable for countries like Japan, Italy and the Netherlands, where for various reasons most of the heavy manufacturing industry is already so located.

Soviet Ports on the Pacific

Eastern Siberia and the Far East are sparsely populated parts of the Soviet Union. Due to its severe climate, its mountainous topography

[8] Sadao Yamaguchi, "The Locational Changes of Iron and Steel Industry in Japan", *Proceedings of IGU Regional Conference in Japan 1957*. Tokyo, 1959. Pp. 529 ff.

[9] Lack of charcoal and coke, unsuitable transportation system, too small market for iron, too high prices compared with imported pig iron, and insufficient knowledge of the new technique were serious deficiencies found by a Government Investigation Committee.

[1] Saburo Okita, "Japan's Economic Prospects", *Foreign Affairs*, October, 1960. Pp. 123 ff.

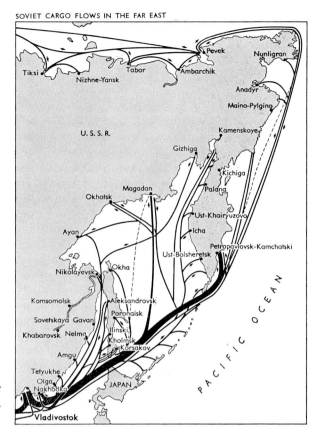

SOVIET CARGO FLOWS IN THE FAR EAST

Source: *Transport SSSR, Morskoj Transport* (V. G. Bakaev and S. M. Baev, eds.). Moskva, 1961.

and its peripheral location, the eastern part of the huge Soviet landmass offers poor conditions for agriculture. It is, however, rich in other natural resources, minerals, forests and fish. The urban population accounts for a higher percentage than in other parts of the Soviet Union. The Far East has three large cities: Khabarovsk, Vladivostok and Komsomolsk. The diversified manufacturing industries of these three cities have a regional monopoly for their products, to use a Western term, due to the long distances to competing industries in western Siberia and European Russia.

Eastern Siberia and the Far East were settled by immigrants from the European part of

Russia, who arrived on the long overland route; the indigenous people were few. The construction of the Trans-Siberian Railroad (1892–1905) had a tremendous impact; it opened these areas to settlement on a relatively large scale. The Soviet Government is continuing the policy of developing the eastern regions and the railroad is still the backbone of the transportation system[1] except for passenger transport which is now dominated by air traffic. Coastal shipping is important, however, and for Sakhalin and Kamchatka and most coastal settlements on the mainland there is no alternative to the sea route for the movement of cargo.

Vladivostok, the Pacific terminal of the Trans-Siberian Railroad, on the same latitude as Batumi, Rome and Boston, traditionally has been the hub of the Soviet Pacific sea routes.

---

[1] The original line ran from Chita through Manchuria to Vladivostok. During World War I an all-Russian link was constructed between Chita and Vladivostok following the Amur and Ussuri rivers.

In 1935–37 the construction of a new port was begun at Nakhodka, some 100 kilometers to the southeast of Vladivostok. It has been growing rapidly after the war. Vladivostok and Nakhodka now have about the same cargo turnover.[2] They are the eastern terminals of the northern sea route and they also have regular sailings to Odessa. The traffic with other Soviet ports on the Pacific is the most important while foreign trade with Pacific nations, other than North Korea and China, was neglible in the 1950s. Coal, petroleum, lumber, fish and salt are the leading cargoes on the Soviet Pacific sea routes.

In spite of its coastal location Vladivostok has a continental climate. The average January temperature is $-13°C$ (9°F) and the average for the warmest month $+19°C$ (66°F). No other major port in the world has such a wide temperature range. However, the waters around Vladivostok are relatively warm, for a branch of the warm Kuroshio current enters the Sea of Japan from the south. Consequently the port of Vladivostok can be kept open by ice-breakers and Nakhodka is seldom blocked by ice.

After the loss of Port Arthur in 1905 Vladivostok became the Russian naval base on the Pacific. It is also the base of a whaling fleet and a fish canning center.

The leading port of Kamchatka is Petropavlovsk. On Sakhalin the two largest ports, Korsakov and Kholmsk, are located in the southernmost part of the island. Of the mainland ports, Magadan on the Nagaevo Bay and Sovetskaya Gavan (Vanino) are important. Magadan, a rapidly expanding town, is the administrative center of the Kolyma gold fields. Sovetskaya Gavan is connected by railroad to Komsomolsk. The port of Nikolayevsk at the mouth of the Amur is the transshipment point for cargo from river to ocean vessels.

[2] I. V. Nikol'skij (*Geografija transporta SSSR,* Moskva, 1960), states that Vladivostok has the largest turnover with Nakhodka in second place; N. J. Ljalikov (*Ėkonomičeskaja geografija SSSR,* Moskva, 1961) lists Nakhodka as the leading commercial port in the Far East.

OCEANIA

Australia

Australia has a short European history. The island-continent was discovered by Dutch explorers in the early seventeenth century. But the European merchants of the day did not establish their trading posts on uninhabited coasts and the discovery was soon "forgotten". Australia had no permanent settlement until Captain Cook had surveyed the east coast in 1770. Eighteen years later—after the American War of Independence had sealed off the old dumping-ground for England's criminals—the first settlement, a penal establishment with 770 convicts and 250 soldiers, was formed at Sydney as a result of Captain Cook's reports. In the ensuing years other groups followed; about 160,000 convicts were transported to Australia in 80 years.[1] Large-scale immigration started with the Gold Rush in the early 1850s. The timing of European settlement in Australia thus closely parallels that of California.

The location of settlements on the coasts of Australia was influenced by the availability of natural harbors or navigable river entrances. Today it is characteristic of Australia that the capital city of each state contains a very large share of the state's population, manufacturing capacity and commercial activities. All state capitals rank among the ten leading ports: Sydney, Melbourne, Perth-Fremantle, Adelaide, Brisbane and Hobart. Since the main centers

of population lie along the coast at great intervals and the interior, economically speaking, is a huge void, coastwise shipping is relatively more important than in other countries of continental dimensions. With the development of railroads and highways many of the smallest ports or landing stages, which played an important role in the early days of the settlement of Australia, have disappeared or remained small.

The discovery of gold brought many vessels to Australia in the years following 1850. Coastwise shipping also increased greatly as at that time overland travel was both very slow and expensive. Most of the present coastal shipping companies have their origins in this period. The number of vessels arriving in Australia from overseas trebled between 1850 and 1900 (650 and 1,860 respectively).[2] Measured in net tonnage the increase was much greater, from 213 to 2,947 thousand tons. The number of vessels entering Australian ports from abroad was roughly the same in the mid-1950s as around the turn of the century but the tonnage had more than trebled (9,162 thousand tons in 1954–55; 1,940 vessels).

Australia has long been known as an important contributor of raw materials to the world market. Although having become remarkably urbanized according to any standards[3] Australia has been able through mechanization to maintain large outputs of her traditional export products from the range, farm and mine. Her close ties with the United Kingdom and other Commonwealth countries are reflected by the direction of her trade. Australians and New Zealanders are often said to be "more British than the British" and to look upon their antipode mother country as "home".

[1] Clifford M. Zierer, "Australia: The Cultural Development", in *Geography of the Pacific* (Otis W. Freeman, Editor). New York, 1951.

[2] "Ports and Shipping", *Atlas of Australian Resources*. Department of National Development, Canberra, 1958.

[3] In 1954 no less than 77 per cent of the population were living in cities and towns, and 54 per cent in the six state capitals.

Oceania

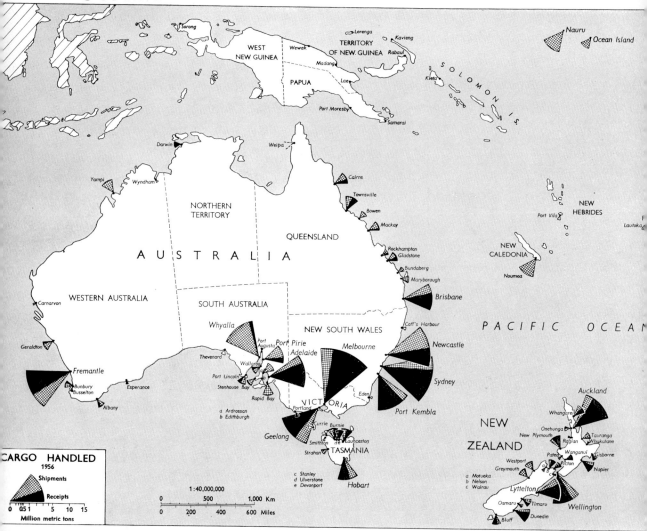

CARGO HANDLED
1956

Shipments

Receipts

0 0.5 1   5   10   15
Million metric tons

1 : 40,000,000

0   500   1,000 Km

0   200   400   600 Miles

The Australian Government early adopted a "white-Australia" policy to prevent their empty continent from being swamped with people from densely settled Java, India, China and Japan. Immigration from the United Kingdom and other countries in Europe with easily assimilated people has been encouraged by the government, especially since World War II. For a couple of years, 1949 and 1950, net immigration exceeded the natural increase,[4] which percentagewise is higher than in the United Kingdom. The population, though still small (10 million in 1960), is thus increasing fairly rapidly.

Australian ports in the mid-1950s handled about 50 million tons a year. Coastal trade accounted for somewhat larger quantities than overseas trade. Overseas trade receipts were about twice as large as shipments. Petroleum,

[4] O. H. K. Spate, "Australia and its Dependencies". In *The Changing World* (W. G. East and A. E. Moodie, editors). London, 1956.

452

crude and refined products in bulk, accounted for 52 per cent of discharged tons from overseas, followed by phosphatic rock (8 per cent), vehicles, timber and iron and steel. The principal exports were grains (30 per cent), sugar (10 per cent), wool and ores. Coastwise trade was dominated by coal (36 per cent) and iron ore (28 per cent) followed by refined petroleum products[5] and iron and steel. Petroleum is now imported almost exclusively in the form of crude for Australian refineries located in or near the capital cities. Exports mainly consist of primary products, chiefly agricultural.

Railways still provide the main links between hinterlands and ports but trucking has increased considerably in recent years. Proximity to the producing area is a basic consideration in the choice of export port but differences in railway gauge[6] and differential rates offered by adjacent railway systems sometimes may send export goods to ports other than those

[5] The tonnage of petroleum products in cabotage has increased substantially in the last few years with the expansion of Australian refining capacity.

[6] More than 40,000 of the 45,000 kilometers of railroad in Australia are owned and operated by the individual states; only 3,500 kilometers belong to the Commonwealth. The different railway systems were built with different gauges, a disadvantage which was especially brought out in the national emergency of World War II when tremendous demands were placed upon the interior transportation system.

[7] The annual production of raw sugar is 1.3 million tons of which 90 per cent is shipped overseas or in coastal freighters to the refineries at Sydney, Melbourne, Adelaide and Fremantle. It used to be shipped in bags as general cargo from ten ports along the Queensland "sugar coast". After 1954 a rapid conversion to bulk movement was organized following the pattern introduced at Hawaii in 1940. The largest terminals are at Mackay, Townsville and Mourilyan (opened in 1960, south of Cairns). Smaller terminals are at Lucinda Point (north of Townsville) and Bundaberg. Freighters which required three weeks in port to load 10,000 tons of bagged sugar are now loaded in two days. This has created employment problems in the port towns. The savings in transport costs will make Australian sugar more competitive and thus benefit the industry which remains the mainstay of settlement in eastern Queensland. E. C. Chapman, "Queensland Ports and the Bulk Shipment of Australian Raw Sugar", *Geography*, 1962. Pp. 310 ff.

[8] Griffith Taylor, *Australia*. 7th Edition, London, 1959.

which would have been justified by distance and port services. In coastwise trade the iron and steel industry, the thermo-electric plants (which supply 90 per cent of Australia's electricity) and the oil refineries are the main traffic generators. Coastwise trade is normally limited to Australian vessels but they do not to any great extent participate in overseas trade.

The principal commodity handled in ports of northern Queensland is sugar from the coastal plains but some ports, particularly Cairns and Townsville, serve a wider area and handle a variety of cargoes.[7] Townsville has rail connections with Mount Isa, Australia's largest copper mine, about 1,000 kilometers to the west, where the 1961 production will be doubled by 1964. The diversified port of Brisbane dominates southern Queensland. It is the only center in the state at which wool sales are held. The leading wool-exporting center of the world is, however, Sydney, which ships more than one million bales a year. Wool[8] continues to be Australia's most important export by value, accounting for 35–40 per cent of total exports and over 10 per cent of the national income. Australia in the 1930s and 1950s normally produced one-fourth of the world's wool. About 2.5–3 million bales are shipped annually.

Sydney, one of the largest cities in the southern hemisphere, has one of the best natural harbors in the world. It is located 20 kilometers to the north of Botany Bay where Cook landed. The site of Sydney Cove was chosen by the commander of the First Fleet, Captain Arthur Phillip, who first went to Botany Bay. Sydney is not the only principal center of population in Australia that originated as a penal establishment; Hobart, Newcastle, and Brisbane are others.

The two large ports north and south of Sydney, Newcastle and Port Kembla, are specialized bulk cargo ports. Both are centers for heavy manufacturing, chiefly iron and steel,

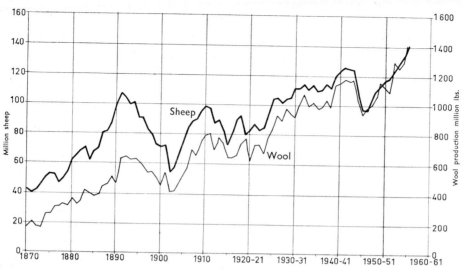

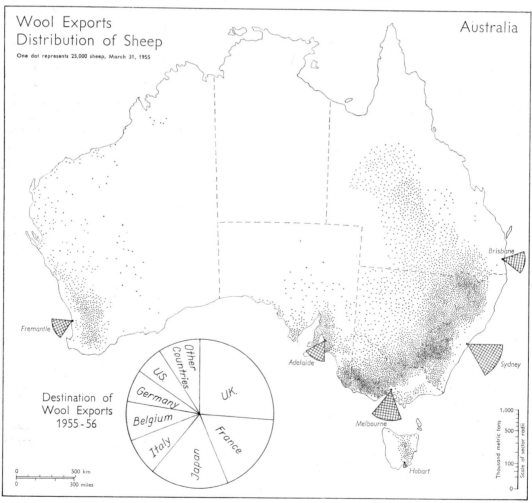

Wool Exports
Distribution of Sheep

One dot represents 25,000 sheep, March 31, 1955

Australia

Destination of
Wool Exports
1955-56

Sources: Graph and distribution of sheep from the *Yearbook of the Commonwealth of Australia*, 1957; wool exports from the *Atlas of Australian Resources*, where the exports of each state are shown as shipped through the major port of that state.

A section of the port of Melbourne on the Yarra River with the city in the background. In bottom left corner the new Appleton Dock with sheds for general cargo and open storage for coal and phosphate rock. In the center the Victoria Dock with wharves for overseas general cargo and interstate passengers and cargo. The main overseas passenger terminal is not on the river but at Port Melbourne on Hobsons Bay east of the river mouth. (Melbourne Harbor Trust Commissioners)

based on the large coal basin which centers on Sydney and is worked north, west and south of the city. Four-fifths of Australia's bituminous coal output (24.4 million tons in 1961) are produced in this field. As Australia has no petroleum field in operation and only a small hydro-electric power potential (except in Tasmania) but large deposits of high quality coal which can easily be mined, coal has been prominent in its energy balance. The peripheral

location of the country has, however, kept coal exports at a minimum. Most of the coal is used near the mines but about 4 million tons are shipped through Newcastle.[9] This quantity had been reached before World War I. Most of the coal is sent coastwise and only small

[9] Neville R. Mills, *Australian Steel Industry*. Sydney, 1948; R. G. Golledge, "Observations on the Urban Pattern and Functional Role of Newcastle, N.S.W.", *Tijdschrift voor Economische en Sociale Geografie*, 1962. Pp. 72 ff.

quantities are exported, the largest customer being New Zealand, which already in 1913 took half a million tons but since has bought somewhat less. Almost two million tons go to nearby Sydney where the large power plant on Botany Bay is the largest customer. Melbourne and Adelaide also receive considerable quantities of coal by collier.

The Australian iron and steel industry is operated by a single firm, the Broken Hill Proprietary Company, Ltd., or B.H.P. as it is usually referred to. Large integrated steel plants are located at Port Kembla and Newcastle. They receive iron ore from Whyalla and recently also from Yampi on the north-west coast. The Newcastle works went into operation in 1915. B.H.P. at that time was a producer of lead, zinc and silver. Port Kembla became a steel center in 1928 when a company that had previously been engaged in iron and steel manufacturing at Lithgow (an inland coal mining center, west of Sydney) transferred its works to the coast on the southern coal field. Port Kembla's history as a center for heavy manufacturing goes back to 1907, when a copper refinery was located here. Later production of sulphuric acid and superphosphate was started. Before 1907 Port Kembla was just a jetty used for loading coal.

Melbourne vies with Sydney as the largest city and the leading port of Australia. The trade structures of the two ports are very similar; both are typical big city ports. The foreign trade of Australia, especially general cargo trade, is strongly concentrated on these two ports.

The Melbourne area was settled in the 1830s. A large boom came with the Gold Rush in the 1850s, when Melbourne was the principal point of entry to the Victorian gold fields. Australia's population almost trebled in ten years and mining became firmly established as a major industry.

The other large port in Victoria, Geelong, also located on Port Phillip Bay, competes with Melbourne for the trade of the western part of the state. It is a leading grain port; most of its tonnage, however, is generated by a petroleum refinery.

The island state of Tasmania, dependent on mainland Australia for manufactured goods and markets for its agricultural products, has many small and medium-sized ports on the northern coast facing Melbourne. The western part of Tasmania is too rugged and wet for agriculture. Interstate trade clearly dominates all Tasmanian ports. Fruit (especially apples) and vegetables are the leading exports of Hobart, the state capital and the largest port.

Among the many ports on Spencer and St. Vincent Bays of South Australia the ore-port of Whyalla and the great-city port Adelaide account for the largest tonnages. Whyalla receives iron ore by rail from the B.H.P. ore fields at Iron Knob (the Middleback Ranges) some 50 kilometers to the northwest. The ore is sent by B.H.P. ore carriers to Port Kembla and Newcastle. As return cargo from Port Kembla some ships carry coke for a blast furnace which was completed at Whyalla in the beginning of World War II. It produces pig iron for the foundries of Australia.[10] Opposite Whyalla on the Bay is Port Pirie, the port of Broken Hill, one of the spectacular mining centers of the arid interior and one of the world's leading lead and zinc producers, in operation since 1883. A smelter and refinery for lead-silver concentrates is located at Port Pirie but zinc is refined near Hobart, Tasmania, by electrolysis. From Rapid Bay south of Adelaide limestone is shipped to Whyalla and the steelworks in New South Wales. Most of the cereal producing areas in this region are adjacent to the ports. This is in marked contrast to New South Wales, Victoria and Western Australia, where the wheat is generally hauled long distances to the ports.

[10] Rupert J. Best (Editor), *Introducing South Australia*. Melbourne, 1958.

Southwestern Australia, isolated by vast areas of almost uninhabited land from the "Fertile Crescent", stretching from the "Sugar Coast" of northern Queensland to the Spencer Gulf area of South Australia, has a dominating capital port, Fremantle.[11] It shares its hinterland, served by the rather dense railway net, with some small or medium-sized ports, Albany, Bunbury and Geraldton. Wheat is the leading export item from this region. Fremantle's traffic volume has increased considerably with the construction of a large petroleum refinery at Kwinana about 20 kilometers south of the port but included in its statistics. Fremantle is an important bunker port and much oil is consumed by calling vessels. The local market of this isolated part of Australia could hardly have warranted such a large refinery.

On the northwest coast of Australia are two ports, Yampi and Darwin. Some small islands in Yampi Sound have high-grade iron ore deposits which are now being mined on a limited scale to supplement the ore flow from Whyalla. Darwin, with a population of somewhat less than ten thousand, is the capital of the Northern Territory and an important trade center in this sparsely populated part of Australia.

The area around the small mission station at Weipa on Cape York Peninsula has been recognized as one of the world's largest deposits of bauxite. Exploitation of the deposit started in 1961. An alumina plant will be built at Lorim Point and a mining town at Jessica Point, both within two miles of Weipa. By 1966 alumina will be regularly shipped to aluminum smelters at Bluff, New Zealand and Bell Bay a few miles north of Launceston, Tasmania.[12]

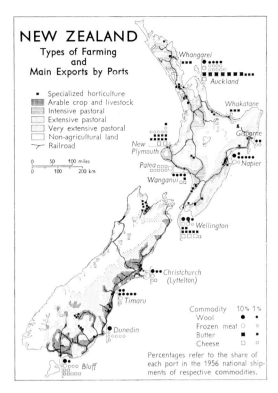

NEW ZEALAND
Types of Farming
and
Main Exports by Ports

- Specialized horticulture
- Arable crop and livestock
- Intensive pastoral
- Extensive pastoral
- Very extensive pastoral
- Non-agricultural land
- Railroad

0   50   100 miles
0   100   200 km

Whangarei
Auckland
Whakatane
Gisborne
New Plymouth
Patea
Napier
Wanganui
Wellington
Christchurch (Lyttelton)
Timaru
Dunedin
Bluff

Commodity	10%	1%
Wool	●	•
Frozen meat	○	∘
Butter	■	▪
Cheese	□	▫

Percentages refer to the share of each port in the 1956 national shipments of respective commodities.

Sources: (1) Types of farming: William H. Wallace, "Railway Traffic and Agriculture in New Zealand", *Economic Geography*, 1958. Pp. 170, 171.
Sources: (2) Port data: *New Zealand Official Yearbook*, 1958.

New Zealand

Organized settlement by Europeans started in 1840 which makes New Zealand an even younger country than Australia. New Zealand had its gold rush in the 1860s which helped to lure thousands of prospective settlers to South Island. After a disastrous depression in the 1880s the introduction of refrigerated shipping and cold storage gave New Zealand an opportunity to sell fresh meat, butter, cheese and eggs in the antipode markets of Great Britain. North Island soon surged ahead in population and economic importance. Now two-thirds of the New Zealanders live on North Island. The population is overwhelmingly British by descent

[11] Perth, the state capital, and Fremantle, its outport at the mouth of the Swan River, have merged into one continuous built-up area.
[12] E. M. Driscoll, "Weipa: A New Bauxite Mining Area in North Queensland", *Geography*, 1962. Pp. 309–310.

Principal exports by value through Wellington are wool, frozen and chilled meat, cheese and butter and the leading imports motor vehicles, iron and steel and textiles. The general cargo wharves are in close proximity to the railway station and the city business area.

The shortest distance from Wellington to Plymouth, England, is through the Panama Canal and the longest via Cape of Good Hope. The four alternative routes range from 11,060 to 12,850 nautical miles. The Cape Horn route is shorter than the Suez route. (Wellington Harbour Board)

and a deliberate restrictive policy has limited its numbers. For decades successive New Zealand Governments have favored selective immigration.[1]

New Zealand's economy is based upon agriculture. The products of pastoral farming constitute more than nine-tenths of its export value. Cattle and sheep and their products are the mainstay of New Zealand's agriculture, each contributing roughly equal shares to the value of the Dominion's agricultural production. The two islands, almost completely covered by natural vegetation a little more than a century ago, have been transformed

into a country of highly productive pastures. The intensive pastoral farms on the plains of North Island are the most productive agricultural units in the country. Agriculture is here based upon the grazing of permanent pastures which have been established by plowing and planting grasses.[2] On the plains of the eastern coast of South Island arable land predominates. Farmers have their land in semipermanent pastures or they grow fodder crops and cash crops. Most of New Zealand's wheat is grown here. But less than half the Dominion's wheat requirement is met within the country, the deficit usually being made up by imports from Australia.

Auckland is the largest city and port of New Zealand followed by the capital, Wellington. Auckland handles about two-fifths of the im-

[1] Robert G. Bowman, "New Zealand". In *Geography of the Pacific*. (Otis W. Freeman, editor.) New York, 1951;

Eila M. J. Campbell, "New Zealand and its Dependencies". In *The Changing World* (W. G. East and A. E. Moodie, editors). London, 1956.

[2] William H. Wallace, "Railway Traffic and Agriculture in New Zealand", *Economic Geography,* 1958. Pp. 168–184.

ports and one-third of the exports by value and Wellington one-third of the imports and one-fifth of the exports. Both ports have somewhat smaller shares of foreign trade expressed in volume. The two chief cities of South Island, Christchurch and Dunedin, are both smaller than the largest cities of North Island. Lyttelton, the port of Christchurch, has a larger foreign traffic than Dunedin both by volume and by value. Lyttelton, Napier, Bluff, Dunedin and New Plymouth account for 5–10 per cent of the export value. The ranking of these ports varies from year to year. Lyttelton normally has close to 15 per cent of the imports by value and Dunedin 5–10 per cent. No other port even approaches five per cent.

New Zealand's exports have gradually become less one-sidedly directed towards the United Kingdom. Immediately before and after World War II the mother country took three-fourths of New Zealand's exports but in 1960 no more than 53 per cent. Shipments to other Commonwealth countries have remained rather stable at 6 to 8 per cent but exports to the markets of Continental Europe have increased and in 1960 amounted to almost one-fifth of the total value.

In the postwar period imports from the United Kingdom have amounted to about 50 per cent. Vehicles and machinery, textile products, iron and steel, books and magazines are among the leading commodity groups.

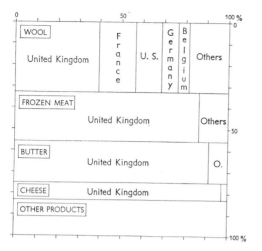

Destination of New Zealand's four main export commodities in 1956. The United Kingdom takes less than 40 per cent of the wool, which accounts for 33 per cent of the total export value, but she takes over 80 per cent of the frozen meat, butter and cheese.

Source: *The New Zealand Official Yearbook.*

Other Commonwealth countries loom larger on the import side than in the exports. Australia is normally the second trade partner accounting

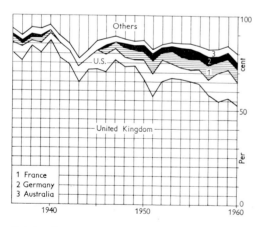

Destination of New Zealand's exports by value, 1936–1958. The United Kingdom is becoming less dominant as a customer, while France and Germany have become more important than before the Second World War especially for wool. Australia's share is small but stable.

Source: *The New Zealand Official Yearbook.*

for 10–15 per cent of the import value. It comes ahead of the United States. Australia supplies raw materials like wheat and sugar but also manufactures like iron and steel and refined petroleum products. This is an important commodity group for a country with one of the world's highest levels of living. The imports of fertilizer materials, rock phosphate from Nauru, basic slag from Belgium, potash from France and the United States and sulphur from the United States amount to large quantities but relatively small values.

Handicraft and manufacturing have existed in New Zealand from the beginning of its European history, strongly encouraged by the remoteness of the country. According to the 1956 census, manufacturing, mining and construction employed 35 per cent of the actively engaged population and various service industries 49 per cent but agriculture and ancillary industries, so important in the export trade, a mere 16 per cent.

The Pacific Islands

The Pacific Ocean covers more than one-third of the surface of the globe. The populated island groups are small, both in area and population. The Hawaiians, the Fijis, Samoa, and Tahiti are regular ports of call for liner shipping and most of the others are served by tramps as cargoes accumulate. Inter-island transportation within groups is carried out by small coasters, auxiliary schooners and, particularly in Hawaii, barges.

Hawaii, since 1959 the fiftieth American state, predominantly trades with the forty-eight conterminous states, which account for over 90 per cent of Hawaii's commodity exchange. Pineapples and sugar produced on a large scale for the mainland market are the islands' chief shipments and petroleum, manufactured goods and food are received in even larger quantities from the mainland. This trade is reserved for American flag vessels. Honolulu is the economic hub of the island group and it is also the crossroads of the Pacific, the major port of call on the long shipping routes across the ocean. Many vessels passing through the Panama Canal en route to or from Japan follow the shorter great circle route which skirts the Aleutians and which allows calls with only short detours at the American west coast ports. For routes other than the northern one Honolulu is the great hub of the Pacific.

Fiji is after Hawaii the most populous of the island groups in the Pacific. The cosmopolitan city of Suva (40,000 inhabitants) is situated on a sheltered harbor on the southeast coast of Viti Levu, the largest island in the group. Nearby Nadi airport is used by planes operating between North America, Australia and New Zealand. The city of Suva is thus the counterpart of Honolulu in the northern Pacific.

Sugar, Fiji's leading export product accounting for two-thirds of the export value, was introduced in the 1870s and has later become almost a monoculture. Indians were brought in for the sugar plantations and today the Indian population outnumbers all others combined. From indentured laborers the East Indians have developed into the economically dominant group. Practically all the sugar is produced by Indian farmers, half of whom are tenants of the Colonial Sugar Refining Company, which has established crushing mills in the cane growing areas on the dry western sides of Viti Levu and Vanua Levu.[1]

Suva is Fiji's leading port handling over half of its trade. Lautoka, built around the largest sugar mill, is the second port of entry.

Noumea, the capital of New Caledonia, is located on an excellent harbor. With a population of about 15,000 it is second only to Suva among the south Pacific island towns. The metamorphic rocks of New Caledonia are highly mineralized, but only nickel, chrome and cobalt have so far been mined in sizable quantities. As a nickel producer New Caledonia ranks third in the world after Canada and the Soviet Union. In the early years of the mining industry labor was supplied by convicts; later by indentured labor recruited in many countries. The contract system of labor was abolished near the end of World War II.

The small, isolated coral islands of Nauru and Ocean Island have large deposits of phosphate, first developed by a private company and since 1919 by the governments of Australia, New Zealand and the United Kingdom. The difficult loading situation was solved at Nauru by the construction of a huge cantilever loader extending 500 meters offshore beyond the reef. Most of the phosphate moves to Australia and New Zealand. Workers are recruited in Hong Kong.

[1] K. W. Robinson, *Australia, New Zealand and the Southwest Pacific*. London, 1960. Pp. 252 ff.

FRONTISPIECES

Page 2: The Japanese turbine tanker *Nissho Maru* (131,000 tons dwt) makes eight or nine voyages a year between Kuwait and the Tokuyama refinery in Japan. (Sasebo Heavy Industries Co., Ltd.)

Page 12: Captain Helge Söderman of the icebreaker *Sankt Erik,* which is owned and operated by the Port of Stockholm to keep the approach channels open throughout the winter, here represents the hundreds of thousands of men who keep the flow of cargo and passengers moving between the ports of the world. (The Port of Stockholm.)

Page 122: View of Stockholm, one of the many cities which grew up as ports, where wholesale trade and shipping are major industries but where the casual visitor now sees only a small part of the port as the modern installations, for lack of space, have been assigned peripheral locations within the city area. The old port (Skeppsbron and Stadsgården) in the heart of the city has been downgraded to handle only short-distance cargo and passenger traffic. (The Port of Stockholm.)

Page 463: The general cargo and passenger facilities of the Port of New York are traditionally highly concentrated to Manhattan and Brooklyn in the state of New York. Only recently were new facilities of a radically different layout constructed in the state of New Jersey. See pages 277–287. (The Port of New York Authority.)

Index

Glossary

Tonnage Measurements

Gross Register Tonnage (GRT), Gross Tonnage, is a measurement of the enclosed volume of a vessel, 100 cubic feet (2.83 m³) being taken as 1 ton.

Net Register Tonnage (NRT), Net Tonnage, is Gross Register Tonnage less an allowance for machinery and crew space. It is usually used for the calculation of port dues and charges, and in statistics of entrances and clearances.

Deadweight Tonnage (dwt tons), measures the maximum carrying capacity of a vessel in long tons (1.016 metric tons) of cargo and fuel, when the vessel is down to its summer load line.

There is no simple relationship between the three measurements. It depends on the size and type of ship. For ocean-going tramps it has been put by Kendall at 100 NRT = 165 GRT = 250 dwt tons. Isserlis in 1938 gave as rough and ready ratios the following: 100 NRT = 160 GRT = 240 dwt tons. See Kendall, *Journal of the Royal Statistical Society,* Vol. CXI, Part II, 1948; Isserlis, *Journal of the Royal Statistical Society,* Vol. CI, 1938.

Coastwise Shipping and *Coastal Shipping.* When not otherwise stated these terms are synonymous with domestic shipping or shipping by sea between two points in the same country. They thus include intercoastal trade (U.S.) or *grand cabotage* (U.S.S.R. and France) and noncontiguous trade (U.S.) as well as interisland trade (Indonesia, Japan, the Philippines).

Tidal Basin, an enclosed area of water in which the tide ebbs and flows, provided with quays, warehouses, etc.

Wet Dock, enclosed basin into which vessels are admitted at high water and in which the gates are closed when the tide begins to fall. Inside the basin the water is maintained at a fairly uniform level.

Statistical Sources

Data for the port maps have been compiled from the following sources:

ADEN: *Port of Aden Annual, 1961–1962,* Aden Port Trust,
United Nations, *Yearbook of International Trade Statistics 1960,* New York, 1962.

ALGERIA: *Annuaire statistique de l'Algérie 1956*

ANGOLA: Information provided by Serviços de Portos, Caminhos de Ferro e Transportes, Exploração do Porto do Lobito e Fiscalização do Caminho de Ferro de Benguela. Irene S. van Dongen, "Coffee Trade, Coffee Regions, and Coffee Ports in Angola", *Economic Geography,* 1961. Pp. 320 ff.

ARGENTINA: Dirección Nacional de Estadística y Censos, *Comercio Exterior 1951–1954.* Buenos Aires, 1959.

AUSTRALIA: Commonwealth Bureau of Census and Statistics, *Transport and Communications,* Bulletin for 1955–1956. Canberra.
"Ports and Shipping", *Atlas of Australian Resources.* Department of National Development, Canberra, 1958.

BAHRAIN: *World Oil,* August 15, 1961.

BARBADOS: Estimate calculated from United Nations, *Yearbook of International Trade Statistics 1960.* New York, 1962.

BELGIUM: Institut National de Statistique, *Statistique annuelle du Trafic international des Ports.* Année 1956.

BRAZIL: *Anuário Estatístico do Brasil,* 1958. Rio de Janeiro, 1958. *Brazilian Technical Studies: Prepared for the Joint Brazil — United States Economic Development Commission.* Washington, D.C., 1954. Foreign trade by port and coastwise shipping by state from the yearbook. Total traffic by port from the report.

BRITISH GUIANA: Estimates based on *Yearbook of International Trade Statistics* and various magazine articles.

BULGARIA: Werner Gumpel, "Die Seeverkehrspolitik des Comecon und ihre Bedeutung für Hamburg", *Geographische Rundschau,* 1962, Pp. 45 ff.

CAMEROONS: Estimate calculated from United Nations, *Yearbook of International Trade Statistics, 1960.* New York, 1962.

CANADA: Dominion Bureau of Statistics, Public Finance and Transportation Division, Transportation and Public Utilities Section. *Shipping Report,* Year ended December 31, 1956. Sections II and III, Ottawa, 1957.

CANARY ISLANDS: Josef Matznetter, *Der Seeverkehr der Kanarischen Inseln.* Wien, 1958. Se also Spain.

CEYLON: Estimate calculated from United Nations, *Yearbook of International Trade Statistics, 1960.* New York, 1962.

CHILE: Servicio Nacional de Estadística y Censos, *Comercio Exterior Año 1956.*

COLOMBIA: Departamento Administrativo Nacional de Estadística, *Anuario de Comercio Exterior de 1956.* Colombia, 1957.

CONGO, former French: *Bulletin mensuel de statistique de l'Afrique Equatoriale Française,* 1956–1957.

CONGO: former Belgian: *Bulletin mensuel du commerce exterieur du Congo belge et du Ruanda-Urundi,* 1956–1957, here taken from A. Krarup Mogensen,

"Belgisk Afrikas havne", *Kulturgeografi,* Nr. 60, 1958.

COSTA RICA: *Anuario Estadístico de Costa Rica, 1956.* San José, 1957.

CUBA: Ministerio de Hacienda, *Comercio Exterior 1955–1956.* La Habana, 1957.

CYPRUS: Estimates based on data from *Cyprus: An Economic Survey,* Barclays Bank, London, 1960.

DAHOMEY: see WEST AFRICA

DENMARK: *Statistisk Årbog 1957.* København, 1957.

DOMINICAN REPUBLIC: Dirección General de Estadística, *Comercio exterior de la Republica Dominicana,* Vol. VI, No. 12. 1958.

EAST GERMANY: *Statistisches Jahrbuch der DDR 1959,* Berlin, 1960.

ECUADOR: Banco Central del Ecuador.
Comercio Exterior Ecuatoriano, Octubre, noviembre y diciembre de 1956.

EGYPT: *Annual Return of Shipping, Cargo and Passenger Traffic in the Ports of Egypt and Suez Canal Transits, 1956.* Cairo, 1958.

EL SALVADOR: see SALVADOR

ETHIOPIA: *Economic Handbook,* December 1958. Issued by the Imperial Ethiopian Government, Ministry of Commerce & Industry, Addis Ababa, 1958.

FALKLAND ISLANDS: Estimates calculated from United Nations, *Yearbook of International Trade Statistics 1960.* New York, 1962.

FIJI: Estimates calculated from United Nations, *Yearbook of International Trade Statistics 1960.* New York, 1962.

FINLAND: Official Statistics of Finland, *Navigation: Shipping between Finland and Foreign Countries, 1956.* Helsinki, 1958. Foreign trade only.

FRANCE: Direction général des Douanes, *Tableau général de la navigation maritime et des transports.* Paris, 1956.
Atlas de France (Métropole), Comité National de Géographie.

FRENCH GUIANA: *Annuaire Statistique de la Guyane 1957–1959.*

FRENCH SOMALILAND: Charles Robequain, *Madagascar et les bases dispersées de l'Union française.* Paris, 1958.

GABON: *Bulletin Mensuel de Statistique de l'Afrique Equatoriale Française.* 1956–1957.

GAMBIA, see WEST AFRICA

GERMANY, see EAST and WEST GERMANY

GHANA: E. A. Boateng, *A Geography of Ghana.* Cambridge, 1959.

GREECE: National Statistical Service of Greece, *Foreign Trade of Greece, 1956–1957.* Foreign trade only.

GUADELOUPE: *Annuaire Statistique de la Guadeloupe 1953–1957.*

GUATEMALA: *Anuario de comercio exterior 1956.*

GUINEA, see WEST AFRICA

HAITI: Estimates based on data from *Overseas Economic Surveys: Hayti, August, 1956.* H.M.S.O., London, 1956.
Miragoâne added, based on data of bauxite shipments.

HONDURAS: *Anuario estadístico.*

HONG KONG: *Hong Kong: Report for the year 1960,* Hong Kong, 1961.

ICELAND: *Nefndarálit um hafnamál og 10 ára áætlun um hafnaframkvæmdir.* Skýrslut atvinnutækjanefndar III (Stencil). 1957.

INDIA: *Statistical Abstract, India, 1961.* Information provided by port authorities.

INDONESIA: *Statistical Pocket Book of Indonesia, 1961.* (Total cargo shipments reported for the two petroleum ports, Palembang and Balikpapan, were 10 million tons in 1960, but Indonesia's oil production was 21 million tons.)

IRAN: Information provided by the Ports and Navigation Organisation, Tehran, Iran.

IRAQ: *World Oil,* August 1960.

IRELAND, REPUBLIC OF: Data provided by port authorities.

ISRAEL: Information provided by Israel Ports Authority, Public Relations Officer. See also Central Bureau of Statistics, *Statistical Bulletin of Israel,* Dec., 1957, Vol. VIII, No. 12.
Central Bureau of Statistics, *Statistical Abstract of Israel 1956/57.* No. 8. Jerusalem, 1957.

ITALY: Istituto Centrale di Statistica, *Statistica della Navigazione Marittima 1956.* Roma, 1958.

IVORY COAST, see WEST AFRICA

JAMAICA: *Jamaica: Report for the year 1959,* Her Majesty's Stationery Office (London, 1962) and various company reports.

JAPAN: Port & Harbour Bureau, Ministry of Transportation, *Statistical Yearbook of Ports and Harbours, 1956.* (Published in Japanese; data extracted by Mr. Ryoji Moriwaki, Institute of Geography, Tohoku University, Sendai. Mr. Moriwaki also provided a base map with about 600 ports.)

JORDAN: George B. Cressey, *Crossroads, Land and Life in Southwest Asia.* Chicago, 1960.

KENYA: East African Railways & Harbours, *Annual Report 1961.*

KOREA, see SOUTH KOREA

KUWAIT: *Annual Review of Operations,* Kuwait Oil Company Limited. 1960.
Petroleum Times, Aug. 1962.

LEBANON: *Bulletin statistique trimestriel.* Vol. VIII, No. 4. Beyrouth, 1957.

LIBERIA, see WEST AFRICA

LIBYA: *The Economic Development of Libya.* The International Bank for Reconstruction and Development. Baltimore, 1960.
John I. Clarke, "Oil in Libya: Some Implications", *Economic Geography,* 1963.

MALTA: Estimate calculated from United Nations, *Yearbook of International Trade Statistics, 1960.* New York, 1962.

MARTINIQUE: *La Martinique 1952–1956.*

MADAGASCAR: *Bulletin mensuel de statistique,* avril 1958. Tananarive, 1958.

MALAGASY REPUBLIC, *see* MADAGASCAR

MALAYA, FEDERATION OF: D. F. Allen, *Minor Ports of Malaya* (Singapore, 1953) and information provided by port authorities.

MAURITANIA: Michael Crowder, "Iron Ore from Mauritania", *Steel Review* 19, 1960.

MAURITIUS: Estimates calculated from United Nations, *Yearbook of International Trade Statistics 1960.* New York, 1962.

MEXICO: *Anuario Estadístico de los Estados Unidos Mexicanos,* 1956–57. Mexico 1958. Foreign trade only.

MOROCCO: *Statistiques du mouvement commercial et maritime du Maroc 1956.*

MOZAMBIQUE: Information provided by Direcção dos Serviços dos Portos, Caminhos de Ferro e Transportes de Moçambique.

NETHERLANDS: Centraal bureau voor de statistiek, *Maandstatistiek van de zeevart en van het havenverkeer.* 1957.

NETHERLANDS ANTILLES: Estimate calculated from United Nations, *Yearbook of International Trade Statistics 1960* (New York, 1962), and total divided according to refinery capacity.

NEUTRAL ZONE: *Petroleum Times,* May, 1962.
World Oil, August, 15, 1961.

NEW CALEDONIA: Estimate calculated from *Minerals Yearbook.*

NEW ZEALAND: *The New Zealand Official Year-Book 1958,* Wellington, 1958.

NIGERIA, see WEST AFRICA

NORWAY: *Statistisk Årbok for Norge, 1960.* Oslo, 1960. Foreign and coastwise traffic for Oslo (1956) and Bergen (estimate) and foreign trade (1959) for other ports.

PAKISTAN: *Pakistan Statistical Yearbook 1957.* Karachi, 1959.

PANAMA: Estimates based on *Yearbook of International Trade Statistics* and various magazine articles.

PANAMA CANAL ZONE: Estimates calculated from Panama Canal Company, Canal Zone Government, *Annual Report,* Fiscal Year ended June 30, 1961.

PERU: *Anuario Estadístico del Perú,* 1956–1957.

PHILIPPINES: Bureau of the Census and Statistics, *Foreign Trade Statistics of the Philippines 1960.* Manila. Foreign trade only.

POLAND: Transactions of the Maritime Intitute at Gdańsk, Series III, Economics and Law Problems of Sea Transport. No. 17. Czesław Wojewódka, *Structural Changes in the traffic of Polish Seaports, 1945–1960.* Part 2. Gdańsk, 1961. (In Polish with English summary.)

PORTUGAL: *Anuário Estatístico 1956,* Lisboa, 1957

PORTUGESE GUINEA, see WEST AFRICA

PUERTO RICO, *see* UNITED STATES

QATAR: *World Oil,* August, 1960

REUNION: Estimates calculated from United Nations, *Yearbook of International Trade Statistics, 1960.* New York, 1962.

SALVADOR: *Anuario Estadístico 1956.* San Salvador, 1958.

SARAWAK: Estimate calculated from United Nations, *Yearbook of International Trade Statistics 1960.* New York, 1962.

SAUDI ARABIA: Information provided by the Saudi Government Railroad, Dhahran, Saudi Arabia; and *World Oil,* August 15, 1961.

SENEGAL, see WEST AFRICA

SIAM, see THAILAND

SIERRA LEONE: H. Reginald Jarrett, "Lunsar: A Study of an Iron Ore Mining Center in Sierra Leone", *Economic Geography,* 1956.

SIERRA LEONE, see WEST AFRICA

SINGAPORE: The Singapore Chamber of Commerce, *Report on the year ended 31st December, 1961.*

SOUTH AFRICA, REPUBLIC OF: *Foreign Trade Statistics. Volume III: Supplementary Trade Statements (Including Shipping and Excise). Calendar Year, 1956.* Department of Customs and Excise, Pretoria.

SOUTH KOREA: *Annual Economic Review 1958.*

SOUTH VIETNAM: Estimate calculated from United Nations, *Yearbook of International Trade Statistics, 1960.* New York, 1962.

SOUTH WEST AFRICA, see SOUTH AFRICA.

SOVIET UNION: Estimates based on *Narodnoe Chozjajstvo SSSR v 1958 godu;*
V. G. Bakaev and S. M. Baev (eds.), *Transport SSSR: Morskoj Transport,* Moskva, 1961;
I. V. Nikol'skij, *Geografija Transporta SSSR,* Moskva, 1960.

SPAIN: *Estadística del Impuesto de transportes por mar, aereo y a la entrada y salida por las fronteras. Estadística del impuesto de tonelaje 1956.* Madrid.

SPANISH SAHARA: Reported planned capacity according to *Norwegian Shipping News.*

SUDAN: Information provided by the Sudan Railways, Atbara, Sudan.
Also *Annual Foreign Trade Report 1956.*

SURINAM: Data provided by the Port of Maracaibo.

SWEDEN: Sveriges Officiella Statistik, *Sjöfart 1956.* Stockholm 1958.
Gunnar Sidenvall, "Goods Traffic at Swedish Ports 1954", *Atlas över Sverige,* sheets 117–118, Stockholm, 1956.

SYRIA: *Statistical Abstract of Syria 1956.* Damascus, 1957.

TAIWAN: *China Handbook 1955–56.* Taipei, 1955.

TANGANYIKA: East African Railways & Harbours, *Annual Report 1961.*

TANGER: Information provided by Le chef des services maritimes, Société du Port de Tanger, Tanger.

THAILAND: Port Authority of Thailand, *Annual Reports 1960–1959. Port of Bangkok.* (An abridged translation.)

TRINIDAD AND TOBAGO: *Annual Statistical Digest,* No. 6, 1956. Port-of-Spain, 1958.

TUNISIA: *Annuaire statistique de la Tunisie, 1956.* Ed. 1957.

TURKEY: Central Statistical Office, *Monthly Bulletin of Statistics,* No. 37, March 1957. Ankara.
Statistique Annuelle du Commerce Exterieur 1956. Parti: 3. Ankara 1957.

UNITED KINGDOM: Data for total traffic of major ports from Henry Rees, *British Ports and Shipping,* London, 1958. For other ports estimates of foreign trade (tonnage) based on *Annual Statement of the Trade of the United Kingdom, Vol. IV: Supplement,* 1955–1957, and coastwise trade (1948) from P. Ford and J. A. Bound, *Coastwise Shipping and Small Ports,* Oxford, 1951.

UNITED STATES: Department of the Army, Corps of Engineers, *Waterborne Commerce of the United States,* Calendar Year 1956.
Only seaports and Great Lakes ports included; data refer to foreign and coastwise trade, lakewise trade (i.e. on the Great Lakes), internal trade (i.e. the entire movement betwen ports takes place on inland waterways), and intraterritory trade (i.e. between ports within a territory or possession). Intraport and local traffic have been excluded.

URUGUAY: Estimate calculated from United Nations, *Yearbook of International Trade Statistics, 1960.* New York, 1962.

VENEZUELA: Dirección General de Estadística y Censos Nacionales, *Estadística Mercantil y Marítima de Venezuela 1955.* Caracas, 1960.

WEST AFRICA: H. P. White, "The Ports of West Africa", *Tijdschrift voor Economische en Sociale Geografie,* 1959. P. 7.

WEST GERMANY: Statistik der Bundesrepublik Deutschland. Band 190. *Die Seeschiffahrt im Jahre 1956.* Band 193. *Die Binnenschiffahrt im Jahre 1956.*

VIRGIN ISLANDS (U. S.) *see* UNITED STATES

YUGOSLAVIA: *Statistički godišnjak FNRJ 1957.* Beograd, 1957.

Author Index

Persons, Vessels and Corporations

Persons

Vessels

Corporations

Ports and Places

Italicized figures indicate a page where the place-name occurs only on map or diagram.
Figures followed by n indicate a page where the place-name occurs only in a footnote.
Country and province names are not included.
Major rivers and waterways accessible to seagoing vessels have been listed.

A

Aachen, W. Germany, *169*
Abadan, Iran, 65, 398, 399–400, 408, *410*
Abbeville, France, *171*
Abdul Aziz, Saudi Arabia, 404
Åbenrå, Denmark, *127*, 139
Aberdeen, Scotland, *111*, *183*, 170, 200
Aberdeen, Wash., U.S., 315
Abidjan, Ivory Coast, 371, 375–76, *facing 384*
Abqaiq, Saudi Arabia, 399, 404, 405
Abu Dhabi, Trucial Oman, *399*
Abu Hadriya, Saudi Arabia, *399*
Aburatsu, Japan, *411*, *441*
Abu Zenima, Egypt, *facing 384*
Acapulco, Mexico, *252*, 321, 428
Acari, Peru, 367
Accra, Ghana, 376, 377, *facing 384*
Acre, Israel, 237 n
Adabiya, Egypt, *230*, *facing 384*
Adana, Turkey, 234
Addis Ababa, Ethiopia, 396
Adelaide, S. Austr., Australia, *93*, *94*, 451, 452, 453 n, *454*, 456
Aden, Aden Colony, *64*, 69, 406–408, 414
Æbeltoft, Denmark, *127*
Ærøskøbing, Denmark, *127*
Affobakka, Surinam, 346
Agadir, Morocco, 246, 370, *facing 384*
Agger, Denmark, *127*
Agha Jari, Iran, 398, 399
Agracha, Spanish Sahara, 371
Aguilas, Spain, *83*, *217*
Ahmadi, Yemen, 409
Ahmadabad, India, *412*
Ahr, Sweden, *127*
Åhus, Sweden, *127*
Ahwaz, Iran, *399*
Aígion, Greece, *230*
Aigle, Switzerland, *61*, 227
Aigues-Mortes, France, 218
Aioi, Japan, *111*, *441*
Ait Amar, Morocco, 246
Ajaccio, Corsica, France, *171*, *217*, 222
Akçay, Turkey, *82*, *230*
Aketi, Congo (f. Belgian), 382
Akiho, Japan, *411*
Akita, Japan, *411*
Akoumapé, Togo, 377
Akranes, Iceland, *127*
Akron, Ohio, U.S., 313
Akureyri, Iceland, *127*
Akyab, Burma, *410*, 416
Ala, Sweden, *127*

Alabaster, Mich., U.S., *253*, 257
Alanya, Turkey, *230*
Albany, W. Austr., Australia, *93*, 457
Albany, N.Y., U.S., 89, *250*, 253
Albert Canal, Belgium, 157, *169*, 170, 172
Albertville, Congo (f. Belgian), *382*
Alblasserdam, Netherlands, *111*
Ålborg, Denmark, *127*, 137, 139
Aleksandrovsk, U.S.S.R., *142*, *449*
Aleppo, Syria, 236, 237, 401 n
Ålesund, Norway, *127*
Alexandretta, Turkey, *see* Iskenderun
Alexandria, Egypt, *65*, *230*, 242, 243, 288, *facing 384*, 429
Alexandria, Va., U.S., 292
Alexandroúpolis, Greece, *230*
Algeciras, Spain, *217*
Alger, Algeria, *83*, *217*, 245, 246, *facing 384*, 396
Alghero, Italy, *217*
Algonac, Mich., U.S., *253*
Alicante, Spain, *83*, 216, *217*
Alleppey, India, *410*
Allinge, Denmark, *127*
Alloa, Scotland, *170*
Almería, Spain, *83*, 216, *217*
Almirante, Panama, *252*
Alpena, Mich., U.S., *253*, *263*, 266
Alton, Ill., U.S., *251*
Ålvik, Norway, *127*
Amagasaki, Japan, *411*, *441*, 445, 447
Åmål, Sweden, *127*
Amapala, Honduras, *252*
Amasra, Turkey, *230*
Amazon R., Brazil, 348–49, 368
Ambarchik, U.S.S.R., *142*, *449*
Ambès, France, *65*, *171*, *217*
Amboina, Moluccas, Indonesia, *410*
Ambriz, Angola, *facing 384*
Amgu, U.S.S.R., *449*
Amherstsburg, Ont., Canada, *253*
Amman, Jordan, 239
Åmmeberg, Sweden, *127*
Amoy, China, *410*, 432 n, 434
Ampenan, Lumbok, Indonesia, *410*
Amrum, Germany, *171*
Amsterdam, Netherlands, *83*, *111*, 152, 156, 162, 164–66, 167, *169*, *171*, 277 n
Amsterdam — Rhine Canal, Netherlands, 164, *169*
Am Timan, Chad, *381*
Amuay Bay, Venezuela, *64*, *339*, 341, 342, *343*
Amur R., U.S.S.R.-China, 437, 449 n
Anacortes, Wash., U.S., *64*, *252*

Anadyr, U.S.S.R., *142*, *449*
Analalava, Madagascar, *facing 384*
Anchorage, Alaska, U.S., *252*
Ancona, Italy, *65*, *217*
Ancud, Chile, *338*
Anenäset, Sweden, *127*
Angle Bay, Milford Haven, Wales, *61*, 193, 194
Ango Ango, Congo (f. Belgian), 382
Angra dos Reis, Rio de Janeiro, Brazil, *338*
Ankara, Turkey, 234, 401 n
Annapolis, Md., U.S., *253*, 289
Annapolis Royal, N.S., Canada, *252*
Anniston, Ala., U.S., *250*
Anshan, China, 437
Antalaha, Madagascar, *facing 384*
Antalya, Turkey, *230*
Antibes, France, *171*, *217*
Antigua, W. Indies, *330*, *338*
Antilla, Cuba, *252*
Antioquía, Colombia, 335, *336*
Antofagasta, Chile, *338*, 364, 365, 366
Antonina, Paraná, Brazil, *338*
António Enes, Mozambique, *facing 384*
Antung, China, *410*, 437
Antwerp, Belgium, *65*, *83*, 116, 120, 152, 156, 157, 162, 166–173, 178, 183, 184, 203, 207, 222, 277 n, 283, 288
Anvers, Belgium, *see* Antwerp
Anzio, Italy, *217*
Aomori, Japan, *411*, *441*
Apalachicola Bay, Fla., U.S., *252*
Apostle Islands, Wis., U.S., *253*
Apsheronski Port, U.S.S.R., *232*
Aqaba, Jordan, *230*, 238, 239
Aracajú, Sergipe, Brazil, *338*
Arbatax, Sardinia, Italy, *217*
Arcachon, France, *171*, *217*
Ardrossan, S. Aust., Australia, *452*
Ardrossan, Scotland, *83*, *93*, *170*
Areia Branca, Rio Grande do Norte, Brazil, *338*, 350
Arendal, Norway, *127*, 128, 129
Arequipa, Peru, 367
Argentia, Nfld., Canada, *252*
Århus, Denmark, *127*, 137, 138, 139
Arica, Chile, *338*, 366
Arkhangelsk, U.S.S.R., *142*, 143, 144, 145, 149
Arles, France, 218, 220
Aruba, Neths. Antilles, 62, *64*, 65, *330*, 334–35, *339*, *343*, 399
Arvida, Que., Canada, 274
Arvika, Sweden, *127*
Arzew, Algeria, 73, *183*, *217*, *facing 384*
Ashdod, Israel, *230*, 237

473

Subject Index